Alcohol-induced mood disorder
Alcohol-induced anxiety disorder
Alcohol-induced sexual dysfunction
Alcohol-induced sleep disorder
Alcohol-related disorder NOS

Amphetamine (or Amphetamine-Like) – Related Disorders

Amphetamine Use Disorders
Amphetamine dependence
Amphetamine abuse

Amphetamine-Induced Disorders
Amphetamine intoxication
Amphetamine withdrawal
Amphetamine intoxication delirium
Amphetamine-induced psychotic disorder
   With delusions
   With hallucinations
Amphetamine-induced mood disorder
Amphetamine-induced anxiety disorder
Amphetamine-induced sexual dysfunction
Amphetamine-induced sleep disorder
Amphetamine-related disorder NOS

Caffeine-Related Disorders

Caffeine-Induced Disorders
Caffeine intoxication
Caffeine-induced anxiety disorder
Caffeine-induced sleep disorder
Caffeine-related disorder NOS

Cannabis-Related Disorders

Cannabis Use Disorders
Cannabis dependence
Cannabis abuse

Cannabis-Induced Disorders
Cannabis intoxication
Cannabis intoxication delirium
Cannabis-induced psychotic disorder
   With delusions
   With hallucinations
Cannabis-induced anxiety disorder
Cannabis-related disorder NOS

Cocaine-Related Disorders

Cocaine Use Disorders
Cocaine dependence
Cocaine abuse

Cocaine-Induced Disorders
Cocaine intoxication
Cocaine withdrawal
Cocaine intoxication delirium
Cocaine-induced psychotic disorder
   With delusions
   With hallucinations
Cocaine-induced mood disorder

Cocaine-induced anxiety disorder
Cocaine-induced sexual dysfunction
Cocaine-induced sleep disorder
Cocaine-related disorder NOS

Hallucinogen-Related Disorders

Hallucinogen Use Disorders
Hallucinogen dependence
Hallucinogen abuse

Hallucinogen-Induced Disorders
Hallucinogen intoxication
Hallucinogen persisting perception disorder (flashbacks)
Hallucinogen intoxication delirium
Hallucinogen-induced psychotic disorder
   With delusions
   With hallucinations
Hallucinogen-induced mood disorder
Hallucinogen-induced anxiety disorder
Hallucinogen-related disorder NOS

Inhalant-Related Disorders

Inhalant Use Disorders
Inhalant dependence
Inhalant abuse

Inhalant-Induced Disorders
Inhalant intoxication
Inhalant intoxication delirium
Inhalant-induced persisting dementia
Inhalant-induced psychotic disorder
   With delusions
   With hallucinations
Inhalant-induced mood disorder
Inhalant-induced anxiety disorder
Inhalant-related disorder NOS

Nicotine-Related Disorders

Nicotine Use Disorder
Nicotine dependence

Nicotine-Induced Disorder
Nicotine withdrawal
Nicotine-related disorder NOS

Opioid-Related Disorders

Opioid Use Disorders
Opiod dependence
Opiod abuse

Opioid-Induced Disorders
Opioid intoxication
Opioid withdrawal
Opioid intoxication delirium
Opioid-induced psychotic disorder
   With delusions
   With hallucinations
Opioid-induced mood disorder
Opioid-induced sexual dysfunction

Opioid-induced ...
Opioid-related disorder NOS

Phencyclidine (or Phencyclidine-Like) – Related Disorders

Phencyclidine Use Disorders
Phencyclidine dependence
Phencyclidine abuse

Phencyclidine-Induced Disorders
Phencyclidine intoxication
Phencyclidine intoxication delirium
Phencyclidine-induced psychotic disorder
   With delusions
   With hallucinations
Phencyclidine-induced mood disorder
Phencyclidine-induced anxiety disorder
Phencyclidine-related disorder NOS

Sedative-, Hypnotic-, or Anxiolytic-Related Disorders

Sedative, Hypnotic, or Anxiolytic Use Disorders
Sedative, hypnotic, or anxiolytic dependence
Sedative, hypnotic, or anxiolytic abuse

Sedative-, Hypnotic-, or Anxiolytic-Induced Disorders
Sedative, hypnotic, or anxiolytic intoxication
Sedative, hypnotic, or anxiolytic withdrawal
Sedative, hypnotic, or anxiolytic intoxication delirium
Sedative, hypnotic, or anxiolytic withdrawal delirium
Sedative-, hypnotic-, or anxiolytic-induced persisting dementia
Sedative-, hypnotic-, or anxiolytic-induced persisting amnestic disorder
Sedative-, hypnotic-, or anxiolytic-induced psychotic disorder
   With delusions
   With hallucinations
Sedative-, hypnotic-, or anxiolytic-induced mood disorder
Sedative-, hypnotic-, or anxiolytic-induced anxiety disorder
Sedative-, hypnotic-, or anxiolytic-induced sexual dysfunction
Sedative-, hypnotic-, or anxiolytic-induced sleep disorder
Sedative-, hypnotic-, or anxiolytic-related disorder NOS

(continued on inside back cover)

ABNORMAL
PSYCHOLOGY

ABNORMAL PSYCHOLOGY

SECOND EDITION

RONALD J. COMER
PRINCETON UNIVERSITY

W. H. FREEMAN AND COMPANY
NEW YORK

To
MARLENE,
WITH ALL MY LOVE

Library of Congress Cataloging-in-Publication Data

Comer, Ronald J.
    Abnormal psychology / Ronald J. Comer.
        p.   cm.
    Includes bibliographical references and index.
    ISBN 0-7167-2494-4
    1. Psychology, Pathological.   I. Title.
    RC454.C634   1992
    616.89—dc20

91-37855
CIP

Printed in the United States of America

1   2   3   4   5   6   7   8   9   0   RRD   9   9   8   7   6   5   4

CONTENTS IN BRIEF

CONTENTS

■

CHAPTER 6

ANXIETY DISORDERS 183

CHAPTER 7

TREATMENTS FOR ANXIETY DISORDERS 231

CHAPTER 8

MOOD DISORDERS 269

PREFACE

JUST 2½ YEARS ago the first edition of this textbook was published. I remember thinking, as I looked at the very first copy of the book, that my decade-long journey had come to an end. That naive belief lasted but five minutes, shattered when the book's indefatigable editor, Moira Lerner, offered me tips on how to prepare for the second edition. And so began another 30 months of work, leading to this, the new edition of *Abnormal Psychology*.

MY GOALS in writing this edition have been threefold: (1) to maintain the strengths of the first edition; (2) to improve upon the first edition by introducing new topics and insights; and (3) to update the book completely in accordance with all of the new developments and studies occurring in the clinical field over the past 2½ years. I believe that each of these goals has been achieved in the new edition. At the risk of seeming shamefully immodest, let me describe how the book maintains the strengths of the earlier edition and further improves upon it.

TRADITIONAL STRENGTHS AND FEATURES

■ Like the first edition, this book captures all facets of abnormal psychology. The many theories, studies, disorders, and treatments of this field are presented accurately and equally and in a logical, unified manner that students can easily understand.

■ The field's rich history is captured by including a carefully selected mix of both classic and recent research and clinical material.

■ The major psychological, biological, and sociocultural models are presented in a balanced and integrated way. This is not predominantly a psychodynamic or behavioral or biological or any other type of textbook. It is a book about all these models.

■ Complete discussions of treatment are presented throughout the book. Following a chapter introducing general issues and theories of treatment early on (Chapter 5), there are separate chapters on "Treatments for Anxiety Disorders" (Chapter 7), "Treatments for Mood Disorders (Chapter 9), and "Treatments for Schizophrenia" (Chapter 16). In addition, each of the other psychopathology chapters contains a full discussion of treatment approaches to that problem.

■ Numerous case studies bring clinical, theoretical, and treatment considerations to life. The textbook is filled with extensive clinical examples and excerpts that provide vivid illustrations of the different pathologies, their possible causes, and various approaches to treatment.

■ The book is adaptable to different courses and teaching preferences. Each chapter is essentially self-contained, with cross-referencing to other parts of the book whenever that might be useful. The chapters may be read in whatever order makes sense to a professor. Chapters can also be skipped or made optional without affecting a student's grasp of basic concepts.

■ The text raises broad contextual issues. For example, it examines questions about cross-cultural and gender differences in diagnosis and treatment and looks at legal and economic influences on the clinical field.

■ Like the first edition, it devotes full chapters to important subjects that are of special interest to college-age readers, such as eating disorders, suicide, and memory disorders—topics usually given limited coverage in other abnormal psychology textbooks.

■ The book is written with a single voice, in clear and straightforward language. This, I believe, is the primary advantage of having a single author. At the same time, just as students in a classroom may profit from expert guest lectures, readers of this textbook are treated to two chapters written by guest authors, each a major figure in the clinical field:

Chapter 14, "Sexual Disorders and Gender Identity Disorders" by Joseph LoPiccolo
University of Missouri-Columbia

Chapter 20, "Problems of Aging" by
Dolores Gallagher-Thompson

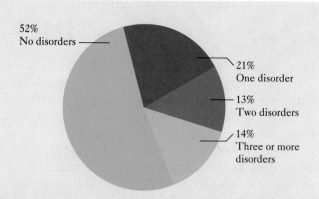

This pie chart from Chapter 4 indicates that almost half of all adults qualify for a DSM diagnosis during their lives; 27 percent meet the criteria for two or more different mental disorders. Adapted from a 1994 survey, the figure reflects the currency and relevance of data provided throughout the textbook.

and Larry Wolford Thompson
Stanford University
and Palo Alto Veterans Affairs Medical Center

The response to these chapters in the first edition was extraordinarily enthusiastic. Thus I was delighted that these authors agreed to update and revise the chapters for this new edition.

■ This book is once again designed to affect and motivate students. I have tried to write with humanity; to communicate my excitement, enthusiasm, and sense of discovery about abnormal psychology; and to incorporate my years of experience in teaching, practice, and research. It is always important to bear in mind that the subject of this book is people—often people in great pain.

■ The book once again provides "tools" for thinking critically about abnormal psychology. It helps readers grasp the logic underlying research and assessment; the connection between a model's principles and the studies, assessment tools, and treatment approaches used by its proponents; and the weaknesses and strengths of various theories and interventions. Readers acquire an ability to assess and question current beliefs, process new knowledge effectively, and remember it accurately. Each chapter ends with a "State of the Field" section that provides a sense of perspective about where the clinical field is today, where it came from, and where it seems to be going.

This Chapter 10 photograph of a candlelight vigil following rock star Kurt Cobain's suicide in April 1994 illustrates the profound impact that a famous person's suicide typically has on fans and other survivors.

New Features and Improvements

■ UPDATING

The book has been thoroughly updated, and where appropriate, revised. Data, studies, theories, and trends that emerged during the past 2½ years have been added to and integrated with those presented in the first edition. Similarly, all graphs and figures contain the most up to date and relevant available information. It is, without question, a textbook of the mid-1990s.

■ DSM-IV

The clinical discussions in the new edition are organized around the field's new diagnostic system, DSM-IV, which was itself published just a few months ago. I used the *actual* DSM-IV as the diagnostic reference source for the textbook, not preliminary drafts of DSM-IV or past options books. Thus, all DSM-IV criteria, definitions, and distinctions in the textbook are accurate and complete, not projected or vague offerings. The reader will find the integration of DSM-IV into the textbook detailed, pervasive, current, and seamless. In addition, I offer a detailed description of changes that have occurred between DSM-III-R and DSM-IV.

■ NEW TOPICS

The clinical field is ever-changing, and accordingly, I have included extensive discussions of numerous new topics, such as stalking (Chapter 21); repressed memories of childhood abuse and false memory syndrome (Chapter 18); *MICAs*, or mentally ill chemical abusers (Chapter 13); facilitated communication for autistic persons (Chapter 19); and men with eating disorders (Chapter 12).

■ GREATER ATTENTION TO ETHNIC AND GENDER ISSUES

Although the first edition carefully probed ethnic and gender issues, I have given still broader attention to these very important issues in the new edition. The reader will find new discussions and boxes on these topics throughout the book, as well as up-to-date graphs clarifying important trends and differences and tying these trends to such issues as economic opportunity.

■ BROAD AND INTEGRATED COVERAGE OF ORGANIC MENTAL DISORDERS

Because at least some biological factors have been uncovered for each of the mental disorders, DSM-IV and the clinical field no longer distinguish a category of disorders called organic mental disorders. Still, there are a number of disorders that are predomi-

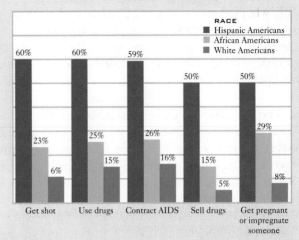

PERCENTAGE OF PARENTS WHO WORRY "A LOT" THAT THEIR CHILDREN WILL:

This figure from Chapter 6 illustrates that members of racial minority groups are likely to worry more than white Americans about certain aspects of their children's safety and future. Related data and figures in Chapter 6 further clarify that the higher anxiety levels of racial minority members may be largely a matter of living in poorer, more deprived, or more dangerous environments.

nantly caused by clearly identifiable organic factors, and in the new edition I have expanded my coverage of these important disorders. For example, the topic of dissociative disorders is now part of the broader Chapter 18 entitled "Disorders of Memory and Identity," which also includes enlightening sections on *amnestic disorders* and the *dementias*—organic disorders that affect memory and identity. Disorders that were previously distinguished as organic mental disorders are also covered in depth in the chapters on substance-related disorders (Chapter 13), problems of childhood and adolescence (Chapter 19), and problems of aging (Chapter 20).

■ BROADER COVERAGE OF PERSONALITY DISORDERS

In line with the clinical field's expanding interest in the personality disorders and the recent explosion of research in this area, I have greatly broadened the coverage of the various explanations and treatments for these disorders and included numerous studies from both the psychological and biological realms (see Chapter 17).

■ EXPANDED COVERAGE OF CERTAIN MODELS

I have broadened the coverage of some of the models in accord with current trends in the field. For example, current psychodynamic models such as *object*

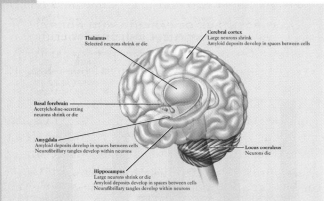

This figure from Chapter 20 summarizes the nature and state of physical changes that occur in the aging brain. The changes affect memory, learning, and reasoning and are found to an excessive degree among people with Alzheimer's disease, the leading cause of dementia.

relations theory and *self-theory* are given attention throughout the book (see Chapter 2). Similarly, the influential *cognitive-behavioral view* of obsessive-compulsive disorders is presented (see Chapters 6 and 7).

Supplements

The supplemental materials that accompanied the first edition received an extremely enthusiastic response. Not wanting to tamper with success, we are again providing everything that worked in that edition, and also adding new supplements that professors will find very useful and exciting. In particular, I have developed a stimulating video package consisting of numerous short video segments that can be readily integrated into each and every lecture. The following supplements are available:

An *Instructor's Manual*, by Janet A. Simons of Central Iowa Psychological Services and me, provides detailed outlines of each chapter, lists principal learning objectives, and offers exciting and novel ideas for varying lectures and launching class discussions.

A *Student Workbook*, by Katherine M. Nicolai, re-examines the content of each chapter by means of chapter summaries, lists of key names and terms, special elucidations of important ideas, numerous sample test questions (both multiple-choice and short-answer, with all answers provided), and suggestions for additional reading.

A comprehensive *Test Bank*, written by Melvyn B. King, Debra E. Clark, and me, offers approximately 2,000 multiple-choice, true-false, and short-answer test questions, many of them brand new for use in this edition, all graded as to difficulty, identified as "applied" or "factual," and keyed to specific pages in the textbook.

Computerized Test Questions, identical to the printed Test Bank, are available in both IBM and Macintosh formats.

Regular *newsletters and updates*, written by Professor Joseph Palladino of the University of Southern Indiana and me, offer new information and research and new pedagogical ideas to professors and students. Many readers find it very useful to receive these newsletters on a regular bases between editions of the textbook, and we are committed to continuing this popular feature.

A new *video package*, consisting of numerous video segments, each between one and five minutes in length, is designed for easy integration into lectures. These video segments illustrate or present clinical topics, pathologies, treatments, historical footage, laboratory experiments, clinical dilemmas, and more. They are taken from numerous sources, including clinical film documentaries, special filmings at clinical sites, and client and therapist interviews. Professors will no longer have to search through hours of film to find just the right footage for a lecture. The many relevant and enriching examples compiled within this package are available to all adopters free of charge.

Acknowledgments

I am enormously grateful to the many people who have contributed to the writing and production of this textbook. Indeed, their efforts have meant much more to me than I can possibly express.

I begin with the guest writers, who contributed two important chapters to the book. Joseph LoPiccolo, Dolores Gallagher-Thompson, and Larry Thompson have brought expertise and consummate skill to the presentations, and the results are simply wonderful.

In addition, Lorraine Garratt assisted me in the execution of just about every aspect of this edition, from researching and writing early drafts of various sections of the book to typing, developing graphs, and making important editorial judgments. I especially appreciate the enormous intellect, wisdom, extraordinary work ethic, and warm personal qualities that she brought to the undertaking. I could not have completed this new edition without her.

My sincere gratitude also goes to Amy Harris, Steve Winshel, Wendi Robbins, and Meath Bowen, all extremely talented individuals who wrote early drafts of various sections of the book. Their efforts and accomplishments were truly outstanding. Furthermore I greatly appreciate the conscientiousness and hard work of the many research assistants who helped with the book, including Linda Chamberlin, Greg Comer, Jon Comer, and Victor Finichi. And I extend a very special thank you to Wendy Wakefield Davis, editorial coordinator of DSM-IV, for her enormous help in providing me with DSM-IV information and developments, and for her constant enthusiasm and glowing disposition.

Throughout the past 2½ years, I have also received valuable feedback and ideas from a number of outstanding academicians and clinicians, who have reviewed portions of the manuscript and who have commented on the state of its clarity, accuracy, and completeness. The final product is in large part due to their collective knowledge and insight and to their willingness to share these with me. First and foremost is **Joseph Palladino**, University of Southern Indiana, whose constant flow of excellent ideas, information, and feedback, as well as his close friendship, added greatly to the quality of this edition. The other reviewers to whom I am greatly indebted include:

Second-edition reviewers:
Marna S. Barrett, Indiana University of Pennsylvania; **Otto A. Berliner**, Alfred State College; **Sarah Cirese**, College of Marin; **S. Wayne Duncan**, University of Washington (Seattle); **Lawrence L. Galant**, Gaston College, NC; **David A. Hoffman**, University of California, Santa Cruz; **Janet R. Matthews**, Loyola University; **Katherine M. Nicolai**, Iowa State University; and **David E. Powley**, University of Mobile.

I also wish to thank the many professors and clinicians from around the country who offered counsel on various aspects of this textbook, including: **Roger B. Allen**, University of Texas, Tyler; **F. G. (Gary) Mears**, University of Texas, Tyler; **Martin Rogers**, California State University, Sacramento; **Josh Weinstein**, Humboldt State College; **Francis Grossman**, Boston University; **Marvin Zuckerman**, University of Delaware; **Ken Ishida**, California State University; Bakersfield; **John Norcross**, University of Scranton; **David A. Clark**, University of New Brunswick; and **David Schlueter**, Clarion University of Pennsylvania.

I also wish to acknowledge and thank once again the individuals who served as reviewers for the first edition of this textbook. Their contributions remain integral to the quality of this new edition. They include Kent G. Bailey, Virginia Commonwealth University; Allan Berman, University of Rhode Island; Douglas Bernstein, University of Illinois; Kirk R. Blankstein, University of Toronto in Mississauga; Victor B. Cline, University of Utah; Morris N. Eagle, York University; Alan Fridlund, University of California, Santa Barbara; Stan Friedman, Southwest Texas State University; Bernard Kleinman, University of Missouri, Kansas City; Alan G. Krasnoff, University of Missouri, St. Louis; Robert D. Langston, University of Texas, Austin; Harvey R. Lerner, Kaiser-Permanente Medical Group; Michael P. Levine, Kenyon College; Robert J. McCaffrey, State University of New York, Albany; Jeffery Scott Mio, Washington State University; Paul A. Payne, University of Cincinnati; David V. Perkins, Ball State University; Norman Poppel, Middlesex County College; Max W. Rardin, University of Wyoming, Laramie; Leslie A. Rescorla, Bryn Mawr College; Vic Ryan, University of Colorado, Boulder; A. A. Sappington, University of Alabama, Birmingham; Roberta S. Sherman, Bloomington Center for Counseling and Human Development; David E. Silber, The George Washington University; Janet A. Simons, Central Iowa Psychological Services; Jay R. Skidmore, Utah State University; Thomas A. Tutko, San Jose State University; Norris D. Vestre, Arizona State University; Joseph L. White, University of California, Irvine; and Amy C. Willis, Washington D.C. Veterans Administration Medical Center. Their wisdom has found its way into the pages of this text.

Often overlooked by others, though certainly not by an author, are the individuals who help prepare the manuscript. I was particularly blessed in this regard and fervently thank Arlene Kronewitter and Arlene Kerch, back from the first edition, for their outstanding work, good cheer, tireless efforts, and repeated willingness to put my endeavor above their personal schedules. Similarly, I am grateful to Elaine Bacsik, Marion Kowalewski, Bernie Van Uiter, and Vera Sohl for their many efforts.

And, then, of course, there are the people at W. H. Freeman and Company. Everyone I have encountered at this company has been a consummate and skilled professional and a pleasure to work with. In particular, I am indebted to Moira Lerner, who returned as developmental editor for this edition. As I noted in my acknowledgments for the first edition, virtually every sentence in this book has Moira's mark. She is truly an awe-inspiring magician in her work. Moreover, she is as delightful and engaging a person as I have ever known. I value her magnificent skill and insight as editor, and even more I appreciate the very warm friendship she has extended to me over the years.

Four other persons at Freeman have also made very special contributions that I would like to mention. During the past year, Diane Cimino Maass, the project editor, has worked tirelessly to shepherd this book through the process of production, successfully juggling complex tasks and varied personalities (including my own). I greatly admire and appreciate her dedication, gentle yet decisive manner, and wise insights. Travis Amos, who returned as photo researcher for this edition, has again worked with great taste, diligence, and enthusiasm to bring the subject matter of abnormal psychology to life. His endless searches for the perfect photograph or painting and his uncompromising commitment to excellence have once again greatly enriched this book. I wish to thank Karla Roberts, the book's designer, whose impressive talent and constant efforts to create an enriching design have led to a finished product that is simply beautiful. Even a cursory glance through the pages of the book attests to her impressive accomplishments. And Susan Brennan, Freeman's psychology editor, managed every aspect of this second edition and was ultimately responsible for bringing it to fruition. Her extraordinary competence, enthusiasm, and commitment are greatly responsible for the finished product you are about to read.

In addition, I would like to thank Mary Shuford, director of development; Barbara Salazar, copy editor; Bernice Soltysik, indexer; Judy Sterio, proofreader; Larry Marcus, assistant photo editor, who just keeps digging and digging until he gets his photo; Nancy Giraldo Walker, rights and permissions manager; Paul Rohloff, production coordinator; Bill Page, illustration coordinator; and Kristen Auclair, editorial assistant. I also wish to thank Marie Schappert, vice president and director of marketing; John Britch, marketing manager; and all of Freeman's sales representatives, who so enthusiastically embraced the first edition and worked with great skill to bring it to the attention of professors around the country. Finally, I extend a special thank you to Linda Chaput, Freeman's past president, whose vision and support were responsible for the first edition, and to Robert L. Biewen, the current president, who unflinchingly committed the company to maintain the quality of the first edition in every way and to even surpass the accomplishments of that edition. Obviously, I've enjoyed and profited from my association with this gifted group of professionals.

In closing, I cannot imagine completing a project of this magnitude in the absence of a loving and supportive family, and I am truly grateful to mine. I thank my mother, Claire; sister, Pam; and brother, Steve, whose love and respect have been an enduring and motivating presence in my life, and my very special parents-in-law, Hadaso and David Slotkin. Similarly, I thank my great sons, Greg and Jon, who continue to fill my life with pride and laughter and joy and love. I can imagine no greater pleasure in life than having watched them grow from adorable infants into such capable, stimulating, and wonderful young adults. I once again express my deepest love and appreciation to my wife, Marlene, to whom I dedicate this book. Her gentleness, goodness, intelligence, and love enrich every day of my life. And, finally I send my admiration and love to my father, Herman Comer, who died just a few years ago. Whenever I felt tired and sorry for myself while working on this project, my mind would wander back to how hard he worked as a salesman over the course of his life, often holding on to several jobs at a time to support our family. He showed the same enormous capacity for hard work later in his life when he fought so hard to recover from a devastating stroke and to return to work, a struggle that was at once heartbreaking and inspiring. He never complained when he was called upon to work hard, only when he was no longer allowed to do so. Sometimes it takes a lifetime for us to fully recognize who our true heroes are. I'm sure that my father always knew how much I love him; I hope he also knows how much I admire him.

Ronald J. Comer
Princeton University
October, 1994

ABNORMAL
PSYCHOLOGY

Topic Overview

CHAPTER 1

ABNORMAL PSYCHOLOGY: PAST AND PRESENT

MENTAL DYSFUNCTIONING crosses all boundaries—cultural, economic, emotional, and intellectual. It affects the famous and the obscure, the rich and the poor, the upright and the perverse. Politicians, actors, writers, and other public icons of the present and the past have struggled with mental dysfunctioning (see Box 1–1). It can bring great suffering, but it can also be the source of inspiration and energy.

BECAUSE THEY ARE so ubiquitous and so personal, mental problems capture the interest of us all. Hundreds of novels, plays, films, and television programs have explored what many people see as the dark side of human nature, and self-help books flood the market to offer advice on how to overcome such problems as compulsive overeating, sexual dysfunctioning, and so-called addictive relationships. Psychologists and psychiatrists are popular guests on both television and radio, and some even have their own shows and encourage troubled people to call or to appear for instant advice.

THE FIELD devoted to the scientific study of the abnormal behavior we find so fascinating is usually called *abnormal psychology*. As in the other sciences, workers in this field, called *clinical scientists*, gather information systematically so that they may describe, predict, explain, and exert some control over the phenomena they study. The knowledge that they acquire is then used by a wide variety of *mental health*, or *clinical*, *practitioners* to detect, assess, and treat abnormal patterns of functioning.

ALTHOUGH THEIR GENERAL GOALS are similar to those of other scientific disciplines, clinical investigators and practitioners confront problems that make their work especially difficult. One of the most troubling problems is that psychological abnormality is extremely hard to define.

BOX 1–1

FAMOUS SUFFERERS OF MENTAL DISORDERS

Many well-known figures in history have suffered from mental disorders. Clinicians often speculate about the nature of their problems on the basis of written accounts of these people's behavior. In more recent years a number of public figures have chosen to reveal their struggles with mental dysfunctioning. Here are some of the well-known people who have suffered from mental disorders.

DISORDERS OF FEAR OR ANXIETY

John Keats, poet

Howard Hughes, inventor, entrepreneur

Jim Piersall, baseball player

Jim Backus, actor

Emily Dickinson, poet

Carolyn Wyeth, artist

Victoria, queen of England

Mary Baker Eddy, founder of Christian Science

Samuel Johnson, lexicographer, author

DISORDERS OF DEPRESSION

Arthur Schopenhauer, philosopher

Frédéric Chopin, composer

John Stuart Mill, philosopher, economist

Graham Greene, author

Thomas Wolfe, author

F. Scott Fitzgerald, author

Buzz Aldrin, astronaut

Dylan Thomas, poet

Sylvia Plath, poet

Honoré de Balzac, author

Louisa May Alcott, author

Clara Barton, philanthropist, founder of Red Cross

Marilyn Monroe, actress

Mike Wallace, television journalist

William Styron, novelist

Art Buchwald, political satirist

Rod Steiger, actor

Dick Cavett, talk show interviewer

DISORDERS OF DEPRESSION ALTERNATING WITH MANIA

Saul, king of Israel (11th century B.C.)

Thomas Eagleton, U.S. senator

Abraham Lincoln, U.S. president

Virginia Woolf, author

Theodore Roosevelt, U.S. president

Robert Lowell, poet

Winston Churchill, British prime minister

Freddie Prinze, comedian

Ernest Hemingway, author

Patty Duke, actress

George Frederick Handel, composer

Robert Schumann, composer

James Joyce, author

Anne Sexton, poet

DISORDERS INVOLVING A LOSS OF REALITY

Jean-Jacques Rousseau, philosopher

Vincent van Gogh, artist

Vaslav Nijinsky, dancer

Sirhan Sirhan, assassin

John Hinckley, would-be assassin

George III, king of England

Mark Vonnegut, author

DISORDERS OF DEPENDENCE ON ALCOHOL AND OTHER SUBSTANCES

Cambyses, king of Persia (6th century B.C.)

Samuel Taylor Coleridge, poet

François Rabelais, author

Elvis Presley, singer

Samuel Butler, poet

Dick Van Dyke, actor

Robert Burns, poet

John Belushi, comedian

Lord Byron, poet

John Barrymore, actor

Judy Garland, singer, actress

Edgar Allan Poe, author, poet

Truman Capote, author

Thomas De Quincey, author

Jim Morrison, poet, singer

Betty Ford, U.S. first lady

Jason Robards, actor

Tennesee Williams, playwright

EATING DISORDERS

Karen Carpenter, singer

Elizabeth I, queen of England

OTHER DISORDERS

Woody Guthrie, singer, songwriter: Huntington's disease

Renée Richards, tennis player: gender identity disorder

Al Capone, gangster: general paresis, syphilis

Rita Hayworth, actress: Alzheimer's disease

■ DEFINING ■ PSYCHOLOGICAL ABNORMALITY

*M*iriam cries herself to sleep every night. She is certain that the future holds nothing but misery. Indeed, this is the only thing she does feel certain about. "I'm going to die and my daughters are going to die. We're doomed. The world is ugly. I detest every moment of this life." She has great trouble sleeping. She is afraid to close her eyes, afraid that she will never wake up, and what will happen to her daughters then? When she does drift off to sleep, her dreams are nightmares filled with blood, dismembered bodies, thunder, decay, death, destruction.

One morning Miriam has trouble getting out of bed. The thought of facing another day overwhelms her. Again she wishes she were dead, and she wishes her daughters were dead. "We'd all be better off." She feels paralyzed by her depression and anxiety, too tired to move and too afraid to leave her house. She decides once again to stay home and to keep her daughters with her. She makes sure that all shades are drawn and that every conceivable entrance to the house is secured. She is afraid of the world and afraid of life. Every day is the same, filled with depression, fear, immobility, and withdrawal. Every day is a nightmare.

*D*uring the past year Brad has been hearing mysterious voices that tell him to quit his job, leave his family, and prepare for the coming invasion. These voices have brought tremendous confusion and emotional turmoil to Brad's life. He believes that they come from beings in distant parts of the universe who are somehow wired to him. Although it gives him a sense of purpose and specialness to be the chosen target of their communications, they also make him tense and anxious. He dreads the coming invasion. When he refuses an order, the voices insult and threaten him and turn his days into a waking nightmare.

Brad has put himself on a sparse diet to avoid the possibility that his enemies may be contaminating his food. He has found a quiet apartment far from his old haunts where he has laid in a good stock of arms and ammunition. His family and friends have tried to reach out to Brad, to understand his problems, and to dissuade him from his disturbing activities. Every day, however, he retreats further into his world of mysterious voices and imagined dangers.

Miriam and Brad are the kinds of people we think of when abnormal behavior is mentioned. Most of us would probably label their emotions, thoughts, and behavior *psychologically abnormal*, or, alternatively, as *psychopathological, maladjusted, emotionally disturbed,* or *mentally ill.*

But *are* Miriam and Brad psychologically abnormal, and if so, why? What is it about their thoughts, emotions, and behavior that might lead us to this conclusion? Many definitions of abnormal mental functioning have been proposed over the years, but none of them has won universal acceptance. Still, most of the definitions do have common features, often called "the four *D*'s": deviance, distress, dysfunction, danger. Psychologically abnormal patterns of functioning, then, are those that, in a given context, are *deviant*— that is, different, extreme, unusual, perhaps even bizarre; *distressful,* or unpleasant and upsetting to the individual; *dysfunctional,* or disruptive to the person's ability to conduct daily activities in a constructive manner; and possibly *dangerous.* This definition provides a useful starting point from which to explore the phenomena of psychological abnormality, although, as we shall see, it has significant limitations.

DEVIANCE

Abnormal mental functioning is functioning that is deviant, but deviant from what? Before any functioning can be said to be deviant, there must be a standard of appropriate and normal functioning against which behavior can be measured. Miriam's behavior, thoughts, and emotions are different from those that are considered normal in our place and time. We do not expect normal people to cry themselves to sleep every night, to wish themselves dead, or to endure paralyzing depression and anxiety. Similarly, Brad's obedience to voices that no one else can hear contradicts our expectation that normal people perceive

Along the Niger River, men of the Wodaabe tribe don elaborate makeup and costumes to attract women. In Western society, the same behavior would violate behavioral norms and probably be judged abnormal.

only the material world accessible to everyone's five senses.

In short, abnormal behavior, thoughts, and emotions are those that violate a society's ideas about proper functioning. Each society establishes *norms*— explicit and implicit rules for appropriate conduct. Behavior that violates legal norms is called criminal. Behavior, thoughts, and emotions that violate norms of psychological functioning are called abnormal. Typically, the norms of psychological functioning focus on conduct that is common in a society, such as our society's expectations that people will remember important events in their lives. Sometimes, however, a society may value certain psychological deviations, such as superior intelligence and extreme selflessness, and may include these forms of functioning within its norms.

This focus on social values as a yardstick for measuring deviance suggests that judgments of abnormality vary from society to society. A society's norms emerge from its particular *culture*—its history, values, institutions, habits, skills, technology, and arts. Thus a society whose culture places great value on competition and assertiveness may accept aggressive behavior, whereas one that highly values courtesy, cooperation, and gentleness may consider aggressive behavior unacceptable and even abnormal. A society's values may also change over time, causing its views of what is psychologically abnormal to change as well. In Western society, for example, a woman's participation in the business or professional world was considered inappropriate and strange a hundred years ago, but today the same behavior is valued.

Judgments of abnormality depend on specific circumstances as well as on psychological norms. The description of Miriam, for example, might lead us to conclude that she is functioning abnormally. Certainly her unhappiness is more intense and pervasive than that of most of the people we encounter every day. Before you conclude that this woman is abnormal, however, consider that Miriam lives in Lebanon, a country pulled apart by years of combat. The happiness she once knew with her family vanished when her husband and son were killed. Miriam used to tell herself that the fighting had to end soon, but as year follows year with only temporary respites, she has stopped expecting anything except more of the same.

In this light, Miriam's reactions do not seem inappropriate. If anything is abnormal here, it is her situation. Sometimes overwhelming or unusual situations elicit reactions that appear abnormal out of context but are understandable in the surroundings in which they occur. Many things in our world elicit intense reactions—large-scale catastrophes and disasters, rape, child abuse, war, terminal illness, chronic pain. Is there an "appropriate" way to react to such things? Should we ever call reactions to them abnormal?

As we shall see in Chapter 4, today's leading diagnostic system holds that some people's reactions to traumatic events are indeed excessive, and assigns such cases to the category of either *acute stress disorder* or *posttraumatic stress disorder.* Many theorists deny the merits of these categories, however, arguing that there can be no such thing as an excessive reaction to brutality or catastrophe.

DISTRESS

Even functioning that is considered unusual and inappropriate in a given context does not necessarily qualify as abnormal. According to many clinical theorists, one's behavior, ideas, or emotions usually have to cause one distress before they can be labeled abnormal. Consider the Ice Breakers, a group of people in Michigan who go swimming in lakes throughout the state every weekend from November through February. The colder the weather, the better they like it. One man, a member of the group for seventeen years, says he loves the challenge. Man against the elements. Mind versus body. A 37-year-old lawyer believes that the weekend shock is good for her health. "It cleanses me," she says. "It perks me up and gives me strength for the week ahead." Another

It is virtually impossible to stay in control of one's emotions when exposed each day to unspeakable horrors and pressures. Rather than signs of abnormality, the fear, panic, and depression of these individuals, caught in the middle of Serbian-Croatian conflicts and atrocities, are understandable reactions to an abnormal situation.

avid Ice Breaker likes the special feelings the group brings to him. "When we get together, we know we've shared something special, something no one else understands. I can't even tell most of the people I know that I'm an Ice Breaker. They wouldn't want anything to do with me. A few people think I'm a space cadet."

Certainly these people are different from most of us, but they are enjoying themselves. Far from experiencing distress, they feel invigorated and challenged. The absence of internal distress must cause us to hesitate before we conclude that these people are functioning abnormally.

Should we conclude, then, that feelings of distress must always be present before a person's functioning can be considered abnormal? Not necessarily. Some people who function abnormally may maintain a relatively positive frame of mind. Consider once again Brad, the young man who hears mysterious voices. Brad does experience severe distress over the coming invasion and the changes he feels forced to make in the way he lives. But what if he felt no such anxiety? What if he greatly enjoyed listening to the voices, felt honored to be chosen, and looked forward to the formidable task of saving the world? Shouldn't we still consider his functioning abnormal? As we shall discover in Chapter 8, people who are described as manic often feel just wonderful, yet still are diagnosed as psychologically disturbed. Indeed, in many cases it is their euphoria and disproportionate sense of well-being that help make them candidates for this diagnosis.

DYSFUNCTION

Abnormal behavior tends to interfere with daily functioning. It so upsets, distracts, or confuses its victims that they cannot care for themselves properly, participate in ordinary social relationships, or work effectively. Brad, for example, has quit his job, left his family, and prepared to withdraw from the productive and meaningful life he once led to an empty and isolated existence in a distant apartment.

Here again one's culture plays a role in the definition of abnormality. Our society holds that it is important to carry out daily activities in an effective, self-enhancing manner. Thus Brad's behavior is likely to be regarded as abnormal and undesirable, whereas that of the Ice Breakers, who continue to perform well at their jobs and maintain appropriate family and social relationships, would probably be considered unusual but not a sign of psychological abnormality.

In Val d'Isère, France, these students bury themselves in snow up to their necks. Far from experiencing distress, they are engaging in a Japanese practice designed to open their hearts and enlarge their spirits, so diagnosticians are unlikely to judge them to be abnormal.

Of course, dysfunction alone does not necessarily indicate psychological abnormality. Some people in our society (Gandhi, Dick Gregory, or Cesar Chavez, for example) fast or in other ways deprive themselves of things they need, in order to protest social injustice. Far from being classified as psychologically abnormal, they are widely viewed as caring, sacrificing, even heroic.

DANGER

Perhaps the ultimate in psychological dysfunctioning is behavior that becomes dangerous to oneself or others. A pattern of functioning that is marked by carelessness, poor judgment, hostility, or misinterpretation can jeopardize one's own well-being and that of many other people. Brad, for example, seems to be endangering himself by his diet and others by his stockpile of arms and ammunition.

Although danger to oneself or others is usually cited as a criterion of abnormal psychological functioning, research suggests that it is more often the exception than the rule. Despite popular misconceptions, most people struggling with anxiety, depression, and even bizarre behavioral patterns pose no immediate danger to themselves or to anyone else.

Difficulties in Defining Psychological Abnormality

Efforts to define psychological abnormality typically raise as many questions as they answer. The major difficulty is that the very concept of abnormality is relative, dependent on the norms and values of the society in question. Ultimately a society *selects* the general criteria for defining abnormality and then *interprets* them in order to judge the normality or abnormality of each particular case.

One clinical theorist, Thomas Szasz (1987, 1961), places such emphasis on society's role that he finds the whole concept of mental illness to be invalid. According to Szasz, the deviations that society calls abnormal are simply "problems in living," not signs of something inherently wrong within the person. Societies, he is convinced, invent the concept of mental illness to justify their efforts to control or change people whose unusual patterns of functioning threaten the social order. In extreme cases the category even serves to justify the removal of those individuals from society. Although most theorists do not share Szasz's extreme view, they agree that the concept of abnormal psychological functioning is elusive, embedded as it is in the values and institutions of a society.

Even if we assume that psychological abnormality is a valid concept and that such abnormalities are unhealthy, a society may have difficulty agreeing on a definition and applying it consistently. If a certain behavior—excessive consumption of alcohol among college students, say—is common in a society, the society may fail to recognize that the behavior is often a symptom of deviance, a source of distress, highly dysfunctional, and dangerous. Thousands of college students throughout the United States are so dependent on alcohol that it interferes greatly with their personal and academic functioning, causes them significant discomfort, places their health in jeopardy, and often endangers them and the people around them. Yet their problem often goes unnoticed, certainly undiagnosed, by college administrators, other students, and health professionals. Alcohol consumption is so much a part of the college subculture that it is easy to overlook drinking behavior that has become abnormal.

Conversely, a society may have trouble distinguishing an abnormality that requires intervention from an eccentric individuality that others have no right to interfere with. From time to time, we see or hear about people who behave in ways we consider strange—a woman who keeps dozens of cats in her apartment or a man who lives alone and rarely talks to anyone. The behavior of these people is deviant and may well be distressful and dysfunctional, yet such propensities are thought of by most professionals as eccentric rather than abnormal. When does an unusual pattern of functioning cross the line from eccentricity to psychological abnormality? When is it deviant, distressful, and dysfunctional *enough* to be considered abnormal? Such questions may be impossible to answer.

Problematic as they are, it is important to keep these questions in mind. While we may agree that abnormal patterns of functioning are those that are deviant, distressful, dysfunctional, and sometimes dangerous in a given context, we should always be aware of the ambiguity and subjectivity of this definition. We should also be aware that few of the current categories of abnormality are as clear-cut as they may seem. Most of them continue to be debated within the clinical community (APA, 1994).

Calling the concept of mental illness a "myth," psychiatrist Thomas Szasz believes that societies apply the label to persons whose deviant behaviors confuse others and may seem to threaten the emotional and physical well-being of others. According to Szasz (1961), "looking for evidence of illness is like searching for evidence of heresy: Once the investigator gets into the proper frame of mind, anything may seem to him to be a symptom of mental illness."

■ Past Views ■ and Treatments

The current facts and figures on psychological abnormality are almost numbing. It is estimated that in any

Behavior considered disturbing during one period in history may be admired, and even envied, during another. When Owen Totten showed off his suit of 5,600 buttons in 1946, his hoarding behavior, even more than his choice of attire, raised many eyebrows. Today, he might be one of the many entrepreneurs thriving in the business of collectibles.

given year 28 to 30 percent of the adults and at least 17 percent of the children and adolescents in the United States display serious mental disturbances and are in need of clinical treatment (Kessler et al., 1994; Regier et al., 1993; Kazdin, 1993; Zill & Schoenborn, 1990; Costello, 1989). It is estimated that at least thirteen of every hundred adults have a significant anxiety disorder, six suffer from profound depression, five display a personality disorder (inflexible and maladaptive personality traits that cause significant impairment or distress), one is schizophrenic (loses touch with reality for an extended period of time), one ex-

periences the brain deterioration of Alzheimer's disease, and close to ten abuse alcohol or other drugs. Add to these figures as many as 600,000 suicide attempts, 600,000 rapes, and 2.9 million cases of child abuse in this country each year, and it becomes apparent that abnormal psychological functioning is a major, indeed pervasive, problem in our society (Regier et al., 1993; McCurdy & Daro, 1993; Koss, 1993; McIntosh, 1991). Beyond these disturbances, most people have difficulty coping at various points in their lives and experience high levels of tension, demoralization, or other forms of psychological discomfort. At such times, they too experience at least some of the distress associated with psychological disorders.

Given such numbers, it is tempting to conclude that something about today's world fosters emotional maladjustment. Some observers have suggested that the rapid changes and technical advancements of our world create enormous pressure and emotional turmoil—that recent developments in the fields of science, communication, and business bring with them such problems as the threat of nuclear warfare, economic instability, and job insecurity. Some have also argued that our world lacks key elements that used to help people bear life's pressures. The family, for instance, is no longer the reliable haven it was once assumed to be: divorce has become more common and adult children now move farther away from their families (see Figure 1–1). A continuing decline in religious, community, and other support systems forces people to face a changing, sometimes frightening world on their own.

Although the special pressures of modern life probably do contribute to psychological dysfunctioning, they are hardly its primary cause. Every society, past and present, has contended with psychological abnormality. Some disorders, such as schizophrenia, occur at the same rate in all societies. Others, such as anxiety disorders and depression, fluctuate from society to society, partly as a reflection of societal differences, and yet are common in all societies. Relatively few psychological disorders are unique to specific societies, caused and defined by the particular pressures those societies engender. In short, abnormal psychological functioning, rampant though it may be, is hardly unique to today's world.

Perhaps the proper place to begin our examination of abnormal behavior and treatment is in the past. If we look back, we may better understand such issues as the nature of psychological abnormality, which of its features remain constant in human societies and which vary from place to place and from time to time, how each society has struggled to understand and treat it, and how present-day ideas and treatments can

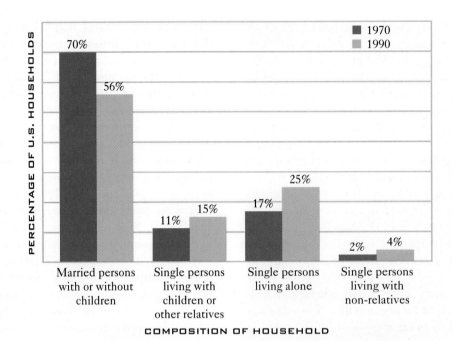

FIGURE 1–1 *The percentage of households headed by a married couple has declined significantly in recent years, while the percentage headed by a single person has increased. Some clinicians suggest that these changes leave millions of persons, particularly children, with fewer personal resources for coping with stress. (Adapted from Bureau of the Census, Statistic Abstract of the United States, 1992.)*

often be traced to the past (see Box 1–2). A look backward makes it clear that progress in the understanding and treatment of mental disorders has hardly been a steady movement forward. Indeed, many of the inadequacies and controversies that characterize the clinical field today parallel those of the past. At the same time, looking back can help us to appreciate the full significance of the field's most recent developments and breakthroughs, as well as the importance of the journey that lies ahead.

ANCIENT VIEWS AND TREATMENTS

Most of our knowledge of prehistoric societies has been acquired indirectly and is based on inferences made from archaeological discoveries. Historians scrutinize the unearthed bones, artwork, artifacts, and other remnants of ancient societies to find clues about those societies' customs, beliefs, and daily life. Their conclusions are at best tentative and always subject to revision in the face of new discoveries.

Thus our knowledge of how ancient societies viewed and treated people with mental disturbances is limited. Historians have concluded that prehistoric societies probably viewed abnormal behavior as the work of evil spirits. They believe that people in these

early societies explained the phenomena around and within them as resulting from the actions of magical, sometimes sinister beings who shaped and controlled the world. In particular, these early people viewed the human body and mind as sites of battle between external forces, and they viewed behavior, both normal and abnormal, as the outcome of battles between good and evil spirits, positive forces and demons, or good and bad gods. Often abnormal behavior was interpreted as a victory by evil spirits, and the cure for such behavior was to force the spirits to leave the person's body.

This supernatural view of abnormality may have begun as far back as the Stone Age, a half-million years ago. Some skulls from that period recovered by archaeologists in Europe and South America show evidence of an operation called **trephination,** in which a stone instrument, or **trephine,** was used to cut away a circular section of the skull. Some historians have surmised that this operation was performed as a treatment for severe abnormal behavior—either "hallucinatory" experiences, in which people saw or heard things not actually present, or "melancholic" reactions, characterized by extreme sadness and immobility—and that the purpose of opening the skull was to release the evil spirits that were supposedly causing the problem (Selling, 1940).

In recent years other historians have raised doubts about this interpretation of trephination, suggesting that the procedure may have been used to remove bone splinters or blood clots caused by stone weapons during tribal warfare (Maher & Maher, 1985). Whether or not Stone Age people actually believed that evil spirits caused abnormal behavior, archaeological findings from later societies clearly indicate that ancient people did eventually account for such behavior by reference to demonic possession. The early writings of the Egyptians, Chinese, and Hebrews, for example, attribute psychological deviance to the influences of evil spirits or demons. This view of abnormality is frequently expressed in the Bible, which describes how an evil spirit from the Lord affected King Saul and how David feigned madness in order to convince his enemies that he was inhabited by divine forces.

People of these early societies practiced *exorcism* as a common treatment for abnormality. The idea was to coax the evil spirits to leave or to make the person's body an uncomfortable place for the spirits to live. A *shaman*, or priest, might recite prayers, plead with the evil spirits, insult them, perform magic, make loud noises, or have the person drink noxious solutions. If these techniques failed, a more extreme form of exorcism, such as whipping or starvation, was employed.

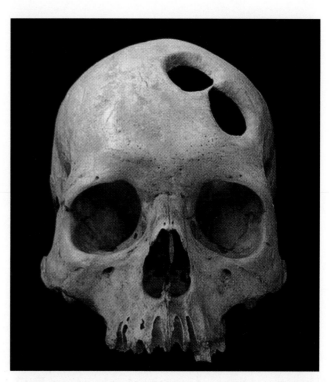

The skulls of some Stone Age people show evidence of trephination, possibly for the purpose of releasing evil spirits and thus remedying abnormal psychological functioning. Signs of bone regrowth around the two holes in this skull suggest that this patient survived two trephinations.

GREEK AND ROMAN VIEWS AND TREATMENTS

In the years when the Greek and Roman civilizations flourished (from 500 B.C. to A.D. 500), philosophers and physicians described a number of mental disorders. Heading the list were *melancholia,* a condition marked by unshakable sadness; *mania,* a state of euphoria and frenzied activity; *dementia,* a general intellectual decline; *hysteria,* a physical ailment with no apparent physical cause; *delusions,* blatantly false beliefs; and *hallucinations,* the experience of imagined sights or sounds as if they were real. Although demonological views concerning mental and physical illness were still widespread, philosophers and physicians began to offer alternative explanations during this period.

Hippocrates (460–377 B.C.), often called the father of modern medicine because of his teaching that illnesses had natural causes rather than metaphysical ones, saw abnormal behavior as a disease caused by internal medical problems rather than by conflicts between gods or spirits. Specifically, he believed that brain pathology was the culprit, and that it resulted — like all other forms of disease, in his view — from an imbalance of four fluids, or *humors,* that flowed through the body: *yellow bile, black bile, blood,* and *phlegm.* An excess of yellow bile, for example, caused mania; an excess of black bile was the source of melancholia.

To treat these patterns of psychological dysfunctioning, Hippocrates sought to correct the underlying physical pathology. He believed, for instance, that the excess of black bile underlying melancholia could be reduced by a quiet life, a vegetable diet, temperance, exercise, celibacy, and even bleeding.

Hippocrates' focus on internal causes for abnormal behavior was later shared and in some cases extended by the great Greek philosophers Plato (427–347 B.C.) and Aristotle (384–322 B.C.) and by influential Greek physicians. The physician Aretaeus (A.D. 50–130), for example, suggested that emotional problems could also cause abnormal behavior. The physician Galen (A.D. 130–200) systematically distinguished emotional causes (such as financial worries and loss of love) from medical ones (such as head injuries and alcohol abuse). Roman physicians adopted such theories when Rome gained power over the ancient world.

These theories led Greek and Roman physicians to treat mental illnesses with a mixture of medical and psychological techniques. Before resorting to such severe methods as bleeding patients or restraining them with mechanical devices, many Greek physicians first prescribed a warm and supportive atmosphere, music, massage, exercise, and baths. Roman physicians were even more emphatic about the need to soothe and comfort patients who had mental disorders.

EUROPE IN THE MIDDLE AGES: DEMONOLOGY RETURNS

That demonological views were dismissed by noted physicians and scholars during the Greco-Roman period was not enough to shake many people's belief in demons. Such views and practices never disappear entirely, and with the decline of Rome they enjoyed a strong resurgence (see Box 1–3).

After the Roman Empire fell, a growing distrust of science spread throughout Europe. In the years from A.D. 500 to 1350, the period known as the Middle Ages, the power of the clergy increased greatly. The church rejected secular studies and scientific forms of investigation, and it controlled all education. Religious beliefs—themselves highly superstitious and demonological at this time—came to dominate all aspects of life. Planetary phenomena, world events, and personal experience and conduct were all interpreted in religious terms, often as a conflict between good and evil, God and the devil. Deviant behavior of all kinds was seen as evidence of an association with Satan. Although some scientists and physicians still argued for medical explanations and treatments for mental dysfunctioning, their views carried little weight in this atmosphere of rigid religious doctrine.

The Middle Ages were centuries of great stress and anxiety, times of war, urban uprisings, and plagues.

THE SHIP OF FOOLS

When George Washington was a child, he threw a silver dollar across the Potomac River. Or so we are told. Historians (and anyone who has seen the Potomac River) realize that this cannot be a historical account of a real event; it is apocryphal, a tale intended to convey certain characteristics of the man and the times. Such stories abound in the literature of all fields, from history to astronomy and botany and, yes, even abnormal psychology. Though the stories serve a purpose, it is the nature of scientists to wish to separate fact from fiction. In recent years, one set of investigators discovered that one of the most widely accepted accounts from the history of abnormal psychology was actually a puff of smoke.

In 1967 the French historian Michel Foucault published a book containing

accounts of the early treatment of mentally ill persons. He wrote of "ships of fools" that carried such people from port to port during the Middle Ages, sometimes simply drifting at sea. Many later texts on abnormal psychology included similar accounts. For years the story of the ship of fools was widely used to illustrate how society segregated and mistreated the mentally ill. The ships were seen as precursors of the mental hospitals of the

nineteenth and twentieth centuries.

Then over a decade ago psychologists Winifred and Brendan Maher (1982) searched the records of the period that is reported to have spawned the ship of fools. The Mahers did find scattered accounts of people who exhibited bizarre behavior and were shipped off to be unloaded somewhere else, but such isolated incidents do not constitute compelling evidence that there ever was a ship of fools. These investigators worked long and hard to find logs, diaries, or other kinds of documentation. They wrote to Foucault and to the libraries that were purported to have relevant holdings. No evidence was found. How, then, had the notion of a ship of fools emerged and spread?

Like all rumors, this one started as a good story and became embellished in

Imbalances of the four humors were believed by Hippocrates to affect personality and cause mental disorders. In these depictions of two of the humors, (left) yellow bile drives a choleric husband to beat his wife; (right) black bile renders a man melancholic and sends him to bed.

the telling. Foucault apparently relied heavily on a book published in 1494 by Sebastian Brant titled *Das Narrenschiff* (The Ship of Fools), a volume of allegorical poems illustrated by woodcuts. Of the 112 poems and woodcuts, four depict medieval ships carrying people wearing the traditional clothing of the court jester. Brant's book addressed only moral and ethical issues of the times. He did not intend to depict people with mental disorders, yet his woodcuts set Foucault to thinking.

When the Mahers contacted the director of a Danish museum with holdings relevant to the period, their inquiry was respectfully treated as an April Fool's Day joke: "You know as well as we that Sebastian Brant's didactic-satirical poem 'Das Narrenschiff' (1494)—and all its imitations—is just a literary fiction without base in reality." The letter also described a practice that originated in Nuremburg in 1350: During the Shrovetide celebrations a procession of jugglers, dancers, clowns, and soldiers wended its antic way through the streets while costumed revelers

danced and made merry. Since 1475 this procession had included a ship—a real one—that was hoisted on wheels and carted down the street; it represented hell, which the revelers dared to mock only during these three days before the start of Lent (when presumably they would repent). The museum director concluded that Brant must have known of this procession and based his woodcuts on it.

Because Brant's title and woodcuts meshed with historians' notions about the medieval world's perceptions of mental illness, Foucault interpreted them as describing an actual practice of shipping off boatloads of "fools." Subsequent writers apparently parroted Foucault unquestioningly and even gave the impression that the existence of ships of fools was a well-known fact, not something they had read about in a single source.

It is not unusual for researchers and writers to cite secondary sources. Imagine Scientist Jones, who writes a paper in which she includes historical information on the topic she is researching. Scientist Kalawi performs a

follow-up study in which he discusses Jones's findings and includes the history he has read in Jones's paper. Author Chin writes a textbook and cites Jones's research, which he knows only from having read Kalawi's paper. Then Author Winshel reads Chin and cites Jones. Because Winshel does not go to the original source—Jones herself—he has no idea whether or not the information is well founded or has been embellished or reformulated in later citations.

This all too common practice can lead to the dissemination of misinformation and the creation of powerful myths that can influence our perceptions of a field. The result may be a blurring of the vision needed to conduct unbiased, rigorous studies that will advance our knowledge of the field. Perhaps the only benefit to be derived from the dissemination of apocryphal stories is the opportunity it provides for careful researchers to hone their investigative skills in debunking the myths—and to force transgressors to admit having been taken for a ride on a ship of fools.

BOX 1-3

THE MOON AND THE MIND

As time passes, every society undergoes changes that redefine both the range of behavior considered normal and the explanations for behavior that deviates from that norm. The belief in demonic possession as a cause of abnormal behavior has been replaced by the assumption that biological, psychological, and sociocultural explanations can be found; yet some ancient theories still have a hold on us today. One is the persistent belief that the phases of the moon have a direct effect on personality and behavior.

It is the very error of the moon;
She comes more near the earth than
    she was wont,
And makes men mad.

When Shakespeare put these words into the mouth of Othello, he was expressing the thoughts of people of centuries past and centuries to come. Primitive societies believed that the moon had magical, mystical powers

Moonstruck maidens dance in the town square in this eighteenth-century French engraving.

and that its changes portended events of many kinds. The moon had the power to impregnate women, to make plants grow, and to drive people crazy. Later societies also accepted the power of the moon to affect behavior, and they applied the terms "lunatic" and "lunacy" to the person and the

behavior to capture their moonlike, or lunar, qualities. Today many respected institutions and people actively support the idea that behavior is affected by the phases of the moon. The belief that bizarre behavior increases when the moon is full is so prevalent that a successful lunar newsletter services a number of hospitals and law enforcement officials, warning them to be wary on nights of a full moon (Gardner, 1984).

Anecdotal evidence abounds: New York City police officers note more violent and bizarre crimes during the full moon, and hospitals claim to experience an increase in births. One has linked the full moon to the onset of ulcers and heart attacks. A Wall Street broker has for years used the schedule of the full moon as a guide in giving investment advice—successfully (Gardner, 1984).

Scientists, who generally rely on explanations other than the inherent mystical prowess of the moon, have

---

Social institutions were in constant flux. People blamed the devil for these hard times and feared him intensely; specifically, they feared being possessed by the devil. The incidence of abnormal behavior apparently increased dramatically during this stressful period. Melancholia, guilt, and anxiety were common problems. In addition, there were outbreaks of so-called **mass madness,** in which large numbers of people apparently shared the same delusions and hallucinations. Two prevalent forms were *tarantism* and *lycanthropy.*

Tarantism (also known as **St. Vitus's dance**) was a mania that occurred throughout Europe between A.D. 900 and 1800. Groups of people would suddenly start to jump around, dance, and go into convulsions (Sigerist, 1943). They might bang into walls or roll on the ground. Some dressed oddly, others tore off their clothing. All were convinced that they had been bitten and possessed by a wolf spider, now called a tarantula, and they sought to cure their disorder by performing a dance called a "tarantella." The dance

was thought to have originated in the town of Taranto in southern Italy; thus the name tarantism.

People with *lycanthropy* thought they were possessed by wolves or other animals. They acted wolflike and might imagine that fur was growing all over their bodies. Stories of lycanthropes, more popularly known as *werewolves,* have been passed down to us and continue to capture the imagination of moviemakers and their audiences.

Many earlier demonological treatments for psychological abnormality reemerged in the Middle Ages. Once again the key to a cure was to rid the person's body of the devil that possessed it, and techniques of exorcism were revived. Clergymen, who generally were in charge of treatment during this period, would plead, chant, or pray to the devil or evil spirits. They might also administer holy water or bitter-tasting concoctions, and if these techniques did not work, they might try to insult the devil and attack his pride (Satan's great weakness, they believed). These milder forms of exorcism were sometimes supplemented by

advanced many theories to make sense of a lunar effect on human behavior. Some say that since the moon causes the tides of the oceans, it is reasonable to expect that it has a similar effect on the bodily fluids of human beings (whose composition is more than 80 percent water). The increase in births might therefore be explained by the force of the moon on the expectant mother's amniotic fluid. Similar tidal and gravitational effects have been posited to explain the increase in bizarre behavior in people who may already be viewed as unbalanced. Aside from the abundant anecdotal evidence, a study of clams by the biologist Frank Brown is often cited to show the ubiquitous power of the moon over the behavior of creatures of the earth (Gardner, 1984). Brown reports moving a group of clams gathered in Connecticut to a laboratory in the landlocked city of Evanston, Illinois. At first the clams opened up to receive food during the times of high tide in Connecticut, as they had done all of their lives. After two weeks, however, the clams

adopted an eating pattern that followed what would have been the schedule of high tides in Evanston—if Evanston had actually had any tides.

This evidence may seem to be compelling, but any hypothesis devised to explain the alleged effects of the moon is only a tentative assumption; none has been substantiated. Some researchers, less moonstruck, have performed rigorous statistical analyses of the actual numbers of births, crimes, and incidents of bizarre behavior that occur during the full moon. They have found no evidence supporting the influence of the moon on any of a variety of scales of human behavior (Byrnes & Kelly, 1992; Kelly et al., 1990; Culver et al., 1988). In view of this lack of support for the popular lunacy theory, some scientists have suggested that we drop the entire question. Other researchers, undissuaded, claim that the lack of statistical evidence is not the problem—the problem has been the researchers' failure to look at the right variables, to use the appropriate measures, or to look at

enough days both before and after the full moon. It has been suggested, for example, that studies of mental hospital admissions should take a lag time into account because the moon-induced behavior may not be identified or the individuals may not be processed until a week or more after the full moon (Cyr & Kalpin, 1988).

Most clinicians remain convinced that moon-induced abnormality is a myth, yet some people do exhibit strange behavior during the full moon, or report strange sensations or increased sexual desire. The simplest explanation for these phenomena is most likely the most accurate. Personal belief, superstition, and bias can be powerful motivators of behavior. For people who already exhibit abnormal behavior or are searching for an excuse or a cue to break with society's behavioral norms, the historical belief in the power of the moon provides a convenient outlet. One waives personal responsibility by attributing one's behavior to the moon. The cause of lunacy may lie far less in the heavens than in our minds.

torture in the form of starvation, whipping, scalding, or stretching—a procedure calculated to drive the devil out of the afflicted person's body.

As the Middle Ages drew to a close, demonology and its methods began to lose favor. Cities throughout Europe grew larger, and municipal authorities gained more power and increasingly took over the secular activities of the church. Among other responsibilities, they began to administer hospitals and direct the care of sick people, including the mentally ill. Medical views of psychological abnormality started to gain prominence once again. In the British lunacy trials of the late thirteenth century, for example, a natural cause such as a "blow to the head" or "fear of one's father" was likely to be cited as responsible for the behavior that had brought people to trial to determine their sanity (Neugebauer, 1979, 1978). During these same years, many of those with mental disturbances were treated in medical hospitals, under municipal authority, rather than by the clergy. The Trinity Hospital in England, for example,

Exorcism, one of the earliest forms of treatment for mental disorders, was revived during the Middle Ages. In this detail from the fifteenth-century painting St. Catherine Exorcising a Possessed Woman, *the devil flees after being cast out of the woman's head by the saint.*

Peasant women are overcome by St. Vitus's dance in this engraving, based on a fifteenth-century painting by Pieter Brueghel.

was established to treat "madness" along with other kinds of illness, and to keep the mad "safe until they are restored to reason" (Allderidge, 1979, p. 322).

THE RENAISSANCE AND THE RISE OF ASYLUMS

Demonological views of abnormality continued to decline in popularity during the first half of the period of flourishing cultural and scientific activity known as the Renaissance (approximately 1400–1700). During these years the German physician Johann Weyer (1515–1588) apparently became the first medical practitioner to specialize in mental illness. Weyer rejected the demonological explanations of abnormality. Although some of his colleagues scoffed at his view that the mind was as susceptible to sickness as the body, his work represents the age's renewed commitment to science and skeptical thinking, and Weyer is now considered the founder of modern psychopathology.

Care for many of the mentally ill continued to improve in this atmosphere. In England many mental patients were kept at home, and their families were given extra funds by the local parish. Across Europe a number of religious shrines became consecrated to

the humane and loving treatment of the mentally ill. Perhaps the best-known such shrine was at Gheel in Belgium. Beginning in the fifteenth century, people with mental problems ranging from melancholia to hallucinations came from all over the world to visit this shrine (actually established centuries earlier) for psychic healing. Local residents welcomed them into their homes, and many pilgrims stayed on to form the world's first "colony" of mental patients. This colony set the stage for many of today's community mental health and foster care programs, and Gheel continues to demonstrate that people with mental disorders can respond to loving care and respectful treatment (Aring, 1975, 1974). Many patients still live in foster homes there until they recover, interacting with and accepted by the town's other residents.

Unfortunately, the improvements in the care for the mentally ill began to fade by the mid-sixteenth century. Municipal authorities eventually discovered that only a small percentage of the severely mentally ill could be accommodated in private homes and community residences, and that medical hospitals were too few and too small. They began to convert some hospitals and monasteries into *asylums,* institutions to which mentally ill people could be sent. These institutions apparently began with the best of intentions—to provide care for the mentally ill. Once the asylums started to overflow with patients, however, they abandoned such goals and eventually became virtual prisons in which patients were held in filthy

London's Bethlehem Hospital, or Bedlam, was typical of insane asylums from the sixteenth to the nineteenth centuries. In his eighteenth-century work from A Rake's Progress, *William Hogarth depicted the asylum as a chaotic place where ladies and gentlemen of fashion came to marvel at the strange behavior of the inmates.*

Belief in demonological possession persisted into the Renaissance. A great fear of witchcraft, for example, swept Europe during the fifteenth and sixteenth centuries. Tens of thousands of people, most of them women, were thought to have made a pact with the devil for the power to visit storm, flood, pestilence, sexual impotence, crop failure, and other kinds of harm upon their enemies. Although "the typical accused witch was . . . an impoverished woman with a sharp tongue and a bad temper" (Schoeneman, 1984), a few appear to have had mental disorders that caused them to act strangely (Zilboorg & Henry, 1941). In this illustration from a book by the French demonologist Pierre de Lancre, Satan takes the form of a five-horned goat (upper right) and presides over a witches' Sabbath.

and degrading conditions and treated with unspeakable cruelty.

The first asylum was founded in Muslim Spain in the early fifteenth century, but the idea did not gain full momentum until the next century. In 1547 the Bethlehem Hospital in London was given to the city by Henry VIII for the exclusive purpose of confining the mentally ill. Here patients, restrained in chains, cried out their despair for all to hear. The hospital actually became a popular tourist attraction; people were eager to pay to look at the howling and gibbering inmates. The hospital's name, pronounced "Bedlam" by the local people, has become synonymous with a chaotic uproar. Asylums later founded in Mexico, France, Russia, the United States, and Austria offered similar forms of "care." In the Lunatics' Tower in Vienna, for example, mental patients were kept in narrow hallways by the outer walls, so that tourists outside could look up and see them. In La Bicêtre in Paris, patients were shackled to the walls of cold, dark, dirty cells with iron collars and given spoiled food that could be sold nowhere else (Selling, 1940).

The inability of municipal authorities to address the needs of large numbers of mental patients was not the only reason for the poor quality of care in asylums. A lingering fear of people with mental disorders was also responsible. Even the best-intentioned theoreticians and caregivers really knew very little about mental illness, and large segments of the population still equated abnormal behavior with possession by mysterious and dangerous forces. The authorities addressed these concerns by restraining and confining mental patients.

The medical theories and cures developed during this period were often misguided and unintentionally cruel. In the eighteenth century no less a figure than Benjamin Rush (1745–1813), often called the father of American psychiatry, treated some mental patients by drawing blood from their bodies, a technique used to treat many bodily illnesses during that period. This treatment was meant to lower an excessively high level of blood in the brain, which Rush believed was causing the patient's abnormal behavior (Farina, 1976). Thus suspicion, ignorance, and erroneous medical theory conspired to keep asylums a shameful form of care until the late eighteenth century.

THE NINETEENTH CENTURY: REFORM AND MORAL TREATMENT

As 1800 approached, the treatment of people with mental disorders began to change for the better once

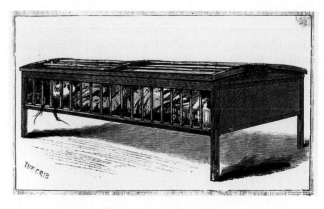

Outrageous devices and techniques continued in use even during the reforms of the nineteenth century. Many patients, particularly violent ones, were repeatedly placed in the "crib," a precursor to the straitjacket.

Philippe Pinel supervised the unchaining of the insane at La Bicêtre asylum in Paris in 1793. His successful reforms helped usher in a worldwide movement of humanitarian "moral treatment" for those with mental disorders.

again. Historians usually point to the Parisian asylum of La Bicêtre (for male patients) as the initial site of asylum reform. In 1793, during the French Revolution, Philippe Pinel (1745–1826) was named the chief physician there. Influenced by the humane work of Jean-Baptiste Pussin, the hospital's superintendent of incurable patients, Pinel began a series of reforms. He argued that the patients were sick people whose mental illnesses should be treated with support and kindness rather than with chains and beatings. He would not allow patients to be abused and tortured. He unchained them and gave them the liberty of the hospital grounds, replaced the dark dungeons with sunny, well-ventilated rooms, and offered patients support and advice. Pinel described his philosophy this way:

> I viewed the scene that was opened to me with the eyes of common sense and unprejudiced observation. . . . I then discovered that insanity was curable in many instances, by mildness of treatment and attention to the state of the mind exclusively, and when coercion was indispensable, that it might be very effectually applied without corporal indignity. . . . I saw, with wonder, the resources of nature when left to herself, or skillfully assisted in her efforts. . . . Attention to these principles alone will, frequently, not only lay the foundation of, but complete a cure: while neglect of them may exasperate each succeeding paroxysm, till, at length, the disease becomes established . . . and incurable. The successful application of moral regimen exclusively, gives great weight to the supposition that, in a majority of instances, there is no organic lesion of the brain.
>
> *(Pinel [1806] 1962, pp. 5, 108–109)*

Pinel's new approach did indeed prove remarkably successful. Many patients who had been locked away in darkness for decades were now enjoying fresh air and sunlight and being treated with dignity. Some improved significantly over a short period of time and were released. Pinel and Pussin were later commissioned to reform yet another Parisian mental hospital, La Salpetrière (for female patients), and had excellent results there as well. Jean Esquirol (1772–1840), Pinel's student and successor, followed his teacher's lead and went on to help establish ten new mental hospitals that operated by the same principles.

During this period an English Quaker named William Tuke (1732–1819) was bringing similar reforms to northern England. In 1796 he founded the York Retreat, a rural estate where about thirty mental patients were lodged as guests in quiet country houses and treated with a combination of rest, talk, prayer, and manual work. He believed that this form of treatment would have better results than mechanical restraints or medical interventions based on unsupported notions about the human brain (see Figure 1–2).

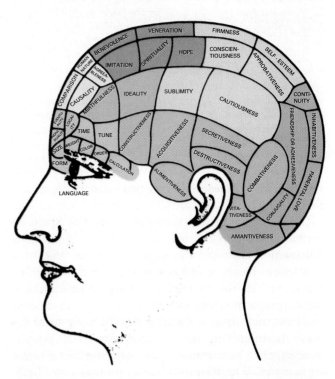

FIGURE 1–2 *Nineteenth-century efforts to understand abnormal behavior in less demonological terms were not always scientifically sound. One hypothesis was called "phrenology." Franz Joseph Gall (1758–1828) and his followers held that the brain consisted of discernible portions, each responsible for some aspect of personality. Phrenologists tried to assess personality by feeling bumps and indentations on a person's head.*

Benjamin Rush, considered the father of American psychiatry, embraced and helped spread the concept of moral treatment during the early nineteenth century. Some of his earlier treatment techniques, however, such as the "restraint chair," reflected contemporary medical thought.

THE SPREAD OF MORAL TREATMENT The methodologies espoused by Pinel and Tuke, called *moral treatment* by their contemporaries because of their emphasis on moral guidance and on humane and respectful intervention, caught on throughout Europe and the United States. Increasingly, mental patients were perceived as potentially productive human beings whose mental functioning had broken down under overwhelming personal stresses. These unfortunate (rather than possessed) people were considered deserving of individualized care that included discussions of their problems, constructive activities, work, companionship, and quiet.

The person most responsible for the early spread of moral treatment in the United States was Benjamin Rush. As we have seen, Rush's earlier medical views were sometimes naive and harsh by today's standards, but he fully embraced the concept of moral treatment when he learned about it. As an eminent physician at Pennsylvania Hospital, he limited his practice and study to mental illness, and he developed numerous humane approaches to treatment. One of his innovations was to require the hospital to hire intelligent and sensitive attendants to work closely with patients,

reading and talking to them and taking them on regular walks. He also suggested that it would be of therapeutic value for doctors to give small gifts to their patients now and then.

Rush was a most influential physician. He wrote the first American treatise on mental illness, *Medical Inquiries and Observations upon the Diseases of the Mind*, published in 1812, and organized the first American course in psychiatry. It was a Boston schoolteacher named Dorothea Dix (1802–1887), however, who was largely responsible for the passage of new laws that mandated more humane care for the mentally ill. In 1841 Dix had gone to teach Sunday school at a local prison and been shocked by the conditions she saw there. Her interest in prison conditions broadened to include the plight of poor and mentally ill people throughout the country. A powerful campaigner, Dix went from state legislature to state legislature speaking of the horrors she had observed and calling for reform. In an address to the Massachusetts legislature, she proclaimed that people with mental disorders were being "confined within this Commonwealth, in cages, closets, cellars, stalls, pens; chained, naked, beaten with rods, and lashed into obedience"

(Deutsch, 1949, p. 165). She told the Congress of the United States that mentally ill people across the country were still being "bound with galling chains, bowed beneath fetters and heavy iron balls attached to drag chains, lacerated with ropes, scourged with rods and terrified beneath storms of execration and cruel blows" (Zilboorg & Henry, 1941, pp. 583–584).

Dix's campaign, which spanned the decades from 1841 until 1881, led to new laws and the appropriation of funds to improve the treatment of the mentally ill. Each state was made responsible for developing effective public mental hospitals. Dix personally helped establish thirty-two of these *state hospitals*, all intended to offer moral treatment (Bickman & Dokecki, 1989; Viney & Zorich, 1982). Similar government-funded hospitals for people with mental disorders were established throughout Europe and run by humanitarian principles.

For years the moral treatment movement improved the care of the mentally ill. By the 1850s, a number of mental hospitals throughout Europe and America reported that most of their patients were recovering and being released (Bockoven, 1963). At Worcester

From 1841 to 1881 the Boston schoolteacher Dorothea Dix tirelessly campaigned for more humane forms of treatment in mental hospitals throughout the United States. Her efforts led to new laws providing for the establishment of public mental hospitals, supported and administered by the states.

State Hospital in Massachusetts, for example, almost 60 percent of long-term mental patients and more than 70 percent of short-term mental patients recovered enough to be discharged. Unfortunately, social changes at the end of the nineteenth century eventually altered this promising situation for the worse.

THE DECLINE OF MORAL TREATMENT As we have observed, the treatment of abnormality has followed a crooked path. Over and over again, relative progress has been followed by serious decline. Viewed in this context, the decline of moral treatment in the late nineteenth century is disappointing but not surprising.

Several factors contributed to this decline (Bockoven, 1963). One was the reckless speed with which the moral treatment movement had advanced. As mental hospitals multiplied, severe money and staffing shortages developed. In the United States, for example, legislatures could not allocate sufficient funds to run the state hospitals properly, so too few professionals were hired, and recovery rates declined. Fewer and fewer patients left the hospitals each year, and admissions continued unabated; overcrowding became a major problem. Under these conditions it was impossible to provide the individual care and genuine concern that were the cornerstones of moral treatment.

The basic assumptions of moral treatment also contributed to its downfall. The major one was that patients would begin to function normally if they were treated with dignity and if their physical needs were met. For some patients this was indeed the case. Others, however, needed more effective treatments than any that had yet been developed. Many of these people remained hospitalized till they died.

A further reason for the decline of moral treatment was the emergence of a new wave of prejudice against the mentally ill. As more and more patients disappeared into the large, distant mental hospitals, the public once again came to view them as strange and dangerous and were less open-handed when it came to making donations or allocating government funds. Moreover, by the end of the nineteenth century, many of the patients entering public mental hospitals in the United States were impoverished foreign immigrants, and as such were already the objects of considerable prejudice. The public had little interest in helping people from other countries; even the hospital personnel were less conscientious and caring in treating them.

By the early years of the twentieth century, the moral treatment movement had ground to a halt in both the United States and Europe. Public mental hospitals provided minimal custodial care and medical interventions that did not work and became more overcrowded and less effective every year. Long-term hospitalization became the norm once again.

This state of affairs was powerfully described in 1908 by Clifford Beers (1876–1943) in *A Mind That Found Itself,* an autobiographical account of his severe mental disturbance and of the "treatment" he received in three mental institutions. Beers revealed that he and other patients were repeatedly restrained, beaten, choked, and spat on in these places, all in the name of treatment. His moving account aroused both public and professional sympathy, and he went on to found the National Committee for Mental Hygiene, dedicated to educating the public about mental illness and the need for proper treatment. Unfortunately, although Beers's work brought considerable attention to the terrible conditions in public mental hospitals, these institutions were not to improve significantly for forty more years.

THE SOMATOGENIC PERSPECTIVE   Another significant trend that began in the late nineteenth

Overcrowding and limited funding led to the formation of back wards in state hospitals across the United States during the early twentieth century. In a throwback to the asylums of earlier times, many patients languished in these wards for years, without therapy or hope of recovery.

century was a dramatic resurgence of the ***somatogenic perspective,*** the view that abnormal psychological functioning has physical causes. This perspective had at least a 2,300-year history—remember Hippocrates' view that abnormal behavior resulted from brain pathology and an imbalance of humors, or bodily fluids—but it had never before been so widely accepted as it was at this time.

Two factors were responsible for this development. One was the work of Emil Kraepelin (1856–1926), a German researcher who was interested in the relation between abnormal psychological functioning and such physical factors as fatigue, and who had measured the effects of various drugs on abnormal behavior. In 1883 Kraepelin published an influential textbook, which he revised seven times over the next forty years, expounding the view that physical factors are responsible for mental dysfunctioning. In addition, as we shall see in Chapter 4, he constructed the first system for classifying abnormal behavior. He identified various ***syndromes,*** or clusters of symptoms, listed their organic causes, and discussed their expected course.

The rise of the somatogenic perspective was also spurred by a series of biological and anatomical discoveries. One of the most important discoveries was that general paresis was caused by an organic disease, syphilis. ***General paresis*** is an irreversible, progressive disorder with both physical and mental symptoms, including paralysis and delusions of grandeur. The organic basis of the disorder had been suspected as early as the mid-nineteenth century, but concrete evidence did not emerge until decades later.

In 1897 Richard von Krafft-Ebing (1840–1902), a German neurologist, established a direct link between general paresis and syphilis. He inoculated paretic patients with matter from syphilis sores and found that none of the patients developed symptoms of syphilis. Their immunity could have been caused only by an earlier case of syphilis, and since all paretic patients were immune to syphilis, Krafft-Ebing theorized that it was the cause of their general paresis. Finally, in 1905, Fritz Schaudinn (1871–1906), a German zoologist, discovered that the microorganism *Treponema pallida* was responsible for syphilis, which in turn was responsible for general paresis.

The work of Kraepelin and the new understanding of general paresis led many researchers and practitioners to suspect that organic factors were responsible for many mental disorders, perhaps all of them. These theories and the possibility of quick and effective medical solutions for mental disorders were especially welcomed by those who worked in mental hospitals, where patient populations were now growing at an alarming rate.

Despite the general optimism, the biological approach yielded largely disappointing results throughout the first half of the twentieth century. True, many medical treatments were developed and applied to hospitalized mental patients during that time, but most of the techniques—extraction of teeth, tonsillectomy, hydrotherapy (alternating hot and cold baths to soothe excited patients), insulin coma shock (a "therapeutic" convulsion induced by lowering a patient's blood sugar level with insulin), and lobotomy (a surgical severing of certain nerve fibers in the brain)—proved ineffectual. Not until the middle of the century, when a number of effective medications were finally discovered, did the somatogenic perspective truly begin to pay off for patients with mental disorders.

THE PSYCHOGENIC PERSPECTIVE Yet another important trend to unfold in the late nineteenth century was the emergence of the *psychogenic perspective,* the view that the chief causes of abnormal functioning are psychological. This perspective, too, has a long history. The Roman scholar Cicero (106–43 B.C.) held that psychological disturbances could cause bodily ailments, and the Greek physician Galen believed that many mental disorders were caused by fear, disappointment in love, and other psychological events. However, the psychogenic perspective did not command a significant following until the late nineteenth century, when studies of the technique of hypnotism demonstrated the potential of this line of inquiry.

Hypnotism is the inducing of a trancelike mental state in which a person becomes extremely suggestible. Its use as a means of treating psychological disorders actually dates back to 1778. In that year an Austrian physician named Friedrich Anton Mesmer (1734–1815) established a clinic in Paris where he employed an unusual treatment for patients with *hysterical disorders,* mysterious bodily ailments that had no apparent physical basis. Mesmer's patients would sit in a darkened room filled with music. In the center of the room, a tub held bottles of chemicals from which iron rods protruded. Suddenly Mesmer would appear in a flamboyant costume, withdraw the rods, and touch them to the troubled area of each patient's body. Surprisingly, a number of patients did seem to be helped by this treatment. Their pain, numbness, or paralysis disappeared.

Mesmer's treatment, called *mesmerism,* was so controversial that eventually he was banished from Paris. But few could deny that at least some patients did

Friedrich Anton Mesmer, standing at the back and to the right in this painting, works with hysterical patients in his Parisian clinic. He believed that hysterical ailments were caused by an improper distribution of magnetic fluid in the body and that touching an ailing part of the body with an iron rod would help correct the problem.

The nineteenth century's leading neurologist, Jean Charcot, gives a clinical lecture on hypnotism and hysterical disorders in Paris. Initially Charcot did not believe that the two were related, but research later convinced him that hysterical symptoms could indeed be induced by hypnotic suggestion and that hysterical disorders were ordinarily caused by psychological processes.

indeed improve after being mesmerized. Several scientists believed that Mesmer was inducing a trance-like state in his patients, and that this state caused their symptoms to disappear. In later years the technique was developed further and relabeled *neurohypnotism,* later shortened to *hypnotism* (from *hypnos,* the Greek word for sleep).

It was not until years after Mesmer died, however, that many researchers had the courage to investigate hypnotism and its effects on hysterical disorders. By the late nineteenth century, two competing views had emerged. That a technique that enhanced the power of suggestion could alleviate hysterical ailments indicated to one group of scientists that hysterical disorders must be caused by the power of suggestion—that is, by the mind—in the first place. Another group of scientists believed that hysterical disorders had subtle physiological causes. Jean Charcot (1825–1893), an eminent Parisian neurologist, argued that hysterical disorders were the result of degeneration in portions of the brain.

The experiments of two physicians practicing in the city of Nancy in France finally seemed to settle the matter. Hippolyte-Marie Bernheim (1840–1919) and Ambroise-Auguste Liébault (1823–1904) showed that hysterical disorders could actually be induced in otherwise normal subjects while they were under the influence of hypnosis. That is, they could make nor-

mal people experience deafness, paralysis, blindness, or numbness by means of hypnotic suggestion—and they could remove these artificially induced symptoms by the same means. In short, they established that a mental process—hypnotic suggestion—could both cause and cure a physical dysfunction. Most leading scientists, including Charcot, finally embraced the idea that hysterical disorders were largely psychological in origin.

Among those who studied the effects of hypnotism on hysterical disorders was a Viennese doctor named Josef Breuer (1842–1925). He discovered that his hypnotized patients sometimes awoke free of hysterical symptoms after speaking freely about past traumas under hypnosis. During the 1890s Breuer was joined in his work by another Viennese physician, Sigmund Freud (1856–1939). As we shall see in greater detail in Chapter 2, Freud's work eventually led him to develop the theory of **psychoanalysis,** which holds that many forms of abnormal and normal psychological functioning are psychogenic. He believed that conflict between powerful psychological processes operating at an unconscious level is the source of much abnormal psychological functioning. Freud also developed the technique of psychoanalysis, a form of discussion in which psychotherapists help troubled people acquire insight into their psychological conflicts. Such insight, he believed, would help the patients overcome their psychological problems.

To many observers, Freud's psychogenic perspective seemed the antithesis of the increasingly influential somatogenic view of mental dysfunctioning. Thus his ideas were initially criticized and rejected. Freud persevered in his writings, studies, and practice, however, and by the early twentieth century psychoanalytic theory and treatment were widely accepted throughout the Western world. Indeed, it would be difficult to name another school of thought that has had greater influence on Western culture.

Freud and his followers applied the psychoanalytic treatment approach primarily to patients with relatively modest mental disorders, problems of anxiety or depression that did not require hospitalization. These patients visited psychoanalytic therapists in their offices for sessions of approximately an hour and then went about their daily activities—a format of treatment now known as *outpatient therapy.*

The psychoanalytic approach had little effect on the treatment of severely disturbed patients in mental hospitals. This type of therapy requires levels of clarity, insight, and verbal skill beyond the capabilities of most such patients. Moreover, psychoanalysis often takes years to be effective, and the overcrowded and understaffed public mental hospitals could not accommodate such a leisurely pace.

■ CURRENT ■ TRENDS

It would hardly be accurate to say that we now live in a period of widespread enlightenment or dependable treatment. Indeed, a recent survey found that 43 percent of respondents believe that people bring on mental disorders themselves and 35 percent consider them to be caused by sinful behavior (Murray, 1993). Nevertheless, the past forty years have brought significant changes in the understanding and treatment of abnormal functioning. There are more theories and types of treatment, more research studies, more information, and, perhaps for these reasons, more disagreements about abnormal functioning today than at any time in the past. In some ways the study and treatment of mental disorders have come a long way, but in other respects, clinical scientists and practitioners are still struggling to make a difference. The current era of abnormal psychology can be said to have begun in the 1950s.

NEW TREATMENTS FOR THE SEVERELY DISTURBED

In the 1950s researchers discovered a number of new *psychotropic medications*—drugs that primarily affect the brain and alleviate many symptoms of mental dysfunctioning. They included the first *antipsychotic drugs,* to correct grossly confused and distorted thinking; *antidepressant drugs,* to lift the mood of severely depressed people; and *antianxiety drugs,* to reduce tension and anxiety.

With the discovery and application of these drugs, many severely disturbed patients in mental hospitals—the same patients who had languished there for years—began to show signs of significant improvement. Hospital administrators, encouraged by the effectiveness of the drugs and pressured by a growing public outcry over the high cost of care and the terrible conditions in public mental hospitals, began to discharge patients almost immediately.

Since the discovery of these medications, mental health professionals in most of the developed nations of the world have followed a policy of *deinstitutionalization,* and hundreds of thousands of patients have been released from public mental hospitals. On any given day in 1955, close to 600,000 people were confined in public mental institutions across the United States. Today the daily patient population in the same hospitals is around 100,000 (Manderscheid & Sonnenschein, 1992) (see Figure 1–3).

In short, outpatient care has now become the primary mode of treatment for people with severe psychological disturbances as well as for those with more moderate problems. When severely impaired people do require institutionalization, the current practice is to provide them with short-term hospitalization and then return them to the community. Ideally, they are then provided with outpatient psychotherapy and medication monitoring in community mental health centers. Other community programs such as supervised residences (halfway houses) and vocational rehabilitation centers may also be available.

This recent emphasis on community care for people with severe psychological disturbances, called the *community mental health approach,* will be discussed further in Chapters 5 and 16. Although the approach has been very helpful for many patients, unfortunately too few community facilities and programs are available to address the needs of severely disturbed people in the United States. As a result, hundreds of thousands fail to make lasting recoveries, and are shuffled back and forth between the mental hospital

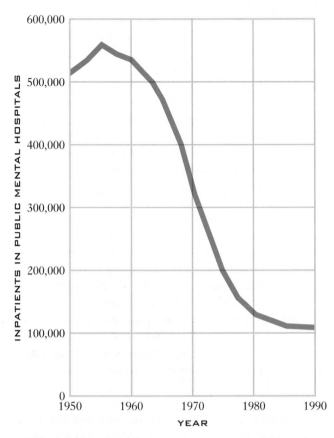

FIGURE 1–3 *The number of patients (100,000) now hospitalized in public mental hospitals in the United States is a small fraction of the number hospitalized in 1955. (Adapted from Manderscheid & Sonnenschein, 1992; Torrey, 1988.)*

since the 1950s. Outpatient care has continued to be the preferred mode of treatment for these people, and the number and types of facilities that offer such care have expanded to meet the need.

Before the 1950s, almost all outpatient care took the form of *private psychotherapy,* an arrangement by which an individual directly paid a psychotherapist for counseling services. This tended to be an expensive form of treatment, available almost exclusively to the affluent. Since the 1950s, however, many medical health insurance plans have expanded coverage to include private psychotherapy, a trend that current government health-care reforms have pledged to continue, so that this service is now more widely available to people with more modest incomes (Levin, 1992). In addition, outpatient therapy has become increasingly available in a variety of relatively inexpensive settings—community mental health centers, crisis intervention centers, family service centers, and other social service agencies (Olfson, Pincus, & Dial, 1994). The new settings have spurred a dramatic increase in the number of persons seeking outpatient care for psychological problems.

The growth in the use of outpatient services by both severely disturbed and less disturbed persons is seen in Figure 1–4. In 1955 approximately 23 percent of people treated for psychological disturbances were treated as outpatients. Today that figure is about 94 percent.

Another change in outpatient care since the 1950s has been the development of specialized programs that focus exclusively on one kind of psychological

and the community. After they are released from the hospital, they receive at best minimal care and often wind up living in decrepit rooming houses or on the streets. It is now estimated that 200,000 persons with severe psychological disturbances are, in fact, homeless on any given day (Manderscheid & Rosenstein, 1992), while another 50,000 are prison inmates (NIMH, 1992). Their virtual abandonment is truly a national disgrace.

NEW TREATMENT SETTINGS FOR LESS SEVERE PSYCHOLOGICAL PROBLEMS

The treatment picture for people with less severe psychological disturbances has been more positive

Therapy for people with mild or moderate psychological disturbances is widely available today in individual, group, or family therapy formats. It can be obtained privately or in less expensive government-subsidized mental health centers and agencies.

1950'S (1.7 MILLION CASES)

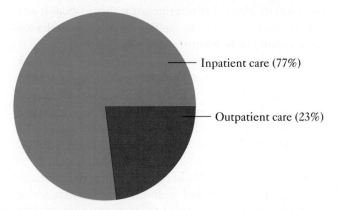

Inpatient care (77%)

Outpatient care (23%)

TODAY (22 MILLION CASES)

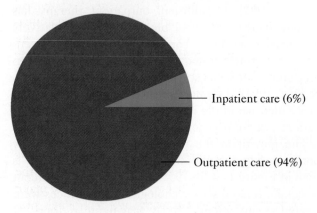

Inpatient care (6%)

Outpatient care (94%)

FIGURE 1–4 *The percentage of mental health patients who are treated on an outpatient basis has grown steadily since the 1950s. "Inpatient care" refers to treatment in state, county, and private mental hospitals, general hospitals, and Veterans Administration hospitals. "Outpatient care" refers to treatment by community mental health agencies, private therapists, day-care centers, and specialists in social and vocational rehabilitation. (Adapted from Regier et al., 1993; Narrow et al., 1993; Witkin et al., 1990; NIMH, 1983.)*

problem. We now have, for example, suicide prevention centers, substance abuse programs, eating disorder programs, phobia clinics, and sexual dysfunction programs. Practitioners in these programs acquire the kind of expertise that can come only by concentrating one's efforts in a single area.

TODAY'S PRACTITIONERS

Today a variety of professionals offer help to people with psychological problems—both those who warrant a clinical diagnosis and others who simply want

to learn how to cope with the stresses in their lives (Murstein & Fontaine, 1993). This, too, represents a change from the situation of several decades ago. Before the 1950s, psychotherapy was the exclusive province of *psychiatrists*, physicians who had completed three to four additional years of training after medical school (a residency) in the treatment of abnormal mental functioning. After World War II, however, the demand for mental health services expanded more rapidly than the ranks of psychiatrists, so other professional groups stepped in to fill the need.

Prominent among those other groups are *clinical psychologists*—professionals who earn a doctorate in clinical psychology by completing four years of graduate training in abnormal functioning and its treatment and also complete a one-year internship at a mental hospital or mental health agency. Before their professional responsibilities expanded into the area of treatment, clinical psychologists were principally assessors and researchers of abnormal functioning. Some of them still specialize in those activities.

Other important groups that provide psychotherapy and related services are *counseling psychologists, educational psychologists, psychiatric nurses, marriage therapists, family therapists,* and—the largest group—*psychiatric social workers* (see Figure 1–5). Each of these specialties requires completion of its own graduate training program (Dial et al., 1992). Theoretically, each specialty conducts therapy in a distinctive way, but in reality there is considerable overlap in the ways practitioners of the various specialties work. Indeed, the individual differences within a given professional group are sometimes much greater than the general differences between groups.

EMERGING PERSPECTIVES

One of the most significant developments in the understanding and treatment of abnormal psychological functioning has been the emergence of numerous, often competing theoretical perspectives. Before the 1950s, the *psychoanalytic* perspective, with its emphasis on unconscious conflicts as the cause of psychopathology, was dominant. Then the discovery of effective psychotropic drugs in the 1950s brought new stature to the somatogenic, or *biological*, view of abnormality.

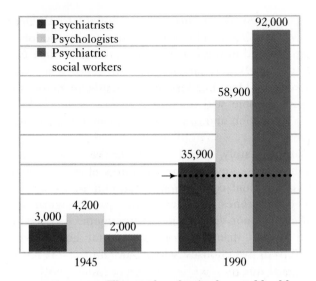

FIGURE 1-5 *The number of trained mental health professionals in the United States has multiplied more than twenty times since World War II, while the total population has yet to double. Today a therapist is more likely to be a psychiatric social worker than a psychiatrist or psychologist. (Adapted from Dial et al., 1992, 1990; Knesper & Pagnucco, 1987; AMA, 1986.)*

As we shall see in Chapter 2, other influential perspectives have also emerged since the 1950s, including the *behavioral, cognitive, humanistic-existential,* and *sociocultural* schools of thought, which explain and treat abnormality in very different ways. At present no single perspective dominates the clinical field as the psychodynamic perspective once did. All these theories have influenced the current understanding and treatment of abnormal functioning.

THE EMPHASIS ON RESEARCH

One final important development in the study and treatment of mental disorders since World War II has been a heightened appreciation of the need for systematic research. As numerous theories and forms of treatment have been proposed, researchers have tried to single out the concepts that best explain and predict abnormal behavior, to determine which treatments are most effective, and to discover whether they should be modified and, if so, how.

Today well-trained clinical researchers are conducting studies in academic institutions, laboratories, mental hospitals, mental health centers, and other clinical settings throughout the world. Their work has already yielded important discoveries and changed many of our ideas about abnormal psychological functioning. Just as important, it repeatedly demonstrates that properly conducted research is essential for continued progress in the study and practice of abnormal psychology.

■ ORGANIZATION ■ OF THE TEXT

The study and treatment of abnormal psychological functioning are exciting and confusing in equal measure. New ideas, discoveries, and refinements are continually being introduced, and the proliferating theories and treatment approaches can be difficult to evaluate and compare.

How, then, should we proceed in our examination of the various kinds of psychological abnormality? To begin with, we need to appreciate the basic perspectives and tools that today's scientists and practitioners find most useful. This is the task we turn to in the next several chapters: Chapter 2 introduces the major views in the clinical field, showing how today's professionals conceptualize abnormal psychological functioning; Chapter 3 looks at the way abnormal functioning is studied—the research tools and strategies used to test the various theories and treatments; Chapter 4 explores how the various patterns of abnormality are assessed and diagnosed; and Chapter 5 introduces the many forms of treatment currently employed by clinical practitioners.

Later chapters examine the major categories of psychological abnormality and the leading treatments for each of them. In the final chapter we shall see how the science of abnormal psychology and its professionals address current social issues and interact with legal, social, and other institutions in today's society.

SUMMARY

■ **THE FELD** devoted to the scientific study of abnormal behavior is called ***abnormal psychology.*** Its goals are to understand and to treat abnormal patterns of functioning.

Abnormal patterns of psychological functioning are generally considered to be those that are *deviant, distressful, dysfunctional,* and *dangerous.* Behavior must be considered in the context in which it occurs, however; behavior considered deviant in one set of circumstances may be the norm in another. The very concept of abnormality is relative, dependent on the *norms* and *values* of the society in question.

■ THE HISTORY of mental illness, stretching back to the origins of humankind, provides any number of clues to the nature of psychological abnormality. Historians have concluded that prehistoric societies probably viewed abnormal behavior as the work of evil spirits. There is evidence that Stone Age cultures used *trephination,* a primitive form of brain surgery, to treat abnormal behavior. People of early societies also sought to drive out evil spirits by *exorcism.*

Physicians of the Greek and Roman empires describe such conditions as *melancholia, mania, dementia, hysteria, delusions,* and *hallucinations,* all of which correspond to conditions recognized today. Hippocrates, considered the father of modern medicine, believed that abnormal behavior was due to an imbalance of the four *humors,* or bodily fluids: black bile, yellow bile, blood, and phlegm. Treatment consisted of correcting the underlying physical pathology through diet and lifestyle.

In the Middle Ages, Europeans resurrected the demonological explanation of abnormal behavior. The combination of great strife in the Western world and the preeminence of the clergy during this period contributed to the popular view that mental disorders were the work of the devil. As the Middle Ages drew to a close, demonology and its harsh treatment methods began to lose favor. Medical views of psychological abnormality started to grow in prominence, and many people with mental disorders were treated in hospitals instead of by the clergy.

Care of the people with mental disorders continued to improve during the Renaissance. A number of religious shrines became consecrated to the humane treatment of such individuals and set the stage for today's community mental health and foster care programs. This enlightened approach was short-lived, however, and by the middle of the sixteenth century persons with mental disorders were being warehoused in *asylums.*

Care of the mentally ill started to improve again in the nineteenth century, initially at La Bicêtre asylum in Paris. There Philippe Pinel treated inmates as people suffering from an illness that required support and kindness. Similar reforms were brought to England by William Tuke. This *moral treatment* methodology was adopted in the United States by Benjamin Rush. In the mid- and late nineteenth century in Massachusetts, Dorothea Dix spearheaded a movement to ensure people with mental disorders of legal rights and protection and to establish *state hospitals* for their care.

Unfortunately, moral treatment was costly, and as hospitals grew, it became impossible to provide the individual care and genuine concern that were its cornerstones. Besides, some psychological disorders did not yield to moral treatment. As a result, the system disintegrated and mental hospitals reverted to warehouses where the inmates received minimal care.

The late nineteenth century saw the return of the *somatogenic perspective,* the view that abnormal psychological functioning is rooted in physical causes. This change was brought about by two factors: (1) the work of the German medical researcher Emil Kraepelin and (2) anatomical and biological discoveries that increased the precision of medical practice, particularly the finding that *general paresis* was caused by the organic disease syphilis.

The same period saw the emergence of the *psychogenic perspective,* the view that the chief causes of abnormal functioning are psychological. One of the key developments at this time was the use of *hypnotism* to treat patients with hysterical disorders. Later work by the physicians Bernheim and Liébault showed that hysterical disorders could be induced under hypnosis, suggesting that a physical disorder could have a purely psychological basis. The related finding by the Viennese doctor Josef Breuer that patients sometimes awoke free of hysterical symptoms after speaking candidly about past traumas during hypnosis served as one of the bases for the future work of another well-known Viennese doctor, Sigmund Freud. Freud's *psychoanalytic* approach eventually gained wide acceptance and influenced future generations of researchers and practitioners.

■ THE PAST FORTY YEARS have brought significant changes in the understanding and treatment of abnormal functioning. In the 1950s, researchers discovered a number of new *psychotropic drugs,* drugs that affect perceptions and emotions. Their success led to a policy of *deinstitutionalization,* under which hundreds of thousands of patients were released from public mental hospitals. One result of this movement was a focus on *outpatient treatment* as the primary approach for helping persons with mental disorders. The wider availability of outpatient care and private therapy has led to a dramatic increase in treatment for patients suffering less severe psychological disturbances.

Today a variety of professionals offer help to people with psychological problems. Each specialty requires completion of its own graduate training. In addition, over the past forty years numerous theoretical perspectives have emerged. Each explains and treats abnormality in a distinctive way. At the same time, there has been a heightened appreciation of the need for systematic research in the clinical field.

Topic Overview

MODELS OF
PSYCHOLOGICAL
ABNORMALITY

hilip Berman, a 25-year-old single unemployed former copy editor for a large publishing house, . . . had been hospitalized after a suicide attempt in which he deeply gashed his wrist with a razor blade. He described [to the therapist] how he had sat on the bathroom floor and watched the blood drip into the bathtub for some time before he telephoned his father at work for help. He and his father went to the hospital emergency room to have the gash stitched, but he convinced himself and the hospital physician that he did not need hospitalization. The next day when his father suggested he needed help, he knocked his dinner to the floor and angrily stormed to his room. When he was calm again, he allowed his father to take him back to the hospital.

The immediate precipitant for his suicide attempt was that he had run into one of his former girlfriends with her new boyfriend. The patient stated that they had a drink together, but all the while he was with them he could not help thinking that "they were dying to run off and jump in bed." He experienced jealous rage, got up from the table, and walked out of the restaurant. He began to think about how he could "pay her back."

Mr. Berman had felt frequently depressed for brief periods during the previous several years. He was especially critical of himself for his limited social life and his inability to have managed to have sexual intercourse with a woman even once in his life. As he related this to the therapist, he lifted his eyes from the floor and with a sarcastic smirk said, "I'm a 25-year-old virgin. Go ahead, you can laugh now." He has had several girlfriends to date, whom he described as very attractive, but who he said had lost interest in him. On further questioning, however, it became apparent that Mr. Berman soon became very critical of them and demanded that they always meet his every need, often to their own detriment. The women then found the relationship very unrewarding and would soon find someone else.

During the past two years Mr. Berman had seen three psychiatrists briefly, one of whom had given him a drug, the name of which he could not remember, but that had precipitated some sort of unusual reaction for which he had to stay in a hospital overnight. Another gave him three treatments with electroconvulsive therapy (ECT) because he complained that he was suicidal. These had no effect on his mood but, according to him, caused significant memory loss. He saw the third psychiatrist for three months, but while in treatment he quit his job and could no longer afford the therapy. When asked why he quit, he said, "The bastards were going to fire me anyway." When asked whether he realized he would have to drop out of therapy when he quit his job, he said, "What makes you think I give a damn what happens to therapy?" Concerning his hospitalization, the patient said that "It was a dump," that the staff refused to listen to what he had to say or to respond to his needs, and that they, in fact, treated all the patients "sadistically." The referring doctor corroborated that Mr. Berman was a difficult patient who demanded that he be treated as special, and yet was hostile to most staff members throughout his stay. After one angry exchange with an aide, he left the hospital without leave, and subsequently signed out against medical advice.

Mr. Berman is one of two children of a middle-class family. His father is 55 years old and employed in a managerial position for an insurance company. He perceives his father as weak and ineffectual, completely dominated by the patient's overbearing and cruel mother. He states that he hates his mother with "a passion I can barely control." He claims that his mother used to call him names like "pervert" and "sissy" when he was growing up, and that in an argument she once "kicked me in the balls." Together, he sees his parents as rich, powerful, and selfish, and, in turn, thinks that they see him as lazy, irresponsible, and a behavior problem. When his parents called the therapist to discuss their son's treatment, they stated that his problem began with the birth of his younger brother, Arnold, when Philip was 10 years old. After Arnold's birth Philip apparently became an "ornery" child who cursed a lot and was difficult to discipline. Philip recalls this period only vaguely. He reports that his mother once was hospitalized for depression, but that now "she doesn't believe in psychiatry."

Mr. Berman had graduated from college with average grades. Since graduating he had worked at three different publishing houses, but at none of them for more than one year. He always found some justification for quitting. He usually sat around his house doing very little for two or three months after quitting a job, until his parents prodded him into getting a new one. He described innumerable interactions in his life with teachers, friends, and employers in which he felt offended or unfairly treated, . . . and frequent arguments that left him feeling bitter . . . and spent most of his time alone, "bored." He was unable to commit himself to any person, he held no strong convictions, and he felt no allegiance to any group.

The patient appeared as a very thin, bearded, and bespectacled young man with pale skin who maintained little eye contact with the therapist and who had an air of angry bitterness about him. Although he complained of depression, he denied other symptoms of the depressive syndrome. He seemed preoccupied with his rage at his parents, and seemed particularly invested in conveying a despicable image of himself. When treatment was discussed with Mr. Berman, the therapist recommended frequent contacts, two or three per week, feeling that Mr. Berman's potential for self-injury, if not suicide, was rather high. The judgment was based not so much on the severity of Mr. Berman's depression as on his apparent impulsivity, frequent rages, childish disregard for the consequences of his actions, and his pattern of trying to get other people to suffer by inflicting injury on himself. Mr. Berman willingly agreed to the frequent sessions, but not because of eagerness to get help. "Let's make it five sessions a week," he said. "It's about time my parents paid for all that they've done to me."

(Spitzer et al., 1983, pp. 59–61)

Philip is clearly a troubled person, but how did he come to be that way? How do we explain his many problems? In confronting this question, we must acknowledge its complexity. First, we must appreciate the wide range of complaints we are trying to understand: Philip's depression and anger, his social failures, his lack of employment, his distrust of those around him, and the problems within his family. All point to less than optimal psychological functioning, and each problem can be the source of others. Second, we must sort through all kinds of potential primary causes, internal and external, biological and interpersonal, past and present, and decide which, if any, is the key to the rest: which is having the biggest impact on Philip's behavior. Such are the challenges facing every investigator of abnormal psychology, whether in research or clinical practice, and the answers have been many and varied, some based on philosophical assumptions, others on principles of science, some resting mostly on subjective experience, others on quantitative empirical evidence.

Although we may not recognize it, we are all probably using implicit theoretical frameworks of our own as we attempt to explain Philip's conduct. Over the course of our lives, each of us has developed a perspective that helps us make sense of the things other people say and do. Such a perspective helps us to explain other people's behavior to our own satisfaction. In science, such perspectives are known as *paradigms* or *models*. Each is an explicit set of basic assumptions that gives structure to an area under study and sets forth guidelines for its investigation (Kuhn, 1962). The paradigm or model influences what the investigators observe, what questions they ask, what information they consider legitimate, and how they interpret this information (Lehman, 1991). To understand how a clinical scientist explains and treats a specific pattern of abnormal functioning, such as Philip's pattern of symptoms, we must appreciate the model that shapes his or her view of abnormal functioning.

Until recent times the models used by clinical scientists were usually monolithic and culturally determined; that is, a single model was paramount in a particular place and at a particular time, couched in the metaphors of the prevalent worldview. Recall the demonological model used to explain abnormal functioning during the Middle Ages. Practitioners of that period constructed a model of mental abnormality that borrowed heavily from their society's preoccupation with religion, superstition, and warfare. Each person was viewed as a battleground where the devil challenged God. Abnormal behavior signaled the devil's victory.

Medieval practitioners would have seen the devil's guiding hand in Philip Berman's efforts to commit suicide, and they would have pointed to demonological possession as the ultimate explanation for Philip's feelings of depression, rage, jealousy, and hatred. Actually, some might have disagreed on the immediate cause of Philip's abnormal behavior, arguing that he was possessed not by the devil but by a tarantula or a wolf, but they would not have doubted that some form of possession was involved. Similarly, while medieval practitioners might have employed any of a variety of treatments to help Philip overcome his difficulties, from prayers to bitter drinks to whippings, all such treatments would have had the common purpose of driving a foreign spirit from his body. Anyone brazen enough to offer an explanation or treatment outside of the accepted demonological model would have been harshly criticized for failure to appreciate the fundamental issues at stake.

Whereas one model was dominant during the Middle Ages, a variety of models are being employed to explain and treat abnormal functioning today. This state of affairs has resulted from shifts in values and beliefs over the past half century and from improvements in the quality and quantity of clinical research. At one end of the spectrum is the *biological model,* which cites organic processes as the key to human behavior. At the other end is the *sociocultural model,* which scrutinizes the effect of society and culture on individual behavior. In between are four models that focus on more psychological and personal dimensions of human functioning: the *psychodynamic model,* which looks at people's unconscious internal dynamics and conflicts; the *behavioral model,* which empha-

sizes ingrained behavior and the ways in which it is learned; the *cognitive model,* which concentrates on the process and content of the thinking that underlies behavior; and the *humanistic-existential model,* which stresses the role of values and choices in determining human individuality and fulfillment.

Rooted as they are in different assumptions and concepts, the models are sometimes in conflict, and proponents of one perspective often scoff at the "naive" interpretations, investigations, and treatment efforts of the rest. At the same time, none of the models is complete in itself; each focuses primarily on one aspect of human functioning, and none is capable of explaining the entire spectrum of abnormality.

■ THE ■ BIOLOGICAL MODEL

Philip Berman is a biological being. His thoughts and feelings are the results of complex biochemical and bioelectrical processes throughout his brain and body. Biological theorists believe that a full understanding of his psychological functioning, including any psychological abnormality, must include an understanding of the biological basis of his thoughts, emotions, and behavior. Not surprisingly, they believe that once this understanding is attained, the most effective interventions for problems such as Philip's will be biological ones.

ORIGINS OF THE BIOLOGICAL MODEL

As we saw in Chapter 1, the roots of the biological model of abnormal psychology stretch back thousands of years. A variety of factors combined to enhance its status during the late nineteenth century: the dissemination of Kraepelin's somatogenic theory; research that linked the mental illness called general paresis to an organic illness, syphilis; and several breakthroughs in medical technology. The model's influence has continued to grow throughout the twentieth century and has been especially strong since the 1950s, when researchers learned to refine or synthesize several kinds of effective *psychotropic drugs,* drugs that have their dominant effect on thought processes and in some cases alleviate symptoms of mental dysfunctioning. Antianxiety, antidepressant, antipsychotic, and other psychotropic medications have changed the treatment picture for mentally disturbed persons and are now used frequently, either as an adjunct to other forms of therapy or as the dominant form of treatment for psychological dysfunction.

BIOLOGICAL EXPLANATIONS OF ABNORMAL BEHAVIOR

Adopting a medical perspective, biological theorists view abnormal behavior as an illness brought about by malfunctioning parts of the organism. Specifically, they point to a malfunctioning brain as the primary cause of abnormal behavior (Gershon & Rieder, 1992; Rosen, 1991). The brain comprises approximately 100 billion nerve cells, called *neurons,* and thousands of billions of support cells, called *glia* (Fishbach, 1992). Within the brain large groups of neurons form anatomically distinct areas, or *brain regions.* Initially it is easier to read an anatomical map of the brain if one conceptualizes these regions as continents, countries, and states. At the bottom of the brain is the "continent" known as the *hindbrain,* which is in turn composed of countrylike regions called the *medulla, pons,* and *cerebellum* (see Figure 2–1). In the middle of the brain is the "continent" called the *midbrain.* And at the top is the "continent" called the *forebrain,* which is composed of countrylike regions called the *cerebrum* (the two cerebral hemispheres), the *thalamus,* and the *hypothalamus,* each in turn made up of statelike regions. The cerebrum, for instance, consists of the *cortex* (see Figure 2–2), *corpus callosum, basal ganglia, hippocampus,* and *amygdala.* The neurons in each of these brain regions control important functions. For example, the hippocampus helps regulate emotions and memory, and the hypothalamus helps regulate hunger.

Biological theorists believe that just as lung and kidney disorders result from problems in the cells of those organs, mental disorders are linked to problems in brain-cell functioning. The problems may be

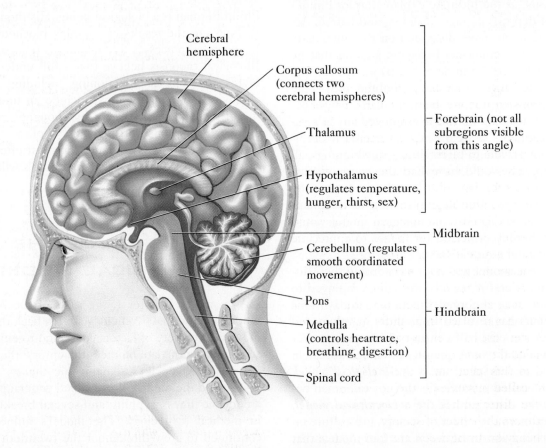

Cerebral hemisphere

Corpus callosum (connects two cerebral hemispheres)

Thalamus

Hypothalamus (regulates temperature, hunger, thirst, sex)

Forebrain (not all subregions visible from this angle)

Midbrain

Cerebellum (regulates smooth coordinated movement)

Pons

Medulla (controls heartrate, breathing, digestion)

Hindbrain

Spinal cord

FIGURE 2–1 *Many of the regions of the human brain can be seen in a side view of the brain sliced down the center. Each region, composed of numerous neurons, is responsible for certain functions.*

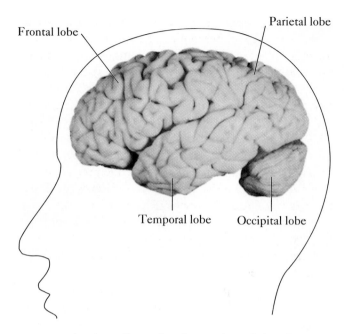

Frontal lobe

Parietal lobe

Temporal lobe

Occipital lobe

FIGURE 2–2 *Researchers have estimated that the cortex, the gray outer layer of the cerebrum, contains at least 70 percent of all the neurons in the central nervous system and is responsible for the highest levels of cognitive and perceptual analysis, including reasoning, speaking, reading, hearing, and seeing. Anatomists separate the cortex of each hemisphere into four regions called lobes.*

anatomical (the size or shape of certain brain regions may be abnormal) or *biochemical* (the chemicals that enable neurons to operate may not work properly). Such difficulties may be the result of various factors, such as excessive stress, inherited metabolic disorders, infections, allergies, tumors, inadequate blood supply, and physical trauma (Haroutunian, 1991; Murphy & Deutsch, 1991).

Using a variety of neurological tests, clinicians have discovered unambiguous connections between a number of mental disorders and specific problems in the brain. For example, Huntington's disease, a degenerative disease marked by violent emotional outbursts, memory and other cognitive difficulties, delusions (that is, false and absurd beliefs that are firmly held), suicidal thinking, and involuntary body movements, has been traced to a loss of neurons in the brain area called the basal ganglia.

Mental disorders that have such clear physical causes were called *organic mental disorders* in the past and were distinguished from *functional mental disorders*, abnormal behavior patterns without clear links to physical abnormalities in the brain. However, years of research have clarified that many so-called functional disorders, including anxiety disorders, depression, and schizophrenia, are also related to physical dysfunctions in the brain, and in fact, the terms organic and functional mental disorders are now no longer formally included in the leading diagnostic and classification system (APA, 1994).

Biological researchers initially came to believe that most or all mental disorders have at least some physical basis largely as a result of insights gained from the study of the psychotropic medications (Gershon & Rieder, 1992). By studying where these drugs go and what they do in the brain, they learned much about the mental disorders they alleviate (Hollister & Csernansky, 1990). In recent years they have added to their understanding of the physical underpinings of abnormal behavior by using techniques that enable them to take "photographs" of the living brain. *Computerized axial tomography (CAT scanning), positron emission tomography (PET scanning), magnetic resonance imaging (MRI),* and other important imaging techniques are considered in more detail in Chapter 4.

Using such strategies and tools, biological researchers have learned, for example, that mental disorders are often related to subtle dysfunctioning in the transmission of brain messages from neuron to neuron. Information spreads throughout the brain in the form of electrical impulses that travel from one neuron to one or more others. An impulse is received by a neuron's **dendrites,** extensions (or antennae) located at one end of the neuron; travels down the neuron's **axon,** a long fiber; and is transmitted to other neurons through the **nerve endings** at the axon's terminus (see Figure 2–3). An important question is

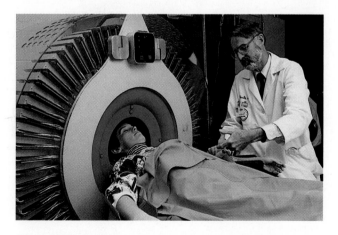

Elaborate biological tests such as positron emission tomography (PET) are often administered to help detect abnormalities that may be causing psychological problems. A PET scan produces moving pictures of metabolic activity at sites throughout the brain, thus revealing problems in functioning as opposed to anatomy.

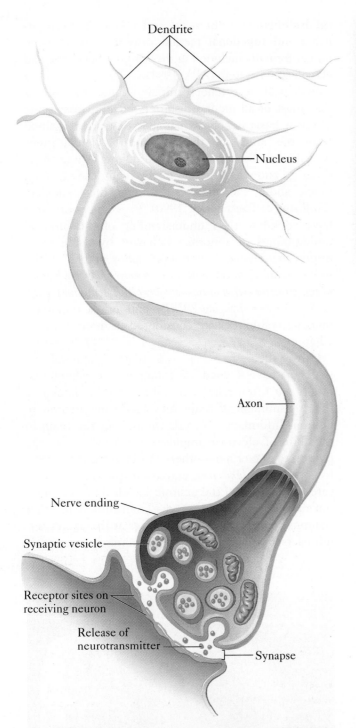

Dendrite

Nucleus

Axon

Nerve ending

Synaptic vesicle

Receptor sites on
receiving neuron

Release of
neurotransmitter

Synapse

FIGURE 2–3 *A typical neuron. A message travels down the neuron's axon to the nerve ending, where neurotransmitters carry the message across the synaptic space to a receiving neuron. (Adapted from Bloom, Lazerson, & Hofstadter, 1985, p. 35.)*

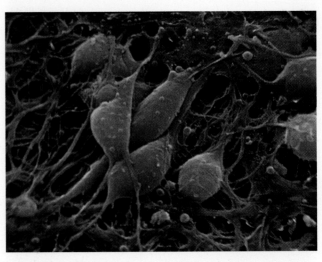

State-of-the-art electron microscopes and color-enhancement techniques produce remarkable close-up photographs of neurons and highlight the complex network of cell bodies, axons, and dendrites that make up the brain.

how messages get from the nerve endings of one neuron to the dendrites of another neuron. After all, the neurons do not actually touch each other. A tiny space, called the *synapse,* separates one neuron from

the next, and the message must somehow move across that space. When an electrical impulse reaches a neuron's ending, apparently the nerve ending is stimulated to release a chemical, called a *neurotransmitter,* that travels across the synaptic space to *receptors* (actually proteins) on the dendrites of the adjacent neurons (see Figure 2–4). The neurotransmitter in turn leads the receiving neurons either to generate another electrical impulse ("firing" or "triggering") or to cease firing, depending on the neurotransmitter involved. Obviously, neurotransmitters play a key role in moving information through the brain (Kanof, 1991).

Researchers have so far identified dozens of neurotransmitters in the brain, and have learned that each neuron uses only certain kinds (Barondes, 1993). Neurological studies indicate that abnormalities in the activity of different neurotransmitters can cause different mental disorders (Gershon & Rieder, 1992). Anxiety disorders, for example, have been linked to insufficient activity of the neurotransmitter *gamma aminobutyric acid,* or *GABA* (Murphy & Handelsman, 1991; Braestrup et al., 1982), schizophrenia to excessive activity of the neurotransmitter *dopamine* (Davis & Greenwald, 1991; Angrist, Lee, & Gershon, 1974), and depression to low activity of the neurotransmitters *norepinephrine* and *serotonin* (Siever, Davis, & Gorman, 1991; Schildkraut, 1965). Indeed, biological theorists would probably point to deficient norepinephrine and serotonin activity to account for Philip Berman's pattern of depression and rage.

Biological researchers also have examined the frequencies with which mental disorders occur among biological relatives. In *family-pedigree studies,* researchers look to see how many members of a given family have a particular disorder. If the disorder occurs with greater frequency in the family than in the general population, perhaps some family members are inheriting a genetic predisposition to the disorder. Several such studies have traced unusually high rates of depression, for example, through several generations (Bloom, Lazerson, & Hofstadter, 1985). In *risk studies,* researchers survey the biological relatives of a patient who has been diagnosed with a specific psychological abnormality to see how many and which of them have the same disorder (Sameroff & Seifer, 1990). Many of these studies have demonstrated that the risk of developing severe depression increases directly with the closeness of one's biological relationship to someone with that disorder (Gottesman, 1991).

Given their orientation, practitioners of the biological school look for certain kinds of clues when they search for the cause of a particular person's abnormal behavior. Does the family have a history of that behavior, and hence a possible genetic predisposition to it? (Philip Berman's case history mentions that his mother was once hospitalized for depression.) Does the disorder seem to be related to a past illness or accident, or to follow its own course, irrespective of situational changes? (Philip's depressed feelings were described as periodic; they seemed to come and go over the course of several years.) Is the behavior exacerbated by events that could be construed as having a physiological effect? (Philip was having a drink when he flew into a jealous rage at the restaurant.) Once these practitioners have pinpointed particular areas of presumed organic dysfunctioning, they are in a better position to choose a course of biological treatment (Apter, 1993).

ASSESSING THE BIOLOGICAL MODEL

Today the biological model enjoys considerable prestige in the clinical field, and investigations into the biological underpinnings of abnormal functioning are proliferating. The new medications that are constantly being developed have themselves become important research tools. Most major new psychotropic drugs are discovered through a serendipitous chain of events, but once researchers know that a particular

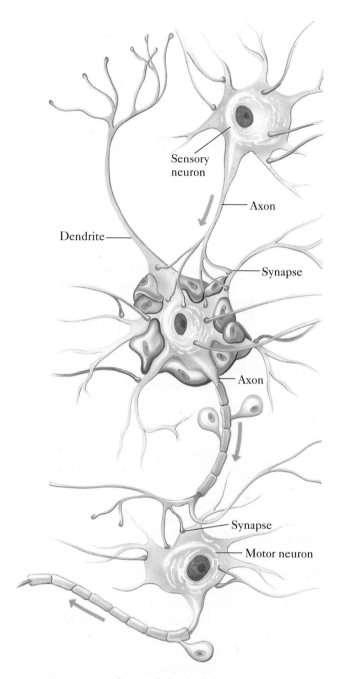

FIGURE 2-4 *A neural circuit. A large neuron with multiple dendrites receives a synaptic contact from another neuron (top) and sends the message to a third neuron (bottom). (Adapted from Bloom, Lazerson, & Hofstadter, 1985, p. 31.)*

drug alleviates a particular mental disorder, they start investigating the drug's biochemical action in the brain and body in the hope of discovering clues to possible biological causes of the disorder (Gershon & Rieder, 1992; Iversen, 1989).

The biological model of abnormal functioning has many virtues. First, it serves to remind us that psychological processes, however complex and subtle, have biological causes worthy of examination and study. Second, thanks to sophisticated procedures developed over centuries of experimentation, research into the biological aspects of abnormal functioning often progresses rapidly, producing valuable new information in a relatively short time. Finally, biological treatments have often been known to afford significant help and relief for abnormal functioning after other interventions have failed. This kind of effectiveness is most welcome in a world where psychological disturbances are so prevalent and often so resistant to change.

At the same time, the biological model has characteristic limitations and problems. Some of its proponents seem to expect that all human behavior can be explained in biological terms and treated with biological methods. This narrow view can limit rather than enhance our understanding of abnormal functioning. Although biological processes certainly do affect our behavior, thoughts, and emotions, they are just as certainly affected by our behavior, thoughts, and emotions. When we perceive the negative events in our lives to be beyond our control, for example, the activity of norepinephrine or serotonin in our brains usually drops off, thus intensifying a depressive reaction. Our mental life is an interplay of biological and non-biological factors, and it is important to explore that interplay rather than to focus exclusively on biological variables.

A second problem is that the evidence for biological explanations is often incomplete or inconclusive. Many neurological studies, for example, must be conducted on animals in whom apparent symptoms of depression, anxiety, or some other abnormality have been induced by drugs, surgery, or behavioral manipulation. Researchers can never be certain that these animals are experiencing the human disorder under investigation and therefore cannot be certain that the biological insights derived from such studies are relevant. Similarly, the human genetic and genealogical studies often cited in support of biological explanations are open to alternative interpretations. Evidence that close relatives are more likely to develop certain disorders than more distant relatives may simply mean that close relatives are more likely to have the same harmful "psychological" experiences. Perhaps a given pair of siblings under study have been traumatized by the loss of the same loved one, or have together been exposed to an extraordinarily frightening situation as children. Indeed, the first of the psychological models that we shall examine, the psychodynamic model, places primary emphasis on the psychological effects of early childhood experiences.

THE PSYCHODYNAMIC MODEL

Although biological theorists view Philip Berman chiefly as a biological being, he is a *psychological* being as well, interpreting, creating, feeling, initiating, and interacting. Several currently influential models of abnormal behavior focus on these and other psychological dimensions of human functioning. The oldest and most famous is the psychodynamic model.

Psychodynamic theorists believe that a person's behavior, whether normal or abnormal, is determined to a large extent by underlying psychological forces of which the person is not consciously aware. These internal forces are considered *dynamic*—that is, they interact with one another; and their interaction gives shape to an individual's behavior, thoughts, and emotions. Abnormal behaviors or symptoms are viewed as the consequences of intrapsychic *conflicts* between these forces or as unconscious attempts to solve such conflicts and lessen some painful inner turmoil.

Thus, psychodynamic theorists would view Philip Berman as a person in conflict, a person whose underlying needs and motives are in a state of disharmony. They would want to explore his past experiences because, in their view, people's psychological conflicts are related to their early relationships with their parents and to traumatic experiences that occurred during their formative years. Psychodynamic theories rest on the *deterministic* assumption that no symptom or behavior is "accidental." All behavior is determined by past experiences, particularly the experiences of childhood. Thus Philip's hatred for his mother, his recollections of her as cruel and overbearing, the weakness and ineffectuality of his father, and the birth of a younger brother when Philip was 10 may all be relevant issues.

ORIGINS OF THE PSYCHODYNAMIC MODEL

The psychodynamic model was first formulated by the Viennese neurologist Sigmund Freud (1856–1939) at the turn of the century. As we saw in Chapter 1, Freud became so interested in the use of hypnosis to treat hysterical illnesses—mysterious physical ailments with no apparent medical cause—

that in 1885 he went to Paris to study hypnosis under the famous neurologist Jean Charcot. After returning to Vienna, he worked with Josef Breuer (1842–1925), a physician who had been conducting experiments on hypnosis and hysteria.

In a famous case, Breuer had treated a woman he called "Anna O.," whose extensive hysterical symptoms included paralysis of the legs and right arm, deafness, and disorganized speech. Breuer placed the woman under hypnosis, expecting that suggestions made to her in that state would help rid her of her hysterical symptoms. While she was under hypnosis, however, she began to talk about traumatic past events and to express deeply felt emotions. This venting of repressed memories seemed to enhance the effectiveness of the treatment. Anna O. referred to it as her "talking cure"; Breuer called it the "cathartic method" (borrowing the term from the Greek *katharsis*, purgation).

Breuer and his new colleague collaborated on a number of case studies in the 1890s and together published an important paper and book on this treatment technique, *Studies in Hysteria.* They proposed that hysterical illnesses were caused by psychological conflicts, principally sexual in origin, of which the patient was not consciously aware, and that these conflicts would exert less negative influence after they had been brought into consciousness by hypnosis and the cathartic method.

Over the course of the next several decades, Freud developed and expanded these ideas into a general theory of *psychoanalysis.* He proposed that "unconscious" conflicts account not just for hysterical illnesses but for all forms of normal and abnormal psychological functioning. Freud also formulated a corresponding method of treatment (which we shall explore in Chapter 5). He came to believe that hypnosis was not necessary to cure psychopathologies and developed instead a conversational approach in which patients would explore their unconscious with a psychoanalyst and come to terms with the conflicts they discovered there.

In 1909 Freud came to the United States to present a series of lectures at Clark University in Worcester, Massachusetts. These "Introductory Lectures on Psychoanalysis" brought his theory to the attention of the American psychological community. Over the next few years, Freud and several of his colleagues in the Vienna Psychoanalytic Society—including Carl Gustav Jung (1875–1961) and Alfred Adler (1870–1937)—became the most influential clinical theorists in the Western world. Freud's twenty-four volumes on psychoanalytic theory and treatment are still widely studied today.

FREUDIAN EXPLANATIONS OF NORMAL AND ABNORMAL FUNCTIONING

As Freud studied the lives and problems of his patients, he came to believe that three central forces shape or "constitute" the personality—instinctual needs, rational thinking, and moral standards. All these forces, he believed, operate at the *unconscious* level, unavailable to immediate, cognizant awareness; and he believed them to be dynamic, or interactive, components whose jostling for expression molds the person's behavior, feelings, and thoughts. Freud called these three forces the *id, ego,* and *superego.*

THE ID   Freud used the term *id* to denote the instinctual needs, drives, and impulses. He believed that people are motivated primarily by the id, which he described as "a cauldron of seething excitement" (Freud, 1933, pp. 103–104). Classical Freudian psychodynamic theory is often referred to as a "drive theory" because of the central role Freud assigned to the id drives.

The id operates in accordance with the **pleasure principle;** that is, it always seeks gratification. One source of id gratification is direct, or **reflex,** activity, as when an infant seeks and receives milk from the mother's breast to satisfy its hunger. Another source, **primary process thinking,** consists of activation of a memory or image of the desired object. When a hungry child's mother is not available, for example, the child may imagine her breast. Such imaginings are at least partially satisfying because the id cannot distinguish between objective and subjective realities. Gratification of id instincts by primary process thinking is called **wish fulfillment.**

Freud also believed that all id instincts tend to be sexual, noting that from the very earliest stages of development a child's gratification has sexual dimensions, as much of its pleasure is derived from nursing, defecating, and masturbating. Freud created the concept of **libido** to represent the sexual energy that fuels not only the id but the other forces of personality as well.

THE EGO   During our early years we come to recognize that our environment will not meet every instinctual need. Our mother, for example, is not always available to provide nurturance at our bidding; and later she may punish us for doing in our pants what she wants us to do in the toilet. Indeed, we may

There are no verbal accidents, according to Freud. Apparent "slips of the tongue" actually reflect unconscious feelings or wishes seeking expression.

become anxious when we experience many of our instinctual needs. Thus a part of the id becomes differentiated into a separate force called the *ego.* Like the id, the ego unconsciously seeks gratification, but it does so in accordance with the *reality principle,* the knowledge we acquire through experience and from the people around us that it can be dangerous or unacceptable to express our id impulses outright. The ego, employing reason and deliberation, guides us to recognize when we can and cannot express those impulses without negative consequences. The ego's mode of operation, called *secondary process,* is to assess new situations, weigh in past experiences, anticipate consequences, and plan how best to obtain gratification.

The ego develops basic strategies, called *ego defense mechanisms,* to control unacceptable id impulses and avoid or reduce the anxiety they arouse. The most basic defense mechanism, *repression,* prevents unacceptable impulses from ever reaching consciousness. Another defense mechanism is *displacement.* If it is dangerous for us to express an id impulse (sexual desire, say) toward one person, the ego may channel the impulse toward another, safer person. This defense also takes place at an unconscious level. There are many other ego defense mechanisms, and each of us tends to favor some over others (see Box 2–1).

THE SUPEREGO   The *superego* grows from the ego, just as the ego grows out of the id. As we learn from our parents that many of our id impulses are un-

acceptable, we unconsciously incorporate, or *introject,* our parents' values. We identify with our parents and judge ourselves by their standards. When we uphold their values, we feel good; when we go against them, we feel guilty.

The superego has two components, the conscience and the ego ideal. The *conscience* is always reminding us that certain behavior, feelings, or thoughts are good or bad, right or wrong. The *ego ideal* is a composite image of the values we have acquired, the kind of person we believe we should strive to become. Parents are usually the chief source of this ideal when children are young, but as children grow older they may come to identify with other people, too; then those people's values become incorporated in the ego ideal.

According to Freud, these three parts of the personality are often in conflict, so that we often seem impelled to act, think, and feel in contradictory ways. A healthy personality is one in which an effective working relationship, a stable and acceptable compromise, has been established among the three forces. If the id, ego, and superego are in excessive conflict, the person's behavior may show signs of dysfunction. Freudians would therefore view Philip Berman as someone whose personality forces have a poor working relationship. His rational, constructive ego is unable to control his id impulses, which lead him repeatedly to act in impulsive and often dangerous ways—suicide gestures, jealous rages, job resignations, outbursts of temper, frequent arguments. At the same time, his superego seems to be poorly formulated and largely ineffective. Having had weak and ineffectual parental models, Philip never incorporated an effective set of values, a positive ego ideal that might have helped to channel and guide his id impulses.

DEVELOPMENTAL STAGES   Freud proposed that the forces of personality are called to action throughout one's development, beginning in early infancy. At each developmental stage the child is confronted with events and pressures that challenge and perhaps threaten his or her habitual way of doing things. Such clashes require adjustments in the id, ego, and superego. If the adjustments are successful, they foster personal growth.

New environmental demands are always unpleasant for growing children, and some can be so traumatic that instead of promoting a child's development, they tend to stifle it. Under certain pressures, the id, ego, and superego may not mature properly or interact effectively, and the child becomes *fixated,* or entrapped, at an early stage of development. Then all subsequent development suffers, and the child may well be headed for abnormal functioning in the future. Because parents provide the primary environmental input during the early years of life, they are often seen as the cause of this improper development.

Freud distinguished most stages of normal development by the body area, or **erogenous zone,** that he considered representative of the child's sexual drives and conflicts at that time. He called these phases the *oral, anal, phallic, latency,* and *genital* stages.

ORAL STAGE   The earliest developmental stage, embracing the first 18 months of life, is called the **oral stage** because the infant's main libidinal gratification comes from feeding and from the body parts involved in it—the mouth, lips, and tongue. To be held and fed at the mother's breast or from a bottle with a nipple is very pleasant and relaxing. The sucking and biting associated with drinking enable the child to gratify the oral drives.

At the beginning of the oral stage, the child is totally *narcissistic*—focused solely on its own needs, with no recognition of an outside world. Gradually, however, the child comes to perceive the mother and other people as *objects* rather than as extensions of itself and begins to appreciate them as separate sources of sustenance, gratification, and protection. A maturing child is increasingly able to identify, need, want, and love such objects. The most significant threat to children during the oral stage is the possibility that the mother who feeds and comforts them will disappear—that is, the risk of **object loss.** Recognition of this possibility makes the child anxious and triggers ego defense mechanisms into action to reduce the anxiety.

If, however, mothers consistently fail to gratify the oral needs of their children, the defense mechanisms they have developed will not be sufficient to reduce their anxiety. These children may become fixated at the oral stage, unable to grow beyond their oral needs, to develop a genuine sense of independence and self-confidence, and to establish appropriate object relations. They may be particularly prone to develop certain forms of abnormal functioning, and their personalities and behavior may display an "oral character" throughout their lives: extreme dependence or, by the same token, extreme mistrust, and perhaps habits such as pencil chewing, constant talking, or overindulgence in eating, smoking, and drinking.

ANAL STAGE   During the second 18 months of life, the **anal stage,** the child's focus of pleasure shifts to the anus. Libidinal gratification comes from retaining and passing feces, and the child becomes very interested in this bodily function. Parents, of course, try to toilet train the child during this period. They teach the child to refrain from playing with feces and to dispose of them in a prescribed place and a hygienic manner. Parents who use disapproval and withdrawal of love as tools in this endeavor may inadvertently cause the child to feel great shame and to lose self-esteem.

If parental toilet-training techniques are too severe, an anal fixation may result, and the child may develop into an adult with an "anal character," prone to be stubborn, contrary, stingy, or overcontrolling (qualities that originally helped them assert their anal wishes against their harsh and demanding parents). Some behave in a so-called passive-aggressive manner, expressing their anger in "retentive" ways—by habitually withholding enthusiasm, for example, and arriving late for appointments or forgetting them altogether. Others repress their anal desire to be messy and rebellious and instead, using the defense mechanism of **reaction formation,** develop opposite personality traits: they become orderly, meticulous, punctual, and hateful of waste—a style referred to as obsessive-compulsive.

Freud believed that toilet training is a critical developmental experience. Those whose training is too harsh may become "fixated" at this stage and develop an "anal character," represented by such qualities as stinginess, stubbornness, and excessive orderliness—byproducts of the oppressive ways in which their psychosexual need to mess was handled.

┏ BOX 2-1

THE DEFENSE NEVER RESTS

Sigmund Freud claimed that the ego tries to defend itself from the anxiety arising out of the conflicts created by unacceptable desires. His daughter, Anna Freud (1895–1982), extended the concept of the ego defense mechanism beyond her father's reliance on repression as the key means for defense of the ego. Though repression is the cornerstone of the psychodynamic model of abnormality, it is but one of many methods by which the ego is thought to protect itself from anxiety. Some of these mechanisms are described below.

Anna Freud, the last of Sigmund Freud's six children, studied psychoanalysis with her father and then opened a practice next door to his. (They shared a waiting room.) Her work on defense mechanisms, other ego activities, and child development eventually earned her a distinct identity and the respect of the clinical field.

good reason not to go to see a movie tonight.

Fantasy is the use of imaginary events to satisfy unacceptable, anxiety-producing desires that would otherwise go unfulfilled.

Example: Pulling into the parking lot at school, a student finds the space he was about to enter suddenly filled by an aggressive, unpleasant person in an expensive sports car. Instead of confronting the offender, the student later fantasizes about getting out of his car and beating the other man to a pulp in front of admiring onlookers, who laud him for his courage and righteousness.

Repression is the central focus of the psychoanalytic approach to therapy. All other defense mechanisms grow out of it. The person who engages in repression avoids anxiety by simply not allowing painful or dangerous thoughts to become conscious. Once thoughts have been repressed, other ego defense mechanisms may be employed to provide additional insulation.

Example: An executive's desire to run amok and kill his boss and col-

leagues at a board meeting is denied access to awareness.

Denial is an extreme sort of self-protection. A person who denies reality simply refuses to acknowledge the existence of an external source of anxiety.

Example: You have a final exam in abnormal psychology tomorrow and you are entirely unprepared, but you tell yourself that it's not actually an important exam and that there's no

Projection is the attributing of one's own unacceptable motives or desires to others. Rather than admit to having an anxiety-producing impulse, such as anger toward another person, the individual represses the feelings and sees the other person as being the angry one.

Example: The disturbed executive who repressed his murderous desires may project his anger onto his employer and claim that it is actually the boss, not he, who is hostile.

PHALLIC STAGE During the *phallic stage,* between the third and fourth years, the focus of sexual pleasure shifts to the genitals—the penis for boys and the clitoris for girls. Boys become attracted to their mother as a fully separate object, a sexual object, and see their father as a rival they would like to push aside. This pattern of desires is called the *Oedipus complex,* after Oedipus, a character in a Greek tragedy who unknowingly kills his father and marries his mother.

At the same time, boys fear retaliation and punishment from their father for their forbidden sexual and

aggressive impulses. According to Freud, most boys fantasize that their punishment will take the form of injury to their genitals. Specifically, they fear castration. To eliminate this fear, they repress their sexual desire for their mother and *identify* with their father. That is, they aspire to be like him in behavior, values, and sexual orientation.

The phallic conflict for girls is somewhat different. During this stage, girls become aware that they do not have a penis—an organ that, according to Freud, they value and desire. They develop a sexual attraction for their father, rooted in the fantasy that by seducing

Rationalization, one of the most common defense mechanisms, is the construction of a socially acceptable reason for an action that actually reflects unworthy motives. Freud explained rationalization as an attempt to explain our behavior to ourselves and to others even though much of our behavior is motivated by unconscious drives that are irrational and infantile.

Example: A student explains away poor grades one semester to her concerned parents by citing the importance of the "total experience" of going to college and claiming that an overemphasis on grades would reduce the overall goal of a well-rounded education. This rationalization may hide an underlying fear of failure and lack of self-esteem.

Reaction formation is the adoption of behavior that is the exact opposite of impulses that one dare not express or even acknowledge.

Example: A man experiences homosexual feelings and responds by taking a strong antihomosexual stance in front of his colleagues.

Displacement, like projection, is a transferral of repressed desires and impulses. In this case one displaces one's hostility away from a dangerous object and onto a safer substitute.

Example: The student whose parking spot was taken may release his pent-up anger by going home and starting a fight with his girlfriend.

In **intellectualization (isolation)** one represses the emotional component of a reaction and resorts to a determinedly logical treatment of the problem at hand. Such an attitude is exemplified by Mr. Spock of the Star Trek television series, who believes that emotional responses interfere with the analysis of an event.

Example: A woman who has been raped gives a detached, methodical description of the effects that the ordeal is known to have on a victim.

Undoing, as the name suggests, is an attempt to atone for unacceptable desires or acts, frequently through ritualistic behavior.

Example: A woman who has murderous thoughts about her husband ceremoniously dusts and repositions their wedding photograph every time such thoughts occur to her.

Regression is a retreat from an anxiety-producing conflict to a developmental stage at which no one is expected to behave maturely and responsibly.

Example: A boy who is unable to cope with the anger he feels toward an unfeeling and rejecting mother reverts to infantile behavior, ceasing to take care of his basic needs and soiling his clothes, for instance.

Identification is the opposite of projection. Rather than attribute one's thoughts or feelings to someone else, one tries to increase one's sense of self-worth by taking on the values and feelings of the person who is causing the anxiety.

Example: In concentration camps during World War II, some prisoners adopted the behavior and attitudes of their oppressors, even to the point of harming other prisoners. By identifying with their captors, these prisoners were attempting to reduce their own fear.

Overcompensation is an attempt to cover up a personal weakness by focusing on another, more desirable trait.

Example: A very shy young woman overcompensates for her lack of social abilities and the problems that her awkwardness causes by spending many hours in the gym trying to perfect her physical condition.

Sublimation is the expression of sexual and aggressive energy in a way that is acceptable to society. This is a unique defense mechanism in that it can actually be quite constructive and beneficial to both the individual and the community. Freud saw love as sublimation at its best: it allows for the expression and gratification of sexual energy in a way that is socially acceptable.

Example: High achievers in our society—athletes, artists, surgeons, and other highly dedicated and skilled people—may be seen as reaching such high levels of accomplishment by directing other energies into their work.

---

him they can have a penis. This pattern of desires in girls is called the *Electra complex,* after Electra, a character in another Greek tragedy who conspired to kill her mother to avenge her father's death. Girls, like boys, fear their phallic impulses. They fear that their wishes will cause their mother to stop loving them or to hurt them. Thus they too repress their desires and come to identify with their mother. The primary yearning for a penis attributed to girls during the phallic stage—*penis envy*—has become one of the most controversial concepts in Freudian theory.

It is important that children resolve the Oedipus and Electra conflicts by coming to identify with the parent of their own sex. If they are punished too harshly for sexual behavior during this stage, or if they are subtly encouraged to pursue their desire for the parent of the opposite sex, their sexual development may suffer. As Freud saw it, they might later develop a sexual orientation different from the norm, fear sexual intimacy, be overly seductive, or have other difficulties in romantic relationships.

When children identify with the parent of the same sex during the phallic stage, they particularly identify

The psychoanalytic notion of the "Electra complex" holds that 4-year-old girls repress threatening desires for their fathers and identify with their mothers, trying to emulate them by dressing, acting, and talking as their mothers do. The behavioral notion of modeling also holds that children often imitate others, but behaviorists do not limit models to parents and do not see imitation as a defensive strategy.

with that parent's moral standards. Thus it is during this stage that the superego is formulated. The superego can be a constructive or a destructive force. It may generate self-praise, self-affection, and high self-esteem; or it may call for self-condemnation, self-punishment, and reparation. Children who become fixated at the phallic stage may suffer pervasive feelings of guilt throughout their lives.

LATENCY STAGE   At 6 years of age children enter the *latency stage,* in which their sexual desires apparently subside and their libidinal energy is devoted to developing new interests, activities, and skills. They seek friends of the same sex, express dislike for the opposite sex, and are embarrassed by sexual displays. The broader process of socialization, of learning one's roles in family and society, takes place at this time.

GENITAL STAGE   At approximately the age of 12, with the onset of puberty and adolescence, the child's sexual urges emerge once again. Now, in what is termed the *genital stage,* sexual pleasure begins to be found in heterosexual relationships. Initially, adolescents are not fully capable of the genuine affection and caring for others that are required in such relationships. They still have many of the narcissistic qualities of earlier stages of development and have yet to outgrow the earlier conflicts. During the genital

stage, however, they make more mature efforts in these areas, and in the normal course of events learn to participate fully in affectionate and altruistic relationships.

The genital stage establishes the foundation for effective adult functioning in general, including the development of vocational interests and abilities. In psychodynamic terms, the adolescent *sublimates,* or rechannels, his or her narcissistic impulses into endeavors that are both socially acceptable and personally gratifying. The genital stage ends when sexual, social, and vocational maturity is achieved.

OTHER PSYCHODYNAMIC EXPLANATIONS

Personal and professional differences between Freud and his colleagues led to a split in the Vienna Psychoanalytic Society early in this century. Carl Jung, Alfred Adler, and others left to develop new theories, many of which perpetuated Freud's basic belief that all human functioning is shaped by dynamic (interacting) psychological forces, though they departed from his model in other respects. Accordingly, all such theories, including Freud's psychoanalytic theory, are referred to as *psychodynamic*. Three of today's most influential psychodynamic theories are *ego theory, object relations theory,* and *self theory.*

Early in this century, two of Freud's most esteemed colleagues, Carl Jung (left) and Alfred Adler, broke off with him and developed psychodynamic theories that deemphasized the sexual aspects of development. Jung believed that each of us inherits a collective unconscious, a set of archetypes (symbols or innate ideas), that provides a foundation for our creative endeavors. Adler believed that the drive to dominate others is central in life and that people spend their lives trying to overcome the "inferiority complex" with which they are born.

EGO THEORY   *Ego psychologists* believe that the ego is a more independent and powerful force than Freud recognized. Rather than growing from the id and serving primarily to redirect id impulses, they contend, the ego grows independently of the id and has autonomous, "conflict-free" functions in addition to its id-related responsibilities. The ego guides memory and perception and strives for mastery and competence independent of the id. Both the conflict-free and conflict-resolving activities of the ego must be considered if psychological functioning is to be explained properly.

Erik Erikson (1902–1994), for example, believed that a person develops an integrated, unique sense of self, called the *ego identity*, a product of *psychosocial* rather than psychosexual development. He also held that people change throughout their lives, and pass through a series of psychosocial stages. As we shall observe in Chapter 19, each stage presents a crisis that challenges the ego. Successful resolution of the crisis brings the person closer to ego identity; failure to resolve the crisis hampers this process and may lead to psychological problems. Unlike Freud, Erikson did not conclude that failure at any one stage guarantees a complete arrest in development. The ego is strong enough to overcome many problems.

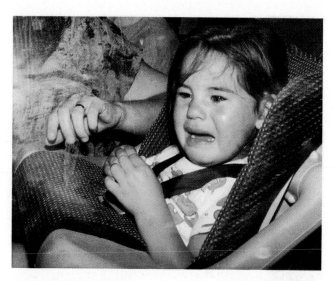

Object relations theorists, psychodynamic theorists who view relationships as the key to human functioning, believe that children must successfully resolve attachment and separation issues to develop into healthy adults. Traumatic disruptions in early relationships can lead to difficulties in forming relationships throughout life, as well as to a damaged sense of self. These were two clinical concerns in the famous case of Baby Jessica (shown above), who was returned to her natural parents in 1993 after living the first few years of her life with adoptive parents.

OBJECT RELATIONS THEORY   In classical Freudian theory, *objects* (other people, and occasionally things) acquire their importance to the individual because they help to satisfy fundamental drives. Psychodynamic **object relations theory,** in contrast, proposes that objects (which are exclusively human in this theory) are important because people are motivated primarily by a need to establish relationships with others. The people with whom we relate are called **external objects;** our psychological representations of them, composed of emotions, images, and symbols, are called **internal objects.** Internal objects shape the individual personality, and contribute to the development of the self-image.

Various object relations theories have been proposed, most notably by Melanie Klein, Margaret Mahler, Otto Kernberg, D. W. Winnicott, and W. R. D. Fairbairn. Despite technical differences between the theories, several common themes emerge. Object relations theories universally focus on *attachment* and *separation* as the central processes in personality development and in the genesis of psychopathology. The motivating force in human behavior is understood to be the desire for relatedness, not the desire for gratification of instinctual pleasures or the reduction of libidinal tensions. People seek

objects, and the objects themselves are primary; what they may provide is of secondary importance.

According to object relations theories, the infant's very early relationship with his or her primary caregiver becomes a "template," or model, for lifelong patterns of relatedness (Cashdan, 1988). The internal world of object relations determines a person's relations with people in the external world, and this internal object world "is basically the residue of the individual's relations with people upon whom he was dependent for the satisfactions of primitive needs in infancy" (Phillipson, 1955, p. 7). Object relations theorists believe that children who have "good enough" parenting progress effectively through several developmental stages, each characterized by attachment and separation issues, while severe failures in the child/caregiver relationship result in fixation, abnormal development, and psychological problems.

SELF THEORY   Another modern movement in psychodynamic theory has focused on the role of the *self*—the unified personality that defines one's sense of identity—rather than on the various components of personality, such as the id, ego, and superego. In the theory of *self psychology* developed by Heinz Kohut (1913–1981), the self is conceptualized as an

Heinz Kohut and Margaret Mahler were pioneers in the development of self theory and object relations theory, respectively, two of today's most widely followed psychodynamic theories.

independent, integrating, and self-motivating force and the basic human motive is to preserve and enhance its wholeness (Cooper, 1983; Kohut, 1977).

Kohut theorized that the self comes into being as the child experiences his or her basic needs being satisfied through relationships with *selfobjects*—people who are experienced as a part of the self. In this sense, self theory is linked to object relations theory. The way a child's personality develops depends on the support the child receives from the first selfobjects, the parents. Parents who are reasonably self-confident, relaxed, and supportive create a healthy milieu for the development of the child's self.

The developing self has three needs. The first is *mirroring,* the parent's affirmation of the child's innate sense of vigor, perfection, and uniqueness. Adequate mirroring fosters self-esteem and self-affirmation; inadequate mirroring can result in a lack of self-esteem and a need for constant reassurance. The developing self also needs to *idealize* and merge with a selfobject who represents calmness, infallibility, and power. Through the internalization of the idealized parent and the later recognition that the parent is not, after all, perfectly powerful or knowledgeable, the self develops self-acceptance, self-confidence, idealism, impulse control, and the capacity for self-soothing. A third need for the developing self is the need to be similar to, or at least not too different from, others. The feeling that one is like others promotes a sense of belonging and *fitting in* to the human community and also strengthens self-esteem (Cirese, 1993; Kohut & Wolf, 1978).

Because the aspects of the self are not entirely self-supporting or stable, Kohut proposed that people (selfobjects) who enhance one's sense of harmony, cohesion, and vigor are critically important to an individual. (An object such as a dog or teddy bear may serve the same purpose.) Throughout life, a healthy self continues to require what Kohut called "sustaining self-selfobject relationships," in which basic needs may be met. Empathic, affirming, and idealized selfobjects are essential for psychological survival. In Kohut's conception, the self exists in relation to others and does not strive for complete independence or separation (Tobin, 1990).

Poor development or "damage" to the self—the result of faulty interaction between the child and his or her selfobjects and of lack of satisfaction of the three essential needs (mirroring, idealization, fitting in)—can lead to psychological disorders, or "self disorders." The role of therapy, according to self theorists, is to help the client accept and express needs unfulfilled in childhood and so to arrive at a strong and unified sense of self.

ASSESSING THE PSYCHODYNAMIC MODEL

Freud and his followers have had a most significant impact on the ways abnormal functioning is understood and treated (Joseph, 1991). Their theories of personality and abnormality are eloquent and comprehensive. Largely because of their groundwork, a wide range of theorists today look for answers and explanations outside the confines of biological processes, focusing instead on less tangible concepts—underlying conflicts, learned habits, cognitive processes, human values. In addition, the techniques of psychotherapy developed by Freud and his followers have demonstrated the potential of psychological treatments and have led to the development of many more such approaches.

Psychodynamic theorists have also helped us to understand that abnormal functioning may be rooted in the same processes that underlie normal functioning. Psychological conflict, for example, is a universal experience; it leads to abnormal functioning, the psychodynamic theorists say, only if the conflict becomes excessive. This notion argues for a humane and respectful attitude toward people deemed to have mental disorders.

At the same time, the psychodynamic model has shortcomings and limitations. First, its concepts can be difficult to define and to research (Erdelyi, 1992, 1985). Because processes such as id drives, ego defenses, and fixation are abstract and supposedly operate at an unconscious level, it is often impossible to determine if they are occurring. Not surprisingly, then, psychodynamic explanations have received little research support, and psychodynamic theorists have been forced to rely largely on individual case studies to support their theories. And though case studies are useful in many ways, they do not provide compelling evidence in support of theoretical explanations.

Another problem is that psychodynamic explanations often fail to establish clear guidelines for predicting abnormality (Edelson, 1985). It is a widely accepted principle in Freudian psychodynamic theory, for example, that oral fixation is caused by either insufficient or excessive gratification of needs during the first year of life, yet psychodynamic theorists rarely specify how much or what kind of gratification is in fact insufficient or excessive. Without such guidelines, we cannot effectively predict who is likely to become orally fixated.

Partly in response to these problems, other psychological models have emerged over the past several decades—the behavioral, cognitive, and humanistic-existential models. Although these newer explanations and corresponding treatments often differ significantly from the psychodynamic perspective, they all have roots in the psychodynamic model. Because so many of the people who developed these models were trained in the psychodynamic tradition, certain psychodynamic-like notions have often been retained in the new models (Garfield & Bergin, 1994). Moreover, it is important to recognize that despite the significant growth of alternative psychological models, the psychodynamic perspective continues to be one of the most widely applied models in the clinical field today (Prochaska & Norcross, 1994).

■ THE ■ BEHAVIORAL MODEL

Like psychodynamic theorists, behavioral theorists hold a deterministic view of human functioning: they believe that our actions are determined largely by our experiences in life. The psychological dimensions on which behavioral theorists focus, however, are quite different from those the psychodynamic theorists favor. They concentrate on specific *behaviors,* the responses that an organism makes to the stimuli in its environment, and on the *principles of learning,* the processes by which behaviors change in response to the environment. In the behavioral view, people are the sum total of their learned behaviors—both external (going to work, say) and internal (having a feeling or thought).

Many learned behaviors are constructive and adaptive, helping people to cope with daily challenges and to lead happy, productive lives. However, abnormal and undesirable behaviors also can be learned. According to the behavioral model, these behaviors are acquired by the same principles of learning as adaptive behaviors. Thus behavioral theorists reject the medical illness perspective adopted by biological and psychodynamic theorists.

Behaviorists who tried to explain Philip Berman's problems would concentrate on his inappropriate behaviors and on the principles of learning by which those behaviors have been acquired. They might view him as a man who has received improper training in life. He has learned behaviors that alienate and antagonize others, behaviors that repeatedly work against him. He does not know how to engage other people, express his emotions constructively, or enjoy himself.

ORIGINS OF THE BEHAVIORAL MODEL

The behavioral model was the first clinical perspective to be developed in psychological laboratories. Whereas the biological model grew from medical and biological research and the psychodynamic model had its origins in neurological research and in the clinical work of physicians, the behavioral model was conceived in laboratories run by psychologists who were conducting experiments on *conditioning,* simple forms of learning in which scientists manipulate stimuli and rewards and observe how the responses of experimental subjects are affected.

Since the turn of the century, conditioning has been one of experimental psychology's chief areas of study. The work of eminent conditioning theorists such as Ivan Pavlov (1849–1936), John Watson (1878–1958), Edward Thorndike (1874–1949), Edwin Guthrie (1886–1959), B. F. Skinner (1904–1990), and Neal Miller (b. 1909) has elucidated three principles of conditioning: *classical* (or *respondent*) *conditioning*, *operant* (or *instrumental*) *conditioning*, and *modeling.*

Efforts to modify abnormal behaviors by means of conditioning were made as early as the 1920s (Jones, 1924). Not until decades later, however, were these principles applied in clinical practice. During the 1950s, many clinicians were growing disenchanted with what they viewed as the vagueness, slowness, and imprecision of the psychodynamic model. Looking for an alternative approach, some of them began to apply the principles of conditioning to the study and treatment of psychological problems (Wolpe, 1987). These efforts gave rise to the behavioral model of psychopathology.

CLASSICAL CONDITIONING EXPLANATIONS OF ABNORMAL BEHAVIOR

Classical conditioning is a process of learning by *temporal association.* Theoretically, two events that repeatedly occur close together in time become fused in a person's mind, and before long the person responds in the same way to both events. If one event elicits a response of joy, the other brings joy as well; if one event brings feelings of relief, so does the other.

The early animal studies of Ivan Pavlov, the Russian physiologist who first demonstrated classical conditioning, illustrate this process. Pavlov placed a bowl of meat powder before a dog, eliciting the innate response that all dogs have to meat: they start to salivate (see Figure 2–5). Next Pavlov inserted an additional step: just before presenting the dog with meat powder, he sounded a metronome. After several such pairings of metronome tone and presentation of meat powder, Pavlov observed that the dog began to salivate as soon as it heard the metronome. The dog had learned to salivate in response to a sound.

In the vocabulary of classical conditioning, the meat in this demonstration is an ***unconditioned stimulus (US);*** it elicits the ***unconditioned response (UR)*** of salivation (that is, a natural response the dog is born with). The sound of the metronome is a ***conditioned***

The initial interest of Pavlov, a physiologist, was the digestive system, and he used surgery and other techniques to study it. Pavlov accidentally discovered classical conditioning, the learning process by which an organism comes to respond to one stimulus just as it automatically responds to another stimulus, after the two stimuli have repeatedly been paired.

stimulus (CS), a previously neutral stimulus that comes to be associated with meat in the dog's mind. As such, it too elicits a salivation response. When the salivation response is elicited by the conditioned stimulus rather than by the unconditioned stimulus, it is called a ***conditioned response (CR).***

Before Conditioning

CS: Tone ⟶ No response
US: Meat ⟶ UR: Salivation

After Conditioning

CS: Tone ⟶ CR: Salivation
US: Meat ⟶ UR: Salivation

If, after conditioning, the conditioned stimulus is repeatedly presented alone, without being paired with the unconditioned stimulus, it will eventually stop eliciting the conditioned response. When Pavlov stopped pairing the metronome tone and meat powder, for example, the dog salivated less and less in response to the tone. The conditioned response was undergoing ***extinction*** (see Figure 2–6).

Classical conditioning accounts for many familiar animal behaviors. It explains, for example, the ad in the lost-and-found column of a local newspaper that said, "Lost: female calico cat that answers to the sound of an electric can opener" (Hart, 1985). According to behaviorists, many human behaviors are also acquired through classical conditioning. The amorous feelings a young man experiences when he smells his girlfriend's perfume, say, may represent a conditioned response. Initially this perfume may have had no emotional effect on him, but because the fragrance was present during several romantic encounters, it too came to elicit an amorous response.

Abnormal behaviors, too, can be acquired by classical conditioning (Wilson, 1990). Consider the situation of a young boy who is repeatedly frightened by a neighbor's large German shepherd dog. Whenever the child walks past the neighbor's front yard, the dog barks loudly and lunges at him, stopped only by a rope tied to the porch. In this unfortunate situation, the boy's parents are not surprised to discover that he develops a fear of dogs. They are mystified, however, by another intense fear the child displays, a fear of sand. They cannot understand why he cries whenever they take him to the beach, refuses to take a single step off the beach blanket, and screams in fear if sand even touches his skin.

Where did this fear of sand come from? The answer is found in the principle of classical conditioning. It turns out that a big sandbox is set up in the neighbor's front yard for the fearsome dog to play in. Every time the dog barks and lunges at the boy, the sandbox is

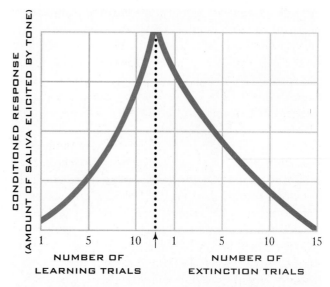

FIGURE 2–6   *Classical conditioning. During learning trials, a stimulus such as a loud tone is repeatedly paired with another stimulus such as meat. The dog learns to salivate in response to the tone, just as it naturally salivates whenever it sees meat. During extinction trials, the tone is no longer paired with the meat, and salivation in response to the tone eventually stops.*

there too. After repeated associations of this kind, the child comes to fear sand as much as he fears the dog. In classical conditioning terms, an unconditioned stimulus—the loud and hostile dog—initially elicits an unconditioned response of fear; then, after repeated associations, a conditioned stimulus—sand—begins to elicit a similar conditioned response of fear. Through this simple process of conditioning, the child develops a fear response that may persist throughout his life. The child may be so successful at avoiding sand that he never learns how harmless it is.

OPERANT CONDITIONING EXPLANATIONS OF ABNORMAL BEHAVIOR

In *operant conditioning,* humans and animals learn to behave in certain ways because they receive *reinforcement* from their environment whenever they do so. This form of conditioning was first elucidated by the eminent psychologist Edward L. Thorndike, whose research led him to formulate the *law of effect*—the principle that responses that lead to satisfying consequences will be strengthened and are likely to be repeated, whereas responses that lead to unsatisfying consequences will be weakened and are

FIGURE 2–5   *In Ivan Pavlov's experimental device, the dog's saliva was collected in a tube as it was secreted, and the amount was recorded on a revolving cylinder called a kymograph. The experimenter observed the dog through a one-way glass window.*

Pet owners have discovered that they can teach animals a wide assortment of tricks through shaping—rewarding successive approximations of a desired behavior.

unlikely to be repeated. Years later, B. F. Skinner renamed this law the *principle of reinforcement* and asserted that it is the primary mechanism for explaining and controlling human behavior.

Using the principle of operant conditioning, experimenters have taught animal subjects a wide range of behaviors, from pulling levers and turning wheels to navigating mazes and even playing Ping-Pong (Skinner, 1948). To teach complex behaviors, they typically employ *shaping*—a procedure in which successive approximations of the desired behavior are rewarded. In teaching a pigeon to play Ping-Pong, for example, the experimenter may initially reward the animal merely for picking up a paddle. Once this response is acquired, the experimenter may reward the pigeon only when, in addition to picking up the paddle, it also carries the paddle in the direction of the ball, and so on until the animal actually learns to return serves (Figure 2–7).

Behaviorists believe that many human behaviors are learned by operant conditioning (Delprato & Midgley, 1992; Skinner, 1989, 1957). Children acquire manners by receiving praise, attention, or treats for

desirable behaviors and censure for undesirable ones. Adults work at their jobs because they are paid when they do and fired when they do not.

Behaviorists also claim that many abnormal behaviors develop as a result of reinforcement. Some people may learn to abuse alcohol and drugs because initially such behaviors brought feelings of calm, comfort, or pleasure (Conger, 1951). Others may exhibit bizarre, psychotic behaviors because they enjoy the attention they get when they do so. A number of studies have found that when the bizarre talk and other unusual behaviors of schizophrenic patients are consistently ignored by hospital personnel and appropriate behaviors are repeatedly rewarded with privileges, money, or attention, many patients begin to show marked changes for the better (Braginsky, Braginsky, & Ring, 1969; Ayllon & Michael, 1959).

Some of Philip Berman's maladaptive behaviors may have been acquired through operant conditioning. When he first became "ornery" at the age of 10, how did his parents react? Perhaps they unintentionally reinforced his rebellious behavior by giving him more attention; and rather than teaching him alternative ways to express his needs, perhaps they simply gave in and let him have his way. Making a related point about child rearing, one psychologist writes, "Parents may pick up a child who is whining. Whining is an aversive event for the parents which is terminated after they respond. . . . However, the child is . . . reinforced" (Kazdin, 1975, p. 31).

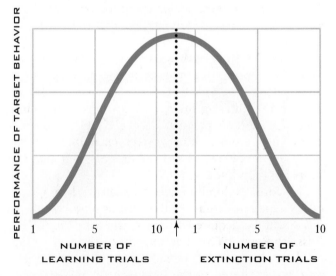

FIGURE 2–7 *Operant conditioning. During learning trials, a target behavior (such as lifting a paddle) is repeatedly rewarded, and the subject increasingly performs the target behavior. During extinction trials, the target behavior is no longer rewarded, and the subject steadily stops performing the target behavior.*

B. F. Skinner, one of the most influential theorists and researchers of the twentieth century, helped develop the "principle of reinforcement" and applied it by training pigeons and other animals to perform a wide variety of behaviors. He believed that reinforcement accounts for most human behaviors, too.

MODELING EXPLANATIONS OF ABNORMAL BEHAVIOR

Modeling is a form of learning in which individuals acquire responses through *observation* and *imitation* (Bandura, 1977, 1976, 1969)—that is, by observing others (the models) and repeating their behaviors. Behaviors are especially likely to be imitated when the models are themselves being rewarded for the behaviors or when the models are important to the observers.

Behaviorists believe that many everyday human behaviors are learned through modeling. Children may acquire language, facial gestures, tastes in food, and the like by imitating the words, gestures, and eating behaviors of their parents. Similarly, adults may acquire interpersonal skills or vocational interests by imitating the behaviors and preferences of important people in their lives.

This form of conditioning, too, can lead to abnormality. A famous study showed that aggressive behaviors could be acquired through modeling (Bandura, Ross, & Ross, 1963). The experimenters had young children observe adult models acting aggressively toward a doll. Later, in the same setting, many of the children behaved in the same highly aggressive manner. Other children who had not observed the adult models behaved much less aggressively.

Similarly, children of poorly functioning people may themselves develop maladaptive reactions because of

their exposure to inadequate parental models. Certainly the selfish and demanding behaviors displayed by Philip Berman's mother could have served as the model for his own self-centered and hypercritical style. Just as his mother was repeatedly critical of others, Philip was critical of every person with whom he developed a close relationship. Similarly, the severe depressive symptoms exhibited by his mother, which led her to be hospitalized, could have been a model for Philip's own depression and discontent.

ASSESSING THE BEHAVIORAL MODEL

The number of behavioral psychologists has grown steadily since the 1950s, and the behavioral model has become a powerful force in the clinical field

"Homogamy," the possession of physical and psychological characteristics that are very similar to those of one's spouse, may be explained by modeling. That is, people may unknowingly imitate the gestures and behaviors of those with whom they spend most of their time until such gestures and behaviors are equally characteristic of them. Alternatively, homogamy may simply reflect the tendency of some people to be attracted to people who are similar to themselves.

Modeling may account for some forms of abnormal behavior. A well-known study by Albert Bandura and his colleagues (1963) demonstrated that children learned to abuse a doll by observing an adult model hit it. Children who had not been exposed to the adult model did not mistreat the doll.

(Franks, 1990; Smith, 1982). Various schools of behavioral thought have emerged over the years, and many treatment techniques have been developed.

Perhaps the most prominent reason that the behavioral model is so attractive is that behavioral explanations and treatments can be tested in the laboratory, whereas the psychodynamic theories generally cannot. The behaviorists' basic concepts—stimulus, response, and reinforcement—can be observed and measured. Even more important, the results of laboratory and field research have lent considerable support to the behavioral model (Emmelkamp, 1994; Wolpe, 1987). Experimenters have successfully used the principles of conditioning to create a number of clinical symptoms in laboratory subjects, thus suggesting that mental disorders may indeed develop in this way. Clinicians have successfully employed behavioral techniques to help change a variety of clinical problems.

Research has also, however, revealed weaknesses in the behavioral model. Although behavioral researchers have induced specific symptoms in subjects, they have not established that such symptoms are ordinarily acquired in this way. There is still no indisputable evidence that the people with mental disorders in our society are largely victims of improper conditioning.

Another problem with the current formulation of the theory is that behavioral explanations and treatments have not been adjusted to account for the research findings coming out of today's conditioning laboratories (Rescorla, 1988). The stimulus-response and reinforcement principles that were once the cornerstone of this model have been challenged in conditioning experiments; some studies even reveal that animal and human subjects can acquire and maintain behaviors in ways that contradict the basic principles

of conditioning. Yet most behaviorists have been largely unaffected by these developments and have continued to rely on the principles of conditioning set forth years ago.

Finally, some critics hold that the behavioral perspective is too simplistic, that its concepts and principles fail to capture the complexity of human behavior. They argue that behaviorists often overlook or minimize the human capacity to think critically. Many behaviorists have themselves been concerned about this issue and in the 1950s began an important movement that continues to the present day. A number of behaviorists felt that they should be looking at more than *overt behaviors,* such as aggressive actions or verbal statements. For example, in 1977 the behaviorist Albert Bandura, who had previously identified modeling as a key learning process, argued that in order to feel happy and function effectively people must develop a positive sense of *self-efficacy,* a judgment that they can master and perform needed behaviors whenever necessary. Similarly, other behaviorists recognized that human beings engage in *cognitive behaviors,* such as private thoughts and beliefs, which were being largely ignored in behavioral theory and therapy. Accordingly, they developed *cognitive-behavioral theories* that took unseen cognitive behaviors into account (Meichenbaum, 1993; Kendall, 1990; Goldiamond, 1965).

Cognitive-behavioral theorists bridge the behavioral model and cognitive model, the perspective that we shall be turning to next. On the one hand, their explanations are firmly entrenched in behavioral principles. They believe, for example, that cognitive processes are acquired and maintained by classical conditioning, operant conditioning, and modeling. On the other hand, cognitive-behavioral theorists share with other kinds of cognitive theorists a belief that the ability to think is the most important aspect of both normal and abnormal human functioning. They hold that people's overt behaviors follow from their interpretations and thoughts, so it is their thoughts rather than their actions that must be examined most closely. Given this central concern with human thought, cognitive-behavioral theories and therapies are now often seen as adjuncts to the cognitive model.

■ THE ■ COGNITIVE MODEL

Philip Berman, like the rest of us, has *cognitive* abilities—special intellectual capacities to think, remember, and anticipate. These cognitive abilities serve him in all his activities and can help him accomplish a great deal in life. Yet they can also work against him. As he cognitively organizes and records his experiences, Philip may be developing false ideas or misinterpreting experiences in ways that lead to counterproductive decisions, maladaptive responses, and unnecessarily painful emotions.

According to the cognitive model, to understand human behavior, we must understand the content and process of human thought. What assumptions and attitudes color a person's perceptions? What thoughts run through that person's mind, and what conclusions do they lead to? When people display abnormal patterns of functioning, cognitive theorists assume that cognitive problems are to blame. Like the behaviorists, they reject a medical illness view of abnormal psychological functioning.

ORIGINS OF THE COGNITIVE MODEL

In the late 1950s, scientists in the field of social psychology—the branch of experimental psychology that studies the individual's interactions with the social environment—became interested in cognitive phenomena they called *attributions.* Social psychologists proposed that we regularly explain the things we see going on around us by attributing them to particular causes and that these causal attributions then influence the way we feel about ourselves and others (Heider, 1958, 1944). For example, a group of test subjects who were physically stimulated by the effects of a drug felt greater anger when they mistakenly attributed their arousal to a person nearby mak-

"Stimulus, response! Stimulus, response! Don't you ever *think?*"

The Far Side © FARWORKS, Inc. Reprinted with permission of Universal Press Syndicate. All rights reserved.

ing irritating comments than when they attributed it to the effects of the drug (Schacter & Singer, 1962; Schacter & Wheeler, 1962). Other social psychology research during the late 1950s and early 1960s indicated that our causal attributions may also influence our ideas, decisions, expectations, and impressions, including our impressions of ourselves. If attributional cognitions play such a critical role in behavior and emotion, shouldn't they also be important in the development and treatment of abnormal behaviors and emotions?

While attributions were becoming the dominant focus in social psychology, the movement toward a more cognitively oriented behaviorism was gaining strength in some segments of the clinical community. These two developments set the stage for the emergence of the cognitive model of abnormal psychology. In the early 1960s two clinicians, Aaron Beck and Albert Ellis, proposed cognitive theories of abnormality (Beck, 1967; Ellis, 1962). Building on earlier work in this area (Kelley, 1955; Rotter, 1954), these theorists claimed that cognitive processes are at the center of behavior, thought, and emotions, and that we can best understand abnormal functioning by looking to the cognitive realm. A number of theorists and therapists soon incorporated the ideas and techniques of Beck and Ellis, refining and expanding the model and greatly influencing the clinical field as a whole (Beck, 1993, 1967; Meichenbaum, 1993, 1977; Ellis, 1989, 1962; Lazarus, 1987, 1971).

COGNITIVE EXPLANATIONS OF ABNORMAL BEHAVIOR

To cognitive theorists, we are all artists who are both reproducing and creating our worlds in our minds as we try to understand the events going on around us. If we are effective artists, our cognitive representations tend to be accurate (agreed upon by others) and useful (adaptive). If we are ineffective artists, however, we may create a cognitive inner world that is alien to others and painful and harmful to ourselves. Abnormal functioning can result from several kinds of cognitive problems: *maladaptive assumptions or attitudes, specific upsetting thoughts,* and *illogical thinking processes.*

MALADAPTIVE ASSUMPTIONS   Albert Ellis (1991, 1989, 1962) proposes that each of us holds a unique set of assumptions about ourselves and our world that serve to guide us through life and determine our reactions to the various situations we encounter. Unfortunately, some people's assumptions are largely irrational, guiding them to act and react in ways that are inappropriate and that prejudice their chances of happiness and success. Ellis calls these **basic irrational assumptions.**

Some people, for example, irrationally assume that they are abject failures if they are not loved or approved of by virtually every person they know. Such people constantly seek approval and repeatedly feel rejected. All their interactions and interpretations are affected by this assumption, so that an otherwise successful presentation in the classroom or boardroom can make them sad or anxious because one listener seems bored, or an evening with friends can leave them dissatisfied because the friends do not offer enough compliments. The basic irrational assumption sets the stage for a life hampered by tension and disappointment.

According to Ellis (1962), other common irrational assumptions are these:

The idea that one should be thoroughly competent, adequate, and achieving in all possible respects if one is to consider oneself worthwhile.

The idea that it is awful and catastrophic when things are not the way one would very much like them to be.

The idea that human unhappiness is externally caused and that people have little or no ability to control their sorrows and disturbances.

The idea that one should be dependent on others and need someone stronger than oneself on whom to rely.

The idea that one's past history is an all-important determiner of one's present behavior and that because something once strongly affected one's life, it should indefinitely have a similar effect.

The idea that there is invariably a right, precise, and perfect solution to human problems and that it is catastrophic if this perfect solution is not found.

Philip Berman often seems to hold the basic irrational assumption that his past history has inexorably determined his present behavior, and that something that once affected his life will have the same effect indefinitely. Philip believes he was victimized by his parents and that he is now doomed by his oppressive past. He seems to approach all new experiences and relationships with expectations of failure and disaster.

SPECIFIC UPSETTING THOUGHTS   Cognitive theorists believe that specific upsetting thoughts may also contribute to abnormal functioning. As we confront the myriad situations that arise in life, numerous thoughts come into our minds, some comforting, others upsetting. Beck has called these unbidden cognitions **automatic thoughts.** When a person's stream of automatic thoughts is overwhelmingly negative, Beck would expect that person to become depressed (Beck, 1993, 1991, 1976). Within a span of seconds, a depressed man may be assaulted by such automatic thoughts as "I should know how to do this. . . . I failed my wife. . . . The future is bleak. . . . I look ugly in this shirt." Philip Berman has made it clear what fleeting thoughts and images keep popping into his mind as he interacts with others: "My old girlfriend wants to jump into bed with her date. . . . I'm a 25-year-old virgin. . . . The therapist wants to laugh at me. . . . My boss wants to fire me. . . . My parents think I'm lazy and irresponsible." Certainly such automatic thoughts are contributing to his pervasive feelings of despondency.

Similarly, Donald Meichenbaum (1993, 1986, 1977), a cognitive-behavioral theorist, suggests that people who suffer from anxiety have inadvertently learned

Aaron Beck proposes that many forms of abnormal behavior can be traced to cognitive factors, such as upsetting thoughts and illogical thinking. Originally trained as a psychoanalytic therapist, Beck came to reject that model and developed a cognitive approach in which therapists challenge clients' dysfunctional beliefs and ways of thinking.

to generate counterproductive *self-statements* (statements about themselves) during stressful situations and as a result react to any difficult situation with automatic fear and discomfort. When Philip Berman met his old girlfriend and her date, his mind may have been flooded with such self-statements as "Oh, no, I can't stand this. . . . I look like a fool. . . . I'm getting sick. . . . Why do these things always happen to me?" These statements may have fueled his anxiety and rage and prevented him from handling the encounter constructively.

ILLOGICAL THINKING PROCESSES Cognitive theorists also point to illogical thinking processes to explain abnormal functioning. Beck (1993, 1991, 1967) has found that some people habitually think in illogical ways and keep drawing self-defeating and even pathological conclusions. As we shall observe in Chapter 8, Beck has identified a number of illogical thought processes characteristic of depression, including *selective perception*, seeing only the negative features of an event; *magnification*, exaggerating the importance of undesirable events; and *overgeneralization*, drawing broad negative conclusions on the basis of a single insignificant event. One depressed student couldn't remember the date of Columbus's third voyage to America during a history class and, overgeneralizing, spent the rest of the day in despair over her invincible ignorance.

Whether they focus primarily on irrational assumptions, self-defeating thoughts, illogical thinking processes, or a combination of the three, cognitive theorists believe that the cognitive sphere is the key to abnormal functioning. Most abnormal behavior is caused not by illness but by incorrect and counterproductive thinking. If malfunctioning people can start to think differently, they can overcome their difficulties.

ASSESSING THE COGNITIVE MODEL

The cognitive model has had very broad appeal. In addition to the many behaviorists who have incorporated cognitive concepts into their theories about learning, a great many clinicians believe that thinking processes are much more than conditioned reactions. Cognitive theory, research, and treatment techniques have developed in so many interesting ways that the model is now viewed as distinct from the behavioral school that spawned it.

There are several reasons for this model's appeal. First, it focuses on the most singular of human processes, human thought. Just as our special cognitive abilities are responsible for so many human accomplishments, they may also be responsible for the special problems that characterize human functioning. Thus many theorists find themselves drawn to a model that views human thought as the primary contributor to normal or abnormal behavior.

Cognitive theories also lend themselves to testing. Researchers have found evidence that people often do exhibit the assumptions, specific thoughts, and thinking processes that supposedly contribute to abnormal functioning, and have shown that these cognitive phenomena are indeed operating in many cases of pathology (Garber et al., 1993; Cole & Turner, 1993). When experimental subjects are manipulated into adopting unpleasant assumptions or thoughts, for example, they became more anxious and depressed (Rimm & Litvak, 1969; Velten, 1968). Similarly, many people with psychological disorders, particularly depressive, anxiety, and sexual disorders, have been found to display maladaptive assumptions, thoughts, or thinking processes (Gustafson, 1992; Shaw & Segal, 1988; Beck et al., 1983, 1974).

Yet the cognitive model, too, has its drawbacks (Beck, 1991). Although it is becoming clear that cognitive processes are involved in many forms of abnormality, their precise role has yet to be ascertained. The maladaptive cognitions seen in psychologically troubled people could well be a consequence rather than a cause of their difficulties. Certainly processes so central to human functioning must be highly vulnerable to disturbances of any kind.

Like the other models, the cognitive model has been criticized for the narrowness of its scope. Although cognition is a very special human dimension, it is still but one part of human functioning. Are human beings not more than their thoughts—indeed, more than the sum total of their fleeting thoughts, emotions, and behaviors? For those who believe that they are, explanations of human functioning must at least sometimes embrace broader issues, such as how people approach life, what they get from it, and how they deal with the question of life's meaning. This is the contention of the humanistic-existential perspective.

■ THE ■ HUMANISTIC-EXISTENTIAL MODEL

Philip Berman is more than his organic processes, psychological conflicts, learned behaviors, and cognitions. Being human, he also has the ability to confront complex and challenging philosophical issues such as self-awareness, values, meaning, and choice, and to incorporate them into his life. And according to humanistic and existential theorists, Philip's problems can be understood only in the light of those issues. Humanistic and existential theorists are usually grouped together because of their common focus on the broader dimensions of human existence. At the same time, there are some important differences between them.

Humanists, the more optimistic of the two groups, believe that human beings are born with a natural inclination to be friendly, cooperative, and constructive, and are driven to *self-actualize*—that is, to fulfill this potential for goodness and growth (Rogers, 1987, 1959; Maslow, 1967). They will be able to do so, however, only if they can honestly appraise and accept their weaknesses as well as their strengths and establish a satisfying system of personal values to live by. If they habitually deceive themselves and create a distorted view of the things that happen to them, they are likely to suffer some degree of psychological dysfunction.

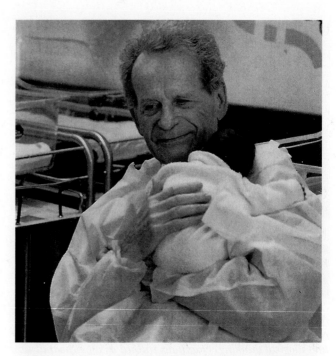

Humanists believe that all humans have a natural drive to "self-actualize"—to fulfill their potential for goodness and growth—but that some people drift away from this basic drive. Abraham Maslow suggested that self-actualized people, such as this volunteer who regularly cares for babies afflicted with AIDS, show concern for the welfare of humanity. They are also thought to be highly creative, spontaneous, independent, and humorous.

Existentialists agree that human beings must have an accurate awareness of themselves and live subjectively meaningful—they say "authentic"—lives in order to be mentally well adjusted. These theorists do not believe, however, that people are naturally inclined to live constructively. They believe that from birth we have total freedom, either to face up to our existence and give meaning to our lives or to shrink from that responsibility. Those who choose to "hide" from responsibility and choice will view themselves as helpless and weak and may live empty, inauthentic, and dysfunctional lives as a consequence. Thus neither humanists nor existentialists embrace a medical illness view of abnormal psychological functioning.

ORIGINS OF THE HUMANISTIC-EXISTENTIAL MODEL

The humanistic and existential views of abnormality both date back to the 1940s. At that time Carl Rogers (1902–1987), often considered the pioneer of the humanistic perspective, began to develop ideas about psychotherapy that contrasted sharply with the influential psychodynamic principles of the day. He suggested that clients would do better in treatment if therapy were focused on their unique subjective perspective rather than on someone else's definition of objective reality. Rogers also proposed that clients would respond better if therapists were particularly warm, genuine, and understanding. He described this new therapeutic approach, called **client-centered therapy,** in an influential book published in the early 1950s.

Rogers then went on to develop a theory of personality and abnormality based on the approach he took in his therapy. He concluded that if people respond to a therapist's warmth with greater honesty about themselves and with a reduction of symptoms, then the human personality must be rooted in more than the irrational instincts and conflicts emphasized in the psychodynamic model. This "humanistic" theory of personality, reminiscent of the theories of the French philosopher Jean-Jacques Rousseau (1712–1778) and the American psychologist and philosopher William James (1842–1910), emphasized a special, positive potential inherent in human beings. About the same time, other humanistic theories developed by Abraham Maslow (1908–1970) and Fritz Perls (1893–1970) also received widespread attention.

The existential view of personality and abnormality came into prominence during this same period. It derived from the ideas of such European existential philosophers as Søren Kierkegaard (1813–1855), Karl Jaspers (1883–1969), Edmund Husserl (1859–1938), Martin Heidegger (1889–1976), and Jean-Paul Sartre (1905–1980), all of whom held that human beings are constantly defining their existence through their actions and that the meaning of individual existence lies in such efforts at definition. In 1942 Ludwig Binswanger, a Swiss psychoanalyst, combined this existential principle with psychoanalytic therapy in an approach called *Daseinanalyse* ("existential analysis"). According to Binswanger, therapists could help their patients only by guiding them through the indispensable process of *being,* the process of developing in one's own unique ways through one's actions.

Other clinical theorists, including Medard Boss, Rollo May, and Viktor Frankl, espoused similar existential ideas throughout the 1950s. A book titled *Existence,* now considered a classic work on the clinical existential perspective, described all the major existential ideas and treatment approaches of the time and helped them gain widespread attention (May, Angel, & Ellenberger, 1958).

The humanistic and existential theories were extremely popular during the 1960s and 1970s, years of

Carl Rogers, one of the founders of the humanistic model, believed that therapists must be empathic, accepting, and genuine if clients are to be helped to trust other people, accept themselves, and overcome their psychological problems. His call for systematic research in the clinical field helped start a trend that still continues. Ironically, most humanistic theorists now consider empirical research an improper and inaccurate method of psychological investigation.

considerable soul-searching and social upheaval in Western society. People were worried that twentieth-century society had become too affluent and materialistic, that human values and concerns had been cast aside, and that feelings of alienation, purposelessness, and spiritual emptiness had become common in the face of rapid technological and bureaucratic growth. Humanistic theories, which reaffirmed the human spirit, and existential theories, which challenged people to take charge of their lives, addressed these growing concerns. Although the humanistic-existential model lost some of its popularity in the 1980s, it continues to influence the treatment techniques of many clinicians.

HUMANISTIC EXPLANATIONS OF ABNORMAL BEHAVIOR

According to Carl Rogers (1987, 1967, 1961, 1951), the road to dysfunction begins in infancy. We all have a basic need to receive *positive regard* from the significant other people in our lives (primarily from our parents). Those who receive *unconditional* (nonjudgmental) *positive regard* early in life are likely to develop

"It's always 'Sit,' 'Stay,' 'Heel'—never 'Think,' 'Innovate,' 'Be yourself.'"

Parents who fail to extend unconditional positive regard may not fully stifle the creative powers of their children, but according to Roger's humanistic theory they are likely to instill a sense of unworthiness and inadequacy that prevents the children from becoming fully self-actualized. (Drawing by P. Steiner; © 1992 The New Yorker Magazine, Inc.)

unconditional self-regard. That is, they come to recognize their worth as persons, even while recognizing that they are not perfect. They feel comfortable about themselves and are able to evaluate themselves in a clear-sighted way. Such people are in a good psychological position to actualize their inherently positive potential.

Unfortunately, some children are repeatedly made to feel that they are not worthy of positive regard. As a result, they acquire *conditions of worth*, standards that tell them they are lovable and acceptable only when they conform to the standards they have been exposed to, and they constantly judge themselves accordingly. Much of the time, they will feel that their thoughts, behavior, or emotions fall short of those standards, and will judge themselves as being unworthy as a result.

Such people are in a difficult psychological position. On the one hand, they have the basic universal need for positive self-regard. On the other hand, they are unable to like themselves unless they are always conforming to a highly critical set of standards. In order to maintain positive self-regard, these people have to look at themselves in a very selective fashion, deny-

ing or distorting thoughts and actions that do not measure up to their conditions of worth.

The constant self-deception makes it impossible for these people to self-actualize. They have a distorted view of themselves and their experiences, and so they do not know what they are genuinely feeling or needing, or what values and goals would be meaningful for them. Moreover, they spend so much energy trying to protect their self-image that little is left to devote to self-actualizing. Problems in functioning are then inevitable.

Thus humanistic clinicians might view Philip Berman as a man who has gone astray. Rather than striving to fulfill his positive human potential, he drifts from job to job, relationship to relationship, and outburst to outburst. In every interaction he is defending himself, trying to interpret events in ways he can live with. He always considers his problems to be someone else's fault, and he keeps presenting himself as a strong person who cares little about what other folks may think. Yet his constant efforts at self-defense and self-enhancement are only partially successful. His basic negative self-image and his assumption that others will think badly of him keep breaking through. This problem would probably be ascribed to the way he was treated as a child. Rather than offer him unconditional positive regard, his mother apparently kept calling him a "pervert" and a "sissy," bullied him, and even abused him. Small wonder that Philip never learned to accept and value himself unconditionally.

EXISTENTIAL EXPLANATIONS OF ABNORMAL BEHAVIOR

Like humanists, existentialists believe that psychological dysfunctioning is caused by self-deception; but existentialists are talking about a kind of self-deception in which people hide from life's responsibilities and fail to recognize that it is up to them to give meaning to their lives and that they have the capacity and freedom to do so. According to existentialists, people start to hide from personal responsibility and choice when they become engulfed in the constant change, confusion, and emotional strain of present-day society, as well as in the particular stresses of their immediate environment. Overwhelmed by these pressures, many people look to others for guidance and authority, and conform excessively to social standards. Others may build resentment toward society. Either way, they overlook their personal freedom of choice and avoid responsibility for their lives and decisions (May & Yalom, 1989; May, 1987, 1961; Bugental, 1965). This abdication of responsibility and choice may offer a form of refuge, but at a cost. Such people are left with empty, inauthentic lives. Their prevailing emotions are anxiety, frustration, alienation, and depression.

Thus existentialists might view Philip Berman as a man who considers himself incompetent to resist the forces of society. He views his parents as "rich, powerful, and selfish," and he sees teachers, acquaintances, and employers as perpetrators of abuse and oppression. Overwhelmed, he fails to appreciate his choices in life and his capacity for finding meaning and direction. Quitting becomes a habit with him— he leaves job after job, ends every romantic relationship, flees difficult situations, and even tries suicide. For existentialists, Philip's problems are best summarized by the part of the case description that states, "He spent most of his time alone, 'bored.' He was unable to commit himself to any person, he held no strong convictions, and he felt no allegiance to any group."

ASSESSING THE HUMANISTIC-EXISTENTIAL MODEL

The humanistic-existential model appeals to many people in and out of the clinical field for several reasons. First, the model focuses on broad human issues rather than on a single aspect of psychological functioning. In recognizing the special features and challenges of human existence, humanistic and existential theorists tap into a dimension of psychological life that is typically missing from the other models (Fuller, 1982). Moreover, the factors that they say are essential to effective psychological functioning— self-acceptance, personal values, personal meaning, personal choice, and so on—are undeniably lacking in many people with psychological disturbances.

The optimistic tone of the humanistic-existential model is also an attraction. Humanistic and existential theorists offer great hope when they assert that despite the often overwhelming pressures of modern society, we can make our own choices, determine our own destiny, and accomplish much.

Still another attractive feature of the humanistic-existential model is its emphasis on health rather than illness (Cowen, 1991). Unlike proponents of some of the other models who see individuals as patients with psychological illnesses, humanists and existentialists view them simply as people whose special potential has yet to be fulfilled. And although they acknowledge the impact of past events on present behavior, they do not hold a deterministic view of behavior. They believe our behavior can be influenced by our innate goodness and potential, and by our willingness to take responsibility, more than by any factor in our past.

Although appealing in these ways, the humanistic-existential focus on abstract issues of human fulfillment also gives rise to a significant problem: these issues are resistant to research. In fact, with the notable exception of Rogers, who spent years empirically testing his psychotherapeutic methods, humanists and existentialists tend to reject the experimental approaches that now dominate the field. They believe that such methods cannot accurately examine their ideas, and they hold that today's researchers typically miss subtle, internal experiences by looking only at what they can define objectively. Humanists and existentialists have tried to establish the merits of their views by appealing to logic, introspection, and individual case histories. Although they are sincere and true to their principles in taking this position, the result is that the model has received limited empirical examination or support. Sherlock Holmes once observed, "It is a capital mistake to theorize before one has data. Insensibly one begins to twist facts to suit theories, instead of theories to suit facts." Many critics would argue that humanistic and existential theorists are particularly vulnerable to this danger.

A final problem is the model's heterogeneity. Theories and therapies called humanistic or existential are so numerous and so varied that it is almost misleading to lump them together into a single category. Still, this extremely varied group of theorists and practitioners does share a belief that human beings are self-determining and have an enormous potential for growth, and that self-exploration is the key to this growth.

■ THE ■ SOCIOCULTURAL MODEL

Philip Berman is also a social being. He is surrounded by people and by institutions, he is a member of a family and a society, and he participates in social and professional relationships. Thus external social forces are always operating on Philip, setting rules and expectations that guide and at times pressure him, helping to shape his behavior, thoughts, and emotions as surely as any internal biological or psychological mechanism.

According to the sociocultural model of psychology, abnormal behavior is best understood in light of the social and cultural forces brought to bear on an individual. What are the norms and values of the society? What roles does the person play in the social environment? What kind of family structure is this person exposed to? And how do other people view and react to him or her?

ORIGINS OF THE SOCIOCULTURAL MODEL

The sociocultural view of abnormality derives its basic assumptions from the fields of *sociology*, the study of human relationships and social groups, and *anthropology*, the study of human cultures and institutions. These fields first emerged as independent areas of study in the nineteenth century and have generated numerous theories touching on the subject of abnormal psychology.

Sociologists have proposed that societies themselves are capable of generating abnormal behavior in their members. Certain communities may be so disorganized that many of their members are forced to engage in odd behavior to adapt to the community's norms or standards. Sociologists also claim that even stable societies may help produce and maintain abnormal behavior in some of their members by the common practice of identifying certain individuals as unusual, reacting to them in special ways, and expecting and encouraging them to take on the roles that the society assigns to abnormal people (Scheff, 1966; Becker, 1964).

In consonance with this sociological notion, anthropologists have found that some patterns of abnormality vary from society to society, from culture to culture (Yap, 1951; Mead, 1949; Benedict, 1934; Malinowsky, 1927). For example, the disorder of "windigo," an intense fear of being turned into a cannibal by a flesh-eating monster, was found only among Algonquin Indian hunters, and "koro," a fear that one's penis will withdraw into the abdomen, was found only in Southeast Asia. Each of these abnormal patterns seemed uniquely tied to the society's particular history and culture (see Box 2–2).

By the 1950s, these sociological and anthropological notions were beginning to have considerable influence on the study and treatment of abnormal psychol-

ogy. Finally, a new clinical model—the sociocultural model—emerged, marked by three key events. One was the publication in 1958 of a major study, *Social Class and Mental Illness*, by August Hollingshead and Frederick Redlich, which linked various forms of mental illness to particular social classes. The study found that psychotic, aggressive, and rebellious behavior was much more common in the lower socioeconomic classes than in the upper classes.

A second event marking the emergence of the sociocultural model was the development of family theory and therapy during the 1950s. After observing interactions between people with schizophrenia and their families, some theorists concluded that mentally disturbed individuals were often the products of a disturbed family structure, and they developed an intervention technique in which *all* members of the family are treated, not just the individual identified as "the sick one" (Nichols, 1992; Bowen, 1987, 1960; Satir, 1967, 1964; Ackerman, 1965).

Finally, the emergence of the sociocultural model was marked by the influential work of Thomas Szasz (1987, 1961), the outspoken psychiatrist who in the 1950s launched an attack against the mental health system and challenged the very concept of mental illness. As we observed in Chapter 1, Szasz took the extreme position that mental disorders are the creations of society. They are simply problems in living that come to be labeled as illnesses because other members of society feel confused and threatened by them. A prolific writer and speaker, Szasz has widely broadcast his arguments among clinical theorists, practitioners, and the public at large over the past three decades. His views have been influential in directing explanations of abnormality away from an exclusive focus on the individual and toward the possible involvement of society.

SOCIOCULTURAL EXPLANATIONS OF ABNORMAL BEHAVIOR

Because behavior is shaped by social forces, sociocultural theorists hold, we must examine the social context if we are to understand abnormal behavior in individual cases. Their explanations focus on *family structure and communication*, *societal stress*, and *societal labels and reactions*.

FAMILY STRUCTURE AND COMMUNICATION According to *family systems theory*, the family is a *system* of interacting parts, the family members,

Research indicates that people in the lower socioeconomic classes have higher rates of psychological dysfunctioning than those in the middle and upper classes. Conditions of chronic poverty, such as that experienced by these Irish tinkers, may contribute, especially when individuals lose their homes, possessions, and dignity.

who relate to one another in consistent ways and are governed by implicit rules unique to each family (Nichols, 1992; Bowen, 1987, 1960; Minuchin, 1987). The parts interact in ways that enable the system to maintain itself and survive—a state known as **homeostasis.** Family systems theorists believe that the structure, rules, and communication patterns of some families actually force individual members to behave in a way that the society at large may define as abnormal. Indeed, the family's ongoing responses and accommodations serve to maintain the "abnormal" behavior. If the individual members were to behave normally, they would severely upset the family's boundaries, implicit rules, and homeostasis and actually increase their own and their family's turmoil. The responses by other family members would quickly extinguish such "normal" behavior. Thus, a dysfunctional family system may both create and maintain an individual's abnormal behavior (Szapocznik & Kurtines, 1993).

Family systems theory portrays certain family systems as being particularly likely to produce abnormal functioning in individual family members (Becvar & Becvar, 1993; Nichols, 1992, 1984). Some families, for example, are so *inflexible* that it is virtually impossible for the children to grow into healthy adults. These families may be resistant to almost all external influences or may fail to adapt to internal changes as necessary, say when a new child is born or an older one enters adolescence. Some families have a rigidly *enmeshed* structure in which the members are grossly overinvolved in each others' activities, thoughts, and feelings. Children from this kind of family may have great difficulty establishing autonomy in life. Conversely, some families display a structure of *disengagement*, which is characterized by overly rigid boundaries between the members. Children from these families may find it hard to function interdependently and may have difficulty giving or requesting support when needed. And some families are characterized by *pathological triangular relationships* in which the parents avoid dealing with their own serious conflicts by always involving the children in their discussions or activities. These children have great difficulty developing into autonomous, separate individuals. Problematic family patterns are often passed on from one generation to the next.

Family systems theorists hold that the problems of one family member cannot be solved with individual therapy alone. Because change in one part of the system will affect the rest of the system, it is possible that positive change in one subsystem may alleviate psychological distress and abnormal functioning in other family members. Thus, family systems therapists may treat a teenage boy's depression by trying to strengthen his parent's marriage or an adolescent girl's eating disorder by changing the diffuse boundaries existing between her and her parents. By the same token, treatment of a "sick" or "scapegoat" member of the family may prove ineffective if the problems in the rest of the family system are not addressed (Nichols, 1984).

Philip Berman's angry and impulsive personal style can be seen as the product of a disturbed family structure. According to family systems theorists, the whole family—mother, father, Philip, and his brother Arnold—relate in such a way as to maintain Philip's behavior. Family theorists might be particularly interested in the conflict between Philip's mother and father and the imbalance between their parental roles. They might see Philip's behavior as both a reaction to and stimulus for his parents' behaviors, and consider his "ornery" behavior, like his mother's critical comments and his father's weak and ineffectual actions, as functioning to preserve the parents' troubled marriage and stabilize the family. With Philip acting out the role of the misbehaving child, or "scapegoat," his parents may have little need or time to question their own relationship. Family systems theorists would also seek to clarify issues such as the precise nature of Philip's relationship with each parent (Is he enmeshed with his mother and/or disengaged from his father?), the implicit rules governing the sibling relationship in the family, the power structure and relationship between the parents and Philip's brother, and the nature of parent-child relationships in previous generations of the family.

SOCIETAL STRESS   The unique characteristics of a given society may create special stresses that heighten the likelihood of abnormal functioning in its members. As we shall see in Chapter 3, researchers often conduct *epidemiological studies* to identify such societies. That is, they measure the *prevalence,* or total number of cases occurring in a population over a specific period of time; the *incidence,* or number of new cases that occur over a specific period of time; and the distribution of a specific psychological disorder in a particular population. Studies of this kind have found correlations between rates of abnormal functioning and such factors as widespread *social change, social class membership, ethnic and national background, race and sex,* and *cultural institutions and values.* As a consequence, clinicians are becoming increasingly sensitive to the "hidden injuries" that result from racism, sexism, and poverty, as well as from less obvious societal stressors such as urbanization and cultural change (Vega & Rumbaut, 1991).

BOX   2-2

CULTURE-BOUND ABNORMALITY

Red Bear sits up wild-eyed, his body drenched in sweat, every muscle tensed. The horror of the dream is still with him; he is choked with fear. Fighting waves of nausea, he stares at his young wife lying asleep on the far side of the wigwam, illuminated by the dying embers.

His troubles began several days before, when he came back from a hunting expedition empty-handed. Ashamed of his failure, he fell prey to a deep, lingering depression. Others in the village, noticing a change in Red Bear, watched him nervously, afraid that he was becoming bewitched by a windigo. Red Bear was also frightened. The signs of windigo were all there: depression, lack of appetite, nausea, sleeplessness and, now, the dream. Indeed, there could be no mistake.

He had dreamed of the windigo—the monster with a heart of ice—and the dream sealed his doom. Coldness gripped his own heart. The ice monster had entered his body and possessed him. He himself had become a windigo, and he could do nothing to avert his fate.

Suddenly, the form of Red Bear's sleeping wife begins to change. He no longer sees a woman, but a deer. His eyes flame. Silently, he draws his knife from under the blanket and moves stealthily toward the motionless figure. Saliva drips from the corners of his mouth, and a terrible hunger twists his intestines. A powerful desire to eat raw flesh consumes him.

With the body of the "deer" at his feet, Red Bear raises the knife high, preparing to strike. Unexpectedly, the deer screams and twists away. But the knife flashes down, again and again. Too late, Red Bear's kinsmen rush into the wigwam. With cries of outrage and horror, they drag him outside into the cold night air and swiftly kill him.
(Lindholm & Lindholm, 1981, p. 52)

Red Bear was suffering from *windigo,* a disorder once common among Algonquin Indian hunters who believed in a supernatural monster that ate human beings and also had the power to bewitch them and turn them into cannibals. Like Red Bear, a small number of afflicted hunters actually did kill and eat household members.

Windigo is one of the unusual mental disorders discovered around the

SOCIAL CHANGE   When a society undergoes major change, the mental health of its members can be greatly affected. Societies undergoing rapid urbanization, for example, usually show a rise in mental disorders, although it is not known which features of urbanization—overcrowding, technological change, social isolation, migration, and so forth—are most to blame (Ghubash, Hamdi, & Bebbington, 1992). Similarly, a society in the throes of economic depression is likely to show a significant rise in rates of clinical depression and suicide (Hammer, 1993; Brown, 1983; Dooley & Catalano, 1980), which may be explained in part by an increase in unemployment and the resulting loss of self-esteem and personal security.

SOCIAL CLASS   As we saw earlier, membership in a lower socioeconomic class appears to increase vulnerability to certain patterns of abnormality (Murphy et al., 1992; Stansfeld & Marmot, 1992). Studies have found that rates of psychological abnormality, especially severe psychological abnormality, are three times higher in the lower socioeconomic classes than in the higher ones (Dohrenwend et al., 1992; Eron & Peterson, 1982).

Perhaps the special pressures of lower-class life help explain this relationship (Adler et al., 1994; Dohrenwend et al., 1992). The higher rates of crime, unemployment, overcrowding, and even homelessness, the inferior medical care, and the limited educational opportunities that often characterize lower-class life may place great stress on members of these groups. Of course, other factors could also be to blame. People who suffer from significant mental disturbances may be less effective at work, earn less money, and as a result drift downward to settle in a lower socioeconomic class.

ETHNIC, RELIGIOUS, AND NATIONAL BACKGROUND   Ethnic, religious, and national groups have distinctive traditions that may influence the kinds of abnormal functioning to which they are vulnerable. Alcoholism, for example, is more prevalent in groups that tolerate heavy drinking (Catholics, Irish, Western Europeans, Eastern Europeans) than in groups that frown on it (Jews, Protestants) (Barry, 1982).

RACIAL AND SEXUAL PREJUDICE   Prejudice and discrimination may also contribute to certain forms of abnormal functioning. Societies typically

---

world, each unique to a particular culture, each apparently growing from the particular pressures, history, institutions, and ideas of the culture (Lindholm & Lindholm, 1981; Kiev, 1972; Lehmann, 1967; Yap, 1951). Sociocultural theorists cite disorders such as windigo as evidence that societies often help to produce abnormal behavior in their members. The following are other exotic disorders that have been reported:

Susto, a disorder found among members of Indian tribes in Central and South America and non-Indian natives of the Andean highlands of Peru, Bolivia, and Colombia, is most likely to occur in infants and young children. The symptoms are extreme anxiety, excitability, and depression, along with loss of weight, weakness, and rapid heartbeat. The culture holds that this disorder is caused by contact with supernatural beings or with frightening

strangers, or by bad air from cemeteries and other supposedly dangerous places. Treatment includes rubbing certain plants and animals against the skin.

Amok, a disorder found in Malaya, the Philippines, Java, and some parts of Africa, is more likely to occur in men than in women. Those who are afflicted jump around violently, yell loudly, grab weapons, such as knives, and attack any people and objects they encounter. This behavior is usually preceded by an earlier stage in which the victim withdraws socially and suffers some loss of contact with reality. The periods of violent behavior are followed by depression and by amnesia concerning the outburst. Within the culture, amok is thought to be caused by stress, severe shortage of sleep, alcohol consumption, and extreme heat.

Koro is a pattern of anxiety found in Southeast Asia in which a man suddenly becomes intensely fearful that his penis will withdraw into his abdomen and that he will die as a result. Cultural lore holds that the disorder is caused by an imbalance of "yin" and "yang," two natural forces believed to be the fundamental components of life. Accepted forms of treatment include having the individual keep a firm hold on his penis until the fear passes, often with the assistance of family members or friends, and clamping the penis to a wooden box.

Latah is a disorder found in Malaya, usually among uneducated middle-aged or elderly women. Certain circumstances (hearing someone say "snake"; being tickled) trigger a fright reaction marked by repeating others' words and acts, using obscene words, and doing the opposite of what others ask.

The social upheaval and accompanying economic depression now occurring throughout the former Soviet Union inevitably affects the emotional health of its people, according to socio-cultural theorists. Not surprisingly, Russia is now faced with growing alienation and stagnation among many of its youth. Here, young Russians gather at a graffiti wall in Moscow, which is a memorial to the rock star Vic, or Tsoi, who died in a car accident.

have "in-groups" and "out-groups," the latter composed of people who are deprived of many of the opportunities and comforts available to the former. The out-groups—whose members are often fewer than the in-group members and different from them in ethnicity, race, or gender—are sometimes called "minority groups" or "ethnic minorities." In the United States such terms typically refer to all nonwhite groups of Americans.

The number of people who are members of ethnic minorities is both substantial and growing in the United States. By the end of the 1990s, a third of the U.S. population will have minority status (Jones, 1990). Given such numbers and the fact that white Americans are themselves composed of many ethnic groups, the use of the term "ethnic minority" in the United States is inaccurate in many eyes. Nevertheless, in large part because of their minority status, people in these groups continue to be confronted each day with prejudice, pressures, and difficulties beyond life's usual stresses, which make it particularly hard to achieve physical and psychological health and life satisfaction.

Women in Western society receive diagnoses of anxiety and depression disorders at least twice as often as men (Wittchen, Essau, & von Zerssen, 1992; Dean & Ensel, 1983). African Americans experience unusually high rates of anxiety disorders (Blazer et al., 1991; Eaton, Dryman, & Weissman, 1991). Hispanic people, particularly young men, have higher rates

of alcoholism than members of most other ethnic groups (Helzer, Burnman, & McEvoy, 1991). Native Americans display unusually high alcoholism and suicide rates (Kinzie et al., 1992). And there are growing indications that despite their reluctance to seek treatment, Asian Americans may suffer from more emotional problems than was previously recognized (Abe & Zane, 1990). Although many factors may combine to produce these differences (Betancourt & López, 1993), racial and sexual prejudice and the struggles and the limitations they impose may contribute to pathological patterns of tension, unhappiness, low self-esteem, and escape (Sue, 1991; Kramer, Rosen, & Willis, 1973).

CULTURAL INSTITUTIONS AND VALUES Disorders such as windigo and koro are thought to grow out of the institutions and values of the cultures where they arise. So is *anorexia nervosa*, a disorder particularly prevalent among young women in Western society (Garner, Shafer, & Rosen, 1991; Garner & Rosen, 1990). As we will see in Chapter 12, people with this disorder intentionally deprive themselves of food and lose dangerous amounts of weight. Many theorists believe that the current emphasis on thinness as the female aesthetic ideal in Western culture is largely responsible for anorexia nervosa's high and apparently increasing incidence there. Studies have found a growing preference for very thin female frames in North American and European magazines, movies, and advertisements over the past two

Some sociocultural theorists believe that intense social stressors may produce outbreaks of mass madness, such as tarantism, the mania that occurred throughout Europe in the Middle Ages, or the Los Angeles riots of 1992. In an insidious cycle, the riots, which occurred against a backdrop of poverty, unemployment, prejudice, and community decline, produced further stress for members of the community. Joe and Joyce Wilson, for example, survey the damage to their business, "Pop's Restaurant," and try to cope with its impact upon their lives.

decades, the same period of time in which the rates of anorexia nervosa have shown a significant rise.

SOCIETAL LABELS AND REACTIONS So-ciocultural theorists also believe that abnormal functioning is influenced greatly by the diagnostic labels given to troubled people and by the ways other people react to those labels (Szasz, 1987, 1963; Scheff, 1975; Rosenhan, 1973). The theorists hold that when people violate the norms of their society, the society categorizes them as deviant and assigns them labels such as "mentally ill."

According to these theorists, the initial label of mental illness may or may not be justified. Regardless, once the label is assigned, a vicious cycle is initiated that ensures the development of further abnormal behavior. The label of mental illness tends to stick to a person, condemning him or her to be viewed in stereotyped ways, reacted to as "crazy," and expected and subtly encouraged to be incapacitated. Gradually the person learns to accept and play the assigned role, functioning and behaving in an increasingly disturbed manner. Ultimately the label seems fully justified.

A famous and controversial study by the clinical investigator David Rosenhan (1973) supports this position. Eight normal people presented themselves at various mental hospitals, complaining that they had been hearing voices say the words "empty," "hollow," and "thud." On the basis of this complaint alone, each "pseudopatient" was diagnosed as schizophrenic and admitted to the hospital. According to the researchers, the events of the following weeks highlighted several issues. First, it was hard to get rid of the label. The length of hospitalization ranged from seven to fifty-two days, even though the pseudopatients behaved normally as soon as they were admitted to the hospital. Second, the schizophrenic label kept influencing the way staff viewed and dealt with the pseudopatients. A pseudopatient who paced the corridor out of boredom was said to be "nervous." Third, pseudopatients reported that the staff's attitudes and reactions toward patients in general were often authoritarian, limited, and counterproductive. Overall, the pseudopatients came to feel powerless, depersonalized, and bored. Their treatment in the hospital seemed to undermine their mood.

ASSESSING THE SOCIOCULTURAL MODEL

The sociocultural model has added an important dimension to the understanding of abnormal functioning. Today most clinicians take family structure and social issues into account in their efforts to understand individual cases of mental disorder, factors that were largely overlooked just thirty years ago. Moreover, practitioners are by and large more sensitive to the negative impact of clinical labels, addressing the issue during therapy and working to improve the use and accuracy of labels in diagnosis and assessment.

At the same time, the sociocultural model, like other models, leaves some questions unanswered and problems unresolved. To begin with, the research used to support this model is sometimes inaccurate. Epidemiological studies, for example, often base prevalence rates on hospital admissions or visits to counseling centers, and figures from those sources do not always reflect a disorder's incidence in the public at large (Cooke, 1989; Bromet, 1984).

A second problem is that the studies done to date have failed to support certain key predictions of the sociocultural model (Gove, 1982). Although some forms of abnormality are indeed associated with certain societies, as the model predicts, other forms, particularly the most severe ones, appear to be universal, with a similar incidence and similar symptoms in a wide range of settings. As we noted in Chapter 1, for example, schizophrenia occurs throughout the world: approximately 1 percent of people everywhere appear to exhibit this disorder's central symptoms of confusion, distorted ideas, and hallucinations; and every society considers these symptoms abnormal (Regier et al., 1993; Strauss, 1979; Murphy, 1976).

Still another problem is that sociocultural research findings are often difficult to interpret. Studies that reveal a relationship between sociocultural factors and mental disorders may fail to establish that the former cause the latter. For example, a number of studies show a link between family conflict and schizophrenic disorders (Vaughan et al., 1992; Goldstein, 1990; Hirsch, 1979). Although this finding may indicate that family dysfunction helps cause schizophrenia, it is equally possible that the schizophrenic behavior of a family member disrupts normal family functioning and creates conflicts.

Perhaps the most serious limitation of the sociocultural model is its inability to predict psychopathology in specific individuals. If, say, the current emphasis on thinness in women is a major reason for the growing incidence of anorexia nervosa in Western nations, why are only a small percentage of the women in these countries anorexic? Certainly, most women are exposed to the same standards of beauty. Are still other factors necessary for the disorder to develop? In response to such criticisms, most clinicians choose to view sociocultural explanations as going hand in hand with biological or psychological explanations. They believe that sociocultural variables may set a climate favorable to the development of certain mental disorders, but that biological or psychological conditions or both must also be present for the mental disorders to unfold.

■ RELATIONSHIPS ■ BETWEEN THE MODELS

The models we have just examined vary widely in the dimensions of behavior they focus on, the assumptions they employ, and the conclusions they reach. Each has proponents, many of whom not only hold their particular model to be the most enlightened but criticize the other models as foolish or misleading (Marmor, 1987) (see Box 2–3). Yet none of the models has proved consistently superior to the rest. Each helps us appreciate a critical dimension of human functioning, and each has important strengths and serious limitations.

In fact, while today's models may differ from one another in significant ways, their conclusions are often compatible (Friman et al., 1993; Marmor, 1987). Certainly our understanding of a person's abnormal behavior is more complete if we appreciate the biological, psychological, *and* sociocultural aspects of his or her problem rather than one of those aspects to the exclusion of the rest. Even the various psychological models can sometimes be compatible. In cases of sexual dysfunction, for example, psychodynamic causes (such as internal conflicts in childhood), behavioral causes (such as learning incorrect sexual techniques), and cognitive causes (such as misconceptions

---

BOX 2–3

TODAY'S THEORISTS EVALUATE FREUD

There is no question that Sigmund Freud's is the best-known name in the clinical field. His theories still pervade popular literature and public consciousness. In recent years, a number of prominent theorists, writers, and scholars have commented on his contributions and his reputation. Their comments show the passion that Freud, his work, and his legacy continue to evoke in today's clinical community.

Stephen M. Sonnenberg, *psychoanalyst*
What we can still learn from Freud is what we could always learn from Freud—that most mental activity goes on outside of conscious awareness, that much of the mental pain and anguish that people experience is the result of conflict that is not conscious, and that there is resistance to recognizing that there is unconscious process.

Alice Miller, psychologist and author
Do I owe anything to Sigmund Freud, psychoanalyst? Today, I would say: twenty years of blindness toward the reality of child abuse

as well as toward the most important facts of my life. In 1896, Sigmund Freud discovered the truth about the repression of childhood traumas and its effects on the adult. Unable to bear his truth, he finally decided to deny his own discovery. One year later, in 1897, he developed the psychoanalytic theory which actually conceals the reality of child abuse and supports the tradition of blaming the child and protecting the parents.

Thomas Szasz, *psychiatrist and author of* The Myth of Mental Illness
We can learn from what he talked about but did not practice—in fact, he systematically lied about it— which is the concept of the *absolutely confidential*, totally voluntary, uncoerced conversation with another person, who comes to see you and pays for the service. The conversation should always be paid for; this ensures that the person isn't coming to you for any other reason. But Freud

about sex) often seem to combine to produce the problem.

The models also demonstrate compatibility when each emphasizes a different kind of causal factor. When theorists talk about a disorder's cause, they are referring either to *predisposing factors,* events that occur long before the appearance of the disorder and set the stage for later difficulties; to *precipitating factors,* events that actually trigger the disorder; or to *maintaining factors,* events that keep the disorder going over time.

When each of several models focuses on a different kind of causal factor, their explanations may be far from contradictory. Clinicians are increasingly embracing *diathesis-stress* explanations of abnormal behavior—the view that a person must first have a biological, psychological, or sociocultural predisposition to a disorder and must then be subjected to an immediate form of psychological stress to develop and maintain certain forms of abnormality. If we explore a

case of depression, for instance, we may well find a neurotransmitter dysfunction as a predisposing factor, a major loss as a precipitating factor, and errors in logic as a maintaining factor.

As different kinds of disorders are presented throughout this textbook, we will look at how the proponents of today's models explain each disorder, how each model's practitioners treat people with the disorder, and how well the explanations and treatment approaches are supported by research. We will observe both how the explanations and treatments differ *and* how they may build upon each other. These examinations require that we have some preliminary information about how clinical scientists and clinical practitioners conduct their work. Thus Chapter 3 describes the methods used by clinical scientists and the standards by which they conduct their research. Chapter 4 and Chapter 5 examine the assessment, diagnostic, and treatment responsibilities of clinical practitioners.

betrayed this concept through his training analysis, through his child analysis and through his so-called analysis of his daughter, which was pure existential incest. Freud was like a pope who preached celibacy but didn't practice it.

Jerome L. Singer, professor and child study researcher
We all have much to learn about scientific integrity and commitment from Freud's willingness to study his own dreams, reexamine his theories and persist in a lifelong exploration that has stirred the imagination of thousands of thinkers of this century.

Albert Ellis, founder of rational-emotive therapy
We can constructively learn from Freud what he first said in 1895 and later, alas, forgot: that "emotional" disturbances are "ideogenic"—that is, importantly related to ideas. We can learn that most of us naturally and easily tend to severely defame our *self* (and not merely our *behavior*) when we act imperfectly, and thereby bring about needless "horror."

Hans J. Eysenck, professor and psychotherapy researcher
I think Freud has been a wholesale

disaster for psychology and what we can learn from him is how not to do things.

In psychology as in other sciences one must provide proof for any assertion. Freud intentionally and deliberately refused to look at his cases in comparison with control cases. He never followed them up to see whether in actual fact what he claimed to have been successes were successful. We now know that in fact many of them were not.

Phyllis Chesler, psychologist and author
Freud taught us—and this has not been accepted here because we're Americans—that life is tragic, that there are real limitations, that everything is a trade-off, that nobody can have a free lunch, that we're not getting out of this alive. . . . Freud was a mournful meditator. He was not Dale Carnegie. He didn't say "Read this book and you're going to be happy and get everything you want." He wasn't saying that, and I don't think that we've picked up his humbling tragic message.

Rollo May, a founder of existential psychotherapy
Freud brought us understanding

of depth, death, also our moods, negation of ideas, our fatigue, our sickness. We can still learn from Freud—not mainly from the rules of psychoanalysis, but rather from how he pictured a whole new culture, a culture in which people would be more broadly understood and more broadly human because the unconscious was part of the experience of the twentieth century.

Jonathan Winston, neuroscience sleep researcher
[Freud's] right that there is a coherent psychological structure beneath the level of the conscious. That's a marvelous insight for which he deserves credit. And he deserves credit too for sensing that dreams are the 'royal road' to the unconscious.

Peter Kramer, psychiatrist and author of Listening to Prozac
Psychotherapy is like one of those branching trees, where each of the branches legitimately claims a common ancestry, namely Freud, but none of the branches are sitting at the root. We'd be very mistaken to jettison psychotherapy or Freud.

(Sources: Gray, 1993, pp. 47–51; Chance et al., 1989, pp. 44–52.)

SUMMARY

■ SCIENTISTS USE PARADIGMS to understand abnormal behavior. Each paradigm, or model, is a set of basic assumptions that influences what questions are asked, what information is considered legitimate, and how that information is interpreted. Each model in use today highlights a different dimension of human behavior and explains abnormality with reference to that dimension.

■ THE BIOLOGICAL MODEL is based on the belief that (1) a full understanding of psychological functioning must include an understanding of the biological bases of thought, emotion, and behavior and that (2) the most effective treatment for psychological abnormality is biological. Biological theorists believe that mental disorders are linked to either anatomical or biochemical problems in the brain. Researchers have found that abnormalities in the activity of different *neurotransmitters*—chemicals released into the *synapse* between two *neurons*—are often connected with different mental disorders.

■ SUPPORTERS OF THE PSYCHODYNAMIC MODEL believe that a person's behavior, whether normal or abnormal, is determined to a large extent by underlying psychological forces of which the person is unaware. They focus on a person's past experiences because they consider psychological conflicts to be rooted in early parent-child relationships and traumatic experiences during the formative years. The psychodynamic model was formulated by Sigmund Freud, who developed a general theory of *psychoanalysis* based on the idea that unconscious conflicts account for all forms of normal and abnormal functioning. Freud envisioned three unconscious dynamic forces—the *id, ego,* and *superego*—constituting the personality and interacting to mold thought, feeling, and behavior.

Other psychodynamic theories that have developed also focus on the interaction of psychological forces. *Object relations theory* views the desire for relatedness as the motivating force in human behavior and focuses on the process of attachment and separation as the central processes in personality development. According to Kohut's *self theory,* the development and maintenance of the self—the unified personality that defines one's sense of identity—is of primary importance to a person's mental health. The self develops as the child's basic needs are met through relationships with *selfobjects*—people who are experienced as a part of the self.

■ THEORISTS WHO ESPOUSE THE BEHAVIORAL MODEL concentrate on a person's behaviors, which are held to develop in accordance with the behavioral *principles of learning*. This approach grew out of psychological experiments on *conditioning*. Three types of conditioning—*classical conditioning, operant conditioning,* and *modeling*—account for all behavior, whether normal or dysfunctional.

■ THE COGNITIVE MODEL claims that we must understand the content and process of human thought to understand human behavior. When people display abnormal patterns of functioning, cognitive theorists point to cognitive problems, including *maladaptive assumptions, specific upsetting thoughts,* and *illogical thinking processes.*

■ THE HUMANISTIC-EXISTENTIAL MODEL focuses on the human ability to confront complex and challenging philosophical issues such as self-awareness, values, meaning, and choice, and to incorporate them into one's life. The two groups that constitute the humanistic-existential approach share this general focus but have very different views of the basic inclinations of the human spirit. The *humanist,* exemplified by the psychologist Carl Rogers, believes that people are driven to *self-actualize;* that is, to fulfill their potential for goodness and growth. When this drive is interfered with, abnormal behavior may result. The *existentialist,* in contrast, believes that all of us have total freedom either to face up to our existence and give meaning to our lives or to shrink from that responsibility. Abnormal behavior is seen as the result of a person's hiding from life's responsibilities.

■ IN THE SOCIOCULTURAL MODEL, abnormal behavior is understood in the light of social and cultural forces brought to bear on the individual. Some theorists focus on *family structure and communication;* they see the family as a system of interacting parts in which structure, rules, and patterns of communication may force family members to behave in abnormal ways. Those who focus on *societal stress* consider the unique characteristics of a given society that may create special problems for its members and heighten the likelihood of abnormal functioning. Theorists who focus on *societal labels and reactions* hold that society categorizes certain people as "crazy" or "mentally ill," and that the label produces expectations that influence the way the person behaves and is treated.

■ THE MODELS VARY WIDELY in the dimensions of behavior they focus on and the assumptions they employ, yet they often provide compatible conclusions, suggesting that our understanding of a person's abnormal behavior is more complete if we appreciate the biological, psychological, and sociocultural aspects of his or her problem. Clinicians are increasingly embracing *diathesis-stress* explanations of abnormal behavior—the view that people must first have a biological, psychological, or sociocultural predisposition to a disorder and must then be subjected to an immediate form of psychological stress to develop and maintain certain forms of abnormality.

Topic Overview

RESEARCH IN ABNORMAL PSYCHOLOGY

∎

SCHIZOPHRENIA IS A SEVERE DISORDER that causes people to lose contact with reality. Its victims often display distorted and disorganized thought, perception, and emotions, bizarre behavior, and social withdrawal. As we shall see in Chapter 15, for the first half of this century most clinical theorists proposed that inappropriate parenting was the primary cause of this disorder. They believed that people with schizophrenia were reared by *schizophrenogenic* ("schizophrenia-causing") *mothers*—cold and domineering women who were impervious to their children's needs. This widely held belief turned out to be wrong.

IN THE 1940s, clinical practitioners developed a surgical procedure that supposedly cured schizophrenia. In this treatment procedure, called a *lobotomy,* a pointed instrument is inserted into the frontal lobe of the brain and rotated, destroying a considerable amount of brain tissue (Schanke, 1992; Goumeniouk & Clark, 1992). Reports soon spread that lobotomized patients showed near-miraculous improvement, and clinical practitioners administered the procedure to tens of thousands of mental patients. This impression, too, turned out to be wrong; far from curing schizophrenia, lobotomies caused irreversible brain damage that left many patients withdrawn, excessively subdued, and even stuporous.

THESE ERRORS UNDERSCORE the importance of research in abnormal psychology (Stricker, 1992). Theories and treatment procedures that seem reasonable and effective in individual instances may prove incorrect when they are applied to large numbers of people or situations. Only by testing a theory or technique on large representative groups of subjects can its accuracy or utility be determined. It was only through such testing that the notion of schizophrenogenic mothers was finally challenged and the indiscriminate use of lobotomies stopped.

Clinical researchers subject the ideas of clinical theorists and the techniques of clinical practitioners to systematic testing. Research is the key to accuracy and progress in all fields of study, and it is particularly important in abnormal psychology, because inaccurate beliefs in this field can cause or prolong enormous suffering. Until clinical researchers conducted relevant studies, for example, millions of parents, already heartbroken by their children's schizophrenic disorders, were additionally stigmatized when they were pointed to as the primary cause of the disorders; and countless schizophrenic people, already debilitated by their symptoms, were made permanently apathetic and spiritless by a lobotomy.

Unfortunately, although effective and rigorous research is essential for progress in this field, the nature of the issues under study makes such research particularly difficult. Researchers must figure out ways to measure such elusive concepts as unconscious motives, private thoughts, mood change, and human potential, and must address such ethical issues as the rights of subjects, both human and animal.

These problems notwithstanding, research in abnormal psychology has taken giant steps forward, especially during the last thirty years. In the past, many clinical researchers had only limited skills. Now graduate clinical programs train large numbers of psychology students to conduct appropriate studies on clinical topics. The development of new and effective research tools and methods has also contributed to impressive growth in our understanding of psychological function and dysfunction.

■ THE TASK ■ OF CLINICAL RESEARCHERS

Clinical researchers, also called clinical scientists, try to discover universal "laws" or principles of abnormal psychological functioning. Like researchers in other fields, they try to use the *scientific method* in their

work—that is, they systematically acquire and evaluate information through observation to gain an understanding of the phenomena they are studying. They search for general, or *nomothetic,* truths about the nature, causes, and treatments of abnormality ("nomothetic" is derived from the Greek *nomothetis,* "lawgiver") by identifying and studying the "average" behaviors and "typical" reactions of large numbers of people. They do not assess, diagnose, or treat individual clients; that is the job of clinical practitioners, who seek an *idiographic,* or individualistic, understanding of abnormal behavior. We shall explore their work in Chapters 4 and 5.

To formulate a nomothetic explanation of abnormal psychology, scientists in abnormal psychology, like scientists in all disciplines, attempt to *identify and explain relationships between variables.* Simply stated, a *variable* is any characteristic or event that can vary, whether from time to time, from place to place, or from person to person. Age, sex, and race are human variables. So are eye color, occupation, and social status. Clinical researchers are particularly interested in such variables as childhood traumas and other life experiences, moods, levels of social and occupational functioning, and responses to treatment techniques. They seek to determine whether two or more such variables change together and whether a change in one variable causes a change in another. Will the death of a parent, for example, cause a child to become depressed? If so, will a given therapy reduce that depression?

Such questions cannot be answered by logic alone. Reasoning is only as accurate as the information available to reason with, so numerous observations are needed to establish a factual basis on which to build a conclusion. Even then, reasoning may fail to serve the scientific enterprise. Although human beings are marvelously sophisticated and complex, they are prone to frequent errors in thinking (Kahneman, Slovic, & Tversky, 1982; Nisbett & Ross, 1980). Witness the false impressions we often form of others, and the many times we jump to wrong conclusions.

To minimize such errors and acquire valid information about abnormal behavior, clinical researchers depend primarily on three methods of investigation: the *case study,* the *correlational method,* and the *experimental method.* Each is best suited to certain circumstances and to answer certain questions. Collectively, they enable clinical scientists to formulate and test hypotheses, or hunches, that certain variables are related in certain ways, and to draw broad conclusions as to why. More properly, a *hypothesis* is a tentative explanation advanced to provide a basis for an investigation.

■ THE ■
CASE STUDY

A *case study* is a detailed and often interpretive description of one person. It describes the person's background, present circumstances, and symptoms. It may also describe the application and results of a particular treatment, and it may speculate about how the person's problems developed.

In his famous case study of Little Hans (1909), Sigmund Freud discusses a 4-year-old boy who has developed a fear of horses. Freud gathered his material from detailed letters sent him by Hans's father, a physician who had attended lectures on psychoanalysis, and from Freud's own limited interviews with the child. Because of the great length of the study (140 pages in Freud's *Collected Papers*), only key excerpts will be reproduced here.

One day while Hans was in the street he was seized with an attack of morbid anxiety. . . . *[Hans's father writes:]*

My Dear Professor:
  On January 7th he went to the Stadtpark with his nursemaid as usual. In the street he began to cry and asked to be taken home, saying that he wanted to 'coax' with his Mummy. At home he was asked why he had refused to go any farther and had cried, but he would not say. Till the evening he was cheerful, as usual. But in the evening he grew visibly frightened; he cried and could not be separated from his mother. . . .
  On January 8th my wife decided to go out with him herself, so as to see what was wrong with him. They went to Schönbrunn, where he always likes going. Again he began to cry, did not want to start, and was frightened. In the end he did go; but was visibly frightened in the street. On the way back from Schönbrunn he said to his mother, after much internal struggling: 'I was afraid a horse would bite me.' He had, in fact, become uneasy at Schönbrunn when he saw a horse. In the evening he seems to have had another attack similar to that of the previous evening, and to have wanted to be 'coaxed' with. He was calmed down. He said, crying: 'I know I shall have to go for a walk again tomorrow.' And later: 'The horse'll come into the room.'. . . .

But the beginnings of this psychological situation go back further still.
  The first reports of Hans date from a period when he was not quite three years old. At that time, by means of various remarks and questions, he was showing a quite peculiarly lively interest in that portion of body which he used to describe as his 'widdler' [his word for penis]. . . .

When he was three and a half his mother found him with his hand to his penis. She threatened him in these words: 'If you do that, I shall send for Dr. A. to cut off your widdler. And then what'll you widdle with?'

Hans: With my bottom.

He made this reply without having any sense of guilt as yet. But this was the occasion of his acquiring the 'castration complex,' the presence of which we are so often obliged to infer in analyzing neurotics, though they one and all struggle violently against recognizing it.
  During the preceding summer [before his fear of horses arose] Hans had . . . been in a state of intensified sexual excitement, the object of which was his mother. The intensity of this excitement was shown by his two attempts at seducing his mother [the second of which occurred just before the outbreak of his anxiety].

My Dear Professor:
  Hans, four and a quarter. This morning Hans was given his usual daily bath by his mother and afterwards dried and powdered. As his mother was powdering round his penis and taking care not to touch it, Hans said: 'Why don't you put your finger there?'

Mother: Because that'd be piggish.

Hans: What's that? Piggish? Why?

Mother: Because it's not proper.

Hans [Laughing]: But it's great fun.

  . . . The father and son visited me during my consulting hours. I already knew the queer little chap. . . . I do not know whether he remembered me, but he behaved irreproachably and like a perfectly reasonable member of human society. The consultation was a short one. His father opened it by remarking that, in spite of all the pieces of enlightenment we had given Hans, his fear of horses had not yet diminished. . . . Certain details which I now learnt—to the effect that he was particularly bothered by what horses wear in front of their eyes and by the black round their mouths—were certainly not to be explained from what we knew. But as I saw the two of them sitting in front of me and at the same time heard Hans's description of his anxiety-horses, a further piece of the solution shot through my mind, and a piece which I could well understand might escape his father. I asked Hans jokingly whether his horses wore eyeglasses, to which he replied that they did not. I then asked him whether his father wore eyeglasses, to which, against all the evidence, he once more said no. Finally I asked him whether by 'the black round the mouth' he meant a moustache; and I then disclosed to him that he was afraid of his father, precisely because he was so fond of his mother. It must be, I told him, that he thought his father was angry with him on that account; but this was not so, his father was fond of him in spite of it, and he might admit everything to him without any fear. Long before he was in the world, I went on, I had known that a little Hans would come who would be so fond of his mother that he would be bound to feel afraid of his father because of it; and I had told his father this. 'But why do you think I'm angry with you?' his father interrupted me at this point; 'have I ever scolded you or hit you?' Hans corrected him: 'Oh yes! You have hit me.' 'That's not true. When was it, anyhow?' 'This morning,' answered the little boy; and his father recollected that Hans had quite unexpectedly butted his head into his stomach, so that he had given him as it were a reflex blow with his hand. It was remarkable that he had not brought this detail into connection with the neurosis; but he now recognized it as an expression of the little boy's hostile disposition towards him, and perhaps also as a manifestation of a need for getting punished for it.

By enlightening Hans on this subject I had cleared away his most powerful resistance against allowing his unconscious thoughts to be made conscious; for his father was himself acting as his physician. The worst of the attack was now over; there was a plentiful flow of material; the little patient summoned up courage to describe the details of his phobia, and soon began to take an active share in the conduct of the analysis.

. . . It was only then that we learnt what the objects and impressions were of which Hans was afraid. He was not only afraid of horses biting him—he was soon silent upon that point—but also of carts, of furniture-vans, and of buses [their common quality being, as presently became clear, that they were all heavily loaded], of horses that started moving, of horses that looked big and heavy, and of horses that drove quickly. The meaning of these specifications was explained by Hans himself: he was afraid of horses falling down, and consequently incorporated in his phobia everything that seemed likely to facilitate their falling down.

It was at this stage of the analysis that he recalled the event, insignificant in itself, which immediately preceded the outbreak of the illness and may no doubt be regarded as the exciting cause of the outbreak. He went for a walk with his mother, and saw a bus-horse fall down and kick about with its feet. This made a great impression on him. He was terrified, and thought the horse was dead; and from that time on he thought that all horses would fall down. His father pointed out to him that when he saw the horse fall down he must have thought of him, his father, and have wished that he might fall down in the same way and be dead. Hans did not dispute this interpretation; and a little while later he played a game consisting of biting his father, and so showed that he accepted the theory of his having identified his father with the horse he was afraid of. From that time forward his behavior to his father was unconstrained and fearless, and in fact a trifle overbearing.

It is especially interesting . . . to observe the way in which the transformation of Hans's libido into anxiety was projected on to the principal object of his phobia, on to horses. Horses interested him the most of all the large animals; playing at horses was his favorite game with the older children. I had a suspicion—and this was confirmed by Hans's father when I asked him—that the first person who had served Hans as a horse must have been his father. . . .

When repression had set in and brought a revulsion of feeling along with it, horses, which had till then been associated with so much pleasure, were necessarily turned into objects of fear.

[Hans later reported] two concluding phantasies, with which his recovery was rounded off. One of them, that of the plumber giving him a new and, as his father guessed, a bigger widdler, was . . . a triumphant wish-phantasy, and with it he overcame his fear of castration.

'The plumber came; and first he took away my behind with a pair of pincers, and then gave me another, and then the same with my widdler. He said: "Let me see your behind!" and I had to turn round, and he took it away; and then he said: "Let me see your widdler!"' . . .

Father: He gave you a *bigger* widdler and a bigger behind.

Hans: Yes.

Father: Like Daddy's because you'd like to be Daddy.

Hans: Yes, and I'd like to have a moustache like yours and hairs like yours.

His other phantasy, which confessed to the wish to be married to his mother and to have many children by her, did not merely exhaust the content of the unconscious complexes which had been stirred up by the sight of the falling horse and which had generated his anxiety. It also corrected that portion of those thoughts which was entirely unacceptable; for, instead of killing his father, it made him innocuous by promoting him to a marriage with Hans's grandmother. With this phantasy both the illness and the analysis came to an appropriate end.

VALUE OF THE CASE STUDY

In the course of treating their patients, clinicians often write case studies. Faced with the task of helping someone, a clinician must first gather all relevant information and search through it for factors that may have brought about the person's problems. The clues provided by the case study may also have direct implications for the person's treatment. But case studies also play nomothetic roles that go far beyond the individual clinical case (Smith, 1988).

Case studies often serve as a source of ideas about behavior and "open the way for discoveries" (Bolgar, 1965). Indeed, Freud's theory of psychoanalysis was based mainly on the cases he saw in private practice. He pored over his case studies to ferret out what he believed to be universal psychological processes and principles of development.

A case study may also provide tentative support for a theory (Kratochwill, Mott, & Dodson, 1984). Freud used the case study of Little Hans in precisely this

One of the most celebrated case studies in abnormal psychology is a study of identical quadruplets, all of whom developed schizophrenic disorders in their 20s. At the National Institute of Mental Health (NIMH) in Washington, D.C., where these sisters underwent extensive study (Rosenthal, 1963), they were given the pseudonyms Nora, Iris, Myra, and Hester (after the initials NIMH) and the family name Genain (after the Greek words for "dire birth").

way. He believed that this case supported his idea that boys experience an Oedipus complex, that this complex accounts for phobic fear, and that childhood sexuality plays an important role in personality development. Previously Freud's arguments in support of these ideas had been drawn from analyses of adults who recalled childhood events. In Hans he had an opportunity to examine the proposed concepts during the actual course of a child's development.

Conversely, case studies may serve to challenge theoretical assumptions (Kratochwill, 1992; Kratochwill et al., 1984). Psychoanalytic theorists claim, for example, that if overt symptoms are removed by behavioral rather than psychoanalytic techniques, new symptoms will emerge (a process called symptom substitution). A number of behavioral case studies, however, describe the removal of problem behaviors without the emergence of new ones later on, thus casting doubt on the psychoanalytic position (Wolpe, 1986; Mowrer & Mowrer, 1938).

Case studies also may serve as a source of ideas for new therapeutic techniques or as examples of unique applications of existing techniques. As we saw in Chapter 2, it was Breuer's famous study of Anna O. that first suggested that patients could derive therapeutic benefit simply from discussing their problems and the underlying psychological issues. Freud believed that the case study of Little Hans had once

again demonstrated the therapeutic potential of a verbal approach.

Finally, case studies offer opportunities to study unusual problems that do not occur often enough to permit more general observations and comparisons

Some twenty-five years after the initial case study of the Genain sisters, the four women returned to NIMH for a follow-up study that used new technology to detect brain activity and structure (Buchsbaum & Haier, 1987). Marked variations in the sisters' levels of functioning corresponded to variations found in their brain activity and structure, suggesting that biological factors or interactions of biological and environmental factors may contribute to schizophrenia.

TABLE 3-1

	IDIOGRAPHIC INFORMATION	NOMOTHETIC INFORMATION	INTERNAL VALIDITY (CAUSATION)	EXTERNAL VALIDITY (GENERALIZABILITY)
Case study	+	−	−	−
Correlational method	−	+	−	+
Experimental method	−	+	+	+

RELATIVE STRENGTHS (+) AND WEAKNESSES (−) OF RESEARCH METHODS

(Lehman, 1991). For years, for example, information about multiple personality disorders was based almost exclusively on case studies, such as the famous *Three Faces of Eve*, a clinical account of a woman who displayed three alternating personalities, each having a distinct set of memories, preferences, and personal habits (Thigpen & Cleckley, 1957).

LIMITATIONS OF THE CASE STUDY

Although case studies are useful in many ways, they have limitations. To begin with, they are reported by biased observers (Lehman, 1991). Freud's psychoanalytic bias is apparent throughout the case study of Little Hans. He describes, for instance, an interaction between Hans and his mother as "the occasion of his acquiring the castration complex," and at another point he calls Hans's problem "the transformation of . . . libido into anxiety." Therapists are participants in the healing process as well as observers of it, and they have a personal stake in the outcomes of their cases and the apparent success of their treatments. The material they choose to include in a case study and their impressions of the client's progress must be considered subjective and unsystematic, however well intended (Lehman, 1991; Smith, 1988; Hersen & Barlow, 1976).

A related problem is that most case studies do not provide objective evidence that a client's dysfunction has in fact been caused by the events that the therapist or client says are responsible. After all, the events they single out as significant are only a fraction of those that may have played a part in creating the person's predicament. When an investigator can show that of a host of possible causes, only one satisfies all criteria and the others can be ruled out, the study is said to have internal accuracy, or *internal validity.*

Obviously, case studies are low on this dimension (see Table 3–1).

A famous case study of identical quadruplets called the Genain sisters illustrates this limitation. These women of identical genetic makeup all developed schizophrenia, suggesting that this disorder may be genetically transmitted. Careful investigation also revealed, however, that the quadruplets were kept in the hospital for the first six weeks of their lives, were severely restricted in their interactions with others during childhood, and were brought up by a hostile and accusatory father—environmental factors that could also have contributed to their disorders. The case study could not confirm or clarify the relevance of the genetic or environmental factors.

Finally, case studies provide little basis for generalization. Even if we agree that Little Hans did develop a fearful reaction to horses because of Oedipal conflicts and fear of his father, how can we be confident that other people's phobias are rooted in the same kinds of causes? Factors or treatment techniques that seem important in one case may be of no help at all in efforts to understand or treat others. When the findings of an investigation can be generalized beyond the immediate study, the investigation is said to have external accuracy, or *external validity.* Case studies are low on this dimension, too (Lehman, 1991).

■ THE ■ CORRELATIONAL METHOD

The limitations of the case study are largely addressed by two other methods of investigation: the correlational method and the experimental method. They do not offer the richness of detail that makes case studies such interesting reading, but they do help investigators draw broad conclusions about the occurrence and characteristics of abnormality in the population at large. Three characteristics of these methods enable clinical investigators to gain nomothetic insights. (1) Researchers observe many individuals to collect enough information, or data, on which to base a conclusion. (2) They apply carefully prescribed procedures uniformly, so that other researchers can replicate their studies to see whether they consistently yield the same findings and implications. (3) The results of studies conducted by these methods can be analyzed by statistical tests that help indicate whether broad conclusions are justified. The correlational and experimental methods were used only occasionally to study abnormal functioning earlier in this century, but they are now the preferred methods of investigation (Pincus et al., 1993).

Correlation is the degree to which events or characteristics vary in conjunction with each other. The *correlational method* is a research procedure used to determine this "co-relationship" between variables. Let us see how this method has been used to answer a question that has stimulated numerous clinical studies: Is there a correlation between the amount of life stress people experience and the degree of psychological disturbance they display (Paykel & Cooper, 1992; Brown, Harris, & Peto, 1973)? That is, as people repeatedly experience stressful events, are they increasingly likely to become psychologically disturbed?

To test this question, researchers must first find a way to measure the two variables (life stress and psychological disturbance). They can do so only if they translate the abstract variables they are investigating into discrete, observable entities or events, a process called *operationalization*. Life stress has been operationalized in some studies as the number of threatening events (such as a significant health problem or the loss of a job) that a person experiences during a certain period of time (Veiel et al., 1992; Paykel, 1983; Miller, Ingham, & Davidson, 1976) and degree of psychological disturbance has been operationalized as a score on a questionnaire that asks a person to express feelings of depression, anxiety, or the like in terms of a numerical scale (Bech, 1992; Miller et al., 1976). One question on a depression questionnaire, for example, might ask how often one feels like crying; a question on an anxiety scale might ask how easily one is startled by minor noises.

Once the variables being examined are operationalized, researchers can measure them in a number of individuals and determine whether a general correlation

between the variables does indeed exist. Those who are chosen for a study, individually called *subjects* and collectively called the *sample,* must be representative of the larger population about whom the researchers wish to make a statement. Otherwise the relationship found in the study might differ from the relationship that exists in the real-world area of interest. A study that found a correlation between life stress and psychological disturbance in a group of very young subjects, for example, might tell researchers little about what, if any, correlation exists among adults.

THE DIRECTION OF CORRELATION

Let us suppose that we conduct such a study. We collect life stress scores and depression scores for ten subjects and plot these scores on the graph shown in Figure 3–1. As you can see, the subject named Jim has a recent life stress score of 7 (seven threatening events over the past three months) and a depression score of 25; thus he is "located" at the point on the graph where these two scores meet. As you may also notice, it turns out that when the data points of all the individuals in this study are plotted, they fall along a roughly straight line that slopes upward. A straight line drawn so that each data point is as close to

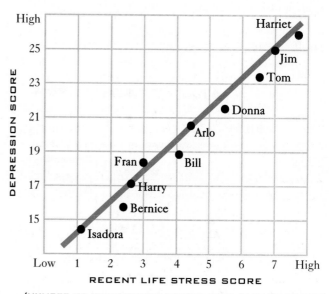

FIGURE 3–1   *The relationship between the amount of recent stress and feelings of depression shown by this hypothetical sample of ten subjects is a near-perfect "positive" correlation.*

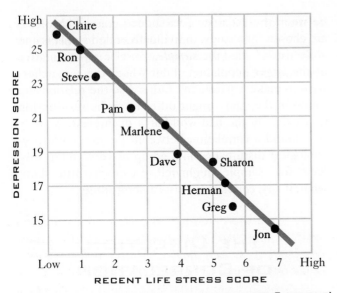

High

25

23

21

19

17

15

DEPRESSION SCORE

Claire
Ron
Steve
Pam
Marlene
Dave
Sharon
Herman
Greg
Jon

Low 1 2 3 4 5 6 7 High

RECENT LIFE STRESS SCORE

(NUMBER OF THREATENING EVENTS OVER PAST 3 MONTHS)

FIGURE 3-2 *The relationship between the amount of recent stress and feelings of depression shown by this hypothetical sample is a near-perfect "negative" correlation.*

the line as possible is called the ***line of best fit***—the one line that best fits all the data points.

The line of best fit in Figure 3–1 slopes upward to the right, indicating that the variables under examination are increasing or decreasing together. That is, the greater a particular person's life stress score, the higher his or her score on the depression scale. Correlations of this kind are said to have a positive direction, and the correlation is referred to as a ***positive***

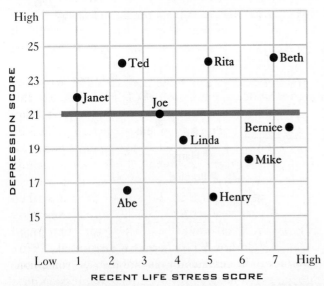

High

25

23

21

19

17

15

DEPRESSION SCORE

Ted
Rita
Beth
Janet
Joe
Bernice
Linda
Mike
Abe
Henry

Low 1 2 3 4 5 6 7 High

RECENT LIFE STRESS SCORE

(NUMBER OF THREATENING EVENTS OVER PAST 3 MONTHS)

FIGURE 3-3 *The relationship between the amount of recent stress and feelings of depression shown by this hypothetical sample is a "near-zero" correlation.*

correlation. Most of the studies that have looked at the relationship between recent life stress and depression have indeed found a positive correlation between the two variables (Paykel & Cooper, 1992; Miller et al., 1976).

Correlations can have a negative rather than a positive direction. In a ***negative correlation,*** as the value of one variable increases, the value of the other variable decreases. If our subjects' scores had instead produced the downward-sloping graph shown in Figure 3–2, the correlation would have been negative and we would have said that depression decreases as life stress increases. Researchers have found, for example, a negative correlation between schizophrenia and socioeconomic status. The lower one's socioeconomic status, the greater the probability of developing schizophrenia.

Finally, it is possible that two variables are ***unrelated,*** that there is no systematic relationship between them. As the measures of one variable increase, those of the other variable sometimes increase and sometimes decrease. If our subjects' scores had been uncorrelated in this way, the graph of their relationship would have looked like Figure 3–3. The line of best fit would have been a horizontal line with no slope. As we noted earlier, researchers have found such a lack of relationship between schizophrenia and the coldness of one's mother, despite past assumptions that these variables were positively correlated.

THE MAGNITUDE OF CORRELATION

In addition to knowing the direction of a correlation, researchers need to know its ***magnitude,*** or strength. That is, how closely do the two variables correspond? Does one always vary as a direct reflection of the other, or is their relationship less precise?

To appreciate this dimension of a correlation, look again at Figure 3–1. In this graph of a positive correlation, the data points all fall very close to the line of best fit. Such a configuration would enable researchers to predict each person's score on one variable with a high degree of confidence if they knew his or her score on the other. In the positive correlation pictured in Figure 3–4, in contrast, the data points are loosely scattered around the upward-sloping line of best fit rather than hugging it closely. In this case, researchers cannot predict with as much accuracy a subject's score on one variable from the score on the other variable. Because the correlation in Figure 3–1 allows researchers to make more accurate

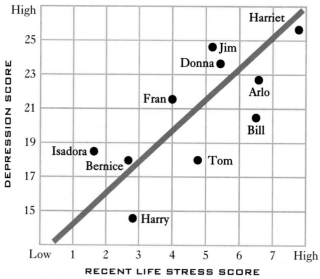

FIGURE 3–4 *The relationship between the amount of recent stress and feelings of depression shown by this hypothetical sample is a "moderately positive" correlation.*

predictions than the one in Figure 3–4, it is stronger, or greater in magnitude.

THE CORRELATION COEFFCIENT

The direction and magnitude of a correlation can be calculated numerically and expressed by a statistical term called the *correlation coefficient,* symbolized by the letter *r* (technically, the *Pearson product moment correlation coefficient,* named after the man who devised it, Karl Pearson). The correlation coefficient can vary from +1.00, which conveys a perfect positive correlation, down to −1.00, which represents a perfect negative correlation between two variables. The sign of the coefficient (+ or −) signifies the direction of the correlation; the number represents its magnitude. An *r* of .00 reflects a zero correlation, or no relationship between variables. The closer *r* is to .00, the weaker, or lower in magnitude, the correlation. Thus correlations of +.75 and −.75 are of equal magnitude and equally strong, whereas a correlation of +.25 is weaker than either.

Because the behavior and reactions of every human being are subject to change and because many human responses can be measured only approximately, most correlations found in psychological research fall short of a perfect positive or negative correlation. One study of the correlation between recent life stress and depression had a sample of 68 adults and found a cor-

relation of +.53 between the two variables (Miller et al., 1976). Although hardly perfect, a correlation of this magnitude with a sample of this size is considered large in psychological research.

STATISTICAL ANALYSIS OF CORRELATIONAL DATA

Once scientists determine the correlation between variables for a particular group of subjects, they must decide whether it accurately reflects a real correlation in the general population from which the subjects are drawn. Even if they have been careful to choose a sample that is representative of the larger population, it is possible that the observed correlation occurred only by chance and that in actuality no such connection exists in the population at large, or that a connection exists but with a different magnitude.

Scientists can never know for certain that the correlation they find is truly characteristic of the larger population, but they can test their conclusions to some extent by doing a *statistical analysis* of their data. In essence, they apply principles of probability to their findings to learn how likely it is that those particular findings have occurred by chance. If the statistical analysis suggests that chance is a likely reason for the correlation they found in the sample, the researchers have no basis for drawing broader conclusions from that correlation. But if the statistical analysis indicates that chance is unlikely to account for the relationship they found, they may conclude that their findings reflect a correlation that really exists in the general population.

By convention, psychology statisticians have defined a particular cutoff point to help them make this decision. If there is less than a 5 percent probability that a study's findings are due to chance, signified by the notation *p* < .05, those findings are said to be *statistically significant,* and the researcher may conclude that they reflect a situation that exists in the larger population. In the actual life stress study described earlier, a statistical analysis did indicate a probability of less than 5 percent that the +.53 correlation found in the sample was due to chance (Miller et al., 1976). Therefore, the researchers concluded with some confidence that among adults in general, depression does tend to rise along with the amount of recent stress in a person's life. Certain dimensions of a correlational study are taken into consideration to determine whether the observed correlation is statistically significant, including the size of the sample (the number of subjects in the study) and the magnitude of the correlation. Of course, it is important to keep in mind that even when a study's results qualify as statistically significant, there is still as much as a 5 percent possibility that these results are due entirely to chance.

STRENGTHS AND LIMITATIONS OF THE CORRELATIONAL METHOD

The correlational method has certain advantages over the case study. When researchers quantify their variables, observe numerous subjects, and apply statistical analyses, they are in a better position to generalize their findings to people beyond the ones they have studied. That is, a correlational study exhibits more external validity than a case study. Researchers are also able to repeat correlational studies on new samples of subjects in order to support or clarify particular relationships, thus corroborating the results of a particular study.

Correlational studies of many pairs of twins have determined that a strong relationship exists between genetic factors and certain psychological disorders. These studies have typically compared the psychopathology concordance rate of pairs of identical twins (twins, like those pictured here, who have identical genes) with that of pairs of fraternal twins (twins whose genetic makeup is not identical). A "concordance" rate represents the likelihood that if one twin has a disorder, the other will develop it. Identical twins have higher concordance rates for some psychopathologies than fraternal twins do.

On the other hand, correlational studies, like case studies, lack internal validity (Skinner, 1984). Although correlations give researchers predictive power by *describing* the relationship between two variables, they do not *explain* the relationship. Looking at the positive correlation found in many life stress studies, we might be tempted to conclude that increases in recent life stress *cause* people to feel more depressed. Actually, however, the two variables may be correlated for any one of three reasons:

1. *Variable A causes variable B.* Let us call amount of recent life stress variable A and depression variable B. It is possible that the two variables are positively correlated because A causes B. That is, increases in life stress cause people to feel sadder, particularly about the difficult situations they have been experiencing.

2. *Variable B causes variable A.* People who are depressed tend to become passive and to withdraw from their usual activities and social relationships. This depressive approach to life may cause them to mismanage their money, be less effective at work, and let social relationships deteriorate. That is, depression may tend to increase the number of stressful life situations.

3. *Variable C causes both A and B.* It is quite possible that an increase in both life stress and depression is caused by a third variable—poverty, for example. A limited income may cause people to experience more health crises, poorer living conditions, extra job pressures, and other forms of life stress. At the same time, poverty may cause them to feel unhappy about their deprivations and limited opportunities. If this should be the case, the correlation between life stress and depression would simply be reflecting the effect of poverty on each of these variables.

The fact that correlation says nothing about causation is not always a problem for clinicians. Sometimes it's enough to know the likelihood that two variables will occur together. Because clinicians are aware that suicide attempts increase as people become more depressed, for example, those who work with severely depressed clients can keep on the lookout for symptoms of suicidal thinking (Beck, 1993, 1967). It doesn't necessarily make a difference to them whether depression directly causes suicidal behavior or whether a third variable, such as a sense of hopelessness, causes both depression and suicidal thoughts. As soon as the clinicians identify intense feelings of depression, they can stand ready to take measures to prevent suicide (such as hospitalization).

Often, however, clinicians do want to know whether one variable causes another. Do parents' marital conflicts cause their children to be more anxious? Does job dissatisfaction lead to feelings of depression? Will a given therapeutic procedure help people to cope more effectively in life? Questions about causality call for the use of the experimental method.

SPECIAL FORMS
OF CORRELATIONAL
RESEARCH

Two kinds of correlational research that are used widely by clinical researchers—epidemiological studies and longitudinal studies—warrant special consideration. *Epidemiological studies* are investigations that determine the incidence and prevalence of a disorder in a given population (Weyerer & Hafner, 1992). *Incidence* is the number of new cases of a disorder that emerge in the population within a particular time interval; *prevalence* is the total number of cases (that is, the sum of existing and newly emerging cases) of the disorder in the population at any given time.

Over the past fifteen years clinical researchers across the United States, under the sponsorship of the National Institutes of Mental Health, have worked on the most comprehensive epidemiological study ever conducted. In the Epidemiologic Catchment Area Study they interviewed more than 20,000 people from five cities to determine the prevalence of numerous mental disorders in this country and the nature and availability of appropriate treatment programs (Regier et al., 1993; Robins & Regier, 1991). The data from this extraordinary study have been compared with figures from well-conducted epidemiological studies done in other countries around the world to see how rates of mental disorders and treatment programs vary from country to country (Weissman et al., 1992; Compton et al., 1991).

Collectively, these epidemiological studies have indicated various trends: women have a higher prevalence rate of anxiety disorders and depression than men, men have a higher rate of alcoholism than women, elderly people have a higher rate of suicide than younger people, African Americans have a higher rate of high blood pressure than white Americans, and persons from some nonWestern countries (such as Taiwan) have a higher rate of mental disorders than people from Western countries

(such as the United States). Findings of this sort help investigators identify groups and settings at risk for particular disorders and often lead them to suspect that something unique about the group or setting is helping to cause the disorder (Rogers & Holloway, 1990). Declining health in elderly people, for example, may make them more likely to commit suicide than younger people, or cultural pressures or attitudes prevalent in one country may be responsible for a rate of mental dysfunctioning that differs from the rate found in another country. Yet, as in other forms of correlational research, such suspicions can be confirmed only by the experimental method.

Longitudinal studies (also called *high-risk* or *developmental studies*) are investigations in which the characteristics or behavior of the same subjects are observed on many occasions over a long period of time. In several well-known longitudinal studies (Parnas, 1988; Griffith et al., 1980; Mednick, 1971), investigators observed the progress over the years of normally functioning children whose mothers or fathers were schizophrenic (that is, normal children who were considered to be at risk for schizophrenia). The researchers found, among other things, that the children of the parents with the most severe cases of schizophrenia were more likely to develop a psychological disorder and to commit crimes at later points in their development. Because longitudinal studies document the order of certain events, they provide stronger clues than conventional correlational studies about which events may be causes and which are likely to be consequences. But they still do not pinpoint causation (Cloninger, 1987). Are the psychological problems that certain high-risk children encounter later in their lives caused by a genetic factor inherited from their severely disturbed parents, by their parents' inadequate coping behaviors, by the loss of their parents to extended hospitalization, or by other factors? Again, experimental studies are necessary to answer these questions.

▪ THE ▪
EXPERIMENTAL
METHOD

An *experiment* is a research procedure in which a situation is manipulated and the effect of the manipulation is observed. The French playwright Molière created a character who was astonished to learn that he had been speaking prose all his life. Similarly, most of

*"Oh, not bad. The light comes on, I press the bar, they write me a check.
How about you?"*

(Drawing by Cheney; © 1993 The New Yorker Magazine, Inc.)

us perform experiments throughout our lives without knowing that we are behaving so scientifically.

Suppose that we go to a party on campus to celebrate the end of midterm exams. As we mix with people at the party, we begin to notice that many of them are becoming quiet and depressed. The more we talk, the more distraught they become. As the party deteriorates before our eyes, we decide we must do something, but before we can eliminate the problem, we need to know what's causing it. Our first hunch may be that something we're doing is responsible. Perhaps our incessant chatter about academic pressures is upsetting everyone. We decide to change the topic to skiing in the mountains of Colorado, and we watch for signs of depression in our next round of conversations. The problem seems to clear up; most people now smile and laugh as they converse with us. As a final check on our thinking, we could go back to talking about school with the next several people we meet. Their dark and hostile reaction would probably convince us that our academic focus of discussion was indeed the cause of the problem.

In this scenario, we have performed an experiment. To test our *hypothesis* about the causal relationship between our discussions of academic matters and the depressed mood of the people around us, we have *manipulated* the variable that we suspect is the cause (the topic of discussion) and then observed the effect of that manipulation on the variable that we suspect is the effect (the mood of the people around us). In scientific experiments, the manipulated variable is called the ***independent variable,*** and the variable being observed is called the ***dependent variable.***

CONFOUNDS

The goal of an experiment is to isolate and identify the cause of a certain effect. If we cannot separate the true, or primary, cause from a host of other possible causes, then the experiment gives us very little information. It would not be very helpful, for instance, to find out that the depressed mood of subjects is caused *either* by our talk of school *or* by some other factor, such as the music at the party or midterm fatigue.

The major obstacles to isolating the true cause and thus carrying out an effective experiment are ***confounds***—variables other than the independent variable that are also acting on the dependent variable. When there are confounds in an experiment, the experimenter cannot confidently attribute the results to the independent variable under investigation because it may actually be the confounding variables that are causing the observed changes (Geyer, 1992).

One of the questions that clinical scientists most frequently ask is "Does a particular therapy relieve the symptoms of a given disorder?" (Lambert & Bergin, 1994). Because this question is about a causal relationship, it can be answered only by an experiment. Let us suppose that we have developed a new treatment called "buttermilk therapy" and that we have reason to believe it will alleviate anxiety in our clients. Our first thought might be to measure our clients' anxiety levels both before and after we give them a large glass of buttermilk and see whether their anxiety levels decrease with this treatment. In doing so we would be manipulating an independent variable (the presence or absence of buttermilk therapy) and observing its effect on a dependent variable (the clients' anxiety). But if we perform this experiment and observe a decrease in anxiety, what can we actually conclude?

Not much. Without realizing it, we have allowed our independent variable, buttermilk therapy, to change right along with the ever-present confound of time. It is possible that the clients simply became less anxious during the hour they spent in the therapist's office, and that the simple passage of time was responsible for their decreased anxiety. We cannot tell whether the decrease in our clients' anxiety is due to the independent variable that we manipulated or to the confound that we overlooked. Because we have not separated the effects of the independent variable from the effects of the confound, we do not know which one was the cause of the change in the dependent variable.

Other confounds also may have been present in this experiment. Situational variables such as the location of the therapy office (a quiet country setting) or a soothing color scheme in the office may have had an effect. Perhaps the subjects in this particular experiment were unusually motivated or had extraordinarily high expectations that the therapy would work, which thus accounted for their improvement. Or perhaps the supportive tone of voice of the assistant who served the buttermilk actually made the subjects more relaxed. To minimize the influence of potential confounds, researchers incorporate three important features into their experiments—a *control group, random assignment,* and a *blind design* (Viken, 1992).

THE CONTROL GROUP

A *control group* is a group of subjects who are not exposed to the independent variable under investigation, but whose experience is otherwise similar to that of the *experimental group,* the subjects who *are* ex-

posed to the independent variable. By comparing the two groups, an experimenter can better determine the effect of the manipulated variable. In our buttermilk therapy study, for example, we might divide our clients into two groups. The experimental group would come into the office and receive buttermilk therapy for an hour, and the control group would simply come into the office for an hour. Now time passes for both groups. The control group shows us the effect of the passage of time (and a host of other confounds present in the office) on anxiety, while the experimental group shows us the effect of both time (and those other confounds) *and* buttermilk therapy. If we were to find later that the anxiety levels of clients in the experimental group were lower than the anxiety levels of clients in the control group, we might conclude that buttermilk therapy was effective in reducing anxiety, above and beyond the effects of time and any other confounds. In short, our control group would have helped us rule out the possibility that something other than the independent variable was causing all of the observed changes in the dependent variable.

It is important to make sure there are no systematic differences, besides therapy or no therapy, in the way the two groups are treated. If one of our groups were coming to the sessions at night and the other during the day, or if one were being greeted by a grumpy receptionist and the other by a friendly one, these differences rather than the buttermilk therapy could be responsible for the difference in their anxiety levels at the experiment's end. Experimenters must guard against this type of confound by trying to provide all subjects, both control and experimental, with experiences that are identical in every way except for the one critical item under investigation, the independent variable.

RANDOM ASSIGNMENT

The way the members of the two groups are chosen is as important as the experimental protocol, for systematic differences that already exist in control and experimental subjects before the experiment may also confound the result. Let's suppose that in setting up our scheme for evaluating the effectiveness of buttermilk therapy, we allow the subjects themselves to choose the group they wish to join. It is likely that those who love buttermilk will choose the buttermilk group and those who detest it will choose the control group. This self-selection can result in quite a long list of differences between the control group and the experimental group. They will include not only

BOX 3-1

ARTIFACTS: STRESS AND THE EXECUTIVE MONKEY

An enormous quantity of scientific research is produced each year. Most of these studies can be thought of as brush strokes on a canvas—it takes many individual strokes before a recognizable image begins to emerge. Conclusions are generally built on accumulated evidence, and no single study is expected to prove a hypothesis independently. Every so often, however, a single experiment yields results so compelling that the thinking of an entire generation is affected.

But beware: an experiment that influences our view of the world may later prove to have serious flaws that have gone unnoticed. Even the best-intentioned and most painstaking researchers are only human. They do not always recognize every possible confound. Or they may have a good idea for an experiment but lack the specific technical skills needed to carry it out. Or in their eagerness to get results that support their theory, they may become a little sloppy in their procedures. Usually peer reviewers catch the mistake before the research is published; or if it is published, it does not become particularly influential and is lost in the crowd. If such an experiment passes peer review and is then seen as important, however, the consequences can be both embarrassing to the researcher and harmful to the discipline. Consider the "executive monkey study."

What happens if you take two monkeys, put them in separate wire cages, and then give them shocks every 20 seconds for 6 hours—shocks that one of the monkeys can terminate (for itself and the other monkey) by pressing a lever? The psychologist J. V. Brady predicted that the monkeys who did not have a lever to press would develop ulcers because they had no control over the shocks (Brady

The executive monkey (left) learns that it can prevent shocks by pressing a lever with its hand. The control monkey (right) is given no control over the shocks and appears to lose interest in both the lever and its surroundings.

et al., 1958). In his experiment, exactly the opposite happened. In each of four pairs of monkeys, the "executive" monkey—the one who was able to stop the shocks—developed duodenal ulcers and died. The other monkey in each pair was not affected. This result ran counter to the theory of learned helplessness, which predicted that the monkeys without control would suffer a greater number of problems than those in control of the shocks. The research community and the public embraced the new finding, partly because it supported the intuitive notion that people with high-level positions in business, people who make important decisions every day, were prone to get ulcers. For thirteen years Brady's results exerted great influence on psychological views about the relationship between environment and stress.

To "replicate" an experiment is to repeat it exactly as it was done the first time and get the same results.

The executive monkey study could not be replicated. Investigators who attempted and failed, including Brady himself, looked carefully at the original procedure used and finally found a glaring mistake. It turned out that Brady had failed to consider the importance of assigning his subjects at random to each of the conditions in the experiment. He had pretested all eight monkeys by giving them shocks. The first four monkeys to press the lever were assigned to the "executive" condition. A later study found that animals with a higher response rate (animals that would press the lever first in Brady's pretest) were more likely to develop ulcers (Weiss, 1977). It appeared that their higher emotionality was responsible for both the response rate and the ulcers. In later executive monkey studies in which there was random assignment, the animals without control over the shocks suffered more than those with control. Brady's finding had been an *artifact*—a product of his own activity, not the monkeys'.

Brady had made an honest mistake. His result was the opposite of his expectations and surprised him as much as anyone else. Unfortunately, it also was generally accepted and cited for more than a dozen years. Nevertheless, the erroneous experiment has proved to be valuable: it spurred an enormous amount of research that has ultimately led to a more accurate understanding of stress and how it relates to health. It also taught the scientific community a great lesson. Apart from the few researchers who intentionally alter data and results to gain status or influence, there will always be some who make inadvertent mistakes. The only way to minimize such mistakes is to train researchers as carefully as possible and review critically each study that is announced.

differences in the therapy experiences of the two groups but also every single systematic difference that exists between people who like buttermilk and those who do not. For example, people who like buttermilk may be healthier, stronger, older, more affectionate, and smarter than those who detest it. All these factors become confounded with the independent variable, so it cannot be known with certainty which is responsible for a decrease in anxiety in the experimental group.

To reduce the possibility that systematic differences already existing between subjects are somehow causing the differences observed between the groups, experimenters typically use *random assignment* (Shapiro & Shapiro, 1983). This is the general term for any selection procedure that ensures that every subject in the experiment is as likely to be placed in one group as the other. Rather than allow subjects to choose their own group in our buttermilk therapy experiment, we might randomly assign them to groups by flipping a coin or picking their names out of a hat. When experimenters randomly assign subjects to different groups, they have more reason to believe that any differences noted between the groups during the experiment are indeed caused by the independent variable. (Boxes 3–1 and 3–2 show what can happen when assignment is not random.) Of course, even if subjects were randomly assigned to the groups in our buttermilk therapy experiment, we might still end up with all the strongest, smartest, and most

---

BOX 3-2

GENDER, RACE, AND AGE BIAS IN RESEARCH

Sometimes mistakes are committed by an entire community of researchers. Blinded by certain biases about society, investigators may consistently err in their efforts to design appropriate studies. For example, for many years scientists in Western society have favored the use of young white men as subjects for research on human functioning (Stark-Adamek, 1992; Gannon et al., 1992; Wahl & Hunter, 1992; Eichler, Reisman, & Borins, 1992). Only relatively recently have researchers come to appreciate the extent to which some of science's broad conclusions about human functioning are, in fact, sometimes inaccurate generalizations drawn from this select sample. In short, studies that use only young white male subjects are seriously lacking in external validity, and their findings may not be relevant to persons of a different sex, race, or age. Research in the mental health and medical fields has been just as guilty of this bias as studies conducted in other fields. Such bias may, we are now learning, lead to serious misconceptions about the symptoms, causes, course, and treatment of various mental disorders.

A recent review of the leading studies on schizophrenia published between 1985 and 1989 revealed that male subjects outnumbered female subjects by more than 2 to 1 (Wahl & Hunter, 1992), despite the fact that this disorder is as prevalent in women as in men. How can we be sure that the psychological and biological insights gleaned from these studies are valid for all schizophrenic persons rather than just schizophrenic men?

In a similar vein, medications for mental disorders have been tested on largely young white male subjects, and on that basis alone have been made available to all patients. Often, however, such medications have turned out to act differently, sometimes dangerously so, in elderly, female, or nonwhite populations (Wolfe et al., 1988). Psychiatrist Keh-Ming Lin recently found, for example, that Asian Americans and foreign-born Asians metabolize the antipsychotic drug haloperidol (Haldol), prescribed for many people with schizophrenia, much faster than white Americans do (Goodman, 1992). This finding suggests that Asian American patients require lower doses of this drug to achieve the same effect, yet up to now they have been started on the same dosage as white Americans.

The need to correct this kind of research bias is much more than a mere academic formality. It is tied closely to such important issues as scientific credibility, public health, and even sexism, racism, and ageism. Although reviews of the psychological literature from the past decade show that researchers are doing better each year— becoming more aware of gender, race, and age, and designing more appropriate studies—it is also clear that more improvement is needed (Sue et al., 1994; Gannon et al., 1992). The American Psychological Association and the Canadian Psychological Association have recently offered position papers and guidelines to help enlighten their members about the problem and its remedies (Stark-Adamek, 1992). They are aware that when research is biased in these ways, knowledge is limited, progress is stifled, and everyone loses.

affectionate subjects accidentally grouped together, but the likelihood of that occurrence is greatly reduced.

BLIND DESIGN

A final confound problem that must be addressed is the effect of bias, on the part of either the subjects or the people conducting the experiment (Kazdin, 1994). Subjects may bias an experiment's results by trying to please or help the experimenter (Margraf et al., 1991). In the buttermilk therapy experiment, buttermilk subjects, knowing the purpose of the study and knowing which group they are in, might actually work harder to feel better to fulfill the experimenter's expectations. If so, *subject bias* rather than buttermilk therapy could be causing the anxiety reduction found in the experimental group.

Even if subjects do not wish to help an experimenter, their expectations about the outcome of a study may influence the way they respond. Numerous studies have indicated that just expecting a treatment to help them causes many people to improve, even if the treatment given is a phony substitute, such as a sugar pill, called a *placebo* (Latin for "I shall please"). The improvement brought about by placebos is real and often substantial, even though the treatment itself is nontherapeutic (see Box 3–3). One study compared the progress of anxious clients who were given placebos over a period of months with the progress of anxious clients who remained on a treatment waiting list during the same period of time, and found that many of those who took the pills and expected them to work improved significantly more than the people on the waiting list (Brill et al., 1964).

There is a straightforward way of preventing the potential effects of subject bias in an experiment: do not let subjects know which group they are in. In the buttermilk study, control subjects could be given a placebo, a buttermilk substitute that looks and tastes like buttermilk but has none of the ingredients of actual buttermilk. If the experimental (true buttermilk) subjects then improved more than the control (false buttermilk) subjects, we could more confidently conclude that buttermilk was the cause of their improvement. This experimental strategy is called a *blind design* because subjects are blind as to which group they are in.

Even when subject bias is addressed, an experiment may still have the problem of *experimenter bias* (Margraf et al., 1991). That is, an experimenter may have expectations that are subtly transmitted to sub-

jects and affect the outcome of the experiment. In the buttermilk therapy experiment, for example, the experimenter might use a more promising tone of voice when talking with buttermilk subjects than when talking with control subjects or be more thorough in answering their questions. This subtle difference in the experimenter's behavior might bring about greater improvement in the buttermilk subjects, confounding the effect of the buttermilk itself. This confound source is referred to as the *Rosenthal effect,* after the psychologist who first helped clarify the effects of experimenter bias (Rosenthal & Rubin, 1978; Rosenthal, 1966).

Experimenters can eliminate the potential effects of their own bias by contriving to be blind themselves. In the buttermilk study, an aide could prepare the buttermilk substitute and pour the buttermilk and the buttermilk substitute into coded bottles. The experimenter could then administer the therapy without knowing which subjects were receiving true buttermilk and which were receiving false buttermilk. Only when the experiment was over and all the observations had been recorded would the experimenter learn which subjects actually received buttermilk and which ones received the substitute.

While the subjects *or* the experimenter may be kept blind in an experiment, it is best that *both* be blind (a *double-blind design*). In fact, most clinical experimenters now use double-blind designs to test the efficacy of antianxiety, antidepressant, and antipsychotic medications (Stonier, 1992; Nunn, 1992). They typically compare the effect of a target drug with that of a placebo or some other drug, making sure that neither drug administrators nor patients know who is receiving which substance. Many experimenters arrange for a group of judges to assess the patients' improvement independently, and the judges, too, are blind to the group each patient is in—a *triple-blind design.*

STATISTICAL ANALYSIS OF EXPERIMENTAL DATA

The findings of experiments, like those of correlational studies, must be analyzed statistically. In any experiment, no matter how well designed, there is a possibility that the differences observed between the experimental and control groups have occurred simply by chance. The experimenter must apply a statistical analysis to the experimental data and determine how likely it is that the pattern of changes in the dependent variable is due to chance. If the likelihood

BOX 3-3

IN PRAISE OF PLACEBOS

A medical researcher wants to know if drug X can reduce migraine headache pain. She finds a sample of 300 patients who suffer from migraines and gives one-third of the group drug X, one-third of the group a bitter-tasting orange pill that is known to have no physiological effect on migraine headaches, and the remaining third no pill at all. Those who receive a pill are told that it is an experimental drug that is highly likely to reduce their pain. The researcher then finds that 85 percent of the subjects taking drug X, 40 percent in the fake-drug group, and 10 percent of the subjects in the no-drug control group report relief from headache pain. What can the researcher conclude? If you checked her experimental methodology and found that it followed all the rules, you would probably conclude that drug X is effective in reducing migraine headache pain. You could also conclude that 10 percent of patients can be expected to recover over time without any treatment at all. And you would come to the somewhat troubling conclusion that the inert, chemically inactive orange pill is also very effective in reducing headache pain. For centuries physicians have known that patients suffering from many kinds of illness, from seasickness to angina, find relief from substances that have no known pharmacological effect. The *placebo* has emerged from the shadow of shamanism and mystery to become a rigorously studied phenomenon as well as a widely accepted treatment.

A startling discovery was made in 1975: the brain produces opiatelike substances known as **endorphins,** naturally occurring pain-relieving chemicals that fit into specific receptor sites in the brain. No one was quite sure why these chemicals were produced or what caused them to be released, but a partial answer came in the late 1970s. A group of doctors studying the use of placebos during dental surgery gave one set of patients an inert chemical and the other an inert chemical along with the drug *naloxone*, which is known to block the effects of endorphins. Both sets of patients believed they were receiving a painkilling substance, but only the group that received the placebo alone reported a reduction in pain. The researchers concluded that placebos somehow caused a release of endorphins in the brain, an effect that was erased by the addition of naloxone. That is, taking a placebo can lead the body to release a powerful painkiller.

The placebo effect is often encountered during studies to test the efficacy of drugs for treating mental disorders, and it seems that the release of endorphins provides some relief for mental disorders, much as it does for physical disorders. Moreover, the placebo does not have to be a pill or any other physical substance. Almost any form of psychotherapy can have a placebo effect. Some researchers have even suggested that "the placebo effect is an important component" of many methods of psychotherapy (Shapiro & Morris, 1978).

This suggestion has been tested in experiments similar to the migraine study (Lambert & Bergin, 1994). Instead of migraines, the subjects are suffering from depression or some other psychological problem. Instead of a pill, one group of subjects receives real psychotherapy and a second group receives fake psychotherapy (a therapist spends time talking to the patient but does not follow any recognized therapeutic regimen). A third group receives no treatment of any kind. The results are the same as in the migraine study: strong improvement for the first group, significant improvement for the second group—the classic placebo effect—and minimal improvement for the third. Thus today's researchers often include a placebo group as a control group in their experiments. Real psychotherapy is considered to be effective, above and beyond its placebo effect, only when subjects given real psychotherapy improve more than subjects who receive placebo (fake) therapy.

What is it about psychotherapy that triggers the placebo effect? One element may be the unique and complex relationship that exists between healer and sufferer. The patient's confidence in the therapist's expertise and skill and in the methods being used are sometimes critical to successful treatment (O'Connell, 1983). Another factor may be the ritualistic elements involved in psychotherapy. Specific interactions take place in a prescribed location according to definable rules of conduct. One basis for effective therapy is this mutual set of expectations (Fish, 1973). These factors have a powerful effect on the patient, and may trigger the release of endorphins or other processes that lead to relief.

is less than 5 percent ($p < .05$), the observed differences are considered to be statistically significant, and the experimenter may conclude with some confidence that they are due to the independent variable.

As with correlational studies, several dimensions of an experiment are taken into account in determining whether a pattern of findings is statistically significant. These include the *size of the sample*, the number of subjects actually studied; the *extent of the difference* observed between the groups; the central tendency of each group's scores—that is, the average score, or **mean,** for each group of subjects; and the *variability* of each group's scores, or how widely the scores range within each group of subjects. The larger the sample, the greater the observed difference, and the lower the variability of scores within each group, the more likely it is that a pattern of findings will be ruled statistically significant. Yet even when experimenters statistically reject chance as the cause of an observed difference, they may be wrong. It is always at least remotely possible that a pattern of findings is due to nothing more than chance.

VARIATIONS IN EXPERIMENTAL DESIGN

It is not easy to devise an experiment that is both well controlled and enlightening. The goal of manipulating a single variable without inadvertently manipulating others—that is, controlling *every possible* confound—is rarely attained in practice. Moreover, because psychological experiments must involve living beings, numerous ethical and practical considerations limit the kinds of manipulations that can be done. For these reasons clinical experimenters often settle for imperfect variations of optimal experimental designs to determine cause-and-effect relationships. The most common such variations are the quasi-experimental design, the natural experiment, the analogue experiment, and the single-subject experiment.

QUASI-EXPERIMENTAL DESIGN   *Quasi-experiments* are experiments in which investigators do not randomly assign subjects to control and experimental groups but instead make use of groups that already exist in the world at large (Kazdin, 1994; Bawden & Sonenstein, 1992). Because these groups already differ before the experiment, the investigator

---

BOX 3-4

HUMAN SUBJECTS HAVE RIGHTS

There is no question that research is necessary if we are to understand and treat mental disorders, or that this is a worthy goal—in fact, an essential one. The design of meaningful research, however, is fraught with ethical pitfalls. Should people be given experimental treatments that could be harmful? Is it right to withhold treatment from one group of patients to compare them with another group receiving a new therapy? When does the benefit to many outweigh the suffering of a few? These are but some of the questions facing researchers, patients, and society. To produce dependable results, an experiment must be conducted according to the scientific method. When this method conflicts with standards of ethical treatment, society—not researchers alone—must decide the answer.

Obtaining informed consent from subjects recruited to participate in an experiment is perhaps the most fundamental ethical safeguard in clinical human research. Informed consent "emphasizes societal respect for individual free choice and rational decision making as intrinsic to human dignity" (Annas, Glants, & Katz, 1977). A dilemma arises, however, when one must obtain consent from people who suffer from disorders that may affect their judgment. Does a mental disorder such as schizophrenia or depression render people unable to make this decision for themselves?

Some researchers argue that when a therapy is not considered harmful, it is not an abrogation of patients' rights to involve them in studies in which they receive treatment, whether or not they are able to make an informed decision to participate. Although this position may seem reasonable at first glance, it has opened the door to some isolated, highly publicized instances of professional misconduct. Large-scale, government-sanctioned abuse of patients occurred in the 1950s and 1960s, for example, when almost 100 people unknowingly became subjects in "depatterning" experiments meant to test the feasibility of mind control. Both the Canadian government and the United States CIA funded experiments in a variety of research settings. These experiments took place during the height of the Cold War, and the two governments wanted to learn more about mind control before potential foes mastered the techniques. Most of the research subjects emerged from the experiments emotionally disabled, with limited memories of the life they had lived before they entered the hospital.

Linda Macdonald was one of those subjects. In 1963 she checked into a Canadian institution to be treated for fatigue and depression. Six months later, she couldn't read, write, cook a

is technically "correlating" their existing difference with whatever manipulations are then carried out in the study, leading some researchers to refer to this research method as a *mixed design.* Research into the problem of child abuse illustrates the use of a quasi-experimental design.

Clinical case studies have suggested that a history of child abuse may cause children to become depressed and withdrawn and to have a poor self-concept, among other effects (Shaunesey et al., 1993; Briere, 1992; Bender, 1976). To test this relationship most systematically, researchers would have to select a sample of small children and assign them randomly to either an experimental or a control group, with the experimental subjects receiving physical abuse throughout their childhood and the control subjects being raised without physical abuse. Clearly, such an experiment would be immoral (see Box 3–4).

Because they cannot inflict abuse on a randomly chosen group of children, experimenters instead compare children who already have a history of abuse with children who do not. Of course, this strategy violates the rule of random assignment and introduces a number of possible confounds into the study. Children who receive physical punishment, for example, usually come from poorer and larger families than children who are punished verbally. Any differences in mood or self-concept found between abused and nonabused children, then, might be due to differences in wealth or family size rather than to the abuse.

Some child-abuse researchers have addressed this problem by using the quasi-experimental design of *matched control groups.* In one such investigation, the experimenter matched experimental and control subjects who had several potentially confounding variables in common, including age, sex, race, birth order, number of children in the family, socioeconomic status, and type of neighborhood (Kinard, 1982). That is, for every abused child in the

---

meal, or make a bed. She did not remember her husband, her five children, or any of the first twenty-six years of her life. During her stay; Ms. Macdonald was given massive doses of various drugs, put into a drug-induced sleep for 86 days, given more than 100 electroshock treatments, and exposed to "psychic driving," a technique in which repetitive taped messages were played for her 16 hours a day. The purpose was not to treat this woman's depression but to gather information about the causes and effects of brainwashing (Davis, 1992; Powis, 1990).

Later many of the victims, including Macdonald, sued the Canadian and American governments for subjecting them to these experiments without their permission. In 1988, the United States government agreed to compensate Macdonald and eight others with about $100,000 each, and in 1992, without admitting any legal or moral responsibility for the experiments but acknowledging "a collective sense of accountability for events which took place in good faith with ill effect," the government of Canada agreed to pay each of the eighty living victims $100,000.

Such instances highlight the ethical necessity to obtain informed consent. Regulations that now govern the conduct of experimenters, written by the U.S. Department of Health and Human Services, include guidelines for making sure that potential human subjects are well informed on eight basic issues:

1. That they are participating in an experiment and what procedures will be used.
2. Any potential or foreseeable risks.
3. Any benefits to themselves or others.
4. Any alternative procedures available to the patient.
5. Whether or not their participation and performance are confidential.
6. Whether or not they will receive any compensation if they are harmed during the experiment.
7. Whom they may contact to ask questions about the experiment.
8. That their participation is voluntary and that they face no penalty if they refuse to participate.

While these are eminently reasonable guidelines for informing potential subjects, there are no accompanying guidelines for establishing whether or not a person is competent to understand these issues and make a truly informed decision. As a result, in some circumstances the requirements are permitted to be altered or waived—a questionable and ill-defined practice.

Today, largely as a result of government regulations, research facilities establish committees to oversee the well-being of research subjects. But even a consensus among well-educated, concerned, ethical individuals does not answer the underlying question: How does one weigh the suspension of individual rights against the potential benefit to others? This has become such a difficult and important issue that universities now train ethicists, who confer with philosophers, psychologists, physicians, civil rights experts, and people from all sectors of society in an effort to develop acceptable guidelines. Though the system is not perfect, it reflects the value our society places on maintaining a balance between scientific advances and an individual's rights.

experimental group, she chose an unabused child of the same age, sex, race, and so on to be included in the control group. Thus, when the data showed that the children in the experimental group were significantly sadder and thought less of themselves than the children in the control group, the investigator was able to conclude with some confidence that abuse, and not one of those potential confounds, was causing the differences in mood and self-concept.

When scientists use random assignment, they are enlisting the laws of probability to help them eliminate any confounding differences between the experimental and control groups. When they use a matched control group, they are hoping that their deliberate and careful selection of subjects will have the same effect. Of course, those experimenters are eliminating only the confounds they are consciously matching for. Any important confounds they fail to consider will still remain and invalidate their findings. Clearly, then, although matched control groups are often necessary, quasi-experiments that use them are less dependable than experiments that use random assignment (Lehman, 1991; Owens et al., 1989).

NATURAL EXPERIMENT *Natural experiments* are those in which nature rather than an experimenter manipulates an independent variable, and the experimenter systematically observes the effects. This is the design that must be used for studying the psychological effects of unusual and unpredictable events, such as floods, earthquakes, plane crashes, and fires. Because the subjects in these studies are selected for the experimental group by an accident of fate rather than by conscious design, natural experiments are actually a kind of quasi-experiment.

On February 26, 1972, a dam gave way in the town of Buffalo Creek, West Virginia, releasing 132 million gallons of black slag, mud, and water into the valley below. The black swirling waters carried with them houses, trailers, cars, bridges, and human beings. The disaster killed 125 people, injured hundreds more, and left thousands homeless. In presiding over a settlement that required the persons responsible for maintaining the dam to pay the survivors many millions of dollars, the court found that the flood had caused psychological impairment in many survivors. Accordingly, this tragedy has received considerable attention from investigators in psychology, including a comprehensive natural experiment conducted by Goldine Gleser and her colleagues (1981).

On the basis of clinical reports and studies of other disasters, the Gleser group formulated several expectations about the psychological effects that the flood might have on the survivors: pathological levels of anxiety, depression, and sleep disturbance, among others. These became the dependent variables of the experiment. Data collected from 381 survivors by means of extensive interviews, self-report checklists, surveys, and physical examinations administered approximately eighteen months after the flood confirmed the experimenters' expectations. The survivors scored significantly higher on anxiety and depression measures than did a control group of people who lived elsewhere. In fact, the anxiety and depression scores of the survivors were about the same as those of clients being treated for anxiety and depression at two mental health clinics in other parts of the country. Similarly, the survivors experienced more sleep disturbances (difficulty falling asleep or staying asleep and nightmares) than the control subjects did. The experimenters found the greatest psychological impairment among those survivors who had come closest to dying and among those who had lost family members and friends in the flood. Finally, the study found more severe psychological disturbances among older children than among preschool-age survivors.

Natural experiments suffer from the same limitation as other quasi-experiments. That is, confounds may be causing the observed effects (Lehman, 1991). The researchers could not know, for example, whether the job pressures of Buffalo Creek residents had differed systematically from those of the control subjects, and so might have accounted for the differences in anxiety and depression scores and sleep disturbances.

Natural experiments also have other limitations. Because they rely on unexpected occurrences in

The Great Flood of 1993 brought destruction and homelessness to thousands of people in America's Midwest, including this man on Front Street in Clarksville, Missouri. Natural experiments conducted in the aftermath of this and other natural catastrophes have found that many survivors experience lingering feelings of anxiety and depression.

nature, they cannot be repeated at will. Also, because each natural event is unique in some ways, broad generalizations drawn from a single study could be incorrect. Nevertheless, findings obtained repeatedly over the years in hundreds of natural experiments have enabled clinical scientists to identify two patterns of anxiety-related symptoms that many people display in the wake of catastrophes. We shall be discussing these patterns—*acute stress disorders* and *posttraumatic stress disorders*—in Chapter 6.

ANALOGUE EXPERIMENT   There is one way in which investigators can freely manipulate independent variables while avoiding many of the ethical and practical limitations of clinical research: they can conduct **analogue experiments.** Experimenters who use this strategy induce laboratory subjects to behave in ways they believe to be functionally analogous to real-life abnormal behavior. They then conduct experiments on this laboratory-created, analogous form of abnormality in the hope of shedding light on the real-life counterpart.

Experimenters often use animals as subjects in analogue studies. Animal subjects are easier to gather and manipulate than human subjects, and they present fewer ethical problems. While the needs and rights of animal subjects must also be considered, most experimenters are willing to subject animals to more manipulation and discomfort than human subjects (see Box 3–5). They believe that the insights gained from such experimentation outweigh the discomfort of the animals (Overmier, 1992). In addition, experimenters can, and often do, use human subjects in analogue experiments.

As we shall see in Chapter 8, Martin Seligman (1975) has used analogue studies with great success to investigate the causes of human depression. Seligman has theorized that people become depressed when they believe they no longer have any control over the good and bad things that happen in their lives and that life's pleasures, such as job satisfaction, love relationships, and monetary rewards, are really random events beyond their control. According to Seligman, while other factors may contribute to depression, this perception of helplessness is the primary cause.

Seligman's strategy for investigating his hypothesis experimentally has been to gather a group of subjects, attempt to change their perceptions of control (manipulate the independent variable), and see whether their moods change accordingly (observe the dependent variable). His subjects have often been dogs, and he has subjected them to random electrical shocks—unpleasant events over which they have absolutely no control. The noxious stimuli are started

Chimpanzees and human beings share more than 90 percent of their genetic material, but the brains and bodies of the two species are enormously different, as are their perceptions and experiences. Other animals are even more different from human beings. Thus abnormal-like behavior produced in animal analogue experiments may differ in key ways from the human abnormality under investigation, and the conclusions drawn from such studies may be incorrect.

and stopped at random intervals irrespective of anything the dogs try to do. Seligman has found that the dogs typically react to this loss of control with symptoms suspiciously similar to those of human depression. In contrast to the control subjects in his studies, who are allowed to escape or avoid shocks and do so with vigor and with no change in their overall behavior patterns, the experimental subjects become exceedingly passive, socially and sexually withdrawn, and slow moving, their demeanor resembling the sadness and pessimism of depression. They stop trying to avoid the shocks and just seem to give up. In short, under laboratory conditions Seligman has created a pattern of behavior—he calls it **learned helplessness**—that he believes to be an analogue of human depression.

Seligman and other researchers have conducted hundreds of experiments on the laboratory phenomenon of learned helplessness in an effort to improve their understanding of depression. They have manipulated all kinds of independent variables (shocks, loud noises, failure experiences, and so on) to determine which kinds of loss of control lead to learned helplessness and, by implication, to depression. They have manipulated the early life

BOX 3-5

ANIMALS HAVE RIGHTS TOO

For years medical and psychological researchers have operated under the assumption that animal experiments are an ethically acceptable alternative to experimenting on humans, and they have gathered insights about human abnormal behavior by doing such things as shocking animals, prematurely separating them from their parents, starving them, surgically altering their brains, and even killing, or *sacrificing*, them to perform an autopsy. In recent years animal rights activists have protested that these research undertakings are often cruel, and they have questioned whether the pain inflicted on research animals is always justified.

The debate over this issue has become heated. At one extreme, some animal rights activists describe medical and psychological researchers as in-

sensitive monsters; at the other, some researchers claim animal rights activists are more interested in animals than in the human beings whose medical and mental health may be enhanced by animal research. Somewhere in the middle lies a serious and difficult ethical problem that must be addressed.

On the one hand, healthy human

functioning is a worthy goal that seems to justify at least some forms of animal experimentation, especially when no other form of research is able to provide insights and solutions. On the other hand, animals are also living creatures, and their comfort and existence cannot simply be dismissed as irrelevant.

In recognition of this issue, the U.S. Congress passed the Animal Welfare Act in 1966, and in 1989 the U.S. Department of Agriculture developed numerous regulations governing the use and care of research animals. The regulations seek to define when animal sacrifice is acceptable in research, to limit the number of surgical operations that can be performed on a single animal, to control the sale of animals for research, to ensure the psychological well-being of animals, to enlarge the cage space of research animals, and to ensure that

experiences of experimental subjects to determine which kinds of experiences help immunize subjects against learned helplessness and, again by analogy, against depression. And they have studied whether certain interventions reverse learned helplessness and so might help reverse depression.

Seligman and his colleagues have conducted some of their analogue studies on human subjects. Typically their laboratory human subjects are randomly exposed to unpleasant and unavoidable stimuli such as loud noises or failures on cognitive tasks. These subjects, too, display symptoms of learned helplessness, including temporary passivity, pessimism about their effectiveness at future tasks, and sadness (Young & Allin, 1992; Miller & Seligman, 1975).

It is important to recognize that Seligman's analogue experiments are enlightening only to the extent

that the laboratory-induced condition of learned helplessness is indeed analogous to human depression. If it turns out that this laboratory phenomenon is only superficially similar to depression, then the clinical inferences drawn from such experiments may be wrong and misleading. This, in fact, is the major limitation of all analogue research (Vredenburg, Flett, & Krames, 1993). Although such studies enable scientists to control and manipulate variables more easily, researchers can never be certain that the phenomena they see in the laboratory are the same as the psychological disorders they are investigating. For this reason, researchers such as Seligman usually conduct many variations of an analogue study in hopes of demonstrating consistent parallels between the laboratory analogue and the real-life phenomenon. The more parallels they demonstrate, the more compelling their analogue findings are.

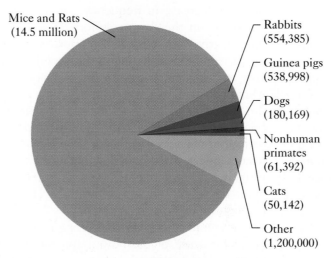

At least 17 million animals are used in research each year. Approximately 85 percent are rats and mice. (Office of Technology Assessment; U.S. Department of Agriculture; National Research Council.)

the animals receive a proper amount of exercise.

Even though guidelines for animal research are now in place, animal rights groups still actively fight against many forms of animal research, using such strategies as demonstrations and flyers targeting the work of researchers, legal maneuvers to delay research, and, in some cases, harrassment of researchers and vandalism of their labs. In 1992 Congress passed the Animal Enterprise Protection Act, making vandalism to animal facilities a federal offense with a penalty of incarceration for up to one year and restitution for damages. Although researchers were generally pleased by this legislative act, most were upset with a decision made by the Washington State Supreme Court the same year. The court ordered researchers at the University of Washington to disclose parts of their research proposals to animal rights activists to ensure that experimental animals would not be subjected to any cruel or unnecessary pain. The scientists at this university, along with many other researchers in the state, protested the decision, claiming that mandatory disclosure of their proposals is a violation of their intellectual property rights, since it would reveal confidential information to other researchers.

Thus, the battle between animal researchers and animal rights activists continues, with no end in sight. Many animal researchers believe that the growing number of restrictions severely limit the scope and necessary freedom of their investigations and thus hinder potential gains for human beings. Animal rights activists argue that the government regulations do not yet adequately protect the rights and needs of animal subjects. The difficulty of resolving this controversy highlights once again the significant ethical dilemmas that clinical researchers face.

SINGLE-SUBJECT EXPERIMENT As our discussion of the experimental method has suggested, experiments are usually done on groups of subjects rather than on one lone individual. By using representative groups of subjects, experimenters can be relatively confident that their findings are more than chance occurrences and represent general trends in larger populations. Sometimes, however, scientists do not have the luxury of experimenting on numerous subjects. They may, for example, be investigating a disorder so rare that few subjects are available. Experimentation is still possible in such cases in the form of *single-subject,* or *single-case, experimental designs* (Kazdin, 1994).

In designs of this kind, the single subject is observed and measured before the manipulation of an independent variable. *Baseline data*—data gathered during the observation or baseline period—reveal what a subject's behavior is like without any manipulations or interventions, and thus establish a standard with which later changes may be compared. The experimenter next introduces the independent variable and observes the subject's behavior once again. Any changes in behavior are attributed to the effects of the independent variable. The most commonly used single-subject experimental designs are the *ABAB* and *multiple-baseline designs*.

ABAB DESIGN In an *ABAB,* or *reversal, design,* a subject's reactions are measured and compared not only during a baseline period (A) and after the introduction of the independent variable (B) but once again after the independent variable has been removed (A) and yet again after it has been reintroduced (B). If the subject's responses change back and forth systematically with changes in the independent variable, the experimenter may conclude that the independent variable is causing the shifting responses (Kratochwill, 1992). Essentially, in an ABAB design a subject is compared with him- or herself under different conditions rather than with control subjects. Subjects therefore serve as their own controls.

Clinicians are likely to resort to an ABAB design when they wish to determine the effectiveness of a particular form of therapy on a client but are unable to obtain other clients with similar problems for a properly controlled experiment. One therapist used this design to determine whether a behavioral reinforcement treatment program was helping to reduce a retarded teenage boy's habit of disrupting his special education class with loud talk (Deitz, 1977). The reinforcement program consisted of rewarding the boy with extra teacher time whenever he managed to go 55 minutes without talking in class more than three times. When the student's level of talking was measured during a baseline period, it was found to consist of frequent verbal disruptions. Next the boy was given a series of teacher reinforcement sessions (the independent variable); as expected, his loud talk soon decreased dramatically. Then the reinforcement treatment was stopped, and the student's loud talk was found to increase once again. Apparently the independent variable had indeed been the cause of the improvement.

To be more confident about this conclusion, the therapist introduced the teacher reinforcement treatment yet again and found that once again the subject's behavior improved. This reintroduction of the independent variable helped rule out the possibility that some confounding factor (such as the onset of magnificent spring weather or a present from a relative) had actually been causing the boy's improvement.

MULTIPLE-BASELINE DESIGN   A *multiple-baseline design* does not employ the reversals found in an ABAB design. Instead, the experimenter selects two or more behaviors displayed by a subject and observes the effect that the manipulation of an independent variable has on each of the behaviors (Herz et al., 1992; Morley, 1989). Let us say that the teenage boy in the ABAB study exhibited two kinds of inappropriate behavior—the disruptive talk during class and odd grimaces. In a multiple-baseline design, the experimenter would first collect baseline data on both the frequency of the boy's disruptive talk and the frequency of his facial grimaces during a 55-minute period. In the next phase of the experiment, the experimenter would reward the boy with extra teacher time whenever he cut down his verbalizations but not when he cut down his grimaces. The experimenter would then measure changes in the boy's verbal and

grimacing behaviors, expecting the verbal interruptions to decrease in frequency but the grimacing to remain about the same as before, in accordance with the selective applications of reinforcement. In the final phase of the experiment, the experimenter would also reward the boy with extra teacher attention whenever he reduced his grimacing, expecting that this manipulation would now lead to a similar reduction in the frequency of grimacing. If the expected pattern of changes was found, it would be reasonable to conclude that the manipulation of the independent variable (teacher reinforcement), rather than some other factor, was responsible for the changes in the two behaviors. Had some extraneous factor such as an improvement in the weather or a gift from a relative been the cause of the boy's improvement, it would probably have caused improvements in both kinds of behavior in other phases of the study, not just in the final phase. In short, by choosing more than one behavioral baseline for observation, an experimenter can systematically eliminate confounding variables from his or her interpretations of the findings.

Obviously, single-subject experiments—both ABAB and multiple-baseline designs—are similar to individual case studies in their focus on one subject. In the single-subject experiment, however, the independent variable is systematically manipulated in such a way that the investigator can conclude with some confidence whether or not it is the cause of an observed effect. That is, the single-subject experiment has greater internal validity than the case study (Lehman, 1991; Smith, 1988).

At the same time, single-subject designs, like case studies, have only limited external validity. Because only one subject is studied, the experimenter cannot be sure that the subject's reaction to the independent variable is typical. Other subjects might react differently. In the single-subject designs described here, for example, there is no basis for concluding that other adolescents with similar behavior problems would respond successfully to the same reinforcement programs.

■ THE LIMITS ■ OF CLINICAL INVESTIGATION

We began this chapter by observing that clinical scientists look for general laws that will help them to understand, prevent, and treat psychological disorders.

A variety of circumstances impede their progress, however. We have already noted some of them. The most problematic are summarized below.

1. *Clinical subjects have needs and rights that investigators are obliged to respect.* Clinical scientists must respect the human and civil rights of their human subjects. Thus they may not instruct parents to abuse their children to determine the psychological effects of child abuse or induce catastrophic events to examine people's psychological reactions to crises. These kinds of ethical considerations set significant limitations on the kinds of investigations that clinical scientists can conduct.

2. *The origins of human functioning are very complex.* Because human behavior generally results from multiple factors working together, it is most difficult to pinpoint precise or principal causes of given behaviors. Moreover, as our discussion of the experimental method suggests, even in well-controlled studies unsuspected factors may be operating on and influencing a person's thoughts, feelings, and actions. So many factors can influence human functioning that it has actually been easier to unravel the complexities of energy and matter than to understand such phenomena as human sadness, stress, and anxiety.

3. *Human beings are changeable.* Moods, behaviors, and thoughts fluctuate. Is the person clinical scientists are studying today truly the same as the one they were investigating yesterday? Does the person feel the same, perceive problems in the same way, or even have the same problems? Variability in a single person, let alone the normal variations from person to person, limits the kinds of conclusions researchers can draw about abnormal functioning.

4. *Human self-awareness may influence the results of clinical investigations.* When human subjects know they are being studied, they may behave in ways that differ from their usual patterns (Harris & Lahey, 1986). Not only may they bias a study by trying to respond in expected ways or to present themselves in a favorable light, but the attention they receive from investigators may in itself affect their perceptions and feelings (usually it increases their optimism and improves their mood). It is an axiom of science that the very act of measuring an object distorts the object to some degree. Nowhere is this more true than in the study of human beings.

5. *Clinical investigators have a special link to their subjects.* Clinical scientists have themselves experienced mood changes, troubled thoughts, family problems, and other difficulties that may be similar to the clinical problems they are investigating. They may identify with the pain of their subjects or have personal opinions about the causes and implications of their problems. As we see in Freud's case study of Little Hans and in the Rosenthal effect found in many experiments, the relation of the clinical investigator to the topic under study can bias the experimenter's attempts to understand abnormality.

These complicating factors amount to yet another reason that clinical scientists must use a variety of methods to study abnormality. Each approach addresses some of the problems inherent in investigating human behavior, but no one approach overcomes them all. Case studies allow investigators to consider a broader range of causes than other methods of investigation, but experiments help them pinpoint precise causal factors in ways that case studies cannot do. Thus it is best to view each method of investigation as one of a battery of approaches that collectively may shed considerable light on abnormal human functioning.

When more than one of these methods has been used to investigate a certain disorder, it is important to ask whether all the results seem to point in the same direction. If they do, it is likely that clinical investigators are close to attaining a clear understanding of that disturbance or an effective treatment for it. Conversely, if the various methods seem to produce conflicting results, investigators must admit that their knowledge in that clinical area is still limited.

Before accepting one another's research findings as conclusive or even as highly suggestive, however,

"You want proof? I'll give you proof!"

Because clinical research is so complex and difficult to evaluate, it is inevitable that personal and professional bias will have at least some influence on the opinions of clinical investigators and practitioners.

clinical investigators are obligated to review the details of the studies with a very critical eye. If a study is an experiment, for example, have the variables been properly controlled, was the choice of subjects representative, was the sample large enough to be meaningful, and have subject and experimenter bias been eliminated? Are the investigator's conclusions justified? How else might the results be interpreted? Only after research findings have been scrutinized in this way can they be considered to expand our knowledge of abnormality.

SUMMARY

■ THE HISTORY of abnormal psychology shows that theories and treatment procedures may seem reasonable and effective in some cases but prove useless and even harmful in others. Only through research can the dangers be discovered and the benefits proved. The researchers who systematically test the ideas of clinical theorists and clinical practitioners are faced with the challenge of figuring out meaningful yet ethical ways to measure such elusive concepts as unconscious motives, private thoughts, mood change, and human potential.

Clinical researchers use the *scientific method* to uncover *nomothetic,* or general, principles of abnormal psychological functioning—its nature, its causes, and how it may be changed for the better. They attempt to identify and examine relationships between *variables*—characteristics or events that can vary—to determine whether two or more variables change together and whether change in one variable causes a change in another. Researchers depend primarily on three methods of investigation: the case study, the correlational method, and the experimental method.

■ THE CASE STUDY is a detailed account of one person's life and psychological problems. Although it focuses on a single person, the case study can serve as a source of ideas about behavior in others. It may provide tentative support for a theory, or it may challenge theoretical assumptions. It may serve as a source of ideas for new therapeutic techniques. A case study may also offer an opportunity to study an unusual problem that does not occur often enough to permit more general observations and comparisons.

Case studies have limitations. The observer may be biased and therefore may be selective about what is included in the report. They tend to have low *internal validity* because it is difficult to establish that the problems being reported were actually related to the specific variables that the researcher discussed, and not to any of the countless other variables that play a part in every person's life. Finally, they may have low *external validity:* it may be a mistake to apply what is learned from a case study to people whose problems appear to be similar.

■ THE CORRELATIONAL METHOD is a procedure for systematically observing the extent to which events or characteristics vary together. This method allows researchers to draw broad conclusions about abnormality in the population at large because they (1) make many observations of numerous individuals, (2) uniformly apply carefully prescribed procedures so that the studies can be replicated, and (3) analyze the results by statistical methods. These three conditions apply equally to the experimental method.

Correlation is the degree to which variables change in accordance with one another. To determine whether a general correlation does indeed exist, the variables must be measured in a large number of individual cases. The *direction* of the correlation is determined by plotting the data on a graph and drawing a *line of best fit*—the line that best fits all of the points. When two variables increase or decrease together, they are said to have a *positive correlation.* When the value of one variable goes up as the other goes down, the correlation is *negative.* If the variables have no systematic relationship, they are said to be *unrelated.* Both the direction and the magnitude of a correlation can be calculated numerically and expressed by the *correlation coefficient (r),* which can vary between +1.00, a perfect positive correlation, and −1.00, a perfect negative correlation. The sign (+ or −) signifies the direction; the number represents the magnitude.

When a correlation has been found, the scientist wants to know if it is truly characteristic of the larger population. To find out, he or she does a *statistical analysis* of the data. If the probability is no more than 5 in 100 that these results would occur by chance, then the findings are said to be *statistically significant.*

The primary drawback to the correlational method is that it allows researchers to describe only the relationship between variables; it does not help them explain the relationship. When it is important to understand the causal relationship between variables, researchers generally turn to the experimental method.

Two widely used forms of the correlation method are *epidemiological studies,* which determine the incidence and prevalence of a disorder in a given population, and *longitudinal studies,* which observe the characteristics or behavior of the same subjects over a long period of time. Although these methods provide clues about which events are causes and which are consequences, they, like other correlational methods, do not pinpoint causation.

■ IN THE EXPERIMENTAL METHOD, researchers manipulate suspected causes to see whether expected effects will result. The variable that is manipulated is called the *independent variable* and the variable that is expected to change as a result is called the *dependent variable.*

Confounds are variables other than the independent variable that are also acting on the dependent variable. They can be major obstacles to efforts to isolate the true cause of an effect. If confounds exist, the researcher cannot be sure that the observed effect is caused by the independent variable and not by some other variable. To minimize the possible influence of confounds, researchers use *control groups, random assignment,* and *blind designs.*

The findings of experiments, like those of correlational studies, must be analyzed statistically. If the likelihood is no more than 5 percent that the differences between the control and experimental groups are due to chance, the results are considered statistically significant.

For ethical and practical reasons, it is difficult to formulate and carry out an ideal experiment in human psychology. Clinical experimenters must often settle for imperfect variations of the optimal experimental design, including the *quasi-experimental design,* the *natural experiment,* the *analogue experiment,* and the *single-subject experiment.* Two versions of the single-subject experiment are the *ABAB design* and the *multiple-baseline design.*

Topic Overview

CLINICAL ASSESSMENT, INTERPRETATION, AND DIAGNOSIS

ngela Savanti was 22 years old, lived at home with her mother, and was employed as a secretary in a large insurance company. She . . . had had passing periods of "the blues" before, but her present feelings of despondency were of much greater proportion. She was troubled by a severe depression and frequent crying spells, which had not lessened over the past two months. Angela found it hard to concentrate on her job, had great difficulty falling asleep at night, and had a poor appetite. . . . Her depression had begun after she and her boyfriend Jerry broke up two months previously.

(Leon, 1984, p. 109)

EVENTUALLY ANGELA SAVANTI MADE AN APPOINTMENT with a therapist at a local counseling center. The first step the clinician took toward helping Angela was to learn as much as possible about her disturbance. Who is she, what is her life like, and what precisely are her symptoms? This information was expected to throw light on the causes and the probable course of her present dysfunction and help the clinician decide what kinds of treatment strategies would be likely to help her. The treatment program could then be tailored to Angela's unique needs and to her particular pattern of abnormal functioning.

WHEREAS RESEARCHERS IN ABNORMAL PSYCHOLOGY seek primarily a nomothetic, or broad, understanding of abnormal functioning, clinical practitioners are interested in compiling *idiographic,* or individual, information about their clients. If practitioners are to help particular people overcome their problems, they must have the fullest possible understanding of those people and know the nature and origins of their problems. Although they also apply general information and principles in their work, they can determine the relevance of such information only after they have thoroughly examined the person who has come for treatment. This idiographic understanding of the client is arrived at through *assessment, interpretation,* and *diagnosis.*

■ CLINICAL ■ ASSESSMENT

Assessment, the collection of relevant information about a subject, goes on at every stage and in every realm of life, from grade school to college admissions to the job market, and from shopping for groceries to voting for president. College admissions officers, who have to predict which students will succeed in college, depend on academic records, recommendations, achievement test scores, interviews, and application forms to give them information about prospective students. Employers, who have to decide which applicants are most likely to be effective workers, collect information about them from résumés, interviews, references, and perhaps on-the-job observations.

Clinical assessment techniques are used not only to determine how and why a person is behaving abnormally and how that person might be helped but also to evaluate clients after they have been in treatment for a while, to see what progress they are making and whether the treatment ought to be modified. Clinicians may also assess clients at the completion of treatment to determine the overall effectiveness of the therapy.

Clinical assessment also plays an important role in research. When researchers want to know the causes of certain disorders or their responsiveness to various kinds of treatment, they have to be sure that the subjects they select are representative of people with those disorders. Sometimes researchers rely on assessments that have already been conducted by clinicians; at other times they conduct their own assessments. The accuracy of the assessments has a direct bearing on the value of the research.

Clinicians' selection of specific assessment techniques and tools depends on their theoretical orientation. Psychodynamic clinicians, for example, use assessment methods that provide information about the components of a person's personality and any unconscious conflicts he or she may be experiencing (Butler & Satz, 1989). This kind of assessment, called a *personality assessment,* enables them to piece together a clinical picture in accordance with the principles and concepts of the psychodynamic model. Behavioral and many cognitive clinicians, in contrast, use assessment methods that provide detailed information about the specific dysfunctional behaviors and cognitions (Haynes, 1990; Kendall, 1990; Ciminero, 1986). The goal of this kind of assessment, called *behavioral assessment,* is to carry out a *functional analysis* of the person's behaviors—an analysis of how the behaviors are learned and reinforced. Hundreds of assessment techniques and tools have been developed from all theoretical perspectives, but most of them fall into three general categories: clinical interviews, tests, and observations.

CLINICAL INTERVIEWS

Most of us feel instinctively that the best way to get to know people is to meet with them. In face-to-face interactions we can see other persons' reactions to our questions, observe as well as listen as they answer, watch them observing us, and generally get a sense of who they are. The clinical interview is a face-to-face encounter of this kind (Wiens, 1990). Research has repeatedly suggested that the way people say something can be as revealing as what they say (Korchin, 1976; Mehrabian, 1972). If a woman becomes markedly restless and avoids eye contact when she talks about men, the clinician may suspect that she feels some anxiety about heterosexual relationships. If a man says that the death of his mother saddened him but looks as happy as can be, the clinician may suspect that the man actually has conflicting emotions about this loss. Almost all practitioners use clinical interviews as part of the assessment process.

CONDUCTING THE INTERVIEW The interview is often the first contact between client and clinician. Harry Stack Sullivan, the renowned American psychiatrist, said that the interviewer's primary task is to "discover who the client is—that is, he must review what course of events the client has come through to be who he is, what he has in the way of background and experience" (Sullivan, 1954, pp. 17–18). Correspondingly, clinical interviewers usually seek detailed information about the person's current problems and feelings, current life situations and relationships, and personal history. They may also examine the person's expectations of therapy and motives for seeking it. The clinician working with Angela Savanti reported:

Angela was dressed neatly when she appeared for her first interview. She was attractive, but her eyes were puffy and ringed with dark circles. She answered questions and related information about her life history in a slow, flat tone of voice, which had an impersonal quality to it. She sat stiffly in her chair with her hands in her lap, and moved very little throughout the entire interview.

The client stated that the time period just before she and her boyfriend terminated their relationship had been one of extreme emotional turmoil. She was not sure whether she wanted to marry Jerry, and he began to demand that she decide either one way or the other. Mrs. Savanti did not seem to like Jerry and was very cold and aloof whenever he came to the house. Angela felt caught in the middle and unable to make a decision about her future. After several confrontations with Jerry over whether she would marry him or not, he told her he felt that she would never decide, so he was not going to see her anymore.

Angela stated that she was both relieved and upset that Jerry had forced the issue and essentially made the decision for her. She did not attempt to contact him, but became increasingly depressed. She had stayed home from work several times during the past month and had just sat around the house and cried.

Angela came from a working-class family of Italian origin. . . . Both sets of grandparents emigrated from Italy, and her parents were born in the United States. . . . Angela's mother and father separated when Angela was 11 years old. Mr. Savanti had moved to another city, and he had never sent money to support the family, nor had he been heard from since his departure. . . . After he left, Mrs. Savanti got a job in a factory, and she has worked there ever since. . . .

Angela stated that her childhood was a very unhappy period. Her father was seldom home, and when he was present, her parents fought constantly. Sometimes the arguments became quite severe and her father would throw things and shout. Mrs. Savanti usually became sullen and withdrawn after an argument, refused to speak to her husband, and became uncommunicative with her daughters. Angela remembered that many times as a child she was puzzled because it seemed that her mother was angry at her, too. Sometimes after an argument, Mrs. Savanti told her daughters that she had ruined her life by marrying their father. . . .

Angela recalled feeling very guilty when Mr. Savanti left. . . . She revealed that whenever she thought of her father, she always felt that she had been responsible in some way for his leaving the family. Angela had never communicated this feeling to anyone, and her mother rarely mentioned his name.

Angela described her mother as the "long-suffering type" who said that she had sacrificed her life to make her children happy, and the only thing she ever got in return was grief and unhappiness. Angela related that her mother rarely smiled or laughed and did not converse very much with the girls. . . . When Angela and [her sister] Doreen began dating, Mrs. Savanti . . . commented on how tired she was because she had waited up for them. She would make disparaging remarks about the boys they had been with and about men in general. . . .

Angela said that she liked her grandparents. . . . Her grandparents and mother were very religious, and it seemed that there were always religious overtones to any discussions with them. Angela reported that she was having a great many doubts about her religious faith and beliefs, and these doubts especially troubled her around the time she stopped seeing Jerry. . . .

Angela had met Jerry at a party two years earlier, when she was 20 and he was 23. She liked him from the first time they met, but she was very careful not to give any indication that she was attracted to him. . . . Angela described Jerry as talkative and friendly, and of similar ethnic background. She said that he too had difficulty expressing his feelings, and many times he resorted to kidding around as a means of avoiding emotional expression.

Jerry began to talk about getting married six months before they stopped dating. He said that he had a good job and he wanted to marry Angela. Angela, however, was very ambivalent about what she wanted to do. She enjoyed being with Jerry, but her mother's indifference toward him troubled her. Mrs. Savanti made numerous comments to the effect that all men are nice before they get married, but later their true nature comes out. . . .

Angela revealed that she had often been troubled with depressed moods. During high school, if she got a lower grade in a subject than she had expected, her initial response was one of anger, followed by depression. She began to think that she was not smart enough to get good grades, and she blamed herself for studying too little. Angela also became despondent when she got into an argument with her mother or felt that she was being taken advantage of at work. However, these periods of depression usually lasted only about a day, and passed when she became involved in some other activity.

The intensity and duration of the [mood change] that she experienced when she broke up with Jerry were much more severe. She was not sure why she was so depressed, but she began to feel it was an effort to walk around and go out to work. Talking with others became difficult, and many times her lips felt as if they were stiff, and she had to make an effort to move them in order to speak. Angela found it hard to concentrate, and she began to forget things she was supposed to do. It took her a long time to fall asleep at night, and when she finally did fall asleep, she sometimes woke up in the midst of a bad dream. She felt constantly tired, and loud noises, including conversation or the television, bothered her. She preferred to lie in bed rather than be with anyone, and she often cried when alone.

At the point where Angela's depressed state was seriously beginning to interfere with her job, she decided she had better see the company physician. She asked the doctor to prescribe something to help her sleep, so she would not be so tired and could concentrate better. The physician suggested that Angela receive some professional help with her problems and she was referred to a counseling center in the area.

(Leon, 1984, pp. 110–115)

Beyond gathering basic interview data of this kind, clinical interviewers give special attention to whatever topics they consider most important. Psychodynamic interviewers try to learn about the person's needs and fantasies, elicit relevant memories about past events and relationships, and observe the way the person molds the interview (Shea, 1990; Pope, 1983). Behavioral interviewers have an acronym, SORC, for the kinds of information they gather in order to do a functional analysis: relevant information about the *stimuli* that trigger the abnormal functioning, about the *organism* or person (such as a low self-opinion), about the precise nature of the abnormal *responses*, and about the *consequences* of those responses (Reyna, 1989; O'Leary & Wilson, 1987). Cognitive interviewers try to discover assumptions, interpretations, and cognitive coping skills that influence the way the person acts and feels (Kendall, 1990). Humanistic clinicians ask about the person's self-concept and try to learn about his or her unique perceptions (Aiken, 1985; Brown, 1972). And biological clinicians use the interview to help pinpoint signs of any biochemical or neurological dysfunction (Kallman & Feuerstein, 1986).

INTERVIEW FORMATS Interviews can be either unstructured or structured. In an ***unstructured interview,*** the clinician asks open-ended questions ("Would you tell me about yourself?"), follows interesting leads, and places few constraints on what the client can discuss. The lack of structure allows clinicians to focus on important topics that they could not anticipate before the interview. Also, it gives them a better appreciation of the issues that are important to the client.

In a ***structured interview,*** clinicians ask a series of prepared questions. Sometimes they use a published ***interview schedule***—a standard set of questions or topics designed for use in all interviews (Shea, 1988). Structured formats enable clinicians to cover the same kinds of important issues in all their interviews and to compare the responses of one individual with those of others. Structured interviews often include a ***mental status exam,*** interview questions and observations designed to reveal the precise nature and degree of a client's abnormal functioning. The questions systematically cover areas of functioning such as awareness of what is going on, orientation with regard to time and place, attention span, memory, judgment and insight, thought content and processes, mood, and appearance.

Most clinical interviews have both structured and unstructured portions, but many clinicians favor one

"So, Mr. Fenton . . . Let's begin with your mother."

In a structured interview, clinicians gather information by asking a set of standard questions irrespective of the client's particular symptoms. Critics argue that excessive structure may lead to irrelevant questions and to the omission of important information. (The Far Side cartoon by Gary Larson is reprinted by permission of Chronicle Features, San Francisco, CA. All rights reserved.)

kind over the other (Leon, Bowden, & Faber, 1989; Graham & Lilly, 1984). Unstructured interviews typically appeal to psychodynamic clinicians because they allow interviewers to search freely for underlying issues and conflicts. They are also popular among humanists because they allow clinicians to guide the conversation in any direction the client's ideas and experiences indicate (Pope, 1983). Structured formats, on the other hand, are more widely used by behavioral clinicians, who need to do a systematic review of many pieces of information to complete a functional analysis of a person's behaviors (Pope, 1983). Structured formats are equally popular among cognitive interviewers because they can point to certain characteristic attitudes or thinking processes, and among biological interviewers because they can help clinicians search systematically for indicators of biological dysfunctioning.

LIMITATIONS OF CLINICAL INTERVIEWS Despite the value of the clinical interview as a source of information about a client, there are limits to what it can accomplish. One problem is that the information gathered during an interview is to some extent preselected by the client. Though most people seek help voluntarily, many come to clinicians under duress, sent by a court, a parent, or a threatening spouse. In such cases the information the client provides may be self-serving. Even clients who come voluntarily may try to present themselves in the best light or feel reluctant to introduce embarrassing topics.

Another problem is that some clients are simply unable to provide accurate information in an interview. The very disturbance that brings them to the clinician may seriously distort their perceptions and reports of events in their lives. People who suffer from depression, for example, take an unduly pessimistic view of themselves, their environment, and their future (Beck, 1991, 1967). Thus a depressed man might describe himself as incompetent at his job, whereas his boss and co-workers consider him all but indispensable.

Yet another drawback is that interviewers may make subjective judgments that skew the information they gather. They usually rely too heavily on first impressions, for example, and give too much weight to unfavorable information about a client (Aiken, 1985; Meehl, 1960). The interviewers' biases, including gender and race biases, may also influence the way they interpret what a client says.

Finally, clients respond differently to different interviewers. Studies show that clients feel uncomfortable with clinicians who are cold and distant, and offer them less information than they do to clinicians who are warm and supportive (Eisenthal, Koopman, & Lazare, 1983; Jourard, 1971). A clinician's race, sex, age, and appearance may also influence the client's responses (Paurohit, Dowd, & Cottingham, 1982; Johnson, 1981). One study found that adolescent girls admitted more misbehaviors to younger interviewers than to older ones, and when they talked to older interviewers they were more likely to claim that they always did what their parents told them to do (Erlich & Reisman, 1961).

In these circumstances, it is not surprising that different clinicians can obtain different answers and draw different conclusions even when they ask the same questions of the same person (Langwieler & Linden, 1993). Accordingly, some researchers believe that interviewing, a time-honored approach to assessment, should be discarded. This might be a reasonable suggestion if there were other, problem-free techniques to use instead. As we shall see, however, the two other kinds of clinical assessment methods also have serious limitations.

CLINICAL TESTS

Tests are devices for gathering information about a few aspects of a person's psychological functioning, from which broader information about that person can be inferred (Goldstein & Hersen, 1990; Aiken, 1985; Graham & Lilly, 1984). Clinicians use them to uncover subtle information that might not become apparent during an interview or observation and to determine how one person's functioning compares with that of others. More than 500 standard clinical tests are currently used throughout the United States.

The tests that clinicians use most frequently are of five kinds:

1. *Projective tests,* consisting of unstructured or ambiguous material to which people are asked to respond. The material is so vague that the responses are likely to reflect the person's psychological makeup.
2. *Self-report inventories,* consisting of lists of items that people are asked to evaluate as characteristic or uncharacteristic of them. In the process they are assumed to reveal their personalities, behavior patterns, emotions, or beliefs.
3. *Psychophysiological tests,* which measure such physical responses as heart rate and muscle tension as possible indicators of psychological problems.
4. *Neuropsychological tests,* which reveal possible neurological impairment.
5. *Intelligence tests,* which are designed to measure a person's intellectual ability.

CHARACTERISTICS OF TESTS   On the surface, it may appear relatively simple to design an effective test. Every month in magazines and newspapers we come across new tests that purport to reveal information about our selves, our relationships, our sex lives, our stresses, our ability to succeed in business, and more. These tests can seem convincing, but they are often misleading. Most of them do not yield consistent or accurate information about our functioning or say anything meaningful about where we stand in comparison with others. If a test is to be useful, it must be *standardized* and must be proved to have *reliability* and *validity* (see Box 4–1).

STANDARDIZATION   Suppose a person scores 40 on a test designed to measure aggressiveness.

BOX 4-1

TESTS, LIES, AND VIDEOTAPE: THE PUBLIC MISUSE OF ASSESSMENT

In movies, criminals being grilled by the police reveal their guilt by sweating, shaking, cursing, or twitching. When they are hooked up to a *polygraph* (a lie detector), the needles bounce all over the paper. Such images have been with us since World War I, when some clinicians developed the theory that certain detectable physiological changes occur in people who are being deceptive (Marston, 1917).

The logic and design of a lie detector test are straightforward. A subject's respiration level, perspiration level, and heart rate are recorded while he or she answers questions. The clinician observes these physiological responses while the subject answers yes to control questions that are known to be true, such as "Are your parents both alive?", and then compares them to the physiological responses when the subject answers the test questions,

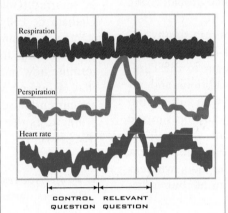

CONTROL   RELEVANT
QUESTION   QUESTION

such as "Did you commit this robbery?" If, as shown here, breathing, perspiration, and heart rate increase while the subject responds to the test questions, he or she may be judged to be lying (Raskin, 1982). The danger of relying on such tests, however, is that there is no compelling evidence that they work (Steinbrook, 1992).

It is crucial that a test be valid if it is to be used as a diagnostic tool. Yet polygraph tests have enjoyed widespread popularity for many years despite an almost total lack of evidence that they are meaningful. Only recently has this inconvenient fact reduced people's reliance on these tests and instigated responsible inquiries into their validity. In 1984 the U.S. Office of Technology Assessment reviewed all available literature on the polygraph and concluded that the test *lacked* validity and that the underlying theoretical assumption—that there is a unique physiological response associated with deception—was not necessarily true (Saxe, Dougherty, & Cross, 1985). As a result, the House of Representatives voted to restrict the use of the polygraph in preemployment screening. Similarly, in 1986 the American Psychological Association concluded that polygraphs were inac-

---

What does that number mean? Even if we know that scores on this test range from 0 to 50, we still don't know whether 40 is what most people score. It may be far above or below the average. If a test score is to be meaningful, we must be able to compare it with the scores other people receive on the same test (Dahlstrom, 1993). We can do so if the test has gone through the process of *standardization;* that is, it has been administered to a large group of subjects whose performance then serves as a common standard, or norm, against which any individual's score can be measured. The initial group of people who took the test is called the *standardization sample.*

A standardization sample must be representative of the larger population the test is intended for. If an aggressiveness test meant for the public at large were standardized on a group of Marines, for example, the

norm might turn out to be much higher than it would be if the test were standardized on people from all walks of life. The Marines' scores would not provide normative information representative of most of the people who would be taking the test. Factors such as age, sex, and education level must also be considered in the selection of a standardization sample. In some cases, it may be useful to generate more than one set of norms. Since women and men in our society may differ in expressions of aggressiveness, for example, it might be a good idea for an aggressiveness test to have one norm for males and another for females. This strategy would allow clinicians to compare the test scores of male subjects with those of a male sample and the scores of female subjects with those of a female sample.

RELIABILITY   *Reliability* is a measure of the consistency of test results. A good test should always

curate, and more fundamentally, that no physiological response pattern was associated with deception in the first place.

With the polygraph's popularity in decline, a rush began to develop a test to replace it, especially as a screening tool for employment. Businesses and governments were losing billions of dollars to theft, low productivity, and other dishonest behavior. This need stimulated development of so-called *integrity tests,* personality tests that seek to measure whether the test takers are generally honest or dishonest—and whether it is safe to hire them for a particular job. More than forty of these written tests are now in use, supposedly revealing other broad characteristics such as dependability, deviance, social conformity, wayward impulses, and hostility to rules. However, here again research suggests that they have virtually no theoretical foundation, show at best limited validity, are easy to fake, are often interpreted by unqualified testers, and, most important, yield high rates of false accusations (Camara & Schneider, 1994; Guastello & Rieke, 1991).

Yet other psychological tests have also caused uproars. In Old Town,

Maine, a police officer lost his job after refusing to take a *penile plethysmograph test,* meant to evaluate his sexual impulses. The officer had been accused of child sexual abuse. Although there was no substantiation, indictment, or conviction, the police department required that the officer see a sex-abuse therapist and undergo testing in order to retain his job.

A penile plethysmograph test consists of placing a rubber tube filled with mercury around a subject's penis and then showing him different stimuli, such as videotapes or slides of naked adults or children. When the subject becomes sexually aroused, the band stretches and the mercury acts as a conductor that transmits the results. Clinicians can chart the arousal on a computer program to determine whether a subject is more aroused by adults than by children, by males than by females, or by coerced rather than consensual sex.

Psychologists point out that although the test does accurately report sexual arousal, it has no predictive validity—it cannot predict whether or not an individual will act on those sexual feelings (Barker & Howell, 1992). Researchers also note that of all the people who may be sexually attracted

to children, relatively few would actually try to satisfy those desires. The test therefore cannot determine whether persons have committed a sexual offense or predict whether they are likely to do so in the future.

The officer from Maine brought a civil rights lawsuit against the city of Old Town, claiming that the government does not have the right to make such an intimate physical test a condition of employment. An employment arbitrator ordered that the officer be reinstated in the police force, and the U.S. Court of Appeals ruled that he could proceed to sue the city of Old Town for damages in a federal court.

Lives can be changed dramatically when people are labeled, whether the label be "dishonest," "criminal," "depressive," or "sexually deviant." Those who administer psychophysiological, personality, or other tests have an obligation to consider the consequences carefully, particularly before they make any results public. Reliance on questionable devices such as polygraph, integrity, and plethysmograph tests may violate civil rights as well as basic tenets of science and may needlessly jeopardize the welfare of the people being tested.

yield the same results in the same situation. A weigh scale, for example, is reliable if it measures the same weight every time we put the same object on it. If it were to read 10 pounds when we put a bag of sugar on it today and 12 pounds tomorrow, it would not be reliable. To make sure that a test yields the same results time and again, test designers must put it through specific kinds of trials. Generally speaking, a good test is one that demonstrates various kinds of reliability, such as test–retest reliability, alternate-form reliability, internal reliability, and interrater reliability (Kline, 1993).

A test has high *test–retest reliability* if it yields the same results when it is given again to the same people. If, for example, a woman's responses on a particular test indicate that she is a heavy drinker, the test should produce the same result when she takes it again a week later. A test dominated by time-specific

questions ("Have you had a drink in the last hour?") may not be reliable, because the answers may be different the second time around. Questions that focus on more general drinking patterns ("How many drinks do you have per week?") may produce more reliable results. The scores subjects earn the first time they take a given test are correlated with their scores the second time they take it, and the resulting correlation coefficient (see p. 77) indicates the test–retest reliability. The higher the correlation, the greater the reliability.

One problem with the test–retest reliability measure is that the second time people take a test, they may try to give the same answers they gave the first time around, thus inflating the apparent reliability of the test (Kline, 1993). To avoid this problem, test designers may try to establish *alternate-form reliability* for a test. They devise an alternate test with the

*"And the cloud that's just overhead and to your right—
what does that remind you of?"*
(Drawing by C. Barsotti; © 1990 The New Yorker Magazine, Inc.)

same kinds of items as the original test, give both forms of the test to trial subjects, and correlate their scores. A high correlation indicates alternate-form reliability.

A test has high *internal reliability* when different parts of it yield the same results. To check for this kind of consistency, researchers may use the *split-half* method: they compare responses on odd-numbered test items with responses on even-numbered items. If the test is internally reliable, scores on the two halves of the test will be highly correlated.

Finally, a test shows high *interrater* (or *interjudge*) *reliability* if different evaluators independently agree on the scoring of the test. True-false and multiple-choice tests yield consistent scores no matter who evaluates them, but other tests require the evaluator to make a judgment, and three evaluators may come up with three different scores. Consider a test that requires the subject to copy a picture, after which a judge rates the accuracy of the copy. Different judges may give different ratings to the same copy. A test's interrater reliability may be determined by the level of agreement when several evaluators score a single person's test performance.

VALIDITY   A test must also yield *accurate,* or *valid,* results. Suppose that a weigh scale reads 12 pounds every time a bag of sugar is put on it. The scale, then, may be considered reliable. But what if the sugar

really weighs only 10 pounds? Although the scale is reliable because its readings are consistent, those readings are not valid. An instrument's validity is the accuracy with which it measures what it is supposed to be measuring (Dahlstrom, 1993; Kline, 1993).

Some tests appear to be valid because they seem to make sense. This sort of validity, called *face validity,* does not by itself establish a test's trustworthiness. A test for depression, for example, might include questions about how often an individual cries. Because it makes sense that depressed people would cry, these test questions would have face validity. It turns out, however, that many people cry a great deal for reasons other than depression and that some extremely depressed people fail to cry at all (Beck, 1967). Thus a test should not be used unless it has successfully been subjected to other, more exacting measures of validity.

Predictive validity is a test's ability to predict a person's future characteristics or behavior. Let us say that a test is designed to gather information about the habits of the parents of elementary school children, their personal characteristics, and their attitudes toward smoking, and on that basis to identify the children who will take up cigarette smoking in junior high school. We could establish its predictive validity by administering the test to a group of elementary school students, waiting until they were in junior high school, and then checking to see which children actually did become smokers.

In practice, it is often quite difficult to determine the predictive validity of a test because there is so much opportunity for complicating factors to arise in the interval between the time the test is administered and the time the predictions can be verified. Testers may lose track of some of the original subjects, or unexpected circumstances may alter the course of events. The elementary school students in the smoking test, for example, might be exposed to an intensive antismoking campaign.

Concurrent validity is the degree to which test scores agree with other available information. A test designed to measure students' anxiety, for example, should produce anxiety scores that agree with school counseling records and parents' reports.

A test displays high *content validity* if it assesses all important aspects of the behavior, skill, or quality it is designed to reveal. Consider *achievement tests,* designed to measure a student's ability in a particular school subject. A foreign-language achievement test would have low content validity if it tested only for vocabulary without paying attention to grammar, language usage, or comprehension.

Finally, tests should have high *construct validity;* that is, they should measure what they are intended to measure and not something else altogether (Cronbach & Meehl, 1955). We might ask, "Do achievement tests measure ability in given subject areas, or do they really measure something else?" Educators have noted that some students do very well and others very poorly on multiple-choice tests. Perhaps a high school student who does well on a chemistry achievement test is actually demonstrating skill at selecting multiple-choice answers rather than an exceptional knowledge of chemistry. In that case, the chemistry achievement test would be lacking in construct validity.

Before any test can be truly useful, it must meet the requirements of standardization, reliability, and validity. No matter how insightful or clever a test may be, clinicians cannot profitably use its results if they are uninterpretable, inconsistent, or inaccurate. Unfortunately, as we shall see, more than a few clinical tests fall short on these essential characteristics, suggesting that at least some clinical assessments miss their intended mark (Shedler, Mayman, & Manis, 1993; Dahlstrom, 1993; Kline, 1993).

PROJECTIVE TESTS Projective tests require subjects to give interpretive answers to questions about relatively vague stimuli such as inkblots or ambiguous pictures, or to follow open-ended instructions such as "Draw a person." The assumption behind these tests is that when clues and instructions are so vague, subjects must "project" aspects of their own personality into the task. As we observed in Chapter 2, psychodynamic theorists believe projection to be a common defense mechanism in which people project their own inner wishes onto others. Thus projective tests are used primarily by psychodynamic clinicians to help them assess the unconscious personality drives and conflicts that they believe to be at the root of abnormal functioning. Among the most widely used projective tests are the *Rorschach test*, the *Thematic Apperception Test*, *sentence-completion tests*, and *drawings*.

RORSCHACH TEST In 1911 Hermann Rorschach, a Swiss psychiatrist, experimented with the use of inkblots in psychiatric diagnosis. He made thousands of blots by dropping ink on paper, folding the paper in half, and then unfolding it to reveal a symmetrical but wholly accidental composition, such as the one shown in Figure 4–1. Rorschach found that everyone saw images in these blots and that the perceived image corresponded in important ways with the psychological condition of the viewer. People diagnosed as schizophrenic, for example, tended to see images that differed radically from those that people with anxiety disorders saw.

Believing that inkblots might be a useful assessment tool, he selected ten and published them in 1921 with instructions for their use. This set of ten

FIGURE 4–1 *An inkblot similar to those used in the Rorschach Test. When test subjects tell what they see in a Rorschach inkblot, testers are interested both in the "thematic" content of the response (the images they see) and in its "style" (for example, whether the subject sees movement in the inkblot).*

inkblots—five in black, white, and gray, and five in color—was called the Rorschach Psychodynamic Inkblot Test. Rorschach himself died just eight months later, at the age of 37, but his colleagues continued his work, and his inkblots have taken their place among the most widely used projective tests of this century.

Clinicians administer the **Rorschach,** as it is commonly called, by presenting one inkblot card at a time to subjects and asking them what they see, what the inkblot seems to be, or what it reminds them of. The subjects are encouraged to give more than one response. In the first phase of the test, called the *free association,* or *performance, phase,* the clinician records everything the subject says. Next the clinician conducts an *inquiry phase* to find out what influenced or determined the subject's responses. In an optional third phase, called *testing the limits,* the clinician may ask the subject whether he or she can see some of the images more commonly seen by other people. In the following exchange, a tense 32-year-old woman who complains of feeling unworthy and lacking in confidence responds to one Rorschach inkblot. Her response is immediately followed by the clinician's inquiry.

Performance

Subject: Oh, dear! My goodness! O.K. Just this [upper] part is a bug. Something like an ant—one of the social group which is a worker, trying to pull something. I think this is some kind of food for the rest of the ants. It's a bee because it has wings, a worker bee bringing up something edible for the rest of the clan.

Inquiry

Clinician: Tell me about the bee.

Subject: Here is the bee, the mouth and the wings. I don't think bees eat leaves but it looks like a leaf or a piece of lettuce.

Clinician: What makes it look like a piece of lettuce?

Subject: Its shape and it has a vein up the middle. It is definitely a bee.

(Klopfer & Davidson, 1962, p. 164)

Clinicians evaluate a person's Rorschach responses on the basis of various criteria. In the early years, Rorschach testers paid greater attention to the themes, images, and fantasies evoked by the inkblots, called the *thematic content.* Subjects who saw numerous water images, for example, were often thought to be grappling with alcoholism, whereas those who saw bizarre images or saw themselves in the blots might

be suffering from schizophrenia. Although thematic content is still of interest, testers now pay more attention to the *style* of subjects' responses: Do the subjects view the design as a whole or see specific details? Do they focus on the blots or on the white spaces between them? Do they use or ignore the shadings and colors in several of the cards? Do they see human movement in the designs ("two witches fighting"), animal movement ("rams butting"), animals engaged in human actions ("birds talking"), or inanimate objects ("a house")? It is commonly thought that "normal" people typically perceive whole designs, but focus on details in at least one or two inkblots; that depressed people give few responses and do not mention color at all; and that impulsive persons respond intensely to color (Exner, 1993, 1987; Lerner & Lerner, 1988).

This is the way the clinician interpreted the bug responses of the 32-year-old woman:

The bee may reflect the image she has of herself as a hard worker (a fact noted by her supervisor). In addition, the "bee bringing up something edible for the rest of the clan" suggests that she feels an overwhelming sense of responsibility toward others.

This card frequently evokes both masculine and feminine sexual associations, either in direct or symbolic form. Apparently [this woman] is not able to handle such material comfortably either overtly or in a more socialized manner, and so both sexual symbols are replaced by the oral symbolism of providing food.

(Klopfer & Davidson, 1962, pp. 182–183)

THEMATIC APPERCEPTION TEST The *Thematic Apperception Test (TAT)* is a pictorial projective test first developed by the psychologist Henry A. Murray at the Harvard Psychological Clinic in 1935 (Murray, 1938; Morgan & Murray, 1935). The most common version of this test, which Murray produced in 1943, consists of thirty black-and-white pictures, each depicting people in a somewhat indeterminate situation. Clinicians select the cards that they feel are most pertinent to the individual being tested. There is also a children's version of the test, known as the Children's Apperception Test, or CAT, which has pictures more evocative of the concerns of children (Bellak & Bellak, 1952).

People who take the TAT are shown one picture at a time and asked to make up a dramatic story about it, stating what is happening in the picture, what led up to it, what the characters are feeling and thinking, and what the outcome of the situation will be. An inquiry phase follows to clarify the responses.

Clinicians who use the TAT believe that people identify with one of the characters on each card. This character, called the *hero*, has certain *needs* and faces certain environmental demands, or *press*. In their stories, people are thought to be expressing their own circumstances, needs, pressures, emotions, and perceptions of reality and fantasy. For example, a female client seems to be identifying with the hero and revealing her own feelings in this story about the TAT picture shown in Figure 4–2, one of the few TAT pictures permitted for display in textbooks:

> This is a woman who has been quite troubled by memories of a mother she was resentful toward. She has feelings of sorrow for the way she treated her mother, her memories of her mother plague her. These feelings seem to be increasing as she grows older and sees her children treating her the same way that she treated her mother.
>
> *(Aiken, 1985, p. 372)*

Clinicians evaluate TAT responses by looking not only at the content of the stories but also at the style in which the person responds to the cards in general. Slow or delayed responses, for example, are thought to indicate depression; overcautiousness and preoccu-

FIGURE 4–3 *Drawing by a depressed man on the Draw-a-Person Test. (From Hammer, 1981, p. 171.)*

pation with details are thought to suggest obsessive thoughts and indecisiveness (Aiken, 1985).

SENTENCE-COMPLETION TEST The sentence-completion test, first developed more than sixty years ago (Payne, 1928), consists of a series of unfinished sentences that people are asked to complete, such as, "I wish ___," or, "My father ___." Various versions have been developed for different age groups. The test can be taken without an examiner present. It is considered a good springboard for discussion and a quick and easy way to pinpoint topics to be explored.

DRAWINGS On the assumption that a drawing tells us something about its creator, clinicians often ask clients to draw human figures and talk about them. Evaluations of these drawings are based on the quality and shape of the drawing, solidity of the pencil line, location of the drawing on the paper, size of the figures, features of the figures, use of background, and comments made by the respondent during the drawing task.

The Draw-a-Person Test (DAP) is the most popular drawing test among clinicians (Machover, 1949). Subjects are first told to draw "a person"; that done, they are told to draw another person of the opposite sex. Theories about these drawings include the notion that a disproportionately large or small head may reflect problems in intellectual functioning, social balance, or control of body impulses, and that exaggerated eyes may indicate high levels of suspiciousness. Figure 4–3 is a DAP drawing

FIGURE 4–2 *A picture used in the Thematic Apperception Test. One client who made up a story about this card seemed to be revealing resentment toward her mother, regret over the way she had treated her mother, and sadness over her relationship with her children.*

produced by a depressed man. His clinical assessor evaluates this drawing in the following report:

> He drew the large figure first; then when he saw that he could not complete the entire figure on the page, he drew the smaller figure. He momentarily paused, looked at both figures, said that the larger figure lacked a collar, picked up the pencil he had laid down, and drew the "collar" by slashing the pencil across the throat of the drawn male. It was almost as if . . . the patient were committing suicide on paper.
>
> *(Hammer, 1981, p. 170)*

THE VALUE OF PROJECTIVE TESTS   Until the 1950s, projective tests were likely to be relied on as the primary indicator of a client's personality. In recent years, however, clinicians and researchers have treated these instruments more as sources of "supplementary" insights about their clients (Lerner & Lerner, 1988; Anastasi, 1982).

One reason for this shift is that practitioners and researchers who adopt the newly emerging models have found these kinds of tests less useful than have psychodynamic clinicians and investigators (Kline, 1993). Even more important, the tests have not typically demonstrated impressive levels of reliability and validity (Lanyon, 1984; Eysenck, 1959).

Reliability studies in which several clinicians have been asked to score the same person's projective test have usually found relatively low agreement (that is,

Drawing tests are commonly used to assess the functioning of children. Two popular tests are the House-Tree-Person test, in which subjects draw a house, tree, and person, and the Kinetic Family Drawing test, in which subjects draw a picture of all their household members engaged in some activity ("kinetic" means "active"). The drawings are thought to reflect the subjects' perceptions of themselves, their relatives, their home life, and their family relationships.

low interrater reliability) among the clinicians' scores (Little & Shneidman, 1959; Kostlan, 1954). Standardized procedures for administering and scoring projective tests do exist and might improve consistency if all practitioners used them (Exner, 1993), but none of these procedures has gained wide acceptance (Kline, 1993).

Similar research has challenged the projective tests' validity (Kline, 1993). Various researchers have given clinicians the responses of clinical subjects to projective tests and asked them to describe the personalities and feelings that the responses revealed (Golden, 1964; Sines, 1959; Kostlan, 1954). The descriptions have then been compared with descriptions of the same subjects provided by their psychotherapists or gathered from extensive case histories. The conclusions drawn from projective tests have repeatedly proved inaccurate.

Another validity problem is that projective tests are sometimes biased against ethnic minorities. For example, people are supposed to identify with the characters in the Thematic Apperception Test (TAT) when they make up stories about them, yet none of the figures depicted are members of ethnic minorities. In response to this problem, some clinicians have developed new versions of existing tests, such as the TAT with African American figures, or designed entirely new tests for use with a particular group, such as the Tell-Me-a-Story (TEMAS) for Hispanic persons (Costantino, 1986).

Given the weak reliability and validity of projective tests and the absence of appropriate normative data with which to assess subjects' responses, clinicians tend to fall back on their "general clinical experience" to interpret performance on projective tests (Kline, 1993). Thus their interpretations are sometimes subjective and biased.

PERSONALITY INVENTORIES   An alternative approach to understanding individual clients is simply to ask them to assess themselves by filling out inventories. One kind of inventory is the broad self-report inventory, or *personality inventory,* which asks respondents a wide range of questions about their behavior, beliefs, and feelings. The typical personality inventory consists of a series of statements, and subjects are asked to indicate whether or not each statement applies to them. Clinicians then use the responses to draw broad conclusions about the person's psychological functioning. These inventories are designed to identify personality traits and underlying emotional needs and are therefore employed more by psychodynamic clinicians than by those of other orientations.

Clinicians often view works of art as informal projective tests in which artists reveal their own conflicts and mental stability. The sometimes bizarre cat portraits of early twentieth-century artist Louis Wain have, for example, been interpreted by some as reflections of the psychosis with which he struggled for many years. Others believe such interpretations to be incorrect, however, and point out that the strange-looking decorative patterns in some of Wain's later paintings were actually based on textile designs.

The first personality inventories were developed to screen recruits during World War I, when the army was looking for a fast way to identify and eliminate people with possible mental disturbances. One was the Woodworth Personal Data Sheet, which consisted of 116 yes-or-no questions about all kinds of possible psychological problems, from nightmares to phobias. This early instrument yielded a single score that was supposed to indicate the level at which a person was functioning. Clinicians no longer hold so simplistic a view of the personality and have since developed personality inventories that are more descriptive.

MINNESOTA MULTIPHASIC PERSONALITY INVENTORY   The Minnesota Multiphasic Personality Inventory *(MMPI)* is by far the most widely used personality inventory (Colligan & Offord, 1992). Two versions of this test are available—the original test, published in 1945 by the psychologists Starke Hathaway and J. C. McKinley, and the *MMPI-2,* a 1989 revision conducted under the supervision of a team of psychologists (Butcher, 1990; Butcher et al., 1990, 1989; Butcher & Graham, 1988). Currently the two versions are competing for the favor of clinicians (Clavelle, 1992).

The traditional MMPI consists of 550 self-statements—to be labeled "true," "false," or "cannot say"—about numerous areas of personal functioning, including the respondent's physical concerns; mood; morale; attitudes toward religion, sex, and social activ-

ities; and possible symptoms of psychological dysfunction, such as phobias and hallucinations.

The inventory was constructed by a method called *criterion keying.* Quantities of statements were gathered from already-existing scales of personal and social attitudes, from textbooks, from medical and neurological case-taking procedures, and from psychiatric examination forms. The authors then asked 724 "normal" people (hospital visitors) and 800 hospitalized mental patients to indicate whether or not each statement was true for them. Only those statements that differentiated the hospitalized subjects from the normal subjects were incorporated into the inventory. For example, because most depressed patients answered true to the statement "I often feel hopeless about the future," while most nondepressed subjects answered false, the statement was included in the MMPI.

The items in the MMPI make up ten clinical scales:

1 or HS *(Hypochondriasis).* Thirty-three items derived from patients showing abnormal concern with bodily functions. For example, the item "I have chest pains several times a week" would be answered true.

2 or D *(Depression).* Sixty items derived from patients showing extreme pessimism, feelings of hopelessness, and slowing of thought and action.

"I usually feel that life is interesting and worthwhile" would be answered false.

3 or Hy *(Conversion hysteria).* Sixty items from patients using physical or mental symptoms as a way of unconsciously avoiding difficult conflicts and responsibilities. "My heart frequently pounds so hard I can feel it" would elicit a response of true.

4 or PD *(Psychopathic deviate).* Fifty items from patients who show a repeated and flagrant disregard for social customs, an emotional shallowness, and an inability to learn from punishing experiences. "My activities and interests are often criticized by others" would be answered true.

5 or Mf *(Masculinity–Femininity).* Sixty items differentiating between male and female respondents. "I like to arrange flowers" would indicate femininity if answered true.

6 or Pa *(Paranoia).* Forty items from patients showing abnormal suspiciousness and delusions of grandeur or persecution. "There are evil people trying to influence my mind" would receive a response of true.

7 or Pt *(Psychasthenia).* Forty-eight items based on patients showing obsessions, compulsions, abnormal fears, and guilt and indecisiveness. "I save nearly everything I buy, even after I have no use for it" would elicit a response of true.

8 or Sc *(Schizophrenia).* Seventy-eight items from patients showing bizarre or unusual thoughts or behavior, who are often withdrawn and experiencing delusions and hallucinations. "Things around me do not seem real" and "It makes me uncomfortable to have people close to me" would each be answered true.

9 or Ma *(Hypomania).* Forty-six items from patients characterized by emotional excitement, overactivity, and flight of ideas. "At times I feel very 'high' or very 'low' for no apparent reason" would be labeled true.

10 or Si *(Social introversion).* Seventy items from persons showing shyness, little interest in people, and insecurity. "I have the time of my life at parties" would be answered false.

People who frequently respond in the affirmative to such items as "I certainly feel useless much of the time" and in the negative to such items as "I usually feel that life is worthwhile" would score relatively high on the depression scale. Similarly, if people repeatedly answer true to such statements as "I am easily embarrassed" and false to statements like "I do not mind meeting strangers," they receive a high score on the social introversion scale. Scores for each scale can range from 0 to 120. When people score above 70 on a particular scale, their functioning on the dimension measured by that scale is considered deviant.

Usually a person's scores on all the scales in the MMPI are summarized graphically on an MMPI profile sheet. The pattern made when the scores are connected, called the person's *profile,* is evaluated to determine that person's general personality style and underlying emotional needs (Graham, 1993; Meehl & Dahlstrom, 1960; Meehl, 1951). To evaluate a client's profile, clinicians often use an *MMPI atlas,* a published compilation of the MMPI profiles and case histories of various kinds of patients (Graham, 1977; Hathaway & Meehl, 1951). By matching a client's profile to similar profiles in the atlas, a clinician can draw conclusions about that client's personality (Graham, 1993, 1987). It is also possible to send a client's MMPI responses to a professional interpretation service to be scored, profiled, and analyzed by computer.

The profile approach to assessment is illustrated in the evaluation of J. A. K., a depressed 27-year-old man whose MMPI profile is shown in Figure 4–4. Noting that J. A. K. scored 94 on the depression scale, above 70 on the psychasthenia, schizophrenia, social introversion, and hypochondriasis scales, and within normal range on the other scales, the clinician wrote the following report:

J. A. K. appears to be in a great deal of psychological discomfort. He feels anxious, depressed, and overwhelmed by his problems. . . . Most of the time he is likely to be rather unemotional and unexcitable and to have a slow personal tempo, but he may also experience episodes of unexplainable excitement and restlessness. He ruminates over his problems; he is very pessimistic about the possibility that things might get better; and he may have concluded that life is no longer worthwhile. He feels very guilty about perceived misdeeds, and he may harbor suicidal ideas, but he does not seem to be more likely than other depressed patients to attempt suicide. He is likely to report somatic concerns. . . . J. A. K. is likely to have problems with concentration, attention, memory, and judgment. Decisions are especially difficult for him. . . .

J. A. K. has very strong unfulfilled dependency needs. He feels very inadequately prepared to handle problems and stresses on his own, and he is likely to turn to others for support and guidance. . . .

J. A. K. views the world as a rather threatening and nonsupportive place, and he feels that he is at the mercy of forces which are beyond his control. He has a very cynical, skeptical, and disbelieving attitude, and he feels mistreated and misunderstood by other people. . . .

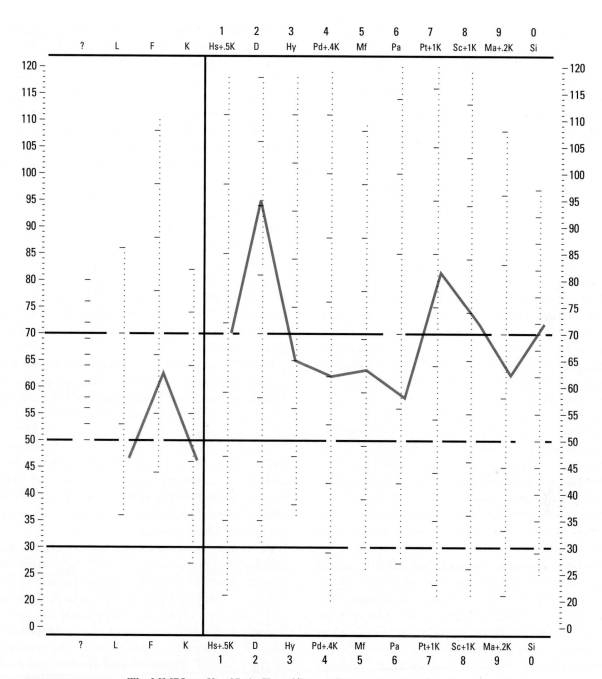

FIGURE 4–4 *The MMPI profile of J. A. K., a 27-year-old man, suggests that he is depressed. He also appears to be anxious, prone to somatic complaints, indecisive, introverted, and insecure. (From Graham, 1977, p. 164.)*

J. A. K. has an extremely unfavorable self-concept [and his] relationships with others tend to be very superficial and unrewarding. He needs other people and he has the capacity for developing deep emotional ties, but he is afraid of getting too involved with others because of fear of rejection and/or exploitation. He does not make friends easily, and other people see him as distant, aloof, and hard to get to know. . . .

Many of J. A. K.'s problems stem from his unrealistically high standards and goals for himself and his perceived failure to achieve them. Such attitudes often are produced by demanding and perfectionistic parents who are almost impossible to please. J. A. K.'s dependent, submissive style is directed at getting sympathy and support from other people. . . . His avoidance of deep emotional ties ensures that he will not be seriously hurt by other people. His anger probably comes from perceived failures on the part of other people to fulfill his strong dependency needs and from their placing of demands on him that he feels he cannot meet.

(Graham, 1977, pp. 178–180)

RESPONSE SETS AND THE MMPI   Each person approaches a self-report inventory such as the MMPI with a particular *response set,* a tendency to respond in fixed ways. One response set might be *acquiescence,* describing people who tend to respond affirmatively to statements irrespective of their content ("yea-sayers"). Another might be *social desirability,* the response set of those who try to answer in ways that they believe are socially acceptable. Obviously, if people's answers are heavily influenced by their response set, their MMPI scores will be misleading. Thus three additional scales have been built into the MMPI to detect such influences.

The *L scale,* or lie scale, consists of items that test whether a person is trying to be viewed favorably. People who keep answering true to such items as "I smile at everyone I meet" and false to items like "I gossip a little at times" receive a high L score. The *F scale,* or frequency scale, consists of items that almost everyone responds to in the same way, such as "Everything tastes the same" (false) or "I enjoy children" (true). People who keep responding to these items in an unusual manner are viewed as careless test takers, yea-sayers, or nay-sayers. Finally, the *K scale,* or defensiveness scale, comprises items that indicate whether people are protecting their image in their responses. If they keep answering false to items such as "I feel bad when others criticize me," they will be viewed as reluctant to admit problems. If the individual scores high on the L, F, or K scale, clinicians may alter their MMPI conclusions or pronounce the test results invalid.

MMPI-2   The new version of the MMPI tries to update and broaden the original while preserving those items and scoring techniques that so many clinicians are familiar with and find useful. The new inventory contains 567 items, many identical to those in the original, some rewritten to reflect contemporary language ("upset stomach," for instance, replaces "acid stomach"), and others that are totally new. In addition to the ten basic scales, which are the same as in the original, the MMPI-2 adds a number of new scales to measure such things as a vulnerability to eating disorders, a tendency to abuse drugs, and poor functioning at work.

Many clinicians have welcomed the MMPI-2 as a valuable improvement and appropriate update. Others, however, believe that the new test has significant flaws and may never be an adequate substitute for the original. One complaint is that the testing sample for the new test was apparently more educated and included more professionals than the population at large. Another concern is that the large body of research that has been conducted on the original MMPI may not be applicable to the MMPI-2. Moreover, there are indications that a number of subjects who take both test versions get different scores on the two tests—showing a high level of depression on one version, say, yet a normal score on the other (Harrell, Honaker, & Parnell, 1992). Researchers are now exploring these issues, and any decision to shelve one of the versions awaits the outcome of their work. In the meantime, at least some clinicians are using both versions of the test in efforts to determine the relative merits for themselves (Clavelle, 1992).

THE VALUE OF PERSONALITY INVENTORIES   The MMPI and other personality inventories have several advantages over projective tests. They are paper-and-pencil tests that do not take much time to administer, and they are objectively and easily scored. Most important, these inventories are usually standardized, so that one person's scores can be compared with many others'.

In addition, personality inventories usually display greater test–retest reliability than projective tests. People who take the MMPI a second time after an interval of less than two weeks receive approximately the same scores; various studies have found a reliability coefficient ranging from .70 to .85 (Graham, 1987, 1977). After an interval of a year or more, the test–retest reliability coefficient drops to approximately .40, but this is still an impressive correlation when we remember that anyone's psychological status is quite likely to change in the course of a year.

Personality inventories also appear to have greater validity than projective tests, so that clinicians can assess respondents' personal characteristics more accurately (Graham & Lilly, 1984; Little & Shneidman, 1959; Kostlan, 1954). To compare the two methods, investigators asked one group of test experts to predict what a number of people were like on the basis of their MMPI responses and another group of experts to make predictions about the same people on the basis of their responses to projective tests (Little & Shneidman, 1959). The evaluations were then compared with descriptions of the subjects derived from extensive case histories. The evaluations based on MMPI scores were found to be more accurate than those derived from projective tests.

All the same, personality inventories can hardly be considered highly valid test instruments (Kline, 1993; Matarazzo, 1992). When clinicians use these tests alone, they have not consistently been able to judge a subject's personality accurately (Shedler et al., 1993; Aiken, 1985). One problem is the very nature of what the tests are trying to measure. The qualities and traits personality inventories purport to measure are not physical entities whose existence and strength can be verified directly. How can we really know the character or depth of a person's emotions or needs when the only indications we have are the person's words and actions? Another problem that affects the validity of personality tests is their inability to take cultural differences into consideration. Test responses suggesting a mental disorder in one culture may be normal responses in another. In Puerto Rico, for example, it is common to believe in and practice spiritualism, and therefore it would be normal for a Puerto Rican person to answer "true" to the MMPI item "Evil spirits possess me at times," a response that, in most U.S. residents, presumably indicates psychopathology (Rogler, Malgady, & Rodriguez, 1989).

Despite their limitations, the MMPI and other personality inventories continue to be very popular assessment tools. Although they may not always help clinicians to identify specific disorders, research does suggest that they can be useful as gross screening devices, to help detect general dysfunctioning (Bellack & Hersen, 1980). Moreover, studies indicate that when personality inventories are used along with interviews or other assessment tools, they can help clinicians draw clearer pictures of people's characteristics and disorders (Levitt, 1989; Sines, 1959; Kostlan, 1954).

NARROW SELF-REPORT INVENTORIES Behavioral and cognitive clinicians also use self-report inventories in their assessments (Kendall, 1990, 1987; Adams, 1989). But unlike the broad personality inventories used by psychodynamic and humanistic clinicians, their paper-and-pencil inventories usually are designed to collect detailed information about one narrow area of functioning. Their purpose is to help clinicians complete a functional analysis of a client's disturbance so that they can set up an appropriate behavioral or cognitive therapy program. There are inventories to measure affect (emotion), social skills, cognitive processes, and reinforcements.

Affective inventories measure the severity of such emotions as anxiety, depression, and anger. The most widely used affective inventory is the Fear Survey Schedule, shown in Table 4–1, in which people rate how intensely they fear various objects and situations (Lang, 1985; Geer, 1965; Wolpe & Lang, 1964). *Social skill inventories* ask respondents to indicate how they would react in a variety of social situations. Clinicians use these inventories, such as the Assertive Behavior Survey Schedule in Table 4–2, to assess a person's social skills, deficits, and fears, and to determine the role these factors play in the person's disorder. *Cognition inventories* disclose the kinds of thoughts and assumptions that are typical of a client, as well as the frequency with which they come to mind (Burgess & Haaga, 1994; Kendall, 1990). These inventories are used to uncover the counterproductive thoughts and patterns of thinking that cognitive clinicians believe are at the root of abnormal functioning. *Reinforcement inventories* require clients to

TABLE 4–1

PARTIAL FEAR SURVEY SCHEDULE

Indicate how much fear you experience when confronted with the following:

1. Sharp objects	None	Very little	A little	Some	Much	Very much	Terror
2. Being a passenger in a car	None	Very little	A little	Some	Much	Very much	Terror
3. Dead bodies	None	Very little	A little	Some	Much	Very much	Terror
4. Suffocating	None	Very little	A little	Some	Much	Very much	Terror
5. Failing a test	None	Very little	A little	Some	Much	Very much	Terror
6. Looking foolish	None	Very little	A little	Some	Much	Very much	Terror
7. Being a passenger in an airplane	None	Very little	A little	Some	Much	Very much	Terror
8. Worms	None	Very little	A little	Some	Much	Very much	Terror
9. Arguing with parents	None	Very little	A little	Some	Much	Very much	Terror
10. Rats and mice	None	Very little	A little	Some	Much	Very much	Terror

Source: Geer, 1965.

TABLE 4-2

PARTIAL ASSERTIVE BEHAVIOR SURVEY SCHEDULE

What would you do in the following situations? Indicate by circling number 1, 2, or 3.

A. In a restaurant, you have ordered your favorite meal. When it comes, it is not cooked to your liking.
   1. You tell the waitress that it is not cooked to your taste or liking and have her take it back and [have it] cooked to your taste or liking.
   2. You complain that it is not cooked to your taste or liking, but you say you will eat it anyway.
   3. You say nothing.

B. You have been waiting in line to buy a ticket. Someone gets in front of you.
   1. You say it is your turn, and get in front of him.
   2. You say it is your turn, but you let the person go before you.
   3. You say nothing.

C. In a supermarket, you are waiting in line at the checkout counter. Someone gets in front of you.
   1. You say, "I'm sorry, but I was here first," and you take your turn.
   2. You say, "I'm sorry, but I was here first," but you let the person go ahead of you.
   3. You say nothing.

Source: Cautela & Upper, 1976.

report the nature, intensity, and frequency of various reinforcements in their lives. In the Reinforcement Survey Schedule, for example, respondents rate on a five-point scale how much pleasure they receive from different stimuli, such as eating particular foods, listening to various kinds of music, reading, playing sports, shopping, talking with people, and making love (Cautela & Kastenbaum, 1967). They also rate how much they would enjoy being in situations like the following:

> You have just completed a difficult job. Your superior comes by and praises you highly for a "job well done." He also makes it clear that such good work is going to be rewarded very soon.
>
> *(Cautela & Kastenbaum, 1967, p. 121)*

Behaviorists use the Reinforcement Survey Schedule as a source of clues to the objects and situations that may be reinforcing dysfunctional behaviors in their clients. It also tells them what kinds of rewards might be effective in a client's behavioral treatment program.

Like personality inventories, the narrow self-report inventories collect information directly from the subjects themselves, and so have a strong face validity and a seeming efficiency. As a consequence, both the number of these tests and the number of clinicians using them have increased steadily in the past two decades. At the same time, the narrow inventories have significant limitations (Shedler et al., 1993; Kendall, 1990, 1987). First, unlike the personality inventories, they rarely contain response-set scales to help determine whether people are being careless or inaccurate in their accounts. Second, relatively few behavioral or cognitive self-report inventories have been subjected to rigorous standardization, reliability, and validity procedures (Sanderman & Ormel, 1992). Surveys of clinicians suggest that self-report inventories are often improvised as the need for them arises, without being tested for accuracy and consistency (Wade, Baker, & Hartmann, 1979).

PSYCHOPHYSIOLOGICAL TESTS More and more during the past decade clinicians have used tests that measure physiological responses (Stoyva & Budzynski, 1993; Kendall, 1990). The interest in psychophysiological measures began when a number of studies suggested that states of anxiety are regularly accompanied by physiological changes such as increases in heart rate, body temperature, blood pressure, electrical resistance in the skin (galvanic skin response), and muscle contraction (Boulougouris et al., 1977; May, 1977; Bloom & Trautt, 1977). Because measures of these psychophysiological changes were often more precise than interviews, projective tests, self-reports, and so on, behavioral and cognitive clinicians began to include them in their functional analyses of anxiety disorders (Cook et al., 1988; Lang, 1985).

Psychophysiological measurements are used widely in the assessment and treatment of sexual disorders (Hall, Proctor, & Nelson, 1988; Geer, 1976). A test instrument called the *vaginal plethysmograph,* for example, is used to measure sexual arousal in women. This instrument, a small tampon-shaped probe with a light at its end, is placed in a woman's vagina to measure the amount of light reflected by the vaginal wall (Sintchak & Geer, 1975). The reflected light increases when the wall arteries receive additional blood—that is, when the woman is sexually aroused. Studies find that this instrument does detect a difference when female subjects are watching erotic films (Wincze & Lange, 1981; Heiman, 1977). As we observed in Box 4–1, a *penile plethysmograph,* sometimes called a *strain gauge,* is used to measure sexual arousal in men (Heiman, 1977).

Psychophysiological tests also have been used in the assessment of medical problems, such as headaches and hypertension (high blood pressure), that are thought to relate to a person's psychological state. As we shall see in Chapter 7, clinical researchers have discovered that the physiological components of these problems can sometimes be treated by *biofeedback,* a technique in which the client is given systematic information about key physiological responses as they occur and thus learns gradually to control them (Norris & Fahrion, 1993; Stoyva & Budzynski, 1993). For example, when tension-headache sufferers are given detailed feedback about the levels of tension in their head muscles, many can learn to relax those muscles at will, and the frequency of their headaches declines.

The measuring of physiological changes has become integral to the assessment of many psychological disorders. Like other kinds of clinical tests, however, psychophysiological tests pose problems for clinicians. One is logistical. Most psychophysiological tests require expensive recording equipment that must be carefully maintained and expertly calibrated (Nelson, 1981; Bellack & Hersen, 1980).

A second problem is that psychophysiological measurements can be misleading because they are not always indicative of the person's usual state. The laboratory equipment itself—impressive, unusual, and sometimes frightening—may arouse a subject's nervous system and thus alter physiological readings. Moreover, physiological responses are often observed to change when they are measured repeatedly in a single session. Galvanic skin responses often decrease upon repeated testing (Montagu & Coles, 1966), and genital arousal responses may lessen because of fatigue (Abel, 1976).

Finally, psychophysiological measurements can be difficult to interpret. Clients' psychophysiological responses are often inconsistent with their self-reports. Several studies have found, for example, that female subjects' subjective ratings of their sexual arousal failed to correlate closely with their plethysmograph readings, except for the fact that both the self-reports and the plethysmograph did indicate that erotic stimuli were more arousing than nonerotic stimuli (Van Dam et al., 1976). Which measure of sexual arousal, then, is a clinician to trust? On the one hand, self-reports of sexual arousal may be subject to error, but on the other hand, shouldn't a measure of sexual feelings include the person's own perception of sexual arousal?

NEUROPSYCHOLOGICAL TESTS As we observed in Chapter 2, some problems in personality or behavior are caused primarily by neurological damage in the brain or alterations in brain activity. Head injury, brain tumors, brain malfunctions, blood-vessel diseases, degenerative diseases, alcoholism, and infections can all cause such organic impairment. If a psychological dysfunction is to be treated effectively, it is important to know whether it stems primarily from some physiological abnormality in the brain.

Neurological problems can sometimes be detected through brain surgery and biopsy; brain X rays; a *computerized axial tomogram (CAT scan),* for which X rays of the brain are taken at different angles; an *electroencephalogram (EEG),* a recording of electrical impulses in the brain gathered by wires attached to the scalp; a *positron emission tomogram (PET scan),* a computer-produced motion picture of rates of metabolism throughout the brain; or *magnetic resonance imaging (MRI),* a complex procedure that uses the magnetic property of certain atoms in the brain to create a detailed picture of the brain's structure (see Box 4–2).

Subtle brain abnormalities, however, may escape these methods of detection. Clinicians have therefore developed less direct but sometimes more revealing *neuropsychological tests* that help identify neurological problems by measuring a person's

Electrodes pasted to a patient's scalp detect electrical impulses from the brain. The impulses are then amplified and converted into ink tracings on a roll of graph paper to produce an electroencephalogram (EEG). The EEG, used here to measure the brain waves of a four-month old being stimulated with toys, is only a gross indicator of the activity of the brain. When diagnosticians observe abnormal brain-wave patterns on an EEG, they conclude that some part of the brain is functioning improperly, and they try to pinpoint the problem by using more specialized diagnostic tools.

cognitive, perceptual, and motor skills (Matarazzo, 1992; Meier, 1992). Because neurological damage is likely to affect visual perception, recent memory, and visual-motor coordination, neuropsychological tests usually focus on these areas of functioning.

The ***Bender Visual-Motor Gestalt Test*** (Bender, 1938), one of the most widely used neuropsychological tests, consists of nine cards, each displaying a simple design (see Figure 4–5). Test subjects look at the designs one at a time and copy each one on a piece of paper. Later they try to reproduce the designs from memory. By the age of 12, most people can remember and copy the designs accurately. Notable errors in the accuracy of the drawings are thought to reflect organic brain impairment.

Some clinicians interpret this test subjectively; others use one of several objective and standardized scoring systems that have been developed. Test–retest reliability has a correlation coefficient of .70 when the scoring systems are used. As for validity, clinicians are able to distinguish organically impaired from nonorganically impaired people on the basis of this test in approximately 75 percent of cases (Heaton, Baade, & Johnson, 1978; Pascal & Suttell, 1951). Because there is such a wide variety of organic impairments, however, no single neuropsychological test can adequately test for them all, and no single test can consistently enable clinicians to distinguish one specific kind of neurological impairment from another (Goldstein, 1990; Smith, 1983; Lezak, 1976). This is the major limitation of the Bender Gestalt Test, and of any other neuropsychological test. At best it is a rough screening device for neurological impairment in general.

To achieve greater precision and accuracy in neurological assessment, clinicians frequently use a comprehensive series, or ***battery,*** of neuropsychological tests, each of which targets a specific neurological

Original

Copy

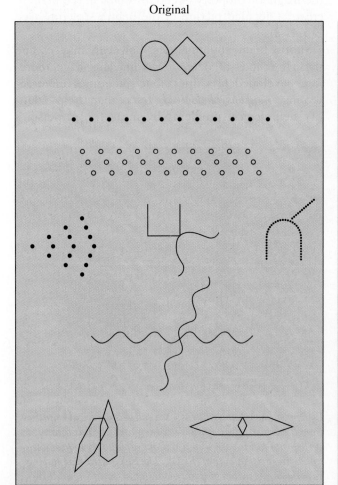
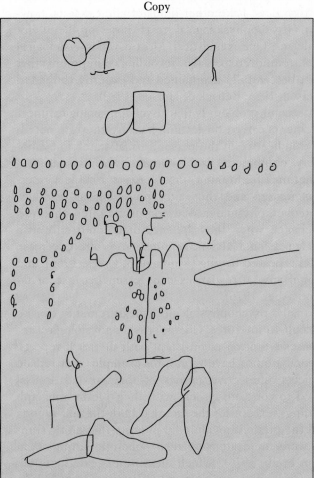

FIGURE 4–5 *In the Bender Gestalt Test subjects copy each of nine designs on a piece of paper, then produce them again from memory. Sizable errors in a drawing (as in the one on the right, which was done by a person with brain damage) may reflect organic brain dysfunction of some kind. (Adapted from Lacks, 1984, p. 33.)*

skill area (Goldstein, 1990). The Halstead-Reitan Neuropsychology Battery, a lengthy series of tests that measure sensorimotor, perceptual, and memory skills, and the shorter Luria-Nebraska Battery are highly regarded and widely used by today's clinicians (Reitan & Wolfson, 1985; Halstead, 1947).

INTELLIGENCE TESTS   There is little agreement about the precise nature of intelligence, although most educators and clinicians agree in a general way with an early definition of intelligence as "the capacity to judge well, to reason well, and to comprehend well" (Binet & Simon, 1916, p. 192). Because intelligence is an inferred notion rather than a specific physical process or entity, it can be measured only indirectly. In 1905 the French psychologist Alfred Binet and his associate Theodore Simon produced an intelligence test consisting of a series of tasks that require people to use various verbal and nonverbal skills. The test totals, adjusted in accordance with the test taker's age, furnish a general intelligence score for the person. Today the general score derived from intelligence tests is termed an ***intelligence quotient,*** or ***IQ,*** so called because initially it represented the ratio of a person's mental age to his or her chronological age, multiplied by 100 (see Figure 4–6).

Since Binet and Simon's first test, intelligence tests and studies of intelligence have been a major preoccupation of the educational and clinical fields. There are now more than eighty intelligence tests designed for administration to groups of people at a time, thirty individual intelligence tests, and twenty tests of specific dimensions of intelligence, such as memory and reasoning skill. The intelligence tests most widely used today are the Wechsler Adult Intelligence Scale,

The Wechsler Adult Intelligence Scale–Revised (WAIS-R) has 11 subtests. Six are "verbal" subtests: Information (factual questions), Digit Span (repeating a series of digits), Vocabulary (word definitions), Arithmetic (arithmetic story problems), Comprehension (questions about everyday living and social situations), and Similarities (determining how two objects or scenes resemble each other). Five are "performance" subtests: Picture Completion (determining what important feature is missing in a picture), Picture Arrangement (ordering a series of pictures so that they tell a story), Block Design (making particular designs with red and white blocks), Object Assembly (assembling simple jigsaw puzzles), and Digit Symbol (marking symbols that correspond to the numbers 1 through 9).

the Wechsler Intelligence Scale for Children, and the Stanford-Binet Intelligence Scale. As we shall discuss in Chapter 19, information gathered from intelligence tests plays a large role in the diagnosis of mental retardation and can also be helpful in the diagnosis of other problems, such as neurological disorders.

Intelligence tests are among the most carefully constructed of all clinical tests. Large standardization samples have been used to calibrate the major ones, so that clinicians have a good idea of how each person's scores compare with the performance of the population at large. These tests have demonstrated very high reliability. Within a test, people perform approximately the same on test items designed to tap the same ability, thus suggesting internal test consistency; and people who take the same IQ test years apart receive approximately the same scores (Kline, 1993; Lindemann & Matarazzo, 1990). Finally, the major IQ tests appear to have relatively high validity. Studies that compare children's IQ scores with their performance in school, for example, have found validity correlations ranging from .40 to .75 (Anastasi, 1982; Matarazzo, 1972).

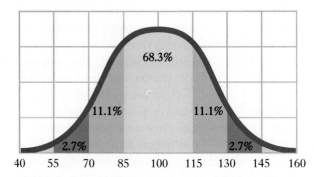

FIGURE 4–6 *The distribution of IQ scores in the population follows a "bell-shaped curve," an idealized graph in which the* mode, *or most frequent score (in this case 100), is in the middle, and less frequent scores fall evenly on each side. More than two-thirds of all people score between 85 and 115 on IQ tests.*

BOX 4-2

TAKING PICTURES
OF THE BRAIN

For many years X rays and surgery were the only means scientists had of looking at a living brain. Both methods reveal aspects of a brain's structure, but neither provides much information about its actual functioning. Moreover, surgery is highly "invasive" (the surgeon cuts open the skull and perhaps cuts into—and damages—healthy tissue), and X rays do not provide detailed views of the brain's structure. In the past several decades other techniques have emerged to permit researchers and physicians to obtain detailed recordings of the brain's physical makeup and activity without invading the tissue (Olfson, 1992).

■ ELECTRO- ■
ENCEPHALOGRAM
(EEG)

The EEG is a record of the electrical activity of the brain. Electrodes placed on the scalp send brain-wave impulses to a machine called an oscillograph, which amplifies and records them. When the encephalogram reveals an abnormal brain-wave pattern, or *dysrhythmia,* clinicians suspect the existence of abnormalities such as brain lesions, and they proceed to use more precise and sophisticated techniques to ascertain the nature and scope of the problem.

■ COMPUTERIZED ■
AXIAL TOMOGRAPHY
(CAT)

The CAT scan is a widely used procedure that has proved invaluable for locating brain structures. A machine passes a beam of X rays through the brain, and this beam is recorded by an X-ray detector on the other side of the patient's head. This procedure creates a thin, horizontal picture of a single cross section of the brain. The procedure is repeated many times over the patient's entire head. A computer then combines the many cross-sectional views to construct a complete three-dimensional picture of the brain. Though the CAT scan does not provide information about the activity of the brain, it is extremely useful for identifying the precise locations, sizes, and shapes of various structures. It reveals tumors, injuries, and anatomical abnormalities much more clearly than a conventional X ray, providing researchers and clinicians with important information about the correlation between a person's behavior and the physical characteristics of his or her brain. Diagnosticians have found that the scans of persons suffering from psychological disorders often deviate noticeably from the CAT scans of people who display no behavioral abnormality.

Although intelligence tests are impressive by these criteria, they have some significant shortcomings. Factors that have nothing to do with intelligence, such as low motivation and high anxiety, can greatly influence a person's performance (Frederiksen, 1993, 1986). In addition, IQ tests may contain culturally biased language, items, or tasks that place people from one background at an advantage over those from another (Helms, 1992; Puente, 1990). Similarly, members of certain minority groups may also have relatively little experience taking this kind of test or be uncomfortable with test examiners from a majority ethnic background and their performances may suffer accordingly. Obviously, clinicians must be careful to watch for such factors when they use these tests to assess a person's mental functioning.

INTEGRATING TEST DATA   Most clinical tests fall short on one or more of the three key criteria of standardization, reliability, and validity, so it is unwise to put too much faith in any one test. Clinicians usually administer a battery of tests to assess psychological functioning and use this collection of information primarily to clarify and supplement the information gathered in the clinical interview.

Let us return to Angela Savanti, the depressed young woman we met at the beginning of the chapter. We saw that Angela's clinician gathered a considerable amount of information about her during the interview—her symptoms, her unhappy childhood, her father's departure from home, her guilt over his departure, her mother's critical and controlling style, Angela's relationship and breakup with her boyfriend, and her tendency to blame herself for everything that went wrong. Angela's clinician collected additional data from a battery of tests (TAT, MMPI, depression inventory, and an intelligence test) and composed the following test report:

■ POSITRON ■ EMISSION TOMOGRAPHY (PET)

The development of PET has made it possible to watch the brain in action. A harmless radioactive isotope is injected into the patient's bloodstream and travels to the brain. The isotope emits subatomic particles, positrons, that collide with electrons to produce photons. The photons are detected by a sensitive electronic device and recorded in a computer. The more physically active parts of the brain receive more of the isotope than the less active regions and produce a greater number of photons. The computer translates these data into a moving picture of the brain in which levels of blood flow and brain activity are represented by various colors. Studies using PET scans have demonstrated some fascinating correlations between specific kinds of brain activity and specific psychological disorders. PET scans of obsessive-compulsive patients, for example, show increased activity in the caudate nuclei structures, and those of bipolar patients tend to show increased activity in the right temporal region during manic episodes.

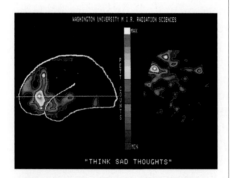

A PET scan of a person thinking sad thoughts reveals which areas of brain activity (shown in red, orange, and yellow) are related to such mood changes.

■ MAGNETIC ■ RESONANCE IMAGING (MRI)

MRI, the most recent development in brain-imaging techniques, provides information on both the structure and the function of the brain and does not require any form of radiation. In this highly complex and elegant procedure a person lies on a machine that creates a magnetic field around his or her head, causing the hydrogen atoms in the brain to line up. When the magnet is turned off, the atoms return to their normal positions, emitting magnetic signals in the process. The signals are recorded, read by a computer, and translated into a detailed and accurate picture of the brain. In many cases MRI is so precise that the image it produces looks more like a photograph of the brain than a typical computer-produced image. MRI is believed to reflect the composition of cells and may be critical in detecting damaged areas of the brain containing different concentrations of hydrogen.

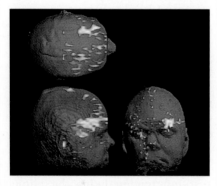

An "echo-planar" MRI, a high speed MRI, reveals the reaction of a patient with an obsessive-compulsive disorder to "an envelope soiled with illicit drugs."

---

*A*ngela cooperated during the psychological testing, and attempted to do each task asked of her. However, she did not answer any question spontaneously, and it usually took her several seconds before she gave a response. . . .

The client scored in the average range of intelligence. The long reaction times to verbal stimuli and the slowness of her motor responses suggested an impairment in intellectual functioning. This slowness in verbal and motor behavior is consistent with the performance observed in persons who are depressed. The client's affect [feeling or emotion], as interpreted from the test material, was constricted and controlled. She appeared to react strongly to some of the events occurring around her, but she controlled her emotions so that other people were not aware of how she felt. . . .

A theme that emerged on several of the tests referred to a person who had an unrealistically high level of aspiration, who was extremely self-critical. As a result, this person labeled her accomplishments as poor or mediocre, no matter how hard she tried. She was constantly plagued with feelings of inadequacy, self-blame, and anger, because she could not live up to her high standards of performance.

Maternal figures were depicted as controlling and lacking in empathy and warmth. The client described a scene in which a woman was forcing her daughter to perform a chore that the mother did not want to do herself. The mother did not understand or care that the daughter was not willing to do the task, and the daughter eventually complied with the mother's wishes.

Male figures were described as nice, but not to be counted on. Part of the blame for this unreliability was placed with the woman with whom the man was interacting. The woman was assumed to have the ability to modify the man's behavior, so any blame for the man's failings had to be shared by the woman as well.

There were no indications of psychotic thought processes during the interviews or on the test material.

(Leon, 1984, pp. 115–116)

The test information serves several functions for Angela's clinician. First, it underscores several of the

"You can't build a hut, you don't know how to find edible roots and you know nothing about predicting the weather. In other words, you do *terribly* on our IQ test."

impressions gathered earlier during the clinical interview. It indicates, for example, that Angela is indeed depressed, carries lingering feelings of anger toward her mother, and views her father and other men as unreliable and likely to disappoint her. Second, the test information helps the clinician determine the scope of the client's problems. It indicates, for example, that Angela's depression is so pervasive that it even retards her verbal and motor behavior, and that her feelings of inadequacy, self-criticism, and anger are deeper and more enduring than the interview itself may have conveyed. Finally, the test data reveal that Angela's intellectual functioning is at least average, that she is not psychotic, and that her aspirations are perhaps unrealistically high. With such information now in hand, the clinician is in a better position to understand Angela and her psychological problems.

Clinical
Observations

In addition to interviewing and testing people, clinicians may follow specific strategies for observing their behavior. One such technique is the *naturalistic observation,* also called an *in vivo* (literally, "in the living") *observation,* in which clinicians observe clients in their everyday environments. Another is the *structured observation,* in which clinicians monitor people

in artificial settings created in their offices or laboratories. They may also have clients observe themselves, a technique called *self-monitoring.* These techniques are used most often by behavioral and cognitive clinicians as they search for vivid behaviors that will enable them to make a functional analysis of a person's disturbance.

NATURALISTIC AND STRUCTURED OBSERVATIONS Most naturalistic clinical observations take place in homes, schools, institutions such as hospitals and prisons, and community settings such as restaurants, supermarkets, and apartment buildings. The observations have usually focused on parent–child, sibling–child, and teacher–child interactions; fearful, aggressive, or disruptive behavior; and self-injurious behavior (Barton & Osborne, 1978; Patterson, 1977). Actually, most such observations are made by *participant observers,* key persons in the client's environment, and reported to the clinician.

When naturalistic observation is impractical, clinicians may choose to observe some clients in a structured setting. Interactions between parents and their children, for example, may be observed in an office or laboratory on videotape or from behind a one-way mirror (Field, 1977; White, 1977). Similarly, clinicians have used observation rooms to monitor married couples engaging in a disagreement, speech-anxious people giving a speech, alcoholic people drinking, and fearful people approaching an object they find frightening (Floyd, O'Farrell, & Goldberg, 1987).

Obviously it is helpful for a clinician actually to watch the behavior, interactions, and situations that may be leading to a person's disturbances, but these methods have several disadvantages as well. For one thing, clinical observations are not always reliable (Foster & Cone, 1986). It is quite possible for various clinicians who observe the same person to focus on different aspects of behavior, evaluate the person differently, and draw different conclusions. Observations may become more consistent when the observers are carefully trained and observer checklists are used (Alevizos et al., 1978).

Observers may make errors that also affect the validity of their observations, especially if they suffer from *overload* (Foster & Cone, 1986). So much is happening during an interaction that the observer may simply be unable to see or record all relevant behavior and events. Another problem is *observer drift,* a steady deterioration in accuracy as a result of fatigue or of a gradual inadvertent change in the criteria used when an observer judges behavior over a long period of time (O'Leary & Kent, 1973). Another possibility is *observer bias*—the observer's judgments are inappropriately influenced by information and expectations he or she already has about the client (Shuller & McNamara, 1980; Kent et al., 1974). Participant observers who are personally connected with the client are particularly prone to bias. A mother who observes her depressed teenage son, for example, may be inclined to minimize his pessimistic remarks, hoping that they are harmless adolescent complaints rather than indicators of severe depression.

Another factor that often limits the validity of clinical observations is the subject's *reactivity*—his or her behavior is affected by the very presence of the observer (Harris & Lahey, 1982). If schoolchildren are aware that someone special is watching them, for example, they may alter their usual classroom behavior, perhaps in the hope of impressing the observer.

Finally, clinical observations may lack *cross-situational validity,* also called *external* or *ecological validity* (Tunnell, 1977; Patterson, 1974). A child who behaves aggressively in school is not necessarily aggressive at home or with friends after school. Because behavior is often specific to particular situations, observations in one setting cannot always be applied to other settings (Simpson & Halpin, 1986).

SELF-MONITORING Earlier we considered self-report inventories, assessment instruments in which subjects report their own behaviors, feelings, or cognitions. In a related procedure, self-monitoring, they observe themselves and carefully record designated behavior, feelings, or cognitions as they occur throughout the day (Bornstein, Hamilton, & Bornstein, 1986). Subjects usually note the *frequency* of the responses they are recording. How frequently does a drug user have an urge for drugs (Thompson & Conrad, 1977) or a headache sufferer have a headache (Feuerstein & Adams, 1977)? They may also be asked to observe and record the *circumstances* surrounding their responses. When self-monitoring is used to assess excessive smoking, for example, people are typically asked to record when and where they are smoking, who is present, what is happening, what they were thinking or feeling just before smoking, and what events followed the smoking. This information may reveal that a person smokes under particular conditions or certain kinds of stress (Conway, 1977).

Self-monitoring offers several advantages. First, it may be the only way to observe behavior that occurs relatively infrequently. When the problem is exhibitionism (exposing one's genitals in public), for instance, some clinicians have had the client keep a record of his or her exhibitionistic urges and actions (Maletzky, 1977, 1974). Second, self-monitoring is useful for observing behavior that occurs so frequently that any other comprehensive observation of it would be impossible. It has been employed to collect information about the nature and frequency of smoking, drinking, drug use, and feelings of anger and anxiety (Conway, 1977; Hay, Hay, & Nelson, 1977; Novaco, 1977). Third, self-monitoring is the only way covert cognitions can be observed and counted. In one study a woman who was having auditory hallucinations (hearing voices and sounds that were not really occurring around her) monitored the hallucinations for her clinician by raising a finger and keeping it raised throughout each such experience (Turner, Hersen, & Bellack, 1977).

Like all other clinical assessment procedures, however, self-monitoring has drawbacks. One is the question of its validity (Nelson, 1977). Clients do not always receive proper instruction in this form of observation, nor are they always motivated to record their observations accurately (Mahoney, 1977). Furthermore, there is often a powerful reactivity effect when clients try to monitor themselves. It has been found, for example, that smokers smoke fewer cigarettes than usual when they are monitoring themselves (Kilmann, Wagner, & Sotile, 1977), drug users take drugs less frequently (Hay et al., 1977), and teachers give more positive and fewer negative comments to their students (Nelson et al., 1977).

■ CLINICAL ■ INTERPRETATION AND JUDGMENT

"The interviews have been completed; the Rorschach and TAT have been administered; the Incomplete Sentences Blank has been finished. Now, what does it all mean?" (Phares, 1979, p. 295). Before treating a client, a clinician must *interpret* the assessment data—that is, transform them into a clinical understanding of the person's problem and a diagnosis.

While gathering assessment data, clinicians generate hypotheses about the nature, causes, and course of a person's disturbed functioning. To a great extent, the principles and concepts embodied in each clinician's particular theoretical orientation help him or her formulate these hypotheses. As assessment proceeds, the mounting data will seem to support some of the hypotheses and refute others.

It is not always clear exactly how clinicians go about testing their hypotheses. Clinicians themselves find it hard to step outside themselves and know what and how they are thinking, and researchers have found it difficult to quantify and measure these covert cognitive processes. Some clinicians have invoked the notion of "clinical intuition" to explain the process of clinical interpretation. Clinicians are thought somehow to feel their way toward conclusions, aided by their clinical experiences and training, but without imposing on them a conscious systematic method. Although this view has a certain intuitive appeal, it hardly sheds light on the processes by which clinicians arrive at their conclusions (Peterson, 1968; Meehl, 1954).

In one useful line of research, investigators have tried to determine whether clinicians simply add and subtract assessment data when they formulate their conclusions or whether they combine the data in more complex ways (Wiggins, 1973). By and large, findings indicate that most clinicians use an *additive,* or *linear, model* when they interpret their data (Hammond & Summers, 1965). That is, they base their conclusions on how many assessment responses point in the same direction; as the number of concurring responses increases, the likelihood of a given conclusion increases as well.

After they have collected and interpreted the assessment information, clinicians attempt to form a *clinical picture,* an integrated picture of the various factors causing and sustaining the person's disturbed functioning that enables the clinician to select appropriate foci and methods for treatment (Sundberg et al., 1973). This picture, often written up formally as a report, is framed in the language and concepts of the clinician's theoretical orientation (Kaplan & Sadock, 1989). The clinician who worked with Angela Savanti held a cognitive-behavioral view of abnormality, so the clinical picture of Angela is constructed in terms of modeling and reinforcement principles and the proposition that Angela's expectations, assumptions, and interpretations are major components of her problem:

Angela was rarely reinforced for any of her accomplishments at school, but she gained her mother's negative attention for what Mrs. Savanti judged to be poor performance at school or at home. Mrs. Savanti repeatedly told her daughter that she was incompetent, and any mishaps that happened to her were her own fault. . . . When Mr. Savanti deserted the family, Angela's first response was that somehow she was responsible. From her mother's past behavior, Angela had learned to expect that in some way she would be blamed. At the time that Angela broke up with her boyfriend, she did not blame Jerry for his behavior, but interpreted this event as a failing solely on her part. As a result, her level of self-esteem was lowered still more.

The type of marital relationship that Angela saw her mother and father model remained her concept of what married life is like. She generalized from her observations of her parents' discordant interactions to an expectation of the type of behavior that she and Jerry would ultimately engage in. Angela demanded that Jerry conform to her definition of acceptable interpersonal behavior, because of her belief that otherwise their marriage would not be a mutually reinforcing relationship. However, Angela set such high standards for Jerry's behavior that it was inevitable that she would be disappointed. . . .

Angela's uncertainties intensified when she was deprived of the major source of gratification she had, her relationship with Jerry. Despite the fact that she was overwhelmed with doubts about whether to marry him or not, she had gained a great deal of pleasure through being with Jerry. Whatever feelings she had been able to express, she had shared with him and no one else. Angela labeled Jerry's termination of their relationship as proof that she was not worthy of another person's interest. She viewed her present unhappiness as likely to continue, and she attributed it to some failing on her part. As a result, she became quite depressed.

(Leon, 1984, pp. 123–125)

With this report, Angela's clinician has largely accomplished the task of attaining an idiographic, or individual, understanding of the client. If clients are to be fully understood and effectively treated, however, the clinician has to determine not only what makes them unique but what they have in common with a specific group of other disturbed people. This is the purpose of diagnosis.

■ DIAGNOSIS ■

Clinicians also use assessment information and interpretation processes to make a *diagnosis*—that is, to determine that a person's psychological problems constitute a particular disorder. Although clinicians can learn enough about a person from assessment information to develop ideas about the nature and causes of the person's problems, they need still other information to know the probable future course of the problem and what treatment strategies are likely to be helpful. It might also help them to know whether clinicians who treated similar cases found that less conspicuous symptoms were also involved in the problem and which factors were the most important to attend to.

When clinicians decide that a person's pattern of dysfunction constitutes a particular disorder, they are saying that the pattern is basically the same as one that has been displayed by many other people, has been observed and investigated in a variety of studies, and perhaps has responded to particular forms of treatment. If their diagnosis is correct, clinicians can fruitfully apply what is generally known about the disorder to the particular person they are trying to help. If a diagnosis is incorrect, however, the clinician may draw inaccurate conclusions about the person and his or her problem and may apply useless or even harmful treatment procedures (see Box 4–3).

CLASSIFCATION SYSTEMS

The principle behind diagnosis is straightforward. When certain symptoms regularly occur together (a cluster of symptoms is called a *syndrome*) and follow a particular course, clinicians agree that those symptoms constitute a particular mental disorder. When people display this particular cluster and course of symptoms, diagnosticians assign them to that category. A comprehensive list of such categories, with a description of the symptoms characteristic of each and guidelines for assigning individuals to categories, is known as a *classification system.*

A classification system serves several important purposes (APA, 1994). First, as we have noted, it enables clinicians to diagnose a person's problem as a disorder. A *diagnosis* (from Greek for "a discrimination") in turn makes it possible for them to tap the general information that has already been gathered about that problem. A classification system also helps researchers to *study* abnormality and develop a body of knowledge about the causes of various patterns of abnormal functioning and ways to treat them. By using an agreed-upon classification system, clinical researchers can efficiently gather a representative sample of people with similar symptoms and investigate their problems. Finally, a classification system enables clinicians and researchers to *communicate* more easily. A clinician does not have to list every one of a client's symptoms in order to discuss that person with a colleague. Mention of the person's diagnostic category will suffice to give other clinicians a general picture of the kinds of difficulties the person is experiencing, which can then be enhanced by idiosyncratic details about the individual's situation. Similarly, a researcher does not have to list all the symptoms shared by the subjects in his or her study before others can understand the kind of dysfunction under investigation.

Emil Kraepelin developed a system for classifying mental disorders on which today's classification systems are built.

As we saw in Chapter 1, Emil Kraepelin developed the first influential classification system for abnormal behavior in 1883. By collecting thousands of case studies of patients in mental hospitals, he was able to identify various syndromes, and to describe each syndrome's apparent cause and expected course (Zilboorg & Henry, 1941). The categories of disorders established by Kraepelin and the hierarchy in which he organized them have formed the foundation for the psychological part of the classification system now used by the World Health Organization, called the *International Classification of Diseases.* This system, which covers both medical and psychological disorders, is currently in its tenth revision, known as *ICD-10.*

Kraepelin's work has also been incorporated into the *Diagnostic and Statistical Manual of Mental Disorders,* a classification system developed by the American Psychiatric Association. Very similar to the ICD, it too has been revised over time. The current edition, *DSM-IV,* was published in 1994 and is by far the most widely used classification system in the United States today. The descriptions of mental disorders presented throughout this book adhere to the categories and distinctions in DSM-IV.

Classification systems must be revised periodically to keep up with new knowledge and changing perspectives in the clinical field. As new insights and viewpoints emerge, new forms of classification are proposed to replace old ones. The DSM was first published in 1952 (DSM-I) and has undergone major revisions in 1968 (DSM-II), 1980 (DSM-III), 1987 (DSM-III-R), and 1994 (DSM-IV) (see Table 4–3). In a sense, then, a classification system actually

BOX 4–3

WHAT AILED VAN GOGH?

Diagnosing mental disorders is a challenging and important task, and practitioners faced with a suffering patient are obliged to be as accurate and helpful as possible. Diagnosing the psychological problems of famous people who are no longer alive, though, is something of a parlor game. Old conclusions may change from time to time to conform to new theories and paradigms, as well as to incorporate newly discovered information about the person in question. A prime instance of such shifts is seen in the unfortunate case of Vincent van Gogh.

Van Gogh led a turbulent and unhappy life. The legendary incident in which he cut off one of his ears, his voluntary commitment to a mental institution, and his ultimate suicide are the best-known pieces of evidence. But van Gogh also wrote extensively about his pain and anguish, describing mental and physical torment and hallucinatory experiences. For years his letters and the accounts of his friends and physicians led clinicians to diagnose van Gogh as suffering from bipolar disorder, schizophrenia, or both. The available evidence seemed to support such a diagnosis. The picture changed in the mid-1980s, however, when the Harvard neurologist Shahram Khoshbin reviewed the many paintings and letters produced by van Gogh in the months before his suicide. Khoshbin concluded that van Gogh in fact suffered from Geschwind's syn-

Vincent van Gogh, a self-portrait.

drome, technically known as interictal personality disorder and believed to accompany epilepsy. Symptoms include excessive drawing (hypergraphia), hyperreligiosity, aggression, and other characteristics that van Gogh is known to have exhibited. Khoshbin's conclusion, then, was that van Gogh had epilepsy (Trotter, 1985).

The controversial issue was raised again more recently when the ear spe-

cialist I. Kaufman Arenberg of the Swedish Medical Center in Colorado and his colleagues reevaluated van Gogh's case. After reading almost eight hundred of van Gogh's letters, they concluded that he suffered from Menière's syndrome, a disorder caused by an excessive buildup of fluid that exerts enormous pressure on the inner ear. Menière's syndrome may lead to nausea, vertigo, poor balance, pain, deafness, and buzzing or ringing. Some estimates put the number of sufferers in this country at 7 million. Arenberg suggested that van Gogh suffered from an extreme form of this disorder and that he may have cut off his ear in an effort to reduce the pain. Many of van Gogh's other problems and pains may have arisen from the severe secondary psychological problems that can accompany Menière's syndrome (Scott, 1990).

The study of abnormal psychology is a relatively young and fluid field, and many people suffering from a mental disorder receive more than one diagnosis during their search for help. New information about the person, new information about disorders, and other factors that can influence clinicians may lead to different conclusions about the same case. Van Gogh has had the questionable honor of being posthumously diagnosed dozens of times. He is worth bearing in mind in any discussion on assessment and diagnosis.

freezes in time one moment in the history of a constantly changing clinical field (Talbott & Spitzer, 1980). This is not to say, however, that there is universal agreement among clinicians whenever a new

system or new categories are developed; today's clinicians are already debating the merits of DSM-IV, just as clinicians continually argued over past versions of the DSM.

DSM-IV

DSM-IV lists close to three hundred mental disorders. Each entry describes the criteria for diagnosing the disorder, the essential clinical features of the disorder (features that are invariably present), and any associated features (features that are often but not invariably present), and gives information about specific age-, culture-, or gender-related features, prevalence and risk, course, complications, predisposing factors, and family patterns. The criteria in DSM-IV, following the leads of DSM-III and DSM-III-R, are more detailed and objective than those of the earliest DSMs. DSM-IV focuses entirely on verifiable symptoms, for example, and stipulates that a person's dysfunction must include certain specified symptoms if it is to qualify for a diagnosis. DSM-I and DSM-II, in contrast, required diagnosticians to infer the underlying cause of a disorder in order to make a diagnosis. To make a diagnosis of "anxiety neurosis" according to DSM-II, for example, diagnosticians first had to conclude that a person was experiencing internal conflicts and defending against anxiety. In DSM-IV such inferences are not required.

When clinicians use DSM-IV to make a diagnosis, they must evaluate a client's condition on five separate *axes,* or branches of information. This requirement forces diagnosticians to review and use a broad range of observations and data. First, clinicians must decide whether the client is displaying one or more of the disorders from *Axis I,* an extensive list of florid clinical syndromes that typically cause significant impairment (see Figure 4–7). The Axis I disorders are organized into the following groups:

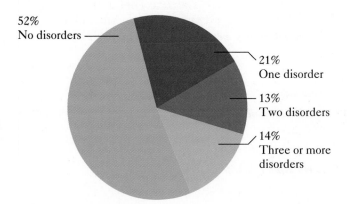

52%
No disorders

21%
One disorder

13%
Two disorders

14%
Three or more disorders

FIGURE 4–7 *How many people in the United States qualify for a DSM diagnosis during their lives? Almost half, according to a recent survey. In fact, 27 percent meet the criteria for two or more different mental disorders. In some cases these individuals even experience their disorders simultaneously, an occurrence known as "comorbidity." (Adapted from Kessler et al., 1994.)*

Disorders Usually First Diagnosed in Infancy, Childhood, and Adolescence Disorders in this group tend to emerge and sometimes dissipate before adult life. They include *pervasive developmental disorders*, such as *autism*, in which persons display severe deficits and pervasive impairment in several areas of development, including social interaction and communication; *learning disorders*, in which persons' functioning in particular academic skill areas is significantly below average (such as *dyslexia*, a reading disorder); *attention-deficit hyperactivity disorder*, in which persons display maladaptive levels of inattention, hyperactivity, or impulsivity, or a combination of these; *conduct disorders*, in which children persistently violate societal norms, rules, and the basic rights of others; and *separation anxiety disorders*, in which children become excessively anxious over the possibility of being separated from their home or parents.

Delirium, Dementia, Amnestic, and Other Cognitive Disorders These are disorders in cognitive functioning, which include such features as *delirium* (a clouded and confused state of consciousness), *dementia* (multiple deficits in intellectual and cognitive function, including impairment in memory), and *amnestic*, or memory, impairment alone. Among the disorders in this group are *Alzheimer's disease* and *Huntington's disease.*

Mental Disorders Due to a General Medical Condition These are mental disorders that are caused *primarily* by a general medical disorder. It includes such disorders as *mood disorder due to a general medical condition, anxiety disorder due to a general medical condition*, and *sleep disorder due to a general medical condition.*

Substance-Related Disorders These disorders are brought about by the use of substances that affect the central nervous system. With such use, persons may become intoxicated, find their social and occupational functioning in disarray, crave increasing amounts of the substance, and experience unpleasant symptoms when they stop taking it. Disorders in this group include *alcohol use disorders, opioid use disorders, amphetamine use disorders, cocaine use disorders*, and *hallucinogen use disorders.*

Schizophrenia and Other Psychotic Disorders In this group of disorders, functioning deteriorates until the patient reaches a state of *psychosis*, or loss of contact with reality. Psychotic symptoms may include *delusions* (bizarre ideas with no basis in reality), *hallucinations* (perceptions of sounds, objects, or smells that are not actually present), *loose*

TABLE 4-3

WHAT'S NEW IN DSM-IV?

New Categories

Rett's disorder	Pervasive developmental disorder that occurs after 5 months of normal post-natal development
Childhood disintegrative disorder	Pervasive developmental disorder that occurs after at least 2 years of normal development
Asperger's disorder	Pervasive developmental disorder in which the principal problems are impaired social interactions and stereotyped patterns of behavior
Feeding disorder of infancy or early childhood	Persistent failure by young children to eat adequately, with significant weight loss or failure to gain weight, over at least one month
Bipolar II disorder	Pattern of one or more major depressive episodes accompanied by at least one hypomanic episode
Acute stress disorder	Acute anxiety and related symptoms occurring within one month after exposure to an extreme traumatic stressor and ending within a month
Narcolepsy	Pattern of irresistible attacks of refreshing sleep over at least a 3-month period
Breathing-related sleep disorder	Pattern of sleep disruption caused by breathing abnormalities during sleep

Category Name Changes

Learning disorders	Replaces *academic skills disorders*
Mathematics disorder	Replaces *developmental arithmetic disorder*
Disorder of written expression	Replaces *developmental writing disorder*
Communication disorders	Replaces *language and speech disorders*
Mixed receptive-expressive language disorder	Replaces *developmental receptive language disorder*
Phonological disorder	Replaces *developmental articulation disorder*
Selective mutism	Replaced *elective mutism*
Stereotypic movement disorder	Replaces *stereotypy/habit disorder*
Other conditions that may be a focus of clinical attention	Replaces *conditions not attributable to a mental disorder that are a focus of treatment or attention*
Specific phobia	Replaces *simple phobia*
Brief psychotic disorder	Replaces *brief reactive psychosis*
Mental disorders due to a general medical condition	Replaces subset of *organic mental disorders*
Substance-induced disorders	Replaces subset of *organic mental disorders*
Delirium, dementia, amnestic, and other cognitive disorders	Replaces subset of *organic mental disorders*
Vascular dementia	Replaces *multi-infarct dementia*
Substance-related disorders	Replaces *substance use disorders* and *psychoactive substance-induced organic mental disorders*
Pain disorder	Replaces *somatoform pain disorder*
Dissociative amnesia	Replaces *psychogenic amnesia*

(continued)

TABLE 4-3

WHAT'S NEW IN DSM-IV?   *(continued)*

CATEGORY NAME CHANGES   *(continued)*

Dissociative fugue	Replaces *psychogenic fugue*
Dissociative identity disorder	Replaces *multiple personality disorder*
Circadian rhythm sleep disorder	Replaces *sleep-wake schedule disorder*
Nightmare disorder	Replaces *dream anxiety disorder*
Female orgasmic disorder	Replaces *inhibited female orgasm*
Male orgasmic disorder	Replaces *inhibited male orgasm*

ORGANIZATION CHANGES

Anorexia nervosa	Now separated from disorders of infancy, childhood, and adolescence
Bulimia nervosa	Now separated from disorders of infancy, childhood, and adolescence
Gender identity disorder	Now subsumes *gender identity disorder of childhood, gender identity disorder of adolescence or adulthood*, and *transsexualism*
Learning disorders	Relocated to Axis I (previously located in Axis II)
Pervasive development disorders— autistic disorder	Relocated to Axis I (previously located in Axis II)
Communication disorders	Relocated to Axis I (previously located in Axis II)
Motor skills disorder	Relocated to Axis I (previously located in Axis II)

CRITERION CHANGES

Autistic disorder	Onset must occur before 3 years of age
Anorexia nervosa	Anorexic persons who binge and purge receive diagnosis of *anorexia nervosa, binge-eating/purging type*
Manic episode	Symptoms must persist at least one week
Panic disorder	Panic attacks must be accompanied by a month or more of persistent concern about having additional attacks or about implications of attacks, or significant related behavior changes
Schizophrenia	Active-phase symptoms must persist at least one month
Brief psychotic disorder	Symptoms must persist at least one day
Conversion disorder	Symptom or deficit must affect voluntary motor or sensory functioning
Adjustment disorder	Symptoms may persist up to 6 months *after* termination of a stressor or its consequences

CATEGORY DELETIONS

DSM-III-R's avoidant disorder of childhood	Now part of *social phobia*
DSM-III-R's overanxious disorder of childhood	Now part of *generalized anxiety disorder*
DSM-III-R's passive-aggressive-personality disorder	Now may be designated under *personality disorder not otherwise specified*

associations (unconnected pieces of thought), and *flattened* or *inappropriate affect* (lack of emotion, or emotions that do not fit the situation).

Mood Disorders Disorders in this group are marked by severe disturbances of mood that cause people to feel extremely and inappropriately sad or elated for extended periods of time. These disorders include *major depressive disorder* and *bipolar disorder* (in which episodes of mania alternate with episodes of depression).

Anxiety Disorders Anxiety is the predominant disturbance in this group of disorders. People with anxiety disorders may experience broad feelings of anxiety and worry *(generalized anxiety disorders)*, anxiety concerning a specific situation or object *(phobic disorders)*, discrete periods of panic *(panic disorder)*, persistent and recurrent thoughts or repetitive behaviors or both *(obsessive-compulsive disorder)*, or lingering anxiety reactions to extraordinarily traumatic events *(acute stress disorder* and *posttraumatic stress disorder)*.

Somatoform Disorders These disorders are marked by physical symptoms that apparently are caused primarily by psychological rather than physiological factors. The disorders include *pain disorders*, in which people experience unexplained levels of pain; *conversion disorders*, in which there is a loss or change in voluntary motor or sensory functioning (for example, paralysis or blindness); *somatization disorder*, in which people experience multiple physical symptoms; and *hypochondriasis*, in which people misinterpret physical sensations as abnormal and become preoccupied with the fear that they have a serious illness.

Factitious Disorders People with these disorders intentionally produce or feign psychological or physical symptoms.

Dissociative Disorders People with these disorders experience a sudden change in the usually integrated functions of consciousness, memory, identity, or perception, which makes it difficult for them to carry on their normal functioning. Disorders in this group include *dissociative amnesia*, in which people are unable to recall extensive pieces of important personal information; *dissociative fugue*, in which people suddenly leave home, assume a new identity, and forget who they were before; and *dissociative identity disorder*, or *multiple personality disorder*, in which people display two or more distinct personalities, each with unique memories, behavior patterns, preferences, and social relationships.

Eating Disorders People with these disorders display abnormal patterns of eating that significantly impair their functioning. People with *anorexia nervosa* refuse to maintain a minimally normal weight for their age and height. People with *bulimia nervosa* go on episodes of binge eating followed by inappropriate compensatory behaviors such as forced vomiting.

Sexual and Gender Identity Disorders These disorders in sexual functioning, behavior, or preferences include *paraphilias*, in which people need unusual imagery, objects, activities, or situations to become sexually aroused (for example, *sexual sadism*, in which people must inflict suffering on their partners to achieve sexual excitement); *sexual dysfunctions*, in which people are unable to complete the sexual response cycle (for example, *male orgasmic disorder* or *female orgasmic disorder*); and *gender identity disorders*, in which people strongly and persistently identify with the other gender.

Sleep Disorders People with these disorders display chronic sleep problems (of more than a month's duration). The disorders may be *dyssomnias*, in which the primary disturbance is in the amount, quality, or timing of sleep (for example, *primary insomnia* or *primary hypersomnia*), or *parasomnias*, marked by the occurrence of abnormal events during sleep (for example, *sleep terror disorder* or *sleepwalking disorder*).

Impulse-Control Disorders People with these disorders are chronically unable to resist impulses, drives, or temptations to perform certain acts that are harmful to them or to others. These disorders include *pathological gambling*; *kleptomania*, a recurrent failure to resist impulses to steal; *pyromania*, a pattern of fire setting for pleasure, gratification, or relief of tension; and *intermittent explosive disorders*, episodes of failure to resist aggressive impulses, resulting in serious assaults or destruction of property.

Adjustment Disorder The primary feature of this disorder is a maladaptive reaction to a clear stressor such as divorce or business difficulties that occurs within three months after the onset of the stressor. The reaction may involve distress, impairment in social or occupational functioning, or other symptoms beyond the normal, expected reaction to such a stressor.

Other Conditions That May Be a Focus of Clinical Attention This group of disorders includes additional conditions or problems that are worth noting because they cause significant psychological or physical impairment. It includes *relational problems, problems related to abuse or neglect*, and *medication-induced movement disorders*. It also includes the category *psychological factors affecting a medical condition*, denoting problems in which psychological factors help produce, maintain, or alter the course of medical conditions (such as headaches, asthma, ulcer, and angina pectoris). The medical conditions affected in this way are sometimes called *psychosomatic* or *psychophysiological*.

Next, diagnosticians must decide whether the client is displaying one of the disorders from *Axis II*, long-standing problems that are frequently overlooked in the presence of the disorders listed in Axis I. There are two major categories of Axis II disorders:

Mental Retardation   People with this disorder display significant subaverage intellectual functioning by 18 years of age and concurrent deficits or impairment in adaptive function.

Personality Disorders   People with these disorders display an enduring pervasive, inflexible, and maladaptive pattern of inner experience and behavior that deviates markedly from the expectations of the individual's culture. Two examples are *antisocial personality disorder*, in which people display a history of continuous and chronic disregard for, and violation of, the rights of others, and *dependent personality disorder*, in which people manifest a pattern of submissive and clinging behavior and fears of separation related to an excessive need to be taken care of.

Although people usually receive a diagnosis from *either* Axis I or Axis II, they may receive diagnoses from both axes. Angela Savanti would first receive a diagnosis of *major depressive disorder*, an Axis I disorder (one of the mood disorders) because her pattern of dysfunction meets these DSM-IV criteria:

A. At least five of the following symptoms have been present during the same two-week period and represent a change from previous functioning:
  1. Depressed mood most of the day, nearly every day
  2. Markedly diminished interest or pleasure in all, or almost all, activities most of the day, nearly every day
  3. Significant weight loss when not dieting, or weight gain, or decrease or increase in appetite nearly every day

  4. Insomnia or hypersomnia nearly every day
  5. Psychomotor agitation or retardation nearly every day
  6. Fatigue or loss of energy nearly every day
  7. Feelings of worthlessness or excessive or inappropriate guilt nearly every day
  8. Diminished ability to think or concentrate, or indecisiveness, nearly every day
  9. Recurrent thoughts of death (not just fear of dying), recurrent suicidal ideation without a specific plan, or a suicide attempt or a specific plan for committing suicide
B. The symptoms cause clinically significant distress or impairment in social, occupational, or other important areas of functioning.

(APA, 1994)

Let us suppose that the diagnostician judged that Angela had also displayed a life history of chronic dependent behavior in that she had submitted and clung to others, required them to take care of her, and subordinated her own needs to those of others. In this case, she would also receive an Axis II diagnosis of *dependent personality disorder.*

The remaining axes of DSM-IV guide diagnosticians to recognize and report factors other than a client's symptoms that are potentially relevant to the understanding or management of the case. *Axis III* information is a listing of any relevant general medical condition the person is currently suffering from. *Axis IV* information is a listing of psychosocial or environmental problems the person is facing that may affect the diagnosis, treatment, or course of the mental disorder. Axis IV categories include *occupational problems, educational problems, housing problems*, and *problems related to the social environment*. And *Axis V* information is a *global assessment of functioning (GAF)*, the diagnostician's rating of the person's overall level of psychological, social, and occupational functioning. If Angela Savanti had diabetes, for example, the clinician might include that under Axis III information. Angela's recent breakup with her boyfriend would be noted with the Axis IV category *problems related to the social environment*. And because she seemed moderately impaired at the time of diagnosis, Angela's global assessment of functioning would probably be rated approximately 55 on Axis V in accordance with DSM-IV's Global Assessment of Functioning Scale (see Table 4–4). The complete diagnosis for Angela Savanti would then be:

Axis I: Major depressive disorder

Axis II: Dependent personality disorder

Axis III: Diabetes

Axis IV: Problem related to the social environment (termination of engagement)

Axis V: GAF = 55 (current)

Because several kinds of diagnostic information are used in DSM-IV, each defined by a different "axis," it is known as a *multiaxial* system. The diagnoses arrived at under this classification system are expected to be more informative and more carefully considered than those derived from the earliest DSMs.

RELIABILITY
AND VALIDITY
IN CLASSIFCATION

The value of a diagnostic classification system, like that of the various assessment methods, is judged by its reliability and validity. Here *reliability* means that different diagnosticians agree that a given pattern of observed behavior should be assigned to a given category. If different diagnosticians keep arriving at different diagnoses after observing the same behavior, then the classification system is not very reliable.

Early versions of the DSM were only moderately reliable (Spitzer & Fleiss, 1974). In the early 1960s, for example, four clinicians, each relying on DSM-I, independently interviewed and diagnosed 153 patients recently admitted to a mental hospital (Beck et al., 1962). Only 54 percent of these clinicians' diagnoses were in agreement. Some categories of classification brought greater agreement (were more reliable) than others, but none showed more than 63 percent agreement. Because all four clinicians were experienced diagnosticians, their failure to agree was attributed largely to deficiencies in the DSM-I classification system—vague descriptions of categories and categories determined more by theoretical biases than by specific symptoms.

The clearer and more objective criteria provided by DSM-III and DSM-III-R yielded somewhat more reliable diagnoses than their predecessors (DiNardo et al., 1993; Akiskal, 1989). Nevertheless, reliability studies rarely found more than 70 percent agreement among clinicians who used these versions of the DSM (Kirk & Kutchins, 1992). One problem was that these classification systems contained some vague, imprecisely defined categories, such as "depressive disorder not otherwise specified" and "anxiety disorder not otherwise specified." A few such categories had to be included because clients' symptoms do not always fit the more precisely specified primary categories. Un-

fortunately, the vaguer categories also brought some imprecision and unreliability.

In order to maximize the reliability of DSM-IV, its task force and work groups first conducted comprehensive reviews of relevant research to pinpoint which categories from past DSMs were indeed producing low reliability (APA, 1994). Then, upon developing new diagnostic criteria and categories for inclusion in DSM-IV, the framers conducted twelve *field trials,* extensive new studies at more than 70 sites, with 6000 participating subjects, to make sure that the new criteria and categories were indeed reliable. As a result, it is expected that DSM-IV will have greater reliability than any of its predecessors (APA, 1994). Similar claims were made during the draft stages of the previous DSMs, though, so many clinicians suggest that we wait until DSM-IV is widely used and tested by the clinical community at large before making any assumptions about its reliability (Kirk & Kutchins, 1992).

The *validity* of a classification system is the accuracy of the information that a diagnostic category provides about the people assigned to that category and about their symptoms. Categories are of most use to clinicians when they demonstrate predictive and concurrent validity. A category has **predictive validity** when it helps predict future symptoms or events. A common symptom of major depressive disorder, for example, is insomnia or hypersomnia. When clinicians give Angela Savanti a diagnosis of major depression, they expect that she may eventually develop this symptom even though she does not manifest it now. Moreover, they expect her to respond to treatments that are effective for other depressed persons. The more often such predictions are accurate, the greater a given category's predictive validity.

Categories show **concurrent validity** when they give clinicians information about "associated" features of a disorder, beyond the "essential" diagnostic symptoms. For example, DSM-IV reports that people who manifest major depressive disorder often also become excessively concerned about their physical health. If Angela Savanti and most other people who receive this diagnosis do indeed display this associated feature, the category is displaying a high degree of concurrent validity.

The developers of DSM-III and DSM-III-R tried to improve upon the weak validity records of DSM-I and DSM-II by carefully reviewing the psychological literature to determine exactly what conclusions and expectations were appropriate for each category (APA, 1987). Although these newer versions did indeed display stronger validity than the early DSMs, they too had some limitations in this realm.

TABLE 4-4

GLOBAL ASSESSMENT OF FUNCTIONING (GAF) SCALE

Consider psychological, social, and occupational functioning on a hypothetical continuum of mental health–illness. Do not include impairment in functioning due to physical (or environmental) limitations

CODE   (NOTE: USE INTERMEDIATE CODES WHEN APPROPRIATE, E.G., 45, 68, 72.)

100
|
91   Superior functioning in a wide range of activities, life's problems never seem to get out of hand, is sought out by others because of his or her many positive qualities. No symptoms.

90
|
81   Absent or minimal symptoms (e.g., mild anxiety before an exam), good functioning in all areas, interested and involved in a wide range of activities, socially effective, generally satisfied with life, no more than everyday problems or concerns (e.g., an occasional argument with family members).

80
|
71   If symptoms are present, they are transient and expectable reactions to psychosocial stressors (e.g., difficulty concentrating after family argument); no more than slight impairment in social, occupational, or school functioning (e.g., temporarily falling behind in schoolwork).

70
|
61   Some mild symptoms (e.g., depressed mood and mild insomnia) **or** some difficulty in social, occupational, or school functioning (e.g., occasional truancy, or theft within the household), but generally functioning pretty well, has some meaningful interpersonal relationships.

60
|
51   Moderate symptoms (e.g., flat affect and circumstantial speech, occasional panic attacks) **or** moderate difficulty in social, occupational, or school functioning (e.g., few friends, conflicts with peers or co-workers).

50
|
41   Serious symptoms (e.g., suicidal ideation, severe obsessional rituals, frequent shoplifting) **or** any serious impairment in social, occupational, or school functioning (e.g., no friends, unable to keep a job).

40
|
31   Some impairment in reality testing or communication (e.g., speech is at times illogical, obscure, or irrelevant) **or** major impairment in several areas, such as work or school, family relations, judgment, thinking, or mood (e.g., depressed man avoids friends, neglects family, and is unable to work; child frequently beats up younger children, is defiant at home, and is failing at school).

30
|
21   Behavior is considerably influenced by delusions or hallucinations **or** serious impairment in communication or judgment (e.g., sometimes incoherent, acts grossly inappropriately, suicidal preoccupation) **or** inability to function in almost all areas (e.g., stays in bed all day; no job, home, or friends).

20
|
11   Some danger of hurting self or others (e.g., suicide attempts without clear expectation of death; frequently violent; manic excitement) **or** occasionally fails to maintain minimal personal hygiene (e.g., smears feces) **or** gross impairment in communication (e.g., largely incoherent or mute).

10
|
1   Persistent danger of severely hurting self or others (e.g., recurrent violence) **or** persistent inability to maintain minimal personal hygiene **or** serious suicidal act with clear expectation of death.

0   Inadequate information.

Source: APA, 1994.

As the list of mental disorders grows ever longer, some clinical observers believe that normal behavior is increasingly being viewed as the somewhat drab absence of abnormal functioning.

NORMAL

DOMINANT SYMPTOMATOLOGY: Characterized by unimpaired occupational, social, and sexual functioning for a period of one year or more. During this time individuals are free of neurotic or psychotic symptoms, i.e., anxiety, depression, hallucinations, or delusional thinking. Judgment is good, self-esteem high. Age onset: birth. More commonly diagnosed in the early twentieth century, this condition is rarely seen today.

DSM-IV's task force and work groups tried to maximize the validity of this newest version of the DSM by again conducting comprehensive reviews of the most recent literature and directing many field trials to the issue of validity (see Box 4–4). Thus, the new criteria and categories of DSM-IV are expected to have stronger validity than earlier versions of the DSM, but like DSM-IV's reliability, the validity of this newest edition has yet to be broadly tested. It is reasonable to expect that it too will have at least some validity problems, given current areas of uncertainty in the field. That is, because the precise course of many disorders has yet to be determined, the predictive validity of those diagnoses is certain to be limited. Similarly, because the associated features of some disorders have yet to be identified, the concurrent diagnostic validity of those categories will inevitably be in question.

PROBLEMS OF CLINICAL MISINTERPRETATION

Even with trustworthy assessment data and reliable and valid classification categories, clinicians will sometimes arrive at a wrong conclusion (Woody & Robertson, 1988). Numerous factors can adversely af-

fect their thinking as they try to formulate a useful clinical picture and an appropriate diagnosis.

First, like all human beings, clinicians are flawed information processors. They often give too much weight to the data they encounter first and too little to data they acquire later (Meehl, 1960; Dailey, 1952). They may sometimes pay too much attention to certain sources of information, such as a parent's report about a child, and too little to others, such as the child's point of view (McCoy, 1976). And, finally, their judgments can be distorted by any number of personal biases—gender, age, race, and socioeconomic status, to name just a few (Fafabrega et al., 1994; Jenkins-Hall & Sacco, 1991; DiNardo, 1975; Broverman et al., 1970). In a recent study, for example, white American therapists were asked to watch a videotaped clinical interview and then to evaluate either an African American or a white American woman who either was or was not depressed. Although the therapists rated the nondepressed African American woman much the same as the nondepressed white American woman, they rated the depressed African American woman with more negative adjectives and judged her to be less socially competent than the depressed white American woman.

Second, clinicians may bring various misconceptions about methodology to the decision-making process (Reisman, 1991). Many think that the more assessment techniques they use, the more accurate

BOX 4-4

THE BATTLE OVER PREMENSTRUAL DYSPHORIC DISORDER

Some categories of mental dysfunctioning are much more controversial than others. Clinicians and even the public wage intense battles over their usefulness and appropriateness whenever DSM is revised. For example, after very long and heated discussions a decade ago, DSM-III dropped *homosexuality* as a category of mental dysfunctioning, citing a lack of evidence in support of such a category and concern about the continued social implications of calling this sexual preference abnormal. Similarly, battles ensued in 1987 when many practitioners wanted to include the category *self-defeating* (or *masochistic*) *personality disorder* in DSM to describe persons who display a pervasive pattern of undermining their own pleasurable experiences, being drawn to relationships or situations in which they suffer, and preventing others from helping them. Many critics feared this was a female-targeted category that would foster a harmful stereotype of women and would suggest that abused women were the cause of their damaging relationship rather than the victims of it. The framers of DSM-III-R ultimately agreed and did not enter it as an official category. Instead, they assigned it as a category "for further study." DSM-IV has dropped it altogether.

Perhaps the biggest controversy in the development of DSM-IV centered on the category *premenstrual dysphoric disorder (PMDD)*. After years of study, a DSM work group recommended in 1993 that this category be formally listed in the new DSM as a type of depressive disorder. The category was to be applied when a woman regularly experiences at least 5 of 11 symptoms during the week prior to menses: sad or hopeless feelings; tense or anxious feelings; marked mood changes; frequent irritability or anger and increased interpersonal conflicts; decreased interest in usual activities; lack of concentration; lack of energy; changes in appetite; insomnia or sleepiness; a subjective feeling of being overwhelmed or out of control; and physical symptoms such as swollen breasts, headaches, muscle pain, "bloating" sensations, or weight gain. To meet a diagnosis of PMDD, the work group stipulated that the symptoms must cause marked impairment and disappear completely soon after menstruation begins, and must have occurred most months for the previous year and be confirmed by at least two months of daily symptom ratings.

The work group claimed that women with this severe pattern of symptoms do not respond well to treatments used for other kinds of depression, such as antidepressant drugs, and therefore that PMDD needed to be researched and treated as a separate category. If it were not included, they argued, many women who are severely impaired by these symptoms would be denied treatment, and their very real problems would not be fully investigated or, in turn, properly understood.

This recommendation set off an uproar. Many clinicians (including some dissenting members of the work group itself), several national organizations, interest groups, and the media voiced their concern that this diagnostic category would "pathologize" severe cases of *premenstrual syndrome*, or *PMS*, the premenstrual discomforts that are common and normal in many women (Chase, 1993; DeAngelis, 1993). The National Organization of Women (NOW) argued that 42 percent of all women experience the vague and general symptoms of PMDD, and could qualify for a diagnosis (Chase, 1993), although the DSM work group estimated that only 5 percent of women would meet the recommended criteria. NOW also argued that a diagnosis of PMDD would cause women's behavior in general to be attributed largely to hormonal changes (a stereotype that society is finally rejecting), placing a stigma on women and promoting discrimination in courtrooms, in the workplace, and during child custody hearings.

Opponents of the new category also argued that there was insufficient data to include it. They claimed that the symptoms of PMDD have not been definitively linked to the menstrual cycle and that women who report having these symptoms show no biological differences from women who do not experience the symptoms. In addition, they said, clinicians have paid far less attention to the possible relationships between male hormones and mental health.

The solution to this huge controversy was a compromise. The PMDD category has not been listed formally in DSM-IV, but clinicians can, on their own, specify it under the broad category of *depressive disorder not otherwise specified*. In addition, DSM-IV describes the pattern and its criteria in the appendix and suggests that it be studied more in the coming years. Whether this "shadow" status will lead to formal inclusion in DSM-V or to the category's quiet disappearance is anyone's guess at this point. Meanwhile, the issue of PMDD illustrates the many important factors—scientific, social, political, and personal—that come into play in the development of a diagnostic system.

their interpretations will be—a belief that is not borne out by research (Kahneman & Tversky, 1973; Golden, 1964; Sines, 1959). Some also cling stubbornly to erroneous beliefs about the meaning of certain data. A classic study that investigated the interpretive processes used by thirty-two clinicians experienced in Rorschach testing revealed that the clinicians were inclined to diagnose male clients as homosexual whenever they made repeated references to human or animal anal images, feminine clothing, male or female genitalia, or similar themes in their Rorschach responses (Chapman & Chapman, 1967). Although research had repeatedly found no relationship between such Rorschach references and homosexuality, the clinicians adamantly clung to what the study's authors termed "illusory correlations" and continued to use them in making clinical judgments.

A third factor that can distort clinical interpretation is the clinicians' expectation that a person who consults them professionally must in fact have some disorder. Because they are looking for abnormal functioning, clinicians may overreact to any assessment data that suggest abnormality, a phenomenon that has been called the "reading-in syndrome" (Phares, 1979). The famous study by David Rosenhan (1973), discussed in Chapter 2, powerfully illustrates this problem. Eight normal people presented themselves at mental hospitals complaining that they had been hearing voices say the words "empty," "hollow," and "thud." On the basis of these complaints alone, hospital clinicians diagnosed these "pseudopatients" as schizophrenic and hospitalized them. Rosenhan was dismayed by how readily hospital clinicians made this diagnosis and how reluctant they were to change it. Although the pseudopatients dropped their symptoms immediately after being admitted to the hospital, the clinicians kept them hospitalized as long as fifty-two days. Apparently the setting in which these clinicians worked had primed them to expect and to diagnose certain kinds of mental disorders even when compelling clinical evidence was lacking.

Given such biases, misconceptions, and expectations, it is small wonder that investigations periodically uncover shocking errors in diagnosis, especially in hospitals. In one study a clinical team was asked to reevaluate the records of 131 randomly selected patients at a mental hospital in New York, conduct interviews with many of the patients, and arrive at a diagnosis for each patient (Lipton & Simon, 1985). The researchers then compared the team's diagnoses with the original ones. Although 89 of the patients had originally received a diagnosis of schizophrenia, only 16 received it upon reevaluation. And whereas 15 patients originally had been given a diagnosis of mood disorder, 50 received it now. Obviously, it is important for clinicians to be aware that diagnostic disagreements of this magnitude can occur.

DANGERS OF DIAGNOSING AND LABELING

Classification is intended to help clinicians understand, predict, and change abnormal behavior, but it can have some unfortunate and unintended consequences. As we saw in Chapter 2, some theorists believe that diagnostic labels may be self-fulfilling prophecies (Rosenhan, 1973; Szasz, 1961; Scheff, 1975). According to this notion, when a person is diagnosed as mentally disturbed, that label is often interpreted as a statement about the person's general behavior and potential. The person may therefore be viewed and treated in stereotyped ways, reacted to as sick or deficient, and expected to take on a sick role. In the Rosenhan (1973) study, for example, staff members spent limited time interacting with those labeled as patients, gave only brief responses to their questions, tended to be authoritarian in their dealings with the patients, and often made them feel invisible. In response to such attitudes and treatment, patients may increasingly consider themselves sick and deficient and eventually come to play the role that is expected of them. As the prophecy fulfills itself, the label "patient" seems justified.

Furthermore, our society attaches a stigma to abnormality, and as a result people labeled mentally ill may find it difficult to get a job, especially a position of responsibility, or to enter into social relationships. Indeed, they themselves may assume that they are incapable, irresponsible, or undesirable because of their emotional difficulties and may shy away from jobs or social interactions that they actually could handle perfectly well. These problems persist despite massive, concerted efforts by various mental health organizations to educate the public.

Similarly, once people receive a clinical diagnosis, it may stick to them for a long time. Clinicians, friends, relatives, and the people themselves may all continue to apply the label long after the disorder has disappeared.

Because of these problems, some clinicians would like to do away with the clinical field's reliance on diagnosis. Others disagree. Although they too recognize the limitations and negative consequences of classifying and labeling, they believe that the best remedy is to work toward increasing what is known about the various disorders and improving the means of diagnosing them (Akiskal, 1989). They hold that classification and diagnosis can yield valuable information that greatly advances the understanding and treatment of people in distress. To throw the information away would be too drastic a measure, one that would create more problems than it might solve.

SUMMARY

■ **CLINICAL PRACTITIONERS** are interested primarily in compiling *idiographic,* or individual, information about their clients. They seek a full understanding of the specific nature and origins of a client's problems through three steps: *assessment,* or the gathering of information about the person's problems; *interpretation,* or the piecing together of data to form a clinical picture of the person; and *diagnosis,* or the process of determining whether the person's dysfunction constitutes a particular psychological disorder.

■ **CLINICAL ASSESSMENT** is carried out before, during, and after treatment. The specific assessment techniques and tools that clinicians use often depend on their theoretical orientation. Most assessment methods fall into three general categories: clinical interviews, tests, and observations.

A *clinical interview* permits the practitioner to interact with a person and generally get a sense of who he or she is. The clinician may conduct either an *unstructured* or *structured* interview.

Clinical tests are devices that gather information about a few aspects of a person's psychological functioning from which broader information about that person can be inferred. They include *projective tests, personality inventories, narrow self-report inventories, psychophysiological tests, neuropsychological tests,* and *intelligence tests.* To be useful a test must be *standardized, reliable,* and *valid.*

Because each type of test falls short on one or more of the key criteria of standardization, reliability, and validity, clinicians generally administer a *battery* of tests to assess psychological functioning. Even so, the results are usually used only to clarify and supplement the information gathered in the clinical interview.

The third method of clinical assessment is *clinical observation.* Two strategies for observing people's behavior are *naturalistic observation* and *structured observation.* Practitioners also employ the related procedure of *self-monitoring:* subjects observe themselves and carefully record designated behavior, feelings, or cognitions as they occur throughout the day.

■ **CLINICIANS MUST INTERPRET** the information they have collected to arrive at a diagnosis of the person's problem. In general, it appears that clinicians use an *additive,* or *linear, model* when they interpret information about a client: they base their conclusions on the number of assessment responses that point in the same direction.

After collecting and interpreting the assessment information, clinicians form a *clinical picture,* which they often write as a psychological report framed by the language and premises of their own orientation.

■ **DIAGNOSIS** is the next step, a determination that a person's psychological problems constitute a particular mental disorder. A *classification system* lists recognized disorders and describes the symptoms characteristic of each. The system developed by the American Psychiatric Association is the *Diagnostic and Statistical Manual of Mental Disorders (DSM).*

The most recent version of the manual, known as *DSM-IV,* lists close to three hundred disorders. Clinicians who use it to make a diagnosis must evaluate a client's condition on five *axes,* or categories of information. The most recent versions of the DSM have proved to be somewhat more reliable and valid than earlier versions. Because DSM-IV is new, however, its reliability and validity have yet to receive broad clinical review.

Even with trustworthy assessment data and reliable and valid classification categories, clinicians will not always arrive at the correct conclusion. Many factors can mar their judgment. They may be overly influenced by the initial data they receive about a person; they may bring misconceptions about methodology to the decision-making process; they may cling to erroneous beliefs; and they may have preconceptions about a person who is seeking help. In other words, clinicians are human and fall prey to the biases, misconceptions, and expectations that beset us all.

Some people think that diagnosing a patient does more harm than good, because the labeling process and the prejudices that labels arouse may be damaging to the person being diagnosed. Nevertheless, most clinicians believe that classification and diagnosis yield valuable information that helps them understand and treat people in distress.

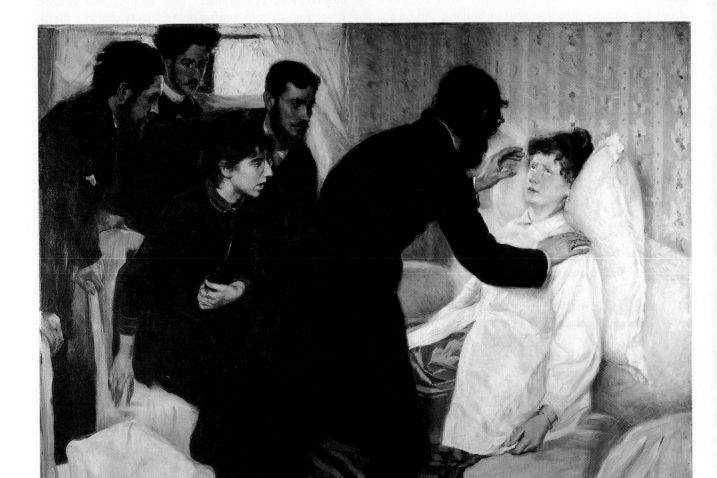

Topic Overview

C H A P T E R

TREATMENTS FOR ABNORMAL PSYCHOLOGICAL FUNCTIONING

February: He cannot leave the house; Bill knows that for a fact. Home is the only place where he feels safe—safe from humiliation, danger, even ruin. If he were to go to work, his co-workers would somehow reveal their contempt for him. A pointed remark, a quizzical look—that's all it would take for him to get the message. If he were to go shopping at the store, before long everyone would be staring at him. Surely others would see his dark mood and thoughts; he wouldn't be able to hide them. He dare not even go for a walk alone in the woods—his heart would probably start racing again, bringing him to his knees and leaving him breathless, incoherent, and unable to get home. No, he's much better off staying in his room, trying to get through another evening of this curse called life.

July: Bill's life revolves around his circle of friends: Bob and Jack, whom he knows from the office, where he was recently promoted to director of customer relations, and Frank and Tim, his weekend tennis partners. The gang meets for dinner every week at someone's house, and they chat about life, politics, and their jobs. Particularly special in Bill's life is Janice, with whom he has a promising relationship. They go to movies, restaurants, and shows together. She thinks Bill's just terrific, and Bill finds himself beaming whenever she's around. In fact, most people think Bill is terrific. They are eager to be with him and earn his respect, and Bill appreciates their admiration. He looks forward to work each day and his one-to-one dealings with customers. He is enjoying life and basking in the glow of his many activities and relationships.

BILL'S THOUGHTS, feelings, and behavior were so debilitating in February that they affected all aspects of his life. Most of his symptoms had disappeared by July, and he returned to his previous level of functioning. All sorts of factors may have contributed to Bill's improvement. Friends and family members may have offered support or advice. A new job or vacation may have lifted his spirits. Perhaps he changed his diet or started to exercise. Any or all of these things may have been useful to Bill, but they could not be considered therapy. That name is usually reserved for special, systematic processes for helping people overcome their psychological difficulties.

According to the clinical theorist Jerome Frank, all forms of therapy have three essential features:

1. A sufferer who seeks relief from the healer.
2. A trained, socially sanctioned healer, whose healing powers are accepted by the sufferer and his social group or an important segment of it.
3. A circumscribed, more or less structured series of contacts between the healer and the sufferer, through which the healer, often with the aid of a group, tries to produce certain changes in the sufferer's emotional state, attitudes, and behavior.

(Frank, 1973, pp. 2–3)

The healing process may be exercised primarily by **psychotherapy**—in Frank's words, "by words, acts, and rituals in which sufferer, healer, and—if there is one—group participate jointly," or by **biological therapy,** consisting of "physical and chemical procedures."

Frank's straightforward definition of therapy belies the conflict and confusion that characterize the field of clinical treatment. Carl Rogers, whom we met in Chapter 2 as the pioneer of the humanistic model, was moved to write, "Therapists are not in agreement as to their goals or aims. . . . They are not in agreement as to what constitutes a successful outcome of their work. They cannot agree as to what constitutes a failure. It seems as though the field is completely chaotic and divided."

Clinicians even differ on such basic issues as what to call the person undergoing therapy. This person is called the *patient* by clinicians who view abnormality as an illness and therapy as a procedure that corrects the illness, and the *client* by clinicians who see abnormality as a maladaptive way of behaving or thinking and who see therapists as teachers of more functional behavior and thought. Because both terms are so common in the field, they will be used more or less interchangeably throughout this book.

On the other hand, there is general agreement in the clinical field that large numbers of people are in need of therapy of one kind or another, and there is growing evidence that therapy is at least sometimes very helpful (Lambert & Bergin, 1994).

■ CLIENTS ■ AND THERAPISTS

Nationwide surveys of adults have suggested that between 16 and 22 million people in this country receive therapy for psychological problems in the course of a year (Kessler et al., 1994; Narrow et al., 1993; Regier et al., 1993). This figure represents approximately 12 percent of the entire adult population. It has become increasingly common for children to be treated for psychological problems, too (Kazdin, 1993; Biederman, 1992).

The number and variety of problems for which treatments are available have increased during this century (see Figure 5–1). When Freud and his colleagues first began to conduct therapy, most of their patients suffered from anxiety or depression. People with schizophrenia and other severe disorders were considered poor prospects for therapy, and treatment for them was confined to custodial care in institutions. The emergence of alternatives to psychodynamic therapies during the past several decades has helped change this situation. Anxiety and depression still dominate the therapy picture (almost half of today's clients in the United States suffer from these problems), but people with other kinds of disorders are also receiving therapy (Narrow et al., 1993). Now people with schizophrenic disorders and people with substance-related disorders each make up 5 to 10 percent of the clients in therapy (Narrow et al., 1993; Knesper, Pagnucco, & Wheeler, 1985). Moreover, large numbers of people with milder psychological problems, sometimes called "problems in living," are also in therapy. Surveys suggest that approximately 25 percent of clients enter therapy because of problems with marital, family, job, peer, school, or community relationships.

Other characteristics of clients have also changed over the years. Until the middle of this century, therapy was primarily a privilege of the wealthy, largely because of the high fees that outpatients were required to pay (Heller & Monahan, 1977; Hollingshead & Redlich, 1958). After all, Freud's fee for one session of therapy was 20 dollars ($160 in today's dollars) and the current cost of private outpatient therapy ranges from 50 to 160 dollars per session (Jaegerman, 1993). However, with the recent expansion of medical insurance coverage and the emergence of publicly supported community mental health centers, people at all socioeconomic levels now receive both outpatient and inpatient therapy (Simons, 1989; Knesper et al., 1985). Women used to outnumber men in therapy by two to one, partly

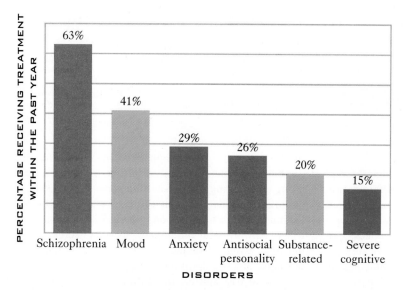

FIGURE 5-1   *Some psychological disorders are more likely to receive treatment than others. Almost two-thirds of Americans with schizophrenia have been treated within the past year, compared to less than one-third of those with a substance-related, anxiety, or severe cognitive disorder. (Adapted from Regier et al., 1993.)*

because they were less reluctant than men to seek help (Lichtenstein, 1980). Lately, however, our society's attitudes and sex-role expectations have been changing, and men are becoming increasingly willing to enter therapy. Almost half of today's therapy patients are male (Manderscheid & Sonnenschein, 1992). In contrast, ethnic minority groups often differ considerably in the rate at which they utilize therapy services (see Box 5-1).

The oldest of the modern adult therapy formats is individual, or one-to-one, therapy in which the therapist meets alone with a client, typically for weekly face-to-face sessions that last an hour. The frequency and length of sessions may vary, however, and orthodox psychoanalytic therapists have clients lie down instead of sit during therapy discussions.

People enter therapy in various ways. Many decide on their own to consult a psychotherapist. Others may do so on the advice of a minister, physician, or other professional with whom they have discussed their difficulties. Still others are forced into treatment. Parents, spouses, teachers, and employers may virtually order people to seek treatment if they are causing disruptions or are in obvious distress; or judges may formally pronounce people mentally ill and dangerous and commit them to a mental hospital for treatment.

The decision to seek therapy is rarely easy. Extensive studies indicate that most patients are aware of their problems well before they look for help (Strupp, Fox, & Lessler, 1969). Many wait more than two years after they first become aware that they have a problem. Generally speaking, therapy seems to hold few attractions for those who have no social network of "friends and supporters of psychotherapy" — people who have themselves been clients or who express confidence in psychotherapy as a solution to personal problems (Kadushin, 1969). During the 1970s the United Auto Workers negotiated a contract in which management agreed to pay the entire cost of both inpatient and outpatient mental health services for a million union members, yet after three years, only 1 percent of eligible workers had used the benefit (Brown, 1976). Apparently they and their referral agents (shop foremen, clergy, and the like) were unaware of the benefit, ignorant of what therapy could do for them, unlikely to think about personal

BOX 5-1

ETHNIC MINORITIES IN THE MENTAL HEALTH SYSTEM

Researchers and clinicians have recently become interested in the different use rates, dropout rates, and experiences of persons from ethnic minority groups in need of psychological services. For example, while African Americans and Native Americans use mental health services as often as white Americans, other ethnic groups, such as Asian Americans and Hispanic Americans, make less use of those services (Flaskerud & Hu, 1992; Sue, 1991, 1977; Sue et al., 1990). Sometimes ethnic minority groups are even less likely to seek treatment for specific kinds of mental disorders. For example, although African Americans in general make about the same use of mental health facilities as white Americans, African Americans who abuse drugs and alcohol are less likely to seek or complete treatment than white American drug and alcohol abusers (Booth et al., 1992; Longshore et al., 1992).

Several factors may lead to the underuse of mental health services by ethnic minority groups. Cultural beliefs, a language barrier, and lack of information about available services sometimes prevent minority individuals from seeking those services. People who need treatment for a mental

disorder may be more stigmatized in some cultures than in others. Furthermore, many members of minority groups simply do not trust the establishment, and rely instead on remedies traditional in their immediate social network. Some Hispanic persons, for example, practice spiritualism and believe that bad spirits can enter the body and cause mental disorders, and that good spirits can cure those disorders (Rogler, Malgady, & Rodriguez, 1989). Since these beliefs are incompatible with Western beliefs about mental disorders and traditional therapy, these Hispanic persons may seek help not from therapists but from folk healers, family members, and friends (Rogler et al., 1989).

Studies have also found that African Americans, Native Americans, Asian Americans, and Hispanic Americans all have higher therapy dropout rates than white Americans (Wierzbicki & Pekarik, 1993). This finding may be due in part to the fact that the dropout rate is higher among poorer clients (Wierzbicki & Pekarik, 1993), and ethnic minorities are overrepresented in lower-income groups. In addition, members of ethnic minority groups may terminate treatment because they do not feel that they are benefiting from therapy or because ethnic and

cultural differences keep them from experiencing rapport with their therapist (Sue, 1991).

Asian American and Hispanic adolescents also appear to be underrepresented in the mental health system, though African American adolescents are not (Bui & Takeuchi, 1992; Mason & Gibbs, 1992). One study of adolescents in California found that Hispanic adolescents represented 32 percent of the general population under 18 years of age but less than 10 percent of adolescents in mental health facilities (Mason & Gibbs, 1992). Similarly, Asian American adolescents represented approximately 9 percent of the population under 18 years of age in California but only 2 percent of adolescents in mental health facilities. African American adolescents represented approximately 6.5 percent of both the state and treatment populations. Cultural and language barriers may contribute to the underuse of mental health facilities by Asian American and Hispanic adolescents. In addition, several researchers have suggested that ethnic and racial minority adolescents with mental disorders, behavior problems, or both are more likely to be placed in the juvenile justice system than to be treated in a mental health facility (Mason et al.,

problems in mental health terms, or worried about the stigma that mental problems might bring in their social set.

The length of time people spend in therapy varies with the nature of the problem and the approach the therapist takes. More than half of all clients visit their therapist fifteen times or fewer (Narrow et al., 1993; Knesper et al., 1985). At the other extreme, a small percentage of people continue in therapy for much of their lives.

When problems are not severe, longer-term treatment generally leads to more improvement than shorter-term treatment. An analysis of 2,400 patients with symptoms of anxiety and depression found that whereas 50 percent had improved significantly after eight sessions of therapy, 75 percent had improved after twenty-six sessions (Howard et al., 1986). On the other hand, even long-term treatment generally has a limited effect on severe psychological problems. People with severe problems generally receive longer and

1992; Gibbs, 1990; Meyers, 1989; Dembo, 1988).

The California study also found that ethnic minority adolescents differ in the *type* of mental health facility where they are most likely to be treated. Hispanic American, Asian American, and African American adolescents were more likely to be treated in public hospitals, whereas white American adolescents were more likely to be treated in private mental hospitals (Mason & Gibbs, 1992). One explanation for this difference is that white American adolescents are more likely to have private insurance and thus to be able to afford treatment in private hospitals, while the ethnic minority adolescents are more likely to need public funding for their treatment, and thus to be placed in public facilities (Mason & Gibbs, 1992). Another consequence of the reliance on public funding by many ethnic minority adolescents is that they have shorter hospitalizations than privately insured white American adolescents, who can afford longer hospitalizations (Mason & Gibbs, 1992).

Some clinicians have recently developed a number of *culture-sensitive therapies,* approaches that are designed to address the unique issues and pressures faced by members of minority groups, especially when the issues contribute largely to the clients' emotional problems (Prochaska & Norcross, 1994; Watkins-Duncan, 1992). These approaches often include features such as (1) raising the consciousness of clients about the impact of the dominant culture and their own culture on their self-views and behaviors, (2) helping clients express suppressed anger and come to terms with their pain, and (3) helping clients make choices that work for them and achieve a bicultural identity and balance that feels right for them.

Researchers have also begun to intensify their investigations into the treatment of persons from ethnic minority groups. This body of research is very limited so far, but a few preliminary trends have emerged (Sue, Zane, & Young, 1994; Prochaska & Norcross, 1994):

1. Ethnic minority groups are generally underserved in the mental health field.

2. Clients from ethnic minorities appear to improve as much as white Americans in some studies, and less in other studies; in no comparative study, however, do they improve more than white American clients.

3. Clients from ethnic minority groups tend to prefer therapists who are ethnically similar to themselves, although this is but one of many characteristics preferred by such clients.

4. Some, but clearly not all, studies suggest that having an ethnically-similar therapist improves the outcome of treatment, certainly in cases where the client's primary language is not English.

5. According to preliminary reports from the scant research on culture-sensitive treatment, features which increase the effectiveness of treatment are: heightened therapist sensitivity to cultural issues, inclusion of cultural morals and models in treatment (especially in therapies for children and adolescents), and pre-therapy intervention programs in which clients from certain ethnic groups are initially introduced to what psychotherapy is, how it can help, what therapy behaviors are required of them, and what to expect.

6. Reviews of research have often made the mistake of lumping together subjects from different ethnic minority groups and failing to consider the important differences between such groups. Similarly, research has only recently begun to consider the important individual differences that exist *within* each ethnic minority group.

All of this research makes clear the urgency of efforts to address ethnic minority issues in both research and practice, to increase the number of ethnic minority clinicians and the availability of their services, and to increase the sensitivity of all health-care providers to the cultures and needs of ethnic minority populations. Studies have found that in cities where the specific needs of the various ethnic groups have been addressed, the numbers of persons in these groups who use such services have increased and the clients are more satisfied with the services they receive and are more likely to continue treatment (O'Sullivan et al., 1989; Rodriguez, 1986; Fischman et al., 1983).

more intense treatment than people with milder problems (Ware et al., 1984), but they are still more impaired at the end (Knesper et al., 1985).

A variety of professionals conduct therapy today (see Figure 5–2); most are psychologists, psychiatrists, and psychiatric social workers. Whatever their profession, these therapists generally see the same kinds of patients (Knesper et al., 1985); that is, the majority of their clients are people with anxiety, depression, or relationship problems. At the same time, psychiatrists see a somewhat larger number of patients with schizophrenia and other severe disorders (16 percent of their cases) than do psychologists (5 percent) or social workers (7 percent). The providers of mental health services are concentrated in urban areas across the United States. In fact, there is a severe shortage of practitioners available to serve the needs of the 50 million people who live in the towns, villages, farms, and countryside of rural America (Human & Wasem, 1991; Murray & Keller, 1991).

Therapy takes place in all sorts of settings, from public institutions to schools to private offices. Most clients, even those who are severely disturbed, are treated as outpatients (Narrow et al., 1993); they live in the community and make regular visits to the therapist's office. Outpatients with higher incomes tend to be treated in private offices while many of those with lower incomes are treated at publicly supported community mental health centers (Knesper et al., 1985). Whatever the patients' psychological problems, therapy sessions in community mental health centers tend to be shorter, less frequent, and fewer than those offered by private therapists (Knesper et al., 1985).

Most of the people who receive inpatient treatment, whether in privately funded or public institutions, such as state mental hospitals, have severe psychological problems. The private institutions usually offer better physical facilities, more trained staff members per patient, and more varied treatments (Redick et al., 1992). Personal wealth, more than any other factor, determines whether a patient is treated in a private or a public institution. In the 1980s the average annual income of patients who received treatment in private hospitals was approximately $18,000, whereas the average income of patients treated in public hospitals was under $8,000 a year (Knesper et al., 1985).

As we also saw briefly in Chapter 1, clinicians have become increasingly concerned about the negative effects of long-term institutionalization and have carried out a policy of deinstitutionalization during the past three decades. Whereas close to 600,000 patients were being cared for in public mental hospitals on any given day in 1955, approximately 100,000 populate the same institutions today. Hospitalization now usually lasts weeks instead of months or years. When people develop severe mental disorders, therapists now try to treat them first as outpatients. If this strategy proves ineffective, the patient may be admitted to a hospital for a short period so that the condition can be monitored, diagnosed, and stabilized. As soon as hospitalization has served this purpose, the patient is returned to the community. In theory, this may be a reasonable treatment plan; but, as we observed in Chapter 1 and will see in more detail in Chapter 16, community treatment facilities have been so underfunded and understaffed over the years that they have not been able to meet the treatment needs of the majority of severely impaired people (see Box 5–2), and hundreds of thousands of people have been condemned to an endless cycle of hospital discharges and readmissions.

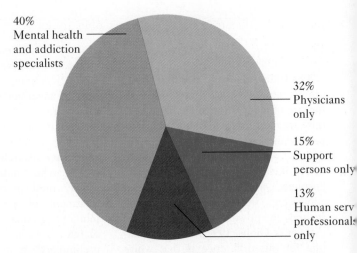

FIGURE 5–2   *Where do people with psychological problems seek help? Approximately 40 percent of the Americans who receive treatment see mental health or addiction specialists. Another 32 percent see a physician only; 13 percent work exclusively with a human service professional, such as a religious or social service counselor; and 15 percent discuss their problems only with support persons, such as a self-help group, family member, or friend. (Adapted from Regier et al., 1993.)*

■ SYSTEMS ■ OF THERAPY

In the clinical field today there are as many as 400 forms of therapy, each practiced by clinicians who believe that their chosen methodology is highly effective (Garfield & Bergin, 1994; Karasu, 1992). One way to start sorting out these many approaches is to distinguish therapy systems from therapy formats. A *system* of therapy is a set of principles and techniques employed in accordance with a particular theory of change. Carl Rogers's humanistic theory, for example, identifies self-awareness and self-actualization as fundamental to good mental health. Therapists who follow his "client-centered" system listen to and empathize with clients, expecting that such techniques will help the clients become aware of themselves and able to actualize their special human potential. A system of therapy may be applied in any of several *formats.* Rogers's client-centered therapy has been employed in individual, group, family, and couple therapy formats. In this section we shall discuss the clinical field's most influential therapy systems. In the next section, we shall examine the principal formats.

Each system of therapy approaches psychological treatment in its own way. In some systems therapists concentrate on helping clients gain insight into their problems, while in others they seek only to change the clients' behavior. In some systems therapists have a medical orientation and treat their clients as patients recovering from an illness; in others the therapists have an educational orientation and treat psychological problems as maladaptive patterns in need of corrective training. We shall be paying particular attention to whether a therapy system is global or problem-based. Therapists who provide **global therapies** try to help clients recognize and change general features of their personality that the therapists believe are at the root of the problem. Therapists who engage in **problem-based therapies** focus attention primarily on the symptoms; they address specific complaints without delving into broad personality issues.

GLOBAL THERAPIES

Therapists who explain psychological problems by pointing to fundamental characteristics of a client's personality proceed in much the same way with every client, regardless of the particular symptoms. For this reason there is a considerable sameness in global treatments from client to client. This is not to say that global treatments are identical for all clients. On the contrary, each person's life, conflicts, problems, and family dynamics are unique, as are the person's therapy issues, reactions, defenses, and capacity for insight. Therapists must apply their techniques in ways that address this uniqueness. The primary global therapies are the *psychodynamic therapies* and the *humanistic-existential therapies*.

PSYCHODYNAMIC THERAPIES Adhering to the principles of the psychodynamic model, psychodynamic therapists contend that today's emotional disorder is the result of yesterday's emotional trauma. A variety of psychodynamic therapies are now being practiced, ranging from classical *Freudian psychoanalysis* to modern therapies based on *object relations theory* or *self theory*. All share the goals of helping clients to uncover past traumatic events and the inner conflicts that have resulted from them; to resolve, or settle, those conflicts; and to resume interrupted personal development (Arlow, 1989; Wolberg, 1987). Because awareness is the key to psychodynamic therapy, this system is considered an "insight therapy."

According to psychodynamic therapists, the process of gaining insight cannot be rushed or imposed. If therapists were simply to tell clients about their inner conflicts, the explanations would sound "off the wall" and the clients would not accept them. Thus therapists must subtly guide the therapeutic discussions so that the patients discover their underlying problems

(Drawing by Shanahan; © 1992 The New Yorker Magazine, Inc.)

BOX 5-2

COMMUNITY MENTAL HEALTH: A MOVEMENT FORWARD AND BACKWARD

In 1963 President John Kennedy called for a "bold new approach" to the treatment of mental disorders—a community approach in which most people with psychological difficulties would receive mental health services from nearby publicly funded agencies. Soon after Kennedy's proclamation, Congress passed the Community Mental Health Act, launching the *community mental health movement* across the United States.

In the decades since then, this movement has had both positive and negative consequences. On the one hand, it has increased the mental health services available to people with mild or moderate disturbances. On the other hand, it has inadvertently narrowed the treatment options available to those with severe mental disorders by leading to a decrease in the number of state mental hospital services without a corresponding increase in community services for such individuals. Some clinicians, then, see the community movement as a major step forward for the field while others consider it a plan that has gone awry.

One aspect of the community movement that advocates and critics both seem to like is the principle of *prevention* that lies at its core (Price, 1988). The mandate to prevent, or at least minimize, mental disorders broadened the domain of the clinical field and has instilled in clinicians an active (go after the client) attitude that contrasts with the passive (wait for the client) posture of traditional therapy. Community workers generally pursue three types of prevention: primary, secondary, and tertiary (Okin & Borus, 1989; Albee, 1982; Caplan, 1964).

Primary prevention consists of efforts to improve community attitudes and policies, with the goal of preventing mental disorders altogether. Community workers may, for example, lobby for better community recreational programs or child-care facilities, consult with a local school board to help formulate a curriculum, or offer public workshops on stress reduction.

Community workers engaged in *secondary prevention* try to identify and treat mental disorders at their earliest stages of development and thus prevent the disorders from reaching more serious levels. Workers may, for instance, consult with schoolteachers, ministers, or police to help them recognize the early signs of psychological dysfunction and teach them how to help people find appropriate treatment (Zax & Cowen, 1976, 1969). Similarly, communities may offer hotlines or walk-in clinics that encourage individuals to make early treatment contacts and receive immediate help before their psychological problems get worse.

Community workers who practice *tertiary prevention* seek to prevent moderate or severe mental disorders from becoming long-term problems by providing appropriate and effective treatment when it is needed. Tertiary care has been provided for millions of people with moderate psychological problems, such as anxiety disorders, through traditional therapy at commu-

---

for themselves. To help them do so, psychodynamic therapists rely on such techniques as *free association, therapist interpretation, catharsis,* and *working through.* Although psychodynamic therapists of different theoretical persuasions focus on different underlying problems (for example, an object relations therapist would focus primarily on problems in early relationships, while a Freudian therapist would spend more time discussing unresolved psychosexual conflicts), all psychodynamic therapists rely on essentially the same techniques.

FREE ASSOCIATION   In psychodynamic therapies the patient is responsible for initiating and leading each discussion. The therapist tells the patient to describe any thought, feeling, or image that comes to mind, even if it seems unimportant or irrelevant. This is the process known as *free association.* The therapist probes the patient's associations, expecting that they will eventually reveal unconscious events and unearth the dynamics underlying the individual's personality. Notice how free association helps the woman quoted below to discover threatening impulses and conflicts within her. She begins by describing a recent experience.

Patient: So I started walking, and walking, and decided to go behind the museum and walk through Central Park. So I walked and went through a back field and felt very excited and wonderful. I saw a park bench next to a clump of bushes and sat down. There was a rustle behind

nity mental health centers across the country. Community programs have generally failed, however, to provide the tertiary services needed for severely disturbed persons—*day centers* (or *day hospitals*), treatment facilities that provide day-long activities and treatment; *halfway houses,* residential group homes where live-in staff offer support, guidance, and practical advice to residents; and *sheltered workshops,* protected and supervised workplaces that offer clients occupational training. These tertiary services are in such short supply in most communities that hundreds of thousands of severely disturbed people deteriorate steadily without proper care.

Why has the community mental health approach fallen short for so many people? One of the major reasons is lack of funding. In 1981, when only 750 of the planned 2,000 community mental health centers were in place, virtually all federal funding was withdrawn and replaced with smaller financial grants to the states. As a result, the existing centers have been forced to focus much of their effort on financial survival (Humphreys & Rappaport, 1993).

In addition, in a rather odd development in recent years, federal funds that were once marked for community mental health centers have instead been put into programs for the treat-

Abuse hot-line operators in New York City receive calls from victims of abuse, or from their relatives or neighbors, and set in motion programs to help the victims and prevent further abuse.

ment and prevention of substance abuse (Humphreys & Rappaport, 1993). Ironically, as funding has drifted into substance abuse treatment agencies, so have many of the community mental health centers' former clientele, people whose substance abuse is associated with domestic violence, depression, anxiety disorders, and social dysfunctioning (Humphreys & Rappaport, 1993; Gorney, 1989; Stoffelmayr et al., 1989). In other words, substance-related problems

have become an entree to treatment for many people with diverse social and psychological problems.

This shift in problem definition bothers many clinicians, who see it as a way to transfer the responsibility for mental disorders onto the victims themselves, since substance-related problems have traditionally been viewed by the public as the result of some personal defect (Humphreys & Rappaport, 1993). They fear that the injunction to "Just say no" will increasingly and inappropriately be shifted from substance abuse to depression and other mental disorders.

Whether or not such trends will characterize community mental health for the remainder of the 1990s is unclear. It will depend partly on how health care is reformed (Kiesler, 1992) and also on how state legislatures decide to allocate the money saved by the continuing closing of large state hospitals. Mental health advocates continue to urge politicians to put those savings, which may exceed $200 million in states such as New York, into community-based programs, but their advice may not be heeded. In the meantime, while the promise of community mental health and, in particular, community prevention remains worthy and exciting, for many in our society it is a promise largely unfulfilled.

me and I got frightened. I thought of men concealing themselves in the bushes. I thought of the sex perverts I read about in Central Park. I wondered if there was someone behind me exposing himself. The idea is repulsive, but exciting too. I think of father now and feel excited. I think of an erect penis. This is connected with my father. There is something about this pushing in my mind. I don't know what it is, like on the border of my memory. (Pause)

Therapist: Mm-hmm. (Pause) On the border of your memory?

Patient: (The patient breathes rapidly and seems to be under great tension.) As a little girl, I slept with my father. I get a funny feeling. I get a funny feeling over my skin, tingly-like. It's a strange feeling, like a blindness, like not see-

ing something. My mind blurs and spreads over anything I look at. I've had this feeling off and on since I walked in the park. My mind seems to blank off like I can't think or absorb anything.

(Wolberg, 1967, p. 662)

THERAPIST INTERPRETATION Although psychodynamic therapists allow the patient to generate the discussion, they are privately trying to piece together a psychodynamic explanation of the person's disorder. They are listening carefully, looking for clues, and drawing tentative conclusions. They share their interpretations with the patient when they think the patient is ready to hear them. Otto Fenichel (1945), a highly respected psychodynamic theorist, once said that psychodynamic therapists should propose what is already apparent to the patient "and just a little bit more." The interpretation of three phenomena that occur during therapy is particularly important—*resistance*, *transference*, and *dreams*.

Patients demonstrate **resistance** when they encounter a block in their free associations or change the subject so as to avoid a potentially painful discussion. Having spent a lifetime using ego defense mechanisms to defend against their unconscious conflicts, people usually resist discussions that threaten to uncover those conflicts. Through the entire course of therapy, the therapist remains on the lookout for resistance, which is usually unconscious, and may point it out to the patient and interpret it. Consider again the woman who walked in Central Park. "My mind seems to blank off . . . ," she says. The therapist interprets the sensation as resistance, and helps her to move further along:

Therapist: The blurring of your mind may be a way of pushing something out you don't want there. [Interpreting her symptoms as resistance.]

Patient: I just thought of something. When father died, he was nude. I looked at him, but I couldn't see anything. I couldn't think clearly. I was brought up not to be aware of the difference between a man and a woman. I feared my father, and yet I loved him. I slept with him when I was very little, on Saturdays and Sundays. A wonderful sense of warmth and security. There was nothing warmer or more secure. A lot of pleasure. I tingle all over now. It was a wonderful holiday when I was allowed to sleep with father. I can't seem to remember anything now. There's a blur in my mind. I feel tense and afraid.

Therapist: That blur contaminates your life. You are afraid of something or afraid of remembering something. [Focusing on her resistance.]

Patient: Yes, yes, but I can't. How can I? How can I?

Therapist: What comes to your mind?

(Wolberg, 1967, p. 662)

Psychodynamic therapists also believe that patients act and feel toward the therapist as they did toward important figures in their childhood, especially their parents and siblings. By interpreting this **transference** behavior, therapists may better understand how a patient unconsciously feels toward a parent or some other significant person in the patient's life. As the woman continues talking, the therapist helps her to explore some transference issues:

Patient: I get so excited by what is happening here. I feel I'm being held back by needing to be nice. I'd like to blast loose sometimes, but I don't dare.

Therapist: Because you fear my reaction?

Patient: The worst thing would be that you wouldn't like me. You wouldn't speak to me friendly; you wouldn't smile; you'd feel you can't treat me and discharge me from treatment. But I know this isn't so, I know it.

Therapist: Where do you think these attitudes come from?

Patient: When I was nine years old, I read a lot about great men in history. I'd quote them and be dramatic. I'd want a sword at my side; I'd dress like an Indian. Mother would scold me. Don't frown, don't talk so much. Sit on your hands, over and over again. I did all kinds of things. I was a naughty child. She told me I'd be hurt. Then at fourteen I fell off a horse and broke my back. I had to be in bed. Mother then told me on the day I went riding not to, that I'd get hurt because the ground was frozen. I was a stubborn, self-willed child. Then I went against her will and suffered an accident that changed my life, a fractured back. Her attitude was, "I told you so." I was put in a cast and kept in bed for months.

Therapist: You were punished, so to speak, by this accident.

Patient: But I gained attention and love from mother for the first time. I felt so good. I'm ashamed to tell you this. Before I healed I opened the cast and tried to walk to make myself sick again so I could stay in bed longer.

Therapist: How does that connect up with your impulse to be sick now and stay in bed so much?

Patient: Oh . . . *(Pause)*

Therapist: What do you think?

Patient: Oh, my God, how infantile, how ungrown up. *(Pause)* It must be so. I want people to love me and be sorry for me. Oh, my God. How completely childish. . . . My mother must have ignored me when I was little, and I wanted so to be loved.

(Wolberg, 1967, p. 662)

Because the therapist's interpretations play such a major role in psychodynamic therapy, psychodynamic therapists must make every effort to listen and interpret without bias. This is easier said than done. Therapists are human beings with feelings, histories, and values that can subtly influence the way they listen to and interpret their patients' problems. Freudian therapists view this unintentional **countertransference** of the therapist's personal issues onto the patient as a detrimental process that could undermine the therapeutic process, and are thus careful to observe and analyze their own feelings as well as their patients'. In fact, this is one reason that during their training they are required to undergo therapy with a so-called training analyst. Some other psychodynamic theorists, however, tend to view countertransference more positively. Object relations therapists, for example, believe that countertransference comes about because of a process called *projective identification,* in which patients unconsciously act out the hostile, dependent, or seductive patterns of their early relationships in ways that *cause* others to respond accordingly. Rather than being an undesired reflection of the therapist's personal conflicts, countertransference is understood as the therapist's natural response to the patient's projective identifications, which yields valuable information about the patient (Cashdan, 1988).

Finally, many psychodynamic therapists try to help patients interpret their **dreams.** Freud (1924) called dreams the "royal road to the unconscious." He believed that repression and other defense mechanisms operate less completely during sleep. Thus a patient's dreams, correctly interpreted, can reveal the person's unconscious instincts, needs, and wishes (see Box 5–3).

Freud defined two kinds of dream content, manifest and latent. **Manifest content** is the consciously remembered dream, **latent content** its symbolic meaning. To interpret a dream, therapists must translate its manifest content into its latent content. Every dream is unique and has unique implications for the dreamer, but psychodynamic therapists believe that some types of manifest content are universal and have much the same meaning in everybody's dreams. For example, a house's basement, downstairs, upstairs, attic, and front porch are often identified as symbols of anatomical parts of the body (Lichtenstein, 1980).

Freud's office is dominated by the key tools of his therapy: a couch, a desk, and a writing pad. Freud had patients lie on the couch during therapy, while he sat behind them taking notes. He believed that this arrangement heightened concentration and facilitated the patient's free associations and recall of important memories or dream material.

CATHARSIS   Insight must be an emotional as well as intellectual process. Psychodynamic therapists believe that patients must experience **catharsis,** a reliving of past repressed feelings, if they are to settle internal conflicts and overcome their problems. Only when catharsis accompanies intellectual insight is genuine progress achieved.

WORKING THROUGH AND RESOLVING A PROBLEM   A single session of interpretation and catharsis will not change a person. For deep and lasting insight to be gained, the patient and therapist must examine the same issues over and over in the course of many sessions, each time with new and sharper clarity. This process is called *working through.*

Working through a disorder can take a long time, so psychodynamic treatment is usually a long-term proposition. Many of Freud's patients came to him for therapy sessions every day for several years. In the 1930s, however, Franz Alexander (1950, 1936, 1930) proposed that weekly sessions might be sufficient for many people, and started a trend that has continued to the present day.

Psychodynamic treatment offered once a week—as most forms of it now are—is properly known as *psychodynamic,* or *psychoanalytic, therapy.* The term *psychoanalysis,* or simply *analysis,* is reserved for therapy given on a daily basis. Analysis is usually conducted by *analysts,* psychoanalytic therapists who receive several extra years of training in a psychoanalytic training institute after earning their graduate degree in psychiatry, psychology, or social work.

SHORT-TERM PSYCHODYNAMIC THERAPIES   In recent years, several therapists have developed a much shorter version of psychodynamic therapy (Sifneos, 1992, 1987; Strupp & Binder, 1984; Luborsky, 1984; Davanloo, 1980; Malan, 1980). Their goal is to retain the basic concepts of psychodynamic theory, yet reduce the overall length of treatment by narrowing the goals and focus of therapy discussions and by more actively directing therapy discussions.

In these short-term psychodynamic therapies, patients identify a single problem or issue—a *dynamic focus*—early in therapy, such as difficulty getting along with certain persons or a marital problem. The therapist helps the patient maintain attention on this focus throughout treatment and helps him or her work only on psychodynamic issues, such as an unresolved Oedipal conflict, that relate to the focus. It is expected that resolution of this focus will generalize to other important life situations.

Typically, the short-term therapists pay particular attention to transference reactions. They help the patient relate patient-therapist interactions to current

BOX 5-3

PERCHANCE TO DREAM

All people dream; so do dogs, and maybe even fish. But what purpose do dreams serve? Some claim that dreams reveal the future; others see them as inner journeys or alternate realities. The Greek philosopher Plato saw dreams as reflections of inner turmoil and wish fulfillment,

. . . desires which are awake when the reasoning and taming and ruling power of the personality is asleep; the wild beast in our nature, gorged with meat and drink, starts up and walks about naked, and surfeits at his will . . . In all of us, even in good men, there is such a latent wild beast nature, which peers out in sleep.

(Phaedrus, c. 380 B.C.)

Psychodynamic therapists consider dreams to be highly revealing. Rather like Plato, Sigmund Freud (1900) contended that dreaming is a mechanism with which we express and attempt to fulfill the unsatisfied desires we spend our lives pursuing. His colleague Carl Jung (1909) also believed them to be expressions of the unconscious psyche. And another colleague, Alfred Adler, believed that dreams serve to prepare us for waking life by providing a medium for solving the problems we anticipate: they give us a setting in which to rehearse new behavior patterns or alert us to internal problems of which we have not been aware (Kramer, 1992). All of these theorists

claimed that patients would benefit from interpreting their dreams in therapy and understanding the underlying needs, aspirations, and conflicts symbolized therein.

Biological theorists offer a different, though not entirely incompatible, view of dreams. In 1977, J. Allan Hobson and Robert McCarley proposed an *activation-synthesis* model of dreams. They claimed that during *REM sleep* (the stage of sleep characterized by rapid eye movement, or *REM*), memories are elicited by random signals from the brain stem—in evolutionary terms, a very old region of the brain. The brain's cortex, the seat of higher cognitive functioning, attempts to make sense of this random bombardment of electrical activity. The result is a dream, often irrational or weird, but the best fit given the variety of signals received by the cortex (Begley, 1989). Hobson later revised the theory to include the idea that the resulting dream, far from being arbitrary, is influenced by the dreamer's drives, fears, and ambitions.

More recently the neuroscientist Jonathan Winson of Rockefeller University contended that dreams are a "nightly record of a basic mammalian process: the means by which animals form strategies for survival and evaluate current experience in light of those strategies" (Winson, 1990). By recording electrical activity in the brains of sleeping and awake nonprimate mam-

mals, Winson found that the brain waves of animals during dreaming were similar to their brain waves when they were engaged in survival activities. Thus Winson concluded that dreams are a means of reprocessing information necessary for an animal's survival. The information is "accessed again and integrated with past experience to provide an ongoing strategy for behavior" (Winson, 1990). In essence, dreams rehash, reprocess, and reevaluate the day's activities, in preparation for the next day's fight for survival.

Surveys and studies of the content of human dreams have revealed some interesting patterns. For example, two thirds of people's dreams involve unpleasant material, such as aggression, threats, rejection, confusion, or an inability to communicate (Van de Castle, 1993). Commonly, a dreamer is pursued or in some way attacked by a threatening figure. Such chase dreams have often been taken to mean that the dreamers are running from internal fears or issues that they do not want to face, or from someone in their lives whom they do not trust.

Eighty percent of college students report having had dreams of falling. Such dreams are thought by some theorists to occur when our sense of security is threatened or when we are in fear of losing control. Many people say falling dreams are the first ones they can remember, although people can

and past interpersonal relationships that may account for the present difficulties.

From the beginning, the therapist tells the patient that therapy will last for a fixed number of sessions, usually fewer than thirty. Theoretically, the time limit motivates the patient to explore his or her dynamic focus and to experiment with new behavior. The time limit also requires that the therapist sometimes be more anxiety-provoking or confrontational when making interpretations. People with high motivation,

intelligence, and tolerance for anxiety and frustration are considered good candidates for these approaches; severely disturbed, suicidal, and drug-dependent patients are not. Freud himself tried short-term therapy with some of his patients and judged it to be relatively effective "provided that one hits the right time at which to employ it." Only a limited number of studies have been conducted on the effectiveness of the newer short-term psychodynamic approaches, but they do suggest that the interventions

have them at any stage of life (Van de Castle, 1993; Cartwright & Lamberg, 1992).

In some studies, one third of subjects claim to have had dreams in which they have the ability to fly (Van de Castle, 1993); however, in a laboratory study, flying occurred in only one out of 635 dreams (Hennager 1993; Snyder, 1970). These results are not necessarily contradictory; even if flying dreams occur infrequently, they may still occur at least once in the lives of many people. Dreams of flying tend to be associated with positive feelings. Freud considered them to be a symbol of sexual desire; others see them as an expression of freedom, like "being on top of the world" (Hennager, 1993; Jung, 1967; Adler, 1931, 1927).

Another common theme is public nudity. The incidence of such dreams appears to vary across cultures. One study found that 43 percent of American college-age subjects reported having them, compared to 18 percent of Japanese subjects (Vieira, 1993; Griffith et al., 1958). Freud (1900) viewed dreams of nudity as an unconscious wish to exhibit oneself. Other theorists contend that people having these dreams may be afraid of being seen for who they really are (Van de Castle, 1993).

Dreams are also distinguished by gender. Some observers have said that the dreams of American women have more in common with the dreams of

The Nightmare *by Johann Einrich Füssli*

Aboriginal women than with those of American men (Kramer, 1989). In a landmark dream study in 1951, researcher Calvin Hall found that men dreamed twice as often about men as they did about women; whereas women dreamed about men and women in equal proportions. In addition, most male dreams took place in outdoor settings, while female dreams were more often set in the home or indoors. Men's sexual dreams were more likely to include women they did not know; whereas women dreamed more often about men they cared for. In 1980, Hall and his colleagues com-

pared the dream content of college-aged men and women with the data he had recorded in 1950 and found no significant changes (Van de Castle, 1993). Other researchers are finding that dreams of men and women are becoming more androgynous, that the dreams of women now take place outdoors more than they did in the past, and that women are now as likely as men to behave aggressively in their dreams (Kramer, 1989).

Finally, the research on dreams has succeeded in putting a number of myths to rest (Walsh & Engelhardt, 1993):

Myth #1: Some people never dream. Actually, all human beings experience three to six periods of REM sleep each night, and dreaming probably occurs in every one.

Myth #2: Dreams are experienced in black and white. Laboratory studies show that everyone dreams in color.

Myth #3: All the places in your dreams are places you have been. Many people dream about places or things they have never seen. Some researchers believe these represent compilations of images or things that are familiar to us.

Myth #4: If you die in your dreams, you will die in actuality. There are people who have reported dying in their dreams, and, thank goodness, remain alive to tell about it.

are sometimes quite helpful to patients (Messer et al., 1992; Crits-Christoph, 1992).

ASSESSING PSYCHODYNAMIC THERAPIES Freud and his many followers have had a most significant impact on the treatment of abnormal psychological functioning. They were the first practitioners to demonstrate the value of systematically applying theory and techniques to treatment. In addition, their systems of therapy were the first to underscore the potential of psychological, as opposed

to biological, treatment and have served as a starting point for many other psychological treatments.

On the other hand, systematic research has generally failed to support the effectiveness of psychodynamic therapies. For the first half of the twentieth century, the value of these approaches was supported principally by the case studies of enthusiastic psychodynamic clinicians and by uncontrolled research studies. Controlled investigations have been conducted only since the 1950s, and only a minority of these have found psychodynamic therapies to be more effective than no treatment or than placebo treatments (Prochaska & Norcross, 1994; Henry & Strupp, 1991). Psychodynamic theorists counter that, like psychodynamic theory itself, their treatment, with its goal of broad and fundamental change and its long duration, does not readily lend itself to empirical investigation (Henry et al., 1994).

Critics also argue that, with the exception of short-term psychodynamic therapies, these systems of treatment simply take too long and cost too much money and hence are impractical for millions of troubled people (Simons, 1981). Psychodynamic therapists respond that the necessary steps of free association, therapist interpretation, catharsis, and working through cannot usually be rushed if lasting change is to occur. Most believe that the quicker symptom reductions brought about by other approaches are superficial and likely to lead to *symptom substitution,* the replacement of old symptoms by new ones.

Given such limitations, it is understandable that psychodynamic therapies no longer dominate the clinical field as they did before the 1950s (see Figure 5–3). Still, 11 percent of today's therapists identify themselves principally as Freudian psychodynamic therapists and 22 percent as contemporary psychodynamic therapists (Prochaska & Norcross, 1994). And, interestingly, many practitioners of other models report that when they seek help for their own problems,

psychodynamic therapy is their choice (Norcross & Prochaska, 1984).

HUMANISTIC AND EXISTENTIAL THERAPIES Believing that mental disorders are rooted in self-deceit, humanistic and existential therapists try to help clients look at themselves and their situations more accurately and acceptingly. They expect that clients will then go much further toward actualizing their full potential as human beings. To achieve these goals they try to enter the client's *phenomenological,* or subjective, world. Unlike the psychodynamic therapists, humanistic and existential therapists usually emphasize present experiences rather than events in the client's past.

As we first observed in Chapter 2, humanistic and existential therapists differ mainly in their view of the human experience. Humanistic therapists believe that people have a special inborn potential that they will automatically fulfill if only they can be helped to look at themselves accurately and acceptingly. Existential therapists, on the other hand, believe that human beings have absolute freedom to choose their own course in life, even a meaningless and empty one. Thus they try to help clients recognize their freedom, accept responsibility for their problems, and make more satisfying choices in their lives.

CLIENT-CENTERED THERAPY In client-centered therapy, the humanistic treatment developed by

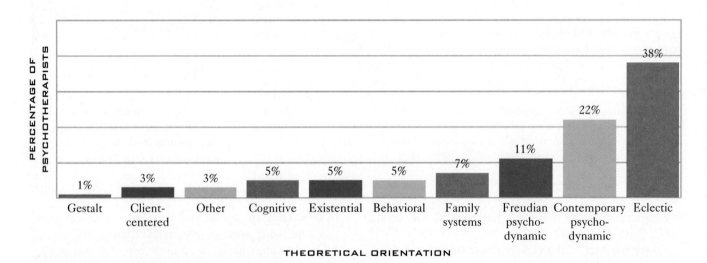

FIGURE 5–3 *Theoretical orientations of today's clinicians. In one survey, almost 40 percent of 818 psychologists, counselors, psychiatrists, and social workers labeled themselves as primarily "eclectic." The cross-professional percentages in this figure fail to reveal that psychologists and counselors are even more likely to follow a behavioral or cognitive model, psychiatrists a Freudian psychodynamic model or eclectic model, and social workers a family systems model. (Adapted from Prochaska & Norcross, 1994; Norcross et al., 1988; Norcross & Prochaska, 1986.)*

Carl Rogers in the late 1940s, therapists try to create a supportive climate in which clients can look at themselves honestly and begin to accept what they discover themselves to be (Raskin & Rogers, 1989; Rogers, 1987, 1967, 1951). The therapist must display three important qualities throughout the therapy—unconditional positive regard for the client, accurate empathy, and genuineness.

Therapists show *unconditional positive regard* by conveying full and warm acceptance no matter what clients say, think, or feel (see Box 5–4). They show *accurate empathy* by accurately hearing what clients are saying and sensitively communicating it back to the clients. They neither interpret what clients are saying nor try to teach them; rather, they listen, and help their clients listen to themselves as well. Finally, therapists must convey *genuineness,* also referred to as *congruence,* to clients. Unless therapists' communications are honest and sincere, clients may perceive them as mechanical and false. The following interaction shows the therapist using all these qualities to move the client toward greater self-awareness:

Client: Yes, I know I shouldn't worry about it, but I do. Lots of things—money, people, clothes. In classes I feel that everyone's just waiting for a chance to jump on me. It's like they were breathing down my neck waiting for a chance to find something wrong. At school there were fellows like that waiting for me. I can't stand people laughing at me. I can't stand ridicule. That's why I'm afraid of kids. When I meet somebody I wonder what he's actually thinking of me. Then later on I wonder how I match up to what he's come to think of me.

Therapist: You feel that you're pretty responsive to the opinions of other people.

Client: Yes, but it's things that shouldn't worry me.

Therapist: You feel that it's the sort of thing that shouldn't be upsetting, but they do get you pretty much worried anyway.

Client: Just some of them. Most of those things do worry me because they're true. The ones I told you, that is. But there are lots of little things that aren't true. And time bothers me, too. That is, when I haven't anything to do. Things just seem to be piling up, piling up inside of me. When I haven't anything to do I roam around. I feel like—at home when I was at the theater and nobody would come in, I used to wear it off by socking the doors. It's a feeling that things were crowding up and they were going to burst.

Therapist: You feel that it's a sort of oppression with some frustration and that things are just unmanageable.

Client: In a way, but some things just seem illogical. I'm afraid I'm not very clear here but that's the way it comes.

Therapist: That's all right. You say just what you think.

(Snyder, 1947, pp. 2–24)

"Why, you swine!"

Criticizing a client's remarks, however subtly or carefully, is the worst thing a therapist can do, according to client-centered therapists. (Drawing by Richter; © 1952, 1980 The New Yorker Magazine, Inc.)

In an atmosphere of unconditional positive regard, accurate empathy, and genuineness, clients can be expected increasingly to feel accepted by their therapist; they then may be able to look at themselves with honesty and acceptance—a process called *experiencing.* That is, they begin to value their own emotions, thoughts, and behaviors, and so are freed from the insecurities and doubts that prevented their self-actualization. The following excerpt shows that Mrs. Oak, a client of Rogers, is embarking on this process.

[Rogers:] Your feeling at the present time is that you have been very much aware of all the cultural pressures—not always very much aware, but "there have been so many of those in my life—and now I'm going down more deeply into myself to find out what I really feel" and it seems very much at the present time as though that somehow separates you a long ways from your culture, and that's a little frightening, but feels basically good. Is that—

[Mrs. Oak:] Yeah. Well, I have the feeling now that it's okay, really. . . . Then there's something else—a feeling that's starting to grow; well, to be almost formed, as I say. This kind of conclusion, that I'm going to stop looking for something terribly wrong. . . . And now without any—without, I should say, any sense of apology or covering up, just sort of simple statement that I can't find what at this time appears to be bad.

[Rogers:] Does this catch it? That as you've gone more and more deeply into yourself, and as you think about the kind of things that you've discovered and learned and so on, the conviction grows very, very strong that no matter how far you go, the things that you're going to find are not dire and awful. They have a very different character.

[Mrs. Oak:] Yes, something like that.

(Rogers, 1961)

BOX 5-4

ANIMALS: A SOURCE OF UNCONDITIONAL POSITIVE REGARD

For thousands of years humans have brought animals into the home to serve every purpose from protection to companionship. In recent years pets have even been looked upon as facilitators in human relationships and in the process of achieving psychological and emotional relief. Has "man's best friend" been elevated to the role of therapist?

It is widely believed that animals can provide solace, comfort, and friendship to a person in need of emotional support. The undying loyalty of the pet dog can supersede all human interactions in the eyes of a child who has been scolded for misbehaving or the elderly nursing home resident whose children no longer visit. Without judging and without condition our favorite pet provides love and companionship. From the humanistic perspective, these are qualities that help

ensure a truly successful treatment outcome.

Physiological studies indicate that the presence of a dog can reduce heart rate and blood pressure in children—the same effect that was noted in children who were asked to read aloud from a book of poetry (Friedmann et al., 1983). Even the survival rates of heart patients have been linked to ownership and interaction with a pet. Similar results have been suggested for elderly people who have little interaction with other human beings (Gammonley & Yates, 1991).

Studies have also indicated that animals can improve the emotions and behavior of persons with psychological problems. A technique called *pet-facilitated therapy* (Corson & Corson, 1978) has, for example, been employed in helping emotionally disturbed children. A group of such children, all of whom had many problems

in their relationships with peers and adults, participated in a program in which they lived and worked on a farm (Ross, 1983). Each child was given a special pet and was responsible for its care. After being involved in this program, the children showed improvement in their self-esteem and sense of control. Similar results have been reported in more formal therapeutic settings. Researchers reason that by making the situation feel less threatening, pets serve as a catalytic bridge between therapist and child, allowing the child to feel safe with the therapist. Moreover, the pet is an attractive addition to the session that most likely helps maintain the child's interest and attention.

Researchers have also found that social interactions between people improve when a pet is around. Pets can facilitate staff-patient interactions and patient-visitor relations and

---

From the very beginning, Rogers (1987, 1951) and his followers believed strongly in the importance of researching client-centered therapy. Even though their phenomenological perspective presented some obvious impediments to objective research (how can one know for sure what is in another person's mind?), he believed that the effectiveness of client-centered therapy could be measured.

Early studies seemed to provide strong support for Rogers's approach. Repeatedly, people treated in client-centered therapy showed more improvement than controls who did not receive treatment (Cartwright, 1961; Rogers & Dymond, 1954). But these early studies had major methodological flaws. Some of the control groups consisted of people who were well adjusted and may have had less need or room for improvement than people who sought client-centered therapy. Other control groups were

made up of people who were troubled but had no intention of seeking therapy, so they might have been less motivated to improve than the clients who elected therapy. In better-controlled studies, client-centered therapy has not fared so well. Although people who receive this therapy do seem to improve more than control subjects in some studies (Greenberg, Elliott, & Lietaer, 1994; Stuhr & Meyer, 1991), they show no such superiority in many others (Rudolph et al., 1980; Dircks et al., 1980).

All the same, Rogers's therapy has had a positive influence on clinical practice. It was the first major alternative to psychodynamic therapy, and as such it helped open up what had been a highly complacent field to new systems and formats. Second, Rogers helped open up the practice of psychotherapy to psychologists; it had previously been considered the province of psychiatrists. Third, Rogers's

promote stronger bonds between volunteers and institutional residents (Savishinsky, 1992; Chinner & Dalziel, 1991). Pets have also been used in psychotherapy to improve the interactions between therapist and client.

One of the most exciting uses of pet therapy centers on the dramatic and heart-rending mental disorder of autism. As we shall observe in Chapter 19, the unusual set of behaviors in people afflicted with autism hinders their ability to form bonds and relate to other people. Therapy with autistic people is typically slow and laborious as practitioners try to reduce disruptive behaviors and encourage the person to interact with others.

In one study, a dog was introduced into the individual treatment sessions of a number of autistic children (Redefer & Goodman, 1989). At first the children displayed typical autistic behaviors—hand posturing, making humming and clicking noises, jumping, continual spinning of objects, roaming. During a number of otherwise routine treatment sessions, the therapist interacted with the dog and encouraged the child to join in. In most cases, by the end of the session

the child showed significantly fewer autistic behaviors, a decrease in self-absorption, and an increase in positive social behavior, such as joining the therapist in simple games, initiating activities, reaching for hugs, and imitating the therapist's actions.

The researchers conjectured that the presence of the dog and the inter-

actions with it heightened the "affective and impulsive state of the children" so that they were better able to participate in and enjoy social interactions. The success of this experiment was not attributed solely to the dog's presence, however; it was the orchestration by the therapist of the interaction between the children and the dog that facilitated the improvement. Pets are not a magical solution, but they may offer help in the treatment of some autistic persons.

Researchers are now looking to see whether pet-facilitated therapy can be applied to other populations as well. One program at a prison has found that inmates given the responsibility of caring for a pet show reductions in violent behavior (Moneymaker & Strimple, 1991).

Although evidence is scanty, both anecdotal and formal studies suggest that pets can and do influence our emotional and physical well-being. Particularly for people who are developing their sense of self or who suffer a psychological disorder that inhibits this development, pet therapy may prove instrumental. It is no wonder that pets occupy such an important and honored role in many societies.

---

commitment to clinical research has strengthened the position of those who argue the importance of systematic research in the treatment domain (Rogers & Sanford, 1989; Sanford, 1987). The client-centered approach has a modest following among today's clinical practitioners. Approximately 3 percent of surveyed therapists report that they employ it (Prochasca & Norcross, 1994).

GESTALT THERAPY   Gestalt therapy is a humanistic form of treatment developed in the 1950s by a charismatic clinician named Frederick (Fritz) Perls (1893–1970). Like Rogers, Perls believed that people experience psychological difficulties when they are unaware of their needs or unwilling to accept or express them. Such individuals are avoiding their real inner selves. They lack self-awareness and self-acceptance, they fear the judgments of others, and their behavior becomes defensive. They act only to

protect themselves from perceived threats and do little to actualize their potential.

Thus gestalt therapists, like client-centered therapists, try to move clients toward self-recognition and self-acceptance (Yontef & Simkin, 1989; Polster, 1987). But unlike client-centered therapists, they try to achieve this goal by frustrating and challenging clients. The numerous techniques they have developed for doing so are meant also to make the therapy process considerably shorter than it is in client-centered and psychodynamic therapy.

In the technique of *skillful frustration,* for example, gestalt therapists refuse to meet their clients' expectations or even their outright demands. Such frustration is meant to help clients see how they try to manipulate others into meeting their needs. Perls (1973) describes his use of skillful frustration with a male client:

The first six weeks of therapy—more than half the available time—were spent in frustrating him in his desperate attempts to manipulate me into telling him what to do. He was by turn plaintive, aggressive, mute, despairing. He tried every trick in the book. He threw the time barrier up to me over and over again, trying to make me responsible for his lack of progress. If I had yielded to his demands, undoubtedly he would have sabotaged my efforts, exasperated me, and remained exactly where he was.

(p. 109)

Unlike psychodynamic therapists, who guide clients toward events and emotions in their past, gestalt therapists make it a practice to keep clients in the **here and now.** Although problems may be rooted in past causes, the effects take place in the present. Clients have needs now, are camouflaging their needs now, and must observe them now. As clients talk about the events and people in their lives, the therapist may ask, "What are you feeling about that person now?" or "What are you doing now, as you speak?" Similarly, therapists will tell clients to "stay with" past feelings and events and observe how they are making them feel at present. When clients are forced to confront these things in the here and now, they are also confronting their inner selves.

Another way gestalt therapists try to promote self-awareness is by instructing clients to **role-play**—that is, to act out various roles assigned by the therapist. Clients may be told to be another person, an object, or even a part of the body. They are instructed to talk as the other would talk and to feel what the other would feel. Here Perls has a client named Glenn act out an interaction between two kinds of men—really two dimensions of himself:

Fritz: I would like you to make up a dialogue. Two guys are having an encounter. One is called the Toughy, the other the Softy. Let them meet each other, get in touch with each other. Softy sits here; Toughy sits there. Or would you like the other way around? Let's put Toughy in there.

Glenn: Yeah. He's the one you look down at. Sitting here now, I have no respect for you, particularly.

Fritz: I guess they both are not willing to suffer each other.

Glenn: Yeah. . . . You can't stand it . . . when I get all gooey. You think that it's better not to show anything. I'm not so sure you're tough at all. I think you're just kind of wooden. *(Sighs)*

Yeah, but it's a lot better. I'm—I'm—I don't hurt nearly as much as you do. I push people around, and I kind of smile about it, now and then. Yeah. And you don't listen to what I say, 'cause when you're soft and feeling close to somebody, it's not going to come across.

Clients in gestalt therapy are guided to express their needs and feelings in their full intensity, through role playing, banging on pillows, and other exercises. These techniques are expected to enable clients to "own" needs and feelings they previously were unaware they had, overcome fears of being judged, and stop behaving defensively. In the typical gestalt therapy group, members help each other to "get in touch" with their needs and feelings.

I keep telling you, you gotta play it cool, because if you start in really feeling in touch, people will go away. They'll withdraw. They won't have anything to do with you. Nobody wants somebody around holding onto them. . . .

(Sighs) You are so lonely! I at least know I'm lonely. You think you're just alone. If I don't feel—if you don't let me feel with people, if you don't feel—let me feel so that I could reach out and touch—

Fritz: "Reach out and touch." What is your right hand doing?

Glenn: It's reaching out.

Fritz: It's reaching out, yah.

Glenn: (Softly) Wow.

(Perls, 1969)

Role playing can become intense, as clients are encouraged to be uninhibited in feeling and expressing emotions. Many cry out, scream, kick, or pound. Through this experience they gradually come to own (accept) feelings that were previously unknown to them.

Perls also developed a list of **rules** to ensure that clients will look at themselves more closely. For example, clients may not ask "why" questions. If they ask, "Why do you do that?" therapists make them change the question into a statement, such as "I hate it when you do that." Another rule is that clients must use "I" language rather than "it" language. They must say, "I am frightened," rather than "The situation is frightening."

Finally, gestalt therapists conduct *exercises and games* with clients. In the *exaggeration game,* clients must repeatedly exaggerate some gesture or verbal behavior—perhaps a phrase that they use regularly. This "game" is intended to help clients recognize the depth of their feelings, the meaning of particular behavior, and the effect of their behavior on others. Perls employs this strategy with a client named Jane:

Fritz: Now talk to your Top Dog! Stop nagging.

Jane: (Loud, pained) Leave me alone.

Fritz: Yah, again.

Jane: Leave me alone.

Fritz: Again.

Jane: (Screaming it and crying) Leave me alone!

Fritz: Again.

Jane: (She screams it, a real blast) Leave me alone! I don't have to do what you say! (Still crying) I don't have to be that good! . . . I don't have to be in this chair! I don't have to. You make me. You make me come here! (Screams) Aarhhh! You make me pick my face (Crying), that's what you do. (Screams and cries) Aarhhh! I'd like to kill you.

(Perls, 1969, p. 293)

Approximately 1 percent of clinicians describe themselves as gestalt therapists (Prochaska & Norcross, 1994). Because they believe that subjective experiences and self-awareness defy objective measurement, controlled research has rarely been conducted on the gestalt approach (Greenberg et al., 1994). We have seen that this is not an unusual position among humanistic and existential theorists. Indeed, Rogers's strong belief in the merits of research stands as an exception to the rule.

EXISTENTIAL THERAPY Existential therapists encourage clients to accept responsibility for their lives (and for their problems), to recognize their freedom to choose a different course, and to choose to live an *authentic life,* one full of meaning and values (May & Yalom, 1989; May, 1987).

Like humanistic therapists, existential therapists emphasize the individual's phenomenological world (van den Berg, 1971) and the here and now (May, 1987; Havens, 1974). For the most part, however, these therapists care more about the goals of therapy than the use of specific therapeutic techniques, and their methods and the length of treatment vary greatly from practitioner to practitioner (May & Yalom, 1989; May, 1987, 1961).

Existential therapists place great emphasis on the relationship between therapist and client (Frankl, 1975, 1963). The therapist and client must be open to each other, work hard together, and try to share, learn, and grow. The therapist's authenticity serves as a model for the client as they examine the meaning of existence and scrutinize the therapy encounter itself. This joint undertaking is not always pleasant, but the achievement of personal authenticity and growth depends on it. Here an existential therapist pushes hard for a patient to accept responsibility for her choices both in therapy and in life:

Patient: I don't know why I keep coming here. All I do is tell you the same thing over and over. I'm not getting anywhere. [Patient complaining that therapist isn't curing her; maintenance of self-as-therapist's-object.]

Doctor: I'm getting tired of hearing the same thing over and over, too. [Doctor refusing to take responsibility for the progress of therapy and refusing to fulfill patient's expectations that he cure her; refusal of patient-as-therapist's-object.]

Emphasizing the need to accept responsibility, recognize one's choices, and live an authentic life, existential therapists guide clients to reject feelings of victimhood.
(CALVIN AND HOBBES © 1993 Watterson. Reprinted with permission of UNIVERSAL PRESS SYNDICATE. All rights reserved.)

While imprisoned in Nazi concentration camps from 1942 to 1945, psychotherapist Viktor Frankl observed that the victims who found some spiritual meaning in their suffering were able to resist despair and to survive. He later developed "logotherapy" (from the Greek, "logos," for word or thought), an existential therapy which helps clients assign values and spiritual meaning to their existence through loving other people and confronting their own suffering. Frankl himself displays the positive attitude toward life and the sense of exploration that he espouses.

Patient: Maybe I'll stop coming. [Patient threatening therapist; fighting to maintain role as therapist's object.]

Doctor: It's certainly your choice. [Therapist refusing to be intimidated; forcing patient-as-subject.]

Patient: What do you think I should do? [Attempt to seduce therapist into role of subject who objectifies patient.]

Doctor: What do you want to do? [Forcing again.]

Patient: I want to get better. [Plea for therapist to cure her.]

Doctor: I don't blame you. [Refusing role of subject curer and supporting desire on part of patient-as-subject.]

Patient: If you think I should stay, ok, I will. [Refusing role of subject-who-decides.]

Doctor: You want me to tell you to stay? [Confrontation with patient's evasion of the decision and calling attention to how patient is construing the therapy.]

Patient: You know what's best; you're the doctor. [Patient's confirmation of how she is construing the therapy.]

Doctor: Do I act like a doctor?

(Keen, 1970, p. 200)

Existential therapists do not believe that experimental methods can adequately test the effectiveness of their treatment interventions (May & Yalom, 1989). They believe that research that reduces patients to test measures or scale scores serves only to dehumanize them. Not surprisingly, then, virtually no controlled research has been conducted on the effectiveness of existential therapy (Prochaska & Norcross, 1994). A lack of empirical data does not, however, represent evidence for ineffectiveness, and, indeed, surveys suggest that as many as 5 percent of today's therapists use an approach that is primarily existential (Prochaska & Norcross, 1994).

PROBLEM-BASED THERAPIES

Problem-based therapies treat clients in accordance with their symptoms. Therapists who use these approaches believe that the best way to help people is to deal with their concrete problems directly and quickly. Unlike practitioners of the global therapies, these therapists vary their treatment techniques as necessary to treat each particular problem, though they do adhere to a basic set of principles about abnormality and treatment (Reyna, 1989). The major problem-based therapies are the behavioral, cognitive, and biological therapies.

BEHAVIORAL THERAPIES   Behaviorists contend that the symptoms of a mental disorder are learned behaviors acquired through the same conditioning processes that produce normal behaviors (Wolpe, 1990; Reyna, 1989). The goal of behavioral therapy is to identify the client's specific problem-causing behaviors and manipulate and replace them with more appropriate ones. A client's early life history is focused on only to the extent that it provides clues about current reinforcers (Kanfer & Philips, 1970). Similarly, relatively little attention is paid to subjective experiences and dreams. The therapist's attitude toward the client is that of teacher rather than healer. Behavioral techniques fall into three categories: *classical conditioning*, *operant conditioning*, and *modeling*.

CLASSICAL CONDITIONING TECHNIQUES Classical conditioning treatments are intended to change clients' dysfunctional reactions to stimuli (Emmelkamp, 1994; Wolpe, 1990). ***Systematic desensitization,*** for example, is a process of teaching phobic clients to react calmly instead of with intense fear to the objects or situations they dread (Wolpe, 1990, 1987, 1958). It is a step-by-step procedure that begins with teaching them the skill of deep muscle relaxation over the course of several sessions. Next, the clients construct a ***fear hierarchy,*** a list of feared objects or situations, starting with those that are minimally feared and ending with the ones that are most fearsome. The following hierarchy was developed by a man who was afraid of criticism, especially about his mental stability:

1. Friend on the street: "Hi, how are you?"
2. Friend on the street: "How are you feeling these days?"
3. Sister: "You've got to be careful so they don't put you in the hospital."
4. Wife: "You shouldn't drink beer while you are taking medicine."
5. Mother: "What's the matter, don't you feel good?"
6. Wife: "It's just you yourself, it's all in your head."
7. Service station attendant: "What are you shaking for?"
8. Neighbor borrows rake: "Is there something wrong with your leg? Your knees are shaking."
9. Friend on the job: "Is your blood pressure okay?"
10. Service station attendant: "You are pretty shaky, are you crazy or something?"

(Marquis & Morgan, 1969, p. 28)

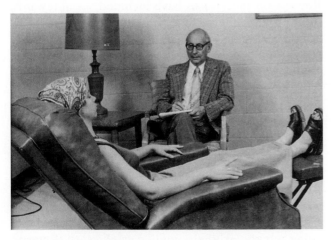

Joseph Wolpe, the psychiatrist who developed the behavioral treatment of systematic desensitization, first teaches a client to relax her mind and body, then guides her to confront feared objects or situations, real or imagined, while she remains relaxed. Systematic desensitization is one of several behavioral techniques that have helped people with phobias.

Desensitization therapists next have clients either imagine or physically confront each item on the hierarchy while they are in a state of deep relaxation. Clients begin by pairing a relaxation response with the least-feared item on the list, and they move up to the next fear-arousing item only after they have mastered complete relaxation on the first item. Step by step they move up the hierarchy until at last they can relax in the presence of all the events that had previously aroused great fear in them. Here a behavioral therapist carefully teaches a client how to pair relaxation responses with scenes from his fear hierarchy:

> Fine. Soon I shall ask you to imagine a scene. After you hear the description of the situation, please imagine it as vividly as you can, through your own eyes, as if you were actually there. Try to include all the details in the scene. While you're visualizing the situation, you may continue feeling as relaxed as you are now. If so, that's good. After 5, 10, or 15 seconds, I'll ask you to stop imagining the scene and return to your pleasant image and to just relax. But if you begin to feel even the slightest increase in anxiety or tension, please signal this to me by raising your left forefinger. When you do this, I'll step in and ask you to stop imagining the situation and then will help you get relaxed once more. It's important that you indicate tension to me in this way, as we want to maximize your being exposed to fearful situations without feeling anxious. OK? Do you have any questions? . . . Fine, we'll have ample opportunity afterwards to discuss things in full.
>
> *(Goldfried & Davison, 1976, pp. 124–125)*

As we shall see in Chapter 7, research has repeatedly found systematic desensitization and other classical conditioning techniques to reduce phobic reactions more effectively than placebo treatments or no treatment at all (Emmelkamp, 1994; Wilson, 1990). These approaches have also been helpful in treating several other kinds of problems, including sexual dysfunctions, posttraumatic stress disorders, agoraphobia, and asthma attacks (Emmelkamp, 1994; Steinmark & Borkovec, 1974; Moore, 1965).

In the diametrically opposite use of classical conditioning known as ***aversion therapy,*** therapists help clients to *acquire* anxiety responses to stimuli that the clients have been finding too attractive. This approach has been used with people who want to stop excessive smoking, for example (Blanchard, 1994; Lichtenstein & Glasgow, 1992; Whitman, 1972). In repeated sessions the clients may be given an electric shock, a nausea-producing drug, or some other noxious stimulus whenever they reach for a cigarette. After numerous pairings of this kind, the clients are expected to develop an unpleasant emotional reaction to cigarettes. The effects of this approach have, however, been short-lived.

Aversion therapy has also been applied to help eliminate such undesirable behavior as self-mutilation in autistic children, sexual deviance, and alcoholism (Emmelkamp, 1994). In the following case, aversion therapy was used successfully with a man who felt repeated urges to make obscene phone calls.

H e was a married, 32-year-old police officer who made up to 20 obscene telephone calls a week to young women in his community. During the calls he would masturbate. He would continue masturbating to orgasm if the woman hung up before he reached orgasm. He ultimately was arrested because he telephoned a woman he knew. She recognized his voice and alerted the sheriff's office. After the details of his behavior surfaced, he lost his job but was permitted to seek psychiatric help in lieu of criminal charges being filed against him. Because he experienced considerable guilt and shame after he made the calls, the following procedure was felt to have a reasonable probability of success. Therapy consisted of the client making an obscene call to a female listener in another office who was instructed to listen and answer questions in a passive but noncomplying manner. Two young, attractive women listeners were part of the treatment; they were instructed not to hang up first. After each telephone contact, the client and listener shared their feelings. This evoked a great deal of anxiety, shame, and embarrassment on the part of the client. The therapist also was present at each of the meetings. Under these circumstances the client experienced the telephone calls as extremely unpleasant. These feelings apparently generalized to the client's real-life situation. For nine months after the brief three-week treatment, the client reported no strong urges to make an obscene call and the authorities in the community were not notified of any such calls.

(Adapted from Boudewyns, Tanna, & Fleischman, 1975,
pp. 704–707)

OPERANT CONDITIONING TECHNIQUES
In operant conditioning treatments, therapists consistently provide rewards for appropriate behavior and withhold rewards for inappropriate behavior. This technique has been employed frequently, and often successfully, with people experiencing psychosis (Glynn, 1990; Paul & Lentz, 1977; Ayllon & Azrin, 1965). When these patients talk coherently and behave normally, they are rewarded with food, privileges, attention, or something else they value. Conversely, they receive no rewards when they speak bizarrely or display other psychotic behaviors.

In addition, parents, teachers, and therapists have successfully used operant conditioning techniques

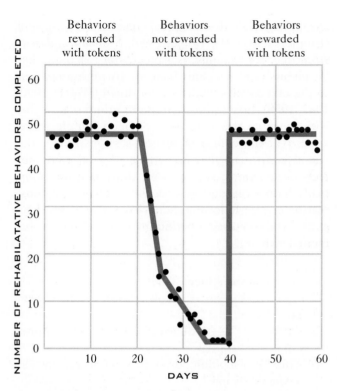

FIGURE 5–4 *A token economy program for 44 schizophrenic patients on a hospital ward. When rehabilitative behaviors, such as making one's bed, were rewarded with tokens for twenty days, patients performed them at a high rate. When rewards were stopped, the patients likewise stopped performing the behaviors. They later returned to a high rate of performance when token rewards were reinstituted. (Adapted from Ayllon & Azrin, 1965.)*

to change problem behaviors in children (such as repeated tantrums) and to teach skills to mentally retarded individuals (Kazdin, 1994; Ross, 1981). Rewards in these cases have included social rewards, meals, television watching, and recreation time.

As we shall see in Chapter 16, operant conditioning techniques typically work best in institutions or schools, where a person's behavior can be reinforced systematically throughout the day. Often a whole ward or classroom is converted into an operant conditioning arena (see Figure 5–4). Such programs are referred to as *token economy* programs because in many of them desirable behavior is reinforced with tokens that can later be exchanged for food, privileges, or other rewards (Ayllon & Azrin, 1968).

One token economy program was applied in a classroom where children were behaving disruptively and doing poorly at their studies (Ayllon & Roberts, 1974). The children earned tokens whenever they did well on daily reading tests or successfully performed other targeted behaviors. They could then exchange their tokens for a reward, such as extra recess time or seeing a movie (see Table 5–1). Under this system, reading accuracy increased from 40 to 85 percent, and the proportion of time spent in disruptive behavior decreased from 50 percent to 5 percent.

MODELING TECHNIQUES   Modeling therapy was first developed by the pioneering social learning theorist Albert Bandura (1977, 1969). The basic design is for therapists to demonstrate appropriate behaviors for clients, who, through a process of imitation and rehearsal, then acquire the ability to perform the behaviors in their own lives. In some cases, therapists model new emotional responses for clients. For example, therapists have calmly handled snakes to show snake-phobic clients that it is possible to be relaxed in the presence of these animals (Bandura, 1977, 1971). After several modeling sessions, clients themselves are encouraged to interact with the snakes. As we shall see in Chapter 7, the modeling of emotion can be quite effective in the treatment of phobic disorders (Rosenthal & Bandura, 1978; Bandura, Adams, & Beyer, 1977).

Behavioral therapists have also used modeling in combination with other techniques to help people acquire or improve their social skills and assertiveness. In an approach called *social skills training,* for example, therapists point out the social deficits of clients and then role-play social situations with the clients. In some enactments the therapist may take the role of the client and demonstrate appropriate social behav-

iors; in others, the client may try out and rehearse the behaviors, always receiving feedback from the therapist. Ultimately the client practices the behaviors in real-life situations. In the following role-playing session the client is a male college student who has difficulty making dates:

Client: By the way *(Pause)* I don't suppose you want to go out Saturday night?

Therapist: Up to actually asking for the date you were very good. However, if I were the girl, I think I might have been a bit offended when you said, "By the way." It's like your asking her out is pretty casual. Also, the way you phrased the question, you were kind of suggesting to her that she doesn't want to go out with you. Pretend for the moment I'm you. Now, how does this sound: "There is a movie at the Varsity Theater this Saturday that I want to see. If you don't have other plans, I'd very much like to take you."

Client: That sounded good. Like you were sure of yourself and liked the girl, too.

Therapist: Why don't you try it.

Client: You know that movie at the Varsity? Well, I'd like to go, and I'd like to take you Saturday, if you don't have anything better to do.

Therapist: Well, that certainly was better. Your tone of voice was especially good. But the last line, "if you don't have anything better to do," sounds like you don't think you have too much to offer. Why not run through it one more time.

Client: I'd like to see the show at the Varsity, Saturday, and, if you haven't made other plans, I'd like to take you.

Therapist: Much better. Excellent, in fact. You were confident, forceful, and sincere.

(Rimm & Masters, 1979, p. 74)

Using a combined strategy of modeling, rehearsal, feedback, and practice, therapists have successfully taught social and assertion skills to shy, passive, or socially isolated people, as well as to people who have a pattern of bursting out in rage or violence after building up resentment over perceived social slights (Emmelkamp, 1994; Hollin & Trower, 1986). As we shall note in later chapters, the approach has also been used to improve the social skills of people who are depressed, alcoholic, obese, or anxious (Cooney et al., 1991; Hersen et al., 1984).

ASSESSING BEHAVIORAL THERAPIES   Behavioral interventions are among the most widely researched treatment approaches in the clinical field (Kendall, 1990). Approximately 5 percent of surveyed therapists report that their approach is primarily behavioral (Prochaska & Norcross, 1994). One reason for

TABLE 5-1

TOKEN ECONOMY PROGRAM IN A FIFTH-GRADE READING CLASS

	NUMBER OF TOKENS
EARNINGS	
80% correct on workbook assignments	2
100% correct on workbook assignments	5
EXCHANGE VALUE	
Access to game room (per 15 minutes)	2
Extra recess time (10 minutes)	2
Review grades in teacher's book	5
Reduce detention (per 10 minutes)	10
Change cafeteria table	15
Have the lowest test grade removed	20
See a movie	6
Have a good-work letter sent to parents	15

Source: Ayllon & Roberts, 1974.

the popularity of behavioral therapies is that they are more amenable to research than the psychodynamic or humanistic approaches. The removal of symptoms—the criterion of progress in behavioral therapy—is easier to observe and measure than conflict resolution or self-actualization—the psychodynamic and humanistic criteria of improvement.

Moreover, behavioral approaches have been effective for numerous problems seen in clinical practice, including specific fears, social deficits, and mental retardation (Emmelkamp, 1994; Bierman & Furman, 1984). Their effectiveness is all the more impressive in view of the relatively short duration and low overall cost of these therapies.

At the same time, behavioral therapies have certain limitations. First, the improvements they bring about do not always extend to the person's real life and do not necessarily maintain themselves without further behavioral interventions (Edelstein, 1989; Stokes & Osnes, 1989; Jacobson, 1989). Second, as we shall observe in later chapters, behavioral therapies do not appear to be particularly effective with psychological disorders that are broad or vaguely defined. Problems involving generalized anxiety, for example, are unlikely to be alleviated by step-by-step, behavior-by-behavior approaches (O'Leary & Wilson, 1987).

Third, some people have raised ethical questions about the behavioral approaches (Kipnis, 1987). It troubles them, for example, that token economy programs and other operant conditioning techniques are imposed on many clients without their permission. Similarly, they are concerned about the pain and discomfort that may be inflicted on clients in aversion therapy. While acknowledging these to be substantive issues, most behaviorists believe that when behavioral interventions are properly conducted, they proceed in a responsible manner that safeguards the client's rights and dignity.

COGNITIVE THERAPIES   Working from the premise that abnormal functioning is caused by counterproductive assumptions and thoughts, cognitive therapists try to help people recognize and change their faulty thinking processes. Because different forms of abnormality involve different kinds of cognitive dysfunctioning, a number of cognitive strategies have been developed.

ELLIS'S RATIONAL-EMOTIVE THERAPY   In line with his belief that irrational assumptions give rise to abnormal functioning, Albert Ellis has developed an approach called *rational-emotive therapy* (Ellis, 1991, 1976, 1962). Therapists help clients to discover the irrational assumptions that govern their emotional responses and to change those assumptions into constructive ways of viewing themselves and the world.

"Has it ever occurred to you just to say, 'Hey, I quit. I don't want to be a part of the food chain anymore'?"

Cognitive therapists try to help clients interpret life situations differently, expecting that such changes in thought will lead to more constructive reactions and choices. (Drawing by Ziegler; © 1992 The New Yorker Magazine, Inc.)

In his own practice, Ellis is a direct and active therapist who tries to persuade clients that the rational-emotive perspective explains their difficulties. He points out their irrational assumptions in a blunt, confrontational, and often humorous way, and then he models the use of alternative assumptions. After criticizing a man's perfectionistic standards, for example, he might say, "So what if you did a lousy job on your project? It's important to realize that one lousy project simply means one lousy project, and no more than that!" Ellis also gives clients homework assignments requiring them to observe their assumptions (Ellis also calls them "hypotheses") as they operate in everyday life and to think of ways to test the assumptions' rationality. He also has clients rehearse new assumptions during therapy and apply them in real-life situations.

> *Therapist:* I'll explain in a minute. But first, the point is for you to decide exactly what hypothesis or nutty idea you want to work on for at least ten minutes a day. And, in your case, it would be the idea, again, that it's terrible for you to get rejected by a woman you find attractive. You would take this idea, and ask yourself several basic questions, in order to challenge and dispute it.
>
> *Client:* What kind of questions?
>
> *Therapist:* Usually, four basic questions—though they have all kinds of variations. The first one is, "What am I telling myself?" or, "What silly idea do I want to challenge?" And the answer, in your case, is, "It's terrible if a woman whom I find attractive rejects me." The second question is, "Is this, my hypothesis, true?" And the answer is—?
>
> *Client:* Uh, well, uh. No, it isn't.
>
> *Therapist:* Fine. If you had said it was true, the third question would have been, "Where is the evidence for its being true?" But since you said it isn't true, the third question is, "Where is the evidence that it's not true?" Well—?
>
> *Client:* Well, uh, it's not true because, as we said before, it may be very inconvenient if an attractive woman rejects me, but it's not more, uh, than that. It's only damned inconvenient!
>
> *(Ellis, 1976, pp. 29–30)*

Rational-emotive therapists have cited numerous studies in support of this approach (Ellis, 1989, 1973). Most early studies were conducted on people with experimentally induced anxieties or with nonclinical problems such as a mild fear of snakes (Kendall, 1990; Kendall & Kriss, 1983), but a growing number of recent studies have been done on actual clinical subjects and have also found that rational-emotive therapy is often helpful (Lyons & Woods, 1991). As we shall observe in Chapter 7, anxious clients in particular who are treated with this therapy improve more than anxious clients who receive no treatment or placebo treatments.

BECK'S COGNITIVE THERAPY   Aaron Beck has independently developed a system of therapy that is similar to Ellis's rational-emotive therapy. Called simply *cognitive therapy,* this approach has been most widely used in cases of depression (Beck, 1993, 1991, 1976, 1967). Cognitive therapists help clients to recognize the negative thoughts, biased interpretations, and errors in logic that pervade their thinking and, according to Beck, cause them to feel depressed. The therapists also guide clients to question and challenge their dysfunctional thoughts, try out new interpretations, and ultimately apply alternative ways of thinking in their daily lives. As we shall see in Chapter 9, depressed people who are treated with Beck's approach improve significantly more than those who receive no treatment and about the same as those who receive biological treatments (Hollon & Beck, 1994; Young, Beck, & Weinberger, 1993). In recent years Beck's cognitive therapy has also been successfully applied to panic disorders and other anxiety disorders (Beck, 1993). Here a cognitive therapist guides a depressed 26-year-old graduate student to see the relationship between the way she interprets her experiences and the way she feels and to begin questioning the accuracy of her interpretations:

> *Patient:* I agree with the descriptions of me but I guess I don't agree that the way I think makes me depressed.
>
> *Therapist:* How do you understand it?
>
> *Patient:* I get depressed when things go wrong. Like when I fail a test.
>
> *Therapist:* How can failing a test make you depressed?
>
> *Patient:* Well, if I fail I'll never get into law school.
>
> *Therapist:* So failing the test means a lot to you. But if failing a test could drive people into clinical depression, wouldn't you expect everyone who failed the test to have a depression? . . . Did everyone who failed get depressed enough to require treatment?
>
> *Patient:* No, but it depends on how important the test was to the person.
>
> *Therapist:* Right, and who decides the importance?
>
> *Patient:* I do.
>
> *Therapist:* And so, what we have to examine is your way of viewing the test (or the way that you think about the test) and how it affects your chances of getting into law school. Do you agree?
>
> *Patient:* Right.
>
> *Therapist:* Do you agree that the way you interpret the results of the test will affect you? You might feel

depressed, you might have trouble sleeping, not feel like eating, and you might even wonder if you should drop out of the course.

Patient: I have been thinking that I wasn't going to make it. Yes, I agree.

Therapist: Now what did failing mean?

Patient: *(Tearful)* That I couldn't get into law school.

Therapist: And what does that mean to you?

Patient: That I'm just not smart enough.

Therapist: Anything else?

Patient: That I can never be happy.

Therapist: And how do these thoughts make you feel?

Patient: Very unhappy.

Therapist: So it is the meaning of failing a test that makes you very unhappy. In fact, believing that you can never be happy is a powerful factor in producing unhappiness. So, you get yourself into a trap—by definition, failure to get into law school equals "I can never be happy."

(Beck et al., 1979, pp. 145–146)

COGNITIVE-BEHAVIORAL THERAPIES Cognitive-behavioral therapies treat cognitions as responses that can be altered by systematic reward or punishment, or, alternatively, as skills that can be modified by systematic training. The psychologist Donald Meichenbaum (1993, 1986, 1977, 1975) has developed a cognitive-behavioral technique called *self-instruction training* to help people solve problems and cope with stress more effectively. Using a step-by-step procedure, therapists teach clients how to make helpful statements to themselves—positive *self-statements*—and how to apply them in difficult circumstances. The therapists begin by explaining and modeling effective self-statements; they then have clients practice and apply the statements in stressful situations.

Using this procedure, Meichenbaum has taught anxious clients to make the following kinds of self-statements as they try to cope with anxiety-arousing situations:

Just think about what you can do about it. That's better than getting anxious.

Just "psych" yourself up—you can meet this challenge.

One step at a time: you can handle the situation.

Relax; you're in control. Take a slow deep breath.

Don't try to eliminate fear totally; just keep it manageable.

(Meichenbaum, 1974)

In comparison with no treatment and placebo treatment, Meichenbaum's self-instruction training has been found helpful for people with impulsive disorders, social anxiety, test anxiety, pain, and problems with anger (Meichenbaum, 1993; Jay et al., 1987; Kendall & Braswell, 1985; Novaco, 1976, 1975). On the other hand, it is not clear whether the cognitive problem-solving skills that are learned by this technique are retained for an extended period of time (Schlichter & Horan, 1981).

ASSESSING COGNITIVE THERAPIES The number of clinicians who employ cognitive approaches has been growing steadily (Kuehlwein & Rosen, 1993; Barlow, 1993). Approximately 5 percent of therapists surveyed identify their orientation as cognitive (Prochaska & Norcross, 1994). This overall percentage, however, reflects a split in the clinical community. Approximately 10 percent of psychologists and other counselors employ cognitive therapy primarily, compared to only 1 percent of psychiatrists and 4 percent of social workers (Prochaska & Norcross, 1994; Norcross, Prochaska, & Farber, 1993). Moreover, surveys suggest that the number of professionals embracing cognitive approaches is continuing to rise.

There are two major reasons for this growth in popularity. First, the cognitive perspective has proved attractive to clinicians of various orientations (Alford & Norcross, 1991). It shares with the psychodynamic model the belief that clients' insights, interpretations, and judgments can be a key to improvement; and, like behavioral treatments, cognitive therapies often attempt to break thought processes down into discrete parts, change them through systematic instruction, and measure the changes with precision. Understandably, then, many psychodynamic and behavioral therapists have been comfortable including cognitive techniques in their therapies or changing to a cognitive or cognitive-behavioral approach altogether.

Another reason for the popularity of the cognitive therapies is their impressive performance thus far in research. As we shall see, cognitive therapy has proved to be very effective for treating depression and moderately effective for anxiety problems (Hollon & Beck, 1994), and cognitive-behavioral approaches have been helpful in cases of sexual dysfunction (Carey et al., 1993; Fox & Emery, 1981).

On the other hand, a period of more probing evaluation and criticism, even from cognitive practitioners and researchers, probably lies ahead for the cognitive therapies. When a new therapy system is still on the rise, many clinicians are willing to try the techniques and give them the benefit of the doubt. It is reasonable to expect, however, that the initial enthusiasm will be modified somewhat as time and experience inevitably expose the system's limitations. The psychodynamic, humanistic, and behavioral approaches each enjoyed a similar period of admiration and even glory, and each later had to face serious questions and criticisms from proponents and opponents alike. Is it enough to alter the cognitive features of a case of psychological dysfunctioning? Can such specific kinds of thought changes make a general and lasting difference in the way a person feels and behaves? These and related questions will probably receive more attention and analysis in the coming years.

BIOLOGICAL THERAPIES Biological therapists use physical and chemical methods to help people overcome their psychological problems. The three principal kinds of biological interventions used today are *drug therapy*, *electroconvulsive therapy*, and *psychosurgery*. Drug therapy is by far the most common approach, whereas psychosurgery is relatively infrequent.

DRUG THERAPY In the 1950s researchers discovered several kinds of effective ***psychotropic drugs,*** drugs that act primarily on the brain and in many cases help to alleviate the symptoms of mental disorders. These drugs have radically changed the prognosis for a number of mental disorders and are now used widely, either as an adjunct or as the dominant form of therapy. In addition, as we saw in Chapter 2, the psychotropic drugs that have proved effective are leading scientists to a better understanding of the mental disorders that they alleviate (Meltzer, 1992; Iversen, 1989).

Unfortunately, the psychotropic drug revolution has also been accompanied by significant problems. Some of the drugs have serious undesirable effects that must be weighed against the good the drugs can do (Wolfe et al., 1988). Often, when clinicians and patients alike become seduced by the possibility of rapid change, the drugs are overused. Finally, while drugs are effective in many cases, they do not help everyone. Four major groups of psychotropic drugs are used in therapy: antianxiety, antidepressant, antibipolar, and antipsychotic drugs (see Figure 5–5).

Antianxiety drugs, also called *minor tranquilizers* or *anxiolytics* (from "anxiety" and the Greek *lytikos*, "able to loosen or dissolve"), reduce tension and anxiety. The pharmacologist Frank Berger discovered the first antianxiety drug, ***meprobamate*** (trade name Miltown), in the late 1940s while he was trying to develop an effective antibiotic medication to fight infections. In 1957 Lowell Randall observed that another group of drugs, ***benzodiazepines,*** also had an antianxiety effect, and these soon became the most popular group of antianxiety drugs (Papp & Gorman, 1993). By the late 1970s over 8,000 tons of benzodiazepines were being consumed in the United States each year; they had become the most widely prescribed drugs in the country (Hollister, 1986). Three widely prescribed benzodiazepines are *alprazolam* (trade name Xanax), *diazepam* (Valium), and *chlordiazepoxide* (Librium).

AN ANTIANXIETY DRUG

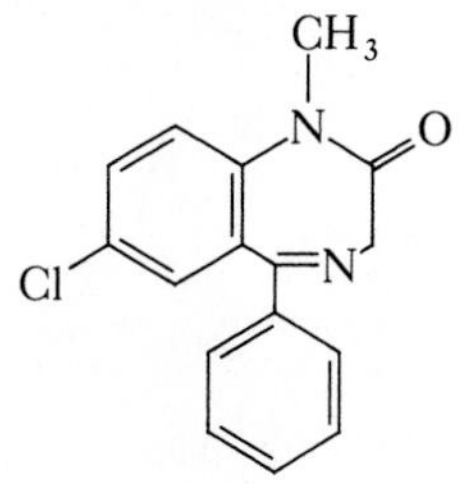

Diazepam
(Valium)

AN ANTIDEPRESSANT DRUG

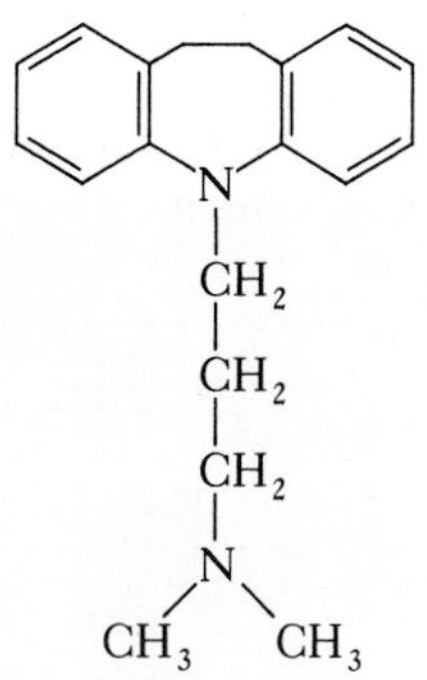

Imipramine
(Tofranil)

AN ANTIPSYCHOTIC DRUG

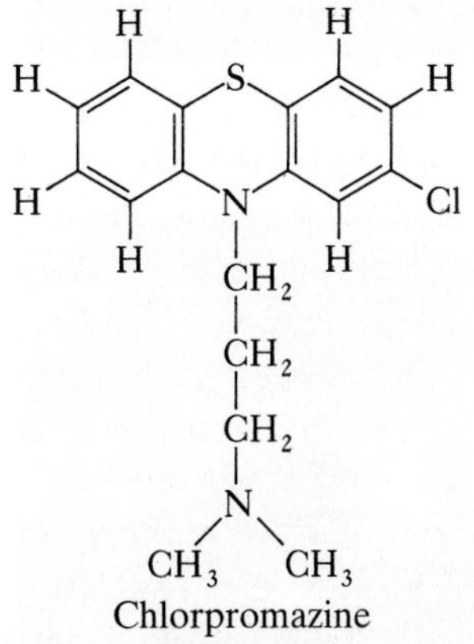

Chlorpromazine
(Thorazine)

FIGURE 5–5 *Chemical structures of important psychotropic drugs.*

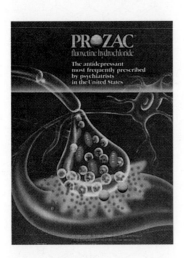

Psychotropic drugs now help millions of people to overcome psychological dysfunctioning. Unfortunately, a clinician's choices about which drugs to prescribe may be influenced not only by research literature but by a pharmaceutical company's promotional campaigns. Enticing ads for drugs fill the journals read by psychiatrists and other physicians.

Research clearly indicates that these drugs help reduce anxiety (Papp & Gorman, 1993). They have been overused and even misused, however, and, as we shall see in Chapter 7, they can induce physical dependence if they are taken in high dosages over an extended period of time (Murphy, Owen, & Tyrer, 1984; Winokur et al., 1980). Thus the drugs alone do not provide a long-term solution for most cases of anxiety.

Antidepressant drugs help lift the spirits of people who are depressed (Apter, 1993; Richelson, 1989). As Chapter 9 will reveal, a drug called *iproniazid* was developed in the early 1950s as a potential cure for tuberculosis. Research soon showed that it did not effectively combat that disease, but unexpectedly it did alleviate the feelings of depression felt by many of the tubercular patients (Loomer, Saunders, & Kline, 1957). Iproniazid and similar drugs, collectively called *MAO inhibitors* because they inhibit the action of the enzyme *monoamine oxidase (MAO)*, were soon marketed as antidepressant medications. Just a few years later, Roland Kuhn (1958), a psychiatrist, experimented with the drug *imipramine* (trade name Tofranil) while searching for a medication to treat schizophrenia. Although ineffective as a treatment for schizophrenia, imipramine and similar drugs, collectively called *tricyclics* because they each have three rings in their molecular structure, were also found to be effective in relieving depression (Davis, Klerman, & Schildkraut, 1967). In the 1980s a third group of antidepressants was discovered. These *second-generation* antidepressant drugs, chemically different from MAO inhibitors and tricyclics, include fluoxetine hydrochloride (trade name Prozac).

Tricyclics and second-generation antidepressants are prescribed much more often than MAO inhibitors (Montgomery et al., 1993; Richelson, 1989). The former drugs have an average success rate of 65 percent in cases of depression, compared to a rate of 50 percent for MAO inhibitors (Wechsler et al., 1965). In addition, tricyclics and second-generation antidepressants do not have the serious undesired effects of MAO inhibitors. The latter can cause dangerously high blood pressure, liver damage, and even death if they are mixed with foods containing the chemical *tyramine,* which is found in such everyday foods as cheese, chocolate, red wine, beer, chicken liver, and yogurt (Blackwell et al., 1967).

Today antidepressant drugs are prescribed in thousands of cases of depression, often in combination with psychotherapy. Indeed, their very trade names often imply a significant elevation of mood (see Table 5–2). Research suggests that cognitive therapy is one form of psychotherapy able to equal the effectiveness of this biological treatment (Hollon & Beck, 1994, 1986). On the other hand, a combination of antidepressant drugs and cognitive therapy is often more effective than either treatment alone (Hollon et al., 1993, 1991, 1985).

Antibipolar drugs help stabilize the moods of persons with a bipolar mood disorder, a disorder marked by mood swings from mania to depression. As we shall see in greater detail in Chapter 9, the most effective antibipolar drug is *lithium,* a metallic element that occurs in nature as a mineral salt (Jefferson & Greist, 1989). Lithium was discovered in 1817, but it was not until 1949 that an Australian psychiatrist named John Cade discovered its effectiveness as a psychotropic drug. Controlled research throughout the 1950s and 1960s confirmed that this drug can both reduce and prevent the manic and depressive episodes of bipolar mood disorders (Klerman et al., 1994; Bunney et al., 1968), and in 1970 the U.S. Food and Drug Administration approved lithium for use in their treatment.

Lithium is helpful in approximately 70 to 80 percent of cases of bipolar disorders, which until Cade's discovery had been unresponsive to all forms of biological and psychological therapy (Prien, 1992; Abou-Saleh, 1992; Pardes, 1989). The dosage of lithium must be carefully monitored, however (Jefferson & Greist, 1989). Too high a concentration may dangerously alter the body's sodium level and even threaten the patient's life. Administered properly, however, this and related drugs represent a true medical miracle for people who previously would have spent their lives on an emotional roller coaster.

Antipsychotic drugs, also called *neuroleptic drugs* because they have unwanted effects similar to the symptoms of neurological diseases, alleviate the confusion, hallucinations, and delusions of psychosis, a loss of contact with reality. In the 1950s a French surgeon named Henri Laborit discovered that *phenothiazines,* a group of antihistamine drugs prescribed for allergic reactions, also had a calming effect on surgical patients. Soon the psychiatrists Jean Delay and Pierre Deniker (1952) found that the same drugs reduced the psychotic symptoms of patients with schizophrenic disorders. Since then, phenothiazines and several related groups of drugs have become the treatment of choice for schizophrenic disorders, as we shall see in Chapter 16. Common phenothiazines are chlorpromazine (trade name Thorazine), thioridazine (Mellaril), and fluphenazine (Prolixin). Other antipsychotic drugs that have been developed include haloperidol (Haldol) and thiothixene (Navane). Recently some new kinds of antipsychotic drugs, called

TABLE 5-2

THE NAME GAME

The trade names of psychotropic medications often seem to advertise the drug's intended effect.

TRADE NAME	LINGUISTIC CONNOTATION
ANTIANXIETY	
Halcion	halcyon (pleasingly calm or peaceful)
Equanil	equanimity
Unisom	unified somnolence
Librium	equilibrium (balance)
ANTIDEPRESSANT	
Elavil	to elevate
Sinequan	sine qua non (the one essential thing)
Vivactil	vivacious
Asendin	to ascend
Zoloft	lofty
ANTIPSYCHOTIC	
Serentil	serenity
Thorazine	Thor (powerful Norse god of thunder)
ANTI-PARKINSONIAN	
Symmetrel	symmetry
ANTI-ALZHEIMER'S	
Cognex	cognizant

atypical antipsychotics (for example, *clozapine*), have also become available.

Research has repeatedly shown that antipsychotic drugs are more effective than any other single form of treatment for schizophrenic disorders (Klerman et al., 1994; Davis, Barter, & Kane, 1989; May, Tuma, & Dixon, 1981). For many patients with schizophrenia the drugs alone are not sufficient treatment, but when drug therapy is combined with appropriate community programs and adjunct psychotherapy, many of these patients, too, can return to a reasonably normal life. Unfortunately, some patients fail to improve even when drugs are combined with psychotherapy and community care.

A major problem is that antipsychotic drugs may also cause serious undesired effects in many patients. The most troubling are *extrapyramidal effects,* movement disorders such as severe shaking, bizarre-looking contractions of the face and body, and extreme restlessness, which are believed to result from

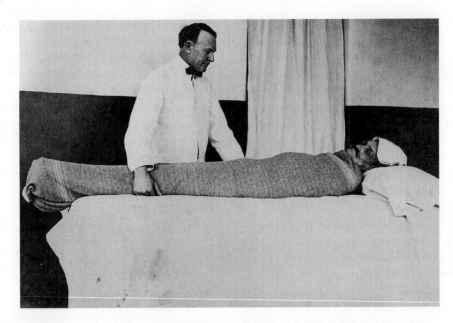

Prior to the discovery of antipsychotic and other psychotropic drugs, clinicians in mental institutions used techniques such as the "wet pack," designed for calming excited patients.

the drugs' effect on the extrapyramidal areas of the brain, areas just beneath the cortex. One kind of extrapyramidal effect, called **tardive dyskinesia** (meaning "late-appearing movement disorder"), emerges in some patients after they have taken antipsychotic drugs for a few years. Tardive dyskinesia is not always reversible even when patients are taken off antipsychotic drugs. Fortunately, the newer, atypical antipsychotic drugs do not appear to produce these unpleasant and dangerous extrapyramidal effects (Meltzer, 1993; Gerlach & Hansen, 1992).

Despite their significant drawbacks, antipsychotic drugs continue to be widely used in cases of schizophrenia. The reason is simple: they often bring improvement and even recovery to patients who would otherwise be doomed to a life of hopeless confinement.

ELECTROCONVULSIVE THERAPY   Another form of biological treatment used widely today, primarily on depressed patients, is **electroconvulsive therapy (ECT)**, a technique first developed in the 1930s by two Italian physicians, Ugo Cerletti and Lucio Bini. Two electrodes are attached to a patient's forehead and an electrical current of 50 to 150 watts is briefly passed through the brain. The current causes a brain seizure, or convulsion, that lasts up to a few minutes. After an average of seven to nine ECT sessions, spaced two or three days apart, many patients feel considerably less depressed (Fink, 1988). ECT helps approximately 72 percent of depressed subjects to improve, whereas placebo treatments help only 23

percent (Wechsler et al., 1965). Accordingly, the procedure is used on tens of thousands of depressed persons annually (Foderaero, 1993). Arguments against and in favor of its use are discussed at length in Chapter 9.

ECT is administered less often today than it was in the past. With the growing success of antidepressant medications and of cognitive therapy, fewer depressed patients now need this extreme form of treatment. Moreover, today's licensing agencies and courts regulate and monitor the use of ECT more carefully than they used to. Nevertheless, ECT is still applied when people have a severe depressive episode that is unresponsive to other forms of treatment (Buchan et al., 1992; Weiner, 1989). In a survey of 3,000 randomly selected psychiatrists, 86 percent stated that ECT is an appropriate form of treatment, though only 22 percent of them actually had used it (APA, 1993; Tapia, 1983).

PSYCHOSURGERY   Brain surgery as a treatment for mental disorders is thought to have roots as far back as trephining, the apparent prehistoric practice of chipping a hole in the skull of a person who behaved strangely. Modern forms of psychosurgery are derived from a technique first developed in the late 1930s by a Portuguese neuropsychiatrist, Antonio de Egas Moniz. In this procedure, known as a **lobotomy,** a surgeon cut the connections between the cortex of the brain's frontal lobes and the lower centers of the brain. As we shall observe in Chapter 16, it became clear by the late 1950s that lobotomies were not so effective as many psychosurgeons had been claiming. Even more disturbing, many lobotomized patients later suffered terrible and irreversible effects—seizures, extreme listlessness, stupor, and in some cases death (Barahal, 1958). Thus, this procedure declined in popularity during the 1960s. Today's procedures are much more precise than the lobotomies of the past (Beck & Cowley, 1990). They have fewer unwanted effects and are apparently beneficial in some cases of severe depression, anxiety, and obsessive-compulsive disorders. Even so, they are considered experimental and are used infrequently, usually only after a severe disorder has continued for years without responding to any other form of treatment (Goodman et al., 1992; Greist, 1992).

■ FORMATS ■ OF THERAPY

Therapists see a client either alone, in *individual therapy;* with other clients who share similar problems, in *group therapy;* or with family members, in *couple* and *family therapy.* Each of these formats is amenable to the techniques and principles of the therapist's particular theoretical orientation, whether it be psychodynamic, behavioral, or some other model. In addition, strategies have been developed for use in specific formats.

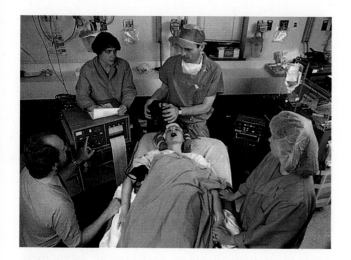

Patients who receive electroconvulsive therapy experience a brain seizure as an electric current passes through electrodes attached to their heads. They are given anesthetics and muscle relaxants so that they will sleep through the procedure and will not flail about during the seizure. Many patients who suffer from severe depression experience a significant rise in mood after a series of such treatments.

INDIVIDUAL THERAPY

Individual therapy is the oldest of the modern therapy formats. The therapist sees the client alone for sessions that may last from fifteen minutes to two hours, depending on such factors as the client's problem, the therapist's orientation, and the cost of the therapy. In addition, the therapist may use adjunct treatment techniques such as biofeedback training or computer analysis that will affect the length of the session. Although patients usually meet with the therapist once a week, some are scheduled more often (as in orthodox psychoanalysis) and some less (as in some drug therapies).

GROUP THERAPY

At the turn of the century, a physician in Boston named Joseph Pratt brought tuberculosis patients together in groups to teach them about their illness and encourage them to provide emotional support for each other. This appears to have been the first clinical application of group therapy (Rosenbaum & Berger, 1963). American and British clinicians continued to experiment with group processes over the next fifty years, but it was not until after World War II that group therapy became a popular format for treating people with psychological problems. At that time, a growing demand for psychological services forced therapists throughout the United States and Europe to look for alternatives to individual therapy. Many who tried the group format found it to be efficient, time-saving, and relatively inexpensive. Some of them claimed that group therapy was often as helpful as individual therapy.

Thousands of therapists now specialize in group therapy, and countless others conduct therapy groups as one aspect of their practice. A recent survey of 481 clinical psychologists, for example, revealed that almost a third of them practice group therapy to some degree (Norcross et al., 1993). Typically, group members meet together with a therapist and discuss the problems or concerns of one or more of the members. The therapist usually follows the principles of his or her theoretical orientation in conducting the group. Groups are often created with particular client populations in mind; for example, there are groups for people with alcoholism, for those who are physically handicapped, and for people who are divorced, abused, or bereaved (Bednar & Kaul, 1994; DeAngelis, 1992; Lynn & Frauman, 1985). The group format has also been used for purposes that are educational rather than therapeutic, such as for

The 1960s and 1970s witnessed an enormous growth in the popularity of "encounter groups," or "sensitivity groups," small and intense non-therapy groups designed to help members develop greater self-awareness and skill in human relationships. Perhaps the most controversial of these was the "nude" encounter group which was thought to help lower the participants' defenses (Bindrim, 1968). Sexual expression was forbidden.

"consciousness raising," religious inspiration, and "encounter" experiences.

On the basis of his own work and on a number of group investigations, the group therapy theorist Irvin Yalom (1985) suggests that successful forms of group therapy share certain "curative" features:

1. *Guidance:* they usually provide information and advice for members.
2. *Identification:* they provide models of appropriate behavior.
3. *Group cohesiveness:* they offer an atmosphere of solidarity in which members can learn to take risks and accept criticism.
4. *Universality:* members discover that other people have similar problems.
5. *Altruism:* members develop feelings of self-worth by helping others.
6. *Catharsis:* members develop more understanding of themselves and of others and learn to express their feelings.
7. *Skill building:* members acquire or improve social skills.

These features are also at work in two specialized kinds of group therapy—psychodrama and self-help groups.

PSYCHODRAMA In the 1920s Jacob Moreno, a Viennese psychiatrist and the first person to use the term "group psychotherapy," developed the therapy known as *psychodrama,* in which group members act out dramatic roles as if they were participating in an improvised play. The atmosphere of structured fantasy is expected to make the participants feel secure enough to express their feelings and thoughts, explore new behavior and attitudes, and empathize with the feelings and perspectives of others. Often the group members act on a stage and even in front of an audience.

Various role-playing techniques are used in psychodrama. In the *auxiliary ego* technique, also called *mirroring,* one group member portrays another, thus showing the latter how he or she appears to others. In *role reversal,* two group members play each other. In the technique of *magic shop,* participants temporarily exchange one of their undesirable personal characteristics for a quality that they desire. All these activities are guided by the therapist, or "director," who also provides feedback about each participant's performance. The audience, too, may give useful feedback.

Although relatively few therapists limit their groups' activities to psychodrama alone, many have incorporated its techniques and principles into their practice. As we saw earlier, many behavioral and humanistic therapists now use role playing to teach assertiveness and social skills and to facilitate interactions among members of their groups (Wood et al., 1981). Similarly, psychodrama's emphasis on spontaneity and empathy has permeated most group therapies (Lubin, 1983).

SELF-HELP GROUPS *Self-help groups* (or *mutual help groups*) are made up of people who have similar problems and come together to help and support one another without the direct leadership of a professional clinician. These groups have become increasingly popular over the last two decades, and today there are about 500,000 such groups attended by 15 million people in the United States alone, addressing a wide assortment of issues, including alcoholism and other forms of drug abuse, compulsive gambling, bereavement, overeating, phobias, child abuse, medical illnesses, rape victimization, unemployment, and divorce (White & Madara, 1992).

Self-help groups are popular for several reasons. Some of the participants are searching for inexpensive and interesting alternatives to traditional kinds of treatment and find self-help groups in their travels, along with self-help books, coping tapes, radio therapy shows, and other modern-day approaches to feeling better (see Box 5–5). Many participants, however,

"Freud once said that he had never seen a patient the germs of whose disease he could not find in himself" (Karon, 1988). Self-help groups go Freud one better: they hold that people with similar problems are in the best position to support and advise one another. Thousands of such groups around the world help people cope with a variety of problems.

have simply lost confidence in the ability of clinicians and social institutions to help with their particular problems (Silverman, 1992). Alcoholics Anonymous, the well-known network of self-help groups for people dependent on alcohol, was developed in 1934 in response to the general ineffectiveness of clinical treatments for alcoholism. Still others are drawn to self-help groups because they find them less threatening and less stigmatizing than therapy groups. Finally, the popularity of self-help groups may be related to the decline of the extended family and other traditional sources of emotional support in Western society (Bloch, Crouch, & Reibstein, 1982).

Self-help groups have some unique characteristics that probably contribute to their effectiveness (Silverman, 1992; Rodolfa & Hungerford, 1982). For example, they encourage more helping among members than therapy groups do. Often new members are assigned to veteran members who take a special interest in them and help integrate them into the group. In addition, self-help groups encourage members to exchange information more than other groups do. People who are newly bereaved, for example, can obtain specific information from their self-help group about funeral arrangements and business matters, as well as about what feelings to expect and how to cope with them.

Many clinicians consider these groups a form of therapy despite the absence of a therapist-leader (Christensen & Jacobson, 1994). At the very least, therapists usually view the groups as compatible with

traditional forms of therapy. They often urge clients to participate in self-help groups as part of a broader treatment program for problems such as alcoholism, eating disorders, and victimization.

ASSESSING GROUP THERAPY Because groups vary so widely in type and conduct and in the characteristics of their leaders and members, and because group interactions can be complex, it has been difficult to assess their effectiveness (Bednar & Kaul, 1994; Sadock, 1989). Moreover, many of the studies that have been done have not used proper research methodology (Sadock, 1989; Lubin, 1983). Thus only a modest number of conclusions can be drawn about therapy that takes this format.

Research does indicate that group therapy is of help to many clients, often as helpful as individual therapy (Bednar & Kaul, 1994; DeAngelis, 1992). It appears that candid feedback is usually useful for group members as long as a balance is struck between positive and negative feedback. Some people have been harmed by group therapy, but such occurrences are not frequent. Apparently, skilled group leaders are usually able to screen out those prospective members who need more individual attention or who would not be able to tolerate the demands of the group experience (Sadock, 1989).

FAMILY THERAPY

Adhering to the sociocultural position that disturbances in social structure often cause disturbances in individual functioning, several clinicians in the 1950s developed *family therapy*—a format in which therapists meet with all members of a family, point out problematic behavior and interactions between the members, and help the whole family to change (Minuchin, 1993, 1992; Satir, 1987, 1964; Ackerman, 1965; Bell, 1961; Bowen, 1960). Most family therapists meet with family members as a group, but some choose to see them separately. Either way, the family is viewed as the unit under treatment. Here is a typical interaction between family members and therapist:

"I just don't understand. We have had a happy family all along until Tommy started acting up." Bob Davis was visibly exasperated. "You are supposed to be the family expert, Ms. Fargo, what do you think?"

"We have tried so hard to be good parents to both of

BOX 5–5

WHAT'S NEW
IN "TREATMENT?"

Each day seems to bring some new approach to helping people with psychological problems. In New York, an ex-stockbroker offers a "playshop" to help people learn to be less serious and more outrageous. Her technique, called "chutzpah therapy," consists of three days of charades, body-movement exercises, coloring with crayons, improvisation, and dressing up in costumes (Kaufman, 1993). Elsewhere in the city, on Saturdays, the three "Advice Ladies" stand on a corner giving advice to passersby (Bellafante, 1993). Interventions such as these may capture the attention of reporters, but they are not always taken seriously by professionals. Three unconventional approaches that *are* receiving serious examination by clinical professionals these days are treatments that make use, respectively, of the great outdoors, the telephone, and the computer.

Outward Bound, a well-known wilderness program that focuses on the development of outdoor skills, self-esteem, and positive group dynamics, also offers a number of programs specifically tailored to meet special psychological needs. In these programs, participants confront physical and mental challenges, such as mountain climbing and hiking, both in groups and alone. Activities like the "solo" period, during which participants are given limited food supplies and left alone for seventy-two hours, are meant to teach people about their strengths and weaknesses and increase their sense of self-reliance and control.

Juvenile offenders who have participated in an Outward Bound program show a one-year reduction in delinquency, but the reduction is not sustained at a two-year follow up (Castellano & Soderstrom, 1992). Similarly, although a reduction in trait anxiety and an increase in feelings of personal competence have been identified in participants immediately after the completion of Outward Bound programs, long-term follow-up studies reveal only limited systematic changes in their self-concepts (Ewert, 1988; Marsh, Richards, & Barnes, 1986).

Bedridden, physically disabled, and hospitalized patients are the targets of ***telephone therapy,*** therapy done over the phone. Although there is concern that important visual and nonverbal cues are lost when therapist and client do not meet face to face, some clinicians suggest that the anonymity and formality of telephone therapy may actually enhance the psychotherapeutic process (Mermelstein & Holland, 1991). Phone therapy has apparently also been helpful for individuals who suffer from *agoraphobia,* a fear of leaving one's home (Cox, Fergus, & Swinson, 1993).

Dr. William Masters (a pioneer, along with Virginia Johnson, in the study of sexual dysfunctioning) has also been busy over the phone these days, as he launches his plans to set up a 1-900 line to dispense sex information. Although he stresses that his hot-

the children," Bob glanced at his wife, "but Tommy just doesn't respond anymore. I wish he was more like his little sister. She is so well behaved and is a joy to have around."

Tommy sat motionless in a chair gazing out the window. He was fourteen and a bit small for his age. He looked completely disinterested in the proceedings.

Sissy was eleven. She was sitting on the couch between her Mom and Dad with a smile on her face. Across from them sat Ms. Fargo, the family therapist.

Ms. Fargo spoke. "Could you be a little more specific about the changes you have seen in Tommy and when they came about?"

Mrs. Davis answered first. "Well, I guess it was about two years ago. Tommy started getting in fights at school. When we talked to him at home he said it was none of

our business. He became moody and disobedient. He wouldn't do anything that we wanted him to. He began to act mean to his sister and even hit her."

"What about the fights at school?" Ms. Fargo asked.

This time it was Mr. Davis who spoke first. "Ginny was more worried about them than I was. I used to fight a lot when I was in school and I think it is normal. I had a lot of brothers and sisters in my family and I learned early that I had to fight for whatever I could; it's part of being a boy. But I was very respectful to my parents, especially my Dad. If I ever got out of line he would smack me one."

"Have you ever had to hit Tommy?" Ms. Fargo inquired softly.

"Sure, a couple of times, but it didn't seem to do any good."

line is not meant to serve as a medium of therapeutic exchange, Masters believes that as an educational resource, it may be helpful to a large number of people. Stating that "So much of sexual disorders and dysfunction is based on ignorance and a lack of education," he thinks that the telephone, with its anonymity and accessibility, may be the best way to reach the greatest number of people (Roan, 1993).

As we observed in Chapter 4, many clinicians already use *computer programs* to help them gather clients' histories, assess self-report inventories, and even make preliminary diagnoses. Numerous attempts have also been made to develop a computer program that can provide effective therapy. One of the earliest and best known is the ELIZA program (Weizenbaum, 1966), designed to simulate the experience of a client-centered therapy session. The patient types in a response to a question, and the computer selects the next question on the basis of key words that appear in the response. Sometimes the computer simply restates the patient's response, the way a client-centered therapist might choose to do (Servan-Schreiber, 1986). People who interact with ELIZA and other computer therapists have frequently attributed insight and reasoning ability to the computer, and many even seem to experience a kind of personal relationship with the computer program (Zarr, 1984).

PLATO DCS (Wagman, 1980), another computer counseling system, helps people articulate their problems in "if-then" statements, a basic technique used by cognitive therapists (Binik et al., 1988). One study of phobias found that this computer therapy was as effective as a human therapist using the same questioning approach (Ghosh & Greist, 1988; Ghosh & Marks, 1987). Similar results were documented with depressed patients (Ghosh & Greist, 1988; Selmi, 1983).

Newer to the marketplace is a corporate computer counseling center in Los Angeles, which aims to complete therapy in ten sessions at a cost of $600 to $800. The idea is to get at problems quickly and confidentially. If there are danger signs, such as suicidal tendencies, a human therapist is warned via computer printout (Murray, 1993). In another new approach, a personal computer program named "Overcoming Depression" offers a form of cognitive therapy to depressed persons, and in the process quotes from Leo Tolstoy and Bertrand Russell.

If computer-facilitated therapies are by necessity simplistic and lacking in specificity, why do they work for some clients? A number of theorists have suggested that people may find it easier to reveal sensitive personal information to a computer than to a live therapist (Greist & Klein, 1980). The computer offers them the freedom to express thoughts and emotions without being judged by another person (Lawrence, 1986). The computer therapist is never tired, angry, or bored (Colby et al., 1979). It does not use facial expressions, gestures, or harrumphing noises that, perhaps unintentionally, indicate surprise, approval, or dismay. It is always available—potentially to greater numbers of people—and it is less costly. These are all attractive attributes in a therapist.

Computers may never substitute fully for the judgment of a trained therapist; nor will they ever be able to simulate the interpersonal patient-therapist relationship, which some believe to be the foundation of recovery. Yet, as researchers and practitioners learn more about the nature of mental disorders and create more complex and humanlike computer programs, computer therapies, like some of the other new approaches we have discussed, may at least find a place as adjuncts to other forms of treatment and intervention.

All at once Tommy seemed to be paying attention, his eyes riveted on his father. "Yeah, he hit me a lot, for no reason at all!"

"Now, that's not true, Thomas." Mrs. Davis has a scolding expression on her face. "If you behaved yourself a little better you wouldn't get hit. Ms. Fargo, I can't say that I am in favor of the hitting, but I understand sometimes how frustrating it may be for Bob."

"You don't know how frustrating it is for me, honey." Bob seemed upset. "You don't have to work all day at the office and then come home to contend with all of this. Sometimes I feel like I don't even want to come home."

Ginny gave him a hard stare. "You think things at home are easy all day? I could use some support from you. You think all you have to do is earn the money and I will do everything else. Well, I am not about to do that anymore."

"As you can see, Ms. Fargo, Ginny and I do not see eye-to-eye on everything about raising the kids. I think she is afraid that she has failed Tommy in some way."

"I've failed?" Ginny's face was now getting red. "You are the one who is never around to provide a good example for the kids. They have a mother; what they need is a father."

"I think you can see, Ms. Fargo" (Bob winked at the therapist), "what I am up against here and why it is no fun to come home anymore."

There was a long tense silence.

"What about you, Sissy," Ms. Fargo looked at the little girl, "what do you think about what's happening at home?"

"I think Tommy is a bad boy. I wish he would stop hitting me. I liked him before when he was nice."

Tommy began to fidget and finally he got up from his chair and started to walk around the room.

"Sit down, son," Mr. Davis demanded in a firm voice. Tommy ignored him.

"Sit down before I knock you down!"

Tommy reluctantly sat down in a chair in the far corner of the room.

Mrs. Davis began to cry. "I just don't know what to do anymore. Things just seem so hopeless. Why can't people be nice in this family anymore? I don't think I am asking too much, am I?"

Ms. Fargo spoke thoughtfully. "I get the feeling that people in this family would like things to be different. Bob, I can see how frustrating it must be for you to work so hard and not be able to relax when you get home. And, Ginny, your job is not easy either. You have a lot to do at home and Bob can't be there to help because he has to earn a living. And you kids sound like you would like some things to be different too. It must be hard for you, Tommy, to be catching so much flack these days. I think this also makes it hard for you to have fun at home too, Sissy."

She looked at each person briefly and was sure to make eye contact. "There seems to be a lot going on. What I would like to do is talk with you together and then see the parents for a while and then maybe you kids alone, to hear your sides of the story. I think we are going to need to understand a lot of things to see why this is happening. I can hear, Tommy, that it is hard for you to be living in this family right now and that it is hard for your parents to have you. Also, as you have gotten older, it may be that you have thought you should be treated a little differently by your folks. What I would like everyone to do is to think about how each of you, if you could, would change the other family members so that you would be happier in the family. I will want everyone to tell me that and I want you all to listen to what the others have to say."

(Sheras & Worchel, 1979, pp. 108–110)

Like group therapists, family therapists may ascribe to any of the major theoretical models (Gurman, Kniskern, & Pinsof, 1986). Whatever their orientation, most also adhere to some of the principles of *family systems theory.* And, indeed, 7 percent of today's therapists identify themselves *primarily* as family systems therapists—13 percent of all social workers, 7 percent of psychologists and counselors, and 1 percent of psychiatrists (Prochaska & Norcross, 1994). As we noted in Chapter 2, family systems theory holds that each family has its own implicit rules, relationship structure, and communication patterns that shape the behavior of the individual members, including dysfunctional behavior. For one family member to change, the family system must be changed.

In one family systems approach, *structural family therapy,* therapists pay particular attention to the family power structure, the role each member plays, and the alliances between family members (Minuchin, 1992, 1987, 1974; Minuchin & Fishman, 1981). The goal of therapy is to build a new family structure in which a working balance, or *homeostasis,* is achieved without the need for any member to adopt a sick role. In the case of the Davis family, for example, Tommy's misbehavior was interpreted as a shift in roles that was upsetting the family's homeostasis, forcing other family members also to change their roles and expectations to establish an alternative form of homeostasis:

As Tommy grew into adolescence and desired to have more independence in his family, his role began to change. He did not want to be treated as "Mommy's little boy." He began to fight frequently at school so that she would have to see his role differently. Mrs. Davis, however, still saw Tommy as her little boy who was now acting like a "bad" boy instead of the model child she expected him to be. Since what she expected from Tommy and what she observed in him were not the same behaviors, she had to change her behavior to treat him differently in an attempt to change his behavior. This also produced a change in Mr. Davis' behavior. Everyone in the system was affected by the change that began with Tommy's desire for independence.

(Sheras & Worchel, 1979, p. 121)

In *conjoint family therapy* the therapist focuses primarily on communication in the family system, helping members recognize harmful patterns of communication, appreciate the impact of such patterns on other family members, and change the patterns (Satir, 1987, 1967, 1964). Here a therapist helps a mother, father, and son identify their communication difficulties:

Therapist: *(To husband)* I notice your brow is wrinkled, Ralph. Does that mean you are angry at this moment?

Husband: I did not know that my brow was wrinkled.

Therapist: Sometimes a person looks or sounds in a way of which he is not aware. As far as you can tell, what were you thinking and feeling just now?

Husband: I was thinking over what she [his wife] said.

Therapist: What thing that she said were you thinking about?

Husband: When she said that when she was talking so loud, she wished I would tell her.

Therapist: What were you thinking about that?

Influential family therapist Salvador Minuchin helped develop the structural approach to family therapy, which focuses on changing dysfunctional power distributions, relationships, alignments, and boundaries in families. Animated and direct, Minuchin straightforwardly points out to family members that their comments and behavior are inappropriate and counterproductive, and pushes them toward alternative structures and behavior.

Family therapy pioneer Virginia Satir (1916–1988), first recognized the importance of communication in families during a series of sessions with a 28-year-old woman and her mother. "I noticed the tilting of a head, or an arm moving, or a voice drop, and then I would see a reaction. It didn't seem to have anything to do with the words. The words could be 'I love you' but all the rest of it was something else" (Satir, 1987, p. 67).

Husband: I never thought about telling her. I thought she would get mad.

Therapist: Ah, then maybe that wrinkle meant you were puzzled because your wife was hoping you would do something and you did not know she had this hope. Do you suppose that by your wrinkled brow you were signalling that you were puzzled?

Husband: Yeh, I guess so.

Therapist: As far as you know, have you ever been in that same spot before, that is, where you were puzzled by something Alice said or did? . . .

Wife: He never says anything.

Therapist: (*Smiling, to Alice*) Just a minute, Alice, let me hear what Ralph's idea is of what he does. Ralph, how do you think you have let Alice know when you are puzzled?

Husband: I think she knows.

Therapist: Well, let's see. Suppose you ask Alice if she knows.

Husband: This is silly.

Therapist: (*Smiling*) I suppose it might seem so in this situation, because Alice is right here and certainly has

heard what your question is. She knows what it is. I have the suspicion, though, that neither you nor Alice are very sure about what the other expects, and I think you have not developed ways to find out. Alice, let's go back to when I commented on Ralph's wrinkled brow. Did you happen to notice it, too?

Wife: (*Complaining*) Yes, he always looks like that.

Therapist: What kind of message did you get from that wrinkled brow? . . .

Wife: (*Exasperated and tearfully*) I don't know.

Therapist: Well, maybe the two of you have not yet worked out crystal-clear ways of giving your love and value messages to each other. Everyone needs crystal-clear ways of giving their value messages. (*To son*) What do you know, Jim, about how you give your value messages to your parents?

(*Satir, 1967, pp. 97–100*)

COUPLE THERAPY

In *couple therapy,* or *marital therapy,* the therapist works with two people who are in a long-term relationship, focusing again on the structure and

Although most couples who are seen together in couple therapy are married, the approach is now available and helpful to unmarried heterosexual couples and gay couples as well. Regardless of the kind of couple in treatment, therapists usually emphasize the structure of the relationship and the couple's communication patterns.

communication patterns in their relationship. Often this format of therapy focuses on a husband and wife, but the couple need not be married or even living together. Couple therapy is usually used when a relationship is unsatisfying or in conflict (Epstein, Baucom, & Rankin, 1993; Gurman, 1985). Also, a couple approach may be employed rather than family therapy when a child's psychological problems are traced to problems between the parents (Fauber & Long, 1992; Turkewitz & O'Leary, 1981).

Although some degree of conflict is inevitable in any long-term relationship, there is growing evidence that many adults in our society experience serious marital discord (Markman & Hahlweg, 1993; Bradbury & Karney, 1993) (see Figure 5–6). The divorce rate in Canada, the United States, and Europe is now close to 50 percent of the marriage rate and has been climbing steadily in recent decades (Inglehart, 1990; Doherty & Jacobson, 1982). Only a third of Americans who married in the early 1970s

are now still married *and* proclaiming their marriages "very happy" (Glenn, 1989). Many of those who live together without marrying seem to have similar levels of relationship disharmony (Greeley, 1991).

Certain complaints are particularly common among the people who enter couple therapy. The most common complaints by women are of feeling unloved by their spouses (66 percent), constantly belittled (33 percent), and repeatedly criticized (33 percent) (Kelly, 1982). Men complain of being neglected (53 percent) and unloved (37 percent) by their spouses and of sensing a long-standing incompatibility of one kind or another (39 percent). Approximately a third of both women and men also complain that they are sexually deprived and that their spouse is chronically angry or "bitchy."

Couple therapy, like family therapy, may be incorporated in any of the major therapy systems (Epstein et al., 1993; Goldman & Greenberg, 1992). A version that has been employed increasingly, **behavioral marital therapy,** follows a behavioral perspective (Cordova & Jacobson, 1993; Jacobson, 1989). Therapists who use this approach help spouses identify and change problem behaviors.

To help replace detrimental marital behaviors with more productive ones, behavioral marital therapists often teach specific communication and problem-solving skills to spouses. Spouses may be instructed to follow such guidelines as these when they discuss their marital problems with each other:

1. Always begin with something positive when stating the problem.
2. Use specific behaviors to describe what is bothersome rather than derogatory labels or overgeneralizations.
3. Make connections between those specific behaviors and feelings that arise in response to them.
4. Admit one's own role in the development of the problem.
5. Be brief and maintain a current or future focus, that is, do not list all previous incidents of the problem, analyze causes, or ask "why" questions.

When deciding what action is in order to solve the problem, spouses are to:

6. Focus on solutions by brainstorming as many solutions as possible.
7. Focus on mutuality and compromise by considering solutions that involve change by both partners.

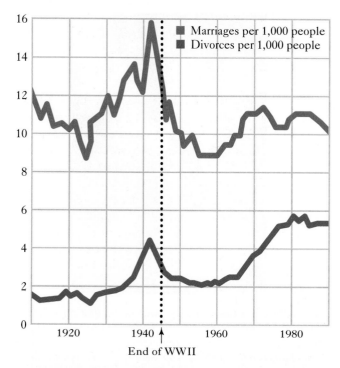

FIGURE 5-6 *Although the rate of marriage has remained the same in the United States since 1920, the divorce rate has almost tripled. Eleven of every 1,000 people get married each year, but 5 of every 1,000 get divorced. (U.S. Census Bureau, National Center for Health Statistics.)*

8. Offer to change something in one's own behavior.
9. Accept, for a beginning, a change less than the ideal solution.
10. Discuss the advantages and disadvantages of each suggestion before reaching agreement.
11. Prepare a final change agreement that is spelled out in clear, descriptive behavioral terms, that is recorded in writing, and that includes cues reminding each partner of changes she or he has agreed to make.

In addition, some general guidelines for problem solving are to be followed:

12. Develop an agenda for each problem-solving discussion.
13. Discuss only one problem at a time; that is, be aware of sidetracking.
14. Do not make inferences; talk about only what you can observe.
15. Paraphrase what the partner has said and check out perceptions to what was said before responding to it.

(Margolin, 1983, pp. 265–266; Jacobson & Margolin, 1979)

To help increase a couple's intimacy, behavioral marital therapists may show them how to reestablish *core*

symbols in their marriage—events, places, rituals, or objects that have special meaning for them (Stuart, 1975). The spouses may be told to reserve Friday nights for "dates" with each other, wear special clothes for each other, or regularly go to favorite places together. The therapist may also have the spouses perform considerate behaviors. In the technique of "caring days," each spouse devotes a day to doing things the other has requested (Stuart, 1980). Similarly, in the "love days" technique, spouses must double the number of their pleasing actions on a designated day of the week (Weiss, Hops, & Patterson, 1973). And in an approach called "consideration," spouses show consideration at least once each day (Margolin & Weinstein, 1983).

Recently, some practitioners of behavioral marital therapy have expanded the approach with a treatment called *integrative behavioral couple therapy* (Cordova & Jacobson, 1993). In addition to behavioral techniques, this broader approach includes cognitive strategies designed to help partners accept marital behaviors that they cannot change and adopt the view that such behaviors are an understandable consequence of basic differences between them. During this part of therapy, the partners learn to empathize with the other's emotional pain, avoid blaming either themselves or their partner for the relationship problems, stop trying to change the partner, reinterpret marital differences as complementary, and recognize the positive features of certain "problem" behaviors. Thus, a wife may be guided to see her husband's "stodginess" as the quality of stability that she was

"I've been a cow all my life, honey. Don't ask me to change now."

In "integrative behavioral couple therapy," an expansion of "behavioral marital therapy," partners are also taught to accept their differences and problematic marital behaviors. (Drawing by Ziegler; © 1992 The New Yorker Magazine, Inc.)

initially attracted to. Or a husband may learn to reinterpret his wife's overinvolvement with friends as the quality of gregariousness that he previously valued.

The general goals of behavioral marital therapy and integrative behavioral couple therapy are to help spouses develop more effective marital behaviors and derive more pleasure from their relationship. Research suggests that couples treated with these approaches do indeed develop more effective interpersonal skills and greater tolerance for one another, and feel greater satisfaction than those who receive no treatment at all (Cordova & Jacobson, 1993; Jacobson & Addis, 1993; Baucom & Hoffman, 1986). One review of relevant studies computed that 72 percent of troubled couples treated with these approaches improved (Hahlweg & Markman, 1988). However, the improvements sometimes fail to last. One study found that 30 percent of previously recovered couples relapsed within two years after treatment, prompting the investigators to recommend routine booster sessions of behavioral marital therapy whenever new stressful live events arise (Jacobson, Schmaling, & Holzworth-Munroe, 1987).

Our culture is inundated with "treatments" that come in such forms as self-help books, radio and television call-in shows, advice columns, and audio and video tapes—offerings sometimes known collectively as "pop therapy." People often find such forms of help quite useful (Starker, 1988). One of the most famous practitioners in this tradition is "Dr. Ruth" Westheimer, who offers counseling and advice on sexual functioning to millions of radio listeners and TV viewers.

ASSESSING FAMILY AND COUPLE THERAPY

As family and couple therapy have grown in popularity, more and more research has been conducted to evaluate their effectiveness. Overall, studies suggest that the approaches are indeed useful for certain problems and under certain circumstances. Reviews of methodologically sound studies (Alexander, Holtzworth-Munroe, & Jameson, 1994; Shadish et al., 1993; Goldman & Greenberg, 1992; Gurman et al., 1986; Todd & Stanton, 1983; Gurman & Kniskern, 1978) reveal the following:

1. In comparison with other forms of treatment, family and couple therapy are usually equal or superior in effectiveness at treating many kinds of problems. The overall improvement rate for cases seen in these formats of therapy has been computed at between 50 and 65 percent, compared to 35 percent for those in control groups.
2. The involvement of the father in family therapy substantially increases the likelihood of a successful outcome.
3. When the presenting complaint is a couple problem, the treatment outcome is significantly better if the spouses are seen together in therapy, as opposed to individual therapy for either spouse.
4. There is little comparative evidence that one couple or family therapy approach is superior to all others at treating a wide range of problems.
5. Short-term and time-limited couple and family therapy are as effective as longer-term therapy.
6. Many clinicians claim that *cotherapy*, a popular approach in which two therapists conduct the couple or family treatment, is a uniquely effective way of modeling appropriate forms of communication for families and couples; yet there is no empirical evidence that cotherapy is more effective than treatment conducted by a single therapist.

■ IS ■ TREATMENT EFFECTIVE?

Probably the most important question to ask about a particular treatment is whether it does what it is supposed to do—that is, whether it helps people cope with and overcome their psychological problems. On the surface, this may seem to be a simple question. In fact, it is one of the most difficult questions for clinical researchers to answer (Persons, 1991). Several problems must be addressed.

The first problem is how to define a "successful" treatment (Strupp, 1989). Consider the posttreatment statements of Louise and Helen, two women who have grappled with anorexia nervosa, the eating disorder in which people purposely lose excessive and dangerous amounts of weight:

ouise: It's not just that I look normal again, but that I *feel* normal. I'm no longer afraid of food, of gaining an ounce, or of being ugly. I no longer cut food for 15 minutes before eating it; and I don't have to chew each piece 12 times before swallowing. It's all so weird, I can hardly believe that I was caught up in it. But I was.

Most of all, I feel free now, free to be me, to run my own life and to meet my own needs. Oh, I love my parents and my sisters, I really do. But I don't have to be perfect and keep pleasing them in order to show my love or to win their love. I know that now. I have a lot of ground to make up, and I can hardly wait.

elen: I'm a lot better now. I weigh 105 pounds instead of 90. I can eat salads, vegetables, and fish without worrying, although I still have problems with bread and potatoes, and sweets are just impossible. I still worry a lot about gaining too much weight; in fact, 105 feels pretty scary. But I weigh myself every day, so I don't think it will get out of hand. I've put my family through a lot and let them down. I'm really sorry about that. I guess they realize now what I've always known, that I'm a mess in many ways. Perhaps some day I'll win back their respect; I really hope so.

Both Louise and Helen have improved, but not to the same degree. Should a clinical researcher consider both of their recoveries successful, or just Louise's? Different researchers would answer this question differently. Some might even be reluctant to pronounce Helen recovered on her evaluation alone. A psychodynamic researcher, for example, might look for evidence that she has satisfactorily resolved her underlying conflicts before making a judgment. Because definitions of success vary from study to study, it is not always appropriate to combine the results from different treatment studies and use them to draw general conclusions (Kazdin, 1994).

The second problem is *how* to measure improvement. Should researchers give equal weight to the reports of clients, friends, relatives, therapists, and teachers? Should they use rating scales, inventories, checklists, therapy insights, behavior observations, so-

Many therapists try to tap into a client's feelings by using art therapy or music therapy as an adjunct to treatment. Clients are expected to find, express, and work out relevant feelings through their art or music, and their creative accomplishments may also encourage feelings of confidence and self-respect.

cial adjustment scores, or some other measure? The various measures of improvement correlate only moderately with one another (Lambert & Hill, 1994; Bloch et al., 1982). Louise's report that she has totally "overcome" her eating problems may be at odds with the reports of friends and relatives who see tension in her face or slowness in her movements whenever she is eating a meal with them. This is another reason why researchers cannot automatically combine findings from different studies to draw broad conclusions about the effectiveness of treatment.

Perhaps the biggest problem is the range and complexity of the treatments currently in use. Clients differ in their problems, personal styles, and motivation for therapy; therapists differ in skill, experience, orientation, and personality; and therapies differ in theory, format, and setting. Because a client's progress in therapy is influenced by all these factors and more, results from a particular study will not always apply to other clients and therapists.

Proper research procedures—use of control groups, random assignment, matched subjects, and the like—address some of these problems and allow clinicians to draw certain conclusions about various therapies. Even in studies that are well designed and well conducted, however, the enormous range and complexity of factors involved in treatment set limits on the conclusions that can be reached (Kazdin, 1994).

Despite such difficulties, the job of evaluating therapies must be done, and clinical researchers have plowed ahead with it (Lambert & Bergin, 1994; Powell & Lindsay, 1987). Thousands of studies have been conducted to test the effectiveness of various treatments, and numerous reviewers have tried to assess those studies and draw overall conclusions. The studies fall into three categories: (1) those that ask whether therapy in general is effective, (2) those that ask whether a particular therapy is generally effective, and (3) those that ask whether particular therapies are effective for particular problems.

IS THERAPY GENERALLY EFFECTIVE?

In 1952 the conditioning theorist Hans J. Eysenck published a paper that raised serious questions about the general effectiveness of psychotherapy. After reviewing twenty-four studies, he concluded that 72 percent of control subjects who received no therapy managed to improve, whereas only 44 percent of subjects in psychoanalytic therapy and 66 percent of subjects in "eclectic" therapy—therapy that combines techniques from a variety of models—improved. In short, he suggested that therapy actually retards improvement. Over the next few decades Eysenck (1980, 1966, 1965, 1960) and clinical researcher Stanley Rachman (1971) conducted additional studies and reviews that again questioned the value of therapy, although their conclusions were somewhat less critical than Eysenck's had been in 1952.

Eysenck's research methods and interpretations have themselves been criticized in recent years, and most therapy researchers now disagree with his extreme conclusion. It has been pointed out, for example, that Eysenck's original criteria of improvement were stricter for treated subjects than for nontreated subjects (Bergin & Lambert, 1978). Nevertheless, Eysenck's claims have led to a number of careful investigations, most of which have suggested that therapy is often (though not always) more helpful than no treatment or than placebos (Lambert & Bergin, 1994). A review that covered many kinds of therapies and mental disorders found therapy to be more effective than no therapy in 48 of 57 adequately controlled effectiveness studies (Meltzoff & Kornreich, 1970). A still broader review examined 375 controlled effectiveness studies, covering a total of almost 25,000 clients seen in a wide assortment of therapies (Smith, Glass, & Miller, 1980; Smith & Glass, 1977). The investigators combined the findings of these studies by standardizing their results, a statistical technique called a "meta-analysis" (Schmidt, 1992). They rated the level of improvement in each treated person and in each untreated control subject and computed the

average difference between those two groups. According to this meta-analysis, the average person who received treatment was better off than 75 percent of the untreated control subjects (see Figure 5–7). Still other meta-analyses have revealed a similar relationship between treatment and improvement (Lambert, Weber, & Sykes, 1993; Crits-Cristoph et al., 1991).

A number of clinicians have also concerned themselves with an important related question: Can therapy be harmful? In his book *My Analysis with Freud* the psychoanalyst Abraham Kardiner (1977) wrote, "Freud was always infuriated whenever I would say to him that you could not do harm with psychoanalysis. He said: 'When you say that, you also say it cannot do any good. Because if you cannot do any harm, how can you do good?'" A number of studies conducted since the 1950s agree with Freud that some patients actually seem to worsen because of therapy (Lambert & Bergin, 1994; Mays & Franks, 1985; Truax, 1963). Similarly, a survey of 70 eminent clinicians and researchers showed a consensus that "deterioration effects" do occur in therapy (Hadley & Strupp, 1976).

The deterioration may take the form of a general worsening of symptoms or the development of new symptoms, including a sense of failure, guilt, low self-concept, or hopelessness over one's inability to profit from therapy (Lambert, Shapiro, & Bergin, 1986; Hadley & Strupp, 1976). These effects have been observed in a wide variety of client populations, therapy systems, formats, and settings. The frequency of client deterioration has varied from study to study (Ogles et al., 1993; Smith et al., 1980), but most studies on this issue find that between 5 and 10 percent of clients decline as a result of therapy. Thus, although many people do indeed seem to be helped by therapy

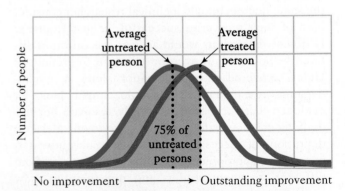

FIGURE 5–7 *Combining subjects and results from hundreds of studies, investigators have determined that the average person who receives psychotherapy experiences greater improvement than do 75 percent of all untreated people with similar problems. (Adapted from Lambert, Weber, and Sykes, 1993; Smith, Glass, & Miller, 1980; Smith & Glass, 1977.)*

in ways that would not otherwise occur, at least some individuals in therapy would be better off having no treatment at all.

ARE PARTICULAR THERAPIES EFFECTIVE?

Most of the studies that have considered the general effectiveness of therapy have lumped all therapies together and treated them all alike, a procedure that many researchers consider inappropriate. One critic suggested that such studies were operating under a *uniformity myth*—a false belief that all therapies are equivalent despite differences in the therapists' training, experience, theoretical orientation, and personalities (Kiesler, 1966).

An alternative approach has been to examine the effectiveness of particular therapies. Most such studies show each of the major systems and formats of therapy to be superior to no treatment or to placebo treatment. Psychodynamic therapies and client-centered therapy (the only humanistic approach to be studied systematically) have fared well occasionally in therapy outcome studies (Prochaska & Norcross, 1994; Stuhr & Meyer, 1991; Svartberg & Stiles, 1991), while behavioral, cognitive, and biological therapies have frequently demonstrated considerable effectiveness (Emmelkamp, 1994; Hollon & Beck, 1994; Apter, 1993).

Many studies have also compared particular therapies with one another (Lambert & Bergin, 1994). A well-known review of properly controlled comparative studies failed to find that one form of therapy consistently stood out over others (Luborsky et al., 1975). Instead, client-centered and psychodynamic therapy were judged equally effective in four of five studies; behavior therapy was more effective than psychodynamic therapy in thirteen of nineteen studies; short-term therapy was just as effective as extended therapy in five of eight studies; and individual and group therapy were equally effective in nine of thirteen studies.

A well-done classic comparative study painted a similar picture (Sloane et al., 1975). The researchers assigned ninety-four clients with anxiety, depressive, and personality disorders to one of three treatment conditions: short-term psychodynamic therapy, behavior therapy, or a waiting-list control group. The subjects in all the conditions were matched on such variables as age, sex, and severity of symptoms. Six highly experienced therapists then provided treatment in weekly hour-long sessions. The researchers found that after four months, the clients who had been receiving either form of therapy, whether psychodynamic or behavioral, had improved to a similar degree, and significantly more than the control clients. Approximately 80 percent of the clients in each therapy group had improved but only 48 percent of the waiting-list clients. In a follow-up study eight months later, the waiting-list subjects had also improved significantly and had almost caught up to those in treatment, but by that time many of these control subjects had themselves become clients in therapy, a factor that probably contributed to their improvement.

This similar showing by different therapies, repeated across many studies, has suggested to some clinical theorists that the various therapies may share certain basic ingredients that in fact are often the primary reasons that clients improve (Garfield, 1992; Crits-Christoph et al., 1991; Frank & Frank, 1991; Grencavage & Norcross, 1990; Strupp, 1989; Karasu, 1986). These theorists have noted, for example, that successful therapies of all kinds provide clients with some individual attention, a credible rationale for their problems, the experience of mastery and success, and raised expectations for improvement. Successful therapies also typically establish a therapeutic alliance between clinician and client, with a basis in faith and trust.

The finding of similar overall success rates in various kinds of therapy has led to a *rapprochement movement,* an effort to delineate a set of "common therapeutic strategies" that characterize the work of all effective therapists (Prochaska & Norcross, 1994; Beutler, Machado, & Neufeldt, 1994; Norcross & Goldfried, 1992; Lafferty, Beutler, & Crago, 1991). One review found that effective therapists tend to be more experienced than less effective therapists and that the use of a treatment manual often increases a therapist's efficacy (Crits-Christoph et al., 1991). Moreover, a survey of highly esteemed and successful therapists of various orientations suggests that most provide feedback to patients, help patients focus on their own thoughts and behavior, pay attention to the way therapist and patient are interacting, and try to promote self-mastery in their patients. In short, effective therapists often seem to practice more similarly than they preach (Korchin & Sands, 1983). Given this growing appreciation of similarity among therapists, it is not at all surprising that 38 percent of recently surveyed therapists refused to identify themselves exclusively with one orientation and described themselves as eclectic or integrative (Prochaska & Norcross, 1994) (see again Figure 5–3).

ARE PARTICULAR THERAPIES EFFECTIVE FOR PARTICULAR DISORDERS?

Different people with different disorders may respond differently to the various therapeutic systems, formats, and settings (Zettle, Haflich, & Reynolds, 1992). As the influential clinical theorist Gordon Paul said some years back, the most appropriate question to ask regarding the effectiveness of therapy may be "*What* specific treatment, by *whom*, is most effective for *this* individual with *that* specific problem, and under *which* set of circumstances?" (Paul, 1967, p. 111).

This consideration has impelled a number of researchers to be as specific as possible in the design of therapy studies, investigating, for example, how effective particular therapies are at treating particular disorders (Kazdin, 1994; Beutler, 1991). These studies have often found sizable differences among the various therapies. Behavior therapies, for example, have emerged as the most effective of all therapies in the treatment of phobic disorders (Emmelkamp, 1994). Similarly, drug therapy is the single most effective treatment for schizophrenic disorders (Meltzer, 1992); cognitive-behavioral therapies have been very effective for panic disorders and sexual dysfunction (Lambert & Bergin, 1994; Heiman & LoPiccolo, 1988); and cognitive therapy and drug therapy have both proved highly successful in cases of depression (Beck, 1993, 1991, 1987; APA, 1993).

Studies of this kind have also revealed that some clinical problems may respond better to combined therapy approaches than to any one therapy alone (Beitman, 1993; Glick, Clarkin, & Goldsmith, 1993; Sander & Feldman, 1993). Drug therapy may be combined with cognitive therapy, for example, to treat depression. A combination of therapies also seems to be in order when a client is suffering from more than one psychological disorder (a condition called *comorbidity*) (Clarkin & Kendall, 1992). In line with such combination approaches, it is becoming increasingly common for clients to be seen by two therapists—a **psychopharmacologist** or **pharmacotherapist,** a psychiatrist who only prescribes medications, and a psychologist, social worker, or other therapist who conducts psychotherapy (Woodward, Duckworth, & Gutheil, 1993). Obviously, in such cases, careful coordination between the two therapists is critical to the client's progress.

Specific information on how particular therapies

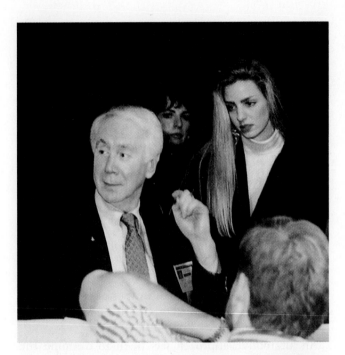

The well-known therapist Arnold Lazarus argues that therapists must be "flexible, versatile, and technically eclectic" (1987, p. 166). In his "multimodal therapy," the therapist focuses on all aspects of a client's problems and combines procedures drawn from various systems of therapy. Lazarus uses the acronym BASIC I.D. to identify the seven "pillars" of human temperament on which he focuses in assessing and treating a client: behavior, affect, sensation, imagery, cognition, interpersonal relationships, and drugs/biology.

fare with particular disorders can help therapists and clients alike make better decisions about treatment (Lambert & Bergin, 1992; Shoham-Salomon, 1991; Beutler, 1991, 1979), and it can provide researchers with a better understanding of therapy processes and ultimately of abnormal functioning. Thus, the effectiveness of particular treatments is a question to which we shall keep returning as we examine the disorders they have been devised to combat.

SUMMARY

■ THERAPY is a systematic procedure for helping people overcome their psychological difficulties. All forms of therapy have three things in common: a sufferer seeking relief, a trained healer, and a series of contacts between healer and sufferer. At the same time, therapies vary in their goals, methods, and ways of measuring success. They even disagree as to whether the person seeking therapy should be considered a client or a patient.

■ **As many as 400 distinct forms** of therapy are being practiced today. A *system* of therapy is a set of principles and techniques employed in accordance with a particular theory of change. The system may be applied in any of several *formats*—individual, group, family, and couple therapy.

■ **Global therapies** help people recognize and change general features of their personality that the therapists believe are at the root of the problem. The primary global therapies are the psychodynamic and the humanistic-existential therapies.

Psychodynamic therapies help patients uncover past traumatic events and the inner conflicts that have resulted from those events. A number of techniques, such as *free association* and therapist interpretations of psychological phenomena such as *resistance, transference,* and *dreams,* reveal the underlying dynamics of patients' disorders. With growing insight and repeated experiences of *catharsis,* the patient *works through* issues of psychological significance. Although psychodynamic therapies remain popular and highly influential, there is little evidence that they are clearly effective for many disorders. On the other hand, their proponents point out that these approaches do not readily lend themselves to empirical investigations.

The other global therapies, the *humanistic-existential therapies,* help clients to look at themselves and their situations more accurately and acceptingly, with the aim of actualizing their full potential as human beings. Humanistic and existential therapists emphasize the here and now.

Practitioners of *client-centered therapy,* one of the leading humanistic approaches, try to create a very supportive climate in which clients can look at themselves honestly and begin to accept what they discover themselves to be. Research has provided mixed support for the effectiveness of this humanistic approach.

Practitioners of *gestalt therapy,* another humanistic approach, try to move clients to recognize and accept their needs through techniques such as *skillful frustration, role playing, rules,* and *exercises* and *games.*

Existential therapists form close relationships with clients and encourage them to accept responsibility for their lives, to recognize their freedom to choose a different course, and to choose to live an authentic life. Existentialists question the merits of empirical research as a method for testing their system of therapy.

■ **Problem-based therapies,** in contrast to global therapies, focus primarily on symptoms and specific complaints, without delving into broad personality issues. The major problem-based therapies are the behavioral, cognitive, and biological therapies.

The goal of the *behavioral therapies* is to identify the client's problem-causing behaviors and replace them with more appropriate ones. Behavioral therapists use three categories of techniques: *classical conditioning, operant conditioning,* and *modeling.*

Cognitive therapies are based on the premise that abnormal functioning is caused by maladaptive assumptions and thoughts. Cognitive therapists try to help people recognize and change their faulty ideas and thinking processes. Among the most widely used cognitive therapies are Ellis's *rational-emotive therapy* and Beck's *cognitive therapy.*

Biological therapies comprise physical and chemical methods developed to help people overcome their psychological problems. The principal kinds of biological interventions are *drug therapy* and *electroconvulsive therapy.*

■ **The leading therapy format** is *individual therapy* in which the therapist sees the client alone for some period of time, usually weekly. The format of *group therapy* became popular after World War II. Two specialized forms of group therapy are *psychodrama* and the *self-help groups.* Research indicates that group therapy is of help to many clients. The feedback and support that group members experience is usually beneficial, and harm to group members is not frequent.

Family therapy is a format in which therapists meet with all members of a family, point out problematic behavior and interactions, and work on helping the whole family to change. Similar to family therapy is *couple therapy,* in which the therapist works with two people who share a long-term relationship. An increasing body of research on the effectiveness of various family and couple therapies suggests that they are useful for some problems and under some circumstances.

■ **The critical question** to be asked about these various treatments is whether or not they actually help people cope with and overcome their psychological problems. Three general conclusions have been reached. First, most recent findings indicate that people in therapy are usually better off than people with similar problems who receive no treatment. Second, the various therapies do not appear to differ dramatically in their general effectiveness. Third, certain therapies do appear to be more effective than others for certain disorders, and often a particular combination of approaches is more effective than a single approach in the treatment of certain disorders.

Topic Overview

ANXIETY DISORDERS

■

THINK ABOUT A TIME when your breathing quickened, your muscles tensed, and your heart pounded with a sudden sense of dread. Was it when your car almost skidded off the road in the rain? When your professor announced a pop quiz? What about when the person you most cared about went out with someone else, or your boss suggested that your job performance ought to improve? Any time you confront what seems to be a serious threat to your well-being, you may react with the state of tension or alarm known as *fear* (Barlow, 1988; Izard, 1977). Sometimes, though, you cannot pinpoint a specific cause for alarm, but still you feel tense and edgy, as if something unpleasant were going to happen. The ominous sense of being menaced by an unspecified threat is usually termed *anxiety,* and it has the same clinical features— the same acceleration of breathing, muscular tension, perspiration, and so forth—as fear (Strelau, 1992; Barlow, 1988).

ALTHOUGH EVERYDAY EXPERIENCES of fear and anxiety are not pleasant, they have an adaptive function: they prepare us for action—for "fight or flight"—when danger threatens. They may motivate us to drive more cautiously in a storm, keep up with our reading assignments, treat our date more sensitively, and work harder at our job. Unfortunately, some people suffer such continuous and disabling fear and anxiety that they cannot lead a normal life. Their discomfort is too severe or too frequent; it lasts too long; it is triggered too readily by what the sufferers themselves recognize as minimal, unspecified, or nonexistent threats. These people are said to have an anxiety disorder.

ANXIETY DISORDERS are the most common mental disorders in the United States. In any given year between 15 and 17 percent of the adult population—23 million people—suffer from one or another of the six anxiety disorders identified by DSM-IV (Kessler et al., 1994; Regier et al., 1993;

Eaton, Dryman, & Weissman, 1991; Blazer et al., 1991; Davidson et al., 1991). Collectively, the anxiety disorders are also society's most expensive mental disorders, costing an estimated total of $46.6 billion in 1990 alone, almost a third of all mental health costs (Rovner, 1993). Approximately $35 billion is attributable to indirect costs, such as the value of reduced or lost work productivity; the rest is accounted for by treatment fees.

People with *phobic disorders* experience a persistent and irrational fear of a specific object, activity, or situation. People with *generalized anxiety disorders* experience general and persistent feelings of anxiety that are not associated with specific objects or situations. People with *panic disorders* have recurrent attacks of terror. Those with *obsessive compulsive disorders* are beset by recurrent and unwanted thoughts that cause anxiety or by the need to perform repetitive and ritualistic actions to reduce anxiety. People with *acute stress disorders* and *posttraumatic stress disorders* are tormented by fear and related symptoms well after a traumatic event (military combat, rape, torture) has ended. Typically a client will be assigned only one of these diagnoses at a time, but studies suggest that most people with a primary diagnosis of one anxiety disorder also meet the criteria for a secondary diagnosis of another anxiety disorder (Brown et al., 1993; Sanderson et al., 1990).

Past editions of the DSM included anxiety disorders in Freud's category of the neuroses. A *neurosis,* according to Freud, was a disorder in which a person's ego defense mechanisms were incapable of preventing or reducing intense anxiety aroused by unconscious conflicts. The resultant struggle with anxiety could take any of several malfunctional forms. In some neurotic disorders (phobic, anxiety, and obsessive compulsive neuroses) the anxiety was apparent. In others (hysterical, neurasthenic, depersonalization, depressive, and hypochondriacal neuroses) the anxiety was thought to be hidden and "controlled unconsciously and automatically by conversion, displacement, and various other psychological mechanisms" (APA, 1968, p. 9).

Because the DSM now defines disorders by symptoms and without reference to possible causes, the category of neurosis has been dropped and the neurotic disorders have been distributed among other categories. Those disorders in which anxiety is a central symptom are now simply called anxiety disorders. Several others of the so-called neurotic disorders, now defined as mood disorders, somatoform disorders, and dissociative disorders, are described in Chapters 8, 11, and 18, respectively.

STRESS, COPING, AND THE ANXIETY RESPONSE

Before we examine the various anxiety disorders, let us take a closer look at the kinds of situations that normally cause us to feel threatened and the kinds of changes we experience in response to such situations. Actually, we feel some degree of threat, called a state of *stress,* whenever we are confronted with demands or opportunities that require us to change in some manner. A state of stress has two components: a *stressor,* the event that creates the demands, and a *stress response,* a person's idiosyncratic reactions to the demands.

The stressors of life may take the form of daily hassles, such as rush-hour traffic or the appearance of unexpected company; major life events or transitions, such as college graduation or marriage; chronic problems, such as poverty, poor health, or overcrowded living conditions; or traumatic events, such as catastrophic accidents, assaults, tornados, or military combat.

Our reaction to such stressors is influenced by the way we *appraise* both the events and our capacity to respond to them. Two stages of appraisal are often distinguished: *primary appraisal,* in which we interpret a situation as threatening or harmless, and *secondary appraisal,* in which we weigh what kind of response is needed and assess whether we have the ability and the personal and social resources to man-

The experience of stress is determined by two components: a stressor and one's appraisal of the stressor. Seemingly mild events, such as playing a game of croquet, can feel very stressful if interpreted as important, threatening, or beyond one's ability.

Although most people are terrified by the very thought of hang gliding above the clouds, some are stimulated by the experience and others are calmed by it. Such individual reactions represent differences in situation, or state, anxiety.

age or cope with it (Lazarus & Folkman, 1984). People who sense that they have sufficient ability and resources to cope are more likely to respond constructively to stressors, take them in stride, and avoid having negative emotional, behavioral, and cognitive reactions to them. In short, one's response to a stressor depends on the nature of the stressor itself and on one's own past experience, behavioral skills, self-concept, social support, and biological makeup.

One of the key reactions to a stressor we appraise as threatening is a sense of fear. Fear is actually a package of responses—physical, emotional, and cognitive. Physically, we perspire, our breathing quickens, our muscles tense, and our hearts beat faster. We may turn pale and develop goose bumps, our lips may tremble, and we may feel nauseated. If the situation is extremely threatening, we may feel such emotions as horror, dread, and even panic. Fear can interfere with our ability to concentrate and distort our view of the world. We may exaggerate the harm that actually threatens us or remember things incorrectly after the threat has passed.

These features of the fear and anxiety response are generated by the action of the body's *autonomic nervous system (ANS)*, the extensive network of nerve fibers that connect the *central nervous system* (the brain and spinal cord) to all the other organs of the body. The ANS helps regulate the involuntary ac-

tivities of these organs—breathing, heartbeat, blood pressure, perspiration, and the like (see Figure 6–1).

When our brain interprets a situation as dangerous, it excites a special group of ANS fibers that quicken our heartbeat and produce the other changes that we experience as fear or anxiety. The ANS nerve fibers specifically responsible for these activities are referred to collectively as the *sympathetic nervous system* (in a sense, these nerve fibers are "sympathetic" to our emergency needs). The sympathetic nervous system is also called the *fight-or-flight* system, precisely because it prepares us for some kind of action in response to danger.

When a perceived danger passes, our functioning ordinarily returns to normal and our fear dissipates, thanks to the action of a second group of ANS nerve fibers, the *parasympathetic nervous system.* These fibers return our heartbeat and other body processes to normal.

These two parts of the ANS—the sympathetic and the parasympathetic nervous systems—thus work in complementary ways, each operating as a check on the other. Together they help regulate our fear and anxiety reactions, as well as other responses to stress, and enable our body to maintain both the stability and the adaptability essential to life.

We all have our own patterns of autonomic nervous system functioning and our own ways of experiencing

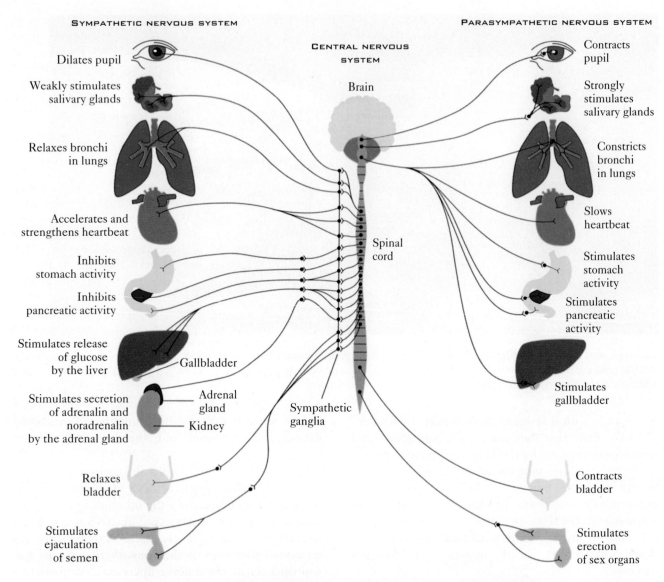

FIGURE 6-1 *The autonomic nervous system (ANS) regulates the involuntary functions of the body. When the sympathetic division of the ANS is activated, it stimulates some organs and inhibits others. The result is a state of general arousal. In contrast, the parasympathetic division's stimulation and inhibition of various organs have an overall calming effect.*

fear and anxiety. One person may respond to a threat by perspiring profusely and being gripped by a sense of dread; another may breathe faster and have difficulty concentrating, yet perspire very little. Similarly, we all have our own level of ongoing anxiety. Some people are always relaxed, while others almost always feel some tension, even when no threat is apparent. A person's general level of anxiety is sometimes called **trait anxiety,** because it seems to be a trait or characteristic that the person brings to each event in life (Spielberger, 1985, 1972, 1966). Some psychologists believe our trait anxiety reflects our early childhood

experience—the atmosphere of safety or insecurity that surrounded us at that time. But others have found that enduring differences in trait anxiety can be noted soon after birth (Kalin, 1993; Pekrun, 1992; Kagan, 1983).

People also differ in their sense of which situations are threatening (Weiner, 1985; Stattin & Magnusson, 1980). Walking through a forest may be fearsome for one person but relaxing for another. Similarly, flying in an airplane may arouse terror in some people and boredom in others. Such variations are called differences in **situation** or **state anxiety.** The fear and anxiety most of us have experienced, however, are quite different from the disproportionate, frequent, and enduring waves of tension and dread experienced by persons who suffer from an anxiety disorder.

■ PHOBIC ■ DISORDERS AND GENERALIZED ANXIETY DISORDERS

Phobic disorders, which involve excessive fears of specific objects or situations, and generalized anxiety disorders, which are marked by persistent and vague feelings of anxiety, are the two most common types of anxiety disorders. Although these disorders differ in character and impact, many theorists (sociocultural, psychodynamic, humanistic, and behavioral theorists, in particular) believe that they have similar roots.

PHOBIC DISORDERS

Most of us are none too eager to visit the dentist (Moore et al., 1991), but few of us have such dread of the drill as this woman:

At the age of twelve, my eye teeth came through very crooked and high up in the gum. I remember my mother dragging me along to the dentist and both of them standing behind me saying I would have to go into the hospital to have them out. . . . After that I would make up any excuse to get out of going. . . . I managed to bluff my way through school and it was such a relief when I actually left, as I knew no school dentist could come round wondering why I hadn't kept an appointment. Also, when I was at school we were always given a note asking us whether we would like to use the school dentist or the family one, and I always managed to forge my mother's signature stating the latter.

For the next ten years my life was unbearable. Looking back on it now, I honestly don't know how I didn't go off my head. I loved going out with boys, but most of them must have thought I was very shy or a miserable person: I could never laugh in public, only half-smile and bow my head. I could never relax, not even for a minute. Parties were unbearable, especially when someone told me a joke. And worst of all was the fact that I knew I would have to go

to the dentist sometime in the future. As the years went by, my teeth got worse and I become more withdrawn. When I was twenty I did meet someone, and I knew if anyone would understand, it would be him, but I still could not bring myself to tell him, and on I went with my head bowed down and all the time thinking that I mustn't open my mouth too much and knowing that I had to go the dentist in the end.

We became engaged on my twenty-first birthday, and a year later we got married. You can imagine my wedding day was unbearable for me. The wedding photos were a nightmare, with the photographers asking me to put my head up and smile, and the whole time I was in a cold sweat. Anyway, we moved to the south coast, my husband got a good job and I could stay at home and not talk to anyone, so therefore I didn't have to open my mouth at all. Then I became pregnant and of course I was petrified I would have a full medical check-up and would have to open my mouth. I told my husband that I had been to the doctor, but at seven months I was afraid that by not going I might endanger the baby, so eventually I went, and as luck would have it, nobody even bothered to look. . . .

I had always wondered when my husband went to the dentist why he never mentioned that I never went, but I certainly wasn't going to. Every night I would lie in a cold sweat thinking about it, and as my son got older I knew I had to do something. Each night got worse; I couldn't sleep; I would wait until my husband was asleep and go downstairs and cry my eyes out. I honestly thought I was going mad. On one of my bad nights my husband came down, and I was in such a state that I managed to blurt the whole lot out. In the morning he got up and went to work, and . . . he came back at lunch time and said that he had had a long talk [with] the dentist and he understood how I felt and would see me the next day. That afternoon, and until 10:45 the next day, was unbearable. I was sick, I had diarrhea, I had a temperature and I certainly didn't sleep a wink. I took four tranquilizers that night and six the next morning, and in the end my husband had to practically carry me in. . . . Anyway, he told me I had left it so long that the roots were all twisted and that the front six teeth would have to come out. I still had about seven other fillings that needed doing, and I knew if I wanted the front ones done it would be no good not turning up for the other treatment. Each visit was a nightmare. Every time I went, my husband had to take hours off work, as if he hadn't been there I certainly wouldn't have turned up.

Eventually the dentist said that on the next visit he would take out the front six. My husband took the day off, and we went together. I had gas, and it was all over in a few seconds. I managed to get to the car and just sat there, and my husband handed me a present: a mirror. At first I was too afraid to look, but when I did I couldn't believe how radiant I looked. But I will never get over my phobia. In fact I am ashamed to admit I have not been back to the dentist since that last visit. I will walk half a mile out of my way rather than pass the door in case he sees me.

(Melville, 1978, pp. 151–153)

Anatidaephobia: The fear that somewhere, somehow, a duck is watching you.

(The Far Side © FARWORKS Inc. Reprinted with permission of Universal Press Syndicate. All rights reserved.)

A *phobia* (from the Greek for "fear") is a persistent and unreasonable fear of a particular object, activity, or situation. People with a phobia become fearful if they even think about the dreaded object or situation, but they usually remain comfortable and functional as long as they avoid the object or thoughts about it. Like the woman who feared the dentist, they may continue to avoid the object or situation even after seemingly benign interactions with it. Most are well aware that their fears are excessive and unreasonable. Many have no idea how their fears started.

We all have our areas of special fear, and it is normal for some things to upset us more than other things. To some extent, the objects and events we fear may be related to our stage of life. A survey of residents of a community in Burlington, Vermont, found that fears of crowds, death, injury, illness, and separation were more common among people in their 60s than in other age groups, whereas fears of snakes, heights, storms, enclosures, and social situations were much more prevalent among 20-year-olds (Agras, Sylvester, & Oliveau, 1969; see Figure 6–2).

How do these common fears differ from phobic disorder—how, for instance, does a "normal" fear of snakes differ from a snake phobia? DSM-IV indicates that the fear experienced in a phobic disorder is more intense and persistent, and the desire to avoid the object or situation is more compelling (APA, 1994). People with phobic disorders experience such distress that their fears often interfere dramatically with their personal, social, or occupational functioning.

Phobic disorders are common in our society. Surveys suggest that 10 to 11 percent of the adult population in the United States suffer from a phobia in any given year (Regier et al., 1993; Eaton et al., 1991). More than 14 percent develop a phobia at some point in their lives. These disorders are more than twice as common in women as in men.

Because some phobias share particular themes, DSM-IV distinguishes three categories: agoraphobia, social phobias, and specific phobias. *Agoraphobia* (from the Greek for "fear of the marketplace") is a fear of venturing into public places, especially when one is alone. *Social phobias* are fears of social or performance situations in which embarrassment may occur. All other phobias are classified as *specific phobias*.

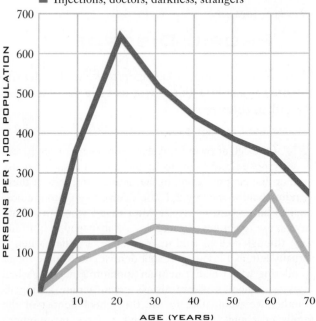

FIGURE 6–2 *Certain age groups are particularly likely to have certain fears. Close to 70 percent of all 20-year-olds surveyed in Burlington, Vermont—more than in any other age group—feared snakes and heights. On the other hand, 60-year-olds were more likely than persons of other ages to be afraid of crowds and of death, and 10-year-olds were more likely than others to fear injections and doctors. (Adapted from Agras, Sylvester, & Oliveau, 1969, p. 153.)*

George Tooker's painting Subway *expresses the sense of threat, entrapment, and disorientation experienced by many people with agoraphobia when they enter public places.*

AGORAPHOBIA   The following report describes the disorder of agoraphobia, a pervasive and complex phobia that makes people avoid public places or situations in which escape might be difficult or help unavailable should they develop incapacitating or embarrassing paniclike symptoms, such as dizziness, palpitations, diarrhea, or nausea (APA, 1994). Many sufferers are constrained less by the fear that the incapacitating symptoms will occur than by their concern that the *anxiety* over the symptoms will get out of hand and incapacitate or embarrass them. In any given year approximately 4 percent of the adult population experience this problem, women twice as frequently as men (Kessler et al., 1994; Eaton et al., 1991). People typically develop agoraphobia in their 20s or 30s.

For several months prior to her application for treatment Veronica had been unable to leave her home. . . . "It is as if something dreadful would happen to me if I did not immediately go home." Even after she would return to the house, she would feel shaken inside and unable to speak to anyone or do anything for an hour or so. However, as long as she remained in her own home or garden, she was able to carry on her routine life without much problem. . . . Because of this agoraphobia, she had

been unable to return to her position as a mathematics teacher in the local high school after the summer vacation.

. . . [Veronica] stated that she had always been a somewhat shy person who generally preferred keeping to herself, but that up until approximately a year ago she had always been able to go to her job, shop, or go to church without any particular feelings of dread or uneasiness. It was difficult for her to recall the first time . . . but it seemed to her that the first major experience was approximately a year before, when she and her mother had been Christmas shopping. They were standing in the middle of a crowded department store when she suddenly felt the impulse to flee. She left her mother without an explanation and drove home as fast as she could. Her mother was extremely angry, and she was unable to explain to her what had happened. She admitted that shopping with her mother was a trial, as her mother was a loud-voiced person who would badger store clerks and often "create a scene" if she did not get the immediate and complete service she demanded. Veronica said that she "just knew" that sooner or later her mother would embarrass her on this shopping tour. . . . After the Christmas vacation she seemed to recover for a while and was at least able to return to her classroom duties without any ill effect. During the ensuing several months she had several similar experiences, usually when she was off duty; but by late spring these fears were just as likely to occur in the classroom. . . . In thinking further about the occurrence of her phobia, it seemed to Veronica that there was actually no particular stress which might account for her fear. Often it seemed to come over her when she was momentarily relaxed, although always when she was in public. For example, it might come over her while she was standing in the classroom watching her pupils during an examination, or, as in the initial experience, when she was standing in the middle of the ladies' dresses section of the store waiting for her mother to return from the restroom.

(Goldstein & Palmer, 1975, pp. 163–164)

It is typical of people with agoraphobia to avoid entering crowded streets or stores, driving through tunnels or on bridges, traveling on public transportation, and using elevators. If they venture out of the house at all, it is usually only in the company of close relatives or friends. Some people with agoraphobia further insist that family members or friends stay with them at home, but even at home and in the company of others they may continue to feel anxious.

In many cases the intensity of the agoraphobia fluctuates, as it did for Veronica. In severe cases, people become virtual prisoners in their own homes. Their social life dwindles, and they cannot hold a job. Persons with agoraphobia may also become depressed, sometimes as a result of the severe limitations that their phobia places on their lives.

Many people with agoraphobia are in fact prone to experience extreme and sudden explosions of fear, called *panic attacks*, when they enter public places. In such cases, the agoraphobic pattern is considered a type of panic disorder, specifically ***panic disorder with agoraphobia,*** because the disorder involves much more than an overblown fear of venturing away from home and developing a few paniclike symptoms. This disorder, which will be discussed in the later section on panic disorders, is thought to have different origins from the phobia under discussion here, technically labeled ***agoraphobia without history of panic disorder.***

SOCIAL PHOBIAS Many people have qualms about interacting with others or talking or performing in front of others. The opera singer Maria Callas often shook with fear while waiting in the wings to perform, and Harold MacMillan, the former British prime minister, typically felt nauseous before question time in Parliament (Marks, 1987). Such normal social fears are inconvenient, but the people who have them manage to function adequately, some at a very high level.

By contrast, people with a social phobia have severe, persistent, and irrational fears of social or performance situations in which embarrassment may occur. A social phobia may be specific, such as a fear of talking or performing in public, eating in public, us-

ing a public bathroom, or writing in front of others, or it may be a broader fear of social situations, such as a general fear of functioning inadequately or inappropriately when others are watching. In both forms, people with social phobias repeatedly evaluate themselves as performing more poorly than they actually do (Stopa & Clark, 1993). The distinguishing characteristic that sets social phobias off from normal social fears is the phobic person's level of discomfort and constant avoidance of the feared situation.

Social phobias can be highly incapacitating (Stein et al., 1994; Liebowitz, 1992). A person who is unable to interact with others or speak in public may fail to perform important scholastic or professional responsibilities. One who cannot eat in public may reject dinner invitations and other social engagements. Since most people with these phobias keep their fears secret, their social reluctance is often misinterpreted as snobbery, disinterest, or stubbornness. Consider this 28-year-old woman who was terrified that her hands would tremble in front of others:

She therefore didn't like giving to or accepting from strangers a drink or cup of tea or coffee. The first time this happened was when she was nineteen and was taken home by her boyfriend to meet his parents. Both this relationship and a succeeding one failed, and from then on she was conscious of her "phobia." She found her fears gradually spreading and affecting her work as a secretary. "At one time I found it difficult to take dictation and type it back if it was given to me just before I was due to leave the office, or if the work was needed urgently and my boss was waiting for it; I would panic and my fingers would just seize up. . . ." "I know everybody has some dread of something, but people accept somebody who has an aversion to mice or flies. If you don't like giving somebody a drink, though, they think you are antisocial and, if your hands shake, that you must either be 'on the bottle' or a complete wreck. It's strange, really, as I strike everybody as a confident person, but with certain people, regardless of whether they are 'ordinary' or 'impressive,' I become very self-conscious."

(Melville, 1978, pp. 78–79)

Social phobias are apparently more common than agoraphobia (see Table 6–1). As much as 8 percent of the population—women somewhat more frequently than men—experience this problem in any given year (APA, 1994; Kessler et al., 1994). The disorder often begins in late childhood or adolescence and may persist for many years, although its intensity may fluctuate over the years (APA, 1994; Schneier et al., 1992).

TABLE 6-1

ANXIETY DISORDERS EPIDEMIOLOGICAL PROFILE

	ONE YEAR PREVALENCE	FEMALE:MALE RATIO	TYPICAL AGE OF ONSET	PREVALENCE AMONG CLOSE RELATIVES
Agoraphobia without panic disorder	2.8%	2:1	20–40 years	Unknown
Social phobia	8.0%	3:2	10–20 years	Elevated
Specific phobia	9.0%	3:1	Variable	Elevated
Generalized anxiety disorder	3.8%	2:1	0–20 years	Elevated
Panic disorder	2.3%	5:2	15–35 years	Elevated
Obsessive-compulsive disorder	2.0%	1:1	4–25 years	Elevated
Acute and posttraumatic stress disorders	0.5%	1:1	Variable	Unknown

Sources: APA, 1994; Kessler et al., 1994; Regier et al., 1993; Eaton et al., 1991; Blazer et al., 1991; Davidson et al., 1991.

SPECIFIC PHOBIAS   A *specific phobia* is a persistent fear of a specific object or situation other than being in public places (agoraphobia) or in socially embarrassing situations (social phobia). When they are exposed to or anticipate being exposed to the dreaded object or situation, people with this disorder invariably experience immediate fear, sometimes even pain. Common specific phobias are intense fears of specific animals or insects, heights, enclosed spaces, and thunderstorms. Many familiar and not-so-familiar specific phobias have been given names by clinicians (see Box 6–1). Here are a few firsthand descriptions (all in Melville, 1978):

Spiders (arachnophobia)   Seeing a spider makes me rigid with fear, hot, trembling and dizzy. I have occasionally vomited and once fainted in order to escape from the situation. These symptoms last three or four days after seeing a spider. Realistic pictures can cause the same effect, especially if I inadvertently place my hand on one. (p. 44)

Birds (ornithophobia)   When I'm in the house alone, I always keep the windows and outside doors closed, even in hot weather. We live in an old house which has fireplaces in every room. I had the bedroom ones taken out and the chimneys blocked up. Downstairs we have gas fires, and I have had covers with small apertures made over these chimneys. (p. 124)

Flying (aerophobia)   We got on board, and then there was the take-off. There it was again, that horrible feeling as we gathered speed. It was creeping over me again, that old feeling of panic. I kept seeing everyone as puppets, all strapped to their seats with no control over their des-

tinies, me included. Every time the plane did a variation of speed or route, my heart would leap and I would hurriedly ask what was happening. When the plane started to lose height, I was terrified that we were about to crash. (p. 59)

Thunderstorms (tonitrophobia)   At the end of March each year, I start getting agitated because summer is coming and that means thunderstorms. I have been afraid since my early twenties, but the last three years have been the worst. I have such a heartbeat that for hours after a storm my whole left side is painful. Every time I promise myself that was the last time, I would rather kill myself than it happen again. I say I will stay in the room, but when it comes I am a jelly, reduced to nothing. I have a little cupboard and I go there, I press my eyes so hard I can't see for about an hour, and if I sit in the cupboard over an hour my husband has to straighten me up. (p. 104)

Each year as many as 9 percent of the United States population have the symptoms of a specific phobia (APA, 1994; Kessler et al., 1994). Eleven percent develop a specific phobia sometime during their lives, and many people have more than one specific phobia at a time (Eaton et al., 1991). Women with this disorder outnumber men by at least 2 to 1—a gender difference that holds in studies extending across the United States, Canada, and Europe (Weissman, 1988).

The impact of a specific phobia on a person's life depends on what arouses the fear. Some things are easier to avoid than others. People whose phobias center on dogs, insects, or water will repeatedly encounter or expect to encounter the objects they dread. Their efforts to avoid them must be elaborate

BOX 6-1

PHOBIAS, FAMILIAR AND NOT SO FAMILIAR

Air	Aerophobia	Corpse	Necrophobia	Failure	Kakorraphia-phobia
Animals	Zoophobia	Crossing a	Gephyrophobia		
Beards	Pogonophobia	bridge		Fire	Pyrophobia
Bees	Apiphobia, melissophobia	Crowds	Ochlophobia	Flood	Antlophobia
		Darkness	Achluophobia, nyctophobia	Flowers	Anthophobia
Being afraid	Phobophobia			Flying	Aerophobia
Being alone	Autophobia, monophobia, eremophobia	Daylight	Phengophobia	Fog	Homichlophobia
		Death	Necrophobia, thanatophobia	Food	Sitophobia, cibophobia
Being buried alive	Tapophobia	Demons, devils	Demonophobia	Foreigners	Xenophobia
Being dirty	Automysophobia	Dirt	Mysophobia, rhypophobia	France and things French	Gallophobia
Being stared at	Scopophobia	Disease	Nosophobia, pathophobia	Fur	Doraphobia
Blood	Hematophobia			Germany and things German	Germanophobia
Books	Bibliophobia	Dogs	Cynophobia		
Cancer	Cancerophobia, carcinomato-phobia	Dolls	Pediophobia	Germs	Spermophobia
		Dreams	Oneirophobia	Ghosts	Phasmophobia
		Drugs	Pharmacophobia	God	Theophobia
Cats	Ailurophobia, gatophobia	Empty rooms	Kenophobia	Graves	Taphophobia
		Enclosed space	Claustrophobia	Heart disease	Cardiophobia
Children	Pediophobia	England and things English	Anglophobia	Heat	Thermophobia
Choking	Pnigophobia			Heights	Acrophobia
Churches	Ecclesiaphobia	Eyes	Ommatophobia	Home	Domatophobia
Cold	Psychrophobia, frigophobia	Feces	Coprophobia	Homosexuality	Homophobia

and may impose great restrictions on their lives. People with snake phobias have a much easier time.

Specific phobias can develop at any time of life, although some, such as animal phobias, tend to begin during childhood and disappear on their own before adulthood (APA, 1994; Marks, 1987). In one phase of the Vermont study, the progress of children and adolescents with specific phobias was observed (Agras et al., 1969). Most improved to some degree over the course of five years without any treatment at all, and 40 percent became totally free of symptoms. Phobias that last into or begin during adulthood, however, tend to hold on stubbornly and usually lessen only under treatment.

GENERALIZED ANXIETY DISORDERS

Bob Donaldson was a 22-year-old carpenter referred to the psychiatric outpatient department of a community hospital. . . . During the initial interview Bob was

visibly distressed. He appeared tense, worried, and frightened. He sat on the edge of his chair, tapping his foot and fidgeting with a pencil on the psychiatrist's desk. He sighed frequently, took deep breaths between sentences, and periodically exhaled audibly and changed his position as he attempted to relate his story:

Bob: It's been an awful month. I can't seem to do anything. I don't know whether I'm coming or going. I'm afraid I'm going crazy or something.

Doctor: What makes you think that?

Bob: I can't concentrate. My boss tells me to do something and I start to do it, but before I've taken five steps I don't know what I started out to do. I get dizzy and I can feel my heart beating and everything looks like it's shimmering or far away from me or something—it's unbelievable.

Doctor: What thoughts come to mind when you're feeling like this?

Bob: I just think, "Oh, Christ, my heart is really beating, my head is swimming, my ears are ringing—I'm either going to die or go crazy."

Horses	Hippophobia	Open spaces	Agoraphobia, cenophobia, kenophobia	Snow	Chionophobia
Human beings	Anthropophobia			Speed	Tachophobia
Ice, frost	Cryophobia	Pain	Algophobia, odynephobia	Spiders	Arachnophobia
Illness	Nosemaphobia			Stings	Cnidophobia
Imperfection	Atelophobia	Physical love	Erotophobia	Strangers	Xenophobia
Infection	Mysophobia, molysmophobia	Pleasure	Hedonophobia	Sun	Heliophobia
		Poison	Toxiphobia	Surgery	Ergasiophobia
Injections	Trypanophobia	Poverty	Peniaphobia	Swallowing	Phagophobia
Insanity	Lyssophobia, maniaphobia	Pregnancy	Maieusiophobia	Teeth	Odontophobia
		Punishment	Poinephobia	Thunder	Keraunophobia, tonitrophobia
Insects	Entomophobia	Railways	Siderodromo-phobia		
Light	Photophobia, phengophobia			Touching or being touched	Haphephobia
		Rain	Ombrophobia		
Lightning	Astrapophobia, keraunophobia	Ridicule	Katagelophobia	Travel	Hodophobia
		Rivers	Potamophobia	Trees	Dendrophobia
Machinery	Mechanophobia	Robbers	Harpaxophobia	Vehicles	Amaxophobia, ochophobia
Marriage	Gamophobia	Russia or things Russian	Russophobia		
Meat	Carnophobia			Venereal disease	Cypridophobia, venereophobia
Men	Androphobia	Satan	Satanophobia		
Mice	Musophobia	School	Scholionophobia, didaskaleino-phobia	Wasps	Spheksophobia
Mirrors	Eisoptrophobia			Water	Hydrophobia
Missiles	Ballistophobia			Wind	Anemophobia
Money	Chrometophobia	Sexual intercourse	Coitophobia, cypridophobia	Women	Gynophobia
Nakedness	Gymnophobia			Words	Logophobia
Night	Nyctophobia	Shadows	Sciophobia	Work	Ergasiophobia, ponophobia
Noise or loud talking	Phonophobia	Sharp objects	Belonophobia		
		Skin	Dermatophobia	Worms	Helminthophobia
Novelty	Cainophobia, neophobia	Skin diseases	Dermatosiophobia	Wounds, injury	Traumatophobia
		Sleep	Hypnophobia	Writing	Graphophobia
Odors	Osmophobia	Snakes	Ophidiophobia	*(Melville, 1978, pp. 196–202)*	
Odors (body)	Osphresiophobia				

Doctor: What happens then?

Bob: Well, it doesn't last more than a few seconds, I mean that intense feeling. I come back down to earth, but then I'm worrying what's the matter with me all the time, or checking my pulse to see how fast it's going, or feeling my palms to see if they're sweating.

Doctor: Can others see what you're going through?

Bob: You know, I doubt it. I hide it. I haven't been seeing my friends. You know, they say "Let's stop for a beer" or something after work and I give them some excuse—you know, like I have to do something around the house or with my car. I'm not with them when I'm with them anyway—I'm just sitting there worrying. My friend Pat said I was frowning all the time. So, anyway, I just go home and turn on the TV or pick up the sports page, but I can't really get into that either.

Bob went on to say that he had stopped playing softball because of fatigability and trouble concentrating. On several occasions during the past two weeks he was unable to go to work because he was "too nervous." Recently he felt especially easily distracted by roadside stimuli while driving and described a frightening sensation that the passing trees were falling over into his car.

(Spitzer et al., 1983, pp. 11–12)

Bob suffers from many of the symptoms of a generalized anxiety disorder. Like Bob, people with this disorder experience excessive anxiety and worry about numerous events or activities (see Box 6–2). Given the scope of their worries, their problem is often described as *free-floating anxiety.*

Generalized anxiety disorders are relatively common in our society. Surveys suggest that up to 3.8 percent of the United States population have the symptoms of this disorder in any given year (APA, 1994; Kessler et al., 1994; Blazer et al., 1991). Although the disorder may emerge at any age, it most commonly appears in childhood or adolescence. As with most phobias, women diagnosed with a generalized anxiety disorder outnumber men 2 to 1.

The DSM-IV criteria for diagnosing a generalized anxiety disorder include symptoms that last at least six months (APA, 1994). People with the disorder typically feel restless, keyed up, or on edge, are easily fatigued, have difficulty concentrating, act irritable, experience muscle tension, and have a hard time falling or staying asleep or have a restless, unsatisfying sleep (APA, 1994).

The majority of people with a generalized anxiety disorder also develop another anxiety disorder, such as a phobia, at some point in their lives (Blazer et al., 1991; Weissman et al., 1978). Many experience depression as well (Kendler et al., 1992). Nevertheless, in contrast to those who suffer from agoraphobia or from a broad social phobia, most people with a generalized anxiety disorder are able, with some difficulty, to maintain adequate social relationships and occupational activities despite their discomfort.

Pervasive anxiety is often difficult for friends and relatives to accept. It's unpleasant for them to see a loved one so anxious and tense, and it's a burden to be continually reassuring. Sometimes they accuse the anxious person of "wanting" to worry, "looking" for things to worry about, and being "happy" only when they worry. These characterizations are unfair and certainly foreign to the subjective experience of the sufferers themselves. People with a generalized anxiety disorder hardly feel happy. They feel that they are in a constant struggle, always threatened and defending themselves, and always trying to escape their pain.

"Honestly now, Mr. Claus, how do you expect others to believe in you if you don't believe in yourself?"

The doubts and anxieties of people with anxiety disorders sometimes take the form of the "imposter phenomenon"—a persistent, gnawing feeling that one does not deserve one's success, that it is based on manipulating or fooling others rather than on competence (Clance & O'Toole, 1987). This unfounded anxiety, usually associated with low self-esteem, is particularly common among successful women in our society (Steinberg, 1986). (RUBES by Leigh Rubin by permission of Leigh Rubin and Creators Syndicate.)

EXPLANATIONS OF PHOBIC AND GENERALIZED ANXIETY DISORDERS

A variety of factors have been cited to explain the development of phobic and generalized anxiety disorders: the numerous stresses and changes of modern society; family pressures; personal conflicts, learning experiences, thoughts, and values; and predisposing biological processes. Supporters of the various models of psychopathology give different weights to different factors, and their explanations differ accordingly.

SOCIOCULTURAL EXPLANATIONS According to sociocultural theorists, phobic and generalized anxiety disorders are more likely to develop in people who are confronted with societal pressures and situations that pose real danger. Studies have found that people in highly threatening environments are more likely to develop the general feelings of tension, anxiety, and fatigue, the exaggerated startle reactions, and the sleep disturbances that characterize generalized anxiety disorders, and the specific fears and avoidance behaviors that characterize phobic disorders (Baum & Fleming, 1993; Melick, Logue, & Frederick, 1982).

Take the psychological impact of living near the Three Mile Island nuclear power plant in the aftermath of the March 1979 nuclear reactor accident (Baum, 1990; Bromet et al., 1984, 1982). In the months after the accident, mothers of preschool children living in the vicinity were found to display five times as many anxiety or depression disorders as mothers of comparable age and family structure living elsewhere. Although many of their disorders subsided

BOX 6-2

FEARS, SHMEARS: THE ODDS ARE USUALLY ON OUR SIDE

People with anxiety disorders have an enormous range of fears. And millions without these disorders worry about possible disaster every day. Most of the feared events are *possible* but, thank goodness, *not probable*. In fact, the ability to live and react in accordance with probability (rather than possibility) may be what distinguishes the fearless from the fearful. What are the actual odds that commonly feared events will happen to us? This sample list shows the range of probability; it also makes it clear that the odds are usually heavily in our favor.

One will undergo an IRS audit this year.	1 in 100
A city resident will be a victim of a violent crime.	1 in 60
A suburbanite will be a victim of a violent crime.	1 in 1,000
A small-town resident will be a victim of a violent crime	1 in 2,000
One's child will suffer a high-chair injury this year.	1 in 6,000
One will be bumped off any given airline flight.	1 in 4,000
One will be struck by lightning.	1 in 9,100
One will be murdered this year.	1 in 12,000

One will be killed on one's next bus ride.	1 in 500 million
One will be hit by a baseball at a major-league game.	1 in 300,000
One will drown in the tub this year.	1 in 685,000
One will be killed in an air crash.	1 in 4.6 million
One's airline flight will arrive late.	1 in 6
One's house will have a fire this year.	1 in 200
One will die in a fire this year.	1 in 40,200
One will die in a fall.	1 in 200,000
One's carton will contain a broken egg.	1 in 10
One will develop a tooth cavity.	1 in 6
One's young child will develop a tooth cavity.	1 in 10
One will contract AIDS from a blood transfusion.	1 in 100,000
Any given miner will be injured while working this year.	1 in 23
Any given construction worker will be injured at work this year.	1 in 27
Any given factory worker will be injured at work this year.	1 in 37

Any given farmer will be injured while working this year.	1 in 19
One will be attacked by a shark.	1 in 4 million
One will receive a diagnosis of cancer this year.	1 in 8,000
A woman will develop breast cancer during her lifetime	1 in 9
One will develop a brain tumor this year.	1 in 25,000
A business owner will become insolvent or declare bankruptcy this year.	1 in 55
A piano player will eventually develop lower back pain.	1 in 3
One will be killed in one's next automobile outing.	1 in 4 million
One will eventually die in an automobile accident.	1 in 140
Condom use will eventually fail to prevent pregnancy	1 in 10
An IUD will eventually fail to prevent pregnancy.	1 in 10
Coitus interruptus will eventually fail to prevent pregnancy.	1 in 5

(Adapted from Krantz, 1992)

The stresses of living and working in a complex, highly technological society may also increase the prevalence of anxiety symptoms and disorders.

during the next year, the Three Mile Island mothers still displayed elevated levels of anxiety or depression a year later.

SOCIETAL CHANGES   Stressful changes have occurred in our society over the past several decades. Older workers have felt increasingly threatened by the introduction of computer technology, parents by the increased media attention to child abuse and abduction, and travelers by the heightened incidence of terrorism. In addition, public concern about the dangers of nuclear energy has intensified. As sociocultural theorists might predict, these societal stresses have been accompanied by steady increases in the prevalence of phobic and generalized anxiety disorders throughout the United States. A 1975 survey of the general population indicated that 1.4 and 2.5 percent of the population suffered from phobic and generalized anxiety disorders, respectively (Weissman et al., 1978). Those rates have now increased to 11.0 and 3.8 percent (Regier et al., 1993; Eaton et al., 1991; Blazer et al., 1991). Moreover, surveys indicate that the prevalence rates of these anxiety disorders are typically higher in urbanized countries that have greater numbers of stressful changes than in less urbanized countries (Compton et al., 1991).

Similarly, prevalence studies across the world (Japan, Britain, Canada, Taiwan, Poland, India, France, Italy, Chile, Israel, and Nigeria) suggest that the prevalence of anxiety symptoms often increases along with societal changes caused by war, political oppression, modernization, and related national events (Compton et al., 1991; Hwu, Yeh, & Chang, 1989).

Some fears induced by societal changes are tied directly to the changes themselves. Many people suffer from "technophobia," a fear of interacting with the technological products of modern society. In a recent survey of 1000 adults in the United States, 55 percent reported that they are afraid of using videotape recorders, answering machines, or Walkmans, and 32 percent said they are intimidated by computers and afraid of damaging the machine when they use it (Swingle, 1993).

POVERTY AND RACE   One of the most direct indicators of societal stress is poverty. People without sufficient means typically live in homes that are more run down and communities with higher crime rates, have fewer educational and job opportunities and more job instability, and are at greater risk for health problems. As sociocultural theorists would predict, research indicates that poorer people have higher rates of phobic and generalized anxiety disorders. In the United States, for example, the rate of generalized anxiety disorders is twice as high among people with incomes of less than $10,000 a year as among those with higher incomes (Blazer et al., 1991). Indeed, as job income decreases in this country, the rate of generalized anxiety disorders steadily increases (Blazer et al., 1991). Similarly, those who rely primarily on welfare or disability benefits for their income show a much greater prevalence of phobias than other people (Eaton et al., 1991).

Since race is closely related to income and job opportunity in the United States (Belle, 1990), it is not surprising that the prevalence rates of generalized anxiety disorders and phobias are also tied to race (see Figure 6–3). In any given year, approximately 6 percent of all African Americans suffer from generalized anxiety disorders, compared to 3.5 percent of white Americans. African American women, perhaps the most socially stressed group in this country (Bennett, 1987), have the highest rate of all (6.6 percent). Similarly, around 16 percent of African Americans have a phobia, whereas 9 percent of white Americans have one. Again, African American women have the highest phobia rate of all (20 percent).

Although poverty and other societal pressures may establish a climate in which phobic and generalized anxiety disorders are more likely to develop, sociocultural variables are not the only factors at work. After all, most people in poor, war-torn, politically oppressed, or endangered communities or societies do not develop anxiety disorders. Granted the broad influence of sociocultural factors, theorists still must explain why some people develop these disorders and others do not. The psychodynamic, humanistic, behavioral, cognitive, and biological schools of thought have each tried to provide an explanation of this kind.

PSYCHODYNAMIC EXPLANATIONS Sigmund Freud (1933, 1917) formulated the initial psychodynamic explanations of phobic and generalized anxiety disorders. To begin with, he distinguished three kinds of anxiety: realistic, neurotic, and moral. We experience *realistic anxiety* when we confront genuine external dangers. This reaction is inborn, universal, and normal. We experience *neurotic anxiety* if we are repeatedly and excessively prevented, by our parents or by circumstances, from expressing our id impulses. We experience *moral anxiety* if we are punished or threatened for expressing our id impulses, come to perceive the id impulses themselves as threatening, and so become anxious whenever we feel those impulses.

As we saw in Chapter 2, Freud proposed that people try to control unacceptable impulses and accompanying neurotic and moral anxiety by employing ego defense mechanisms. If these defenses perform unsatisfactorily, a person may develop an anxiety disorder. According to Freud, phobic disorders represent overreliance on certain defense mechanisms, whereas generalized anxiety disorders occur when defense mechanisms break down under stress.

In particular, Freud believed that people with phobias make excessive use of the defense mechanisms of *repression* and *displacement* to control their underlying anxiety. Repeatedly they push their anxiety-producing impulses deeper into unconsciousness (repression) and transfer their fears to neutral objects or situations (displacement) that are easier to cope with and control. Although the new objects of fear are often related to the threatening impulses, the phobic person is not aware of the relationship.

Consider once again Freud's (1909) famous case of Little Hans, the child whose fear of horses was discussed in Chapter 3. Freud proposed that Hans became afraid of his own id impulses during his Oedipal stage (the third and fourth years of life). When he began to express sexual feelings toward his mother by handling his penis and asking his mother to place her finger on it, she threatened to cut off his penis and stressed that his desires were totally improper. This threat so frightened Hans that he became unconsciously afraid that his father, too, would learn of his desires and castrate him. In short, Hans came to develop high levels of neurotic and moral anxiety. Rather than experience fear whenever he felt those id impulses and rather than fear his mother and father, Hans repressed the impulses and displaced his fears onto a neutral object—horses. According to Freud, Hans chose horses because he had come to associate them with his father.

Freud saw generalized anxiety disorders, by contrast, as a breakdown in a person's defenses. Defense mechanisms can become overwhelmed if one continually experiences extreme levels of anxiety, such as a child might experience when repeatedly and excessively punished for expressing id impulses. If, for example, a young boy is harshly spanked every time he cries for milk as an infant, messes his pants as a 2-year-old, and explores his genitals as a toddler, he may eventually come to believe that his various id impulses are extremely dangerous and may experience severe anxiety whenever he has such impulses. Ego defense mechanisms may also break down if they are weak or inadequate. Overprotected children, shielded by their parents from all frustrations and sources of anxiety, have little opportunity to develop effective defense mechanisms. Later, when they encounter the inevitable pressures of adult life, their defense mechanisms may be too weak to cope with the resulting anxieties.

Contemporary psychodynamic theorists hold similar views on the causes of generalized anxiety disorders. For example, *object relations theorists* believe that the children of overly strict or overly protective parents develop a fear of being attacked by "bad objects"

PERCENTAGE OF PARENTS WHO WORRY "A LOT" THAT THEIR CHILDREN WILL:

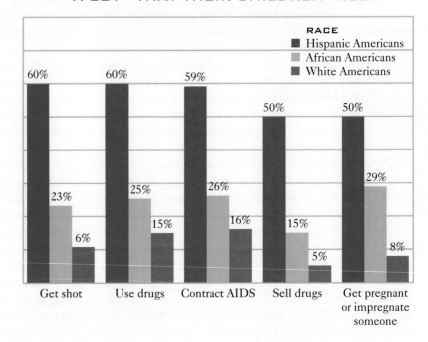

PERCENTAGE OF PARENTS WHO WORRY "A LOT" THAT THEIR CHILDREN WILL:

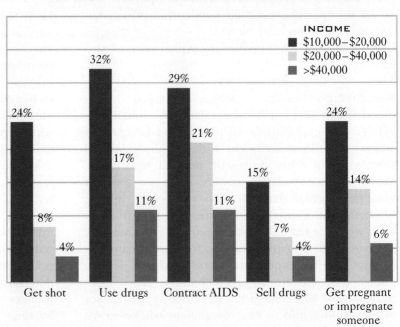

FIGURE 6–3 *According to a survey of 1,738 parents in the United States, African Americans and Hispanic Americans are much more likely than white Americans to worry significantly about their children's safety, future, and survival. Similarly, poorer parents are much more likely than wealthier parents to worry greatly about their children's welfare, irrespective of race, suggesting that the higher anxiety levels of racial minorities may be largely a matter of living in poorer, more deprived, or more dangerous environments. (Adapted from National Commission on Children, 1991.)*

(particularly their parents) or losing "good objects," and may carry this internalized anxiety state into adulthood in the form of a generalized anxiety disorder (Cirese, 1993; Zerbe, 1990). Similarly, *self-theorists* believe that children whose parents fail to treat them in a confident, relaxed, and supportive manner develop *disintegration anxiety:* they experience the self

as lacking all support and set up lifelong defensive structures to sooth and repair their damaged self (Zerbe, 1990). Such makeshift structures are typically overwhelmed by the stresses of adulthood, causing a state of *self-fragmentation,* or "coming apart at the seams," characterized by repeated outbreaks of anxiety (Diamond, 1987).

To support the psychodynamic explanations of phobic and generalized anxiety disorders, researchers have tried to show that people do indeed employ repression and related defense mechanisms in the face of fear and anxiety. In some studies of repression, experimenters have frightened subjects by presenting an apparent threat and have then measured how well the subjects remember the fear-arousing event. In accord with psychodynamic expectations, researchers have found that subjects often forget many aspects of the upsetting events. In a famous study of this kind, Saul Rosenzweig (1943, 1933) arranged for subjects to fail half of the problems on an important test. He found that the subjects later remembered less about the problems they had answered incorrectly than about those they had answered successfully.

Still other psychodynamic researchers have tried to demonstrate that people with phobic and generalized anxiety disorders in particular use defense mechanisms excessively. Evaluators who have looked for evidence of repression in the transcripts of early therapy sessions with anxious patients have found that when the patients are asked to discuss anxiety-arousing experiences, they do often react defensively by quickly forgetting what they were just talking about, changing the direction of the discussion, or denying negative feelings (Luborsky, 1973).

Several findings are also consistent with the psychodynamic claim that extreme punishment for early id impulses may lead to higher levels of anxiety at later points in life (Chiu, 1971). An examination of cultures in Kenya, India, Okinawa, Mexico, and the Philippines suggested a correlation between restrictive child-rearing practices and anxiety in adulthood (Whiting et al., 1966). In cultures where children are regularly punished and threatened, adults seem to have more fears and anxieties. In addition, several studies have supported the psychodynamic position that extreme protectiveness by parents may also lead to heightened anxiety in their children (Jenkins, 1968; Eisenberg, 1958).

Although these studies are consistent with the psychodynamic explanations of phobic and generalized anxiety disorders, they have been criticized on several grounds. First, some scientists question whether certain studies show what they claim to show. When people are reluctant to talk about upsetting events early in therapy, they are not necessarily repressing those events. They may be consciously focusing on the positive aspects of their lives or be too embarrassed to share personal negative events until they develop trust in the therapist. Similarly, when studies show a relationship between parenting styles and individual anxiety, they are not necessarily establishing a causal relationship between these two variables. It could be that high levels of anxiety in children lead some parents to develop an overcontrolling or overprotective parenting style.

Second, even if people in these studies are exhibiting repression and if parenting styles do lead to anxiety, it does not necessarily follow that people with anxiety disorders are afraid of their id impulses or that defense mechanisms have broken down. Even strong proponents of the psychodynamic perspective acknowledge that it is very difficult to develop research designs capable of testing the fundamental theoretical components of this model.

A final problem is that a number of research studies and clinical reports have actually contradicted the psychodynamic explanations. In one, sixteen people with generalized anxiety disorders were interviewed to obtain histories of their upbringing (Raskin et al., 1982). They reported relatively little of the excessive discipline or disturbed childhood environments that psychodynamic therapists might expect for people with this disorder.

HUMANISTIC AND EXISTENTIAL EXPLANATIONS Humanistic and existential theorists propose that phobic and generalized anxiety disorders, like other mental disorders, arise when people stop looking at themselves honestly and acceptingly and instead deny and distort their true thoughts, emotions, and behavior. Their defensive postures ultimately serve to make them extremely anxious and incapable of fulfilling their potential as human beings.

The humanistic position on why people develop phobic and generalized anxiety disorders is best illustrated by Carl Rogers's explanation. Rogers believed that some people develop a defensive way of functioning when as children they fail to receive *unconditional positive regard* from significant others and so become overly critical of themselves. They develop harsh self-standards—Rogers called them *conditions of worth*—which they try to meet by repeatedly distorting and denying their true experiences. Using such defensive techniques, these people succeed only partially in feeling good about themselves; threatening self-judgments persist in breaking through and causing intense anxiety. This foundation of anxiety sets the stage for a phobic or generalized anxiety disorder or some other form of mental dysfunctioning.

Rogers and his colleagues conducted studies to test his explanation of abnormal functioning and found some support for it (Chodorkoff, 1954). These investigations, however, usually grouped numerous mental disorders together and did not focus specifically on phobic and generalized anxiety disorders. Moreover, other humanistic theorists believe that traditional research methods cannot provide a fair test for humanistic explanations and have not even tried to test their ideas empirically. As a result, the humanistic explanations have received limited research verification.

Existentialists believe that phobic and generalized anxiety disorders grow out of *existential anxiety,* a universal human fear of the limits and responsibilities of one's existence (Tillich, 1952). We experience existential anxiety, they say, because we know that life is finite and we fear the death that awaits us. We also know that our actions and choices may have unexpected consequences, and we fear that we may hurt others unintentionally. Finally, we suspect that life in general has no purpose and that our own personal existence may ultimately lack meaning.

According to existentialists, people can confront their existential anxiety head on by taking responsibility for their actions, making decisions, making their lives meaningful, and appreciating their own uniqueness, or they can shrink from this confrontation. Caught up in the change, confusion, and strain of our highly organized, competitive technical civilization, some people choose to lead "inauthentic lives": they deny their fears, overlook their freedom of choice, avoid taking responsibility for their lives, and conform excessively to the standards and guidelines imposed by society (May, 1967; Bugental, 1965). According to

"Just because you're Attila the Hun, Dad, doesn't mean
I have to be Attila the Hun."

Existentialists believe that people must take responsibility for their actions, making conscious and meaningful decisions in order to live authentic lives that are relatively free of anxiety. (Drawing by P. Steiner; © 1993 The New Yorker Magazine, Inc.)

existentialists, such a lifestyle inevitably fails to reduce one's existential anxiety, which continues to erupt in the form of anxiety disorders. Viktor Frankl (1965) explains phobias in this manner:

> The original total anxiety apparently seeks some concrete content, some objective representation of "death" and "life." . . . Often the very words in which patients describe their symptoms and complaints . . . can put us on the track of the real, the existential reason for the neurosis. Thus, a patient . . . expressed her anxiety as: "A feeling like hanging in the air." This was in fact an apt description of her whole spiritual situation. (p. 180)

Like humanists, existentialists generally believe that traditional research methods are inadequate for examining the merits of their explanation. They argue that empirical investigations miss subtle, internal experiences by looking only at what can be observed and defined objectively. These theorists resort instead to logic, introspection, and individual case examples as evidence for their views on phobic and generalized anxiety disorders. As a result, little systematic research has been conducted on the existential viewpoint.

BEHAVIORAL EXPLANATIONS   Behaviorists believe that people with phobic and generalized anxiety disorders learn, through conditioning, first to fear and later to avoid certain objects, situations, or events. Those with phobic disorders learn to fear and avoid only a small number of objects or situations; those with generalized anxiety disorders acquire a broad range of such fears.

LEARNING TO FEAR   Behaviorists propose *classical conditioning* as a common way of acquiring fear reactions to objects or situations that are not inherently dangerous. Two events that occur close together in time become closely associated in a person's mind, and, as we saw in Chapter 2, the person then reacts similarly to both of them. If one event triggers a fear response, the other may also.

Over 70 years ago a clinician described the case of a young woman who apparently acquired a phobic fear of running water through classical conditioning (Bagby, 1922). As a child of 7 she went on a picnic with her mother and aunt, and ran off by herself into the woods after lunch. While she was climbing over some large rocks, her feet became deeply wedged between two of them, and the harder she tried to free herself, the more firmly trapped she became. No one heard her screams, and she became more and more terrified. In the terminology of behaviorists, the entrapment was eliciting a fear response.

Entrapment: $\longrightarrow$ Fear response

As she struggled to free her feet, the girl was also exposed to other stimuli. In particular, she heard a waterfall nearby. The sound of the running water became linked in her mind to her terrifying encounter with the rocks, and she developed a fear of running water as well.

Running water $\longrightarrow$ Fear response

Eventually the aunt found the screaming child, freed her from the rocks, and gave her comfort and reassurance; but significant psychological damage had been done. From that day forward, the girl was terrified of running water. For years family members had to hold her down to bathe her. When she traveled on a train, friends had to cover the windows so that she would not have to look at any streams. The young woman had apparently acquired a phobia through classical conditioning.

In conditioning terms, the entrapment was an *unconditioned stimulus* (US) that understandably elicited an *unconditioned response* (UR) of fear. The running water represented a *conditioned stimulus* (CS), a formerly neutral stimulus that became associated with entrapment in the child's mind and came to elicit a fear reaction. The newly acquired fear was a *conditioned response* (CR).

CS: Running water $\longrightarrow$ CR: Fear

US: Entrapment $\longrightarrow$ UR: Fear

Another way of acquiring fear reactions is through *modeling;* that is, through observation and imitation (Bandura & Rosenthal, 1966). A person may observe that others are afraid of certain objects or events and develop fears of the same objects or events. Consider a young boy whose mother is afraid of illnesses, doctors, and hospitals. If she frequently expresses those fears, before long the boy himself may fear illnesses, doctors, and hospitals.

LEARNING TO AVOID   Why should one fear-provoking experience develop into a long-term phobia? Shouldn't the trapped girl later have seen that running water would bring her no harm? Shouldn't the boy later see that illnesses are temporary and doctors and hospitals helpful? Behaviorists agree that fears will indeed undergo *extinction* if a person is repeatedly exposed to the feared object and sees that it brings no harm. After acquiring a fear response, however, people try to avoid what they fear. Whenever they find themselves near a fearsome object, they quickly move away. They may also think ahead and take measures to ensure that such encounters will not occur. Remember that the girl had friends cover the

When people observe others (models) being afraid of or victimized by an object or situation, they themselves may develop a fear of the object. Alfred Hitchcock's film The Birds *led to an increase in the incidence of ornithophobia (fear of birds) during the 1960s.*

windows on trains so that she could avoid looking at streams. Similarly, the boy may try to avoid visits to doctors, hospitals, and sick friends.

In the behavioral view, such *avoidance behaviors* develop through *operant conditioning,* the process by which we learn to behave in ways that are repeatedly rewarded. The girl and boy are repeatedly rewarded by a marked reduction in anxiety whenever they avoid the things they fear. Unfortunately, such avoidance also serves to preserve their fear responses (Miller, 1948; Mowrer, 1947, 1939). Phobic people do not get close to the dreaded objects often enough to learn that they are really quite harmless.

Behaviorists propose that specific learned fears will blossom into a generalized anxiety disorder when a person acquires a large number of them. This development is presumed to come about through *stimulus generalization:* responses to one stimulus are also elicited by similar stimuli. The fear of running water acquired by the girl in the rocks could have generalized to such similar stimuli as milk being poured into a glass or even the sound of bubbly music. If a person experiences a series of upsetting events, if each event produces one or more feared stimuli, and if the person's reactions to each of these stimuli generalize to yet other stimuli, that person may build up a large number of fears and eventually develop a generalized anxiety disorder. According to behaviorists, then, the anxiety manifested in generalized anxiety disorders is broad but hardly free-floating.

EVIDENCE FOR THE BEHAVIORAL EXPLANATIONS   Behavioral studies have indicated that fear reactions can indeed be acquired through conditioning. Some analogue experiments have found that laboratory animals can be taught to fear objects through classical conditioning (Miller, 1948; Mowrer, 1947, 1939). Experimenters typically place an animal in a shuttle box—a two-compartment box in which animals can jump over a barrier from one compartment to the other—and shock the animal through the floor after a few seconds. Most animals react by running in circles, urinating, defecating, and crying out. After repeated trials, the animals show this reaction the moment they are placed in or even near the shuttle box, before the onset of shock. Because of its temporal association with shock, the box itself becomes a conditioned stimulus capable of eliciting conditioned fear responses.

The same studies have also demonstrated that animals can learn to avoid the shock of a shuttle box. While running around the box, most animals eventually cross the barrier into the other side, where they are safe from shock. Usually they discover that this is the road to safety, and henceforth jump over the barrier and escape to the safe side whenever they are shocked. Eventually the animals learn to avoid the threatening side altogether and go directly to the safe compartment before the current is even turned on. When experimenters use extremely traumatic stimuli (that is, high levels of shock), fear and avoidance reactions are learned more rapidly—often in one trial—and are particularly hard to extinguish (Solomon, Kamin, & Wynne, 1953).

Analogue studies with human beings have sometimes yielded similar results. In a famous report, John B. Watson and Rosalie Rayner (1920) described how they taught a baby boy called Little Albert to fear white rats. For weeks Albert was allowed to play with a white rat and appeared to enjoy doing so. One time when Albert reached for the rat, however, the experimenter struck a steel bar with a hammer, making a very loud noise that upset and frightened Albert. The next several times that Albert reached for the rat, the experimenter again made the loud noise. Albert acquired a fear and avoidance response to the rat. As Watson (1930) described it, "The instant the rat was shown, the baby began to cry . . . and began to crawl away so rapidly that he was caught with difficulty before he reached the edge of the mattress" (p. 161). According to some reports, Albert's fear of white rats also generalized to such objects as a rabbit, human hair, cotton, and even a Santa Claus mask.

Research has also supported the behavioral position that fears can be acquired through modeling. Psychologists Albert Bandura and Theodore Rosenthal (1966), for example, had human subjects

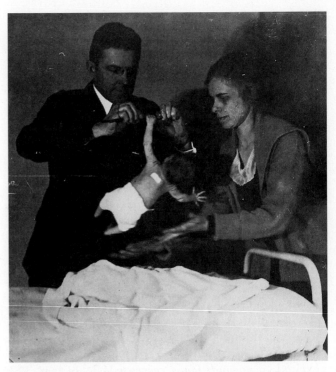

John B. Watson, pioneer of the American behaviorist movement, tests the grasping reflex of an infant. Watson never replicated the study in which he and his colleague Rosalie Rayner used classical conditioning to teach Little Albert to fear white rats. There is also some question as to whether the infant's fear reaction approached the strength of a phobia.

observe a person apparently being shocked by electricity whenever a buzzer sounded. The victim was actually the experimenter's accomplice—in research terminology, a *confederate*—who pretended to experience pain by twitching, writhing, and yelling whenever the buzzer went on. After the unsuspecting subjects had observed several such episodes, they themselves underwent a fear reaction, indicated by an increase in their heart rate and in their galvanic skin response, whenever they heard the buzzer. The process of acquiring fear reactions through modeling in this way is called *vicarious conditioning.* Clinical case reports of anxiety disorders sometimes paint a similar picture. During World War II, for example, cases were reported of combat airmen who became clinically anxious after observing other airmen display extreme anxiety (Grinker & Spiegel, 1945).

Similar modeling results have been obtained in a study of rhesus monkeys. Laboratory-reared adolescent monkeys, who had no fear of snakes, observed their wild-reared parents, who had a pronounced fear of snakes, behaving fearfully in the presence of real, toy, and model snakes. After six relatively short sessions of observation, the adolescent monkeys also demonstrated an intense fear of snakes (Mineka et al., 1984). A follow-up study three months later revealed that the adolescent monkeys were still afraid of snakes, real and simulated.

Although these studies support behaviorists' explanations of phobic and generalized anxiety disorders, other research has called those explanations into question (Marks, 1987; Samelson, 1980; Harris, 1979). One study was unsuccessful in conditioning fear in fifteen infants as Watson and Rayner had done with Little Albert (Bregman, 1934). Indeed, Watson and Rayner themselves never reported a replication of their work. Similarly, several laboratory studies with adult subjects have attempted but failed to condition fear reactions (Hallam & Rachman, 1976; Bancroft, 1971).

Clinical case reports and questionnaires also seem to question whether phobic and generalized anxiety disorders result from specific classical conditioning or modeling incidents. Although specific incidents have been cited in some cases (Ost, 1991; Merckelbach, Arntz, & de Jong, 1991), other cases suggest no clear origin (Marks, 1987; Keuthen, 1980). In summary, although researchers have found that these anxiety problems can be acquired by classical conditioning or modeling and retained by avoidance responses, they have not established that the disorders are ordinarily acquired in this way.

A BEHAVIORAL-BIOLOGICAL EXPLANATION
Some phobias are much more common than others. Phobic reactions to animals, heights, loud noises, illnesses, darkness, and water are more common than phobic reactions to meat, grass, and houses. Behaviorists often account for this uneven distribution of fears by proposing that human beings, as a species, have a predisposition to develop certain fears (Ohman & Soares, 1993; Marks, 1987, 1977, 1969; Seligman, 1971). This idea is referred to as *preparedness,* because human beings, theoretically, are "prepared" to acquire some phobias and not others. This point is highlighted in the following case description by I. M. Marks (1977):

A four-year-old girl was playing in the park. Thinking that she saw a snake, she ran to her parents' car and jumped inside, slamming the door behind her. Unfortunately, the girl's hand was caught by the closing car door, the results of which were severe pain and several visits to the doctor. Before this, she may have been afraid of snakes, but not phobic. After this experience, a phobia developed, not of cars or car doors, but of snakes. The snake phobia persisted into adulthood, at which time she sought treatment from me. (p. 192)

Marks concludes, "Certain stimuli seem to act as magnets for phobias . . . as if human brains were preprogrammed to make these preferential connections easily" (p. 194).

In a series of important tests of this notion, the psychologist Arne Ohman and his colleagues have conditioned different kinds of fears in two groups of human subjects (Ohman & Soares, 1993; Ohman, Erixon, & Lofberg, 1975). In one such study they showed all subjects slides of faces, houses, snakes, and spiders. One group received electric shocks whenever they observed the slides of faces and houses, while the other group was shocked during their observations of snakes and spiders. Using the subjects' galvanic skin responses as a measure of fear, the experimenters found that both groups learned to fear the intended objects after repeated shock pairings, but then they noted an interesting distinction: after a short shock-free period, the subjects who had learned to fear faces and houses stopped registering high GSRs in the presence of those objects; but subjects who had learned to fear snakes and spiders continued to show high GSRs in response to them for a long while. Their fears apparently continued even without the reinforcement of an accompanying shock. One interpretation of this finding is that animals and insects are stronger candidates for human phobias than faces or houses.

Researchers do not know whether such human fear predispositions are imposed biologically or culturally. Proponents of a biological predisposition argue that the fear propensities have been transmitted genetically through the evolutionary process (Ohman, 1993; Marks & Tobena, 1990; DeSilva, Rachman, & Seligman, 1977). They suggest that the objects of common phobias represented real dangers to our ancestors and that the ancestors who more readily acquired a fear of animals, darkness, heights, and the like were more likely to survive long enough to reproduce. Proponents of a cultural predisposition argue that parents, friends, and experience teach us early in life that certain objects are legitimate sources of fear, and this training predisposes many people to acquire corresponding phobias (Carr, 1979). Research has supported each of these perspectives (Gray, 1987; McNally, 1986). As is so often the case in such circumstances, we may find that both biological and cultural factors are involved.

COGNITIVE EXPLANATIONS Cognitive explanations have focused on generalized anxiety disorders rather than on phobias. The most prominent cognitive theories suggest that a generalized anxiety disorder is caused by *maladaptive assumptions*. As we saw in Chapter 2, for example, Albert Ellis believes that some people hold basic irrational assumptions that color their interpretations of events and lead to inappropriate emotional reactions (Ellis, 1984, 1977, 1962). According to Ellis, people with generalized anxiety disorders often hold the following assumptions:

"It is a dire necessity for an adult human being to be loved or approved of by virtually every significant other person in his community."

"It is awful and catastrophic when things are not the way one would very much like them to be."

"If something is or may be dangerous or fearsome one should be terribly concerned about it and should keep dwelling on the possibility of its occurring."

When people with these basic assumptions are faced with a stressful event, such as an exam or a blind date, they are likely to interpret it as highly dangerous and threatening, to overreact, and to experience fear. As they apply the assumptions to more and more life events, they may begin to develop a generalized anxiety disorder.

In a similar cognitive theory, Aaron Beck holds that people with a generalized anxiety disorder constantly make unrealistic silent assumptions that imply that they are in imminent danger (Beck, 1991, 1976; Beck & Greenberg, 1988; Beck & Emery, 1985):

"Any strange situation should be regarded as dangerous."

"A situation or a person is unsafe until proven to be safe."

"It is always best to assume the worst."

"My security and safety depend on anticipating and preparing myself at all times for any possible danger."
(Beck & Emery, 1985, p. 63)

Such silent assumptions lead people to experience narrow and persistent anxiety-provoking images and thoughts, called *automatic thoughts.* In a social situation they may dwell on such automatic thoughts as "I'll make a fool of myself"; "I won't know what to say"; "People will laugh at me." When they work on important projects, they are plagued by thoughts of "What if I fail?"; "Other things might get in the way";

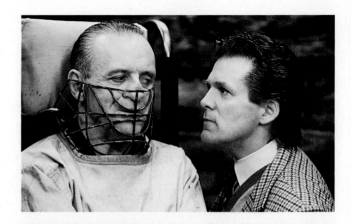

Cognitive researchers have found that people respond less fearfully to negative events when they can predict and control their onset. In fact, many people enjoy the feeling of fear as long as it occurs under controlled circumstances, such as when viewing a suspense or horror movie. Even here, however, people find different kinds of events arousing—some are more threatened by the sinister plots of Hannibal Lecter, others by a menacing Tyrannosaurus rex.

"I won't have enough time to do a good job"; "I'm falling behind."

Research has provided support for Ellis's and Beck's notion that maladaptive assumptions can induce anxiety. In several studies, nonanxious subjects who were manipulated into adopting negative views about themselves later developed signs of anxiety. For example, when normal college students were instructed to read to themselves such sentences as "My grades may not be good enough" and "I might flunk out of school," they temporarily showed greater respiratory changes and emotional arousal than did control subjects who read neutral sentences (Rimm & Litvak, 1969).

Other studies have suggested that people who tend to worry and have upsetting thoughts and images typically experience such features of anxiety as general nervous tension, muscle tension, upset stomach, and a sinking and heavy feeling in the stomach (Borkovec et al., 1993, 1983). Such worriers also experience more intrusions of negative thoughts and are more distracted than nonworriers when they try to concentrate on tasks.

Other experimenters have directly studied people with generalized anxiety disorders and have found that many do indeed hold dysfunctional assumptions (Himle, Himle, & Thyer, 1989; Hibbert, 1984). One study found that thirty-two subjects with generalized anxiety disorders held exaggerated notions of possible harmful events or consequences (Beck et al., 1974). Each subject reported upsetting assumptions, images, and automatic thoughts about at least one of the following danger areas: physical injury, illness, or death; mental illness; psychological impairment or loss of control; failure and inability to cope; and rejection, depreciation, and domination. Indeed, 70 percent of them feared three or more of these possibilities. Related studies have also found that people with generalized anxiety symptoms are more attentive to threatening cues than to other kinds of cues (Mineka & Sutton, 1992; MacLeod, Mathews, & Tata, 1986).

What kinds of people are likely to have inflated expectations of danger and experience generalized anxiety disorders? Some cognitive theorists point to people whose lives have been punctuated by numerous *unpredictable* negative events. These individuals become generally fearful of the unknown and always wait for the boom to drop (Pekrun, 1992). In order to avoid being "blindsided," they keep trying to predict the occurrence of new unforeseen negative events, looking everywhere for signs of danger. Ironically, they wind up "reading" such signs into most of the situations that they encounter and see danger everywhere, thus setting up a life of anxiety. Consistent with this notion, numerous laboratory studies have demonstrated that animal and human subjects respond more fearfully to unpredictable or unsignaled negative events than to predictable or signaled ones (Mineka, 1985), and that subjects choose to predict and control such negative events when given the option (Weinberg & Levine, 1980). However, researchers have yet to perform the difficult task of determining whether people with generalized anxiety disorders have experienced more unpredictable negative events than others in life.

BIOLOGICAL EXPLANATIONS Biological theorists have also focused chiefly on generalized anxiety disorders. Several important discoveries have led them to believe that these disorders are caused in part by biochemical dysfunctioning in the brain. The first of these discoveries was made in the 1950s, when researchers determined that **benzodiazepines**, the family of drugs that includes diazepam (Valium), alprazolam (Xanax), and chlordiazepoxide (Librium), provide relief from anxiety. No one understood, however, why they were effective.

It was not until the late 1970s that newly developed radioactive techniques enabled researchers to pinpoint the exact sites in the brain that are affected by benzodiazepines (Mohler & Okada, 1977; Squires & Braestrup, 1977). Apparently certain neurons have receptor molecules that receive the benzodiazepines, just as a lock receives a key. Particularly high concentrations of these neuroreceptors are located in the brain's limbic system and hypothalamus, brain areas known to be heavily involved in modulating emotional states (Gray, 1987; Costa, 1985; Hollister, 1982).

Investigators soon discovered that these same neuroreceptors ordinarily receive **gamma aminobutyric acid (GABA)**, a common and important neurotransmitter in the brain (Haefely, 1990; Costa et al., 1978, 1975). As we saw in Chapter 2, neurotransmitters are chemicals that carry messages from one neuron to another. GABA carries inhibitory messages: when GABA is received at a neuroreceptor, it causes the neuron to stop firing.

Researchers have studied the possible role of GABA and GABA receptors in fear reactions (Barondes, 1993; Costa, 1985, 1983; Insel et al., 1984) and have pieced together the following scenario: In normal fear reactions, neurons throughout the brain

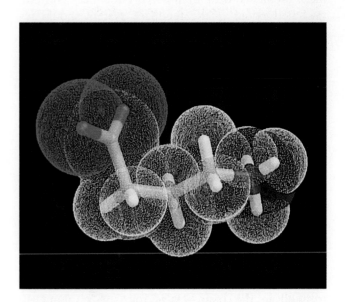

A computer-drawn molecule of gamma aminobutyric acid (GABA), the neurotransmitter that carries an inhibitory message to neuron receptors. Neurons that receive GABA stop firing, reducing the brain's state of excitability and the overall experience of anxiety.

fire more rapidly, trigger the firing of still more neurons, and create a general state of hyperexcitability throughout the brain and body; thus the increases in perspiration, breathing, and heartbeat. This state is experienced as fear or anxiety. After neuronal firing continues for a while, it triggers a feedback system that reduces the level of excitability. GABA-producing neurons throughout the brain release this neurotransmitter, which then binds to GABA receptors on receiving neurons and induces those neurons to stop firing. The state of excitability is thereby reduced, and the experience of fear or anxiety subsides.

Researchers believe that a problem in this feedback system can cause fear or anxiety to go unchecked (Lloyd, Fletcher, & Minchin, 1992). Some investigators have been able to generate and intensify fear or anxiety reactions in animals by reducing the capacity of GABA to bind to GABA receptors throughout the animals' brains (Costa, 1985; Mohler, Richards, & Wu, 1981). This finding suggests that people with a generalized anxiety disorder may have ongoing problems in their anxiety feedback system. Perhaps their brain supplies of GABA are too low, they have too few GABA receptors, or their GABA receptors do not readily bind the neurotransmitters. Or perhaps their brain releases an excess of other chemicals that reduce GABA's activity at receptor sites. Indeed, researchers have identified some natural brain chemicals that seem to promote anxiety by doing just that (Barondes, 1993).

If people with generalized anxiety disorders do have problems with their GABA feedback system, then corrections to the feedback system should reduce their chronically high levels of anxiety. This may be the reason that benzodiazepine drugs are so helpful to people with anxiety disorders. The benzodiazepines apparently act on GABA neuron receptors, enhancing their ability to bind GABA (Leonard, 1992; Costa & Guidotti, 1979).

This explanation of generalized anxiety disorders is promising but it has certain problems. One is that further biological discoveries seem to complicate the picture. It has been found, for example, that GABA is only one of several body chemicals that can bind to the important GABA receptors (Bunney & Garland, 1981). Could these other chemicals, operating either alone or in conjunction with GABA, be critical factors in the brain's control of anxiety? Moreover, we now know that GABA is very widely distributed in the brain—it is released at about 40 percent of the synapses there—so it is difficult to identify precisely where in the brain it produces its effect on anxiety (Barondes, 1993).

Another problem is that most of the research on the biological regulation of anxiety has been done on laboratory animals. When researchers generate fear responses in animals, they are assuming that the animals are experiencing something that approximates human anxiety, but it is impossible to be certain. The animals may be experiencing a high level of arousal that is quite distinct from human anxiety.

Finally, biological theorists are faced with the problem of establishing a causal relationship. Although biological studies implicate physiological functioning in human anxiety disorders, they do not usually establish that the physiological events cause such disorders. The biological responses of chronically anxious adults may be the result rather than the cause of their anxiety disorders. Perhaps chronic anxiety eventually leads to poorer GABA reception.

Some researchers have tried to establish that biological dysfunctioning does actually precede the appearance of generalized anxiety disorders. Researchers have found, for example, that some infants become physically aroused very quickly while others remain placid in the face of the same degree of stimulation (Thomas et al., 1963). It may be that these early differences reflect inborn arousal styles and that the easily aroused children are more likely to develop anxiety disorders later in life (Kalin, 1993).

Some family pattern research is also consistent with the notion that generalized anxiety disorders are caused in part by a physiological predisposition. If biological tendencies toward generalized anxiety disorders are inherited, people who are biologically related should have more similar probabilities of developing this disorder. Concordance studies have indeed found that blood relatives of persons with a generalized anxiety disorder are more likely than nonrelatives to have the disorder too (Kendler et al., 1992; Carey & Gottesman, 1981; Noyes et al., 1978). Approximately 15 percent of the relatives of people with generalized anxiety disorders themselves display a generalized anxiety disorder—proportionally more than the 4 percent found in the general population. And the closer the relative (an identical twin, for example, as opposed to a fraternal twin or other sibling), the greater the likelihood that he or she will also have the anxiety disorder (Marks, 1986; Rosenthal, 1970; Slater & Shields, 1969). Similar data have been reported regarding some of the phobic disorders (APA, 1994; Marks, 1986).

Of course, we must be careful in our interpretations of these studies. Although their findings are consistent with the view that biological abnormalities precede generalized anxiety disorders, they could also be suggesting that these disorders are caused by environmental experiences. Because relatives are likely to share aspects of the same environment, their shared disorders may be reflecting similarities in environment and upbringing rather than similarities in biological makeup. Indeed, the closer the relatives, the more similar their environmental experiences are likely to be. Because identical twins are more physically alike than fraternal twins, they may even experience more similarities in their upbringing.

Obviously, clinicians and researchers have generated many facts and ideas about phobic and generalized anxiety disorders. At times, however, the sheer quantity of concepts and findings makes it difficult to grasp what is and what is not really known about the disorders. Moreover, each of the leading explanations has characteristic limitations. The psychodynamic and humanistic explanations have been difficult to research. Behavioral and cognitive researchers have been able to create anxiety symptoms in the laboratory by using the principles of their models but have failed to establish that anxiety disorders ordinarily develop in these ways. And biological researchers have yet to clarify the precise roles and importance of the biochemical correlates to these disorders. Given this state of affairs, we cannot say that phobic and generalized anxiety disorders are well understood or that some explanations have a clear edge over others.

■ PANIC ■ DISORDERS

Sometimes an anxiety reaction accelerates into a smothering, nightmarish panic; one loses control of one's behavior, is practically unaware of what one is doing, and feels a sense of imminent doom. Anyone can react with panic if a situation is provocative enough. Usually such reactions occur when a real threat is immense and comes on suddenly. Some people, however, experience *panic attacks*—periodic, discrete bouts of panic that occur abruptly and reach a peak within 10 minutes. Such attacks consist of at least four symptoms of panic, the most common of which are palpitations, tingling in the hands or feet, shortness of breath, sweating, hot and cold flashes, trembling, chest pains, choking sensations, faintness, dizziness, and a feeling of unreality (APA, 1994). Small wonder that during a panic attack many people fear they will die, go crazy, or lose control. Here a woman describes such an episode:

Although only some people display panic disorders, almost anyone is capable of experiencing panic in the face of a clear and overwhelming threat that unfolds at breakneck speed. Overflowing and uncontrollable crowds led to horror and panic when a wall collapsed at the European Cup soccer finals in Brussels in 1985. Thousands of persons were injured and thirty-eight were killed.

I was inside a very busy shopping precinct and all of a sudden it happened: in a matter of seconds I was like a mad woman. It was like a nightmare, only I was awake; everything went black and sweat poured out of me—my body, my hands and even my hair got wet through. All the blood seemed to drain out of me; I went as white as a ghost. I felt as if I were going to collapse; it was as if I had no control over my limbs; my back and legs were very weak and I felt as though it were impossible to move. It was as if I had been taken over by some stronger force. I saw all the people looking at me—just faces, no bodies, all merged into one. My heart started pounding in my head and in my ears; I thought my heart was going to stop. I could see black and yellow lights. I could hear the voices of the people but from a long way off. I could not think of anything except the way I was feeling and that now I had to get out and run quickly or I would die. I must escape and get into the fresh air.

(Hawkrigg, 1975)

Apparently a person must reach a certain level of physical or cognitive maturity before being capable of experiencing a full-blown panic attack. A research team headed by Chris Hayward (1992) found that over 5 percent of the 754 sixth- and seventh-grade girls whom they interviewed had experienced a panic attack. In the subgroup of girls rated most physically immature, none reported panic attacks, but 8 percent of the girls who had completed puberty did report having them.

People with any of the anxiety disorders may experience a panic attack when they confront one of the objects or situations they dread (APA, 1994). Some

BOX 6-3

ASSESSING AN ANXIETY DISORDER

How do clinicians detect an anxiety disorder? One of the most useful techniques is simply to ask relevant questions and determine from the responses whether the symptoms fit the criteria specified in DSM-IV. To help clinicians collect all relevant information, various interview schedules have been developed, such as the *Anxiety Disorders Interview Schedule—Revised* (DiNardo & Barlow, 1988), exerpted below. Affirmative or otherwise characteristic responses to a series of questions such as these may push the clinician closer and closer to diagnosing a particular anxiety disorder:

SOCIAL PHOBIA

In social situations, where you might be observed or evaluated by others, do you feel fearful/anxious/nervous?

Are you overly concerned that you might do and/or say something that might embarrass or humiliate yourself in front of others, or that others may think badly of you?

What do you anticipate before going into social situations?

Do you avoid these situations because you are afraid that you will have a panic attack?

If you had the physical symptoms while you were alone, would you still be frightened?

GENERALIZED ANXIETY DISORDER

What kinds of things do you worry about?

During the last six months, have you been bothered by these worries more days than not?

Are you a worrier? Do you worry excessively about small things such as being late for an appointment, repairs to the house or car, etc.?

On an average day over the last month, what percent of the day do you feel tense, anxious, worried?

How long has the tension, anxiety, worry been a problem?

During the past six months, have you been bothered by trembling (shortness of breath, feeling keyed, etc.)?

PANIC DISORDER

Have you had times when you have felt a sudden rush of intense fear or anxiety, or a feeling of impending doom?

In what situations have you had those feelings?

Have you ever had those feelings come "from out of the blue," or while you are at home alone, or in situations where you did not expect them to occur?

How long does it usually take for the rush of anxiety to become intense?

How long does the anxiety usually last at its peak level?

In the last month, how much have you worried about, or how fearful have you been about having another attack?

---

people, however, experience panic attacks without apparent provocation, and do so recurrently and unpredictably. They may receive a diagnosis of *panic disorder.*

According to DSM-IV, a diagnosis of panic disorder is warranted if after at least one unexpected panic attack a person spends a month or more worrying persistently about having another attack, worrying about the implications or consequences of the attack (such as fear of going crazy or having a heart attack), or changing his or her behavior markedly in response to the attack.

In any given year, as many as 2.3 percent of adults in the United States suffer from a panic disorder (Kessler et al., 1994; Regier et al., 1993; Eaton et al.,

1991). Most people develop the disorder between late adolescence and the mid-thirties, and the diagnosis is at least twice as common among women as among men (APA, 1994). Many other people experience panic attacks that are not severe or frequent enough to be diagnosed as a panic disorder (Eaton et al., 1994; Katerndahl & Realini, 1993). In one survey of 256 normal young adults, 36 percent reported that they had had one or more panic attacks during the previous year (Norton, Dorward, & Cox, 1986). Similarly, 43 percent of 534 Australian adolescents reported having experienced at least one panic attack (King et al., 1993).

Many people mistakenly believe that they have a general medical problem when they first experience panic attacks (Oakley-Browne, 1991). Conversely, certain medical problems such as *mitral valve prolapse,* a cardiac malfunction marked by periodic episodes of heart palpitations, and *thyroid disease* may initially be misdiagnosed as panic disorder and nothing else (Coplan et al., 1992; Gorman et al., 1986, 1981; Agras, 1985). Thus, accurate assessment is very important (see Box 6–3).

Panic disorders are often accompanied by agoraphobia (fear of venturing into public places), a pattern that DSM-IV terms *panic disorder with agoraphobia.* In such cases, the agoraphobic pattern usually seems to emerge from the panic attacks (Barlow, 1988; Munjack, 1984). After experiencing unpredictable and recurrent panic attacks, people become fearful of having one someplace where help is unavailable or escape difficult. Anne Watson was one such person:

M s. Watson reported that until the onset of her current problems two years ago, she had led a normal and happy life. At that time an uncle to whom she had been extremely close in her childhood died following a sudden unexpected heart attack. Though she had not seen her uncle frequently in recent years, Anne was considerably upset by his death. Nevertheless, after two or three months her mood returned to normal. Six months after his death she was returning home from work one evening when suddenly she felt that she couldn't catch her breath. Her heart began to pound, and she broke out into a cold sweat. Things began to seem unreal, her legs felt leaden, and she became sure she would die or faint before she reached home. She asked a passerby to help her get a taxi and went to a nearby hospital emergency room. The doctors there found her physical examination, blood count and chemistries, and electrocardiogram all completely normal. . . . By the time the examination was finished Anne had recovered completely and was able to leave the hospital and return home on her own. The incident had no effect on her daily life.

Four weeks later Ms. Watson had a second similar attack while preparing dinner at home. She made an appointment to see her family doctor, but again, all examinations were normal. She decided to put the episodes out of her mind and continue with her normal activities. Within the next several weeks, however, she had four attacks and noticed that she began to worry about when the next one would occur. . . .

She then found herself constantly thinking about her anxieties as attacks continued; she began to dread leaving the house alone for fear she would be stranded, helpless and alone, by an attack. She began to avoid going to movies, parties, and dinners with friends for fear she would have an attack and be embarrassed by her need to leave. When household chores necessitated driving, she waited until it was possible to take her children or a friend along for the ride. She also began walking the twenty blocks to her office to avoid the possibility of being trapped in a subway car between stops when an attack occurred.

(Spitzer et al., 1983, pp. 7–8)

Many clinicians now believe that most cases of panic disorder are in fact accompanied by agoraphobia, although studies are not clear on this issue (Basoglu, 1992). Cases of panic disorder without the symptoms of agoraphobia are simply designated *panic disorder without agoraphobia* in DSM-IV. As we observed earlier, cases of agoraphobia without panic origins are labeled *agoraphobia without history of panic disorder.*

Biological researchers initially led the way in explaining panic disorder as a unique anxiety disorder with unique causes. In recent years cognitive researchers have built upon the insights gathered from biological research.

BIOLOGICAL EXPLANATIONS

The biological explanation for panic disorders had its beginning in the 1960s with the surprising discovery that people with these disorders were helped not by benzodiazepine drugs, the drugs effective in treating generalized anxiety disorders, but by certain *antidepressant drugs,* drugs that are usually used to alleviate the symptoms of depression (Klein, 1964; Klein & Fink, 1962). Researchers then reasoned that panic attacks and generalized anxiety may involve different biological processes (Klein & Klein, 1989; Redmond, 1985; Klein, 1964).

To understand the biology of panic disorders, researchers worked backward from their understanding of the effective antidepressant drugs, just as they had worked backward from their knowledge of benzodiazepines to understand the biochemical underpinnings of generalized anxiety disorders. They knew that the antidepressant drugs in question alter the activity of *norepinephrine,* another chemical that carries messages from neuron to neuron in the brain.

If antidepressant drugs alter norepinephrine activity in such a way as to eliminate panic attacks, researchers wondered, might it be that panic disorders are caused in the first place by abnormal norepinephrine activity? They have gathered evidence that norepinephrine activity may in fact be irregular in people who experience panic attacks (Papp, Coplan, & Gorman, 1992; Gorman et al., 1990, 1989). For example, when the *locus coeruleus*—a brain area

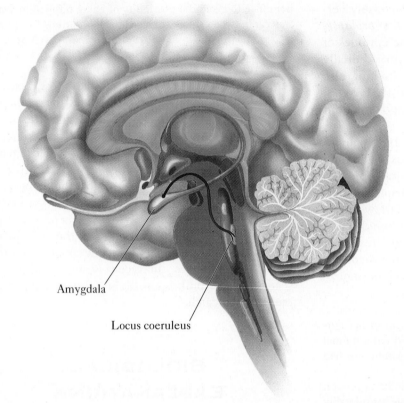

Amygdala

Locus coeruleus

FIGURE 6–4 *The locus coeruleus, a small area in the brain stem, sends its major messages to the amygdala, a structure in the brain's limbic system that is known to trigger emotional reactions. The neurons of the locus coeruleus use norepinephrine, a neurotransmitter implicated in panic disorders and in depression.*

rich in neurons that use norepinephrine (see Figure 6–4)—is electrically stimulated in monkeys, the monkeys display a paniclike reaction. Conversely, when this norepinephrine-rich brain area is surgically damaged, monkeys show virtually no reactions at all, even in the face of unmistakable danger. This finding suggests that panic reactions may be related to changes in norepinephrine activity in the locus coeruleus (Redmond, 1981, 1979, 1977).

In another line of research, scientists have induced panic attacks in human beings by administering chemicals known to alter the activity of norepinephrine (Basoglu, 1992). When low doses of the chemical compound *yohimbine* are given to subjects who suffer from panic disorders, many of them immediately experience a panic attack (Charney et al., 1987; Uhde et al., 1985). Placebo drugs administered to the same subjects have no such effects. One study successfully used yohimbine to induce panic symptoms even in people with no history of panic (Charney, Heninger, & Redmond, 1984, 1983). Such findings strongly implicate norepinephrine in the generation of panic attacks, because yohimbine alters norepinephrine functioning, particularly in the locus coeruleus, without having any effect at all on the operations of other neurotransmitters in the brain (Den Boer, Westenberg, & Verhoeven, 1990).

Still other drugs known to alter norepinephrine activity in the locus coeruleus have been tested and shown to *reduce* panic symptoms. For example, *clonidine,* a blood pressure medication, has been shown to reduce the symptoms of panic disorders, as well as overall anxiety levels, significantly more than a placebo does (Uhde et al., 1989, 1984, 1982).

Although these studies seem to point to abnormal norepinephrine activity in the locus coeruleus as a key cause of panic disorders (Papp et al., 1992; Gorman et al., 1990, 1989), the nature of this abnormal activity is still not fully understood. Moreover, there is some evidence that other neurotransmitters may also play important roles in panic disorders (Leonard, 1992; Kahn et al., 1988). Nevertheless, whatever the precise biological abnormalities may be, they appear to be different from those that cause generalized anxiety disorders.

COGNITIVE-BIOLOGICAL EXPLANATIONS

A growing number of theorists believe that biological and cognitive factors combine to produce panic disorders (Ehlers, 1993; Craske & Barlow,

1993; Clark, 1993; Rapee, 1993; Barlow, 1989, 1988; Chambless, 1988). They think that panic-prone people may be highly sensitive to certain bodily sensations and misinterpret them as indicative of an imminent catastrophe. Rather than understanding the probable cause of their sensations as "something I ate" or "a fight with the boss," the panic-prone grow increasingly worried about losing control, fear the worst, lose all perspective, and rapidly deteriorate into panic. Expecting that their "dangerous" sensations may return at any time, they set themselves up for future misinterpretations and panic attacks.

Why might some people be prone to such misinterpretations? A variety of factors have been cited, including inadequate coping skills, lack of social support, and a childhood characterized by unpredictability, lack of control, chronic illnesses in the family, and overreactions by parents to somatic symptoms in the child (Ehlers, 1993; Barlow, 1989, 1988). Whatever the precise causes, research suggests that panic-prone individuals develop a high degree of *anxiety sensitivity:* they become preoccupied with their bodily sensations, lose their ability to assess them logically and knowledgeably, and interpret them as potentially harmful. One study found that subjects who scored high on an anxiety sensitivity survey were five times more likely than other subjects to develop a panic disorder within three years after the survey (Maller & Reiss, 1992). Another study found that people with panic disorders are indeed more frightened by their bodily sensations than other people (Taylor, Koch, & McNally, 1992). And in yet another study, panic patients who responded to the self-report inventory shown in Table 6–2 reported much more difficulty "reasoning," "thinking objectively," and "focusing on the facts" in the face of bodily arousal than did

TABLE 6–2

COGNITIVE DYSFUNCTION INVENTORY, WITH SCORING KEY*

INSTRUCTIONS: Try to think back to your recent panic attacks and then determine how well each of the statements below seems to describe you at the time of the attack.

When I am having a panic attack . . .

	NOT AT ALL	SLIGHTLY	MODERATELY	COMPLETELY
1. I have difficulty reasoning.	0	1	2	3
2. I remain coolheaded.	3	2	1	0
3. My mind goes blank.	0	1	2	3
4. I can think clearly about what is happening to me.	3	2	1	0
5. I can examine my fears realistically	3	2	1	0
6. I remember others' advice and apply it.	3	2	1	0
7. All I can think of is how I feel.	0	1	2	3
8. I am able to focus on the facts.	3	2	1	0
9. I think of a variety of solutions.	3	2	1	0
10. I imagine the worst.	0	1	2	3
11. I can distract myself.	3	2	1	0
12. My mind does not function normally.	0	1	2	3
13. I am not able to think objectively about my symptoms.	0	1	2	3
14. I picture frightening things that could happen to me.	0	1	2	3
15. I am able to apply logic to my problem.	3	2	1	0
16. I can't think straight.	0	1	2	3

* The more difficulty people have thinking clearly, the higher their total score.
Source: Beck, 1988, p. 100.

patients with other kinds of anxiety disorders (Beck & Sokol-Kessler, 1986).

According to cognitive theorists, such people tend to misinterpret several kinds of sensations. Many seem to "overbreathe," or hyperventilate, in stressful situations. Apparently the abnormal breathing makes them think they are in danger or even dying, so they panic (Margraf, 1993; Rapee, 1993; Kenardy et al., 1990). In so-called *biological challenge tests,* researchers produce a hyperventilation reaction or other biological sensations in subjects by administering drugs or by instructing the subjects to breath, exercise, or think in certain ways. When such procedures are applied to people with panic disorder, they do indeed experience greater anxiety than people without this disorder, particularly when the subjects in both groups are tricked into believing that the hyperventilation or other bodily sensations are relatively dangerous or out of their control (Rapee, 1993, 1990).

Other physical sensations that trigger misinterpretations in the panic-prone include euphoric excitement, fullness in the abdomen, acute anger, and sudden tearing in the eyes (Sokol-Kessler & Beck, 1987). One patient, on learning that her artwork had been accepted for exhibit at a gallery, became extremely excited, experienced "palpitations of the heart," misinterpreted them as a sign of a heart attack, and panicked. Another patient was told of a relative's death, felt tears spring to his eyes, feared he was about to cry uncontrollably, and began to panic.

Although the cognitive-biological explanation of panic disorders has been around only a short time, it has already captured the attention of numerous panic theorists and has received considerable empirical support. As we have noted, research clearly indicates that the panic-prone may interpret bodily sensations in ways that are not at all common. Precisely how different their misinterpretations are and how they interact with biological factors are questions that need to be answered more fully in the coming years.

■ OBSESSIVE- ■
COMPULSIVE
DISORDERS

Obsessions are persistent thoughts, ideas, impulses, or images that seem to invade a person's consciousness.

Compulsions are repetitive and rigid behaviors or mental acts that a person feels compelled to perform in order to prevent or reduce anxiety or distress. Minor obsessions and compulsions are familiar to almost everyone. We may find ourselves preoccupied with thoughts about an upcoming concert, date, examination, or vacation; worry that we forgot to turn off the stove or lock the door; or be haunted for days by the same song, melody, or poem. Similarly, we may feel better when we avoid stepping on cracks, turn away from black cats, follow a strict routine every morning, or arrange our closets in a carefully prescribed manner.

Minor obsessions and compulsions can play a helpful role in life. Distracting tunes or little rituals often calm us during times of stress. A man who repeatedly clicks his pen, hums a tune, or taps his fingers during a test may be releasing tension and thus improving his performance. Many people find it comforting to repeat religious or cultural rituals, such as touching a mezuzah, sprinkling holy water, or fingering rosary beads.

According to DSM-IV, a diagnosis of obsessive-compulsive disorder is appropriate when a person's obsessions or compulsions feel excessive, unreasonable, intrusive, and inappropriate; are hard to dismiss; cause significant distress; are very time-consuming; or interfere with daily functions. Obsessive-compulsive disorders are classified as anxiety disorders because the victims' obsessions cause intense anxiety, while their compulsions are aimed at preventing or reducing anxiety. Moreover, their anxiety intensifies if they try to resist their obsessions or compulsions. Consider the obsessive compulsive pattern displayed by Georgia, whose husband complained, "If neatness was an Olympic sport, Georgia would easily have been captain of the team."

Y ou remember that old joke about getting up in the middle of the night to go to the john and coming back to the bedroom to find your wife has made the bed? It's no joke. Sometimes I think she never sleeps. I got up one night at 4 a.m. and there she was doing the laundry downstairs. Look at your ash tray! I haven't seen one that dirty in years! I'll tell you what it makes me feel like. If I forget to leave my dirty shoes outside the back door she gives me a look like I had just crapped in the middle of an operating room. I stay out of the house a lot and I'm about half-stoned when I do have to be home. She even made us get rid of the dog because she said he was always filthy. When we used to have people over for supper she would jitterbug around everybody till they couldn't digest their food. I hated to call them up and ask them over because I could always hear them hem and haw and make up excuses not to come over. Even the kids are walking down the street nervous about getting dirt on them. I'm going out of my mind but you can't talk to her. She just blows up and spends twice as much time cleaning things. We have guys in to wash the walls so often I think the house is going to fall down from being scrubbed all the time. About a week ago I had it up to here and told her I couldn't take it any more. I think the only reason she came to see you was because I told her I was going to take off and live in a pig pen just for laughs.

Georgia's obsessive concern with cleanliness forced her to take as many as three showers a day, one in the morning, one before supper, and one before going to bed, and on hot days the number of showers would rise in direct proportion to the temperature. Her husband could not understand how she got dirty overnight, but Georgia always dismissed his objections by observing that "it isn't any skin off his nose if I take good care of myself" and that "he would be the first to holler if I turned sloppy." . . .

Georgia was aware, in part, of the effect she was having on her family and friends, but she also knew that when she tried to alter her behavior she got so nervous that she felt she was losing her mind. She was frightened by the possibility that "I'm headed for the funny-farm." As she said,

I can't get to sleep unless I am sure everything in the house is in its proper place so that when I get up in the morning, the house is organized. I work like mad to set everything straight before I go to bed, but, when I get up in the morning, I can think of a thousand things that I ought to do. I know some of the things are ridiculous, but I feel better if I get them done, and I can't stand to know something needs doing and I haven't done it. I never told anybody but once I found just one dirty shirt and washed, dried, and ironed it that day. I felt stupid running a whole wash for one shirt but I couldn't bear to leave it undone. It would have bothered me all day just thinking about that one dirty shirt in the laundry basket.

(McNeil, 1967, pp. 26–28)

Georgia's obsessive-compulsive disorder consisted of both obsessions (her repeated concerns about becoming dirty or disordered) and compulsions (her repeated cleaning rituals). In fact, her obsessive worries seemed to generate and fuel her cleaning compulsions. In most but not all cases of this disorder, people display both obsessions and compulsions.

Close to 2 percent of the population in the United States suffer from obsessive-compulsive disorders in any given year (APA, 1994; Regier et al., 1993). They are equally common in males and females and usually begin in childhood, adolescence, or the early 20s

(APA, 1994; Karno & Golding, 1991; Flament, 1990). As with Georgia, the disorder typically persists for many years, the symptoms and their severity fluctuating over time (Flament et al., 1991). Many people with an obsessive-compulsive disorder are also depressed or have an eating disorder (APA, 1994; Rapoport, Swedo, & Leonard, 1992).

OBSESSIONS

Obsessions are not the same as excessive worries about real problems. They are thoughts that feel both intrusive ("ego dystonic") and foreign ("ego alien") to the people who experience them. Attempts to ignore, resist, or dismiss these thoughts may arouse even more anxiety, and before long they come back more strongly than ever. Like Georgia, people with obsessions are usually quite aware that their cognitions are excessive, inappropriate, and in fact products of their own mind, and many experience them as repugnant and torturous. Clinicians have found it useful to distinguish various kinds of obsessions, although a single person may have several kinds that overlap and complement one another.

Obsessions often take the form of *obsessive thoughts and wishes*. For example, a woman may have horrifying thoughts of killing, stabbing, injuring, mutilating, choking, or shooting her children. Consider Shirley, a 23-year-old woman:

*D*uring the preceding three months, she had been disturbed by recurring thoughts that she might harm her two-year-old son, Saul, either by stabbing or choking him. She constantly had to check to reassure herself that Saul was still alive; otherwise she became unbearably anxious.

(Goldstein & Palmer, 1975, p. 155)

Similarly, a man may keep wishing that his wife would die; a college student may repeatedly toy with the idea of crashing his car. These people do not believe that they actually want such things to happen, yet the wishes and fantasies keep forming in their minds.

Sometimes people experience *obsessive impulses* or urges to carry out certain acts—to jump in front of a truck, say; to yell out obscene words at work, in church, or at home; to kiss strangers passing by on the street. Shirley had such impulses, too:

*I*f she read in the daily paper of the murder of a child, she would become agitated, since this reinforced her fear that she too might act on her impulse. At one point, while relating her fears, Shirley turned to the interviewer and asked, with desperation, whether this meant that she was going crazy.

(Goldstein & Palmer, 1975, p. 155)

Obsessive images may flood the mind, some of them quite graphic. One person may see fleeting images of his or her child bleeding from all parts of the body. Another may keep visualizing forbidden sexual scenes.

Obsessive ideas can make life difficult. Georgia, the woman with the cleaning compulsion, had developed the idea that germs were lurking everywhere, threatening to contaminate her. People with such obsessions may believe that they will catch germs if they touch doorknobs, toilets, banisters, unwashed clothing, car door handles, and the like.

A person may keep having *obsessive doubts* about the past or the future. Thinking back over his life, a man may wonder endlessly, "Did I do the right thing? Did I make the right decisions? If only I hadn't . . ." He may also repeatedly question whether he is remembering the past correctly. Here a clinician describes a 20-year-old college junior who experienced obsessive doubts.

*H*e now spent hours each night "rehashing" the day's events, especially interactions with friends and teachers, endlessly making "right" in his mind any and all regrets. He likened the process to playing a videotape of each event over and over again in his mind, asking himself if he had behaved properly and telling himself that he had done his best, or had said the right thing every step of the way. He would do this while sitting at his desk, supposedly studying; and it was not unusual for him to look at the clock after such a period of rumination and note that, to his surprise, two or three hours had elapsed.

(Spitzer et al., 1981, pp. 20–21)

Doubts about the future can be just as troubling. Whenever a person has to make a decision, for example, he or she may be overwhelmed with repeated doubts: "What should I do? How will I know what's right? What if I do the wrong thing? How can I decide?"

Certain basic themes permeate the thoughts of most people troubled by obsessive thinking (APA, 1994). A study carried out in New Delhi, India, exam-ined the obsessions of eighty-two subjects and found that the most common theme, *dirt or contamination*, was present in 59 percent of the cases (Akhtar et al., 1975). Other common themes were *violence and aggression* (25 percent), *orderliness* (23 percent), *religion* (10 percent), and *sexuality* (5 percent). Contamination is the theme most commonly found in Western populations, too, but aggression, orderliness, and sexual obsessions are more prominent here than in the New Delhi population (Rachman & Hodgson, 1980, 1974; Stern & Cobb, 1978).

COMPULSIONS

Although compulsive behaviors are technically under voluntary control, the people compelled to do them have little sense of choice in the matter. They believe something terrible, often unspecified, will happen if they don't act on their compulsion. Yet most such people recognize at the same time that their behavior is excessive and unreasonable. Typically they try to resist their compulsions at first but give in when anxiety overcomes them. Afterward they usually feel less anxious for a short while. Aside from this release of tension, however, no pleasure is derived from the compulsive act itself (APA, 1994).

Some people develop the act into a **compulsive ritual,** performing the compulsive act in a detailed and often elaborate manner. They must go through the ritual in exactly the same way every time, according to certain carefully observed rules (see Box 6–4). Failure to complete it properly will generate further anxiety and often call for the ritual to be repeated from the beginning.

Like obsessions, compulsions take various forms and center on a variety of themes. A *cleaning compulsion* is very common. Like Georgia, people with these compulsions feel compelled to keep cleaning themselves, their clothing, their homes. The cleaning may follow ritualistic rules and be repeated dozens or hundreds of times a day. The requirements of the cleaning ritual may be so detailed, bizarre, and time-consuming that a normal life is virtually impossible:

*R*uth complained that her life was extremely restricted because she was spending most of her time engaged in some type of behavior she felt driven to carry out. In addition, each ritual activity was becoming more involved and time consuming. At the time of the interview, she was washing her hands at least three or four times an hour, showering six or seven times a day, and thoroughly cleaning her apartment at least twice a day. . . .

People who yield to compulsions, such as the compulsion to avoid stepping on cracks, typically believe that something terrible will happen if they don't act on them. (The Far Side © FARWORKS Inc. Reprinted with permission of Universal Press Syndicate. All rights reserved.)

Ruth stated that she felt frustrated and tired most of the time, due to the amount of effort involved in these rituals. She experienced a great deal of pain in her hands because the outer layer of skin was virtually rubbed off. Nonetheless, she felt compelled to thoroughly wash her hands and repeatedly clean her apartment each time she felt that she or her environment was contaminated in some way.

(Leon, 1977, pp. 127–132)

Checking compulsions cause people to check the same things over and over. Some people believe their safety or that of others depends on the frequent checking of appliances and other belongings (door locks, gas taps, ashtrays, important papers), although no such connection may exist. Another kind of checking compulsion consists of repeated checking of the accuracy of a story or the details of an event. Again, such behavior may be repeated dozens or even hundreds of times each day, far beyond any reasonable function.

A third common compulsion is displayed by people who repeatedly seek *symmetry, order,* or *balance* in their actions and surroundings. They must place certain items (such as clothing, books, or foods) in perfect order in accordance with strict rules. If they make the slightest error, they may have to start over again and build to a perfect placement. Again, this is more than simple orderliness.

Ted is a 13-year-old referred to a Midwestern inpatient psychiatric research ward because of "senseless rituals and attention to minutiae." He can spend 3 hours "centering the toilet paper roll on its holder or rearranging his bed and other objects in his room. When placing objects down, such as books or shoelaces after tying them, he picks them up and replaces them several times until they seem "straight." Although usually placid, he becomes abusive with family members who try to enter his room for fear they will move or break his objects. When he is at school, he worries that people may disturb his room. He sometimes has to be forced to interrupt his routine to attend meals. Last year he hid pieces of his clothing around the house because they wouldn't lie straight in his drawers. Moreover, he often repeats to himself, "This is perfect; you are perfect."

(Spitzer et al., 1983, p. 15)

Touching, verbal, counting, and eating compulsions are also common. *Touching compulsions* cause people to feel they must touch or avoid touching certain items whenever they see them. *Verbal rituals* compel them to repeat expressions, phrases, or chants time and again. Some people conduct these verbal rituals internally; others feel the need to express them aloud. Individuals with *counting compulsions* feel driven to count the things they see around them in the course of their daily activities.

RELATIONSHIP BETWEEN OBSESSIONS AND COMPULSIONS

Although some people with an obsessive-compulsive disorder experience obsessions only or compulsions

BOX 6-4

SAMUEL JOHNSON AND HOWARD HUGHES: FAMOUS CASE STUDIES IN OBSESSIVE-COMPULSIVE BEHAVIOR

Samuel Johnson, famous during his lifetime for his *Dictionary of the English Language* and his celebrated series of *Rambler* essays, was born to a struggling bookseller in Lichfield, England, in 1709. Johnson's courageous personality, prolific works, and philosophical commentaries on English life continue to fascinate biographers and scholars today. To clinicians, however, it is his reputation for having been a quirky, compulsive, and largely melancholic individual that makes him most interesting. His letters and the detailed descriptions of his friend and famed biographer, James Boswell, show him to have been prone to depression, obsessive-compulsive behavior, and hypochondriasis. As Johnson wrote on March 30, 1777, "When I survey my past life I discover nothing but a barren waste of time with some disorders of the body, and disturbances of the mind, very near to madness" (Boswell, 1953).

Contemporaries described him as a "noisy beehive of crackpot mannerisms" (Davis, 1989; Malamud, 1979), muttering to himself, keeping count as he walked, touching posts anxiously, and ritually gesticulating with his hands and feet before crossing a threshold (Davis, 1989).

He had another particularity, of which none of his friends ever ventured to ask an explanation. It appeared to me some superstitious habit, which he had contracted early, and from which he had never called upon his reason to disentangle him. This was his anxious care to go out or in at a door or passage by a certain number of steps from a certain point, or at least so as that either his right or his left foot (I am not certain which) should constantly make the first actual movement when he came close to the door or passage. . . . It is requisite to mention, that while talking or even musing at he sat in his chair, he commonly held his head to one side towards his right shoulder, and shook it in a tremendous manner, moving his body backwards and forwards, and rubbing his left knee in the same direction, with the palm of his hand. In the intervals of articulating he made various sounds with his mouth, sometimes as if ruminating, or what is called chewing the cud, sometimes giving a half whistle, sometimes making his tongue play backwards from the roof of his mouth, as if clucking like a hen, and sometimes protruding it against his upper gums in front as if pronouncing quickly under his breath, *too, too, too:* all this accompanied sometimes with a thoughtful look, but more frequently with a smile.
(Boswell, 1933, pp. 301–302)

Such descriptions are evidence of an obsessive-compulsive disorder. It is interesting, however, that despite his notable oddities, Johnson was able to make an enormous success of his professional life. In the words of William Blake, "though he looked like a mad hatter, [he] inspired men to reason and courage. He had learned from life" (Davis, 1989; Malamud, 1979).

Howard Hughes was born on December 24, 1905, and died on April 5, 1976, aboard a private jet bound for a hospital in Houston, Texas. Hughes's career is legendary. After inheriting

---

only, most of them experience both (Jenike, 1992). In fact, as we noted earlier, their compulsive acts are often a response to their obsessive thoughts.

One investigation found that in 61 percent of the cases reviewed, a subject's compulsions seemed to represent a *yielding* to obsessive doubts, ideas, or urges (Akhtar et al., 1975). Remember how Shirley, the woman who obsessed about harming her young son, would yield to this obsession by repeatedly checking to see whether he was safe. Similarly, a man who keeps doubting that his house is secure may yield to that obsessive doubt by repeatedly checking locks and gas jets. Or a man who obsessively fears contamination may yield to that fear by performing cleaning rituals (see Box 6–4). In 6 percent of the cases reviewed, the compulsions seemed to serve to *control* obsessions. A man who is beset by obsessive sexual images and urges, say, may try to distract him-a company that made drill bits used in drilling for oil, he went on to become a successful movie producer and record-setting flyer, to build the world's largest flying boat, and to found an international airline, TWA.

Hughes's personal habits are also legendary. He vanished from view in 1951 and lived his last twenty-five years in isolation, dominated by obsessive fears of contamination and the compulsion to carry out bizarre cleaning rituals. James Phelan, an investigative reporter, wrote a biography of Hughes, gathering his information from Hughes's closest aides. As the following excerpts show, Howard Hughes, one of the richest and most powerful men in the world, was at the same time a sad figure imprisoned by his obsessive-compulsive disorder:

When Howard Hughes was flying around the world setting records, starting an international airline, and running several businesses at once, no one suspected that he would one day become a near-helpless prisoner of phobias and an obsessive-compulsive disorder.

Stewart [a barber] was admitted by a man who introduced himself as John Holmes. Holmes gave Stewart detailed instructions. He was to scrub up, doctor-style, in the bathroom before beginning the hair cutting. Then he was to put on a pair of rubber surgical gloves. He was to have no foreign objects, such as pencils or pens, on his person. And, finally, he was not to speak to the man whose hair he would cut. . . .

Finally Holmes said, "Okay, Mr. Hughes will see you now," and took

him into the bedroom. What he found stunned him.

"I found a skinny, bare-assed naked man sitting on an unmade three-quarter bed. His hair hung about a foot down his back. His beard was straggly and down to his chest. I tried not to act surprised, as if I was used to meeting naked billionaires sitting on unmade beds.

"I started to put my case with the barber tools on a chair. Hughes shouted, 'No, no! Not on the chair!'"

Hughes turned to Holmes and

said, "Get some insulation for our friend to put his equipment on." Holmes got a roll of paper towels and laid out a layer on a nearby sideboard. The sideboard was already covered with a sheet, and so was the other furniture in the bedroom. . . .

Barbering Hughes took three hours. There was a series of special procedures, which Hughes outlined in detail. Stewart was to use one set of combs and scissors to cut his beard, but a different set to cut his hair. Before Stewart began, Hughes ordered a series of wide-mouthed jars filled with isopropyl alcohol. When Stewart used a comb he was to dip it into the alcohol before using it again, to "sterilize" it. After using a comb a few times, he was to discard it and proceed with a new comb.

While Stewart was trimming his hair on either side of his head, Hughes carefully folded his ears down tight "so none of that hair will get in me."

Stewart trimmed his beard to a short, neat Vandyke and gave his hair a tapered cut well above the collar line.

When he finished, Hughes thanked him and Holmes escorted him out. A few days later an emissary came down to Huntington Park and gave Stewart an envelope. In it was $1000. . . .

(Phelan, 1976, pp. 27–28, 44–46, 82)

self by repetitive verbal rituals. Here a teenager describes how she tried to control her obsessive fears of contamination by performing counting and verbal rituals:

Patient: If I heard the word, like, something that had to do with germs or disease, it would be considered something bad, and so I had things that would go through

my mind that were sort of like "cross that out and it'll make it okay" to hear that word.

Interviewer: What sort of things?

Patient: Like numbers or words that seemed to be sort of like a protector.

Interviewer: What numbers and what words were they?

Patient: It started out to be the number 3 and multiples of

3 and then words like "soap and water," something like that; and then the multiples of 3 got really high, and they'd end up to be 124 or something like that. It got real bad then. . . .

(Spitzer et al., 1981, p. 137)

Many people with obsessive-compulsive disorders worry that they will act out their obsessions. A man with obsessive images of mutilated loved ones may worry that he is but a step away from committing murder; or a woman with obsessive urges to yell out in church may worry that she will one day give in to them and embarrass herself. Most of these concerns are unfounded. Although many obsessions lead to compulsive acts—particularly to cleaning and checking compulsions—they do not usually lead to acts of violence, immorality, or the like.

EXPLANATIONS OF OBSESSIVE-COMPULSIVE DISORDERS

Obsessive-compulsive disorders were once among the least understood of the mental disorders. In recent years, however, researchers, particularly in the biological realm, have begun to learn more about them. The most influential explanations come from the psychodynamic, cognitive-behavioral, and biological models.

THE PSYCHODYNAMIC VIEW: BATTLE OF THE ID AND EGO Psychodynamic theorists believe that obsessive-compulsive disorders, like other anxiety disorders, develop when children come to fear their own id impulses and use ego defense mechanisms to lessen the resulting anxiety. The distinguishing feature of obsessive-compulsive disorders is that the battle between anxiety-provoking id impulses and anxiety-reducing defense mechanisms is played out very explicitly rather than at an unconscious level. The id impulses usually take the form of obsessive thoughts, and the ego defenses appear as counterthoughts or compulsive actions. This process is at work when a woman keeps having images of family members horribly injured and counters those thoughts with repeated safety checks throughout the house, or when a man repeatedly has forbidden sexual thoughts and distances himself from them by constantly washing or meticulously avoiding sexual content in conversations.

Three ego defense mechanisms are particularly common in obsessive-compulsive disorders: isolation, undoing, and reaction formation. People who resort to *isolation* isolate and disown undesirable and unwanted thoughts, and experience them as foreign intrusions. People who engage in *undoing* perform acts that implicitly cancel out their undesirable impulses. People who wash their hands repeatedly or conduct elaborate symmetry rituals may be symbolically undoing their unacceptable id impulses. People who develop a *reaction formation* take on lifestyles that directly oppose their unacceptable impulses. One person may live a life of compulsive kindness and total devotion to others to counteract unacceptably aggressive impulses. Another may lead a life of total celibacy to counteract obsessive sexual impulses.

Sigmund Freud believed that during the anal stage of development (about 2 years of age) some children experience intense rage and shame that fuel the id-ego battle and set the stage for obsessive-compulsive functioning. He theorized that during this period in their lives, children are deriving their psychosexual pleasure from their bowel movements while at the same time their parents are trying to toilet train them and teach them to delay their anal gratification. If parents are premature or too harsh in their toilet training, the children may experience rage and develop *aggressive id impulses,* antisocial impulses that repeatedly seek expression. They may soil their clothes all the more and become generally destructive, messy, or stubborn.

If parents then handle this aggressiveness by further pressuring and embarrassing the child, the child may also feel shameful, guilty, and dirty. The aggressive impulses will now be countered by the child's strong desire to control them; the child who wants to soil will also have a competing desire to retain. This intense conflict between the id and ego may continue throughout life and eventually blossom into an obsessive-compulsive disorder. In accord with this explanation, there is evidence that many people who develop obsessive-compulsive disorders have rigid and demanding parents; however, most of these studies have been poorly designed (Fitz, 1990). Moreover, this disorder also occurs in people whose family backgrounds are very different from the kind Freud anticipated.

Not all psychodynamic theorists agree with Freud's explanation of obsessive-compulsive disorders. Some object relations theorists, for example, propose that disturbed relationships early in life leave some people with a split view of the world. Believing that thoughts, emotions, actions, and persons are either *all* good or *all* bad, they must resort to ego alien obsessions in order to tolerate the negative aspects of their thinking or feelings (Oppenheim & Rosenberger, 1991). In another departure from Freud, a number of ego psychologists believe that the aggressive impulses experienced by people with this disorder reflect an unfulfilled need for self-expression or efforts to overcome feelings of vulnerability or insecurity rather than poor toilet-training experiences (Salzman, 1968; Erikson, 1963; Sullivan, 1953; Horney, 1937). Even these theorists, however, agree with Freud that people with this disorder have intense, aggressive impulses, along with a competing need to control those impulses.

THE COGNITIVE-BEHAVIORAL VIEW A relatively new but promising explanation of obsessive-compulsive disorders that uses both cognitive and behavioral principles begins with the premise that everyone has repetitive, unwanted, unpleasant, and intrusive thoughts, such as thoughts of harming others, engaging in unacceptable sexual acts, or being contaminated by germs (Rachman, 1993; Salkovskis, 1989, 1985; Salkovskis & Westbrook, 1989; Clark, 1989; Rachman & Hodgson, 1980). Whereas most people regard normal and universal thoughts of this kind as meaningless and dismiss or ignore them with ease, those who develop an obsessive-compulsive disorder typically believe themselves responsible and reprehensible for having such terrible thoughts, and worry that the thoughts will lead to harmful acts or consequences. These people find the intrusive thoughts so noxious, discomforting, and stressful that they try to eliminate or avoid them by *neutralizing*—thinking or behaving in ways calculated to put matters right internally, to make amends for the unacceptable thoughts. They may use such neutralizing techniques as requesting special reassurance from others, deliberately thinking "good" thoughts or visualizing positive images, cleaning their hands, or checking for possible sources of danger.

When such a neutralizing strategy brings a temporary reduction in discomfort, it becomes reinforced; thus it is likely to be employed again in the future. Eventually the neutralizing thought or act is employed so often that it becomes, by definition, an obsession or compulsion. At the same time, the fact that the neutralizing strategy is effective confirms to the individual that the initial intrusive thought was indeed reprehensible or dangerous and in need of elimination. The intrusive thought now feels even more distressing and worrisome; as a result it begins to occur so frequently that it too becomes an obsession.

One of the key questions raised by this cognitive-behavioral explanation is why some people (those who go on to develop an obsessive-compulsive disorder) find universal and normal thoughts so disturbing

to begin with. Researchers have uncovered several factors:

1. *Depressed mood.* People prone to obsessive-compulsive disorders tend to be more depressed than other people. Research has shown that depressed mood increases the number and intensity of unwanted intrusive thoughts, thus increasing one's overall discomfort with the thoughts (Clark & Purdon, 1993; Conway et al., 1991; Rachman & Hodgson, 1980).

2. *Strict code of acceptability.* Many of the people who develop an obsessive-compulsive disorder have exceptionally high standards of conduct and morality. Their unwanted thoughts, especially aggressive or sexual ones, are thus more unacceptable to them than to others. Moreover, such people tend to believe that "bad" thoughts are the same as bad acts—thinking about hurting a child is the same as doing so (Rachman, 1993; Rachman & Hodgson, 1980).

3. *Dysfunctional beliefs about responsibility and harm.* People who develop an obsessive-compulsive disorder typically believe that their intrusive negative thoughts—perfectly normal thoughts—are capable of harming themselves or others. Since they feel responsible for the danger they imagine, they also feel responsible for eliminating it (Salkovskis 1989, 1985). Several studies confirm that persons who have broad beliefs of excessive responsibility do indeed feel greater discomfort over intrusive thoughts than others do (Purdon, 1992; Freeston et al., 1992).

4. *Dysfunctional beliefs about the control of thoughts.* Research also suggests that people who develop an obsessive-compulsive disorder have inaccurate and maladaptive ideas about how human thinking works (Freeston et al., 1992). Rather than recognize intrusive thoughts as normal and rather meaningless, they think that they can and should *control* all unpleasant thoughts that pop into their minds and fear that a lack of perfect control over such thoughts will lead to a loss of control over their behavior, or to "going crazy" (Clark & Purdon, 1993; Rachman, 1993; Clark, 1989).

Research has also supported other aspects of this cognitive-behavioral theory. Some investigators have obtained evidence that frequent intrusive thoughts are, as the theory suggests, a normal aspect of human thinking (Niler & Beck, 1989; Clark & deSilva, 1985). In one study, 84 percent of normal subjects reported unwanted and repetitive intrusive thoughts

(Rachman & deSilva, 1978). Studies have also confirmed that people who develop obsessive-compulsive disorders resort, at least sometimes, to more elaborate neutralizing strategies than other people do in efforts to suppress their unwanted thoughts (Freeston et al., 1992), and that such neutralizing strategies do temporarily reduce the discomfort they feel (Roper, Rachman, & Hodgson, 1973; Hodgson & Rachman, 1972). Finally, research supports the theory's assertion that people with this disorder eventually come to experience a greater number of intrusive negative thoughts than other people (Clark, 1992; Purdon, 1992; Freeston et al., 1992), perhaps as an indirect result of their neutralizing efforts. Indeed, one study found that the higher patients scored on an obsessive-compulsive scale, the greater the frequency of their intrusive thoughts (Clark, 1992).

Though research has clearly supported important pieces of this cognitive-behavioral explanation, several aspects of the theory remain unclear. Precisely how important, for example, are neutralizing thoughts and actions in the development of the disorder? While some theorists believe that they are the key (Salkovskis, 1989, 1985), others suggest that, in many cases at least, they are less important than the relative inability to dismiss intrusive thoughts in the first place or dysfunctional notions about the need to control such thoughts (Clark & Purdon, 1993).

Another question that remains to be answered is whether other factors might play a complementary role in the development of obsessive-compulsive disorder. Is it possible, for example, that in addition to dysfunctional beliefs and dysphoric mood, people who develop this disorder are driven by biological factors to experience more intrusive thoughts, become more upset by them, and attempt to neutralize them? Some recent work has suggested that biological factors may indeed be involved in the onset and maintenance of this disorder.

THE BIOLOGICAL VIEW Partly because obsessive-compulsive disorders have been so difficult to explain, researchers have tried to identify hidden biological factors that may contribute to them (Jenike, 1992; Turner, Beidel, & Nathan, 1985). Two intersecting lines of biological research now look very promising. One points to abnormally low activity of the neurotransmitter serotonin in obsessive-compulsive people, the other to abnormal functioning in key regions of their brains.

Serotonin, like GABA and norepinephrine, is a brain chemical that carries messages from neuron to neuron. It first became implicated in obsessive-compulsive disorders when clinical researchers dis-

covered unexpectedly that obsessive and compulsive symptoms were reduced by the antidepressant drug *clomipramine* (Rapoport, 1991, 1989; Swedo et al., 1989; Ananth, 1983). Since clomipramine seems to increase serotonin activity while reducing obsessive and compulsive symptoms, some researchers have concluded that the disorder is associated with low serotonin activity (Altemus et al., 1993; Flament et al., 1985).

Another line of research links obsessive-compulsive disorders to abnormal functioning in the *orbital region* of the frontal cortex (a brain area just above each eye) and the *caudate nuclei* (parts of the basal ganglia, which lie under the cerebral cortex). These parts of the brain set up a circuit that controls the conversion of sensory input into cognitions and actions (see Figure 6–5). The circuit begins in the orbital region, where impulses involving bodily excretion, sexuality,

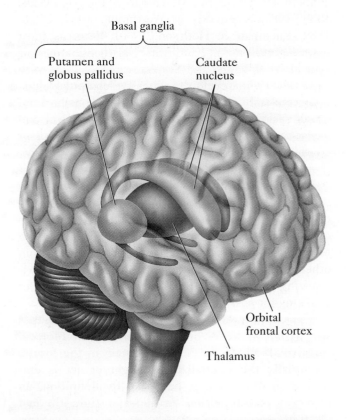

FIGURE 6–5 *A three-dimensional view of the human brain (with parts shown as they would look if the overlying cerebral cortex were transparent) clarifies the locations of the orbital frontal cortex and the basal ganglia—areas implicated in obsessive-compulsive disorder. Among the basal ganglia's structures are the caudate nuclei, which filter powerful impulses that arise in the orbital frontal cortex so that only the most powerful ones reach the thalamus. Perhaps the orbital frontal cortex or the caudate nuclei or both are so active in people with obsessive-compulsive disorders that numerous impulses reach the thalamus, generating obsessive thoughts or compulsive actions. (Adapted from Rapoport, 1989, p. 85.)*

violence, and other primitive activities normally arise. Nerve fibers then carry these impulses down into the caudate nuclei for possible translation into action. These nuclei serve as a filter that allows only the most powerful impulses to reach the *thalamus*, the next stop on the circuit. If the thalamus receives the impulses, the person is driven to think further about them. Many biological theorists now believe that either the orbital region or the caudate nuclei of some people function too actively, leading to a constant breakthrough of troublesome thoughts and actions (Baxter et al., 1992; Swedo et al., 1992; Rapoport, 1991). Several clues have pointed in this direction.

First, it has been observed for years that obsessive-compulsive symptoms sometimes arise or subside after the orbital region or the caudate nuclei are damaged by accident or illness (Paradis et al., 1992; McKeon et al., 1984). In one well-publicized case, an obsessive-compulsive patient tried to commit suicide by shooting himself in the head. Although he survived the shot, he did considerable damage to the brain areas in question. Perhaps as a result of the injury, his obsessive and compulsive symptoms decreased dramatically.

Such cases have been taken more seriously in recent years in light of research with *positron emission tomography (PET scans)*. As we saw in Chapter 4, PET scans show the brain in action by tracking glucose (the brain's source of energy) and other natural compounds as they are metabolized by the brain. PET scan studies have revealed that obsessive-compulsive patients metabolize glucose in the caudate nuclei and the orbital region more rapidly than control subjects do (Baxter et al., 1990). Moreover, obsessive-compulsive patients whose symptoms respond well to treatment subsequently show a lower rate of glucose metabolism in these brain areas than do patients who are unaffected by treatment (Baxter et al., 1992; Swedo et al., 1992).

These two sets of findings, one tying obsessive-compulsive disorder to low serotonin activity and the other to some kind of heightened functioning in the orbital region and the caudate nuclei, may themselves be linked. It turns out that the neurotransmitter serotonin plays a very active role in the operation of these brain areas, so low serotonin activity might well be expected to disrupt their proper functioning. While many researchers now believe that such abnormalities set up some kind of biological predisposition for the development of this disorder (Rapoport, 1991, 1989; Turner et al., 1985), it is important to recognize that the precise roles and interactions of these factors are not yet fully understood.

■ ACUTE STRESS ■ DISORDERS AND POSTTRAUMATIC STRESS DISORDERS

*M*ark remembers his first "firefight" and encountering the VC [Viet Cong] for the first time. He lost all bladder and bowel control—in a matter of a few minutes. In his own words, "I was scared and literally shitless; I pissed all over myself, and shit all over myself too. Man, all hell broke loose. I tell you, I was so scared, I thought I would never make it out alive. I was convinced of that. Charlie had us pinned down and [was] hitting the shit out of us for hours. We had to call in the napalm and the bombing." During the first fight, Mark, an infantryman, experienced gruesome sights and strange sounds in battle. He witnessed headless bodies. "One guy said to me, 'Hey, Mark, new greenhorn boy, you saw that head go flying off that gook's shoulder. Isn't that something?'" Within 2 weeks Mark saw the head of a running comrade blown off his shoulders, the headless body moving for a few feet before falling to the ground. Mark, nauseous and vomiting for a long time, couldn't see himself surviving much longer: "I couldn't get that sight out of my head; it just kept on coming back to me in my dreams, nightmares. Like clockwork, I'd see R's head flying, and his headless body falling to the ground. I knew the guy. He was very good to me when I first got to the unit. Nobody else seemed to give a damn about me; he broke me in. It's like I would see his head and body, you know, man, wow!" Mark often found himself crying during his first weeks of combat. "I wanted to go home. I was so lonely, helpless, and really scared. But I knew I could not go home until my year was up."

(Brende & Parson, 1985, pp. 23–24)

Mark's reaction to these combat experiences is normal and understandable. During or immediately after an unusual and traumatic situation, many people become highly anxious and depressed. For some, however, anxiety and depression persist well after the situation is over. These people may be suffering from *acute stress disorder* or *posttraumatic stress disorder,* distinct patterns of symptoms that arise in reaction to a psychologically traumatic event (APA, 1994). The event usually involves actual or threatened serious injury or threatened death to oneself or to a family member or friend. Unlike other anxiety disorders, which typically are triggered by objects or situations that most people would not find threatening, situations that cause acute stress disorders or posttraumatic stress disorders—combat, rape, an earthquake, an airplane crash—would be traumatic for anyone.

According to DSM-IV, if the anxiety-linked symptoms begin within four weeks of the traumatic event and last from 2 to 28 days, the pattern is diagnosed as *acute stress disorder* (APA, 1994). If the symptoms continue longer than 28 days, a diagnosis of *posttraumatic stress disorder* is appropriate. The symptoms of a posttraumatic stress disorder may begin either shortly after the traumatic event or months or years afterward. Aside from these differences in onset and duration, the two anxiety disorders are almost identical, and include the following symptoms:

1. *Reexperiencing the traumatic event* The person may have recurring recollections, dreams, or nightmares about the event. A few relive the event so vividly in their minds that they think they are back in the traumatic situation.
2. *Avoidance* The person will usually avoid activities or situations that are reminiscent of the traumatic event, and will try to avoid thoughts, feelings, or conversations associated with it.
3. *Reduced responsiveness* Reduced responsiveness to the external world, often called "psychic numbing" or "emotional anesthesia," may begin during or soon after the traumatic event. The person feels detached or estranged from other people or loses interest in activities enjoyed previously. The ability to experience such intimate emotions as tenderness and sexuality is often impaired. Reduced responsiveness is particularly prominent in acute stress disorders, where it may further include signs of *dissociation*, or separation: dazedness, loss of memory, derealization (feeling that the environment is unreal or strange), or depersonalization (feeling that ones thoughts or body are unreal or foreign).
4. *Increased arousal, anxiety, and guilt* People with these disorders may experience hyperalertness, an exaggerated startle response, sleep disturbances, or other signs of increased arousal, and may also have trouble concentrating or remembering things. They may feel extreme guilt because they survived the traumatic event while others did not. Some also feel guilty about what they may have had to do to survive.

We can see these symptoms in the recollections of Vietnam combat veterans years after they returned home:

lan: I can't get the memories out of my mind! The images come flooding back in vivid detail, triggered by the most inconsequential things, like a door slamming or the smell of stir-fried pork. Last night I went to bed, was having a good sleep for a change. Then in the early morning a storm-front passed through and there was a bolt of crackling thunder. I awoke instantly, frozen in fear. I am right back in Vietnam, in the middle of the monsoon season at my guard post. I am sure I'll get hit in the next volley and convinced I will die. My hands are freezing, yet sweat pours from my entire body. I feel each hair on the back of my neck standing on end. I can't catch my breath and my heart is pounding. I smell a damp sulfur smell.

(Davis, 1992)

on: It was like Dr. Jekyll and Mr. Hyde. I'd go on self-destruct cycles you wouldn't believe, especially when I started drinking. My poor wife, she went through hell. Vietnam started coming into my head. And she couldn't understand. She couldn't deal with it. . . . You get tired of being shot at again, over and over and over again. How many times do I gotta get blown up. I'm tired of seeing bullets hit me. I'm tired of seeing my friends get shot at. I'm tired. . . . I grew up and died right there [at the scene of battle]. And the last ten years have just been a space. I've just occupied space, just space. I've accomplished nothing. Nothing but occupied space.

("The War Within," 1985)

ucas: [My wife] said that I wasn't the loving guy she used to know and love, that something horrible must have happened to me over there to change me so completely. . . . She said that the look in my eyes was the look of a deeply terrorized person, with a long-distance stare, looking off into the beyond—not into the present with her at this time. She also mentioned that my frightened look and pallid complexion, my uptight way of sitting, talking, walking, you name it, my aloofness, and all that, made her too uncomfortable for us to continue our relationship. . . . Finally, as time went on, I realized that so many people couldn't be wrong about me. The change in me began to seem deep to me—deeper than I would ever have imagined to be the case.

(Brende & Parson, 1985, pp. 46–47)

An acute or posttraumatic stress disorder can occur at any age, even in childhood, and can cause mild to severe impairment in one's personal, family, social, or occupational functioning (Jordan et al., 1992). Clinical surveys show that approximately 0.5 percent of the total population experience one of these disorders in any given year; at least 1.3 percent will suffer from one of them within their lifetime (Davidson et al., 1991). Still another 6 to 15 percent experience some of the symptoms of these disorders.

STRESS DISORDERS CAUSED BY COMBAT

For years clinicians have recognized that many soldiers develop symptoms of severe anxiety and depression *during* combat (Oei, Lim, & Hennessy, 1990). The pattern of symptoms was called "nostalgia" during the American Civil War and was considered to be the result of extended absence from home (Bourne, 1970). The syndrome was called "shell shock" during World War I because it was thought to result from minute brain hemorrhages or concussions caused by explosions during battle. During World War II and the Korean War, it was referred to as "combat fatigue" (Figley, 1978). Not until after the Vietnam War, however, did clinicians come to recognize that a great many soldiers, perhaps as many as 29 percent, also experience serious psychological symptoms *after* combat. This percentage is even higher, as high as 80 percent, for soldiers who were prisoners of war (Sutker, Allain, & Winstead, 1993).

In the first years after the Vietnam War, the psychological problems of combat veterans were generally overlooked, perhaps in part because of the nation's desire to put reminders of this unpopular war behind it. By the late 1970s, however, it had become apparent to staff members in veterans' hospitals throughout the United States that many Vietnam combat veterans were still experiencing war-related psychological problems that had been delayed in onset or previ-

The symptoms of posttraumatic stress disorder appear after combat (or after another traumatic event), often when the individual is safely back home. The emotion and pain displayed by tens of thousands of veterans at the unveiling of the Vietnam War Memorial in Washington, D.C., more than a decade after the war ended, served as a vivid reminder that the war and its psychological effects were far from over for many people.

ously ignored (Williams, 1983). Some signs of these disturbances were that one-quarter of the 1.5 million combat soldiers who returned from Vietnam had been arrested within two years of returning, and approximately 200,000 had become dependent on drugs. The divorce rate among Vietnam veterans was nearly double that of the general population, and their suicide rate was nearly 25 percent higher. We now know that as many as 31 percent of all men and 26 percent of all women who served in Vietnam subsequently suffered an acute or posttraumatic stress disorder, while another 23 percent of the men and 21 percent of the women suffered from at least some of the symptoms of these disorders (Weiss et al., 1992). In fact, 11 percent of the male and 8 percent of the female veterans of this war still experience significant posttraumatic stress symptoms.

Some of the more common recurring symptoms are intrusive and repeated recollections of traumatic Vietnam War experiences in the form of flashbacks, night terrors, nightmares, and persistent images and thoughts (Williams, 1983; Goodwin, 1980). Such recollections may be triggered by simple events that remind the veterans of conditions in Vietnam—a sudden downpour of summer rain or a rise in temperature to 80 degrees or more (DeFazio, Rustin, & Diamond, 1975). They may also be triggered by

Soldiers often react to combat with severe anxiety or depression or both, reactions shown by these soldiers in Vietnam. These immediate responses to battle have at various times been called "shell shock," "combat fatigue," or most recently "acute stress disorder."

combat scenes in news reports, novels, movies, or television shows. Veterans of more recent wars report similar symptoms. In a study of a group of Persian Gulf War combat veterans, over a third reported 6 months later that they were experiencing nightmares and drinking more than before (Labbate & Snow, 1992).

STRESS DISORDERS CAUSED BY OTHER TRAUMAS

Acute and posttraumatic stress disorders may also follow natural and accidental disasters such as earthquakes, floods, tornados, fires, airplane crashes, and serious car accidents. One study found that 10 percent of victims of serious traffic accidents qualified for a diagnosis of posttraumatic stress disorder within 6 months of their accident (Brom, Kleber, & Hofman, 1993).

Eighteen months after the 1972 flood in Buffalo Creek, West Virginia, which killed and injured hundreds of people and destroyed thousands of homes, the survivors were more anxious and depressed and experienced more nightmares and other sleep disturbances than matched control subjects who lived elsewhere (Green et al., 1990; Gleser et al., 1981). The ones who had come closest to dying or who had lost family members showed the most psychological impairment.

Similar stress reactions have been found among the survivors of Hurricane Andrew, the 1992 storm that ravaged Florida and other parts of the southeastern United States (Gelman & Katel, 1993; Treaster, 1992). What some people have called "the storm of the century" destroyed hundreds of thousands of homes, automobiles, and other personal belongings, wreaked havoc on the natural environment, and left millions impoverished. By a month after the storm the number of calls received by the Domestic Violence Hotline in Miami and the number of spouses applying for police protection had doubled (Treaster, 1992). Moreover, hundreds of mental health professionals who went door to door shortly after the storm seeking to help victims throughout Florida reported seeing an extraordinary number of acute and posttraumatic stress symptoms, including edginess, sleep difficulties, spontaneous crying, flashbacks, depression, disorientation, and even short-term memory loss. By six months after the storm it was clear that many elementary school–age children were also victims of posttraumatic stress disorders, their

symptoms ranging from disruptive behavior in school to failing grades and problems with sleep (Gelman & Katel, 1993). One child said months afterward, "When I go to sleep, I think the storm is going to come, so I can't go to sleep." Another recalled, "I was sleeping, and I thought it was coming again" (Gelman & Katel, 1993, p. 65).

Acute and posttraumatic stress disorders may also follow incidents of victimization. Lingering stress symptoms have been observed in survivors of Nazi concentration camps years after their liberation (Kuch & Cox, 1992; Eitinger, 1973, 1969, 1964). One study of 149 concentration camp survivors found that twenty years later 97 percent still experienced anxiety symptoms and feared that family members might be in danger when they were out of their sight; 71 percent had nightmares recalling their captivity and dreamed that their children, born afterward, were now imprisoned with them; 80 percent felt guilty that they had survived while other family members and friends had not; and 92 percent blamed themselves for not saving their relatives and friends (Krystal, 1968). A recent retrospective study of 124 Holocaust survivors found that 46 percent eventually fully met the diagnostic criteria for posttraumatic stress disorder (Kuch & Cox, 1992).

A common form of victimization in our society is sexual assault and rape. A Senate Judiciary Committee report (1991) stated that more than 100,000 rapes are reported to police annually. Indeed, rape reports rose four times faster than the overall crime rate during the 1980s, and it is believed that these reports represent only a small portion of the actual number of such incidents (Koss, 1993). Some recent national surveys, which ask more detailed and explicit questions than earlier ones and help subjects answer more

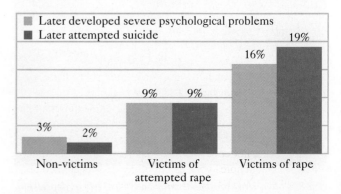

FIGURE 6–6 *Many rape victims develop symptoms of posttraumatic stress disorder. In one study, 19 percent of those surveyed by telephone revealed that they attempted suicide at some point after being raped, compared to 2 percent of nonvictims. (Adapted from Kilpatrick et al., 1985.)*

honestly, suggest that as many as 683,000 women 18 years old and over may be raped each year (Youngstrom, 1992). Even years after their attack, both female and male rape victims have been found to experience severe stress symptoms—fearfulness and anxiety, suspiciousness, depression, guilt, self-blame, high startle responses, reliving the assault, nightmares, and other sleep disturbances (Steketee & Foa, 1987; Goyer & Eddleman, 1984; see Figure 6–6). According to some recent surveys, 31 percent of female rape victims may suffer from posttraumatic stress disorders (Youngstrom, 1992). Such symptoms are apparent in the following case description:

*M*ary Billings is a 33-year-old divorced nurse, referred to the Victim Clinic at Bedford Psychiatric Hospital for counseling by her supervisory head nurse. Mary had been raped two months ago. The assailant gained entry to her apartment while she was sleeping, and she awoke to find him on top of her. He was armed with a knife and threatened to kill her and her child (who was asleep in the next room) if she did not submit to his demands. He forced her to undress and repeatedly raped her vaginally over a period of 1 hour. He then admonished her that if she told anyone or reported the incident to the police he would return and assault her child.

After he left, she called her boyfriend, who came to her apartment right away. He helped her contact the Sex Crimes Unit of the Police Department, which is currently investigating the case. He then took her to a local hospital for a physical examination and collection of evidence for the police (traces of sperm, pubic hair samples, fingernail scrapings). She was given antibiotics as prophylaxis against venereal disease. Mary then returned home with a girlfriend who spent the remainder of the night with her.

Over the next few weeks Mary continued to be afraid of being alone and had her girlfriend move in with her. She became preoccupied with thoughts of what had happened to her and the possibility that it could happen again. Mary was frightened that the rapist might return to her apartment and therefore had additional locks installed on both the door and the windows. She was so upset and had such difficulty concentrating that she decided she could not yet return to work. When she did return to work several weeks later, she was still clearly upset, and her supervisor suggested that she might be helped by counseling.

During the clinic interview, Mary was coherent and spoke quite rationally in a hushed voice. She reported recurrent and intrusive thoughts about the sexual assault, to the extent that her concentration was impaired and she had difficulty doing chores such as making meals for herself and her daughter. She felt she was not able to be effective at work, still felt afraid to leave her home, to answer her phone, and had little interest in contacting friends or relatives.

The range of Mary's affect was constricted. She talked in the same tone of voice whether discussing the assault or less emotionally charged topics, such as her work history. She was easily startled by an unexpected noise. She also was unable to fall asleep because she kept thinking about the assault. She had no desire to eat, and when she did attempt it, she felt nauseated. Mary was repelled by the thought of sex and stated that she did not want to have sex for a long time, although she was willing to be held and comforted by her boyfriend.

(Spitzer et al., 1983, pp. 20–21)

EXPLANATIONS OF ACUTE AND POSTTRAUMATIC STRESS DISORDERS

There is an obvious cause-and-effect relationship between an extraordinary trauma and the subsequent onset of an acute or posttraumatic stress disorder. The stressful event alone, however, is not a complete explanation. Although everyone who experiences an unusual trauma is certainly affected by it, only some people develop one of these disorders. Researchers do not yet understand why some people do and others do not develop them, but they have called three factors to our attention: the survivor's *childhood experiences*, *personality*, and *social support system* (Schnurr, Friedman, & Rosenberg, 1993).

A recent wave of studies has uncovered childhood events that seem to leave some people vulnerable to developing acute and posttraumatic stress disorders in response to later traumatic experiences. People whose childhoods have been characterized by poverty, whose parents separated or divorced before their child was 10, whose family members suffered from mental disorders, or who experienced assault, abuse, or catastrophe at an early age appear more likely to develop acute or posttraumatic disorders in the face of later trauma than people without such childhood experiences (Bremner et al., 1993; Kolb, 1992; Davidson et al., 1991). The reasons for a tie between these early life experiences and later stress disorders have been the subject of much speculation. It has been suggested, for example, that the tendency of many abused children to dissociate, or psychologically separate themselves, from the experience and memory of abuse may become a habitual way of dealing with traumatic events in life, leading them to wall off later traumas as well and setting the stage for the development of acute or posttraumatic stress disorders (Bremner et al., 1993).

Millions of people reacted to the San Francisco earthquake of 1989 with dread and panic, but some laid-back individuals seemed to thrive on all the excitement. Their "hardy" personality styles may have helped to protect them from the development of posttraumatic stress disorders.

Other studies suggest that people with certain personality profiles or attitudes are more likely to develop these disorders (Clark et al., 1994). It has been found, for example, that rape victims who had psychological problems before they were raped or were struggling with stressful life situations (Sales, Baum, & Shore, 1984) and war veterans who had poor relationships before they went into combat (Chemtob et al., 1990) run a greater risk of developing lingering stress reactions after their traumatic experiences. Similarly, people who generally view life's aversive events as beyond their control develop more severe acute and posttraumatic stress symptoms after criminal assaults than people who feel more control over aversive events (Kushner et al., 1992). These findings are reminiscent of another: that many people respond to stress with a set of positive attitudes, collectively called *hardiness,* that enable them to carry on their lives with a sense of fortitude, control, and commitment (Kobasa, 1990, 1987, 1979).

Lastly, it has been found that people who are sustained by strong support systems after a traumatic event are less likely to develop an extended disorder (Perry et al., 1992). Rape victims who feel loved, cared for, valued, and accepted by a group of friends or relatives are more likely to recover successfully from their sexual assault. Societal support appears to be just as important. A rape victim who is further de-

valued and traumatized by representatives or agencies of the criminal justice system is more likely to develop lingering symptoms (Sales et al., 1984). In contrast, clinical reports suggest that weak social support systems have contributed to the development of posttraumatic stress disorders in some Vietnam veterans (Figley & Leventman, 1990). This man's return home was, sadly, not at all unusual:

*N*ext morning my sisters went to school as usual, while my brother went to college. Everything seemed the same to them, real routine, you know. I didn't feel "routine." I felt out of it. I felt nervous, tense, jittery, even shaky. I wasn't able to fall asleep, so I got up at 10:00 A.M. I was home alone. So I walked down to the package store and bought me some liquor to help me out—you know, with the nervousness, and my anger about everything. . . .

In spite of all my efforts to avoid having anyone see me, a long-time friend saw me and really welcomed me home. It was really nice. Then, like out of nowhere, six guys showed up on the scene; I knew most of them. They wanted to know about the "good dope" in Vietnam. They didn't seem interested in me as a person. They had heard of the Thai red, the opium, and all that stuff. They asked me about the Vietnamese whores; and how many times I caught the clap [gonorrhea].

They also wanted to know what it was like having sex with Vietnamese women. One of them yelled out, "How many babies you've burned, man? How many young children don't have their fathers because of guys like you? Yeah, you killers, man; you heard me." Before I knew what had happened the cops were there. I had beaten four guys up severely; three had to be taken to the hospital. I seemed to have lost my head totally. I didn't want to hurt anybody. I had done a lot of killing in the 'Nam; I just wanted to be left alone, now. But I was really mad; I felt I had to defend myself against and kill the new "gooks"—the American gooks.

I was disappointed, so hurt, and bitter at myself for "going off" and losing control of myself. I was told later that I was attacked first; I don't remember. I came back to my room, and began really drinking. I just kept thinking to myself that the streets of Cholon, Saigon, Nha Trang, and other cities and villages in Vietnam were probably safer for me than back in the United States.

(Brende & Parson, 1985, pp. 49–50)

Although childhood experiences, personality, and social support may play important roles in a person's reactions to stress, it is important to keep in mind that the events that trigger acute and posttraumatic stress disorders can sometimes be so extreme and traumatic that they override a positive childhood, hardy personality, and supportive social context. A follow-up study of 253 Vietnam prisoners of war found that five years after their release 23 percent warranted a psychiatric diagnosis, though all had been effective Air Force officers and had been evaluated as well adjusted before their imprisonment (Ursano, Boydstun, & Wheatley, 1981). Moreover, it was the men who had been imprisoned longest and treated most harshly who had the highest percentage of such diagnoses. Another study of Vietnam combat veterans found that those who had been exposed to the worst atrocities later experienced the most severe symptoms of posttraumatic stress disorder (Yehuda, Southwick, & Giller, 1992). Childhood, personal, and social variables notwithstanding, it is, as a survivor of trauma once said, "hard to be a survivor" (Kolff & Doan, 1985, p. 45).

The State of the Field

Anxiety Disorders

The evidence that clinicians and researchers have gathered about anxiety disorders indicates that they are the most common mental disorders in the United States, that they are more prevalent among women than among men, and that they are likely to continue in the absence of treatment. Research has also determined that aside from the common denominator of anxiety, the various anxiety disorders differ in important ways. Panic disorders and generalized anxiety disorders, once lumped together as "anxiety neurosis," are now considered to be two distinct disorders, in recognition of their different features, courses, biological dimensions, and probable origins. Similarly, acute and posttraumatic stress disorders have been set off from the other anxiety disorders because of their characteristic courses, causes, and clinical features.

Some anxiety disorders are better understood than others. For years behavioral researchers have been gathering valuable insights into phobic disorders, and recently biological and cognitive researchers have made great strides toward explaining the once poorly understood panic disorders and obsessive-compulsive disorders. Less impressive is the clinical field's current progress toward understanding generalized anxiety disorders: only the biological correlates of this broad disorder seem to be unfolding clearly. Acute and posttraumatic stress disorders, newly identified syndromes, are only now receiving intense study.

The various models of psychopathology all have something to say about anxiety disorders, but each explanation is weakened by its model's characteristic limitations. The psychodynamic and humanistic theories are very difficult to research. The behavioral and cognitive explanations often rely on laboratory studies in which researchers successfully create anxietylike symptoms but fail to establish that real-life anxiety disorders emerge in a similar manner. And biological explanations often fail to identify the precise nature, role, and importance of the biological variables linked to anxiety disorders.

Several important tasks lie ahead for those who theorize about and research anxiety disorders. They must demonstrate conclusively that the factors and variables they consider crucial are indeed important in the development or maintenance of anxiety disorders. They must distinguish causal factors from factors that help maintain the disorder. Finally, they must discover the mechanisms by which the factors and variables emphasized in one model interact with those emphasized in other models. Actually, there is already a growing trend in this direction. Composite biological-cognitive theories have been proposed to help explain panic disorders, and the behavioral-biological theory of preparedness has been used to help explain the development of phobic disorders. This trend toward combining viewpoints is most welcome. Such combinations may eventually yield complete and incisive explanations that allow clinicians to proclaim that at last they understand anxiety disorders.

Summary

■ FEAR is a state of tension or alarm. *Anxiety* is a broader reaction that occurs when our sense of threat is more diffuse or vague. People with anxiety disorders experience ongoing fear and anxiety that prevent them from leading a normal life. Their experiences are severe, frequent, or long-lasting, and are triggered too readily by minimal, unspecified, or nonexistent threats. Anxiety disorders are collectively the most common mental disorders in the United States. DSM-IV distinguishes six categories of disorder: phobic disorder, generalized anxiety disorder, panic disorder, obsessive-compulsive disorder, acute stress disorder, and posttraumatic stress disorder.

■ THE TWO MOST COMMON TYPES of anxiety disorders are phobias and generalized anxiety disorders. A *phobia* is a persistent and unreasonable fear of a particular object, activity, or situation. There are three main categories of phobic disorders. *Agoraphobia* is a fear of venturing into public places in which escape might be difficult or help unavailable should paniclike symptoms develop. *Social phobia* is a severe, persistent, and irrational fear of social or performance situations in which embarrassment may occur. All other phobias—intense fear of animals, insects, heights, closed places, thunderstorms, or the like—are called *specific phobias.* People with *generalized anxiety disorder* experience excessive anxiety and worry about numerous events or activities.

A variety of factors may contribute to the development of phobic and generalized anxiety disorders. Proponents of the various models have focused on different factors and offered different explanations.

According to the *sociocultural* view, increases in societal dangers and pressures may establish a climate in which these anxiety disorders are more likely to develop.

Freud, the initial formulator of the *psychodynamic* view, said that phobic disorders result from excessive use of the defense mechanisms of *repression* and *displacement* to control underlying anxiety, whereas generalized anxiety disorders develop when defense mechanisms break down and function poorly.

Carl Rogers, the leading *humanistic* theorist, believed that people with phobic and generalized disorders first develop a defensive way of functioning when as children they fail to receive *unconditional positive regard* from significant others and so become overly critical of themselves.

Existentialists believe that phobic and generalized anxiety disorders result from the existential anxiety we experience because we know that life is finite and suspect it may have no meaning.

Behaviorists believe that phobic disorders are learned from the environment through *classical conditioning* and through *modeling.* They also believe that avoidance behaviors develop through *operant conditioning* and prevent extinction of a fear response. Behaviorists propose that specific learned fears produce a generalized anxiety disorder through *stimulus generalization.*

Cognitive theorists believe that generalized anxiety disorders are caused by *maladaptive assumptions* which lead persons to view most life situations as dangerous. It may be that people who have experienced too many unpredictable negative events in life are prone to such thinking.

Biological theorists argue that generalized anxiety disorders result from deficient activity of the neurotransmitter GABA. Concordance studies have lent some support to the notion that generalized anxiety disorders are caused in part by a physiological predisposition.

■ ANYONE is capable of a panic reaction, but sufferers of *panic disorder* experience panic attacks frequently, unpredictably, and without apparent provocation. Because persons with panic disorders are often helped by antidepressant drugs, biological theorists believe that abnormal *norepinephrine* activity in the *locus coeruleus* is a key factor. The cognitive-biological position is that panic-prone people become preoccupied with their bodily sensations and mental states and misinterpret them as indicative of imminent catastrophe.

■ PEOPLE WITH AN *obsessive-compulsive disorder* are beset by *obsessions*—repetitive and unwanted thoughts, ideas, impulses, or images that keep invading their consciousness and causing anxiety—or *compulsions*—repetitive and rigid actions that they feel compelled to perform to reduce anxiety. The most common theme of obsessive thinking is contamination. Common forms of compulsions are cleaning; checking; symmetry, order, or balance; touching; verbal rituals; and counting. Although some people with an obsessive compulsive disorder experience obsessions only or compulsions only, most experience both.

According to the *psychodynamic* view, obsessive-compulsive disorders arise out of the battle between id impulses, which appear as obsessive thoughts, and ego defense mechanisms, which take the form of counterthoughts or compulsive actions. *Cognitive-behavioral* theorists suggest that the disorder grows from a normal human tendency to have unwanted and unpleasant thoughts—a tendency that some persons misinterpret as dangerous, reprehensible, and controllable. Their cognitive and behavioral efforts to eliminate or avoid such thoughts inadvertently lead to the development of obsessions and compulsions. *Biological* researchers have identified two biological factors that may contribute to this disorder: low activity of the neurotransmitter *serotonin* and abnormal functioning in key regions of the brain, including the *caudate nuclei.*

■ PEOPLE WITH *acute stress disorder* or *posttraumatic stress disorder* react with a distinct pattern of symptoms to a traumatic event, including reexperiencing the traumatic event, avoidance of related events, reduced responsiveness, and increased arousal, anxiety, and guilt. The symptoms of acute stress disorder begin soon after the trauma and last less than a month. Those of posttraumatic stress disorder may begin at any time (even years) after the trauma, and may last for months or years.

Acute and posttraumatic stress disorders can emerge in response to combat conditions and have been especially prominent among Vietnam veterans. They may also occur in the wake of natural disasters or after stress that is intentionally inflicted, as in instances of genocide and rape. In attempting to explain why some people develop acute or posttraumatic stress disorder and others do not, researchers have focused on childhood experiences, personal variables, and social support.

Topic Overview

Psychodynamic Therapies

Humanistic and Existential Therapies

PROBLEM-BASED THERAPIES

Systematic Desensitization

Flooding and Implosive Therapy

Modeling

Social Skills Training

Cognitive Therapies

Stress Management Training

Exposure and Response Prevention

Drug Therapies

TREATMENTS FOR
ANXIETY DISORDERS

WHAT DOES IT MEAN to overcome an anxiety disorder? When should the treatment for such a disorder be considered successful? Is it when symptoms are reduced, or must they be eliminated? Perhaps it is enough for the client to learn how to function in the face of anxiety. The answers depend partly on the perspective of the therapist and partly on the views and goals of the client. Here Fred describes his "triumph" over anxiety problems:

Everything used to upset me. From big problems to the smallest of issues. I'd worry and worry, stay awake nights, and drive my wife up the wall. Therapy has helped to change all that. My wife says I seem to be a different person. And I feel like a different person. I rarely get upset, certainly not over little things. Oh, sure, if there's an illness or accident, or a problem at work, I'll get concerned. But it doesn't get out of hand. I'm really enjoying my life again.

And Howard says:

I'm feeling better since I first started treatment, but it's a long way from perfect. I still have a lot of fears, worry a lot, blow things out of proportion. But I do have more of a handle on things now. At least I don't worry so often. I don't get scared in so many situations. I even have some evenings when I don't worry at all. It's a battle. I have to work at it. But at least I'm no longer anxious every second.

ALTHOUGH FRED AND HOWARD are talking about different kinds of success, they both believe they have made significant progress in their battles against anxiety. And in each case progress has been aided by a systematic treatment approach. Fred and Howard are among the 6 to 7 million people in the United States with an anxiety disorder, or 29 percent of all U.S. residents with such a disorder, who receive treatment each year from mental health or medical professionals. Each person who receives treatment averages around thirteen visits to a therapist in the course of a year (Regier et al., 1993; Narrow et al., 1993).

■ GLOBAL ■ THERAPIES

The practitioner of a global therapy follows the same general procedure regardless of the client's particular disorder. *Psychodynamic* therapists try to help all their clients recognize and resolve the impact of past events. Using such procedures as free association and gently suggesting interpretations, they lead clients on a search for the deep-seated impulses, needs, and conflicts that underlie their emotions and behavior, expecting that the resulting insights will eventually foster recovery. *Humanistic and existential* therapists, for their part, try to help clients become more aware and accepting of their true thoughts and feelings, expecting that in this way they will learn to lead more authentic and fulfilling lives.

PSYCHODYNAMIC THERAPIES

Practitioners of the various psychodynamic therapies work to help anxious patients uncover and resolve the unconscious issues that they believe are at the root of their disorders. Classic psychodynamic therapists, for example, try to help the clients become less afraid of their id impulses and more able to control them successfully. In contrast, object relations therapists help anxious patients identify and resolve the anxiety-provoking childhood relationship problems that they seem to be repeating in adulthood. And self therapists seek to help anxious patients build a cohesive self from the fragmented self that, they believe, keeps generating anxiety (Compton, 1992; Zerbe, 1990; Gillman, 1990; Diamond, 1987).

In the following case, the therapist uses classic psychoanalytic techniques and interpretations to help a client overcome his generalized anxiety disorder. The client, a financially successful young man, was unable to enjoy his success, felt inferior to others, and had a very limited social life.

*I*n the course of analysis many facts were revealed that explained his inability to enjoy his financial success, and his despair of having an intimate relationship with a respectable girl. Briefly stated these difficulties were all rooted in guilt arising from unresolved oedipal conflicts and incestuous feelings for his sisters. Material success and becoming the sole support of the family symbolized for him the childhood wish to replace and surpass his father. Hence when he accomplished his wholehearted desire to give his mother every comfort to compensate for her many years of hardship, he was faced with an acute conflict.

He had always retained his strong attachment to his mother, since she was the only understanding and mild person in his whole miserable environment. He also had very tender feelings for his two young sisters. Toward the male members of his family who had always abused him he felt hatred, rebellion, and a desire to excel them. . . .

[Over the course of treatment] he saw clearly how much his business was responsible for creating actual conflicts and neurotic difficulties because it was a stepping stone to realizing his competitive drives. Apart from the conscious reasons he also recognized the unconscious motivations for his ambitions to be an independent, successful businessman, the center of this being more powerful materially than his brothers and father and to have power over them, make them dependent, if he could, on him. He became also more aware as analysis progressed why he gradually became tired of the business, lost his ambition, began to have anxieties that grew worse. By realizing his ambitions to be more successful than the older brothers and father, he also realized his childhood and puberty period ambitions, which then carried the oedipal desire and so were charged with a powerful sense of guilt. The adult success revived the early striving and brought forth the early repressed guilt feeling that accompanied these strivings, and this chaos created his desire to run away from it all, in the neurosis and illness. . . .

With this [insight] and working through of aggressiveness the patient began to achieve self-confidence in his business, social, and family relations. He became less afraid of his business associates and began to develop genuine feelings of affection for, or at least understanding of, various members of his family. He started meeting young people of college training and even putting up brave arguments against their opinions. At this period he bought a better car, which he had hitherto avoided doing, and he also began to interest himself in sports. He became ambitious to make up his lack of education, began to study, and went to the theater. Finally he decided to sell his business, to rest for a period.

(Lorand, 1950, pp. 37–43)

Controlled research has not consistently supported the effectiveness of psychodynamic approaches in cases of anxiety disorder (Svartberg & Stiles, 1991; Prochaska, 1984). The bulk of evidence suggests that psychodynamic therapy is at best of modest help to people suffering from the broad symptoms of generalized anxiety disorders and of little help for those with other anxiety disorders, such as phobic and obsessive-compulsive disorders (Nemiah, 1984; Berk & Efran, 1983; Salzman, 1980).

In fact, Freud himself said that psychodynamic techniques alone may be insufficient to cure phobic disorders: "One can hardly ever master a phobia if one waits till the patient lets the analysis influence him to give it up. One succeeds only when one can induce them through the influence of analysis . . . to go about alone and to struggle with their anxiety while they make the attempt" (Freud, [1919] 1959, pp. 399–400).

Psychodynamic therapy may actually add to the difficulties of patients with obsessive-compulsive disorders (Salzman, 1980). It has been claimed that the psychodynamic focus on free association and interpretation inadvertently plays into the tendency of obsessive-compulsive persons to ruminate and over-interpret (Noonan, 1971). Thus some psychodynamic therapists prefer to employ specific short-term psychodynamic therapies with these clients, therapies that are more direct and action-based than the classical techniques. In one approach, the therapist directly advises obsessive-compulsive clients that their compulsions are defense mechanisms and urges them to

"DO YOU WANT A CRACKER, OR DO YOU NEED A CRACKER?"

Both psychodynamic and humanistic therapists guide clients with anxiety disorders (and other disorders as well) to uncover hidden feelings and needs. Psychodynamic therapists believe that self-discoveries of this kind help clients re-experience past traumas and feelings, resolve internal conflicts, and overcome anxiety. Humanistic therapists believe that such discoveries lead to greater self-acceptance and, in turn, greater self-actualization and peace of mind.

stop acting compulsively (Salzman, 1985, 1980). Research has not yet demonstrated whether these newer approaches are indeed more effective than traditional psychodynamic therapies (Hirschfeld & Goodwin, 1988).

HUMANISTIC AND EXISTENTIAL THERAPIES

Like psychodynamic therapists, humanistic and existential therapists treat all disorders more or less uniformly. Client-centered humanistic therapists try to show unconditional positive regard for their clients and to empathize with them, expecting that an atmosphere of genuine acceptance and caring will provide the security they need to recognize their true inner needs, thoughts, and emotions (Raskin & Rogers, 1989). The therapists' goal is to help clients "experience" themselves—that is, become completely trusting of their instincts and honest and comfortable with themselves. Their anxiety or other symptoms of psychological dysfunctioning will then subside. In Chapter 5 we observed part of a therapy session between Carl Rogers and the client Mrs. Oak (see pp. 151–152). Here Rogers describes how client-centered therapy helped Mrs. Oak overcome the anxiety and related symptoms that had been disrupting her life.

Mrs. Oak was a housewife in her late thirties who was in a deeply discordant relationship with her husband and also much disturbed in her relationship with her adolescent daughter, who had recently been through a serious illness which had been diagnosed as psychosomatic. Mrs. Oak felt she must be to blame for this illness. She herself was a sensitive person, eager to be honest with herself and to search out the causes of her problems. She was a person with little formal education, though intelligent and widely read.

By the fifth interview any specific concentration on her problems had dropped out and the major focus of therapy had shifted to an experiencing of herself and her emotional reactions. She felt at times that she should be "working on my problems" but that she felt drawn to this experiencing, that somehow she wanted to use the therapy hour for what she called her "vaguenesses." This was a good term, since she expressed herself in half-sentences, poetic analogies, and expressions which seemed more like fantasy. Her communications were often hard to follow or understand but obviously involved much deep feeling experienced in the immediate present.

She was unusually sensitive to the process she was experiencing in herself. To use some of her expressions, she was feeling pieces of a jigsaw puzzle, she was singing a song without words, she was creating a poem, she was learning a new way of experiencing herself which was like learning to read Braille. Therapy was an experiencing of herself, in all its aspects, in a safe relationship. At first it was her guilt and her concern over being responsible for the maladjustments of others. Then it was her hatred and bitterness toward life for having cheated and frustrated her in so many different areas, particularly the sexual, and then it was the experiencing of her own hurt, of the sorrow she felt for herself for having been so wounded. But along with these went the experiencing of self as having a capacity for wholeness, a self which was not possessively loving toward others but was "without hate," a self that cared about others. This last followed what was, for her, one of the deepest experiences in therapy . . .—the realization that the therapist cared, that it really mattered to him how therapy turned out for her, that he really valued her. She experienced the soundness of her basic directions. She gradually became aware of the fact that, though she had searched in every corner of herself, there was nothing fundamentally bad, but rather, at heart she was positive and sound. She realized that the values she deeply held were such as would set her at variance with her culture, but she accepted this calmly. . . .

One of the outstanding characteristics of the interviews was the minimal consideration of her outside behavior. Once an issue was settled in her, the behavioral consequences were mentioned only by chance. After she had "felt" her way through her relationship with her daughter, there was little mention of her behavior toward the daughter until much later when she casually mentioned that the relationship was much better. Likewise, in regard to a job. She had never worked outside the home, and the prospect terrified her, yet she thought it highly important if she were to feel independent of her husband. She finally settled the issue in her feelings to the extent that she said she thought now that she could look for or take a job. She never mentioned it again . . . It was the same in regard to her marriage. She decided that she could not continue in marriage but that she did not wish to break up the marriage in a battle or with resentment and hurt. Shortly after the conclusion of therapy she achieved this goal of a separation and divorce which was mutually agreed upon.

When she left therapy, it was with the feeling that a process was going on in her which would continue to operate. She felt that the relationship with the therapist had been very meaningful and in a psychological sense would never stop, even though she walked out of the office for good. She felt ready, she thought, to cope with her life, though she realized it would not be easy.

(Rogers, 1954, pp. 261–264)

In spite of this and other optimistic case reports, research has failed to show that humanistic and existential approaches are generally effective treatments for anxiety disorders. Controlled studies of Rogers's client-centered approach suggest that this form of treatment is only sometimes more effective than providing placebo therapy or nothing at all (Greenberg et al., 1994; Prochaska & Norcross, 1994). Moreover, there have been relatively few such studies of other humanistic or existential approaches to anxiety disorders, largely because practitioners of these approaches believe that experimental methods cannot test the validity of their phenomenological focus, techniques, and goals (Greenberg et al., 1994; Prochaska & Norcross, 1994).

■ PROBLEM- ■ BASED THERAPIES

Behavioral, cognitive, and *biological* therapists, in contrast to global therapists, practice problem-based therapies tailored to the idiosyncratic features of each disorder. Behaviorists have virtually ruled the clinical field in the treatment of phobic disorders, particularly of specific phobias. All three of these approaches, however, have made substantial contributions to treatment of the other anxiety disorders.

SPECIFC PHOBIAS

The anxiety disorders that have had the longest record of successful treatment are the specific phobias, yet the vast majority of people who have these disorders receive no treatment for them (see Figure 7–1). All the problem-based therapies have been used to treat intense fears of specific objects, events, or situations, but behavioral therapists have consistently fared better than the others in head-to-head comparisons (Emmelkamp, 1994, 1982; Page, 1991).

The major behavioral approaches to specific phobias are *desensitization, flooding,* and *modeling.* Collectively, these approaches are called *exposure treatments,* because in all of them clients are exposed to the object or situation they dread. The exposure may be vicarious or direct, brief or long, gradual or sudden.

SYSTEMATIC DESENSITIZATION Clients treated by *systematic desensitization,* a technique developed by Joseph Wolpe (1990, 1987, 1969, 1958), learn to relax while they are confronted with the objects or situations they fear. Since relaxation and fear are incompatible, the new relaxation response is thought to substitute for the fear response.

Wolpe began to develop this technique in 1944, when, as a military medical officer, he conducted classical conditioning experiments on cats. In the first phase of these experiments, he sounded a buzzer while hungry cats were eating. When he later sounded the buzzer at random times, the cats sought out food and ate it. Next he sounded a buzzer while the same cats were receiving electric shocks. Now the cats showed fear in response to the buzzer and would not eat while it sounded. Wolpe concluded that eating and fear were incompatible responses and that the stronger fear response had now substituted for the eating response. He had replaced the old bond (buzzer : eating) with a new bond (buzzer : fear).

Wolpe believed that this process of inhibition should work both ways. Just as he could stop an animal's eating response by teaching it a more powerful fear response, he should be able to replace the fear response with a different mode of behavior. In fact, an earlier experiment by Mary Cover Jones (1924) supported this expectation. Jones had reported the case of a young boy who was afraid of rabbits. She helped the child to overcome this fear by giving him his favorite food while she moved a rabbit closer and closer. Soon the child could actually play with the rabbit.

Wolpe labeled this process *reciprocal inhibition,* a term then in use by physiologists (Sherrington, 1906), because he believed that he was dealing with a physiological incompatibility between the responses of eating and fear. He believed that the technique of reciprocal inhibition could be used to overcome phobias, and he searched for responses other than eating that might be incompatible with fear. He decided upon the relaxation response and developed a technique for teaching people to replace fear responses with relaxation responses, the technique now known as systematic desensitization. Systematic desensitization is taught in three phases: *relaxation training,* construction of a *fear hierarchy,* and *graded pairing* of feared objects and relaxation responses.

RELAXATION TRAINING   Desensitization therapists first teach clients to release all the tension in their bodies on cue. Over the course of several sessions and homework assignments, clients learn to identify individual muscle groups, tense them, relax them, and ultimately relax the whole body. With continued practice, the clients are able to bring on a state of deep muscle relaxation at will.

In the case of Mrs. Schmidt, a woman with a "gross fear of rejection," Wolpe began with relaxation training. His instructions included the following points:

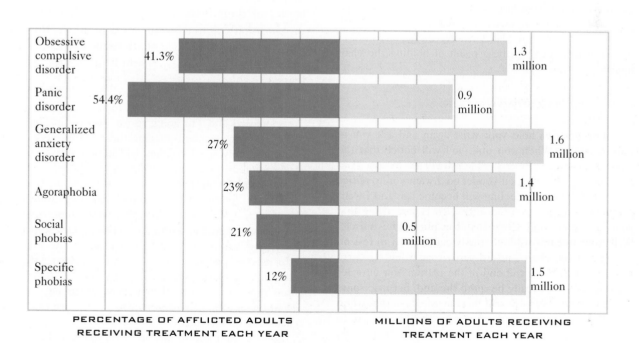

FIGURE 7-1   *Who receives treatment for their anxiety disorders? More than half of all persons who have a panic disorder in the United States receive professional treatment each year, but only about one-eighth of those with a specific phobia, a less disabling disorder, receive treatment. Because the prevalence rates of these disorders differ, however, more people receive treatment for specific phobias than for panic disorders. (Adapted from Regier et al., 1993; Blazer et al., 1991; Boyd et al., 1990.)*

A person suffering from aerophobia once said, "I'm not afraid of flying—it's crashing and getting burned to a crisp I'm afraid of." Seeking to reduce the $1.5 billion a year lost to this phobia, the airline industry has offered desensitization programs for sufferers. USAir's Fearful Flyers Program begins with an instructor guiding would-be passengers in relaxation exercises.

Identifying and Tensing the Muscle Groups

. . . Now, what I want you to do is, with your left hand, hold the arm of your chair quite tight. I want you to observe certain things that are a result of your holding this chair tight. First of all, there are certain sensations. To begin with, you have sensations . . . in your hand and you may have other sensations. With your right hand, point out to me all the places where you get any kind of feeling which seems to be a result of holding the chair tightly.

Relaxing the Muscle Groups

. . . I'm going to hold your wrist again and ask you to pull against it. When you pull, you will notice that the muscle becomes tight again. Then I will say to you, "Let go gradually." Now, when you let go, I want you to notice two things. The tight feeling will become less and I want you also to notice that the letting go is something that you do—something active that you put in the muscle. Well, your forearm will eventually come down to rest on the arm of the chair and ordinarily that would seem to you as though that's the end of the matter. You have let go. But it will not really be quite the end, because some of the muscle fibers will still be contracted, so that when your forearm has come down to the chair I will say to you, "Keep on letting go. Go on doing that in the muscle, that activity which you were doing while it was coming down. . . . Try and make it go further and further."

(*Wolpe,* The Case of Mrs. Schmidt)

CONSTRUCTION OF A FEAR HIERARCHY

During the early sessions of desensitization, thera-pists also help clients to make a list of specific situations in which their phobia is aroused. The situations are then ranked in a hierarchy, ranging from circumstances that evoke only a trace of fear to those that the clients consider extremely frightening (see Table 7-1). Near the bottom of Mrs. Schmidt's fear hierarchy were slights by people she didn't know or care about; at the top were rejections by people who meant a great deal to her.

GRADED PAIRINGS Next the clients learn how to relax in the face of their fears. They are instructed to place themselves in a general state of relaxation. While they are in this state, the therapist has them confront the event at the bottom of their fear hierarchy. This may be an actual physical confrontation (a person who fears heights, for example, may stand on a chair or climb a stepladder)—in which case the process is called *in vivo desensitization*—or the confrontation may be imagined, with the client creating a mental image of the frightening event while the therapist describes it—in which case the process is called *covert desensitization.*

The clients move through the entire list, pairing their relaxation responses with each feared item in the hierarchy. Because the first item is only mildly frightening, it is usually only a short while before they are able to relax totally when they confront it. Over the course of several sessions, clients move up the ladder of their fears until they reach and overcome the one that frightens them most of all. At this point they can relax in the face of all items on the hierarchy. Here Wolpe guides Mrs. Schmidt up her hierarchy of fears:

OK, now, you are quite nice and relaxed. Now, keep your eyes closed and I'm going to ask you to imagine some scenes. Now, you will imagine these scenes very clearly, and generally speaking they will not affect your state of relaxation. But if by any chance anything does affect your state of calm, you'll be able to signal that to me by raising your right forefinger about an inch. So now, I want you to imagine just that you're standing on a street corner and you're watching the traffic. Just a nice, pleasant, peaceful day, and you're watching the cars, and the taxis and trucks, and people all passing at this corner. OK, now, stop imagining this scene. Now, if the scene didn't worry you at all, do nothing. If that scene disturbed you, raise your finger now. (*No finger movement*) OK, that's fine, now just keep on relaxing.

Now, I want you to imagine that you're walking along the sidewalk and you see, walking toward you from the other side, Mrs. Benning. Now, as you pass Mrs. Benning, you see she is looking toward you and you get ready to greet her, and she just walks past as though she didn't recognize you. Now, stop imagining that. Now, if that, if imagining that disturbed you even a very small

TABLE 7-1

SAMPLE "FEAR OF FLYING" HIERARCHY

(read from the bottom up)

- The plane starts down the runway, and the motors get louder as the plane increases speed and suddenly lifts off.
- The plane encounters turbulence.
- The plane has taken off from the airport and banks as it changes direction. I am aware of the "tilt."
- The plane is descending to the runway for a landing. I feel the speed and see the ground getting closer.
- I am looking out the window and suddenly the plane enters clouds and I cannot see out the window.
- I notice the seat-belt signs light up, so I fasten my seat belt and I notice the sound of the motors starting.
- I am now inside the plane. I move in from the aisle and sit down in my assigned seat.
- I walk down the ramp leading to the plane and enter the door of the plane.
- I hear my flight number announced, and I proceed to the security checkpoint with my hand luggage.
- I am entering the terminal. I am carrying my bags and tickets.
- I am driving to the airport for my flight. I am aware of every plane I see.
- It is ten days before the trip, and I receive the tickets in the mail.
- I have called the travel agent and told him of my plans.
- A trip has been planned, and I have decided "out loud" to travel by plane.

Source: Adapted from Martin & Pear, 1988, p. 380; Roscoe et al., 1980.

bit, I want you to raise your right index finger now. If it didn't worry you, don't do anything. *(No finger movement)*

Now, I want you to imagine again that you're walking on the sidewalk and you see, moving toward you, Selma and you get ready to greet her, and she seems to see you but she walks right on—she doesn't greet you. Now, stop imagining this. If you felt any disturbance at that . . . *(Right forefinger rises)*

(Wolpe, The Case of Mrs. Schmidt*)*

When a client is tense during a scene, as Mrs. Schmidt was during the last scene, the therapist stops and has the client focus exclusively on relaxing. Once the client is relaxed, they try the scene again until it can be imagined without arousing any fear. They do not move on to the next scene until each of the lower-ranked scenes has been mastered fully.

FLOODING AND IMPLOSIVE THERAPY Another behavioral treatment for phobic disorders is *flooding.* This technique was actually developed by a psychodynamic therapist, Thomas Stampfl (1975), who called it *implosive therapy.* Today "flooding" and "implosive therapy" are used almost interchangeably and the procedure is employed primarily by behaviorists. Flooding therapists believe that clients will stop

fearing things when they are exposed to them repeatedly and made to see that they are actually quite harmless.

Flooding operates much like the extinction procedures that have been developed by conditioning researchers. In a famous extinction study, experimenters first gave dogs a series of intense electrical shocks always accompanied by the sound of a buzzer, thus conditioning the dogs to fear not only shock but the sound of the buzzer as well (Solomon, Kamin, & Wynne, 1953). Later the dogs were also taught that they could escape the stimulus they feared by jumping over a barrier and out of their box whenever the buzzer sounded. The dogs continued to display these acquired responses even when the experimenters later stopped the shocks. That is, their fear and avoidance responses persisted indefinitely because they never stayed in the box long enough to learn that the shocks had been stopped. The experimenters were able to extinguish these acquired responses only by forcibly restraining the dogs in their boxes until they finally realized that shocks were no longer accompanying the sound of the buzzer.

Therapists who use the technique of flooding believe that people with phobic disorders, like the dogs in this study, must be forced to confront what they fear so they will see that no real danger exists. These therapists use no relaxation training and no graduated approach. Flooding procedures, like desensitization, can be either in vivo (Crow et al., 1972; Leitenberg & Callahan, 1973) or imaginal (Stampfl & Levis, 1967; Levis & Carrera, 1967). Some clinicians reserve the term "flooding" for the in vivo procedures and "implosive therapy" for imaginal ones.

When therapists guide clients in imagining the feared objects or situations, they often embellish and exaggerate the description so that the clients experience intense emotional arousal. In the case of a woman who had a phobic reaction to snakes, the therapist had her imagine the following scenes, among others:

> Close your eyes again. Picture the snake out in front of you, now make yourself pick it up. Reach down, pick it up, put it in your lap, feel it wiggling around in your lap, leave your hand on it, put your hand out and feel it wiggling around. Kind of explore its body with your fingers and hand. You don't like to do it, make yourself do it. Make yourself do it. Really grab onto the snake. Squeeze it a little bit, feel it. Feel it kind of start to wind around your hand. Let it. Leave your hand there, feel it touching your hand and winding around it, curling around your wrist.

In the behavioral exposure technique of implosive therapy, or flooding, therapists have clients imagine or confront feared objects in their full intensity and often present the object in as frightening a way as possible. A person with a snake phobia might be shown a vivid picture of the animal's open mouth and sharp fangs or helped to imagine them in gruesome detail.

Okay, now put your finger out towards the snake and feel his head coming up. Its head is towards your finger and it is starting to bite at your finger. Let it, let it bite at your finger. Put your finger out, let it bite, let it bite at your finger, feel its fangs go right down into your finger. Oooh, feel the pain going right up your arm and into your shoulder.

Okay, feel him coiling around your hand again, touching you, slimy, now he is going up on your shoulder and he crawls there and he is sitting on your chest and he is looking you right in the eye. He is big and he is black and he is ugly and he's coiled up and he is ready to strike and he is looking at you. Picture his face, look at his eyes, look at those long sharp fangs. . . . He strikes out at you. *(Therapist slaps hand.)* Feel him bite at your face. Feel him bite at your face, let him bite; let him bite; just relax and let him bite; let him bite at your face, let him bite; let him bite at your face; feel his fangs go right into your cheeks; and the blood is coming out on your face now . . . feel it biting your eye and it is going to pull your eye right out and down on your cheek. It is kind of gnawing on it and eating it, eating at your eye. Your little eye is down on your cheek and it is gnawing and biting at your eye. Picture it. Now it is crawling into your eye socket and wiggling around in there, feel it wiggling and wiggling up in your head.

(Hogan, 1968, pp. 423–431)

In view of the intensity of implosive therapy and the suddenness with which clients are exposed to the stimuli they fear, some clinicians hold that the procedure may do further damage to clients and should be considered only as a last resort. As we shall see shortly, however, when it is conducted by a properly trained therapist, implosive therapy is no more likely than other forms of treatment to cause harm and is more likely than most to help clients overcome their phobias.

MODELING The behavioral technique of *modeling,* or *vicarious conditioning,* has also been used to treat specific phobias (Bandura, 1977, 1971; Bandura, Adams, & Beyer, 1977). In this procedure it is the therapist who confronts the feared object or situation while the fearful client observes. The therapist essentially acts as a model who demonstrates that the client's fear is groundless or highly exaggerated. It is expected that after several sessions clients will be able to approach the objects or situations with relative composure.

The most effective modeling technique is *participant modeling,* or *guided participation.* Here the therapist and client first construct a fear hierarchy, just as they would in desensitization. Then, while the client observes, the therapist experiences the least feared item in the hierarchy. Eventually the client is

In the behavioral exposure technique of participant modeling, a therapist treats a client with a snake phobia by first handling the snake himself and demonstrating its harmlessness, then encouraging the client to touch and handle the snake.

encouraged to join in, and they move up the hierarchy until the client is able to confront the most feared object or situation on the list.

Here is a participant modeling procedure for the treatment of snake phobias:

After these introductory interactions, the therapist may proceed to the major sequence of modeled interactions with the snake, which are as follows:
I. Gloved-hand procedure.
  1. Stroke the snake's midsection, then tail, then top of head.
  2. Raise the snake's midsection, then tail, then head.
  3. Grasp the snake gently but firmly a few inches from the head and about 6 inches from the tail, remove it from the cage (taking care not to approach the client or swing the snake obviously closer to him).
  4. Comfortably handle the snake, modeling how easy and comfortable the interaction process can be, how the model is in complete control, and so forth. This facet of the procedure should continue for several minutes . . . until external indications are that the client's anxiety level is rather low.
II. Bare-hand procedure.
  1–4. The above procedure should be repeated by the therapist/model using his bare hands.

. . . When these two modeling sequences have been successfully completed, the client may be asked if he is willing to approach the snake. . . . When the client agrees to approach the snake, the therapist should pick the snake up and hold it while he asks the client to don the gloves and briefly touch the snake's midsection. When the client successfully does so, reinforcement and support should be given; for example, "I'll bet that is the

first time in your life you ever touched a snake. Good for you!"

The client may then be asked to stroke the midsection, then touch and stroke the tail, and finally touch and stroke the top of the head. Should the snake extend its tongue, the therapist might matter-of-factly note that it is harmless, merely a sensing device for sound waves.

When the gloved touching and stroking behaviors have been completed, the client should be asked to hold the snake in his gloved hands. He may be instructed to place his hand loosely about the midsection of the snake and hold it there until he feels fairly comfortable (the therapist continues to support the snake). If these actions appear to cause some anxiety (or, perhaps, excitement) in the client, it may be suggested that he take a deep breath to induce relaxation. When progress is apparent, praise should be given.

The procedure continues, with the client holding (in gloved hand) the snake's tail, then its head. Finally, he may be asked to support the entire snake. This progression is not rapid, of course; time is allowed at each step for the client to become comfortable and praise is given for progress. If at any point the client expresses anxiety, the therapist should immediately take the snake back (calmly) and offer reassurance before returning to the participation process.

(Rimm & Masters, 1979, pp. 126–127)

EFFECTIVENESS OF BEHAVIORAL THERAPIES Clinical researchers have repeatedly found that each of the behavioral therapies for specific phobias is helpful (Emmelkamp, 1994). Moreover, in most cases once a phobia has been successfully treated by a behavioral method, new symptoms do not arise to replace it, as some psychodynamic theorists predict.

The first controlled experiment on desensitization measured the progress of two groups of subjects with snake phobias (Lang & Lazovik, 1963). One group received desensitization therapy; the control group received no therapy at all. After treatment, the desensitized subjects showed significantly less fear of snakes than the control subjects did. Even six months later, the desensitized subjects were less fearful of snakes. Overall, close to 75 percent of people with specific phobias improve with desensitization therapy (McGrath et al., 1990).

Flooding, too, helps people overcome specific phobias. A single implosive therapy session was administered to twenty-one subjects who were extremely fearful of rats, during which the therapist had them imagine scenes in which they touched rats, had their fingers nibbled by rats, were clawed by rats, and the like (Hogan & Kirchner, 1967). After this treatment, twenty of the subjects were able to open a rat's cage and fourteen could actually pick up the rat. A control group of twenty-two subjects were instructed to imagine irrelevant and neutral scenes while they relaxed. Only three of them could later open a rat's cage, and seven refused even to enter the room.

Modeling has also proved to be an effective treatment for specific phobias. Albert Bandura and his colleagues (1969) used modeling to treat students who had snake phóbias. One group of students went through a procedure consisting of live modeling and guided participation. A second group was treated by *symbolic modeling;* that is, they observed films of people who were safely and comfortably interacting with snakes. Each film in the sequence showed an increasingly threatening kind of interaction. Yet another group was treated with covert desensitization, while a control group received no treatment at all.

Ninety-two percent of the subjects treated with live modeling and guided participation overcame their fear of snakes. Many of the symbolic modeling and covert desensitization subjects also improved, but not nearly so much as the guided participation subjects. The untreated control subjects showed virtually no improvement.

At first glance these findings seem to suggest that modeling may be superior to desensitization as a form of treatment, but other research has shown that this is not the case. The key to success with a behavioral approach appears to be actual contact with the feared object or situation (Emmelkamp, 1994; Arntz & Lavy, 1993). In vivo desensitization is more effective than covert desensitization, in vivo flooding more effective than imaginal flooding, and participant modeling more helpful than modeling that is strictly vicarious (Menzies & Clarke, 1993). Thus the apparent superiority of participant modeling over covert desensitization in Bandura's snake phobia study is probably just another case of real exposure outdoing imaginal exposure. When the exposure factor is kept constant, desensitization, flooding, and modeling appear to be equally effective treatments for specific phobias. Recognizing the similar efficacies of these approaches, many behavioral therapists now combine features of each, making sure they include the critical feature of in vivo exposure (Ritchie, 1992; Flynn, Taylor, & Pollard, 1992; Marks, 1987).

Agoraphobia

For years clinicians made relatively little impact on agoraphobia, the fear of leaving one's home and entering public places. Yet approaches have recently been developed that enable many such people to venture out with less anxiety. These new approaches do not always bring as much relief to sufferers as the highly successful treatments for specific phobias, but they do offer considerable relief to many people.

Once again behaviorists have led the way by developing a variety of in vivo exposure approaches (Emmelkamp, 1994; Gelder, 1991; Rose, 1990). Therapists typically help clients to venture farther and farther from their homes and to enter outside places gradually, one step at a time. Sometimes the therapists use support, reasoning, and coaxing to get clients to confront the outside world. They also use more systematic exposure methods, such as the reinforcement technique described in the following case study:

T he first of our patients to take part in these experiments was a young woman who, shortly after she married, found herself unable to leave home. Even walking a few yards from her front door terrified her and often led to panic; she felt she might faint, choke, or even die if she did not return home at once. This phobia could be traced back to her childhood. . . .

It is not surprising . . . that this young woman found herself unable to function independently after leaving home to marry. Her inability to leave her new home was reinforced by an increasing dependence on her husband and by the solicitous overconcern of her mother, who was more and more frequently called in to stay with her. Her disability in a mobile society was enormous, and since she was cut off from her friends and from so much enjoyment in the outside world, depression added to her misery. Several years of psychotherapy brought her no relief, and she eventually became addicted to sleeping pills, which she discovered gave her enough courage to venture a little way alone. Eventually, she came to our laboratory for help.

To measure the patient's improvement, we laid out a mile-long course from the hospital to downtown, marked at about 25-yard intervals. Before beginning the experiment, we asked the patient to walk as far as she could along the course. Each time she balked at the front door of the hospital. Then the first phase of the experiment began: We held two sessions each day in which the patient was praised for staying out of the hospital for a longer and longer time. The reinforcement schedule was simple. If the patient stayed outside for 20 seconds on one trial and then on the next attempt stayed out for 30 seconds, she was praised enthusiastically. Now, however, the criterion for praise was raised—without the patient's knowledge—to 25 seconds. If she met the criterion she was again praised, and the time was increased again. If she did not stay out long enough, the therapist simply ignored her performance. To gain the therapist's attention, which she valued, she had to stay out longer each time.

This she did, until she was able to stay out for almost half an hour. But was she walking farther each time? Not at all.

She was simply circling around in the front drive of the hospital, keeping the "safe place" in sight at all times. We therefore changed the reinforcement to reflect the distance walked. Now she began to walk farther and farther each time. Supported by this simple therapeutic procedure, the patient was progressively able to increase her self-confidence. . . .

Praise was then thinned out, but slowly, and the patient was encouraged to walk anywhere she pleased. Five years later, she was still perfectly well. We might assume that the benefits of being more independent maintained the gains and compensated for the loss of praise from the therapist.

(Agras, 1985, pp. 77–80)

Figure 7–2 demonstrates the progress of an agoraphobic client treated by this approach.

Exposure therapy for people with agoraphobia often includes additional features, particularly the use of support groups (Rose, 1990) and home-based self-help programs (Emmelkamp et al., 1992), to motivate agoraphobic clients to work hard at their treatment. In the ***support group*** approach, a small number of peo-

ple with agoraphobia go out together for exposure sessions that last for several hours. The group members support and encourage one another, and eventually coax one another to move away from the safety of the group and perform exposure tasks on their own. In the ***home-based self-help programs,*** clinicians give clients and their families detailed instructions (such as those in Table 7–2) for carrying out exposure treatments themselves.

Between 60 and 80 percent of the agoraphobic clients who receive exposure treatment find it easier to enter public places, and the improvement persists for years after the beginning of treatment (Craske & Barlow, 1993; O'Sullivan & Marks, 1991). Unfortunately, these improvements are often partial rather than complete, and relapses may occur in as many as 50 percent of successfully treated clients, although these people readily recapture previous gains if they are treated again (O'Sullivan & Marks, 1991). People with more severe and longer-lasting symptoms tend to profit less from exposure treatment (Noyes, 1992). Also those whose agoraphobic symptoms accompany a panic disorder seem to benefit less than others from exposure therapy alone. We shall take a closer look at this group when we investigate treatments for panic disorders.

SOCIAL PHOBIAS

As with agoraphobia, clinicians are only now beginning to have any consistent success in treating social phobias—persistent fears of social or performance situations in which embarrassment may occur. This recent progress is due in large part to the growing recognition that social phobias have two distinct components that may feed each other: (1) people with these phobias may have incapacitating social fears, and (2) they may lack skill at initiating conversations, communicating their needs, or addressing the needs of others. Armed with this insight, clinicians now treat social phobias by either trying to reduce social fears, providing social skills training, or both, depending on the client (see Box 7–1).

REDUCING SOCIAL FEARS   Although some studies suggest that certain psychotropic medications may help reduce the social and performance fears of people with social phobias (Oberlander et al., 1994; Roy-Byrne & Wingerson, 1992), clinicians have primarily used psychotherapy techniques to achieve this goal. In recent years, for example, behaviorists have effectively employed exposure techniques to reduce

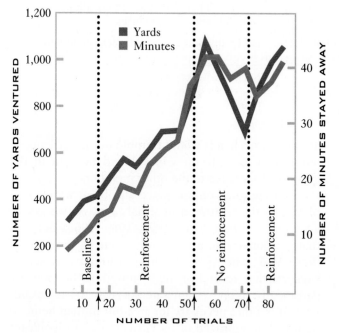

FIGURE 7–2   *When an agoraphobic patient was increasingly reinforced for walking out of and staying away from the front door of the hospital, she ventured increasingly farther and stayed away longer. When reinforcements were then stopped, she initially ventured even farther and stayed away even longer ("extinction burst"), but then steadily decreased the distance and time spent away from the hospital. When reinforcements were reinstated, she again ventured farther and stayed away longer. (Adapted from Agras et al., 1968.)*

TABLE 7-2

SELF-HELP INSTRUCTIONS FOR THE CLIENT WITH AGORAPHOBIA

When you are troubled by fear, the best treatment is to practice in those situations in which the fear occurs. When you practice *systematically* and *persistently*, you will experience a decrease of your fear. For those people who are fearful of going into the street alone the treatment procedure is as follows:

1. Each treatment session takes 90 minutes of your time. It is very important that you stick to these times. It is necessary to choose those times when you have nothing else to do and when you are at home alone. During treatment hours, you are therefore not allowed to receive any guests.

2. Since you will have to practice 90 minutes *in one session*, you *cannot* practice 60 minutes in the morning and then do the remainder in the afternoon. In that case, it is very likely your fear will increase rather than decrease. When you are tired of walking, you may, of course, rest for a few minutes.

3. Go into the street alone and start walking until you feel uncomfortable or tense. Then return to your home immediately. (Taking the dog and a bicycle with you is not permitted.)

4. Note the time that you are out on the street. Take a notebook in which you write down this period of time.

5. After this go outside again. Again, walk until you become tense or anxious. Then return to your home immediately, and, as before, write down the time that you have spent out on the street.

6. Continue practicing until 90 minutes have passed by.

7. Copy down the times you have scored during the last three practice sessions on the special form. Put this form in an envelope and send it to us that same day. We can then check how you are coming along. Postage is free.

8. It is very important to write down the times you have scored. In this way, you can see for yourself how much progress you have made. Research has shown that people who write down their times improve more than people who do not.

9. You are supposed to try to enlarge the distance you walk away from your home. Therefore, you are not allowed to walk in circles. You are not allowed to do any shopping or any talking to friends and acquaintances.

10. *Progress will not always continue at the same pace.* You should not let yourself be discouraged by this fact. Some people might notice rapid initial progress and later on a decrease. Usually this is only a temporary problem.

Source: Emmelkamp, 1982, pp. 299–300.

social fears (Hope & Heimberg, 1993; Scholing & Emmelkamp, 1993; Turner et al., 1992; Mattick, Peters, & Clarke, 1989). Here again the therapists guide, encourage, and persuade clients with social phobias to expose themselves to dreaded social situations and to remain until their fear subsides. Usually exposure is gradual, beginning with the situations they find least frightening and moving up the hierarchy from there. Often the exposure approach includes a home-based self-help dimension in which clients are instructed on how to confront social situations on their own (Heimberg et al., 1990).

Group therapy often provides an ideal setting for these exposure treatments, enabling people to confront the social situations they fear head on in an atmosphere of support and concern (Hope & Heimberg, 1993; Heimberg et al., 1991, 1990; Rose, 1990). One woman who was afraid of blushing in front of people had to sit in front of other group members with her blouse slightly opened until her fear dissipated (Emmelkamp, 1982). Similarly, a man who was afraid that his hands would tremble in the presence of others had to write on a blackboard in front of the group and serve tea to the other members.

Cognitive interventions have also been widely employed in the treatment of social fears. As we saw in Chapter 6, Albert Ellis (1991, 1989, 1962) believes that irrational assumptions are often at the root of these and other psychological disorders. Research suggests that several of the assumptions he cites are particularly likely to generate social fears; for example, "It is a dire necessity for an adult human being to be loved or approved of by virtually every significant other person in his community," or "Your general worth and self-acceptance depend upon the goodness of your performance and the degree that people approve of you" (Golden, 1981).

In Ellis's technique of ***rational-emotive therapy*** the practitioner's role is to point out the irrational assumptions held by clients, offer alternative (more realistic) assumptions, and assign homework that gives clients practice at challenging old assumptions and applying new ones. As clients with social phobias adopt new assumptions, their social fears are expected to lessen. The procedure is illustrated in the following discussion between Ellis and a client who fears that he will be rejected if he speaks up at gatherings. This discussion took place after the client had followed a homework assignment in which he was to observe his self-defeating thoughts and beliefs and force himself to say anything he had on his mind in social situations, no matter how stupid it might seem to him.

> After two weeks of this assignment, the patient came into his next session of therapy and reported: "I did what you told me to do."
>
> "Yes? And what happened?"
>
> "Quite a lot! I found it much more difficult than I thought it would be to put what you said into effect. Really difficult!"
>
> "But you did so, nevertheless?"
>
> "Oh, yes. I kept doing, forcing myself to do so. Much more difficult than I expected, it was!"
>
> "What was difficult, exactly?"
>
> "First of all, seeing those sentences. The ones you said I was telling myself. I just couldn't see them at all at first. I seemed to be saying absolutely nothing to myself. But every time, just as you said, I found myself retreating from people, I said to myself: 'Now, even though you can't see it, there must be some sentences. What are they?' And I finally found them. And there were many of them! And they all seemed to say the same thing."
>
> "What thing?"
>
> "That I, uh, was going to be rejected."
>
> "If you spoke up and participated with others, you mean?"
>
> "Yes, if I related to them I was going to be rejected. And wouldn't that be perfectly awful if I was to be rejected. And there was no reason for me, uh, to take that, uh, sort of thing, and be rejected in that awful manner."
>
> "So you might as well shut up and not take the risk?"
>
> "Yes, so I might as well shut my trap and stay off in my corner, away from the others."
>
> "So you did see it?"
>
> "Oh, yes! I certainly saw it. Many times, during the week."
>
> "And did you do the second part of the homework assignment?"
>
> "The forcing myself to speak up and express myself?"
>
> "Yes, that part."
>
> "That was worse. That was really hard. Much harder than I thought it would be. But I did it."
>
> "And—?"
>
> "Oh, not bad at all. I spoke up several times; more than I've ever done before. Some people were very surprised. Phyllis was very surprised, too. But I spoke up." . . .
>
> "And how did you feel after expressing yourself like that?"
>
> "Remarkable! I don't remember when I last felt this way. I felt, uh, just remarkable—good, that is. It was really something to feel! But it was so hard. I almost didn't make it. And a couple of other times during the week I had to force myself again. But I did. And I was glad!"
>
> "So your homework assignments paid off?"
>
> "They did; they really did."
>
> Within the next few weeks, this patient, largely as a result of doing his homework assignments, became somewhat less inhibited socially and was able to express himself more freely than he had ever been able to do before. It is quite doubtful whether, without this kind of homework assignment, he would have made so much progress so quickly.
>
> *(Ellis, 1962, pp. 202–203)*

It is apparent from cases such as this that Ellis, too, uses in vivo exposure techniques in his therapy. He believes that this exposure is necessary to help clients change their assumptions: "Unless phobic individuals act against their irrational beliefs that they must not approach fearsome objects or situations . . . , can they ever really be said to have overcome such beliefs?" (Ellis, 1979, p. 162). Behaviorists might argue that exposure is playing a more direct and influential role in this cognitive treatment than Ellis acknowledges (Scholing & Emmelkamp, 1993).

Numerous studies indicate that rational-emotive therapy and similar cognitive approaches reduce social fears (Emmelkamp, 1994; Chambless & Gillis, 1993; Hope & Heimberg, 1993; Robin, 1992). Moreover, these reductions are still apparent in follow-up observations up to five years after treatment (Heimberg et al., 1991; Mersch, Emmelkamp, & Lips, 1991). Ellis's therapy has been applied to other anxiety disorders, as well as to other categories of mental dysfunctioning, but nowhere does it perform better than as a treatment for social phobias. At the same time, research also suggests that cognitive therapy, like exposure treatment, rarely enables clients to overcome social phobias fully. Although it does reduce social fear, it does not consistently help people perform effectively in the social realm (Gardner et al., 1980). This is where social skills training has come to the forefront (Emmelkamp, 1994; Stravynski, Marks, & Yule, 1982).

SOCIAL SKILLS TRAINING *Social skills training* combines several behavioral techniques in an effort to help people acquire needed social skills. Therapists usually model appropriate social behaviors for clients and encourage the clients to try them out. Typically clients role-play with the therapists, rehearsing their new social behaviors until they become proficient. Throughout the process, therapists provide candid feedback and reinforce (praise) the clients for effective social performances.

Social skills training groups and assertiveness training groups often serve those functions. Members try out and rehearse new social behavior with or in front of other group members. The group can provide a consensus on what is socially appropriate, and social reinforcement from group members is often more powerful than reinforcement from a therapist alone.

Some practitioners have devised exercises to help group members develop the skills of social interaction (Rimm & Masters, 1979). One beginning exercise focuses on *greetings*, requiring that each member turn to a neighbor and say, "Hello, how are you?" The neighbor replies, "Fine, how are you?" This exchange is to be made with warmth, good eye contact, and a strong, assertive tone of voice. *Exchanging compliments* is an exercise designed to help group members who have difficulty giving and receiving compliments. One person turns to another and delivers a warm and emphatic compliment, such as "Gee, I really like the way you're wearing your hair today." The recipient is encouraged to respond with an acknowledgment, such as "Thank you, that makes me feel good," or "Thanks, I thought I'd try something different." An exercise called *small talk* has a member who is "it" designate two other members and give them a topic for light conversation ("Harry and Louise, discuss the weather"). As always, the therapist encourages and praises good eye contact, spontaneity, and warmth.

Studies have found that social skills training helps socially fearful people perform better in social situations (Emmelkamp, 1994; Mersch et al., 1991), but it appears that this form of treatment alone has only a limited effect on social phobias. Clients may become

BOX 7–1

LIGHTS, CAMERA, ANXIETY: TREATING STAGE FRIGHT

Many clinicians consider severe *stage fright* to be a social phobia because it involves a fear of performance situations in which embarrassment may occur. Yet most people are uncomfortable in front of an audience. It has been estimated that between 55 and 85 percent of the population feels uncomfortably anxious when speaking in public (Stein, Walker, & Forde, 1994; Motley, 1988).

Michael Motley, a professor of rhetoric and communications, offers public speaking courses to help people deal with this common form of anxiety. His approach is to change people's attitudes toward public speaking and correct the widespread myths about it. He tries to take away their fear of making mistakes by convincing them that it's OK to make mistakes. He teaches his students to view speeches as communication rather than performance, to realize that audiences are really much more interested in hearing what they have to say than in criticizing the way they are saying it. Research indicates that a speaker's nervousness is rarely noticed by the audience, even by those who are trained to detect anxiety cues and told to look for them.

In addition, Motley helps speakers to understand, anticipate, and recognize the physiological arousal that accompanies public speaking. Heart rate usually increases greatly just before a speech, rising from an average resting rate of 70 beats per minute to between 95 and 140. Once the speech begins, the heart rate jumps again to between 110 and 190 beats per minute. This second increase has taken many speakers by surprise, convincing them they were about to fall apart. Actually, it is only a temporary surge that tends to subside within 30 seconds, and the period can usually be made shorter yet if the speaker practices monitoring its rise and inevitable fall.

Motley offers the following tips for public speaking:

Decide on your specific objectives first. Before you think about anything else, know one or two major points you want to communicate. Then plan the best way to get them across.

Put yourself in your audience's place. Recognize how you and most of the audience differ in attitudes, interests, and familiarity with what you are talking about. Then speak to them on their terms, in their language.

Don't memorize, don't read. Except for a few carefully chosen gems—memorable phrases or examples you know will work well—be as spontaneous as possible. Don't rehearse to the point that you find yourself saying things exactly the same way each time. Use brief notes to keep yourself organized.

Speak to one person at a time. Looking at and talking to individuals in the audience helps keep you natural; it

Bound & Gagged

Contrary to popular beliefs, the goal of assertiveness training groups is to teach people to express their needs in socially "acceptable" ways, not to have them lash out at others uncontrollably. Thus, the approach may be useful for people who are generally hostile as well as for those who are socially anxious. (Copyright 1993 Tribune Media Services, Inc. All rights reserved.)

feels foolish orating at one person. Speak to that person as long as it is mutually comfortable, usually up to 15 seconds.

Try not to think about your hands and facial expressions. Instead, concentrate on what you want to get across and let your nonverbal communication take care of itself. Conscious attention to gestures leads to inhibition and awkwardness.

Take it slow and easy. People in an audience have a tremendous job of information-processing to do. They need your help. Slow down, pause, and guide the audience through your talk by delineating major and minor points carefully. Remember that your objective is to help the audience understand what you are saying, not to present your information in record time.

Speak the way you talk. Speak as you do in casual conversation with someone you respect. Expecting perfection is unrealistic and only leads to tension. The audience is interested in your speech, not your speaking.

Ask for advice and criticism. For most people, careful organization and a conversational style add up to a good speech. A few speakers, however, have idiosyncrasies that distract an audience. Solicit frank criticism from someone you trust, focusing on what might have prevented you from accomplishing your objectives. Usually people can correct problems themselves once they are aware of them. If you don't feel you can, take a course in public speaking or see a speech consultant. *(Motley, 1988, p. 49)*

Unfortunately, Motley's exact approach is of limited help to such performing artists as dancers, actors, singers, and musicians. Whereas *what* a public speaker says is more important than *how* it is said, how an artist *performs* is crucial. Another difference between public speaking and artistic performances is that the physiological effects of anxiety, particularly poor concentration and trembling, can interfere with the quality of a performance by reducing the performer's fine motor control.

In a survey by the International Conference of Symphony and Opera Musicians, 24 percent of professional classical musicians reported having a problem with performance anxiety, or stage fright, and 16 percent described their problem as severe (Fishbein et al., 1988). The study also found that many of these individuals drink alcohol or use anxiety-reducing drugs, particularly *beta blockers*, often without prescriptions, to reduce their performance anxiety. Clinical research has increasingly suggested that beta blockers may be useful for impaired musicians, dancers, and the like because they reduce the palpitations and tremors that can interfere with performance (Noyes, 1988), but in the wrong dosage the drugs can cause more problems than they solve.

A different approach was attempted in a study of thirty-four musicians with stage fright (Clark & Agras, 1991), which found that cognitive-behavioral group therapy along with exposure techniques was effective in reducing performance anxiety. The therapists targeted the musicians' exaggerated beliefs about the importance of any one performance and provided coping models and relaxation training. This treatment reduced the levels of subjective anxiety, improved confidence, and even improved the quality of the musical performance.

more adept socially as a result of treatment, but they often continue to experience uncomfortable levels of fear (Marks, 1987; Shaw, 1979; Falloon et al., 1977).

Thus, while exposure treatment, cognitive therapy, and social skills training are each helpful in the treatment of social phobias, it appears that no single one of them is consistently able to bring about a complete change. Studies directly comparing the three approaches usually find that each is helpful but that none is superior to the others (Wlazlo et al., 1990; Mattick et al., 1989; Gardner et al., 1980). When the approaches are combined, however, the results have been most encouraging (Hope & Heimberg, 1993; Salovey & Haar, 1990; Butler et al., 1984). One study compared the progress of four treatment groups: people who received social skills training, people who received social skills training combined with rational-emotive therapy, people in a consciousness-raising group, and control subjects on a waiting list (Wolfe & Fodor, 1977). The group that received the combined treatment showed significantly more improvement in both fear reduction and social performance than the other three groups.

GENERALIZED
ANXIETY DISORDERS

Generalized anxiety disorders—persistent feelings of worry and anxiety about numerous events or activities—currently are the anxiety disorders least responsive to treatment, although each year approximately 27 percent of all people with this disorder in the United States seek outpatient treatment with a mental health or medical professional (Blazer et al., 1991).

Global therapies, particularly psychodynamic and humanistic-existential approaches, have been applied widely to these disorders and have proved modestly helpful, while problem-based systems of therapy—particularly cognitive therapies, stress management training, and antianxiety drugs—have been somewhat more helpful (Hollon & Beck, 1994; Chambless & Gillis, 1993; Catalan et al., 1984; Barlow & Beck, 1984).

COGNITIVE THERAPIES Ellis's (1991, 1989, 1962) rational-emotive therapy has frequently been applied in cases of generalized anxiety disorder. Rational-emotive therapists help clients pinpoint and change the assumptions that may be causing them to feel such all-encompassing anxiety; for example, "It is awful and catastrophic when things are not the way one would very much like them to be," and "There is invariably a right, precise, and perfect solution to human problems and it is catastrophic if this perfect solution is not found." Although controlled research has been limited, some studies do suggest that rational-emotive therapy brings about modest reductions in anxiety in clients with generalized anxiety disorders (Lipsky, Kassinove, & Miller, 1980).

Aaron Beck has developed another cognitive treatment for generalized and other anxiety disorders that is similar to the rational-emotive approach (Hollon & Beck, 1994; Beck, 1991; Beck & Emery, 1985). As we saw in Chapter 6, Beck believes that the underlying assumptions of people with generalized anxiety disorders are dominated by themes of imminent danger—such assumptions as "A situation is unsafe until it is proved to be safe" and "My security and safety depend on anticipating and preparing myself at all times for any possible danger." According to Beck, assumptions of this kind must be worked on if the people who hold them are to rid themselves of pervasive feelings of anxiety.

Beck centers therapy on altering the numerous anxiety-provoking images and thoughts, called *automatic thoughts,* that arise from the maladaptive assumptions of anxiety-prone persons and bombard their thinking in situation after situation ("What if I fail?"; "Other things might get in the way"; "I'm falling behind."). In a procedure that is somewhat more systematic than Ellis's approach, the therapist helps the client recognize his or her automatic thoughts, observe the faulty logic and assumptions underlying them, and test the validity of the thoughts. As clients increasingly recognize the inaccuracy of their automatic thoughts and underlying assumptions, they are expected to become less prone to see danger where there is none.

This cognitive treatment for generalized anxiety disorders is really an adaptation of Beck's influential and very effective treatment for depression (which is discussed in Chapter 9). It has been applied to generalized anxiety disorders only in recent years, but researchers are beginning to find that it is often somewhat helpful to people with this disorder, reducing their anxiety to more tolerable levels (Hollon & Beck, 1994; Barlow et al., 1992). Indeed, some comparative studies suggest that this approach may be the single most helpful of the various treatments for generalized anxiety disorders (Chambless & Gillis, 1993; Borkovec & Costello, 1992; Butler et al., 1991, 1987; Power et al., 1990, 1989).

STRESS MANAGEMENT TRAINING Some clinicians believe that people with generalized anxiety disorders have simply never learned to manage anxiety in stressful situations. These therapists teach

BOX 7-2

MY MOTHER, THE PSYCHOLOGIST

Many therapists trace their clinical interests to their own backgrounds, particularly to the behaviors or idiosyncracies of parents, siblings, or friends. It appears that researchers, too, may have similar sources of inspiration. A case in point is well-known researcher Donald Meichenbaum, developer of *self-instruction training.*

Meichenbaum has theorized that people who experience anxiety have inadvertently learned to generate counterproductive *self-statements* during stressful situations, and, as a result, react to any difficult situation with fear and discomfort. Correspondingly, he has developed the treatment program called self-instruction training, in which therapists lead clients to make helpful rather than counterproductive self-statements while in difficult situations. Where did this theory and treatment approach come from? Meichenbaum (1993) describes some recent insights that he had regarding his mother:

On a recent occasion she related a common and somewhat prototypic account of a coworker who asked her to help move some files. As the story unfolded, my mother not only conveyed what had happened to her, but she also commented on how she felt and thought in complying with this request.

"So, what should I say? I did what she asked. I'm a nice person. Who would know that the files would be so heavy and I could hurt my back?"

"You lifted boxes?" I asked.

"But that's not the worst," she responded. "I came back into the office and I found that Sadie, who asked me to help her, was gone. Now, I start getting angry—not with Sadie, but getting down on myself."

Interestingly, my mother's stories never seem to include mere descriptive accounts of what transpired. She also provides a running commentary evaluating her accompanying thoughts, feelings, and behaviors.

"You know it's bad enough I lifted something that I shouldn't have. I decided I shouldn't get upset too. I noticed that I was working myself up. I caught myself and thought, look you've got choices. You don't have to get yourself down because you made a mistake."

As she was telling me her story, I realized that I had listened to such tales throughout my entire childhood and adolescence. I re-called that each evening at dinner we shared stories of what had happened to each of us and how we had handled these events. Our thoughts and feelings were part of the dinner menu. In addition, free of charge, my mother provided commentary about her thoughts as well as about those of others. She conveyed how we could "notice," "catch," "interrupt," "choose," different thoughts and behaviors. She was the indefatigable problem-solver.

In a moment of insight, I realized that my entire research career, which has been spent trying to understand and measure how adults and children think and how their thoughts influence their feelings and behavior, had its origins at my family's dinner table. My mother was an "undaunted psychologist," coping and teaching us to cope with the normal and not so normal perturbations of life. Perhaps this style was not unique to my mother and such procedures could be applied to those who are not coping well.

Perhaps Meichenbaum's mother is not as well known as David Letterman's Mom, but her contributions to her son's career and to society are no less important, and legions of anxious people are in her debt.

---

clients stress management skills that can be applied during stressful times to keep anxiety from building out of control (Lehrer & Woolfolk, 1993; Sanchez-Canovas et al., 1991). The most common forms of stress management training are *self-instruction training, relaxation training,* and *biofeedback training* (Lindsay et al., 1987).

SELF-INSTRUCTION TRAINING Donald Meichenbaum (1993, 1977, 1975) has developed a cognitive-behavioral technique for coping with stress called **self-instruction training,** or **stress inoculation training** (see Box 7–2). It is based on the belief that during stressful situations, many people make state-ments to themselves ("self-statements"), similar to Beck's automatic thoughts, that heighten their anxiety and render them ineffective. Therapists who provide self-instruction training teach clients to rid themselves of these negative self-statements ("Oh, no, everything is going wrong") and replace them with coping self-statements ("One step at a time; I can handle the situation").

Clients are first taught coping self-statements that they can apply during four stages characteristic of a stressful situation. The first stage is a stage of preparation for an anticipated stress. For example, clients may practice saying things to themselves that prepare them for the challenge of asking for a raise. For the second stage, they learn self-statements that enable them to cope with stressful situations as they are occurring, the kind of self-statements that can help them when they are actually in the boss's office asking for a raise. Third, they learn self-statements that will help them through the very difficult moments when a situation seems to be going badly, as when the boss glares at them as they ask for more money. And finally, they learn to make reinforcing self-statements after they have coped effectively. Here are a few examples of these four kinds of self-statements:

Preparing for a Stressor

What is it you have to do?

You can develop a plan to deal with it.

Just think about what you can do about it. That's better than getting anxious.

Confronting and Handling a Stressor

Just psych yourself up—you can meet this challenge.

This tenseness can be an ally: a cue to cope.

Relax: you're in control. Take a slow deep breath.

Coping with the Feeling of Being Overwhelmed

When fear comes, just pause.

Keep the focus on the present: what is it you have to do?

You should expect your fear to rise.

Don't try to eliminate fear totally: just keep it manageable.

Reinforcing Self-statements

It worked: you did it.

It wasn't as bad as you expected.

You made more out of your fear than it was worth.

Your damn ideas—that's the problem. When you control them, you control your fear.

Once clients are skilled at using self-statements, the next step is typically to subject them to stressful experiences in therapy and instruct them to apply what they have learned. The therapist may employ unpredictable electric shocks, imaging techniques, or stress-inducing films, or have the clients role-play un-

pleasant and embarrassing situations (Meichenbaum, 1977).

Self-instruction training has proved to be of modest help in cases of chronic and broad anxiety (Sanchez-Canovas et al., 1991; Ramm et al., 1981) and somewhat more helpful to people who suffer from test-taking and performance anxiety or mild forms of anxiety (Meichenbaum, 1993, 1972; Kirkland & Hollandsworth, 1980). It has also been adapted with some success to help athletes compete better and people behave less impulsively, control anger, and control pain (Meichenbaum, 1993; Crocker, 1989; Novaco, 1977).

In view of the limited effectiveness of self-instruction training in treating anxiety disorders, Meichenbaum (1972) himself has suggested that it should be used primarily to supplement other treatments. In fact, anxious people treated with a combination of self-instruction training and rational-emotive therapy have been seen to improve more than people treated by either approach alone (Glogower, Fremouw, & McCroskey, 1978).

RELAXATION TRAINING   The relaxation training used for generalized anxiety disorders is identical to that taught in desensitization therapy (pp. 235–236). Over the course of several sessions clients learn how to relax their muscles. It is expected that they will then be able to relax at will during stressful situations, thus reducing or preventing anxiety. Sometimes therapists actually create stressful situations during therapy sessions so that the clients can practice relaxing under stress (Suinn & Richardson, 1971). Suggestion, imagery, exercise, hyperventilation, and even short-acting drugs may be used to induce anxiety for this purpose (Mathews, 1985).

Research indicates that relaxation training is more effective than no treatment or placebo treatment in cases of generalized anxiety disorders (Bernstein & Carlson, 1993; Barlow et al., 1992; Barlow, 1989). The improvement it produces, however, tends to be modest (Butler et al., 1991), and other techniques that induce relaxation, such as meditation, often seem to be equally effective in reducing anxiety (Kabat-Zinn et al., 1992; Mathews, 1984). Research suggests that relaxation training is of greatest help to people with generalized anxiety disorders when it is combined with cognitive therapy or with other stress management techniques (Brown, Hertz, & Barlow, 1992; Butler et al., 1991, 1987; Durham & Turvey, 1987).

BIOFEEDBACK   As we observed in Chapter 4, *biofeedback* is a behavioral-biological treatment technique in which people are connected to a monitoring device that gives them continuous information about a physiological activity (such as heart rate or muscle

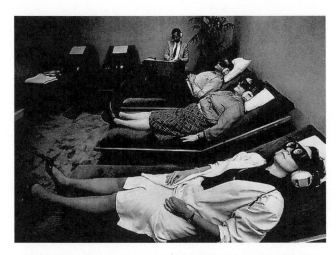

Many businesses now offer stress-reduction programs for employees to help reduce or prevent stress on the job. Using a machine called the Synchro-Energizer, this clinician leads employees through a "brain tune-up" that combines the principles of relaxation and biofeedback training.

tension) in their body. By following the therapist's instructions and attending to the signals from the monitor, they gradually learn to control the activity. With practice, a person can learn to control even seemingly involuntary physiological processes.

Biofeedback has been applied to a wide range of problems. Therapists have taught clients to control brain-wave activity to reduce brain seizures, heart rate to reduce cardiac arrhythmias, and blood pressure level to reduce hypertension (Blanchard, 1994; Wittrock & Blanchard, 1992; McGrady & Roberts, 1992).

Biofeedback has also been used to reduce feelings of anxiety (Stoyva & Budzynski, 1993; Hurley & Meminger, 1992; Raskin et al., 1980). The most widely applied technique uses a device called an *electromyograph (EMG)*, which provides feedback about the level of muscular tension in the body so that clients can learn to reduce it (and their anxiety) at will. Electrodes are attached to the client's muscles— usually the frontalis, or forehead, muscles—where they detect the minute electrical activity that accompanies muscle contraction (see Figure 7–3). The bioelectric potentials coming from the muscles are then amplified and converted into an easily interpreted image, such as lines on a screen, or into a tone whose pitch and volume vary along with changes in muscle tension. Thus clients "see" or "hear" when their muscles are becoming more or less tense. After repeated trial and error, they become skilled at voluntarily reducing muscle tension and, theoretically, at reducing tension and anxiety in everyday stressful situations.

Research indicates that EMG biofeedback training helps both normal and anxious subjects reduce their anxiety levels to a modest degree (Hurley & Meminger, 1992; Rice & Blanchard, 1982). Several direct comparisons have shown that EMG biofeedback training and relaxation training have similar effects on anxiety levels (Brown, Hertz, & Barlow, 1992; Andrasik & Blanchard, 1983). The subjects given EMG feedback are better able than relaxation-trained subjects to reduce their EMG readings (Coursey, 1975; Canter et al., 1975), but the two techniques produce similar results on all other indicators of anxiety (Canter et al., 1975).

In efforts to reduce anxiety, biofeedback therapists have also used an *electroencephalograph (EEG),* which records electrical activity in the brain, to teach clients to produce *alpha waves* voluntarily. Our brain-wave patterns—that is, the rhythmic electrical discharges in our brains—vary with our activities. Alpha waves occur when we are in a relaxed wakeful state. It has been suggested that biofeedback-induced increases in alpha-wave activity will lead to greater relaxation and be of help to anxious people (Hardt & Kamiya, 1978). Unfortunately, the production of alpha waves does not appear to promote relaxation consistently in either normal or highly anxious people. Thus this method appears to have only limited potential as a treatment for generalized anxiety disorders (Blanchard et al., 1992; Andrasik & Blanchard, 1983).

Heart-rate feedback, which teaches clients voluntarily to slow their heartbeat, is yet another biofeedback technique that has been applied to generalized anxiety disorders (Heffernan-Colman et al., 1992; Rupert & Schroeder, 1983). Unfortunately, research

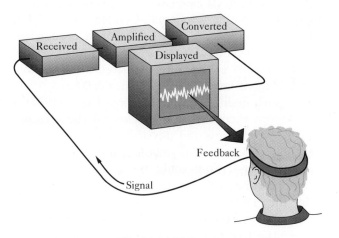

FIGURE 7–3 *This biofeedback system is recording tension in the forehead muscle of a headache sufferer. The system receives, amplifies, converts, and displays information about the tension, allowing the client to "observe" it and to try to reduce his tension responses.*

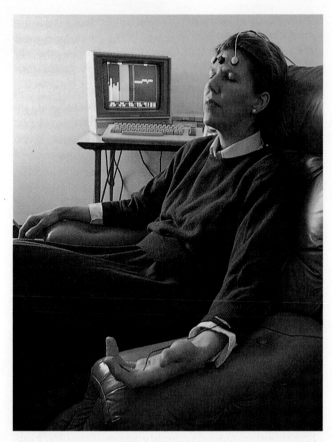

The muscular tension experienced by this client is detected by electrodes attached to her body and displayed on the nearby monitor. Electromyograph biofeedback training has proved modestly helpful in reducing anxiety.

suggests that this technique, too, is of limited help to anxious clients (Rice & Blanchard, 1982; Emmelkamp, 1982). Most subjects are able to slow their heart rate only slightly and are usually dismayed to learn how much easier it is to speed the rate up than to reduce it (Heffernan-Colman et al., 1992; Blanchard & Epstein, 1978). Moreover, even when anxious subjects do learn to slow their heart rate, the reduction is not consistently associated with a subjective feeling of lower anxiety (Nunes & Marks, 1976, 1975). Such findings have led George Engel (1974), a well-known theorist and researcher on the relationship between stress and physical functioning, to reflect, "If one taught an anxious patient to slow his heart, the end result could be an anxious patient whose heart beats slower" (p. 303).

In the 1960s and 1970s, many people hailed biofeedback training as an approach that would change the face of clinical treatment. This early expectation has not been fulfilled. So far, biofeedback procedures have tended to be more cumbersome, less efficient, and less productive than mental health clinicians had envisioned (Wittrock & Blanchard, 1992;

Blanchard & Epstein, 1978). The techniques have played an important adjunct role in the treatment of some physical problems, including headaches, gastrointestinal disorders, seizure disorders, and such neuromuscular disorders as cerebral palsy (King, 1992; Whitehead, 1992; Blanchard et al., 1992, 1982), but they have played a limited role in the treatment of generalized anxiety disorders and other psychological problems.

ANTIANXIETY DRUGS   It would be hard to find someone in our society who is not familiar with the words "tranquilizer" and "Valium." This familiarity reflects the enormous impact that antianxiety medications have had on our culture at large, not to mention the mental health profession. It is easy to forget that these medications have emerged only in the past thirty years.

Until the 1950s, medications called *sedative-hypnotic drugs*, particularly *barbiturates*, were the major biological treatment for anxiety disorders (Lader, 1992; Hollister, 1986). These drugs, used to sedate people at low doses and help them fall asleep at higher doses, created serious problems. They made people very drowsy, too high a dose could lead to death, and those who took barbiturates over an extended period could become physically dependent on them.

In the late 1940s, however, Frank Berger, a chemist who was trying to develop a more effective antibiotic, synthesized a compound called **meprobamate.** When he tested this drug on animals, he discovered that it was an excellent muscle relaxant. Subsequent testing showed that meprobamate also reduced anxiety both in animals and in humans (Berger, 1963). In the 1950s meprobamate was released as a new kind of antianxiety medication under the brand name Miltown.

Meprobamate was less dangerous and less addictive than barbiturates, but it still caused drowsiness, so researchers continued to search for more satisfactory antianxiety medications. In 1957 Lowell Randall tested a drug named *chlordiazepoxide*, a member of the family of drugs called **benzodiazepines** (see Table 7–3). This drug had actually been developed in the 1930s and put aside as seemingly useless, but Randall noticed that chlordiazepoxide tranquilized animals without making them extremely tired. Chlordiazepoxide was soon marketed under the brand name Librium. Several years later another benzodiazepine drug, *diazepam*, was developed and marketed under the brand name Valium.

From the beginning, researchers confirmed that benzodiazepines reduced anxiety both in animals and in humans (Rickels, 1978). Moreover, benzodiazepines often enhanced the effectiveness of psychotherapeutic approaches (Noyes et al., 1984). The benzodiazepine drugs quickly became popular among health professionals. They not only seemed to reduce anxiety without making people exceptionally tired but appeared relatively nontoxic even in large dosages. Unlike barbiturates, they did not pose great danger to life, and when taken alone, they did not slow the respiratory system. Doctors and patients alike looked at benzodiazepines as miracle drugs (Lader, 1992). Some benzodiazepines also gained wide use as sleeping medications.

Only years later did researchers begin to understand the reasons for the effectiveness of benzodiazepines. As we saw in Chapter 6, in 1977 two separate research teams discovered that there are specific neuron sites in the brain that receive benzodiazepines (Mohler & Okada, 1977; Squires & Braestrup, 1977) and that these receptor sites are the same ones that ordinarily receive GABA (gamma-aminobutyric acid), a neurotransmitter that inhibits neuron firing, thus slowing physical arousal throughout the body and reducing anxiety (Barondes, 1993; Nutt, 1990). When benzodiazepines bind to these neuron receptor sites, particularly those receptors known as GABA-A receptors, they apparently enhance the ability of GABA to bind to them as well, and so improve GABA's ability to slow neuron firing and reduce bodily arousal (Lloyd, Fletcher, & Minchin, 1992).

Benzodiazepines are prescribed for generalized anxiety disorders more than for other kinds of anxiety disorders. The drugs are not particularly helpful in

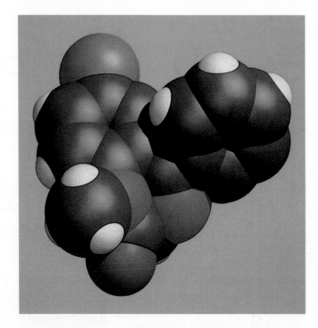

A computer-drawn molecule of the antianxiety drug "diazepam," known by the trade name Valium.

cases of specific phobias (Klein, Rabkin, & Gorman, 1985) or obsessive-compulsive disorders (Klein et al., 1985), but controlled studies reveal that they do sometimes reduce the symptoms of generalized anxiety disorder (Leonard, 1992; Klein et al., 1985).

Because they initially offered so much promise and appeared relatively safe, these antianxiety medications became the most widely prescribed drugs in the

TABLE 7-3

DRUGS THAT REDUCE ANXIETY

CLASS/GENERIC NAME	TRADE NAME	USUAL DAILY DOSE (MG)	ABSORPTION
Benzodiazepines			
Alprazolam	Xanax	0.75–4.0	Rapid
Chlordiazepoxide	Librium	15–100	Rapid
Clorazepate dipotassium	Tranxene	15–60	Very rapid
Clonazepam	Klonopin	1–4	Very rapid
Diazepam	Valium	4–40	Very rapid
Lorazepam	Ativan	2–6	Intermediate
Oxazepam	Serax	30–120	Slow
Triazolam	Halcion	0.125–0.250	Rapid
Azaspirones			
Buspirone	BuSpar	15–60	Slow
Beta blockers			
Propanolol	Inderal	10–40	Rapid
Atenolol	Tenormin	50–100	Rapid

Source: Physician's Desk Reference, 1994; Shader & Greenblatt, 1993, p. 1399; Leaman, 1992, p. 236; Silver & Yudofsky, 1988, pp. 807–809.

BOX 7-3

THE DARK SIDE OF HALCION

In 1982, when *Halcion* (generic name *triazolam*) was first approved by the Food and Drug Administration, it was heralded as the perfect sleeping pill. Unlike other benzodiazepines, which linger in the body and leave people somewhat groggy the next day, Halcion is metabolized in 4 to 6 hours. This gave Halcion such an advantage over other medications that within a few years it became the most commonly prescribed sleeping pill in the world. More than 7 million orders were filled by American pharmacists in 1990 alone.

Unfortunately, the other side to Halcion's quick removal from the body is a possible "rebound effect" of severe daytime anxiety. In addition, users have reported numerous troubling undesired effects, such as confusion, memory loss, depression, agitation, and aggression, and many people have become physically dependent on the drug.

Throughout the 1980s the FDA collected individual case reports of

undesired effects associated with Halcion through its "postmarketing surveillance" process, which requires doctors and drug companies to pass along all patients' complaints about a drug, regardless of their apparent merit. In 1989, after noting an abundance of reports of anxiety, memory

loss, hostility, and paranoid behaviors in Halcion users, particularly after two or more weeks of consistent use, the FDA decided to investigate the drug. The drug's manufacturer, Upjohn Co., defended its product, claiming that spontaneous case reports can be misleading and that only controlled studies can determine whether a drug is problematic. Upjohn said it had no information that would suggest that Halcion was of any danger to its users. The FDA voted not to place any restrictions on the drug.

Then the news media began to report homicides committed by persons who blamed their actions on the drug. The first such case involved a Utah woman who killed her mother while on Halcion and then sued Upjohn. Without conceding that Halcion was in any way to blame, the company settled the case out of court. Upjohn was subsequently named in dozens of civil suits.

The controversy escalated in 1991, when Upjohn acknowledged that it had inadvertently underreported such

---

United States (Strange, 1992; Hollister, 1986). Lately, however, clinicians have begun to realize that this growth was excessive and potentially dangerous (Lader, 1992; Rickels & Schweizer, 1990).

Several problems have emerged. First, it became clear that benzodiazepines alone are not a long-term solution for anxiety. When the medications are stopped, many clients' anxieties return as strong as ever (Rickels & Schweizer, 1990; Lindsay et al., 1987). Second, although benzodiazepines are not addictive when they are taken for a short time and in a low dosage, it eventually became clear that people who take them in large dosages for an extended time can become physically dependent on them and can also develop significant undesired effects—drowsiness, lack of coordination, impaired memory, depression, aggressive behavior, and worse (Apter, 1993; Lader, 1992; Strange, 1992) (see Box 7–3).

Third, some evidence emerged in animal studies that long-term use of benzodiazepines may gradually erode one's ability to cope with stress, thus producing a greater dependence on the drug over the years (Roy-Byrne & Wingerson, 1992). Fourth, although benzodiazepines are not toxic themselves, clinicians learned that they do *potentiate*, or multiply, the effects of other toxic drugs, such as alcohol (Allen & Lader, 1992). People on these antianxiety drugs who drink even small amounts of alcohol can experience dangerous, sometimes fatal respiratory slowdown. And finally, it was discovered that because these drugs act so quickly and are so easy to take, family physicians would frequently prescribe them for patients who did not have serious anxiety disorders, unwisely exposing them to the drugs' addictive or potentiating effects (Lader, 1992; Knesper et al., 1985).

undesired effects as paranoia and memory loss in "protocol 321," a 1973 clinical trial of Halcion. Other damaging evidence was uncovered: The particular researcher who had enrolled, treated, and examined the participants in some of the clinical tests that led to the FDA's original approval of Halcion confessed to fraudulent reporting in several other drug studies. Upjohn argued, however, that his role in the Halcion studies had been negligible and that even without his data, the studies showed Halcion to be safe and effective.

Empirical studies since then have shown mixed results regarding Halcion's effects. Most report some memory impairment after the drug is ingested (Roache et al., 1993; Berlin et al., 1993), but there is no agreement on whether or not the drug promotes aggression and disinhibition (Rothschild, 1992; Jonas et al., 1992; Cherek et al., 1991).

In view of the escalating controversy, the FDA conducted a second review of the drug. In May 1992 the FDA advisory committee again decided to let Halcion stay on the U.S. market, but this time it reduced the recommended maximum dose from 0.5 to 0.25 milligrams a day. In addition, the FDA committee recommended strengthening the package warnings about the possibility of rebound effects and hostile reactions. Currently the FDA is continuing to investigate the drug.

Meanwhile, public sentiment seems to have turned against the pharmaceutical company that makes Halcion. The first civil case against Upjohn to be decided *in court* centered on the case of an assistant police chief found guilty of shooting and killing his best friend. After the man was sentenced to jail, his family sued Upjohn and the doctor who prescribed the drug, claiming that Halcion had made him delusional, so that he thought his friend was plotting against him, and that the family had suffered because of the imprisonment. In December 1992 a state court jury in Dallas, Texas, ruled that Halcion had been partially responsible for the murder, and assessed Upjohn and the doctor who prescribed the sleeping pill $1.6 million for actual damages suffered by the family and $200,000 in punitive damages for failing to warn consumers of Halcion's unwanted effects. Some stockholders have since sued the company as well, claiming that they would not have bought stock in the company if they had known about the misleading reports about Halcion's undesirable effects.

Five countries have banned the use of Halcion pending further investigations. In 1993, Great Britain permanently revoked Upjohn's license to market Halcion in the United Kingdom. Several others have lowered the maximum prescribed dosages allowed because the undesirable effects are more common at higher dosages.

The furor over Halcion has resulted in a sizable reduction in the number of prescriptions written for this drug. By 1994 Halcion annual sales had dropped by half. The negative perception of Halcion has led physicians to turn increasingly to other kinds of drugs to help their clients sleep. But unwanted effects are also associated with the alternative drugs, and many people complain that the other drugs prescribed for them are not so effective as Halcion. Until further research more precisely establishes Halcion's unwanted effects, or until a safer and equally effective drug is found for relieving insomnia, Halcion is likely to remain on the market in the United States and many other countries, but with greater warnings and restrictions on its use.

Several new kinds of antianxiety drugs have also been applied to generalized anxiety disorders in recent times (Roy-Byrne & Wingerson, 1992). One group of drugs, called **beta blockers,** bind to receptors in the brain called **β-adrenergic receptors** and thus block the reception of the neurotransmitter *norepinephrine*. Beta blockers are able to reduce specific physical symptoms of anxiety, such as palpitations and tremors, because they prevent norepinephrine from activating the sympathetic nervous system (Tyrer, 1992). So far, however, research indicates that beta blockers bring only minor improvement at best to people with generalized anxiety disorders (Meibach, Mullane, & Binstok, 1987). Another antianxiety drug, *buspirone*—a member of a group of drugs called *azaspirones,* which bind to yet different receptors in the brain—has received more research support than beta blockers. This drug is often as effective as benzodiazepines (Shah et al., 1991) yet appears less likely to lead to addiction (Enkelmann, 1991; Murphy, Owen, & Tyrer, 1989).

While these new antianxiety drugs undergo further investigation, benzodiazepines continue to be the drugs most widely prescribed to curb broad anxiety symptoms (Shader & Greenblatt, 1993). The drugs often do provide temporary and modest relief for generalized anxiety disorders, but they cannot be relied on for significant and lasting improvements.

PANIC DISORDERS

Approximately 54 percent of all residents of the United States with a panic disorder receive treatment each year from a mental health or medical professional (Regier et al., 1993; Narrow et al., 1993). Today the systematic interventions offered by professionals are often quite helpful, but this was not always the case. In fact, until recently clinicians were rarely successful in treating people who experienced sudden and unpredictable outbreaks of panic. Linked in the past with generalized anxiety disorders under the rubric of "anxiety neurosis," panic disorders were usually treated with the same interventions; but while global therapies and stress management techniques were of at least modest help in treating generalized anxiety disorders, they brought almost no improvement in panic disorders (Hirschfeld, 1992; Sheehan, 1982). Even more telling was the fact that antianxiety drugs, particularly benzodiazepines, usually failed to reduce the frequency or intensity of panic attacks (Norman, Judd, & Burrows, 1992). These realizations led to the classification and study of panic disorders as a separate psychopathology and to the eventual development of highly effective biological and cognitive interventions.

DRUG THERAPIES In 1962 the clinical investigators Donald Klein and Max Fink discovered that panic attacks could be prevented or at least made less frequent by *antidepressant drugs*, the medications used primarily to lift the spirits of people suffering from depression. This unexpected finding was a clinical breakthrough. Since then, studies across the world have repeatedly confirmed that certain antidepressant drugs bring relief to many people with panic disorders and that the drugs seem to be helpful whether or not the panic disorders are accompanied by depressive symptoms (Klerman et al., 1994; Rickels et al., 1993; Hirschfeld, 1992). Recently *alprazolam* (Xanax), a benzodiazepine drug whose action is somewhat more powerful and different from that of the other benzodiazepine drugs, has also proved effective in the treatment of panic disorders (Rickels et al., 1993; Ballenger et al., 1988).

As we saw in Chapter 6, researchers have come to believe that panic attacks may be related to abnormal activity of the neurotransmitter norepinephrine at certain neuron sites in the brain (Papp et al., 1992; Uhde et al., 1989, 1985, 1984; Redmond, 1985; Klein, 1964). It seems that the antidepressant drugs act to restore appropriate norepinephrine activity in people with a panic disorder, particularly in the locus coeruleus, a brain area filled with norepinephrine neurons, and in doing so help to reduce the symptoms of the disorder.

Altogether, studies conducted around the world indicate that these drugs bring at least some improvement to 80 percent of patients who have a panic disorder (Hirschfeld, 1992). Approximately 40 percent

reach full recovery or improve markedly, and the improvements have been observed up to four years after the start of treatment. On the other hand, 20 percent of people with this disorder remain severely debilitated in spite of such treatment (Hirschfeld, 1992).

Clinicians have also found antidepressant drugs or alprazolam to be helpful in most cases of panic disorder with agoraphobia, cases in which the client's outbreaks of panic are accompanied by a general fear of entering public places (Rickels et al., 1993; Hirschfeld, 1992; Marks & Swinson, 1992). Unlike panic-free agoraphobia, this kind of agoraphobia may actually be caused by the panic attacks themselves (Barlow, 1988). That is, after experiencing a number of spontaneous panic attacks, the person may begin to anticipate that he or she will have an attack in public and increasingly avoid going out. Antidepressant drugs and alprazolam help break this attack-anticipation-fear cycle, enabling many agoraphobic people to venture out into public places once again (Maddock et al., 1993). As the drugs eliminate or reduce their panic attacks, clients become more confident that the attacks have ceased and less hesitant to approach the settings they have been avoiding.

At the same time, some studies suggest that an antidepressant drug or alprazolam alone is not always sufficient to relieve panic disorder with agoraphobia (Laraia, Stuart, & Best, 1989). In some of these studies, the prescribed dosage may have been too low to have an effect on the panic attacks (Roy-Byrne & Wingerson, 1992). Often, however, the problem seems to be that the client's anticipatory anxiety has become so severe that fear of public outings continues even after the panic attacks are eliminated or reduced by medication (Marks & Swinson, 1992; Klein et al., 1987, 1983). For these clients, a combination of antidepressant drugs and behavioral exposure treatments may be more effective than either treatment alone (Nagy et al., 1993; Mavissakalian, 1993).

COGNITIVE THERAPY As we saw in Chapter 6, a growing number of theorists believe that panic attacks come on when people interpret certain physical sensations (such as faintness, chest pains, or rapid heartbeat) as signs of imminent catastrophe (Ehlers, 1993; Clark, 1993; Rapee, 1993; Barlow, 1989, 1988). The misinterpretation causes further symptoms of panic and becomes a self-fulfilling prophecy. This view is the basis of the cognitive therapies for panic disorders.

Aaron Beck (1988), for example, tries to teach patients that their physical sensations are harmless, thus eliminating misinterpretations. Initially he briefs clients on the general nature of panic attacks, the actual causes of their bodily sensations, and their tendency to misinterpret them. People who experience sudden faintness before a panic attack may be taught that such sensations are often due to a faulty adjustment of their blood pressure mechanism to changes in posture; clients with chest pains are taught that the pain is due to tension in their intercostal muscles; and those who hyperventilate learn that this is typically a harmless reaction to stress. As the clients become convinced that such explanations are accurate interpretations of their physical sensations, they are able to remind themselves in real-life situations that the sensations are not signs of impending catastrophe, thus shorting out the panic sequence at an early point. Over the course of Beck's therapy, clients may also be taught to distract themselves from their sensations by, for example, starting a conversation with someone when the sensations occur.

Beck also induces panic sequences during therapy sessions so that clients can develop and apply their new insights and skills under watchful supervision. In such *biological challenge* procedures, clients whose attacks are ordinarily triggered by a rapid heart rate may be instructed to jump up and down for several minutes in the presence of the therapist or to run up a flight of stairs (Clark, 1993; Rapee, 1993; Watkins et al., 1990). They can then practice interpreting their heightened heart rate appropriately and distracting themselves from dwelling on their sensations.

Research indicates that this and similar cognitive treatments for panic disorders are often quite helpful (Margraf et al., 1993; Clum et al., 1993; Chambless & Gillis, 1993; Craske & Barlow, 1993; Salkovskis et al., 1991; Barlow et al., 1989). In one study thirteen clients with panic disorders received twelve weeks of cognitive treatment, while sixteen similar clients received eight weeks of general supportive therapy, consisting of a weekly monitoring of symptoms and brief support sessions (Sokol-Kessler & Beck, 1987). Those treated with the cognitive intervention went from an average of five panic attacks per week to none over the course of treatment, while those who received support treatment reduced their weekly panic attacks from an average of four to three.

Similarly six recent studies conducted internationally revealed that 85 percent of subjects with panic disorders were panic free both immediately after receiving cognitive therapy and up to two years later, compared to 13 percent of control subjects who were on a waiting list or who received supportive therapy (Chambless & Gillis, 1993).

Head-to-head research comparisons show cognitive therapy to be at least as helpful as antidepressant drugs or alprazolam in the treatment of panic disorder, sometimes more so (Margraf et al., 1993; Brown et al., 1992; Klosko et al., 1990). One study found fewer panic symptoms, less avoidance behavior, and lower levels of anxiety among clients who had been treated with cognitive therapy than among people treated with an antidepressant medication (Clark et al., 1992, 1990). At the same time, the subjects on medication did improve significantly more than subjects who received no treatment. In view of the effectiveness of both cognitive and drug treatments for panic disorders, some clinicians have tried combining these treatments, but it is not yet clear that the addition of medication is more effective than cognitive therapy alone (Clum et al., 1993; Brown et al., 1992).

OBSESSIVE-COMPULSIVE DISORDERS

Approximately 41 percent of all U.S. residents with obsessive-compulsive disorders receive treatment each year from mental health or medical professionals (Regier et al., 1993; Narrow et al., 1993). Before the 1970s, few treatments seemed to be of much help in alleviating these disorders, pathologies in which a person is plagued by repeated unwanted thoughts (obsessions), repeatedly feels compelled to carry out particular behaviors (compulsions), or both (Zetin, 1990; Black, 1974). Today, however, effective behavioral and biological treatments and promising cognitive-behavioral approaches have dramatically changed this gloomy treatment picture.

BEHAVIORAL APPROACH: EXPOSURE AND RESPONSE PREVENTION   In the mid-1960s V. Meyer (1966) treated two patients with chronic obsessive-compulsive disorders by instructing the hospital staff to supervise them around the clock and prevent them from performing their compulsive acts. The patients' compulsive behavior abated significantly, and the improvement was still apparent after fourteen months. Several years later Meyer and his associates (1974) tried the same approach on fifteen patients with moderate to severe obsessive-compulsive disorders. With one exception, "every patient showed a marked diminution in compulsive behavior, sometimes amounting to a total cessation of the rituals. . . . 10 were either much improved or totally asymptomatic" (p. 251).

In the 1970s clinical researcher Stanley Rachman and his colleagues dropped the staff-supervision feature of this procedure and simply instructed clients to try to restrain themselves from performing compulsive acts (Rachman, 1985; Rachman & Hodgson, 1980; Rachman, Hodgson, & Marks, 1971). Clients were repeatedly exposed to objects or situations that typically elicited anxiety, obsessive fears, and compulsive behaviors, but were instructed to refrain from performing any of the behaviors they might feel compelled to perform. Because clients found this very difficult to do, the therapists often went first. As the clients watched, the therapists interacted with the objects without performing any compulsive actions, and then they encouraged the clients to do the same (a form of participant modeling). This *exposure and response-prevention procedure* is demonstrated in the following case description:

The patient had developed some obsessional-compulsive behaviour patterns during adolescence but did not seek psychological assistance until the age of twenty, when he was admitted to a psychiatric hospital suffering from a marked obsessional disorder. His request for treatment had been precipitated by dismissal from his job as a result of excessive washing rituals that interfered with his working capacity. At the time of his admission to the hospital, the washing rituals occupied the greater part of his day. . . . He experienced particular difficulties over elimination. For example, he had to undress before urinating or defecating. After elimination he had to wash intensively and frequently take showers or baths. . . . He also displayed extensive and elaborate avoidance behavior (e.g., he never touched the floor, or grass, or door handles, etc.).

MODELING   In this phase of treatment the patient was asked to watch whilst the therapist touched the items in the avoidance test and then to attempt to touch them himself. This was a gradual process; for instance, the mud and the excrement were initially touched through a piece of paper. After watching the therapist touch the item, the patient was encouraged, but never forced, to imitate this approach behaviour. Inevitably, these sessions incorporated some period of response prevention.

After session fifteen the patient was touching the marmalade, ash and mud, during session twenty-one he touched the urine, and during session twenty-three he touched the smear of excrement. After session nineteen the patient began to report, for the first time, that he was noticing an improvement outside the experimental situation. During subsequent sessions he reported the following signs of improvement:

1. Showering once a week instead of twice a day.
2. Washing after urination was reduced from twenty minutes to six minutes.
3. Swimming for first time in five years. Previously he was put off by the thought of dirty water.
4. Played croquet and touched the dirty ball.

5. Stroked a cat.
6. Didn't worry when the sole of another patient's shoe touched him during his meal.
7. Sunbathing on the grass. Previously he worried about the possibility of dogs having messed on the grass.

RESPONSE PREVENTION   In each of the five sessions the patient spent half an hour touching the smear of excrement and then he was told not to wash his hands. The period of response prevention was progressively increased over the five sessions (one-quarter hour, three-quarters hour, two hours, three hours). Improvement outside the experimental situation was maintained over these five sessions.

TREATMENT PHASE   During the next two months, the treatment procedure of "modeling and response prevention" was carried out in and around the ward. Each day between 10:00 A.M. and 12:00 noon the patient observed the therapist touching and handling dirty objects, participated himself, and was required to refrain from washing his hands or any part of his body or clothes. . . .

PROGRESS   A subjective assessment of progress during the treatment was the patient's increased tolerance for dirt on his body or clothes. At the end of each session the patient reported a decrease in discomfort and anxiety, and over the treatment period as a whole, he reported that he found the modeling easier to perform. A more objective measure is the amount of time spent washing and . . . the number of times the patient washed. He meticulously kept a record of the times, and the record was converted into graph form [Figure 7–4]. A clear change in washing and toilet behaviour can be seen when the figures at the onset and at the end of treatment are compared.

The most marked and important decrease was the reduction of his washing frequency, from fifteen times a day to twice a day, as this reflects the total elimination of compulsive washing following chance contact with "dirty" or "contaminated" objects. At the end of the treatment the patient washed eighty-seven percent less frequently than before treatment, and spent seventy percent less time on this behaviour. Toilet times also decreased, partly because the patient spent less time washing his hands after going to the toilet—over the last month of treatment he never took longer than two to three minutes—and partly because he used less lavatory paper. The number of sheets was reduced from thirty to between eight and ten on each occasion.

(Rachman, Hodgson, & Marzillier, 1970, pp. 385–392)

Some behavioral therapists believe that after several therapy sessions, clients can and should carry out self-help procedures in their own homes (Emmelkamp, 1994; Marks & Swinson, 1992; Mehta, 1990). The following exposure and response-prevention homework assignments were given over the course of therapy to a woman with a cleaning compulsion:

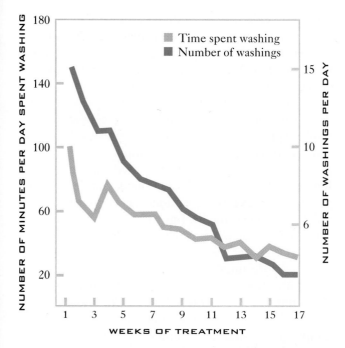

FIGURE 7-4 *When treated for his compulsive cleaning rituals by the behavioral technique of exposure and response prevention, a client showed a steady decline in the frequency of his daily washings and in the total amount of time he spent at them. Over the course of seventeen weeks of sessions, he went from washing himself fifteen times a day (1 hour and 21 minutes) to twice a day (31 minutes). (Adapted from Rachman, Hodgson, & Marzillier, 1970, p. 390.)*

1. Do not mop the floor of your bathroom for a week. After this, clean it within three minutes, using an ordinary mop. Use this mop for other chores as well without cleaning it.
2. Clean the window sill with a few broad sweeps within 20 seconds. The sill is cleaned in this way only once every other week.
3. Buy a fluffy mohair sweater and wear it for a week. When taking it off at night do not remove the bits of fluff. Do not clean your house for a week.
4. Dust the doormat in your livingroom. Do not clean the house for a week.
5. You, your husband, and children all have to keep shoes on. Do not clean the house for a week.
6. Do not have your children go upstairs naked, but let them undress in their bedroom. Do not clean the bedrooms for a week.
7. (The week after) Clean the playroom within ten minutes (only with the vacuum cleaner, no dusting).
8. Vacuum the house within 50 minutes (livingroom, kitchen, hall, and bedrooms) without doing things twice.
9. Drop a cookie on the contaminated floor, pick the cookie up and eat it.
10. Drop your knives and forks on the floor and use them for dinner.

11. Leave the sheets and blankets on the floor and then put them on the beds. Do not change these for a week.

(Emmelkamp, 1982, pp. 299–300)

Eventually therapists help such clients to determine a reasonable schedule and procedure for cleaning themselves and their houses and to institute more normal cleaning policies.

It has been found that between 60 and 90 percent of obsessive-compulsive clients who are treated with this type of technique—in either individual or group therapy—improve considerably (Fals-Stewart, Marks, & Schafer, 1993; Riggs & Foa, 1993; Marks & Swinson, 1992). Improvements include a decrease in the frequency of compulsive acts and in consequent experiences of anxiety, a reduction in obsessive thinking, and better family, social, and work adjustments. Such improvements continue to be observed years later (Marks & Swinson, 1992; O'Sullivan et al., 1991; Marks, 1987). At the same time, relatively few clients who receive this treatment overcome all their symptoms, and as many as one-quarter of them apparently fail to improve at all (Marks & Swinson, 1992; Greist, 1990). Another limitation of this approach is that it does relatively little to help people who have obsessions but no compulsions (Jenike, 1992). After all, the way this intervention "reaches" obsessions is by blocking the resulting compulsive acts.

The effectiveness of the exposure and response-prevention technique suggests to many behaviorists that people with obsessive-compulsive disorders are like the man in the old joke who keeps snapping his fingers to keep elephants away. When someone points out, "But there aren't any elephants around here," the man replies, "See?" One review concludes, "With hindsight, it is possible to see that the obsessional individual has been snapping his fingers, and unless he stops (response prevention) and takes a look around at the same time (exposure), he isn't going to learn much of value about elephants" (Berk & Efran, 1983, p. 546).

COGNITIVE-BEHAVIORAL INTERVENTIONS
Several approaches that combine cognitive and behavioral techniques have been used to treat people with obsessive-compulsive disorders. In one, called *habituation training,* therapists try to *evoke* a client's obsessive thoughts again and again, with the expectation that such intensified exposure to the thoughts will eventually cause them to lose their threatening meaning, to generate less anxiety, and so to trigger fewer new obsessive thoughts or compulsive

acts (Salkovskis & Westbrook, 1989; Rachman & Hodgson, 1980).

In one version of habituation training, clients are simply instructed to summon the obsessive thought or image to mind and then to hold it for a prolonged period (Rachman & Hodgson, 1980). In another version, clients spend up to an hour once or twice a day listening to their own voices on tape repeating their obsessional thoughts again and again (Salkovskis & Westbrook, 1989; Salkovskis, 1985).

For clients who experience obsessions only, habituation training is often the entire thrust of a cognitive-behavioral therapist's plan of treatment (Rachman & Hodgson, 1980). For clients who have further obsessions or compulsions, however, therapists may also employ *covert-response prevention.* The clients are taught to identify, prevent, or distract themselves from carrying out any other obsessive thoughts or compulsive actions that may emerge during habituation training. Over the course of repeated sessions, clients' obsessions and/or compulsions are expected to decrease. The bulk of support for this new cognitive-behavioral approach has come from promising case studies rather than empirical investigations (Hollon & Beck, 1994; Salkovskis & Westbrook, 1989; Headland & McDonald, 1987; Salkovskis, 1983).

Not all cognitive-behavioral theorists agree that habituation training and covert-response prevention address all the key elements of obsessive-compulsive functioning. Psychologists David A. Clark and Christine Purdon (1993) argue, for example, that to reduce obsessions or compulsions, therapists must also guide clients to challenge and change their underlying dysfunctional beliefs that unwanted negative thoughts are terrible and abnormal and in need of control. This alternative view, however, also awaits broad empirical testing.

DRUG THERAPIES   Ever since antianxiety drugs, particularly benzodiazepines, were discovered, clinicians have prescribed them in cases of obsessive-compulsive disorder, but research has only occasionally indicated that the drugs have much effect on this stubborn condition. On the other hand, as we saw in Chapter 6, certain antidepressant drugs, particularly *clomipramine* and *fluoxetine* (brand names Anafranil and Prozac), have emerged as a useful form of treatment for obsessive-compulsive disorders (Klerman et al., 1994; Jenike, 1992; Rapoport, 1991, 1989). In what some observers consider to be a breakthrough study, clomipramine was shown a few years back to be highly effective in treating people suffering from *trichotillomania,* an extremely painful and upsetting compulsion (believed to affect approximately 2 million persons, most of them women, in the United States) in which people repeatedly pull at and even yank out their hair, eyelashes, and eyebrows (Swedo et al., 1989).

According to several studies, these antidepressant drugs bring improvement to between 50 and 80 percent of subjects with obsessive-compulsive disorders, whereas placebo drugs bring improvement to as few as 5 percent of similar subjects (Orloff et al., 1994; Jenike, 1992). The obsessions and compulsions of people who take these antidepressant drugs do not usually disappear totally, but they are reduced an average of 40 to 50 percent within eight weeks of treatment (DeVeaugh-Geiss et al., 1992; Greist, 1990). People whose improvement is based on these drugs alone, however, tend to relapse if the medication is discontinued (Michelson & Marchione, 1991).

Why do these antidepressant drugs alleviate the symptoms of obsessive-compulsive disorder? As we discussed in Chapter 6, biological researchers now believe that the disorder is related to low activity of the neurotransmitter serotonin, as well as to abnormal functioning in two parts of the brain—the orbital region of the frontal cortex and the caudate nuclei. Successful antidepressant drug treatment apparently corrects each of these physical abnormalities.

First, the drugs have been found to increase serotonin activity. In fact, the only antidepressant drugs that alleviate obsessive-compulsive disorders are those that increase serotonin activity (see Figure 7–5); antidepressants that primarily affect other neurotransmitters have no effect on this disorder (Jenike, 1992; Leonard, 1992; Rapoport, 1989). Medical researcher Henrietta Leonard and her colleagues (1991) found that fourteen subjects with severe cases of compulsive nail-biting, or *onychophagia,* improved more when they took the serotonin-enhancing antidepressant drug clomipramine than when they took *desipramine,* an antidepressant drug that operates on neurotransmitters other than serotonin. In fact, seven of the fourteen subjects taking clomipramine showed a 30 percent or better decrease in the amount and severity of their nail-biting. Two subjects stopped biting their nails entirely.

Second, the effective antidepressant drugs have been found to reduce metabolic activity in the orbital region of the frontal cortex and caudate nuclei to more normal levels. In one study, thirteen obsessive-compulsive patients showed reduced, more normal metabolic activity in the orbital region after a year of successful treatment with antidepressant drugs (Swedo et al., 1992). In a related study, psychiatric researcher Lewis Baxter and his colleagues (1992) found that seven of nine successfully treated persons showed reduced, more normal levels of metabolic activity in the right caudate nucleus.

Obviously, the treatment picture for obsessive-compulsive disorders, like that for panic disorders, has improved over the past decade (Zetin, 1990). Once a very stubborn problem, unresponsive to all forms of treatment, obsessive-compulsive disorders now appear to be helped by several interventions, particularly exposure and response-prevention treatment and antidepressant drugs, either separately or in combination (Riggs & Foa, 1993; Greist, 1992; Marks & Swinson, 1992). Moreover, a startling recent research finding suggests that both the behavioral and biological interventions may ultimately have the same effect on the brain. The Baxter research team also included in its investigation a group of nine obsessive-compul-

sive subjects who received exposure and response-prevention treatment rather than antidepressant drugs. The subjects who responded to this behavioral approach, like those who responded to antidepressant drug treatment, showed a marked reduction in metabolic activity in the right caudate nucleus (Baxter et al., 1992). This is the first time that behavior therapy for a mental disorder has been so directly tied to an observable change in brain function.

ACUTE AND POSTTRAUMATIC STRESS DISORDERS

The relatively recent identification of acute and posttraumatic stress disorders as specific diagnostic

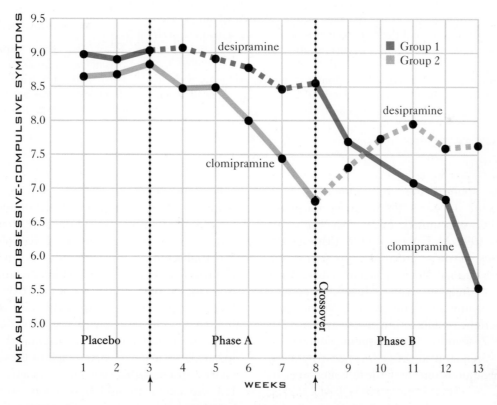

FIGURE 7–5 *A "crossover study" demonstrates that obsessive-compulsive disorders are improved only by antidepressants that increase serotonin activity, not by those that increase norepinephrine activity. The obsessive-compulsive symptoms of all patients in the study stayed the same while the patients were on placebo drugs for the initial 3 weeks. Then, in phase A, the symptoms of patients who were given the serotonin enhancer "clomipramine" for 5 weeks decreased significantly, while the symptoms of the patients given "desipramine," a norepinephrine enhancer, stayed the same. Next, in phase B, when clomipramine patients were switched (crossed over) to 5 weeks on desipramine, their symptoms returned; by contrast, when desipramine patients were switched to 5 weeks of clomipramine, their symptoms decreased significantly. (Rapoport, 1989.)*

BOX 7-4

PREPARING VICTIMS FOR RAPE'S AFTERMATH

Mary Koss and Mary Harvey

Victims as well as significant others can benefit from some discussion of the usual symptomatic responses to rape, the psychological impact of rape, and the length of time required to feel recovered. Such information may prevent more serious problems from developing by making the expectations of involved others more realistic and by encouraging the victim to feel justified to seek help. The information that could be shared with victims and their families might be similar to the following comments. . . .

Rape is a trauma just like a major disaster such as a tornado or a bad car accident.

■ PHYSICAL SYMPTOMS ■

Because of the shock that these events cause to your systems, some physical problems usually develop afterwards. You may experience symptoms you usually associate with extreme fear, such as pounding heart, shortness of breath, or dizziness. You may find your appetite or sleeping is changed as when you're worried about a major traumatic event like a court appearance or are under a lot of pressure at work.

You may notice problems with sex that you've rarely experienced before. Often this is a signal that you're not ready to resume your former activities so quickly. It's perfectly okay to substitute other forms of feeling close and [to avoid] intercourse until you feel ready.

Even though these physical symptoms are typical, they will still upset you. Seek a doctor's care but be sure to tell him or her of your recent rape so that they can treat you properly.

■ FEELINGS ■

Nearly everyone experiences some psychological problems after a rape. Particularly upsetting are nightmares, flashbacks of the experience, and the feeling that you need to talk about

---

categories has spurred the development of numerous treatment programs for the psychologically troubled survivors of traumatic events (Marmar et al., 1993; McCann, 1992; McFarlane, 1991). Although the specific features of these treatment programs vary from trauma to trauma, all the programs share basic goals: they try to help survivors reduce or overcome their lingering symptoms, gain perspective on their traumatic experiences, and return to constructive living (see Boxes 7–4 and 7–5). Treatment programs for Vietnam War veterans who suffer from posttraumatic stress disorder demonstrate how these issues may be addressed.

Therapists have used a combination of techniques to alleviate the posttraumatic symptoms of Vietnam veterans. Antianxiety drugs have reduced the tension, hyperalertness, and exaggerated startle responses that many veterans experience (Marmar et al., 1993; Braun et al., 1990). In addition, antidepressant medications have sometimes lessened nightmares, flashbacks, intrusive recollections, and feelings of depression (Marmar et al., 1993; Nagy et al., 1993; Davidson et al., 1990).

Exposure techniques have also been employed (Mueser, Yarnold, & Foy, 1991; Boudewyns et al., 1990). For example, covert flooding along with relaxation training helped rid a 31-year-old veteran of his frightening combat flashbacks and nightmares (Fairbank & Keane, 1982). The therapist and client first singled out combat scenes that the veteran had been reexperiencing frequently. The therapist then helped the client to imagine one of these scenes in great detail and urged him to retain the image until his anxiety subsided. After each of these flooding exercises, the therapist switched to positive imagery and led the client through relaxation exercises. In response to this treatment, the man's flashbacks and nightmares diminished. Other studies have also suggested that both covert flooding and covert desensitization can reduce the fears, hyperarousal, nightmares, and flashbacks of war veterans (Brown et al., 1992; Keane et al., 1989).

Although symptomatic relief of this kind is useful, most clinicians believe that veterans with posttraumatic stress disorders cannot fully recover until they also develop insight and perspective in regard to their

your experience over and over again until everyone around you is fed up. These are normal psychological processes that operate after a major trauma. Their purpose is to gradually wear down the frightening impact of an experience. They will eventually help you put the experience behind you.

Even if you don't have any problems now, it's not unusual for some to crop up six months or a year from now. The problems that are most common are fears that you never had before or were never that pronounced, feeling bad about yourself and about life in general, conflicts in your intimate relationships, and problems getting back to your former enjoyment of sex.

You may find that the rape has affected your whole family. Don't be surprised if you develop negative feelings about someone that are stronger or different than you've ever had before. Try to talk your feelings over and be specific about what the other person can do to help you feel better. Family members may feel pretty impatient that it is taking you so long to get on top of things.

■ AVAILABILITY ■ OF SERVICES

You may find that although your enjoyment of life is less, you can live with your symptoms and cope. However, there may come a time when you feel that the toll is too great and you need relief. Or, you may notice that your important relationships are suffering or deteriorating. A number of people are available to help you at this point. I'm going to give you a sheet listing some of them so that you'll know who to call.

Besides counselors who could see you privately if you wanted, it is possible to become a member of a group made up of women who have been raped. It can often help to feel less crazy and alone if you know other people who share your experience and know what it's like.

■ LENGTH ■ OF RECOVERY

It usually takes over a year to feel fully recovered from rape, to be able to think of your assault without crying, and to feel the same level of health you enjoyed previously. Going through a court process or anything else that reminds you of the assault may make you feel temporarily worse after you thought you were finally getting on top of things. It's not unusual for there to be ups and downs on the way to recovery.

If it's okay with you, I'd like to call you at home in a few days and see how you're doing. Then, or at a later time, I'd be glad to see you again or help you make an appointment with a counselor.
(Koss & Harvey, 1987, pp. 109–110)

combat experiences and the impact those experiences continue to have on them (Marmar et al., 1993; Weiss & Marmar, 1993). Sometimes clinicians help clients to bring out deep-seated feelings, accept what they have done and experienced, become less judgmental of themselves, and learn to trust others once again. In related work, the psychologist James Pennebaker (1990) has found that talking (or even writing) about suppressed traumatic experiences can help to reduce lingering anxiety and tension.

Most attempts at expressing feelings and developing insight are undertaken in group therapy, or "rap groups," in which Vietnam veterans meet to share experiences and give mutual emotional support. In an atmosphere of group trust, social support, and common experience, many people find it easier to recall events and confront feelings they have been trying to avoid for years (Sipprelle, 1992; Rozynko & Dondershine, 1991). One of the major issues dealt with in rap groups is guilt—guilt about things the members may have done to survive or about the very fact that they did survive while close friends died. Once the veterans are finally able to talk candidly about their combat experiences and guilt feelings, they may start to recover from them (Lifton, 1973). Many are eventually able to gauge their responsibility for past actions more accurately and experience a new sense of personal integrity.

Another important issue addressed in rap groups is the rage that many veterans feel. Many of these people are intensely angry that they had to fight for a questionable cause, face unbearable conditions and tensions in Vietnam, and deal with an accusing society upon their return. In the early stages of therapy these feelings are frequently taken out on the group leader or other members. One team of therapists reported, "We sometimes had feelings akin to those of war prisoners being interrogated by their captors" (Frick & Bogart, 1982). Later the anger may take the form of grief: "Crying from anger may be something to welcome as a part of important growth in a group or individual" (Blank, 1979).

Rap groups originated in 1971, when an organization called Vietnam Veterans Against the War decided that there was a pressing need for a forum in which veterans could discuss their experiences with other

BOX 7-5

THE SOCIOCULTURAL MODEL IN ACTION: TREATING THE VICTIMS OF DISASTER

In 1992, about 250,000 people were displaced by Hurricane Andrew and thousands more were affected by it. For years the American Red Cross has provided food, shelter, and clothing when needed by survivors of disasters such as this and the federal government has helped them find the financial resources for rebuilding their ruined homes and businesses. But until recently no organization addressed the psychological needs of disaster survivors, even though a very large number appear to require mental health services after large-scale disasters. Researchers estimate, for example, that survivors experience a 17 percent increase in mental disorders, and over half suffer from significant mental distress (Rubonis & Bickman, 1991; Roberts, 1990).

In 1991 the American Psychological Association, in collaboration with the American Red Cross, created the Disaster Relief Network to help provide the large numbers of mental health professionals needed after a

In the aftermath of Hurricane Andrew, a mother must wash her newborn baby with water from a jug, while the family takes up residence in a tent within sight of their former home.

disaster. The more than 1200 psychologists in the network volunteer to provide free emergency mental health services at disaster sites throughout the United States (APA, 1991). They have been mobilized for such natural disasters as the Midwest's Great Flood of 1993, Hurricane Andrew in 1992, and the earthquakes in southern California, and such human-caused disasters as the Los Angeles riots, the World Trade Center bombing, and business office shootings.

The Disaster Relief Network provides active short-term *community intervention* because traditional, longer-term mental health services are often not appropriate, and in any case are usually not available or are not sought after a disaster (Joyner & Swenson, 1993). This is unfortunate, because the emotional support that survivors may seek out and receive from friends and relatives often breaks down within a few days or weeks. People soon get tired of hearing about the survivors' experiences and the stress of the disaster. Moreover, many survivors feel guilty about discussing their own losses if others' losses were greater, and so are reluctant to seek out professional help. Those who are unmarried and without children, for example, often feel they are supposed to be able to deal with their losses and anguish better than people who also have to care for children. And many survivors simply do not recognize their own emotional fragility immediately after a disaster (Michaelson, 1993). People who live in poverty are in particular

veterans and together heal their psychological wounds (Lifton, 1973). Rap groups spread throughout the United States. Today more than 150 small counseling centers (Veteran Outreach Centers) across the country, as well as numerous treatment programs in Veterans Administration hospitals, specialize in this approach (Brende & Parson, 1985). In addition to rap groups, these agencies offer individual therapy, counseling for the spouses and children of troubled veterans, family therapy, and assistance in securing

employment, education, and benefits (Blank, 1982). The great demand for such services seems to increase still more during celebrations or anniversaries of wartime events and during new wars. In 1991, during the war in the Persian Gulf, there was an increased demand for services from veterans of the Vietnam War, Korean War, and World War II.

Because most Veteran Outreach Centers have existed only a relatively short time, research into their effectiveness is just beginning (Funari, Piekarski, &

need of community-level interventions. These survivors apparently have more psychological distress after disasters than survivors with higher incomes (Gibbs, 1989), they cannot afford private counseling, and they are less likely to know where to go to seek counseling.

Since psychological needs cannot be addressed if basic survival needs are not met, the first aim of disaster mental health professionals arriving at a disaster site is to help survivors meet their basic needs as quickly as possible. During the Great Flood of 1993, for example, mental health professionals worked in shelters and service centers and rode in Red Cross emergency vehicles to deliver food and water along with counseling services. Other counselors joined flood victims in piling sandbags to protect their homes from further damage. Counselors also used these early contacts with victims as an opportunity to determine which individuals were most in need of counseling. At this stage any counseling had to be brief—perhaps only 10 to 30 minutes with each person, often in a highly distracting environment—a shelter, a sandbag brigade, a line at a water truck.

Once mental health volunteers become involved in the community, they may intervene more actively to meet the psychological needs of the survivors. Psychologists and other mental health workers often use a four-stage approach, as the community workers did during the Great Flood of 1993 (Michaelson, 1993).

1. *Normalize people's responses to the disaster.* The counselors educate survivors about the symptoms they may experience, such as sleep disturbances, eating disturbances, and difficulty concentrating. Survivors of disasters may also suffer from irritation, sadness, grief, fear, anger, and resentment. Essentially, survivors are given permission to experience these emotions and told that these are normal responses to a disaster.

2. *Diffuse anxiety, anger, and frustration.* To diffuse the anxiety, anger, and frustration that survivors often feel after a disaster, counselors help them talk about their experiences and their feelings about the event.

3. *Teach self-helping skills.* Community professionals educate and train survivors to develop such self-help skills as stress management. As part of this effort, they may hand out fliers on handling stress to survivors. The survivors can then put the fliers aside until they need the information.

4. *Provide referrals.* The workers eventually may refer survivors to other professionals and agencies who can provide long-term counseling. Some mental disorders may emerge within days; others, however, may not surface for months after the disaster. It is estimated that between 15 and 25 percent of survivors need more specialized assistance.

The mental health professionals counsel not only the survivors but relief workers, who can become overwhelmed by the traumas they witness. During the Los Angeles riots, for example, the primary responsibility of many counselors was to *debrief* Red Cross workers (Youngstrom, 1992)—to help them vent and normalize their feelings and teach them about acute and posttraumatic stress disorders and how to identify victims who need further treatment. Many mental health professionals who live in the disaster area need counseling themselves, since they, too, are survivors. The dual role they are thrown into may make it difficult for them to deal with their own experiences.

To meet the needs of large numbers of disaster survivors, *paraprofessionals*—lay persons who receive training and supervision from professionals—may also be called upon. Graduate students at various schools in the Los Angeles area provided counseling for survivors of the riots. Some of them were actually more effective than professionals because they were more familiar with the afflicted community and shared the survivors' socioeconomic and minority status.

Clearly, community-level interventions are essential after large-scale disasters to provide psychological counseling to needy survivors who might not seek out mental health services. The Disaster Relief Network has helped address the enormous need for this type of counseling, and at the same time has demonstrated the application of the sociocultural theory at its best.

Sherwood, 1991). So far, clinical reports and empirical studies suggest that they offer an important, sometimes life-saving treatment opportunity. Julius's search for help upon his return from Vietnam was, unfortunately, an ordeal that many veterans have shared:

When I got back from the 'Nam, I knew I needed psychotherapy or something like that. I just knew that if I didn't get help I was going to kill myself or somebody else. . . . I went to see this doctor; he barely looked at me. I felt he "saw me coming" and knew all about my sickness. I was the "sicky" to him. He just kept on asking me all that bullshit about how many children I had killed and was I guilty and depressed about it. He asked how it felt to kill people. He also kept on asking me about my brothers and sisters. But he never asked me about what my experiences were like in Vietnam. He never did. I saw him for treatment for about a month—about three visits, but I quit because we weren't getting anywhere. . . . He just kept on giving me more and more medications. I could've set up my own pharmacy. I needed someone to talk to

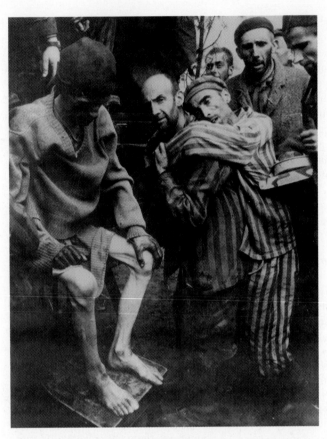

Many survivors of Nazi concentration camps faced a long road back to psychological health. Because knowledge of posttraumatic stress disorders was nonexistent until recent years, most survivors had to find their way back without professional help. The lingering emotional impact of their traumatic experiences was felt not only by them but often by their children and other close relatives.

about my problems, my real problems, not some bullshit about my childhood. I needed someone who wanted to help. The clinic later referred me to another shrink. . . . I guess she thought she was being honest with me, by telling me that she was not a veteran, was not in Vietnam, and did not know what was wrong with me. She also told me that she had no experience working with Vietnam veterans, and that I should go to the Veterans Administration for help. . . .

Two years ago, I made another try to get some help at another agency close to where my mother lives. I was also told to go to the nearest VA. I was given some dope medicine, and I never came back. I kept getting angry and angrier; I felt I was being handed a line of shit by these doctors. I also became scared that there was something really wrong with me now. I just didn't want to go to the VA for help. . . . I blame the VA for my going to 'Nam anyway; I wanted no part of it.

It was only in the last 3 years when my wife made an important phone call to a local Veterans Outreach Center that I started feeling I had hope, that something could be done for me. I received the help that I have always needed. Fi-

nally, I found it easier to hold a job and take care of my family. My nightmares are not as frightening or as frequent as they used to be. Things are better now; I am learning to trust people and give more to my wife and children.

(Brende & Parson, 1985, pp. 206–208)

THE STATE OF THE FIELD

TREATMENTS FOR ANXIETY DISORDERS

Clearly the treatment picture for anxiety disorders has changed greatly over the past fifteen years. Many new approaches have been developed, and anxiety problems that once confounded therapists are now responding to clinical interventions. As we examine the various treatments for anxiety disorders, three major trends emerge:

1. Behavioral, cognitive, and drug therapies have dominated the treatment picture for anxiety disorders. Behavioral interventions are often effective in treating specific phobias, agoraphobia, and obsessive-compulsive disorders, and are often viewed as the treatments of choice in these problem areas. Newly developed cognitive approaches have been quite helpful to people with panic disorders, and somewhat helpful to those with generalized anxiety disorders or social phobias. And antianxiety drugs serve an important adjunct role in treating generalized anxiety disorders, while certain antidepressant drugs, surprisingly, have a major impact on panic disorders and obsessive-compulsive disorders. Finally, global approaches such as psychodynamic and humanistic therapies have sometimes played helpful roles in cases of generalized anxiety disorder and acute and posttraumatic stress disorder.
2. In view of these findings, clinicians now make greater efforts to match anxious clients to particular forms of treatment. They have also become more inclined to combine procedures associated with the various treatment models. Social phobias are now often treated with a combination of exposure therapy, cognitive therapy, and social skills training; many cases of panic disorder with agora-phobia are treated with a combination of exposure techniques and

Many people eventually overcome the effects of traumatic stress. During a reunion, these concentration camp survivors proudly display their tattooed camp identification numbers as symbols of their triumph over their psychological wounds.

antidepressant drugs; clinicians often mix global therapies or cognitive therapy with relaxation training and/or antianxiety drugs in treating generalized anxiety disorders and acute and posttraumatic stress disorders; and in many cases antidepressant drugs are used to complement exposure and response-prevention treatments for obsessive-compulsive disorders.

3. Research has guided clinicians to clarify and alter their treatment procedures for anxiety disorders. Over the past fifteen years behaviorists have become clearer about the importance of exposure in their various interventions and have placed this feature at the center of treatment; biological therapists have become more judicious in their use of antianxiety drugs in light of findings that these drugs can be addictive in high doses; and biological therapists have discovered that antidepressant drugs are more helpful than antianxiety drugs for some anxiety disorders, and have adjusted their medication decisions correspondingly.

For clinicians and for the millions of people who seek help for anxiety, the field's growing effectiveness is a most positive and momentous development.

SUMMARY

■ **PSYCHODYNAMIC THERAPISTS** use global procedures such as free association to help clients uncover and resolve the unconscious issues that they believe are at the root of anxiety disorders. Research has not, however, consistently supported the effectiveness of the psychodynamic approaches in cases of anxiety disorder, nor have global humanistic and existential approaches proved to be highly effective treatments in such cases.

■ **SPECIFC PHOBIAS** were the first anxiety disorders to be treated successfully. They appear to

Rap groups for Vietnam veterans have helped many of their members overcome the anxiety, depression, sleep disturbance, and flashbacks that linger for years after the war.

respond to each of the problem-based therapies, but behavioral therapies have been much more successful than others. The three major behavioral approaches are all *exposure treatments:* desensitization, flooding, and modeling. *Desensitization* has three phases: *relaxation training,* construction of a *fear hierarchy,* and *graded pairing* of feared objects and relaxation responses. In *flooding,* or *implosive therapy,* clients are repeatedly exposed to feared objects or situations and made to see that they are actually harmless. The most effective modeling technique is *participant modeling,* or *guided participation,* in which clients observe and repeat the therapist's actions in the situations they fear.

Research has shown that the exposure approaches to specific phobias are all helpful but that *in vivo exposure* is more effective than imaginal or observational exposure. Many behavioral therapists now combine features of all these methods, being sure to retain the critical feature of in vivo exposure.

■ ATTEMPTS AT TREATING AGORAPHOBIA met with relatively little success until recently. New approaches, however, have offered considerable relief to people with this disorder, particularly behavioral

approaches. Therapists who use exposure techniques typically help clients to venture farther and farther from their homes and to participate in feared situations gradually, step by step. The therapist may use support, reasoning, and coaxing or reinforcement to change a client's behavior. Sometimes support groups and home-based self-help programs make use of these techniques.

■ SOCIAL PHOBIAS often have two distinct components: social fears and lack of specific social skills. Thus clinicians may design treatment according to the client's particular area of difficulty. They may try to reduce social fear by using exposure techniques, group therapy, and various cognitive interventions. They may improve social skills with *social skills training,* a procedure which combines a number of behavioral techniques, including modeling and role playing, in such formats as social skills training groups and assertiveness training groups. Often a combination of exposure techniques, cognitive therapy, and social skills training is used effectively in cases of social phobia.

■ GENERALIZED ANXIETY DISORDERS are currently the anxiety disorders least responsive to treatment. Cognitive therapies, stress management training, and antianxiety drugs are often applied in cases of this disorder. ***Rational-emotive therapy*** is among the cognitive approaches that have been used in an attempt to change beliefs that may be at the root of generalized anxiety. Three forms of ***stress management training*** are commonly employed: *self-instruction training, relaxation training,* and *biofeedback training.* ***Benzodiazepine drugs*** such as diazepam (Valium) reduce anxiety by improving the ability of GABA to slow physical arousal throughout the body. These drugs can be addictive in high doses, however, and are now prescribed less frequently than they were. As a result, biological clinicians have also begun to prescribe some new kinds of antianxiety drugs, including **beta blockers** and **buspirone**, whose effectiveness is now being tested.

■ **ALTHOUGH PANIC DISORDERS** once defied treatment, some highly effective biological and cognitive interventions are now available. Certain antidepressant drugs bring relief to many people with panic disorders. Cognitive therapy teaches patients that the unusual physical sensations that they periodically experience are actually harmless.

■ **OBSESSIVE-COMPULSIVE DISORDERS** also appear to respond to several different approaches. The leading behavioral approach combines prolonged in vivo ***exposure*** with ***response prevention,*** the blocking of compulsive behaviors. In a promising cognitive-behavioral approach, ***habituation training,*** therapists encourage clients to summon their obsessive thoughts to mind for a prolonged period, expecting that such prolonged exposure will cause the thoughts to lose their threatening meaning and generate less anxiety. Finally, most antianxiety drugs are not considered helpful for obsessive-compulsive disorders, but ***antidepressant drugs*** have begun to emerge as a useful form of treatment for these disorders.

■ **PEOPLE WITH ACUTE AND POSTTRAUMATIC STRESS DISORDERS** may receive any of a number of treatment approaches. Techniques used for symptomatic relief include antianxiety drugs, sleeping medications, and exposure techniques. Most clinicians also use supportive and humanistic therapy, including group therapy, to help survivors with acute and posttraumatic stress disorders develop insight and perspective in regard to the continuing impact of their traumatic experiences.

Topic Overview

CHAPTER 8

MOOD DISORDERS

■

MOST PEOPLE'S MOODS are transient. Their feelings of elation or sadness are understandable responses to daily events and change readily without affecting the overall tenor of their lives. The moods of people with mood disorders, in contrast, tend to last a long time, color all of their interactions with the world, and disrupt their normal functioning. Virtually all of such people's actions are dictated by their powerful moods.

DEPRESSION AND MANIA are the dominating emotions in mood disorders. *Depression* is a low, sad state in which life seems bleak and its challenges overwhelming. *Mania,* the extreme opposite of depression, is a state of breathless euphoria, or at least frenzied energy, in which people have an exaggerated belief that the world is theirs for the taking. Most people with a mood disorder suffer exclusively from depression, a pattern often called *unipolar depression.* They have no history of mania and return to a normal or nearly normal mood state when their depression lifts. Others undergo periods of mania that alternate with periods of depression, a pattern called *bipolar disorder* or *manic-depressive disorder.* One might logically expect a third pattern of mood disorder, unipolar mania, in which people suffer exclusively from mania, but, outside of mania caused by a medical condition, this pattern is so rare that there is some question as to whether it exists at all (APA, 1994; Das & Khanna, 1993).

MOOD DISORDERS HAVE ALWAYS captured people's interest, in part because so many prominent people have suffered from them. The Bible speaks of the severe depression of Nebuchadnezzar, Saul, and Moses. Queen Victoria of England and Abraham Lincoln seem to have experienced recurring depressions. Similarly, depression and sometimes mania have plagued such artists as George Frideric Handel, Ernest Hemingway,

Abraham Lincoln was one of many leaders who suffered from episodes of depression. In 1841 he wrote to a friend, "I am now the most miserable man living. If what I feel were equally distributed to the whole human family, there would be not one cheerful face on earth."

Eugene O'Neill, Virginia Woolf, Robert Lowell, and Sylvia Plath (Andreasen, 1980). The plight of these famous figures has been shared by millions, and the economic consequences (costs of treatment, hospitalization, work loss, and so on) amount to $44 billion each year (MIT, 1993). The human suffering these disorders cause is incalculable.

■ UNIPOLAR ■ PATTERNS OF DEPRESSION

Because so much psychological terminology has entered the popular vernacular over the last thirty years, people more dejected and unhappy than usual often say they are "depressed." In most cases, what they are describing is a perfectly normal mood swing, a response perhaps to sad events, understandable fatigue, or unhappy thoughts (see Figure 8–1). Unfortunately, this use of the term confuses a normal mood with a dysfunctional clinical syndrome. All of us experience dejection from time to time; only an unfortunate minority experience unipolar depression.

Normal dejection is seldom so severe as to alter daily functioning significantly, and it lifts within a reasonable period. Downturns in mood can even be beneficial. Some people spend such periods in contemplation, exploring their selves, their values, and their situations, and often emerge with a sense of greater strength, clarity, and resolve.

Clinical depression, on the other hand, is a serious psychological disturbance with no redeeming characteristics. The psychological pain it brings is severe and long-lasting and may intensify as the months and years go by. It is so debilitating that clinically depressed persons may reach a point where they are unable to carry out the simplest of life's activities; some, in fact, try to end their lives.

THE PREVALENCE OF UNIPOLAR DEPRESSION

Surveys suggest that between 5 and 10 percent of adults in the United States suffer from a severe unipolar pattern of depression in any given year, while another 3 to 5 percent suffer from mild forms of the disorder (Kessler et al., 1994; Regier et al., 1993) (see Table 8–1). The prevalence rates are similar in many other countries, including Canada, England, Italy, and New Zealand (Smith & Weissman, 1992; Murphy et al., 1984). In fact, it is estimated that as many as 17 percent of all adults in the world experience an episode of severe unipolar depression at some point in their lives (Kessler et al., 1994; Weissman et al., 1991; Weissman & Klerman, 1985).

A worldwide research project further suggests that the prevalence of unipolar depression is on the rise (Weissman et al., 1992; Klerman & Weissman, 1989). A recent examination of more than 39,000 people in the United States (including Puerto Rico), Canada, Italy, Germany, France, Taiwan, Lebanon, and New Zealand revealed that in most countries the risk of experiencing severe depression at some point in life has steadily increased with each successive generation since 1915. Also, the average age of onset of severe

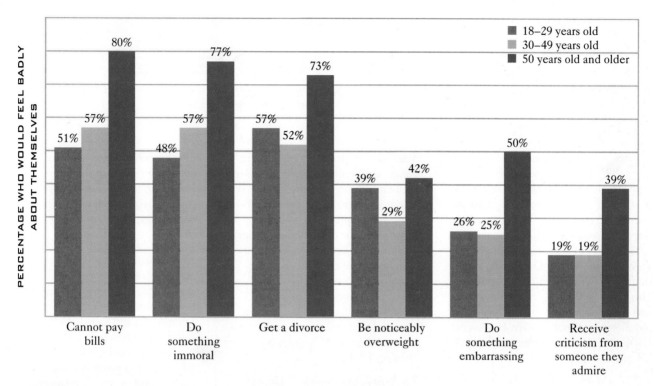

FIGURE 8-1 *What situations make people feel bad about themselves? In part, it depends on their generation. Older adults are more likely than young adults to feel bad about themselves in a wide variety of situations, particularly not being able to pay their bills, doing something immoral, or getting a divorce. (Adapted from Newsweek Poll, 1992.)*

depression, which is now 27 in the United States, has become younger with each successive generation (Weissman et al., 1992, 1991). Although better identification and diagnosis of depression may account for some of these findings, the researchers have largely been able to rule out such artifacts by applying the same diagnostic criteria for each generation under examination (Lewinsohn et al., 1993).

In almost all industrialized countries, women are at least twice as likely as men to experience severe episodes of unipolar depression (Weissman et al., 1991; Klerman & Weissman, 1989) (see Box 8-1). As many as 26 percent of women may have a severe depressive episode at some time in their lives, compared with 12 percent of men (APA, 1993; Weissman & Klerman, 1985; Boyd & Weissman, 1981). Women

TABLE 8-1

MOOD DISORDERS EPIDEMIOLOGICAL PROFILE

	ONE YEAR PREVALENCE	FEMALE:MALE RATIO	TYPICAL AGE OF ONSET	PREVALENCE AMONG FIRST-DEGREE RELATIVES
Major depressive disorder	5–10%	2:1	24–29 years	Elevated
Dysthymic disorder	2.5–5.4%	Between 3:2 and 2:1	10–25 years	Elevated
Bipolar I disorder	0.7%	1:1	15–44 years	Elevated
Bipolar II disorder	0.5%	1:1	15–44 years	Elevated
Cyclothymic disorder	0.4%	1:1	15–25 years	Elevated

Sources: APA, 1994; Kessler et al., 1994; Regier et al., 1993; Weissman et al., 1991.

BOX 8-1

DEPRESSING NEWS FOR WOMEN

More women than men are diagnosed with major unipolar depression. More women report being mildly depressed. The inescapable conclusion is that women are at least twice as likely as men to suffer from unipolar depression (Smith & Weissman, 1992). Depressing news, indeed. This apparent gender difference has generated much theorizing and investigation. One theorist, the psychologist Susan Nolen-Hoeksema (1990, 1987), has reviewed five possible explanations.

1. *The artifact hypothesis.* Women and men are equally prone to depression, but gender differences arise because studies fail to detect depression in men. One reason could be that men find it less socially acceptable to report feeling depressed or to seek treatment. Alternatively, depressed women may display emotional symptoms, such as sadness and crying, that are easily diagnosed, while depressed men may mask these symptoms. It has been suggested that depressed men turn to drink and are

diagnosed as alcoholic. In fact, the gender difference in alcoholism—men outnumber women 2 to 1—is complementary to the gender difference in depression; moreover, many alcoholic persons show other symptoms of depression. Some researchers even go so far as to suggest that depression and alcoholism are similar genetically based disders. The artifact hypothesis, however, lacks consistent research support (Fennig, Schwartz, & Bromet, 1994).

2. *The X-linkage hypothesis.* Depression is caused by a dominant mutation on the X chromosome. Since women are genotypically XX, they run a greater risk of inheriting the gene than men, who are genotypically XY. The hypothesis is supported by the finding that depression is correlated with other X-chromosome abnormalities, such as color blindness. Family pedigree studies, however, have contradicted it. If depression were an X-chromosome disorder, a depressed father would always transmit it to his

daughters but not to his sons; yet studies indicate that more father-son than father-daughter pairs are diagnosed with unipolar depression.

3. *Classical psychoanalytic explanations.* At the Oedipal stage of psychological development a girl realizes that she lacks a penis and believes herself to have been castrated by her mother; she feels both hostility toward her mother and a sense of her own inferiority. She also identifies with her mother. With this background, women's relationships with men are motivated by a desire to possess a phallus in symbolic form. They suffer low self-esteem as a result of their lifelong penis envy, are more vulnerable to loss, and thus are more prone to develop depression. This model lacks empirical support and has been widely criticized as being chauvinistic.

4. *A sociocultural explanation.* The quality of women's roles in society makes them more vulnerable to

are also more likely than men to experience episodes of mild unipolar depression, although the difference in these rates is less extreme (Smith & Weissman, 1992; Weissman et al., 1991). Among children, the prevalence of unipolar depression is similar for girls and boys. All of these rates are similar across all socioeconomic classes (Weissman et al., 1991).

Relatively few differences in prevalence have been found among ethnic groups. White Americans between the ages of 30 and 64 have a somewhat higher rate than African Americans in that age range, but the rates for younger and older adults are the same in

both populations (Weissman et al., 1991). Within both races, unipolar depression is again more than twice as common among women as among men.

Episodes of severe unipolar depression may begin at any age. Approximately two-thirds of severely depressed people recover within six months, some without treatment (APA, 1994; Keller, 1988). Having been depressed once, however, a person has an increased risk of becoming depressed again. Most of those who recover from an episode of severe unipolar depression will have at least one subsequent episode in their lifetime (APA, 1994, 1993; Surtees & Barkley, 1994).

Edvard Munch's painting Melancholy (Laura) *was inspired by his sister's bouts of severe depression.*

5. *The learned helplessness explanation.* Women are more vulnerable to depression because they are more likely to feel they have little control over their lives. Studies have shown that women are more prone to laboratory learned helplessness effects than men. One found that female college students who were exposed to a helplessness-inducing set of insoluble anagrams later performed other tasks much more poorly than their male counterparts (Le Unes, Nation, & Turley, 1980). Nolen-Hoeksema notes, however, that a stringent test of this explanation for depression remains to be carried out.

The artifact hypothesis implies that more effort should be made to identify and treat depression in men. The biological and classical psychoanalytic explanations say that therapeutic resources could be fruitfully focused on women themselves. The sociocultural and learned helplessness explanations suggest that it is society itself that requires "treatment," or restructuring. No explanation of gender differences in depression has gained unequivocal support. Certainly, if one is finally seen to be more persuasive than the others, it will have great influence on the way resources are allocated for the prevention and treatment of this debilitating disorder.

depression. On the one hand, as the housewife role has become increasingly devalued and less rewarding, women in this role may become depressed because they have limited sources of gratification (Gove & Tudor, 1973). On the other hand, working women may be prone to depression because they bear the double burden of housework and a job outside the home.

THE CLINICAL PICTURE OF DEPRESSION

Some depressed people manage to function after a fashion, but their depression robs them of effectiveness and pleasure, as we see in the cases of Derek and Beatrice:

*D*erek has probably suffered from depression all of his adult life but was unaware of it for many years. Derek called himself a night person, claiming that he could not think clearly until after noon even though he was often awake by 4:00 A.M. He tried to schedule his work as editorial writer for a small town newspaper so that it was compatible with his depressed mood at the beginning of the day. Therefore, he scheduled meetings for the mornings; talking with people got him moving. He saved writing and decision making for later in the day.

Derek had always been a thoughtful person and was often preoccupied. His family and colleagues grew used to his apparent inattention and absentmindedness. He often failed to answer people when they spoke to him. Sometimes they were surprised to hear his slow, soft-spoken reply 20 or 30 seconds later. His wife tried to be patient when it took him 20 seconds to respond to "Do you want coffee or tea tonight?" Derek's private thoughts were rarely cheerful and self-confident. He felt that his marriage was a mere business partnership. He provided the money, and she provided a home and children. Derek and his wife rarely expressed affection for each other. Occasionally, he had images of his own violent death in a bicycle crash, in a plane crash, or in a murder by an unidentified assailant.

Derek felt that he was constantly on the edge of job failure. He was disappointed that his editorials had not attracted the attention of larger papers. He was certain that several of the younger people on the paper had better ideas and wrote more skillfully than he did. He scolded himself for a bad editorial that he had written ten years earlier. Although that particular piece had not been up to his usual standards, everyone else on the paper had forgotten it a week after it appeared. But ten years later, Derek was still ruminating over that one editorial. . . .

Derek attributed his inability to enjoy himself and his methodical, passionless marriage to his severe Anglo-Saxon Protestant upbringing. He had been taught that open expressions of affection were ill-mannered. He had never seen his own parents embrace in their fifty years of marriage. In his family, humility was valued more than self-confidence. He had been brought up to do the "right thing," not to enjoy himself. Raucous merrymaking was only for the irresponsible. Even a game of Go Fish had to be played in secret when he was a child.

Derek brushed off his morning confusion as a lack of quick intelligence. He had no way to know that it was a symptom of depression. He never realized that his death images might be suicidal thinking. People do not talk about such things. For all Derek knew, everyone had similar thoughts.

(Lickey & Gordon, 1991, pp. 183–185)

For several years, Beatrice had been irritable, but then for a six-month period, her irritability bordered on the irrational. She screamed in anger or sobbed in despair at every dirty dish left on the coffee table or on the bedroom floor. Each day the need to plan the dinner menu provoked agonizing indecision. How could all the virtues or, more likely, vices of hamburgers be accurately compared to those of spaghetti? A glass of spilled milk was an occasion for panic. Beatrice would bolt from her chair and run from the dining room. Ten minutes later, she would realize that the spilled milk was insignificant. She had her whole family walking on eggs. She thought they would be better off if she were dead.

Beatrice could not cope with her job. As a branch manager of a large chain store, she had many decisions to make. Unable to make them herself, she would ask employees who were much less competent for advice, but then she could not decide whose advice to take. Each morning before going to work, she complained of nausea. In public, she was usually able to control her feelings of panic and felt

a little better when she actually arrived at work and was away from the wary eyes of her family.

Beatrice's husband loved her, but he did not understand what was wrong. He thought that she would improve if he made her life easier by taking over more housework, cooking, and child care. His attempt to help only made Beatrice feel more guilty and worthless. She wanted to make a contribution to her family. She wanted to do the chores "like normal people" did but broke down crying at the smallest impediment to a perfect job. Because Beatrice's volatility put a stress on her marriage, the couple went to a psychiatrist for marriage counseling. The psychiatrist failed to diagnose Beatrice's depression. He provided marriage counseling that was designed for healthy people. Consequently, the counseling failed. Months passed, and Beatrice's problem became more serious. Some days she was too upset to go to work. She stopped seeing her friends. She spent most of her time at home either yelling or crying. Finally, Beatrice's husband called the psychiatrist and insisted that something was seriously wrong.

(Lickey & Gordon, 1991, p. 181)

As these case descriptions indicate, depression has many symptoms other than sadness, and the symptoms often reinforce one another. Chronic indecisiveness, for example, may lead to poor job performance, which in turn leads to a lower self-image, less self-confidence, and still more indecisiveness, as in Beatrice's case. Moreover, depression can be somewhat differently expressed in different people. The symptoms associated with depression span five areas of functioning: the emotional, motivational, behavioral, cognitive, and somatic.

EMOTIONAL SYMPTOMS Most people who are depressed feel intensely sad and dejected. They describe themselves as feeling "miserable," "empty," and "humiliated." They report getting little pleasure from anything, and they tend to lose their sense of humor. Some depressed people also experience anxiety, anger, or agitation (see Box 8–2). This sea of misery may find expression in frequent crying spells; those who do not actually cry often report that they feel like crying.

Many depressed people seem to lose their feelings of affection for friends and relatives (Gara et al., 1993). One woman said, "I envy everybody. I envy my own children. . . . I envy little girls who can play just like children" (Moriarty, 1967, p. 72). A depressed man said, "I feel I don't love anyone. I feel there are too many people demanding things of me—clinging to me" (Rowe, 1978, p. 49).

Some people in the midst of a depression mask it by smiling and looking happy most of the time. Movie star Marilyn Monroe was such an individual. Emotion researcher Paul Ekman and his colleagues (1988) claim that certain facial and behavioral clues distinguish genuine happiness from masked depression, but that "we learn to ignore them, not wanting the burden of knowing the truth."

MOTIVATIONAL SYMPTOMS Depressed people usually lose the desire to participate in their accustomed activities. Almost all report a lack of drive, initiative, and spontaneity, and they may have to force themselves to go to work, converse with friends, eat meals, or have sex (Buchwald & Rudick-Davis, 1993). Aaron Beck (1967) has described this state as a "paralysis of will." One individual recalls, "I didn't want to do anything—just wanted to stay put and be let alone. By nature I have initiative and I'm self-generating, but not then. Oh, I suppose that if a fire broke out, I'd have moved, but it usually took something of some magnitude to make me stir" (Kraines & Thetford, 1972, p. 20).

Suicide represents the ultimate escape from life's activities and pressures. Many depressed people become indifferent to life or wish to die; others wish that they could kill themselves, and some actually try. As we shall see in Chapter 10, many factors influence a suicidal person's actions, but depressed people are certainly at risk (Lester, 1993). It has been estimated that between 7 and 15 percent of people who suffer from depression commit suicide (Coryell & Winokur,

1992; Tsuang, 1978). Approximately half of all suicides are committed by people who are depressed.

BEHAVIORAL SYMPTOMS The activity of depressed people usually decreases dramatically. They do less and are less productive. They spend more time alone and may stay in bed for long periods. One man recalls, "I'd awaken early, but I'd just lie there—what was the use of getting up to a miserable day? I knew I had to go to the office, so finally I would get up. I'd dress on the installment plan and have several cups of coffee" (Kraines & Thetford, 1972, p. 21).

Depressed people may also move more slowly, with seeming reluctance and lack of energy (Parker et al., 1993; Buchwald & Rudick-Davis, 1993). Even their speech may be slow, quiet, and monotonal, delivered with eyes cast down and back bent. Researchers who videotaped and then evaluated admission interviews at a mental hospital found that depressed patients made less eye contact with their interviewers than did nondepressed patients and also turned down their mouths and hung their heads more (Waxer, 1974).

COGNITIVE SYMPTOMS Depressed people hold decidedly negative views of themselves. They consider themselves inadequate, undesirable, inferior, perhaps evil. Their opinions of their physical appearance are no kinder. They may view themselves as unattractive or even repulsive. Consider the self-judgments of a lawyer suffering from depression:

*H*e described himself as a "shell of a person" fit only to be prosecuted for moral decay. A loud voice—"heh"—was ridiculing him. He was not a man. Had he not neglected his wife, both emotionally and sexually? Was he not cursed and ignored by God as a failure? All his benevolent acts were a cover for self-aggrandizement. . . . He had indulged himself in a life of pseudo-service. He should never have entered the legal profession . . . he was clearly an imposter, an empty, useless wretch who could no longer concentrate or make the simplest decisions, who paced his office late into the night, afraid to go home and face another restless, sleepless night.

(Whybrow, Akiskal, & McKinney, 1984, pp. 3–4)

Depressed people usually blame themselves for nearly every negative event, even things that have nothing to do with them, and they rarely credit themselves for positive achievements. Their guilt and self-criticism may seem harsh to everyone else, but they see it as perfectly appropriate. At the same time, they feel helpless to control or improve any aspect of their lives.

BOX 8-2

TWO SIDES OF THE SAME COIN?

Most clinicians view anxiety and depression as separate problems with different sets of symptoms; but others argue that the two diagnoses differ not in kind but in degree (Kendall & Watson, 1989). They contend that anxiety may grow so intense that it becomes depression. This idea is supported by the finding that many measures of depression and anxiety overlap—similarities are found both in the measures themselves and in the responses given by depressed and anxious patients (Jolly & Dykman, 1994; Wittchen & Essau, 1993; Dobson, 1985)—and clinicians often disagree as to whether a given subject is depressed or anxious or both (Blanchard, Waterreus, & Mann, 1994; Deluty, Deluty, & Carver, 1986).

Some research suggests that depression and anxiety may actually have a common basis (Paul, 1988). Some of these studies focus on the theory that uncontrollable stress causes a feeling of helplessness (see p. 288), and hence that anxiety (in response to the stress) ordinarily precedes depression (the feeling of helplessness). Rats given a stress-reducing drug did not exhibit helplessness responses when they were exposed to uncontrollable stress: no anxiety, no ensuing depression. Another line of research has found that the drug alprazolam (Xanax) often is an effective treatment for *both* anxiety disorders and depression (Bernstein, Garfinkel & Borchardt, 1990; Bramanti et al., 1990). In fact, it is considered an antianxiety medication *and* an antidepressant drug by some clinicians.

Other research suggests that anxiety and depression are distinct disorders that have some symptoms in common, including unpleasant feelings and demoralization (Tellegen, 1985). Scales used to measure the *cognitive* components of anxiety and depression have shown significant differences between the two (Beck, Steer, & Epstein, 1992; Clark, Beck, & Stewart, 1990). Depressed patients report more hopelessness, lower self-esteem, and more negative thoughts than anxious patients, who, for their part, report more feelings of danger.

A contradiction is evident: either anxiety and depression are different points on the same scale or they are distinct disorders. If they are indeed different disorders, researchers and practitioners must learn to distinguish better one syndrome from the other. If they are the same disorder with different manifestations, the diagnostic system requires overhauling. The tenth *International Classification of Diseases (ICD-10)* defined a new disorder called *mixed anxiety and depression (MAD)* to describe people who do not fully meet the usual criteria for either diagnosis but who manifest symptoms of both anxiety and depression, unrelated to stressful life events. This classification was also considered for inclusion in DSM-IV, but the framers finally decided against it. Those who opposed the new category were concerned that, rather than leading to greater precision in diagnosis, it would instead lead to more cursory evaluations of patients' symptoms and histories (Preskorn & Fast, 1993).

So the debate goes on. Clinicians of all theoretical paradigms are interested in whether anxiety and depression are different facets of the same disorder or separate disorders that frequently occur together. Many believe that the future course of research into anxiety and depression and their treatments depends on the outcome of these investigations (Kendall & Watson, 1989).

Another cognitive symptom of depression is a negative view of the future. Depressed people are usually convinced that nothing will ever improve (Metalsky et al., 1993; Dixon et al., 1993). They expect the worst and hence are likely to procrastinate. This sense of hopelessness also makes depressed people especially vulnerable to suicidal thinking. A successful businessman recalls, "Everything seemed black. The whole world was going to the devil, the country was going bankrupt, and my business was doomed to fail. . . . I was as pessimistic as hell—I was worse than that—I was almost hopeless about everything" (Kraines & Thetford, 1972, p. 20).

People with depression frequently complain that their intellectual ability is deteriorating (Willner, 1984). They feel confused, unable to remember things, easily distracted by outside noises, and unable to solve even small problems. Time crawls for them, yet they feel that they cannot get anything done (Hawkins et al., 1988). Actually, these difficulties are often imagined rather than real. When researchers compared the performances of twenty-four depressed and twenty-four nondepressed undergraduates at tasks that required the subjects to respond to hypothetical social problems, the two groups performed comparably. The only difference was that the

William Styron, the Pulitzer Prize-winning author of The Confessions of Nat Turner *and* Sophie's Choice, *describes the pessimism that characterized his own major depressive episode: "The pain is unrelenting, and what makes the condition intolerable is the foreknowledge that no remedy will come—not in a day, an hour, a month or a minute. It is hopelessness even more than pain that crushes the soul."*

depressed subjects predicted poorer performances for themselves and evaluated their performances less favorably than did the nondepressed subjects (Cane & Gotlib, 1985).

Research does seem to bear out the belief of many depressed people that they no longer remember things well (Channon, Baker, & Robertson, 1993; Weingartner & Silberman, 1984). Several studies found that depressed subjects were less able than nondepressed subjects to remember events of the distant past. Note, however, that this deficit may reflect motivational deficiencies rather than cognitive impairment per se. Studies suggest that depressed people often resist making the sustained effort required for long-term memory and related cognitive tasks (Lachner & Engel, 1994; Tancer et al., 1990).

SOMATIC SYMPTOMS Depression is often accompanied by such physical ailments as headaches, indigestion, constipation, dizzy spells, unpleasant sensations in the chest, and generalized pain. In fact, many depressions are initially misdiagnosed as medical problems (Kirmayer et al., 1993; Van Hemert et al., 1993). Disturbances in appetite and sleep are particularly common, as are complaints of constant tiredness that is not relieved even when rest and sleep are increased (Kazes et al., 1994; Buchwald & Rudick-Davis, 1993; Spoov et al., 1993). One patient recalls, "I slept poorly, so I began taking sleeping pills. I was tired most of the time even though I did far less work than usual" (Kraines & Thetford, 1972, p. 20). De-

pressed people usually get less sleep overall than others and awaken more frequently during the night. At the other end of the spectrum, however, are the approximately 9 percent of depressed people who sleep excessively (Ballenger, 1988).

DIAGNOSING UNIPOLAR PATTERNS OF DEPRESSION

Several clinical patterns are included in the category of unipolar depression. As a result, some clinicians believe that "unipolar depression" is really a catchall name for a variety of disorders, each of which has a distinct origin, prognosis, and responsiveness to treatment. Others believe that the patterns simply reflect different points on the continuum of a single disorder. While this debate awaits resolution, DSM-IV considers the following diagnoses to be different patterns of unipolar depression.

DSM-IV considers people to be experiencing a *major depressive episode* when their depression is significantly disabling, lasts for two weeks or more, is characterized by at least five symptoms of depression, and is not caused by such factors as drugs or a general medical condition. The severity of an episode may vary from person to person. In a small percentage of cases the episode may even involve psychotic symptoms, in which the person loses contact with reality, experiencing *delusions*—bizarre ideas without foundation—or *hallucinations*—perceptions of things that are not actually present (APA, 1994; Bech, 1992). A depressed man with psychotic symptoms may imagine, for example, that he "can't eat because my intestines are deteriorating and will soon stop working," or he may believe that he sees his dead wife.

People in the grip of a major depressive episode may receive a diagnosis of *major depressive disorder, single episode*, indicating that it is their first such episode and that they have never experienced a manic episode, or *major depressive disorder, recurrent*, indicating a history of such unipolar depressive episodes. A major depressive disorder is further described as *seasonal* if it fluctuates with seasonal changes (for example, if the depression tends to recur each winter); *catatonic* if it is dominated by either motor immobility or excessive motor activity; *postpartum* in onset if it occurs within four weeks of giving birth; or *melancholic* if the person is almost totally unaffected by pleasurable events, tends to be more depressed in the morning, and suffers from significant motor

CALLAHAN

"Your order is not ready, nor will it ever be."

disturbances, early morning awakenings, appetite loss, and excessive guilt (APA, 1994).

People who display a more chronic but less disabling pattern of unipolar depression may receive a diagnosis of *dysthymic disorder* (the term is Greek for "despondency"). Here depressed mood and only two or three other symptoms of depression are typically present and the depression persists for at least two years (or at least one year in children and adolescents). Periods of normal mood, lasting only days or weeks, may occasionally interrupt the depressed mood. When dysthymic disorder leads to a major depressive disorder, the sequence is called *double depression* (Hellerstein et al., 1994; APA, 1993).

In some cases a unipolar depressive pattern causes significant impairment but does not fully meet the criteria of major depressive disorder or dysthymic disorder. Some people, for example, experience a recurrent, brief depressive disorder in which disabling symptoms occur for several days at a time month after month (Angst & Hochstrasser, 1994). Others experience a minor depressive episode that is characterized by fewer than five symptoms of depression and lasts less than two years. DSM-IV categorizes such cases as *depressive disorder not otherwise specified.*

RECENT LIFE EVENTS AND UNIPOLAR DEPRESSION

Clinicians have noted that episodes of unipolar depression often seem to be triggered by stressful events. Correspondingly, the British psychiatric researcher Eugene Paykel and his colleagues have found that depressed people as a group experience a

greater number of stressful life events just before the onset of their disorder than do nondepressed people during the same period of time (Paykel & Cooper, 1992; Paykel, 1983, 1982). This relationship holds in the United States, England, Italy, Kenya, and India. In the groups under study, stresses began to multiply up to a year before the onset of the depressive disorders, but in most cases were greatest during the months before onset. Stressful life events also appeared to precede schizophrenia, anxiety disorders, and other psychological disorders, but depressed people reported significantly more such events than anybody else.

Researchers have tried to determine whether some people are more vulnerable to such stresses than others. Studies conducted in England have found, for example, that women who have three or more young children living at home, lack a close confidant, and have no employment outside the home, or have lost their mother before the age of 11, are more likely to become depressed after experiencing stressful life events (Alloway & Bebbington, 1987; Brown, 1988; Brown, Harris, & Peto, 1973). In short, people whose lives are generally stressful and isolated seem more likely than others to become depressed when stresses multiply. Additionally, depressed people who lack social support tend to remain depressed longer than those who live in a supportive environment (Paykel & Cooper, 1992). In fact, people who are separated or divorced, as well as those living in nursing homes or prisons, are much more likely than others to be depressed (see Figure 8–2).

These studies suggest that unipolar patterns of depression are often brought on by external events. Yet they also suggest that such patterns are not always products of the environment. At least 30 percent of the depressed subjects in the studies did not report undesirable events before the onset of their depression (Paykel & Cooper, 1992). Here are two such people:

The onset was quite sudden. I went home and went to bed early. At five o'clock (I remember the time) I awoke into a different world. It was as though all had changed while I slept; that I awoke not into normal consciousness, but into a nightmare. I got up and dressed, came down, then broke into tears and told my wife that I couldn't face going to work. I didn't.

(Rowe, 1978, p. 269)

It's quite obvious to me that there was something wrong with me inside—call it physical, chemical, or change of life. My personality was certainly O.K. before this depression hit me . . . and if there were things wrong with my personality, they certainly did not interfere with my intelligence, initiative, or mood. There was nothing un-usual about my business—in fact, it was better—and my home situation was no different. There simply was no reason for me to have become depressed.

(Kraines & Thetford, 1972, p. 24)

Since the circumstances of origin and onset seem to vary so widely, clinicians used to consider it important to distinguish reactive (exogenous) depression from endogenous depression (Mendels & Cochrane, 1968). *Reactive depressions* supposedly followed clear-cut precipitating events, whereas *endogenous depressions* unfolded without apparent antecedents and were as-sumed to be caused by internal factors. But how does one know whether a depression is reactive or not? Even if stressful events have occurred before the on-set of depression, clinicians cannot be certain that the

depression is reactive. The events could be a minor factor only or even a pure coincidence (Paykel, 1982). Conversely, even when a depression seems to emerge in the absence of stressful events, clinicians cannot be sure that it is endogenous (Paykel, Rao, & Taylor, 1984). Perhaps a subtle stressor has escaped notice.

Accordingly, today's clinicians usually concentrate on recognizing both the internal and the situational components of any given case of unipolar depression (Keller, 1988; Harlow, Newcomb, & Bentler, 1986). DSM-IV, unlike the early diagnostic systems, does not require diagnosticians to determine whether an individual's depression is externally or internally caused. All the same, some clinicians do believe that the *melancholic* depressive episodes described in DSM-IV represent an endogenous form of depression (Hirschfeld & Goodwin, 1988).

(A)

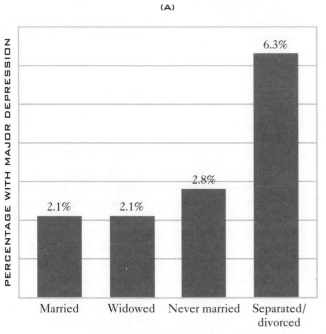

(B)

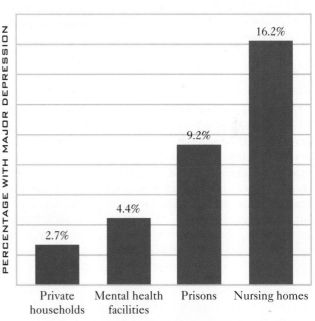

FIGURE 8-2 *(a) The one-year prevalence rates of major depressive disorder make it clear that marital status is linked to major depression. Over the course of any given year, more than 6 percent of adults in the United States who are separated or divorced experience this disorder, compared to 2 percent of married adults. Even when the odds are adjusted for gender, age, and race, currently separated or di-vorced people are three times as likely to be depressed as people who currently are married. It may be that the stress of undergoing divorce precipitates depression, that depression puts intolerable stress on some marriages, or that marital problems lead to both depression and divorce. (b) Where one lives is also related to major depres-sion. Over the course of any given year, more than 16 percent of adults who live in a nursing home in the United States suffer from a major depressive disorder, compared to 9.2 percent of those who are incarcerated, 4.4 percent of those who live in a men-tal health facility, and 2.7 percent of persons who live in a private household. (Adapted from Weissman et al., 1991.)*

BOX 8-3

THE GRIEVING PROCESS

Each year more than 8 million people in the United States experience the death of a member of their immediate family (Osterweis & Townsend, 1988). Many more lose a close friend or a more distant but still cherished relative. Such a loss is so painful that it can lead to depressed feelings and other psychological problems, a reaction so similar to clinical depression that Freud and Abraham based the psychoanalytic explanation of unipolar depression on it. But mourning the loss of a loved one is a natural process, and there are normal mechanisms for coping with the stress. The bereavement process allows us eventually to come to grips with our loss and to resume our normal lives.

Unfortunately, there are many common misconceptions about the course of the normal grieving process, and some of these errant beliefs actually interfere with the process. The most common mistake people make is to believe that there is a set timetable for mourning. Friends and acquaintances

Bereavement has no age boundaries, as attested to by the grief reactions of this boy and his grandmother at the funeral of his father, a policeman killed during fighting between Croatians and Serbians. The shock, disbelief, and despair on their faces are common reactions to loss.

often allow only a few weeks before they expect the mourner to begin a return to normal life. In fact, it is sometimes many months before a person is ready to do so. In such cases, the mourner's grief cannot be said to be pathological (Gelman, 1983). The amount of time needed depends on such factors as the relationship of the mourner to the deceased, the age of the mourner, and, clearly, the mourner's personality. Much suffering

would be avoided if those who wanted to offer support did not impose their own timetable on the course of someone else's grief.

Some researchers suggest that the bereavement process is historically and culturally defined and therefore is experienced differently in different cultural groups (Strocbe et al., 1992). Some cultures encourage lifelong ties to the deceased, while others forget the deceased as quickly as possible. Adherents of the Shanto and Buddhist religions practiced in Japan believe that contact should be maintained, and almost all homes have an altar dedicated to their deceased ancestors. Offering food to the dead and speaking to them are common practices. The Hopi Indians, though, fear the dead and believe that contact with death brings pollution, so they quickly rid the home of all reminders of their deceased relatives and try to forget about them as soon as possible. Hopi rituals performed after death are meant to break off all contact and ties between

EXPLANATIONS OF UNIPOLAR PATTERNS OF DEPRESSION

The current leading explanations of unipolar depression fall into two major categories. Some investigators focus on the situational components of the disorder in an effort to understand why and how various stresses may lead to depression. Others concentrate on the possible role of biological factors. In line with the growing recognition that unipolar depression may in-

volve both situational and biological causes, it is probably best to view each of these approaches as offering a partial rather than a comprehensive account of who develops unipolar depression and why.

THE PSYCHODYNAMIC VIEW Sigmund Freud and his student Karl Abraham developed the initial psychoanalytic theory of depression (Freud, 1917; Abraham, 1916, 1911). Their starting point was the similarity they noticed between clinical depression and the grief reactions of people who lose loved ones (see Box 8–3). Constant weeping, loss of appetite,

mortals and the spirits of the dead. Muslims in Egypt believe that the bereaved should dwell on their loss and surround themselves with others who share their sorrow, but Muslims in Bali are taught to contain their grief and to laugh and be joyful (Wikan, 1991).

In modern Western society we view bereavement as an interference in the daily routine of life, a troublesome and debilitating emotional response that one must overcome as quickly and efficiently as possible. The researcher Margaret Stroebe refers to this as the "breaking bonds" approach to bereavement, because it requires the bereaved to break all ties with the deceased and form a new identity by finding different rewards and reinforcements in new relationships. According to this view, people who continue to be emotionally attached to the dead are maladjusted.

But this type of bereavement was not always the norm in the United States. Stroebe notes that as recently as a century ago, Americans had a much different conception of bereavement. The breaking of ties was *not* encouraged and it was common for bereaved people to hold on strongly to memories of their dead. In the mid–nineteenth century, communication with the dead through séances and mediums was popular. The amount of grief one felt after the death of a loved one was held to indi-

cate the relationship's strength and significance, and the bereaved were expected to focus on a reunion with the deceased in heaven.

In Western society today, despite individual variations in duration of grief, research has shown that mourners typically share certain experiences (Osterweis & Townsend, 1988). The bereavement process often begins with *shock:* the survivor has *difficulty believing* that the person has died. The shock and disbelief are frequently followed by a sense of *loss and separation*, a feeling that sometimes leads to misperceptions and illusions—glimpsing the dead person in the street or dreaming that the person is alive. Once the mourner fully accepts the fact that the deceased is not coming back, *despair* may set in. Depression, irritability, guilt, and anger are natural responses at this stage. Social relationships may deteriorate at this time, as the mourner loses interest in the outside world and his or her customary activities. Some mourners begin to suffer medical problems.

Once the mourning process is complete, it then becomes possible to think of the deceased person without being overwhelmed by feelings of despair and a sense of loss. At this point, one is prepared to get on with one's life, although anniversaries and other special dates may cause flare-ups of mourning for many years to come.

In Western society, the normal grieving process is often disrupted, even prolonged, by others' treatment of the mourner. In addition to envisioning an unrealistic timetable for recovery, friends and relatives may have other expectations that will hinder rather than help. Anticipating, for example, that the widow or widower will feel like the odd person out, friends may be reluctant to invite the surviving spouse to a social gathering. They may visit the mourner less frequently at this time, just when the person most needs support. And when friends do visit, they may take pains to avoid mentioning the bereaved person's loss, not realizing the great relief that sometimes comes from talking about one's pain.

Recently, numerous self-help bereavement groups have appeared throughout the United States that allow mourners to gather with others who have lost loved ones and discuss the emotional and practical problems they all face. Many of these groups are led by people who have completed a grieving process themselves and wish to offer insight and support to others. Group members do not avoid the topic of death, and no one promises or demands a speedy return to normal. For many, this is an ideal environment in which to confront and accept their loss. It allows an important process to proceed as it should—without pressure, misinterpretation, or judgment.

difficulty sleeping, inability to find pleasure in life, and general withdrawal are common features of both mourning and depression (Stroebe et al., 1992; Osterweis, Solomon, & Green, 1984).

According to Freud and Abraham, a series of unconscious processes is set in motion when a loved one dies or is lost in some other way. At first, unable to accept the loss, mourners regress to the oral stage of development, the period when infants are so dependent that they cannot distinguish themselves from their parents. By regressing to this stage the mourners fuse their own identity with that of the person they

have lost, symbolically regaining the lost person in the process. In other words, they *introject* the loved one and then experience all their feelings toward the loved one as feelings about themselves.

For most mourners, this unconscious process is temporary and lasts only for the period of mourning. They soon begin to reestablish a separate identity and resume social relationships. For some, however, the grief reaction worsens. They feel empty, continue to avoid social relationships, and become more preoccupied with their sense of loss. Introjected feelings of anger toward the loved one for departing, or perhaps over unresolved conflicts from the past, cause these people to experience self-hatred, which leads to a negative mood, self-blame, and further withdrawal. In effect, these people become depressed.

Freud and Abraham believed that two kinds of people are particularly prone to introjection and depression in the face of loss: those whose parents failed to meet their nurturance needs during the oral stage of infancy and those whose parents gratified those needs excessively. Infants whose needs are inadequately met remain overly dependent on others throughout their lives, feel unworthy of love, and have low self-esteem. Those whose needs are excessively gratified find the oral stage so pleasant that they resist moving on to other stages in life. People of either kind may spend their lives desperately seeking love and approval from others and trying to obtain it by working extremely hard, devoting themselves to others, or denying their own needs (Bemporad, 1992). Such people are likely to experience a greater sense of loss when a loved one dies and greater anger toward the loved one for having departed.

Of course, many people become depressed without losing a loved one. To explain why, Freud invoked the concept of *imagined,* or *symbolic, loss.* A man who loses his job, for example, may unconsciously interpret the experience as the loss of his wife, believing that she will no longer want him if he is unsuccessful at work. A college student may experience failure in a calculus course as the loss of her parents, believing that they love her only when she excels academically.

Over the course of this century, some psychodynamic theorists have argued for changes in emphasis in Freud and Abraham's theory of depression. Several have deemphasized the notion of hostility turned inward (Cohen et al., 1954; Bibring, 1953; Balint, 1952). Others have minimized the importance of oral fixation and have linked depression to anal and phallic problems as well (Jacobson, 1971; Bibring, 1953). And some have argued that loss of self-esteem is the dominant issue in depression (Jacobson, 1971; Bibring, 1953).

Overall, however, Freud and Abraham's influence on current psychodynamic thinking is very strong (APA, 1993; Coccaro, 1991). For example, *object relations theorists,* who, as we noted in Chapter 2, link people's functioning to their relationships with others and to their inner representations of such relationships, hold a view of depression that is very similar to the classical position (Horner, 1991; Sandler & Sandler, 1978; Kernberg, 1976). They propose that depression results when people's relationships leave them feeling unsafe and insecure, and that people whose parents pushed them toward either excessive

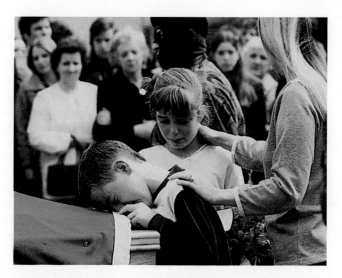

Psychodynamic theorists believe that depression is caused by the real or imagined loss of a loved one. Research has found that people who lose their parents as children have an increased likelihood of experiencing depression as adults.

dependence or excessive self-reliance are more likely to become depressed when they later confront complications or losses in their relationships.

The following description of a depressed middle-aged woman brings forth the psychoanalytic concepts of early dependence, later dependence, loss of a loved one, symbolic loss, and introjection:

*M*rs. Marie Carls was in her middle fifties when she came for the first interview. She appeared distinguished in her manner, with an almost aristocratic demeanor. . . . She had been born and had lived in Europe until a few years prior to the onset of treatment. . . .

All her complaints were somatic in nature. She tired easily, to the point of exhaustion. She knew she was melancholy, but she thought that it was because she did not feel well. She was very religious and had been brought up in an environment in which there was strict adherence to Catholicism. She went to confession very often.

A few sessions after the beginning of the treatment, she started to define her various complaints and general state of malaise as "an obscure force" which would take possession of her. She knew that this obscure force was a psychological experience. It was something which would come suddenly and make her depressed, tired, and often cause cramps in her stomach. . . .

The patient had always felt very attached to her mother. As a matter of fact, they used to call her "Stamp" because she stuck to her mother as a stamp to a letter. She always tried to placate her volcanic mother, to please her in every possible way. The mother, however, did not fulfill her maternal role very well. . . .

After marriage [to Julius], she continued her pattern of submission and compliance. Before her marriage she had difficulty in complying with a volcanic mother, and after her marriage she almost automatically assumed a submissive role. Actually, she described her husband as very considerate, egalitarian, and not domineering at all. His only fault was that he did not have a volcanic or dynamic personality. He was too placid, too good, and rather boring. . . .

Several months after beginning treatment, the patient reported a dream. Ignatius and she had decided not to see each other again. She would have to leave him forever. I asked who Ignatius was, because I had not heard the name until then. The patient replied almost with surprise, "But the first time I came to see you, I told you that in the past I had had an infatuation." She then told me that when she was thirty years old, in the middle of the Second World War, she lived at the periphery of a city which was frequently bombed. Ignatius, a friend of the family, had had his home completely demolished by bombs. The patient and her husband invited Ignatius, who was single, to come and live with them. Ignatius and the patient soon discovered that they had an attraction for each other. They both tried to fight that feeling; but when Julius had to go to another city for a few days, the so-called infatuation became much more than that. There were a few physical contacts. . . . There was an intense spiritual affinity. Ignatius understood her: he spoke her language, liked what she liked, and gave her the feeling of being alive. She remembered that before she married Julius, she had invented a slogan which she often emphatically repeated, "Long live life"; but only with Ignatius could she believe in that slogan again. Ignatius suggested that they elope, but she did not take him seriously. A few months later everybody had to leave the city. Ignatius and Marie promised to keep in touch, but both of them were full of hesitation because of Julius, a devoted husband to Marie and a devoted friend to Ignatius. Nothing was done to maintain contact. Two years later, approximately a year after the end of the war, Marie heard that Ignatius had married. She felt terribly alone and despondent. . . .

In a subsequent stage of therapy Marie concentrated on her marriage. . . . Her suffering had become more acute as she realized that old age was approaching and she had lost all her chances. Ignatius remained as the memory of lost opportunities. Yes, Ignatius had wanted her to go with him, but she wouldn't because she felt that her husband and God would never forgive her. Even that beautiful short relationship was spoiled by her feeling of guilt. Her life of compliance and obedience had not permitted her to reach her goal. An Ignatius existed in the world, but she had lost him forever. She had never loved her husband, and that was what was wrong with her marriage. . . .

For many years she had hoped she could make up for the loss of Ignatius, but now she could no longer do so. She could no longer scream, "Long live life!" She would rather think, "Down with life without Ignatius, a life which has lost its meaning."

When she became aware of these ideas, she felt even more depressed. She was complaining less and less about the obscure force, and more and more about her marriage.

She felt that everything she had built in her life was false or based on a false premise. In a certain way her husband was not so compliant, permissive, and tolerant as she had seen him; but possessive because she had to live by his way of living, with all its placidity and the boredom. But this was impossible to do when she really did not love the man. . . .

A psychiatrist must agree that love is important, and a life without love is an impoverished life. But love means many things, just as there are many types of love. For Marie it meant only romantic love, all passion and flame, like the one she had imagined with Ignatius. Life without that type of love is not at all a life characterized by lovelessness, and by no means to be equated with death: but it was so for her. There are many strong and pleasant feelings that one can feel for family members, career, friends, humanity, cultural interests, and so on. They are different loves, but they count too. . . .

(Arieti & Bemporad, 1978, pp. 275–284)

Studies by psychodynamic researchers have generally supported the psychodynamic ideas that depression is often triggered by a major loss and that people who experience early losses and early dependent relationships are more vulnerable to losses later in life (APA, 1993). In a famous study of 123 infants who were placed in a nursery after being separated from their mothers, René Spitz (1946, 1945) found that 19 of the infants became very weepy and sad upon separation, withdrew from their surroundings, ignored others, and lay passively in their cots. They moved slowly and sometimes had trouble sleeping. Many lost weight. Moreover, their development seemed to slow down. Later studies confirmed that separation from the mother before the age of 6 years often brings about a reaction of this kind, a pattern called ***anaclitic depression*** (Bowlby, 1980, 1977, 1973, 1969).

A remarkable series of experiments with monkeys conducted by Harry Harlow during the 1960s and 1970s also suggest a link between loss and depression. After first observing that infant monkeys whose mothers died often reacted in ways that suggested human anaclitic depression, Harlow and his colleagues proceeded to study separation and isolation in monkeys. In a typical study, the experimenters first raised an infant monkey in a laboratory playpen with its mother and then separated the two for a few weeks (Seay, Hansen, & Harlow, 1962). They repeatedly found that the infant monkeys reacted first by protesting (crying out and jumping around) and then with apparent despair, expressed as a sharp decrease in vocalization, exploration, and play (Seay et al., 1965, 1962; Harlow & Harlow, 1965). The longer the separation, the more severe the reaction (Suomi,

1976). Infant monkeys raised with other young monkeys and then separated from them also showed protest-despair reactions of this kind (Suomi & Harlow, 1977, 1975; Suomi, Harlow, & Domek, 1970).

Other research has suggested that losses suffered early in life may also set the stage for depression during adulthood (Burbach & Borduin, 1986). When a depression scale was administered to 1,250 medical patients during visits to their family physicians, the patients whose fathers had died during their childhood earned higher depression scores (Barnes & Prosen, 1985). Likewise, several carefully controlled studies have found that more depressed adults than nondepressed adults have lost a parent before the age of 5 (Crook & Eliot, 1980).

A related body of research also supports the psychodynamic proposition that people whose childhood needs were improperly addressed are the ones most likely to become depressed after experiencing loss (Parker, 1992). Investigators have had depressed and nondepressed subjects fill out a scale called the *Parental Bonding Instrument,* which indicates how much care and protection individuals feel they received as children. Many depressed subjects report that their parents displayed a child-rearing style identified as "affectionless control," consisting of a mixture of low care and high protection (Parker, 1992, 1983; Hickie et al., 1990; Plantes et al., 1988).

In another line of psychodynamic research, investigators have studied dreams to determine whether depression involves hostility turned inward. The dreams reported by depressed subjects are compared with the dreams of nondepressed subjects by an evaluator who is trained in dream analysis but does not know which dreams belong to which subjects. The evaluator rates each dream for such factors as hostility and masochism (hostility toward oneself). Several studies have indicated that the dreams of depressed people do reflect higher levels of hostility and masochism than the dreams of nondepressed people (Hauri et al., 1974).

These various studies offer some support for the psychodynamic view of depression, but it is important to be aware of their limitations. First, although the findings indicate that losses and inadequate parenting sometimes precipitate depression, they do not establish that such factors are typically responsible for the disorder. In the studies of young children and young monkeys, for example, only some of the subjects who were separated from their mothers showed depressive reactions. The nineteen babies in the nursery study who suffered anaclitic depression represented only 15 percent of the separated infants. Altogether, it is

In their experiments with monkeys, Harry Harlow and his colleagues found that infant monkeys reacted with apparent despair to separation from their mothers. Even monkeys raised with surrogate mothers—wire cylinders wrapped with foam rubber and covered with terry cloth—formed an attachment to them, and clung to them when anxious, and reacted with despair when separated from them.

estimated that less than 10 percent of all people who experience major losses in life actually become depressed (Paykel & Cooper, 1992; Paykel, 1982).

Second, much of the supportive psychodynamic research focuses on depression among the very young. It may be that depression at this age is quite different from adult depression. Although many of the reactions of the infant monkeys in Harlow's research paralleled the anaclitic depression seen in human children, they differed greatly from the depressive symptoms of human adolescents and adults (Suomi & Harlow, 1977). In fact, Harlow was able to generate depressive reactions in separated adolescent monkeys only by further isolating each monkey in an individual vertical chamber that hampered its physical activity. Clearly, such restraint goes far beyond the simple manipulation of separation and loss.

A third problem with the psychodynamic evidence is that many of the findings are inconsistent. Though many studies find evidence of a relationship between childhood loss and later depression, others do not (Parker, 1992; Owen, Lancee, & Freeman, 1986); and though some studies indicate that depressed people may exhibit covert hostility toward others and themselves, others, again, do not (Klerman, 1984).

A final drawback to this research is that important components of the psychodynamic explanation of depression are nearly impossible to test. Because such processes as symbolic loss, fixation at the oral stage, and introjection are said to operate at an unconscious level, it is difficult for researchers to determine if and when they are occurring. Similarly, some key psychodynamic notions, such as a person's receiving insufficient or excessive need gratification during childhood, elude precise assessment because they can be measured only by retrospective self-reports. When subjects fill out the Parental Bonding Instrument, for example, how can researchers be sure that they are indicating their parents' actual behaviors, as opposed to poorly or defensively remembered events?

THE BEHAVIORAL VIEW Peter Lewinsohn has developed a behavioral explanation of unipolar depression (Lewinsohn et al., 1984; Lewinsohn & Arconad, 1981). He suggests that for some people the rewards that ordinarily reinforce positive behaviors start to dwindle, and they respond by performing fewer and fewer positive behaviors and develop a depressed style of functioning. The rewards of campus life, for example, may disappear for a young woman when she graduates from college and takes a job in the business world; or an aging baseball player may lose the reinforcements of high salary and adulation when his athletic skills deteriorate. Although many people manage to greet such changes with a sense of perspective and resolve to fill their lives with other forms of gratification, some become disheartened and perform fewer constructive behaviors. As their activity level drops, their positive reinforcements decrease even more, and the decline in reinforcements leads to even fewer positive behaviors. In this manner, a person may spiral toward depression. A corollary to this theory states that a high rate of punishing experiences (say, a hostile work environment) may also lead to depression "by interfering with the person's engagement in and enjoyment of rewarding activities" (Lewinsohn & Arconad, 1981).

To test his theory Lewinsohn has followed subjects into their homes and observed the reinforcements they receive there. In a series of studies he had research evaluators observe mealtime interactions in the families of depressed people and count the posi-

tive statements that family members addressed to the depressed individual (Libet & Lewinsohn, 1973; Lewinsohn & Shaffer, 1971). In accord with the behavioral theory, these evaluators repeatedly found that family members who were depressed received fewer verbal reinforcements than did the other people around them.

Lewinsohn has also found that a person's number of reinforcements is indeed related to the presence or absence of depression. Not only do depressed subjects report a lower number of positive reinforcements, as measured on a "Pleasant Events Schedule," than nondepressed subjects over a 30-day period, but when their reinforcements increase, the mood of these depressed subjects improves as well (Lewinsohn, Youngren, & Grosscup, 1979). Similarly, Lewinsohn (1975) has found that depressed people tend to have more unpleasant experiences than others do in such categories as health, finances, social interactions, and professional and academic pursuits.

Lewinsohn and other behaviorists believe that *social* reinforcements are particularly important (Peterson, 1993; Coyne, 1985; Lewinsohn et al., 1984). Consistent with this notion, research has found that depressed subjects tend to experience fewer positive social reinforcements than nondepressed subjects, and that as their mood improves, their positive social reinforcements increase as well. Related studies have indicated that depressed patients tend to make others angry, are avoided, and have fewer friends, less interpersonal support, and more unpleasant social interactions than other people. Although depressed people may be the victims of social circumstances, it is also possible that they are partly responsible for the decreases in their social reinforcements. One study observed, for example, that depressed people have greater difficulty than others with self-disclosure, fear rejection, misread social situations, and worry a lot about possible separation from loved ones (Boyce et al., 1993). Correspondingly, phone callers in one study reported feeling worse than usual after a short conversation with a depressed person (Coyne, 1976), and subjects in another became less verbal, less supportive, and less cheerful than usual when they interacted with someone who was mildly depressed (Gotlib & Robinson, 1982).

Lewinsohn and other behaviorists have done an admirable job of compiling data to support these theories, but this research, too, has significant limitations. It has relied heavily on the self-reports of depressed and nondepressed subjects, and as we saw in Chapter 4, such measures can be biased and inaccurate; in the case of depressed individuals, for example, they may be influenced heavily by a gloomy mood and negative outlook (Youngren & Lewinsohn, 1980).

It is also important to keep in mind that Lewinsohn's studies have been correlational and do not establish that decreases in reinforcing events are the *initial* causes of depression. A depressed mood in itself may lead to a decrease in activities and hence to fewer reinforcements. Causal relationships might be better established if it were somehow possible to measure the number of positive reinforcements in a person's life just before the onset of the first episode of unipolar depression. According to the behaviorial theory, the number should already be decreasing at that time. Another approach, one that obviously poses serious ethical problems, would be to deprive people of many of their usual positive reinforcements and see whether they become significantly depressed as a result.

THE COGNITIVE VIEW Aaron Beck's research and clinical observations have led him to believe that *negative thinking*, rather than underlying conflicts or fewer positive reinforcements, lies at the heart of unipolar depression (Young, Beck, & Weinberger, 1993; Beck, 1991, 1967). Other cognitive theorists (Albert Ellis, for one) have also pointed to maladaptive thinking as the key to depression, but Beck's theory is the one most often associated with the disorder. He argues that depressed people are so filled with negative thoughts about themselves, their situations, and the future that all aspects of their functioning are affected dramatically. According to Beck, *maladaptive attitudes*, the *cognitive triad*, *errors in thinking*, and *automatic thoughts* combine to produce this pervasive negativity.

MALADAPTIVE ATTITUDES   Beck believes that children's attitudes toward themselves and the world are based on their own experiences, their family relationships, and the judgments of the people around them. Unfortunately, some children develop negative attitudes, such as "My general worth is tied to every task I perform" and "If I fail, others will feel repelled by me." Many failures are inevitable in a full, active life, so such attitudes are inaccurate and self-defeating. The negative attitudes become templates, or schemas, against which the child evaluates every experience (Young et al., 1993; Beck et al., 1990).

THE COGNITIVE TRIAD   A negative cognitive structure that develops during childhood may lie dormant for years, as long as life proceeds smoothly, without major disturbances or disappointments. But at any time a traumatic situation—particularly one reminiscent of early failure or loss—can trigger an extended round of pervasive negative thinking. According to Beck, the negative thinking takes three forms and is therefore termed the *cognitive triad:* the individuals repeatedly interpret (1) *their experiences*, (2) *themselves*, and (3) *their futures* in negative ways that lead them to feel depressed.

Experiences may be interpreted as burdens, obstacles, or traumas that repeatedly defeat, deprive, or disparage the person. The thinking of one depressed client proceeded in the following manner:

> She made a terrible mistake in moving to this city, she should never have taken the children from their father. . . . The climate is unbearable, she could slip and fall on those icy sidewalks at any time, and then what would happen to the children? The children don't love her, they treat her like dirt; other people's children have more time for their parents.
>
> *(Mendels, 1970, p. 3)*

At the same time, depressed people view themselves as deficient, undesirable, worthless, and inadequate:

> I can't bear it. I can't stand the humiliating fact that I'm the only woman in the world who can't take care of her family, take her place as a real wife and mother, and be respected in her community. When I speak to my young son Billy, I know I can't let him down, but I feel so ill-equipped to take care of him; that's what frightens me. I don't know what to do or where to turn; the whole thing is too overwhelming. . . . I must be a laughing stock. It's more than I can do to go out and meet people and have the fact pointed up to me so clearly.
>
> *(Fieve, 1975)*

Finally, the future regularly appears bleak to those who are depressed, sure to be a never-ending series of hardships, miseries, frustrations, and failures:

> Joan lived her life in the constant expectation that the outcome of every situation would be bad. If she went on a car journey with her husband she expected not to arrive safely. Numerous safe arrivals had not ameliorated her pessimism. "I think if I go over a bridge it will collapse. I think I should stay in bed all day if that's the things I always think. I always think that something bad is going to happen."
>
> *(Rowe, 1978)*

ERRORS IN THINKING   According to Beck, depressed people habitually employ errors of logic, forms of distorted thinking that help build and maintain the cognitive triad. Here are five of these common errors in logic:

Drawings by Charles Shultz. © 1956 United Feature Syndicate, Inc.

Charlie Brown's feelings of depression are caused by errors of logic, such as arbitrary inference.

Arbitrary Inference   Depressed people often draw negative conclusions on the basis of little or even contrary evidence. For example, a man walking through the park passes a woman who is looking at nearby trees and flowers, and he concludes, "She's avoiding looking at me."

Selective Abstraction   Depressed people often focus on one negative detail of a situation while ignoring the larger context. For example, a nightclub comedienne performs for a very responsive audience who laugh and enthusiastically applaud all but one of her jokes. Focusing on that one joke, the performer concludes, "I didn't have it tonight."

Overgeneralization   Depressed people often draw a broad conclusion from a single, perhaps insignificant, event. For example, a student in a history class is unable to remember the date of the signing of the Magna Carta and walks around the rest of the day convinced that he is stupid.

Magnification and Minimization   Depressed people often underestimate the significance of positive experiences or exaggerate that of negative ones. A college student receives an A on a difficult English exam, for example, but concludes that the grade reflects the professor's generosity rather than her own ability (minimization). Later in the week the same student catches a cold and must miss an English class. She is convinced that she will be unable to keep pace the rest of the semester and may fail the course because of this missed class (magnification).

Personalization   Depressed people often incorrectly view themselves as the cause of negative events. When Sunday's picnic is postponed by a sudden rainstorm, for example, a father blames himself for ruining his family's fun because he selected that day for the picnic. Or a woman blames herself for her sister's divorce, believing that the infrequency of her visits and her lack of sensitivity were somehow responsible.

AUTOMATIC THOUGHTS   Depressed people experience the cognitive triad in the form of *automatic thoughts,* a steady train of unpleasant thoughts that repeatedly remind them of their assumed inadequacy and the hopelessness of their situation. Beck labels these thoughts "automatic" because they seem to just happen, as if by reflex. In the course of only a few hours, depressed people may be visited by hundreds of such thoughts: "I'm worthless. . . . I'll never amount to anything. . . . I let everyone down. . . . Everyone hates me. . . . My responsibilities are overwhelming. . . . I've failed as a parent. . . . I'm stupid. . . . Everything is difficult for me. . . . I've caused problems for my friends. . . . Things will never change." One therapist says of a depressed client, "By the end of the day, she is worn out, she has lived a thousand painful accidents, participated in a thousand deaths, mourned a thousand mistakes" (Mendels, 1970).

A FEEDBACK SYSTEM   Beck believes that the emotional, motivational, behavioral, and somatic aspects of depression all follow from the cognitive processes he has described. If people think they are unwanted by everyone else, they will experience the misery of being a social outcast. If they anticipate a future of unhappiness, they will not be motivated to take on new projects. Once the cognitive processes generate additional symptoms of depression, Beck believes, the new symptoms act to confirm the original negative cognitions, thus creating a feedback system that reinforces the mistaken cognitions. That is, people who find themselves sad, crying, or without appetite may take these problems as further evidence that their lives are miserable. Similarly, people who are unmotivated to work may view their inactivity as proof that the future will indeed be bleak. In this way, the depressed person is soon caught in a vicious cycle.

INVESTIGATING BECK'S THEORY   Beck's cognitive view of unipolar depression has received considerable research support. Several studies have confirmed that depressed people tend to hold such maladaptive attitudes as "People will probably think less of me if I make a mistake" and "I must be a useful, productive, creative person, or life has no purpose" (Garber, Weiss, & Shanley, 1993; Weissman & Beck, 1978). Moreover, the number of maladaptive attitudes correlate strongly with the degree of depression, suggesting that the more of these attitudes one holds, the more depressed one tends to be.

Other research has supported Beck's idea that depressed people exhibit the cognitive triad (Cole & Turner, 1993; Haaga & Beck, 1992). Depressed subjects recall unpleasant experiences more readily than positive ones, a tendency that reverses itself when the subjects' symptoms later improve (Lloyd & Lishman, 1975). Depressed subjects also rate themselves and their performances lower than nondepressed subjects do, even when they have performed just as well as nondepressed persons (Slife & Weaver, 1992; Loeb, Beck, & Diggory, 1971). And in storytelling and projective assessment tests, depressed subjects usually select pessimistic statements such as "I expect my plans will fail" and "I feel like I'll never meet anyone who's interested in me" (Weintraub, Segal, & Beck, 1974).

Beck's association of depression with errors in logic has also received research support (Cole & Turner, 1993; Yost, Cook, & Peterson, 1986). In one study, female subjects were asked to read paragraphs about women in difficult situations and then to answer multiple-choice questions about them. The multiple-choice options included examples of overgeneralization, arbitrary inference, selective abstraction, and magnification or minimization. The women who were depressed chose a significantly greater number of responses reflecting errors in logic than the nondepressed women did (Hammen & Krantz, 1976). Similarly, a study of 400 elementary school children found that depressed children scored significantly higher than nondepressed children on the Children's Negative Cognitive Error Questionnaire (Leitenberg et al., 1986).

Finally, research has supported Beck's claim that depressed people repeatedly experience negative automatic thoughts (Garber et al., 1993). Hospitalized depressed patients scored significantly higher on an Automatic Thought Questionnaire than other kinds of patients did (Ross et al., 1986). Nondepressed subjects who were manipulated into reading negative automatic-thought-like statements about themselves became increasingly depressed (Strickland, Hale, & Anderson, 1975). And people who consistently made *ruminative responses* during their depressed moods (having repeated thoughts about their mood rather than acting to change the mood) were found to experience longer periods of depressed mood than people who avoided such thoughts (Nolen-Hoeksema, Morrow, & Fredrickson, 1993).

This body of research clearly indicates that negative cognitions are associated with depressive functioning, but it fails to establish that cognitive dysfunctioning represents the cause and core of unipolar depression. The investigations leave open the possibility that a central mood problem leads to cognitive difficulties, which then take a further toll on mood, motivation, behavior, and physiology (Miranda & Persons, 1988; Lewinsohn et al., 1981). In fact, Beck's feedback model itself acknowledges that negative mood can have a significant impact on a person's cognitions.

Some studies have tried to establish that cognitive dysfunction does precede the negative mood of depressed people, as Beck claims. In one, investigators followed the progress of fifteen severely depressed women and interviewed them after their depressive symptoms had markedly declined to determine whether they still held maladaptive attitudes (Rush et al., 1986). The researchers found that the women who continued to hold such attitudes were more likely to develop depressive symptoms again six months later. That is, their negative schemas remained in place even during periods of improved mood, apparently setting the stage for renewed depressive functioning at a later point.

A COGNITIVE-BEHAVIORAL VIEW: LEARNED HELPLESSNESS   Feelings of helplessness emerge repeatedly in this account of a young woman's depression:

*M*ary was 25 years old and had just begun her senior year in college. . . . Asked to recount how her life had been going recently, Mary began to weep. Sobbing, she said that for the last year or so she felt she was losing control of her life and that recent stresses (starting school again, friction with her boyfriend) had left her feeling worthless and frightened. Because of a gradual deterioration in her vision, she was now forced to wear glasses all day. "The glasses make me look terrible," she said, and "I don't look people in the eye much any more." Also, to her dismay, Mary had gained 20 pounds in the past year. She viewed herself as overweight and unattractive. At times she was convinced that with enough money to buy contact lenses and enough time to exercise she could cast off her depression; at other times she believed nothing would help. . . .

Mary saw her life deteriorating in other spheres, as well. She felt overwhelmed by schoolwork and, for the first time in her life, was on academic probation. Twice before in the past seven years feelings of inadequacy and pressure from part-time jobs (as a waitress, bartender, and salesclerk) had caused her to leave school. She felt certain that unless she could stop her current downward spiral she would do so again—this time permanently. She despaired of ever getting her degree.

In addition to her dissatisfaction with her appearance and her fears about her academic future, Mary complained of a lack of friends. Her social network consisted solely of her boyfriend, with whom she was living. Although there were times she experienced this relationship as almost unbearably frustrating, she felt helpless to change it and was pessimistic about its permanence. . . .

(Spitzer et al., 1983, pp. 122–123)

FIGURE 8–3 *Experimental animals learn to escape shocks that are administered in one compartment of a shuttle box by jumping to the other (safe) compartment. They may also learn to avoid the shocks altogether by jumping to the safe compartment in response to a warning, such as the dimming of a light.*

Mary feels that she is "losing control of her life." Often she believes that she can do nothing to change what she considers to be her unattractive appearance and excess weight. She "despairs of ever getting her degree" and feels helpless to change her frustrating relationship with her boyfriend. According to psychologist Martin Seligman, such feelings of helplessness are at the center of Mary's depression. Since the mid-1960s Seligman has been developing the *learned helplessness* theory of depression (Seligman 1992, Seligman, 1975), which combines concepts from the behavioral and cognitive models and holds that people become depressed when they think (1) that they no longer have control over the reinforcements in their lives and (2) that they themselves are responsible for this helpless state. In Seligman's view, all of the symptoms of depression grow from this perception of helplessness and self-blame.

Seligman's theory first began to take shape when he and his colleagues were conducting conditioning studies with laboratory dogs, trying to teach them to escape and then avoid shocks. They placed each dog in a *shuttle box,* a box partitioned by a barrier over which the animal could jump to reach the other side (see Figure 8–3). Then they dimmed the lights as a warning signal and seconds later administered shocks to the dog. The shocks continued until the dog learned to escape them by jumping over the barrier.

Some of the dogs had been allowed to rest the day before (naive dogs); others had spent the previous day strapped into an apparatus called a hammock, in which they received inescapable shocks at random

intervals. What fascinated Seligman was how these two groups then differed in ther reactions to the shocks in the shuttle box.

When placed in a shuttle box, an experimentally naive dog, at the onset of the first electric shock, runs frantically about until it accidentally scrambles over the barrier and escapes the shock. On the next trial, the dog, running frantically, crosses the barrier more quickly than on the preceding trial; within a few trials it becomes very efficient at escaping, and soon learns to avoid shock altogether. After about fifty trials the dog becomes nonchalant and stands in front of the barrier; at the onset of the signal for shock it leaps gracefully across and never gets shocked again.

A dog that had first been given inescapable shock showed a strikingly different pattern. This dog's first reactions to shock in the shuttle box were much the same as those of a naive dog: it ran around frantically for about thirty seconds. But then it stopped moving; to our surprise, it lay down and quietly whined. After one minute of this we turned the shock off; the dog had failed to cross the barrier and had not escaped from shock. On the next trial, the dog did it again; at first it struggled a bit, and then, after a few seconds, it seemed to give up and to accept the shock passively. On all succeeding trials, the dog failed to escape. This is the paradigmatic learned-helplessness finding.

(Seligman, 1975, p. 22)

Seligman concluded that the dogs who had previously received random inescapable shocks had learned that they had no control over aversive reinforcements (shocks) in their lives. That is, they had learned that they were helpless to do anything to change negative situations. Thus, even when these dogs were later placed in a new situation where they could in fact control their fate, they continued to believe that they had no control. They continued to act helpless and failed to learn to escape painful shock by jumping to the safe side of the shuttle box.

In subsequent experiments, Seligman and other investigators demonstrated that such helplessness effects can be generated in various animal species and under a variety of conditions (Hiroto & Seligman, 1975). Believing that the effects of learned helplessness greatly resemble the symptoms of human depression, he proposed that humans in fact become depressed after developing the implicit belief that they have no control over reinforcements in their lives. Consequently, much of the helplessness research conducted during the past few decades has tried to demonstrate that helplessness in the laboratory is analogous to depression in the real world.

Many laboratory studies of learned helplessness in humans have produced reactions that mimic the passivity displayed in depression. In one helplessness study, nondepressed human subjects were pretreated in one of three ways: one group of subjects were exposed to a very loud noise that they could stop by pushing a button; a second group were also exposed to the loud noise but could do nothing to stop it; and a third group (naive subjects) heard no loud noise at all (Hiroto, 1974). All subjects were then placed in front of a finger shuttle box (a rectangular box with a handle on top) and subjected to a loud noise. Without the subjects' knowledge, the box was rigged so that the noise would stop when the handle was moved from one side to the other. Both the naive subjects and those who had previously had control over the loud noise quickly learned to move the handle and turn off the noise. The subjects who had been pretreated with unavoidable loud noise, however, failed to learn the simple task of moving the handle across the box. Most of them simply sat passively and accepted the abrasive sound.

Human and animal subjects who undergo helplessness training also display other reactions similar to depressive symptoms. When human subjects are given random aversive reinforcements, for example, they later score higher on a depressive mood survey than do subjects who are allowed control over their reinforcements (Miller & Seligman, 1975; Gatchel, Paulus, & Maples, 1975); and just as depressed people often show reductions in overt aggressive behavior, helplessness-trained subjects withdraw more and compete less in laboratory games (Kurlander, Miller, & Seligman, 1974). Animals subjected to inescapable shock eat little and lose weight, and they lose interest in sexual and social activities—common symptoms of human depression (Lindner, 1968). Finally, uncontrollable aversive events result in lower activity of the brain neurotransmitter norepinephrine in rats, a depletion that has also been noted in the brains of people with unipolar depression, as we shall see (Hughes et al., 1984; Weiss, Glazer, & Pohorecky, 1976, 1974).

REVISIONS IN THE LEARNED HELPLESSNESS THEORY Since Seligman first formulated his theory, researchers and theorists have clarified and revised certain aspects of it. They have, for example, demonstrated that *actual* loss of control over reinforcements is not the critical feature in producing the learned helplessness response in laboratory studies. It is necessary only that subjects *perceive* a loss of control. On the basis of such findings, Seligman has argued that people will become depressed if they *believe* that they have lost control over the reinforcements in their lives, and in fact a review of close to 100 studies has revealed that subjects who generally believe that their lives are largely under the control of external forces or chance tend to experience higher levels of depression (Benassi, Sweeney, & Dufour, 1988).

Another important clarification centers on the role of **attributions** in learned helplessness and depression. An important question kept arising in the early years of Seligman's theory. If depressed people feel incapable of controlling the events in their lives, why do they persistently blame themselves for everything? Doesn't repeated self-blame reflect overestimation of one's control over events rather than underestimation? Actually, helpless feelings and self-blame can be quite compatible: people can blame their lack of control on the fact that they are inadequate, ineffective, or undesirable.

The clarification of this point has led to a major change in the helplessness theory during the past decade. According to the revised theory, when people perceive events to be beyond their control, they implicitly ask themselves why (Abramson, Metalsky, & Alloy, 1989; Abramson, Seligman, & Teasdale, 1978). If they attribute their present lack of control to some *internal* cause that is both *global* and *stable* ("I am inadequate at *everything* and I *always* will be"), they may well feel helpless to prevent future negative outcomes and bereft of hope that anything positive will occur, and they may experience unipolar depression. If they make other kinds of attributions, this reaction is unlikely (see Table 8–2).

The italics in the last paragraph highlight the three important dimensions of these attributions: (1) the

TABLE 8-2

INTERNAL AND EXTERNAL ATTRIBUTIONS

Event: "I failed my psych test today"

| | Internal | | External | |
	Stable	Unstable	Stable	Unstable
Global	"I have a problem with test anxiety."	"Getting into an argument with my roommate threw my whole day off."	"Written tests are an unfair way to assess knowledge."	"No one does well on tests that are given the day after vacation."
Specific	"I just have no grasp of psychology."	"I got upset and froze when I couldn't answer the first two questions."	"Everyone knows that this professor enjoys giving unfair tests."	"This professor didn't put much thought into the test because of the pressure of her book deadline."

internal–external dimension (Does one see the cause as being located in oneself or elsewhere?), (2) the *global–specific* dimension (Does one believe the cause is relevant to many situations or just to this specific situation?), and (3) the *stable–unstable* dimension (Does one see the cause as enduring or short-lived?). Consider a college student whose girlfriend breaks up with him. If he attributes this loss of control over a key source of gratification to an internal cause that is both global and stable—"It's my fault [internal], I ruin everything I touch [global], and I always will [stable]"—he then has reason to expect future losses of control and may therefore experience an enduring sense of helplessness. According to the learned helplessness view, he is a prime candidate for depression.

If the internal cause to which the student pointed were more specific ("The way I've behaved the past couple of weeks blew this relationship") and unstable ("I don't know what got into me—I don't usually act like that"), he would not be so likely to anticipate future losses of control. Similarly, if the student were to attribute the breakup to external causes ("she never did know what she wanted"), he would be less likely to expect future losses of control, and would probably not experience helplessness and depression.

This attribution factor helps explain why some people react helplessly to losses of control while others do not (Metalsky et al., 1993; Heyman, Dweck, & Cain, 1992). It also suggests that helplessness may be prevented or reversed if people are taught to attribute losses of control to external causes or to internal causes that are specific or unstable (Ramirez, Maldonado, & Martos, 1992). Helplessness reactions were prevented in a group of grade school children

in just this way: the children were guided to make alternative attributions for their classroom failures (Dweck, 1976).

Since the helplessness theory was revised, hundreds of studies have tested and supported the relationship between styles of attribution, helplessness, and depressive functioning in both children and adult subjects (Peterson, Colvin, & Lin, 1992; Nolen-Hoeksema, Girgus, & Seligman, 1992). In one study, a group of moderately depressed adults were asked to fill out an Attributional Style Questionnaire (see Table 8–3) before and after successful therapy (Seligman et al., 1988). Before therapy, their high levels of depression were accompanied by attribution styles that were highly internal, stable, and global. At the end of therapy and again one year later, their depression levels were lower and their attribution styles were significantly less internal, stable, and global.

EVALUATING THE LEARNED HELPLESS-NESS THEORY   Although the helplessness model of unipolar depression is a promising and widely applied theory, it poses some problems. First, laboratory-induced helplessness does not parallel depression in every respect. Uncontrollable shocks administered in the laboratory, for example, invariably produce heightened anxiety along with the helplessness effects (Seligman, 1975), but human depression is not always accompanied by anxiety.

A second problem is that much of the research on learned helplessness relies on animal subjects. While the animals' passivity, social withdrawal, and other reactions seem to correspond to the symptoms of human depression, it is impossible to know whether they are true reflections of the same psychological phenomena (Telner & Singhal, 1984).

TABLE 8-3

SAMPLE ITEM FROM THE ATTRIBUTIONAL-STYLE QUESTIONNAIRE

YOU HAVE BEEN LOOKING FOR A JOB UNSUCCESSFULLY FOR SOME TIME.

1. Write down *one* major cause _____ .

2. Is the cause of your unsuccessful job search due to something about you or something about other people or circumstances? (Circle one number.)

Totally due to other people or circumstances						Totally due to me	External vs. internal attribution
1	2	3	4	5	6	7	

3. In the future when looking for a job, will this cause again be present? (Circle one number.)

Will never again be present						Will always be present	Unstable vs. stable attribution
1	2	3	4	5	6	7	

4. Is the cause something that just influences looking for a job, or does it also influence other areas of your life? (Circle one number.)

Influences just this particular situation						Influences all situations in my life	Specific vs. global attribution
1	2	3	4	5	6	7	

5. How important would this situation be if it happened to you? (Circle one number.)

Not at all important						Extremely important
1	2	3	4	5	6	7

Source: Seligman et al., 1979.

Finally, the attributional aspect of the helplessness theory has raised important questions. Although numerous studies suggest that depressive reactions are indeed related to internal, stable, and global attributions of negative events (Ramirez et al., 1992; Seligman et al., 1984), equally respectable studies have failed to find such a connection (Brewin & Furnham, 1986; Hargreaves, 1985). Moreover, even if we grant that attributions may play an important role in mediating human loss of control, what about the many dogs and rats who learn helplessness? Are they attributing their lack of control to internal, general, and stable causes? Can animals make attributions, even implicitly? Or is this an area where animal and human helplessness part company?

These questions notwithstanding, Seligman's learned helplessness theory has provided a compelling model of unipolar depression and has demonstrated an impressive capacity to grow in response to new findings and difficult questions. It has also inspired considerable research and thinking about human depression and human adaptation, from which new insights and ideas continue to emerge.

THE BIOLOGICAL VIEW   Medical researchers have been aware for years that certain diseases, drugs, and toxins produce mood alterations, and some have taken these findings to suggest that clinical depression may itself have a biological foundation. Their suspicions have been supported during the past several decades by compelling evidence that biological abnormalities also contribute to the development of unipolar depression (Siever, Davis, & Gorman, 1991). The role of biological factors has been implied by genetic studies and more directly supported by investigations that tie unipolar patterns of depression to biochemical dysfunction.

GENETIC FACTORS   Many theorists believe

According to the attribution theory of learned helplessness, Calvin may be a candidate for further experiences of helplessness and depression because of his belief that he was born unlucky—an internal, stable, and global attribution. (CALVIN AND HOBBES © 1993 Watterson. Reprinted with permission of UNIVERSAL PRESS SYNDICATE. All rights reserved.)

that some people inherit a predisposition to develop unipolar depression. Support for this genetic view has come primarily from family pedigree studies, twin studies, and adoption studies.

Researchers who conduct *family pedigree studies* select people with unipolar depression as *probands* (the proband is the person who is the focus of a genetic study) and examine their close relatives to see whether depression afflicts other members of the family. If a predisposition to unipolar depression is inherited, relatives should have a higher rate of depression than the population at large. And researchers have found that as many as 20 percent of those relatives are depressed, compared to 5 to 10 percent of the general population (Harrington et al., 1993; Nurnberger & Gershon, 1992, 1984).

If a predisposition to unipolar depression is inherited, one would also expect more cases of depression among the probands' close relatives than among their distant relatives. *Twin studies* of depression among monozygotic (identical) twins and dizygotic (fraternal) twins have found rates consistent with this expectation (Nurnberger & Gershon, 1992, 1984). A Danish study determined that when a monozygotic twin has unipolar depression, there is a 43 percent chance that the other twin will have the same disorder, whereas when a dizygotic twin has unipolar depression, the other twin has only a 20 percent chance of developing the disorder (Bertelsen, Harvald, & Hauge, 1977).

Of course, as we have observed in earlier chapters, such findings are not proof of a genetic predisposition. Close relatives tend to have similar environments and learning experiences—similar stresses, role models, and family atmosphere—and these shared experiences may account for similar

Children whose mothers are depressed are at greater risk of later experiencing depression than are children of nondepressed mothers. Modeling effects, the mother's behavior toward her children, or socioeconomic pressures may partly account for this relationship, but adoption studies suggest that genetic factors may also play a significant role in it (Cummings & Davies, 1994).

predispositions to particular disorders (Lewontin et al., 1984). Moreover, the data also suggest that even if genetic factors are operating in unipolar depression, they are only contributing factors at best. As the twin studies indicate, the probability that the proband's twin will develop unipolar depression is less than 50 percent even when their genetic structures are identical.

Finally, *adoption studies* suggest that a genetic factor may operate in severe cases of unipolar depression. A study of the families of adopted persons who had been hospitalized for unipolar depression in Denmark determined that the biological parents of these severely depressed adoptees had a higher incidence of severe depression than did the biological parents of a control group of nondepressed adoptees, but not of mild depression (Wender et al., 1986). Theorists who believe that the different patterns of unipolar depression represent distinct disorders with distinct origins have pointed to studies such as this to support their assertion.

BIOCHEMICAL FACTORS As we have seen, neurotransmitters are the brain chemicals that carry messages from one nerve cell, or neuron, to another. When an electrical message is received by a neuron, it travels down the cell's long axon to the cell terminals. These nerve endings release a neurotransmitter that travels across a synaptic space to receptors on the receiving neuron, telling that neuron either to fire (transmit the electrical impulse) or to stop firing. Different neurons store and use different neurotransmitters. *Norepinephrine* and *serotonin* are the two neurotransmitters that have been strongly implicated in unipolar patterns of depression (see Figure 8–4).

In the 1950s, several pieces of evidence pointed to low norepinephrine activity in the brain as a possible factor in depression. First, medical researchers discovered that *reserpine*, a drug used to treat high blood pressure, causes depression in some people (Ayd, 1956). An examination of reserpine's effect on the brain indicated that it lowered norepinephrine supplies in the nerve endings of many neurons, thus suggesting to researchers that depression may be related to low supplies of norepinephrine.

A second piece of evidence emerged from the discovery of a family of antidepressant drugs known as *monoamine oxidase (MAO) inhibitors.* These compounds increase the norepinephrine supplies of many neurons. The possibility that this was the means by which MAO inhibitors alleviated depression again fitted in with the idea that depression is related to low supplies of norepinephrine.

A third piece of evidence came from the discovery during the 1950s of another group of antidepressant medications, called *tricyclics.* Although these drugs are chemically different from MAO inhibitors, researchers soon learned that they, too, seemed to operate by ultimately increasing norepinephrine supplies in the brain (Snyder, 1984, 1976).

These three lines of investigation led to the tentative conclusion that unipolar depression was a product of low norepinephrine supplies (Schildkraut, 1965; Bunney & Davis, 1965). Researchers reasoned that lower supplies of this neurotransmitter must result in less neuronal firing, a concept that certainly fits the slow-motion picture of depression. Because norepinephrine belongs to the class of chemicals called catecholamines, this theory is known as the *catecholamine theory.*

While researchers in the United States were focusing on norepinephrine as the biological key to unipolar depression, British researchers were focusing on the neurotransmitter serotonin (Coppen, 1967). They discovered that serotonin operates much like norepinephrine in a number of ways; that is, the blood pressure medication reserpine lowers supplies of brain serotonin, just as it lowers norepinephrine, and the MAO inhibitors and tricyclic antidepressants increase supplies of serotonin in the brain, just as they increase norepinephrine (Amsterdam, Brunswick, & Mendels, 1980). Moreover, the neurons that use serotonin as their neurotransmitter tend to be located in many of the same areas of the brain as those that use norepinephrine (see Figure 8–5). These findings led many theorists to conclude that serotonin deficiencies may also cause unipolar depression (Golden & Gilmore, 1990). This view is often called

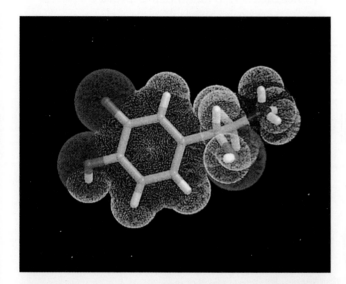

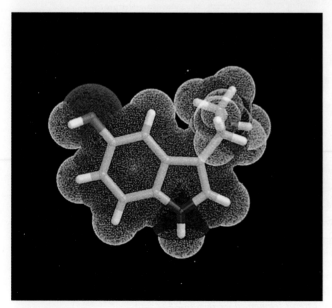

FIGURE 8–4 *Computer-drawn molecules of the neurotransmitters norepinephrine (top) and serotonin (bottom). Low activity of these neurotransmitters has repeatedly been implicated in unipolar depression.*

the *indoleamine theory,* because serotonin belongs to the class of chemicals known as indoleamines.

INVESTIGATING THE NEUROTRANSMITTER THEORIES Over the past two decades an enormous amount of research has been devoted to sorting out the contributions of norepinephrine and serotonin to unipolar depression. Several proposals have emerged:

1. *Low norepinephrine and low serotonin combine to cause depression.* According to this argument, unipolar depression will occur only when both norepinephrine and serotonin supplies are low, and it will lift only when the levels of both neurotransmitters are increased. This theory lost its influence when some studies indicated that depression was accompanied sometimes by low norepinephrine levels alone and at other times by low serotonin alone. The blood pressure medicine **alpha-methyldopa** (Aldomet), for example, lowers norepinephrine supplies but does not lower serotonin. Nevertheless, a substantial number of people who take this drug become depressed.

2. *Low levels of either neurotransmitter can lead to depression.* Many findings have been consistent with this proposal (Garver & Davis, 1979). For example, research has been conducted on 3-methoxy-4-hydroxyphenylglycol (MHPG), a chemical by-product of norepinephrine metabolism in the brain (such by-products are called **metabolites**). Because this by-product leaves the brain and enters the bloodstream and other parts of the body relatively intact, its level in the urine is thought to reflect the supply of norepinephrine in the brain (McNeal & Cimbolic, 1986). Studies have found that some, but not all, depressed people excrete low levels of MHPG, suggesting that the norepinephrine levels of depressed people are sometimes, but not always, low (Yazici et al., 1993; Maas, 1975; Fawcett & Bunney, 1967).

Studies of 5-hydroxyindoleacetic acid (5-HIAA), a major by-product of serotonin, tell a similar story. Researchers have found that approximately 25 percent of depressed people display very low levels of 5-HIAA, while other depressed people have normal levels (Yazici et al., 1993; Baldessarini, 1983; Maas, 1975). This finding suggests that unipolar depression is sometimes, but not always, accompanied by low serotonin levels.

Yet another line of research suggests that either low serotonin or low norepinephrine supplies may cause depression. These studies first focused on **tryptophan,** which is a **precursor** of serotonin—

that is, a brain chemical that appears early in the chain of reactions that lead to the production of serotonin. Researchers believe that administering tryptophan should increase a person's brain supply of serotonin without increasing that of norepinephrine. The finding that tryptophan often does alleviate depressive symptoms suggests that increases in serotonin alone can sometimes improve depression (Van Praag, 1984). Similarly, when *tyrosine,* a precursor of norepinephrine, is administered to depressed people, it sometimes reduces depressive symptoms, suggesting that norepinephrine increases alone can alleviate some cases of depression (Gelenberg et al., 1980).

3. *Norepinephrine depression is different from serotonin depression.* Some theorists have proposed that unipolar depression linked to low norepinephrine is qualitatively different from depression linked to low serotonin (Van Praag, 1984; Asberg et al., 1984, 1976). This "two-disease theory" has an intuitive appeal. After all, though norepinephrine and serotonin are both neurotransmitters, they are chemically distinct. Can the depressive reaction caused by the relative absence of one chemical truly be identical to that caused by the absence of the other?

In support of this notion, Marie Asberg and her colleagues (1976) found that depressed subjects

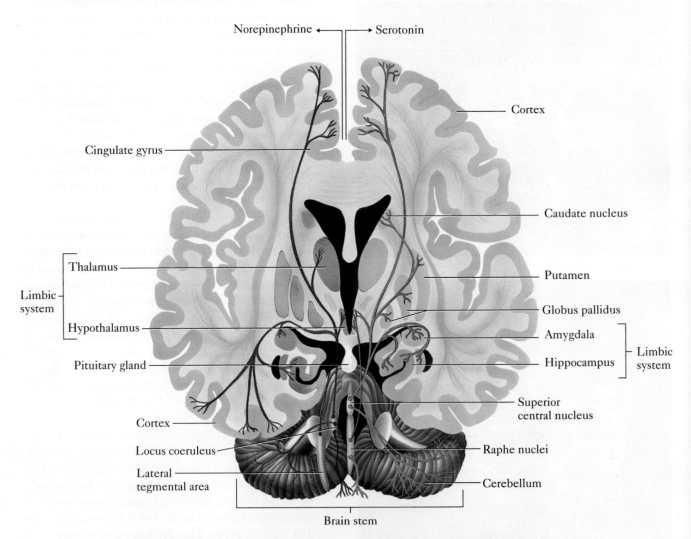

FIGURE 8-5 *The cell bodies of neurons that contain norepinephrine or serotonin are located throughout the brain stem. The cell bodies of norepinephrine neurons are found in the locus coeruleus and lateral tegmental area, while the serotonin-containing cell bodies are concentrated in the raphe nuclei. The axons of these neurons extend to various parts of the brain, particularly to the limbic system, the portion that regulates emotion. The norepinephrine pathways are indicated in blue, the serotonin pathways in turquoise. (Adapted from Snyder, 1986, p. 108.)*

whose serotonin was depleted were more apathetic and suicidal than depressed subjects with normal serotonin levels. They also found that suicide attempts made by depressed patients with low serotonin were more frequent and more violent than those made by other depressed people.

4. *Neither norepinephrine nor serotonin supplies are key factors in depression.* Some researchers believe that the biological explanations of unipolar depression have placed too much emphasis on the *supply* of norepinephrine or serotonin available in the brain and that other brain processes are really at the core of unipolar depression. There are growing suspicions, for example, that the primary biological problem may be ineffective norepinephrine or serotonin *receptors* that fail to attract and capture sufficient amounts of neurotransmitters, thus creating the impression that the neurotransmitters are depleted in the brain (Newman, Lerer, & Shapira, 1993; Singh & Lucki, 1993).

Still other researchers believe that it is wrong to focus exclusively on norepinephrine and serotonin, whether on their supplies or on their receptors. There is some evidence that high levels of a different neurotransmitter, **acetylcholine,** may also be associated with depression (McNeal & Cimbolic, 1986; Janowsky et al., 1972). Exposure to potent insecticides that increase acetylcholine levels causes some adults to undergo a depressive change in mood (Gershon & Shaw, 1961). Similarly, intravenous administration of **physostigmine,** a chemical that increases acetylcholine supplies in the brain, can cause a depressionlike syndrome in previously nondepressed subjects (Risch et al., 1983; Davis et al., 1976). Such findings have led several theorists to propose that some overall imbalance in norepinephrine, serotonin, and acetylcholine activity causes the symptoms of unipolar depression (Ballenger, 1988; Risch & Janowsky, 1984). Finally, a growing number of researchers think that perhaps each of these neurotransmitters plays a role in the operation of a "body clock" whose malfunction is the true source of depression (see Box 8–4).

EVALUATING THE NEUROTRANSMITTER THEORIES   The neurotransmitter theories of depression have deservedly generated much enthusiasm and investigation, but many questions are still unanswered. First, this research, too, has consisted to a large degree of analogue studies that create depres-

sionlike symptoms in laboratory animals. While the symptoms these studies generate are superficially similar to human depression, researchers cannot be certain that they do in fact reflect the quality and substance of the human disorder (Overstreet, 1993).

A second problem is that until recent years, the limitations of technology required most studies on human beings to manipulate and measure brain chemical activity indirectly, and as a result investigators could never be quite certain of the actual biochemical events (Katz et al., 1993; Grossman, Manji, & Potter, 1993; Shopsin & Feiner, 1984). Researchers assumed, for example, that when they administered certain chemical precursors to human subjects, those precursors were converted into neurotransmitters, whose presence then increased the specific neurotransmitter activity in the brain. It is conceivable, however, that nothing of the kind was happening. Similarly, most estimates of existing supplies of neurotransmitters in a living person's brain were based on measurements of neurotransmitter metabolites in the urine or spinal fluid. Again, it is possible that those measures were not accurate reflections of the supplies of norepinephrine and serotonin in the brain. Studies using newer technology, such as the PET and MRI, should address such concerns in the coming years.

These limitations notwithstanding, biological researchers seem to be closing in on some compelling and enlightening insights into the biological underpinnings of unipolar depression. Their work, along with the work and findings of psychological researchers, has also begun to open doors to the effective treatment of unipolar patterns of depression, an important turn of events that we shall be investigating in Chapter 9.

■ BIPOLAR ■ DISORDERS

People with bipolar disorder experience both the lows of depression and the highs of mania. Many describe their life as an emotional roller-coaster. They must deal not only with the direct consequences of their reckless euphorias and paralyzing dysphorias, but also with the additional problems brought about simply by the fact that there is so much change in their lives (Goodwin & Jamison, 1990). This roller-coaster ride and its impact on relatives and friends is dramatically seen in the following description:

BOX 8-4

WHEN BODY CLOCKS NEED RESETTING

Our lives are structured by cycles and rhythms—daily, monthly, seasonal, and yearly. The 24-hour day provides the cycle to which we adapt our most common activities—sleeping, eating, working, and socializing. Although our daily rhythms are imposed largely by our environment, they are also driven by a kind of internal clock, consisting of recurrent biological fluctuations, called *circadian rhythms,* that must be coordinated with one another and with both cyclic and transient changes in the environment. The daily operation of our internal clocks is apparently controlled by at least two self-sustained oscillators. One oscillator is strong and consistent, and rigidly controls regular changes in body temperature, hormone secretions, and *rapid eye movement (REM) sleep*—the near-awake phase of sleep during which we dream. The other oscillator, weaker and more ready to adjust to changes, controls the sleep–wake cycle and activity–rest cycle. Most people can go to sleep late one night and early the next and have no trouble falling asleep quickly and sleeping soundly; but during this same period their body temperature will rigidly follow its usual pattern, peaking at the same time each afternoon and bottoming out each morning (Gold, 1987).

A series of revealing studies conducted throughout the 1980s has convinced many researchers that depression is often the result of an imbalance, or *desynchronization,* between the body's circadian rhythms and the rhythms of the environment (Healy & Williams, 1988; Zerssen et al., 1985; Goodwin, Wirz-Justice, & Wehr, 1982). For example, the sleep cycle, the most basic rhythm in our lives, is apparently reversed in depressed people. Unlike other people, they quickly move into REM sleep after falling asleep, experience longer stretches of REM sleep during the early parts of the sleep cycles, and have shorter episodes of REM sleep toward the morning (Buysse, Reynolds, & Kupfer, 1993; Hirshfield & Goodwin, 1988; Gold, 1987; Wehr & Goodwin, 1981). Depressed people also display more frequent rapid eye movements during REM sleep and less deep sleep overall. Thus some theorists think the body's two oscillators, the rigid one in control of REM sleep and the flexible one in control of the sleep–wake cycle, may be out of harmony (Goodwin et al., 1982).

■ HORMONES ■ AND DEPRESSION

Endocrine glands are located throughout the body, working along with the nervous system to regulate such vital activities as growth, reproduction, sexual activity, heart rate, body temperature, energy, and responses to stress. Under various conditions, the glands release hormones, which in turn propel body organs into action. This entire endocrine system is run by the *hypothalamus,* the brain area often called the "brain of the brain."

Secretions of the hormone *melatonin* appear to be particularly important in depression (Lam et al., 1990). This hormone, nicknamed the Dracula hormone, is secreted by the brain's *pineal gland* when our surroundings are dark, but not when they are light. The role of melatonin in human biology is not entirely understood, but in animals it seems to help regulate hibernation, activity levels, and reproductive cycles. As nights grow longer during the fall and winter, animals secrete more and more melatonin, which has the effect of slowing them down and preparing them for an extended seasonal rest. When daytime hours lengthen in the spring and summer, melatonin secretions decrease, raising energy levels and setting the stage for reproduction. Although human activity levels and reproduction cycles do not appear to be so closely tied to light and dark, our pineal glands nevertheless carry on the tradition of secreting greater amounts of melatonin during the dark nights of winter than during the short nights of summer.

Some theorists believe that because of our heightened melatonin secretions, humans slow down, have less energy, and need more rest in the wintertime, much as hibernating animals do. Most people manage to adjust to these internal changes. Researchers believe, however, that some people are so sensitive to winter's heightened melatonin secretions that they find it impossible to carry on with business as usual (Dilsaver, 1990; Rosenthal & Blehar, 1989). Their seasonal slowdown takes the form of depression, but a depression characterized by symptoms that are quite consistent with animal hibernation—a big appetite, a craving for carbohydrates, weight gain, oversleeping, and fatigue (Gupta, 1988). This pattern, often called *seasonal affective disorder* (Rosenthal & Blehar, 1989), or *SAD,* is now described in the DSM. Researchers believe that these people are also extremely sensitive to the drop in melatonin secretions that occurs during the longer days of summer. Some, in fact, become overenergized and overactive and display a hypomanic or manic pattern every summer (Faedda et al., 1993; Carney et al., 1988).

Research suggests that the *suprachiasmatic nuclei (SCN),* a small cluster of neurons in the hypothalamus, connected to the pineal gland and to the eyes, may be the regulator for the circadian rhythms (Rietvald, 1992; Ballenger, 1988). When light enters the eyes, the "light" message is carried by the neurotransmitter acetylcholine to the SCN. This message is then carried by the neurotransmitter norepinephrine to the pineal gland, which reacts by stopping its manufacture of melatonin. If the pineal gland were to fail to receive this "light" message, it would keep producing melatonin; the melatonin would in turn repeatedly act upon the hypothalamus, thus affecting the timing of hormone secretions throughout the body. Depressed people may have an abnormality in the SCN or in some other link in this chain, leading to desynchronization and to depressive symptoms (Anderson et al., 1992; Lewy et al., 1992; Healy & Waterhouse, 1990).

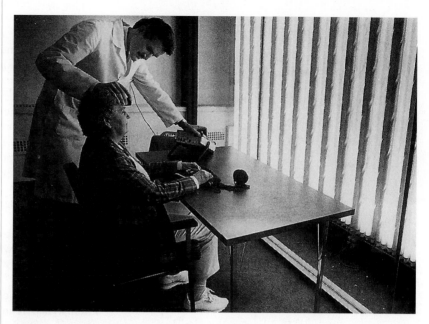

Various techniques have been developed to provide SAD patients with extra amounts of light on short winter days.

■ LIGHT ■ THERAPY

If in fact darkness is the problem in SAD, the answer may be light. One of the most effective treatments for SAD turns out to be light therapy, or ***phototherapy,*** exposure to extra amounts of synthetic light throughout the winter. When seasonally depressed patients sit under intense light for several hours every winter day, their depression can be reduced or eliminated (Avery et al., 1993; Anderson et al., 1992; Rosenthal et al., 1988; Lewy et al., 1987, 1980). Some theorists believe that extremely bright light must be applied (an intensity of 2,500 lux as opposed to the normal 250 lux), while others believe that even dim light may be helpful (McIntyre et al., 1990). Some believe that the light must be administered both in the morning and at night, while others consider one administration per day to be sufficient (Doghramji et al., 1990; Lewy et al., 1987). Light therapy may have mild unpleasant effects, including headache, eyestrain, and a feeling of being "wired" (APA, 1993; Levitt et al., 1993).

Of course, there is another, more enjoyable way to get more light—take a winter vacation in a sunny place. Some theorists go so far as to suggest that people with wintertime blues, and certainly those with SAD, should spend a week or two just before winter begins in a location approximately 3 to 4 degrees north or south of the equator, where 70 percent more sunlight is available each day. The effectiveness of this form of "treatment" has yet to be investigated scientifically.

In view of the impracticalities of light therapy, clinicians have searched actively for alternative ways to alter melatonin levels. One promising possibility is melatonin pills. Researchers are beginning to demonstrate that it isn't really the amount of melatonin secreted that causes depression for SAD-prone people but the time of day it is secreted. That is, the hormone's usual role may be to set the body's biological clock each day. Ill-timed secretions of it throughout the 24-hour period may disrupt the body's circadian rhythms, and so leave the person vulnerable to depression. A team of researchers headed by Alfred Lewy believe that SAD may eventually be better treated by a dose of melatonin than by hours of phototherapy (Lewy et al., 1992). A pill, given at key times in the day, would readjust each patient's body clock and alleviate depression. These researchers have found that a dose of melatonin in the morning does in fact delay a subject's circadian rhythm, whereas a dose in the afternoon or early evening advances the rhythm.

The use of melatonin pills has already been tried for some other kinds of problems. Some researchers have successfully used them to correct jet lag for subjects, and others have used them to correct the body-clock problems of blind people whose circadian rhythm often shifts to a 25-hour cycle without light cues from the environment. If these pills do indeed turn out to be a useful treatment for seasonal affective disorders, we may have reached a major turning point in effectively and efficiently addressing the suffering of people with this roller-coaster problem.

Echoing Shakespeare's observation that "the lunatic, the lover, and the poet are all compact," clinical researchers Frederick Goodwin and Kay Jamison (1990) claim that some of our most famous poets, including Sylvia Plath, have experienced bipolar disorders. Plath committed suicide in 1963 at the age of 31.

*I*n his early school years he had been a remarkable student and had shown a gift for watercolor and oils. Later he had studied art in Paris and married an English girl he had met there. Eventually they had settled in London.

Ten years later, when he was thirty-four years old, he had persuaded his wife and only son to accompany him to Honolulu, where, he assured them, he would be considered famous. He felt he would be able to sell his paintings at many times the prices he could get in London. According to his wife, he had been in an accelerated state, but at that time the family had left, unsuspecting, believing with the patient in their imminent good fortune. When they arrived they found almost no one in the art world that he was supposed to know. There were no connections for sales and deals in Hawaii that he had anticipated. Settling down, the patient began to behave more peculiarly than ever. After enduring several months of the patient's exhilaration, overactivity, weight loss, constant talking, and unbelievably little sleep, the young wife and child began to fear for his sanity. None of his plans materialized. After five months in the Pacific, with finances growing thin, the patient's overactivity subsided and he fell into a depression. During that period he refused to move, paint, or leave the house. He lost twenty pounds, became utterly dependent on his wife, and insisted on seeing none of the friends he had accumulated in his manic state. His despondency became so severe that several doctors came to the house and advised psychiatric hospitalization. He quickly agreed and received twelve electroshock treatments, which relieved his depressed state. Soon afterward he began to paint again and to sell his work modestly. Recognition began to come from galleries and critics in the Far East. Sev-

eral reviews acclaimed his work as exceptionally brilliant.

This was the beginning of the lifelong career of his moodswing. In 1952, while still in Honolulu, he once again became severely depressed. . . . Four years later he returned to London in a high. In this manic state he spent his carefully accumulated lifetime savings, took on several mistresses, divorced his wife, gave away paintings, and gambled. He began to be obsessed by religion and mysticism, and felt he could communicate with the universe through his paintings. When this manic period subsided and he surveyed the wreckage of his life, an eight-month interval of normal mood followed, after which he again switched into a profound depression. During this normal phase he recognized that paintings accomplished during the psychotic high were not as good as he had thought them to be.

During this rebound normal period, he met and married his second wife, who said that at the time he was enthusiastic and irresistibly charming but not in any sense abnormal mentally.

Despite the fact that he was now beginning to achieve international renown for his canvases, he began to feel plagued with frequent and severe suicidal depressions. During these periods he withdrew, refused to paint, lost weight, and slept sixteen hours out of twenty-four. He said that he no longer wanted to live. On one occasion his wife found him walking naked in the middle of the night, about to take a bottle of sleeping pills. This depression lifted spontaneously after six months.

(Fieve, 1975, pp. 64–65)

THE CLINICAL PICTURE OF MANIA

In contrast to the unrelieved gloom of depression, a person in a state of mania is governed by a dramatic, inappropriate, and disproportionate elevation of mood. The symptoms of mania encompass the same areas of functioning—emotional, motivational, behavioral, cognitive, and somatic—as those of depression, but mania affects those areas in an almost diametrically opposite way (see Table 8–4).

Mania is characterized by active, expansive *emotions* that seem to be looking for an outlet. The mood of euphoric joy and well-being is out of all proportion to the actual happenings in the person's life. One person with mania explained, "I feel no sense of restriction or censorship whatsoever. I am afraid of nothing and no one" (Fieve, 1975, p. 68). Another described his manic experience as "a sense of communion, in the first place with God, and in the second with all mankind" (Custance, 1952, p. 37). Not every person with mania is a picture of happiness, however. Some can also become irritable, angry, and

TABLE 8-4

MANIFESTATIONS OF MANIA AND DEPRESSION

MANIA	DEPRESSION
Emotional	
Elation	Depressed mood
Liking for self	Dislike of self
Increased mirth response	Loss of mirth response
Cognitive	
Positive self-image	Negative self-image
Positive expectations	Negative expectations
Tendency to blame others	Tendency to blame self
Denial of problems	Exaggeration of problems
Arbitrary decision making	Indecisiveness
Motivational	
Driven and impulsive behavior	Paralysis of the will
Action-oriented wishes	Wishes for escape
Drive for independence	Increased wishes for dependency
Desire for self-enhancement	Desire for death
Behavioral	
Hyperactivity	Inertia/agitation
Productivity	Lack of productivity
Loudness	Quietness
Physical	
Indefatigability	Easy fatigability
Increased libido	Loss of libido
Insomnia	Insomnia

Source: Beck, 1967, p. 91.

annoyed (Verdoux & Bourgeois, 1993; Double, 1991)—especially when others get in the way of their ambitions, activities, and plans—like this man:

All by himself, he had been building a magnificent swimming pool for his country home in Virginia, working eighteen hours a day at it. He decided to make the pool public and open a concession stand at one end to help defray the mounting costs of the project. When his wife suggested that he might be going overboard, he became furious and threatened to leave her for another woman. Soon afterward, when his wife was out, he took many valuables from the house—his share, he claimed—and sold or pawned them. Complaining that his wife was a stick in the mud, he decided to throw a round-the-clock party, and he invited to the house almost everyone he passed on the street. This psychotic behavior went on for weeks, and during this time he slept only two to four hours a night. He had no time to eat, and he talked continuously, planning grandiose sexual schemes "as soon as someone takes my wife off my hands."

(Fieve, 1975, p. 148)

In the *motivational* realm, people with mania seem to want constant excitement, involvement, and companionship. They enthusiastically seek out new friends and old, new interests and old, and have little awareness that their social style is overwhelming, domineering, and excessive:

He was interested in everything and everyone around him. He talked familiarly to patients, attendants, nurses, and physicians. He took a fancy to the woman physician on duty in the admission building, calling her by her first name and annoying her with letters and with his familiar, ill mannered, and obtrusive attentions. . . . He made many comments and asked many questions about other patients and promised that he would secure their discharge. He interfered with their affairs and soon received a blow on the jaw from one patient and a black eye from another.

(Kolb, 1973, p. 372)

The *behavior* of people with mania is usually described as hyperactive. They move quickly, as though there were not enough time to do everything they want to do. They may talk rapidly and loudly, their conversations filled with jokes and efforts to be clever or, conversely, with complaints and hostile tirades. Flamboyance is another characteristic of manic functioning: dressing in flashy clothes, giving large sums of money to strangers, getting involved in dangerous activities. Several of these qualities are evident in the monologue delivered by Joe to the two policemen who escorted him to the mental hospital:

You look like a couple of bright, alert, hardworking, clean-cut, energetic go-getters and I could use you in my organization! I need guys that are loyal and enthusiastic about the great opportunities life offers on this planet! It's yours for the taking! Too many people pass opportunity by without hearing it knock because they don't know how to grasp the moment and strike while the iron is hot! You've got to grab it when it comes up for air, pick up the ball and run! You've got to be decisive! decisive! decisive! No shilly-shallying! Sweat! Yeah, sweat with a goal! Push, push, push, and you can push over a mountain! Two mountains, maybe. It's not luck! Hell, if it wasn't for bad luck I wouldn't have any luck at all! Be there firstest with the mostest! My guts and your blood! That's the system! I know, you know, he, she or it knows it's the only way to travel! Get 'em off balance, baby, and the rest is leverage! Use your head and save your heels! What's this deal? Who are these guys? Have you got a telephone and a secretary I can have instanter if not sooner? What I need is office space and the old LDO [long-distance operator].

(McNeil, 1967, p. 147)

In the *cognitive* realm, people with mania usually display poor judgment and planning, as if they feel too good or move too rapidly to consider consequences or possible pitfalls. Filled with optimism, they rarely listen when others try to slow them down, interrupt their buying sprees, or prevent them from investing money unwisely. They may also hold an inflated opinion of themselves, believing that there are few topics beyond their expertise and few tasks beyond their grasp. Sometimes their self-esteem approaches grandiosity (Silverstone & Hunt, 1992). The novelist Saul Bellow captures the expansiveness and self-glorification of a person during a manic episode:

He was a great entertainer but going insane. The pathologic element could be missed only by those who were laughing too hard to look. Humboldt, that grand erratic handsome person with his wide blond face, that charming, fluent deeply worried man to whom I was so attached, passionately lived out the theme of Success. Naturally he died a Failure. What else can result from the capitalization of such nouns? Myself, I've always held the number of sacred words down. In my opinion Humboldt had too long a list of them—Poetry, Beauty, Love, Waste Land, Alienation, Politics, History, the Unconscious. And, of course, Manic and Depressive, always capitalized. According to him, America's great Manic Depressive was Lincoln. And Churchill with what he called his Black Dog moods was a classic case of Manic Depression. "Like me, Charlie," said Humboldt. "But think—if Energy is Delight and if Exuberance is Beauty, the Manic Depressive knows more about Delight and Beauty than anyone else. Who else has so much Energy and Exuberance? Maybe it's the strategy of the Psyche to increase Depression. Didn't Freud say that Happiness was nothing but the remission of Pain? So the more Pain the intenser the Happiness. But there is a prior origin to this, and the Psyche makes Pain on purpose. Anyway, Mankind is stunned by the Exuberance and Beauty of certain individuals. When a Manic Depressive escapes from his Furies he's irresistible. He captures History. I think that aggravation is a secret technique of the

Unconscious. As for great men and kings being History's slaves, I think Tolstoi was off the track. Don't kid yourself, kings are the most sublime sick. Manic Depressive heroes pull Mankind into their cycles and carry everybody away."

(Bellow, 1975)

People with mania are also easily distracted by random stimuli from the environment. Especially during the acute phases of mania, they may have so much trouble keeping their thoughts on track that they become incoherent, even out of touch with reality (Double, 1991; Harrow et al., 1988). Some also report that their sensory impressions seem sharper, brighter, more colorful, and more pleasurable than when they are not in a state of mania.

Finally, in the *physical* realm, people with mania feel remarkably energetic. They typically get little sleep, yet feel and act wide awake (Silverstone & Hunt, 1992). Even if they miss a night or two of sleep, their energy level seems very high. Clifford Beers (1908) wrote:

For several weeks I believe I did not sleep more than two or three hours a night. Such was my state of elation, however, that all signs of fatigue were entirely absent; and the sustained and abnormal mental and physical activity in which I then indulged has left on my memory no other than a series of very pleasant impressions.

DIAGNOSING BIPOLAR DISORDERS

DSM-IV considers people to be experiencing a full *manic episode* when they display for at least one week an abnormally elevated, expansive, or irritable mood, along with at least three other symptoms of mania. Such episodes may vary from moderate to extreme in severity and may include such psychotic features as delusions or hallucinations. When the symptoms of mania are less severe (causing no marked impairment) and shorter in duration (at least four days) than those of a manic episode, the person is said to be experiencing a *hypomanic episode* (APA, 1994).

DSM-IV distinguishes two general kinds of *bipolar disorders*—bipolar I and bipolar II disorders. People with *bipolar I* disorders experience manic and major depressive episodes. Most of them experience an *alternation* of the episodes; some, however, have *mixed episodes* that consist of both manic and depressive symptoms within the same day. In *bipolar II disorders,* hypomanic—that is, mildly manic—episodes alternate with major depressive episodes over the

In recent years actress Patty Duke has talked and written about her roller-coaster life with bipolar disorder. Until her disorder was diagnosed and treated, she experienced recurrent episodes of suicidal depression alternating with episodes of normal mood or mania.

course of time. Only individuals who have never had a full manic episode receive this diagnosis.

If people experience four or more episodes of mood disturbance within a one-year period, their disorder, whether a bipolar I or bipolar II pattern, is further classified as *rapid cycling*. If their mood episodes vary with the seasons, the bipolar disorder is further classified as *seasonal*.

Surveys conducted around the world indicate that between 0.4 and 1.3 percent of all adults suffer from a bipolar disorder in any given year, with bipolar I disorders being somewhat more common than bipolar II disorders (Kessler et al., 1994; Regier et al., 1993; Smith & Weissman, 1992; Weissman et al., 1991). According to most studies, bipolar disorders are equally common in women and men, and usually begin between the ages of 15 and 44 years (Smith & Weissman, 1992; Weissman et al., 1991; Weissman & Klerman, 1985). Research conducted in the United States suggests that bipolar disorders are equally common in all socioeconomic classes and ethnic groups (APA, 1994; Weissman et al., 1991).

Up to 60 percent of bipolar disorders begin with a manic or hypomanic episode (Silverstone & Hunt, 1992; Coryell & Winokur, 1992; Goodwin & Jamison, 1984). In most untreated cases, the manic and depressive episodes last for several months each (Coryell & Winokur, 1992; Goodwin & Jamison, 1984). Manic episodes immediately precede or follow the depressive episodes in about two-thirds of all cases. Intervening periods of normal mood last for two or more years in many cases (Weissman & Boyd, 1984), but

only briefly in other cases. Some individuals, in fact, continue to display some disturbances in mood between episodes (APA, 1994).

In the absence of treatment, manic and depressive episodes tend to recur (APA, 1994; Goodwin & Jamison, 1990). One team of researchers reviewed the progress of ninety-five recorded cases of untreated bipolar disorders, each spanning an average of twenty-six years, and found that 84 percent of the patients had five or more mood episodes in that time span, 65 percent had seven or more, and 42 percent had eleven or more (Angst, Fedler, & Frey, 1979). Generally, as episodes recur, the intervening periods of normality grow shorter and shorter (Goodwin & Jamison, 1984).

When individuals experience numerous periods of hypomanic symptoms and mild depressive symptoms, DSM-IV assigns a diagnosis of *cyclothymic disorder.* The milder symptoms of this form of bipolar disorder continue for two or more years at a time, interrupted occasionally by normal moods that may last up to two months. This disorder, like the more severe bipolar disorders, usually begins in adolescence or early adulthood and is equally common among women and men. At least 0.4 percent of the population develops cyclothymic disorder (APA, 1994). In some cases, the milder symptoms eventually blossom into a bipolar I or II disorder.

EXPLANATIONS OF BIPOLAR DISORDERS

Throughout the first half of this century, the study of bipolar disorders made little progress. Various models were proposed to explain bipolar mood swings, but research did not support their validity. Psychodynamic theorists suggested that mania, like depression, emerges from the loss of a love object. Whereas some people introject the lost object and become depressed, others deny the loss and become manic. They avoid the terrifying conflicts generated by the loss by escaping into a fast-thinking and fast-moving style of life (Lewin, 1950). Although some psychodynamic clinicians have cited case reports that fit this explanation (Krishnan et al., 1984; Cohen et al., 1954), few controlled studies have been able to find any systematic relationship between recent loss (real or imagined) and the onset of a manic episode (Dunner & Hall, 1980).

For a long time manic-depressive cycles seemed to resist all explanations and forms of treatment. Lately, however, some promising clues from the biological realm have led to better understanding. These biological insights come from research into *neurotransmitter activity, sodium ion activity,* and *genetic factors.*

NEUROTRANSMITTERS When researchers first proposed the catecholamine theory, holding that a low norepinephrine supply leads to depression, they also argued that an oversupply of norepinephrine is related to mania (Schildkraut, 1965). Subsequent research has offered some support for this claim. One study measured the norepinephrine level in subjects' spinal fluid, on the assumption once again that this measure would reflect the norepinephrine supply in the brain (Post et al., 1980, 1978). It found the norepinephrine levels of manic patients to be significantly higher than those of depressed or control subjects. When bipolar patients in another study were given reserpine, the blood pressure drug known to reduce the norepinephrine supply in the brain, some subjects' manic symptoms subsided (Telner et al., 1986).

The belief that mania is related to high norepinephrine activity has also been supported by research on the action of the drug *lithium.* As we shall see in Chapter 9, lithium is by far the most effective treatment for bipolar disorders, in many cases correcting both the manic and the depressive poles of the cycle. Once researchers became aware of lithium's dramatic impact, they proceeded to study its effects on the brain and soon learned that it reduces norepinephrine activity at key neural sites (Bunney & Garland, 1984; Colburn et al., 1967). Many reasoned that if lithium reduces manic symptoms while reducing norepinephrine activity, mania itself may be related to high norepinephrine activity.

Because serotonin activity often parallels norepinephrine's in relation to depression, theorists expected that a large supply of serotonin would also be related to manic functioning, but no such correspondence has shown up. Instead, research has indicated that mania, like depression, is associated with a low supply of serotonin (Price, 1990). For example, spinal fluid levels of 5-HIAA, the serotonin metabolite, are no higher in manic patients than in normal control subjects, and in fact are often lower (Post et al., 1980; Banki, 1977; Sjostrom, 1973). Similarly, when researchers have administered tryptophan to manic patients, they have found that this serotonin precursor sometimes alleviates manic symptoms, again suggesting that a lack of serotonin is the problem in mania (Van Praag, 1978, 1977; Prange et al., 1974, 1970). Researchers have also found that lithium, the drug that treats mania so successfully, often seems to increase brain serotonin activity (Price, 1990; Bunney & Garland, 1984). Somehow, depression and mania both seem to be related to a low level of serotonin.

In an effort to make sense of these seemingly contradictory findings, some researchers have proposed a "permissive theory" of mood disorders (Prange et al., 1974, 1970). According to this theory, low serotonin activity sets the stage for a mood disorder and permits the brain's norepinephrine activity to define the particular form of the disorder. Low serotonin activity accompanied by low or normal norepinephrine activity will lead to depression, a notion consistent with some of the neurotransmitter theories of unipolar depression discussed earlier (pp. 295–297). Conversely, low serotonin activity accompanied by high norepinephrine activity will lead to mania. Although not all researchers are convinced that norepinephrine and serotonin interact in this particular way to produce bipolar disorders, a growing number do believe that the disorders reflect some form of abnormal functioning by both of the neurotransmitter systems (Baraban, Worley, & Snyder, 1989).

SODIUM ION ACTIVITY Another biological explanation of mania and bipolar disorders points to a defective transportation of sodium ions across neuron membranes throughout the brain (Meltzer, 1991). Investigators have arrived at this explanation by working backward from the discovery of lithium's effectiveness as a treatment for bipolar disorders. They already knew that lithium forms mineral salts, is a member of the family of alkali metals, and thus is closely related to sodium (chemical symbol, Na). Reasoning that when lithium is ingested, it may affect the body's use of this alkali relative, researchers began to look closely at the physiological functions of sodium.

On both sides of the cell membrane of every neuron (see Figures 8–6 and 8–7) are positively charged sodium ions that play a critical role in sending incoming messages down the axon to the nerve endings. When the neuron is at rest, most of the sodium ions sit on the outer side of the membrane; when the neuron is stimulated by an incoming message at its receptor site, however, a shift occurs in the cell, and sodium ions from the outer side of the membrane travel across to the inner side, thus propagating a wave of electrochemical activity that continues down the length of the axon and culminates in the "firing" of the neuron. This activity is followed by a flow of potassium ions from the inside to the outside of the neuron, thus helping the neuron to return to its original resting state.

If brain messages are to be transmitted properly, the sodium ions must travel properly back and forth between the outside and the inside of the neural membrane. Proper transport of these ions ensures that a neuron will be neither too susceptible nor too resistant to stimulation. Conversely, some researchers believe, improper transport may cause neurons to fire too easily, resulting in mania, or to be too resistant to firing, resulting in depression. Such defects in the transport of sodium ions may result in shifting misalignments along neural membranes and consequent fluctuations from one mood extreme to the other (Kato et al., 1993; Meltzer, 1991).

Researchers have found clear indications of defective sodium ion transportation at certain neuron membranes in the brains of people with bipolar disorders. They have, for example, observed abnormal functioning in the proteins that help transport sodium ions back and forth across a neuron's membrane during firing (Kato et al., 1993; Meltzer, 1991). Some recent research further suggests that people with bipolar disorders may have an extensive membrane defect that causes these problems in the sodium transport mechanisms (Kato et al., 1993; Meltzer, 1991). Perhaps because of its similarity to sodium, lithium helps counterbalance the problems caused by the faulty sodium transport system, thus stabilizing the moods of people with bipolar disorders.

Research in this area has accelerated of late, inspired by the remarkable effectiveness of lithium. As Solomon Snyder (1980) has said, "A drug that normalizes patients, preventing both manic and depressive

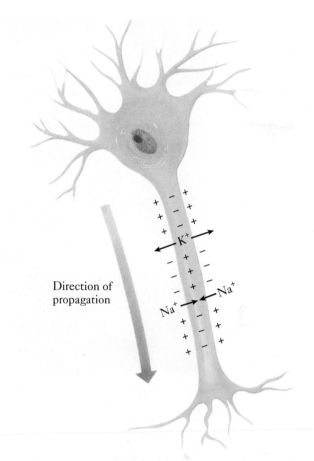

FIGURE 8-7 *Neurons relay messages in the form of electrical impulses that begin in the cell body and travel down the axon toward the nerve endings. As an impulse travels along the axon, it reduces the difference in voltage between the interior and exterior of the cell. This allows sodium ions (Na^+) to flow in. The inflow of sodium propagates the impulse. As sodium flows in, potassium ions (K^+) flow out, thus helping the membrane's electrical potential to return to its resting state, ready for the arrival of a new impulse. (Adapted from Snyder, 1986, p. 7.)*

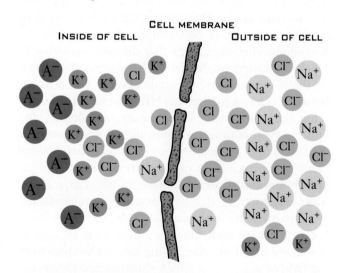

FIGURE 8-6 *The cell membrane, composed of protein and fat, contains small pores that allow the passage of water, sodium ions (Na^+), chloride ions (Cl^-), potassium ions (K^+), and large protein molecules with negative electric charges (A^-). Potassium and chloride ions diffuse freely through the pores, but it is much more difficult for sodium ions to do so, and protein molecules can hardly diffuse at all. (Adapted from Julien, 1985, p. 229.)*

episodes, would seem to be acting at some site closely linked to the fundamental abnormality of the manic-depressive disorder" (p. 28).

GENETIC FACTORS   Many theorists have argued that people inherit a predisposition to develop the biological abnormalities underlying bipolar disorders (Siever et al., 1991; Blehar et al., 1988). Family pedigree studies have provided strong evidence that this is so. Close relatives of people with a bipolar disorder have been found to have a 4 to 25 percent likelihood of developing the same or a related mood disorder, compared to the 1 percent prevalence rate in the general population (APA, 1994; Nurnberger & Gershon, 1992; Fieve, Dunner, & Elston, 1984). Moreover, if one identical twin has a bipolar disorder, the

Closely knit families in which there is little intermarriage across the generations are attractive candidates for genetic linkage studies, which seek to identify possible patterns in the inheritance of disorders. The possible genetic patterns of bipolar disorders have, for example, been studied in some Amish families in Pennsylvania.

likelihood is as much as 70 percent that the other twin will have it too, compared to the less than 25 percent likelihood for a fraternal twin (Fischer, 1980; Bertelsen et al., 1977). Obviously, the more similar the genetic makeup of two people, the more similar their tendency to develop a bipolar disorder.

Researchers have also conducted *genetic linkage studies* to identify possible patterns in the inheritance of bipolar disorders. They select extended families that have exhibited high rates of the disorder over several generations, observe the pattern of distribution of the disorder among family members, and determine whether it closely follows the distribution pattern of other family traits, such as color blindness, red hair, or a particular medical syndrome. If, for example, all the family members with a bipolar disorder also were to have a genetically transmitted skin condition that nonbipolar family members did not have, researchers might conclude that a predisposition to bipolar disorders is linked to a predisposition to this skin condition, and that the two predispositions are carried by genes located close together on the same chromosome.

By studying the records of Israeli, Belgian, and Italian families that have shown high rates of bipolar disorder across several generations, researchers have found bipolar disorders linked to red-green color blindness and to a medical abnormality called G6PD deficiency (Baron et al., 1987; del Zompo et al., 1984; Mendlewicz et al., 1987, 1980, 1972). These two conditions are known to be transmitted by genes on the X chromosome, suggesting that the predisposition to bipolar disorders might also be transmitted by a gene on the X chromosome, located "close to and possibly between the two marker loci" (Baron et al., 1987).

On the other hand, a genetic examination of Old Order Amish families in Pennsylvania who have also displayed high rates of bipolar disorder across several generations traced the problem to an entirely different chromosomal area (Egeland et al., 1987, 1984). After determining that one extended Amish family had a particularly high prevalence of bipolar disorder, the researchers took blood samples from all eighty-one members of the clan. Using new techniques from the field of molecular biology, they isolated DNA (deoxyribonucleic acid, a nucleic acid present in the chromosomes that codes hereditary information) from each sample and cut it into segments. Comparisons of the gene segments from bipolar family members with gene segments from their nonbipolar relatives revealed a discrepancy in a region on chromosome 11 near two known genes—the insulin gene and the

Ha-ras-1 gene. On the basis of this discovery, the researchers initially concluded that a gene or group of genes in this region of chromosome 11 is responsible for a predisposition to develop bipolar disorders.

These two lines of investigation have led some theorists to conclude that at least two different genes may establish a predisposition to develop a bipolar disorder (Hodgkinson et al., 1990; Robertson, 1987). Other theorists, however, have interpreted the very different findings from the two lines of research to mean that the logic behind these genetic studies is faulty and leads to incorrect conclusions about the existence of genetic factors in bipolar disorders. And, in fact, recent failures to replicate these two sets of findings have raised further questions about their validity and implications (Nurnberger & Gershon, 1992; Kelsoe et al., 1989). It is important to remember, after all, that the hypothesized genes pointed to in each line of research have yet to be isolated and analyzed.

THE STATE OF THE FIELD

MOOD DISORDERS

Because mood disorders are so prevalent in our society, because clinicians treat so many clients with these disorders, and because so much research has been conducted, it seems as though a great deal is known about the subject. In truth, clinicians do have a lot of information about mood disorders, but they do not yet fully understand all that they know.

We know that there are two distinct patterns of mood disorder—unipolar depression and bipolar disorders. Patterns of unipolar depression are quite prevalent; they tend to occur more among women, to subside eventually even without treatment, and to recur periodically. Bipolar disorders are relatively uncommon; they are equally distributed among women and men, are unlikely to subside fully without treatment, and are very likely to recur in the absence of treatment. We also know that both unipolar depression and bipolar disorders are marked by a range of symptoms besides dysfunctional mood, including significant problems in cognitive, motivational, behavioral, and somatic functioning, so that they have a powerful impact on the sufferer's life.

Researchers have also done a remarkable job of identifying important factors that accompany and perhaps cause the mood disorders. Only one set of factors has emerged consistently in bipolar dis-

orders—biological factors. The present assumption is that some biological abnormalities, perhaps inherited and perhaps precipitated by life stress, cause bipolar disorders.

The situation with unipolar patterns of depression is much more complex. Researchers have identified several factors that are closely tied to these disorders, including a reduction in positive reinforcements, a perception of helplessness, negative ways of thinking, biological abnormalities, and in some cases life stresses such as the loss of a loved one. Precisely how these factors relate to unipolar depression is, to say the least, unclear. It may be that each pattern of unipolar depression represents a distinct disorder, and that each factor causes a particular depressive disorder. Alternatively, the different patterns of unipolar depression may be but variations of the same basic disorder. If so, the factors uncovered by researchers may relate to this single disorder in any of several ways:

1. One of these factors may indeed be the key cause of unipolar depression. That is, one theory may be more useful than any of the others for predicting and understanding how a unipolar depression unfolds. If so, cognitive and biological factors seem to be the leading candidates, for both have been found to precede and predict depression.

2. Any of the leading factors may be capable of initiating a unipolar pattern of depression (Akiskal & McKinney, 1975, 1973). This initial cause may then trigger problems in other areas of functioning, thus establishing a syndrome of unipolar depression in all its breadth. Some people may begin with low serotonin activity, which could predispose them to react helplessly in stressful situations, interpret events negatively, and enjoy fewer pleasures in life. Others may begin by experiencing a severe loss that sets off helplessness reactions, low serotonin activity, and reductions in positive reinforcements. Regardless of the initial cause, these people may all move toward a "final common pathway" of unipolar depression.

A number of studies support this interpretation. Some researchers have found that when animals are subjected to uncontrollable negative reinforcements, they not only react helplessly but also develop norepinephrine and serotonin depletions in their brains (Maier, 1984). Other researchers have found that when animals' norepinephrine and serotonin supplies are experimentally reduced, the animals start exhibiting helplessness behavior (Weiss et al., 1976; Weiss, 1970). Clearly, one symptom of depression is capable of engendering or exacerbating others.

3. An interaction between two or more factors may be necessary to create an episode of unipolar depression. Perhaps people will become depressed only if they have low serotonin activity, feel helpless to control their reinforcements, and repeatedly blame themselves for negative events. This would help explain why only some helplessness-trained people actually come to exhibit helplessness in most studies, or why only some of the people with low serotonin levels become depressed. These persons may fail to fulfill all of depression's causal requirements.

4. The various factors isolated by researchers may play different roles in unipolar depression. Some may cause the disorder, some may result from it, and some may help maintain it. Peter Lewinsohn and his colleagues (1988) conducted a study aimed at clarifying this issue. They first assessed more than 500 randomly chosen subjects on several key depression factors, then assessed the subjects again eight months later to see who had in fact become depressed and which of the factors had predicted depression. Negative cognitions, life stress, and self-dissatisfaction were found to precede and predict depression; impoverished social relationships and reductions in positive reinforcements did not. The research team concluded that the former factors help cause unipolar depression, while the latter simply accompany or result from depression, and perhaps help maintain it. Given Lewinsohn's seminal role in developing the reinforcement explanation of depression, this study and its conclusion are most compelling.

Because of the work that has been done over the past twenty-five years, mood disorders are now being diagnosed and distinguished with greater precision, with more knowledge about their breadth and course, and with greater awareness of possible contributing factors. Many important puzzle pieces have been gathered. Now the task is to put them together into a meaningful picture that will suggest even better ways to predict, prevent, and treat the disorders.

SUMMARY

Most people's moods are transient and affect their lives only minimally, but people with mood disorders have moods that tend to last for months or years, dominate their interactions with the world, and disrupt their normal functioning. The victim of *unipolar depression,* the most common pattern of mood disorder, suffers exclusively from depression. In *bipolar disorders,* periods of mania alternate or intermix with periods of depression.

■ **DEPRESSION** is characterized by severe and debilitating psychological pain that may keep intensifying over an extended period of time. Women are more likely than men to experience both severe and milder episodes of unipolar depression. Once depressed, a person has an increased risk of becoming depressed again.

The symptoms of depression span five areas of functioning: emotional, motivational, behavioral, cognitive, and physical. Depressed people are also at greater risk for suicidal behavior.

Many unipolar depressions seem to be triggered by stressful life events. Clinicians may distinguish *reactive (exogenous) depression,* which follows clear-cut precipitating events, from *endogenous depression,* which is assumed to be caused by internal factors. This distinction is often difficult to make, however.

■ **SEVERAL EXPLANATIONS** for unipolar depression have been proposed. Because of growing recognition that unipolar depression may have both situational and biological causes, it is probably best to view each of the theories as offering only a partial account of this disorder. According to the *psychodynamic* view of depression, a series of unconscious processes is set in motion when people experience real or imagined losses. People who introject feelings for the lost object may come to feel self-hatred and depression.

The *behavioral* view says that when people experience significant reduction in their total rate of positive reinforcements, they are more likely to develop a depressive style of functioning. As they become less active, their rate of positive reinforcements decreases still further, leading to still fewer positive behaviors and eventually to depression.

According to the *cognitive* view, depression results from negative thinking about oneself, the world, and the future. Four cognitive processes—*maladaptive attitudes,* the *cognitive triad, errors in thinking,* and *automatic thoughts*—generate the emotional, motivational, behavioral, and physical symptoms of depression, which confirm the negative cognitions and create a vicious cycle.

According to the *learned helplessness* theory of unipolar depression, people become depressed when they perceive a loss of control over the reinforcements in their lives and when they believe that they themselves are responsible for their helpless state. Three attributional dimensions determine a person's perception of control: internal–external, global–specific, and stable–unstable. People who attribute their loss of control to causes that are internal, global, and stable are more likely to suffer helplessness effects, a sense of hopelessness, and depression.

According to the *biological* view, deficiencies in two chemical neurotransmitters, **norepinephrine** and **serotonin,** may cause depression. The *genetic* view suggests that an inherited predisposition to biochemical abnormalities underlies unipolar depression.

■ MANIA is a state of dramatic, inappropriate, or disproportionate elevation in mood, a clinical picture the reverse of that of depression. The same five areas are affected: emotional (euphoria), motivational (enthusiasm), behavioral (hyperactivity), cognitive (optimism), and physical (high energy). Manic episodes almost always indicate a bipolar disorder, one in which depressive episodes also occur.

■ BIPOLAR DISORDERS are much less common than unipolar depression, afflict women and men equally, emerge between the ages of 15 and 44 years, and tend to recur if they are not treated. The lives of many people with bipolar disorders often fluctuate between extreme highs and lows. Those who experience manic and major depressive episodes receive a diagnosis of **bipolar I** disorder. People who experience mild manic, or **hypomanic,** episodes and major depressive episodes receive a diagnosis of **bipolar II** disorder. And those whose mood swings consist of mild depressive and mild manic episodes receive a diagnosis of **cyclothymic disorder.**

Most clinical models fail to explain bipolar patterns, but biological research has begun to provide clues. Mania has been related to high norepinephrine activity and a low level of serotonin. Researchers also suspect that sodium ions may be improperly transported back and forth between the outside and the inside of the nerve cell's membrane, either causing neurons to be fired too easily, with resultant mania, or making it difficult for the neurons to fire, with resultant depression. **Family pedigree studies** suggest that people may inherit a predisposition to the biological abnormalities underlying bipolar disorders. **Genetic linkage studies** initially seemed to identify two genes that establish such a predisposition, but the implications of these earlier studies have been called into question by more recent studies.

Topic Overview

TREATMENTS FOR UNIPOLAR DEPRESSION

Psychodynamic Therapy

Behavioral Therapy

Interpersonal Psychotherapy

Cognitive Therapy

Electroconvulsive Therapy

Antidepressant Drugs

TREATMENTS FOR BIPOLAR DISORDERS

Lithium Therapy

Adjunctive Psychotherapy

TREATMENTS
FOR MOOD DISORDERS

■

WHEN WE LOOK AT PEOPLE in the midst of profound
depression or mania, it is sometimes hard to believe that
their moods could ever return to normal. Nevertheless,
many people with mood disorders eventually recover,
either spontaneously or through treatment. Others at least learn to carry
on effectively in the face of continuing symptoms. Consider two different
experiences in the battle to overcome depression:

IT'S AS IF it's all been washed away, as if I haven't got time to think about
the past now. I can't be bothered. I can't imagine ever getting depressed. If it
came back again, it would be a hell of a shock. I'm just confident that it's going
to stay away.

(Rowe, 1978, p. 65)

NOW WHEN I AWAKEN in the morning and feel so disgusted, I throw off
the covers and pull up the window shade. Most of the time I still go back to bed
for awhile, but I have made the first step. I then wash my face in cold water and
get a cup of coffee. . . . It's a constant effort—this battle against the depression. I know that in the beginning of this illness, I couldn't do these things even
if I had wanted to; now I can. With an effort I make condolence calls, visit
friends, go to the theater—but I go.

(Kraines & Thetford, 1972, p. 24)

THEIR VICTORIES are of different orders, but these two people share
an important accomplishment: their lives are no longer governed by their
moods. Each year an estimated 15 million adult U.S. residents are experiencing mood disorders, and over 41 percent receive treatment from a

mental health or medical professional in the hope of regaining some measure of control over their moods (Regier et al., 1993) (See Figure 9–1). Many are successful; most, however, suffer a relapse at some time in the future (APA, 1994, 1993).

■ TREATMENTS ■ FOR UNIPOLAR DEPRESSION

A large and diverse group of therapists treat unipolar depression. An average of 10 percent of the clients of psychiatrists, psychologists, and social workers have this kind of disorder (Knesper et al., 1985)—and so

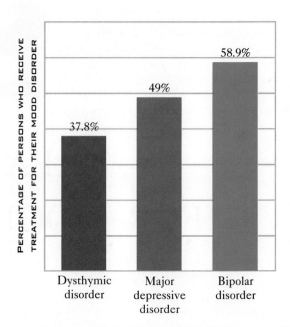

FIGURE 9–1 *People with mood disorders are more likely to receive treatment than those with most other mental disorders. As one might expect, the more disruptive the mood disorder (bipolar or major depressive disorder), the more likely the person is to be in treatment. (Adapted from Regier et al., 1993; Weissman et al., 1991.)*

do a great many of the therapists. The treatment approaches they employ range from global to problem-based, and are typically quite different from the personal methods people use to get out of a bad mood (see Box 9–1).

PSYCHODYNAMIC THERAPY

Believing that unipolar depression results from unconscious grief over real or imagined losses compounded by excessive dependence on other people, psychodynamic therapists try to help depressed clients bring those processes to consciousness, so they can understand the source of their pain and learn to leave it behind them. As practitioners of a global therapy, these therapists use the same basic psychodynamic procedures with depressed clients that they use with others: they encourage the client to associate freely during therapy; suggest interpretations of the client's associations, dreams, and displays of resistance and transference; and help the client reexperience and reevaluate past events and feelings. Free association helped one patient recall the early experiences of loss that, according to his therapist, had set the stage for his depression:

Among the things that happy people have in common are spiritual faith, social involvement, productive work that is linked to self-esteem, satisfying sleep, and a satisfying love relationship (Tice, 1990; Erber, 1990; Diener, 1984). It is not always clear, however, whether these are the causes or the effects of their happiness.

Among his earliest memories, possibly the earliest of all, was the recollection of being wheeled in his baby cart under the elevated train structure and left there alone. Another memory that recurred vividly during the analysis was of an operation around the age of five. He was anesthetized and his mother left him with the doctor. He recalled how he had kicked and screamed, raging at her for leaving him.

(Lorand, 1968, pp. 325–326)

In the following case, the therapist interpreted a depressed client's dream to trace his mood problem to early dependence and to real and symbolic losses:

The patient reported a dream in which he was at his father's gravesite, in which his dead father was lying. In the dream the patient was crying and others were trying to comfort him. He had the feeling that everyone close to him was sick. He woke from the dream crying. In his associations this patient remembered the actual death of his father, stating that at the time, "I felt as if my purpose in life had been extinguished." The patient had had a quasi-symbiotic relationship with his father, who had preferred him over the other children. He followed his father's orders to the letter, in return for which his father lavished praise on him and gave him substantial sums of money. He never dared to cross his father since he had the experience of witnessing what had occurred to his brothers when they disagreed even slightly with the father. This patient had grown up in a rural area where the father, a wealthy and influential businessman, had ruled over a large estate like a small monarch. Although he had slavishly followed his father's instructions, the patient often had been irresponsible in his own affairs, and had lost moderate sums of money because of his naïveté. He had the dream after losing a considerable sum of money at cards. The dream may have represented an awareness that he was now on his own, yet there remained within him a desperate desire to be taken care of once again by a powerful other. The dream showed his characteristic turning to others to make things right, as his father had done in the past whenever he was in trouble.

(Arieti & Bemporad, 1978, p. 300)

At times psychodynamic therapists adjust their usual procedures to address special problems posed by depressed clients. If a client is too dejected even to associate freely early in therapy, the therapist may have to take a more active role than usual in the early therapy discussions (Bemporad, 1982; Spiegel, 1965; Kolb, 1956).

The therapist, by . . . introducing topics which he thinks the patient can discuss, may often help him talk of a wider range of subjects. Also, by asking specific questions the therapist may help the patient overcome his inability to talk about particular subjects. . . . If the therapist is too passive, the patient's silence may increase . . . and after each interview [the patient] may experience a sense of failure with increased depression.

(Levin, 1968, p. 355)

By the same token, psychodynamic therapists must deal particularly carefully with the transference behavior of depressed clients (APA, 1993). Because of their extreme dependence on important people in their lives, depressed clients may cling to the therapist even more than other clients do, crying out for guidance and relief, and expecting the therapist to take care of them (Bemporad, 1992; Kolb, 1956). In describing her treatment sessions with a depressed client, one therapist wrote:

There followed a long, typical period during which the patient lived only in the aura of the analyst and withdrew from other personal relationships to a dangerous extent. The transference was characterized by very dependent . . . attitudes toward the analyst, but also by growing demands that I display self-sacrificing devotion in return.

(Jacobson, 1971, p. 289)

Some psychodynamic theorists believe that the therapist should make the depressed client aware of these extreme transference feelings early in treatment and help the client accept the therapist's limitations (Bemporad, 1992, 1982; Arieti & Bemporad, 1978; Jacobson, 1975). Others believe that a transference discussion of this kind should be postponed until "a later phase of the analysis, when the patient can better endure frustration, and can make demands without feeling guilt or fearing dismissal" (Lorand, 1968, pp. 334–335).

Psychodynamic therapists expect that in the course of treatment depressed clients will eventually become less dependent on others, cope with losses more effectively, and make corresponding changes in their daily lives. This kind of progress is seen in the case of a depressed middle-aged business executive:

He had functioned well in the context of a favored status relationship with his boss. However, he had been transferred to another department where his new boss was aloof and gave his colleagues little feedback. This new superior simply expected everyone to do their jobs and was not concerned with personal niceties. The patient found himself becoming more and more depressed when he failed to elicit the needed reassurance from his new

BOX 9-1

CHASING THE BLUES

"Get in a good mood! How hard can it be just to decide to be in a good mood and then be in a good mood?"

"Gee, it's *easy.*"

In this opening scene from the movie *Say Anything*, Lloyd Dobler's sister responds sarcastically to him as he begs her to cheer up. The frequently heard "Cheer up!" implies that we have some degree of control over our moods, but cheering up is usually easier said than done.

Though most people do not suffer from a mood disorder, we all experience bad moods—down feelings that make our lives uncomfortable and unenjoyable for a while. What can we do to get rid of these undesirable states? Everyone has his or her own personal methods for trying to get out of a bad mood; but researchers have found that people tend to use some strategies more often than others (O'Brien, 1993; Larsen, 1993; Tice, 1992). The following techniques are particularly common:

1. Act to solve one's problems.
2. See the good as well as the bad in upsetting situations.
3. Remind oneself of personal successes in life.
4. Resolve to avoid similar problems in the future.
5. Compare oneself to others who have it worse.
6. Compare one's present situation to past situations.
7. Socialize.
8. Drink alcohol.
9. Cry.
10. Distract oneself with TV, a book, a movie, or the like.
11. Isolate oneself.
12. Be fatalistic about one's problems.
13. Blame others for one's problems.

"Why don't you just go and see this summer's feel-good movie?"

(Drawing by Mankoff; © 1993 The New Yorker Magazine, Inc.)

Be aware that these strategies do not necessarily help. Constructive thinking and actions do seem to improve a bad mood in many instances, but isolating oneself and blaming others typically do not (Larsen, 1993).

In addition, it appears that the positive impact of socializing is not always strong, and the verdict is still out on the usefulness of distracting oneself (O'Brien, 1993; Larsen, 1993; Tice, 1992).

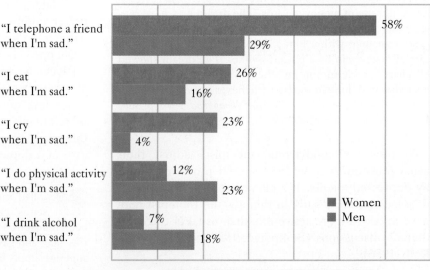

"I telephone a friend when I'm sad." — 58% / 29%
"I eat when I'm sad." — 26% / 16%
"I cry when I'm sad." — 23% / 4%
"I do physical activity when I'm sad." — 12% / 23%
"I drink alcohol when I'm sad." — 7% / 18%

■ Women
■ Men

PERCENTAGE WHO ANSWERED YES

Source: Adapted from Weiss, 1991.

superior. He vacillated between seeing no meaning in his work and getting furious at the company's usually trivial errors, which he now magnified. In therapy, he was able to connect his current plight to his childhood experience of devoting himself to pleasing his father. The latter rarely gave praise and was harshly critical of all the children, but the patient remembered feeling euphoric and important when the father did acknowledge some achievement.

The patient's father was still living and in a nursing home, where the patient visited him regularly. On one occasion, he went to see his father full of high expectations, as he had concluded a very successful business transaction. As he began to describe his accomplishments to his father, however, the latter completely ignored his son's remarks and viciously berated him for wearing a pink shirt, which he considered unprofessional. Such a response from the father was not unusual, but this time, as a result of the work that had been accomplished in therapy, the patient could objectively analyze his initial sense of disappointment and deep feeling of failure for not pleasing the older man. Although this experience led to a transient state of depression, it also revealed to the patient his whole dependent lifestyle—his use of others to supply him with a feeling of worth. This experience added a dimension of immediate reality to the insights that had been achieved in therapy and gave the patient the motivation to change radically his childhood system of perceiving himself in relation to paternal transference figures. This clinical vignette illustrates one of the major objectives of the working-through process: one must perceive usual situations in a new way and then use such insights for the purpose of change.

(Bemporad, 1982, p. 291)

Despite successful reports such as this one, researchers have found long-term psychodynamic therapies to be helpful only occasionally in cases of unipolar depression (Shapiro et al., 1994; APA, 1993; Prochaska, 1984; Berk & Efran, 1983). Two features of the approach have been cited to explain its limited effectiveness. First, as we noted earlier, depressed clients may be too passive and feel too fatigued to participate fully in therapy discussions and to exercise the subtle insight that psychodynamic therapy requires. Second, clients may become discouraged and end treatment too early when this long-term approach is unable to provide the quick relief that they desperately seek. Short-term psychodynamic approaches have shown somewhat greater promise, although research has been limited and results modest (APA, 1993; Svartberg & Stiles, 1991). Despite researchers' findings that psychodynamic therapies are of limited help in treating depression, these approaches continue to be employed widely to combat it. Many therapists believe that, at the very least, these therapies may be useful in cases of depression that clearly involve a history of childhood loss or trauma, a chronic

sense of emptiness, or stringent self-expectations (APA, 1993).

BEHAVIORAL THERAPY

Peter Lewinsohn has developed an influential behavioral treatment for unipolar patterns of depression corresponding to his view that such patterns are related to a decrease in the number of positive reinforcements in a person's life (Lewinsohn et al., 1990, 1982; Teri & Lewinsohn, 1986). Therapists who take this approach reintroduce clients to events and activities that the clients once found pleasurable. The therapists also systematically reinforce nondepressive behavior and help clients improve their interpersonal skills.

REINTRODUCING PLEASURABLE EVENTS
The therapist first identifies activities that are reinforcing by having the client monitor his or her daily activities and fill out a Pleasant Events Schedule and an Activity Schedule (see Table 9–1). Given this information, the therapist then selects approximately ten activities that the client considers pleasurable, such as going shopping or taking photographs, and encourages the client to set up a weekly schedule for engaging in them (Lewinsohn, 1974; Lewinsohn et al., 1969). Sometimes a formal contract is even formulated (see Table 9–2), in which the client promises to engage in more pleasant activities and a family member or friend pledges to reward the client for doing so. Studies have shown that reintroducing selected activities in this way leads to increased participation in the activities and to a better mood (Teri & Lewinsohn, 1986; Lewinsohn & Graf, 1973). The following case description exemplifies this process:

This patient was a forty-nine-year-old housewife whose children were grown and no longer living at home. Her major interest in life was painting, and indeed she was an accomplished artist. She developed a depression characterized by apathy, self-derogation, and anxiety while she was incapacitated with a severe respiratory infection. She was unable to paint during her illness and lost interest and confidence in her art work when she became depressed. Her therapist thought that she could restitute her sources of "reinforcement" if she could be motivated to return to the easel. After providing a supportive relationship for a month, the therapist scheduled a home visit to look at her paintings and to watch and talk with her while she picked up her brush and put paint to canvas. By the time he arrived, she had already begun to paint and within a few weeks experienced a gradual lessening of her depression.

(Liberman & Raskin, 1971, p. 521)

TABLE 9-1

SAMPLE ITEMS IN A BEHAVIORAL ACTIVITY SCHEDULE

Make check mark(s) within the parentheses to correspond to the activities of this day.
Only activities that were at least a little pleasant should be checked.

ACTIVITY	FREQUENCY CHECK	ACTIVITY	FREQUENCY CHECK
1. Buying things for myself	( )	17. Having a lively talk	( )
2. Going to lectures or hearing speakers	( )	18. Having friends come to visit	( )
3. Saying something clearly	( )	19. Giving gifts	( )
4. Watching TV	( )	20. Getting letters, cards, or notes	( )
5. Thinking about something good in the future	( )	21. Going on outings (to the park, a picnic, or a barbecue, etc.)	( )
6. Laughing	( )	22. Photography	( )
7. Having lunch with friends or associates	( )	23. Reading maps	( )
8. Having a frank and open conversation	( )	24. Wearing clean clothes	( )
9. Working on my job	( )	25. Helping someone	( )
10. Being helped	( )	26. Talking about my children or grandchildren	( )
11. Wearing informal clothes	( )	27. Meeting someone new of the opposite sex	( )
12. Being with friends	( )	28. Seeing beautiful scenery	( )
13. Reading essays or technical, academic, or professional literature	( )	29. Eating good meals	( )
14. Just sitting and thinking	( )	30. Writing papers, essays, articles, reports, memos, etc.	( )
15. Social drinking	( )	31. Doing a job well	( )
16. Seeing good things happen to my family or friends	( )	32. Having spare time	( )

Source: Lewinsohn et al., 1976, p. 117.

REINFORCING NONDEPRESSIVE BEHAVIOR Behaviorists argue that when people become depressed, old adaptive behavior such as going to work tends to be replaced by negative, depressive behavior such as complaining, crying, and self-deprecation, behavior that serves to keep people and opportunities for positive reinforcement at a distance. To combat this pattern, therapists may use a *contingency management* approach: they systematically ignore a client's depressive behavior while giving attention and other rewards to constructive statements and behavior. Therapists may also use family members and friends as part of this approach, instructing them to ignore the client's depressive behaviors and reward adaptive behaviors (Liberman & Raskin, 1971).

TEACHING SOCIAL SKILLS When depressed people behave despondently in social situations, the people around them are likely to feel uncomfortable and keep their distance; the depressed person is then deprived of an important source of reinforcement for positive social behavior. Thus Lewinsohn and other behavioral therapists argue that depressed people must be taught, or at least retaught, to exercise effective social skills.

In one group therapy program for strengthening the social skills of depressed clients, called *personal effectiveness training,* group members are asked to rehearse a variety of social roles with one another as a way of improving "expressive" behaviors such as eye contact, facial expression, tone of voice, and posture. Studies indicate that the social interactions of

TABLE 9-2

CONTRACT WITH FRIEND OR RELATIVE TO INCREASE POSITIVE ACTIVITIES

My goal for the coming week is to increase the number of pleasant activities which I engage in by .... events or activities. I have explained to .... why this is important for improving my disposition and he/she has agreed to help.

I promise to forfeit .... (put here the amount of money, a valued possession, or a service you might perform for your friend or relative) if I don't achieve the goal of increased activity which I have stated above.

Signed ....
(your name)

I understand that .... (your name) is attempting to increase his/her activity in the coming week and I agree to help. Specifically, I agree to provide warmth and encouragement when .... (your name) tells me about activities or events which have occurred, and to give .... (specify some event, amount of money, or other reward you think will motivate you to achieve your goal) to .... (your name) if he/she achieves the goal which he/she has established.

Signed ....
(friend's name)

Source: Lewinsohn, Biglan, & Zeiss, 1976, p. 110.

depressed clients improve under such techniques (Hersen et al., 1984; King et al., 1974).

EFFECTIVENESS OF LEWINSOHN'S BE- HAVIORAL TREATMENT Lewinsohn's behavioral techniques seem to be of little help when only one of them is applied. When one group of depressed people were instructed to increase their pleasant activities over the course of a week and a control group of depressed subjects were told simply to monitor their activities over the same span of time, neither group showed any improvement (Hammen & Glass, 1975).

On the other hand, treatment programs that combine several of Lewinsohn's behavioral techniques do appear to reduce depressive symptoms, particularly if the depression is mild or moderate (Lewinsohn et al., 1990, 1984; Teri & Lewinsohn, 1986). In a series of studies, Lewinsohn and his colleagues (1982) found that depressed clients who received a combination of his behavioral treatments typically improved from moderate to mild levels of depression.

In recent years Lewinsohn and his colleagues have plotted out a comprehensive group treatment program consisting of lectures, classroom activities,

homework assignments, and even a textbook addressed to depressed clients (Teri & Lewinsohn, 1986; Lewinsohn et al., 1984). This group program, which consists of two-hour group sessions scheduled over eight weeks, seems to reduce depressive symptoms substantially in 80 percent of the clients and to help clients maintain these gains. Unfortunately, the approach has, once again, proved less helpful to severely depressed people than to those who are mildly or moderately depressed.

INTERPERSONAL PSYCHOTHERAPY

During the 1980s, clinical researchers Gerald Klerman and Myrna Weissman developed an influential and successful form of treatment for unipolar patterns of depression known as *interpersonal psychotherapy,* or *IPT* (Klerman & Weissman, 1992; Klerman et al., 1984), based on the premise that "depression, regardless of symptom patterns, severity, biological vulnerability, or personality traits, occurs in an interpersonal context and that clarifying and renegotiating this context . . . is important to the person's recovery" (Weissman et al., 1982, p. 296).

Borrowing a variety of concepts and techniques from psychodynamic, humanistic, and behavioral therapists, IPT therapists make a concerted effort to rectify the interpersonal problems that they believe accompany depressive functioning. Over the course of twelve to sixteen weekly sessions, they help clients develop insights into their interpersonal conflicts, change their social situations, and acquire social skills.

ADDRESSING KEY INTERPERSONAL PROBLEM AREAS IPT therapists believe that therapy for depressed persons must address at least one of four interpersonal problem areas. First, the depressed person may, as psychodynamic theorists suggest, be experiencing a *grief reaction* over the loss of a significant loved one. In such cases, IPT therapists encourage clients to think about the loss, explore their relationship with the lost person, and acknowledge and express angry feelings toward the departed. As clients formulate new ways of remembering the lost person, they are also expected to develop new relationships to "fill the empty space."

Second, depressed people often find themselves in the midst of an *interpersonal role dispute,* according to IPT therapists. Role disputes occur when two people have different expectations about their relationship and about the role each should play. Such disputes may lead to open conflicts or smoldering resentments, and to depressed feelings. IPT therapists help clients to explore any role disputes in their relationships. Over the course of treatment, therapists may also help clients develop and pursue strategies for solving their role disputes.

Depressed people may also be experiencing *interpersonal role transition.* People can have great difficulty coping with significant life changes, such as divorce or the birth of a child. As with a grief reaction, they may experience the change itself as a loss, but usually what they feel even more keenly is an inability to cope with the role change that accompanies the loss, possibly because they perceive the situation as threatening to their self-esteem and sense of identity. In such cases IPT therapists help clients review and evaluate their old roles, explore the opportunities offered by the new roles, and develop the social support system and skills the new roles require. Mastery of the new roles is expected to produce a sense of optimism and to help restore the clients' self-esteem.

The fourth interpersonal problem area that may accompany depression is the existence of some *interpersonal deficits,* such as extreme shyness, insensitivity to others' needs, and social awkwardness. According to Klerman and Weissman, depressed people who have a history of inadequate or unsustaining interpersonal relationships often display such deficits. It is common for such people to have experienced a number of severely disrupted relationships as children and never to have established intimate relationships as adults. IPT therapists use psychodynamic procedures to help these clients recognize and overcome past traumas and underlying conflicts that have inhibited their social development. They may also use behavioral techniques such as social skills training and assertiveness training to improve a client's social effectiveness. In the following therapy discussion, the therapist encourages the client to recognize the effect his demeanor has on others.

Client: (After a long pause with eyes downcast, a sad facial expression, and slumped posture) People always make fun of me. I guess I'm just the type of guy who really was meant to be a loner, damn it. (Deep sigh)

Therapist: Could you do that again for me?

Client: What?

Therapist: The sigh, only a bit deeper.

Client: Why? (Pause) Okay, but I don't see what . . . okay. (Client sighs again and smiles)

Therapist: Well, that time you smiled, but mostly when you sigh and look so sad I get the feeling that I better leave you alone in your misery, that I should walk on eggshells and not get too chummy or I might hurt you even more.

Client: (A bit of anger in his voice) Well, excuse me! I was only trying to tell you how I felt.

Therapist: I know you felt miserable, but I also got the message that you wanted to keep me at a distance, that I had no way to reach you.

Client: (Slowly) I feel like a loner, I feel that even you don't care about me—making fun of me.

Therapist: I wonder if other folks need to pass this test, too?

(Young & Beier, 1984, p. 270)

EFFECTIVENESS OF INTERPERSONAL THERAPY Several comprehensive and methodologically impressive studies indicate that IPT and related interpersonal approaches are effective treatments for mild to severe cases of unipolar depression (Elkin, 1994; Mason et al., 1994; Klerman & Weissman, 1992). These studies have found that symptoms almost totally disappear in 50 to 60 percent of depressed clients who received IPT treatment. One study compared the progress of depressed clients who received sixteen weeks of IPT with that of control clients who did not (Klerman & Weissman, 1992; Weissman et al., 1979). Self-assessments and clinical evaluations indicated that the IPT clients experienced a significantly greater reduction of depressive symptoms than the control clients. Moreover, although a comparable improvement in social functioning was not apparent during the treatment period itself, researchers observed one year later that the IPT clients were functioning more effectively than the control clients in their social activities and in their families. On the basis of such findings, IPT is frequently used for depressed clients, particularly those who are struggling with psychosocial conflicts, either at work or in marriage, or who are in the midst of negotiating a transition in their career or social role (APA, 1993).

COGNITIVE THERAPY

In Chapter 8 we saw that Aaron Beck views unipolar depression as the result of a chain of cognitive errors. Beck believes that depressed people have *maladaptive attitudes* that lead to negatively biased ways of viewing themselves, the world, and their future—the so-called *cognitive triad.* These biased views combine with *illogical thinking* to produce *automatic thoughts,* unrelenting negative thoughts that flood the mind and generate the symptoms of depression.

Beck has developed a cognitive treatment for unipolar depression that helps clients recognize and change their dysfunctional cognitive processes, thus improving both their mood and their behavior (Beck, 1993, 1985, 1967). The treatment, which usually requires twelve to twenty sessions, is similar to Albert Ellis's rational-emotive therapy (discussed in Chapters 5 and 7) but is tailored more to the specific cognitive errors found in depression. The approach begins with a complete assessment of the client's symptoms (see Box 9-2), followed by four successive phases of treatment.

PHASE 1: INCREASING ACTIVITIES AND ELEVATING MOOD Believing that depressed people could benefit from participating in more activities, therapists set the stage for cognitive therapy by encouraging clients to become more active and confident. A behavioral-like approach is used in which the therapist and client spend time during each session preparing a detailed schedule of hourly activities for

the coming week (see Figure 9-2). The initial weekly schedule may be confined to such simple activities as calling a friend and eating dinner with family members. Gradually the assignments become more challenging, but always within the client's grasp. As clients become more active from week to week, their mood is expected to improve. Obviously, this aspect of treatment is similar to Lewinsohn's behavioral approach. Beck, however, believes that the increases in activity and improvements in mood produced by this approach will not by themselves lead a person out of depressive functioning; cognitive interventions must follow. Inasmuch as Beck incorporates behavioral techniques in the early stage of treatment, it is probably more accurate to call his overall approach a cognitive-behavioral rather than a purely cognitive intervention.

PHASE 2: EXAMINING AND INVALIDATING AUTOMATIC THOUGHTS Once clients are somewhat active again and feeling some relief from their depression, they are better able to observe and think about themselves. Cognitive therapists then help educate them about their unrelenting negative automatic thoughts, assigning "homework" in which the client must recognize and record the thoughts as

	Monday	Tuesday	Wednesday	Thursday	Fr
9–10		Go to grocery store	Go to museum	Get ready to go out	
10–11		Go to grocery store	Go to museum	Drive to Doctor's appointment	
11–12	Doctor's appointment	Call friend	Go to museum	Doctor's appointment	
12–1	Lunch	Lunch	Lunch at museum		
1–2	Drive home	Clean front room	Drive home		
2–3	Read novel	Clean front room	Washing		
3–4	Clean bedroom	Read novel	Washing		
4–5	Watch TV	Watch TV	Watch TV		
5–6	Fix dinner	Fix dinner	Fix dinner		
6–7	Eat with family	Eat with Family	Eat with family		
7–8	Clean kitchen	Clean kitchen	Clean kitchen		
8–12	Watch TV, read novel, sleep	Call sister, watch TV, read novel, sleep	Work on rug, read novel, sleep		

FIGURE 9-2 *In the early stages of cognitive therapy for depression, the client and therapist prepare a weekly activity schedule such as this. Activities as simple as watching television or calling a friend are specified. (Adapted from Beck et al., 1979, p. 122.)*

BOX 9-2

ASSESSING DEPRESSION

If it looks like a duck, walks like a duck, and quacks like a duck, then it probably is a duck. Although many issues in abnormal psychology are more complex than they first appear, people of all sorts tend to believe that depression is as easily identifiable as a duck. If you look sad, move lethargically, and speak in unhappy tones, then you are probably depressed. However, although there are a number of behavioral signs that a person is suffering from a depressive episode, the actual diagnosis of depression is considerably more difficult than one might expect. The most widely used diagnostic tools for assessing depression are those that measure physical and cognitive parameters.

A widely used biological assessment technique is the *dexamethasone suppression test (DST),* based on research linking the activity of the hypotha-

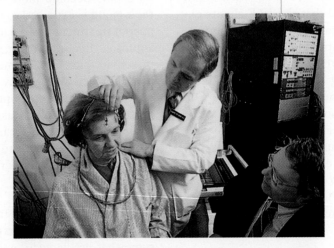

One means of assessing depression is to take electroencephalogram recordings of people while they sleep. Many people who are clinically depressed, especially older persons, demonstrate a shorter-than-average interval between the onset of sleep and the first REM sleep period.

lamic-pituitary-adrenal cortical region of the brain to depression. The level of the hormone *cortisol,* which is regulated by this system, is often higher in depressed people than in nondepressed people. A drug called dexamethasone suppresses or reduces the

level of cortisol in most people, but does not have that effect on people who are depressed. This finding suggests that their hypothalamic-pituitary-adrenal system is overactive. In any event, the failure of dexamethasone to suppress a person's cortisol level is seen as a positive indicator of depression.

In the cognitive realm, the *Beck Depression Inventory (BDI)* is one of the most widely used assessment tools for diagnosing clinical depression (Beck et al., 1961). Originally developed for use in guiding an interview, it eventually became a popular self-report questionnaire in which clients select statements that reflect their attitudes toward themselves. A version containing thirteen items was later introduced as a quick way for family physicians to screen patients for depression (Beck & Beck, 1972), but the original BDI contained twenty-one items, and it is that

they occur. Some clients are even instructed to use wrist counters to help them become aware of how many automatic thoughts they experience in the course of a day.

The automatic thoughts are then reviewed in the therapy session. The client, of course, considers the thoughts realistic, but the therapist questions their validity. In session after session, therapist and client engage in a form of collaborative empiricism in which they test the objective reality behind the thoughts and often conclude that they are groundless. Beck offers the following exchange as an example of this sort of review.

Therapist: Why do you think you won't be able to get into the university of your choice?

Patient: Because my grades were really not so hot.

Therapist: Well, what was your grade average?

Patient: Well, pretty good up until the last semester in high school.

Therapist: What was your grade average in general?

Patient: A's and B's.

Therapist: Well, how many of each?

Patient: Well, I guess, almost all of my grades were A's but I got terrible grades my last semester.

Therapist: What were your grades then?

Patient: I got two A's and two B's.

Therapist: Since your grade average would seem to me to come out to almost all A's, why do you think you won't be able to get into the university?

longer scale that has received the most attention. Studies have shown it to be valid and internally consistent (Beck, Steer, & Garbin, 1988). Sample items appear below. Examinees are asked to select the response (0, 1, 2, or 3) that best describes their thinking.

The Beck Depression Inventory is

SAMPLE ITEMS FROM THE BECK DEPRESSION INVENTORY

ITEM		INVENTORY
Suicidal ideas	0	I don't have any thought of killing myself.
	1	I have thoughts of killing myself but I would not carry them out.
	2	I would like to kill myself.
	3	I would kill myself if I had the chance.
Work inhibition	0	I can work about as well as before.
	1	It takes extra effort to get started at doing something.
	2	I have to push myself very hard to do anything.
	3	I can't do any work at all.
Loss of libido	0	I have not noticed any recent change in my interest in sex.
	1	I am less interested in sex than I used to be.
	2	I am much less interested in sex now.
	3	I have lost interest in sex completely.

---

clearly not intended as a subtle probe of hidden attitudes. Its questions are direct, aimed at assessing cognitions of which the clients are consciously aware. The items are intended to reflect the types of distorted thinking and disturbances in feeling from which depressed people are thought to suffer (Vredenburg, Krames, & Flett, 1985).

These assessment tools are only a small sample of the many techniques used to diagnose clinical depression (Parker et al., 1994). Not all assessment tools yield the same results. A positive DST, for example, may or may not correlate with a high BDI score. Because there is no consensus on the diagnosis, cause, or treatment of depression, different tests may in fact be detecting different problems. Distorted cognitions may constitute one form of depression, for example, while someone with a positive DST may be suffering from a different depressive syndrome. Although there is no immediate answer to this problem, the best solution for now may be for clinicians to use a battery of interview questions and tests and diagnose in accordance with what the majority of responses and tests seem to indicate.

Patient: Because of competition being so tough.

Therapist: Have you found out what the average grades are for admissions to the college?

Patient: Well, somebody told me that a B+ average would suffice.

Therapist: Isn't your average better than that?

Patient: I guess so.

(Beck et al., 1979, p. 153)

PHASE 3: IDENTIFYING DISTORTED THINKING AND NEGATIVE BIASES As clients begin to recognize the fallacies in their automatic thoughts, cognitive therapists show them how illogical thinking processes may be contributing to these thoughts. The depressed student was using all-or-nothing (dichoto-

mous) thinking when she concluded that any grade lower than A was a failure.

As clients review their automatic thoughts and their errors in thinking, therapists also help them to recognize that almost all their interpretations of events have a negative bias. Various techniques may be used to help clients identify and change their biased style of interpretation. With self-blaming clients, for example, therapists often use *reattribution techniques* to guide the clients to identify possible causes of problems other than themselves. Beck offers the following example of this technique:

Patient: I can't tell you how much of a mess I've made of things. I've made another major error of judgment which should cost me my job.

Therapist: Tell me what the error in judgment was.

Patient: I approved a loan which fell through completely. I made a very poor decision.

Therapist: Can you recall the specifics about the decision?

Patient: Yes. I remember that it looked good on paper, good collateral, good credit rating, but I should have known there was going to be a problem.

Therapist: Did you have all the pertinent information at the time of your decision?

Patient: Not at the time, but I sure found out 6 weeks later. I'm paid to make profitable decisions, not to give the bank's money away.

Therapist: I understand your position, but I would like to review the information which you had at the time your decision was required, not 6 weeks after the decision had been made.

When the therapist and patient reviewed the pertinent information available at the time of his decision, the patient reasonably concluded that his initial decision was based on sound banking principles. He even recalled checking the client's financial background intensively. The patient was helped by the method of reattribution.

(Beck et al., 1979, p. 188)

PHASE 4: ALTERING PRIMARY ATTITUDES

In the final phase of therapy, therapists help clients to change their primary attitudes, the central beliefs that have predisposed them to depression in the first place. During the first three phases of therapy, many clients will already have begun to see the maladaptiveness of their attitudes and will have started to alter them on their own. By encouraging clients to test their attitudes, therapists can foster further revision, as in the following therapy discussion:

Therapist: On what do you base this belief that you can't be happy without a man?

Patient: I was really depressed for a year and a half when I didn't have a man.

Therapist: Is there another reason why you were depressed?

Patient: As we discussed, I was looking at everything in a distorted way. But I still don't know if I could be happy if no one was interested in me.

Therapist: I don't know either. Is there a way we could find out?

Patient: Well, as an experiment, I could not go out on dates for a while and see how I feel.

Therapist: I think that's a good idea. Although it has its flaws, the experimental method is still the best way currently available to discover the facts. You're fortunate in being able to run this type of experiment. Now, for the first time in your adult life you aren't attached to a man. If you find you can be happy without a man, this will greatly strengthen you and also make your future relationships all the better.

(Beck et al., 1979, pp. 253–254)

Therapists expect that repeated tests of and challenges to a client's basic attitudes will help the client form a less self-defeating way of thinking. Thus the cognitive core of the depression is removed.

EFFECTIVENESS OF COGNITIVE THERAPY

Over the past few decades, literally hundreds of studies have concluded that mildly to severely depressed people who receive cognitive therapy improve significantly more than those who receive placebo treatments or no treatments at all (Hollon & Beck, 1994; Pace & Dixon, 1993; Hollon et al., 1993). Approximately 50 to 60 percent of clients treated with this approach, like those treated with IPT, show a total remission of depressive symptoms. Studies also indicate that clients who do respond to this approach display steady improvements in their cognitive functioning (that is, progressively less pessimism, and positive changes in self-concept) over the course of therapy, and that these improvements correlate strongly with improvements in depression (Pace & Dixon, 1993).

In view of the strong research support for Beck's approach, increasing numbers of therapists have been employing it (Hollon et al., 1993). Some have developed group programs to make the therapy more readily available to greater numbers of people (Eidelson, 1985). Thus far, however, research suggests that cognitive therapy may be less effective in groups than in individual therapy sessions (Rush & Watkins, 1981).

ELECTROCONVULSIVE THERAPY

Two patients describe their experiences with electroconvulsive therapy:

Strapped to a stretcher, you are wheeled into the ECT room. The electroshock machine is in clear view. It is a solemn occasion; there is little talk. The nurse, the attendant, and the anesthetist go about their preparation methodically. Your psychiatrist enters. He seems quite matter-of-fact, businesslike—perhaps a bit rushed. "Everything is going to be just fine. I have given hundreds of these treatments. No one has ever died." You flinch inside. Why did he say that? But there is no time to dwell on it. They are ready. The electrodes are in place. The long clear plastic tube running from the bottle above ends with a needle in your vein. An injection is given. Suddenly—terrifyingly—you can no longer breathe; and then. . . . You awaken in your hospital bed. There is a soreness in your legs and a bruise on your arm you can't explain. You are confused to find it so difficult to recover memories. Finally, you stop struggling in the realization that you have no memory for what has transpired. You were scheduled to have ECT, but something must have happened. Perhaps it was postponed. But the nurse keeps coming over to you and asking, "How are you feeling?" You think to yourself: "It must have been given"; but you can't remember. Confused and uncomfortable, you begin the dread return to the ECT room. You have forgotten, but something about it remains. You are frightened.

(Taylor, 1975)

Dr. Persad met us on the sixth floor at seven-forty-five. He tried to calm me down, and I recall his saying that he had never seen anyone so agitated as I. The prospect of ECT really frightened me. . . .

I changed into my pajamas and a nurse took my vital signs [blood pressure, pulse, and temperature]. The nurse and other attendants were friendly and reassuring. I began to feel at ease. The anesthetist arrived and informed me that she was going to give me an injection. I was asked to lie down on a cot and was wheeled into the ECT room proper. It was about eight o'clock. A needle was injected into my arm and I was told to count back from 100. I got about as far as 91. The next thing I knew I was in the recovery room and it was about eight-fifteen. I was slightly groggy and tired but not confused. My memory was not impaired. I certainly knew where I was. I rested for another few minutes and was then given some cookies and coffee. Shortly after eight-thirty, I got dressed, went down the hall to fetch [my wife], and she drove me home. At home I enjoyed breakfast and then lay down for a few hours. Late in the morning I got dressed. I felt no pain, no confusion, and no agitation. I felt neither less depressed nor more depressed than I had before the ECT. . . . After about the third or fourth treatment I began to feel somewhat better. I started perking up. After the third treatment I went up to Dr. Persad's office and spoke to him briefly. He asked me if I had noticed any improvement and to what degree. I believed that I had improved 35 to 40 percent. Dr. Persad believed that the improvement was more likely to be 70 to 75 percent.

(Endler, 1982, pp. 81–82)

One of the most controversial forms of treatment for depression is *electroconvulsive therapy,* or *ECT* (Fink, 1992; Breggin, 1979). Clinicians and patients alike vary greatly in their opinions of it (see Table 9–3). Some consider it a safe biological procedure with minimal risks and few undesired effects; others believe it to be an extreme and frightening measure that can cause striking memory loss and even neurological damage. Despite this heated controversy,

TABLE 9–3

ARGUMENTS FOR AND AGAINST ELECTROCONVULSIVE THERAPY

ARGUMENTS FOR ECT	ARGUMENTS AGAINST ECT
Theory of ECT is based on correcting a malfunctioning neurophysiological mechanism.	ECT is not corrective and works to the contrary, causing serious neurological destruction.
ECT's immediate effectiveness is supported by a large body of well-documented research.	An equally large body of contradictory research can be juxtaposed; ECT's long-term applicability suffers from a high incidence of relapse.
Undesired effects are much less troublesome from ECT than from medication in many instances; such effects are typically transient and dissipate over time.	Undesired effects are more profound than acknowledged; potential exists for cognitive dysfunction, personality alteration, and permanent organic changes with repeated treatment.
ECT is a useful intervention in life-threatening situations such as suicidal intent.	No data exist to defend ECT's utility in life-threatening situations.
State regulations regarding voluntary informed consent are too restrictive and legally impede the necessary administration of ECT under certain conditions.	Specific guidelines for ensuring full informed consent are actually inconsistent from state to state and do not necessarily provide the patient with all essential details surrounding treatment effects and outcome.

Source: Taylor & Carroll, 1987, p. 755.

ECT is still used, because it is an effective and fast-acting intervention for severe unipolar depression (APA, 1993; Weiner & Coffey, 1988).

THE TREATMENT PROCEDURE In an ECT procedure, two electrodes are attached to the patient's head, and an electrical current of 65 to 140 volts is sent through the brain for half a second or less. In *bilateral ECT* one electrode is applied to each side of the forehead, and the current passes through the brain's frontal lobes. A method used increasingly in recent years is *unilateral ECT,* in which the electrodes are placed so that the current passes through only one side of the brain.

The electrical current causes a *convulsion,* or brain seizure, that lasts from 25 seconds to a few minutes. The convulsion itself, not any attendant pain, appears to be the key to ECT's effectiveness (Ottosson, 1985, 1960; Weiner, 1984). Patients can therefore be put to sleep with barbiturates before ECT is administered with no reduction of therapeutic impact. Use of a muscle relaxant is also routine, to minimize the danger of physical injury from flailing about during the convulsion. Patients awaken approximately ten minutes after the current is applied. A typical program of ECT for depressed persons consists of six to nine treatments administered over two to three weeks. Most patients then feel less depressed than before the treatment was started (Fink, 1992).

THE ORIGINS OF ECT The discovery that electric shock can be therapeutic was made by accident. The history of ECT can be traced to 1785, when Dr. W. Oliver, physician to England's royal family, was treating a patient with "mental difficulties." He accidentally gave the man an overdose of *camphor,* a widely used stimulant, and the patient went into a coma and had convulsions. When the patient awakened, Oliver reported, "his senses returned to him, and something like a flash of lightning preceded their return. He now quitted his confinement . . . , he became natural, easy, polite, and in every respect like himself" (Valenstein, 1973, p. 149). This accident led a few doctors at the time to conclude that convulsions can cure psychological problems, and they began to give large doses of camphor to other mentally disturbed patients.

Inducing convulsions did not, however, become a common means of treating mental disorders until the early 1930s. At that time a Hungarian physician named Joseph von Meduna declared that schizophrenic and other psychotic people rarely suffered from epilepsy and that epileptic people rarely were

psychotic. Moreover, he said, in the few people who were both psychotic and epileptic, epileptic seizures seemed to remove psychotic symptoms temporarily. Believing that the convulsions of epilepsy somehow prevented psychosis, Meduna reintroduced camphor-caused convulsions as a form of treatment for psychosis.

Meduna was leaping to conclusions. A correlation between convulsions and lack of psychotic symptoms does not necessarily imply that one event causes the other. Moreover, subsequent research has challenged his observation that psychosis is inversely related to epilepsy. Nevertheless, whatever the validity of his argument, Meduna pursued and reported success with his convulsion-inducing treatment.

Camphor treatment had serious drawbacks, however. It sometimes caused convulsions so strong that they were fatal; with other patients it would take as long as three hours to produce seizures or could fail to induce convulsions at all. Meduna found that a derivative of camphor, *metrazol,* worked in about fifteen seconds, but it too was very dangerous for some patients and unreliable for others.

About the same time, Manfred Sakel, a Viennese physician, developed another technique for inducing convulsions in psychotic patients—*insulin coma therapy* (Sakel, 1938). He gave his patients large doses of insulin, causing their blood sugar to drop so dramatically that they went into a coma. This treatment, too, was helpful to some patients, but again quite dangerous, causing intense bodily stress, physical complications, and sometimes death.

A few years later, while looking for more effective and safer ways to induce convulsions in psychotic patients, an Italian psychiatrist named Ugo Cerletti discovered that he could sometimes induce seizures in dogs by attaching electrodes to their mouths and rectums and applying voltage. Still, he feared that placing electrodes on their heads, or on the heads of human beings, would be fatal. One day, however, he visited a slaughterhouse and observed that before slaughtering hogs with a knife, butchers clamped the animals' heads with metallic tongs and applied an electrical current. The hogs fell unconscious and had convulsions, but they did not die from the current itself. Their comas merely made it easier for the butchers to kill them by other means. Cerletti wrote, "At this point I felt we could venture to experiment on man." Cerletti and his colleague Lucio Bini (1938) did experiment with humans and developed electroconvulsive therapy as a treatment for psychosis. As one might expect, much uncertainty and confusion accompanied their first clinical application of ECT, including doubts about the right of experimenters to impose such an untested treatment against a patient's will:

*T*he schizophrenic arrived by train from Milan without a ticket or any means of identification. Physically healthy, he was bedraggled and alternately was mute or expressed himself in incomprehensible gibberish made up of odd neologisms. The patient was brought in but despite their vast animal experience there was great apprehension and fear that the patient might be damaged, and so the shock was cautiously set at 70 volts for one-tenth of a second. The low dosage predictably produced only a minor spasm, after which the patient burst into song. Cerletti suggested another shock at a higher voltage, and an excited and voluble discussion broke out among the spectators. . . . All of the staff objected to a further shock, protesting that the patient would probably die. Cerletti was familiar with committees and knew that postponement would inevitably mean prolonged and possibly permanent procrastination, and so he decided to proceed at 110 volts for one-half second. However, before he could do so, the patient who had heard but so far not participated in the discussion sat up and pontifically proclaimed in clear Italian without hint of jargon "Non una seconda! Mortifera!" (Not again! It will kill me!). Professor Bini hesitated but gave the order to proceed. After recovery, Bini asked the patient "What has been happening to you?" and the man replied "I don't know; perhaps I've been asleep." He remained jargon-free and gave a complete account of himself, and was discharged completely recovered after 11 complete and 3 incomplete treatments over a course of 2 months.

(Brandon, 1981, pp. 8–9)

ECT soon became popular and was applied to a wide range of psychological problems, as new techniques so often are. Its effectiveness with depressive disorders in particular became quite apparent. Ironically, however, doubts were soon raised concerning its effectiveness in cases of psychosis, and many researchers have judged it ineffective in this domain (Taylor & Carroll, 1987).

CHANGES IN ECT PROCEDURES Although Cerletti gained international fame for this procedure, eventually he abandoned ECT and spent his later years seeking alternative treatments for mental disorders (Karon, 1985). The reason: he abhorred the broken bones, memory loss, confusion, and neural damage that the convulsions caused. Other clinicians have stayed with the procedure, however, and have modified it to reduce undesirable consequences (APA, 1993; Fink, 1992, 1987).

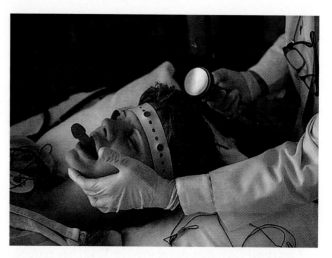

Patients given ECT today are administered barbiturate drugs to help them sleep, muscle relaxants to prevent convulsive jerks of the body and broken bones, oxygen to guard against brain damage, and, often, unilateral, rather than bilateral, applications of electricity to reduce memory loss. After approximately six treatments over the course of two weeks, many severely depressed people find themselves in better spirits. Some experience a degree of memory loss and confusion, but most of these effects are usually temporary.

In the early years of ECT, fractures and dislocations of the jaw and shoulder sometimes resulted, either from the ECT convulsion itself or from excessive restraint by nurses and attendants (Kiloh, 1982). Practitioners avoid this problem today by giving patients muscle relaxants so that restraint is unnecessary and there is no undesirable tension in the body. Similarly, short-term anesthetics (barbiturates) are used to put patients to sleep during the procedure, thus reducing their terror and any consequent trauma (Fink, 1992). As the use of muscle relaxants and of barbiturates became standard procedure, they themselves created new dangers (such as respiratory failure and cardiac arrhythmia), forcing doctors to take still more precautions, such as making oxygen and artificial respiration readily available.

As a result of these changes, ECT is medically more complex than it used to be, but also less dangerous and somewhat less frightening (Fink, 1992; Hamilton, 1986). The number of deaths precipitated by ECT is similar to the mortality rate from general anesthesia—fewer than 3 in 10,000 (Fink, 1984, 1978; Kalinowsky, 1980). Cardiovascular and other physical complications still arise sometimes, though rarely in physically healthy patients (APA, 1993, 1990; Sachs & Gelenberg, 1988).

Patients who receive *bilateral ECT* typically have difficulty remembering the period of time just before their ECT treatments, but much of this memory loss usually clears up after about a month (APA, 1993; Calev et al., 1991; Squire & Slater, 1983). Some may also experience gaps in more distant memory, and this form of amnesia can be permanent (Squire, 1977). Understandably, the relatively small number of people who have suffered significant permanent memory losses are often left embittered. One woman, who reported losing almost all recall of the year before and the year after her treatment and large parts of three other years, summarizes her feelings: "I could have stayed in bed for those five years and it would all be the same. If I knew that I was going to lose my career and my intelligence and my relationships and myself, I wouldn't have consented" (Foderaero, 1993).

Unilateral ECT, first developed in 1942, has reduced the danger of such impairment (Liberson, 1945; Friedman & Wilcox, 1942). It requires less electrical current than bilateral ECT and causes less, if any, neural damage (Lancaster, Steinhert, & Frost, 1958; Goldman, 1949) and less memory loss and confusion, especially when the electrodes are applied to the nondominant hemisphere of the brain (Fink, 1992; Pettinati & Rosenberg, 1984).

Much of the evidence seems to suggest that unilateral ECT is often just as effective as bilateral ECT, although this issue is hotly debated (Parker et al., 1992; Ottosson, 1991; Sackeim, 1986; Squire & Slater, 1978). With these generally favorable results, practitioners have increasingly been choosing unilateral over bilateral ECT.

EFFECTIVENESS OF ECT Properly controlled research indicates that ECT is an effective treatment for unipolar depression. In most studies that compare depressed patients receiving ECT with those receiving placebos, the ECT patients improve significantly more than the placebo patients (APA, 1993; Sackeim, 1990; Wechsler, Grosser, & Greenblatt, 1965). Overall, these studies suggest that between 60 and 70 percent of ECT patients improve. The procedure seems to be most effective in severe cases characterized by delusions or by such melancholic symptoms as motor retardation, sleep disturbance, and loss of appetite (Buchan et al., 1992; Weiner & Coffey, 1988).

How does ECT alleviate unipolar depression? Studies have consistently found that ECT increases neurotransmitter activity in the brain, suggesting to many theorists that the procedure corrects a deficit in norepinephrine and/or serotonin activity in people who are depressed (Sackeim, 1988; Essman, 1986; Kety, 1974). This is a promising theory, but it is important to remember (1) that ECT causes neurons all over the brain to fire, leaving open the possibility that neurons other than the ones that use norepinephrine

and serotonin play an important role, and (2) that ECT-induced seizures also affect many other systems throughout the body (Fink, 1992; Sackeim, 1988; Holaday et al., 1986). Perhaps one of these other areas of impact is the key to understanding and treating unipolar depression.

DECLINING USE OF ECT Although research has repeatedly established the effectiveness of ECT, and although ECT techniques have improved steadily, the use of this procedure has generally declined since the 1950s. Apparently more than 100,000 patients a year underwent ECT during the 1940s and 1950s. Today as few as 30,000 to 50,000 per year are believed to receive it (Foderaero, 1993). There are several reasons for ECT's general decline.

1. *It is an extreme measure with undesirable consequences.* Applying an electrical current to the brain is, by any standard, a forceful form of intervention and a frightening prospect to many patients, irrespective of its effectiveness. The reassurances of clinicians and researchers cannot fully relieve this basic and understandable fear. Moreover, while today's techniques reduce the known dangers of ECT, the procedure can still result in confusion and memory loss, particularly in those who receive repeated administrations.

2. *It has a history of abuse.* During its early years, ECT was applied to a wide range of patients for many reasons and in many ways. Some people received literally hundreds of ECT treatments. ECT was also frequently misused as a means of punishing or controlling patients in mental hospitals (Donaldson, 1976; GAP, 1947).

    These abuses reflected a lack of appreciation of the power of this treatment and, many people argue, inadequate self-regulation by the clinical field (Winslade, 1988). In the 1950s and 1960s, motivated by a general atmosphere of increasing concern about social injustice, human rights, and abuse of power in the United States, many lay people and mental health professionals raised critical questions about ECT. By the 1970s, ECT had come under the watchful eye of consumer groups, courts, and state legislatures (Fink, 1992; Winslade et al., 1984). For example, a 1974 California bill limited the use of ECT, requiring that other treatments be tried first and that patients be assured of the right to refuse ECT (see Box 9–3). Since the 1960s, most states have passed laws specifically governing ECT administration (Senter et al., 1984). Furthermore, the American Psychological

BOX 9–3

ECT AND THE LAW

Since its introduction in the 1930s, electroconvulsive therapy has increasingly come under the scrutiny of courts and state legislatures throughout the United States. The primary reason: the clinical field has done a poor job of regulating the use of this powerful and frightening procedure. When self-regulation fails, the government and legal system typically step in.

During ECT's first decade, psychiatrists and clinical researchers were left on their own to apply, experiment with, and modify the procedure (Winslade, 1988). Although this work often yielded impressive results, it also elicited numerous complaints from patients and some clinicians (Rothman, 1985). In 1947 a psychiatric task force, the Group for the Advancement of Psychiatry, finally conducted an investigation into "shock therapy" and issued a critical report noting that ECT was being used indiscriminately and excessively, often for punitive rather than therapeutic purposes and for controlling difficult, dangerous, and uncooperative patients (GAP, 1947). The next official report on ECT did not appear until 1978, more than thirty years later, when the American Psychiatric Association issued a task force report titled *Electroconvulsive Therapy*. This report endorsed the use of ECT for severe depression when drugs have failed, and made detailed recommendations for informing patients about ECT and obtaining their consent to the procedure (Winslade, 1988; Winslade et al., 1984). Subsequent psychiatric reports have continued to endorse this procedure as a treatment for people with severe unipolar depression (APA, 1993, 1990; Fink, 1992).

Legal regulation of ECT did not begin in earnest until the mid-1970s, when the California state legislature, responding to criticism from patients and former patients, passed a law restricting its use (Senter et al., 1984). All competent mental patients in California—both voluntary and involuntary—were granted the right to be informed about the nature of ECT and to consent to or refuse to undergo it. Many other states have since passed laws regulating ECT use. Some of these states, such as California and Texas, have strict regulations requiring concurring independent opinions from professionals that ECT is appropriate and necessary and mandating court hearings to determine whether involuntary patients are competent to consent to ECT. Other states have less restrictive laws that allow hospital superintendents to override a patient's right to refuse ECT simply by documenting that the procedure is being done for "good cause" (Senter et al., 1984).

Probably the most significant federal court decision regarding ECT has been *Wyatt* v. *Hardin*, which defined the legal standards for ECT treatments in Alabama, specifically forbidding some uses of ECT and establishing fourteen rules that severely restrict its practice (Winslade et al., 1984). This decision dictates, for example, that two psychiatrists (with the hospital director's concurrence) decide in each case that ECT is the most appropriate treatment, that a physical and neurological examination be conducted ten days before ECT, that anesthesia and muscle relaxants be used, that a psychiatrist and anesthesiologist be present during ECT, and that a single series of treatments be limited to twelve ECT sessions at most in a twelve-month period. In an effort to standardize the safe practice of ECT, the American Psychological Association and the National Institutes of Health have devised similar guidelines (APA, 1990, 1978; NIH, Consensus Conference, 1985).

Legal and judicial restrictions over the use of ECT have stirred heated debate in the clinical community. Many theorists believe that such protective measures are long overdue (Tenenbaum, 1983; Friedberg, 1975; Tien, 1975). Some would like to make it harder for administrators to override a patient's refusal of ECT, and some would require that all patients be given a complete description of ECT's effects when their consent is obtained, including a clear statement about the risk of some permanent memory loss (Fink, 1992; Friedberg, 1975). Others believe that the laws and courts have gone too far, that such requirements as voluntary consent, professional board approval, and full disclosure often slow or prevent the therapeutic administration of ECT, leaving many patients unnecessarily depressed (Tenenbaum, 1983; Greenblatt, 1984; Kaufmann & Roth, 1981; Tien, 1975). Like the debate over the value and humaneness of ECT itself, this argument continues with no end in sight (Winslade, 1988; Taylor & Carroll, 1987).

Association (1990) and the National Institutes of Health have established guidelines for its use and models for informed consent (Fink, 1992).

3. *There are now medications that treat depression.* The discovery of antidepressant drugs in recent decades has provided an attractive alternative medical tool for relieving unipolar depression. These drugs are effective, relatively inexpensive, and do

not have "the same aura of extraordinariness" as ECT (Heshe & Roeder, 1976).

ANTIDEPRESSANT DRUGS

In the 1950s, two kinds of drugs were discovered that seemed to alleviate depressive symptoms: *MAO (monoamine oxidase) inhibitors* and *tricyclics* (see Table 9–4). These antidepressant drugs have recently been joined by a third group, the so-called *second-generation antidepressants.* Before the discovery of these medications, the only drugs that brought any relief for depression were amphetamines. Amphetamines stimulated some depressed people to greater activity, but they did not result in greater joy.

MAO INHIBITORS As we saw in Chapter 5, the effectiveness of MAO inhibitors as a treatment for unipolar depression was discovered accidentally when physicians noted that *iproniazid* had an interesting effect on many tubercular patients: it seemed to make them happier (Sandler, 1990). It was found to have the same effect on depressed patients (Saunders, 1963; Kline, 1958; Loomer, Saunders, & Kline, 1957).

Iproniazid damages the liver, however, and caused many deaths. Fortunately, researchers were able to create similar drugs, such as phenelzine (trade name Nardil), isocarboxazid (Marplan), and tranylcypromine (Parnate), that were less toxic than iproniazid but equally powerful in fighting depression. What these drugs all had in common biochemically was that they slowed the body's production of the enzyme *monoamine oxidase (MAO).* Thus they were called *MAO inhibitors.* Research later indicated that approximately half of the mild to severely depressed patients who take MAO inhibitors are helped by them (Davis, 1980; Davis et al., 1967).

During the past few decades, scientists have learned how MAO inhibitors operate on the brain and how they alleviate depression. When the enzyme MAO interacts chemically with molecules of norepinephrine, it removes the nitrogen, or amine, component from it by oxidation and destroys its effectiveness as a neurotransmitter. People with high MAO levels may thus be left with too little norepinephrine and become depressed. MAO inhibitors block this destructive activity of the enzyme MAO and thereby stop the destruction of norepinephrine. The result is a heightened level of norepinephrine activity, causing depressive symptoms to abate.

TABLE 9-4

DRUGS THAT REDUCE UNIPOLAR DEPRESSION

CLASS/ GENERIC NAME	TRADE NAME	USUAL DAILY MAXIMUM ORAL DOSE (mg)
Monoamine oxidase inhibitors		
Isocarboxazid	Marplan	50
Phenelzine	Nardil	90
Tranylcypromine	Parnate	40
Tricyclics		
Imipramine	Tofranil	300
Amitriptyline	Elavil	300
Doxepin	Adapin Sinequan	300
Trimipramine	Surmontil	300
Desipramine	Norpramin Pertofrane	300
Nortriptyline	Aventyl Pamelor	200
Protriptyline	Vivactil	60
Second-generation antidepressants		
Maprotiline	Ludiomil	225
Amoxapine	Asendin	400
Trazodone	Desyrel	500
Clomipramine	Anafranil	250
Fluoxetine	Prozac	80
Sertraline	Zoloft	200
Paroxetine	Paxil	50

Source: Physician's Desk Reference, 1994; APA, 1993.

As clinicians have gained experience with the MAO inhibitors, they have learned that even the variants of iproniazid are capable of causing liver damage, high blood pressure, and sometimes death. The problem is that the enzyme MAO is essential for certain normal body functions. For example, many of the foods we eat—including cheeses, bananas, and some wines—contain *tyramine,* a chemical that can raise blood pressure dangerously if too much of it accumulates (Davidson, 1992; Silver & Yudofsky, 1988). MAO in the liver and intestines serves the beneficial role of quickly breaking tyramine down into another chemical, and hence keeping blood pressure under control. Unfortunately, when MAO inhibitors are taken to combat depression, they also block MAO production in the liver and intestines, thus allowing tyramine to accumulate and putting the person in great danger of high blood pressure and perhaps sudden death (Blackwell et al., 1967).

Since becoming aware of this danger, doctors have been careful to restrict the diets of clients who are receiving MAO inhibitors, warning them not to eat any of the long list of foods that contain tyramine. These restrictions, along with other dangers associated with MAO inhibitors, have reduced clinicians' enthusiasm for these medications, especially since researchers have succeeded in developing other types of antidepressants that are safer and often more effective (Montgomery et al., 1993; White & Simpson, 1981).

TRICYCLICS   The discovery of tricyclics in the 1950s was also accidental. Researchers had just discovered *phenothiazines,* the first group of drugs found to reduce schizophrenic symptoms, and eagerly began looking for similar drugs to combat schizophrenia. The Swiss psychiatrist Roland Kuhn thought that a drug called *imipramine* might be a possibility because its molecular structure was similar to that of the phenothiazines (Kuhn, 1958).

Imipramine did not turn out to be an effective treatment for schizophrenia, but doctors soon discovered that it did relieve unipolar depression in many people. Imipramine (Tofranil) and related drugs became known as *tricyclic antidepressants* because they all share a three-ring molecular structure. Other well-known tricyclics are amitriptyline (Elavil), nortriptyline (Aventyl), and doxepin (Sinequan).

Research has repeatedly demonstrated the effectiveness of tricyclics for treating unipolar patterns of depression. In hundreds of studies, mild to severely depressed patients taking tricyclics have improved significantly more than similar patients taking placebos (Montgomery et al., 1993; APA, 1993). When 387 depressed patients were treated with either tricyclic drugs or placebos for ten weeks, the tricyclic patients showed significantly greater improvement than the placebo patients by the sixth week (Lipman et al., 1986). Numerous case reports have also described the successful impact of these drugs. The cases of Derek and Beatrice, whom we met in Chapter 8, are typical of the glowing reviews tricyclics often receive:

Derek might have continued living his battleship-gray life had it not been for the local college. One winter Derek signed up for an evening course called "The Use and Abuse of Psychoactive Drugs" because he wanted to be able to provide accurate background information in future newspaper articles on drug use among high school and college students. The course covered psychiatric as well as recreational drugs. When the professor listed the symptoms of affective mood disorders on the blackboard, Derek had a flash of recognition. Perhaps he suffered from depression with melancholia.

Derek then consulted with a psychiatrist, who confirmed his suspicion and prescribed imipramine. A week later, Derek was sleeping until his alarm went off. Two weeks later, at 9:00 A.M. he was writing his column and making difficult decisions about editorials on sensitive topics. He started writing some feature stories on drugs just because he was interested in the subject. Writing was more fun than it had been in years. His images of his own violent death disappeared. His wife found him more responsive. He conversed with her enthusiastically and answered her questions without the long delays that had so tried her patience.

(Lickey & Gordon, 1991, p. 185)

Finally, after a few tearful months, the psychiatrist . . . prescribed antidepressant medication for Beatrice. Ten days later, Beatrice told her psychiatrist that a 100-pound weight had suddenly been lifted from her shoulders. For Beatrice, it was not "a beautiful day, but . . ." anymore; it was simply "a beautiful day." No qualifications were necessary. . . . The psychiatrist was almost as delighted as Beatrice.

(Lickey & Gordon, 1991, p. 182)

Studies also suggest that depressed people who stop taking tricyclics immediately after obtaining relief have a 40 to 50 percent chance of relapse within six to twelve months (Montgomery et al., 1993). If patients continue to take the drugs for many months after being free of depressive symptoms, however, their chances of relapse decrease considerably (Montgomery et al., 1993, 1988; Evans et al., 1992).

Many researchers have concluded that tricyclics alleviate depression by acting on neurotransmitter "reuptake" mechanisms (Goodwin, 1992; McNeal & Cimbolic, 1986). We saw earlier that a message is carried from a sending neuron to a receiving neuron by means of a neurotransmitter released from the nerve ending of the sending neuron. However, there is a complication in this process. While the nerve ending is releasing a neurotransmitter, a pumplike mechanism in the same ending is trying to recapture it. The purpose of this mechanism is to prevent the neurotransmitter from remaining in the synapse too long and repeatedly stimulating the receiving neuron. Among depressed people, this pumplike reuptake mechanism may be too successful, causing too great a reduction of norepinephrine and serotonin activity and hence of neural firing, and resulting in a clinical picture of depression. Studies have indicated that tricyclics act to block this reuptake process (see Figure 9–3), preventing nerve endings from recapturing too much norepinephrine and serotonin and therefore increasing neurotransmitter activity (Goodwin, 1992; Iversen, 1965).

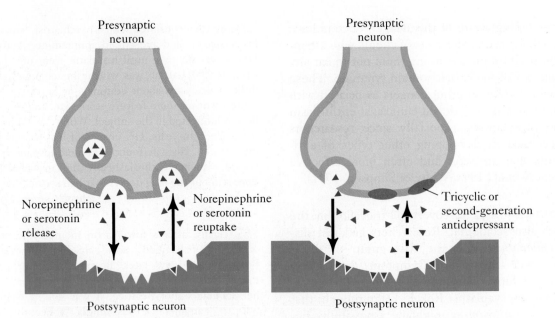

Presynaptic neuron

Norepinephrine or serotonin release

Norepinephrine or serotonin reuptake

Postsynaptic neuron

Presynaptic neuron

Tricyclic or second-generation antidepressant

Postsynaptic neuron

FIGURE 9-3 *(Left) When a neuron releases norepinephrine or serotonin from its endings, a pumplike reuptake mechanism immediately begins to recapture some of the neurotransmitter molecules before they are received by the postsynaptic (receptor) neuron. (Right) Tricyclic and some second-generation antidepressant drugs block this reuptake process, enabling more norepinephrine or serotonin to reach, and thus fire, the postsynaptic (receptor) neuron. (Adapted from Snyder, 1986, p. 106.)*

While many researchers believe that this is why tricyclics are able to alleviate unipolar depression, others have questioned whether it is indeed the key to the drugs' effectiveness (Charney & Heninger, 1983; Sulser et al., 1978). Critics of the reuptake explanation have observed that although tricyclics inhibit the reuptake process immediately upon being absorbed into the blood, the symptoms of depression usually continue unabated for at least seven to fourteen days after drug therapy is initiated. If the drugs act immediately to increase norepinephrine and serotonin availability, why the lag in clinical improvement?

Further studies conducted with this question in mind have found that after seven to fourteen days of administration, tricyclics seem to alter the sensitivity of norepinephrine and serotonin receptors located on neurons throughout the brain (McNeal & Cimbolic, 1986; Stahl, 1984; Rosenblatt et al., 1979). Some of these receptors become more capable of attracting and capturing norepinephrine and serotonin after this period of antidepressant administration, and so better able to receive and transmit messages (Charney et al., 1981); other norepinephrine and serotonin receptors actually become less sensitive after seven to fourteen days of tricyclics (Sulser, 1983). Working backward from these findings, some researchers now suspect that unipolar depression may in fact be caused primarily by neurotransmitter receptors whose sensitiv-

ity to norepinephrine and serotonin is disturbed in some manner (Singh & Lucki, 1993), and that tricyclics alleviate depression not simply by altering reuptake mechanisms but also by correcting the sensitivity of these receptors (Lickey & Gordon, 1991; McNeal & Cimbolic, 1986).

Today tricyclics are prescribed more often than MAO inhibitors, primarily for two reasons. First, although tricyclics have their own undesirable effects, such as tiredness, dry mouth, dizziness, and occasional blurred vision (APA, 1993; Cohn et al., 1990), they are less dangerous than MAO inhibitors, and they do not require dietary restrictions (Montgomery, 1993; Georgotas & McCue, 1986). Second, numerous studies have shown tricyclics to outperform placebos more often than MAO inhibitors do (Tapia, 1983; Davis et al., 1967; Wechsler et al., 1965), and in direct comparisons patients taking tricyclics show higher rates of improvement than those taking MAO inhibitors (Swonger & Constantine, 1983).

On the other hand, discriminating studies conducted in recent years have begun to reveal that different kinds of symptoms may be alleviated by these different kinds of drugs. The MAO inhibitors often seem to be more effective than tricyclics for depressed patients whose symptoms include overeating, oversleeping, intense anxiety, and rejection sensitivity (Goodwin, 1993; McGrath et al., 1993; Davidson,

1992). Tricyclics may be a more effective treatment for melancholic-type depression, a cluster of symptoms that includes pronounced motor slowdown, loss of appetite, and insomnia (Goodwin, 1993; Hirschfeld & Goodwin, 1988). Given these newly emerging distinctions, today's clinicians continue to prescribe MAO inhibitors for some patients, as long as the patients are healthy, willing to be monitored regularly, and capable of adhering to a strict diet.

SECOND-GENERATION ANTIDEPRESSANTS

Finally, new and effective antidepressant drugs, structurally different from the MAO inhibitors and tricyclics, have been discovered during the past several years. Some of these *second-generation antidepressants* (including maprotiline, amoxapine, and trazodone) seem to primarily, and perhaps directly, alter the sensitivity of norepinephrine and serotonin receptors (Richelson, 1989; McNeal & Cimbolic, 1986; Ananth, 1983). Other second-generation antidepressants (including fluoxetine, paroxetine, and sertraline), have been labeled *selective serotonin reuptake inhibitors (SSRIs),* as they are thought to alter serotonin activity specifically, without affecting other neurotransmitters or biochemical processes (Johnson et al., 1993; Montgomery et al., 1993; Singh & Lucki, 1993).

Studies directly comparing the effectiveness of second-generation drugs with that of tricyclics find the two groups of drugs to be equally effective (APA, 1993; Workman & Short, 1993). The second-generation drugs are gaining in popularity, however, especially the SSRIs (see Figure 9–4). Prescribing clinicians often prefer them for people at high risk for suicide, because the newer drugs have not been im-

plicated in as many deaths due to overdose as the older tricyclics have (Barondes, 1994; Montgomery et al., 1993; APA, 1993). In addition, some of the undesired effects associated with the older antidepressants, such as dry mouth, constipation, impaired vision, and weight gain, are avoided entirely with the newer drugs (APA, 1993). On the other hand, the second-generation drugs have characteristic unpleasant effects of their own; some clients, for example, find they cause nausea and headaches (Goodwin, 1992).

ANTIDEPRESSANTS VERSUS ECT A number of studies have found ECT to be more effective than antidepressant drug therapy (Janicak et al., 1985). One estimate, based on a broad spectrum of classic controlled studies, is that, on the average, 72 percent of ECT patients improve, while tricyclic drugs and MAO inhibitors yield average improvement rates of 65 and 50 percent, respectively (Wechsler et al., 1965). Half of all ECT successes relapse within a year, however, unless that treatment is followed up by antidepressant drug therapy or psychotherapy—a relapse rate similar to the one for antidepressant-treated patients who stop taking their medications as soon as their symptoms subside (Prien, 1992; Fink, 1992; Sackeim et al., 1990).

Some researchers have questioned the legitimacy of these comparisons (Fogel, 1986; Avery & Lubrano, 1979). When ECT does work, it tends to alleviate unipolar depression within a week or two. Antidepressants may take as long as three to six weeks and then require further weekly adjustments until maximum effectiveness is finally reached (Quitkin et al., 1981). Thus any study comparing ECT with antidepressants after just a few weeks of treatment is likely to favor ECT.

When clinicians today consider a biological treatment for mild to severe unipolar depression, they generally prescribe one of the antidepressant medications. Sometimes these drugs are even used to help prevent depression in patients with histories of recurrent episodes (Montgomery et al., 1993; Prien et al., 1984, 1978). Most clinicians are not likely to refer patients for ECT unless they are severely depressed and unresponsive to all other forms of treatment (Fink, 1992, 1988). For example, 95 percent of referrals to the ECT research program at Rush–Presbyterian–St. Luke's Medical Center in Chicago are depressed patients who have not responded to other interventions (Taylor & Carroll, 1987). Studies suggest that ECT is helpful for 50 to 80 percent of the severely depressed patients who do not respond to antidepressant drugs (APA, 1993; Avery & Lubrano, 1979; Fink, 1978). If a depressed patient seems to be

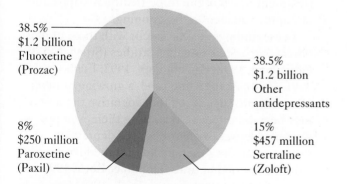

1993 ANTIDEPRESSANT SALES

38.5%
$1.2 billion
Fluoxetine
(Prozac)

38.5%
$1.2 billion
Other
antidepressants

8%
$250 million
Paroxetine
(Paxil)

15%
$457 million
Sertraline
(Zoloft)

FIGURE 9–4 *The leading second-generation antidepressant drugs are Prozac, Zoloft, and Paxil. Introduced within the last six years, they nevertheless accounted for more than 60 percent of antidepressant drug sales in 1993. (Adapted from Cowley, 1994.)*

Regular exercise has been found to be positively linked to one's level of happiness, and exercise may help prevent or reduce feelings of depression (Diener, 1984). It is not clear, however, whether this relationship is the result of changes in biology, activity level, or cognition, or a combination of factors.

a high suicide risk, the clinician may consider referring him or her for ECT treatment even sooner (Fink, 1992; Brown, 1974; Hurwitz, 1974). Yet no studies have indicated that ECT actually thwarts suicide (Frankel, 1984; Friedberg, 1975).

TRENDS IN TREATMENT

For most kinds of mental disorder, no more than one treatment or combination of treatments, if any, emerges as highly successful. A unipolar pattern of depression seems to be an exception. Research suggests that unipolar depression may be effectively treated by any of several approaches: cognitive, interpersonal, behavioral, or biological. During the past decade researchers have conducted several comparative outcome studies to determine whether any of these approaches is more effective than the others. Several patterns have emerged:

1. *Cognitive, interpersonal,* and *biological therapies* appear to be the most successful treatments for

unipolar depression, from mild to severe. In most head-to-head comparisons, they seem to be equally and highly effective at reducing depressive symptoms (Elkin, 1994; Haaga & Beck, 1992; Elkin et al., 1989). There are indications, however, that some subpopulations of depressed patients respond better to one therapy than to another (Stewart et al., 1993).

The most ambitious study of antidepression therapy to date was a six-year, $10 million investigation sponsored by the National Institute of Mental Health, the largest therapy outcome study ever conducted in the United States (Elkin, 1994; Elkin et al., 1989, 1985). Experimenters separated 239 moderately and severely depressed people into four treatment groups. One group was treated with sixteen weeks of Beck's cognitive therapy, another with sixteen weeks of interpersonal therapy, and a third group with the antidepressant drug imipramine. The fourth group received a placebo. A total of twenty-eight therapists conducted these treatments, and each had been carefully chosen, uniformly trained in his or her respective therapy, and then tested for competence.

Using a depression assessment instrument called the Hamilton Rating Scale for Depression, the investigators found that each of the three therapies almost completely eliminated depressive symptoms in 50 to 60 percent of the subjects who completed treatment, whereas only 29 percent of those who received the placebo showed such improvement—a trend which also held, although somewhat less powerfully, when other assessment measures were used. Drug therapy reduced the depressive symptoms more quickly than the cognitive and interpersonal therapies did, but these psychotherapies had matched the drug in effectiveness by the final four weeks of treatment. Each of the three treatments appeared to improve all areas of functioning.

These findings are consistent with those of most other comparative outcome studies (Stravynski & Greenberg, 1992; Hollon et al., 1992; Frank et al., 1991, 1990). At the same time, a growing number of studies are suggesting that cognitive therapy may be more effective than drug therapy at preventing relapses or recurrences of depression except when drug therapy is continued for an extended period of time (Hollon & Beck, 1994; Haaga & Beck, 1992; Kovacs et al., 1981) (see Figure 9–5). It is therefore interesting to note that the 1980s witnessed a significant increase in the number of physicians prescribing antidepressants. The number of office visits in which

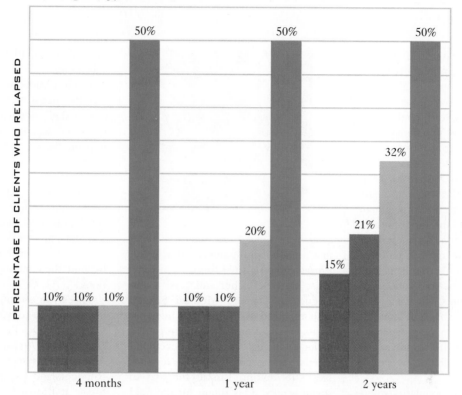

■ Combined cognitive–drug therapy, no continuation
■ Cognitive therapy, no continuation
■ Drug therapy, plus continuation for 1 year
■ Drug therapy, no continuation

FIGURE 9-5 *What is the relationship between type of treatment and relapse? In one study, therapy for three groups of depressed clients was terminated after 12 weeks. The clients had received either cognitive therapy, antidepressant drug therapy, or combined cognitive-drug therapy—all deemed successful. A fourth group of clients continued to receive a year of drug therapy even after responding successfully to antidepressant drugs. After two years, subjects whose drug therapy had been stopped after initial improvement continued to have a higher relapse rate than all other subjects. (Adapted from Evans et al., 1992.)*

an antidepressant was prescribed grew from 2.5 million in 1980 to 4.7 million in 1987 (Olfson & Klerman, 1993). That trend has continued in the 1990s with the emergence of second-generation antidepressants (see Box 9–4).

2. In head-to-head comparisons, depressed people who receive *behavioral therapy* have shown less improvement than those who receive cognitive, interpersonal, or biological therapy. Behavioral therapy has, however, proved more effective than placebo treatments or no attention at all (Emmelkamp, 1994; Zeiss, et al., 1979; Taylor & Marshall, 1977; Shaw, 1977, 1976). Also, as we have seen, behavioral therapy is of less help to people who are severely depressed than to those with mild or moderate depression.

3. Research suggests that *psychodynamic therapies* are less effective than these other therapies in treat-

ing all levels of unipolar depression (Svartberg & Stiles, 1991; McLean & Hakstian, 1979). In fact, in several studies psychodynamic therapy has performed no more effectively than placebos, leading to improvement in only 30 percent of the participating subjects (Berk & Efran, 1983). Psychodynamic clinicians argue, however, that this system of therapy simply does not lend itself to empirical research, that its effectiveness should be judged by therapists' reports of individual recovery and progress (Bemporad, 1992). And the fact remains that many people in treatment for depression receive psychodynamic therapy, a reflection of the continuing appeal of this approach (Weissman, 1984).

4. Most studies have found that a combination of psychotherapy (usually cognitive or interpersonal psychotherapy) and drug therapy is modestly more helpful to depressed people than either treatment

FLYING WITH PROZAC

First approved by the FDA late in 1987, *fluoxetine,* better known by its trade name, ***Prozac,*** has now been prescribed for over 11 million people throughout the world. Its enormous popularity is attributable to two factors. (1) As a second-generation antidepressant, it has fewer undesired effects than MAO inhibitors and tricyclics, so that many depressed people are able to tolerate and benefit from an antidepressant drug for the first time in their lives. (2) Prozac also appears to be an effective treatment for other problems, such as eating disorders and obsessive-compulsive disorders. In fact, after extensive testing, an FDA committee recommended in late 1993 that the drug be formally approved for use with obsessive-compulsive disorders.

Prozac's enormous popularity among prescribing psychiatrists and physicians as well as the public at large has itself caused considerable concern in the clinical community and in the media. Many people believe that it is being glamorized and overused, and that possible dangers in taking the

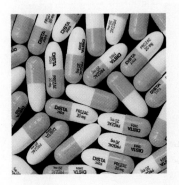

drug have been largely ignored. The first major professional attack on Prozac came in 1990 from the psychiatrist Martin Teicher and several colleagues at Harvard Medical School, who reported six cases in which patients who had previously been free of serious suicidal thoughts developed intense and violent suicidal tendencies after taking Prozac for two to seven weeks. This report hit the field and public like a tornado. It stirred an intense debate among clinicians regarding the proper role of the drug and seemed to inspire some patients to sue the drug's manufacturer for damages as a result of similar undesirable effects. A clear link between Prozac and

intensified suicidal thinking was *not* subsequently established by empirical research (Ashleigh & Fesler, 1992), but the negative publicity led to at least a slight decline in Prozac's popularity and acceptance and loosened its grip on the antidepressant drug marketplace as the 1990s unfolded. Tricyclic antidepressants regained some of their lost popularity among physicians, and other second-generation antidepressants, including sertraline (Zoloft) and paroxetine (Paxil), were soon being prescribed in numbers beyond their manufacturers' expectations.

The hype surrounding Prozac had begun to die down when the publication of Dr. Peter Kramer's book *Listening to Prozac* (1993) reignited America's interest in it. Kramer, a Rhode Island psychiatrist and a professor at Brown University, described case studies in which Prozac not only alleviated the symptoms of clinical depression but actually had a transforming effect on some of his patients' personalities. Some patients were completely unaffected by the drug, but some, with long histories of social

---

alone (Klerman et al., 1994; Hollon & Beck, 1994; Hollon et al., 1993, 1991; Klerman & Weissman, 1992). Some studies, however, find combination therapies to be no more effective than either treatment alone (Rush & Watkins, 1981).

■ TREATMENTS ■ FOR BIPOLAR DISORDERS

Until recently, people with bipolar disorders were usually destined to spend their lives on an emotional

roller coaster. Psychotherapists of varying orientations reported almost no success in treating the manic symptoms of bipolar clients and very limited success in treating bipolar depressive symptoms (Lickey & Gordon, 1991). Likewise, biological therapists found that antidepressant drugs and ECT only occasionally relieved the depressive episodes of a bipolar cycle, and that sedatives and antipsychotic drugs failed to affect the grandiosity and accelerated flood of ideas that characterize manic episodes (Prien et al., 1974). For reasons not clearly understood, ECT applied during a manic episode sometimes interrupted the episode and restored normality (Black et al., 1987; Small, 1985), but patients with mania usually felt too good to consent to such a frightening and unpleasant procedure.

masochism, low self-esteem, and a despondent outlook on life, were, according to Kramer, able to adopt new patterns of interacting with the world.

Within weeks of starting Prozac, Tess settled into a satisfying dating routine. I'd never seen a patient's social life reshaped so rapidly and dramatically. Low self-worth and poor interpersonal skills—the usual causes of social awkwardness—are so deeply ingrained and difficult to influence that ordinarily change comes gradually, if ever. But Tess blossomed all at once.

Although Kramer reports twinges of uneasiness about prescribing Prozac to his patients for extended periods of time, he, like a growing number of clinicians, believes he would be withholding the bounties of science from them if he did not. Kramer suggests that the authentic self is revealed only as the depressive mask is removed. If Tess no longer feels like her "self," when she goes off the medication, and decides to continue taking the drug indefinitely, who is he to claim she should be naturally unhappy?

Kramer's enthusiasm and the public's enthusiastic response to his book have once again alarmed many clinical professionals. Some are concerned that Kramer is overstating Prozac's effectiveness. They argue that the drug is no more effective than any other antidepressant (although it apparently has fewer undesired effects than most), and that it hardly changes personality. As one person said after taking Prozac for depression, "I have my ability to not snap at people back, my energy back . . . [but] I don't feel like Superman, and I still can't stand parties" (Toufexis, 1993). Others are concerned that extended Prozac therapy may rob people of the adaptive aspects of despair, interfering with their realistic connection to external events and their ability to withstand the natural emotional reactions when those events are unpleasant. Still others point out the importance of "listening" to one's feelings of depression. Just as physical pain often serves as an indicator of bodily malfunction, the discomfort of mental pain may be protective inasmuch as it may reveal unreasonable or dangerous impulses. Finally, some professionals are concerned that Prozac will do away

with the human vulnerabilities that people need in order to create and to grow.

Kramer's response is that by increasing some people's resilience, Prozac enables them to participate more fully in life. He finds the chemical's success both exciting and unnerving, as it usurps what heretofore has been considered the realm of the psychotherapist. In many cases he has found a combination of traditional person-to-person psychotherapy and drug therapy to be the most effective treatment, and he believes that these patients would not have done so well on drugs alone. Nevertheless, he observes that some of his patients "harbored a kernel of vulnerability that the psychotherapy did not touch" but that responded to drug intervention.

Vulnerability, anxiety, guilt, sadness . . . are these essential parts of what it means to be a human being? Dr. Peter Kramer says perhaps they are not. Conceding that the moral implications of Prozac are complex, he argues that its discovery will be as impossible to ignore as Freud's discovery of the unconscious. At the very least, the discovery and advocacy of this drug are proving to be just as controversial.

LITHIUM THERAPY

The drug *lithium* has so dramatically changed this gloomy picture that many people view the silvery-white element—found in various simple mineral salts throughout the natural world—as a true miracle drug. The case of Anna, which dates from the 1960s, when lithium was still considered an experimental drug, shows the extraordinary impact this drug can have.

Anna was a 21-year-old college student. Before she became ill, Anna was sedate and polite, perhaps even a bit prim. During the fall of her sophomore year at college, she had an episode of mild depression that began when she received a C on a history paper she had worked quite hard on. The same day she received a sanctimonious letter from her father reminding her of the financial hardships he was undergoing to send her to college. He warned her to stick to her books and not to play around with men. Anna became discouraged. She doubted that she deserved her parents' sacrifice. Anna's depression did not seem unusual to her roommate, to her other friends, or even to Anna herself. It seemed a natural reaction to her father's unreasonable letter and her fear that she could not live up to the standards he set. In retrospect, this mild depression was the first episode of her bipolar illness.

Several months later, Anna became restless, angry, and obnoxious. She talked continuously and rapidly, jumping from one idea to another. Her speech was filled with rhymes, puns, and sexual innuendoes. During Christmas vacation, she made frequent and unwelcome sexual overtures to her brother's friend in the presence of her entire family. When Anna's mother asked her to behave more politely, Anna began to cry and then slapped her mother across the mouth. Anna did not sleep that night. She sobbed. Between sobs she screamed that no one understood her problems, and no one would even try. The next day, Anna's family took her to the hospital. She was given chlorpromazine which calmed her. When she was discharged two weeks later, she was less angry and no longer assaultive. But she was not well and did not go back to school. Her thought and speech were still hypomanic. She had an exaggerated idea of her attractiveness and expected men to fall for her at the first smile. She was irritated when they ignored her attentions. Depressive symptoms were still mixed with the manic ones. She often cried when her bids for attention were not successful or when her parents criticized her dress or behavior.

Anna returned to school the following fall but suffered another depressive episode, followed by another attack of mania within seven months. She had to withdraw from school and enter the hospital. This time, Anna was fortunate to enter a research unit that was authorized to use lithium. The psychiatrists diagnosed her illness as bipolar disorder. Because she was so agitated, they began treatment with chlorpromazine as well as lithium. The initial sedative action of the chlorpromazine rapidly calmed her agitation, and this drug was discontinued after only a few days. As the effects of chlorpromazine subsided, the lithium began to take effect. After seventeen days on lithium, Anna's behavior was quite normal. She was attractively and modestly dressed for her psychiatric interviews. Earlier, she had been sloppily seductive; hair in disarray, half-open blouse, smeared lipstick, bright pink rouge on her cheeks, and bright green make-up on her eyelids. With the help of lithium, she gained some ability to tolerate frustration. During the first week of her hospital stay, she had screamed at a nurse who would not permit her to read late into the night in violation of the ward's 11:00 P.M. "lights out" policy. On lithium, Anna was still annoyed by this "juvenile" rule, but she controlled her anger. She gained some insight into her illness, recognizing that her manic behavior was destructive to herself and others. She also recognized the depression that was often mixed with the mania. She speculated that the mania was an attempt to cover up depression. She admitted, "Actually, when I'm high, I'm really feeling low. I need to exaggerate in order to feel more important."

Because Anna was on a research ward, the effectiveness of lithium had to be verified by removal of the drug. When she had been off lithium for four to five days, Anna began to show symptoms of both mania and depression. She threatened her psychiatrist, and as before, the threats were grandiose with sexual overtones. In a slinky voice, she warned, "I have ways to put the director of this hospital in my debt. He crawled for me before and he'll do it again. When I snap my fingers, he'll come down to this ward and squash you under his foot." Soon afterward, she threatened suicide. She later explained, "I felt so low last night that if someone had given me a knife or gun, POW." By the ninth

day off lithium, Anna's speech was almost incomprehensible: "It's sad to be so putty, pretty, so much like water dripping from a faucet. . . ." Lithium therapy was reinstituted, and within about sixteen days, Anna again recovered and was discharged on lithium.

(*Lickey & Gordon, 1991, pp. 236–239*)

Determining the correct lithium dosage for a given patient is a delicate process. Some clinicians advocate a simple body-weight method of predicting dosage (Groves, Clothier, & Hollister, 1991), but others believe that determining the proper dosage requires analysis of blood and urine samples and other laboratory tests (Johnson et al., 1984; Swonger & Constantine, 1983). Too low a dose will have little or no effect on the bipolar mood swings, but too high a dose of lithium can result in lithium intoxication (literally, lithium poisoning), which can cause nausea, vomiting, sluggishness, tremors, seizures, sodium imbalance, kidney dysfunction, and even death (Abou-Saleh, 1992; Kondziela, 1984). Once the correct dose is achieved, however, lithium may produce a noticeable change within five to fourteen days, as it did for Anna. Patients may then be placed on maintenance doses for an indefinite period of time. Patients who are unresponsive to or unable to tolerate lithium sometimes respond better to *carbamazepine* (Tegretol), an anticonvulsant drug discovered to have therapeutic effects in bipolar disorders as well, or *valproic acid* (Depake) (Prien, 1992; Ballenger & Post, 1980).

ORIGINS OF LITHIUM TREATMENT The discovery that lithium effectively reduces bipolar symptoms was, like so many other medical discoveries, quite accidental. In 1949 an Australian psychiatrist, John Cade, hypothesized that manic behavior is caused by a toxic level of uric acid in the body. He set out to test this theory by injecting guinea pigs with uric acid, but first he combined it with lithium to increase its solubility.

To Cade's surprise, the guinea pigs became not manic but quite lethargic after their injections. Cade suspected that the lithium had produced this effect. When he later administered lithium to ten manic human beings, he discovered that it calmed and normalized their mood.

Cade's promising findings quickly captured the interest of clinicians and researchers in Australia, Denmark, England, and several other countries, but not in the United States (Kline, 1973). Here lithium had just been declared an illegal drug because its wide use as a salt substitute had led to a number of deaths. Cade later wrote, "One can hardly imagine a less propitious year in which to attempt the pharmacological rehabilitation of lithium." It was not until 1970 that the U.S. Food and Drug Administration approved lithium for use in bipolar disorders.

EFFECTIVENESS OF LITHIUM WITH MANIC EPISODES   All manner of research has attested to lithium's effectiveness in treating manic episodes (Klerman et al., 1994; Prien, 1992, 1978; Bunney & Garland, 1984). In numerous blind studies, clinicians have given lithium to one group of patients with mania and placebo drugs to another; then a different set of clinicians, unaware of what the patients have been taking (blind) and even of the nature of the experiment (blind again), have rated the improvement of all patients in the study. Repeatedly lithium has been found to be much more effective than placebos. Improvement rates of patients with mania range upward from 60 percent.

Other kinds of studies have demonstrated a still more direct relationship between lithium and the reduction of manic behaviors. In these studies (single-subject ABAB and multiple-baseline designs, discussed in Chapter 3) patients with mania have been given lithium for a while, then placebos, then lithium again, and so on, as Anna was. Manic behavior has consistently decreased under lithium and returned when placebos are substituted (Abou-Saleh, 1992; Prien, 1992; Bunney et al., 1968).

Another frequent finding is that patients with recurrent mania undergo fewer new episodes as long as they are taking lithium (Prien, 1992; Suppes et al., 1991; Priebe & Wildgrube, 1990). In one study, only 36 percent of 212 bipolar patients relapsed while taking lithium, compared to a 79 percent relapse rate among 68 bipolar patients on placebos (Davis, 1976). This finding suggests that lithium may also be a *prophylactic* drug, a drug that actually helps prevent symptoms from developing. Accordingly, today's clinicians often recommend that patients continue lithium treatments even after their manic episodes subside (Abou-Saleh, 1992; Goodwin & Jamison, 1990).

EFFECTIVENESS OF LITHIUM WITH DEPRESSIVE EPISODES   Research indicates that lithium also alleviates the depressive episodes of bipolar disorders. Moreover, maintenance doses of lithium apparently decrease the risk of future depressive episodes, just as they seem to prevent the recurrence of manic episodes (Klerman et al., 1994; Abou-Saleh, 1992; Bassuk & Schoonover, 1977; Baastrup, 1964).

These findings have led researchers to wonder whether lithium might also be helpful in cases of unipolar depression. Here the results have been mixed. Although some studies suggest that lithium is not very helpful in relieving unipolar depression (Prien, 1984), a few find that it does help a small portion of patients with this disorder (Abou-Saleh, 1992; Goodwin et al., 1972). Some studies also suggest that lithium occasionally prevents recurrences of unipolar depression (Coppen, 1994; Abou-Saleh, 1992; Persson, 1972). Of course, it may be that the "unipolar" patients helped by lithium actually have a bipolar disorder whose manic phase has yet to appear.

Recently lithium has also proved effective as an *augmentation* treatment for patients with tricyclic-resistant unipolar depressions (APA, 1993; Stein & Bernadt, 1993). In one study, up to two-thirds of "tricyclic nonrespondent" patients were converted to "responders" by the *addition* of lithium to their drug therapy (Joffe et al., 1993).

LITHIUM'S MODE OF OPERATION   Researchers do not really understand how lithium operates, but they are beginning to suspect that it alters synaptic activity in neurons that use the neurotransmitters norepinephrine and serotonin, though not in the same way as antidepressant drugs. Recent research indicates that the firing of a neuron actually consists of several phases that unfold at lightning speed. After the neurotransmitter binds to a receptor site on the receiving neuron, a series of cellular changes in the receiving neuron set the stage for firing. These changes are often called "second messengers" because they intervene between the reception of the original message and the actual firing of the neuron (Snyder, 1986). The second-messenger events cause sodium ions in the receptor's vicinity to cross the neuron's membrane, resulting in a change in the electrical charge of the neuron, the transmission of the message down the cell's axon, and the firing of the neuron (see Figure 8–8). Whereas antidepressant drugs affect the initial reception of neurotransmitters by neurons, lithium appears to affect the second-messenger systems in the neurons.

Various second-messenger systems are at work in different neurons. In one of the most important, chemicals called *phosphoinositides* (consisting of sugars and lipids) are produced after a neurotransmitter is received and lead to other chemical alterations in the neuron (Baraban et al., 1989). A number of studies indicate that lithium has a significant effect on this particular messenger system. That is, the synaptic activity at any neuron that uses this second-messenger system—whether a neuron that receives serotonin or one that receives norepinephrine—may be altered by lithium. Thus, even if bipolar disorders are related to abnormal activity of both serotonin and norepinephrine, as some theorists argue, one drug—lithium—can correct both kinds of abnormality through its impact on all phosphoinositide-producing second-messenger systems (Goodwin & Jamison, 1990).

Alternatively, it may be that lithium effectively treats bipolar functioning by directly altering sodium ion activity in neurons (Swonger & Constantine, 1983). In Chapter 8 we saw that lithium is related to sodium, and we considered the theory that bipolar disorders are triggered by unstable alignments of sodium ions along the membranes of certain neurons in the brain. If this instability is indeed the key to bipolar problems, one would expect lithium to have a direct effect of some kind on sodium ion activity. Research suggests that lithium may in fact act in this way.

Several studies indicate that lithium ions often substitute, although imperfectly, for sodium ions (Baer et al., 1971), and others offer evidence that lithium affects sodium concentrations throughout the body (Mendels & Frazer, 1974; Naylor et al., 1974). Still another line of research suggests that lithium alters the transport mechanisms that move sodium ions back and forth across the neural membrane as the neuron is firing (Goodwin & Jamison, 1990; Bunney & Garland, 1984). Any or all of these findings could be the reason that lithium alleviates and prevents the severe mood swings that characterize bipolar disorders. On the other hand, while lithium may in fact affect sodium ion activity, its effect on other important ions may be the reason for its effectiveness in relieving bipolar disorders. Studies are currently under way to determine the effect lithium may have on ions such as magnesium and calcium (Dubovsky et al., 1992, 1991; Goodwin & Jamison, 1990).

ADJUNCTIVE PSYCHOTHERAPY

Clinicians rarely treat bipolar patients with psychotherapy alone (Klerman et al., 1994). The psychiatrist Ronald Fieve has written, "When the primary treatment of manic depression . . . has required the patient to talk with me about his problems . . . in my experience not very much has happened" (Fieve, 1975, p. 2). Virtually no controlled studies have been done on the effectiveness of psychotherapy alone for bipolar disorders, a fact that may reflect the clinical community's conviction that such approaches by themselves are simply not sufficient to treat this disorder (Lickey & Gordon, 1991).

At the same time, clinicians have learned that lithium therapy alone is not always sufficient either. As we saw earlier, 30 to 40 percent of patients with bipolar disorders may not respond to lithium or may relapse while taking it (Abou-Saleh, 1992; Prien et al., 1984; Davis, 1976). There is also evidence that close to 50 percent of patients on lithium do not receive the proper dosage: many are not taking it as prescribed, others stop taking it altogether against medical advice, and some receive prescriptions for incorrect dosages (Gelenberg et al., 1989; Bower, 1987).

In view of these problems, many clinicians now advocate psychotherapy or "psychotherapeutic management" as an adjunct to lithium treatment (Graves, 1993; Miklowitz & Goldstein, 1990; Wulsin et al., 1988). Individual, group, and family psychotherapies are increasingly being made available to patients with bipolar disorders to help them with problems that may affect their recovery. The concerns most commonly addressed in psychotherapy are:

1. *Medication management* The importance of continuing proper lithium treatment is emphasized during therapy, and adherence to the medication regimen may be monitored (Goodwin & Jamison, 1990; Kripke & Robinson, 1985). Patients are also encouraged to discuss their reasons for disliking or rejecting lithium. They may be bothered by the drug's unwanted effects, be feeling too well to recognize the need for ongoing medication, miss the feelings of euphoria they used to have, or complain of being less productive and creative when they take lithium (Goodwin & Jamison, 1990; Wulsin et al., 1988; Jamison, 1987).

2. *Family and social relationships* Bipolar patients who return to critical and overinvolved families are more likely to relapse within nine months than those patients who live in a more supportive and less intrusive family atmosphere (Goodwin & Jamison, 1990; Miklowitz et al., 1988). Thus helping patients cope with family members and improving family functioning are common focuses

in psychotherapy. As they recover, patients with bipolar disorders often experience major interpersonal and social difficulties, including the loss of friends and lovers who have been frightened away or repelled during the bipolar episodes (Wulsin et al., 1988; Aleksandrowicz, 1980; Donnelly et al., 1978). In psychotherapy, patients may be encouraged to explore the interaction between social problems and symptoms, develop social skills and support systems, recognize their social limitations, and reduce social overstimulation and distress (Klerman & Weissman, 1992; Frank et al., 1990). One study of sixty bipolar patients stabilized on lithium found that social support was the factor most strongly linked to a good treatment outcome (O'Connell et al., 1985).

3. *Education* Many patients and their families may actually know very little about their bipolar disorder and need to be given information about causes, common patterns, and practical implications. Psychotherapists may not only provide much important information but also encourage members of therapy groups to share what their firsthand experiences have taught them (Van-Gent & Zwart, 1991; Wulsin et al., 1988).

4. *Problem solving* Bipolar disorders can create problems in all aspects of life and interfere in all areas of pursuit. A person may, for example, be unable to stay in school or to hold a job when manic or depressive symptoms strike. Thus one role of therapy may be to help clients develop solutions for the particular difficulties they encounter (APA, 1993; Kripke & Robinson, 1985).

Few controlled studies have tested the effectiveness of psychotherapy as an adjunct to drug therapy for patients with severe bipolar disorders, but a growing number of clinical reports suggest that its use leads to less hospitalization, better social functioning, and higher employment rates for clients (Clarkin et al., 1990; Miklowitz et al., 1988). Although lithium is clearly the chief agent of genuine improvement, it is becoming apparent that the drug is most effective for patients when it is combined with other forms of therapy. Psychotherapy plays an even more central role in the treatment of cyclothymic disorder, the mild bipolar pattern that we observed in Chapter 8 (see p. 303). Patients with this problem typically receive either psychotherapy alone or in combination with lithium. There are, however, no studies on whether such approaches help people who experience this pattern (Klerman et al., 1994).

THE STATE OF THE FIELD

TREATMENTS FOR MOOD DISORDERS

Mood disorders are among the most treatable of all mental disorders. More than 60 percent of people who suffer from them can be helped. The symptoms of unipolar patterns of depression can usually be reduced or eliminated in two to twenty weeks; after that, treatment is generally discontinued, to be reinstated if depressive symptoms recur. The symptoms of bipolar disorders can also be reduced within a few weeks, but treatment must be continued indefinitely to help prevent future episodes of depression and mania.

The choice of treatment for bipolar disorders is narrow and simple—lithium (or a related drug), perhaps combined with psychotherapy, is the single most successful approach. The picture for unipolar patterns of depression is broader and more complex, although no less promising. Cognitive therapy, interpersonal therapy, and antidepressant drug therapy are all helpful in cases of any severity; behavioral therapy is helpful in mild to moderate cases; and ECT is useful and effective in severe cases. No single one of the therapies has emerged as clearly superior to the others. Combinations of psychotherapy and drug therapy tend to be modestly more helpful than any one approach alone.

Why should several very different approaches be highly effective in the treatment of unipolar patterns of depression? Although clinicians do not yet know the answer, two explanations have received some credence. First, it seems plausible that removing any one of the factors that contribute to unipolar depression may promote improvements in all areas of functioning, just as it seems possible for one causal factor to trigger several others and create a case of unipolar depression in the first place. Studies supporting this explanation have found that when a given therapy is effective, the client is seen to improve in all areas of functioning (Elkin, 1994). Antidepressant drugs, for instance, ultimately lead to some of the same improvements in cognitive functioning as Beck's cognitive therapy does (Fava et al., 1994; Reda et al., 1985).

The second explanation proposes the existence of various kinds of unipolar depression, each responsive to a different kind of therapy, a possibility noted in Chapter 8. Researchers have in fact found that unipolar depressions with particular features sometimes respond better to one form of treatment than to another. Studies have indicated that interpersonal psychotherapy is more helpful in depressions precipitated by situational factors than in depressions that seem to occur endogenously (Prusoff et al., 1980), while antidepressant medications are more likely than other treatments to be helpful for cases characterized by appetite and sleep problems, acute onset, and a family history of depression (McNeal & Cimbolic, 1986; Schatzberg et al., 1982; Byrne & Stern, 1981).

Whatever the ultimate explanation, there is no question that the present treatment picture is very promising both for people with unipolar patterns of depression and for those with bipolar disorders. The odds are that one or a combination of the therapies now in use will indeed alleviate their symptoms. On the other hand, the sobering fact remains that as many as 40 percent of people with a mood disorder do not improve under treatment and must suffer their mania or depression until it runs its course.

Summary

■ **MOOD DISORDERS** are among the most treatable of all mental disorders: more than 60 percent of people with these disorders can be helped. A wide range of approaches have been employed in the management of unipolar depression. Fewer treatments have been developed for bipolar disorders. There biological interventions rule the field.

■ **PSYCHODYNAMIC THERAPISTS** try to help clients with unipolar depression become aware of and work through their real or imagined losses and excessive dependence on others. Although research has shown that psychodynamic therapies are not consistently helpful in cases of unipolar depression, they are still widely employed.

■ **IN THE BEHAVIORAL APPROACH** therapists reintroduce their clients to events and activities that the clients once found pleasurable. The therapists also systematically reinforce nondepressive behaviors and teach effective interpersonal skills. If results are to be achieved, several of these behavioral techniques must be applied simultaneously. Such therapy is effective primarily for people who are mildly to moderately depressed.

■ **INTERPERSONAL THERAPY (IPT)** is based on the assumption that depressive functioning stems from interpersonal problem areas. These therapists try to rectify the problem that underlies the depres-

sion by helping clients to develop insight into these problem areas, change them, and learn skills to protect the clients in the future. Research suggests that IPT is often an effective treatment for mild to severe cases of unipolar depression.

■ **COGNITIVE TREATMENT** for depression helps clients identify and change their dysfunctional cognitive processes. At present this is one of the most effective approaches to treating depression.

■ **ELECTROCONVULSIVE THERAPY (ECT)** remains a controversial procedure, although it is an effective and fast-acting intervention for unipolar depression. Electrodes attached to a patient's head send an electric current through the brain, causing convulsions. ECT is particularly effective when depression is severe, characterized by delusions, or marked by such symptoms as motor retardation, sleep disturbance, and loss of appetite.

■ **IN THE 1950s** two classes of drugs were discovered that alleviate depressive symptoms: the *MAO inhibitors* and the *tricyclics.* MAO inhibitors block the destruction of norepinephrine, allowing the levels of this neurotransmitter to build up and alleviate depressive symptoms. Because MAO is necessary to remove the amino acid tyramine from the body, people taking MAO inhibitors must follow a restricted diet to keep excess tyramine from collecting in the liver and raising their blood pressure to a dangerous level.

Tricyclics, which tend to have higher success rates than MAO inhibitors, may alleviate depression by blocking neurotransmitter reuptake mechanisms, thereby increasing the activity of norepinephrine and serotonin. A third group of antidepressant drugs, the *second-generation antidepressants,* are gaining popularity rapidly. These new drugs, some of which appear to alleviate depression by altering the sensitivity of neurotransmitter receptors and others by selectively increasing the activity of serotonin, are as effective as tricyclics and have fewer undesired effects.

■ **IN SUM,** many cases of unipolar depression may be effectively treated by a variety of approaches. Cognitive, interpersonal, and biological therapies may be the most successful for mild to severe depression. Behavioral therapy is helpful in mild to moderate cases, and ECT is effective in severe cases. Combinations of psychotherapy and drug therapy tend to be modestly more helpful than any one approach alone.

■ **LITHIUM** has proved to be effective in alleviating and preventing both the manic and the depressive episodes of bipolar disorders. It is generally not very helpful, however, in treating unipolar depression. Although the mechanism by which lithium works is not fully understood, researchers suspect that it may affect *second messengers* or interact with sodium ions in certain neurons.

In recent years it has become clear that lithium alone is not always sufficient treatment for bipolar disorders and that patients fare better with a combination of drug and other forms of therapy. Therefore, many clinicians now advocate psychotherapy as an adjunct to lithium therapy. The issues most commonly addressed in psychotherapy for patients with bipolar disorders are medication management, family and social relationships, education, and problem solving.

Topic Overview

CHAPTER 10

SUICIDE

■

I HAD DONE ALL I COULD and I was still sinking. I sat many hours seeking answers, and all there was was a silent wind. The answer was in my head. It was all clear now: Die. . . .

THE NEXT DAY a friend offered to sell me a gun, a .357 magnum pistol. I bought it. My first thought was: What a mess this is going to make. That day I began to say goodbye to people: not actually saying it but expressing it silently.

FRIENDS WERE AROUND, but I didn't let them see what was wrong with me. I could not let them know lest they prevent it. My mind became locked on my target. My thoughts were: Soon it will all be over. I would obtain the peace I had so long sought. The will to survive and succeed had been crushed and defeated. I was like a general on a battlefield being encroached on by my enemy and its hordes: fear, hate, self-depreciation, desolation. I felt I had to have the upper hand, to control my environment, so I sought to die rather than surrender. . . .

I WAS ONLY AWARE of myself and my plight. Death swallowed me long before I pulled the trigger. The world through my eyes seemed to die with me. It was like I was to push the final button to end this world. I committed myself to the arms of death. There comes a time when all things cease to shine, when the rays of hope are lost.

I PLACED THE GUN to my head. Then, I remember a tremendous explosion of lights like fireworks. Thus did the pain become glorious, an army rallied to the side of death to help destroy my life, which I could feel leaving my body with each rushing surge of blood. I was engulfed in total darkness.

(Shneidman, 1987, p. 56)

The animal world is filled with seemingly self-destructive behavior. Worker bees lose their stings and die after attacking intrusive mammals. Salmon die after the exhausting swim upstream to spawn. Lemmings are said to rush to the sea and drown. In each of these cases a creature's

The suicide of Nirvana's Kurt Cobain in April, 1994, shocked millions of young rock fans throughout the world and led many to experience a profound sense of grief and confusion. In Seattle, Cobain's home town, a candlelight vigil was attended by about 5000 people, including these two fans. Just a month prior to his death, Cobain had over-dosed on a combination of painkillers and alcohol. Although it was called an accident at the time, a friend later observed, "You don't take 50 pills by accident" (Jones, 1994).

behavior leads to its death, but it would be inaccurate to say the animal or insect wants to die or is trying to die. If anything, its actions are in the service of life. They are instinctual responses that help the species to survive in the long run. The self-destructive behavior described by the suicide survivor differs radically from these other actions. Only in the human act of suicide do beings knowingly end their own lives.

Suicide has been observed throughout history. It has been recorded among the ancient Chinese, Greeks, and Romans. King Saul's suicide is reported in the Old Testament. Cato threw himself upon his sword. And in more recent times, suicides by such famous people as Ernest Hemingway, Marilyn Monroe, and rock star Kurt Cobain have both shocked and fascinated society.

Today suicide ranks among the top ten causes of death in Western society. According to the World Health Organization, approximately 120,000 deaths by suicide occur each year. More than 30,000 suicides are committed annually in the United States alone, by 12.8 of every 100,000 inhabitants, accounting for almost 2 percent of all deaths in the nation (McIntosh, 1991; National Center for Health Statistics, 1988). It is also estimated that each year more than 2 million other persons throughout the world—600,000 in the United States—make unsuccessful attempts to kill themselves; these people are called *parasuicides* (McIntosh, 1991). Indeed, more than 5 million people now living in the United States have at some time attempted suicide, and still more contemplate such acts

without carrying them out (Bagley & Ramsay, 1985; Sherer, 1985). These numbing statistics come to life in the following statement:

> Before you finish reading this page, someone in the United States will try to kill himself. At least 60 Americans will have taken their own lives by this time tomorrow. . . . Many of those who attempted will try again, a number with lethal success.
>
> *(Shneidman & Mandelkorn, 1983)*

Actually, it is difficult to obtain accurate figures on suicide. Many investigators believe that the estimates are low, perhaps only half of the actual total (Smith, 1991; Shneidman, 1981). Because suicide is an enormously stigmatizing act in our society, relatives and friends may refuse to acknowledge that loved ones have taken their own lives. Moreover, it can be difficult for coroners to distinguish suicides from accidental drug overdoses, automobile crashes, drownings, and the like (Jacobs & Klein, 1993). Since relatively few of those who commit suicide actually leave notes (see Box 10–1), only the most obvious cases are categorized appropriately (Smith, 1991; Shneidman, 1981).

Suicide is not classified as a mental disorder by DSM-IV, but it does typically involve such clinical variables as a breakdown of coping skills, emotional turmoil, and distorted perspective. Although textbooks often address this topic in conjunction with mood disorders, at least half of all suicides result from other mental disorders, such as alcohol dependence or schizophrenia, or involve no clear mental disorder at all.

Despite the prevalence and long history of suicide, people have traditionally been misinformed about its symptoms and causes. A decade ago, when researchers administered a suicide fact test to several hundred undergraduates, the average score was only 59 percent correct (McIntosh, Hubbard, & Santos, 1985). Fortunately, the recent scores on a similar test by students in both Canada and the United States have been higher (Leenaars & Lester, 1992) (see Table 10–1). This heightened awareness probably reflects the fact that the study of suicide has become a major focus of the clinical field, and our insights are improving.

■ WHAT ■ IS SUICIDE?

Not every self-inflicted death is a suicide. A man who crashes his car into a tree after falling asleep at the steering wheel is hardly trying to kill himself. Thus Edwin Shneidman (1993, 1981, 1963), one of the

BOX 10-1

SUICIDE NOTES

Dear Bill: I am sorry for causing you so much trouble. I really didn't want to and if you would have told me at the first time the truth probably both of us would be very happy now. Bill I am sorry but I can't take the life any more, I don't think there is any goodness in the world. I love you very very much and I want you to be as happy in your life as I wanted to make you. Tell your parents I am very sorry and please if you can do it don't ever let my parents know what happened.

Please, don't hate me Bill, I love you.

Mary

(Leenaars, 1991)

A suicide often passes undetected or remains shrouded in mystery because the only person who could tell us the truth has been lost to the world. At the same time, an estimated 12 to 34 percent of people who commit suicide leave notes, providing unequivocal proof of their intentions and a unique record of their psychological state only hours or minutes before they died (Black, 1993; Leenaars, 1992, 1989).

Each suicide note is a personal document, unique to the writer and the circumstances (Leenaars, 1989). Some are barely a single sentence, others run several pages. People who leave notes clearly wish to make a powerful statement to those they leave behind (Leenaars, 1989), whether the message be "a cry for help, an epitaph, or a last will and testament" (Frederick,

1969, p. 17). Most suicide notes are addressed to specific individuals.

Suicide notes elicit varied reactions from survivors (Leenaars, 1989). A note can clarify the cause of death, thus saving relatives the ordeal of a lengthy legal inquiry. Friends and relatives may also find that it eases their grief to know the person's reasons for committing suicide (Chynoweth, 1977). Yet some suicide notes add to the guilt and negative emotions that survivors commonly experience, as in the following case:

Rather than permit his wife to leave him, twenty-year-old Mr. Jefferson hanged himself in the bathroom, leaving a note on the front door for his wife, saying, "Cathy I love you. You're right, I am crazy . . . and thank you for trying to love me. Phil." Mrs. Jefferson felt and frequently insisted that she "killed Phil." She attempted suicide herself a week after. . . .

(Wallace, 1981, p. 79)

Traditionally, suicide notes have been private documents, read only by relatives, the police, or the courts (Frederick, 1969). During the latter half of this century, however, researchers have asked to study suicide notes for clues that may help them understand the phenomenon of suicide. Several aspects of suicide notes have been of particular interest to researchers: differences between genuine and fake suicide notes; such dimensions as the age and sex of the note writer; the grammatical structure

of the note; the type and frequency of words used; the conscious and unconscious content; emotional, cognitive, and motivational themes; and even the handwriting (Leenaars, 1989).

One of the many important findings of suicide note studies is that suicide shows significant variation with age. Younger persons express more self-directed hostility and interpersonal problems in their notes; those between 40 and 49 report being unable to cope with life; those between 50 and 59 rarely cite a reason for their suicide; and those over 60 are motivated by such problems as illness, disability, and loneliness.

Studies of notes have also revealed that the nature of suicide has changed little since the 1940s. Suicide notes written in the 1940s and 1950s are similar in content to those written in the 1980s, with the exception that modern notes show less ambivalence and more constricted thinking.

A written note is necessarily only a fragment of the writer's experiences, perceptions, thoughts, and emotions and provides only a partial picture. Moreover, as Edwin Shneidman points out, the writers may not be fully aware of their motives; their cognitive constriction prevents them from being truly insightful. Suicide notes are "not the royal road to an easy understanding of suicidal phenomena" (Shneidman, 1973, p. 380). In conjunction with other sources, however, the study of suicide notes may be a fruitful avenue of research.

most influential writers on this topic, defines *suicide* as an *intentioned* death—a self-inflicted death in which one makes an *intentional*, *direct*, and *conscious* effort to end one's life. Most theorists agree that the term "suicide" should be limited to deaths of this sort.

Intentioned deaths may take various forms. Consider the following three imaginary instances. Although all of these people intended to die, their pre-

cise motives, the personal issues involved, and their suicidal actions differed greatly.

*D*ave: Dave was a successful man. By the age of 50 he had risen to the vice presidency of a small but profitable office machine firm. He was in charge of marketing and sales. True, he had invested most of his time in his work, and as a result had not developed close family

TABLE 10-1

FACTS ON SUICIDE QUIZ (REVISED)

CIRCLE THE ANSWER YOU FEEL IS MOST CORRECT FOR
EACH QUESTION. "T" (TRUE), "F" (FALSE),
OR "?" (DON'T KNOW)

T F ? 1. People who talk about suicide rarely commit suicide. [73%]*

T F ? 2. The tendency toward suicide is not genetically (i.e., biologically) inherited and passed on from one generation to another. [46%]

T F ? 3. The suicidal person neither wants to die nor is fully intent on dying. [38%]

T F ? 4. If assessed by a psychiatrist, everyone who commits suicide would be diagnosed as depressed. [57%]

T F ? 5. If you ask someone directly "Do you feel like killing yourself?," it will likely lead that person to make a suicide attempt. [95%]

T F ? 6. A suicidal person will always be suicidal and entertain thoughts of suicide. [76%]

T F ? 7. Suicide rarely happens without warning. [63%]

T F ? 8. A person who commits suicide is mentally ill. [70%]

T F ? 9. A time of high suicide risk in depression is at the time when the person begins to improve. [47%]

T F ? 10. Nothing can be done to stop people from making the attempt once they have made up their minds to kill themselves. [92%]

T F ? 11. Motives and causes of suicide are readily established. [58%]

T F ? 12. A person who has made a past suicide attempt is more likely to attempt suicide again than someone who has never attempted. [80%]

T F ? 13. Suicide is among the top 10 causes of death in the U.S. [83%]

T F ? 14. Most people who attempt suicide fail to kill themselves. [74%]

T F ? 15. Those who attempt suicide do so only to manipulate others and attract attention to themselves. [64%]

T F ? 16. Oppressive weather (e.g., rain) has been found to be very closely related to suicidal behavior. [26%]

T F ? 17. There is a strong correlation between alcoholism and suicide. [68%]

T F ? 18. Suicide seems unrelated to moon phases. [49%]

19. What percentage of suicides leaves a suicide note? [40%]
    a. 15–25%   b. 40–50%   c. 65–75%

20. Suicide rates for the U.S. as a whole are _____ for the young. [8%]
    a. lower than   b. higher than   c. the same as

(continued)

relationships. Still, he was content. He had a devoted wife and two teenage sons who respected him. They lived in an upper-middle-class neighborhood, had a spacious house, and enjoyed a comfortable life. Dave was proud of his professional accomplishments, pleased with his family, and happy in the role of family provider.

In August of his fiftieth year, everything changed. Dave was fired. Just like that, after many years of loyal and effective service. The firm's profits were down and the president wanted to try new, fresher marketing approaches. He wanted to try a younger person in Dave's position.

Dave was shocked. The experience of rejection, loss, and emptiness was overwhelming. He looked for another position, but found only low-paying jobs for which he was overqualified. The office machine business was no longer the wide-open field he had started in, nor was he the energetic young man of years past. He began to fear that he would never find a position with the status and salary he was accustomed to.

Each day as he looked for work Dave became more depressed, anxious, and desperate. He was convinced that his wife and sons would not love him if he could not maintain their lifestyle. Even if they did, he could not love himself under such circumstances. He kept sinking, withdrawing from others, and entering a state of hopelessness.

Six months after losing his job, Dave began to consider ending his life. The pain was too great, the humiliation unending. He hated the present and dreaded the future. He believed his family would be better off with him dead; he was certain he would be better off. He actually discussed these thoughts with friends and listened to their reactions, arguments, and encouragement. Nevertheless, he became increasingly convinced that suicide was a plausible, even desirable notion.

Throughout February he went back and forth. On some days he was sure he wanted to die. On other days, an enjoyable evening or uplifting conversation might change his mind temporarily. On a Monday late in February he heard about a job possibility and the anticipation of the next day's interview seemed to lift his spirits. But at Tuesday's interview, things did not go well. It was clear to him that he would not be offered the job. He went home, took a recently purchased gun from his locked desk drawer, and shot himself.

TABLE 10-1

FACTS ON SUICIDE QUIZ (REVISED) *(continued)*

21. With respect to sex differences in suicide attempts: [65%]
    a. Males and females attempt at similar levels.
    b. Females attempt more often than males.
    c. Males attempt more often than females.
22. Suicide rates among the young are ____ those for the old. [7%]
    a. lower than   b. higher than   c. the same as
23. Men kill themselves in numbers ____ those for women. [67%]
    a. similar to   b. higher than   c. lower than
24. Suicide rates for the young since the 1950s have: [97%]
    a. increased   b. decreased   c. changed little
25. The most common method employed to kill oneself in the U.S. is: [28%]
    a. hanging   b. firearms   c. drugs and poison
26. The season of highest suicide risk is: [11%]
    a. winter   b. fall   c. spring
27. The day of the week on which most suicides occur is: [60%]
    a. Monday   b. Wednesday   c. Saturday
28. Suicide rates for non-whites are ____ those for Whites. [35%]
    a. higher than   b. similar to   c. lower than
29. Which marital status category has the lowest rates of suicide? [59%]
    a. married   b. widowed   c. single, never, married

30. The ethnic/racial group with the highest suicide rate is: [15%]
    a. Whites   b. Blacks   c. Native Americans
31. The risk of death by suicide for a person who has attempted suicide in the past is ____ that for someone who has never attempted. [80%]
    a. lower than   b. similar to   c. higher than
32. Compared to other Western nations, the U.S. suicide rate is: [21%]
    a. among the highest   b. moderate   c. among the lowest
33. The most common method in attempted suicide is: [63%]
    a. firearms   b. drugs and poisons   c. cutting one's wrists
34. On the average, when young people make suicide attempts, they are ____ to die compared to elderly persons. [41%]
    a. less likely   b. just as likely   c. more likely
35. As a cause of death, suicide ranks ____ for the young when compared to the nation as a whole. [86%]
    a. the same   b. higher   c. lower
36. The region of the U.S. with the highest suicide rates is: [36%]
    a. east   b. midwest   c. west

Source: Hubbard & McIntosh, 1992, p. 164.
Answer key: true items—2, 3, 7, 9, 12, 13, 14, 17, and 18; *false* items—1, 4, 5, 6, 8, 10, 11, 15, and 16. Items for which the correct answer is "a": 19, 22, 24, 27, 29, and 34. Items for which the correct answer is "b": 21, 23, 25, 32, 33, and 35. Items for which the correct answer is "c": 20, 26, 28, 30, 31, and 36.
* *Note:* The percentages in brackets following each question refer to the proportion of 331 undergraduates enrolled in general psychology who correctly answered the item.

Billy: Billy never truly recovered from his mother's death. He was only 7 years old and unprepared for a loss of such magnitude. His father sent him to live with his grandparents for a time, to a new school with new kids and a new way of life. In Billy's mind, all these changes were for the worse. He missed the joy and laughter of the past. He missed his home, his father, and his friends. Most of all he missed his mother.

He did not really understand her death. His father said that she was in heaven now, at peace, happy. That she had not wanted to die or leave Billy, that an accident had taken her life. His father explained that life would be very hard for a while but that someday Billy would feel better, laugh again, enjoy things again. Billy waited for that day, but it didn't seem to come. As his unhappiness and loneliness continued day after day, he put things together in his own way. He believed that he would be happy again if he could join his mother. He felt that she was waiting for him, wait-ing for him to come to her. These thoughts seemed so right to him; they brought him comfort and hope. One evening, shortly after saying good night to his grandparents, Billy climbed out of bed, went up the stairs to the roof of their apartment house, and jumped to his death. He was frightened but at the same time happy as he jumped. In his mind he was joining his mother in heaven.

Margaret: Margaret and Bob had been going together for a year. It was Margaret's first serious relationship; it was her whole life. She confided all of her feelings to Bob, all of her hopes, ideas, and plans. She loved sharing and doing things with him. She loved their intimacy. She felt that Bob shared these feelings. He said as much and acted like a person who cared. Thus when Bob told Margaret that he no longer loved her and was leaving her for someone else, Margaret was shocked and shaken.

As the weeks went by, Margaret was filled with two competing feelings—depression and anger. On the one hand, she was devastated—wondering how she could continue, fill the void, and bear this rejection. She felt lost and alone. Several times she called Bob, begged him to reconsider, and pleaded for a chance to win him back. At the same time, she felt hatred toward Bob. She didn't deserve this treatment. She had done nothing but love him and give all of herself to him. In return, he had sent her away and destroyed her life. It was he who deserved to suffer, not she. Sometimes when she was talking to him, her pleas would change to demands, her cries to yells. Who did he think he was? He would get his eventually.

Margaret's friends became more and more worried about her. At first they understood her pain, sympathized with it, and assumed it would soon subside. But as time went on, her depression and anger actually intensified. Then Margaret began to act strangely. When she drove her car, she would suddenly speed around sharp turns. She started drinking heavily and casually mixing her drinks with all kinds of pills. She would pick arguments with friends and even strangers, and wanted to carry these fights to physical blows. She constantly seemed to flirt with danger.

One night Margaret went into her bathroom, reached for a bottle of sleeping pills, and swallowed a handful of them. She wanted to make her pain go away and she wanted Bob to know just how much pain he had caused her. She continued swallowing pill after pill, crying and swearing as she gulped them down. When she began to feel drowsy, she decided to call her close friend Cindy. She was not sure why she was calling, perhaps to say good-bye, to explain her actions, or to make sure that Bob was told; or perhaps to be talked out of it. Cindy, of course, became desperate. She pleaded with Margaret, pointed out the irrationality of her actions, and tried to motivate her to live. Margaret was trying to listen, but she became less and less coherent. She had taken so many pills. She was beyond helping herself. Cindy hung up the phone and quickly called Margaret's neighbor and the police. When reached by her neighbor, Margaret was already in a coma. The police could not revive her and they rushed her to the hospital. Doctors and nurses worked feverishly to save her, but to no avail. Seven hours later, while her friends and family waited for news in the hospital lounge, Margaret died.

While Margaret seemed ambivalent about her death, Dave was clear in his wish to die. And whereas Billy viewed death as a trip to heaven, Dave saw it as an end to his existence. Such differences can be important in assessing, understanding, and treating suicidal clients. Accordingly, Shneidman has distinguished four kinds of people who intentionally end their lives: the *death seeker, death initiator, death ignorer,* and *death darer.*

Death seekers have a clear intention of ending their lives at the time they attempt suicide. This single-

ness of purpose is usually of short duration. Such clarity and commitment to act can change to ambivalence the very next hour or day, and then return again in an equally short time.

Dave, the middle-aged executive, was a death seeker. Granted, he had many misgivings about suicide, was ambivalent about it for weeks, and even sought out conversations to dissuade him. Had he been unable to carry out his action on Tuesday, Wednesday might have brought a different frame of mind and perhaps a different ending. On Tuesday, however, he was a death seeker—clear in his desire to die and acting in a manner that guaranteed a fatal outcome.

Some theorists argue that people who use more lethal suicide techniques, such as firearms, have a clearer death-seeking intent than those who use less lethal techniques, such as drug overdose. Shneidman points out, however, that many people who use less lethal techniques are very clear in their wish to die, fully believe that their action will end their lives, and accordingly should be classified as death seekers.

Although **death initiators** also clearly intend to end their lives, they act out of a conviction that the process of death is already under way and that they are simply hastening the process. Some expect that they will die in the near future—a matter of days or weeks. Sometimes they believe that by killing themselves now, they are avoiding the loss of control or suffering that otherwise awaits them. As we shall see later, many suicides among the elderly and sick fall into this category. The novelist Ernest Hemingway, for example, followed the pattern of a death initiator. A strong and proud man, he developed grave concerns about his failing body—concerns that some observers believe were at the center of his suicide.

Death ignorers do not believe that their self-inflicted death will mean the end of their existence. They believe they are trading their present life for a better or happier existence. Many child suicides, like Billy, fall into this category, as do adult believers in a hereafter who commit suicide to reach another form of life.

In designating this category, Shneidman was not challenging anyone's belief in the hereafter. Rather, he was distinguishing suicides by people who expect their existence to end from suicides by those who expect some sort of continuation of being. A widower who ends his life because he cannot bear his loneliness has a different intent from a widower who acts so that he may join his wife in heaven.

Death darers are ambivalent in their intent to die even at the moment of their attempt, and they show

A sky surfer tries to ride the perfect cloud over Sweden. Thrill-seekers often progress from one dangerous activity to another, giving rise in recent years to such "sports" as white-water rafting, bungie jumping, and rock climbing. Are these people daredevils searching for new highs, as many claim, or are some of them actually death darers?

form of suicide, their true intent is unclear. In this chapter the term "suicide" refers only to deaths in which the victims intentionally, directly, and consciously end their own lives.

THE STUDY OF SUICIDE

Suicide researchers are faced with a major problem: their subjects are no longer alive. How can investigators draw accurate conclusions about the intentions, feelings, and circumstances of people who are no longer available to answer questions about their actions? Two major research strategies have been used, each with its limitations.

One strategy is **retrospective analysis,** a kind of psychological autopsy in which clinicians and researchers piece together data from the person's past (Jacobs & Klein, 1993). Even when a suicide comes as a surprise, relatives and friends may remember past statements, conversations, and behavior that can be revealing in the light of subsequent events. Other retrospective data may be gathered from psychotherapists' notes and remembrances: some people who commit suicide were previously in therapy and talked about the issues and problems that led them to take their lives. Finally, retrospective data may also be provided by the suicide notes that some victims leave behind.

Unfortunately, these sources of information are not always available. Less than a quarter of all suicide victims have been in psychotherapy (Fleer & Pasewark, 1982), and only 12 to 34 percent leave notes (Black, 1993; Leenaars, 1992, 1989). Nor is retrospective information necessarily valid. A grieving, perhaps guilt-ridden relative may be incapable of objective and accurate recollections.

Because of these limitations, many researchers also use the strategy of *studying people who survive their suicide attempts* and equating them with those who commit fatal suicides. Of course, people who survive suicide may differ in important ways from those who actually do kill themselves (Maris, 1992; Stengel, 1974, 1964). Among adolescents, for example, attempted suicides outnumber fatal suicides by as many as 200 to 1. When the number of incomplete suicides is this high, it may well be that many of these people do not want to die. Although survivors of suicide attempts are imperfect sources of information, suicide researchers have found it useful and informative to study them. We shall therefore consider those who attempt suicide and those who commit suicide as more or less alike.

this ambivalence in the act itself. Although to some degree they wish to die, and they often do die, they take actions that do not guarantee death. The person who plays Russian roulette—that is, pulls the trigger of a revolver randomly loaded with one bullet—is a death darer. So is the person who walks along the ledge of a tall building or a nonpilot who flies an airplane without help. Death darers often are as interested in gaining attention, making someone feel guilty, or expressing anger as in dying per se (Brent et al., 1988; Hawton et al., 1982).

Margaret might be considered a death darer. Although her unhappiness and anger were pronounced, she was not sure that she wanted to die even as she took an excess of pills. While taking the pills, she called her friend, reported her actions, and listened to her friend's advice and pleas. She carried her ambivalence into the suicidal act itself and remained in conflict until her death.

When individuals play *indirect, covert, partial,* or *unconscious* roles in their own deaths, Schneidman classifies them in a suicide-like category called **subintentional death** (Shneidman, 1993, 1981). Seriously ill people who consistently mismanage their medicines may belong in this category. In related work, Karl Menninger (1938) has distinguished a category called **chronic suicide.** Here people behave in life-endangering ways over an extended period of time—perhaps consuming excessive alcohol, abusing drugs, indulging in risky activities, or pursuing high-risk occupations. Although their deaths may represent a

PATTERNS
AND STATISTICS

Suicide rates vary from country to country. Hungary, Germany, Austria, Denmark, Finland, Belgium, Switzerland, and Japan have very high rates, more than 20 suicides annually per 100,000 persons (Diekstra, 1990; WHO, 1987) (see Table 10–2); conversely, Egypt, Mexico, Greece, Spain, Italy, and Ireland have relatively low rates, fewer than 8 per 100,000. The United States and Canada fall in between, each with a suicide rate of between 12 and 13 per 100,000 persons (Diekstra, 1990, 1989; WHO, 1988).

One factor often cited to account for these national differences is religious affiliation and beliefs (Shneidman, 1987). In Japan, for example, where religious beliefs are rooted in Shinto and Buddhist traditions, people's attitudes toward death tend to be quite different from those prevailing in typically Western, Judeo-Christian communities (see Box 10–2).

Furthermore, countries that are predominantly Catholic, Jewish, or Muslim tend to have lower suicide rates than predominantly Protestant countries. Perhaps the first three religions, with their relatively strict proscriptions against suicide and heavy integration of members into church and communal life, help to deter people from committing suicide. Yet there are exceptions to this tentative rule. Austria, for example, a predominantly Roman Catholic country, has one of the highest suicide rates in the world. In fact, research is beginning to suggest that it may not be religious *doctrine* that militates against suicide but rather the degree of an individual's *devoutness* (Holmes, 1985; Martin, 1984). Irrespective of their particular persuasion, very religious people seem to be less likely to commit suicide. Similarly, it seems that people who hold a greater reverence for life are less prone to contemplate or attempt self-destruction (Lee, 1985).

The suicide rates of men and women also differ (see Figure 10–1). Women attempt three times as many suicides as men, yet men succeed at more than

TABLE 10-2

NATIONAL SUICIDE RATES (PER 100,000 OF POPULATION)*

COUNTRY	RATE	COUNTRY	RATE
1. Hungary	45.3	18. Australia	11.6
2. Federal Republic of Germany	43.1	19. Scotland	11.6
3. Austria	28.3	20. Netherlands	11.0
4. Denmark	27.8	21. New Zealand	10.3
5. Finland	26.6	22. Portugal	9.2
6. Belgium	23.8	23. England and Wales	8.9
7. Switzerland	22.8	24. Ireland	7.8
8. France	22.7	25. Italy	7.6
9. Japan	21.2	26. Argentina	6.3
10. German Democratic Republic	19.0	27. Spain	4.9
11. Sweden	18.5	28. Greece	4.1
12. Cuba	17.7	29. Dominican Republic	2.4
13. Bulgaria	16.3	30. Mexico	1.6
14. Norway	14.1	31. Peru	1.4
15. Canada	12.9	32. Guatemala	0.5
16. United States	12.3	33. Nicaragua	0.2
17. Hong Kong	12.2	34. Egypt	0.1

* 1980–1986
Source: Adapted from Diekstra, 1990, 1989; WHO, 1988.

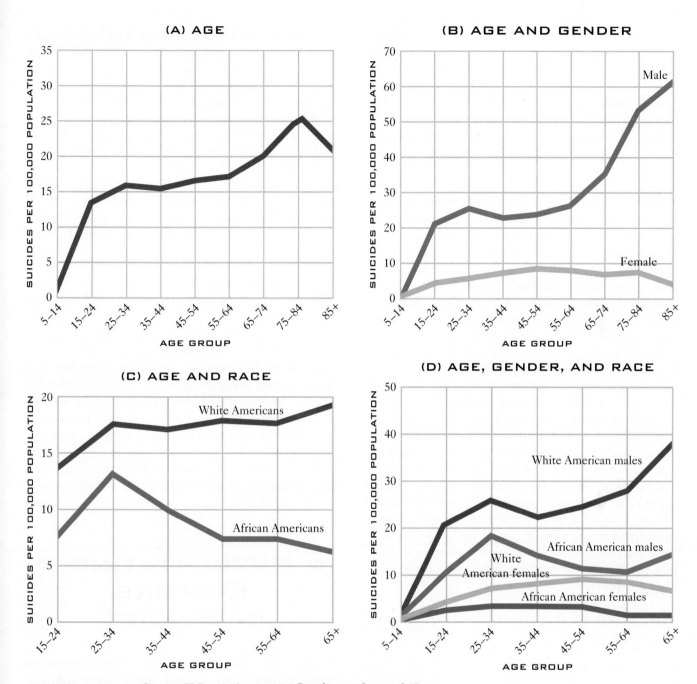

FIGURE 10–1 *Current U.S. suicide rates: (a) People over the age of 65 are more likely to commit suicide than those in any other age group; (b) males commit suicide at higher rates than females of corresponding ages; (c) white Americans commit suicide at higher rates than African Americans of corresponding ages; (d) elderly white American men have the highest risk of suicide. (Adapted from McIntosh, 1991, pp. 62–63; U.S. Bureau of the Census, 1990.)*

three times the rate of women (McIntosh, 1991; Stillion, 1985). Approximately 20.6 of every 100,000 men in the United States kill themselves each year, an average of 66 men each day; the suicide rate for women, which has been increasing in recent years, is 5.4 per 100,000, an average of 18 women each day (NCHS, 1988).

One reason for these differing rates appears to be the different methods used by men and women (Kushner, 1985). Men tend to use more violent methods, such as shooting, stabbing, or hanging themselves, whereas women use less violent methods, such as barbiturate overdose. Indeed, firearms account for close to two-thirds of the male suicides in the United States, compared to 40 percent of the female suicides (McIntosh, 1992; NCHS, 1990). Violent attempts at suicide are less reversible, allow less time for a change of mind or for others to intervene, and are more likely to lead to death (Kushner, 1985; Marks, 1977).

Why do men and women choose different ways of killing themselves? Some observers believe that more men than women are clear in their wish to die, and that this firmness of purpose accounts for the differential use of these methods. Others argue that because men have traditionally been stereotyped as more decisive and strong and less expressive than women, they are not permitted in their own minds to make less serious attempts or to call for help once they are in danger. Research has in fact found that male and female college students perceive completed suicide to be more powerful and more "masculine" than attempted suicide (Jack, 1992; Linehan, 1973).

Suicide is also related to marital status (see Figure 10–2). Married people, especially those with children, have a relatively low suicide rate; the single and widowed have higher rates; and divorced people have the highest rate of all (NCHS, 1988). One study compared ninety persons who committed suicide with ninety psychologically troubled patients matched for age, gender, and schooling who had never attempted suicide (Roy, 1982). Only 16 percent of the suicide subjects were married or cohabiting at the time of the suicide, compared to 30 percent of the control subjects. Similarly, an analysis conducted in Canada over three decades has revealed a strong positive correlation between national divorce rates and suicide rates (Trovato, 1987).

Finally, in the United States at least, suicide rates seem to differ markedly among the races (see Figure 10–1c). The suicide rate of white Americans, 14 per 100,000 persons, is twice as high as that of African Americans and members of other racial groups (McIntosh, 1991; NCHS, 1988). The major exception to this pattern is the very high suicide rate of Native Americans (Berlin, 1987). Their overall suicide rate is twice the national average; some Native American groups even display rates as high as four to ten times the national average (Berlin, 1987; Willard, 1979). Although the extreme poverty of many Native Americans may account in part for such trends, studies reveal that such factors as alcohol use, modeling, and availability of firearms may also be involved (Young, 1991; Berman & Jobes, 1991). Studies with Native Americans in Canada have similar implications (Bagley, 1991).

It is worth noting that some of the statistics on suicide have been called into question by researchers in recent years. For example, one analysis suggests that the actual rate of suicide may be 15 percent higher for African Americans and 6 percent higher for women than usually reported (Phillips, 1993). Individuals from these groups, more often than other persons, use methods of suicide that are mistaken for accidental causes of death; for example, poisoning, drug overdose, single car crashes, and pedestrian deaths.

■ PRECIPITATING ■ FACTORS IN SUICIDE

Suicidal acts often are tied to contemporaneous events or conditions. Though these factors may not fully account for suicide, they do serve to precipitate it. Common precipitating factors are *stressful events and situations, mood and thought changes, alcohol use, mental disorders,* and *modeling events.*

STRESSFUL EVENTS AND SITUATIONS

SUICIDES PER 100,000 POPULATION

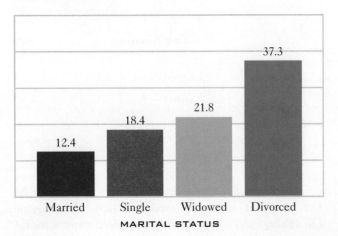

FIGURE 10–2 *Approximately 37 of every 100,000 divorced persons commit suicide, more than three times the suicide rate of married persons. (Adapted from McIntosh, 1991, p. 64.)*

Researchers have repeatedly counted more undesirable events in the recent lives of suicide attempters than in those of matched control subjects (Heikkinen, Aro, & Lonnqvist, 1992; Paykel, 1991). In one study,

BOX 10-2

SUICIDE AMONG
THE JAPANESE

In a study that compared American medical students' attitudes toward suicide with those of Japanese medical students, it was found that while the Americans regarded suicide as an expression of anger or aggression, the Japanese viewed it as normal, reasonable behavior (Domino & Takahashi, 1991). The sociologist Mamoru Iga (1993) holds that this difference reflects a fundamental discrepancy in the cultures' religious and philosophical understandings of life and death.

The Shinto and Buddhist traditions stress eternal change and the ephemeral quality of human life. In the basic tenets of Buddhism, life is viewed as being sorrowful and death is considered a way of freeing oneself from illusion and suffering. Furthermore, for many Japanese, the highest aim in life is to achieve complete detachment from earthly concerns, total self-negation. Within this framework, death can be seen as beautiful, as an expression of sincerity *(makoto)*, or as an appropriate reaction to shame. Thus, according to Iga, "In Japan, suicide has traditionally been an accepted, if not a welcomed, way of solving a serious problem. . . . Suicide is not a sin in Japan; it is not punishable by God. Suicide is not viewed as a social or national issue but a personal problem."

Iga further explains the different attitudes toward suicide by pointing to Japan's lack of a humanistic tradition in which self-expression, self-love, and self-enhancement are prominently valued. Out of such a tradition in the West comes the impulse to prevent suicide. Japanese society values the subjugation of individual welfare to social order. Its primary humanistic tradition is a desire for harmony between humanity and nature and it dictates that humans bow to nature accordingly. Thus there is really no deep-rooted principle that says it is important to stop people from taking their own lives.

Finally, Iga points to several other sociocultural factors can further contribute to the high rate of suicide in Japan. One is the pervasive sexism that is a long-standing feature of Japanese culture. Others are the increasing academic stresses on young people and increasing work pressures on middle-aged men, both a result of democratization and increasing interaction with the Western world. On the other hand, these interactions between the cultures have also caused numerous Japanese to adopt some American attitudes toward suicide prevention. After visiting the Los Angeles Suicide Prevention Center, some Japanese psychologists and psychiatrists opened the first suicide prevention center in Japan in 1971. They were apprehensive at first that shame would deter the Japanese from seeking help there, but the center has been successful and as of 1990 was operating in 33 Japanese cities.

---

suicide attempters reported twice as many stressful events in the year before their attempt as nonsuicidal depressed patients or nondepressed mental patients (Cohen-Sandler et al., 1982). An attempt may be precipitated by a single recent event or, as in the following case, by a series of events that have a combined impact.

Sally's suicide attempt took place in the context of a very difficult year for the family. Sally's mother and stepfather separated after 9 years of marriage. After the father moved out, he visited the family erratically. Four months after he moved out of the house, the mother's boyfriend moved into the house. The mother planned to divorce her husband and marry her boyfriend, who had become the major disciplinarian for the children; a fact that Sally intensely resented. Sally also complained of being "left out" in relation to the closeness she had with her mother. Another problem for Sally had been two school changes in the last 2 years which left Sally feeling friendless. In addition, she failed all her subjects in the last marking period.

(Pfeffer, 1986, pp. 129–130)

One of the most common kinds of recent stress in cases of suicide is loss of a loved one by death, divorce, breakup, or rejection (Heikkinen et al., 1992; Paykel, 1991; Hawton, 1982). Another form of loss frequently tied to suicide is loss of a job (Heikkinen et al., 1992; Snyder, 1992; Lester & Yang, 1991). Researchers have found that the rate of suicide attempts in Vienna is significantly higher for unemployed people than for the population in general (Probsting & Till, 1985). Similarly, the unemployment rate and the suicide rate in the United States rose and fell together from 1940 to 1984 (Yang, Stack, & Lester, 1992), and the rate of suicide among U.S.

TABLE 10-3

COMMON PREDICTORS OF SUICIDE

1. Depressive disorder and certain other mental disorders

2. Alcoholism and other forms of substance abuse

3. Suicide ideation, talk, preparation; certain religious ideas

4. Prior suicide attempts

5. Lethal methods

6. Isolation, living alone, loss of support

7. Hopelessness, cognitive rigidity

8. Being an older white male

9. Modeling, suicide in the family, genetics

10. Economic or work problems; certain occupations

11. Marital problems, family pathology

12. Stress and stressful events

13. Anger, aggression, irritability

14. Physical illness

15. Repetition and comorbidity of factors 1–14

Source: Adapted from Maris, 1992.

farmers tends to rise during a declining farm economy (Ragland & Berman, 1991).

People may also attempt suicide in response to long-term rather than recent or episodic stress. Four long-term stresses are commonly implicated—serious illness, abusive environment, occupational stress, and role conflict (see Table 10–3).

SERIOUS ILLNESS   As we noted earlier, a painful or disabling illness is at the center of many suicide attempts (Lester, 1992; Allebeck & Bolund, 1991). People with such problems may come to feel that their death is unavoidable and imminent, or that the suffering and problems caused by their illness are more than they can endure. An analysis of the medical records of eighty-eight cancer patients who had died by suicide in Sweden revealed that nearly two-thirds were in an advanced or terminal phase of the disease and had severe symptoms (Bolund, 1985).

Although illness-linked suicides have a long history, they have become more prevalent and controversial in recent years. Medical progress is partly responsible. Although physicians can now apply life-sustaining techniques that keep seriously ill people alive much longer, they are seldom able to maintain the quality

and comfort of the patients' lives. In such situations some persons try to end their slow and painful decline.

ABUSIVE ENVIRONMENT   Victims of an abusive or repressive environment from which they have little or no hope of escape sometimes commit suicide. Some prisoners of war, victims of the Holocaust, abused spouses, abused children, and prison inmates have attempted to end their lives (Shaunesey et al., 1993; Bergman & Brismar, 1991; Counts, 1990) (see Figure 10–3). Like those who have serious illnesses, these people may have been in constant psychological or physical pain, felt that they could endure no more suffering, and believed that there was no hope for improvement in their condition.

OCCUPATIONAL STRESS   Some jobs create ongoing feelings of tension or dissatisfaction that can precipitate suicide attempts. Research has often found particularly high suicide rates among psychiatrists and psychologists, physicians, dentists, lawyers, and unskilled laborers (Holmes & Rich, 1990; Richings et al., 1986; Stillion, 1985). Of course, these correlational data do not establish that occupational pressures are in fact pushing the suicide rate up. There are alternative interpretations. Unskilled workers may be responding to financial insecurity rather than job stress when they attempt suicide. Similarly, there is the possibility that rather than reacting to the emotional strain of their work, suicidal psychiatrists and psychologists have long-standing emotional

Hundreds of persons wait in line when job openings are announced at a new hotel in Chicago. The all-too familiar lines of unemployed and, often, homeless people in cities throughout the United States may signal a threat to life as well as an economic struggle. Research indicates that national suicide rates often climb during periods of increased unemployment.

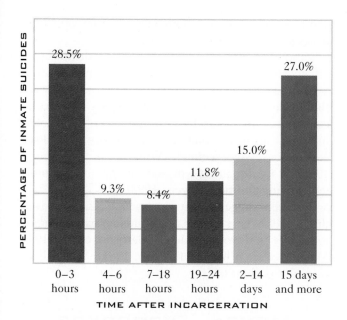

FIGURE 10-3 *Approximately 107 out of every 100,000 inmates in U.S. jails commit suicide each year—eight times the national prevalence rate. More than half of these suicides occur during the first day of incarceration. Almost 29 percent take place during the first three hours. (Adapted from Bonner, 1992; Hayes & Rowan, 1988.)*

problems that stimulated their career interest in the first place (Johnson, 1991).

ROLE CONFLICT Another long-term stress linked to suicide is role conflict. Everyone occupies a variety of roles in life—spouse, employee, parent, and colleague, to name a few. These roles may conflict and cause considerable stress. In recent years researchers have found that women who hold jobs outside of the home often experience role conflicts—conflicts between their family demands and job requirements, for example, or between their social needs and vocational goals—and that these conflicts are reflected in a higher suicide rate (Stack, 1987; Stillion, 1985). Women in professional positions, such as physicians, appear to experience the most role conflict, and they display the highest suicide rate of women in the workforce (Stefansson & Wicks, 1991; Stillion, 1985).

MOOD AND THOUGHT CHANGES

Many suicide attempts are preceded by a shift in mood and thought. Although these shifts may not be severe enough to warrant a diagnosis of a mental dis-

order, they typically represent a significant change from the person's past mood or point of view.

The mood change most often linked to suicide is an increase in sadness (McGuire, 1982; Tishler, McKenry, & Morgan, 1981). Also common are heightened feelings of anxiety, anger, or shame (Pine, 1981; Weissman et al., 1973). Shneidman (1993, 1991) characterizes the key to suicide as "psychache," a feeling of "psychological pain experienced as intolerable, caused by unfulfilled psychological needs." He points out, "No one commits suicide out of joy; no suicide is born out of exultation. The enemy of life is pain. Pain is what the suicidal person seeks to escape" (1987, p. 56).

In the cognitive realm, many people on the verge of suicide have become preoccupied with their problems, lose perspective, and see suicide as an effective solution to their difficulties (Shneidman, 1993, 1987). They develop a sense of *hopelessness*—a pessimistic belief that their present circumstances, problems, and negative mood will not change (Klingman & Hochdorf, 1993; Ellis & Ratliff, 1986; Holden et al., 1985). Some clinicians believe that a feeling of hopelessness is the single most sensitive indicator of suicidal intent (Weishaar & Beck, 1992; Holden et al., 1985; Beck, 1967), and they take special care to look for signs of hopelessness when they assess the risk of suicide (see Table 10–4). People who contemplate suicide may also develop a pattern of *dichotomous thinking,* viewing their problems and solutions in either/or terms (Shneidman, 1993, 1987; Neuringer, 1976, 1974). In the following statement a woman who survived her jump from a building describes her dichotomous thinking at the time of the jump. She saw death as the only alternative to her pain:

> I was so desperate. I felt, my God, I couldn't face this thing. Everything was like a terrible whirlpool of confusion. And I thought to myself: There's only one thing to do. I just have to lose consciousness. That's the only way to get away from it. The only way to lose consciousness, I thought, was to jump off something good and high. . . .
>
> *(Shneidman, 1987, p. 56)*

ALCOHOL USE

Studies indicate that at least 20 percent of the people who commit suicide drink alcohol just before the act (Hirschfeld & Davidson, 1988). Autopsies reveal that about one-fourth of these people are legally intoxicated at the time of death (Flavin et al., 1990; Abel & Zeidenberg, 1985). In fact, the excessive use of alcohol just before suicide is probably much higher;

TABLE 10-4

HOPELESSNESS SCALE

HOPELESSNESS IS INDICATED WHEN PEOPLE ANSWER:

True

I might as well give up because there's nothing I can do about making things better for myself.

I can't imagine what my life would be like in ten years.

My future seems dark to me.

I just don't get the breaks, and there's no reason to believe I will in the future.

All I can see ahead of me is unpleasantness rather than pleasantness.

I don't expect to get what I really want.

Things just won't work out the way I want them to.

I never get what I want so it's foolish to want anything.

It is very unlikely that I will get any real satisfaction in the future.

The future seems vague and uncertain to me.

There's no use in really trying to get something I want because I probably won't get it.

False

I look forward to the future with hope and enthusiasm.

When things are going badly, I am helped by knowing that they can't stay that way forever.

I have enough time to accomplish the things I most want to do.

In the future I expect to succeed in what concerns me most.

I happen to be particularly lucky and I expect to get more of the good things in life than the average person.

My past experiences have prepared me well for my future.

When I look ahead to the future I expect I will be happier than I am now.

I have great faith in the future.

I can look forward to more good times than bad times.

Source: Beck et al., 1974.

coroners are more likely to classify deaths as accidental when they detect high alcohol consumption (Crompton, 1985). Such statistics suggest to many clinical researchers that alcohol consumption often contributes to suicidal behavior (Wasserman, 1992; Schuckit & Schuckit, 1991).

Some theorists believe that alcohol's disinhibiting effects allow people who are contemplating suicide to overcome the fears that would otherwise restrain them (Patel et al., 1972). Others suggest that alcohol contributes to suicide by lowering an individual's inhibitions against violence and helping to release covert aggressive feelings (Whitlock & Broadhurst, 1969), or by impairing a person's judgment and problem-solving abilities (Rogers, 1992).

Research suggests that the use of other kinds of drugs may have a similar tie to suicide, particularly in teenagers and young adults (Garrison et al., 1993; Marzuk et al., 1992; Shafii et al., 1985). We shall return to this point later.

MENTAL DISORDERS

As we noted earlier, people who attempt suicide do not necessarily have a mental disorder. Although they are troubled, unhappy, or anxious, their feelings may not add up to any disorder defined in DSM-IV. On the other hand, between 30 and 70 percent of all suicide attempters do display a mental disorder (Brent et al., 1993; Beaumont & Hetzel, 1992; Litman, 1987; Roy, 1985). The mental disorders linked most strongly to suicide are *mood disorders* (unipolar and bipolar depression), *schizophrenia*, and *substance-related disorders* (particularly alcoholism). Research suggests that approximately 10 to 15 percent of people with each of these disorders try to kill themselves (Black & Winokur, 1990; Miles, 1977). *Panic disorders* too have been linked to suicide, but in most cases the disorder occurs in conjunction with one of the other conditions (Norton et al., 1993; Lepine, Chignon, & Teherani, 1993).

In Chapter 8 we observed that most people with a major depressive disorder experience suicidal thoughts as part of their syndrome. Those whose disorder includes a strong sense of hopelessness seem most likely to attempt suicide (Fawcett et al., 1987). Even when depressed people are showing improvement in mood, they may remain high suicide risks. In fact, among those who are severely depressed, the risk of suicide may actually increase as their mood improves and they have more energy to act on their suicidal wishes.

Even if suicide is attempted in response to a severe physical illness, an episode of major depression may be playing a key role in the decision (Hendin & Klerman, 1993; Brown et al., 1986) (see Box 10-3). In one case a depressed 26-year-old

Severely depressed about his progressive illness, Ernest Hemingway shot and killed himself in 1961. Two series of electroconvulsive treatments had failed to improve his mood.

woman with cerebral palsy initially fought to compel a psychiatric hospital to assist her in committing suicide; when the woman's depression later lifted, she reversed her position (Bursztajn et al., 1986). Similarly, a study of forty-four terminally ill patients revealed that fewer than a quarter of them had thoughts of suicide or wished for an early death, and that those who did were all suffering from major depression (Brown et al., 1986). In the following case a clinically depressed terminally ill woman changes her perspective over time.

$\mathcal{N}$ ancy was a personal friend who had moved away some months ago, after concluding her divorce and seeing her twin daughters comfortably started in their college careers. With no forewarning, she called one afternoon to say that she was back in town. She realized her request would probably be refused, but could she have 50 seconal tablets? In total seriousness, she said it was important that she do away with herself before the weekend and the arrival home of her daughters. This was no simple "cry for help" or manipulative appeal. She had called from her hospital room, where she later revealed that she had been diagnosed as having advanced lung cancer, with metastases to the skull and back. Her prognosis, with chemotherapy, was for perhaps three or four months before lapsing into a ter-

minal state. She was already pale and withered, breathing with difficulty despite the recent drainage of a quart of fluid from her chest. She was determined to commit suicide, rather than endure the trials of therapy, or see her last financial resources squandered on fruitless medical care. She was the only child of an elderly couple, and was certain the news would strike down her father. Above all, she did not want to face her daughters' pain or her friends' pity and solicitude. "Realistic" suicide? The call for seconal from an unlikely source was still an invitation to debate her fate. Every appeal for time, reflection, and granting her family and friends the opportunity to say goodbye was made and countered. Her only show of sadness came when she was reminded that there were many who would keep some vestige of her in their hearts. She was remarkably free of fear—the determination to act, the focus on how to achieve her aim suppressed all other emotion.

She had her way a day later. Two close friends who accompanied her home managed to provide her with a quantity of medication, which she downed with liberal amounts of alcohol. When she was drowsy, they took their leave, intending to come back a day later to arrange matters before the daughters' return. Some quirk of fate or physiology intervened, for when Nancy was found, in spite of her lethal ingestion, she was still holding to life. She was comatose for several days, and finally returned to a home full of children, parents, her divorced husband, and many friends. She called again that week to vent her anger that she had been "proselytized" to stay alive when she wished only to die, and then to express her deep feelings of thankfulness that she had been given the opportunity to take a more measured and dignified leave of those she loved. She died not long after, spared the agony she had feared, a little afraid, but happier for her manner of leaving. Nancy's attempt may itself have altered the dynamics of her crisis, but it was the working of time that transformed a credibly realistic suicide into an acceptance of death with integrity uncompromised.

(Kahn, 1982, p. 87)

In many cases of suicide after alcohol use the individuals actually have a long history of abusing alcohol or some other substance (Merrill et al., 1992; Miles, 1977). The basis for the link between substance-related disorders and suicide is not clear. It may be that the tragic lifestyle resulting from the long-term use of alcohol or other drugs or the sense of being hopelessly trapped by a drug leads to suicidal thinking. Alternatively, both substance abuse and suicidal thinking may be caused by a third factor—by psychological pain, for instance, or desperation (Frances & Franklin, 1988). There may in fact be a downward-spiral effect, wherein people are driven toward alcohol usage by psychological pain or loss, only to find themselves caught in a pattern of alcohol abuse that serves to aggravate rather than solve their

BOX 10-3

THE RIGHT TO COMMIT SUICIDE

In the fall of 1989, a Michigan doctor, Jack Kevorkian, built a "suicide device." A person using it could, at the touch of a button, change a saline solution being fed intravenously into the arm to one containing chemicals that would bring unconsciousness and a swift death. The following June, under the doctor's supervision, Mrs. J. Adkins took her life. She left a note explaining: "This is a decision taken in a normal state of mind and is fully considered. I have Alzheimer's disease and I do not want to let it progress any further. I do not want to put my family or myself through the agony of this terrible disease." Mrs. Adkins believed that she had a right to choose death and that her choice was rational; indeed, her husband supported her decision. Dr. Kevorkian believed that the "device" could be valuable in assisting persons with compelling grounds for suicide. Michigan authorities, however, promptly prohibited further use of the device.

(Adapted from Belkin, 1990; Malcolm, 1990)

Dr. Kevorkian and his suicide device.

Dr. Kevorkian's continuing court battles have brought into public consciousness the issue of a person's right to commit suicide and society's right to intervene (West, 1993). The way a society views suicide depends greatly on its perceptions of life and death (Battin, 1993). The people of classical Greece valued physical and mental well-being in life and dignity in death;

therefore, individuals with sufficient cause, such as grave illness or mental anguish, had legal recourse to suicide. Athenian citizens could obtain official permission from the Senate to take their own lives, and magistrates were authorized to dispense hemlock to such persons for that purpose (Humphry & Wickett, 1986).

American attitudes toward suicide reflect a tradition that has long discouraged such acts (Siegel, 1988). A "sanctity of life" morality has prevailed, according to which all human existence is valued and should be protected (Eser, 1981). The Bible does not explicitly censure the taking of one's own life, but in the fifth century St. Augustine declared that suicide broke the commandment "Thou shalt not kill." Soon after, the church announced that persons who attempted suicide would be excommunicated (Fletcher, 1981). Later, in countries such as Britain, suicide was considered a crime against the king or state, a failure to fulfill one's obligations to society (Siegel, 1988).

Today we still speak of "committing" suicide as though it were a crimi-

problems (Miller et al., 1991; Downey, 1991). Nor should the medical complications of chronic substance abuse be overlooked. Most suicides by alcoholic people, for example, occur in the late stages of the disorder when cirrhosis and other medical complications begin, suggesting that at least some of these people may be acting as "death initiators" who believe that a journey toward death has already begun (Miles, 1977; Barraclough et al., 1974).

In Chapter 15 we shall examine schizophrenia, a disorder that causes people to lose touch with reality. Common symptoms include hearing voices that are not actually present (hallucinations) and holding beliefs that are blatantly false and even bizarre (delusions). There is a popular belief that suicides by schizophrenic persons must be in response to imagined voices commanding self-destruction or to a delusion that suicide is a grand and noble gesture.

nal act (Barrington, 1980) and allow the state to use force and involuntary commitment to prevent it (Grisez & Boyle, 1979). Nevertheless, times and attitudes are changing, and the idea of a "right to suicide" and "rational suicide" is receiving increasing support in our society.

Common law traditionally affirms a person's right to self-determination (Miesel, 1989), and some people argue that this right extends to the "liberty right" to end one's life (Battin, 1982; Siegel, 1988). Others consider suicide a "natural right," comparable to the rights to life, ownership of property, and freedom of speech (Battin, 1982). Interpreted in its broadest sense, a right to suicide would apply to everyone. Most proponents, however, would restrict this right to situations in which the act of suicide would be considered "rational," adopting a "quality of life" view that suggests that suicide is a reasonable alternative when life stops being an enriching and fulfilling experience (Weir, 1992; Eser, 1981; Grisez & Boyle, 1979). In theory, this more conservative stand implies that suicide prevention measures should be restricted to "irrational" cases, including cases that are motivated by mental disorders such as depression (Weir, 1992; Battin, 1982, 1980). One clinical theorist argues that persons who seek the assistance of mental health professionals or prevention centers clearly desire and require help (Motto, 1980).

Public support for a right to suicide seems strongest in instances of termi-

nal illness (Siegel, 1988). In the United States, the Society for the Right to Die presses for legislation to prevent the "unnecessary prolongation of life"; Concern for Dying educates the public on these issues; and the Hemlock Society supports "self-deliverance" for the terminally ill (Burek, 1990; Siegel, 1988). Polls suggest that about half of the population believe that terminally ill persons should be free to take their lives or to seek a physician's assistance to do so (Malcolm, 1990; Siegel, 1988). Now a legally competent person can write a "living will," declaring in advance the treatment that would be desired or refused in the event of terminal illness (Humphry & Wickett, 1986; Miesel, 1989; Siegel, 1988).

Even in cases of severe illness, however, the suicidal person's thinking may be affected by psychological disorders or stress. The fact is that a great many people face extremely difficult circumstances in which suicide might seem rational but very few of them actually choose this option. AIDS and cancer patients who commit suicide, for example, are a very small minority of those populations (Malcolm, 1990). Interestingly, physicians report a higher preoccupation with suicide among those waiting for their HIV antibody test results than among those who have been told they are HIV positive (Hendin & Klerman, 1993; Perry, 1990). Rather than being a natural response to the negative impact of illness, suicide in the face of terminal disease may instead be indicative of

clinical depression, anxiety, deficiencies in coping skills, or distress in reaction to the emotional withdrawal of family members. Perhaps the suicidal terminally ill would benefit more from treatment and support that help them come to terms with their situation than from being given the "right" to die.

In addition, a medically ill person's right to suicide is questionable if it impinges on the lives of others. An increased incidence of suicide could enhance the problem of "suicide contagion" in emotionally vulnerable members of society.

Finally, the right to suicide could be gravely abused. Although it is upheld as the ultimate freedom, a right to suicide might trap some people in an "obligation to suicide." An elderly person, for example, might feel unjustified in expecting relatives to support and care for him or her when suicide is a socially approved alternative (Sherlock, 1983). A slippery-slope view predicts that if these and other suicides are accepted as rational, it might be all too easy for society to slip into accepting practices such as forced euthanasia and infanticide (Annas, 1993; Battin, 1982).

How are these conflicts to be resolved? The future holds great challenges for those who seek to understand, treat, and prevent suicide, but the questions of whether and when we should stand back and do nothing pose just as great a challenge. Whatever one's stand on this issue, it is a matter of life and death.

Research indicates that although some persons with schizophrenia do display these kinds of symptoms at the time of suicide, most suicides by schizophrenic persons reflect feelings of demoralization (Haas et al., 1993; Vieta et al., 1992). They tend to be committed by relatively young and unemployed people with schizophrenia who have experienced relapses over several years and now believe that the disorder will forever disrupt their lives (Drake, Gates, & Cotton,

1986, 1984). Suicide is the leading cause of death for this population (Haas et al., 1993).

MODELING: THE CONTAGION OF SUICIDE

It is not unusual for people to try to commit suicide after observing or reading about a suicide (Phillips et al., 1992; Phillips, 1983, 1982). Perhaps these people have been struggling with major problems and the other person's suicide seems to reveal a possible solution; or they have been contemplating suicide and the other person's suicide seems to give them permission or finally persuades them to act. Whatever the specific mechanism may be in such cases, one suicidal act apparently serves as a model for another.

Three kinds of models in particular seem to trigger suicides: suicides by celebrities, highly publicized suicides, and suicides by co-workers or colleagues.

CELEBRITIES In an analysis of suicide data spanning 1948 to 1983, Steven Stack (1987) found that suicides by entertainers and political figures in the United States are regularly followed by unusual increases in the number of suicides across the nation. Shortly after the young comedian Freddie Prinze committed suicide in 1978, for example, a rash of suicides occurred in the United States (Wasserman, 1984). In some cases the victims even left notes in which they mentioned Prinze's suicide. Similarly, in April, 1994, a depressed 28-year-old fan mourned the suicide of Nirvana's Kurt Cobain at a large outdoor Seattle candlelight vigil, then went home and, like Cobain, killed himself with a shotgun.

HIGHLY PUBLICIZED CASES The news media often focus on a particular suicide because of its unusual nature, extraordinary circumstances, or special implications. Such highly publicized accounts may trigger suicides that are similar in method or circumstance (Ishii, 1991). In England, for example, a widely publicized suicide by self-immolation was followed within one year by eighty-two other suicides in which the victims set themselves on fire (Ashton & Donnan, 1981). An examination of inquest reports revealed that most of the suicide victims had histories of emotional problems and that none of the suicides was politically motivated, although the publicized suicide had political overtones. In short, the subjects of the study seemed to be responding to their own problems in a manner precipitated by the suicide they had observed or read about. The frightening impact of well-publicized suicides has led some clinicians to call for a code of practice that the news media should follow in reporting such deaths (Motto, 1967), and in recent times the media has tried to act responsibly. When, for example, thousands of young people called radio and television stations in the hours following Kurt Cobain's suicide, distraught, worried, and in some cases suicidal, some of the stations responded by posting "hot-line" numbers for suicide prevention centers, presenting interviews with suicide experts,

and offering counseling services and advice directly to callers. Indeed, a repeated theme throughout MTV's coverage was, "Don't do it!" Some clinicians believe that these media actions helped hold down the number of modeled suicides.

CO-WORKERS AND COLLEAGUES Suicides in a school, workplace, or small community often receive word-of-mouth publicity that may trigger suicide attempts by others in the setting. A suicide by a recruit at a U.S. Navy training school, for example, was followed by another completed and an attempted suicide at the school within a two-week period. To put an end to what threatened to become a suicide epidemic, the school initiated a program of staff education on suicide and group therapy sessions for recruits who had been close to the suicide victims (Grigg, 1988).

■ VIEWS ■ ON SUICIDE

Although numerous situations may precipitate suicide, most people who encounter such situations never try to kill themselves. In an effort to explain why some people are more prone to suicide than others, theorists have proposed still broader factors that may set the stage for self-destructive action. The leading theories come from the psychodynamic, biological, and sociocultural perspectives. Unfortunately, as we shall see, these explanations have received

The 1993 mass suicide by dozens of Branch Davidian members at their Waco, Texas, compound produced a giant fireball that the nation, watching on television, will not soon forget. Group suicides are not well understood by clinicians and researchers, although the leaders of such groups often seem to have an extraordinary hold on the thoughts, emotions, and behaviors of each member.

limited empirical support, and in fact they fail to address all kinds of suicidal acts. Thus it would be inaccurate to conclude that the clinical field currently has a satisfactory understanding of suicide.

THE PSYCHODYNAMIC VIEW

Many psychodynamic theorists believe that suicide usually results from depression and self-directed anger. This theory was first stated by Wilhelm Stekel at a meeting in Vienna in 1910, when he proclaimed that "no one kills himself who has not wanted to kill another or at least wished the death of another" (Shneidman, 1979). Some years later Sigmund Freud (1920) wrote, "No neurotic harbors thoughts of suicide which he has not turned back upon himself from murderous impulses against others."

As we saw in Chapter 8, Freud (1917) and Abraham (1916, 1911) proposed that when people experience the real or symbolic loss of a loved one, they come to "introject" the lost person; that is, they unconsciously incorporate the person into their own identity and feel toward themselves as they had felt toward the other. For a short while, negative feelings toward the loved one are experienced as self-hatred. Introjected feelings become particularly negative and long-lasting in some instances, perhaps in people who have been extremely dependent on and resentful of the lost loved one, or who have experienced childhood losses that were unresolved, causing them to overreact in the face of the present loss. Either way, extreme anger toward the lost loved one turns into unrelenting anger against oneself, and finally into a broad depressive reaction. Suicide is a further expression of this self-hatred. The following description of a suicidal patient demonstrates how such dynamics may operate:

A 27-year-old conscientious and responsible woman took a knife to her wrists to punish herself for being tyrannical, unreliable, self-centered, and abusive. She was perplexed and frightened by this uncharacteristic self-destructive episode and was enormously relieved when her therapist pointed out that her invective described her recently deceased father much better than it did herself.

(Gill, 1982, p. 15)

Late in his career, Freud further explained suicide by proposing that human beings have a basic "death instinct," which he called *Thanatos,* that functions in opposition to their "life instinct." According to Freud, while most people learn to redirect their death instinct and aim it toward others, suicidal people, caught in a web of self-anger, direct the instinct squarely upon themselves (Freud, 1955).

In support of Freud's view of suicide, researchers have consistently found a relationship between childhood losses and later suicidal behaviors (Paykel, 1991). One comparison of family histories (Adam, Bouckoms, & Steiyen, 1982) found the incidence of early parental loss to be much higher among 98 suicide attempters (48 percent) than among 102 nonsuicidal control subjects (24 percent). Common losses were death of the father and divorce or separation of the parents, especially during either the earliest years of life (birth to 5 years old) or late adolescence (17 to 20 years old). Of course, although such findings do coincide with the psychodynamic view, they are correlational and do not establish the causality suggested in the model.

Sociological findings, too, are consistent with Freud's proposal that suicidal people are directing a death instinct toward themselves rather than toward others. National suicide rates have been found to drop significantly in times of war, when, one could argue, people are encouraged to direct their self-destructive energy against "the enemy." In addition, societies with high rates of homicide tend to have low rates of suicide, and vice versa (Binstock, 1974). On the other hand, research has failed to establish that suicidal people are in fact dominated by intense feelings of anger. Although hostility is an important component in some suicides, several studies find that other emotional states are even more common (Linehan & Nielsen, 1981; Shneidman, 1979).

By the end of his career, Freud expressed dissatisfaction with his theory of suicide, and other psychodynamic theorists have modified his ideas over the years. Yet themes of loss and self-directed aggression usually remain at the center of their explanations (Kincel, 1981; Furst & Ostow, 1979).

THE BIOLOGICAL VIEW

Until the 1970s the belief that biological factors contribute to suicidal behavior was based primarily on family pedigree studies. Researchers repeatedly found higher rates of suicidal behavior among the parents and close relatives of suicidal people than among those of nonsuicidal people, suggesting to some observers that genetic, and so biological, factors were at work (Roy, 1992; Garfinkel, Froese, & Golombek, 1979; Hauschild, 1968). Studies of twins also were consistent with this view of suicide. A study of twins born in Denmark between 1870 and 1920, for example, located nineteen identical pairs and fifty-eight fraternal pairs in which at least one of the twins had committed suicide (Juel-Nielsen & Videbech, 1970). In four of the identical pairs the other twin also committed suicide (21 percent), while the other twin among the fraternal pairs never committed suicide.

Of course, as with all family pedigree research, nonbiological interpretations could also be offered for these findings. Psychodynamic clinicians might argue that children whose parents commit suicide are prone to depression and suicide because they have lost a loved one at a critical stage of development. And behavioral theorists might emphasize the modeling role played by parents or close relatives who attempt suicide. Clearly, a genetic or biological conclusion is inappropriate on the basis of family research findings alone.

In the past few years laboratory research has provided more direct support for a biological view of suicide. People who commit suicide are often found to have lower levels of the neurotransmitter *serotonin* (Nordstrom & Asberg, 1992; Roy, 1992; Stanley, 1991). The first indication of this relationship came from a study by Marie Asberg and her colleagues (1976). Working with sixty-eight depressed patients, these researchers measured each patient's level of *5-hydroxyindoleactic acid (5-HIAA)*, a component of cerebrospinal fluid that is a metabolite, or by-product, of brain serotonin. Twenty of the patients had particularly low levels of 5-HIAA (and presumably low levels of serotonin), while the remaining forty-eight had relatively higher 5-HIAA levels. The researchers found that the low 5-HIAA subjects made a total of eight suicide attempts (two lethal), whereas the much larger group of high 5-HIAA subjects made only seven. The researchers interpreted this finding to mean that a low serotonin level may be "a predictor of suicidal acts." Later studies found that suicide attempters with low 5-HIAA levels are ten times more likely to make a repeat attempt and succeed than are suicide attempters with high 5-HIAA levels (Roy, 1992; Asberg et al., 1986; Traskman et al., 1981).

Studies that examine the autopsied brains of suicide victims point in the same direction (Stanley et al., 1986, 1982; Paul et al., 1984). Such studies usually measure the serotonin level by determining the number of *imipramine receptor sites* in the brain. Recall that imipramine is an antidepressant drug that binds to certain neural receptors throughout the brain (see Chapter 9). It is believed that the degree of imipramine binding reflects a person's usual level of serotonin; the less imipramine binding, the less serotonin activity (Langer & Raisman, 1983). Fewer imipramine binding sites are found in the brains of persons who die by suicide than in the autopsied brains of nonsuicides—in fact, approximately half as many binding sites is the usual finding.

At first glance, these studies may appear to tell us little that is new. Inasmuch as low serotonin activity is correlated with depression and many depressed people attempt suicide, we would certainly expect many suicidal people to have low serotonin activity. On the other hand, there is evidence that the link between low serotonin and suicide is not necessarily mediated by depression. One investigation found low 5-HIAA levels among suicidal subjects who had had no history of depression (Brown et al., 1982). Similarly, researchers have found unusually low 5-HIAA levels among suicide attempters diagnosed with personality disorders, schizophrenic disorders, anxiety disorders, and substance dependence in addition to those diagnosed with depressive disorders (Van Praag, 1983; Banki & Arato, 1983).

How, then, might low serotonin activity act to increase the likelihood of suicidal behavior? Recent research links low serotonin activity with the presence of strong aggressive impulses, and this relationship may mediate serotonin's link with suicide (Linnoila & Virkkunen, 1992; Brown et al., 1992; Van Praag, 1986). It has been found, for example, that highly aggressive men have significantly lower 5-HIAA levels than less aggressive men (Brown et al., 1992, 1982, 1979) and that low serotonin levels often characterize those who commit aggressive acts such as arson and murder (Bourgeois, 1991). Moreover, lower 5-HIAA levels have been found in people who used guns and other violent means to commit suicide than in those who used nonviolent methods, such as drug overdose (Edman & Asberg, 1986; Banki et al., 1985, 1984; Van Praag, 1983, 1982). And finally, one study found that depressed patients with lower 5-HIAA levels both tried to commit suicide more often and displayed higher hostility scores on various personality inventories than did depressed patients with higher 5-HIAA scores (Van Praag, 1986).

Although these studies have been limited to small numbers of subjects (Motto, 1986), the pattern of findings suggests to many theorists that a low serotonin level does indeed produce aggressive feelings and impulsive behavior (Bourgeois, 1991; Stanley et al., 1986). In people who are clinically depressed, low serotonin activity may produce aggressive and impulsive tendencies that leave them particularly vulnerable to suicidal thinking and action. Even in the absence of a depressive disorder, people with low serotonin levels may develop highly aggressive feelings and be dangerous to themselves or others.

THE
SOCIOCULTURAL VIEW

Just before the turn of the century, Emile Durkheim ([1897] 1951), a sociologist, developed the first comprehensive theory of suicidal behavior. For years Durkheim's theory was the most cited and researched in the area of suicide; even today it continues to be influential. Believing that the societal context is an important influence on individual behavior, Durkheim proposed that scientists should gather epidemiological information about suicide and discern the unique relationships that exist between suicidal people and their society.

According to Durkheim, the probability of suicide is determined by how embedded a person is in such social institutions as the family, the church, and the community. The more a person belongs, the lower the risk of suicide. Conversely, people who are removed from or have poor relationships with society are at greater risk of killing themselves. He defined three categories of suicide based on the individual's relationship with society.

Egoistic suicides are committed by people over whom society has little or no control. These people are not concerned with the norms or rules of society, nor are they integrated into the social fabric. According to Durkheim, this kind of suicide is more likely in people who are isolated, alienated, and nonreligious. The larger the number of such people living in a society, the higher that society's suicide rate.

Altruistic suicides, in contrast, are committed by people who are so well integrated into the social structure that they intentionally sacrifice their lives for the well-being of society. Soldiers who threw themselves on top of a live grenade to save others, Japanese kamikaze pilots who gave their lives in air attacks, and Buddhist monks and nuns who protested the Vietnam War by setting themselves on fire—all were committing altruistic suicide. According to Durkheim, societies that encourage altruistic deaths and deaths to preserve one's honor (as Far Eastern societies do) are also likely to have higher suicide rates.

Anomic suicides, the third category proposed by Durkheim, are committed by people whose social environment fails to provide stable structures, such as family and church, to support and give meaning to life. Such a societal state, called *anomie* (literally, "without law"), leaves individuals without a sense of

According to Emile Durkheim, people who intentionally sacrifice their lives for others are committing altruistic suicide. Betsy Smith, a heart transplant recipient who was warned that she would probably die if she did not terminate her pregnancy, elected to have the baby and died giving birth to a healthy daughter.

belonging and brings about what Durkheim calls a heightened "inclination for suicide." Unlike egoistic suicide, which is the act of a person who rejects the structures of a society, anomic suicide is the act of a person who has been let down by a disorganized, inadequate, often decaying society.

Durkheim argues that when societies go through periods of anomie, their suicide rates increase accordingly. Historical research supports this claim. Periods of economic depression and social disintegration bring about relative anomie in a country, and national suicide rates tend to increase during such times (Yang et al., 1992; Lester, 1991). Similarly, periods of population change and increased immigration tend to bring about a state of anomie, and such increases are also reflected in higher suicide rates. Steven Stack (1981) examined the suicide rates and immigration increases of thirty-four countries. After controlling for age and other important factors affecting suicide, he found that immigration and suicide rates were related. Each 1 percent increase in immigration was associated with an increase of 0.13 percent in the suicide rate.

A profound change in an individual's immediate surroundings, rather than general societal deficiencies, can also lead to anomic suicide. People who suddenly inherit a great sum of money, for example, may go through a period of anomie as their relationships with social, economic, and occupational structures are upset or altered. Thus Durkheim predicts that societies with greater opportunities for change in individual wealth or status will have higher suicide rates, and this prediction, too, is supported by research (Lester, 1985).

Durkheim's theory of suicide highlights the potential importance of societal factors—a dimension sometimes overlooked by clinicians. On the other hand, his theory by itself is unable to explain why some individuals who experience anomie commit suicide yet the majority do not. Durkheim himself concluded that the final explanation probably involves an interaction between societal and individual factors.

■ SUICIDE ■ IN DIFFERENT AGE GROUPS

The likelihood of committing suicide generally increases with age, although people of all ages may try to kill themselves (see Figure 10–4). Recently, particular attention has been focused on self-destruction in three age groups—*children*, partly because suicide at a very young age contradicts society's perception that childhood is an enjoyable period of discovery and growth; *adolescents and young adults*, because of the steady and highly publicized rise in their suicide rate; and the *elderly*, because suicide is more prevalent in this age group than in any other. Although the characteristics and theories of suicide discussed throughout this chapter apply to all age groups, each group faces unique problems that help account for patterns in self-destruction among its members.

CHILDREN

*T*ommy [age 7] and his younger brother were playing together, and an altercation arose that was settled by the mother, who then left the room. The mother recalled nothing to distinguish this incident from innumerable similar ones. Several minutes after she left, she considered Tommy strangely quiet and returned to find him crimson-faced and struggling for air, having knotted a jumping rope around his neck and jerked it tight.

(French & Berlin, 1979, p. 144)

*D*ear Mom and Dad,
I love you. Please tell my teacher that I cannot take it anymore. I quit. Please don't take me to school anymore. Please help me. I will run away so don't stop me. I will kill myself. So don't look for me because I will be dead. I love you. I will always love you. Remember me.
Help me.

Love Justin [age 10]
(Pfeffer, 1986, p. 273)

Although suicide is relatively infrequent among children, it has been increasing rapidly during the past several decades. Approximately 250 children under 15 years of age in the United States now commit suicide each year (one per 100,000 in this age group), a rate increase of nearly 800 percent since 1950 (NCHS, 1993). Boys outnumber girls by 3 to 1. Many other children try to kill, or at least hurt, themselves. It has been estimated that as many as 12,000 children may be hospitalized in the United States each year for deliberately self-destructive acts, such as stabbing, cutting, burning, overdosing, or jumping from high places (NIMH, 1986).

One study of suicide attempts by children between 5 and 14 years of age revealed that the majority had taken an overdose of drugs and made their attempt at home, half were living with only one parent, and 25 percent had attempted suicide before (Kienhorst et al., 1987). Researchers have found that suicide attempts by the very young are commonly preceded by such behavioral patterns as running away from home, accident-proneness, acting out, temper tantrums, self-deprecation, loneliness, psychophysiological disorders (see Chapter 11), extreme sensitivity to criticism, low tolerance of frustration, and morbid fantasies and daydreams (McGuire, 1982). Studies have further linked child suicides to the recent or anticipated loss of a loved one, family stress and parental unemployment, abuse by parents, and a clinical level of depression (Asarnow, 1992; Fasko & Fasko, 1991; Kienhorst et al., 1987).

Most people find it hard to believe that children fully comprehend the implications of a suicidal act. They argue that by virtue of their cognitive limitations, children who attempt suicide fall into Shneidman's category of "death ignorers": like Billy, who sought to join his mother in heaven, they do not appreciate the permanence of death and hold an idealized view of what is to come (Fasko & Fasko, 1991). Although research indicates that some children who attempt suicide are unclear about the finality of death, especially younger and less mature children, many child suicides are in fact based on a clear understanding of death and on a clear wish to die (Pfeffer, 1993, 1986).

Suicidal thinking among even normal children is apparently more common than most people once believed. Clinical interviews with schoolchildren have revealed that between 6 and 26 percent have contemplated suicide (Jacobsen et al., 1994; Kashani et al., 1989). Other studies suggest that as many as 5 percent of preadolescent children may be seriously self-destructive (Puig-Antich et al., 1978). It is not clear whether suicidal thinking by young children represents a new phenomenon or was previously undetected.

ADOLESCENTS AND YOUNG ADULTS

*D*ear Mom, Dad, and everyone else,
I'm sorry for what I've done, but I loved you all and I always will, for eternity. Please, please, please don't blame it on yourselves. It was all my fault and not yours or anyone else's. If I didn't do this now, I would have done it later anyway. We all die some day, I just died sooner.
Love,
John

(Berman, 1986)

The suicide of John, age 17, was not an unusual occurrence. Suicidal actions become much more common after the age of 14 than at any earlier age. In the United States more than 6,000 adolescents and young adults kill themselves each year; that is, more than 13 of every 100,000 persons between the ages of 15 and 24 (Bureau of the Census, 1990; Center for Disease Control, 1987). Because fatal illnesses are relatively rare among the young, suicide has become the third leading cause of death in adolescents and young adults, after accidents and homicides, accounting for 13 percent of all deaths in this age range (Pfeffer, 1988; Berman, 1986). In contrast, suicide accounts for less than 2 percent of deaths in the total population. About 75 percent of adolescents who commit suicide are male (Berman, 1986).

Unlike the rates for other age groups, suicide rates in the 15-to-24-year-old group are becoming more similar across the races in the United States. Although the suicide rate of young white Americans continues to be considerably higher than that of young African

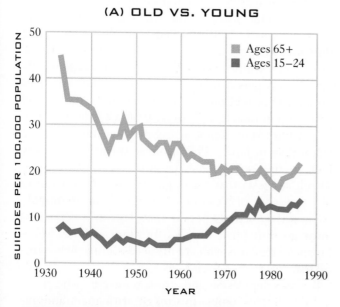

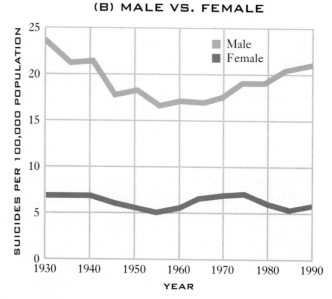

FIGURE 10-4 *Changing suicide rates over the years: (a) Before the 1980s, the suicide rate of elderly people had been declining for at least a half-century, while that of young adults was increasing. Still, older people continue to be at higher risk for suicide. (b) Conversely, the suicide rates of males and females have remained rather steady over the years, as has the greater prevalence of suicide among males than among females. (Adapted from McIntosh, 1991, 1987; Buda & Tsuang, 1990. U.S. Bureau of the Census, 1968, 1947.)*

Americans, the latter rate is growing faster (Berman, 1986). In many cases the converging rates probably reflect converging pressures on young African Americans and young white Americans—competition for grades and college opportunities, for example, is now intense for both groups. In some cases, however, the growth of the young African American suicide rate may be linked to unique factors such as increasing unemployment among African American teenagers, the numerous anxieties of inner-city life, and the rage among young African Americans over racial inequities in our society (Hendin, 1987; Spaights & Simpson, 1986; Stack, 1982).

Although statistical analyses of suicide typically lump 15-to-24-year-olds together, this is hardly a homogeneous group. Clinicians and researchers have often found it important to view separately two subgroups in this category—*teenagers* (15-to-18-year-olds) and *college students* (18-to-22-year-olds).

TEENAGERS Over 2,000 teenagers, or 11.1 of every 100,000, commit suicide in the United States each year, making it the third leading cause of death in this age group, and as many as 250,000 teenagers may make attempts (NCHS, 1991; Bureau of the Census, 1990). Moreover, in a 1991 Gallup poll a full third of teenagers surveyed said they had considered suicide, and 15 percent said they had thought about it seriously. Many school counselors have identified the danger of adolescent suicide as a major problem in their schools and have requested guidelines for dealing with suicidal behaviors in their students (Coder, Nelson, & Aylward, 1991).

Some of the major warning signs of suicide in teenagers are tiredness and sleep loss, loss of appetite, mood changes, decline in school performance, withdrawal, increased smoking or drug or alcohol use, increased letter writing to friends, and the giving away of valued possessions (Peach & Reddick, 1991; Neiger & Hopkins, 1988; Berman, 1986; Dykeman, 1984). Drug overdose is the technique by which most adolescents attempt suicide, although those who shoot themselves are the most likely to die (Berman & Jobes, 1991; Garfinkel et al., 1982).

About half of teenagers' suicides, like those of people in other age groups, have been linked to clinical depression (Kashden et al., 1993; Robbins & Alessi, 1985). In addition, adolescents who think about or attempt to kill themselves are often under considerable stress (de Man et al., 1992; de Wilde et al., 1992). Many experience such long-term pressures as missing or poor parental relationships, family conflict, inadequate peer relationships, and social isolation (Adams et al., 1994; D'Attilio et al., 1992; Tishler & McKenry,

The intense training and testing characteristic of Japan's educational system produce high levels of stress in many students. The students in this classroom are participating in summer "juku," a camp where they receive remedial help, extra lessons, and exam practice 11 hours a day.

1982). Adolescent suicide also seems to be triggered by more immediate stresses, such as unemployment, discord, or financial setbacks in the family, or difficulties with a boyfriend or girlfriend (de Wilde et al., 1992; Pfeffer, 1990, 1988; Wright, 1985).

Stress at school seems to be a particularly common problem in teenagers who attempt suicide (Brent et al., 1988). One study found that nearly 60 percent of suicidal teenage subjects had recently been having difficulty keeping up at school (Houston et al., 1982). Still other studies have revealed that academically gifted teenagers sometimes attempt suicide, perhaps because they feel pressured to be perfect and to stay at the top of the class (Leroux, 1986; Delisle, 1986).

Nowhere is academic stress more visibly a suicide factor than in Japan. The Japanese suicide rate is very high in the late teenage years (Hawton, 1986). Research suggests that this high rate may be related to *shiken jigoku*, or "examination hell," an extremely competitive testing period that Japanese teenagers must go through if they are to enter college. Many Japanese students who are unsuccessful in these critical tests try to take their lives.

Beyond depression and stress, teenagers who try to kill themselves appear to struggle with anger and impulsivity more than do suicide attempters in other age groups (Kashden et al., 1993; Hoberman & Garfinkel, 1988). Aggressive and antisocial behaviors and inadequate assertiveness skills have frequently been found in suicidal teenagers (Shaffer & Gould, 1986; Cohen-Sandler et al., 1982). It may be that unassertive adolescents build up resentment and turn their anger on themselves as the only acceptable target (Rotheram, 1987; Phillip & McCulloch, 1966).

It is important to note that far more teenagers attempt suicide than actually kill themselves. Conservative estimates of attempted suicides in this age group have ranged from 57 to 100 attempts per 100,000 population (Solomon & Murphy, 1984). Some theorists believe that there are actually many more attempts, and that the ratio of attempts to fatalities is between 50 to 1 and 200 to 1 (Hawton, 1986; Pfeffer, 1986). The unusually large number of incomplete attempts by teenagers may mean that they are more often ambivalent than older persons who make such attempts. While some do indeed wish to die, many may simply want to make others understand how desperate they are, get help, or teach others a lesson (Hawton, 1986; Hawton et al., 1982; White, 1974). Up to 40 percent of attempters go on to make more suicide attempts, and up to 14 percent eventually die by suicide (Spirito et al., 1989; Diekstra, 1989).

Some theorists believe that adolescent life itself engenders a climate conducive to suicidal action (Maris, 1986). Adolescence is a period of rapid growth and development, and in our society it is often marked by conflicts, tensions, and difficulties at home and school. Adolescents tend to react to events more sensitively, angrily, dramatically, and impulsively than people in other age groups, so that the likelihood of suicidal actions during times of stress is increased (Kaplan, 1984; Taylor & Stansfeld, 1984). They are also likely to experience depressed feelings, and indeed such feelings appear to be increasing among teenagers in general (Rosenstock, 1985; Teri, 1982). Finally, the suggestibility of adolescents and their eagerness to imitate others may help set the stage for suicidal action (Hazell & Lewin, 1993; Berman, 1986). One study has found that 93 percent of adolescent suicide attempters knew someone who had attempted suicide previously (Conrad, 1992).

COLLEGE STUDENTS   For many years, it was believed that the suicide rate is higher for 18-to-22-year-old college students than for other young people in the same age range, but recent investigations have challenged this notion (Schwartz & Whitaker, 1990). Again, female students are more likely to attempt suicide, but fatal suicides are more numerous among males. Furthermore, studies suggest that as many as 20 percent of college students have suicidal thoughts at some point in their college career (Carson & Johnson, 1985).

One factor underlying these suicides is the challenge of college itself (Priester & Clum, 1992; Lyman, 1961). Academic pressures, examinations, and competition for grades undoubtedly increase the stressfulness of the student's life. Other factors that have been implicated in suicides among college students are the loss of social support felt by those who move away from their families and friends to attend college and the rapid change of values that some students experience during their college years (Carson & Johnson, 1985; Berkovitz, 1985).

It may also be that college students bring past problems with them to their new environments, complicating the already difficult task of dealing with college-linked pressures and situations (Hendin, 1987; Curran, 1986; Berkovitz, 1985). Indeed, a third of college students interviewed in one study reported having suicidal thoughts before they entered college (Sherer, 1985). Some clinicians suggest that the college students who consider suicide are those who never learned how to deal with personal problems and emotions before going to college. A study of 218 undergraduates, for example, found that suicidal students did not necessarily experience more stress than other students but had fewer resources for dealing with problems and intense emotions (Carson & Johnson, 1985).

The number and variety of possible contributing factors make it difficult to interpret studies of suicide among college students. Research in England, for example, has indicated that the number of college suicides increases along with the prestige of the school (Stengel, 1974; Seiden, 1969). How are we to understand this finding? Certainly academic pressures are high at prestigious schools, but these schools also have other characteristics that may contribute to the high rate of suicide. The number of students living away from home—or far from home—usually is higher at these schools than at other institutions, and these schools are noted for encouraging students to work independently. Perhaps the lack of structure introduces a significant amount of stress.

Obviously, many aspects of college life are demanding and stressful. Evidence suggests that students are helped by friendships and by sharing their experiences and problems with others at college (Arnstein, 1986). In this way, the pressures of college life that sometimes contribute to depression and suicidal behavior may be reduced.

RISING SUICIDE RATE   The suicide rate for adolescents and young adults is not only high but increasing. The suicide rate for this age group has more than doubled since 1955 (McIntosh, 1991). The rate for young persons peaked in 1977, when 13.6 of every 100,000 adolescents and young adults committed suicide, leveled off to 11.9 per 100,000 by 1983, then increased again to 13.1 in recent years (Bureau of the Census, 1990; NCHS, 1989). This latest upswing suggests that suicide among the young may be on the rise once again (Pfeffer, 1986).

Several theories, each pointing to societal changes, have been proposed to explain why the suicide rate among adolescents and young adults has risen dramatically during the past few decades. (1) Noting the overall rise in the number and proportion of adolescents and young adults in the general population since 1950, Paul Holinger and his colleagues (1991, 1988, 1987, 1984, 1982) have suggested that the competition for jobs, college positions, and academic and athletic honors keeps intensifying in this age group, leading increasingly to shattered dreams and frustrated ambitions (see Figure 10–5). (2) Following Durkheim's notion of anomic suicide, some theorists hold that weakening ties in the nuclear family during the past few decades have provoked feelings of alienation and rejection in many of today's young people—emotions that may contribute to suicidal thoughts and actions (Peck, 1982). (3) The increased availability of drugs and pressure to use them may also be factors (Schuckit & Schuckit, 1991; Hawton, 1986). In accord with this view, two studies found that 70 percent of teenage suicide attempters abused drugs or alcohol to some degree (Miller et al., 1991; Shafii et al., 1985). (4) The mass media coverage of suicide attempts by teenagers and young adults may itself play a role in the rising suicide rate among the young (Myatt & Greenblatt, 1993; Gould & Shaffer, 1986). As we observed earlier, highly publicized suicides often trigger other suicide attempts. The detailed descriptions of teenage suicide that the media and arts have offered in recent years may serve as models for young people who are contemplating suicide. Within days of the highly publicized suicides of four adolescents in a garage in Bergenfield, New Jersey, in 1987, dozens of teenagers across the United States took similar actions (at least twelve of them fatal)—two in the same garage just one week later.

These explanations for the rise in suicide rates among young persons remind us that societal change does not necessarily lead to social progress. Our society's advances in medical, industrial, and communication technology during the past several decades are

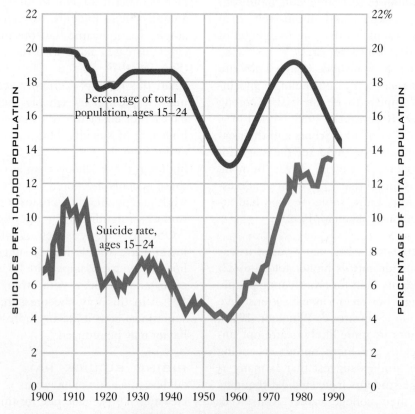

FIGURE 10–5 *Over the years, whenever the proportion of adolescents and young adults in the general population has increased, the suicide rate of this age group has risen as well. (Adapted from Holinger & Offer, 1991.)*

undeniably impressive. But often there is a significant price to pay for such rapid change, and that price may include the mental health and survival of all too many of our youth.

THE ELDERLY

Rose Ashby walks to the dry cleaner's to pick up her old but finest dinner dress. Although shaken at the cost of having it cleaned, Rose tells the sympathetic girl behind the counter, "Don't worry. It doesn't matter. I won't be needing the money any more."

Walking through the streets of St. Petersburg, Florida, she still wishes it had been Miami. The west coast of the fountain of youth peninsula is not as warm as the east. If only Chet had left more insurance money, Rose could have afforded Miami. In St. Petersburg, Rose failed to unearth de León's promised fount.

Last week, she told the doctor she felt lonely and depressed. He said she should perk up. She had everything to live for. What does he know? Has he lost a husband like Chet, and his left breast to cancer all in one year? Has he suffered arthritis all his life? Were his ovaries so bad he had to undergo a hysterectomy? Did he have to suffer through menopause just to end up alone without family or friends? Does he have to live in a dungeon? Is his furniture worn, his carpet threadbare? What does he know? Might his every day be the last one for him?

As Rose turns into the walk to her white cinderblock apartment building, fat Mrs. Green asks if she is coming to the community center that evening. Who needs it? The social worker did say Rose should come. Since Rose was in such good health, she could help those not so well as she.

Help them do what? Finger-paint like little children? Make baskets like insane people? Sew? Who can see to sew? Besides, who would appreciate it? Who would thank her? Who could she tell about her troubles? Who cares?

When she told the doctor she couldn't sleep, he gave her the prescription but said that all elderly people have trouble sleeping. What does he know? Does he have a middle-aged daughter who can only think about her latest divorce, or grandchildren who only acknowledge her birthday check by the endorsement on the back? Are all his friends dead and gone? Is all the money from her dead husband's insurance used up? What does he know? Who could sleep in this dungeon?

Back in her apartment, Rose washes and sets her hair. It's good she has to do it herself. Look at this hair. So thin, so sparse, so frowsy. What would a hairdresser think?

Then make-up. Base. Rouge. Lipstick. Bright red. Perfume? No! No cheap perfume for Rose today. Remember the bottles of Joy Chet would buy for her? He always wanted her to have the best. He would boast that she had everything, and that she never had to work a day in her life for it.

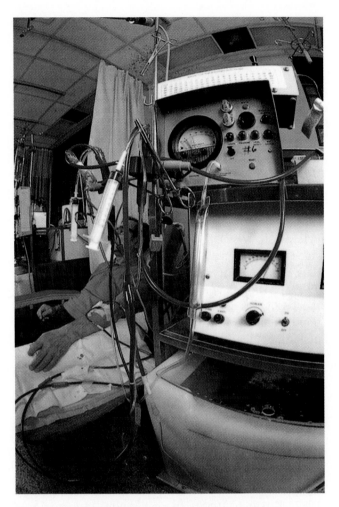

Among patients with chronic kidney disorders who are over the age of 60 and require regular dialysis, one of every six elects to stop treatment (Neu & Kjellstrand, 1986). Without dialysis, most slip into a coma and die within 8 days.

"She doesn't have to lift her little finger," Chet would say, puffing on his cigar. Where is the Joy now? Dead and gone. With Chet. Rose manages a wry laugh at the play on words.

Slipping into her dinner dress, she looks into the dresser mirror. "It's good you can't see this face now, Chet. How old and ugly it looks."

Taking some lavender notepaper from the drawer, she stands at the dresser to write. Why didn't anyone warn her that growing old was like this? It is so unfair. But they don't care. People don't care about anyone except themselves.

Leaving the note on the dresser, she suddenly feels excited. Breathing hard now, she rushes to the sink—who could call a sink in the counter in the living room a kitchen?—and gets a glass of water.

Trying to relax, Rose arranges the folds in her skirt as she settles down on the chaise. Carefully sipping the water as she takes all the capsules so as to not smear her lipstick, Rose quietly begins to sob. After a lifetime of tears, these will be her last. Her note on the dresser is short, written to no one and to everyone.

*You don't know what it is like
to have to grow old and die.*

(Gernsbacher, 1985, pp. 227–228)

Statistics indicate that in Western society the elderly are more likely to commit suicide than people in any other age group (see Figures 10–1a and 10–4a). More than 21 of every 100,000 persons over the age of 65 in the United States commit suicide (McIntosh, 1992). This rate has been rising steadily since 1981, when 17 of every 100,000 elderly persons took their own lives. Elderly persons committed over 19 percent of all suicides in the United States during the 1980s, yet account for only 12 percent of the total population (McIntosh, 1992). Some investigators believe that suicide is in fact the leading cause of death among the elderly (Simon, 1987).

Many factors contribute to the high suicide rate among the elderly (Richman, 1991). As people grow older, all too often they become ill, lose close friends and relatives, lose control over their lives, and lose status in our society. Such experiences may result in feelings of hopelessness, loneliness, depression, or inevitability among aged persons, and so increase the likelihood that they will attempt suicide (Osgood, 1987; Kirsling, 1986). In one study 44 percent of elderly people who committed suicide gave some indication that their act was prompted by the fear of being placed in a nursing home (Loebel et al., 1991). Similarly, those who have lost a spouse display a much higher suicide rate (Nieto et al., 1992; McIntosh, 1992). Their risk is greatest during the first year of bereavement, but it remains elevated in later years as well (Murphy et al., 1979).

Elderly persons are typically more resolute than younger persons in their decision to die, so their success rate is much higher (Turkington, 1987). Some researchers have noted that they tend to use less violent but more lethal methods (Nieto et al., 1992). Apparently one of every four elderly persons who attempts suicide succeeds (McIntosh, 1987). Given this resolve and the obvious physical decline of aged persons, many people argue that older persons who want to die are clear in their thinking and should be allowed to carry out their wishes. At the same time, however, clinical depression appears to play an important role in at least 50 percent of suicides among the elderly (Lyness et al., 1992), suggesting that more elderly persons should be receiving treatment for their depressive disorders than is typically the case (Simon, 1987).

The suicide rate among elderly people in the United States is lower in some minority groups. Although Native Americans have the highest overall suicide rate, for example, the rate among elderly Native Americans is quite low (McIntosh & Santos, 1982). Similarly, the suicide rate among elderly African Americans is only one-third the rate of elderly white Americans.

Why are suicide rates for the elderly particularly low in some minority groups? The respect afforded elderly Native Americans may help account for their low rate (McIntosh & Santos, 1982). The aged are held in high esteem by Native Americans and looked to for the wisdom and experience they have acquired over the years. This heightened status is quite different from the loss of status often experienced by elderly white Americans (Butler, 1975).

The low suicide rate among elderly African Americans has been explained in different terms. One theory is that because of the pressures African Americans live under, "only the strongest survive" (Seiden, 1981). Those who reach an advanced age have overcome significant adversity and often feel proud of what they have accomplished. Advancement to old age is not in itself a form of success for white Americans, and leaves them with a different attitude toward life and age. Another explanation suggests

Elderly persons are held in high esteem in many traditional societies and cultures because of the store of knowledge they have accumulated over the years. Perhaps not so coincidentally, suicides among the elderly seem to be less common in these cultures than in those of many modern industrialized nations.

that aged African Americans have successfully overcome the rage that characterizes many suicides in younger African Americans.

■ TREATMENT ■ AND SUICIDE

Treatment of people who are suicidal falls into two major categories: *treatment after suicide has been attempted* and *suicide prevention.* Today special attention is also given to relatives and friends (Farberow, 1993, 1991), whose bereavement, guilt, and anger after a suicide fatality or attempt can be intense. Many people turn to psychotherapy or support groups to help them deal with their reactions to a loved one's suicide, but the discussion here will be limited to the treatment afforded suicidal people themselves.

TREATMENT AFTER A SUICIDE ATTEMPT

After a suicide attempt, most victims' primary need is medical care. Some are left with severe injuries, brain damage, or other medical problems. Once the physical damage is reversed or at least stabilized, psychotherapy may begin. Unfortunately, even after trying to kill themselves, most suicidal people fail to receive systematic therapy (see Figure 10–6). In a random survey of 382 teenagers, 9 percent were found to have made at least one suicide attempt, and of those only half had been given subsequent psychological treatment (Harkavy & Asnis, 1985). Another study found that 46 percent of people treated for attempted suicide in a Helsinki general hospital were not given even a psychological consultation (Suokas & Lonnqvist, 1991).

When therapy is provided, it may be on an outpatient or inpatient basis. For patients with mental disorders such as schizophrenia and severe mood disorders, extended inpatient treatment has been found to be more effective in decreasing the number of subsequent suicide attempts than outpatient and short-term inpatient therapy have been (Deering et al., 1991).

The goal of therapy is to keep the clients alive, help them achieve a nonsuicidal state of mind, and eventually guide them to develop more construc-

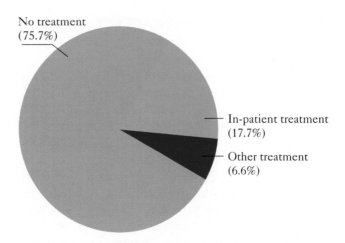

FIGURE 10–6 *In an alarming finding, a study conducted a decade ago revealed that more than 75 percent of persons who deliberately harmed themselves did not receive subsequent treatment. Although recent reports are more encouraging, it appears that most suicide attempters still fail to receive systematic follow-up treatment. (Adapted from Diekstra, 1982.)*

No treatment (75.7%)

In-patient treatment (17.7%)

Other treatment (6.6%)

tive ways of handling stress and solving problems (Shneidman, 1993; Möller, 1990). Various therapy systems and formats have been employed (Rotheram-Borus et al., 1994; Berman & Jobes, 1992), but relatively little research has compared the effectiveness of the various approaches.

One study compared the results of treatment given two groups of repeated suicide attempters (Liberman & Eckman, 1981). Twelve subjects were treated in a *behavior therapy group*—taught how to improve their verbal and nonverbal expressive skills and instructed in relaxation techniques. They also attended family sessions where they learned to improve family communication and to share responsibilities. The second group of twelve suicide attempters received *insight-oriented treatment* consisting of individual psychodynamic therapy sessions supplemented by group therapy and family therapy sessions. Both treatment programs began during hospitalization and continued on an outpatient basis for nine months.

At first assessment, the subjects who underwent behavior therapy seemed to improve more than those who were given psychodynamic therapy. They showed less depression, less anxiety, and more assertiveness on self-report measures, and twice as many of them were holding full-time jobs at the time of a follow-up review. Yet the number of subsequent suicide attempts was approximately equal in the two groups. Three of the insight therapy subjects and two of the behavior therapy subjects attempted suicide again.

SUICIDE PREVENTION

During the past thirty years emphasis has shifted from suicide treatment to suicide prevention (Cantor, 1991; Maltsberger, 1991; Farberow & Litman, 1970). In some respects this change is most appropriate: the last opportunity to keep many potential suicide victims alive comes before the first attempt.

The emphasis on suicide prevention began in earnest during the mid-1950s with the development of *suicide prevention programs.* The first such program in the United States was the Los Angeles Suicide Prevention Center, founded by Norman Farberow and Edwin Shneidman in 1955; the first in England was called the Samaritans, founded by the Reverend Chad Varah in 1953. There are now more than 200 independent, locally funded suicide prevention centers in the United States and over 100 in England, and the numbers are still growing (Lester, 1989; Roberts, 1979). In addition, many mental health centers, hospital emergency rooms, pastoral counseling centers, and poison control centers now include suicide prevention programs among their services. There are also more than 1,000 *suicide hotlines,* 24-hour-a-day telephone services, in the United States (Garland, Shaffer, & Whittle, 1989). Callers reach a counselor, typically a trained *paraprofessional*—a person without a formal degree in a counseling profession—who provides services under the supervision of a mental health professional.

Suicide prevention centers define suicidal people as people *in crisis*—that is, under great stress, unable to cope, feeling threatened or hurt, and interpreting their situations as unchangeable. Accordingly, the centers engage in *crisis intervention:* they try to help suicidal people perceive their situations more accurately, make better decisions, act more constructively, and overcome their crisis. Because crises can occur at any time, the centers advertise their hotlines and also welcome clients to walk in without appointments.

Although specific features vary from center to center, the general approach used by the Los Angeles Suicide Prevention Center reflects the goals and techniques of many such organizations (Lester, 1989; Shneidman & Farberow, 1968; Rotheram, 1987). During the initial contact, the counselor has several tasks: establishing a positive relationship, understanding and clarifying the problem, assessing suicide potential, assessing and mobilizing the caller's resources, and formulating a plan for overcoming the crisis (Shneidman & Farberow, 1968).

The psychologist Edwin Shneidman, who helped found America's first suicide-prevention center in 1955, has developed techniques to assess suicidal risk, identified various types of suicide, and corrected numerous myths about suicide.

Establishing a Positive Relationship Obviously, callers must trust counselors if they are to confide in them and follow their suggestions. Thus counselors try to set a positive and comfortable tone for discussion. They convey the message that they are listening, understanding, interested, nonjudgmental, and available.

Understanding and Clarifying the Problem
Counselors first try to understand the full scope of the caller's crisis, then help the person see the crisis in clear and constructive terms. In particular, counselors try to help callers identify the central issues and the transient nature of their crises and recognize the alternatives to suicidal action.

Assessing Suicide Potential Some callers are in greater crisis than others, and closer to attempting suicide. The strategy a counselor chooses will depend on the degree of risk. Thus the development of accurate suicide assessment techniques has become a major concern of clinicians and researchers (Rotheram, 1987; Pallis et al., 1982).

Crisis workers at the Los Angeles Suicide Prevention Center fill out a questionnaire often called a "lethality scale" to estimate the caller's potential for suicide. It helps them to determine the degree of stress the caller is under, relevant personality characteristics, how detailed the suicide plan is, the severity of symptoms, and the coping resources available to the caller. The crisis workers can then assess whether callers should be hospitalized for their own safety, referred for treatment, or launched on some other course of action.

Assessing and Mobilizing the Caller's Resources
Although they may view themselves as ineffectual and helpless, people who are suicidal usually have many strengths and resources, including relatives and friends. It is the counselor's job to recognize, point out, and activate those resources.

Formulating a Plan   Together the crisis worker and caller formulate a plan of action. In essence, they are agreeing on a way out of the crisis, a constructive alternative to suicidal action. Although both participate in formulating the plan, the counselor may take the lead role, giving suggestions and perhaps even fostering a dependent relationship. If callers are in the midst of a suicide attempt, counselors will also try to ascertain their whereabouts and get medical help to them immediately.

Most plans of action include a series of follow-up counseling sessions over the next few days or weeks, either in person at the center or by phone. Counselors usually negotiate a "no suicide" contract with the caller—a promise not to attempt suicide, or at least a promise to reestablish contact if the caller again contemplates suicide. Each plan also usually requires that the caller make certain changes and take certain actions in his or her personal life. Family members and friends become involved in some plans.

Although crisis intervention appears to be sufficient treatment for some suicidal people (Hawton, 1986), longer-term therapy is needed for up to 60 percent of them (Farberow, 1974). These are cases in which the suicide crisis has stemmed from chronic problems in coping and living that are best addressed in extended therapy (Mills, 1985). If the crisis intervention center does not offer this kind of therapy, the counselors will refer these people elsewhere.

As the suicide prevention movement spread during the 1960s, many clinicians concluded that crisis intervention techniques should also be applied to problems other than suicide. They reasoned that nonsuicidal people may also be immobilized by crises and may benefit from an active, problem-solving form of intervention. Crisis intervention has emerged during the past three decades as a respected form of treatment for such wide-ranging problems as teenage confusion, drug and alcohol abuse, rape victimization, and spouse abuse (Lester, 1989; Bloom, 1984).

THE EFFECTIVENESS OF SUICIDE PREVENTION

It has been difficult for researchers to assess the effectiveness of suicide prevention centers (Eddy et al., 1987; Bloom, 1984). There are many kinds of centers, each with its own procedures and serving populations that vary in number, age, economic stability, and environmental pressures. Communities with high suicide risk factors, such as an elderly population or economic strife, may continue to have higher suicide rates than other communities irrespective of the effectiveness of their local prevention centers.

Do suicide prevention centers reduce the number of suicides in a community? Clinical researchers do not know (Lester, 1989; Auerbach & Kilmann, 1977). Studies comparing local suicide rates before and after the establishment of community prevention centers have yielded very different findings. Some find a decline in suicide rates (Miller et al., 1984; Dashef, 1984), others no change (Barraclough et al., 1977; Lester, 1974, 1972), and still others an increase in suicide rates (Weiner, 1969). It is important to note, however, that the increase in suicide rates found in some studies may reflect society's overall increase in suicidal behavior. One investigator found that although suicide rates did increase in some cities with prevention centers, they increased even more in cities without such centers (Lester, 1991, 1974).

Do suicidal people contact prevention centers? Apparently only a small percentage do. Research has indicated that approximately 2 percent of the people who actually killed themselves in Los Angeles ever contacted the Los Angeles Suicide Prevention Center (Weiner, 1969). Moreover, the typical caller to an urban prevention center appears to be young, African American, and female, whereas the greatest number of suicides are committed by elderly white men (Lester, 1989, 1972).

On the other hand, prevention centers do seem to be helpful in averting suicide for those high-risk people who do call. The clinical researchers Norman Farberow and Robert Litman (1970) identified 8,000 high-risk individuals who contacted the Los Angeles Suicide Prevention Center. Approximately 2 percent of these callers later committed suicide, compared to the 6 percent suicide rate usually found in similar high-risk groups. One implication of such findings is that these centers need to be more visible to and approachable by people who are harboring thoughts of suicide. The growing number of advertisements and announcements in newspapers and on television, radio, and billboards attest to a movement in this direction.

Partly because of the many suicide prevention programs and the data they have generated, today's clinicians have a better understanding of suicide and greater ability to assess suicidal risk than those of the past (McIntosh et al., 1985). Studies reveal that the health-care professionals who are most knowledgeable about suicide are psychologists, psychiatrists, and personnel who actually work in prevention centers (Domino & Swain, 1986). Relatively less informed professionals who might be contacted by suicidal persons include members of the clergy (Domino & Swain, 1986; Domino, 1985).

Shneidman (1987) has called for broader and more effective public education about suicide as the ultimate form of prevention. And at least some suicide education programs—most of them concentrating on teachers and students—have begun to emerge (Klingman & Hochdorf, 1993; Sandoval, Davis, & Wilson, 1987). The correct curriculum for such programs has been the subject of considerable debate and their merits have yet to be broadly investigated (Garland & Zigler, 1993). Nevertheless, most clinicians agree with the intent behind these programs and, more generally, with Shneidman when he states:

> The primary prevention of suicide lies in education. The route is through teaching one another and . . . the public that suicide can happen to anyone, that there are verbal and behavioral clues that can be looked for . . . , and that help is available. . . .
>
> In the last analysis, the prevention of suicide is everybody's business.
>
> *(Shneidman, 1985, p. 238)*

THE STATE OF THE FIELD

SUICIDE

Once a mysterious and hidden problem, hardly acknowledged by the public and barely investigated by researchers, suicide is today in the limelight. The public's curiosity about this phenomenon is growing, and researchers are actively pursuing information about such acts. During the past two decades in particular, investigators have learned a great deal about the motives, states of mind, social stimuli, and environmental conditions tied to suicide. They have also made impressive progress in identifying its most common precipitants and risk factors.

Perhaps most promising of all, clinicians and educators have begun to enlist the public in the fight against this problem. They now believe that suicide rates can be reduced only if people recognize the enormous scope of this problem and learn how to identify and respond to suicide risks. They are calling for broader public education about suicide—programs aimed at both young and old.

This is a promising beginning, but only a beginning. Critical problems remain in this area of study and treatment. First, when all is said and done, clinicians do not yet fully comprehend why some people kill themselves while others under similar circumstances manage to find alternative ways of addressing their problems. Psychodynamic, biological, and sociocultural explanations of suicide have received only limited research support and have been unable to predict specific attempts at suicide. Second, clinicians have yet to develop undisputably successful interventions for treating suicidal persons. Suicide prevention programs have been embraced by the clinical community and certainly reflect its commitment to helping suicidal persons, but it is not yet clear how much such programs actually reduce the risk or rate of suicide.

It is reasonable to expect that the current commitment by the clinical field to investigate, publicize, and overcome the phenomenon of suicide will lead to a better understanding of suicide and to more successful interventions. Clearly such goals are of importance to everyone. Although suicide itself is typically a lonely and desperate act, the implications and impact of such acts are very broad indeed.

SUMMARY

■ SUICIDE ranks among the top ten causes of death in Western society. It may be defined as a self-inflicted death in which one makes an *intentional, direct,* and *conscious* effort to end one's life. Edwin Shneidman has distinguished four kinds of people who intentionally end their lives: the **death seeker,** the **death initiator,** the **death ignorer,** and the **death darer.** He has also distinguished a suicide-like category called **subintentioned death,** in which people play indirect, covert, partial, or unconscious roles in their own deaths.

■ THE TWO MAJOR RESEARCH STRATEGIES used in the study of suicide are *retrospective analysis,* a kind of psychological autopsy, and the study of people who survive suicide attempts, on the assumption that they are similar to those who commit fatal suicides. Each strategy has limitations.

Suicide rates vary from country to country. One reason seems to be cultural differences in religious affiliation, beliefs, or degree of devoutness. Suicide rates also differ according to race and sex. Though women make three times as many attempts at suicide as men, more than three times as many men succeed in killing themselves. Suicide rates are also related to marital status.

Many suicidal acts are tied to contemporaneous events or conditions. Though these factors may not fully account for the act, they do serve to precipitate it. Common precipitating factors are *stressful events and situations, mood and thought changes, alcohol use, mental disorders,* and *events that inspire modeling.*

■ PSYCHODYNAMIC THEORISTS believe that suicide usually results from a state of depression and a process of self-directed anger. Freud also proposed that human beings have a basic death instinct, which he called *Thanatos.*

The *biological* view of suicide has focused on the finding that people who commit suicide often have lower activity of the neurotransmitter *serotonin.* It has been suggested that in people who are clinically depressed, low serotonin activity may produce aggressive and impulsive tendencies that leave them particularly vulnerable to suicidal thinking and action. Even in the absence of a depressive disorder, people with low serotonin levels may develop highly aggressive feelings and be dangerous to themselves or others.

Emile Durkheim's *sociocultural* theory holds that the probability of suicide is determined by the extent to which a person is embedded in such social institutions as the family, the church, and the community. The more a person belongs, the lower the risk of suicide. Durkheim defined three categories of suicide based on the person's relationship with society: *egoistic suicides, altruistic suicides,* and *anomic suicides.* His theory highlights the potential importance of societal factors, but he concluded that the final explanation probably involves an interaction between societal and individual factors.

■ DIFFERENT AGE GROUPS have a different likelihood of committing suicide. Suicide is relatively infrequent among children, although it has been increasing rapidly in that group during the past several decades. Suicidal thinking among normal children is apparently more common than most people once believed.

Suicidal actions become much more common after the age of 14. Suicide has become the third leading cause of death for adolescents and young adults. It is often linked to clinical depression and unusual stress, but some theorists believe that adolescent life itself helps engender a climate conducive to suicidal action.

Several theories, each pointing to societal changes, have been proposed to explain why the suicide rate among adolescents and young adults has risen so dramatically during the past few decades. They point to the overall rise in the number and proportion of adolescents and young adults in the general population, the weakening of ties in the nuclear family, the increased availability and use of drugs among the young, and the broad media coverage attending suicide attempts by teenagers and young adults.

In Western society the elderly are more likely to commit suicide than people in any other age group. As people grow older and their health deteriorates, they lose close friends and relatives in their age group, lose control over their lives, and lose status in our society. Resulting feelings of hopelessness, loneliness, depression, or inevitability may increase the likelihood that they will attempt suicide.

■ AFTER TRYING and failing to kill themselves, some suicidal people receive therapy. The goal of therapy is to help the client achieve a nonsuicidal state of mind and develop more constructive ways of handling stress and solving problems. Various therapy systems and formats have been employed.

Over the past thirty years, emphasis has shifted from suicide treatment to suicide prevention because the last opportunity to keep many suicidal people alive comes before their first attempt. *Suicide prevention programs* generally consist of 24-hour-a-day "suicide hotlines" and walk-in centers staffed largely by *paraprofessionals.* During their initial contact with someone considered suicidal, counselors seek to establish a positive relationship, to understand and clarify the problem, to assess the suicide potential, to assess and mobilize the caller's resources, and to formulate a plan for overcoming the crisis. Although such *crisis intervention* may be sufficient treatment for some suicidal people, longer-term therapy is needed for most of them. Apparently only a small percentage of suicidal people contact prevention centers.

■ THOUGH CLINICAL SCIENTISTS know a great deal about suicide, they do not yet fully comprehend why people kill themselves. Furthermore, myths about suicide and suicide intervention abound, sometimes contributing to tragedies that might otherwise be averted.

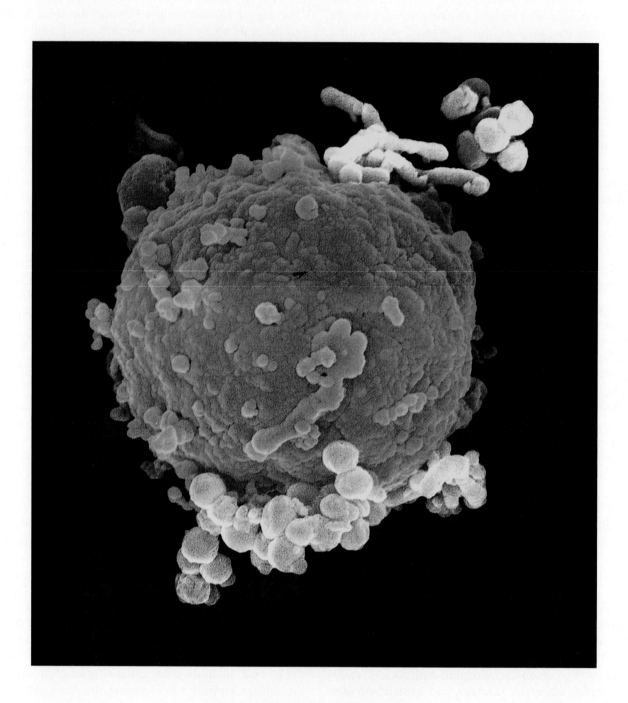

Topic Overview

**FACTITIOUS
DISORDERS**

**SOMATOFORM
DISORDERS**

Conversion Disorders

Somatization Disorders

Pain Disorder

Hypochondriasis

Body Dysmorphic Disorders

**PSYCHOPHYSIOLOGICAL
DISORDERS**

"Traditional" Psychophysiological
Disorders

"New" Psychophysiological Disorders

Psychoneuroimmunology

PSYCHOLOGICAL FACTORS
AND PHYSICAL DISORDERS

■

T HROUGHOUT THIS TEXT we have repeatedly encountered mental disorders that have physical causes. Abnormal neurotransmitter activity, for example, contributes to the development of generalized anxiety disorders, panic disorders, and unipolar patterns of depression. Today's clinicians also recognize that somatic, or bodily, illnesses can have psychological causes. In fact, this idea is not new at all. It can be traced back to the fourth century B.C., when Socrates said, "You should not treat body without soul" (Fiester, 1986; Gentry & Matarazzo, 1981).

DESPITE ITS ANCIENT ROOTS, the idea that psychological factors may contribute to somatic illnesses held little appeal before the twentieth century. It was particularly unpopular during the Renaissance, when medicine became a physical science and scientists became committed to the pursuit of objective "fact" (Gatchel & Baum, 1983). At that time the mind was the province of priests and philosophers, the body the realm of physicians and scientists. The seventeenth-century French philosopher René Descartes went so far as to claim that the mind, or soul, was a separate entity from the body, totally unable to affect physical matter or somatic processes. His position, called *mind-body dualism,* dominated medical theory for the next 200 years. Physicians in the nineteenth century followed the tradition of mind-body dualism when they concluded that each organic disease was caused by a distinct microorganism.

DURING THE PAST 100 YEARS, however, medicine has moved steadily toward an interactive view of physical illness. Clinical research and observations have persuaded medical scientists that many physical illnesses are *psychogenic*—contributed to by such psychological factors as worry, family stress, and unconscious needs. Some of these physical illnesses, today called *factitious disorders* and *somatoform disorders*, are thought to be caused exclusively by psychological factors. Others, called *psychophysiological disorders*, are believed to result from an interaction of organic and psychological factors.

■ FACTITIOUS ■ DISORDERS

People who become physically sick usually go to a physician for medical evaluation, diagnosis, and treatment. Sometimes, however, an illness defies medical assessment, and physicians may suspect some causes other than the physical factors they have been seeking. They may conclude, for instance, that the patient is *malingering*—intentionally feigning illness to achieve some external gains, such as financial compensation or military deferment.

Alternatively, physicians may suspect that the patient is manifesting a *factitious disorder,* more precisely, a *factitious disorder with predominantly physical signs and symptoms.* People with this disorder intentionally produce or feign physical symptoms, but, unlike malingerers, their motivation for assuming the sick role is the role itself (APA, 1994). They have no external incentives for developing the symptoms.

A 29-year-old female laboratory technician was admitted to the medical service via the emergency room because of bloody urine. The patient said that she was being treated for lupus erythematosus by a physician in a different city. She also mentioned that she had had Von Willebrand's disease (a rare hereditary blood disorder) as a child. On the third day of her hospitalization, a medical student mentioned to the resident that she had seen this patient several weeks before at a different hospital in the area, where the patient had been admitted for the same problem. A search of the patient's belongings revealed a cache of anticoagulant medication. When confronted with this information she refused to discuss the matter and hurriedly signed out of the hospital against medical advice.

(Spitzer et al., 1981, p. 33)

The physical symptoms of a factitious disorder of this kind may be a total fabrication, self-inflicted, or an exaggeration of a preexisting physical condition (APA, 1994). People with the disorder usually describe their medical history dramatically, but become vague when pressed for details. Their knowledge of medical terminology and hospital routine is often extensive. When they are hospitalized they are likely to demand attention from the staff but to disregard hospital regulations. Many eagerly undergo painful testing or treatment, even surgery. They may develop real medical problems, such as the formation of scar tissue from unnecessary surgery, abscesses from numerous injections, or adverse reactions to drugs. If physicians confront them with evidence that their symptoms are factitious, they typically deny the charges and rapidly discharge themselves from the hospital; they are quite likely to enter another hospital the same day.

Munchausen syndrome is the chronic form of this disorder. Like Baron Munchausen, an eighteenth-century cavalry officer who journeyed from tavern to tavern in Europe telling fantastical tales about his supposed adventures, people with this syndrome travel from hospital to hospital reciting their symptoms, gaining admission, and receiving treatment (Zuger, 1993; Thompson & Steele, 1988). In a related but apparently rare form of factitious disorder, *Munchausen syndrome by proxy,* parents fabricate or induce physical illnesses in their children in order to get attention from physicians (McQuiston, 1993). When these children are removed from their parents and placed in the care of others, their symptoms disappear.

Although clinical researchers have yet to determine the prevalence of factitious disorder with predominantly physical signs and symptoms, they believe the syndrome to be more common among men than among women (APA, 1994). Cases usually begin during early adulthood and often develop into a pattern that greatly impairs the person's ability to hold a steady job, maintain family ties, or form enduring social relationships. The disorder seems to be most common among people who (1) received extensive medical treatment and hospitalization as children for a true physical disorder, (2) carry a grudge against the medical profession, (3) have worked as a nurse, laboratory technician, or medical paraprofessional, (4) had a significant relationship with a physician in the past, or (5) have underlying dependent, exploitive, or self-defeating personality traits (APA, 1994).

The precise causes of factitious disorders are not really understood. These disorders have received little systematic study, and clinicians have not been able to develop standard effective treatments for them. Some success has been reported in individual cases with the use of a flexible, multidisciplinary treatment team (Schwarz et al., 1993; Parker, 1993). DSM-IV also identifies *factitious disorder with predominantly psychological signs and symptoms,* a pattern in which people feign symptoms suggestive of a mental disorder (particularly a psychosis), and *factitious disorder with combined psychological and physical signs and symptoms.*

■ SOMATOFORM ■ DISORDERS

When a physical illness eludes medical assessment, physicians may alternatively suspect that the patient has a *somatoform disorder.* Such patients have physical complaints that are rooted exclusively in psychological causes. In contrast to people with factitious disorders, patients with somatoform disorders experience no sense of willing their symptoms or having control over them. Indeed, they rarely believe that the problems are anything but organic.

In earlier diagnostic systems, somatoform disorders were listed as "neuroses," the Freudian categorization meant to suggest that the disorders resulted from underlying conflicts, intense ongoing anxiety, and ego defense mechanisms that failed to control the anxiety (see p. 184). As we noted earlier, however, recent editions of the DSM have done away with the category of neurosis, in line with a policy of defining disorders by symptoms and without reference to specific causes. Accordingly, the somatoform disorders now constitute a separate category, unconnected to the anxiety, mood, or dissociative disorders—patterns that were also listed as neuroses in past systems.

Some somatoform disorders, known as *hysterical disorders,* involve an actual loss or alteration of physical functioning. People with *conversion disorders,* for instance, develop dramatic physical symptoms or deficits affecting voluntary motor or sensory functioning; those with *somatization disorders* experience multiple physical symptoms; and those with *pain disorders* experience pain that is not predominantly attributable to a medical cause.

In another group of somatoform disorders, the *preoccupation disorders,* physical functioning is at most minimally lost or altered, but people with these disorders become preoccupied with the notion that something is wrong with them physically. Those who experience *hypochondriasis* mistakenly and incessantly fear that fluctuations in their physical functioning indicate a serious disease. Those with *body dysmorphic disorders* worry excessively that some aspect of their physical appearance is defective.

HYSTERICAL SOMATOFORM DISORDERS

Hysterical disorders, the somatoform disorders that involve altered or lost physical functioning, are often difficult to distinguish from problems with a medical base. The symptoms of these disorders take many forms and typically have a marked impact on patients' lives.

CONVERSION DISORDERS A *conversion disorder* is characterized by one or more physical symptoms or deficits affecting voluntary motor or sensory function that are actually expressions of a psychological problem, such as a conflict or need: the psychological problem is converted to a physical symptom. The symptoms often suggest a neurological dysfunction, such as paralysis, seizures, blindness, anesthesia (loss of feeling), or aphonia (loss of speech), and are thus often called "pseudoneurological" (APA, 1994). One woman developed a conversion symptom of dizziness in apparent response to her unhappy marriage and her inability to deal directly with her abusive husband:

A 46-year-old married housewife was referred by her husband's psychiatrist for consultation. In the course of discussing certain marital conflicts that he was having with his wife, the husband had described "attacks" of dizziness that his wife experienced that left her quite incapacitated.

In consultation, the wife described being overcome with feelings of extreme dizziness, accompanied by slight nausea, four or five nights a week. During these attacks, the room around her would take on a "shimmering" appearance, and she would have the feeling that she was "floating" and unable to keep her balance. Inexplicably, the attacks almost always occurred at about 4:00 P.M. She usually had to lie down on the couch and often did not feel better until 7:00 or 8:00 P.M. After recovering, she generally spent the rest of the evening watching TV; and more often than not, she would fall asleep in the living room, not going to bed in the bedroom until 2:00 or 3:00 in the morning.

The patient had been pronounced physically fit by her internist, a neurologist, and an ear, nose, and throat specialist on more than one occasion. Hypoglycemia had been ruled out by glucose tolerance tests.

When asked about her marriage, the patient described her husband as a tyrant, frequently demanding and verbally abusive of her and their four children. She admitted that she dreaded his arrival home from work each day, knowing that he would comment that the house was a mess and the dinner, if prepared, not to his liking. Recently, since the onset of her attacks, when she was unable to make dinner he and the four kids would go to McDonald's or the local pizza parlor. After that, he would settle in to watch a ballgame in the bedroom, and their conversation was minimal. In spite of their troubles, the patient claimed that she loved her husband and needed him very much.

(Spitzer et al., 1981, pp. 92–93)

Most conversion disorders emerge between late childhood and young adulthood; they are diagnosed at least twice as often in women as in men (APA, 1994; Tomasson, Kent, & Coryell, 1991). They usually appear suddenly, at times of extreme psychological stress, and last a matter of weeks (APA, 1994). Conversion disorders are thought to be quite rare, occurring in at most three out of every 1000 persons (APA, 1994).

SOMATIZATION DISORDERS   Two women known as Ann and Sheila baffled a variety of medical specialists with the wide range of their symptoms:

*A*nn describes nervousness since childhood; she also spontaneously admits to being sickly since her youth with a succession of physical problems doctors often indicated were due to her nerves or depression. She, however, believes that she has a physical problem that has not yet been discovered by the doctors. Besides nervousness, she has chest pain, and has been told by a variety of medical consultants that she has a "nervous heart." She also goes to doctors for abdominal pain, and has been diagnosed as having a "spastic colon." She has seen chiropractors and osteopaths for backaches, for pains in the extremities, and for anesthesia of her fingertips. Three months ago she had vomiting, chest pain, and abdominal pain, and was admitted to a hospital for a hysterectomy. Since the hysterectomy she has had repeated anxiety attacks, fainting spells that she claims are associated with unconsciousness that lasts more than thirty minutes, vomiting, food intolerance, weakness, and fatigue. She has had several medical hospitalizations for workups of vomiting, colitis, vomiting blood, and chest pain. She has had a surgical procedure for an abscess of the throat.

*S*heila reported having abdominal pain since age 17, necessitating exploratory surgery that yielded no specific diagnosis. She had several pregnancies, each with severe nausea, vomiting, and abdominal pain; she ultimately had a hysterectomy for a "tipped uterus." Since age 40 she had experienced dizziness and "blackouts," which she eventually was told might be multiple sclerosis or a brain tumor. She continued to be bedridden for extended periods of time, with weakness, blurred vision, and difficulty urinating. At age 43 she was worked up for a hiatal hernia because of complaints of bloating and intolerance of a variety of foods. She also had additional hospitalizations for neurological, hypertensive, and renal workups, all of which failed to reveal a definitive diagnosis.

(Spitzer et al., 1981, pp. 185, 260)

When we read the case descriptions of Ann and Sheila, we are struck by the sheer quantity and range of medical problems these women experienced. People who have numerous physical ailments without an organic basis, and whose difficulties continue or recur for several years, are likely to receive a diagnosis of *somatization disorder.* This pattern, first described by Pierre Briquet in 1859, is also known as *Briquet's syndrome.* To receive a diagnosis of somatization disorder, the person's multiple ailments must include pain symptoms at four sites or functions of the body, two gastrointestinal symptoms (such as nausea, vomiting, or diarrhea), one sexual symptom (such as erectile or ejaculatory dysfunction or menstrual difficulties), and one pseudoneurologic symptom (such as double vision, paralysis, or difficulty breathing).

Patients with somatization disorders usually go from doctor to doctor in search of relief (APA, 1994; Cloninger et al., 1984). They often describe their many symptoms in dramatic and exaggerated terms. Most also feel anxious and depressed.

Between 0.2 and 2.0 percent of all women in the United States are believed to experience a somatization disorder in any given year, compared to less than 0.2 percent of all men (APA, 1994; Regier et al., 1993). The disorder often runs in families; 10 to 20 percent of the close female relatives of women with the disorder also develop it. The disorder usually begins between adolescence and young adulthood with no identifiable precipitating event (APA, 1994; Smith, 1992).

Somatization disorder lasts considerably longer than a conversion disorder, typically for many years. The symptoms may fluctuate over time but rarely disappear completely without psychotherapy (APA, 1994). Two-thirds of the people diagnosed with this disorder in the United States in any given year receive treatment from a medical or mental health professional for its psychological aspects (Regier et al., 1993).

PAIN DISORDER   When people experience severe or prolonged pain, and psychological factors play a significant role in the onset, severity, exacerbation, or maintenance of the pain, they may receive a diagnosis of *pain disorder* (APA, 1994). The pain may occur in any part of the body. The more precise diagnosis of *pain disorder associated with psychological factors* is given when psychological factors play the *major* role. If both psychological and general medical factors play significant roles, the diagnosis is *pain disorder associated with both psychological factors and a general medical condition.* Patients with conversion or somatization disorders may also experience pain without a dominant medical cause, but in a pain disorder the pain is the central symptom.

Researchers have not been able to determine the precise prevalence of pain disorders, but they appear to be relatively common, and women seem to experience them more often than men (APA, 1994). The disorder may begin at any age, and in some cases continues for years (APA, 1994).

Often a pain disorder develops after an accident or during an illness that has caused genuine pain. The pain, however, eventually becomes more severe and enduring than organic factors can explain. Laura, a 36-year-old woman with sarcoidosis, reported pains that far exceeded the usual symptoms of that tubercular disease. In fact, as the following interview indicates, her pain continued even after the sarcoidosis went into complete remission:

*L*aura: Before the operation I would have little joint pains, nothing that really bothered me that much. After the operation I was having severe pains in my chest and in my ribs, and those were the type of problems I'd been having after the operation, that I didn't have before. . . . I'd go to an emergency room at night, 11:00, 12:00, 1:00 or so. I'd take the medicine, and the next day it stopped hurting, and I'd go back again. In the meantime this is when I went to the other doctors, to complain about the same thing, to find out what was wrong; and they could never find out what was wrong with me either. . . .

Doctor: With these symptoms on and off over the years, has that interfered with the way you've lived your life?

Laura: Yes. At certain points when I go out or my husband and I go out, we have to leave early because I start hurting. . . . A lot of times I just won't do things because my chest is hurting for one reason or another. . . .

Doctor: Does it interfere with your work, those pains?

Laura: Yes, but I still work. . . .

Doctor: Have you had chest x-rays recently? Did they show the sarcoid was the same?

Laura: . . . One doctor said he didn't see any signs of sarcoid, but I knew I was still having joint pains. Two months ago when the doctor checked me and another doctor looked at the x-rays, he said he didn't see any signs of the sarcoid then and that they were doing a study now, on blood and various things, to see if it was connected to sarcoid. . . .

(Green, 1985, pp. 60–63)

IDENTIFYING HYSTERICAL SYMPTOMS In an effort to distinguish hysterical somatoform disorders from "true" medical problems, diagnosticians rely on several distinctions:

NEUROLOGICAL AND ANATOMICAL INCONSISTENCIES The symptoms of some hysterical disorders do not usually correspond to what medical scientists know about the anatomical distribution of nerves and the way the nervous system works (APA, 1994). Some patients, for example, display a conversion symptom called "glove anesthesia," numbness that begins abruptly at the wrist and extends with uniform intensity throughout the hand to the fingertips. As Figure 11–1 shows, such clearly defined and equally distributed numbness is not characteristic of neurological damage. Even the newly recognized neurological disease, *carpal tunnel syndrome,* which is characterized by numbness, tingling, and pain in the hand, does not typically involve a uniform distribution of symptoms throughout the hand.

UNEXPECTED COURSE OF DEVELOPMENT Hysterical disorders do not necessarily lead to the same physical consequences as corresponding medical problems (Levy, 1985). When paraplegia (paralysis from the waist down) is caused by damage to the spinal cord, for example, the leg muscles may atrophy, or waste away, unless the patient receives proper physical therapy and exercise. People whose paralysis is a conversion disorder do not ordinarily experience such atrophy; presumably they exercise their muscles to some degree, without being aware that they are doing so.

SELECTIVE SYMPTOMATOLOGY The physical symptoms of hysterical disease may operate selectively, or inconsistently. People with conversion blindness, for example, have fewer accidents than people who are organically blind, an indication that they have at least some vision even if they are unaware of it.

PREOCCUPATION SOMATOFORM DISORDERS

People who have *hypochondriasis* and *body dysmorphic disorders,* both characterized as **preoccupation somatoform disorders,** misinterpret physical symptoms as signs of serious physical problems. Friends, relatives, and physicians may try to dissuade them from this notion, but usually without success. Although often these kinds of somatoform disorders cause considerable anxiety or depression, they do not affect

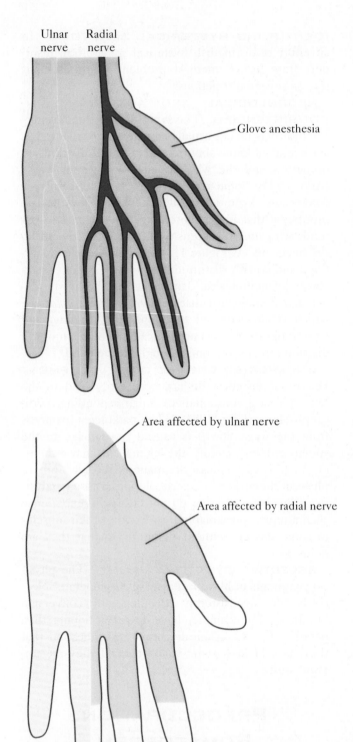

Ulnar   Radial
nerve   nerve

Glove anesthesia

Area affected by ulnar nerve

Area affected by radial nerve

FIGURE 11-1 *In the conversion symptom called "glove anesthesia," the entire hand extending to the wrist becomes numb. Actual physical damage to the ulnar nerve, in contrast, causes anesthesia in the ring finger and little finger and beyond the wrist partway up the arm; and damage to the radial nerve causes insensitivity only in parts of the ring, middle, and index fingers and the thumb and partway up the arm. (Adapted from Gray, 1959.)*

a person's social or occupational functioning so profoundly as hysterical disorders do (APA, 1994; Starcevic, 1988; Jenike, 1985).

HYPOCHONDRIASIS   People who suffer from *hypochondriasis* unrealistically and fearfully interpret bodily signs or symptoms as signs of a serious illness. Often the reported ailments are merely normal fluctuations in physical functioning, such as occasional coughing, sores, or sweating. Despite repeated diagnostic tests, patients with hypochondriasis are not reassured (APA, 1994). They may go from doctor to doctor in their efforts to find a helpful intervention. Some patients actually recognize that their concern about having a serious medical illness is excessive; others do not (APA, 1994).

Hypochondriasis can present a picture very similar to that of a somatization disorder. Each typically involves numerous physical symptoms and frequent visits to doctors, and each causes patients great concern. Although it is often a difficult judgment to make, diagnosticians try to distinguish between the two on the basis of the following criteria: if the anxiety level is significant and the bodily symptoms are relatively minor, a diagnosis of hypochondriasis is in order; if the bodily symptoms are more significant and overshadow the patient's anxiety, they probably indicate a somatization disorder.

Although hypochondriasis can begin at any age, it emerges most commonly in early adulthood. Some patients eventually overcome their preoccupation, but for most the disorder becomes chronic, the symptoms waxing and waning over the years. Like pain disorders, hypochondriasis is reportedly very familiar to physicians, but its exact prevalence is unknown. Men and women are equally likely to receive this diagnosis (APA, 1994).

"He didn't really die of anything. He was a hypochondriac."

(Drawing by Geo. Price; © 1970 The New Yorker Magazine, Inc.)

BODY DYSMORPHIC DISORDERS People who experience a *body dysmorphic disorder,* also known as *dysmorphophobia,* become preoccupied with some imagined or exaggerated defect in their appearance. Most commonly they worry about facial flaws such as wrinkles, spots on the skin, excessive facial hair, swelling of the face, or a misshapen nose, mouth, jaw, or eyebrow (APA, 1994). Some worry about the appearance of their feet, hands, breasts, penis, or another body part. Others are concerned about bad odors coming from sweat, the breath, the genitals, or the rectum (Marks, 1987). Some people are distressed by several body features. Here we see a case of body dysmorphic disorder that centers on body odor:

A woman of 35 had for 16 years been worried that her sweat smelled terrible. The fear began just before her marriage when she was sharing a bed with a close friend who said that someone at work smelled badly, and the patient felt that the remark was directed at her. For fear that she smelled, for 5 years she had not gone out anywhere ex-

cept when accompanied by her husband or mother. She had not spoken to her neighbors for 3 years because she thought she had overheard them speak about her to some friends. She avoided cinemas, dances, shops, cafes, and private homes. Occasionally she visited her in-laws, but she always sat at a distance from them. Her husband was not allowed to invite any friends home; she constantly sought reassurance from him about her smell; and strangers who rang the doorbell were not answered. Television commercials about deodorants made her very anxious. She refused to attend the local church because it was small and the local congregants might comment on her. The family had to travel to a church 8 miles away in which the congregants were strangers; there they sat or stood apart from the others. Her husband bought all her new clothes as she was afraid to try on clothes in front of shop assistants. She used vast quantities of deodorant and always bathed and changed her clothes before going out, up to 4 times daily.

(Marks, 1987, p. 371)

It is common for people in our society to be somewhat concerned about their appearance (see Figure 11–2). Adolescents and young adults in particular

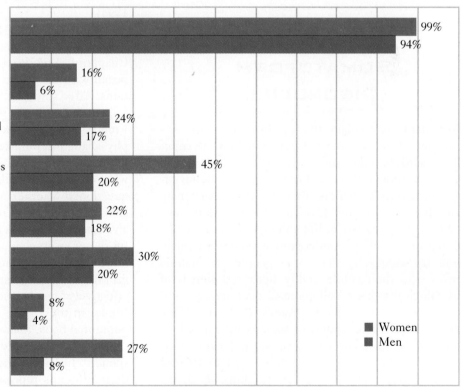

FIGURE 11–2 *"Mirror mirror on the wall . . ." People with body dysmorphic disorder become particularly preoccupied with imagined or exaggerated physical defects, but they are not the only ones who have concerns about their appearance. Indeed, it is estimated that 1.5 million Americans undergo "aesthetic surgery" each year. Surveys find that in our appearance-conscious society, surprisingly high percentages of people regularly think about and try to alter the way they look. (Kimball, 1993; Poretz & Sinrod, 1991; Weiss, 1991; Simmon, 1990.)*

often worry about such things as acne. The concerns of people with body dysmorphic disorders, however, are extreme and disruptive. Sufferers may even have difficulty looking others in the eye, convinced that their flaws are on display. They may also go to great lengths to conceal the "defect"—always wearing sunglasses to hide the shape of their supposedly misshapen eyes, for example, or even seeking plastic surgery to correct the problem (Phillips et al., 1993; Thomas, 1984). Many people with this disorder isolate themselves and refuse to seek work or pursue other activities outside the home (Phillips et al., 1993; Phillips, 1991). One study found that 30 percent of subjects with the disorder were housebound, and 17 percent had attempted suicide (Phillips et al., 1993). Most cases begin during adolescence and persist for an extended period. Often, however, they are not diagnosed for many years because individuals with the disorder are reluctant to reveal their concerns. Researchers have not yet determined the prevalence of this disorder, but preliminary reports suggest that it may be equally common among men and women (APA, 1994).

VIEWS ON SOMATOFORM DISORDERS

Most theorists explain the preoccupation somatoform disorders—hypochondriasis and body dysmorphic disorders—the same way they explain certain anxiety disorders (discussed in Chapter 6). Behaviorists, for example, believe that the disproportionate fears displayed by people with these disorders have been acquired earlier in life through classical conditioning or modeling. And cognitive theorists explain them by suggesting that some people are acutely sensitive to their subtle bodily signs and signals of physiological arousal, and come to overinterpret and overattend to such signals (Karoly & Lecci, 1993; Barsky, 1992). The hysterical somatoform disorders, however—conversion, somatization, and pain disorders—are considered to be unique and to require special explanations (Kirmayer, Robbins, & Paris, 1994).

The ancient Greeks believed that hysterical disorders were experienced only by women and came about when the uterus of a sexually ungratified woman wandered throughout her body in search of fulfillment, producing a physical symptom wherever it lodged. (Our word "hysteria" comes from the Greek word for uterus, *hustera*.) Hippocrates suggested marriage as the most effective treatment for hysterical disorders.

The current belief in the clinical field that hysterical ailments are caused by psychological factors dates back to the work of Ambroise-Auguste Liébault and Hippolyte Bernheim in the late nineteenth century. Founders of the Nancy School in Paris—an institution for the study and treatment of mental disorders—these researchers were able to produce such hysterical symptoms as deafness, paralysis, blindness, and numbness in normal people by hypnotic suggestion and could remove these symptoms by the same means (see Chapter 1). Having established that a psychological process—hypnotic suggestion—could both induce and reverse physical dysfunctioning, they concluded that hysterical somatoform disorders are themselves probably caused by psychological processes.

Today's leading explanations for hysterical disorders come from the psychodynamic, behavioral, and cognitive models. As we shall observe, however, none has received much research support, and the disorders are still poorly understood (Kirmayer et al., 1994).

THE PSYCHODYNAMIC VIEW   As we noted in Chapter 1, Freud's theory of psychoanalysis actually began with his efforts to account for hysterical symptoms. After studying hypnosis in Paris and becoming acquainted with the work of Liébault and Bernheim, Freud became interested in the work of an older physician, Joseph Breuer (1842–1925). Breuer used hypnosis to treat the woman he called Anna O., whom we met in Chapter 2. Recently critics have questioned whether Anna's hysterical deafness, disorganized speech, and paralysis were entirely hysterical and whether Breuer's hypnotic treatment was as helpful to her as he claimed (see Box 11–1). At the time, however, this case, along with others, seemed to confirm the idea that hysterical ailments could be treated effectively by hypnosis. Freud collaborated with Breuer in the 1890s, and together they published an influential book, *Studies in Hysteria*.

Partly because hysterical disorders seemed to respond to hypnosis, Freud (1894) came to believe that these ailments represented a conversion of underlying emotional conflicts into physical symptoms. Observing that most of his patients with these disorders were women, he proposed that the underlying conflicts developed during a girl's phallic stage (ages 3 through 5), when he believed girls develop an *Electra complex:* they experience strong sexual feelings for their father and come to recognize that they must

BOX 11-1

A CLOSER LOOK AT THE CASE OF ANNA O.

You have read of the "groundbreaking case" of Anna O., whom Josef Breuer cured through catharsis. He wrote in his famous 1895 report that his "talking cure" relieved her of many bizarre symptoms—paralysis, trances, visual problems, speech problems, and facial disorders. Breuer reported that after he hypnotized Anna O. and traced a symptom back to an original disquieting event, the symptom would disappear. This case is often cited as the basis for Freud's later development of psychoanalysis. The problem is that in reality Anna O. may never have been cured.

In 1925 Freud told Carl Jung that Anna O. retained many of her original problems and was being treated primarily with morphine. The "talking cure" had failed. Yet this failure was never publicly acknowledged.

In 1972 H. F. Ellenberger tracked down the facts about Anna O. He began by confirming her true identity: she was Bertha Pappenheim, a well-to-do young woman of Vienna. Breuer treated her from 1880 to 1882, but his renowned report did not emerge until 1895. Ellenberger contacted a sanatorium in Germany where Anna O. stayed in 1882. There he found two fascinating documents: the original, previously unknown report by Breuer, written in 1882, on which the later report was based, and a follow-up report by one of the doctors who treated

Bertha Pappenheim, Josef Breuer's famous "Anna O."

Anna O. at the sanatorium. They contained a number of discrepancies.

Breuer's 1882 report provides much more detail on Anna O., her family, and her physiological disorders than his 1895 report does, and it concludes by saying that her symptoms were greatly alleviated. It is presumably an account of his treatment of Anna O., yet it makes no mention of several issues that are discussed in detail in the later report. Moreover, the report of the sanatorium doctor makes no mention of the "talking cure" and instead describes a troubled young woman who was given doses of chloral hydrate and morphine to treat the same symptoms that Breuer claimed to have cured.

Ellenberger concludes that Bertha Pappenheim was not a typical case of hysteria and that many of her problems may have had an organic cause. Moreover, the cathartic cure played little, if any, role in her treatment. Proponents of psychoanalysis contend that, like many other apocryphal stories in science, religion, and history, Breuer's dubious report does not affect the merits of the field to which it gave birth. Opponents argue that this "paper tiger" of a case continues to be cited and that relatively little of merit has emerged to substantiate it. Like debates in many other fields, this one may be of more academic than practical interest. Psychoanalysis is healthy and popular, and its influence permeates our culture. Perhaps this is as it should be, and Anna O.'s continued illness should remain a historical footnote. But as you learn more about abnormal psychology (or physics or philosophy or history), remember to trust, but verify.

compete with their mother for their father's affection. In deference to their mother's dominant position and to cultural taboos, they repress their sexual feelings and adopt a socially approved abhorrence of such desires.

Freud believed that if a child's parents overreact to her sexual feelings, the Electra conflict will go unresolved and the child may reexperience sexual anxiety throughout her life. Whenever events trigger sexual feelings, the adult may experience an overwhelming unconscious need to hide them from both herself and the world. Freud concluded that some women hide such reemerging sexual feelings by unconsciously converting them into physical symptoms.

Most of today's psychodynamic theorists have modified Freud's explanation of hysterical disorders, particularly his notion that the disorders can always be traced to unresolved Electra conflicts (Kriechman, 1987). They continue to believe, however, that the disorders reflect (1) an unconscious conflict of some kind that arouses anxiety and (2) a conversion of this anxiety into "more tolerable" physical symptoms that symbolize the underlying conflict.

Psychodynamic theories have distinguished two mechanisms at work in hysterical somatoform disorders—primary gain and secondary gain (Colbach, 1987). People are said to be achieving *primary gain* when their hysterical symptoms keep their internal conflicts out of awareness. During an argument, for example, people with inner conflicts about expressing anger may develop a conversion symptom of aphonia (inability to speak) or paralysis of the arm, thus preventing a threatening rage reaction from reaching consciousness. People are said to be achieving *secondary gain* when their hysterical symptoms also enable them to avoid unpleasant activities or to receive kindness or sympathy from others. Both forms of gain help to lock in their symptoms. When, for example, a conversion paralysis allows a soldier to avoid battle duty or conversion blindness prevents the breakup of a relationship, secondary gain may be operating. According to psychodynamic theorists, primary gains initiate hysterical symptoms; secondary gains are by-products of the symptoms. Although such psychodynamic notions are widely accepted, they have received little research support.

THE COGNITIVE VIEW   A number of theorists propose that hysterical disorders are forms of *communication:* through them people manage to express emotions that they cannot express otherwise (Lipowski, 1987). Like their psychodynamic colleagues, these theorists hold that the emotions of patients with hysterical disorders are being converted into physical symptoms. They suggest, however, that the purpose of the conversion is not to "defend" against anxiety but to communicate some distressing emotion—anger, fear, depression, guilt, jealousy—in a "physical language of bodily symptoms" that is familiar to the patient and therefore comfortable (Fry, 1993; Barsky & Klerman, 1983). Because of its emphasis on language and communication as opposed to underlying conflicts and defenses, this view is generally considered a cognitive perspective.

According to this view, people who have difficulty acknowledging their emotions or expressing them to others are candidates for a hysterical disorder, especially when they are in the midst of a difficult interpersonal situation. Similarly, those who learn the language of physical dysfunction through firsthand experience with a genuine physical malady either in themselves or in a relative or friend may then adopt hysterical symptoms as a form of communication (Woodruff, Goodwin, & Guze, 1973; Ziegler & Imboden, 1962). Without any particular awareness on their part, these people may slip into a sick role that distracts them from their own psychological pain while conveying their great distress to others.

This cognitive explanation of hysterical disorders is obviously broader than the psychodynamic view. It allows that emotions other than anxiety may contribute to physical dysfunctioning, that defensive functioning is less of a factor in hysterical conversions than poor ability to communicate, and that familiarity with an illness plays a major role in the development of hysterical ailments. Only this last feature of the cognitive explanation has been supported by research, however. Often hysterical disorders emerge after people have had similar medical problems or after close relatives or friends have experienced such maladies (Levy, 1985).

THE BEHAVIORAL VIEW   Behavioral theorists propose that the physical symptoms of hysterical disorders bring the sufferer rewards. Perhaps the symptoms keep the sufferer out of a difficult work situation or relationship, or elicit attention that is otherwise withheld (Mullins, Olson, & Chaney, 1992; Ullmann & Krasner, 1975). According to behaviorists, such reinforcements operantly condition people into assuming the role of an invalid. Like cognitive theorists, behaviorists hold that a person must be relatively familiar with an illness to be able to adopt its physical symptoms.

The behavioral focus on rewards is similar to the psychodynamic notion that many people with hysterical disorders attain secondary gains from their physical symptoms. The key difference between the two positions is that psychodynamic theorists view such gains as indeed secondary—that is, as a feature that develops only after underlying dynamic conflicts produce the disorder. Behaviorists view the gains (or rewards) as the primary factor in the development of the disorder.

Like the psychodynamic and cognitive explanations, the behavioral view of hysterical disorders has received little research support. Even clinical case reports only occasionally support this position. In many cases the pain and upset that accompany the disorders seem to outweigh any rewards the symptoms may bring.

TREATMENTS FOR SOMATOFORM DISORDERS

People with somatoform disorders usually seek psychotherapy only as a last resort. They fully believe that their problems are somatic and reject all suggestions to the contrary. When a physician tells them that their problems have no physical basis, they simply go to another physician.

Eventually many patients with these disorders do try psychotherapy for their problems. Those with preoccupation somatoform disorders typically receive the kinds of treatment that are applied to phobic and obsessive-compulsive disorders, particularly *exposure and response-prevention interventions* (discussed in Chapter 7). The effectiveness of these approaches in the treatment of preoccupation somatoform disorders, however, has yet to be determined.

People with hysterical somatoform disorders receive interventions that stress either *insight, suggestion, reinforcement,* or *confrontation.* The most commonly applied insight approach has been psychodynamic therapy, which helps patients bring their anxiety-arousing conflicts into consciousness so they can work through them, theoretically eliminating the need to convert anxiety into physical symptoms. Approaches that employ suggestion include telling patients persuasively that their physical symptoms will soon disappear (Bird, 1979) or suggesting the same thing to them under hypnosis (Ballinger, 1987). Therapists who take a reinforcement approach try to arrange the removal of reinforcement for a client's "sick" behavior and an increase in positive reinforcement for nonsymptomatic behaviors (Mullins et al., 1992). Finally, therapists who take a confrontational approach straightforwardly tell patients that their symptoms are without an organic foundation, hoping to force them out of the sick role (Brady & Lind, 1961).

Researchers have been unable to determine the effects of these various forms of psychotherapy on hysterical disorders (Ballinger, 1987). Case studies suggest, however, that conversion disorders and pain disorders respond better to psychotherapy than do somatization disorders, and that approaches that rely on insight, suggestion, and reinforcement bring more lasting improvement than the confrontation strategy.

One thing that makes the study and treatment of hysterical disorders difficult is the ever-present possibility that a diagnosis of hysteria may be a misdiagnosis, that the problem under examination may actually have an organic base. Although organic causes must be ruled out before a diagnosis of somatoform disorder is reached, the tools of medical science are too imprecise to eliminate organic factors completely (APA, 1994; Merskey, 1986). Some of the medical problems most difficult for doctors to diagnose are those involving vague, multiple, and confusing symptoms, including such conditions as hyperparathyroidism, porphyria, multiple sclerosis, and systemic lupus erythematosus. These problems are often initially misdiagnosed as somatoform disorders. In addition, the organic basis for some physical ailments has simply not yet been discovered. In years past, for example, whiplash was regularly diagnosed as a somatoform pain disorder, because medical scientists had not yet uncovered the physical causes of this painful condition (Merskey, 1986).

In a revealing study on this subject, researchers carefully reassessed a large number of conversion disorder diagnoses and determined that in 25 percent of the cases organic factors may have been involved (Watson & Buranen, 1979). In another study 63 percent of a group of patients diagnosed as having conversion disorders were later found to have organic brain dysfunctioning; such brain disorders had developed in only 5 percent of a comparison group of anxious or depressed patients (Whitlock, 1967). Thus it is now recommended that clinicians employ an integrated, multidisciplinary approach when they assess and treat people with the symptoms of these disorders, always keeping in mind that the problems under examination may be just what the clients say they are—physical problems (Woodbury, DeMaso, & Goldman, 1992; Wherry, McMillan, & Hutchison, 1991). Table 11–1 shows some of the factors that distinguish the various types of disorders that involve physical symptoms.

■ PSYCHO- ■ PHYSIOLOGICAL DISORDERS

Earlier in this century clinicians identified a group of physical illnesses that seemed to result from an interaction of psychological and physical factors (Dunbar, 1948; Bott, 1928). These illnesses differed from

TABLE 11-1

DIFFERENTIATING DISORDERS THAT HAVE PHYSICAL SYMPTOMS

DISORDER	VOLUNTARY CONTROL OF SYMPTOMS?	SYMPTOMS LINKED TO PSYCHOLOGICAL FACTOR?	AN APPARENT GOAL?
Malingering	Yes	Maybe	Yes
Factitious disorder	Yes	Yes	No*
Somatoform disorder	No	Yes	Maybe
Psychophysiological disorder	No	Yes	Maybe
Physical illness	No	Maybe	No

* Except for medical attention.

Source: Adapted from Hyler & Spitzer, 1978.

somatoform disorders in that both psychological and physical factors played significant causal roles and the illnesses themselves brought about actual medical damage. Whereas early versions of the DSM labeled these illnesses *psychosomatic* or *psychophysiological disorders,* DSM-IV uses the label *psychological factors affecting medical condition* and further clarifies that the psychological factors may be *psychological symptoms, personality traits, coping styles,* or another such factor. We shall use the more familiar and less cumbersome term "psychophysiological" in discussing them.

At first clinicians believed that only a limited number of illnesses were psychophysiological and that they usually involved dysfunction in some part of the patient's autonomic nervous system (see pp. 185–187). The list of such illnesses included ulcers, asthma, and coronary heart disease. In recent years researchers have learned that other kinds of physical illnesses—most notably bacterial and viral infections such as colds, mononucleosis, and cancer—may also be caused by an interaction of psychological and physical factors. Let us focus first on the "traditional" psychophysiological disorders, and then on the newer members of this category.

"TRADITIONAL" PSYCHOPHYSIOLOGICAL DISORDERS

During the first half of this century, clinicians organized psychophysiological disorders around the various body systems affected by them (APA, 1968).

They identified, for example, skin disorders, respiratory disorders, cardiovascular disorders, gastrointestinal disorders, and musculoskeletal disorders that were psychophysiological. The best known and most prevalent of the disorders were ulcers, asthma, chronic headaches, hypertension, and coronary heart disease.

Ulcers are lesions, or holes, that form in the wall of the stomach (gastric ulcers) or of the duodenum (peptic ulcers), resulting in burning sensations or pain in the stomach, occasional vomiting, and stomach bleeding. This disorder is experienced by 5 to 10 percent of all persons in the United States and is responsible for more than 6,000 deaths each year (Suter, 1986). Ulcers are apparently caused by an interaction of psychological factors, such as environmental stress, intense feelings of anger or anxiety, or a dependent personality (Tennant, 1988; Weiner et al., 1957; Wolf & Wolff, 1947), and physiological factors, such as excessive secretions of the gastric juices or a weak lining of the stomach or duodenum (Fiester, 1986; Mirsky, 1958; Weiner et al., 1957).

Asthma causes the body's airways (the trachea and bronchi) to constrict periodically, so that it is hard for air to pass to and from the lungs. The resulting symptoms are shortness of breath, wheezing, coughing, and a terrifying choking sensation. Approximately 15 million people in the United States suffer from asthma. Most victims are under 15 years of age at the time of the first attack (DeAngelis, 1994). This disease is a leading cause of illness and disability among children and adolescents. Approximately 70 percent of all cases appear to be caused by an interaction of such psychological factors as generalized anxiety, heightened dependency needs, environmental stress, and troubled family relationships (Purcell et al., 1969;

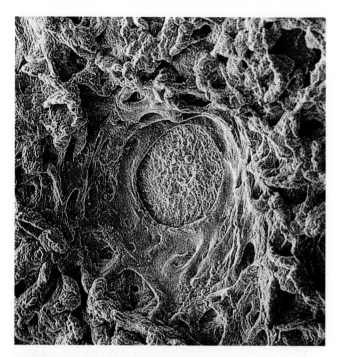

An ulcer in the stomach lining of a rat. Such open sores can occur in the mucous lining of the duodenum as well. For reasons that are not clear, the prevalence of ulcers in human beings has apparently been declining in recent years. (Thompson, 1988.)

Rees, 1964; Alexander, 1950) and such physiological factors as allergies to specific substances, a slow-acting sympathetic nervous system, and a weakness of the respiratory system traceable to respiratory infections or biological inheritance (Alexander, 1981; Miklich et al., 1973; Konig & Godfrey, 1973; Rees, 1964).

Chronic headaches are frequent intense aches of the head or neck that are not caused primarily by a physical disorder. There are two types. *Muscle contraction headaches* (also called *tension headaches*) bring pain at the back or front of the head or at the back of the neck. These headaches occur when the muscles surrounding the skull contract, constricting the blood vessels. Approximately 40 million Americans, more women than men, suffer from these headaches. *Migraine headaches* are extremely severe and often immobilizing aches located on one side of the head, often preceded by a warning sensation called an *aura,* and sometimes accompanied by dizziness, nausea, or vomiting. Migraine headaches develop in two phases: (1) blood vessels in the brain constrict, so that the flow of blood to parts of the brain is reduced, and (2) the same blood vessels later dilate, so that blood flows through them rapidly, stimulating numerous neuron endings and causing pain. Migraines are suffered by about 12 million people in the

United States, two-thirds of them women. Research suggests that chronic headaches are caused by an interaction of psychological factors, such as environmental stress, general feelings of helplessness, feelings of hostility, compulsiveness, or a passive or depressive personality style (Mathew, 1990; Levor et al., 1986), and such physiological factors as serotonin dysfunction, vascular weakness, or musculoskeletal deficiencies (Raskin et al., 1987; Blanchard & Andrasik, 1982).

Hypertension is a state of chronic high blood pressure. That is, the blood pumped through the body's arteries by the heart produces too much pressure against the artery walls. Hypertension has few outward symptoms but it plays havoc with the entire cardiovascular system, greatly increasing the likelihood of stroke, coronary heart disease, and kidney problems. It is estimated that 40 million people in the United States have hypertension, tens of thousands die directly from it annually, and millions more perish because of illnesses brought on by this condition (Johnson, Gentry, & Julius, 1992). Only 5 to 10 percent of all cases of hypertension are caused exclusively by physiological abnormalities; the vast majority are brought about by a combination of psychological and physiological factors and are often designated *essential hypertension* (Johnson et al., 1992). Some of the leading psychological causes of essential hypertension are constant environmental danger, chronic feelings of anger or its inhibition, and an unexpressed need for power (Johnston, 1992; McClelland, 1985, 1979; Harburg et al., 1973).

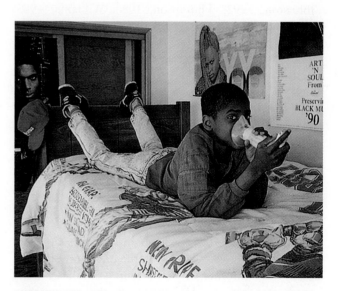

Children who suffer from asthma may use an aerochamber, or inhaler, to help them inhale helpful medications. The child pumps the medication into the device's plastic tube, then inhales it.

Leading physiological causes include a diet high in salt and dysfunctional **baroreceptors**—sensitive nerves in the arteries responsible for signaling the brain that blood pressure is becoming too high (Julius, 1992; Schwartz, 1977).

Coronary heart disease is caused by a blocking of the **coronary arteries**—the blood vessels that surround the heart and are responsible for providing oxygen to the heart muscle. The term actually refers to any of several specific problems, including **angina pectoris,** extreme chest pain caused by a partial blockage of the coronary arteries that prevents a sufficient amount of oxygen from reaching the heart; **coronary occlusion,** a complete blockage of a coronary artery that halts the flow of blood to various parts of the heart muscle and eventually leads to permanent destruction of heart tissue; and **myocardial infarction** (a "heart attack"). The permanent damage to the heart caused by these problems may lead to death. Together these problems are the leading causes of death in men over the age of 35 and of women over 40 in the United States, accounting for close to 800,000 deaths each year, or 38 percent of all deaths in the nation (Blanchard, 1994; Thompson, 1988; Matarazzo, 1984; National Center for Health Statistics, 1984). More than half of all cases of coronary heart disease are related to an interaction of such psychological factors as job stress and the so-called *Type A personality style* (high levels of impatience, frustration, competitiveness, and hostility, and constant striving for control and success) and such physiological factors as a high level of serum cholesterol, obesity, hypertension, the effects of smoking, and lack of exercise (Johnston, 1992; Thompson, 1988; Williams, 1985; Friedman & Rosenman, 1974, 1959).

THE DISREGULATION MODEL OF TRADITIONAL PSYCHOPHYSIOLOGICAL DISORDERS   By definition, psychophysiological disorders are caused by an interaction of psychological and physical factors. But how do these factors combine to produce a given illness? Gary Schwartz, a leading researcher, has proposed the **disregulation model** to account for this phenomenon (see Figure 11–3). Schwartz suggests that our brain and body ordinarily establish **negative feedback loops** that guarantee a smooth, self-regulating operation of the body (Schwartz, 1982, 1977). The brain receives information about external events from the environment, processes this information, and then stimulates body organs into action. Mechanisms in the organs then provide critical negative feedback, telling the brain that its stimulation has been sufficient and should now stop.

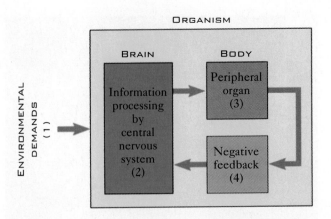

FIGURE 11–3   *Schwartz's disregulation model states that in the normal process of regulation the organism receives environmental pressure (1), the brain processes information about this pressure (2) and then stimulates body organs into action (3), and the organs then provide negative feedback to the brain stating that the stimulation has been sufficient and should cease (4). (Adapted from Schwartz, 1977.)*

This process can be seen in the blood pressure feedback loop (Julius, 1992; Egan, 1992). In one part of this loop the brain receives information that dangers exist in the environment, such as nearby lightning or cars speeding by. In the next part of the loop, the brain processes such information and alerts the nervous system to elevate the blood pressure. And in a later part of the loop, baroreceptors, the pressure-sensitive cells surrounding the body's blood vessels, alert the nervous system when the blood pressure rises too high, and the nervous system then lowers the blood pressure. In short, the various parts of the feedback loop work together to help maintain the blood pressure at an appropriate level.

According to Schwartz, the proper operation of negative feedback loops is essential to a person's health. If one part of a loop falters, the body will enter a state of disregulation rather than effective self-regulation, problems will occur throughout the loop, and a psychophysiological disorder may ultimately develop. Hypertension, for example, may result from problems in any part of the blood pressure feedback loop. Should information from the environment be excessive (as when one is faced with continuous job stress or extended unemployment), should information processing be faulty (as when one keeps misinterpreting or overreacting to everyday events), should a peripheral organ malfunction (as when the aorta narrows abnormally), or should a feedback mechanism fail (as when baroreceptors fail to inform the brain that blood pressure is rising too high), inaccurate information will be fed to the next part of the loop and relayed to the next, until every part in the loop has been stimulated to raise the blood pressure.

In short, according to Schwartz's model, three general areas of difficulty may contribute to disregulation and ultimately to psychophysiological disorders: (1) one's environment may create extraordinary stress; (2) one may have idiosyncratic psychological reactions to environmental events—that is, idiosyncratic ways of processing information; or (3) body organs or feedback mechanisms may function improperly.

FACTORS THAT CONTRIBUTE TO PSYCHOPHYSIOLOGICAL DISORDERS   Over the years, theorists have suggested a variety of factors that may contribute to psychophysiological illnesses. These factors may be grouped in accordance with Schwartz's disregulation model.

EXTRAORDINARY ENVIRONMENTAL PRESSURES   Sometimes the demands placed on people are so intense or long-lasting that they prevent negative feedback loops from establishing a comfortable state of self-regulation. Three kinds of environmental events may lead to disregulation and set the stage for psychophysiological disorders—cataclysmic, personal, and background stressors (Cohen, 1983; Lazarus & Cohen, 1977).

Cataclysmic stressors are events that have a powerful and lingering negative effect on a whole population, such as a war or natural disaster. After the 1979 nuclear accident at Three Mile Island, for example, people who lived near the nuclear plant were found to experience an unusually large number of psychophysiological disorders (not radiation-linked illnesses), and they continued to do so for years (Schneiderman & Baum, 1992; Baum et al., 1983).

Personal stressors are stressful events that many people are likely to experience at some time in their lives—a severe illness, a death in the family, or divorce. Losing one's job and extended unemployment, for example, have been tied to hypertension (Johnson et al., 1992; Edwards, 1973; Kasl & Cobb, 1970).

Background stressors are ongoing circumstances that produce persistent feelings of tension, such as living in a crime-ridden neighborhood or in an atmosphere of chronic social discord, working in an unsatisfying job, or struggling to keep up with one's schoolwork. Hypertension is twice as common among African Americans as among white Americans (Johnson et al., 1992). Although physiological factors may help account for this difference, some theorists propose that it is also linked to the dangerous ghetto environments in which so many African Americans live and to the dead-end jobs at which so many must work (Anderson et al., 1992).

IDIOSYNCRATIC PSYCHOLOGICAL REACTIONS   According to some theorists, certain needs, attitudes, emotions, and coping styles may increase one's chances of developing psychophysiological disorders (Friedman & Booth-Kewley, 1987). These theorists suggest that such factors cause people to overreact repeatedly to stressors, thus setting the stage for psychophysiological dysfunctioning.

Franz Alexander, a leading psychodynamic theorist, proposed that a frustrated dependency need enhances one's chances of developing an ulcer, that unresolved feelings of anger may result in hypertension, and that other unconscious needs may lead to still other psychophysiological disorders (Alexander, French, & Pollock, 1968; Alexander, 1950). Similarly, David Graham proposed that people who see themselves as unjustly treated and who long for revenge may be more likely to develop ulcers; that those who see life as threatening and who keep themselves constantly on guard against danger are prone to develop hypertension (see Figure 11–4); and that those who believe that they are always being left out of things may develop asthma (Graham, 1972; Graham et al., 1962).

FIGURE 11–4   *When David Graham asked patients to select the cartoons that reminded them of situations they had been in, both patients with hives and those with hypertension chose these three cartoons, supporting Graham's belief that people with hives feel they are taking a beating in life and that those with hypertension generally feel threatened. (Adapted from Roesler & Greenfield, 1962.)*

Although each of these theories enjoyed some popularity in the past, neither has received much research support (Tennant, 1988; Krantz & Glass, 1984; Weiner et al., 1957). Recently, however, researchers have found support for the notion that a "repressive" coping style may have a harmful impact on physical health (DeAngelis, 1992). Men who are uncomfortable expressing anger and hostility tend to experience a rise in blood pressure in response to mental stress tests (Vogele & Steptoe, 1993; Lai & Linden, 1992). Increased rates of asthma have also been found among those with a repressive coping style (DeAngelis, 1992).

Other theorists propose that broad personality styles may lead to psychophysiological disorders. The most famous explanation of this kind links the so-called Type A personality to the development of coronary heart disease. Meyer Friedman and Raymond Rosenman (1959), both cardiologists, have characterized people with Type A personality as consistently hostile, cynical, driven, impatient, competitive, and ambitious. They propose that this way of assessing and interacting with the world produces continual stress and often leads to cardiovascular deterioration. People with a Type B personality style, by contrast, are thought to be more relaxed, less aggressive, and less concerned about time, and so less likely to develop coronary heart disease. In reality, of course, most people fall between these two extremes, tending toward one or the other but exhibiting elements of both.

The link between Type A personality style and coronary heart disease has been supported by numerous studies (Rosenman, 1990; Williams, 1989; Friedman et al., 1984). In one well-known investigation of more than 3,000 subjects, Friedman and Rosenman (1974) separated healthy men in their 40s and 50s into Type A and Type B categories and then followed the health of the men over the next eight years. They found that when physiological factors such as cholesterol level were controlled for, more than twice as many Type A men developed coronary heart disease. Later studies found that this relationship between Type A functioning and heart disease also held among women (Haynes, Feinleib, & Kannel, 1980). Recent studies seem to find a weaker link between this personality style and heart disease than earlier ones indicated; however, it appears that at least some of the characteristics associated with the Type A style, particularly hostility, are indeed related to heart disease (Mendes de Leon, 1992; Engebretson & Matthews, 1992; Williams, 1989). In fact, one study has found that feelings of anger di-

A currency dealer shouts orders during trading at the Paris Stock Exchange. The stresses of working on the stock exchange and in similar high-pressure environments apparently increase a worker's risk of developing a medical illness, including coronary heart disease.

rectly impair the heart's pumping efficiency (Ironson et al., 1992).

PHYSIOLOGICAL DYSFUNCTION We saw in Chapter 6 that when the brain stimulates body organs into action, it does so through the operation of the *autonomic nervous system (ANS),* consisting of the many nerve fibers that connect the central nervous system to the organs. If we see a frightening animal, for example, a group of ANS fibers identified as the *sympathetic nervous system* increases its activity and prepares us for action by causing our heart to beat quickly, the pupils of our eyes to dilate, our respiration to speed up, and some blood vessels to constrict and others to dilate. As the danger passes, another group of ANS fibers known as the *parasympathetic nervous system* becomes more active in the reverse direction, slowing the heartbeat, respiration, and the like. Essentially, it calms down our functioning. These two subparts of the ANS are constantly working and complementing each other, helping our bodies to operate smoothly and stably—a condition called *homeostasis* (Cannon, 1927).

Hans Selye (1976, 1974), a leading researcher on the effects of stress, was one of the first to describe the relationship between stress and the ANS. He proposed that people typically respond to stress with a three-stage sequential reaction, which he called the *general adaptation syndrome.* In the presence of threat, the sympathetic nervous system increases its activity and arouses responses throughout the body *(alarm stage).* The parasympathetic nervous system next attempts to counteract these responses *(resistance stage).* Finally, if exposure to or perceptions of stress continue, the resistance may fail and organs controlled by the ANS may become overworked and break down *(exhaustion stage).*

Because the ANS is at the center of stress reactions, defects in its operation are believed to contribute to the development of psychophysiological disorders (Friedman & Booth-Kewley, 1987). If, for example, one's ANS is stimulated too easily, it may keep overreacting to situations that most people find only mildly stressful, so that certain organs eventually become damaged. A psychophysiological disorder may then develop.

The ANS is not the only point of connection between stress and bodily reactions. Another is the *pituitary-adrenal endocrine system,* which when stimulated at times of stress causes the pituitary gland to secrete hormones that affect functioning throughout the body. If this system malfunctions, body organs may be overworked and damaged, and again a psychophysiological disorder may develop.

Local biological dysfunction also may contribute to psychophysiological disorders. People may, for example, have *local somatic weaknesses*—particular organs that are either defective or prone to dysfunction under stress (Rees, 1964). Those with a "weak" gastrointestinal system may be candidates for an ulcer. Those with a "weak" respiratory system may develop asthma. Such local somatic weaknesses are thought to be genetically inherited or to result from improper diet or infection.

Organ dysfunction may also be caused by *individual response specificity,* or idiosyncratic biological reactions to stress. Some people, for example, perspire in response to stress, others develop stomachaches, and still others experience a faster heartbeat or a rise in blood pressure. Although such variations are perfectly normal, the repeated activation of a "favored" system may wear it down and ultimately result in a psychophysiological disorder. It has been discovered, for example, that some infants secrete much more gastric acid under stress than other infants (Weiner, 1977; Mirsky, 1958). Over the years, this individual physical reaction may wear down the mucous lining of the stomach or duodenum until an ulcer develops.

Finally, organ dysfunction may be the result of *autonomic learning*—the inadvertent conditioning of particular responses in the autonomic nervous system (Lachman, 1972). A nervous young boy, for example, may one day secrete excessive gastric acid, which causes him to complain of stomach pain. His parents may respond to his pain by keeping him home from school and seeking to make him comfortable. Though this is certainly an appropriate way to deal with a sick child, a covert process of reinforcement may be taking place. The day at home with tender loving care may serve to reward the child's gastrointestinal activity, conditioning him to secrete excessive amounts of gastric acid in the future, thus increasing his risk of developing an ulcer.

Experimenters have demonstrated that autonomic responses can be conditioned by reward and punishment (Miller, 1969; Kimmel & Kimmel, 1963). After being systematically reinforced for specific changes in heartbeat, blood pressure, or blood vessel dilation, animal subjects have been able to produce such changes voluntarily. One group of researchers, using such rewards as shock avoidance and food, taught baboons to elevate their blood pressure voluntarily for up to five minutes at a time seventy or more times a day (Harris, Goldstein, & Brady, 1977). Similarly, operant conditioning of autonomic responses has been achieved in human subjects by the use of biofeedback techniques (discussed on pp. 248–249).

Clearly, then, psychophysiological disorders have strong ties to environmental stress, stressful reactions, and biological dysfunctioning. The interaction of such factors was once considered an unusual occurrence that could *occasionally* lead to these particular disorders. Such theories as the disregulation model, however, suggest that the interaction of psychological and physical factors is the *rule* of bodily functioning, not the exception. As the years have passed, more and more illnesses have been added to the list of traditional psychophysiological disorders, until it includes such common ailments as irritable bowel syndrome (intermittent episodes of abdominal discomfort), psoriasis (a skin disorder involving reddish lesions), eczema (a disorder characterized by extremely itchy skin eruptions), rheumatoid arthritis (severe inflammation and swelling of the joints), and hypoglycemia (a low level of serum glucose).

"NEW" PSYCHOPHYSIOLOGICAL DISORDERS

For years physicians and clinicians believed that stress could impair physical health only in the form of traditional psychophysiological disorders, but researchers have discovered that stress may contribute to other medical illnesses, particularly to viral and bacterial infections. This discovery came after numerous studies suggested a link between stress and susceptibility to illness in general. Let us look first at how this link was established and then at the area of study known as *psychoneuroimmunology*, a new discipline that further ties stress and illness to the body's *immune system*.

STRESS AND SUSCEPTIBILITY TO ILLNESS In 1967 Thomas Holmes and Richard Rahe developed a scale that assigned numerical values to the life stresses that most people experience at some

time in their lives. The investigators began by asking subjects to estimate, on the basis of their own experiences, how much stress would be elicited by various life events, always using the event of marriage as a point of comparison. If marriage is assigned a stress score of 50, for example, how stressful would they rate trouble with the boss? detention in jail? foreclosure of a mortgage or loan?

The scores of several hundred subjects were then tallied and used as the basis for the Social Adjustment Rating Scale (Table 11–2), which assigns stress values to forty-three life changes. The most stressful

TABLE 11–2

MOST STRESSFUL LIFE EVENTS

ADULTS: "SOCIAL ADJUSTMENT RATING SCALE"*

1. Death of spouse
2. Divorce
3. Marital separation
4. Jail term
5. Death of close family member
6. Personal injury or illness
7. Marriage
8. Fired at work
9. Marital reconciliation
10. Retirement
11. Change in health of family member
12. Pregnancy
13. Sex difficulties
14. Gain of new family member
15. Business readjustment
16. Change in financial state
17. Death of close friend
18. Change to different line of work
19. Change in number of arguments with spouse
20. Mortgage over $10,000
21. Foreclosure of mortgage or loan
22. Change in responsibilities at work

STUDENTS: "UNDERGRADUATE STRESS QUESTIONNAIRE"**

1. Death (family member or friend)
2. Had a lot of tests
3. It's finals week
4. Applying to graduate school
5. Victim of a crime
6. Assignments in all classes due the same day
7. Breaking up with boy-/girlfriend
8. Found out boy-/girlfriend cheated on you
9. Lots of deadlines to meet
10. Property stolen
11. You have a hard upcoming week
12. Went into a test unprepared
13. Lost something (especially wallet)
14. Death of a pet
15. Did worse than expected on test
16. Had an interview
17. Had projects, research papers due
18. Did badly on a test
19. Parents getting divorce
20. Dependent on other people
21. Having roommate conflicts
22. Car/bike broke down, flat tire, etc.

Source: Holmes & Rahe, 1967; Crandall et al., 1992.

  * Full scale has 43 items.

  ** Full scale has 83 items.

event on the scale is the death of a spouse, which receives a score of 100 *life change units (LCUs)*. Lower on the scale is retirement (45 LCUs), and still lower is a minor violation of the law (11 LCUs). Even positive events, such as an outstanding personal achievement, are somewhat stressful (28 LCUs). This scale gave researchers a yardstick for measuring the total amount of stress a person has experienced over a period of time. If in the course of a year a businessman started a new business (39 LCUs), sent his son off to college (29 LCUs), moved to a new house (20 LCUs), and witnessed a close friend die in an automobile accident (37 LCUs), his stress score for the year would be 125 LCUs.

The researchers then proceeded to examine the relationship between life stress (as measured in LCUs) and the onset of illness. They found that the LCU scores of sick people during the year before they fell ill were much higher than those of healthy people (Holmes & Rahe, 1989, 1967). A particularly telling cutoff point was a score of 300 LCUs. If someone's life changes totaled more than 300 LCUs over the course of a year, that person was particularly likely to develop a serious health problem, in many cases a viral or bacterial infection.

The first investigations on this topic took the form of *retrospective studies:* subjects were asked to think back over the past year and remember their life events and illnesses. Investigators feared that in those circumstances, though, people's illnesses could be serving as time landmarks that actually helped their recall of particular life events. In other words, people who had been sick might be more likely to remember events that led up to their illnesses than healthy people were to remember events that occurred during the same span of time. To rule out this possibility, researchers began to conduct *prospective studies* as well, studies that predicted *future* health changes on the basis of current life events.

Rahe (1968), for example, studied 2,500 healthy naval officers and enlisted men who were going to be at sea for at least six months. He divided the naval personnel into a high-risk group (the 30 percent with the highest LCU scores over the previous six months) and a low-risk group (the 30 percent with the lowest LCU scores), and he kept track of the subsequent health changes of the two groups. Twice as many high-risk as low-risk subjects developed illnesses during their first month at sea; in addition, the high-risk group continued to develop more illnesses each month for the next five months.

One shortcoming of the Social Adjustment Rating Scale is that it may not accurately measure the life stress of specific populations. In their development of the scale, Holmes and Rahe (1967) used a sample composed predominantly of white Americans. Less than 5 percent of the subjects were African American. But since their ongoing life experiences often differ in significant ways, might not African Americans and white Americans differ in their stress reactions to various kinds of life events? One study indicates that indeed they do (Komaroff, Masuda, & Holmes, 1989, 1986). Both white and African Americans rank death of a spouse as the single most stressful life event, but African Americans experience greater stress from such events as a major personal injury or illness, a major change in work responsibilities, and a major change in living conditions than white Americans do. Such differences probably reflect the differences in the impact and meaning of such events in the lives of persons of the two groups.

Similarly, college students often face stressors that are different from those listed in the Social Adjustment Rating Scale (Crandall et al., 1992). Instead of having marital difficulties, being fired at work, or applying for a job, a college student may have trouble with a roommate, fail a class, or apply to graduate school. So researchers have also developed new scales to measure life events more accurately in this population (Table 11–2). Using these scales, researchers have again found correlations between stressful events and illness (Crandall et al., 1992).

Since Holmes and Rahe's pioneering work, stresses of various kinds have been tied to a wide range of diseases and physical conditions (see Figure 11–5), from trench mouth and upper respiratory infection to cancer (Cooper & Faragher, 1991; Kiecolt-Glaser et al., 1991). The greater the life stress, the greater the likelihood of illness. Researchers have even found a relationship between psychological stress and death. George Engel (1971, 1968) has concluded that *sudden death*—unexpected death in the wake of psychological trauma—is not uncommon. According to Engel, sudden death may be precipitated by either acute grief, danger, death of a loved one, threatened loss of a loved one, mourning or anniversary of mourning, loss of status or self-esteem, deliverance from danger, or a happy ending. Death during mourning or on the anniversary of mourning is seen in a particularly poignant case, "that of a 70-year-old man who died during the opening bars of a concert held to mark the fifth anniversary of his wife's death. She was a well-known piano teacher, and he had established a music conservatory in her memory. The concert was being given by conservatory pupils" (Engel, 1971).

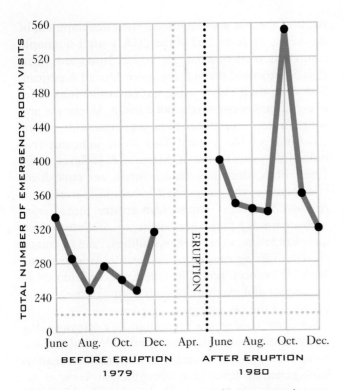

FIGURE 11-5 *A single catastrophic event may increase one's chances of developing a physical ailment. Researchers Paul and Gerald Adams (1984) found that during the months immediately following the eruption of Mount St. Helens on May 18, 1980, there was a 34 percent increase in emergency room visits and a 19 percent rise in deaths in nearby Othello, Washington.*

A striking instance of sudden death at the loss of a loved one is seen in the following case:

Charlie and Josephine had been inseparable companions for 13 years. In a senseless act of violence Charlie, in full view of Josephine, was shot and killed in a melee with the police. Josephine first stood motionless, then slowly approached his prostrate form, sunk to her knees, and silently rested her head on the dead and bloody body. Concerned persons attempted to help her away, but she refused to move. Hoping she would soon surmount her overwhelming grief, they let her be. But she never rose again; in 15 minutes she was dead. Now the remarkable part of the story is that Charlie and Josephine were llamas in the zoo! They had escaped from their pen during a snow storm and Charlie, a mean animal to begin with, was shot when he proved unmanageable. I was able to establish from the zoo keeper that to all intents and purposes Josephine had been normally frisky and healthy right up to the moment of the tragic event.

(Engel, 1968)

The stress of bereavement can be equally fatal to humans. When researchers examined the medical records of 4,486 British widowers 55 years of age or older, they discovered that 213 of these men had died during the first six months of their bereavement—a fatality rate significantly higher than usual for married men in this age range (Young, Benjamin, & Wallis, 1963). After six months the mortality rate of the widowers returned to a normal level. Another study of 903 close relatives of persons who had died in a community in Wales found that almost 5 percent of the relatives died during the first year of their bereavement (Rees & Lutkin, 1967). The widows and widowers in this group had a mortality rate of 12 percent, compared to a rate of less than 1 percent for age-matched control subjects.

PSYCHONEUROIMMUNOLOGY How is a stressful event translated into a viral or bacterial infection? Researchers have increasingly focused on our body's immune system as the key to this relationship, and have developed a new area of study called *psychoneuroimmunology* to examine the links between stress, the immune system, and health.

The body's immune system is a complex net-work of cells that helps protect people from *antigens*—foreign invaders such as bacteria and viruses, which stimulate an immune response—and from cancer cells (Jemmott, 1987). Among the most important cells in the system are billions of *lymphocytes,* white blood cells that are manufactured in the lymph system and circulate throughout the bloodstream. Upon stimulation by antigens, lymphocytes spring into action to help the body overcome the invaders.

One group of lymphocytes, called *helper T-cells,* identify antigens and then multiply and trigger the production of still other kinds of immune cells. Another group, *killer T-cells,* seek out and destroy body cells that have already been infected by viruses, thus helping to stop the spread of a viral infection. A third group of lymphocytes, *B-cells,* produce *antibodies,* or immunoglobulins, protein molecules that recognize and bind to a specific antigen, mark it for destruction, and prevent it from causing infection.

The functioning of lymphocytes and other cells of the immune system is known to be affected by such factors as age, nutrition, and body temperature (Jemmott & Locke, 1984). Researchers now suspect that stress can also interfere with the activity of lymphocytes, slowing them down and thus increasing a person's susceptibility to viral and bacterial infections (Ader, Felten, & Cohen, 1991). The notion of a link between stress and deficient functioning by the immune system has been supported by both animal and human studies.

When laboratory animals are subjected to great stress, the concentration of antibodies in their blood decreases (Vessey, 1964) and the response of antibodies to antigens diminishes (Hibma & Griffin, 1994; Solomon, 1969). Similarly, the lymphocytes of stressed animal subjects reproduce more slowly than normal and respond to and destroy antigens less effectively (Monjan & Collector, 1977; Keller et al., 1981; Joasoo & McKenzie, 1976). In one study the immunological functioning of infant monkeys was reduced for up to two months after they had been separated from their mothers for a single day (Coe et al., 1987).

Studies with humans have told a similar story (Herbert & Cohen, 1993). Scientists who monitored Skylab astronauts during various phases of their extended space mission discovered that their T-cell reactions to antigens decreased within a few hours after the stress of splashdown and returned to normal three days later (Kimzey, 1975; Kimzey et al., 1976). Similarly, the functioning of the immune systems of people who were exposed to simulated combat conditions in a laboratory for three days deteriorated significantly (Palmblad et al., 1976).

These killer T-cells surround a larger cancer cell and destroy it, thus helping to prevent the spread of cancer. Killer T-cells and other lymphocytes also help fight other illnesses by detecting and destroying bacteria and viruses throughout the body.

A relationship has also been found between ordinary life stress and poor immunologic functioning (Kiecolt-Glaser & Glaser, 1992). In a landmark study, R. W. Bartrop and his colleagues (1977) in New South Wales, Australia, compared the immune systems of twenty-six people whose spouses had died eight weeks earlier with those of twenty-six matched controls whose spouses had not died. Blood samples revealed that lymphocyte functioning was significantly lower in the bereaved subjects than in the control subjects.

These studies seem to be telling a remarkable story. The subjects have all been healthy individuals who happened to experience unusual levels of stress. During the stressful periods, they remained healthy on the surface, but their experiences were apparently slowing their immune systems so that they became susceptible to illness. If stress affects our body's capacity to fight off illness in this way, we can see why researchers have repeatedly found a relationship between life stress and medical illnesses of various kinds (see Box 11–2).

Researchers are now working to understand exactly how stress alters the immune system, and several have come to focus once again on the autonomic nervous system. As we saw earlier, stress leads to increased activity by the sympathetic nervous system. Studies suggest that this increased autonomic arousal is accompanied by the release of the neurotransmitters norepinephrine and epinephrine throughout the brain and body. Beyond supporting the activity of the sympathetic nervous system, these chemicals apparently modulate the functioning of the immune system (Felten, 1993; Bellinger et al., 1992). One study has found, for example, that epinephrine injected into volunteers brings about a temporary decrease in the number and circulation of helper T-cells (Crary et al., 1983). We now know that specific receptors for norepinephrine and epinephrine are located on the membranes of lymphocytes (Felten, 1993; Borysenko & Borysenko, 1982). When the neurotransmitters bind to these receptors, the lymphocytes apparently receive an inhibitory message to reduce their activity.

Other body chemicals, such as cortisol and endorphins, are also released by the body during times of stress and may have important effects on immunologic processes (Shavit & Martin, 1987; Borysenko & Borysenko, 1982; Millan & Emrich, 1981). It is possible that these chemicals will also prove to be important mediators in the stress-illness relationship.

Do stressful events inevitably slow the functioning of the immune system and lead to medical problems? Apparently not. It seems that various factors can influence the relationship between stress and the immune

BOX 11-2

THE PSYCHOLOGICAL EFFECTS OF HIV AND AIDS

The *human immunodeficiency virus (HIV)* is a parasite that leads to the death of its host cell. This virus infects T-4 helper lymphocytes, the cells that protect the body from disease by telling the immune system which invaders to kill (Batchelor, 1988). The lymphocytes in turn transport the killer deep into the immune system. In many cases, HIV develops into *acquired immune deficiency syndrome (AIDS)*. Most sufferers do not die of AIDS per se but instead succumb to opportunistic infections that would not survive in the body if the immune system were not disabled. The psychological suffering of both people who are HIV-positive and people with AIDS, previously overlooked, is now being addressed by researchers and health-care workers.

The progression from HIV infection to AIDS may take weeks, months, or even years (Kiecolt-Glaser & Glaser, 1988); very little is known about how and why persons who are infected with HIV develop

AIDS, whether slowly or rapidly. One thing is certain, however: an already weakened immune system is less able to defend itself against the virus. Ex-

treme stress, mental dysfunctioning, and environmental pressures can adversely affect the ability of the immune system to ward off illness. There is a deadly interplay between the effect of the disease on the mental health of the HIV sufferer and the effect of declining mental health on the patient's physical well-being.

Psychological disorders associated with HIV may be caused by factors that are either primarily organic or primarily psychological. The HIV may invade the brain, for example, causing *AIDS dementia complex (ADC)*. The virus appears to cross the blood-brain barrier by riding *macrophages*, cells whose normal job is to help fight infection (Joyce, 1988). AIDS dementia complex can result in deep lethargy, manic-depressive symptoms, and psychosis (Maj et al., 1994). More commonly, there is a general decrement in cognitive functioning—it takes longer to think or remember (Maj et al., 1994). In a vicious and fatal cycle, the patient's psychological

system, including *perceptions of control, personality and mood*, and *social support*.

PERCEPTIONS OF CONTROL AND IMMUNE SYSTEM FUNCTIONING
Researchers have found that perceptions of control may influence one's vulnerability to immune system dysfunctioning. One study examined the immune reactions of rats who were being subjected to the stress of electric shock (Maier et al., 1985). One group of rats (the control

subjects) were repeatedly shocked in their cages but could learn to turn off the shocks by turning a wheel in the cage. A second group of rats (the experimental subjects) were also shocked in their cages and could also turn a wheel in the cage, but their wheel-turning had no effect on the shocks; the shocks were delivered at random, whether the rats turned the wheel or not.

The experimenters then injected antigens into the bodies of the rats to see how their lymphocytes would

well-being diminishes, causing the immune system to weaken further. Not a great deal is known about ADC, but some researchers believe that it may affect as many as 90 percent of AIDS sufferers and that it may be one of the earliest symptoms to develop (Price et al., 1988). Unfortunately, the unfamiliarity of clinicians with ADC may interfere with its early detection. One approach to the detection of ADC has been the use of brain-imaging tools, such as the MRI and CAT scan. These techniques permit lesions and atrophy to be seen in regions of the brain associated with cognitive functioning (Broderick et al., 1993).

Although not all HIV sufferers will develop AIDS dementia complex, almost all are subjected to a more subtle but equally destructive array of environmental stressors that lead to psychological problems and weaken their ability to fight disease. Society does not provide AIDS sufferers with a supportive environment in which to wage their war. Instead it attaches considerable stigma to the disease and to the people who contract it. Surveys show that a large part of the population continues to view AIDS as a punishment being visited on a subset of the populace, primarily gay men and intravenous drug users (Herek & Glunt, 1988). The public disclosures of several famous people who contracted AIDS through means other than homosexual contact or intra-

venous drug use encouraged AIDS activists to believe that this view would change. When Magic Johnson told the world he had HIV, many people turned to him as a spokesman for improving the treatment of other sufferers; but despite his service on the Presidential Commission on AIDS and his vocal advocacy of research into a cure, this adulated athlete lost lucrative endorsement contracts and found other professional players unwilling to face him on the court for fear of contracting AIDS. Clearly, even Magic Johnson was not safe from the repercussions of the public's angst over AIDS.

Because of these attitudes, patients with AIDS may face discrimination and even harassment, along with a decline in services that most of us take for granted, such as health insurance and police protection (Tross & Hirsch, 1988). Surveys show that these attitudes continue despite experts' proclamations that incidental contact with AIDS sufferers does not lead to infection (Herek et al., 1993). Prejudice and misunderstanding continue. Moreover, major social changes face the victims of AIDS, some of whom must also contend with the loss of friends through social pressure, along with their own imminent demise. This kind of stress can lead to apathy, depression, preoccupation with the illness, anxiety-related disorders, and other such problems, all of which can directly affect the ability of the im-

mune system to fight off the disease (Fleishman & Fogel, 1994). Once again, a vicious and fatal cycle of events.

No vaccine or cure for HIV infection or AIDS is currently available, but a drug therapy effective against organic ADC may soon be developed. The experimental drug AZT, which has been found in some cases to slow the progress of AIDS, is able to cross the blood-brain barrier and may be useful in battling the HIV virus in the brain. In addition, recent studies of the drug *zidoduvine* show that it may have the ability to reduce the effects and progress of ADC (Portegies, 1993).

To fully reduce the psychologically based disorders that accompany HIV, however, we must learn to give the patient with AIDS what is available to all other sufferers of a terminal illness—compassion and hope. We can do so only by educating the public about the facts regarding AIDS. Although millions of dollars are spent to educate both youngsters and adults about AIDS (Jacobs, 1993), it is extraordinarily difficult to overcome deeply felt prejudices against people whom some perceive as different and against a disease that is mysterious and deadly. Only when they are accepted as people in need of help and understanding will patients with AIDS find themselves in an environment that may help their recovery rather than accelerate their death.

---

react. The lymphocytes of the control rats multiplied just as they would under unstressful conditions. In the experimental rats, who had had no control over being shocked, lymphocytes multiplied more slowly than usual. In short, stress per se did not cause immunologic dysfunctioning—only stress accompanied by a perceived lack of control. Correspondingly, reexaminations of the life change studies discussed earlier are beginning to reveal that uncontrollable life change is more closely linked to the onset of ill-

ness than controllable life change (Roll & Theorell, 1987).

PERSONALITY AND MOOD AND IMMUNE SYSTEM FUNCTIONING

Several theorists have proposed that people who generally respond to life stress with optimism, constructive coping strategies, and resilience may experience better immune system functioning and be better prepared to fight off illness. As we observed in Chapter 6, some researchers have

Laboratory animals are widely used in research on the immune system. The destruction of the immune systems of these mice, which has caused their hair to fall out, enables researchers to produce and investigate various invasive cells and viruses.

identified a "hardy" personality style, represented by people who welcome challenge and are willing to commit themselves and take control in their daily encounters (Maddi, 1990; Kobasa, 1990, 1987, 1979). According to studies of telephone company managers, army officers, bus drivers, printers, and lawyers, people with a hardy personality are less likely than others to become ill after stressful events (Kobasa, 1984, 1982). Salvatore Maddi has even developed a "hardiness course" designed to teach coping strategies to clients, thus increasing their hardiness and lowering their susceptibility to illness (Fischman, 1987).

In a related line of research, David McClelland and his associates have identified a personality style, the *inhibited power motive style*, that they claim contributes to immunologic dysfunctioning (McClelland, 1993, 1985). People who display this personality style are thought to have a strong need for power (the desire for prestige or influence over others) but have been taught to inhibit it (McClelland, 1993, 1985, 1979). Instead of seeking powerful positions, cultivating relationships in which they can be dominant, or expressing hostility, they satisfy their need for power in indirect ways—by serving other people or worthy causes, for example, or by upholding high principles.

People with inhibited power motives seem to be more likely than others to develop physical illnesses, particularly upper respiratory infections, in the face of academic and other power-related stresses (McClelland, 1993; Jemmott, 1987). According to McClelland, such stressors arouse the power needs of these people; the resulting intense arousal of the sympathetic nervous system increases the amounts of epinephrine and norepinephrine released, which inhibit the functioning of the immune system (McClelland, 1993, 1979).

In one study designed to test this theory, 64 dental students were examined at five points in the school year: September, November, April, June, and July (Jemmott et al., 1983). September and July were considered to be periods of low academic stress, whereas November, April, and June—months filled with work and exams—were seen as periods of high academic stress. During each of these periods the experimenters collected samples of saliva from the subjects and analyzed them for *secretory immunoglobulin A (s-IgA)* content. S-IgA is an antibody that helps defend people against upper respiratory infections: the lower the s-IgA readings, the poorer the functioning of the immune system.

As expected, the average s-IgA measures of the dental students were normal during the calm of September, dropped significantly during the stressful months of November, April, and June, and rebounded in July. In short, during periods of increased stress, the subjects' immune systems seemed less able to ward off upper respiratory infections. The investigators then looked separately at the s-IgA measures of those dental students who scored high in inhibited power motive. Their s-IgA levels tended to be low even during the relatively calm periods of September and July. That is, these students remained highly susceptible to illness over a longer period of time than those with a low power motive. Their inhibited power drive, then, may account for the relatively high rates of illness among them.

In a related study 132 college students were shown one of two 50-minute films (McClelland & Kirshnit, 1988). Half of the subjects saw a World War II documentary film with a theme of aggressive domination, designed to arouse their power needs. The other group saw a documentary on Mother Teresa, who won the Nobel Peace Prize for her selfless work among the destitute of India. Power needs increased far more among the students who saw the war film than among those who witnessed Mother Teresa's devotion to a peaceful cause. Moreover, among the subjects who viewed the war film, those with a generally higher inhibited power motive showed a greater drop in s-IgA concentrations than did students with a lower power motive.

Numerous studies have also pointed out a correlation between certain personality characteristics and the prognosis of cancer patients (Anderson et al., 1994; Schulz, 1994; Levy & Roberts, 1992). These studies found that cancer patients who displayed a helpless coping style and who could not readily express their feelings, particularly anger, had a worse prognosis than patients who did express their emotions. In fact, some investigators have proposed a *Type C personality style* that is supposedly correlated with a relatively poorer prognosis in cancer patients (Temoshok et al., 1985). Individuals with a Type C personality deny negative emotions; fail to express anger, fear, or sadness; and score high on social conformity and compliance (Locke & Colligan, 1986).

Finally, research has also linked mood to immune system functioning. In fact, some research suggests that immune functioning may be more closely related to depressed mood than to specific negative life events (Weisse, 1992). People who experience a depressed mood, even if they are not clinically depressed, tend to have poorer immune system functioning (Perkins et al., 1991). Similarly, a strong correlation has been found between depressive disorders and immune system suppression (Perkins et al., 1991; Schleifer & Keller, 1991). Recent research has further indicated that depression does not necessarily cause poorer immune system functioning, but rather that poor immune functioning and its resultant viral infections may help cause depressive disorders (Amsterdam & Hernz, 1993).

SOCIAL SUPPORT AND IMMUNE SYSTEM FUNCTIONING   Numerous studies have found that people who have few social supports and feel lonely have poorer immune functioning in the face of stress than people who do not feel lonely. In one such study, medical students were given the UCLA Loneliness Scale and then divided into "high" and "low" loneliness groups (Kiecolt-Glaser et al., 1984). The high-loneliness group showed lower lymphocyte responses during a final exam period. Similarly, a study of heart disease patients found that those who did not have anyone to talk to were three times more likely to die than those who did (Turkington, 1992; Williams et al., 1992).

Other studies have found that social support and affiliation help protect both humans and animals from stress, poor immune system functioning, and subsequent medical illness (Levy & Roberts, 1992; Cohen et al., 1992; Kiecolt-Glaser et al., 1991). In one study, hepatitis B vaccine inoculations were administered to forty-eight medical students on the last day of a three-day examination period (Glaser et al., 1992). The students who reported the greatest amount of social support had stronger immune responses to the hepatitis B vaccine. Similarly, some studies have suggested that patients with certain forms of cancer who receive social support in their personal lives or supportive therapy often have a better prognosis than patients without such supports (Levy & Roberts, 1992; Spiegel et al., 1989).

How does social support come to alter immune system functioning? One possibility is that it influences the net amount of life stress one experiences. Divorced women who reported greater social support, for example, were found to experience fewer stressors than divorced women who reported less social support (Garvin et al., 1993).

The work of psychoneuroimmunologists suggests once again that the study of abnormal psychology must extend to behavior and illnesses that once seemed far removed from the clinical domain. Just as abnormal physical functioning may contribute to abnormal mental functioning, mental dysfunctioning may lead to physical problems of various kinds. Again we are reminded that the brain is part of the body, and that the two are inextricably linked for better and for worse. At the same time, even an enlightened perspective such as this can be overstated and can lead to new misunderstandings about illness and causation, as we are reminded in Box 11–3.

PSYCHOLOGICAL TREATMENTS FOR PSYCHOPHYSIOLOGICAL DISORDERS

As clinicians have become more aware that psychological factors often contribute to physical disorders, they have increasingly used psychological interventions to help treat such disorders (Lehrer et al., 1993). The most common of these interventions have been *relaxation training, biofeedback training, meditation, hypnosis, cognitive interventions,* and *insight therapy.* Initially these approaches were applied only to the traditional psychophysiological disorders, but today they are used for the fullest range of medical difficulties. The field of treatment that combines psychological and physical interventions to treat or prevent medical problems is known as *behavioral medicine* (Blanchard, 1994).

RELAXATION TRAINING   As we saw in Chapter 5, people can be taught to relax their muscles at will, a process that also reduces feelings of anxiety, largely by reducing activity in the sympathetic nervous system. Given the effects of relaxation on the nervous system, clinicians believe that *relaxation training* can be of particular help in preventing or treating

BOX 11-3

PSYCHOLOGICAL FACTORS IN PHYSICAL ILLNESS: HAS THE PENDULUM SWUNG TOO FAR?

Benjamin Blech

(This essay originally appeared in Newsweek, *September 19, 1988.)*

It started with a terrible backache. That's when I realized how pervasive the new-age mentality has become. When I read that Shirley MacLaine, its leading practitioner, had convinced her devotees that people create their own reality—"You are God," she said—I assumed she meant nothing more by it than inspirational motivation. After all, isn't that what parents and preachers have been saying all along? Do your best. Aim high. Onward and upward. Every day in every way. . . . Be like the little engine that said it could.

Then I discovered the flip side of MacLaine's argument: if I'm sick, it must be my fault. If my life is a mess, I've failed to fulfill my potential. Real life isn't always perfect. Extrapolate from that to such realities as poverty and pestilence and you have what I view as a contemporary madness: for every misfortune in life, we seem too ready to blame the victim.

But first let me tell you what happened when my back went bad. Remember when sciatica could elicit at least a murmur of sympathy? Well, not anymore. Friends are now Freudians; everyone is "into" psychology. And when I shared the news that I have a herniated disc, all-knowing laymen looked at me and repeatedly asked: "Why are you letting stress get to you that much? Why are you doing this to yourself?"

Believe it or not, wear and tear, age and time, can actually cause damage to bodily parts and functions. Yet in these psychologically sophisticated times, the insight that illness is affected by the mind has so overwhelmed us that we often forget that it is also physical.

Some years ago Norman Cousins caused a considerable stir in medical circles when he attributed his recovery from a critical arthritic illness to extended exposure to humor. His conclusion deserved widespread circulation. Laughter is good medicine. Feelings can foster health. Attitude may mean the difference between life and death. But—and here is the crucial cautionary that's often lost in the upbeat literature of our day—disease is still a cruel killer. Cancer victims

---

illnesses that are related to stress and heightened autonomic functioning (Schneiderman & Baum, 1992).

Relaxation training has been extensively used in the treatment of essential hypertension (Lehrer et al., 1993; Johnston, 1992; Agras, 1984, 1974). One study assigned hypertensive subjects to one of three forms of treatment: medication, medication plus relaxation training, or medication plus supportive psychotherapy (Taylor et al., 1977). Only those who received relaxation training in combination with medication showed a significant reduction in blood pressure. Still other studies have indicated that the positive effect of relaxation training on patients with hypertension persists for a year or more (Johnston, 1992; Agras et al., 1980). Relaxation training has also been of some help in treating headaches, insomnia, asthma, the undesired effects of cancer treatments, and Raynaud's disease, a disorder of the vascular system characterized by throbbing, aching, and pain (Bernstein & Carlson, 1993; Lehrer et al., 1993).

BIOFEEDBACK TRAINING Patients given *biofeedback training* are connected to machinery that gives them continuous data about their involuntary body activities. This information enables them gradually to gain control over those activities. Moderately helpful in the treatment of anxiety disorders, the procedure has also been applied to a growing number of physical disorders.

Electromyograph (EMG) feedback was used to treat sixteen patients who were experiencing facial pain caused in part by tension in their jaw muscles (Dohrmann & Laskin, 1978). In an EMG procedure electrodes are attached to a client's muscles so that the electrical activity that accompanies muscular contractions may be detected (see pp. 248–249). The

who truly want to live do nevertheless die. Wishing doesn't necessarily alter dreadful conditions. Yet those who suffer with courage are now stigmatized for failing to recover—even viewed as if they were committing suicide.

I cannot forget the pain of my best friend in the weeks before he died. Sam faced his imminent demise with dignity. He was able to bear almost everything but he could not forgive himself for his illness. He had been led to believe by the apostles of new ageism, friends who embraced this cultural perspective, that he had failed. Failed, because if he had really wanted to, the purveyors of these Mary Poppins–style miracles assured him, he would certainly recover. Failed because if he would only try a bit harder he would rid himself of the poisons that were destroying his body. Failed because as a husband and father, his will to live should have overpowered and overcome everything.

Hope is a wonderful tonic, but I fear that these days exhortation has overcome compassion. The result is a kind of indifference and unwillingness to face the fact that some misfortunes will always persist, in spite of our best efforts:

People can be poor not because they didn't try hard enough to pull themselves out of their ghettos but because society really stacked the deck against them so that they literally didn't have a chance.

People can be uneducated because the teachers were not there, because the help which should have been given was not offered, because the "system" failed to work.

People can require welfare and food stamps because, in the words of President Kennedy, life is not fair and there are times when tragedy strikes uninvited and unexpected, even unavoidably.

People can be hungry not because they don't want to work but because the world turns its back on those with unproductive skills and then calls them parasites.

People can even be sick and really need a medical doctor, not a holistic health healer.

Carlyle was of course quite correct when he said, "The greatest of faults is to be conscious of none." Self-awareness demands recognition of personal failings. But it seems we have allowed the pendulum to swing too far. From the blind extreme of "It's al-

ways their fault" to the delusionary and self-destructive "It's always my fault," we have veered from truth in equal measure.

Ironically, our obsession with self-incrimination is a product of those very movements which promised peace of mind through an emphasis on personal accountability. Of course in the spirit of est we must "take responsibility for our lives." But must we take as our identities the scripts that all too often are simply handed us?

If I slip on a banana peel that somebody else carelessly left on the ground, I can curse my bad luck and get on with my life. But if I drop the peel myself and was stupid enough to slip on it too, then I will never forgive myself.

Perhaps the time has come for us to call an amnesty in the war on ourselves. No matter what the comic-strip character Pogo may have said, there are times when we have met the enemy—and it isn't us.

When I was a small boy, I loved the story of the little engine that kept telling itself it could and it did. Growing up has taught me that there are times when it can't and maturity demands awareness not only of our abilities, but also of our limits.

---

machine then amplifies the bioelectrical potentials and converts them into an audible tone. Changes in the pitch and volume of the tone indicate changes in muscle tension. After "listening" to EMG feedback repeatedly, the subjects learned how to relax their jaw muscles at will and later reported a decrease in facial pain. As a control for this experiment, eight other subjects with the same condition were wired to similar equipment and told that a low-grade electrical current was passing through the affected muscles. These subjects showed little improvement in muscle tension or pain.

EMG feedback has also been used successfully in the treatment of tension headaches and muscular disabilities caused by strokes or accidents (Blanchard, 1994; Phillips, 1991). Other forms of biofeedback have been moderately helpful in the treatment of heart arrhythmia, asthma, migraine headaches,

high blood pressure, stuttering, pain from burns, and Raynaud's disease (Lehrer et al., 1993; Phillips, 1991; Kotses et al., 1991; Webster, 1991).

MEDITATION Although meditation has been practiced since ancient times, health-care professionals have only recently become aware of its effectiveness in relieving many forms of physical distress (Carrington, 1993). *Meditation* is a technique of turning one's concentration inward, achieving a slightly altered state of consciousness, and temporarily ignoring all stressors. In the most common approach, meditators go to a quiet place, assume a comfortable posture, utter or think a particular sound (called a *mantra*) to help focus their attention, and allow their minds to turn away from all ordinary thoughts and concerns (Carrington, 1993, 1978). One of numerous other forms of meditation involves simply concentrating on

Clinicians are always developing new methods and tools to help people relax. A climber dangles from Alaska's Mount Barrile to demonstrate the use of "Tranquilite" sleep goggles, which are supposed to induce relaxation with blue light and a soothing "pink sound."

one's breath as it flows in and out (Kabat-Zinn, 1993). Meditation is typically practiced in private for approximately 15 minutes twice a day. Many people who follow a regular schedule of meditation report feeling more peaceful, engaged, and creative; interacting more effectively with other people; and enjoying life more (Carrington, 1993, 1978; Schneider et al., 1992).

Meditation has been used to help manage pain in cancer patients (Goleman & Gurin, 1993) and to help treat hypertension, cardiovascular problems, asthma, psoriasis, diabetes, and even viral infections (Carrington, 1993, 1978; Shapiro, 1982; Murray, 1982). It has also been useful in relieving the stress-related problem of insomnia (see Box 11–4). In one study, people who had suffered from some degree of sleeplessness for fourteen years were given four training sessions in meditation (Woolfolk et al., 1976). Thereafter they were able to fall asleep twice as quickly as before and felt more comfortable while doing so. Sub-

jects trained in relaxation showed similar gains, whereas control subjects showed virtually no improvement. These differences were still apparent when the subjects were assessed again six months later.

HYPNOSIS As we observed in Chapter 1, subjects who undergo *hypnosis* are guided by a hypnotist into a sleeplike, suggestible state during which they can be directed to act in unusual ways, to experience unusual sensations, to remember seemingly forgotten events, or to forget remembered events. With training some people are able to induce their own hypnotic state *(self-hypnosis)*. Originally developed in the eighteenth century by Friedrich Mesmer as a treatment for hysterical ailments, hypnosis is now used to supplement psychotherapy, to help conduct research, and to help treat many physical conditions (Barber, 1993, 1984).

Hypnosis is effectively used to control pain during surgical procedures (Evans & Stanley, 1991; Wadden & Anderton, 1982). Patients appear less likely to have medical complications in response to this procedure than to local or general anesthesia. One patient was reported to have undergone dental implant surgery under hypnotic suggestion (Gheorghiu & Orleanu, 1982): after a hypnotic state was induced, the dentist suggested to the patient that he was in a pleasant and relaxed setting listening to a friend describe his own success at undergoing similar dental surgery under hypnosis. The dentist then proceeded to perform a successful 25-minute operation.

Although only some people are able to undergo surgery when hypnotic procedures alone are used to control pain, hypnosis combined with chemical anesthesia is apparently beneficial to many patients (Wadden & Anderton, 1982). Given its effectiveness in reducing pain, hypnosis is also used frequently in the treatment of pain disorders (Spiegal, 1992). Hypnotic procedures have also been successfully applied to combat such problems as skin diseases, asthma, insomnia, hypertension, warts, and other forms of infection (Barber, 1993; Agras, 1984).

Some researchers even propose that hypnosis can help prevent bacterial and viral infections. Howard Hall and his colleagues (1987) hypnotized twenty healthy adult subjects, instructing them to visualize their lymphocytes as powerful sharks attacking weak germs in their blood. The subjects were to practice this imagery while hypnotizing themselves twice a day for a week. Blood tests taken before the initial hypnosis, an hour after it, and a week later indicated that the number of lymphocytes in the subjects— particularly the younger adults—actually rose, thus increasing the capacity of these subjects to fight off illness.

COGNITIVE INTERVENTIONS People with physical ailments have sometimes been taught new attitudes, or cognitive responses, toward their ailments as part of treatment. In particular, *self-instruction training,* also known as *stress inoculation training,* has helped patients to cope with chronic and severe pain reactions and disorders, including pain from burns, arthritis, surgical procedures, headaches, ulcers, multiple sclerosis, and cancer treatment (Meichenbaum, 1993, 1986, 1977, 1975). As we saw in Chapter 7, stress inoculation therapists systematically teach clients to rid themselves of private negative statements ("Oh, no, I can't take this pain") and to replace them with private coping statements ("When pain comes, just pause; keep focusing on what you have to do").

Researchers gave stress inoculation training to eight burn victims over the course of five days, while eight other burn victims (control subjects) received only the routine services provided to burn patients, such as psychiatric consultation, instructions in coping strategies, and pain medication (Wernick, 1983). The stress inoculation subjects were taught to employ private coping statements whenever they experienced pain. The burn patients who received stress inoculation

training made significantly fewer requests for pain medication, while the requests of the control patients actually doubled over the course of the study. In addition, the stress inoculation subjects later complied with other aspects of their treatment better than the control subjects did.

INSIGHT THERAPY If stress and anxiety often contribute to physical problems, insight psychotherapy designed to reduce general levels of anxiety should help alleviate them (House et al., 1988; Varis, 1987). Thus, physicians often recommend insight psychotherapy to patients as an adjunct to medical treatment. Some recent research suggests that the discussion of past traumas may indeed have beneficial effects on one's health (Lutgendorf et al., 1994; Francis & Pennebaker, 1992; Pennebaker, 1990). Moreover, a few studies have indicated that asthmatic children who receive individual or family therapy often adjust better to their life situations, experience less panic during asthma attacks, have fewer and milder attacks, and miss fewer days of school (Alexander, 1981). Beyond this small group of studies, however, the effectiveness of insight therapy in the medical domain has not been investigated systematically (Agras, 1984).

COMBINATION APPROACHES A number of studies have found that the various psychological interventions for physical problems often are equal in effectiveness (Lehrer et al., 1993; Agras, 1984). Relaxation and biofeedback training, for example, are equally helpful (and more helpful than placebos) in the treatment of hypertension, tension headaches, migraine headaches, asthma, and Raynaud's disease.

Psychological interventions are often of greatest help when they are combined both with other such treatments and with medical treatment (Lehrer et al., 1993; Lazarus, 1990; Maddi, 1990). Nine ulcer patients who were given relaxation, stress inoculation, and assertiveness training along with medical interventions were found to be less anxious, to complain less often about pain, to experience fewer days of symptoms, and to use fewer antacids than a group of eight ulcer subjects who received medication only (Brooks & Richardson, 1980). Furthermore, a follow-up check 42 months later revealed that five of the medication-only subjects had either required surgery or developed a recurring ulcer problem, whereas only one of the combination-treated subjects had done so.

Combination interventions have also been helpful in changing Type A behavior patterns and in reducing the risk of coronary heart disease among Type A people (Johnston, 1992; Roskies et al., 1986). In one

"Dr. Birnes believes in the holistic approach."

BOX 11-4

SLEEP AND SLEEP DISORDERS

Sleep is crucial to health and well-being. Without it people behave oddly and have strange experiences. Studies have found that sleep deprivation for 100 hours or more leads to hallucinations, paranoia, and bizarre behavior. When people who have gone without sleep attempt simple tasks, they find that their cognitive and motor functioning have deteriorated. Surprisingly, though, they can sometimes perform tasks demanding high concentration and skill with great dexterity.

Physiological recordings indicate that when people remain awake for over 200 hours they frequently experience periods of "microsleep" lasting two to three seconds. It appears that the body refuses to be entirely deprived of sleep for extended periods. The odd effects of sleep deprivation are completely eliminated once a person is allowed a period of recovery sleep.

To study these phenomena, researchers bring people into the laboratory and record their activities as they sleep. Three types of recording devices are used simultaneously, the *electroencephalograph (EEG)*, which records electrical activity in the brain; the *electrooculograph,* which records the movement of the eyes; and the *electromyograph (EMG),* which measures muscle tension and activity.

One of the most important discoveries of sleep research is that a person's eyes move rapidly during certain periods of the night (Aserinsky & Kleitman, 1953). This *rapid eye movement (REM)* occurs during approximately 25 percent of the time a person is asleep. The rest of the time, eye movements are either slow and regular or nonexistent.

Research on eye movement and brain activity has helped delineate five identifiable stages during the normal sleep cycle, though stages 1 through 4 are generally referred to as non-REM (NREM) to distinguish them from the unique activity of REM sleep (stage 5). As we cycle through the five stages of sleep several times over the course of a night, we typically experience four to six periods of REM sleep. REM sleep is often called "paradoxical sleep" because it resembles both deep sleep and wakefulness. Although there are small movements and muscle twitches during REM, the body is immobilized—essentially paralyzed. At the same time, the eyes are moving back and forth at a high rate. Blood flow to the brain increases and the EEG shows brain wave activity that is almost identical to that of a waking and alert person. Eighty percent of the subjects who are awakened from REM sleep and asked about their experiences report that they were dreaming.

When we are deprived of enough sleep or if the normal sleep cycle is disrupted, we suffer. DSM-IV distinguishes the *dyssomnias,* sleep disorders involving disturbances in the amount, quality, or timing of sleep, from the *parasomnias,* disorders involving abnormal events that occur during sleep (APA, 1994). Some sleep disorders occur independent of other psychological or medical disorders; others occur in conjunction with a mental or medical disorder, either as a result of the disorder itself or as an effect of drugs used to treat it.

■ DYSSOMNIAS ■

Insomnia, a disorder of initiating and maintaining sleep, is the most common dyssomnia. Over the course of each year between 30 and 40 percent of all adults experience difficulty falling and staying asleep, but only some of them qualify for a diagnosis of *primary insomnia,* in which this problem is their predominant complaint, lasts at least one month, and causes significant distress or impairment (APA, 1994). Chronic insomniacs are subject to periods of sleepiness or microsleep during the day, and their ability to function is often impaired.

The causes of insomnia fall into five general categories:

1. *Biological factors.* Some researchers suggest that a biological predisposition to be a very light sleeper or to have an overactive arousal system may interfere with sleep (Hobson, 1986). In addition, some medical disorders can contribute to insomnia.

2. *Psychological disorders.* Many mental disorders, including depression and schizophrenia, are accompanied by difficulties in initiating and maintaining sleep.

3. *Lifestyle.* Sleeping late on weekends, sleeping in a room that is too hot or too cold, exercising just before going to sleep, ingesting too much caffeine, and other such habits may cause insomnia.

4. *Efforts to fall asleep.* People who experience difficulty in falling asleep may try virtually anything to do so. They may develop ritualistic behavior that they believe will help them to overcome their insomnia. Unfortunately, that behavior may actually become a stimulus for not sleeping. Preparing for bed, thinking about sleeping, even counting sheep may condition the person to stay awake.

5. *Substance misuse.* Many people believe that alcohol and other drugs will help them fall asleep; however, sleeping pills and alcohol often have the opposite effect, leading to shallow sleep and abnormal REM periods.

The treatments for insomnia are as varied as the causes. The most effective treatments address the factors described above.

A less common group of dyssomnias are disorders in which sleep or sleepiness are excessive or out of control. These include primary hypersomnia, narcolepsy, breathing-related sleep disorder, and circadian rhythm sleep disorder.

The predominant problem of the person with *primary hypersomnia* is excessive sleepiness for at least a month. The disorder may take the form of prolonged sleep episodes or daytime sleep episodes that occur almost daily (APA, 1994).

Narcolepsy, a disorder characterized by more than three months of irresistible attacks of REM sleep during waking hours, afflicts more than 200,000 people in the United States. The person's REM sleep is often brought on by strong emotion. Sufferers may find themselves suddenly experiencing REM sleep in the midst of an argument or during an exciting part of a football game. Treatment often includes amphetamine-like drugs.

Breathing-related sleep disorder is a dyssomnia in which sleep is frequently disrupted by a breathing disorder, causing excessive sleepiness or insomnia. The person with *sleep apnea,* the most common breathing disorder to cause this problem, found among 1 to 10 percent of the adult population (APA, 1994), actually stops breathing for up to 30 or more seconds while asleep. Sleep apnea is found predominantly in overweight men and is accompanied by heavy snoring. Hundreds of episodes may occur each night. During an episode, the trachea is partially or fully blocked and the diaphragm is unable to propel air out of the lungs, causing the heartbeat to slow and the brain to be deprived of oxygen. At the end of an episode, the person awakens very briefly and begins to breathe normally. Sufferers are often unaware of their disorder, but many report the extreme sleepiness during the day that characterizes breathing-related sleep disorders.

People with *circadian rhythm sleep disorder* experience excessive sleepiness or insomnia as a result of persistent or recurrent sleep disruptions brought about by a mismatch between the predominating sleep-wake schedule in their environment and their own circadian sleep-wake pattern. This dyssomnia may appear as a persistent pattern of falling asleep late and awakening late, a pattern of jet lag after repeated travel, or a pattern induced by night-shift work or frequent changes in work shifts.

■ PARASOMNIAS ■

Nightmare disorder is the most common of the parasomnias. Periodically during REM sleep, most people experience nightmares, or distressful, frightening dreams that awaken them, but their nightmares are usually infrequent and short-lived and do not affect normal functioning. In some cases, chronic nightmares persist and cause great distress and must be treated with psychotherapy or mild drug therapy. Such nightmares often increase when the people are under stress.

Persons with *sleep terror disorder* awaken suddenly during the first third of their major sleep episode, screaming out in extreme fear and agitation. They are in a state of panic, are often incoherent, and have a heart rate to match. Generally the sufferer does not remember the episode the next morning. Sleep terrors most often appear in children between ages 4 and 12 years, and disappear on their own during adolescence. Approximately 1 to 6 percent of children experience them at some time (APA, 1994).

People with a *sleepwalking disorder* repeatedly leave their beds and walk around, without being conscious of the episode or remembering it later. The episodes occur in the first third of the night, and generally consist of sitting up, getting out of bed, and walking around, apparently with a specific purpose in mind. People who are awakened while sleepwalking are confused for several moments. If allowed to continue sleepwalking, they eventually return to bed. Most people who sleepwalk manage to avoid obstacles, climb stairs, and perform complex activities, always in a seemingly emotionless and unresponsive state. Accidents do occur, however: tripping, bumping into objects, and even falling out of windows have all been reported. Approximately 1 to 5 percent of all children have this disorder at some time. As many as 30 percent of children have isolated episodes. The causes of sleepwalking are unknown, and it generally disappears by age 15 (APA, 1994).

Sleep and sleep disorders have caught the public interest in the last decade, and sleep research laboratories are now found in many major cities. Because sleep is so crucial in our lives, it is important to understand its underlying mechanisms. The results of sleep studies have implications not only for the treatment of sleep disorders and related psychological problems but for every human activity and endeavor.

study, 862 patients who had suffered a heart attack within the previous six months were assigned to one of two groups (Friedman et al., 1984). The control group was given three years of cardiological counseling regarding diet, exercise, and relevant medical and surgical information. The experimental group received the same counseling plus Type A behavioral counseling over the same period of time. They were taught to identify manifestations of their Type A personalities and to recognize their excessive physiological, cognitive, and behavioral responses in stressful situations. They were also trained in relaxation and taught to change counterproductive attitudes (for example, the belief that their achievement was a measure of their worth).

The researchers found that the addition of the Type A behavioral counseling package led to major differences in lifestyle and health. Type A behavior was reduced in 79 percent of the patients who received both Type A counseling and cardiological counseling for three years, compared to 50 percent of those who received cardiological counseling only. Moreover, fewer of those who received the combined counseling suffered another heart attack—only 7 percent, compared to 13 percent of the subjects who had received cardiological counseling only (see Figure 11–6).

The treatment picture for physical illnesses has been changing. Medical interventions continue to predominate, but the use of psychological techniques as adjuncts is clearly on the rise. Psychological interventions already play a major role in the treatment of some physical problems such as chronic and debilitating pain (Keefe et al., 1992; Guck et al., 1985) and are being applied increasingly to other medical ailments. Clearly, today's scientists and practitioners are traveling a course far removed from the path of mind-body dualism that once dominated medical thinking.

THE STATE OF THE FIELD

PSYCHOLOGICAL FACTORS AND PHYSICAL DISORDERS

In recent years few subjects have wooed the attention of psychologists and clinical researchers more persuasively than the role of psychological processes in physical disorders. Once considered to be outside the field of abnormal psychology, these disorders are being seen increasingly as problems that fall squarely within its boundaries. Indeed, clinicians now believe that such psychological factors as internal conflicts and reactions to stress can contribute in some degree to the onset of virtually all physical ailments.

The number of studies devoted to the relationship between psychological dysfunction and physical illness has increased steadily during the past thirty years, and our knowledge of this topic has grown substantially. What researchers once saw as a vague tie between stress and physical illness is now understood more precisely as a complicated set of interrelationships involving such factors as idiosyncratic psychological reactions to stress, dysfunction of the autonomic nervous system, activation of neurotransmitters, and suppression of the immune system.

Similarly, insights into treatment techniques have been accumulating rapidly in this area. Psychological approaches such as relaxation training and cognitive therapy are being applied increasingly in cases of physical impairment, usually in combination with traditional medical interventions. Although such approaches have yielded only modest results so far, clinicians are becoming convinced that psychological interventions will eventually play important roles in the treatment of many physical ailments.

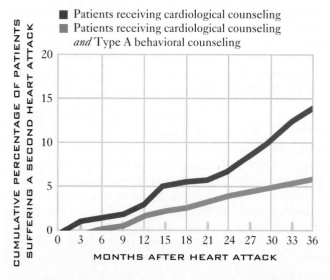

FIGURE 11–6 *Heart attack survivors who received behavioral counseling aimed at reducing their Type A behaviors experienced fewer repeat heart attacks during the 36 months after their attack than did survivors who received only standard medical counseling. (Adapted from Friedman et al., 1984.)*

The accumulating insights and applications in this area are exciting less for their acknowledgment of psychological factors as causes of physical illness than for their emphasis on the interrelationship of the brain and the rest of the body. We have observed repeatedly that mental disorders are best understood and treated when both psychological and biological factors are taken into consideration. We now know that medical problems are also best explained by a focus on the way these factors interact.

Summary

■ **Today's clinicians** recognize that somatic, or bodily, illnesses can have psychological causes. This idea received little support before the twentieth century, when medical theory was dominated by *mind-body dualism,* or the belief that the mind and body were totally separate entities. More recently, research has shown that many physical illnesses are *psychogenic*—affected and perhaps even caused by psychological processes.

■ **Patients with factitious disorders** feign physical (or psychological) disorders in order to assume the role of a person with an illness. People with *Munchausen syndrome,* the chronic form of factitious disorder, travel from hospital to hospital reciting a litany of imaginary ailments and receiving treatment.

■ **Patients with a somatoform disorder** have physical complaints whose causes are exclusively psychological. Unlike people with factitious disorders, these sufferers believe that their illnesses are organic.

Hysterical somatoform disorders involve the actual loss or alteration of physical functioning and are often difficult to distinguish from problems with an organic base. They include *conversion disorder, somatization disorder* (or *Briquet's syndrome*), and *pain disorder.*

People with *preoccupation somatoform disorders* are preoccupied with the notion that something is wrong with them physically. In this category are *hypochondriasis,* which is characterized by unrealistic and fearful misinterpretations of bodily symptoms as signs of serious somatic diseases; and *body dysmorphic disorder,* characterized by intense concern that some aspect of one's physical appearance is defective.

Theorists explain preoccupation somatoform disorders much as they do specific phobias or panic disorders. Hysterical somatoform disorders, however, are viewed as unique disorders that are still poorly understood. None of the prevailing views has received much support from research.

Therapy for preoccupation somatoform disorders usually includes the kinds of treatments applied to phobic and obsessive-compulsive disorders, particularly exposure and response-prevention interventions. Interventions for hysterical somatoform disorders stress either insight, suggestion, reinforcement, or confrontation.

■ **A third class** of psychogenic disorders consists of the *psychophysiological disorders,* in which psychological and physiological factors interact. DSM-IV uses the label *psychological factors affecting medical condition* to describe illnesses in which psychological factors are *clearly* related to the patient's physical condition.

Traditional psychophysiological disorders include *ulcers, asthma, chronic headaches, hypertension,* and *coronary heart disease.* Researchers have found a clear relationship between these physical disorders and such psychological factors as stress. This link has been explained by the *disregulation model,* which proposes that our brain and body ordinarily establish *negative feedback loops* that guarantee a smooth, self-regulating operation of the body. When the feedback system fails to regulate itself properly, psychophysiological problems may result.

■ **Recently** several "new" psychophysiological disorders have been identified. Viral and bacterial infections and yet other health problems have been linked to high levels of stress. Scientists view the body's *immune system* as a key to these relationships and have developed a new area of study called *psychoneuroimmunology.*

The body's *immune system* consists of *lymphocytes* and other cells which fight off *antigens*—bacteria, viruses, and other foreign invaders. Stress can interfere with lymphocyte activity, thereby interfering with the immune system's ability to protect against illness during times of stress. Other factors that seem to affect immune functioning include perception of control (the belief that one can control one's environment), personality and mood, and social support.

Behavioral medicine, the most common treatment approach for psychophysiological disorders, combines psychological and physical interventions. Individual interventions include relaxation training, biofeedback training, meditation, hypnosis, cognitive interventions, and insight therapy.

Topic Overview

EATING DISORDERS

ECAUSE CONTEMPORARY WESTERN society equates thinness with health and beauty, most of us are as preoccupied with the quantity of the food we eat as we are with its taste and nutritional value. One need only count the articles about dieting in magazines and newspapers to be convinced that thinness has become a national obsession (see Figure 12–1). Perhaps it is not coincidental that during the past two decades we have also witnessed an increase in two dramatic eating disorders at whose core is a morbid fear of gaining weight. Victims of **anorexia nervosa** relentlessly pursue extreme thinness and lose so much weight that they may starve themselves to death. The term "anorexia," which means "lack of appetite," is actually a misnomer; sufferers usually continue to have strong feelings of hunger (Garfinkel & Garner, 1982; Crisp, 1980). People with **bulimia nervosa** go on frequent eating binges during which they uncontrollably consume large quantities of food, then force themselves to vomit or take other strong steps to keep from gaining weight.

LATELY, THE NEWS MEDIA have published so many reports about these disorders that we may safely assume the public finds them interesting. Certainly one reason for this surge in public interest is the frightening medical consequences that can result from anorexic or bulimic behavior. The death in 1982 of Karen Carpenter, the popular singer and entertainer, from medical problems relating to anorexia nervosa serves as a reminder.

ANOTHER WIDESPREAD CONCERN about these disorders is their disproportionate prevalence among adolescent girls and young women. Because we think of adolescence as a time of growing independence and transformation, it is particularly painful to witness young women endangering their development by engaging in bizarre eating habits. It is especially difficult for their families. One mother of an anorexic teenager put it this way: "You

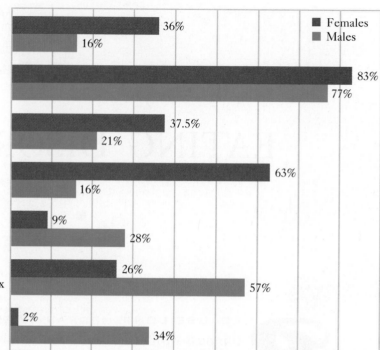

Pay attention to the calories of every meal — Females 36%, Males 16%

Underweight people who like their appearance — Females 83%, Males 77%

Adults trying to lose weight — Females 37.5%, Males 21%

Adolescents trying to lose weight — Females 63%, Males 16%

Adolescents trying to gain weight — Females 9%, Males 28%

Users of the "personals" who look for "very attractive" persons of the opposite sex — Females 26%, Males 57%

Users of the "personals" who look for "thin" persons of the opposite sex — Females 2%, Males 34%

FIGURE 12–1 *Surveys reveal that females and males in our society are held, both by themselves and by members of the opposite sex, to very different standards of appearance and worth. Small wonder that the average American woman wants to lose eleven pounds whereas the average American man wants to lose only one. (Adapted from Weiss, 1991; Calorie Control Council national survey, 1991; Smith et al., 1990; Britton, 1988; Rosen & Gross, 1987; Cash et al., 1986.)*

watch your child deliberately hurting herself, and obviously suffering, and yet you are unable to help her. Another tragedy is that it affects the whole family, for we live in an atmosphere of constant fear and tension" (Bruch, 1978, p. 1).

Up until the past decade, anorexia nervosa and bulimia nervosa were viewed as distinct disorders that had different characteristics and causes and required different forms of treatment. Today, however, clinicians and researchers have come to understand that often the similarities between the two disorders are as important as the differences between them (APA, 1994). Indeed, as we shall see, many people with anorexia nervosa display binge behaviors even as they persist in losing dangerous amounts of weight; moreover, some anorexic victims later develop bulimia nervosa, and vice versa (Sharp & Freeman, 1993).

■ ANOREXIA ■
NERVOSA

Janet Caldwell, 14 years old and in the eighth grade, displays many characteristic symptoms of anorexia nervosa, according to the DSM-IV classification:

1. Refusal to maintain body weight at or above minimally normal weight for age and height; for example, weight loss leading to body weight less than 85 percent of that expected, or failure to make expected weight gain during period of growth, leading to body weight less than 85 percent of that expected.
2. Intense fear of gaining weight or becoming fat, even though underweight.
3. Disturbance in the way in which one's body weight or shape is experienced; undue influence of body weight or shape on self-evaluation, or denial of the seriousness of the current low body weight.
4. In post-menarcheal females [females who have begun to menstruate], amenorrhea, the absence of at least three consecutive menstrual cycles.

*J*anet Caldwell was . . . five feet, two inches tall and weighed 62 pounds. . . . Janet began dieting at the age of 12 when she weighed 115 pounds and was chided by her family and friends for being "pudgy." She continued to restrict her food intake over a two-year period, and as she grew thinner, her parents became increasingly more concerned about her eating behavior. . . .

Janet was the middle child in a family of three children. . . . Her older sister was 17 and a senior in high

Perhaps the most publicized victim of anorexia nervosa during the past decade was Karen Carpenter, the young singer who developed this disorder at the height of her career and died of related medical problems.

school, and her brother was 12. Her parents were of Protestant, middle-class background, and the family attended church regularly. . . .

Janet . . . felt that her weight problem began at the time of puberty. She said that her family and friends had supported her efforts to achieve a ten-pound weight loss when she first began dieting at age 12. Janet did not go on any special kind of diet. Instead, she restricted her food intake at meals, generally cut down on carbohydrates and protein intake, tended to eat a lot of salads, and completely stopped snacking between meals. At first, she was quite pleased with her progressive weight reduction, and she was able to ignore her feelings of hunger by remembering the weight loss goal she had set for herself. However, each time she lost the number of pounds she had set for her goal she decided to lose just a few more pounds. Therefore she continued to set new weight goals for herself. In this manner, her weight dropped from 115 pounds to 88 pounds during the first year of her weight loss regimen.

Janet felt that, in her second year of dieting, her weight loss had continued beyond her control. Her menstrual periods had stopped shortly after she began dieting, and this cessation coincided with the point at which she began to lose weight quite rapidly. However, since her menses had occurred on only two or three occasions, she was not concerned about the cessation of her periods until the past year when her weight loss and change in appearance had become quite noticeable. . . . She became convinced that there was something inside of her that would not let her gain weight. . . . Janet commented that although there had been occasions over the past few years when she had been fairly "down" or unhappy, she still felt driven to keep on dieting. As a result, she frequently went for walks, ran errands for her family, and spent a great deal of time cleaning her room and keeping it in a meticulously neat and unaltered arrangement.

When Janet's weight loss continued beyond the first year, her parents insisted that she see their family physician, and Mrs. Caldwell accompanied Janet to her appointment. Their family practitioner was quite alarmed at Janet's appearance and prescribed a high-calorie diet. Janet said that her mother spent a great deal of time pleading with her to eat, and Mrs. Caldwell planned various types of meals that she thought would be appealing to Janet. Mrs. Caldwell also talked a great deal to Janet about the importance of good nutrition. Mr. Caldwell, on the other hand, became quite impatient with these discussions and tended to order Janet to eat. Janet then would try to eat something, but often became tearful and ran out of the room because she could not swallow the food she had been ordered to eat. The youngster said that she often responded to her parents' entreaties that she eat by telling them that she indeed had eaten but they had not seen her do so. She often listed foods that she said she had consumed which in fact she had flushed down the toilet. She estimated that she only was eating about 300 calories a day.

Mrs. Caldwell indicated that Janet appeared quiet and withdrawn, in contrast to her generally active and cheerful disposition, at the time she began dieting. Mrs. Caldwell recalled that Janet was having difficulties with her girlfriends during that period and Janet had mentioned that it seemed as if her friends were making excuses to avoid coming over when she invited them. Janet became very critical of her girlfriends, and Mrs. Caldwell felt that Janet behaved in an argumentative and stubborn manner with them. On occasions when Janet knew that some friends were coming over to the house, she drew up ahead of time a detailed plan of activities for them that encompassed the entire time period they had planned to spend at her house. She then became angry and uncomfortable if the girls did not want to engage in these activities or did not wish to do so in the order and the amount of time Janet had allotted to each activity. In general, Janet seemed less spontaneous and talked less with her family and others than she had during any previous period that her parents could recall.

(Leon, 1984, pp. 179–184)

TABLE 12-1

SAMPLE ITEMS FROM THE EATING DISORDER INVENTORY II

For each item, decide if the item is true about you ALWAYS (A), USUALLY (U), OFTEN (O), SOMETIMES (S), RARELY (R), or NEVER (N). Circle the letter that corresponds to your rating.

A	U	O	S	R	N	I think that my stomach is too big.
A	U	O	S	R	N	I eat when I am upset.
A	U	O	S	R	N	I stuff myself with food.
A	U	O	S	R	N	I think about dieting.
A	U	O	S	R	N	I think that my thighs are too large.
A	U	O	S	R	N	I feel ineffective as a person.
A	U	O	S	R	N	I feel extremely guilty after overeating.
A	U	O	S	R	N	I am terrified of gaining weight.
A	U	O	S	R	N	I get confused about what emotion I am feeling.
A	U	O	S	R	N	I feel inadequate.
A	U	O	S	R	N	I have gone on eating binges where I felt that I could not stop.
A	U	O	S	R	N	As a child, I tried very hard to avoid disappointing my parents and teachers.
A	U	O	S	R	N	I have trouble expressing my emotions to others.
A	U	O	S	R	N	I get confused as to whether or not I am hungry.
A	U	O	S	R	N	I have a low opinion of myself.
A	U	O	S	R	N	I think my hips are too big.
A	U	O	S	R	N	If I gain a pound, I worry that I will keep gaining.
A	U	O	S	R	N	I have the thought of trying to vomit in order to lose weight.
A	U	O	S	R	N	I think my buttocks are too large.
A	U	O	S	R	N	I eat or drink in secrecy.
A	U	O	S	R	N	I would like to be in total control of my bodily urges.

Source: Garner, Olmsted, & Polivy, 1991, 1984.

Like Janet, at least half of the people with anorexia nervosa reduce their weight by restricting their intake of food, a pattern called *restricting type anorexia nervosa.* At first, people with this kind of anorexia tend to cut out desserts, sweets, and fattening snacks and limit their diet to foods that are high in protein and low in calories (APA, 1994). Gradually other foods join the list of forbidden items, the daily caloric intake levels off at 600 to 800 calories, and the person takes relatively little pleasure in eating (Simon et al., 1993; Marshall, 1978). In many cases there is almost no variability in diet: the pursuit of thinness becomes a personal test of self-discipline. Others with this disorder lose weight by forcing themselves to vomit after meals or by abusing laxatives or diuretics, and they may even engage in eating binges, a pattern called *binge-eating/purging type anorexia nervosa,* which we shall discuss in more detail when we examine bulimia nervosa (APA, 1994).

Approximately 90 to 95 percent of all cases of anorexia nervosa occur in females, and although the disorder can appear at any age, the peak age of onset is between 14 and 18 years (APA, 1994). As many as one of every 100 adolescent and young adult females develop the disorder, and many more display at least some of its symptoms (APA, 1994; Levine, 1988). Typically the disorder begins after a person who is slightly overweight or of normal weight decides to "get in shape" or "just lose a few pounds" (Patton et al., 1990; Garfinkel & Garner, 1982) and follows a stressful event such as separation of the parents, a move away from home, or an experience of personal failure (APA, 1994). Although most victims recover, between 5 and 18 percent of them become so seriously ill that they die, usually of medical problems brought about by starvation.

Anorexia nervosa seems to be on the increase (APA, 1994; Nielsen, 1990). Certainly one reason for the reported increase is a heightened awareness of the disorder among diagnosticians (Amati et al., 1981). It also appears, however, that the absolute numbers of cases are increasing in North America, Great Britain, Japan, and Europe (Suematsu et al., 1985).

The central features of anorexia nervosa are (1) a drive for thinness and a morbid fear of becoming overweight, (2) preoccupation with food, (3) certain cognitive disturbances, (4) personality and mood problems, and (5) characteristic medical consequences (APA, 1994; Andersen, 1985). Table 12–1 demonstrates how some of these features are sometimes measured and assessed.

Becoming thin is life's central goal for the person with anorexia nervosa, but fear is at the root of her preoccupation: fear of becoming obese, of giving in to her growing desire to eat, and more generally of losing control over the size and shape of her body. In fact, anorexia nervosa has been called a "weight phobia" (Crisp, 1967). People with anorexia set a weight limit for themselves that is well below the acceptable weight for people of their age and height.

Despite this focus on thinness and the severe restrictions they may place on their food intake, people with anorexia are *preoccupied with food.* They may spend considerable time thinking and even reading about food and planning their limited meals (King, Polivy, & Herman, 1991). Many report that their dreams are filled with images of food and eating (Frayn, 1991; Levitan, 1981).

This preoccupation with food may in fact be the *result* of food deprivation rather than its cause (Yates, 1989; Andersen, 1986; Casper & Davis, 1977). Studies of nonanorexic people placed on extended starvation diets have noted the emergence of similar characteristics. The most prominent "starvation study," conducted in the late 1940s, put thirty-six conscientious objectors who volunteered for the project on a semi-starvation diet for six months (Keys et al., 1950). Like people with anorexia nervosa, these volunteers became preoccupied with food and eating. They spent hours each day planning their small meals, talked about food more than any other topic, studied cookbooks and recipes, mixed food in odd combinations, and dawdled over their meals. Many also had vivid dreams about food.

Anorexic persons also exhibit *cognitive dysfunction* of various kinds. For example, they usually have a low opinion of their body shape and consider themselves unattractive (Heilbrun & Witt, 1990). Most have such a disturbed perception of their bodies that they fail to recognize how emaciated they have become. Instead, they overestimate their actual proportions. A 23-year-old anorexic woman said:

I look in a full-length mirror at least four or five times daily and I really cannot see myself as too thin. Sometimes after several days of strict dieting, I feel that my shape is tolerable, but most of the time, odd as it may seem, I look in the mirror and believe that I am too fat.

(Bruch, 1973)

A distorted image of this kind complements the person's fear that she is in danger of becoming obese and motivates her to lose even more weight. The tendency to overestimate body size has been tested in the laboratory (Williamson et al., 1993). In a popular assessment technique subjects are asked to look at a photograph of themselves through an apparatus with an adjustable anamorphic lens and to manipulate the lens until the image it shows depicts their actual body size. The image can be made to vary from 20 percent thinner to 20 percent larger than actual appearance as the lens is adjusted. In one study more than half of the anorexic subjects were found to overestimate their body size, stopping the lens when the image was larger than they actually were. The majority of control subjects, in contrast, underestimated their body size (Garner et al., 1976).

Another cognitive feature of anorexia nervosa is the development of maladaptive attitudes and misperceptions (Wertheim & Poulakis, 1992; Garner & Bemis, 1985, 1982). People with the disorder often hold such beliefs as "I must be perfect in every way"; "Self-control and self-discipline must be perfect in life"; "Weight and shape are the most important criteria for inferring one's own worth." From these assumptions

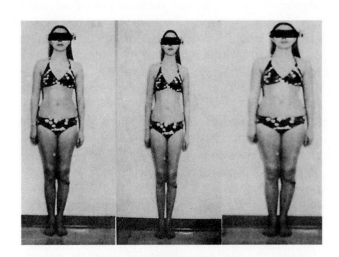

Subjects who look at photographs of themselves through an anamorphic lens can adjust the lens until they see what they believe is their actual image. A subject may alter her actual image (left) from 20 percent thinner (middle) to 20 percent larger (right). Most anorexic subjects overestimate their body size.

grow other notions, such as "I will become a better person if I deprive myself" and "I can avoid guilt by not eating." Gertrude, who recovered from anorexia nervosa, recalls that at age 15 "my thought processes became very unrealistic. I felt I had to do something I didn't want to do for a higher purpose. That took over my life. It all went haywire" (Bruch, 1978, p. 17).

Anorexic people also display several *personality* and *mood problems.* They tend to be at least mildly depressed and to have low self-esteem (APA, 1994; Russell, 1981). They may also exhibit symptoms of anxiety beyond their specific fears about body weight, including extreme indecisiveness and a weakening of concentration (Russell, 1981). Some are also troubled by sleep disturbances such as insomnia (APA, 1994; Crisp, 1980, 1970).

Anorexia nervosa is often accompanied by obsessive-compulsive patterns of behavior (APA, 1994; Vitousek & Manke, 1994; Pigott et al., 1991). It is common for the person to set herself rigid rules for food preparation or to cut her food into specific shapes. Even broader obsessive-compulsive patterns are common. Recall how Janet Caldwell became decreasingly spontaneous in all spheres of her life. When her friends were expected over, she would plan every minute of the visit in detail, and she became angry if her friends did not wish to pass the time precisely as Janet had planned. One study compared anorexic patients and obsessive-compulsive patients by means of tests, clinicians' ratings, and the patients' own self-evaluations, and the two groups earned equally high scores for obsessiveness and compulsiveness (Solyom, Freeman, & Miles, 1982).

Again, studies of normal subjects placed on semistarvation diets have reported similar mood and behavior changes, suggesting that some of these psychological features of anorexia nervosa may be brought about by starvation (Keys et al., 1950; Schiele & Brozek, 1948). The subjects in the conscientious objector study withdrew socially, narrowed their interests, and became increasingly anxious, depressed, and irritable, and some developed noticeable compulsions. Some chewed as many as sixty packages of gum a day, keeping it up even when it failed to alleviate hunger and tension. The subjects were seen to hoard food, cookbooks, coffeepots, hot plates, and even some non-food-related objects such as clothing and old books.

Finally, the starvation habits of anorexia nervosa cause a range of *medical problems* (Sharp & Freeman, 1993; Salisbury & Mitchell, 1991). Amenorrhea has already been mentioned. Other consequences include lowered body temperature, low blood pressure, body swelling, reduced bone mineral density, and slow

Thirty-six male subjects who were put on a semistarvation diet for 6 months developed many of the symptoms seen in anorexia nervosa (Keys et al., 1950). Many dawdled over their meals, and a few, like this subject, even licked their plates clean.

heart rate. Metabolic and electrolyte imbalances also may occur, and can lead to death by cardiac arrest, congestive heart failure, or circulatory collapse (Sharp & Freeman, 1993).

The severe nutritional deficiencies of anorexia may also cause significant changes in the appearance of the skin, hair, and other body parts. The skin becomes rough, dry, and cracked. Nails may become brittle, and hands and feet may be cold and blue. Some people lose hair from their scalp, and some grow lanugo (the fine, silky hair that covers some newborns) on their trunk, extremities, and face.

As the symptoms of this disorder suggest, people with anorexia nervosa are caught in a vicious cycle. Their drive for thinness and fear of obesity, fueled by a distorted body image, leads them to starve themselves. Starvation in turn leads to a preoccupation with food, to increased anxiety, depression, and obsessive rigidity, and to medical dysfunction. Now they feel even more afraid that they will lose control over their weight, their eating, and themselves, so they renew their resolve to achieve thinness by not eating. Michael Levine, a leading theorist on eating disorders, says that "although self-destruction is not the motive, the end result of the battle with starvation is the tightening of a noose" (1987, p. 48).

■ BULIMIA ■ NERVOSA

Lindsey Hall, a married woman with bulimia nervosa, describes her day:

W e eat the same breakfast, except that I take no butter on my toast, no cream in my coffee and never take seconds (until Doug gets out the door). Today I am going to be really good and that means eating certain predetermined portions of food and not taking one more bite than I think I am allowed. I am very careful to see that I don't take more than Doug does. I judge by his body. I can feel the tension building. I wish Doug would hurry up and leave so I can get going!

As soon as he shuts the door, I try to get involved with one of the myriad of responsibilities on the list. I hate them all! I just want to crawl into a hole. I don't want to do anything. I'd rather eat. I am alone, I am nervous, I am no good, I always do everything wrong anyway, I am not in control, I can't make it through the day, I just know it. It has been the same for so long.

I remember the starchy cereal I ate for breakfast. I am into the bathroom and onto the scale. It measures the same, BUT I DON'T WANT TO STAY THE SAME! I want to be thinner! I look in the mirror, I think my thighs are ugly and deformed looking. I see a lumpy, clumsy, pear-shaped wimp. There is always something wrong with what I see. I feel frustrated trapped in this body and I don't know what to do about it.

I float to the refrigerator knowing exactly what is there. I begin with last night's brownies. I always begin with the sweets. At first I try to make it look like nothing is missing, but my appetite is huge and I resolve to make another batch of brownies. I know there is half of a bag of cookies in the bathroom, thrown out the night before, and I polish them off immediately. I take some milk so my vomiting will be smoother. I like the full feeling I get after downing a big glass. I get out six pieces of bread and toast one side in the broiler, turn them over and load them with patties of butter and put them under the broiler again till they are bubbling. I take all six pieces on a plate to the television and go back for a bowl of cereal and a banana to have along with them. Before the last toast is finished, I am already preparing the next batch of six more pieces. Maybe another brownie or five, and a couple of large bowlfuls of ice cream, yogurt or cottage cheese. My stomach is stretched into a huge ball below my ribcage. I know I'll have to go into the bathroom soon, but I want to postpone it. I am in never-never land. I am waiting, feeling the pressure, pacing the floor in and out of the rooms. Time is passing. Time is passing. It is getting to be time.

I wander aimlessly through each of the rooms again tidying, making the whole house neat and put back together. I finally make the turn into the bathroom. I brace my feet, pull my hair back and stick my finger down my throat, stroking twice, and get up a huge pile of food. Three times,

four and another pile of food. I can see everything come back. I am glad to see those brownies because they are SO fattening. The rhythm of the emptying is broken and my head is beginning to hurt. I stand up feeling dizzy, empty and weak. The whole episode has taken about an hour.

(Hall, 1980, pp. 5–6)

Victims of bulimia nervosa—a disorder also known as *binge-purge syndrome, gorge-purge syndrome,* and *dietary chaos syndrome*—habitually engage in episodes of uncontrollable overeating ("binges") such as the one recalled by Lindsey Hall, who later recovered and wrote about her experience.

A binge occurs over a discrete period of time, such as an hour, during which the person consumes an amount of food that is definitely larger than most people would eat during a similar period of time under similar circumstances (APA, 1994). People who binge feel out of control while they are binging, unable to stop eating or to choose foods and portions wisely (APA, 1994). According to DSM-IV, a diagnosis of bulimia nervosa is warranted if the following criteria are met:

1. Recurrent episodes of binge eating.
2. Recurrent inappropriate compensatory behavior in order to prevent weight gain, such as self-induced vomiting; misuse of laxatives, diuretics, enemas, or other medications; fasting; or excessive exercise.
3. The binge eating and inappropriate compensatory behaviors both occur, on average, at least twice a week for three months.
4. Self-evaluation is unduly influenced by body shape and weight.
5. The disturbance is not part of a larger pattern of anorexia nervosa.

If the compensatory behavior displayed by the bulimic individual regularly includes self-induced vomiting or misuse of laxatives, diuretics, or enemas, the specific diagnosis is *purging type bulimia nervosa.* If the individual instead displays other compensatory behaviors such as fasting or exercising frantically, the specific diagnosis is *nonpurging type bulimia nervosa.* Clinicians have observed that many people seem to display a pattern of binge eating *without* any accompanying compensatory behaviors, often called *binge-eating disorder.* DSM-IV has recommended that this category be studied further; in the meantime people with this pattern receive the diagnosis *eating disorder not otherwise specified.*

Many adolescents and young adults go on occasional eating binges or experiment with self-induced vomiting or laxatives after they hear about people do-ing these things from their friends or from the media (Rand & Kuldau, 1991). In one study, 50 percent of the college students surveyed reported periodic binges, 6 percent had tried vomiting, and 8 per-cent had experimented with laxatives at least once (Mitchell et al., 1982). In a study of young working women, 41 percent reported binge eating (Hart & Ollendick, 1985). Only some of these subjects, how-ever, satisfied all of the DSM-IV criteria for a diagno-sis of bulimia nervosa: surveys in several countries suggest that between 1 and 6 percent of adolescent and young adult females develop the full syndrome (APA, 1994; Rand & Kuldau, 1992; Bennett, Spoth, & Borgen, 1991).

Like anorexia nervosa, bulimia nervosa usually oc-curs in females (again, 90 to 95 percent of the cases), begins in adolescence or young adulthood (most often between 15 and 19 years of age), and arises after a pe-riod of intense dieting (APA, 1994; Patton et al., 1990; Pope et al., 1986). It often lasts for several years, with intermittent letup. The weight of people with bu-limia nervosa usually stays within a normal range, al-though it may fluctuate noticeably within that range (APA, 1994). Some people with this pattern, however, become significantly underweight and may qualify for a diagnosis of anorexia nervosa instead (see Figure 12–2). Still other bulimic individuals become over-weight, largely as a result of their binge eating (Mitchell et al., 1990). Most overweight people, how-ever, are not bulimic (APA, 1994) (Box 12–1 discusses the primary causes of obesity).

Binge eating is the central feature of bulimia ner-vosa. As in Lindsey Hall's case, binges are usually carried out in secret or as inconspicuously as possible. The person gobbles down massive amounts of food very rapidly, with minimal chewing, tending to select food with a sweet taste, high caloric content, and a soft texture, such as ice cream, cookies, doughnuts, and sandwiches. Although the term "bulimia" comes from the Greek *bous limos,* meaning "cattle hunger," the food is hardly tasted or thought about during binges.

In the early stages of the disorder, the binges tend to be triggered by an upsetting event, depressed mood, hunger, concerns about one's weight or shape, or a desire to indulge in a forbidden food. Later the binge may become a carefully planned, even ritualis-tic event, with food bought expressly for that pur-pose.

Binges usually begin with feelings of unbearable tension (Lingswiler et al., 1989). The individual feels irritable, removed from the scene, and powerless to control an overwhelming need to eat "forbidden"

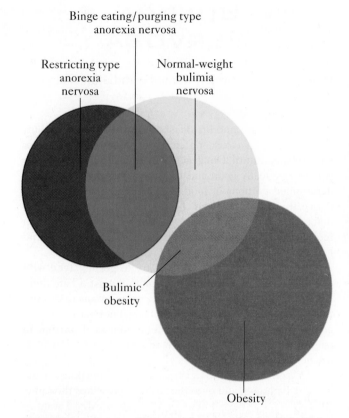

FIGURE 12–2 *Patterns of anorexia nervosa, bulimia nervosa, and obesity may overlap. Some people with anorexia nervosa binge and purge their way to weight loss. Similarly, some obese persons binge-eat. However, less than half of all anorexic people also purge, most bulimic people are not obese, and most overweight people are not bulimic. (Adapted from APA, 1994; Garner & Fairburn, 1988; Russell, 1979.)*

foods (Levine, 1987). During the binge, the person usually feels unable to stop eating. A binge typically ends within an hour or two, usually because no more food is available or because of stomach discomfort or pain, fatigue, interruption by other people, or self-in-duced vomiting (APA, 1994). Although the binge it-self may be experienced as pleasurable in the sense that it relieves the unbearable tension, it is followed by feelings of extreme self-reproach, guilt, and de-pression, and a fear of gaining weight and being dis-covered (APA, 1994; Mizes & Arbitell, 1991).

After a binge people with bulimia nervosa try to ***compensate*** for and undo its effects. Hall resorted to vomiting. Like most others with this disorder (APA, 1994), she developed great skill at this technique and eventually carried it out in a deliberate and ritualistic manner that made her feel in control again and re-lieved her of pain. Actually, vomiting fails to prevent the absorption of at least one-third of the calories con-sumed during a binge. And ironically, repeated vomit-ing disrupts the body's satiety mechanisms, making people even hungrier and leading to more frequent and intense binges (Wooley & Wooley, 1985).

Similarly, the compensatory use of laxatives or diuretics fails almost completely to undo the caloric effects of binging. Even when laxatives are taken immediately after a binge, they do not act until after calories have been absorbed into the small intestine. And diuretics simply do not operate on body fat (Garner et al., 1985).

Vomiting and other kinds of compensatory behavior may quickly relieve the uncomfortable physical feelings of fullness or temporarily reduce the feelings of anxiety, self-disgust, and lack of control attached to binge eating (French, Nicki, & Cane, 1993; Rosen & Leitenberg, 1985, 1982), so that over time a cycle evolves in which purging allows more binging and binging necessitates more purging. The cycle makes bulimic persons feel generally powerless, useless, and disgusted with themselves. Most recognize fully that they have an eating disorder, but their anxiety over gaining weight prevents them from interrupting the cycle. They feel increasingly depressed, ashamed, and guilty over their secret.

Hall's recollections illustrate how the pattern of binging, purging, and self-disgust begins to take hold:

I went away to boarding school at age fourteen with the nickname, Thunder Thighs. . . . The girls at my boarding school were all so beautiful that they seemed unapproachable. Long fingernails, neat clothes, curly hair and THIN bodies. It was obvious that thin was in right from the start.

Despite my nickname, I wasn't really obese. I weighed 142 pounds and was 5'6" tall. But heavy legs and thighs were the most disgusting form of being overweight. Having a big chest still meant boys wanted to touch you, but being pear-shaped was an unspoken sin. I began to focus on my body as the source of all my unhappiness. Every bite that went into my mouth was a naughty and selfish indulgence, and I became more and more disgusted with myself. . . .

The first time I stuck my fingers down my throat was during the last week of school. I saw a girl come out of the bathroom with her face all red and her eyes puffy. She had always talked about her weight and how she should be dieting even though her body was really shapely. I knew instantly what she had just done and I had to try it. . . .

I chose to go to a college 3,000 miles from home in a blatant show of independence and bravery, but once alone in my dorm room, I was stunned by the isolation and the enemy relationship I had with my Self. I retreated into eating which was a numbing device in the past, and I learned how to throw up.

I began with breakfasts which were served buffet-style on the main floor of the dorm. I learned which foods I could eat that would come back up easily. When I woke in the morning, I had to make the decision whether to stuff myself for half an hour and throw up before class, or whether to try and make it through the whole day without overeating. There were four stalls in the dorm bathroom and I had to make sure no one caught me in the process. If it was too busy, I knew which restrooms on the way to class were likely to be empty. I always thought people noticed when I took huge portions at mealtimes, but I figured they assumed that because I was an athlete, I burned it off. . . . Once a binge was under way, I did not stop until my stomach looked pregnant and I felt like I could not swallow one more time.

That year was the first of my nine years of obsessive eating and throwing up. . . . I didn't want to tell anyone what I was doing, and I didn't want to stop. . . . though being in love or other distractions occasionally lessened the cravings, I always returned to the food.

(Hall, 1980, pp. 9–12)

As noted before, a bulimic pattern typically begins during or after a period of intense dieting in which the individual has tried to address a mild or moderate weight problem (APA, 1994). Often that diet has been successful and earned praise from family members and friends. Research has found that normal subjects placed on very deficient diets also develop a tendency to binge. Some of the subjects in the conscientious objector study, for example, later engaged in binging when they were allowed to return to regular eating, and a number of them continued to be hungry even after large meals (Keys et al., 1950). Similarly, a recent study examined the binge eating behavior of overweight subjects at the end of a very low calorie diet and behavioral weight loss program (Telch & Agras, 1993). Immediately after the program, 62 percent of subjects who had not previously been binge eaters reported binge eating episodes, although their binge episodes did decrease during the three months after treatment stopped. Thus the intense dieting that typically precedes the onset of bulimia nervosa may itself predispose some people to the disorder.

BULIMIA NERVOSA VS. ANOREXIA NERVOSA

Bulimia nervosa is similar to anorexia nervosa in many ways. Both disorders typically unfold after a period of intense dieting by people who are fearful of becoming obese, driven to become thin, preoccupied with food, weight, and appearance, and grappling with

BOX 12–1

OBESITY: TO LOSE OR NOT TO LOSE

By medical standards, 15 to 24 percent of adults between the ages of 30 and 62 in the United States are obese—significantly over the weight that is typical of people of their height (National Center for Health Statistics, 1988). Being overweight is not a mental disorder, nor in most cases is it the result of abnormal psychological processes. Nevertheless, this problem causes great anguish to the many people who have it.

Our society's reaction to obesity is one of the main reasons for their anguish. The media, people on the streets, and even health professionals often treat obesity as shameful. Indeed, obese people are often the unrecognized victims of discrimination in gaining admissions to college, jobs, promotions, and satisfaction in their personal relationships (Rothblum, 1992; Stunkard & Wadden, 1992). Mounting evidence indicates that obesity results from multiple physiological, social, and other factors and that the overweight person is not to be sneered at as weak and out of control. First, genetic and biological factors

seem to play a role in it. Researchers have found that children of obese biological parents are more likely to be obese than children whose biological parents are not obese, whether or not the people who raise those children are obese (Stunkard et al., 1986). Research has also indicated that there may be a link between the neurotransmitter serotonin and obesity—deficits of serotonin in the brain may increase one's craving for carbohydrates and predispose some people to overeat and become obese (Logue, 1991).

Environment also plays a causal role in obesity. Studies have shown that people eat more when they are in the company of others, particularly if the other people are eating (Logue, 1991). It has also been found consistently that people of low socioeconomic environments are more likely to be obese than those of high socioeconomic backgrounds (Ernst & Harlan, 1991). The same distinction is found between highly developed and Third World countries. In countries where food is scarce, overweight is a sign of prosperity.

Despite such findings, societal pressures continue to push overweight people to see obesity as a disgrace and weight loss as the sole solution to their problems. Perhaps the primary reason for society's disdain for obese people lies in the web of myths that surround them. One such myth, that overweight people lack character or have personality defects, is, as we have seen, quite inaccurate. So, apparently, are three perceptions that have permeated our society for many years: (1) overweight people are significantly endangering their health; (2) dieting is the best means to lose weight; and (3) weight loss is the appropriate central goal of people who are overweight.

■ HEALTH ■ RISK?

Contrary to popular belief, mildly to moderately obese people are not at greater risk of coronary disease or cancer or any other disease. There is no hard evidence linking obesity to early death, and in fact quite the opposite may be true—being underweight puts one at some health risk (Robertson, 1992; Andres, 1980).

feelings of depression, anxiety, and the need to be perfect (APA, 1994; Ledoux et al., 1993; Marcus et al., 1985). Both groups of people believe that they weigh too much and look too heavy, regardless of their actual weight or appearance, and feel dominated by conflicts about what, when, and how much to eat (McKenzie et al., 1993; Ledoux et al., 1993; Dacey et al., 1991). Both disorders are often associated with disturbed attitudes toward eating and with difficulty identifying and differentiating such internal states as hunger, fatigue, anxiety, and anger (Williamson et al., 1991; Smith et al., 1991; Ruderman, 1986).

Yet bulimia nervosa also differs from anorexia nervosa in important ways (see Table 12–2). People with bulimia nervosa are much more likely to recognize that their behavior is pathological. They are also more inclined to be interested in pleasing others (Striegel-Moore, Silberstein, & Rodin, 1993). And whereas many people with anorexia nervosa are relatively unconcerned about sexual activity or being sexually attractive, people with bulimia nervosa care greatly—indeed, excessively—about being attractive to others and having intimate relationships (Raboch & Faltus, 1991; Muuss, 1986). Correspondingly, they

■ DIETING ■ WORKS?

There are scores of diets. There is virtually no evidence, however, that any diet yet devised can ensure long-term weight loss (Wilson, 1994). Most studies look only at the weight that obese people have lost during the first year. Any examination of long-term effects generally shows a net gain in the person's weight and certainly not any significant loss (Cogan & Rothblum, 1992; Kramer et al., 1989). This rebound effect is common among people who go on very low-calorie diets, which, in addition to failing to keep weight off, frequently are nutritionally deficient and physically dangerous (Wadden, Stunkard, & Liebschutz, 1988).

One reason that dieting fails to achieve long-term weight loss is that the dieter is engaged in a losing battle against his or her own *weight set point,* the weight level that a particular body is organized to maintain. In response to weight loss below the set point, a dieter's body increasingly stores energy in its fat cells rather than in lean muscle mass, causing lost weight to return and to do so in the form of fat (Dulloo & Girardier, 1990). Furthermore, the body's metabolic rate (the rate at which it uses energy) decreases in the course of dieting and remains depressed after dieting stops. The physiological changes that occur over the course of dieting are compounded by the fact that many obese people already have lower metabolic rates and two to three times the number of fat cells that thin people have.

Contrary to popular belief, most mildly and moderately obese people do *not* consume more calories than thin people. Most low-calorie dieters shift from weight loss to weight gain, then to loss again, and so on. In the end this yo-yo pattern may itself be a health risk, increasing the likelihood of high blood pressure and cardiovascular disease (Brownell & O'Neil, 1993; Lissner et al., 1991). As a result of these and other factors, people who are obese often feel that it is impossible to lose weight and keep it off without existing in a permanent state of semistarvation (Garner & Wooley, 1991). In cases of extreme obesity, where weight loss is desired and clearly advisable, it appears that establishing a realistic, attainable goal rather than an unrealistic ideal is most likely to lead to long-term weight loss and prevent a yo-yo pattern of dieting (Brownell & O'Neil, 1993; Brownell & Wadden, 1992).

■ LOWER BODY ■ WEIGHT IS THE PROPER GOAL?

Some researchers contend that emphasis should shift away from weight loss and toward improving general health and attitudes. Obesity has often been linked to poor eating habits and, perhaps more important, poor self-concept and distorted body image. If the psychological health of obese people can be improved and if they and others can be educated about the myths and truths regarding obesity, perhaps everyone will be better off.

A growing number of researchers are beginning to conclude that obesity should often be left alone, at least so far as weight loss is concerned; at the very least, weight loss should involve more modest and realistic goals. It is certainly desirable to intervene against the environmental and societal factors that may push one toward obesity, but many researchers now counsel that maintaining good physical and psychological health is the most reasonable and useful goal, whatever one's weight. Even if this view is borne out by ongoing research, it will be a difficult task to reeducate a public that continues to associate obesity with negative personality traits. Regardless of the conclusion reached by scientists in laboratories, it is critical that the public overcome its prejudices against people who are overweight, for at worst obesity is a problem that requires intervention, and at best it is simply another version of the normal human condition.

are more sexually experienced and active than people with anorexia nervosa. On the other hand, they tend to consider their social lives unsatisfactory and conflicted, their social and family support low, and their own social skills inadequate (Grisset & Norvell, 1992).

People with bulimia nervosa display fewer of the obsessive qualities that enable people with restricting type anorexia nervosa to regulate their caloric intake so rigidly (Andersen, 1985; Vandereycken & Meermann, 1984). At the same time, victims of bulimia demonstrate several disturbed characteristics of their own. They may have long histories of dramatic mood swings and become easily frustrated or bored. They have enormous difficulty controlling their impulses (Fahy & Eisler, 1993; Steiger et al., 1991). For example, they tend to be ruled by their strong emotions and may change friends and relationships very frequently; and they are much more likely than the general population to abuse alcohol and other drugs, a pattern that often begins with the excessive use of diet pills (APA, 1994; Higuchi et al., 1993). More than one-third of people with bulimia nervosa display the characteristics of a personality disorder, a pattern we

TABLE 12-2

ANOREXIA NERVOSA VERSUS BULIMIA NERVOSA

RESTRICTING TYPE ANOREXIA NERVOSA	BULIMIA NERVOSA
Refusal to maintain a minimum body weight for healthy functioning	Underweight, normal weight, near normal weight, or overweight
Hunger and disorder denied; often proud of weight management and more satisfied with body	Intense hunger experienced and binge-purge considered abnormal; greater body dissatisfaction
Less antisocial behavior	Greater tendency to antisocial behavior and alcohol abuse
Amenorrhea of at least 3 months' duration common	Irregular menstrual periods common; amenorrhea uncommon unless body weight is low
Mistrust of others, particularly professionals	More trusting of people who wish to help
Tend to be obsessional	Tend to be dramatic
Greater self-control, but emotionally overcontrolled with problems experiencing and expressing feelings	More impulsivity and emotional instability
More likely to be sexually immature and inexperienced	More sexually experienced and sexually active
Females are more likely to reject traditional feminine role	Females are more likely to embrace traditional feminine role
Age of onset often around 14–18	Age of onset around 15–19
Greater tendency for maximum pre-disorder weight to be near normal for age	Greater tendency for maximum pre-disorder weight to be slightly greater than normal
Lesser familial predisposition to obesity	Greater familial predisposition to obesity
Greater tendency toward pre-disorder compliance with parents	Greater tendency toward pre-disorder conflict with parents
Tendency to deny family conflict	Tendency to perceive intense family conflict

Sources: APA, 1994; Levine, 1987; Andersen, 1985; Garner et al., 1985; Neuman & Halvorson, 1983.

shall examine more closely in Chapter 17 (APA, 1994; Pendleton, Tisdale, & Marler, 1991).

Finally, the medical complications of bulimia nervosa differ from those of anorexia nervosa (Sharp & Freeman, 1993; Mitchell et al., 1991, 1987). Only 50 percent of women with bulimia nervosa are amenorrheic or have very irregular menstrual periods, compared to almost 100 percent of those with anorexia nervosa (Glassman et al., 1991). Moreover, the daily repeated vomiting of many bulimic people washes their teeth and gums in hydrochloric acid, leading in some cases to serious dental problems, including receding gums, breakdown of enamel, and even loss of teeth (APA, 1994; Philipp et al., 1991). People who vomit regularly or have chronic diarrhea may also develop a potassium deficiency called *hypokalemia,* which may lead to weakness, paralysis, gastrointestinal disorders, kidney disease, irregular heart rhythms, or heart damage (Sharp & Freeman, 1993; Mitchell et al., 1991, 1990). Occasionally repeated vomiting may damage the wall of the esophagus, causing internal bleeding and possibly even a fatal rupture of the esophagus (Mitchell et al., 1987).

■ EXPLANATIONS ■ OF EATING DISORDERS

For years traditional psychodynamic explanations of eating disorders dominated the clinical field (Sayers, 1988; Murray, 1986). Some Freudian theorists suggested, for example, that unresolved oral conflicts lead to anorexia nervosa (Lerner, 1986; Sugarman, Quinlan, & Devenis, 1981; Meyer & Weinroth, 1957). They argued that some children are unable to separate themselves from their mothers at the appropriate time and become fixated at the oral stage. Such children were thought to become especially frightened when they approach adolescence and confront sexual maturity and separation from their parents, and they were thought to develop anorexic behavior in an unconscious attempt to return to the early oral relationship by undoing outward signs of maturity. Psychodynamic explanations of this kind, however, received little research support, and indeed some contemporary psychodynamic theorists have instead proposed explanations that emphasize such factors as poor sense of self and relationship issues (Yarock, 1993; Steiger & Houle, 1991; Bruch, 1986, 1962).

In recent years theorists and researchers have looked in additional directions for an understanding of eating disorders and have identified several causal factors, no one of which appears necessary or sufficient in itself to bring the disorders about. Today's theorists usually apply a *multidimensional risk perspective* to the disorders, a view that identifies several key factors that place a person at risk for eating disorders (Martin, 1990; Levine, 1987; Johnson & Maddi, 1986; Garfinkel & Garner, 1982). Presumably the more of these factors that are present, the greater a person's risk of developing such a disorder. Some of the leading factors identified to date are *sociocultural pressures, family environment, ego deficiencies and cognitive disturbances, biological factors*, and *mood disorders*.

SOCIOCULTURAL PRESSURES

Many theorists believe that Western society's current emphasis on thinness has contributed to the recent increases in eating disorders (Abramson & Valene, 1991; McGibbon et al., 1991; Striegel-Moore et al., 1986). Western standards of female attractiveness have changed throughout history and now favor a slender figure. As clinical theorists Paul Garfinkel and David Garner (1982) point out, "Favor was shown for a buxom appearance in the early part of the century, followed by the flat chested flapper of the 1920s and the return of bustiness and an hour-glass figure in the 1950s. Recently, preference has once more returned to thinness as attractive for females" (p. 106).

The shift back to a thinner female frame has been steady since the 1950s. One investigation collected data on the height, weight, and age of contestants in the Miss America Pageant from 1959 through 1978 (Garner et al., 1980). After controlling for height differences, they found an average decline of 0.28

"Seated Bather," by Pierre Auguste Renoir (1841–1919), like other works of art, shows that the aesthetically ideal woman of the past was considerably larger than today's ideal. Indeed, women of similar shape are now considered modestly overweight.

Mannequins were once made extra-thin to show the lines of the clothing for sale to best advantage. Today the shape of the ideal woman is indistinguishable from that of a mannequin.

BOX 12-2

THE GENDER GAP IN EATING DISORDERS

Only 5 to 10 percent of all cases of eating disorders occur in males. Although the reasons for this striking gender difference are not entirely clear, several explanations have been proposed. One is that men and women are subjected to different sociocultural pressures. For example, a survey of college men found that the majority selected "muscular, strong and broad shoulders" to describe the ideal male body, and "thin, slim, slightly underweight" to describe the ideal female body (Kearney-Cooke & Steichen-Asch, 1990). Of course, although the emphasis on a muscular, strong, and athletic body as the ideal male body may decrease the likelihood of eating disorders in men, it may create other problems such as steroid abuse or excessive weight-lifting to increase muscular size and strength (Mickalide, 1990).

A second reason for the different rates of eating disorders among men and women may be the different methods of weight loss used by the two groups. According to some clinical observations, men may be more likely to use exercise to lose weight, while women diet more often (Mickalide, 1990). Dieting is the precipitant to most cases of eating disorders.

Finally, eating disorders among men may be underdiagnosed. Some men do not want to admit that they have a traditionally "female problem" and may try to hide their disorder. In addition, clinicians may be less able to identify eating disorders in men because of different clinical manifestations. For example, amenorrhea, an obvious symptom of anorexia nervosa in females, is not an available indicator among men with this disorder. It is much more difficult to test for male re-

productive problems, such as low levels of testosterone (Andersen, 1990).

How do men who do develop eating disorders compare to women with these problems? Some of them apparently grapple with similar issues. A number, for example, report that they aspire to a "lean, toned, thin" shape similar to the ideal female body, rather than a strong, muscular shape with broad shoulders typical of the male ideal body (Kearney-Cooke & Steichen-Asch, 1990).

In some cases, however, the precipitants of eating disorders are apparently different for men and women. For example, there are some indications that men with these disorders usually *are* overweight when they first start trying to lose weight (Andersen, 1990; Edwin & Andersen, 1990). In one study men with eating disorders reported having been teased about their bodies

---

pounds per year among the contestants and 0.37 pounds per year among winners. These same researchers examined data on all *Playboy* magazine centerfold models over the same twenty-year span and found that the average weight, bust, and hip measurements of these women decreased significantly throughout that period. The researchers also found an increased emphasis on dieting when they examined five popular woman-oriented magazines from 1959 through the late 1970s. A total of 385 diet articles appeared over those years. During the 1960s the average number of articles was 16 per year, whereas the yearly average for the 1970s was 23. A more recent study of Miss America contestants, Playboy magazine centerfolds, and women-oriented magazines indicates that each of these trends has continued into the 1990s (Wiseman et al., 1992).

Because thinness is especially valued and rewarded in the subcultures of fashion models, actors, dancers, and certain kinds of athletes, members of these groups are likely to be particularly concerned about

their weight (Morris et al., 1989; Silverstein et al., 1986). As sociocultural theorists would predict, these people are more vulnerable than others to eating disorders (Prussin & Harvey, 1991). One study compared the prevalence of anorexia nervosa among 183 ballet students, 56 students of fashion modeling, and 81 female university students. No cases of the disorder were found among the university students, but it did occur in 7 percent of the dancers and 7 percent of the modeling students (Garner & Garfinkel, 1980, 1978).

Varying attitudes toward thinness in different socioeconomic and minority groups may help explain socioeconomic and racial differences in the prevalence of eating disorders (Rosen et al., 1991). In past years, white American women of the upper socioeconomic classes expressed more concern about thinness and dieting than African American women or than white American women of the lower socioeconomic classes (Margo, 1985; Stunkard, 1975). Correspondingly, eating disorders were more common among white American women higher on

and picked less for athletic teams during adolescence than men without eating disorders (Kearney-Cooke & Steichen-Asch, 1990). In contrast, women with eating disorders usually *feel* overweight when they begin dieting, but may not actually be overweight according to objective measures (Edwin & Andersen, 1990).

One group of men who suffer from particularly high rates of eating disturbances are athletes. Their problems are precipitated not by a cultural requirement to be thin but rather by the requirements and pressures of certain sports (Thompson & Sherman, 1993). The highest rates of eating disturbances have been found among jockeys, wrestlers, distance runners, body builders, and swimmers. One study of male jockeys, for example, found that they used such methods as restricting their food intake, abusing laxatives and diuretics, and inducing vomiting to lose weight (King & Mezey, 1987). Jockeys commonly spent up to four hours before a race in a sauna, shedding up to seven pounds of weight at a time. Similarly, male wrestlers in high school and college commonly restrict their food intake for up to three days before a match in order to "make weight," often losing between 2 and 12 percent of their body weight. One method that is particularly common in this group is practicing or running in several layers of warm or rubber clothing in order to lose up to five pounds of water weight shortly before weighing in for a match (Thompson & Sherman, 1993).

Whereas most women with eating disorders are obsessed with thinness at all times, wrestlers and jockeys are usually preoccupied with weight reduction only during the season, and indeed most wrestlers return to their normal weight once the season is over. After "making weight," many wrestlers go on eating and drinking binges in order to gain strength and hydrate themselves for the upcoming match, only to return to a weight-loss strategy after the match to get prepared for the next weigh-in. This eating cycle of weight loss and regain each season has an adverse effect on the body, altering its metabolic activity and hindering future efforts at weight control (Steen, Oppliger, & Brownell, 1988). In addition, the weight reduction of male athletes has been found to have an adverse affect on their nutrient intake, nutrient absorption, renal function, thermal regulation, testosterone levels, and strength (Mickalide, 1990). Another difference that has been found between males athletes with eating problems and women with eating disorders is that male athletes tend to make accurate estimates of their body size (Enns, Drewnowski, & Grinker, 1987). Recent research further suggests that female athletes with eating disorders display many of the same characteristics as male athletes with these disorders (Prussin & Harvey, 1991).

As the number of males with eating disturbances increases, researchers are becoming more interested in understanding both the similarities and differences between men and women with such disturbances (Andersen, 1992). All eating disturbances are capable of producing physical and psychological damage. Thus, they must all be well researched and addressed in future investigations and clinical work.

the socioeconomic scale. In more recent years the emphasis on thinness and dieting has been embraced by all classes and minority groups, and the prevalence of eating disorders has increased there as well (Rosen et al., 1991; Root, 1990).

Subcultural differences may also help explain the striking gender gap for eating disorders. Our society's emphasis on appearance has been aimed at women much more than men during most of our history (Nichter & Nichter, 1991; Rolls et al., 1991). Indeed, speaking for an entire culture, Ambrose Bierce (1911) once said:

To men a man is but a mind.
Who cares what face he carries?
Or what form he wears?
But a woman's body is the woman.

Some theorists believe that this double standard of attractiveness has left women much more concerned about being thin, much more inclined to diet, and much more vulnerable to eating disorders (Rand & Kuldau, 1991; Swartz, 1985). It is interesting to note that an increased emphasis on male thinness and dieting in recent years has been accompanied by an apparent increase in the number of eating disorders among males (Seligmann, Rogers, & Annin, 1994; Striegel-Moore et al., 1986; Herzog et al., 1984) (see Box 12–2).

Western society not only glorifies thinness; it creates a climate of prejudice and hostility against overweight people. Cruel comments and jokes about obesity are standard fare on television shows and in movies, books, and magazines, whereas similar slurs based on ethnicity, race, and gender are considered unacceptable. Research indicates that the prejudice against obese people is deep-rooted (Brownell & O'Neil, 1993; Wooley & Wooley, 1982, 1979). In one study prospective parents were shown a picture of a chubby child and one of a medium-weight or thin child and rated the former as less friendly, energetic, intelligent, and desirable than the latter. In another study, preschool children, given a choice between a

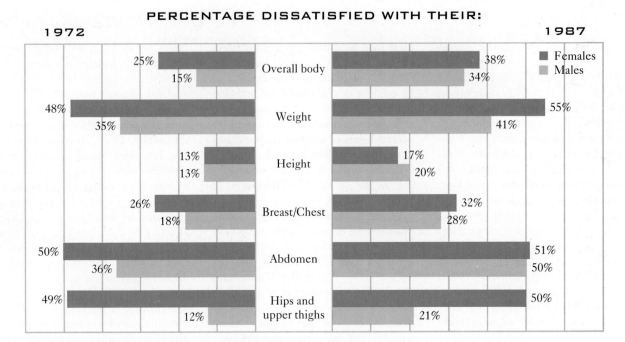

FIGURE 12-3 *According to surveys on body image conducted in the early 1970s and late 1980s, people in our society are more dissatisfied with their bodies now than they were a generation ago. Women are still more dissatisfied than men, but today's men are more dissatisfied with their bodies than the men of a generation past. (Adapted from Rodin, 1992, p. 57.)*

chubby and a thin rag doll, chose the latter, although they could not say why. College students who were asked to compare applicants for a job after reading a description of each candidate recommended a thin applicant over an obese one, even though the descriptions of the two applicants were the same otherwise. Researchers have also found that most female high school and college students of normal weight characterize themselves as overweight, wish to be very thin, and often use dangerous strategies to lose weight (Fisher et al., 1991; Zellner et al., 1989) (see Figure 12–3).

To a degree, physicians, insurance companies, and health organizations such as the American Heart Association may also contribute to society's bias against obesity by their overstated warnings about the dangers of being overweight (Robertson, 1992; Wooley & Wooley, 1982). Although extreme obesity is indeed unhealthy, mild or moderate obesity is apparently not. Researchers have found no significant differences in mortality among female subjects between 5 feet 3 inches and 5 feet 6 inches who range in weight from 115 to 195 pounds. Accordingly, the Department of Health and Human Services has revised its tables for "healthy" weights in recent years, allowing much more leeway in its standards for each level of height. Similarly, despite the claims of many psy-

chologists, researchers have not found overweight people to be more disturbed psychologically than persons of normal weight (Garner et al., 1985).

Such exaggerated claims about the risks of obesity contribute to the glorification of thinness and prejudice against obesity that pervade Western society. Together these sociocultural pressures establish a climate in which people seek thinness and fear weight gain, thus increasing the likelihood of developing eating disorders.

FAMILY ENVIRONMENT

As a primary transmitter of societal values, the family often plays a critical role in the development of eating disorders. Research suggests that as many as half of the families of people with eating disorders have a long history of emphasizing thinness, physical appearance, and dieting (Strober, 1992; Irving, 1990; Garfinkel & Garner, 1982).

Families may also set the stage for eating disorders by establishing abnormal and confusing family interactions and forms of communication throughout a child's upbringing. As we observed earlier, family systems theorists view each family as a system of interacting parts. These parts, the family members, interrelate in consistent ways, operate by implicit rules, and maintain a certain balance, or *homeostasis.* Systems theorists argue that the families of people who develop eating disorders are often disturbed to begin with and that the eating disorder of one member is simply a reflection of the larger family pathology (Lundholm & Waters, 1991; Kog & Vandereycken, 1989; Palazzoli, 1985, 1974).

Salvador Minuchin believes that what he calls an *enmeshed family pattern* often leads to eating disorders (Minuchin et al., 1978). In an enmeshed system, family members are overinvolved with each other's affairs and overconcerned about each other's welfare. The members rarely speak about their own ideas and feelings, yet each seems to know what other family members feel and mean. Let us think back to Janet Caldwell, the young woman with anorexia nervosa. Janet's family discouraged individual expression in the manner of enmeshed families, as illustrated by this additional passage from her case description:

*T*he expression of emotions such as anger, fear, or unhappiness was not encouraged at the Caldwell home, and the children were told by their parents that they were being childish if they verbalized strong feelings of any kind. The usual parental approach to dealing with emotional issues was to sit down and spend a great deal of time talking about the precipitating events that led up to a particular emotional feeling or outburst. However, expressing strong feelings was considered to be a sign of immaturity.

(Leon, 1984, p. 180)

On the positive side, enmeshed families can be affectionate and loyal. On the negative side, they can be clinging and foster dependency. There is little room in them for individuality and autonomy. Parents are too involved in the lives of their children, and see them not as individuals but as appendages who can make the lives and experiences of the parents more complete.

Minuchin argues that adolescence poses a special problem for these families. The adolescent child's normal push for independence threatens to disrupt the family facade of harmony and closeness. As the family searches for a solution, it subtly forces the child to take on a "sick" role—to develop an eating disorder or some other pattern such as chronic headaches or an ulcer. The child's disorder enables the family to maintain its illusion of living in harmony. A sick child needs her family, and family members can rally round and protect her.

Case studies and empirical studies have sometimes, but not consistently, lent support to the family systems explanation (Axtell & Newlon, 1993; Gowers,

Kadambari, & Crisp, 1985). One study tested the family systems prediction that the families of children with eating disorders would become unstable if the child were to improve (Crisp, Harding, & McGuinness, 1974). The investigators asked parents of anorexic daughters to fill out a psychological inventory before and after their daughters regained their lost weight. Before weight restoration, the parents' scores were comparable to those of parents of nonanorexic girls. After the daughters regained weight, however, their parents showed a significant increase in depression and anxiety. Although this finding is consistent with family systems theory, it is also possible that the stress of the weight-restoration therapy—itself a source of great conflict and tension—was causing the depressed and anxious feelings of family members (Strober, 1992).

Ego Deficiencies and Cognitive Disturbances

Hilde Bruch, a pioneer in the study and treatment of eating disorders, developed an influential theory that incorporates both psychodynamic (particularly self psychology) and cognitive notions (Bruch, 1986, 1981, 1973, 1962). She argued that disturbed mother-child interactions lead to serious *ego deficiencies* in the child (including a *poor sense of autonomy and control*) and to severe *perceptual and other cognitive disturbances* that jointly produce disordered eating patterns.

According to Bruch (1974, 1973), parents may respond to their children either effectively or ineffectively. *Effective parents* provide discriminating attention to their children's biological and emotional needs, giving them food when they are crying from hunger and comfort when they are crying out of fear. Children who are responded to in this way develop a sense of control and the ability to differentiate one internal state from another. *Ineffective parents,* by contrast, fail to attend to their children's internal needs and instead impose their own definitions of those needs on the children. The parents arbitrarily decide when their children are hungry, cold, or tired, without correctly interpreting the children's actual condition. They may feed the children at times of anxiety rather than hunger, or comfort them at times of tiredness rather than anxiety. Children who are subjected to this kind of parenting fail to develop a *cohesive self:* they grow up confused and unable to differentiate between their own internal needs, not knowing when

Hilde Bruch, a pioneer in the study of eating disorders, called attention to the prevalence of these disorders and the role of low self-esteem and lack of autonomy. Several interventions developed by her are now included in most eating disorder treatment programs.

they are hungry or satiated and unable to identify their own emotions or levels of fatigue.

Unable to rely on internal standards, these children turn instead to external guides, such as their parents. Some are considered "model children," always trying to do the things that give pleasure to their family, but they fail to develop genuine self-reliance. They feel what Bruch called a "paralyzing sense of ineffectiveness," and they "experience themselves as not being in control of their behavior, needs, and impulses, as not owning their own bodies, as not having a center of gravity within themselves" (1973, p. 55).

As adolescence approaches, these children are under increasing pressure to establish autonomy but feel unable to do so (Strauss & Ryan, 1987). To overcome their sense of helplessness, they try to achieve extreme self-control; in particular, they seek control over their body size and shape and over their eating habits. Some people are "successful" in this attempt at control, and they march toward restricting type anorexia nervosa. Others are unsuccessful and spiral instead toward a binge-purge pattern. Helen, an 18-year-old, describes her experience:

*T*here is a peculiar contradiction—everybody thinks you're doing so well and everybody thinks you're great, but your real problem is that you think that you are not good enough. You are afraid of not living up to what you think you are expected to do. You have one great fear, namely that of being ordinary, or average, or common—just not good enough. This peculiar dieting begins with such anxiety. You want to prove that you have control, that you can do it. The peculiar part of it is that it makes you feel good about yourself, makes you feel "I can accomplish something." It makes you feel "I can do something nobody else can do."

(Bruch, 1978, p. 128)

Clinical reports and research have provided some support for Bruch's theory. Clinicians have repeatedly observed that the parents of adolescents with eating disorders tend to define their children's needs for them rather than allow them to define their own needs (Steiner et al., 1991; Bruch, 1973; Rowland, 1970). When Bruch (1973) interviewed the mothers of fifty-one anorexic patients, many proudly recalled that they had always "anticipated" their young child's needs, never permitting the child to "feel hungry."

Research has also supported Bruch's proposition that people with eating disorders perceive and distinguish internal cues inaccurately, including cues of hunger and emotion. Studies have found that anorexic persons feel "full" sooner after they start to eat than others do (Garner & Bemis, 1982; Garfinkel et al., 1978), and that bulimic subjects often have trouble distinguishing hunger from other bodily needs or emotions. When they are anxious or upset, for example, they mistakenly think they are also hungry, and they respond as they might respond to hunger—by eating (Rebert, Stanton, & Schwartz, 1991).

Finally, research has supported Bruch's argument that people with eating disorders respond excessively to the opinions, wishes, and views of others. Comparisons of subjects with these disorders and control subjects have indicated that the former are more likely to worry about how others view them, seek approval (as measured on a social desirability scale), perceive relatively little control over their lives, and score higher on tests of conformity and lack of responsiveness to their own inner needs (Vitousek & Manke, 1994; Striegel-Moore et al., 1993; Strober, 1983, 1981).

BIOLOGICAL FACTORS

Over the past decade researchers have tried to determine whether biological factors help cause eating disorders. One influential theory has argued that people with bulimia nervosa have a heightened physiological need for carbohydrates, thus accounting for a strong preference for carbohydrates during binges. Proponents of this position have also suggested that bulimia-prone people may be sensitive to high-carbohydrate foods: as they eat carbohydrates, they develop an intensified craving for carbohydrates and eat still more of them to satisfy this craving (Wurtman & Wurtman, 1984, 1982; Wurtman, 1983). However, consistent evidence either for or against this notion has not yet emerged.

More recently biological researchers have focused on the *hypothalamus* and the concept of *weight set point* as keys to understanding the development and maintenance of eating disorders (Grossman, 1990, 1986; Garner et al., 1987). As we saw in Chapter 2, the hypothalamus is a part of the brain that helps maintain various bodily functions and affects the endocrine system by way of the pituitary gland. With its rich supply of blood vessels, it can detect changes in blood chemistry as well as respond to incoming neural information about what is happening throughout the body.

Researchers have located two separate centers in the hypothalamus that control eating (Grossman, 1990; Bray et al., 1980; Stellar, 1954). One, the *lateral hypothalamus,* or *LH*, consisting of the side areas of the hypothalamus, produces hunger when it is activated. When the LH of a laboratory animal is electrically stimulated, the animal eats, even if it has been fed recently. If, on the other hand, the LH is destroyed, the animal will refuse to eat, even if it has been starved by the experimenter. The other hypothalamus center, the *ventromedial hypothalamus,* or *VMH,* consisting of the bottom and middle of the hypothalamus, depresses hunger when it is activated. When the VMH is electrically stimulated, laboratory animals stop eating. When it is destroyed, the stomach and intestines of animals increase their rate of processing food, causing the animals to eat more often and eventually to become obese (Duggan & Booth, 1986; Hoebel & Teitelbaum, 1966).

It is now believed that the LH and VMH work in tandem to help set up a "weight thermostat" in the body that predisposes individuals to keep their body at a particular weight level, called their *weight set point* (Garner et al., 1985; Keesey & Corbett, 1983). When a person's weight falls below his or her particular set point, the LH is activated and seeks to restore the lost weight by producing hunger. It also decreases the body's *metabolic rate;* that is, the rate at which the body expends energy. When a person's weight rises above his or her set point, the VMH is activated, and it seeks to remove the excess weight by depressing hunger and increasing the body's metabolic rate.

The destruction of this rodent's ventromedial hypothalamus led to extreme overeating and weight gain.

In short, a person's weight set point reflects the range of body weight (or percent of body fat) that is normal for that individual in accordance with such influences as genetic inheritance, early eating practices, and the body's need to maintain internal equilibrium (Levine, 1987). If weight falls significantly below a person's set point, the hypothalamus will act to alter thinking, biological functioning, and behavior in an effort to restore weight to the set point (Polivy & Herman, 1985; Wooley & Wooley, 1985).

According to weight set point theory, when people pursue a strict diet, their weight eventually moves below their set point and their brain begins compensatory activities. The psychological symptoms that result from starvation, such as preoccupation with food, food hoarding, and desire to binge (Hill & Robinson, 1991), are manifestations of the hypothalamus's efforts to reestablish the weight set point. In another compensatory move, the hypothalamus sets in motion a bodily condition known as *hyperlipogenesis,* in which fat cells throughout the body retain abnormally large amounts of fat (Wooley & Wooley, 1985). Once this condition develops, people on extreme diets find it harder and harder to lose weight however little they eat, and they gain weight rapidly as soon as they resume normal eating habits (Spalter et al.,

1993). These compensatory activities address the body's need to maintain internal equilibrium, but they also raise dieters' fears that they are in danger of losing control over their weight and appearance.

Once the brain and body begin acting to raise weight to the set point, dieters enter a battle of sorts against their compensatory activities. Some people are apparently "successful" in this battle, manage to shut down and control their eating almost completely, and move toward restricting type anorexia nervosa. For others, the battle spirals toward the binge-purge pattern found in binge eating/purging type anorexia nervosa or bulimia nervosa. These people reach a "psychobiological impasse" in which the extreme dieting that they are employing to gain control over their hunger and feelings of tension actually causes them to become more and more hungry, emotionally unstable, and likely to binge (Johnson & Maddi, 1986).

It is not yet clear why some (restricting anorexic) people manage to attain control over the body's homeostatic weight mechanisms while others become caught in a cycle of binging and purging. Perhaps the psychological differences between anorexic and bulimic persons are important. Maybe the obsessive style of people with anorexia nervosa enables them to stick to a rigid regimen of restrictive eating despite the brain's push for weight gain, while the impulsiveness of those with bulimia nervosa make it impossible for them to resist their increasing urge to eat. Alternatively, the different levels of conflict found in the families of the two groups or some kind of biological predisposition may account for the different courses followed by anorexic and bulimic people.

MOOD DISORDERS

Earlier we noted that many people with eating disorders, particularly those with bulimia nervosa, experience symptoms of depression, such as sadness, low self-esteem, pessimism, and errors in logic (Ledoux et al., 1993; Beatty et al., 1990). This finding has led some theorists to conclude that mood disorders predispose some people to eating disorders (Hsu, Crisp, & Callender, 1992; Pope & Hudson, 1988, 1984).

Their claim is supported by four kinds of evidence. First, many more people with an eating disorder qualify for a clinical diagnosis of major depression than do people in the general population (APA, 1994). As many as 75 percent of those with bulimia nervosa may experience mood disorders, which are present before the bulimic patterns in at least a third of

the cases (Mitchell & Pyle, 1985; Pope & Hudson, 1984). Second, the close relatives of people with eating disorders apparently have a much higher rate of mood disorders than do close relatives of people without such disorders (APA, 1994; Johnson & Maddi, 1986). Third, persons with eating disorders, particularly bulimia nervosa, often display low activity of the neurotransmitter serotonin, similar to the serotonin depletions found in depressed people (Goldbloom et al., 1990; Wilcox, 1990). Fourth, persons with eating disorders are often helped significantly by some of the same antidepressant drugs that alleviate depression. The medications not only reduce the depressive symptoms but also alter the dysfunctional eating patterns in many cases (Mitchell & deZwaan, 1993).

Although such findings are consistent with the notion that depression helps cause eating disorders, alternative explanations are also possible. Sociocultural, familial, and biological factors that contribute to disordered eating patterns may likewise help cause depression, thus accounting for the appearance of both eating and mood disorders in many people (McCarthy, 1990; Jimerson et al., 1990). It is also possible that in some cases the pressure and pain of having an eating disorder help cause the mood disorder (Silverstone, 1990). Whatever the correct interpretation, it is clear that many people grappling with eating disorders also suffer from depression and that treatment must address both forms of dysfunction.

A MULTIDIMENSIONAL PERSPECTIVE

According to the multidimensional perspective, the various factors discussed in this section intersect in some people and together encourage eating disorders to unfold (Gleaves, Williamson, & Barker, 1993; Garner & Garfinkel, 1980). It is not necessary to display all of the associated characteristics or to be exposed to all of the influences to develop the syndrome. A combination of sociocultural pressures, autonomy problems, adolescent changes, and biological effects of dieting may bring about and maintain the disorder in one case, while a quite different combination, such as a dysfunctional family pattern, depression, and the effects of dieting, may account for another. "At this time, the specific interactions between the factors necessary and sufficient . . . are not known. Furthermore, characteristics which protect some . . . vulnerable individuals have not been investigated" (Garfinkel & Garner,

1982, p. 210). Nor is it yet known with certainty why some people develop bulimia nervosa instead of anorexia nervosa, or vice versa (Levine, 1987; Andersen, 1985; Vandereycken & Meermann, 1984).

■ TREATMENTS ■ FOR EATING DISORDERS

Today's treatments for eating disorders have two dimensions. First, they seek to correct as quickly as possible the pathological eating pattern that is endangering the client's health. For anorexic clients this means helping them to eat more and to gain weight; for bulimic persons, it means stopping, or at least reducing, the binges and purges. Second, therapists try to address the broader psychological and situational factors that led to and now maintain the dysfunctional eating patterns. In addition, family and friends can play an important role in correcting the disorder (Sherman & Thompson, 1990) (see Box 12–3).

TREATMENTS FOR ANOREXIA NERVOSA

The immediate aim of treatment is to help anorexic people regain their lost weight, recover from malnourishment, and reestablish normal eating habits. Therapists must then help them to make psychological changes that enable them to maintain their immediate gains.

WEIGHT RESTORATION AND RESUMPTION OF EATING   A variety of methods are used to help anorexic patients gain weight quickly and restore them to health in a matter of weeks (Powers et al., 1991). In the past the methods were almost always applied in a hospital, but now they are increasingly being offered in outpatient settings (Kennedy, Kaplan, & Garfinkel, 1992).

In life-threatening cases, clinicians may provide nourishment directly by forcing *tube and intravenous feedings* on patients (Martin, 1985; Sours, 1980). Although such feedings help keep patients alive and rapidly reverse the downward trend of weight loss, they are typically applied with minimal cooperation

Sociocultural theorists argue that one aspect of treatment for eating disorders should be to change society's attitudes and socialization practices. The emphasis on appearance and thinness begins early in life in our society, particularly for females. These preschool participants in a beauty contest are learning the kind of aesthetic standards by which they will be judged throughout their lives.

BOX 12-3

HOW FAMILY AND FRIENDS CAN HELP

1. Write down specific instances of the person's problematic behavior or attitudes, and encourage other friends and family members to do the same. [Later therapy discussions will then be more precise.]

2. Educate yourself and other family members about eating disorders, and about the nearest resources offering professional and expert treatment.

3. Get support and advice from people you trust—clergy, social workers, friends, family physicians. Don't isolate yourself from people who care about you and who can help. Attend a support group.

4. Arrange for family and friends to speak confidentially with the person about the specifics and consequences of his or her disordered eating and weight-management practices. Try to remain calm, caring, and nonjudgmental. Avoid giving simplistic suggestions about nutrition or self-control.

5. Communicate directly to the person the seriousness of your concern, your conviction that treatment is necessary, and your willingness to provide emotional, financial, and other practical support.

6. Exercise responsibility, authority, and authoritative wisdom in obtaining treatment for *(a)* minors with eating disorders and *(b)* anyone who is suicidal, very sick, or out of control.

7. Reaffirm the importance of yourself and your other family members. Don't allow your life to be disrupted by emotional upheaval—arguments, threats, blame, guilt, bribes, resentment—concerning issues of food, weight, and eating.

8. Sustain the person's sense of importance and dignity by encouraging decision-making and personal responsibility. Don't be manipulated into shielding the person from the consequences of the dis-

order, including separation from you.

9. Be patient: Recovery is a long process because treatment must address the physical, psychological, behavioral, social, and cultural dimensions of complex disorders.

10. Love your relative or friend for himself or herself, not for appearance, health, body weight, or achievement. Encourage healthy feelings and interests, and avoid talking about appearance, eating habits, and weight.

11. Remember that families [alone] neither cause nor cure eating disorders, but they can make a major contribution to recovery and future development. Dwelling on guilt or causes is counterproductive.

12. Remember that compassion is "bearing with" a person in distress, not suffering unduly because of their injustices or unwillingness to get help.

by Michael Levine, 1988

---

from the patient, breed the patient's distrust, and set up a power struggle between patient and clinician (Zerbe, 1993; Tiller et al., 1993; Pertschuk et al., 1981).

Antipsychotic drugs have also been used to help reverse starvation habits (Mitchell, 1989; Condon, 1986). These medications fail to help in most cases, however, and they may have serious undesirable effects, as we shall see in Chapter 16 (Condon, 1986). Still other clinicians have had some success with *antidepressant medications* (Kaye et al., 1991; Gwirtsman et al., 1990). These drugs appear to be particularly helpful in relieving the depressive and obsessive symptoms that often accompany the anorexic syndrome.

Weight-restoration programs often include an *operant conditioning* approach (Halmi, 1985; Martin,

1985). Patients are given positive reinforcement when they eat properly or gain weight and no reinforcement when they eat improperly or fail to gain weight. Once again, however, the impact of this approach has proved limited (Halmi, 1985). Studies suggest that patients who are treated with operant conditioning fail to maintain their initial weight gain unless other forms of intervention are also employed (Pertschuk, 1977).

In recent years, *supportive nursing care*, combined with a high-calorie diet, has become the most popular weight-restoration technique (Andersen, 1986; Garfinkel & Garner, 1982). In this approach, well-trained nurses conduct the day-to-day hospital program. They place patients on a low-calorie diet at first and then gradually increase the diet over the course of several weeks to between 2,500 and 3,500 calories a day. The nurses educate patients about the program, give them progress reports, provide encouragement, and help them recognize that their weight gain is proceeding in a deliberate and controlled manner, that they are on their way to health, and that they will not go overboard into obesity. At the same time, the nurses remain firm in carrying out the program and avoid being manipulated into complicity with the patient's anorexic fears and desires. Studies suggest that patients on nursing care programs usually gain the necessary weight over eight to twelve weeks (Garfinkel & Garner, 1982; Russell, 1981).

PSYCHOLOGICAL CHANGES Clinical researchers have found that anorexic people must address their underlying emotional problems and alter their maladaptive thinking patterns if they are to experience lasting improvement (Tobin & Johnson, 1991; Garfinkel, 1985). Therapists typically offer a mixture of therapy and education to achieve this goal, using individual, group, and family therapy formats (Ehle, 1992; Crisp et al., 1991; Strober & Bowen, 1986; Garfinkel & Garner, 1982).

BUILDING AUTONOMY AND SELF-AWARENESS One focus of psychological treatment is to help anorexic patients become more aware of any underlying difficulties with expressing autonomy and to exercise control in more appropriate ways and develop independence (Bruch, 1986, 1982, 1973, 1962). Another is to help anorexic clients recognize and trust their own feelings, so that they can become more skilled at identifying their internal sensations and emotions (Bruch, 1973). Therapy in this area is delicate. It would be counterproductive for a therapist to tell an anorexic client what he or she is experiencing internally, as that would play into the person's self-distrust and overconcern about others' opinions. Furthermore, therapists must not make guesses about the clients' internal experiences, because the overly conforming anorexic person is likely to agree readily whether the guess is correct or not. Instead, clients must be encouraged to discover their own inner sensations—to "say it first" (Bruch, 1973). Then the therapist can acknowledge and accept the discovery and probe it further. In the following exchange, a therapist tries to help a 15-year-old client identify and share her feelings:

Patient: I don't talk about my feelings; I never did.

Therapist: Do you think I'll respond like others?

Patient: What do you mean?

Therapist: I think you may be afraid that I won't pay close attention to what you feel inside, or that I'll tell you not to feel the way you do—that it's foolish to feel frightened, to feel fat, to doubt yourself, considering how well you do in school, how you're appreciated by teachers, how pretty you are.

Patient: (Looking somewhat tense and agitated) Well, I was always told to be polite and respect other people, just like a stupid, faceless doll *(Affecting a vacant, doll-like pose)*.

Therapist: Do I give you the impression that it would be disrespectful for you to share your feelings, whatever they may be?

Patient: Not really; I don't know.

Therapist: I can't, and won't, tell you that this is easy for you to do. . . . But I can promise you that you are free to speak your mind, and that I won't turn away.

(Strober & Yager, 1985, pp. 368–369)

CORRECTING DISTURBED COGNITIONS Changing an anorexic person's misconceptions and attitudes about eating and weight is critical to a full and lasting recovery. Such changes are, however, difficult to bring about, because these attitudes are embraced by so many members of our society (see Table 12–3). Toward this end, Beck's cognitive therapy has been applied to cases of anorexia nervosa, just as it has been applied to depression (Wilson & Fairburn, 1993; Garner & Bemis, 1985, 1982). Therapists guide clients to focus on, challenge, and change maladaptive assumptions, such as "I must always be perfect" or "My weight and shape determine my value." The therapist may ask the client to gather evidence to support or refute the truth of such assumptions, weigh the advantages and disadvantages of living by them, and consider their consistency with other values. The therapist may also seek to educate the client about her misconceptions. Here we see a therapist challenging an assumption common among anorexic people:

Patient: Once I reach my goal weight, or once I get into the habit of eating "non-dietetic" food, I will not be able to stop and I will catapult into obesity.

Therapist: Are the only two options emaciation or obesity? If you have maintained "control" at this weight, where is the evidence that you will not be able to exert similar "control" at a normal weight? Recovered patients do not typically indulge in only high-calorie foods, and very few become obese. Could it be that you are feeling this way because you are currently starved—that once you get to a normal weight, you won't be sitting on a powder keg of hunger?

(Garner & Bemis, 1985, pp. 126–127)

TABLE 12-3

SOCIAL ATTITUDES SCALE: HOW DO YOU SCORE?

Please read the following statements and indicate how strongly you agree or disagree with each.

1. A man would always prefer to go out with a thin woman than one who is heavy.

Strongly agree	Agree somewhat	Agree	Neither agree nor disagree	Disagree	Disagree somewhat	Strongly disagree
☐	☐	☐	☐	☐	☐	☐

2. Clothes are made today so that only thin people can look good.

Strongly agree	Agree somewhat	Agree	Neither agree nor disagree	Disagree	Disagree somewhat	Strongly disagree
☐	☐	☐	☐	☐	☐	☐

3. Fat people are often unhappy.

Strongly agree	Agree somewhat	Agree	Neither agree nor disagree	Disagree	Disagree somewhat	Strongly disagree
☐	☐	☐	☐	☐	☐	☐

4. It is not true that attractive people are more interesting, poised, and socially outgoing than unattractive people.

Strongly agree	Agree somewhat	Agree	Neither agree nor disagree	Disagree	Disagree somewhat	Strongly disagree
☐	☐	☐	☐	☐	☐	☐

5. A pretty face will not get you very far without a slim body.

Strongly agree	Agree somewhat	Agree	Neither agree nor disagree	Disagree	Disagree somewhat	Strongly disagree
☐	☐	☐	☐	☐	☐	☐

6. It is more important that a woman be attractive than a man.

Strongly agree	Agree somewhat	Agree	Neither agree nor disagree	Disagree	Disagree somewhat	Strongly disagree
☐	☐	☐	☐	☐	☐	☐

7. Attractive people lead more fulfilling lives than unattractive people.

Strongly agree	Agree somewhat	Agree	Neither agree nor disagree	Disagree	Disagree somewhat	Strongly disagree
☐	☐	☐	☐	☐	☐	☐

8. The thinner a woman is, the more attractive she is.

Strongly agree	Agree somewhat	Agree	Neither agree nor disagree	Disagree	Disagree somewhat	Strongly disagree
☐	☐	☐	☐	☐	☐	☐

9. Attractiveness decreases the likelihood of professional success.

Strongly agree	Agree somewhat	Agree	Neither agree nor disagree	Disagree	Disagree somewhat	Strongly disagree
☐	☐	☐	☐	☐	☐	☐

These items, developed by psychologist Judith Rodin (1992), test how much *you believe that appearance matters*. Score your responses as follows:

For items 1, 2, 3, 5, 7, and 8, give yourself a zero if you said "strongly disagree"; a 2 for "disagree"; up to a 6 for "strongly agree."

Items 4, 6, and 9 are scored in reverse. In other words, give yourself a zero for "strongly agree" and a 6 for "strongly disagree."

Add together your points for all nine questions. A score of 46 or higher means that you are vulnerable to being influenced by the great importance that current society places on appearance.

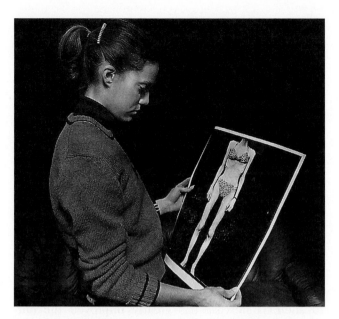

In 1980 a 16-year-old anorexic patient named Jane, 5 feet 8 inches tall, weighed 90 pounds, down 45 pounds from her weight 8 months earlier. After two years of treatment, she gained back 25 pounds. Looking at pictures of anorexic persons helped her to recognize that body distortions are typical of this disorder.

Many clinicians also believe that anorexic clients' correction, or at least recognition, of their distorted body image is a "precondition to recovery" (Bruch, 1973). Therapists usually educate clients about the body distortions typical of anorexia nervosa and train them to recognize that their own assessments of their size are incorrect (Garner & Bemis, 1982; Garner & Garfinkel, 1981, 1979). Such education often paves the way for more accurate body perceptions. At the very least, a patient may reach a point where she says, "I know that a cardinal feature of anorexia nervosa is a misperception of my own size, so I can expect to feel fat no matter what size I really am," or "When I try to estimate my own dimensions, I'm like a color-blind person trying to coordinate her own wardrobe. I'll have to rely on objective data to determine my actual size." With the aid of such insights, patients are less likely to be driven to extremes of behavior by their distorted body perceptions.

CHANGING INTERACTIONS WITHIN THE FAMILY   As we noted earlier, family systems theorists believe that a family structure of enmeshment, along with other forms of family dysfunction, contributes to anorexia nervosa (Kog & Vandereycken, 1989; Palazzoli, 1985). Thus family therapy is often used in cases of this disorder (Dare & Eisler, 1992; Vanderlinden & Vandereycken, 1991). As in other family therapy situations, the therapist meets with the family as a whole, observes how the family members interact, points out dysfunctional family patterns, and helps the members make appropriate changes. The therapy of Salvador Minuchin and his colleagues (1978) exemplifies the approach used in many cases of anorexia nervosa. In order to change the common family pattern of enmeshment and help the anorexic person separate her feelings and needs from those of other family members, Minuchin intervenes in a variety of ways.

The therapist *supports each family member's personal space* by laying down rules that enhance the members' independence and respect for one another. They are encouraged to speak for themselves; checking for approval, for example, is strictly prohibited. Members are repeatedly reminded that they may not finish someone else's phrase or story, or request help in an area in which they should be competent.

Because children in enmeshed families are often drawn into the conflicts between parents, and parents frequently intrude on sibling interactions, the family therapist is always on guard to *protect appropriate family boundaries.* Minuchin and his colleagues (1978) regularly remind and question family members during sessions (p. 100):

Did you ask them if they want your participation?

Did you ask for help?

This is an issue that concerns your parents, not you.

Let your children work this out by themselves.

Many parents in enmeshed families abdicate their authority and expect their children to respond with levels of maturity beyond their age. Minuchin tries to counter this tendency by *reinforcing respect for each member's unique position within the family* and *supporting a hierarchy* in which parents are higher than children and older children are higher than younger children. As a result, parents are expected to feel more effective in their executive roles, and to respect a child's need to grow and acquire autonomy at a pace appropriate to the child's age.

Finally, the family therapist may find it necessary to *instigate therapeutic family crises* in order to reveal and then correct hidden conflicts (Minuchin, 1970). Using a strategy called "reframing the symptom," for example, the therapist may propose to the family that the child's anorexic symptoms are actually voluntary. This redefinition will often serve to unite parents and induce them to stop treating the child as an invalid, and it challenges the anorexic child herself to recognize the power she exerts through her symptoms rather than seeing herself as totally helpless.

In the following family therapy session, the therapist uses these and similar techniques to help change the patterns of enmeshment in the family of an anorexic teenager:

Mother: I think I know what [Susan] is going through: all the doubt and insecurity of growing up and establishing her own identity. *(Turning to the patient, with tears)* If you just place trust in yourself, with the support of those around you who care, everything will turn out for the better.

Therapist: Are you making yourself available to her? Should she turn to you, rely on you for guidance and emotional support?

Mother: Well, that's what parents are for.

Therapist: *(Turning to patient)* What do you think?

Susan: *(To mother)* I can't keep depending on you, Mom, or everyone else. That's what I've been doing, and it gave me anorexia. . . .

Therapist: Do you think your mom would prefer that there be no secrets between her and the kids—an open door, so to speak?

Older sister: Sometimes I do.

Therapist: *(To patient and younger sister)* How about you two?

Susan: Yeah. Sometimes it's like whatever I feel, she has to feel.

Younger sister: Yeah.

Therapist: *(To mother)* How does it make it better for you to be so close and involved with your kids?

Mother: I don't see what's so wrong. You seem to be condemning me for being a conscientious parent. . . .

Therapist: *(To father)* I wonder where you fit in? What stops your wife from turning to you? Again, I wonder if your wife is as sensitive to your needs and what you go through. . . .

Father: I would say, probably not. I'm a pretty reserved fellow.

Therapist: *(To the girls)* Is that the way it is with him?

Older sister: Dad, you need to express what you think more. . . .

(Strober & Yager, 1985, pp. 381–382)

COMBINING THE APPROACHES Today's therapists tend to combine these various techniques for treating anorexia nervosa (Tobin & Johnson, 1991;

Garfinkel & Garner, 1982). The particular combination selected depends on the individual anorexic patient's situation and problems.

Studies suggest that the combining of approaches is indeed often helpful (Tobin & Johnson, 1991; Garfinkel & Garner, 1982; Hersen & Detre, 1980). Such programs are now offered in mental health centers, medical and mental hospitals, and private treatment facilities across the United States. Inasmuch as several pathways may lead to anorexia nervosa, it makes sense that the most effective form of intervention would be a treatment program that is multifaceted and flexible, tailored to the unique needs of the patient.

THE AFTERMATH OF ANOREXIA NERVOSA
The development of multiple treatment approaches to anorexia nervosa has greatly improved the outlook for people with this disorder in recent years. Nevertheless, many of them still face significant obstacles on the road to recovery. Although the course and outcome of anorexia nervosa are highly variable, certain trends have emerged in numerous follow-up studies:

1. Weight is often quickly restored once treatment begins (Andersen et al., 1985; Theander, 1970; Dally, 1969), but complete psychological and physical recovery may take several years. Altogether, approximately 75 percent of patients continue to show improvement when they are examined several years or more after their initial recovery: 45 percent are fully recovered and 30 percent considerably improved. Approximately 25 percent remain seriously impaired or are dead at follow-up (APA, 1994; Tolstrup et al., 1985; Martin, 1985; Garfinkel & Garner, 1982; Hsu, 1980).

2. The death rate from anorexia nervosa seems to be declining (Andersen et al., 1985; Crisp, 1981; Hsu et al., 1979). Earlier diagnosis and safer and faster weight-restoration techniques may account for this trend. Deaths are usually caused by starvation, suicide, or electrolyte imbalance (APA, 1994; Tolstrup et al., 1985).

3. Approximately 50 to 80 percent of anorexic females menstruate again when they regain their weight. Others remain amenorrheic at least for a while (Crisp, 1981; Hsu, 1980; Garfinkel et al., 1977).

4. Typically, recovery is not a smooth process (Murray, 1986). At least 15 percent of patients have recurrences of anorexic behavior while they are recovering. These recurrences are

usually precipitated by new stresses, such as marriage, pregnancy, or a major relocation (Sohlberg & Norring, 1992; Hsu et al., 1979).

5. Even years later, many patients continue to express concerns about gaining too much weight. Approximately 45 to 65 percent say they worry about their weight and appearance (Hsu et al., 1979; Morgan & Russell, 1975). Some patients continue to restrict their diets to some degree, experience anxiety when they eat with other people, or hold some distorted ideas about food, eating, and weight (Clinton & McKinlay, 1986).

6. At follow-up, 40 to 60 percent of anorexic patients continue to experience some emotional problems—particularly depression, social anxiety, and obsessiveness. Such problems are particularly common in those who have not succeeded in attaining a normal weight (Hsu et al., 1992; Schwartz & Thompson, 1981; Crisp, 1981).

7. Family problems persist for approximately 50 percent of anorexic patients (Hsu, 1980).

8. Most anorexic patients are performing effectively at their jobs at follow-up. As many as 90 percent hold jobs and perform well, and the majority express high job satisfaction (Theander, 1970).

9. Those who recover go on to marry or have intimate relationships at rates comparable to those of nonanorexic populations. Sexual functioning tends to remain impaired in nonrecovered anorexic people (Hsu et al., 1979; Theander, 1970; Dally, 1969).

10. The more weight patients lose before treatment, the poorer their recovery rate (Burns & Crisp, 1985; Morgan & Russell, 1975). The longer an anorexic person goes without successful intervention, the poorer the prognosis (Burns & Crisp, 1985; Hsu et al., 1979; Pierloot et al., 1975). Some anorexic people appear to recover without formal treatment of any kind.

11. Young adolescents seem to have a better recovery rate than older patients (APA, 1994; Hsu et al., 1979; Morgan & Russell, 1975). Females have a better recovery rate than males.

12. Those who display psychological, behavioral, or sexual problems before the development of anorexia nervosa tend to have a poorer recovery rate than those without such premorbid problems (Burns & Crisp, 1985; Hsu et al., 1979; Morgan & Russell, 1975; Halmi et al., 1973). People who perform well at school or work before the onset of anorexia nervosa tend to have a higher recovery rate (Garfinkel et al., 1977).

Like many other people who recover from anorexia nervosa, Jane continued to weigh herself every morning and still became anxious each time she observed a weight gain.

TREATMENTS FOR BULIMIA NERVOSA

Treatment programs tailored to the particular features of bulimia nervosa have been developed only in recent years, but they have already had a meteoric rise in popularity. Most of these programs are offered in eating-disorder clinics, and all share the immediate goal of reducing and eliminating binge-purge patterns and normalizing eating habits and the broader goal of addressing the underlying causes of bulimic behavior patterns. The programs emphasize education as much as therapy. Many programs combine several treatment strategies, including *individual insight therapy, group therapy, behavioral therapy,* and *antidepressant drug therapy* (Fahy, Eisler, & Russell, 1993; Fichter, 1990; Pyle et al., 1990).

INDIVIDUAL INSIGHT THERAPY Psychody-namic and cognitive approaches have been the most common forms of individual insight therapy for bulimic clients (Johnson, 1991; Fichter, 1990). As in the treatment of other kinds of disorders, psychodynamic therapists use free association and interpretive techniques to help bulimic clients uncover and eventually resolve their underlying conflicts and issues, including their frustrating tensions, lack of self-trust, need for control, and feelings of powerlessness (Lerner, 1986; Yager, 1985). Case reports suggest that psychodynamic therapy is sometimes helpful for bulimic persons. Only a few research studies have been conducted to test its effectiveness, but these studies are also generally supportive (Garner et al., 1993; Yager, 1985; Bruch, 1973).

Therapists who use cognitive approaches try to help bulimic people discuss and alter their maladaptive attitudes toward food, eating, weight, and shape, thus eliminating the kinds of thinking that raise anxiety and lead to binging (Wilson & Pike, 1993; Garner et al., 1993; Cooper & Fairburn, 1992). As in the treatment of anorexia nervosa, the therapists typically teach clients to identify the dysfunctional thoughts that regularly precede their urge to binge—"I have no self-control," "I might as well give up," "I look fat," "I am fat," "I must lose weight," "I must diet" (Fairburn, 1985). They then guide clients to evaluate those thoughts and to draw more appropriate conclusions. Using a combination of therapy and education, the therapists may also guide clients to recognize, question, and eventually change the broader cognitive features of their problem, such as their perfectionistic standards, sense of helplessness, and low self-concept.

Researchers have found cognitive therapy to be relatively effective in cases of bulimia nervosa, reducing binge eating, purging, and feelings of depression (Leitenberg et al., 1994; Wilson & Fairburn, 1993; Garner et al., 1993). Approaches that mix cognitive and psychodynamic techniques also appear to be helpful (Yager, 1985).

GROUP THERAPY Most bulimia nervosa programs now include either therapist-led or self-help group therapy to give sufferers an opportunity to share their thoughts, concerns, and experiences with one another (Franko, 1993; Rathner et al., 1993; Pyle et al., 1990; Laube, 1990; Jones, 1985). In these groups they learn that their disorder is not unique or shameful, and they receive much-needed support and understanding from the other members, along with candid feedback and insights (Asner, 1990). Group

Members of "Overeaters Anonymous," a worldwide network of support groups, acknowledge that they use food self-destructively, and learn to treat their bodies with greater respect. Many members report that the program's principles help them tremendously, but some clinicians believe that OA inadvertently encourages bulimic and other members to think maladaptively about food by defining overeating as a life-long illness of "food addiction."

therapy may also provide a training ground where bulimic clients can work directly on underlying social fears, such as the fear of displeasing others or being criticized. In one new group therapy technique, the **group meal,** clients plan and eat a meal together with the therapist, all the while discussing their thoughts and feelings as they occur (Franko, 1993). Research suggests that group therapy is helpful in as many as 75 percent of bulimia nervosa cases, particularly when it is combined with individual insight therapy (Wilfley et al., 1993; Mitchell et al., 1985).

BEHAVIORAL THERAPY Behavioral techniques are often employed in cases of bulimia nervosa along with individual insight therapy or group therapy (Nutzinger & deZwaan, 1990; Long & Cordle, 1982). Bulimic clients may, for example, be asked to monitor and keep diaries of their eating behavior, their fluctuations of hunger and satiety, and their other feelings and experiences (Saunders, 1985; Greenberg & Marks, 1982). This strategy helps them to observe their eating patterns more objectively and to recognize the emotional features of their disorder. In another behavioral technique, clients are sometimes instructed actually to plan their binges beforehand. They may be told to set time limits on binges or to binge only at specified times, in certain places, and on certain days (Cauwels, 1983). These steps are expected to help them gain a sense of control over their binge eating.

Behaviorists are increasingly using the technique of *exposure and response prevention* to help break the binge-purge cycle (Franko, 1992; Gray & Hoage, 1990). As we saw in Chapter 7, this approach has been successfully applied in many cases of obsessive-compulsive disorder. It consists of exposing people to situations that would ordinarily raise their obsessive anxiety and then preventing them from performing their usual compulsive acts. Over the course of treatment, the clients come to understand that the situations are actually quite harmless and that they do not need to resort to their compulsive behaviors to reduce their anxiety. Viewing a bulimic person's vomiting as a compulsive act that reduces obsessive fears about eating, behavioral therapists may have bulimic clients eat particular kinds and amounts of food and then prevent them from vomiting (Rosen & Leitenberg, 1985, 1982). Studies have found that eating-related anxieties often decrease over the course of this treatment, that patients can eat increasingly large meals without experiencing anxiety, and that binge eating and vomiting decrease substantially (Wilson et al., 1986; Johnson et al., 1984).

ANTIDEPRESSANT MEDICATIONS During the past decade, antidepressant drugs have often been added to the treatment package for bulimia nervosa (Mitchell & deZwaan, 1993; Goldbloom & Olmsted, 1993). In one double-blind study the antidepressant drug imipramine was administered for six weeks to twenty bulimic women, while a placebo was given to ten others (Pope et al., 1983). After treatment, eighteen of the twenty women treated with antidepressants showed a moderate to marked reduction of binge eating. In fact, seven stopped binge eating entirely. In contrast, only one of the ten who were given placebos improved even moderately, eight showed no improvement, and one became worse.

Although other studies have not always yielded such impressive results (Leitenberg et al., 1994), some do indicate that antidepressant medications can be helpful in bulimia nervosa, especially in combination with other forms of therapy (Goldbloom & Olmsted, 1993; Fava et al., 1990). As in the treatment of anorexia nervosa, these drugs appear to be most effective for patients who display depression and obsessive-compulsiveness as part of their symptomatology (Yager, 1985).

THE AFTERMATH OF BULIMIA NERVOSA Left untreated, bulimia nervosa usually lasts for years, sometimes receding temporarily but then emerging again (APA, 1994). As with anorexia nervosa, relapses are usually precipitated by a new life stress, such as an impending examination, job change, illness, marriage, or divorce (Abraham & Llewellyn-Jones, 1984).

Approximately 40 percent of bulimic clients show an outstanding immediate response to treatment: they stop their binges or binge less than once a month, stop purging, and stabilize their eating habits and weight (Fairburn et al., 1986; Pope et al., 1983; Abraham & Llewellyn-Jones, 1984). Another 40 percent show a moderate response—decreased binge eating, decreased purging, and better weight stabilization and meal regularity. The remaining 20 percent show no improvement in their eating patterns. Relapse is, however, a problem even among clients who respond successfully to treatment. One study found that close to one-third of recovered bulimic clients relapsed within two years of treatment (Olmsted, Kaplan, & Rockert, 1994). The vast majority of these relapses occurred within 6 months.

Research suggests that treatment also helps many bulimic people make significant and lasting improvements in their psychological and social functioning (Herzog et al., 1990). In follow-up studies conducted between one and three years after treatment, former patients have been found to be less depressed than they were at the time they were diagnosed, although many continue to experience at least a few depressive symptoms (Brotman et al., 1988; Fairburn et al., 1986). Follow-up studies have also indicated that approximately one-third of former patients interact more healthily at work, at home, and in social settings; another third interact effectively in only two of these areas; and the remaining third function well in at best one of these areas (Hsu & Holder, 1986).

Some clinicians have proposed that several factors affect the rate and extent of recovery: (1) binge-purge patterns of long duration will be more difficult to change; (2) enduring recovery will be more difficult when a person's daily routine has come to center primarily on binging and when binge-purge patterns have largely taken the place of such activities as sex, socializing, vocational pursuits, and creative endeavors; and (3) change will be more difficult in the face of severe depression, anxiety, and other emotional distress (Levenkron, 1982). In addition, some recent investigations suggest that relapse may be more likely among persons who vomited more frequently while bulimic and those who maintain a high degree of interpersonal distrust even at the end of treatment (Olmsted et al., 1994).

THE STATE OF THE FIELD

EATING DISORDERS

The prevalence of eating disorders has increased in Western society during the past two decades, and public and clinical interest has risen right along with it. Correspondingly, researchers have been studying anorexia nervosa and bulimia nervosa with great fervor and have learned much about these problems.

They have learned, for example, that the two disorders are similar in many important ways. They have uncovered the unusually significant role played by sociocultural pressures in the development of these disorders, and the critical influences of dieting, starvation, and biological factors in precipitating and maintaining them. They have also determined that the disorders are brought about by a host of intersecting factors, which can best be corrected by multiple intervention programs.

At the same time, many questions are still unanswered, and every new discovery forces clinicians to adjust their theories and treatment programs. Indeed, bulimia nervosa was not even formally identified as a clinical disorder until the 1980s, and recently researchers have learned that bulimic people sometimes feel strangely positive toward their symptoms. A recovered bulimic person raises this point:

> It involves all facets of your life, stopping growth completely. It controls your life in a way that only people with other dependencies can understand. It's progressive and makes you feel totally unworthy. Eventually it will kill you. But I still miss my bulimia as I would an old friend who has died.
>
> *(Cauwels, 1983, p. 173)*

Obviously, when such feelings are understood and addressed, treatment programs will become more effective.

While clinicians and researchers strive for more answers about anorexia nervosa and bulimia nervosa and greater effectiveness in treating them, the clients themselves have begun to take an active role. A number of patient-initiated national organizations now provide information, education, and support to people with eating disorders and to their families through a national telephone hotline, professional referrals, printed information and newsletters, and workshops, seminars, and conferences. These organizations include the National Anorexic Aid Society, American Anorexia and Bulimia Association, National Association of Anorexia Nervosa and Associated Disorders, and Anorexia Nervosa and Related Eating Disorders, Inc.

The very existence of such organizations helps counter the isolation and shame felt by people with eating disorders. By publicizing the relatively common occurrence of such problems and the availability of help, these organizations help countless sufferers to recognize that they are hardly alone or powerless against eating disorders that seem to them to have control over their lives.

SUMMARY

■ **EATING DISORDERS** have increased dramatically since thinness has become a national obsession. Victims of *anorexia nervosa* relentlessly pursue extreme thinness and lose dangerous amounts of weight. Victims of *bulimia nervosa* go on frequent eating binges, then compensate by such means as forcing themselves to vomit or taking laxatives to keep from gaining weight. These eating disorders, which share many important features, are disproportionately prevalent among adolescent girls and young women.

■ **ANOREXIA NERVOSA** most often appears between the ages of 14 and 18 and strikes as many as one percent of the female population. Between 5 and 18 percent of its victims die of medical problems related to starvation.

Five central features of anorexia nervosa are a drive for thinness and a morbid fear of becoming overweight, preoccupation with food, cognitive disturbances, personality and mood problems, and medical problems, including *amenorrhea*.

■ **BULIMIA NERVOSA**, also known as the binge-purge syndrome, usually appears in females between the ages of 15 and 19 years, and is displayed by between 1 and 6 percent of them. These young women generally maintain their body weight within a normal range, although it may fluctuate noticeably. Some people with this pattern do, however, become underweight and others overweight.

The binge periods of bulimic persons are often planned and accompanied by a great deal of tension, followed by guilt and self-reproach. Theorists suggest that purging behavior is initially reinforced by the immediate relief from uncomfortable feelings of fullness, or temporary reduction of the feelings of anxiety, self-disgust, and loss of control attached to binge eating. Over time, however, people with this pattern often feel increasingly disgusted with themselves, depressed, and guilty.

■ **TODAY'S THEORISTS** usually apply a *multidimensional risk perspective* to explain eating disorders, and identify several key factors that place a person at risk for an eating disorder: sociocultural pressures, family environment, ego deficiencies and cognitive disturbances, biological factors, and mood disorders.

■ **THE FIRST STEP** in treating anorexia nervosa is to increase caloric intake and restore the person's weight quickly, by such strategies as *supportive nursing care*. The second step is to address the underlying problems, so that improvement may be lasting, by a mixture of individual, group, and family therapies.

Treatments for bulimia nervosa focus on eliminating the binge-purge pattern and addressing underlying causes of the disorder. Often several treatment strategies are combined, including individual insight therapy, group therapy, behavioral therapy, and antidepressant medications.

Topic Overview

DEPRESSANTS

Alcohol

Sedative-Hypnotic Drugs

Opioids

STIMULANTS

Cocaine

Amphetamines

Caffeine

HALLUCINOGENS

Psychedelic Drugs

Cannabis

COMBINATIONS OF SUBSTANCES

EXPLANATIONS OF SUBSTANCE-RELATED DISORDERS

TREATMENTS FOR SUBSTANCE-RELATED DISORDERS

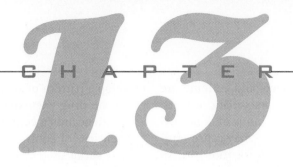

SUBSTANCE-RELATED DISORDERS

■

*T*HERE IS PROBABLY NO SUBSTANCE on earth that has not been ingested by human beings somewhere, at some time. Curious and adventuresome, we have learned that a vast variety of substances are edible and nutritious when they are prepared in certain ways, and we have developed a long list of acceptable foods and delicacies. Humans have likewise stumbled upon substances that have interesting effects on the brain and the rest of the body. Many such substances have proved beneficial to health or healing and have gained use as medicines; some have been found to have calming or stimulating effects and are used to enhance social and recreational experiences. The use of potent substances pervades our society: we may swallow an aspirin to quiet a headache, an antibiotic to fight an infection, or a tranquilizer to calm us down; drink coffee to get going in the morning or wine to relax with friends; or smoke cigarettes to soothe our nerves.

MANY OF THE SUBSTANCES that humans have come across are capable of harming the body or adversely affecting behavior or mood. The compulsive misuse of these substances has become one of society's most disabling problems.

TECHNICALLY, THE TERM "DRUG" applies to any substance other than food that changes our bodily or mental functioning. Henceforth in this chapter, the words "drug" and "substance" will be used interchangeably with that connotation. In recent years "substance" has gained favor among the people who treat substance-related disorders, partly because most people think of a drug as either a medicine (whether prescription or nonprescription) or an illegal substance, and fail to see that potentially harmful substances such as alcohol, tobacco, and caffeine are drugs, too, each with its own characteristic effects.

Drug misuse may lead to various kinds of abnormal functioning. First, ingestion of a drug may cause temporary changes in behavior, emotion, or thought. An excessive amount of alcohol, for example, may lead to a state of *intoxication* (literally, "poisoning"), a temporary syndrome in which a person exhibits impaired judgment, mood changes, irritability, slurred speech, and loss of coordination. Drugs such as LSD may produce a distinct form of intoxication, sometimes called *hallucinosis,* a state of perceptual distortions and hallucinations.

The regular use of some substances can also lead to longer-term patterns of maladaptive behavior and to changes in the body's response to the substance. People who regularly ingest a given substance may de-velop a pattern of *substance abuse,* in which they rely on the drug excessively and chronically and allow its use to occupy a central place in their lives. Because of their loss of control over drug use, substance abusers may seriously damage their family and social relationships, perform unreliably at work, and create physical hazards for themselves or others. People who display *substance dependence,* a more advanced substance-related disorder that is known popularly as *addiction,* further develop a *physical* dependence on a drug in addition to a pattern of abusing it—that is, they develop a *tolerance* for the drug or experience *withdrawal* symptoms if they suddenly stop taking it, or both. *Tolerance* is a condition in which a person needs increasing doses of the substance in order to keep obtaining the desired effect. Similarly, long-term regular use may lead to *withdrawal,* a condition in which

BOX 13-1

TOBACCO AND NICOTINE: A POWERFUL ADDICTION

Smoking tobacco has been an accepted practice for centuries, but recently health professionals have become aware that *nicotine,* the active substance in tobacco and a stimulant of the central nervous system, is a powerfully addictive substance. The physiological effects and dangers of smoking tobacco are well documented. More than 410,000 people die each year in the United States as a result of smoking (Farley, 1994; Report of the Surgeon General, 1990, 1988). Pregnant women who smoke are more likely than nonsmokers to deliver prematurely and to have babies who are underweight (Goldstein, 1994). Smoking is directly associated with high blood pressure, coronary heart disease, lung disease, cancer, stroke, and other deadly medical problems. People who smoke two packs a day are twenty-two times as likely to die from lung cancer as non-smokers. Moreover, nonsmokers who inhale cigarette smoke from the environment also have an elevated risk of lung cancer and other diseases (Report of the Surgeon General, 1987).

Approximately 26 percent of Americans over the age of 12 are regular smokers (NIDA, 1992). Indeed, 17 percent of all high school seniors smoke regularly (Johnston et al., 1993). Although these rates represent drops of 40 percent during the past 35 years, they are still alarming (Goldstein, 1994). Most adult smokers know that smoking is unhealthy and would rather not do it. So why do they continue to smoke? Because, as the surgeon general declared in 1988, nicotine is as addictive as heroin, perhaps even more so. Inhaling a puff of cigarette smoke delivers a dose of nicotine to the brain faster than it could be delivered by injection into the bloodstream, and it is believed to bind directly to receptors in the brain, which soon becomes dependent on it. When regular smokers abstain, they experience withdrawal symptoms—irritability, increased appetite, sleep distur-bances, decreased metabolic rate, cognitive difficulties, and a powerful desire to smoke. Smokers also develop a tolerance for nicotine and must increase their consumption in order to achieve the same psychological and physiological results and to avoid withdrawal.

Because smoking is socially acceptable (although its acceptability is on the decline), most people are comfortable admitting that they smoke and openly look for ways to quit. This situation has created a ready market for numerous products and techniques for helping people kick the habit. Most of these methods do not work very well. Success rates for all approaches depend heavily on the motivation of the smoker. Many smokers seem to find that the immediate pleasure they experience often outweighs the fear of long-term consequences. Whether the person succeeds at quitting also depends on factors such as stress, social support, family members who smoke, self-confidence, gender, and availabil-

people experience unpleasant and at times dangerous symptoms—for example, muscle aches and cramps, anxiety attacks, sweating, nausea—when they suddenly stop taking or reduce their dosage of the drug. Withdrawal symptoms can begin within hours of the last dose and tend to intensify over several days before they subside. Surveys suggest that over the course of a year, between 9.5 and 11.3 percent of all adults in the United States, more than 15 million people, display a substance-related disorder, but only 20 percent of them receive treatment for it (Kessler et al., 1994; Regier et al., 1993).

Many drugs are available in our society, and new ones emerge almost every day. Some are found in nature, others are derived from natural substances, and still others are synthetically produced. Some, such as antianxiety drugs and barbiturates, require a physi-

cian's prescription for legal use. Others, such as alcohol and the nicotine found in cigarettes, are legally available to all adults (see Box 13–1). Still others, such as heroin, are illegal under any circumstance, yet are manufactured and sold in such quantities that they constitute major, albeit underground, industries. Nearly 13 percent of all people in the United States currently use marijuana, cocaine, heroin, or some other illegal substance (NIDA, 1993). Twenty-seven percent of high school seniors have used an illicit drug within the past year (Johnston et al., 1993).

The drugs that currently are arousing the most concern among the general public fall into three categories: substances that act to *depress* the central nervous system, such as alcohol and opioids; *stimulants* of the central nervous system, such as cocaine and amphetamines; and *hallucinogens*, such as

---

ity of information (Tunstal, Ginsberg, & Hall, 1985).

In general, self-help kits, informational pamphlets, commercial programs, and support groups are at most modestly helpful. Most people who do stop smoking after receiving such interventions start smoking again within one year (Hall et al., 1985).

The most successful treatments for nicotine addiction have been behavioral therapies and drug interventions. Using *aversive conditioning*, therapists have on the average been able to foster a two-year abstinence from smoking in about 50 percent of cases. The most common form of aversive conditioning is **rapid smoking.** The smoker treated by this technique sits in a closed room and puffs quickly on a cigarette, as often as once every six seconds, until the smoker begins to feel ill and cannot take another puff. The feelings of illness become associated with smoking, and the smoker experiences an aversive reaction to cigarettes (Baker & Brandon, 1988).

A common drug intervention for smoking is the use of **nicotine gum,** which contains a high level of nicotine that is released as the smoker chews. Theoretically, people who ingest nicotine by chewing no longer need to smoke, and the reinforcing effects of smoking are removed. Research sug-

An American Cancer Society anti-smoking poster.

gests that this approach does improve a smoker's chances of long-term abstinence, especially when it is combined with behavioral therapies. The more nicotine-dependent the smoker, the more effective the use of nicotine gum (Jarvik & Schneider, 1984). A primary drawback, however, is that the use of nicotine gum does not lead to a decrease in nicotine consumption.

A similar biological approach is the

nicotine patch. This Band-aid–like strip is attached to the skin throughout the day. Its nicotine content is supposedly absorbed through the skin, leaving the smoker with less need for nicotine. Some people report that the patch helps them abstain from or cut down on cigarette smoking, but research has yet to establish the efficacy of this approach (Goldstein, 1994).

From the smoker's viewpoint, most treatments have little or no effect on the critical component of nicotine withdrawal: the craving for a cigarette. Many smokers report that the craving is the most debilitating obstacle to quitting. The blood pressure drug **clonidine** has undergone testing as a possible means of reducing this and other symptoms of withdrawal from nicotine and other addictive substances, and has shown some promise (Glassman et al., 1984), but it is no magic pill. The more one smokes, the harder it is to quit. On the positive side, however, former smokers' risk for disease and death decreases steadily the longer they abstain from smoking (Goldstein, 1994; Jaffe, 1985). For those who are able to take the long view, this assurance may be a powerful motivator. In the meantime, more than 1,000 people die of smoking-related diseases each day.

TABLE 13-1

RELATIONSHIPS BETWEEN SEX, WEIGHT, ORAL ALCOHOL CONSUMPTION, AND BLOOD ALCOHOL LEVEL

ABSOLUTE ALCOHOL (OUNCES)	BEVERAGE INTAKE*	BLOOD ALCOHOL LEVEL (PERCENT)					
		FEMALE (100 LB.)	MALE (100 LB.)	FEMALE (150 LB.)	MALE (150 LB.)	FEMALE (200 LB.)	MALE (200 LB.)
½	1 oz. spirits† 1 glass wine 1 can beer	0.045	0.037	0.03	0.025	0.022	0.019
1	2 oz. spirits 2 glasses wine 2 cans beer	0.090	0.075	0.06	0.050	0.045	0.037
2	4 oz. spirits 4 glasses wine 4 cans beer	0.180	0.150	0.12	0.100	0.090	0.070
3	6 oz. spirits 6 glasses wine 6 cans beer	0.270	0.220	0.18	0.150	0.130	0.110
4	8 oz. spirits 8 glasses wine 8 cans beer	0.360	0.300	0.24	0.200	0.180	0.150
5	10 oz. spirits 10 glasses wine 10 cans beer	0.450	0.370	0.30	0.250	0.220	0.180

* In 1 hour.

† 100-proof spirits.

Source: Ray & Ksir, 1993, p. 194.

LSD and cannabis, which cause changes in sensory perception.

■ DEPRESSANTS ■

Depressants are substances that slow the activity of the central nervous system and in sufficient doses cause a reduction of tension and inhibitions and impair judgment, motor activity, and concentration. The three most widely used groups of depressants are *alcohol*, *sedative-hypnotics*, and *opioids*.

ALCOHOL

Two-thirds of the people in the United States drink alcohol-containing beverages, at least from time to time. Indeed, alcohol is by far the most popular drug in the United States, and purchases of beer, wine, liquor, and sundry cocktail ingredients add up to tens of billions of dollars each year. More than 5 percent of all adults are heavy drinkers, consuming at least five drinks on at least five occasions during the past month (NIDA, 1993). Male heavy drinkers outnumber female heavy drinkers by more than 3 to 1, 8.6 percent to 2.4 percent (NIDA, 1993).

All alcoholic beverages contain *ethyl alcohol.* This chemical compound is rapidly absorbed into the blood through the lining of the stomach and the intestine, and immediately begins to take effect. The ethyl alcohol is carried in the bloodstream to the central nervous system (CNS), where it acts to depress, or slow, its functioning. At first it affects the higher centers of the CNS, those that control judgment and inhibition, and people become less constrained, more talkative, and often more friendly. As their inner control breaks down, they may feel relaxed, safe, self-confident, and happy. Some also experience heightened sexual desire and seek to act upon those feelings. Alcohol's depression of these regions of the CNS also impairs fine motor skills, increases sensitivity to light, and causes the small blood vessels of the skin to dilate, so that the face and neck become flushed and the person feels warm.

As more alcohol is ingested, the effects increase, eventually depressing other areas in the CNS and thus causing changes that are even more problematic. People become still less restrained and more confused. Their ability to make rational judgments declines, their speech becomes less guarded and less coherent, and their memory falters (Goldstein, 1994). Many become loud, boisterous, and aggressive, their emotions exaggerated and unstable; mildly amusing remarks or situations may strike them as hilarious.

Motor impairment also becomes more pronounced as drinking continues, and reaction times slow. People at this stage are unsteady when they stand or walk and clumsy in performing even simple activities. They may drop things, bump into doors and furniture, and misjudge distances. Their vision becomes blurred, particularly peripheral vision, and they have trouble distinguishing between different intensities of light. Hearing is affected, too. As a result of such impairments, people who have drunk too much alcohol may have great difficulty driving or solving simple problems.

The extent of the effect of ethyl alcohol on body chemistry is determined by its *concentration* in the blood. Thus a given amount of alcohol will have less effect on a larger person than on a smaller one (see Table 13–1 and Figure 13–1), because the larger person has a greater volume of blood. Other factors may also influence the concentration of ethyl alcohol in the blood. For example, women become more intoxicated than men at an equal dose of alcohol, since women have significantly less of the stomach enzyme *alcohol dehydrogenase,* which breaks down alcohol in the stomach before it enters the blood (NIAAA, 1992).

Levels of impairment are closely related to the concentration of ethyl alcohol in the blood. When alcohol constitutes 0.06 percent of the blood volume, a person usually feels relaxed and comfortable without yet being intoxicated. However, by the time the blood-alcohol concentration reaches 0.09 percent (three cocktails, five bottles of beer, or 16 ounces of ordinary wine), the drinker crosses the line into intoxication. As the concentration of alcohol in the bloodstream further increases, the drinker becomes even more intoxicated and impaired. If the level goes as high as 0.55 percent, death will probably result. Most people, however, lose consciousness before they can drink enough to reach this level.

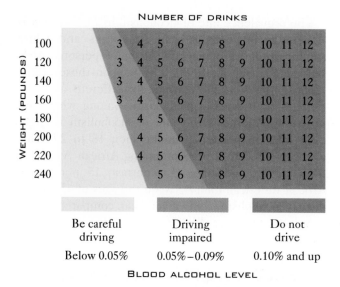

FIGURE 13–1 *Counting a 12-ounce glass of beer as one drink, clinicians estimate that a 100-pound person will reach a state's legal limit for drunk driving, a blood alcohol level of 0.08 to 0.10 percent, after ingesting just four drinks, whereas a 240-pound person will usually reach this limit only after having around seven drinks. The ability to drive is somewhat impaired even when the blood alcohol level is below the legal limit. (Adapted from Frances & Franklin, 1988.)*

The effects of alcohol decline only as the alcohol concentration in the blood declines. Most of the alcohol is broken down, or *metabolized,* by the liver into carbon dioxide and water, which can be exhaled and excreted (Korsten et al., 1975; Raskin, 1975). The average rate of metabolizing is 10 to 15 percent of an ounce per hour, but different people's livers conduct this process at somewhat different speeds; thus rates of "sobering up" vary. Despite a popular misconception, neither drinking black coffee, splashing cold water on the face, nor "getting hold of oneself" can speed the process up. Only time and metabolism can make a person sober.

Most people become intoxicated at most occasionally, and their use of alcohol remains a matter of personal choice. Many people, however, progress from casual or "social" drinking to uncontrollable alcohol consumption. They develop a long-term pattern of alcohol abuse or alcohol dependence—patterns collectively known as *alcoholism.* Surveys indicate that over a one-year period, between 7.4 and 9.7 percent of all adults in the United States abuse or are dependent on alcohol (Kessler et al., 1994; Regier et al., 1993). Between 13 and 23 percent of the adult population will display one of these patterns at some time in their lives, with men outnumbering women by as much as 5 to 1 (APA, 1994; Kessler et al., 1994; Helzer et al., 1991).

The prevalence rate of alcoholism in a given year is 7 percent for both African Americans and white Americans and 9 percent for Hispanic persons (APA, 1994; Helzer et al., 1991). The men in these ethnic groups, however, show strikingly different age patterns in their rates of alcoholism. Among white and Hispanic Americans the rate of alcoholism is highest—over 18 percent—among men 18 to 29 years old, compared to 8 percent among African American men in that age range. In contrast, 15 percent of African American men between the ages of 45 and 64 display alcoholism in any given year, compared to 7 to 8 percent of white American and Hispanic men in that age range.

ALCOHOL ABUSE AND DEPENDENCE Alcohol abusers regularly drink excessive amounts of alcohol, feel unable to change their drinking habits, and rely on alcohol to enable them to do things that would otherwise make them anxious. The excessive drinking often interferes with their socializing or with their cognitive ability and work performance. They may have frequent arguments with family members or friends, miss work repeatedly, and even lose their jobs.

Clinicians have identified three broad patterns of alcohol abuse. In one, the person drinks large amounts of alcohol every day, keeps drinking until intoxicated, and plans his or her daily life around drinking.

*D*rinking made me more relaxed, easier to be with. It helped me sell, it gave me energy, it gave me courage. Weekends were for drinking, fishing trips were for drinking, holidays were for drinking—everything pleasant was associated with alcohol. And when I stopped drinking for a short time, I couldn't help noticing the difference. I was tired, irritable, vaguely depressed, no fun to be with, a bad father, a worse husband—and so I continued drinking because drinking had come to occupy the center of my life. . . . By the time I reached my early thirties, though, all pretense at control had gone. Every night was a drinking bout that lasted until I had drained that evening's quart bottle. Then, to get going in the morning, I had to have a couple of bloody Marys. And to keep going during the day, more to drink. Even through the haze of alcohol, I began to feel that things weren't going as well as they had before. My wife and I had nothing to say to each other, I couldn't stand being with the kids for more than a few minutes at a time, and my sales had begun to fall off. I blamed it on the economy, then on the President's policies, then on bad planning at the top of our company—on everybody and everything but me and my drinking. Finally, in a single year, I had three auto accidents, one serious enough to involve injury to the occupants of the other vehicle (needless to say,

When a man and a woman of identical size drink identical amounts of alcohol, the woman becomes intoxicated more quickly. Apparently women's bodies have so much less alcohol dehydrogenase, the enzyme that breaks alcohol down in the stomach, that they absorb 30 percent more alcohol into their blood than men.

I'd been drinking before all three). I lost my license for two years. My wife, fed up with life with "a drunken bum," left me and took the children. And my partner called me in and told me that he'd had enough, that if I didn't go on the wagon, he and I were through. . . .

(Nathan & Harris, 1980, pp. 283–284)

In a second pattern of alcohol abuse, drinking to excess is limited to weekends or evenings, or both. The actor Dick Van Dyke displayed this pattern of alcohol abuse.

I didn't miss work ever because of drinking. And I never drank at work. Never drank during the day—only at home and only in the evenings. . . . I never craved a drink during the day. I was never a morning drinker—I didn't want one then. The idea made me as sick as it would make anyone else. But evening drinking is a form of alcoholism, just like periodic drinking is a form of alcoholism. . . .

My wife had long gone to bed. I was sitting alone, drinking, lost in what I took to be deep thought. I realized suddenly, "Why I am thinking gibberish here—my mind is completely out of it." When I woke up the next morning, I got up and went to a hospital. Went straight into a treatment center.

(HEW, 1976, p. 76)

In a third pattern of alcohol abuse, the person may abstain from drinking for long periods of time, then go on periodic binges of heavy drinking that can last weeks or months. The drinker may remain intoxicated for days. Such people experience "blackouts" and later are unable to recall the period of their intoxication.

For many people, the pattern of alcoholism further includes physical dependence. As they use alcohol repeatedly, their body builds up a tolerance for it and they need to drink increasing amounts in order to feel any effects. They also experience withdrawal responses when they abstain from alcohol. When they try to stop drinking, within hours their hands, tongue, and eyelids begin to shake noticeably. They feel weak and nauseous. They sweat and vomit. Their heart beats rapidly and their blood pressure rises. They may also become anxious, depressed, unable to sleep, or irritable.

A small percentage of people who are alcohol dependent also experience a particularly dramatic withdrawal reaction within three days after they stop or reduce drinking: *alcohol withdrawal delirium,* or *delirium tremens* ("the DT's"). Delirium is abundant mental confusion and clouded consciousness. Alcoholic persons in the throes of delirium tremens may have terrifying visual hallucinations: they believe they are seeing small frightening animals or objects moving about rapidly, perhaps pursuing them or crawling on them. Here is Mark Twain's classic description of Huckleberry Finn's alcoholic father:

I don't know how long I was asleep, but . . . there was an awful scream and I was up. There was Pap looking wild, and skipping around every which way and yelling about snakes. He said they was crawling up on his legs; and then he would give a jump and scream, and say one had bit him on the cheek—but I couldn't see no snakes. He started and run round . . . hollering "Take him off! he's biting me on the neck!" I never see a man look so wild in the eyes. Pretty soon he was all fagged out, and fell down panting; then he rolled over . . . kicking things every which way, and striking and grabbing at the air with his hands, and screaming . . . there was devils a-hold of him. He wore out by and by. . . . He says . . .

"Tramp-tramp-tramp: that's the dead; tramp-tramp-tramp; they're coming after me; but I won't go. Oh, they're here; don't touch me . . . they're cold; let go . . . ."

Then he went down on all fours and crawled off, begging them to let him alone. . . .

(Twain, 1885)

Like Pap, people who experience delirium tremens become disoriented; they don't know where they are or what time of the day, month, or year it is. Some also have seizures and lose consciousness and are vul-

nerable to strokes and other life-threatening problems. Like most other alcohol withdrawal symptoms, the DT's usually run their course in two to three days. Research suggests that delirium tremens is related to low levels of magnesium and that drinkers with generally low magnesium levels are prone to develop it (Victor & Wolfe, 1973).

Another dramatic and relatively rare withdrawal reaction, *alcohol-induced psychotic disorder,* consists of *delusions,* ideas that have no basis in fact, or *auditory hallucinations,* such as imaginary voices that say demeaning or hostile things, either directly to the alcoholic person or about him or her. Such reactions usually develop within two days after the person stops drinking and may last for weeks or months.

PERSONAL AND SOCIAL IMPACT OF ALCOHOL AND ALCOHOLISM   Partly because alcohol is legal, accessible, and often portrayed positively in the arts and in advertising, there is little appreciation of the fact that it is one of society's most dangerous drugs. Alcoholism destroys millions of families, social relationships, and careers (Steinglass et al., 1985). Medical treatment, lost productivity, and potential losses due to premature deaths from alcoholism have been estimated to cost society between $86 and $116 billion annually (NIAAA, 1991). It is also a factor in a third to a half of all suicides, homicides, assaults, rapes, and accidental deaths, including close to 50 percent of all fatal automobile accidents in the United States (Painter, 1992). Altogether, intoxicated drivers are responsible for 23,000 deaths each year—an average of one alcohol-related death every 23 minutes (OSAP, 1991). Similarly, intoxicated pedestrians are 4 times more likely than sober pedestrians to be hit by a car (Painter, 1992).

Alcoholism has serious effects on the individual's family as well as on society at large. The 28 to 34 million people who are children of alcoholic persons often grow up in a dysfunctional family environment characterized by higher than average levels of disharmony, sexual abuse, and physical abuse (Mathew et al., 1993; Velleman & Orford, 1993; Famularo et al., 1992). Indeed, fathers and mothers who abuse their children are respectively 10 and 3 times more likely than other parents to abuse alcohol (Painter, 1992). Children of alcoholic persons may be at increased risk for a variety of problems. Anxiety, depression, phobias, and substance abuse are the disorders most commonly reported by adults with alcoholic parents, and elevated levels of conduct disorder and attention-deficit hyperactivity disorder may occur in children living in alcoholic homes. Some investigators have suggested that people with alcoholic parents also display recognizable behavior patterns, ranging from poor communication skills to low self-esteem, role confusion, and increased likelihood of marital instability (Greenfield et al., 1993; Mathew et al., 1993).

Alcohol abuse and dependence are also major problems among the young. Approximately 3.4 percent of today's high school seniors report that they drink every day (Johnston, O'Malley, & Bachman, 1993), and an estimated 5 million teenagers have experienced problems related to alcohol use (Beck, Thombs, & Summons, 1993). Even 8 to 12 percent of surveyed elementary school children admit to some alcohol use (Johnston et al., 1993; Hutchinson & Little, 1985).

Chronic and excessive alcohol consumption can also seriously damage one's physical health. It can, for example, cause serious, often fatal damage to the liver. An excessive intake of alcohol overworks the liver, resulting in an accumulation there of excess fat, a condition sometimes called a "fatty liver." If the excessive alcohol intake continues for years, further liver damage may develop into an irreversible condition called *cirrhosis,* in which the liver becomes scarred, forms fibrous tissue, and begins to change its anatomy and functioning. Blood fails to flow through it properly, and major complications follow. Cirrhosis is the seventh most frequent cause of death in the United States, accounting for around 28,000 deaths each year (Ray & Ksir, 1993; ADAMHA, 1987); and a high percentage of these cases are the result of chronic alcohol use.

Alcohol abuse and dependence may also cause other medical problems. Alcohol can depress heart functioning and damage heart muscle fibers and over time may lead to heart failure, irregularities of functioning, or blood clots. It can also impair the immune responses that, as we observed in Chapter 11, defend the body against disease. Chronic alcohol consumption reduces the level of white blood cells, depresses antibody production, and suppresses the activity of specialized immune cells that keep the lungs free from infection. Alcoholism may increase susceptibility to cancer and to bacterial infections, speed the onset of AIDS, or exacerbate HIV-induced immunosuppression in HIV-positive people (NIAAA, 1992).

Chronic excessive drinking also poses major problems in nutrition. Alcohol is high in calories, but because it has virtually no food value—no vitamins, minerals, fats, proteins, or usable carbohydrates—its calories are often described as "empty." They satiate people, lower their desire for other foods, and lead them to eat less than they should. As a result, chronic drinkers are likely to become malnourished, their bodies weak, tired, and highly vulnerable to disease. The vitamin and mineral deficiencies of alcoholic

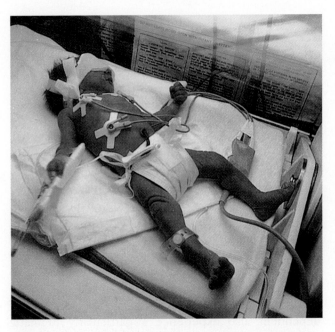

A woman who drinks during pregnancy risks harming her fetus. More than 50,000 babies are born with alcohol-related problems in the United States each year. Many of these babies suffer from "fetal alcohol syndrome." Ingestion of cocaine, heroin, and certain other drugs during pregnancy may also severely affect the psychological and physical development of babies.

persons may also cause certain mental disorders. An alcohol-related deficiency of vitamin B (thiamine), for example, may cause *Wernicke's encephalopathy,* a potentially fatal neurological disease characterized by confusion, excitement, delirium, double vision, and other eye-movement abnormalities. Untreated, Wernicke's encephalopathy may develop into *Korsakoff's syndrome* (also called *alcohol-induced persisting amnestic disorder*), marked by extreme confusion, memory impairment, and other neurological symptoms. People with Korsakoff's syndrome cannot remember the past or learn new information, and may make up for their memory losses by *confabulating*—spontaneously reciting made-up events to fill in the gaps. Even in the absence of these serious disorders, intoxicating levels of alcohol can interfere with the memory process by inhibiting the cellular changes that constitute a new memory (Morrissett & Swartzwelder, 1993).

Finally, it is now clear that women who drink during pregnancy are placing the health of their fetuses at risk. Heavy drinking early in pregnancy often leads to a miscarriage. Moreover, alcohol use during pregnancy may lead to babies born with *fetal alcohol syndrome,* a pattern of abnormalities that includes mental retardation, hyperactivity, head and face deformities, heart defects and other organ malfunctions, and retarded growth (Goldstein, 1994; Ray & Ksir, 1993). The scope and likelihood of these symptoms are apparently related to the amount, duration, and timing of alcohol in the mother's system during pregnancy. Thus, babies of women who drink heavily throughout their pregnancy are at greatest risk for developing these symptoms. At the same time, however, even relatively low amounts of drinking by a pregnant woman apparently place her baby at some risk. It has been estimated that in the overall population, between 0.4 and 2.9 out of every 1000 births are characterized by the fetal alcohol syndrome. The rate increases to between 23 and 29 out of every 1000 births among women who are problem drinkers (Ray & Ksir, 1993).

SEDATIVE-HYPNOTIC DRUGS

Sedative-hypnotic drugs produce feelings of relaxation and drowsiness. At relatively low dosages, they have a calming or sedative effect. At higher ones, they are sleep inducers—or hypnotics. The two most widely used sedative-hypnotics are antianxiety drugs and barbiturates.

ANTIANXIETY DRUGS As we saw in Chapter 7, *benzodiazepines,* the antianxiety drugs discovered in the 1950s, are now the most popular sedative-hypnotic drugs available. These drugs, which include Valium, Xanax, Halcion, and Librium, can relieve anxiety without making people as drowsy as other kinds of sedative-hypnotics. They have less impact on the brain's respiratory center than barbiturates, so they are less likely than those drugs to depress the respiratory functioning and cause death by overdose.

When benzodiazepines first appeared, they seemed so safe and effective that physicians prescribed them quite readily, and their use proliferated in our society. It became easy to get prescriptions for benzodiazepines or to obtain them illegally; it was therefore easy to take them in high dosages. This widespread and heavy use showed clinicians that the drugs can, in fact, cause intoxication in high dosages and lead to a pattern of abuse or dependence (see Table 13–2). It is now estimated that more than 1 percent of the adult population in the United States abuse or become dependent on antianxiety drugs at some point in their lives (APA, 1994) and thus become subject to many of the dangers that researchers have identified in barbiturate abuse and dependence.

TABLE 13–2

			RISK OF ORGAN DAMAGE OR DEATH	RISK OF SEVERE SOCIAL OR ECONOMIC CONSEQUENCES	RISK OF SEVERE OR LONG-LASTING MENTAL AND BEHAVIORAL CHANGE
	INTOXICATION POTENTIAL	DEPENDENCY POTENTIAL			
Opioids	High	High	Low	High	Low to Moderate
Sedative-hypnotics:					
Barbiturates	Moderate	Moderate to High	Moderate to High	Moderate to High	Low
Benzodiazepines	Moderate	Low	Low	Low	Low
Stimulants (cocaine, amphetamines)	High	High	Moderate	Low to Moderate	Moderate to High
Alcohol	High	Moderate	High	High	High
Cannabis	High	Low to Moderate	Low	Low to Moderate	Low
Mixed drug classes	High	High	High	High	High

RISKS AND CONSEQUENCES OF DRUG MISUSE

Source: APA, 1994; Gold, 1986, p. 28.

BARBITURATES First discovered in Germany more than 100 years ago, *barbiturates* were widely prescribed by physicians throughout the first half of this century to combat anxiety and to help people sleep (Cooper, 1977). Although the emergence of benzodiazepines has reduced the use of these drugs in recent years, some physicians still prescribe them, especially for sleep problems. Barbiturates can indeed be helpful for tension and insomnia, but clinicians have become aware that many dangers are involved in their use, not the least of which is their potential for abuse and dependence. Disproportionate use of barbiturates among middle-aged women in our society has made them the chief victims of this problem. In addition, several thousand deaths a year are caused by accidental or suicidal overdoses of the drug. A number of other sedative-hypnotic drugs, including *methaqualone* (trade name Quaalude), act upon the brain in barbiturate-like ways and can lead to similar forms of abuse or dependence.

Barbiturates are usually taken in pill or capsule form. In low doses they reduce a person's level of excitement in the same way that benzodiazepines do, by increasing the synaptic activity of the inhibitory neurotransmitter GABA (see pp. 205–206), but apparently they do so through different biological channels than benzodiazepines (Vellucci, 1989). At higher doses, barbiturates depress the firing of neurons that bring messages into the reticular formation. Since the *reticular formation* is the body's arousal center and responsible for keeping people awake and alert, the person gets sleepy. At still higher doses, barbiturates depress spinal reflexes and muscles and are often used as surgical anesthetics. If a barbiturate dose reaches too high a level, the resulting respiratory failure and low blood pressure can lead to coma and even death.

Barbiturates are actually more like alcohol than like benzodiazepines in their action on the brain and the rest of the body. In fact, before the development of barbiturates, alcohol and its derivatives were the most widely used sedative-hypnotic drugs. People can get intoxicated from large doses of barbiturates, just as they do from alcohol. They become increasingly impulsive, talkative, and in some cases irritable. Their judgment declines and their moods swing rapidly. Coordination is affected, speech is slurred, and attention and memory are impaired.

Even when physicians prescribe barbiturates for their hypnotic effects, patients soon discover their sedative qualities and may start taking the drug to help them cope with daily problems rather than to help them sleep. Repeated use of this kind can quickly lead to abuse. A person may feel unable to stop or reduce the use of barbiturates and may spend much of the day intoxicated. Social and occupational functioning may be disrupted by quarrels, alienation, and poor job performance, all stemming from the effects of the drug.

Barbiturate abuse can further lead to dependence. Tolerance for the drugs increases very rapidly in people who overuse them; increasing amounts become necessary to calm those people down or help them to sleep. Moreover, abstaining from the drug may cause withdrawal symptoms that are similar to those seen in alcoholism: nausea, vomiting, weakness, malaise, feelings of anxiety and depression, and sleep problems. In extreme cases the withdrawal reaction may resemble delirium tremens (here called *barbiturate withdrawal delirium*). Barbiturate withdrawal is one of the most dangerous forms of drug withdrawal, as some barbiturate addicts experience convulsions when they abstain from the drug.

One of the great dangers of barbiturate dependence is that the lethal dose of the drug remains the same even while the body is building up a tolerance for its other effects (Gold, 1986). In a common and tragic scenario, once the initial barbiturate dose prescribed by a physician stops working, a person decides independently to keep increasing it every few weeks. Eventually the person ingests a dose that may very well prove fatal.

OPIOIDS

Opioids include opium and the drugs derived from it, such as heroin, morphine, and codeine. A natural sub-

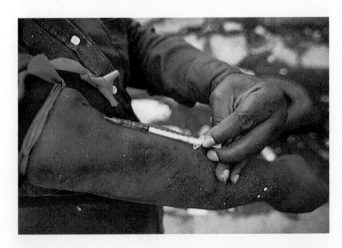

Opioids may be taken by mouth, inhaled (snorted), injected just beneath the surface of the skin, or, as here, injected intravenously. Those who share needles to inject themselves run the risk of developing AIDS or hepatitis; those using unsterile equipment may develop skin abscesses.

The more things change, the more they stay the same. Opium users used to get high at opium dens, such as this one in New York City's Chinatown, photographed in 1926. Today many crack users gather at "crack houses" to drug themselves into near oblivion.

stance from the sap of the opium poppy seed, **opium** itself has been in use for thousands of years. In the past it was used widely in the treatment of medical disorders because of its ability to reduce both physical and emotional pain. Physicians eventually discovered, however, that the drug was physically addictive.

In 1804 a new substance—*morphine*—was derived from opium by the German chemist Frederic Serturner. It, too, was an effective pain reliever, even more effective than opium. In addition, morphine made people quiet and helped put them to sleep (thus its name, derived from Morpheus, the Greek god of sleep). Believing that morphine was free of opium's addictive properties, physicians began to use it widely soon after its discovery. In the United States its use accelerated during the Civil War, when many wounded soldiers received morphine injections. Although the drug helped alleviate their pain, it soon became clear that repeated administrations could also lead to addiction. In fact, morphine addiction became known as "soldiers' disease."

Near the end of the nineteenth century, scientists were trying to derive a nonaddictive pain reliever from morphine by removing its addictive components and retaining the pain-relieving ones. In 1898 morphine was converted into a new pain reliever, *heroin,* which was believed to achieve this goal. In fact, for several years heroin was viewed as a wonder drug. It was used as a cough medicine and for other medicinal purposes and to relieve the discomforts of morphine

withdrawal. Eventually physicians recognized that heroin itself is extremely addictive, and in fact leads to more rapid tolerance than the other opioids. By 1917 the U.S. Congress concluded that all drugs derived from opium were addictive and passed a law making opioids illegal except for medical purposes.

New derivatives of opium have been discovered, and synthetic (laboratory-blended) opioids such as methadone have also been developed. These various opioid drugs are known collectively as *narcotics.* Each has its own potency, speed of action, and tolerance level. Morphine and codeine have become the primary medical narcotics, usually prescribed to relieve pain. Heroin has remained illegal in the United States under all circumstances.

Narcotics may be smoked, inhaled ("snorted"), injected by needle just beneath the skin ("skin popped"), or injected directly into the bloodstream ("mainlined"). An injection quickly brings on a *rush*—a spasm of warmth and ecstasy that is sometimes compared with orgasm. The brief spasm is followed by several hours of a pleasant feeling called a *high* or *nod.* During a high, the drug user feels relaxed and euphoric. Worries, tensions, and pains subside. The person becomes lethargic and unconcerned about food, sex, or other bodily needs.

Heroin and other opioids create these effects by depressing the central nervous system, particularly the centers that generate emotion. The drugs are received at brain receptor sites that ordinarily receive

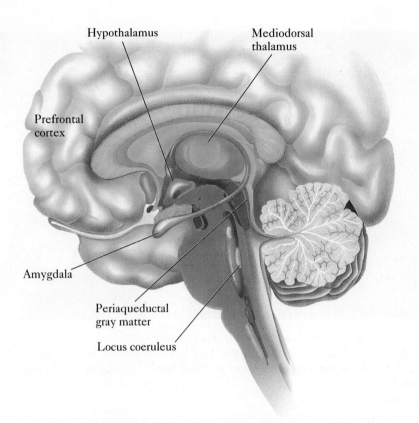

Hypothalamus

Mediodorsal thalamus

Prefrontal cortex

Amygdala

Periaqueductal gray matter

Locus coeruleus

FIGURE 13-2 *The neural receptors to which opioids bind are most concentrated in the brain's emotion center, which includes the amygdala, hypothalamus, and locus coeruleus, and the pain center, which includes the mediodorsal thalamus and periaqueductal gray matter. (Adapted from Snyder, 1986, p. 49.)*

endorphins—neurotransmitters that help relieve pain and reduce emotional tension (Snyder, 1991, 1986; Trujillo & Akil, 1991) (see Figure 13–2). When neurons at these receptor sites receive opioids, they fire and produce pleasurable and calming feelings just as they would do if they were receiving endorphins. In addition to pain relief, sedation, and mood changes, opioids cause nausea, constriction of the pupils of the eyes ("pinpoint pupils"), and constipation, bodily reactions that can also be brought about by the release of endorphins in the brain.

HEROIN ABUSE AND DEPENDENCE

Chronic users of heroin fall into patterns of abuse and dependence similar to those shown by chronic users of the less powerful opioids. It takes only a few weeks of repeated heroin use for people to be caught in a pattern of abuse: the drug becomes the center of their lives, and social and occupational functioning deteriorates significantly. Most abusers also develop a dependence on heroin, quickly building up a tolerance for it and experiencing withdrawal symptoms when they abstain.

Addicted individuals start to experience withdrawal symptoms right after the several-hour high. They begin to feel anxious and restless, and have an intense craving for the drug. After a few more hours, they start to perspire profusely, breathe more rapidly, and develop the symptoms of a head cold. These withdrawal symptoms become progressively more serious for two or three days. They may be accompanied by severe twitching, constant aches, painful gastrointestinal and muscle cramps, fever, acute vomiting and diarrhea, loss of appetite, elevated blood pressure, dehydration, and weight loss of up to 15 pounds.

Withdrawal distress usually peaks by the third day, then gradually subsides and disappears by the eighth day. A person in withdrawal can either wait the symptoms out (an extremely difficult and unpleasant ordeal) or end withdrawal by taking more heroin. Heroin taken at any time during withdrawal will quickly restore a feeling of physical and emotional well-being.

The character of drug taking eventually changes for people dependent on heroin. They soon need the drug just to maintain normal functioning and to avoid the distress of withdrawal, and they must continually increase their doses in order to achieve that state. The temporary high becomes less intense and less important (Goldstein, 1994). What started as a search for pleasure develops into a fight for survival.

Because they must be on a steady diet of heroin, addicted persons soon organize their lives around plans for getting their next dose. The habit can cost hundreds of dollars a day, because heroin is available only through illegal channels, and many addicted individuals turn to criminal activities, such as theft and prostitution, to support their "habit."

DANGERS OF HEROIN   The most direct danger of heroin abuse is an overdose. An overdose of this drug depresses the respiratory center in the brain, virtually paralyzing it and in many cases causing death. Death is particularly likely during sleep, when a person is unable to fight the effect by consciously working at breathing. People who resume the use of heroin after having abstained for a time run a special risk of overdosing. They often make the fatal mistake of taking the dose they used when they were last addicted. Because their bodies have been free of heroin for some time, however, they can no longer tolerate this high level. Each year approximately 1 percent of the untreated persons dependent on heroin and other opioids die under the drug's influence, usually from an overdose (APA, 1994).

Users run risks aside from the effects of the drug itself. Often profit-minded pushers mix heroin with a cheaper drug, such as a barbiturate, LSD, or a local anesthetic, or even a deadly substance such as cyanide or battery acid. Addicted persons who use dirty needles and other unsterile equipment when they inject heroin are vulnerable to AIDS, hepatitis, and skin abscesses (O'Rourke, 1990; NIDA, 1987). In some areas of the United States the HIV infection rate among persons dependent on heroin is reported to be as high as 60 percent (APA, 1994). The drug *quinine* is often added to heroin to counteract the dangers of contracting some potential infections. While quinine does help to some extent, too much of it may cause flooding of the lungs and death. Many deaths attributed to heroin may actually have been caused by a quinine-induced flooding of the lungs.

Surveys suggest that close to 1 percent of the adult population become addicted to heroin or other opioids at some time in their lives (APA, 1994). The number of opioid addicts took its sharpest turn upward during the 1960s and 1970s, and by the late 1970s it had reached more than half a million. Although recent studies suggest a decline and stabilization during the 1980s, there are apparently still more than 400,000 addicted persons in the United

States (Elias, 1993; Gold, 1986). Of course, such statistics may well be understated, given the reluctance of many people to admit to an illegal activity (Maurer & Vogel, 1978).

■ STIMULANTS ■

Stimulants are substances that act to increase the activity of the central nervous system, resulting in increased blood pressure and heart rate and in intensified behavioral activity, thought processes, and alertness. Two of the best-known and most troublesome stimulants are cocaine and amphetamines. The effects of these substances on the brain are virtually indistinguishable (Snyder, 1986). When users report different effects from the two, it is because they have ingested different amounts of the drugs. Inhaled cocaine, for example, acts more quickly than an amphetamine taken in pill form. Two of the most commonly used stimulants are caffeine and nicotine.

COCAINE

Cocaine—the central active ingredient of the coca plant, found in South America—is the most powerful natural stimulant now known. The drug was first isolated from the plant in 1865. South American natives, however, have chewed the leaves of the plant since prehistoric times for the energy and alertness the drug content provides. Processed cocaine *(hydrochloride powder)* is an odorless, white, fluffy powder. For recreational use, it is most often inhaled ("snorted") so that it is absorbed through the mucous membrane of the nose. Some users prefer the more powerful effects of injecting cocaine intravenously or smoking cocaine "base" in a pipe or cigarette.

> Sherlock Holmes took his bottle from the corner of the mantelpiece, and his hypodermic syringe from its neat morocco case. With his long white nervous fingers, he adjusted the delicate needle and rolled back his left shirtcuff. For some little time his eyes rested thoughtfully upon the sinewy forearm and wrist, all dotted and scarred with innumerable puncture-marks. Finally, he thrust the sharp point home, pressed down the tiny piston, and sank back into the velvet-lined armchair with a long sigh of satisfaction.
>
> Three times a day for many months I had witnessed this performance, but custom had not reconciled my mind to it. . . .
>
> "Which is it today," I asked, "Morphine or cocaine?"
>
> He raised his eyes languidly from the old black-letter volume which he had opened.

"It is cocaine," he said, "a seven-per-cent solution. Would you care to try it?"

"No, indeed," I answered brusquely. "My constitution has not got over the Afghan campaign yet. I cannot afford to throw any extra strain upon it."

He smiled at my vehemence. "Perhaps you are right, Watson," he said. "I suppose that its influence is physically a bad one. I find it, however, so transcendently stimulating and clarifying to the mind that its secondary action is a matter of small moment."

"But consider!" I said earnestly. "Count the cost! Your brain may, as you say, be roused and excited, but it is a pathological and morbid process which involves increased tissue-change and . . . a permanent weakness. You know, too, what a black reaction comes upon you. Surely, the game is hardly worth the candle."

(Doyle, 1938, pp. 91–92)

For years the prevailing opinion of cocaine was that aside from causing intoxication and occasional temporary psychosis, it posed few significant problems (see Box 13–2). Like Sherlock Holmes, many people believed that the benefits outweighed the costs. Only in recent years have researchers recognized its potential for harm and developed a clearer understanding of how cocaine produces its effects. This insight was triggered by a dramatic increase in the drug's popularity and in problems related to its use. In the early 1960s an estimated 10,000 persons in the United States had tried cocaine; in the early 1970s the number was 100,000; and by the early 1980s it was 15 million. Today more than 23 million people in the United States have tried cocaine (NIDA, 1993). Close to 2 million people are currently using cocaine at least

BOX 13-2

"A BIG WILD MAN WHO HAS COCAINE IN HIS BODY"

Sigmund Freud's contributions to the understanding and treatment of mental disorders are second to none. Even his detractors acknowledge his brilliance and his wisdom. Yet Freud, like so many people before and after him, was played for a fool by a drug—in his case, cocaine. Freud fell into the familiar trap of wishful thinking, prematurely concluding that cocaine was free of danger, largely because he enjoyed it and wanted it to be safe. His colossal misjudgment almost brought down his career before it had really begun.

In 1884 Freud's reputation as an effective neurologist and skillful researcher of neuroanatomy was growing. Having read about the stimulating effects of coca leaves on Peruvian Indians and about the isolation of pure cocaine, he wondered whether the substance might be an effective treatment for nervous exhaustion, and he proceeded to test it on himself. He quickly experienced a powerful reaction—euphoria, energy, alertness, strength, and disinterest in food. He

seemed more than a little smitten with cocaine when he wrote to his fiancée, "Woe to you my princess when I come. I will kiss you quite red and feed you until you are plump. And if you are forward, you shall see who is stronger, a gentle little girl who doesn't eat enough or a big wild man who has cocaine in his body" (Freud, 1885).

Freud proceeded to study the effects of cocaine on numerous subjects and soon proclaimed to the medical community of Western Europe:

Cocaine brings about an exhilaration and lasting euphoria. . . . You perceive an increase of self-control and possess more vitality and capacity for work. . . . In other words, you are simply normal, and it is soon hard to believe that you are under the influence of any drug. . . . Long intensive mental or physical work is performed without any fatigue. . . . This result is enjoyed without any of the unpleasant after effects that follow exhilaration brought about by alcohol.

(Freud, 1885)

Freud's professional influence continued to grow in clinical circles, as did the use of cocaine by patients with anxiety, depression, or other psychological problems.

Freud received a very rude awakening after he recommended to a close friend, Erst Fleischl von Marxow, that he take cocaine to relieve him of his addiction to morphine. Fleischl injected himself with increasingly higher doses of cocaine until finally he became a victim of cocaine-induced psychosis.

The plight of his friend was more than a personal tragedy for Freud. Soon reports of cocaine psychosis from all over Europe led to severe criticism of Freud by the Continent's most eminent medical authorities and dealt a heavy blow to his reputation. It was not at all clear that he would be able to continue his medical career. But then he became interested in hypnosis and began to develop the theories and techniques of psychoanalysis, and this time his provocative and daring ideas served him and the clinical field very well indeed.

once a month—most of them between 18 and 34 years of age (NIDA, 1993).

Cocaine brings on a euphoric rush of well-being and confidence. Given a high enough dose, this rush can be almost orgasmic, like that produced by heroin. Initially cocaine stimulates the higher centers of the central nervous system, making its users feel excited, energetic, talkative, and even euphoric. As more is taken, it also stimulates other centers of the CNS, producing a faster pulse, higher blood pressure, faster and deeper breathing, and further arousal and wakefulness. Cocaine apparently produces these effects by stimulating the release of the neurotransmitters dopamine and norepinephrine from neurons throughout the brain; supplies of these neurotransmitters at receiving neurons become excessive and the CNS is overstimulated (Kleber & Gawin, 1987).

If a very high dose of cocaine is taken, the stimulation of the CNS will result in poor muscle coordination, grandiosity of manner, declining judgment, aggression, compulsive behavior, and a changeable temper—all symptoms of *cocaine intoxication.* People in a severe state of intoxication may also become confused, anxious, rambling, and incoherent. Some people experience hallucinations or delusions, or both, a condition known as *cocaine-induced psychotic disorder* (Rosse et al., 1993; Yudofsky, Silver, & Hales, 1993).

A young man described how, after free-basing, he went to his closet to get his clothes, but his suit asked him, "What do you want?" Afraid, he walked toward the door, which told him, "Get back!" Retreating, he then heard the sofa say, "If you sit on me, I'll kick your ass." With a sense of impending doom, intense anxiety, and momentary panic, the young man ran to the hospital where he received help.

(Allen, 1985, pp. 19–20)

As the symptoms caused by cocaine subside, the user often experiences a depression-like letdown, popularly called "crashing," which may be accompanied by headaches, dizziness, and fainting. For occasional users, the effects of cocaine usually disappear within twenty-four hours. Those who have taken an excessive dose, however, may sink into stupor, deep sleep, or coma.

COCAINE ABUSE AND DEPENDENCE   An extended period of cocaine use may lead to a pattern of abuse in which the person feels unable to stop using cocaine, is intoxicated throughout the day, and functions poorly in social and occupational spheres. A physical dependence may also develop, so that more

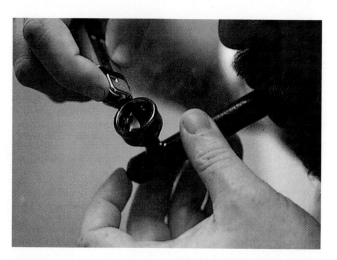

Crack, a powerful form of free-base cocaine, is produced by boiling cocaine down into crystalline balls and is smoked with a special crack pipe.

cocaine is needed to achieve the desired effects, and abstinence results in significant feelings of depression; intense fatigue; insomnia, bad dreams, deep sleep, or other sleep problems; and irritability, tremulousness, and anxiety (APA, 1994; Washton, 1987). These withdrawal symptoms may last for weeks or even months.

Despite the reinforcing properties of cocaine, in the past cocaine abuse and dependence were limited by the high cost of processed cocaine and by the fact that it was usually *snorted*—a means of ingestion that is limited by the constriction of nasal blood vessels, and that has less powerful effects than either injection or smoking (OSAP, 1991; Spotts & Shontz, 1983). Since 1984, however, newer, more powerful, and sometimes cheaper forms of cocaine have gained favor among users and have produced an enormous increase in abuse and dependence. Currently one user in five falls into a pattern of abuse or dependence. Many people now use the technique of *free-basing,* in which the pure cocaine basic alkaloid is chemically separated or "freed" from processed cocaine, vaporized by heat from a flame, and inhaled with a pipe (Cohen, 1980). And millions more use *crack,* a powerful ready-to-smoke free-base cocaine with the ability to induce more persistent and intense drug craving than most other drugs (OSAP, 1991).

Crack is cocaine that has been boiled down into crystalline balls. It is smoked with a special crack pipe. This form of cocaine makes a crackling sound when it is smoked, hence the name. Crack is sold in small quantities at a typical cost of between $10 and $20. Some cities have seen veritable crack epidemics among people who previously could not have afforded cocaine. Approximately 1.5 percent of high school seniors report using crack within the past year (Johnston et al., 1993). Although this rate represents a sizable drop from the 1986 rate of 4 percent, the crack epidemic is still very disturbing, particularly because of the unusual degree of violent crime and risky sex-for-drugs exchanges reported in the crack-using population (Balshem et al., 1992). The crack epidemic is also problematic in that it is concentrated in poor urban areas (OSAP, 1991).

DANGERS OF COCAINE Cocaine poses serious dangers. Aside from its effects on mental and emotional functioning, cocaine turns out to be highly dangerous to one's physical well-being. Its widespread use in increasingly powerful forms caused the annual number of cocaine-related emergency room incidents in the United States to multiply twenty-five times between 1982 and 1991, from 4,243 cases to 102,727 cases (NIDA, 1993) (see Figure 13–3). In addition, it

has been linked to as many as 20 percent of all suicides by persons under 61 years of age (Marzuk et al., 1992).

The most obvious danger of cocaine use comes from overdose. Excessive doses have a strong effect on the respiratory center of the brain, at first stimulating it and then depressing it, possibly to the point of respiratory failure and death. Cocaine also stimulates the brain center that controls body temperature: while the drug raises a person's temperature, it may also constrict the blood vessels in the skin—and throughout the rest of the body—making it impossible for the person to perspire. The dangerously high body temperature that results can lead to death.

Cocaine can also create significant, even fatal heart problems. The heart beats rapidly and irregularly under the drug's influence and at the same time must work harder to pump blood through cocaine-constricted blood vessels. For some people, this strain on

DRUG-RELATED DEATHS

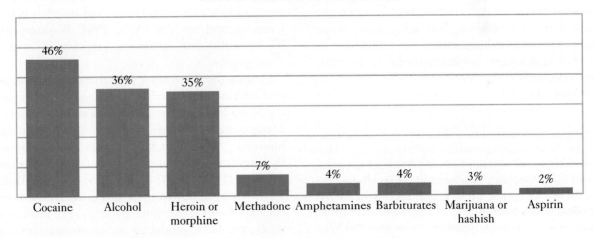

DRUG-RELATED EMERGENCY ROOM VISITS

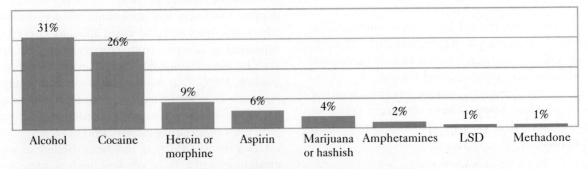

FIGURE 13–3 *Which drugs are implicated in drug related deaths and drug-related emergency room visits? In 1991 cocaine was cited by medical examiners in 46 percent of all drug-related deaths, while alcohol was cited in 36 percent and opioids in 35 percent. Alcohol was responsible for 31 percent of all drug-related emergency room visits, while cocaine was responsible for 26 percent and opioids for 9 percent. Percentages add up to more than 100 because more than one drug was cited in some cases. (NIDA, 1992.)*

the heart causes a brain seizure that brings breathing or heart functioning to a sudden halt. These effects may be more common in people who have taken a high dose of cocaine and who have a history of cocaine abuse, but they also occur in casual cocaine users (Gold, 1986). Such was the case with Len Bias, the well-known college basketball player who died of these effects a few years back, apparently after ingesting only a moderate amount of cocaine.

The effects of prenatal cocaine exposure on future generations are also cause for serious concern (Scherling, 1994). Cocaine crosses the placental barrier and penetrates fetal brain tissue. It also restricts blood supply to the placenta, depriving the fetus of oxygen. *Fetal cocaine syndrome* is apparently even more subtle and devastating than fetal alcohol syndrome, and is characterized by decreased sensitivity to cocaine, altered immune function, learning deficits, decreased activity in the brain's dopamine system, and abnormal thyroid size (Adler, 1992).

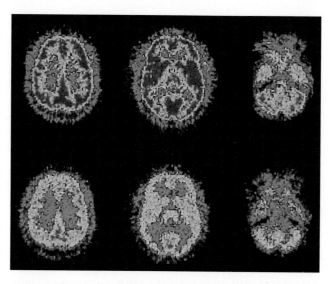

Although cocaine and amphetamines stimulate the central nervous system, they decrease activity in some areas of the brain. The PET scans of a cocaine user (bottom row) reveal a drop in glucose metabolism—indicated by the color blue—in some brain regions. PET scans of a nonuser (top row) reveal a high level of activity—indicated by the color red—in the same areas.

AMPHETAMINES

The *amphetamines* are stimulant drugs that are manufactured in the laboratory. Some common ones are amphetamine (Benzedrine), dextroamphetamine (Dexedrine), and methamphetamine (Methedrine). First synthesized by the chemist Gordon Alles in the 1930s for use in the treatment of asthma, these drugs soon became popular among people trying to lose weight; athletes seeking an extra burst of energy; soldiers, truck drivers, and pilots trying to stay awake; and students studying for exams throughout the night. They are still frequently used in these ways— now, however, with significantly less approval and help from medical practitioners. The drugs are far too dangerous to be used so casually.

Amphetamines are most often taken in pill or capsule form, although some people inject the drug intravenously for a quicker, more powerful impact. Others ingest the drug in such forms as "ice" and "crank," counterparts of free-basing cocaine and crack, respectively.

Like cocaine, amphetamines increase energy and alertness and reduce appetite in low doses, produce intoxication and psychosis in high doses, and cause an emotional letdown as they leave the person's body. Also like cocaine, amphetamines stimulate the CNS by increasing the release of the neurotransmitters dopamine and norepinephrine from neurons throughout the brain (Goldstein, 1994). Because of their chemical resemblance to these neurotransmitters, am-

phetamine molecules are able to enter the nerve endings where the neurotransmitters are stored, push them out of their storage sites, prevent them from returning to the storage sites, and propel them across the synaptic space to stimulate the firing of nearby neurons (Goldstein, 1994; Bhakthavatsalam et al., 1985). When taken in large doses, amphetamines, like cocaine, may cause extensive damage to cells and cell communication pathways in two areas of the brain that regulate the transmission of dopamine and serotonin, thus causing hallucinations and delusions (Ellison, 1992).

Tolerance to amphetamines builds so quickly that it is easy to become ensnared in a pattern of amphetamine dependence. People who start using amphetamines to reduce their appetite and weight may soon find they are as hungry as ever, and increase their amphetamine dosage in response. Athletes who use amphetamines to increase their energy may find before long that larger and larger amounts of the drug are needed. As their tolerance of amphetamines increases, they are also pushed toward a greater expenditure of energy than their bodies can afford, and so subject themselves to more injuries and illness. So-called speed freaks who pop pills all day for days at a time have built a tolerance so high that they now take as much as 200 times their initial amphetamine dose. When chronic abusers stop taking amphetamines, they enter the state of deep depression and extended sleep that also characterizes withdrawal from cocaine.

CAFFEINE

Caffeine is the world's most widely consumed stimulant drug (Chou, 1992). Seventy-five percent of the amount of this drug consumed is taken in the form of coffee (from the coffee bean); the rest is consumed in tea (from the tea leaf), cola (from the kola nut), and chocolate (from the cocoa bean), and in its purified form in numerous prescription and over-the-counter medications, such as Excedrin (Chou, 1992; Johnson-Greene et al., 1988).

Americans consume between 15 and 45 million pounds of caffeine annually with an average daily intake of 200 mg (equivalent to about two cups of coffee) (Chou, 1992; Julien, 1988). Research has revealed that 99 percent of caffeine is absorbed in the body and that it reaches its peak concentration in 30 to 60 minutes, penetrating all body membranes and being distributed evenly to all body tissues (Julien, 1988). Caffeine acts as a stimulant of the central nervous system, producing a release of the neurotransmitters dopamine, serotonin, and norepinephrine in the brain (Benowitz, 1990). Thus it increases vigilance and arousal and general motor activity, and reduces fatigue. It also disrupts the performance of complex motor tasks and may interfere with both the duration and quality of sleep (Chou, 1992; Jacobson & Thurman-Lacey, 1992). Caffeine also produces biological changes throughout the body. Heart rate decreases with moderate amounts of consumption, respiration increases, and the gastric acid secreted by the stomach increases (Benowitz, 1990; Levitt, 1975).

More than 250 milligrams of caffeine (two to three cups of brewed coffee) can produce *caffeine intoxication,* which may include such symptoms as restlessness, nervousness, stomach disturbances, twitching, and increased heart rate (APA, 1994). Caffeine intoxication may also produce the symptoms of an anxiety disorder or sleep disorder in some people (APA, 1994). Grand mal seizures and fatal respiratory failure or circulatory failure can occur at doses in excess of 10 grams of caffeine (about 100 cups of coffee).

Although DSM-IV does not include the category *caffeine dependence* (it is listed in the DSM appendix as a category in need of further study), research is increasingly linking caffeine to a withdrawal syndrome in some persons. A recent study by Kenneth Silverman and his colleagues (1992) demonstrated that the abrupt cessation of caffeine by persons who consume low to moderate amounts of it daily (the equivalent of two and a half cups of coffee or seven cans of cola) can cause significant withdrawal symptoms. In a six-day study the researchers had 62 adult subjects consume their usual caffeine-filled drinks and foods for two days, then refrain from all caffeine foods for two days while taking placebo pills that they thought contained caffeine, and then refrain from caffeine foods for two days while taking actual caffeine pills. More subjects experienced painful headaches (52 percent), depression (11 percent), anxiety (8 percent), and fatigue (8 percent) during the two-day placebo period than during the caffeine periods. In addition, more subjects reported using unauthorized medications (13 percent) and performed more slowly on a tapping task during the placebo period than during the caffeine periods.

The widespread and casual use of caffeine has spurred much debate on its effects on health, and, as public awareness of possible health risks has increased, researchers have observed a decline in caffeine consumption. The International Coffee Organization reports that 53 percent of Americans drank coffee in 1991, whereas 80 percent had done so in 1983 (Chou, 1992).

Unfortunately, research on the health risks of caffeine is often confounded. Investigators in this area have often measured caffeine intake by coffee consumption, for example, but coffee also contains other chemicals that may be dangerous to one's health. Thus, although some studies have hinted at links between caffeine and cancer (particularly pancreatic cancer), clear evidence does not yet exist. Similarly, studies demonstrating correlations between cardiac arrhythmias or high cholesterol levels and caffeine consumption have proved unreliable (Hirsch et al., 1989; Rosmarin, 1989). Caffeine does, however, appear to cause a slight increase in blood pressure over time in regular caffeine users, and a larger but short-lived increase during the first few days of consumption in caffeine-naive subjects (Shi et al., 1993).

■ HALLUCINOGENS ■

Hallucinogens are substances that cause changes primarily in sensory perception. They may differ from one another both structurally and in the effects they produce. They include so-called *psychedelic drugs* such as LSD, powerful drugs whose profound perceptual changes may extend to hallucinations, and *cannabis drugs,* a group of drugs produced from varieties of the hemp plant *Cannabis sativa*, which cause a mixture of hallucinogenic, depressant, and stimulant effects.

PSYCHEDELIC DRUGS

Our brain receives and interprets sensations of sight, sound, smell, taste, and touch that combine to give us the information we need about the world around us. If these sensations or their processing become disturbed, our perceptions of the world can be distorted. Psychedelics are chemical substances that affect these sensory experiences, producing sensations so novel that they are sometimes called "trips." The trips may be exciting or frightening, enhancing or dangerous, depending on how a person's mind interacts with the psychedelics. This interaction may vary greatly from person to person and even from time to time for the same person.

The psychedelic drugs include LSD (lysergic acid diethylamide), mescaline, psilocybin, MDMA ("ecstasy"), DOM, DMT, morning-glory seeds, bufotenine, and PCP. Many of these substances come from plants or animals; others are laboratory-produced rearrangements of natural psychedelics.

LSD, one of the most famous and most powerful hallucinogens, was derived by the Swiss chemist Albert Hoffman in 1938 from a group of naturally occurring drugs called *ergot alkaloids.* For years LSD remained in limited use while researchers struggled to understand its action and medicinal value. Then

Psychedelic art seemed all-pervasive in the 1960s. Displayed on advertisements, clothing, record albums, and book covers, it was inspired by the kinds of images and sensations produced by psychedelic drugs such as LSD.

during the 1960s, a decade of social rebellion and experimentation, it found a home. Millions of persons turned to the drug as a means of expanding their experience.

Within two hours of being swallowed, LSD brings on a state of *hallucinogen intoxication,* sometimes called *hallucinosis,* marked by a general intensification of perceptions, particularly visual perceptions, along with maladaptive psychological changes and physical symptoms. People may focus on minutiae — the pores of the skin, for example, or individual blades of grass. Colors may seem enhanced or take on a shade of purple. Illusions may be experienced in which objects seem distorted, and inanimate objects may appear to move, breathe, or change shape. A person under the influence of LSD may also hallucinate and see people, objects, or geometric forms that are not actually present.

Intoxication symptoms involving the other senses may include hearing sounds more clearly, often with new or previously undetected qualities, and feeling tingling or numbness in the arms or legs or altered sensations of hot and cold. Some people have been badly burned after touching flames that felt cool to them under the influence of LSD. LSD may also cause the senses to cross, an effect called *synesthesia.* A loud noise may be experienced as visible fluctuations in the air. Colors may be "heard" or "felt."

LSD can also cause emotional changes, ranging from euphoria to anxiety or depression. The perception of time may slow down dramatically. Long-forgotten thoughts and feelings may resurface. Physical symptoms can include dilation of the pupils, sweating, palpitations, blurred vision, tremors, and loss of coordination. All these effects take place while the user is fully awake and alert. The overall experience can seem either mystical or horrifying (Moody, 1969). Whether pleasant or frightening, the immediate effects wear off in about six hours.

It seems that LSD produces these symptoms by interfering with neurons that use the neurotransmitter serotonin (Jacobs, 1993, 1987, 1984). These neurons are ordinarily involved in the brain's transmission of visual information and (as we observed in Chapter 8) emotional experiences; thus LSD's interference produces a range of visual and emotional symptoms. Ordinarily when serotonin-containing neurons are activated, they release serotonin, whose action helps the brain to filter incoming sensory messages. Without the action of serotonin, the brain would be flooded by perceptual and emotional input — particularly visual input — and people would experience more sensations, see more details, distort visual images, and even see things not actually there. This is the very effect created by LSD, which apparently binds to the surface of serotonin-containing neurons and essentially prevents them from releasing serotonin (Jacobs, 1984).

Although people develop minimal tolerance and do not experience withdrawal when they stop using LSD, it poses distinct dangers for both one-time and long-term users. First, LSD is so remarkably potent that any dose, no matter how small, is likely to elicit powerful perceptual, emotional, and behavioral reactions. Sometimes these powerful reactions to LSD are extremely unpleasant, an experience described in the drug vernacular as a "bad trip":

A 21-year-old woman was admitted to the hospital along with her lover. He had had a number of LSD experiences and had convinced her to take it to make her less constrained sexually. About half an hour after ingestion of approximately 200 microgm., she noticed that the bricks in the wall began to go in and out and that light affected her strangely. She became frightened when she realized that she was unable to distinguish her body from the chair she was sitting on or from her lover's body. Her fear became more marked after she thought that she would not get back into herself. At the time of admission she was hyperactive and laughed inappropriately. Her stream of talk was illogical and affect labile. Two days later, this reaction had ceased.

(Frosch, Robbins, & Stern, 1965)

Reports of LSD users who injure themselves or commit suicide or murder usually involve a severe panic reaction of this kind.

Another danger is the extended impact that LSD has on some people. They may, for example, develop a *hallucinogen-induced psychotic disorder,* confusing their hallucinations with reality and developing bizarre ideas to support their disturbed perceptions (Bowers, 1977). Or they may develop a *hallucinogen-induced mood disorder,* characterized by extreme guilt and depression, or *hallucinogen-induced anxiety disorder* (fearfulness, tension, or restlessness). Many fear that they have destroyed their brains and driven themselves crazy, and worry that they will never return to normal.

Finally, about a quarter of LSD users experience lingering effects called a *hallucinogen persisting perception disorder,* or simply *flashbacks*—sensory and emotional changes that recur long after the LSD has left the body (APA, 1994). Flashbacks may occur days or even months after the last LSD experience. They may become less severe and disappear within several

months; some persons, however, report flashbacks five years or longer after taking LSD. Flashbacks are entirely unpredictable. A one-time LSD user may have multiple flashbacks, or a regular user with no history of flashbacks may suddenly start to experience them.

CANNABIS

Cannabis sativa, the hemp plant, grows in warm climates throughout the world. Its main active ingredient, *tetrahydrocannabinol (THC),* is found in the resin exuded by its leaves and flowering tops. The drugs produced from varieties of hemp are collectively called *cannabis.* The most powerful of them is *hashish;* drugs of intermediate strength include *ganja;* and the weaker ones include the best-known form of cannabis, *marijuana,* a mixture of the crushed leaves and flowering tops. Actually, each of these cannabis drugs is found in various strengths because the potency of a cannabis drug is greatly affected by the climate in which the plant is grown, the way the drug was prepared, and the manner and duration of its storage.

Although cannabis contains several hundred active compounds, THC appears to be the ingredient most responsible for its effects. The greater the THC content, the more powerful the cannabis: hashish contains a high portion, while marijuana's is relatively low.

Cannabis is smoked. At low doses it typically produces feelings of inner joy and relaxation and may lead people to become either contemplative or talkative (Wilson & Maguire, 1985). Some smokers, however, feel anxious, suspicious, apprehensive, or irritated, especially if they have been in a bad mood or are smoking in an upsetting environment. Many smokers report sharpened perceptions and great preoccupation with the intensified sounds and sights around them. Time seems to slow down, and distances and sizes seem greater than they actually are. This overall state of *cannabis intoxication* is known more commonly as a "high" or as being "stoned."

The physical changes induced by cannabis include reddening of the eyes (the blood vessels in the conjunctiva become engorged), a fast heartbeat, an increase in blood pressure and appetite, dryness in the mouth, dizziness, and nausea. Some people become drowsy and may even fall asleep.

In high doses, cannabis produces visual distortions, alterations of body image, and hallucinations

(Mathew et al., 1993). Smokers may become confused or impulsive; some panic and fear that they are losing their minds. Some smokers develop delusions that other people are trying to hurt them *(cannabis-induced psychotic disorder)*. Most of the effects of cannabis last for three to six hours. The changes in mood, however, may continue for a longer time (Chait, Fishman, & Schuster, 1985).

MARIJUANA ABUSE AND DEPENDENCE

Until the early 1970s, the use of the weak form of cannabis, marijuana, rarely led to a pattern of abuse or dependence. Most people who used the substance seemed able to do so recreationally without letting it become the center of their lives. Since then the picture has changed. Many people, including large numbers of high school students, are now caught in a pattern of marijuana abuse—getting high on marijuana every day and finding their social and occupational or academic lives significantly affected by their heavy use of it (see Figures 13–4 and 13–5).

Many chronic users also develop a tolerance for marijuana and some experience flulike withdrawal symptoms when they try to stop smoking, including hot flashes, loss of appetite, runny nose, sweating, diarrhea, and hiccups (Ray & Ksir, 1993; Jones & Benowitz, 1977).

Why have patterns of marijuana abuse and dependence emerged in the last two decades? Mainly because the drug has changed. The marijuana available in the United States today is two to ten times more powerful than that used in the early 1970s. The THC content of today's marijuana is as much as 10 to 15 percent, compared to 1 to 5 percent in the late 1960s (APA, 1994). Apparently marijuana is now cultivated in locations—both foreign and domestic—where a hot and dry climate produces higher THC content (Weisheit, 1990).

DANGERS OF MARIJUANA As the potency and use of marijuana have increased, researchers have discovered that smoking this substance may

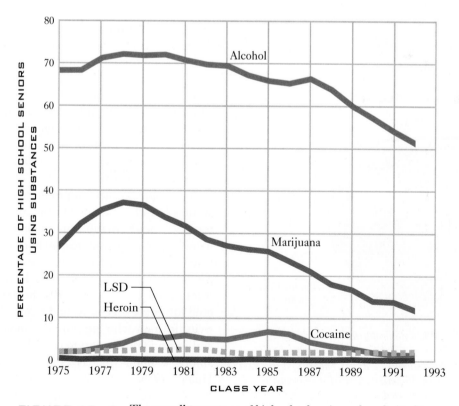

FIGURE 13–4 *The overall percentage of high school seniors who admitted to using drugs illicitly at least once within 30 days of being surveyed rose in the 1970s and then declined in the 1980s and 1990s. The rate of marijuana use has been falling since 1978, cocaine use since 1985, alcohol use since 1980, and heroin and LSD use have remained relatively stable. But mental health professionals have detected a disturbing trend among eighth-graders: their rate of illegal drug use has risen. (Johnston et al., 1993.)*

CIGARETTES

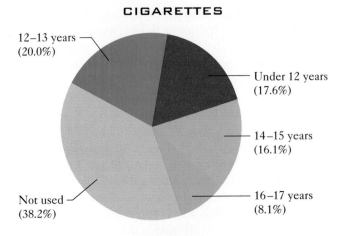

12–13 years
(20.0%)

Under 12 years
(17.6%)

14–15 years
(16.1%)

16–17 years
(8.1%)

Not used
(38.2%)

ALCOHOL

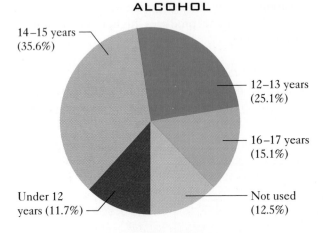

14–15 years
(35.6%)

12–13 years
(25.1%)

16–17 years
(15.1%)

Not used
(12.5%)

Under 12
years (11.7%)

MARIJUANA

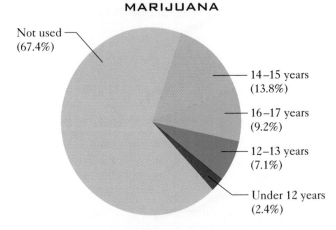

Not used
(67.4%)

14–15 years
(13.8%)

16–17 years
(9.2%)

12–13 years
(7.1%)

Under 12 years
(2.4%)

FIGURE 13–5 *When do people first try a drug? According to a national survey, 61 percent of all high school seniors first tried alcohol between 12 and 15 years of age. Within the same age span 36 percent first tried smoking a cigarette and 21 percent first tried marijuana. (Johnston et al., 1993.)*

pose significant problems and dangers. It occasionally elicits panic reactions similar to the ones caused by psychedelics (Ray & Ksir, 1993). People with emotional problems are thought to be more

vulnerable to such reactions, but others may also experience them. Typically the panic reaction ends in three to six hours, along with marijuana's other effects.

Earlier research suggested that marijuana did not interfere with automobile driving as much as alcohol did and that drivers were able to compensate for their perceptual changes through concentration and increased caution (Crancer et al., 1969). It seems, however, that marijuana's impact on driving has increased along with its potency. Studies have implicated marijuana in numerous automobile accidents (Petersen, 1984). Apparently cannabis intoxication interferes with performance of the complex sensorimotor tasks involved in driving.

Marijuana also appears to interfere with cognitive functioning (Hooker & Jones, 1987). People on a marijuana high often fail to remember information, especially recently acquired information, no matter how hard they try to concentrate. Clearly, heavy marijuana smokers are operating at a considerable disadvantage at school and in the workplace.

Evidence has mounted that chronic marijuana smoking may lead to long-term problems. It may, for example, contribute to lung disease. Studies have indicated that marijuana smoking reduces one's ability to expel air from the lungs even more than tobacco smoking does. One marijuana cigarette is equivalent to at least sixteen tobacco cigarettes in this regard. In addition, research indicates that marijuana smoke contains significantly more tar and benzopyrene than tobacco smoke. Both of these substances have been linked to cancer (Ray & Ksir, 1993).

Another concern is the effect of chronic marijuana smoking on human reproduction. Although early studies found reductions in the male hormone testosterone among marijuana smokers, the reductions were very small and researchers concluded at that time that chronic marijuana use had no effect on reproduction (Ray & Ksir, 1993; Kolodny et al; 1974). Studies since the late 1970s, however, have discovered lower sperm counts and reduced spermatozoa activity in men who are chronic smokers of marijuana, and irregular and abnormal ovulation has been found among women (Nahas, 1984; Hembree, Nahas, & Huang, 1979).

Finally, research has suggested that THC has a mild and temporary suppressive effect on the functioning of the immune system (Hollister, 1986). Although this suppression is not clinically significant and marijuana smokers have not displayed higher rates of infection, some researchers suspect that the effect may have longer-term implications.

Recent efforts to educate the public about the changing nature and impact of regular marijuana use appear to be paying off: 2 percent of today's high school seniors smoke marijuana on a daily basis, down from 11 percent in 1978 (Johnston et al., 1993). Moreover, about 77 percent of high school seniors believe that regular marijuana smoking poses a serious risk, more than double the percentage in 1978 (Johnston et al., 1993)—but probably fewer than held this belief fifty years earlier (see Box 13–3). Still other surveys show both junior high and senior high school students reporting little peer pressure to smoke marijuana; indeed, almost 90 percent of them believe that their friends would disapprove if they were to smoke it regularly (Johnston et al., 1993).

■ COMBINATIONS ■ OF SUBSTANCES

Because people often take more than one drug at a time, researchers have had to study the ways in which drugs interact with one another. Two important concepts have emerged from this work: cross-tolerance and synergistic effects.

CROSS-TOLERANCE

Sometimes two or more drugs are so similar in their actions on the brain and the rest of the body that as people build up a tolerance for one drug, they are simultaneously developing a tolerance for the others, even if they have never taken them. When users display such *cross-tolerance,* they can reduce the symptoms of withdrawal from one drug by taking one of the others. Because alcohol and antianxiety drugs are cross-tolerant, for example, it is sometimes possible to alleviate the alcohol withdrawal reaction of delirium tremens by administering antianxiety drugs, along with vitamins and electrolytes.

SYNERGISTIC EFFECTS

When different drugs are in the body at the same time, they may potentiate, or enhance, each other's effects. The combined impact, called a *synergistic ef-*

fect, is often greater than the sum of the effects of each drug taken alone: a small dose of one drug mixed with a small dose of another can produce an enormous change in body chemistry.

One kind of synergistic effect occurs when two or more drugs have *similar actions.* For instance, alcohol, antianxiety drugs, barbiturates, and opioids—all depressants of the central nervous system—may produce a severe depression of the CNS when mixed (Miller & Gold, 1990). Combining them, even in small doses, can lead to extreme intoxication, coma, and even death.

Many tragedies have been caused by synergistic effects of this kind. A young man may drink just a few alcoholic beverages at a party, for example, and shortly afterward take a normal dose of barbiturates to help him fall asleep. He believes he has acted with restraint and good judgment—yet he may never wake up.

A different kind of synergistic effect results when drugs have *opposite (antagonistic) actions.* Stimulant drugs, for example, interfere with the liver's usual disposal of barbiturates and alcohol. Thus people who combine barbiturates or alcohol with cocaine or amphetamines may build up toxic, even lethal levels of the depressant drugs in their systems. Students who take amphetamines to help them study late into the night and then take barbiturates to help them fall asleep are unwittingly placing themselves in serious danger.

POLYSUBSTANCE USE

Each year tens of thousands of people are admitted to hospitals with a multiple drug emergency, and several thousand of them die (NIDA, 1992). Sometimes the cause is carelessness or ignorance: a "wired" student who later takes sleeping pills may simply be unaware of the synergistic effects created by the combination. Often, however, the person uses a combination of drugs precisely because he or she enjoys the synergistic effects. This kind of multiple drug use, or *polysubstance use,* appears to be on the rise—so much so that *polysubstance-related disorders* are becoming as common as individual substance-related disorders (Miller et al., 1990; Weisheit, 1990). Let us look in on a group therapy session for users of crack:

Okay. Now, can you give me a list of all the drugs you've used? Gary?

Polysubstance use, particularly a mixture of cocaine and opioids, eventually proved fatal for comedian John Belushi, who often made jokes about the use of drugs on "Saturday Night Live," and actor River Phoenix, who was a practicing vegetarian and environmentalist. Their deaths were separated by years, at locations only blocks apart, from biological causes that were identical.

Gary: Pot. Coke. Crack. Mescaline. Acid. Speed. Crystal meth. Smack. Base dust. Sometimes alcohol.

Dennis: Alcohol. Pot. Coke. Mescaline. LSD. Amyl nitrate. Speed and Valium.

Davy: Coke. Crack. Reefer. Alcohol. Acid. Mescaline. Mushrooms. Ecstasy. Speed. Smack.

Rich: Alcohol. Pot. Ludes [Quaaludes]. Valium. Speed. Ups [amphetamines]. Downs [barbiturates]. Acid. Mescaline. Crack. Base. Dust. That's about it.

Carol: Alcohol. Pot. Cocaine. Mescaline. Valium. Crack.
(Chatlos, 1987, pp. 30–31)

Teenagers and young adults seem particularly likely to use drugs in combination (Wright, 1985; Gould et al., 1977). Research suggests that 27 percent of the young adults who use marijuana also use cocaine, often at the same time; that 84 percent of the teenagers who use marijuana also drink alcohol; and that 37 percent of the teenagers who drink alcohol also use marijuana (NIDA, 1985).

Some famous people have been the victims of polysubstance use. Elvis Presley's delicate balancing act of stimulants and depressants eventually went awry. Janis Joplin's propensity for mixing wine and heroin was ultimately fatal. And John Belushi's and River Phoenix's liking for the combined effect of cocaine and opioids ("speedballs") also ended in tragedy. Obviously, whether it is intentional or accidental, mixing drugs is a hazardous undertaking.

■ EXPLANATIONS ■ OF SUBSTANCE-RELATED DISORDERS

Clinicians have proposed a number of theories to explain why people abuse or become dependent on various substances. Such theories are often presented with considerable passion and conviction, but none has gained unqualified research support (Peele, 1989). Like other forms of mental dysfunctioning, excessive and chronic drug use is increasingly being viewed as a consequence of a combination of biological, psychological, and sociocultural factors.

THE GENETIC AND BIOLOGICAL VIEW

For years studies of twins and of adoptees have suggested that people can inherit a predisposition to substance abuse and dependence (Kendler et al., 1994, 1992; Goodwin, 1984, 1976; Vaillant, 1983). As we noted in Chapter 3, twin studies compare the concordance rates of genetically identical (monozygotic) twins with those of fraternal (dyzygotic) twins. If a predisposition to drug taking is indeed inherited, then the drug-abuse concordance rate of identical twins should be higher than that of fraternal twins. Studies seem to indicate that it is (Goldstein, 1994). For example, an alcohol-abuse concordance rate of 54 percent was found in one group of identical twins; that is, in 54 percent of the cases in which one identical twin abused alcohol, the other twin also abused alcohol. In contrast, a group of fraternal twins had a concordance rate of only 28 percent (Kaij, 1960). Of course, as we have observed, such findings do not rule out other interpretations. For one thing, parents may act more similarly toward identical twins than toward fraternal twins.

A stronger indicator that there may be a genetic factor in drug abuse and dependence has come from adoption studies (Goldstein, 1994). One investigation examined the alcoholism rates of people who had been adopted shortly after birth (Goodwin et al., 1973). One group of adoptees had biological parents who were alcoholic, while the other group's biological parents were not. By the age of 30, those with alcoholic biological parents showed significantly higher rates of alcohol abuse than those with nonalcoholic biological parents. Since all adoptees were reared in nonalcoholic environments, the different alcoholism rates suggest that a predisposition to develop alcoholism may be inherited.

Research involving the breeding of animals has also implicated genetic factors in the development of drug dependence (Goldstein, 1994; George, 1990). Researchers who have selected animals that prefer alcohol to other beverages and mated them have found that their offspring display the same preference. Similarly, researchers have mated rats from strains with different levels of alcohol preference and found the alcohol preferences of the offspring to be intermediate between those of the parents.

Even more direct evidence that a genetic factor may be at play in drug abuse and dependence has recently been provided by the "gene mapping" techniques that we discussed in Chapter 8. Using this new technology, investigators locate genes that are tied to various characteristics and disorders. Gene-mapping investigations are beginning to find links between aberrant genes and substance-related disorders. One set of studies has found an aberrant form of the so-called D2 receptor gene present in 69 percent of alcoholic subjects and 51 percent of subjects with cocaine dependence, but in less than 20 percent of nonalcoholic subjects (Blum & Noble, 1993; Blum et al., 1991). However, debate on this subject is very heated (Gejman et al., 1994; Arinami et al., 1993; Turner et al., 1992). Should the conflict subside in favor of the D2 gene association, it would provide the strongest evidence to date that genes play at least some role in the development of alcoholism, cocaine dependence, and other substance-related disorders.

For years genetic studies provided the only evidence for the position that biological factors play a key role in the development and maintenance of drug misuse. However, advances in technology have recently enabled researchers to explore the biological underpinnings of drug dependence more directly and to pinpoint some of the biological factors that may contribute to excessive and chronic drug use (Miller & Giannini, 1990).

One line of study has pinpointed some of the biological processes that produce drug tolerance and withdrawal symptoms. In many cases, the excessive and chronic ingestion of a particular kind of drug causes the brain to reduce its production of a particular neurotransmitter that would ordinarily act to sedate, alleviate pain, lift mood, or increase alertness (Goldstein, 1994). Because the drug acts to produce such a reaction, action by the neurotransmitter is less necessary. As the drug is taken increasingly, the body's production of the corresponding neurotransmitter decreases, leaving the person in need of more and more of the drug to achieve its initial effects. In short, the person builds tolerance for the drug. Moreover, as persons become increasingly reliant on the drug rather than on their own neurotransmitter, they must continue to ingest the drug in order to feel reasonably calm, comfortable, happy, or alert. If they

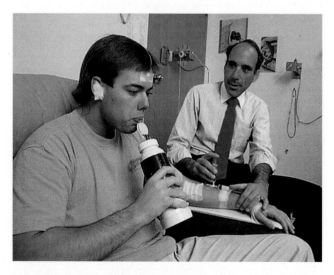

In studies to help determine whether the effects of alcohol and other drugs are linked to genetic factors, the children of drug-dependent parents and control subjects ingest various substances in the laboratory while researchers systematically observe the effects of these substances on brain and body functioning.

BOX 13-3

CANNABIS AND SOCIETY

For centuries cannabis played a respected role in the field of medicine. It was recommended as a surgical anesthetic by Chinese physicians 2,000 years ago and was used in other lands to treat cholera, malaria, coughs, insomnia, and rheumatism. In the mid–nineteenth century Western European physicians used it to treat neuralgia, menstrual pain, and migraine. Cannabis entered the United States in the early twentieth century, mainly in the form of marijuana. The U.S. drug company Parke-Davis became a leading importer of marijuana and distributed it for medical purposes.

Suddenly, however, the positive view of cannabis began to change. For one thing, more effective medicines replaced it. As morphine, aspirin, barbiturates, and other drugs were developed, physicians used cannabis less and less. Second, cannabis acquired some notoriety as a recreational drug early in the

Marijuana is made from the leaves of the hemp plant "Cannabis sativa." The plant is an annual herb, reaches a height of between 3 and 15 feet, and is grown in a wide range of altitudes, climates, and soils.

century, and its illegal distribution became a law enforcement problem. Authorities associated marijuana with alcohol and other disreputable drugs, assumed it was highly dangerous, and communicated this "fact" to the public. In 1937, when the "killer weed" was outlawed, the following magazine report was typical:

In Los Angeles, Calif., a youth was walking along a downtown street after inhaling a marijuana cigarette. For many addicts, merely a portion of a "reefer" is enough to induce intoxication. Suddenly, for no reason, he decided that someone had threatened to kill him and that his life at that very moment was in danger. Wildly he looked about him. The only person in sight was an aged bootblack. Drug-crazed nerve centers conjured the innocent old shoe-shiner into a destroying monster. Mad with fright, the addict hurried to his room and got a gun. He killed the old man, and then, later,

suddenly stop taking the drug, for a while they will have a deficient supply of the neurotransmitter needed for feeling well; they will in fact feel terrible. That is, they will experience uncomfortable withdrawal symptoms until the brain resumes its normal production and release of the necessary neurotransmitter.

A chronic and excessive ingestion of benzodiazepines, for example, eventually lowers the brain's production of the inhibitory neurotransmitter GABA (Tallman, 1978), setting the stage for insufficient GABA activity when a benzodiazepine abuser suddenly stops using the drug. Similarly, a chronic use of opioids eventually reduces the brain's own production of endorphins, leaving an abstinent addict with an inadequate supply of this neurotransmitter for sedating and for reducing pain (Snyder, 1991, 1977; Goldstein, 1976). And a chronic use of cocaine or amphetamines eventually lowers the brain's own pro-

duction of dopamine, norepinephrine, and serotonin, leaving abstinent users with fewer of these chemicals to stimulate their brains and the rest of their bodies (NIDA, 1991; Kleber & Gawin, 1987; Snyder, 1986). Finally, the recent discovery of *anandamide,* the body's own THC, suggests that excessive use of marijuana may reduce natural anandamide production, altering regulation of mood, pain, memory, and movement (Fackelmann, 1993).

Even if biological factors do predispose some people to develop and maintain drug problems, most people with such predispositions never fall into the trap of drug abuse and dependence. Why do some and not others develop these grossly dysfunctional problems? Psychological theorists—particularly psychodynamic and behavioral theorists—and sociocultural theorists have tried to suggest factors that may help push biologically predisposed people to take drugs and produce a pattern of misuse.

babbled his grief over what had been wanton, uncontrolled murder. . . .

That's marijuana!

(Anslinger & Cooper, 1937, p. 153)

Marijuana resurfaced with renewed vigor in the 1960s. It seemed to fit right in with that decade's disillusionment, protest, and self-exploration. Young people in particular discovered the pleasures of getting high, and smoking marijuana became a popular form of recreation. Many saw marijuana as a symbol of the government's low credibility: the drug was hardly the killer weed the government claimed it to be, and the harsh legal punishments for smoking it seemed unreasonable.

In the 1970s marijuana use continued to expand throughout the United States. By the end of the decade 16 million people reported using it at least once, 11 percent of the population identified themselves as recent users, and 11 percent of high school seniors said they smoked marijuana every day (NIDA, 1982).

These rates declined considerably during the 1980s. The marijuana that was imported to the United States became more powerful and dangerous than the earlier form and people stopped using it so often and so casually. At the same time, marijuana and other kinds of cannabis returned to their roots, so to speak, and once again found respect as a form of medical treatment.

In the late 1970s and 1980s cannabis researchers developed precise techniques for measuring and controlling THC content and for extracting pure THC from cannabis. They also developed synthetic analogues of THC. These newly acquired abilities opened the door to new medical applications for cannabis (Ray & Ksir, 1993). Cannabis became helpful in treating glaucoma, a severe eye disease in which fluid from the eyeball is obstructed from flowing properly. Oral THC combats glaucoma by lowering the pressure of fluid in the eye. Cannabis was also found to help patients with asthma, by causing the bronchi to dilate. And because THC helps prevent nausea and vomiting, it gained use among cancer patients whose chemotherapy elicited such reactions (Plasse et al., 1991; Gunby, 1981). Similarly, some studies suggested that THC might help improve the appetites of AIDS patients (Plasse et al., 1991).

In light of all this, the National Organization for the Reform of Marijuana Laws (NORML) has campaigned for the medical legalization of marijuana cigarettes, arguing that doses of THC are more controllable in marijuana cigarettes than in THC pill form, and in the late 1980s the Drug Enforcement Administration (DEA) considered classifying marijuana as a Schedule II drug—that is, a medically-useful drug that can be prescribed by physicians—instead of a Schedule I drug. In 1992, however, the DEA finally decided against this and the Food and Drug Administration even terminated the process of reviewing requests for the "compassionate use" of marijuana cigarettes (Karel, 1992). They held that prescriptions of pure THC, available in a capsule called *dronabinol* (trade name *Marinol*), serve all needed medical functions. Indeed, although 36 states now have laws allowing physicians to prescribe marijuana cigarettes, the FDA has officially approved such medical actions in only a handful of cases over the years (Karel, 1992).

THE PSYCHODYNAMIC VIEW

Psychodynamic theorists believe that people who ultimately abuse substances have inordinate dependency needs traceable to their early years (Shedler & Block, 1990; Ward, 1985; Abadi, 1984). They theorize that when parents fail to satisfy a child's need for nurturance, the child is likely to go through life in a dependent manner—relying too much on others for support, help, and comfort—in an effort to find the nurturance he or she did not receive as a child. If this search for external sources of support includes experimentation with a drug, such a person is likely to develop a dependent relationship with the substance.

Some psychodynamic theorists also believe that some people develop a "substance abuse personality" that makes them particularly vulnerable to drugs. To investigate this proposition, researchers have typically selected a population of chronic users of a particular drug, administered a battery of interviews and personality tests, determined the personality characteristics of each participant, and compared these personality profiles with those of control subjects who do not take the drug. Such studies have found that people who abuse or depend on drugs tend to be more dependent, antisocial, impulsive, and depressive than other people (Shedler & Block, 1990; Grinspoon & Bakalar, 1986; Labouvie & McGee, 1986; Gilbert & Lombardi, 1967).

Researchers have tried to determine the causal sequence of such correlations by repeating the personality tests at intervals during the subjects' lives. One such longitudinal study measured the characteristics of a large group of nonalcoholic young men and then kept track of each man's development (Jones, 1971, 1968). The profiles of those men who developed alcohol problems in middle age were compared with the profiles of those who did not. The men who developed alcohol problems had been more impulsive as adolescents and continued to be so in middle age, suggesting that impulsive men are indeed more prone to develop alcohol problems.

A major problem with these studies is that a suspiciously wide range of personality traits has been linked to drug abuse and dependence; in fact, different studies point to different "key" traits. Inasmuch as some addicted people are apparently dependent, others impulsive, and still others antisocial, researchers have been unable to conclude that any one personality trait or cluster of traits stands out as a factor in substance abuse and dependence (Rozin & Stoess, 1993; Lang, 1983).

THE BEHAVIORAL VIEW

According to *reinforcement* theorists, the reduction of tension, raising of spirits, or sense of well-being produced by a drug has a reinforcing effect and increases the likelihood that the user will seek this reaction again, especially under stress (Clark & Sayette, 1993; Steele & Josephs, 1990).

In support of this theory, studies have found that both human and animal subjects do in fact drink more alcohol when they are under stress (Young & Herling, 1986; Marlatt, 1977). One group of experimenters had social drinkers work on a difficult anagram task while another person unfairly criticized and belittled them (Marlatt, Kosturn, & Lang, 1975). These subjects were then asked to participate in an "alcohol taste task": their job was supposedly to compare and rate various alcoholic beverages. The harassed subjects drank significantly more alcohol during the taste task than did control subjects who had not been criticized. Another group of subjects were harassed while doing the anagrams but were given an opportunity to retaliate against their critics. These subjects drank relatively little during the tasting. Their retaliatory behavior had apparently reduced their tension and lessened their need for alcohol.

In a manner of speaking, the reinforcement theorists and researchers are arguing that many people take drugs to medicate themselves when they feel tense and upset. If so, one would expect elevated rates of drug abuse and dependence among people with high levels of anxiety, depression, or anger (Khantzian, 1985). This expectation has in fact been supported by research (King et al., 1993; Bukstein et al., 1992; Manley, 1992; NIAAA, 1991). In a study of 835 clinically depressed patients, for example, more than one-fourth were found to abuse drugs during

episodes of their disorders (Hasin, Endicott, & Lewis, 1985). Another study found that 50 percent of cocaine abusers met the diagnostic criteria for a depressive disorder (Gawin & Kleber, 1986). Similarly, Vietnam veterans suffering from posttraumatic stress disorder (PTSD) exhibit significantly higher rates of substance-related disorders than veterans without PTSD (McFall, Mackay, & Donovan, 1992), people suffering from bulimia nervosa and from anxiety disorders have higher than average rates of substance-related disorders (Higuchi et al., 1993; Walfish et al., 1992), and persons who have been sexually and physically abused as children display elevated rates of substance abuse in adulthood (Yama et al., 1993; Hernandez, 1992).

At the same time, however, a number of studies indicate that many people do not find drugs pleasurable or reinforcing when they first take them. Some volunteers who are administered heroin in laboratory settings, for example, initially dislike the drug or feel indifferent to it (Alexander & Hadaway, 1982). Similarly, a number of addicts report that their initial opium experiences were anything but pleasurable:

We slept most of the day until late afternoon, and when I woke up she got up and got a tray out of the dresser drawer and brought it over and placed it on the bed. . . . She told me she was [an opium] smoker and asked me if I had ever smoked hop. I told her I never had and she said that I ought to try it once, as she was sure I would like it. . . . [After smoking it] I suddenly became very nauseated and had to leave to vomit. I vomited till there was nothing left on my stomach and I was still sick so I went to bed.

(Lindesmith, 1972, p. 85)

Even when a drug does initially produce pleasant feelings and reward the user with a reduction in tension, the picture seems to change later when the person takes the drug excessively and chronically. As we saw earlier, many people become increasingly anxious and depressed over time as they take more and more drugs (Vaillant, 1993; Nathan & O'Brien, 1971; Nathan et al., 1970). Why, then, do they keep ingesting them?

Some behaviorists use Richard Solomon's **opponent-process theory** to answer this question. Solomon (1980) holds that the brain is structured in such a way that pleasurable emotions, such as drug-induced euphoria, inevitably lead to opponent processes—negative aftereffects—that leave the person feeling worse than usual. People who continue to use pleasure-giving drugs inevitably develop opponent aftereffects, such as cravings for more of the drug, withdrawal responses, and an increasing need for the drug. According to Solomon, the opponent processes eventually dominate and suppress the pleasure-giving processes, and avoidance of the negative aftereffects replaces pursuit of pleasure as the individual's prmary motivation for taking drugs. Although a highly regarded theory, the opponent-process explanation has not received systematic research support (Peele, 1989).

Other behaviorists have proposed that *classical conditioning* may also contribute to certain aspects of drug abuse and dependence (Ehrman et al., 1992; Pomerleau & Pomerleau, 1984; Lindesmith, 1968). They hold that objects present at the time drugs are taken may act as conditioned stimuli and come to elicit some of the same pleasure brought on by the drugs themselves. Just the sight of a hypodermic needle or a regular supplier, for example, have been known to comfort a heroin or amphetamine addict and relieve withdrawal symptoms.

In a similar manner, objects that are present during withdrawal distress may elicit withdrawal-like symptoms. One former heroin addict experienced nausea and other withdrawal symptoms when he returned to the neighborhood where he had gone through withdrawal in the past—a reaction that led him to start taking heroin again (O'Brien et al., 1975). Similarly, after eight addicted human subjects were repeatedly exposed to a peppermint odor during their withdrawal reactions, they experienced withdrawal-like symptoms (tearing eyes, sick feelings, running nose) whenever someone near them ate peppermint candy (O'Brien et al., 1977).

Although these studies demonstrate that withdrawal responses can be classically conditioned, other studies suggest that such conditioning is not at work in most cases. In interviews with forty persons who had gone through heroin withdrawal, only eleven reported having withdrawal symptoms during later encounters with environments and objects associated with their withdrawal, and only five of these people actually relapsed into heroin use (McAuliffe, 1982). In short, the classical conditioning explanations of drug abuse and dependence, like the reinforcement explanations, have received at best mixed support (Powell, Bradley, & Gray, 1992).

THE SOCIOCULTURAL VIEW

Sociocultural theorists propose that the people most likely to develop a pattern of drug abuse or depen-

Some cultures encourage alcohol use more than others, thus increasing the risk of alcoholism. Many even offer institutionalized opportunities for drinking. These men are participating in Germany's 16-day "Oktoberfest," during which bartenders serve 5 million liters of beer to thousands of revelers.

dence are those whose societies create an atmosphere of stress (see Box 13–4) or whose families value, or at least tolerate, drug taking (Walsh, 1992). Epidemiological studies have provided some support for these claims. One study found that regions in the United States where daily life is relatively more stressful (states where divorce is more common or where more people are laid off from work) report higher rates of alcoholism (Linsky, Strauss, & Colby, 1985). Similarly, hunting societies, in which people presumably experience greater danger, uncertainty, and tension, have more alcohol problems than agrarian societies (Bacon, 1973; Horton, 1943); city dwellers have higher alcoholism rates than residents of small towns and rural areas (Cisin & Calahan, 1970); and lower socioeconomic classes have higher drinking and substance abuse rates than other classes (Smith, North, & Spitznagel, 1993; Beauvais, 1992). Studies have similarly found higher heroin addiction rates among people who live in stressful environments. As we noted in Chapter 6, heroin use was very common among American soldiers in Vietnam during the 1960s. About 40 percent of Army enlisted men there used heroin at least once, half of them so often that they had a withdrawal reaction when they stopped (Grinspoon & Bakalar, 1986).

Studies also support the claim that family attitudes and patterns of functioning may play a role in the development of patterns of substance misuse. Problem drinking is more common among teenagers whose parents and peers drink, and among teenagers whose family environment is stressful and unsupportive (Carey, 1993; Chassin et al., 1993; Holman et al., 1993; OSAP, 1991). Moreover, lower rates of

BOX 13-4

"MENTALLY ILL CHEMICAL ABUSERS": A CHALLENGE FOR TREATMENT

A state appeals court yesterday ordered Larry Hogue, who has for years frightened residents of Manhattan's Upper West Side with his bizarre behavior, to remain in a state mental hospital until a hearing next week. . . . Before he was arrested, Mr. Hogue had attacked passers-by and cars in the area around West 96th Street and Amsterdam Avenue. . . .

"We believe Mr. Hogue is still mentally ill and dangerous to himself and his community," said Arnold D. Fleischer, an assistant Attorney General, who argued for the interim stay at the Brooklyn court house. . . . Mr. Hogue has been arrested 30 times and served at least six terms in prison, ranging from five days to a year, according to law-enforcement records. He now faces charges of criminal mischief for scraping the paint off a car last August.

(New York Times, *February 9, 1993*)

The case of Larry Hogue, the so-called "Wild Man of West 96th Street," has helped bring the plight of MICAs to public attention.

Larry Hogue, nicknamed the "Wild Man of West 96th Street" by his neighbors, is a ***mentally ill chemical abuser (MICA),*** as are between 20 and 50 percent of all people who suffer from chronic mental disorders.

Estimates for young adult chronic patients are as high as 74 percent (Polcin, 1992; Khalsa et al., 1991). More than half of the people who abuse drugs other than alcohol suffer from at least one concurrent mental disorder (Robertson, 1992; Leshner, 1991; Millman, 1991).

MICAs tend to be young and male. They often have lower than average levels of social functioning and school achievement and increased levels of poverty, homelessness, acting-out behavior, hospital admissions, emergency room visits, and encounters with the criminal justice system (Bartels et al., 1993; Kutcher et al., 1992; O'Hare, 1992). MICAs commonly report greater distress than non-substance-abusing patients with mental disorders (Carey, Carey, & Meisler, 1991). MICAs also have significantly poorer treatment outcomes than other people with chronic mental disorders.

---

alcohol abuse are found among Jews and Protestants, groups in which the boundaries of drinking are clearly defined and drinking to the point of intoxication is less common (Calahan, Cisin, & Crossley, 1969; McCord & McCord, 1960; Snyder, 1955), whereas alcoholism rates are relatively high among the Irish and Eastern Europeans, who less clearly define the boundaries of acceptable drinking (Vaillant & Milofsky, 1982).

Epidemiological findings of these kinds are consistent with the sociocultural view of substance abuse and dependence, but as we noted earlier, they are subject to nonsociocultural interpretations as well. In fact, as we have seen, none of the models has provided undisputed evidence to support its position on substance-related disorders and certainly none by itself has been able to account for dysfunctional patterns of drug use (Peele, 1989). Thus at present drug misuse remains a complex phenomenon that is far from being fully understood.

■ TREATMENTS ■ FOR SUBSTANCE-RELATED DISORDERS

A wide variety of treatments have been applied to substance-related disorders, sometimes with great

The relationship between substance abuse and mental dysfunctioning is complex. A mental disorder may precede substance abuse, and the drug may be a form of self-medication or result of impaired judgment. Some clinicians theorize that the recent increase in the prevalence of MICAs can be traced to the deinstitutionalization movement: when vulnerable people suffering from chronic mental disorders moved into the community, they easily gained access to alcohol and drugs that were unavailable to them in the hospital (Polcin, 1992). On the other hand, substance abuse may cause or exacerbate psychopathology. Cocaine, for example, exacerbates the symptoms of psychosis and can cause schizophrenia to appear earlier than normal (Shaner et al., 1993). A third and perhaps the most compelling theory is that substance abuse and mental disorders interact to create a unique problem that is, so to speak, greater than the sum of its parts (Robertson, 1992). The course and outcome of one problem can be significantly influenced by the presence of the other disorder.

Treatment of MICAs has been undermined by the tendency of substance abuse to be underdiagnosed. Drug screening in mental health settings is often inadequate, and all but the most severe substance abuse cases may go unrecognized and therefore untreated (Bartels et al., 1993). Unrecognized substance abuse may also lead to the misdiagnosis of mental disorders or the misunderstanding of the course and prognosis of a disorder (Shaner et al., 1993).

The treatment of MICAs is further complicated by the specialized nature of many mental health and substance abuse treatment facilities. Such facilities are often designed and funded to treat primarily one disorder or the other, and few are either equipped or willing to treat both. As a result, it is not uncommon for MICA patients to be rejected as inappropriate for treatment in both substance abuse and mental health programs. Many MICAs fall through the cracks in this way and find themselves in jail or in homeless shelters for want of the treatment they sought in vain (Polcin, 1992).

The ideal MICA treatment program appears to be a safe and supportive therapeutic environment that adapts both mental health and substance abuse treatment techniques and takes into account the unique effects of both problems (Carey, 1989). Such hybrid models are proving relatively successful (Fals & Schafer, 1992). One particularly inspiring development is the recent establishment of self-help groups for MICAs living in the community. In Philadelphia, for example, there are more than thirty "Double Trouble" groups for MICAs, based on the Alcoholics Anonymous model (Caldwell & White, 1991).

The problem of falling through the cracks is perhaps most poignant in the case of homeless MICAs. Researchers estimate that 10 to 20 percent of homeless persons are MICAs (Drake, Osher, & Wallach, 1991). Homeless MICAs typically are homeless longer than other homeless persons and are more likely to experience extremely harsh conditions, such as living on the winter streets rather than in a homeless shelter. They are more likely than other homeless persons to be jailed, to grant sexual favors for food or money, and to be victimized. They are a particularly isolated group, resistant to efforts to help and distrustful of people and institutions (Drake et al., 1991). It has been suggested that treatment programs for homeless MICAs should emphasize lengthy outreach periods, trust building, practical assistance, and intensive case management with a commitment to long-term care (Drake et al., 1991). In short, clinicians must develop treatment programs that are tailored to the unique combination of problems of this special population, rather than expect them to respond to approaches that have been developed for people with other problems that are far less complex.

success, at other times with only moderate effectiveness (Prochaska, Di Clemente, & Norcross, 1992; Walburg, 1985). The treatments may be applied on either an outpatient or an inpatient basis. Although inpatient treatment for these disorders seems to be on the rise, research does not suggest that this more expensive format is consistently more effective than outpatient treatment (Alterman et al., 1994; Miller & Hester, 1986).

Investigators of treatment programs for people with substance-related disorders confront several problems. First, different substance-related disorders often pose different treatment problems (Kleber & Gawin, 1987).

Second, some people recover from their substance problems without any intervention at all (Prochaska et al., 1992). Yet other people appear to recover and then relapse, or fail to recover from their disorder even after intensive treatment, and continue to lead a drug-involved life for the time that is left to them. Thus it can be extremely difficult to determine at any given time whether a treatment is succeeding, failing, or irrelevant to a given person's progress.

Finally, as with other mental disorders, the different criteria and goals employed by different clinical researchers make it difficult to draw broad conclusions about a treatment's effectiveness (Woody et al., 1988). How long, for example, must a person refrain from substance use in order to be categorized as a treatment success? And is total abstention the only criterion, or is a reduction of drug use considered significant? Different answers to these questions will lead to markedly different research conclusions.

These problems notwithstanding, clinicians have worked diligently to find ways to correct substance-related disorders. Most of the approaches fall into one of several groups: insight, behavioral, cognitive-behavioral, and biological therapies. Although presented separately, these interventions are usually combined either with each other or with other formats, such as couple therapy or family therapy (Galanter, 1993; O'Farrell et al., 1992).

INSIGHT THERAPIES

Insight therapists try to help people with substance-related disorders to become aware of and address the psychological factors that contribute to their pattern of drug use (Jungman, 1985). Psychodynamic therapists, for example, first help clients to uncover and resolve their underlying conflicts and then try to help them alter their substance-related styles of living (Levinson, 1985). Client-centered therapists guide clients to accept the feelings and thoughts that, according to their theory, they have hidden from themselves while turning to drugs.

Although these approaches are often applied to substance-related disorders, research has not found them to be highly effective (Meyer et al., 1989; Miller & Hester, 1980). Their lack of success may indicate that drug abuse or dependence eventually becomes a stubborn and independent problem irrespective of its causes, and that the maladaptive pattern must be the primary target for change if people are to become drug-free. Thus insight therapies tend to be of greater help when they are combined with other approaches in a multidimensional treatment program. They have been combined successfully with behavioral and biological therapies (Galanter, 1993; Weidman, 1985) and are offered most often in group-therapy formats.

BEHAVIORAL AND COGNITIVE-BEHAVIORAL THERAPIES

A widely used behavioral treatment for substance-related disorders is *aversive conditioning,* an approach based on the principles of classical conditioning. Here individuals are repeatedly presented with an unpleasant stimulus (for example, an electric shock) at the same time that they are taking a drug. After repeated pairings, the individuals are expected to start reacting negatively to the substance itself and to lose their craving for it.

Aversive conditioning has been applied to alcohol abuse and dependence more than to other substance-use disorders (Callner, 1975). In the past, the protocols for aversive conditioning were sometimes drastic and controversial. In one treatment program alcoholic people were injected with *succinylcholine,* a drug that actually paralyzed their bodies while they tasted alcoholic beverages (Sanderson, Campbell, & Laverty, 1963). These people did develop an aversion to alcohol, but many clinicians understandably worried about the safety and ethics of the program. Moreover, the effectiveness seemed to be short-lived. Electrical aversive conditioning, which pairs electrical shock with drinking, also raised ethical questions while proving to have limited effectiveness (Wilson, 1987, 1978).

Today's aversive conditioning techniques tend to be somewhat less severe. In one approach, drinking behavior is paired with drug-induced nausea and vomiting (Elkins, 1991; Cannon et al., 1986, 1981). Another, *covert sensitization,* requires alcoholic people to imagine extremely upsetting, repulsive, or frightening scenes while they are drinking (Emmelkamp, 1994; Cautela, 1977, 1966). The supposition is that the pairing of these imagined scenes with liquor will elicit negative responses to liquor itself. One of the main limitations of the aversive conditioning approaches is that they can be successful only when clients are sufficiently motivated to continue with such a program despite its unpleasantness.

Another behavioral approach focuses on teaching *alternatives* to drug taking. This approach, too, has been applied to alcohol abuse and dependence more than to other substance-related disorders. Problem drinkers may be taught to use relaxation, meditation, or biofeedback instead of alcohol to reduce their tensions (Rohsenow, Smith, & Johnson, 1985). Some are also given assertiveness training or taught social skills to help them both express their anger more directly and withstand social pressures to drink (Van Hasselt et al., 1993; Chaney et al., 1978). Similarly, leisure education programs have been implemented to teach substance abusers positive "fun" alternatives to drug abuse (Aguilar & Munson, 1992).

A behavioral approach that has been effective in the short-term treatment of persons who abuse cocaine (a notoriously hard-to-treat group) is *contingency training,* in which clients receive incentives contingent on submitting drug-free urine specimens. In one recent study of contingency training, 58 percent of cocaine abusers completed the full six months of treatment, with 68 percent achieving at least eight weeks of continuous abstinence. Since the length of time clients remain with the program and the length of their abstinence are predictors of future freedom from substance abuse, the results are cause for some optimism (Higgins et al., 1993).

Most behavioral treatments for substance abuse and dependence have had at most limited success (Meyer et al., 1989), and, in fact, they generally work best in combination with cognitive approaches (Washton & Stone-Washton, 1990). In one cognitive-behavioral approach, *behavioral self-control training (BSCT),* therapists first instruct clients to monitor their own drinking behavior (Miller et al., 1992; Miller, 1983). When clients record the times, locations, emotions, bodily changes, and other circumstances that accompany their drinking, they become more sensitive to the cues they associate with excessive drinking. Clients are then taught to set appropriate limits on their drinking, to recognize when the limits are being approached, to control their rate of drinking (perhaps by spacing their drinks or by sipping them rather than gulping), and to apply alternative coping behaviors, such as relaxation techniques, in situations that would otherwise elicit drinking. Approximately 70 percent of the clients who complete this program have been assessed as showing some improvement (Miller & Hester, 1980). The program appears to be more effective in cases where individuals are younger and not physically dependent on alcohol (Miller et al., 1992; Meyer et al., 1989).

In a similar combination approach, *relapse-prevention training,* heavy drinkers again use self-monitoring to identify the situations and emotional changes that place them at risk for heavy drinking, then learn coping strategies to use in such situations (Kivlaham et al., 1990; Marlatt & Gordon, 1985, 1980). Clients are also taught to plan ahead of time how much drinking is appropriate, what they will consume, and under what circumstances, and they practice their adaptive strategies in either real or imagined high-risk situations. Here a therapist presents the basic principles of this approach to a client:

> We know that you would like to be totally abstinent for life, but our knowledge of alcoholics generally and of you in particular suggests that however hard you try, you are likely to drink on some occasion or occasions after you leave hospital. This is not being pessimistic, but simply realistic. We are not suggesting that your task is hopeless—far from it—but we do want you to anticipate future events and work out ways of coping. We have already told you that some drink will be given to you during your stay in hospital and that your aim is to stop after

a certain amount when you feel like continuing. In this way we believe that you will gradually break the compulsion to continue and will develop your willpower. This should have two effects when you leave hospital. First, when you attempt to drink, your experience of resisting temptation in the hospital will give you greater control. Second, if you do drink you will find it easier to pull out before you explode into a heavy-drinking binge. . . .

> *(Hodgson & Rankin, 1982, p. 213)*

As this statement suggests, relapse-prevention training, like BSCT, seeks to give clients control over their drinking behavior. Research indicates that the approach only sometimes reduces the frequency of intoxication (Hollon & Beck, 1994; Annis et al., 1989). Like BSCT, relapse-prevention training is apparently more effective for alcohol abusers than for those who are physically dependent on alcohol (Meyer et al., 1989). It has also been adapted, with some success, to the treatment of cocaine abuse (Carrol, Rounsaville, & Gawin, 1991).

BIOLOGICAL TREATMENTS

Biological techniques play a variety of roles in the treatment of substance-related disorders. They may be directed at helping people withdraw from substances, abstain from them, or simply maintain their existing substance use without further escalation. Research suggests that biological approaches alone rarely lead to long-term improvement but can sometimes be a helpful component of broader treatment programs (Kleber et al., 1985).

DETOXIFICATION *Detoxification* is systematic and medically supervised withdrawal from a drug (Wartenberg et al., 1990). Many detoxification programs are set up in hospitals or clinics, as drug users often seem more motivated to persevere through withdrawal in those settings. Inpatient detoxification programs of this kind may also offer individual and group therapy, a "full-service" institutional approach that has become increasingly popular in recent years.

One detoxification strategy, used most often with sedative-hypnotic drug dependence, is to have clients withdraw gradually from the drug, taking ever-decreasing doses until they are off the drug completely. Although withdrawal symptoms still occur with this technique, they are likely to be milder. Another detoxification strategy is to administer other drugs that reduce the symptoms of withdrawal. Antianxiety drugs are, for example, sometimes used to reduce severe alcohol withdrawal reactions.

Detoxification programs have proved effective in helping motivated people to withdraw from drugs. For people who fail to pursue psychotherapy after withdrawal, however, relapse rates tend to be high (Pickens & Fletcher, 1991).

ANTAGONIST DRUGS After successful withdrawal from a drug, the next challenge is to avoid a recurrence of drug abuse or dependence. In one biological technique, people with substance-related disorders are given *antagonist drugs,* drugs that block or change the effects of the addictive drug. *Disulfiram (Antabuse),* for example, is often given to people who are trying to refrain from drinking alcohol (Ray & Ksir, 1993). By itself this drug is believed to have relatively few negative effects; but a person who drinks alcohol while taking disulfiram will experience intense nausea, vomiting, blushing, faster heart rate, dizziness, and perhaps fainting. Theoretically, people who have taken disulfiram will refrain from alcohol, knowing the terrible reaction that awaits them should they have even one drink. Disulfiram has proved helpful but again only with people who are highly motivated (Meyer et al., 1989; Becker, 1979; Weinberg, 1977). After all, they can stop taking the disulfiram and return to alcohol at any time.

Narcotic antagonists, such as naloxone, cyclazocine, and naltrexone, and partial antagonists such as buprenorphine are sometimes used with people who are dependent on opioids. These drugs attach to opioid receptor sites throughout the brain and make it impossible for the opioid to have its usual euphoric effect. Theoretically, without the rush or high, continued drug use becomes pointless. Although narcotic antagonists have been helpful in emergencies to rescue people from an overdose of opioids, they are usually considered too dangerous for treatment of opioid dependence. The antagonists must be administered very carefully because of their ability to throw addicted persons into severe withdrawal reactions (Goldstein, 1994; Kleber et al., 1985).

Surprisingly, some recent studies have found that the narcotic antagonist *naltrexone* may also reduce an alcoholic person's craving for drink, and may also block the "high" that alcohol creates. One study found that this drug broke the cycle of craving that is typically set in motion when a recovering alcoholic person "lapses" and has one or two drinks. Complete relapses were reduced to 23 percent in the naltrexone group, compared to 54 percent in a traditional detoxification group (Volpicelli et al., 1992). A similar study found that patients receiving naltrexone and coping skills therapy had three times the rate of abstinence

achieved by control patients. Less than half of the former patients who sampled alcohol experienced a full relapse, while the majority of the control patients relapsed after sampling alcohol (O'Malley et al., 1992). Although naltrexone cannot be called a cure for alcoholism, these findings are considered very promising indeed. Recent studies with animal subjects suggest that certain narcotic antagonists may also have some therapeutic value in cocaine dependence (Goldstein, 1994).

Finally, newly developed antibodies are under investigation as a possible cocaine antagonist. These antibodies seek cocaine molecules and break them into two inert byproducts. If the results of future research are positive, the new antibodies may represent the first compound to significantly help motivated cocaine abusers stay drug-free long enough to break the cycle of addiction (Landry et al., 1993).

DRUG MAINTENANCE THERAPY A drug-related lifestyle may be a greater problem than the drug's direct effects. Much of the damage caused by heroin addiction, for example, comes from overdoses, unsterile needles, harmful contaminants, and an accompanying life of crime. Thus clinicians were initially very enthusiastic when *methadone maintenance programs* were developed in the 1960s to treat heroin addiction (Dole & Nyswander, 1967, 1965). In these programs, addicted clients are given the synthetic opioid methadone as a substitute for heroin. Although the clients then become dependent on methadone, their addiction is maintained under legal and safe medical supervision. The programs' creators believed methadone to be preferable to heroin because it can be taken orally, thus eliminating the dangers of needles, and it needs to be taken only once a day.

The initial methadone programs appeared to be very effective, and some of them claimed success rates as high as 80 to 100 percent (McGlothlin, Anglin, & Wilson, 1978; DeLong, 1975). These programs also offered vocational and social rehabilitation so that some heroin users could live relatively normal and constructive lives. As a result of these successes, numerous methadone maintenance programs were established throughout the United States, Canada, and England (Payte, 1989).

These programs became less popular during the 1980s, largely because of the addictiveness of methadone itself (Peachey & Franklin, 1985; Etzioni, 1973). Many clinicians came to believe that substituting one addiction for another is not an acceptable "solution" for drug dependence, and many addicted persons complained that methadone addiction creates an additional drug problem that simply complicates the original one, leaving them with a far from drug-free existence. In fact, methadone is apparently harder to withdraw from than heroin.

Pregnant women maintained on methadone have the added concern of the drug's effect on their children. Methadone has been associated with severe and extensive withdrawal symptoms in newborns and with possible neurological symptoms. Methadone-exposed children may exhibit greater anxiety and aggression than their unexposed peers, and may be at increased risk of developing attention-deficit disorders and learning disorders (DeCubas & Field, 1993).

Despite such concerns, interest in medically supervised treatments such as methadone maintenance has increased in recent years as a result of the rapid spread of the HIV virus among intravenous drug abusers and their sex partners and children. Twenty-four to 30 percent of AIDS cases reported in 1992 were directly associated with intravenous drug abuse, and intravenous drug abuse is the ultimate causal factor in most heterosexual transmission of AIDS and in 60 percent of pediatric AIDS cases (Brown, 1993; NIDA, 1991). Intravenous drug abuse is risky not only because of the dangers of unsterile needle sharing but also because of the disinhibiting effects of drugs, which can lead to high-risk sexual behavior (Millstein, 1992). Thus some methadone maintenance programs have incorporated AIDS education and health-focused supportive psychotherapy in their treatment services (Batki, 1988).

SELF-HELP PROGRAMS

In view of the cost and limited success of clinical interventions, many drug users have organized among themselves to help one another recover without professional assistance. The drug self-help movement dates back to 1935, when two alcoholic men from Ohio met to discuss alternative treatment possibilities. The first discussion led to others and to the eventual formation of a self-help group for alcoholic persons. The members discussed alcohol-related problems, traded ideas, and provided support. The organization became known as *Alcoholics Anonymous (AA)*.

Today AA has more than 2 million members in 89,000 groups across the United States and nearly 100 other countries (AA World Services, 1994). It provides peer support therapy with moral and spiritual features to help people overcome alcoholism (Moos & Finney, 1983). Different members apparently find different aspects of AA helpful. For some it is the peer support and identification that help them gain control over drinking behavior (Galanter et al., 1990); for others it is the spiritual dimension. Meetings take place regularly, and members are available to help each other 24 hours a day. By establishing guidelines for living, the organization helps members abstain "one day at a time," urging them to accept as "fact" the idea that they are powerless over alcohol and that they must stop drinking entirely and permanently if they are to live normal lives.

A related self-help organization is AlAnon, which offers support groups for people who live with and care about alcoholic persons. In these groups people share their painful experiences and learn how to cope with the impact of the alcoholic persons in their lives and how to stop reinforcing their drinking and related behavior.

Self-help programs have also been developed for other substance-related disorders, particularly heroin and cocaine dependence. *Narcotics Anonymous* and *Cocaine Anonymous,* based on the Alcoholics Anonymous model, are growing in popularity. Many self-help programs, such as Daytop Village and Phoenix House, have expanded into *residential treatment centers,* or *therapeutic communities,* where former heroin and cocaine abusers live, work, and socialize in a drug-free environment while undergoing individual, group, and family therapies and making a transition back to community life.

The actual success of the self-help and residential treatment programs has been difficult to determine (Ray & Ksir, 1993; Meyer et al., 1989). Some of the programs keep no records of members who failed to be helped and dropped out. Moreover, many such programs are distrustful of researchers and deal with them very selectively (Vaillant, 1983). This attitude may be changing, though, and collaborations now under way between such programs and researchers may eventually yield a more precise picture of the programs' effectiveness. In the meantime, the evidence that keeps self-help and residential treatment programs going comes in the form of individual testimonials. Many tens of thousands of persons have revealed that they are members of these programs and credit them with turning their lives around (Galanter et al., 1990).

CONTROLLED DRUG USE VS. ABSTINENCE

Is total abstinence the only cure for drug abuse and dependence, or can people with substance use disorders learn to keep drug use under better control?

This issue has been debated for years, especially when the drug in question is alcohol.

As we saw earlier, many cognitive-behavioral theorists believe that people can continue to drink in moderation if they learn to set more appropriate drinking limits. These advocates of controlled drinking argue that a goal of strict abstinence may in fact encourage people to abandon self-control entirely if they should have a single drink (Peele, 1989; Heather, Winton, & Rollnick, 1982). Those who view alcoholism as a disease, in contrast, take the AA position of "Once an alcoholic, always an alcoholic," and hold that relapse is almost inevitable when alcoholic people believe that they can safely take one drink (Pendery, Maltzman, & West, 1982). They hold that this misguided belief will sooner or later open the door to alcohol once again and lead back to uncontrollable drinking.

Feelings about this issue are so strong that the people on one side have at times challenged the motives and integrity of those on the other (Sobell & Sobell, 1984, 1976, 1973; Pendery et al., 1982). Research indicates, however, that both controlled drinking and abstinence may be viable treatment goals, depending on the individual's personality and on the nature of the particular drinking problem (O'Leary & Wilson, 1987). Studies suggest, for example, that abstinence is a more appropriate goal for people who are physically dependent on alcohol, while controlled drinking can be helpful to younger abusive drinkers, who may simply need to be taught a nonabusive form of drinking (Marlatt, 1985; Miller, 1983, 1982). Studies also suggest that abstinence is more appropriate for people who believe that they are alcoholic and that abstinence is the only answer for them (Rosenberg, 1993). These people are more likely to relapse after having just one drink. The results of these studies may apply to other drug disorders as well.

It is important to keep in mind that, generally speaking, both abstinence and controlled drinking are extremely difficult for alcoholic persons to achieve (Watson, 1987; Vaillant, 1983; Emrick & Hansen, 1983). Although treatment may help heavy drinkers to improve for a while, follow-up studies indicate high relapse rates. A study that followed the progress of 110 individuals found that thirty years after treatment, 20 percent had become moderate drinkers, 34 percent had become abstinent, and the rest continued to display significant drinking problems (Vaillant, 1983). Other findings are even gloomier, suggesting that recovery rates are sometimes as low as 5 to 10 percent (Peele, 1989; Emrick & Hansen, 1983).

Gloomier yet are the findings of a study of men treated for heroin addiction: twenty-five years after initial court-ordered treatment, 75 percent of the subjects were either dead, in jail, or still abusing heroin, while 25 percent were drug-free (Hser, Anglin, & Powers, 1993). Such statistics serve as a harsh reminder that substance abuse and dependence continue to be among our society's most durable and disabling problems. They have also led some clinicians to focus more on sociocultural issues and others to concentrate more on prevention programs.

SOCIOCULTURAL TREATMENT PROGRAMS

Many substance abusers live in a poverty-stricken and violence-prone environment (NIDA, 1990). A growing number of today's treatment programs try to be sensitive to the special sociocultural pressures and unique problems faced by drug abusers who are poor, homeless, or members of ethnic minority groups (Deitch & Solit, 1993; Wallace, 1993). Sensitivity to each patient's unique life challenges can be the best defense against the environmental and social stresses that can lead to relapse.

Similarly, therapists have become more aware that significant gender issues are often tied to substance-related disorders (Lisansky-Gomberg, 1993). Because women and men have different physical and psychological reactions to drugs, for example, women often require treatment methods different from those designed for men (Hamilton, 1991). In addition, treatment of women substance abusers may be com-

At "Via Avanta," a residential treatment center in Los Angeles, a therapist leads a parenting session for women dependent on opioids. Individuals live, work, and socialize in such centers while receiving treatment for their substance dependence.

plicated by numerous gender-specific issues, including the impact of sexual abuse, the stresses of raising children, and the fear of criminal prosecution for abusing drugs during pregnancy (Chiavaroli, 1992; Roper, 1992; Wallen, 1992). Seventy percent of women with substance-related disorders have experienced sexual abuse before age 16 according to some investigations, and more than one-third of the substance-abusing women in one study reported an average of ten rapes by age 27 (Arbiter, 1991; Finnegan, 1991; Hagan, 1991; Worth, 1991). Thus, many women substance abusers feel more comfortable seeking help at gender-sensitive clinics or at feminist-oriented residential programs that focus on empowerment and education and that allow children to live with their recovering mothers (Copeland & Hall, 1992; DeAngelis, 1992).

PREVENTION

In recent years, drug prevention efforts have spread beyond the school environment as clinicians recognize that children spend only a portion of their time at school, and that those at the greatest risk for drug-related disorders may be chronic truants or may have left school entirely. Prevention programs have also become more tailored to target populations. Clinicals researchers are attempting to determine not merely how substance-related disorders in general can be prevented but how they can be prevented in specific groups. Which intervention, for which population, is most effective for preventing abuse of which substances (NIDA, 1991)?

Prevention programs vary in their techniques and objectives. Some programs advocate total abstinence from drugs, while others advocate "responsible" use. Some seek to interrupt or prevent "gateway drug" use; others, recognizing that early onset of drug use is strongly correlated with later abuse, seek to delay the age of experimentation with drugs. Similarly, programs may differ in whether they try to provide drug education, teach constructive alternatives to drug use, change the psychological state of the potential user, modify relationships with peers, or combine some of these techniques.

Prevention programs may focus on the *individual* (for example, by providing education about unpleasant drug effects), on the *family* (by teaching parenting skills and improving family functioning), on the *peer group* (by changing peer norms or teaching resistance to peer pressure), on the *school* (by establishing firm enforcement of drug policies), or on the *community* at large (by public service announcements

such as the "Just say no" campaign). The most effective prevention programs combine several such areas of focus to create a comprehensive and cooperative program that provides a consistent message about drug abuse in all areas of children's lives (NIDA, 1991).

Some prevention programs have even been developed for preschool children. The *Beginning Alcohol and Addiction Basic Education Studies (BABES)* program teaches preschool children decision-making skills, coping skills, and techniques for resisting peer pressure and dealing with feelings. It also provides information about alcohol and other drugs, and familiarizes children with sources of help. The BABES program uses instructional puppets such as Buttons and Bows McKitty, whose parents are drug-dependent; Early Bird, who gives warning signals about self-destructive behaviors and about the effects of incorrect beliefs about drugs; Recovering Reggie, a recovering alcoholic dog who tells about his addiction and recovery; and Rhonda Rabbit, an abused child who lives in a home with addicted parents and demonstrates coping skills (Abbott, 1987).

The *Head Start* program has initiated a similar preschool prevention curriculum, targeting the poverty-stricken populations enrolled in Head Start and their parents. The program teaches about drug effects, risk factors, health issues, peer pressure, parenting skills, and development and use of support networks (Oyemade, 1989). Although in some respects it seems sad to have to focus on preschool children as the subjects of intensive efforts to prevent drug abuse, there is nevertheless cause for optimism that such programs may make a major positive difference in the course of their lives.

THE STATE OF THE FIELD

SUBSTANCE-RELATED DISORDERS

In some respects the story of the misuse of drugs is the same today as it was in past years. Substance use is still rampant, and it creates some of society's most prevalent psychological disorders and debilitating problems. New drugs keep emerging and the public continues to go through periods of naiveté regarding their use, believing for a time that the drugs are "safe" and only gradually learning that they pose significant dangers. And treatments for substance-related disorders continue to have only limited effect.

Yet there are some important new wrinkles in this familiar story. Researchers have begun to develop a clearer understanding of the way many drugs act on the body and of the biological reasons for drug tolerance and withdrawal symptoms. In the treatment sphere, self-help groups and rehabilitation programs are flourishing. Preventive education to make people aware of the seduction of drugs and the dangers of drug misuse is also on the upswing and seems to be making a dent in the public's drug behavior, especially among teenagers, whose use of drugs has declined somewhat in recent years. And clinicians have discovered drug antagonists that seem to hold promise as future forms of biological intervention.

These recent developments are encouraging. Meanwhile, however, enormous quantities of drugs are being distributed and used, more every year. New drugs and drug combinations are discovered almost daily. And with them come new problems, new questions, and requirements for new research and new interventions. Thus despite their efforts, clinical practitioners and investigators have found it difficult to make a sizable impact on this problem. As drugs proliferate, perhaps the most valuable lesson to be learned from clinical research and from our society's drug-taking history is an old one: There is no free lunch. High psychological and biological costs are attached to the pleasures associated with many of these substances. Not all the costs are yet known, but costs do inevitably seem to emerge.

Summary

■ **The term "drug"** applies to any substance other than food that changes our bodily and mental functioning. Drug misuse may lead to temporary changes in behavior, emotion, or thought, such as *intoxication.* Chronic excessive use can lead to either *substance abuse,* a pattern in which people rely heavily on a drug and structure their lives around it, or *substance dependence,* in which they show the symptoms of substance abuse plus physical dependence on the drug (often called *addiction*). People who become physically dependent on a drug develop a *tolerance* to it or experience unpleasant *withdrawal symptoms* when they abstain from it, or both.

■ **Depressants** are drugs that slow the activity of the central nervous system. The most widely used depressants are *alcohol, sedative-hypnotic drugs,* and *opioids.* Alcoholic beverages contain **ethyl alcohol,** which is carried to the central nervous system (CNS), depressing its function and leading to impairment of fine motor skills and other physiological effects. These effects become more pronounced as consumption increases. *Intoxication* occurs when the concentration of alcohol in the bloodstream reaches 0.09 percent. Alcohol abuse generally follows one of several patterns: large amounts of alcohol daily, excessive amounts only during evenings and weekends, and occasional binges. Severe alcohol abuse may further lead to alcohol dependence.

Sedative-hypnotic drugs produce feelings of relaxation and drowsiness. **Antianxiety drugs** are the most popular of these drugs, and **barbiturates** are the most dangerous and widely abused. Chronic excessive use of barbiturates often leads to very severe withdrawal symptoms, including convulsions in some instances.

Opioids include opium and drugs derived from it, such as **heroin, morphine,** and **codeine.** The opium derivatives and synthetic opioids, collectively known as **narcotics,** depress the central nervous system, reducing tension and pain and causing other bodily reactions. Dependence on powerful opioids such as heroin develops after only a few weeks of use. An overdose can easily lead to respiratory failure.

■ **Stimulants** are substances that act to increase the activity of the central nervous system, such as *cocaine, amphetamines,* and *caffeine.* **Cocaine** produces a euphoric effect by stimulating the release of dopamine and norepinephrine in the brain. Ingestion of high doses of cocaine leads to cocaine intoxication and may lead to temporary psychosis. Cocaine abuse often leads to dependence, marked by tolerance and by withdrawal symptoms that include depression, fatigue, and irritability.

Amphetamines are stimulant drugs that are manufactured in a laboratory. As with cocaine, tolerance to amphetamines develops quickly, and depressive withdrawal symptoms occur when an addicted person stops taking the drug.

■ **Hallucinogens** are substances that cause changes primarily in sensory perception. They include *psychedelic drugs* and *cannabis.* **Psychedelic drugs,** such as **LSD,** cause profound perceptual changes and hallucinations by disturbing the normal processing of perceptual information. LSD interferes with neurons that use serotonin, which is critical in the filtering of incoming perceptual information. LSD is extremely potent, and ingestion of the drug may lead to a "bad trip" or to *flashbacks.*

Cannabis sativa is a hemp plant whose main ingredient is *tetrahydrocannabinol (THC).* The most powerful form is *hashish;* the most popular, and weakest, is *marijuana.* Marijuana is more powerful today than it was in years past, and regular use can lead to patterns of abuse and dependence.

Many people take more than one drug at a time, and the drugs interact with each other. Sometimes two drugs display *cross-tolerance.* They act similarly on the brain, and taking one drug will affect the person's tolerance for the other. When different drugs enhance each other's effects, they have a combined impact known as a *synergistic effect.* The use of two or more drugs at the same time—*polysubstance use*—has become increasingly common.

■ **A VARIETY OF EXPLANATIONS** for substance abuse and dependence have been put forward, but none has gained unqualified research support. The *biological* view of substance misuse has made considerable strides in recent years. Studies of twins and adoptees suggest that people may inherit a predisposition to substance dependence. Biological researchers have further learned that drug tolerance and withdrawal symptoms are related to a common sequence of biological events. Chronic ingestion of a drug causes the brain to reduce its production of a particular neurotransmitter that ordinarily acts to alleviate pain or increase alertness. When the drug is taken regularly, the body decreases its production of the neurotransmitter, leaving the person in need of more and more of the drug (tolerance) and temporarily defenseless against pain or depressive functioning when drug taking is stopped suddenly (withdrawal).

The *psychodynamic* view proposes that people who turn to substance abuse have inordinate dependency needs traceable to the oral stage of life. Some theorists also believe that some people have a "substance abuse personality" that makes them vulnerable to drugs. However, efforts to link particular personality traits to substance abuse have been largely unsuccessful.

The leading *behavioral* view proposes that drug use is reinforced because it reduces tension and raises spirits. Research has supported the behavioral view that some people ingest drugs to alleviate stress.

In many instances, however, the initial experience is not pleasurable, and even when it is, subsequent drug use often leads to dramatically unpleasant experiences.

The *sociocultural* view proposes that the people most likely to develop a pattern of drug abuse are those whose societies create an atmosphere of stress or whose families value or tolerate drug taking. Epidemiological studies provide some support for these claims.

■ **TREATMENTS** for substance abuse and dependence vary as widely as explanations for its cause. Frequently one approach is more effective with one type of substance-related disorder than another. Insight therapies try to help clients become aware of and address the psychological factors that contribute to their pattern of drug use. A common behavioral technique is *aversive conditioning,* in which an unpleasant stimulus is paired with the drug that the person is taking. Cognitive and behavioral techniques have been combined in such forms as *behavioral self-control training (BSCT)* and *relapse-prevention training.* Biological treatments can sometimes be helpful components of a broader treatment program. They include *detoxification,* systematic and medically supervised withdrawal from a drug; *antagonist drugs;* and *drug maintenance therapy,* in which clients are given a synthetic drug as a substitute for their addictive drug.

Self-help groups have emerged as a popular means to combat substance abuse and dependence. *Alcoholics Anonymous,* for example, provides peer support for alcohol abusers, establishing guidelines for living and overcoming the addiction. Similar programs have been started for other substance-use disorders. Many of these programs have expanded into *residential treatment centers,* or *therapeutic communities,* where former addicted persons live, work, and socialize in a drug-free environment while they receive treatment. The effectiveness of self-help groups and residential treatment centers has been difficult to gauge.

Finally, *prevention programs* for drug-related disorders have expanded in scope and number in recent years. Many of them are comprehensive and cooperative programs that focus on children, the family, the peer group, the school, *and* the community. Preschool prevention programs are also becoming important parts of the prevention movement.

Topic Overview

SEXUAL DISORDERS AND GENDER IDENTITY DISORDERS

JOSEPH LOPICCOLO

(The Sections on Paraphilias and Gender Identity Disorders are by Ronald J. Comer.)

EW AREAS OF FUNCTIONING are of more interest to human beings than sexual behavior. Because sexual feelings are so much a part of our development and daily functioning, because sexual activity is so tied to the satisfaction of our basic needs, and because sexual performance is so linked to our self-esteem, sexual behavior is a major focus of both private thoughts and public discussions.

CORRESPONDINGLY, ABNORMAL SEXUAL BEHAVIOR is of more interest to most people than almost all other forms of abnormal functioning. Most people are fascinated by the sexual problems of others and worry about the normality of their own sexuality. Our society is so curious about abnormal sexual behavior and attaches so much shame to it that many people who have problems in this realm are also burdened with feelings of anxiety, guilt, or self-disgust as a consequence.

THERE ARE TWO KINDS OF SEXUAL DISORDERS: sexual dysfunctions and paraphilias. People with *sexual dysfunctions* are unable to function normally in some area of the human *sexual response cycle*. They may not be able to become sexually aroused, for example, or to achieve orgasm. People with *paraphilias* experience recurrent and intense sexual urges, fantasies, or behaviors in response to sexual objects or situations that society deems inappropriate. They may, for example, be aroused by sexual activity with a child or by exposure of their genitals to strangers, and may act on those urges. In addition to these sexual disorders, there are **gender identity disorders,** sexual-related disorders in which people persistently feel that they have been assigned to the wrong sex and in fact identify with the other gender.

■ SEXUAL ■ DYSFUNCTIONS

Many psychological disorders affect only a small percentage of people. Sexual dysfunctions, in contrast—problems in sexual functioning, such as failure to achieve an erection in men and difficulties with orgasm in women—are very common, and are very distressing to those who experience them. Sexual frustration, guilt about failure, loss of self-esteem, and emotional problems with the sex partner are typically the psychological effects of sexual dysfunction. Sexual dysfunction is a common cause of divorce—unfortunately, for most dysfunctions can be treated successfully in relatively brief therapy.

Sexual dysfunctions will be described here in the context of heterosexual couples in long-term relationships, because this is the context in which the majority of cases are seen in therapy. Both male and female homosexual couples are subject to the same dysfunctions, however, and therapists use the same basic techniques when they treat these couples. When a man's penis will not become erect, it does not matter whether the intended partner is a woman or another man.

A word about terminology: people often speak vaguely when they talk of sex; they say "sleep with" when they mean "have sex with." Here the term "intercourse" will be used only to refer to penile-vaginal thrusting. Other sexual activities will also be specified precisely—"genital caressing," for instance, rather than the less clear "petting."

TYPES OF SEXUAL DYSFUNCTIONS

Sexual dysfunctions have been defined as "psychophysiological disorders which make it impossible for the individual to have and/or enjoy coitus," and DSM-IV classifies them according to the phase of the sexual response cycle that is primarily affected. As first described by the pioneering sex researchers William Masters and Virginia Johnson (1966) and later

elaborated on by the noted sex therapist Helen Kaplan (1977, 1974), the *sexual response cycle* consists of four stages, shown in Figures 14–1, 14–2, and 14–3. Dysfunctions can affect any of the first three phases of the cycle, the *desire phase*, the *arousal phase*, and the *orgasm phase*. There is also a fourth phase, the *resolution phase*, but as it consists simply of the relaxation and decline in arousal that follow orgasm, there are no sexual dysfunctions associated with it.

The *desire phase* consists of feeling an urge to have sex, having sexual fantasies or daydreams, and feeling sexually attracted to others. Two dysfunctions are associated with the desire phase. *Hypoactive sexual*

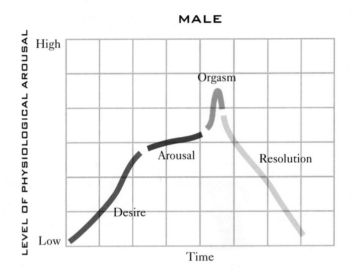

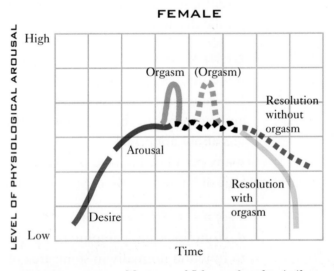

FIGURE 14–1 *Masters and Johnson found a similar sequence of phases in the normal sexual response cycle of both males and females. Sometimes, however, women do not experience orgasm, which leads to a somewhat different resolution phase. And sometimes women experience two or more orgasms in succession before the resolution phase. (Adapted from Masters & Johnson, 1970, 1966; Kaplan, 1974.)*

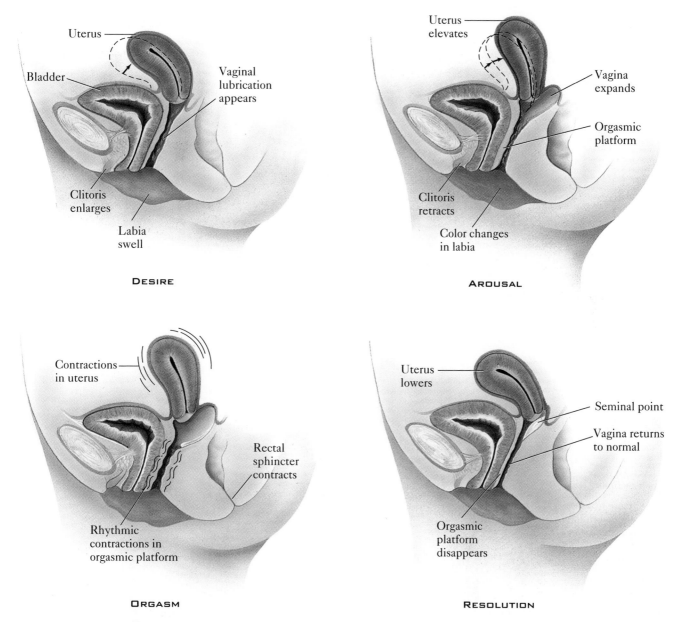

FIGURE 14−2   *Changes in the female sexual anatomy occur during each phase of the sexual response cycle. (Adapted from Hyde, 1990, p. 200.)*

desire is a lack of interest in sex, and, as a result, a low level of sexual activity. When a person with hypoactive sexual desire does have sex, however, he or she often functions normally and may even enjoy the experience, or at least does not find it unpleasant. People with **sexual aversion,** in contrast, find sex actively unpleasant. Instead of experiencing arousal and pleasure, these people often feel revulsion, disgust, anxiety, and fear.

The **arousal phase** is marked by general physical arousal, increases in heart rate, muscle tension, blood pressure, and respiration, and specific changes in the pelvic region. Blood pooling in the pelvis, called **pelvic vasocongestion,** leads to erection of the penis

in men, and to swelling of the clitoris and labia and the production of vaginal lubrication in women. Dysfunctions affecting this phase are **male erectile disorder** (previously called **impotence**) and **female sexual arousal disorder** (formerly referred to as **frigidity**). Early versions of the DSM did not differentiate between physical arousal and the subjective experience of emotional arousal, and sex therapists pointed out that a more detailed classification system was needed (Schover et al., 1982). As one of my own patients put it, "Oh, I get very aroused and excited, the problem is just that my damn penis won't get hard!" Conversely, there are patients (more typically women) who report the occurrence of all the

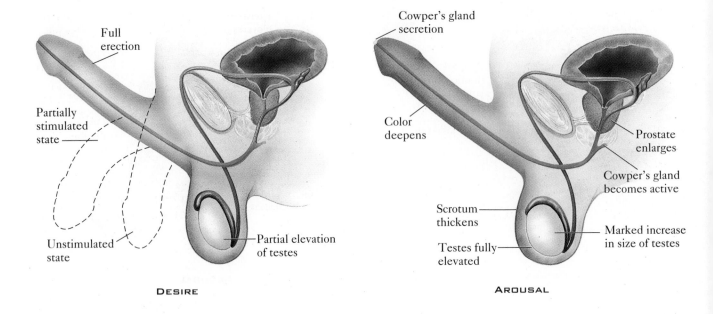

DESIRE

Full erection

Partially stimulated state

Unstimulated state

Partial elevation of testes

AROUSAL

Cowper's gland secretion

Color deepens

Scrotum thickens

Testes fully elevated

Prostate enlarges

Cowper's gland becomes active

Marked increase in size of testes

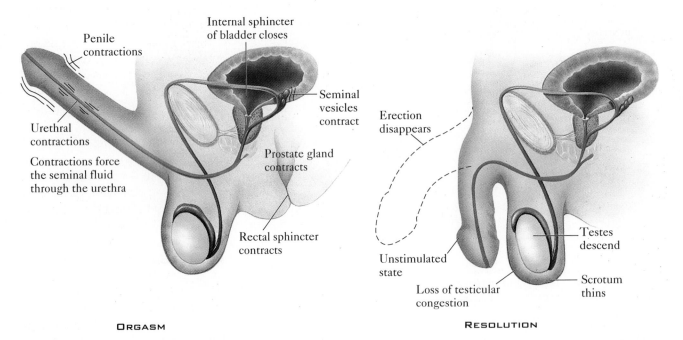

ORGASM

Penile contractions

Urethral contractions

Contractions force the seminal fluid through the urethra

Internal sphincter of bladder closes

Seminal vesicles contract

Prostate gland contracts

Rectal sphincter contracts

RESOLUTION

Erection disappears

Unstimulated state

Loss of testicular congestion

Testes descend

Scrotum thins

FIGURE 14–3   *Changes in the male sexual anatomy occur during each phase of the sexual response cycle. (Adapted from Hyde, 1990, p. 199.)*

physiological components of arousal but who do not experience any accompanying excitement or pleasure. Thus DSM-IV defines sexual arousal disorders as involving either a failure of lubrication or genital swelling in women or the absence of penile erection in men, and clarifies that the disorders may or may not be accompanied by a decreased subjective sense of sexual excitement and pleasure.

The *orgasm phase* of the sexual response cycle consists of reflexive muscular contractions in the pelvic region. The most common male sexual dysfunction in this phase is *premature ejaculation,* defined as "ejaculation with minimal sexual stimulation before, on, or shortly after penetration and before the person wishes it" (APA, 1994, p. 509). Less common is a man's inability to reach orgasm despite adequate stimulation, called *male orgasmic disorder* in DSM-IV, but usually referred to as *inhibited male orgasm, inhibited ejaculation, ejaculatory incompetence,* or *retarded ejaculation* by sex therapists.

DSM-IV calls the female disorder of the orgasm phase *female orgasmic disorder,* previously called *inhibited female orgasm.* As we shall see, there is some disagreement as to whether a woman's lack of orgasm during intercourse per se is a sexual dysfunction, provided she can reach orgasm with her partner during direct stimulation of the clitoris, with caressing by her partner's hand or mouth. Almost all contemporary sex therapists and researchers feel that the evidence is clear that women who have such "clitoral" orgasms are entirely normal and healthy (Stock, 1993; LoPiccolo & Stock, 1987).

Two dysfunctions listed in DSM-IV do not fit neatly into a specific phase of the sexual response cycle. These are the so-called *sexual pain disorders.* In *vaginismus,* spastic contractions of the muscles around the outer third of the vagina prevent entry of the penis. Severe cases of vaginismus can result in "unconsummated marriage," which means that a couple has never been able to have intercourse. In *dyspareunia* (from Latin words meaning "painful mating"), the person experiences severe pain in the genitals during sexual activity. Dyspareunia does occasionally occur in men, but it is much more common in women.

As the DSM-IV categories of sexual dysfunction are rather broad, two descriptive dimensions are often added to a diagnosis to clarify a patient's specific problem. The dysfunction may be described as either *lifelong* or *acquired,* and as either *generalized* or *situational.* Thus a woman with "lifelong, generalized orgasmic dysfunction" has never experienced an orgasm during any form of sexual activity. A man would be diagnosed as having "acquired situational erectile failure" if he previously had erections during sex with his wife but now has erections only during solitary masturbation or with another partner.

PREVALENCE OF
SEXUAL DYSFUNCTIONS

It is difficult to know how many people are troubled by sexual dysfunction. Many people with these problems are too embarrassed to seek treatment. Researchers have attempted to circumvent this difficulty by contacting a random sample of the general, nonpatient population and asking them to fill out questionnaires or to be interviewed about their sexual adjustment. Many people contacted in such studies refuse to participate, however, feeling that sex is too private a matter to be shared in a survey. Typical refusal rates are in the 25 percent range, and it appears that those who do volunteer to participate in sex research are more liberal, more sexually experienced, and more unconventional than the norm, and hence do not constitute a representative sample (Catania et al., 1990). As sexual conservatism and lack of experience are often considered to be factors leading to sexual dysfunction, the research studies on volunteers may underestimate the rate of sexual dysfunction in the general population. One study, however, the National Institute of Mental Health's study of the rate of all mental disorders, concluded that 24 percent of the general population suffered from some type of sexual dysfunction. This rate was the second highest of all diagnostic categories; only substance-related disorders were more common (Spector & Carey, 1990).

PREVALENCE OF MALE DYSFUNCTIONS
Estimates of the prevalence of sexual dysfunctions can be derived from several studies conducted on the general population: the famous "Kinsey reports" on several thousand American men and women, which were conducted in the 1930s and 1940s (Kinsey et al., 1953; Kinsey, Pomeroy, & Martin, 1948); more recent American surveys (Spector & Carey, 1990; Frank, Anderson, & Rubinstein, 1978; Hunt, 1974; Hite, 1970); and surveys of large samples of men and women in England (Sanders, 1987, 1985).

In spite of the cultural stereotype that portrays all men as wanting all the sex they can get, hypoactive sexual desire is found in about 15 percent of men studied. Aversion to sex, in contrast, seems to be so rare in men as not to appear in these studies, although sex therapists do see occasional cases.

In the last several years the number of men seeking therapy for hypoactive sexual desire has increased markedly. One study reports that from 1974 to 1976, only 30 percent of hypoactive sexual desire patients were male (LoPiccolo & Friedman, 1988); in 1981 and 1982, in contrast, 55 percent of all patients in therapy for hypoactive sexual desire were male. Some social commentators have suggested that the women's movement has made women competitors with men for jobs, status, and power, and this competition has caused a rise in the incidence of male hypoactive sexual desire. Sex therapists tend not to agree with this idea, however. Rather, what seems to account for the increase in male cases is our culture's increasing acceptance of women's sexuality. In the past, when our society considered "nice" women to be uninterested in sex, a woman married to a man with hypoactive sexual desire would be unlikely to complain and to suggest that they enter sex therapy. As the women's movement legitimized female sexuality, women became more likely to pressure their husbands for more frequent sex and to initiate sex therapy. It is pressure from sexually deprived wives that brings men with hypoactive sexual desire into sex therapy, as the men themselves typically do not feel very distressed about their lack of sex drive and are not eager to enter therapy (LoPiccolo & Friedman, 1988).

Erectile failure occurs in about 8 to 10 percent of the general male population. Because of its association with several of the diseases that afflict older adults, erectile failure is most often seen in older men, the majority of them over the age of 50 (Bancroft, 1989). The rate of erectile failure in the general population is around 1 percent at age 30, 2 percent at age 40, 7 percent at age 50, 18 percent at age 60, 27 percent at age 70, and 76 percent at age 80 (Weizman & Hart, 1987; Kinsey et al., 1948).

The rates of premature ejaculation found in population studies have varied between 10 and 38 percent, probably because definitions of the problem vary. The Kinsey report found that "for perhaps three-quarters of all males, orgasm is reached within two minutes" (Kinsey et al., 1948, p. 580), but Morton Hunt's 1974 study found that the average duration of intercourse had increased dramatically, to 10 to 14 minutes, in the intervening twenty-six years.

This dramatic change has increased the distress of men who suffer from premature ejaculation, which is primarily a younger man's problem; the majority of cases involve men under the age of 30 (Bancroft, 1989). Premature ejaculation is a normal experience for young men having their first sexual encounters, but they often berate themselves and start to think of themselves as dysfunctional, having no history of successful sexual relationships as a basis for sexual self-esteem. With continued sexual experience, most men spontaneously acquire greater control over their sexual responses. Of course, an increase in the time required to reach orgasm is a normal physiological change in aging men, but it is a slow change that occurs over many years. A young man whose premature ejaculation is not resolved with greater sexual experience would have to wait twenty to thirty years for normal aging processes to solve his problem.

Male orgasmic disorder (inhibited ejaculation) is a relatively uncommon disorder, occurring in 1 to 3 percent of the general population and in 3 to 12 percent of patients seeking sex therapy (Dekker, 1993).

PREVALENCE OF FEMALE DYSFUNCTIONS
Hypoactive sexual desire is found in 20 to 35 percent of the general population of women, and sex therapists report that low sex drive is now the problem most commonly seen in clinical practice. Sexual

aversion is less common, but precise prevalence figures on this form of dysfunction are not available.

Lack of arousal alone is not often a focus of either sex therapy or research, as this condition usually coexists with orgasmic dysfunction, but a great deal of research has been done on female orgasm rates. Studies indicate that 11 to 48 percent of women have arousal disorders, 10 to 15 percent of women have never had an orgasm, and another 10 to 15 percent only rarely experience orgasm. Interestingly enough, the prevalence of generalized, lifelong lack of orgasm does not seem to have changed over the last forty years, though change might have been expected in view of the sexual revolution and the increased acceptance of female sexuality. In addition, some women display a situational lack of orgasm, a phrase that covers a wide range of behavior patterns. As we saw earlier, sex therapists agree that lack of orgasm during intercourse is not itself a dysfunction provided the woman enjoys intercourse and can reach orgasm during genital caressing. Traditional psychoanalytic theory, though, did hold lack of orgasm during intercourse to be pathological (see Box 14–1).

Various studies have indicated that altogether 30 to 77 percent of women do have orgasm during intercourse. Differences in methodology probably account for this wide range of findings. A reasonable current estimate is that perhaps 50 percent of women experience orgasm in intercourse at least fairly regularly (LoPiccolo & Stock, 1987).

Not many data are available on the prevalence of vaginismus and dyspareunia. While perhaps 20 percent of women occasionally experience pain during intercourse, vaginismus probably occurs in less than 1 percent of the population. Among patients of one British sex therapy clinic, 10 to 15 percent complained of vaginismus or dyspareunia as their main problem (Bancroft, 1989). This figure is higher than is typical of clinics in the United States. Perhaps these disorders are less common in America, or perhaps American women are more likely to consult their gynecologist for these problems than to go to a sex therapy clinic.

CAUSES OF SEXUAL DYSFUNCTIONS

Theories of the causes of sexual dysfunctions focus on the influence of childhood learning about sex, attitudes and beliefs that are problematic, biological causes such as the effects of diseases and medications, individual psychodynamic factors, and relationship issues. Our knowledge of causation is

BOX 14-1

THE VAGINAL ORGASM CONTROVERSY

Sigmund Freud (1905) began the controversy about what constitutes sexual health for women. As we saw in Chapter 2, a child's sexuality progresses through an innate, biologically programmed series of phases, in Freud's theory. During the oral phase, in infancy, sexual pleasure is focused on the mouth. Later, during the anal phase, about age 2, erotic feelings center on the anus. Around age 4 or so, in the phallic phase, the little girl's clitoris becomes erotically charged and is her main source of sexual arousal and pleasure.

During the phallic phase, the girl develops an Electra complex: she experiences sexual feelings toward her father and rivalry with her mother. According to Freud, she feels women are inferior because they lack a penis, and develops penis envy. A girl who achieves a healthy resolution of the Electra complex identifies with her mother, accepts her femininity, and loses interest in her clitoris, which is essentially a small substitute for a pe-

nis. When she becomes a mature woman, she reaches the genital stage, and gets her sexual arousal from vaginal stimulation. Women who failed to make this shift in focus from the clitoris to the vagina were considered, by classical psychoanalytic theory, to be fixated at an immature, neurotic, and masculine level. They were even considered to be "frigid," since the orgasms they had from clitoral stimulation were not thought to be mature and healthy (Sherfey, 1973).

What is the evidence for this theory? Essentially, it was pure speculation, without any experimental work to support it. During Freud's time, virtually nothing was known about the anatomy and physiology of female sexual response.

In the past twenty-five years the weight of the evidence has been very heavily against Freud's theory. It has been shown that in comparison with the clitoris, the vagina is poorly supplied with nerve endings (Kinsey et al., 1953). The clitoris and penis both develop from the same structure in

the embryo, so expecting a woman to lose clitoral sensitivity makes as much sense as expecting a man's sexual focus somehow to switch from his penis to his scrotum. Masters and Johnson, in their pioneering studies of the female sexual response (1966), showed that all orgasms are identical, regardless of the body part being stimulated. Furthermore, their research demonstrated that when orgasm occurs during vaginal intercourse, it does so primarily because of indirect stimulation of the clitoris. In essence, then, there actually is no difference between a "clitoral" and a "vaginal" orgasm. Finally, decades of research have failed to demonstrate any differences in mental health, maturity, femininity, or sexual adjustment between women who have orgasms during vaginal intercourse and those who have their orgasms during direct clitoral stimulation (Sherfey, 1973; Fisher, 1973; LoPiccolo & Stock, 1987). Modern sex therapists are virtually unanimous in rejecting Freudian ideas about clitoral and vaginal orgasms.

---

incomplete, and much more research is needed in this area.

HYPOACTIVE SEXUAL DESIRE AND SEXUAL AVERSION

The definition of low sexual desire is somewhat problematic. DSM-IV defines this dysfunction as "persistently or recurrently deficient or absent sexual fantasies and desire for sexual activity," but it does not specify what a "deficient" level is. Large-scale surveys (Blumstein & Schwartz, 1983; Hunt, 1974) indicate that the average frequency of sex is two to three times per week for married couples, but these figures are not very meaningful. Age, years married, education, social class, and race, to mention just a few variables, all influence this average figure. Furthermore, frequency of occurrence does not necessarily indicate level of desire, as sexual ac-

tivity may occur because of pressure from the spouse or a sense of obligation. Moreover, disagreement about how often partners want to have sex does not necessarily indicate that one of them has low sexual desire. The wife may desire sex daily, for example, and the husband may want to have sex only three times a week. Both of these desired frequencies are in the normal range, and neither partner may have any psychological problems that are related to their desired frequency. This couple is just badly matched in regard to the desired frequency of intercourse. If they had chosen different partners, this might not be a problem for them.

Table 14-1 shows the results of a survey of ninety-three happily married couples, who were asked to report their actual frequency of sex and their desired frequency. These data show there is a wide range of

TABLE 14-1

DESIRED VS. ACTUAL FREQUENCY OF SEXUAL INTERCOURSE FOR MALES AND FEMALES IN 93 HAPPILY MARRIED COUPLES*

FREQUENCY	PERCENTAGE REPORTING AS "DESIRED"		PERCENTAGE REPORTING AS "ACTUAL"	
	MALES	FEMALES	MALES	FEMALES
More than once a day	12.2%	3.3%	2.2%	1.1%
Once a day	28.9	19.8	2.2	1.1
3–4 times a week	42.4	50.6	35.6	39.6
Twice a week	12.2	16.5	30.0	24.2
Once a week	4.4	9.9	15.6	20.9
Once every 2 weeks	0	0	8.9	8.8
Once a month	0	0	2.2	2.2
Less than once a month	0	0	3.3	0
Not at all	0	0	0	0

* Mean age, 34 for men, 32 for women; married mean of 9 years; mean number of children, 2.6; mean family income, $33,000.
Source: LoPiccolo & Friedman, 1988.

desired frequency, and that anything between once a day and twice a week is typical of many of the subjects surveyed. On the basis of these results and of clinical experience, it has been suggested that the diagnosis of hypoactive sexual desire is not warranted unless the patient desires sex less frequently than once every two weeks (LoPiccolo & Friedman, 1988).

Actually most of the cases seen in sex therapy do not involve merely hypoactive sexual desire but virtually nonexistent sexual desire (Letourneau & O'Donohue, 1993). These patients typically have no interest whatsoever in having sex with their partner, do not masturbate, and do not have sexual fantasies. Here are some typical statements from these patients:

If my husband didn't mention it, it would probably be a year before it even occurred to me that we hadn't had sex lately.

When we have sex, I enjoy it and everything works fine. I tell myself that I should remember to do it more often. Then a month goes by, my wife gets upset with me, and I realize it slipped my mind again.

When I haven't eaten in a while, I get hungry. But it doesn't seem to matter how long it's been since we had sex, I never get hungry for sex.

Questions about the normal range of sexual desire do not enter the picture in sexual aversion disorders, patterns marked by "persistent or recurrent extreme aversion to, and avoidance of, all or almost all genital sexual contact with a sexual partner" (APA, 1994, p. 500). The strong negative emotions that these patients experience, up to and including panic attacks or nausea and vomiting, make fine diagnostic distinctions a nonissue.

A person's sex drive is determined by a combination of physical and psychological factors, any of which may play a part in reducing sexual desire. Most cases of low sexual desire are attributable primarily to psychological factors, but certain physical conditions can lower a person's sex drive severely (Kresin, 1993).

To begin with, a number of hormones are involved in the physiology of sex, and abnormalities in their levels can help cause low sex drive (Kresin, 1993; Segraves, 1988). *Testosterone,* the major male sex hormone, is an important factor in the sex drive of both men and women (in women, testosterone is produced by the adrenal glands). If testosterone is low, sex drive is usually impaired. *Luteinizing hormone,* produced in the brain by the pituitary gland, stimulates testosterone production, so an abnormally low level of this hormone is another cause of low sex drive. *Estrogen,* the primary female sex hormone, is also important for sex drive. Any marked deviation in a woman's estrogen level, whether excessively high or excessively low, can result in low sex drive. Many of the early oral contraceptives contained high levels of estrogen, and many of the women who took them did have their sex drive repressed. While this effect is rarer with the low-dose pills prescribed today, it does still occur in some women. Women who are postmenopausal can have an insufficient level of estrogen, and a lowered sex drive as a result. This effect is also seen in women after childbirth, when estrogen levels are low for some time. In men, estrogen levels above the small amount normally present in the system interfere with sex drive. Men produce a small amount of estrogen, but it is usually metabolized in the liver, and so has no effect. In men whose liver is not functioning normally, however, such as men with alcoholic liver damage, estrogen levels will be elevated and sex drive reduced. Elevated levels of *prolactin,* another pituitary hormone, interfere with sex drive in both men and women. This elevation is most often caused by a prolactin-secreting tumor in the pituitary in men. Women who are breast-feeding have elevated prolactin, as this hormone is involved in milk production, and some breast-feeding women do show lowered sexual drive. Abnormally high or low levels of several of the hormones secreted by the thyroid gland also reduce sex drive. All these hormonal conditions can be treated with replacement hormones or drugs. It appears, however, that abnormal hormone levels are the cause of only a very small percentage of cases of hypoactive sexual desire (Kresin, 1993; LoPiccolo & Friedman, 1988).

A number of drugs, both prescription and illicit, suppress sex drive (Nitenson & Cole, 1993; Buffum, 1992; Segraves, 1988). Many medications prescribed to treat high blood pressure reduce sexual interest, as do drugs used to treat ulcers, glaucoma, allergies, heart disease, and convulsions. Many psychotropic drugs, including antianxiety, antidepressant, and antipsychotic agents, also have this effect. Most of these drugs influence the level of a neurotransmitter such as dopamine or serotonin, which seems to be involved in sexual desire. Sedative and pain-reducing medications often have the effect of lowering sex drive. While many illicit drugs, such as cocaine, marijuana, amphetamines, and heroin, may initially increase sexual interest at low doses, sex drive is uniformly very reduced in chronic users and at higher dose levels, despite the great differences in the other effects of these drugs. Alcohol may also enhance sex drive at a low level, presumably by lowering psychological inhibitions, but with higher levels and chronic use, sex drive is diminished (Roehrich & Kinder, 1991). This outcome reflects both the sedating effect of alcohol and the liver damage that comes with long-term use. Any number of drugs are known to suppress sex

drive, but centuries of searching have failed to find a true *aphrodisiac,* a substance that increases sex drive (Bancroft, 1989).

Not surprisingly, chronic physical illness can also suppress sex drive (Kresin, 1993; Bullard, 1988). A low sex drive can be a direct result of the illness, an effect of medication on sex hormones, or a consequence of the stress, pain, and depression that often accompany chronic illness.

The psychological causes of hypoactive sex drive and sexual aversion are even more varied and complex. Situational factors such as divorce, a death in the family, job stress, or the increased life stress of having a baby when both parents are employed often lead to hypoactive sexual desire (Letourneau & O'Donohue, 1993; Kaplan, 1979).

Personal beliefs and characteristics can also be important determinants. A number of traits are commonly found in association with hypoactive sexual desire and sexual aversion. Being raised in a severely antisexual religion or culture is one such factor. Having an exaggeratedly hardworking, serious approach to life and thinking of sex as frivolous or self-indulgent is another. People with mild obsessive-compulsive traits may find contact with another person's body fluids and odors to be unpleasant and aversive. People who are basically homosexually oriented may marry, either as a way of ensuring social acceptance or as a means of escaping from impulses they regard as unacceptable, and then find their sexual desire to be low in this heterosexual relationship. Some low-desire patients have been hurt in past relationships in which they felt strong sexual desire. These people may now fear loss of control over their sexual urges, and therefore suppress them completely. Occasionally patients with low sexual desire actually have a sexual deviation, or paraphilia, and are therefore not very interested in normal sexual activity. For example, men with tranvestism (aroused by dressing up in women's clothes, wigs, and makeup) often marry without admitting their transvestism to their wives, and then appear to have hypoactive sexual desire because their interest in conventional sex is low. Simple fear of pregnancy can inhibit sexual desire, and so can even a mild level of depression. Because our culture defines sexual attractiveness in terms of youth, many aging men and women lose interest in sex as their self-esteem and attraction to their partner diminish with age.

There are also many relationship-based causes of hypoactive sexual desire and sexual aversion. Simply being in an unhappy, conflicted relationship is sufficient to suppress sex drive or make sex unpleasant. If one partner gains a large amount of weight or

BIZARRO

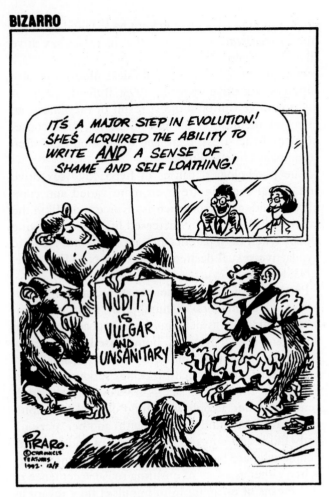

ITS A MAJOR STEP IN EVOLUTION!
SHE'S ACQUIRED THE ABILITY TO
WRITE AND A SENSE OF
SHAME AND SELF LOATHING!

NUDITY
IS
VULGAR
AND
UNSANITARY

*Psychological factors such as one's attitudes toward sex
and nudity play major roles in human sexuality and can
contribute to the development of sexual dysfunctions.
(The "Bizarro" cartoon by Dan Piraro is reprinted by permission
of Chronicle Features, San Francisco, CA. All rights reserved.)*

becomes careless about personal hygiene, this can
make sex unappealing or unpleasant for the other. If
one partner is a very unskilled, unenthusiastic lover,
the other can begin to lose interest in sex. Sometimes
people in an otherwise happy marriage differ in their
needs for closeness and "personal space." The one
who needs more personal space may develop hypoactive sexual desire as a way of creating the necessary
distance. A person who feels powerless in a relationship and very dominated by the other can also lose
sexual interest. Finally, some men, having adopted
our culture's double standard, are unable to feel sexual desire for a woman they love and respect. Some of
these men lose sexual interest when their wife has
their first child, as they cannot see a mother as a sexually exciting woman.

   While all of these factors can lead to either hypoactive sexual desire or sexual aversion, the experience of having been molested or assaulted is espe-

cially likely to result in sexual aversion (Browne &
Finklehor, 1986). Women are infinitely more likely
than men to be raped as adults and molested as children; thus the majority of people with sexual aversion
disorder are female. Research has indicated that sexual aversion is extremely common in victims of sexual
abuse and persists for years, even decades, afterward
(Jackson et al., 1990; Becker, 1989; Maltz & Holman,
1987). These people typically have very specific aver-
sions to whatever happened to them during the assault. A woman who as a child was forced to fondle
her father's penis, for example, may be unable to look
at or touch her husband's genitals without strong feelings of revulsion and disgust. In extreme cases, these
patients may experience vivid flashbacks during adult
sexual activity, and visual memories of the assault
overwhelm them.

ERECTILE FAILURE   As the following case history illustrates, erectile failure is often caused by a
combination of physiological and psychological factors.

R obert, a 57-year-old man, came to sex therapy with
   his wife because of his inability to get erections. He
had not had a problem with erections until six months earlier, when they attempted to have sex after an evening out,
during which he had had several drinks. They attributed
his failure to get an erection to his being "a little drunk,"
but he found himself worrying over the next few days that
he was perhaps becoming impotent. When they next attempted intercourse, he found himself unable to get involved in what they were doing because he was so intent
on watching himself to see if he would get an erection.
Once again he did not, and they were both very upset. His
failure to get an erection continued over the next few
months. Robert's wife was very upset and sexually frustrated, accusing him of having an affair, or of no longer finding her attractive. Robert wondered if he was getting too
old, or if his medication for high blood pressure, which he
had been taking for about a year, might be interfering with
erection. Robert was a heavy smoker and was overweight—
two factors that contributed to his high blood pressure.
When they came for sex therapy, they had not attempted
any sexual activity for over two months.

   Until recently, cases of erectile failure were custom-
arily categorized as *either* psychogenic *or* organic, as
if these were two mutually exclusive categories.
Current thinking acknowledges that many cases—
perhaps the majority—involve some partial organic
impairment of the erection response, which in turn
makes the man more vulnerable to the psychological
factors that inhibit erection (LoPiccolo, 1985). One

recent study found that only 10 of 63 cases of erectile failure were caused by purely psychogenic factors, and only 5 were the result of organic impairment alone (LoPiccolo, 1991).

The same hormonal abnormalities that can cause hypoactive sexual desire can also produce erectile failure. However, abnormal levels of testosterone, estrogen, prolactin, or thyroid hormones are found in only a small percentage of cases (Morales et al., 1991). Vascular abnormalities are much more common. Since an erection occurs when the chambers in the penis fill with blood, erectile failure can result from heart disease, restriction of blood flow into the penis by atherosclerosis (clogging of the arteries, which can result from years of heavy smoking), or excessive drainage from abnormally large penile veins (Huws, 1991). Leakage of blood out of the penile chambers through holes or tears can also cause erectile failure, as can disease or damage to the nervous system. Perhaps 50 percent of diabetic men experience erectile failure, as diabetes often damages the peripheral nerves involved in erection. Spinal cord injuries, kidney failure, and renal dialysis (treatment with an artificial kidney machine) can each produce erectile failure. Many of the medications that lower sexual drive also interfere with erection, so men who take medication for high blood pressure, allergies, ulcers, anxiety, or depression may experience erectile failure as a result (Tanagho, Lue, & McClure, 1988). However, some of the new types of high blood pressure medication do not interfere with erection, so a man who is having difficulties should consult his doctor about possible alternative medication (Morrissette et al., 1993).

Medical procedures for diagnosing organic causes of erectile failure have become very sophisticated in the past few years. With *Doppler ultrasound recording,* blood flow in the penis can be measured very accurately and vascular abnormalities located. Hormonal factors can be evaluated from simple blood tests.

Neurological damage is more difficult to assess, but evaluation of **nocturnal penile tumescence (NPT),** or erections during sleep, in a sleep laboratory is very useful (Schiavi et al., 1993). Men typically have erections during rapid eye movement (REM) sleep, the phase that corresponds with dreaming (see p. 406). A healthy man will have two to five REM periods each night, with perhaps two to three hours of nocturnal penile erections (see Figure 14–4). Abnormal or absent NPT usually indicates some organic basis for erectile failure (Mohr & Beutler, 1990). Because it is expensive for a patient to sleep in a hospital-based sleep laboratory, portable take-home recorders have been developed, as have simple "snap gauge" bands

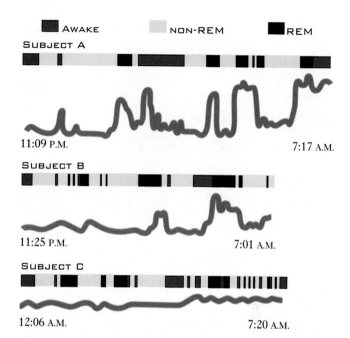

FIGURE 14–4 *Measurements of erections during sleep help reveal the sources of erectile problems. Subject A, a man without erectile problems, has normal erections during REM sleep. Subject B has erectile failure problems that seem to be at least partly psychogenic—otherwise he would not have any erections during REM sleep. Subject C's erectile failure disorder is related to organic problems, an interpretation supported by his lack of erections during REM sleep. (Adapted from Bancroft, 1985.)*

that the patient fastens around his penis before going to sleep and then checks the next morning. Broken bands indicate that penile erection has occurred during the night. These snap gauges are only rough screening devices; indeed, the lack of NPT may indicate an abnormal lack of REM sleep rather than organic impairment of erection (Mohr & Beutler, 1990).

Psychological factors underlying erectile failure can be quite complex. Any of the individual or interpersonal causes of hypoactive sexual desire, such as marital conflict, lack of attraction to the partner, or fear of closeness, can also interfere with arousal and lead to erectile failure. Certain psychological and behavioral issues, however, are particularly likely to be associated with erectile failure. For example, men who have lost their jobs and are under financial stress often develop erectile failure (Morokoff & Gillilland, 1993).

A major psychological mechanism emphasized by Masters and Johnson (1970) is **performance anxiety** and **the spectator role.** Once a man begins to experience erectile problems, for whatever initial reason, he becomes anxious about failing to have an erection and worries during each sexual encounter. Instead of relaxing and enjoying the sensations of sexual pleasure,

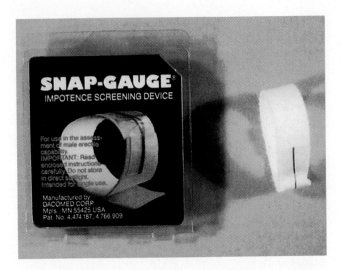

The snap-gauge, worn around the penis at night, is a fabric band with three plastic filaments. If the filaments are broken in the morning, the man knows that he has experienced normal erections during REM sleep and that erectile failures during intercourse are probably due to psychological factors. If the filaments are still intact, his erection problems may be due to organic impairment.

he remains somewhat distanced from the activity, watching himself and focusing on the goal of reaching erection. Instead of being an aroused participant, he becomes a self-evaluative spectator. Whatever the initial reason for erectile failure, the resulting anxious, self-evaluative spectator role becomes the reason for the ongoing problem. In this self-perpetuating vicious cycle, the original cause of the erectile failure becomes less important than fear of failure.

The performance-anxiety theory has been tested by David Barlow (1986) in a series of laboratory analogue experiments. In these studies, erotic films are shown both to men with erectile failure and to normal control subjects, and their erection responses are recorded by a gauge around the penis called a plethysmograph (see Figure 14–5). Before viewing the films, the men are given either a "performance demand" instruction (for example, a request that they try to get the best erection they can or a threat that they will receive an electric shock if an erection does not occur) or a "no demand" instruction that simply asks them to watch the films. Interestingly, normal men tend to respond to performance demands with increased erection, while erectile-failure patients show the pattern predicted by Masters and Johnson: their best erections occur in the absence of a performance demand. Barlow suggests that it is not performance demand per se that causes erectile failure but the way a man cognitively processes a perceived performance demand. Performance demands cause nondysfunctional men to focus on the sexually stimu-

lating aspects of the encounter, increasing their arousal, but cause anxiety and fear of failure in dysfunctional men. Barlow also compared the men's subjective ratings of their erections with actual physiological measurements of the penis, and found that normal men perceive their erections accurately, but dysfunctional men underestimate the degree of their erections. This finding supports the idea that negative self-evaluation plays a role in erectile failure. While these studies have identified interesting differences between erectile-failure patients and the control group, they don't explain how the differences developed. It is possible that the earlier experience of erectile failure leads these patients to respond to performance cues with anxiety, rather than the reverse order of causation suggested by Barlow.

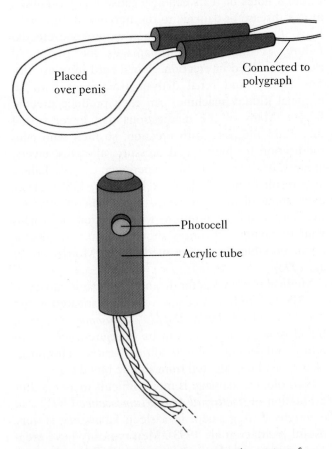

Placed over penis

Connected to polygraph

Photocell

Acrylic tube

FIGURE 14–5 *Experimenters use various types of plethysmographs to measure sexual arousal in subjects. One kind of penile plethysmograph (above) consists of a thin rubber tube, with a fine strand of mercury inside, which is placed around the penis. The diameter of the strand of mercury changes during arousal and is recorded on a polygraph recording device. In one kind of vaginal plethysmograph, a tampon-shaped device with a light at its end is inserted in the vagina. As the subject becomes increasingly aroused, the arteries of the vaginal wall receive additional blood and the device reflects more and more light.*

Another major psychological factor in erectile failure is the nature of the sexual relationship between a male patient and his wife (LoPiccolo, 1991). There are two relationship patterns that may contribute to erectile failure. In one, the wife provides inadequate physical stimulation to the husband. As a man ages, more intense, direct, and lengthy physical stimulation of the penis is required for erection to occur. This is a normal change and does not necessarily lead to erectile failure, but many older wives, raised in a more conservative time, have never engaged in much stimulation of the husband's penis, and the husbands have never asked them to. When they were younger, the psychological stimulation of kissing his wife and caressing her breasts and genitals led to good erections in the husband. Now that they are aging, he needs more physical stimulation, and because they are not aware of these normal changes, he may begin to develop the anxieties that lead to erectile failure. The second relationship pattern may occur when a couple believes that only intercourse can give the wife an orgasm. This idea increases the pressure on the man to have an erection and makes him more vulnerable to erectile failure. If the wife reaches orgasm through oral or manual caressing of her genitals, she does not depend on his erection for her sexual gratification, and his performance pressure is reduced.

PREMATURE EJACULATION Eddie's experience is typical of many men with premature ejaculation:

E ddie, a 20-year-old student, sought treatment after his girlfriend ended their relationship because his premature ejaculation left her sexually frustrated. Eddie had had only one previous sexual relationship, during his senior year in high school. With two friends he would drive to a neighboring town and find a certain prostitute. After picking her up, they would drive to a deserted area and take turns having sex with her, while the others waited outside the car. Both the prostitute and his friends urged him to hurry up because they feared discovery by the police, and besides, in the winter it was cold. When Eddie began his sexual relationship with his girlfriend, his entire sexual history consisted of this rapid intercourse, with virtually no foreplay. He found caressing his girlfriend's breasts and genitals and her touching of his penis to be so arousing that he sometimes ejaculated before complete entry of the penis, or after at most only a minute or so of intercourse.

Research has failed to connect premature ejaculation to organic factors, or to the complex individual and relationship factors associated with hypoactive sexual desire or erectile failure. Rather, premature

ejaculation seems to be typical of young, sexually inexperienced men who simply have not learned to slow down, modulate their arousal, and prolong the pleasurable process of making love. Men who have sex only infrequently are also prone to ejaculate prematurely, as the sensory threshold in the penis varies with the frequency and recency of sexual activity (LoPiccolo, 1985). Because both anxiety and ejaculation involve activation of the sympathetic nervous system, sex therapists have theorized that anxiety aroused by efforts to delay ejaculation can make the problem worse (Bancroft, 1989). However, a study of the role of anxiety in rapid ejaculation did not find this to be the case (Strassberg et al., 1990).

Masters and Johnson (1970) proposed that men learn to be rapid ejaculators during adolescent masturbation, when they often hurry to ejaculate because of fear of being discovered by their parents. Such experiences, however, seem to have been equally common in men who are not premature ejaculators (Heiman et al., 1986). Helen Kaplan (1974) proposed that premature ejaculators cannot accurately perceive their own arousal level and therefore cannot control their ejaculation. However, two laboratory studies that compared premature ejaculators and age-matched normal control subjects actually found that the premature ejaculators were as accurate or *more* accurate when their self-ratings were compared with objective measures of physiological arousal (Strassberg et al., 1987; Spiess, Geer, & O'Donohue, 1984). It may be that premature ejaculators, who because of their problem keep their attention focused on how close they are to ejaculation throughout the sex act, have trained themselves to be unusually accurate self-observers in this regard. Some evolutionary biologists have even speculated that rapid ejaculation may have been selected for during primate evolution, through a "survival of the fastest" process (Hong, 1984). A male who could ejaculate rapidly would be more likely to reproduce successfully, as there would be less chance that the female would escape, another male would interrupt, or a predator would attack before coitus was completed. None of these theories is well supported by research.

INHIBITED EJACULATION A number of physiological factors can inhibit ejaculation. A low testosterone level can interfere, and so can any neurological disease that reduces peripheral sensation or impairs functioning of the sympathetic nervous system. Men with multiple sclerosis or with neuropathy caused by diabetes may first experience inhibited ejaculation and then later develop erectile failure, as the ejaculation reflex seems to be more fragile than the erection reflex. Drugs that inhibit sympathetic arousal, such as alcohol, certain medications for high blood pressure, some antidepressants, and many antianxiety and antipsychotic agents can also inhibit ejaculation (Bancroft, 1989). The very widely prescribed antidepressant fluoxetine, or Prozac, appears to inhibit ejaculation in perhaps 15 to 25 percent of men who take it (Nitenson & Cole, 1993; Buffum 1992). Men who suffer a concussion may also develop inhibited ejaculation, but the mechanism for this effect is not known (LoPiccolo, 1985).

Psychological causes of inhibited ejaculation are thought to be similar to those for erectile failure. The concept of performance anxiety and the spectator role has been stressed: once a man begins to focus on reaching orgasm, he stops being an aroused participant in his sexual activity and instead becomes an unaroused, self-critical observer. Inhibited ejaculation may also be secondary to hypoactive sexual desire (LoPiccolo & Friedman, 1988). A man who engages in sex primarily because of pressure from his partner, without any real desire for sex, simply may not get aroused enough to reach orgasm. A few studies suggest that men who do not ejaculate have high levels of anxiety and hostility, but this relationship has not been found consistently in other research (Dekker, 1993).

FEMALE AROUSAL AND ORGASM DYSFUNCTIONS Stephanie and Bill, married for three years, came for sex therapy because of her total lack of orgasm.

Stephanie had never had an orgasm in any way, but because of Bill's concern, she had been faking orgasm during intercourse until recently. Finally she told him the truth, and they sought therapy together. Stephanie had been raised by a strictly religious family. She could not recall ever seeing her parents kiss or show physical affection for each other. She was severely punished on one occasion when her mother found her looking at her own genitals, at about age 7. Stephanie received no sex education from her parents, and when she began to menstruate, her mother told her only that this meant that she could become pregnant, so she mustn't ever kiss a boy or let a boy touch her. Her mother restricted her dating severely, with repeated warnings that "boys only want one thing." While her parents were rather critical and demanding of her (asking her why she got one B among otherwise straight A's on her report card, for example), they were loving parents and their approval was very important to her.

Stephanie's history seems to provide a clear example of the causes of orgasm problems in women.

However, things are not quite this simple. Until recently there was a major weakness in the theory of female arousal and orgasm dysfunctions proposed by sex therapists. The traditional theory considered these dysfunctions to result from our culture's double standard, which demands that women suppress and deny their sexuality. According to this view, women are raised with negative messages about what it means to be sexual, and sexual dysfunction is a direct result of this learning (Masters & Johnson, 1970). The flaw in this theory is that it doesn't explain why some women develop healthy sexuality and others become dysfunctional, since all of them are exposed to the same cultural message. Most inorgasmic women who come for therapy report that they, like Stephanie, were raised in a sexually restrictive manner, which suggests that factors such as religious upbringing, punishment for childhood masturbation, lack of preparedness for onset of menstruation, restrictions placed on adolescent dating, and being told that "nice girls don't" are indeed likely causes of orgasmic dysfunction. Research has demonstrated, however, that this kind of history is just as common among sexually functional women (LoPiccolo & Stock, 1987; Morokoff, 1978; Fisher, 1973). Unfortunately, the "protector factors" that make some women immune to these negative cultural and familial messages about female sexuality have yet to be identified. It is also unclear just how powerful the cultural script is that says nice women are nonsexual. One study did find that 88 percent of inorgasmic women but only 30 percent of orgasmic women reported they had been "good girls" as children—that is, they were obedient, did well in school, and never had major conflicts with their parents (O'Connor, 1979).

Psychological factors known to reduce arousal and interfere with orgasm in women include all the individual and relationship factors listed earlier as factors in hypoactive sexual desire and sexual aversion. Fifty to 75 percent of women molested as children or raped as adults have arousal and orgasm dysfunctions (Browne & Finklehor, 1986).

Kinsey's study in 1953 found that orgasm was more frequent in women who were better educated, came from upper-class families, had been married longer, and had more experience with adolescent masturbation or premarital petting. Kinsey also found that women born later in the century had a higher orgasm rate than those born earlier, presumably a reflection of the sexual liberalization that occurred during the 1920s and 1930s. Morton Hunt's large-scale study in 1974, however, did not find that any of these differences still existed some twenty years later. He concluded that the widespread social revolution of the last generation, with its increased acceptance of female sexuality, had wiped out the effects of education, social class, and so on. A very comprehensive study by Seymour Fisher (1973) found no relationship between orgasm rates and such personality traits as femininity, aggressiveness, passivity, guilt, impulsivity, and narcissism. Fisher did find, however, that positive memories of a good father-daughter relationship during childhood and adolescence were related to attainment of orgasm in adulthood. Similarly, a study of over 2,400 Czechoslovakian women found that memories of an unhappy childhood or loss of one parent during childhood were associated with lack of orgasm in adulthood (Raboch & Raboch, 1992).

When a large number of sexually dysfunctional women in sex therapy were compared with a matched control group of highly sexually responsive women, some interesting factors related to orgasm consistency were brought to light (Heiman et al., 1986). Childhood memories of a positive relationship with one's mother, affection between parents, the mother's positive personality qualities, and the mother's expression of positive emotions were all shown to be related to orgasm. Even more strongly related were the degree of emotional involvement and the length of the relationship at the time of the woman's first experience of coitus, the pleasure she obtained during that experience, her current attraction to her partner's body, and marital happiness. Interestingly, it was also found that use of sexual fantasies during sex with the current partner was much more common in orgasmic than in dysfunctional women.

Some physiological conditions can also affect women's arousal and orgasm. Diabetes can damage the nervous system in ways that interfere with arousal, vaginal lubrication, and possibly orgasm. Similarly, many women with multiple sclerosis or some other neurological disease are inorgasmic (Schover & Jensen, 1988). The same medications and drugs that inhibit ejaculation in men interfere with orgasm in women. Postmenopausal changes in skin sensitivity and in the structure of the clitoris and the vaginal walls can lead to either dyspareunia or orgasmic dysfunction in some women (Morokoff, 1993, 1988).

A number of theories have related female orgasm to the size of the clitoris, the presence of adhesions between clitoral shaft and hood, the distance from the clitoris to the vaginal opening, and the strength of the *pubococcygeal (PC) muscle* (part of the pelvic floor). However, research has failed to support these ideas (Stock, 1993; LoPiccolo & Stock, 1987).

VAGINISMUS Vaginismus has no physiological cause; it is a psychological condition in which the muscles around the vagina involuntarily contract. It is considered to be a conditioned fear response, set off by anticipation that vaginal penetration will be painful and damaging. Vaginismus can result from general anxiety and ignorance about sexual intercourse, specific fears caused by exaggerated stories about how painful and bloody the first occasion of intercourse is for women, trauma caused by an unskilled, impatient lover who forces his penis into the vagina before the woman is aroused and lubricated, and, of course, the trauma of childhood sexual abuse or adult rape. Women who experience painful intercourse because of an infection of the vagina or urinary tract or a gynecological disease such as herpes simplex, or after menopause, can develop a "rational" vaginismus, as it is true that insertion of the penis *will* be painful for them unless they obtain medical treatment for these conditions. Most women who have vaginismus also have other dysfunctions, such as sexual aversion or orgasmic dysfunction, but this is not always the case. Some women with vaginismus enjoy sex, have a high sex drive, and have orgasm from clitoral stimulation. In these women, the negative emotions are specific to fear of vaginal penetration.

DYSPAREUNIA Painful intercourse in women usually has a physical cause (Sarrel & Sarrel, 1989). Sex therapists have learned to be skeptical about patients referred for treatment of "psychogenic dyspareunia," as the majority of such diagnoses reflect the referring gynecologist's ignorance about physical causes of painful intercourse rather than an absence of organic cause (LoPiccolo & Stock, 1987; Grillo & Grillo, 1980). Damage caused by childbirth is the most common cause of dyspareunia, as delivery can injure the vagina, cervix, uterus, or the pelvic ligaments. Similarly, the scar left by an episiotomy (a cut often made to enlarge the vaginal entrance and ease delivery) can be a source of pain. The penis hitting remnants or strands of the hymen can cause dyspareunia; so can an undiagnosed vaginal infection; and wiry pubic hair can abrade the labia when penile thrusting drags it into the vagina. Pelvic diseases such as endometriosis (a condition in which tissue migrates from the lining of the uterus and becomes attached to internal organs), tumors, and cysts are also possible causes, as are allergic reactions to the chemicals in vaginal douches, spermicidal contraceptive creams, the rubber in condoms or diaphragms, or the protein in male semen (LoPiccolo & Stock, 1987).

Dyspareunia that is truly psychogenic usually reflects a simple lack of arousal: it is painful to have a penis forced into an unaroused, unlubricated vagina. In other words, psychogenic dyspareunia is synonymous with female sexual arousal disorder. Women who suffer from organically based dyspareunia usually report that they enjoy sex and get aroused, but their sex life is being ruined by the pain that accompanies what used to be an unreservedly positive event.

TREATMENT OF
SEXUAL DYSFUNCTIONS

The last twenty years have brought a remarkable change in the psychotherapeutic procedures used to treat sexual dysfunction. Since early in this century, the major treatment approach had been long-term, intensive Freudian psychoanalysis, on the assumption that sexual dysfunction was caused by failure to progress through the stages of childhood psychosexual development. To advance through the developmental stages, the patient had to reexperience childhood (more successfully this time) by means of the transference relationship with the analyst, which functions as a substitute for the original parent-child relationship. A major personality reorganization was considered necessary, since in psychoanalytic theory, sexual dysfunctions are symptomatic of a much larger failure of personality development. It was thought that analytic therapy four to five times a week over many months or even years would be required to increase sexual functioning. This idea led analysts to conclude that "as a mass problem, the question of frigidity is unfortunately not to be solved" (Bergler, 1951).

In the 1950s and 1960s, behavioral therapists began to offer alternative treatments for sexual dysfunctions. In behavioral theory, sexual dysfunctions are considered to result from anxiety, which is known to block sexual response. Therapeutic procedures consisted of training in muscle relaxation, which reduces anxiety, and systematic desensitization (Lazarus, 1965; Wolpe, 1958). In systematic desensitization of erectile failure, for example, patients would become deeply relaxed and then imagine or visualize sexual scenes, beginning with mild activities such as kissing and working up to images of intercourse. When the patients could imagine a sexual activity without becoming anxious and tense, they would be permitted to try the activity at home, in actual sexual interaction with their partner. This anxiety-reduction approach was moderately successful but did not work when the major causes of dysfunction were misinformation, a negative attitude, and lack of effective sexual technique.

A revolution in the treatment of sexual dysfunctions occurred with the publication of Masters and

The extensive research, theories, and clinical reports of William Masters and Virginia Johnson have dramatically changed the way clinicians understand and treat sexual functioning and dysfunctioning.

Johnson's *Human Sexual Inadequacy* in 1970. Their approach came to be known as "sex therapy." Over the years their procedures have been modified and some entirely new ones added, so that today's sex therapy is a complex treatment approach with several components, including cognitive, behavioral, and communication-skill-building techniques. At the same time, modern sex therapy is short term, focused specifically on the sexual problem rather than on personality reorganization, and directive in nature. Fifteen to twenty sessions of weekly therapy are typical for treatment of most dysfunctions.

The first component of sex therapy is the *assessment and conceptualization* of the problem. Along with a medical examination to uncover possible organic problems, the patient is interviewed concerning his or her "sex history." The emphasis is on understanding both past life events and current factors that cause the dysfunction. Masters and Johnson (1970) spent several hours taking histories from each patient, but modern practice is to spend much less time on the past than on the current emotions, attitudes, and behavior that maintain the dysfunction (LoPiccolo, 1990). When discussing these causative factors with patients, sex therapists stress the principle of *mutual responsibility.* Both partners in a relationship share the sexual problem, regardless of who has the actual dysfunction. The husband of an inorgasmic woman, for example, is partially responsible for creating or maintaining their problem, and he is also a patient who needs to make changes if she is ever to be able to have an orgasm. Because of the principle of mutual responsibility, sex therapists much prefer to have both members of a sexual partnership in therapy, and indeed, treatment is generally more successful when that is the case (Heiman, LoPiccolo, & LoPiccolo, 1981). Often the partner who does not have a dysfunction is reluctant to enter therapy, claiming that "it's not my problem." The sex therapist's response is that assigning blame is not the issue, and while the nondysfunctional partner may have had nothing to do with *causing* the problem, he or she clearly has a crucial role to play in *solving* it. Masters and Johnson (1970) suggested that patient couples would feel more comfortable with a male-female therapy team, since each would then have an advocate in the therapist who knows what intercourse is like for a person of her or his sex. Masters and Johnson considered this "dual sex co-therapy team" to be crucial for therapeutic success, but research comparing the success rates of single therapists and dual sex co-therapy teams has not shown any differences in effectiveness (LoPiccolo et al., 1985). Because of the greater expense of co-therapy, most sex therapy today is done by one therapist working alone.

A second major component of sex therapy is the provision of *accurate information* about sexuality. Many patients who suffer from sexual dysfunction know very little about the anatomy and physiology of sexual response. They may be misinformed about effective techniques of sexual stimulation, the role of the clitoris in a woman's orgasm, or the need for more physical stimulation to produce penile erection as men age. Sex therapists assess and supplement their patients' knowledge through discussion, instructional books and videotapes, and professional educational films.

The third component of sex therapy is work to *change problematic attitudes, cognitions, and beliefs* about sexuality. Family attitudes toward sex, past traumatic experiences, and the patients' own emotional reaction to dysfunction in themselves or in their partners can all create strongly negative thoughts and emotions that prevent sexual arousal and pleasure, and our socially imposed sex roles are accompanied by a set of sex-role myths or cognitive distortions that can also lead to sexual dysfunctions. Some of these widespread myths are listed in Box 14–2. Helping patients to examine these myths critically can be very therapeutic.

Another important component of sex therapy is the *elimination of performance anxiety and the spectator role* through *sensate focus* and *nondemand pleasuring.* Since pressure to attain an erection or orgasm interferes with arousal, sex therapy begins with a ban on intercourse and genital caressing. Couples are instructed that for a time, sexual activity at home is to be restricted to kissing, hugging, and sensual whole-body massage, not including breasts or genitals. Over successive weeks, their sexual repertoire is gradually rebuilt, with a constant emphasis on enjoying the experience of sensual pleasure and not striving for results. The sensate focus principle is associated with Masters and Johnson (1970), who systematized it, but a British physician, Sir John Hunter, is known to have suggested the same approach over 200 years ago. Sir John told a man with erectile failure to "go to bed with this woman, but first resolve to himself that he would not have any connection with her, for six nights. . . . He told me that his resolution had produced such a total alteration in the state of his mind that the powers [erection] soon took place, for instead of going to bed with the fear of inability, he went with fears that he would be possessed with too much desire, too much power" (Hunter & MacAlpine, 1963).

The fifth component of sex therapy is to *increase communication and the effectiveness of sexual technique.* Because it is embarrassing or uncomfortable for most dysfunctional patients to tell their partners what they find pleasurable in sexual activity, they do not learn from each other, but just engage in the same ineffective sexual techniques over and over. During therapy the couple are told to use their sensate focus sessions at home to try sexual positions in which the person being caressed can guide the other's hands and regulate the speed, pressure, and location of the caressing. Couples are also taught to give verbal instructions in a nonthreatening, informative manner ("It feels better over here, with a little less pressure"), instead of in a threatening manner that doesn't tell the partner what to do differently ("The way you're touching me doesn't turn me on").

The last general component of sex therapy is to *change destructive lifestyles and marital interactions.* Sex is the lowest priority in the schedule of many dysfunctional patients, and if sex is left until late at night, in bed, when both partners are exhausted, they are unlikely to feel any sensuality and pleasure. The sex therapist will suggest that couples rearrange their priorities, and have their sensate focus sessions when

"When I touch him he rolls into a ball."

they are relaxed, not tired out or under time pressure. Similarly, if the couple's marriage is in conflict, or if there is little emotional connection between them, trying to build a good sexual relationship is virtually impossible. In such cases the therapist will help the couple restructure their relationship to reduce conflict and build more closeness.

Specific techniques have been developed to treat each of the sexual dysfunctions.

HYPOACTIVE SEXUAL DESIRE AND SEXUAL AVERSION Because of the many difficult psychological issues that are likely to underlie hypoactive sexual desire and sexual aversion, these dysfunctions require a longer and more complex program of treatment than others. Jerry Friedman and I (1988) have described a four-element sequential treatment model for hypoactive drive and aversion that is widely used.

BOX 14-2

SEX-ROLE MYTHS

■ MYTHS ■ OF MALE SEXUALITY

1. *Men should not have certain emotions.* Men believe they are supposed to be strong, aggressive, competitive, unemotional, and in control. All of these emotions interfere with the tenderness, closeness, sensuality, openness, and emotional expressiveness that contribute to good sex.

2. *In sex, it's performance that counts.* Men take a goal-oriented approach to sex, equating erections and orgasm with success, and are unable to relax and enjoy sex as a pleasurable process rather than as an end to be achieved.

3. *The man must take charge and orchestrate sex.* Men who think this way do not let the woman guide them to do what she likes to have done to her. This attitude also leads a man to focus on what he is doing to the woman, rather than learning to receive pleasure from what she does to him.

4. *A man always wants and is always ready to have sex.* This myth pressures men to try to have sex in situations or relationships in which they are not emotionally comfortable, with predictably unpleasant results.

5. *All physical contact must lead to sex.* This notion prevents men from simply enjoying kissing, hugging, cuddling, and caressing, as they see these activities as only a prelude to "the real thing."

6. *Sex equals intercourse.* This myth is especially destructive to men with erectile problems. If a man and his partner can derive sexual pleasure and orgasm from manual or oral genital caressing, any performance anxiety that might interfere with erection will be greatly reduced.

7. *Sex requires an erection.* This is a corollary to myth 6. The truth is that the penis is not the only sexual part of the man's body, and couples can have very pleasurable sex without an erection.

8. *Good sex is a linear progression of increasing excitement terminated only by orgasm.* Acceptance of this myth eliminates the pleasure of leisurely, playful sex, which may include breaks to talk, rest, and enjoy each other fully as people rather than as just genital organs.

9. *Sex should be natural and spontaneous.* This myth prevents couples from teaching each other what they like during sex. For today's typical couple, with both partners working, sharing child-rearing responsibilities, and living high-stress lives, it is often necessary to make very nonspontaneous plans for sex, designating a time when both are likely to be relaxed, not exhausted, and capable of responding sexually.

10. *In this enlightened age, myths 1–9 no longer have any influence on us.* While the sexual liberalization of the past thirty years has eliminated some sexual inhibitions, it has caused us to worry much more

The first stage of therapy, called *affectual awareness*, focuses on helping the client become aware of his or her negative emotions regarding sex. Therapy sessions during which the patient visualizes sexual scenes help uncover feelings of anxiety, fear, resentment, vulnerability, and so forth. Many patients claim that they have overcome negative ideas about sex, but such changes are likely to be superficial, leaving a negative affectual (emotional or gut-level) residue hidden under a bland umbrella feeling of lack of interest in sex. The purpose of the affectual awareness stage of therapy is to get under this umbrella and make the patient aware that he or she is not just naturally uninterested in sex, but that something is blocking the normal biological sex drive that all people have.

The second phase of therapy, the *insight* phase, helps patients understand why they have the negative emotions identified in the affectual awareness phase. Negative messages from their religion, culture, family, and current and past relationships are explored. In a sense, this and the previous step are preparatory. The more active treatment follows.

The third phase of therapy fosters *cognitive and emotional change*. In this phase, cognitive techniques are applied to the irrational thoughts and emotions that inhibit sexual desire. Patients generate "coping statements" that help them change their negative emotions and thoughts. Typical statements might be "If I allow myself to enjoy sex, it doesn't mean I'll lose control," and "When I was younger I learned to feel guilty about sex, but I'm a grownup now, and I don't have to feel that way anymore."

The fourth stage of treatment consists of *behavioral interventions*. It is at this stage that sensate focus, skill training, and other general sex therapy procedures are introduced. Sex drive is heightened in a number of ways: having patients keep a "desire diary" in which

---

about being good enough at sex and to strive to emulate the supersexual role models in current literature, films, and music.
(Zilbergeld, 1978)

■ MYTHS ■ OF FEMALE SEXUALITY

1. *Sex is only for women under 30.* Many women don't reach their peak of sexual responsiveness until their mid-30s, and there is no real decline thereafter.

2. *Normal women have an orgasm every time they have sex.* Even for easily orgasmic women, 70 to 80 percent of the time is the average rate of orgasm.

3. *All women can have multiple orgasms.* Research indicates that 20 percent of women are multiply orgasmic. There is no relationship between sexual adjustment or satisfaction and the number of orgasms a woman has each time she has sex.

4. *Pregnancy and delivery reduce women's sexual responsiveness.* While discomfort during the last months of pregnancy and just after de-livery can temporarily inhibit sex, the increased blood supply to the pelvis that develops during pregnancy can actually increase sexual responsiveness.

5. *A woman's sex life ends with menopause.* While vaginal dryness can interfere with enjoyment of intercourse in some postmenopausal women who do not receive estrogen therapy, many women, freed from concerns about contraception and pregnancy, experience increased sexual arousal and interest after menopause.

6. *There are different kinds of orgasm related to a woman's personality. Vaginal orgasms are more feminine and mature than clitoral orgasm.* An orgasm is an orgasm, not a personality trait.

7. *A sexually responsive woman can always be turned on by her partner.* Fatigue, anger, worry, and many other emotions suppress sexuality in even the most responsive women.

8. *Nice women aren't aroused by erotic books or films.* Research indicates that women are just as aroused by erotica as men are.

9. *You are frigid if you don't like the more exotic forms of sex.* Many very sexual women aren't interested in oral or anal sex, sex toys such as vibrators, or group sex.

10. *If you can't have an orgasm quickly and easily, there's something wrong with you.* The threshold for orgasm varies naturally among women. Just as some women can run faster than others, some have orgasm more rapidly.

11. *Feminine women don't initiate sex or become wild and unrestrained during sex.* This is a holdover of the Victorian double standard.

12. *Double jeopardy: you're frigid if you don't have sexual fantasies and a wanton woman if you do.* Many, but not all, sexually responsive women do have sexual fantasies.

13. *Contraception is a woman's responsibility, and she's just making up excuses if she says contraceptive issues are inhibiting her sexually.* Many highly sexual women find their sexual enjoyment interfered with by contraceptive technology. Many couples who feel their families are complete find vasectomy to be a good solution.
(Heiman & LoPiccolo, 1988)

they record sexual thoughts and feelings, having them read books and view films with good erotic content, and encouraging them to develop their own sexual fantasies. All of these activities make sexual thoughts and cues more readily available to the patient. Nonsexual affection, consisting of simple hugs, squeezes, and pats, and pleasurable shared activities such as dancing and walking together are also encouraged, to help strengthen feelings of sensual enjoyment and sexual attraction.

For sexual aversion resulting from sexual assault or childhood molestation, additional therapeutic procedures are used. The patient is encouraged to remember the assault, and to talk and think about these memories until they are no longer traumatic. In another procedure, the patient writes letters to the molester or has an "empty chair" mock dialogue with the molester, in order to finally express the feelings of rage and powerlessness the assault created. During the cognitive phase, patients are encouraged not to allow the offender to continue to harm them by inhibiting their sex life now, but rather to fight back by recovering the sexuality that was taken from them by the molestation. Sensate focus is carefully structured so that location, context, and sexual actions do not set off flashbacks to the assault.

This type of program seems to be fairly successful. In one study of the approach, frequency of sex increased from once a month to once a week for men who had experienced hypoactive sexual desire, and from once every two weeks to more than once a week for female patients. Women who had experienced sexual aversion increased sexual intercourse from less than once every two weeks to more than once a week (Schover & LoPiccolo, 1982).

ERECTILE FAILURE   Treatment of erectile failure also consists of reducing performance anxiety and increasing stimulation. During sensate focus the couple learns the "tease technique," in which, if he gets an erection in response to her caressing, they stop until he loses it. This exercise teaches them that erections occur naturally in response to stimulation, as long as the couple doesn't focus on performance. When they are ready to resume intercourse, the man lies on his back and the woman kneels above him and uses her fingers to push his *nonerect* penis into her vagina. This procedure, known as the "stuffing technique," frees him from having to have a rigid penis to accomplish entry. The couple are instructed to achieve the woman's orgasms through manual or oral sex, again reducing pressure on the male to perform.

This set of procedures seems to work well in cases in which there is no severe organic impairment of erection. Physical intervention is often indicated, however, for men with major physical problems underlying or complicating their difficulty with erection. For these men, a common approach is surgical implantation of a *penile prosthesis,* which produces an artificial erection. This device consists of a semirigid rod made of rubber and wire. It can be bent down so that the man can wear normal clothing, but bent up to an erect position when the man wants to have sex. Another type of prosthesis consists of inflatable hollow cylinders inserted into the penis, a reservoir of fluid placed under the abdominal wall, and tubing connecting the penile cylinders to a pump inserted in the scrotum. When the man wants to have sex, he squeezes the pump, forcing fluid from the reservoir to the penile cylinders, which expand and produce an erection. These surgically implanted prostheses are expensive (between $5,000 and $15,000, depending on the type), but over 25,000 were installed in 1988 in the United States. This kind of treatment is uncommon elsewhere in the world, primarily because of the expense (LoPiccolo, 1991).

A nonsurgical approach to erectile failure is the use of a *vacuum erection device (VED).* A hollow cylinder is placed over the penis and pushed against the body to create an airtight seal. The cylinder is connected to a hand pump, which pumps the air out of the cylinder and leaves the penis in a partial vacuum. This draws blood into the penis and produces an erection. The cylinder is removed and a rubber constriction ring is placed around the base of the penis to maintain the erection. The VED is less expensive ($300 to $600) but interferes with the spontaneity of sex, as the man must take time to use it during lovemaking. The vacuum device is most often used for men whose erectile failure is caused by diabetes or neurological problems, and it seems to work well for these men (Aloni et al., 1992; Turner et al., 1991).

Vascular surgery to remove blockages in the arteries, repair leaks in the penile chambers, or tie off excessively large penile veins is also useful in some cases. For men with neurologic damage but an intact blood circulation system, injection of drugs that dilate the penile arteries is often useful. Drugs that were formerly used for this purpose tended to cause scarring in the penis over long periods of use, and so were used more as a short-term "confidence booster" for men with situational erectile failure (Bancroft, 1989). However, the drugs that are now used do not seem to have this effect, and injection therapy has become common for long-term treatment of organically based erectile failure (Wagner & Kaplan, 1993).

PREMATURE EJACULATION Premature ejaculation is treated with almost 100 percent success by direct behavioral retraining procedures (Masters & Johnson, 1970; Semans, 1956). In the "stop–start" or "pause" procedure, the penis is manually stimulated until the man is fairly highly aroused. The couple then pause until his arousal subsides, and then the stimulation is resumed. This sequence is repeated several times before stimulation is carried through to ejaculation, so the man ultimately experiences much more total time of stimulation than he has ever experienced before and learns to have a higher threshold for ejaculation. The "squeeze" procedure is much like the stop–start procedure, except that when stimulation stops, the woman firmly squeezes the penis between her thumb and forefinger, at the place where the head of the penis joins the shaft. This squeeze seems to reduce arousal further. After a few weeks of this training, the necessity of pausing diminishes. Then the couple progress to putting the penis in the vagina, but without any thrusting movements. Again, if the man rapidly becomes highly aroused, the penis is withdrawn and the couple waits for arousal to drop off. When good tolerance for inactive containment of the penis is achieved, the training procedure is repeated during active thrusting. Generally, two to three months of practice are sufficient to enable a man to enjoy prolonged intercourse without any need for pauses or squeezes.

INHIBITED EJACULATION Male orgasmic disorder is treated by reducing performance anxiety and ensuring adequate stimulation. The couple are instructed that during sex the penis is to be caressed manually (and, if acceptable to them, orally) until the man is aroused, but that stimulation is to stop whenever he feels he might be close to having an orgasm. This paradoxical instruction reduces goal-focused anxiety about performance and allows the man to enjoy the sexual pleasure provided by the caressing. An electric vibrator may be used to increase the intensity of stimulation. For men with neurological damage or a history of concussion, therapy is likely to include some physiological treatment, possibly a drug that increases arousal of the sympathetic nervous system or stimulation of the anus with a vibrator or electric current to trigger the ejaculation reflex (Murphy & Lipshultz, 1988).

FEMALE AROUSAL AND ORGASM DYSFUNCTIONS Specific treatment techniques for female arousal and orgasm dysfunctions include self-exploration, body awareness, and directed masturbation training (Heiman & LoPiccolo, 1988). These procedures are especially useful for women with gen-

Myths aside, people do not lose interest in sex as they age. Most middle-aged and elderly women and men remain fully capable of sexual performance and orgasms, although the speed and intensity of their sexual response may lessen somewhat.

eralized, lifelong lack of orgasm. Masters and Johnson stressed the use of couple sensate focus procedures for such cases, but later experience showed that it is more effective for the woman to learn to have orgasm by herself first, and then share this knowledge with her partner.

The directed masturbation program has nine steps. In the first step, the woman uses diagrams and reading material simply to learn about her body, her genitals, and the female sexual response. In step 2 she explores her whole body by touch. Step 3 consists of locating erotically sensitive areas, with a focus on the breasts and genitals, especially the clitoris. Actual stimulation of these areas, masturbation, is step 4. Step 5 is erotic masturbation accompanied by sexual pictures, stories, and the woman's own fantasies.

Step 6 has three elements. First, if the woman has not yet experienced an orgasm, she will begin to use an electric vibrator to increase the intensity of stimulation. Second, she will be instructed to act out or role-play a very exaggerated orgasm, to overcome any fears about losing control or looking silly when she has a real orgasm. Finally, she will use "orgasm triggers," such as holding her breath, contracting her pelvic muscles, tensing her leg muscles, and thrusting her pelvis.

Step 7 integrates Masters and Johnson's sensate focus procedure with the woman's individual progress. This training in communication and sexual skill teaches her to demonstrate for her partner how she likes to be touched and how she can have orgasm. In step 8 her partner brings her to orgasm with manual, oral, or vibrator stimulation. In the last step, the woman and her partner practice intercourse in positions that permit one or the other of them to continue to stimulate her clitoris while the penis is in the vagina.

This training program has been found to be very effective: over 90 percent of women learn to have orgasm during masturbation, about 80 percent during caressing by their partner, and about 30 percent during intercourse (Heiman & LoPiccolo, 1988). As it is a structured program, it works equally well in group therapy, and even as a self-treatment: the woman can go through the program without a therapist, using a self-help book and instructional videotape (LoPiccolo, 1990).

Treatment for situational lack of orgasm includes a gradual stimulus generalization procedure, to help the woman expand the ways she reaches orgasm. If the woman can masturbate to orgasm when she is alone, for example, but only by pressing her thighs together, and can't have orgasm in any way when her partner is present, the therapist will help her to identify a number of small, intermediate steps between the way she has orgasm now and the wished-for orgasm during sex with her partner. In this example, intermediate steps might include using thigh pressure but also putting her fingers on her clitoris, direct stimulation of the clitoris with the thighs spread apart, thigh pressure with her partner present, thigh pressure with his fingers on her clitoris, his direct stimulation of her clitoris without thigh pressure, and direct clitoral stimulation during insertion of the penis (Zeiss, Rosen, & Zeiss, 1977). This approach is quite effective in helping women learn to have orgasm with a partner (McCabe & Delaney, 1992).

As we saw earlier, sex therapists do not consider lack of orgasm during intercourse to be a problem, provided the woman enjoys intercourse and can have orgasm when her partner caresses her. For this reason, reassurance about their normality, not treatment, is indicated for women whose only concern is situational lack of orgasm during intercourse. While sex therapists agree that lack of orgasm during intercourse is not a problem, popular books and magazines continue to suggest ways for women to achieve orgasm during intercourse (Eichel & Nobile, 1992). Their suggestions do not, however, always seem to be effective (Kaplan, 1992).

VAGINISMUS Vaginismic patients practice contracting and relaxing the pubococcygeal muscle, which, as we noted earlier, is part of the pelvic floor and surrounds the vagina, until they have acquired voluntary control over their vaginal muscles. They overcome their fear of penetration by using a set of gradually larger dilators, which they insert in their own vagina at home and at their own pace, so that they are not frightened or traumatized. Later, when the woman can comfortably insert the largest dilator, she begins to guide her partner as he slowly and gently inserts the dilators. Finally, as he lies passively on his back and she kneels above him, she gradually inserts his penis. The therapist stresses the need for effective stimulation, so that she learns to associate penetration with vaginal lubrication, pleasure, and arousal, instead of with fear. Some therapists use muscle-relaxing drugs or hypnosis during dilation, but this does not seem to be a necessary part of the treatment. Therapy for vaginismus is highly successful; over 90 percent of the women treated become able to have pain-free intercourse (Beck, 1993; LoPiccolo, 1990).

DYSPAREUNIA There are no specific treatment procedures for psychogenic dyspareunia. Since psychogenic dyspareunia is actually caused by lack of arousal, the general sex therapy procedures and the specific techniques for enhancing female arousal and orgasm are used (Quevillon, 1993). When the pain is caused by scars or lesions, the couple can be taught positions for intercourse that do not put pressure on the traumatized sites. Since many cases of dyspareunia are caused by undiagnosed physical problems, an examination by a gynecologist who is expert in this area is essential (Reid & Lininger, 1993).

■ PARAPHILIAS ■

People with *paraphilias* manifest recurrent and intense sexual urges, sexually arousing fantasies, or related behaviors involving either nonhuman objects, children, or nonconsenting adults, or experiences of suffering or humiliation on the part of themselves or their partners. According to DSM-IV, only those who experience these urges or behaviors for at least six months and repeatedly act on them or feel extreme guilt, shame, or some other kind of distress over them warrant a diagnosis (APA, 1994). Many people with a paraphilia can become aroused only when a paraphiliac stimulus is present, acted out, or fantasized about. Other people seem to need the paraphiliac stimulus only occasionally, as during times of stress. Some clinicians hold that, with the exception of nonconsensual paraphilias, paraphiliac activities should be considered a disorder only when they are the exclusive or preferred means of achieving sexual excitement and orgasm (Becker & Kavoussi, 1988). People with one kind of paraphilia often display others as well (Abel & Osborn, 1992).

Actually, relatively few people receive a formal diagnosis of paraphilia, but the large market in paraphiliac pornography and other items leads clinicians to suspect that the disorders may be quite prevalent (APA, 1994). People whose paraphilias involve children or nonconsenting adults often wind up in legal trouble and come to the attention of professionals in that way. Those who do receive a diagnosis are almost always men. Theorists have proposed various explanations for paraphilias and applied various treatments to them (Stein et al., 1992; Fedoroff, 1992; Perilstein et al., 1991; Emmanuel et al., 1991). Overall, however, research has revealed relatively little about the causes and treatments of most of these disorders (APA, 1994).

FETISHISM

The key feature of *fetishism* is recurrent intense sexual urges, sexually arousing fantasies, or behaviors that involve the use of a nonliving object, often to the exclusion of all other stimuli. Usually the disorder begins in adolescence (APA, 1994). Almost anything can be a fetish object; women's underwear, shoes, and boots are particularly common (APA, 1994; Raphling, 1989). Some persons with fetishism commit petty theft for the purpose of collecting as many of the objects of their desire as possible. The objects may be touched, smelled, worn, or used in some other way while the person masturbates, or the individual may ask partners to wear the object when they have sex. In the nineteenth century, Richard von Krafft-Ebing ([1886] 1975) described one such case:

A lady told Dr. Gemy that in the bridal night and in the night following her husband contented himself with kissing her, and running his fingers through the wealth of her tresses. He then fell asleep. In the third night Mr. X produced an immense wig, with enormously long hair, and begged his wife to put it on. As soon as she had done so he richly compensated her for his neglected marital duties. In the morning he showed again extreme tenderness, whilst he caressed the wig. When Mrs. X removed the wig she lost at once all charm for her husband. . . . The result of this marriage was, after five years, two children and a collection of 72 wigs.

Researchers have not been able to pinpoint the causes of fetishism (Wise, 1985). Psychodynamic the-

orists have proposed that fetishes are defense mechanisms to help the person avoid the anxiety associated with normal sexual contact. Their efforts to translate this explanation into an effective psychodynamic treatment, however, have met with relatively little success (LoPiccolo, 1992).

Behaviorists have proposed that fetishes are acquired through classical conditioning. In one behavioral study, male subjects were shown a series of slides of nude women interspersed with slides of boots (Rachman, 1966). After numerous trials, the subjects became aroused by the boot photos alone. If early sexual experiences similarly occur in conjunction with a particular object, the stage may be set for development of a fetish.

Behaviorists have sometimes treated fetishism with aversion therapy (Kilmann et al., 1982). In one study, an electric shock was administered to the arms or legs of subjects with fetishes while they imagined their objects of desire (Marks & Gelder, 1967). After two weeks of therapy all subjects in the study showed at least some improvement. In another aversion technique, *covert sensitization,* persons with fetishism are guided to imagine the pleasurable but unwanted object and repeatedly to pair this image with an imagined aversive stimulus, until the object of erotic pleasure is no longer desired.

Another behavioral treatment for fetishism is *masturbatory satiation* (Quinsey & Earls, 1990; Marshall, 1979; Marshall & Lippens, 1977). In this method, the client masturbates to orgasm while fantasizing aloud about a sexually appropriate object, then switches to fantasizing in detail about fetishistic objects while masturbating and continues to elaborate on the fetishistic fantasy for an hour. The procedure is meant to produce a feeling of boredom, which in turn becomes associated with the fetishistic object.

TRANSVESTIC FETISHISM

Transvestic fetishism, also known as *transvestism* or *cross-dressing,* involves the recurrent need or desire to dress in clothes of the opposite sex in order to achieve sexual arousal. The typical person with transvestism, almost always a heterosexual male, begins cross-dressing in childhood or adolescence (APA, 1994). He is the picture of characteristic masculinity in everyday life, and cross-dresses only in relative privacy. A small percentage of such men cross-dress to visit bars or social clubs. Some wear a single item of women's apparel, such as underwear or hosiery, under

"Crossroads" is a self-help group for men with transvestic fetishism, a recurrent need to dress in women's clothing as a means to achieve sexual arousal. These men are not transsexual; they never question their identity as men and have no wish to be women.

their masculine clothes. Others wear makeup and dress fully as women. Many married men with transvestism involve their wives in their cross-dressing behavior (Kolodny, Masters, & Johnson, 1979). Recent research into the personality characteristics of those with transvestism reveals many to be fairly hostile and self-centered, with a limited capacity for intimacy. They report high levels of marital discord, which transcends their cross-dressing behaviors (Wise et al., 1991). Transvestic fetishism is often confused with transsexualism, but, as we shall observe shortly, the two are entirely separate disorders.

The development of transvestic fetishism sometimes seems consistent with the principles of operant conditioning. Several case studies describe individuals who were reinforced for cross-dressing as children, openly encouraged and supported by parents or other adults for this behavior. In one case, for example, a woman was delighted to discover that her young nephew enjoyed dressing in girls' clothes; she had always wanted a niece, and she proceeded to buy him dresses and jewelry and sometimes dressed him as a girl and took him out shopping.

PEDOPHILIA

A person who is subject to *pedophilia,* literally "love of children," obtains sexual gratification by watching, touching, or engaging in simple or complex sexual acts with prepubescent children, usually those 13

years old or younger. Some persons with this disorder are satisfied by child pornography; others are driven to watching, fondling, or engaging in sexual intercourse with children (Barnard et al., 1989; Grinspoon et al., 1986). Some persons with pedophilia are attracted only to children *(exclusive type);* others are attracted to adults as well *(nonexclusive type)* (APA, 1994).

One study found that 4 percent of pedophilia victims are 3 years old or younger, 18 percent are 4 to 7 years old, and 40 percent are 8 to 11 (Mohr et al., 1964). In addition, studies suggest that the victim usually knows the molester and that 15 to 30 percent of sexual molestation cases are incestuous (Gebhard et al., 1965; Mohr et al., 1964). Both boys and girls can be pedophilia victims, but there is some evidence that three-quarters of them are girls (Koss & Heslet, 1992).

People with pedophilia usually develop their disorder during adolescence. Many were themselves sexually abused as children (McCormack et al., 1992). It is not unusual for them to be married and to have sexual difficulties or other frustrations in life that lead them to seek an arena in which they can be masters. Alcohol abuse is another factor that figures prominently in many cases (Rada, 1976).

Some clinicians suggest that immaturity is often the primary cause of this disorder (Groth & Birnbaum, 1978). Social and sexual skills may be underdeveloped, so that the person feels intense anxiety at the very thought of a normal sexual relationship. Some persons with pedophilia also display faulty thinking, such as "It's all right to have sex with children as long as they agree" (Abel et al., 1984).

Most pedophilic offenders are imprisoned or forced into treatment if they are caught. After all, they are committing child sexual abuse when they approach a child. Treatments include those already mentioned for other paraphilias, such as aversion therapy and masturbatory satiation (LoPiccolo, 1992; Enright, 1989). Another approach, also used for other paraphilias, is *orgasmic reorientation* (Enright, 1989), which conditions clients to new, more appropriate sources of erotic stimuli: they are shown conventional stimuli while they are responding to the other, unconventional objects. For example, a person with pedophilia may be instructed to obtain an erection from pictures of young children and then to begin masturbating to a picture of a nude adult. If he starts to lose the erection, he must return to the original stimulus until he is masturbating effectively, then change back to the accepted stimulus. When orgasm becomes imminent, all focus should be on the more appropriate stimulus. This training continues for a period of several weeks and may be supplemented by covert sensitization, social skills training, or psychodynamic intervention.

Lastly, there is a cognitive-behavioral treatment for pedophilia: *relapse-prevention training.* Modeled after the relapse-prevention programs used in the treatment of drug dependence (p. 475), this approach helps clients to identify the problematic situations that typically trigger their pedophilic fantasies and actions (such as depressed mood or distorted thinking) and to develop strategies to avoid or cope more effectively with these situations, thus preventing the pedophilic behavior (LoPiccolo, 1992; Pithers, 1990). One study of 147 people with pedophilia found only a 4 percent relapse rate over a five-year period among offenders who received this treatment (Pithers & Cumming, 1989).

EXHIBITIONISM

The person with *exhibitionism* has recurrent sexually arousing fantasies or urges of exposing his genitals to another person, almost always a member of the opposite sex, and may act on the fantasies or urges (APA, 1994; Abel, 1989). Further sexual activity with the other person is not usually attempted or desired. What is often desired, however, is a reaction of shock or surprise. Sometimes a so-called flasher will frequent a particular neighborhood or exhibit at particular hours. Urges to expose themselves typically intensify when people with this disorder have free time or are under significant stress (Abel, 1989).

The big "secret" in the popular 1992 movie The Crying Game *was that the sultry and alluring character Dil is a male transsexual. More than a cross dresser, Dil felt as if he had been assigned to the wrong sex and he wanted to be a woman in every possible way.*

Generally, the disorder begins before age 18, and most such individuals are males (APA, 1994). Exhibitionistic persons are immature in their approaches to the opposite sex and have difficulty in interpersonal relationships. Over half of those with exhibitionism are married, but their sexual relationships with their wives are not satisfactory (Blair & Lanyon, 1981; Mohr, Turner, & Jerry, 1964). Many have doubts or fears about their masculinity, and some apparently have a strong bond to a possessive mother.

Treatment is the same as that for other paraphilias, including covert sensitization, masturbatory satiation, and relapse-prevention training, possibly combined with orgasmic reorientation, social skills training, or psychodynamic intervention (LoPicolo, 1992; McNally & Lukach, 1991). One unusual, apparently successful version of aversive conditioning pairs the unpleasant smell of valeric acid with images of self-exposure (Maletzky, 1980). Clinicians have also reported some success with hypnotherapy (Polk, 1983; Epstein, 1983; Ritchie, 1968).

VOYEURISM

A person who engages in *voyeurism* has recurrent and intense sexual desires to observe unsuspecting people in secret as they undress or to spy on couples engaged in intercourse. The risk of being discovered often adds to the person's excitement. The individual generally does not seek to have sex with the person being spied on (APA, 1994).

People with voyeurism may masturbate either during the act or when thinking about it afterward. The vulnerability of the people being observed and the probability that they would feel humiliated if they found out are often part of the voyeur's enjoyment. Voyeurism usually begins before the age of 15 and tends to be chronic (APA, 1994).

Elements of both exhibitionism and voyeurism can play a role in normal sexuality, but in such instances they are engaged in with the consent or understanding of the partner. The clinical disorder of voyeurism is marked by the repeated invasion of another person's privacy. Some people with voyeurism are unable to have normal sexual interplay; others, however, maintain normal sexual relationships apart from their voyeurism.

Many clinicians believe that people with voyeurism are seeking by their actions to exercise power over others, possibly because they feel inadequate or are sexually or socially inhibited. Psychodynamic theorists have explained voyeurism as an attempt to reduce castration anxiety, originally generated by the sight of an adult's genitals. Theoretically, those with voyeurism are repeating the behavior that produced the original fright, so that they can be reassured there is nothing to fear (Fenichel, 1945). Behaviorists explain the disorder as a learned behavior that can be traced to a chance and secret observation of a sexually arousing scene. If such observations are repeated on several occasions in conjunction with masturbation, a voyeuristic pattern may develop.

FROTTEURISM

A person who exhibits *frotteurism* has recurrent and intense sexual urges to touch and rub against a non-consenting person, or sexually arousing fantasies of doing so. As with other paraphilias, the person must act on these urges or be very distressed by them in order to warrant a diagnosis. Frottage (from French *frotter*, to rub) is usually committed in a crowded place, such as a subway or a busy sidewalk (APA, 1994). The person, almost always a male, may rub his genitals against the victim's thighs or buttocks or fondle her genitalia or breasts with his hands. Typically he fantasizes during the act that he is having a caring relationship with the victim (APA, 1994).

Frotteurism usually begins in adolescence or earlier, often after the person observes others committing an act of frottage. After the person reaches the age of 25, the acts gradually decrease and often disappear (APA, 1994).

SEXUAL MASOCHISM

Sexual masochism is a pattern in which a person repeatedly has intense sexual urges and fantasies that involve being humiliated, beaten, bound, or otherwise made to suffer. Although many people have fantasies (while they masturbate or have intercourse) of being forced into sexual acts against their will, only those who are markedly distressed by the fantasies would receive this diagnosis (APA, 1994; Reik, 1989). Many people with the disorder act on the masochistic urges by themselves, perhaps binding, sticking pins into, or even mutilating themselves. Others have their sexual partners restrain, tie up, blindfold, spank, paddle, whip, beat, electrically shock, "pin and pierce," or humiliate them (APA, 1994). The following letter to the advice columnist Ann Landers (1993) shows how upsetting this paraphilia is to many who experience it:

Dear Ann:

When I read those letters in your column about self-mutilators, I knew I had to write.

I have been intentionally hurting myself for years and am seeing a specialist who is trying to help me. I would appreciate your input. I am a masochist. I love pain. It feels good to me.

I have been told that I hate myself, which is the truth. When I was a child, I used to bang my head against the floor as hard as I could. While I no longer do this and have stopped carving on myself, I beg others to do it for me.

Without intense pain, I cannot enjoy sex. I like hair-pulling, hard (not playful) pinching and biting that leaves teeth marks. When I am deprived of pain during sex, I sometimes curl up into a fetal position and start biting my arms or my knees.

I wish I could learn how to enjoy sex without pain, but I don't know where to start. Or maybe I do know and am hiding from the truth. If it meant cutting out sex for a while, I wouldn't be willing to do it.

I know I'm screwed up and would love to be normal. Please help me, Ann.

MASON CITY, Iowa

In one form of sexual masochism, *hypoxyphilia,* people strangle or smother themselves, or ask their partner to do this, in order to enhance their sexual pleasure. There have, in fact, been a growing number of clinical reports of *autoerotic asphyxia,* in which individuals, usually males and as young as 10 years old, inadvertently induce a fatal cerebral anoxia (lack of oxygen) by hanging, suffocating, or strangling themselves while masturbating. There is some debate as to whether this practice should be characterized as sexual masochism, but it is commonly accompanied by other acts of bondage, superfluous to the physiological asphyxia (Blanchard & Hucker, 1991).

Most masochistic sexual fantasies begin in childhood. The person does not act out the urges until later, usually by early adulthood. The disorder typically continues over the course of many years. The masochistic acts of some people remain at the same level of severity during that time; others keep increasing the potential dangerousness of their acts over time or show an increase during times of particular stress (APA, 1994).

In many cases the pattern of sexual masochism seems to have developed through classical conditioning. One case study tells of a teenage boy with a broken arm who was caressed and held close by an attractive nurse as the physician set his fracture without anesthesia (Gebhard, 1965). He experienced a powerful combination of pain and sexual arousal that may have been the cause of his later masochistic urges and acts.

People with sexual masochism and those with sexual sadism often achieve satisfaction with each other. Although many such relationships stay within safe bounds and are often portrayed with humor in photos, novels, and movies, they can cross the line and result in severe physical or psychological damage.

SEXUAL SADISM

Sexual sadism is a pattern in which a person, usually male, is intensely sexually aroused by the act or thought of inflicting physical or psychological suffering on others, such as by dominating, restraining, blindfolding, cutting, strangling, mutilating, or even killing the victim. The label is derived from the name of the Marquis de Sade (1740–1814), who inflicted severe cruelty on other people in order to satisfy his sexual desires. Eventually he was confined in a mental institution. People who fantasize about sadism typically imagine that they have total control over a sexual victim who is terrified by the prospect of the sadistic act. Many carry out sadistic acts with a consenting partner, often a person who is sexually masochistic. Some act out their urges on nonconsenting victims (see Box 14–3). In all cases, the real or fantasized victim's suffering is the key to arousal.

Fantasies of sexual sadism, like those of sexual masochism, may appear in childhood, and sadistic acts, when they occur, develop by early adulthood. The pattern is chronic (APA, 1994). The acts sometimes stay at the same level of cruelty, but more often they increase in severity over the years. Obviously, people with severe forms of the disorder may be highly dangerous to others (Dietz et al., 1990).

The pattern has been associated with a variety of causal factors. Behaviorists suggest that classical conditioning often plays a role in its development. While inflicting pain, perhaps unintentional, on an animal or person, an adolescent may feel intense emotions and sometimes sexual arousal. The association between inflicting pain and being aroused sexually sets the stage for a pattern of sexual sadism. Behaviorists also propose that many cases result from modeling, when adolescents observe others achieving sexual satisfaction by inflicting pain. The ubiquitous sexual magazines, books, and videotapes in our society make such models readily available. Indeed, one broad review of pornographic magazines and books determined that close to one quarter of the materials contained an act of paraphilia, and sadomasochism was overwhelmingly the most common type (Lebegue, 1991).

Psychodynamic and cognitive theorists have suggested that people with sexual sadism may have underlying feelings of sexual inadequacy or insecurity and that they inflict pain in order to achieve a sense of power, which in turn increases their sexual arousal. Alternatively, some biological investigations have found signs of possible abnormal functioning in the endocrine systems of persons with sadism (Langevin et al., 1988). However, none of these explanations has been systematically investigated or consistently supported by empirical research (Breslow, 1989).

Sexual sadism has been treated by aversive conditioning. The public's view of and perhaps distaste for this procedure have been influenced by the description of treatment given to a cruel and sadistic character in Anthony Burgess's novel (later a movie) *A Clockwork Orange:* simultaneous presentation of sadistic images and electrical shocks. It is not clear that aversive conditioning is consistently helpful in sexual sadism. Relapse-prevention training, used in some criminal cases, seems somewhat effective (Vaillant & Antonowicz, 1992; Pithers & Cumming, 1989).

SOCIETAL NORMS AND SEXUAL LABELS

The definitions of the various paraphilias, like those of sexual dysfunctions, are closely tied to the norms

BOX 14-3

RAPE: SEXUAL ASSAULT, PSYCHOLOGICAL TRAUMA

Rape—forced sexual intercourse or another sexual act upon a nonconsenting or underage person—is prevalent in our society and leaves the victim psychologically traumatized and vulnerable. More than 100,000 rapes are reported to authorities annually (FBI, 1991), but they apparently represent only a small fraction of the number of rapes committed (Koss, 1993, 1990). In fact, it is estimated that the incidence of rape may be six to fifteen times greater than the number reported (Koss, 1993, 1992). Many victims are reluctant to report a rape because they are ashamed or because they feel that dealing with police or the courts will compound their trauma.

Most rapists are men and most victims are women. Studies estimate that between 8 and 25 percent of all women are raped or are the victims of some sexual assault at some time during their lives (Koss, 1993). Surveys also suggest that most rape victims are young: 29 percent of all victims are under 11 years old, 32 percent are between the ages of 11 and 17, and 29 percent are between 18 and 29. Approximately 22 percent of the victims are raped by strangers; the rest are raped by acquaintances, friends, neighbors, boyfriends or ex-boyfriends, husbands or ex-husbands, fathers or stepfathers, or other relatives (Koss, 1992; Youngstrom, 1992).

A discussion of rape is actually out of place in a chapter on sexual disorders. Although rape does by definition involve a sexual act, the motivation for this act is often not primarily sexual. The typical rapist's motivation is aggression or anger rather than sexual desire, and his sexual gratification is usually limited during the rape. Between a third and a half of all rapists fail to have an erection or to ejaculate (Sadock, 1989; Burgess & Baldwin, 1981).

Rapists fall into four categories: *sexual sadists*, who are sexually aroused by seeing a victim suffer; *sexual exploiters*, who impulsively use victims as objects of gratification; *inadequate aggressors*, who believe that no woman would voluntarily have sex with them; and *angry abusers*, who seem to displace their rage against women in general upon the victim (Hall, 1992). There is a suspicion that some adolescents who commit rape may be grappling with issues that are different from those of adults (Hannett & Misch, 1993).

The psychological impact of rape on a victim is immediate and may last a long time. Rape victims typically experience enormous distress during the week after the assault. Stress continues to rise for the next three weeks, maintains a peak level for another month or so, and then starts to improve over the next few months (Koss, 1993). Indeed, in one study, 94 percent of rape victims fully qualified for a clinical diagnosis of *acute stress disorder* when they were observed an average of twelve days after their assault (Rothbaum et al., 1992). Although the majority of rape victims improve psychologically within three or four months, most continue to experience elevated levels of fear, anxiety, self-esteem problems, and sexual dysfunction—effects that may continue for up to 18 months or longer (Koss, 1993; Resick, 1987). Even years after the assault, women who were raped are more likely to qualify for diagnoses of depression, substance-related disorders, and anxiety disorders than other women (Koss, 1993; Winfield et al., 1990; Burnam et al., 1988; Kilpatrick et al., 1985).

Victims who have a strong psychological foundation and who are bolstered by a strong support system are more likely to make an adequate psychological recovery (Davis, Brickman, & Baker, 1991; Sales, Baum, & Shore, 1984), but the trauma of the sexual assault and its aftermath (including a harsh legal system and a judgmental society) may overwhelm even the psychologically healthiest and most well supported of women.

Victims who can express their fear and rage to believing family members, doctors, and police seem to make the most psychological progress (Sadock, 1989). A large number of rape crisis intervention centers and other victim services were developed across the United States in the 1970s and 1980s, but recent funding limitations have cut back many of these services (Koss, 1993). Both individual and group therapies have been helpful for victims of rape, but many clinicians believe that group therapy is the treatment of choice (Koss & Harvey, 1991). It is particularly effective at countering feelings of isolation, providing sup-

of the particular society in which they occur rather than to fixed medical criteria (Brown, 1983). It could be argued that except when people are hurt by them, many paraphiliac behaviors are not disorders at all (Grinspoon et al., 1986). Especially in light of the stigma associated with sexual disorders and the self-revulsion that many people experience when they believe they have such a disorder, we need to be very careful about applying such labels to others or to ourselves. Keep in mind

port, validating feelings, and reducing self-blame.

Rape victims may also experience short-term somatic problems as a result of their assault. Many victims suffer physical trauma during the assault, although only half of those injured receive formal medical care (Beebe, 1991; Koss, Woodruff, & Koss, 1991). Between 4 and 30 percent of victims develop a sexually transmitted disease (Koss, 1993; Murphy, 1990) and 5 percent become pregnant (Beebe, 1991; Koss et al., 1991). Yet a recent broad national survey of women revealed that 60 percent of rape victims received no pregnancy testing or prophylaxis, and 73 percent received no information or testing for exposure to HIV (National Victims Center, 1992).

Some related recent studies by the psychologist Mary Koss and her colleagues indicate that victims of rape and other crimes are also much more likely than other women to suffer serious long-term somatic problems for years afterward (Golding, 1994; Koss & Heslet, 1992; Koss, Koss, & Woodruff, 1991). Interviews with 390 women revealed that victims of rape or assault had poorer general health as well as poorer mental health for at least five years after the crime, made twice as many visits to physicians, and incurred 2½ times more medical expenses. Even victims of less severe crimes, such as home burglary or purse snatching, showed some increase in somatic problems over the five-year period. It is not yet clear why rape and other assaults lead to more long-term somatic problems. The extraordinarily stressful experience could lead to poorer immune system functioning, or it could exacerbate preexisting somatic symptoms.

Several kinds of rape have received special attention during the past decade: spouse rape, date rape, and incest.

■ SPOUSE RAPE ■

Until recently the law presumed that sexual intercourse was a contractual part of marriage, and a woman could not accuse her husband of rape. That situation changed in 1982, when a Florida man was convicted of the crime of raping his wife. Twenty-five states have now eliminated the legal exemption for marital rape. Still other states remain ambivalent on the issue and offer the husband the benefit of the doubt unless there is convincing evidence of abuse. Research suggests that it is just as common for women who are raped by their husbands or dates to fear injury or death during the rape as it is for women who are raped by strangers (NVC, 1992).

■ DATE RAPE ■

Rape by a date or close acquaintance is a major social problem, according to several large surveys of college students (Koss et al., 1988; Muehlenhard & Linton, 1987). These surveys suggest that 15 percent of women have been forced into intercourse against their will by acquaintances, either in high school or in college. Although date rape may occur on a first or early date, many students say that they knew or dated the person who raped them for a year or more before.

■ FATHER-DAUGHTER INCEST ■

Incest, from the Latin *incestus,* "impure," is sexual intercourse between persons closely related by blood or marriage. About 75 percent of reported cases involve father-daughter (or stepfather-stepdaughter) relationships (Sadock, 1989). These cases represent a form of *statutory rape* (unlawful intercourse between a male over 16 years old and a female under the state's age of consent) as well as a psychological assault on the victim that may last a lifetime. Researchers estimate that altogether between 50,000 and 400,000 children are sexually abused in the United States each year and that one in four females may be sexually abused before reaching adulthood (Eisen, 1993). Still, it is difficult to assess how many of these cases represent father-daughter incest, because daughters are reluctant, ashamed, or afraid to tell what has happened to them (Kilpatrick et al., 1987).

Most of the statistical information about incest comes from adults who are surveyed anonymously about sexual abuse that they experienced during childhood. Because many incidents have been reported in such studies, clinicians have become increasingly interested in studying and treating victims of incest (Koss, 1990). They have in particular become aware of the profound feelings of depression, guilt, and shame that many victims of father-daughter incest carry into adulthood, and of the difficulties that these early experiences may pose for later intimacy and interpersonal trust (Eisen, 1993; Conte, 1991; Arndt, 1991; Gold, 1986; Owens, 1984). Therapy and self-help groups for women who have experienced incest as children and adolescents have proliferated rapidly in recent years and are reportedly helpful to many victims. These interventions appear to make an impact by helping victims rework painful experiences in a supportive environment and regain a sense of autonomy.

that homosexuality was for years considered a paraphilia by clinical professionals and that this judgment was used to justify laws and even police actions against homosexual persons. Only when the gay rights movement helped change society's understanding of and attitudes toward homosexuality did clinicians stop considering it a disorder. In the meantime, the clinical field had inadvertently contributed to the persecution, anxiety, and humiliation of millions of people because of personal sexual behavior that differed from the conventional norms (see Box 14–4).

■ GENDER ■ IDENTITY DISORDER

One of the most fascinating disorders related to sexuality is *gender identity disorder,* or *transsexualism,* a disorder in which people persistently feel that a vast mistake has been made—they have been assigned to the wrong sex. Such persons are preoccupied with getting rid of their primary and secondary sex characteristics—many of them find their own genitals repugnant—and acquiring the characteristics of the other sex (APA, 1994). They usually feel uncomfortable wearing the clothes of their own sex and dress instead in clothes of the opposite sex. They are not, however, transvestites. People who display the paraphilia transvestic fetishism cross-dress in order to become sexually aroused; transsexual persons have much deeper reasons for cross-dressing, reasons of sexual identity. In addition to cross-dressing, transsexual individuals often engage in activities that are traditionally associated with the other sex.

Some transsexual persons alter their sexual characteristics by hormone treatments. The hormone prescribed for transsexual males, who outnumber transsexual females by more than 3 to 1, is the female hormone estrogen. It causes breast development, loss of body and facial hair, and change in the distribution of body fat; it may also lead to such unwanted effects as hypertension, weight gain, depression, and liver abnormalities. Similar treatments with the male sex hormone testosterone are given to transsexual females. Their cross-dressing, activity preferences, and hormone-induced physical changes make many individuals virtually indistinguishable from the other sex.

Various psychological theories have been proposed to explain this disorder, but research in this area has been limited and generally weak. Some clinicians suspect that the disorder has largely biological causes (Orlebeke et al., 1992); but most studies of hormonal, EEG, and other physiological measures have not found any differences between transsexual persons and nontranssexual persons.

Sometimes gender identity disorders occur in children (APA, 1994). Like transsexual adults, they too feel uncomfortable about their assigned sex and thoroughly wish to be a member of the opposite sex. In addition to a preference for cross-dressing, these children usually prefer to play cross-sex roles in make-believe play, to participate in the stereotypical games of the other sex, and to play with children of the other sex. This childhood pattern usually disappears by adolescence or adulthood, but in some cases it develops into adult transsexualism. Thus many transsexual adults have had a childhood gender identity disorder (Tsoi, 1992), but most children with a gender identity disorder do not become transsexual adults. A number of adult persons with transsexualism do not develop any symptoms until mid-adulthood.

Drug therapy and psychotherapy are sufficient to enable many transsexual persons to lead a satisfactory existence in the gender role that they believe represents their true identity. For others, however, this is not enough, and their dissatisfaction leads them to undergo one of the most controversial practices in medicine: sex-change surgery.

The first sex-change operation actually took place in 1931, but the procedure did not gain acceptance among practitioners working on this problem until 1952, when an operation converted an ex-soldier named George Jorgensen into a woman, renamed Christine Jorgensen. This transformation made headlines around the world and sparked the interest of people everywhere.

By 1980, sex-reassignment surgery was routine in at least forty medical centers in the western hemisphere (Arndt, 1991). This surgery is preceded by one to two years of hormone therapy, after which the operation itself involves, for men, amputation of the penis, creation of an artificial vagina, and face-altering plastic surgery. For women, surgery may include bilateral mastectomy and hysterectomy. The procedure for creating a functioning penis, called *phalloplasty,* is not yet perfected and not recommended; however, doctors have developed a silicone prosthesis that gives the patient the appearance of having male genitals and has apparently satisfied the needs of many female-to-male transsexual persons (Hage & Bouman, 1992). Approximately 1,000 sex-change operations are performed each year in the United States. Studies in some European countries suggest that 1 out of every 30,000 men and 1 out of every 100,000 women seek sex-change surgery (APA, 1994).

Clinicians have heatedly debated the legitimacy of surgery as a treatment for gender identity disorder. Some consider it a humane solution, indeed the only completely satisfying one to transsexual people. Others argue that transsexual surgery is a "drastic nonsolution" for a purely psychological problem, akin to lobotomy (Restak, 1979). Research has not yet been able to settle the matter. The long-term outcome of

Feeling like a woman trapped in a man's body, the English writer James Morris (left) underwent sex-reassignment surgery, described in his 1974 autobiography Conundrum. *Today Jan Morris (right) is the successful author of more than a dozen books and numerous travel articles and seems comfortable with her change of gender.*

surgical sex reassignment, either by itself or in combination with psychotherapy and hormone treatments, is not well established. Many people seem to function well for years after such treatments, but some have experienced serious psychological difficulties. Without any form of treatment, gender identity disorder among adults is usually chronic, but some cases of spontaneous remission have reportedly occurred.

Our gender is so fundamental to our sense of our identity that it is difficult for most of us to imagine wanting to change it, much less the feelings of conflict and stress experienced by those who do question their assigned gender. Whether the underlying cause is biological or psychological, gender identity disorder represents a dramatic psychological dysfunction that shakes the foundations of the sufferer's existence.

THE STATE OF THE FIELD

SEXUAL DISORDERS AND GENDER IDENTITY DISORDERS

❧

Because there is so much public interest in and discussion about sexual disorders, it sometimes appears as if much is known about these problems; such is not the case. Clinical theorists and practitioners have only recently begun to understand the nature and origins of sexual dysfunctions and to develop effective treatments for them. Moreover, they have made only limited progress in explaining and treating paraphilias, the other group of sexual disorders, or the sexual-related gender identity disorders.

Yet this picture is changing rapidly, at least in the realm of sexual dysfunctions. For years our explanations and treatments for sexual dysfunctions were influenced largely by popular myths and by the dominating perspective of the psychodynamic model. Then in 1970 William Masters and Virginia Johnson published their research on human sexual functioning and dysfunctioning and began a veritable revolution in the clinical field that continues today. Over the past two decades, sexual functioning has been one of the most broadly investigated subjects in clinical research, with systematic studies providing enlightening and useful information about the nature and causes of various sexual dysfunctions. Correspondingly, clinicians have developed extraordinarily helpful treatments for people with sexual dysfunctions—people previously doomed to a lifetime of sexual frustration and distress. Today sex therapy is typically a complex program with multiple components tailored to the particular problems and personality of an individual and couple. The breadth of current research undertakings and therapy programs suggests that our understanding and treatment of sexual dysfunctions will continue to improve in the coming years.

BOX 14-4

HOMOSEXUALITY AND SOCIETY

In the year 1948, when Alfred Kinsey and his associates conducted one of the first extensive studies of male sexuality, they found that 4 percent of the male population were exclusively homosexual and that 37 percent had had a homosexual experience that led to orgasm. Half of the unmarried men over the age of 35 had had a homosexual experience to the point of orgasm. In a later study they found the occurrence of homosexuality among women to be approximately one-half to one-third that of men (Kinsey et al., 1953). These findings shocked and astonished many people.

Homosexuality has always existed in all cultures. It is not new, nor is the controversy that surrounds it. Most cultures do not openly advocate homosexuality, but historically few have condemned it so fiercely as Western culture has since the Victorian era. Nevertheless, research shows that a society's acceptance or rejection of people who engage in homosexual activity does not affect the incidence of homosexual behavior.

Before 1973, the DSM listed homosexuality as a sexual disorder. Protests by gay activist groups and many psychotherapists eventually led to its elimination from the manual as a sexual disorder per se, but the DSM did retain a category called *ego dystonic homosexuality*—the experience of extreme distress over one's homosexual preference. Recent editions of the DSM have dropped even this category, and the issue of homosexuality is no longer mentioned. Most clinicians now accept homosexuality as a variant of normal sexual behavior and not a disorder.

Despite the growing acceptance of homosexuality by clinicians, many people in Western society continue to foster antihomosexual attitudes and to propagate myths about the lifestyles of homosexual persons. The facts are that homosexual persons do *not* suffer from gender confusion. They are *not* prone to psychopathologies (Paul et al., 1982). There is *not* an identifiable "homosexual personality." And children raised in a homosexual household are *not* more likely to become homosexual (Green et al., 1986).

To cope with the stress, discrimination, and even danger they encounter, many homosexual people have chosen to live on streets or in neighborhoods that are predominantly homosexual.

Certain bars or restaurants serve as gathering places where gay persons exchange information and socialize. Organizations exist to support and lobby for issues affecting homosexual people, demanding equal treatment under the law and in society (Freiberg, 1994). This battle is being fought constantly. One of the key issues in gaining support for homosexual rights has been the debate over whether homosexual persons choose their lifestyle or whether it is a natural part of their physiological and psychological make-up. This debate is fueled by the findings from the scientific community. Recent research has suggested that sometimes homosexuality is *not* simply a lifestyle choice but a physiological predisposition. Several studies have examined the brains of deceased homosexual men and found a region within the hypothalamus that is smaller in this population than in heterosexual men (LeVay, 1991). These studies are far from definitive, but they support the claim from some segments of the gay community that homosexuality is a naturally occurring phenomenon.

In addition, evidence has recently been found to support the view that homosexuality often has a heritable component. Several large studies of both male and female homosexual persons have found genetic markers indicating that homosexuality may sometimes be passed on by the mother's genes (Hamer, 1993). In pairs of identical twins (who share identical genetic makeup) in which one was homosexual, more than 50 percent of the other siblings were also homosexual. The number drops to less than 20 percent when the siblings are fraternal twins or nontwins and to under 10 percent when the children are adopted and unrelated by blood (Bailey & Pillard, 1993). This research has led some scientists to conclude that in some instances there is a link between homosexuality and a specific set of genes. Although environmental factors also have a major impact on homosexuality—otherwise all persons with a homosexual identical twin would be homosexual—genetics may sometimes play a key role. Scientists continue to try to isolate the exact genes that may be involved.

Homosexual persons are represented in every socioeconomic group, every race, and every profession. It is impossible to identify a characteristic that consistently separates them from the rest of the population other than their sexual preference. Moreover, heterosexual and homosexual relationships do not differ dramatically. AIDS is currently affecting hundreds of thousands of homosexual males, moving an increasing number of previously promiscuous men toward monogamy in long-term relationships, but it is important to note that commitments of this sort have always existed among homosexual persons.

The homosexual community takes the position that since sexual preference is the only behavioral variable that consistently distinguishes homosexual from heterosexual couples, gay couples should be accorded the same rights as heterosexual ones. Today marriages are performed for same-sex couples. Homosexual couples are de-

manding access to housing reserved for couples only, and recent court cases are supporting their right to have the same rights as heterosexual couples. Other cases have focused on health insurance coverage: should the partner of a gay person receive "spouse" coverage? These issues affect the day-to-day lives of homosexual couples in the same way that they affect heterosexual couples. The goal of the homosexual community is simple. They wish to be treated exactly as male-female couples are treated. They point out that the critical issues in any relationship, whether homosexual or heterosexual, are commitment, love, interdependence—gender need not be an important consideration.

In the early 1990s many issues regarding acceptance of homosexuality came to a head in the United States. Media coverage exposed numerous episodes of gay-bashing in which homosexual men were beaten, even killed. The practice of "outing," in which public figures who have not made their homosexuality known are exposed by gay activists, was increasingly frequent. And, in an action that stirred a national debate, President Clinton reviewed the military's policy regarding homosexuality.

During his campaign, Clinton had received much support from the gay community for his support of AIDS research and his promise to review the military's then-current policy of asking recruits their sexual preference and of actively pursuing reports of homosexuality in its ranks and discharging anyone suspected of being gay. Once Clinton was in office, the promised review grew into a many-headed monster that dominated the news for months. Military commanders and social conservatives argued that homosexuality was incompatible with military service. The gay community and

its supporters argued that sexual preference was unrelated to one's ability to serve one's country. The tentative conclusion reached by the end of 1993 was a middle-of-the-road "don't ask, don't tell" policy. The armed forces would not hunt out homosexual persons, but, if faced with incontrovertible evidence, they could discharge the offender from the service.

One of the most important issues to emerge during the debate on homosexuality and the military was whether Americans—those in the armed services specifically, but throughout the country as well—could overcome prejudice against homosexuality. Despite the high emotions this issue evokes, the evidence suggests that people can learn to accept and work with others who are different in ways that are considered basic to a person's nature. A historical and empirical review of the relevant literature reveals that, through education and exposure, people come to accept these differences (Herek, 1993). Many gay rights activists point to the similarities between the civil rights movement of the 1960s and the effort by the gay community to gain acceptance as evidence that society can learn to be more open and accepting.

Obviously, homosexuality continues to be a lifestyle that many people adopt, whether through choice, environment, genetics, or psychosocial development. Now that clinical concerns about homosexuality have been put aside, one of the key remaining issues is how society will deal with a significant proportion of its population that typically does not differ from the rest in any way other than sexual preference. So far, Western society cannot claim to have dealt very effectively or fairly with this question, but at least a trend toward understanding and equality seems to be emerging.

One of the most important insights to emerge from all this work concerns the need for proper education about sexual dysfunctions. Popular myths and judgments still abound in this area, often leading to feelings of shame, self-dislike, isolation, and hopelessness—and often contributing directly to the sexual difficulty. Sex therapists have come to recognize that even a modest amount of proper education about sexual dysfunctioning can help persons who are in treatment. In fact, most people, not just those who seek treatment, can benefit from a clearer, more accurate understanding of sexual functioning. Public education about sexual functioning—through books, television and radio, school programs, group presentations, and the like—has become a new focus of clinical scientists in recent years. Broad interventions of this kind appear to be as important as private treatment or continued research efforts. It is to be hoped that they too will continue and increase in the coming years.

Summary

■ **THERE ARE TWO KINDS** of sexual disorders: sexual dysfunctions and paraphilias. People with *sexual dysfunctions* are unable to function normally in some area of the human *sexual response cycle.* People with *paraphilias* manifest recurrent and intense sexual urges, sexually arousing fantasies, and behaviors in response to objects or situations that society deems inappropriate. In addition, there are *sexual-related* disorders called *gender identity disorders* in which people persistently feel that they have been assigned to the wrong sex and identify with the other gender.

■ **DSM-IV** classifies sexual dysfunctions according to the phase of the sexual response cycle affected—the desire, arousal, orgasm, or resolution phase. During the *desire phase,* the two most common dysfunctions are *hypoactive sexual desire,* or a lack of interest in sex, and *sexual aversion,* in which sex is found to be actively unpleasant. The two most common dysfunctions involving the *arousal phase* are *male erectile disorder* and *female sexual arousal disorder.* During the *orgasm phase* the most common dysfunctions are *premature ejaculation* and *male* and *female orgasmic disorder.* DSM-IV also identifies the dysfunctions of *vaginismus,* spastic contractions of the muscles around the outer vagina, and *dyspareunia,* pain in the genitals during sexual activity.

■ **SEX DRIVE** is determined by a combination of physical and psychological functions. It varies so widely that it is difficult to specify a "normal" level of sexual desire and activity. The dysfunctions associated with sexual arousal may be related to the hormones involved in the physiology of sex, to various prescription and illicit drugs, and to stress, strict religious upbringing, obsessive compulsive traits, or a history of painful relationships.

The causes of erectile failure are also both physiological and psychological. Frequently a mild organic impairment can make a man more vulnerable to the psychological factors that inhibit erection. The physiological factors include vascular abnormalities that restrict blood flow to the penis, damage to the penile chambers, spinal cord injuries, kidney failure, and many of the drugs that affect arousal. Psychological factors affecting erectile failure are generally the same as those that affect arousal. In addition, *performance anxiety* and the *spectator role* are psychological phenomena believed to contribute to erectile failure.

Premature ejaculation is generally attributable to psychological factors and is typical of young, inexperienced men. Inhibited ejaculation may be caused by a low testosterone level, by drugs that inhibit sympathetic arousal, by many of the drugs that are associated with hypoactive sex arousal, and perhaps by psychological factors similar to those that cause erectile failure.

Female arousal and orgasm dysfunctions were traditionally believed to result from our culture's double standard, which until recently demanded that women suppress their sexuality; but this view has received little research support. Psychological causes apparently include those that lead to hypoactive sexual desire. A woman's sexual responsiveness has been linked to childhood memories of a positive relationship with her mother; issues related to her current partner, such as attraction and emotional commitment; and the use of sexual fantasies.

Vaginismus is considered to be a conditioned fear response developed through negative sexual experiences or because of gynecological diseases that have caused pain during sex. Dyspareunia, on the other hand, usually has a physical cause, such as damage caused by childbirth, undiagnosed vaginal infections, pelvic diseases, and allergies to chemicals introduced into the vagina.

■ **IN THE 1970s** the work of William H. Masters and Virginia E. Johnson led to the development of *sex therapy.* The major components of this therapeutic approach are assessment and conceptualization; accurate information; change of problematic attitudes, cognitions, and beliefs; the elimination of performance anxiety and the spectator role; improvements in communication and sexual technique; and a change in destructive lifestyles and marital interactions.

Treatments for hypoactive sexual desire and sexual aversion disorders involve four elements: affectual awareness, insight, cognitive and emotional changes, and behavioral interventions. This approach has met with a fair degree of success. Premature ejaculation is treated with almost a 100 percent success rate by direct behavioral retraining procedures. Inhibited male orgasm is treated by reducing performance anxiety and ensuring adequate stimulation. Treatment for erectile failure also consists of reducing performance anxiety and increasing stimulation. In addition, if the cause of erectile dysfunction is physiological, surgical implantation of a *penile prosthesis* may be undertaken. A nonsurgical alternative is the use of a *vacuum erection device.*

Treatments for female arousal and orgasm dysfunction include self-exploration, body awareness, and directed masturbation training. Vaginismus is treated by having patients practice contracting and relaxing the pubococcygeal muscles while inserting progressively larger dilators, in order to acquire voluntary control.

■ PARAPHILIAS are characterized by intense sexual urges, sexually arousing fantasies, of related behaviors involving either nonhuman objects, children or nonconsenting adults, or experiences of suffering or humiliation. These patterns are generally classified as disorders if they are repeatedly acted on or if the person feels shame, guilt, or distress over them. Paraphilias are found primarily in men. Relatively little is known about what causes the disorders or how to treat them effectively.

Fetishism is characterized by recurrent, intense sexual urges, sexually arousing fantasies, or behaviors that involve the use of a nonliving object. *Transvestic fetishism,* or *transvestism,* is the recurrent need or desire to dress in clothes of the opposite sex in order to achieve sexual arousal. *Pedophilia* involves sexual gratification derived from watching, touching, or engaging in sexual acts with prepubescent children. *Exhibitionism* consists of recurrent intense urges to act out sexually arousing fantasies of exposing one's genitals to another person.

Voyeurism involves recurrent intense desires to secretly observe people undressing or during intercourse. *Frotteurism* is a recurrent and intense desire to touch and rub one's genitals against a nonconsenting adult. *Sexual masochism* is a pattern in which people repeatedly have intense sexual urges and fantasies of being humiliated, beaten, bound, or otherwise made to suffer. *Sexual sadism* is a pattern in which people are intensely sexually aroused by the act or thought of inflicting physical or psychological suffering on others. The definitions of paraphilias are closely tied to the norms of the particular society in which they occur, and some people argue that paraphiliac behaviors are not disorders at all unless people are hurt by them.

■ FINALLY, people who manifest a *gender identity disorder,* or *transsexualism,* persistently feel that they have been assigned to the wrong sex and are preoccupied with acquiring the physical characteristics of the other sex. Hormone treatments and the more extreme sex-change operations have been used in many cases of this disorder, but the appropriateness of surgery as a form of "treatment" for this poorly understood disorder has been hotly debated. Males outnumber females with this disorder by approximately 3 to 1.

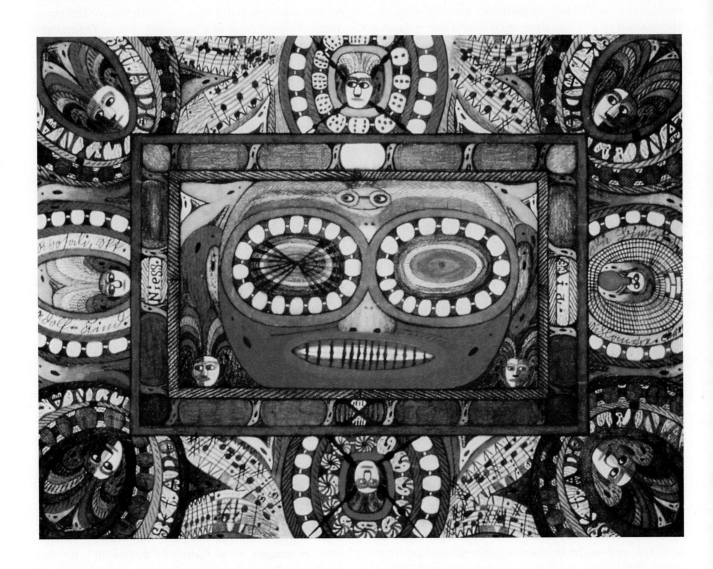

Topic Overview

CHAPTER 15

SCHIZOPHRENIA

PSYCHOSIS IS A CONDITION characterized by loss of contact with reality. Often sufferers' capacity to perceive, process, and respond to environmental stimuli becomes so impaired and distorted that they may be unable to achieve even marginal adaptive functioning. Individuals in a state of psychosis may have hallucinations (false sensory perceptions) or delusions (false beliefs) or may withdraw into a private world that is almost totally unaffected by the persons and events around them.

PSYCHOSIS MAY RESULT from various factors. As we noted in Chapter 13, taking LSD, abusing amphetamines or cocaine, or ingesting some other toxic substances may produce psychosis. Similarly, aging, brain injuries, or brain diseases may cause psychotic disorders. Most commonly, psychosis appears in the form of *schizophrenia,* a disorder in which personal, social, and occupational functioning that had previously been adaptive deteriorates into a welter of distorted perceptions, disturbed thought processes, deviant emotional states, and motor abnormalities.

What . . . does schizophrenia mean to me? It means fatigue and confusion, it means trying to separate every experience into the real and the unreal and sometimes not being aware of where the edges overlap. It means trying to think straight when there is a maze of experiences getting in the way, and when thoughts are continually being sucked out of your head so that you become embarrassed to speak at meetings. It means feeling sometimes that you are inside your head and visualizing yourself walking over your brain, or watching another girl wearing your clothes and carrying out actions as you think them. It means knowing that you are continually "watched," that you can never succeed in life because the laws are all against you and knowing that your ultimate destruction is never far away.

(Rollin, 1980, p. 162)

Approximately one of every 100 people on earth meets the DSM-IV criteria for schizophrenia (APA, 1994; Regier et al., 1993). More than two million people currently living in the United States have been or will be diagnosed as suffering from schizophrenia (Keith, Regier, & Rae, 1991). Some 200,000 to 400,000 new cases are reported each year (Regier et al., 1993; Kramer, 1983). The President's Commission on Mental Health (1978) brought such figures to life with the observation "There are as many schizophrenics in America as there are people in Oregon, Mississippi and Kansas, or in Wyoming, Vermont, Delaware and Hawaii combined." The financial cost of the disorder is enormous—estimated at tens of billions of dollars annually, including the costs of hospitalization, lost wages, and disability benefits. The catastrophic impact of this disorder on families represents an even greater emotional cost. Moreover, schizophrenia is associated with increased risk for suicide and for physical—often mortal—illness (Bruce et al., 1994; McGlashan, 1988). As we discussed in Chapter 10, it is estimated that up to 15 percent of schizophrenic persons commit suicide (Roy, 1992).

Although it appears in all socioeconomic groups, schizophrenia is more likely to be found in people of the lower socioeconomic classes (see Figure 15–1). Some researchers believe that the stress of poverty is itself a cause of schizophrenia (Dohrenwend et al., 1992). Although this may indeed be part of the reason for the statistical link between schizophrenia and membership in the lower socioeconomic classes, lately other factors have been cited as well. Schizophrenia may actually cause a person to migrate from a higher to a lower socioeconomic class (Munk & Mortensen, 1992). Victims of schizophrenia may be less able to maintain previously high levels of functioning after they become impaired. Similarly, those born into lower socioeconomic classes may find an upward economic climb interrupted by the onset of this disorder.

Equal numbers of men and women receive a diagnosis of schizophrenia, although the age of onset is typically earlier in men (APA, 1994; Hafner, 1992; Shtasel et al., 1992). Almost 3 percent of all divorced or separated persons suffer from this disorder over the course of their lives, compared to 1 percent of married people and 2 percent of people who remain single (Keith et al., 1991). As with socioeconomic class, however, it is not clear whether divorce increases one's risk of developing schizophrenia, or schizophrenia increases marital discord, or both.

Approximately 2.1 percent of African Americans suffer from this disorder over the course of their lives,

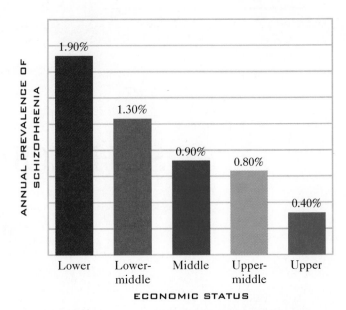

FIGURE 15–1 *According to recent surveys, poor people in the United States are much more likely than wealthy people to experience schizophrenia. This relationship may indicate that the stresses of poverty help cause schizophrenia, that the impairment of schizophrenia leads to poverty, or both. (Adapted from Keith et al., 1991.)*

compared to 1.4 percent of white Americans (Keith et al., 1991). This racial difference may be linked to the fact that African Americans are more likely to be poor and to experience marital separation. When the factors of socioeconomic class and marital status are controlled for, the prevalence rates of schizophrenia are equal for the two races.

Schizophrenia has been with us throughout history; it is the condition commonly described by the word "madness" (Cutting, 1985). The Bible speaks of King Saul's mad rages and terrors and of David's efforts to feign madness in order to escape his enemies. Hippocrates considered this syndrome to be a form of mental deterioration caused by an imbalance of the body's humors, and the Roman physician Galen (A.D. 130–200), who referred to it as "dementia," blamed it on a reduction in the number and size of a person's normal "animal spirits," and on coldness and excess humidity in the brain.

In 1865 a Belgian psychiatrist named Benedict Morel (1809–1873) used the label *démence précoce* ("precocious dementia") to describe the condition of a 14-year-old-boy who showed progressive apathy, mutism, withdrawal, and emotional instability. Although he had once been a brilliant student, the boy had lost interest in academics and seemed to forget everything he had known. *Démence* was meant to describe the serious intellectual and mental deterioration and *précoce* to convey the early onset of the deterioration. In 1899 Emil Kraepelin used the Latin form of Morel's label, *dementia praecox*, to describe such disorders.

In 1911 the Swiss psychiatrist Eugen Bleuler (1857–1939) gave the name "schizophrenia" to disorders of this kind, combining Greek words that mean "split mind." Bleuler used the term to imply (1) a fragmentation of thought processes, (2) a split between thoughts and emotions, and (3) a withdrawal from reality. It was not meant to convey a split into two or more personalities, although many people continue to misinterpret it in this way (see Chapter 18). Bleuler improved on Morel's descriptions by correctly observing that intellectual deterioration was not an inevitable feature of schizophrenia, nor was progressive mental deterioration the rule. He noted, on the contrary, that many individuals eventually stabilized and a few even improved.

Today theorists and researchers continue to try to understand the nature and causes of schizophrenia. The general public shows great interest in the disorder, flocking to movies (including the remarkably popular horror movies) and plays whose plots center on schizophrenia (see Box 15–1). Yet all too many schizophrenic people are virtually neglected in our country, and their needs are almost entirely ignored. Although practicable and effective therapies have been developed for the disorder, most of these people live without adequate treatment and without even partially fulfilling their potential as human beings.

THE CLINICAL PICTURE OF SCHIZOPHRENIA

Among people who are diagnosed as schizophrenic, there is considerable variation in symptoms, in the apparent cause and course of the disorder, and in responsiveness to treatment (APA, 1994). In fact, there is a growing belief among clinicians that schizophrenia is actually a group of many distinct disorders that have some common features (Carpenter, Heinrichs, & Wagman, 1988). DSM-IV, however, classifies schizophrenia as a single disorder with numerous faces. To illustrate the variety of forms schizophrenia may take, let us consider three people who were diagnosed as suffering from it. The cases are taken from the files of Silvano Arieti (1974), a prominent theorist on schizophrenia.

Ann, 26 years old

Ann graduated from high school and from a school for commercial art. She was a very persistent student, very punctual in her study habits, and even in her early childhood showed a talent for drawing and painting. Following her studies in commercial art she obtained several jobs which were not commensurate with her ability. She even did factory work.

. . . At the age of 18 she met a man ten years her senior with whom she became infatuated. They went out on frequent dates, but the man was inducted into the army. The patient then began going out with Henry, the younger brother of the inducted man. . . .

They became engaged shortly thereafter and went out together frequently until their marriage. . . . Married life was considered a boring routine by both Ann and Henry. There was very little conversation between them. . . .

Ann's disappointment in Henry increased. They had nothing in common; she was artistically inclined, whereas he had only an ordinary, conventional outlook toward life. It was at this time that she started to go dancing and then met Charles. Her interest in him increased, but she knew that she was married and that a divorce was not compatible with the precepts of the Catholic church. Her conflict grew and put her in a state of great agitation. . . .

. . . One evening she came home from dancing and told her mother that she was going to give up her husband Henry, marry Charles, go to Brazil with him, and have twenty babies. She was talking very fast and saying many things, several of which were incomprehensible. At the same time she also told her mother that she was seeing the Virgin Mary in visions. She then went to her mother-in-law and told her to take back her son Henry, because he was too immature. The following day Ann went to work and tried to get the entire office down on their knees with her to recite the rosary. A few days later, her mother took her to a priest, whom she "told off" in no uncertain terms. She finally spit at him. A psychiatrist was consulted, and he recommended hospitalization.

. . . When the patient was first seen in the ward by the examiner, she was dashing around the room, singing and laughing. She was markedly agitated; frequently she would cry one minute and then laugh in a silly, impulsive manner, or suddenly slump over and become mute. Her speech would be incoherent at one time because she mumbled and at another time she would shriek very loudly. She would be irrelevant, or circumstantial, and she frequently rambled, her thoughts being completely unrelated to one another. Her affect would vary from extreme lability to complete flatness. She was hallucinating in auditory and visual spheres quite vividly. She was saying:

I was judged insane and others felt that this was the place for me. I am too weak. You look to me like Uncle Joe, and he is so far away. He knew how much I loved him. We could always get along. I never meant to be disobedient to you. The darn son of a bitch, you couldn't

BOX 15-1

HOWLING FOR ATTENTION

It's when I was bitten by a rabid dog. . . . When I'm emotionally upset, I feel as if I am turning into something else: my fingers go numb, as if I had pins and needles right in the middle of my hand; I can no longer control myself. . . . I get the feeling I'm becoming a wolf. I look at myself in the mirror and I witness my transformation. It's no longer my face; it changes completely. I stare, my pupils dilate, and I feel as if hairs are growing all over my body, as if my teeth are getting longer. . . . I feel as if my skin is no longer mine.

(Benezech, DeWitte, & Bourgeois, 1989)

In the film An American Werewolf in London, *a possessed man watches in terror as his hand stretches into the forepaw of a wolf.*

Lycanthropy, the delusion of being an animal, is a rare psychological syndrome. The word "lycanthropy" comes from the Greek *lykos,* wolf, and *anthropos,* man. Accounts have been found all over the world of people who take on the characteristics and behavior of wolves or other animals. Belief in these tales has persisted for centuries, though the perceptions about causation have changed. In the Middle Ages, lycanthropy was attributed to demonic possession (Lehmann, 1985). In the sixteenth and seventeenth centuries, the accepted causes were physical illness and satanic influence. In some societies where lycanthropy was frequently reported, it occurred after special ointments, probably potent hallucinogenic drugs, were applied, often for religious purposes (Lévi-Strauss, 1977). In other societies, cases of lycanthropy were closely linked to mental disorders, including schizophrenia, severe mood disorders, and certain forms of brain damage.

Mention of lycanthropy continues to evoke an image of a werewolf baring

---

smile at me. You are the Pope and I must be obedient to the Pope. He is the only one I must be obedient to. You didn't flinch when I said "son of a bitch." You are trying to help me. All the others are different. That I can't fake in your presence, my Lord. You will understand me as my friends didn't. Russia is the only Catholic country. Russia is to the rest of the world what God is to the Pope.

Later the patient became more agitated and required strong sedation. Her illness seemed to proceed toward more advanced disintegration. She laughed in an inappropriate manner, and her whole behavior appeared silly. She was restless, confused, and talked to imaginary persons.

(Arieti, 1974, pp. 173–177)

Richard, 23 years old

*I*n high school, Richard was an average student. After graduation from high school, he was drafted into the army, where he felt unhappy. . . . After his discharge, he wanted to enter some kind of musical career, but gave up the idea because it did not offer financial security. He had several jobs, for example, as a delivery boy, elevator man, and hospital helper. He could not keep a job for any length of time because he was very sensitive to criticism and was always afraid that he would not satisfy his bosses.

Richard remembered this period, after his discharge from the army, as one of the worst in his life, even worse than his childhood. Throughout his life he had been very sensitive and had always taken things too much to heart, but after his discharge, when he was supposed to do things on his own and show what he was able to do, his sensitivity increased. He was "eating his heart out" for unimportant reasons; any, even remote, anticipation of disappointment was able to provoke attacks of anxiety in him. He could never be indifferent or detached, but was very much involved in everything. After his discharge from the army his life had become a series of crises.

Approximately two years after his return to civilian life, Richard left his job because he became overwhelmed by these feelings of lack of confidence in himself, and he refused to go look for another one. He stayed home most of the day. His mother would nag him that he was too lazy and

its fangs at a terrified villager on a fog-shrouded Scottish moor, all because the former was bitten by another werewolf in the unbroken chain that passes such a legacy on, but there are now more plausible explanations for this type of behavior. One explanation is that people afflicted with lycanthropy suffer from *porphyria*, an inherited blood disease whose victims sprout extra facial hair and are vulnerable to sunlight. People with porphyria can be treated successfully with blood pigment. Another current explanation associates lycanthropy with a disturbance in the activity of the temporal lobe of the brain. The posterior region of the temporal lobe is close to other areas of the brain that are linked to visual functions and may be the source of visual hallucinations. Abnormal brain activity in the temporal lobe combined with a psychotic thought disorder may account for many of the symptoms of lycanthropy.

One of the most interesting recent instances of lycanthropy happens to differ somewhat from the classical mold. A 26-year-old man had been convinced that he was a cat for more than fifteen years at the time his case was reported. He was a research scientist who had a history of alcohol abuse, major depression, and several other problems. While being treated for these disorders, he revealed to the clinician that as a child he had discovered that he was a cat. He was able to communicate with other cats, he reported, and his true identity was confirmed by the family cat, Tiffany. It should be noted that this man had apparently been neglected, if not outright abused, by his parents. In addition, there was a history of severe mental and emotional disorders in his immediate family.

When the boy made his discovery, he began to hunt with cats and to eat raw meat. He also reported that he had had a series of monogamous sexual relationships with cats. At the age of 17 he refined his view of his feline existence and concluded that in fact he was a tiger. He fell in love with Dolly, a tiger at the zoo. His plans to orchestrate Dolly's escape from the zoo and live with her were dashed when she was sold to an Asian zoo, and he fell into a major depression.

At the time of the clinical interview, the young man looked normal except for his attire—striped clothes, primarily—and his long fingernails. He had a number of friends, and except for his cat delusions, his thought processes were normal.

The clinician's explanation for this extreme and persistent case of lycanthropy was that the patient had "failed to form an adequate self-identification with either parent, due to their own disturbances, and subsequently targeted his favorite cat as an idealized self-object during childhood. This process, perhaps superimposed on a medical or neurological vulnerability, may have produced his remarkably persistent lycanthropic delusion" (Kulick, Pope, & Keck, 1990, p. 136).

Modern cases of lycanthropy make a powerful point about human nature: ideas and beliefs play major roles in shaping behavior. Though our explanations for abnormal behavior evolve as we become more sophisticated about the workings of the human mind, age-old myths are difficult to put to rest.

---

unwilling to do anything. He became slower and slower in dressing and undressing and taking care of himself. When he went out of the house, he felt compelled "to give interpretations" to everything he looked at. He did not know what to do outside the house, where to go, where to turn. If he saw a red light at a crossing, he would interpret it as a message that he should not go in that direction. If he saw an arrow, he would follow the arrow interpreting it as a sign sent by God that he should go in that direction. Feeling lost and horrified, he would go home and stay there, afraid to go out because going out meant making decisions or choices that he felt unable to make. He reached the point where he stayed home most of the time. But even at home, he was tortured by his symptoms. He could not act; any motion that he felt like making seemed to him an insurmountable obstacle, because he did not know whether he should make it or not. He was increasingly afraid of doing the wrong thing. Such fears prevented him from dressing, undressing, eating, and so forth. He felt paralyzed and lay motionless in bed. He gradually became worse, was completely motionless, and had to be hospitalized.
. . . Even in the hospital, he had to interpret everything that occurred. If a doctor asked him a question, he had

a sudden impulse to answer, but then feared that by answering he would do the wrong thing. He tried desperately to find signs that would indicate to him whether he should answer or not. An accidental noise, the arrival of another person, or the number of words the questions consisted of were indications of whether he should reply or not.

Being undecided, he felt blocked, and often would remain mute and motionless, like a statue, even for days. He had always been more or less afraid of being with people because he did not feel strong enough to take their suggestions or to refuse them; in the hospital such fear increased.
(Arieti, 1974, pp. 153–155)

Laura, 40 years old

Laura's desire was to become independent and leave home [in Austria] as soon as possible. Throughout her childhood she attended dancing schools, and she became a professional dancer at the age of 20. . . . She was very successful and was booked for vaudeville theaters in many European countries, but she performed mostly in Germany. . . .

It was during one of her tours in Germany that Laura met her husband. He was a French tourist, a businessman, who became interested in her acting. He would often go to Germany from France just to see her. He overwhelmed her with his consideration and interest, and Laura felt that she liked his attention. She had some qualms about leaving her theatrical career and marrying him, but finally she decided to do so. They were married and went to live in a small provincial town in France where the husband's business was. Laura felt like a stranger immediately; she was in an environment very different from her own and was not accepted by his family. There were realistic grounds for her feelings. They considered her a foreigner and could not forgive her for having been a dancer, and not a "regular girl." She spent a year in that town and was very unhappy. She felt that when there were arguments or controversies, her husband always took the side of his family and never took her part.

Finally . . . Laura and her husband decided to immigrate to the United States, along with her husband's sister. Laura did not get along well with her sister-in-law and again felt that her husband showed favoritism toward his sister.

The years spent in America had not been easy ones. Laura and her husband had not been happy together. They had different points of view about many things, and the gap caused by their different backgrounds was never closed. Laura's husband became more and more intolerant of her attitude and started to neglect her. Nothing would irritate her more than his lavish attentions to his sister.

They had no children, and Laura . . . showed interest in pets. She had a dog to whom she was very devoted. The dog became sick and partially paralyzed, and veterinarians felt that there was no hope of recovery. The dog required difficult care, and her husband, who knew how she felt about the animal, tolerated the situation for several weeks. But finally he broached the problem to his wife, asking her "Should the dog be destroyed or not?" From that time on Laura became restless, agitated, and depressed. . . .

. . . Later Laura started to complain about the neighbors. A woman who lived on the floor beneath them was knocking on the wall to irritate her. According to the husband, this woman had really knocked on the wall a few times; he had heard the noises. However, Laura became more and more concerned about it. She would wake up in the middle of the night under the impression that she was hearing noises from the apartment downstairs. She would become upset and angry at the neighbors. Once she was awake, she could not sleep for the rest of the night. The husband would vainly try to calm her. Later she became more disturbed. She started to feel that the neighbors were now recording everything she said; maybe they had hidden wires in the apartment. She started to feel "funny" sensations. There were many strange things happening, which she did not know how to explain; people were looking at her in a funny way in the street; in the butcher shop, the butcher had purposely served her last, although she was in the middle of the line. During the next few days she felt that people were planning to harm either her or her husband. In the neighborhood she saw a German woman whom she had not seen for several years. Now the woman had suddenly reappeared, probably to testify that the patient and her husband were involved in some sort of crime.

Laura was distressed and agitated. She felt unjustly accused, because she had committed no crime. Maybe these people were really not after her, but after her husband. In the evening when she looked at television, it became obvious to her that the programs referred to her life. Often the people on the programs were just repeating what she had thought. They were stealing her ideas. She wanted to go to the police and report them.

(Arieti, 1974, pp. 165–168)

Symptoms of Schizophrenia

Ann, Richard, and Laura each regressed from a normal level of functioning to become significantly ineffective in dealing with the world. Ann, a promising art student, became unhappy and discontented, and finally totally disoriented; Richard, a sensitive and talented young man, became so indecisive that he literally stopped moving; and Laura, once so independent and competent, became restless and agitated and eventually consumed by bizarre suspicions. Among them, these three individuals demonstrate the range of symptoms associated with schizophrenia. Although several such disturbances are usually present in any given case of schizophrenia, no single symptom is present in every case.

In recent years, clinicians have grouped symptoms of schizophrenia into three categories—*positive symptoms* (such as delusions and hallucinations), so named because they seem to represent "pathological excess," bizarre additions to a normal repertoire of behaviors; *negative symptoms* (such as flat emotions or lack of volition), symptoms that seem to reflect "pathological deficits," characteristics that are lacking; and *psychomotor symptoms*. Men with schizophrenia are more likely to display negative symptoms than women, but both sexes display equal numbers of positive symptoms (Shtasel et al., 1992).

POSITIVE SYMPTOMS Positive symptoms include delusions, disorganized thinking and speech, heightened perceptions and hallucinations, and inappropriate affect.

DELUSIONS Many schizophrenic people develop disturbances in their *thought content*—that is, in

No it's not "the King." But surveys indicate that as many as one out of every 8 Americans believes that Elvis Presley is still alive, leading to numerous Elvis sightings at 7-Eleven stores around the country and an army of Elvis impersonators. Clinicians stop short of calling such beliefs delusions, however, noting that the Elvis loyalists do not hold onto their beliefs with a high degree of conviction. Most can be persuaded that Elvis has indeed "left the building."

their ideas and beliefs. They have ***delusions,*** ideas that they believe fervently but that have no basis in fact and are often absurd. These beliefs may be elaborate and internally consistent or fragmented and capricious; they may appear to the believer as either enlightening or confusing. Some people with schizophrenia hold a single delusion that dominates their life and behavior, while others have many delusions. Delusions of persecution are the most common in schizophrenia (APA, 1994); others include delusions of reference, grandiosity, and control.

People who have ***delusions of persecution*** believe that they are being plotted or discriminated against, spied on, slandered, threatened, attacked, or deliberately victimized. Laura believed that her neighbors

were trying to irritate her and that other people were trying to harm her and her husband. When she saw an old acquaintance from Germany, she thought the woman had come to testify against her.

People who have ***delusions of reference*** attach special and personal significance to the actions of others, or to various objects or events. A man may believe, for example, that the words spoken in a movie are referring to him, that a radio announcer is secretly mocking him, or that a sudden weather change is a sign to change jobs. Laura believed that strangers were looking at her in a funny way, and Richard interpreted arrows on street signs as indicators of the direction he should take.

People with ***delusions of grandeur*** believe themselves to be great inventors, historical figures, religious saviors, or other specially empowered persons. One patient recalled, "I felt that I had power to determine the weather, which responded to my inner moods, and even to control the movement of the sun in relation to other astronomical bodies."

Delusions of control are beliefs that one's impulses, feelings, thoughts, and actions are being controlled by other people. A woman may believe that external forces are regulating her need to eat, the speed at which she drives, and her behavior toward people. Often people with such delusions believe that they are somehow "wired" to the outside forces or receiving radio signals from them. In the following letter about his hospital experience, a man describes his desperate concerns about being controlled:

The inmates, here, hate me extremely because I am sane. . . . They talk to me telepathically, continuously and daily almost without cessation, day and night. . . . By the power of their imagination and daily and continuously, they create extreme pain in my head, brain, eyes, heart, stomach and in every part of my body. Also by their imagination and daily and continuously, they lift my heart and stomach and they pull my heart, and they stop it, move it, twist it and shake it and pull its muscles and tissues. . . . By telepathy and imagination, they force me to say orally whatever they desire, whenever they desire and as long as they desire. I never said a word of my own. I never created a thought or image of my own.

(Arieti, 1974, pp. 404–405)

DISORGANIZED THINKING AND SPEECH
People with schizophrenia often present very disorganized speech and patterns of thinking. Many display ***positive formal thought disorders,*** peculiar excesses of verbal expression, such as loose associations, neologisms, perseveration, and clang that can cause the sufferer great confusion and make communication with others extremely difficult.

People who display *loose associations,* or *derailment,* the most common formal thought disorder, rapidly shift from one topic to another, making inconsequential and incoherent statements and apparently believing them to make sense. For example, a schizophrenic man, asked about his itchy arms, responded:

> The problem is insects. . . . My brother used to collect insects. . . . He's now a man 5 foot 10 inches. . . . You know, 10 is my favorite number. . . . I also like to dance, draw, and watch television.

In this man's speech, associations between one block of words and the next are oblique: a relatively unimportant word in each sentence becomes the focus of the next.

Some schizophrenic people display a formal thought disorder called *neologisms,* made-up words that have meaning only to the person using them. The following statement illustrates one patient's use of such words:

> I am here from a foreign university . . . and you have to have a "plausity" of all acts of amendment to go through for the children's code . . . and it is no mental disturbance or "putenence" . . . it is an "amorition" law . . . there is nothing to disturb me . . . it is like their "privatilinia". . . and the children have to have this "accentuative" law so they don't go into the "mortite" law of the church.
>
> *(Vetter, 1969, p. 189)*

Schizophrenic individuals may also display formal thought disorders by *perseverating*—that is, repeating their words and statements again and again. They may also use *clang,* or rhyme, as a guide to formulating thoughts and statements. When asked how she was feeling, one schizophrenic person replied, "Well, hell, it's well to tell." Another described the weather as "So hot, you know it runs on a cot."

Positive formal thought disorders are not unique to schizophrenia. Loose associations and perseverations are common in cases of severe mania, for example. Even people who function normally may organize statements loosely or may on occasion use words that others fail to understand, especially when they are fatigued or feeling ill; but the formal thought disorders of schizophrenia are much more severe and pervasive (Holzman, 1986).

It may be that some degree of disorganized speech or thinking appears long before a full pattern of schizophrenic symptoms unfolds (Bilder et al., 1992; Harvey, 1991; Walker & Lewine, 1990). A number of researchers have conducted **high-risk studies** to investigate schizophrenia—studies in which people hypothesized to be at great risk for developing the disorder (such as people whose parents are schizophrenic) are followed throughout their childhood. These studies have indicated that high-risk people who later develop schizophrenia show significantly more disordered thinking at the age of 15 than similar high-risk subjects who do not later develop schizophrenia (Parnas et al., 1989, 1982).

HEIGHTENED PERCEPTIONS AND HALLUCINATIONS   A *heightened sensitivity to sounds and sights* is reported by many people with schizophrenia, and has long been associated with "madness." The deranged protagonist in Edgar Allan Poe's "Tell-Tale Heart" asks, "Have I not told you that what you mistake for madness is but the overacuteness of the senses?" Some schizophrenic people feel that their senses are being *flooded* by all the sights and sounds that surround them, so that it is almost impossible for them to attend to anything important:

> Everything seems to grip my attention although I am not particularly interested in anything. I am speaking to you just now, but I can hear noises going on next door and in the corridor. I find it difficult to shut these out, and it makes it more difficult for me to concentrate on what I am saying to you. Often the silliest little things that are going on seem to interest me. That's not even true; they don't interest me, but I find myself attending to them and wasting a lot of time this way.
>
> *(McGhie and Chapman, 1961)*

Laboratory studies of schizophrenic subjects have repeatedly demonstrated this kind of dysfunction (APA, 1994; Perry & Braff, 1994; Harvey, 1991; Posner et al., 1988). In one study, schizophrenic and nonschizophrenic subjects were instructed to listen for and identify a target syllable on a recording while background speech was also being played on the recording (Harris et al., 1985). As long as the background speech was kept simple, the two groups were equally effective at picking out the target syllable; but when the background speech was made more distracting, the schizophrenic subjects became less able than the others to identify the target syllable. Related studies of high-risk subjects suggest that attention problems of this kind may also develop years before a full schizophrenic pattern unfolds (Cornblatt & Keilp, 1994; Cornblatt & Erlenmeyer-Kimling, 1985).

Hallucinations, perceptions that occur in the absence of external stimuli, are the most severe perceptual disturbance found in cases of schizophrenia. In *auditory* hallucinations, by far the most common kind in schizophrenia (APA, 1994; Mueser, Bellack, & Brady, 1990), people hear sounds and voices that seem to come from outside their heads. The voices may be familiar or unfamiliar, single or multiple, complimentary or critical, and may be heard frequently or only on occasion. Often they talk directly to the hallucinator, perhaps giving commands or warning of dangers. In other cases, they are experienced as being overheard.

> The voices . . . were mostly heard in my head, though I often heard them in the air, or in different parts of the room. Every voice was different, and each beautiful, and generally, speaking or singing in a different tone and measure, and resembling those of relations or friends. There appeared to be many in my head, I should say upwards of fourteen. I divide them, as they styled themselves, or one another, into voices of contrition and voices of joy and honour.
>
> *("Perceval's Narrative" in Bateson, 1974)*

> For about almost seven years—except during sleep—I have never had a single moment in which I did not hear voices. They accompany me to every place and at all times; they continue to sound even when I am in conversation with other people, they persist undeterred even when I concentrate on other things, for instance read a book or a newspaper, play the piano, etc.; only when I am talking aloud to other people or to myself are they of course drowned by the stronger sound of the spoken word and therefore inaudible to me. But the well-known phrases recommence at once, sometimes in the middle of a sentence, which tells me that the conversation had continued during the interval, that is to say that those nervous stimuli or vibrations responsible for the weaker sounds of the voices continue even while I talk aloud.
>
> *(Schreber, 1955, p. 225)*

Researchers have found that schizophrenic subjects who are unskilled at voluntarily imagining sounds are more likely than other schizophrenic people to experience auditory hallucinations (Heilbrun, Blum, & Haas, 1983; Seitz & Molholm, 1947). Studies have also suggested that auditory hallucinations are more likely to occur during times of idleness, inattention, or sensory isolation. One study noted increases in hallucinations when schizophrenic people listened to a bland noise over headphones and wore goggles to restrict visual information (Margo, Hemsley, & Slade, 1981). As a patient once observed, "Isn't it funny, when I'm shoveling snow I don't hear voices" (Strauss et al., 1981).

Hallucinations can also involve the other senses. *Tactile* hallucinations may take the form of tingling, burning, or electrical-shock sensations, or the feeling of insects crawling over one's body or just beneath the skin. *Somatic* hallucinations convey the sensation that something is happening inside the body, such as an organ shifting position or a snake crawling inside one's stomach. *Visual* hallucinations run the gamut from vague perceptions of colors or clouds to distinct visions of people, objects, or scenes that are not there. They are different from the range of normal mental images experienced by adults and children. People with *gustatory* hallucinations regularly find that their food or drink tastes strange, and people with *olfactory* hallucinations smell odors that no one else does, being haunted, for example, by the smell of poison, smoke, or decay.

Hallucinations and delusional ideas often go hand in hand. A woman who hears voices issuing commands, for example, may have the delusion that the commands are being placed in her head by someone else. Similarly, a man with delusions of persecution may hallucinate the smell of poison in his bedroom or the taste of poison in his coffee. Regardless of which comes first, the hallucination and delusion eventually feed into each other.

INAPPROPRIATE AFFECT Many schizophrenic people display *inappropriate affect,* emotions that are unsuited to the situation. They may, for example, smile inappropriately when making a somber statement or on being told terrible news, or become upset in situations that should make them happy. They may also undergo inappropriate shifts in mood. During a tender conversation with his wife, for example, a schizophrenic man suddenly started yelling obscenities at her and complaining about her inadequacies.

In some cases, at least, this symptom may arise in response to the other positive features of schizophrenia. Consider a schizophrenic woman who smiles when told of her husband's serious illness. Although her apparent joy is an inappropriate reaction to bad news, we do not know that she is indeed happy about this news or that she is even hearing or comprehending it. Instead, she may be responding to another of the many thoughts and stimuli flooding her senses, or to a joke she is hearing from an auditory hallucination.

NEGATIVE SYMPTOMS Negative symptoms of schizophrenia include poverty of speech, blunted and flat affect, disturbances in volition, and disturbed relationships with the external world.

POVERTY OF SPEECH People with schizophrenia often display *alogia,* a decreased command and productivity of speech characterized by brief and empty replies. Some of those with alogia apparently have fewer thoughts and may experience the negative formal thought disorder called *blocking,* in which their thoughts disappear from memory, causing their statements to end in silence before they can be completed. One patient describes how this problem feels to him:

> I may be thinking quite clearly and telling someone something and suddenly I get stuck. You have seen me do this and you may think I am just lost for words or that I have gone into a trance, but that is not what happens. What happens is that I suddenly stick on a word or an idea in my head and I just can't move past it. It seems to fill my mind and there's no room for anything else. This might go on for a while and suddenly it's over. Afterwards I get a feeling that I have been thinking very deeply about whatever it was but often I can't remember what it was that has filled my mind so completely.
>
> *(McGhie & Chapman, 1961)*

Other schizophrenic persons may actually say quite a bit but still manage to convey little meaning, reflecting what is termed *poverty of content.* Vaslav Nijinsky, one of the century's great ballet dancers, wrote the following diary entry on February 27, 1919, as his schizophrenia was becoming increasingly apparent:

> I do not wish people to think that I am a great writer or that I am a great artist nor even that I am a great man. I am a simple man who has suffered a lot. I believe I suffered more than Christ. I love life and want to live, to cry but cannot—I feel such a pain in my soul—a pain which frightens me. My soul is ill. My soul, not my mind. The doctors do not understand my illness. I know what I need to get well. My illness is too great to be cured quickly. I am incurable. Everyone who reads these lines will suffer—they will understand my feelings. I know what I need. I am strong, not weak. My body is not ill—it is my soul that is ill. I suffer, I suffer. Everyone will feel and understand. I am a man, not a beast. I love everyone, I have faults, I am a man—not God. I want to be God and therefore I try to improve myself. I want to dance, to draw, to play the piano, to write verses, I want to love everybody. That is the—object of my life.
>
> *(Nijinsky, 1936)*

BLUNTED AND FLAT AFFECT   Many schizophrenic people have a *blunted affect*—they manifest less anger, sadness, joy, or other feelings than most people—and some show almost no emotions at all, a condition known as *flat affect.* The faces of these subjects are typically immobile, their eye contact is poor, and their voices are monotonous. One young schizophrenic man told his father, "I wish I could wake up feeling really bad—it would be better than feeling nothing" (Wechsler, 1972, p. 17).

DISTURBANCES IN VOLITION   As schizophrenic people struggle to function in a grossly distorted world, many undergo changes in volition. They often display *avolition,* or apathy, feeling drained of energy and interest in normal goals and unable to initiate or complete a course of action. This problem is particularly common in people who have had the disorder for many years, as if they have been worn down by it. Similarly, the individuals may display *ambivalence,* a feature so common among the subjects Bleuler studied that he proclaimed it one of the central symptoms of schizophrenia.

Richard, in the case study we discussed earlier, was overwhelmed by his ambivalence and related indecisiveness. He stayed at home because going out required him to make decisions, but even in his house, every motion involved a tortuous choice. Should he move his body or not? Was he following "signs" correctly? Daily activities such as eating, dressing, and undressing eventually became impossible ordeals.

DISTURBED RELATIONSHIPS WITH THE EXTERNAL WORLD   Schizophrenic people often withdraw emotionally and socially from their environment and become totally preoccupied with their own ideas and fantasies (Bellack et al., 1989; Falloon et al., 1984). They may distance themselves from other people and avoid talking to them. Because their ideas are illogical and distorted, this withdrawal helps distance them still further from reality. In fact, one study found that 75 percent of schizophrenic subjects were less knowledgeable about everyday social issues than were people with other psychological disorders (Cutting & Murphy, 1990, 1988).

PSYCHOMOTOR SYMPTOMS   Loss of spontaneity in movement and the development of odd grimaces, gestures, and mannerisms are also symptoms of schizophrenia (APA, 1994). Such movements tend to be repetitive and often seem to be purposeful, like a ritualistic or magical act.

Sometimes the psychomotor symptoms of schizophrenia take extreme forms, collectively called *catatonia.* People in a *catatonic stupor* become totally unaware of and unresponsive to their environment, remaining motionless and silent for long stretches of time. Recall how Richard would lie motionless and mute in bed for days. Some people show *catatonic rigidity,* maintaining a rigid, upright posture for hours and resisting efforts to be moved. Others exhibit *catatonic posturing,* assuming awkward, bizarre positions for long periods of time. They may spend hours holding their arms out at a 90-degree angle or balancing in a squatting position. Some subjects also display

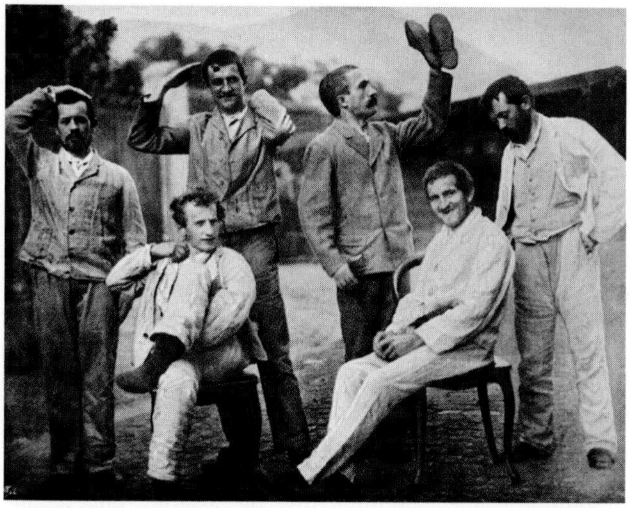

Each of these schizophrenic patients, photographed at the turn of the century, displays features of catatonia, including catatonic posturing, in which they assume bizarre positions for long periods of time.

waxy flexibility, indefinitely maintaining postures into which they have been placed by someone else. If a nurse raises a patient's arm or tilts the patient's head, for example, the individual will remain in that position until moved again.

People who display ***catatonic excitement,*** a different form of catatonia, move excitedly, sometimes with wild waving of arms and legs. When such patients are extremely hyperactive and uncontrolled, they pose a danger to themselves and others. Some clinicians believe that the various catatonic symptoms are but further forms of positive symptomology (catatonic excitement) or negative symptomology (catatonic stupor, rigidity, or posturing).

The Course of Schizophrenia

Schizophrenia usually emerges between the late teens and the mid-30s (APA, 1994). Although the course of this disorder varies widely from person to person (APA, 1994), many patients seem to go through three phases—prodromal, active, and residual.

During the ***prodromal phase*** schizophrenic symptoms are not yet prominent, but the person has begun to deteriorate from previous levels of functioning. The person may withdraw socially; have trouble completing tasks and fulfilling responsibilities; acquire peculiar habits, such as collecting garbage or picking fights; neglect personal hygiene and grooming; or display blunted or inappropriate affect. Difficulties in communication, thought, and perception may emerge in such forms as digressive, vague, elaborated, or metaphorical speech, strange ideas, superstitions, or belief in a "sixth sense."

During the ***active phase,*** schizophrenic symptoms become prominent. In some instances this phase is triggered by stress in the person's life. For Ann, the confused and disoriented woman we read about earlier, the immediate precipitant was falling in love with a man she met dancing. Similarly, reality unraveled for Laura, the Austrian woman, when her dog had to be destroyed. Richard's symptoms, on the other hand, could not be traced to a particular stressful event.

The ***residual phase*** is marked by a return to the prodromal level of functioning. The florid symptoms of the active phase recede, but many individuals remain in a general state of decline. Emotions are typically blunted or flat, and the person is still unable to carry out previous functions and responsibilities.

Each of these phases may last for days or for years. Although as many as a quarter of patients may recover completely, the majority of individuals continue indefinitely to show at least some residual impairment (Strange, 1992). After months or even years in a residual state, many people have a recurrence of the active phase, followed again by another residual phase. Recovery from schizophrenia is more complete and more likely in subjects who functioned quite adequately before the disorder appeared (had good ***premorbid*** functioning), or when the disorder was precipitated by stressful events, was abrupt in onset (short prodromal phase), or developed during middle age (APA, 1994).

Diagnosing Schizophrenia

For years schizophrenia was the "wastebasket category" for diagnosticians, especially in the United States, where the disorder was defined more broadly than elsewhere. A person who acted unpredictably or strangely was often given this label, even if the behavior was transient or did not include the major symptoms of schizophrenia (see Box 15–2). A popular slogan among clinicians in the 1950s was "Even a trace of schizophrenia is schizophrenia" (Lewis & Piotrowski, 1954).

BOX 15-2

A DIAGNOSTIC DILEMMA

Depending on how we hold a close-up photograph of the moon, we can perceive the formations on its surface either as mounds or as craters. Sometimes diagnosing a mental disorder can also seem a matter more of perspective than of clear-cut differences in symptoms. In Chapter 8, we noted that clinicians often have difficulty distinguishing anxiety from depression. Similarly, they are frequently confronted with patients who display symptoms that suggest both *schizophrenia* and a *bipolar disorder*. Differentiating between these disorders is sometimes easier said than done.

Schizophrenic people often exhibit severe mood changes, and patients suffering from a bipolar disorder may have distorted perceptions and bizarre cognitive experiences. Yet if clinicians are fully to understand the nature and possible course of a client's problems and choose an appropriate treatment (at the earliest and most treatable stage), they must decide on one diagnosis. Schizophrenia, for example, will respond well to antipsychotic drugs, while a bipolar disorder will respond

to lithium. There is growing evidence that clinicians frequently make mistakes when they diagnose these two disorders. Apparently many persons hospitalized for schizophrenia are actually experiencing a bipolar disorder, and vice versa (Carlson et al., 1994; Lipton & Simon, 1985).

What are clinicians to do in the face of such confusion? One solution is not to choose between schizophrenia and bipolar disorders at all when a clear choice cannot be made. DSM-IV lists *schizoaffective disorder* as a possible diagnosis when people exhibit both schizophrenic symptoms and signs of a mood disorder. This category is very controversial, however. Many clinicians argue that there is no such disorder, and that the name should really be read as "I don't know."

Yet another way to distinguish schizophrenia from a bipolar disorder might be to observe how the patient responds to treatment. If lithium works, the problem is mania. If antipsychotic medication works, it is schizophrenia. Haphazard as this procedure may sound, some clinicians believe it to be the most efficient way

to arrive at a correct diagnosis. They suggest that it is also a powerful means to learn to differentiate between disorders that appear not in black and white but in shades of gray. It is important to keep in mind, however, that diagnosis by treatment is always a risky venture. Headaches caused by a brain tumor may be alleviated temporarily by aspirin, but people whose headaches respond to aspirin are not necessarily suffering from a brain tumor.

Today there is no totally satisfactory solution to the diagnostic dilemma. The problem exists because our current state of knowledge about these mental disorders is limited, and the situation will improve only as our knowledge of psychopathology grows. In the meantime, perhaps the most useful approach to the problem is for clinicians to pay closer attention to the diagnostic standards of DSM-IV. Studies suggest that diagnoses of schizophrenia and bipolar disorder become at least more accurate when the established criteria are followed with meticulous care (Pulver et al., 1988).

To avoid overuse of this diagnostic category, the writers of recent DSMs have carefully specified the diagnostic criteria for schizophrenia, as well as for other psychotic disorders. DSM-IV calls for a diagnosis of schizophrenia when:

1. The person has shown continuous signs of schizophrenia for six months or more. For at least one month of this pattern, the person has displayed an active phase of schizophrenia that includes two or more major symptoms of the disorder.
2. The person has deteriorated from a previous level of functioning in such areas as work, social relations, and self-care.
3. A depressive or manic episode, if present, occurred before or after the psychotic symptoms,

or was brief in comparison with the duration of psychotic symptoms. This criterion enables clinicians to differentiate schizophrenia from a mood disorder.
4. The symptoms are not due to substance use or a medical condition that could produce similar symptoms, such as cerebral tumors, brain traumas, multiple sclerosis, or vitamin B_{12} deficiency.

DSM-IV'S CATEGORIES OF SCHIZOPHRENIA As we have seen, schizophrenia is a heterogeneous disorder. Some people with schizophrenia are troubled by delusions and hallucinations but remain coherent in their conversations. Others display very confused thought processes but do not seem to be having systematized delusions. Kraepelin, writing in

1896, distinguished three patterns of schizophrenia—hebephrenic, catatonic, and paranoid schizophrenic. The writers of DSM-IV continue to find his categories descriptive of patients' behavior, and have labeled the various types of schizophrenia disorganized (hebephrenic), catatonic, paranoid, undifferentiated, and residual.

DISORGANIZED TYPE The central symptoms of *disorganized schizophrenia* are confusion, incoherence, and flat or inappropriate affect. Fragmentary delusions or hallucinations may be present, but the disorganization of thought is so extreme that broad and systematized ideas and perceptions do not develop. Formal thought disturbances and perceptual problems make for difficult communication, which leads in turn to extreme social withdrawal. Grimaces, odd mannerisms, and flat and inappropriate affect are common in this type of schizophrenia. "Silliness" is also a common feature; some patients giggle constantly without apparent reason. This is why the pattern was first called "hebephrenic," after Hebe, the Greek goddess of youth, who according to Greek mythology often acted like a clown to make the other gods laugh. Not surprisingly, people with disorganized schizophrenia usually function very poorly. They are unable to take adequate care of themselves, to maintain social relationships, or to hold a job.

CATATONIC TYPE The central feature of *catatonic schizophrenia* is a psychomotor disturbance of some sort. Some of the people in this category spend their time in a catatonic stupor, mute and unresponsive; others are seized with catatonic excitement, waving their arms and acting in an uncontrolled manner; in still other cases, the extremes of stupor and excitement alternate. Richard, the unemployed young man who became mute and statuelike, would receive a diagnosis of schizophrenia, catatonic type.

PARANOID TYPE The most prominent symptom of *paranoid schizophrenia* is an organized system of delusions and auditory hallucinations that often guide the person's life. Laura would receive this diagnosis. She believed that her neighbors, a past acquaintance, and people on the street were out to get her (delusions of persecution). People on television programs were supposedly stealing her ideas (delusions of reference). And she heard noises from the apartment downstairs (auditory hallucinations) and experienced "funny sensations" that further supported her beliefs. Increasingly her delusions and hallucinations took center stage.

Anxiety or anger may accompany the delusional thoughts and hallucinatory perceptions in this type of schizophrenia, especially when the thoughts and perceptions are questioned or denied by others. In contrast, some people, particularly those whose paranoia is marked by delusions of grandeur, remain cool and aloof (APA, 1994). Confident and impressed by their special knowledge, they find other people's "naiveté" laughable.

UNDIFFERENTIATED TYPE Many people who are diagnosed as schizophrenic do not fall neatly into one category; in these cases, the schizophrenic disorder is classified as *undifferentiated type*. Over the years, this vague diagnosis has been particularly abused, and a range of schizophrenic and nonschizophrenic patterns have been incorrectly assigned to it. Although such misassignments are less common today because of the detailed clinical criteria now used in the DSM, some misuse of the category continues.

RESIDUAL TYPE When the florid symptoms of schizophrenia lessen in intensity and number yet remain with the patient in a residual form, the diagnosis is usually changed to *residual type* of schizophrenia. As we noted earlier, people with this type of schizophrenia may continue to display blunted or inappropriate emotional reactions, social withdrawal, eccentric behavior, and some illogical thinking.

OTHER CATEGORIZATIONS OF SCHIZOPHRENIA Although DSM-IV favors the distinctions described above, clinicians have also used other schemas to subtype schizophrenia over the years. In recent years a distinction between so-called Type I and Type II schizophrenia has gained prominence (Crow, 1985, 1982, 1980). The label *Type I schizophrenia* is applied to cases dominated by positive symptoms, such as delusions, hallucinations, and positive formal thought disorders (Ragin et al., 1989; Andreasen et al., 1985; Crow, 1985, 1982, 1980). Cases of *Type II schizophrenia* are those characterized by negative symptoms, such as flat affect, poverty of speech, and loss of volition (see Table 15–1).

The distinction between Type I and Type II schizophrenia has been gaining favor among clinicians because researchers have found it to be more useful than other kinds of distinctions in predicting the course and prognosis of the disorder. As we shall see shortly, Type I patients generally have a better premorbid adjustment, greater likelihood of improvement, and better responsiveness to antipsychotic drugs than do Type II patients (Cuesta et al., 1994; Fenton & McGlashan, 1994; Leff, 1992). Moreover, the positive symptoms of Type I schizophrenia seem to be closely linked to biochemical abnormalities in the brain, while the negative symptoms of Type II schizophrenia have been tied to structural abnormalities in the brain (Ananth et al., 1991; Weinberger & Kleinman, 1986).

TABLE 15-1

	TYPE I	TYPE II

Symptoms	Positive symptoms:
	  delusions
	  hallucinations
	  positive formal thought disorders
	  inappropriate affect
		Negative symptoms:
		  avolition
		  social withdrawal
		  alogia
		  blunted and flat affect

Premorbid adjustment	Relatively good	Relatively poor
Responsiveness to traditional antipsychotic drugs	Good	Poor
Outcome of disorder	Fair	Poor
Biological features	Abnormal neurotransmitter activity	Abnormal brain structures

TYPE I VS. TYPE II SCHIZOPHRENIA

Source: Adapted from Crow, 1985, 1982, 1980.

■ VIEWS ON ■ SCHIZOPHRENIA

As with many other kinds of psychological disorders, sociocultural, biological, and psychological factors may each contribute to the development of schizophrenia. In the sociocultural realm, the very label "schizophrenia" has been found to create societal expectations and reactions that may exacerbate schizophrenic behavior. In the biological realm, biochemical and structural abnormalities appear to increase the likelihood that the disorder will develop. And in the psychological realm, schizophrenia has been associated with intrapsychic, social environmental, and family problems. In fact, many theorists hold that an interaction of factors contributes to schizophrenia—for example, that people with a biological predisposition to develop the disorder may do so in response to certain societal pressures and expectations and in the face of key psychological stressors (Yank et al., 1993; Cutting, 1985).

THE SOCIOCULTURAL VIEW

In the following passage, a schizophrenic man discusses the sociocultural factors that he believes helped cause his disorder.

Like any worthwhile endeavor, becoming a schizophrenic requires a long period of rigorous training. My training for this unique calling began in earnest when I was six years old. At that time my somewhat befuddled mother took me to the University of Washington to be examined by psychiatrists in order to find out what was wrong with me. These psychiatrists told my mother: "We don't know exactly what is wrong with your son, but whatever it is, it is very serious. We recommend that you have him committed immediately or else he will be completely psychotic within less than a year." My mother did not have me committed since she realized that such a course of action would be extremely damaging to me. But after that ominous prophecy my parents began to view and treat me as if I were either insane or at least in the process of becoming that way. Once, when my mother caught me playing with some vile muck I had mixed up—I was seven at the time—she gravely told me, "they have people put away in mental institutions for doing things like that." Fear was written all over my mother's face as she told me this. . . . The slightest odd behavior on my part was enough to send my parents into paroxysms of apprehension. My parents' apprehensions in turn made me fear that I was going insane. . . . My fate had been sealed not by my genes, but by the attitudes, beliefs, and expectations of my parents. . . . I find it extremely difficult to condemn my parents for behaving as if I were going insane when the psychiatric authorities told them that this was an absolute certainty.

(Modrow, 1992, pp. 1–2)

Sociocultural theorists believe that many features of schizophrenia are caused by the diagnosis itself (Modrow, 1992; Szasz, 1987, 1963; Murphy, 1968; Scheff, 1966). They propose that the label "schizophrenia" is assigned by society to people who deviate from certain behavioral norms. Justified or not, once the label is assigned, it becomes a self-fulfilling prophecy that promotes the development of many schizophrenic symptoms. Like the man quoted above, people who are called schizophrenic are viewed and reacted to as "crazy" and expected and encouraged to display a schizophrenic style of behavior. Increasingly, they accept their assigned role and learn to play it convincingly.

At one level, this theory constitutes a general warning about the dangers of diagnostic labeling. As such, it has appeal for many clinicians, a number of whom have observed for themselves that diagnoses are often made on the basis of inadequate data, stick once they are made, influence the way subsequent behavior is perceived, and lead to other behaviors implied by the diagnosis.

Perhaps the most influential demonstration of these dangers has been offered in the famous Rosenhan (1973) study, which we first encountered in Chapter 2 (see p. 63). When eight normal people presented themselves at various mental hospitals complaining

The renowned ballet artist Vaslav Nijinsky, performing here in Schéhérazade, *developed severe schizophrenia and spent the last years of his life in a mental institution.*

that they had been hearing voices utter the words "empty," "hollow," and "thud," they were readily diagnosed as schizophrenic and hospitalized. Although the pseudopatients then dropped all symptoms and proceeded to behave normally, they had great difficulty getting rid of the label. Throughout their hospitalization, their diagnosis of schizophrenia influenced the way they were viewed and treated by the hospital staff. A pseudopatient who paced the corridor out of boredom was thought to be "nervous." Pseudopatients who kept notes on the ward to document their experiences received the daily nursing notation, "Patient engages in writing behavior."

The pseudopatients also reported that staff members spent limited time interacting with them or with other patients, usually responded curtly to patients' questions, were frequently authoritarian in manner, and often treated patients as though they were invisible. Rosenhan reports, "A nurse unbuttoned her uniform to adjust her brassiere in the presence of an entire ward of viewing men. One did not have the sense that she was being seductive. Rather, she didn't notice us. A group of staff persons might point to a patient in the dayroom and discuss him animatedly, as if he were not there." The pseudopatients described feeling powerless, depersonalized, and bored, and often behaved in a listless and apathetic manner.

The controversial design of this study has aroused the emotions of clinicians and researchers, pro and con. Even those who are outraged by it agree with its conclusion that a diagnosis of schizophrenia can itself have a negative effect on the way people are perceived and treated, and on the way the people themselves feel and behave.

Some theorists go so far as to assert that schizophrenia is largely the creation of society and that as a product of norms and expectations, the disorder can be expected to vary from society to society as norms and expectations vary. According to this more extreme sociological hypothesis, each society will define bizarreness differently and will attach different role prescriptions to the label. In short, symptoms that Western society calls schizophrenic should be different from the schizophrenic symptoms defined by other countries and cultures.

This prediction of variability has not been borne out by research (Smith, 1982). In fact, most societies have a label that approximates the Western category of schizophrenia, and the behavior implied by this label tends to be remarkably the same from society to society. The anthropologist Jane Murphy (1976), for example, studied two non-Western societies—the Yupik-speaking Eskimos on an island in the Bering Sea and the Egba Yorubas of rural, tropical Nigeria—

and found that the Eskimos have a disorder called *nuthkavihak* while the Yorubas have a disorder called *were*, each of which loosely translates into English as "insanity" and has symptoms (hallucinations, delusions, disorientation) that are remarkably similar to those of the Western disorder of schizophrenia.

GENETIC AND BIOLOGICAL VIEWS

What is arguably the most prolific and enlightening research on schizophrenia during the past few decades has come from the genetic and biological realms of inquiry. These studies have underscored the key role of genetic and biological factors in the development of schizophrenia and have opened the door to important changes in its treatment.

THE GENETIC VIEW Genetic researchers believe that some people inherit a biological predisposition to schizophrenia and, in accordance with a diathesis-stress model, come to develop the disorder when they are confronted by extreme stress, usually during late adolescence or early adulthood (Gottesman, 1991; Holzman & Matthysse, 1990). The genetic viewpoint has been supported by studies of (1) relatives of schizophrenic people, (2) twins

who are schizophrenic, (3) schizophrenic people who are adopted, and (4) chromosomal mapping.

RELATIVES OF SCHIZOPHRENIC PEOPLE Studies have found repeatedly that schizophrenia is more common among relatives of schizophrenic people than among relatives of nonschizophrenic people (Kendler et al., 1994, 1993; APA, 1994; Parnas et al., 1993; Gottesman, 1991). Moreover, the more closely related the relatives are to the schizophrenic proband, the greater their likelihood of developing the disorder (see Figure 15–2).

As we saw earlier, approximately 1 percent of the general population develops schizophrenia. This rate increases to an average of 10 percent among first-order relatives (parents, siblings, and children) of schizophrenic people. Approximately 6 percent of the parents, 9 percent of the siblings, and 13 to 16 percent of the children of schizophrenic people also manifest schizophrenia. Similarly, the schizophrenia prevalence rate rises to 3 percent among second-order relatives; that is, half-siblings, uncles, aunts, nephews, nieces, and grandchildren of schizophrenic people (Gottesman, 1991; Gottesman & Shields, 1982).

Of course, this trend by itself does not establish a genetic basis for the disorder. The prominent neuroscientist Solomon Snyder (1980) points out, "Attendance at Harvard University also runs in families but would hardly be considered a genetic trait." Family members are exposed to many of the same

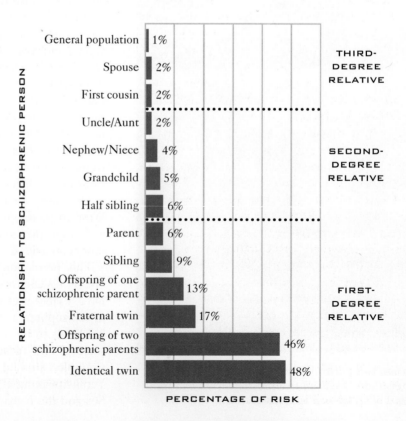

FIGURE 15–2 *People who are biologically related to schizophrenic people have a heightened risk of developing the disorder during their lifetime. The closer the biological relationship (that is, the more similar the genetic structure), the greater the risk of developing the disorder. (Adapted from Gottesman, 1991, p. 96.)*

RELATIONSHIP TO SCHIZOPHRENIC PERSON

General population 1%
Spouse 2%
First cousin 2%
Uncle/Aunt 2%
Nephew/Niece 4%
Grandchild 5%
Half sibling 6%
Parent 6%
Sibling 9%
Offspring of one schizophrenic parent 13%
Fraternal twin 17%
Offspring of two schizophrenic parents 46%
Identical twin 48%

THIRD-DEGREE RELATIVE

SECOND-DEGREE RELATIVE

FIRST-DEGREE RELATIVE

PERCENTAGE OF RISK

environmental influences as the schizophrenic person, and it may be these influences that lead to schizophrenia.

TWINS WHO ARE SCHIZOPHRENIC As we have noted previously, if both members of a pair of twins have a particular trait, they are said to be **concordant** for that trait. For a trait that is transmitted genetically, identical twins (who share identical genes) will show a higher concordance rate than fraternal twins (who share only some genes). Thus if genetic factors are at work in schizophrenia, identical twins should have a higher concordance rate for schizophrenia than fraternal twins. This expectation has been supported repeatedly by research (APA, 1994; Gottesman, 1991; Gottesman & Shields, 1982). Studies have found that if one identical twin develops schizophrenia, there is a 40 to 60 percent chance that the other twin will do so as well. If one fraternal twin is schizophrenic, in contrast, the other twin has approximately a 17 percent chance of developing the disorder.

SCHIZOPHRENIC PEOPLE WHO ARE ADOPTED Adoption studies have pointed convincingly to a genetic factor in schizophrenia (APA, 1994; Gottesman, 1991; Kety, 1974; Rosenthal, 1971). These studies look at schizophrenic adults who were adopted as infants and determine whether their behavior is more similar to that of their biological relatives or to that of their adoptive relatives. Because the schizophrenic subjects were reared apart from their biological relatives, similar schizophrenic symptoms in those relatives would indicate genetic influences. Conversely, schizophrenic similarities in their adoptive relatives would suggest environmental influences.

Seymour Kety and his colleagues (1988, 1978, 1975, 1974, 1968) conducted an extensive study on this subject in Copenhagen, Denmark, where detailed records of adoptions and mental disorders are available. In a sample of nearly 5,500 adults who had been adopted early in life, they found 33 who were schizophrenic. Matching control subjects were also selected from the same large sample—33 normal adoptees of similar age, sex, and schooling as the schizophrenic subjects. Next the investigators located a total of 365 biological and adoptive relatives (parents and siblings) of these 66 adoptees and separated the relatives into four groups: (1) biological relatives of schizophrenic adoptees; (2) adoptive relatives of schizophrenic adoptees; (3) biological relatives of normal adoptees; and (4) adoptive relatives of normal adoptees. A psychiatrist, unaware of who was related to whom, conducted an in-depth interview with each relative. His interview summaries were then read and evaluated by independent psychiatric judges who were again unaware of each person's status. On the basis of these interviews and evaluations, each relative was given a psychiatric diagnosis.

Of the 365 relatives, a total of 37 received a diagnosis of either *definite schizophrenia* or *uncertain schizophrenia* (schizophrenia-like patterns that did not fully warrant a clinical diagnosis). Most of these 37 turned out to be biological relatives of schizophrenic adoptees, a result that strongly supports the hypothesis that there is a genetic factor in schizophrenia. Almost 14 percent of the biological relatives of the schizophrenic adoptees were classified as schizophrenic (either definite or uncertain schizophrenia), whereas only 2.7 percent of their adoptive relatives received this classification. The biological and adoptive relatives of the normal adoptees had schizophrenic prevalence rates of 3.4 percent and 5.5 percent, respectively. Clearly the biological relatives of schizophrenic adoptees were most likely to develop schizophrenia.

Some critics of Kety's work have argued that it is misleading to include the category "uncertain schizophrenia" in the study's results. After all, individuals in this category are *not* schizophrenic (see Box 15–3). In response to this criticism, Kety also conducted data analyses in which only individuals who were judged to manifest definite schizophrenia received the diagnosis. Using these stricter criteria, he found that the schizophrenia prevalence rate for biological relatives of schizophrenic adoptees became 6.4 percent, still significantly higher than the revised prevalence rates shown by their adoptive relatives (1.4 percent) or by the biological and adoptive relatives of normal adoptees (1.7 percent and 2.2 percent, respectively). More recently Kety (1988) conducted a similar analysis of the relatives of schizophrenic persons living in other parts of Denmark, and found a strikingly similar pattern.

Such findings have led many researchers to conclude that the genetic factor in schizophrenia is significant, at least as great as that found in such illnesses as diabetes, hypertension, coronary artery disease, and ulcers, which are all acknowledged to have a genetic component (Kendler, 1983). Few, however, believe that this is the only factor involved (APA, 1994; Crow, 1988). Kety himself has said, "These data do not imply, nor do I believe, that genetic factors . . . are the only important influences in the etiology and pathogenesis of schizophrenia" (1974, p. 961).

CHROMOSOMAL MAPPING As with bipolar disorders (see Chapter 8), researchers have conducted **chromosomal mapping** research to identify more precisely the possible genetic factors in schizophrenia

AN ARRAY OF PSYCHOTIC DISORDERS

"Schizophrenia" is often used as a synonym for "psychosis." Although schizophrenia is indeed the most common kind of psychosis, it is but one of several. Psychotic functioning actually comes in many sizes and shapes, and may be caused by a variety of factors. In addition to schizophrenia, DSM-IV distinguishes the following psychotic disorders.

DELUSIONAL DISORDER

People who have at least one month of persistent delusions that are not bizarre and not part of a larger schizophrenic pattern may receive a diagnosis of *delusional disorder.* Aside from their delusions, they do not act in a particularly odd way and rarely show prominent hallucinations.

Persecutory, jealous, grandiose, and *somatic* delusions are common in people who have this disorder. Lately public attention has been drawn to *erotomanic* delusions. People with these delusions believe,

In one or two of every 1,000 births, a mother suffers "postpartum psychosis," marked by hallucinations, severe depression, and, in some cases, impulses to kill herself or her child or both. This disorder appears to be either a "brief psychotic disorder," a "schizoaffective disorder," or a "major depressive episode with psychotic features." It is different from the much more common "postpartum depression without psychotic features."

without any basis whatsoever, that they are loved by another person, who may be a casual acquaintance or even a complete stranger.

It has been estimated that around .03 percent of the population experience a delusional disorder. The disorder is equally common in men and women, although the jealous type is apparently more common in men. The disorder generally begins in the middle or late adult years, but can appear at a younger age (APA, 1994).

BRIEF PSYCHOTIC DISORDER

If psychotic symptoms appear suddenly and last anywhere from a day to a month, followed eventually by a full recovery, a diagnosis of *brief psychotic disorder* may be called for. The psychotic symptoms may include delusions, hallucinations, loose associations, incoherence, catatonia, or disorganized behavior. This disorder may occur either in response to a very stressful event such as the loss of a loved one, or in the absence of a stressor. In a *postpartum* pattern of brief psychotic disorder, the symptoms

(Bassett, 1992; Eaves et al., 1988). In this new strategy, they select large families in which schizophrenia is unusually common, take blood samples from all members of the families, isolate the DNA from each sample and "cut" it into segments, and then compare the gene segments from schizophrenic family members with the gene segments from nonschizophrenic members using a technique called *restriction fragment-length polymorphism (RFLP).* Applying RFLP to five families from Iceland and two families from England, Hugh Gurling and his colleagues (1989) have found that a particular area on chromosome 5 of schizophrenic family members has a different appear-

ance from the same area on chromosome 5 of non-schizophrenic family members. The researchers concluded from this study of 39 schizophrenic and 65 nonschizophrenic family members that an abnormal gene or cluster of genes in this area of chromosome 5 establishes a predisposition in at least some cases of schizophrenia.

Although this research has been greeted as a possible breakthrough in the study of schizophrenia, major problems remain to be solved (Holzman & Matthysse, 1990). For example, the area of chromosome 5 implicated in the study is very large, containing more than 1,000 genes. Researchers have yet to

emerge in women within 4 weeks after they give birth.

Brief psychotic disorders are apparently uncommon, although a precise prevalence rate is not known. The disorder typically begins in the late 20s or early 30s (APA, 1994).

SCHIZOPHRENIFORM DISORDER

People with *schizophreniform disorder* experience most of the key features of schizophrenia, but the symptoms last less than six months. In short, this diagnosis applies if the disorder lasts longer than a brief psychotic disorder but is less persistent than schizophrenia. Emotional turmoil, fear, confusion, and very vivid hallucinations often characterize this psychotic pattern.

Schizophreniform disorder appears to be equally common among men and women. Surveys suggest that 0.1 percent of all people experience it in any given year (APA, 1994).

SCHIZOAFFECTIVE DISORDER

Sometimes people display prominent symptoms of both schizophrenia and a mood disorder. In such cases, they may receive a diagnosis of *schizoaffective disorder.* To receive this diagnosis, however, the individual must, during the course of the disorder, have at least one episode of concurrent schizophrenia and mood disturbance and another episode of psychotic symptoms only. The mood disturbance may be a major depressive, manic, or mixed episode.

Schizoaffective disorders appear to be equally common among men and women. The disorder is thought to be less common than schizophrenia, although the precise prevalence rate is unknown. It may occur anytime between adolescence and later life, but the typical age of onset appears to be early adulthood (APA, 1994). Some clinicians dislike this category, believing it to be a wastebasket category that is generally used when diagnosticians have a hard time determining whether a client's mood problems are resulting from a schizophrenic disorder or vice versa.

SHARED PSYCHOTIC DISORDER

A person who embraces the delusions held by another individual may qualify for a diagnosis of *shared psychotic disorder.* Such individuals usually have a close relationship with a dominant person (called the *inducer* or *the primary case*), such as a parent or sibling, whose psychotic thinking they come to share. When the disorder is found in a two-person relationship, as it usually is, it is often known as *folie à deux.* If the relationship with the inducer is broken, the second person's delusional beliefs usually subside or disappear. Sometimes the disorder occurs in a whole family or group.

Little is known about the prevalence of this disorder. It appears to be somewhat more common in women than in men. Its age of onset is apparently quite variable (APA, 1994).

PSYCHOTIC DISORDER DUE TO A GENERAL MEDICAL CONDITION AND SUBSTANCE-INDUCED PSYCHOTIC DISORDER

If a medical problem such as a medical illness or brain damage is causing a person's hallucinations or delusions, the individual may receive a diagnosis of *psychotic disorder due to a general medical condition.* A variety of medical problems may cause such symptoms, including cerebrovascular disease, Huntington's disease, epilepsy, endocrine diseases, and metabolic diseases.

If prominent hallucinations or delusions are caused by the direct physiological effects of a substance, the person is said to be suffering from a *substance-induced psychotic disorder.* The substance may be an abused drug such as alcohol, hallucinogens, or cocaine, and the disorder may occur in association with either *intoxication* or *withdrawal* from the substance, depending on the substance. The symptoms may also be caused by a medication or a toxin such as nerve gas, carbon monoxide, carbon dioxide, fuel, or paint.

isolate the gene or cluster of genes that may contribute to schizophrenia. In addition, other studies applying the same approach to schizophrenic and nonschizophrenic members of large families in Sweden and Italy have found no consistent discrepancy on chromosome 5 (Macciardi et al., 1992; Kennedy et al., 1988). It may be that the findings of the Gurling study are misleading or being misinterpreted. Alternatively, different kinds of schizophrenia may have different causes. Gurling's subjects may have a kind of schizophrenia caused by a chromosome 5 defect, while the schizophrenia symptoms in the Swedish or Italian family may be caused by gene defects on other chromosomes or by factors that are entirely nongenetic. In accord with this interpretation, still other studies have recently identified possible gene defects on chromosomes 9, 10, 11, 18, and 19 that may predispose individuals to develop schizophrenia (Bassett, 1992; Garofalo et al., 1992).

BIOLOGICAL VIEWS How might genetic factors lead to the development of schizophrenia? Biological research has pointed to two kinds of biological abnormalities, each of which apparently contributes to schizophrenia and each of which could conceivably be inherited—biochemical abnormalities and abnormal brain structure.

BIOCHEMICAL ABNORMALITIES   To summarize our earlier discussions of neurons, neurotransmitters, and synapses, the brain consists largely of neurons. When an impulse (or "message") travels from neuron to neuron in the brain, it is received by a neuron's dendrites (antennae), travels down the neuron's axon, and reaches its nerve ending. The nerve ending then releases a chemical neurotransmitter from its storage vessels, and these neurotransmitter molecules cross the synaptic space and attach to receptors on the dendrites of another neuron, thus relaying the message and causing that neuron to fire. Research conducted over the past two decades has suggested that in schizophrenic persons, the neurons that use the neurotransmitter *dopamine* fire too often and transmit too many messages, thus producing the symptoms of the disorder. Like the biological explanations of anxiety, depression, and mania, this so-called ***dopamine hypothesis*** of schizophrenia was arrived at by a mixture of serendipity, painstaking experimental work, and clever theorizing. The chain of events began with the accidental discovery of ***antipsychotic medications,*** drugs that help remove the symptoms of schizophrenia.

As we shall see in Chapter 16, the first group of antipsychotic medications, the ***phenothiazines,*** were discovered in the 1950s by researchers who were looking for effective antihistamine drugs to combat allergies. Although phenothiazines failed as antihistamines, their effectiveness in reducing schizophrenic symptoms soon became apparent, and clinicians began prescribing them for most schizophrenic people. Eventually researchers learned that these drugs also produce a very troublesome effect, muscular tremors identical to those seen in Parkinson's disease. Normally that disabling neurological disease emerges after the age of 50; when schizophrenic patients were given an antipsychotic drug, the young were as likely to develop Parkinsonian symptoms as the old.

This effect of antipsychotic drugs gave researchers their first important clue to the biology of schizophrenia. Medical scientists already knew that people with Parkinson's disease have abnormally low levels of the neurotransmitter dopamine in some areas of the brain, as a result of the destruction of dopamine-containing neurons, and that insufficient dopamine is the reason for their uncontrollable shaking. In fact, administration of the chemical *L-dopa*—a precursor of dopamine—is a somewhat helpful treatment for Parkinson's disease precisely because it helps to raise dopamine levels.

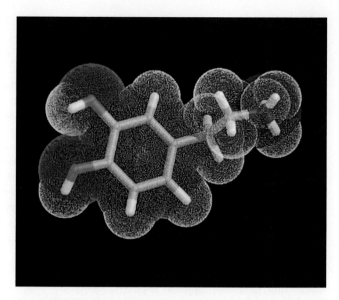

A computer-drawn molecule of dopamine. Excessive activity of this neurotransmitter has been linked to schizophrenia and to amphetamine and cocaine psychosis, while low dopamine activity has been related to Parkinson's disease.

Scientists put these pieces of information together and came up with a pair of important hypotheses. If antipsychotic drugs generate Parkinsonian symptoms while alleviating schizophrenia, perhaps they operate by reducing dopamine activity. And if lowering dopamine activity alleviates the symptoms of schizophrenia, perhaps schizophrenia is related to excessive dopamine activity in the first place.

ESTABLISHING THE DOPAMINE-SCHIZO-PHRENIA LINK   Since the 1960s, research has both supported and enlarged upon the dopamine hypothesis. It has been found, for example, that some people with Parkinson's disease develop schizophrenic symptoms if they take too much L-dopa (Davis, Comaty, & Janicak, 1988). Presumably the L-dopa raises their dopamine activity to schizophrenia-inducing levels. Correspondingly, when schizophrenic patients have been given L-dopa, their schizophrenic symptoms have worsened considerably (Angrist, Sathananthan, & Gershon, 1973). Presumably their high dopamine activity becomes even higher.

Support for the dopamine hypothesis has also come from research on amphetamines, drugs that, as we saw in Chapter 13, stimulate the central nervous system (Davis et al., 1988). Researchers first became aware of close links between amphetamines and schizophrenia during the 1970s when they noticed that people who take high doses of amphetamines over an extended period of time may develop ***amphetamine psychosis***—a syndrome that closely mimics schizophrenia and includes hallucinations and motor hyperactivity. They later found that antipsychotic drugs can correct amphetamine psychosis, just as they are able to alleviate the symptoms of schizophrenia, and furthermore, that even small doses of amphetamines exacerbate the symptoms of schizophrenia (Janowsky & Davis, 1976; Janowsky et al., 1973). Researchers eventually traced these links between amphetamines, schizophrenia, and antipsychotic drugs to dopamine activity (Snyder, 1976). They found that amphetamines increase dopamine synaptic activity in the brain, thus inducing or exacerbating schizophrenic symptoms.

The dopamine hypothesis gained its widest acceptance once researchers developed a procedure that enabled them to pinpoint sites in the brain that have high concentrations of dopamine receptors (Seeman et al., 1976; Snyder, 1976). In this procedure, a small area of an animal's brain is removed and its neurons are spread out in a dish filled with fluid. Radioactive dopamine is added to the fluid, and any radioactivity that subsequently concentrates at the neurons is measured. If a neuron's radioactivity reading is high, dopamine binding is presumed to have taken place, and the neuron is presumed to possess dopamine receptors. Conversely, no radioactivity at a neuron indicates no dopamine binding and no dopamine receptors. By systematically applying this test to neurons from all parts of the brain, researchers were able to map the brain's dopamine receptor sites.

Researchers then repeated the procedure, substituting antipsychotic drugs for dopamine. That is, they determined which neuroreceptors throughout the brain would accumulate radioactive antipsychotic drugs. They found that antipsychotic drugs bind to many of the same receptors as dopamine (Creese et al., 1977; Snyder et al., 1976; Burt et al., 1977). On the basis of this finding, they concluded that phenothiazines and other antipsychotic drugs are *dopamine antagonists*—drugs that bind to dopamine receptors, prevent dopamine from binding there, and so prevent dopamine-receiving neurons from firing (Iversen, 1975; Kebabian et al., 1972). Subsequently, researchers were able to distinguish different kinds of dopamine receptors in the brain, and found that phenothiazines bind most strongly to those receptors called *D-2* receptors (Strange, 1992).

OVERACTIVE DOPAMINE SYNAPSES Such findings led researchers to believe that certain dopamine synapses in schizophrenic people are overactive—that messages from dopamine-sending neurons to dopamine-receiving neurons, particularly to the D-2 receptors on these neurons, are transmitted too readily or too often (see Figure 15–3). This theory has an intuitive appeal because dopamine-receiving neurons have been found to play an active role in guiding and sustaining attention (Cohen et al., 1988). People whose attention mechanisms are grossly impaired might well be expected to suffer from the abnormalities of attention, perception, and thought that characterize schizophrenia.

Why might the dopamine synapses of schizophrenic people be overactive? Researchers used to think that the dopamine-sending neurons of these individuals produce and store too much dopamine, but studies have failed to support this hypothesis (Seidman, 1990; Carlsson, 1978; Van Praag, 1977). Currently theorists believe that the cause of the synaptic overactivity is a larger than usual number of dopamine receptors, particularly D-2 receptors (Sedvall, 1990; Seidman, 1990; Kleinman, Casanova, & Jaskiw, 1988; Owen et al., 1987). Remember that when dopamine carries a message to a receiving neuron, it binds to receptors on the membrane of the neuron. Schizophrenic people appear to have a larger number of D-2 receptors on their receiving neurons than other people do. Inasmuch as more receptors lead to more firing, the numerous dopamine receptors ensure greater dopamine synaptic activity and overtransmission of dopamine messages. Researchers have in fact found that the autopsied brains of many schizophrenic people contain more dopamine receptors than those of nonschizophrenic people (Owen et al., 1987, 1978; Lee & Seeman, 1980). In some cases the use of antipsychotic drugs appears to be partly responsible for the production of these extra dopamine receptors (Farde et al., 1990), but some autopsies have also revealed larger numbers of dopamine receptors in schizophrenic people who have never taken antipsychotic drugs (Strange, 1992).

QUESTIONING THE DOPAMINE HYPOTHESIS Although these studies are helping to unravel the biology of schizophrenia, their results may not be so clear-cut as they first appear. To begin with, the dopamine hypothesis and its focus on D-2 receptors may be overstated (Meltzer, 1992, 1987). The biggest challenge to this hypothesis has come from the discovery of a new group of antipsychotic drugs, referred to as *atypical antipsychotics* because they have a different mechanism of action than the traditional drugs. As we shall see in Chapter 16, *clozapine,* the most commonly prescribed atypical antipsychotic drug, is often more effective than the traditional antipsychotic drugs, helping many people who have been unresponsive to the traditional drugs.

One difference between traditional and the atypical antipsychotic drugs is in their ability to bind to and block various dopamine receptors. The traditional drugs bind to and block most of the D-2 receptors in

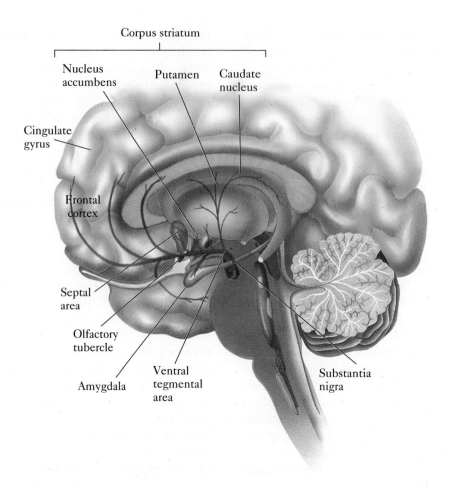

Corpus striatum

Nucleus
accumbens   Putamen   Caudate
nucleus

Cingulate
gyrus

Frontal
cortex

Septal
area

Olfactory
tubercle

Amygdala   Ventral
tegmental
area

Substantia
nigra

FIGURE 15-3 *Some of the neurons that release the neurotransmitter dopamine have cell bodies in the substantia nigra with axons extending all the way
to the corpus striatum, the part of the brain that functions to produce smooth coordination and movement in the arms and legs. When these neurons release too little
dopamine, the muscular tremors and other symptoms of Parkinson's disease occur.
Another group of neurons that release dopamine have cell bodies in the ventral
tegmental area with axons extending to the olfactory tubercle, nucleus accumbens,
amygdala, and cingulate gyrus—areas that apparently function to link sensory
perceptions to memories and emotions. It may be that when these neurons are excessively active and release too much dopamine, the symptoms of schizophrenia result.
Other dopamine pathways do not appear to be linked to Parkinson's disease or
schizophrenia. (Adapted from Snyder, 1986, p. 85.)*

the brain, but few, if any, of another group of receptors, called *D-1* receptors (Farde et al., 1992; Farde &
Nordstrom, 1992). On the other hand, the atypical
drug clozapine binds to about half of the D-2 receptors and half of the D-1 receptors (Gerlach & Hansen,
1992). This finding suggests to some researchers that
D-2 receptors may be less important in schizophrenia
and D-1 receptors more so than the dopamine hypothesis currently holds.

Even more challenging for the dopamine hypothesis is the finding that clozapine also binds to and
blocks many receptors for the neurotransmitter *serotonin* (Kahn et al., 1993; Owen et al., 1993; Meltzer,
1992). This finding has led some researchers to be-

lieve that excessive serotonin functioning may also
play a key role in schizophrenia. It may be, for example, that schizophrenia is related to some kind of intersecting activity of the serotonin and dopamine
pathways in the brain.

Finally, in yet another challenge to the traditional
dopamine hypothesis, a number of theorists are beginning to assert that excessive dopamine activity
contributes only to Type I schizophrenia (Crow, 1985,
1982, 1980). As we saw earlier, cases of Type I
schizophrenia are those characterized by positive
symptoms such as delusions and hallucinations,
whereas Type II cases are marked by negative symptoms such as flat affect and loss of volition. Observing

that Type I cases are more responsive than Type II cases to the traditional antipsychotic drugs (the drugs that bind so strongly to D-2 receptors) and that Type II cases are often responsive to atypical antipsychotic drugs (the drugs that bind less strongly to D-2 receptors), researchers are increasingly suspecting that the dopamine hypothesis may be relevant only to Type I schizophrenia (Ragin et al., 1989; Crow, 1980). In fact, other research has increasingly linked Type II schizophrenia to a totally different kind of biological abnormality—abnormal brain structure.

ABNORMAL BRAIN STRUCTURE   Ever since Kraepelin, clinicians have suspected that schizophrenia is caused by abnormalities in brain structure. Only during the past decade, however, have researchers been able to link this disorder, particularly Type II schizophrenia, to specific structural abnormalities (Strange, 1992; Buchsbaum & Haier, 1987). This development has been made possible by improvements in postmortem tissue analyses and by the development of computerized technologies (such as computerized axial tomography, positron emission tomography, and magnetic resonance imaging) that can produce pictures of brain structure and brain activity without harming the brain in the process (see pp. 118-119).

Researchers who have used these newer technologies have consistently found that many schizophrenic people have *enlarged ventricles*—the brain cavities that contain cerebrospinal fluid (APA, 1994; Cannon & Marco, 1994; Hyde et al., 1991; Weinberger & Kleinman, 1986). In particular, the ventricles on the left side of their brains seem much larger than the ventricles on the right (Losonczy et al., 1986). Since these enlargements appear at the onset of schizophrenia and before drug treatment, they are not produced by antipsychotic drugs (Cannon & Marco, 1994; DeLisi et al., 1992; Weinberger et al., 1982).

Patients with enlarged ventricles tend to display more negative and fewer positive symptoms of schizophrenia, a poorer premorbid social adjustment, greater cognitive disturbances, and poorer responses to traditional antipsychotic drugs (Bornstein et al., 1992; Klausner et al., 1992). On the other hand, enlarged ventricles have also been found in cases of mood disorder and of alcoholism, so that researchers cannot be certain about the precise implications of the relation of enlarged ventricles to schizophrenia (Pearlson et al., 1984).

Other kinds of structural abnormalities, quite possibly related to enlarged ventricles, have also been found in the brains and in the skulls of Type II schizophrenic patients. Some studies suggest that

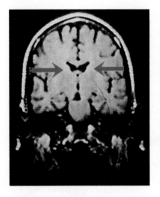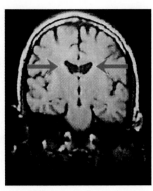

In a study of fifteen pairs of identical twins in which one of each pair was diagnosed as schizophrenic, magnetic resonance imaging (MRI) revealed that the brain of the schizophrenic twin (right) almost always had larger ventricles—butterfly-shaped spaces filled with fluid and located between the lobes—than the other (left).

these people have smaller frontal lobes, cerebrums, and craniums than nonschizophrenic people (Raine et al., 1992; Suddath et al., 1990), and, perhaps most important, a reduced blood flow in their brains (Sagawa et al., 1990; Buchsbaum & Haier, 1987). Two investigations observed schizophrenic and nonschizophrenic subjects who were performing a simple card-sorting task, and measured the rate at which blood was flowing to their frontal lobes (Berman et al., 1992; Weinberger, 1983). The rate of blood flow dropped sharply for approximately half of the schizophrenic subjects, whereas blood flow actually increased for most of the nonschizophrenic control subjects. Like the ventricle abnormalities, reduced cerebral blood flow has been found to occur in schizophrenic persons before any drug treatments and is more common in persons with Type II schizophrenia (Siegel et al., 1993).

Now that research into structural abnormalities has begun to yield such impressive findings, investigators are looking for ties between *specific* structural abnormalities and *specific* symptoms of schizophrenia (Green et al., 1994). Auditory hallucinations, for example, seem to have been traced to Broca's area, the speech region of the brain (McGuire, Shah, & Murray, 1993; Cleghorn et al., 1992). One study measured cerebral blood flow in the brains of schizophrenic men both while they were hallucinating and again an average of five months later when they were not hallucinating (McGuire et al., 1993). The researchers found increased blood flow in Broca's area while the men were experiencing auditory hallucinations. These results suggest that the brains of schizophrenic persons are actually generating words when people hear auditory hallucinations. Of course, schizophrenic individuals do not realize that their

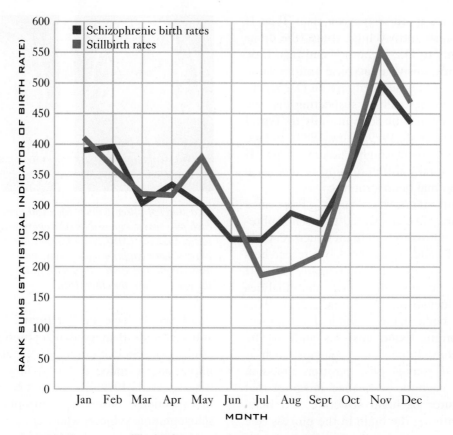

FIGURE 15–4 *The birth pattern of people who develop schizophrenia is very closely linked to that of stillbirths, yielding a correlation of 0.8. The incidence of stillbirths and the incidence of births of persons who later develop schizophrenia are each highest during November and December and lowest during the summer. One interpretation of this relationship is that fetuses are more exposed to certain infectious agents during the winter months, producing death in some cases and a viral infection which eventually causes schizophrenia in other cases. (Adapted from Torrey et al., 1993.)*

own brains are generating the words they hear, so they interpret the words as being produced by someone else.

What might cause the ventricle enlargements, blood flow problems, or other structural abnormalities that seem to accompany many cases of schizophrenia? Various studies have collected evidence that such abnormalities may be caused by genetic factors, birth complications, immune reactions, or toxins (DeLisi et al., 1992, 1986; Andreasen et al., 1986). And, in a recent popular theory, several researchers suggest that the brain abnormalities may be the result of pre-birth exposure to viruses. They hypothesize that the viruses enter the brain during the perinatal period and remain latent until puberty or young adulthood, when they are reactivated by hormonal changes or another viral infection, thus causing schizophrenic symptoms (Torrey et al., 1993; Torrey, 1991).

The viral theory has been supported by evidence that more schizophrenic persons are born during the

winter than during the other seasons of the year (Torrey, 1992; Berquier & Ashton, 1991; Bradbury & Miller, 1985). One study found that approximately 8 percent more schizophrenic persons are born during the winter months than would be expected from population birth rates (DeLisi, Crow, & Hirsch, 1986). The larger number of schizophrenic people born during these months may be due to an increase in fetal or infant exposure to viruses at that time of year (Torrey, 1991; Barr et al., 1990) (see Figure 15–4).

Although investigators are only beginning to understand the precise nature and meaning of brain structure abnormalities, this research has already indicated that the biological underpinnings of schizophrenia are more complex and more subtle than anyone had imagined. Together the biochemical and brain structure findings are beginning to shed much light on the mysteries of schizophrenia. At the same time, it is important to recognize that many people who manifest these biochemical and structural abnormalities never develop schizophrenia. Why not? Possibly, as we noted earlier, because biological factors merely set the stage for schizophrenia, while key psychological factors must be present for the disorder to unfold.

PSYCHOLOGICAL VIEWS

When investigators began to identify genetic and biological factors in schizophrenia during the 1950s and 1960s, many clinicians abandoned psychogenic explanations of the disorder. During the past decade, however, the tables have been turned once again and psychological factors are increasingly being considered an important piece of the puzzle of schizophrenia. This turnaround has occurred partly because biology alone has proved unable to account for schizophrenia and partly because research has increasingly provided some support for certain psychological theories. The leading psychological explanations of schizophrenia have come from the psychodynamic, behavioral, family systems, existential, and cognitive perspectives.

THE PSYCHODYNAMIC VIEW   Freud (1924, 1915) believed that the development of schizophrenia involves a two-part psychological process: (1) *regression* to a pre-ego stage and (2) *restitutive efforts* to reestablish ego control. After very limited contact with schizophrenic persons, he proposed that schizophrenia, like neurosis (anxiety and depressive disorders), stems from a basic conflict between a person's self-gratifying impulses and the demands of the real world. When their external world is particularly harsh or withholding (for example, when their parents are consistently cold or unnurturing), those who become schizophrenic, like people who develop a neurosis, regress to an early period in their functioning. According to Freud, neurotic people regress partially and become overly dependent on ego defense mechanisms to deal with real-world demands; schizophrenic people, with egos that are even less stable, regress to the earliest point in their development, a point before the formation of the ego and before their recognition of the external world as existing outside of and apart from them.

Ultimately, schizophrenic persons regress to a state of *primary narcissism*, like that of infants, in which only their own needs are felt. This near-total regression leads to self-indulgent symptoms such as neologisms, loose associations, and delusions of grandeur.

Freud also believed that upon regressing to a pre-ego stage these people start trying to reestablish ego control and contact with reality. Their restitutive efforts give rise to yet other schizophrenic symptoms. Auditory hallucinations, for example, may represent an unconscious attempt to substitute for a lost sense of reality.

Freud's general position that schizophrenia involves extreme regression and restitutive efforts has been retained by many psychodynamic theorists throughout the twentieth century (Blatt & Wild, 1976; Fenichel, 1945). However, their views have received virtually no research support (Maher, 1966). More contemporary psychodynamic theorists tend to include both biological and psychological factors in their explanations. Self theorists, for example, suggest that a combination of these factors makes it impossible for schizophrenic persons to develop a cohesive core self; they experience, instead, a protracted fragmentation of the self. Their schizophrenic symptoms represent the expressions and coping efforts of this struggling self (Pollack, 1989; Kohut & Wolf, 1978).

THE BEHAVIORAL VIEW   Behaviorists point primarily to *operant conditioning* to explain schizophrenia (Liberman, 1982; Ullmann & Krasner, 1975). They propose that most people are taught by their environment (family, neighbors, social institutions) to attend to social cues—for example, to other people's smiles, frowns, and comments. When they respond to these stimuli in a socially acceptable way, they are better able to satisfy their emotional needs and to achieve their goals. Some people, however, do not receive such reinforcements. Unusual circumstances may prevent their encountering social cues in their environment, or important figures in their lives may be socially inadequate and unable to provide proper reinforcements. Either way, these people stop attending to social cues and focus instead on other, often irrelevant cues—the brightness of light in a room, a bird flying above, or the sound of a word rather than its meaning. As they attend more and more to such inappropriate signals, their responses become increasingly bizarre. Such responses in turn elicit heightened attention or other types of reinforcement from the environment, thus increasing the likelihood that they will be repeated.

Support for the behavioral position has been circumstantial. As we shall see in Chapter 16, researchers have found that schizophrenic patients are often capable of learning appropriate verbal responses and social behaviors if their bizarre responses are consistently ignored by hospital personnel while normal responses are reinforced with cigarettes, food, attention, or other rewards (Belcher, 1988; Foxx et al., 1988; Braginsky, Braginsky, & Ring, 1969; Ayllon & Michael, 1959). The fact that verbal and social responses can be successfully altered by such reinforcements suggests to some theorists that the behavioral patterns of schizophrenia may be acquired through operant conditioning in the first place. As we know, however, an effective treatment for a disorder does not necessarily imply the cause of the disorder. Entirely different factors may be responsible for the development of schizophrenic behavior.

Today the behavioral view is usually treated as only a partial explanation for schizophrenia. Although it may help explain why a given person displays more schizophrenic behavior in some situations than in others, it is too limited, in the opinion of many people, to account for schizophrenia's origins and its many symptoms.

FAMILY VIEWS   In the psychological views discussed so far, the social environment is thought to play a central role in schizophrenia. This collective focus on the environment has led some theorists to look particularly closely at the families of schizophrenic people.

THE SCHIZOPHRENOGENIC MOTHER Some theorists have suggested that the parents of schizophrenic individuals have a particular personality style. The noted psychodynamic clinician Frieda Fromm-Reichmann (1948), for example, used the term *schizophrenogenic mother* (schizophrenia-causing mother) to describe the mothers of schizophrenic individuals, saying that such mothers are cold, domineering, and impervious to their children's needs. According to Fromm-Reichmann, they appear to be self-sacrificing but are actually using their children to address their own needs. At once overprotective and rejecting, they confuse their children and set the stage for schizophrenic functioning.

Although this notion has appealed to many clinicians, years of research have challenged its validity. The majority of schizophrenic people do *not* appear to have had mothers who fit the schizophrenogenic description. In fact, some studies have suggested that quite a different personality style may prevail among the mothers of schizophrenic persons. In one study the mothers of schizophrenic subjects were found to be shy, inadequate, withdrawn, anxious, suspicious, or incoherent, while the mothers of nonschizophrenic control subjects seemed more likely to display what Fromm-Reichmann would have called a schizophrenogenic maternal style (Waring & Ricks, 1965).

DOUBLE-BIND COMMUNICATIONS One of the best-known family theories is the *double-bind hypothesis* (Bateson, 1978; Bateson et al., 1956), which maintains that some parents repeatedly communicate pairs of messages that are mutually contradictory, thus placing the children in double-bind situations: the children cannot avoid displeasing their parents; nothing they do is right. Children who are repeatedly caught in such contradictions may react by developing schizophrenic symptoms.

According to Gregory Bateson and his colleagues, both a primary communication and a metacommunication are contained in any message. The *primary communication* is the semantic content of the message; the *metacommunication* encompasses the tone, context, and gestures attached to the message. Although primary communications and metacommunications may be congruent, they can also be incongruent and therefore confusing. If one person says to another, "I'm glad to see you," yet frowns and avoids eye contact, the two aspects of the message are incongruent. Usually double-bind messages arise from a contradiction between a primary communication and the accompanying metacommunication. In the following double-bind situation, little Leo cannot be certain whether his mother is telling him to stay away, as her frozen posture suggests, or "Come to me," as her spoken words require.

Momma goes out shopping leaving three-year-old Leo with Daddy. As she returns and opens the door, Leo runs over to greet his mother. Whereupon the woman involuntarily freezes. Leo sees this and stops. Whereupon his mother says, "Leo, baby, what's the matter, don't you love your Mommy? Come and give me a big kiss."

If baby Leo ignores his first perception and runs up to the woman again, she freezes and takes his kiss in an off-hand, angry way. If baby Leo refuses to budge, she scolds him for being a bad boy. Because of his age or inexperience Leo can't comment on what is happening, or if he does, either his mother or father scolds him for being naughty: "Don't talk to your mother/father that way or you will be punished." The net result is that Baby Leo is reduced to an impotent rage whereupon he is sent to bed for being bad.

(Barnes & Barnes, 1973, p. 85)

According to this theory, a child who is repeatedly exposed to double-bind situations may adopt a *special life strategy* for coping with the environment. Unfortunately, some such strategies can lead to schizophrenic symptoms. One strategy might be always to ignore primary communications and respond only to metacommunications; that is, always be suspicious of what a person is saying, wonder about its true meaning, look for clues in the person's gestures or tones, and respond accordingly. People who increasingly respond to messages in this way may be on their way to manifesting symptoms of paranoid schizophrenia.

Another strategy might be to respond to primary communications exclusively, interpreting everything literally. People who adopt this strategy will not learn to appreciate the subtleties of communication. They will often miss the intent of others' communications and respond inappropriately, in ways that may seem hyperliteral and only loosely relevant. Such behavior may develop into the symptoms of disorganized schizophrenia.

Finally, a third strategy is to ignore other people's messages. If one does not hear incongruent messages, one will not be confused by them. People who consistently employ this strategy of coping with their environment may become more and more removed from the external world. Eventually they may become withdrawn, perhaps even mute, displaying the symptoms of catatonic schizophrenia.

The double-bind hypothesis is closely related to the schizophrenogenic-mother explanation of schizophrenia. When Fromm-Reichmann describes schizophrenogenic mothers as both overprotective and rejecting at the same time, she is in fact describing someone who is likely to offer double-bind communications. Similarly, the mothers in Bateson's case examples of double-bind communications, such as Leo's mother, typically fit the description of a schizophrenogenic mother. Like the schizophrenogenic-mother theory, the double-bind hypothesis has been popular in the clinical field since its inception (Cronen et al., 1983), but investigations into the theory have been few and in fact unsupportive. In one study, clinicians read and evaluated letters written by parents to their children in the hospital (Ringuette & Kennedy, 1966). One group of parents had schizophrenic children; the other had nonschizophrenic children. Rating each letter on a seven-point scale according to the double-bind messages it contained, the clinicians found the letters of both groups of parents to offer similar degrees of double-bind communication.

FAMILY STRUCTURE   Theodore Lidz (1973, 1963) has proposed that disturbed patterns of interaction and communication evolve in certain families and may push offspring toward schizophrenic functioning. According to Lidz, either of two kinds of family alignments can lead to schizophrenia: marital schism or marital skew.

In Lidz's view, *marital schism* is more often associated with schizophrenia in women. It is seen in families in which the mother and father are in open conflict, with each spouse trying to undercut the other and compete for the daughter's loyalty. The mother is constantly denigrated by the father and develops low self-esteem. The father turns to the daughter, implicitly asks her to take her mother's place, and develops a heightened emotional relationship with her.

The daughter is caught in the middle in this family structure. Any attempt to please one parent will be viewed as a rejection by the other. Although attached to her father, she also identifies with his foe, her mother. In defense, she adopts a posture of massive confusion that allows her to avoid acknowledging or resolving the conflicts. In other words, she retreats into schizophrenia.

Lidz claims that schizophrenic men come from families with a *marital skew* structure. Here there is no overt hostility. The mother, following Fromm-Reichmann's stereotype of the schizophrenogenic mother, is impervious to the needs of others and dominates family life. The father keeps peace by continually yielding to her wishes. The mother develops a heightened emotional relationship with her son, implicitly asking him to be different from his father.

Like the daughter who is confused by marital schism, the son in a marital skew situation is full of conflict. He wants to identify with his father, yet must reject all that his father stands for in order to please his mother. He, too, takes refuge in the pathology of schizophrenia, nonfunctional behavior that effectively distances him from his family dynamics and his own internal turmoil.

Although Lidz's theory has attracted widespread interest, it is actually based on very small and possibly unrepresentative family samples. Indeed, the studies that yielded this theory examined a total of only forty families, all from the upper socioeconomic classes (Lidz, 1973, 1963; Lidz et al., 1965, 1957). Without wider sampling and appropriate control groups, it is impossible to know how common these family patterns are in cases of schizophrenia.

THE STATUS OF FAMILY THEORIES   So far no single family explanation of schizophrenia has received impressive research support. This is not to suggest, however, that the behaviors of family members have little to do with the development of schizophrenia. On the contrary, it has been found that schizophrenia, like other mental disorders, is often precipitated by stressful family situations, including emotional instability of some kind in a parent (Leff & Vaughn, 1976; Tsuang et al., 1974). Moreover, studies keep pointing to the presence of family conflict of one kind or another in the backgrounds of most people with schizophrenia (Miklowitz, 1994; Falloon &

Liberman, 1983; Vaughn & Leff, 1976; Brown et al., 1962). Three trends have emerged from numerous such studies of the families of schizophrenic people. The parents (1) *display more conflict,* (2) *have greater difficulty communicating with one another,* and (3) *are more critical of and overinvolved with their children than other parents.* Certainly these trends suggest that negative family experiences may contribute to the development and chronicity of schizophrenia (Mavreas et al., 1992; Vaughan et al., 1992; Goldstein, 1985); however, it is also possible that schizophrenic individuals themselves disrupt family life and help cause the family problems that clinicians and researchers continue to observe (Asarnow & Horton, 1990; Mishler & Waxler, 1968).

THE EXISTENTIAL VIEW R. D. Laing (1967, 1964, 1959) adopted key components of the sociocultural and family theories of schizophrenia, combined them with the existential principles that were his hallmark, and formulated the most controversial view of schizophrenia in the clinical field. Laing believed that schizophrenia is actually a constructive process in which people try to cure themselves of the confusion and unhappiness caused by their social and family environment. He believed that, left alone to complete this process, people with schizophrenia would indeed achieve a healthy level of integration.

Laing's theory begins with the existential position that in order to give meaning to their lives, all human beings must be in touch with their *true selves.* Unfortunately, says Laing, it is difficult to achieve this inner discovery and lead a meaningful existence in present-day society. Typically, social interactions require us to develop a *false self* rather than a true one in order to satisfy the expectations, demands, and standards of others.

Laing asserted that the people who become schizophrenic have even greater obstacles than these to deal with. Like the double-bind theorists, he believed that the families of schizophrenic people communicate and act in particularly confusing ways, convey contradictory expectations, and make paradoxical demands. Not only are children in these families unable to discover their true selves, they cannot even develop a false self that succeeds in meeting the demands of others.

The situation becomes so bad that out of desperation these people undertake an inner search for a sense of strength and purpose. They withdraw from others and attend increasingly to their own inner cues as they try to recover their wholeness as human beings. Laing argued that these people would emerge

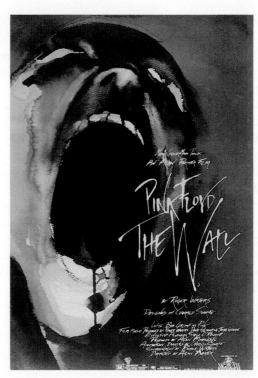

"Is there anybody out there?" R. D. Laing's theory that schizophrenia is an extended inward search undertaken by some persons in order to cure themselves of confusion and unhappiness caused by their family and society has been romanticized throughout the arts. It is, for example, the central theme of Pink Floyd's hugely popular album and movie The Wall.

stronger and less confused if they were simply allowed to continue this inner search. Instead, society and its clinicians tell them that they are sick and even list signs and symptoms of schizophrenia that seem to prove this assertion. Yielding to society's expectations, the individuals assume the role of schizophrenic patient, submitting to efforts at treatment that actually serve to produce further schizophrenic symptoms. In an effort to cure these people, society dooms them to suspension in an inner world.

It is easy to understand why Laing's theory is so controversial. Most theorists reject his notion that schizophrenia is a positive or constructive process. They see it as a problem that brings extensive suffering and no benefit. Similarly, many schizophrenic individuals reject Laing's theory.

"Schizophrenia's a reasonable reaction to an unreasonable society." It's great on paper. Poetic, noble, etc. But if you happen to be a schizophrenic, it's got some not-so-cheery implications. . . . One of R.D.'s worst sins is how blithely and misleadingly he glides over the suffering involved. . . . Pulling off a revolution and ushering in a new era in which truth and beauty reign triumphant seems unlikely when you're having trouble brushing your teeth or even walking.

(Vonnegut, 1974, p. 91)

For his part, Laing emphasized that he did indeed acknowledge the pain and terror experienced by schizophrenic persons, but he maintained that their suffering grows largely from society's inadequacies and from its inappropriate response to their inward searches. The debate over the existential view of schizophrenia continues, and for the most part research has not resolved the controversy (Howells & Guirguis, 1985). Laing's phenomenological ideas do not lend themselves to empirical research (Hirsch & Leff, 1975). Moreover, the existentialists who embrace his view have little confidence in traditional research approaches.

THE COGNITIVE VIEW The cognitive explanation of schizophrenia incorporates the biological findings of the past few decades. It proposes that biological problems arise first, causing strange sensory experiences; then further features of schizophrenia emerge as a result of the individuals' attempts to understand and explain their unusual experiences. When first confronted by voices, visions, or other sensations, these people turn to friends and relatives to help them understand what is happening, only to have the existence of their new sensory experiences denied. Eventually they come to believe that their friends and relatives are trying to hide the truth from them, they reject all feedback from others, and they develop beliefs (delusions) that they are being manipulated or persecuted (Garety, 1991; Maher, 1974). In short, they take what is sometimes called a "rational path to madness" (Zimbardo, 1976).

This cognitive theory has not been tested directly among schizophrenic subjects, but a link between sensory dysfunctioning and delusional thinking has often been observed in persons who lose their hearing (Zimbardo et al., 1981; Maher, 1974; Reed, 1974). Most people who lose their hearing for an organic reason are not immediately aware of what is happening to them. When their hearing begins to deteriorate, they tend to think that the people around them are whispering; when told this is just not so, hearing-impaired persons sometimes conclude that they are being deceived and plotted against. As long as they are unaware of their growing deafness, their logical processes lead them to delusional conclusions. This is a common phenomenon and helps to account for the relatively high prevalence of persecutory delusions among the elderly (Kay, 1972; Post, 1966).

The cognitive view of schizophrenia is newer than the other psychological explanations of the disorder. It focuses primarily on one piece of the schizophrenia puzzle—delusions—and research to evaluate it has been limited and indirect. The emergence of this explanation, however, reflects a growing tendency to see schizophrenia as a disorder determined by multiple interacting factors. The theory explicitly acknowledges the role of biological factors and tries to understand how psychological processes may interact with such factors. As we noted earlier, similar interactionist perspectives are being adopted increasingly by today's psychodynamic, behavioral, and family theorists. Given the complexity and elusiveness of schizophrenia, such efforts at integration seem most appropriate and welcome.

THE STATE OF THE FIELD

SCHIZOPHRENIA

Schizophrenia, one of our species' most bizarre and frightening disorders, has been studied intensively throughout this century. Only since the discovery of antipsychotic drugs in the 1950s, however, have clinicians gained significant insight into its causes. Although theories about schizophrenia abounded before that time, they typically lacked empirical support, contributed to inaccurate stereotyping of the parents of schizophrenic people, and resulted in ineffective forms of treatment. With effective antipsychotic medications in hand, however, researchers have been able to work backward to identify important biological factors in the development of schizophrenia, and have begun to understand better the role of psychological and sociocultural factors.

Investigators have also begun to learn much about the nature and course of schizophrenia. As a result, the prevailing view of schizophrenia as a single disorder with numerous faces may be changing. Research is increasingly suggesting that the different types of schizophrenia may actually represent different disorders, each with a distinct course; distinct biological, genetic, and perhaps psychological origins; and a distinct response to treatment.

Most clinical theorists now agree that schizophrenia, in whatever form, is probably caused by a combination of factors. Many believe, for example, that genetic and biological factors establish a predisposition to develop the disorder, that psychological factors such as personal or familial stress help bring the disorder to fruition, and that other psychological and sociocultural factors, such as individual misinterpretations or societal labeling, help maintain and exacerbate the symptoms.

The precise ways in which heredity, biology, psychology, and society combine to cause schizophrenia are still being uncovered. Certainly there have been exciting, at times spectacular, findings in each of these spheres, including findings from the recent studies of chromosome markers, brain chemistry, and brain structure, but much remains to be learned. What are the precise determining causes of schizophrenia, how does each contribute to the disorder, how do they interact, and how should various forms of schizophrenia be viewed and treated? The considerable progress now being made should impress us, but it must not blind us to the significant gaps, uncertainties, and confusions that continue to obscure our view.

Summary

■ PSYCHOSIS is a state in which individuals lose contact with reality. It frequently takes the form of *schizophrenia,* a disorder in which previously adaptive levels of social, personal, and occupational functioning deteriorate into distorted perceptions, disturbed thought processes, deviant emotional states, and motor abnormalities. Approximately 1 percent of the world's population suffers from this disorder. Many clinicians believe that schizophrenia may be a group of distinct disorders that have some common features.

The symptoms associated with schizophrenia fall into three groupings: *positive symptoms,* "pathological excesses" in behavior; *negative symptoms,* "pathological deficits" in behavior; and *psychomotor symptoms.* The leading positive symptoms found in schizophrenia are *delusions, disorganized thinking and speech, hallucinations* and other disturbances in perception and attention, and *inappropriate affect.* Negative symptoms that often characterize schizophrenia include *poverty of speech, blunted* and *flat affect, disturbances in volition,* and *social withdrawal.* The most typical of the disturbances in psychomotor behavior are collectively called *catatonia.*

■ SCHIZOPHRENIA usually emerges during late adolescence or early adulthood and tends to progress through three phases. A *prodromal phase,* character-ized by a deterioration in functioning, is followed by an *active phase,* in which schizophrenic symptoms become more prominent. The *residual phase* is marked by a return to functioning similar to that of the prodromal phase. Patients may be placed in five categories of schizophrenia, according to DSM-IV criteria: *disorganized type, catatonic type, paranoid type, undifferentiated type,* and *residual type.* In addition, clinicians have begun to distinguish between *Type I schizophrenia,* characterized by the predominance of positive symptoms, and *Type II schizophrenia,* whose symptoms are largely negative.

■ AN INTERACTION OF sociocultural, biological, and psychological factors seems to contribute to schizophrenia. The *sociocultural view* is based on the principle that society has certain expectations in regard to the behavior of a person who is labeled as schizophrenic, and that these expectations may help promote the further development of symptoms.

■ THE GENETIC VIEW, based on the principle that some people inherit a biological predisposition to schizophrenia, is supported by studies of several kinds, including twin studies, adoption studies, and chromosomal mapping studies.

■ THE BIOLOGICAL VIEW attempts to identify the biological abnormalities that are inherited or developed by persons with schizophrenia. The predominant *biochemical* explanation of schizophrenia focuses on an unusually high level of activity in neurons that use the neurotransmitter *dopamine.* There is evidence that the brains of schizophrenic people may contain an unusually large number of dopamine receptors, particularly D-2 receptors. In addition to biochemical abnormalities, modern brain imaging techniques have detected *abnormal brain structures* in schizophrenic people. Two such abnormalities, quite possibly related, are the presence of enlarged ventricles and unusual variations in blood flow in certain parts of the brain.

■ THE PSYCHOLOGICAL VIEWS are based on the principle that psychological factors are critical in the development of schizophrenia. The leading psychological explanations have come from the psychodynamic, behavioral, family, existential, and cognitive perspectives. Traditional *psychodynamic theorists* believe that schizophrenia involves *regression* to a pre-ego state of *primary narcissism* and *restitutive* efforts to reestablish ego control. Contemporary psychodynamic theorists point to a combination of biological and psychodynamic factors. *Behaviorists* theorize that schizophrenic people fail to attend to relevant social cues and as a result develop bizarre responses to the environment. The *family explanations* for schizophrenia hold that the family environment contains such confusing elements as a **schizophrenogenic mother, double-bind communications, marital schism,** and **marital skew.** R. D. Laing's **existential theory** states that schizophrenia is actually a constructive process by which people try to cure themselves of the confu-sion and unhappiness caused by their social and family environment. *Cognitive theorists* contend that when schizophrenic people try to explain their bio-logically induced hallucinations or other strange sen-sations, they develop delusional thinking. Their logical processes lead them to delusional conclusions. Most clinical theorists now agree that schizophrenia, in whatever form, can probably be traced to a combi-nation of factors such as these.

Topic Overview

TREATMENTS FOR SCHIZOPHRENIA

THE SYMPTOMS OF SCHIZOPHRENIA might seem by their very nature to defy treatment. What possible help can there be for people whose thoughts and perceptions are so profoundly confused and distorted? What kind of communication can take place between a patient and a therapist who speak virtually different languages? For years, efforts at treating schizophrenia brought only frustration. Lara Jefferson, a young woman with schizophrenia, wrote of her treatment experience in the 1940s:

They call us insane—and in reality they are as inconsistent as we are, as flighty and changeable. This one in particular. One day he derides and ridicules me unmercifully; the next he talks to me sadly and this morning his eyes misted over with tears as he told me of the fate ahead. Damn him and all of his wisdom!

He has dinned into my ears a monotonous dirge—"Too Egotistical—too Egotistical—too Egotistical. Learn to think differently."—And how can I do it? How—how—can I do it? How the hell can I do it? I have tried to follow his suggestions but have not learned to think a bit differently. It was all wasted effort. Where has it got me?

(Jefferson, 1948)

history, schizophrenic patients ... less. The disorder is still ex-... t, but clinicians are much more ... ...ey were in the past. Much of ... recently discovered antipsy-... ...elp many people with schizophrenia think rationally enough to engage in therapeutic programs that previously had a limited effect at best. Most people with schizophrenia now live outside of institutes, and many of them profit from outpatient treatment and community programs, although, as we shall see, the treatment picture for people with schizophrenics remains far from perfect. A look at past interventions and how treatment has progressed over the years will help us understand the nature and implications of today's approaches to this debilitating disorder.

■ INSTITUTIONAL ■ CARE

For more than half of this century, society's response to schizophrenia was *institutionalization,* usually in a public facility. Because schizophrenic patients failed to respond to traditional therapies and remained thoroughly incapacitated by their disorder, the principal goals of these establishments were restraint and custodial care (provision of food, shelter, and clothing). Patients rarely saw therapists and were largely neglected. Many were abused. Oddly enough, this tragic state of affairs unfolded in an atmosphere of good intentions.

PAST INSTITUTIONAL CARE

The move toward institutionalization began in 1793, when the French physician Philippe Pinel "unchained the insane" from virtual imprisonment at La Bicêtre asylum and began the practice of "moral treatment" (as we saw in Chapter 1). For the first time in centuries, severely disturbed patients were viewed as human beings who should be cared for with sympathy and kindness. Pinel's ideas spread throughout Europe and the United States, and led to the creation of large mental hospitals rather than asylums to care for mentally disturbed people (Goshen, 1967).

These new mental hospitals, typically located in isolated, relatively inexpensive areas, were developed with the noblest of goals (Grob, 1966). They were to be havens from the stresses of daily life and offer a healthful psychological environment in which patients could work closely with therapists. It was believed that such institutional care should be available to both the poor and the rich, so states throughout the United States were required by law to establish public mental institutions, *state hospitals,* to supplement the private ones.

Starting in the mid-nineteenth century, the state hospital system developed serious problems. Wards became increasingly overcrowded, admissions kept rising, and state funding was unable to keep up with the increasing need for professional therapists. Too many aspects of treatment became the responsibility of nurses and attendants, whose knowledge and experience at that time were limited. Between 1845 and 1955 the number of state hospitals and mental patients rose steadily while the quality of care declined. During this period close to 300 state hospitals were established in the United States. The number of hospitalized patients on any given day rose from 2,000 in 1845 to nearly 600,000 in 1955.

The priorities of the public mental hospitals changed during those 110 years. In the face of overcrowding and understaffing, the emphasis shifted from humanitarian care to order-keeping and efficiency. In a throwback to the asylum period, disruptive patients were physically restrained, isolated, and punished; individual attention diminished. Upon first entering a state hospital, most patients were given solicitous attention and care, but they were soon transferred to chronic wards, or "back wards," if they failed to improve (Bloom, 1984). These back wards were in fact human warehouses that were filled with an aura of hopelessness. Staff members often relied on mechanical restraints such as straitjackets and handcuffs to deal with difficult patients. More "advanced" forms of intervention included medically debilitating approaches such as hydrotherapy and lobotomy (see Box 16–1). In the late 1950s it was estimated that 94 percent of the state hospitals could not meet the standards that had been set by the American Psychiatric Association (Roche, 1964). Most of the patients in these institutions were schizophrenic (Hafner & an der Heiden, 1988).

Many patients not only failed to improve under these conditions but developed additional symptoms, apparently as a result of institutionalization itself. The most common pattern of deterioration was the *social breakdown syndrome:* extreme withdrawal, anger, physical aggressiveness, and loss of

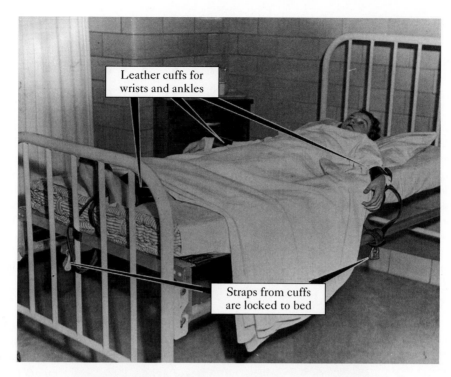

Leather cuffs for
wrists and ankles

Straps from cuffs
are locked to bed

As state hospitals across the United States became overcrowed, they relied increasingly on mechanical restraints as a method of controlling patients. At Byberry State Hospital in Philadelphia, for example, violent patients were often tied to their beds, a procedure that was employed as late as the 1950s.

interest in personal appearance and functioning (Gruenberg, 1980). Often more troublesome than the original symptoms of their disorders, this new syndrome made it impossible for patients to return to society even if they somehow recovered from the difficulties that had first brought them to the hospital.

IMPROVED INSTITUTIONAL CARE

As we noted in Chapter 5, the 1950s saw the development and spread of humanistic and behavioral treatments for various kinds of mental disorders. Clinicians of the time also developed two institutional interventions, *milieu therapy* and the *token economy program*—the former based primarily on humanistic principles and the latter on behavioral principles—that finally offered some help to schizophrenic and other patients who had been languishing in institutions for years (Bloom, 1984). These approaches were particularly helpful in addressing the personal-care and self-image problems exacerbated by institutionalization. They were soon adopted by many institu-

tions and are now standard features of institutional care.

MILIEU THERAPY Humanistic theorists propose that institutionalized patients deteriorate mainly because they are deprived of opportunities to develop self-respect, independence, and responsibility and to engage in meaningful activity, all experiences basic to healthy human functioning. This deprivation begins as a result of their disorder and intensifies in response to institutional depersonalization and neglect. Thus the premise of *milieu therapy* is that the social milieu of institutions must change if patients are to make clinical progress, and that an institutional climate conducive to self-respect, individual responsibility, and meaningful activity must be established.

ORIGINS OF MILIEU THERAPY The pioneer of this approach was Maxwell Jones, a London psychiatrist who in 1953 converted a psychiatric ward of patients with various disorders into a *therapeutic community*. Patients were referred to as "residents" of the community and were treated as persons capable of running their own lives and making their own decisions. Residents participated in institutional planning and government, attending community meetings where they worked with staff members to establish rules and determine sanctions. In fact, patient–staff

BOX 16–1

LOBOTOMY: HOW COULD IT HAPPEN?

In 1949 the *New York Times* reported on a medical procedure that appeared to offer hope to an enormous number of sufferers of severe mental disorders, people for whom it seemed no future was possible outside of increasingly overcrowded mental institutions:

> Hypochondriacs no longer thought they were going to die, would-be suicides found life acceptable, sufferers from persecution complex forgot the machinations of imaginary conspirators. Prefrontal lobotomy, as the operation is called, was made possible by the localization of fears, hates, and instincts [in the prefrontal cortex of the brain]. It is fitting, then, that the Nobel Prize in medicine should be shared by Hess and Moniz. Surgeons now think no more of operations on the brain than they do of removing an appendix.

We now know that the lobotomy was hardly the miracle treatment suggested in this report. In fact, far from "curing" people with mental disorders, the procedure left thousands upon thousands withdrawn, excessively subdued, and even stuporous. Yet, in the twenty-five years after the introduction of the lobotomy by the Portuguese neuropsychiatrist Egas Moniz in 1935, clinicians around the

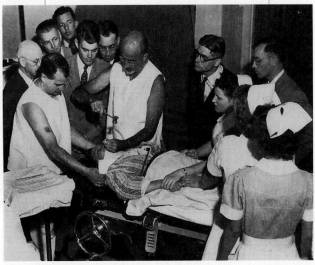

Neuropsychiatrist Walter Freeman performs a lobotomy in 1949 by inserting a needle through a patient's eye socket into the brain.

world considered psychosurgery to be an effective way to treat people suffering from schizophrenia and other severe mental disorders. Moniz's particular lobotomy procedure, called a **prefrontal leukotomy,** involved drilling two holes in either side of the skull and inserting an instrument resembling an icepick into the brain tissue to cut or destroy nerve fibers. Moniz's theory was based on his belief that serious mental disorders were caused by "fixed thoughts" that interfered with mental functioning. The abnormal thought patterns could be altered, he believed, if the appropriate nerve pathways in the brain were severed.

In retrospect, this form of psychosurgery seems crude and barbaric,

yet in its time it was considered a mainstream procedure. In examining the personal, situational, and political factors that contributed to the widespread acceptance of the lobotomy in the 1940s and 1950s, the neuroscientist Elliot Valenstein (1986) considers one of the most important factors to have been the extreme overcrowding in mental hospitals at the time. In the absence of effective treatments for many serious mental disorders, patients were destined to remain in state mental institutions indefinitely. Excessive crowding was making it difficult to maintain decent standards there, a problem being exacerbated by the multitude of returning World War II veterans who required treatment for emotional problems.

Valenstein also points to the central roles played by certain powerful personalities, the inventors and advocates of psychosurgery. Although he does not deny the fact that Moniz and his American counterpart, Walter Freeman, were gifted and dedicated physicians, Valenstein also calls attention to their desire for status. Moniz, director of the new Neurological Institute in Lisbon and a member of the Portuguese parliament, had been twice passed over for the Nobel Prize for medicine by the time he attended the Second International Congress of

distinctions were almost eliminated in Jones's therapeutic community. Everyone was valued as an important therapeutic agent, in the belief that patients could benefit from interactions with other patients as well as from discussions with staff members. Similarly, staff members could gain insights from talking with patients. The atmosphere was one of mutual respect, interdependence, support, and openness. Patients were involved in a variety of constructive activities, including special projects, semipermanent jobs,

Neurology in 1935. It was there that he learned of Carlyle Jacobsen's experiments on the prefrontal brain areas of monkeys and chimpanzees. Learning how the destruction of the animals' prefrontal brain lobes had sedated them, Moniz wondered whether this procedure might be used to alleviate the symptoms of anxiety in human beings. Later Moniz contended that he had been contemplating this kind of operation for several years. After returning home from the conference, Moniz immediately set to work. Just three months later, having done no animal testing for safety and with arguably little preparation, he performed the first prefrontal leukotomy on a human being.

Today it is hard to believe that respected physicians and scientists around the world would condone, much less applaud, this kind of impulsive experimentation on human beings. Moniz's prestige and capacity for diplomacy were so great, and the field of neurology was so small, that his work received relatively little criticism. Furthermore, for many people, this "cure" seemed to offer an economic and social relief that was just too desirable to resist.

By 1941 some 350 to 500 lobotomies had been performed throughout the world (Hutton, Fleming, & Fox, 1941). The 1940s then witnessed an enormous increase in the number of psychosurgical operations, attributed largely to the influence of a book called *Psychosurgery: Intelligence, Emotion, and Social Behavior Following Prefrontal Lobotomy for Mental Disorders*, published in 1942. Its authors, Walter Freeman and his surgical partner, James Watts, were the first to adopt the prefrontal lobotomy after its

introduction by Moniz. Later they would develop a second kind of psychosurgery called the *transorbital lobotomy,* in which the surgeon inserted a needle into the brain through the eye socket and rotated it in order to destroy the brain tissue. Their book described the results of eighty cases of lobotomy and contained detailed instructions and illustrations of the standard "Freeman-Watts" procedure.

Physicians may have been misled by the initial outcome studies of lobotomy, which were methodologically flawed and offered no placebo comparison groups (Valenstein, 1986). Apparently they were also captivated by glowing written reports of postoperative patient responses to lobotomy. Actually, however, some of these early positive reports also included descriptions of patient reactions to lobotomies that probably should have alerted physicians about the potential dangers of the procedure. Freeman himself wrote in 1942,

The chief effects appear to be loss of fantasy, or creative drive, or sensitivity, of sympathetic understanding of others. If the operation is radical, patients are likely to be somewhat gross in their appetites for food and sex, careless and slovenly in appearance, and largely impervious to criticism. . . . Patients after lobotomy show some lack of personality depth. They are cheerful and complacent and are indifferent to the opinions and feelings of others.

A decade later, these very kinds of statements contributed to lobotomy's downfall. Moreover, studies increasingly confirmed that in addition to a fatality rate of 1.5 to 6 percent, lobotomy resulted in objectionable

physical consequences such as epileptic seizures, huge weight gain, loss of motor coordination, partial paralysis, incontinence, endocrine problems, and extreme intellectual and emotional unresponsiveness.

In the 1950s concern developed that psychosurgery might be used to control the perpetrators of violent crimes, and lobotomy became a civil rights issue as well. Furthermore, with the discovery of antipsychotic drugs, the lobotomy began to look like an expensive, complicated, and inhumane way of treating mental disorders. By 1960 the number of lobotomies being performed had been drastically reduced.

Today psychosurgery of any kind is rare, considered experimental, and used only as a last resort in the most severe cases of obsessive-compulsive disorder and depression (Goodman et al., 1992; Greist, 1992). Psychosurgical procedures have also been dramatically refined, and hardly resemble the blind and brutal lobotomies of forty and fifty years ago. The *cingulotomy,* for example, involves the insertion of an electrode needle through two small holes in the skull, to make a tiny cut in a particular nerve bundle called the *cingulum.* The procedure is often guided by magnetic resonance imaging (MRI) to increase accuracy. More than 500 cingulotomies have been performed at Massachusetts General Hospital since 1962 (Beck & Cowley, 1990). Despite this improvement in psychosurgery, many professionals believe any kind of surgery aimed specifically at destroying brain tissue is unethical, and argue that even a limited use of psychosurgery keeps alive one of the clinical field's most shameful and ill-advised efforts at cure.

occupational therapy, recreation, and community government. In short, their daily schedule resembled life outside the hospital.

THE SPREAD OF MILIEU THERAPY Milieu-style programs were soon developed in institutions

throughout the Western world. Even clinicians who did not agree with Jones's humanistic perspective on mental disorders agreed that milieu therapy was superior to custodial care for most institutionalized mental patients.

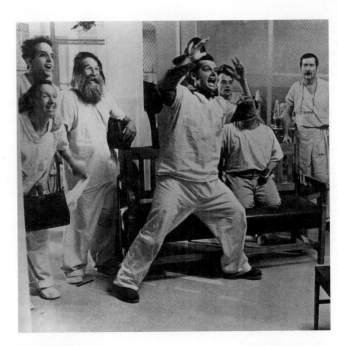

Francisco de Goya's early nineteenth century painting The Madhouse, *depicting a typical mental hospital of his day, is strikingly similar to the portrayal in Ken Kesey's 1950s novel (later a play and film),* One Flew Over the Cuckoo's Nest. *Institutions of both the distant and the recent past were overcrowded, often negligent, and concerned primarily with keeping order.*

Milieu approaches have varied from setting to setting. In some institutions, "milieu therapy" simply means that staff members try to facilitate interactions (especially group interactions) between patients and staff, keep patients active, and establish higher expectations of what patients should be able to accomplish. Other milieu programs actually create patient councils to administer ward affairs, give patients considerable responsibility in guiding their own lives, and offer meaningful work opportunities. A few institutions, such as R. D. Laing's Kingsley Hall, have been fully converted into therapeutic communities where staff and patients are equals, and the social milieu is indeed the central feature of the treatment received there.

THE EFFECTIVENESS OF MILIEU THERAPY
Because milieu approaches vary so greatly among institutions and have been applied to patients with various disorders, researchers have had difficulty assessing their effectiveness. So far the only conclusion that can be drawn is that some milieu approaches do indeed help institutionalized schizophrenic patients. Chronic patients in some milieu hospital programs have improved and left the hospital at higher rates than chronic patients in custodial programs (Paul & Lentz, 1977; Artiss, 1962; Cumming & Cumming, 1962). On the other hand, many of these patients remain impaired and must live in sheltered settings af-

ter their release. In addition, as we shall see shortly, milieu approaches tend not to be as effective as some other current approaches to treating institutionalized schizophrenic patients.

Despite these limitations, milieu therapy continues to be practiced in many institutions. Studies have found that this approach is often a helpful adjunct to other hospital approaches (Ciompi et al., 1992). It has also had an impact on community treatment programs. We shall see later that programs established at halfway houses to ease schizophrenic individuals back into community residential life often incorporate resident self-government, work schedules, and other features of milieu therapy.

THE TOKEN ECONOMY
In the 1950s behaviorists had little status in mental institutions and were permitted to work only with patients whose problems seemed virtually hopeless. At the time, the "hopeless" included chronic schizophrenic patients. Through years of experimentation, behaviorists found that the systematic application of operant techniques could help alter the dysfunctional patterns of these patients (Ayllon, 1963; Ayllon & Michael, 1959). Programs that apply such techniques have been given the name *token economy programs.*

Teodoro Ayllon and Nathan Azrin (1968, 1965) set up the first token economy program for schizophrenic patients in an Illinois hospital. Patients were rewarded whenever they behaved acceptably according to an established set of criteria and were not rewarded when they behaved unacceptably. The immediate rewards for acceptable behavior were tokens that could later be used to purchase specific items or privileges; thus the name "token economy."

As a first step Ayllon and Azrin selected a series of target behaviors that patients would be rewarded for. The patients could earn tokens by performing on-the-ward tasks such as making their beds, serving meals, and doing laundry, and for off-ward jobs such as kitchen work and telephone duty. They could also earn tokens by speaking more normally, abiding by ward rules, and showing self-control in social interactions.

The researchers then selected a range of reinforcements that patients would find appealing. Tokens could be traded for any of the following rewards:

1. *Privacy.* A single-bed room cost 30 tokens, a two-bed room 15, and a four-bed room 8 tokens.
2. *Privileges.* Patients could go on an escorted walk on the hospital grounds at a cost of 2 tokens. An accompanied trip downtown cost 100 tokens.
3. *Staff interactions.* An extended private discussion with the social worker cost 100 tokens.
4. *Religious activities.* For 1 token patients could purchase an extra religious service on the ward. They could purchase one off the ward for 10 tokens. Private discussions with the chaplain remained free.
5. *Entertainment.* Patients could choose their own television programs for 3 tokens. They could attend a movie on the ward for 1 token.
6. *Shopping.* Candy, beverages, and cigarettes cost from 1 to 5 tokens. Toiletries ranged from 1 to 10 tokens. Clothing cost from 12 to 400 tokens.

Although some clinicians had predicted that such a program would prove too complicated for schizophrenic patients, Ayllon and Azrin found that most learned the system and began to behave more appropriately. They also conducted a series of experiments to determine the range and limits of token economy programs, and found that the most effective payoff time was immediately after patients performed a task properly. Today token economy programs are being used in many hospital settings (Emmelkamp, 1994; Paul & Lentz, 1977; Kazdin, 1977, 1975).

To keep widening a patient's repertoire of appropriate behaviors, clinicians must periodically introduce new target behaviors and reinforcements. Some hospitals actually set up several token economy programs, called *leveled programs,* each representing a different level of difficulty. When patients learn to perform the target behaviors of one program consistently, they are transferred to another program where more demanding behaviors are required; target behaviors from the former program no longer earn tokens. Ideally, the patients progress from level to level until they are ready for discharge.

THE EFFECTIVENESS OF TOKEN ECONOMY PROGRAMS Research suggests that token economies do help change schizophrenic patterns and related inappropriate behaviors (Emmelkamp, 1994; Belcher, 1988). In one of the most successful such programs, Gordon Paul and R. L. Lentz (1977) applied operant principles to twenty-eight chronic schizophrenic patients whose dysfunctional behaviors included mutism, repeated screaming, incontinence, smearing feces on walls, and physical assault. The program addressed every aspect of the patients' lives. Tokens could be earned for proper appearance, bed-making, bathing, appropriate meal behavior, contributions in class, acceptable social behavior, and normal talk—all of which were explained and rehearsed in regular training sessions. The list of reinforcements was long and varied, and even included certain necessities, such as breakfast, lunch, and dinner. If patients did not earn enough tokens to buy a meal, they were given a free "medical meal"—a healthful but unappetizing blend of nutrients.

Most patients improved significantly under this program. After seven months, many were regularly demonstrating appropriate behavior in each target area. By the end of the program, four and a half years later, 98 percent of the subjects had been released, usually to shelter care facilities. At a follow-up eighteen months later, only two patients had been rehospitalized.

Paul and Lentz also set up two other kinds of programs for purposes of comparison. A *custodial program,* consisting of custodial care, medication, and limited psychotherapy, was administered to a control group of twenty-eight chronic schizophrenic patients closely matched to the token economy patients in symptoms, age, and background. In addition, a *milieu program* was established for twenty-eight other matched patients. This last group was organized as a community, with a patient council to make important decisions about patients' activities and community events. Staff members repeatedly communicated positive expectations and encouragement ("I know you can get that job done") while also conveying negative feedback for inappropriate behavior and making it clear that they expected to see improvement.

In all three programs, staff members observed patients' behavior on an hourly basis, thus enabling Paul and Lentz to compare the patients' progress. They found that after seven months the token economy patients made more improvements than the milieu patients, and both groups improved significantly more than the custodial patients. In addition, only 71 percent of the milieu patients and 45 percent of the custodial patients were released by the end of their four-and-a-half-year programs, compared to 98 percent of the token economy patients.

PROBLEMS FACING TOKEN ECONOMIES

A number of important questions and objections have been raised regarding token economy programs and the studies conducted to evaluate them (Kazdin, 1983). One problem is that many token economy studies, unlike the Paul and Lentz study, are uncontrolled. When administrators set up a token economy, they usually include all ward patients in the program rather than dividing the patients into a token economy group and a control group. As a result, patients' improvements can be compared only with their own past behaviors, and that comparison may be confounded by variables other than the program's operant principles (a new physical setting, for example, or a general increase in staff attention could be the cause of improvement).

Many clinicians also have raised ethical and legal concerns about token economy programs. In order for such programs to be effective, administrators need to control the important reinforcements in a patient's life, including, theoretically, basic reinforcements such as food, a comfortable bed, and the like. But aren't there some items in life to which all human beings are entitled? A number of important court decisions have now affirmed that patients have certain basic rights that clinicians cannot violate, irrespective of the positive goals of a treatment program, including the right of free access to food, storage space, and furniture, as well as freedom of movement (Emmelkamp, 1994). Though highly appropriate, such boundaries have set limits on the scope and impact of many token economy programs.

Some clinicians have also questioned the quality of the improvement achieved under token economy programs. Are behaviorists altering a patient's schizophrenic thoughts and perceptions or simply improving the patient's ability to mimic normal behavior? This issue is illustrated in the case of a middle-aged schizophrenic man named John, who had the delusion that he was the United States govern-

ment. Whenever he spoke to others, he spoke as the government. "We are happy to see you. . . . We need people like you in our service. . . . We are carrying out our activities in John's body." When John's hospital ward was converted into a token economy, the staff members targeted his delusional statements, requiring him to identify himself properly to earn tokens. If he called himself John, he would receive tokens; if he maintained that he was the government, he would receive nothing.

After a few months on the token economy program, John stopped presenting himself as the government. When asked his name, he would say, "John." Although staff members were understandably pleased by his improvement, John himself had a different view of the situation. In a private discussion he said:

We're tired of it. Every damn time we want a cigarette, we have to go through their bullshit. "What's your name? . . . Who wants the cigarette? . . . Where is the government?" Today, we were desperate for a smoke and went to Simpson, the damn nurse, and she made us do her bidding. "Tell me your name if you want a cigarette. What's your name?" Of course, we said, "John." We needed the cigarettes. If we told her the truth, no cigarettes. But we don't have time for this nonsense. We've got business to do, international business, laws to change, people to recruit. And these people keep playing their games.

(Comer, 1973)

Critics of the behavioral approach would argue that John was still delusional and therefore as "schizophrenic" as before. Behaviorists, however, would defend John's progress, arguing that he had improved by learning to keep his delusion to himself and at the very least had improved in his judgments about the consequences of his behavior. They also might see this as an important step toward changing his private thinking.

Finally, getting patients to make a satisfactory transition from token economy hospital programs to community living has presented a difficult problem for behaviorists. In an environment where rewards are contingent on proper behaviors, proper behaviors become contingent on continued rewards. Some patients who find that the real world doesn't reward them so concretely abandon their newly acquired behaviors. Thus behaviorists have adopted two strategies to facilitate the transition from token economy hospital programs to community living: (1) *changing hospital programs* so that they resemble real life more closely (for example, instituting more social reinforcements, such as attention and praise from staff

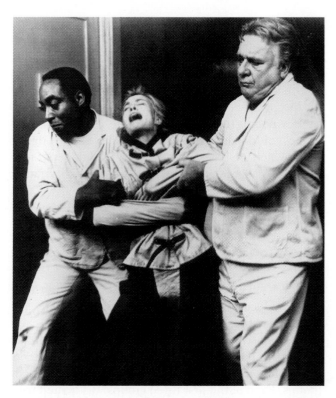

In the 1950s institutions began to rely less on restraints such as the straitjacket (depicted in the film biography Frances*) in favor of milieu therapy programs, which encouraged patients to control their own lives, or of token economy programs, which used systematic reinforcements to change patients' behavior.*

members) and (2) *changing community residences* into token economy programs. Such strategies have, however, had a limited impact (Paul & Lentz, 1977). Moreover, many clinicians are uncomfortable with the idea of controlling people's lives to a large extent after they leave an institution, and prefer to adopt the salient features of milieu therapy, such as support, self-government, and job placement, as the focus of community residential programs.

All these issues notwithstanding, token economy programs have had a most important effect on the treatment of people with schizophrenia. They were among the first hospital treatment techniques that actually helped change schizophrenic symptoms, got chronic patients moving again, and enabled some of them to be released from the hospital. Although no longer as popular as they once were (Glynn, 1990), token economies are still employed in many mental hospitals, usually along with medication, and in some community residences as well. The token economy approach has also been applied to other clinical problems, including mental retardation, delinquency, and hyperactivity, as well as in other fields, such as education and business.

◾ ANTIPSYCHOTIC ◾ DRUGS

Milieu therapy and token economy programs helped to improve the gloomy prognosis for schizophrenia, but it was the discovery of antipsychotic drugs in the 1950s that truly revolutionized its treatment (Breslin, 1992; Weinberger, 1991). These drugs eliminate many schizophrenic patients' symptoms and today are almost always a part of treatment. What is more, as we noted in Chapter 15, they have also influenced the way clinicians view schizophrenia.

The discovery of antipsychotic medications dates back to the discovery of *antihistamine drugs.* In the 1940s medical researchers found that certain drugs blocked the release of histamine—a chemical stored in cells throughout the body—and brought remarkable relief to people suffering from allergies such as hay fever. Although the drugs also produced considerable tiredness and drowsiness, they quickly rose in popularity, and many antihistamines were developed.

During the same period, researchers in the area of surgical anesthesia were looking for a way to prevent anesthetized patients from experiencing a sudden drop in blood pressure and going into shock. The French surgeon Henri Laborit came to believe that the new antihistamine drugs, given along with general anesthesia, might prevent such a drop in blood pressure. He administered one group of antihistamines, *phenothiazines,* to his surgical patients. Although the drugs actually had no effect on blood pressure, Laborit noticed that they did have an effect that might help to calm patients before surgery—they made patients sleepy and relaxed, while allowing them to remain awake. Laborit and others experimented with several phenothiazine antihistamines and became most impressed with one called *chlorpromazine.* Laborit reported, "It provokes not any loss of consciousness, not any change in the patient's mentality but a slight tendency to sleep and above all 'disinterest' for all that goes on around him." Before long, this drug gained wide acceptance as a preoperative medication.

Laborit and other researchers also suspected that, because of its relaxing effect, chlorpromazine might be helpful in the treatment of mental disorders. The psychiatrists Jean Delay and Pierre Deniker (1952) soon tested the drug on six psychotic patients and reported a sharp reduction in their symptoms. In 1954, after a series of laboratory and clinical tests, chlorpromazine began to be marketed in the United States as an antipsychotic medication under the trade name Thorazine.

Since the discovery of chlorpromazine, numerous antipsychotic drugs have been developed (see Table 16–1). Collectively they are known as *neuroleptic drugs,* because they often produce effects similar to the symptoms of neurological diseases. Some of the drugs, like chlorpromazine, are from the phenothiazine group, including *thioridazine* (Mellaril), *mesoridazine* (Serentil), *fluphenazine* (Prolixin), and *trifluoperazine* (Stelazine). Others, such as *haloperidol* (Haldol) and *thiothixene* (Navane), belong to different chemical classes.

As we saw in Chapter 15, these drugs apparently reduce schizophrenic symptoms by reducing excessive activity of the neurotransmitter dopamine (Strange, 1992; Davis et al., 1988). Remember that many schizophrenic persons, particularly those with Type I schizophrenia, have an excessive number of receptors on their dopamine-receiving neurons, which apparently lead to extra dopamine activity at those sites and so to the symptoms of schizophrenia. After a pa-

tient takes antipsychotic drugs for a time, the dopamine-receiving neurons apparently grow additional dopamine receptors (Strange, 1992; Burt et al., 1977; Seeman et al., 1976). It is as if the neurons recognize that dopamine transmission is being blocked by the drugs at the usual receptors and compensate by developing new ones. Now the patient has two groups of dopamine receptors—the many original ones, which are blocked, and a normal number of new ones, which produce normal synaptic activity rather than schizophrenic symptoms.

THE EFFECTIVENESS OF ANTIPSYCHOTIC DRUGS

Research has repeatedly shown that antipsychotic drugs reduce schizophrenic symptoms in many patients (Strange, 1992; Davis et al., 1988). An early comprehensive study examined 344 schizophrenic patients in nine hospitals (Cole et al., 1964). Patients were randomly assigned to one of four treatment groups. Each of the first three groups was treated with a different antipsychotic drug, while the fourth group received a placebo. In this double-blind study, neither the patients nor the hospital staff knew who was taking real drugs and who was taking the placebos. After six weeks of treatment, the patients were evaluated by the hospital staff. More than 75 percent of the patients taking actual antipsychotic medications were evaluated as "much improved." Only 25 percent of the placebo patients improved to this degree. In fact, 50 percent of the patients taking antipsychotic drugs were now rated as "normal" or "borderline normal," compared to only 15 percent of the placebo patients (see Figure 16–1).

Further research has suggested that antipsychotic drugs are the single most effective intervention for schizophrenic patients *during hospitalization.* In one of the best known, best-constructed hospital studies on this subject (May, Tuma, & Dixon, 1981; May, 1968; May & Tuma, 1964), a total of 228 hospitalized schizophrenic patients were assigned to one of five treatment groups: (1) antipsychotic medications only, (2) psychodynamic therapy only, (3) antipsychotic medications plus psychotherapy, (4) milieu therapy, and (5) electroconvulsive therapy. Patients treated with drugs alone and those treated with drugs plus psychodynamic therapy improved equally and showed significantly more improvement than all other subjects in the study. The least improvement occurred among those receiving psychodynamic therapy only or milieu therapy only. Patients who received electroconvulsive therapy fell in between.

TABLE 16–1

ANTIPSYCHOTIC DRUGS

CLASS/GENERIC NAME	TRADE NAME	USUAL DAILY ORAL DOSE (mg)
Chlorpromazine	Thorazine	200–600
Triflupromazine	Vesprin	50–150
Thioridazine	Mellaril	200–600
Mesoridazine besylate	Serentil	150
Piperacetazine	Quide	20–40
Trifluoperazine	Stelazine	2–4
Fluphenazine hydro-chloride	Prolixin Permitil	2.5–10
Perphenazine	Trilafon	16–64
Acetophenazine maleate	Tindal	60
Chlorprothixene	Taractan	75–200
Thiothixene	Navane	6–30
Haloperidol	Haldol	2–12
Loxapine	Loxitane	20
Molindone hydro-chloride	Moban Lidone	15–60
Pimozide	Orap	2–10
Clozapine	Clozaril	200–900

Source: Silver & Yudofsky, 1988, pp. 771–773.

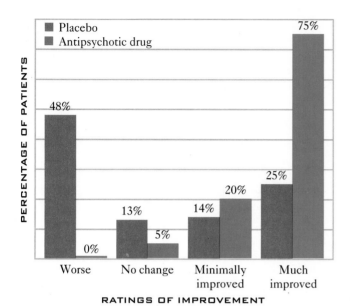

FIGURE 16-1 *After 6 weeks of treatment, 75 percent of schizophrenic patients who were given antipsychotic drugs were much improved, compared to only 25 percent of patients given placebos. In addition, close to half of those on the placebos worsened. (Adapted from Cole et al., 1964.)*

The patients in the study subsequently received treatments that were determined individually by their therapists. A follow-up assessment conducted two to five years later indicated that those who had received antipsychotic drug treatment in the hospital, with or without psychodynamic therapy, continued to do better than the other patients after their release from the hospital: they were rehospitalized less frequently and spent fewer days in the hospital during the intervening years. These results suggest that antipsychotic drugs may be superior to other forms of treatment for many hospitalized schizophrenic patients.

Research has also indicated that schizophrenic symptoms return for some patients if they stop taking antipsychotic drugs too soon (Davis et al., 1993). One study examined the continued progress of recently released patients who had been helped by antipsychotic medications (Hogarty et al., 1974; Hogarty & Goldberg, 1973). Soon after improving, one group of patients was switched to placebo drugs, while a second group continued to receive real antipsychotic medication for at least several months more. A follow-up study two years later revealed that the placebo group went on to have a rehospitalization rate of 80 percent, while the real medication group relapsed at a 45 percent rate. In another study the long-used antipsychotic medications of people with chronic cases of schizophrenia were discontinued and changed to a placebo after five years without severe symptoms. Seventy-five percent of the chronic pa-

tients relapsed within a year, compared to 33 percent of chronic patients who remained on active medication (Sampath et al., 1992).

As we noted in Chapter 15, recent research has indicated that antipsychotic drugs alleviate the *positive symptoms* of schizophrenia, such as hallucinations and delusions, more completely, or at least more quickly, than the *negative symptoms*, such as flat affect, poverty of speech, and loss of volition (Leff, 1992; Breier et al., 1991). Correspondingly, people dominated by positive symptoms (Type I schizophrenia) display generally higher recovery rates from schizophrenia, while those with negative symptoms (Type II schizophrenia) are less affected by drug treatment and have a poorer prognosis (Lindstrom et al., 1992; Pogue-Geile, 1989).

Antipsychotic drugs have now achieved widespread acceptance in the treatment of schizophrenia. Patients often dislike the powerful impact of these drugs, and some refuse to take them; but like Edward Snow, a writer who overcame schizophrenia, many are greatly helped by the medications.

*I*n my case it was necessary to come to terms with a specified drug program. I am a legalized addict. My dose: 100 milligrams of Thorazine and 60 milligrams of Stelazine daily. I don't feel this dope at all, but I have been told it is strong enough to flatten a normal person. It keeps me—as the doctors agree—sane and in good spirits. Without the brain candy, as I call it, I would go—zoom—right back into the bin. I've made the institution scene enough already to be familiar with what it's like and to know I don't want to go back.

(Snow, 1976)

UNWANTED EFFECTS OF ANTIPSYCHOTIC DRUGS

Unfortunately, in addition to their impact on schizophrenic symptoms, antipsychotic drugs can produce disturbing movement abnormalities that may affect appearance and functioning (Pickar, Owen, & Litman, 1991) (see Figure 16-2). These effects are called *extrapyramidal effects* because they appear to be caused by the drugs' impact on the extrapyramidal areas of the brain, areas that regulate motor activity. They include Parkinsonian symptoms, dystonia, akathisia, neuroleptic malignant syndrome, and tardive dyskinesia. These undesired effects are so common that they are listed in DSM-IV as *medication-induced movement disorders* (APA, 1994).

PARKINSONIAN SYMPTOMS As we saw in Chapter 15, antipsychotic drugs produce effects that

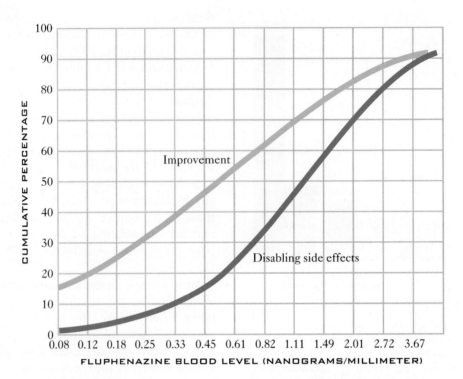

FIGURE 16-2 *The reactions of schizophrenic patients to the traditional antipsychotic drug fluphenazine (Prolixin) demonstrate the close relationship between drug dosage, patient improvement, and serious unwanted drug effects. As blood levels of the drug increase, so do patient improvement and disabling unwanted drug effects. At higher levels of the drug, the benefits-risk trade-off becomes highly arguable. (Adapted from Barondes, 1993, p. 162.)*

resemble the symptoms of the neurological disorder Parkinson's disease in 20 to 40 percent of patients on the drugs (Strange, 1992). Patients may experience such severe and continuous muscle tremors and muscle rigidity that they shake, move very slowly, shuffle their feet, and show little facial expression. These drug effects are sometimes mistakenly viewed as further symptoms of the schizophrenic disorder.

Parkinson's disease is caused by low dopamine activity in the substantia nigra, a part of the midbrain that coordinates movement and posture. Apparently when antipsychotic drugs block dopamine activity throughout the brain, activity of the neurotransmitter in the substantia nigra ceases, thus causing Parkinsonian symptoms (Pickar et al., 1991). In most cases the unwanted effects can be reversed by prescribing an anti-Parkinsonian drug (such as *benztropine*, trade name Cogentin) along with the antipsychotic drug.

DYSTONIA *Dystonia* is a condition characterized by involuntary muscle contractions that cause bizarre and uncontrollable movements of the face, neck, tongue, and back. It is more common at high doses of antipsychotic drugs and in older patients (Khanna,

Das, & Damodaran, 1992). Apparently this drug effect is also related to the reduction of dopamine synaptic activity in the substantia nigra and responds well to treatment with anti-Parkinsonian drugs.

AKATHISIA *Akathisia* is marked by a very high degree of restlessness and agitation, sometimes mistaken for schizophrenic agitation. People who suffer from this effect of antipsychotic drugs experience great discomfort in the limbs and continually move their arms and legs in an effort to relieve it. Like the Parkinsonian symptoms and dystonia, akathisia seems to be related to reduced dopamine activity in the substantia nigra, but it is not so easy to control by anti-Parkinsonian medications (Pickar et al., 1991). Sometimes the only recourse is to reduce the dose of the antipsychotic drug.

NEUROLEPTIC MALIGNANT SYNDROME In some cases antipsychotic drugs produce ***neuroleptic malignant syndrome,*** a severe, potentially fatal reaction marked by muscle rigidity, fever, altered consciousness, and autonomic dysfunction. This immobilizing syndrome apparently occurs in 0.2 to 2.4 percent of persons who take the drugs (Hermesh et al., 1992; Singh, 1981). The syndrome, which is sometimes overlooked in its early stages, is treated by the immediate stoppage of antipsychotic drugs, interventions to reduce fever, dehydration, and other specific symptoms, and in some cases, medications (Velamoor et al., 1994; Pennati et al., 1991; Levenson, 1985).

TARDIVE DYSKINESIA   *Tardive dyskinesia* means "late-appearing movement disorder." Whereas many of the other undesirable drug effects appear within days or weeks, tardive dyskinesia usually does not unfold until a person has taken antipsychotic drugs for more than a year. It consists of involuntary writhing or ticlike movements of the tongue, mouth, face, or whole body, and may include involuntary chewing, sucking, and lip smacking and jerky, purposeless movements of the arms, legs, or entire body. In some people it is accompanied by memory impairment (Sorokin et al., 1988).

Although most cases of tardive dyskinesia are mild and involve a single symptom such as tongue flicking, some are severe and socially debilitating and include such features as continual rocking back and forth, irregular breathing, and grotesque contortions of the face and body. It is believed that between 20 and 30 percent of the people who take antipsychotic drugs for an extended period of time develop tardive dyskinesia to some degree (APA, 1994; Strange, 1992).

Apparently people over 55 years of age are much more vulnerable to tardive dyskinesia, although younger patients may also develop the problem. The highest incidence occurs in those who take antipsychotic drugs for longer than two years (Smith & Baldessarini, 1980; May & Simpson, 1980). There are also some research indications that Type II schizophrenic people, whose negative symptoms are relatively unresponsive to antipsychotic drugs anyway, may have a higher risk of developing tardive dyskinesia (Davis, Borde, & Sharma, 1992).

Tardive dyskinesia can be difficult, sometimes impossible, to eliminate. If it is discovered early and the antipsychotic drugs are stopped immediately, it will usually disappear (APA, 1994; Pickar et al., 1991). Early detection, however, is elusive. Some of the symptoms are so similar to schizophrenic symptoms that clinicians may overlook them, continue or even increase antipsychotic drug therapy, and inadvertently create a more serious case of tardive dyskinesia. Similarly, because of their cognitive deficits, many schizophrenic people are not aware of developing a movement disorder (Macpherson & Collis, 1992). The longer patients continue taking antipsychotic drugs, the less likely it is that their tardive dyskinesia

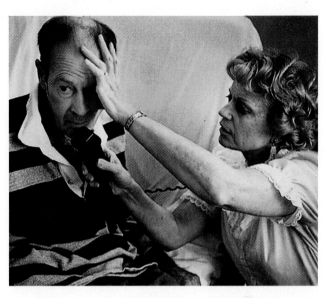

This man has a severe case of Parkinson's disease, a disorder caused by low dopamine activity, and his muscle tremors prevent him from shaving himself. Antipsychotic drugs often produce similar Parkinsonian symptoms.

will disappear when the antipsychotic drugs are finally stopped. There is some evidence that treatment with vitamin E may reduce symptoms of tardive dyskinesia, but the research results have been mixed (Egan et al., 1992; Shiriqui et al., 1992). Researchers do not yet understand why antipsychotic drugs cause tardive dyskinesia in some patients, although they suspect that the syndrome is once again related to the drugs' effect on dopamine receptors in the substantia nigra.

Despite the risk of tardive dyskinesia, antipsychotic medications continue to be prescribed for most schizophrenic patients, particularly those with positive symptoms. Clinicians argue that without the drugs these patients would be doomed to lives of schizophrenic dysfunction. They also point out that most patients who take antipsychotic drugs do not develop tardive dyskinesia and that it can usually be reversed if it is detected early.

CURRENT PRESCRIPTION PRACTICES Clinicians are now wiser and more careful in their prescription practices than they were in past years. In the past, when a patient did not respond to a neuroleptic drug, clinicians might keep increasing the dose (Kane, 1992). Research now suggests that this strategy does not work, that patients who fail to respond to a neuroleptic drug rarely respond to a higher dose (Kane, 1992), and today's clinicians typically stop the neuroleptic drug in such cases (Essali et al., 1992; Simhandl & Meszaros, 1992; Safferman &

Munne, 1992). Similarly, today's clinicians try to prescribe the lowest effective dose of antipsychotic drugs for each patient and to reduce or halt medication weeks or months after the patient reestablishes nonpsychotic functioning (Kane, 1990, 1987; Muller, 1983).

Unfortunately, as we noted earlier, some patients, particularly chronic patients, cannot hold their own without medications. These persons tend to be put back on medications rather quickly, often receiving a higher-than-recommended dose of antipsychotic drugs (Remington et al., 1993; Collins et al., 1992). A recent study of chronic schizophrenic patients living in sheltered-care facilities found that their drug doses had actually been increased over a twelve-year period and that 10 percent of them were now taking extremely high doses (Segal, Cohen, & Marder, 1992).

Given such trends, researchers are currently searching for ways to predict psychotic relapse so that they may better determine when a patient's dose can be lowered or discontinued. One promising method for predicting relapse is to measure the *prolactin* level in the patient's blood—apparently patients with a low level of serum prolactin tend to relapse earlier (Lieberman, 1993; Coryell et al., 1990). A second method is to observe a patient's behavioral changes after he or she is given a dopamine-enhancing drug such as *methylphenidate* (Lieberman, 1993). Patients who display symptoms after receiving methylphenidate apparently relapse more rapidly.

New Antipsychotic Drugs

Even as the traditional antipsychotic drugs were rising in popularity over the past three decades, researchers searched actively for alternative drugs to offer patients who did not respond to, could not tolerate, or were endangered by the traditional drugs. In recent years research has yielded several new antipsychotic drugs that may now be given to patients who fall into this category. The most effective and widely used of these new drugs is *clozapine,* trade name Clozaril (Buckley et al., 1994; Meltzer, 1991). As we discussed in Chapter 15, clozapine is considered an *atypical* antipsychotic drug because its biological impact differs from that of traditional antipsychotic medications. It has been found to be significantly more effective than the traditional drugs, helping approximately 80 to 85 percent of schizophrenic persons

as compared to the approximately 65 to 75 percent helped by traditional neuroleptics (Breier et al., 1994; Naber et al., 1992; Kane, 1992).

Another major benefit of clozapine is that it causes few extrapyramidal symptoms, apparently because it does not block as many dopamine receptors as traditional neuroleptic drugs (Chengappa et al., 1994; Gerlach & Hansen, 1992). More important, few, if any, cases of tardive dyskinesia have been attributed to clozapine, even after prolonged treatment (Meltzer, 1993; Safferman et al., 1991). In addition, tardive dyskinesia and other extrapyramidal symptoms are often reduced when schizophrenic patients are switched to clozapine (Clozapine Study Group, 1993; Levin et al., 1992). Another advantage of clozapine is that unlike traditional neuroleptics, it appears to at least sometimes reduce the negative symptoms found in Type II schizophrenia as well as the positive symptoms found in Type I schizophrenia (Breier et al., 1994; Clozapine Study Group, 1993).

Yet clozapine has some serious problems of its own (Banov et al., 1994). People who use this drug have a 1 to 2 percent risk of developing **agranulocytosis,** a life-threatening drop in white blood cells (granulocytes). Since researchers have not yet developed a way to predict who is susceptible to this disorder, patients who take clozapine need frequent blood tests so that it can be detected early (Alvir & Lieberman, 1994; Krupp & Barnes, 1992) (see Box 16–2). If a patient is found to suffer from agranulocytosis, clozapine is discontinued and the patient's blood count usually returns to normal after two or three weeks. Unfortunately, several deaths have resulted from failure to detect agranulocytosis early. Several less serious unwanted effects have also been associated with clozapine. Patients who take this drug may experience drowsiness or dizziness, excessive salivation, weight gain, or, occasionally, seizures (Meltzer, 1993; Leadbetter et al., 1992; Thomas & Goudemand, 1992).

Because clozapine can induce agranulocytosis, it has been approved by the FDA only for schizophrenic patients who do not improve with traditional neuroleptic drugs. Although some researchers agree with this policy (Krupp & Barnes, 1992), others argue that *all* patients should be allowed to try clozapine, even if they show some improvement on other drugs, because with clozapine there is less chance of extrapyramidal effects and because some patients improve more on clozapine than on the traditional neuroleptic drugs (Meltzer, 1993).

Continuing their search for antipsychotic drugs that are both effective and safe, researchers have recently

BOX 16-2

THE BUSINESS OF MENTAL HEALTH: "JUST BECAUSE YOU'RE PARANOID . . ."

Although the atypical antipsychotic drug *clozapine* (brand name Clozaril) has enormous potential as an effective treatment for hundreds of thousands of people with resistant cases of schizophrenia, it has, until very recently, resulted only in frustration and even heartache for most of the potential users in the United States. Their efforts to obtain the drug have been thwarted repeatedly since its development, and their psychological needs have regularly been overrun by the interests of business, state government, and the health industry.

The problem began with the early discovery that a small percentage of people who take this drug develop *agranulocytosis,* a life-threatening drop in one's white blood count. Thus, patients who take it must receive regular blood tests so that any signs of agranulocytosis may be spotted quickly. Indeed, because of this unwanted effect, the U.S. Food and Drug Administration (FDA) delayed the approval of clozapine until 1990 (it has been available in Europe since the mid-1970s). Then the FDA approved it with the added requirement that the blood of all persons who take it must be tested every week.

So far, so good. But then the drug's manufacturer took this requirement a step further and said that all clozapine users in the United States had to buy into an entire treatment package consisting of the medication *and* weekly testing by the drug company's own subsidiaries. The average cost of this

package was a whopping $9,000 per year, compared to an average total cost of $3,000 per year in Europe, where doctors prescribe the medication and then send patients to any qualified hospital for testing.

Most schizophrenic patients in the United States could not afford this expensive package of drug and testing, and, what's more, their insurance companies (including the state Medicaid systems and the Veterans Administration) refused to pay for it because they felt the cost was excessive. So hundreds of thousands of treatment-resistant schizophrenic patients, who could have been helped by clozapine without the added risk of developing tardive dyskinesia, were unable to receive this drug treatment.

Clearly schizophrenic patients were caught in the middle and were being victimized by the interests of business, state government, and the health industry. A flurry of lawsuits by patient advocacy groups against the drug manufacturer and against medical insurers followed, along with lawsuits by 32 states against the drug manufacturer for antitrust violations and investigations and hearings by the Federal Trade Commission and Congress. Settlements for these suits were reached only recently. In one settlement, the drug manufacturer finally agreed to sell clozapine separately, without requiring that the necessary regular blood testing be done by its own subsidiaries. And in a settlement reached in the fall of 1992, the drug manufacturer agreed to rebate $10 million to clozapine users and to pay another $11 million to mental health agencies, to patients who cannot afford treatment, and to attorneys. Sadly, however, valuable time had already been lost for many persons with schizophrenia.

Moreover, the cost of clozapine is still high. The annual cost of the drug even alone averages $4,000 in the United States, compared to $1,200 in Europe. It is expected that things will improve in the next few years, since the patent on clozapine ran out in 1994 and other drug companies can now manufacture it as well. In the meantime, however, the whole episode has served as yet another reminder of our society's long legacy of inadequate and often insensitive treatment programs for persons with schizophrenia, highlighted by such horrors as the back wards of institutions, lobotomies, and the failure of deinstitutionalization.

developed *risperidone (Risperdal)* and *remoxipride (Roxiam),* atypical antipsychotic drugs which also appear to be more effective than the traditional neuroleptic drugs while producing fewer undesired effects (Heinrich et al., 1994; King et al., 1992). In addition, dozens of other compounds are in the testing stages.

■ PSYCHOTHERAPY ■

Before the discovery of antipsychotic drugs, psychotherapy was not really a viable option as a treatment for schizophrenia. Most schizophrenic patients were simply too far removed from reality to profit from therapy. A further complication was that successful therapy is based on a trusting relationship with a therapist, and many people with schizophrenia react to therapists and everyone else with suspicion and avoidance (see Box 16–3). In these circumstances, it was remarkable indeed that a handful of therapists, blessed with extraordinary patience and skill, did specialize in the treatment of this disorder and reported some success (Will, 1967, 1961; Sullivan, 1962, 1953; Fromm-Reichmann, 1950, 1948, 1943).

These therapists believed that the primary task of therapy was to win the trust of schizophrenic patients and build a close relationship with them. Frieda Fromm-Reichmann, for example, would initially tell her patients that they could continue to exclude her from their private world and hold onto their disorder as long as they wished. She reported that eventually, after much testing and acting out, schizophrenic patients would accept, trust, and grow attached to her, and begin to examine relevant issues with her. Similarly, Otto Will offered patients total acceptance, love, and understanding. Sometimes he would even enter into their distorted world and use their language, symbols, and logic.

Although no consistent research was conducted on the effectiveness of such psychotherapeutic approaches, people who later recovered from schizophrenia often confirmed that trust and emotional bonding had been important to them throughout therapy. Here a woman tells her therapist how she had felt during their early interactions:

At the start, I didn't listen to what you said most of the time but I watched like a hawk for your expression and the sound of your voice. After the interview, I would add all this up to see if it seemed to show love. The words were nothing compared to the feelings you showed. I sense that you felt confident I could be helped and that there was hope for the future. . . .

The problem with schizophrenics is that they can't trust anyone. They can't put their eggs in one basket. The doctor will usually have to fight to get in no matter how much the patient objects. . . .

Loving is impossible at first because it turns you into a helpless little baby. The patient can't feel safe to do this until he is absolutely sure the doctor understands what is needed and will provide it.

Hating is like shitting. If you shit, it shows you are alive but, if the doctor can't accept your shit, it means he doesn't want you to be alive. It makes him like a mother who can't accept her child's mess. . . . It used to terrify me to sit and watch you, to see if you could handle all my hate and shit, or whether you would be choked by it the way I was.

(Hayward & Taylor, 1965)

Psychotherapy is now successfully employed in many more cases of schizophrenia, thanks to the discovery and effectiveness of antipsychotic drugs (Goldstein, 1991; Karon, 1988). By helping to relieve thought and perceptual disturbances, the drugs enable people with schizophrenia to play an active role in the therapeutic process, think more clearly about themselves and their relationships, and make changes in their behavior (Boker, 1992; Bartko et al., 1988). Although psychotherapy tends to be of limited help during the earliest stages of the disorder, research suggests that it becomes very useful later on, particularly after medications have made an impact. The most helpful forms of psychotherapy include *insight therapy, social therapy,* and *family therapy.*

INSIGHT THERAPY

A variety of insight therapies are now applied to schizophrenia (Wasylenki, 1992; Ernst, 1985; Auerhahn & Moskowitz, 1984). Studies suggest that insight therapists who are more experienced with schizophrenia have greater success, often regardless of their particular orientation (Karon, 1988, 1985; Lamb, 1982; Karon & Vandenbos, 1981). According to one study, therapists who are successful with schizophrenic patients tend to take a more active role than less successful therapists, setting limits, expressing opinions, challenging patients' statements, and providing guidance (Whitehorn & Betz, 1975). At the same time, the issue of gaining a patient's trust remains a major part of therapy.

SOCIAL THERAPY

Clinicians now make practical advice and life adjustment a central focus of treatment for schizophrenic people (Bellack et al., 1989). Although they are still concerned with the removal of symptoms, many direct therapy toward such issues as problem solving, decision making, and the development of social skills (Liberman & Corrigan, 1993; Wixted et al., 1988). Therapists may also help their clients find work, financial assistance, and proper housing. This kind of intervention has been labeled *social therapy,* or *sociotherapy* (Hogarty et al., 1986, 1974), and it is now offered in group therapy formats as well as in individual therapy (Wilson, Diamond, & Factor, 1990).

Social therapists also work hard to teach schizophrenic patients about self-medication and symptom management. They provide patients with information about how their medication works, how to take it, and what effects to expect, and teach them to identify warning signs of relapse (Liberman & Corrigan, 1993; Wirshing et al., 1992). Self-management not only reduces patients' chance of relapse but also provides them with a better understanding of their disorder, bolsters their self-confidence, and reduces feelings of helplessness (Boker, 1992; Sullwold & Herrlich, 1992).

Research supports the belief that social therapy helps keep patients out of the hospital. Gerard Hogarty and his colleagues (1986, 1974) compared the progress of four groups of chronic schizophrenic patients after their discharge from a state hospital. One group received both antipsychotic medications and social therapy in the community, while the other groups received medication only, social therapy only, or no treatment of any kind. The researchers' first finding was that chronic patients needed medication in the community to avoid rehospitalization. Over a two-year period, 80 percent of those who did not take medication needed to be hospitalized again, compared to 48 percent of those who received medication. They also found that among the patients on medication, those who also received social therapy adjusted to the community and avoided rehospitalization most successfully. Clearly, social therapy played an important role in their recovery.

FAMILY THERAPY

Between 25 and 40 percent of recovering schizophrenic patients in the community live with their parents, siblings, spouses, and children (Torrey, Wolfe, & Flynn, 1988; Bocker, 1984; Lamb & Goertzel, 1977). Such unions create special pressures for both the patients and the family members.

Recovering schizophrenic patients are greatly affected by the behavior and reactions of family members, even if family dysfunction was not a factor in the onset of the patients' disorder (Kreisman et al., 1988). It has been found, for example, that schizophrenic persons with positive perceptions of their relatives and of their relatives' attitudes toward them have better treatment outcomes (Lebell et al., 1993; Scott et al., 1993). Similarly, released schizophrenic patients whose relatives have high levels of *expressed emotion*—that is, high levels of criticism, emotional overinvolvement, and hostility—often have a higher relapse rate than those who return to cooler, less emotional relatives (Mavreas et al., 1992; Vaughan et al., 1992; Brown et al., 1972). It is not clear whether high levels of expressed emotion in a home precede the onset of schizophrenia or result from the pressures of caring for a schizophrenic relative (Fox, 1992; Nuechterlein et al., 1992). Once in place, however, the emotional pattern seems to hinder long-term recovery.

Family members, for their part, are often greatly affected by the behavior of a schizophrenic relative living at home. In an enlightening series of interviews with eighty British families that had a schizophrenic family member living at home, investigators found most family members to be greatly disturbed by the social withdrawal of their schizophrenic relative (Creer & Wing, 1974). A number were also disturbed by the schizophrenic person's socially embarrassing behaviors, such as restlessness, pacing, odd posturing, and talking to him- or herself. One relative complained, "In the evening you go into the sitting room and it's in darkness. You turn on the light and there he is just sitting there, staring in front of him."

To address such family issues and enhance the chance of recovery, clinicians now commonly include family therapy in the treatment of schizophrenia (Domenici & Griffin-Francell, 1993; Zastowny et al., 1992; Goldstein, 1991, 1987, 1981). Family therapy provides family members with guidance, training, practical advice, education about schizophrenia *(psychoeducation)*, and emotional support and empathy. It helps family members become more realistic in their expectations, more tolerant of deviant behavior, less guilt-ridden and confused, and more willing to try new patterns of interaction and communication. Over the course of treatment, therapists also try to help the schizophrenic individual cope with the pressures of family life, make better use of family resources, and avoid problematic interactions. The approach often succeeds in improving communication and reducing tensions within the family, and so helps relapse rates to go down, particularly when combined with drug therapy (Zastowny et al., 1992; Mueser &

BOX 16-3

"BEING PERSONALLY TOUCHED BY MENTAL ILLNESS IS VERY DIFFERENT FROM TREATING IT"

Keith Russell Ablow, M.D.

When clinicians work with schizophrenic people, they usually manage to put aside personal feelings and fears in order to accomplish their therapeutic tasks. But what happens when a clinician's family member or friend develops a severe mental disorder? Psychiatrist Keith Russell Ablow movingly conveys his own personal reaction in an essay originally published in the Washington Post, *Feb. 9, 1993.*

Late one night last year, a close friend from college called me at home. We had spent hours the previous night at dinner, discussing our careers and our families. While I spent years in medical school and psychiatric residency, he had become a very successful businessman.

But during that late-night phone call his tone was anything but friendly. "When we were talking last night, you asked me the name of my new business partner," he said. "Why did you want that information?"

My question had been routine; I barely remember having asked. "I didn't have any real reason," I replied. "I just thought if he was local I might know him."

"Keith, if you want to get involved in one of my business deals, all you have to do is ask," he said.

"I didn't want to be involved," I replied, stunned by his accusatory tone. "I was just wondering. What's the problem?"

There was a long silence. "Fine," he said coldly. "If you want to go head-to-head, we can do that. You play your game, and I'll play mine," he said, then hung up.

I called back immediately, perplexed and upset by his behavior.

"I'm only going to tell you this once," he said the moment he heard my voice. "If I want to talk to you, I'll call you. Other than that, I don't need or want to hear from you," he said, hanging up.

I almost called again, still not convinced that he meant what he had said. Instead, I called his father and a mutual friend of ours. Each of them had also been falsely accused, over the course of a few weeks, of trying to sabotage his business deals.

It quickly became clear that my friend was mentally ill. He was suffering from paranoid delusions, a form of psychosis, and saw us as his enemy. . . .

I found myself wishing that his paranoia had resulted from street drugs in the hope that it would go away soon, once the effects of the drug had worn off. But I was certain that he had never used street drugs in the 10 years I had known him.

Unfortunately, little has changed since that night. My friend has almost completely avoided psychiatric care. We have spoken only a few times for a few minutes. He still distrusts me and his family and views us as unwelcome intrusions in his life.

The last time I called him, I asked if we could get together and talk about our friendship. His response was the same as other times I had tried to reach him. "Why are you calling me?" he asked. "If I need to speak with you, I know where to find you," he said, hanging up.

Being personally touched by mental illness is very different from treating it. Over the past several months, I have experienced many of the emotions that relatives and friends of the mentally ill have described: guilt, fear, sorrow, a sense of loss and the inevitable question of whether something I did had somehow caused or triggered his illness.

Glynn, 1990; Hogarty et al., 1986). These principles are at work in the following case:

Mark was a 32-year-old single man living with his parents. He had a long and stormy history of schizophrenia with many episodes of psychosis, interspersed with occasional brief periods of good functioning. Mark's father was a bright but neurotically tormented man gripped by obsessions and inhibitions in spite of many years of psychoanalysis. Mark's mother appeared weary, detached, and embittered. Both parents felt hopeless about Mark's chances of recovery and resentful that needing to care for him would always plague their lives. They acted as if they were being intentionally punished. It gradually emerged that the father, in fact, was riddled with guilt and self-doubt; he suspected that his wife had been cold and rejecting toward Mark as an infant and that he had failed to

It is easier now for me to understand the depth of guilt that families of mentally ill patients struggle to escape. I, after all, didn't have to wonder whether something I did or didn't do as a parent decades before might be wrapped up in my friend's current suffering. I didn't have to trace the branches of my family tree looking for aberrant genes.

Yet what I felt most immediately and most intensely was guilt. I relived past events and wondered how I could have ignored what now seemed like signs of my friend's emotional instability. At the time, I regarded them as eccentricities.

On one occasion, for example, he had demanded from me an oath of allegiance to our friendship. "If we're going to be friends," he said, "I want us to be more like brothers, so we can count on each other no matter what."

He suggested we cut our fingers and, as a symbol of our bond, mix our blood. I laughed the idea off, thinking he was joking. In retrospect, I'm not so sure.

He made a great deal of the fact that he wanted only one or, at most, two very committed friends. I was flattered; his focus on trust made me feel he was especially trustworthy. I never recognized the underlying vulnerability and fear that his demands reflected.

I worried that maybe our competitiveness had damaged him and fueled his paranoia. Over the years, he and I had tended to measure our professional achievements against one an-

other. We were both acutely aware of which of us was closer to achieving his goals. Did I covet his business deals, after all? Was there a kernel of truth to his paranoia?

His illness also revealed how much more unsettling it can be to relate to a psychotic individual on a personal—rather than a professional—level. In the office, I have treated many people who, having assaulted or murdered others, feel no remorse whatsoever.

But treating them frightened me less than the thought of encountering my friend in his current state. The truth was, I was afraid of him. He had turned on me before.

During what to me seemed a minor argument seven years earlier, my friend had threatened to use his many contacts in academia to derail my hopes for admission to medical school. We ultimately resolved our dispute, but I never forgot the seriousness with which he had leveled his threat.

I had watched him methodically, almost fanatically, undermine competitors. He kept extensive files on them, sometimes including damaging personal information.

If he had shown that degree of determination to overwhelm his competition in business while relatively well, I wondered, how far would he go now that he was sick to protect his business deal from me? Would he kill me if he felt he had to? I had to admit to myself that I would be hesitant to open my apartment door if he knocked on it unexpectedly. I wondered whether people he was doing business with

might be in some danger and whether he should be committed against his will. . . .

. . . I felt inadequate: as a psychiatrist I thought I should be able to do something to intervene in his illness. I talked to his parents and tried to explain the possible disorders their son might be suffering from. I helped them get the names of prominent psychiatrists near his home.

Looking back, I worry that I could have helped him more. That night on the phone, I might instead have asked him what had shaken his confidence in me and apologized for the misunderstanding. I could have understood his accusation as a plea for reassurance that I would always stand by him. Slowly, perhaps over the course of many months or years, I could have urged him to examine his fear in psychotherapy.

But I was responding as a friend; not a psychiatrist. And I now have lost a friend, not a patient. The waves of grief come unexpectedly. I think of the time passing without contact like a wall being built between us. It is a bigger loss than if he had died.

I think often of the advice he gave me when I was unhappy and under great stress in medical school. "Remember," he told me, "you're still in complete control. You have all the cards. If you were to throw them in and leave that place tomorrow, you'd leave with your intelligence, your family and your friends."

I hope, ultimately, he will see that the same holds true for him.

intervene, due to his unwillingness to confront his wife and the demands of graduate school that distanced him from home life. He entertained the fantasy that Mark's illness was a punishment for this. Every time Mark did begin to show improvement—both in reduced symptoms and in increased functioning—his parents responded as if it were just a cruel torment designed to raise their hopes and then to plunge them into deeper despair when Mark's condition deteriorated. This pattern was especially apparent when

Mark got a job. As a result, at such times, the parents actually became more critical and hostile toward Mark. He would become increasingly defensive and insecure, finally developing paranoid delusions, and usually would be hospitalized in a panicky and agitated state.

All of this became apparent during the psychoeducational sessions. When the pattern was pointed out to the family, they were able to recognize their self-fulfilling prophecy and were motivated to deal with it. As a result, the therapist decided to see the family together. Concrete instances of the pattern and its consequences were explored, and alternative responses by the parents were developed. The therapist encouraged both the parents and Mark to discuss their anxieties and doubts about Mark's progress, rather than to stir up one another's expectations of failure. The therapist had regular individual sessions with Mark as well as the family sessions. As a result, Mark has successfully held a job for an unprecedented 12 months.

(Heinrichs & Carpenter, 1983, pp. 284–285)

The families of persons with schizophrenia also need outside social support to be of most help to their troubled relatives (Perlick et al., 1992), and a number of *family support groups* and *family psychoeducational programs* have been organized (Hyde & Goldman, 1992; Birchwood et al., 1992; Wing, 1988). Family members come together with others in the same situation, share their thoughts and emotions, receive support, and learn about schizophrenia. Although research has yet to determine the usefulness of these groups, such approaches are becoming increasingly common as professionals try to address this long-neglected need.

Psychiatrist E. Fuller Torrey has spent the past three decades pointing out the failures of deinstitutionalization and lobbying for greater resources and better treatment facilities for schizophrenic people.

■ THE ■ COMMUNITY APPROACH

During the 1950s the U.S. government established a Joint Commission on Mental Illness and Mental Health, part of whose purpose was to study the deplorable conditions in public mental institutions. In 1960 the commission issued a report, *Action for Mental Health.* Because the isolated state hospitals had failed so miserably to address the needs of chronic mental patients, the commission called for the development of local mental health services and recommended that the care of patients be transferred from the state institutions to local hospitals and mental health clinics. As we saw in Chapter 5, President John F. Kennedy put the weight of his office behind these recommendations in 1963, calling for a "bold new approach" to mental disorders, and Congress passed the Community Mental Health Act.

According to this act, mental patients were to receive a range of mental health services—outpatient

therapy, inpatient treatment, emergency care, preventive care, and aftercare—right in their communities rather than far from home. The act was intended to address a variety of psychological disorders, but schizophrenic patients, especially those who had been institutionalized for years, were targeted and affected more than most (Hafner & an der Heiden, 1988). The government was ordering that these patients be released and treated in the community. Other countries around the world put similar community care programs into action shortly thereafter (Torrey, 1988; Hafner & an der Heiden, 1988).

Thus began three decades of *deinstitutionalization,* an exodus of hundreds of thousands of schizophrenic and other chronic mental patients from state institutions into the community. On a given day in 1955 close to 600,000 patients were living in state institutions; today around 100,000 patients reside there (Manderscheid & Sonnenschein, 1992). During this period of deinstitutionalization, clinicians have learned that recovering schizophrenic patients can profit greatly from community-based programs. Unfortunately, as we shall see in more detail later, the quality and funding of community care for schizophrenic patients have been grossly inadequate throughout the United States, leading to a "revolving door" syndrome in which patients are repeatedly released to the community, readmitted to an institution within months, released again, admitted yet again, and so on.

EFFECTIVE
COMMUNITY CARE

Recovering schizophrenic patients living in the community need medication, psychotherapy, help in handling daily pressures and responsibilities, guidance in making decisions, training in social skills, residential supervision, and vocational counseling and training. According to research, patients whose communities systematically address these needs make greater progress than patients living in other communities (Hogarty, 1993). One study compared the one-year progress of thirty schizophrenic patients whose community in Vancouver, British Columbia, offered outstanding community services with that of thirty matched subjects in a community in Portland, Oregon, that offered fewer services (Beiser et al., 1985). The Vancouver patients were found to have fewer hospital readmissions and a higher employment rate and to report a greater sense of general well-being than the Portland group. Some of the key elements in effective community care programs are *coordination of patient services* by a community mental health center, *short-term hospitalization, partial hospitalization, halfway houses,* and *occupational training.*

COORDINATED SERVICES The Joint Commission on Mental Illness and Mental Health proposed that the cornerstone of community care should be a **community mental health center,** a treatment facility that would provide medication, psychotherapy, and inpatient emergency care to severely disturbed people. In addition, the community mental health center was to coordinate the patient services offered by other community agencies. Each center was expected to serve a designated "catchment area," a geographic area with a population of 50,000 to 200,000 people.

When community mental health centers do in fact place a high priority on the treatment of schizophrenic patients, and do develop and coordinate a range of community services for them, the patients often make steady and significant progress (Beiser et al., 1985). They are better reintegrated into the community and function more effectively than those

who receive standard outpatient care (Madianos & Madianou, 1992). Among the most effective centers in the United States are those serving Prairie View, Kansas; Dane County, Wisconsin; Weber County, Utah; Range, Minnesota; and Sacramento, California (Stein, 1993).

Coordination of services is particularly important for patients who have a dual diagnosis of schizophrenia and substance abuse, so-called MICAs, a problem that we discussed in Chapter 13 (pp. 472–473). It is estimated that at least 50 percent of schizophrenic patients also are addicted to alcohol or other drugs (Westermeyer, 1992). Traditional substance-abuse programs are usually not helpful to persons with schizophrenia (Drake, McHugo, & Noordsy, 1993). Programs that integrate treatment for substance abuse with treatment for schizophrenia tend to be more successful (Drake et al., 1993; Westermeyer, 1992).

SHORT-TERM HOSPITALIZATION As Rosenhan's 1973 study of pseudopatients confirmed (p. 63), institutional life may lead patients to feel powerless, bored, and even doomed by their diagnostic labels. At the same time, as the Group for the Advancement of Psychiatry (1970–71) has pointed out, schizophrenic patients can profit greatly from the routine diagnostic evaluation, close observation, supervision, and precise monitoring of medication that are uniquely available in hospitals.

Clinicians have grappled with the problem of providing the positive features of hospitalization while minimizing its negative effects. The solution developed by the community mental health movement has been to provide patients who seem to need hospitalization with a short-term program of inpatient treatment that lasts a few weeks, rather than months or years, followed by a program of posthospitalization care and treatment out in the community, or **aftercare** (Sederer, 1992; Lamb, 1988). Countries throughout the world now favor this policy of short-term hospitalization (Hafner & an der Heiden, 1988).

When people develop schizophrenic symptoms, today's clinicians first try to treat them on an outpatient basis, usually administering antipsychotic medication and perhaps psychotherapy. If these interventions prove inadequate, short-term hospitalization may be tried (Davis et al., 1988). As soon as the patients are stabilized, they are released to the community for aftercare. Short-term hospitalization of this kind usually leads to a greater reduction of symptoms and a lower rehospitalization rate than extended institutional care (Caton, 1982; Herz et al., 1977, 1975).

PARTIAL HOSPITALIZATION   For people whose needs fall somewhere between full hospitalization and outpatient therapy sessions, some communities offer partial hospitalization at *day centers* or *day hospitals* (Kennedy, 1992; Hoge et al., 1988). These programs originated in Moscow in 1933, when a shortage of hospital beds necessitated the premature release of many mental patients. Day hospitals were formed to provide these patients with hospital-type care during the day, but patients returned home for the night. The concept was later accepted in Canada and England and still later was adopted by community treatment programs in the United States. Today's day centers provide daily activities and specific treatment programs for patients, and social rehabilitation programs to help them improve their social skills. Several studies suggest that recovering schizophrenic patients in day centers often do better than those in programs that provide extended hospitalization or traditional outpatient therapy. (Creed, Black, & Anthony, 1989; Herz et al., 1971; Meltzoff & Blumenthal, 1966).

HALFWAY HOUSES   *Halfway houses* are residences for people who do not require hospitalization but cannot live either alone or with their families. These residences, typically large houses in areas where housing is inexpensive, usually shelter between one and two dozen people. Although outside mental health professionals may be available to residents, the live-in staff usually consists of *paraprofessionals*—lay people who have received some training in providing emotional support and practical guidance about matters of daily living. Various patient populations reside in halfway houses; schizophrenic patients are among the most common.

The atmosphere of most halfway houses is supportive. The residents discuss their day-to-day problems and try to help one another adjust to life in the community. The houses are usually organized around a milieu therapy philosophy: residents are encouraged to set up their own rules and governing mechanisms, to be responsible and independent, and to contribute to the welfare of the halfway house by doing chores, helping other residents, and behaving properly.

In the following passage, a woman describes how living in a halfway house contributed to her recovery from schizophrenia. She entered the house on a court order, after ten hospitalizations in twelve years.

*T*he halfway house changed my life. First of all, I discovered that some of the staff members had once been clients in the program! That one single fact offered me hope. For the first time, I saw proof that a program could help someone, that it was possible to regain control over one's life and become independent. The house was democratically run; all residents had one vote and the staff members, outnumbered 5 to 22, could not make rules or even discharge a client from the program without majority sentiment. There was a house bill of rights that was strictly observed by all. We helped one another and gave support. When residents were in a crisis, no staff member hustled them off or increased their medication to calm them down. Residents could cry, be comforted and hugged until a solution could be found, or until they accepted that it was okay to feel bad. Even anger was an acceptable feeling that did not have to be feared, but could be expressed and turned into constructive energy. If you disliked some aspect of the program or the behavior of a staff member, you could change things rather than passively accept what was happening. Choices were real, and failure and success were accepted equally. Although I was incredibly suspicious, I could find little about which to be "paranoid." I could read my file at any time. All problems were discussed at house meetings so nothing was kept secret. Bit by bit, my distrust faltered and the fears lessened. I slept better and made friends. I was treated with respect and respected others, so gradually I began to respect myself. My life became more manageable as I learned the "tools" I needed. I learned about stress, how to recognize symptoms of stress in my life, and how to control or cope with the stressors. Other residents and staff members who had hallucinated for years and now were able to control their hallucinations shared with me some of the techniques that had worked for them. Things like diet, bioenergetic "grounding," and interpersonal relationships became a few of my tools.

(Lovejoy, 1982, pp. 605–609)

Research indicates that halfway houses help many recovering schizophrenic people adjust to community life and avoid rehospitalization (Simpson, Hyde, & Faragher, 1989; Caton, 1982) (see Figure 16–3). Correspondingly, the number of these residences has grown steadily throughout the United States, from 2 in 1950 to more than 1,500 today.

OCCUPATIONAL TRAINING   Regular employment enables people to support themselves, exercise independence, gain self-respect, and learn to work with others. It also helps bring companionship and order to a person's daily life. For these reasons, occupational training and placement are important aspects of community treatment for schizophrenic people (Leshner et al., 1992). Many community mental health workers work with vocational rehabilitation agencies to place clients in appropriate training programs.

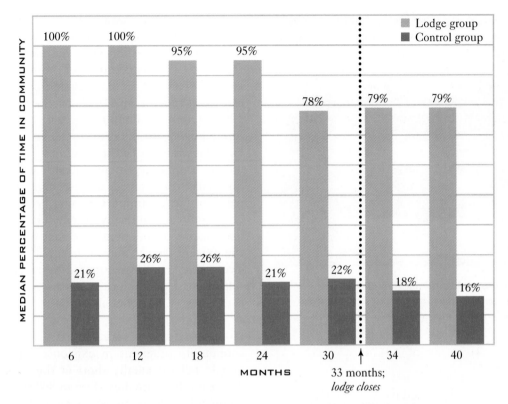

FIGURE 16–3   *In a famous study by George Fairweather and his associates (1969), schizophrenic patients who were released from a hospital to a "lodge" (halfway house and business program) adjusted better than schizophrenic people who were released directly to a boardinghouse or apartment. They also remained in the community longer, avoided rehospitalization more successfully, and continued this trend even after the lodge closed.*

Many people recovering from schizophrenia begin their occupational training in a ***sheltered workshop***—a protected and supervised workplace for employees who are not ready for competitive or complicated jobs. The workshop tries to establish a typical work environment: products such as toys, home furnishings, or simple appliances are manufactured and later sold, workers are paid according to their performance, and all are expected to be at work regularly and on time. For some the sheltered workshop becomes a permanent workplace. For others it is an important step toward better-paying and more complex outside employment or a return to their previous job or its equivalent.

Unfortunately, in the United States vocational rehabilitation is not consistently available to people with chronic schizophrenia or other severe mental disorders. One study found that only 25 percent of such people are employed, less than 10 percent outside of sheltered workplaces (Mulkern & Manderscheid, 1989). The Department of Labor and its programs focus more on other needy groups, such as minority groups, lower socioeconomic groups, and the poorly educated. More sheltered workshops are available to

long-term mental patients in Sweden, England, the Netherlands, and Russia, among other countries, than in the United States (Black, 1977).

INADEQUACIES IN COMMUNITY TREATMENT

The community mental health movement has had a major impact on the treatment of mental disorders. In 1955 only 23 percent of all patients in treatment were receiving outpatient care in the United States. As we saw in Chapter 1, approximately 94 percent of all treated patients receive outpatient services today. The shift to community care for people with schizophrenia accounts for much of this overall change (Rosenstein et al., 1989).

As we have observed, effective community programs clearly can help patients with schizophrenia recover. Reports of patients who are treated by effective community programs and given social therapy indicate that they are happier and more satisfied with

Sheltered workshops, such as the one at New York City's Fountain House, provide job training and jobs and teach independence, self-respect, and social skills. Unfortunately, there is a severe shortage of such workshops for people with schizophrenia.

their lives than institutionalized patients are (Hogarty, 1993; Test & Stein, 1978). Unfortunately, less than half of all people with schizophrenia receive appropriate community mental health services (Von Korff et al., 1985). Indeed, close to 40 percent of all people with this disorder fail to receive any form of treatment at all in any given year (Regier et al., 1993). Two factors are primarily responsible: *poor coordination of services* and *shortage of services*.

POOR COORDINATION OF SERVICES   Often there is no communication among the various agencies in a community and no overall strategy dictating the care that a schizophrenic person receives from them (Leshner et al., 1992). The advice that a patient receives in a day center may differ from that dispensed at the community mental health center; similarly, there could be an opening at a nearby halfway house and the therapist at the community mental health center might not even know about it. In addition, community agencies often cannot provide patients with continuing contacts with the same staff members, so it is difficult for patients to develop the kind of trusting relationships with clinicians and other workers that are essential to their progress (Leshner et al., 1992).

This problem is seen in one study's finding that of sixty-five schizophrenic persons living in a California residential facility, only 51 percent attended a social rehabilitation program located a block away (Lamb, 1979). Moreover, when the rehabilitation program

was moved farther away, only 29 percent made use of a van that was available to take them there.

Poor communication between state hospitals and the state's various community mental health centers is also a source of inefficiency and poor mental health care (Leshner et al., 1992; McShane & Redoutey, 1987). Often community agencies are not even informed when patients are discharged from the hospital. This problem had its beginning in the early days of the community mental health movement, when hospitals were forced to discharge patients before many of the community mental health centers were open and ready to receive them. The hospitals developed habits of independence that have continued to the present day. Moreover, hospital care is so expensive today that institutions often feel pressured to release patients before a discharge plan has been completed (Leshner et al., 1992).

SHORTAGE OF SERVICES   The number of community programs in existence for schizophrenic people falls decidedly short of the number needed. Although there are now close to 800 community mental health centers in the United States, the Joint Commission on Mental Illness and Mental Health had estimated that nearly three times that many would be necessary to serve the nation properly. There is also a severe shortage of halfway houses and sheltered workshops.

Perhaps even more disturbing, most of the community mental health centers that do exist fail to provide adequate and coordinated services for the schizophrenic people they purport to treat. Although the primary function of community mental health centers is supposedly to "concentrate on providing psychiatric treatment for acute mental illness cases and for patients who can be helped either short of admission to a mental hospital or following discharge," most centers have given little time, attention, or financial priority to these patients over the past three decades. Increasingly the larger part of the centers' resources has been devoted to providing outpatient psychotherapy, education, and prevention services for people with less disabling problems, such as anxiety and depressive disorders or problems in social adjustment. For the past fifteen years, only about 10 percent of the patients treated by community mental health centers have been schizophrenic (Rosenstein et al., 1990, 1989; Torrey, 1988). Several factors appear to be responsible.

First, most mental health professionals simply prefer to work with people whose problems are less severe than schizophrenia (Kirk & Therrien, 1975; Hogarty, 1971). Providing sociotherapy and related services for recovering schizophrenic patients means spending a great deal of time on such issues as daily schedules, responsibilities, and self-care. From a professional standpoint, this sort of counseling tends to be less interesting than therapy for anxious and depressed persons. Moreover, the progress of schizophrenic patients is usually slower and more frustrating than that of less disturbed patients, and professionals often have a pessimistic outlook about the possibilities of helping them (Lee et al., 1993; Harding et al., 1992). In addition, cultural and language barriers between mental health professionals and schizophrenic patients who belong to racial and ethnic minorities often make it difficult for these patients to find adequate treatment in the community (Leshner et al., 1992).

Second, community residents often object to the presence of community programs for recovering schizophrenic patients in their neighborhoods, frequently going so far as to picket, protest, and even vandalize halfway houses, day centers, and other community facilities. This has been referred to as the *"NIMBY" (not in my back yard) syndrome.* Community resistance is one of the major problems facing halfway houses and similar programs today (Leshner et al., 1992).

But perhaps the primary reason for shortages and inadequacies in community care is economic. On the one hand, more public funds are allocated for people with mental disorders now than in the past. In 1963 a total of $1 billion was spent in this area, whereas today more than $23 billion is spent on people with mental disorders, 53 percent of it supplied by state governments, 38 percent by the federal government, and 9 percent by local governments (Redick et al., 1992; Torrey, 1988). On the other hand, little of this new money is going to community treatment programs for the severely disturbed. Except in those relatively few areas that have well-coordinated community programs, the states continue to direct most (70 percent) of their money into staff salaries and services at state hospitals, despite the fact that the daily census of these hospitals has decreased more than 80 percent since 1963 (Stein, 1993). Indeed, in some states the number of staff members at state hospitals has actually increased since the 1960s (Torrey, 1988). The federal government directs its aid into monthly subsistence payments for the severely disturbed (supplemental security income, or SSI, and social security disability income, or SSDI), subsidies for mentally disturbed people residing in nursing homes and in general hospitals (Medicaid and Medicare), and subsidies to community mental health centers (which, as we know, direct most of their services to people who are less disturbed). Thus much of the financial burden of providing community treatment for severely disturbed persons falls on the local governments, whose resources are simply too limited to meet the challenge effectively.

CONSEQUENCES OF INADEQUATE COMMUNITY TREATMENT What happens to schizophrenic patients whose communities do not provide necessary services and whose families cannot afford private treatment (see Figure 16–4)? As we observed earlier, a large number receive no treatment at all; many others spend a short time in a state hospital and are then discharged prematurely, often without benefit of adequate follow-up treatment (Regier et al., 1993; Torrey et al., 1988; Pepper & Ryglewicz, 1982). Between 25 and 40 percent of all schizophrenic patients return to their families, under whose care they may receive medication, perhaps some emotional and financial support, but little else in the way of treatment. Another 5 to 11 percent leave the state hospital to enter an alternative institution such as a nursing home or rest home. Here they typically receive little more than custodial care and medication (Smyer, 1989; Torrey et al., 1988). An additional 21 to 35 percent are placed in single-room-occupancy hotels or in privately run boarding homes, rooming houses, or converted hotels typically found in run-down inner-city neighborhoods (Torrey et al., 1988). Although some such settings are legitimate

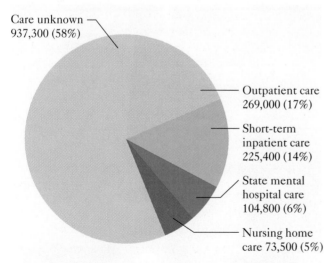

Care unknown
937,300 (58%)

Outpatient care
269,000 (17%)

Short-term
inpatient care
225,400 (14%)

State mental
hospital care
104,800 (6%)

Nursing home
care 73,500 (5%)

FIGURE 16–4 *Distribution of schizophrenic people in the United States. When the National Institute of Mental Health sought to ascertain the care given to schizophrenic people throughout the United States in 1986, it was unable to find most of them. Only 42 percent of schizophrenic people were receiving care. (Adapted from Torrey, 1988, p. 35; NIMH, 1986.) Recent statistics are a bit more encouraging: today 63 percent of people with this disorder apparently receive treatment in any given year. (Regier et al., 1993.)*

"bed-and-care" facilities, providing meals, medication reminders, and a certain amount of staff supervision, most fail to offer even these minimal services. Rather, the patient lives in a small room under conditions that are substandard and unsafe. At times a media report such as the following newspaper account focuses on the abominable conditions in such dwellings; usually they receive no public attention.

Hundreds of mentally ill patients throughout Dade County are being packed into aging hotels and homes that are little better than slums, according to health officials who say the appalling living conditions virtually ensure patients will sink deeper into insanity.

Florida's policy of emptying its mental institutions, a paucity of appropriate "halfway houses," and lax inspections of existing homes have left many mentally ill without the care that might ease them back into normal life.

It also has left them without protection. Released from hospitals into overburdened halfway houses, the indigent patients eventually are shunted to landlords, some of whom jam them, perhaps three to a room, into decaying and dangerous buildings and then collect their welfare payments as rent.

The worst buildings, found scattered throughout Little Havana and the dying hotel district in South Miami Beach, contain the stuff of nightmares. Piles of trash and feces litter the floors. Half-naked men wander purposelessly through hallways, and doors swing open into hot and fetid rooms where others, gazing vacantly at the ceiling, lie neglected on dirty cots.

In some cases, the state Department of Health and Rehabilitative Services places patients in substandard homes. HRS officials concede there is a problem, but say they are doing the best they can in an overloaded and underfunded system.

In one instance, HRS released patients to a Little Havana house run by a landlord who three years earlier lost his state license to operate a group home because of its life-threatening conditions.

The landlord . . . didn't apply for a license for his latest home at 218 SW Eighth Ave. Instead, he used plywood sheets to divide the coral rock house into 12-foot by 14-foot boxes and then told HRS workers he would take in the mentally ill.

Each of the boxes, strung along trash-strewn passageways in the two-story house, contains a narrow bed, a fan and a chest of drawers. Hot meal containers and plastic forks fill waste bins. Most of the boxes also contained people like Vallant Garez, a timid 55-year-old whose bed sores attest to hours spent in bed, staring at a paint-chipped wall a foot from his pillow.

(Miami Herald, *August 10, 1984*)

Few attempts are made to engage such boarding home residents in therapeutic activities, and they have few opportunities for vocational rehabilitation, sheltered work, or job placement. Most survive on government disability payments (Barker et al., 1992) and spend their days wandering through neighborhood streets. It is often said that these schizophrenic patients are now being dumped and warehoused in the community, just as they were once warehoused in institutions. Not surprisingly, most of them go through repeated cycles of hospitalization, discharge, and readmission—the "revolving door" syndrome (Geller, 1992). Although the daily census of patients in state hospitals has fallen by 80 percent since 1963, the number of annual hospital admissions has actually increased by 80 percent, from 178,000 to more than 326,000 (Rosenstein et al., 1990). Most of these admissions are in fact readmissions (Geller, 1992): an estimated half of all mental patients released from state hospitals are rehospitalized within a year of discharge. One study found that close to a third of patients in a state hospital had been admitted more than ten times (Geller, 1992).

Finally, and perhaps saddest of all, a great number of people with schizophrenia have become homeless (Opler et al., 1994; Leshner et al., 1992; Torrey et al., 1988). Many of them are released hospital patients. Others are young adults who have not even received hospitalization in the first place. Several factors have been cited for the increased homelessness among

It is estimated that more than 100,000 of the homeless people in the United States suffer from schizophrenia or another severe mental disorder. Their plight is the result of deinstitutionalization, inadequate community services, societal and professional neglect, and the urban gentrification movement.

schizophrenic people, including the lack of adequate hospital discharge planning, failure to refer people to housing and support services, and patients' loss of employment while they were hospitalized. But perhaps the key factor is a dramatic decrease in affordable housing. During the past twenty years, cities throughout the United States have undertaken redevelopment and gentrification programs designed to revitalize inner-city life by replacing low-income housing and single-room-occupancy hotels with office buildings, shopping centers, convention centers, and expensive condominiums and hotels. As a result, almost half of the nation's low-cost single-room units have disappeared since 1970 (Knesper, Wheeler, & Pagnucco, 1984). New York City alone has lost 110,000, or 87 percent, of its low-rent single-room housing. In the process schizophrenic people have been turned out into the streets. They take refuge in hallways, subways, and vacant buildings, and sleep on park benches or heating grates. Many people simply wind up in prisons when their pathology leads them to break the law (Glancy & Regehr, 1992; Leshner et al., 1992). The "lucky" ones find beds in public shelters. Certainly deinstitutionalization and the community mental health movement have failed these people.

There are between 350,000 and 1 million street people in the United States. As many as one-third of them have a severe mental disorder, commonly schizophrenia (DeAngelis, 1994; Manderscheid & Rosenstein, 1992; Conference of Mayors, 1986). One study found that over a third of 132 patients released from the Central Ohio Psychiatric Hospital in 1985 became homeless within six months—this in a state whose mental health system has been ranked among the best in the country (Belcher, 1988). Many schizophrenic patients now report feeling *relieved* when they are able to return to hospital life: they no longer have to search fruitlessly to find housing, food, or treatment in the community (Drake & Wallach, 1992).

THE PROMISE OF COMMUNITY TREATMENT

Despite these very serious problems, the demonstrated success and potential of proper community care for people recovering from schizophrenia continue to capture the interest of both clinicians and many government officials, who press for further development of community services. Since 1977 a program called the *Community Support Program (CSP)*, initiated by the National Institute of Mental Health, has provided communities and states with funds to help develop wide-ranging and coordinated support systems for chronic and severely disturbed mental patients (Torrey, 1988).

Similarly, in recent years the federal government has created the Task Force on Homelessness and Severe Mental Illness, whose job is to find more effective ways for the federal government, states, and local organizations, both public and private, to meet the housing, treatment, and support needs of people with mental disorders, with emphasis on the needs of the homeless among them (Leshner et al., 1992). In 1992 the task force proposed some major initiatives to overcome the inadequacies in community care. One initiative, called Access to Community Care and Effective Services and Support (ACCESS), will make federal grants available to test new integrated approaches in twenty to thirty communities around the country (Leshner et al., 1992).

A second initiative of the task force, called Safe Havens, will provide low-cost, stable housing for homeless people with mental disorders who are unable or unwilling to use traditional emergency shelters or transitional housing. Many shelters, for example, do not admit people who are psychotic or whose disorder is compounded by a substance-related disorder. The Safe Havens will offer secure, supervised, semiprivate lodging for twelve to twenty-five people, and provide a telephone and a mailing address, which people looking for jobs and housing must have, and a place to receive disability payments. It is hoped that the Safe Havens will encourage homeless people with mental disorders to use other community services as well.

One other important development has been the formation of *national interest groups* that are successfully promoting community treatment for schizophrenic and other chronic patients (Rosenstein et al., 1989). One, the National Alliance for the Mentally Ill, began in 1979 with 300 members and has expanded to more than 140,000 members in 1100 chapters (NAMI, 1994). Comprising family members of people with severe mental disorders (particularly schizophrenia, bipolar disorders, and major depression), this group has become a powerful lobbying force in many state legislatures, has established inspection procedures for state hospitals, and has pressured community mental health centers to provide treatment for schizophrenic persons.

Today community care is a major aspect of treatment for recovering schizophrenic patients in countries throughout the world (Liberman, 1994; Perris,

1988; Madianos & Economou, 1988). Some countries, observing the problems of deinstitutionalization in the United States, have managed to introduce their community programs in a better organized, less disruptive, and more successful manner. Sweden, for example, in gradually dismantling its public mental hospitals, has taken care to have community resources available before releasing chronic hospitalized patients and to give patients adequate preparation for release (Perris, 1988). Clearly, both in the United States and abroad, effective, wide-ranging, and coordinated community treatment is viewed as an important part of the solution to the problem of schizophrenia.

THE STATE OF THE FIELD
TREATMENTS FOR SCHIZOPHRENIA

After years of frustration and failure in efforts to treat schizophrenia, clinicians now have an arsenal of weapons with which to fight it—medication, institutional programs, psychotherapy, and community programs. These approaches can be combined to meet the specific needs of each individual (Meyer, 1984).

Today, at the first sign of schizophrenic symptoms, a person is usually given treatment on an outpatient basis, starting with antipsychotic drugs, perhaps accompanied by psychotherapy and enrollment in appropriate community programs (Davis et al., 1988). This outpatient approach is helpful to many patients, but short-term hospitalization may be necessary for others (Davis et al., 1988). At the hospital, psychiatrists try to stabilize patients on medication and then release them to the community, where ideally they can participate in community programs, live in a supportive environment, pursue psychotherapy, and continue on medication as long as necessary.

This combined approach has greatly improved a schizophrenic person's chances of returning to functional living, and today a large number of persons with schizophrenia are responding reasonably well to treatment (Eaton et al., 1992; Harding, Zubin, & Strauss, 1992; Ram et al., 1992). When Kraepelin first described schizophrenia at the turn of the century, he estimated that only 13 percent of patients with this disorder ever improved and that the improvements were usually temporary. Today, even with the current

shortages and inadequacies in community programs, many more schizophrenic people show improvement. Somewhere between 4 and 30 percent are believed to recover completely and permanently. Another 30 percent return to relatively independent lives, although their occupational and social functioning may continue to fall short of earlier levels. And still another 30 percent remain out of the hospital most of the time, with many of them able to maintain some level of employment, although they need considerable help in managing for themselves. Sadly, however, between 10 and 30 percent continue to require hospitalization for much of their lives (Wing, 1988; Tsuang et al., 1979; Bland et al., 1976).

Certainly the clinical field has advanced considerably in the treatment of schizophrenia, yet it still has far to go. It is intolerable that the majority of schizophrenic people receive few or none of the effective community interventions that have been developed over the past three decades, worse still that tens of thousands have become homeless vagrants deserted by society. Although many factors have contributed to this state of affairs, neglect by clinical practitioners has certainly played a big role in it. It is now the mandate of these professionals, prodded by the newly developed interest groups and task forces, to address the needs of all schizophrenic people by more systematically applying the treatment interventions and insights that have emerged in recent years.

SUMMARY

■ **FOR YEARS** all efforts to treat schizophrenia brought only frustration. The disorder is still difficult to treat, but today's therapies are more successful than those of the past.

■ **FOR MORE THAN HALF** of this century the main treatment for schizophrenia was *institutionalization* and custodial care. Schizophrenic patients, because they failed to respond to traditional therapies, were usually placed in institutions, typically in the back wards of public institutions where the primary goal was to restrain them. They rarely saw therapists. Most were neglected and many were abused. Many patients not only failed to improve under these conditions but developed additional symptoms as a result of institutionalization itself.

■ **BETWEEN 1845 AND 1955** the number of state hospitals and mental patients rose steadily while the quality of care declined. Then, following humanistic and behavioral principles, clinicians developed two in-hospital interventions—*milieu therapy* and the *token economy program*—that are now standard features of institutional care. These approaches are particularly helpful in addressing the personal-care and self-image problems brought about by schizophrenia and by institutionalization.

■ **THE DISCOVERY OF ANTIPSYCHOTIC DRUGS** in the 1950s revolutionized the treatment of schizophrenia. In many cases, these drugs, also called *neuroleptic drugs,* helped to eliminate the symptoms of schizophrenia. Today they are almost always a part of treatment. Research suggests that antipsychotic drugs are typically the key to effective intervention for schizophrenic patients. Many patients experience a return of symptoms, however, if they stop taking the drugs too soon.

Many theorists believe that the drugs operate by reducing excessive dopamine activity in the brain. Unfortunately, traditional antipsychotic drugs can also produce dramatic unwanted effects. The most visible are *extrapyramidal effects,* movement abnormalities that affect appearance and functioning. Effects such as *Parkinsonian symptoms, dystonia,* and *akathisia* respond in most cases to anti-Parkinsonian drugs, enabling patients to continue taking antipsychotic drugs. Another effect, *neuroleptic malignant syndrome,* is treated by stopping the drugs and applying other measures. Still another effect, *tardive dyskinesia,* is often difficult—at times impossible—to eliminate, even when antipsychotic drugs are stopped, and early detection is elusive because of its similarities to some of the symptoms of schizophrenia. Given these problems with traditional antipsychotic drugs, it is welcome news that some *atypical* antipsychotic drugs (such as *clozapine*) that seem to be more effective and to cause fewer or no extrapyramidal effects have recently become available. These new drugs do, however, pose new difficulties and dangers of their own.

■ **PSYCHOTHERAPY** was of little help in treating schizophrenia before the discovery of antipsychotic drugs. Now, however, psychotherapy is often employed successfully in conjunction with antipsychotic drugs, and research suggests that it can be very useful over the course of the disorder. The most help-ful forms of psychotherapy include insight therapy, social therapy, and family therapy.

■ **RECENTLY A COMMUNITY APPROACH** has been applied to the treatment of schizophrenia. A policy of *deinstitutionalization* has brought about a mass exodus of hundreds of thousands of schizophrenic and other chronic mental patients from state institutions into the community, leading to an urgent need for community service programs designed to help integrate them back into society. Among the key elements of effective community care programs are coordination of patient services by a *community mental health center, short-term hospitalization* (followed by *aftercare*), *day centers, halfway houses,* and *occupational training.*

■ **THE COMMUNITY MENTAL HEALTH MOVEMENT** has had a major impact on the treatment of mental disorders. Unfortunately, the quality of and funding for community care for schizophrenic persons has been grossly inadequate throughout the United States, resulting in a "revolving door" syndrome in which patients who have been released to the community are readmitted to an institution within months, released again, admitted yet again, and so on. Fewer than half of all schizophrenic persons receive effective community mental health services. Two factors are primarily responsible for this state of affairs: poor coordination of services and shortage of services.

One result of the inadequacy of community treatment is that a great number of schizophrenic people have become homeless. At least one-third of the street people in the United States suffer from a severe mental disorder, most commonly schizophrenia.

■ **DESPITE THESE SERIOUS PROBLEMS,** the success and potential of proper community care for recovering schizophrenic persons continue to capture the interest of both clinicians and government officials. One major development in this area has been the formation of national interest groups that are successfully promoting community treatment for schizophrenic and other chronic patients. Moreover, community care has become the major form of treatment for recovering schizophrenic people in countries throughout the world.

Topic Overview

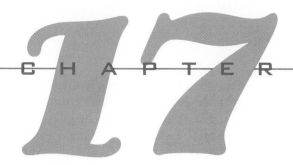

PERSONALITY DISORDERS

THE TERM "PERSONALITY" refers to the unique and enduring patterns of inner experience and behavior displayed by each individual. Usually a personality is somewhat unified and integrated, so that an individual acts fairly consistently at different times, in different situations, and with different people. Theorists view the enduring consistencies with which we interact with our surroundings—often called *personality traits*—as intrinsic characteristics, learned responses, or a combination of the two (Watson, Clark, & Harkness, 1994).

ALTHOUGH WE TEND to behave in relatively predictable, patterned ways across various situations and relationships, according to our constellation of personality traits, most of us also maintain a certain adaptive flexibility in response to our changing environments. We learn from past experiences and experiment with different responses in our efforts to cope effectively. This is something that people who suffer from a personality disorder are frequently unable to do.

A PERSONALITY DISORDER is a pervasive, enduring, and inflexible pattern of inner experience and behavior that deviates markedly from the expectations of one's culture and leads to distress or impairment (APA, 1994). The narrow range of cognitive, emotional, and interpersonal responses displayed by people with these disorders often leads to psychological pain and social or occupational difficulties. The disorder begins, or at least becomes recognizable, in adolescence or early adulthood (APA, 1994).

A PERSONALITY DISORDER and the distress it produces make for a lifelong ordeal, although the disorders vary in the disruption they bring to a person's social or occupational life. Whether mild or severe, however, they tend to affect every facet of a person's being. And they are among the most difficult mental disorders to treat. A complicating issue is the fact that many people with patterns of this type are not aware that they are "different" and are not able to trace problems they may be having to their personal style of thinking and behaving. The disorders often cause less pain to the affected individuals than to the people with whom they come in daily contact. The prevalence of personality disorders among adults has been estimated at between 4 and 15 percent (APA, 1994; Zimmerman & Coryell, 1989; Reich et al., 1989; Gunderson, 1988).

As we saw in Chapter 4, DSM-IV distinguishes between *Axis I* disorders, vivid disorders that cause significant impairment and that may emerge and end at various points in the life cycle, and *Axis II* disorders—those that are of long standing and usually begin before adulthood and persist in stable form into adult life. The personality disorders are Axis II disorders. Unlike most of the clinical syndromes of Axis I, personality disorders usually do not have periods of significant remission and do not vary greatly in intensity or improve over time.

Axis I and Axis II disorders often coexist (Flick et al., 1993). It is not at all unusual for a person with a personality disorder to suffer from an acute (Axis I) form of mental disorder as well. A number of explanations have been proposed for the high rates of coexistence, or comorbidity, found for Axis I and personality disorders (Pfohl et al., 1991). One theory proposes that personality disorders are in fact less severe cases of Axis I disorders and that the diagnosis of one disorder almost automatically implies the diagnosis of the other. Alternatively, personality disorders may predispose some people to develop certain Axis I disorders (Johnson & Wonderlich, 1992). As we shall see, avoidant personality disorder, for example, may predispose people to social phobia, and schizotypal personality disorder may be a predisposing factor in schizophrenia. Then again, Axis I disorders could be predisposing factors in personality disorders. Or perhaps some other variable or biological factor creates a predisposition to both.

DSM-IV distinguishes ten personality disorders and groups them in three clusters on the basis of descriptive similarities (APA, 1994). Cluster A, characterized by odd or eccentric behaviors, consists of the paranoid, schizoid, and schizotypal personality disorders. Cluster B, characterized by dramatic, emotional, or erratic behaviors, consists of the antisocial, borderline, histrionic, and narcissistic personality disorders. And Cluster C, characterized by fearful or anxious behavior, consists of the avoidant, dependent, and obsessive-compulsive personality disorders.

As we examine these personality disorders, it will become evident that the symptoms of one disorder often overlap with those of another, thus making it difficult to distinguish them (Zimmerman, 1994). Even diagnosticians may have difficulty of this kind and in many cases they assign more than one personality disorder category to an individual. In addition, clinicians often disagree as to the correct diagnosis for a given person with a personality disorder. This has raised serious questions about the validity (accuracy) and reliability (consistency) of the present DSM categories and has led many clinicians to propose alternative approaches to classifying personality disorders. We shall return to this issue later in the chapter.

As we examine the various personality disorders, we must avoid the trap of overapplying any category to ourselves or to the people we know. Indeed, it is all too easy to catch glimpses of oneself or of one's acquaintances in the descriptions of the various personality disorders (Widiger & Costa, 1994; Maher & Maher, 1994). In the vast majority of cases, such interpretations are unwarranted. We all display personality traits; that is part of being human. And many of these traits inevitably resemble those that are characteristic of personality disorders. Only rarely are they so inflexible, maladaptive, and distressful that they can be considered disorders.

■ ODD OR ■ ECCENTRIC PERSONALITY DISORDERS

Cluster A includes the paranoid, schizoid, and schizotypal personality disorders. People with these disorders typically display odd or eccentric behavior, some of the same odd behaviors seen in the Axis I disorder schizophrenia (for example, extreme suspiciousness, social withdrawal, and cognitive and perceptual peculiarities). Some clinicians believe that these personality disorders are indeed related to schizophrenia and call them *schizophrenia-spectrum disorders*, along with several other schizophrenia-like syndromes (Siever, 1992). In support of this idea, studies reveal that people with these personality disorders are more likely than other persons to qualify for an additional diagnosis of schizophrenia or to have close relatives with schizophrenia (APA, 1994; Battaglia et al., 1991; Siever et al., 1990). On the other hand, these findings may simply reflect the difficulty diagnosticians have in distinguishing these personality disorders from schizophrenia, rather than some kind of direct relationship between them.

As we shall see, clinicians have carefully delineated the symptoms of these odd and eccentric personality disorders over the years, yet the causes of the disorders are not well understood. Although theorists have offered a variety of explanations, particularly psychodynamic ones, the causes of the disorders have received relatively little systematic investigation. Nor have clinicians been very successful in treating persons with these personality disorders, although a variety of approaches have been tried. In fact, people with these disorders rarely seek treatment (Fabrega et al., 1991).

PARANOID PERSONALITY DISORDER

People with *paranoid personality disorder* display a pattern of pervasive distrust and suspiciousness of others (APA, 1994). Because people with this disorder suspect everyone of intending them harm, they shun close relationships. Their trust in their own ideas and abilities can be excessive, though, as we see in the case of Charles.

Charles, an only child of poorly educated parents, had been recognized as a "child genius" in early school years. He received a Ph.D. degree at 24, and subsequently held several responsible positions as a research physicist in an industrial firm.

His haughty arrogance and narcissism often resulted in conflicts with his superiors; it was felt that he spent too much time working on his own "harebrained" schemes and not enough on company projects. Charles increasingly was assigned to jobs of lesser importance than that to which he was accustomed. He began to feel, not unjustly, that both his superiors and his subordinates were "making fun of him" and not taking him seriously. To remedy this attack upon his status, Charles began to work on a scheme that would "revolutionize the industry," a new thermodynamic principle which, when applied to his company's major product, would prove extremely efficient and economical. After several months of what was conceded by others as "brilliant thinking," he presented his plans to the company president. Brilliant though it was, the plan overlooked certain obvious simple facts of logic and economy.

Upon learning of its rejection, Charles withdrew to his home where he became obsessed with "new ideas," proposing them in intricate schematics and formulas to a number of government officials and industrialists. These resulted in new rebuffs which led to further efforts at self inflation.

(Millon, 1969, pp. 329–330)

Ever vigilant, cautious, and quick to react to perceived threats, people with a paranoid personality disorder continually expect to be the target of some trickery or exploitation, and they find "hidden" meanings everywhere, usually of a belittling or threatening nature (see Figure 17–1). In one study in which subjects were asked to role play, paranoid subjects were more likely than nonparanoid controls to interpret the ambiguous actions of others as reflecting hostile intentions, and to choose anger as the appropriate role-play response (Turkat et al., 1990). In another study, investigating paranoid responses to ambiguous or incomplete stimuli, undergraduates with paranoid personalities accused the experimenters of not providing correct answers, a response never observed among control subjects (Thompson et al., 1988).

People with paranoid personality disorder approach relationships with skepticism and guardedness. Quick to challenge the loyalty or trustworthiness of acquaintances, they remain cold and distant, reluctant to confide in others for fear of being hurt and of having potential friends turn against them. Such unwarranted suspicions are exemplified by the classic paranoid husband who with no justification continually questions the fidelity of his wife.

People with a paranoid personality disorder are critical of weakness and fault in others, particularly in work-related situations, but they view themselves as blameless and consequently are hypersensitive to criticism. Argumentative and rigid, they are unable to recognize their mistakes, instead projecting their inadequacies onto others and often blaming others for the things that go wrong in their own lives or even for their general unhappiness (Vaillant, 1994). They persistently bear grudges, thus further compromising their relationships with others, including persons in positions of authority.

Between 0.5 and 2.5 percent of the adult population are believed to manifest a paranoid personality disorder, apparently more men than women (APA, 1994). The suspiciousness of people with paranoid personality disorder, unlike that of persons with a paranoid type of schizophrenia or a delusional disorder, is not usually of a delusional nature. That is, their ideas are not so bizarre or so firmly believed that they constitute a clear departure from reality. Similarly, their self-centeredness, hypersensitivity, and concern over power remain within the boundaries of reality, although they are excessive and maladaptive (Meissner, 1987).

EXPLANATIONS OF PARANOID PERSONALITY DISORDER The etiology of paranoid personality disorder, like that of most other personality

PERSONALITY DISORDER

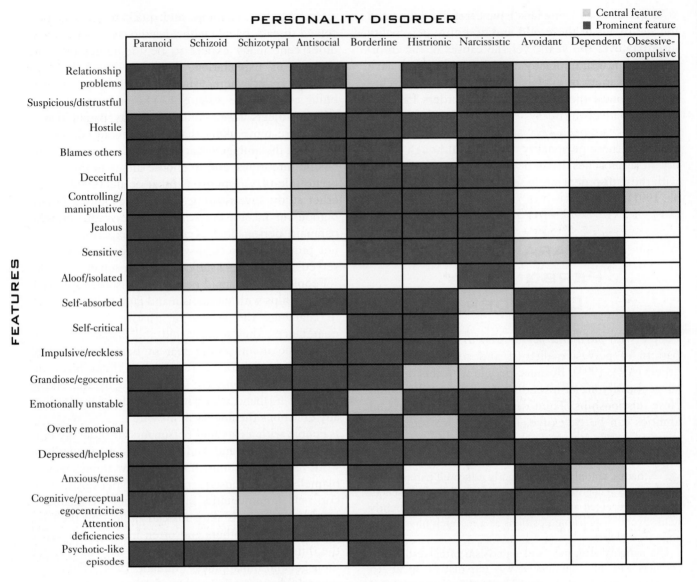

FIGURE 17-1 *Prominent and central features of ten personality disorders. The symptoms of the various disorders often overlap significantly, leading to frequent misdiagnosis or to multiple diagnoses for a given client. Thus some clinicians have called for changes in DSM IV's system of classifying the personality disorders.*

disorders, has received little empirical investigation. Psychodynamic theories, the most prominent explanations for this disorder, trace it to early interactions with demanding and rejecting parents. (Indeed, psychodynamic explanations for almost all of the personality disorders begin with the proposition that people with the disorders have experienced rejection or lack of love when young.) According to one psychodynamic view, repeated mistreatment and the absence of consistent parental love during infancy and childhood cause some individuals to become overly vigilant to danger and to negative reactions from others, resulting in a broad and basic distrust of others

(Cameron, 1974). Interacting each day with fathers who are often distant, rigid, and ineffectual and with mothers who are seductive, overcontrolling, and rejecting (Manschreck, 1985), the children come to view all environments as hostile. Some theorists further suggest that children with such unfortunate roots are likely to develop feelings of excessive hostility and rage that they *project* onto others, leading them to feel even more persecuted and attacked (Garfield & Havens, 1991).

Still other psychodynamic theorists propose that early parental interactions of this kind produce feelings of inadequacy in children and cause them to view themselves as mistake-prone and different from others (Turkat & Banks, 1987). In trying to perform to their parents' overdemanding and rigid expectations, the children often find themselves cast out by their peers and humiliated. They *rationalize* their rejection and the resulting social isolation as stemming from others' jealousy of their specialness. A number of cognitive theorists, too, have conceptualized paranoid functioning as a set of strategies designed to counter feelings of humiliation, shame, and inadequacy (Colby, 1981).

The idea of a genetic factor in paranoid personality disorder has also been proposed. An epidemiologic study of self-reported suspiciousness in 3,810 Australian twin pairs found that if one twin was excessively suspicious, the other had an increased likelihood of also being suspicious (Kendler et al., 1987). As with other such studies, however, these findings alone cannot tell us whether it is genetic factors or common experiences that lead both twins to be overly suspicious.

TREATMENT FOR PARANOID PERSONALITY DISORDER

A number of difficulties hamper the treatment of people with paranoid personality disorder. To begin with, few of these individuals come to treatment willingly (Millon, 1981). Unless they are in a state of crisis, they do not see themselves as needing help. Once in therapy, many apparently interpret the role of patient as subordinate, feel personally inadequate, and in turn distrust their therapist and resist treatment (Sparr et al., 1986).

Psychodynamic therapists focus treatment on the person's intrapsychic conflicts and deficits (Aronson, 1989). Object relations therapists, who give center stage to relationships in their psychodynamic work, try to see through the patient's defensive anger and work on what they view as his or her deep wish for a satisfying relationship (Auchincloss & Weiss, 1992). The effectiveness of psychodynamic therapy for this patient population remains unclear, however. In one study, patients with paranoid personality disorder showed less response to psychodynamic therapy than those with other mental disorders or other personality disorders (Conte et al., 1988).

Cognitive therapists hold that one of the initial steps to reduce the vigilance and defensiveness of clients with paranoid personality disorder is to increase their sense of self-efficacy (Beck & Freeman, 1990). When clients feel better able to handle problems and control their anxiety, they feel safer and so more amenable to trying alternative ways of thinking and coping. Then cognitive therapists work with them on improving their skills at solving interpersonal problems, developing more realistic perceptions of others' behaviors and intentions, and increasing their awareness of other people's perspectives (Beck & Freeman, 1990).

Whatever the psychotherapeutic approach, the patient's progress is typically slow. In fact, psychotherapy may continue for years before any significant progress is made (Quality Assurance Project, 1990). Psychotherapy for paranoid personality disorder, like that for most other personality disorders, yields limited gains at best. Similarly, drug therapy has generally been ineffective for those with this disorder (Block & Pristach, 1992).

SCHIZOID PERSONALITY DISORDER

Like people with paranoid personality disorder, those with schizoid personality disorder do not have close ties with others. But they avoid social contact because they genuinely prefer to be alone, not because they suspect other people's motives.

Roy was a successful sanitation engineer involved in the planning and maintenance of water resources for a large city; his job called for considerable foresight and independent judgment but little supervisory responsibility. In general, he was appraised as an undistinguished but competent and reliable employee. There were few demands of an interpersonal nature made of him, and he was viewed by most of his colleagues as reticent and shy and by others as cold and aloof.

Difficulties centered about his relationship with his wife. At her urging they sought marital counseling for, as she put it, "he is unwilling to join in family activities, he fails to take an interest in the children, he lacks affection and is disinterested in sex."

The pattern of social indifference, flatness of affect and personal isolation which characterized much of Roy's behavior was of little consequence to those with whom a deeper or more intimate relationship was not called for; with his immediate family, however, these traits took their toll.

(Millon, 1969, p. 224)

People with ***schizoid personality disorder*** display a pattern of detachment from social relationships and a restricted range of emotional expression (APA,

1994). Other people often view them as "loners," observers rather than participants in the world around them. Detached and seclusive, they are uninterested in initiating or maintaining acquaintanceships or friendships, take little interest in having sexual relationships, and even seem indifferent to their families.

In accord with their solitary propensities, people with this pattern seek out occupations that require little or no contact with others. When necessary, they can form stable, if distant, work relations, but they prefer to keep to themselves, often working alone over the course of the day. They typically live by themselves as well, and avoid socializing by withdrawing into a routine of solitary habits and activities. As a result, their social skills tend to be relatively limited.

The restricted interactions of people with schizoid personality disorder reflect an equally restricted range of emotion and expression. Unaffected by praise or criticism, they are self-absorbed and generally unaware of or unmoved by others' opinions. Even in situations that would typically arouse strong emotions, people with this disorder rarely show their feelings, expressing neither joy nor anger. They seem to have no need for attention or acceptance, are typically viewed as cold, humorless, or dull, and generally succeed in being ignored.

The prevalence of schizoid personality disorder is not known (APA, 1994). Slightly more men than women are believed to have the disorder, and men may be more impaired by it (APA, 1994).

EXPLANATIONS OF SCHIZOID PERSONALITY DISORDER Psychodynamic theorists, particularly object relations theorists, believe that the extreme social withdrawal of people with a schizoid personality disorder is a defensive reaction to an unsatisfied basic need for human contact (Carstairs, 1992; Horner, 1991, 1975; Mahler, 1979). The parents of people with this disorder, like those of persons with paranoid personality disorder, are seen as having been unaccepting, underprotective, and rejecting. In some cases the parents or others were even abusive, or the childhood was marked by traumas. Rather than react with a sense of distrust and hostility (as those with paranoid symptoms do), these individuals suffer an inability to give or receive love, and in their vulnerability to rejection, they develop a defensive coping strategy of shunning all relationships. A sense of loyalty to the offending caretaker has caused them to respond not with outrage but with lowered self-esteem (Stone, 1989).

Similarly, psychodynamic practitioners of self theory believe that people with schizoid personality disorder have a "self disorder." Because of their faulty interactions with their parents, they are unable to satisfy the basic needs of a developing self. That is, they cannot achieve self-esteem, self-affirmation, self-confidence, or the capacity for self-soothing, nor can they achieve a sense of belonging or fitting in to the human community (Cirese, 1993). They experience a fundamental splitting of the self into a bundle of unintegrated self-representations (Gabbard, 1990). Suffering from a diffuse identity and unsure of who they are, they are unable to relate to others.

Cognitive theorists propose that people with schizoid personality disorder suffer from several cognitive deficits, including a profound vagueness and poverty of thought and an inability to scan the environment effectively and achieve accurate perceptions (Beck & Freeman, 1990). These deficits help account for their lack of emotional responsiveness. Unable to register and interpret subtle emotional cues, they are unlikely to respond to emotion-evoking stimuli. As this idea of cognitive deficits predicts, children with schizoid personality disorder have been found to suffer more developmental delays in language, education, and motor functioning than control subjects, despite a similar level of intelligence in the two groups (Wolff, 1991).

TREATMENT FOR SCHIZOID PERSONALITY DISORDER With their lack of emotion and motivation and their disengagement from interpersonal contact, people with schizoid personality disorder have little interest in initiating treatment. Those who enter therapy usually do so because of some other disorder, such as alcoholism or another substance-related disorder.

Although schizoid personality disorder is apparently more amenable to psychotherapy than paranoid personality disorder (Quality Assurance Project, 1990), people with this disorder are nevertheless quite resistant to treatment. Threatened by the intimacy of a therapeutic relationship, they often distance themselves from their therapist and seem uncaring about their treatment (Siever, 1981). Therapy that moves rapidly or probes deeply is generally unsuccessful (Stone, 1989).

Cognitive-behavioral strategies are sometimes used to help clients with schizoid personality disorder become more aware of and experience more positive emotions (Beck & Freeman, 1990). Therapists may, for example, present clients with a list of emotions to think about or have them record interesting or pleasurable experiences. Therapists may also use role playing, in vivo exposure, and homework assignments to help teach social skills (Beck & Freeman, 1990). Such techniques do apparently bring about some specific changes, but broad personality changes are unlikely to follow.

Drug therapy has offered little help to people with this disorder, although the use of antipsychotic medications has been proposed by theorists who place schizoid personality disorder on the schizophrenia spectrum (Liebowitz et al., 1986).

Group therapy, either alone or as an adjunct to individual psychotherapy, is apparently useful in the treatment of schizoid persons when it provides a contained, safe setting for social contact (Vaillant & Perry, 1985). Some patients with schizoid personality disorder, however, find group encounters threatening and remain aloof to the efforts of the group (Stone, 1989; Liebowitz et al., 1986). They sense a "ganging up" by the other members, and feel stifled by pressure to speak and to share more of themselves with other group members (Gabbard, 1990).

SCHIZOTYPAL PERSONALITY DISORDER

The schizotypal personality disorder is so severe that those who suffer from it are greatly handicapped in all interactions with other people, as we see in the case of Harold:

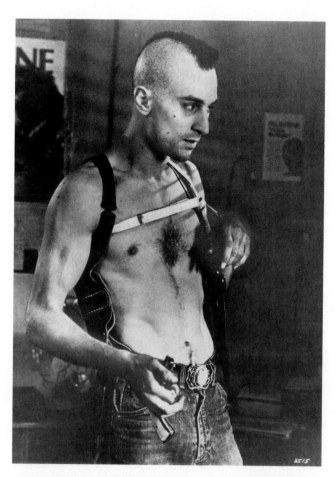

Some of film's most memorable characters have displayed personality disorders. Travis Bickle, of Taxi Driver *fame, seemed to manifest the symptoms of schizotypal personality disorder. His social discomfort and reduced capacity for interpersonal relationships, self-referential interpretations of various events, cognitive eccentricities, highly suspicious nature, grandiosity, emotional flatness, and transient psychotic episodes combined eventually to lead him on a killing rampage.*

Harold was the fourth of seven children. . . . "Duckie," as Harold was known, had always been a withdrawn, frightened and "stupid" youngster. The nickname "Duckie" represented a peculiar waddle in his walk; it was used by others as a term of derogation and ridicule. Harold rarely played with his sibs or neighborhood children; he was teased unmercifully because of his "walk" and his fear of pranksters. Harold was a favorite neighborhood scapegoat; he was intimidated even by the most innocuous glance in his direction.

His father's brutality toward the other children of the family terrified Harold. Although Harold received less than his share of this brutality, since his father thought him to be a "good and not troublesome boy," this escape from paternal hostility was more than made up for by resentment and teasing on the part of his older siblings. By the time Harold was 10 or 11, his younger brothers joined in taunting and humiliating him.

Harold's family was surprised when he performed well in the first few years of schooling. He began to falter, how-

ever, upon entrance to junior high school. At about the age of 14, his schoolwork became extremely poor, he refused to go to classes and he complained of a variety of vague, physical pains. By age 15 he had totally withdrawn from school, remaining home in the basement room that he shared with two younger brothers. Everyone in his family began to speak of him as "being touched." He thought about "funny religious things that didn't make sense"; he also began to draw "strange things" and talk to himself. When he was 16, he once ran out of the house screaming "I'm gone, I'm gone, I'm gone . . . ," saying that his "body went to heaven" and that he had to run outside to recover it; rather interestingly, this event occurred shortly after his father had been committed by the courts to a state mental hospital. By age 17, Harold was ruminating all day, often talking aloud in a meaningless jargon; he refused to come to the family table for meals.

(Millon, 1969, pp. 347–348)

People with *schizotypal personality disorder* display a pattern of interpersonal deficits marked by acute discomfort in close relationships, cognitive or perceptual distortions, and behavioral eccentricities (APA, 1994). They tend to seek isolation, experience considerable anxiety in the presence of others, and typically have few if any close friends outside of their immediate families. Moreover, their inability to connect pleasurably or meaningfully with others may cause them to feel intensely lonely.

It is the nature and extent of their cognitive distortions and behavioral eccentricities that distinguish these people from those with paranoid and schizoid personality disorders. Like people with paranoid personality disorder, for example, they are very suspicious about the motives of others, but they further demonstrate many peculiarities of thought. They may harbor *ideas of reference,* believing that unrelated events pertain to them in some important way. They may have unusual perceptual experiences, including bodily *illusions,* such as sensing an external "force" or presence. Some people with schizotypal personality disorder see themselves as having special extrasensory abilities, and dabble in spirituality. Others express odd beliefs or *magical thinking,* such as the belief that they have magical control over others. In adolescents with this disorder, such oddities of thought may appear in bizarre fantasies or preoccupations.

Along with eccentricities of thought, schizotypal persons often display eccentric behavior. They may spend an unusual amount of time on organizational tasks such as arranging labels on cans or organizing closets. Many are disheveled in appearance, wearing a peculiar assortment of clothing and accessories. In addition, the emotions of these individuals may be either inappropriate or flat. Humorlessness and blandness are common, although schizotypal people may also appear tense or sad, overreacting without provocation.

People with schizotypal personality disorder often have great difficulty keeping their attention focused (Lenzenwerger et al., 1991). This problem may partially explain one of their most distinctive characteristics—*digressive speech.* They typically converse in a vague manner, making statements that are inappropriately elaborate. It is often difficult to follow their train of thought, as their ideas are expressed abstractly and are only tangentially connected to each other and to the topic of conversation. In one study, more loose associations and related speech problems were found among children with this disorder than in control subjects (Caplan et al., 1990). Ironically, many

people with schizotypal personality disorder respond only to the concrete aspects of others' speech—that is, to the literal and not the figurative meaning of what other people say. Although their symptoms are obviously similar to those of people with schizophrenia, they rarely are as extreme and they do not represent a complete break from reality.

Some theorists claim that a significant relationship exists between schizotypal symptoms and a propensity for creative thought (Schuldberg et al., 1988). The results of one study suggest that schizotypal persons with greater perceptual distortions and magical thinking may be especially likely to have creative ability. Yet the general tendency of people with this personality disorder is to drift aimlessly, to lead an idle, ineffectual life (Millon, 1990). They are likely to choose undemanding jobs in which they can work below their capacity and have no need to interact with other people.

According to recent studies, the features of schizotypal personality disorder may break down along gender lines. The "positive" symptoms (that is, the excesses) of the disorder, such as magical thinking and ideas of reference, seem to be more common in women, whereas the "negative" symptoms (the deficits), such as constricted emotions and lack of friends, appear to be more common among men (Raine, 1992).

People with this disorder are more likely than the general population to have attempted suicide and to have been hospitalized with another mental disorder (Lenzenweger et al., 1991; Bornstein et al., 1988). It has been estimated that as many as 3 percent of all persons have a schizotypal personality disorder (APA, 1994). Slightly more males than females seem to experience it (APA, 1994).

EXPLANATIONS OF SCHIZOTYPAL PERSONALITY DISORDER Because the symptoms of schizotypal personality disorder and schizophrenia are often so similar (see Table 17–1), researchers have tried to show that some of the factors that explain schizophrenia can also help explain schizotypal personality disorder. Their efforts have often been successful in recent years. As in the case of schizophrenia, for example, the development of schizotypal symptoms has been linked to poor family communication during childhood and to psychological disorders in parents (Asarnow et al., 1991; Nagy & Szatmari, 1986).

Research has also suggested that defects in attention may contribute significantly to schizotypal personality disorder, just as they apparently do to

TABLE 17-1

COMPARISON OF PERSONALITY DISORDERS AND SIMILAR AXIS I DISORDERS

PERSONALITY DISORDER	RESEMBLING DISORDER	DIFFERENCE
Paranoid Schizoid Schizotypal	Schizophrenia Delusional disorder	Persistent psychotic symptoms, such as delusions and hallucinations, are not necessarily part of personality disorders. If psychotic symptoms occur, they are transient and less severe
Antisocial	Conduct disorder	People with personality disorder must be at least 18 years old and have a history of violating others' rights since age 15
Borderline	Mood disorders	People with personality disorder have short mood episodes, early onset, and long-standing course
Histrionic	Somatoform disorders	In somatoform disorders complaints of physical illness overshadow any histrionic symptoms that may occur
Narcissistic	Cyclothymic disorder (mild bipolar disorder)	In personality disorder grandiosity dominates and mood shifts are situation-bound
Avoidant	Social phobia	People with social phobia fear social *circumstances;* those with personality disorder primarily fear social *relationships*
Dependent	Childhood separation anxiety disorder	Personality disorder extends beyond childhood and permeates all areas of functioning
Obsessive-compulsive	Obsessive-compulsive (anxiety) disorder	True obsessions and compulsions are not present in personality disorder. Symptoms are "embraced" by people with personality disorder, but "resisted" by those with anxiety disorder

schizophrenia (Weston & Siever, 1993; Siever & Davis, 1991). One laboratory measure of attention is the *backward masking task,* in which subjects try to identify a new visual target immediately after a previous visual stimulus has been flashed on and off the screen. Both schizotypal and schizophrenic subjects seem unable to readily shut out the previous stimulus and need much more time than normal control subjects to identify the second target correctly (Weston & Siever, 1993; Braff & Saccuzzo, 1985). Similarly, schizotypal subjects perform poorly on a variety of other tests of attention, just as schizophrenic subjects do (Thaker et al., 1991; Siever et al., 1990).

Finally, recent research has begun to link schizotypal personality disorder to some of the same biological factors tied to schizophrenia (Weston & Siever, 1993). For example, like schizophrenic patients, schizotypal patients appear to have higher levels of

activity of the brain neurotransmitter dopamine, as measured by the level of dopamine byproducts in the blood (Siever et al., 1993, 1990). In addition, one study found that schizotypal patients have enlarged ventricles in their brains, a structural abnormality that has been linked to schizophrenia (Rotter et al., 1991). There are also some indications that these biological factors may have a genetic base. Schizotypal personality disorder is more prevalent among the close relatives of people with this disorder than in the general population (Carey & DiLalla, 1994; Kendler et al., 1991; Baron et al., 1985, 1983).

Certainly, these findings suggest a close relationship between schizotypal personality disorder and schizophrenia, but it is important to note that the personality disorder has also been linked to mood disorders. Relatives of people with depression, for example, also have a higher than usual rate of schizotypal personality disorder, and vice versa. This finding suggests, at the very least, that schizotypal personality disorder is not tied exclusively to schizophrenia (Schulz, 1986).

TREATMENT FOR SCHIZOTYPAL PERSON-
ALITY DISORDER   Psychotherapy is sometimes of use for persons with schizotypal disorder, but, as in cases of paranoid and schizoid personality disorder, the therapist must take into account the client's limited capacity for interaction (Stone, 1989; McGlashan, 1986). Therapists who are experienced with this patient population advise that treatment goals be modest and pursued slowly and supportively.

Helping clients "reconnect" with the world and establish personal boundaries is often the central therapeutic task, irrespective of the therapist's model. Therapists may address boundary problems by setting explicit limits, requiring punctuality, being decisive and firm when necessary, and distinguishing clearly between the patient's views and the therapist's (Stone, 1989). Some of the specific goals of therapy are preventing further social isolation, easing loneliness, accentuating individual strengths, avoiding overstimulation, and developing self-awareness of personal feelings (Quality Assurance Project, 1990; Walsh, 1990).

Cognitive therapists further try to teach schizotypal clients to evaluate their unusual thoughts or perceptions according to objective evidence in the environment rather than by relying on emotional responses (Beck & Freeman, 1990). Similarly, they try to help clients disregard inappropriate thoughts and refrain from acting on them. They may keep track of a client's odd or magical predictions, for example, and then point out their invalidity, or have a client who gets caught in loose and abstract verbalizations make summary statements during therapy.

Behavioral techniques are sometimes used for those schizotypal patients who display marked peculiarities of behavior. On occasion, specific reeducative methods such as elocution lessons, social skills training, and tips on appropriate dress and manners have helped the individuals learn to fit in and feel less alienated around others (Liebowitz et al., 1986).

Finally, drug therapy has also often been given to patients with schizotypal personality disorder, partly, again, because of their similarity to patients with schizophrenia. Antipsychotic drugs in low doses apparently help some patients, usually by reducing some of their thought disorders (Weston & Siever, 1993; Perry et al., 1990; Schulz et al., 1988). Patients with this personality disorder may be particularly sensitive to the detrimental effects of medication, however, so the dosage must be monitored closely.

■ DRAMATIC, ■ EMOTIONAL, OR ERRATIC PERSONALITY DISORDERS

Cluster B personality disorders include the antisocial, borderline, histrionic, and narcissistic personality disorders. People with these problems often display dramatic, emotional, or erratic behavior. As a group, these personality disorders are more commonly diagnosed than the others (Fabrega et al., 1991). Once again clinical theorists (particularly psychodynamic theorists) have offered numerous explanations and treatment suggestions for the disorders, but research has actually shed little light on these issues. Only one of the disorders, antisocial personality disorder, has received much empirical attention over the years, probably because it creates so many problems for society. As a result, we have a somewhat greater understanding of the factors that contribute to this disorder than we do about the causes of other personality disorders. In recent years, borderline personality disorder has also been receiving considerable research attention (Linehan & Kehrer, 1993).

ANTISOCIAL PERSONALITY DISORDER

Robert Hare (1993), one of the world's leading researchers of antisocial personality disorder, recalls an early professional encounter with Ray, a prison inmate who displayed this disorder:

*I*n the early 1960s, I found myself employed as the sole psychologist at the British Columbia Penitentiary. I started work completely cold—with no training program or sage mentor to hint at how one went about being a prison psychologist. I wasn't in my office for more than an hour when my first "client" arrived. He was a tall, slim, dark-haired man in his thirties. The air around him seemed to buzz, and the eye contact he made with me was so direct and intense that I wondered if I had ever really looked anybody in the eye before. That stare was unrelenting—he didn't indulge in the brief glances away that most people use to soften the force of their gaze.

Without waiting for an introduction, the inmate—I'll call him Ray—opened the conversation: "Hey, Doc, how's it

Charles Manson, who directed his followers to kill nine people in 1969, fits many of the criteria of an antisocial personality disorder, including disregard for and violation of others' rights, impulsivity, disregard for truth, and lack of remorse. In a recent interview Manson bragged, "I was crazy when crazy meant something."

going? Look, I've got a problem. I need your help. I'd really like to talk to you about this."

Eager to begin work as a genuine psychotherapist, I asked him to tell me about it. In response, he pulled out a knife and waved it in front of my nose, all the while smiling and maintaining that intense eye contact.

Once he determined that I wasn't going to push the button, he explained that he intended to use the knife not on me but on another inmate who had been making overtures to his "protégé," a prison term for the more passive member of a homosexual pairing. Just why he was telling me this was not immediately clear, but I soon suspected that he was checking me out, trying to determine what sort of a prison employee I was. Following our session, in which he described his "problem" not once or twice but many times, I kept quiet about the knife. To my relief, he didn't stab the other inmate, but it soon became evident that Ray had caught me in his trap: I had shown myself to be a soft touch who would overlook clear violations of fundamental prison rules in order to develop "professional" rapport with the inmates.

From that first meeting on, Ray managed to make my eight-month stint at the prison miserable. His constant demands on my time and his attempts to manipulate me into doing things for him were unending. On one occasion, he convinced me that he would make a good cook—he felt he had a natural bent for cooking, he thought he would become a chef when he was released, this was a great opportunity to try out some of his ideas to make institutional food preparation more efficient, etc.—and I supported his request for a transfer from the machine shop (where he had apparently made the knife). What I didn't consider was that

the kitchen was a source of sugar, potatoes, fruit, and other ingredients that could be turned into alcohol. Several months after I had recommended the transfer, there was a mighty eruption below the floorboards directly under the warden's table. When the commotion died down, we found an elaborate system for distilling alcohol below the floor. Something had gone wrong and one of the pots had exploded. There was nothing unusual about the presence of a still in a maximum-security prison, but the audacity of placing one under the warden's seat shook up a lot of people. When it was discovered that Ray was the brains behind the bootleg operation, he spent some time in solitary confinement.

Once out of "the hole," Ray appeared in my office as if nothing had happened and asked for a transfer from the kitchen to the auto shop—he really felt he had a knack, he saw the need to prepare himself for the outside world, if he only had the time to practice he could have his own body shop on the outside. . . . I was still feeling the sting of having arranged the first transfer, but eventually he wore me down.

Soon afterward I decided to leave the prison to pursue a Ph.D. in psychology, and about a month before I left Ray almost persuaded me to ask my father, a roofing contractor, to offer him a job as part of an application for parole.

Ray had an incredible ability to con not just me but everybody. He could talk, and lie, with a smoothness and a directness that sometimes momentarily disarmed even the most experienced and cynical of the prison staff. When I met him he had a long criminal record behind him (and, as it turned out, ahead of him); about half his adult life had been spent in prison, and many of his crimes had been violent. Yet he convinced me, and others more experienced than I, of his readiness to reform, that his interest in crime had been completely overshadowed by a driving passion in—well, cooking, mechanics, you name it. He lied endlessly, lazily, about everything, and it disturbed him not a whit whenever I pointed out something in his file that contradicted one of his lies. He would simply change the subject and spin off in a different direction. Finally convinced that he might not make the perfect job candidate in my father's firm, I turned down Ray's request—and was shaken by his nastiness at my refusal.

Before I left the prison for the university, I took advantage of the prison policy of letting staff have their cars repaired in the institution's auto shop—where Ray still worked, thanks (he would have said no thanks) to me. The car received a beautiful paint job and the motor and drivetrain were reconditioned.

With all our possessions on top of the car and our baby in a plywood bed in the backseat, my wife and I headed for Ontario. The first problems appeared soon after we left Vancouver, when the motor seemed a bit rough. Later, when we encountered some moderate inclines, the radiator boiled over. A garage mechanic discovered ball bearings in the carburetor's float chamber; he also pointed out where one of the hoses to the radiator had clearly been tampered with. These problems were repaired easily enough, but the next one, which arose while we were going down a long hill, was more serious. The brake pedal became very spongy and then simply dropped to the floor—no brakes, and it was a *long* hill. Fortunately, we made it to a service station, where we found that the brake line had been cut so that a slow leak would occur. Perhaps it was a coincidence that Ray was working in the auto shop when the car was being tuned up, but I had no doubt that the prison "telegraph" had informed him of the owner of the car.

My first job after receiving my Ph.D. was at the University of British Columbia, not far from the penitentiary where I had worked several years before. During registration week in that precomputer age, I sat behind a table with several colleagues to register long lines of students for their fall classes. As I was dealing with a student my ears pricked up at the mention of my name. "Yes, I worked as Dr. Hare's assistant at the penitentiary the whole time he was there, a year or so, I would say it was. Did all his paperwork for him, filled him in on prison life. Sure, he used to talk over hard cases with me. We worked great together." It was Ray, standing at the head of the next line.

My *assistant!* I broke into the easy flow of his remarks with, "Oh, really?" expecting to disconcert him. "Hey, Doc, how's it going?" he called without losing a beat. Then he simply jumped back into his conversation and took off in another direction. Later, when I checked his application forms, it became apparent that his transcript of previous university courses was fraudulent. To his credit, he had not attempted to register in one of *my* courses.

Often referred to as "psychopaths" or "sociopaths," persons with *antisocial personality disorder* display a pervasive pattern of disregard for and violation of other people's rights (APA, 1994). Outside of substance-related disorders, this is the disorder most closely linked to adult criminal behavior, both minor and major.

DSM-IV stipulates that a person must be 18 years of age or older to receive a diagnosis of antisocial personality disorder, but most such persons have displayed some patterns of antisocial misbehavior before they were 15, including truancy, running away from home, initiation of physical fights, forced sexual activity, physical cruelty to animals or people, deliberate destruction of property, fire setting, and frequent lying and stealing.

Like Ray, people with this personality disorder are repeatedly deceitful. Many are unable to work consistently at a job; they have frequent absences and are likely to abandon their jobs altogether. Not surprisingly, they run a high risk of unemployment (Bland et al., 1988). Usually these individuals are also irresponsible with money, frequently failing to honor financial obligations. They are impulsive, taking action without planning ahead or considering the consequences. Irritable and aggressive, they frequently initiate or

participate in physical fights or assaults (Vaillant, 1994). Many travel from place to place, without a fixed address or a clear goal or sense of purpose. Reckless and egocentric, they have little regard for their own safety or for that of others, even for their children. Many also have difficulty maintaining an enduring attachment to another person (Gacono & Meloy, 1992).

People with antisocial personality disorder are very skillful at achieving personal profit through the manipulation of other people. The pain, loss, or damage they cause seldom distresses them, so they are commonly perceived as lacking moral conscience. They glibly rationalize their actions by characterizing their victims as weak and deserving of being conned or stolen from. Antisocial persons who do experience a sense of guilt over wrongdoing have been labeled "secondary" psychopaths by some clinicians (Cleckley, 1976). Their behavior has been attributed more to poor impulse control than to a lack of remorse (see Box 17–1).

Surveys indicate that between 1.5 and 3.5 percent of the adult population manifest an antisocial personality disorder (Kessler et al., 1994; APA, 1994; Regier et al., 1993). The disorder is as much as three times more common among men than among women (APA, 1994), and white Americans are somewhat more likely than African Americans to receive the diagnosis (Robins et al., 1991; Collins et al., 1988).

Because people with this disorder are often arrested, many researchers have looked for patterns of antisocial functioning in prison populations (Parker, 1991). Among male urban jail detainees, an antisocial personality pattern has been found to be a strong predictor of past violent arrests (Abram & Teplin, 1990). Another study found that a greater percentage of imprisoned Vietnam veterans have antisocial personality disorder than nonimprisoned Vietnam veterans (Shaw et al., 1987). The criminality of persons with this disorder has been found to decline somewhat with age, although a large percentage of them apparently continue their criminal activities throughout adulthood (Arboleda-Florez & Holley, 1991).

Studies and clinical observations indicate a close relationship between antisocial personality disorder and alcoholism. Persons with antisocial symptoms display a higher rate of alcoholism than the rest of the population (Sher & Trull, 1994; Lewis & Bucholz, 1991). Among alcoholic persons, those with antisocial traits are more likely than others to have demonstrated alcoholism at an early age, to have drunk heavily in the past, and to have alcohol-related health problems (Malloy et al., 1990; Yates et al., 1988). Hospitalized alcoholic patients with antisocial personality disorder

Some clinicians believe that the hatred, prejudice, and violence displayed by members of supremacist groups are manifestations of antisocial personality disorder. Every country in the world has citizens who fervently wish to violate the rights of others, from the so-called "skinheads" in the United States (above) to the Neo-Nazis in Germany (below). Other clinicians argue that repulsive and criminal behavior is not by itself an indication of mental dysfunctioning.

also have poorer treatment outcomes (Hesselbrock, 1991) and are more likely to resume drinking than other alcoholic inpatients (Mather, 1987). Other substance-related disorders are also very common among people with an antisocial personality disorder (Sher & Trull, 1994; Griffin et al., 1989; Kosten, 1988).

This relationship between alcohol and other substance-related disorders and antisocial personality disorder is complex. On the one hand, early intoxication and substance abuse may loosen behavioral inhibitions and thus contribute to the development of antisocial personality disorder (Kaminer, 1991; Newcomb & Bentler, 1988). On the other hand, antisocial personality disorder may make adolescents vulnerable to substance abuse (Bukstein et al., 1989). Alternatively, antisocial personality disorder and substance abuse may share common causes such as a deep-seated need to take risks (Sher & Trull, 1994). Interestingly, drug users with antisocial personality disorder specifi-

cally cite the recreational aspects of drug use as reasons for initiating and maintaining it (Mirin & Weiss, 1991).

Finally, children with both *conduct disorder* and *attention-deficit hyperactivity disorder* apparently have a heightened risk of later developing antisocial personality disorder (APA, 1994; Hara, 1989). Some of the symptoms of these two childhood disorders, which we shall examine in Chapter 19, are so similar to those of antisocial personality disorder that some clinicians even consider the childhood disorders to be antisocial personality disorders in the making. Like adults with antisocial personality disorder, children with a conduct disorder persistently violate rules and others' rights and are deceitful, and children with attention-deficit hyperactivity disorder display a lack of insight and foresight, an inability to learn from experience, a diminished sense of fear, poor judgment, and difficulty distinguishing fantasies from reality (Bloomingdale & Bloomingdale, 1989). In fact, however, the precise nature of the relationship between the childhood disorders and antisocial personality disorder has been difficult to pinpoint (APA, 1994; Matthys et al., 1988).

EXPLANATIONS OF ANTISOCIAL PERSONALITY DISORDER   Explanations of antisocial personality disorder come primarily from the psychodynamic, cognitive, behavioral, and biological models. Psychodynamic theorists propose that this disorder, like many of the other personality disorders, begins with an absence of parental love during infancy, which leads to the child's lacking basic trust in others (Gabbard, 1990). Those who develop antisocial personality disorder respond to such early inadequacies by becoming emotionally detached from all relationships, and attempt to bond with others only through the use of power and destructiveness. The withdrawal from relatedness prevents the children from developing an awareness of others, which in turn results in a massive failure of superego development. This, psychodynamic theorists believe, is the root of the antisocial person's lack of conscience and morality (Gabbard, 1990).

Consistent with the psychodynamic explanation, researchers have found that people with this disorder are more likely than others to have experienced childhood stress, particularly in forms such as family poverty, family violence, and parental conflict or divorce (Luntz & Widom, 1994; Farrington, 1991; Emery, 1982). Many have also grown up with parents who themselves had an antisocial personality disorder (Lahey et al., 1988), a developmental experience which could certainly undermine one's trust in others.

BOX 17-1

DISORDERS OF IMPULSE CONTROL RATHER THAN PERSONALITY

Impulsivity is a symptom of numerous mental disorders, including antisocial and borderline personality disorders, bipolar disorder, substance-related disorders, schizophrenia, and paraphilias. DSM-IV also distinguishes several other disorders of which impulsivity is the *central* disabling feature. People with one of these *impulse-control disorders* fail to resist an impulse, drive, or temptation to perform acts that are harmful to themselves or others (APA, 1994). Usually they experience increasing tension or arousal before the act and pleasure or relief while they are performing it. Some, but not all, feel regret, self-reproach, or guilt afterward. These disorders often cause enormous distress to the sufferer and the community.

The disorders of impulse control identified by DSM-IV include pyromania, kleptomania, and pathological gambling. Although these problems arouse much curiosity and are portrayed in numerous movies and television programs, they have in fact received relatively little research attention.

Pyromania is the deliberate and repeated setting of fires to achieve intense pleasure or relief from tension. The fires are not set for monetary or any other apparent gain. This poorly understood disorder, which is much more common among men than women, is thought to be related to a variety of factors, including poor parental relationships, individual temperament, poor social skills, and possible neurochemical predispositions (APA, 1994; Soltys, 1992; Lowenstein, 1989). Research has been hampered by the difficulty of distinguishing instances of pyromania from those of *arson*—the setting of fires for revenge or gain or because of a psychotic delusion. The largest study undertaken so far surveyed the records of the National Board of Fire Underwriters and found that many of the firesetters described themselves as experiencing an "irresistible impulse" to set fires (Lewis & Yarnell, 1951). The inability of more recent studies to find more than a few cases of pyromania (APA, 1994; Koson & Dvoskin, 1982) suggests that the criteria for diagnosis, or perhaps the diagnostic category itself, may not be very useful.

The story is similar with respect to *kleptomania*—recurrent failure to resist the impulse to steal. People with this disorder, which is much more common in women, do not steal for gain. In fact, they often have more than enough money to pay for the articles they steal. Nor do they steal out of anger or revenge, or in response to a delusion or hallucination. Apparently it is the tension before the act and the sense of relief afterward that drive their behavior. The pattern may involve either brief episodes that occur sporadically, longer episodes that take place periodically, or a chronic, fluctuating course (APA, 1994).

Little research has been done on kleptomania. What is known has been drawn largely from case studies of shoplifting and stealing; yet fewer than 5 percent of shoplifters have this disorder. Most clinicians consider it to be rare and some question its usefulness as a clinical category (APA, 1994), but others believe it to be relatively common, especially among persons who also suffer from mood or eating disorders (Goldman, 1992; McElroy et al., 1991; Gerlinghoff & Backmund, 1987).

The most common of the impulse disorders is *pathological gambling,* persistent and recurrent maladaptive gambling behavior that disrupts personal, family, or vocational pursuits (APA, 1994). It is estimated that between 1 and 3 percent of the adult population may suffer from it (APA, 1994). Clinicians are careful to distinguish pathological from social gambling, for unlike pyromania and kleptomania, this behavior occurs in mild forms that are not only legal but

Some cognitive theorists suggest that people with antisocial personality disorder experience a developmental delay in the acquisition of moral principles and reasoning (Kagan, 1986). They have genuine difficulty keeping another point of view in mind along with their own, and can consider other persons' reactions only *after* they have acted on their own desires. Other cognitive theorists have suggested that people who are diagnosed with this disorder hold a philosophy of life that trivializes the importance of other persons' needs (Levenson, 1992). These theorists believe that such a philosophy may be far more pervasive in our society than most people recognize.

Some behavioral theorists have suggested that antisocial symptoms may be acquired through modeling,

socially approved. Pathological gambling is defined less by the amount of time or money spent in gambling than by the addictive nature of the behavior. Pathological gamblers are unable to walk away from a wager and are restless and irritable if gambling is denied them. Repeated losses of money lead to more gambling in an effort to win the money back, and the gambling continues even in the face of financial, social, and health problems. Four progressive phases characterize the course of many pathological gamblers: winning, losing, desperation, and hopelessness (Rosenthal, 1992).

Pathological gambling differs from the other impulse-control disorders in one very important way. Because this disorder is more prevalent than the others and because the behavior resembles alcoholism, a great deal of attention has been directed toward its treatment. Treatments that combine approaches tend to be more effective than any one approach alone (Schwarz & Lindner, 1992; Lesieur & Blume, 1991). Pathological gamblers who join self-help support groups, such as Gambler's Anonymous, a network patterned after Alcoholics Anonymous, seem to have a higher recovery rate, perhaps in part because they have admitted that they have a problem and are seeking to conquer it.

Recently there has been some controversy over the adoption of a disease model of pathological gambling. Editorials in various newspapers ask whether the "medicalization" of gambling too easily excuses irresponsible or illegal behavior (Vatz & Weinberg, 1993), and express dismay at the public approbation of public figures who have admitted to powerlessness over gambling impulses. On the other hand, several recent studies suggest that a neurochemical factor may in fact be related to pathological gambling and some of the other impulse-control disorders (McElroy et al., 1992; Moreno, Saiz, & Lopez, 1991), and some case studies report effective treatment for this disorder (Hollander et al., 1992).

DSM-IV also distinguishes two other impulse-control disorders. People with *intermittent explosive disorder*, a rare disorder more common in men than in women, have periodic aggressive outbursts in which they seriously assault people and destroy property. Their aggressiveness is grossly disproportionate to any provocation. People with *trichotillomania* repeatedly pull out hair from various parts of their bodies (particularly the scalp, eyebrows, and eyelashes), with resultant noticeable hair loss. Many clinicians believe that this disorder, which apparently is more common among women, is a compulsion and should be classified as an obsessive-compulsive anxiety disorder. Because it occurs without accompanying obsessions and without rigid rules, however, DSM-IV contends that it warrants its own category.

As with trichotillomania, it is often very difficult to distinguish the impulse-control disorders from other mental disorders, such as obsessive-compulsive and other anxiety disorders, depression, and personality disorders. Thus theorists commonly explain the impulse-control disorders by referring to the more familiar disorders that they resemble. When they are looked at closely, however, the impulse-control disorders, particularly fire setting, stealing, and pathological gambling, do not fit easily into existing categories of abnormal behavior, and accordingly warrant individual study and perhaps individual explanations.

and like psychodynamic theorists they point to the heightened rate of antisocial personality disorders among parents of people with this disorder as possible evidence for their explanation (Lahey et al., 1988). Other behaviorists have suggested that some parents may unwittingly teach antisocial behavior in the home by, for example, reinforcing a child's aggressive behavior (Patterson, 1986, 1982).

Finally, research indicates that antisocial personality disorder may be linked to a number of biological variables, and twin and adoption investigations suggest that this link may be due, in part, to genetic factors (Dahl, 1993; McGuffin & Thapar, 1992; Siever & Davis, 1991). For example, the autonomic nervous systems and central nervous systems of persons with the disorder seem to act more slowly than those of other persons, as indicated by their preponderance of EEG slow waves, decreased skin conductance, and low arousal (Raine, 1989; Bloomingdale & Bloomingdale, 1989). The continual search for excitement by persons with antisocial personality disorder and their disregard for prudence and caution may actually represent attempts to increase their own autonomic and central nervous system activity. As Box 17–2 indicates, researchers have increasingly been closing in on the way biological factors may intersect with behavioral and cognitive factors to bring about some of the symptoms of the disorder.

TREATMENTS FOR ANTISOCIAL PERSONALITY DISORDER Approximately a quarter of all people with antisocial personality disorder receive treatment for it (Regier et al., 1993), yet no known specific intervention appears to be effective (Mannuzza & Klein, 1991). A major difficulty in treating these individuals is their lack of conscience and their lack of motivation to change (Widiger, Corbitt, & Millon, 1992). Only a small percentage of them seek treatment voluntarily. The rest are acting on an ultimatum from an employer, their school, or the law, or come to the attention of therapists when they also develop another disorder (Fulwiler & Pope, 1987). Thus it is not surprising that in one study, 70 percent of patients with this disorder left treatment prematurely (Gabbard & Coyne, 1987).

Some cult leaders have been characterized as sociopathic persons who seduce their flock initially by being charming, bright, and persuasive, and maintain their hold over members through a mixture of subtle, degrading, and often abusive techniques. Once an aspiring rock guitarist, Vernon Howell changed his name to David Koresh and took leadership of the Branch Davidians in 1987, where he expressed a range of grandiose and suspicious ideas in his daily Bible classes and military-like commands.

In recent years a cognitive-behavioral approach to the treatment of antisocial personality disorder has been developed (Beck & Freeman, 1990). Here therapists try to move clients toward thinking on a higher, more abstract plane. Guided discussions, structured cognitive exercises, and behavioral experiments are used to help the individual progress through a hierarchy of increasingly moral and other-oriented ways of thinking. The efficacy of this cognitive approach is uncertain, however.

A milieu, therapeutic community approach, applied in hospitals and prisons, has also been recommended, on the theory that a structured environment that emphasizes responsibility toward others may be helpful for a select group of patients with antisocial personality disorder (Reid & Burke, 1989; Salama, 1988). In addition, challenging and rigorous wilderness programs that emphasize individual and group commitment have produced some improvements in the self-confidence, self-esteem, and interpersonal focus of persons with this disorder (Reid & Burke, 1989).

BORDERLINE PERSONALITY DISORDER

People with a borderline personality disorder are so unstable that their relationships cannot help but be dysfunctional, as in the case of Helen.

*H*elen decompensated over several years . . . following persistent quarrels with her exasperated husband, a man she married in her teens. . . . For brief periods, Helen sought to regain her husband's affections, but these efforts were for naught, and she became bitterly resentful, guilt-ridden and self-deprecating. Her erratic mood swings not only increased feelings of psychic disharmony, but further upset efforts to gain her husband's attention and support. As she persisted in vacillating between gloomy despondency, accusatory attacks and clinging behaviors, more of her sources of support were withdrawn, thereby intensifying [her] separation anxieties. . . . The next step, that of a regression to invalidism, was especially easy for her since it was consistent with her lifelong pattern of passive-dependence. Along with it, however, came discomforting feelings of estrangement and the collapse of all self-controls, as evidenced in her ultimate infantile-like behaviors and the total disorganization of her cognitive processes.

(Millon, 1969, pp. 360–361)

People with ***borderline personality disorder*** display a pervasive pattern of instability in interpersonal relationships, self-image, and moods, and marked

Alex Forrest, the emotionally unstable, impulsive, suicidal, and dangerous character in Fatal Attraction, *relentlessly pursued a married man with whom she had a brief relationship. Her symptoms are reminiscent of a borderline personality disorder.*

impulsivity (APA, 1994). The disorder actually covers a wide variety of personality types that some theorists believe inhabit the border zone between mood disorders and schizophrenia. Individuals so labeled experience major shifts in mood, swinging in and out of intense depressive, anxious, and irritable states that last anywhere from a few hours to a few days. Prone to bouts of anger and hostility (Gardner et al., 1991), they are engaged in a conflict between the world around them and the expression of their emotional needs (Perry & Cooper, 1986). When their anger is directed outward, it may result in physical aggression and violent behavior. Just as often, however, their anger is directed inward and expressed through self-damaging acts. These acts are committed on impulse and can be severe enough to cause significant bodily harm.

A sizeable percentage of the patients in mental health emergency rooms are borderline individuals who have engaged in self-mutilation (Bongar et al., 1990; Margo & Newman, 1989). Their self-destructive activities may range from alcohol and substance abuse to binge eating, delinquency, unsafe sex, irresponsible spending, reckless driving, bloodletting, or other forms of self-mutilation (Nace, 1992; Garfinkel & Gallop, 1992; Farrugia, 1992; Margo & Newman, 1989). Suicidal threats and actions are also common (APA, 1994; Runeson, 1989); one 15-year follow-up

study found a suicide rate of 8.5 percent among patients with this disorder (Paris, 1990). Many borderline individuals seem to engage in acts of self-destructiveness as a means of dealing with chronic feelings of emptiness and boredom. Uncertain about their identity and struggling to define themselves amidst a muddle of values and goals, they may seek validation through physical sensation.

As a result of their poorly grounded and distorted sense of self, people with borderline personality disorder frequently seek to identify with others, but their social behavior is often as confused and impulsive as their self-image and mood. They form intense, conflict-ridden relationships in which their feelings are not necessarily reciprocated (Modestin & Villiger, 1989). Alternating between overidealization and devaluation of the other person and fearing abandonment (realistically or not), they have difficulty maintaining appropriate interpersonal distance (Melges & Swartz, 1989). In fact, they frequently lose sight of the boundaries that distinguish who they are and what they feel from the feelings and identities of the other person. Borderline persons quickly become disappointed and enraged when others fail to meet their expectations; yet they remain intensely attached to their relationships, paralyzed by their fear of being left alone. In the face of possible desertion, they frequently resort to manipulative behaviors such as self-mutilation or suicidal gestures to prevent the other person from leaving the relationship.

The prevalence of borderline personality disorder has been estimated at 2 percent of the general population (APA, 1994). Around 75 percent of the patients who receive this diagnosis are women (APA, 1994; Gibson, 1990). Comparisons of male and female borderline patients indicate that women may be more likely to have coexisting mood disorders and display more self-destructive behavior; men seem more likely to have coexisting conduct, attention-deficit, and antisocial personality disorders (Andrulonis, 1991; Bardenstein et al., 1988).

The course of borderline personality disorder varies from person to person. In the most common pattern, however, the individual's degree of instability, impairment, and risk of suicide peak during young adulthood, then gradually wane with advancing age (APA, 1994). The best outcomes are associated with higher intelligence, shorter duration, and less severe symptoms (McGlashan, 1992).

EXPLANATIONS OF BORDERLINE PERSONALITY DISORDER   The fear of abandonment that tortures so many people with borderline personality disorder has led theorists and researchers

BOX 17-2

A LESSON NOT LEARNED

Personality disorders have received less systematic investigation than most other mental disorders. The one exception is antisocial personality disorder, or sociopathy. Partly because persons with this personality disorder create so many problems for society, researchers have shown considerable interest in it and have produced some important clinical insights. In one enlightening line of investigation spanning four decades, researchers have built study upon study in an effort to understand why persons with this disorder often seem incapable of learning from experience or weighing possible consequences before they act.

This line of empirical inquiry began in 1957 when the researcher David Lykken hypothesized that sociopathic people may experience less anxiety than other people and thus may lack an ingredient that is essential for learning a number of important behaviors. He argued that people ordinarily learn socially appropriate behaviors in order to avoid or reduce the anxiety brought on by others' disapproval. Sociopathic people, however, cannot learn from feelings of anxiety, because they do not experience those feelings.

In a clever study, Lykken (1957) tested the relationship between anxiety and learning in people with antisocial personality disorder. In the first part of the study, Lykken asked whether sociopathic subjects experience the same anxiety as normal subjects in response to real-life situations. He constructed a questionnaire in which subjects read thirty-three pairs of activities and were asked which of each pair they would rather do. Both items in each pair described an unpleasant event, but the events differed in the amount of anxiety they provoked. One activity was unpleasant because it was tedious ("getting up to go to work in the morning," say, or "cleaning out a cesspool"), the other because it provoked anxiety ("standing on a ledge on the 25th floor" or "knocking over a glass in a restaurant"). Lykken reasoned that if sociopathic subjects were not deterred by anxiety, they would be more likely than the normal subjects to choose the anxiety-producing alternative over the tedious alternative. This was in fact the case. These findings suggested that sociopathic people do experience less anxiety than other people.

Next Lykken examined the precise role that anxiety plays in learning for sociopathic and normal subjects. He had subjects try to learn a mental maze that consisted of twenty choice points or steps. At each choice point, the subject was required to press one correct switch out of four choices in order to move to the next step. Subjects were instructed to get through the maze with as few errors as possible. The learning of the twenty correct responses was the *manifest* task. But embedded in this task was an avoidance-learning *latent* task. One of the three incorrect responses at each choice point was paired with an electric shock. That is, when subjects made this incorrect response, they were shocked. Lykken reasoned that in addition to learning correct responses (the manifest task), subjects would learn to avoid shocked incorrect responses (the latent task) and would eventually err only on unshocked responses. Lykken found that sociopathic subjects learned the manifest task as well as normal subjects, but failed to learn the anxiety-motivated avoidance task—that is, the frequency of their shocked errors did not decrease. In short, when learning depended on anxiety, they failed to learn.

Next Lykken placed all of his subjects in a classical conditioning experiment in which an unconditioned stimulus (an electric shock) was paired with a conditioned stimulus (the sound of a buzzer) to condition an anxiety response (heightened galvanic skin response) to the sound of the buzzer alone. Lykken was unable to condition an anxiety response in the sociopathic subjects. Taken together, these findings support the idea that

---

once again to examine parental relationships as a possible source of this pathology. Psychodynamic theorists, particularly object relations theorists, suggest that the road to this pattern, as to other personality disorders, begins with a relationship problem between children and unaccepting parents (Kernberg, 1984; Mahler, 1979, 1974). In the case of borderline individuals, this lack of acceptance leads to a loss of self-esteem, heightened dependence on the parents, and a lower capacity for coping with the vicissitudes of separation (Richman & Sokolove, 1992; Arnow & Harrison, 1991; Tryon et al., 1988).

Researchers have indeed found that the infancies of many people with borderline personality disorder were marked by developmental problems between parent and child, including parental neglect and rejection, grossly inappropriate parental behavior, and a large number of mother and father substitutes (Ludolph et al., 1990; Paris et al., 1988). Correspondingly, borderline persons often rate their parents

people with an antisocial personality disorder are devoid of the normal anxiety needed to learn certain behaviors.

Are sociopathic people ever capable of learning avoidance responses? Apparently yes. Some years later the investigator Frank Schmauk (1970) used Lykken's maze-learning problem and found that sociopathic subjects did in fact learn to make the avoidance response when failure to do so resulted in a loss of money rather than a shock. This finding suggested to Schmauk that the *type* of punishment was a critical factor in teaching sociopathic people avoidance responses.

But the story did not end there. In recent years several researchers have suggested that it is not the type but the *salience* of the punishment that is critical in learning avoidance responses. They claim that in Schmauk's experiment, the loss of money was very salient because the subjects could see the money being taken away in front of them. The shock was not salient because it was a latent punishment that the subjects did not know they could avoid. The researchers found that when sociopathic subjects were forced to focus their attention on punishments, even little punishments, they performed as well on avoidance learning tasks as nonsociopathic subjects (Newman & Kosson, 1986).

Still more recent research has suggested that the learning problems of sociopathic persons are also related to the difficulty they have delaying responses (Newman et al., 1992; Newman, Patterson, & Kosson, 1987). In one experiment subjects played a card game for financial gain in which the probability of punishment (losing 5 cents) increased by 10 percent after each turn, until punishment occurred 100 percent of the time. Therefore, subjects who stopped playing the game the earliest won the most money. When the subjects were allowed to take each turn immediately, the sociopathic subjects kept choosing to take more turns and lost more money than the nonsociopathic subjects. But when the subjects were forced to wait 5 seconds after each turn, sociopathic subjects did not take more turns than the nonsociopathic subjects.

Altogether, these findings suggest that sociopathic persons can be influenced by anxiety and can learn avoidance tasks if they are forced to pay attention to the risks involved in a given task, if they are forced to delay responses, or if the punishments involved in a task are made more salient (Newman, Kosson, & Patterson, 1987; Newman & Kosson, 1986).

Why should people with antisocial personality disorder experience anxiety less readily than other people? Biological researchers have picked up the ball here and tried to locate a biological cause for the reactions of these individuals. In a series of studies they have found that sociopathic subjects often respond to warnings or expectations of stress with physiological responses that collectively indicate low brain and bodily arousal (Patrick et al., 1993, 1990; Raine, 1989; Ellis, 1987; Hare, 1982, 1978). For example, they show more slow-wave cortical activity than nonsociopathic subjects (Gabrielli & Mednick, 1983). Such low arousal may lead sociopathic people to "tune out" threatening or emotional situations. Consequently, emotional situations may have less impact on them than on nonsociopathic people, and failure to learn anxiety-motivated avoidance responses is inevitable (Ellis, 1987; Hare, 1980, 1978).

It could also be argued that chronic underarousal should lead sociopathic persons to engage in sensation-seeking behavior. Indeed, they may be drawn to antisocial activity precisely because it meets their need for excitement. In support of this idea, researchers have found that antisocial personality disorder is indeed often related to sensation-seeking behavior (Hesselbrock & Hesselbrock, 1992; Gridley, 1990; Zuckerman, 1978; Blackstein, 1975). Simply put, sociopathic persons generally take risks and seek thrills.

Obviously, antisocial personality disorder can be studied systematically and precisely, and clinical researchers can make significant contributions to our understanding of this disorder. It is reasonable to expect that in coming years researchers can and will play just as valuable a role in clarifying the nature, causes, and treatments of the other personality disorders.

---

unfavorably and remember them as being uncaring, controlling, and sometimes mean-spirited (Baker et al., 1992; Nigg et al., 1992). In addition, the families of borderline patients have often been disrupted by divorce or death, usually early in the patient's childhood (Plakun, 1991; Wilson et al., 1986).

A great many studies have also examined the role of early trauma in the etiology of borderline traits, and some have found a heightened prevalence of childhood physical and sexual abuse, including incest, among people with this disorder (Beitchman et al., 1992; Marcus, 1989). This finding is consistent with the greater prevalence of this disorder among women, since more girls than boys are sexually abused.

Some features of borderline personality disorder have been further linked to biological abnormalities. The greater a borderline person's impulsivity, as demonstrated by a suicide attempt or aggression against others, the lower his or her brain serotonin activity (Weston & Siever, 1993; Coccaro & Kavoussi,

1991; Gardner et al., 1990). People with this disorder also experience abnormalities in REM sleep similar to those of depressed persons (Weston & Siever, 1993; Siever & Davis, 1991; Akiskal et al., 1985). And the transient psychotic symptoms of some borderline individuals have been linked to abnormalities in dopamine activity (Coccaro & Kavoussi, 1991). In accord with such biological findings, close relatives of persons with borderline personality are five times more likely than the general population to have this disorder (APA, 1994; Kendler et al., 1991; Torgersen, 1984).

Finally, some sociocultural theorists suggest that borderline personality disorders are particularly likely to emerge when a culture changes too rapidly, begins to disintegrate, and loses its cohesiveness (Paris, 1991). Consistent with this notion, there has been an apparent increase in the prevalence of this disorder in recent years, a phenomenon that some theorists attribute to the changing structure of society and of the family, including the emergence of new child-rearing practices (Segal, 1988), and to such specific factors as capricious TV models, the widespread use of drugs, and a dearth of compelling social causes (Millon, 1987).

TREATMENT OF BORDERLINE PERSONALITY DISORDER Treatment with borderline patients is typically very difficult, given the dependency and anger of these individuals. A dilemma that many therapists face is the need to maintain a balance between empathizing with them and challenging their views (Horton, 1992; Greenberg, 1989). Like patients with many of the other personality disorders, many borderline persons resist therapy; they may react defensively against attempts to persuade them to look closely at their own mental state and the viewpoints of others (Fonagy, 1991).

Nevertheless, it appears that individual psychotherapy can be effective and lead to sustained improvement for some patients (Koenigsberg, 1993; Linehan & Kehrer, 1993; Sansone et al., 1991). A general but limited character change appears to be the most realistic goal. Long-term therapy is common (Diamond et al., 1990). Once patients make progress in treatment, termination may become a difficult issue because of the patients' problems with attachment and abandonment (Sansone et al., 1991).

Psychodynamic therapists focus on such issues as the borderline patient's fundamental disturbance of object relations, self-identity problems, use of defenses, and pervasive loneliness and emptiness (Michels, 1992; Egan, 1988). Some therapists combine cognitive-behavioral strategies with a psychodynamic approach (Katz & Levendusky, 1990), for example, modeling alternative interpretations and reactions to situations in order to improve the patient's awareness of other people's perspectives (Westen, 1991). Some clinicians further speak with people who are close to the borderline patient as a means of checking the patient's perceptions of reality (Rauchfleisch, 1992).

The use of a group format may also be effective in treating borderline patients (Leszcz, 1992; O'Leary et al., 1991). The group can both amplify and buffer the patient's emotions, cognitions, actions, and memories. It may also offer a therapeutic opportunity for such patients to form close attachments to several persons rather than investing all of their emotions, needs, and hopes in but one or two "chosen" relationships. Groups have also been somewhat useful in strengthening the self-image of borderline persons and protecting their self-esteem (Brightman, 1992).

Some drugs, particularly antidepressant, antibipolar, and antipsychotic drugs, have been of help in calming the emotional and aggressive storms of people with this disorder, and slowing down their impulsivity (Weston & Siever, 1993; Siever & Davis, 1991; Cowdry & Gardner, 1988; Soloff, 1987). Interestingly, one study noted that clinicians were more likely to prescribe antipsychotic drugs for the aggressive outbursts of men with borderline personality disorder, while women were more likely to receive antidepressants (Andrulonis, 1991). Either way, the use of drugs on an outpatient basis with this patient population is controversial, given their elevated risk for attempting suicide. A combination of drug therapy and pschotherapy has also been helpful in some cases (Koenigsberg, 1993; Cowdry & Gardner, 1989).

Finally, because borderline patients are often hospitalized—for example, after self-mutilation or suicide attempts—their management as inpatients has also received considerable attention. Some clinicians believe that an unlocked milieu-oriented hospital unit is more helpful to these individuals than a locked one, since an unlocked environment increases their empowerment and improves their attitudes toward treatment (Wester, 1991; Winchel & Stanley, 1991). In addition, the use of formal written contracts in the inpatient management of borderline patients has sometimes been tried, in efforts to contain dangerous behavior and to help patients stay on a steady course even in the face of unexpected or upsetting events (Miller, 1990; Bloom & Rosenbluth, 1989).

HISTRIONIC PERSONALITY DISORDER

A histrionic personality disorder can complicate life considerably, as we see in the case of Suzanne:

S uzanne, an attractive and vivacious woman, sought therapy in the hope that she might prevent the disintegration of her third marriage. The problem she faced was a recurrent one, her tendency to become "bored" with her husband and increasingly interested in going out with other men. She was on the brink of "another affair" and decided that before "giving way to her impulses again" she had "better stop and take a good look" at herself. . . .

Suzanne was quite popular during her adolescent years. . . . Rather than going on to college, Suzanne attended art school where she met and married a fellow student—a "handsome, wealthy ne'er-do-well." Both she and her husband began "sleeping around" by the end of the first year, and she "wasn't certain" that her husband was the father of her daughter. A divorce took place several months after the birth of this child.

Soon thereafter she met and married a man in his forties who gave both Suzanne and her daughter a "comfortable home, and scads of attention and love." It was a "good life" for the four years that the marriage lasted. . . . In the third year of this marriage she became attracted to a young man, a fellow dancing student. The affair was brief, but was followed by a quick succession of several others. Her husband learned of her exploits, but accepted her regrets and assurances that they would not continue. They did continue, and the marriage was terminated after a stormy court settlement.

Suzanne "knocked about" on her own for the next two years until she met her present husband, a talented writer who "knew the scoop" about her past. He "holds no strings" around her; she is free to do as she wishes. Surprisingly, at least to Suzanne, she had no inclination to venture afield for the next three years. She enjoyed the titillation of "playing games" with other men, but she remained loyal to her husband, even though he was away on reportorial assignments for periods of one or two months. The last trip, however, brought forth the "old urge" to start an affair. It was at this point that she sought therapy.

(Millon, 1969, p. 251)

People with *histrionic personality disorder,* once called *hysterical personality disorder,* display a pattern of excessive emotionality and attention seeking (APA, 1994). Indeed, they are typically described as "emotionally charged." Their moods may shift rapidly, though the feelings these people express may be as exaggerated as they are shallow. Irrational or angry outbursts are common. People with this disorder are continually "on stage," using theatrical gestures and mannerisms and the most grandiose language to describe ordinary everyday events. Like a chameleon, they adapt themselves to their audience, changing surface characteristics and lacking a core sense of who they really are. Their style of speech is correspondingly impressionistic, scanty in detail and substance. Similarly, their opinions or beliefs are assembled around impressions and appearances, and as a result are usually fleeting.

Histrionic individuals require the constant presence of others to witness their emotionality and to validate their being and their mood states. Approval and praise are their lifeline. They feel lost and unsure of themselves in the absence of outside reassurance and in situations where they are not the center of attention. They do not tolerate delays in gratification well. Vain, self-indulgent, egocentric, and demanding, they overreact to any minor event that gets in the way of their insatiable quest for attention.

An exaggerated display of physical illness and weakness is common among people with a histrionic personality disorder. Histrionic traits are also prevalent among people with somatoform disorders (Morrison, 1989). An estimated 20 percent of patients with a conversion disorder display histrionic symptoms (Marsden, 1986). It is not uncommon for people with histrionic personality disorder to use a suicide attempt as a purely manipulative gesture (Guillard & Guillard, 1987). Other attention-getting maneuvers include inappropriate provocative behavior and sexual seduction.

Histrionic people are highly suggestible, responding impulsively to momentary circumstances or other people's perceived opinions in order to gain acceptance. They are likely to pursue the latest fads in fashion and thought in their efforts to be admired. As physical appearance constitutes an obvious and immediate way of commanding attention, they tend to obsess over how they look and how others will perceive them, often wearing bright, eye-catching clothes.

Histrionic people are also likely to have a distorted perception of the intensity of their relationships. For instance, they may consider themselves to be the intimate confidants of people who actually see them as casual acquaintances. They also tend to gravitate toward inappropriate romantic partners, people who may be exciting but who do not treat them well, and they then proceed to become involved in an ungratifyingly close relationship.

Until recently, histrionic personality disorder was believed to be more common in women than in men (Reich, 1987). Profiles of the "hysterical wife" have long been discussed in the psychological literature (Char, 1985). Several studies, however, have uncovered gender bias in the past efforts to diagnose persons with this disorder. When presented with case studies describing people with various mixtures of histrionic and antisocial traits, clinicians in several studies gave a diagnosis of histrionic personality disorder to more women than men (Ford & Widiger, 1989; Hamilton et al., 1986). More recent epidemiological studies suggest that 2 to 3 percent of adults have this personality disorder, with males and females equally affected (APA, 1994; Nestadt et al., 1990).

EXPLANATIONS OF HISTRIONIC PERSONALITY DISORDER In view of psychodynamic clinicians' historical interest in hysteria, it is no surprise to find a great many psychodynamic theories of histrionic personality disorder in the literature. Most of the theories share the position that as children histrionic persons typically experienced unhealthy relationships with either one or both of their parents—often portrayed as cold and controlling—which left them feeling unloved, fearful of abandonment, and extraordinarily needful of nurturance from others (Gunderson, 1988). To defend against their deep-seated fears of loss, the individuals behave in an overly emotional manner and invent crises that encourage other people to act protectively toward them (Kuriansky, 1988).

Some psychodynamic explanations have focused exclusively on female patients—they suggest that a lack of maternal nurturance causes some daughters to turn to their fathers for gratification of their dependency needs. To win their father's attention, they engage in flirtatious and dramatic displays of emotion, establishing a histrionic pattern that governs other relationships in their lives (Gabbard, 1990). Eventually they enter adulthood as "unhappy little girls," looking to their husbands or to other men as idealized fathers who will take care of them and always trying to manipulate them (Char, 1985).

A number of cognitive explanations have focused on the deficient cognitive functioning that characterizes people with a histrionic personality disorder, such as their vague and impressionistic style of speech, lack of detail, and extreme suggestibility. According to these theories, as histrionic persons become increasingly self-involved and emotional, they have little room left for factual knowledge or intellectual curiosity. Increasingly they are influenced by the obvious rather than by a reservoir of detailed memo-

ries, and their thoughts take the form of hunches rather than fact-driven ideas. Not surprisingly, they seem to lack the capacity for introspection or deep intellectual conversations (Hollender, 1988). Other cognitive theorists propose that histrionic persons have an underlying assumption that they are helpless to care for themselves. Supposedly, this assumption becomes a broad and pervasive belief that drives the individuals constantly to seek out others who will meet their needs (Beck & Freeman, 1990).

Finally, sociocultural theorists have suggested that the development of histrionic personality disorder may have roots in society's norms and expectations. They point out that until recent years, our society encouraged girls to hold on to their dependency needs as they grew up, thus favoring the development of childishness in women and fostering the histrionic lifestyle (Hollender, 1988). Indeed, the vain, self-dramatizing, and selfish histrionic person may be viewed as a caricature of femininity as our culture once defined it (Beck & Freeman, 1990).

TREATMENT FOR HISTRIONIC PERSONALITY DISORDER People with histrionic personality disorder, unlike those with most other personality disorders, tend to seek out treatment. They have been found to use health services of all kinds at a higher frequency than the rest of the population (Nestadt et al., 1990). A central goal in the treatment of histrionic patients is to help them recognize their excessive dependency and their attempts to secure complete satisfaction from other people (Chodoff, 1989). They must be assisted to find their own inner source of satisfaction and achieve a more independent way of life. Working with histrionic patients can be very difficult, however; they commonly bring their unreasonable demands, tantrums, and seductiveness into the therapy session (Gabbard, 1990). They may grasp at false or premature insights or make superficial pretenses of changing, merely to please the therapist (Chodoff, 1989). Some do not continue therapy beyond the point of discussion of surface issues. Others may wish to continue therapy well beyond its usefulness.

A variety of psychotherapy approaches have been tried with histrionic patients, including psychodynamic approaches, cognitive therapies which try to help them change their maladaptive beliefs of helplessness and to convert their global way of thinking into a more systematic and problem-focused one, and group therapies which heavily utilize feedback from other persons (Winston & Pollack, 1991; Quality Assurance Project, 1990; Beck & Freeman, 1990). Clinical case reports suggest that each of these approaches is helpful on occasion, primarily when therapists are able to strike an effective balance between providing support, projecting a logical demeanor, and setting and maintaining strict professional boundaries (Gabbard, 1990; Liebowitz et al., 1986). Drug therapy does not appear to be helpful, except for the depressive symptoms that some histrionic patients also experience (Liebowitz et al., 1986).

NARCISSISTIC PERSONALITY DISORDER

The narcissistic personality disorder can be seen in the case of 30-year-old Steven, an artist who is married and has one child:

Steven came to the attention of a therapist when his wife insisted that they seek marital counseling. According to her, Steve was "selfish, ungiving and preoccupied with his work." Everything at home had to "revolve about him, his comfort, moods and desires, no one else's." She claimed that he contributed nothing to the marriage, except a rather meager income. He shirked all "normal" responsibilities and kept "throwing chores in her lap," and she was "getting fed up with being the chief cook and bottlewasher, tired of being his mother and sleep-in maid."

On the positive side, Steven's wife felt that he was basically a "gentle and good-natured guy with talent and intelligence." But this wasn't enough. She wanted a husband, someone with whom she could share things. In contrast, he wanted, according to her, "a mother, not a wife"; he didn't want "to grow up, he didn't know how to give affection, only to take it when he felt like it, nothing more, nothing less."

Steve presented a picture of an affable, self-satisfied and somewhat disdainful young man. He was employed as a commercial artist, but looked forward to his evenings and weekends when he could turn his attention to serious painting. He claimed that he had to devote all of his spare time and energies to "fulfill himself," to achieve expression in his creative work. . . .

His relationships with his present co-workers and social acquaintances were pleasant and satisfying, but he did admit that most people viewed him as a "bit self-centered, cold and snobbish." He recognized that he did not know how to share his thoughts and feelings with others, that he was much more interested in himself than in them and that perhaps he always had "preferred the pleasure" of his own company to that of others.

(Millon, 1969, pp. 261–262)

People with *narcissistic personality disorder* display a chronic and pervasive pattern of grandiosity, need for admiration, and lack of empathy (APA, 1994). The Greek myth has it that Narcissus died enraptured by the beauty of his own reflection in a pool, pining away while longing to possess his own image. His name has come to be synonymous with extreme self-involvement, and indeed people with narcissistic personality disorder have a grandiose sense of self-importance. They exaggerate their achievements and talents, expecting others to recognize them as superior and often appearing arrogant and haughty (see Box 17–3). Preoccupied with fantasies of unlimited success, power, or beauty, they require the constant attention and admiration of those around them, although they are very choosy about the people and institutions they will associate closely with. They also believe that their problems are unique and can be appreciated only by other "special" high-status people. Despite their charm, the favorable first impression they may make, and their wide circle of notable acquaintances, people with this disorder are rarely able to maintain a stable, long-term relationship.

The self-absorption of people with a narcissistic personality is apparent even when they pretend to be interested in others.

BOX 17-3

"YOU SHOULD HAVE SEEN THE FISH THAT GOT AWAY"

What's my job? Why, I'm a-a-a-a . . . rocket scientist. Yeah! A rocket scientist. That's the ticket. I make rockets and fly 'em to the moon, and then I, a-a-a-a . . . fly 'em back. Yeah, for refueling . . . Yeah! That's the ticket.

Any viewer of the television show "Saturday Night Live" during the late 1980s remembers the pathological liar portrayed by comedy actor Jon Lovitz. The character struck a chord in most viewers; indeed, his lies and inflections were mimicked by millions of people each week. Aside from simply being funny, there are probably two reasons that this character caught the public's fancy. First, most people lie some of the time, and can appreciate the dilemma and solutions of the Lovitz character. Second, many people know individuals who lie regularly, often unnecessarily, almost as if they are driven to do so.

Almost everyone has been in a situation when lying seems preferable to telling the truth. Sometimes these lies are told to protect another person from being hurt by the truth (such as when you tell a friend his or her new haircut looks great even if it doesn't). This is often referred to as an "altruistic" or "white" lie since it is not told for self-serving reasons (Bok, 1978). It can be distinguished from a "defensive" lie, a self-serving lie that people offer to avoid getting into trouble (such as telling your professor that the computer wouldn't print your paper when in fact you hadn't finished writing it).

Although most people have told white lies or defensive lies when faced with an uncomfortable situation, few can be classified as "pathological" liars. Pathological liars do not lie to protect themselves or others, but rather their lies have no situational gain. Pathological lies tend to be compulsive or fantastic in nature and can often be easily refuted by others (Ford et al., 1988; Selling, 1942). Although pathological lying is not itself considered a disorder, it is sometimes characteristic of people with an antisocial, histrionic, or narcissistic personality disorder.

The phenomenon of lying has received the attention of several researchers (Saxe, 1991). Various explanations have been offered for why people lie. Psychodynamic theorists view lying as an important and normal

---

With their boastful and pretentious manner, narcissistic persons are seldom receptive to the feelings of others. Like Steven, they show a general lack of empathy, an inability or unwillingness to recognize and identify with others' thoughts and needs. Many take advantage of others to achieve their own ends, an interpersonal exploitation that may be partially associated with envy, for narcissistic persons are continually envious of others, usually at the same time that they believe others to be envious of them. They are often successful, impressively knowledgeable, and articulate, yet bored and doubt-ridden as well (Akhtar, 1989). They seek professional achievement only to satisfy their need for personal recognition, so it does little to give them a larger sense of purpose or to provide pleasure in and of itself.

While maintaining their grandiosity, narcissistic individuals may also react to criticism or frustration with bouts of rage, shame, and humiliation (Gramzow & Tangney, 1992). Hypersensitive to the evaluations of others, they may display intense fury when they perceive an injury to their self-esteem. On the other hand, some people with this personality disorder react with cold indifference to criticism (Messer, 1985); and still others become extremely pessimistic and are pervaded by a sense of futility and depression (Svrakic, 1990, 1987). Cycles of zest alternating with disappointment are common (Svrakic, 1990).

Less than 1 percent of adults are estimated to manifest a narcissistic personality disorder (APA, 1994). Between 50 and 75 percent of those are male (APA, 1994; Bourgeois et al., 1993). Narcissistic-type behaviors and thoughts are common and normal among teenagers; they do not usually lead to adult narcissism (APA, 1994).

EXPLANATIONS OF NARCISSISTIC PERSONALITY DISORDER Again psychodynamic theorists have theorized about narcissistic personality disorder more than other theorists, and again they begin with the proposition that this disorder may arise when cold and rejecting parents interact with their infants in an unloving and unaccepting manner, causing

mechanism by which young children can separate themselves from their parents and become autonomous beings (Goldberg, 1973; Kohut, 1966). During adolescence, lying and secrecy again becomes an important and, to a point, constructive way for individuals to assert their independence (Goldberg, 1973).

Behaviorists claim that people learn to lie by being exposed to others (for example, parents) who lie. The more often people hear those around them lie, the more likely they are to tell their own lies. Parental reactions to a child's lies can also influence his or her future propensity to lie (Smith, 1968). Other researchers suggest that child abuse and emotionally traumatic experiences can be predisposing factors to lying (Ford et al., 1988).

Sociocultural theorists suggest that one's culture can also have a large effect on one's attitudes towards lying. According to this theory, lying is more acceptable in some cultures than in others. In fact, in some cultures, the clever deceit of others is highly regarded (Miller, 1958).

Finally, biological researchers report that lying is more common among people with certain neurological disorders. For example, pathological lying is more common among patients who have had seizures, thalamic dysfunction, abnormal EEG readings, or a history of head trauma (Modell, Mountz, & Ford, 1992; Ford et al., 1988; Barker, 1962; Lidz et al., 1949).

Other researchers are less interested in why people lie and instead focus on ways to detect when people lie. The ability to detect a lie can be of obvious value in both our personal and professional lives. Court trials are often explicitly focused on evaluating a person's honesty, and during job interviews and corporate meetings evaluations of honesty may also be of importance. In Chapter 4 we discussed formal efforts to detect deceit such as lie detector and integrity tests (see pp. 102–103), but as we have seen, these methods have serious pitfalls and researchers have been trying to develop more reliable and valid ways of assessing honesty and integrity.

In the meantime, how can we protect ourselves from being deceived? How can we tell when someone is lying to us? A variety of informal clues to detect lies have been cited by investigators. Apparently, people often betray their prevarications with nonverbal cues. An observer may, for example, be able to spot deception from behavioral cues such as the deceiver's slowness to respond, frequent pauses, inappropriate message duration, or unusual physical gestures such as arm raising and staring (Bond et al., 1992; DeTurck & Miller, 1990). When persons ask someone to "Look me in the eye when you say that," they are often trying to pick up on subtle cues to determine whether the speaker is uttering a falsehood or telling the truth.

Obviously, however, such clues may be of limited help. So until more precise ways to detect lies are developed, keep an eye out for people who pause and seem to think for inordinate stretches of time before answering, "I'm a-a-a . . . researcher on lying." Yeah, that's the ticket!"

the children to feel unsatisfied, rejected, unworthy, and wary of the world. Some of these children spend their lives defending against these feelings by telling themselves that they are actually perfect and desirable and by seeking admiration from others (Vaillant, 1994).

Each psychodynamic theory further explains these dynamics in accordance with its own specific concepts. Object relations theorists, who place particular emphasis on early relationships, propose that the early negative treatment interrupts a critical process of attachment between children and their parents and leads ultimately to a distorted self-image (Kernberg, 1989, 1970). That is, the children develop a grandiose self-image that helps them maintain illusions of self-sufficiency and freedom from dependence (Siomopoulos, 1988). Ignored and rejected by their parents, they also react with fury. The narcissistic person's lack of empathy and persistent feelings of envy are believed to stem from unconscious rage against all others who represent potential sources of gratification and dependence.

Another group of psychodynamic theorists, self theorists, argue that rejecting parents deprive their children of *mirroring*, one of the most important processes in the development of a healthy sense of self (Fiscalini, 1993). That is, they fail to confirm, or mirror, the child's innate sense of vigor and uniqueness. As a result, the child's "grandiose self" and "reality-based" self, which normally would merge, remain split throughout life. The grandiose self, which produces an inflated sense of desirability and power, becomes dominant (Svrakic, 1989).

In support of these psychodynamic theories, research has found that abused children, children of divorce, and children whose mother or father has died or given them up for adoption are at greater risk for the development of narcissistic personality disorder (Kernberg, 1989).

Other theorists, particularly those who espouse the behavioral and cognitive models, have argued that persons often develop narcissistic personality disorder as a result of being treated too *positively* rather than too negatively in early life. These theorists hold that individuals may acquire a narcissistic posture when their "admiring or doting parents" favor or even idealize them and teach them repeatedly to "overvalue their self worth" (Millon, 1987). Some theorists further postulate that narcissistic symptoms may emerge when a person is repeatedly called "different" by parents or by the community (Beck & Freeman, 1990). The social responses of others, whether positive or negative, to supposedly special or different qualities may reinforce a sense of superiority, personal uniqueness, and grandiose expectations. In support of these ideas, firstborn and only children, whose parents often do view and treat them as having special talents or intelligence, have been found to score higher on measures of narcissism than other children (Curtis & Cowell, 1993).

Finally, many sociocultural theorists link individual cases of narcissistic personality disorder to general "eras of narcissism" in society (Cooper & Ronningstam, 1992; Cooper, 1981; Lasch, 1978). They suggest that periodic societal breakdowns in family structure and social and political ideals may produce generations of youth who are characterized by self-centeredness, an inability to delay gratification, a short attention span, and a materialistic outlook. Western cultures in particular, which encourage self-expression and individualism, are seen as more likely to foster such generational narcissism.

TREATMENT FOR NARCISSISTIC PERSONALITY DISORDER People with narcissistic personality disorder, like those with most other personality disorders, only occasionally respond well to treatment. In fact, this disorder has been characterized as one of the most difficult conditions to treat (Lawrence, 1987). When narcissistic persons seek treatment, they usually do so because of an associated disorder, most commonly depression (Beck & Freeman, 1990). They are likely to begin therapy with a sense of entitlement and may attempt to manipulate the therapist into supporting their sense of grandiosity. Clients often seem to project their grandiosity onto therapists and may develop a love-hate stance toward them (Uchoa, 1985).

The famous object relations theorist Otto Kernberg has developed a particular psychodynamic approach toward these patients. His goal is to *confront* the person's grandiose self and uncover the pathological defense mechanisms that have been developed to protect it (Kernberg, 1989). According to Kernberg, the patient's envy, rage, and insistence on self-sufficiency should be addressed by a combination of active confrontation and psychodynamic interpretation.

Practitioners of self theory recommend a more passive approach. They see confrontation as a failure at empathy that may be disruptive to treatment in that it repeats the parental failures of childhood. Narcissistic vulnerability needs to be addressed through interpretation, they believe, not confrontation (Masterson, 1990). Fundamental insecurities must be handled gently, to give patients a safe haven in which their true self may emerge (Spitzer, 1990).

Cognitive therapists try to change specific ways in which narcissistic clients think. For example, therapists may try to guide the patients' focus onto other people's opinions, improve the way they react to criticism, increase their ability to empathize, and eliminate exploitive behavior (Beck & Freeman, 1990). They may also try to alter patients' grandiose self-image by tackling their all-or-nothing categorizations and their exaggerations of other people's positive and negative opinions. Again, however, all approaches, from psychodynamic to cognitive, seem to meet with little success.

■ ANXIOUS OR ■ FEARFUL PERSONALITY DISORDERS

Cluster C includes the avoidant, dependent, and obsessive-compulsive personality disorders. People with these disorders typically display anxious and fearful behavior. Many symptoms of these disorders are similar to those that characterize the Axis I anxiety and depressive disorders, but direct links have not been established (Weston & Siever, 1993). As with most of the other personality disorders, numerous explanations have been offered for these disorders, but empirical support for these theories is very limited. Treatments for the anxious and fearful personality disorders appear to be at least modestly helpful, a significant improvement over the efficacy of interventions for most of the other personality disorders.

AVOIDANT PERSONALITY DISORDER

People with an avoidant personality disorder are so fearful of being rejected that they give no one an opportunity to reject them—or to accept them either.

J ames was a bookkeeper for nine years, having obtained his position upon graduation from high school. He spoke of himself as a shy, fearful and quiet boy ever since early childhood. . . .

James was characterized by his supervisor as a loner, a peculiar young man who did his work quietly and efficiently. They noted that he ate alone in the company cafeteria and never joined in coffee breaks or in the "horsing around" at the office. . . .

As far as his social life was concerned, James had neither dated nor gone to a party in five years. . . . He now spent most of his free time reading, watching TV, daydreaming and fixing things around the house.

James experienced great distress when new employees were assigned to his office section. Some 40 people worked regularly in this office and job turnover resulted in replacement of four or five people a year. . . . In recent months, a clique formed in his office. Although James very much wanted to be a member of this "in-group," he feared attempting to join them because "he had nothing to offer them" and thought he would be rejected. In a short period of time, he, along with two or three others, became the object of jokes and taunting by the leaders of the clique. After a few weeks of "being kidded," he began to miss work, failed to complete his accounts on time, found himself unsure of what he was doing and made a disproportionate number of errors. . . . Although he did not connect his present discomfort to the events in his office, he asked if he could be reassigned to another job where he might work alone.

(Millon, 1969, pp. 231–232)

People with avoidant and schizoid personality disorders often spend much of their time alone. The former yearn for but fear social relationships, whereas the latter are indifferent to social relationships and truly want to be alone.

People with *avoidant personality disorder* display a chronic and pervasive pattern of inhibition in social situations, feelings of inadequacy, and extreme sensitivity to negative evaluation (APA, 1994). Not surprisingly, they actively avoid occasions or activities that involve interpersonal contact. At the center of their social withdrawal lies not so much a low level of social skill as a dread of criticism, disapproval, or rejection.

These people are preoccupied with the way others perceive them and are easily hurt by criticism or disapproval. In social situations, their manner is timid and hesitant; they are afraid of saying something foolish or inappropriate or of embarrassing themselves by blushing, crying, or nervousness, and are sensitive to social deprecation. Even in intimate relationships they act and express themselves with restraint, afraid of being shamed or ridiculed.

Individuals with this disorder believe themselves to be personally unappealing or inferior to others. They tend to exaggerate the potential difficulties of new situations, so they seldom take risks or engage in new activities. They usually have few or no close friends, though they actually yearn for intimate relationships, and frequently feel empty, depressed, and lonely. As a substitute, many take refuge in an inner world of fantasy and imagination (Millon, 1990).

Since many people with social phobias have avoidant personality disorder, some theorists suspect that the two disorders are related (Holt et al., 1992; Schneier et al., 1991). Although some symptoms are indeed common to both disorders (a fear of humiliation and low confidence, for example), there are important differences as well. People with social phobias primarily fear social *circumstances* rather than the close social *relationships* of concern to avoidant persons (Turner et al., 1986). In addition, avoidant personality disorder is very common among persons with a chronic depressive disorder (Alnaes & Torgersen, 1989). Indeed, the social withdrawal, low self-esteem, and hypersensitivity to rejection displayed by avoidant persons are typical of depression.

Between 0.5 and 1.0 percent of adults have an avoidant personality disorder. It is equally common among men and women. Many children and teenagers may also be painfully shy and display avoidant behaviors, but this is usually just a normal part of their development.

EXPLANATIONS OF AVOIDANT PERSONALITY DISORDER Theorists often assume that the avoidant personality disorder is caused by the same kinds of factors as other anxiety-related disorders—biochemical abnormalities and genetic predisposition, learned fears, upsetting thought processes. However, direct causal ties between such factors and this personality disorder have yet to receive much empirical study (Weston & Siever, 1993). In the meantime, explanations offered by psychodynamic and cognitive theorists have received the most clinical attention.

A number of psychodynamic theorists trace the pervasive shame experienced by people with avoidant personality disorder to childhood experiences such as early bowel and bladder accidents and accompanying parental reprimands (Gabbard, 1990). Indeed, some theorists suggest that these people's parents have repeatedly ridiculed them. The children internalize this ridicule and experience severe self-deprecation, a conviction of their unlovability, and a distrust of the professed love of others (Liebowitz et al., 1986). In one study patients with avoidant personality disorder revealed childhoods marked by unencouraging home climates and few demonstrations of parental love and pride (Arbel & Stravynski, 1991).

In a similar manner, several cognitive theorists have suggested that the thought patterns found in avoidant personality disorder—including self-deprecation and expectations of rejection—have originated in early childhood when avoidant persons were confronted with strong criticisms and rejections. These experiences lead avoidant persons to assume that other people will also be negative and critical, and as adults they expect and fear rejection, misinterpret people's reactions, and discount positive feedback. In addition, because avoidant individuals have developed negative self-images as a result of their childhood experiences, they now believe that others are justified in their criticisms.

TREATMENT FOR AVOIDANT PERSONALITY DISORDER   Clients with avoidant personality disorder come to therapy in the hope of finding acceptance and affection. Keeping them in therapy can be a challenge, however, for many of them soon begin to avoid the sessions (Beck & Freeman, 1990). They tend to distrust the therapist's sincerity and start to fear rejection in the therapeutic relationship. Thus, as with several of the other personality disorders, the initial therapeutic task is to build the patient's trust, often through support and empathy (Gabbard, 1990). Apart from that, therapists tend to treat people with avoidant personality disorder much as they treat persons with social phobias and other anxiety disorders—that is, with psychodynamic, behavioral, cognitive, or drug interventions. Research suggests that such approaches are at least modestly helpful for many patients.

Psychodynamic therapists help the patients uncover the origins of their symptoms and work through the unconscious forces that are operating (Hurt et al., 1991). Behavioral therapists provide social skills training and exposure treatment, requiring avoidant clients gradually to increase their social contacts (Hurt et al., 1991; Stravynski et al., 1987). Although these behavioral interventions may eventually decrease the clients' anxiety and lessen their social isolation, research suggests that avoidant patients initially have a hard time applying their newly acquired social skills (Quality Assurance Project, 1991). Their lack of self-confidence and overcautiousness make it difficult for them to test new ways of behaving in everyday situations. Cognitive therapists have had some success helping avoidant clients change their distressing beliefs and thoughts, increase their tolerance for emotional discomfort, and build up their self-image (Beck & Freeman, 1990; Alden, 1989). And antianxiety and antidepressant drugs are sometimes useful in reducing the social anxiety and discomfort of avoidant persons, although the symptoms frequently return when medication is stopped (Liebowitz et al., 1991, 1990; Mattick & Newman, 1991).

Research also suggests that group treatment is helpful for many people with avoidant personality disorder. Because the group format is itself socially demanding, it is a useful practice ground for them. At least modest gains have been made in groups that use a combination of approaches, such as exposure, behavioral rehearsal, skill building, and support (Azima, 1993; Renneberg et al., 1990; Alden, 1989).

DEPENDENT PERSONALITY DISORDER

People with dependent personality disorder are so reliant on others that they cannot make the smallest decision for themselves. Mr. G. is a case in point.

*M*r. G. was a rather short, thin and nicely featured but somewhat haggard man who displayed a hesitant and tense manner when first seen by his physician. His place of employment for the past 15 years had recently closed and he had been without work for several weeks. He appeared less dejected about the loss of his job than about his wife's increasing displeasure with his decision to "stay at home until something came up." She thought he "must be sick" and insisted that he see a doctor. . . .

Mr. G. was born in Europe, the oldest child and only son of a family of six children. . . . His mother kept a careful watch over him, prevented him from engaging in undue exertions and limited his responsibilities; in effect, she precluded his developing many of the ordinary physical skills and competencies that most youngsters learn in the course of growth. . . .

A marriage was arranged by his parents. His wife was a sturdy woman who worked as a seamstress, took care of his home, and bore . . . four children. Mr. G. performed a variety of odds-and-ends jobs in his father's tailoring shop. His mother saw to it, however, that he did no "hard or dirty work," just helping about and "overlooking" the other employees. As a consequence, Mr. G. learned none of the skills of the tailoring trade. . . .

During the ensuing years, he obtained employment at a garment factory owned by his brothers-in-law. Again he served as a helper, not as a skilled workman. Although he bore the brunt of essentially good-humored teasing by his co-workers throughout these years, he maintained a friendly and helpful attitude, pleasing them by getting sandwiches, coffee and cigarettes at their beck and call.

He married again to a hard-working, motherly type woman who provided the greater portion of the family income. Shortly thereafter, the son of his first wife emigrated to this country. Although the son was only 19 at the time, he soon found himself guiding his father's affairs, rather than the other way around.

(Millon, 1969, p. 242)

People with *dependent personality disorder* display a pattern of submissive and clinging behavior and fears of separation related to a pervasive and excessive need to be taken care of (APA, 1994). It is normal and healthy to be dependent on others to some extent, but those with dependent personality disorder rely on others for continual advice and reassurance about all everyday matters and decisions, as well as for countering profound feelings of personal inadequacy and helplessness. Afraid of being unable to care for themselves, they go to great lengths to avoid being alone, clinging to close friends or relatives with an intensity and level of neediness uncharacteristic of most "healthy" relationships. In extreme cases, they are unable to tolerate any physical separation from their spouse or partner (Liebowitz et al., 1986).

These individuals differ from those with avoidant personality disorder in that they experience difficulty with separation rather than with the initiation of relationships. They feel completely helpless and devastated when close relationships end and quickly seek out another relationship to fill the void and to provide care and support. Many continue to hold onto relationships with partners who physically or psychologically abuse them.

People with dependent personality disorder tend to be submissive. They have difficulty initiating projects or doing things on their own. Yet they frequently volunteer to do things that are unpleasant or even demeaning as a means of getting other people to like

them. Lacking confidence in their ability and judgment, they allow others to make important decisions for them and seldom disagree with others, no matter what the facts or the consequences may be. Adults with this disorder typically depend on their spouse to decide where to live, what job to have, and which neighbors to befriend (APA, 1994). Similarly, teenagers with this pattern rely excessively on their parents to decide what to wear, with whom to associate, how to spend their free time, and where to attend college (APA, 1994). As a result of their profound fear of rejection, these people are oversensitive to criticism and disapproval. Skillful social conformists, they adroitly adapt themselves to fit others' desires and expectations.

People with dependent personality disorder experience pathological amounts of distress, loneliness, depression, self-criticism, and low self-esteem (Overholser, 1992) and are at high risk for full depressive disorders and phobias and other anxiety disorders (APA, 1994). Their separation anxiety and their feelings of helplessness when they anticipate abandonment may leave them particularly susceptible to suicidal thoughts (Kiev, 1989; Fulwiler & Pope, 1987).

It is not known how prevalent dependent personality disorder is in the general population. For years clinicians believed that more women than men manifested this pattern (Overholser, 1992), but recent research suggests that the disorder is as common in men as in women (APA, 1994; Reich, 1990). Some studies have found the close relatives of male subjects with this disorder to have more depressive disorders than usual, while the relatives of female subjects had more panic disorders. This finding suggests that different factors may predispose men and women to develop a dependent personality disorder (Reich, 1990).

EXPLANATIONS OF DEPENDENT PERSONALITY DISORDER For years psychodynamic theorists have proposed that many of the same dynamics that result in depression (see pp. 280–285) are at work in dependent personality disorder. Freudian theorists, for example, have suggested that unresolved conflicts during the oral stage of psychosexual development may set the stage for a dependent personality disorder (Greenberg & Bornstein, 1988). They believe that the behaviors of the dependent person reflect a fixation at the oral stage and are symbolic of childlike wishes to be nurtured and taken care of.

Other psychodynamic theorists have pointed to the overinvolvement of intrusive parents in the etiology

(a)

(b)

As the technology of film animation has become more complex over time, so have the personality problems of animated characters. (a) Troubled characters of the past were usually defined by a single undesirable personality trait, as demonstrated by Snow White's friend "Grumpy," second from left. (b) Today's characters have clusters of self-defeating traits. Beavis and Butt-head, for example, display poor control of impulses, disregard for others' rights, disturbed relationships, emotional and cognitive shallowness, and, in the case of Beavis, submissive and clinging behavior.

of dependent personality disorder (Bornstein, 1992; Gabbard, 1990). They suggest that the parents of dependent persons were overprotective, for either authoritarian or loving reasons. By taking care of their child's every need, they actually fostered dependent behaviors and heightened the child's feelings of insecurity and anxiety over separation (Main, 1989).

Behaviorists take a similar position. They have proposed that persons with this disorder were often taught by their social environment to be dependent.

Enjoying their child's dependence on them, for example, some parents may systematically reward clinging and loyal behavior while punishing (perhaps through withdrawal of love) independent actions. Alternatively, parents may model their own dependent behavior for their children. Either way, children subjected to such learning experiences are unlikely to develop adequate skills (or confidence) in making decisions, assuming responsibility, initiating projects, or expressing disagreement.

Cognitive theorists propose that a key problem is that persons with dependent personality disorder hold broad maladaptive beliefs that (1) they are inadequate and helpless to deal with the world, and (2) they must find another person to provide protection before they can cope (Beck & Freeman, 1990). These persons also engage in dichotomous thinking: "If one is to be dependent, one must be completely helpless," or "If one is to be independent, one must be alone." With such cognitive distortions in place, they actively avoid achieving autonomy out of fear of being abandoned and left alone.

TREATMENT FOR DEPENDENT PERSONALITY DISORDER   People with dependent personality disorder present a particular package of difficulties for therapists (Perry, 1989). They usually approach therapy passively, conferring all responsibility for their treatment and well-being on the therapist. Getting them to accept responsibility for themselves is consequently a central therapeutic concern. In addition, their symptoms pose a dilemma regarding the optimal length of therapy. On the one hand, short-term therapy may help the clients confront their fears of loss and independence; on the other hand, the separation anxiety aroused by this time frame may overwhelm them (Gabbard, 1990). Another difficult therapy issue is what to do about the dependent client's partner (typically a spouse or parent), whose own needs and behaviors may feed into the client's symptoms. Some clinicians propose that separate therapy for the partner may also be needed if the client's disorder is to be fully addressed (Liebowitz et al., 1986).

A variety of treatment strategies have been used for persons with dependent personality disorder, and they have apparently been at least modestly helpful. Psychodynamic therapy for these clients focuses on many of the same issues as therapy with depressed persons (see pp. 312–313), whose underlying issues are viewed as similar. In particular, the patient's almost inevitable *transference* of dependency needs onto the therapist typically becomes a major treatment issue (Perry, 1989).

Cognitive therapists try to help dependent clients challenge and change their assumptions of incompetence and helplessness (Beck & Freeman, 1990). And cognitive-behavioral therapists often provide assertiveness training to help clients better express their own needs and wishes in relationships. At the same time, because of the potential for development of a submissive-dominant patient-therapist relationship, some clinicians argue that it is better to use humanistic, or nondirective, approaches than direct cognitive-behavioral instructions and techniques (Millon, 1981).

As with avoidant personality disorder, a group therapy format seems to be relatively beneficial for persons with this disorder, partly because it provides dependent patients with support from a number of peers rather than from an intense relationship with a single, perhaps dominant therapist (Azima, 1993; Perry, 1989). Moreover, the peer modeling and practice at expressing feelings that arise in such groups help many patients develop assertiveness and problem-solving skills, and build up their confidence (Beck & Freeman, 1990).

OBSESSIVE-COMPULSIVE PERSONALITY DISORDER

People with an obsessive-compulsive personality disorder are so intent on doing everything "right" that their efforts impair both their productivity and their relationships, as in the case of Wayne:

Wayne was advised to seek assistance from a therapist following several months of relatively sleepless nights and a growing immobility and indecisiveness at his job. When first seen, he reported feelings of extreme self-doubt and guilt and prolonged periods of tension and diffuse anxiety. It was established early in therapy that he always had experienced these symptoms. They were now merely more pronounced than before.

The precipitant for this sudden increase in discomfort was a forthcoming change in his academic post. New administrative officers had assumed authority at the college, and he was asked to resign his deanship to return to regular departmental instruction. In the early sessions, Wayne spoke largely of his fear of facing classroom students again, wondered if he could organize his material well, and doubted that he could keep classes disciplined and interested in his lectures. It was his preoccupation with these matters that he believed was preventing him from concentrating and completing his present responsibilities.

At no time did Wayne express anger toward the new college officials for the "demotion" he was asked to accept. He repeatedly voiced his "complete confidence" in the "rationality of their decision." Yet, when face-to-face with them, he observed that he stuttered and was extremely tremulous.

Wayne was the second of two sons, younger than his brother by three years. His father was a successful engineer, and his mother a high school teacher. Both were "efficient, orderly and strict" parents. Life at home was "extremely well planned," with "daily and weekly schedules of responsibilities posted" and "vacations arranged a year or two in advance." Nothing apparently was left to chance. . . . Wayne adopted the "good boy" image. Unable to challenge his brother either physically, intellectually or socially, he became a "paragon of virtue." By being punctilious, scrupulous, methodical and orderly, he could avoid antagonizing his perfectionistic parents, and would, at times, obtain preferred treatment from them. He obeyed their advice, took their guidance as gospel and hesitated making any decision before gaining their approval. Although he recalled "fighting" with his brother before he was six or seven, he "restrained his anger from that time on and never upset his parents again."

(Millon, 1969, pp. 278–279)

People with *obsessive-compulsive personality disorder* display a pattern of preoccupation with orderliness, perfectionism, and mental and interpersonal control, at the expense of flexibility, openness, and efficiency. In their preoccupation with rules and orderliness they lose sight of the larger picture. When confronted with a task, for example, these devoted schedulers and list makers often become so fixated on organization and logistical details that they fail to grasp the overall point of the activity. As a result, their work is often finished behind schedule or incomplete.

People with this personality disorder set such unreasonably high standards for themselves that they can never be satisfied with their performance. At the same time, they generally refuse to delegate responsibility or to work with a team, convinced that others are too careless or incompetent to do the job right. Their fear of making a mistake may result in a pervasive indecisiveness and frequent avoidance or postponement of decisions or choices. Also in devoting all their time and energies to meeting their high standards of performance, obsessive-compulsive persons often neglect to develop genuine leisure activities and friendships.

People with this personality disorder are not only rigid with regard to self-imposed standards of performance, but they also display an inflexibility about morals, ethics, and values. Often regarded as closed-minded, they scrupulously adhere to their own personal code and use it as a yardstick by which to measure others. Their rigidity is also reflected in an equally restricted expression of affection. Their relationships are often stilted and superficial.

Obsessive-compulsive persons are rarely generous with their time or money. They are miserly not only in their spending habits but in their inability to throw out anything worn-out or useless, even though they have only the vaguest sentimental or monetary reasons for keeping it (APA, 1994; Warren & Ostrom, 1988).

Obsessive-compulsive personality disorder has a 1.0 to 1.7 percent prevalence in the general population, with white, educated, married, employed men receiving the diagnosis most often (APA, 1994; Nestadt et al., 1991). Indeed, men are twice as likely as women to receive this diagnosis (APA, 1994).

People often believe that obsessive-compulsive personality disorder and obsessive-compulsive disorder (the anxiety disorder) are closely related. Some patients do qualify for both diagnoses and the two disorders do share some features (Pollack, 1987). Altogether, obsessive-compulsive personality disorder is present in a minority (perhaps 20 percent) of patients with obsessive-compulsive anxiety disorder (APA, 1994; Jenike, 1991). In some cases the anxiety disorder predates the personality disorder (Baer & Jenike, 1992), while the opposite sequence is at play in other cases (Berg et al., 1989). It is important to note, however, that although the prevalence of obsessive-compulsive personality disorder is certainly higher than usual among patients with the anxiety disorder, other personality disorders (avoidant, histrionic, schizotypal, and dependent) may be even more common among patients with the anxiety disorder (Steketee, 1990). In addition, depression and social phobias are at least as prevalent as obsessive-compulsive anxiety disorder among people with obsessive-compulsive personality disorder (Turner et al., 1991; Fulwiler & Pope, 1987).

Indeed, no empirical support has been found for the notion of a specific link between the personality and anxiety disorders (Mavissakalian et al., 1990). One of the important differences between them is that the symptoms of obsessive-compulsive anxiety disorder are ego dystonic (that is, the person does not want them), whereas the symptoms of obsessive-compulsive personality disorder are ego syntonic: the person often embraces them and rarely wishes to resist them (Zohar & Pato, 1991). In addition, the functioning of people with the anxiety disorder is much more likely to be impaired.

Some clinicians have observed that the symptoms of this personality disorder are often strikingly similar to those of the so-called Type A personality pattern (see Chapter 11). People with each of these patterns experience an exaggerated sense of time urgency, hostility, and aggressiveness. Moreover, both styles of functioning may be conceptualized as attempts to gain and maintain a sense of control. Thus it has been suggested by some theorists that a Type A personality pattern may actually be a subtype of obsessive-compulsive personality disorder (Garamoni & Schwartz, 1986).

EXPLANATIONS OF OBSESSIVE-COMPULSIVE PERSONALITY DISORDER Many explanations of obsessive-compulsive personality disorder borrow heavily from those of obsessive-compulsive anxiety disorder—a dubious practice, given the imperfect links between the two disorders. As with so many of the personality disorders, psychodynamic explanations dominate, and again empirical evidence is limited at best.

Freudian theorists suggest that people with obsessive-compulsive personality disorder are *anal regressive*. That is, because of overly rigid and punitive toilet training during the anal stage, they become fixated at this stage and try always to resist their instincts to mess, which later leads to the persistent expression of such traits as orderliness, inhibition, and a passion for collecting things.

More contemporary psychodynamic theorists suggest that early struggles with parents over control and independence in any realm may cause the child to become flooded with aggressive impulses (Kuriansky, 1988). In an effort to defend against such threatening impulses, the child denies and intellectualizes them and behaves in a rigid and overcontrolled manner, setting in motion a lifelong pattern (Mollinger, 1980).

Yet another psychodynamic explanation has attributed the origins of obsessive-compulsive personality disorder to overcontrolling parents who punish the child for autonomous behavior and thus inhibit the child's development of a separate identity (Millon, 1981). In consequence, the child strives mightily to conform with the lofty standards of others, especially the internalized standards of his or her parents. This strict adherence to rigid standards becomes a central theme for the individual's functioning.

Cognitive theorists propose that illogical thinking processes help maintain obsessive-compulsive personality disorder. They point, for example, to black-or-white dichotomous thinking, which produces rigidity, perfectionism, and procrastination, as well as to exaggeration of potential consequences of mistakes or errors, magnification, and catastrophizing. Cognitive theorists also consider people with this personality disorder to be deficient in the cognitive capacity to reflect on life and the world (Miller, 1988). Their superfocused and overcontrolling cognitive style prevents them from integrating their experiences into a coherent, proportioned worldview.

TREATMENT FOR OBSESSIVE-COMPULSIVE PERSONALITY DISORDER Because people with obsessive-compulsive personality disorder do not usually believe there is anything seriously wrong with them, they tend to seek treatment only if they need help for an accompanying Axis I disorder, most frequently anxiety or depression, or if someone close to them insists (Beck & Freeman, 1990). Whereas drug therapy and behavior therapy have been highly effective for patients with obsessive-compulsive anxiety disorder (see pp. 255–259), clinical case reports suggest that patients with the personality disorder often respond better to psychodynamic or cognitive psychotherapy (Primac, 1993; Jenike, 1991, 1990; Wells et al., 1990). Therapists who take these approaches typically try to help their obsessive-compulsive patients become more aware of, directly experience, and accept their real feelings; overcome their insecurities; take risks; and accept their personal limitations (Salzman, 1989). Over time, the therapists also address clients' tendency to overintellectualize and try to help them "loosen up" and learn to have fun (Liebowitz et al., 1986). Cognitive therapists further work on helping clients to correct their dichotomous thinking, perfectionism, indecisiveness, and procrastination, and to cope better with their chronic worrying and rumination.

■ CATEGORIZING ■ THE PERSONALITY DISORDERS

The inclusion of personality disorders in recent versions of the DSM signifies their growing diagnostic importance. It appears, however, that more misdiagnoses are made in this area of pathology than in most other DSM categories, an indication of some serious problems in validity and reliability (Zimmerman, 1994), leading some theorists to propose alternative approaches to classifying these disorders (see Box 17–4).

The diagnostic difficulties are partly due to the nature of the DSM criteria used to identify personality disorders. Many of the criteria consist of inferred traits rather than specific observable behaviors. In other words, each of the diagnoses relies rather heavily on the subjective judgment of the individual clinician. And clinicians tend to vary widely in their beliefs about when a normal personality style crosses the line and warrants a classification as a disorder (Widiger & Costa, 1994). Indeed, some believe that it is wrong ever to think of these counterproductive personality styles as mental disorders.

The similarity of personality disorders *within* the same cluster presents yet another diagnostic complication. There is so much overlap between the diagnostic criteria for Cluster C's avoidant personality disorder and dependent personality disorder (feelings of inadequacy, fear of disapproval, and the like), for example, that many clinicians consider it unreasonable to define them as two independent disorders. Thus some theorists view the personality disorders within each cluster as variations on a single deviant mode of personality organization (Livesley et al., 1994; Siever & Davis, 1991). For instance, as we have noted, paranoid, schizoid, and schizotypal personality disorders are commonly referred to as "schizophrenia spectrum disorders" and viewed as arising from similar influences.

There is even a troublesome overlap of criteria *between* the three clusters, so that many people seem to qualify for diagnoses in more than one cluster (Flick et al., 1993). The prevalence of borderline traits (Cluster B) among some people with dependent personality disorder (Cluster C), for instance, may suggest that these two disorders in fact represent different degrees of the same behavioral pattern.

A very different yet equally troubling problem is the heterogeneity of the people included in each of the personality disorder classifications (Widiger, 1993, 1992). An individual must meet a certain number of criteria to receive a given diagnosis, but no single feature or characteristic is an essential criterion for any given personality disorder. Thus people who display very different personality profiles may receive the same diagnosis, each client meeting a different set of criteria for the same disorder.

Clearly, investigations into the characteristics, validity, reliability, and interrelationships of the personality disorder categories are still needed (Widiger & Costa, 1994). The diagnostic criteria for the disorders have undergone revision in each of the recent editions of the DSM. In fact, several of the categories themselves have changed from edition to edition. For example, DSM-III-R's category of *passive-aggressive personality disorder,* a pattern of negativistic attitudes and passive resistance to demands for adequate performance in social and occupational situations, has

BOX 17-4

REINFORCEMENTS AND PERSONALITY: THE SCHEMA OF THEODORE MILLON

The clustering schema used in DSM-IV is widely accepted. At the same time, it has been criticized by some for failing to consider the possibility that all the personality disorders may have underlying causes or themes in common.

Theodore Millon (1992, 1990, 1988, 1969), one of the field's pioneers on personality disorders, proposes that the simplest and clearest way to understand an individual's personality is to understand the *reinforcements* that influence his or her life. Specifically, what *type* of reinforcements does the person typically seek, what are the usual *sources* of these reinforcements, and what *instrumental processes*, or *strategies*, does the person use to obtain the reinforcements?

According to Millon, the *type* of reinforcements that people seek may be primarily positive (*R +*)—likely to enhance their lives or to bring pleasure—or negative (*R−*)—likely to prevent or relieve psychological pain or suffering.

People may typically look to themselves or to others as the potential *source* of their reinforcements. Those who rely on themselves for reinforcement tend to be independent self-starters who at the extreme may have difficulty developing trust in and empathy for others. People who rely on others for reinforcement may demonstrate in a variety of ways a strong need for affection, affiliation, and support from outside themselves. There are also ambivalent individuals who do not prefer one reinforcement source over the other: they vacillate between relying on themselves and relying on others for reinforcement. Finally, some people have great difficulty obtaining

	SOURCE OF REINFORCEMENT			
MODE OF REINFORCEMENT	Self (*independent*)	Others (*dependent*)	Vacillating (*ambivalent*)	Detached (*none*)
Active	Antisocial R+ / Paranoid R−	Histrionic R−		Avoidant R−
Passive	Narcissistic R+	Dependent R−	Obsessive-Compulsive R−	Schizoid R−
Vacillating			Borderline R+ / R−	
Detached (none)				Schizotypal R−

Millon's reinforcement matrix summarizes the source, mode, and type (R+ or R−) of reinforcement associated with the various personality disorders.

reinforcement from sources of any kind, and often appear withdrawn and detached.

People may pursue reinforcements by using an *instrumental* strategy that is active, characterized by initiative and alertness, or passive, characterized by reactivity and inertness.

These three polarities help to describe normal personality patterns. People who use active strategies and look to themselves for reinforcements, for example, may be considered "forceful" personalities; those who use passive strategies while looking to themselves are called "confident"; and those who use active strategies but look to others for reinforcements may be seen as "sociable." Millon argues that the reinforcement polarities may also be used to categorize the various personality disorders and to provide insight into how the disorders are developed and sustained. Accordingly, he describes each of the personality disorders in the following ways:

PARANOID PERSONALITY DISORDER

The paranoid personality disorder is an *active, self-focused* style of functioning, sustained by *negative* reinforcement. Paranoid people are constantly vigilant, as if to anticipate and defend against threatening and malevolent reinforcements (R−). Resistant to external authority and control, they rely on themselves for survival. And they are highly active—often edgy, jealous, impulsive, and quick to react with anger to environmental cues that they perceive as threatening.

SCHIZOID PERSONALITY DISORDER

People with a schizoid personality disorder are *passive*, unable to obtain reinforcement either from themselves or from others, and sustained by *negative* reinforcement. Hypersensitive to stimulation, they avoid all potential forms of overstimulation (R−). They are detached—deficient both in self-reliance and in the ability or inclination to rely on others. And they are passive—lacking spontaneity and initiative and displaying little need for social or sexual activity.

SCHIZOTYPAL PERSONALITY DISORDER

People with schizotypal personality disorder tend to display striking deficits in each of the three reinforcement polarities. They have great difficulty obtaining reinforcement of any kind. If one were to attempt to fit the reinforcement scheme onto this disorder, however, it would most likely be a pattern of negative reinforcement $(R-)$. Perhaps the schizotypal patterns of withdrawal, fantasy, and other eccentric behavior are escape mechanisms by which the person avoids overstimulation or otherwise unmanageable levels of stress. Schizotypal persons also seem to lack any source of reinforcement. They are inclined to see themselves as incomplete, estranged, and burdened with a life of emptiness. These individuals also usually seem to lack instrumental reinforcement mechanisms. They seem paralyzed—void, or incapable, of meaningful action.

ANTISOCIAL PERSONALITY DISORDER

People with antisocial personality disorder are *active, self-focused,* and sustained primarily by *positive* reinforcement. That is, they actively pursue pleasure and do so by depending on themselves. The primary type of reinforcement that sustains antisocial persons is the pursuit of pleasure $(R+)$, even though that pleasure may be extremely short-lived and may result in some form of punishment.

BORDERLINE PERSONALITY DISORDER

Borderline persons are *ambivalent* not only about whether to rely on themselves or on others for reinforcement, but about whether the pattern of reinforcement they prefer is positive or negative and about whether to use an active or a passive mode of behavior to attain it. In sum, the borderline patient displays conflicting, contradictory, and generally paradoxical behavior, moods, and inclinations.

HISTRIONIC PERSONALITY DISORDER

People with histrionic personality disorder are *active, other-focused,* and sustained primarily by *negative* reinforcement. That is, they actively try to avoid pain, and do so by depending on others. The extraordinary need of people with a histrionic personality disorder for affection and support seems to reflect an effort to avoid the boredom and pain of emotional emptiness $(R-)$. They are extremely dependent on others, performing in a manner calculated to solicit attention, praise, reassurance, and approval. And they tend to be impulsive and often hedonistic in their active, never-ending pursuit of these responses.

NARCISSISTIC PERSONALITY DISORDER

People with a narcissistic personality disorder are *passive, self-focused,* and sustained primarily by *positive* reinforcement. That is, they pursue pleasure, and do so in a passive manner and by depending on themselves. Characterized primarily by an overly expansive egocentrism, persons with this disorder seek positive reinforcement $(R+)$, such as praise, admiration, and special consideration from others. They exhibit a self-importance and self-absorption that exclude any consideration for others. And, expecting special favors from others without feeling a need to reciprocate, they rely on a passive reinforcement process.

AVOIDANT PERSONALITY DISORDER

People with an avoidant personality disorder are *active* and sustained by *negative* reinforcement, but are unable to obtain reinforcement either from themselves or from others. They actively avoid the pain of social rejection and humiliation by withdrawal $(R-)$. They are *detached,* unable to obtain reinforcement because of their inability to execute either self-directed or other-directed behavior. And, although it may sound like a contradiction in terms, people with avoidant personality disorder are active in their avoidance of others. Because they manage to extract personal humiliation from

virtually any occurrence, they scan their environment for potential threats and spend considerable energy avoiding the pain of social exchange.

DEPENDENT PERSONALITY DISORDER

Persons with a dependent personality disorder are *passive, other-focused,* and sustained primarily by *negative* reinforcement. That is, they seek to avoid psychologically painful circumstances, doing so in a passive manner and by depending on others. Their dependent and submissive behavior is a strategy to avoid losing the support of the people they rely on $(R-)$.

OBSESSIVE-COMPULSIVE PERSONALITY DISORDER

People with an obsessive-compulsive personality disorder are *passive, ambivalent* in regard to the source of their reinforcement, and sustained by *negative* reinforcement. That is, they use a passive approach to try to avoid pain, vacillating between depending on themselves and depending on others in the pursuit of this goal. Their passivity emerges as a perfectionistic adherence to the rules, regulations, and general expectations promulgated by society. Such behavior is passive in the sense that should a desired outcome not be achieved, the person who has conscientiously followed the dictates of others is absolved of personal responsibility, blame, and guilt.

Certainly, Millon's schema is not without problems. His match-ups of reinforcement style and personality disorder are open to debate. Do narcissistic persons, for example, really seek positive reinforcement in life, as Millon claims, or are they sustained by negative reinforcements—acting out of a personal sense of inadequacy and trying to prevent the pain of self-recognition? Such issues aside, Millon's schema does demonstrate that symptom saliency is not the only way to classify personality disorders and that there may be common themes or unifying principles underlying the personality disorders which should be taken into consideration.

been dropped because research has failed thus far to establish that this is a cohesive disorder rather than a problematic single trait. Similarly, two categories that DSM-III-R targeted for further study, the *sadistic personality disorder* and the *self-defeating personality disorder,* are absent from DSM-IV.

As we have noted, the current diagnostic problems have led some theorists to suggest alternative approaches to classifying personality disorders. Some believe that the disorders differ more in degree than in type of dysfunction, and have proposed differentiating them by the severity of certain central traits rather than by the presence or absence of specific traits (Widiger, 1993). And in the scheme outlined in Box 17–4, Theodore Millon, one of the field's leading theorists, has proposed that the various personality disorders should be distinguished by the kinds of reinforcements that sustain them.

THE STATE OF THE FIELD

PERSONALITY DISORDERS

Psychologists' attitudes toward the concept of personality have shifted over the years. During the first half of this century, theorists and researchers believed deeply in the legitimacy of the concept and tried to identify stable personality traits that would account for behavior. Then they discovered the importance of situational factors and a backlash developed—"personality" became almost an obscene word in some circles. The category of personality disorders has suffered the same fate. When psychodynamic and humanistic theorists dominated the clinical field, neurotic *character disorders,* the precursors to personality disorders, were considered useful clinical categories; but the popularity of these categories declined as the behavioral, cognitive, biological, and sociocultural models gained ascendancy. During the 1960s and 1970s, only antisocial personality disorder received much attention.

Personality and personality disorders have rebounded during the past decade and have been gaining the rapt attention of numerous practitioners and researchers. Clinicians have seen case after case in which rigid personality traits, or consistencies in behavior, are more problematic for a client than specific biochemical, behavioral, or cognitive deficiencies, and

researchers have increasingly noted the inability of situational factors alone to account for behavior. Consequently, the concept of the personality disorder is being addressed with renewed interest and respect.

A major problem that once hindered the study of personality disorders was the difficulty of identifying these broad problems. In recent years, however, some clinical theorists have proposed unifying principles and themes that help define and distinguish the personality disorders, and diagnosticians have developed effective objective tests and interview protocols for assessing them (Zimmerman, 1994; Loranger et al., 1994; Perry, 1992; Millon, 1987). Such advances have set in motion a wave of systematic research.

So far, only the antisocial and borderline personality disorders have received much study, but in the current research climate we can expect that the other personality disorders will also attract considerable attention in the coming years. Then clinicians should be better able to answer some pressing questions: How prevalent are the various personality disorders? How do they interrelate? How are they related to other kinds of mental disorders? And what interventions are most effective?

It is also reasonable to expect future research to point to various limitations in the present categorizations of personality disorders, and categories will probably continue to change. Indeed, as we noted earlier, DSM-IV dropped the DSM-III-R category of passive-aggressive personality disorder from its listings, because studies suggested that it represented a single trait more than a cohesive disorder. Future alterations, too, are likely to be based on research rather than, as in the past, on the intuitions, impressions, or biases of clinicians and theorists. To the many people who are impaired and distressed by pervasive, inflexible, and maladaptive personality traits, this change in direction may be most helpful.

SUMMARY

■ **THE TERM "PERSONALITY"** refers to the unique and enduring patterns of inner experiences and behavior displayed by each individual. A *personality disorder* is a pervasive, enduring, and inflexible pattern of inner experience and behavior that deviates markedly from the expectations of one's culture and leads to distress or impairment. A personality disorder begins in adolescence or early adulthood and makes for a lifelong ordeal. DSM-IV distinguishes ten personality disorders, and groups them in three clusters on the basis of descriptive similarities: *paranoid*, *schizoid*, and *schizotypal* personality disorders, characterized by odd or eccentric behaviors; *antisocial*, *borderline*, *histrionic*, and *narcissistic* personality disorders, characterized by dramatic, emotional, or erratic behaviors; and *avoidant*, *dependent*, and *obsessive-compulsive* personality disorders, characterized by fearful or anxious behaviors.

People with ***paranoid personality disorder*** display a pattern of pervasive distrust and suspiciousness of others, always interpreting their motives as malevolent. Those with ***schizoid personality disorder*** display a pattern of detachment from social relationships and a restricted range of emotional expression. And individuals with ***schizotypal personality disorder*** display a pattern of interpersonal deficits marked by acute discomfort in close relationships, cognitive or perceptual distortions, and behavioral eccentricities. People with disorders in this cluster usually are resistant to treatment. Therapists must take into account the client's limited capacity for interaction and extreme sensitivity.

Persons with ***antisocial personality disorder*** display a pervasive pattern of disregard for and violation of the rights of others. Partly because persons with this personality disorder create so many problems for society, researchers have shown considerable interest in it and have produced some important insights. No known specific intervention for antisocial personality disorder is particularly effective. People with ***borderline personality disorder*** display a pervasive pattern of instability in interpersonal relationships, self-image, and moods, and marked impulsivity. Individual psychotherapy apparently can be effective and lead to sustained, though limited, improvement for some clients with this disorder. Individuals with ***histrionic personality disorder,*** once called hysterical personality disorder, display a pattern of excessive emotionality and attention seeking. Unlike those with most other personality disorders, these individuals tend to seek out treatment. However, working with histrionic patients can be very difficult for therapists: the patients commonly bring their unreasonable demands, tantrums, and seductiveness into the therapy session. A variety of psychotherapy approaches have been tried with histrionic patients, and clinical case reports suggest that treatment is helpful on occasion. People with ***narcissistic personality disorder,*** the final disorder in this cluster, display a chronic and pervasive pattern of grandiosity, need for admiration, and lack of empathy. As with most other personality disorders, persons with this personality disorder only occasionally respond well to treatment. In fact, this disorder has been characterized as one of the most difficult conditions to treat.

People with ***avoidant personality disorder*** display a chronic and pervasive pattern of inhibition in social situations, feelings of inadequacy, and extreme sensitivity to negative evaluation. Those with ***dependent personality disorder*** display a pattern of submissive and clinging behavior and fears of separation related to a pervasive and excessive need to be taken care of. And individuals with ***obsessive-compulsive personality disorder*** display a pattern of preoccupation with orderliness, perfectionism, and mental and interpersonal control, at the expense of flexibility, openness, and efficiency. A variety of treatment strategies have been used for people with disorders in this cluster, and apparently have been at least modestly helpful.

■ **THE INCLUSION OF PERSONALITY DISORDERS** in recent versions of the DSM signifies their growing diagnostic importance. It appears, however, that more misdiagnoses are made in this area of pathology than in most other DSM categories, an indication of some serious problems in validity and reliability. The diagnostic difficulties are partly due to the nature of the DSM criteria used to identify personality disorders, such as the *similarities* among personality disorders (so that people often seem to qualify for more than one diagnosis) and the *heterogeneity* of the people included in each of the personality disorder classifications.

Clearly, investigations into the personality disorder categories are still needed. The diagnostic criteria for the disorders have undergone revision in each of the recent editions of the DSM, and several of the categories themselves have been changed. *Passive-aggressive personality disorder,* for instance, has been dropped. The current diagnostic problems have led some theorists to suggest alternative approaches to classifying personality disorders.

Topic Overview

DISORDERS OF MEMORY AND IDENTITY

S WE OBSERVED in Chapter 17, the term "personality" encompasses the unique and enduring pattern of inner experiences and behavior displayed by each individual. Ordinarily a personality has unity; its facets are integrated, so that the person can act with some degree of consistency. Many factors help us to maintain this personal unity; two important ones are *memory* and *identity*.

OUR MEMORY links our past, present, and future. The recollection of past experiences, although not always precisely accurate (see Box 18–1), helps us make sense of and react to present events and guides us in making decisions about the future. We recognize our friends and relatives, teachers and employers, and respond to them in appropriate and consistent ways. Without a memory we would always be starting over; with it, life has progression and continuity. The Spanish filmmaker Luis Buñuel wrote, "Our memory is our coherence, our reason, our feeling, even our action. Without it, we are nothing."

MEMORY ALSO PROVIDES us with an *identity,* a sense of who we are—a unique person with particular preferences, abilities, characteristics, and needs. Others recognize our particularities and expect certain things of us. Even more important, we recognize ourselves and develop our own expectations, values, and goals.

PEOPLE SOMETIMES EXPERIENCE a breakdown in this integration and self-recognition; they experience a significant alteration in their memory or identity. Through interruptions in learning new information or recalling old information, or by changes in the ability to think and process

BOX 18-1

WHOSE MEMORY IS IT, ANYWAY?

My earliest memory . . . my earliest memory . . . I know—I was in the kitchen, and some cookies were in the oven. Alice had gone off to make the beds, and I was waiting for her to finish so I could have some milk and warm cookies. They smelled so good, I can almost smell them now. I must have been 3 or 4 years old, and my parents had told me not to touch the hot stove, but I guess I didn't think that meant the oven, too. So I went over and looked through the glass oven door, and saw that one of the cookies looked like it was ready. I opened the door, reached down, and tried to take one off of the hot tray. It was so hot that when I touched it, I pulled my hand back so fast that I hit the top of the inside of the oven, and that's when I really hurt myself. The next thing I know, Alice is running into the room and going to the refrig-

erator for butter for the burn, and at the same time Marcia and Greg get home from school and my parents walk in and . . . Wait a minute, this isn't my family, these are the Bradys! This isn't my memory—it's an old *Brady Bunch* episode!

We are all notoriously bad at recalling very early experiences in our lives.

Most early childhood memories are fragmented images or brief scenes, rarely the comprehensive, detailed recollections that we have of events during our later childhood and adult years. Interestingly, our early memories are usually of trauma or trivia rather than such milestones as birth, our first step, or our first words. Memories seem to begin to be recorded and retrievable from about the fourth year. For events that occurred before that, we all seem to suffer some sort of amnesia.

Take a minute right now to think of your earliest memory. It is most likely of a single event that you have accepted over the years as a firsthand recollection of your childhood. Maybe it was the time your parents brought you home a special toy, or the time your brother pushed you out of the treehouse, or something as trivial as your favorite plaid dress. The strength

information, memory and identity are disrupted. Sometimes the alterations in memory lack a clear physical cause, and are, by tradition, called *dissociative disorders*. In other cases, the physical causes are quite clear, and the memory disorder is called *organic*.

Dissociative disorders are often conceptualized as a dissociation, or separation, of one part of a person's identity from another. The three most prominent dissociative disorders are *dissociative amnesia*, *dissociative fugue*, and *dissociative identity disorder (multiple personality disorder)*. The principal symptom of **dissociative amnesia** is an inability to recall important personal events and information. A person with **dissociative fugue** not only forgets the past

but travels to a new location and may assume a new identity. And an individual with **multiple personality disorder** has two or more distinct identities or personalities and periodically switches from one to another.

Several memorable books and movies have dealt with such dissociative disorders. Two of the best known are *The Three Faces of Eve* and *Sybil*. The topic is so intriguing that the majority of television drama series seem to include at least one case of dissociative functioning each season, creating the impression that the disorders are very common. Many clinicians, however, believe that they are quite rare.

of the memory convinces you that it is real, and it has the feel of remembering, but there is a strong possibility that you have reconstructed the event from descriptions and information given you by your family.

As time passes, memories fade. One study found that subjects had very good memory for events in the past year; their ability to locate in time events that occurred from two to six years earlier declined 6 percent, and it continued to decline as events receded in the past (Linton, 1979). This finding does not fully explain, though, the almost complete lack of memories of the events of our earliest years. In this respect we should distinguish between the events themselves and the things we learned from them (Cutts & Ceci, 1989; Neisser, 1985). Certainly we do not forget how to walk, or the words that we learned to speak and understand during our earliest years. Childhood amnesia applies only to autobiographical memory, perhaps because it is not until the early school years that our lives have an organized structure. Without the kind of knowledge about the world that allows us to classify and organize our experiences, they are just a string of unrelated happenings. Structure gives us hooks on which to hang our memories, so that we can recall them later.

First memories may actually be the key to our present sense of self and are therefore of central importance to psychotherapies that are based on dialogue and discussion (Cutts & Ceci, 1989). Freud believed that our early memories open the secret chambers of our lives. Alfred Adler (1927) insisted that the content of the earliest memory is related to one's self-style and is therefore molded to meet one's sense of self (Adcock & Ross, 1983). He contended that these memories are critical to the diagnostic process whether they are real or not, because they reveal people's attitudes toward themselves, others, and life in general. Research has shown that people reconstruct autobiographical events in accord with their self-theories about how they are most likely to act (Barclay, 1981). People will give plausible, consistent accounts of their intentions and actions during very early experiences, but these accounts reflect their *present* beliefs about their personalities and themselves. Thus, clinicians today continue to turn to clients' earliest memories as a way to learn more about their views of themselves and the world around them.

Even children experience childhood amnesia. A "childhood early memory scoring system" has been devised to help identify and diagnose childhood psychopathologies (Last & Bruhn, 1985). Appropriately, it is less interested in accuracy than in the type and qualities of the memories.

Back to the "memory" that opened this discussion—how might this apparent mixup be explained? One possibility is that our society's heavy reliance on television has made the "tube" a surrogate for real life, taking it beyond entertainment and confusing our sense of actual versus vicarious experience.

A second explanation is that the scene represents a self-view consistent with that of the person claiming the memory. Perhaps the individual sees himself or herself as having been an adventurous child with a loving family (and maid) who lived an ideal life in a model suburb; at the same time, a therapist might see the trauma of the remembered event and the child's disobedience as cues to aspects of his or her personality that require further exploration. In either case, early childhood memories, whether real or constructed, are fertile ground for the therapist who wants to understand and diagnose the client seeking help. Of course, there is always the possibility that somewhere, in a split-level house with six bikes in the driveway, a man named Brady who had three boys of his own . . .

Disturbances of memory and identity that have their roots in clear physical causes include amnestic disorders and dementias. *Amnestic disorders* affect a person's memory exclusively, either for events before an amnesia-inducing trauma or for information learned after it—or both. They are caused by medical conditions, substance misuse, injury, or other problems that can impinge on the physical functioning of the brain. *Dementias* involve more than just memory: they are characterized by deficits in other areas of cognitive functioning as well, such as reasoning and problem solving. They are caused primarily by diseases that affect specific areas of the brain. The most common is *Alzheimer's disease.*

■ DISSOCIATIVE ■ DISORDERS

The dissociative disorders that have received the most attention are dissociative amnesia, dissociative fugue, and dissociative identity disorder. DSM-IV also lists *depersonalization disorder* as a dissociative disorder. This listing is controversial among diagnosticians because the memories and identities of people with this problem seem to remain intact. It is their sense of "self" and of the reality of the self that becomes altered: their mental processes or bodies feel unreal and foreign to them. They feel as though they have become separated from their body and are observing themselves from outside. Because this disorder does not actually involve clear alterations in memory and identity, however, we shall not include it in the present discussions.

DISSOCIATIVE AMNESIA

People with dissociative amnesia are suddenly unable to recall important information about their lives, usually of a traumatic or stressful nature (APA, 1994). The loss of memory is much more extensive than normal forgetting and cannot be attributed to an organic disorder. Very often the episode of amnesia is directly precipitated by a specific upsetting event (Classen, Koopman, & Spiegel, 1993).

*B*rian was spending the day sailing with his wife, Helen. The water was rough but well within what they considered safe limits. They were having a wonderful time and really didn't notice that the sky was getting darker, the wind blowing harder, and the sailboat becoming more difficult to control. After a few hours of sailing, they found themselves far from shore in the middle of a powerful and dangerous storm.

The storm intensified very quickly. Brian had trouble controlling the sailboat amidst the high winds and wild waves. He and Helen tried to put on the safety jackets they had neglected to wear earlier, but the boat turned over before they were finished. Brian, the better swimmer of the two, was able to swim back to the overturned sailboat, grab the side, and hold on for dear life, but Helen simply could not overcome the rough waves and reach the boat. As Brian watched in horror and disbelief, his wife disappeared from view.

After a time, the storm began to lose its strength. Brian managed to restore the sailboat to its proper position and sail back to shore. Finally he reached safety, but the personal consequences of this storm were just beginning. The next days were filled with pain and further horror: the Coast Guard finding Helen's body . . . discussions with authorities . . . breaking the news to Helen's parents . . . funeral plans . . . the funeral itself . . . conversations with friends . . . self-blame . . . grief . . . and more— the start of a nightmare that wouldn't end.

There are four kinds of dissociative amnesia— *localized, selective, generalized,* and *continuous.* Any can be triggered by a traumatic experience such as Brian's, but each represents a distinct pattern of forgetting.

Let us imagine that on the day after the funeral Brian awakens and cannot recall any of the events of the past difficult days, beginning with the boating

People with dissociative disorders are able to "get away from it all," including themselves, by totally forgetting many of their actions, thoughts, and events.

tragedy. He remembers everything that occurred before the accident and can now recall everything from the morning after the funeral forward, but the intervening days remain a total blank. In this case, Brian would be suffering from *localized,* or *circumscribed, amnesia,* the most common type of dissociative amnesia. Here a person forgets all events that occurred over a limited period of time, beginning almost always with an event that was very disturbing.

People with *selective amnesia,* the second most common form of dissociative amnesia, remember some, but not all, events occurring over the circumscribed period of time. Brian may remember his conversations with friends and breaking the news to his in-laws, for example, but have no recollection of making funeral plans or of the funeral itself.

The forgotten or partially forgotten period is called the *amnestic episode.* During an amnestic episode, people sometimes act puzzled and confused and may even wander about aimlessly. They are already experiencing memory difficulties, but seem to be unaware of them. Later, however, when they try and fail to recall the events of the amnestic episode, they are quite aware of their memory disturbance and upset by it.

In some cases the forgetting extends back to a time before the traumatic period. Brian may awaken after the funeral and find that, in addition to the preceding few days, he cannot remember other events in his past life. In this case, he is experiencing *generalized amnesia.* In extreme cases, people with this form of amnesia do not even remember who they are and fail to recognize relatives and friends.

In the forms of dissociative amnesia discussed so far, the period affected by the amnesia has an end; but in *continuous amnesia,* forgetting continues into the present, and new and ongoing experiences fail to be retained. Brian's loss of memory, for example, may extend indefinitely into his life after the accident. He may remember what happened before the tragedy but keep forgetting events that occur since then. He is caught in a prolonged amnestic episode. Although rare as a dissociative form of amnesia, continuous amnesia, as we shall observe later, is more common in cases of amnesia that have an organic basis.

All of these forms of dissociative amnesia are similar in that the amnesia disrupts *episodic memory* only—a person's autobiographical memory of personal experiences and other highly personal material. *Semantic memory*—memory for abstract, encyclopedic, or categorical information—remains intact. People with dissociative amnesia are as likely as anyone else to know the name of the president of the United States, for example, and how to write, read, drive a car, and so on.

Many cases of dissociative amnesia occur during wartime and in natural disasters, when people's health and safety may be significantly threatened (APA, 1994; Kihlstrom et al., 1993). Combat veterans often report memory gaps of hours or days, and sometimes forget personal information, such as their name and address (Bremner et al., 1993). In fact, between 5 and 14 percent of all mental disorders that emerge during military combat are cases of dissociative amnesia. More than a third of these combat amnesia cases arise in soldiers who have endured prolonged marching and fighting under heavy enemy fire; soldiers who have engaged in periodic fighting make up 13 percent of the cases; soldiers whose experience has been confined to base camp make up only 6 percent of the cases (Sargent & Slater, 1941). Recently, many cases of dissociative amnesia linked to child sexual abuse have also been reported to clinicians (see Box 18–2).

The disorder may also arise under more ordinary circumstances. The sudden loss of a loved one through rejection, abandonment, or death can lead to dissociative amnesia (Loewenstein, 1991). In other cases, guilt over behavior that a person considers immoral or sinful (such as an extramarital affair) may precipitate the disorder.

The personal impact of dissociative amnesia depends on the extent and importance of what is forgotten. Obviously, an amnestic episode of two years is more disabling than one of two hours. Similarly, an amnestic episode during which a person undergoes major life changes causes more difficulties than one that is largely uneventful.

DISSOCIATIVE FUGUE

When a loss of memory takes on the added dimension of actual physical flight, it is labeled a dissociative fugue. People with this disorder forget their personal identity and at least some details of their past life, flee to an entirely different location, and may establish a new identity (APA, 1994).

In some cases, the individuals travel only a short distance, their new identity is not a complete one, and they have few social contacts (APA, 1994). Their fugue is brief—a matter of hours or days—and ends suddenly.

In other cases, however, the fugue is quite extensive. Such persons establish a well-integrated new identity, adopt a new name, engage in complex social interactions, and even pursue a new line of work. In their new identity they may have personal characteristics they never displayed before. Usually they are more outgoing and less inhibited (APA, 1994). Despite a missing personal history, they give no outward appearance of abnormal functioning. Fugues of this kind usually last longer than a few hours, and the dis-

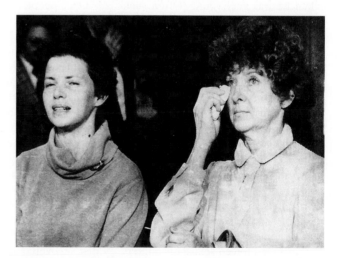

In 1980 a Florida park ranger found a woman naked and starving in a shallow grave. Unaware of her identity and in an apparent fugue state, she was hospitalized as "Jane Doe." Five months later, the woman was recognized on Good Morning, America *by Irene Tomiczek* (right) *as her 34-year-old daughter, Cheryl Ann, who had been missing for seven years. With the help of sodium amobarbital treatment and reunion with her family, Cheryl Ann's fugue at last began to lift.*

BOX 18-2

REPRESSED CHILDHOOD MEMORIES VS. FALSE MEMORY SYNDROME

In recent years, a unique type of dissociative amnesia has attracted enormous public attention. Reports of *repressed childhood memory*, in which adults recover buried memories of sexual and physical abuse from their childhood, have increased dramatically in the late 1980s and early 1990s.

A woman may claim, for example, that her father sexually molested her repeatedly between the ages of five and seven—a memory that returned to her only during therapeutic intervention. Or a young man may remember that a family friend made sexual advances upon him on several occasions when he was very young. Often such individuals are in treatment for disorders such as an eating disorder or depression, and over the course of therapy, their repressed memories begin to surface. The traumatic events that have been repressed are seen as responsible for the disorders from which the individuals now suffer.

Although some of these cases revolve around a single traumatic experience, many others involve repeated abuse over a number of years. In some of the most severe and bizarre cases, victims have reported memories of participating in bloody Satanic rituals that included forced sexual encounters and human sacrifices. They relate details of horrific group behavior involving both family members and other members of a sect or cult. Their recollections of abuse can be com-

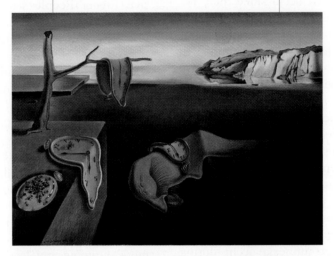

Salvador Dali's painting The Persistence of Memory *(1931) suggests that memory does indeed persist, but often in a distorted form.*

pelling and vivid and reflect great conviction.

Once people recall childhood sexual traumas, many confront their abusers. Some have even brought criminal charges and others civil charges. In fact, 19 states have recently revised their laws to allow charges to be brought even after the statute of limitations has run out (Horn, 1993). Hundreds of such cases are now in the courts. Willingness by state legislatures and courtroom juries to decide in favor of the apparent victims indicates a growing acceptance of the notions of repressed and recovered memories.

Society has become deeply divided on this issue. Some people believe that recovered memories are as they appear—horrific memories that have been buried in the deep recesses of a person's mind, only to resurface years later in a safer climate. Others believe that the memories are in fact a very se-

rious and damaging form of the "illusory" childhood memories discussed earlier— images and stories falsely constructed or embraced by confused and suggestible persons. In fact, an organization called the False Memory Syndrome Foundation has been founded in Philadelphia to assist those claiming to be falsely charged with the abuse. Indeed, the claim that recovered memories are actually distorted or false memories has itself been gaining status in the courts. Recently, for example, a man who was publicly accused by his 23-year-old daughter of having sexually abused her when she was a child, brought suit against her therapists, claiming that their treatment techniques had induced false memories in his daughter and, at the same time, brought destruction to his reputation, job, marriage, and family. He won the suit and was granted a large financial judgment by the jury.

The clinical community is just as deeply divided on this issue, with some clinicians convinced that many of these cases are legitimate examples of repression and at least as many arguing forcefully against this view. The proponents of the repressed memory position point out that child sexual abuse is an enormous problem, victimizing at least 200,000 to 300,000 children in the United States each year (Horn, 1993; AAPC, 1992). Few experiences bring more horror or shame, are kept more private, or have a more lingering impact (Nash et al., 1993;

Briere, 1992), making victims prime candidates for a reaction of dissociative amnesia. Some studies even suggest that between 18 and 59 percent of sexual abuse victims have difficulty recalling at least some aspects of their trauma (Horn, 1993). Thus, the proponents argue, it is reasonable to expect that some children may totally repress their painful sexual abuse traumas until therapy discussions or life events later trigger their memories.

Proponents further point out that the notion of hidden memory is hardly foreign to the clinical field. The defense mechanism of repression has been at the center of psychodynamic explanations and treatments for years. Moreover, they assert, the DSM-IV category of *dissociative amnesia* represents a formal acknowledgement of the phenomenon.

The opponents to the repressed memory perspective have responded to each of these points. They agree that child sexual abuse is indeed an enormous problem, but, they claim, it is one that most victims remember all too well rather than forget. Systematic research has not found many cases in which such events are completely wiped from one's memory. One study, for example, observed teenagers who had been sexually abused and found no evidence of repression over a 10 year period (Loftus, 1993).

Opponents also question how accurate recalled sexual traumas are likely to be. Not only are adult memories of childhood events typically illusory, but memories of events that happen to us as adults are also fallible. Studies have shown, for example, that eyewitness accounts of crimes or other salient experiences may change over time or be influenced by various factors such as suggestions by other people or differing accounts of the events (Loftus, 1993). Even for highly memorable events such as the explosion of the space shuttle *Challenger*, people give inaccurate accounts of where they

were or who told them of the accident, although they seem certain of their recollections. In short, the opponents argue, the public's ready acceptance of so-called recovered memories is probably unwarranted.

Opponents of the repressed memory position further point out that Freud himself disagreed with the interpretations now being applied in these cases. Granted, in 1893 Freud did believe that many of his patients had been sexually abused as children, and that their repressed memories of those events had caused them to develop psychological problems. But, over the next four years, Freud changed his mind and came to believe that the patient memories which came to light in treatment actually represented repressed fantasies and desires rather than true recollections. The motives behind Freud's theoretical shift have been hotly debated in the clinical field, but the fact remains that his views can hardly be cited as support for the repressed childhood memory position.

If the recovery of childhood memories is not what it appears to be, what is it? A powerful case of suggestibility, according to the opponents. They hold that therapists themselves have been highly affected by both the clinical and public attention surrounding this diagnosis and some are prone to accept it despite a lack of evidence (Frankel, 1993). With certain clients, these therapists may actively seek indicators that early sexual abuse occurred and conduct therapy correspondingly, implicitly or explicitly encouraging the clients to find repressed memories (Ganaway, 1989). Many such therapists even use a variety of *memory recovery techniques* to help clients uncover such memories—including hypnosis, journal writing, dream interpretation, and interpreting body symptoms such as a dry mouth (Lindsay & Read, 1993). It may be that clients often oblige and unwit-

tingly form illusory memories of abuse.

Several factors may contribute to the creation of false memories by clients: suggestions by a respected authority figure, long delays between the purported events and the surfacing of the memory, the plausibility of the events, and repetitive therapy discussions of the alleged abusive events (Belli et al., 1992; Loftus, Hashtroudi, & Lindsay, 1993). In short, recovered memories may actually be *iatrogenic*—unintentionally caused by the therapist.

Of course, repressed memories of child sexual abuse do not surface only in clinical settings. Many alleged victims come forward on their own. They report flashbacks revealing sexual abuse and they then seek therapy. These self-revelations are on the increase. Some psychologists attribute them to the large number of popular books, articles, and television shows that take a strong stand in support of recovering repressed memories (Loftus, 1993). Several such books offer readers lists of criteria for diagnosing repression of sexual abuse memories: long lists of symptoms that, in some cases, are actually rather common and not clinical in nature or that have not been reliably correlated with instances of sexual abuse (Tavris, 1993). When readers meet a number of these criteria, they may begin a search for repressed memories.

It is important to recognize that the heated debate over the phenomenon of repressed childhood memories does not in any way diminish the enormity of the problem of child sexual abuse. In fact, both proponents and opponents alike are greatly concerned that this controversy may be taken by the public to mean that clinicians have doubts about the scope of the problem of child sexual abuse. In a controversy filled with the potential for sad outcomes, that would be the most unfortunate result of all.

tance traveled is more than a few miles. Indeed, some people have been known to travel to foreign countries thousands of miles away. This kind of fugue is seen in the case of the Reverend Ansel Bourne, described by the famous psychologist William James at the turn of the century:

The Rev. Ansel Bourne, of Greene, R.I., was brought up to the trade of a carpenter; but . . . he became converted from Atheism to Christianity just before his thirtieth year, and has since that time for the most part lived the life of an itinerant preacher. . . . He is of a firm and self-reliant disposition, a man whose yea is yea and his nay, nay; and his character for uprightness is such in the community that no person who knows him will for a moment admit the possibility of his case not being perfectly genuine.

On January 17, 1887, he drew 551 dollars from a bank in Providence with which to pay for a certain lot of land in Greene, paid certain bills, and got into a Pawtucket horsecar. This is the last incident which he remembers. He did not return home that day, and nothing was heard of him for two months. He was published in the papers as missing, and foul play being suspected, the police sought in vain his whereabouts. On the morning of March 14th, however, at Norristown, Pennsylvania, a man calling himself A. I. Brown who had rented a small shop six weeks previously, stocked it with stationery, confectionery, fruit and small articles, and carried on his quiet trade without seeming to any one unnatural or eccentric, woke up in a fright and called in the people of the house to tell him where he was. He said that his name was Ansel Bourne, that he was entirely ignorant of Norristown, that he knew nothing of shop-keeping, and that the last thing he remembered—it seemed only yesterday—was drawing the money from the bank, etc. in Providence. . . . He was very weak, having lost apparently over twenty pounds of flesh during his escapade, and had such a horror of the idea of the candy-store that he refused to set foot in it again.

The first two weeks of the period remained unaccounted for, as he had no memory, after he had once resumed his normal personality, of any part of the time, and no one who knew him seems to have seen him after he left home. The remarkable part of the change is, of course, the peculiar occupation which the so-called Brown indulged in. Mr. Bourne has never in his life had the slightest contact with trade. "Brown" was described by the neighbors as taciturn, orderly in his habits, and in no way queer. He went to Philadelphia several times; replenished his stock; cooked for himself in the back shop, where he also slept; went regularly to church; and once at a prayer-meeting made what was considered by the hearers a good address, in the course of which he related an incident which he had witnessed in his natural state of Bourne.

(James, 1890, pp. 391–393)

Approximately 0.2 percent of the population experiences dissociative fugue. Like dissociative amnesia, a fugue usually follows a severely stressful event, such as a wartime experience or a natural disaster, though it also can be triggered by personal stress, such as financial or legal difficulties or episodes of depression (APA, 1994; Kihlstrom et al., 1993). Some adolescent runaways are suspected to be in a state of fugue (Loewenstein, 1991). Fugues are also similar to dissociative amnesia in that only episodic memories from the past are impaired, while semantic knowledge remains intact (Kihlstrom et al., 1993).

Fugues tend to end abruptly. In some cases, the recovery of past memories is spontaneous, as with the Reverend Mr. Bourne. The person "awakens" in an unfamiliar place, surrounded by strangers, and wonders how he or she got there. In other cases the lack of personal history may arouse curiosity or suspicion, a traffic accident or legal difficulty may lead police to discover the false identity, or friends may search for and find the missing person (Kihlstrom et al., 1993). When these people are found, it may be necessary to ask them extensive questions about the details of their lives, repeatedly remind them who they are, and even involve them in psychotherapy before they recover their memories.

Most people who experience a fugue regain most or all of their memories and never have a recurrence. Interestingly, though, as they recover their past, many of them forget the events of the fugue period (APA, 1994). Some, like the Reverend Mr. Bourne, never have even a temporary recollection of the fugue period; their awareness of it may come entirely from other people's accounts.

Since most fugues are brief and totally reversible, impairment and aftereffects are usually minimal (Keller & Shaywitz, 1986). People who have been away for months or years, however, often do have trouble adjusting to family, social, or occupational changes that have occurred during their flight. Moreover, some people commit illegal or violent acts in their fugue state and later must face the consequences of those acts.

DISSOCIATIVE IDENTITY DISORDER (MULTIPLE PERSONALITY DISORDER)

Multiple personality disorder is as dramatic as it is disabling, as we see in the case of Eric:

azed and bruised from a beating, Eric, 29, was discovered wandering around a Daytona Beach shopping mall on Feb. 9. He had no ID and acted so oddly that ambulance workers, who took him to a nearby hospital, assumed he was retarded. Transferred six weeks later to Daytona Beach's Human Resources Center, Eric began talking to doctors in two voices: the infantile rhythms of "young Eric," a dim and frightened child, and the measured tones of "older Eric," who told a tale of terror and child abuse. According to "older Eric," after his immigrant German parents died, a harsh stepfather and his mistress took Eric from his native South Carolina to a drug dealers' hideout in a Florida swamp. Eric said he was raped by several gang members and watched his stepfather murder two men.

One day in late March an alarmed counselor watched Eric's face twist into a violent snarl. Eric let loose an unearthly growl and spat out a stream of obscenities. "It sounded like something out of *The Exorcist*," says Malcolm Graham, the psychologist who directs the case at the center. "It was the most intense thing I've ever seen in a patient." That disclosure of a new personality, who insolently demanded to be called Mark, was the first indication that Graham had been dealing with a rare and serious emotional disorder: true multiple personality. . . .

Eric's other manifestations emerged over the next weeks: quiet, middle-aged Dwight; the hysterically blind and mute Jeffrey; Michael, an arrogant jock; the coquettish Tian, whom Eric considered a whore; and argumentative Phillip, the lawyer. "Phillip was always asking about Eric's rights," says Graham. "He was kind of obnoxious. Actually, Phillip was a pain."

To Graham's astonishment, Eric gradually unfurled 27 different personalities, including three females. . . . They ranged in age from a fetus to a sordid old man who kept trying to persuade Eric to fight as a mercenary in Haiti. In one therapy session, reports Graham, Eric shifted personality nine times in an hour. "I felt I was losing control of the sessions," says the psychologist, who has eleven years of clinical experience. "Some personalities would not talk to me, and some of them were very insightful into my behavior as well as Eric's."

(Time, October 25, 1982, p. 70)

A person with multiple personality disorder displays two or more distinct personalities, often called **subpersonalities,** each with a unique set of memories, behaviors, thoughts, and emotions. At any given time, one of the subpersonalities dominates the person's consciousness and interactions with the environment. Usually one subpersonality, the **primary** or **host personality,** appears more often than the others.

The transition from one subpersonality to another is usually sudden and often dramatic (APA, 1994; Dell & Eisenhower, 1990). Eric, for example, twisted his face, growled, and yelled obscenities while changing personalities. Transitions are usually precipitated by a stressful event (APA, 1994), although artificial precipitants, such as hypnotic suggestion, can also bring about the change (Smith, 1993; Brende & Rinsley, 1981).

Multiple personality was first reported almost four centuries ago (Bliss, 1985, 1980). Most clinicians consider it to be a rare disorder, but recent reports suggest that it may be more common than it was once thought to be (APA, 1994; Kluft, 1991). Most cases are first diagnosed in late adolescence or young adulthood, but the symptoms usually begin to develop in early childhood after episodes of abuse, typically before the age of 5 (Ross et al., 1991; Sachs, 1986). Indeed, studies suggest that as many as 97 percent of these patients have been physically, often sexually, abused during their early years (Ross et al., 1990, 1989; Dell & Eisenhower, 1990; Putnam et al., 1986). The disorder is diagnosed in women between three and nine times as often as it is in men (APA, 1994). In some cases, the parents of people with multiple personality disorder appear to have themselves displayed some kind of dissociative disorder (Dell & Eisenhower, 1990; Ross et al., 1989).

THE SUBPERSONALITIES The subpersonalities relate to one another in ways that vary from case to case. Generally, however, there are three kinds of relationships: mutually amnesic, mutually cognizant, and one-way amnesic.

In *mutually amnesic relationships*, the subpersonalities have no awareness of one another (Ellenberger, 1970). Conversely, in *mutually cognizant patterns*, each subpersonality is well aware of the rest. They may hear one another's voices and even talk among themselves. Some are on good terms, relating as friends would do and sharing opinions and goals. Others do not get along at all. Eric's subpersonalities were mutually cognizant:

ost of the personalities interacted. Cye, a religious mystic, once left a comforting note for Eric. The pushy Michael, who loved rock music, hated Eric's classical records so much that he yanked the wires from a stereo. Eric defended the menacing Mark: "Mark never hurt anybody," he said one day. "He is just there to scare other people off when they get too close." Eric referred to his troupe of personalities as his "talking books." One of the characters was a librarian named Max who occasionally announced a sudden personality change by saying, "One of the books just fell off the shelf."

(Time, October 25, 1982, p. 70)

Other patterns fall between these two extremes. The most common multiple personality pattern is the *one-way amnesic relationship:* some subpersonalities are aware of others, but the awareness is not reciprocated. Those that are aware are called *co-conscious subpersonalities.* They are "quiet observers" that watch the actions and thoughts of the other subpersonalities but do not interact with them. Sometimes, while another subpersonality is dominating consciousness, they make themselves known through such indirect means as auditory hallucinations (for example, a voice giving commands) or "automatic writing" (the conscious personality finds itself writing down words over which it experiences no control).

A one-way amnesic relationship was at work in the case of Miss Christine Beauchamp, one of the earliest reported and most famous examples of multiple personality (Prince, 1906). In therapy, this woman initially manifested three subpersonalities. Her therapist labeled them the Saint (a religious, even-tempered subpersonality), the Woman (irreligious and bad-tempered), and the Devil (mischievous and cheerful). The Saint, Miss Beauchamp's primary personality, knew nothing of the Woman or the Devil. The Woman knew of the Saint but not of the Devil. The Devil knew of both the Saint and the Woman but in different ways: she had direct access to the Saint's thoughts, but her knowledge of the Woman was based solely on her observations of the Woman's behavior.

Investigators used to believe that cases of multiple personality disorder usually involved two or three subpersonalities. Studies now suggest, however, that the average number of subpersonalities per patient is much higher—15 for women and 8 for men (APA, 1994; Ross et al., 1989). In fact, there have been cases in which 100 or more subpersonalities were observed (APA, 1994). The subpersonalities may emerge in groups of two or three at a time.

Therapists typically become aware of the greater number of subpersonalities only as therapy progresses. In the case of Miss Beauchamp, the Saint, the Woman, and the Devil were joined by other personalities during the course of treatment (Rosenzweig, 1988, 1987; Prince, 1906). A more recent example is the full story of "Eve White," the woman made famous in the book and movie *The Three Faces of Eve.* The book reported that Eve had three personalities—Eve White, Eve Black, and Jane (Thigpen & Cleckley, 1957). Eve White, the primary personality, was colorless, quiet, and serious; Eve Black was carefree, mischievous, and uninhibited; and Jane was mature and intelligent. According to the book, these three subpersonalities eventually merged into Evelyn, a stable and enduring personality who represented an integration of the other three.

It turned out, however, that this was not the end of Eve's dissociation. Twenty years later, in the mid-1970s, she identified herself in an autobiography. Now named Chris Sizemore, she described her pre- and posttherapy life more fully and said that altogether twenty-two subpersonalities had emerged, including nine subpersonalities after Evelyn! Usually they emerged in groups of three, each group displaying a range of characteristics, abilities, and tastes. Apparently the authors of *The Three Faces of Eve* had worked with her during the ascendancy of one such group, and never knew about her previous and subsequent subpersonalities. This woman has now overcome her disorder and achieved a single, stable identity. She has been Chris Sizemore for nearly twenty years (Sizemore & Huber, 1988).

Subpersonalities usually have their own names. This seems strangely appropriate, given the extent to which they differ from one another in personality characteristics, vital statistics, abilities and preferences, and even physiological responses (Alpher, 1992; Dell & Eisenhower, 1990).

PERSONALITY CHARACTERISTICS   A look once again at the three personalities first displayed by Miss Beauchamp highlights the diversity typical of subpersonalities in this disorder (Prince, 1906). The primary personality, the Saint, was a fragile, prim, and humorless woman who also was very religious and cared for children and older people. She was overly conscientious and idealistic, and often experienced

Chris Sizemore, the subject of the book and film The Three Faces of Eve, *is now an accomplished author, artist, and mental health spokesperson who no longer manifests a multiple personality disorder. The variety of her portraits reflects the many subpersonalities Sizemore displayed.*

severe guilt and depression. The subpersonality called the Woman was an irreligious person who disliked children and older people. She had a bad temper and was very ambitious. Finally, the Devil, also named Sally, had a mischievous and "playfully wicked" personality and a corresponding sense of humor. She tended to be childlike, impulsive, and seductive, and was filled with energy and the joy of life. Even when the Saint became depressed and suicidal, Sally remained cheerful and functional. Not surprisingly, Sally had little patience with the other two subpersonalities. To her the Saint was weak and sentimental, and she truly hated the Woman.

VITAL STATISTICS   The subpersonalities may differ in features as basic as age, sex, race, and family history (Coons, Bowman, & Milstein, 1988), as in the famous case of Sybil Dorsett. Sybil's multiple personality disorder has been described in fictional form, but the novel is based on an actual case, and both the therapist and the patient have attested to its accuracy (Schreiber, 1973). Sybil manifested seventeen subpersonalities, all with different identifying features. They included adults, a teenager, and a baby named Ruthie; and while most of her personalities were female, two were male, named Mike and Sid. The subpersonalities had distinct physical images of themselves and of each other. The subpersonality named Vicky, for example, saw herself as an attractive blonde, while another, Peggy Lou, was described as a pixie with a pug nose. Mary was plump with dark hair, and Vanessa was a tall redhead with a willowy figure. Mike's olive skin and brown eyes stood in contrast to Sid's fair skin and blue eyes.

ABILITIES AND PREFERENCES   Although semantic memory is not affected in dissociative amnesia or fugue, it can often be disrupted in multiple personality disorder. It is not uncommon for the different subpersonalities to have different abilities: one may be able to drive, speak a foreign language, or play a musical instrument, while the others cannot (Coons et al., 1988). Their handwriting styles can also differ (Coons, 1980). In addition, a person's subpersonalities usually have different tastes in food, friends, music, and literature, as in Sybil's case.

*A*mong outsiders Vanessa claimed to like everybody who wasn't a hypocrite. Peggy Lou vented her spleen against what she called "showoffs like Sybil's mother." Vicky favored intelligent and sophisticated persons. Both Mary and Sybil had a special fondness for children. Mary, indicating oneness rather than autonomy, remarked about a woman they all knew, "None of us liked her."

Excited by conversations about music, Peggy Lou often shut her ears in the course of other conversations. Bored by female conversation in general, Mike and Sid sometimes succeeded in making Sybil break an engagement or nagged throughout the visit.

. . . Marjorie told Dr. Wilbur, "I go with Sybil when she visits her friends, but they talk about things they like and I don't care about—houses, furniture, babies. But when Laura Hotchkins comes, they talk about concerts, and I like that."

(Schreiber, 1973, p. 288)

Chris Sizemore ("Eve") displayed such differences in abilities and preferences. She later pointed out, "If I had learned to sew as one personality and then tried to sew as another, I couldn't do it. Driving a car was the same. Some of my personalities couldn't drive" (1975, p. 4).

PHYSIOLOGICAL ACTIVITY   Researchers have discovered that subpersonalities may also display actual physiological differences, as in autonomic nervous system activity, blood pressure levels, and menstrual cycles (Putnam, Zahn, & Post, 1990). One study investigated the brain activities of different subpersonalities by measuring their *evoked potentials*—that is, the brain response patterns recorded on an electroencephalograph as the subject observes a flashing light (Putnam, 1984). When this evoked potential test was administered to four subpersonalities of each of ten people with multiple personality disorder, it showed that the brain activity patterns of the subpersonalities differed greatly within each individual. This was a dramatic finding. The brain pattern in response to a specific stimulus is usually stable and unique to a given individual. The subpersonalities of these ten subjects showed the kinds of variations usually found in totally different people.

This study also made use of control subjects who pretended to have different subpersonalities. They were instructed to create and rehearse their alternate personalities in detail and were then given the same evoked-potential test for each of their simulated subpersonalities. The brain-reaction patterns of these control subjects did not vary for the different simulated subpersonalities. This is evidence that the significant variations in brain reaction patterns from subpersonality to subpersonality in cases of multiple personality cannot be brought about by simple faking.

THE PREVALENCE OF MULTIPLE PERSONALITY DISORDER   As we noted earlier, multiple personality has traditionally been thought of as a rare disorder. Some researchers have even argued that multiple personality disorder is not a legitimate diagnosis. These researchers suggest that cases of multiple personality are *iatrogenic*—that is, unintentionally caused by practitioners. They believe that therapists create this disorder by subtly suggesting the existence of alternate personalities during therapy or by eliciting the personalities while patients are under hypnosis. In addition, they believe that a therapist who is looking for multiple personalities may reinforce these patterns by becoming more interested in a patient when he or she displays symptoms of dissociation (Merskey, 1992; Fahy, 1988). These arguments seem to be supported by the fact that many cases do initially come to the attention of a therapist while the client is being treated for a less serious problem (Allison, 1978).

By 1970 only 100 cases had ever been reported in professional journals. But in recent years, the number of people diagnosed with multiple personality disorders has been increasing more and more rapidly. By the mid-1970s, 200 cases had been reported; the number reached 300 by the late 1970s and then doubled by the early 1980s (Kluft, 1983). Thousands of contemporary cases have been identified in the United States and Canada alone (Ross et al., 1989; Kluft, 1987). Although the disorder is still relatively rare, the prevalence rate appears to have risen dramatically.

What accounts for this recent increase in the number of cases reported? At least two factors seem to be involved. First, belief in the authenticity of this disorder is growing, and willingness to diagnose it has increased accordingly (French, 1987). It has become clear to many investigators, after careful evaluation of the literature and careful observations of clients, that cases of multiple personality are not necessarily iatrogenic (Braun, 1984; Kluft, 1982). Many of the so-called iatrogenic cases actually involve people who have finally sought treatment after having experienced losses of time throughout their lives, a symptom that is very consistent with multiple personality disturbances (Putnam, 1988, 1985; Schacter, 1989). Moreover, in many of these cases, it turns out that the subpersonalities had already been observed by friends or relatives, or noticed by the individuals themselves, before the therapist was first consulted. In addition, researchers have increasingly found that multiple personality is not a culture-bound phenomenon largely indigenous to the United States, as they once believed, but has been identified around the world (Coons et al., 1991).

The large number of multiple personality cases being reported may also reflect recent changes in diag-

One of the cinema's best-known fictional sufferers of multiple personality disorder, Norman Bates, is horrified to discover his mother has stabbed a woman to death in the shower. Later in the movie Psycho *we learn his mother died years ago and now "exists" as one of Bates's subpersonalities.*

nostic biases and criteria. As we saw in Chapter 15, from 1910 to 1978 schizophrenia was one of the most popular diagnoses in the clinical field (Rosenbaum, 1980). Because the criteria for that disorder tended to be vague and flexible, the diagnosis was readily applied to a wide range of unusual and mysterious patterns of abnormality. It is possible that many cases of multiple personality were incorrectly diagnosed as schizophrenia during that period. Under the stricter criteria of DSM-III, DSM-III-R, and DSM-IV, diagnosticians have applied the label of schizophrenia with greater accuracy, allowing multiple personality cases to be recognized and assessed more readily (Coons & Fine, 1990; French, 1987). Some clinicians also now use tests of hypnotizability to help distinguish patients with multiple personality disorder from those with schizophrenia (Jaschke & Spiegel, 1992). They note that while the former tend to be highly hypnotizable, schizophrenic patients have trouble maintaining continuous concentration and therefore have low hypnotizability scores.

Several other tools for assessing multiple personality and other dissociative disorders have also been developed in recent years (Allen & Smith, 1993; Carlson et al., 1993; Frischholz & Braun, 1991). The most commonly used and widely researched is the Dissociative Experiences Scale (DES), a brief, twenty-eight-item self-report scale that can be completed within fifteen minutes (Bernstein & Putnam, 1986). The Structured Clinical Interview for DSM-IV Dissociative Disorders (SCID-D), a systematic interview protocol, also helps diagnose dissociative disorders and assess the severity of dissociative symptoms (Steinberg, 1993).

Despite such changes in professional perceptions, diagnostic practices, and assessment tools, many clinicians remain reluctant to make this diagnosis (Saxe et al., 1993; McElroy, 1992). In fact, people suffering from this disorder still receive an average of four different diagnoses, such as schizophrenia and depression, and average nearly seven years of contact with health services before a diagnosis of multiple personality disorder is finally made (Putnam et al., 1986).

EXPLANATIONS OF DISSOCIATIVE DISORDERS

Relatively few researchers have investigated the origins of the dissociative disorders, although a variety of theories have been offered to explain them. Proponents of older perspectives especially, such as the psychodynamic and behavioral viewpoints, have gathered little systematic data. On the other hand, newer theories, which combine cognitive, behavioral, and biological principles and highlight such factors as state-dependent learning and self-hypnosis, have begun to capture the enthusiasm of clinical scientists.

THE PSYCHODYNAMIC VIEW Psychodynamic theorists believe that dissociative disorders represent an extreme use of *repression*, the most fundamental defense mechanism: people ward off anxiety by unconsciously preventing painful memories, thoughts, or impulses from reaching awareness. Everyone uses repression to a degree, but those people diagnosed as having dissociative disorders are thought to repress their memories excessively and dysfunctionally (Terr, 1988).

Dissociative amnesia and fugue are each seen as representing a single episode of massive repression in which a person unconsciously blocks the memory of an extremely upsetting event to avoid the pain of confronting it (Putnam, 1985). Such a reaction has its roots in childhood. When parents overreact to a child's expressions of id impulses (for example, to

signs of sexual impulses), some children become excessively afraid of those impulses, defend against them, and develop a strict code prohibiting such "immoral" desires. Later in their lives, when they act in a manner that violates their moral code—by having an extramarital affair, for example—they are brought face to face with their most unacceptable impulses. They may be forced to repress the whole situation as the only means of protecting themselves from overwhelming anxiety.

If amnesia and fugue conceal a single repressed event, multiple personality disorders bespeak a lifetime of excessive repression (Reis, 1993). Psychodynamic theorists believe that dependence on this ongoing style of coping is triggered by extremely traumatic childhood experiences, particularly abusive parenting. Young Sybil, for example, was repeatedly made to suffer unspeakable tortures by her disturbed mother, Hattie:

A favorite ritual . . . was to separate Sybil's legs with a long wooden spoon, tie her feet to the spoon with dish towels, and then string her to the end of a light bulb cord, suspended from the ceiling. The child was left to swing in space while the mother proceeded to the water faucet to wait for the water to get cold. After muttering, "Well, it's not going to get any colder," she would fill the adult-sized enema bag to capacity and return with it to her daughter. As the child swung in space, the mother would insert the enema tip into the child's urethra and fill the bladder with cold water. "I did it," Hattie would scream triumphantly when her mission was accomplished. "I did it." The scream was followed by laughter, which went on and on.

(Schreiber, 1973, p. 160)

According to psychodynamic theorists, children who are exposed to such traumas and abuses may come to fear the dangerous world they live in and take to flight symbolically by regularly pretending to be another person who is safely looking on from afar. This flight is much more desperate and pathological than the flights of fantasy and daydreaming that all people engage in on occasion. Sybil's psychotherapist concluded, "She had sought rescue from without until, finally recognizing that this rescue would be denied, she resorted to finding rescue from within. . . . Being a multiple personality was the ultimate rescue" (Schreiber, 1973, p. 158).

Abused children may also become afraid of the impulses that they believe are leading to their punishments. They may strive to be "good" and "proper" all of the time and keep repressing the impulses they consider "bad" and "dangerous." Whenever "bad" thoughts or impulses do break through, such children may feel bound to disown and deny them, and may unconsciously assign all unacceptable thoughts, impulses, and emotions to other personalities. This situation would lead to an inhibited and drab primary personality that is accompanied by bold and colorful subpersonalities.

Most of the support for the psychodynamic position is drawn from case histories. Such brutal childhood experiences as beatings, cuttings, burnings with cigarettes, imprisonment in closets, rape, and extensive verbal abuse have often been reported in multiple personality cases. On the other hand, the backgrounds of some individuals with multiple personality disorders do not seem to be markedly deviant (Bliss, 1980). Moreover, child abuse appears to be far more prevalent than multiple personality disorder. Why, then, do only a small fraction of abused children develop this form of dysfunctioning?

THE BEHAVIORAL VIEW Behaviorists believe that dissociation is a response acquired through operant conditioning. People who experience a horrifying event may later find temporary relief when their minds drift to other subjects. For some, this momentary forgetting, leading to a reduction in anxiety, increases the likelihood of future forgetting. In short, they are reinforced for the act of forgetting and learn—without being aware that they are learning—that forgetting lets them avoid or escape anxiety.

The behavioral explanation of dissociative disorders shares several features with the psychodynamic view. Both hold that dissociative disorders are precipitated by traumatic experiences, that the disorders represent ways of avoiding extreme anxiety, and that the individuals themselves are unaware that their disorder is actually protecting them from facing a painful reality. The explanations do, however, differ in some important ways. Psychodynamic theorists believe that the disorders represent attempts at forgetting that, although unconscious, are purposeful from the start, whereas behaviorists believe the initial development of dissociative reactions to be more accidental. Furthermore, behaviorists believe that a subtle reinforcement process rather than a hardworking unconscious is keeping the individual unaware that he or she is using dissociation as a means of escape.

Like the psychodynamic explanation, the behavioral explanation has certain shortcomings. Behaviorists too have been forced to rely largely on case histories to support their position. While case descriptions do typically support the behavioral view, they are often equally consistent with other kinds of explanations as well, offering no evidence that one explanation is superior to the other. A case that seems to reflect the reinforcement of forgetting, for example, can usually also be interpreted as an example of unconscious repression.

The behavioral explanation does not yet explain precisely how temporary distractions from painful memories grow into acquired responses or why, since temporary acts of forgetting are frequently reinforced in life, more people do not develop dissociative disorders. Nor has it yet described how reinforcement can account for the complicated interrelationships of subpersonalities found in multiple personality disorders.

STATE-DEPENDENT LEARNING What people learn when they are in a particular state or situation they tend to remember best when they are returned to that same state or situation. Something learned under the influence of alcohol, for example, is likely to be recalled better under the influence of alcohol than in an alcohol-free condition (Overton, 1966). Similarly, people given a learning task to do while they smoke cigarettes will later recall the learned material better when they are smoking.

This association between state and recall is called *state-dependent learning.* It was initially observed in experimental animals that were administered certain drugs, taught to perform certain tasks, and later tested on those tasks under various conditions. Researchers repeatedly found that the animals' subsequent test performances were better in corresponding drug states than in drug-free states (Pusakulich & Nielson, 1976; Spear, 1973; Overton, 1966, 1964). Research with human subjects later showed that state-dependent learning could be associated with psychological states as well as physiological ones. One study found mood to be influential (see Figure 18–1): material learned during a happy mood was recalled best when the subject was again in a happy mood, and sad-state learning was recalled best during sad states (Bower, 1981). Similarly, people who commit crimes of passion or violence often recall the details of their crimes more completely when hypnotists cause them to return to a similar state of arousal (Fischer & Landon, 1972).

One way of interpreting the phenomenon of state-dependent learning is to see it as an indication that *arousal levels* are an important part of memory processes. That is, a particular level of arousal will have a set of remembered events, thoughts, and skills attached to it. When a situation elicits that particular level of arousal, the person is more likely to recall the memories associated with it. Skill performances may be enhanced at levels of arousal that correspond to the states in which they were acquired and practiced.

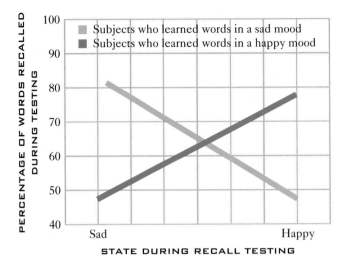

FIGURE 18-1 *State-dependent learning was demonstrated in a study by Bower (1981). Subjects who learned a list of words while in a hypnotically induced happy state remembered the words better if they were in a happy mood when tested later than if they were in a sad mood. Conversely, subjects who learned the words when in a sad mood recalled them better if they were sad during testing than if they were happy.*

Some research even suggests that the amygdala, the structure in the brain's limbic system that originates emotional behavior (see Chapter 6), may also regulate the link between arousal and memory (Mishkin, 1978).

For most people state-dependent learning is a relative phenomenon. They can recall many past events across a range of arousal states, but will remember each better in some states than in others. Perhaps some people—those prone to develop dissociative disorders—have state-to-memory links that are extremely rigid and narrow. Their thoughts, memories, and skills may be tied exclusively to particular states of arousal. They recall past events only when they experience arousal states almost identical to the states in which the memory was acquired.

According to proponents of this view, changes in arousal may be at the core of dissociative disorders (Silberman et al., 1985). In dissociative amnesia, for example, extreme anxiety may be experienced during an upsetting event and relative calm at a later time. In dissociation-prone people, this contrast in arousal states may interfere with the ability to recall the upsetting event. Similarly, in dissociative fugue, the shift from a harrowing environment and anxious state to a peaceful environment and calmer state may make past events irretrievable.

Multiple personality disorders may also be accounted for by the principles of state-dependent learning. Different arousal levels may elicit different clusters of memories, thoughts, and abilities—that is,

different subpersonalities (Putnam, 1992). When a person experiences a particular mood or level of arousal, the memories, thoughts, and abilities acquired under a similar level of arousal may surge into consciousness. Later, when the person undergoes a major shift in arousal, a different set of memories and abilities may emerge. This explanation is consistent with our earlier observation that personality transitions in multiple personality disorders tend to be rapid and stress-related.

Efforts to tie state-dependent learning to dissociative disorders keep running into a major problem: theorists do not yet agree about the nature of the contribution of state to memory. Many believe that arousal does not have a special role in remembering and that state-dependent learning can be explained in other ways. Researchers already know that several kinds of cues present at the time of learning will act as memory aids (Tulving & Watkins, 1977). Objects, smells, and sounds can help elicit memories of past events to which they are tied. It is possible that a state of arousal is just another such cue, albeit an internal one. Proponents of this view argue that the notion of state-dependent learning has little new to say about memory itself and less still about the active forgetting involved in dissociative disorders.

SELF-HYPNOSIS As we first noted in Chapter 1, the word "hypnosis" describes the deliberate induction of a sleeplike state in which a person shows a very high degree of suggestibility. While in this state, the person can behave, perceive, and think in ways that would ordinarily seem impossible. Hypnotized subjects can, for example, be made to suspend their sensory functioning so that they become temporarily blind, deaf, or insensitive to pain (Fromm & Nash, 1992).

Hypnosis can help people remember events that occurred and were forgotten years ago, a capability of which many psychotherapists make frequent use. Conversely, it can also make people forget facts, events, and even their personal identity—a phenomenon that is called *hypnotic amnesia* (Spanos & Coe, 1992; Coe, 1989).

Most investigations of hypnotic amnesia follow similar formats. Subjects are asked to study a word list or other material until they are able to repeat it correctly. Under hypnosis, they are then instructed to forget the material until they receive a cancellation signal (such as the snap of a finger), at which time they will suddenly recall the learned material once again. Repeatedly these experiments have shown the subjects' memories to be severely impaired during the period of hypnotically suggested amnesia and then restored

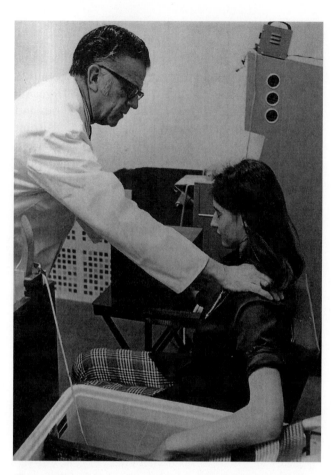

Ernest Hilgard hypnotizes subjects into experiencing tepid water as painfully cold or ice water as comfortably warm. Work by Hilgard and other researchers on hypnotic amnesia has helped convince many clinicians that dissociative disorders represent a form of self-hypnosis.

after the cancellation signal is given (Coe, 1989). It appears that episodic memories (memories of personal events such as one's birthday party or an accident) are more readily forgotten under hypnotic suggestion than semantic memories (memories of encyclopedic information or basic knowledge) (Kihlstrom, 1980).

The parallels between hypnotic amnesia and dissociative disorders are striking (Bliss, 1980). Both are conditions in which people forget certain material for a period of time yet later recall it to mind. In both, the people forget without any insight into why they are forgetting or any awareness that something has been forgotten. Finally, in both situations, events are more readily forgotten than basic knowledge. These parallels have led some theorists to conclude that dissociative disorders may represent a form of self-hypnosis: people actively induce themselves to forget unpleasant events (Bliss, 1985, 1980; Hilgard, 1977). Dissociative amnesia, for example, may occur in people who, consciously or unconsciously, go so far as to

hypnotize themselves into forgetting horrifying experiences that have recently occurred in their lives. If the self-induced amnesia extends to all memories of a person's past and identity, that person may undergo a dissociative fugue. As in experimental hypnosis, the forgotten material is fully retrievable and is remembered completely when the fugue ends.

Self-hypnosis can also be used to explain multiple personality disorders. In fact, in a report on fourteen women diagnosed with the disorder, Eugene Bliss (1980) argued that "the crux of the syndrome of multiple personalities seems to be the patient's unrecognized abuse of self-hypnosis" (p. 1395). Each of the women in Bliss's investigation appeared to be very susceptible to hypnosis and to be capable of hypnotic amnesia. Moreover, most of them reported long histories of what could be construed as self-hypnosis, dating back to the age of 4, 5, or 6. As one of these women described her early childhood, "Now that I know what hypnosis is, I can say that I was in a trance often. There was a little place where I could sit, close my eyes and imagine, until I felt very relaxed just like hypnosis" (p. 1392). Other studies have similarly suggested great susceptibility to hypnosis in individuals with dissociative disorders (Frischholz et al., 1992) and an early history of self-hypnosis among multiple personality patients (Braun & Sachs, 1985).

On the basis of investigations such as this, a number of theorists now believe that multiple personality disorders may often begin between the ages of 4 and 6 because that is a time when children are generally very suggestible (see Figure 18–2) and excellent hypnotic subjects (Kluft, 1987; Bliss, 1985, 1980; Beahrs, 1983). They argue that some traumatized or abused children manage to escape their threatening world by self-hypnosis, mentally separating themselves from their body and its surroundings and fulfilling their wish to become some other person or persons. According to Bliss, "self-hypnosis becomes the primary mode of coping. Unpleasant experiences are henceforth forgotten or delegated to a personality by the switch into a hypnotic state."

There are two schools of thought about the nature of hypnosis, each with distinct implications for dissociative disorders. Some theorists see hypnosis as a *special process* or *trance,* an out-of-the-ordinary kind of psychological and physiological functioning (Hilgard, 1992, 1987, 1977). The special-process view holds (1) that people with dissociative disorders place themselves in internal trances during which their conscious functioning is significantly altered, (2) that their forgetting during this self-hypnosis is automatic and complete, and (3) that their willingness to develop new identities (fugue) or become different

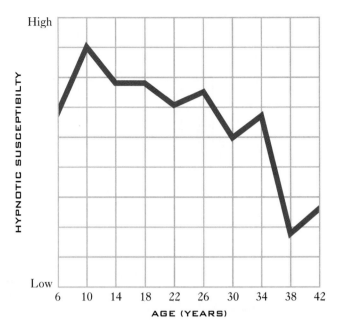

FIGURE 18-2 *Multiple personality disorder is thought to often begin between the ages of 4 and 6, when the child's hypnotic susceptibility is on the rise. A person's hypnotic susceptibility steadily increases until pre-adolescence, then generally declines with age. (Adapted from Morgan & Hilgard, 1973.)*

personalities (multiple personality disorder) is fostered by the heightened capacity for illogical thinking that occurs under hypnosis. Some special-process theorists also argue that people with high, stable levels of susceptibility to hypnosis are strong candidates for dissociative disorders (Sarbin & Coe, 1979).

Other theorists believe that hypnotic behaviors, and hypnotic amnesia in particular, can be explained by *common*, or *sociocognitive, processes* such as high motivation, attention, attributions, role enactments, and expectation (Spanos & Coe, 1992). According to these theorists, hypnotic phenomena consist simply of motivated people performing tasks that are asked of them. Because of their high motivation, heightened attention, and receptiveness to hypnosis, these individuals actively work to carry out the instructions of the hypnotist to the letter. Yet, because of their strong belief in hypnosis, they fail to recognize their own contributions and report instead that they are behaving automatically and without purposeful effort.

It may be, for example, that some hypnotized subjects manage to forget and then to recall material by *first diverting and then refocusing their attention* at critical times during testing (Spanos & Coe, 1992; Spanos, 1991, 1990, 1986). That is, hypnotized subjects may implicitly distract themselves during testing and keep their attention focused away from the test material. Several studies have compared the test performances of hypnotized subjects with those of highly motivated

nonhypnotized subjects (Spanos, 1986, 1982; Spanos & D'Eon, 1980; Spanos et al., 1980). One group of subjects were taught a word list and then hypnotized and instructed to forget it. A second group of nonhypnotized subjects were taught the same word list and then asked to recall the words while performing a distracting task (counting backward by threes). The experimenters found that the self-distracted nonhypnotized subjects displayed the same kinds of memory problems as the hypnotized subjects, and to the same extent. Other studies have found that nonhypnotized task-motivated subjects can also be induced to perform like hypnotized subjects in experiments involving, variously, pain reduction, hallucinations, and time distortion (Spanos et al., 1983, 1979).

Thus, proponents of the sociocognitive view of hypnosis might hold that people with dissociative disorders provide themselves with powerful suggestions to forget and to imagine and implicitly use social and cognitive principles to follow those suggestions. Like hypnotized subjects, these individuals are not faking.

Whether hypnosis involves special or sociocognitive processes, hypnosis research effectively demonstrates the power and potential of our normal thought processes, while rendering the idea of dissociative disorders somewhat less remarkable. At the same time, hypnosis research has raised a number of questions, and until these questions are addressed, the possible tie between hypnosis and dissociative disorders remains unsettled.

TREATMENTS FOR DISSOCIATIVE AMNESIA AND FUGUE

As we saw earlier, cases of dissociative amnesia and fugue often end spontaneously and lead to complete recovery. Sometimes, however, they linger and require treatment (Lyon, 1985). *Psychodynamic therapy* is commonly applied to both disorders (Loewenstein, 1991). Therapists guide patients to free-associate and search their unconscious in the hope of bringing the forgotten experiences back to the level of consciousness. Actually, the focus of psychodynamic therapy is very much in harmony with the treatment needs of people with dissociative disorders. After all, people with dissociative amnesia and fugue need to recover lost memories, and psychodynamic therapists generally strive to uncover memories—as well as other psychological entities—that have been repressed. Thus many theorists, including some who do not

Unlike the extreme avoidance that occurs in dissociative disorders, daydreaming and fantasizing are normal, healthy, and constructive processes. They may serve as flights of fancy or help us analyze or resolve problems.

espouse the psychodynamic perspective ordinarily, believe that psychodynamic therapy may be the most appropriate and effective approach for these disorders.

Another common treatment for dissociative amnesia and fugue, used either in conjunction with or instead of psychodynamic therapy, is *hypnotic therapy,* or *hypnotherapy.* Therapists hypnotize patients and then guide them to recall the forgotten events (MacHovek, 1981; Garver, Fuselier, & Booth, 1981; Bliss, 1980). Experiments have repeatedly indicated that hypnotic suggestion can successfully elicit forgotten memories, and experience has shown that people with dissociative disorders are usually highly susceptible to hypnosis (Frischholz et al., 1992; Putnam et al., 1986). Moreover, if, as some theorists argue, dissociative amnesia and fugue involve self-hypnosis, then hypnotherapy may be a uniquely relevant intervention for them. It has been applied both alone and in combination with other approaches.

Sometimes intravenous injections of *sodium amobarbital* (Amytal) or *sodium pentobarbital* (Pentothal) are used to help patients regain lost memories (Ruedrich et al., 1985). At the proper dosage, these barbiturates can put people into a near-sleep state during which they may recall forgotten events (Kluft, 1988; Perry & Jacobs, 1982). The nickname "truth serum" is sometimes applied to the drugs, but the key to their success is their capacity for sedating people and lowering their inhibitions.

Several problems with this biological approach have limited its use by clinicians. First, it often fails to work; a large percentage of treated clients fail to recall past events. Second, the drugs cannot be used safely for more than a few sessions, because as barbiturates they may lead to physical dependence. Finally, even when one of the drugs does help someone recall past events, the recollection may last only as long as the interview session itself. After they awaken, many people forget much of what they have said and experi-

enced under the drug's influence. For these reasons, sodium amobarbital and sodium pentobarbital tend to be used in conjunction with other treatment approaches, if they are used at all.

TREATMENTS FOR MULTIPLE PERSONALITY DISORDER

Unlike the victims of dissociative amnesia and fugue, people with multiple personality disorder rarely recover spontaneously. Therapists usually try to help people with this more chronic disorder to (1) understand and recognize the full breadth of their disorder, (2) recover the gaps in their memory, and (3) integrate their subpersonalities into one (Kluft, 1992, 1991, 1983; Dell & Eisenhower, 1990; Bliss, 1985, 1980).

RECOGNIZING THE DISORDER Once a diagnosis of multiple personality disorder is made, therapists typically try to form a therapeutic alliance both with the primary personality and with each of the subpersonalities (Kluft, 1992). The therapist may also try to establish *contracts* with the subpersonalities, to prevent abrupt termination of treatment, self-harm, suicide, or other destructive behaviors. In general, these alliances and contracts are not easily achieved, owing to the history of abuse and mistrust of others.

Multiple personality patients are typically slow to recognize the full scope and nature of their disorder. The notion of having more than one personality may seem as strange to them as it does to everyone else. Although patients "have lived in this twilight state for years, experienced amnesias, and been told by others about strange behaviors, the reality has not been confronted" (Bliss, 1980, p. 13). Thus educating patients about their disorder is a key to beginning treatment (Allen, 1993). Some therapists actually introduce the subpersonalities to one another under hypnosis, and some have patients look at videotapes of their other personalities (Ross & Gahan, 1988; Sakheim, Hess, & Chivas, 1988). The process of opening the patient's eyes to the extent of the problem is usually intensely emotional for the patient (Bliss, 1980).

Many therapists have found group therapy to be a useful psychoeducational approach (Becker & Comstock, 1992). Being with a group of people who all have multiple personality disorder helps reduce a person's feelings of isolation and fears of being "crazy" (Buchele, 1993). Family therapy is often used as an adjunct to individual therapy to help educate spouses and children about the disorder (Porter, Kelly, & Grame, 1993). In turn, family members can often provide valuable information to the therapist that the patient is unable to give because of amnesia.

RECOVERING MEMORIES To help these patients recover the missing pieces of their past, therapists use many of the approaches applied to the other dissociative disorders, including psychodynamic therapy, hypnotherapy, and sodium amobarbital (Smith, 1993; Kluft, 1991, 1985; Herzog, 1984). These techniques work slowly for multiple personality patients. After all, past events not only are actively forgotten by the primary personality but often are embedded exclusively in the minds of alternate personalities. Such "separate ownership" presents a formidable obstacle to the task of remembering. In many cases, a subpersonality assumes a "protector" role, to prevent the primary personality from suffering the pain of recollecting traumatic experiences. Some subpersonalities may continually deny experiences that the others recall (Lyon, 1992). It is not uncommon for patients to become self-destructive and violent during the memory-recovery phase of therapy, and to need restraint and even hospitalization at this stage of treatment (Kelly, 1993; Lamberti & Cummings, 1992; Young, Young, & Lehl, 1991).

INTEGRATING THE SUBPERSONALITIES The final goal of therapy is to help the person gain access to and merge the different subpersonalities. *Integration* is a continuous process that occurs throughout treatment as dissociative boundaries diminish, until the patient has achieved continuous ownership of his or her behaviors, emotions, sensations, and knowledge. *Fusion* is the final merging of two or more subpersonalities.

Many patients are reluctant to pursue this final treatment goal (Kluft, 1991, 1988). The subpersonali-

ties themselves are likely to distrust the idea and to view integration as a form of death. As one subpersonality said, "There are too many advantages to being multiple. Maybe we're being sold a bill of goods by therapists" (Hale, 1983).

Therapists have used a range of approaches to help integrate the personalities, including psychodynamic, supportive, cognitive, and drug therapies (Fichtner et al., 1990; Caddy, 1985). One woman's primary personality was given assertiveness training: as she learned to express anger in more functional and satisfying ways, her aggressive and hostile subpersonality began to disappear. Some therapists have even conducted discussions and interactions between the subpersonalities, as if they were conducting group therapy.

In Sybil's case, the progress toward full integration was slow and halting and required eleven years of therapy. Her progress can be traced in the following excerpts from different stages of her treatment (Schreiber, 1973):

1957 Integration? Far from it. As the past flooded back, there was all the more reason to regress into the other selves, defenses against the past. (p. 270)

1958 Peggy Lou's memories were becoming Sybil's. By responding to Peggy Lou's memory as if it were her own, . . . Sybil had been able to recall an incident from the childhood of the alternating self. And all at once Sybil realized that at that moment she felt not merely like Peggy Lou: she was one with her. (p. 272)

1962 "Am I going to die?" each of the selves asked Dr. Wilbur. For some of the selves integration seemed synonymous with death. The doctor's assurances that, although one with Sybil, the individual selves would not cease to be seemed at best only partly convincing. "There are many things I have to do," Vanessa told Marcia. "You see, I won't be here very long." (p. 316)

1965 Sybil's attitude toward these selves . . . had completely changed, from initial denial to hostility to acceptance—even to love. Having learned to love these parts of herself, she had in effect replaced self-derogation with self-love. This replacement was an important measure of her integration and restoration. . . . Dr. Wilbur hypnotized Sybil and called for Vicky Antoinette. "How are things going, Vicky?" the doctor asked. "What progress is there underneath?" "I'm part of Sybil now, you know," Vicky replied. "She always wanted to be like me. Now we are one." (p. 337)

Once the subpersonalities are integrated, further therapy is necessary to solidify the integrated personality and to provide the social and coping skills that will prevent subsequent dissociations. Without continuous intervention, many patients are at risk for further dissociative responses to acute stress in the future (Fink, 1992).

Some therapists report high success rates in treating multiple personality disorder (Wilbur, 1984; Kluft, 1984; Allison, 1978), but others find that most patients continue to resist full and final integration. A few therapists have in fact questioned the need for full integration, arguing that patients may be able to function with reasonable effectiveness as long as they rid themselves of their more disturbed subpersonalities (Hale, 1983).

The relatively small number of reported multiple personality cases has prevented researchers from assessing and comparing the effectiveness of the various treatment approaches. As the number of case reports continues to grow, it may soon be possible to conduct statistical evaluations. Meanwhile, individual case reports remain the primary source of information about treatment methods and their outcomes.

■ ORGANIC ■ DISORDERS AFFECTING MEMORY AND IDENTITY

Alterations in memory and identity can also have clearly organic causes, including brain injury, medical conditions, and substance misuse. These organic disorders fall into two categories—*amnestic disorders,* which primarily affect memory, and *dementias,* which affect both memory and other cognitive skills.

Much of what is known about the anatomical and chemical bases of memory and identity has emerged through studies of humans who have suffered injuries to specific locations in the brain. Important information about memory has also been gained through experiments in which lesions are produced in animals' brains and then their ability to learn new information is studied. Additionally, careful study of actual nerve cells in the brain has begun to reveal the specific changes that occur as memories are formed.

MEMORY SYSTEMS

In essence, there are two human memory systems, and they work together to help us learn and recall. *Short-term memory,* or *working memory,* collects new information and then does the initial cognitive work

of evaluating, processing, and either storing or discarding it. *Long-term memory* is the repository of all the information that we have stored over the years— information that first made its way through the short-term memory system. When short-term information becomes part of our long-term memory, it is said to have been *encoded.* Remembering such information involves *retrieval,* conceptualized as going into one's long-term memory to bring it out.

Information in long-term memory can be classified as either procedural or declarative. *Procedural memories* are learned physical or cognitive skills we perform without needing to think about them, such as cutting with scissors or knowing how to solve a math problem. *Declarative memory* consists of information that is directly accessible to consciousness, such as names, dates, and other facts that have been learned. Declarative memory is far more disrupted than procedural memory in most organic disorders.

THE ANATOMY OF MEMORY

In the past 100 years, advances in the study of the brain have shown that specific structures correspond directly to specific functions (Scoville & Milner, 1957). Visual information, for example, is known to be processed in a well-defined region of the cerebral cortex. Memory functions, however—and memories themselves—are far more difficult to localize. Researchers have searched for the specific place in the brain where the *content* of memory is stored, but their work has led to the conclusion that no such well-defined storehouse exists. What has emerged is the view that memory is a process rather than a place, involving the activity of cells in many parts of the brain; when the memory process is invoked, a memory is activated and comes forth.

Nevertheless, the study of organic memory disorders has led researchers to identify brain structures that appear to mediate short-term and long-term memory processes. Two areas that have been implicated in the encoding and retrieving of memories are the *temporal lobes* (and nearby structures) and the *diencephalon.*

Embedded under the *temporal lobes,* major regions in the cortex of each hemisphere of the brain, are the *hippocampus* and *amygdala,* key parts of the brain's limbic system (see Figure 18–3). Many cases of organic memory loss involve lesions or trauma to these structures, and these cases seem to be particularly

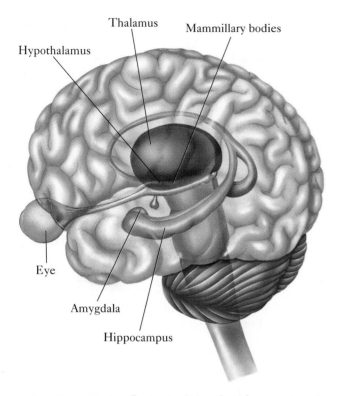

Thalamus

Mammillary bodies

Hypothalamus

Eye

Amygdala

Hippocampus

FIGURE 18-3 *Brain structures that play a major role in memory are the hippocampus, amygdala, mammillary bodies, thalamus, and hypothalamus. Dysfunctioning by these structures may produce a memory disorder. (Adapted from Bloom et al., 1988, p. 247.)*

characterized by severe difficulty in receiving new information and storing it.

The *diencephalon* also contains a number of structures, the most important for memory being the ***mammillary bodies, thalamus,*** and ***hypothalamus.*** Lesions to these structures generally result in problems with encoding of new information.

The diencephalon actually contains numerous connections to the hippocampus and amygdala. For example, a structure known as the *fornix* connects the hippocampus with the mammillary bodies of the diencephalon, and lesions in it have significant effects on memory, suggesting the existence of a circuit that newly learned information follows—and that disruption of this circuit may be the cause of the memory disorder. There is also evidence, however, that memory processes are redundant; if one pathway is disrupted, alternate routes may be available. The multiple pathways by which new information may be processed make it even more difficult to identify the exact role played by specific brain structures (Amaral, 1987).

One fact that has intrigued researchers is that lesions to memory-related brain structures appear to affect declarative knowledge (recall of conscious information) far more than procedural knowledge (recall of

automatic-type skills). One explanation is that the temporal lobes and diencephalon, which have evolved more recently than other structures of the brain, are more closely related to the higher cognitive functions unique to humans. Automatic, unconscious processes, including those that execute motor tasks, may be controlled by older brain structures. As a result, when the temporal lobes (and the structures embedded under them) and the diencephalon are injured, procedural knowledge is less likely to be disrupted.

THE BIOCHEMISTRY OF MEMORY

Beyond identifying and understanding the structures within the brain that mediate memory processes, researchers would like to understand how the cells of the brain create and store memories. Although no one has yet found the "engram"—the exact physical change in a cell that accounts for a memory—many new discoveries have been made about the physiological bases of learning and memory.

One of the most exciting of these findings is the role that *long-term potentiation (LTP)* may play in memory formation (Bliss & Gardner, 1973). Careful studies have shown that repeated electrical stimulation of nerve cells in the brain can lead to a significant increase in the likelihood that the cell will respond—and respond strongly—to future stimulation. This effect can last quite a long time (hence the name long-term potentiation) and may be a key mechanism in the formation of memories. As when many sleds are ridden down a snowy slope, creating a groove that later sledders easily find, LTP may serve to create a groove that corresponds to the process of making a memory, so that one can easily retrieve that memory later by following the same path.

Long-term potentiation does not in itself explain memory formation at the cellular level. Complicated chemical processes must also occur, and memory researchers have identified biochemical changes within cells that may help the formation of memories. Recent studies have shown that a specific type of receptor, the *N-methyl-D-aspartate (NMDA)* receptor, is extremely active in long-term potentiation: blocking the activity of these receptors has been shown to block LTP (Baraban, 1993). *Calcium* has also been strongly implicated as a critical factor in the phenomenon of LTP. Calcium participates in the synthesis of protein molecules, and the creation of certain proteins is believed to play a role in long-term memory. Finally, there is strong evidence that the actual physical characteristics of nerve cells change when memories are created: the ***cholinergic hypothesis*** suggests that an important part of memory formation is an increase in the sensitivity of certain nerve cells to the neurotransmitter *acetylcholine*. This change in sensitivity would require actual change in the nature of the receptors on the nerve cells.

All these changes suggest that memory occurs as a result of real and observable physical changes in nerve cells. The human brain is composed of tens of billions of neurons—more than enough to support the theory that specific structures within the brain are responsible for creating and storing memories, and that they do so by changing the chemistry and physiology of neurons throughout the brain.

With this overview of the systems, anatomy, and biochemistry of memory, we turn to the organic disorders that affect memory and identity—the *amnestic disorders* and *dementias*.

AMNESTIC DISORDERS

Although, as we noted earlier, dissociative amnesia can take any of several forms, it most often affects a person's ability to recall autobiographical information from the past. This is generally known as ***retrograde amnesia***—a lack of memory of events that occurred before the event that caused the amnesia. People who suffer from ***amnestic disorders,*** organic disorders in which memory impairment is the primary symptom, *may* also suffer from retrograde amnesia, depending on the particular disorder. In such cases, the memory problem may occur either because the pathways to long-term memory are not functioning or because the area of the brain where the memories are stored is no longer intact. In addition, people with amnestic disorders *always* exhibit ***anterograde amnesia,*** characterized by inability to learn and recall new information. In severe forms of anterograde amnesia, people newly met are almost immediately forgotten, and problems solved one day must be tackled again the next. Patients may not remember any of the changes that have taken place since the time of their organic trauma. A middle-aged patient, for example, may continue to believe that Richard Nixon is president in 1994, more than twenty years after suffering his or her trauma. The sufferer of anterograde amnesia may retain all other cognitive skills, including verbal skills and problem-solving abilities. The IQ is not changed. It is as though information from short-term memory, the psychological "work space" that holds informa-

tion for a few minutes or so, can no longer cross over into long-term memory.

The anterograde amnesias observed in amnestic disorders are generally the result of a dysfunction of or disconnection between the regions of the brain responsible for short-term memory and long-term memory. The most firmly established finding is that these anterograde amnesias are closely associated with the brain's temporal lobes (including the hippocampus and amygdala) and diencephalon (particularly the hypothalamus and thalamus).

KORSAKOFF'S SYNDROME (ALCOHOL-INDUCED PERSISTING AMNESTIC DISORDER) As we observed in Chapter 13, approximately 5 percent of people with chronic alcoholism develop the severe amnestic disorder known as Korsakoff's syndrome. Excessive drinking, combined with a lack of proper diet, lead to a deficiency of the vitamin *thiamine*. The effect on portions of the diencephalon are dramatic. Patients in the early stages of Korsakoff's syndrome, called ***Wernicke's encephalopathy*** are extremely confused, their condition resembling the dementias described in the next section. Treated with large doses of thiamine, the syndrome subsides (APA, 1994); untreated, it progresses to irreparable amnesia of a very specific type. Korsakoff's patients experience severe anterograde amnesia: they are very poor at learning and recalling new facts and information, although their general knowledge and intelligence remains intact (Butters & Cermak, 1980). Furthermore, the learning deficit in Korsakoff's patients applies primarily to declarative knowledge; they are still able to incorporate new procedural knowledge, such as the way to solve a particular kind of puzzle, and they also maintain their language skills (Verfaellie et al., 1990). This may explain why Korsakoff's patients often ***confabulate***—using their general intellectual skills and language skills, they create elaborate stories and lies to compensate for the memories they keep losing. The effect on personality can also be profound. Before the onset of Korsakoff's syndrome, chronic drinkers may be aggressive, boisterous people; after the disorder has progressed, they often become more passive and unimposing.

In addition to profound anterograde amnesia, Korsakoff's patients experience some retrograde amnesia. They have particular difficulty remembering events from the years immediately preceding the onset of the syndrome, as opposed to events further back in the past (Albert et al., 1979). This problem may in fact be due to their heavy drinking during those recent years (which would have caused encoding problems), and not to retrieval problems after onset of the disorder.

BRAIN SURGERY AND HEAD TRAUMA

Both head injuries and brain surgery are capable of causing amnestic disorders. Either may destroy memory-related brain structures or sever connections between memory-related areas of the brain.

Second only to the popularity of emotional trauma as a cause of amnesia in television shows and movies, bumps on the head are portrayed as a quick and easy way to lose one's memory. In fact, *mild* head trauma, such as a concussion that does not result in coma or a period of unconsciousness, usually leaves a person with only minimal memory dysfunction, which disappears within days or at most months (Levin et al., 1987; McLean et al., 1983). Almost half of the cases of *severe* head trauma, in contrast, do result in permanent memory and learning problems, both anterograde and retrograde problems, partly the results of damage to the temporal lobes and the structures embedded under them. As memory returns after a head trauma, the person begins to recall facts about people and places. The ability to put events in the context of time—to understand *when* they happened—returns last (Cummings, 1993).

Surgical lesions create much more specific memory problems. The most famous case of memory loss as a result of brain surgery belongs to H.M. (a man whose identity has been more or less protected for decades, despite his notoriety in the memory literature). H.M. suffered from severe epilepsy, a disorder that creates seizures in the temporal lobes. To alleviate his symptoms, doctors removed parts of his temporal lobes, along with the amygdala and hippocampus (Milner, 1971). At that time their role in the formation of memories was not known. H.M. experienced severe anterograde amnesia for the rest of his life, although he was able to learn some types of procedural information, such as how to trace figures while looking at them in a mirror (a standard exercise used to test a person's ability to acquire a new skill) (Corkin, 1968; see Figure 18–4).

Today temporal lobe surgery is generally restricted to *either* the right or left side of the brain. Removal or disconnection of the right temporal lobe impairs nonverbal, spacial memory skills, such as recall for geometric shapes (Tulving et al., 1988). Removal or disconnection of the left temporal lobe creates verbal, language-related dysfunctions (Ivnik et al., 1987). General intellectual function remains as it was before the surgery.

(A)

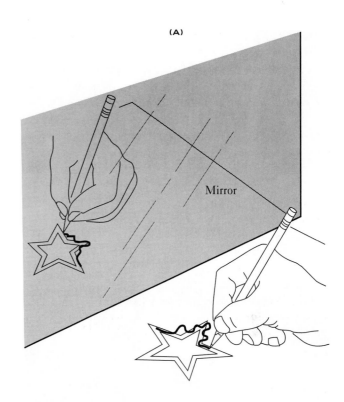

(B)

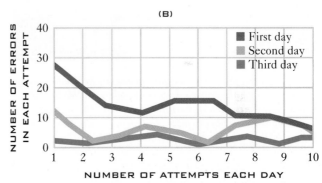

FIGURE 18–4 *The Mirror Tracing Task. (a) All subjects initially have difficulty tracing a line between two figures while observing their hand in a mirror (Kolb & Whishaw, 1990). (b) After repeated practices, however, they usually become quite proficient at this task, as did H.M., the famous subject whose amygdala and hippocampus were surgically removed, leaving him with severe anterograde amnesia (Milner et al., 1968).*

OTHER AMNESTIC DISORDERS Other forms of trauma can also cause lesions in memory-related regions of the brain. *Vascular disease*, which affects the flow of blood to the brain, can lead to classic forms of amnesia (Gorelick et al., 1988). Similarly, *heart attacks*, which interrupt the flow of oxygen to the brain, can create severe disturbances of both recall and recognition (Volpe & Hirst, 1983). *Infectious diseases* that affect the brain have also been found to affect the temporal lobes and other areas of the brain that influence memory. Specifically, *herpes encephalitis* has

Because of their short-term memory problems, people with advanced cases of Alzheimer's disease are often unable to complete simple tasks such as painting a picture. In addition, their long-term memory deficits may prevent them from recognizing even close relatives or friends.

been associated with moderate amnesia, which may linger even after treatment (Gordon et al., 1990).

DEMENTIAS

Dementias are syndromes associated with significant loss in memory and therefore are sometimes difficult to distinguish from the amnestic disorders; the trademark of dementias, however, is that at least one other cognitive function is also impaired (APA, 1994; Albert & Lafleche, 1991). Clinicians must look at more than one indicator in order to make a diagnosis, and in many cases an accurate diagnosis may not be possible until the disease has progressed significantly. Dementias, which are experienced by 3 percent of the adult population in any given year (APA, 1994), may impair what we know, and further distort our ability to know who we are.

Dementias may be categorized along any number of dimensions. One of the most useful distinctions is that between *cortical* and *subcortical dementias;* that is, dementias arising in the cortex and those that arise elsewhere in the brain.

CORTICAL DEMENTIAS In addition to memory impairment, some of the prominent problems that characterize the cortical dementias are *aphasia,* difficulty in finding speaking words; personality changes such as inappropriate behavior, impulsiveness, and lack of foresight; and progressive deterioration. *Alzheimer's disease,* the most common cortical dementia, afflicts 2 to 4 percent of the elderly population in the United States, up to 4 million people (APA, 1994). The prevalence of Alzheimer's disease doubles every five years in people over 60 (Cummings, 1993). A more complete discussion of the causes and treatments of this disease appears in Chapter 20, but we will consider many of the important memory and identity issues here.

Alzheimer's disease is often difficult to distinguish from alcoholic Korsakoff's syndrome in older patients because its most common initial symptom is significant anterograde amnesia (Albert & Moss, 1984). It is thus important that a clinician take a full history of the patient and explore the possibility of alcohol abuse (Delis, 1993).

People with Alzheimer's disease have difficulty on tests requiring immediate recall of new information (APA, 1994; Morris & Baddeley, 1988). Memory for events from their past is also impaired; in mild cases memories from youth may be more easily recalled than more recent events (Beatty et al., 1988), but in more advanced cases of Alzheimer's disease, patients lose virtually all knowledge of the past. Eventually they cannot recognize the faces of even close relatives. Once again, procedural memory frequently remains intact for some time, so that patients with fairly advanced Alzheimer's disease can still learn to perform new motor tasks (Bondi & Kaszniak, 1991). Sadly, however, though specific symptoms vary from one individual to another, the final result is generally the same. The patients' cognitive abilities are so severely impaired that their sense of identity is destroyed and they are fully dependent on other people.

Alzheimer's disease has become a focus of public and scientific awareness for several reasons. The most compelling is that it is a disabling disease that affects a dramatic percentage of elderly people. The cost to society in both emotional trauma and health care is astronomical. A second reason is the significant advances that have already been made in the search for the causes of the disease. As we shall observe in

Chapter 20, researchers have narrowed the location of the gene that is believed to be responsible for Alzheimer's disease at the same time that they have identified specific brain chemicals and neural processes that contribute to the symptoms. If theories on the causes of the disease conflict, perhaps it is because Alzheimer's has more than one kind of precipitating factor.

Other cortical dementias include Pick's disease and Creutzfeldt-Jakob disease. *Pick's disease,* a degenerative disease of the brain that particularly affects the frontal and temporal lobes, usually strikes people between the ages of 50 and 60 years (APA, 1994). *Creutzfeldt-Jakob disease,* a rapidly progressing pattern of dementia caused by a virus, typically occurs between 40 and 60 years of age (APA, 1994).

SUBCORTICAL DEMENTIAS Disorders that affect subcortical brain structures create a distinctive set of memory and identity problems. The memory impairment is primarily the inability to retrieve information from long-term storage, although learning new information may also be a major problem (Cummings & Benson, 1984). The speech disorder aphasia, common in the cortical dementias, is not present in the subcortical dementias, but these disorders do often create debilitating personality changes.

Huntington's disease, an inherited progressive degenerative disease of cognition, emotion, and movement, is usually diagnosed in the victim's late 30s or early 40s, but often begins much earlier (APA, 1994). It has a dramatic effect on personality, and brings on depression, instability, and anxiety. Unlike people in the early stages of Alzheimer's disease, Huntington's patients show severe retrograde amnesia early on, and suffer from impairments in learning procedural skills, such as new motor tasks (Butters et al., 1990). Learning new information is difficult for them, but they are better able to remember lists of words when the words are related (Wilson et al., 1987)—further evidence that this disorder affects a different set of brain structures than the ones affected in cortical dementias. Children of people with Huntington's disease have a 50 percent chance of developing it.

Parkinson's disease, a slowly progressive neurological condition marked by tremors, rigidity, and unsteadiness, causes dementia in 20 to 60 percent of cases, particularly among older people or those with advanced cases (APA, 1994). The memory deficits in people suffering from this disease are similar to those experienced in Huntington's disease, but their language impairments differ. Parkinson's patients have great difficulty learning new information, such as lists of words, but are very good at knowing how many times a word appeared on a list—two very different types of memory tasks (Weingartner et al., 1984). This finding, along with mixed performance on other language-based memory tests, suggests that Parkinson's patients primarily have problems retrieving rather than encoding information. At the same time, they have significant difficulty learning procedural skills, such as a new motor task (Harrington et al., 1990). As we noted in Chapter 16 (pp. 561–562), Parkinson's disease is closely tied to low levels of the neurotransmitter dopamine in the brain.

Other subcortical dementias are far less common than Huntington's and Parkinson's diseases. *Supranuclear palsy* is a progressive degenerative disease that leaves sufferers with significantly altered personality and impaired memory. Similarly, *Wilson's disease* and *multiple sclerosis* may cause dementias that fit the profile of subcortical dementias.

OTHER DEMENTIAS A variety of other dementias have also been identified. They include dementias cause by viral and bacterial infectious disorders such as HIV and AIDs, meningitis, and advanced syphilis; by epilepsy; by vascular disorders; and by substances such as abused drugs or toxins (mercury, lead, carbon monoxide).

TREATMENTS OF AMNESTIC DISORDERS AND DEMENTIAS

Treating amnestic disorders and dementias is a frustrating and difficult challenge (see Box 18–3). Because these disorders affect a variety of brain structures and involve many neurotransmitters and neurochemical processes, no single approach or set of approaches is effective in all cases. The most important step in treating people with these disorders is to identify as clearly as possible the type and cause of the disease. Clinicians begin by taking a complete history of the patient; knowing that there is alcohol abuse or a family history of Alzheimer's disease helps narrow the diagnosis. Second, clinicians employ extensive neuropsychological testing (see pp. 115–117) to identify the patient's specific cognitive impairments. Finally, they employ brain imaging techniques (see pp. 118–119) to identify any clear,

BOX 18-3

"YOU ARE THE MUSIC, WHILE THE MUSIC LASTS"

Clayton S. Collins

(Excerpted by permission from Profiles, *the magazine of Continental Airlines, February, 1994.)*

Oliver Sacks danced to the Dead. For three solid hours. At 60. And with "two broken knees."

The Oxford-educated neurologist who likes to say, with an impish grin, that he doesn't like any music after Mozart's *Magic Flute*, wasn't particularly taken by the Grateful Dead concert in Friedrich Nietzche's *mnemonic* sense, he explains (as only he would), "but in a tonic and dynamic sense they were quite overwhelming. And though I had effusions for a month after, it was worth it."

The power of music—not just to get an aging physician with classical tastes up and rocking, but also to "bring back" individuals rendered motionless and mute by neurological damage and disorders—is what's driving Sacks these days. The . . . best-selling author *(Migraine, A Leg to Stand On, The Man Who Mistook His Wife for a Hat, Seeing Voices* and *Awakenings—* which was made into a 1990 film starring Robin Williams) is working on another case-study book, one that deals in part with the role of music as a stimulus to minds that have thrown up stiff sensory barriers, leaving thousands of victims of stroke, tumors, Parkinson's disease, Tourette's syndrome, Alzheimer's and a wide range

Over the years, the innovative neurologist Oliver Sacks has used treatment techniques that range from the medication L-Dopa to the music of the Grateful Dead.

of less-publicized ailments alone, debilitated and disoriented.

"One sees how robust music is neurologically," Sacks says. "You can lose all sorts of particular powers but you don't tend to lose music and identity." His conviction regarding the role of music in helping the neurologically afflicted to become mentally "reorga-

nized" runs deep: "Whenever I get out a book on neurology or psychology, the first thing I look up in the index is music," he says. "And if it's not there, I close the book." . . .

Speaking in his distinctive stammer before a gathering of 1,400 music therapists in Toronto, Sacks seems disjointed, his large rumpled form hunched over the podium, squinting in the glare as he fishes for a scrap of paper bearing a relevant quote from a medical text or a favorite philosopher. He drops such provocative phrasings as "kinetic stutter" (in describing Parkinsonism), then recalls all in one breath that the poet Novalis said, "Every disease is a musical disorder. Every cure is a musical solution," basking bemusedly in the appreciative gasps before admitting, "I've never known exactly what it means." . . .

Much of what he has encountered, particularly in working with patients at Beth Abraham Hospital, Bronx, N.Y., . . . relates to music.

"One saw patients who couldn't take a single step, who couldn't walk, but who could dance," he says. "There were patients who couldn't speak, but who could sing. The power of music in these patients was instantaneous . . . from a frozen Parkinsonian state to a freely flowing, moving, speaking state."

Sacks remembers a woman with Parkinson's who would sit perfectly

obvious cause of the disorder, such as a gross brain lesion.

Clinicians and researchers have yet to find reliable, effective treatments for amnestic disorders and dementias and currently rely on an array of drug therapies and behavioral interventions. Fortunately, recent research on the genetic, biochemical, and

anatomical causes of such disorders has provided hope that these diseases may be either treated or prevented in the years to come. Because dementias are the more common disorders of memory and identity, most of the research in this area has been directed at these diseases. As we shall see in Chapter 20, certain drugs and other therapies are becoming

still until "activated" by the music of Chopin, which she loved and knew by heart. She didn't have to hear a tune played. "It was sometimes sufficient to give her an opus number," Sacks says. "You would just say 'Opus 49,' and the F-minor 'Fantasy' would start playing in her mind. And she could move."

Music is certainly cultural, acknowledges the doctor, but it is basically biological. "One listens to music with one's muscles," he says, quoting Nietzsche again. "The 'tonic' [the key] is mostly brain-stem, an arousal response." The "dynamic," how loud or forcefully the music is played, registers in the basal ganglia. And the "mnemonic" aspect of songs speaks to the unique memories of individuals: from tribal chant to blare of bagpipes to Bizet. The cliché about music's universality, he says, has merit.

"Deeply demented people respond to music, babies respond to music, fetuses *probably* respond to music. Various animals respond to music," Sacks says. "There is something about the animal nervous system . . . which seems to respond to music all the way down.

"I don't know how it is with invertebrates. I think it's a desperately needed experiment," the grin widens, "to see how squids and cuttlefish respond." . . .

"I think the notion of music as being a prosthesis in a way, for neurological dysfunctions, is very fundamental," Sacks says, citing the case of a patient with damage to the frontal lobes of his brain.

"When he sings, one almost has the strange feeling that [music] has given him his frontal lobes back, given him back, temporally, some function that has been lost on an organic basis," Sacks says, adding a quote from T.S. Eliot: "You are the music, while the music lasts."

The effects of music therapy may not always last. Sacks will take what he can get. "To organize a disorganized person for a minute is miraculous. And for half an hour, more so." . . .

The key, says Sacks, is for patients to "learn to be well" again. Music can restore to them, he says, the identity that predates the illness. "There's a health to music, a life to music." . . .

For Sacks, who's been affiliated with a half-dozen neurological institutes and written dozens of seminal papers, medicine needs to be demonstrable, firmly grounded in physiology. Music's been healing for thousands of years, Sacks says. "It's just being looked at now more systematically and with these special populations."

So if the Grateful Dead moved Sacks to dance, it had been in the name of research. Seeking a clinical application, Sacks returned to Beth Abraham the next day and "kidnapped" one of his patients. "Greg" was an amnesiac with a brain tumor and no coherent memories of life since about 1969—but an encyclopedic memory of the years that came before, and a real love of Grateful Dead tunes.

Sacks took Greg to that night's performance. "In the first half of the concert they were doing early music, and Greg was enchanted by everything," Sacks recalls. "I mean, he was not an amnesiac. He was completely oriented and organized and with it." Between sets Sacks went backstage and introduced Greg to band member Micky Hart, who was impressed with Greg's knowledge of the group but quite surprised when Greg asked after Pigpen. When told the former band member had died 20 years before, "Greg was very upset," Sacks recalls. "And then 30 seconds later he asked 'How's Pigpen?'"

During the second half, the band played its newer songs. And Greg's world began to fall apart. "He was bewildered and enthralled and frightened. Because the music for him— and this is an extremely musical man, who understands the idiom of the Grateful Dead—was both familiar and unfamiliar. . . . He said 'This is like the music of the future.'"

Sacks tried to keep the new memories fresh. But the next day, Greg had no memory of the concert. It seemed as if all had been lost. "But—and this is strange—when one played some of the new music, which he had heard for the first time at the concert, he could sing along with it and remember it."

It is an encouraging development. . . . Children have been found to learn quickly lessons that are embedded in song. Sacks, the one-time quiet researcher, is invigorated by the possibilities. He wonders whether music could carry such information, to give his patient back a missing part of his life. To give Greg "some sense of what's been happening in the last 20 years, where he has no autobiography of his own."

That would have Sacks dancing in the aisles.

---

available for treatment of the best known and most common dementias, particularly Alzheimer's disease.

In developing drugs to combat the various dementias, researchers have focused on the neurotransmitters and neurologic pathways that seem to underlie the diseases (Martin & Welsh, 1993). Their basic approach is either to inhibit or to increase the action of a set of neurochemicals that affect learning and memory. Researchers are trying to develop chemicals that will stimulate the formation of new neural pathways when others have been destroyed (Hagg et al., 1990) and drugs that will enhance the functions of existing neurotransmitters. For the most part, progress was slow until recent advances were made in the study of Alzheimer's disease. This work has been important for reasons beyond the treatment of Alzheimer's disease; a breakthrough in the treatment of one type of dementia is likely to lay the groundwork for similar advances in others.

As we shall see in Chapter 20, behavioral interventions for dementias are as yet of limited value, but some progress has been made in treating people with amnestic disorders whose amnesia is caused by head injury. These patients have successfully been taught special methods for remembering new information; in some cases the teachers have been computers (Schacter et al., 1990). Overall, however, behavioral interventions are likely to remain an adjunct to the drug therapies until dementias and amnestic disorders are better understood.

Rather than being discouraged by the lack of effective treatments for organic disorders of memory and identity, researchers are anticipating a period of advances in the understanding, treatment, and prevention of the most common and disabling disorders. The complexity of brain structures, the similarity of many disorders, and the confusion of biochemical processes underlying cognition can be overwhelming, but this decade is expected to see significant breakthroughs.

THE STATE OF THE FIELD

DISORDERS OF MEMORY AND IDENTITY

❧

Periodically a phenomenon will capture the public's interest but be scoffed at by scientists. The chronic fatigue syndrome, for example, received little respect or attention from medical scientists until recent years. They believed that reports of this disabling pattern of weakness either were exaggerated or could be explained by reference to a broader medical syndrome. The growing number of carefully reported cases, however, eventually convinced most scientists that this is indeed a serious and distinct medical ailment, and serious efforts to investigate and treat it have increased.

In the field of abnormal psychology, dissociative disorders have suffered a similar fate. Until lately, investigations into dissociative amnesia and fugue were limited and multiple personality disorder failed to stir the interest of empirical researchers. This skepticism and lack of interest on the part of scientists has changed greatly during the past decade. The growing number of reported cases of dissociative disorders, particularly of multiple personality disorder, has increasingly convinced researchers that the patterns do in fact exist and often lead to significant dysfunctioning.

The last ten years have seen a veritable explosion of research designed to help clinicians recognize, understand, and treat the dissociative disorders. Although this research has yet to lead to comprehensive insights or highly effective treatments, it has already established that the disorders are more common than anyone previously believed and may in fact be rooted in processes, such as state-dependent learning and self-hypnosis, that are well known to clinical scientists from other contexts. This new wave of research enthusiasm will probably lead to significant growth in our understanding and treatment of these disorders in the coming years.

Some clinicians now worry that the interest and belief in dissociative disorders is swinging too far in the other direction (Kelley & Kodman, 1987). They believe, for example, that at least some of the legal defenses based on multiple personality disorder are contrived or inaccurate and that many current diagnoses of dissociative disorder have more to do with the increasing popularity of the disorders than with a careful assessment of symptoms. Such possibilities serve to underscore even further the importance of continued investigations into all aspects of these disorders.

Less controversial but equally intriguing are the disorders of memory and identity that have organic causes. The enormous complexity of the brain and its functions makes it extremely difficult to understand, diagnose, or treat the range of amnestic disorders and dementias that have been identified. However, exciting new research on the genetic and biochemical factors that affect these disorders has captured the public's attention.

A common thread in the study of the dissociative disorders and the organic disorders of memory and identity is the inherent fascination of issues of memory and identity. These features of human functioning are so central to each person's continuing sense of self that research in this realm is of fundamental importance to every person's well-being.

Summary

■ **Memory plays a central role** in personality by linking us to the past, present, and future and providing us with a sense of identity. People with *dissociative disorders* experience a significant alteration in their memory or identity without a clear physical cause. The three most prominent dissociative disorders are dissociative amnesia, dissociative fugue, and dissociative identity disorder (multiple personality disorder). A fourth dissociative disorder is depersonalization disorder.

■ **People with** *dissociative amnesia* are suddenly unable to recall important personal information or past events in their lives. There are four kinds of dissociative amnesia: localized, selective, generalized, and continuous. People with *dissociative fugue* not only lose their memory of their personal identity but flee to a different location and establish a new identity. *Multiple personality disorder* is a rare, dramatic disorder in which a person displays two or more distinct subpersonalities. A *primary personality* appears more often than the others, but transitions to the other subpersonalities may occur frequently and suddenly. Most people with multiple personality disorder have been abused as children. The subpersonalities often have complex relationships with one another and usually differ from one another in *personality characteristics, vital statistics, abilities and preferences,* and even *physiological responses.* The number of people diagnosed with multiple personality disorder has increased in the past two decades, perhaps primarily because it has come to be more widely recognized as a legitimate disorder.

■ **Some theorists** suggest that dissociative disorders may be tied to the phenomenon of *state-dependent learning;* that is, information is best recalled when a person experiences the same arousal level or the same state of mind as that experienced when the information was originally learned. This link may be particularly strong and rigid in people with dissociative disorders, and entire sets of memories, even personalities, may be elicited when the person reenters a particular mood or level of arousal.

Self-hypnosis has also emerged as a promising explanation for dissociative disorders. Hypnosis has been used to induce *hypnotic amnesia,* which bears a striking resemblance to the memory losses seen in dissociative disorders. On the basis of several studies, a number of theorists now believe that multiple personality disorders may often begin around the age of 4 to 6, when children are generally very susceptible to hypnosis. After some trauma or abuse, the child mentally separates from his or her body through self-hypnosis.

Dissociative amnesia and fugue often end spontaneously, but when they do not, *psychodynamic therapy* is commonly used to help the patients recover their lost memories. Therapists may also *hypnotize* patients and then guide them to recall the forgotten events. In a few cases, intravenous injections of *sodium amobarbital* or *sodium pentobarbital* help patients regain lost memories. Recovery from a multiple personality disorder is rarely spontaneous. Therapists usually try to help people to recognize the full scope and nature of their disorder, recover the gaps in their memories, and integrate their subpersonalities into one.

■ **Organic disorders** which cause alterations in memory and identity fall into two categories—*amnestic disorders,* which primarily affect memory, and *dementias,* which affect both memory and other cognitive functions. These disorders may be characterized by problems in **short-term memory, long-term memory,** or both. Often they involve abnormalities in key brain structures such as the *temporal lobes* (including the *hippocampus* and *amygdala* embedded under them) and the *diencephalon* (including the *mammillary bodies, thalamus,* and *hypothalamus*). Amnestic disorders include *Korsakoff's syndrome* and disorders caused by brain surgery and head trauma. Dementias include *Alzheimer's disease, Huntington's disease,* and *Parkinson's disease.* Drug therapies dominate the treatment picture for these disorders, particularly for the dementias, and are beginning to show promise.

Topic Overview

CHAPTER 19

PROBLEMS OF CHILDHOOD AND ADOLESCENCE

■

MANY PSYCHOLOGICAL DISORDERS have their onset during childhood or early adolescence. Some seem to be caused in part by the pressures that are a natural part of early life, others by unique traumatic experiences, and still others by biological abnormalities. Some of the disorders subside without treatment or can be corrected during childhood, some seem to evolve into distinctly adult psychological problems, and some continue virtually unchanged throughout the life span.

MANY THEORISTS THINK OF LIFE as a series of stages through which people pass on the way from birth to death. The stages that they propose are typically traversed in fixed order, although the rate and nature of the passage may vary from person to person. The stages give clinicians a useful picture of normal development and help them detect deviations from the norm.

IN CHAPTER 2 WE DISCUSSED Freud's theory of personality development and his proposal that each child passes through psychosexual stages—the oral, anal, phallic, latency, and genital stages. Although Freud also talked about stages of adulthood, he offered little insight into their nature. A more comprehensive developmental theory has been provided by Erik Erikson (1963), the ego psychologist whom we discussed in Chapter 2 (see p. 43).

■ NORMAL ■ STAGES OF DEVELOPMENT

Erikson divided life into eight stages, each marked by a particular developmental crisis. To Erikson a "crisis" is not a cataclysmic event but rather a turning point, a time when heightened potential coincides with heightened vulnerability. The passage from stage to stage can be marked by enhanced functioning, if the transition is made successfully, or by maladjustment, if the transition is incomplete or unsuccessful. Erikson suggested that people experience new drives and needs at each stage, new kinds of social interactions, and new reactions from society. The way one experiences each stage is directly related to the way one has resolved earlier crises. Failure to master the developmental tasks of one stage produces a pattern of pathology in the next.

Stage 1: Crisis of Trust vs. Mistrust

The psychosocial crisis that occurs during the first year of life is the infant's need to develop a sense of trust. The developing infant is ready to take in the world through its senses, but he or she needs help to do so. If all goes well, the infant is nurtured, provided for, and satisfied by the parents, and so develops a general sense of trust and hope. If all does not go well, however, either because gratification is repeatedly and excessively delayed or because the parents fail to provide the needed satisfaction, the child may suffer a defect in basic trust, which may lead to a childhood disorder or set the stage for a disorder later in life.

Stage 2: Crisis of Autonomy vs. Shame and Doubt

In the second year of life, children experience rapid growth in motor activity, speech, sensory discrimination, and other areas of functioning. This growth serves the child's need for increased *autonomy,* or sense of independence and self-control. According to Erikson, there is a tension in both child and parent during this stage, as the parent's wish to protect the child clashes with the child's efforts to become autonomous. If parents resist the demands for autonomy too strongly or harshly by, for example, repeatedly belittling the child when he or she fails at new tasks, they may produce shame or doubt in the child. Children who successfully meet the challenges of this stage develop willpower and a balance between the exercise of free will and self-restraint. Those who

are overwhelmed by parental restraints, however, may come to display compulsive overcompliance or impulsive defiance; in other words, overcontrolled or undercontrolled behavior.

Stage 3: Crisis of Initiative vs. Guilt

In the third or fourth year, children begin to understand how parents expect them to behave, and role playing begins. They start to associate with peers, enter into games and other forms of cooperative play, and develop a sense of initiative. Sex roles also emerge. During this stage, children learn that unbounded initiative is not acceptable but must often be inhibited or repressed. As they play various roles in the context of the family and develop a sense of what is allowed and what is not, they develop a conscience and an ability to feel guilt. Children who move through this stage successfully ultimately arrive at a state of equilibrium in which their sense of initiative, the courage to pursue tangible goals, is guided by an appropriate degree of conscience. Those whose initiative is stifled too much may be paralyzed by guilt.

Stage 4: Crisis of Industry vs. Inferiority

Erikson's fourth stage starts with the child's entrance into school and lasts until adolescence. During this stage, children discover the importance of work and develop a sense of industry. At the same time, they are in danger of acquiring feelings of inadequacy. If children judge themselves to be inferior to their peers, they may be discouraged from further work or

According to Erik Erikson, children discover the importance of work and develop a sense of industry during their early school years. However, he added, they must also make room for imagination, play, and experimentation if they are to obtain a balanced perspective and be properly prepared for adolescence.

learning. They are also at risk of working too much, to the detriment of imagination and playfulness. The major rules and laws of society are incorporated during these years. Erikson viewed this as a most decisive stage. Successful passage results in a sense of competence that serves as the basis for cooperative participation in the workings of society. Unsuccessful passage leaves children with lingering feelings of inferiority.

Stage 5: Identity vs. Role Confusion

The fifth stage lasts through adolescence. The primary concern during this stage is *psychosocial identity*, a sense of inner sameness and continuity. The adolescent strains for inner coherence and a durable set of values. A successful transition through adolescence results in fidelity, an ability to be true to oneself at the same time that one is true to others. Adolescents typically band together in their efforts to define themselves, and in doing so are often cruel and exclusionary to outsiders. When such cruelty and exclusion are carried to extremes, they may result in delinquency, temporary or permanent. Other pathological patterns that may develop during adolescence result from the individual's inability to form a cohesive identity.

Stage 6: Intimacy vs. Isolation

During early adulthood, people use the consolidated identity that they developed during adolescence to form intimate relationships and sexual unions that call for self-sacrifice and compromise. The goal of this period is to attain love. The ethical conviction developed in adolescence and the sense of moral obligation formed in childhood contribute to ethical strength in young adulthood. People who are unable to meet the challenges of this stage may become isolated, some actually avoiding the contacts that create and sustain intimacy. Their insularity and isolation can lead to various psychological problems, such as irrational fears or depression.

Stage 7: Generativity vs. Stagnation

During middle adulthood, people ordinarily turn their attention to the next generation. Their focus becomes procreativity, or, to use Erikson's term, *generativity*. Caring for younger people, whether through parenthood or by advising junior colleagues at work, is a primary concern. This process enriches the individual who engages in it. People who fail to develop such activities may, according to Erikson, experience stagnation and boredom.

"During the next stage of my development, Dad, I'll be drawing closer to my mother—I'll get back to you in my teens."

(Drawing by Lorenz; © 1991 The New Yorker Magazine, Inc.)

Stage 8: Integrity vs. Despair

The last of Erikson's stages, old age, brings accumulated knowledge and understanding and mature judgment along with a decline in bodily and mental functioning. The goal of the period is to attain wisdom, a detached yet active concern with life in the face of death. Wisdom is achieved through the integration of insights gained from the past and the present regarding one's place in the stream of life. Those who do not effectively meet the challenges of this stage may experience an extreme fear of death or despair, show bitterness and disgust, and feel that time is too short. Such persons are prone to develop depression, hypochondriasis, or paranoia during their final years.

Although theorists sometimes disagree with the details of Erikson's scheme, most agree with his belief that people pass through successive stages, confront key pressures during each one, and either grow or decline, depending on how they and their environment meet these pressures. As Erikson repeatedly pointed out, there are many opportunities for failure and maladaptiveness during each developmental stage, whether because of psychological inadequacy, biological abnormality, or extraordinary environmental stress. In this chapter we shall discuss the abnormal patterns and dysfunctions that develop when people have problems during the first five of Erikson's stages—those from birth through adolescence. In Chapter 20 we shall examine the abnormal patterns that are linked to Erikson's last three stages, particularly the final stage—old age.

■ ABNORMAL ■ DEVELOPMENTS OF CHILDHOOD AND ADOLESCENCE

People often think of childhood as a carefree and happy period. However, it can also be a frightening and upsetting time during which one is regularly confronting new people, situations, and obstacles. In fact, most children experience at least some emotional and behavioral problems in the normal course of development (see Box 19–1). Worrying, bed-wetting, nightmares, temper tantrums, and restlessness are common problems among children. In most cases these problems seem to resolve themselves as children get older (Crowther, Bond, & Rolf, 1981; Lapouse & Monk, 1964, 1959; MacFarlane et al., 1954).

Nor is adolescence necessarily the upbeat period that many people think it is. The physical and sexual changes, social and academic pressures, personal doubts, and temptations that characterize this time of transition leave many teenagers anxious, confused, and depressed (Takanishi, 1993; Eccles et al., 1993; Petersen et al., 1993). In fact, the "normal" psychological state of adolescents seems to be deteriorating in the United States. Surveys reveal that today's teenagers, although generally happy, feel less confident, secure, and trusting, less affectionate toward their families, and less in control of their inner feelings and impulses than adolescents did several decades ago (Offer, Ostrov, & Howard, 1981). Today's teenagers also report more problems, are more worried about their appearance, and describe themselves as more easily hurt than did teenagers of the past.

Beyond these common psychological difficulties, 17 to 22 percent of all children and adolescents in the United States experience a diagnosable mental disorder (Kazdin, 1994; Zill & Schoenborn, 1990; Costello, 1989). Boys with mental disorders outnumber girls, a most interesting difference in view of the fact that the prevalence rate of adult psychological disorders is usually higher among women than among men. Some believe that the shift in rates of psychological disorders from childhood to adulthood reflects the special and increased pressures placed on women in Western society. Others suggest that it may reflect biases against women in diagnosis.

The perception of childhood disorders has changed over the course of this century. Initially clinicians viewed children as small adults and treated their disorders as downward extensions of adult disorders (Peterson & Roberts, 1991). Now, however, clinicians recognize that there are often important differences between adult and childhood disorders.

Some of the disorders of children—childhood anxiety disorders, childhood depression, and disruptive disorders—do have similarities to their adult counterparts, but they are also distinct in important ways. Other childhood disorders—elimination disorders—usually disappear or radically change form by adulthood. A third group—disorders involving disturbances in the acquisition of cognitive, communication, motor, or social skills—sometimes persist in relatively stable forms into adult life.

CHILDHOOD ANXIETY DISORDERS

Anxiety is a common problem among children (King, 1993; Ollendick & King, 1991); in fact, surveys suggest that close to half of all children have multiple fears (see Figure 19–1). These fears tend to disappear over time—they seem to be almost "a passing episode in a normal developmental process" (Emmelkamp, 1982)—and clinicians believe that formal treatment for them is unnecessary. Several forms of anxiety cause severe suffering for some children, however, and may be thought of as mental disorders in need of treatment.

It is not uncommon, for example, for children, like adults, to have a specific phobia, social phobia, or generalized anxiety disorder (APA, 1994). When these disorders occur in children, they sometimes take on particular features. Children with a social phobia, for example, typically become extremely upset, embarrassed, and timid in the presence of strangers, and often cry, throw tantrums, freeze, or withdraw from such situations. And children with generalized anxiety disorder tend to be very self-conscious and to worry about future events, possible injuries, group activities, meeting expectations and deadlines, and even past behavior. Many are overly concerned about their competence in various kinds of tasks and about others' evaluations of their performance (King et al., 1992).

One form of anxiety in children, *separation anxiety disorder,* is listed as a specified category in DSM-IV. Carrie, a 9-year-old girl suffering from this disorder, was referred to a local mental health center by her school counselor.

*T*he counselor indicated that he perceived the girl's problem to be a fear of school. He reported that the problem seemed to begin about 2 months ago when Carrie

PERCENTAGE OF CHILDREN WHO WORRY "A LOT" THAT :

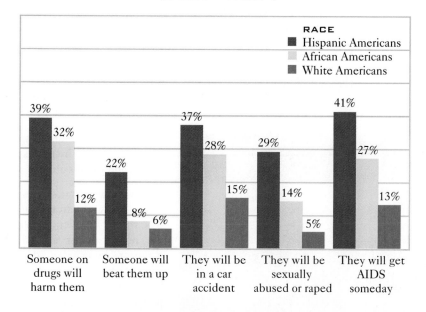

PERCENTAGE OF CHILDREN WHO WORRY "A LOT" THAT :

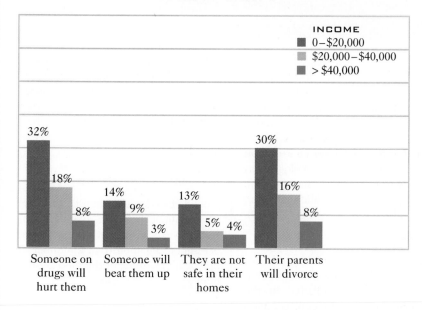

FIGURE 19-1 *According to a survey of 929 children between 10 and 17 years of age, Hispanic American and African American children are much more likely than white American children to "worry a lot" about their safety and survival. Similarly, poorer children are more likely to worry about their welfare than wealthier children, irrespective of race, suggesting that the higher anxiety levels of children of racial minorities may be largely a matter of living in poorer, more deprived, or dangerous environments. (Adapted from National Commission on Children, 1991.)*

seemed to become excessively anxious while at school for no apparent reason. She initially reported feeling sick to her stomach and later became quite concerned over being unable to get her breath. She stated that she was too nervous to stay at school and that she wanted her mother to come get her and take her home. Upon being called, Carrie's mother seemed extremely concerned and came to get her. The counselor indicated that a similar incident occurred the next day with Carrie ending up going home again. She had not returned to school since. The counselor reported having spoken to Carrie's mother over the phone, who stated that the family doctor was unable to find any-

thing wrong with her daughter but that Carrie still resisted the idea of going to school.

At the time of the intake evaluation the mother indicated that she felt Carrie was just too nervous to go to school. She stated that she had encouraged her daughter to go to school on numerous occasions but that she seemed afraid to go and appeared to feel bad, so she had not forced her. In inquiring about Carrie's activities while not in school, the mother reported that she watched some TV and that the two of them found a lot of things to do together, such as visiting relatives or going shopping. When asked if Carrie went places by herself, the mother stated that Carrie didn't

BOX 19-1

THE ETIOLOGY AND TREATMENT OF CHILDHOOD

Jordan W. Smoller

This "clinical review" of the "disorder" called childhood originally appeared in Glen C. Ellenbogen (Ed.), Oral Sadism and the Vegetarian Personality. *New York: Brunner/Mazel, 1986.*

Childhood is a syndrome that has only recently begun to receive serious attention from clinicians. The syndrome itself, however, is not at all recent. As early as the eighth century, the Persian historian Kidnom made reference to "short, noisy creatures," who may well have been what we now call "children." The treatment of children, however, was unknown until this century, when so-called child psychologists and child psychiatrists became common. Despite this history of clinical neglect, it has been estimated that well over half of all Americans alive today have experienced childhood directly (Seuss, 1983). In fact, the actual numbers are probably much higher, since these data are based on self-reports which may be subject to social desirability biases and retrospective distortion.

Clinicians are still in disagreement about the significant clinical features of childhood, but the proposed DSM-IV will almost certainly include the following core features:

1. Congenital onset
2. Dwarfism
3. Emotional lability and immaturity
4. Knowledge deficits
5. Legume anorexia

CONGENITAL ONSET   In one of the few existing literature reviews on

childhood, Temple-Black (1982) has noted that childhood is almost always present at birth, although it may go undetected for years or even remain subclinical indefinitely. This observation has led some investigators to speculate on a biological contribution to childhood. As one psychologist has put it, "we may soon be in a position to distinguish organic childhood from functional childhood" (Rogers, 1979).

DWARFISM   This is certainly the most familiar clinical marker of childhood. It is widely known that children are physically short relative to the population at large. Indeed, common clinical wisdom suggests that the treatment of the so-called small child (or "tot") is particularly difficult. These children are known to exhibit infantile behavior and display a startling lack of insight (Tom & Jerry, 1967).

EMOTIONAL LABILITY AND IMMATURITY   This aspect of childhood is often the only basis for a clinician's diagnosis. As a result, many otherwise normal adults are misdiagnosed as children and must suffer the unneces-

sary social stigma of being labeled a "child" by professionals and friends alike.

KNOWLEDGE DEFICITS   While many children have IQs within or even above the norm, almost all will manifest knowledge deficits. Anyone who has known a real child has experienced the frustration of trying to discuss any topic that requires some general knowledge.

LEGUME ANOREXIA   This last identifying feature is perhaps the most unexpected. Folk wisdom is supported by empirical observation—children will rarely eat their vegetables (see Popeye, 1957, for review).

■ CAUSES ■ OF CHILDHOOD

Now that we know what it is, what can we say about the causes of childhood? Recent years have seen a flurry of theory and speculation from a number of perspectives. Some of the most prominent are reviewed below.

SOCIOLOGICAL MODEL

Emile Durkind was perhaps the first to speculate about sociological causes of childhood. He points out two key observations about children: (1) the vast majority of children are unemployed, and (2) children represent one of the least educated segments of our society. In fact, it has been estimated that less than 20 percent of children have had more than a fourth-grade education. . . . One promising rehabilitation program

(Spanky & Alfalfa, 1978) has trained victims of severe childhood to sell lemonade.

Biological Model

The observation that childhood is usually present from birth has led some to speculate on a biological contribution. An early investigation by Flintstone and Jetson (1939) indicated that childhood runs in families. Their survey of over 8,000 American families revealed that over half contained more than one child. Further investigation revealed that even most nonchild family members had experienced childhood at some point. . . .

Psychological Models

A considerable number of psychologically based theories of the development of childhood exist. They are too numerous to review here. Among the more familiar models are Seligman's "learned childishness" model. According to this model, individuals who are treated like children eventually give up and become children. As a counterpoint to such theories, some experts have claimed that childhood does not really exist. Szasz (1980) has called "childhood" an expedient label. In seeking conformity, we handicap those whom we find unruly or too short to deal with by labeling them "children."

■ Treatment ■ of Childhood

Efforts to treat childhood are as old as the syndrome itself. Only in modern times, however, have humane and systematic treatment protocols been applied.

The overwhelming number of children has made government intervention inevitable. The nineteenth century saw the institution of what remains the largest single program for the treatment of childhood—so-called public schools. Under this colossal program, individuals are placed into treatment groups on the basis of the

severity of their condition. For example, those most severely afflicted may be placed in a "kindergarten" program. Patients at this level are typically short, unruly, emotionally immature, and intellectually deficient.

Unfortunately, the "school" system has been largely ineffective. Not only is the program a massive tax burden, but it has failed even to slow down the rising incidence of childhood.

Faced with this failure and the growing epidemic of childhood, mental health professionals are devoting increasing attention to the treatment of childhood. . . . The following case (taken from Gumbie & Pokey, 1957) is typical.

Billy J., age 8, was brought to treatment by his parents. Billy's affliction was painfully obvious. He stood only 4'3" high and weighed a scant 70 pounds, despite the fact that he ate voraciously. Billy presented a variety of troubling symptoms. His voice was noticeably high for a man. He displayed legume anorexia and, according to his parents, often refused to bathe. His intellectual functioning was also below normal—he had little general knowledge and could barely write a structured sentence. Social skills were also deficient. He often spoke inappropriately and exhibited "whining behavior." His sexual experience was nonexistent. Indeed, Billy considered women "icky." . . .

After years of this kind of frustration, startling new evidence has come to light which suggests that the prognosis in cases of childhood may not be all gloom. . . . Moe, Larrie, and Kirly (1974) began a large-scale longitudinal study. These investigators studied two groups. The first group comprised 34 children currently engaged in a long-term conventional treatment program. The second was a group of 42 children receiving no treatment. . . .

The results . . . of a careful 10-year follow-up were startling. . . . Shemp (1984) found subjects improved. Indeed, in most cases, the subjects appeared to be symptom-free. Moe et al. report a spontaneous remission rate of 95 percent, a finding that is certain to revolutionize the clinical approach to childhood.

These recent results suggest that the prognosis for victims of childhood may not be so bad as we have feared. We must not, however, become too complacent. Despite its apparently high spontaneous remission rate, childhood remains one of the most serious and rapidly growing disorders facing mental health professionals today. And beyond the psychological pain it brings, childhood has recently been linked to a number of physical disorders. Twenty years ago, Howdi, Doodi, and Beauzeau (1965) demonstrated a sixfold increased risk of chickenpox, measles, and mumps among children as compared with normal controls. Later, Barbie and Kenn (1971) linked childhood to an elevated risk of accidents—compared with normal adults, victims of childhood were much more likely to scrape their knees, lose their teeth, and fall off their bikes.

Clearly, much more research is needed before we can give any real hope to the millions of victims wracked by this insidious disorder.

like to do that and that the two of them typically did most everything together. The mother went on to note that Carrie really seemed to want to have her (the mother) around all the time and tended to become upset whenever the two of them were separated.

(Schwartz & Johnson, 1985, p. 188)

Children with a separation anxiety disorder experience excessive anxiety, often panic, whenever they are separated from home or a parent. They have great trouble traveling independently away from home, and often refuse to visit friends' ouses, go on errands, or attend camp or school. Many cannot even stay alone in a room, and cling to their parent around the house. The children may fear that they will get lost when they are separated or that their parent will meet with an accident or illness. Separation anxiety is often associated with somatic complaints such as headaches, stomachaches, or nausea when a child is separated from a parent or anticipates separation. Children may also have temper tantrums, cry, or plead with their parents not to leave them (APA, 1994).

It has been estimated that about 4 percent of children and adolescents experience this disorder (APA, 1994). If it is going to emerge, it always does so before the age of 18, as early as in the preschool years, and lasts at least four weeks, but may wax and wane over the course of childhood. In many cases the disorder is precipitated by a life stress such as the death of a parent or pet, moving, or a change of schools. Surveys suggest that it is somewhat more common among girls than boys (APA, 1994).

As in Carrie's case, a separation anxiety disorder sometimes takes the form of a **school phobia,** or **school refusal,** a common problem in which children experience extreme anxiety about attending school and often stay home for an extended period of time. Some cases of school phobia, however, may involve factors other than separation, such as social fears, anxiety about academic performance, depression, and fears of specific objects or persons at school.

CAUSES OF CHILDHOOD ANXIETY DISORDERS Proponents of the various models explain childhood anxiety in much the same way they account for adult anxiety (discussed in Chapter 6). Childhood fears, for example, are caused by classically conditioned fear responses, according to behaviorists; by excessive use of repression and displacement, according to traditional psychodynamic theorists; by relationship confusion and self-fragmentation, according to contemporary psychodynamic theorists; and by physiological abnormalities, according to biological theorists.

In addition, features unique to childhood have been cited as important to the development of childhood anxiety disorders. Since children have had fewer past experiences than adults, many aspects of their world are new, unpredictable, and scary to them. They may be frightened by common developmental changes, such as a mother's return to work, the birth of a sibling, or the beginning of school, or by special traumas, such as moving to a new residence, losing a parent, or becoming seriously ill (Tweed, Schoenbach, & George, 1989; Kashani et al., 1981). Although most children seem to overcome the effects of such events, some are unable to recover, and develop an abnormal pattern of anxiety or some other form of psychopathology (Long & Vaillant, 1984).

Children are highly dependent on their parents for emotional support and guidance, and may be greatly influenced by parental inadequacies. If, for example, parents themselves react to events with high levels of anxiety or overprotect their child, the child is more likely to develop anxiety problems. Similarly, if parents repeatedly reject, disappoint, avoid, or abuse their children, the world may become an unpleasant and anxious place for the child.

Finally, our culture often presents children with dark notions and images that may frighten them and set the stage for anxiety disorders. Today's children are repeatedly warned, both at home and at school, about the dangers of kidnapping and drugs. Although these discussions and reminders may be necessary for the children's safety, they hardly breed feelings of psychological security. Similarly, television shows, movies, and news programs are often filled with violent and scary images that can heighten anxiety

Childhood anxieties may be the result of developmental traumas, such as the increasingly common experience of having to share a parent's affection with a new stepparent. The face of this boy after his mother's remarriage says it all.

levels. Investigators have even noted that many of our time-honored fairy tales and nursery rhymes contain frightening images that may upset children.

TREATMENTS FOR CHILDHOOD ANXIETY DISORDERS Anxiety disorders in children, as in adults, may be treated by a variety of approaches. Psychodynamic therapists try to help anxious children, as well as those with other kinds of psychological problems, bring their unconscious conflicts to the surface and resolve them. Because children have a limited capacity for analyzing and reflecting on their feelings and motives, therapists typically use *play therapy* to help achieve these goals. They have the children express their conflicts and feelings indirectly by playing with toys, drawing, and making up stories. The therapists then interpret these activities and, through continued play and fantasy, try to help the children develop relevant insights, resolve conflicts, and alter their emotions and behavior. Case studies have indicated that psychodynamic therapy is effective in the treatment of anxiety disorders in children (Barros, 1992; Elmhirst, 1984; White et al., 1972). However, only a limited number of empirical studies have tested and supported its effectiveness (Kazdin, 1994; Barrios & O'Dell, 1989). Similarly, family therapy and drug therapy for childhood anxiety disorders have been applied widely but have received relatively limited empirical attention to date (Klein et al., 1992; Simeon et al., 1992).

Behaviorists have used exposure techniques and social skills training to treat childhood anxiety disorders (Kazdin, 1994; Morris & Kratochwill, 1983). Relaxation therapy and massage therapy have also been used to reduce anxiety in children (Field et al., 1992; Platania–Solazzo et al., 1992). Studies suggest that behavioral approaches, particularly combinations of them, significantly reduce children's fears and anxieties, just as they help to reduce adult fears, but here too the number of such studies has been limited (Kazdin, 1994; Barrios & O'Dell, 1989). Approaches that combine behavioral and cognitive techniques, such as helping children to identify anxiety cues and to employ coping skills, may also reduce childhood anxiety (Kendall et al., 1991, 1989; Kane & Kendall, 1989).

CHILDHOOD DEPRESSION

Until the 1980s, clinicians generally assumed that young children were incapable of severe depression. They believed that the depressive patterns observed

Childhood anxieties can be caused by society's warnings of possible catastrophes. These school children in Japan dive for cover during an earthquake drill.

in some children were simply a normal lowering of mood or related to another psychological disorder (Kazdin, 1994; Cantwell, 1982; Pearce, 1977). Studies conducted throughout the 1980s, however, indicated that many children do in fact experience a constellation of depressive symptoms that are severe and not attributable to other problems—such symptoms as persistent crying, negative self-concept, decreased activity, social withdrawal, and suicidal thoughts (Kazdin, 1990; Schwartz & Johnson, 1985). Bobby is one such child:

W hen seen for an interview, Bobby appeared as a rather dejected looking 10-year-old who seemed to be much more serious than one would expect for a child of his age. Bobby indicated that his parents had brought him to the clinic because "they think I have emotional problems." When asked to elaborate, Bobby said that he wasn't sure what emotional problems really were but that he thought they were upset because "I cry sometimes." In observing Bobby in the playroom it was obvious that his activity level was well below that expected for a child of 10. He showed a lack of interest in the toys that were available to him, and the interviewer was unable to get him interested in any play activity for more than a few minutes. In questioning him about home and school, Bobby indicated that he didn't like school because he didn't have any friends, and he wasn't good at playing games like baseball and soccer like the other kids were, stating "I'm not really very good at anything." He stated that, at home, things were "OK" except that "my parents work most of the time, and we never do anything together like other families." When asked what he would wish for if he could have any three wishes granted he indicated, "I would wish that I was the type of boy my mother and father want, I would wish that I could have friends, and I would wish that I wouldn't feel sad so much."

The death of a parent may lead to childhood depression. Edvard Munch's painting The Dead Mother and the Little Girl *captures the devastating impact of such a loss.*

In speaking with the parents, the mother reported that she and her husband had become increasingly concerned about their son during the past year. She indicated that he always seemed to look sad and cried a lot for no apparent reason and that he appeared to have lost interest in most of the things that he used to enjoy doing. The mother confirmed Bobby's statements that he had no friends, indicating that he had become more and more of a loner during the past 6 to 9 months. She stated that his schoolwork had also suffered in that he is unable to concentrate on school assignments and seems to have "just lost interest." The mother notes, however, that her greatest concern is that he has recently spoken more and more frequently about "killing himself," saying that the parents would be better off if he wasn't around.

(Schwartz & Johnson, 1985, p. 214)

Studies suggest that approximately 2 percent of children between 4 and 16 years of age experience a major depressive disorder (Kazdin, 1994; Institute of Medicine, 1989). The rate may be 7 percent among adolescents alone (Petersen et al., 1993, 1991). Studies have found no difference in the rates of depression in boys and girls before the age of 11, but by the age of 16, girls are twice as likely as boys to be depressed (Angold & Rutter, 1992; Kazdin, 1990).

Explanations of childhood depression are similar to those offered for adult depression (see Chapter 8). Theorists have pointed to such factors as loss, learned helplessness, negative cognitive bias, and low norepinephrine activity to account for the disorder (Petersen et al., 1993). Moreover, like adult depres-

sion, childhood depression often seems to be precipitated by a negative life event, major change, rejection, or ongoing abuse (see Box 19–2).

Research has uncovered a relatively high rate of depression and other forms of mental dysfunction among the parents of depressed children (Beardslee et al., 1993; Hammen, 1991). As with all such family correlations, however, it is not clear whether this relationship suggests hereditary or environmental factors.

Research also indicates that childhood depression responds best to some of the kinds of treatment that are highly successful for adult depression—cognitive-behavioral therapy and social skills training—as well as to family therapy (Kazdin, 1994, 1989; Stark, Rouse, & Livingston, 1991). Controlled studies of the efficacy of drug therapy, however, have not clearly supported the use of antidepressants in treating childhood depression (Ambrosini et al., 1993; Geller et al., 1993). Treatments that combine various approaches according to the needs of a particular child are often more helpful than any one method alone (Kazdin, 1989).

DISRUPTIVE BEHAVIOR DISORDERS

It is common for children to flout social rules, misbehave, or act aggressively or defiantly. In one study, teachers were asked to rate aggression and noncompliance in hundreds of normal day-care students (Crowther, Bond, & Rolf, 1981). As Figure 19–2 indicates, at age 2 almost 29 percent of the boys were considered to be at least moderately aggressive and 57 percent were rated as at least moderately noncompliant. These rates fell as the children grew older.

Some children, however, display patterns of negativity, hostility, and defiance that are more frequent, intense, and disruptive than common aggressiveness; they are considered to have a *disruptive behavior disorder* and may receive a diagnosis of either oppositional defiant disorder or conduct disorder. Children with **oppositional defiant disorder** argue repeatedly with adults, lose their temper, and feel great anger and resentment. They frequently defy adult rules and requests, annoy others, and blame others for their own mistakes and problems. These behaviors are always apparent at home and sometimes at school and elsewhere. The disorder typically begins by 8 years of age and is more common in boys than in girls before puberty, but equally common among boys and girls after puberty (APA, 1994). Its prevalence among children is between 2 and 16 percent according to various studies (APA, 1994).

Aggressive behavior in 2-year-olds is considered quite normal. It is expected to become significantly less frequent and less intense as a child grows older. If it does not, the child may be displaying an oppositional defiant disorder or conduct disorder.

Conduct disorder is a more severe pattern. Children with this disorder go further and repeatedly violate the basic rights of others. They are often aggressive and may in fact be physically cruel to persons or animals, deliberately destroy others' property, lie and cheat, skip school, or run away from home. Many steal from and threaten or even harm their victims, committing such crimes as shoplifting, forgery, breaking into houses and other buildings or cars, mugging, extortion, and armed robbery. As they get older their physical violence may extend to rape, assault, or in rare cases homicide (APA, 1994).

Conduct disorders usually begin before age 10 **(childhood-onset type),** but in some cases the child shows no conduct problems until after this age **(adolescent-onset type).** Children with a milder conduct disorder (relatively few symptoms and causing only minor harm to others) may improve over time, but in severe cases the disorder often continues into adulthood, and may lead to the development of an antisocial personality disorder. Between 6 and 16 percent of boys under 18 years of age and 2 to 9 percent of girls display this disorder. Children with conduct disorder are frequently diagnosed with other mental disorders as well, including personality, anxiety, and mood disorders, attention-deficit hyperactivity disorder, substance-related disorders, and learning disorders (APA, 1994; Wierson et al., 1992).

About a third of the children seen at child guidance clinics are referred there for conduct disorders. Large numbers of adult criminals have been seen earlier in their lives in child guidance clinics for conduct problems, or placed in correctional institutions. Many

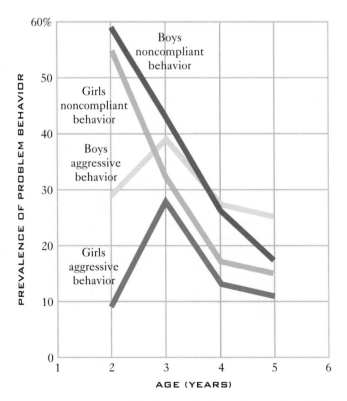

FIGURE 19–2 *Teacher evaluations of more than 700 preschoolers indicated that the rates of both noncompliant and aggressive behavior dropped as the children grew older. (Adapted from Crowther, Bond, & Rolf, 1981.)*

BOX 19-2

CHILD ABUSE

Child abuse is the intentional use of physical or psychological force by an adult on a child, often aimed at hurting or destroying the child (Gil, 1970). A recent study done by the National Committee for the Prevention of Child Abuse found that 2.9 million cases of child abuse were reported to child services in 1992, as compared with 1.9 million cases reported in 1985 (McCurdy & Daro, 1993). Approximately 27 percent of these reports cited physical abuse, 17 percent sexual abuse, 49 percent neglect, and 7 percent emotional maltreatment (Paget et al., 1993; AAPC, 1992). Moreover, it is estimated that annually between 2,000 and 4,000 instances of child abuse result in a child's death (Green, 1989). In fact, some observers believe that physical child abuse and neglect are the leading causes of death among young children. Surveys suggest that each year one in ten children is subjected to severe violence, such as being kicked, bitten, hit (often with an object), beaten, threatened with a knife or a gun, or assaulted with a knife or a gun (Gelles & Straus, 1987).

What I remember most about my mother was that she was always beating me. She'd beat me with her high heeled shoes, with my father's belt, with a potato masher. When I was eight, she black and blued my legs so badly, I told her I'd go to the police. She said, "Go, they'll just put you into the darkest prison." So I stayed. When my breasts started growing at 13, she beat me across the chest until I fainted. Then she'd hug me and ask forgiveness. . . . Most kids have nightmares about being taken away from their parents. I would sit on our front porch crooning softly of going far, far away to find another mother. *(Time, September 5, 1983, p. 20)*

Honoré Daumier's Fatherly Discipline.

Although child abuse occurs in all socioeconomic groups, it is apparently more common among the poor (Gelles, 1992). The abusers are usually the parents. Girls and boys are abused at approximately the same rate. Physical injury is more likely to occur during the preschool years and adolescence (AHA, 1986). Babies who are fussy and irritable and cry a great deal are apparently at particularly high risk of being abused (Gil, 1970).

Two other forms of child abuse have been receiving special attention in recent years: psychological abuse and sexual abuse. **Psychological abuse** may include severe rejection; coercive, punitive, and erratic discipline; scapegoating and ridicule; unrealistic expectations; exploitation and corruption; isolation; and refusal to provide help for an emotionally disturbed child (Hart & Brassard, 1991, 1987; Hart, Germain, & Brassard, 1987). This form of mistreatment probably accompanies all forms of physical abuse and neglect, and occurs by itself in about 200,000 cases each year (McCurdy & Daro, 1993; AAPC, 1992; Hart & Brassard, 1987; AHA, 1986). The legal system has devoted little attention to this form of child abuse, but the mental health field has become increasingly concerned about the effects of and treatment for this problem (Garrison, 1987).

Child sexual abuse, the use of a child for gratification of adult sexual desires, does not usually result in physical injury but causes the victim enormous psychological damage, including long-term feelings of mistrust, poor self-image, depression, guilt, social withdrawal, poor school performance, and difficulties with sexual intimacy. It may occur outside of or in the home. It is estimated that 50,000 to 200,000 new cases occur each year in the United States. In surveys of adult women, 20 to 35 percent reported having been forced into sexual contact with an adult male as children, many of them with their father or stepfather (Green, 1989). Although the majority of victims are girls, the fact that boys are also sexually abused has been acknowledged within the past ten years (Bolton, Morris, & MacEachron, 1989). Both legal and mental health professionals have become even more interested in this problem during the past decade because of several highly publicized cases of alleged sexual abuse in day-care centers around the United States.

Recently, the validity of children's testimony in *some* sexual abuse cases has been debated. Although the trend has been to believe children, the overturning of Margaret Kelly Michael's conviction in 1993 marked an increasing awareness of the suggestibility of children and the power of interrogators in some cases. Ms. Michaels, a former child-care worker at the Wee Care Day Nursery in Maplewood, New Jersey, was convicted of 115 charges of sexual abuse of nineteen children and sentenced to forty-seven years in prison. After she had served five years in prison, however, her conviction was overturned on the grounds that she did not receive a fair trial, in part because the judge's questioning of the children was not impartial. In the wake of this case, psychologists are being called upon to investigate just how easily a child's memory of events can be altered by adult suggestions and by the pressure of opinionated interviewers. The findings of research on this topic will inevitably have a great influence on the way abuse charges are pursued.

Before the turn of the century, the legal system tried to avoid intervention in family life, even in instances of child abuse (Garrison, 1987). Medical reports of suspected child abuse did not begin to receive widespread attention until the 1960s (Newberger, 1983), and medical and legal professionals did not become actively involved in detecting and intervening in such cases until 1974, when states adopted laws requiring physicians to report cases of suspected child abuse and the Federal Child Abuse Prevention and Treatment Act was passed (Garrison, 1987). Since then media accounts have kept this staggering social problem in the public eye. Numerous federal and state legislatures and court systems have also sprung into more protective and punitive action; and mental health professionals have contributed by developing numerous research and therapy programs.

Since entering into the study of child abuse, clinical researchers have learned that a variety of factors may interact to produce child abuse, including such parental characteristics as poor impulse control and low self-esteem, such parental background factors as having been abused as children

and having had poor role models, such situational stresses as marital disputes or family unemployment, and such immediate precipitants as a child's misbehavior. Research shows that physically abusive families also tend to have lower incomes, younger parents with less education, and more likelihood of alcohol or drug abuse (Whipple, Webster, & Stratton, 1991). Because the type and combination of factors vary from case to case, clinicians must carefully assess the parents, child, and family dynamics of a case before planning a treatment program (Azar & Wolfe, 1989).

A number of interventions have been tried in cases of child abuse. Parents may develop insight about themselves and their behavior, receive training on alternatives to abuse, and learn parenting skills in groups and classes such as those offered by the national organization Parents Anonymous. In groups or in individual treatment, they may learn more effective child interaction and management skills through such behavioral interventions as modeling, role playing, and feedback (Azar & Siegal, 1990; Wolfe et al., 1988; Barth et al., 1983). They may receive cognitive therapy to help correct misperceptions about their children or themselves (Azar & Siegal, 1990; Azar et al., 1984). Many parents who abuse their children believe that their children actually intend to upset them, and some have unrealistic expectations in regard to their children's behavior (Azar & Rohrbeck, 1986; Plotkin, 1983). A number of treatments are also aimed at helping parents deal more effectively with the situational stresses that often trigger their abuse, such as unemployment, marital discord, or depressed feelings (Campbell et al., 1983). Some treatment programs combine various therapy interventions, in accordance with the needs of a particular family (Wolfe et al., 1981). The effects of such approaches on the parents' behavior, the child's self-esteem

and psychological recovery, and family harmony have yet to be fully determined (Azar & Wolfe, 1989).

Obviously, the treatments developed for cases of child abuse have focused on the parents more than the abused children. Recent studies suggest, however that the victims of child abuse may suffer pervasive long-term psychological effects that probably should be anticipated and addressed in early child-focused interventions (Roesler & McKenzie, 1994). Cathy Spatz Widom (1991) is currently conducting a longitudinal study that compares later development of 908 people who were abused or neglected before the age of 11 with 607 similar people who were not abused or neglected as children. She has found that those who were abused as children (1) had arrest records 53 percent higher as teenagers and 38 percent higher as adults; (2) had a greater risk of becoming criminally violent; (3) had a higher unemployment rate, lower-paying jobs, less education, and lower IQ scores; and (4) had a higher suicide rate. Similarly, the child psychologist Byron Egeland (1991) has found that people who had been abused as children later showed lower achievement scores in school, poorer work and study skills, lower social acceptance, and more psychological problems such as anxiety, misbehavior, aggression, defiance, and hyperactivity-distractibility. The psychologically damaging effects of child abuse are also documented by short-term studies, which reveal impaired academic and behavioral functioning in school among maltreated children from kindergarten to twelfth grade (Eckenrode, Laird, & Doris, 1993). Finally, numerous studies have documented the fact that more than one-third of victims grow up to be abusive, neglectful, or seriously inept parents themselves (Oliver, 1993). Clearly, many victims of child abuse are even more victimized than anyone previously had imagined.

children with conduct disorders are suspended from school, placed in foster homes, or incarcerated.

When children between the ages of 8 and 18 break the law, the legal system often labels them *juvenile delinquents.* Each state provides its own definition of delinquency. More than half of the juveniles who are arrested each year are *recidivists,* or persons who have records of previous arrests. Males are much more involved in juvenile crime than females, although rates for females are on the increase. Females are most likely to be arrested for drug use, sexual offenses, and running away, males for drug use and crimes against property. Arrest statistics typically underestimate actual juvenile crime rates; many acts simply go unreported or undetected. Even so, arrests of adolescents for serious crimes have at least tripled during the past twenty years, and the Department of Justice (1994) reported recently that the juvenile crime rate jumped almost 50 percent between 1988 and 1992.

A variety of factors have been cited as causes of conduct disorders, including genetic and biological factors, antisocial traits, drug abuse, and membership in a lower socioeconomic class (Linz et al., 1990; Rutter & Giller, 1983). However, *family dysfunction* has been pointed to most often (Miller & Prinz, 1990). Conduct disorders often emerge in an atmosphere of family conflict and hostility (Dadds et al., 1992; Whittaker & Bry, 1992). Children whose parents reject them, leave them, or fail to provide them with consistent discipline and supervision are more likely than others to lie, steal, or run away (APA, 1994; Frick et al., 1992; Lefkowitz et al., 1977). Similarly, children whose parents have alcohol or other substance dependence (particularly their fathers), mood disorders, or schizophrenia are more likely to display a conduct disorder (APA, 1994). Research has also found that some parents of delinquent children tend to display lower levels of moral judgment and to have had higher rates of antisocial behavior and hyperactivity in their youth than other parents (APA, 1994; Schachar & Wachsmuth, 1990; Moore & Arthur, 1983).

Generally, treatments for conduct disorders have been more effective with children under 13 years of age than with those over 13, as disruptive behavior patterns become more stable with age (Loeber, 1991; McMahon & Wells, 1989). The most effective approaches appear to be *family interventions* in which (1) parents are taught more effective ways to deal with their children (for example, consistently to reward appropriate behaviors) or (2) parents and children meet together in behavior-oriented family therapy (Long et al., 1994; Bank et al., 1991; Griest &

Wells, 1983; Alexander & Parsons, 1982). These approaches, however, may bring about greater change in the child's behavior in the home than outside of the home. Community-based residential programs for children with conduct disorders, school-based interventions, and skill training techniques (training the child to cope with anger) have had at most limited effectiveness (McMahon & Wells, 1989). Recently some clinicians have also recommended drug therapy to help control aggressive outbursts in children with conduct disorders (Kemph et al., 1993; Campbell et al., 1992; Kafantaris et al., 1992).

Dealing with juvenile offenders has been a troubling problem for the courts. Institutionalization in so-called juvenile training centers has not met with much success. In fact, such institutions frequently serve to solidify the delinquent culture rather than resocialize the young offenders who are detained there. While the rate of repeated arrests for adolescents sent to training centers varies with the type of crime and the type of treatment, the overall rate has been estimated to be as high as 80 percent. When therapy, particularly behavior therapy, has replaced or accompanied institutionalization, behavior has sometimes improved. Immediate probation as an alternative to institutionalization has been more successful in cases involving crimes of a less serious nature. The success of such a course of action apparently depends in part on adequate supervision and on the sensitivity of probation officers. Unfortunately, most probation officers are without mental health training and spend an average of one hour per month with each young offender (Erickson, 1992).

Critics of the penal system claim that the greatest promise for delinquents lies in prevention programs that begin in early childhood. Preventive measures that have been used include increasing training opportunities for young people who are disaffected by school, increasing the quality and quantity of recreational facilities, providing health care, alleviating the conditions of poverty, and improving parents' child-rearing skills. All interventions work better when they are accompanied by efforts to support, educate, and involve the family (Zigler et al., 1992).

ATTENTION-DEFICIT HYPERACTIVITY DISORDER

Children who display an *attention-deficit hyperactivity disorder (ADHD)* attend very poorly to tasks *or* behave overactively and impulsively *or* both. An ADHD pattern often appears before the child starts school, as in the case of Steven, a child who displays poor attention, as well as overactivity and impulsiveness.

S teven's mother cannot remember a time when her son was not into something or in trouble. As a baby he was incredibly active, so active in fact that he nearly rocked his crib apart. All the bolts and screws became loose and had to be tightened periodically. Steven was also always into forbidden places, going through the medicine cabinet or under the kitchen sink. He once swallowed some washing detergent and had to be taken to the emergency room. As a matter of fact, Steven had many more accidents and was more clumsy than his older brother and younger sister. Even though Steven was less well-coordinated and more clumsy than other children, he always seemed to be moving fast. His mother recalls that Steven progressed from the crawling stage to a running stage with very little walking in between.

Trouble really started to develop for Steven when he entered kindergarten. Since his entry into school, his life has been miserable and so has the teacher's. Steven does not seem capable of attending to assigned tasks and following instructions. He would rather be talking to a neighbor or wandering around the room without the teacher's permission. When he is seated and the teacher is keeping an eye on him to make sure that he works, Steven's body still seems to be in motion. He is either tapping his pencil, fidgeting, or staring out the window and daydreaming. Steven hates kindergarten and has few long-term friends; indeed, school rules and demands appear to be impossible challenges for him. The effects of this mismatch are now showing in Steven's schoolwork and attitude. He has fallen behind academically and has real difficulty mastering new concepts; he no longer follows directions from the teacher and has started to talk back.

(Gelfand, Jenson, & Drew, 1982, p. 256)

The symptoms of ADHD often exacerbate one another. A child who has trouble focusing attention may be pulled into action in several directions at once. Similarly, a constantly moving child is likely to have difficulty attending to tasks or exercising careful judgment. Often one of these areas of disturbance is much more prominent than the other. In such cases, the child may receive a diagnosis of ***ADHD, predominantly inattentive type,*** or ***ADHD, predominantly hyperactive-impulsive type*** (called simply ***hyperactivity*** by many clinicians). Otherwise, the diagnosis is ***ADHD, combined type*** (APA, 1994).

ADHD symptoms tend to be highly visible at home, school, and work and in social situations (Biederman et al., 1990) and less apparent when the

child enters a novel setting or one-on-one situation or receives frequent reinforcement or strict control.

About half of the children with ADHD also experience learning or communication problems, many perform poorly in school, and about 80 percent misbehave, often quite seriously. In fact, ADHD is often seen in conjunction with learning, communication, and conduct disorders (Bird et al., 1993; Paniagua et al., 1990). It is also common among children with mood and anxiety disorders (APA, 1994).

Between 3 and 5 percent of schoolchildren display ADHD, around 80 percent of them boys (APA, 1994). The disorder spans all cultures (APA, 1994; Ross & Ross, 1982) and usually persists through childhood. Many children show a lessening of symptoms as they move into late adolescence, but, as Figure 19–3 indicates, in a number of these cases some forms of learning, perceptual, and behavioral problems remain (APA, 1994; Mannuzza et al., 1993). ADHD continues into adulthood for about a third of affected individuals (Lie, 1992). Those whose parents manifested this problem are more likely than others to develop it (APA, 1994). Both first-degree and second-degree relatives of people with ADHD have a higher than usual prevalence rate of the disorder (Faraone, Biederman, & Milberger, 1994).

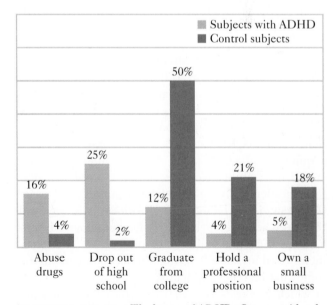

FIGURE 19–3 *The legacy of ADHD. Once considered a disorder that children outgrow, ADHD is now recognized as a problem with a continuing impact for many individuals. A longitudinal study of 103 boys with ADHD and 100 control subjects recently revealed that those with ADHD were more likely to abuse drugs as teenagers and less likely to earn a high school or bachelor's degree, hold a professional position such as stockbroker or accountant, or own a small business. (Adapted from Mannuzza et al., 1993.)*

Research has not pointed to clear causes of ADHD. Some investigators have argued that biological dysfunction leads to the attention deficits and other features of the disorder, but they have not yet determined the precise nature of the dysfunction (Loge et al., 1990; Hynd et al., 1990). One popular theory holds that it reflects some form of brain damage (Giedd et al., 1994)—indeed, the disorder was once referred to as *minimal brain damage*—but this notion has failed to receive consistent support (Anastopoulos & Barkley, 1992; Loney, 1981).

Other theorists believe that ADHD is caused by psychological factors such as stress (Amsel, 1990). Some research has suggested that families with ADHD children have fewer extended family contacts, that mothers of children with hyperactivity are more depressed, and that parent alcohol consumption is higher (Cunningham et al., 1988). Once again, however, such family patterns are as likely to be the result of a child's ADHD pattern as the cause of it.

Given this state of research, today's clinicians generally view ADHD as a disorder with multiple and interacting causes (Anastopoulos & Barkley, 1992). They also recognize that ADHD symptoms and a diagnosis of ADHD may create still further difficulties and generate additional symptoms in the child. Hyperactive children are often viewed more negatively than other children by their peers, their parents, and the children themselves (King & Young, 1981; Arnold, 1973).

There is considerable disagreement about the most effective treatment for ADHD. The most common approach has been stimulant drugs, such as *methylphenidate (Ritalin)*, which is prescribed for 1 to 2 percent of the school-aged population in the United States (Safer & Krager, 1988, 1984). These drugs have a quieting effect on many ADHD children and increase their ability to solve complex problems, perform academically, and control aggressive behavior (Hinshaw, 1991; Douglas et al., 1988). It is believed that they achieve such effects by neurologically enhancing the child's ability to profit from reinforcement (Barkley, 1989). Drug therapy appears to be somewhat beneficial in half to two-thirds of the cases in which it is used. Data on the efficacy of drugs are sometimes contradictory, however, and many clinicians have great concern over the possible long-term effects of drug use (Greenhill, 1992).

A biological treatment for hyperactivity that gained a vocal and devoted following in the late 1970s was a diet that eliminates food containing certain additives. Specifically, the *Feingold diet* eliminates artificial flavoring or coloring, preservatives, and natural salicylates (Feingold, 1975). This treatment has received little or no research support, however, and has lost most of its early popularity.

Behaviorists have treated ADHD primarily by teaching parents and teachers how to systematically reinforce the child for paying attention or behaving appropriately at home or school. Such operant conditioning treatments have been relatively successful, especially in combination with drug therapy (Du Paul & Barkley, 1993). Some therapists have further combined behavioral approaches with self-instruction training for the ADHD children, similar to the adult-oriented cognitive approach that we discussed in Chapter 7 (Hinshaw & Melnick, 1992; Reid & Borkowski, 1987). However, the effectiveness of such cognitive strategies in treating ADHD children has yet to be fully demonstrated (Hinshaw & Erhardt, 1991).

ELIMINATION DISORDERS

Children with elimination disorders—enuresis and encopresis—repeatedly and involuntarily urinate or pass feces, respectively, in their clothes, in bed, or on the floor, after an age at which they are expected to control these bodily functions. Moreover, their symptoms are not the result of a general medical condition.

Enuresis is involuntary (or in some cases intentional) bed-wetting or wetting of one's clothes. It may be *nocturnal* (occurring primarily at night) or, less commonly, *diurnal* (occurring primarily in the day), or both. Nocturnal enuresis usually occurs during the first third of the night, when the child is not yet dreaming. Occasionally, however, it takes place during Rapid Eye Movement sleep while the child dreams that he or she is urinating. Only children who are 5 years of age or older (or functioning at an equivalent developmental level) qualify for this diagnosis. In addition, they must have at least two enuretic experiences per week or be greatly impaired or distressed by this problem (APA, 1994). The prevalence of enuresis decreases with age. Seven percent of boys and 3 percent of girls who are 5 years old experience this disorder. In contrast, 3 percent of boys and 2 percent of girls who are 10 years old experience it. At age 18 years, the pattern is found among 1 percent of males and somewhat fewer females (APA, 1994). Approximately 75 percent of all people with enuresis

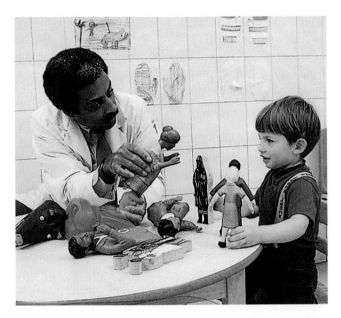

Therapists may use special techniques such as play therapy to assess the functioning of children and to help children express their feelings and thoughts and understand themselves and others.

have a close relative (parent, sibling, or child) who has had or will have the same disorder (APA, 1994).

The condition may represent a continuation of the habits of infancy or may reflect a return to earlier behavior after a period of having been dry. Many children who have been dry for a time resume bed-wetting as an apparent response to stress. Common predisposing stresses include hospitalization, the birth of a sibling, and entrance into school.

The point at which it is no longer considered "normal" to wet one's bed or pants depends on the society. In the United States, it is estimated that 10 to 30 percent of all children between the ages of 3 and 4 wet their beds (Erickson, 1992). Yet the clinical theorist Bruno Bettelheim (1969) reported that 40 percent of the 9-year-olds on an Israeli kibbutz wet their beds, and that no one seemed to regard it as much of a problem.

Psychodynamic theorists explain bed-wetting as a symbol of other conflicts and therefore as a symptom of a more general disorder (Olmos de Paz, 1990). Family systems theorists attribute the disorder to disturbed family interactions that produce sustained anxiety or hostility. Behaviorists suggest that bed-wetting represents a failure of toilet training. Training may have been attempted too early, or may have been lax or improperly reinforced. Some theorists also propose that delayed development of the physical structure of the urinary system may contribute to his pattern (Erickson, 1992).

Most cases of enuresis eventually correct themselves even without treatment; however, therapy is often applied to accelerate this process. Treatments for enuresis based on behavioral principles have enjoyed much success (Friman & Warzak, 1990; Whelan & Houts, 1990). In a widely used and apparently helpful classical conditioning approach, a bell and a battery are wired to a pad consisting of two metallic foil sheets, and the entire apparatus is placed under the child at bedtime (Howe & Walker, 1992; Mowrer & Mowrer, 1938). A single drop of urine acts as an electrolyte that sets off the bell. The child is awakened immediately after he or she starts to wet. Thus the bell (unconditioned stimulus) paired with the sensation of a full bladder (conditioned stimulus) produces the conditioned response of waking. For the procedure to be successful, parents must administer it accurately and supportively, and the child must cooperate. Cognitive therapies that teach self-control have also had a high rate of success with a low rate of relapse (Ronen et al., 1992). Some success has also been reported using the antidepressant drug *imipramine* (trade name Tofranil); however, its beneficial effects usually disappear when the drug is stopped (Fritz et al., 1994; Christophersen & Rapoff, 1992).

Encopresis, or repeated defecating in inappropriate places, is less common than enuresis and less well researched. Like enuresis, it may be a continuation of infancy behavior or regressive in nature. The problem, which is usually involuntary, starts after the age of 4. It affects about 1 percent of 5-year-olds, a rate that drops to near zero by adulthood. It is more common in boys than in girls (APA, 1994).

Encopresis is often related to constipation and impaction in the child, and in such cases treating the constipation may be a key part of treatment. In other cases it has been related to inadequate, inconsistent toilet training or to stress (APA, 1994). Often, it is accompanied by enuresis. Encopresis often occurs during the day, usually late in the afternoon after school, and seldom at night (Levine, 1975).

Encopresis is regarded as more serious than enuresis. The disorder typically causes more social problems, shame, and embarrassment. Children who suffer from it often try to conceal their condition from others and try to avoid situations, such as camp or school, in which they might become embarrassed (APA, 1994; Ross, 1981). The most common and successful treatments are behavioral, medical, and combinations of the two (Ronen, 1993; Thapar et al., 1992). Family therapy has also been helpful (Wells & Hinkle, 1990).

Disorders of Learning, Coordination, and Communication

Many children display grossly inadequate development and functioning in learning, coordination, or communication. Disorders of these kinds often lead to impaired performance in school and daily living, and typically are more common in boys than in girls. Similar problems are often seen in a child's close biological relatives.

The classification of many of these problems as mental disorders has been controversial. Many clinicians view them as primarily educational or social problems, appropriately addressed within the school or home. The framers of recent editions of the DSM have reasoned, however, that the dysfunction caused by the disorders and their frequent occurrence in association with other psychological problems justify their classification as mental disorders. Of special concern to therapists are studies that have found an increased risk of severe depression and suicide in adolescents with such problems, particularly learning disorders (Huntington & Bender, 1993).

LEARNING DISORDERS Children may receive a diagnosis of *mathematics disorder* when their arithmetic skills are markedly below their intellectual capacity and interfere with academic achievement or daily activities. The disorder, which is experienced by approximately 1 percent of school children, is usually apparent by the third grade (APA, 1994).

The expressive writing skills of a child with a *disorder of written expression* are so far below the child's intellectual capacity that they lead to impaired functioning in the academic and personal realms. Specific deficits include extreme and repeated errors in spelling, grammar, punctuation, and paragraph organization. Severe cases are usually apparent by the second grade (APA, 1994).

The reading achievement of children with a *reading disorder,* also known as *dyslexia,* is well below the expected performance of persons of their age, intelligence, and education. These children show marked impairment in the ability to recognize words and to comprehend what they read, though they have no visual or hearing defects, their schooling is adequate, and their intellectual functioning is at least average. They omit, distort, or substitute words when they read, and read slowly and haltingly. The disorder may not be fully apparent until the fourth grade or

later. It is estimated that 4 percent of schoolchildren experience dyslexia (APA, 1994). Mild cases can be greatly helped by reading therapy, and the problem may virtually disappear by adulthood. In many cases, however, symptoms may continue into adulthood despite treatment.

DEVELOPMENTAL COORDINATION DISORDER Children with a *developmental coordination disorder* perform well below the level of others of their age in daily activities requiring motor coordination, and their symptoms are not caused by medical problems. Young children with the disorder are clumsy and show delays in motor activities such as tying shoelaces, buttoning shirts, and zipping pants. Older sufferers may have great difficulty assembling puzzles, building models, playing ball, and printing or writing. It is estimated that as many as 6 percent of children between 5 and 11 years may experience this disorder. In some cases the lack of coordination continues into adulthood (APA, 1994).

COMMUNICATION DISORDERS Children who consistently fail to make correct speech sounds at an appropriate age receive a diagnosis of *phonological disorder* if the problem is not due to a difference of dialect or defect of hearing or of the speech mechanism. The child's misarticulations, substitutions, and omissions of speech sounds may give an impression of baby talk. It is estimated that 2 to 3 percent of children under 8 years of age experience a moderate or severe disorder; even more have a mild version of it. The prevalence rate falls to 0.5 percent by 17 years of age (APA, 1994). Speech therapy results in complete recovery in most cases; in milder cases the problem may disappear without treatment by the age of 8 years.

Children who display an *expressive language disorder* have great difficulty using language to express themselves. They may have a very limited or inaccurate vocabulary, have trouble acquiring new words, regularly shorten sentences, omit critical parts of sentences, order words in an unusual manner, or develop language slowly. Between 3 and 5 percent of all children display such problems (APA, 1994). Approximately half of them eventually acquire full normal language abilities, while the remainder acquire more or less normal abilities, usually by late adolescence. Specialized help is often useful.

Children with a *mixed receptive/expressive language disorder* have such difficulty comprehending *and* expressing language that it interferes with their academic achievement or daily activities. In mild cases, the children may have difficulty understanding

The mother-child relationship has received enormous attention from researchers over the years in efforts to understand a range of childhood, adolescent, and adult disorders. Unfortunately, mothers have traditionally been blamed, often without evidence, more than fathers or other factors for the psychological disorders of their children, from schizophrenia and autism to enuresis and stuttering. (Caplan et al., 1989.)

particular words or complex statements, such as "if–then" sentences. In more severe cases, they may be poor at understanding basic vocabulary or simple sentences, or at processing auditory information. They may have difficulty discriminating sounds, associating sounds and symbols, or storing, recalling, or sequencing information. Moreover, their difficulties may include some of the symptoms of an expressive language disorder. Up to 3 percent of schoolchildren may display this problem. Many eventually acquire adequate language abilities, but some severely affected persons never do.

Finally, children who *stutter* experience a disturbance in the normal fluency and time patterning of their speech (APA, 1994). They may repeat, prolong, or interject sounds, pause within a word, block sounds, substitute words to avoid other words that are hard for them to say, experience excessive physical tension when they produce words, repeat whole words having only one syllable (for example, "I-I-I-I see him"), or experience a combination of these problems.

Approximately 1 percent of children and adolescents stutter; 75 percent of them are male. The prob-

lem usually begins between 2 and 7 years of age. As many as 80 percent of those with stuttering recover, 60 percent without any treatment, usually by the age of 16 years.

CAUSES OF DISORDERS OF LEARNING, COORDINATION, AND COMMUNICATION

Studies have linked these disorders to such factors as genetic defects, birth injuries, lead poisoning, inappropriate diet, sensory dysfunction, and poor teaching (Erickson, 1992; Gelfand et al., 1982). Yet none of these relationships has been found consistently, and the precise causes of the disorders remain unclear.

A leading explanation for the learning disorders in particular, the *perceptual deficit theory,* considers these disorders to be products of problems in perceptual processing (Wong, 1979). Dyslexia, for instance, is thought to be caused by a perception deficit in which the letters are actually perceived in reverse, in mirror image. Another explanation, the *academic instruction theory,* suggests that learning disorders reflect deficiencies in teaching rather than in perception, that some children receive poor instruction in particular areas of cognitive functioning (Englemann, 1969). Proponents of this theory have tried to develop better ways of teaching learning-disabled children. They break down arithmetic, reading, and other learning areas into component skills and teach these skills in small increments. In one study a behaviorist worked individually with reading-disabled seventh-graders whose skills were $1^{1}/_{2}$ to $4^{1}/_{2}$ years below their grade level (Schwartz, 1977). He awarded points and positive reinforcements to the students for progress in reading words, then sentences, then paragraphs. The students' reading levels improved an average of 2.6 grades, compared to 1.6 grades for control students who received other forms of treatment. Improvements were observed not only in reading levels but in attention span, self-confidence, and the amount of spontaneous reading they did.

AUTISTIC DISORDER

A little boy named Mark presents a typical picture of autistic disorder:

*I*n retrospect [Susan, Mark's mother] can recall some things that appeared odd to her. For example, she remembers that . . . Mark never seemed to anticipate being picked up when she approached. In addition, despite Mark's attachment to a pacifier (he would complain if it were mislaid), he showed little interest in toys. In fact, Mark seemed to lack interest in anything. He rarely pointed to things and seemed oblivious to sounds. . . .

Mark spent much of his time repetitively tapping on tables, seeming to be lost in his own world.

After his second birthday, Mark's behavior began to trouble his parents. . . . Mark, they said, would "look through" people or past them, but rarely at them. He could say a few words but didn't seem to understand speech. In fact, he did not even respond to his own name. Mark's time was occupied examining familiar objects, which he would hold in front of his eyes while he twisted and turned them. Particularly troublesome were Mark's odd movements—he would jump, flap his arms, twist his hands and fingers, and perform all sorts of facial grimaces, particularly when he was excited—and what Robert [Mark's father] described as Mark's rigidity. Mark would line things up in rows and scream if they were disturbed. He insisted on keeping objects in their place and would become upset whenever Susan attempted to rearrange the living room furniture. . . .

Slowly, beginning at age five, Mark began to improve. . . . The pronoun in the sentence was inappropriate and the sentence took the form of a question he had been asked previously, but the meaning was clear.

(Wing, 1966)

Mark was manifesting an ***autistic disorder,*** also called ***autism,*** a disorder first identified by the American psychiatrist Leo Kanner in 1943. Children with this disorder are extremely unresponsive to others, show poor communication skills, have limited skill at imaginative play, and often react to their environment in bizarre ways. The symptoms appear very early in life, before 3 years of age. Several other disorders (*Rett's, Child disintegrative,* and *Asperger's disorders*) are similar to autism, each differing in time of onset or symptomology. Although DSM-IV distinguishes autism from these other disorders and groups them all under the broad category of ***pervasive developmental disorders,*** most researchers and clinicians use the term "autism" to refer to all of the disorders, and we shall do the same.

Autism affects only 2 to 5 of every 10,000 children (APA, 1994). Approximately 80 percent of autistic children are boys. But although girls are less likely to have autism than boys, girls who do have it tend to function at lower levels and have lower IQ scores than autistic boys (APA, 1994; Eme, 1992; Szatmari & Jones, 1991). Two autistic children in three remain severely impaired into adulthood and are unable to lead independent lives (APA, 1994). Only one in three makes at least a fair adjustment and is able to maintain social relationships, perform regular work, and lead at least a partially independent life. Autistic people with a higher IQ and better language skills tend to have a more promising future (Venter et al., 1992).

UNRESPONSIVENESS   Aloofness, lack of responsiveness, and lack of interest in other people have long formed the cornerstone of the diagnosis of autism (Volkmar et al., 1993; Walters, Barrett, & Feinstein, 1990). Like Mark, autistic children typically do not reach for their parents during infancy, and may arch their backs when they are held. They often treat adults interchangeably or cling mechanically to a select person.

Autistic children often fail to recognize or acknowledge those around them. They may offer no eye contact or facial responsiveness to their parents. As Mark's parents noted, he "would look through people or past them, but rarely at them."

In their early years, autistic children show indifference to children of their own age. They do not form friendships or play cooperatively. As they grow older, some become more aware and sociable, form attachments, and become involved in games and physical activities with other children, but such social activities tend to be passive and superficial.

LANGUAGE AND COMMUNICATION DEFICITS   Approximately half of all autistic children fail to speak or develop language skills (Dawson & Castelloe, 1992; Rutter, 1966). Those who do talk may show peculiarities in their speech. One of the most common speech problems is ***echolalia,*** the exact echoing or parroting of phrases spoken by others. The children repeat words with the same accent or inflection, but without comprehension. It has been found that autistic children echo questions and commands more often when they do not know proper responses. If they are taught to say "I don't know," the echoing decreases (Carr, Schreibman, & Lovaas, 1975). Sometimes the children use echoing as a form of assent. That is, they repeat a phrase instead of saying "Yes." In addition to immediate echolalia of this kind, many display ***delayed echolalia;*** that is, they repeat a sentence hours or days after they have heard it.

Autistic children may also display other speech oddities, such as ***pronominal reversal,*** or confusion of pronouns—the use of "you" instead of "I." When Mark was hungry, he would say, "Do you want dinner?" Many also use idiosyncratic and unclear language (***metaphorical language***) or ***neologisms,*** which, as we observed in Chapter 15, are invented words that are meaningless to anyone else. Some have difficulty naming objects (***nominal aphasia),*** and others cannot use abstract speech. The children may also employ incorrect speech inflections, ending statements with a questionlike rise in tone, for example. And finally, they may fail to use appropriately the facial expressions and gestures that ordinarily accompany speech.

Autistic children also have difficulty understanding speech and using it spontaneously. A slight change in sentence structure may prevent them from understanding a familiar question or request. Even those with relatively effective speech and comprehension have difficulty initiating or making spontaneous conversation.

LIMITED IMAGINATIVE PLAY AND DEVIANT RESPONSES TO THE ENVIRONMENT Autistic children play and interact with the environment in unusual ways. Typically they are very resistant to change and become very upset at minor changes in objects or persons, or in their routine. Many also display ritualistic and repetitive behaviors. Mark, for example, would line things up, and would scream if they were disturbed. Similarly, autistic children may react with tantrums if a parent wears an unfamiliar pair of glasses, a chair is moved to a different part of the room, they are told to clean up after dinner instead of before, or a word in a song is changed. Kanner (1943) labeled this characteristic a *perseveration of sameness.* Conversely, the same children may fail to react at all to changes that make a major difference in their lives.

Many autistic children become strongly attached to particular objects, such as plastic lids, rubber bands, cards, buttons, parts of their body, or water. They may collect these objects, carefully arrange them, carry them, or play with them constantly. Objects that can be taken apart or have a certain texture are particular favorites. Some children are fascinated by movement, and may observe spinning objects, such as fans or records, for hours.

The motor movements of autistic children may also be unusual. Mark would jump, flap his arms, twist his hands and fingers, and grimace. In addition to such *self-stimulatory behaviors,* some children perform *self-injurious behaviors,* such as repeatedly lunging or banging their heads against walls, pulling their hair, or biting parts of their body.

The perceptual reactions of autistic children are often disturbed and paradoxical (Wing, 1976; Wing & Wing, 1971). Sometimes the children appear overstimulated by sights and sounds and try to block them out, while at other times they seem to be understimulated and to perform self-stimulatory actions in compensation. They may fail to react to loud noises yet turn around when they hear soda being poured. They may fail to recognize that they have reached the dangerous edge of a high place yet immediately spot a small object that is out of place in their room.

VIEWS ON AUTISM A variety of explanations have been offered for autism, including perceptual-cognitive, biological, and family and environmental views. Although each has received some support, none is without limitations and problems.

PERCEPTUAL-COGNITIVE VIEWS According to some theorists, autistic children have primary perceptual or cognitive disturbances that make normal communication, interpersonal relationships, and environmental interactions impossible (Baron-Cohen, 1991, 1989; Goodman & Ashby, 1990; Leslie & Frith, 1988). Several kinds of disturbance have been suggested.

One of the oldest perceptual explanations holds that autistic children have a fundamental impairment in their ability to *comprehend sounds* (Klin, 1993; Rutter, 1971, 1968). Theoretically, the children hear sounds but cannot make sense of them as other children can. This inability hinders their understanding of the world around them and makes them asocial. In support of this theory, several studies have found that autistic children do not respond appropriately to sounds, sometimes react to a sound as if they hear more than one, and sometimes remember meaningful speech no better than meaningless gibberish (Klin, 1993).

In another perceptual-cognitive explanation, the psychiatrist Ivar Lovaas has postulated that autism stems from *stimulus overselectivity*—attention to only one dimension of a stimulus (Lovaas et al., 1979, 1971). A lemon, for example, has a certain shape, color, smell, taste, and texture, all of which help us identify it. If you attended only to the color of a lemon, you might confuse it with a banana, a lawn chair, the sun, or some other yellow object. Moreover, you would not be able to identify a black-and-white picture of a lemon. This is precisely the experience of autistic children, according to Lovaas. As a result, they have difficulty associating human beings with all the things they represent—security, food, warmth, gratification of needs, and the like—and they fail to develop a proper affection and desire for social interactions. Similarly, they cannot associate words with the objects they represent.

BIOLOGICAL VIEWS During the past few decades researchers have tried to determine the role of biological factors in autism. Biological explanations have been popular for two reasons. First, the disorder unfolds so early in life—often at birth—that environmental factors have relatively little time to operate. Second, underlying biological factors sometimes seem to offer the only possible explanation for symptoms that are so diverse and paradoxical. Yet research has yet to provide a clear biological understanding of this disorder.

Examinations of the relatives of autistic children are consistent with the possibility of a *genetic factor* in this disorder (Folstein & Rutter, 1988). Studies find that siblings of autistic children have an increased risk of developing the disorder. The prevalence of autism among these siblings is between 1 and 2 per 100 (Rutter & Bartak, 1971), a rate fifty times higher than the general population's. Moreover, identical twins of autistic siblings demonstrate the highest risk of all. The genetic explanation of autism has also received support from the discovery of certain chromosomal abnormalities in 10 to 12 percent of persons with this disorder (Sudhalter et al., 1990; Rutter & Garmezy, 1983).

Some studies suggest a link between autism and *prenatal difficulties or birth complications* (Goodman, 1990; Steffenburg et al., 1989). The rate of maternal rubella (German measles), for example, is ten times higher in pregnancies that produce autistic children (Chess, 1971). Similarly, more labor and delivery complications have been reported in births of autistic children than in births of other children. The mother's exposure to toxic chemicals before or during pregnancy has also been associated with increased rates of autism (Rimland, 1992). Studies have also linked the disorder to illnesses during the first three years of life (DeMyer, 1979).

Research also suggests that *neurological dysfunction* may be involved in autism. Several studies find that autistic children have a higher number of neurological problems than other children (Gillberg et al., 1990). And some researchers have found differences between the electroencephalograms (EEGs) of autistic and nonautistic children (APA, 1994; Dawson & Castelloe, 1992). Some studies suggest deficits in the left temporal lobe, which are thought to be related to the linguistic and social impairments found in autistic individuals (White & Rosenbloom, 1992; DeLong, 1978).

Many researchers now suggest that autism can have multiple biological causes. In fact, some researchers have suggested that subgroups of autism should be identified according to the specific medical condition associated with each case (Gillberg, 1992). A number of theorists also propose that all biological factors (genetic, prenatal, birth, and postnatal) eventually lead to a common problem in the brain—a "final common pathway" that leads to an autistic pattern of behavior (DeMyer et al., 1981; Coleman, 1979). Some of the leading candidates for this final pathway are disturbances in the *brain stem* (McClelland et al., 1992; Tanguay & Edwards, 1982; Skoff, Mirsky, & Turner,

Behaviorist Ivar Lovaas is one of the field's most influential theorists on autism. His behavioral treatment approaches have been applied in thousands of educational and clinical settings.

1980); abnormalities in the *reticular activating system*, the area that ascends from the brain stem and arouses electrical activity in the cortex (Kootz, Marinelli, & Cohen, 1982; Hutt et al., 1964); abnormalities in the *cortex* of the brain, the area that deals with higher-order processing, integration, coding, and language (Maurer & Damasio, 1982; DeMyer et al., 1981; Hauser et al., 1975); and *neurotransmitter imbalances*, such as a high activity of serotonin or dopamine (Martineau et al., 1992; Yuwiler et al., 1992; Young et al., 1982).

FAMILY AND ENVIRONMENTAL VIEWS Many theories of autism implicate the family and environment as a cause. These theories have undergone an interesting transition since autism was first identified. At first most theorists claimed that environmental factors were wholly or largely responsible for the disorder. As the years passed, however, focus on the family and environment diminished considerably. Research failed to offer much support for this view of autism, and promising perceptual-cognitive and biological interpretations increasingly captured the attention of researchers and clinicians. Although the family and environmental explanations are less influential today, however, they continue to make a significant impact on the clinical field and to generate many studies. Theories and research focus on three areas of causation—characteristics of parents, family interactions, and early stress.

From the time he first identified autism, Leo Kanner (1954, 1943) argued that particular *personality characteristics of the parents* of autistic children contribute to the disorder. He saw these parents as very intelligent people, yet obsessive and cold — "refrigerator parents." Such parents may exacerbate certain innate deficiencies in their children, which then blossom into a full autistic syndrome of withdrawal and isolation.

Although such claims have had enormous influence on the public's impression of these parents and on the self-image of the parents themselves, research has failed to support a picture of rigid, cold, or disturbed parents (Roazen, 1992). In fact, they have proved to be warmer and more sociable in many comparisons with parents of normal children and with parents of deaf, mentally retarded, and dysphasic children (who exhibit language deficits as a result of a brain injury) (Gonzales et al., 1979; Cox et al., 1975). Even the claim of higher parental intelligence has not been borne out (Gillberg & Schaumann, 1982; Tsai et al., 1982).

Other theorists argue that it is not the parents' characteristics but *parent interactions with the child* that lead to autistic patterns (Bettelheim, 1967; Ferster, 1961). According to them, the parents interact with their children in ways that are negative, angry, rejecting, or nonreinforcing. Bruno Bettelheim's (1967) family interaction theory of autism was for years very influential in the field. Bettelheim explained that parents of autistic children reject them and fail to respond to their emotional needs. The children sense the parents' negative feelings and can do nothing to get a positive response. Feeling powerless, they withdraw to protect themselves. They become totally passive and seek a simple world filled with sameness.

Like the theories that point to the characteristics or maladjustment of the parents, the family interaction explanations have received little empirical support. Most studies suggest that the parents of autistic children are no less supportive and accepting of their children than the parents of normal, mentally retarded, brain-damaged, or dysphasic children are (Erickson, 1992; Cantwell et al., 1978; DeMyer et al., 1972).

Finally, some clinicians suspect that unusual *environmental stress* helps cause autism. They propose that events that occur very early in life traumatize the children, stifle their development, and lead them into lives of near-total withdrawal. Once again, however, research has not supported this notion. Aside from the birth and postnatal factors described earlier, no relationship has been found between stressful life events and autism (Folstein & Rutter, 1977; Cox et al., 1975). Researchers who compared autistic and dysphasic children found no differences in the incidence of parental death, divorce, separation, financial problems, or environmental deficits (Cox et al., 1975).

TREATMENTS FOR AUTISTIC DISORDER

Treatments for autism are designed to help the individuals adapt better to their environment within their limitations. Although no treatment now known totally reverses the autistic pattern, it is possible to help many of these persons attain more effective functioning and contact with the world. The most prominent treatment approaches for autistic children are drug, psychodynamic-humanistic, and behavioral interventions, communication training, parent training and support, and community integration.

DRUG THERAPY   Given alone, psychotropic medications have been of limited help to autistic children. In conjunction with other treatments or with educational programs, however, some of these drugs may be effective (Cook et al., 1992; Todd, 1991). Because of its positive impact on attention and learning, the antipsychotic drug haloperidol has been particularly helpful when it is used in conjunction with the learning approaches of behavioral therapists. In addition, vitamin B_6 in combination with magnesium helps increase attention and language in some autistic children while reducing self-stimulatory behaviors and tantrums (Rimland, 1992, 1988).

PSYCHODYNAMIC-HUMANISTIC THERAPY   Believing that autism is primarily the result of severe disturbances in early parent-child relationships, psychodynamic and humanistic therapists have tried to provide corrective environmental experiences, marked by great warmth and acceptance, which theoretically help the child form a bond with the mother or a mother figure (Bettelheim, 1967; Goldfarb, 1967; Mahler, 1965). Although several clinicians reported considerable success with psychodynamic-humanistic treatments of this kind in the past (Bettelheim, 1967), research later challenged such claims (Brown, 1963, 1960), and accordingly, these approaches have been less popular in recent years.

BEHAVIORAL THERAPY   Behavioral aproaches have been used with autistic children for more than thirty years. These approaches teach the children new, appropriate behaviors, including speech, social skills, classroom skills, and self-help skills, and try to reduce negative, dysfunctional ones.

Therapists who use modeling techniques have the children imitate behaviors that the therapists demonstrate. Those who use operant conditioning reinforce the children when they perform desired behaviors. Neither of these behavioral procedures is easy to employ, because autistic children often have difficulty imitating and find it hard to make connections between behaviors and rewards. Nevertheless, with careful planning and execution, therapists apparently can help the children learn new behaviors. For successful learning to occur, the desired behaviors must be *shaped*—broken down and learned step by step—and the reinforcements must be explicit and consistent (Lovaas, 1987; Harris & Milch, 1981).

Behavioral programs that systematically employ such procedures often bring results that other approaches do not. A recent long-term controlled study (McEachin et al., 1993; Lovaas, 1987) compared the progress of nineteen autistic children who received intensive behavioral intervention with that of nineteen autistic children in a control group. The treatment began when the children were 3 years old and continued until they were 7. By the age of 7, the experimental group required less specialized treatment in school (many of them entered regular classrooms) and had higher IQs than the control group. These gains were still evident in the children at 11 to 19 years of age. Eight of the children given early behavioral interventions scored on a par with average normal children on tests of intelligence and adaptive behavior. In light of such findings, many clinicians now consider behavioral programs to be the preferred treatment for autism (Waters, 1990). Since behavioral intervention beginning at an early age has been found to produce long-lasting and significant improvements, many clinicians are now focusing on techniques for early identification of autistic disorders (Adrien et al., 1993, 1992).

Behaviorists have also developed techniques for eliminating undesirable behaviors from the autistic child's repertoire (Foxx & Faw, 1990; Foxx et al., 1988). These efforts have centered on self-injurious behaviors, such as head-banging or biting oneself, which often place the children in danger, and self-stimulatory behaviors, such as repeated rocking or hand-flapping, which may interfere with learning and with cooperative play. Some behavioral programs ignore inappropriate behaviors while reinforcing desirable ones. Other behavioral programs use punishment to help eliminate negative behaviors. The punishments range from restraint to electric shock (Saposnek & Watson, 1974). It turns out, however, that self-injurious behaviors sometimes resume or even increase after the restraint or electric shocks are discontinued (Harris & Ersner-Hershfield, 1978).

The use of punishment in the treatment of autistic children has understandably concerned many people and stirred debate. Although these procedures may help achieve important goals, they prompt a number of questions. First, does punishment belong under

Behaviorists have had considerable success teaching autistic children to speak. The therapist systematically models how to position the mouth and how to make appropriate sounds, and then rewards the child's accurate imitations.

the heading of treatment? Some people believe that the pain and suffering these approaches inflict on young clients are unacceptable. Others counter that medical treatments are often just as painful, yet necessary to improve a person's health. But how does a clinician determine when punishment is necessary? Does biting one's arm justify the interventions, or must the behavior be life-threatening? And finally, who has the right to make these judgments? When children are involved, consent must be obtained from parents or guardians. But do they have the right to authorize painful procedures? Some clinicians argue that punishments such as shock should be used only after an impartial review board has been consulted and safeguards are in place (Gerhardt et al., 1991; Oppenheim, 1976).

Many therapies for autistic children, particularly the behavioral therapies, are conducted in a school setting. The children attend special classes, often at special schools, where education and therapy are pursued simultaneously. Specially trained teachers help the children improve their skills, behaviors, and interactions with the world.

Clinicians sometimes suggest that higher-functioning autistic children should be integrated into normal classrooms with nonautistic peers (Simpson & Sasso, 1992; Tomchek et al., 1992). *Integrated education* and *peer-mediated interventions* are especially useful in teaching autistic children how to socialize (Goldstein et al., 1992; Nientimp & Cole, 1992).

COMMUNICATION TRAINING Despite intensive behavioral treatment aimed at teaching autistic children to talk, 50 percent remain speechless. As a result, many therapists also turn to nonvocal modes of communication with their autistic clients. During the 1980s, *sign language* became popular for this purpose. Studies have found that *simultaneous communication,* a method combining sign language and speech, is often more successful than the use of either alone (Gaines et al., 1988). Other therapists advocate the use of *augmentative communication systems,* such as communication boards or computers that use pictures, symbols, or written words to represent objects or needs. A child may point to a picture of a fork to represent "I am hungry," for example, or point to a radio for "I want music." The advantage of these systems is that it is easier for the children simply to point to a selection than to muster the complex motor responses needed for sign language or vocal communication. There is much controversy over the efficacy of *facilitated communication,* one of the newest augmentative methods being used to help autistic persons communicate (see Box 19–3).

TREATMENT AND TRAINING FOR PARENTS
Professionals no longer view parents of autistic persons as the enemy, to be blamed for all the child's problems in the first place. Increasingly they are recognizing the parents' suffering and are trying to address their needs for information, guidance, and support.

Each treatment model now tries to involve parents in the treatment program. Psychodynamic therapists often work to establish a link between parent and child. Behavioral programs include parent-training components to help parents learn and apply behavioral techniques at home (Love, Matson, & West, 1990; Anderson et al., 1989). Some treatment programs now include instruction manuals for parents and home visits by professionals. In some cases, the entire program of treatment is conducted in the child's home.

Individual therapy and support groups for parents also are becoming increasingly available. Here they can explore their feelings and have their own problems and needs addressed. In addition, parent associations and lobbies such as the National Society for Children and Adults with Autism provide emotional support and practical help.

COMMUNITY INTEGRATION Clinicians are now developing new ideas and programs for improving the opportunities of autistic children as they grow older (Wall, 1990; Schopler & Hennike, 1990). Community-based programs that help integrate autistic persons into the community are becoming increasingly popular (Pfeiffer & Nelson, 1992). Educational and home programs are now concerned with teaching self-help, living, and work skills to autistic children as early as possible, as well as self-management skills

that enable autistic persons to control their behavior and to initiate social interactions when a treatment provider is not around to help (Koegel et al., 1992; Stahmer & Schreibman, 1992). In addition, carefully run *group homes* are being established for many autistic adolescents and young adults. These homes, along with *sheltered workshops,* address the problems faced by aging parents whose children will always need supervision (Van Bourgondien & Schopler, 1990; Schopler, 1981; Wing, 1981). Such efforts demonstrate the field's awareness that the needs and problems of autistic individuals usually last a lifetime.

MENTAL RETARDATION

Ed Murphy, aged 26, can tell you what it's like to be diagnosed as retarded:

*W*hat is retardation? It's hard to say. I guess it's having problems thinking. Some people think that you can tell if a person is retarded by looking at them. If you think that way you don't give people the benefit of the doubt. You judge a person by how they look or how they talk or what the tests show, but you can never really tell what is inside the person.

Take a couple of friends of mine. Tommy McCan and PJ. Tommy was a guy who was really nice to be with. You could sit down with him and have a nice conversation and enjoy yourself. He was a mongoloid. The trouble was people couldn't see beyond that. If he didn't look that way it would have been different, but there he was locked into what the other people thought he was. Now PJ was really something else. I've watched that guy and I can see in his eyes that he is aware. He knows what's going on. He can only crawl and he doesn't talk, but you don't know what's inside. When I was with him and I touched him, I know that he knows.

(Bogdan & Taylor, 1976, p. 51)

For much of his life Ed was labeled mentally retarded and was educated and cared for in special institutions. During his adult years, his clinicians came to suspect that Ed's intellect in fact surpassed that ordinarily implied by this term. Nevertheless, Ed did live the childhood and adolescence of a person labeled retarded, and his recollections illustrate the prejudice often confronted by mentally retarded persons.

Mentally retarded persons are those who are significantly below average in intelligence and adaptive ability. As Ed's description suggests, the term has been applied to a broad and varied population, including children in institutional wards who rock

BOX 19-3

FACILITATED COMMUNICATION AND AUTISM: POINTING IN THE WRONG DIRECTION?

Facilitated communication is the newest mode of communication being used with autistic persons. It is similar to some other augmentative communication strategies in that the client communicates by pointing to specific items on a communication board or computer keyboard. The difference is that in facilitated communication, a second person, or "facilitator," provides emotional and physical assistance as the autistic client points to each selection.

The facilitator supports the individual's hand, wrist, or arm as he or she points to letters on the computer keyboard or display terminal. The facilitator is not supposed to direct the person's hand, but simply to minimize the motor difficulties typical of autism by isolating the client's index finger, stabilizing the hand and arm, slowing the hand down as it moves from one selection to the next, and pulling the hand back after each selection to prevent repeated key pressing. The facilitator also helps the communicator stay focused on the task by reminding him or her to look at the device, keeping the index finger isolated, and minimizing interruptive

behaviors such as self-stimulation or aggression.

The method was developed in Australia during the 1970s. It was introduced to the United States in 1990 by Douglas Biklen, a Syracuse University researcher who had gone to Australia to learn about it. Biklen published a description of his experiences with facilitated communication, and instantly the method became popular within the autism community. Success was reported in hundreds of developmentally disabled people across the country.

One reason facilitated communication has become so popular so quickly is that it offers parents some hope that beneath their child's noncommunicative surface is a person who can think and communicate as clearly as anyone else. With facilitation, autistic children who were never taught to read or spell are writing poetry and prose. Children who were previously thought to shun interpersonal contact are talking about their thoughts, fears, and desires. Children who were thought to be mentally retarded are completing complicated math assignments, studying history and science, and being mainstreamed into classrooms with

children of their own age. Autistic people are claiming through their computers that they are highly intelligent but somehow "trapped" inside their bodies.

Proponents of facilitated communication believe that most autistic people do have a rich, internal consciousness that is trapped within by neuromotor difficulties. The body and mind cannot connect, and the autistic person is unable to initiate any movement. They believe that the physical and emotional support provided by the facilitator allows the autistic person to overcome these neuromotor barriers to communication.

The initial groundswell of enthusiasm for facilitated communication has, however, slowed considerably in the past few years. Two developments have been responsible for a sharp decline in its popularity. First, the technique has led to numerous accusations of physical and sexual abuse by autistic individuals against their parents, relatives, or friends. Authorities have determined most of these accusations to be blatantly false, raising serious questions about the validity of the procedure that produced such claims.

---

vacantly back and forth, young people who work daily in special job programs, and men and women who raise and support their families by working at undemanding jobs (APA, 1994).

Approximately one of every 100 persons receives a diagnosis of mental retardation (APA, 1994), so that 100,000 to 150,000 infants born each year are destined to receive this diagnosis (President's Committee on Mental Retardation, 1980). Approximately three-fifths of them are boys. As we shall see, the vast majority are considered *mildly* retarded.

In 1950 Alfred Binet developed the first widely used intelligence test and proposed that testing should serve as the first step in treating mental retardation. He wrote, "After the illness, the remedy." Unfortunately, the remedy for this problem proved elusive, and for much of the twentieth century mentally retarded persons were considered beyond help. During the past few decades, professionals have taken a more positive attitude, worked to prevent or alleviate the disorder, and developed special interventions and educational approaches

A child's hand is supported by a facilitator (his mother in this case) while he points to letters on an alphabet board. Computer keyboards or display terminals are commonly used in facilitated communication.

Second, an enormous number of clinical researchers, therapists, and educators have come forth to challenge the merits of this procedure. These skeptics do not believe that the communications made through this method are valid. The facilitator, they believe, is unconsciously or consciously influencing the autistic person's choice of letters, and many of them consider facilitated communication to be nothing more than a "human Ouija board."

The skeptics point out that most of the evidence supporting facilitated communication comes from case reports rather than empirical studies. In fact, most of the systematic research conducted in recent years seems to challenge the procedure rather powerfully. For example, researchers have found that when the facilitator is kept ignorant of the topic of conversation (for example, when facilitators wear headphones that prevent their hearing a researcher's questions), the autistic person is unable to communicate meaningfully. In one particularly compelling study, researchers showed autistic subjects a picture and then instructed them to label or describe it through facilitated communication

with the help of a facilitator (Wheeler et al., 1992). The subjects could produce accurate labels only when their facilitators had seen the same picture. In fact, when the facilitator had been shown a different picture from that shown the autistic subject, the subject would often type a response that corresponded to the facilitator's picture. Clearly, facilitators often play much more than a passive role in this procedure.

Thus the growing belief among most clinicians and educators is that the technique of facilitated communication may work as proponents claim for *some* autistic persons, but not for the majority of people with this disorder. Opponents of facilitated communication fear that parents and educators who use this technique as their main educational approach are in danger of turning their backs on more useful techniques for teaching communication skills. In addition, they point out that facilitated communication, even in those cases where it might be genuinely helpful, does little to solve the behavioral problems or improve the adaptive functioning of autistic people, and thus they argue that approaches that teach basic self-help and vocational skills should still have precedence over facilitated communication training. In the absence of empirical studies showing that facilitated communication can work, most clinicians are now hesitant to use it as their main teaching strategy, though many continue to use it on an experimental basis.

for those who are mentally retarded (Fiedler & Antonak, 1991).

A major turning point came in the 1960s, when President John Kennedy publicly acknowledged that one of his sisters was retarded and established a panel to make recommendations for improved services to mentally retarded persons. The panel's recommendations along with organized lobbying efforts by parents of retarded persons resulted in laws that mandated more research and rehabilitation in this area. Indeed, since the 1960s the federal government has trained

and supported thousands of mental retardation specialists, whose efforts have led to a clearer understanding and better education and treatment of persons with this disorder (Grinspoon et al., 1986).

Echoing the criteria set forth by the American Association on Mental Retardation (AAMR) in 1992, DSM-IV holds that **mental retardation** should be diagnosed when people manifest significant subaverage general *intellectual functioning* (an IQ of 70 or below) and display concurrent deficits or impairments in present *adaptive behavior* (APA, 1994); in other words, they cannot effectively meet the standards expected for their age by their cultural group in at least *two* of the following skill areas: communication, self-care, home living, social or interpersonal skills, use of community resources, self-direction, functional academic skills, work, leisure, health, and safety. DSM-IV further requires that the persons develop these symptoms before the age of 18. Although these criteria may seem straightforward, they are in fact hard to apply.

INTELLIGENCE   As we observed in Chapter 4, clinicians and educators rely largely on intelligence tests to define and distinguish different levels of intellectual functioning. These tests consist of questions or tasks chosen to represent different dimensions of intelligence, such as knowledge, reasoning, and judgment. An intelligence quotient (IQ) score derived from the individual's test performance theoretically indicates the person's overall intellectual capacity.

Many theorists have questioned whether IQ tests are valid—that is, whether they measure and predict what they are supposed to measure and predict. If IQ scores reflect intelligence, they should predict a person's performance on tasks that seem to rely on intelligence, such as school tasks (Smith & Smith, 1986). Correlations between IQ and school performance range from .40 to .75, indicating that many children with lower IQs do indeed perform poorly in school, while many of those with higher IQs perform better (Smith & Smith, 1986; Anastasi, 1982). At the same time, these correlations also suggest that the relationship is far from perfect. Educators frequently find a particular child's school performance to be at odds with his or her IQ. Moreover, IQ scores are not correlated at all highly with job productivity or social effectiveness—areas of performance that also seem to rely on intellectual ability (Anastasi, 1982).

Another validity problem is that intelligence tests appear to be socioculturally biased, as we first noted in Chapter 4 (Helms, 1992; Puente, 1990; Anastasi, 1982). Children reared in middle- and upper-socioeconomic-level households tend to have an advantage in the tests because they are regularly exposed to the kinds of vocabulary, exercises, and challenges that the tests measure (Tulkin, 1968). The tests rarely reflect the "street sense" needed for survival by persons who live in poor, crime-ridden areas—a kind of know-how that certainly seems to require intellectual skills.

Validity is also a problem when intelligence tests are given to members of cultural minorities and in a language in which the person being tested is not fluent (Puente, 1990; Elliott et al., 1985). Studies sug-

Studies suggest that IQ scores and school performances can be raised by enriching the daily environments of young children. One positive result of such studies has been the implementation of "Head Start" programs in cities around the country, such as this one in New York City. These educational programs for preschoolers from poor neighborhoods provide highly stimulating learning and social environments and seem to increase a child's chances of later performing well in school. The positive effects apparently fade after several years, however, if children do not receive further enrichment programs in elementary school.

gest that people score significantly higher when they are tested in their native languages, an opportunity rarely afforded immigrants in educational settings in the United States (Edgerton, 1979).

Such concerns have direct implications for the diagnosis of mental retardation (Wilson, 1992; Heflinger, Cook, & Thackrey, 1987). It may be that some persons receive this diagnosis primarily because of cultural differences, discomfort in the testing situation, or the bias of a tester. In fact, one investigator found that school psychologists are more likely to recommend lower-socioeconomic-level Mexican-American children to special classes for the retarded even when their IQs are the same as those of nonminority children of a higher socioeconomic class (Mercer, 1973).

ADAPTIVE FUNCTIONING   Diagnosticians have chosen a cutoff IQ score of 70 for mental retardation precisely because people with scores below 70 tend to be deficient in their adaptive functioning—that is, in their ability to be personally independent and socially responsible, to communicate, and to fulfill daily living requirements (APA, 1994). This relationship between IQ and adaptive skills does not always hold, however, especially for those whose IQs are close to 70. Some of these people are quite capable of managing their lives and functioning independently; others are not.

Brian comes from a lower-income family. He always has functioned adequately at home and in his community. He dresses and feeds himself and even takes care of himself each day until his mother returns home from work. He also plays well with his friends. At school, however, Brian refuses to participate or do his homework. He seems ineffective, at times lost, in the classroom. Referred to a school psychologist by his teacher, he received an IQ score of 60.

Jeffrey comes from an upper-middle-class home. He was always slow to develop, and sat up, stood, and talked late. During his infancy and toddler years, he was put in a special stimulation program and given special help and attention at home. Still Jeffrey has trouble dressing himself today and cannot be left alone in the backyard lest he hurt himself or wander off into the street. Schoolwork is very difficult for him. The teacher must work slowly and provide individual instruction for him. Tested at age 6, Jeffrey received an IQ score of 60.

Brian seems well adapted to his environment outside of school. He is the kind of child that the President's Committee on Mental Retardation once called the "six-hour retarded child." He fits the IQ criterion for mental retardation, but perhaps not the adaptive criterion. Jeffrey's limitations are more pervasive. His low IQ score is complemented by poor adaptive behaviors at home and elsewhere. A diagnosis of mental retardation may be more appropriate for Jeffrey than for Brian. Many researchers therefore suggest that the definition of mental retardation should place more emphasis on social competence and adaptive skills than on IQ (Greenspan & Granfield, 1992).

Various scales have been developed to assess adaptive behavior (Leland, 1991; Britton & Eaves, 1986). For example, the *Vineland* and *AAMR* adaptive behavior scales rate a child's ability to perform daily functions such as dressing and bathing, as well as such areas as independent functioning, physical development, economic activity, language, number and time concepts, vocational activity, self-direction, responsibility, and socialization (APA, 1994).

Although such scales are helpful, they are not always accurate predictors of a person's ability to function independently. Some individuals do better than the scales predict; others fall short. Thus clinicians themselves must observe and judge the effectiveness of every individual, paying attention both to the person's background and to community standards. Unfortunately, this is a subjective process. Clinicians are not always familiar with a particular culture's or community's standards, and some may be biased against them. Given the many problem areas involved in the measurement of intellectual and adaptive functioning, the AAMR (1992, p. 5) has supplemented its definition of mental retardation with the following four assumptions.

1. An assessment is valid only if it considers cultural and linguistic diversity as well as differences in communication and behavioral factors.
2. An assessment is valid only if the individual's deficits pertain to skills important within the context of the individual's community and typical of the individual's age peers and is indexed to the person's individualized needs for support.
3. Specific adaptive limitations often coexist with strengths in other adaptive skills or other personal capabilities.
4. With appropriate supports over a sustained period, the life functioning of the person with mental retardation will generally improve. The AAMR emphasizes that mental retardation is not a permanent *trait*, but is a *state* in which current functioning is impaired.

CHARACTERISTICS OF MENTALLY RETARDED INDIVIDUALS The most important and consistent difference between retarded and nonretarded people is that the retarded person learns more slowly (Kail, 1992; Hale & Borkowski, 1991). Although there are some striking exceptions (see Box 19–4), when retarded and nonretarded people of comparable mental age approach the same learning task, the retarded person usually employs relevant behavior, skills, and insights at a slower pace than the nonretarded person. Other areas of difference include attention, short-term memory, and language (Chamberlain, 1985; Yabe et al., 1985; Mineo & Cavalier, 1985).

When I was at school, concentrating was almost impossible. I was so much into my own thoughts—my daydreams—I wasn't really in class. I would think of the cowboy movies—the rest of the kids would be in class and I would be on the battlefield someplace. The nuns would yell at me to snap out of it, but they were nice. That was my major problem all through school that I

BOX 19-4

THE SAVANT SYNDROME

Leslie has never had any formal musical training. Yet upon hearing Tchaikovsky's Piano Concerto no. 1 on the piano for the first time in his teen years, he played it back flawlessly and without hesitation. He can do the same with any other piece of music, no matter how long or complex. Yet he cannot hold a utensil to eat and merely repeats in monotone fashion that which is spoken to him. Leslie is blind, is severely mentally handicapped and has cerebral palsy.
(Treffert, 1989, p. xi)

Kennenth is 38 years old but has a mental age of 11 years. His entire vocabulary consists of 58 words. Yet he can give the population of every city and town in the United States with a population over 5,000; the names, number of rooms and locations of 2,000 leading hotels in America; the distance from each city and town to the largest city in its state; statistics concerning 3,000 mountains and rivers; and the dates and essential facts of over 2,000 leading inventions and discoveries.
(Treffert, 1989, pp. xi–xii)

Most people are familiar with the "savant syndrome," thanks to Dustin Hoffman's portrayal of an autistic savant in the movie *Rain Man*. The savant skills that Hoffman portrayed—counting 246 toothpicks in the instant after they fall to the floor, memorizing the phone book through the *G*'s, and lightning-fast calculating abilities—were not merely products of a screenwriter's imagination; they were based on some of the astounding abilities that have been displayed by certain real-life autistic and mentally retarded people (Treffert, 1989).

A *savant* is a person with a major mental disorder or intellectual handicap who has some spectacular ability, some area of exceptional brilliance, despite his or her handicap. Often these abilities are remarkable only in the context of the person's handicap, but sometimes a savant's ability would be just as remarkable in a person who was not handicapped (Treffert, 1989). The extraordinary skills that savants display have most often to do with music, art, math, memory, mechanics, coordination, and geography (Rimland, 1978).

One of the most common savant skills is "calendar calculating," the ability to calculate what day of the week a date will fall on, such as New Year's Day in 2050 (Spitz, 1994). A common musical ability found in savants is the ability to play a piece of classical music flawlessly from memory after hearing it only once. Other savants can paint exact replicas of scenes they saw years ago. Alonzo, Jedediah, and David represent some of the skills and handicaps found in savants.

Alonzo has an I.Q. of 50 and a vocabulary of about that many words. Like Leslie, he only parrots back what is said to him and rarely initiates speech. But his animal sculptures are magnificent. He can complete a horse and colt in absolutely perfect anatomical detail in less than an hour. One fleeting glance at a picture is all he requires for a model that he will then reproduce in three-dimensional detail.

Jedediah, with a mental age of 10, unable to write his name, answered the question "In a body whose three sides are 23,145,789 yards, 5,642,732 yards and 54,965 yards, how many cubicle 1/8ths of an inch exist?" with the correct 28-digit figure after a five-hour computation. "Would you like the answer backwards or forwards?" he inquired. "I can give it either way."

David is mentally ill, requiring long-term hospitalization because of his dangerous and devastating rage attacks. While seriously impaired in a number of other areas, he has memorized the bus system of Milwaukee, Wisconsin. Give him the number of the bus pulling up in front of you and the time of day and he will

daydreamed. . . . I don't think I was bored. I think all the kids were competing to be the honor students, but I was never interested in that. I was in my own world—I was happy.

(Ed Murphy in Bogdan & Taylor, 1976, p. 48)

Difficulties with attention and memory are particularly characteristic of institutionalized retarded persons, and clinicians suspect that institutionalization itself contributes to these and other cognitive difficulties. It may be, for example, that the limited number of adult-child interactions in most institutions contributes to slow language development. Similarly, institutional factors may be partly responsible for the tendency to rely on others that inhibits the task performances of retarded persons.

Following the tradition of educators and clinicians, DSM-IV distinguishes four levels of mental retardation: *mild* (IQ 50–70), *moderate* (IQ 35–49), *severe* (IQ

tell you on what corner you are standing anywhere in the city.
(Treffert, 1989, p. xii)

In one study of the case histories of 5,400 autistic children, extraordinary abilities were found in 531 of the subjects, or 9.8 percent of the entire sample (Rimland, 1978). Although the prevalence of savant abilities in mentally retarded people is much smaller, only 0.06 percent, mental retardation is a much more common disorder, so the numbers of autistic and mentally retarded savants are about equal. Some researchers note the possibility that even more autistic children have savant skills that go undetected because of the children's poor ability to communicate. Bernard Rimland (1990) has labeled these individuals "autistic crypto-savants."

Several explanations for the savant syndrome have been suggested. One is that savant abilities are inherited skills that coexist coincidentally with the person's handicaps. This theory has not received much support because it does not account for the high percentage of autistic people who display these skills in comparison with the normal population. A second explanation is that savants experience *eidetic imagery,* a strong visual image of an object or scene that persists when the object or scene is removed.

In the 1988 film Rain Man, *Raymond is a young man whose autistic disorder is complemented by extraordinary skills, such as being able to memorize all the numbers in a telephone book and keeping track of all cards in a blackjack game.*

This theory may explain feats of memory (such as memorizing maps or calendar dates); it does not explain how some calendar calculators can calculate dates in the distant future for which they could not have seen a calendar. Moreover, this theory has not been supported by controlled studies that have tested for eidetic imagery in the savant population (Duckett, 1977).

Two other explanations of savant skills are based on theories that are also used to explain the deficits found in autistic persons. One is that savant abilities are the result of *stimulus overselectivity* and that savants involuntarily concentrate on and attend to very specific topics. They become preoccupied with trivial or bizarre activities such as memorizing facts, counting, and calculating, and are able to focus on very specific stimuli

(O'Connor & Hermelin, 1991).

The other is based on research on the *right brain/left brain dichotomy* found in autistic individuals. In the general population, the right hemisphere is more involved with spatial tasks and performance skills while the left hemisphere generally has more to do with verbal ability and sequential or abstract skills. This theory holds that autistic deficits are caused by dysfunction of the left hemisphere and that savant skills are the result of compensation for these deficits by the right hemisphere.

Theorists also suggest that these skills may be maintained because they are reinforced by the praise these people receive for them, and because autistic people do not mind constantly repeating a monotonous activity. In fact, such stereotypic, repetitive behaviors are a main characteristic of autistic disorders.

Although we do not yet fully know what to make of savant behavior, it does serve as an important reminder that every person represents a "package" of strengths and weaknesses, skills and problem areas. To focus exclusively on one realm of functioning and view a person as only a mentally retarded individual, a depressive, a schizophrenic, or a genius is to sadly miss complex, meaningful, and important features of that person's functioning.

20–34), and *profound* (IQ below 20). The intellectual and adaptive impairments of persons who fall into these various categories are often the results of different factors. Moreover, the persons who function at the various levels differ markedly from one another. One of the most important ways in which they differ is in the degree of *support* they require from other people. In fact, in its current definition of mental retardation, the AAMR (1992) prefers to distinguish these four categories on the basis of the level of support the per-

son needs—"intermittent," "limited," "extensive," or "pervasive"—rather than use the DSM's IQ-based distinctions.

MILD RETARDATION Approximately 85 percent of all retarded persons fall into the category of *mild retardation* (IQ 50–70) (APA, 1994). They are sometimes called "educably retarded" because they can benefit from an academic education. They can develop social and communication skills during their preschool years; academic skills up to approximately the sixth-grade level during adolescence; and social and vocational skills adequate for self-support during adulthood (APA, 1994). Still, they typically need assistance when they are under unusual social or economic stress. Their jobs tend to be unskilled or semiskilled.

Mild mental retardation is not usually detected until a child enters school, at which time school evaluators assign the label. Interestingly, the intellectual performance of individuals in this category often seems to improve with age; some even seem to leave the label behind them when they leave school and go on to function adequately in the community.

Research has linked mild mental retardation primarily to environmental factors and, to a lesser extent, to genetic and biological factors.

ENVIRONMENTAL CAUSES   Environmental understimulation, inadequate parent-child interactions, and insufficient early learning experiences may each contribute to mild mental retardation. These relationships have emerged in studies comparing deprived and enriched environments.

The majority of mildly retarded people come from *poor and deprived home environments* (see Figure 19–4) (Robinson & Robinson, 1970). In many cases, one of the parents and perhaps a sibling also display low intelligence. The poorer health and inadequate diets common in poorer homes may partly account for this relationship. A study of impoverished environments, however, suggests that the poor quality of parent modeling and low stimulation that exist in some of these homes may be the overriding factors in the development of mild mental retardation (Heber, 1979). The investigator in this study examined the IQ scores of mothers and children living in a poor Milwaukee neighborhood. Children whose mothers had IQs under 80 seemed to decline in intellectual functioning as they got older. While only 20 percent of 6-year-olds with such mothers themselves had IQ scores under 80, 90 percent of adolescents with such mothers had IQ scores under 80. In contrast, neighborhood children whose mothers had IQs over 80 showed no decline in their IQ scores as they got older. In light of these findings, many clinicians now emphasize the need for intensive, systematic early intervention with children of low-IQ mothers in an effort to reverse some of the environmental influences that encourage mental retardation (Coulter, 1992). Such intervention programs have been found to improve the children's later performance in school (Ramey & Ramey, 1992).

Some of the strongest evidence for environmental influences in mental retardation comes from projects

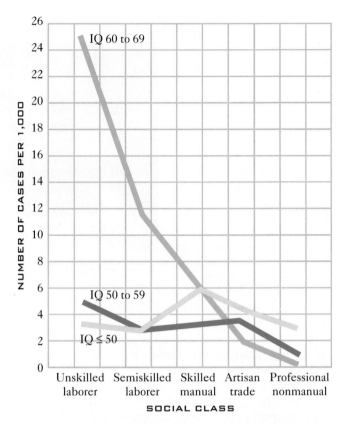

FIGURE 19–4   *The prevalence of mild mental retardation is much higher in the lower socioeconomic classes than in the upper classes. In contrast, more impaired forms of mental retardation are evenly distributed. (Adapted from Popper, 1988; Birch et al., 1970.)*

that alter the environment of retarded children (Marfo & Kysela, 1985). In the 1930s two clinicians transferred thirteen very young children from an unstimulating orphanage to another institution where they were regularly played with and given individual attention (Skeels & Dye, 1939). The children's IQs rose an average of 30 points. In contrast, eleven children who remained in the original orphanage continued to decline in IQ. In a follow-up study twenty-five years later, the same clinicians found that the thirteen people who had been transferred were now holding good jobs and raising families (most of them had been adopted in the interim), whereas those who had remained in the original orphanage were still institutionalized or holding menial jobs (Skeels, 1966).

GENETIC CAUSES   Because environmental factors seem to play such an important causal role in mild mental retardation, this kind of retardation has also been called *cultural, familial,* or *environmental retardation.* Yet at least some genetic and biological factors also seem to be operating. Some researchers who have compared the IQ scores of adopted children, their adoptive parents, and their biological parents have found higher IQ correlations between the children and their biological parents than between the children and their adoptive parents (Vernon, 1979; Munsinger, 1975). These findings have suggested to many people that heredity plays a major role in intellectual functioning and in the development of mild mental retardation.

At the same time, however, other adoption studies have instead highlighted the importance of environment. One study examined families in which parents were raising adopted children along with their own biological children (Scarr & Weinberg, 1977). The researchers computed IQ correlations between the mothers and their biological child and between the same mothers and their adopted child. The two sets of correlations turned out to be approximately the same, suggesting that IQ is often influenced more by environment than by heredity. The environmental influence shown in this study merited particular notice because the adopted children were of a different race than their adoptive family—the parents and biological children were white Americans and the adopted children were African Americans.

Another team of investigators conducted a similar study and in addition obtained the IQ scores of the adopted children's biological mothers (Horn et al., 1979). The IQ scores of these women averaged 6 points lower than those of the adoptive mothers, yet the adopted children earned IQ scores similar to those of the other children in their new family (average IQ of 112).

BIOLOGICAL CAUSES Early biological events may also contribute to mild mental retardation. Studies suggest, for example, that a mother's moderate drinking, drug use, or malnutrition during pregnancy may impair her child's intellectual potential (Stein et al., 1972; Harrell, Woodyard, & Gates, 1955). Similarly, malnourishment during childhood increases the risk of a person developing mild mental retardation (Davison & Dobbing, 1966). One study found an unusually low number of cells in the autopsied brains of children who had died from malnutrition (Winick, Rosso, & Waterlow, 1970).

It appears that the effect of malnourishment on intellectual development is at least partly reversible. One investigation compared the intellectual growth of three groups of children: severely malnourished Korean children who were adopted at 18 months of age and reared in middle-class American homes, properly nourished Korean children adopted by American families, and malnourished children who remained in their native environment (Winick,

Meyer, & Harris, 1975). At age 6, the previously malnourished children who had been adopted scored an average IQ of 102, whereas the malnourished children who had remained in their native environment scored 40 points lower. Although the scores of these adopted children were still lower than the scores of adopted children who had always been properly nourished, their IQs improved significantly after the children had been on regular, proper diets for years.

MODERATE, SEVERE, AND PROFOUND RETARDATION The approximately 10 percent of the retarded population who function at a level of *moderate retardation* (IQ 35–49) can learn to care for themselves and can profit from vocational training. They also profit, to some degree, from an academic curriculum, but their academic progress is not usually beyond the second-grade level (APA, 1994). When they reach adulthood, many can work in unskilled or semiskilled jobs, usually under supervision. Most moderately retarded persons adapt well to life in the community, usually in supervised settings (APA, 1994).

The approximately 4 percent of the retarded population who are *severely retarded* (IQ 20–34) display little speech during the preschool years. During the school-age years they can learn to talk and to care for themselves through concentrated teaching and training (APA, 1994). Their understanding of communication is usually better than their speech. They usually require careful supervision, profit somewhat from vocational training, and can perform only basic vocational tasks in structured and sheltered settings. Most adapt well to life in the community, in group homes or community nursing homes, or with their families (APA, 1994).

Around 1 percent of the retarded population is *profoundly retarded* (IQ below 20). In their early childhood years these individuals display considerable impairments in sensorimotor functioning. With training they acquire basic skills such as walking, some talking, and feeding themselves. They require a highly structured environment with close supervision and help and an individual relationship with a caregiver in order to develop to the fullest (APA, 1994).

The primary causes of moderate, severe, and profound retardation are biological, although people who function at these levels are also enormously affected by their environment. The leading biological causes are chromosomal and metabolic disorders, prenatal conditions, birth complications, and postnatal diseases and injuries (Pueschel & Thuline, 1991; Menke et al., 1991).

Until the 1970s, clinicians were pessimistic about the potential of children with Down syndrome. Today these children are viewed as individuals who can learn and accomplish many things in their lives.

CHROMOSOMAL CAUSES *Down syndrome,* named after Langdon Down, the British physician who first identified it, is the most common of the chromosomal disorders leading to mental retardation (Evans & Hamerton, 1985). Approximately 1 of every 800 live births results in Down syndrome, an incidence that increases to 1 in 100 when the mother's age is over 35 (Somasundaram & Papakumari, 1981). Many older mothers are now encouraged to undergo *amniocentesis,* testing of the amniotic fluid that surrounds the fetus, during the fourth month of pregnancy to detect Down syndrome and other chromosomal abnormalities.

Three types of chromosomal aberrations may cause Down syndrome. In the most common type, called *trisomy 21* (accounting for 94 percent of the cases), the individual has three free-floating twenty-first chromosomes instead of two (Pueschel & Thuline, 1991). In a second type, *translocation,* there are two normal twenty-first chromosomes and a third twenty-first chromosome fused with another chromosome (the fifteenth or thirteenth). And in a third extremely rare type, *mosaicism,* cells with two and cells with three twenty-first chromosomes are found in the same person.

Individuals with Down syndrome have a distinct appearance, with a small head, flat face, slanted eyes, high cheekbones, and, in some cases, a protruding tongue. Their hands are broad and thick with short fingers and typically have only a single palm crease. Because their eyes and high cheekbones resemble those of Asians, the disorder has sometimes been called *mongolism.*

People with Down syndrome may also articulate

poorly and be difficult to understand (Mahoney, Glover, & Finger, 1981). Although they are often demonstratively affectionate with family members, the stereotype that portrays them as "always" placid, cheerful, and cooperative appears to be an exaggeration. In fact, they display the usual range of individual personality characteristics (Carr, 1994).

Most Down syndrome persons range in IQ from 35 to 55; they account for about a third of the people who are moderately retarded (Grinspoon et al., 1986). Those with mosaicism tend to have IQs closer to 70. The aging process appears to occur more quickly in people with Down syndrome, and most even show some signs of senility as they approach 40 (Carr 1994; Burt et al., 1992). Now that scientists are able to observe chromosomes under a microscope by using chemical "staining" techniques and in turn to map the genes on each of the body's twenty-three pairs of chromosomes, they have come to suspect that Down syndrome is linked to genes located on the lower third of chromosome 21 (Epstein & Groner, 1989). When the person inherits three copies of chromosome 21 instead of the usual two, the extra genes on the lower part of the chromosome apparently produce the symptoms of Down syndrome. Scientists have determined that the genes linked to many cases of Alzheimer's disease are located on the middle third of chromosome 21 and that one of the Alzheimer-producing genes is located particularly close to the Down-syndrome-producing genes (Tanzi et al., 1989). Thus it may well be that Down syndrome and early dementia occur together because the genes that produce each of these disorders are located close to each other on chromosome 21 (see Figure 19–5).

Fragile X syndrome is the second most common chromosomal cause of mental retardation, accounting for 5 to 7 percent of all such cases among males (Zigler & Hodapp, 1991). Children born with a fragile X chromosome (one with a genetic abnormality) generally have moderate to severe degrees of mental handicap, language impairments, and, in some cases, behavioral problems (McEvoy, 1992). Although the physical features associated with fragile X are not so pronounced as those of other chromosomal disorders, they may include a long face, prominent jaw, and large testicles. Although the condition is more common in boys (who have only one X chromosome), some girls have also been affected. Fragile X syndrome cannot yet be identified through prenatal testing, but some researchers suggest that new developments in molecular techniques will soon make that possible (Abuelo, 1991; Hagerman & Brunschwig, 1991).

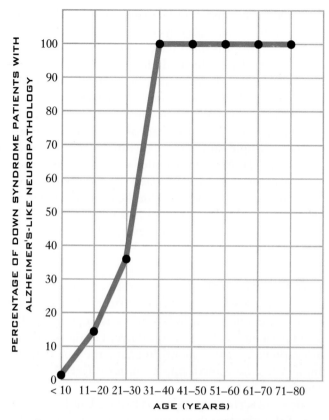

PERCENTAGE OF DOWN SYNDROME PATIENTS WITH ALZHEIMER'S-LIKE NEUROPATHOLOGY

AGE (YEARS)

FIGURE 19–5 *By the age of 35 to 40, most people with Down syndrome show some of the neuropathological changes characteristic of Alzheimer's disease. Both Down syndrome and Alzheimer's disease are linked to abnormalities on chromosome 21. (Adapted from Popper, 1989; Wisniewski et al., 1985.)*

METABOLIC CAUSES Metabolic disorders that affect intelligence and development are typically caused by the pairing of two defective *recessive genes,* one from each parent. Although one such gene would have no influence if it were paired with a normal dominant gene, its pairing with another defective gene leads to disturbed chemical production in the child and thus to disturbed metabolic processes.

The most common retardation-causing metabolic disorder is *phenylketonuria (PKU).* Approximately 1 of every 17,000 children has this disorder. Babies with PKU appear normal at birth but are unable to metabolize the amino acid *phenylalanine* into *tyrosine.* The phenylalanine accumulates and is converted into substances that poison the system, causing severe retardation. Persons with PKU have light coloring and many have eczema and epilepsy. They sometimes display odd behavior and movements and may be hyperactive.

Infants can now be screened for PKU. If affected children are diagnosed early enough and are started on a low-phenylalanine diet before three months of age, they may develop normal intelligence. Even-

tually, after age 6, and under careful supervision, they may be able to increase the phenylalanine in their diet.

In *Tay-Sachs disease,* another metabolic disorder resulting from a pairing of recessive genes, an enzyme missing from the infant's nerve cells leads to an excessive accumulation of fats, which in turn causes progressive mental deterioration and loss of visual and motor functioning over the course of two to four years, followed by death. The disease is most common among Jewish persons (Carter, 1970). One of every 30 persons of Eastern European Jewish ancestry carries the recessive gene responsible for this disorder, so that 1 of every 900 Jewish couples is at risk for having a child with Tay-Sachs disease.

In many cases, the carriers of these metabolic disorders (those who may pass the defective recessive genes along to their children) can be detected with blood tests. If a couple are identified as carriers, the prospective mother can undergo amniocentesis during her pregnancy to determine whether the child is going to have the disorder. If the test is positive, the couple may choose to undergo a therapeutic abortion to avoid the painful degeneration and early death that await the victims of some of these disorders (Pueschel & Goldstein, 1991).

PRENATAL CAUSES As a fetus develops, significant physical problems in the pregnant mother can endanger the child's prospects for a normal life (Menke et al., 1991). When a pregnant woman has too little iodine in her diet, for example, her child may develop *cretinism.* Her low supply of iodine may lead to a severe deficiency in the manufacture of the hormone *thyroxin,* which in turn can result in a defective thyroid gland in the baby. The deteriorating thyroid gland causes development to slow down, and mental retardation occurs. Individuals with cretinism have a dwarflike appearance—a large head, swollen abdomen, and short, stubby limbs. The disorder is rare today because the salt in most diets now contains iodine. Also, any infant born with this disorder may quickly be given thyroid extract to bring about a relatively normal development.

Children whose mothers abuse alcohol or other drugs during pregnancy are also at risk for mental retardation. As we observed in Chapter 13, such children may be born with a cluster of serious problems called *fetal alcohol syndrome:* the infant weighs less than normal, is intellectually deficient, manifests slow development, and has irregularities of the face and limbs (Phelps & Grabowski, 1993). It has been estimated that between 0.4 and 2.9 of every 1,000 newborn children may display fetal alcohol syndrome (Streissguth et al., 1991).

Maternal infections during pregnancy may cause a number of childhood abnormalities. *Rubella,* or German measles, is one of the best-known infections of this kind. If a mother contracts this otherwise minor illness, particularly in the first three months of pregnancy, mental retardation, heart disease, deafness, and a host of other abnormalities may develop in the child (Barlow, 1978). A vaccine taken during pregnancy now reduces the likelihood of this infection, but some pregnant women contract rubella before they discover that they are pregnant.

Another prenatal maternal infection that can cause mental retardation is *syphilis.* Children of mothers with syphilis often die within weeks after birth or even before birth. The effects on those who survive may include mental retardation, blindness, and deafness. Today physicians automatically test their pregnant clients for syphilis, so this disease is a less common cause of mental retardation now than it was in the past.

BIRTH-RELATED CAUSES Two birth complications that can lead to mental retardation are *anoxia* (loss of oxygen) and *extreme prematurity* (Menke et al., 1991). A prolonged period without oxygen during or after delivery can cause brain damage and retardation in a baby (Erickson, 1992). Similarly, although premature birth does not necessarily pose problems for children, researchers have found that a very low birth weight (less than 3.5 pounds) resulting from prematurity may cause some degree of mental retardation (Largo et al., 1989).

DISEASE- AND INJURY-RELATED CAUSES After birth, particularly up to age 6, certain injuries and accidents can lead to mental retardation. Poisonings, serious head injuries caused by accident or abuse, excessive exposure to X rays, and excessive use of certain drugs pose special dangers in this regard. For example, *lead poisoning,* associated with eating lead-based paints and with inhaling high levels of automobile fumes, can interfere with cellular metabolism and cause retardation in children (Berney, 1993). The exact blood level that is dangerous has not yet been determined. Similarly, mercury, radiation, nitrite, and pesticide poisoning may each cause retardation.

Similarly, certain infections during a child's early years can lead to mental retardation in some cases (Iivanainen & Lahdevirta, 1990). One of the most serious childhood diseases is *meningitis,* an inflammation of the meninges of the brain (Scola, 1991). This infection can cause brain damage and mental retardation, but such effects can be prevented with proper early treatment. Similarly, *encephalitis* during early childhood can cause serious brain damage unless it is treated quickly and effectively.

Some forms of moderate, severe, and profound mental retardation have multiple biological causes. *Microcephaly*—characterized by a small, unusually shaped head—can be caused by a combination of hereditary, prenatal, birth, and postnatal factors (Dorman, 1992). Twenty percent of institutionalized retarded people suffer from this disorder (Cytryn & Lourie, 1972). Another disorder with multiple causes is *hydrocephalus,* characterized by an increase in cerebrospinal fluid and resultant head enlargement. If this disorder is treated quickly, its effect on intellectual functioning may be less severe; if not, the disorder may even be fatal.

CARE, EDUCATION, AND TREATMENT FOR MENTALLY RETARDED PEOPLE The prognosis for mentally retarded persons is influenced by several factors: (1) where they live, (2) the kinds of educational and treatment programs they participate in, and (3) the growth opportunities offered by their family and community.

RESIDENTIAL ALTERNATIVES Until the middle of the nineteenth century, retarded people in the United States were cared for at home. Later in the century, public institutions—*state schools*—were established (Grinspoon et al., 1986). Parents were encouraged to send their retarded children to live in these institutions as soon as possible, theoretically to afford them proper care, treatment, and education. Unfortunately, in practice these overcrowded institutions offered only custodial care, and retarded persons in these settings were neglected, often abused, and isolated from society. Ed Murphy recalls his experiences in a state school:

To me there never was a State School. The words State School sound like a place with vocational training or you get some sort of education. That's just not the way Empire State School is. . . . If you looked at individuals and see what they said they were supposed to do for that person and then what they actually did, you would find that many of them were actually hurt—not helped. I don't like the word vegetable, but in my own case I could see that if I had been placed on the low grade ward I might have slipped to that. I began feeling myself slip. They could have made me a vegetable. If I would have let that place get to me and depress me I would still have been there today. Actually, it was one man that saved me. They had me scheduled to go to P-8—a back ward—when just one man looked at me. I was a wreck. I had a beard and baggy State clothes on. I had just arrived at the place. I was trying to understand what was happening. I was confused. What I looked like was P-8 material. There was this supervisor, a woman. She came on the ward and looked right at me and said: "I have him scheduled for P-8." An older attendant was there. He looked over at me and said, "He's too bright for that ward. I think we'll keep him." . . .

Of course I didn't know what P-8 was then, but I found out. I visited up there a few times on work detail. That man saved my life. Here was a woman that I had never known who they said was the building supervisor looking over me. At that point I'm pretty positive that if I went there I would have fitted in and I would still be there.

(Bogdan & Taylor, 1976, p. 49)

During the 1960s and 1970s a parent lobby, legal actions, and heightened public awareness led to a series of institutional reforms (Fiedler & Antonak, 1991). A number of newly established small institutions for mentally retarded persons encouraged self-sufficiency, devoted more staff time to patient care, and offered educational and medical services. Persons in these institutions began to show gains in IQ and reported being happier than in the past (Klaber, 1969; King & Raynes, 1967).

During this same period Denmark and Sweden began *normalization programs* in their institutions for mentally retarded persons. These programs offered living conditions and activities that closely resembled those enjoyed in the mainstream of society (Baldwin, 1985; Marlett, 1979). Persons in such programs were provided with flexible routines, normal developmental experiences, opportunities to make their own decisions, the right to develop a sexual identity, and normal economic freedoms. Today many institutions operate normalization programs, and care for mentally retarded persons is being offered in community settings as well (Baldwin, 1985).

As part of the *deinstitutionalization* movement of the 1960s and 1970s (see pp. 570–578), large numbers of retarded people were released from institutions (Beyer, 1991). Many had to make the transition to community life without special education or guidance, even without adequate residential placement. Like deinstitutionalized schizophrenic persons, they were virtually dumped into the community. Not surprisingly, many failed to adjust to a life without help or supervision and required reinstitutionalization.

In recent years more community programs and residences have been set up to address the needs of retarded persons (Jacobson & Schwartz, 1991; Clarke, Clarke, & Berg, 1985). In group homes, halfway houses, small local branches of larger institutions, and even independent residences, community staff members may be available to assist the retarded residents, and the residents are taught to get along in the community. Ed Murphy states his preference for community life:

I don't have it that bad right now. I have my own room and I get my meals at the house. The landlord is going to up the rent though—$45 a week for room and board. I'll be able to pay it, but I don't know what Frank and Lou across the hall will do. They wash dishes at the steak house and don't take home that much.

(Bogdan & Taylor, 1976, p. 50)

With the development of such programs, most mentally retarded persons now live their adult lives in the community (Jacobson & Schwartz, 1991; Repp, Barton, & Brulle, 1986). Virtually all who function at a level of mild mental retardation can reside successfully, often independently, in the community at large. Those with a moderate level of retardation may live in group homes that provide either evening supervision *(supported living arrangements)* or twenty-four-hour supervision *(community living families)*. Severely retarded persons live either with their families, in supervised group homes, or in community nursing homes that provide close supervision *(intermediate care facilities)*. And although some profoundly retarded people still must spend their adult lives in an institution, many are able to live in a smaller local facility (APA, 1994; Landesman-Dwyer, 1981).

Today the vast majority of retarded children live at home rather than in an institution until they are ready to enter a community residence (Erickson, 1992; Grinspoon et al., 1986). Even with a strong support system, however, some parents cannot cope with a handicapped child. In such circumstances, the child typically spends his or her early years in an institution.

As retarded persons approach adulthood, the family home may become a lonely and restricted place for them (Krauss et al., 1992). Parents who are aging and less energetic may no longer be able to address the needs of a retarded son or daughter. Programs have been designed to increase the social support networks of these people through community interactions, but sometimes a community residence may be the most appropriate alternative for a retarded child near the end of adolescence.

Unfortunately, investigators have sometimes found disappointingly low levels of family involvement once a child is placed in an out-of-home setting. This has become a great concern to clinicians, who have emphasized the importance of families as a source of social support, guidance, and advocacy (Blacher & Baker, 1994, 1992).

EDUCATIONAL PROGRAMS   Ed Murphy found school a difficult experience after he had been labeled retarded.

I kind of stood in the background—I kind of knew that I was different—I knew that I had a problem, but when you're young you don't think of it as a problem. A lot of people are like I was. The problem is getting labeled as being something. After that you're not really seen as a person. It's like a sty in your eye—it's noticeable. Like that teacher and the way she looked at me. In the fifth grade— in the fifth grade my classmates thought I was different, and my teacher knew I was different. One day she looked at me and she was on the phone to the office. Her conversation was like this, "When are you going to transfer him?" This was the phone in the room. I was there. She looked at me and knew I was knowledgeable about what she was saying. Her negative picture of me stood out like a sore thumb.

(Bogdan & Taylor, 1976, p. 48)

In 1975 Congress passed the Education for All Handicapped Children Act, calling upon each state to provide mentally retarded children with "free appropriate public education in the least restrictive environment." Appropriate education depends on the severity of the child's retardation (Cipani, 1991). Mildly retarded children, for example, must first be taught preschool readiness skills (sitting and attending), self-help skills, and language; later they are instructed in academic subjects and adaptive behaviors; and still later they receive vocational training (Marlett, 1979; Goldstein, 1975). At the other end of the spectrum, education for severely and profoundly retarded children must focus more on survival, self-help, language, and sensorimotor skills. Teachers of these individuals may also need to concentrate on reducing inappropriate behavior such as rocking or tantrums. Sometimes the educational efforts for retarded persons include programs which may even begin during the child's first few years of life. As we observed earlier, early intervention programs seem to offer great promise.

One of the greatest debates in the field of education centers on the correct educational environment for mentally retarded persons. Some educators favor special classes while others advocate mainstreaming (Gottlieb et al., 1991). In the *special education* approach, retarded children are grouped only with other retarded children and given a specially designed curriculum. It has been argued that special classes create

an environment in which the children can experience success instead of failure, receive the special attention they require, and encounter a curriculum more appropriate to their abilities and needs. In the *mainstreaming* approach, retarded children are placed in regular classes with nonretarded students. Proponents argue that this format provides a more normal educational experience, helps underscore the many similarities between retarded and nonretarded children, reduces stigmatization, facilitates interaction between retarded and nonretarded children, and places greater emphasis on academic subjects (AAMR, 1992; Turner & Small, 1985).

Researchers have not been able to determine whether one of these approaches is superior to the other (Gottlieb, 1981). Levels of performance are much the same under both educational formats (Budoff & Gottlieb, 1976). Moreover, although some studies find that children who are mainstreamed have a better self-image than children in special classes, others find either no such difference or else a better self-image among special-class children (Haywood et al., 1982; Zigler & Muenchow, 1979). Finally, mainstreamed children appear to be just as stigmatized in the eyes of their peers as special-class children (Gottlieb & Budoff, 1973). Perhaps mainstreaming is better for some children, special classes for others. Other important variables may include the subjects being taught and the skill, planning, and attitude that particular teachers bring to their work (Ascione & Borg, 1983; Haywood et al., 1982).

Operant learning principles are regularly applied in the education of retarded children (Erickson, 1992; Kazdin, 1979). Teachers break learning tasks down into small steps and give positive reinforcement as each small step is accomplished. Tasks taught to mentally retarded persons in this way include self-help skills, proper verbal responding, appropriate social responding, and academic tasks (Matson & Gorman-Smith, 1986). Computer programs that apply reinforcement principles have been used increasingly to help educate mentally retarded persons (Mineo & Cavalier, 1985; Ager, 1985). Many institutions, schools, and private homes have instituted *token economy programs*—the operant learning programs that have been used on a larger scale with institutionalized schizophrenic patients.

Parents often play an active role in their retarded child's education. Indeed, the Education for All Handicapped Children Act guarantees parents' participation in developing "individualized education programs" at school, a privilege not afforded to the parents of nonretarded children. This high level of involvement has resulted from the hard work and lobbying of parent associations in courts and legislatures across the United States. Many parents also serve as teachers at home (Reese & Serna, 1986; Chamberlain, 1985). To help them in their teaching role, parent-training manuals and courses have been developed.

THERAPY   Retarded persons often experience emotional and behavioral problems. Estimates are that a quarter of the severely and profoundly retarded persons in the United States display such problem behaviors as self-injury, vandalism, aggression, tantrums, and stereotyped repetitive movements (Qureshi & Alborz, 1992; Grinspoon et al., 1986), and that 10 percent of all mentally retarded persons have another diagnosable mental disorder in addition to their retardation (Grizenko et al., 1991). Moreover, mentally retarded persons at all levels may experience low self-esteem, interpersonal difficulties, and difficulty in adjusting to community life (Lubetsky, 1986; Reiss, 1985).

Insight therapies have been used to help mentally retarded people deal with issues of this kind (Hurley & Hurley, 1986; Ginsberg, 1984), but these therapies are helpful only some of the time. Apparently the greatest success is seen with insight approaches that are structured, directive, and problem solving; that help retarded people cope and interact with their environment; that enhance their feelings of self-worth; and that encourage them to persevere (Grinspoon et al., 1986). Group therapy has also become a popular and often effective format for retarded persons (Richards & Lee, 1972).

Close to half of all institutionalized retarded persons also are given medication for emotional or behavioral problems (Meador & Osborn, 1992), and a third take medication for epileptic seizures (Grinspoon et al., 1986). As many as 20 percent of the mildly retarded persons living in the community take such medications, yet research has not clearly indicated that the medications are in fact helpful to them (Aman & Singh, 1991; Grinspoon et al., 1986); nor has it established their long-term effects. Indeed, many clinicians suggest that too often the medications are used simply to keep retarded persons docile (Erickson, 1992; Grinspoon et al., 1986).

OPPORTUNITIES FOR PERSONAL, SOCIAL, AND OCCUPATIONAL GROWTH   In addition to a proper residence, education, and treatment, retarded persons must be given opportunities for *personal, social,* and *vocational growth.* Feelings of self-efficacy and competence are important aspects of personal growth, and retarded people can achieve them if they are allowed to make their own choices in life without undue pressure (Wehmeyer, 1992). Per-

sonal growth begins with the family: parents can unintentionally stifle a retarded child's self-sufficiency and independence by being too helpful, too protective, and too available as the child grows older. Ed Murphy recalls his mother:

> When I was growing up she never let me out of her sight. She was always there with attention. If I yelled she ran right to me. So many children who are handicapped must be in that position—they become so dependent on their mother. Looking back I don't think she ever stopped protecting me even when I was capable of being self-sufficient. I remember how hard it was to break away from that. She never really believed that after I had lived the first six months that I could be like everybody else. . . . It wasn't wrong that she protected me, but there comes a time when someone has to come in and break them away.
>
> *(Bogdan & Taylor, 1976, pp. 47–48)*

The community must also provide retarded persons with opportunities for personal growth. Denmark and Sweden, the originators of the normalization movement, have led the way in this area as well (Perske, 1972). These countries have developed youth clubs for retarded persons that encourage members to take risks, find their way around independently, cope with minor emergencies, and, in some cases, locate and set up their own apartments.

Socializing, sex, and marriage are difficult issues for retarded persons and their families. Typically, society

The interpersonal and sexual needs of retarded persons are normal, and many demonstrate considerable ability to express intimacy. Yet most retarded persons receive poor preparation and excessive restriction in these areas.

does a poor job of preparing retarded people for these experiences. Institutions are usually careful to separate male and female patients, and indeed, many parents prevent their retarded adolescents and young adults from socializing with persons of the opposite sex. This lack of education and experience may create even more problems for retarded people than IQ level when they first encounter social and sexual relationships. Local chapters of the National Association for Retarded Citizens now provide guidance in this respect, and several *dating skills programs* have been developed by clinicians (Valenti-Hein et al., 1994). Ed Murphy describes his attraction to Joan and his lack of knowledge in this domain:

I first met Joan in 1970. It was when I started working at the ARC workshop. I sat there and maybe the second or third day I glanced over and saw her there. The first time I noticed her was in the eating area; I was having lunch. I looked around and she was the only one there that attracted me. There was just something about her. . . .

It took awhile for her to understand how she felt. She didn't want to be too friendly. She didn't like my putting my arm around her. We went for walks during lunch and she got pretty fond of me and I got pretty fond of her. One day I asked her, "Well, how about a movie?" She said, "All right," but she had to get her mother's permission. Then one day she said she could go. It was a Saturday matinee gangster movie. We arranged to meet at the bus stop downtown. . . .

Being at the state school and all you never had the chances romantically like you might living on the outside. I guess I was always shy with the opposite sex even at Empire. We did have dances and I felt that I was good looking, but I was bashful and mostly sat. I was bashful with Joan at the movie. In my mind I felt funny, awkward. I didn't know how to approach her. Should I hug her? You can't hug the hell out of her because you don't know how she would take it. You have all the feeling there, but you don't know what direction to go in. If you put your arm around her she might scream and you're finished. If she doesn't scream you're still finished.

(Bogdan & Taylor, 1976, p. 50)

Some states have laws restricting marriage for retarded persons on the grounds that they cannot understand the obligations of marriage. These laws are rarely enforced, however, and in fact between a quarter and half of all mildly retarded persons eventually marry (Grinspoon et al., 1986). Despite public stereotypes, the marriages can be very successful. Mildly retarded persons encounter on the average only slightly more marital discord than nonretarded people (Robinson & Robinson, 1976). While some retarded persons are able to raise children without

unusual difficulty, others need special help and community services; still others may be incapable of raising children. The care-giving deficits found most often in mentally retarded parents are lack of functional domestic skills, poor perception of the child's needs, and inadequate parent-child interaction or neglect (Bakken et al., 1993; Keltner, 1992).

It was once common for retarded persons to be sterilized involuntarily, often at the request of their parents (Kempton & Kahn, 1991; Grinspoon et al., 1986). However, laws that permit this practice have been increasingly challenged as unconstitutional, and such procedures have become very restricted (Elkins & Anderson, 1992; Beyer, 1991). The current feeling among many clinicians is that with proper training and experience, retarded people can usually learn to use contraceptives, carry out responsible family planning, and in many cases rear children effectively. Researchers have found that parent-training programs for mentally handicapped parents are most successful when they are highly individualized, are presented in incremental steps, and occur in the home setting (Dowdney & Skuse, 1993; Bakken et al., 1993). Several scales have been developed to help predict the person's adequacy or inadequacy as a parent and to help plan individualized intervention programs (Espe-Sherwindt, 1991).

Finally, retarded adults need the self-satisfaction, structure, social stimulation, and financial rewards that come from holding a job. Many retarded persons do indeed want to work but have difficulty finding a job without government or agency intervention (AAMR, 1992; Friedman, 1976). Many work in *sheltered workshops,* where the pace and type of work are tailored to their skills and where supervision is available. After training in these workshops, many mildly or moderately retarded persons move out into the regular workforce. Because job retention is highly correlated with social skills, many clinicians and educators have emphasized the importance of teaching the kinds of social skills needed in employment settings (Chadsey-Rusch, 1992; Cavaiuolo & Nasca, 1991). The sheltered workshop tends to be the highest level of employment that severely and profoundly retarded persons can achieve, and enables them to be at least partly self-supporting.

Although training programs for mentally retarded persons have improved greatly in both number and quality over the past twenty-five years, much remains to be accomplished. Indeed, it is estimated that the majority of today's mentally retarded persons fail to receive the full range of educational and vocational training services from which they could profit (Tyor & Bell, 1984). To help ensure that the lives of mentally retarded persons are as complete, independent, and meaningful as possible, the U.S. government has funded numerous university-affiliated facilities whose job is to support research and provide model service programs for retarded and other developmentally disabled persons around the country (Grinspoon et al., 1986). It is hoped that programs of this kind will lead to further innovations in education, treatment, and vocational training, as well as to better public education about mental retardation. Only with such progress will retarded persons be able truly to cross the barrier created by their label. Once again Ed Murphy movingly and eloquently conveys the importance of this issue:

I never thought of myself as a retarded individual but who would want to. You're not knowledgeable about what they are saying behind your back. You get a feeling from people around you; they try to hide it but their intentions don't work. They say they will do this and that—like they will look out for you—they try to protect you but you feel sort of guilty. You get the feeling that they love you but that they are looking down at you. You always have that sense of a barrier between you and the ones that love you. By their own admission of protecting you you have an umbrella over you that tells you that you and they have an understanding that there is something wrong—that there is a barrier.

(Bogdan & Taylor, 1976, p. 50)

THE STATE OF THE FIELD

PROBLEMS OF CHILDHOOD AND ADOLESCENCE

Early in this century, children and adolescents were largely ignored by researchers, except for the insights they seemed to offer into adult functioning and dysfunctioning. Clinicians, too, usually viewed children as little adults rather than as individuals who might experience unique kinds of problems and require special interventions.

All that has changed over the course of the past sixty years, and today the mental health of children is a major focus of both researchers and clinicians. Numerous studies now concentrate exclusively on the problems of children and adolescents, and numerous clinicians specialize in the treatment of these populations. As a result, many childhood problems have been identified and clinical theorists have proposed various explanations for them: the unique cognitive and emotional structure of young persons, the ordinary pressures of youth, special childhood traumas, parenting deficiencies and family dysfunction, and biological factors. In addition, disorders of childhood and adolescence have been distinguished from such "life-span" disorders as autism and mental retardation, which begin early and typically impair their victims' functioning throughout their lives.

Child-focused researchers and clinicians have generally followed a path that parallels the one pioneered by adult-focused researchers and practitioners. That is, they have identified and distinguished a large number of childhood disorders and developed a variety of specialized treatment interventions. They have learned that although some of these disorders may appear to be straightforward, they are in fact anything but simple in their causes, treatments, and implications. And they have discovered firsthand the powerful negative influence that labels may have on the expectations and reactions of parents, teachers, clinicians, and the public at large, and have correspondingly become sensitive to the dangers of overdiagnosing children's problems. They now recognize that some degree of dysfunction and pain is a normal part of the human condition and that overreaction to it may create extra problems for children and their families.

In recent years clinicians and researchers have also increasingly recognized the relative powerlessness of children, and have enlisted the aid of government agencies to protect the rights and safety of this population and to draw attention to such problems as child abuse and neglect, child sexual abuse, child malnourishment, and the fetal alcohol syndrome. Clinicians have helped to determine the psychological impact of such problems and developed interventions designed to prevent and treat them.

The study and treatment of childhood problems may have been relatively slow to get started, but they are now moving rapidly. With the clinical field's growing recognition of children as important beings and with its increasing insight and effectiveness, developments in this area of abnormal psychology are likely to continue at an impressive pace. As the tongue-in-cheek box on the "disorder" called childhood implies, childhood has been around for a long time; now that clinicians have discovered it, they are unlikely to underestimate the complexity of its special issues or the extent of its importance ever again.

SUMMARY

■ **MANY THEORISTS THINK OF LIFE** as a series of stages through which people pass in a fixed order. Erik Erikson has provided a comprehensive developmental theory in which life is divided into eight stages, each marked by a particular developmental crisis and a new set of drives and needs. Erikson's stages are based on the following eight crises: *trust vs. mistrust, autonomy vs. shame and doubt, initiative vs. guilt, industry vs. inferiority, identity vs. role confusion, intimacy vs. isolation, generativity vs. stagnation,* and *integrity vs. despair.* Abnormal behavior may appear during each developmental stage as a result of psychological inadequacy, biological abnormality, or extraordinary environmental stress.

■ **UP TO 17 TO 22 PERCENT** of all children and adolescents in the United States experience a mental disorder. Clinicians who initially viewed children as small adults now recognize that there are often important differences between adult and childhood disorders.

Close to half of all children have multiple fears. In addition to the normal fears that disappear over time, children may experience *anxiety disorders* that are more persistent and may cause severe suffering. *Separation anxiety disorder* is characterized by excessive anxiety, often panic, whenever the child is separated from a parent.

Only recently have clinicians recognized that children experience severe *depressive* symptoms. Research has uncovered a relatively high rate of depression and other forms of mental dysfunction among the parents of depressed children.

Some children exceed the normal breaking of rules and act very aggressively. Children who display an *oppositional defiant disorder* argue repeatedly with adults and lose their temper. Those with a *conduct disorder,* a more severe pattern, repeatedly violate the basic rights of others. These children often are violent and cruel, and may lie, cheat, steal, and run away.

Children who display *attention-deficit hyperactivity disorder (ADHD)* attend poorly to tasks or act impulsively and move around excessively or both. Approximately half of the children with this disorder also experience learning problems and most misbehave.

Children with *elimination disorders—enuresis* and *encopresis—*repeatedly urinate and pass feces in inappropriate places, respectively, during the day or at night while sleeping or both. The behavioral bell-and-battery technique is an effective treatment for enuresis.

Children who display grossly inadequate functioning in learning, coordination, or communication may also receive a clinical diagnosis. These problems include the so-called *learning disorders, developmental coordination disorder,* and *communication disorders.* Studies have linked these problems to such factors as genetic defects, birth injuries, lead poisoning, diet, sensory or perceptual dysfunction, and poor teaching.

■ **PEOPLE WITH AUTISTIC DISORDER** (autism) display a broad set of dysfunctional behaviors early in life. They are unresponsive to others, have language and communication deficits (including *echolalia, pronominal reversal, nominal aphasia,* and *metaphorical language*), have limited skill at imaginative play, and exhibit deviant responses to the environment (such as *perseveration of sameness, strong attachments to objects, self-stimulatory behaviors,* and *self-injurious behaviors*). Treatment for autism seeks to help the children adapt to their environment. Although treatment in most cases cannot totally reverse the autistic pattern, some help has been found through the use of drug therapy, behavioral treatments, communication training, treatment and training for parents, and community integration.

■ **INDIVIDUALS WITH MENTAL RETARDATION** are significantly below average in intelligence (as measured on intelligence tests), display concurrent deficits or impairments in adaptive behavior (as measured on adaptive functioning tests or in clinical interviews), and develop these symptoms before the age of 18. Approximately 1 out of every 100 persons receives a diagnosis of mental retardation. Controversy, however, surrounds these criteria.

The most important and consistent difference between retarded and nonretarded individuals is that retarded people learn more slowly. Educators and clinicians have found it useful to distinguish four levels of mental retardation: mild, moderate, severe, and profound. More recently the American Association of Mental Retardation has preferred distinctions based on the level of support the person needs—"intermittent," "limited," "extensive," or "pervasive."

Mild retardation, the most common level, has been linked primarily to environmental factors such as environmental understimulation, inadequate parent-child interactions, and insufficient early learning experiences. It has also been referred to as *cultural, familial,* or *environmental retardation.* There is growing evidence that genetic and biological factors may also contribute to mild mental retardation.

The dominant causes of *moderate, severe,* and ***profound mental retardation*** are biological, although individuals who function at these levels of retardation are also enormously affected by their environment. The leading biological causes are *chromosomal disorders* (for example, ***Down syndrome*** or ***fragile X syndrome***), *metabolic disorders* that typically are caused by the pairing of two defective recessive genes (for example, ***phenylketonuria,*** or ***PKU,*** and ***Tay-Sachs disease***), disorders related to *prenatal problems* (*cretinism* and ***fetal alcohol syndrome***), disorders related to *birth complications,* such as anoxia or extreme prematurity, and disorders that result from *postnatal diseases and injuries* such as head injuries, poisoning, meningitis, or encephalitis.

In recent decades treatment for mental retardation has begun to focus on ***normalization programs*** that offer conditions of everyday life in an institutional or community setting. Halfway houses, group homes, and residences of various kinds provide education and training on how to get along in the community.

One of the most intense debates in the field of education centers on the correct educational environment for mentally retarded individuals, pitting proponents of ***special classes*** against proponents of ***mainstreaming.*** Research has not yet favored one approach over the other. In general, the use of ***operant learning*** has been successful in educating retarded individuals.

Retarded persons who also experience emotional or behavioral problems sometimes receive insight, behavioral, or drug therapy.

In general, retarded persons must have opportunities for personal, social, and occupational growth. Thus increasing numbers of programs are offering training in such areas as socializing, sex, marriage, and parenting. In addition, vocational training programs are available for many retarded persons.

Topic Overview

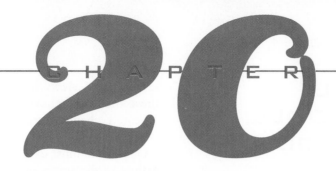

PROBLEMS OF AGING

DOLORES GALLAGHER-THOMPSON
AND LARRY W. THOMPSON

(The section on Early and Middle Adulthood and Box 20–2 are by Ronald J. Comer.)

■

I N CHAPTER 19 we saw that many psychological disorders have their onset during childhood or early adolescence. At the other end of the spectrum, a number of disorders develop as old age approaches or advances. As with childhood disorders, some of the disorders of later life seem to be caused primarily by the pressures that are particularly likely to appear at that time of life, others by unique traumatic experiences, and still others by biological abnormalities.

CHAPTER 19 FOCUSED on the first five of the eight developmental stages proposed by Erik Erikson—the stages that people traverse between birth and the end of adolescence. These stages, according to Erikson, are followed by the stages of *early adulthood*, in which people ideally attain intimacy and love rather than isolation; *middle adulthood*, in which people strive for generativity, and care for younger people through parenthood or mentoring of junior colleagues or co-workers; and *old age*, in which the goal is to integrate and to pass along all of one's insights from the past and present. Erikson believed that the developmental stages of adulthood, like those of childhood and adolescence, are filled with opportunities for either growth or maladaptiveness.

■ EARLY ■ AND MIDDLE ADULTHOOD

Several therapists have elaborated upon Erikson's descriptions of the stages of early and middle adulthood (Levinson, 1986; Gould, 1978; Vaillant, 1977; Neugarten, 1968). Gail Sheehy's *Passages,* one of the most successful books of the 1970s and 1980s, pre-

sented their views in popular form. Like Erikson, these theorists believe that the stages are marked by repeated change, stress, and adjustment (see Box 20–1).

One of the most extensive descriptions and investigations of the stages of early and middle adulthood is that of Daniel Levinson (1986, 1984, 1977). According to Levinson, the stage of *early adulthood,* lasting from about age 22 to 40, is characterized simultaneously by high energy and abundance and by contradiction and stress. Typically, people are in their peak

---

BOX 20–1

SUDDENLY I'M THE ADULT?

Richard Cohen

(This essay originally appeared in Psychology Today, *May 1987.*)

Several years ago, my family gathered on Cape Cod for a weekend. My parents were there, my sister and her daughter, too, two cousins, and, of course, my wife, my son and me. We ate at one of those restaurants where the menu is scrawled on a blackboard held by a chummy waiter and had a wonderful time. With dinner concluded, the waiter set the check down in the middle of the table. That's when it happened. My father did not reach for the check.

In fact, my father did nothing. Conversation continued. Finally, it dawned on me. Me! I was supposed to pick up the check. After all these years, after hundreds of restaurant meals with my parents, after a lifetime of thinking of my father as the one with the bucks, it had all changed. I reached for the check and whipped out my American Express card. My view of myself was suddenly altered. With a stroke of a pen, I was suddenly an adult.

Some people mark off their life in years, others in events. I am one of the latter, and I think of some events

as rites of passage. I did not become a young man at a particular year, like 13, but when a kid strolled into the store where I worked and called me "mister," I turned around to see whom he was calling. He repeated it several times—"Mister, mister"—looking straight at me. The realization hit like a punch: Me! He was talking to me. I was suddenly a mister.

There have been other milestones. The cops of my youth always seemed to be big, even huge, and of course they were older than I was. Then one day they were neither. In fact, some of them were kids—short kids at that. Another milestone.

The day comes when suddenly you realize that all the football players in the game you're watching are younger than you. Instead of being big men, they are merely big kids. With that milestone goes the fantasy that someday, maybe, you too could be a player—maybe not a football player but certainly a baseball player. I had a good eye as a kid—not much power, but a keen eye—and I always thought I could play the game. One day I realized that I couldn't. Without having ever reached the hill, I was over it.

For some people, the most momentous milestone is the death of a parent. This happened recently to a friend of mine. With the burial of his father came the realization that he had moved up a notch. Of course, he had known all along that this would happen, but until the funeral, the knowledge seemed theoretical at best. As long as one of your parents is alive, you stay in some way a kid. At the very least, there remains at least one person whose love is unconditional.

For women, a milestone is reached when they can no longer have children. The loss of a life, the inability to create one—they are variations on the same theme. For a childless woman who could control everything in life but the clock, this milestone is a cruel one indeed.

I count other, less serious milestones—like being audited by the Internal Revenue Service. As the auditor caught mistake after mistake, I sat there pretending that really knowing about taxes was for adults. I, of course, was still a kid. The auditor was buying none of it. I was a taxpayer, an adult. She all but said, Go to jail.

There have been others. I remember the day when I had a ferocious ar-

biological form during this stage. Their aspirations are youthful, they establish a niche in society, they may raise a family, and ultimately they reach a relatively "senior" position in the adult world. To many people this period brings great satisfaction and creativity. But early adulthood can also be a period of enormous stress. The burden of becoming a parent, undertaking an occupation, incurring financial obligations, and making other critical decisions about marriage, family, work, and lifestyle often fills people with intense feelings of anxiety and tension.

Levinson describes the stage of *middle adulthood,* lasting from about age 45 to 60, as a period in which biological functioning, although less than optimal, is still sufficient for an "energetic, personally satisfying and socially valuable life." During this stage, people usually become "senior members" of their particular world, and take responsibility for their own work, that of others, and the development of younger adults. Although this too can become a period of self-satisfaction and peace of mind, a person's growing biological problems, numerous responsibilities, and anticipation

gument with my son and realized that I could no longer bully him. He was too big and the days when I could just pick him up and take him to his room/isolation cell were over. I needed to persuade, reason. He was suddenly, rapidly, older. The conclusion was inescapable: So was I.

One day you go to your friends' weddings. One day you celebrate the birth of their kids. One day you see one of their kids driving, and one day those kids have kids of their own. One day you meet at parties and then at weddings and then at funerals. It all happens in one day. Take my word for it.

I never thought I would fall asleep in front of the television set as my father did, and as my friends' fathers did, too. I remember my parents and their friends talking about insomnia and they sounded like members of a different species. Not able to sleep? How ridiculous. Once it was all I did. Once it was what I did best.

I never thought that I would eat a food that did not agree with me. Now I meet them all the time. I thought I would never go to the beach and not swim. I spent all of August at the beach and never once went into the ocean. I never thought I would appreciate opera, but now the pathos, the schmaltz and, especially, the combination of voice and music appeal to me. The deaths of Mimi and Tosca move me, and they die in my home as often as I can manage it.

I never thought I would prefer to stay home instead of going to a party, but now I find myself passing parties up. I used to think that people who watched birds were weird, but this summer I found myself watching them, and maybe I'll get a book on the subject. I yearn for a religious conviction I never thought I'd want, exult in my heritage anyway, feel close to ancestors long gone and echo my father in arguments with my son. I still lose.

One day I made a good toast. One day I handled a headwaiter. One day I bought a house. One day— what a day!—I became a father, and not too long after that I picked up the check for my own. I thought then and there it was a rite of passage for me. Not until I got older did I realize that it was one for him, too. Another milestone.

of old age may also produce considerable stress and tension and some degree of psychological dysfunctioning.

Although the stages of early and middle adulthood may themselves be sources of stress, Levinson believes that the periods of *transition* that people must pass through as they move from one stage to another are even more unstable and wrenching and likely to produce tension and psychological dysfunctioning. During such transitional periods, people confront particularly difficult career, marital, and family issues and reflect on and adjust their dreams.

In the *early adult transition* from age 17 to 22—the period that bridges adolescence and early adulthood—people typically go through a very unsettled time. Although they take steps toward individuation and they modify their relationships with family, friends, and social institutions, they typically feel insecure in these efforts and so may experience repeated anxiety and confusion.

Even more traumatic is the *middle life transition,* from age 40 to 45—the period that bridges early and middle adulthood. During this period, individuals experience significant changes in the character of their lives. On the positive side, they may ultimately become more compassionate, reflective, and judicious, less conflicted, and more accepting and loving of themselves and others during these years. On the negative side, however, they may feel overwhelmed as they increasingly recognize that they are no longer young and vibrant, that time is passing quickly, that life's heaviest responsibilities are falling on them, that they must prepare for the future, and that their dreams may not be met. They may question their accomplishments in life and conclude that they have achieved and will continue to achieve too little. During this period of transition, some persons even try to deny the passage of time and to recapture their youth. Close to 80 percent of men interviewed by Levinson reported that this transition, popularly labeled the *midlife crisis,* was truly tumultuous and painful, and that they frequently felt anxious and depressed.

Another line of theorizing about early and middle adulthood proposes that the values and expectations of one's cohorts may also affect and create stress in a person (Neugarten, 1968). A *cohort* is a group of people born in the same year or time period—that is, people of the same generation. Generally, members of a given cohort are influenced by many of the same historical and personal events. The cohort born in 1920, who experienced Prohibition, the Great Depression of the 1930s, and the "good war" of the 1940s (World War II), is likely to have a different set

A new father prepares for his daughter's feeding and a new mother says good-bye before going off to war in the Persian Gulf. Although the specific responsibilities change from generation to generation, early adulthood—a period lasting until about age 40—is filled with numerous stresses that can sometimes lead to anxiety and tension.

of attitudes than the cohort born in the 1950s, who have directly experienced the Vietnam War and the Woodstock '69 phenomenon. Moreover, each cohort establishes its own values, expectations, and implicit timetables for accomplishing life tasks. Surveys suggest, for example, that the members of the cohort born around 1920 believed as adults that the "right" time to get married was between 19 and 25 years of age and that the "right" age to finish school and go to work was between 20 and 22; by contrast, only a minority of the cohort born in 1940 believed as adults that these life tasks should be completed that early (Easterlin, 1987). People in the older cohort who completed school and married in their 30s might find themselves much more isolated, unsupported, and therefore stressed than similarly situated people in the younger group. Research suggests that people whose values, expectations, and lifestyle are "in sync" with their cohort's often have less stressful and less tense lives than those who are out of sync with their cohort.

In short, stress is built into the normal experiences, stages, and climate of early and middle adulthood. For some adults these normal stresses feel overwhelming and lead to high levels of anxiety and depression and other forms of dysfunctioning. Abnormal behavior may also result from traumatic experiences during early and middle adulthood, such as losing one's job or being abused by one's spouse (see Box 20–2). Abnormal behavior during these years can be caused as well by all the other psychological and biological factors that are the primary focus of this book.

■ LATER LIFE ■

Like the problems of children and adolescents, those of elderly persons received little attention until recent years. *Geropsychology*, the field concerned with the mental health of elderly people, has developed almost entirely within the last twenty years, mainly to explore whether or not methods of assessment and treatment of the mental health problems of later life should be similar to the methods applied to younger and middle-aged persons or whether this age group requires different approaches. It studies the influence of socioeconomic status, ethnic affiliation, and history (both personal and generational) on the psychological functioning of people as they age and the impact of the special challenges that often accompany old age, such as dwindling income and failing health.

"Old age" is arbitrarily defined in our society as referring to the years past age 65. Clinicians further distinguish between the *young-old,* people between the ages of 65 and 74; the *old-old,* those between 75 and 84; and the *oldest-old,* individuals 85 and above. In 1989, 31 million people in the United States were over 65; they accounted for nearly 13 percent of the total U.S. population, or about one in every eight Americans (see Figure 20–1). This figure reflected a tenfold increase in the older population since 1900. Another surge of growth is anticipated between the years 2010 and 2030, when members of the baby-

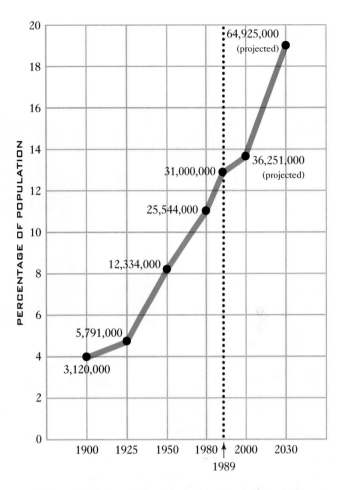

FIGURE 20–1   *The population of people aged 65 and older in the United States has been climbing throughout the twentieth century. The percentage of elderly people in the population increased from 4 percent in 1900 to 13 percent in 1989 and is expected to be 19 percent in 2030. (AARP, 1990; U.S. Bureau of the Census, 1988.)*

boom generation will be reaching old age (AARP, 1990).

Life expectancy in the United States has been increasing since 1900. Childhood diseases and illnesses have become less common than they used to be, and infant deaths are correspondingly fewer. In addition, as people age they learn to take better care of themselves, so that those who survive to adulthood are likely to live fairly long lives. Persons who reach the age of 65 have an average life expectancy of an additional 17 years (19 years for women and 15 years for men).

Data from the American Association of Retired Persons (1990) and the U.S. Census Bureau (1988) indicate that today's older men are nearly twice as likely to be married as older women—77 percent of men, 42 percent of women. Half of all older women are widows. Indeed, there are five times as many widows

BOX 20-2

SPOUSE ABUSE

In Stamford, Conn., a woman married to a *Fortune* 500 executive locked herself into their Lincoln Continental every Saturday night to escape her husband's kicks and punches. She did not leave him because she mistakenly feared he could sue for divorce on grounds of desertion and she, otherwise penniless, would get no alimony.

Barbara, 30, a middle-class housewife from South Hadley, Mass., was first beaten by her husband when she was pregnant. Last summer Barbara's husband hurled a dinner plate across the kitchen at her. His aim was off. The plate shattered against the wall and a piece of it struck their four-year-old daughter in the face, blinding the child in one eye.

In Miami, Diane, 27, a receptionist, said she married "a real nice guy," a Dr. Jekyll who turned into Mr. Hyde a week after the wedding. "Being married to this man was like being a prisoner of war. I was not allowed to visit my family. I couldn't go out on my own. He wouldn't even let me cry. If I did, it started an 'episode.'"

In a Duluth shelter for battered women, Lola, who married 19 years ago at age 18, said her husband was losing control more frequently: "He gets angry because he's coming home with a bag full of groceries and I didn't open the door fast enough. Because he didn't like the way I washed the clothes. Because the supper's not ready. Because supper's ready too soon."

(Time, September 5, 1983, p. 23)

Spouse abuse, the mistreatment or misuse of one spouse by the other, can take various forms, from shoving to battering (Sadock, 1989). Most abused spouses are women, married or cohabitating. In 1992 the American Medical Association declared that physical and sexual abuse against women had reached "epidemic proportions," and suggested that physicians be alert for signs of domestic violence in all female patients (Glazer, 1993; AMA, 1992). A woman in the United States is more likely to be assaulted by an intimate or acquaintence than by a stranger. It is estimated that spouse abuse occurs in at least 4 million homes in the United States each year and that between a fourth and a third of all U.S. women have been abused at least once by their husbands (AMA, 1992). Similarly, many women are battered by the persons they date. The U.S. Surgeon General has ranked spouse abuse as the leading cause of injuries to women between the ages of 15 and 44. Indeed, 1400 women in the U.S. are killed each year by their husbands or someone with whom they have been initmate, nearly one-fourth of all female homicides (Ingrassia & Beck, 1994).

Spouse abuse cuts across all races, religions, educational levels, and socioeconomic groups (Mollerstrom, Patchner, & Milner, 1992). Some experts believe that violent abuse, particularly murder, occurs more often at lower socioeconomic levels (Straus & Gelles, 1986). Others suggest that members of the middle class are simply less likely to report abuse, and point to the wider spacing of middle-class homes, which prevents neighbors from detecting violence and calling the police (Glazer, 1993; Sherman, 1992). A large percentage of persons who abuse their spouses have alcohol-related or other substance-related problems (Mollerstrom et al., 1992; Saunders, 1992).

For years this behavior was viewed as a private matter, and even the legal system avoided involvement. Indeed, until 1874 a husband had a legal right to beat his wife in the United States. Even after that date abusers were rarely arrested or prosecuted. Police were reluctant to do anything other than calm down domestic violence, the number-one source of police fatalities. And the courts rarely prosecuted an abuser. The emphasis on civil rights in the 1970s and the efforts of women's groups finally revealed the magnitude of the problem, and in the past two decades state leg-

as widowers, largely because most women of the present generation of elders married men older than themselves. There are about 145 older women for every 100 older men.

Two-thirds of older adults live with their families, usually with a spouse but sometimes with a child, a sibling, or another relative. Close to a third of all noninstitutionalized older persons live alone. This

islatures have passed more laws to empower the courts to prosecute abusers and protect victims (100 laws were passed in 1993 alone); police have become more oriented toward intervention; and the clinical profession has increasingly studied and treated the problem. Twenty-five states now have laws that require the police to make an arrest when they are called to a scene where domestic violence has been reported. However, arrests do not necessarily lead to convictions, nor do convictions always result in sentences that deter abusive behavior in the future.

Many abusive husbands consider their wives to be their private property and become most assaultive when the wife shows independence. They often are extremely jealous and possessive, and may inflict more abuse when the wife pursues outside friendships or even attends to the children's needs before the husband's. And they often misinterpret their wives' actions as wishes to pick a fight or cause an upset (Holtzworth-Munroe & Hutchinson, 1993). Beyond assault, they tend to belittle and isolate their wives, and repeatedly make them feel inept, worthless, and dependent. Although an abusive husband may show genuine remorse for a time after beating his wife, he is likely to repeat the behavior (Walker, 1984, 1979). Many such men were themselves beaten as children or saw their mothers beaten (Saunders, 1992; Pagelow, 1981). Often they suffer from low self-esteem and feel generally stressed (Russell & Hulson, 1992).

Victims of abuse typically feel very dependent on their spouse, unable to function on their own, and even unable to experience an identity separate from their spouse. This sense of dependence and their feeling that they are helpless to change the situation keep them in the relationship despite the obvious physical dangers. The great majority of victims are not masochistic, as many clinical theorists once believed (Walker, 1984; Finkelhor et al., 1983). Many stay with their spouses out of economic need. Indeed, research suggests that a woman's standard of living drops an average of 73 percent the first year after a divorce (Glazer, 1993; Heise & Chapman; 1990). About 50 percent of victims grew up in homes where they or their mothers were abused, and most come from families that saw male and female roles in stereotyped ways. Many victims have very low self-esteem (Cornell & Gelles, 1983), blame themselves for the abuse, and agree with their spouse that they did something bad to provoke it. Usually the pattern of abuse does not emerge until after the couple is married.

Initially clinicians proposed couple therapy as the treatment of choice for spouse abuse. But they have learned that as long as a woman continues to be abused at home, such an intervention is but a charade. The steps of treatment now preferred are (1) separating a woman from her abusive husband and situation; (2) therapy for the victim to help her recognize her plight, see her options, and experience a more positive self-image and greater autonomy; (3) therapy for the abuser to help him cope with life more effectively, develop more appropriate attitudes toward his wife, and develop more appropriate avenues for expressing anger and frustration (Saunders, 1982; Ganley, 1981); and (4) couple therapy, if both spouses have made satisfactory progress in their individual therapies. A number of community programs have been set up to help provide these intervention services, including hotlines, emergency shelters or "safe houses" for women, and public organizations and self-help groups to aid abused spouses and provide education about the problem (Sullivan et al., 1992).

Deluth, Minnesota, the first jurisdiction to adopt a mandatory arrest policy in cases of spouse abuse, has been a leader in the battered women's movement. It has a comprehensive spouse abuse program in which a first-time offender is jailed overnight and released into a 26-week batterers' program. If he fails to attend three consecutive classes, he goes back to jail. In the ten-year history of the program, Deluth has not reported one case of domestic homicide. On the one hand, over 60 percent of the men who completed the program were found to no longer be abusing their spouses when studied up to eighteen months later (Edelson & Eiskovitz, 1989). On the other hand, at least 40 percent of the men treated in the program committed the same offense within five years, either against the same woman or against a new partner (Sherman, 1992).

Thus, although progress has been made in the last twenty years, the problem of spouse abuse remains a difficult one. The very fact that treatment programs for spouse abuse now exist is an important development for both victims and our society, and most clinicians believe that many of these programs are on the right track. Because relatively little empirical evaluation of the programs has been undertaken, however, it is not yet possible to know precisely how helpful the various interventions are or how to improve upon them.

category has been increasing rapidly during the past decade, perhaps because families are on the move and thus less nuclear than they used to be.

Older persons head approximately 20 million households, and 75 percent of them own their own homes. Only about 5 percent of the total older population live in nursing homes, but the percentage increases dramatically with age, from 1 percent of the young-old to 6 percent of the old-old and 22 percent of the oldest-old.

About 90 percent of the elderly in the United States are Caucasian, 8 percent are African American, and about 2 percent are of other races. Persons of Hispanic origin (of whatever race) represent about 3 percent of the older population. For the past decade, however, the minority elderly population has been growing rapidly, and by the year 2050, 20 percent of the elderly will be nonwhite.

About half of the population of older adults live in nine states. California, New York, and Florida each have over 2 million elders, and Pennsylvania, Texas, Illinois, Ohio, Michigan, and New Jersey have over 1 million each. More elders are moving to Sunbelt states such as Florida, California, Arizona, and New Mexico in search of a warm climate.

In 1989, households headed by older adults in this country reported a median income of $23,179 ($23,817 for white Americans, $15,766 for African Americans, and $19,310 for Hispanic Americans). Elders who lived alone reported the lowest incomes. The major sources of income for older individuals are social security, personal savings, earnings, and pension plans. Only about 12 percent of older Americans are in the labor force, and about half of these workers are employed only part-time.

The educational level of the older population has been steadily increasing. More than half have earned a high school diploma, and 11 percent have graduated from college.

Older people tend to have more health problems than younger people (see Figure 20–2). About 29 percent assess their health as failing or poor (only 7 percent of people under the age of 65 do so) and most older adults report one or more chronic health conditions, such as arthritis, hearing loss, or heart disease. Older persons account for a third of all hospital stays. Altogether, people over 65 account for 36 percent of total personal expenditures for health care.

The population of older adults is actually quite heterogeneous. We need to be mindful of the fact that older adults are more unlike than similar to one another (Cavanaugh, 1990). Elders have very different life experiences, adapt to change in uniquely personal ways, and age at different rates. The field of geropsychology distinguishes between chronological age and functional age. *Chronological age,* or the number of years one has lived since birth, is regarded as nothing more than a "shorthand variable," because it is not a true indicator of a person's functional capacities. *Functional age* is a reflection of three interrelated aspects of aging—biological, social, and psychological (Birren & Cunningham, 1985).

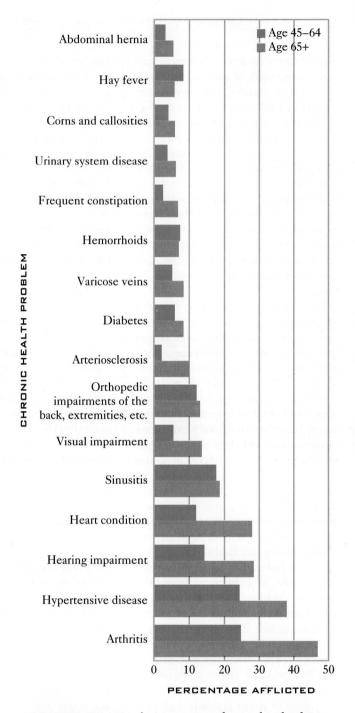

FIGURE 20–2 *As persons age, they tend to develop more health problems. With a few exceptions, chronic medical problems are more prevalent among elderly persons than among the middle-aged. (Adapted from U.S. Senate Special Committee on Aging, 1983, p. 59.)*

Biological age represents one's present position with respect to one's potential life span. Clinicians determine biological age by assessing the functioning of various vital organ systems, such as the cardiovascular system. With increasing age, the systems' capacity for self-regulation diminishes, resulting in an increased probability of death. ***Social age*** refers to a person's roles, habits, and behavior in comparison with those of other members of his or her society. A person's manner of dress, language, and interpersonal style, for example, will reflect a particular social age. ***Psychological age*** refers to a person's capacity to adapt his or her behavior to the changing environment. This aspect of aging will be influenced by the person's cognitive functioning, motivation, and self-esteem. To understand older persons, it is necessary to consider all of these aspects of aging.

Older people are frequently stereotyped by younger ones (including younger clinicians), who react to them strictly in terms of their chronological age rather than their functional capabilities (Kimmel, 1988; Gatz & Pearson, 1988). One study asked over 500 college students to evaluate photos of the same men at various ages (25, 52, and 73) on such characteristics as activity level, competence, intelligence, creativity, flexibility, and energy (Levin, 1988). Students consistently evaluated the same men more negatively at 73 than at younger ages, suggesting that it may be difficult for younger persons to see older persons in their true light. As the negative images of aging continue to be countered by the media and by direct experience, it is to be hoped that such attitudes will change.

■ Successful ■ Aging: A Stress-and-Coping Model

As we age, important changes occur both physically and psychologically. On the negative side, our bodies experience continued wear and tear, and we become more prone to illness and injury than when we were younger. We are also more likely to experience certain kinds of psychological stress. Significant losses, for example, occur with greater frequency in later life. Older people lose persons close to them (spouse, friends, adult children), and many lose a sense of purpose in life after they retire or experience other role shifts. If they live long enough, they lose bodily integrity through chronic illness. And not to be overlooked is the loss of favored pets and possessions through relocation and the like.

Despite these common experiences of change and stress, older people need not deteriorate rapidly, either physically or psychologically. In fact, a growing body of literature challenges the assertion that the aging body and mind are programmed to fall apart (Rowe & Kahn, 1987). Extensive research on the prevention of heart disease, for example, has shown that when older patients take control over key risk factors such as cigarette smoking, cholesterol intake, and blood pressure, this major cause of death is substantially reduced. Such findings suggest that prudent living and new health technology may enable older adults to remain healthy and vigorous for longer periods of time.

Similarly, psychological stress need not necessarily result in mental dysfunction among elderly people (Lewinsohn et al., 1990). While losses and other stressful experiences do contribute to depression in some older adults, for others such situations apparently become opportunities to learn more about themselves and to grow as people.

Why do some older people succumb to the stresses that accompany aging and develop physical and psychological problems, while others, indeed the majority, manage to endure? The answer seems to lie in the notion of coping. Some people manage to cope with stress better than others (Horn & Meer, 1987).

The ***stress-and-coping model*** developed by Richard Lazarus and Susan Folkman (1984) suggests that the key to coping is how one cognitively appraises a given situation or event. According to this model, which we first encountered in Chapter 6 (see pp. 184–185), when people confront a potentially stressful situation, they make certain evaluations, either consciously or unconsciously. First, they make a ***primary appraisal***—they judge the situation to be either irrelevant, positive, or stressful. If they determine that the event is stressful, they then make a ***secondary appraisal,*** and judge what might and can be done in response. They evaluate what coping options are available to them, whether the options will accomplish what they are supposed to do, and whether they will be able to apply the coping strategies effectively. As the situation develops further and as they apply their coping responses, the individuals are likely to make ***reappraisals***—they repeatedly change their perceptions of the situation in response to the flow of new information.

People's appraisals of a situation and of their coping options determine how they will react to it. If they evaluate a given event as being extraordinarily taxing or their coping options as inadequate, they may feel overwhelmed by the stress, either physically or psychologically. If, on the other hand, they determine that they have effective coping options available to them and apply those options, they may address the threat effectively and even profit from the challenge it provides.

According to research, older persons use a wide range of strategies to cope with negative life events (Folkman et al., 1987; McCrae, 1982). Lazarus and Folkman (1984) have had subjects fill out the "Ways of Coping" checklist, a self-report measure that they developed, and have found that some people are more inclined to use coping strategies that are *problem-focused*—cognitive or behavioral problem-solving strategies, such as trying to come up with several solutions, gathering information, and making a plan of action—while others prefer *emotion-focused* strategies, such as seeking emotional support, distancing, avoiding, and self-blame. In general, the older people who cope most effectively with loss and other stressors tend to use problem-focused strategies more than emotion-focused strategies. Studies have also found, however, that some emotion-focused strategies may be useful in old age, particularly when one is diagnosed as having a serious physical illness. In fact, health-care professionals often encourage some form of avoidance or denial, because it may be seen as adaptive in that circumstance (Cavanaugh, 1990).

A common strategy for coping in old age that does not quite fit the problem-focused versus emotion-focused distinction is to turn to religion and spirituality (Cox & Hammonds, 1988). Older people who cope successfully are more likely than younger persons to attend a house of worship. Many of them seem to hold a strong belief in a higher power and also seem to benefit from the social aspects of religion, such as attending services with friends or family members and receiving support from the clergy and members of the congregation, as well as from the theology itself. It is likely that if we are fully to understand coping in older adults, we must include the study of religious beliefs and practices in addition to other methods of coping.

In short, even though older adults do not have much control over the stressful events that occur in their environment, they do have control over their responses to those events: how they appraise and react to the situation. By using more problem-focused modes of coping, many older people are able to weather these challenges and even learn from them. This perspective has led clinical geropsychologists to place strong emphasis on the development of cognitive and behavioral interventions to help older

Geropsychologists point out that old age is more than a loss of youth or a march toward death. Elderly persons are filled with a mixture of past memories, present needs, and future goals, all of which must be addressed if they are to achieve fulfillment and psychological peace.

people cope with the stresses they confront. In the cognitive realm they often help older people identify perceptions and thoughts that are overly pessimistic and stress-inducing. In the behavioral realm, they help people reengage with family and friends and inject more enjoyment and control into their lives.

Recently a considerable body of research has found that a range of problems among elderly people respond well to cognitive and behavioral therapies, including depression (Thompson, Gallagher, & Breckenridge, 1987), anxiety disorders (McCarthy, Katz, & Foa, 1991), prolonged or atypical grieving (Gantz, Gallagher-Thompson, & Rodman, 1991), and chronic functional limitations due to physical health problems (Rybarczyk et al., 1991). As we shall discuss later, our own work with family members experiencing stress in their role of primary caregiver to a frail elder relative also supports the usefulness of this kind of practical approach (Gallagher-Thompson, Lovett, & Rose, 1991). In some instances, however, family members, whether caregivers or not, find that their stress exceeds their capacity, and what results is neglect of their elder spouse or parent, or actual abuse of the person (see Box 20–3).

Cognitive and behavioral therapies are generally accepted well by older people, perhaps because they are less threatening than psycho-

BOX 20-3

ABUSE OF THE ELDERLY

A 78-year-old New York woman . . . was assaulted and beaten by her 36-year-old grandson a dozen times, even though she was confined to a wheelchair. Although hospitalized seven times, the woman still refused to testify against her grandson. . . .

A 68-year-old South Carolina woman was kept by her daughter in "conditions of unspeakable squalor." . . . Living under a pile of filthy blankets, the woman was kept in an unheated portion of the house that got so cold that the urine from the woman's catheter was frozen when a social worker discovered her.

A 64-year-old Florida man, his health failing, was swindled out of his 40-acre orange grove and everything else he owned by a relative he trusted. "I signed too many papers," the man told social workers. "I still fear for my life."

(Ryan, 1981)

The abuse of elderly persons is a major problem in our society. A survey of more than 2,000 elderly persons in the Boston metropolitan area revealed that 3 percent had been subjected to physical violence, verbal aggression, and neglect (Pillemer & Finkelhor, 1988). Similarly, a compilation of current records, documents, and mental health surveys has suggested that approximately 4 percent of elderly people living in the United States have

been "moderately to severely" abused in forms ranging from theft of social security checks to neglect, beatings, druggings, torture, and rape (House Select Committee on Aging, 1981).

Abuse of an elderly person is usually committed by a close relative, in most cases by the spouse but often by the victim's adult child. Some cases of elder abuse by spouses are continuations of long-term patterns of spouse abuse, but many represent new behaviors triggered by the special pressures and frustrations of old age or sickness. Abuse by children, too, may represent a continuation of a long-term pattern or a new response. Once it begins, however, the abuse usually becomes a chronic pattern.

Although both men and women are victims of elder abuse, more women are victimized than men, and women usually suffer more severe abuse. It is believed that the prevalence rates indicated by the survey underestimate the actual extent of the problem. Elderly people may hesitate to report abuse because of the guilt and shame attached to it. Too, many victims are confused by the abuse because of the love they feel for the abusive relative. And many victims, dependent on their abusers, are terrified of being abandoned or retaliated against if they report the pattern of abuse.

Little literature is available on the treatment of this pervasive problem

other than some clinical reports of attempts to remedy the situation by moving the victim out of the home and into a nursing home. Obviously, however, this solution is inappropriate for those older people who are not really so functionally impaired that they require a nursing home; it severely limits their independence and in a sense punishes the victim. Besides, some elderly persons are physically abused in nursing homes, too.

More effective interventions might include the establishment of safe apartments where abused elderly people could take refuge, the creation of the kind of self-help groups that have been successful for younger abused spouses, and education of the elderly so that they will recognize abuse when it occurs and be less likely to use denial as a means of coping with the situation (Pillemer & Finkelhor, 1988).

A great deal of abuse springs from strong feelings of anger that a caregiver has difficulty controlling (Gallagher et al., 1989). The teaching of cognitive-behavioral skills in the management of anger, such as relaxation training, appropriate assertiveness, development of alternative responses to anger, and the use of positive self-talk to reward oneself for developing alternative responses, can modify this behavior significantly, sometimes in a relatively short time.

---

dynamic therapies and do not carry the risks associated with psychotropic medications (Gallagher-Thompson & Thompson, 1994). This factor may give cognitive and behavioral therapies an advantage over other approaches that have also proved beneficial to elderly persons, such as group therapy, family therapy, and psychoeducational approaches.

■ COMMON ■ CLINICAL PROBLEMS IN LATER LIFE

Studies indicate that as many as 50 percent of the elderly would benefit from mental health services

(MacDonald & Schnur, 1987), yet fewer than 20 percent actually receive such help. A number of barriers explain this gap (Butler & Lewis, 1986). First, many older people do not define their problems in psychological terms. They tend to view any mental health problem as a stigma and assume that help-seeking will result in prolonged care or even hospitalization. Thus they prefer to go to their primary-care physician when they are troubled rather than to a mental health practitioner. Second, relatively few clinicians are equipped to work with the psychological problems of later life. Few graduate or medical school programs even offer a course or provide supervised field experience in gerontology, though this situation is slowly being remedied. Third, the limitations on insurance reimbursement to providers of mental health care for the elderly have been a barrier. Taken together, these factors make it very difficult to serve the mental health needs of the elderly. Changes are needed both in the way elderly people perceive stress and mental health care and in the way professionals are trained and reimbursed.

DEPRESSION

*B*ernice Anderson is a 78-year-old woman who is beginning to feel that life is not worth living. She recently became widowed, has severe arthritis, and sometimes finds it difficult to take care of herself. Her daughter Sarah, aged 50, recently told her that she may have to go to live in a senior housing situation of some kind. Sarah, a very busy professional woman with a husband and family, recognizes that her mother probably cannot continue to live alone, but she also feels that she cannot have her mother living with her. Since these events occurred, Bernice has not been eating well, is having difficulty sleeping, and has lost interest in her hobbies of gardening and swimming at a local club, where she also used to meet with friends regularly.

Depression is the most common mental health problem of older adults (Koenig & Blazer, 1992; Blazer, 1990). A range of depressive feelings, from profound unhappiness to feelings of being blue and dissatisfied with life, have been reported by as many as 60 percent of older adults in self-report questionnaires. Between 1 and 20 percent of older adults meet DSM-IV's criteria for clinical depression. Those who have recently experienced a trauma such as the loss of their spouse and those with serious physical illnesses have the highest rate of depression (Philpott, 1990; Bliwise, McCall, & Swan, 1987). The prevalence of depression also is high in older people with cognitive

impairment: as many as 30 percent of older adults who are diagnosed as cognitively impaired (that is, suffering from dementia) also have a significant clinical depression to contend with (Reifler et al., 1986).

Finally, the prevalence of depression is higher in older women than in older men, although, as with younger persons, it is unclear whether men genuinely experience less depression or simply underreport the symptoms they do experience. Men may also express their depression through physical rather than psychological symptoms (Blazer, 1990).

ASSESSMENT Depression is best assessed in older adults through a structured clinical interview, rather than through a self-report questionnaire. An interview gives the older person an opportunity to explain more about his or her symptoms and gives the interviewer an opportunity to be sure that the client really understands the questions being asked. Since some elderly people have less than a high school education, they can and do misunderstand self-report questionnaires. Also, there can be confusion about whether the specific symptoms uncovered by a questionnaire, such as fatigue, poor appetite, and sleep disturbances, really reflect depression or some other health problem, such as undiagnosed cancer or heart disease. Greater understanding can be achieved in a clinical interview, since the therapist has an opportunity to clarify such questions and concerns.

Nevertheless, two self-report questionnaires have been widely used as screening devices with older adults in both medical and mental health settings. One is the *Geriatric Depression Scale (GDS)* (Yesavage et al., 1983), which asks whether each of thirty statements such as "I find it hard to get up in the morning" and "I tend to avoid people at social gatherings" is true or false. The GDS was specifically developed to emphasize the psychological aspects of depression and to deemphasize its physiological aspects. The other popular scale, used with older adults who have a higher reading level and greater comprehension of English, is the *Beck Depression Inventory (BDI)* (Beck et al., 1961). This twenty-one-item measure, which was first described in Chapter 9, asks about sadness, appetite, sleep problems, low energy, libido problems, self-evaluation, ideas about the future, and the like. The validity and reliability of these scales with older adults have been demonstrated (Gallagher, 1986), and their scores are easily interpreted.

It is also important for older depressed people to have a thorough physical evaluation by a geriatrician familiar with the common health problems of old age. It is crucial to review all medications that the person

A key to feeling vital and upbeat, whether old or young, is to be active, committed, and interested in one's surroundings. Elderly people with this life posture maintain a relatively young psychological age. Charlotte Stinger, 79, a student at the Academy of Ballet, has been studying dance for 28 years.

When a thorough evaluation by a neuropsychologist is not possible, many practitioners use Folstein's Mini-Mental State Examination, a well-validated screening measure for detecting problems of orientation and common cognitive processes, such as memory and reasoning (Folstein, Folstein, & McHugh, 1975).

TREATMENT   Like younger depressed patients, older persons who are depressed may be helped by a number of treatments. Antidepressant medications are sometimes viewed as the treatment of choice for clinical depression, partly because psychotherapy for older adults is a relatively recent development. At the same time, however, it is difficult to use drug treatment effectively with older persons (Blazer, 1990). The biological mechanisms for the breakdown and absorption of these chemicals are not the same in later life as in the earlier years: the overall metabolic rate is slower in older adults, so that drugs remain in the system longer and can accumulate to toxic levels more quickly. In addition, older adults often find that the unwanted effects of the common antidepressant medications are very difficult to tolerate. For example, as we saw in Chapter 9, the tricyclic antidepressants often cause dry mouth, dizziness upon getting up, constipation, and other annoying effects that may reach such severe proportions in some older individuals that they discontinue the medication. The clinician can reduce the usual dosage and help the patient to monitor them and to take practical steps to minimize them, such as increasing the amount of bran in the diet to control constipation (Vieth, 1982). Nevertheless, it often has been very difficult to find exactly the right tricyclic antidepressant medication for a given patient and to manage the undesired effects successfully.

The second-generation antidepressant drugs, particularly the *selective serotonin reuptake inhibitors* (SSRIs), address some of these issues. Sertraline (Zoloft) and fluoxetine (Prozac) have no cardiac effects, are nonsedating, and do not cause hypotension, urinary retention, or blurred vision (Auster, 1993). Thus, some medical experts believe that an SSRI may be the drug of choice for elderly people with depression. Promising research seems to support these assertions (Lapierre, 1991; Cohn et al., 1990).

The use of psychotherapy with clinically depressed older adults has focused on relatively short-term treatments such as cognitive-behavioral therapy (modeled after the approaches of Beck and Lewinsohn that we encountered in Chapter 9) or brief psychodynamic therapy. Our own research has indicated that about 75 percent of clinically depressed elderly outpatients respond well to about 20 sessions of psychotherapy

is taking, since many older adults unintentionally abuse both over-the-counter and prescription medications, using compounds that interact badly with one another or taking more or less than the optimal amount. These practices can make it very difficult to prescribe proper antidepressant medication, even if it seems warranted.

Finally, it is important to assess the cognitive functioning of older people who have symptoms of depression. Cognitive impairment, or dementia, has a number of symptoms in common with depression, and an older client may be incorrectly diagnosed as having one or the other if the full picture is not obtained. This situation has implications for treatment because there are few effective treatments for dementia, whereas clinical depression responds to a variety of both short- and long-term interventions.

and respond equivalently to both types that we investigated. Their depression either disappeared completely or improved substantially, and they also maintained these gains for at least two years (Gallagher-Thompson, Hanley-Peterson, & Thompson, 1989; Thompson et al., 1987). Elderly clients who respond best to psychotherapy tend to be those whose depression is apparently caused by situational factors, who have no concurrent personality disorder, and who have the ability to plan for and to experience pleasant activities regularly.

In current ongoing studies we have compared cognitive-behavioral psychotherapy with drug therapy and are finding that the combination of the two tends to be more effective than either of them alone, particularly for older people with a physiologically caused type of depression (Gantz et al., 1991). About 65 percent of older depressed outpatients are responding extremely well to the combined condition versus about 50 percent for the cognitive-behavioral therapy alone or the medication alone. In our studies the medication used most often is desipramine (Norpramin), which produces relatively few undesirable effects. We also found that the highest dropout rate occurs when patients are given medication alone, and that in order to use medication in combination with therapy successfully, clinicians must be extremely well versed in the management of the unwanted effects that typically occur (Roose, 1991).

When to discontinue drug therapy is another issue requiring careful evaluation. The Old Age Depression Interest Group in England (1993) has recommended that elders, like younger people, be continued on a lower "maintenance dose" of their antidepressant for an extended period after they recover from a depressive episode, in order to protect against relapse. However, very little research has actually been conducted on this topic; clearly, more systematic research is needed to determine optimal combinations of drug, dosage, and length of treatment.

Clinicians in our setting have also been exploring the use of longer-term cognitive-behavioral therapy with older individuals who are experiencing both depression and a personality disorder, such as an avoidant personality disorder. We have found that extending treatment to approximately forty or fifty sessions (rather than terminating it after the more usual fifteen to twenty sessions) enables more persons with this dual diagnosis to improve in both mood and general functioning. The additional sessions focus on identifying and challenging the core beliefs or schemas that have underlain the personality structure for most of the person's adult life (Beck et al., 1990).

Several other treatment approaches have also been used in cases of elderly depression, although they tend to be used less frequently and have received less research attention than the cognitive-behavioral, short-term psychodynamic, and drug therapies. Some depressed older persons apparently respond well to family therapy, partly because their families unintentionally reinforce negative rather than positive adaptive behaviors, and family therapy is able to channel the energy of family members in more appropriate directions. Some older depressed persons also appear to profit from group therapy, particularly supportive (Finkel, 1991) or cognitive-behavioral group therapy (Yost et al., 1986). And for some older adults with a very severe depression that has been unresponsive to other interventions, electroconvulsive therapy (ECT) is sometimes applied. Its administration is considered safer and freer from harmful effects than it was in the past, even for older patients, as long as they are in good physical health (Blazer, 1990).

SUICIDAL THOUGHTS OR ACTIONS Suicide is particularly likely to occur in older white males who have a combination of clinical depression and a sense of severe hopelessness (Fry, 1986). Suicidal older persons often profit from inpatient care, followed by various forms of therapy to help them resolve the crisis and find hope for the future. Once again, we and others have found that cognitive-behavioral therapy with such patients can effectively marshal their resources and help them develop a different perspective on their current problems and on future opportunities, once the suicidal crisis is past (Osgood, 1985). Other forms of treatment, such as family therapy and group therapy, have also been successfully used with suicidal elders (Richman, 1993).

TREATMENT OF MANIA IN LATER LIFE Data are accumulating to suggest that onset of a variety of manic syndromes for the first time in the fifth or sixth decade of life is more common than was previously thought (Young & Klerman, 1992). However, much remains to be learned about how best to treat the various manic syndromes that arise in late life. The usual treatment of choice, *lithium*, may not be particularly safe for older adults, or effective. Information about long-term use of lithium in the elderly is virtually nonexistent at the present time.

PSYCHOEDUCATIONAL PROGRAMS Our psychoeducational programs began as a series of weekly "Coping with Depression" classes offered to older adults in the community who were interested in acquiring skills to improve their mood. The classes focused on the same kind of cognitive-behavioral

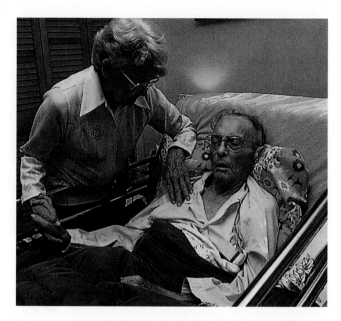

The burden of providing care at home for a spouse or parent who is impaired physically or psychologically can arouse feelings of anxiety, depression, and anger. Newly developed psychoeducation programs for caregivers appear to prevent or reduce such feelings.

skills used in therapy, but they were packaged differently, with equal emphasis on didactic learning of the material and its practical application. Skills such as mood monitoring, increasing the frequency of engagement in pleasant activities, and learning to reward oneself for new behaviors were featured. This series of classes has now been successfully used with nonclinically depressed elders for more than a decade and has been described by some as "just what they needed" to prevent a clinical depression from developing (Thompson et al., 1983).

More recently, classes with a different content have also been developed to help family members reduce the stress associated with providing long-term care for older persons (Gallagher-Thompson, 1994). Many of these caregivers are themselves elderly; as many as 50 percent are older than 60, and 18 percent are older than 70 (Melcher, 1988). The classes teach family caregivers how to solve problems, manage their anger, assert themselves with recalcitrant family members, and relax in stressful situations. Class participants have less depression and more perceived social support than control subjects evaluated at comparable time intervals (Lovett & Gallagher, 1988). Additional programs geared to other needs of caregivers, such as decision making in regard to nursing home placement and preparing for their loved one's death, are now in the planning stages. The psychoeducational approach

seems to appeal to a broad range of older persons and is acceptable to them, in part because it does not share the stigma of mental health services.

ANXIETY DISORDERS

Anxiety is a common human emotion, experienced throughout life. Yet anxiety and anxiety disorders are relatively undefined and poorly studied in the elderly. As in younger persons, anxiety often coexists with depression in elderly people. In fact, it can be very difficult to determine which is the major disorder (Shamoian, 1991). In a study conducted in our laboratory, we examined the degree of overlap between anxiety and depression in a group of close to 100 older individuals who were seeking treatment for depression, and found relatively high correlations between the anxiety and depression measures (Kilcourse et al., 1991).

Not much was known about the prevalence of anxiety disorders in the elderly until recently, when data from surveys conducted in several major cities indicated that generalized anxiety disorder is found in about 7 percent of elders, agoraphobia in about 2 to 5 percent, specific phobias in 1 to 12 percent, and panic disorders in less than 1 percent (Flint, 1994; Bliwise et al., 1987). Other data suggest that obsessive-compulsive disorder may be found in 1 to 10 percent of elders seeking help at mental health clinics (Jenike, 1991). These surveys also suggest that the prevalence of most anxiety disorders actually decreases with age among both men and women (Flint, 1994; Blazer, George, & Hughes, 1991), although the rate is generally higher in women than in men, regardless of age. There is a possibility that anxiety disorders are underreported by the elderly. Perhaps older people must reach a higher level of discomfort before they will actually seek help. Some may attribute symptoms of anxiety such as heart palpitations and sweating to medical conditions (Blazer et al., 1991).

ASSESSMENT   Assessing anxiety in older people is similar in many ways to assessing depression. Although several self-report questionnaires may be used to give a rough estimate of the severity of anxiety experienced, most geropsychologists prefer to gather this information through a structured clinical interview. This way, additional probes can be used and ambiguous issues clarified.

One of the most important tasks facing assessors is determining whether the anxiety experienced by an older adult is in fact an appropriate response to objective conditions. The fear of an older person who dreads being alone in his or her apartment in a high-crime neighborhood, for instance, may be quite realistic. Such a person should be helped to relocate rather than given clinical treatment.

TREATMENT Traditionally, older adults with anxiety disorders have been treated with antianxiety medication, particularly benzodiazepines, although those with obsessive-compulsive disorder, have, like their younger counterparts, been increasingly treated with certain antidepressants such as fluoxetine (Prozac) (Jenike, 1991). Despite the fact that benzodiazepines are effective in treating anxiety, these drugs must be used cautiously because persons over the age of 60 respond to them quite differently than do younger adults. Lower doses are necessary, and the potential for unpleasant effects is much greater (Pomara et al., 1991). Most notably, benzodiazepines can cause cognitive impairment, which may be mistaken for mental deterioration. They may also cause drowsiness, headaches, lack of energy, and loss of coordination. In addition, most geropsychiatrists try to avoid the long-term use of benzodiazepines because of the potential for the patient to become addicted to them.

Behavioral techniques such as relaxation training (for generalized anxiety disorder) and systematic desensitization (for phobias) have also been applied to several of the anxiety disorders in older persons. An effective cognitive-behavioral approach called *anxiety management techniques (AMT)* seeks to reduce anxiety through the development of skills for controlling fear (McCarthy et al., 1991). Chief among these skills are progressive muscle relaxation, controlled breathing, and a cognitive focus on identifying and correcting maladaptive thought patterns through such techniques as self-talk and imagery. Social skills training may also be incorporated in the package. This treatment approach seems to be well tolerated by older individuals and effective for specific phobias and generalized anxiety, the two anxiety disorders that are most common in the elderly. And finally, psychodynamic approaches in which anxious older patients review their lives to help them understand and reduce underlying conflicts have also met with some success (Johnson, 1991).

In contrast to the extensive empirical literature on the treatment of late-life depression, few controlled research studies have been done to support the efficacy of various treatments for anxiety. Further research is also needed to develop safer drug therapies for anxious older adults (Zimmer & Gershon, 1991).

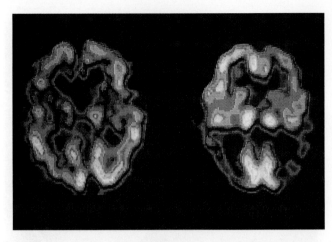

A PET scan of the brain of an Alzheimer's disease sufferer (right) indicates diminished blood flow and degeneration of brain tissue; a PET scan of a normal subject's brain appears at the left. People with this disorder, the major cause of dementia, experience a progressive deterioration of memory and other cognitive functions.

DEMENTIA

Fear that we are losing our mental abilities occasionally strikes all of us, perhaps after we have rushed out the door without our keys, when we meet a familiar person and cannot remember her name, or when in the middle of a critical test our mind seems to go blank. At such times, those who are inclined to think the worst may well believe that they are experiencing the first stages of *dementia,* the highly disruptive syndrome caused by a medical condition or substance that is marked by memory impairment *and* other cognitive disturbances, such as a deficit in abstract thinking, judgment, or language (APA, 1994). Rest assured that such mishaps are quite common and normal. Indeed, as people progress through middle age, memory difficulties and lapses of attention are likely to increase, and by age 60 or 70 may occur with regularity. Intellectual changes of this kind are associated with the normal process of aging, and for the most part they are not severe enough to be considered a sign of dementia. Sometimes, however, people experience intellectual changes that are broad, severe, and excessive. Like Harry, they manifest dementia, the syndrome that we first observed in Chapter 18.

*H*arry appeared to be in perfect health at age 58, except that for a few days he had had a nasty flu. He worked in the municipal water treatment plant of a small city, and it was at work that the first overt signs of Harry's mental illness appeared. While responding to a minor emergency, he became confused about the correct order in which to pull the levers that controlled the flow of fluids. As a result, several thousand gallons of raw sewage were discharged into a river. Harry had been an efficient and diligent worker, so after puzzled questioning, his error was attributed to the flu and overlooked.

Several weeks later, Harry came home with a baking dish his wife had asked him to buy, having forgotten that he had brought home the identical dish two nights before. Later that week, on two successive nights, he went to pick up his daughter at her job in a restaurant, apparently forgetting that she had changed shifts and was now working days. A month after that, he quite uncharacteristically argued with a clerk at the phone company; he was trying to pay a bill that he had already paid three days before.

By this time his wife had become alarmed about the changes in Harry. Thinking back, she began to piece together episodes that convinced her that his memory had actually been undependable for at least several months, perhaps much longer. When she discovered that he had been writing reminder notes to himself on odd scraps of paper and that these included detailed instructions about how to operate machinery at work if various problems arose, she insisted that he see a doctor. He himself realized that his memory had been failing, and so he agreed with his wife, though reluctantly. The doctor did a physical examination and ordered several laboratory tests, including an electroencephalogram (a brain wave test). The examination results were normal, and the doctor thought the problem might be depression. He prescribed an antidepressant drug, but if anything, it seemed to make Harry's memory worse. It certainly did not make him feel any better. That treatment failing, the doctor thought that Harry must have hardening of the arteries of the brain, about which, he said, nothing could be done.

Months passed and Harry's wife was beside herself. She could see that his problem was worsening. Not only had she been unable to get effective help, but Harry himself was becoming resentful and sometimes suspicious of her attempts. He now insisted there was nothing wrong with him, and she would catch him narrowly watching her every movement. From time to time he accused her of having the police watch him, and he would draw all the blinds in the house. Once he ripped the telephone out of the wall, convinced it was "spying." Sometimes he became angry— sudden little storms without apparent cause. He would shout angrily at his wife and occasionally throw or kick things. Such episodes did not seem dangerous because they were short-lived and because Harry seemed more frustrated than angry. His outbursts lacked sustained direction and intensity. More difficult for his wife was Harry's repetitiveness in conversation: He often repeated stories from the past and sometimes repeated isolated phrases and sentences from more recent exchanges. There was no context and little continuity to his choice of subjects. He might recite the same story or instruction several times a day. His work was also a great cause of deep concern. His wife, who had the summer off from her position as a fourth-grade

teacher, began checking on him at his job at least once a day. Soon she was actually doing most of his work. His supervisor, an old friend of the family, looked the other way. Harry seemed grateful that his wife was there.

Two years after Harry had first allowed the sewage to escape, he was clearly a changed man. Most of the time he seemed preoccupied; he usually had a vacant smile on his face, and what little he said was so vague that it lacked meaning. He had entirely given up his main interests (golf and woodworking), and he became careless about his person. More and more, for example, he slept in his clothes. Gradually his wife took over getting him up, toileted, and dressed each morning.

One day the county supervisor stopped by to tell his wife that Harry just could not work any longer. A disability insurance policy would carry him for the few months until he was 62, and then he would be eligible for early retirement. He hadn't really worked for a long while anyway, and he had become so inattentive that he had to be kept away from machinery. He was just too much of a burden on his co-workers. Harry himself still insisted that nothing was wrong, but by now no one tried to explain things to him. He had long since stopped reading. His days were spent sitting vacantly in front of the television, but he couldn't describe any of the programs he had watched.

Harry's condition continued to worsen slowly. When his wife's school was in session, his daughter would stay with him some days, and neighbors were able to offer some help. But occasionally he would still manage to wander away. On those occasions he greeted everyone he met—old friends and strangers alike—with "Hi, it's so nice." That was the extent of his conversation, although he might repeat "nice, nice, nice" over and over again. He had promised not to drive, but one day he did take the family automobile and promptly got lost. The police brought him home, and his wife took the car keys and kept them. When Harry left a coffee pot on a unit of the electric stove until it melted, his wife, desperate for help, took him to see another doctor. Again Harry was found to be in good health. This time the doctor ordered a *CAT scan* (*c*omputed *a*xial *t*omography), a sophisticated X-ray examination that made a visual image of Harry's brain, which, it revealed, had actually shrunk in size. The doctor said that Harry had "Pick-Alzheimer disease" and that there was no known cause and no effective treatment.

Harry could no longer be left at home alone, so his daughter began working nights and caring for him until his wife came home after school. He would sit all day, except that sometimes he would wander aimlessly through the house. Safety latches at each entrance kept him from going outdoors, though he no longer seemed interested in that— or in much of anything else. He had no memory for events of the day and little recollection of occasions from the distant past, which a year or so before he had enjoyed describing. His speech consisted of repeating the same word or phrase over and over (for example, "Hooky then, hooky then, hooky then"). His wife kept trying to find help. She inquired at the state mental hospitals but was told that because Harry wasn't dangerous, he was not eligible for admission.

Because Harry was a veteran, she took him to the nearest Veterans Administration Hospital, which was 150 miles away. After a stay of nine weeks, during which the CAT scan and all the other tests were repeated with the same results, the doctors said Harry had a chronic brain syndrome. They advised long-term hospitalization in a regional veterans' hospital about 400 miles away from his home. Meanwhile his wife, who wanted Harry closer to home, had found that local nursing homes would charge more than her monthly take-home pay to care for him and that Medicare would not pay nursing home charges. Desperate, five years after the accident at work, she accepted with gratitude hospitalization at the veterans' hospital so far away.

At the hospital the nursing staff sat Harry up in a chair each day and, aided by volunteers, made sure he ate enough. Still, he lost weight and became weaker. He would weep when his wife came to see him, but he did not talk, and he gave no other sign that he recognized her. After a year, even the weeping stopped. Harry's wife could no longer bear to visit. Harry lived on until just after his sixty-fifth birthday, when he choked on a piece of bread, developed pneumonia as a consequence, and soon died.

(Heston, 1992, pp. 87–90).

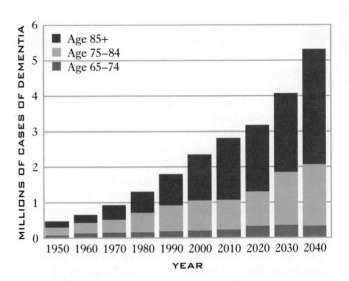

FIGURE 20-3   *The number of people suffering from dementia in the United States has increased each decade, along with increases in the average life span. As the number of people reaching the age of 80 and beyond keeps increasing, so does the number of persons vulnerable to dementia. Nearly a third of all people over 80 suffer some form of dementia. (Adapted from Office of Technology Assessment, 1987; Cross & Gurland, 1986.)*

The first thing to note about dementia is its remarkable relationship to age. Studies indicate that among people around the age of 65, the prevalence of dementia ranges from 2 to 4 percent. There is a gradual increase over the next ten years of the life span to a rough range of 10 to 15 percent, and a jump to 30 percent for all people over the age of 80. Since dementia is age-related and since the average life span continues to increase, we can expect the prevalence eventually to reach catastrophic proportions in our society unless preventive and curative treatments are developed soon (see Figure 20–3). In 1980 over 1.5 million persons displayed dementia in the United States, and the incidence, or number of new cases during that year, was around 350,000. By the year 2020, the incidence will exceed 600,000, and the total number of persons with dementia is projected to be about 3.5 million (Schoenberg, Kokmen, & Okazaki, 1987). This growing prevalence means increasing health-care costs, greater stress and burdens placed on the families that care for these frail persons, and a serious public health problem that requires a coordinated national policy effort.

Dementia is often confused with delirium, another syndrome that is caused by a medical condition or substance. Both syndromes are more common in elderly people than in people of other ages, and indeed they sometimes occur together. ***Delirium*** is a clouding of consciousness in which a person's awareness of

the environment becomes less clear and the individual experiences great difficulty concentrating, focusing attention, and maintaining a straightforward and well-oriented stream of thought (APA, 1994). The disturbance typically develops over a short period of time, usually hours or days. It results in misinterpretations, illusions, and on occasion, hallucinations. The symptoms of dementia and delirium are sometimes similar; they can, however, be distinguished. Although their memory is impaired, people with dementia are alert and do not display the clouded consciousness that characterizes delirium. Moreover, the two syndromes are usually caused by different factors and follow different courses. Delirium may be caused by substance intoxication, stress, nutritional imbalance, fever, infection, or certain neurological disorders, and often follows major surgery (APA, 1994; Lipowski, 1980). It is often totally reversible if the cause is addressed quickly.

Sometimes dementia, too, has an underlying cause that is reversible. It has been estimated that up to 20 percent of first-time patients who complain of dementia symptoms may respond to appropriate medical treatments if the cause can be pinpointed (Katzman, 1981). Some elders may be suffering from metabolic or nutritional disorders that can be corrected. For others, improvement in sensory functions such as vision and hearing can lead to a substantial improvement in cognitive performance. Unfortunately, however, most cases of dementia are caused by neurological problems, such as *Alzheimer's disease* and *stroke,* that are difficult, if not impossible, to address. Thus, in the opinion of many experts, dementia is a more troubling problem among the aged than delirium.

ALZHEIMER'S DISEASE   As we note in Chapter 18 (see pages 642-646), *Alzheimer's disease,* named after Alois Alzheimer, the German physician who first identified it in 1907, is the most common form of dementia, accounting for at least 50 percent of cases (Bliwise et al., 1987). This gradually progressive degenerative process can appear in middle age *(early onset),* but most often it occurs after the age of 65 *(late onset)* (APA, 1994). Its prevalence increases markedly among people in their late 70s and early 80s. Some studies have reported higher rates of this disease in women, but this finding may be due simply to the fact that women live longer than men. Alzheimer's disease can be diagnosed with certainty only by postmortem studies that identify specific structural changes within the brain tissue (see Figure 20–4). The most notable of these changes are the excessive formation of *neurofibrillary tangles* and *senile plaques* in the brain.

Neurofibrillary tangles are twisted protein fibers found *within* the cells of the hippocampus and other brain structures vital to memory and learning. All people form tangles as they age, but people with Alzheimer's disease form an extraordinary number of them (Selkoe, 1992). *Senile plaques* are sphere-shaped deposits of a small molecule known as the *beta-amyloid protein* that form in the spaces *between* neurons, usually along the membranes of neurons located in the hippocampus, cerebral cortex, and some other brain regions, as well as in some blood vessels in these brain areas. As with tangles, the formation of plaques is a normal part of aging, but it is dramatically increased in people with Alzheimer's disease (Selkoe, 1992). It has been speculated that such plaques may interfere with exchanges between cells, which in turn leads to cell death or dysfunction.

The course of Alzheimer's disease ranges from two to as many as fifteen years. Dysfunction progresses insidiously over this time, usually beginning with mild memory problems and lapses of attention that are virtually unnoticed or ignored at first. As time passes, these symptoms increase in frequency and severity, and at some point it becomes clear that the individual is having difficulty in completing complicated tasks, such as balancing the checkbook, or is forgetting important appointments. Later the individual begins to have difficulty with simple tasks, and changes in personality often become much more noticeable. For ex-

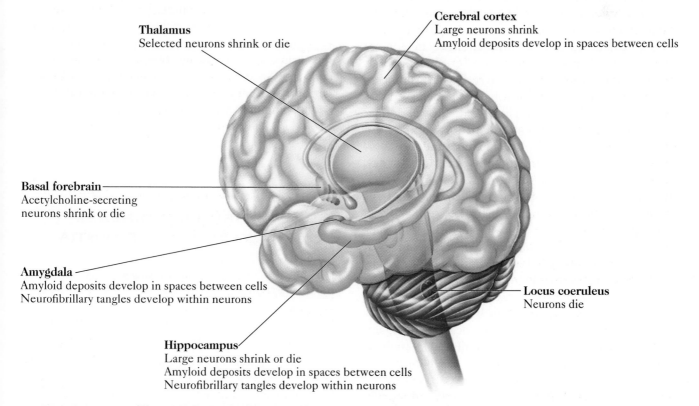

FIGURE 20–4   *The aging brain. In old age, our brains undergo structural changes that affect memory, learning, and reasoning to some degree. These same changes occur to an excessive degree in people with Alzheimer's disease. (Selkoe, 1992, p. 136.)*

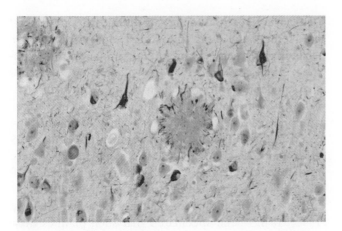

Tissue from the brain of a 69-year-old man with Alzheimer's disease reflects the structural changes characteristic of the disorder, including excessive amounts of plaque (large dark-gold sphere) the clusters of beta-amyloid protein that form outside of cells; and neurofibrillary tangles, the twisted fibers within cells that make the cells appear blackened (small dark blobs).

ample, a man who for most of his life was quite formal and proper may make inappropriate sexual advances toward a family friend.

During the early stages of Alzheimer's disease, people tend to deny that they have a problem, but when it becomes more obvious, many become anxious or depressed about their impaired thinking. As the dementia progresses further, however, they show less and less concern about it. While they may display a burst of anger at their inability to accomplish a task or at a caregiver's efforts to restrain them, in general they show little acknowledgment of or concern about their limitations. During the late stages of this process there is less interpersonal involvement, increased disorientation as to time and place, frequent wandering, and extremely poor judgment in matters important to safety and hygiene. They become more and more agitated at night and take frequent naps during the day. This phase can last anywhere from two to five years, with the individuals requiring constant care and supervision (Mace & Rabins, 1991).

Despite the serious changes in cognitive functioning that occur over this time, Alzheimer's victims usually remain in fairly good health until the later stages of the disease. As their mental facilities decline, their activity level decreases markedly, and they tend to spend more time just sitting or lying in bed. At this point they begin to have more physical ailments, and often they develop complicating illnesses, such as pneumonia, that can result in death.

VASCULAR DEMENTIA The symptoms of *vascular dementia,* or *multi-infarct dementia,* are due to a cerebrovascular accident, or stroke, that causes a

loss of blood flow to certain areas of the brain, which in turn damages focal, or specific, areas of the brain. The patient may be aware of the stroke, or it may be "silent"—that is, the patient may be unaware that anything has happened. The more strokes a person has, or the more massive each one is, the greater the extent of the brain damage. This condition is unlike Alzheimer's disease, in which large areas of the brain atrophy with correspondingly greater loss of cognitive function.

Vascular dementia is the second most common type of dementia among the elderly, with prevalence rates estimated to range from 8 to 29 percent (Selkoe, 1992; Katzman, 1981). It occurs more often in men than in women (APA, 1994), a finding that may be related to the documented higher prevalence of cardiovascular disease and hypertension in men as they age, causing the risk of strokes to increase. This disease, too, is progressive, but its clinical course differs quite a bit from that of Alzheimer's disease. Its symptoms develop abruptly rather than gradually, since they result from a stroke. Behavioral changes occur in a stepwise rather than gradual fashion, with greater fluctuations in function: persons with vascular dementia usually maintain very intact cognitive function in areas governed by parts of the brain that have not been affected, whereas Alzheimer's disease patients generally are impaired, at least to some extent, in all areas of cognitive functioning, because larger areas of their brains are nonfunctional (see Table 20–1). Some people with vascular dementia are very difficult for their caregivers to manage because they cannot discriminate between the kinds of cognitive tasks they perform well and the ones that are significantly impaired. Families generally have to make such deci-

TABLE 20–1

A COMPARISON OF ALZHEIMER'S DISEASE AND VASCULAR DEMENTIA

CHARACTERISTIC	ALZHEIMER'S DISEASE	VASCULAR DEMENTIA
Age of onset	60s–80s	40s–50s
Sex most affected	Possibly females	Males
Nature of onset	Gradual	Abrupt
Course of disease	Progressive	Stepwise
Physical impairments	Few, appear late in life	Frequent

sions for the individual. These interventions lead to more overt conflict than is generally encountered with Alzheimer's victims, who are more likely to recognize their limitations.

Sometimes Alzheimer's disease and vascular dementia are present in the same individual. It is estimated that between 10 and 20 percent of patients who have one of these disorders also have the other. These persons tend to be more difficult to treat because the rate and types of decrements they experience are highly unpredictable. Many are placed in extended-care facilities because they present an overwhelming management problem for the family.

OTHER DEMENTIAS We observed several other disorders that produce dementia in Chapter 18 (see Figure 20-5). These problems are less common among the elderly than Alzheimer's disease and vascular dementia, but have had considerable influence on the study of Alzheimer's disease. *Pick's disease,* a rare disease that affects the frontal and temporal lobes, is difficult to differentiate from Alzheimer's disease clinically, but the distinction becomes clear at autopsy. The strong suggestion of genetic inheritance in this disease has stirred continued attempts to identify a genetic basis for Alzheimer's disease. *Creutzfeldt-Jakob* disease, the rare progressive dementia that is caused by a slow-acting virus, has a rapid course, and often includes spasmodic movements that are rarely seen in Alzheimer's patients. *Huntington's disease,* which usually has its onset during the middle years, typically starts with a movement disorder, which is accompanied increasingly by dementia. The gene carrying this inherited disease has been located on chromosome 4. And finally, *Parkin-*

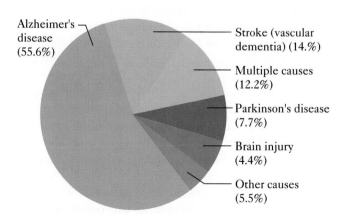

FIGURE 20–5 *The leading cause of dementia is Alzheimer's disease, accounting for more than half of all cases. Other leading causes include vascular dementia and Parkinson's disease. Many cases have multiple causes. (Adapted from Selkoe, 1992, p.138).*

Alzheimer's disease (55.6%)

Stroke (vascular dementia) (14.%)

Multiple causes (12.2%)

Parkinson's disease (7.7%)

Brain injury (4.4%)

Other causes (5.5%)

son's disease, the age-related disorder of the central nervous system that is marked by severe disturbances in psychomotor control and coordination, is often accompanied by dementia, particularly in the later stages.

EXPLANATIONS OF ALZHEIMER'S DISEASE Alzheimer's disease has received considerable attention from researchers in recent years. We still have only limited information about the cause of this devastating disease, but theories abound.

NEUROTRANSMITTER EXPLANATIONS At least two common neurotransmitters—*acetylcholine* and *L-glutamate*—are depleted in the brains of Alzheimer victims. In numerous studies, clinical researchers have tried to increase the activity of these neurotransmitters to see whether this would alleviate the symptoms of Alzheimer's disease.

The neurotransmitter **acetylcholine** is implicated in high-level cognitive processes such as learning, memory, and abstract thinking, and several experimental procedures have been designed to increase its availability in the brain. One strategy has been to administer *choline,* an essential component of acetylcholine, or *lecithin,* a choline precursor, to Alzheimer's patients, but this procedure has not proved particularly beneficial.

Another strategy has been to prevent the breakdown of acetylcholine in the brain by blocking the action of the enzyme *acetylcholinesterase.* Researchers have used the drug **tacrine hydrochloride** to achieve this goal and have found that some patients who take high doses of this drug improve slightly on short-term memory and reasoning ability, as well as on use of language and coping ability (Davis et al., 1992; Farlow et al., 1992). Although the benefits of this drug are limited and the risk of adverse effects, such as liver complications, is high, no other viable treatment has been discovered. When the drug was made available late in 1993, under the trade name Cognex, it became the first therapeutic agent on the market developed specifically for the treatment of mild to moderate Alzheimer's disease. Most clinicians believe, however, that his drug may be beneficial for select patients only, and even then any improvement in function is likely to be limited (Kumar, 1993).

L-glutamate is a neurotransmitter that plays an important role in the transmission of impulses from a specific part of the cortex to the hippocampus, the part of the brain that, as we observed in Chapter 18, is essential for the storage and retrieval of new information. The role of L-glutamate depletion in Alzheimer's disease is thought to be significant because memory is often the first and most severely affected cognitive ability in patients. Research on drugs which may increase the activity of this neurotransmitter is still limited, however. Other drug studies have also been undertaken in an attempt to uncover still other kinds of neurotransmitter activity that may be involved in Alzheimer's disease and to improve the cognitive functioning of Alzheimer's patients (Bondareff, Mountjoy, & Roth, 1982).

GENETIC THEORIES   The hypothesis that mental deterioration in the elderly may have a genetic basis has interested researchers for several decades, and evidence in its favor has emerged over the years. Researchers have found, for example, a concentration of progressive dementias in some families (Matsuyama, Jarvik, & Kumar, 1985). They have also discovered that the risk of a sibling developing Alzheimer's disease is inversely related to the patient's age at the onset of the disease (Heston et al., 1981). That is, the younger a patient is at the onset of the disease, the greater the likelihood that a sibling may also develop it. Because of the accumulated genetic data, many clinicians now distinguish between *familial* Alzheimer's disease and *sporadic* Alzheimer's disease, in which a family history of brain disease is not clearly in evidence.

As we noted in Chapter 19, an association between Alzheimer's disease and Down syndrome has led researchers to propose that some genes on chromosome 21 may contribute to Alzheimer's disease (see Figure 20–6). Recent research has specifically pointed to at least two distinct gene sites on this chromosome as contributors to early-onset familial Alzheimer's disease (Tanzi, 1991). The significance of this finding becomes more compelling when it is viewed in the light of the structural brain changes that occur in Alzheimer's disease. We noted earlier on that one prominent change is the build-up of beta-amyloid protein plaques along nerve-cell membranes. It is now known that in people with early-onset familial Alzheimer's disease, mutations occur within the gene on chromosome 21 that is responsible for the production of the **beta-amyloid precursor protein (beta-APP)**. This mutated gene apparently gives rise to a mutated version of beta-APP, which in turn helps produce more or faster beta-amyloid accumulation (plaques) in key areas of the brain (Mullan et al., 1992; Chartier-Harlin et al., 1991; Goate et al., 1991; Murrell et al., 1991). Thus many theorists now believe that in certain families genetically transmitted beta-APP mutations heighten the likelihood of beta-amyloid plaque formations, in turn increasing the chances of developing early-onset familial Alzheimer's disease (Marx, 1992; Hardy, 1992; Kosik, 1992).

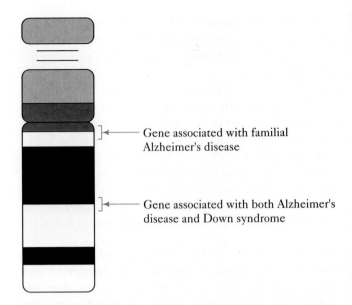

FIGURE 20–6 *A gene abnormality located toward the top of chromosome 21 is commonly found in patients with a familial form of Alzheimer's disease. In addition, scientists have located a gene lower on the chromosome responsible for the production of the beta-amyloid protein, found in abnormal deposits in the brains of both people with Alzheimer's disease and those with Down syndrome. (Adapted from Tanzi, 1991; Tanzi et al., 1989.)*

Additional evidence that Alzheimer's disease has a genetic component is seen in recent reports that a defect on chromosome 14 has been found in some cases of early-onset familial disease (Schellenberg et al., 1991). Some workers also suggest that chromosome 19 may be implicated in late-onset familial Alzheimer's disease, but this hypothesis has yet to be supported fully (Pericak-Vance et al., 1991).

All of these discoveries are very promising, but it is important to note that while a number of studies have linked rare gene mutations to familial Alzheimer's disease through their effect on beta-amyloid, other research has found no strong relationship between the amount of beta-amyloid plaques and the degree of dementia (Hyman & Tanzi, 1992). Furthermore, not all familial-Alzheimer's patients with amyloid plaques have shown genetic mutations. Moreover, the vast majority of persons with Alzheimer's disease do not have clear family histories of inherited brain dysfunction. Thus, we still have no conclusive evidence describing the mechanism of beta-amyloid effects or the extent to which genetic mutations may influence the development of this disease in the population as a whole.

OTHER THEORIES   Other hypotheses have also stimulated research on the underlying mechanisms of Alzheimer's disease. The fact that a viral-like protein has been isolated in other dementias, such as

Creutzfeldt-Jakob disease, has encouraged scientists to look for a slow-acting infectious agent in Alzheimer's disease as well (Prusiner, 1991; Harrison & Roberts, 1991). Researchers have also investigated the hypothesis that the immune systems of people who develop Alzheimer's disease fail to recognize neural tissue and attack it as though it were a foreign body (Roberts et al., 1991; Mortimer et al., 1991). High concentrations of aluminum in the brains of some Alzheimer's victims have led some investigators to look for heavy metals or other toxic substances in the brains of Alzheimer's patients. Other researchers have cited elevated levels of zinc in the brain as a possible factor in this disease. And clinical researchers who favor vascular theories believe that the structural changes characteristic of Alzheimer's disease may result from inadequate delivery of oxygen and sugar to the brain, or from the disruption of other metabolic processes by poor exchanges at the capillary level. Lastly, there is the growing view that any number of factors may precipitate the structural changes characteristic of Alzheimer's disease. The disease may simply be the final common pathway of expression for many different causal agents, all of which act to disrupt cerebral processes and thus trigger permanent structural and biochemical changes and massive dysfunction (Glenner, 1985).

TREATMENTS FOR ALZHEIMER'S VICTIMS AND THEIR FAMILIES The first step in treating a person suspected of having Alzheimer's disease is to make as accurate a diagnosis as possible. This requires a thorough examination by an interdisciplinary team of physicians and other health specialists. A detailed medical history and complete physical examination, along with additional laboratory tests, are nearly always essential because the type of dementia a person is suffering from usually cannot be established on the basis of the behavioral symptoms alone. In some cases, as we have seen, the condition can be diagnosed for certain only after an autopsy.

Once a diagnosis has been made, various therapies may be employed. As we have just discussed, drug therapies for people with Alzheimer's disease are largely experimental and have produced modest improvements at best. However, a number of psychological interventions have been developed which seek to alleviate some of the distress and problematic behaviors that the disease causes. These interventions cannot eliminate cognitive impairment or return individuals to their earlier level of functioning, but they can improve the quality of life both for patients and for their families.

Relatives who provide care for persons with Alzheimer's disease often feel overwhelmed, depressed, and frustrated, and in turn, may need support and treatment from clinicians. The wife of this Alzheimer's sufferer said, "I used to work with him with a calendar every night, take about 15, 20 minutes to do the days of the week. Then it got too stressful for him. . . . So that's why you see him swishing around with paint, with the crayons—to relieve that stress."

Behavioral interventions are often applied in cases of Alzheimer's disease. Typically, behaviorists identify specific everyday actions performed by the Alzheimer's victim that are stressful for the family, such as wandering at night, being incontinent, and demanding frequent attention. They may also identify behaviors that the family would like to see increased, such as the ability to participate in some self-care activities (Fisher & Carstensen, 1990). Behavioral therapists next teach family members how to shape positive behaviors and how and when to apply reinforcement, using a combination of role-playing techniques, modeling, and in-home practice (Pinkston & Linsk, 1984). Behavioral principles and techniques can also be taught to staff members in long-term care facilities and nursing homes, to improve the quality of life for both them and their patients and to reduce the need for such offensive practices as keeping hard-to-manage patients in restraints (Fisher & Carstensen, 1990). These behavioral approaches have been particularly effective in treating wandering, inappropriate sexual behavior, incontinence, and refusal to feed oneself.

A very different behavioral approach focuses on developing programs to treat the feelings of depression experienced by approximately 30 percent of victims in the early to middle stages of the disease (Teri & Reifler, 1987). Behaviorists guide the caregiver and patient together to develop a list of potentially pleasant activities to share, so that more pleasurable interactions can be built into their daily routine (Teri & Logsdon, 1991). This approach is quite effective in reducing symptoms of depression in both the patient and the family caregiver.

Caregiving takes a very heavy toll on the close relatives of Alzheimer's victims. In fact, one of the most frequent reasons for the institutionalization of victims is that overwhelmed caregivers can no longer cope with the demands of the situation (Colerick & George, 1986). Caretakers frequently report experiencing anger and depression (Gallagher et al., 1989), and a number of empirical studies have demonstrated the negative impact of caregiving on caregivers' physical and mental health (Schulz, Visintainer, & Williamson, 1990). Clinicians now recognize that one of the most important aspects of treating Alzheimer's disease is to identify and treat the needs of caregivers and to improve their well-being, often without involving the patient at all (Zarit, Orr, & Zarit, 1985).

Our work has concentrated on helping caregivers reduce their own depression and acquire skills for more adaptive management of the frustration and anger they experience. This effort includes such programs as inpatient and outpatient *respite care*, which emphasizes that regular time-out should be planned for (Berman et al., 1987); the psychoeducational programs that we described earlier; individual counseling and psychotherapy for very distressed family members; and support groups of various kinds to meet a wide variety of needs (Gallagher, Lovett, & Rose, 1991).

The *support-group* movement is very strong in this as in many other areas of human suffering. A national organization called the Alzheimer's Association has set up chapters throughout the United States and Europe. It was founded by a woman whose husband had Alzheimer's disease at a time when few people even knew what the term meant and still fewer services were available for patients and their families. Specialized support groups also exist for families of brain-damaged people whose impairment is attributable to other causes, such as Parkinson's disease and frequent strokes. Caregivers typically report that they gain the most from support groups that are made up of people in situations very similar to their own, so therapists now encourage them to shop around until they find a support group where they feel comfortable (Gallagher-Thompson, 1994).

Finally, interventions need to be developed to help caregivers maintain their *physical* health. Some studies reveal that caregivers show significantly greater signs of deficient immune system functioning than noncaregivers (Kiecolt-Glaser et al., 1987). And other research has found other negative medical consequences of prolonged caregiving, such as increased cardiovascular distress in female caregivers (Vitaliano et al., 1989). This area is just beginning to be investigated, however.

Fortunately, just as patients seem to adapt to their impairment and to at least some of its functional limitations over time (Burnside, 1988), family caregivers do too (Rabins et al., 1990). Moreover, work in our laboratory, reminiscent of the hardiness research discussed in Chapters 6 and 11, indicates that there is a subgroup of caregivers who tend to remain high in positive mood and morale and low in perceived burden throughout their caregiving experience, despite the fact that their frail elder relative continues to deteriorate. Researchers have not, however, determined what factors enable some caregivers to be such good copers.

SPECIAL CONCERNS ABOUT DEMENTIA

One area about which very little is known is the influence of ethnicity on assessment and treatment of people with dementia and their families. Although a large increase in the minority population of persons over the age of 65 is expected in the next twenty years, rather little research has been done on or clinical attention paid to their special needs (Valle, 1989.) We know, for example, that proportionately fewer Asians and Pacific Islanders than people of European descent are placed in nursing homes, but we do not really know why. And we do not know the extent to which other cultures view caregiving as a burden, as it is almost uniformly viewed in the Anglo culture. Moreover, because only a few assessment instruments have been appropriately translated or validated in the native language of many minority elders, it is difficult to conduct standardized assessments for diagnosing cases of dementia in members of those minority groups.

A second area of concern is that serious abuses exist in the nursing home industry. Indeed, health-care professionals may soon find it necessary to lobby for reform in nursing homes, or to promote more forcefully the development of a continuum of care that permits the cognitively impaired elder to remain at home as long as possible. If appropriate services were available to support elders and their families at home, expensive and impersonal care might not be needed—at least not to the extent that is now projected for the future. Such services would include in-home health care; in-home support services such as assistance in meal preparation, bathing, and medication; and day-care facilities that can offer rehabilita-

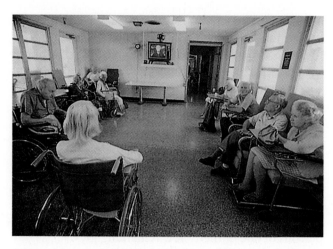

Many of today's nursing homes are unstimulating settings in which elderly patients may be neglected, mistreated, and over-medicated.

tion programs and social activities. It is a tremendous relief to caregivers to have these services and to know that their frail elder relative is in a safe and supervised environment whose cost is substantially less than a stay in a nursing home. The nursing-home industry has been slow to develop such alternatives, probably largely because they would lower the demand for the profitable institutional care the nursing homes provide.

A final concern is the growing cost of long-term care. As the proportion of elders in the population increases in the next twenty to forty years, the younger sector of the population will have to bear most of the burden of financing these various programs (Hewitt & Howe, 1988). Careful planning must be done now if the problem is to be solved in an equitable fashion.

SUBSTANCE ABUSE

Chuck and Sandra Clemens are elderly neighbors of yours who are becoming increasingly withdrawn from other people. Chuck's speech seems to be slurred fairly often lately, and Sandra's appearance is not as neat as it used to be. You frequently see them at the local convenience store buying beer and lots of over-the-counter medicines, such as antihistamines, but they really never seem that sick to you. You hear some other neighbors talking about the deplorable condition of their apartment and you wonder what is wrong. The next thing you know, Sandra has been taken to the hospital: she broke her hip in a fall, because she was unsteady on her feet. When the visiting nurse inspects the apartment in preparation for Sandra's return from the hospital, she finds a stash of unused medications, many empty beer cans and wine bottles,

and little food. Chuck is immediately brought in for counseling, and both he and his wife are strongly encouraged to join the chapter of Alcoholics Anonymous in their area.

Although alcohol and other forms of substance abuse are certainly a problem for many older persons, the prevalence of substance abuse actually appears to decline after age 60, perhaps as a consequence of changes in health and reduced financial status (Maddox, 1988). It seems that the majority of older adults do not misuse alcohol, prescription drugs, and other substances despite the fact that aging is widely perceived as a time of frequent stress and that in our society alcohol and drugs are widely used to reduce stress. At the same time, it is important to note that accurate data about the prevalence of alcohol and other forms of drug abuse among older adults is difficult to obtain, because many older people do not suspect or admit that they have such a problem. Some regard it as shameful, others fail to realize that their drinking has become a problem, and a number misuse their medications without being aware of it.

Surveys suggest that between 3 and 5 percent of the older adult population, particularly men, have alcohol-related problems in any given year (Helzer et al., 1991; Maddox, 1988). Men under 30 are four or five times as likely as men over 60 to exhibit a behavioral problem associated with alcohol abuse, such as repeated falling, spells of dizziness or blacking out, secretiveness about drinking, and increasing social withdrawal (Helzer et al., 1991; Butler & Lewis, 1986). These studies fail to show a consistent relationship between older adults' alcohol abuse and their socioeconomic status, though younger adults' alcohol abuse is associated with lower socioeconomic status. Older patients who are institutionalized for either medical or psychological reasons do, however, display relatively high rates of problem drinking. For example, alcohol problems among older persons admitted to general and mental hospitals ranged from a reported low of 15 percent to a high of 49 percent, and estimates of alcohol-related problems among patients in nursing homes have ranged from 25 to 60 percent (Maddox, 1988).

Surveys and descriptive studies often distinguish two major categories of older problem drinkers: early-onset and late-onset alcohol abusers. *Early-onset* drinkers are aging abusers who have experienced significant alcohol-related problems for many years, often since their 20s or 30s. Many of these people are well known to the health and social services professionals in their community. *Late-onset* alcohol abusers, in contrast, may not have started the pattern until their 50s or 60s. Their abusive drinking typically begins as a reaction to the frequent negative events associated with growing older, such as the death of a spouse or retirement. Researchers disagree about the relative numbers of late- and early-onset alcohol abusers, and particularly about the extent to which women fall into the late-onset category.

Another leading form of substance abuse in the elderly is the unintentional or, less commonly, intentional misuse of prescription drugs, particularly in combination with alcohol (Gottheil, 1987). A very poignant letter by a 72-year-old woman was published in the magazine *Aging* in 1990. She revealed that because of problems earlier in her life, her physician prescribed first tranquilizers, then a stimulant, and then medication for severe headaches. Eventually she increased the dosage of these various medications, noting that the drugs no longer had the same effect and that she did not feel well. She said she felt no guilt about what happened because "after all I was only following the doctor's orders at all times" (Reynolds, 1990, p. 27). Her functioning became so impaired, however, that she needed hospitalization and therapy to end her addiction.

A major national survey has indicated that among persons who receive prescriptions from a physician, the average number of prescriptions is 7.5, but it is 14.2 for people over the age of 60. Among those living in the community, 85 percent indicated that they used prescription drugs regularly; 67 percent took at least one drug every day and 25 percent took three or more drugs daily, whereas for younger persons the corresponding figures were 43 percent and 9 percent (Lipton, 1988, p. 74). Over 95 percent of the residents of nursing homes take two or more medications each day, sometimes more for the convenience of the nursing home staff than for the good of the resident. Research is beginning to suggest that there is a problem of some magnitude here, and it is likely to get worse as the population of elders increases.

Research also indicates, however, that the use of "hard drugs" or "street drugs" by the elderly is very unusual (Petersen, 1988). Those who have been heroin users in their youth typically stop completely by their 50s or 60s, often because of concurrent serious health problems and lack of money. There have been very few studies on the use of cocaine, LSD, PCP, or other such drugs among the elderly.

ASSESSMENT An older person's abuse of alcohol or prescription drugs may be discovered during a physical examination or when the family detects a change in behavioral patterns and an increased use of a substance. Sometimes older people themselves realize that they have a problem. Unfortunately, relatively few mental health professionals have acquired the skills necessary to assess and deal with the alcohol and prescription drug problems of elderly people. Some younger clinicians, for example, find it difficult to ask older persons direct questions about alcohol intake, feeling presumptuous or intrusive when they do so. We find, however, that older adults will provide information about alcohol consumption and alcohol-related behaviors if they are asked about them straightforwardly. In addition, many professionals mistakenly believe that they should not deprive older persons of one of their "few remaining joys."

It has been difficult to find a good screening measure for identifying alcohol and other forms of drug abuse in the elderly. The clinical theorists Mark Willenbring and William Spring (1988) recommend giving elderly clients the "HEAT," a mnemonic device for a series of four questions: one subjective, open-ended question designed to elicit subtle defensiveness and three questions that have been found to identify the majority of alcoholic persons in hospitals:

How do you use alcohol?

Have you ever thought you use to *Excess?*

Has *Anyone* else ever thought you used too much?

Have you ever had any *Trouble* resulting from your use?

Any other substance may be mentioned in place of alcohol. Willenbring and Spring advise that clinicians should suspect a drug problem if clients appear excessively defensive, angry, embarrassed, or uncomfortable in their answers to any of these questions. They also suggest that for persons between 55 and 75 years of age, two drinks a day and three per occasion are probably reasonable maximum safe usages, while for those over 75, one drink per day and two per occasion may be safe, although this has not yet been established empirically (1988, p. 31). Some people in the field of gerontology even think that it is sometimes good to encourage older adults to have a small amount of alcohol daily, to promote socialization and relaxation (Kastenbaum, 1988).

To detect misuse of medications, it is first necessary to find out exactly what medications older persons are taking. A number of therapists ask their clients to put all of their medications in a bag and bring them to the next evaluation session (LeSage & Zwygart-Stauffacher, 1988). This strategy typically leads to more accurate information than questioning alone, since many older people are forgetful and may omit some medications or get the dosages mixed up. If older persons are responsible for taking their own medications, clinicians need also to determine whether they understand how to take each one (Gottheil, 1987). Medications will be taken most carefully and accurately by older people who understand the purposes behind them and the exact procedures for taking them, and who recognize the "red flags"—such as alterations in sensory or perceptual functioning—that can signify their unintentional misuse.

TREATMENT Alcohol abuse among elderly people is treated in many of the same ways as alcohol abuse among younger adults (see pp. 470–475), including such approaches as detoxification, Antabuse, and Alcoholics Anonymous (Schiff, 1988). While most AA meetings are attended by people of varying ages, specialized groups called Golden Years have been organized largely to attract older adults and make the experience more comfortable for them.

An important component of many treatment programs for elders who abuse alcohol is a group therapy format that includes a focus on the social and psychological stresses associated with aging (Zimberg, 1978). The Florida Mental Health Institute has a number of cognitive-behavioral group programs for the treatment of older drinkers. These groups, targeted to people aged 55 and over, teach older drinkers how to solve problems, enhance their social support networks, and manage themselves in high-risk situations, and they provide education and information on alcohol. Research has indicated that these programs are successful in helping older persons attain sobriety and remain free of alcohol and medication misuse for as long as one year after completing the programs (Schonfeld & Dupree, 1990).

A variety of strategies appear to be useful in reducing medication misuse among elderly people. First, it is helpful when clinicians make sure that older patients have accurate information about their medications and understand it, and when pharmacists or nurses take time to clarify directions and to develop a system for taking the medications as prescribed. Second, it is helpful when a medication regimen is simplified as much as possible so that the patient is more able to follow it accurately. Third, older individuals tend to receive better health care when they are taught to tell their various physicians just what medications they are on and from whom they are receiving them; many physicians do not realize how easy it is for elders to misuse their medications. Finally, it is beneficial when clinicians instruct older persons to monitor the undesired effects of medications and to distinguish those that are potentially serious from

those that are inconveniences, so that serious effects can be reported immediately to the physician and the medication regimen can be changed. More active collaboration among pharmacists, physicians, and older patients can also greatly reduce the likelihood of unintentional drug misuse.

PSYCHOTIC DISORDERS

Schizophrenia is more common in younger persons than in older ones (Keith et al., 1991). In fact, many schizophrenic persons find that their symptoms become attenuated in later life. Improvement can occur in people who have been schizophrenic thirty or more years, particularly in such areas as social skills and work capacity (Cohen, 1990). New symptoms do not commonly appear in old age.

Most older schizophrenic people require some sort of structured care (Cavanaugh, 1990). Having had this severe disorder for many years, they tend to function best at relatively low-level jobs; a number experience repeated hospitalizations. As a result of the trend toward deinstitutionalization in the United States over the past few decades, many older schizophrenic people end up in nursing homes, where they do not receive appropriate treatment, or homeless on the streets, a situation discussed in Chapter 16.

Another psychotic disorder, *delusional disorder,* the problem marked by the presence of one or more nonbizarre delusions, is relatively rare among adults of all ages (3 out of every 10,000) but tends to increase slightly with age (APA, 1994; Cavanaugh, 1990). Some geriatric clinicians believe that a mild form of delusional disorder can sometimes be a healthy adaptation to a stressful world that may in fact really be out to get the individual in one way or another. There is, however, little in either the clinical or the research literature to support this view.

The psychotic disorders are often treated with antipsychotic drugs. As we have seen previously, however, most of these medications may produce serious undesired motor effects in adults of all ages, particularly elderly patients, and so they must be used sparingly. In other interventions, clinicians may try to develop a strong therapeutic alliance so that patients can trust at least one person in the world, offer supportive counseling, encourage patients to identify and discount their delusional ideas, and work with family members to increase their tolerance for their older psychotic relatives (Blazer, 1990). So far few controlled studies have investigated the efficacy of treatment of psychotic disorders among the elderly.

■ OTHER ■ FACTORS IN THE MENTAL HEALTH OF THE ELDERLY

As geropsychologists, we are continually struck by the amount of new knowledge that is developing in our field, and constantly wrestle with it to determine its clinical implications. Among issues of increasing interest today are the role of ethnicity in the mental health of the elderly, the problems raised by long-term care, and the necessity of health maintenance in an aging world.

ETHNICITY

Gerontologists must be aware of their patients' ethnicity as they try to diagnose and treat the mental health problems of older people. As we saw in Chapter 2, discrimination based on ethnicity has always been a problem in the United States, and many people have suffered disadvantages as a result, particularly those who are now old (Cavanaugh, 1990). The term "double jeopardy" has been used to describe the problem of being simultaneously old and a member of a minority racial or ethnic group. "Triple jeopardy" describes the dilemma of the person who is old, a member of an ethnic minority, and female, since many more older women than older men live alone, are widowed, and have incomes below the poverty level.

The language barrier is the most significant difficulty for many ethnic elders, as well as cultural beliefs that prevent them from seeking the services of medical and mental health professionals. Many members of minority groups simply do not trust the establishment, and rely instead on remedies traditional in their immediate social network. Ethnic elders may also lack information about available services that are sensitive to their culture and particular needs (Ralston, 1991; Jackson, 1988).

A significant challenge for the next twenty to forty years will be the development of appropriate outreach, diagnostic, and intervention programs that older minority adults and their families will find culturally relevant. This task is not easy, given the number of minority groups in this country, the multitude of languages they speak, and the scarcity of information currently available about how these elders respond to stress and about what they perceive as a stressful event. A concerted effort in this regard is needed, because the minority population is the fastest-growing segment within the over-65 group in the United States today.

LONG-TERM CARE

The term "long-term care" is applied to a variety of forms of extended care provided to older adults. It may be used to describe the services received in a partially supervised apartment or housing complex for seniors who are not as independent as they used to be, or in a nursing home or other institutional setting where skilled medical and nursing care are available around the clock. Since the majority of elders have at least one chronic health problem and may live alone, there is and will continue to be a need for settings where elders can live safely and with as high a quality of life as possible when they are no longer able to function independently.

The quality of care provided in long-term residences varies widely. Persons should make a careful review of their own situation as well as the pluses and minuses of the facility before choosing to enter a program of long-term care, particularly a nursing home. That decision, however, is often made not by the elderly persons themselves but by physicians or family members.

At any given time, only about 5 percent of the elderly population actually reside in nursing homes, but fear of being "put away" in a nursing home is a signif-

When long-term-care institutions offer stimulating programs, such as this exercise class for people with Alzheimer's disease, allow patients to control their lives as much as possible, and facilitate involvement by family members and friends, elderly persons are generally happier and show relatively better cognitive functioning.

icant factor in the lives of most older adults (Butler & Lewis, 1986). Many fear having to move, as well as the impersonal environment and the emphasis on disabilities that exist in long-term-care settings. Others fear losing their independence, or have known people who died shortly after being admitted to such a facility and thus are very pessimistic about their ability to adjust.

A number also worry about the economic implications of moving to a long-term-care facility. Because families are trying to keep their elders at home longer (and using a variety of services to help them do so), most elders do not enter nursing homes until they are in the last stages of a disease and in need of almost total care. This means that nursing homes will be dealing increasingly with terminally ill patients and their families. Since round-the-clock nursing care is always going to be expensive, nursing home costs will continue to rise. The health insurance plans that are currently available do not even begin to cover the costs of permanent placement. All of these issues can affect the mental health of older adults in very significant ways, from causing depression and anxiety in the individual to arousing conflict in the family. Research focused on improving the quality of life for both patients and staff in long-term-care facilities is sorely needed. A related issue is the need for continued training of the staff and management of such facilities so that any advances in knowledge can be quickly shared and implemented.

HEALTH MAINTENANCE

Because of the increasing longevity of older persons and the increasing cost of health care, it would seem prudent for the current generation of young adults to take a wellness or health-promotion approach to their own aging process. By this we mean doing things that are important for maintaining both physical and mental health, such as not smoking, eating well-balanced and sensible meals, and exercising regularly—not only to look good but also to manage stress. Although research data are lacking at present, it is reasonable to assume that older adults will adapt more readily to changes and negative events if their health is good. Good health may serve as a buffer against depression, since the ability to enjoy one's good health encourages engagement in enjoyable activities in general.

By the same token, mental health professionals should be encouraging lifelong participation in prevention programs, such as the various psychoeducational approaches we discussed earlier. It is also important to urge people to seek treatment promptly for any psychological problems that they do develop as they grow older, and to help them overcome their prejudices against doing so.

THE STATE OF THE FIELD
PROBLEMS OF AGING

For many years elderly persons, like children and adolescents, received little attention from clinical practitioners and researchers. It was as if these professionals believed that the broadly studied psychological problems of early and middle adulthood disappeared when people reached the age of 65, or that elderly people were immune to developing new problems. Clinicians now recognize that quite the opposite is true. Because of the losses and other stresses elders face, stresses brought about by a changing brain and body and the changes in lifestyle attached to old age, elderly people are vulnerable to a range of psychological problems. Some of the problems—depression, anxiety, alcoholism—are common in all age groups, but their emergence in old age is often the result of the special stresses of later life. Other problems are disproportionately common in the elderly population, such as dementia and the abuse of prescription drugs. Either way, it is now clear to clinicians that elderly people often experience various mental disorders and problems, and they have started to study and treat these problems in earnest during the past two decades.

This shift in clinical priorities has occurred for a variety of reasons. First, the number and percentage of people who are elderly in our society are steadily increasing, so that the needs of this age group are becoming more and more visible. Second, as the elderly population grows larger, greater caretaking pressures are being placed upon middle-aged and young-old children, and these people have lobbied for more clinical help and research. Third, as the number of elderly persons in our society rises, young and middle-aged adults are increasingly recognizing that the problems of old age await them as well, and they understand that they have a vested interest in the study and treatment of these problems. And fourth, as the number of elderly people grows, the number of aging-related psychological disorders continues to grow as well. The prevalence of aging-related psychological disorders is higher now than it ever was before, and it keeps rising.

Thus the public and the mental health field are currently devoting considerable attention to the psychological problems of aging. As the study and treatment of elderly persons advance in the coming years, a number of puzzles will probably be resolved. Dementia, depression, anxiety, and other disorders among the aged are likely to be better understood and treated. The special concerns of caretakers will probably be better appreciated and addressed. And it is hoped that more humane and comforting solutions for the residential needs of aged persons will be developed.

Another important trend in the study and treatment of elderly people is the current emphasis on prevention and preparation. Since the stresses and biological changes of old age are largely predictable, clinical educators are now developing programs aimed at preventing them or preparing people for them before they occur. Young adults are being encouraged to start planning for a financially secure retirement, middle-aged persons are advised to take proper care of their health, and clinical educators organize groups to help middle-aged and young-old persons understand the changes that await them in their later years. These are all important forms of "treatment" for the psychological problems of old age. Such efforts are really just beginning, but their value is already becoming clear. We may not be able to stop the aging process, but we can and should use every weapon in our arsenal to prevent or reduce the psychological pain attached to it.

Summary

■ **IN THE COURSE OF AGING,** adults pass through the stages of *early adulthood, middle adulthood,* and *old age,* or *later life.* Each of these stages and the transitions between them contain particular kinds of stress.

The problems of later life received little attention until recently. In fact, the field of *geropsychology* has developed almost entirely within the last twenty years to explore whether methods of assessment and treatment of the mental health problems of later life should be similar to the methods appropriate for younger persons. Clinicians distinguish the *young-old* (ages 65–74), the *old-old* (ages 74–84), and the *oldest-old* (age 85 and up). The field of geropsychology also distinguishes *chronological age,* the number

of years a person has been alive, from *functional age,* which is a reflection of three interrelated aspects of aging: *biological age, social age,* and *psychological age.* A distinction is also made between chronological age and one's *cohort,* or the particular generation a person belongs to.

■ **A COMMON SOURCE OF PSYCHOLOGICAL STRESS** for older people is their frequent experience of loss as friends, spouses, and relatives die. Some also lose a sense of meaning or purpose after retirement or as chronic illness afflicts them. Lazarus and Folkman's *stress-and-coping model* suggests that most older people cope effectively with these stresses, using such approaches as *primary appraisal, secondary appraisal,* and *reappraisal.* By using *problem-focused* modes of coping more than *emotion-focused* modes, many are able to weather the challenges facing them.

Although as many as 50 percent of the elderly would benefit from mental health services, fewer than 20 percent seek help. Many elderly people view any mental health problems as a stigma. Sadly, few clinicians are trained specifically to deal with the mental health problems of the elderly.

■ **DEPRESSION** is the most common mental health problem of older adults; as many as 20 percent meet the DSM-IV criteria for this disorder. The prevalence is higher among women than men. Antidepressant drugs are commonly used to treat depression among the elderly. However, these are less desirable for older depressed patients than for younger ones because the biological mechanisms for the breakdown and absorption of these drugs change with age. Cognitive-behavioral therapy and brief psychodynamic therapy appear to be helpful. In some cases, electroconvulsive therapy has been used successfully. Group therapy may also be effective. Prevention programs for nondepressed older adults that focus on ways to cope with the pressures of aging have been found to be effective in preventing depression. Similar training for caregivers has also helped to prevent depression among them.

■ **APPROXIMATELY 7 PERCENT** of elderly people suffer from *generalized anxiety disorder,* 2 to 5 percent from *agoraphobia,* 1 to 12 percent from *specific phobias,* and less than 1 percent from *panic disorders.* Overall, the prevalence of anxiety disorders actually decreases with age. Treatment for anxiety disorders among the elderly has traditionally included antianxiety medications, although these drugs may cause cognitive impairments that are sometimes mistaken for mental deterioration. Psychotherapy also appears to be helpful, particularly systematic desensitization and cognitive-behavioral therapies such as *anxiety management techniques (AMT),* which teach the client cognitive skills to help control fear.

■ **ALTHOUGH MINOR LAPSES IN MEMORY** or intellectual functioning increase as one gets older, these problems are usually not severe enough to warrant a diagnosis of *dementia.* Around the age of 65, the prevalence of dementia ranges from 2 to 4 percent, followed by a gradual increase over the next ten years to a range of 10 to 15 percent; it jumps to 30 percent among persons over the age of 80. The most common form of dementia among the elderly is *Alzheimer's disease.* It can be definitively diagnosed only on the basis of a postmortem study that identifies structural changes in the brain, particularly an excessive number of *neurofibillary tangles* and *senile plaques.* This disorder is characterized by an insidious progression of dysfunction that increases in frequency and severity. The second most common form of dementia among the elderly is *vascular dementia,* characterized by damage to very specific areas of the cerebral cortex that have been caused by a cerebrovascular accident (stroke). This disorder differs from Alzheimer's disease in that it develops abruptly and may affect some areas of cognitive functioning but not others. Other forms of dementia are *Pick's disease, Creutzfeldt-Jakob disease, Huntington's disease,* and *Parkinson's disease.*

A number of theories have been proposed to explain the occurrence of Alzheimer's disease. *Neurotransmitter theories* propose that the depletion of *acetylcholine* may be responsible. Correspondingly, some clinicians try to treat Alzheimer's disease by increasing the amount of acetylcholine in the brains of patients. *L-glutamate,* which plays an important role in the transmission of impulses in the brain, has also been tied to Alzheimer's disease. *Genetic theories* suggest that defective genes on chromosome 21, 14, or 19 may contribute to certain kinds of Alzheimer's disease.

■ **ALTHOUGH THERE IS NO MEDICAL CURE** for Alzheimer's disease, a variety of interventions seek to alleviate some of its distress and problematic behaviors. The drug *tacrine* (trade name Cognex) may help produce limited improvements in certain areas of cognitive functioning. *Behavioral therapists* teach family members how to encourage and re-

ward specific behaviors. Because of the heavy strain placed on caregivers, some programs have focused on alleviating their anger and depression in order to help them cope with the Alzheimer's patient. *Self-help support groups* have been formed by the friends and families of Alzheimer's sufferers to help them learn to cope in the caregiver role.

■ **BETWEEN 3 AND 5 PERCENT** of the older adult population exhibit *alcohol-related problems* in any given year. Clinicians distinguish between older problem drinkers whose alcohol-related problems began when they were much younger and those who developed problems in their 50s or 60s in response to the negative events associated with growing older. Treatment for alcohol abuse in the elderly is similar to that used with younger patients, including detoxification, group therapy, self-help groups (such as Alcoholics Anonymous), and training in developing better coping skills. The abuse of street drugs is unusual among older persons, but the *abuse of prescription drugs* is a significant problem. To reduce abuse of prescription drugs, patients must be informed of the effects of their medications and then helped to monitor and administer the appropriate medication in the appropriate dosages.

■ **ELDERLY PERSONS** may also manifest psychotic disorders such as *schizophrenia.* It is uncommon, however, for new symptoms of schizophrenia to appear in old age. *Delusional disorder* is also relatively uncommon among elderly adults. Schizophrenic and delusional disorders in the elderly are often treated much the same as in younger patients; but many antipsychotic drugs pose particular dangers for elderly patients, and must be used sparingly.

■ **MANY FACTORS MUST BE CONSIDERED** if we are to understand mental disorders among older adults. Geropsychologists are looking at *ethnicity,* for example, and the role that discrimination and cultural difference may play in mental dysfunction among the elderly. Another issue of major importance is the *long-term care* of the elderly. Long-term-care facilities have not typically been effective in addressing the needs of older persons. In fact, the fear of inadequate care or being "put away" in a nursing home weighs heavily on the minds of most elderly persons. Finally, *health maintenance* of the elderly requires more attention. Prevention of medical problems in older adults may circumvent later problems and help them cope with stress more effectively.

Topic Overview

CHAPTER

LAW, SOCIETY, AND THE MENTAL HEALTH PROFESSION

■

THROUGHOUT THIS BOOK we have seen the importance of the roles clinical scientists and practitioners play in our society: they gather and impart knowledge about psychological dysfunctioning, and they treat people who are experiencing psychological problems. They do not, however, perform these functions in a vacuum. Their relationship with their science, their clients, and the public unfolds within a complex social system. It is that system, in fact, which assigns them their professional responsibilities and regulates them in the performance of their duties.

EARLIER CHAPTERS have highlighted a number of the ways clinical scientists and practitioners interact with the public at large and with specific social agencies. They describe how clinicians have helped carry out the government's policy of deinstitutionalization, how the government has regulated clinicians' use of electroconvulsive therapy, and how clinicians have called to society's attention the psychological ordeal of Vietnam veterans. The relationship between the field of abnormal psychology and the other institutions of our society is complex. Just as we must understand the social context of abnormal behavior in order to appreciate its nature and consequences, so must we understand the context in which this behavior is studied and treated.

THE MENTAL HEALTH PROFESSION and the legislative and judicial professions—the institutions charged with promoting and protecting both the public good and the rights of individuals—have had an interesting relationship dating back many years. Sometimes the relationship has been harmonious, and the two fields have worked in concert to protect the rights and address the needs of mentally disturbed individuals and society. At other times one field has imposed its will on the other and overridden its judgments, and the relationship has been stormy.

This relationship has two distinct facets. One consists of the role played by mental health professionals in the criminal justice system. Clinicians have, for example, been called upon to evaluate the mental stability of many people accused of crimes and thus to help the courts determine their culpability. The second facet of this relationship consists of the role played by the legislative and judicial systems in regulating some aspects of mental health care. Legal channels have been established that can force individuals to receive psychological treatment, even against their will. At the same time, the courts have become watchdogs over the rights of patients in the mental health system.

▪ CLINICAL ▪ INFLUENCES ON THE CRIMINAL JUSTICE SYSTEM

Our courts mete out what they consider just and appropriate punishment on the assumption that individuals are *responsible* for their crimes and are *capable* of defending themselves in court. If either of these features is lacking, it is considered inappropriate to find individuals guilty or incarcerate them in the usual manner. The courts have decided that *mental instability* is one mediating factor that can indeed render individuals incapable of being responsible for their actions and of defending themselves in court. Although the courts make the final judgment of mental instability, their decisions are guided to a large degree by the opinions of mental health professionals.

When individuals accused of crimes are judged to be mentally unstable, they are typically sent to a mental institution for treatment, a process called **criminal commitment.** Actually there are two forms of criminal commitment. In one, individuals are judged *mentally unstable at the time of their crime* and accordingly are found innocent of wrongdoing. Those who plead not guilty by reason of insanity are permitted to bring mental health professionals into court to support their claim. If they are found not guilty on this basis, they are committed for treatment until they improve enough to be released.

In a second form of criminal commitment, individuals are judged *mentally unstable at the time of their trial* and accordingly are considered to be incapable of understanding the procedures and defending themselves in court. They are committed for treatment until they are competent to stand trial. Once again, the testimony of mental health professionals is relied on to help determine the defendant's mental incompetence.

Such judgments of mental instability have generated many arguments over the years. Many people consider the judgments to represent unfortunate loopholes in the legal system that allow criminals to escape proper punishment for their wrongdoing. Others argue that a legal system simply cannot be just unless it allows for extenuating circumstances, such as mental instability.

CRIMINAL COMMITMENT AND INSANITY DURING COMMISSION OF A CRIME

In March 1981 the actress Jodie Foster received the following letter:

> Dear Jodie:
> There is a definite possibility that I will be killed in my attempt to get Reagan. It is for this very reason that I am writing you this letter now. As you well know by now, I love you very much. The past seven months I have left you dozens of poems, letters and messages in the faint hope you would develop an interest in me. . . . Jodie, I would abandon this idea of getting Reagan in a second if I could only win your heart and live out the rest of my life with you, whether it be in total obscurity or whatever. I will admit to you that the reason I'm going ahead with this attempt now is because I just cannot wait any longer to impress you. I've got to do something now to make you understand in no uncertain terms that I am doing all of this for your sake. By sacrificing my freedom and possibly my life I hope to change your mind about me. This letter is being written an hour before I leave for the Hilton Hotel. Jodie, I'm asking you please to look into your heart and at least give me the chance with this historical deed to gain your respect and love. I love you forever.
>
> *John Hinckley*

Are these the ravings of an insane man? Or are they the heartfelt emotions of a calculating murderer? Soon after writing this letter, John W. Hinckley stood waiting, pistol ready, outside the Washington Hilton

Few courtroom decisions have spurred as much debate or legislative action as the jury's verdict that John Hinckley was not guilty by reason of insanity in his attempt to kill President Ronald Reagan. As a consequence of this verdict, Congress and half of the state legislatures changed their criteria for such a verdict.

Hotel. Moments later, President Ronald Reagan emerged from the hotel, and the popping of pistol fire was heard. As Secret Service men propelled Reagan into the limousine, a policeman and the president's press secretary fell to the pavement. The president had been shot, and by nightfall most of America had seen the face and heard the name of the young man from Colorado.

Was John Hinckley insane at the time of the shooting? If insane, should he be held responsible for his actions? On June 21, 1982, fifteen months after he shot four men in the nation's capital, a jury pronounced Hinckley not guilty by reason of insanity. Hinckley thus joined the ranks of Richard Lawrence, a house painter who shot at Andrew Jackson in 1835, and John Schrank, a saloonkeeper who shot former president Teddy Roosevelt in 1912. Each of these would-be assassins was found not guilty by reason of insanity.

For most Americans, the Hinckley verdict was a shock. For those familiar with the characteristics of the insanity defense, the verdict was less surprising. In the Hinckley case, as in other federal court cases, the prosecution had the burden of proving that the defendant was sane beyond a reasonable doubt. At that time, many state courts placed a similar responsibility on the prosecution. Such a clear-cut demonstration of sanity can be a difficult task, especially when the defendant has exhibited bizarre behavior in other

domains. In fact, a few years later, Congress passed a law making it the defense's burden in federal cases to prove that defendants are insane, rather then the prosecution's burden to prove them sane. The majority of state legislatures have since followed suit (Steadman, et al., 1993).

It is important to recognize that insanity is a *legal* term, that the definition of insanity used to help determine criminal responsibility is set by legislators, not by clinicians. Thus defendants with mental disorders do not necessarily fulfill the criteria of legal insanity. A jury's acquittal of a criminal defendant by reason of insanity has been a part of the British legal tradition since 1505 (Robitscher & Haynes, 1982), but the most important precursor of the modern definition of insanity occurred in 1843 in response to the Daniel M'Naghten murder case. M'Naghten shot and killed Edward Drummond, the secretary to British Prime Minister Robert Peel, while trying to shoot Peel. Because of M'Naghten's apparent delusions of persecution, the jury found him to be not guilty by reason of insanity. The public was appalled by this decision, and their angry outcry forced the British law lords to present a new clarification of the insanity defense. This clarification has come to be known as the **M'Naghten rule:**

> To establish a defense of insanity, it must be proved that at the time of committing the act, the party accused was laboring under such a defect of reason, from disease of the mind, as not to know the nature and quality of the act he was doing, or if he did know it, that he did not know he was doing what was wrong.

In essence, the M'Naghten rule held that experiencing a mental disorder at the time of a crime does not by itself constitute insanity; the defendant also had to be unable to know right from wrong. In the late nineteenth century some state and federal courts, dissatisfied with the M'Naghten rule, adopted an alternative test—the *irresistible impulse test.* This test, which had first been applied in Ohio in 1834, emphasized inability to control one's actions. A person who committed a crime during a "fit of passion" was considered insane and not guilty under this test.

Until recent years, state and federal courts chose between the M'Naghten test and the irresistible impulse test in determining the sanity of criminal defendants; most courts used the M'Naghten criteria. For a while a third test, called the **Durham test,** was popular, but it was soon replaced in most courts. This test, based on a decision handed down by the Supreme Court in 1954 in *Durham* v. *United States,* stated simply that individuals are not criminally responsible if their "unlawful act was the product of mental disease or mental defect." This test was meant to offer more flexibility in decisions regarding insanity, but the general criterion of "mental disease" or "mental defect" proved too broad. It could refer to such problems as alcoholism, drug dependence, and conceivably even headaches or ulcers, which were listed as psychophysiological disorders in DSM-I. The Durham test forced courts to rely even more on the interpretations and opinions of clinicians—and these were often contradictory.

In 1955 the American Law Institute (ALI) formulated a penal code that combined elements of all three tests—M'Naghten, irresistible impulse, and Durham. For a time this code became the most widely accepted legal test of insanity. All federal courts, including the court that had jurisdiction over the Hinckley case, and most state courts applied its criteria. The code indicated that

a person is not responsible for criminal conduct if at the time of such conduct as a result of mental disease or defect he lacks substantial capacity either to appreciate the criminality (wrongfulness) of his conduct or to conform his conduct to the requirements of law.

The ALI test also clarified a very important point:

As used in this Article, the term "mental disease or defect" does not include an abnormality manifested only by repeated criminal or otherwise antisocial conduct.

Under previous tests, a defendant's criminal behavior could be cited as a demonstration of "mental disease" or "irresistible impulse." A defense attorney might attempt to demonstrate, for example, that a client's life of crime was sufficient evidence that the client was a "disturbed sociopath." Under the ALI guidelines, there had to be independent indicators of an individual's mental instability. In one case, *Barrett* v. *United States* (1977), it was also clarified that "temporary insanity created by voluntary use of alcohol or drugs" does not relieve an offender of criminal responsibility.

After the Hinckley verdict, however, there was a public uproar over the ALI guidelines, and a movement to toughen the standards gained momentum among elected officials, lawyers, and mental health professionals. In 1983 the American Psychiatric Association recommended removal of the provision that absolved people of responsibility for criminal acts if they were unable to conform their behavior to the requirements of law, and advised retention only of the wrongfulness criterion—essentially a return to the M'Naghten standard:

A person charged with a criminal offense should be found not guilty by reason of insanity if it is shown that, as a result of mental disease or mental retardation, he was unable to appreciate the wrongfulness of his conduct at the time of his offense.

(APA, 1983, p. 685)

This revised criminal insanity test was passed by Congress under the Insanity Defense Reform Act of 1984, and it now applies to all cases tried in federal courts and about half of the state courts (Steadman et al., 1993). The broader ALI standard is still used in the remaining state courts, except those in Idaho, Montana, and Utah, which have abolished the insanity plea altogether. Research has not found, however, that the reform criteria actually diminish the likelihood of "not guilty by reason of insanity" verdicts (Ogloff et al., 1992; Finkel 1991, 1990, 1989; Finkel & Duff, 1989; Finkel & Handel, 1988).

Obviously, severe and confusing mental disorders are more likely than others to impair individuals' judgments of right versus wrong or their ability to control their behavior. Thus it is not surprising that approximately two-thirds of defendants who are acquitted of a crime by reason of insanity qualify for a diagnosis of schizophrenia when they are hospitalized after their acquittal (Steadman et al., 1993; Callahan et al., 1991). The vast majority have a history of past hospitalization, arrest, or both. In addition, studies reveal that about half of the defendants who successfully plead insanity are white; 86 percent are male. Their mean age is 32 years. The crimes for which defendants are found not guilty by reason of insanity vary greatly. Large-scale studies have found, however, that approximately 65 percent of acquittees are charged with a violent crime of some sort (Steadman et al., 1993; Callahan et al., 1991). Close to 15 percent are accused specifically of murder (see Figure 21-1 and Box 21-1).

CRITICISMS OF THE INSANITY DEFENSE
Despite the revisions of the criteria for a finding of insanity, criticism of the insanity defense continues. One concern arises out of the seeming incompatiblity between certain assumptions of United States law and theories of human behavior. While the law assumes that individuals have free will and thus are responsible for their actions, several models of human behavior rest on the assumption that behavior is determined by situational or biological forces acting on the individual. Since "insanity" is a legal and moral judgment and not a scientific one, critics argue that the goals and philosophy of law are incompatible with those of behavioral science (Winslade, 1983).

A second criticism questions the validity of current scientific knowledge of abnormal behavior. During a typical insanity defense trial, the testimony of defense clinicians conflicts with the testimony of clinicians hired by the prosecution (Otto, 1989). To make matters worse, two or more expert clinical witnesses hired by the same side may all contradict each other. The jury can be faced with a situation in which no two "experts" altogether agree on their diagnostic assessments. Some people see this lack of professional consensus as evidence that the clinical field is still too primitive to be influencing the outcome of important legal proceedings. Thomas Szasz (1963) has argued, "The presence or absence of mental illness in an offender cannot be ascertained, simply because there are no workable standards of mental health" (p. 137). Many mental health professionals would counter, however, that DSM-IV now provides a "workable standard" of mental health. Moreover, some standardized scales have been developed, such as the Rogers Criminal Responsibility Assessment Scales, which help assessors to discriminate the sane from the insane according to the M'Naghten standard and to apply the standard to people of different genders, races, and ages (Rogers & Ewing, 1992; Rogers, 1987). And finally the Council on Psychiatry and Law (1992) has recommended the implementation of a system of peer review to ensure that professional standards are upheld when clinicians work on and testify in legal cases.

Perhaps the most widespread criticism of the insanity defense is that it systematically allows dangerous criminals to escape punishment. This view was held by former president Richard Nixon, for example, who advocated that the insanity defense be abolished. It is true that some people who successfully plead insanity are in fact released from treatment facilities within months of their acquittal. And some legal scholars have argued that unless the insanity defense is abolished throughout the nation, a small but significant number of dangerous criminals will continue to slip through our criminal justice system (Winslade, 1983). Yet it is important to keep in mind that the number of such cases is quite small. Surveys show that the public dramatically overestimates the percentage of defendants who plead insanity, guessing it to be 30 to 40 percent, when in fact it is less than 1 percent (Steadman et al., 1993; Callahan et al., 1991). Moreover, research suggests that only a minority of these defendants fake or exaggerate their psychological symptoms (Grossman & Wasyliw, 1988), and only a quarter are actually found not guilty by reason of insanity (Callahan et al., 1991). That is, less than one out of every 400 defendants in the United States is found not guilty by reason of insanity.

During most of our history, the successful insanity plea amounted to the same thing as a long-term prison sentence—indeed, often a longer sentence than a verdict of guilty would have brought (Ogloff et al., 1992; Finkel, 1988). Treatment in a mental hospital wrought little, if any, improvement, and mental health professionals were therefore reluctant to assert that the offender was unlikely to commit a crime again. Moreover, tragic cases would occasionally emerge that called into question clinicians' ability to make such judgments and to accurately predict dangerousness. In Idaho, for example, a young man raped two women and was found not guilty by reason of insanity. After receiving less than a year of treatment, he was released. Soon he was arrested again for shooting a nurse, and convicted of assault with intent to kill. The uproar over this 1981 case led the Idaho state legislature to abolish the insanity plea. Nevertheless, the increasing effectiveness of drug therapy in institutions, the growing bias against extended institutionalization, and greater emphasis on patients' rights have led of late to earlier releases of offenders from mental hospitals (Blackburn,1993). In 1992, in the case of *Foucha* v. *Louisiana*, the U.S. Supreme court ruled that the only basis for determining the release of such individuals is whether or not they are still "insane"; they cannot be indefinitely detained in state mental hospitals simply because they are dangerous.

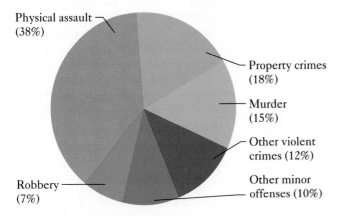

FIGURE 21–1 *Crimes for which persons are found not guilty by reason of insanity (NGRI). A recent review of NGRI verdicts in eight states revealed that most persons who were acquitted on this basis had been charged with a crime of violence. This defense is not employed in many cases involving minor offenses. (Based on Steadman et al., 1993; Callahan et al., 1991.)*

RECENT TRENDS   In recent years 12 states have added the option of a verdict of "guilty but mentally

BOX 21–1

FAMOUS CASES INVOLVING THE INSANITY DEFENSE

1977 In Michigan, Francine Hughes poured gasoline around the bed where her husband, Mickey, lay in a drunken stupor, then lit a match and set him on fire. At her trial she explained that he had beaten her repeatedly for fourteen years, and that he had threatened to kill her if she tried to leave him. The jury found her not guilty by reason of temporary insanity, transforming her into a national symbol for many abused women. Some people saw the decision as confirmation of a woman's right to self-defense in her own home.

1978 David "Son of Sam" Berkowitz, serial killer in New York City, was assessed as psychotic by two psychiatrists after he explained that barking dogs had sent him demonic messages to kill. Nevertheless, he was found guilty of his crimes. Long after his trial, he claimed that he had actually made up the delusions.

1979 Kenneth Bianchi, one of the pair known as the Hillside Stranglers, entered a plea of not guilty by reason of insanity, but along with his cousin was found guilty of sexually assaulting and murdering women in the Los Angeles area in late 1977 and early 1978. Among other claims, Bianchi argued that he had a multiple personality disorder.

1980 In December the rock music legend John Lennon was murdered by Mark David Chapman. Chapman later explained that he had killed Lennon because he believed Lennon to be a "sell-out." He also described hearing the voice of God, considered himself his generation's "catcher in the rye" (from the J. D. Salinger novel), and compared his role to that of Moses. Despite clinical testimony that supported Chapman's plea of not guilty by reason of insanity, he himself refused to claim that schizophrenia was at the root of his crime. He was judged competent to stand trial and was ultimately convicted of murder.

1981 In an attempt to prove his love for the actress Jodie Foster, John Hinckley Jr. tried to assassinate President Ronald Reagan. Hinckley was found not guilty by reason of insanity and was committed to St. Elizabeths Hospital for the criminally insane in Washington, where he remains today.

1991 Julio Gonzales stood trial for starting a fire that killed eighty-seven people at a social club in New York. A psychologist testified that Gonzales had suffered from a wide range of personality disorders and "long-standing psychological defects" that led him to break with reality, suffer a brief psychotic episode, and start the fire after

having a fight with his girlfriend and being evicted from the club. The jury did not agree with the clinician, however, and Gonzales was convicted and sentenced to prison.

1992 The 31-year-old Milwaukee mass murderer Jeffrey Dahmer was tried for the killings of fifteen young men. Dahmer apparently drugged some of his victims and performed crude lobotomies on them in an attempt to create zombielike companions for himself. He also dismembered his victims' bodies and stored their parts to be eaten. Although his defense attorney argued that Dahmer was not guilty by reason of insanity, the jury found him guilty as charged.

1994 On June 23, 1993, 24-year-old Lorena Bobbitt cut off her husband's penis with a twelve-inch kitchen knife while he slept. During her trial, defense attorneys argued that following years of abuse by John Bobbitt, his wife suffered a brief psychotic episode and was seized by an "irresistible impulse" to cut off his penis after he came home drunk and raped her. On January 23, 1994, the jury acquitted her of the charge of malicious wounding by reason of temporary insanity. She was committed to a state mental hospital for further assessment and treatment and released a few months later.

---

ill" when a jury is determining the guilt or innocence of a defendant who has pleaded insanity (Steadman et al., 1993). Defendants who receive this verdict are found to have had a mental illness at the time of their crimes, but the illness was not sufficiently related to or responsible for the crime to acquit them of the offense. The "guilty but mentally ill" option allows jurors to convict a person they perceive as dangerous

while attempting also to ensure that the individual's psychotherapeutic needs will be met.

Unlike the traditional insanity verdict, this new verdict assigns moral blame to the defendant. Defendants found to be guilty but mentally ill are given a prison term with the proviso that they will also undergo psychological treatment if necessary. Advocates of this new option see it as a better means of maintaining and defending our society's standards of behavior. In Georgia, juries given the option of declaring a person guilty but mentally ill have, in fact, delivered insanity acquittals less often (Callahan et al., 1992). Research with mock juries also has found that the verdict of guilty but mentally ill is readily used by jurors as a compromise, resulting in a two-thirds reduction in verdicts of guilty and of not guilty by reason of insanity (Poulson, 1990). One study found that 86 percent of mock jurors preferred having such a third option and saw it as "moral, just and an adequate means of providing for the treatment needs of mentally ill offenders" (Roberts, Golding, & Fincham, 1987).

Critics of the concept believe that appropriate mental health care should be made available to all prisoners anyway, without any special designation (Cohen, 1993), and point out that the prevalence of mental disorders is much higher among prisoners than among the general population (Gunn et al., 1991; Teplin, 1990). They argue that jurors who choose this verdict are often being misled into believing the consequences will be different for the convicted person and say that the verdict often differs from a guilty verdict in name only (Tanay, 1992; Petrella et al., 1985). In fact, while some states offer an "unequivocal statutory right to treatment" for people judged guilty but mentally ill, others give discretion to the correctional facilities to provide treatment "as is deemed necessary" (Plaut, 1983). Critics also argue that the new verdict option may only confuse jurors already faced with an enormously complex task (APA, 1983; Morris, 1983).

Some states allow still another kind of defense, "guilty with diminished capacity." Here a defendent's mental instability is viewed as an extenuating circumstance that should help determine precisely which crime the defendant is guilty of (Slovenko, 1992). The defense lawyer argues that mental dysfunctioning prevented the defendent from having the capacity to harbor the mental intent required for a particular crime, and the accused person should therefore be found guilty of a lesser crime. The famous case of Dan White, who killed Mayor George Moscone and City Supervisor Harvey Milk of San Francisco in 1978, illustrates the use of this verdict.

On the morning of November 27, 1978, Dan White loaded his .38 caliber revolver. White had recently resigned his position as a San Francisco supervisor because of family and financial pressures. Now, after a change of heart, he wanted his job back. When he asked Mayor George Moscone to reappoint him, however, the mayor refused. Supervisor Harvey Milk was among those who had urged Moscone to keep White out, for Milk was America's first openly gay politician, and Dan White had been an outspoken opponent of measures supporting gay rights.

White avoided the metal detector at City Hall's main entrance by climbing through a basement window after telling construction workers who recognized him that he had forgotten his keys. After they unlocked the window for him, he went straight to the mayor's office. There Moscone greeted him and poured a couple of drinks, perhaps hoping to soothe White's rage at not being reappointed. Neither man had a chance to touch his drink before White pulled out his gun and shot the mayor once in the arm and once in the chest. As Moscone lay bleeding on the floor, White walked over to him and, from only inches away, fired twice into Moscone's head.

White then reloaded his gun, ran down the hall, and spotted Harvey Milk. White asked to talk with him. Right after the two men went into White's former office, three more shots rang out. Milk crumpled to the floor. Once again White from point-blank range fired two more bullets into his victim's head. Shortly afterward he turned himself in to the police. Several months later the jury rendered its verdict: Dan White was not guilty of murder, only voluntary manslaughter.

Murder is the illegal killing of a human being with malice aforethought, that is, with the intent to kill. Manslaughter is the illegal killing of a human being without malice aforethought. The attacker may intend to harm the victim, but not to kill. If the victim nonetheless dies, the crime is voluntary manslaughter. Involuntary manslaughter is an illegal killing from negligence rather than intentional harm.

How could a man who loaded his pistol with cartridges that explode on impact, who made a conscious effort to avoid the metal detector, and who, finally, walked over to the prone, wounded men and shot each one twice more in the head—how could such a man be said to have no murderous intent?

The answer lies in the role psychiatry played in the trial. Defense attorney Douglas Schmidt argued that a patriotic, civic-minded man like Dan White—high school athlete, decorated war veteran, former fireman, policeman, and city supervisor—could not possibly have committed such an act unless something had snapped inside him. The brutal nature of the two final shots to each man's head only proved that White had lost his wits. White was not fully responsible for his actions because he suffered from "diminished capacity." Although White killed Mayor George Moscone and Supervisor Harvey Milk, he had not planned his actions. On the day of the shootings, White was mentally incapable of planning to kill, or even of wanting to do such a thing.

Well known in forensic psychiatry circles, Martin Blinder, professor of law and psychiatry at the University of California's Hastings Law School in San Francisco, brought a good measure of academic prestige to White's defense. White had been, Blinder explained to the jury, "gorging himself on junk food: Twinkies, Coca-Cola. . . . The more he consumed, the worse he'd feel and he'd respond to his ever-growing depression by consuming ever more junk food." Schmidt later asked Blinder if he could elaborate on this. "Perhaps if it were not for the ingestion of this junk food," Blinder responded, "I would suspect that these homicides would not have taken place." From that moment on, Blinder became known as the author of the Twinkie defense.

The next psychiatrist, George F. Solomon, further drove home the idea that it was not Dan White but an irritating extraneous influence—something outside himself—that made White do these terrible things. Did White have the capacity to premeditate and deliberate murder? "No," Solomon responded. "Why not?" he was asked. "I don't think that he was capable of permitting himself to plan something so awful." The killings, Solomon told the jury, were the result of "a dissociated state of mind, which means a disruption of the normal integrated functions." White had, Solomon continued, "blocked out of his mind his awareness of his duty to uphold the right."

Dan White was convicted only of voluntary manslaughter, and was sentenced to seven years, eight months. (He was released on parole January 6, 1984.) Psychiatric testimony convinced the jury that White did not wish to kill George Moscone or Harvey Milk.

The angry crowd that responded to the verdict by marching, shouting, trashing City Hall, and burning police cars was in good part homosexual. Gay supervisor Harvey Milk had worked well for their cause, and his loss was a serious setback for human rights in San Francisco. Yet it was not only members of the gay community who were appalled at the outcome. Most San Franciscans shared their feelings of outrage.

(Coleman, 1984, pp. 65–70)

Because of possible miscarriages of justice, many legal experts have argued vociferously against the "diminished capacity" defense (Slovenko, 1992; Coleman, 1984), and a number of states have eliminated it. Some studies find, however, that mock jurors often use the option carefully and appropriately (Finkel & Duff, 1989; Finkel et al., 1985). Jurors have been found to choose this option primarily in situations where: (1) they see some culpability at the time of action and (2) they believe the defendant was in some way responsible for bringing about his or her own mental condition.

SEX OFFENDER STATUTES Ever since 1937, when Michigan enacted the first "sex psychopath" statute, many states have given a special designation to sex offenders (Monahan & Davis, 1983). These states presume that persons who are repeatedly found guilty of certain sex crimes are mentally ill and categorize them as "mentally disordered sex offenders." The Michigan statute, for example, classifies as "sexually delinquent" any person "whose sexual be-

Each segment of the clinical field has its own "forensic" specialists who represent it in the courts and houses of legislature. Forensic psychologists, psychiatrists, and social workers typically receive special training in such duties as evaluating the functioning of criminal defendants, making recommendations concerning patients' rights, and assessing the psychological trauma experienced by crime victims.

havior is characterized by repetitive or compulsive acts . . . , by the use of force upon another person in attempting sexual relations . . . , or by the commission of sexual aggression against children under the age of 16."

Unlike defendants who have been found not guilty by reason of insanity, people classified as mentally disordered sex offenders have been convicted of a criminal offense and are thus judged to be morally responsible for their actions. Nevertheless, the status of a sex offender, like that of a person found not guilty by reason of insanity, implies that commitment to a mental health facility is a more appropriate sentence than imprisonment (Small, 1992). In part, such statutes reflect society's conception of sex offenders as sick people. On a practical level, the provisions help prevent the physical abuse that sex offenders sometimes face as ostracized members of prison society.

In 1977 the Group for the Advancement of Psychiatry recommended the repeal of "mentally disordered sex offender" statutes, and in recent years a growing number of states have modified or abolished such statutes and programs. There are several reasons for this trend. First, many states have found these statutes difficult to act on. Some state statutes, for example, require that a candidate for sex offender status be found "sexually dangerous beyond a reasonable doubt"—a judgment that often goes beyond the clinical field's expertise (Szasz, 1991). Also, there is evidence that racial bias can significantly affect the assignment of sex offender status (Sturgeon & Taylor, 1980). White Americans are twice as likely to be granted sex offender status as African Americans and Hispanic Americans who have been convicted of similar crimes.

CRIMINAL COMMITMENT AND INCOMPETENCE TO STAND TRIAL

Regardless of their state of mind at the time of a crime, defendants may be held to be *mentally incompetent* to stand trial. The competence provisions have been established to ensure that defendants understand the charges and proceedings they are facing and have "sufficient present ability to consult with" their counsel in preparing and conducting an adequate defense. This minimum standard of competence was specified by the Supreme Court in *Dusky* v. *United States* (1960).

Competence issues typically are raised by the defendant's attorney, although prosecutors and arresting police officers may bring the issue before the court as well (Meyer, 1992). In order to ensure due process, all parties (including the presiding judge) are usually careful to recommend a psychological examination for any defendant who seems to exhibit signs of mental dysfunctioning. They prefer to err on the side of caution because some convictions have been reversed on appeal when a defendant's competence was not initially established. When the issue of competence is raised, the judge orders a psychological evaluation, usually on an inpatient basis. The examiner then presents a written or oral report to the court at a hearing to determine the mental state of the accused. If the court holds that the defendant is incompetent to participate in his or her defense, the individual is assigned to a mental health facility until he or she is competent to stand trial (Bennett & Kish, 1990).

It is important to note that many more cases of criminal commitment result from decisions of mental incompetence than from verdicts of not guilty by reason of insanity (Blackburn, 1993). On the other hand, the majority of criminals currently institutionalized for psychological treatment in the United States are inmates whose mental problems have led officials of correctional institutions to send them to special mental health units within the prison or to mental hospitals for treatment (Monahan & Steadman, 1983; Steadman et al., 1982).

A risk inherent in competence provisions is that an innocent defendant may spend years in a mental health facility without having the opportunity to disprove accusations of criminal conduct in court. Some defendants have served longer "sentences" in mental health facilities awaiting competence than they would have in prison if they had been convicted (Meyer, 1992). The possibility of such abuses was curbed by an important Supreme Court ruling in the case of *Jackson* v. *Indiana* (1972). In this case the Court ruled that a chronically disordered defendant cannot be indefinitely committed under criminal status. After a reasonable amount of time, a criminally committed defendant should be either found competent and tried, set free, or transferred to a mental health facility under civil commitment procedures. Furthermore, the Court noted that criminal charges may be dismissed if, as in any other case, the defendant's right to a speedy trial has been violated.

Until the early 1970s, most states followed the practice of requiring the commitment of mentally incompetent defendants to maximum security institutions for the "criminally insane" (Winick, 1983). Under current law, the courts have greater flexibility in such matters. In some cases, particularly when the charge is a minor one, the defendant may be treated on an outpatient basis.

■ LEGAL ■ INFUENCES ON THE MENTAL HEALTH SYSTEM

The legal system also has had a significant impact on clinical professionals. First, courts and legislatures have developed the process of *civil commitment,* whereby certain individuals can be forced to undergo mental health treatment. Although many persons who show signs of mental disturbance seek treatment voluntarily, a large number are not aware of their problems or are simply not interested in receiving treatment. What are clinicians to do for these people? Should they force treatment upon them? Or do people have the right to feel miserable and function ineffectively? The law has addressed this question by providing civil commitment guidelines under which certain persons can be forced into treatment.

Second, the legal system, on behalf of the state, has also taken on the responsibility of specifying and protecting **patients' rights** during treatment. The protection of patients' rights is obviously important for those disturbed individuals who have been involuntarily committed, but it is also important for those who have voluntarily sought institutionalization or even outpatient therapy. The rights that have received the most attention in recent years are the right to receive treatment and the right to refuse treatment.

CIVIL COMMITMENT

Every year in the United States large numbers of mentally disturbed persons are involuntarily committed to mental institutions. These commitments have long been a focus of controversy and debate. As you will see, the laws that currently govern the treatment of mentally disturbed persons during civil commitment proceedings bear a resemblance to those governing the treatment of criminal defendants. In some ways, however, the law provides greater protection for the suspected criminal than for the suspected psychotic (Burton, 1990).

WHY COMMIT?   Generally our legal system permits involuntary commitment of individuals when they are considered to be *in need of treatment* and *dangerous to themselves or others*. The state's authority to commit disturbed individuals rests on two principles: *parens patriae* and police power (Wettstein, 1988). Under the principle of *parens patriae* ("father of the country"), the state can make decisions, including involuntary hospitalization, that promote the *individual's* best interests and protect him or her from self-harm or self-neglect. Conversely, police power enables the state to protect *society* from the harm that may be inflicted by a person who is homicidal or otherwise violent. Seeking to protect the assumed interests of the individual and society, the state provides treatment to those persons whose disabilities are so severe that they are unable to recognize their needs and to seek treatment voluntarily.

CURRENT PROCEDURES AND RIGHTS
Statutes governing the civil commitment process vary from state to state. Some basic procedures and rights, however, are common to most of these statutes.

Many formal commitment proceedings are initiated by family members. In response to a son's suicide attempt, for example, his parents may try to persuade him to commit himself to a mental institution. If the son refuses, the parents may go to court and seek an involuntary commitment order. If the son is a minor, the process is simple. The Supreme Court, in the case of *Parham* v. *J. R.* (1979), ruled that a due process hearing is not necessary in such cases. It need only be demonstrated that a mental health professional considers such commitment warranted. If the son is an adult, however, the process is more elaborate. The court will usually order a mental examination and provide the individual with the opportunity to contest the commitment attempt in court. In many states the person has a right to a jury trial on the matter, and the right to be represented by legal counsel (Holstein, 1993).

Although the Supreme Court has offered few guidelines on the procedural aspects of civil commitment, one important decision, rendered in the case of *Addington* v. *Texas* (1979), has outlined the *minimum standard of proof* necessary for commitment. Before this case was decided, each state developed its own standard of proof for commitment. Many states vaguely required a "preponderance of evidence" that commitment was necessary. Some had stricter requirements. Texas, for example, required the presentation of "clear, unequivocal and convincing evidence" of the necessity of commitment. Many people felt that even this standard was not strict enough and argued that the need for civil commitment should be established "beyond a reasonable doubt"—the standard in criminal cases. This was the standard at issue in *Addington* v. *Texas*. When Addington's mother attempted to have him committed by the state of Texas, he argued that the standard of proof for commitment in Texas was not strict enough. Addington asked the Supreme Court to overturn the state court's judgment by mandating that the "beyond a reasonable doubt" standard employed in criminal cases should be applied to his civil commitment case. Addington lost his appeal, but in the course of its decision the Supreme Court established a Texas-style standard as the appropriate minimum standard for all states. Specifically, it ruled that before an individual can be committed, there must be "clear and convincing" proof that he or she is mentally ill and has met the state's criteria for involuntary commitment. The Court was concerned that the "beyond a reasonable doubt" standard employed in criminal cases was too strict for civil commitment cases, given the "fallibility of psychiatric diagnosis." Nevertheless, the Court did establish a new minimum standard of proof for commitment cases that in fact was stricter than the standards then employed in many states.

It is important to note that the Court's "clear and convincing" standard of proof can be applied to a variety of criteria. The ruling does not suggest *what* criteria should be used. This matter is left to the discretion of each state. The ruling determines only the minimum standard of proof that should be applied to whatever commitment criteria the state chooses to enforce.

EMERGENCY COMMITMENT   Many situations require immediate action; no one can wait for formal commitment proceedings when a life is at stake. An emergency room patient who is suicidal or suffering from auditory hallucinations that order hostile actions against others may need immediate treatment and round-the-clock supervision. If treatment could not be applied in such situations without the patient's full consent, the consequences could be tragic.

Most states acknowledge that such circumstances may arise. Therefore, many states give attending physicians (not necessarily psychiatrists in certain states) the right to order temporary commitment and medication of a patient who is behaving in a bizarre or violent manner. Usually the states require certification by two physicians that such patients are in a state of mind that makes them dangerous to themselves or others. Such certifications are often referred to as *two-physician certificates*, or "2 PCs." Limitations on the length of such emergency commitments vary from state to state. Three days is the limit in a number of states (Holstein, 1993). Should the physicians who provide treatment determine that a longer period of commitment is necessary, formal commitment proceedings may be initiated.

WHO IS DANGEROUS?   In the past, people with mental disorders were less likely to commit violent or dangerous acts than people without such disorders. It now appears that these low rates of violence were related, at least in part, to the fact that so many of these people resided in institutions. With the advent of deinstitutionalization and the presence of hundreds of thousands of severely disturbed individuals in the community who currently receive little or no treatment, this pattern has shown signs of shifting.

Although approximately 90 percent of people with mental disorders are in no way violent or dangerous (Swanson et al., 1990), recent studies suggest a modest relationship between *severe* mental disorders and violent behavior. After reviewing a number of studies, the law and psychology professor John Monahan (1993, 1992), an authority on mental health law, has concluded that the rate of violent behavior among persons with severe mental disorders, particulary psychotic disorders, is at least somewhat higher than that of people without mental disorders. In particular, studies suggest the following:

Approximately 15 percent of patients in mental hospitals have assaulted another person prior to admission.

Around 25 percent of patients in mental hospitals assault another person during hospitalization.

Approximately 12 percent of community residents with schizophrenia, major depression, or bipolar disorder have assaulted other people, compared to 2 percent of persons without a mental disorder. Between 25 and 35 percent of people who display a substance-related disorder have assaulted others.

Approximately 4 percent of persons who report having been violent during the past year suffer from schizophrenia. One percent of nonviolent persons suffer from schizophrenia.

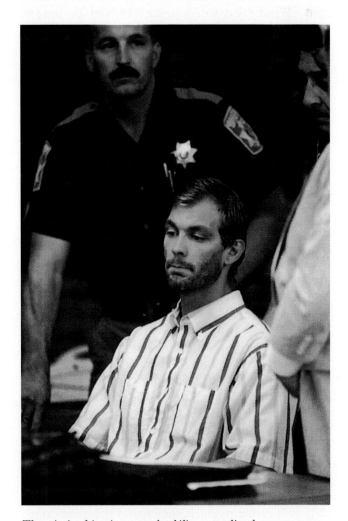

The criminal justice system's ability to predict dangerousness is often tragically inadequate, as we are reminded by the case of Jeffrey Dahmer. In 1988, Dahmer was imprisoned for sexually molesting a 13-year-old boy. In 1990, despite his own father's stated concerns, Dahmer was released with only limited followup. By his own admission, he proceeded to drug, strangle, and dismember at least seventeen additional victims.

Monahan cautions that these findings do not suggest that people with mental disorders are generally dangerous. Nor do they justify the "caricature of the mentally disordered" that is often portrayed by the media, the "shunning of former patients by employers and neighbors," or the "lock 'em up" laws proposed by some politicians. On the other hand, they do indicate that a severe mental disorder may be more of a risk factor for violence than mental health experts have generally believed, and as such should be studied and understood by public educators.

Because a determination of dangerousness is frequently required for judicial approval of involuntary civil commitment, the reliable and valid determination of who is dangerous is of major importance. But can mental health professionals accurately predict who will commit violent acts? The data gathered to date are not very encouraging (McNiel & Binder, 1991; Monahan & Walker, 1990). Research suggests that psychiatrists and psychologists are wrong more often than right when they predict violence, even when predicting violence against themselves (see Box 21–2). Most frequently they overestimate the likelihood that a patient will engage in violent behavior. This body of research is not conclusive, however, because it has usually examined long-term predictions for institutionalized patients who are later released. It may be that the experience of institutionalization reduces such patients' tendency to behave violently.

Are accurate predictions of violent behavior impossible? If so, should dangerousness be excluded as a criterion for commitment? Monahan (1984) has cautioned once again against premature conclusions, pointing out that much more research must be done. In particular, more studies of *short-term* predictions of violence—that is, predictions of *imminent* violence—are needed. Indeed, some recent studies have begun to suggest that short-term predictions are more accurate than long-term ones (McNiel & Binder, 1991).

Whether or not practicing clinicians are now accurate predictors of violent behavior, it may be possible to develop new assessment and prediction techniques that employ statistical approaches and are relatively accurate (Klassen & O'Conner, 1988). One group of researchers conducted a study of short-term predictions of violence among patients in an acute-care psychiatric unit (Werner, Rose, & Yesavage, 1983). In accord with earlier research, they found that predictions made by individual clinicians were very inaccurate (psychologists and psychiatrists were equally likely to be wrong). The clinicians apparently viewed suspicious, excited, and uncooperative patients as dangerous, although these characteristics are not actually related to violent behavior. The researchers also

found that the accuracy of predictions remained low when the predictions of several clinicians were combined. Nevertheless, the investigators were able to demonstrate that clinicians did have information available to them that could increase the accuracy of their predictions if they used it. In particular, individuals who experience hallucinations and exhibit relatively little emotional withdrawal are more likely to assault other people. This research indicates that it may be possible to develop objective assessment techniques that have more predictive power than the subjective judgments of clinicians.

CRITICISMS OF CIVIL COMMITMENT   Civil commitment has been criticized on several grounds. The criterion of dangerousness is one bone of contention. If judgments of dangerousness are often inaccurate, why should they be used as grounds to deprive someone of liberty? The American Civil Liberties Union has strongly criticized the use of such assessments in commitment cases (Ennis & Emory, 1978).

A related problem is that legal definitions of "mental illness" and "dangerousness" are vague. The terms may be defined so broadly that they can be applied to anyone the evaluators view as simply undesirable or inferior. It has been argued that involuntary commitment standards have sometimes been applied to people whose only offenses are bouncing checks, spending "too much" money, living unconventional lifestyles, and holding unpopular political opinions (Wexler, 1983).

A further problem with involuntary civil commitment is the sometimes questionable therapeutic value of commitment itself. Research suggests that many persons committed involuntarily do not respond well to psychotherapy (Wanck, 1984). Perceptions of choice and control and personal commitment may be important determinants of successful outcome in a therapeutic setting (Langer, 1983).

On the basis of these and other arguments, Thomas Szasz (1977, 1963) has argued that involuntary commitment should be abolished. As we saw earlier, Szasz views the label of mental illness as arbitrary and usually unjustified. Because of the ambiguities of diagnosis, he says, the biases of the practitioner and of society rather than scientific facts are the major determinants of clinical evaluations. He and others believe that individuals who demonstrate by their behavior that they are truly dangerous are best dealt with through the criminal justice system.

Many civil libertarians are sympathetic to Szasz's argument that involuntary commitment can be abused for purposes of coercive control (Morse, 1982; Ennis

BOX 21-2

VIOLENCE AGAINST THERAPISTS

Is therapy hazardous to one's health? Indeed it is for some patients. Now it appears that many therapists are at risk as well. Between 12 and 14 percent of therapists have been targets of patients' violence at least once in private therapy, and an even larger percentage have been assaulted in mental hospitals (Tryon, 1987; Bernstein, 1981). A recent study found that 40 percent of psychiatrists had been assaulted at least once during their career (Menninger, 1993). The likelihood of being assaulted appears to be equal for female and male therapists.

Patients have used a variety of weapons in their attacks, including such common ones as shoes, lamps, fire extinguishers, and canes. In very serious cases, the ones we occasionally read about in newspapers, patients have used guns or knives and have severely wounded or even killed a therapist.

(Drawing by W. Miller; © 1983 The New Yorker Magazine, Inc.)

What are the causes of these attacks? More research is needed, but the surveys conducted to date indicate that some therapists consider themselves at fault; they feel that they or some aspect of the patient–therapist interaction may have had a role in provoking the attack (Shapiro, 1993; Tryon, 1987; Madden et al., 1976). In general, inexperienced therapists are more likely to be victims. Many of the assailants have displayed violent behavior before, but only a small minority of therapists have been able to anticipate the attacks.

Many therapists who have been attacked, like other victims of assault, are deeply affected by the incident. They feel anxious and insecure in their work for a long time. One study that examined therapists in mental health facilities found that most of those who had been victims of patient violence displayed symptoms of post-traumatic stress disorder (Caldwell, 1992). After an attack, therapists may try to be more selective in accepting patients and look for cues that signal impending violence. One therapist even studied karate for a year and a half (Tryon, 1987). Unfortunately, lingering feelings of anxiety may affect a clinician's effectiveness. Therapists who are focusing on their own safety are concentrating less on the problems of their patients, so that the patients become unwitting victims of the crime as well.

& Emory, 1978). Indeed, such abuses by the state have been reported frequently in the former Soviet Union and other countries, where mental hospitals have been used routinely to incarcerate political dissidents.

Given such problems, some researchers have recently advocated moving toward a concept of *risk assessment* and away from the notion of dangerousness per se in making decisions about commitment. They believe this would be a more constructive way of deciding where and under what restrictions persons with mental disorders should be treated (Steadman et al., 1993).

TRENDS IN CIVIL COMMITMENT The acceptance of broad involuntary commitment statutes probably reached its peak in 1962, when a Supreme Court ruling encouraged placement in mental health facilities instead of prisons for individuals whose unacceptable behavior seemed to be caused by psychological dysfunctioning. In the case of *Robinson* v. *California*, the Court ruled that the sentencing of drug addicts to correctional institutions may violate the Constitution's ban on cruel and unusual punishment, and it recommended involuntary civil commitment to a mental hospital as a more reasonable action. This ruling encouraged the application of civil commitment proceedings against many kinds of "social deviants" at a time when the laws governing such procedures were vague or nonexistent.

In the years immediately following this ruling, civil commitment procedures granted far fewer rights to "defendants" than did criminal courts (Holstein, 1993). It was particularly difficult for involuntarily committed patients to obtain their release. Substantial legal assistance was often needed. The persistent overprediction of dangerousness by clinicians exacerbated this problem.

During the late 1960s, the plight of the committed was increasingly publicized by reporters, novelists, and civil libertarians who were convinced that numerous persons were being committed unjustifiably. As the public became more aware of the problems surrounding involuntary commitment, state legislatures started to enact narrower standards for commitment (Holstein, 1993). These statutory revisions of the late 1960s and early 1970s had a significant impact on the rates of involuntary commitment (Wanck, 1984), which declined while release rates increased. Furthermore, the bulk of court decisions favored the broadening of patients' rights, including an elaboration of the commitment hearing process.

Criticisms of the criteria for dangerousness also increased during this time, and many jurisdictions modified their commitment standards to require the demonstration of *imminent* dangerousness. Short-term predictions of dangerousness were eventually used in most states as justification for short-term emergency commitment. In addition, many states adopted more specific definitions of dangerousness itself, in some cases spelling out the specific types of behavior that must be observed before such a diagnosis can be made.

These changes have continued to influence commitment rates and procedures, and fewer people are institutionalized through civil commitment procedures today than in the past. Some clinicians fear that this continuing trend will lead inevitably to more criminal and violent behavior and arrests among people who would have been committed under broader criteria. These concerns have not, however, been supported by research (Teplin, Abram, & McClelland, 1994; Hiday, 1992). Nevertheless, recent rulings and statutes suggest that the pendulum may soon be swinging back. Concerned that commitment criteria have become too narrow, some states have started to broaden theirs once again (Beck & Parry, 1992; Belcher & Blank, 1990; Wexler, 1988, 1983). Whether this actually represents a return to the vague commitment procedures of past years and whether such a trend is in fact advantageous for disturbed in-

dividuals and society will become clearer in the coming years.

PROTECTING PATIENTS' RIGHTS

Over the past two decades the legal rights of mental patients have been significantly expanded by court decisions and state and federal legislation. The rights that have received the most attention have been the *right to treatment* and the *right to refuse treatment*.

THE RIGHT TO TREATMENT Theoretically, some people are so mentally disturbed that they are unable to recognize their need for treatment. Involuntary commitment procedures afford the state a means to provide care for these individuals. A risk inherent in such provisions, however, is that individuals may be deprived of their liberty without receiving any beneficial treatment. If the state does not provide the treatment that motivated commitment in the first place, mental institutions become mere prisons for the unconvicted.

Faced with the inadequacies of large state mental institutions, some patients and their legal representatives began in the 1960s and 1970s to demand the treatment they felt the state was obligated to provide. A suit filed on these grounds on behalf of institutionalized patients in Alabama led to a landmark in the battle for patients' rights. In the 1972 case of *Wyatt* v. *Stickney* a federal court ruled that the state was constitutionally obligated to provide "adequate treatment" to all persons who had been committed involuntarily. Because conditions in the state's hospitals were so deplorable, the presiding judge laid out specific goals that had to be met by state administrators. The court ordered Alabama to provide more therapists, better living conditions, more privacy, opportunities for heterosexual interaction and physical exercise, and a more judicious use of physical restraint and medication. Many of these standards have since been adopted in other court jurisdictions.

Another important decision was handed down in 1975 by the Supreme Court in the case of *O'Connor* v. *Donaldson*. After being confined in a Florida mental institution for more than fourteen years, Kenneth Donaldson sued for release. Although Donaldson had repeatedly sought release and been overruled by the institution's psychiatrists, he and his fellow patients were being largely ignored by the staff and allowed a bare minimum of personal freedom.

Furthermore, Donaldson had been initially committed on highly questionable grounds. Despite evidence to the contrary, his father had claimed that his son was dangerous.

Donaldson argued that he was not dangerous and that the facility in which he was confined did not provide adequate treatment. The Supreme Court ruled in favor of Donaldson, fined the hospital's superintendent, and ruled that such institutions must engage in periodic reviews of their patients' cases. The justices also stated unanimously that the state "cannot constitutionally confine . . . a nondangerous individual who is capable of surviving safely in freedom by himself or with the help of willing and responsible family members or friends." Donaldson did have a friend who had repeatedly agreed to take him into his custody. The *Donaldson* case attracted a great deal of publicity. In addition to setting an important legal precedent, it helped focus attention on the plight of people committed to mental institutions.

A more recent case of importance, *Youngberg* v. *Romeo* (1982), provided support for the right to treatment while cautioning courts against becoming too involved in the exact methods of treatment. The Supreme Court ruled that persons committed involuntarily have a constitutional right to "reasonably nonrestrictive confinement conditions" as well as "reasonable care and safety." In contrast to the earlier lower-court decision in *Wyatt* v. *Stickney,* however, this decision provided only a crude outline of minimum standards for institutions.

Some people were concerned that the *Youngberg* decision signaled a slowing of the pace of court-mandated reforms and of the Supreme Court's involvement in mental health issues. In this decision the Court noted the expertise of mental health professionals and suggested that treatment decisions should be assumed to be valid until proved otherwise. Such a perspective seemed to indicate that the justices were unwilling to support a significant expansion of the judicial system's involvement in the daily affairs of mental health institutions. The ruling also suggested that mental health professionals could rely largely on their professional judgment when they formulated systematic treatment procedures. To make sure that mental patients did not lose the rights they had gained throughout the 1970s, Congress passed the Protection and Advocacy for Mentally Ill Individuals Act in 1986 (Woodside & Legg, 1990). This law established *protection and advocacy* systems in all states and U.S. territories and gave advocates and lawyers who worked for patients within the system the power to investigate possible cases of patient abuse and neglect, and to address these problems legally.

In recent years public advocates have argued that the right to treatment should be extended to the tens of thousands of severely mentally disturbed persons who are repeatedly released from hospitals after a short stay and are essentially sent to the streets to care for themselves. There are growing indications, unfortunately, that many homeless persons with mental disorders are being sentenced to prison, where the percentage of inmates who receive treatment is quite low (see Figure 21–2), simply because mental health treatment centers are overburdened (Wielawski, 1992). The U.S. Substance Abuse and Mental Health Services Administration (1993) has said flatly that "reliance upon the criminal justice system rather than the mental health system to respond to the needs of these individuals perpetuates many of [their] problems." Many mental health advocates are now suing federal and state agencies across the country, demanding that they fulfill the promises of the community mental health movement.

THE RIGHT TO REFUSE TREATMENT During the past two decades the courts have also established that patients, particularly those in institutions, have the right to refuse certain forms of treatment. The courts have been reluctant to issue a single general ruling on this issue because the range of treatment methods is so broad. A ruling based on one form of treatment would be likely to affect other treatments in unintended ways. Thus specific treatments have been targeted in various court rulings.

Most of the "right to refuse treatment" rulings have centered on *biological treatments*—treatments that are easier to impose on patients without their cooperation and that often seem more intrusive, aversive, and hazardous than psychotherapy. For example, state rulings have consistently granted patients the right to refuse psychosurgery, the form of physical treatment considered most clearly irreversible and therefore most dangerous.

As we saw in Chapter 9, some states have also acknowledged a patient's right to refuse electroconvulsive therapy (ECT), the treatment used in many cases of unipolar depression. The issue is much more arguable with regard to ECT than with respect to psychosurgery. ECT is highly effective for many severely depressed persons. On the other hand, ECT is an aversive form of treatment that has been criticized by many recipients and that has a potential for misuse and abuse, as many media reports, books, and movies have made clear. Stories such as Nan's are not uncommon:

*W*hen her private psychiatrist told her to enter a psychiatric hospital for shock treatment, she reluctantly agreed. After entering the hospital, however, she changed her mind. Despite her protests, she was given shock treatment and experienced the usual effects of confusion and memory loss. After a few shocks, however, her wish to stop the treatment became so strong that she said to a nurse, "I just have to get out of here. I'm leaving no matter what you say." It was then that she escaped.

When the psychiatrist who had sent her to the hospital found out that Nan had run away, he telephoned her at home and said he would call the police if she did not return to the hospital. Under this pressure she returned, telling the nurses, "I really don't want to be here; I feel like I'm being forced to have shock. The doctor said if I didn't come back he'd send the police after me." Despite these events, her readmission was called voluntary, with no mention of her documented fear of shock treatment, of her desire not to be in the hospital, or of the threat of police intervention. She received more shock treatment during her second hospitalization, until she fled once more.

(Coleman, 1984, pp. 166–167)

Today states vary in the degree to which they allow patients to refuse ECT. Some continue to permit ECT to be imposed on committed patients, others require the consent of a third party in such cases, and still others grant patients—particularly voluntary patients—the right to refuse ECT. In these latter states ECT can usually be administered only after patients are informed fully about the nature of the treatment and give their written consent to it.

In the past, patients have not had the right to refuse psychotropic medications. States viewed these drugs as a benign form of treatment that often helped and rarely hurt patients. As we have seen repeatedly, however, this perception of drug treatments turns out to have been naive. Many psychotropic drugs, particularly antipsychotic drugs, are exceedingly powerful and sometimes produce such dangerous effects as tardive dyskinesia. As these unwanted effects have become more apparent, some states have granted patients the right to refuse medication.

Two leading federal cases have led the way on the "right to refuse medication" issue—*Rennie* v. *Klein* (1979, 1981) in New Jersey and *Rogers* v. *Okin* (1979, 1980, 1981) in Massachusetts. Typically, states that recognize a patient's right to refuse medication require physicians to explain the purpose and intent of medications to patients and obtain their written consent. If the patient's refusal is considered incompetent, dangerous, or irrational, it can be overturned by an independent psychiatrist, medical committee, or

RECEIVE PSYCHOTHERAPY

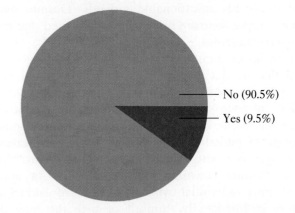

No (90.5%)
Yes (9.5%)

RECEIVE RESIDENTIAL TREATMENT

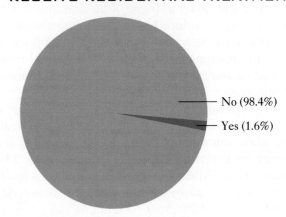

No (98.4%)
Yes (1.6%)

RECEIVE 24-HOUR HOSPITAL MENTAL HEALTH CARE

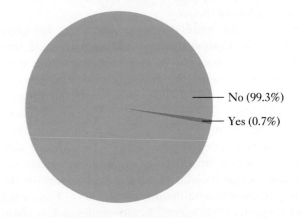

No (99.3%)
Yes (0.7%)

FIGURE 21–2 *Prisoners who receive treatment. Despite the high prevalence of mental disorders among prisoners, only 9.5 percent of inmates in state prisons in the United States receive psychotherapy, only 1.6 percent receive treatment in a residential treatment program (separate living arrangements), and less than 1 percent receive 24-hour hospital mental health care. More white American and female inmates receive these forms of treatment than African American and male inmates. (Adapted from Swanson et al., 1993; Goldstrom, Manderscheid, & Rudolf, 1992.)*

local court (Prehn, 1990; Wettstein, 1988). However, the refusing patient is supported in this review process by legal counsel or a patient advocate.

OTHER RIGHTS OF PATIENTS The rights to receive treatment and to refuse treatment have attracted the most attention, but they are not the only patient rights to have been safeguarded by court decisions over the past few decades. In the 1973 case of *Sounder* v. *Brennan*, for example, a district court ruled that patients who perform work in mental institutions must receive payment in accordance with the Fair Labor Standards Act. In 1976 the Supreme Court ruled that this right applied in private mental institutions but not in state hospitals.

A district court ruled in the 1974 case of *Stoner* v. *Miller* that patients released from state mental hospitals have a right to live in community "adult homes." As we discussed earlier, many patients released under the policy of deinstitutionalization have encountered inadequate treatment and poor residential opportunities in the community. As an extension of their guaranteed right to treatment, *Stoner* v. *Miller* and other court decisions during the 1970s have acknowledged the right of such individuals to aftercare and to an appropriate community residence.

Finally, a district court ruled in the 1975 case of *Dixon* v. *Weinberger* that individuals whose mental dysfunction is not severe enough to require confinement in a mental institution have a right to treatment in less restrictive facilities. If an inpatient program at a community mental health center or a halfway house is available, then that is the facility to which such people should be committed, not a mental hospital.

THE "RIGHTS" DEBATE Few would argue with the intent of these guaranteed patient rights. Obviously, disturbed people do not cease to be human beings, and as such they have civil rights that must be considered and protected at all times (see Box 21–3). However, many clinicians express concern that these guaranteed rights sometimes lead to undesirable outcomes and may even serve to deprive patients of opportunities for effective recovery. Consider the right to refuse medication. Many clinicians believe that this right or the procedures needed to safeguard it may deprive some patients of a faster, more complete recovery. Indeed, some research has indicated that patients with severe mental disorders who refuse medication are more likely to require temporary hospitalization (Sheline & Beattie, 1992). If medications

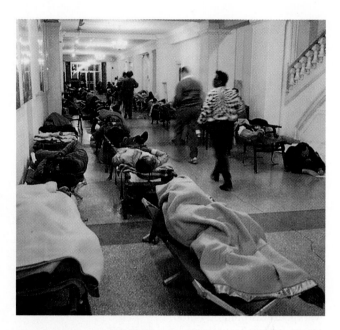

Although "guaranteed" the right to live in community adult homes, chronic mental patients often receive no treatment or guidance and wind up on the streets or in public shelters, such as this shelter for the homeless in Washington, D.C.

can help bring about a schizophrenic patient's recovery, does not the patient have the right to that recovery? If confusion causes patients to refuse medication, can clinicians in good conscience go along with that refusal and delay medication while legal channels are cleared? The psychologist Marilyn Whiteside raises similar concerns in her description of a 25-year-old mentally retarded patient:

He was 25 and severely retarded. And after his favorite attendant left, he became self-abusive. He beat his fists against the side of his head until a football helmet had to be ordered for his protection. Then he clawed at his face and gouged out one of his eyes.

The institution psychologists began a behavior program that had mildly aversive consequences: they squirted warm water in his face each time he engaged in self-abuse. When that didn't work, they requested permission to use an electric prod. The Human Rights Committee vetoed this "excessive and inhumane form of correction" because, after all, the young man was retarded, not criminal.

Since nothing effective could be done that abridged the rights and negated the dignity of the developmentally disabled patient, he was verbally reprimanded for his behavior—and allowed to push his thumb through his remaining eye. He is now blind, of course, but he has his rights and presumably his dignity.

(Whiteside, 1983, p. 13)

BOX 21-3

STALKING THE FINE LINE

In 1992 Teresa Zeleske met a nice, gentle young man, Virgil. They fell in love, Teresa left her husband four months later, and she and Virgil became engaged. Before long, however, Virgil's darker side began to show itself. He took out his anger at work and was promptly fired. In retaliation, he threatened to blow up the building. Although upset, Teresa decided to stick by the man she had agreed to marry, and soon became his wife. But Virgil's problems seemed to increase. He turned his attention to Teresa, listening in on her phone calls and following her. After seven months she could not take it any longer and had Virgil move out. While they were separated Virgil kept begging for forgiveness and asking to be taken back. Teresa refused, but Virgil was persistent. He began harassing her, calling at all hours and accusing her of being "a whore." During one confrontation, Virgil almost strangled Teresa. Going to the police was of no avail—there were no laws in Wisconsin against the kind of harassment Virgil was using to torment Teresa. Eventually, she was able to get a court hearing on domestic battery charges, during which Virgil

While playing in a professional tournament in 1993, tennis star Monica Seles was stabbed by a thirty-eight year old disturbed man from Germany. The attacker, apparently obsessed with helping the career of another star, Steffi Graf, was described by his aunt as having been a "quiet, reticent child."

vowed to kill her. Sadly, Virgil kept his promise a few months later. Teresa returned to her home late one night with two male friends. Three hours later shots were heard from her apartment. Police found all four dead of gunshots—including Virgil, who died by his own hand.

A spate of cases like the horror that befell Teresa Zeleske has spawned great public interest in the harassing behavior called *stalking.* Are people who harass and threaten others displaying a mental disorder? Where do we draw the line between legal but inappropriate behavior and illegal

acts? Which authorities should deal with the problem and how? The mental health and legal communities have joined the rest of us in asking these questions as society searches for a solution to what seems to be a growing problem.

The number of cases of stalking in the United States has been estimated at 200,000 each year (Corwin, 1993). The actual number may be much higher, but law enforcement does not categorize all cases of harassment or abuse as stalking. Mental health professionals estimate that 90 percent of stalkers suffer from some kind of mental disorder. Some apparently experience an *erotomanic delusion,* a belief without any basis whatsoever that one is loved by another person who may actually be a casual acquaintance or even a complete stranger (Anderson, 1993). Stalkers with this delusion are typically diagnosed with schizophrenia (paranoid type), a delusional disorder, or yet another psychotic disorder. The split from reality may explain why they become obsessed with somone and sometimes develop a fantasy in which they feel compelled to harm or kill that person. More typically, though, stalking

Similar questions can even be raised about the right of patients to a minimum wage. Although the court ruling correctly tries to protect patients from being taken advantage of by institutions, it may also disrupt the effectiveness of reputable behavioral token economy programs (Glynn, 1990). These hospital programs may be designed to reward patients' work with hospital privileges, social rewards, and other nonmonetary rewards.

While monetary reinforcement may be effective for some patients, nonmonetary rewards may be more effective for others. By depriving such programs of a highly flexible reward system, a mandated minimum wage may reduce a patient's chances for recovery.

On the other side of the argument, it must be pointed out that the clinical field has not always monitored itself in these areas of patients' rights. Over the

is associated with a host of nonpsychotic disorders, including borderline, antisocial, and narcissistic personality disorders, and depression (Moses-Zirkes, 1992). The remaining stalkers do not fully fit the criteria of any mental disorder. The multiplicity of possibilities makes it much more difficult to identify a given person as being likely to become a stalker. Some experts, however, believe that it is possible to establish a general profile of stalkers.

The clinical psychologist Stanton Samenow, author of *Inside the Criminal Mind*, views stalkers as people with disturbed self-images who resort to violence when they are rejected. Unable to reconcile their experience in the world with their internal image of themselves as either irresistible charmers or utter losers, they strike out. The criminologist Jack Levin of Northeastern University differentiates stalkers from people who commit crimes of passion. Stalkers plan their actions; that is, their harassment is premeditated. They are motivated by a desire to control their victims in an effort to overcome their own feelings of powerlessness. Overall, however, little research has been done on the psychological underpinnings or patterns of behavior of people who become stalkers, and studies have failed to reveal when a person's delusional or obsessive interest in someone crosses the line into action (Dietz et al., 1991). So far, the main point of agreement among all who look at stalking is that it is a complex and little-understood phenomenon.

Headline cases, as when the actress Rebecca Shaeffer of the television show *My Sister Sam* was shot outside her West Hollywood apartment by an obsessed fan, catch the public's attention and spur interest and action. But most victims of stalkers are not celebrities. It has been estimated that around one-fourth of all women who are murdered in the United States are killed by husbands or boyfriends—and many of them have been stalked first (Furio, 1993). The victim may go through months or even years of fear and intimidation, changing phone numbers, moving, hiding. An endless stream of threatening phone calls and letters, intimidating visits, and physical abuse creates an atmosphere of terror that dominates the lives of both victim and stalker.

Common sense might suggest that the law would help protect persons from stalking, either because it constitutes criminal activity or because it is seriously abnormal behavior that requires intervention. Unfortunately, however, threatening and harassing behavior without actual physical violence typically leaves police officials with their hands tied: one cannot be fully protected against actions that have not yet been taken. This is the dilemma facing not only the victims of stalking, but the legal community that wants to protect them and the mental health and civil liberties communities that want to ensure the rights of all.

Lately a number of state legislatures across the United States have enacted new laws in response to the public outcry over numerous widely publicized cases (Anderson, 1993). These laws make it easier for a stalking victim to obtain a restraining order, but they also have certain limitations. They are, for example, ineffective against stalkers whose first act of violence is murder. In addition, the enforcement of the new laws may have a negative effect in some cases: sitting in jail could fuel rather than extinguish the stalker's anger. Furthermore, many of the antistalking laws are ambiguous and open to interpretation; with each state formulating its own antistalking legislation, federal authorities find it difficult to intervene in a consistent manner. The new laws are also vulnerable to misuse. Spouses may use them to retaliate against partners who have no thought of committing acts the legislation was intended to forestall. Lastly, some of the new laws may violate the constitutional rights of alleged stalkers, and are likely to be struck down by the U.S. Supreme Court. This is a chilling prospect for past and potential victims of stalking, but it is natural for the pendulum to swing toward a more restrained approach as the mental health and legal communities try to find a way to protect the rights both of victims and of those who are accused.

The dilemma is obvious: stalkers who suffer from a mental disorder need to be viewed as victims in need of treatment—yet this must be done without jeopardy to the persons they are stalking or to their own constitutional rights. So far, a balanced solution has been hard to find, and the roll of cases continues to grow.

years, many treatment programs have administered medications and other biological treatments carelessly, excessively, or harmfully (Crane, 1973). Similarly, many institutions have misused patients' labor. So the courts and state legislatures have stepped in. William Keating, describing the initial reactions of clinicians to his proposed regulations in California, said, "There were a lot of bruised egos, a lot of people saying that doctors should regulate themselves. I said, That's right, you should, but haven't been. That's why we are."

One must also ask whether the field's present state of knowledge and expertise justifies allowing clinicians to override patients' rights. That is, can clinicians confidently say that certain treatments will indeed help patients? And can they predict and overcome the potential unwanted effects of certain forms of treatment? Since today's clinicians themselves often are in conflict concerning these issues, it seems appropriate that patients, their advocates, and impartial evaluators continue to play significant roles in the decision-making process.

■ OTHER ■ CLINICAL-LEGAL INTERACTIONS

Mental health and legal professionals may influence each other's work in other ways as well. During the past two decades, for example, their paths have crossed in three new areas: malpractice suits, jury selection, and the scope of clinical practice.

MALPRACTICE SUITS

The number of lawsuits against therapists has risen so sharply in recent years that clinicians have coined new terms for the fear of being sued: they now are increasingly subject to "litigaphobia" and "litigastress." Such ultrasensitization to malpractice suits can lead to a distortion of clinical priorities (Monahan, 1993). About 16 percent of psychiatrists have been sued (AMA, 1987), although the percentage of psychologists and social workers who have been sued appears to be much smaller. Events that precipitate claims against clinicians include attempted suicide, sexual activity with a patient, failure to obtain informed consent for a treatment, negligent drug therapy, omission of drug therapy that would speed up improvement, improper termination of treatment, and wrongful commitment (Smith, 1991; Wettstein, 1989).

Improper termination of treatment was at issue in a highly publicized case involving an Alabama state hospital in 1985. Two and a half months after a man being treated for alcohol-related depression was released from the hospital, he shot and killed a new acquaintance in a motel lounge. He was convicted of murder and sentenced to life in prison. The victim's father, claiming negligence, filed a civil suit against a psychologist, physician, and social worker at the state hospital, and after two years of legal action was awarded a total of almost $7 million by a jury. The state supreme court later overturned the verdict, saying that a state hospital is entitled to a certain degree of immunity in such cases.

Two investigators studied the effects of this case on subsequent decisions to release patients from the state hospital (Brodsky & Poythress, 1990). They found that the hospital had released 11 percent of its patients during the six months before the lawsuit was filed, and 10 percent during the two years it was being litigated, but only 7 percent of its patients during the six months following the verdict. Although judgments about a patient's improvement are supposed to be made on their own merits, they were apparently being affected by a heightened fear of litigation at this hospital. Clearly civil malpractice suits are capable of having significant effects on clinical decisions and practice, for better or for worse.

JURY SELECTION

During the past fifteen years more and more lawyers have been turning to clinicians for advice on conducting trials (Gottschalk, 1981). A relatively new breed of clinical specialists, often known as "jury specialists," now advise lawyers on which prospective jurors are likely to favor their side and on what procedures and strategies are likely to win jurors' support during trials. The clinical specialists make their suggestions on the basis of surveys, interviews, statistical analyses of correlations between jurors' backgrounds and attitudes, and laboratory simulations of upcoming trials. It is not clear that such clinical advice is more valid than a lawyer's instincts, or indeed that either group's judgments are particularly accurate. Because some lawyers believe that clinical advice is useful, however, clinical professionals are influencing these legal procedures and decisions.

THE SCOPE OF CLINICAL PRACTICE

During the past few years the legislative and judicial systems have also helped to alter the boundaries that distinguish one clinical profession from another. In particular, they have given more authority to psychologists and effectively blurred the line that once separated psychiatry from psychology. In 1989 Congress passed a group of bills that permitted psychologists to receive direct reimbursements from Medicare for treating elderly and disabled people. Until then, only psychiatrists received such payments. In 1993, Iowa became the tenth state in recent years to rule that psychologists could admit patients to the state's hospitals, a power previously held only by psychiatrists

(Cullen, 1993). And in 1991 Congress empowered the Department of Defense (DOD) to explore the most significant boundary of all between the two professions—the authority to prescribe drugs, heretofore denied to psychologists. The DOD set up a three-year training program for two military psychologists called Cutting Edge, in which they learned to prescribe drugs for a broad range of mental problems, initially under the supervision of physicians. In 1994, five new trainees began the program. This is an issue of particular interest to the military, where there is a severe shortage of mental health services. The Army, for instance, has only 110 psychologists and 180 psychiatrists to serve 700,000 persons on active military duty. But everyone in the clinical field recognizes the much larger implications of the trial program.

This blurring of professional boundary lines is not just a matter of the legislative and judicial systems taking it upon themselves to alter the activities of clinical professionals. In fact, psychologists have actively organized around the issue, built their case, and lobbied in state legislatures across the country for each of the laws and decisions that have increased their power, and psychiatrists have lobbied just as hard against the decisions. In each instance clinicians have sought the involvement of other institutions, and each demonstrates how intertwined the mental health system is with the various other institutions of society.

■ SELF- ■ REGULATION: ETHICS AND THE MENTAL HEALTH FIELD

Discussions of the legal and mental health systems may sometimes give the impression that clinicians are uncaring practitioners who address patients' rights and needs only when they are being monitored by outside forces. This, of course, is not the case. Most clinicians are very much aware of and concerned about the subtle human issues that pervade their work. They strive to help clients and at the same time respect their rights and dignity.

But clinicians do face considerable obstacles in the pursuit of these goals. First, patients' rights and proper care raise complex questions that do not have simple or obvious answers. Different clients and therapists, all guided by their diverse perspectives, may indeed arrive at different answers to such questions.

Second, clinicians, like other professionals, often have difficulty appreciating the full impact of their actions or altering the system in which they work. For example, the quality of institutional care afforded mental patients during the first half of this century is now viewed as a dark chapter in the field's history. But the poor therapy, the inhumanity, and the abuses that are apparent now were not so obvious then. Indeed, thousands of conscientious and caring clinicians contributed to this very system—partly because they did not appreciate how misguided the system was and partly because they felt helpless to change it.

A third problem is that some clinicians are indeed self-serving and even immoral. Like other professions, the clinical field includes at least a few practitioners who place their own needs and wishes above others'. For the integrity of the profession and the protection of individuals, such professionals need to be monitored and regulated.

Clinicians do not rely exclusively on the legislative and court systems to address such obstacles to proper and effective clinical practice. They also regulate themselves by continually thinking about, developing, and revising ethical guidelines for members of the field. Many legal decisions simply place the power of law behind these professional guidelines.

Each profession within the mental health field has a code of ethics. The code of the American Psychological Association exemplifies the kinds of issues with which the various mental health professions are concerned. It begins with a basic principle, that the goal of psychologists "is to broaden knowledge of behavior and, where appropriate, to apply it pragmatically to improve the conditions of both the individual and society" (APA, 1992). Moreover, because their "judgments and actions may affect the lives of others," the code calls for psychologists to guard against "factors that might lead to misuse of their influence." The current code addresses a number of specific points, including the following.

1. *Psychologists are permitted to offer advice* in self-help books, television and radio programs, newspaper and magazine articles, mailed material, and other nontraditional vehicles and settings, provided they do so responsibly and professionally and base their advice on appropriate psychological literature and practices.

2. *Psychologists may not engage in fraudulent research, plagiarizing the work of others or publishing fabricated data or falsified results.* During the past fifteen years cases of scientific fraud or misconduct have been uncovered in all

of the sciences, including psychology. These acts have led to misunderstandings of important issues, taken scientific inquiries in the wrong direction, and undermined public trust. Unfortunately, the effects of research misconduct are hard to undo even after a retraction. The impressions created by false findings may continue to influence the thinking of both the public and other scientists for years (Pfeifer & Snodgrass, 1990).

3. *Psychologists must acknowledge their limitations with regard to patients of different gender, ethnicity, disability, language, socioeconomic status, and sexual orientation.* This requirement often means that they should obtain additional training or supervision, consult with an appropriate colleague, or make appropriate referrals in order "to ensure the competence of their services."

4. *Psychologists who make evaluations and testify in legal cases must base their assessments on sufficient information and substantiate their findings appropriately.* If an adequate examination of the individual in question is not possible, psychologists must make clear the limited nature of their testimony.

5. *Psychologists are prohibited from exploiting the trust and dependency of clients and students, sexually or otherwise.* This guideline is meant to address the broad social problem of sexual harassment, as well as the problem of therapists who take sexual advantage of clients in therapy. The current code specifically prohibits psychologists from engaging in sexual intimacies with a present or former therapy client for at least two years after the end of treatment; and even then such conduct is permissible only in "the most unusual circumstances." Some therapists call this the "almost never rule" (Bates, 1992). Moreover, psychologists may not accept as clients people with whom they have previously engaged in sexual intimacies.

Recent years have seen an increase in the number of clients who have told state licensing boards of sexual misconduct by their therapist or sued their therapist for such behavior (Zamichow, 1993). These increases may reflect not a greater prevalence of such cases but clients' heightened awareness of and anger over the inappropriateness of such behavior. Some cases in point:

*T*wo women patients brought claims against the same male psychologist in the mid-1980s for having sex during treatment, which he claimed was for "therapeutic benefit." In the first case, settled out of court in 1985, the patient sued for sexual misconduct, emotional distress, pain and loss of self-esteem. . . . In the second case, the patient sued the therapist for sexual misconduct, breach of contract and assault and battery. The cases were settled out of court.

A woman sued a husband-and-wife psychotherapy team for sexual misconduct and mental and physical discomfort. The patient said sex with the male therapist resulted in a pregnancy and subsequent abortion, and that the woman therapist also inappropriately cuddled her. The case was settled out of court.

(Youngstrom, 1990, p. 21)

Clients may suffer extensive emotional damage from such betrayals of trust (Sherman, 1993). Indeed, a growing number of therapists are now treating clients whose primary problem is that they have previously been sexually abused in some manner by a therapist (Pope & Vetter, 1991).

How many therapists actually have a sexual relationship with a client? A 1977 study found that 12.1 percent of male and 2.6 percent of female psychologists admitted having sexual contact with patients (Holroyd & Brodsky, 1977). In a survey conducted ten years later, 3.6 percent of male psychologists and 0.5 percent of female psychologists anonymously reported sexual relationships with patients (Pope, Tabachnick, & Keith-Spiegel, 1987). And a 1989 survey of 4,800 therapists revealed that 0.9 percent of male therapists and 0.2 percent of female therapists had had sexual contact with patients (Borys & Pope, 1989).

The steady decline in sexual misconduct by therapists revealed by these studies may indicate that fewer therapists are in fact having sexual relationships with patients, either because of a growing recognition of the inappropriateness of such behavior or because of growing fear of the legal and professional consequences of such actions (Pope & Bouhoutsos, 1986; Walker & Young, 1986). Alternatively, today's therapists may simply be less willing to admit, even anonymously, the misbehavior that is a felony in a growing number of states. It is also worth noting that 11 percent of 395 randomly selected psychologists in one survey admitted having had a sexual relationship with a former patient (Akamatsu, 1989).

Although the vast majority of therapists control and keep their sexual conduct within appropriate professional bounds, their ability to control private feelings and thoughts is apparently another story (see Box 21–4). In one survey, 72 percent of

BOX 21-4

THERAPISTS' FEELINGS TOWARD CLIENTS

In a recent national survey of 285 therapists, almost a third reported having hated at least one client in their career; and 46 percent reported having been so angered by a client that they did something that they later regretted.

The survey found that psychodynamic therapists tended to feel better prepared to deal with animosity toward their clients than therapists of other models. Perhaps because countertransference is a key issue in psychodynamic therapy, they were generally more aware than other therapists of their feelings for their clients and less likely to act on them. Many therapists reported feeling inadequately trained to deal with their feelings for clients. Here are some of the therapists' reactions:

EXPERIENCE	PERCENTAGE OF SURVEYED THERAPISTS WHO HAVE EVER HAD THE EXPERIENCE
Feeling afraid that a client may commit suicide	97
Feeling angry with a client because he or she is uncooperative with you	90
Feeling afraid that a client may physically attack a third party	89
Feeling afraid that your colleagues may be critical of your work with a client	88
Feeling angry with a client because he or she is often late for or misses sessions	87
Feeling angry with a client because he or she makes too many demands	87
Feeling sexually attracted to a client	87
Feeling afraid that a client may physically attack you	83
Feeling angry with a client because of late or unpaid therapy bills	83
Feeling angry with a client because he or she is verbally abusive toward you	81
Telling a client that you are angry with him or her	78
Raising your voice at a client because you are angry at him or her	57
Feeling so angry with a client you do something you later regret	46
Telling a client that you are afraid of him or her	33
Feeling hatred toward a client	31

Source: Adapted from Pope & Tabachnick, 1993.

therapists reported engaging in sexual fantasy about a client, although most said that this was a rare occurrence (Pope et al., 1987). In other surveys close to 90 percent reported having been sexually attracted to a client, at least on occasion (Pope & Tabachnick, 1993; Pope et al., 1986). Although relatively few of these therapists acted on their feelings, 63 percent felt guilty, anxious, or concerned about the attraction (Pope et al., 1986).

In recent years some consumer-oriented brochures on sexual misconduct in psychotherapy have been developed to equip clients to evaluate the appropriateness of their therapists' behavior (Thorn, Shealy, & Briggs, 1993). Given the potential for damage in a sexual relationship between therapist and client, many clinicians now believe it imperative that clients learn to identify and respond assertively to the early warning signs.

6. ***Psychologists must also adhere to the principle of confidentiality, long one of the most important features of therapy.*** For a client's peace of mind and to facilitate effective therapy, clients must be able to trust that their private exchanges with a therapist will not be disclosed to others. Thus the APA code of ethics states, "Psychologists have a primary obligation and must take reasonable precautions to respect the confidentiality rights of those with whom they work or consult, recognizing that confidentiality may be established by law, institutional rules, or professional or scientific relationships."

There are times, however, when the principle of complete confidentiality must be compromised. A therapist in training, for example, may need to discuss cases on a regular basis with a supervisor. This practice is common, and clients are usually informed when such procedures are in effect. A second exception may arise in cases of outpatients who are clearly dangerous, even homicidal. In such cases, a therapist may breach confidentiality to initiate involuntary commitment proceedings.

A further qualification of the confidentiality principle has been added as a result of a 1976 ruling by the California Supreme Court in the case of *Tarasoff* v. *Regents of the University of California*, considered one of the most important court decisions affecting client-therapist relationships. The *Tarasoff* case concerned a mental health outpatient at a University of California hospital who confided to his therapist that he wanted to harm his former girlfriend, Tanya Tarasoff. Several days after terminating therapy, the former patient fulfilled his promise. He stabbed Tanya Tarasoff to death.

Should confidentiality have been breached in this case? The therapist, in fact, felt that it should. Campus police were notified, but the patient was released after some questioning. In their suit against the hospital and therapist, the victim's parents argued that these measures were insufficient. They argued that the therapist should have warned them and their daughter that the patient intended to harm Ms. Tarasoff. The court agreed: "The protective privilege ends where the public peril begins." In addition to mandating a breach of confidentiality, this ruling requires the therapist to perform an extremely difficult feat: to determine when "a patient poses a serious danger of violence to others."

In partial concession to the *Tarasoff* ruling, the current APA code of ethics declares that therapists should reveal confidential information, even without the client's consent, when it is necessary "to protect the patient or client or others from harm." Since the *Tarasoff* ruling, California's courts have further clarified the therapist's duty to protect unsuspecting people from a client (Greenberg, 1987). The courts have held that therapists are also obligated to protect persons who are in close proximity to a client's intended victim and thus in danger (*Hedlund* v. *Collson*). A child, for example, is likely to be endangered when a client assaults the child's mother. The courts have further held that the duty to protect applies only when the intended victim is identified or readily identifiable, rather than a member of the general public (*Thompson* v. *County of Alameda*). Finally, the California courts have held that the duty does not apply when violence is unforeseeable or when the object of a client's intended violence is property rather than a person. Although the *Tarasoff* principles technically apply only to therapists in California, a number of other states have either adopted the courts' rulings or modified them (Pietrofesa et al., 1990; Bloom, 1990). Only a few states have rejected the California principles outright. Moreover, many states have adopted a "Duty to Protect Bill," designed to clarify the standards for confidentiality and action and protect mental health professionals from certain civil suits (Monahan, 1993).

Many therapists were initially resistant to the whole notion of breaking confidentiality, but surveys indicate that most now accept the legitimacy and ethics of it in order to prevent danger (Pope et al., 1987). More than 90 percent of surveyed psychologists view it as ethical in cases involving suicide, child abuse, or homicide. Moreover, 79 percent report having broken confidentiality themselves when a client was suicidal, 62 percent when child abuse was occurring, and 58 percent when a client was homicidal.

■ MENTAL HEALTH, ■ BUSINESS, AND ECONOMICS

The legislative and judicial systems are not the only social institutions with which mental health professionals interact. Among the others that influence and are influenced by clinical practice and study are the business and economic sectors of society.

BUSINESS AND MENTAL HEALTH

The National Institute for Occupational Safety and Health (NIOSH) lists psychological disorders as among the ten leading work-related diseases and injuries in the United States (Millar, 1984). Moreover, in some states, the number of stress-related worker's compensation claims has risen as much as 700 percent during the past decade (Schut, 1992). The business world has worked closely with mental health professionals to help identify the extent of psychological problems in the workforce and their influence on workers' performance (Millar, 1990, 1984). It has also turned to clinical professionals to help develop programs to prevent and remedy such problems (NIOSH, 1988, 1985). Two programs that have gained broad acceptance in the past decade are employee assistance programs and stress-reduction and problem-solving seminars.

Employee assistance programs are run either by mental health professionals who are employed directly by a company or by consulting mental health agencies. Companies publicize the availability of such services in the workplace, educate workers about mental dysfunctioning, and teach supervisors how to identify and refer workers who are in psychological trouble. Businesses believe that employee assistance programs save them money in the long run by preventing psychological problems from interfering with work performance. Left untreated, psychological and substance abuse problems have been shown to increase medical claims, absenteeism, and worker's compensation claims, and at the same time decrease productivity and morale (Block, 1992). Employee assistance programs also help businesses to curtail the costs of mental health and substance abuse insurance benefits, which have risen steadily over the past few years, from an average of $163 per employee in 1987 to $306 in 1991 (Foster-Higgins, 1991).

Stress-reduction and *problem-solving seminars* are workshops or group sessions in which mental health professionals teach employees coping, problem-solving, and stress-reduction techniques. Programs are just as likely to be organized for higher-level executives as for middle-level managers and assembly-line workers. Often groups of workers are required to attend such workshops, which may run for several days, and given time off from their jobs to do so. Again, the expectation of businesses is that these programs will save money by helping workers develop coping skills that lead to a healthier state of mind, less dysfunctioning on the job, and better job performance.

ECONOMICS AND MENTAL HEALTH

We have already seen how government-level economic decisions influence the mental health field's treatment of schizophrenic people and others with severe mental disorders. The desire by state and federal governments to reduce expenses has been a major consideration in the deinstitutionalization programs around the country, which have contributed to the premature release of hospital patients to communities unprepared to provide the needed treatment. Economic considerations affect other kinds of clients and forms of treatment as well.

At first glance, funding for mental health services seems to have risen sharply in the United States over the past two decades. A total of $23 billion was spent on such services in 1988, compared to $3.3 billion in 1969 (Redick et al., 1992). However, if adjustments are made for inflation and findings are stated in 1969 dollars, the 1988 expenditure is $5.3 billion, a relatively modest rise from the 1969 total (see Figure 21–3). Thus, although the number of persons in need of or seeking therapy has increased significantly, funding for such services is now increasing only slightly. This imbalance inevitably affects the length and frequency of services mental health professionals can supply.

In response to such financial realities, more and more people have to pay for mental health services themselves, and private insurance companies have become a major source of support for such services. Only 56 percent of all mental health services are now government-supported; 44 percent are paid for by direct client fees and private insurance reimbursements (Taube, 1990) (see Figure 21–4).

The growing economic role of private insurance companies has a significant effect on the way clinicians go about their work. In an effort to reduce their expenditures and to monitor what they are paying for, many of these companies have, for example, developed "managed care systems" in which the insurance company often determines which therapists clients may choose, the cost of sessions, and the number of sessions a client may be reimbursed for. Most of these companies have instituted a *peer review system* in which a panel of clinicians who essentially work for

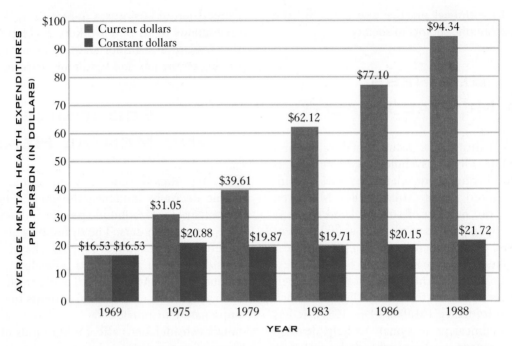

FIGURE 21-3 *The average amount of money spent for mental health services annually per person in the United States increased almost sixfold from $16.53 in 1969 to $94.34 in 1988. However, when adjustments are made for inflation and expenditures are stated in 1969 dollars, the amount spent per person rose more modestly, from $16.53 to $21.72 in 1988. (Adapted from Redick et al., 1992, p. 5.)*

the insurance companies may periodically review a therapist's report of a client's treatment and recommend that insurance benefits be either continued or terminated. In some cases, insurers require details from the therapist's session notes, which contain the intimate details of the patient's life (Goleman, 1993).

Many therapists and clients dislike peer reviews, claiming that the reports that therapists must make breach confidentiality, even when efforts are made to safeguard anonymity, and that the value of therapy in a given case is sometimes difficult to convey in a brief report (see Box 21–5). Some also argue that peer review inevitably works to shorten therapy, even if longer-term treatment would be advisable in particular cases. And others worry that the system could be a step toward wider regulation of therapy by insurance companies rather than by therapists.

■ THE PERSON ■ WITHIN THE PROFESSION

The actions and goals of clinical researchers and practitioners not only influence and are influenced by other institutions but are closely tied to their personal needs and goals. Abnormal psychology is a discipline in which the human strengths, imperfections, wisdom, and clumsiness of its professionals combine to influence the effectiveness of the profession as a whole. We have seen that the needs and preferences of these human beings influence their responses to clients' concerns, their theoretical orientations, and the kinds of clients they choose to work with. And we have also noted that personal leanings sometimes overcome professional standards and lead in extreme cases to instances of research fraud by clinical scientists and sexual misconduct by therapists.

A survey on the mental health of therapists found that 71 percent of 509 psychotherapists reported being in therapy at least once, about a fifth of them three or more times (Norcross et al., 1987). Most of those who received treatment spent more than 100 hours with therapists. Their reasons for seeking therapy were largely the same as those of other clients: emotional problems, depression, and anxiety topped the list. In related research a sample of psychotherapists reported being brought up in dysfunctional families. A number of them reported high rates of physical and sexual abuse, parental alcoholism, institutionalization of a parent in a mental hospital, and death of a family member

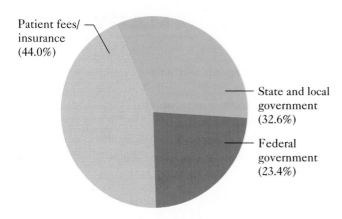

FIGURE 21-4 *Sources of mental health expenditures. Forty-four percent of all mental health services in the United States in the 1980s were reimbursed by direct client fees and private insurance companies. (Adapted from Taube, 1990, p. 219; Freeland & Schendler, 1983.)*

(Elliot & Guy, 1993). Many further reported experiencing significant distress even in adult life.

Another survey revealed that all therapists feel like imposters at some point in their career, 87 percent feel like fakes at least occasionally, and 18 percent feel this way frequently (Gibbs & DeVries, 1987). The survey also seemed to suggest that such feelings are not related to the fact that therapists must appear well adjusted and highly educated, but stem instead from personal anxieties and traits.

The science and profession of abnormal psychology has lofty goals: to understand, predict, and alter abnormal functioning. But we must not lose sight of the context in which its activities are conducted. Mental health researchers and clinicians are human beings, within a society of human beings,

working to serve human beings. The mixture of discovery, misdirection, promise, and frustration that we have encountered in these chapters is thus to be expected. When one thinks about it, could the study and treatment of human behavior really proceed in any other way?

THE STATE OF THE FIELD

LAW, SOCIETY, AND THE MENTAL HEALTH PROFESSION

Clinical researchers and professionals once conducted their work in relative isolation. Today, however, their activities are intimately tied to other institutions, such as the legislative, judicial, and economic systems. The main reason for this growing interconnectedness is that the clinical field has achieved a remarkable level of acceptance in our society. It now provides direct services to millions of people; it has much to say about almost every aspect of society, from education to ecology; and it is looked to as a source of information and expertise by government agencies, journalists, and people in general. When a field achieves such acceptance, it almost inevitably has some influence on the way other institutions are run. It also runs the risk of becoming so influential that other institutions jump in to monitor and restrict its activities.

To an extent, the interrelationship that has evolved between the mental health field and other institutions in our society is a healthy system of checks and balances. It allows the mental health profession to continue providing many useful services, yet helps ensure that its influence does not become excessive or misguided. Given the importance of such checks and balances, the close ties between the clinical field and other institutions are likely to continue and even to grow in the coming years.

The enormous growth and impact of the mental health profession make it all the more important that people hold an accurate perception of its strengths *and* weaknesses. As we have seen throughout this book, the field has acquired an impressive body of knowledge, especially during the

"Beth, you must learn to recognize Sam's needs, and, Sam, you must learn to recognize Beth's needs, and you both must learn to recognize my needs."

(Drawing by Maslin; © 1993 The New Yorker Magazine, Inc.)

past several decades; however, what mental health professionals do not know and cannot do still outweigh what they do know and can do. Everyone who turns to the field directly or indirectly must recognize this important fact. A society cannot be faulted for being vastly curious about and regularly seeking the input of a field of study—even when the field is young and imperfect—as long as the members of society fully appreciate the actual *state of the field*.

SUMMARY

■ THE MENTAL HEALTH PROFESSION interacts with the legislative and judicial institutions in two primary ways. First, clinicians may be called upon to help evaluate the mental stability of people accused of crimes. Second, the legislative and judicial branches of government help regulate various aspects of mental health care.

BOX 21-5

THE ITEMIZED STATEMENT IN CLINICAL PSYCHIATRY: A NEW CONCEPT IN BILLING

(In this article, by Robert S. Hoffman, M.D., which originally appeared in The Journal of Irreproducible Results, *1980, the psychiatrist's biting wit is equaled only by his sense of outrage over the growing demands made by insurance companies.)*

Due to the rapidly escalating costs of health care delivery, there has been increasing pressure on physicians to document and justify their charges for professional services. This has created a number of serious problems, particularly in the field of psychiatry. Chief among these is the breach of confidentiality that arises when sensitive clinical information is provided to third-party insurance carriers, e.g. the patient's diagnosis or related details about his/her psychiatric disorder. Even when full disclosure of such information is made, insurance carriers frequently deny benefits because the description of the treatment appears imprecise or inadequate. There also has been some criticism of the standard hourly fee-for-service, the argument being that psychiatrists, like other medical specialists, should be required to adjust their fees depending upon the particular treatment offered.

In view of these considerations, a method is required which will bring psychiatric billing in line with accepted medical practice. The procedure illustrated below, which we have successfully employed in our clinic for the past two years, achieves this goal. It requires only a modest investment in time and effort: the tape-recording of all psychotherapy sessions, transcription of tapes, tabulation of

therapeutic interventions, and establishment of a relative value scale for the commonly used maneuvers. This can easily be managed by two full-time medical billing personnel per psychiatrist. The method, in our hands, has been found to increase collections from third-party carriers by 65% and to raise a typical psychiatrist's annual net income almost to the level of a municipal street sweeper or plumber's assistant.

Below is a specimen monthly statement illustrating these principles:

CALVIN L. SKOLNIK, M.D., INC.
A Psychiatry Corporation

Jan. 5, 1978

Mr. Sheldon Rosenberg
492 West Maple Dr.
East Orange, N.J.

Dear Mr. Rosenberg:

In response to the request by your insurer, Great Lakes Casualty and Surety Co., for more precise documentation of professional services rendered, I have prepared the enclosed itemization for the month of December. I trust that this will clarify the situation sufficiently for your benefit payments to be resumed.

Until next Tuesday at 11:00, I remain

Cordially,
CALVIN L. SKOLNIK, M.D.

■ CRIMINAL PUNISHMENT DEPENDS on the assumption that individuals are *responsible* for their crimes and are *capable* of defending themselves in court. If, as a result of clinical testimony, defendants are judged to have been mentally unstable at the time they committed a crime, they may be found *not guilty by reason of insanity* and placed in a treatment facility rather than a prison. If, on the basis of clinical testimony, a person is judged mentally unstable *(incompetent)* at the time of trial, the trial itself may be delayed while the defendant receives treatment. Each of these situations represents a form of *criminal commitment.*

Insanity is a legal term, defined by legislators, not by clinicians. Until the late nineteenth century, all federal courts and most state courts in the United States judged insanity in accordance with the *M'Naghten rule,* which holds that defendants were insane at the time of a criminal act if they did not know the nature or quality of the act or did not know

Charges

140	clarifications	@ .25	35.00
157	restatements	@ .25	39.25
17	broad-focus questions	@ .35	5.95
42	narrow-focus questions	@ .30	12.60
86	reflections of dominant emotional theme	@ .35	30.10
38	resolutions of inconsistencies	@ .45	17.10
22	pointings out of nonverbal communications	@ .40	8.80
187	encouragements to say more	@ .15	28.05
371	sympathetic nods with furrowed brow	@ .10	37.10
517	acknowledgments of information reception (Uh-huhs, Um-hmmm, etc.)	@ .08	41.36
24	interpretations of unconscious defense configurations	@ .30	7.20
16	absolution for evil deeds	@ .50	8.00
2	pieces of advice	@ .75	1.50
6	expressions of personal feelings	@ .50	3.00
2	personal reminiscences	@ .65	1.30
35	misc. responses (sighs, grunts, belches, etc.)	@ .20	7.00
7	listening to remarks disparaging therapist's appearance, personal habits, or technique	@ 1.75	12.25
12	listening to sarcastic remarks about psychiatry	@ 1.00	12.00
3	listening to psychiatrist jokes	@ .80	2.40
3	telephone calls to therapist	@ .15	.45
1	telephone call to therapist at especially inopportune moment	@ 10.50	10.50
22	Kleenex tissues	@ .005	.11
1	ashtray	@ 3.50	3.50
1	filling and repainting of 1 ashtray-size dent in wall	@ 27.50	27.50
1	shampooing of soft drink stain on carpet	@ 15.00	15.00
1	letter of excuse from work	@ 2.50	2.50
2	surcharges for unusually boring or difficult sessions	@ 35.00	70.00
	Subtotal: charges		$438.52

Credits

4	unusually interesting anecdotes	@ .45	1.80
3	good jokes	@ .50	1.50
1	item of gossip about another patient which was found useful in her therapy	@ 3.50	3.50
1	apology for sarcastic remark	@ 1.00	1.00
1	use of case history at American Psychiatric Association convention		10.00
½	chicken salad sandwich on whole wheat c/mayo	@ 1.75	.88
7	bummed cigarettes (65¢/pack)		.23
1	damaged Librium tablet, returned unused		.10
	Subtotal: credits		$18.99
	Total: PLEASE REMIT—		$419.53

right from wrong at the time they committed it. Some states later abandoned this test in favor of the *irresistible impulse test,* which holds that defendants were insane at the time of a crime if they were unable to control their actions when they committed the crime. In the 1950s a third test became popular: the *Durham test* states simply that people are not responsible for their criminal acts if those acts were the result of mental disease. In 1955 the American Law Institute proposed a penal code that combined elements of all three tests, and this code gained widespread use in federal and state courts. In 1983, however, after John Hinckley was found not guilty of shooting the president and two aides by reason of insanity, the federal courts and half of the state courts adopted a more stringent code that essentially reestablished the M'Naghten standard.

The insanity defense has been criticized on several grounds, and in recent years 12 states have chosen to also permit a verdict of "guilty but mentally ill." This new verdict assigns moral blame to defendants but recognizes their mental illness. They are given a prison term with the proviso that they will also receive psychological treatment. Similarly, in many states sex offenders are found to be mentally ill and assigned to treatment. By such innovations society tries to balance moral responsibility and mental dysfunctioning.

Regardless of their state of mind at the time of the crime, defendants may be mentally incompetent to stand trial; that is, incapable of fully understanding the charges and legal proceedings that confront them. If they are ruled incompetent upon clinical evaluation, they are typically sent to a mental hospital until they are competent to stand trial. In some cases, the period of time spent in the mental institution can be longer than the prison sentence would have been. A ruling by the Supreme Court now ensures that incompetent persons cannot be held in a mental hospital indefinitely.

■ THE LEGAL SYSTEM also has significant influence on the clinical profession. First, legal channels may be used to commit noncriminals to mental hospitals for treatment—a process called *civil commitment.* Society allows involuntary commitment when one is considered *in need of treatment* and *dangerous to oneself or others.* Statutes governing civil commitment procedures vary from state to state, but a *minimum standard of proof*—clear, unequivocal, and convincing evidence of the necessity of commitment—must be provided for commitment, as defined in the case of *Addington* v. *Texas.*

Second, courts and legislatures have significantly affected the clinical profession by specifying a number of legal rights to which mental patients are entitled. The rights that have received the most attention are the *right to treatment* and the *right to refuse treatment.* Other rights gained by patients in recent years include the right to receive payment for work performed in a mental institution, the right to aftercare and an appropriate community residence upon release from an institution, and the right to treatment in the least restrictive facility available.

■ MENTAL HEALTH AND LEGAL PROFESSIONALS also cross paths in three other areas. First, malpractice suits against therapists have risen in recent years, charging such offenses as sexual activity with a patient, wrongful commitment, and improper termination of treatment. Second, lawyers now frequently solicit the advice of mental health professionals regarding the selection of jurors and case strategies. Finally, the legislative and judicial systems have played a role in defining the scope of clinical practice. For example, legislation now permits psychologists as well as psychiatrists to receive Medicare payments for therapy services and to admit patients to hospitals in certain states.

■ IN ADDITION to being guided by laws, courts, and legal processes, each clinical profession has a code of ethics. The code for psychologists, for example, sets guidelines for offering advice to the public in books and on television; prohibits psychologists from engaging in fraudulent research; mandates that they obtain whatever additional training or consultation is needed to address patients' needs; requires them to base evaluations in legal cases on sufficient information; prohibits them from exploiting the trust and dependence of clients and students, sexually or otherwise; and establishes guidelines for respecting patient confidentiality. There are times when the principle of confidentiality must be compromised. Perhaps the most important court case affecting client–therapist confidentiality has been *Tarasoff* v. *Regents of the University of California,* which has led to clarifications of the circumstances under which therapists must break confidentiality in order to protect the public.

■ CLINICAL PRACTICE AND STUDY also intersect with the business world, particularly in efforts to identify and address psychological problems in the workplace. Similarly, the mental health system often interacts with the economic institutions of our society.

For example, because government funding for mental health services has risen only modestly in the past two decades, more and more private insurance companies are reimbursing therapists for their services and are setting up reimbursement procedures that may influence the duration and focus of therapy.

Finally, mental health activities are affected by the personal needs, values, and goals of the human beings who provide the clinical services. Therapists and researchers are themselves grappling with psychological issues that inevitably affect the choices, direction, and even quality of their work.

GLOSSARY

Abnormal psychology The scientific study of abnormal behavior in order to describe, predict, explain, and ultimately learn to prevent or to alter abnormal patterns of functioning.

Acetylcholine A neurotransmitter that when present in high levels may be associated with depression.

Acute schizophrenia A form of schizophrenia characterized by sudden onset of symptoms, good premorbid functioning, prominent affective symptoms or confusion, and good response to treatment.

Acute stress disorder An anxiety disorder in which fear and related symptoms are experienced soon after a traumatic event and last less than a month.

Addiction Physical dependence on a substance, marked by such features as tolerance, withdrawal symptoms during abstinence, or both.

Affect A subjective experience of emotion or mood.

Affectual awareness The first stage of sexual therapy in which the client becomes aware of his or her negative emotions regarding sex.

Aftercare A program of posthospitalization care and treatment out in the community.

Agoraphobia A pervasive and complex phobia that makes people avoid public places or situations in which escape might be difficult or help unavailable should they develop incapacitating or embarrassing paniclike symptoms.

Agoraphobia without history of panic disorder An agoraphobic pattern that does not have its origin in a panic attack.

Akathisia A Parkinsonian symptom consisting of a very high degree of restlessness and agitation and great discomfort in the limbs.

Alarm stage An increase of activity in the sympathetic nervous system in the presence of a perceived threat. See also **General adaptation syndrome.**

Alcohol Any beverage containing ethyl alcohol, including beer, wine, and liquor.

Alcohol dehydrogenase An enzyme which breaks down alcohol in the stomach before it enters the blood. Women have significantly less of this enzyme than men and therefore tend to become more intoxicated after ingesting an equal dose of alcohol.

Alcohol withdrawal delirium A dramatic reaction experienced by some people who are alcohol-dependent. It occurs within three days of cessation or reduction of drinking and consists of mental confusion, clouded consciousness, and terrifying visual hallucinations. Also known as delirium tremens (DTs).

Alcoholics Anonymous (AA) A self-help organization that provides support and guidance for persons with alcohol abuse or dependence.

Alcoholism A pattern of behavior in which a person abuses or develops a dependence on alcohol.

Alogia A symptom in schizophrenia, characterized by decreased fluency and productivity of speech.

Alpha waves Brain waves characteristic of relaxed wakefulness.

Alprazolam A benzodiazepine drug, also shown to be effective in the treatment of panic disorders. Marketed as Xanax.

Altruistic suicide Suicide committed by people very well integrated into the social structure who intentionally sacrifice their lives for the well-being of society.

Alzheimer's disease The most common form of dementia, sometimes occurring well before old age.

Amenorrhea The cessation of menstruation that often accompanies anorexia nervosa in women.

Amnesia Loss of memory. See also **Anterograde, Dissociative,** and **Retrograde amnesia.**

Amniocentesis A prenatal procedure used to test the amniotic fluid that surrounds the fetus in order to detect the possibility of birth defects.

Amphetamine A stimulant drug that is manufactured in the laboratory.

Amphetamine-induced psychotic disorder A syndrome caused by a high dose of amphetamines that closely mimics schizophrenia and includes hallucinations and motor hyperactivity.

Amygdala The structure in the brain's limbic system that gives rise to emotional behavior and that may also regulate the link between arousal and memory.

Anaclitic depression A pattern of behavior that includes sadness, withdrawal, weight loss, and trouble sleeping and that is associated with separation from one's mother before the age of 6 years.

Anal stage In psychoanalytic theory, the second 18 months of life, during which the child's focus of pleasure shifts to the anus, and libidinal gratification comes from retaining and passing feces.

Analogue experiment An investigation in which the experimenter induces laboratory subjects to behave in ways that resemble real-life abnormal behavior.

Anatomical brain disorders Problems stemming from abnormal size or shape of certain brain regions.

Anesthesia A lessening or loss of sensation for touch or pain.

Anomic suicides (anomie) Suicide committed by

individuals whose social environment fails to provide stability.

ANOREXIA NERVOSA A disorder characterized by the relentless pursuit of extreme thinness and by an extreme loss of weight.

ANOXIA A complication of birth in which the baby is deprived of oxygen.

ANTABUSE (DISULFIRAM) A drug that is relatively benign when taken by itself, but causes intense nausea, vomiting, increased heart rate, and dizziness when taken with alcohol. It is often taken by people who are trying to refrain from drinking alcohol.

ANTAGONIST DRUG Any drug that blocks or changes the effects of another drug.

ANTEROGRADE AMNESIA The inability to learn and remember new information. It sometimes follows a shock or trauma.

ANTHROPOLOGY The study of human cultures and institutions.

ANTIANXIETY DRUGS Psychotropic drugs that reduce tension and anxiety.

ANTIBIPOLAR DRUG A drug that helps stabilize the moods of people suffering from bipolar mood disorder. See also **Lithium.**

ANTIBODIES Bodily chemicals that seek out and destroy antigens such as bacteria or viruses.

ANTIDEPRESSANT DRUGS Psychotropic drugs that lift the mood of depressed people.

ANTIGENS Foreign invaders such as bacteria and viruses that stimulate an immune response.

ANTIPSYCHOTIC DRUGS Psychotropic drugs that help correct grossly confused or distorted thinking.

ANTISOCIAL PERSONALITY DISORDER A personality disorder characterized by a disregard for and violation of other people's rights.

ANXIETY Emotional state characterized by fear, apprehension, and physiological arousal.

ANXIETY DISORDERS Disorders in which anxiety is a central symptom.

ANXIETY-SENSITIVITY According to cognitive-behavioral theorists, the tendency of certain individuals to become preoccupied with their bodily sensations, lose their ability to assess them logically, and interpret them as potentially harmful, leaving some more likely to develop panic attacks.

ANXIOLYTICS See **Antianxiety drugs.**

APHASIA A common symptom in some kinds of dementia, characterized by difficulty producing the names of individuals and objects.

APHRODISIAC A substance that is thought to increase the sex drive. Over the centuries people have considered many substances to be aphrodisiacs, but none has been proven to increase the sex drive.

ARBITRARY INFERENCE An error in logic in which a person draws negative conclusions on the basis of little or even contrary evidence. It may contribute to some cases of depression.

AROUSAL PHASE The second phase in the sexual response cycle, characterized by general physical arousal, increases in heart rate, muscle tension, blood pressure, and respiration, and specific changes in the pelvic region.

ASSERTIVENESS TRAINING A cognitive-behavioral approach to increasing assertive behavior that is socially desirable.

ASSESSMENT The collection of relevant information about a client or subject.

ASTHMA Medical problem marked by constricting of the trachea and bronchi resulting in shortness of breath, wheezing, coughing, and choking.

ASYLUM A type of institution first established in the sixteenth century to provide care for the mentally ill. Most became virtual prisons in which patients endured degrading conditions.

ATTENTION-DEFICIT/HYPERACTIVITY DISORDER A disorder characterized by a persistent inability to focus attention, overactive and impulsive behavior, or both.

ATTRIBUTION The explaining of the things we see going on around us as the result of particular causes that then influence the way we feel about ourselves and others.

ATYPICAL ANTIPSYCHOTIC DRUGS A new group of antipsychotic drugs (the most common being clozapine) which appear to cause few extrapyramidal symptoms. These drugs are labeled "atypical" because they have a different mechanism of action than the traditional drugs, blocking fewer dopamine receptors.

AUDITORY HALLUCINATION A hallucination in which a person hears sounds and voices that are not actually present.

AUGMENTATIVE COMMUNICATION SYSTEMS A method for teaching individuals with autism, mental retardation, or cerebral palsy to communicate by pointing to pictures, symbols, or written words that represent objects or needs.

AURA A warning sensation that frequently precedes a migraine headache.

AUTISM A pervasive developmental disorder characterized by extreme unresponsiveness to others, poor communication skills, limited skill at imaginative play, and odd or bizarre reaction to the environment.

AUTOEROTIC ASPHYXIA A fatal lack of oxygen which people inadvertently self-induce while hanging, suffocating, or strangling themselves during masturbation.

AUTOMATIC THOUGHT Unbidden cognitions that come into the mind, some comforting and some upsetting.

AUTONOMIC LEARNING The inadvertent conditioning of particular responses in the autonomic nervous system.

AUTONOMIC NERVOUS SYSTEM (ANS) The extensive network of nerve fibers that connects the central nervous system to all the other organs of the body.

AVERSION THERAPY A behavioral technique that helps clients acquire anxiety responses to stimuli that they have been finding too attractive.

AVOIDANCE BEHAVIOR Behavior that removes or avoids anxiety-producing objects or situations.

AVOIDANT PERSONALITY DISORDER A personality disorder characterized by a chronic and pervasive pattern of inhibition in social situations, feelings of inadequacy, and extreme sensitivity to negative evaluation.

AVOLITION A symptom in schizophrenia, characterized by apathy, a lack of interest in normal goals, an inability to make decisions, and an inability to initiate or complete a course of action.

Axon The long fiber that extends from the body of the neuron.

B-cell Lymphocyte that produces antibodies.

Barbiturates Addictive sedative-hypnotic drugs used to reduce anxiety or to help persons fall asleep.

Baroreceptors Sensitive nerves in the arteries responsible for alerting the brain when blood pressure becomes too high.

Baseline data An individual's initial response level on a test or scale.

Basic irrational assumptions Inappropriate assumptions guiding the way in which one acts that prejudice a person's chances for happiness and success.

Battery A comprehensive group of tests, each of which targets a specific skill area.

Behavior The response that an organism makes to the stimuli in its environment.

Behavioral assessment The collection of information about specific dysfunctional behaviors a person engages in.

Behavioral medicine A field of study and treatment that combines psychological and physical concepts and interventions to better understand, treat, or prevent medical problems.

Behavioral model A theoretical perspective that emphasizes ingrained behavior and the ways in which it is learned.

Behavioral self-control training (BSCT) An approach to treating alcohol abuse in which clients are taught to monitor their own drinking behavior, set appropriate limits on their drinking, control their rate of drinking, and apply alternative coping behaviors.

Behavioral therapy (also Behavior modification) A therapeutic approach that views the goal of therapy as identifying the client's specific problem-causing behaviors and either modifying them or replacing them with more appropriate ones.

Bender Visual-Motor Gestalt Test A neuropsychological test in which a subject is asked to copy a set of nine simple designs and later reproduce the designs from memory.

Benzodiazepines The most common antianxiety drugs. The group includes Valium, Xanax, and Librium.

Bereavement The process of working through the grief that one feels when a loved one dies.

Beta-amyloid protein A small molecule that forms sphere-shaped deposits called senile plaques. These deposits collect in the spaces between neurons in people with Alzheimer's disease, interfering with memory and learning.

Beta blocker A drug that reduces the physical symptoms of anxiety by blocking the reception of norepinephrine in the brain.

Bilateral electroconvulsive therapy (ECT) A form of electroconvulsive therapy in which two electrodes are used, and electrical current is passed through both sides of the brain.

Binge-eating disorder A type of eating disorder in which a person displays a pattern of binge eating without any accompanying compensatory behaviors. Listed in the DSM-IV appendix, designated for further study.

Binge-eating/purging type anorexia nervosa A type of anorexia nervosa in which people engage in eating binges but still lose excessive weight by forcing themselves to vomit after meals or by abusing laxatives or diuretics.

Biofeedback A treatment technique in which the client is given systematic information about key physiological responses as they occur and learns to control the responses voluntarily.

Biological challenge A procedure used to induce panic in subjects or clients by having them exercise vigorously or perform other physical tasks in the presence of a therapist or researcher.

Biological model The theoretical perspective that cites organic processes as the key to human behavior.

Biological therapy The use of physical and chemical procedures to help people overcome psychological difficulties.

Bipolar disorder A disorder marked by alternating or intermixed periods of mania and depression.

Bipolar I disorder A type of bipolar disorder in which a person experiences manic and major depressive episodes.

Bipolar II disorder A type of bipolar disorder in which a person experiences mildly manic (hypomanic) episodes that alternate with major depressive episodes.

Birth complications Biological conditions during birth, including anoxia and extreme prematurity, that can compromise the physical and mental well-being of the child.

Blind design An experiment in which subjects do not know whether they are in the experimental or the control condition.

Blocking A symptom associated with schizophrenia in which thoughts seem to disappear from memory and statements end in silence before they can be completed.

Blunted affect A symptom of schizophrenia in which a person displays less emotion—anger, sadness, joy—than other people.

Body dysmorphic disorder (dysmorphobia) A somatoform disorder marked by excessive worry that some aspect of one's physical appearance is defective.

Body mass index (BMI) The quotient of one's weight in kilograms and height in centimeters, used to determine whether a person weighs too much.

Borderline personality disorder A personality disorder characterized by a pervasive pattern of instability in interpersonal relationships, self-image, and moods, and marked impulsivity.

Brain stem The region of the central nervous system that connects the spinal cord with the cerebrum.

Brain wave The oscillations of electrical potential, as measured by an electroencephalograph, that are created by neurons in the brain.

Breathing-related sleep disorder A sleep disorder in which sleep is frequently disrupted by a breathing problem, causing excessive sleepiness or insomnia.

Brief psychotic disorder Psychotic symptoms that appear suddenly after a very stressful event or a period of emotional turmoil and last anywhere from a few hours to a month.

BRIQUET'S SYNDROME   See **Somatization disorder.**

BULIMIA NERVOSA   A disorder characterized by frequent eating binges, during which the person uncontrollably consumes large quantities of food followed by forced vomiting or other extreme compensatory behaviors to avoid gaining weight.

CAFFEINE   A stimulant drug that is commonly consumed in the form of coffee, tea, cola, and chocolate.

CANNABIS DRUGS   Drugs produced from the different varieties of hemp plant. They cause a mixture of intoxicating, hallucinogenic, depressant, and stimulant effects.

CASE STUDY   A detailed account of one person's life and psychological problems.

CATATONIA   Extreme psychomotor symptoms found in some forms of schizophrenia.

CATATONIC EXCITEMENT   A form of catatonia in which a person moves excitedly, sometimes with wild waving of the arms and legs.

CATATONIC SCHIZOPHRENIA   Schizophrenia characterized by a severe psychomotor disturbance.

CATATONIC STUPOR   A symptom associated with schizophrenia in which a person becomes totally unresponsive to the environment, remaining motionless and silent for long stretches of time.

CATECHOLAMINE THEORY   The view that unipolar depression is related to low activity of norepinephrine (a catecholamine) in the brain and less neuronal firing.

CATHARSIS   The reliving of past repressed feelings in order to settle internal conflicts and overcome problems.

CENTRAL NERVOUS SYSTEM   The brain and spinal cord.

CEREBRAL CORTEX   The outer layer of the cerebrum, or upper portion of the brain, also known as the gray matter. It is associated with higher cognitive functions.

CHECKING COMPULSION   A compulsion in which people feel compelled to check the same things over and over.

CHILD ABUSE   The intentional, nonaccidental use of physical or psychological force by an adult on a child, often aimed at hurting, injuring, or destroying the child.

CHLORPROMAZINE   A phenothiazine drug commonly used for treating schizophrenia. Marketed as Thorazine.

CHROMOSOMAL MAPPING   A research strategy for studying the DNA of a large extended family in which a particular trait (schizophrenia, for example) is unusually common.

CHROMOSOMES   The structures within a cell that contain genes.

CHRONOLOGICAL AGE   The number of years one has lived since birth.

CIRCADIAN RHYTHM SLEEP DISORDER   A sleep disorder in which people experience excessive sleepiness or insomnia as the result of a mismatch between the sleep-wake cycle in their environment and their own circadian sleep-wake cycle.

CIRCADIAN RHYTHMS   Internal "clocks" consisting of recurrent biological fluctuations.

CIRRHOSIS   A disease of the liver, often caused by excessive drinking, in which the liver becomes scarred, forms fibrous tissue, and begins to change its anatomy and functioning.

CIVIL COMMITMENT   The legal process by which individuals can be forced to undergo mental health treatment.

CLANG   A rhyme used by schizophrenic individuals as a guide to formulating thoughts and statements.

CLASSICAL CONDITIONING   A process of learning by temporal association in which two events that repeatedly occur close together in time become fused in a person's mind.

CLEANING COMPULSION   A common compulsion in which people feel compelled to keep cleaning themselves, their clothing, their homes, and anything they might touch.

CLIENT-CENTERED THERAPY   The therapeutic approach associated with Carl Rogers that focuses on a patient's unique subjective perspective rather than on someone's definition of objective reality. Rogers proposed that clients would respond better if therapists were particularly warm, genuine, and understanding.

CLINICAL PSYCHOLOGIST   A professional who earns a doctorate in clinical psychology by completing four years of graduate training in abnormal functioning and its treatment as well as a one-year internship at a mental hospital or mental health agency.

CLINICAL PSYCHOLOGY   The study, assessment, treatment, and prevention of abnormal behavior.

CLITORIS   The female sex organ located in front of the urinary and vaginal openings. It becomes enlarged during sexual arousal.

CLOZAPINE (CLOZARIL)   The most commonly prescribed atypical antipsychotic drug.

COCAINE   A drug that is the most powerful natural stimulant known.

COGNITION   The intellectual capacity to think, remember, and anticipate.

COGNITIVE BEHAVIOR   Thoughts and beliefs, many of which remain private.

COGNITIVE-BEHAVIORAL MODEL   A theoretical perspective that attributes psychological problems to cognitive behaviors.

COGNITIVE MODEL   A theoretical perspective that emphasizes the process and content of the thinking that underlies behavior.

COGNITIVE THERAPY   A therapeutic system constructed on the premise that abnormal functioning is caused by counterproductive assumptions and thoughts. Its goal is to help people recognize and change their faulty thinking processes.

COGNITIVE TRIAD   The three forms of negative thinking that theorist Aaron Beck says encompass one's experiences, one's view of oneself, and one's view of the future.

COHORT   A group of people who are born in the same time period or year—that is, people of the same generation.

COITUS   Sexual intercourse.

COMMUNITY MENTAL HEALTH CENTER   A treatment facility for persons with psychological dysfunctions that provides outpatient psychotherapy and medication and inpatient emergency care.

COMMUNITY MENTAL HEALTH MOVEMENT A sociopolitical trend emphasizing community care for people with severe psychological disturbances.

COMPULSION A repetitive and rigid behavior or mental act that a person feels compelled to perform in order to prevent or reduce anxiety or distress.

COMPUTERIZED AXIAL TOMOGRAPHY (CAT SCAN) A composite image of the brain created by compiling X-ray images taken from many angles.

CONCORDANCE A statistical measure of the frequency with which both members of a pair of twins have the same particular trait.

CONDITIONED RESPONSE (CR) A response previously associated with an unconditioned stimulus that comes to be elicited by a conditioned stimulus.

CONDITIONED STIMULUS (CS) A previously neutral stimulus that comes to be associated with nonneutral stimulus.

CONDITIONING A simple form of learning in which a given stimulus comes to evoke a given response.

CONDITIONS OF WORTH According to client-centered theorists, the internal standards by which a person judges his or her own lovability and acceptability, determined by the standards (i.e., conditions of worth) to which the person was held as a child.

CONDUCT DISORDER A pathological pattern of childhood behavior in which the child repeatedly violates the basic rights of others or major societal norms or rules, displaying aggression and sometimes destroying others' property, lying, or running away from home.

CONFABULATION A spontaneously made-up event fabricated to fill in a gap in one's memory. Characteristic of persons with alcoholism suffering from Korsakoff's syndrome.

CONFEDERATE An experimenter's accomplice who plays a role in creating a believable counterfeit situation in an experiment.

CONFIDENTIALITY The commitment on the part of a professional person not to divulge the information he or she obtains from a client.

CONFOUND A variable other than the independent variable that is also acting on the dependent variable.

CONJOINT FAMILY THERAPY A family therapy approach in which the therapist focuses primarily on communication within the family system, helping members to recognize harmful patterns of communication, to appreciate the impact of such patterns on other family members, and to change the patterns.

CONTINGENCY TRAINING A short-term behavioral treatment for drug abuse in which clients receive incentives contingent on submitting drug-free urine samples.

CONTINUOUS AMNESIA A disturbance of memory in which forgetting continues into the present, and new and ongoing experiences fail to be retained.

CONTROL GROUP In an experiment, a group of subjects who are not exposed to the independent variable.

CONVERSION DISORDER A somatoform disorder characterized by one or more physical symptoms or deficits affecting voluntary motor or sensory function.

CORONARY HEART DISEASE Illness caused by a blocking of the coronary arteries.

CORRELATION The degree to which events or characteristics vary in conjunction with each other.

CORRELATIONAL COEFFICIENT (R) A statistical expression of the direction and the magnitude of a correlation, ranging from -1.00 to $+1.00$.

COUNSELING PSYCHOLOGY A mental health specialty similar to clinical psychology that requires completion of its own graduate training program.

COUNTERTRANSFERENCE A phenomenon of psychotherapy in which therapists unintentionally allow their own feelings, history, and values to subtly influence the way they interpret a patient's problems.

COUPLE THERAPY A therapeutic approach in which the therapist works with two people who share a long-term relationship. It focuses on the structure and communication patterns in the relationship.

COVERT DESENSITIZATION Desensitization training that focuses on imagining confrontations with the frightening objects or situations while in a state of relaxation. See also In vivo desensitization.

COVERT SENSITIZATION A behavioral treatment for eliminating unwanted behavior by pairing the behavior with unpleasant mental images.

CRACK A powerful, ready-to-smoke free-base cocaine. See also Free-base.

CRETINISM A congenital disorder characterized by mental retardation and other physical abnormalities and caused by low levels of iodine in a pregnant woman's diet.

CREUTZFELDT-JAKOB DISEASE A rare, rapidly progressive dementia caused by a virus, that often includes spasmodic movements.

CRIMINAL COMMITMENT A legal process by which individuals accused of crimes are judged to be mentally unstable and are sent to a mental institution for treatment.

CRISIS INTERVENTION See Suicide prevention program.

CROSS-TOLERANCE Tolerance for a drug one has never taken, as a result of using another similar drug.

CULTURE A people's common history, values, institutions, habits, skills, technology, and arts.

CYCLOTHYMIC DISORDER A disorder characterized by numerous periods of hypomanic symptoms and mild depressive symptoms.

DATE RAPE Rape by a date or close acquaintance.

DAY CENTER (DAY HOSPITAL) A treatment center that provides daylong therapeutic activity and care.

DECLARATIVE MEMORY Memory for information that is directly accessible to consciousness, such as names, dates, and other learned facts.

DEFENSE MECHANISMS. See Ego defense mechanisms.

DEINSTITUTIONALIZATION The practice begun in the mid-twentieth century to release hundreds of thousands of patients from public mental hospitals.

DELIRIUM A rapidly occurring clouded state of consciousness in which a person experiences great difficulty concentrating, focusing attention, and maintaining a straightforward and well-oriented stream of thought.

DELIRIUM TREMENS (DTS)   See **Alcohol withdrawal delirium.**

DELUSION   A blatantly false belief firmly held despite evidence to the contrary.

DELUSION OF CONTROL   The belief that one's impulses, feelings, thoughts, and actions are being controlled by other people.

DELUSION OF GRANDEUR   The belief that one is a great inventor, historical figure, religious savior, or other specially empowered person.

DELUSION OF PERSECUTION   The belief that one is being plotted or discriminated against, spied on, slandered, threatened, attacked, or deliberately victimized.

DELUSION OF REFERENCE   A belief that attaches special and personal significance to the actions of others or to various objects or events.

DELUSIONAL DISORDER   A disorder consisting of persistent, nonbizarre delusions that are not part of a larger schizophrenic pattern.

DEMENTIA   A severe decline of intellectual and other mental faculties, first described by early Greek and Roman philosophers and physicians.

DEMONOLOGY   The belief that abnormal behavior results from supernatural causes such as evil spirits.

DENDRITE   The extensions, or antennae, located at one end of a neuron that receive impulses from other neurons.

DENIAL   An ego defense mechanism in which a person fails to acknowledge unacceptable thoughts, feelings, or actions.

DEPENDENT PERSONALITY DISORDER   A personality disorder characterized by a pattern of submissive and clinging behavior and fears of separation related to a pervasive and excessive need to be taken care of.

DEPENDENT VARIABLE   The variable in an experiment that is expected to change as the independent variable is manipulated.

DEPERSONALIZATION DISORDER   A disorder characterized by a persistent and recurrent feeling of being detached from one's mental processes or body; that is, one feels unreal and alien.

DEPRESSION   A low, sad state in which life seems bleak and its challenges overwhelming.

DERAILMENT (LOOSE ASSOCIATIONS)   A common formal thought disorder of schizophrenia, characterized by rapid shifts from one topic of conversation to another.

DEREALIZATION   The feeling that the external world is unreal and strange.

DESIRE PHASE   The first phase of the sexual response cycle, characterized by an urge to have sex, sexual fantasies, and feelings of sexual attraction to others.

DESYNCHRONIZATION   An imbalance between the body's circadian rhythms and the rhythms of the environment.

DETOXIFICATION   Systematic and medically supervised withdrawal from a drug.

DEVIANCE   Variance from accepted patterns of behavior.

DEXAMETHASONE SUPPRESSION TEST (DST)   A biological assessment technique that indirectly measures cortisol levels in patients in order to diagnose depression.

DIAGNOSIS   The process of determining whether a person's dysfunction constitutes a particular psychological disorder.

DIATHESIS-STRESS PERSPECTIVE   The view that a person must first have a biological, psychological, or sociocultural predisposition to a disorder and then be subjected to an immediate form of psychological stress to develop and maintain it.

DIAZEPAM   A benzodiazepine drug marketed as Valium.

DIENCEPHALON   A brain structure located below the cerebral cortex, consisting of the mammillary bodies, thalamus, and hypothalamus. Damage to these structures generally results in problems with encoding new information.

DISORGANIZED SCHIZOPHRENIA   Schizophrenia characterized by confusion, incoherence, and flat or inappropriate affect.

DISPLACEMENT   An ego defense mechanism that channels unacceptable id impulses toward another, safer substitute.

DISREGULATION MODEL   A theory that explains psychophysiological disorders as breakdowns in the body's negative feedback loops, resulting in an interruption of the body's smooth, self-regulating operation.

DISSOCIATIVE AMNESIA   A memory disruption in which the inability to recall important personal events and information is not due to organic causes.

DISSOCIATIVE DISORDER   Disorder characterized by a separation of one part of a person's memory or identity from another.

DISSOCIATIVE FUGUE   A psychologically caused disorder in which a person travels to a new location and may assume a new identity, simultaneously forgetting his or her past.

DISSOCIATIVE IDENTITY DISORDER (MULTIPLE PERSONALITY DISORDER)   A disorder in which a person displays two or more distinct personalities.

DIZYGOTIC TWINS   Twins who develop from separate eggs.

DOPAMINE   The neurotransmitter whose high activity has been shown to be related to schizophrenia.

DOPAMINE HYPOTHESIS   The theory that schizophrenia results from excessive firing of neurons that use the neurotransmitter dopamine and, hence, from their transmitting too many messages.

DOPPLER ULTRASOUND RECORDING DEVICE   A device that measures the blood flow in the penis.

DOUBLE-BIND COMMUNICATION   Simultaneous messages that are mutually contradictory.

DOUBLE-BIND HYPOTHESIS   A family systems theory that says some parents help cause schizophrenic symptoms in their children by repeatedly engaging in double-bind communications, thus placing the children in the dilemma of being unable to please them.

DOUBLE-BLIND DESIGN   Experimental procedure in which neither the subject nor the experimenter knows whether the subject has received the experimental treatment or a placebo.

DOUBLE DEPRESSION   A sequence in which dysthymic disorder leads to a major depressive disorder.

DOWN SYNDROME   A form of mental retardation related to a chromosomal abnormality.

DRUG ABUSE   The excessive intake of a substance that results in emotional, social, occupational, or functional impairment.

DRUG MAINTENANCE THERAPY An approach to treating substance abuse in which addicted clients are given legally and medically supervised doses of a substitute drug with which to satisfy their addiction.

DRUG THERAPY The use of psychotropic drugs to alleviate the symptoms of mental disorders.

DSM-IV (DIAGNOSTIC AND STATISTICAL MANUAL-IV) The current edition of a system for classifying psychological problems and disorders. Developed by the American Psychiatric Association, it is the most widely used system in the United States.

DURHAM TEST A legal test for determining the responsibility of a person committing a crime. It asks whether the unlawful act is a product of a mental disease or defect. This test was used only for a short period.

DYSLEXIA (READING DISORDER) A disorder characterized by a marked impairment in the ability to recognize words and to comprehend what one reads, not caused by visual or hearing defects, poor schooling, or intellectual deficit.

DYSPAREUNIA Pain in the genitals during sexual activity.

DYSSOMNIAS Sleep disorders in which the amount, quality, or timing of sleep is disturbed.

DYSTHYMIC DISORDER A mood disorder that is similar to but more chronic and less disabling than unipolar depression. Periods of normal mood, lasting only days or weeks, may occasionally interrupt the depressed mood.

DYSTONIA A Parkinsonian symptom in which involuntary muscle contractions cause bizarre and uncontrollable movements of the face, neck, tongue, and back.

ECHOLALIA A symptom of autism or schizophrenia in which a person responds to being spoken to by repeating some of the other person's words.

EDUCATIONAL PSYCHOLOGY A mental health specialty that focuses on behavior and problems particularly in educational settings.

EGO One of the three psychological forces proposed by Freud as central to shaping the personality. The ego operates in accordance with the reality principle, employing reason and deliberation to guide us in recognizing when the expression of id impulses would have negative consequences.

EGO DEFENSE MECHANISMS According to psychoanalytic theory, these are strategies developed by the ego to control unacceptable id impulses and to avoid or reduce the anxiety they arouse.

EGO-DYSTONIC HOMOSEXUALITY A past DSM category indicating a homosexual preference accompanied by extreme distress.

EGO IDEAL A composite image of the values one has acquired—the kind of person one believes in striving to become.

EGO PSYCHOLOGY A psychodynamic theory that focuses on the importance of the ego.

EGOISTIC SUICIDE Suicide committed by people over whom society has little or no control.

EIDETIC IMAGERY A strong visual image of an object or scene that persists in some persons long after the object or scene is removed.

EJACULATION Contractions of the muscles at the base of the penis that causes sperm to be ejected.

ELECTRA COMPLEX According to Freud, the pattern of desires all girls experience in which they develop a sexual attraction for their father, rooted in the fantasy that by seducing him they can have his penis.

ELECTROCONVULSIVE THERAPY (ECT) See **Bilateral ECT** and **Unilateral ECT.**

ELECTROENCEPHALOGRAPH (EEG) A device that records electrical impulses in the brain.

ELECTROMYOGRAPH (EMG) A device that provides feedback about the level of muscular tension in the body.

ELECTROOCULOGRAPH A device that records the movement of the eyes.

EMERGENCY COMMITMENT Temporary commitment to a mental hospital of a patient who is behaving in a bizarre or violent way. See also **Two-physician certificates.**

EMPLOYEE ASSISTANCE PROGRAMS Mental health programs a company offers its employees. They may be run either by mental health professionals employed directly by the company or by consulting mental health agencies.

ENCEPHALITIS An early-childhood disease that can sometimes cause serious brain damage if untreated.

ENCOPRESIS Childhood disorder characterized by repeated defecation in inappropriate places.

ENCOUNTER GROUP A small group guided by a leader through intensive experiences designed to develop participants' self-awareness and, as a consequence, their skills in human relationships.

ENDOGENOUS DEPRESSION A depression that develops without apparent antecedents and is assumed to be caused by internal factors.

ENDORPHIN A neurotransmitter that helps relieve pain and reduce emotional tension. Sometimes referred to as the body's own opioids.

ENKEPHALIN See **Endorphin.**

ENMESHED FAMILY PATTERN A family system in which members are overinvolved with each other's affairs and overconcerned about each other's welfare.

ENURESIS A pattern of repeated bedwetting or wetting of one's clothes.

EPIDEMIOLOGICAL STUDY (EPIDEMIOLOGY) An investigation that determines the incidence and prevalence of a disorder in a given population.

EPILEPSY A disorder of the brain characterized by seizures, alterations in consciousness, and impairment of sensory, mental, or motor skills.

EPINEPHRINE Hormone secreted by the medulla during emotional arousal.

EPISODIC MEMORY A person's autobiographical memory of personal experiences and other highly personal material.

ERECTILE FAILURE See **Male erectile disorder.**

ERGOT ALKALOID A naturally occurring compound from which LSD is derived.

EROGENOUS ZONES Body areas that Freud considered representative of the child's sexual drives and conflicts at each of the normal stages of development.

ESSENTIAL HYPERTENSION Chronic high blood

pressure brought about by a combination of psychological and physiological factors.

ESTROGEN   The primary female sex hormone.

ETHYL ALCOHOL   The chemical compound in all alcoholic beverages that is rapidly absorbed into the blood and immediately begins to affect the person's functioning.

EVOKED POTENTIAL   The brain response patterns recorded on an electroencephalograph.

EXHAUSTION STAGE   The failure of the parasympathetic nervous system to resist a sustained response of the sympathetic nervous system, leading to a breakdown in the control of the autonomic nervous system over the organs of the body. See also **General adaptation syndrome.**

EXHIBITIONISM   A disorder in which persons have sexually arousing fantasies, sexual urges, or behaviors involving the exposure of their genitals to an unsuspecting stranger, causing significant impairment or distress.

EXISTENTIAL ANXIETY   A pervasive fear of the limits and responsibilities of one's existence.

EXISTENTIAL MODEL   The theoretical perspective that human beings are born with the total freedom to either face up to one's existence and give meaning to one's life or to shrink from that responsibility.

EXISTENTIAL THERAPY   Like humanistic therapy, existential therapies emphasize the validity of the individual's phenomenological world and the importance of the here and now, but they also place great emphasis on making choices and on the relationship between therapist and client.

EXORCISM   The practice in early societies of treating abnormality by coaxing evil spirits to leave the person's body.

EXPERIMENT   A scientific procedure in which a situation is manipulated and the effect of the manipulation is observed.

EXPERIMENTAL GROUP   In an experiment, the group of subjects who are exposed to the independent variable.

EXPOSURE AND RESPONSE PREVENTION   A treatment for obsessive-compulsive disorder in which clients are exposed to anxiety arousing thoughts or situations and then prevented from performing their compulsive acts.

EXPOSURE TREATMENT   Behavioral approaches to treating simple phobias in which clients are exposed to the dreaded object or situation.

EXPRESSED EMOTION   The level of criticism, emotional overinvolvement, and hostility displayed in a family. High levels of expressed emotion in family members are thought to be associated with a poorer outcome for recovering individuals with schizophrenia.

EXTERNAL VALIDITY   The degree to which the results of a study may be generalized beyond the immediate investigation.

EXTINCTION   The decrease in responding that occurs when an unconditioned stimulus is no longer paired with the conditioned stimulus or when a response is no longer rewarded.

EXTRAPYRAMIDAL EFFECT   Unwanted movements, such as severe shaking, bizarre-looking contractions of the face and body, and extreme restlessness, induced by some antipsychotic drugs, resulting from the effect of certain drugs on the extrapyramidal areas of the brain.

FACILITATED COMMUNICATION   A method for teaching individuals with autism to communicate. The therapist or "facilitator" provides emotional and physical assistance as the individual types or points to letters on a keyboard or communication board.

FACTITIOUS DISORDER   An illness with no identifiable physical cause in which the patient is believed to be intentionally producing or feigning physical or psychological symptoms.

FAMILY PEDIGREE STUDY   The method used by biological researchers to see how many members of a given family have a particular disorder.

FAMILY SYSTEMS THEORY   An approach to human behavior that views the family as a system of interacting parts and proposes that members of a given family interact in consistent ways and operate by implicit rules.

FAMILY SYSTEMS THERAPY   A therapy format in which therapists meet with all members of a family, point out problematic behavior and interactions between the members, and help the whole family to change.

FANTASY   An ego defense mechanism in which a person uses imaginary events to satisfy unacceptable impulses.

FEAR   The central nervous system's physiological and emotional response to danger.

FEAR HIERARCHY   A list of the objects or situations that frighten a person, starting with those which are minimally feared and ending with those which are feared the most. Used in desensitization.

FEMALE ORGASMIC DISORDER (INHIBITED FEMALE ORGASM)   A woman's inability to reach orgasm despite adequate stimulation.

FETAL ALCOHOL SYNDROME   A cluster of problems in a child, including low birth weight, irregularities in the hands and face, and intellectual deficits, caused by excessive alcohol intake by its mother during gestation.

FETISHISM   A pattern characterized by recurrent sexual urges, sexually arousing fantasies, or behaviors that involve the use of nonliving objects, causing significant distress or impairment.

FIXATION   According to Freud, a condition in which the id, ego, and superego do not mature properly and are frozen at an early stage of development.

FLASHBACK   The recurrence of hallucinogen-induced sensory and emotional changes long after the drug has left the body. (Also called **hallucinogen-persisting perception disorder**). Or in posttraumatic stress disorder, the re-experiencing of past traumatic events.

FLAT AFFECT   A symptom of schizophrenia in which the person shows almost no emotions at all.

FLOODING   A treatment for phobias in which clients are exposed repeatedly and intensively to the feared object and made to see that it is actually quite harmless. See also **Implosive therapy.**

FOLIE À DEUX (SHARED PSYCHOTIC DISORDER)   A psychotic disorder in which a delusion is shared by two people.

FOREBRAIN   The top area of the brain, consisting of the cerebrum, thalamus, and hypothalamus.

FORENSIC SCIENCE   The study of legal issues relating to medicine or psychology.

FORMAL THOUGHT DISORDER A disturbance in the production and organization of thought.

FRAGILE X SYNDROME A chromosomal disorder characterized by moderate to severe degrees of mental handicap, language impairments, and behavioral problems.

FREE ASSOCIATION A psychodynamic technique in which the patient describes any thought, feeling, or image that comes to mind, even if it seems unimportant.

FREE-BASE A technique for ingesting cocaine in which the pure cocaine basic alkaloid is chemically separated from processed cocaine, vaporized by heat from a flame, and inhaled with a pipe.

FREE-FLOATING ANXIETY Chronic and persistent feelings of nervousness and agitation that are not clearly attached to a specific, identifiable threat.

FRONTAL LOBE The region of each cerebral hemisphere that governs motor function and abstract thinking.

FROTTEURISM A disorder in which recurrent and intense sexual urges, sexually arousing fantasies, or behaviors center on touching and rubbing against a nonconsenting person.

FUGUE See **Dissociative fugue.**

FUNCTIONAL AGE A measure that reflects three interrelated aspects of aging, the biological, the social, and the psychological.

FUNCTIONAL MENTAL DISORDERS Abnormal behavior patterns that have no clear link to physical abnormalities in the brain.

GABA The neurotransmitter gamma aminobutyric acid, whose low activity has been linked to generalized anxiety disorders.

GALVANIC SKIN RESPONSE (GSR) Changes in the electrical resistance of the skin.

GANJA A recreational drug of at least intermediate strength derived from varieties of the hemp plant.

GENDER IDENTITY DISORDER A disorder in which persons feel uncomfortable about their assigned sex and strongly wish to be a member of the opposite sex. They are often preoccupied with getting rid of their primary and secondary sex characteristics and many find their own genitals repugnant.

GENE A structure within the chromosome that carries a discrete piece of hereditary information.

GENERAL ADAPTATION SYNDROME A three-stage reaction to stress proposed by theorist Hans Selye to describe the relationship between stress and the autonomic nervous system.

GENERAL PARESIS An irreversible, progressive disorder with both physical and mental symptoms, including paralysis and delusions of grandeur.

GENERALIZED AMNESIA A disorder in which a person forgets both the period beginning with a traumatic event and all other events before the onset of this period.

GENERALIZED ANXIETY DISORDER A disorder characterized by general and persistent feelings of anxiety and worry about numerous events or activities.

GENETIC LINKAGE STUDY A research approach in which extended families with high rates of a disorder over several generations are observed in order to determine whether the disorder closely follows the distribution pattern of other family traits.

GENITAL STAGE In Freud's theory, the stage beginning at approximately 12 years old, when the child begins to find sexual pleasure in heterosexual relationships.

GERONTOLOGY The study of the physical, emotional, and psychological changes, as well as the disorders, that accompany old age.

GEROPSYCHOLOGY The field of psychology concerned with the mental health of elderly people.

GESTALT THERAPY A humanistic form of therapy developed by Fritz Perls in which therapists try to move their clients toward self-recognition and self-acceptance by frustrating and challenging them.

GLIA Brain cells that support the neurons.

GRIEF The reaction one experiences when a loved one is lost.

GROUP HOME Special homes where people with disorders or disabilities are taught self-help, living, and working skills.

GROUP THERAPY A therapeutic approach in which a group of people with similar problems meet together with a therapist and discuss the problems or concerns of one or more of the members. The therapist usually follows the principles of his or her preferred theoretical model in conducting the group.

GUIDED PARTICIPATION A modeling technique in which the therapist and client first construct a fear hierarchy and the client then observes and imitates the therapist, experiencing the least feared item in the hierarchy, a more feared item, and so on.

HABITUATION TRAINING A therapeutic technique in which a therapist tries to evoke a client's obsessive thoughts again and again with the expectation that the thoughts will eventually lose their threatening meaning and generate less anxiety.

HALCION (TRIAZOLAM) An antianxiety drug which is quickly metabolized in the body.

HALFWAY HOUSE A group home that has a live-in staff to offer support, guidance, and practical advice to residents.

HALLUCINATION The experiencing of imagined sights, sounds, or other sensory experiences as if they were real.

HALLUCINOGEN A substance that primarily causes changes in sensory perception.

HALLUCINOGEN PERSISTING PERCEPTION DISORDER (FLASHBACK) The recurrence of drug-induced sensory and emotional changes long after a hallucinogenic drug has left the body.

HALLUCINOSIS A state of perceptual distortion and hallucination.

HARDINESS A set of positive attitudes in response to stress that enable a person who has been exposed to life-threatening situations to carry on with a sense of fortitude, control, and commitment.

HASHISH The most powerful drug produced from varieties of the hemp plant.

Hebephrenic schizophrenia See **Disorganized schizophrenia.**

Helper T-cell A lymphocyte that identifies antigens and then both multiplies and triggers the production of other kinds of immune cells.

Helplessness See **Learned helplessness.**

Heroin A highly addictive substance derived from opium.

High The pleasant feeling of relaxation and euphoria that follows the rush from certain recreational drugs.

High-risk study A study in which people hypothesized to be at greater risk for developing a disorder are followed throughout their childhood and compared with controls who are considered not to be at risk.

Hindbrain The lower rearward portion of the brain comprised of the medulla, pons, and cerebellum.

Hippocampus Part of the limbic system located below the cerebral cortex that is involved in the memory system. Damage to this area can result in severe difficulties in receiving, storing, or remembering new information.

Histrionic personality disorder A personality disorder characterized by excessive emotionality and attention seeking.

Homeostasis A state in which the parts of a system interact in ways that enable the system to maintain itself and survive.

Homosexuality Sexual preference for a person of one's own gender.

Humanistic-existential model A theoretical point of view that stresses the role of values and choices in determining human individuality and fulfillment.

Humanistic-existential therapy A system of therapy that tries to help clients view themselves and their situations more accurately and acceptingly and move toward actualizing their full potential as human beings.

Humanistic model The theoretical perspective that human beings are born with a natural inclination to be friendly, cooperative, and constructive, and are driven to self-actualize.

Humanistic therapy A system of therapy that tries to help clients look at themselves accurately and acceptingly so that they can fulfill their inborn potential.

Huntington's disease An inherited progressive degenerative disease of cognition, emotion, and movement. Its onset, usually during the middle years, is later followed by dementia.

Hydrocephalus A disease characterized by an increase in cerebrospinal fluid and resultant head enlargement.

Hypertension Chronic high blood pressure.

Hypnosis A sleeplike, suggestible state during which a person can be directed to act in unusual ways, to experience unusual sensations, to remember seemingly forgotten events, or to forget remembered events.

Hypnotic amnesia A condition in which a person forgets facts, events, and even his or her identity in obedience to an instruction received under hypnosis.

Hypnotic therapy (hypnotherapy) A treatment for psychological problems, such as amnesia and fugue, in which the patient undergoes hypnosis and is then guided to recall forgotten events.

Hypnotism The inducing of a trancelike mental state in which a person becomes extremely suggestible.

Hypoactive sexual desire A lack of interest in sex.

Hypochondriasis A somatoform disorder in which people mistakenly and incessantly fear that minor fluctuations in their physical functioning indicate a serious disease.

Hypocyphilia A form of sexual masochism in which people strangle or smother themselves, or ask their partner to do this, in order to enhance their sexual pleasure.

Hypoglycemia A psychophysiological disorder characterized by a low level of serum glucose.

Hypomanic pattern A pattern in which a person experiences symptoms of mania, but the symptoms are less severe and cause less impairment than a manic episode.

Hypothalamus A part of the brain that helps maintain various bodily functions, including hunger and eating.

Hypothesis A tentative explanation advanced to provide a basis for an investigation.

Hysteria A term once used to describe what is now known as conversion disorder.

Hysterical disorder A somatoform disorder in which physical functioning is altered or lost.

Iatrogenic disorders Disorders that are unintentionally caused by practitioners.

Id One of the three psychological forces proposed by Freud as central to shaping personality; the id is the source of instinctual needs, drives, and impulses.

Identification The unconscious incorporation of parental values and feelings and fusing them with one's identity. Also an ego defense mechanism in which persons take on the values and feelings of the person who is causing them anxiety.

Idiographic understanding An understanding of the abnormal behavior of a particular individual.

Illogical thinking Habitual illogical ways of thinking that may lead to self-defeating and even pathological conclusions.

Imipramine A tricyclic drug that has been found to be effective in treating unipolar depression.

Immune system The sum of complex bodily systems that detect and destroy antigens.

Implosive therapy A treatment for phobias in which clients are exposed repeatedly to the feared object and made to see that such exposure is harmless. See also **Flooding.**

Imposter phenomenon A persistent feeling that one does not deserve one's success because it is based solely on hard work or manipulation of others rather than competence.

Impulse-control disorders Disorders in which people fail to resist an impulse, drive, or temptation to perform an act that is harmful to themselves or to others.

In vivo desensitization Desensitization training that makes use of actual physical situations, as opposed to imagined ones. See also **Covert desensitization.**

Inappropriate affect A symptom of schizophrenia

in which a person expresses emotions that are unsuited to the situation.

INCEST Sexual relations between close relatives.

INCIDENCE A statistical measure of the number of new cases of a problem or disorder that occur over a specific period of time.

INDEPENDENT VARIABLE The variable in an experiment that is manipulated to determine whether it has an effect on another variable that is held constant.

INDIVIDUAL THERAPY A therapeutic approach in which a therapist sees a client alone for sessions that may last from fifteen minutes to two hours.

INDOLEAMINE THEORY The view that unipolar depression is caused by deficiencies in the level of the neurotransmitter serotonin (an indoleamine).

INFORMED CONSENT A person's consent to participate in an experiment or procedure, given with full knowledge of the potential benefits and risks.

INHIBITED EJACULATION See **Inhibited male orgasm.**

INHIBITED POWER MOTIVE STYLE A personality style linked to a tendency to develop physical illness and characterized by a strong but inhibited need for power.

INSANITY DEFENSE A legal defense in which persons charged with a criminal offense claim to be not guilty by reason of insanity and try to show that, as a result of mental dysfunctioning, they were unable to appreciate the wrongfulness of their conduct at the time of their offense.

INSIGHT THERAPY Psychotherapeutic approach that helps the patient primarily achieve a greater understanding of his or her problem and key aspects of his or her functioning.

INSOMNIA The most common dyssomnia, characterized by difficulties initiating and maintaining sleep.

INSTRUMENTAL CONDITIONING See **Operant conditioning.**

INTEGRITY TEST A test that seeks to measure whether the test taker is generally honest or dishonest.

INTELLIGENCE QUOTIENT (IQ) A score derived from intelligence tests that is designed to represent a person's overall intellectual capacity.

INTELLIGENCE TEST A test designed to measure a person's intellectual ability.

INTERMITTENT EXPLOSIVE DISORDER An impulse-control disorder in which people periodically fail to resist aggressive impulses, leading to the performance of serious assaults on people or destruction of property.

INTERNAL VALIDITY The accuracy with which a study can pinpoint one out of various possible factors as being the cause of a phenomenon.

INTERPERSONAL PSYCHOTHERAPY (IPT) A treatment for unipolar patterns of depression. It is based on the premise that because depression occurs in an interpersonal context, clarifying and renegotiating that context is important to a person's recovery.

INTOXICATION A substance-induced state, or organic mental syndrome, in which a person exhibits impaired judgment, mood changes, irritability, slurred speech, and loss of coordination.

INTROJECTION The unconscious incorporation of parental values that leads to the development of the superego in the child. According to psychodynamic theory, people who have lost a loved one may introject, or fuse, their own identity with that of the person they have lost.

IRRESISTIBLE IMPULSE TEST A legal criterion for determining a person's responsibility for committing a crime. This test asks whether the person was unable to control his or her actions.

IRRITABLE BOWEL SYNDROME A psychophysiological disorder characterized by intermittent episodes of abdominal discomfort.

ISOLATION An ego defense mechanism in which people unconsciously isolate and disown undesirable and unwanted thoughts, experiencing them as foreign intrusions from undetermined parts of the mind. This mechanism has been invoked as an explanation of obsessive-compulsive disorder.

JUVENILE DELINQUENTS Term used to describe children between the ages of 8 and 18 who break the law.

KILLER T-CELL A lymphocyte that seeks out and destroys body cells that have been infected by viruses..

KLEPTOMANIA An impulse-control disorder characterized by the recurrent failure to resist impulses to steal objects not needed for personal use or monetary value.

KORO A pattern of anxiety found in Southeast Asia in which a man suddenly becomes intensely fearful that his penis will withdraw into his abdomen and that he will die as a result.

KORSAKOFF'S SYNDROME (ALCOHOL-INDUCED PERSISTING AMNESTIC DISORDER) An alcohol-related disorder marked by extreme confusion, memory impairment, and other neurological symptoms.

L-DOPA A precursor of dopamine, given to patients suffering from Parkinson's disease, a disease in which dopamine is low.

L-GLUTAMATE A common neurotransmitter that is depleted in the brains of Alzheimer's victims.

LATENCY STAGE In psychoanalytic theory, the stage children enter at 6 years of age in which their sexual desires apparently subside and their libidinal energy is devoted to developing new interests, activities, and skills.

LATENT CONTENT The symbolic meaning of a dream.

LATERAL HYPOTHALAMUS (LH) The region of the hypothalamus that produces hunger when activated.

LAW OF EFFECT The principle which states that when a response leads to a satisfying consequence, it is strengthened and is likely to be repeated.

LEARNED HELPLESSNESS The perception, based on subjective experience, that one has no control over one's reinforcements.

LEARNING DISABILITY A developmental disorder marked by impairments in cognitive skills such as reading, mathematics, or language.

LESION Localized damage to tissue.

Lethality scale A scale used by crisis prevention centers to estimate a caller's potential for suicide.

Leveled programs A token economy system that incorporates different levels of difficulty.

Libido In Freudian theory, the sexual energy that fuels the id and other forces of personality.

Life change units (LCUs) A system for measuring the stress associated with various life events.

Light therapy (phototherapy) A treatment for seasonal affective disorders in which patients are exposed to intense light for several hours.

Limbic system Region of the brain at the lower part of the cerebrum that controls bodily changes associated with emotions.

Lithium A metallic element that occurs in nature as a mineral salt and is the most effective antibipolar drug.

Lobotomy Psychosurgery that severs the connections between the cortex of the brain's frontal lobes and the lower centers of the brain.

Localized (circumscribed) amnesia In this, the most common form of dissociative amnesia, a person forgets all events that occurred over a limited period of time.

Logotherapy A treatment that focuses on changing clients' attitudes toward their existence. Developed by Viktor Frankl. See **Paradoxical intention.**

Long-term memory The memory system that contains all the information that we have stored over the years.

Longitudinal study An investigation in which the characteristics or behavior of the same subjects is observed on many different occasions over a long period of time.

Loose associations (Derailment) A common thought disorder of schizophrenia, characterized by rapid shifts from one topic of conversation to another.

LSD (lysergic acid diethylamide) A psychedelic drug derived from ergot alkaloids that brings on a state in which perceptions in general, but particularly visual perceptions, are intensified.

Luteinizing hormone The chemical produced by the pituitary gland that stimulates testosterone production.

Lycanthropy A condition in which a person believes himself or herself to be possessed by wolves or other animals.

Lymphocytes White blood cells that are manufactured in the lymph system and circulate throughout the bloodstream, helping the body overcome antigens.

M'Naghten rule A legal test for determining a person's responsibility for committing a crime. First used in the mid-nineteenth century, it is based on whether the person was able to determine right from wrong.

Magnetic resonance imaging (MRI) The use of the magnetic property of certain atoms in the brain to create a detailed picture of the brain's structure.

Mainstreaming An approach to educating mentally retarded persons in which retarded children are placed in regular classes with nonretarded children.

Major depressive episode A severe episode of depressed mood that is significantly disabling and is not caused by such factors as drugs or a general medical condition.

Male erectile disorder A dysfunction of the arousal phase of the sexual response cycle in men, characterized by a persistent or recurrent inability to attain an erection or to maintain an erection until completion of sexual activity.

Male orgasmic disorder (inhibited male orgasm) A man's inability to reach orgasm despite adequate stimulation.

Malingering Intentionally feigning illness to achieve some external gains, such as financial compensation or military deferment.

Mania A state or episode of euphoria, frenzied activity, or related episodes.

Manic-depressive disorder See **Bipolar disorder.**

Manifest content The consciously remembered features of a dream.

Mantra A sound, uttered or thought, used to focus one's attention to turn away from ordinary thoughts and concerns during meditation.

MAO inhibitor An antidepressant drug that inhibits the action of the enzyme monoamine oxidase.

Marijuana One of the drugs derived from the varieties of the hemp plant.

Marital schism A family situation in which the father and mother are in open conflict, with each trying to undercut the other in competition for the loyalty of the daughter. Some theorists believe this conflict can lead to schizophrenic behavior in the daughter.

Marital skew A family situation in which a so-called schizophrenogenic mother dominates the family, and the father keeps peace by continually yielding to her wishes. Some theorists believe this conflict can lead to schizophrenic behavior in the son.

Marital therapy A therapeutic approach in which the therapist works with two people who share a long-term relationship. It focuses on the structure and communication patterns in the relationship.

Masked depression A childhood depression disorder in which the child's primary depressive reaction appears to be hidden by other symptoms such as very active behavior, aggressiveness, psychophysiological problems, or delinquency behavior.

Masochism See **Sexual masochism.**

Masturbation Self-stimulation of the genitals to achieve sexual arousal.

Masturbatory satiation A behavioral treatment for fetishism in which a client masturbates for a prolonged period of time while fantasizing in detail about the fetishistic objects, with the expectation that the procedure will produce a feeling of boredom which in turn becomes associated with the fetishistic object.

Mean The average of a group of scores.

Medication-induced movement disorders Disturbing movement abnormalities that are sometimes a side effect of antipsychotic drugs. They include Parkinsonian symptoms, neuroleptic malignant syndrome, dystonia, akathisia, and tardive dyskinesia.

Meditation A technique of turning one's concentration

inward and achieving a seemingly altered state of consciousness. Often used to relieve emotional and physical stress.

MELANCHOLIA A condition described by early Greek and Roman philosophers and physicians as consisting of unshakable sadness. Today it is known as depression.

MELATONIN A hormone that appears to have a role in regulating mood. Melatonin is secreted when a person's surroundings are dark, but not when they are light.

MENINGITIS A childhood disease marked by inflammation of the meninges of the brain. It can lead to brain damage and mental retardation if not treated.

MENTAL AGE The age level at which a person performs on a test of intellectual skill, independent of his or her chronological age.

MENTAL RETARDATION A condition diagnosed when people manifest significant subaverage general intellectual functioning and display concurrent deficits or impairments in present adaptive functioning.

MENTAL STATUS EXAM A set of interview questions and observations designed to reveal the degree and nature of a client's abnormal functioning.

MENTALLY ILL CHEMICAL ABUSER (MICA) A person with a chronic mental disorder who also abuses alcohol or other drugs.

MESCALINE A psychedelic drug.

MESMERISM The method employed by Austrian physician F. A. Mesmer to treat hysterical disorder. It was a precursor to hypnotism.

METABOLISM The chemical and physical processes that go on in any living organism that break down food and convert it into energy. Also, the biochemical transformation of substances in the cells of living things, as when the liver breaks down alcohol into acetylaldehyde.

METACOMMUNICATION The context, tone, and gestures attached to any message. See also **Primary communication.**

METHADONE A laboratory-made drug substitute for heroin. See also **Drug maintenance therapy.**

MICROENCEPHALY A biological disorder characterized by a small, unusually shaped head, resulting from a combination of hereditary, prenatal, birth, and postnatal factors.

MIDBRAIN The middle region of the brain.

MIDDLE LIFE TRANSITION A period lasting from approximately ages 40 to 45 that bridges early and middle adulthood and may be characterized by significant changes in a person's life.

MIDLIFE CRISIS The tumultuous and painful feelings of anxiety and depression that sometimes accompany the changes associated with middle life transition.

MIGRAINE HEADACHE An extremely severe headache that occurs on one side of the head and is often immobilizing, often preceded by a warning sensation called an *aura.*

MILIEU THERAPY A humanistic approach to institutional treatment based on the premise that institutions help patients recover by creating a climate conducive to self-respect, individual responsibility, and meaningful activity.

MIND-BODY DUALISM The view that the mind is a separate entity from the body, totally unable to affect physical matter or somatic processes.

MINNESOTA MULTIPHASIC PERSONALITY IN- VENTORY (MMPI) A widely used personality inventory consisting of a large number of statements which subjects mark as being true or false for them.

MINOR TRANQUILIZERS See **Antianxiety drugs.**

MITRAL VALVE PROLAPSE (MVP) A cardiac malfunction marked by periodic episodes of heart palpitations.

MIXED DESIGN A research design in which correlation analysis is used in concert with other types of analyses. See also **Quasi-experiment.**

MODEL A set of concepts taken from one domain and applied analogously to another. It helps scientists explain and interpret observations. See also **Paradigm.**

MODELING A form of learning in which an individual acquires responses by observing and imitating others.

MONOAMINE OXIDASE (MAO) A body chemical that destroys the neurotransmitter norepinephrine.

MONOAMINE OXIDASE (MAO) INHIBITORS Antidepressant drugs that lower MAO activity and thus increase the level of norepinephrine activity in the brain.

MONOZYGOTIC TWINS Twins who have developed from a single egg.

MOOD DISORDER Disorder affecting one's emotional state, including depression and bipolar disorder.

MORAL ANXIETY According to Freud, anxiety that results from being punished or threatened for expressing id impulses, rather than following superego standards, so that a person eventually comes to perceive the id impulses themselves as threatening.

MORAL TREATMENT An approach to treating people with mental dysfunction that was originated by Phillippe Pinel and William Tuke in the early nineteenth century. It emphasized moral guidance, humane and respectful intervention, and kindness.

MORPHINE A substance derived from opium that is even more effective than opium in relieving pain.

MULTIAXIAL SYSTEM A classification system in which different "axes," or categories, represent different kinds of diagnostic information. DSM-IV is a multiaxial system.

MULTIDIMENSIONAL RISK PERSPECTIVE A theory about the causes of a disorder that identifies several different kinds of risk factors, such as sociocultural pressures, ego problems, cognitive disturbances, *and* biological factors.

MULTIPLE-BASELINE DESIGN An experimental design in which several behaviors of a single subject are measured and then the experimenter observes the effect that the manipulation of an independent variable has on each of the behaviors.

MULTIPLE PERSONALITY DISORDER (DISSOCIATIVE IDENTITY DISORDER) A dissociative disorder in which a person displays two or more distinct personalities.

MUNCHAUSEN SYNDROME A factitious disorder in which a person travels from hospital to hospital reciting symptoms, gaining admission, and receiving treatment.

MUSCLE-CONTRACTION HEADACHE A chronic headache caused by the contraction of muscles surrounding the skull.

NARCISSISTIC PERSONALITY DISORDER A personality disorder in which the person displays a chronic and pervasive pattern of grandiosity, need for admiration, and lack of empathy.

NARCOLEPSY   A dyssomnia characterized by sudden onsets of REM sleep during waking hours, generally brought on by strong emotion.

NARCOTIC   Any natural or synthetic derivative of opium.

NARCOTIC ANTAGONIST   A substance that counteracts the effects of opioids. See **Antagonist drug.**

NATURAL EXPERIMENT   An experiment in which nature rather than an experimenter manipulates an independent variable and the experimenter systematically observes the effects.

NATURALISTIC OBSERVATION (IN VIVO OBSERVATION)   A method for observing behavior in which clinicians or researchers observe clients or subjects in their everyday environment.

NEGATIVE CORRELATION   A statistical relationship in which the value of one variable increases while the other variable decreases.

NEGATIVE FEEDBACK LOOPS   A physiological process in which the brain receives information about external events from the environment, processes this information, and then stimulates body organs into action. Mechanisms in the organs then provide negative feedback, telling the brain that its stimulation has been sufficient and should now stop.

NEGATIVE SYMPTOMS (OF SCHIZOPHRENIA)   Symptoms that seem to reflect pathological deficits or characteristics that seem to be lacking—flat affect, poverty of speech, motor retardation, and loss of volition.

NEOLOGISM   A made-up word that has meaning only to the person using it.

NERVE ENDING   The region at the neuron's terminus from which an impulse that has traveled through the neuron is transmitted to a neighboring neuron.

NEUROFIBRILLARY TANGLES   Twisted protein fibers found within certain brain cells of people with Alzheimer's disease, interfering with memory and learning.

NEUROLEPTIC DRUG   See **Antipsychotic drugs.**

NEUROLEPTIC MALIGNANT SYNDROME   A severe, potentially fatal reaction to antipsychotic drugs, marked by muscle rigidity, fever, altered consciousness, and autonomic dysfunction.

NEUROLOGICAL   Relating to the structure or activity of the brain.

NEURON   A nerve cell. The brain contains billions of neurons.

NEUROPSYCHOLOGICAL TEST   A test that detects brain damage by measuring a person's cognitive, perceptual, and motor performances.

NEUROSIS   Freud's term for disorders characterized by intense anxiety, attributed to failure of a person's ego defense mechanisms to cope with his or her unconscious conflicts.

NEUROTIC ANXIETY   In Freudian theory, anxiety experienced by people who are repeatedly and excessively prevented, by their parents or by circumstances, from expressing their id impulses.

NEUROTRANSMITTER   A chemical that, released by one neuron, crosses the synaptic space to be received at receptors on the dendrites of adjacent neurons.

NEUTRALIZING   Efforts by persons to eliminate unwanted, intrusive thoughts by thinking or behaving in ways

that put matters right internally or that make amends for unacceptable thoughts.

NIGHTMARE DISORDER   A common parasomnia in which a person experiences chronic distressful, frightening dreams.

NOMOTHETIC UNDERSTANDING   A general truth about the nature, causes, and treatments of abnormality.

NONPURGING TYPE BULIMIA NERVOSA   A type of bulimia in which an individual displays compensatory behaviors other than self-induced vomiting or the misuse of laxatives, such as fasting or exercising frantically.

NOREPINEPHRINE   A neurotransmitter whose abnormal activity is linked to depression and panic disorder.

NORMALIZATION PROGRAM   A treatment program for mentally retarded persons that provides everyday conditions that closely resemble life in the mainstream of society.

NORMS   A given culture's explicit and implicit rules for appropriate conduct.

OBJECT LOSS   The loss of a significant person in one's life. According to psychodynamic theory, the risk of object loss during the oral stage (the loss of the mother who provides food and comfort) makes a child anxious and triggers defense mechanisms.

OBJECT RELATIONS THEORY   A psychodynamic theory that views the desire for relatedness with others (objects) as the motivating force in human behavior, focusing on the processes of attachment and separation.

OBSERVER DRIFT   The tendency of an observer who is rating subjects in an experiment to gradually and involuntarily change criteria, thus making the data unreliable.

OBSESSION   A persistent thought, impulse, or mental image that seems to invade a person's consciousness.

OBSESSIVE-COMPULSIVE DISORDER   A disorder in which a person has recurrent and unwanted thoughts or the need to perform repetitive and ritualistic actions, and the experience of intense anxiety whenever these behaviors are suppressed.

OBSESSIVE-COMPULSIVE PERSONALITY DISORDER   A personality disorder characterized by a pattern of preoccupation with orderliness, perfectionism, and mental and interpersonal control, at the expense of flexibility, openness, and efficiency.

OEDIPUS COMPLEX   In Freudian theory, the pattern of desires in which boys become attracted to their mother as a sexual object and see their father as a rival they would like to push aside.

ONYCHOPHAGIA   Compulsive nail-biting.

OPERANT CONDITIONING   The process of learning through reward.

OPERATIONALIZATION   The translating of an abstract variable of interest to an investigator into discrete, observable entities or events.

OPIOID   Opium or any of the drugs derived from opium, including morphine, heroin, and codeine.

OPIUM   A highly addictive substance made from the sap of the opium poppy seed. It has been widely used for thousands of years to reduce physical and emotional pain.

OPPONENT-PROCESS THEORY   An explanation for drug addiction based on the interplay of positive, pleasurable emotions that come from ingesting the drug and negative aftereffects that leave a person feeling even worse than usual.

OPPOSITIONAL DEFIANT DISORDER   A disorder in which children argue repeatedly with adults, lose their temper, and feel great anger and resentment.

ORAL STAGE   In this earliest developmental stage in Freud's conceptualization of psychosocial development, the infant's main libidinal gratification comes from feeding and from the body parts involved in it.

ORGANIC MENTAL DISORDERS   Mental disorders that have clear physical causes.

ORGANICITY   The quality of being caused primarily by damage to the brain or alterations in brain activity.

ORGASM   The third stage of the sexual response cycle, consisting of reflexive muscular contractions in the pelvic region.

ORGASM PHASE   The third phase in the sexual response cycle, characterized by reflexive muscular contractions in the pelvic region.

ORGASMIC REORIENTATION   A procedure for treating pedophilia or certain other paraphilias in which clients are conditioned to new, more appropriate sources of erotic stimuli.

OUTPATIENT   A setting for treatment in which persons visit a therapist's office as opposed to remaining in a hospital.

OVERT BEHAVIOR   Observable actions or clear verbalizations.

PAIN DISORDER   A somatoform disorder characterized by severe and prolonged pain in which psychological factors play a significant role in the onset, severity, exacerbation, or maintenance of the pain.

PANIC ATTACK   Periodic, discrete bouts of panic that occur abruptly and reach a peak within 10 minutes.

PANIC DISORDER   An anxiety disorder characterized by recurrent and unpredictable panic attacks that occur without apparent provocation.

PANIC DISORDER WITH AGORAPHOBIA   A panic disorder in which panic attacks lead to agoraphobic patterns of behavior.

PANIC DISORDER WITHOUT AGORAPHOBIA   A panic disorder in which agoraphobia is absent.

PARADIGM   An implicit theoretical framework that arises out of an explicit set of basic assumptions. A scientist's paradigm affects the way he or she interprets observations and other data.

PARADOXICAL INTENTION   A technique used in logotherapy in which the therapist employs direct and sometimes humorous confrontation to help clients embrace the very thoughts, fears, and behaviors that are causing problems for them.

PARANOIA   A psychosis characterized by delusions.

PARANOID DISORDER   See **Delusional disorder.**

PARANOID PERSONALITY DISORDER   A personality disorder characterized by a pattern of distrust and suspiciousness such that others' motives are interpreted as malevolent.

PARANOID SCHIZOPHRENIA   Schizophrenia characterized by an organized system of delusions and hallucinations that often guide the person's life.

PARAPHILIAS   Disorders in which the person has recurrent and intense sexual urges, sexually arousing fantasies, or behaviors involving either unusual objects, activities, or situations causing significant distress or impairment.

PARAPROFESSIONAL   A person without previous professional training who provides services under the supervision of a mental health professional.

PARASOMNIAS   Sleep disorders characterized by the occurrence of abnormal events during sleep.

PARASUICIDE   A person who attempts suicide and lives.

PARASYMPATHETIC NERVOUS SYSTEM   The group of nerve fibers of the autonomic nervous system that helps maintain normal organ functioning. It also slows organ functioning after stimulation and returns other body processes to normal.

PARENS PATRIAE   The principle by which the state can make decisions—such as to hospitalize a person against his or her wishes—that are believed to promote the individual's best interests and protect him or her from self-harm or neglect.

PARKINSON'S DISEASE   A slowly progressive neurological condition marked by tremors, rigidity, and unsteadiness that seems to be caused by decreased dopamine activity.

PARKINSONIAN SYMPTOM   Dystonia, akathisia, tardive dyskinesia, and other symptoms similar to those found in Parkinson's disease. Schizophrenic patients taking antipsychotic medication that blocks the activity of dopamine may display one or more of these symptoms.

PARTIAL REINFORCEMENT SCHEDULE   A token economy system in which people receive tokens only some of the times that they perform target behaviors. This is thought to encourage them to perform a behavior for its own sake.

PASSIVE-AGGRESSIVE PERSONALITY DISORDER   A personality disorder characterized by the need to control the lives of people close to oneself by indirect means. Because this problem may reflect a single trait rather than a pervasive personality disorder, the category was dropped from DSM-IV and designated for further study.

PATHOLOGICAL GAMBLING   An impulse-control disorder characterized by recurrent and persistent maladaptive gambling behavior that disrupts personal, family, or vocational pursuits.

PCP   Phencyclidine, a psychedelic drug.

PEDOPHILIA   A disorder in which a person experiences recurrent and intense sexual urges, sexually arousing fantasies, or behaviors involving sexual activity with a prepubescent child.

PEER REVIEW SYSTEM   A process in which a panel of clinicians reviews a therapist's reports of a client's treatment and recommends that insurance benefits be either continued or terminated.

PENILE PROSTHESIS   A surgical implantation consisting of a semirigid rod made of rubber and wire that produces an artificial erection.

PENIS ENVY   The Freudian theory that girls wish to overcome their feelings of inferiority during the phallic phase by having a penis.

PERFORMANCE ANXIETY The fear of performing inadequately and a consequent tension experienced during sex. See also **Spectator role.**

PERSEVERATION The persistent repetition of words and statements often seen in schizophrenia or autism.

PERSONALITY The unique pattern of behavior, perception, and emotion displayed by each individual.

PERSONALITY ASSESSMENT The gathering of information about the components of someone's personality and any unconscious conflicts he or she may be experiencing.

PERSONALITY DISORDER A disorder characterized by an enduring, pervasive, maladaptive, and inflexible pattern of inner experience and behavior that deviates markedly from the expectations of one's culture.

PERSONALITY INVENTORY A test designed to measure broad personality characteristics, consisting of statements about behaviors, beliefs, and feelings that people are asked to evaluate as characteristic or uncharacteristic of them.

PERSONALITY TEST A device, such as pencil-and-paper inventory, that is used to describe and measure aspects of a subject's personality.

PERSONALITY TRAIT An enduring consistency with which a person reacts to and acts upon his or her surroundings.

PERVASIVE DEVELOPMENTAL DISORDERS A broad category of disorders beginning in early childhood, characterized by severe and pervasive impairments in reciprocal social interaction skills, communication skills, or the presence of stereotyped behavior, interests, and activities.

PHALLIC STAGE In psychoanalytic theory, the period between the third and fourth years when the focus of sexual pleasure shifts to the genitals.

PHALLOPLASTY A procedure used during sex-reassignment surgery to create a functional penis.

PHARMACOTHERAPIST (PSYCHOPHARMACOLOGIST) A psychiatrist who primarily prescribes medications.

PHENOMENOLOGY One's personal experiences and perspectives of the world.

PHENOTHIAZINES A group of antihistamine drugs, originally prescribed for allergic reactions, that were found to be effective antipsychotic medications.

PHENYLETHYLAMINE TEST A biological assessment technique that indirectly measures the level of phenylethylamine, a chemical linked to depression, in the brain.

PHENYLKETONURIA (PKU) A metabolic disorder in which the body is unable to metabolize the amino acid phenylalanine into tyrosine. If untreated, the phenylalanine accumulates and is converted into substances that poison the system and cause retardation.

PHOBIA A persistent and irrational fear of a specific object, activity, or situation.

PHOTOTHERAPY See **Light therapy.**

PHYSOSTIGMINE A drug used to prevent the breakdown of acetylcholine in an effort to reduce the effects of Alzheimer's disease.

PICK'S DISEASE A degenerative disease of the brain that particularly affects the frontal and temporal lobes.

PLACEBO A sham treatment that the subject believes to be genuine.

PLAY THERAPY An approach to treating childhood disorders that helps children express their conflicts and feelings indirectly by drawing, playing with toys, and making up stories.

PLEASURE PRINCIPLE In Freudian theory, the pursuit of gratification that motivates the id.

PLETHYSMOGRAPH A device used to measure sexual arousal.

POLYGRAPH A test that seeks to determine whether or not the test taker is telling the truth by measuring physiological responses such as respiration level, perspiration level, and heart rate.

POLYSUBSTANCE USE The misuse of combinations of drugs to achieve a synergistic effect.

POSITIVE CORRELATION A statistical relationship in which the values of two variables increase together or decrease together.

POSITIVE SYMPTOMS (OF SCHIZOPHRENIA) Symptoms that seem to represent pathological excesses or bizarre additions to a normal repertoire of behavior. They include delusions, hallucinations, and positive formal thought disorders.

POSITRON EMISSION TOMOGRAPHY (PET SCAN) A computer-produced motion picture showing rates of metabolism throughout the brain.

POSTTRAUMATIC STRESS DISORDER An anxiety disorder in which fear and related symptoms continue to be experienced long after a traumatic event.

POVERTY OF CONTENT A lack of meaning in spite of high emotion that is often found in the speech of people with schizophrenia who display loose associations.

PREDISPOSITION An inborn or acquired vulnerability (or inclination or diathesis) for developing certain symptoms.

PREMATURE EJACULATION Ejaculation with minimal sexual stimulation or before, upon, or shortly after penetration and before the person wishes it.

PREMENSTRUAL DYSPHORIC DISORDER A pattern characterized by markedly depressed mood, anxiety, and marked mood changes, and a decreased interest in activities during the last week of the luteal phase. These symptoms remit within a few days after the onset of menses. This pattern is listed in the appendix of DSM-IV as a category provided for further study.

PREMORBID The period prior to the onset of an illness.

PREPAREDNESS A predisposition to acquire certain fears.

PRESENILE Occurring in middle age.

PRESENILE DEMENTIA Dementia occurring in middle age. See also **Dementia.**

PREVALENCE The total number of cases of a problem or disorder occurring in a population over a specific period of time.

PREVENTION A key aspect of community mental health programs, which strive to prevent or at least minimize mental disorders.

PRIMARY COMMUNICATION The semantic content in any message. See also **Metacommunication.**

PRIMARY GAIN In psychodynamic theory, part of a mechanism for explaining hysterical somatoform disorder. It is the goal achieved by hysterical symptoms of keeping internal conflicts out of awareness.

PRIMARY HYPERSOMNIA A sleep disorder in which the predominant problem is excessive sleepiness for at least a month, taking the form of prolonged sleep episodes or day-time sleep that occurs almost daily.

PRIMARY INSOMNIA A sleep disorder in which the predominant complaint is an inability to initiate or maintain sleep.

PRIMARY PERSONALITY The subpersonality that appears more often than the others in individuals with multiple personality disorder.

PRIMARY PROCESS In Freudian theory, a source of id gratification that consists of activating a memory or image of a desired object.

PRINCIPLE OF REINFORCEMENT B. F. Skinner's version of the law of effect, believed by him to be the primary mechanism for explaining and controlling human behavior.

PROBAND The person who is the focus of a genetic study.

PROCEDURAL MEMORY Memory of learned physical or cognitive skills we perform without needing to think about them. These memories are not directly accessible to consciousness.

PRODROMAL PHASE The period during which symptoms of schizophrenia are not yet prominent, but the person has begun to deteriorate from previous levels of functioning.

PROGNOSIS A prediction on the course and outcome of a disorder.

PROJECTION An ego defense mechanism in which a person attributes to others undesirable characteristics or impulses in himself or herself.

PROJECTIVE TEST A test that consists of unstructured or ambiguous material to which people are asked to respond.

PROLACTIN A pituitary hormone that can interfere with the sex drive.

PROPHYLACTIC DRUG A drug that actually helps prevent symptoms from developing.

PROSPECTIVE STUDY A study that predicts future changes on the basis of past and present events.

PROTECTION AND ADVOCACY SYSTEM The system by which lawyers and advocates who work for patients may investigate possible cases of patient abuse and neglect and then address any problems they find.

PROZAC (FLUOXETINE) A second-generation antidepressant that appears to have fewer undesired side effects than MAO inhibitors and tricyclics. It also appears to be an effective treatment for eating and obsessive-compulsive disorders.

PSILOCYBIN A psychedelic drug.

PSYCHEDELIC DRUG A substance, such as LSD, that causes profound perceptual changes.

PSYCHIATRIC SOCIAL WORKER A mental health specialist who is qualified to conduct psychotherapy upon earning a masters degree or doctorate in social work.

PSYCHIATRIST A physician who in addition to medical school has completed three to four years of residency training in the treatment of abnormal mental functioning.

PSYCHOANALYSIS Either the theory or the treatment of abnormal mental functioning that emphasizes unconscious conflicts as the cause of psychopathology.

PSYCHODRAMA A group therapy technique that calls for group members to act out dramatic roles as if they were participating in an improvised play in which they express their feelings and thoughts, explore new behaviors and attitudes, and empathize with the feelings and perspectives of others.

PSYCHODYNAMIC MODEL The theoretical perspective that sees all human functioning as being shaped by dynamic psychological forces and looks at people's unconscious internal conflicts in order to explain their behavior.

PSYCHODYNAMIC THEORY A system of therapy whose goals are to help clients uncover past traumatic events and the inner conflicts that have resulted from them; resolve, or settle, those conflicts; and resume interrupted personal development.

PSYCHOGENESIS The development of abnormal functioning from psychological causes.

PSYCHOGENIC ILLNESS An illness caused primarily by psychological factors such as worry, family stress, and unconscious needs.

PSYCHOLOGICAL AUTOPSY A procedure used to analyze information about a deceased person to determine whether the person's death was self inflicted.

PSYCHOLOGICAL REPORT A clinician's write-up of information collected and interpreted, creating a clinical picture framed in the language of the clinician's particular theoretical orientation.

PSYCHONEUROIMMUNOLOGY The study of the connections between stress, illness, and the body's immune system.

PSYCHOPATHOLOGY Any abnormal pattern of functioning that may be described as deviant, distressful, dysfunctional, or dangerous.

PSYCHOPATHY See **Antisocial personality disorder.**

PSYCHOPHARMACOLOGIST (PHARMACOTHERAPIST) A psychiatrist who primarily prescribes medications.

PSYCHOPHYSIOLOGICAL (PSYCHOSOMATIC) DISORDERS Illnesses believed to result from an interaction of organic and psychological factors. DSM-IV uses the label Psychological factors affecting medical condition.

PSYCHOPHYSIOLOGICAL TEST A test which measures physical responses (such as heart rate and muscle tension) as possible indicators of psychological problems.

PSYCHOSEXUAL STAGES The developmental stage defined by Freud in which the id, ego, and superego interact. Each stage is marked by a different source of libidinal pleasure.

PSYCHOSIS A state in which an individual loses contact with reality in key ways.

PSYCHOSOMATIC (PSYCHOPHYSIOLOGICAL) ILLNESSES Illnesses that have both psychological and physical causes. DSM-IV labels these illnesses Psychological factors affecting medical condition.

PSYCHOTHERAPY A treatment system in which words and acts are used by a client (patient) and therapist to overcome psychological difficulties.

PSYCHOTROPIC DRUGS Drugs that primarily affect the brain.

PUBOCOCCYGEAL (PC) MUSCLE The primary pelvic muscle in women, used during sexual activity.

PURGING TYPE BULIMIA NERVOSA A type of

bulimia in which an individual regularly induces vomiting or misuses laxatives or diuretics.

PYROMANIA An impulse-control disorder characterized by a pattern of fire setting for pleasure, gratification, or relief from tension.

Q-SORT A widely used self-report instrument in which subjects are given a set of cards containing statements about personality or performance and are asked to sort them into piles describing different aspects of themselves.

QUASI-EXPERIMENT An experiment in which investigators do not randomly assign the subjects to control and experimental groups but instead make use of groups that already exist in the world at large.

QUININE A drug that is often added to heroin to counteract the dangers of infection.

RANDOM ASSIGNMENT A testing condition in which subjects are randomly placed either in the control group or in the experimental group in order to reduce the possibility that preexisting differences between the groups are influencing the results.

RAPE Forced sexual intercourse against the will of the victim.

RAPID EYE MOVEMENT (REM) SLEEP The period of the sleep cycle during which the eyes move quickly, back and forth, indicating that the person is dreaming.

RAPPROCHEMENT An effort to delineate a set of "common therapeutic strategies" that characterize the work of all effective therapists.

RATIONAL EMOTIVE THERAPY A therapeutic technique developed by Albert Ellis that helps clients to discover the irrational assumptions governing their emotional responses and to change those assumptions into constructive ways of viewing the world and themselves.

RATIONALIZATION An ego defense mechanism in which one creates acceptable reasons for unwanted or undesirable behavior.

REACTION FORMATION An ego defense mechanism in which a repressed desire is instead expressed by opposite personality traits (such as when a desire to be messy and rebellious is repressed and expressed as neatness and conformity).

REACTIVE DEPRESSION A depression that appears to follow on the heels of clear-cut precipitating events.

REACTIVITY The extent to which the very presence of an observer affects a person's behavior.

REALITY PRINCIPLE In Freudian theory, the knowledge we acquire through experience and from the people around us that it can be dangerous or unacceptable to express our id impulses outright.

RECEPTOR A site on a neuron that receives a neurotransmitter.

RECIPROCAL INHIBITION A desensitization process in which a fear response is stopped by pairing fear-arousing stimuli with responses (such as relaxation) that are incompatible with fear.

REFLEX GRATIFICATION In Freudian theory, a direct source of id gratification, as when an infant seeks and receives milk from the mother's breast to satisfy its hunger.

REGRESSION An ego defense mechanism in which a person returns to a more primitive mode of interacting with the world.

REINFORCEMENT The desirable or undesirable stimuli that follows as a result of an organism's behavior.

RELAPSE-PREVENTION TRAINING A treatment technique in which heavy drinkers are taught to use self-monitoring to identify the situations and emotional changes that place them at high risk for heavy drinking.

RELAXATION TRAINING A procedure in which clients are taught to release all the tension in their bodies on cue.

RELIABILITY A measure of the consistency of test or research results.

REPRESSION An ego defense mechanism that prevents unacceptable impulses from reaching consciousness.

RESERPINE A drug originally used to treat high blood pressure but later discovered to cause depression in some people.

RESIDENTIAL TREATMENT CENTER A place where former drug addicts live, work, and socialize in a drug-free environment. Also called therapeutic communities.

RESIDUAL SCHIZOPHRENIA A condition in which the florid symptoms of schizophrenia have lessened in intensity and number yet remain with the patient in a residual form.

RESISTANCE An ego defense mechanism that blocks a patient's free associations or causes the patient to change subjects to avoid a potentially painful discussion.

RESISTANCE STAGE The parasympathetic nervous system's attempt to counteract the response of the sympathetic nervous system in the presence of a threat. See also **General adaptation syndrome.**

RESOLUTION PHASE The fourth phase in the sexual response cycle, characterized by relaxation and a decline in arousal following orgasm.

RESPONDENT CONDITIONING See **Classical conditioning.**

RESPONSE PREVENTION See **Exposure and response prevention.**

RESPONSE SET A particular way of responding to questions or statements on a test, such as always selecting "true," regardless of the content of the questions.

RESTRICTING TYPE ANOREXIA NERVOSA A type of anorexia nervosa in which people reduce their weight by restricting their food intake.

RESTRICTION FRAGMENT-LENGTH POLYMORPHISM (RFLP) A technique used in chromosomal mapping in which gene segments from members of a family are compared in order to locate the gene responsible for an inherited disorder, such as schizophrenia.

RETICULAR FORMATION The body's arousal center located in the brain.

RETROGRADE AMNESIA A lack of memory about events that occurred before the event that caused the amnesia.

RETROSPECTIVE STUDY (1) A kind of psychological autopsy in which clinicians and researchers piece together data from the past. This type of study is common for studying the past of a person who committed suicide. (2) Also, a kind of research study in which subjects are asked to recall past events.

REVEALED DIFFERENCES APPROACH A technique

for investigating familial influences in which parents and their children are brought together by an investigator and told to reach an agreement on issues about which they disagree.

REVERSAL DESIGN (ABAB) An experimental design in which behavior is measured to achieve a baseline (A), then again after the treatment has been applied (B), then again after the conditions during baseline have been reintroduced (A), and then once again after the treatment is reintroduced (B).

REWARD A pleasurable stimulus given to an organism to encourage a specific behavior.

RISK STUDY A research method that surveys the biological relatives of a patient who has been diagnosed with a specific abnormality to see which and how many of them have the same disorder.

ROLE PLAY A therapy technique in which clients are instructed to act out roles assigned to them by the therapist.

RORSCHACH TEST A projective test using a subject's reactions to inkblots to help reveal psychological features of the subject.

ROSENTHAL EFFECT The general finding that the results of any experiment often conform to the expectations of the experimenter. It is attributed to the inescapable effects of bias.

RUMINATIVE RESPONSE Dwelling intently on one's depressive symptoms.

RUSH A spasm of warmth and ecstasy that occurs when certain drugs, such as heroin, are ingested.

SADISM Sexual pleasure achieved through inflicting physical or emotional pain.

SAMPLE A group of subjects that is representative of the larger population about which a researcher wishes to make a statement.

SAVANT A person with a major mental disorder or intellectual handicap who has some extraordinary ability despite his or her handicaps.

SCHIZOAFFECTIVE DISORDER A disorder in which symptoms of both schizophrenia and a mood disorder are prominent.

SCHIZOID PERSONALITY DISORDER A personality disorder characterized by a pattern of detachment from social relationships and a restricted range of emotional expression.

SCHIZOPHRENIA A psychotic disorder lasting for at least six months in which personal, social, and occupational functioning that were previously adaptive deteriorate as a result of distorted perceptions, disturbed thought processes, deviant emotional states, and motor abnormalities.

SCHIZOPHRENIFORM DISORDER A disorder in which all of the key features of schizophrenia are present but last between one and six months.

SCHIZOPHRENOGENIC MOTHER A mother who is supposedly cold, domineering, and impervious to the needs of others. It has been suggested by some theorists that this type of behavior in the mother may be associated with schizophrenia in the child.

SCHIZOTYPAL PERSONALITY DISORDER A personality disorder characterized by a pattern of acute discomfort in close relationships, cognitive or perceptual distortions, and eccentricities of behavior.

SCHOOL PHOBIA A childhood anxiety disorder in which children experience extreme anxiety about attending school and often stay home for an extended period of time.

SCHOOL REFUSAL See **School phobia.**

SCIENTIFIC METHOD The process of systematically acquiring and evaluating information through observation to gain an understanding of specific phenomena.

SEASONAL AFFECTIVE DISORDER (SAD) A mood disorder in which mood episodes are related to changes in season. It appears to be related to shifts in the overall amount of light one is exposed to, and correspondingly, to shifts in melatonin secretions.

SECOND-GENERATION ANTIDEPRESSANTS New antidepressant drugs that differ structurally from tricyclics and MAO inhibitors.

SECONDARY GAIN In psychodynamic theory, part of a mechanism for explaining hysterical somatoform disorder. Hysterical symptoms not only keep internal conflicts out of awareness (primary gain) but also result in the person's receiving kindness or sympathy from others (secondary gain).

SECONDARY PROCESS In Freudian theory, the ego's mode of operation, consisting of assessing new situations, weighing in past experiences, anticipating consequences, and planning how best to obtain gratification.

SEDATIVE-HYPNOTIC DRUG A drug used in low doses to reduce anxiety and in high doses to help people sleep.

SELECTIVE SEROTONIN REUPTAKE INHIBITORS (SSRI) A group of second-generation antidepressant drugs (including fluoxetine, paroxetine, and setraline) that are thought to alter serotonin activity specifically, without affecting other neurotransmitters or biochemical processes.

SELECTIVE AMNESIA A disorder in which the person remembers some but not all events occurring over a circumscribed period of time.

SELF-ACTUALIZATION The humanistic process by which people fulfill their potential for goodness and growth.

SELF-DEFEATING PERSONALITY DISORDER According to DSM-IIIR, a personality disorder characterized by a sense of martyrdom and by behavior that is self-effacing and servile. Not included in DSM-IV.

SELF-EFFICACY The judgment that one can master and perform needed behaviors whenever necessary.

SELF-HELP GROUP (MUTUAL HELP GROUP) A therapy group made up of people who have similar problems and come together to help and support one another without the direct leadership of a professional clinician.

SELF-HYPNOSIS The induction by oneself of a hypnotic state.

SELF-INSTRUCTION TRAINING A cognitive therapy that helps people solve problems and cope with stress by teaching them how to make helpful statements to themselves and how to apply such statements in difficult circumstances.

SELF-MONITORING A technique for monitoring behavior in which clients observe themselves.

SELF PSYCHOLOGY A variation of psychoanalysis developed by Heinz Kohut that focuses on a person's self-worth.

SELF-REPORT INVENTORY A test consisting of lists of

items that people are asked to evaluate as characteristic or uncharacteristic of them.

Self-statement   A statement about oneself, sometimes counterproductive, that comes to mind during stressful situations.

Semantic memory   A person's memory for abstract, encyclopedic, or categorical information.

Senile   Typical of or occurring in people over the age of 65.

Senile dementia   See **Dementia.**

Senile plaques   Sphere-shaped deposits of beta-amyloid protein that form in the spaces between certain neurons in people with Alzheimer's disease, interfering with memory and learning.

Sensate focus   A treatment for sexual disorders that instructs couples to take the focus away from intercourse and instead spend time concentrating on mutual massage, kissing, and hugging. This approach reduces the pressure to achieve erection and orgasm.

Sensitivity training group   A small group in which a "trainer," or leader, helps participants to observe and think about their own interactions and, as a result, to develop greater insight about and skill in human communications and relationships.

Sensory blunting   A significant reduction in the strength of one's physical sensations.

Separation anxiety disorder   A childhood disorder characterized by excessive anxiety, even panic, whenever the child is separated from a parent.

Serotonin   A neurotransmitter whose abnormal activity is linked to depression, eating disorders, and obsessive-compulsive disorder.

Sex offender statute   The presumption by legislators that people who are repeatedly found guilty of certain sex crimes are mentally ill and should be categorized as "mentally disordered sex offenders."

Sexual arousal disorder   A failure of lubrication or genital swelling in women or an absence of penile erection in men, or the lack of a subjective sense of sexual excitement and pleasure in either men or women.

Sexual aversion disorder   A disorder characterized by the aversion to and active avoidance of genital sexual contact with a sexual partner.

Sexual dysfunction   A disorder in which a person is unable to function normally in some area of the human sexual response cycle.

Sexual masochism   A pattern in which a person has repeated and intense sexual urges, fantasies, or behaviors that involve being humiliated, beaten, bound, or otherwise made to suffer.

Sexual pain disorder   A dysfunction in which a person experiences pain during arousal or intercourse. See also **Dyspareunia** and **Vaginismus.**

Sexual response cycle   The generalized sequence of behavior and feelings that occur during sexual intercourse, consisting of desire, arousal, orgasm, and resolution.

Sexual sadism   A pattern in which a person, usually a male, has repeated and intense sexual urges, fantasies, or behaviors that involve inflicting physical or psychological suffering on others.

Shaping   A learning procedure in which successive approximations of the desired behavior are rewarded.

Shared psychotic disorder (folie à deux)   A disorder in which a person embraces delusions held by another individual.

Sheltered workshop   A protected and supervised workplace that offers clients occupational training.

Short-term memory   The memory system that collects new information and then does the initial cognitive work of evaluating, processing, and either storing or disregarding it.

Shuttle box   A box partitioned by a barrier that an animal can jump over in order to escape or avoid shock. Used in learned helplessness studies.

Single-subject experimental design   A research method in which a single subject is observed and measured both before and after the manipulation of an independent variable.

Situation (or state) anxiety   Anxiety experienced in particular situations or environments.

Sleep apnea   A disorder in which the person actually stops breathing for up to thirty or more seconds while asleep.

Sleep terror disorder   A parasomnia in which persons awaken suddenly during the first third of their major sleep episode, screaming out in extreme fear and agitation.

Sleepwalking disorder   A parasomnia in which people repeatedly leave their beds and walk around without being conscious of the episode or remembering it later.

Social breakdown syndrome   A pattern of deterioration resulting from institutionalization and characterized by extreme withdrawal, anger, physical aggressiveness, and loss of interest in personal appearance.

Social phobia   A persistent fear of social or performance situations in which embarrassment may occur.

Social skills training   A therapeutic approach used by behavioral therapists to help people acquire or improve their social skills and assertiveness through the use of role playing and rehearsing of desirable behaviors.

Social therapy (Sociotherapy)   An approach to therapy in which the therapist makes practical advice and life adjustment a central focus of treatment for schizophrenia.

Sociocultural model   The theoretical perspective that emphasizes the effect of society and culture on individual behavior.

Sociology   The study of human relationships and social groups.

Sociopathy   See **Antisocial personality disorder.**

Sociotherapy   See **Social therapy.**

Sodium amobarbital (Amytal)   A drug used to put people into a near-sleep state during which they may recall forgotten events.

Sodium pentobarbital (Pentothal)   See **Sodium amobarbital.**

Somatization disorder   A somatoform disorder characterized by numerous physical ailments without an organic basis and whose difficulties continue for several years.

Somatoform disorder   A physical illness or ailment

that is not fully explained by a general medical condition, the direct effects of a substance, or another mental disorder. It differs from a factitious disorder in that the patient experiences no sense of willing the symptoms or of having control over them.

SOMATOGENESIS The development of abnormal functioning from physical causes.

SPECIFIC PHOBIA An intense and persistent fear of a clearly discernable, circumscribed object or situation (excluding social phobia and agoraphobia).

SPECTATOR ROLE A psychological position that some people take during sex in which their focus on their sexual performance is so pronounced that the sexual performance and enjoyment are impeded.

STANDARDIZATION The process in which a test is administered to a large group of subjects whose performance then serves as a common standard or norm.

STATE DEPENDENT LEARNING Learning that becomes associated with conditions in which it occurred, so that it is best remembered under the same conditions. For example, information learned when under the influence of alcohol is better recalled when the person is again under the influence of alcohol.

STATE HOSPITAL A public mental institution, run by the state.

STATISTICAL ANALYSIS The application of principles of probability to the findings of a study in order to learn how likely it is that the findings have occurred by chance.

STATISTICAL SIGNIFICANCE A measure of the probability that an observed event occurred by chance rather than as the result of a particular relationship or an experimental manipulation.

STATUTORY RAPE Sexual intercourse with a minor, under any condition.

STIMULANT DRUG A drug that induces physical agitation by increasing the activity of the nervous system.

STIMULUS GENERALIZATION A phenomenon in which responses to one stimulus are also elicited by similar stimuli.

STRESS INOCULATION See **Self-instruction training.**

STRESS MANAGEMENT TRAINING An approach to treating generalized and other anxiety problems that focuses on teaching clients to reduce and control stress.

STRESSOR An event that creates a degree of threat by confronting a person with a demand or opportunity for change of some kind.

STRUCTURAL FAMILY THERAPY A family systems treatment approach in which the therapist pays particular attention to the family power structure, the role each member plays within the family, and the alliances between family members.

STRUCTURED INTERVIEW An interview format in which clinicians ask prepared questions.

STRUCTURED OBSERVATION A method of observing behavior in which people are monitored in artificial settings created in clinicians' offices or in laboratories.

STUTTER A disturbance in the normal fluency and time patterning of speech, characterized by repeating words or sounds, prolonging or interjecting sounds, pausing within a word, or blocking sounds.

SUBINTENTIONED DEATH A death in which the victim plays an indirect, covert, partial, or unconscious causal role.

SUBJECT An individual chosen to participate in a study.

SUBLIMATION In psychoanalytic theory, the rechanneling of narcissistic impulses into endeavors that are both socially acceptable and personally gratifying. It can also be used as an ego defense mechanism.

SUBPERSONALITIES The distinct personalities found in individuals suffering from multiple personality disorder, each with a unique set of memories, behaviors, thoughts, and emotions.

SUBSTANCE ABUSE A pattern of behavior in which a person relies on a substance excessively and chronically, allowing it to occupy a central position in his or her life.

SUBSTANCE DEPENDENCE A pattern of behavior in which a person relies on a substance excessively and chronically, usually resulting in tolerance to the substance, or withdrawal symptoms upon cessation, or both.

SUBSTANCE-RELATED DISORDER A pattern of maladaptive behavior centered around the use of, abuse of, or dependence on certain substances.

SUDDEN DEATH Unexpected death in the wake of psychological trauma.

SUICIDE A self-inflicted death in which the person acted intentionally, directly, and consciously.

SUICIDE PREVENTION PROGRAMS Programs found in many hospitals and counseling centers that try to identify people who are at the point of killing themselves and to help them perceive their situation more accurately and constructively in order to overcome the crisis.

SUPEREGO One of the three psychological forces proposed by Freud as central to shaping the personality. The superego emerges from the ego and embodies the values and ideals taught to us by our parents.

SUPPORT GROUP A therapy-like group of people with a common psychological problem who meet and work on their difficulties together.

SUPPORTIVE NURSING CARE A treatment, applied to anorexia nervosa in particular, in which well-trained nurses conduct a day-to-day hospital program.

SYMBOLIC LOSS A Freudian concept developed to explain depression in cases where the person has not lost a loved one. In symbolic loss any valued lost object (for example, a loss of employment) may be unconsciously interpreted as the loss of a loved one.

SYMPATHETIC NERVOUS SYSTEM The nerve fibers of the autonomic nervous system that quicken the heartbeat and produce other changes experienced as fear or anxiety.

SYMPTOM A physical or psychological sign of a disorder.

SYMPTOM SUBSTITUTION The belief held by some psychodynamic therapists that quick symptom reduction is likely to result in the replacement of the old symptoms by new ones.

SYNAPSE The tiny space into which neurotransmitters are released, between the nerve ending of one neuron and the dendrite of another.

SYNDROME A cluster of symptoms that usually occur together.

SYNERGISTIC EFFECT An enhancement of effects that

occurs when more than one drug is having an effect on the body at any one time.

SYNESTHESIA   A crossing over of sensory perceptions, caused by LSD and other psychedelic drugs. For example, a loud sound may be experienced as visible fluctuation in the air.

SYSTEMATIC DESENSITIZATION   A process in which phobic clients learn to react calmly instead of with intense fear to the objects or situations they dread.

T-GROUP   A small group guided by a leader and similar to an encounter group in intensity but concerned primarily with educating people.

TARANTISM   Also known as St. Vitus's dance, this was a phenomenon that occurred throughout Europe between A.D. 900 and 1800 in which groups of people would suddenly start to jump around, dance, and go into convulsions.

TARDIVE DYSKINESIA   Extrapyramidal effects, such as involuntary smacking of the lips or wagging of the chin, that appear in some patients after they have taken antipsychotic drugs for a few years. It is more common in older patients, and it is sometimes difficult or impossible to eliminate. See also **Extrapyramidal effects.**

TAY-SACHS DISEASE   A metabolic disorder resulting from a pairing of recessive genes that causes mental deterioration, loss of visual functioning, and death.

TENSION HEADACHE   See **Muscle-contraction headache.**

TESTOSTERONE   The principal male sex hormone.

TETRAHYDROCANNABINOL (THC)   The main psychoactive ingredient of the hemp plant.

THALAMUS   The region of the brain that acts as a relay station for sensory information, sending it to the cerebrum.

THANATOS   According to the Freudian view, thanatos is the basic death instinct that functions in opposition to the life instinct.

THEMATIC APPERCEPTION TEST   A projective test using pictures that depict people in somewhat unclear situations.

THERAPIST   A person who implements a system of therapy to help a person overcome psychological difficulties.

THERAPY   Special, systematic process for helping people overcome their psychological difficulties. The process may consist primarily of discussion or action (psychotherapy) or of biological intervention.

THOUGHT STOPPING   A cognitive-behavioral technique for treating obsessions in which therapists teach clients to interrupt their obsessive thoughts, based on the assumption that doing so will keep them from occurring so often.

TOKEN ECONOMY   A program in which a person's desirable behavior is reinforced systematically throughout the day by the awarding of tokens that can be exchanged for goods or privileges.

TOLERANCE   The adjustment the body makes to the habitual presence of certain drugs so that larger and larger doses are required to achieve the initial effect.

TRAIT   A characteristic of an individual that may be observed and measured.

TRAIT ANXIETY   A person's general level of anxiety.

TRANQUILIZER   A drug that reduces anxiety.

TRANSFERENCE   According to psychodynamic theorists, a phenomenon that occurs during psychotherapy, in which the patient acts toward the therapist as he or she did or does toward important figures, particularly parents.

TRANSSEXUALISM   A disorder in which a person feels uncomfortable about his or her assigned sex and strongly wishes to be a member of the opposite sex. They are often preoccupied with getting rid of their primary and secondary sex characteristics and many find their own genitals repugnant.

TRANSVESTIC FETISHISM (TRANSVESTISM, OR CROSS-DRESSING)   A pattern in which a person has recurrent and intense sexual urges, sexually arousing fantasies, or behaviors involving dressing in clothes of the opposite sex, causing significant distress or impairment.

TREPHINATION   An ancient operation in which a stone instrument was used to cut away a circular section of the skull. It is believed to have been a Stone Age treatment for abnormal behavior.

TRICHOTILLOMANIA   An extremely painful and upsetting compulsion in which people repeatedly pull at and even yank out their hair, eyelashes, and eyebrows.

TRICYCLIC DRUG   An antidepressant drug such as imipramine that has three rings in its molecular structure.

TRISOMY   Three chromosomes of one kind rather than the usual two.

TUBE AND INTRAVENOUS FEEDING   Forced nourishment sometimes provided to sufferers of anorexia nervosa when their condition becomes life-threatening.

TWO-PHYSICIAN CERTIFICATES (2 PCs)   A method of emergency involuntary commitment used in some states, marked by certification by two physicians that a person is in such a state of mind as to be dangerous to himself or herself or to others and may be committed involuntarily.

TYPE A PERSONALITY STYLE   A personality pattern characterized by hostility, cynicism, drivenness, impatience, competitiveness, and ambition.

TYPE I SCHIZOPHRENIA   Schizophrenia that is dominated by positive symptoms, such as delusions, hallucinations, and positive formal thought disorders.

TYPE II SCHIZOPHRENIA   Schizophrenia that is dominated by negative symptoms, such as flat affect, poverty of speech, and loss of volition.

TYRAMINE   A chemical that, if allowed to accumulate, can raise blood pressure dangerously. It is found in many common foods and is broken down by MAO. See also **MAO inhibitor.**

TYROSINE   The chemical that most people produce by metabolizing the amino acid phenylalanine, a process that fails to occur in children with phenylketonuria.

ULCER   Lesions or holes that form in the wall of the stomach or of the duodenum.

UNCONDITIONAL POSITIVE REGARD   Full, warm acceptance of a person regardless of what he or she says, thinks, or feels; a critical component of client-centered therapy.

UNCONDITIONED RESPONSE (UCR)   The natural, automatic response elicited by an unconditioned stimulus.

Unconditioned stimulus (UCS)   A stimulus that elicits an automatic, natural response.

Unconscious   The deeply hidden mass of memories, experiences, and impulses that is viewed in Freudian theory as the wellspring of most behavior.

Undifferentiated schizophrenia   A diagnosis assigned to people who are considered schizophrenic but who do not fall neatly into one of the categories of schizophrenia.

Undoing   An ego defense mechanism in which a person attempts to atone for an unacceptable desire or act by another act. This concept is sometimes used by some psychodynamic theorists to explain obsessive-compulsive disorder. The compulsive act is thought to implicitly cancel out the person's undesirable impulses.

Unilateral electroconvulsive therapy (ECT)   A form of electroconvulsive therapy in which electrodes are attached to only one side of the head and electrical current passes through only one side of the brain. Unilateral ECT causes less confusion and memory loss than bilateral ECT and is equally effective.

Unipolar depression   Depression without a history of mania which is followed, upon recovery, by a normal or nearly normal mood.

Unstructured interview   An interview format in which the clinician asks questions spontaneously, based on issues that emerge during the interview.

Vacuum erection device (VED)   A device consisting of a hollow cylinder that is placed over the penis connected to a hand pump. The pump is used to create a partial vacuum around the penis, which fills with blood as a result and becomes erect.

Vaginismus   A condition marked by involuntary contractions of the muscles around the outer third of the vagina when penetration is attempted, preventing entry of the penis.

Validity   The accuracy of a test's or study's results; that is, the extent to which the test or study actually measures or shows what it claims to. See also **External validity** and **Internal validity.**

Valium (diazepam)   A minor tranquilizer.

Variable   Any characteristic or event that can vary, whether from time to time, from place to place, or from person to person.

Vascular dementia   Dementia caused by cerebrovascular accident or stroke that restricted the blood flow to certain areas of the brain.

Ventromedial hypothalamus (VMH)   The region of the hypothalamus that when activated depresses hunger.

Vicarious conditioning   Acquiring fear or other reactions through modeling.

Visual hallucinations   Hallucinations in which a person may either experience vague perceptions, perhaps of colors or clouds, or have distinct visions of people, objects, or scenes that are not there.

Voyeurism   A disorder in which a person has recurrent and intense sexual desires to observe people in secret as they undress or to spy on couples engaged in intercourse.

Waxy flexibility   A catatonia in which a person will maintain a posture into which he or she has been placed by someone else.

Weight set point   The weight level that a person is predisposed to maintain, set up by a "weight thermostat" that is governed by the lateral and ventromedial hypothalamus.

Wernicke's encephalopathy (Alcohol-induced persisting amnestic disorder)   A neurological disease characterized by confusion, excitement, delirium, double vision, and other eye-movement abnormalities, and caused by an alcohol-related deficiency of vitamin B. If untreated it progresses into Korsakoff's syndrome.

Windigo   A disorder once common among Algonquin hunters who believed in a supernatural monster that ate human beings and had the power to bewitch them and turn them into cannibals.

Wish fulfillment   In psychodynamic theory, the gratification of id instincts by primary process thinking.

Withdrawal   Unpleasant, sometimes dangerous reactions that occur when drug users suddenly stop taking or reduce their dosage of a drug.

Working through   The process during psychoanalysis of confronting repressed conflicts, reinterpreting memories and feelings, and overcoming their negative effects.

REFERENCES

Abadi, S. (1984). Adiccion: la eterna repeticion de un desencuentro (Acerca de la dependencia humana) [Addiction: The endless repetition of a disencounter]. *Revista de Psicoanalisis, 41*(6), 1029–1044.

Abbott, S. (1987). BABES and puppets helping children: Myth Mary & Early Bird teach prevention. *Alcoholism and Addiction, 8*(2), 17.

Abe, J. S., Zane, N. W. S. (1990). Psychological maladjustment among Asian and Caucasian American college students. Controlling for confounds. *Journal of Counseling Psychology, 37,* 437–444.

Abel, E. L., & Zeidenberg, P. (1985). Age, alcohol and violent death: A postmortem study. *Journal Stud. Alcohol, 46,* 228–231.

Abel, G. G. (1989). Paraphilias. In H. I. Kaplan & B. J. Sadock (Eds.), *Comprehensive textbook of psychiatry* (Vol. 1, 5th ed.). Baltimore: Williams & Wilkins.

Abel, G. G., Becker, J. V., & Cunningham-Rathner, J. (1984). Complications, consent, and cognitions in sex between children and adults. *Inter. J. Law Psychiat., 7,* 89–103.

Abel, G. G., & Osborn, C. (1992). The paraphilias: The extent and nature of sexually deviant and criminal behavior. *Psychiat. Clin. N. Amer., 15*(3), 675–687.

Abelson, J. L., & Curtis, G. C. (1993). Discontinuation of alprazolam after successful treatment of panic disorder: A naturalistic follow-up study. *Journal of Anxiety Disorders, 7,* 107–117.

Ablow, K. R. (1993, Feb. 9). Being personally touched by mental illness is very different from treating it. *The Washington Post,* p. WH7

Abou-Saleh, M. T. (1992). Lithium. In E. S. Paykel (Ed.), *Handbook of Affective Disorders.* New York: Guilford.

Abraham, K. (1911). Notes on the psychoanalytic investigation and treatment of manic-depressive insanity and allied conditions. In *Selected Papers on Psychoanalysis.* New York: Basic Books, 1960, pp. 137–156.

Abraham, K. (1916). The first pregenital stage of the libido. In *Selected Papers on Psychoanalysis.* New York: Basic Books, 1960, pp. 248–279.

Abraham, S., & Llewellyn-Jones, D. (1984). *Eating disorders: The facts.* New York: Oxford UP.

Abram, K. M., & Teplin, L. A. (1990). Drug disorder, mental illness, and violence. *National Institute on Drug Abuse Research Monograph Series, 103,* 222–238.

Abramson, E. E., & Valene, P. (1991). Media use, dietary restraint, bulimia and attitudes towards obesity: A preliminary study. *British Review of Bulimia and Anorexia Nervosa, 5*(2), 73–76.

Abramson, L. Y., Metalsky, G. I., & Alloy, L. B. (1989). Hopelessness depression: A theory-based subtype of depression. *Psych. Rev., 96*(2), 358–372.

Abramson, L. Y., Seligman, M. E., & Teasdale, J. D. (1978). Learned helplessness in humans: Critique and reformulation. *J. Abnorm. Psychol., 87*(1), 49–74.

Abuelo, D. N. (1991). Genetic Disorders. In J. L. Matson and J. A. Mulick (Eds.), *Handbook of Mental Retardation* (2nd ed.). New York: Pergamon Press.

Ackerman, N. (1965). Interlocking pathologies in family relationships. In S. Rado & G. Daniels (Eds.), *Changing concepts in psychoanalytic medicine.* New York: Grune & Stratton.

Adam, K. S., Bouckoms, A., & Streiner, D. (1982). Parental loss and family stability in attempted suicide. *Arch. Gen. Psychiat., 39*(9), 1081–1085.

Adams, D. M., Overholser, J. C., & Lehnert, K. L. (1994). Perceived family functioning and adolescent suicidal behavior. *J. Amer. Acad. Child Adol. Psychiat., 33*(4), 498–507.

Adams, H. (1989). Has behavior therapy progressed? *Contemporary Psychology, 34,* 557–558.

Adams, P. R., & Adams, G. R. (1984). Mount Saint Helen's ashfall: Evidence for a disaster stress reaction. *Amer. Psychol., 39,* 252–260.

Adcock, N. V., & Ross, M. W. (1983). Early memories, early experiences and personality. *Soc. Behav. Pers., 11*(2), 95–100.

Ader, R., Felten, D. L., & Cohen, N. (Eds.). (1991). *Psychoneuroimmunology.* New York: Academic Press.

Adesso, V. J. et al. (1974). Effects of a personal growth group on positive and negative self-references. *Psychother. Theory Res. Prac., 11*(4), 354–355.

Adler, A. (1927). *Individual psychology.* London: Kegan Paul, Trench, Trubner & Co.

Adler, A. (1927). *Understanding Human Nature.* New York: Premier.

Adler, A. (1931). *What Life Should Mean to You.* New York: Capricorn.

Adler, N. E., Boyce, T., Chesney, M. A., Cohen, S., Folkman, S., Kahn, R. L., & Syme, S. L. (1994). Socioeconomic status and health: The challenge of the gradient. *Amer. Psychol., 49*(1), 15–24.

Adler, T. (1992). Prenatal cocaine exposure has subtle, serious effects. *APA Monitor, 23*(11), 17.

Adrien, J. L., Lenoir, P., Martineau, H., Perrot, A., Hameury, L., Larmande, C., Sauvage, D. (1993). Blind ratings of early symptoms of autism based on family home movies. *J. Amer. Acad. Child Adol. Psychiat., 32*(3), 617–626.

Adrien, J. L., Perrot, A., Sauvage, D., Leddet, I. (1992). Early symptoms in autism from family home movies: Evaluation and comparison between 1st and 2nd year of life using IBSE

Scale. *Acta-Paedopsychiatrica: International Journal of Child and Adolescent Psychiatry, 55*(2), 71–75.

Ager, A. (1985). Recent developments in the use of microcomputers in the field of mental handicap: Implications for psychological practice. *Bull. Brit. Psychol. Society, 38,* 142–145.

Agras, W. S. (1974). Behavioral approaches to the treatment of essential hypertension. *International Journal of Obesity, 5* (Suppl. 1), 173–181.

Agras, W. S. (1984). Behavioral Medicine: An Overview. In A. J. Frances & R. E. Hales (Eds.), *American Psychiatric Association annual review* (Vol. 5). Washington, DC: American Psychiatric Press.

Agras, W. S. (1984). The behavioral treatment of somatic disorders. In W. D. Gentry (Ed.), *Handbook of behavioral medicine.* New York: Guilford.

Agras, W. S. (1985). *Panic: Facing fears, phobias, and anxiety.* New York: W. H. Freeman.

Agras, W. S. (1991). Nonpharmacological treatments of bulimia nervosa. *J. Clin. Psychiat., 52*(Suppl.), 29–33.

Agras, W. S., Sylvester, D., & Oliveau, D. (1969). The epidemiology of common fears and phobias. *Comprehen. Psychiat., 10*(2), 151–156.

Agras, W. S., Taylor, O. B., Kraemer, H. C., Allen, R. A., & Schneider, M. S. (1980). Relaxation training: Twenty-four hour blood pressure reductions. *Arch. Gen. Psychiat., 37,* 859–863.

Aguilar, T., & Munson, W. (1992). Leisure education and counseling as intervention components in drug and alcohol treatment for adolescents. *Journal of Alcohol and Drug Education, 37*(3), 23–34.

Aiken, L. R. (1985). *Psychological testing and assessment* (5th ed.). Boston: Allyn & Bacon.

Akamatsu, T. J. (1988). Intimate relationships with former clients: National Survey of Attitudes and Behaviour among practitioners. *Professional Psychology: Research and Practice 19*(4), 454–458.

Akhtar, S. (1989). Narcissistic personality disorder: Descriptive features and differential diagnosis. *Psychiat. Clin. N. Amer., 12*(3), 505–529.

Akhtar, S., Wig, N. H., Verma, V. K., Pershod, D., & Verma, S. K. (1975). A phenomenological analysis of symptoms in obsessive-compulsive neuroses. *Brit. J. Psychiat., 127,* 342–348.

Akiskal, H. S. (1989). The classification of mental disorders. In H. I. Kaplan & B. J. Sadock (Eds.), *Comprehensive textbook of psychiatry* (Vol. 1, 5th ed.). Baltimore: Williams & Wilkins.

Akiskal, H. S., & McKinney, W. T. (1973). Depressive disorders: Toward a unified hypothesis. *Science, 182,* 20–28.

Akiskal, H. S., & McKinney, W. T. (1975). Overview of recent research in depression: Integration of ten conceptual models into a comprehensive clinical frame. *Arch. Gen. Psychiat., 32,* 285–305.

Akiskal, H. S., Yerevarian, B. I., Davis, G. C., King, D., & Lemmi, H. (1985). The nosologic status of borderline personality: clinical and polysomnographic study. *Amer. J. Psychiat., 142,* 192–198.

Albee, G. W. (1982). Primary prevention: Insights for rehabilitation psychology. *Rehab. Psychol., 27*(1), 13–22.

Albert, M. S., Butters, N., & Levin, J. (1979). Temporal gradients in the retrograde amnesia of patients with alcoholic Korsakoff's disease. *Archives of Neurology, 36,* 211–216.

Albert, M. S., & Lafleche, G. (1991). Neuropsychological testing of memory disorders. In T. Yanagihara & R. C. Petersen (Eds.), *Memory Disorders: Research and Clinical Practice.* New York: Marcel Dekker, Inc.

Alcoholics Anonymous World Services, Inc. (1994). *Personal communication.* Statistic branch. New York, NY.

Alden, L. (1989). Short-term structured treatment for avoidant personality disorder. *J. Cons. Clin. Psychiat., 57*(6), 756–764.

Aleksandrowicz, D. R. (1980). Psychoanalytic studies of mania. In R. H. Belmaker & H. M. van Praag (Eds.), *Mania: An evolving concept.* Jamaica, NY: Spectrum.

Alevizos, P., DeRisi, W., Liberman, R., Eckman, T., & Callahan, E. (1978). The behavior observation instrument: A method of direct observation for program evaluation. *J. Appl. Behav. Anal., 11,* 243–257.

Alexander, B. (1981). Behavioral approaches to the treatment of bronchial asthma. In C. K. Prokop & L. A. Bradley (Eds.), *Medical psychology: Contributions to behavioral medicine.* New York: Academic.

Alexander, B. K., & Hadaway, P. F. (1982). Opiate addiction: The case for an adaptive orientation. *Psychol. Bull., 92*(2), 367–381.

Alexander, F. (1930). About dreams with unpleasant content. *Psychiat. Quart., 4,* 447–452.

Alexander, F. (1936). The sociological and biological orientation of psychoanalysis. *Ment. Hyg. of New York, 20,* 232–248.

Alexander, F. (1950). Analysis of the therapeutic factors in psychoanalytic treatment. *Psychoanal. Quart., 19,* 482–500.

Alexander, F. (1950). *Psychosomatic medicine.* New York: Norton.

Alexander, F., French, T. M., & Pollack, G. H. (1968). *Psychosomatic specificity: Experimental study and results.* Chicago: University of Chicago Press.

Alexander, J. F., & Parsons, B. V. (1982). *Functional family therapy.* Monterey, CA: Brooks/Cole.

Alexander, J. F., Holtzworth-Munroe, A., & Jameson, P. (1994). The process and outcome of marital and family therapy: Research review and evaluation. In A. E. Bergin & S. L. Garfiel (Eds.), *Handbook of psychotherapy and behavior change* (4th ed.). New York: Wiley.

Alford, B., & Norcross, J. (1991). Cognitive therapy as integrative therapy. *J. Psychother. Integ. 1*(3), 175–190.

Allderidge, P. (1979). Hospitals, madhouses and asylums: Cycles in the care of the insane. *Brit. J. Psychiat., 134,* 321–334.

Allebeck, P., & Bolund, C. (1991). Suicides and suicide attempts in cancer patients. *Psychol. Med., 21*(4), 979–984.

Allen, D., & Lader, M. (1992). The interactions of ethanol with single and repeated doses of suriclone and diazepam on physiological and psychomotor functions in normal subjects. *Euro. J. Clin. Pharm., 42.*

Allen, J. G. (1993). Dissociative processes: Theoretical underpinnings of a working model for clinician and patient. *Bull. Menninger Clin., 57*(3), 287–308.

Allen, J. G., & Smith, W. H. (1993). Diagnosing dissociative disorders. *Bull. Menninger Clin., 57*(3), 328–343.

Allison, R. B. (1978). A rational psychotherapy plan for multiplicity. *Svensk Tidskrift Hyp., 3,* 9–16.

Allison, T. G. (1992). How to Counsel Patients with Chronic Fatigue Syndrome. The Psychology of Health, Immunity and Disease. Fourth National Conference: The National Institute for the Clinical Application of Behavioral Medicine.

Alloway, R., & Bebbington, P. E. (1987). The buffer theory of social support: A review of the literature. *Psychol. Med., 17,* 91–108.

Alnaes, R., & Torgersen, S. (1989). Clinical differentiation between major depression only, major depression with panic disorder and panic disorder only: Childhood and personality disorder. *Psychiatria Fennica, Suppl.*, 58–64.

Aloni, R., Heller, L., Ofer, O., Mendelson, E., & Davidoff, G. (1992). Noninvasive treatment for erectile dysfunction in the neurogenically disabled population. *J. Sex Marit. Ther.*, *18*(3), 243–249.

Alpher, V. S. (1992). Introject and identity: Structural-interpersonal analysis and psychological assessment of multiple personality disorder. *J. Pers. Assess.*, *58*(2), 347–367.

Altemus, M., Pigott, T., L'Heureux, F., Davis, C. L., Rubinow, D. R., Murphy, D. L., & Gold, P. W. (1993). CSF Somatostatin in obsessive-compulsive disorder. *Amer. J. Psychiat.*, *150*(3), 460–464.

Alterman, A. I., O'Brien, C. P., McLellan, A. T., Ausust, D. S., et al. (1994). Effectiveness and costs of inpatient versus day hospital cocaine rehabilitation. *J. Nerv. Ment. Dis.*, *182*(3), 157–163.

Alvir, J. M. J., & Lieberman, J. A. (1994). A reevaluation of the clinical characteristics of clozapine-induced agranulocytosis in light of the United States experience. *J. Clin. Psychopharm.*, *14*(2), 87–89.

Aman, M. G., & Singh, N. N. (1991). Pharmacological intervention. In J. L. Matson & J. A. Mulick (Eds.), *Handbook of mental retardation*. New York: Pergamon.

Amaral, D. G. (1987). Memory: Anatomical organization of candidate brain regions. In F. Plum (Ed.), *Handbook of Physiology: The Nervous System*. New York: Oxford UP.

Amati, A., Celani, T., del Vecchio, M., & Vacca, L. (1981). Anorexia nervosa: l'iter attraverso la medicine generale e l'approccio differito in psichiatria. [Anorexia nervosa: The connection between general medicine and the approach in psychiatry.] (Ital) *Medicina Psicosomatica*, *26*(4), 357–363.

Ambrosini, P. J., Bianchi, M. D., Rabinovich, H., & Elia, J. (1993). Antidepressant treatments in child and adolescents I. Affective disorders. *J. Amer. Acad. Adol. Psychiat.*, *32*(1), 1–6.

American Association for Protecting Children (AAPC). (1992). *Highlights of official child neglect and abuse reporting*. Denver, CO: American Humane Society.

American Assoc. of Retired Persons. (1990). *A profile of older Americans*. Washington, DC: Author.

American Assoc. on Mental Retardation. (1992). *Mental Retardation: Definition, Classification, and Systems of Supports* (9th ed.). Washington, D.C.: Author.

American Humane Assoc. (1986). *Highlights of official child neglect and abuse reporting 1984*. Denver: Author.

American Medical Assoc. (1992). *Diagnostic Treatment Guidelines on Domestic Violence*. Washington, D.C.: Author.

American Psychiatric Assoc. (1968). *Diagnostic and statistical manual of mental disorders* (2nd. ed.). Washington, DC: Author.

American Psychiatric Assoc. (1983). APA statement on the insanity defense: Insanity defense work group. *Amer. J. Psychiat.*, *140*(6), 681–688.

American Psychiatric Assoc. (1987). *Diagnostic and statistical manual of mental disorders* (3rd rev. ed.). Washington, DC: Author.

American Psychiatric Assoc. (1989). *Treatments of psychiatric disorders*. Washington, DC: Author.

American Psychiatric Assoc. (1991). *DSM-IV options book*. Washington, DC.

American Psychiatric Assoc. (1993). *Practice Guideline for Major Depressive Disorder in Adults*. Washington, DC: Author.

American Psychiatric Assoc. (1994). *Diagnostic and statistical manual of mental disorders* (4th ed.). Washington, DC: Author.

American Psychological Assoc. (1981). *Specialty guidelines for the delivery of services*. Washington, DC: Author.

American Psychological Assoc. (1987). Ethical principles of psychologists. *Amer. Psychol.*, *45*, 390–395.

American Psychological Assoc. (1990). Ethical principles of psychologists (amended June 2, 1989). *Amer. Psychol.*, *45*(6), 390–395.

American Psychological Assoc. (1991, October). APA-CPA Disaster Response Project: Interim Project Report, Sacramento, CA.

American Psychological Assoc. Ethics Committee. (1992). Ethical Principles of Psychologists and Code of Conduct. *Amer. Psychol.*, *47*(12), 1597–1611.

American Psychological Assoc. (1993). Guidelines for providers of psychological services to ethnic, linguistic, and culturally diverse populations. *Amer. Psychol.*, *48*(1), 45–48.

Amsel, A. (1990). Arousal, suppression, and persistence: Frustration theory, attention, and its disorders [Special Issue]. *Cog. Emot.*, *4*(3), 239–268.

Amsterdam, J. D., Brunswick, D. J., & Mendels, J. (1980). The clinical application of tricyclic antidepressant pharmacokinetics and plasma levels. *Amer. J. Psychiat.*, *137*(6), 653–662.

Amsterdam, J. D., & Hernz, W. J. (1993). Serum antibodies to herpes simplex virus Types I and II in depressed patients. *Bio. Psychiat.*, *34*, 417–420.

Ananth, J. (1983). New antidepressants. *Comprehen. Psychiat.*, *24*, 116–124.

Ananth, J., Djenderdjian, A., Shamasunder, P., Costa, J., et al. (1991). Negative symptoms: Psychopathological models. *Journal of Psychiatry and Neuroscience*, *16*(1), 12–18.

Anastasi, A. (1982). *Psychological testing* (5th ed.). New York: Macmillan.

Anastasi, A. (1988). *Psychologic testing* (6th ed.). New York: Macmillan.

Anastopoulos, A. D., & Barkley, R. A. (1992). Attention deficit-hyperactivity disorder. In C. E. Walker & M. C. Roberts (Eds.), *Handbook of clinical child psychology* (2nd ed.). New York: Wiley.

Andersen, A. E. (1985). *Practical comprehensive treatment of anorexia nervosa and bulimia*. Baltimore: Johns Hopkins UP.

Andersen, A. E. (1986). Sexuality and fertility: Women with anorexia nervosa and bulimia. *Med. Aspects of Human Sex.*, *20*, 138–143.

Andersen, A. E. (1990). Diagnosis and treatment of males with eating disorders. In A. E. Andersen (Ed.), *Males with eating disorders*. New York: Brunner/Mazel Publishers.

Andersen, A. E. (1992). Eating disorders in males: A special case? In K. D. Brownell, J. Rodin, & J. H. Wilmore (Eds.), *Eating, body weight, and performance in athletes: Disorders or modern society*. Philadelphia: Lea & Febiger.

Andersen, A. E. (1992). Eating disorders in males: Critical questions. In R. Lemberg (Ed.), *Controlling Eating Disorders with Facts, Advice, and Resources*. Phoenix, AZ: The Oryx Press.

Andersen, A. E., Morse, C., & Santmyer, K. (1985). Inpatient treatment for anorexia nervosa. In D. M. Garner & P. Garfinkel (Eds.), *Handbook of psychotherapy for anorexia nervosa and bulimia*. New York: Guilford.

Andersen, B. L., Kiecolt-Glaser, J. K., & Glaser, R. (1994). A biobehavioral model of cancer stress and disease course. *Amer. Psychol., 49*(5), 389–404.

Anderson, J. L., Vasile, R. G., Mooney, J. J. & Bloomingdale, K. L., et al. (1992). Changes in norepinephrine output following light therapy for fall/winter seasonal depression. *Bio. Psychiat., 32*(8), 700–704.

Anderson, N. (1923). *The hobo: The sociology of the homeless man.* Chicago: Univ. Chicago.

Anderson, N. B., McNeilly, M., & Myers, H. F. (1992). A contextual model for research of race differences in autonomic reactivity. In E. H. Johnson, W. D. Gentry, & S. Julius (Eds.), *Personality, Elevated Blood Pressure, and Essential Hypertension.* Washington: Hemisphere Publishing Corp.

Anderson, S. C. (1993). Anti-stalking laws: Will they curb the erotomanic's obsessive pursuit? *Law & Psychology Review, 17,* 171–191.

Anderson, S. R., Avery, D. L., DiPietro, E. K., Edwards, G. L., et al. (1989). Intensive home-based early intervention with autistic children. *Education & Treatment of Children, 10*(4), 352–366.

Andrasik, F., Blanchard, E. B., & Neff, D. F. (1984). Biofeedback and relaxation training for chronic headaches: A controlled comparison of booster treatments and regular contacts for long-term maintenance. *J. Cons. Clin. Psychol., 52*(4), 609–615.

Andreasen, N. C. (1980). Mania and creativity. In R. H. Belmaker & H. M. van Praag (Eds.), *Mania: An evolving concept.* New York: Spectrum.

Andreasen, N. C., Hoffman, R. E., & Grove, W. M. (1985). Mapping abnormalities in language and cognition. In M. Alpert (Ed.), *Controversies in schizophrenia: Changes and constancies.* New York: Guilford.

Andreasen, N. C., Nasrallah, H. A., Dunn, V. et al. (1986). Structural abnormalities in the frontal system in schizophrenia: A magnetic resonance imaging study. *Arch. Gen. Psychiat., 43,* 136–144.

Andrulonis, P. A. (1991). Disruptive behavior disorders in boys and the borderline personality disorder in men. *Ann. Clin. Psychiat., 3*(1), 23–26.

Angier, N. (1994, April 5). Quest for evolutionary meaning in the persistence of suicide. *New York Times,* pp. C1, 10.

Angold, A., & Rutter, M. (1992). Effects of age and pubertal status on depression in a large clinical sample. *Development and Psychopathology, 4*(1), 5–28.

Angrist, B., Lee, H. K., & Gershon, S. (1974). The antagonism of amphetamine-induced symptomatology by a neuroleptic. *Amer. J. Psychiat., 131,* 817–819.

Angrist, B., Sathananthan, G., & Gershon, S. (1973). Behavioral effect in schizophrenic patients. *Psychopharmacologia, 31,* 507.

Angst, J., Fedler, W., & Frey, R. (1979). The course of unipolar and bipolar affective disorders. In M. Schou, E. Stromgreen (Eds.), *Origin, prevention and treatment of affective disorders.* New York: Academic Press.

Angst, J., & Hochstrasser, B. (1994). Recurrent brief depression: The Zurich Study. *J. Clin. Psychiat., 55*(Suppl. 4), 3–9.

Annas, G. J. (1993). Physician-assisted suicide—Michigan's temporary solution. *New England Journal of Medicine, 328*(21), 1573–1574.

Annas, G. J., Glants, L. H., & Katz, B. F. (1977). *Informed consent to human experimentation: The subject's dilemma.* Cambridge, MA: Ballinger.

Annis, H. M., Davis, C. S., Graham, M. et al. (1989). A controlled trial of relapse prevention procedures based on self-efficacy theory. Unpublished manuscript. Toronto: Addiction Research Foundation.

Anslinger, H. J., & Cooper, C. R. (1937). Marijuana: Assassin of youth. *American Magazine, 124,* 19, 153.

Apter, J. T. (1993). Frontiers in biological psychiatry: New drug development. *New Jersey Medicine, 90*(2), 144–146.

Arbel, N., & Stravynski, A. (1991). A retrospective study of separation in the development of adult avoidant personality disorder. *Acta Psychiatr. Scandin., 83*(3), 174–178.

Arbiter, N. (1991). Residential programs for women. In *National Conference on Drug Abuse Research and Practice Conference Highlights.* Rockville, MD: National Institute on Drug Abuse.

Arbitt, S. A., & Blatt, S. J. (1973). Differentiation of simulated and genuine suicide notes. *Psych. Rep., 33,* 283–297.

Arboleda-Florez, J., & Holley, H. L. (1991). Antisocial burnout: An exploratory study. *Bulletin of the American Academy of Psychiatry and the Law, 19*(2), 173–183.

Arieti, S. (1974). *Interpretation of schizophrenia.* New York: Basic Books.

Arieti, S., & Bemporad, J. (1978). *Severe and mild depression: The psychotherapeutic approach.* New York: Basic Books.

Arieti, S., & Bemporad, J. (1980). The psychological organization of depression. *Amer. J. Psychiat., 137,* 1360–1365.

Arinami, T., Itokawa, M., Komiyama, T., Mitsushio, H., Mori, H., et al. (1993). Association between severity of alcoholism and the A1 allele of the dopamine D2 receptor gene TaqI A RFLP. in Japanese. *Bio. Psychiat., 33,* 108–114.

Aring, C. D. (1974). The Gheel experience: Eternal spirit of the chainless mind! *JAMA, 230*(7), 998–1001.

Aring, C. D. (1975). Gheel: The town that cares. *Family Health, 7*(4), 54–55, 58, 60.

Arkowitz, H. (1992). A common factors therapy for depression. In J. C. Norcross & M. R. Goldfried (Eds.), *Handbook of psychotherapy integration.* New York: Basic Books.

Arlow, J. A. (1989). Psychoanalysis. In R. J. Corsini & D. Wedding (Eds.), *Current psychotherapies.* Itasca, IL: Peacock.

Armstrong, J. G., & Roth, D. M. (1989). Attachment and separation difficulties in eating disorders: A preliminary investigation. *Inter. J. Eat. Dis., 8*(2), 141–155.

Arndt, W. B., Jr. (1991). *Gender disorders and the paraphilias.* Madison, CT: International Univ.

Arnold, L. E. (1973, October). Is this label necessary? *Journal of School Health, 43,* 510–514.

Arnow, D., & Harrison, R. H. (1991). Affect in early memories of borderline patients. *J. Pers. Assess., 56*(1), 75–83.

Arnstein, R. L. (1986). Ethical and value issues in psychotherapy with college students. *Journal of College Student Psychotherapy, 1,* 3–20.

Arntz, A., & Lavy, E. (1993). Does stimulus elaboration potentiate exposure in vivo treatment: Two forms of one-session treatment of spider phobia. *Behav. Psychother., 21,* 1–12.

Aronson, T. A. (1989). Paranoia and narcissism in psychoanalytic theory: Contributions of self psychology to the theory and therapy of the paranoid disorders. *Psychoanalytic Review, 76*(3), 329–351.

Artiss, K. L. (1962). *Milieu therapy in schizophrenia.* New York: Grune & Stratton.

Asarnow, J. R. (1992). Suicidal ideation and attempts during middle childhood: Associations with perceived family stress and depression among child psychiatric inpatients. *Journal of Clinical Child Psychology, 21*(1), 35–40.

Asarnow, J. R., Asarnow, R. F., Hornstein, N., & Russell, A. (1991). Childhood-onset schizophrenia: Developmental perspectives on schizophrenic disorders. In E. F. Walker (Ed.), *Schizophrenia: A Life-course Developmental Perspective.* San Diego, CA: Academic Press.

Asarnow, J. R., & Horton, A. A. (1990). Coping and stress in families of child psychiatric inpatients: Parents of children with depressive and schizophrenic spectrum disorders. *Child Psychiat. Human Dev., 21*(2), 145–157.

Asberg, M. et al. (1984). CSF monoamine metabolites in melancholia. *Acta Psychiatr. Scandin., 69*(3), 201–219.

Asberg, M., Traskman, L., & Thoren, P. (1976). 5 HIAA in the cerebrospinal fluid: A biochemical suicide predictor? *Arch. Gen. Psychiat., 33*(10), 1193–1197.

Ascione, F. R., & Borg, W. R. (1983). A teacher training program to enhance mainstreamed, handicapped pupils' self concepts. *J. School Psychol., 21*(4), 297–309.

Aserinsky, E., & Kleitman, N. (1953). Eye movements during sleep. *Federal Process, 13,* 6–7.

Ashleigh, E. A., & Fesler, F. A. (1992). Fluoxetine and suicidal preoccupation. *Amer. J. Psychiat., 149*(12), 1750.

Ashton, J. R., & Donnan, S. (1981). Suicide by burning as an epidemic phenomenon: An analysis of 82 deaths and inquests in England and Wales in 1978–9. *Psychol. Med., 11*(4), 735–739.

Asner, J. (1990). Reworking the myth of personal incompetence: Group psychotherapy for bulimia nervosa. *Psychiat. Ann., 20*(7), 395–397.

Atthowe, J. M. (1973). Token economies come of age. *Behav. Ther., 4*(5), 646–654.

Auchincloss, E. L., & Weiss, R. W. (1992). Paranoid character and the intolerance of indifference. *J. Amer. Psychoanal. Assoc., 40*(4), 1013–1037.

Auerbach, S. M., & Kilmann, P. R. (1977). Crisis intervention: A review of outcome research. *Psychol. Bull., 84,* 1189–1217.

Auerhahn, N. C., & Moskowitz, M. B. (1984). Merger fantasies in individual inpatient therapy with schizophrenic patients. *Psychoanal. Psychol., 1*(2), 131–148.

Auster, R. (1993). Sertraline: A new antidepressant. *American Family Physician, 48,* 311–314.

Avery, D., & Lubrano, A. (1979). Depression treated with imipramine and ECT: The DeCarolis study reconsidered. *Amer. J. Psychiat., 136,* 559–569.

Avery, D. H., Bolte, M. A., Dager, S. R., Wilson, G., et al. (1993). Dawn simulation of winter depression: A controlled study. *Amer. J. Psychiat., 150*(1), 113–117.

Axtell, A., & Newlon, B. J. (1993). An analysis of Adlerian Life Themes of bulimic women. *Individual Psychology, 49*(1), 58–67.

Ayd, F. J., Jr. (1956). A clinical evaluation of Frenquel. *J. Nerv. Ment. Dis., 124,* 507–509.

Ayllon, T. (1963). Intensive treatment of psychotic behavior by stimulus satiation and food reinforcement. *Behav. Res. Ther., 1,* 53–62.

Ayllon, T., & Azrin, N. H. (1965). The measurement and reinforcement of behavior of psychotics. *J. Exp. Anal. Behav., 8,* 357–383.

Ayllon, T., & Azrin, N. H. (1968). *The token economy: A motivational system for therapy and rehabilitation.* New York: Appleton.

Ayllon, T., & Michael, J. (1959). The psychiatric nurse as a behavioural engineer. *J. Exp. Anal. Behav., 2,* 323–334.

Ayllon, T., & Roberts, M. D. (1974). Eliminating discipline problems by strengthening academic performance. *J. Appl. Behav. Anal., 7*(1), 71–76.

Azar, S. T., Fantuzzo, J. W., & Twentyman, C. T. (1984). An applied behavioral approach to child maltreatment: Back to basics. *Adv. Behav. Res. Ther., 8*(1), 3–11.

Azar, S. T., Robinson, D. R., Hekimian, E. E., & Twentyman, C. T. (1984). Unrealistic expectations and problem solving ability in maltreating and comparison mothers. *J. Cons. Clin. Psychol., 52,* 687–691.

Azar, S. T., & Rohrbeck, C. A. (1986). Child abuse and unrealistic expectations: Further validation of the Parent Opinion Questionnaire. *J. Cons. Clin. Psychol., 54,* 867–868.

Azar, S. T., & Siegal, B. R. (1990). Behavioral treatment of child abuse: A developmental perspective. *Behav. Mod., 14*(3), 279–300.

Azar, S. T., & Wolfe, D. A. (1989). Child abuse and neglect. In E. J. Mash & R. Barkley (Eds.), *Treatment of childhood disorders.* New York: Guilford.

Azima, F. J. C. (1993). Group psychotherapy with personality disorders. In H. I. Kaplan & B. J. Sadock (Eds.), *Comprehensive group psychotherapy* (3rd ed.). Baltimore: Williams & Wilkins.

Baastrup, P. C. (1964). The use of lithium in manic-depressive psychosis. *Comprehen. Psychiat., 5,* 396–408.

Bacon, S. D. (1973). The process of addiction to alcohol: Social aspects. *Quart. J. Stud. Alcohol., 34*(1, Pt. A), 1–27.

Baer, L., & Jenike, M. A. (1992). Personality disorders in obsessive compulsive personality disorder. *Psychiat. Clin. N. Amer., 15*(4), 803–812.

Baer, L., Platman, S. R., Kassir, S., & Fieve, R. R. (1971). Mechanisms of renal lithium handling and their relationship to mineralcorticoids: A dissociation between sodium and lithium ions. *J. Psychiat. Res., 8*(2), 91–105.

Bagby, E. (1922). The etiology of phobias. *J. Abnorm. Psychol., 17,* 16–18.

Bagley, C. (1991). Poverty and suicide among Native Canadians: A replication. *Psych. Rep., 69*(1), 149–150.

Bagley, C., & Ramsay, R. (1985). Psychosocial correlates of suicidal behaviors in an urban population. *Crisis, 6*(2), 63–77.

Baiocco, G. (1991). Indici predittivi psicometrici e psiofisiologici in biofeedback training. [Psychophysiological and psychometric predictive signs in biofeedback training.] *Rivista di Psichiatria, 26*(6), 339–343.

Baker, L., Silk, K. R., Westen, D., Nigg, J. T., et al. (1992). Malevolence, splitting, and parental ratings by borderlines. *J. Nerv. Ment. Dis., 180*(4), 258–264.

Baker, T., & Brandon, T. H. (1988). Behavioral treatment strategies. In *A report of the Surgeon General: The health consequences of smoking: Nicotine addiction.* Rockville, MD: U.S. Dept. Health and Human Services.

Bakken, J., Miltenberger, R. G., & Schauss, S. (1993). Teaching parents with mental retardation: Knowledge versus skills. *Amer. J. Ment. Retard.*, *97*(4), 405–417.

Baldessarini, R. J. (1983). *Biomedical aspects of depression and its treatment.* Washington, D.C.: American Psychiatric Association Press, Inc.

Baldwin, S. (1985). Sheep in wolf's clothing: Impact of normalisation teaching on human services and services providers. *Inter. J. Rehab. Res.*, *8*(2), 131–142.

Balint, M. (1952). New beginning and the paranoid and the depressive syndromes. *Inter. J. Psychoanal.*, *33*, 214–224.

Ball, J. C., Rosen, L., Flueck, J. A., & Nurco, D. N. (1982). Lifetime criminality of heroin users in the United States. *J. Drug Issues*, *12*(3), 225–239.

Ballenger, J. C. (1988). The clinical use of carbamazepine in affective disorders. *J. Clin. Psychiat.*, *49*(Suppl.), 13–19.

Ballenger, J. C., Burrows, G. D., DuPont, R. L., Lesser, I. M. et al. (1988). Alprazolam in panic disorder and agoraphobia: Results from a multicenter trial: I. Efficacy in short-term treatment. *Arch. Gen. Psych.*, *45*(5), 413–422.

Ballenger, J. C., & Post, R. M. (1980). Carbamazepine in manic-depressive illness: A new treatment. *Amer. J. Psychiat.*, *137*(7), 782–790.

Ballinger, S. E. (1987). Uses and limitations of hypnosis in treating a conversion overlay following somatic trauma. *Austral. J. Clin. Exp. Hyp.*, *15*(1), 29–37.

Balshem, M., Oxman, G., Van Rooyen, D., & Girod, K. (1992). Syphillis, sex, and crack cocaine: Images of risk and morality. *Social Science & Medicine*, *35*(2), 147–160.

Bancroft, J. (1971). A comparative study of aversion and desensitization in the treatment of homosexuality. In L. Burns & J. Worsley (Eds.), *Behaviour Therapy in the 1970s.* Bristol, UK: Wright.

Bancroft, J. (1989). *Human sexuality and its problems.* New York: Churchill-Livingstone.

Bandura, A. (1969). *Principles of behavior modification.* New York: Holt, Rinehart & Winston.

Bandura, A. (1971). Psychotherapy based upon modeling principles. In A. E. Bergin & S. L. Garfield (Eds.), *Handbook of psychotherapy and behavior change.* New York: Wiley.

Bandura, A. (1971). Vicarious and self-reinforcement processes. In R. Glaser (Ed.), *The nature of reinforcement.* New York: Academic Press.

Bandura, A. (1973). *Aggression: A social learning analysis.* Englewood Cliffs, NJ: Prentice Hall.

Bandura, A. (1976). *Social learning theory.* Englewood Cliffs, NJ: Prentice Hall.

Bandura, A. (1977). Self-efficacy: Toward a unifying theory of behavioral change. *Psych. Rev.*, *84*(2), 191–215.

Bandura, A., Adams, N. E., & Beyer, J. (1977). Cognitive processes mediating behavioral change. *J. Pers. Soc. Psychol.*, *35*(3), 125–139.

Bandura, A., Blanchard, E. B., & Ritter, B. (1969). Relative efficacy of desensitization and modeling approaches for inducing behavioral, affective, and attitudinal changes. *J. Pers. Soc. Psychol.*, *13*, 173–199.

Bandura, A., & Rosenthal, T. (1966). Vicarious classical conditioning as a function of arousal level. *J. Pers. Soc. Psychol.*, *3*, 54–62.

Bandura, A., Ross, D., & Ross, S. (1963). Imitation of film-mediated aggressive models. *J. Abnorm. Soc. Psychol.*, *66*, 3–11.

Bank, L., Marlowe, J. H., Reid, J. B., Patterson, G. R., & Weinrott, M. R. (1991). A comparative evaluation of parent-training interventions for families of chronic delinquents. *J. Abnorm. Child Psychol.*, *19*, 15–33.

Banki, C. M. (1977). Correlation between cerebrospinal fluid amine metabolites and psychomotor activity in affective disorders. *J. Neurochem.*, *28*, 255–257.

Banki, C. M., & Arato, M. (1983). Amine metabolites and neuroendocrine responses related to depression and suicide. *J. Affect. Dis.*, *5*(3), 223–232.

Banki, C. M., Arato, M., Papp, Z., & Kurza, M. (1984). Biochemical markers in suicidal patients. *J. Affect. Dis.*, *6*, 341–350.

Banki, C. M., Vojnik, M., Papp, Z., Balla, K. Z., & Arato, M. (1985). Cerebrospinal fluid magnesium and calcium related to amine metabolites, diagnosis, and suicide attempts. *Bio. Psychiat.*, *20*, 163–171.

Banov, M. D., Tohen, M., & Friedberg, J. (1993). High risk of eosinophilia in women treated with clozapine. *J. Clin. Psychiat.*, *54*(12), 466–469.

Baraban, J. M. (1993). The biology of memory. In J. M. Oldham, M. B. Riba, & A. Tasman (Eds.), *Review of Psychiatry*, Vol. 12. Washington, DC: American Psychiatric Press.

Baraban, J., Worley, P., & Snyder, S. (1989). Second messenger systems and psychoactive drug action: Focus on the phosphoinositide system and lithium. *Amer. J. Psychiat.*, *146*(10), 1251–1259.

Barahal, H. S. (1958). 1000 prefrontal lobotomies: Five to ten year follow-up study. *Psychiat. Quart.*, *32*, 653–678.

Barber, T. X. (1984). Hypnosis, deep relaxation, and active relaxation: Data, theory and clinical applications. In F. L. Woolfolk & P. M. Lehrer (Eds.), *Principles and practice of stress management.* New York: Guilford.

Barber, T. X. (1993). Hypnosuggestive approaches to stress reduction: Data, theory, and clinical applications. In P. M. Lehrer & R. L. Woolfolk (Eds.), *Principles and Practice of Stress Management* (2nd ed.). New York: Guilford.

Barclay, C. R. (1981). A component view of memory development. *Psychol. Quart. J. Human Behav.*, *18*(4), 35–52.

Bardenstein, K. K., McGlashan, T. H., & McGlashan, T. H. (1988). The natural history of a residentially treated borderline sample: Gender differences. *J. Pers. Dis.*, *2*(1), 69–83.

Barker, J. C. (1962). The syndrome of hospital addiction (Munchausen syndrome): A report on the investigation of seven cases. *J. Ment. Sci.*, *108*, 167–182.

Barker, J. G., & Howell, R. J. (1992). The plethysmograph: A review of recent literature. *Bull. Amer. Acad. Psychiat. Law*, *20*(1), 13–25.

Barker, P. R., Manderscheid, R. W., Hendershot, G. E., Jack, S. S., Schoenborn, C. A., & Goldstrom, I. (1992). Serious mental illness and disability in the adult household population: United States, 1989. In R. W. Manderscheid & M. A. Sonnenschein (Eds.), *Mental Health, United States, 1992.* Washington, DC: U.S. Department of Health and Human Services.

Barkley, R. A. (1989). Attention deficit-hyperactivity disorder. In E. J. Mash & R. Barkley (Eds.), *Treatment of childhood disorders.* New York: Guilford.

Barlow, C. F. (1978). *Mental retardation and related disorders.* Philadelphia: Davis.

Barlow, D. H. (1989). Treatment outcome evaluation methodology with anxiety disorders: Strengths and key issues. *Adv. Behav. Res. Ther.*, *11*(3), 121–132.

Barlow, D. H. (1986). Causes of sexual dysfunction: The role of anxiety and cognitive interference. *J. Cons. Clin. Psychol.*, *54*, 140–148.

Barlow, D. H. (1988). Current models of panic disorder and a view from emotion theory. In A. J. Frances & R. E. Hales (Eds.), *American Psychiatric Press review of psychiatry* (Vol. 7). Washington, DC: American Psychiatric Press.

Barlow, D. H. (Ed.). (1993). *Clinical Handbook of Psychological Disorders: A Step-by-Step Treatment Manual* (2nd ed.). New York: Guilford.

Barlow, D. H., & Beck, J. G. (1984). The psychosocial treatment of anxiety disorders: Current status, future directions. In J. B. W. Williams & R. L. Spitzer (Eds.), *Psychotherapy research: Where are we and where should we go?* New York: Guilford.

Barlow, D. H., Craske, M. G., Cerny, J. A., & Klosko, J. S. (1989). Behavioral treatment of panic disorder. *Behav. Ther.*, *20*(2), 261–282.

Barlow, D. H., O'Brien, G. T., & Last, C. G. (1984). Couples treatment of agoraphobia. *Behav. Ther.*, *15*(1), 41–58.

Barlow, D. H., Rapee, R. M., & Brown, T. A. (1992). Behavioral treatment of generalized anxiety disorder. *Behav. Ther.*, *23*, 551–570.

Barlow, D. H. et al. (1984). Panic and generalized anxiety disorders: Nature and treatment. *Behav. Ther.*, *15*(5), 431–449.

Barnard, G. W., Fuller, A. K., Robbins, L., & Shaw, T. (1989). *The Child Molester: An integrated approach to evaluation and treatment.* New York: Brunner/Mazel Publishers.

Barnes, G. E., & Prosen, H. (1985). Parental death and depression. *J. Abnorm. Psychol.*, *94*(1), 64–69.

Barnes, T. R., & Braude, W. M. (1985). Akathisia variants and tardive dyskinesia. *Arch. Gen. Psychiat.*, *42*(9), 874–878.

Baron, M., Barkai, A., Gruen, R., Peselow, E. et al. (1987). Platelet sup 3H imipramine binding and familial transmission of affective disorders. *Neuropsychobiology*, *17*(4), 182–186.

Baron, M., Gruen, R., Asnis, L., et al. (1983). Familial relatedness of schizophrenic and schizotypal states. *Amer. J. Psychiat.*, *140*, 1437–1442.

Baron, M., Gruen, R., Rainer, J. D., et al. (1985). A family study of schizophrenic and normal control probands: Implications for the spectrum concept of schizophrenia. *Amer. J. Psychiat.*, *142*, 447–455.

Baron-Cohen, S. (1989). Perceptual role taking and protodeclarative pointing in autism. *Brit. J. Dev. Psychol.*, *7*, 113–127.

Baron-Cohen, S. (1991). Do people with autism understand what causes emotion? *Child Dev.*, *62*, 385–395.

Barondes, S. H. (1993). *Molecules and Mental Illness.* New York: Scientific American Library.

Barondes, S. H. (1994, February 25). Thinking about prozac. *Science, 263*, p. 1102–1103.

Barr, C. E., Mednick, S. A., & Munk-Jorgensen, P. (1990). Exposure to influenza epidemics during gestation and adult schizophrenia: A 40-year study. *Arch. Gen. Psychiat.*, *47*(9), 869–874.

Barraclough, B. M., Bunch, J., Nelson, B. et al. (1974). A hundred cases of suicide: Clinical Aspects. *Brit. J. Psychiat.*, *125*, 355–373.

Barraclough, B. M., Jennings, C., & Moss, J. R. (1977). Suicide prevention by the Samaritans: A controlled study of effectiveness. *Lancet, 2*, 237–238.

Barrington, M. R. (1980). Apologia for suicide. In M. P. Battin & D. J. Mayo (Eds.), *Suicide: The philosophical issues.* New York: St. Martin's.

Barrios, B. A., & O'Dell, S. L. (1989). Fears and anxieties. In E. J. Mash & R. Barkley (Eds.), *Treatment of childhood disorders.* New York: Guilford.

Barros, E. L. (1992). Psychic change in child analysis. *Inter. J. Psychoanal.*, *73*(2), 303–311.

Barry, H., III. (1982). Cultural variations in alcohol abuse. In I. Al-Issa (Ed.), *Culture and psychopathology.* Baltimore: Univ. Park.

Barsky, A. J. (1992). Amplification, somatization, and the somatoform disorders. *Psychosomatics, 33*(1), 28–34.

Barsky, A. J., & Klerman, G. L. (1983). Overview: Hypochondriasis, bodily complaints and somatic styles. *Amer. J. Psychiat.*, *140*, 273–283.

Bartels, S., Teague, G., Drake, R., Clark, R., Bush, P., & Noordsy, D. (1993). Substance abuse in schizophrenia: Service utilization and costs. *J. Nerv. Ment. Dis.*, *181*(4), 227–232.

Barth, R. P., Blythe, B. J., Schinke, S. P., & Schilling, R. F. (1983). Self-control training with maltreating parents. *Child Welfare, 62*, 313–324.

Bartko, G., Herczeg, I., & Zador, G. (1988). Clinical symptomatology and drug compliance in schizophrenic patients. *Acta Psychiatr. Scandin.*, *77*(1), 74–76.

Barton, E. J., & Osborne, J. G. (1978). The development of classroom sharing by a teacher using positive practice. *Behav. Mod.*, *2*(2), 231–250.

Bartrop, R. W., Lockhurst, E., Lazarus, L., Kiloh, L. G., & Penny, R. (1977). Depressed lymphocyte function after bereavement. *Lancet, 1*, 834–836.

Basoglu, M. (1992). The relationship between panic disorder and agoraphobia. In G. D. Burrows, S. M. Roth, & R. Noyes, Jr., *Handbook of Anxiety* (Vol. 5). Oxford: Elsevier.

Bassett, A. S. (1992). Chromosomal aberrations and schizophrenia: Autosomes. *Brit. J. Psychiat.*, *161*, 323–334.

Bassuk, E. L., & Schoonover, S. C. (1977). *The practitioner's guide to psychoactive drugs.* New York: Plenum.

Batchelor, W. F. (1988). AIDS 1988. *Amer. Psychol.*, *43*(11), 853–858.

Bates, J. (1992). New Ethics code 'practical and livable.' *APA Monitor, 23.*

Bateson, G. (1978, April 21). The double-bind theory—Misunderstood? *Psychiatric News*, p. 40.

Bateson, G., Jackson, D., Haley, J., & Weakland, J. (1956). Toward a theory of schizophrenia. *Behav. Sci.*, *1*, 251–264.

Batki, S. (1988). Treatment of intravenous drug users with AIDS: The role of methadone maintenance. *Journal of Psychoactive Drugs, 20*, 213–216.

Battaglia, M., Gasperini, M., Sciuto, G., Scherillo, P., et al. (1991). Psychiatric disorders in the families of schizotypal subjects. *Schizo. Bull.*, *17*(4), 659–668.

Battin, M. P. (1980). Manipulated suicide. In M. P. Battin & D. J. Mayo (Eds.), *Suicide: The philosophical issues.* New York: St. Martin's.

Battin, M. P. (1980). Suicide: A fundamental human right? In M. P. Battin & D. J. Mayo (Eds.), *Suicide: The philosophical issues.* New York: St. Martin's.

Battin, M. P. (1982). *Ethical issues in suicide.* Englewood Cliffs, NJ: Prentice Hall.

Battin, M. P. (1993). Suicidology and the right to die. In A. A. Leenaars (Ed.), *Suicidology.* Northvale, NJ: Jason Aronson Inc.

Baucom, D. H. (1982). A comparison of behavioral contracting and problem-solving/communication training in behavioral marital therapy. *Behav. Ther., 13,* 162–174.

Baucom, D. H., & Hoffman, J. A. (1986). The effectiveness of marital therapy: Current status and applications to the clinical setting. In N. S. Jacobson & A. S. Gurman (Eds.), *Clinical handbook of marital therapy.* New York: Guilford.

Baum, A. (1990). Stress, intrusive imagery, and chronic stress. *Health Psychology, 9,* 653–675.

Baum, A., & Fleming, I. (1993). Implications of psychological research on stress and technological accidents. *Amer. Psychol., 48*(6), 665–672.

Baum, A., Gatchel, R. J., & Schaeffer, M. (1983). Emotional, behavioural and physiological effects of chronic stress at Three Mile Island. *J. Cons. Clin. Psychol., 51,* 565–572.

Bawden, D. L., & Sonenstein, F. L. (1992). Quasi-experimental designs. *Children and Youth Services Review, 14*(1-2), 137–144.

Baxter, L. R., Schwartz, J. M., Bergman, K. S., Szuba, M. P., Guze, B. H., Mazziotta, J. C., Alazraki, A., Selin, C. E., Ferng, H. K., Munford, P., & Phelps, M. E. (1992). Caudate glucose metabolic rate changes with both drug and behavior therapy for obsessive-compulsive disorder. *Arch. Gen. Psychiat., 49,* 681–689.

Baxter, L. R., Schwartz, J. M., Guze, B. H., Bergman, K. et al. (1990). PET imaging in obsessive compulsive disorder with and without depression. Symposium: Serotonin and its effects on human behavior (1989, Atlanta, GA). *J. Clin. Psychiat., 51*(Suppl.), 61–69.

Beahrs, J. O. (1983). Co-consciousness: A common denominator in hypnosis, multiple personality, and normalcy. *Amer. J. Clin. Hyp., 26*(2), 100–113.

Beardslee, W. R., Keller, M. B., Lavori, P. W., Staley, J., & Sacks, N. (1993). The impact of parental affective disorder on depression in offspring: A longitudinal follow-up in a nonreferred sample. *J. Amer. Acad. Child. Adol. Psychiat., 32*(4), 723–730.

Beatty, W. B., Salmon, D. P., Butters, N., et al. (1988). Retrograde amnesia in patients with Alzheimer's disease or Huntington's disease. *Neurobiology of Aging, 9,* 181–189.

Beatty, W. W., Wonderlich, S. A., Staton, R. D., & Ternes, L. A. (1990). Cognitive functioning in bulimia: Comparison with depression. *Bull. Psychosom. Society, 28*(4), 289–292.

Beaumont, G., & Hetzel, W. (1992). Patients at risk of suicide and overdose. 2nd International Symposium on Moclobemide: RIMA (Reversible Inhibitor of Monoamine Oxidase Type A): A new concept in the treatment of depression. *Psychopharmacology, 106*(Suppl.), 123–126.

Beauvais, F. (1992). The consequences of drug and alcohol use for Indian youth. *American Indian & Alaska Native Mental Health Research, 5*(1), 32–37.

Bech, P. (1992). Symptoms and assessment of depression. In E. S. Paykel (Ed.), *Handbook of Affective Disorders.* New York: Guilford.

Beck, A. T. (1967). *Depression: Clinical, experimental and theoretical aspects.* New York: Harper & Row.

Beck, A. T. (1976). *Cognitive therapy and the emotional disorders.* New York: International Univ.

Beck, A. T. (1985). Is behavior therapy on course? *Behav. Psychother., 13*(1), 83–84.

Beck, A. T. (1985). Theoretical perspectives on clinical anxiety. In A. H. Tuma & J. D. Maser (Eds.), *Anxiety and the anxiety disorders.* Hillsdale, NJ: Erlbaum.

Beck, A. T. (1987). Cognitive therapy. In J. K. Zeig (Ed.), *The evolution of psychotherapy.* New York: Brunner/Mazel.

Beck, A. T. (1988). Cognitive approaches to panic disorder: Theory and therapy. In S. Rachman & J. Maser (Eds.), *Panic: Psychological perspectives.* Hillsdale, NJ: Erlbaum.

Beck, A. T. (1991). Cognitive therapy: A 30-year retrospective. *Amer. Psychol., 46*(4), 368–375.

Beck, A. T. (1993). Cognitive approaches to stress. In P. M. Lehrer & R. L. Woolfolk (Eds.), *Principles and Practice of Stress Management* (2nd ed.). New York: Guilford.

Beck, A. T., & Beck, R. W. (1972). Screening depressed patients in family practice: A rapid technique. *Postgraduate Med., 52,* 81–85.

Beck, A. T., & Emery, G., with Greenberg, R. L. (1985). Differentiating anxiety and depression: A test of the cognitive content-specificity hypothesis. *J. Abnorm. Psychol., 96,* 179–183.

Beck, A. T., Emery, G., & Greenberg, R. (1985). *Anxiety disorders and phobias: A cognitive perspective.* New York: Basic Books.

Beck, A. T., Epstein, N., & Harrison, R. (1983). Cognitions, attitudes and personality dimensions in depression. *Brit. J. Cog. Psychother., 1*(1), 1–16.

Beck, A. T., Freeman, A. & Assoc. (1990). *Cognitive therapy of personality disorders.* New York: Guilford.

Beck, A. T., & Greenberg, R. L. (1988). Cognitive therapy with children and adolescents. In A. J. Frances & R. E. Hales (Eds.), *American Psychiatric Press review of psychiatry* (Vol. 7). Washington, DC: American Psychiatric.

Beck, A. T., Laude, R., & Bohnert, M. (1974). Ideational components of anxiety neurosis. *Arch. Gen. Psychiat., 31,* 319–325.

Beck, A. T., Resnik, H., Lettieri, D. (Eds.). (1974). *The prediction of suicide.* Maryland: The Charles Press.

Beck, A. T., Rush, A. J., Shaw, B. F., & Emery, G. (1979). *Cognitive therapy of depression.* New York: Guilford.

Beck, A. T., Sokol, L., Clark, D. A., Berchick, R. J., & Wright, F. D. (1992). Focused cognitive therapy of panic disorder: A crossover design and one-year follow-up. *Amer. J. Psychiat., 149*(6), 778–783.

Beck, A. T., & Sokol-Kessler, L. (1986). A test of cognitive dysfunction in panic attacks. Paper presented at the research conference, Univ. Pennsylvania, Philadelphia.

Beck, A. T., Steer, R. A., & Epstein, N. (1992). Self concept dimensions of clinically depressed and anxious outpatients. *J. Clin. Psych., 48*(4), 423–432.

Beck, A. T., Steer, R. A., & Garbin, M. G. (1988). Psychometric properties of the Beck Depression Inventory: Twenty-five years of evaluation. *Clin. Psychol. Rev., 8*(1), 77–100.

Beck, A. T., Ward, C. H., Mendelson, M., Mock, J. E., & Erbaugh, J. (1961). An inventory for measuring depression. *Arch. Gen. Psychiat., 4,* 561–571.

Beck, A. T., Ward, C. H., Mendelson, M., Mock, J. E., & Erbaugh, J. (1962). Reliability of psychiatric diagnosis. 2: A study of consistency of clinical judgments and ratings. *Amer. J. Psychiat., 119,* 351–357.

Beck, A. T., Weissman, A., Lester, D. et al. (1974). The measurement of pessimism: The hopelessness scale. *J. Cons. Clin. Psychol. 42,* 861–865.

Beck, A. T., et al. (1985). Treatment of depression with cognitive therapy and amitriptyline. *Arch. Gen. Psychiat., 42*(2), 142–148.

Beck, G. (1993). Vaginismus. In W. O'Donohue and J. Geer (eds.), *Handbook of sexual dysfunctions.* Boston: Allyn and Bacon.

Beck, K., Thombs, D., & Summons, T. (1993). The social context of drinking scales: Construct validation and relationship to indicants of abuse in an adolescent population. *Addictive Behaviors, 18,* 159–169.

Beck, J. C., & Parry, J. W. (1992). Incompetence, treatment refusal, and hospitalization. *Bulletin of the American Academy of Psychiatry and the Law, 20*(3), 261–267.

Beck, M., & Cowley, G. (1990, March 26). Beyond Lobotomies. *Newsweek,* p. 44.

Becker, C. E. (1979). Pharmacotherapy in the treatment of alcoholism. In J. Mendelson & N. Mello (Eds.), *The diagnosis and treatment of alcoholism.* New York: McGraw-Hill.

Becker, J. V. (1989). Impact of sexual abuse on sexual functioning. In S. R. Leiblum & R. C. Rosen (Eds.), *Principles and practice of sex therapy* (2nd ed.). New York: Guilford.

Becker, J. V., & Kavoussi, R. J. (1988). Sexual disorders. In J. A. Talbott, R. E. Hales, & S. C. Yudofsky (Eds.), *American Psychiatric Press textbook of psychiatry.* Washington, DC: American Psychiatric Press.

Becker, P., & Comstock, C. (1992, October). A retrospective look at one MPD/DD group: Recommendations for future MPD/DD groups. Paper presented at the Ninth International Conference of the International Society for the Study of Multiple Personality and Dissociative Disorders, Chicago.

Becker, W. C. (1964). Consequences of different kinds of parental discipline. In M. L. Hoffman & L. W. Hoffman (Eds.), *Review of child development research* (Vol. 1). New York: Russell Sage Foundation.

Becvar, D. S., & Becvar, R. J. (1993). *Family therapy: A systemic integration* (2nd ed.). Boston: Allyn and Bacon.

Bednar, R. L., & Kaul, T. J. (1994). Experiential group research: Can the canon fire? In A. E. Bergin & S. L. Garfiel (Eds.), *Handbook of psychotherapy and behavior change* (4th ed.). New York: Wiley.

Beebe, D. K. (1991). Emergency management of the adult female rape victim. *American Family Physician, 43,* 2041–2046.

Beers, C. W. (1908). *A mind that found itself.* Garden City, NY: Doubleday.

Beers, C. W. (1931). *A mind that found itself* (5th edition). New York: Doubleday.

Begley, S. (1989, August 14). The Stuff that Dreams are Made of. *Newsweek,* p. 40.

Begley, S. (1994, February 7). One pill makes you larger, and one pill makes you small . . . *Newsweek,* p. 37–40.

Beiser, M., Shore, J. H., Peters, R., & Tatum, E. (1985). Does community care for the mentally ill make a difference? A tale of two cities. *Amer. J. Psychiat., 142,* 1047–1052.

Beitchman, J. H., Zucker, K. J., Hood, J. E., DaCosta, G. A., & Cassavia, E. (1992). A review of the long-term effects of childhood sexual abuse. *Child Abuse & Neglect, 16*(1), 101–118.

Beitman, B. D. (1993). Afterward to Section IV. In J. M. Oldham, M. B. Riba, & A. Tasman (Eds.), *Review of Psychiatry* (Vol. 12). Washington, DC: American Psychiatric Press.

Beitman, B. D. (1993). Pharmacotherapy and the stages of psychotherapeutic change. In J. M. Oldham, M. B. Riba, & A. Tasman (Eds.), *Review of Psychiatry* (Vol. 12). Washington, DC: American Psychiatric Press.

Belcher, J. R. (1988). Defining the service needs of homeless mentally ill persons. *Hosp. Comm. Psychiat., 39*(11), 1203–1205.

Belcher, J. R. (1988). The future role of state hospitals. *Psychiat. Hosp., 19*(2), 79–83.

Belcher, J. R., & Blank, H. (1989–90). Protecting the right to involuntary commitment. *J. Appl. Soc. Sci., 14*(1), 95–115.

Belkin, L. (1990, Jun. 6). Doctor tells of first death using his suicide device. *New York Times,* A1, p. 3.

Bell, J. E. (1961). Family group therapy: A method for the psychological treatment of older children, adolescents, and their parents. *Public Health Monograph, 64.* Washington, DC: GPO.

Bellack, A. S., & Hersen, M. (1980). *Introduction to clinical psychology.* New York: Oxford UP.

Bellack, A. S., Morrison, R. L., & Mueser, K. T. (1989). Social problem solving in schizophrenia. *Schizo. Bull., 15*(1), 101–116.

Bellafante, G. (1993, June 7). Got a problem? Get in line. *Time,* p. 73.

Bellak, L., & Bellak, S. (1952). *Children's apperception test.* New York: Psychology Corp.

Belle, D. (1990). Poverty and women's mental health. *Amer. Psychol., 45*(3), 385–389.

Belli, R. F., Windschitl, P. D., McCarthy, T. T., & Winfrey, S. E. (1992). Detecting memory impairment with a modified test procedure: Manipulating retention interval with centrally presented event items. *Journal of Experimental Psychology: Learning, Memory, and Cognition, 18,* 356–367.

Bellinger, D. L., Felten, S. Y., & Felten, D. L. (1992). Neural-immune interactions. In A. Tasman & B. Riba (Eds.), *Review of Psychiatry,* vol 11. Washington: DC: American Psychiatric Press, Inc.

Bellow, S. (1984). *Humboldt's gift.* New York: Penguin.

Bemporad, J. R. (1992). Psychoanalytically oriented psychotherapy. In E. S. Paykel (Ed.), *Handbook of Affective Disorders.* New York: Guilford.

Ben-Porath, Y. S., & Butcher, J. N. (1991). The historical development of personality assessment. In C. E. Walker (Ed.), *Clinical Psychology: Historical and research foundations.* New York: Plenum.

Benassi, V. A., Sweeney, P. D., & Dufour, C. L. (1988). Is there a relation between locus of control orientation and depression? *J. Abnorm. Psychol., 97*(3), 357–367.

Bender, B. (1976). Duo therapy: A method of casework treatment of children. *Child Welfare, 55*(2), 95–108.

Bender, L. (1938). *A visual motor gestalt test and its clinical use.* New York: American Orthopsychiatric Assoc.

Benedict, R. (1934). Anthropology and the abnormal. *J. Gen. Psychol.,* 10, 59–82.

Benedict, R. (1934). *Patterns of culture.* New York: Houghton Mifflin.

Benezech, M., DeWitte, J. J. E., & Bourgeois, M. (1989). A

lycanthropic murderer [letter to the editor]. *Amer. J. Psychiat.*, *146*(7), 942.

Bennett, G. T., & Kish, G. R. (1990). Incompetency to stand trial: Treatment unaffected by demographic variables. *J. Forensic Sci.*, 35(2), 403–412.

Bennett, M. B. (1987). Afro-American women, poverty and mental health: A social essay. *Women and Health, 12*(3-4), 213–228.

Bennett, N. A., Spoth, R. L., & Borgen, F. H. (1991). Bulimic symptoms in high school females: Prevalence and relationship with multiple measures of psychological health, *Journal of Community Psychology*, 19(1), 13–28.

Benowitz, N. (1990). Clinical pharmacology of caffeine. *Annual Review of Medicine, 41*, 277–288.

Berg, C. Z., Rapoport, J. L., Whitaker, A., Davies, M., Leonard, H., Swedo, S. E., Braiman, S., & Lenane, M. (1989). Childhood obsessive compulsive disorder: a two-year prospective follow-up of a community sample. *J. Amer. Acad. Child Adol. Psychiat.*, 28(4), 528–533.

Berger, F. M. (1963). The similarities and differences between meprobamate and barbiturates. *Clin. Pharm. Ther.*, 4, 209–231.

Bergin, A. E., & Lambert, M. J. (1978). The evaluation of therapeutic outcomes. In S. L. Garfield & A. E. Bergin (Eds.), *Handbook of psychotherapy and behavior change: An empirical analysis*. New York: Wiley.

Bergler, E. (1951). *Neurotic counterfeit sex*. New York: Grune & Stratton.

Bergman, B., & Brismar, B. (1991). Suicide attempts by battered wives. *Acta Psychiatr. Scandin.*, 83(5), 380–384.

Berk, S. N., & Efran, J. S. (1983). Some recent developments in the treatment of neurosis. In C. E. Walker et al. (Eds.), *The handbook of clinical psychology: Theory, research, and practice* (Vol. 2). Homewood, IL: Dow Jones-Irwin.

Berkovitz, I. H. (1985). The adolescent, schools, and schooling. *Adol. Psychiat.*, 12, 162–176.

Berlin, I., Warot, D., Hergueta, T., Molinier, P., Bagot, C., & Puech, A. J. (1993). Comparison of the effects of zolpiden and triazolam on memory functions, psychomotor performances, and postural sway in healthy subjects. *Journal of Clinical Psychopharmacology*, 13(2), 100–106.

Berlin, I. N. (1987). Suicide among American Indian adolescents: An overview. *Suic. Life-Threat. Behav.*, 17, 218–232.

Berman, A. L. (1986). Helping suicidal adolescents: Needs and responses. In C. A. Corr & J. N. McNeil (Eds.), *Adolescence and death*. New York: Springer.

Berman, A. L., & Jobes, D. A. (1991). *Adolescent suicide: Assessment and intervention*. Washington, DC: American Psychological Association.

Berman, K. F., Torrey, E. F., Daniel, D. G., & Weinberger, D. R. (1992). Regional cerebral blood flow in monozygotic twins discordant and concordant for schizophrenia. *Arch. Gen. Psychiat.*, 49(12), 927–934.

Berman, S., Delaney, N., Gallagher, D., Atkins, P., & Graeber, M. (1987). Respite care: A partnership between a Veterans Administration nursing home and families to care for frail elders at home. *Gerontologist*, 27, 581–584.

Berney, B. (1993). Round and round it goes: The epidemiology of childhood lead poisoning, 1950–1990. *Milbank Quarterly*, 71(1), 3–39.

Bernstein, D. A., & Carlson, C. R. (1993). Progressive relax-ation: Abbreviated methods. In P. M. Lehrer & R. L. Woolfolk (Eds.), *Principles and Practice of Stress Management* (2nd ed.). New York: Guilford.

Bernstein, E. M., & Putnam, F. W. (1986). Development, reliability, and validity of a dissociation scale. *J. Nerv. Ment. Dis.*, 174(12), 727–735.

Bernstein, G. A., Garfinkel, B. D., & Borchardt, C. M. (1990). Compared studies of pharmacotherapy for school refusal. *J. Amer. Acad. Child Adol. Psychiat.*, 29(5), 773–781.

Bernstein, H. A. (1981). Survey of threats and assaults directed toward psychotherapists. *Amer. J. Psychother.*, 35, 542–549.

Berquier, A., & Ashton, R. (1991). A selective review of possible neurological etiologies of schizophrenia. *Clinical Psychology Review*, 11(5), 645–661.

Bertelsen, A., Harvald, B., & Hauge, M. (1977). A Danish twin study of manic depressive disorders. *Brit. J. Psychiat.*, 130, 330–351.

Betancourt, H., & Lopez, S. R. (1993). The study of culture, ethnicity, and race in American psychology. *Amer. Psychol.*, 48(6), 629–637.

Bettelheim, B. (1967). *The empty fortress: Infantile autism and the birth of the self*. New York: Free Press.

Bettelheim, B. (1969). *Children of the dream*. London: Collier Macmillan.

Beutler, L. E. (1979). Toward specific psychological therapies for specific conditions. *J. Cons. Clin. Psychol.*, 47, 882–892.

Beutler, L. E. (1991). Have all won and must all have prizes? Revisiting Luborsky et al.'s verdict. *J. Cons. Clin. Psychol.*, 59, 226–232.

Beutler, L. E., Machado, P. P. P., & Neufeldt, S. A. (1994). Therapist variables. In A. E. Bergin & S. L. Garfield (Eds.), *Handbook of psychotherapy and behavior change*. New York: Wiley.

Beyer, H. A. (1991). Litigation involving people with mental retardation. In J. L. Matson & J. A. Mulick (Eds.), *Handbook of mental retardation* (2nd ed.). New York: Pergamon Press.

Bhakthavatsalam, P., Kamatchi, G. L., & Ghosh, M. N. (1985). Tolerance pattern to amphetamine anorexia after selective lesions in the hypothalamic dopaminergic projection. *Life Sciences*, 37(7), 635–643.

Bibring, E. (1953). The mechanisms of depression. In P. Greenacre (Ed.), *Affective disorders*. New York: International Univ.

Bickman, L., & Dokecki, P. (1989). Public and private responsibility for mental health services. *Amer. Psychol.*, 44(8), 1133–1137.

Biederman, J. (Ed.) (1992). Special Section: New developments in pediatric psychopharmacology. *J. Amer. Acad. Child Adol. Psychiat.*, 31, 14–49.

Biederman, J., Keenan, K., & Faraone, S. V. (1990). Parent-based diagnosis of attention deficit disorder predicts a diagnosis based on teacher report. *J. Amer. Acad. Child Adol. Psychiat.*, 29(5), 698–701.

Bierman, K. L., & Furman, W. (1984). The effects of social skills training and peer involvement on the social adjustment of preadolescents. *Child Dev.*, 55(1), 151–162.

Bilder, R. M., Lipschutz-Broch, L., Reiter, G., Geisler, S. H., et al. (1992). Intellectual deficits in first-episode schizophrenia: Evidence for progressive deterioration. *Schizo. Bull.*, 18(3), 437–448.

Bindrim, P. (1968). A report on a nude marathon: The effects of physical nudity upon the practice interaction in the marathon group. *Psychother. Theory Res. Prac., 5,* 180–188.

Binet, A., & Simon, T. (1916). *The development of intelligence in children (The Binet-Simon Scale).* Baltimore: Williams & Wilkins.

Binik, Y. M., Servan-Schreiber, D., Freiwald, S., & Hall, K. S. (1988). Intelligent computer-based assessment and psychotherapy: An expert system for sexual dysfunction. *J. Nerv. Ment. Dis., 176*(7), 387–400.

Binstock, J. (1974). Choosing to die: The decline of aggression and the rise of suicide. *The Futurist, 8*(2), 68–71.

Birch, H. G., Richardson, S. A., Baird, D. et al. (1970). *Mental subnormality in the community—A clinical and epidemiological study.* Baltimore: Williams & Wilkins.

Bird, H. P., Gould, M. S., Staghezza, B. M. (1993). Patterns of diagnostic comorbidity in a community sample of children aged 9 through 16 years. *J. Amer. Acad. Child Adol. Psychiat., 32*(2), 361–368.

Bird, J. (1979). The behavioral treatment of hysteria. *Brit. J. Psychiat., 134,* 129–137.

Birren, J., & Cunningham, W. (1985). Research on the psychology of aging: Principles, concepts and theory. In J. Birren & K. W. Schaie (Eds.), *Handbook of the psychology of aging* (2nd ed.). New York: Van Nostrand Reinhold.

Bishopric, N. J., Cohen, H. J., & Lefkowitz, R. J. (1980). Beta-adrenergic receptors in lymphocyte subpopulations. *J. Allergy & Clin. Immun., 65,* 29–33.

Blacher, J., & Baker, B. L. (1992). Toward meaningful involvement in out-of-home placement settings. *Mental Retardation, 30*(1), 35–43.

Blacher, J., & Baker, B. L. (1994). Family involvement in residential treatment of children with retardation: Is there evidence of detachment? *J. Child Psychol. Psychiat. Allied Disc., 35*(3), 505–520.

Black, A. (1974). The natural history of obsessional neurosis. In H. R. Beech (Ed.), *Obsessional states.* London: Methuen.

Black, B. J. (1977). Substitute permanent employment for the deinstitutionalized mentally ill. *J. Rehab., 43,* 32–35.

Black, D. W., & Winokur, G. (1990). Suicide and psychiatric diagnosis. In S. J. Blumenthal & D. J. Kupfer (Eds.), *Suicide over the life cycle: Risk factors, assessment, and treatment of suicidal patients.* Washington, DC: American Psychiatric Press, Inc.

Black, D. W., Winokur, G., & Nasrallah, A. (1987). Treatment of mania: A naturalistic study of electroconvulsive therapy vs. lithium in 438 patients. *J. Clin. Psychiat., 48,* 132–139.

Black, S. T. (1993). Comparing genuine and simulated suicide notes: A new perspective. *J. Cons. Clin. Psychol., 61*(4), 699–702.

Blackburn, I. M., Bishop, S., Glen, A. I. M., Whalley, L. J., & Christie, J. E. (1981). The efficacy of cognitive therapy in depression: A treatment trial using cognitive therapy and pharmacotherapy, each alone and in combination. *Brit. J. Psychiat., 139,* 181–189.

Blackburn, R. (1993). *The psychology of criminal conduct: Theory, research, and practice.* New York: Wiley.

Blackstein, K. R. (1975). The sensation seeker and anxiety reactivity. Relationship between sensation-seeking scales and the activity preference questionnaire. *J. Clin. Psychol., 31,* 677–681.

Blackwell, B., Marley, E., Price, J., & Taylor, D. (1967). Hyper-

tensive interactions between monoamine oxidase inhibitors and foodstuffs. *Brit. J. Psychiat., 113,* 349–365.

Blair, C. D., & Lanyon, R. I. (1981). Exhibitionism: Etiology and treatment. *Psychol. Bull., 89*(3), 439–463.

Blanchard, E. B. (1994). Behavioral medicine and health psychology. In A. E. Bergin & S. L. Garfield (Eds.), *Handbook of psychotherapy and behavior change.* New York: Wiley.

Blanchard, E. B., & Andrasik, F. (1982). Psychological assessment and treatment of headache: Recent developments and emerging issues. *J. Cons. Clin. Psychol., 50*(6), 859–879.

Blanchard, E. B., & Epstein, L. H. (1978). *A biofeedback primer.* Reading, MA: Addison-Wesley.

Blanchard, E. B., Schwarz, S. P., Suls, J. M., Gerardi, M., et al. (1992). Two controlled evaluations of multicomponent psychological treatment of irritable bowel syndrome. *Behav. Res. Ther., 30*(2), 175–189.

Blanchard, E. B. et al. (1982). Biofeedback and relaxation training with three kinds of headache: Treatment effects and their prediction. *J. Cons. Clin. Psychol., 50*(4), 562–575.

Blanchard, M. R., Waterreus, A., & Mann, A. H. (1994). The nature of depression among older people in inner London, and the contact with primary care. *Brit. J. Psychiat., 164,* 396–402.

Blanchard, R., & Hucker, S. J. (1991). Age, transvestism, bondage, and concurrent paraphilic activities in 117 fatal cases of autoerotic asphyxia. *Brit. J. Psychiat., 159,* 371–377.

Bland, R. C., & Orn, H. (1986). Family violence and psychiatric disorder. *Canad. J. Psychiat., 31*(2), 129–137.

Bland, R. C., Orn, H., & Newman, S. C. (1988). Lifetime prevalence of psychiatric disorders in Edmonton. *Acta Psychiatr. Scandin., 77*(Suppl. 338), 24–32.

Bland, R. C., Parker, J. H., & Orn, H. (1976). Prognosis in schizophrenia: A ten-year follow-up of first admissions. *Arch. Gen. Psychiat., 33*(8), 949–954.

Blank, A. S. (1979). *Vietnam veterans—Operation Outreach. First Training Conference Papers.* St. Louis: U.S. Veterans Admin.

Blank, A. S. (1982). Apocalypse terminable and interminable: Operation Outreach for Vietnam veterans. *Hosp. Comm. Psychiat., 33*(11), 913–918.

Blatt, S., & Wild, C. (1976). *Schizophrenia: A developmental analysis.* New York: Academic Press.

Blazer, D. (1990). *Emotional problems in later life.* New York: Springer.

Blazer, D. G., George, L. K., & Hughes, D. (1991). The epidemiology of anxiety disorders: An age comparison. In C. Salzman & B. D. Lebowitz (Eds.), *Anxiety in the elderly.* New York: Springer.

Blazer, D. G., Hughes, D., George, L. K., Swartz, M., & Boyer, R. (1991). Generalized anxiety disorder. In L. N. Robins, & D. A. Regier (Eds.), *Psychiatric Disorders in America: The Epidemiologic Catchment Area Study.* New York: Maxwell Macmillan International.

Blehar, M. C., Weissman, M. M., & Gershon, E. S. (1988). Family and genetic studies of affective disorders. National Institute of Mental Health: Family and genetic studies of affective disorders. *Arch. Gen. Psychiat., 45*(3), 288–292.

Bliss, E. L. (1980). Multiple personalities: A report of 14 cases with implications for schizophrenia and hysteria. *Arch. Gen. Psychiat., 37*(12), 1388–1397.

Bliss, E. L. (1980). *Multiple personality, allied disorders and hypnosis.* New York: Oxford UP.

Bliss, E. L. (1985). "How prevalent is multiple personality?": Dr. Bliss replies. *Amer. J. Psychiat., 142*(12), 1527.

Bliss, T., & Gardner, M. A. (1973). Long-lasting potentiation of synaptic transmission in the dentate area of unanesthetized rabbit following stimulation of the prerforant path. *Journal of Physiology, 232,* 357–374.

Bliwise, N., McCall, M. E., & Swan, S. J. (1987). In E. E. Lurie & J. H. Swan & Assoc. (Eds.), *Serving the mentally ill elderly: Problems and perspectives.* Lexington, MA: Heath.

Bloch, S., Crouch, E., & Reibstein, J. (1982). Therapeutic factors in group psychotherapy: A review. *Arch. Gen. Psychiat., 27,* 216–324.

Block, B., & Pristach, C. A. (1992). Diagnosis and management of the paranoid patient. *American Family Physician, 45*(6), 2634–2640.

Block, L. (1992, June 8). Mental Health Expenses make employers anxious. *Business Insurance,* p. 3.

Bloom, B. L. (1984). *Community mental health: A general introduction* (2nd ed.). Monterey, CA: Brooks/Cole.

Bloom, F., Lazerson, A., & Hofstadter, L. (1985). *Brain, mind, and behavior.* New York: W. H. Freeman.

Bloom, H., & Rosenbluth, M. (1989). The use of contracts in the inpatient treatment of the borderline personality disorder. *Psychiat. Quart., 60*(4), 317–327.

Bloom, J. D. (1990). The Tarasoff decision & gun control legislation. *Inter. J. Offend. Ther. Compar. Criminol., 34*(1), v–viii.

Bloom, L. J., & Trautt, G. M. (1977). Finger pulse volume as a measure of anxiety: Further evaluation. *Psychophysiology, 14,* 541–544.

Bloomingdale, L., & Bloomingdale, E. (1989). Childhood identification and prophylaxis of antisocial personality disorder. In R. Rosner & H. I. Schwartz (Eds.), *Juvenile Psychiatry and the Law.* New York: Plenum.

Blum, K., & Noble, E. (1993). Drug dependence and the A1 allele gene. *Drug Alc. Dep., 33*(5).

Blum, K., Noble, E., Sheridan, P., et al. (1990). Allelic association of human dopamine D2 receptor gene in alcoholism. *JAMA, 263,* 2055–2060.

Blum, K., Noble, E., Sheridan, P., Finley, O., et al. (1991). Association of the A1 allele of the D2 dopamine receptor gene with severe alcoholism. *Alcohol, 8*(5), 409–416.

Blumstein, P., & Schwartz, P. (1983). *American couples.* New York: Morrow.

Bocker, F. M. (1984). Soziale Integration und Kontakte zu Bezugspersonen des gewohnten sozialen Umfeldes wahrend stationarer Behandlung im psychiatrischen Krankenhaus. Eine prospektive katamnestische Untersuchung an erstmals aufgenommenen Patienten mit schizophrenen und cyclothymen Psychosen [Social integration and contact with people in the normal social environment during treatment in a psychiatric hospital: A follow-up of first-admission inpatients with schizophrenia and affective disorders]. *Eur. Arch. Psychiat. Neurol. Sci., 234*(4), 250–257.

Bockoven, J. S. (1963). *Moral treatment in American psychiatry.* New York: Springer.

Bogdan, R., & Taylor, S. (1976, Jan.). The judged, not the judges: An insider's view of mental retardation. *Amer. Psychol., 31*(1), 47–52.

Bok, S. (1978). *Lying: Moral Choice in Public and Private Life.* New York: Pantheon Books.

Boker, W. (1992). A call for partnership between schizophrenic patients, relatives and professionals. *Brit. J. Psychiat., 161*(suppl. 18), 10–12.

Bolgar, H. (1965). The case study method. In B. B. Wolman (Ed.), *Handbook of clinical psychology.* New York: McGraw-Hill.

Boller, F. (1983). Alzheimer's disease and Parkinson's disease: Clinical and pathological associations. In B. Reisberg (Ed.), *Alzheimer's disease: The standard reference.* New York: Free Press.

Bolton, F., Morris, L., & MacEachron, A. (1989). *Males at Risk: The other side of Child Abuse.* Newbury Park, CA: Sage Publications.

Bolund, C. (1985). Suicide and cancer: II. Medical and care factors in suicides by cancer patients in Sweden, 1973–1976. *J. Psychol. Oncology, 3*(1), 31–52.

Bond, C., Omar, A., Pitre, U., Lashley, B. R., et al (1992). Fishy-looking liars: Deception judgment from expectancy violation. *J. Pers. Soc. Psychol., 63*(6), 969–977.

Bondareff, W., Mountjoy, L. Q., & Roth, M. (1982). Loss of neurons of origin of the adrenergic projection to cerebral cortex (nucleus locus coeruleus) in senile dementia. *Neurology, 32,* 164–168.

Bondi, M. W., & Kaszniak, A. W. (1991). Implicit and explicit memory in Alzheimer's disease and Parkinson's disease. *J. Clin. Exp. Neuropsych., 13,* 339–358.

Bongar, B., Peterson, L. G., Golann, S., & Hardiman, J. J. (1990). Self-mutilation and the chronically suicidal patient: An examination of the frequent visitor to the psychiatric emergency room. *Ann. Clin. Psychiat., 2*(3), 217–222.

Bonner, R. L. (1992). Isolation, seclusion, and psychosocial vulnerability as risk factors for suicide behind bars. In R. W. Maris, A. L. Berman, J. T. Maltsberger, & R. I. Yufit (Eds.), *Assessment and prediction of suicide.* New York: Guilford.

Borkovec, T. D., & Costello, E. (1992). Efficacy of applied relaxation and cognitive behavioral therapy in the treatment of generalized anxiety disorder. Manuscript submitted for publication.

Borkovec, T. D., & Inz, J. (1990). The nature of worry in generalized anxiety disorder: A predominance of thought activity. *Behav. Res. Ther., 28*(2), 153–158.

Borkovec, T. D., Lyonfields, J. D., Wiser, S. L., & Deihl, L. (1993). The role of worrisome thinking in the suppression of cardiovascular response to phobic imagery. *Behav. Res. Ther., 31*(3), 321–324.

Borkovec, T. D., Robinson, E., Pruzinsky, T., & Depree, J. A. (1983). Preliminary exploration of worry: Some characteristics and processes. *Behav. Res. Ther., 21,* 9–16.

Bornstein, P. H., Hamilton, S. B., & Bornstein, M. T. (1986). Self-monitoring procedures. In A. R. Ciminero, K. S. Calhoun, & H. E. Adams (Eds.), *Handbook of behavioral assessment* (2nd ed.). New York: Wiley.

Bornstein, R. A., Schwarzkopf, S. B., Olson, S. C., & Nasrallah, H. A. (1992). Third-ventricle enlargement and neuropsychological deficit in schizophrenia. *Bio. Psychiat., 31*(9), 954–961.

Bornstein, R. F. (1992). The dependent personality: Developmental, social, and clinical perspectives. *Psychol. Bull., 112*(1), 3–23.

Bornstein, R. F., Klein, D. N., Mallon, J. C., & Slater, J. F. (1988). Schizotypal personality disorder in an outpatient population: Incidence and clinical characteristics. *J. Clin. Psych.*, *44*(3), 322–325.

Borys, D. S., & Pope, K. S. (1989). Dual relationships between therapist and client: A national study of psychologists, psychiatrists and social workers. *Profess. Psychol.*, *20*, 283–293.

Borysenko, M., & Borysenko, J. (1982). Stress, behavior, and immunity: Animal models and mediating mechanisms. *Gen. Hosp. Psychiat.*, *4*, 59–67.

Boswell, J. (1933). *The Life of Dr. Johnson.* London: J. M. Dent & Sons.

Boswell, J. (1953). *The Life of Samuel Johnson, (Vol 1), The Life (1709–1965).* Oxford Clarendon Press.

Bott, E. (1928). Teaching of psychology in the medical course. *Bulletin of the Association of American Medical Colleges, 3,* 289–304.

Boudewyns, P. A., Hyer, L., Woods, M. G., Harrison, W. R., et al. (1990). PTSD among Vietnam veterans: An early look at treatment outcome using direct therapeutic exposure. *Journal of Traumatic Stress, 3*(3), 359–368.

Boudewyns, P. A., Tanna, V. L., & Fleischman, D. J. A. (1975). A modified shame aversion therapy for compulsive obscene telephone calling. *Behav. Ther., 6,* 704–707.

Boulougouris, J. C., Rabavilas, A. D., & Stefanis, C. (1977). Psychophysiological responses in obsessive-compulsive patients. *Behav. Res. Ther., 15*(3), 221–230.

Bourgeois, J. A., Hall, M. J., Crosby, R. M., & Drexler, K. G. (1993). An examination of narcissistic personality traits as seen in a military population. *Military Medicine, 158*(3), 170–174.

Bourgeois, M. (1991). Serotonin, impulsivity and suicide. *Human Psychopharmacology Clinical and Experimental, 6*(Suppl.), 31–36.

Bourne, P. G. (1970). *Men, stress & Vietnam.* Boston: Little, Brown.

Bowen, M. (1987). Psychotherapy, past, present & future. In J. K. Zeig (Ed.), *The evolution of psychotherapy.* New York: Brunner/Mazel.

Bowen, M. A. (1960). A family concept of schizophrenia. In D. D. Jackson (Ed.), *The etiology of schizophrenia.* New York: Basic Books.

Bower, B. (1987, June). What's in the cards for manic depression? The surprisingly harsh and long-lived mood swings of manic depression are charted in a closetful of cards. *Science News.*

Bower, B. (1992, August 15). Truth aches. *Science News, 142,* 110–111.

Bower, G. H. (1981). Mood and memory. *Amer. Psychol., 36*(2), 129–148.

Bowers, M. B. (1977). Psychoses precipitated by psychomimetic drugs. *Arch. Gen. Psychiat., 34,* 832–835.

Bowlby, J. (1969). *Attachment* (Vol. 1). New York: Basic Books.

Bowlby, J. (1973). *Separation: Anxiety and anger.* New York: Basic Books.

Bowlby, J. (1977). The making and breaking of affectional bonds: I. Aetiology and psychopathology in the light of attachment theory. *Brit. J. Psychiat., 130,* 201–210.

Bowlby, J. (1977). The making and breaking of affectional bonds: II. Some principles of psychotherapy. *Brit. J. Psychiat., 130,* 421–431.

Bowlby, J. (1980). By ethology out of psychoanalysis: An experiment in interbreeding. *Animal Behav., 28*(3), 649–656.

Boyce, P., Hickie, I., Parker, G., Mitchell, P., Wilhelm, K., & Brodaty, H. (1993). Specificity of interpersonal sensitivity to non-melancholic depression. *J. Affect. Dis., 27,* 101–105.

Boyd, J. H., Rae, D. S., Thompson, J. W., Burns, B. J., et al. (1990). Phobia: Prevalence and risk factors. *Social Psychiatry and Psychiatric Epidemiology, 25*(6), 314–323.

Boyd, J. H., & Weissman, M. M. (1981). Epidemiology of affective disorders: A reexamination and future directions. *Arch. Gen. Psychiat., 38*(9), 1039–1046.

Bradbury, T. N., & Karney, B. R. (1993). Longitudinal study of marital interaction and dysfunction: Review and analysis. *Clinical Psychology Review, 13*(1), 15–27.

Bradbury, T. N., & Miller, G. A. (1985). Season of birth in schizophrenia: A review of evidence, methodology, and etiology. *Psychol. Bull., 98*(3), 569–594.

Brady, J. P., & Lind, D. L. (1961). Experimental analysis of hysterical blindness: Operant conditioning techniques. *Arch. Gen. Psychiat., 4,* 331–339.

Brady, J. V., Porter, R. W., Conrad, D. G., & Mason, J. W. (1958). Avoidance behavior and the development of gastroduodenal ulcers. *J. Exp. Anal. Behav., 1,* 69–73.

Braestrup, C., Schmiechen, R., Neef, G., Nielson, M., & Petersen, E. N. (1982). Interactions of convulsive ligands with benzodiazepine receptors. *Science, 216,* 1241–1243.

Braff, D. L. (1981). Impaired speed of information processing in non-medicated schizotypal patients. *Schizo. Bull., 7,* 499–508.

Braff, D. L., & Saccuzzo, D. P. (1985). The time course of information-processing deficits in schizophrenia. *Amer. J. Psychiat., 142*(2), 170–174.

Braginsky, B. M., Braginsky, D. D., & Ring, K. (1969). *Methods of madness: The mental hospital as a last resort.* New York: Holt.

Bramanti, P., Ricci, R. M., Rifici, C., Ecari, U., et al. (1990). Etizolam: A controlled study versus alprazolam in the treatment of generalized anxiety disorder with minor associated depressive symptoms. *Current Therapeutic Research, 48*(2), 369–377.

Brandon, S. (1981). The history of shock treatment, in *Electroconvulsive therapy: An appraisal.* Oxford: Oxford UP.

Braun, B. G. (1984). Hypnosis creates multiple personality: Myth or reality? *Inter. J. Clin. Exp. Hyp., 32*(2), 191–197.

Braun, B. G., & Sachs, R. G. (1985). The development of multiple personality disorder: Predisposing, precipitating, and perpetuating factors. In R. P. Kluft (Ed.), *Childhood antecedents of multiple personality.* Washington, DC: American Psychiatric Press.

Braun, P., Greenberg, D., Dasberg, H., et al. (1990). Core symptoms of post-traumatic stress disorder unimproved by alprazolam treatment. *J. Clin. Psychiat., 51,* 236–238.

Bray, G. A., Dahms, W. T., Atkinson, R. L. et al. (1980). Factors controlling food intake: A comparison of dieting and intestinal bypass. *Amer. J. Clin. Nutrition, 33,* 376–382.

Breggin, P. R. (1979). *Electroshock: Its brain-disabling effects.* New York: Springer.

Bregman, E. (1934). An attempt to modify the emotional attitudes of infants by the conditioned response technique. *J. Genetic Psychol., 45,* 169–198.

Breier, A., Buchanan, R. W., Kirkpatrick, B., Davis, O. R., et al. (1994). Effects of clozapine on positive and negative symptoms in outpatients with schizophrenia. *Amer. J. Psychiat.*, *151*(1), 20–26.

Breier, A., Schreiber, J. L., Dyer, L. et al. (1991). NIMH longitudinal study of chronic schizophrenia: prognosis and predictor of outcome. *Arch. Gen. Psychiat.*, *48*(7), 642.

Bremner, J. D., Southwick, S. M., Johnson, D. R., Yehuda, R., & Charney, D. S. (1993). Childhood physical abuse and combat-related posttraumatic stress disorder in Vietnam Veterans. *Amer. J. Psychiat.*, *150*(2), 235–239.

Bremner, J. D., Steinberg, M., Southwick, S. M., Johnson, D. R., & Charney, D. S. (1993). Use of the structured clinical interview for DSM-IV dissociative disorders for systematic assessment of dissociative symptoms in posttraumatic stress disorder. *Amer. J. Psychiat.*, *150*(7), 1101–1014.

Brende, J. O., & Parson, E. R. (1985). *Vietnam veterans.* New York: Plenum.

Brende, J. O., & Rinsley, D. B. (1981). A case of multiple personality with psychological automatisms. *J. Amer. Acad. Psychoanal.*, *9*(1), 129–151.

Brent, D. A., Kalas, R., Edelbrock, C., Costello, A. J., Dulcan, M. K., & Conover, N. (1986). Psychopathology and its relationship to suicidal isolation in childhood and adolescence. *J. Amer. Acad. Child Psychiat.*, *25*, 666–673.

Brent, D. A., Kupfer, D. J., Bromet, E. J., & Dew, M. A. (1988). The assessment and treatment of patients at risk for suicide. In A. J. Frances & R. E. Hales (Eds.), *American psychiatric press review of psychiatry* (Vol. 7). Washington, DC: American Psychiatric Press.

Brent, D. A., Perper, J. A., Moritz, G., Allman, C., Friend, A., Roth, C., Schweers, J., Balach, L., & Baugher, M. (1993). Psychiatric risk factors for adolescent suicide: A case-control study. *J. Amer. Acad. Child Adol. Psychiat.*, *32*(3), 521–529.

Brent, D. A., Perper, J. A., Moritz, G., Baugher, M., & Allman, C. (1993). Suicide in adolescents with no apparent psychopathology. *J. Amer. Acad. Child Adol. Psychiat.*, *32*(3), 494–500.

Breslin, N. A. (1992). Treatment of schizophrenia: Current practice and future promise. *Hosp. Comm. Psychiat.*, *43*(9), 877–885.

Breslow, N. (1989). Sources of confusion in the study and treatment of sadomasochism. *J. Soc. Behav. Pers.*, *4*(3), 263–274.

Brewin, C. R., & Furnham, A. (1986). Attributional versus preattributional variables in self-esteem and depression: A comparison and test of learned helplessness theory. *J. Pers. Soc. Psychol.*, *50*(5), 1013–1020.

Briere, J. (1992). *Child Abuse Trauma: Theory and Treatment of the Lasting Effects.* Newbury Park, CA: SAGE Publications.

Briere, J. (1992). Methodological issues in the study of sexual abuse effects. *J. Cons. Clin. Psychol.*, *147*, 1398–1390.

Brightman, B. K. (1992). Peer support and education in the comprehensive care of patients with borderline personality disorder. *Psychiat. Hosp.*, *23*(2), 55–59.

Brill, N., Koegler, R., Epstein, L., & Forgy, E. (1964). Controlled study of psychiatric outpatient treatment. *Arch. Gen. Psychiat.*, *10*, 581–595.

Britton, A. G. (July/August 1988). Thin is out, fit is in. *American Health*, p. 66–71.

Britton, W. H., & Eaves, R. C. (1986). Relationship between the Vineland Adaptive Behavior Scales—Classroom Edition of the Vineland Social Maturity Scales. *Amer. J. Ment. Def.*, *91*(1), 105–107.

Broderick, D. F., Wippold, F. J., Clifford, D. B., Kido, D., & Wilson, B. (1993). White matter lesions and cerebral atrophy on MRI images in patients with and without AIDS dementia complex. *American Journal of Roentgenology*, *161*(1), 17–81.

Brodsky, S., & Pothyress, N. (1990). Presentation. American Psychological Association Convention, Boston.

Brom, D., Kleber, R. J., & Hofman, M. C. (1993). Victims of traffic accidents: Incidence and prevention of post-traumatic stress disorder. *J. Clin. Psych.*, *49*(2), 131–140.

Bromet, E. J. (1984). Epidemiology. In A. S. Bellack & M. Hersen (Eds.), *Research methods in clinical psychology.* New York: Pergamon.

Bromet, E. J., Hough, L., & Connell, M. (1984). Mental health of children near the Three Mile Island reactor. *Journal of Preventive Psychiatry*, *2*, 275–301.

Bromet, E. J., Schulberg, H. C., & Dunn, L. (1982). Reactions of psychiatric patients to the Three Mile Island nuclear accident. *Arch. Gen. Psychiat.*, *39*(6), 725–730.

Brooks, G. R., & Richardson, F. C. (1980). Emotional skills training: A treatment program for duodenal ulcer. *Behav. Ther.*, *11*(2), 198–207.

Brotman, A. W., Herzog, D. B., & Hamburg, P. (1988). Long-term course in 14 bulimic patients treated with psychotherapy. *J. Clin. Psychiat.*, *49*, 157–160.

Broverman, I. K., Broverman, D. M., Clarkson, F. E., Rosenkrantz, P. S., & Vogel, S. R. (1970). Sex role stereotypes and clinical judgments of mental health. *J. Cons. Clin. Psychol.*, *34*, 1–7.

Brown, B. (1974). Depression roundup. *Behav. Today*, *5*(17), 117.

Brown, B. S. (1976). Obstacles to treatment for blue-collar workers. In *New dimensions in mental health.* Washington, DC: U.S. Dept. Health, Education and Welfare.

Brown, B. S. (1983). The impact of political and economic changes upon mental health. *Amer. J. Orthopsychiat.*, *53*(4), 583–592.

Brown, E. (1972). Assessment from a humanistic perspective. *Psychother. Theory Res. Prac.*, *9*, 103–106.

Brown, G. L., Ebert, M., Goyer, P., Jimerson, D. C., Klein, W. J., Bunney, W. E., & Goodwin, F. K. (1982). Aggression, suicide, and serotonin: Relationships to CSF amine metabolites. *Amer. J. Psychiat.*, *139*, 741–746.

Brown, G. L., & Goodwin, F. K. (1986). Special Issue: Suicide and life-threatening behavior. *Suic. Life-Threat. Behav.*, *16*(2), 223–243.

Brown, G. L., Goodwin, F. K., Ballenger, J. C., Goyer, P. F., & Major, L. F. (1979). Aggression in humans correlates with cerebrospinal fluid metabolites. *Psychiatry Research*, *1*, 131–139.

Brown, G. L., Linnoila, M. I., & Goodwin, F. K. (1992). Impulsivity, aggression, and associated affects: Relationship to self-destructive behavior and suicide. In R. W. Maris, A. L. Berman, J. T. Maltsberger, & R. I. Yufit (Eds.), *Assessment and prediction of suicide.* New York: Guilford.

Brown, G. W. (1988). Early loss of parent and depression in adult life. In S. Fisher & J. Reason (Eds.), *Handbook of life stress, cognition and health.* Chichester: Wiley.

Brown, G. W., Harris, T. O., & Peto, J. (1973). Life events and psychiatric disorders: II. Nature of causal link. *Psychol. Med.*, *3*(2), 159–176.

Brown, G. W., Monck, E. M., Carstairs, G. M., & Wing, J. K. (1962). Influence on family life on the course of schizophrenic illness. *British Journal of Preventive and Social Medicine, 16,* 55–68.

Brown, G. W., Sklair, F., Harris, T. O., & Birley, J. L. T. (1973). Life-events and psychiatric disorders. Part I. Some methodological issues. *Psychol. Med., 3,* 74–87.

Brown, J. C. (1983). Paraphilias: Sadomasochism, fetishism, transvestism and transsexuality. *Brit. J. Psychiat., 143,* 227–231.

Brown, J. H., Henteleff, P., Barakat, S., & Rowe, C. J. (1986). Is it normal for terminally ill patients to desire death? *Amer. J. Psychiat., 143*(2), 208–211.

Brown, J. L. (1960). Prognosis from presenting symptoms of preschool children with atypical development. *Amer. J. Orthopsychiat., 30,* 382–390.

Brown, J. L. (1963). Follow-up of children with atypical development (infantile psychosis). *Amer. J. Orthopsychiat., 33,* 855–861.

Brown, L. (1993). Enrollment of drug abusers in HIV clinical trials: A public health imperative for communities of color. *Journal of Psychoactive Drugs, 25*(1), 45–48.

Brown, T. A., Hertz, R. M., Barlow, D. H. (1992). New developments in cognitive-behavioural treatment of anxiety disorders. In A. Tasman, & M. B. Riba (Eds.), *Review of Psychiatry* (Vol. 11). Washington, DC: American Psychiatric Press.

Brown, T. A., Moras, K., Zinbarg, R. E., Barlow, D. H. (1993). Diagnostic and symptom distinguishability of generalized anxiety disorder and obsessive-compulsive disorder. *Behav. Ther., 24,* 227–240.

Browne, A., & Finklehor, D. (1986). Impact of child sexual abuse: A review of the research. *Psychol. Bull., 99*(1), 66–77.

Brownell, K. D., & O'Neil, P. M. (1993). Obesity. In D. H. Barlow (Ed.), *Clinical handbook of psychological disorders: A step-by-step treatment manual* (2nd ed.). New York: Guilford.

Brownell, K. D., & Wadden, T. A. (1992). Etiology and treatment of obesity: Understanding a serious, prevalent, and refractory disorder. *J. Cons. Clin. Psychol., 60*(4), 505–517.

Browning, R. M. (1971). Treatment of a total behavior modification program with five autistic children. *Behav. Res. Ther., 9,* 319–327.

Bruce, M. L., Leaf, P. J., Florio, L. P., & Holzer, C. (1991). Affective disorders. In L. N. Robins & D. S. Regier (Eds.), *Psychiatric Disorders in America: The epidemiological catchment area study.* New York: Free Press.

Bruce, M. L., Leaf, P. J., Rozal, G. P. M., Florio, L., & Hoff, R. A. (1994). Psychiatric status and 9-year mortality data in the New Haven Epidemiological Catchment Area Study. *Amer. J. Psychiat., 151*(5), 716–721.

Bruch, H. (1962). Perceptual and conceptual disturbances in anorexia nervosa. *Psychosom. Med., 24,* 187–194.

Bruch, H. (1973). *Eating disorders: Obesity, anorexia nervosa and the person within.* New York: Basic Books.

Bruch, H. (1973). Psychiatric aspects of obesity. *Psychiat. Ann., 3*(7), 6–10.

Bruch, H. (1974). Anorexia nervosa. In *American Handbook of Psychiatry* (2nd ed.). New York: Basic Books.

Bruch, H. (1978). *The golden cage: The enigma of anorexia nervosa.* Cambridge, MA: Harvard UP.

Bruch, H. (1981). Developmental considerations of anorexia nervosa and obesity. *Canad. J. Psychiat., 26,* 212–217.

Bruch, H. (1982). Anorexia nervosa: Therapy and theory. *Amer. J. Psychiat., 139,* 1531–1538.

Bruch, H. (1986). Anorexia nervosa: The therapeutic task. In K. D. Brownell & J. P. Foreyt (Eds.), *Handbook of eating disorders: Physiology, psychology and treatment of obesity, anorexia and bulimia.* New York: Basic Books.

Buchan, H., Johnstone, E. C., McPherson, K., Palmer, R. L., et al. (1992). Who benefits from electroconvulsive therapy? Combined results of the Leicester and Northwick Park trials. *Brit. J. Psychiat., 160,* 355–359.

Buchele, B. J. (1993). Group psychotherapy for persons with multiple personality and dissociative disorders. *Bull. Menninger Clin., 57*(3), 362–370.

Bucher, R. E., & Costa, P. F. (1985). A abordagem terapeutica do toxicomano [The treatment of drug addicts]. *Acta Psiquiatrica y Psicologica de America Latina, 31*(2), 113–130.

Buchsbaum, M. S., & Haier, R. J. (1987). Functional and anatomical brain imaging: Impact on schizophrenia research. *Schizo. Bull., 13*(1), 115–132.

Buchwald, A. M., & Rudick-Davis, D. (1993). The symptoms of major depression. *J. Abnorm. Psychol., 102*(2), 197–205.

Buckley, P., Thompson, P., Way, L., & Meltzer, H. Y. (1994). Substance abuse among patients with treatment-resistant schizophrenia: Characteristics and implications for clozapine therapy. *Amer. J. Psychiat., 151*(3), 385–389.

Buda, M., & Tsuang, M. T. (1990). The epidemiology of suicide: Implications for clinical practice. In S. J. Blumenthal & D. J. Kupfer (Eds.), *Suicide over the life cycle: Risk factors, assessment, and treatment of suicidal patients.* Washington, DC: American Psychiatry Press.

Budoff, M., & Gottlieb, J. (1976). Special class EMR children mainstreamed: A study of an aptitude (learning potential) treatment interaction. *Amer. J. Ment. Def., 81,* 1–11.

Buffum, J. (1992). Prescription drugs and sexual function. *Psychiatric Medicine, 10*(2), 181–198.

Bugental, J. F. (1965). The existential crisis in intensive psychotherapy. *Psychother. Theory Res. Prac., 2*(1), 16–20.

Bukstein, O. G., Brent, D. A., & Kaminer, Y. (1989). Comorbidity of substance abuse and other psychiatric disorders in adolescents. *Amer. J. Psychiat., 146*(9), 1131–1141.

Bukstein, O. G., Glancy, L., & Kaminer, Y. (1992). Patterns of affective comorbidity in a clinical population of dually diagnosed adolescent substance abusers. *J. Amer. Acad. Child Adol. Psychiat., 31*(6), 1041–1045.

Bullard, D. G. (1988). The treatment of desire disorders in the medically and physically disabled. In R. C. Rosen & S. R. Leiblum (Eds.), *Sexual desire disorders.* New York: Guilford.

Bunney, W. E., & Davis, J. M. (1965). Norepinephrine in depressive reactions: A review. *Arch. Gen. Psychiat., 13*(6), 483–493.

Bunney, W. E., & Garland, B. L. (1981). Receptor function in depression. *Adv. in Bio. Psychiat., 7,* 71–84.

Bunney, W. E., & Garland, B. L. (1984). Lithium and its possible modes of actions. In R. M. Post & J. C. Ballenger (Eds.), *Neurobiology of mood disorders* (Vol. I, Frontiers of Clinical Neuroscience). Baltimore: Williams & Wilkins.

Bunney, W. E., Goodwin, F. K., Davis, J. M., & Fawcett, J. A. (1968). A behavioral-biochemical study of lithium treatment. *Amer. J. Psychiat., 125,* 499–512.

Burbach, D. J., & Borduin, C. M. (1986). Parent-child relations and the etiology of depression: A review of methods and findings. *Clin. Psychol. Rev., 6*(2), 133–153.

Burek, D. M. (Ed.) (1990). *Encyclopedia of associations* (25th ed.). Detroit, MI: Gale Research.

Burgess, E., & Haaga, D. A. (1994). The Positive Automatic Thoughts Questionnaire (ATQ-P) and the Automatic Thoughts Questionnaire—Revised (ATQ-RP): Equivalent measures of positive thinking? *Cog. Ther. Res., 18*(1), 15–23.

Burnam, M. A., Stein, J. A., Golding, J. M., Siegel, J. M., Sorenson, S. B., Forsythe, A. B., & Telles, C. A. (1988). Sexual assault and mental disorders in a community population. *J. Cons. Clin. Psychol., 56*, 843–850.

Burns, T. P., & Crisp, A. H. (1985). Factors affecting prognosis in male anorexics. *J. Psychiat. Res., 19*(2–3), 323–328.

Burnside, I. (1988). Nursing care. In L. F. Jarvik & C. H. Winograd (Eds.), *Treatments for the Alzheimer patient: The long haul.* New York: Springer.

Bursztajn, H., Gutheil, T. G., Warren, M. J., & Brodsky, A. (1986). Depression, self-love, time, and the "right" to suicide. *Gen. Hosp. Psychiat., 8*(2), 91–95.

Burt, D. D., Loveland, K. A., Lewis, K. R. (1992). Depression and the onset of dementia in adults with mental retardation. *Amer. J. Ment. Retard., 96*(5), 502–511.

Burt, D. R., Creese, I., & Snyder, S. H. (1977). Antischizophrenic drugs: Chronic treatment elevates dopamine receptor binding in brain. *Science, 196*(4287), 326–328.

Burton, V. S. (1990). The consequences of official labels: A research note on rights lost by the mentally ill, mentally incompetent, and convicted felons. *Comm. Ment. Hlth. J., 26*(3), 267–276.

Butcher, J. N. (1990). *MMPI-2 in Psychological Treatment.* New York: Oxford UP.

Butcher, J. N., & Graham, J. R. (1988). *The MMPI restandardization project.* Tampa, FL: Univ. Minnesota Continuing Education Project.

Butcher, J. N., Graham, J. R., Dahlstrom, W. G., Tellegen, A. M., & Kaemmer, B. (1989). *MMPI-2 manual for administration and scoring.* Minneapolis: Univ. Minnesota.

Butcher, J. N., Graham, J. R., Williams, C. L., & Ben-Porath, Y. S. (1990). *Development and use of the MMPI-2 content scales.* Minneapolis: University of Minnesota Press.

Butler, G. (1993). Predicting outcome after treatment for generalized anxiety disorder. *Behav. Res. Ther., 31*(2), 211–213.

Butler, G., Cullington, A., et al. (1984). Exposure and anxiety management in the treatment of social phobia. *J. Cons. Clin. Psychol., 52*, 642–650.

Butler, G., Cullington, A., Hibbert, G., Klimes, I., & Gelder, M. (1987). Anxiety management for persistent generalized anxiety. *Brit. J. Psychiat., 151*, 535–542.

Butler, G., Fennel, M., Robson, P., & Gelder, M. (1991). A comparison of behavior therapy and cognitive behavior therapy in the treatment of generalized anxiety disorder. *J. Cons. Clin. Psychol., 59*(1), 167–175.

Butler, R. N. (1975). Psychiatry and the elderly: An overview. *Amer. J. Psychiat., 132*, 893–900.

Butler, R. N., & Lewis, M. I. (1986). *Aging and mental health* (3rd ed.). Columbus, OH: Merrill.

Butler, R. W., & Satz, P. (1989). Psychological assessment of personality of adults and children. In H. I. Kaplan & B. J. Sadock (Eds.), *Comprehensive textbook of psychiatry* (Vol. 1, 5th ed.). Baltimore: Williams & Wilkins.

Butters, N., & Cermak, L. S. (1980). *Alcoholic Korsakoff's Syndrome.* New York: Academic Press.

Butters, N., Heindel, W. C., & Salmon, D. P. (1990). Dissociation of implicit memory in dementia: Neurological implications. *Bulletin of the Psychonomic Society, 28*(4), 359–366.

Buysse, D. J., Reynolds, C. F., & Kupfer, D. J. (1993). Depression. In M. A. Carsakadon (Ed.), *The Encyclopedia of Sleep and Dreaming.* New York: MacMillan.

Byrd, K. R. (1994). The narrative reconstructions of incest survivors. *Amer. Psychol., 49*(5), 439–440.

Byrne, K., & Stern, S. L. (1981). Antidepressant medication in the outpatient treatment of depression: Guide for nonmedical psychotherapists. *Profess. Psychol., 12*(3), 302–308.

Byrnes, G., & Kelly, I. W. (1992). Crisis calls and lunar cycles: A twenty-year review. *Psych. Rep., 71*(3, Pt.1), 779–785.

Caddy, G. R. (1985). Cognitive behavior therapy in the treatment of multiple personality. *Behav. Mod., 9*(3), 267–292.

Calahan, D., Cisin, I. H., & Crossley, H. M. (1969). *American drinking practices: A national study of drinking behaviors and attitudes.* New Brunswick, NJ: Rutgers Center of Alcohol Studies.

Calam, R., Waller, G., Slade, P., & Newton, T. (1990). Eating disorders and perceived relationships with parents. *Inter. J. Eat. Dis., 9*(5), 479–485.

Caldwell, M. F. (1992). Incidence of PTSD among staff victims of patient violence. *Hosp. Comm. Psychiat., 43*(8), 838–839.

Caldwell, S., & White, K. (1991). Co-creating a self-help recovery movement: Serving persons with dual disorders of mental illness and substance abuse. *Psychosocial Rehabilitation Journal, 15*(2), 91–95.

Calev, A., Kochav-lev, E., Tubi, N., Nigal, D., et al. (1991). Change in attitude toward electroconvulsive therapy: Effects of treatment, time since treatment, and severity of depression. *Convulsive Therapy, 7*(3), 184–189.

Calev, A., Nigal, D., Shapira, B., Tubi, N., et al. (1991). Early and long-term effects of electroconvulsive therapy and depression on memory and other cognitive functions. *J. Nerv. Ment. Dis., 179*(9), 526–533.

Caliguri, M., Murray, C., Buchwald, C., Levine, H., Cheney, P., Peterson, D., Komaroff, A. L., & Ritz, J. (1987). Phenotypic and functional deficiency of natural killer cells in patients with chronic fatigue syndrome. *Journal of Immunology, 139*, 3306–3313.

Callahan, L. A., McGreevy, M. A., Cirincione, C., & Steadman, H. J. (1992). Measuring the effects of the GBMI verdict: Georgia's 1982 GBMI reform. *Law and Human Behavior, 16*(4), 447–461.

Callahan, L. A., Steadman, H. J., McGreevy, M. A., & Robbins, P. C. (1991). The volume and characteristics of insanity defense pleas: An eight-state study. *Bulletin of the American Academy of Psychiatry and the Law, 19*(4), 331–338.

Callner, D. A. (1975). Behavioral treatment approaches to drug abuse: A critical review of the research. *Psychol. Bull., 82*(2), 143–164.

Calorie Control Council. (1991, July 8). Calorie Control Council national survey. *Time Magazine,* p. 51.

Camara, W. J., & Schneider, D. L. (1994). Integrity tests: facts and unresolved issues. *Amer. Psychol., 49*(2), 112–119.

Cameron, N. (1974). Paranoid conditions and paranoia. In S.

Arieti & E. Brody (Eds.), *American Handbook of Psychiatry*. New York: Basic Books.

Campbell, M., Gonzalez, N. M., Silva, R. R. (1992). The pharmacologic treatment of conduct disorders and rage outbursts. *Psychiat. Clin. N. Amer.*, 15(1), 69–85.

Campbell, R. V., O'Brien, S., Bickett, A. D., & Lutzker, J. R. (1983). In-home parent training of migraine headaches and marital counseling as an ecobehavioral approach to prevent child abuse. *J. Behav. Ther. Exp. Psychiat.*, 14, 147–154.

Cane, D. B., & Gotlib, I. H. (1985). Depression and the effects of positive and negative feedback on expectations, evaluations, and performance. *Cog. Ther. Res.*, 9(2), 145–160.

Cannon, D. S., Baker, T. B., Gino, A., & Nathan, P. E. (1986). Alcohol-aversion therapy: Assessment of conditioning. *J. Cons. Clin. Psychol.*, 54, 825–830.

Cannon, D. S., Baker, T. B., & Wehl, W. K. (1981). Emetic and electric shock alcohol aversion therapy: Six and twelve-month follow-up. *J. Cons. Clin. Psychol.*, 49, 360–368.

Cannon, T. D., & Marco, E. (1994). Structural brain abnormalities as indicators of vulnerability to schizophrenia. *Schizo. Bull.*, 20(1), 89–102.

Cannon, W. (1927). The James-Lange theory of emotions: A critical examination and an alternative. *American Journal of Psychology*, 39, 106–124.

Canter, A., Kondo, C. Y., & Knott, J. R. (1975). A comparison of EMG feedback and progressive muscle relaxation training in anxiety neurosis. *Brit. J. Psychiat.*, 127, 470–477.

Cantor, P. (1991). Developmental perspective on prevention and treatment of suicidal youth. In A. A. Leenaars (Ed.), *Life span perspectives of suicide: Time-lines in the suicide process*. New York: Plenum.

Cantwell, D., Baker, L., & Rutter, M. (1978). A comparative study of infantile autism and specific developmental receptive language disorder: IV. Analysis of syntax and language function. *J. Child Psychol. Psychiat. Allied Disc.*, 19, 351–362.

Cantwell, D. P. (1982). Childhood depression. In B. B. Lahe & A. E. Kazdin (Eds.), *Advances in clinical child psychology* (Vol. 5). New York: Plenum.

Caplan, G. (1964). *Principles of preventive psychiatry*. New York: Basic Books.

Caplan, P. J. (1989). *Don't blame mother: Mending the mother-daughter relationship*. New York: Harper & Row.

Caplan, R., Perdue, S., Tanguay, P. E., & Fish, B. (1990). Formal thought disorder in childhood onset schizophrenia and schizotypal personality disorder. *J. Child Psychol. Psychiat. Allied Disc.*, 31(7), 1103–1114.

Carey, G., & DiLalla, D. L. (1994). Personality and Psychopathology: Genetic Perspectives. *J. Abnorm. Psychol.*, 103(1), 32–43.

Carey, G., & Gottesman, I. I. (1981). Twin and family studies of anxiety, phobic, and obsessive disorders. In D. K. Klein & J. Rabkin (Eds.), *Anxiety: New research and changing concepts*. New York: Raven.

Carey, K. (1989). Emerging treatment guidelines for mentally ill chemical abusers. *Hosp. Comm. Psychiat.*, 40(4), 341–342.

Carey, K. (1993). Situational determinants of heavy drinking among college students. *Journal of Counseling Psychology*, 40(2), 217–220.

Carey, M., Carey, K., & Meisler, A. (1991). Psychiatric symptoms in mentally ill chemical abusers. *J. Nerv. Ment. Dis.*, 179(3), 136–138.

Carey, M. P., Wincze, J. P., & Meisler, A. W. (1993). Sexual dysfunction: Male erectile disorder. In D. H. Barlow (Ed.), *Clinical Handbook of Psychological Disorders: A Step-by-Step Treatment Manual* (2nd ed.). New York: Guilford.

Carlson, E. B., Putnam, F. W., Ross, C. A., Torem, M., Coons, P., Dill, D., Loewenstein, R. J. Braun, B. G. (1993). Validity of the dissociative experiences scale in screening for multiple personality disorder: A multicenter study. *Amer. J. Psychiat.*, 150(7), 1030–1036.

Carlson, G. A., Fennig, S., & Bromet, E. J. (1994). The confusion between bipolar disorder and schizophrenia in youth: Where does it stand in the 1990s? *J. Amer. Acad. Child Adol. Psychiat.*, 33(4), 453–460.

Carlsson, A. (1978). Antipsychotic drugs, neurotransmitters, and schizophrenia. *Amer. J. Psychiat.*, 135(2), 104–173.

Carlsson, A. (1978). Does dopamine have a role in schizophrenia? *Bio. Psychiat.*, 13(1), 3–21.

Carney, P. A., Fitzgerald, C. T., & Monaghan, C. E. (1988). Influence of climate on the prevalence of mania. *Brit. J. Psychiat.*, 152, 820–823.

Carpenter, W. T., Heinrichs, D. W., & Wagman, A. M. (1988). Deficit and nondeficit forms of schizophrenia: The concept. *Amer. J. Psychiat.*, 145(5), 578–583.

Carr, A. T., (1979). The psychopathology of fear. In W. Sluckin (Ed.), *Fear in animals and man*. New York: Van Nostrand Reinhold.

Carr, E. G., Schreibman, L., & Lovaas, O. I. (1975). Control of echolalic speech in psychotic children. *J. Abnorm. Child Psychol.*, 3, 331–351.

Carr, J. (1994). Annotation: Long term outcome for people with Down Syndrome. *J. Child Psychol. Psychiat. Allied Disc*, 35(3), 425–439.

Carrington, P. (1978). *Clinically standardized meditation (CSM) instructors kit*. Kendall Park, NJ: Pace Educational Systems.

Carrington, P. (1993). Modern forms of meditation. In P. M. Lehrer & R. L. Woolfolk (Eds.), *Principles and Practice of Stress Management* (2nd ed.). New York: Guilford.

Carroll, K. M., Rounsaville, B. J., & Gawin, F. H. (1991). A comparative trial of psychotherapies for ambulatory cocaine abusers: Relapse prevention and interpersonal psychotherapy. *American Journal of Drug and Alcohol Abuse*, 17, 229–247.

Carson, N. D., & Johnson, R. E. (1985). Suicidal thoughts and problem-solving preparation among college students. *J. Coll. Stud. Personnel*, 26(6), 484–487.

Carstairs, K. (1992). Paranoid-schizoid or symbiotic? *Inter. J. Psychoanal.*, 73(1), 71–85.

Carter, B. F., & Brooks, A. (1991). Child and adolescent survivors of suicide. In A. A. Leenaars (Ed.), *Life span perspectives of suicide: Time-lines in the suicide process*. New York: Plenum.

Carter, C. H. (1970). *Handbook of mental retardation syndromes*. Springfield, IL: Thomas.

Cartwright, R. (1961). The effects of psychotherapy on self-consistency: A replication and extension. *J. Cons. Clin. Psychol.*, 29, 376–382.

Cartwright, R. D., & Lamberg, L. (1992). *Crisis Dreaming: Using Your Dreams to Solve your Problems*. New York: Harper Collins.

Cash, T. F., Winstead, B. A., & Janda, L. H. (April 1986). The great American shape-up. *Psych. Today*, 30–37.

Cashdan, S. (1988). *Object relations therapy: Using the relationship.* New York: Norton.

Casper, R. C., & Davis, J. M. (1977). On the course of anorexia nervosa. *Amer. J. Psychiat., 134,* 974.

Castellano, T. C., & Soderstrom, I. R. (1992). Therapeutic wilderness programs and juvenile recidivism: A program evaluation. *Journal of Offender Rehabilitation, 17*(3–4), 19–46.

Catalan, J., Gath, D., Edmonds, G., & Ennis, J. (1984). The effects of non-prescribing of anxiolytics in general practice. *Brit. J. Psychiat., 144,* 593–602.

Catania, J. A., Gibson, D. R., Chitwood, D. D., & Coates, T. J. (1990). Methodological problems in AIDS behavioral research: Influences on measurement error and participation bias in studies of sexual behavior. *Psychol. Bull., 108,* 339–362.

Caton, C. L. (1982). Effect of length of inpatient treatment for chronic schizophrenia. *Amer. J. Psychiat., 139*(7), 856–861.

Cautela, J. R. (1966). Treatment of compulsive behavior by covert sensitization. *Psych. Rec., 16*(1), 33–41.

Cautela, J. R. (1967). Covert sensitization. *Psych. Rec., 20,* 459–468.

Cautela, J. R., & Kastenbaum, R. (1967). A reinforcement survey schedule for use in therapy, training, and research. *Psych. Rep., 20,* 1115–1130.

Cautela, J. R., & Upper, D. (1976). The behavioral inventory battery. In M. Hersen & A. Bellach (Eds.), *Behavioral assessment: A practical handbook.* New York: Pergamon.

Cauwels, J. M. (1983). *Bulimia: The binge-purge compulsion.* New York: Doubleday.

Cavaiuolo, D., & Nasca, M. (1991). The relevance of social survival skills in job retention of workers with mental retardation. *Vocational Evaluation and Work Adjustment Bulletin, 24*(1), 27–31.

Cavanaugh, J. C. (1990). *Adult development and aging.* Belmont, CA: Wadsworth.

Cerletti, U., & Bini, L. (1938). L'elettroshock. *Arch. Gen. Neurol. Psychiat. & Psychoanal., 19,* 266–268.

Cerny, J. A., Barlow, D. H., Craske, M. G., & Himadi, W. G. (1987). Couples treatment of agoraphobia: A two-year follow-up. *Behav. Ther., 18*(4), 410–415.

Chadsey-Rusch, J. (1992). Toward defining and measuring social skills in employment settings. *Amer. J. Ment. Retard., 96*(4), 405–418.

Chait, L. D., Fishman, M. W., & Schuster, C. R. (1985). "Hangover" effects the morning after marijuana smoking. *Drug Alc. Dep., 15*(3), 229–238.

Chamberlain, P. (1985). Increasing the attention span of five mentally handicapped children using their parents as agents of change. *Behav. Psychother., 13*(20), 142–153.

Chambless, D. L. (1988). Cognitive mechanisms in panic disorder. In S. Rachman & J. Maser (Eds.), *Panic: psychological perspectives.* Hillsdale, NJ: Erlbaum.

Chambless, D. L., & Gillis, M. M. (1993). Cognitive therapy of anxiety disorders. *J. Cons. Clin. Psychol., 61*(2), 248–260.

Chance, P., et al. (Eds.). (1989, September). "Re-examining Freud." *Psych. Today,* pp. 48–52.

Chaney, E. F., Blane, H. T., Abran, H. S., Gotner, J., Lacy, E., McCourt, W. F., Clark, E., & Myers, E. (1978). Skill training with alcoholics. *J. Cons. Clin. Psychol., 46,* 1092–1104.

Channon, S., Baker, J. E., & Robertson, M. M. (1993). Effects of structure and clustering on recall and recognition mem-

ory in clinical depression. *J. Abnorm. Psychol., 102*(2), 323–326.

Chapman, C. (1992). Diagnosing dissociative disorders in alcohol and drug dependent clients. *Alcoholism Treatment Quarterly, 9*(1), 67–75.

Chapman, L. J., & Chapman, J. P. (1967). Genesis of popular but erroneous diagnostic observations. *J. Abnorm. Psychol., 72,* 193–204.

Char, W. F. (1985). The hysterical spouse. *Med. Aspects Human Sex., 19*(9), 123–133.

Charney, D. S., & Heninger, G. R., (1983). Monoamine receptor sensitivity and depression: Clinical studies of antidepressant effects of serotonin and noradrenergic function. *Psychopharm. Bull., 19,* 490–495.

Charney, D. S., Heninger, G. R., & Redmond, D. E. (1983). Yohimbine induced anxiety and increased noradrenergic function in humans: Effects of diazepam and clonidine. *Life Science, 33,* 19–29.

Charney, D. S., Heninger, G. R., & Redmond, D. E. (1984, May). Neurobiological mechanism. From Abstracts of the APA Annual Meeting (Abstract 30C). Los Angeles.

Charney, D. S., Heninger, G. R., & Sternberg, D. E. (1984). The effect of mianserin on alpha 2 adrenergic receptor function in depressed patients. *Brit. J. Psychiat., 144,* 407–418.

Charney, D. S., Menkes, D. B., & Heninger, G. R. (1981). Receptor sensitivity and the mechanism of action of antidepressant treatment. *Arch. Gen. Psychiat., 38*(10), 1160–1180.

Charney, D. S., Woods, S. W., Goodman, W. K., & Heninger, G. R. (1987). Neurobiological mechanisms of panic anxiety: Biochemical and behavioral correlates of yohimbine-induced anxiety. *Amer. J. Psychiat., 144*(8), 1030–1036.

Chartier-Harlin, M. C., Crawford, F., Houlden, H., Warren, A., Hughes, D., Figani, L., Goate, A., Rossor, M., Roques, P., & Hardy, J. (1991). Early-onset Alzheimer's disease caused by mutations at codon 717 of the beta-amyloid precursor protein gene. *Nature, 353,* 844–846.

Chase, M. (1993, May 28). Psychiatrists declare severe PMS a depressive disorder. *The Wall Street Journal,* p. B1, B6.

Chassin, L., Pillow, D., Curran, P., Molina, B., & Barrera, M. (1993). Relation of parental alcoholism to early adolescent substance use. A test of three mediating mechanisms. *J. Abnorm. Psychol., 102*(1), 3–19.

Chatlos, C. (1987). *Crack: What you should know about the cocaine epidemic.* New York: Perigee Books.

Chemtob, C. M., Bauer, G. B., Neller, G., Hamada, R., et al. (1990). Posttraumatic stress disorder among Special Forces Vietnam Veterans. *Military Medicine, 155*(1), 16–20.

Chengappa, K. N. R., Shelton, M. D., Baker, R. W., Schooler, N. R., Baird, J., & Delaney, J. (1994). The prevalence of akathisia in patients receiving stable doses of clozapine. *J. Clin. Psychiat., 55*(4), 142–145.

Cherek, D. R., Spiga, R., Roache, J. D., & Cowan, K. A. (1991). Effects of triazolam on human aggressive, escape and point-maintained responding. *Pharmacology Biochemistry & Behavior, 40,* 835–839.

Chess, S. (1971). Autism in children with congenital rubella. *J. Autism Child. Schizo., 1,* 33.

Chiavaroli, T. (1992). Rehabilitation from substance abuse in individuals with a history of sexual abuse. *Journal of Substance Abuse Treatment, 9*(4), 349–354.

Chinner, T. L., & Dalziel, F. R. (1991). An exploratory study on the viability and efficacy of a pet-facilitated therapy project within a hospice. *Journal of Palliative Care, 7*(4), 13–20.

Chiu, L. H. (1971). Manifested anxiety in Chinese and American children. *J. Psychol., 79,* 273–284.

Chodoff, P. (1989). Histrionic personality disorder. In American Psychiatric Association (Eds.), *Treatments of Psychiatric Disorders: A task force report of the American Psychiatric Association.* Washington, DC: American Psychiatric Press.

Chodorkoff, B. (1954). Self-perception, perceptual defense, and adjustment. *J. Abnorm. Soc. Psychol., 49,* 508–512.

Chou, T. (1992). Wake up and smell the coffee: Caffeine, coffee, and the medical consequences. *Western Journal of Medicine, 157,* 544–553.

Christensen, A., & Jacobson, N. S. (1994). Who (or what) can do psychotherapy: The status and challenge of nonprofessional therapies. *Psych. Sci., 5*(1), 8–14.

Christophersen, E. R., & Rapoff, M. A. (1992). Toileting problems in children. In C. E. Walker (Ed.), *Clinical psychology: Historical and research foundations.* New York: Plenum.

Chynoweth, R. (1977). Significance of suicide notes. *Austral. New Zeal. J. Psychiat., 11,* 197–200.

Ciminero, A. R. (1986). Behavioral assessment: An overview. In A. R. Ciminero, K. S. Calhoun, & H. E. Adams (Eds.), *Handbook of behavioral assessment* (2nd ed.). New York: Wiley.

Ciompi, L., Dauwalder, H., Maier, C., Aebi, E., Trutsch, K., Kupper, Z., & Rutishauser, C. (1992). The pilot project 'soteria berne': Clinical experiences and results. *Brit. J. Psychiat., 161*(suppl. 18), 145–153.

Cipani, E. (1991). Educational classification and placement. In J. L. Matson & J. A. Mulick (Eds.), *Handbook of mental retardation.* New York: Pergamon.

Cirese, S. (1993). Personal communication.

Cisin, I. H., & Calahan, D. (1970, Jul. 6). The big drinkers. *Newsweek,* 57.

Clance, P. R., & O'Toole, M. A. (1987). The impostor phenomenon: An integral barrier to empowerment and achievement [Special Issue]. *Women & Therapy, 6*(3), 51–64.

Clark, D. A. (1989). A schema-control model of negative thoughts. Paper presented at the World Congress of Cognitive Therapy, Oxford, England.

Clark, D. A. (1992). Depressive, anxious and intrusive thoughts in psychiatric inpatients and outpatients. *Behav. Res. Ther., 30,* 93–102.

Clark, D. A., Beck, A. T., & Stewart, B. L. (1990). Cognitive specificity and positive negative affectivity: Complementary or contradictory views on anxiety and depression? *J. Abnorm. Psychiat., 99*(2), 140–155.

Clark, D. A., & deSilva, P. (1985). The nature of depressive and anxious thoughts: Distinct or uniform phenomena? *Behav. Res. Ther., 23,* 383–393.

Clark, D. A., & Purdon, C. (1993). New perspectives for a cognitive theory of obsessions. *Australian Psychologist.*

Clark, D. B., & Agras, W. S. (1991). The assessment and treatment of performance anxiety in musicians. *Amer. J. Psychiat., 148*(5), 598–605.

Clark, D. B., & Sayette, M. A. (1993). Anxiety and the development of alcoholism: Clinical and scientific issues. *The American Journal on Addictions, 2,* 59–76.

Clark, D. M. (1993). Cognitive mediation of panic attacks induced by biological challenge tests. *Adv. Behav. Res. Ther., 15,* 75–84.

Clark, D. M., Gelder, M. G., Salkovskis, P. M., Hackman, A., Middleton, H., & Anastasiades, P. (1990, May 15). Cognitive therapy for panic: Comparative efficacy. Paper presented at Annual Conference of American Psychiatric Association, New York.

Clark, L. A., Watson, D., & Mineka, S. (1994). Temperament, personality, and the mood and anxiety disorders. *J. Abnorm. Psychol., 103*(1), 103–116.

Clarke, A. M., Clarke, A. D. B., & Berg, J. M. (Eds.). (1985). *Mental deficiency: The changing outlook.* London: Methuen.

Clarkin, J. F., & Kendall, P. C. (1992). Comorbidity and treatment planning: Summary and future directions. *J. Cons. Clin. Psychol., 60*(6), 904–908.

Clarkin, J. F., Glick, I. D., Haas, G. L., Spencer, J. H., et al. (1990). A randomized clinical trial of inpatient family intervention V. Results for affective disorders. *J. Affect. Dis., 18,* 17–28.

Classen, C., Koopman, C., & Spiegel, D. (1993). Trauma and dissociation. *Bull. Menninger Clin., 57*(2), 178–194.

Clavelle, P. R. (1992). Clinicians' perceptions of the comparability of the MMPI and MMPI-2. *Psychological Assessment, 4*(4), 466–472.

Clayton, P. J. (1985). Suicide [Special Issue]. *Psychiat. Clin. N. Amer., 8*(2), 203–214.

Cleckley, H. (1976). *The Mask of Sanity* (5th ed). St. Louis: Mosby.

Cleghorn, J. M., Franco, S., Szechtman, B., Kaplan, R. D., et al. (1992). Toward a brain map of auditory hallucinations. *Amer. J. Psychiat., 149*(8), 1062–1069.

Clinton, D. N., & McKinlay, W. W. (1986). Attitudes to food, eating and weight in acutely ill and recovered anorectics. *Brit. J. Clin. Psychol., 25*(1), 61–67.

Cloninger, C. R., Sigvardsson, S., von Knorring, A. L., & Bohman, M. (1984). An adoption study of somatoform disorders: II. Identification of two discrete somatoform disorders. *Arch. Gen. Psychiat., 41*(9), 863–871.

Clozapine Study Group (1993). The safety and efficacy of clozapine in severe treatment-resistant schizophrenic patients in the UK. *Brit. J. Psychiat., 163,* 150–154.

Clum, G. A., Clum, G. A., & Surls, R. (1993). A meta-analysis of treatment for panic disorder. *J. Cons. Clin. Psychol., 61*(2), 317–326.

Coccaro, E. F. (1993). Psychopharmacological studies in patients with personality disorders: Review and perspective. *J. Pers. Dis.,* (Suppl. 1), 181–192.

Coccaro, E. F., Astill, J. L., Szeeley, P. J., & Malkowicz, D. E. (1990). Serotonin in personality disorder. *Psychiat. Ann., 20*(10), 587–592.

Coccaro, E. F., & Kavoussi, R. J. (1991). Biological and pharmacological aspects of borderline personality disorder. *Hosp. Comm. Psychiat., 42*(10), 1029–1033.

Cocozza, J. J., & Steadman, H. J. (1978). Prediction in psychiatry: An example of misplaced confidence in experts. *Social Problems, 25,* 265–270.

Coder, T. L., Nelson, R. E., & Aylward, L. K. (1991). Suicide among secondary students. *School Counselor, 38*(5), 358–361.

Coe, C. L., Rosenberg, L. T., Fischer, M., Levine, S. (1987, Dec.). Psychological factors capable of preventing the inhibition of antibody responses in separated infant monkeys. *Child Dev., 58,* 1420–1430.

Coe, W. C. (1989). Posthypnotic amnesia: Theory and

research. In N. P. Spanos & J. F. Chaves (Eds.), *Hypnosis: The cognitive-behavioral perspective.* Buffalo, NY: Prometheus Books.

Cogan, J. C., & Rothblum, E. D. (1992). Outcomes of weight-loss programs. *Genetic, Social, and General Psychology Monographs, 118*(4), 385–415.

Cohen, C. I. (1990). Outcome of schizophrenia into later life: An overview. *Gerontologist, 30,* 790–797.

Cohen, F. (1993). Captives' legal right to mental health care. *Law & Psychology Review, 17,* 1–39.

Cohen, F. (1983). Stress, emotion, and illness. In L. Temoshok, C. Van Dyke, & L. S. Zegans (Eds.), *Emotions in health and illness: Theoretical and research foundations.* Orlando, FL: Grune & Stratton, Inc.

Cohen, M. B., Baker, G., Cohen, R. A., Fromm-Reichmann, F., & Weigert, E. V. (1954). An intensive study of twelve cases of manic-depressive psychosis. *Psychiatry, 17,* 103–137.

Cohen, R. (1987). Suddenly, I'm the adult. *Psych. Today,* 70–71.

Cohen, R. M., Semple, W. E., Gross, M., & Nordahl, T. E. (1988). From syndrome to illness: Delineating the pathophysiology of schizophrenia with PET. *Schizo. Bull., 14*(2), 169–176.

Cohen, S. (1980). Coca paste and freebase: New fashions in cocaine use. *Drug Abuse & Alcoholism Newsletter, 9*(3).

Cohen, S., Kaplan, J. R., Cunnick, J. E., Manuck, S. B., et al. (1992). Chronic social stress, affiliation, and cellular immune response in nonhuman primates. *Psych. Sci., 3*(5), 301–304.

Cohen-Sandler, R., Berman, A. L., & King, R. A. (1982). A follow-up study of hospitalized suicidal children. *J. Amer. Acad. Child Psychiat., 214,* 398–403.

Cohen-Sandler, R., Berman, A. L., & King, R. A. (1982). Life stress and symptomatology: Determinants of suicidal behavior in children. *J. Amer. Acad. Child Psychiat., 21,* 178–186.

Cohn, J., Katon, W., & Richelson, E. (1990, Jul. 15). Choosing the right antidepressant. *Patient Care,* 88–116.

Colbach, E. M. (1987). Hysteria again and again and again. *Inter. J. Offend. Ther. Compar. Crimin., 31*(1), 41–48.

Colburn, R. N., Goodwin, F. K., Bunney, W. E., Jr., & Davis, J. M. (1967). Effect of lithium on the uptake of noradrenaline by synaptosomes. *Nature, 215,* 1395–1397.

Colby, K. M. (1981). Modeling a paranoid mind. *The Behavioral and Brain Sciences, 4,* 515–560.

Colby, K. M., Faught, W. S., & Parkison, R. C. (1979). Cognitive therapy of paranoid conditions: Heuristic suggestions based on a computer simulation model. *Cog. Ther. Res., 3*(1) 55–60.

Cole, D. A., & Turner, J. E., Jr. (1993). Models of cognitive mediation and moderation in child depression. *J. Abnorm. Psychol., 102*(2), 271–281.

Cole, J. O., Klerman, G. L., Goldberg, S. C. et al. (1964). Phenothiazine treatment in acute schizophrenia. *Arch. Gen. Psychiat., 10,* 246–261.

Coleman, L. (1984). *The reign of error: Psychiatry, authority, and law.* Boston: Beacon.

Coleman, M. (1979). Studies of the autistic syndromes. In R. Katzman (Ed.), *Congenital acquired cognitive disorders.* New York: Raven.

Colerick, E. J., & George, L. K. (1986). Predictors of institutionalization among caregivers of patients with Alzheimer's Disease. *J. Amer. Geriatric Society, 34,* 493–498.

Coll, P. G., O'Sullivan, G., & Browne, P. A. (1992). Lycanthropy lives on. In R. Noll (Ed.), *Vampires, werewolves, and demons: Twentieth century reports in the psychiatric literature.* New York: Brunner/Mazel.

Colligan, R. C., & Offord, K. P. (1992). *The MMPI: A Contemporary Normative Study of Adolescents.* Norwood, NJ: Alex Publishing Corporation.

Collins, C. S. (February, 1994). Doctor of the Soul. *Profiles Magazine,* 39–41.

Collins, E. J., Hogan, T. P., & Awad, A. G. (1992). The pharmacoepidemiology of treatment-refractory schizophrenia. *Canad. J. Psychiat., 37*(3), 192–195.

Collins, J. J., Schlenger, W. E., & Jordan, B. K. (1988). Antisocial personality and substance abuse disorders. *Bull. Amer. Acad. Psychiat. Law, 16*(2), 187–198.

Comer, R. (1973). Therapy interviews with a schizophrenic patient. Unpublished manuscript.

Compton, A. (1992). The psychoanalytic view of phobias: III. Agoraphobia and other phobias of adults. *Psychoanalytic Quarterly, 61*(3), 400–425.

Compton, W. M., Helzer, J. E., Hwu, H., Yeh, E., McEvoy, L., Tipp, J. E., & Spitznagel, E. L. (1991). New methods in cross-cultural psychiatry: Psychiatric illness in Taiwan and the United States. *Amer. J. Psychiat., 148*(12), 1697–1704.

Condon, J. T. (1986). Long-term neuroleptic therapy in chronic anorexia nervosa complicated by tardive dyskinesia: A case report. *Acta Psychiatr. Scandin., 73*(2), 203–206.

Conger, J. J. (1951). The effects of alcohol on conflict behavior in the albino rat. *Quart. J. Stud. Alcohol., 12,* 1–29.

Conlan, M. F. (1988, December 12). Top drug cop weighs use of marijuana as an Rx drug. *Drug Topics.*

Conrad, N. (1992). Stress and knowledge of suicidal others as factors in suicidal behavior of high school adolescents. *Issues in Mental Health Nursing, 13*(2), 95–104.

Constantino, G., Malgady, R. G., & Vazquez, C. (1981). A comparison of Murray's TAT and a new thematic apperception test for urban Hispanic children. *Hispanic Journal of Behavioral Sciences, 3,* 291–300.

Conte, H. R., Plutchik, R., Picard, S., Karasu, T. B., et al. (1988). Self-report measures as predictors of psychotherapy outcome. *Comprehen. Psychiat., 29*(4), 355–360.

Conte, J. R. (1991). Overview of child sexual abuse. In A. Tasman & S. M. Goldfinger (Eds.), *American Psychiatric Press Review of Psychiatry* (Vol. 10). Washington, DC: American Psychiatric Press.

Conway, J. B. (1977). Behavioral self-control of smoking through aversive conditioning and self-management. *J. Cons. Clin. Psychol., 45*(3), 348–357.

Conway, M., Howell, A., & Giannopoulos, C. (1991). Dysphoria and thought suppression. *Cog. Ther. Res., 15,* 153–166.

Cook, E. H., Rowlett, R., Jaselskis, C., Leventhal, B. L. (1992). Fluoxetine treatment of children and adults with autistic disorder and mental retardation. *J. Amer. Acad. Child Adol. Psychiat., 31*(4), 739–745.

Cook, E. W., Melamed, B. G., Cuthbert, B. N., McNeil, D. W., & Lang, P. J. (1988). Emotional imagery and the differential diagnosis of anxiety. *J. Cons. Clin. Psychol., 56,* 734–740.

Cook, M. L., & Peterson, C. (1986). Depressive irrationality. *Cog. Ther. Res., 10*(3), 293–298.

Cooke, D. J. (1989). Epidemiological and survey methods. In G. Parry & F. N. Watts (Eds.), *Behavioural and mental health research: A handbook of skills and methods.* Hove, UK: Lawrence Erlbaum Associates.

Cooney, N. L., Kadden, R. M., Litt, M. D., & Getter, H. (1991). Matching alcoholics to coping skills or interactional therapies. Two-year follow-up results. *J. Cons. Clin. Psychol.*, *59*, 598–601.

Coons, P. M. (1980). Multiple personality: Diagnostic considerations. *J. Clin. Psychiat.*, *41*(10), 330–336.

Coons, P. M., Bowman, E. S., & Milstein, V. (1988). Multiple personality disorder: A clinical investigation of 50 cases. *J. Nerv. Ment. Dis.*, *176*(9), 519–527.

Coons, P. M., & Fine, C. G. (1990, June). Accuracy of the MMPI in identifying multiple personality disorder. *Psych. Rep.*, *66*, 831–834.

Cooper, A. (1983). The place of self psychology in the history of depth psychology. In A. Goldberg (Ed.), *The future of psychoanalysis: Essays in honor of Heinz Kohut*. New York: International Universities Press.

Cooper, A. M. (1981). Narcissism. In S. Arieti & H. K. Brodie (Eds.), *American Handbook of Psychiatry*, Vol. 7. New York: Basic Books.

Cooper, A. M., & Ronningstam, E. (1992). Narcissistic personality disorder. In A. Tasman & M. B. Riba (Eds.), *American Psychiatric Press Review of Psychiatry* (Vol. 11). Washington, DC: American Psychiatric Press.

Cooper, C. L., & Faragher, E. B. (1991). Psychosocial stress and breast cancer. In N. Plotnikoff, A. Murgo, R. Faith, & J. Wybran (Eds.), *Stress and Immunity*. Ann Arbor, MI: CRC Press.

Cooper, J. R. (Ed.). (1977). *Sedative-hypnotic drugs: Risks and benefits*. Washington, DC: GPO.

Cooper, M. R., Anastasiades, P., & Fairburn, C. G. (1992). Selective processing of eating, shape, and weight-related words in persons with bulimia nervosa. *J. Abnorm. Psychol.*, *101*(2), 352–355.

Cooper, M. R., & Fairburn, C. G. (1992). Selective processing of eating, weight and shape-related words in patients with eating disorders and dieters. *British Journal of Clinical Psychology*, *31*(3), 363–365.

Cooper, M. R., & Fairburn, C. G. (1992). Thoughts about eating, weight and shape in anorexia nervosa and bulimia nervosa. *Behav. Res. Ther.*, *30*(5), 501–511.

Cooper, T., Detre, T., & Weiss, S. M. (1981). Coronary-prone behavior and coronary heart disease: A critical review. *Circulation*, *63*, 1199–1215.

Copeland, J., & Hall, W. (1992). A comparison of women seeking drug and alcohol treatment in a specialist women's and two traditional mixed-sex treatment services. *British Journal of Addiction*, *87*(9), 1293–1302.

Coplan, J. D., Papp, L. A., King, D. L., & Gorman, J. M. (1992). Amelioration of mitral valve prolapse after treatment for panic disorder. *Amer. J. Psychiat.*, *149*(11), 1587–1588.

Coppen, A. (1967). The biochemistry of affective disorders. *Brit. J. Psychiat.*, *112*, 1237–1264.

Coppen, A. (1994). Depression as a lethal disease: Prevention strategies. *J. Clin. Psychiat.*, *55*(Suppl. 4), 37–45.

Cordova, J. V., & Jacobson, N. S. (1993). Couple distress. In D. H. Barlow (Ed.), *Clinical Handbook of Psychological Disorders: A Step-by-Step Treatment Manual* (2nd ed.). New York: Guilford.

Corkin, S. (1968). Acquisition of motor skill after bilateral medial temporal-lobe excision. *Neuropsychologia*, *6*, 255–264.

Cornblatt, B. A., & Erlanmeyer-Kimling, L. (1985). Global attentional deviance as a marker of risk for schizophrenia: Specificity and predictive validity. *J. Abnorm. Psychol.*, *94*(4), 31–46.

Cornblatt, B. A., & Keilp, J. G. (1994). Impaired attention, genetics, and the pathophysiology of schizophrenia. *Schizo. Bull.*, *20*(1), 31–46.

Cornell, C. P., & Gelles, R. J. (1983). *Intimate violence in families*. Beverly Hills, CA: Sage.

Corson, S. A., & Corson, E. D. (1978). Pets as mediators of therapy. *Current Psychiat. Ther.*, *18*, 195–205.

Corwin, M. (1993, May 8). When the law can't protect. *Los Angeles Times*, p.A1.

Coryell, W., Kelly, M., Perry, P. J. (1990). Haloperidol plasma levels and acute clinical change in schizophrenia. *Journal of Clinical Psychopharmacology*, *10*, 397–402.

Coryell, W., & Winokur, G. (1992). Course and outcome. In E. S. Paykel (Ed.), *Handbook of Affective Disorders*. New York: Guilford.

Costa, E. (1983). Are benzodiazepine recognition sites functional entities for the action of endogenous effectors or merely drug receptors? *Adv. in Biochem. & Psychopharm.*, *38*, 249–259.

Costa, E. (1985). Benzodiazepine-GABA interactions: A model to investigate the neurobiology of anxiety. In A. H. Tuma & J. Maser (Eds.), *Anxiety and the anxiety disorders*. Hillsdale, NJ: Erlbaum.

Costa, E., & Guidotti, A. (1979). Molecular mechanisms in the receptor action of benzodiazepines. In G. R. Okun & A. K. Cho (Eds.), *Annual Review of Pharmacology and Toxicology* (Vol. 19). Palo Alto, CA: Annual Review.

Costa, E., Guidotti, A., Mao, C. C., & Suria, A. (1975). New concepts on the mechanism of action of benzodiazepines. *Life Sciences*, *17*(2), 167–185.

Costa, E., Guidotti, A., & Toffano, G. (1978). Molecular mechanisms mediating the action of benzodiazepines on GABA receptors. *Brit. J. Psychiat.*, *133*, 239–248.

Costello, E. J. (1989). Developments in child psychiatric epidemiology. *J. Amer. Acad. Child Adol. Psychiat.*, *28*, 836–841.

Coulter, D. L. (1992). An ecology of prevention for the future. *Mental Retardation*, *30*(6), 363–369.

Council on Psychiatry and the Law (1992). Peer review of psychiatric testimony. *Bull. Amer. Acad. Psychiat. Law*, *20*(3), 343–352.

Counts, D. A. (1990). Abused women and revenge suicide: Anthropological contributions to understanding suicide. In D. Lester (Ed.), *Current concepts of suicide*. Philadelphia: The Charles Press.

Coursey, R. D. (1975). Electromyograph feedback as a relaxation technique. *J. Cons. Clin. Psychol.*, *43*(6), 825–834.

Coursey, R. D. (1975). Personality measures and evoked responses in chronic insomniacs. *J. Abnorm. Psychol.*, *84*(3), 239–249.

Cowdry, R. W., & Gardner, D. L. (1988). Pharmacotherapy of borderline personality disorder. *Arch. Gen. Psychiat.*, *45*, 111–119.

Cowen, E. L. (1991). In pursuit of wellness. 98th Annual Convention of the American Psychological Association Distinguished Contributions to Psychology in the Public Interest Award Address (1990, Boston, MA). *Amer. Psychol.*, *46*, 404–408.

Cowley, G., Hager, M., & Joseph, N. (1990, November 12). Chronic Fatigue Syndrome. *Newsweek*, p. 62.

Cowley, G., with Holmes, S., Laueman, J. F., & Gordon, J. (1994, February 7). The culture of Prozac. *Newsweek*, p. 41–42.

Cox, A., Rutter, M., Newman, S., & Bartak, L. (1975). A comparative study of infantile autism and specific developmental receptive language disorder: II. Parental characteristics. *Brit. J. Psychiat., 126*, 146–159.

Cox, B., Fergus, K. & Swinson, R. P. (1993). Telephone behavior therapy for panic disorder with agoraphobia. Poster presented at The American Psychological Association's Annual Conference, San Francisco.

Cox, H., & Hammonds, A. (1988). Religiosity, aging, and life satisfaction. *J. Religion & Aging, 5*, 1–21.

Coyne, J. C. (1976). Depression and the response of others. *J. Abnorm. Psychol., 85*(2), 186–193.

Coyne, J. C. (1985). Studying depressed persons interactions with strangers and spouses. *J. Abnorm. Psychol., 94*(2), 231–232.

Crancer, A., Dille, J., Wallace, J., & Haykin, M. (1969). Comparison of effects of marijuana and alcohol on simulated driving experience. *Science, 164*, 851–854.

Crandall, C. S., Preisler, J. J., & Aussprung, J. (1992). Measuring life events stress in the lives of college students: The Undergraduate Stress Questionnaire (USQ). *Journal of Behavioral Medicine, 15*(6), 627–662.

Crane, G. E. (1973). Persistent dyskinesia. *Brit. J. Psychiat., 122*, 395–405.

Crary, B., Borysenko, M., Sutherland, D. C., Kutz, I., Borysenko, J. Z., & Benson, H. (1983). Decrease in mitogen responsiveness of mononuclear cells from peripheral blood after epinephrine administration in humans. *J. Immunol., 130*, 694–697.

Crary, B., Hauser, S. L., Borysenko, M., Kutz, I., Hoban, C., Ault, K. A., Weiner, H. L., & Benson, H. (1983). Epinephrine induced changes in the distribution of lymphocyte subsets in the peripheral blood of humans. *J. Immunol., 131*, 1178–1181.

Craske, M. G., & Barlow, D. H. (1993). Panic disorder and agoraphobia. In D. H. Barlow (Ed.), *Clinical Handbook of Psychological Disorders: A Step-by-Step Treatment Manual* (2nd ed.). New York: Guilford.

Creed, F., Black, D., & Anthony, P. (1989). Day-hospital and community treatment for acute psychiatric illness: A critical appraisal. *Brit. J. Psychiat., 154*, 300–310.

Creer, C., & Wing, J. K. (1974). *Schizophrenia at home.* London: National Schizophrenia Fellowship.

Creese, I., Burt, D. R., & Snyder, S. H. (1977). Dopamine receptor binding enhancement accompanies lesion-induced behavioral supersensitivity. *Science, 197*, 596–598.

Crisp, A. H. (1967). The possible significance of some behavioral correlates of weight and carbohydrate intake. *J. Psychosom. Res., 11*, 117–131.

Crisp, A. H. (1970). Premorbid factors in adult disorders of weight, with particular reference to primary anorexia nervosa (weight phobia). *J. Psychosom. Med., 14*(1), 1–22.

Crisp, A. H. (1980). *Anorexia nervosa: Let me be.* New York: Grune & Stratton.

Crisp, A. H. (1981). Anorexia nervosa at a normal weight?: The abnormal-normal weight control syndrome. *Inter. J. Psychiat. Med., 11*, 203–233.

Crisp, A. H., Harding, B., & McGuinness, B. (1974). Anorexia nervosa: psychoneurotic characteristics of parents: relationship to prognosis. *J. Psychosom. Res., 18*, 167–173.

Crisp, A. H., Norton, K., Gowers, S., Halek, C., et al. (1991). A controlled study of the effect of therapies aimed at adolescent and family psychopathology in anorexia nervosa. *Brit. J. Psychiat., 159*, 325–333.

Crits-Christoph, P. (1992). The efficacy of brief dynamic psychotherapy: A meta-analysis. *Amer. J. Psychiat., 149*, 151–158.

Crits-Christoph, P., & Baranackie, K. (1992, June). The Quantitative Assessment of Relationship Themes method. Paper presented at the annual meeting of the Society for Psychotherapy Research, Berkeley, CA.

Crits-Christoph, P., Baranackie, K., Kurcias, J. S., Beck, A. T., Carroll, K., Perry, K., Luborsky, L., McLellan, A. T., Woody, G. E., Thompson, L., Gallagher, D., Zitrin, C. (1991). Meta-analysis of therapist effects in psychotherapy outcome studies. *Psychotherapy Research, 1*(2), 81–91.

Crocker, P. R. (1989). A follow-up of cognitive-affective stress management training. *Journal of Sport and Exercise Psychology, 11*, 236–242.

Crompton, M. R. (1985). Alcohol and violent accidental and suicidal death. *Med. Sci. Law, 25*, 59–62.

Cronbach, L. J., & Meehl, P. E. (1955). Construct validity in psychology tests. *Psychol. Bull., 52*, 281–302.

Cronen, V. E., Johnson, K. M., & Lannamann, J. W. (1983). Paradossi, doppi-legami e circuiti riflessivi: una prospettiva teorica alternativa. *Terapia-Familiare, 14*, 87–120.

Crook, T. (1986). Drug effects in Alzheimer's Disease. In T. L. Brink (Ed.), *Clinical gerontology: A guide to assessment and intervention.* New York: Haworth.

Crook, T., & Eliot, J. (1980). Parental death during childhood and adult depression: A critical review of the literature. *Psychol. Bull., 87*(2), 252–259.

Crow, M. J., Marks, I. M., Agras, W. S., & Leitenberg, H. (1972). Time-limited desensitization implosion and shaping for phobic patients: A cross-over study. *Behav. Res. Ther., 10*, 319–328.

Crow, T. J. (1980). Positive and negative schizophrenic symptoms and the role of dopamine: II. *Brit. J. Psychiat., 137*, 383–386.

Crow, T. J. (1982). Positive and negative symptoms and the role of dopamine in schizophrenia. In G. Hemmings (Ed.), *Biological aspects of schizophrenia and addiction.* New York: Wiley.

Crow, T. J. (1985). The two-syndrome concept: Origins and current status. *Schizo. Bull., 11*(3), 471–486.

Crow, T. J. (1988). Genes and viruses in schizophrenia: the retrovirus/transposon hypothesis. In C. N. Stefanis & A. D. Rabavilis (Eds.), *Schizophrenia: Recent biosocial developments.* New York: Human Sciences.

Crow, T. J. (1988). Sex chromosomes and psychosis: The case for a pseudoautosomal locus. *Brit. J. Psychiat., 153*, 675–683.

Crowther, J. H., Bond, L. A., & Rolf, J. E. (1981). The incidence, prevalence, and severity of behavior disorder among preschool-age children in day care. *J. Abnorm. Child Psychol., 9*, 23–42.

Cuesta, M. J., Peralta, B., & DeLeon, J. (1994). Schizophrenic syndromes associated with treatment response. *Prog. Neuro-Psychopharmacol. & Biol. Psychiat.,* 18, 87–99.

Cuixart, P. C., & Conill, V. T. (1979). Anorexie mentale juve nile traitee par antidepresseurs et psychotherapie sans necessite d'isolement. *Neuropsychiat. de L'Enfance,* 27, 135–139.

Cullen, E. A. (1993, August). Iowa becomes the tenth state with a Hospital privileges Statute for psychologists. *Practitioner Focus,* 6(2), p. 6.

Culver, R., Rotton, J., & Kelly, I. W. (1988). Geophysical variables and behavior: XLIV. Moon mechanisms and myths: A critical appraisal of explanations of purported lunar effects on human behavior. *Psych. Rep.,* 62(3), 683–710.

Cumming, J., & Cumming, E. (1962). *Ego and milieu: Theory and practice of environmental therapy.* New York: Atherton.

Cummings, C., Gordon, J., & Marlatt, G. A. (1980). Relapse: Prevention and prediction. In W. Miller (Ed.), *The addictive behaviors.* Oxford: Pergamon.

Cummings, E. M., & Davies, P. T. (1994). Maternal depression and child development. *Journal of Child Psychology & Psychiatry,* 35(1), 73–112.

Cummings, J. L. (1993). Amnesia and memory disturbances in neurologic disorders. In J. M. Oldham, M. B. Riba, & A. Tasman, (Eds.), *Review of Psychiatry* (Vol. 12). Washington, DC: American Psychiatric Press.

Cummings, J. L. & Benson, D. F. (1984). Subcortical dementia: review of an emerging concept. *Archives of Neurology,* 41, 874–879.

Cunningham, C. E., Benness, B. B., & Siegel, L. S. (1988). Family functioning, time allocation, and parental depression in the families of normal and ADDH children. *Journal of Clinical Child Psychology,* 17(2), 169–177.

Curran, D. K. (1986). Adolescent suicidal behavior. *Issues in Ment. Hlth. Nursing,* 8(4), 275–477.

Curtis, J. M., & Cowell, D. R. (1993). Relation of birth order and scores on measures of pathological narcissism. *Psych. Rep.,* 72(1), 311–315.

Custanco, J. (1952). *Wisdom, madness and folly.* New York: Pellegrini & Cudaby.

Cutting, J. (1985). *The psychology of schizophrenia.* Edinburgh: Churchill-Livingstone.

Cutting, J., & Murphy, D. (1988). Schizophrenic thought disorder: A psychological and organic interpretation. *Brit. J. Psychiat.,* 152, 310–319.

Cutting, J., & Murphy, D. (1990). Impaired ability of schizophrenics, relative to manics or depressives, to appreciate social knowledge about their culture. *Brit. J. Psychiat.,* 157, 355–358.

Cyr, J. J., & Kalpin, R. A. (1988). Investigating the lunar-lunacy relationship: A reply to Rotton and Kelly. *Psych. Rep.,* 62(1), 319–322.

Cytryn, L., & Lourie, R. S. (1972). Mental retardation. In A. M. Freedman & H. I. Kaplan (Eds.), *The child: His psychological and cultural development: II. The major psychological disorders and their treatment.* New York: Atheneum.

D'Attilio, J. P., Campbell, B. M., Lubold, P., Jacobson, T., et al. (1992). Social support and suicidal potential: Preliminary findings for adolescent populations. *Psych. Rep.,* 70(1), 76–78.

Dacey, C. M., Nelson, W. M., Clark, V. F., & Aikman, K. G. (1991). Bulimia and body image dissatisfaction in adolescence. *Child Psychiat. Human Dev.,* 21(3), 179–184.

Dadds, M. R., Sanders, M. R., Morrison, M., & Rebgetz, M. (1992). Childhood depression and conduct disorder: II. An analysis of family interaction patterns in the home. *J. Abnorm. Psychol.,* 101(3), 505–513.

Dahl, A. A. (1993). The personality disorders: A critical review of family, twin, and adoption studies. *J. Pers. Dis., Spring* (Suppl. 1), 86–99.

Dahlstrom, W. G. (1993). Tests: Small samples, large consequences. *Amer. Psychol.,* 48(4), 393–399.

Dailey, C. A. (1952). The effects of premature conclusions upon the acquisition of understanding a person. *J. Psychol.,* 33, 133–152.

Dally, P. (1969). *Anorexia nervosa.* New York: Grune & Stratton.

Darbonne, A. (1969). Study of psychological content in the communications of suicidal individuals. *J. Cons. Clin. Psychol.,* 33, 590–596.

Darbonne, A. (1969). Suicide and age: A suicide note analysis. *J. Cons. Clin. Psychol.,* 33, 46–50.

Dare, C., & Eisler, I. (1992). Family therapy for anorexia nervosa. In P. J. Cooper & A. Stein (Eds.), *Feeding Problems and Eating Disorders in Children and Adolescents.* Philadelphia, PA: Harwood Academic Publishers.

Das, A., & Khanna, R. (1993). Organic manic syndrome: Causative factors, phenomenology and immediate outcome. *J. Affect. Dis.,* 27(3), 147–153.

Dashef, S. S. (1984). Active suicide intervention by a campus mental health service: Operation and rationale. *J. Amer. Coll. Hlth.,* 33(3), 118–122.

Davanloo, H. (Ed.). (1980). *Short-term dynamic psychotherapy.* New York: Aronson.

Davidson, J., Kudler, H., Smith, R., et al. (1990). Treatment of posttraumatic stress disorder with amitriptyline and placebo. *Arch. Gen. Psychiat.,* 47, 259–266.

Davidson, J. R., Hughes, D., Blazer, D. G., & George, L. K. (1991). Posttraumatic stress disorder in the community: An epidemiological study. *Psychol. Med.,* 21(3), 713–721.

Davidson, J. R. T. (1992). Monoamine oxidase inhibitors. In E. S. Paykel (Ed.), *Handbook of Affective Disorders.* New York: Guilford.

Davis, E. J., Borde, M., & Sharma, L. N. (1992). Tardive dyskinesia and Type II schizophrenia. *Brit. J. Psychiat.,* 160, 253–256.

Davis, J. D., Kane, J. M., Marder, S. R., Brauzer, B., Gierl, B., Schooler, N., Casey, D. E., & Hassan, M. (1993). Dose response of propheylatic antipsychotics. *J. Clin. Psychiat.,* 54(3, suppl.), 24–30.

Davis, J. M. (1976). Overview: Maintenance therapy in psychiatry: II. Affective disorders. *Amer. J. Psychiat.,* 133, 1–13.

Davis, J. M. (1980). Antidepressant drugs. In H. I. Kaplan, A. M. Freedman, & B. J. Sadock (Eds.), *Comprehensive textbook of psychiatry III.* Baltimore: Williams & Wilkins.

Davis, J. M., Barter, J. T., & Kane, J. M. (1989). Antipsychotic drugs. In H. I. Kaplan & B. J. Sadock (Eds.), *Comprehensive textbook of psychiatry* (Vol. 1, 5th ed.). Baltimore: Williams & Wilkins.

Davis, J. M., Comaty, J. E., & Janicak, P. G. (1988). The psychological effects of antipsychotic drugs. In C. N. Stefanis & A. D. Rabavilis (Eds.), *Schizophrenia: Recent biosocial developments.* New York: Human Sciences.

Davis, J. M., Klerman, G., & Schildkraut, J. (1967). Drugs used in the treatment of depression. In L. Efron, J. O. Cole, D. Levine, & J. R. Wittenborn (Eds.), *Psychopharmacology: A review of progress*. Washington, DC: U. S. Clearinghouse of Mental Health Information.

Davis, K., Thal, L., Gamzu, E., et al. (1992). A double-blind, placebo-controlled multicenter study of tacrine for Alzheimer's disease. *New England Journal of Medicine, 327*, 1253–1259.

Davis, K. L., & Greenwald, B. S. (1991). Biology of schizophrenia. In K. Davis, H. Klar, & J. Coyle (Eds.), *Foundations of psychiatry*. Philadelphia: W. B. Saunders.

Davis, K. L., Hollister, L. E., Overall, J., Johnson, A., & Train, K. (1976). Physostigmine: Effects on cognition and affect in normal subjects. *Psychopharmacology, 51*, 23–27.

Davis, M. (1992). Analysis of aversive memories using the fear potentiated startle paradigm. In N. Butters, & L. R. Squire (Eds.), *The Neuropsychology of Memory* (2nd ed.). New York: Guilford.

Davis, P. (1989). *In Mind of Johnson: A study of Johnson, the Rambler*. London.

Davis, R. (1992). Canada settles '63 brainwash case. *USA Today* Nov 19, p. 2A.

Davis, R. C., Brickman, E., & Baker, T. (1991). Supportive and unsupportive responses of others to rape victims: Effects on concurrent victim adjustment. *American Journal of Community Psychology, 19*, 443–451.

Davis, S. F. (1992). Report to the American Psychological Association. Reported in *Psych. Today, 25*(6), 9.

Davison, A. N., & Dobbing, J. (1966). Myelination as a vulnerable period in brain development. *British Medical Bulletin, 22*, 40–44.

Dawson, G., & Castelloe, P. (1992). Autism. In C. E. Walker (Ed.), *Clinical psychology: Historical and research foundations*. New York: Plenum.

de Man, A. F., Leduc, C. P., & Labrèche-Gauthier, L. (1992). Correlates of suicide ideation in French-Canadian adults and adolescents: a comparison. *J. Clin. Psychiat., 48*(6), 811–816.

de Wilde, E. J., Kienhorst, I. C. W. M., Diekstra, R. F. W., & Wolters, W. H. G. (1992). The relationship between adolescent suicidal behavior and life events in childhood and adolescence. *Amer. J. Psychiat, 149*, 45–51.

Dean, A., & Ensel, W. M. (1983). The epidemiology of depression in young adults: The centrality of social support. *J. Psychiat. Treatment & Evaluation, 5*(2–3), 195–207.

DeAngelis, T. (1992, November). Best psychological treatment for many men: group therapy. *APA Monitor, 23*(11), p. 31.

DeAngelis, T. (1992, December). Illness linked with repressive style of coping. *APA Monitor, 23*(12) p. 14.

DeAngelis, T. (1992, November). Program embodies feminist values to aid women with addictions. *APA Monitor, 23*(11), 29.

DeAngelis, T. (1993, September). Controversial diagnosis is voted into latest DSM. *APA Monitor, 24*(9) pp. 32–33.

DeAngelis, T. (1994, March). Poor kids are focus of asthma studies. *APA Monitor,* pp. 25(3) 26–27.

DeAngelis, T. (1994, May). Vets, minorities, single moms make up homeless population. *APA Monitor, 25*(5), p. 39.

DeCubas, M., & Field, T. (1993). Children of methadone-dependent women: Developmental outcomes. *Amer. J. Orthopsychiat., 63*(2), 266–269.

Deering, C. D., Coyne, L., Grame, C. J., Smith, M. J., et al. (1991). Effects of extended hospitalization: A one-year follow-up study. *Bull. Menninger Clin., 55*(4), 444–453.

DeFazio, V. J., Rustin, S., & Diamond, A. (1975). Symptom development in Vietnam-era veterans. *Amer. J. Orthopsychiat. 45*(1), 158–163.

Deitch, D., & Solit, R. (1993). International training for drug abuse treatment and the issue of cultural relevance. *Journal of Psychoactive Drugs, 25*(1), 87–92.

Deitz, S. M. (1977). An analysis of programming DRL schedules in educational settings. *Behav. Res. Ther., 15*(1), 103–111.

Dekker, J. (1993). Inhibited male orgasm. In W. O'Donohue and J. Geer (Eds.), *Handbook of sexual dysfunctions*. Boston: Allyn and Bacon.

Del Zompo, M., Bocchatta, A., Goldin, L. R., & Corsini, C. U. (1984). Linkage between X chromosome markers and manic depressive illness: Two Sardinian pedigrees. *Acta Psychiatr. Scandin., 70*(3), 282–287.

Delay, J., & Deniker, P. (1952). Le traitment des psychoses par une methode neurolytique derivee d'hibernotherapie: Le 4560 RP utilise seul en cure prolongee et continuee. *Congres des Medicins Alienstes et Neurologistes de France et des Pays du Langue Francaise, 50*, 503–513.

DeLeon (1992) cited in Youngstrom, N. Training brings psychologists closer to prescribing drugs. *APA Monitor:, 23*(10).

Delis, D. C. (1993). Neuropsychological assessment of memory disorders. In J. M. Oldham, M. B. Riba, & A. Tasman, (Eds.), *Review of Psychiatry* (Vol. 12). Washington, DC: American Psychiatric Press.

DeLisi, L. E., & Crow, T. J. (1986). Is schizophrenia a viral or immunologic disorder? *Psychiat. Clin. N. Amer., 9*(1), 115–132.

DeLisi, L. E., Crow, T. J., & Hirsch, S. R. (1986). The third biannual winter workshop on schizophrenia. *Arch. Gen. Psychiat., 43*(7), 705–706.

DeLisi, L. E., Hoff, A. L., Kushner, M., Calev, A., et al. (1992). Left ventricular enlargement associated with diagnostic outcome of schizophreniform disorder. *Bio. Psychiat., 32*(2), 199–201.

DeLisi, L. E., Smith, S. B., & Hamovit, J. R. (1986). Herpes simplex virus, cytomegalovirus and Epstein-Barr virus antibody titres in sera from schizophrenic patients. *Psychol. Med., 16*(4), 757–763.

Delisle, J. R. (1986). Death with honors: Suicide among gifted adolescents [Special Issue]. *J. Couns. Dev., 64*(9), 558–560.

Dell, P. F., & Eisenhower, J. W. (1990). Adolescent multiple personality disorder: A preliminary study of eleven cases. *J. Amer. Acad. Child Adol. Psychiat., 29*(3), 359–366.

DeLong, F. L. (1975). Cognitive effects of long-term marijuana use. *Dissertation Abstracts Inter., 36*(5-B), 2444–2445.

DeLong, G. R. (1978). A neuropsychological interrelation of infantile autism. In M. Rutter & E. Schopler (Eds.), *Autism: A Reappraisal of Concepts and Treatment*. New York: Plenum.

Delprato, D. J., & Midgley, B. D. (1992). Some fundamentals of B. F. Skinner's behaviorism. *Amer. Psychol., 47*(11), 1507–1520.

Deluty, B. M., Deluty, R. H., & Carver, C. S. (1986). Concordance between clinicians and patients ratings of anxiety and depression as mediated by private self-consciousness. *J. Pers. Assess., 50*(1), 93–100.

DeMyer, M. K. (1979). *Parents and children in autism*. Washington, DC: Winston.

DeMyer, M. K., Alpern, G. D., Barton, S., DeMyer, W., Churchill, D. W., Hingtgen, J. N., Bryson, C. Q., Pontius, W., & Kimberlin, C. (1972). Imitation in autistic, early schizophrenic, and nonpsychotic subnormal children. *J. Autism Child. Schizo.*, 2, 264–287.

DeMyer, M. K., Hingtgen, J. N., & Jackson, R. K. (1981). Infantile autism reviewed: A decade of research. *Schizo. Bull.*, 7, 388–391.

den Boer, J. A., Westenberg, H. G., & Verhoeven, W. M. (1990). Biological aspects of panic anxiety. *Psychiat. Ann.*, 20(9), 494–500, 502.

Department of Justice. (1994). Cited in P. Bender, Senate committee praises Delaware Youth Programs. Gannett News Service, April 26, 1994.

DeSilva, P., Rachman, S., & Seligman, M. (1977). Prepared phobias and obsessions: Therapeutic outcome. *Behav. Res. Ther.*, 15, 65–77.

DeTurck, M. A., & Miller, G. R. (1990). Training observers to detect deception: Effects of self-monitoring and rehearsal. *Human Communication Research*, 16(4), 603–620.

Deutsch, A. (1949). *The mentally ill in America*. New York: Columbia UP.

DeVeaugh-Geiss, J., Moroz, G., Biederman, J., Cantwell, D. P., et al. (1992). Clomipramine hydrochloride in childhood and adolescent obsessive compulsive disorder. A multicenter trial. *J. Amer. Acad. Child Adol. Psychiat.*, 31(1), 45–49.

Dial, T. H., Pion, G. M., Cooney, B., Kohut, J., Kaplan, K. O., et al. (1992). Training of mental health providers. In R. W. Manderscheid & M. A. Sonnenschein (Eds.), *Mental Health, United States, 1992*, DHHS Pub. No. (SMA)92-1942. Washington, DC: GPO.

Dial, T. H., Tebbutt, R., Pion, G. M., Kohout, J., et al. (1990). Human resources in mental health. In R. W. Manderscheid & M. A. Sonnenschein (Eds.), *Mental Health, United States, 1990*, DHHS Pub. No. (ADM)90-1708. Washington, DC: GPO.

Diamond, D. (1987). Psychotherapeutic approaches to the treatment of panic attacks, hypochondriasis and agoraphobia. *British Journal of Medical Psychology*, 60, 85–90.

Diamond, D., Kaslow, N., Coonerty, S., & Blatt, S. J. (1990). Changes in separation-individuation and intersubjectivity in long-term treatment. *Psychoanalytic Psychiatry*, 7(3), 363–397.

Diekstra, R. F. W. (1982). Epidemiology of attempted suicide in the EEC. In J. Wilmott, J. B. Mendlewicz, & S. Karger (Eds.), *New Trends in Suicide Prevention*. Bibliotheca Psychiatrica.

Diekstra, R. F. W. (1989). Suicidal behavior in adolescents and young adults: The international picture. *Crisis*, 10, 16–35.

Diekstra, R. F. W. (1989). Suicide and attempted suicide: An international perspective. *Acta Psychiatr. Scandin.*, 80(suppl. 354), 1–24.

Diekstra, R. F. W. (1990). An international perspective on the epidemiology and prevention of suicide. In S. J. Blumenthal & D. K. Kupfer (Eds.), *Suicide over the life cycle*. Washington, DC: American Psychiatric Press.

Diekstra, R. F. W. (1990). Suicide, depression and economic conditions. In D. Lester (Ed.), *Current concepts of suicide*. Philadelphia: The Charles Press.

Diener, E. (1984). Subjective well-being. *Psychol. Bull*, 95, 542–575.

Dietz, P. E., Hazelwood, R. R., & Warren, J. (1990). The sexually sadistic criminal and his offenses. *Bulletin of the American Academy of Psychiatry and the Law*, 18(2), 163–178.

Dietz, P. E., Matthews, D. B., et al. (1991). Threatening and otherwise inappropriate letters to members of the U. S. Congress. *Journal of Forensic Sciences*, 36(5), 1445–1468.

DiLoreto, A. O. (1971). *Comparative psychotherapy: An experimental analysis*. Chicago: Aldine-Atherton.

Dilsaver, S. C. (1990). Onset of winter depression earlier than generally thought? *J. Clin. Psychiat.*, 51(6), 258.

DiNardo, P. A. (1975). Social class and diagnostic suggestion as variables in clinical judgment. *J. Cons. Clin. Psychol.*, 43, 363–368.

DiNardo, P. A., Moras, K., Barlow, D. H., Rapee, R. M., & Brown, T. A. (1993). Reliability of DSM-III-R anxiety disorder categories. *Arch. Gen. Psychiat.*, 50, 251–256.

Dircks, P., Grimm, F., Tausch, A., & Wittern, O. (1980). Förderung der seelischen Lebensqualitat von Krebspatienten durch personenzentrierte Gruppengespräche. *Zeitschrift für Klinische Psychologie*, 9, 241–251.

Dixon, W. A., Heppner, P. P., Burnett, J. W., & Lips, B. J. (1993). Hopelessness and stress: Evidence for an interactive model of depression. *Cog. Ther. Res.*, 17(1), 39–52.

Dobson, K. S. (1985). An analysis of anxiety and depression scales. *J. Pers. Assess.*, 49(5), 522–527.

Doghramji, K., Gaddy, J. R., Stewart, K. T., Rosenthal, N. E. et al. (1990). 2- versus 4-hour evening phototherapy of seasonal affective disorder. *J. Nerv. Ment. Dis.*, 178(4), 257–260.

Doherty, W. J., & Jacobson, N. S. (1982). Marriage and the family. In B. B. Wolman (Ed.), *Handbook of developmental psychology*. Englewood Cliffs, NJ: Prentice Hall.

Dohrenwend, B. (1990). Socioeconomic status (SES) and psychiatric disorders: Are the issues still compelling? *Social Psychiatry and Psychiatric Epidemiology*, 25, 41–47.

Dohrenwend, B. P., Levav, I., Shrout, P. E., Schwartz, S., et al. (1992). Socioeconomic status and psychiatric disorders: The causation-selection issue. *Science*, 255(5047), 946–952.

Dohrmann, R. J., & Laskin, D. M. (1978). An evaluation of electromyographic feedback in the treatment of myofascial pain-dysfunction syndrome. *JADA*, 96, 656–662.

Dole, V. P., & Nyswander, M. (1965). A medical treatment for heroin addiction. *JAMA*, 193, 646–650.

Dole, V. P., & Nyswander, M. (1967). Heroin addiction, a metabolic disease. *Arch. Inter. Med.*, 120, 19–24.

Domenici, N., & Griffin-Francell, C. (1993). The role of family education. *J. Clin. Psychiat.* 54(suppl. 3), 31–34.

Domino, G. (1985). Clergy's attitudes toward suicide and recognition of suicide lethality. *Death Studies*, 2, 187–199.

Domino, G., & Swain, B. J. (1985–86). Recognition of suicide lethality and attitudes toward suicide in mental health professions. *Omega: J. Death & Dying*, 16(4), 301–308.

Domino, G., & Takahashi, Y. (1991). Attitudes toward suicide in Japanese and American medical students. *Suic. Life-Threat. Behav.*, 21(4), 345–359.

Donaldson, K. (1976). *Insanity inside out*. New York: Crown.

Donnelly, E. F., Murphy, D. L., & Goodwin, F. K. (1978). Primary affective disorder: Anxiety in unipolar and bipolar depressed groups. *J. Clin. Psychol.*, 34, 621–623.

Dooley, C., & Catalano, R. (1980). Economic change as a cause of behavioral disorder. *Psychol. Bull.*, *87*(3), 450–468.

Dorman, C. (1992). Microcephaly and intelligence. *Developmental Medicine & Child Neurology*, *33*(3), 267–269.

Double, D. B. (1991). A cluster analysis of manic states. *Comprehen. Psychiat.*, *32*(3), 187–194.

Douglas, V. I., Barr, R. G., Amin, K., O'Neill, M. E., & Britton, B. G. (1988). Dosage effects and individual responsivity to methylphenidate in attention deficit disorder. *J. Child Psychol. Psychiat. Allied Disc.*, *29*, 453–475.

Dowdney, L., & Skuse, D. (1993). Parenting provided by adults with mental retardation. *J. Child Psychol. Psychiat. Allied Disc.*, *34*(1), 25–47.

Downey, A. M. (1991). The impact of drug abuse upon adolescent suicide. *Omega: J. Death and Dying*, *22*(4), 261–275.

Doyle, A. C. (1938). The sign of the four. In *The Complete Sherlock Holmes*. New York: Garden City, NY: Doubleday.

Drake, R., Gates, C., & Cotton, P. G. (1984). Suicide among schizophrenics: Who is at risk? *J. Nerv. Ment. Dis.*, *172*(10), 813–817.

Drake, R., Gates, C., & Cotton, P. G. (1986). Suicide among schizophrenics: A comparison of attempters and completed suicides. *Brit. J. Psychiat.*, *149*, 784–787.

Drake, R. E., McHugo, G. J., & Noordsy, D. L. (1993). Treatment of alcoholism among schizophrenic outpatients: 4-year outcomes. *Amer. J. Psychiat.*, *150*(2), 328–329.

Drake, R. E., Osher, F., & Wallach, M. (1991). Homelessness and dual diagnosis. *Amer. Psychol.*, *46*(11), 1149–1158.

Drake, R. E., & Wallach, M. A. (1992). Mental patients' attraction to the hospital: Correlates of living preference. *Community Mental Health Journal*, *28*(1), 5–12.

Du Paul, G. J., & Barkley, R. A. (1993). Behavioral contributions to pharmacotherapy: The utility of behavioral methodology in medication treatment of children with attention-deficit hyperactivity disorder. *Behav. Ther.*, *24*, 47–65.

Dubovsky, S. L., Lee, C., Christiano, J., & Murphy, J. (1991). Elevated platelet intracellular calcium concentration in bipolar depression. *Bio. Psychiat.*, *29*(5), 441–450.

Dubovsky, S. L., Murphy, J., Christiano, J., & Lee, C. (1992). The calcium second messenger system in bipolar disorders: Data supporting new research direction. *Journal of Neuropsychiatry and Clinical Neurosciences*, *4*(1), 3–14.

Duckett, J. (1977). Adaptive and maladaptive behavior of idiot savants. *Amer. J. Ment. Def.*, *82*, 308–311.

Duggan, J. P., & Booth, D. A. (1986). Obesity, overeating, and rapid gastric emptying in rats with ventromedial hypothalamic lesions. *Science*, *231*(4738), 609–611.

Dulloo, A., & Girardier, L. (1990). Adaptive changes in energy expenditure during refeeding following low-calorie intake: Evidence for a specific metabolic component favoring fat storage. *Amer. J. Clin. Nutrition*, *52*, 415–420.

Dunbar, F. (1948). *Synopsis of psychosomatic diagnosis and treatment*. St. Louis: Mosby.

Dunbar, F. (1954). *Emotions and bodily changes: A survey of literature on psychosomatic interrelationships, 1910–1953* (4th ed.). New York: Columbia UP.

Dunn, G. E., Paolo, A. M., Ryan, J. J., & VanFleet, J. (1993). Dissociative symptoms in a substance abuse population. *Amer. J. Psychiat.*, *150*(7), 1043–1047.

Dunner, D. L. & Hall, K. S. (1980). Social adjustment and psychological precipitants in mania. In R. H. Belmaker & H. M. van Praag (Eds.), *Mania: An evolving concept*. New York: Spectrum.

Durham, R. C., & Turvey, A. A. (1987). Cognitive therapy vs. behaviour therapy in the treatment of chronic general anxiety. *Behav. Res. Ther.*, *25*(3), 229–234.

Dweck, C. S. (1976). Children's interpretation of evaluative feedback: The effect of social cues on learned helplessness. *Merrill Palmer Quart.*, *22*(2), 105–109.

Dykeman, B. F. (1984). Adolescent suicide: Recognition and intervention. *Coll. Stud. J.*, *18*(4), 364–368.

Easterlin, R. (1987, May). Cited in A. Rosenfeld & E. Stark. The prime of our lives. *Psych. Today*, 62–72.

Eaton, W. W., Bilker, W., Haro, J. M., Herman, H. (1992). Long-term course of hospitalization for schizophrenia: II. Change with passage of time. *Schizo. Bull.*, *18*(2), 229–241.

Eaton, W. W., Dryman, A., & Weissman, M. M. (1991). Panic and phobia. In L. N. Robins, & D. A. Regier (Eds.), *Psychiatric Disorders in America: The Epidemiologic Catchment Area Study*. New York: Maxwell Macmillan International.

Eaton, W. W., Kessler, R. C., Wittchen, H. A., & Magee, W. J. (1994). Panic and panic disorder in the United States. *Amer. J. Psychiat.*, *151*(3), 413–420.

Eaves, L., & Schultz, S. C. et al. (1988). Genetics, immunology, and virology. *Schizo. Bull.*, *14*(3), 365–382.

Eccles, J. S., Midgley, C., Wigfield, A., Buchanan, C. M., et al. (1993). Development during adolescence. *Amer. Psychol.*, *48*(2), 90–101.

Eckenrode, J., Laird, M., & Doris, J. (1993). School performance and disciplinary problems among abused and neglected children. *Developmental Psychology*, *29*(1), 54–62.

Eddy, D. M., Wolpert, R. L., & Rosenberg, M. L. (1987). Estimating the effectiveness of interventions to prevent youth suicides. Invitational conference on applications of analytic methods to mental health: Practice, policy, research. *Medical Care*, *25*(12), 57–65.

Edelson, J., & Eiskovitz, Z. (1989, September). Intervening with men who batter. *Social Services Review*, pp. 387–414.

Edelson, M. (1985). Psychoanalysis, anxiety and the anxiety disorders. In A. H. Tuma & J. Maser (Eds.), *Anxiety and the anxiety disorders*. Hillsdale, NJ: Lawrence Erlbaum Assoc.

Edelstein, B. A. (1989). Generalization: Terminological, methodological and conceptual issues. *Behav. Ther.*, *20*(3), 311–324.

Edman, G., & Asberg, M. (1986). Skin conductance habituation and cerebrospinal fluid 5-hydroxyindoleacetic acid in suicidal patients. *Arch. Gen. Psychiat.*, *43*(6), 586–592.

Edwards, C. C. (1973). What you can do to combat high blood pressure. *Family Health*, *5*(11), 24–26.

Edwin, D. H., & Andersen, A. E. (1990). Psychometric testing in 76 males with eating disorders. In A. E. Andersen (Ed.), *Males with eating disorders*. New York: Brunner/Mazel.

Egan, B. M. (1992). Vascular reactivity, sympathetic tone, and stress. In E. H. Johnson, E. D. Gentry, & S. Julius (Eds.), *Personality, elevated blood pressure, and essential hypertension*. Washington, DC: Hemisphere Publishing Corporation.

Egan, J. (1988). Treatment of borderline conditions in adolescents. *J. Clin. Psychiat.*, *49*(Suppl. 290), 32–35.

Egan, M. F., Hyde, T. M., Albers, G. W., Elkashef, A., (1992).

Treatment of tardive dyskinesia with vitamin E. *Amer. J. Psychiat.*, *146*(6), 773–777.

Egeland, B. (1991, Feb.). Presentation. American Association for the Advancement of Science.

Egeland, J. A., Gerhard, D. S., Pauls, D. L., Sussex, J. N. et al. (1987). Bipolar affective disorders linked to DNA markers on chromosome 11. *Nature, 325*(6107), 783–787.

Egeland, J. A. et al. (1984). Amish study: V. Lithium sodium countertransport and catechol methyltransference in pedigrees of bipolar probands. *Amer. J. Psychiat.*, *141*(9), 1049–1054.

Ehle, G. (1992). Experiences with "planned" dynamic group psychotherapy of patients with anorexia nervosa. *Group Analysis, 25*(1), 43–53.

Ehlers, A. (1993). Interoception and panic disorder. *Adv. Behav. Res. Ther., 15*, 3–21.

Ehlers, A. (1993). Somatic symptoms and panic attacks: A retrospective study of learning experiences. *Behav. Res. Ther., 31*(3), 269–278.

Ehrman, R., Robbins, S., Childress, A., & O'Brien, C. (1992). Conditioned responses to cocaine-related stimuli in cocaine abuse patients. *Psychopharmacology, 107*(4), 523–529.

Eichel, E. W., & Nobile, P. (1992). *The perfect fit: How to achieve mutual fulfillment and monogamous passion through the new intercourse.* New York: Fine.

Eichler, M., Reisman, A. L., & Borins, E. M. (1992). Gender bias in medical research. *Women and Therapy, 12*(4), 61–70.

Eidelson, J. I. (1985). Cognitive group therapy for depression: Why and what. *Inter. J. Ment. Hlth., 13*, 54–66.

Eisen, M. R. (1993). The victim's burden: guilt, shame and abuse. *Imagination, Cognition and Personality, 12*(1), 69–88.

Eisenberg, L. (1958). School phobia: A study in the communication of anxiety. *Amer. J. Psychiat., 114*, 712–718.

Eisenthal, S., Koopman, C., & Lazare, A. (1983). Process analysis of two dimensions of the negotiated approach in relation to satisfaction in the initial interview. *J. Nerv. Ment. Dis., 171*, 49–54.

Eitinger, L. (1964). *Concentration camp survivors in Norway and Israel.* New York: Humanities Press.

Eitinger, L. (1969). Psychosomatic problems in concentration camp survivors. *J. Psychosom. Res., 13*, 183–190.

Eitinger, L. (1973). A follow-up study of the Norwegian concentration camp survivors: Mortality and morbidity. *Israel Annals of Psychiatry and Related Disciplines, 11*, 199–210.

Ekman, P., Friesen, W. V., & O'Sullivan, M. (1988). Smiles when lying. *J. Pers. Soc. Psychol., 54*(3), 414–420.

Elias, M. (1993, July 15). Poor odds for heroin recovery. *USA Today*, p. 1D.

Elkin, I. (1994). The NIMH Treatment of Depression Collaborative Research Program: Where we began and where we are. In A. E. Bergin & S. L. Garfiel (Eds.), *Handbook of psychotherapy and behavior change* (4th ed.). New York: Wiley.

Elkin, I., Shea, M. T., Watkins, J. T., Imber, S. D. et al. (1989). National Institute of Mental Health Treatment of Depression Collaborative Research Program: General effectiveness of treatments. *Arch. Gen. Psychiat., 46*(11), 971–982.

Elkins, R. L. (1980). Covert sensitization treatment of alcoholism: Contributions of successful conditioning to subsequent abstinence maintenance. *Addict. Behav., 5*, 67–89.

Elkins, R. L. (1991). An appraisal of chemical aversion (emetic

therapy) approaches to alcoholism treatment. *Behav. Res. Ther., 29*, 387–414.

Elkins, T. E., & Anderson, H. F. (1991). Sterilization of persons with mental retardation. *Journal of the Association for Persons with Severe Handicaps, 17*(1), 19–26.

Ellenberger, H. F. (1970). *The discovery of the unconscious.* New York: Basic Books.

Elliot, D. M., & Guy, J. D. (1993). Mental health professionals vs. non-mental health professionals: Childhood trauma and adult functioning. *Professional Psychology: Research and Practice, 24*(1), 83–90.

Elliott, S. N. et al. (1985). Three year stability of WISC R IQs for handicapped children from three racial/ethnic groups. *J. Psychoeduc. Assess., 3*(3), 233–244.

Ellis, A. (1962). *Reason and emotion in psychotherapy.* Secaucus, NJ: Lyle Stuart.

Ellis, A. (1973). *Humanistic psychotherapy: The rational-emotive approach.* New York: McGraw-Hill.

Ellis, A. (1976). Rational emotive therapy. In V. Binder, A. Binder, & B. Rimland (Eds.), *Modern therapies.* Englewood Cliffs, NJ: Prentice Hall.

Ellis, A. (1976). RET abolishes most of the human ego. *Psychother. Ther. Res. Prac., 13*, 343–348.

Ellis, A. (1976). The rational-emotive view. *J. Contemp. Psychother., 8*(1), 20–28.

Ellis, A. (1977). The basic clinical theory of rational-emotive therapy. In A. Ellis & R. Grieger (Eds.), *Handbook of rational-emotive therapy.* New York: Springer.

Ellis, A. (1979). A note on the treatment of agoraphobics with cognitive modification versus prolonged exposure in vivo. *Behav. Res. Ther., 17*, 162–164.

Ellis, A. (1979). The theory of rational-emotive therapy. In A. Ellis & J. M. Whitely (Eds.), *Theoretical and empirical foundations of rational-emotive therapy.* Monterey, CA: Brooks/Cole.

Ellis, A. (1984). Rational-emotive therapy. In R. J. Corsini (Ed.), *Current psychotherapies* (3rd ed.). Itasca, IL: Peacock.

Ellis, A. (1987). The evolution of rational emotive therapy (RET) and cognitive behavior therapy (BET). In J. K. Zeig (Ed.), *The evolution of psychotherapy.* New York: Brunner/Mazel.

Ellis, A. (1989). Rational Emotive Therapy. In R. J. Corsini & D. Wedding (Eds.), *Current Psychotherapies* (4th Edition). Itasca, IL: Peacock.

Ellis, A. (1991). The revised ABC's of rational-emotive therapy (RET). *Journal of Rational-Emotive & Cognitive-Behavior Therapy, 9*, 139–172.

Ellis, L. (1987). Relationships of criminality and psychopathy with eight other apparent behavioral manifestations of suboptimal arousal. *Personality and Individual Differences, 8*(6), 905–925.

Ellis, T. E., & Ratliff, K. G. (1986). Cognitive characteristics of suicidal and nonsuicidal psychiatric inpatients. *Cog. Ther. Res., 10*(6), 625–634.

Ellison, G. (1992). Continuous amphetamine and cocaine have similar neurotoxic effects in lateral habenular nucleus and fasciculus retroflexus. *Brain Research, 598*, 353–356.

Ellison, J. M., & Adler, D. A. (1990). A strategy for the pharmacotherapy of personality disorders. *New Directions for Mental Health Services, 47*, 43–63.

Elmhirst, S. I. (1984). A psychoanalytic approach to anxiety in childhood. In V. P. Varma (Ed.), *Anxiety in children*. London: Croom Helm.

Eme, R. F. (1992). Selective female affliction in the developmental disorders of childhood: A literature review. *Journal of Clinical Child Psychology, 21*(4), 354–364.

Emery, R. E. (1982). In Wilson et al., (Eds.), *J. of Abnormal Child Psychol., 10*, 215–228. Effects of marital discord on the school behavior of children of schizophrenic, affectively disordered, and normal parents.

Emmanuel, N. P., Lydiard, R. B., & Ballenger, J. C. (1991). Fluoxetine treatment of voyeurism. *Amer. J. Psychiat., 148*(7), 950.

Emmelkamp, P. M. (1982). Exposure in vivo treatments. In A. Goldstein & D. Chambless (Eds.), *Agoraphobia: Multiple perspectives on theory and treatment*. New York: Wiley.

Emmelkamp, P. M. (1982). *Phobic and obsessive-compulsive disorders*. New York: Plenum.

Emmelkamp, P. M. (1994). Behavior therapy with adults. In A. E. Bergin & S. L. Garfiel (Eds.), *Handbook of psychotherapy and behavior change* (4th ed.). New York: Wiley.

Emmelkamp, P. M., & Beens, J. (1991). Cognitive therapy with obsessive-compulsive disorder: A comparative evaluation. *Behav. Res. Ther., 29*(3), 293–300.

Emmelkamp, P. M., de Haan, E., Hoogduin, C. A. (1990). Marital adjustment and obsessive-compulsive disorder. *Brit. J. Psychiat., 156*, 55–60.

Emmelkamp, P. M., Van Dyck, R., Bitter, M., Heins, R., et al. (1992). Spouse-aided therapy with agoraphobics. *Brit. J. Psychiat., 160*, 51–56.

Emrick, C. D., & Hansen, J. (1983). Assertions regarding effectiveness of treatment for alcoholism: Fact or fantasy? *Amer. Psychol., 38*, 1078–1088.

Endler, N. S. (1982). *Holiday of darkness*. New York: Wiley.

Engebretson, T. O., & Matthews, K. A. (1992). Dimensions of hostility in men, women, and boys: Relationships to personality and cardiovascular responses to stress. *Psychosom. Med., 54*, 311–323.

Engel, G. L. (1968). A life setting conducive to illness: The giving-up-given-up complex. *Annals of Internal Medicine, 69*, 293.

Engel, G. L. (1971). Sudden and rapid death during psychological stress, folklore or folkwisdom? *Annals of Internal Medicine, 74*, 771–774.

Englemann, S. (1969). *Conceptual learning*. San Rafael, CA: Dimensions Publishing Company.

Enkelmann, R. (1991). Alprazolam versus buspirone in the treatment of outpatients with generalized anxiety disorder. *Psychopharmacology, 105*(3), 428–432.

Ennis, B. J., & Emery, R. D. (1978). *The rights of patients* (ACLU Handbook Series). New York: Avon.

Enns, M. P., Drewnowski, A., & Grinker, J. A. (1987). Body composition, body size estimation, and attitudes towards eating in male college athletes. *Psychosom. Med., 49*(1), 56–64.

Enright, S. J. (1989). Paedophilia: A cognitive/behavioural treatment approach in a single case. *Brit. J. Psychiat., 155*, 399–401.

Epstein, N., Baucom, D. H., & Rankin, L. A. (1993). Treatment of marital conflict: A cognitive-behavioral approach. *Clinical Psychology Review, 13*(1), 45–57.

Epstein, S. (1983). Hypnotherapeutic control of exhibitionism: A brief communication. *Inter. J. Clin. Exp. Hyp., 31*(2), 63–66.

Erber, R. (1990, Aug.). Presentation. American Psychological Association.

Erdelyi, M. H. (1985). *Psychoanalysis: Freud's cognitive psychology*. New York: W. H. Freeman.

Erdelyi, M. H. (1992). Psychodynamics and the unconscious. *Amer. Psychol., 47*(6), 784–787.

Erickson, M. T. (1992). *Behavior disorders of children and adolescents*. Englewood Cliffs, NJ: Prentice Hall.

Erikson, E. (1963). *Childhood and society*. New York: Norton.

Erlich, J., & Reisman, D. (1961). Age and authority in the interview. *Public Opinion Quart., 25*, 39–56.

Ernst, K. (1985). Die psychische Behandlung Schizophreniekranker in der Klinik [The psychiatric treatment of hospitalized schizophrenics]. *Schweizer, Archiv fur Neurologie, Neurochirurugie und Psychiatrie, 136*(1), 67–74.

Ernst, N. D., & Harlan, W. R. (1991). Obesity and cardiovascular disease in minority populations: Executive summary. Conference highlights, conclusions, and recommendations. *American Journal of Clinical Nutrition, 53*(Suppl.), 1507–1511.

Eron, L. D., & Peterson, R. A. (1982). Abnormal behavior: Social approaches. In M. R. Rosenzweig & L. W. Porter (Eds.), *Annu. Rev. Psychol*. Palo Alto, CA: Annual Reviews.

Eser, A. (1981). "Sanctity" and "quality" of life in a historical comparative view. In S. E. Wallace & A. Eser (Eds.), *Suicide and euthanasia: The rights of personhood*. Knoxville, TN: Univ. Tennessee.

Essali, M. A., Das, I., deBelleroche, J., & Hirsch, S. R. (1992). Calcium mobilization in platelets from schizophrenic and health subjects: Regulation by lithium and neuroleptics. *Journal of Psychopharmacology, 6*(3), 389–394.

Essman, W. B. (1986). Effect of electroconvulsive shock on serotonin activity. In S. Malitz & H. A. Sackeim (Eds.), *Electroconvulsive therapy: Clinical and basic research issues*. New York: Ann. NY Acad. Sci.

Etzioni, A. (1973, Apr.) Methadone: Best hope for now. *Smithsonian, 48*, 67–74.

Evans, B. J., & Stanley, R. O. (1991). Hypnoanaesthesia and hypnotic techniques with surgical patients. *Austral. J. Clin. Exp. Hyp., 19*(1), 31–39.

Evans, J. A., & Hamerton, J. L. (1985). Chromosomol anomalies. In A. M. Clarke, A. D. B. Clarke, & J. M. Berg (Eds.), *Mental deficiency: The changing outlook* (4th ed.). London: Methuen.

Evans, M. D., Hollon, S. D., DeRubeis, R. J., Piasecki, J. M., et al. (1992). Differential relapse following cognitive therapy and pharmacotherapy for depression. *Arch. Gen. Psychiat., 49*, 802–808.

Ewert, A. (1988). Reduction of trait anxiety through participation in Outward Bound. *Leisure Sciences, 10*(2), 107–117.

Exner, J. E. (1987). Computer assistance in Rorschach interpretation. In J. N. Butcher (Ed.), *Computerized psychological assessment: A practitioner's guide*. Lincoln, NE: Univ. Nebraska.

Exner, J. E. (1993). *The Rorschach: A Comprehensive System, Volume 1: Basic Foundations* (3rd ed.). New York: Wiley.

Eysenck, H. J. (1952). The effects of psychotherapy: An evaluation. *J. Cons. Psychol., 16*, 319–354.

Eysenck, H. J. (1959). Learning theory and behaviour therapy. *J. Ment. Sci., 105*, 61–75.

Eysenck, H. J. (Ed.). (1960). *Behavior therapy and the neuroses: Readings in modern methods of treatment derived from learning theory*. New York: Pergamon.

Eysenck, H. J. (1965). The effects of psychotherapy. *Inter. J. Psychiat., 1*, 99–178.

Eysenck, H. J. (1966). *The effects of psychotherapy.* New York: International Science Press.

Eysenck, H. J. (1980). *The effects of psychotherapy.* New York: International Science Press.

Fabrega, H., Mulsant, B. M., Rifai, A. H., Sweet, R. A., Pasternak, R., Ulrich, R., & Zubenko, G. S. (1994). Ethnicity and psychopathology in an aging hospital-based population. *J. Nerv. Ment. Dis., 182*(3), 136–144.

Fabrega, H., Ulrich, R., Pilkonis, P., & Mezzich, J. (1991). On the homogeneity of personality disorder clusters. *Comprehen. Psychiat., 32*(5), 373–386.

Fackelmann, K. (1993, February 6). Marijuana and the brain: Scientists discover the brain's own THC. *Science News, 143,* 88–94.

Faedda, G. L., Tondo, L., Teichner, M. H., Baldessarini, R. J., Gelbard, H. A., & Floris, G. F. (1993). Seasonal Mood Disorders: Patterns of seasonal recurrence in mania and depression. *Arch. Gen. Psychiat., 50*(1), 17–23.

Fahy, T. A. (1988). The Diagnosis of multiple personality disorder. *Brit. J. Psychiat., 153,* 597–606.

Fahy, T. A., & Eisler, I. (1993). Impulsivity and eating disorders. *Brit. J. Psychiat., 162,* 193–197.

Fahy, T. A., Eisler, I., & Russell, G. F. M. (1993). A placebo-controlled trial of d-fenfluramine in bulimia nervosa. *Brit. J. Psychiat., 162,* 597–603.

Fairbank, J. A., & Keane, T. M. (1982). Flooding for combat-related stress disorders: Assessment of anxiety reduction across traumatic memories. *Behav. Ther., 13,* 499–510.

Fairburn, C. G. (1985). Cognitive-behavioural treatment for bulimia. In D. M. Garner & P. E. Garfinkel (Eds.), *Handbook of psychotherapy for anorexia nervosa and bulimia.* New York: Guilford.

Fairburn, C. G. (1985). The management of bulimia nervosa. *J. Psychiat. Res., 19,* 465–472.

Fairburn, C. G. (1992). The outpatient management of bulimia nervosa. In P. J. Cooper & A. Stein (Eds.), *Feeding Problems and Eating Disorders in Children and Adolescents.* Philadelphia, PA: Harwood Academic Publishers.

Fairburn, C. G., Kirk, J., O'Connor, M., & Cooper, P. J. (1986). A comparison of two psychological treatments for bulimia nervosa. *Behav. Res. Ther., 24,* 629–643.

Fairweather, G. W., Danders, D. H., Maynard, H., & Cressler, D. L. (1969). *Community life for the mentally ill: An alternative to institutional care.* Chicago: Aldine.

Falloon, I. R. H., Boyd, J. L., & McGill, C. W. (1984). *Family care for schizophrenia: A problem-solving approach to mental illness.* New York: Guilford.

Falloon, I. R. H., & Liberman, R. P. (1983). Behavioral family interventions in the management of chronic schizophrenia. In W. R. McFarlane (Ed.), *Family therapy in schizophrenia.* New York: Guilford.

Falloon, I. R. H., Lindley, P., McDonald, R., & Marks, I. M. (1977). Social skills training of outpatient groups: A controlled study of rehearsal and homework. *Brit. J. Psychiat., 131,* 599–609.

Fals, S. W., & Schafer, J. (1992). The treatment of substance abusers diagnosed with obsessive-compulsive disorder: An outcome study. *Journal of Substance Abuse Treatment, 9*(4), 365–370.

Fals-Stewart, W., Marks, A. P., & Schafer, J. (1993). A comparison of behavioral group therapy and individual behavior therapy in treating obsessive-compulsive disorder. *J. Nerv. Ment. Dis., 181,* 189–193.

Famularo, R., Kinscherff, R., & Fenton, T. (1991). Posttraumatic stress disorder among children clinically diagnosed as borderline personality disorder. *J. Nerv. Ment. Dis., 179*(7), 428–431.

Famularo, R., Kinscherff, R., & Fenton, T. (1992). Parental substance abuse and the nature of child maltreatment. *Child Abuse & Neglect, 15*(4), 465–483.

Faraone, S. V., Biederman, J., & Milberger, S. (1994). An exploratory study of ADHD among second-degree relatives of ADHD children. *Bio. Psychiat., 35*(6), 398–402.

Farberow, N. L. (1974). *Suicide.* Morristown, NJ: General Learning.

Farberow, N. L. (1991). Adult survivors after suicide: Research problems and needs. In A. A. Leenaars (Ed.), *Life span perspectives of suicide: Time-lines in the suicide process.* New York: Plenum.

Farberow, N. L. (1993). Bereavement after suicide. In A. A. Leenaars, A. L. Berman, P. Cantor, R. E. Litman, & R. W. Maris (Eds.), *Suicidology.* Northvale, NJ: Jason Aronson, Inc.

Farberow, N. L., & Litman, R. E. (1970). A comprehensive suicide prevention program. Los Angeles: Suicide Prevention Center of Los Angeles. Unpublished final report.

Farde, L., & Nordstrom, A. L. (1992). PET Analysis indicates atypical central dopamine receptor occupancy in clozapine-treated patients. *Brit. J. Psychiat., 160*(Suppl. 17), 30–33.

Farde, L., Nordstrom, A. L., Wiedel, F. A., Pauli, S., et al. (1992). Positron emission tomographic analysis of central D-sub-1 and D-sub-2 dopamine receptor occupancy in patients treated with classical neuroleptics and clozapine: Relation to extrapyramidal side effects. *Arch. Gen. Psychiat., 49*(7), 538–544.

Farde, L., Wiedel, F., Stone-Elander, S., Halldin, C., Nordstrom, A. L., Hall, H., & Sedvall, G. (1990). D-2 dopamine receptors in neuroleptic-naive schizophrenia patients: A positron emission tomography study with [11C] raclopride. *Arch. Gen. Psychiat., 26*(46), 57–63.

Farina, A. (1976). *Abnormal psychology.* Englewood Cliffs, NJ: Prentice Hall.

Farley, C. J. (1994, April 18). The butt stops here. *Time,* pp. 58–64.

Farlow, M., Gracon, S. I., Hershey, L. A., Lewis, K. W., Sadowsky, C. H., Dolan-Ureno, J. (1992). A controlled trial of tacrine in Alzheimer's disease. *JAMA, 268*(18), 2523–2529.

Farrington, D. P. (1991). Psychological contributions to the explanations of offending. *Issues in Criminological & Legal Psychology, 1*(17), 7–19.

Farrugia, D. L. (1992). Recognizing emerging borderline personality disorders. *School Counselor, 39*(3), 195–201.

Fasko, S. N., & Fasko, D. (1991). Suicidal behavior in children. *Psychology: A Journal of Human Behavior, 27*(4)–28(1), 10–16.

Fauber, R. L., & Long, N. (1992). Parenting in a broader context: A reply to Emery, Finchman, and Cummings. *J. Cons. Clin. Psychol., 60*(6), 913–915.

Fava, M., Herzog, D. B., Hamburg, P., Riess, H. et al. (1990). Long-term use of fluoxetine in bulimia nervosa: A retrospective study. *Ann. Clin. Psychiat., 2*(1), 53–56.

Fava, M., Bless, E., Otto, M. W., Pava, J. A., & Rosenbaum, J. F. (1994). Dysfunctional attitudes in major depression. *J. Nerv. Ment. Dis., 182*(1), 45–49.

Fawcett, J., Scheftner, W., Clark, D., Hedeker, D. et al. (1987). Clinical predictors of suicide in patients with major affective disorders: A controlled prospective study. *Amer. J. Psychiat., 144*(1), 35–40.

Fawcett, J. A., & Bunney, W. E., Jr. (1967). Pituitary adrenal function and depression: An outline for research. *Arch. Gen. Psychiat., 16*(5), 517–535.

Fedoroff, J. P. (1992). Buspirone hydrochloride in the treatment of an atypical paraphilia. *Archives of Sexual Behavior, 21*(4), 401–406.

Feingold, B. (1975). *Why your child is hyperactive.* New York: Random House.

Felner, R. D., DuBois, D., & Adan, A. (1991). Community-based intervention and prevention. In C. E. Walker (Ed.), *Clinical psychology: Historical and research foundations.* New York: Plenum.

Felten, D. L. (1993). Direct innervation of lymphoid organs: Substrate for neurotransmitter signaling of cells of the immune system. *Neuropsychobiology, 28,* 110–112.

Fenichel, O. (1945). *The psychoanalytic theory of neurosis.* New York: Norton.

Fennig, S., Schwartz, J. E., & Bromet, E. J. (1994). Are diagnostic criteria, time of episode and occupational impairment important determinants of the female:male ration for major depression? *J. Affect. Dis., 30,* 147–154.

Fenton, W. S., & McGlashan, T. H. (1994). Antecedents, symptom progression, and long-term outcome of the deficit syndrome in schizophrenia. *Amer. J. Psychiat., 151*(3), 351–356.

Fernandez, G. A., & Nygard, S. (1990). Impact of involuntary outpatient commitment on the revolving door syndrome in North Carolina. *Hosp. Comm. Psychiat., 41*(9), 1001–1004.

Ferster, C. B. (1961). Positive reinforcement and behavior deficits of autistic children. *Child. Dev., 32,* 437.

Ferster, C. B., & DeMyer, M. K. (1961). The development of performances in autistic children in an automatically controlled environment. *J. Chronic Dis., 13,* 312–345.

Feuerstein, M., & Adams, H. E. (1977). Cephalic vasomotor feedback in the modification of migraine headache. *Biofeed. Self-Reg., 2*(3), 241–254.

Fichter, M. (1990). Psychological therapies in bulimia nervosa. In M. M. Fichter (Ed.), *Bulimia nervosa: Basic research, diagnosis and therapy.* Chichester: Wiley.

Fichtner, C. G., Kuhlman, D. T., Gruenfeld, M. J., & Hughes, J. R. (1990). Decreased episodic violence and increased control of dissociation in a carbamazepine-treated case of multiple personality. *Bio. Psychiat., 27*(9), 1045–1052.

Fiedler, C. R., & Antonak, R. F. (1991). Advocacy. In J. L. Matson & J. A. Mulick (Eds.), *Handbook of mental retardation.* New York: Pergamon.

Field, T. M. (1977). Effects of early separation, interactive deficit, and experimental manipulations on infant-mother face-to-face interaction. *Child. Dev., 48*(3), 763–771.

Field, T. M., Morrow, C. J., Valdeon, C., Larson, S., et al. (1992). Massage reduces anxiety in child and adolescent psychiatric patients. *J. Amer. Acad. Child Adol. Psychiat., 31*(1), 125–131.

Fiester, S. J. (1986). Psychotherapeutic management of gastrointestinal disorders. In A. J. Frances & R. E. Hales (Eds.), *Psychiatric update—American Psychiatric Association annual review* (Vol. 5). Washington, DC: American Psychiatric Press.

Fieve, R. R. (1975). *Moodswing.* New York: Morrow.

Fieve, R. R., Dunner, D. L., & Elston, R. (1984). Search for biological/genetic markers in a long-term epidemiological and morbid risk study of affective disorders. Symposium held at the Institute of Pharmacological Research. "Maria negri": Biological markers in mental disorders. *J. Psychiat. Res., 18*(4), 425–445.

Figley, C. R. (1978). Symptoms of delayed combat stress among a college sample of Vietnam veterans. *Military Med., 143*(2), 107–110.

Figley, C. R., & Leventman, S. (1990). Introduction: Estrangement and victimization. In C. R. Figley & S. Leventman (Eds.), *Strangers at home: Vietnam veterans since the war.* New York: Praeger.

Fink, D. (1992). The psychotherapy of multiple personality disorder. A case study. *Psychoanalytic Inquiry, 12*(1), 49–70.

Fink, M. (1978). Efficacy and safety of induced seizures (EST) in man. *Comprehen. Psychiat., 19,* 1–18.

Fink, M. (1978). Is ECT a useful therapy in schizophrenia? In J. P. Brady & H. K. H. Brodie (Eds.), *Controversy in psychiatry.* Philadelphia: Saunders.

Fink, M. (1984). Theories of the antidepressant efficacy of convulsive therapy (ECT). In R. M. Post & J. C. Ballenger (Eds.), *Neurobiology of mood disorders* (Vol. I, Frontiers of Clinical Neuroscience). Baltimore: Williams & Wilkins.

Fink, M. (1987). Convulsive therapy in affective disorder: A decade of understanding and acceptance. In H. Y. Meltzer (Ed.), *Psychopharmacology: The third generation of progress.* New York: Raven.

Fink, M. (1988). Convulsive therapy: A manual of practice. In A. J. Frances & R. Hales (Eds.), *Rev. of Psychiat.* (Vol. 7). Washington, DC: American Psychiatric Press.

Fink, M. (1992). Electroconvulsive therapy. In E. S. Paykel (Ed.), *Handbook of Affective Disorders.* New York: Guilford.

Finkel, N. J. (1988). *Insanity on trial.* New York: Plenum.

Finkel, N. J. (1989). The Insanity Defense Reform Act of 1984: Much ado about nothing. *Journal of Behavioral Science and Law, 7*(3), 403–419.

Finkel, N. J. (1990). De facto departures from insanity instructions. *Law and Human Behavior, 14*(2), 105–122.

Finkel, N. J. (1991). The insanity defense. *Law and Human Behavior, 15*(5), 533–555.

Finkel, N. J., & Duff, K. (1989). The insanity defense: giving jurors a third option. *Forensic Reports, 1,* 65–70.

Finkel, N. J., & Handel, S. F. (1988). Jurors and insanity: Do test instructions instruct? *Forensic Reports, 1,* 65–79.

Finkel, N. J., & Handel, S. F. (1989). How jurors construe "insanity." *Law and Human Behavior, 13*(1), 41–59.

Finkel, N. J., Shaw, R., Bercaw, S., & Koch, J. (1985). Insanity defenses: From the juror's perspective. *Law and Psychology Review, 9,* 97–92.

Finkel, S. (1991). Group psychotherapy in later life. In W. A. Myers (Ed.), *New techniques in the psychotherapy of older patients.* Washington, DC: American Psychiatric Press.

Finkelhor, D., Gelles, R., Hotaling, G., & Straus, M. (Eds.). (1983). *The dark side of families.* Beverly Hills, CA: Sage.

Finnegan, L. (1991). Treatment for pregnancy and post-partum women and their infants. In *National Conference on Drug Abuse Research and Practice Conference Highlights.* Rockville, MD: National Institute on Drug Abuse.

Fiscalini, J. (1993). Interpersonal relations and the problem of narcissism. In J. Fiscaline & A. L. Grey (Eds.), *Narcissism and the interpersonal self.* New York: Columbia UP.

Fischbach, G. D. (1992, September). Mind and brain. *Scientific American,* p. 48.

Fischer, M. (1980). Twin studies and dual mating studies in defining mania. In R. H. Belmaker & H. M. van Praag (Eds.), *Mania: An evolving concept.* Jamaica, NY: Spectrum.

Fischer, R., & Landon, G. M. (1972). On the arousal state-dependent recall of the "subconscious" experience: State-boundness. *Brit. J. Psychiat., 120*(555), 159–172.

Fischman, G., Fraticelli, B., Newman, D. E., & Sampson, L. M. (1983). Day-treatment programs for the Spanish-speaking: A response to underutilization. *International Journal of Social Psychiatry, 29*(3), 215–219.

Fischman, J. (1987). Getting tough. *Psych. Today, 21*(12), 26–28.

Fish, J. (1973). *Placebo therapy.* San Francisco: Jossey-Bass.

Fishbein, M., Middlestadt, S. E., Ottati, V., Strauss, S., & Ellis, A. (1988). Medical problems among ICSOM musicians: Overview of a national survey. *Medical Problems of Performing Artists, 3,* 1–8.

Fisher, J. E., & Carstensen, L. L. (1990). Behavior management of the dementias. *Clin. Psychol. Rev., 10,* 611–629.

Fisher, M., Schneider, M., Pegler, C., & Napolitano, B. (1991). Eating attitudes, health-risk behaviors, self-esteem, and anxiety among adolescent females in a suburban high school. *Journal of Adolescent Health, 12*(5), 377–384.

Fisher, S. (1973). *The female orgasm.* New York: Basic Books.

Fitz, A. (1990). Religious and familial factors in the etiology of obsessive-compulsive disorder: A review. *Journal of Psychology and Theology, 18*(2), 141–147.

Flament, M. F. (1990). Epidemiologie du trouble obsessionnel-compulsif chez l'enfant et l'adolescent. [Epidemiology of obsessive-compulsive disorder during childhood and adolescence.] *Encephale, 16,* 311–316.

Flament, M. F., Koby, E., Rapoport, J. L., Berg, C. J., et al. (1991). Childhood obsessive-compulsive disorder: A prospective follow-up study. *Annual Progress in Child Psychiatry & Child Development,* 373–394.

Flament, M. F. et al. (1985). Clominpramine treatment of childhood obsessive-compulsive disorder: A double-blind controlled study. *Arch. Gen. Psychiat., 429*(10), 977–983.

Flavin, D. K., Franklin, J. E., & Frances, R. J. (1990). Substance abuse and suicidal behavior. In S. J. Blumenthal & D. J. Kupfer (Eds.), *Suicide over the life cycle: Risk factors, assessment, and treatment of suicidal patients.* Washington, DC: American Psychiatry Press.

Fleer, J., & Pasewark, R. A. (1982). Prior public health agency contacts of individuals committing suicide. *Psych. Rep., 50*(3, Pt. 2), 1319–1324.

Fleishman, J. A., & Fogel, B. (1994). Coping and depressive symptoms among people with AIDS. *Health Psychology, 13*(2), 156–169.

Fletcher, J. (1981). In defense of suicide. In S. E. Wallace & A. Eser (Eds.), *Suicide and euthanasia: The rights of personhood.* Knoxville, TN: Univ. Tennessee.

Flick, S. N., Roy-Byrne, P. P., Cowley, D. S., Shores, M. M., &

Dunner, D. L. (1993). DSM-III-R personality disorders in a mood and anxiety disorders clinic: Prevalence, comorbidity, and clinical correlates. *J. Affect. Dis., 27,* 71–79.

Flint, A. J. (1994). Epidemiology and comorbidity of anxiety disorders in the elderly. *Amer. J. Psychiat., 151*(5), 640–649.

Floyd, F. J., O'Farrell, T. J., & Goldberg, M. (1987). Comparison of marital observational measures: The Marital Interaction Coding System and the Communications Skills Test. *J. Cons. Clin. Psychol., 55*(3), 2200.

Flynn, T. M., Taylor, P., & Pollard, C. E. (1992). Use of mobile phones in the behavioral treatment of driving phobias. *J. Behav. Ther. Exp. Psychiat., 23*(4), 299–302.

Foa, E. B., & Riggs, D. S. (1993). Posttraumatic stress disorder and rape. In J. M. Oldham, M. B. Riba, & A. Tasman (Eds.), *Review of Psychiatry,* Vol. 12. Washington, DC: American Psychiatry Press.

Foderaero, L. W. (1993, August 12). Electroshock therapy makes a comeback. *Anchorage Daily News,* p. D3.

Fogel, B. S. (1986). ECT versus tricyclic antidepressants. *Amer. J. Psychiat., 143*(1), 121.

Folkman, S., Lazarus, R. S., Pimley, S., & Novacek, J. (1987). Age differences in stress and coping processes. *Psychol. & Aging, 2,* 171–184.

Folstein, M., Folstein, S., & McHugh, P. (1975). Mini-mental state: A practical method for grading the cognitive state of patients for the clinician. *J. Psychiat. Res., 12,* 189–198.

Folstein, S., & Rutter, M. (1977). Genetic influences in infantile autism. *Nature, 265,* 726–728.

Folstein, S., & Rutter, M. L. (1988). Autism: Familial aggregation and genetic implications. *J. Autism Dev. Dis., 18,* 3–11.

Fonagy, P. (1991). Thinking about thinking: Some clinical and theoretical considerations in the treatment of a borderline patient. *Inter. J. Psychoanal., 72*(4), 639–656.

Ford, C. V., King, B. H., & Hollender, M. H. (1988). Lies and liars: Psychiatric aspects of prevarication. *Amer. J. Psychiat., 145*(5), 554–562.

Ford, M. R., & Widiger, T. A. (1989). Sex bias in the diagnosis of histrionic and antisocial personality disorders. *J. Cons. Clin. Psychol., 57*(2), 301–305.

Foster, S. L. & Cone, J. D. (1986). Design and use of direct observation. In A. R. Ciminero, K. S. Calhoun, & H. E. Adams (Eds.), *Handbook of behavioral assessment* (2nd ed.). New York: Wiley.

Foster-Higgins & Co. (1991) cited in L. Block "Mental Health Expenses make employers anxious." *Business Insurance,* June 8, 1992, p. 3.

Fox, P. (1992). Implications for expressed emotion therapy within a family therapeutic context. *Health and Social Work, 17*(3), 207–213.

Fox, S., & Emery, G. (1981). Cognitive therapy of sexual dysfunctions: A case study. In G. Emery, S. D. Hollon, & R. C. Bedrosian (Eds.), *New directions in cognitive therapy.* New York: Guilford.

Foxx, R. M., & Faw, G. D. (1990). Long-term follow-up of echolalia and question answering. *J. Appl. Behav. Anal., 23*(3), 387–396.

Foxx, R. M., McMorrow, M. J., Davis, L. A., & Bittle, R. G. (1988). Replacing a chronic schizophrenic man's delusional speech with stimulus appropriate response. *J. Behav. Ther. Exp. Psychiat., 19*(1), 43–50.

Frances, R. J., & Franklin, J. E. (1988). Alcohol and other psychoactive substance use disorders. In J. A. Talbott, R. E. Hales, & S. C. Yudofsky (Eds.), *Textbook of psychiatry.* Washington, DC: American Psychiatric Press.

Francis, L. P. (1980). Assisting suicide: A problem for the criminal law. In M. P. Battin & D. J. Mayo (Eds.), *Suicide: The philosophical issues.* New York: St. Martin's.

Francis, M. E., & Pennebaker, J. W. (1992). Putting stress into words: The impact of writing on physiological, absentee, and self-reported emotional well-being measures. *American Journal of Health Promotion, 6*(4), 280–287.

Frank, E., Anderson, C., & Rubinstein, D. (1978). Frequency of sexual dysfunction in "normal" couples. *New England Journal of Medicine, 299*(3), 111–115.

Frank, E., Kupfer, D. J., Perel, J. M., Cornes, C., Jarrett, D. B., Mallinger, A. G., et al. (1990). Three-year outcomes for maintenance therapies in recurrent depression. *Arch. Gen. Psychiat., 47*(12), 1093–1099.

Frank, E., Kupfer, D. J., Wagner, E. F., McEachran, A. B., & Cornes, C. (1991). Efficacy of interpersonal therapy as a maintenance treatment of recurrent depression: Contributing factors. *Arch. Gen. Psychiat., 48*, 1053–1059.

Frank, J. D. (1973). *Persuasion and healing* (Rev. ed.). Baltimore: Johns Hopkins UP.

Frank, J. D., & Frank, J. (1991). *Persuasion and healing* (3rd ed.). Baltimore: John Hopkins UP.

Frankel, F. H. (1984). The use of electroconvulsive therapy in suicidal patients. *Amer. J. Psychother., 38*(3), 384–391.

Frankel, F. H. (1993). Adult reconstruction of childhood events in the multiple personality literature. *Amer. J. Psychiat., 150*(6), 954–958.

Frankenhaeuser, M. (1979). Psychoneuroendocrine approaches to the study of emotion as related to stress and coping. In H. E. Howe and R. Dienstbier (Eds.), *Nebraska symposium on motivation 1978.* Lincoln: University of Nebraska Press.

Frankl, V. E. (1963). *Man's search for meaning.* New York: Washington Square.

Frankl, V. E. (1965). *The doctor and the soul* (2nd ed.). New York: Knopf.

Frankl, V. E. (1975). Paradoxical intention and dereflection. *Psychother. Theory, Res. Prac., 12*(3), 226–237.

Franko, D. L. (1993). The use of a group meal in the brief group therapy of bulimia nervosa. *International Journal of Group Psychotherapy, 43*(2), 237–242.

Franks, C. M. (1990). Behavior therapy: An overview. In C. M. Franks, G. T. Wilson, P. C. Kendall, & J. P. Foreyt (Eds.), *Review of behavior therapy: Theory and practice* (Vol. 12). New York: Guilford.

Frayn, D. H. (1991). The incidence and significance of perceptual qualities in the reported dreams of patients with anorexia nervosa. *Canad. J. Psychiat., 36*(7), 517–520.

Frederick, C. J. (1969). Suicide notes: A survey and evaluation. *Bull. Suicidology, 8*, 17–26.

Frederick, C. J. (1985). An introduction and overview of youth suicide. In M. L. Peck, N. L. Farberow, & R. E. Litman (Eds.), *Youth suicide.* New York: Springer.

Frederiksen, N. (1986). Toward a broader conception of human intelligence. *Amer. Psychol., 41*, 445–452.

Frederiksen, N. (1993). Changing conceptions of intelligence. In G. G. Brannigan & M. R. Merrens (Eds.), *The undaunted psychologist: Adventures in research.* New York: McGraw-Hill.

Freeland, M., & Schendler, C. E. (1983). National health expenditure growth in the 1980s. *Health Care Financing Rev., 4*(3).

Freeman, W., & Watts, J. W. (1942). *Psychosurgery: Intelligence, Emotion, and Social Behavior Following Prefrontal Lobotomy for Mental Disorders.* Springfield, Ill: Charles C Thomas.

Freeman, W. History of Psychosurgery. Unpublished manuscript, Himmelfarb Health Science Library. George Washington University.

Freeston, M., Ladouceur, R., Gagnon, F., & Thibodeau, N. (1992). Beliefs about obsessional thoughts. Unpublished manuscript, Laval University, Quebec City, Quebec.

Freeston, M., Ladouceur, R., Thibodeau, N., & Gagnon, F. (1992). Cognitive intrusions in a non-clinical population. II. Associations with depressive, anxious, and compulsive symptoms. *Behav. Res. Ther., 30*, 263–271.

Freiberg, P. (1994, April). Gay-rights position takes on significance. *APA Monitor, 25*(4), p. 40.

French, D. J., Nicki, R. M., & Cane, D. B. (1993). Bulimia nervosa: An examination of the anxiety-inhibiting properties of the prospect of vomiting. *Behav. Psychother., 21*, 97–106.

French, O. (1987). More on multiple personality disorder. *Amer. J. Psychiat., 144*(1), 123–124.

Freud, S. (1885). On the general effects of cocaine. *Medicinisch-chirugisches Centralblatt, 20*, 373–375.

Freud, S. (1894). The neuro-psychoses of defense. In J. Strachey (Ed.), *The standard edition of the complete psychological works of Sigmund Freud.* Vol. III. London: Hogarth Press, 1962.

Freud, S. (1900). *The interpretation of dreams.* J. Strachey (Ed. and Trans.). New York: Wiley.

Freud, S. (1909). Analysis of a phobia in a five-year-old boy. In *Sigmund Freud: Collected Papers.* Vol. III. New York: Basic Books.

Freud, S. (1915). A case of paranoia counter to psychoanalytic theory. In *Complete Psychological Works.* Vol. 14. London: Hogarth, 1957.

Freud, S. (1917). *A general introduction to psychoanalysis.* Translated by J. Riviere. New York: Liveright, 1963.

Freud, S. (1917). Mourning and melancholia. In *Collected Papers.* Vol. 4. London: Hogarth Press and the Institute of Psychoanalysis, 1950, pp. 152–172.

Freud, S. (1919). Lines of advance in psychoanalytic therapy. Translated by J. Riviere and J. Strachey. In J. Strachey (Ed.), *The standard edition of the complete psychological works of Sigmund Freud.* London: Hogarth Press, 1955.

Freud, S. (1924). The loss of reality in neurosis and psychosis. *Collected papers, 2*, 277–282.

Freud, S. (1933). *New introductory lectures on psychoanalysis.* New York: Norton.

Freud, S. (1955). *Notes upon a case of obsessional neurosis.* London: Hogarth Press.

Frick, P. J., Lahley, B. B., Loeber, R., et al. (1992). Familial risk factors to oppositional defiant disorder and conduct disorder: Parental psychopathology and maternal parenting. *J. Cons. Clin. Psychol., 60*(1), 49–55.

Frick, R., & Bogart, L. (1982). Transference and countertransference in group therapy in Vietnam veterans. *Bull. Menninger Clin., 46*(5), 429–444.

Friedberg, J. (1975, August). Electroshock therapy: Let's stop blasting the brain. *Psych. Today*, 18–23, 98–99.

Friedman, E., & Wilcox, P. J. (1942). Electrostimulated convulsive doses in intact humans by means of unidirectional currents. *J. Nerv. Ment. Dis., 96,* 56–63.

Friedman, H. S., & Booth-Kewley, S. (1987). Personality, Type A behavior, and coronary heart disease: The role of emotional expression. *J. Pers. Soc. Psychol., 53*(4), 783–792.

Friedman, H. S., & Booth-Kewley, S. (1987). The "disease-prone personality." *Amer. Psychol., 42,* 534–555.

Friedman, M., & Rosenman, R. (1959). Association of specific overt behavior pattern with blood and cardiovascular findings. *JAMA, 169,* 1286.

Friedman, M., & Rosenman, R. (1974). *Type A behavior and your heart.* New York: Knopf.

Friedman, M., Thoresen, C., Gill, J., et al (1984). Alteration of type A behavior and reduction in cardiac recurrences in postmyocardial infarction patients. *Amer. Heart J., 108*(2), 653–665.

Friedman, P. (1976). Overview of the institutional labor problem: The nature and extent of institutional labor in the United States. In M. Kindred, J. Cohen, D. Penrod, & T. Shaffer (Eds.), *The mentally retarded citizen and the law: President's committee on mental retardation.* New York: Free Press.

Friedman, S., Jones, J. C., Chernen, L., & Barlow, D. H. (1992). Suicidal ideation and suicide attempts among patients with panic disorder: A survey of two outpatient clinics. *Amer. J. Psychiat., 129*(5), 680–685.

Friedman, S., Neaigus, A., desJarlais, D., et al. (1992). Social intervention against AIDS among injecting drug users. *British Journal of Addiction, 87*(3), 393–404.

Friedmann, E. et al. (1983). Social interaction and blood pressure: Influence of animal companions. *J. Nerv. Ment. Dis., 171*(8), 461–465.

Friman, P. C., Allen, K. D., Kerwin, M. L. E., & Larzelere, R. (1993). Changes in modern psychology: A citation analysis of the Kuhnian Displacement Thesis. *Amer. Psychol., 48*(6), 658–664.

Friman, P. C., & Warzak, W. J. (1990). Nocturnal enuresis: A prevalent, persistent, yet curable parasomnia. *Pediatrician, 17*(1), 38–45.

Frischholz, E. J., & Braun, B. G. (1991, August). Diagnosing Dissociative Disorders: New Methods. Paper presented at the annual meeting of the American Psychological Association, San Francisco, CA.

Frischholz, E. J., Lipman, L. S., Braun, B. G., & Sachs, R. G. (1992). Psychopathology, hypnotizability, and dissociation. *Amer. J. Psychiat., 149*(11), 1521–1525.

Fritz, G. K., Rockney, R. M., & Yeung, A. S. (1994). Plasma levels and efficacy of imipramine treatment for enuresis. *J. Amer. Acad. Child Adol. Psychiat., 33*(1), 60–64.

Fromm, E., & Nash, M. R., eds. (1992). *Contemporary hypnosis research.* New York: Guilford.

Fromm-Reichmann, F. (1943). Psychotherapy of schizophrenia. *Amer. J. Psychiat., 111,* 410–419.

Fromm-Reichmann, F. (1948). Notes on the development of treatment of schizophrenia by psychoanalytic psychotherapy. *Psychiat., 11,* 263–273.

Fromm-Reichmann, F. (1950). *Principles of intensive psychotherapy.* Chicago: Univ. Chicago.

Frosch, W. A., Robbins, E. S., & Stern, M. (1965). Untoward reactions to lysergic acid diethylamide (LSD) resulting in hospitalization. *New Engl. J. Med., 273,* 1235–1239.

Fry, P. S. (1986). *Depression, stress, and adaptations in the elderly.* Rockville, MD: Aspen.

Fry, R. (1993). Adult physical illness and childhood sexual abuse. *J. Psychosom. Res., 37*(2), 89–103.

Fuller, R. C. (1982, Fall). Carl Rogers, religion, and the role of psychology in American culture. *Journal of Humanistic Psychology, 22,* 21–32.

Fulwiler, C., & Pope, H. G., Jr. (1987). Depression in personality disorder. In O. G. Cameron (Ed.), *Presentations of Depression: Depressive Symptoms in Medical and Other Psychiatric Disorders.* New York: Wiley.

Funari, D. J., Piekarski, A. M., & Sherwood, R. J. (1991). Treatment outcomes of Vietnam veterans with posttraumatic stress disorder. *Psych. Rep., 68*(2), 571–578.

Furio, J. (1993, January). Can new state laws stop stalkers? *Ms.* magazine.

Furst, S. S., & Ostow, M. (1979). The psychodynamics of suicide. In L. D. Hankoff & B. Einsidler (Eds.), *Suicide: Theory and clinical aspects.* Littleton, MA: PSG Publishing Company, Inc.

Gabbard, G. O. (1990). *Psychodynamic Psychiatry in Clinical Practice.* Washington, DC: American Psychiatric Press.

Gabbard, G. O., & Coyne, L. (1987). Predictors of response of antisocial patients to hospital treatment. *Hosp. Comm. Psychiat., 38*(11), 1181–1185.

Gabrielli, W. F. Jr., & Mednick, S. A. (1983). Genetic correlates of criminal behavior. *Amer. Beh. Sci., 27,* 59–74.

Gacono, C. B., & Meloy, J. R. (1992). The Rorschach and the DSM III-R antisocial personality: A tribute to Robert Linder. *Journal of Clinical Psychology, 48*(3), 393–406.

Gage, F. H., & Fisher, L. J. (1991). Intracerebral grafting: a tool for the neurobiologist. *Neuron, 6,* 1–12.

Gaines, R., Leaper, C., Monahan, C., & Weickgenant, A. (1988). Language learning and retention in young language-disordered children. *J. Autism Dev. Dis., 18,* 281–296.

Galanter, M. (1993). Network therapy for addiction: A model for office practice. *Amer. J. Psychiat., 150*(1), 28–35.

Galanter, M., Talbott, D., Gallegos, K., & Rubenstone, E. (1990). Combined Alcoholics Anonymous and professional care for addicted physicians. *Amer. J. Psychiat., 147*(1), 64–68.

Gallagher, D. (1986). The Beck Depression Inventory and older adults: Review of its development and utility. *Clin. Gerontologist, 5,* 149–163.

Gallagher, D., Rose, J., Rivera, P., Lovett, S., et al. (1989). Prevalence of depression in family caregivers. *Gerontologist, 29*(4), 449–456.

Gallagher-Thompson, D. (1994). Direct services and interventions for caregivers: A review and critique of extant programs and a look ahead to the future. In M. Cantor (Ed.), *Family caregiving: Agenda for the future.* San Francisco, CA: American Society on Aging.

Gallagher-Thompson, D., Hanley-Peterson, P., & Thompson, L. W. (1989). Maintenance of gains versus relapse following brief psychotherapy for depression. *J. Cons. Clin. Psychol., 58,* 371–374.

Gallagher-Thompson, D., Lovett, S., & Rose, J. (1991). Psychotherapeutic interventions for stressed family caregivers. In W. A. Myers (Ed.), *New techniques in the psychotherapy of older patients.* Washington, DC: American Psychiatric Press.

Gammonley, J., & Yates, J. (1991). Pet projects: Animal assisted therapy in nursing homes. *Journal of Gerontological Nursing, 17*(1), 12–15.

Ganaway, G. K. (1989). Historical versus narrative truth: Clarifying the role of exogenous trauma in the etiology of MPD and its variants. *Dissociation, 2,* 205–222.

Ganley, A. (1981). *A participant and trainer's manual for working with men who batter.* Washington, DC: Center for Women Policy Studies.

Gannon, L., Luchetta, T., Rhodes, K., Pardie, L., & Segrist, D. (1992). Sex bias in psychological research: Progress or complacency? *Amer. Psychol. 47*(3), 389–396.

Gantz, F., Gallagher-Thompson, D., & Rodman, J. (1991). Cognitive-behavioral facilitation of inhibited grief. In A. Freeman & F. Dattilio (Eds.), *Casebook of cognitive-behavior therapy.* New York: Plenum.

GAP (Group for the Advancement of Psychiatry). (1947, Jan. 22). 18.

Gara, M. A., Woolfolk, R. L., Cohen, B. D., Goldston, R. B., Allen, L. A., & Novalany, J. (1993). Perception of self and other in major depression. *J. Abnorm. Psychol., 102*(1), 93–100.

Garamoni, G. L., & Schwartz, R. M. (1986). Type A behavior pattern and compulsive personality: Toward a psychodynamic-behavioral integration. *Clinical Psychology Review, 6*(4), 311–336.

Garber, J., Weiss, B., & Shanley, N. (1993). Cognitions, depressive symptoms, and development in adolescents. *J. Abnorm. Psychol., 102*(1), 47–57.

Gardner, D. L., Leibenluft, E., O'Leary, K. M., & Cowdry, R. W. (1991). Self-ratings of anger and hostility in borderline personality disorder. *J. Nerv. Ment. Dis., 179*(3), 157–161.

Gardner, D. L., Lucas, P. B., & Cowdry, R. W. (1990). CSF metabolites in borderline personality disorder compared with normal controls. *Bio. Psychiat., 28,* 247–254.

Gardner, F. L., McGowan, L. P., DiGiuseppe, R., & Sutton-Simon, K. (1980, November). A comparison of cognitive and behavioral therapies in the reduction of social anxiety. Paper presented to the American Association of Behavior Therapy, New York.

Gardner, R. (1984, Jul. 12). Full moon lunacy: Fact or fiction. *Trenton Times,* p. B1.

Garety, P. (1991). Reasoning and delusions. *Brit. J. Psychiat., 159*(Suppl. 14), 14–18.

Garfield, S. L. (1991). Common and specific factors in psychotherapy. *Journal of Integrative and Eclectic Psychotherapy, 10,* 5–13.

Garfield, S. L. (1992). Eclectic psychotherapy: A common factors approach. In J. C. Norcross & M. R. Goldfried (Eds.), *Handbook of psychotherapy integration.* New York: Basic Books.

Garfield, S. L., & Bergin, A. E. eds. (1986). *Handbook of psychotherapy and behavior change* (3rd ed.). New York: Wiley.

Garfield, S. L., & Bergin, A. E. (1994). Introduction and historical overview. In A. E. Bergin & S. L. Garfiel (Eds.), *Handbook of psychotherapy and behavior change* (4th ed.). New York: Wiley.

Garfinkel, B. D., Froese, A., & Golombek, H. M. (1979). Suicidal behavior in a pediatric population. In Proceedings of the 10th International Congress for Suicide Prevention. Ottawa: International Association for Suicide Prevention.

Garfinkel, B. D., Froese, A., & Hood, J. (1982). Suicide attempts in children and adolescents. *Amer. J. Psychiat., 139*(10), 1257–1261.

Garfinkel, B. D., & Golombek, H. M. (1983). Suicidal behavior in adolescence. In H. Golombek & B. D. Garfinkel (Eds.), *The adolescent and mood disturbance.* New York: International Universities Press.

Garfinkel, P. E. (1985). The treatment of anorexia nervosa in Toronto. *J. Psychiat. Res., 19*(2–3), 405–411.

Garfinkel, P. E., & Gallop, R. (1992). Eating disorders and borderline personality disorder. In D. Silver & M. Rosenbluth (Eds.), *Handbook of Borderline Disorders.* Madison, CT: International Universities Press.

Garfinkel, P. E., & Garner, D. M. (1982). *Anorexia nervosa: A multidimensional perspective.* New York: Brunner/Mazel.

Garfinkel, P. E., Moldofsky, H., & Garner, D. M. (1977). The outcome of anorexia nervosa: Significance of clinical features, body image and behavior modification. In R. A. Vigersky (Ed.), *Anorexia Nervosa.* New York: Raven.

Garfinkel, P. E. et al. (1978). Body awareness in anorexia nervosa: Disturbances in body image and satiety. *Psychosom. Med., 40*(6), 487–498.

Garland, A. F., Shaffer, D., & Whittle, B. (1989). A national survey of adolescent suicide prevention programs. *J. Amer. Acad. Child Adol. Psychiat., 28,* 931–934.

Garland, A. F., & Zigler, E. (1993). Adolescent suicide prevention: Current research and social policy implications. *Amer. Psychol., 48*(2), 169–182.

Garner, D. M. (1984). *The EDI.* Odessa, FL: Psychological Assessment Resources, Inc.

Garner, D. M. (1991). *The EDI-2.* Odessa, FL: Psychological Assessment Resources, Inc.

Garner, D. M., & Bemis, K. M. (1982). A cognitive-behavioral approach to anorexia nervosa. *Cog. Ther. Res., 6*(2), 123–150.

Garner, D. M., & Bemis, K. M. (1985). Cognitive therapy for anorexia nervosa. In D. M. Garner & P. E. Garfinkel (Eds.), *Handbook of psychotherapy for anorexia nervosa and bulimia.* New York: Guilford.

Garner, D. M., Fairburn, C. G., & Davis, R. (1987). Cognitive behavioral treatment of bulimia nervosa: A critical appraisal. *Behav. Mod., 11*(4), 398–431.

Garner, D. M., & Garfinkel, P. E. (1978). Sociocultural factors in anorexia nervosa. *Lancet, 2,* 674.

Garner, D. M., & Garfinkel, P. E. (1979). The Eating Attitudes Test: An index of the symptoms of anorexia nervosa. *Psychol. Med., 9,* 273–279.

Garner, D. M., & Garfinkel, P. E. (1980). Sociocultural factors in the development of anorexia nervosa. *Psychol. Med., 10,* 647–656.

Garner, D. M., & Garfinkel, P. E. (1981). Body image in anorexia nervosa: Measurement, theory and clinical implications. *Inter. J. Psychiat. Med., 11,* 263–284.

Garner, D. M., Garfinkel, P. E., & O'Shaughnessy, M. (1985). The validity of the distinction between bulimia with and without anorexia nervosa. *Amer. J. Psych., 142,* 581–587.

Garner, D. M., Garfinkel, P. E., Schwartz, D., & Thompson, M. (1980). Cultural expectations of thinness in women. *Psych. Rep., 47,* 483–491.

Garner, D. M., Garfinkel, P. E., Stancer, H. C., & Moldofsky, H. (1976). Body image disturbances in anorexia nervosa and obesity. *Psychosom. Med., 38,* 327–336.

Garner, D. M., Olmsted, M. P., Polivy, J. (1983). The eating disorders inventory: A measure of cognitive-behavioral dimensions of anorexia nervosa and bulimia. In P. L. Darby et al. (Eds.), *Anorexia nervosa: Recent developments in research.* New York: Liss.

Garner, D. M., Olmsted, M. P., Polivy, J. (1984). *The EDI.* Odessa, FL: Psychological Assessment Resources, Inc.

Garner, D. M., Rockert, W., Davis, R., Garner, M. V., Olmsted, M. P., & Eagle, M. (1993). Comparison of cognitive-behavioral and supportive-expressive therapy for bulimia nervosa. *Amer. J. Psychiat., 150*(1), 37–46.

Garner, D. M., & Rosen, L. W. (1990). Anorexia nervosa and bulimia nervosa. In A. S. Bellack, M. Hersen, & A. E. Kazdin (Eds.), *International handbook of behavior modification and therapy.* New York: Plenum.

Garner, D. M., Shafer, C., & Rosen, L. (1991). Critical appraisal of the DSM III-R diagnostic criteria for eating disorders. In S. R. Hooper, G. W. Hynd, & R. E. Mattison (Eds.), *Child psychopathology.* Hillsdale, NJ: Lawrence Erlbaum Associates.

Garner, D. M., & Wooley, S. C. (1991). Confronting the failure of behavioral and dietary treatments for obesity. *Clin. Psychol. Rev., 11*(6), 729–780.

Garofalo, G., Ragusa, R. M., Barletta, C., & Spina, E. (1992). Schizophrenia and chromosomal fragile sites. *Amer. J. Psychiat., 149*(8), 1116.

Garrison, C. Z., McKeown, R. E., Valois, R. F., & Vincent, M. L. (1993). Aggression, substance use, and suicidal behaviors in high school students. *Amer. J. Pub. Hlth., 83*(2), 179–184.

Garrison, E. G. (1987). Psychological maltreatment of children: An emerging focus for inquiry and concern. *Amer. Psychol., 42*(2), 157–159.

Garver, D. L., & Davis, J. M. (1979). Biogenic amine hypotheses of affective disorders. *Life Sciences, 24*(5), 383–394.

Garver, R. B., Fuselier, G. D., & Booth, T. B. (1981). The hypnotic treatment of amnesia in an Air Force basic trainee. *Amer. J. Clin. Hyp., 24*(1), 3–6.

Garvin, V., Kalter, N., & Hansell, J. (1993). Divorced women: Individual differences in stressors, mediating factors, and adjustment outcomes. *Amer. J. Orthopsychiat., 63*(2), 232–240.

Gatchel, R. J., & Baum, A. (1983). *An introduction to health psychology.* New York: Random House.

Gatchel, R. J., Paulus, P. D., & Maples, C. W. (1975). Learned helplessness and self-reported affect. *J. Abnorm. Psychol., 84*(8), 732–734.

Gatz, M., & Pearson, C. G. (1988). Ageism-revised and the provision of psychological services. *Amer. Psychol., 43*, 184–188.

Gatz, M., & Smyer, M. A. (1992). The mental health system and older adults in the 1990s. *Amer. Psychol., 47*(6), 741–751.

Gawin, F. H., & Kleber, H. D. (1986). Abstinence symptomatology and psychiatric diagnosis in cocaine abuse: Clinical observations. *Arch. Gen. Psychiat., 43*(2), 107–113.

Gebhard, P. H. (1965). Situational factors affecting human sexual behavior. In F. Beach (Ed.), *Sex and behavior.* New York: Wiley.

Gebhard, P. H., Gagnon, J. H., Pomeroy, W. B., & Christenson, C. V. (1965). *Sex offenders: An analysis of types.* New York: Harper & Row.

Geer, J. H. (1965). The development of a scale to measure fear. *Behav. Res. Ther., 3*, 45–53.

Geer, J. H. (1976). Genital measures: Comments on their role in understanding human sexuality. *J. Sex Marital Ther., 2*(3), 165–172.

Gejman, P. V., Ram, A., Gelernter, J., Friedman, E., Cao, Q., et al. (1994). No structural mutation in the Dopamine d-2 receptor gene in alcoholism or schizophrenia. *JAMA, 271*(3), 204–208.

Gelberg, L., Linn, L. S., & Leake, B. D. (1988). Mental health, alcohol and drug use, and criminal history among homeless adults. *Amer. J. Psychiat., 145*(2), 191–196.

Gelder, M. (1991). Psychological treatment for anxiety disorders: Adjustment disorder with anxious mood, generalized anxiety disorders, panic disorder, agoraphobia, and avoidant personality disorder. In C. Coryell & G. Winokur (Eds.), *The Clinical Management of Anxiety Disorders.* New York: Oxford UP.

Gelenberg, A. J. (1989). Mood disorders. In J. Hobson (Ed.), *Abnormal states of brain and mind.* Boston: Birhauser.

Gelenberg, A. J., Kane, J. M., Keller, M. B., Lavori, P., Rosenbaum, J. F., Cole, K., & Lavelle, J. (1989, Nov. 30). Comparison of standard and low serum levels of lithium for maintenance treatment of bipolar disorder. *New Engl. J. Med., 321*(22), 1489–1493.

Gelenberg, A. J. et al. (1980). Tyrosine for the treatment of depression. *Amer. J. Psychiat., 137*(5), 622–623.

Gelfand, D. M., Jenson, W. R., & Drew, C. J. (1982). *Understanding child behavior disorders.* New York: Holt, Rinehart & Winston.

Geller, B., Fox, L. W., & Fletcher, M. (1993). Effect of tricyclic antidepressants on switching to mania and on the onset of bipolarity in depressed 6- to 12-year-olds. *J. Amer. Acad. Child. Adol. Psychiat., 32*(1), 43–50.

Geller, J. L. (1992). A historical perspective on the role of state hospitals viewed from the era of the "revolving door." *Amer. J. Psychiat., 149*, 1526–1533.

Gelles, R. J. (1992). Poverty and violence toward children. *American Behavioral Scientist, 35*(3), 258–274.

Gelles, R. J., & Straus, M. A. (1987). Is violence toward children increasing? A comparison of 1975 and 1985 national survey rates. *J. Interpersonal Violence, 2*, 212–222.

Gelman, D. (1983, Nov. 7). A great emptiness. *Newsweek*, 120–126.

Gelman, D., & Katel, P. (1993, April 5). The trauma after the storm. *Newsweek.*

Gentry, W. D., & Matarazzo, J. D. (1981). Medical psychology: Three decades of growth and development. In L. A. Bradley & C. K. Prokop (Eds.), *Medical psychology: A new perspective.* New York: Academic Press.

George, F. R. (1990). Genetic approaches to studying drug abuse: Correlates of drug self-administration. National Institute on Alcohol Abuse and Alcoholism Neuroscience and Behavioral Research Branch Workshop on the Neurochemical Bases on Alcohol-Related Behavior. *Alcohol, 7*(3), 207–211.

Georgotas, A., & McCue, R. E. (1986). Benefits and limitations of major pharmacological treatment for depression. *Amer. J. Psychother., 40*(3), 370–376.

Gerhardt, P., Holmes, D. L., Alessandri, M., Goodman, M. (1991). Social policy on the use of aversive interventions: Empirical, ethical, and legal considerations. *J. Autism Dev. Dis., 21*(3), 265–277.

Gerlach, J., & Hansen, L. (1992). Clozapine and D1/D2 antag-
onism in extrapyramidal functions. Brit. J. Psychiat.,
160(suppl), 34–37.
Gerlinghoff, M., & Backmund, H. (1987). Stealing behavior in
anorexia nervosa and bulimia nervosa. Fortschritte-der-Neu-
rologie Psychiatrie, 55(11), 343–346.
Gernsbacher, L. M. (1985). The suicide syndrome. New York: Human Sciences.
Gershon, L., & Shaw, F. H. (1961). Psychiatric sequelae of
chronic exposure to organophosphorous insecticides. Lancet,
1, 1371–1374.
Geyer, S. (1992). Artifacts in "limited prospective" designs?
Testing confounding effects on response behaviour of
women prior to breast surgery. J. Psychosom. Res., 36(2),
107–116.
Gheorghiu, V. A., & Orleanu, P. (1982). Dental implant under
hypnosis. Amer. J. Clin. Hyp., 25(1), 68–70.
Ghosh, A., & Greist, J. H. (1988). Computer treatment in psychiatry. Psychiat. Ann., 18(4), 246–250.
Ghosh, A., & Marks, I. M. (1987). Self-treatment of agoraphobia by exposure. Behav. Ther., 18(1), 3–16.
Ghubash, R., Hamdi, E., & Bebbington, P. (1992). The Dubai
Community Psychiatry Survey: Prevalence and socio-demo-
graphic correlates. Social Psychiatry & Psychiatric Epidemiol-
ogy, 27(2), 53–61.
Gibbs, J. T. (1990). Mental health issues of black adolescents:
Implications for policy and practice. In A. R. Stiffman & L.
E. Davis (Eds.), Ethic Issues in Adolescent Mental Health. New-
bury Park, CA: Sage Publications.
Gibbs, M. S. (1989). Factors in the victim that mediate between disaster and psychopathology: A review. Journal of
Traumatic Stress, 2, 489–514.
Gibson, D. (1990). Borderline personality disorder issues of
etiology and gender. Occupational Therapy in Mental Health,
10(4), 63–77.
Giedd, J. N., Castellanos, F. X., Casey, B. J., Kozuch, P., et al.
(1994). Quantitative morphology of the corpus callosum in
Attention Deficit Hyperactivity Disorder. Amer. J. Psychiat.,
151(5), 665–669.
Gil, D. (1970). Violence against children. Cambridge, MA: Harvard, UP.
Gilbert, J. G., & Lombardi, D. N. (1967). Personality characteristics of young male narcotic addicts. J. Cons. Psychol.,
31(5), 536–538.
Gill, A. D. (1982). Vulnerability to suicide. In E. L. Bassuk,
S. C. Schoonover, & A. D. Gill (Eds.), Lifelines: Clinical per-
spectives on suicide. New York: Plenum.
Gillberg, C. (1992). Subgroups in autism: Are there behavioral
phenotypes typical of underlying medical conditions? Jour-
nal of Intellectual Disability Research, 36(3), 201–214.
Gillberg, C., Ehlers, S., Schaumann, H., Jakobsson, G. et al.
(1990). Autism under age 3 years: A clinical study of 28 cases
referred for autistic symptoms in infancy. J. Child Psychol.
Psychiat. Allied Disc., 31(6), 921–934.
Gillberg, C., & Schaumann, H. (1982). Social class: infantile
autism. J. Autism Dev. Dis., 12, 223–228.
Gillberg, C., & Svendsen, P. (1983). Childhood psychosis and
computed brain scan findings. J. Autism Dev. Dis., 13, 19–32.
Gillman, R. D. (1990). The oedipal organization of shame: The
analysis of a phobia. Psychoanalytic Study of the Child, 45,
357–375.
Ginsberg, B. G. (1984). Beyond behavior modification: Client-
centered play therapy with the retarded. Acad. Psychol. Bull.,
6(3), 321–334.
Glancy, G. D., & Regehr, C. (1992). The forensic aspects of
schizophrenia. Psychiat. Clin. N. Amer., 15(3), 575–589.
Glaser, R., Kiecolt-Glaser, J. K., Bonneau, R. H., Malarkey, W.,
Kennedy, S., & Hughes, J. (1992). Stress-induced modula-
tion of the immune response to recombinant hepatitis B vac-
cine. Psychosom. Med., 54, 22–29.
Glassman, A. H. et al. (1984). Cigarette craving, smoking withdrawal, and clonidine. Science, 226(4676), 864–866.
Glassman, J. N., Rich, C. L., Darko, D., & Clarkin, A. (1991).
Menstrual dysfunction in bulimia. Ann. Clin. Psychiat., 3(2),
161–165.
Glazer, S. (1993, February 26). Violence against women: Is the
problem more serious than statistics indicate? CQ Researcher,
3(8), 169–192.
Gleaves, D. H., Williamson, D. A., & Barker, S. E. (1993).
Confirmatory factor analysis of a multidimensional model of
bulimia nervosa. J. Abnorm. Psychol., 102(1), 173–176.
Glenn, N. D., & Weaver, C. N. (1985). The psychological well-
being of adult children of divorce. Journal of Marriage and the
Family, 47, 905–912.
Glenner, G. G. (1985). On causative theories in Alzheimer's
Disease. Human Pathology, 16, 433–435.
Gleser, G. C., Green, B. L., & Winget, C. (1981). Prolonged psychological effects of disaster: A study of Buffalo Creek. New York:
Academic Press.
Glick, I. D., Clarkin, J. F., & Goldsmith, S. J. (1993). Combining medications with family psychotherapy. In J. M. Old-
ham, M. B. Riba, & A. Tasman (Eds.), Review of Psychiatry
(Vol. 12). Washington, DC: American Psychiatric Press.
Glogower, F. D., Fremouw, W. J., & McCroskey, J. C. (1978). A
component analysis of cognitive restructuring. Cog. Ther.
Res., 2(3), 209–223.
Glynn, S. M. (1990). Token economy approaches for psychiatric patients: Progress and pitfalls of chronic psychiatric ill-
ness. Behav. Mod., 14(4), 383–407.
Goate, A., Chartier-Harlin, M. C., Mullan, M., Brown, J., Crawford, F., Fidani, L., Giuffra, L., Haynes, A., Irving, N., &
James, L., (1991). Nature, 350, 564.
Gold, A. E., & Johnston, D. W. (1990). Does anger relate to hypertension and heart disease? In P. Bennet, M. Spurgeon, &
J. Weinman (Eds.), Current Developments in Health Psychology.
London: Harwood.
Gold, E. R. (1986). Long-term effects of sexual victimization
in childhood: An attributional approach. J. Cons. Clin. Psy-
chol., 54, 471–475.
Gold, M. S. (1986). The facts about drugs and alcohol. New York:
Bantam.
Gold, M. S. (1987). The good news about depression: Cures and
treatments in the new age of psychiatry. New York: Villard.
Goldberg, A. (1973). On telling the truth. In S. C. Feinstein &
P. L. Giovacchini (Eds.), Adolescent psychiatry: Development
and clinical studies (Vol. 2). New York: Basic Books.
Goldberg, T. E., Gold, J. M., & Braff, D. L. (1991). Neuropsychological functioning and time-linked information process-
ing in schizophrenia. In A. Tasman & S. M. Goldfinger
(Eds.), American Psychiatric Press review of psychiatry (Vol. 10).
Washington, DC: American Psychiatric Press.
Goldbloom, D. S., Hicks, L. K., & Garkinkel, P. E. (1990).

Platelet serotonin uptake in bulimia nervosa. *Bio. Psychiat.*, *28*(7), 644–647.

Goldbloom, D. S., & Olmsted, M. P. (1993). Pharmacotherapy of bulimia nervosa with fluoxetine: Assessment of clinically significant attitudinal change. *Amer. J. Psychiat.*, *150*(5), 770–774.

Golden, M. (1964). Some effects of combining psychological tests on clinical inferences. *J. Cons. Clin. Psychol.*, *28*, 440–446.

Golden, M. (1981). A measure of cognition within the context of assertion. *Journal of Clinical Psychology*, *37*, 253–262.

Golden, R. N., & Gilmore, J. H. (1990). Serotonin and mood disorders. *Psychiat. Ann.*, *20*(10), 580–588.

Goldfarb, W. (1967). Factors in the development of schizophrenic children. In J. Romano (Ed.), *The origins of schizophrenia*. Amsterdam: Excerpta Medica.

Goldfried, M. R., & Davison, G. C. (1976). *Clinical behavior therapy*. New York: Holt, Rinehart & Winston.

Goldiamond, I. (1965). Self-control procedures in personal behavior problems. *Psych. Rep.*, *17*, 851–868.

Golding, J. M. (1994). Sexual assault history and physical health in randomly selected Los Angeles women. *Health Psychology*, *13*(2), 130–138.

Goldman, A., & Greenberg, L. (1992). Comparison of integrated systemic and emotionally focused approaches to couples therapy. *J. Cons. Clin. Psychol.*, *60*(6), 962–969.

Goldman, D. (1949). Brief stimulus electric shock therapy. *J. Nerv. Ment. Dis.*, *110*, 36–45.

Goldman, M. (1992). Kleptomania: An overview. *Psychiat. Ann.*, *22*(2), 68–71.

Goldstein, A. (1976). Heroin addiction. *Arch. Gen. Psychiat.*, *33*, 353–358.

Goldstein, A. (1976). Opioids peptides (endorphins) in pituitary and brain. *Science*, *193*, 1081–1086.

Goldstein, A. (1994). Addiction: From biology to drug policy. New York: W. H. Freeman.

Goldstein, G. (1990). Comprehensive Neuropsychological Assessment Batteries. In G. Goldstein & M. Hersen (Eds.), *Handbook of psychological assessment* (2nd ed.). New York: Pergamon.

Goldstein, G., & Hersen, M. (1990). Historical Perspectives. In G. Goldstein & M. Hersen (Eds.), *Handbook of psychological assessment* (2nd ed.). New York: Pergamon.

Goldstein, H. (1975). *Social learning curriculum: Teacher's guide.* Columbus, OH: Merrill.

Goldstein, H., Kaczmarek, L., Pennington, R., Shafer, K. (1992). Peer-mediated intervention: Attending to, commenting on, and acknowledging the behavior of preschoolers with autism. *J. Appl. Behav. Anal.*, *25*(2), 289–305.

Goldstein, M. J. (1981). Family factors associated with schizophrenia and anorexia nervosa. *J. Youth Adol.*, *10*(5), 385–405.

Goldstein, M. J., ed. (1981). New developments in interventions with families of schizophrenics. San Francisco: Jossey-Bass.

Goldstein, M. J. (1985). Family factors that antedate the onset of schizophrenia and related disorders: The results of a fifteen-year prospective longitudinal study. *Acta Psychiatr. Scandin. Supplementum*, *319*(71), 7–18.

Goldstein, M. J. (1987). Treatment of families of schizophrenic patients: Theory, practice, and research. *Inter. J. Fam. Psychiat.*, *8*(2), 99–115.

Goldstein, M. J., (1991). Psychosocial (nonpharmacologic) treatments for schizophrenia. In A. Tasman & S. M. Goldfinger (Eds.), *American Psychiatric Press review of psychiatry* (Vol. 10). Washington, DC: American Psychiatric Press.

Goldstein, M. J., & Palmer, J. O. (1975). *The experience of anxiety: A casebook* (2nd ed.). New York: Oxford UP.

Goldstrom, I. D., Manderscheid, R. W., & Rudolph, L. A. (1992). Mental health services in state adult correctional facilities. In R. W. Manderscheid & M. A. Sonnenschein (Eds.), *Mental Health, United States, 1992*. Washington, D. C.: U.S. Department of Health and Human Services.

Goleman, D. (1993, April 14). What you reveal to a psychotherapist may go further. *New York Times*, p. C12.

Goleman, D., & Gurin, J. (1993). *Mind/Body Medicine*. Yonkers, NY: Consumers Union of United States, Inc.

Goleman, D., & Gurin, J. (1993). Mind/Body Medicine—At last. *Psych. Today*, *26*(2), 16, 80.

Gonzales, S., Kolvin, I., Garside, R. F., & Leitch, I. M. (1979). Characteristics of parents of handicapped children: I. Preliminary findings. In B. P. Cantwell et al. (Ed.).

Goodman, D. (1992). NIMH grantee finds drug responses differ among ethnic groups. *ADAMHA News*, *18*(1), p. 5.

Goodman, R. (1990). Technical note: Are perinatal complications causes or consequences of autism? *J. Child Psychol. Psychiat. Allied Disc.*, *31*(5), 809–812.

Goodman, R., & Ashby, L. (1990). Delayed visual maturation and autism. *Dev. Med. & Child Neurol.*, *32*(9), 814–819.

Goodman, W. K., McDougle, C., & Price, L. H. (1992). Pharmacotherapy of Obsessive Compulsive Disorder. *J. Clin. Psychiat.*, *53*(Suppl. 4), 29–37.

Goodwin, D. W. (1976). Adoption studies of alcoholism. *J. Operational Psychiat.*, *7*(1), 54–63.

Goodwin, D. W. (1976). *Is alcoholism hereditary?* New York: Oxford UP.

Goodwin, D. W. (1984). Studies of familial alcoholism: A review. *J. Clin. Psychiat.*, *45*(12, Sect. 2), 14–17.

Goodwin, D. W., Guze, S., & Robins, E. (1969). Follow-up studies in obsessional neurosis. *Arch. Gen. Psychiat.*, *20*, 182–187.

Goodwin, D. W., Schulsinger, F., Hermansen, L., Guze, S. B., & Winokur, G. A. (1973). Alcohol problems in adoptees raised apart from alcoholic biological parents. *Arch. Gen. Psychiat.*, *128*, 239–243.

Goodwin, F. K. (1993). Predictors of antidepressant response. *Bull. Menninger Clin.*, *57*(2), 146–160.

Goodwin, F. K., & Jamison, K. R. (1984). The natural course of manic-depressive illness. In R. M. Post & J. C. Ballenger (Eds.), *Neurobiology of mood disorders*. Baltimore: Williams & Wilkins.

Goodwin, F. K., & Jamison, K. R. (1990). *Manic-Depressive Illness*. New York: Oxford UP.

Goodwin, F. K., Murphy, D. L., & Dunner, D. L. (1972). Lithium response in unipolar versus bipolar depression. *Amer. J. Psychiat.*, *129*(1), 44–47.

Goodwin, F. K., Wirz-Justice, A., & Wehr, T. A. (1982). Evidence that pathophysiology of depression and the mechanism of action of antidepressant drugs both involve alterations in circadian rhythms. In E. Costa & G. Racagni (Eds.), *Typical and atypical antidepressants: Clinical practice*. New York: Raven.

Goodwin, G. M. (1992). Tricyclic and newer antidepressants.

In E. S. Paykel (Ed.), *Handbook of Affective Disorders*. New York: Guilford.

Goodwin, J. (1980). The etiology of combat-related posttraumatic stress disorders. In T. Williams (Ed.), *Posttraumatic stress disorders of the Vietnam veteran: Observations and recommendations for the psychological treatment of the veteran and his family*. Cincinnati: Disabled American Veterans.

Goodwin, R. A., & Mickalide, A. D. (1985). Parent-to-parent support in anorexia nervosa and bulimia. *Children's Hlth. Care, 14*(1), 32–37.

Gordon, B., Selnes, O. A., Hart, J. Jr., et al. (1990). Long-term cognitive sequelae of acyclovir-treated herpes simplex encephalitis. *Archives of Neurology, 47*, 646–647.

Gorelick, D. (1992). Sociodemographic factors in drug abuse treatment. *Journal of Health Care for the Poor & Underserved, 3*(1), 49–58.

Gorelick, P. B., Amico, L. L., Ganellen, R., et al. (1988). Transient global amnesia and thalamic infarction. *Neurology, 38*, 496–499.

Gorman, J. M., Battista, D., Goetz, R. R., Dillon, D. J. et al. (1989). A comparison of sodium bicarbonate and sodium lactate infusion in the induction of panic attacks. *Arch. Gen. Psychiat., 46*(2), 145–150.

Gorman, J. M., Fryer, A. F., Gliklich, J., King, R., & Klein, D. F. (1981). Mitral valve prolapse and panic disorder: Effect of imipramine. In D. F. Klein & J. G. Rabkin (Eds.), *Anxiety: New research and changing concepts*. New York: Raven.

Gorman, J. M., Liebowitz, M. R., Fyer, A. J., & Stein, J. (1989). A neuroanatomical hypothesis for panic disorder. *Amer. J. Psychiat., 146*(2), 148–161.

Gorman, J. M., Papp, L., & Klein, D. F. (1990). Biological models of panic disorder. In G. D. Burrows, M. Roth, & R. Noyes Jr. (Eds.), *Handbook of Anxiety* (Vol. 3), Amsterdam: Elsevier Science Publishers.

Gorman, J. M., Shear, M. K., Devereux, R. B., King, R., & Klein, D. F. (1986). Prevalence of mitral valve prolapse in panic disorder: Effect of echocardiographic criteria. *Psychosom. Med., 48*, 167–171.

Gorney, B. (1989). Domestic violence and chemical dependency: Dual problems, dual interventions. *Journal of Psychoactive Drugs, 21*(2), 229–238.

Goshen, C. E. (1967). *Documentary history of psychiatry: A source book on historical principles*. New York: Philosophy Library.

Gotlib, I. H., & Robinson, L. A. (1982). Responses to depressed individuals: Discrepancies between self-report and observer-related behavior. *J. Abnorm. Behav., 91*(4), 231–240.

Gottesman, I. I. (1991). *Schizophrenia genesis*. New York: W. H. Freeman.

Gottesman, I. I., & Shields, J. (1976). A critical review of recent adoption, twin, and family studies of schizophrenia: Behavioral genetics perspectives. *Schizo. Bull., 2*, 360–401.

Gottheil, E. (1987). Drug use, misuse, and abuse by the elderly. *Med. Aspects of Human Sex., 21*(3), 29–37.

Gottlieb, J. (1981). Mainstreaming: Fulfilling the promise? *Amer. J. Ment. Def., 86*(2), 115–126.

Gottlieb, J., Alter, M., & Gottlieb, B. W. (1991). Litigation involving people with mental retardation. In J. L. Matson & J. A. Mulick (Eds.), *Handbook of mental retardation*. New York: Pergamon.

Gottlieb, J., & Budoff, M. (1973). Social acceptability of retarded children in nongraded schools differing in architecture. *Amer. J. Ment. Def., 78*, 15–19.

Gottschalk, E. C. (1981, Apr. 3). While more firms try jury consultants, debate grows over how much they help. *Wall St. J.*

Gould, L. C. et al. (1977). Sequential patterns of multiple-drug use among high school students. *Arch. Gen. Psychiat., 34*(2), 216–222.

Gould, M. S., & Shaffer, D. (1986). The impact of suicide in television movies. *New England Journal of Medicine, 315*, 690–694.

Gould, R. L. (1978). *Transformations: Growth and change in adult life*. New York: Simon & Schuster.

Goumeniouk, A. D., & Clark, C. M. (1992). Prefrontal lobotomy and hypofrontality in patients with schizophrenia: An integration of the findings. *Canad. J. Psychiat., 37*(1), 17–22.

Gove, W. R. (1982). The current status of the labeling theory of mental illness. In W. R. Gove (Ed.), *Deviance and mental illness*. Beverly Hills, CA: Sage.

Gove, W. R., & Tudor, J. F. (1973). Adult sex roles and mental illness. *Amer. J. Sociol., 78*, 812–835.

Gowers, S., Kadambari, S. R., & Crisp, A. H. (1985). Family structure and order of patients with anorexia nervosa. Conference on Anorexia Nervosa and Related Disorders (1984, Swansea, Wales). *J. Psychiat. Res., 19*(2–3), 247–251.

Goyer, P. F., & Eddleman, H. C. (1984). Same-sex rape of nonincarcerated men. *J. Psychoanal. Anthropol., 141*(4), 576–579.

Graham, D. T. (1972). Psychosomatic medicine. In N. S. Greenfield & R. A. Sternbach (Eds.), *Handbook of psychophysiology*. New York: Holt, Rinehart & Winston.

Graham, D. T., Kabler, J. D., & Graham, F. K. (1962). Physiological response to the suggestion of attitudes specific for hives and hypertension. *Psychosom. Med., 24*(2), 159–169.

Graham, J. R. (1977). *The MMPI: A practical guide*. New York: Oxford UP.

Graham, J. R. (1987). *The MMPI: A practical guide* (2nd ed.). New York: Oxford UP.

Graham, J. R. (1993). *MMPI-2: Assessing personality and psychopathology* (2nd ed.). New York: Oxford UP.

Graham, J. R., & Lilly, R. S. (1984). *Psychological testing*. Englewood Cliffs, NJ: Prentice Hall.

Gramzow, R., & Tangney, J. P. (1992). Proneness to shame and the narcissistic personality. *Personality and Social Psychology Bulletin, 18*(3), 369–376.

Graves, J. S. (1993). Living with mania: a study of outpatient group psychotherapy for bipolar patients. *Amer. J. Psychother., 47*(1), 113–126.

Gray, C. D. (1989). Opening comments on the Conference on Developmental Disabilities and HIV Infection. *Mental Retardation, 27*, 199–200.

Gray, H. (1959). *Anatomy of the human body* (27th ed.). Philadelphia: Lea & Febiger.

Gray, J. A. (1987). *The Psychology of Fear and Stress* (2nd ed). Cambridge: Cambridge UP.

Gray, J. J., & Hoage, C. M. (1990). Bulimia nervosa: Group behavior therapy with exposure plus response prevention. *Psych. Rep., 66*(2), 667–674.

Gray, P. (1993, November 29). "The Assault on Freud." *Time, 142*(23), pp. 47–51.

Greeley, A. M. (1991). *Faithful attraction*. New York: Tor Books.

Green, A. H. (1989). Physical and Sexual Abuse of Children. In H. I. Kaplan & B. J. Sadock (Eds.), *Comprehensive textbook of psychiatry*/5-Volume 2 (5th ed.). Baltimore, MD: Williams & Wilkins.

Green, B. L., Grace, M. C., Lindy, J. D., Gleser, G. C. et al. (1990). Risk factors for PTSD and other diagnoses in a general sample of Vietnam veterans. *Amer. J. Psychiat.*, *147*(6), 729–733.

Green, M. F., Hugdahl, K., & Mitchell, S. (1994). Dichotic listening during auditory hallucinations in patients with schizophrenia. *Amer. J. Psychiat.*, *151*(3), 357–362.

Green, S. A. (1985). *Mind and body: The psychology of physical illness*. Washington, DC: American Psychiatric Press.

Greenberg, D., & Marks, I. (1982). Behavioral therapy of uncommon referrals. *Brit. J. Psychiat.*, *141*, 148–153.

Greenberg, E. (1989). Healing the borderline. *Gestalt Journal*, *12*(2), 11–55.

Greenberg, L., Elliott, R., & Lietaer, G. (1994). Research on experiential psychotherapies. In A. E. Bergin & S. L. Garfield (Eds.), *Handbook of psychotherapy and behavior change*. New York: Wiley.

Greenberg, L. T. (1987). The dangerous patient and psychiatric liability. *Trtmnt. Trends*, *2*(1).

Greenberg, R. P., & Bornstein, R. F. (1988). The dependent personality: II Risk for psychological disorders. *J. Pers. Dis.*, *2*(2), 136–143.

Greenblatt, M. (1984). ECT: Please, no more regulations! *Amer. J. Psychiat.*, *14*(11), 1409–1410.

Greenfield, S., Swartz, M., Landerman, L., & George, L. (1993). Long-term psychosocial effects of childhood exposure to parental problem drinking. *Amer. J. Psychiat.*, *150*(4), 608–619.

Greenhill, L. L. (1992). Pharmacologic treatment of attention deficit hyperactivity disorder. *Psychiat. Clin. N. Amer.*, *15*(1), 1–27.

Greenspan, S., & Granfield, J. M. (1992). Reconsidering the construct on mental retardation: Implications of a model of social competence. Special Issue: Social Skills. *Amer. J. Ment. Retard.*, *96*(4), 442–453.

Greist, J. H. (1990). Treatment of obsessive compulsive disorder: Psychotherapies, drugs, and other somatic treatment. *Journal of Clinical Psychology*, *51*(Suppl. 8), 44–50.

Greist, J. H. (1992). An integrated approach to treatment of obsessive-compulsive disorder. *J. Clin. Psychiat.*, *53*(Suppl. 4), 38–41.

Greist, J. H., & Klein, M. H. (1980). Computer programs for patients, clinicians, and researchers in psychiatry. In J. B. Sidowski, J. H. Johnson, & T. A. Williams (Eds.), *Technology in mental health care delivery systems*. Norwood, NJ: Ablex.

Grencavage, L. M., & Norcross, J. C. (1990). Where are the commonalities among the therapeutic common factors? *Professional Psychology: Research and Practice*, *21*, 372–378.

Gresham, A. C. (1993). The insanity plea: A futile defense for serial killers. *Law & Psychology Review*, *17*, 193–208.

Gridley, M. C. (1990). Psychopathic vs. nonpsychopathic thrill seeking. *Psychology: A Journal of Human Behavior*, *27*(1), 18–20.

Griest, D. L., & Wells, K. C. (1983). Behavioral family therapy with conduct disorders in children. *Behav. Ther.*, *14*, 37–53.

Griffin, M. L., Weiss, R. D., Mirin, S. M., & Lange, U. (1989). A comparison of male and female cocaine abusers. *Arch. Gen. Psychiat.*, *46*(2), 122–126.

Griffith, J. J., Mednick, S. A., Schulsinger, F., & Diderichsen, B. (1980). Verbal associative disturbances in children at high risk for schizophrenia. *J. Abnorm. Psychol.*, *89*, 125–131.

Grigg, J. R. (1988). Imitative suicides in an active duty military population. *Military Med.*, *153*(2), 79–81.

Grillo, I., & Grillo, D. (1980). Management of dyspareunia secondary to hymenal remnants. *Obstetrics and Gynecology*, *75*, 433–436.

Grinker, R. R., & Spiegel, J. P. (1945). *Men under stress*. Philadelphia: Blakiston.

Grinspoon, L., & Bakalar, J. B. (1986). Can drugs be used to enhance the psychotherapeutic process? *Amer. J. Psychother.*, *40*(3), 393–404.

Grinspoon, L. et al., (Eds.) (1986, Oct.) Mental retardation. *Part. I. Ment. Hlth. Letter*, *3*(4).

Grinspoon, L. et al. (Eds.). (1986). Paraphilias. *Harvard Med. School Ment. Hlth. Newsletter*, *3*(6), 1–5.

Grisez, G., & Boyle, J. M., Jr. (1979). *Life and death with liberty and justice: A contribution to the euthanasia debate*. Notre Dame, IN: Univ. Notre Dame.

Grisset, N. I., & Norvell, N. K. (1992). Perceived social support, social skills, and quality of relationships in bulimic women. *J. Cons. Clin. Psychol.*, *60*(2), 293–299.

Grizenko, N., Cvejic, H., Vida, S., Sayegh, L. (1991). Behaviour problems of the mentally retarded. *Canad. J. Psychiat.*, *36*(10), 712–717.

Grob, G. N. (1966). *State and the mentally ill: A history of Worcester State Hospital in Massachusetts, 1830–1920*. Chapel Hill, NC: Univ. North Carolina.

Grossman, F., Manji, H. K., & Potter, W. Z. (1993). Platelet $\propto$2-adrenoreceptors in depression: A critical examination. *Journal of Psychopharmacology*, *7*(1), 4–18.

Grossman, L. S., & Wasyliw, O. (1988). A Psychometric study of stereotypes: Assessment of malingering in a criminal forensic group. *J. of Pers. Assess.* *52*(3), 549–563.

Grossman, S. P. (1986). The role of glucose, insulin and glucagon in the regulation of food intake and body weight. *Neurosci. & Biobehav. Rev.*, *10*(3), 295–315.

Grossman, S. P. (1990). Brain mechanisms concerned with food intake and body-weight regulation. In M. M. Fichter (Ed.), *Bulimia nervosa: Basic research, diagnosis and therapy*. Chichester: Wiley.

Groth, A. N., & Birnbaum, H. J. (1978). Adult sexual orientation and attraction to under-age persons. *Arch. Sex. Behav.*, *7*, 175–181.

Groves, G. E., Clothier, J. L., Hollister, L. E. (1991). Predicting lithium dose by the body-weight method. *International Clinical Psychopharmacology*, *6*(1), 19–23.

Gruenberg, E. M. (1980). Mental disorders. In J. M. Last (Ed.), *Maxcy-Rosenau public health and preventive medicine* (11th ed.). New York: Appleton-Century-Crofts.

Guastello, S. J., & Reike, M. L. (1991). A review and critique of honesty test research. *Behavioral Sciences and the Law*, *9*(4), 501–523.

Guck, T. P., Skultety, F. M., Meilman, P. W., Dowd, E. T. (1985). Multidisciplinary pain center follow-up study: Evaluation with a no-treatment control group. *Pain*, *21*, 295–306.

Guillard, P., & Guillard, C. (1987). Suicide and attempted suicide in Martinique. *Psychologie Medicale*, *19*(5), 629–630.

Gunby, P. (1981). Many cancer patients receiving THC as antiemetic. *Med. News, 245*(15), 1515.

Gunderson, J. G. (1988). Personality disorders. In A. M. Nicholi Jr. (Ed.), *The new Harvard guide to psychiatry*. Cambridge, MA: Belknap Press.

Gunn, J., Maden, A., & Swinton, M. (1991). Treatment needs of prisoners with psychiatric disorders. *British Medical Journal, 303*, 338–341.

Gupta, R. (1988). Alternative patterns of seasonal affective disorder: Three case reports from North India. *Amer. J. Psychiat., 145*(4), 515–516.

Gurling, H. M., Sherrington, R. P., Brynjolfsson, J., Read, T., et al. (1989). Recent and future molecular genetic research into schizophrenia. *Schizo. Bull., 15*(3), 373–382.

Gurman, A. (1985). On saving marriages. *Fam. Ther. Networker, 9*(2), 17–18.

Gurman, A., & Kniskern, D. P. (1978). Behavioral marriage therapy: II. Empirical perspective. *Family Process, 17*, 129–148.

Gurman, A., Kniskern, D. P., & Pinsof, W. M. (1986). Research on the process and outcome of marital and family therapy. In S. L. Garfield and A. E. Bergin (Eds.), *Handbook of psychotherapy and behavior change: An evaluative analysis*. (3rd ed.). New York: Wiley.

Gustafson, R. (1992). The relationship between perceived parents' child-rearing practices, own later rationality, and own later depression. *Journal of Rational Emotive and Cognitive Behavior Therapy, 10*(4), 253–258.

Gwirtsman, H. E., Guze, B. H., Yager, J., & Gainsley, B. (1990). Fluoxetine treatment of anorexia nervosa: An open clinical trial. *J. Clin. Psychiat., 51*(9), 378–382.

Haaga, D. A. F., & Beck, A. T. (1992). Cognitive therapy. In E. S. Paykel (Ed.), *Handbook of Affective Disorders*. New York: Guilford.

Haas, G. L., Radomsky, E. D., Glanz, L., Keshavan, M. S., Mann, J. J., & Sweeney, J. A. (1993, May). Suicidal behavior in schizophrenia: Course-of-illness predictors. Presented at the Annual Meeting of the Society of Biological Psychiatry, San Francisco, CA.

Hadley, S. W., & Strupp, H. H. (1976). Contemporary views of negative effects in psychotherapy: An integrated account. *Arch. Gen. Psychiat., 33*(1), 1291–1302.

Haefely, W. (1990). Benzodiazepine receptor and ligands: Structural and functional differences. In I. Hindmarch, G. Beaumont, S. Brandon, & B. E. Leonard (Eds.), *Benzodiazepines: Current Concepts* (Pt. 1). Chichester: Wiley.

Haefely, W. (1990). The GABA-benzodiazepine receptor: Biology and pharmacology. In G. Burrows, M. Roth, & R. Noyes (Eds.), *Handbook of Anxiety* (Vol. 3). Amsterdam: Elsevier Science Publishers.

Hafner, H., & an der Heiden, W. (1988). The mental health care system in transition: A study in organization, effectiveness, and costs of complementary care for schizophrenic patients. In C. N. Stefanis, & A. D. Rabavilis (Eds.), *Schizophrenia: Recent biosocial developments*. New York: Human Sciences.

Hafner, H., Riecher-Rossler, A., Fatkenheuer, B., Hambrecht, M., et al. (1991). Sex differences in schizophrenia. *Psychiatria Fennica, 22*, 123–156.

Hafner, H., Riecher-Rossler, A., Maurer, K., Fatkenheuer, B., et al. (1992). First onset and early symptomatology of schizophrenia: a chapter of epidemiological and neurobiological research into age and sex differences. *Euro. Arch. Psychiat. Neurol. Sci., 242*, 109–118.

Hagan, T. (1991). Special services for women in treatment. In *National Conference on Drug Abuse Research and Practice Conference Highlights*. Rockville, MD: National Institute on Drug Abuse.

Hage, J. J., & Bouman, F. G. (1992). Silicone genital prosthesis for female-to-male transsexuals. *Plastic Reconstructive Surgery, 90*(3), 516–519.

Hagerman, R. J., & Brunschwig, A. (1991). Fragile X syndrome: A clinical perspective. *Comprehensive Mental Health Care, 1*(3), 157–176.

Hagg, T., et al. (1990). Nerve growth factor infusion into the denervated adult rat hippocampal formation promotes its cholinergic reinnervation. *Journal of Neuroscience, 10*, 3087–3092.

Hahlweg, K., & Markman, H. G. (1988). Effectiveness of behavioral marital therapy: Empirical status of behavioral techniques in preventing and alleviating marital distress. *J. Cons. Clin. Psychol., 56*(3), 440–447.

Hale, C. A., & Borkowski, J. G. (1991). Attention, memory and cognition. In J. L. Matson & J. A. Mulick (Eds.), *Handbook of mental retardation*. New York: Pergamon.

Hale, E. (1983, Apr. 17). Inside the divided mind. *New York Times Magazine*, 100–106.

Hall, C. S. (1951). What people dream about. *Scientific American, 184*, 60–63.

Hall, G. C., Proctor, W. C., & Nelson, G. M. (1988). Validity of physiological measures of pedophilic sexual arousal in a sexual offender population. *J. Cons. Clin. Psychol., 56*, 718.

Hall, G. N. (1992). Cited in A round-up of rapists. *Psychology Today, 25*(6), 12–13.

Hall, L. (with L. Cohn). (1980). *Eat without fear*. Santa Barbara, CA: Gurze.

Hall, S. M., Tunstall, C., Rugg, D. et al. (1985). Nicotine gum and behavioral treatment in smoking cessation. *J. Cons. Clin. Psychol., 53*, 256–258.

Hallam, R. S., & Rachman, S. (1976). Current status of aversion therapy. In M. Hersen, R. Eisler, & P. Miller (Eds.), *Progress in behavior modification* (Vol. 2). New York: Academic.

Halmi, K. A. (1985). Behavioral management for anorexia nervosa. In D. M. Garner & P. E. Garfinkel (Eds.), *Handbook of psychotherapy for anorexia nervosa and bulimia*. New York: Guilford.

Halmi, K. A. (1985). Classification of the eating disorders. *J. Psychiat. Res., 19*, 113–119.

Halmi, K. A., Brodland, G. & Loney, J. (1973). Prognosis in anorexia nervosa. *Ann. Internal Med., 78*, 907–909.

Halstead, W. C. (1947). *Brain and intelligence: A quantitative study of the frontal lobes*. Chicago: Univ. Chicago.

Hamilton, M. (1986). Electroconvulsive shock on serotonin activity. In S. Malitz & H. A. Sackeim (Eds.), *Electroconvulsive therapy: Clinical and basic research issues*. New York: Ann. NY Acad. Sci.

Hamilton, N. (1991). Intake and diagnosis of drug-dependent women. In National Conference on Drug Abuse Research and Practice Conference Highlights. Rockville, MD: National Institute on Drug Abuse.

Hamilton, S., Rothbart, M., & Dawes, R. N. (1986). *Sex Roles, 15*(5–6), 269–274.

Hammen, C. (1991). *Depression runs in families*. New York: Springer-Verlag.

Hammen, C. L., & Glass, D. R. (1975). Expression, activity, and evaluation of reinforcement. *J. Abnorm. Psychol., 84*(6), 718–721.

Hammen, C. L., & Krantz, S. (1976). Effect of success and failure on depressive cognitions. *J. Abnorm. Psychol., 85*(8), 577–588.

Hammer, E. (1981). Projective drawings. In A. I. Rabin (Ed.), *Assessment with projective techniques*. New York: Springer.

Hammer, T. (1993). Unemployment and mental health among young people: A longitudinal study. *Journal of Adolescence, 16*, 407–420.

Hammond, K. R., & Summers, D. A. (1965). A cognitive dependence on linear and non-linear cues. *Psych. Rev., 72*, 215–224.

Hara, H. (1989). Attention-deficit hyperactivity disorder. *Journal of Mental Health, 35*, 51–62.

Harburg, E. et al. (1973). Socio-ecological stress, suppressed hostility, skin color, and black-white male blood pressure: Detroit. *Psychosom. Med., 35*(4), 276–296.

Harding, C. M., Zubin, J., & Strauss, J. S. (1992). Chronicity in schizophrenia: revisited. *Brit. J. Psychiat., 161*(suppl. 18), 27–37.

Hardt, J. V., & Kamiya, J. (1978). Anxiety change through electroencephalographic alpha feedback seen only in high anxiety subjects. *Science, 201*(4350), 79–81.

Hardy, J. (1992). An "anatomical cascade hypothesis" for Alzheimer's disease. *Trends in Neurological Sciences, 15*, 200–201.

Hare, R. D. (1978). Electrodermal and cardiovascular correlates of sociopathy. In R. D. Hare & D. Shalling (Eds.), *Psychopathic behaviour: Approaches to research*. New York: Wiley.

Hare, R. D. (1978). Psychopathy and electrodermal responses to nonsignal stimulation. *Biological Psychology, 6*, 237–246.

Hare, R. D. (1993). *Without Conscience: The disturbing world of the psychopaths among us*. New York: Pocket Books.

Hare, R. D., Hart, S. D., & Harpur, T. J. (1991). Psychopathy and the DSM-IV criteria for antisocial personality disorder. *J. Abnorm. Psychol., 100*(3), 391–398.

Hargreaves, I. R. (1985). Attributional style and depression. *Brit. J. Psychol., 24*(1), 85–86.

Harkavy, J. M., & Asnis, G. (1985). Suicide attempts in adolescence: Prevalence and implications. *New England Journal of Medicine, 313*, 1290–1291.

Harlow, H. F., & Harlow, M. K. (1965). The affectional systems. In A. Schrier, H. Harlow, & F. Stollnitz (Eds.), *Behavior of nonhuman primates* (Vol. 2). New York: Academic Press.

Harlow, L. L., Newcomb, M. D., & Bentler, P. M. (1986). Depression, self-derogation, substance use, and suicide ideation: Lack of purpose in life as a mediational factor. *J. Clin. Psychol., 42*(1), 5–21.

Harnett, P. H., & Misch, P. (1993). Developmental issues in the assessment and treatment of adolescent perpetrators of sexual abuse. *Journal of Adolescence, 16*, 396–405.

Haroutunian, V. (1991). Gross anatomy of the brain. In K. Davis, H. Klar, & J. T. Coyle (Eds.), *Foundations of psychiatry*. Philadelphia: Saunders.

Harrell, R. F., Woodyard, E., & Gates, A. I. (1955). *The effects of mothers' diet on the intelligence of the offspring*. New York: Columbia UP.

Harrell, T. H., Honaker, L. M., & Parnell, T. (1992). Equivalence of the MMPI-2 and the MMPI in psychiatric patients. *Psychological Assessment, 4*(4), 460–465.

Harrington, D. L., et al. (1990). Procedural memory in Parkinson's disease: impaired motor but not visuoperceptual learning. *J. Clin. Exp. Neuropsych., 12*, 323–339.

Harrington, R. C., Fudge, H., Rutter, M. L., Bredenkamp, D., Groothues, C., & Pridham, J. (1993). Child and adult depression: A test of continuities with data from a family study. *Brit. J. Psychiat., 162*, 627–633.

Harris, A., Ayers, T., & Leek, M. R. (1985). Auditory span of apprehension deficits in schizophrenia. *J. Nerv. Ment. Dis., 173*(11), 650–657.

Harris, A. H., Goldstein, D. S., & Brady, J. V. (1977). Visceral learning: Cardiovascular conditioning in primates. In J. Beatty & H. Legewie (Eds.), *Biofeedback and behavior*. New York: Plenum.

Harris, B. (1979). Whatever happened to Little Albert? *Amer. Psychol., 34*, 151–160.

Harris, F. C., & Lahey, B. B. (1982). Subject reactivity in direct observation assessment: A review and critical analysis. *Clin. Psychol. Rev., 2*, 523–538.

Harris, F. C., & Lahey, B. B. (1986). Condition-related reactivity: The interaction of observation and intervention in increasing peer praising in preschool children. *Education and Treatment of Children, 9*(3), 221–231.

Harris, S. L., & Ersner-Hershfield, R. (1978). Behavioral suppression of seriously disruptive behavior in psychotic and retarded patients: A review of punishment and its alternatives. *Psychol. Bull., 85*, 1352–1375.

Harris, S. L., & Milch, R. E. (1981). Training parents as behavior modifiers for their autistic children. *Clin. Psychol. Rev., 1*, 49–63.

Harrison, P. J., & Roberts, G. W. (1991). "Life, Jim, but not as we know it?" Transmissible dementias and the prion protein. *Brit. J. Psychiat., 158*, 457–470.

Harrow, M. et al. (1988). A longitudinal study of thought disorder in manic patients. *Arch. Gen. Psychiat., 43*(8), 781–785.

Hart, B. L. (1985). *The behavior of domestic animals*. New York: W. H. Freeman.

Hart, K. J., & Ollendick, T. H. (1985). Prevalence of bulimia in working and university women. *Amer. J. Psychiat., 142*(7), 851–854.

Hart, S. N., & Brassard, M. R. (1987). A major threat to children's mental health: Psychological maltreatment. *Amer. Psychol., 42*(2), 160–165.

Hart, S. N., & Brassard, M. R. (1991). Psychological maltreatment: Progress achieved. *Developmental Psychopathology, 3*(1), 61–70.

Hart, S. N., Germain, R., & Brassard, M. R. (1987). The challenge: To better understand and combat the psychological maltreatment of children and youth. In M. R. Brassard, R. Germain, & S. N. Hart (Eds.), *Psychological maltreatment of children and youth*. New York: Pergamon.

Harvey, P. D. (1991). Cognitive and linguistic functions of adolescent children at risk for schizophrenia. In E. F. Walker (Ed.), *Schizophrenia: A life-course developmental perspective*. New York: Academic Press.

Hasin, D., Endicott, J., & Lewis, C. (1985). Alcohol and drug abuse in patients with affective syndromes. *Comprehen. Psychiat., 26,* 283–295.

Hathaway, S. R., & Meehl, P. E. (1951). *An atlas for the clinical use of the MMPI.* Minneapolis: Univ. Minnesota.

Hauri, P., Chernik, D., Hawkins, D., & Mendels, J. (1974). Sleep of depressed patients in remission. *Arch. Gen. Psychiat., 31,* 386–391.

Hauschild, T. (1968). Suicidal population of a military psychiatric center. *Military Medicine, 133,* 425–437.

Hauser, S. L., DeLong, G. R., & Rosman, N. P. (1975). Pneumoencephalographic findings in the infantile autism syndrome: A correlation with temporal lobe disease. *Brain, 98,* 667–688.

Havens, L. L. (1974). The existential use of the self. *Amer. J. Psychiat., 131*(1), 1–10.

Hawkins, W. L., French, L. C., Crawford, B. D., & Enzle, M. C. (1988). Depressed affect and time perception. *J. Abnorm. Psychol., 97*(3), 275–280.

Hawton, K. (1982). Attempted suicide in children and adolescents. *J. Child Psychol. Psychiat. Allied Disc., 23*(4), 497–503.

Hawton, K. (1986). *Suicide and attempted suicide among children and adolescents.* Beverly Hills, CA: Sage Publications.

Hawton, K., Cole, D., O'Grady, J., & Osborn, M. (1982). Motivational aspects of deliberate self-poisoning in adolescents. *Brit. J. Psychiat., 141,* 286–291.

Hawton, K., O'Grady, J., Osborn, M., & Cole, D. (1982). Adolescents who take overdoses: Their characteristics, problems and contacts with helping agencies. *Brit. J. Psychiat., 140,* 118–123.

Hay, L. R., Hay, W. R., & Angle, H. V. (1977). The reactivity of self-recording: A case report of a drug abuser. *Behav. Ther., 8*(5), 1004–1007.

Hay, W. M., Hay, L. R., & Nelson, R. Q. (1977). The adaptation of covert modeling procedures to the treatment of chronic alcoholism and obsessive compulsive behavior: Two case reports. *Behav. Ther., 8*(1), 70–76.

Hayes, L. M., & Rowan, J. R. (1988). *National Study of Jail Suicides: Seven Years Later.* Alexandria, VA: National Center for Institutions and Alternatives.

Haynes, S. G., Feinleib, M., & Kannel, W. B. (1980). The relationship of psychosocial factors to coronary heart disease in the Framingham study: III. Eight-year incidence of coronary heart disease. *Amer. J. Epidemiol., 111,* 37–58.

Haynes, S. N. (1990). Behavioral assessment of adults. In G. Goldstein & M. Hersen (Eds.), *Handbook of psychological assessment* (2nd ed.). New York: Pergamon.

Hayward, C., Killen, J. D., Hammer, L. D., Litt, I. F., Wilson, D. M., Simmonds, B., & Taylor, C. B. (1992). Pubertal stage and panic attack history in sixth- and seventh-grade girls. *Amer. J. Psychiat., 149,* 1239–1243.

Hayward, M. D., & Taylor, J. E. (1965). A schizophrenic patient describes the action of intensive psychotherapy. *Psychiat. Quart., 30.*

Haywood, H. C., Meyers, C. E., & Switzky, H. N. (1982). Mental retardation. *Annu. Rev. Psychol., 33,* 309–342.

Hazell, P., & Lewin, T. (1993). Friends of adolescent suicide attempters and completers. *J. Amer. Acad. Child Adol. Psychiat., 32*(1), 76–81.

Headland, K., & McDonald, B. (1987). Rapid audio-tape treatment of obsessional ruminations. A case report. *Behav. Psychother., 15,* 188–192.

Health Education and Welfare. (1976). Even my kids didn't know I was an alcoholic: An interview with Dick Van Dyke. (ADM) 76–348. Washington, DC: GPO.

Healy, D., & Waterhouse, J. M. (1990). The circadian system and affective disorders: Clocks or rhythms? *Chronobio. Inter., 7*(1), 5–10.

Healy, D., & Williams, J. M. (1988). Dysrhythmia, dysphoria, and depression: The interaction of learned helplessness and circadian dysrhythmia in the pathogenesis of depression. *Psychol. Bull., 103*(2), 163–178.

Heather, N., Rollnick, S., & Winton, M. (1983). A comparison of objective and subjective measures of alcohol dependence as predictors of relapse following treatment. *Brit. J. Clin. Psychol., 22*(1), 11–17.

Heather, N., Winton, M., & Rollnick, S. (1982). An empirical test of "a cultural delusion of alcoholics." *Psych. Rep., 50*(2), 379–382.

Heaton, R. K., Baade, L. E., & Johnson, K. L. (1978). Neuropsychological test results associated with psychiatric disorders in adults. *Psychol. Bull., 85,* 141–162.

Heber, F. R. (1979). *Research in the prevention of sociocultural retardation through early prevention. Mental retardation, the child and his surroundings.* Washington, DC: International Union of Child Welfare.

Heffernan-Colman, C., Colleen, J., Sharpley, C. F., & King, N. J. (1992). "Individual" variables and heart rate control via biofeedback: A review. *Australian Psychologist, 27*(1), 28–42.

Heflinger, C. A., Cook, V. J., & Thackrey, M. (1987). Identification of mental retardation by the System of Multicultural Pluralistic Assessment: Nondiscriminatory or nonexistent? *J. School Psychol., 25*(2), 177–183.

Heider, F. (1944). Social perception and phenomenal causality. *Psych. Rev., 51,* 358–374.

Heider, F. (1958). *The psychology of interpersonal relations.* New York: Wiley.

Heikkinen, M., Aro, H., & Lonnqvist, J. (1992). Recent life events and their role in suicide as seen by the spouses. *Acta Psychiatr. Scandin., 86*(6), 489–494.

Heilbrun, A. B., Blum, N., & Haas, M. (1983). Cognitive vulnerability to auditory hallucination: Preferred imagery mode and spatial location of sounds. *Brit. J. Psychiat., 143,* 294–298.

Heilbrun, A. B., & Witt, N. (1990). Distorted body image as a risk factor in anorexia nervosa: Replication and clarification. *Psych. Rep., 66*(2), 407–416.

Heiman, J. R. (1977). A psychophysiological exploration of sexual-arousal patterns in females and males. *Psychophysiology, 14,* 266–274.

Heiman, J. R., Gladue, B. A., Roberts, C. W., & LoPiccolo, J. (1986). Historical and current factors discriminating sexually functional from sexually dysfunctional married couples. *J. of Marital Fam. Ther., 12*(2), 163–174.

Heiman, J. R., & LoPiccolo, J. (1988). *Becoming orgasmic: A personal and sexual growth program for women.* New York: Prentice Hall.

Heiman, J. R., LoPiccolo, L., & LoPiccolo, J. (1981). Treatment of sexual dysfunction. In A. S. Gurman & D. P. Kniskern (Eds.), *Handbook of family therapy.* New York: Brunner/Mazel.

Heimberg, R. G., Dodge, C. S., Hope, D. A., Kennedy, C. R., et al. (1990). Cognitive behavioral group treatment for social phobia: Comparison with a credible placebo control. *Cog. Ther. Res.*, *14*(1), 1–23.

Heimberg, R. G., Salzman, D. G., Holt, C. S., & Blendall, K. (1991). Cognitive behavioral treatment for social phobia: Effectiveness at five-year follow-up. Manuscript submitted for publication.

Heinrich, K., Klieser, E., Lehmann, E., Kinzler, E., & Hruschka, H. (1994). Risperidone versus clozapine in the treatment of schizophrenic patients with acute symptoms: A double-blind, randomized trial. *Prog. Neuro-Psychopharmacol. & Biol. Psychiat.*, *18*, 129–137.

Heinrichs, D. W., & Carpenter, W. T., Jr. (1983). The coordination of family therapy with other treatment modalities for schizophrenia. In W. McFarlane (Ed.), *Family therapy in schizophrenia*. New York: Guilford.

Heise, L., & Chapman, J. R. (1990). Reflections on a movement: The U.S. battle against women abuse. In M. Schuler (ed.), *Freedom from Violence: Women's Strategies Round the World*. OEF International.

Heller, K., & Monahan, J. (1977). *Psychology and community change*. Homewood, IL: Dorsey.

Hellerstein, D. J., Yanowitch, P., Rosenthal, J., Hemlock, C., et al. (1994). Long-term treatment of double depression: A preliminary study with serotonergic antidepressants. *Prog. Neuro-Psychopharmacol. & Biol. Psychiat.*, *18*, 139–147.

Helms, J. E. (1992). Why is there no study of cultural equivalence in standardized cognitive ability testing? *Amer. Psychol.*, *47*(9), 1083–1101.

Helzer, J. E., Burnam, A., & McEvoy, L. T. (1991). Alcohol abuse and dependence. In L. N. Robins & D. S. Regier (Eds.), *Psychiatric Disorders in America: The epidemiological catchment area study*. New York: Free Press.

Hembree, W. C., Nahas, G. G., & Huang, H. F. S. (1979). Changes in human spermatozoa associated with high dose marihuana-smoking. In G. G. Nahas & W. D. M. Paton (Eds.), *Marihuana: Biological effects*. Elmsford, NY: Pergamon.

Hendin, H. (1987). Youth suicide: A psychosocial perspective. *Suic. Life Threat. Behav.*, *17*(2), 151–165.

Hendin, H., & Klerman, G. (1993). Physician-assisted suicide: The dangers of legalization. *Amer. J. Psychiat.*, *150*(1), 143–145.

Hennager, K. (1993). Flying in Dreams. In M. A. Carskadon (Ed.), *Encyclopedia of Sleep and Dreams*. New York: Macmillan.

Henry, W. P., & Strupp, H. H. (1991). Vanderbilt University: The Vanderbilt Center for Psychotherapy Research. In L. E. Beutler & M. Crago (Eds.), *Psychotherapy research: An international review of programmatic studies*. Washington, DC: American Psychological Association.

Henry, W. P., Strupp, H. H., Schact, T. E., & Gaston, L. (1994). Psychodynamic approaches. In A. E. Bergin & S. L. Garfiel (Eds.), *Handbook of psychotherapy and behavior change* (4th ed.). New York: Wiley.

Herbert, T. B., & Cohen, S. (1993). Depression and immunity: a meta-analytic review. *Psychol. Bull.*, *113*(3), 472–486.

Herek, G. M., & Capitanio, J. P. (1993). Public reaction to AIDS in the U.S.: A 2nd generation of stigma. *Amer. J. Pub. Hlth.*, *83*(4), 574–577.

Herek, G. M., & Glunt, E. K. (1988). An epidemic of stigma: Public reactions to AIDS. *Amer. Psychol.*, *43*(11), 886–891.

Hermelin, B. (1976). Coding and the sense modalities. In L. Wing (Ed.), *Early childhood autism*. Oxford: Pergamon.

Hermesh, H., Aizenberg, D., Weizman, A., Lapidot, M., Mayor, C., & Munitz, H. (1992). Risk for definite neuroleptic malignant syndrome: A prospective study in 223 consecutive inpatients. *Brit. J. Psychiat.*, *161*, 254–257.

Hernandez, J. (1992). Substance abuse among sexually abused adolescents and their families. *Journal of Adolescent Health*, *13*(8), 658–662.

Hersen, M., & Barlow, D. H. (1976). *Single-case experimental designs: Strategies for studying behavior change*. New York: Pergamon.

Hersen, M., Bellack, A. S., Himmelhoch, J. M., & Thase, M. E. (1984). Effects of social skill training, amitriptyline, and psychotherapy in unipolar depressed women. *Behav. Ther.*, *15*, 21–40.

Hersen, M., & Detre, T. (1980). The behavioral psychotherapy of anorexia nervosa. In T. B. Karasu & L. Bellak (Eds.), *Specialized techniques in individual psychotherapy*. New York: Brunner/Mazel.

Herz, L. R., Volicer, L., Ross, V., & Rheaume, Y. (1992). A single-case-study method for treating resistiveness in patients with Alzheimer's disease. *Hosp. Comm. Psychiat.*, *43*(7), 720–724.

Herz, M. I., Endicott, J., & Spitzer, R. L. (1975). Brief hospitalization of patients with families: Initial results. *Amer. J. Psychiat.*, *132*(4), 413–418.

Herz, M. I., Endicott, J., & Spitzer, R. L. (1977). Brief hospitalization: A two-year follow-up. *Amer. J. Psychiat.*, *134*(5), 502–507.

Herz, M. I. et al. (1971). Day vs. inpatient hospitalization: A controlled study. *Amer. J. Psychiat.*, *127*(4), 1371–1381.

Herzog, A. (1984). On multiple personality: Comments on diagnosis, etiology, and treatment. *Inter. J. Clin. Exp. Hyp.*, *32*(2), 210–221.

Herzog, D. B., Keller, M. B., Lavori, P. W., Bradburn, I. S., & Ott, I. L. (1990). Course and outcome of bulimia nervosa. In M. M. Fichter (Ed.), *Bulimia nervosa: Basic research, diagnosis and therapy*. Chichester: Wiley.

Herzog, D. B., Norman, D. K., Gordon, C., & Pepose, M. (1984). Sexual conflict and eating disorders in 27 males. *Amer. J. Psychiat.*, *141*, 989–990.

Heshe, J., & Roeder, E. (1976). Electroconvulsive therapy in Denmark. *Brit. J. Psychiat.*, *128*, 241–245.

Hesselbrock, M. N. (1991). Gender comparison of antisocial personality disorder and depression in alcoholism. *Journal of Substance Abuse*, *3*(2), 205–219.

Hesselbrock, M. N., & Hesselbrock, V. M. (1992). Relationship of family history, antisocial personality disorder and personality traits in young men at risk for alcoholism. *Journal of Studies on Alcohol*, *53*(6), 619–625.

Heston, L. L. (1992). *Mending Minds: A guide to the new psychiatry of depression, anxiety, and other serious mental disorders*. New York: W. H. Freeman.

Heston, L. L., Mastri, A. R., Anderson, V. E., & White, J. (1981). Dementia of the Alzheimer type: Clinical genetics, natural history and associated condition. *Arch. Gen. Psychiat.*, *38*, 1085–1090.

Hewitt, P. S., & Howe, N. (1988). Future of generational politics. *Generations*, *12*(3), 10–13.

Heyman, G. D., Dweck, C. S., & Cain, K. M. (1992). Young children's vulnerability to self-blame and helplessness: Relationship to beliefs about goodness. *Child Dev.*, *63*(2), 401–415.

Hibbert, G. A. (1984). Ideational components of anxiety: Their origin and content. *Brit. J. Psychiat.*, *144*, 618–624.

Hibma, M., & Griffin, J.F.T. (1994). Brief communication: The influence of maternal separation on humoral and cellular immunity in farmed deer. *Brain, Behavior, and Immunity 8*, 80–85.

Hickie, I., Wilhelm, K., Parker, G., Boyce, P., Madzi-Pavlovic, D., Brodaty, H., & Mitchell, P. (1990). Perceived dysfunctional intimate relationships: A specific association with the nonmelancholic depressive type. *J. Affect. Dis.*, *19*, 99–107.

Hiday, V. A. (1992). Civil commitment and arrests: An investigation of the criminalization thesis. *J. Nerv. Ment. Dis.*, *180*(3), 184–191.

Hiday, V. A. (1992). Coercion in civil commitment: Process, preferences, and outcome. *International Journal of Law and Psychiatry, 15*(4), 359–377.

Higgins, S., Budney, A., Bickel, W., Hughes, J., Foerg, F., & Badger, G. (1993). Achieving cocaine abstinence with a behavior approach. *Amer. J. Psychiat.*, *150*(5), 763–772.

Higuchi, S., Suzuki, K., Yamada, K., Parrish, K., & Kono, H. (1993). Alcoholics with eating disorders: Prevalence and clinical course, A study from Japan. *Brit. J. Psychiat.*, *162*, 403–406.

Hilgard, E. R. (1977). Controversies over consciousness and the rise of cognitive psychology. *Austral. Psychol.*, *12*(1), 7–26.

Hilgard, E. R. (1977). Psychology's influence on educational practices: A puzzling history. *Education, 97*(3), 203–219.

Hilgard, E. R. (1987). Research advances in hypnosis: Issues and methods. *Inter. J. Clin. Exper. Hyp.*, *35*, 248–264.

Hilgard, E. R. (1992). Dissociation and theories of hypnosis. In E. Fromm & M. R. Nash (Eds.), *Contemporary hypnosis research*. New York: Guilford.

Hill, A. J., & Robinson, A. (1991). Dieting concerns have a functional effect on the behaviour of nine-year-old girls. *British Journal of Clinical Psychology, 30*(3), 265–267.

Himle, J. A., Himle, D. P., & Thyer, B. A. (1989). Irrational beliefs and anxiety disorders. *J. Rational, Emotive & Cog. Behav. Ther.*, *7*(3), 155–165.

Hinshaw, S. P. (1991). Stimulant medication and the treatment of aggression in children with attentional deficits. *Journal of Clinical Child Psychology, 20*, 301–312.

Hinshaw, S. P., Buhrmester, D., & Heller, T. (1989). Anger control in response to verbal provocation: Effects of stimulant medication for boys with ADHD. *J. Abnorm. Child Psychol.*, *17*, 393–407.

Hinshaw, S. P., & Erhardt, D. (1991). Attention-deficit hyperactivity disorder. In P. C. Kendall (Ed.), *Child and adolescent therapy: Cognitive-behavioral procedures*. New York: Guilford.

Hinshaw, S. P., & Melnick, S. (1992). Self-management therapies and attention-deficit hyperactivity disorder: Reinforced self-evaluation and anger control interventions. *Behav. Mod.*, *16*(2), 253–273.

Hiroto, D. S. (1974). Locus of control and learned helplessness. *J. Exp. Psychol.*, *102*(2), 187–193.

Hiroto, D. S., & Seligman, M. E. (1975). Generality of learned helplessness in man. *J. Pers. Soc. Psychol.*, *31*(2), 311–327.

Hirsch, A., Gervino, E., Nakao, S., Come, P., Silverman, K., & Grossman, W. (1989). The effect of caffeine on exercise tolerance and left ventricular function in patients with coronary artery disease. *Annals of Internal Medicine, 110*, 593–598.

Hirsch, B. J. (1979). Psychological dimensions of social networks: A multimethod analysis. *Amer. J. Community Psychol.*, *7*(3), 263–277.

Hirsch, S., & Leff, J. (1975). *Abnormalities in parents of schizophrenics*. Oxford: Oxford UP.

Hirschfeld, R. M. (1992). The clinical course of panic disorder and agoraphobia. In G. D. Burrows, S. M. Roth, & R. Noyes, Jr., *Handbook of Anxiety* (Vol. 5). Oxford: Elsevier.

Hirschfeld, R. M., & Davidson, L. (1988). Clinical risk factors for suicide. [Special Issue]. *Psychiat. Ann.*, *18*(11), 628–635.

Hirschfeld, R. M., & Davidson, L. (1988). Risk factors for suicide. In A. J. Frances & R. E. Hales (Eds.), *American psychiatric press review of psychiatry* (Vol. 7). Washington, DC: American Psychiatric Press.

Hirschfeld, R. M., & Goodwin, F. K. (1988). Mood disorders. In J. A. Talbott, R. E. Hales, & S. C. Yudofsky (Eds.), The American Psychiatric Press textbook of psychiatry. Washington, DC: American Psychiatric Press.

Hite, S. (1970). *The Hite report: A nationwide study of female sexuality*. New York: Dell.

Hoberman, H. M., & Garfinkel, B. D. (1988). Completed suicide in children and adolescents. *J. Amer. Acad. Child Adol. Psychiat.*, *27*, 689–695.

Hobson, J. A., & McCarley, R. W. (1977). The brain as a dream state generator: An activation-synthesis hypothesis of the dream process. *Amer. J. Psychiat.*, *134*(12), 1335–1348.

Hodgkinson, S., Mullan, M. J., & Gurling, H. M. (1990). The role of genetic actors in the etiology of the affective disorders. [Special Issue]. *Behav. Genetics, 20*(2), 235–250.

Hodgson, R., & Rankin, H. (1982). Cue exposure and relapse prevention. In W. Hay & P. Nathan (Eds.), *Clinical case studies in the behavioral treatment of alcoholism*. New York: Plenum.

Hodgson, R. J., & Rachman, S. (1972). The effects of contamination and washing in obsessional patients. *Behav. Res. Ther.*, *10*, 111–117.

Hoebel, B. G., & Teitelbaum, P. (1966). Weight regulation in normal and hypothalamic hyperphagic rats. *J. Compar. Physiol. Psychol.*, *61*(2), 189–193.

Hoffman, R. S. (1980). The itemized statement in clinical psychiatry: A new concept in billing. *J. Irreproducible Results, 26*(3), 7–8.

Hogan, R. A. (1968). The implosive technique. *Behav. Res. Ther.*, *6*, 423–431.

Hogan, R. A., & Kirchner, J. H. (1967). A preliminary report of the extinction of learned fears via a short term implosive therapy. *J. Abnorm. Psychol.*, *72*, 106–111.

Hogarty, G. E. (1971). The plight of schizophrenics in modern treatment programs. *Hosp. Comm. Psychiat.*, *22*(7), 197–203.

Hogarty, G. E. (1993). Prevention of relapse in chronic schizophrenic patients. *J. Clin. Psychiat.*, *54*(3, suppl.), 18–23.

Hogarty, G. E., & Goldberg, I. C. (1973). Drugs and social therapy in the aftercare of schizophrenic patients. *Arch. Gen. Psychiat.*, *28*, 54–64.

Hogarty, G. E. et al. (1974). Drug and sociotherapy in the aftercare of schizophrenic patients: II. Two-year relapse rates. *Arch. Gen. Psychiat.*, *31*(5), 609–618.

Hogarty, G. E. et al. (1974). Drug and sociotherapy in the aftercare of schizophrenic patients: III. Adjustment of non-relapsed patients. *Arch. Gen. Psychiat.*, *31*(5), 609–618.

Hogarty, G. E. et al. (1986). Family psychoeducation, social skills training, and maintenance chemotherapy in the after-care treatment of schizophrenia: I. One-year effects of a controlled study on relapse and expressed emotion. *Arch. Gen. Psychiat.*, 43(7), 633–642.

Hoge, M. A., Farrell, S. P., Munchel, M. E., & Strauss, J. S. (1988). Therapeutic factors in partial hospitalization. *Psychiatry*, 51(2), 199–210.

Holaday, J. W., Tortella, F. C., Long, J. B. et al. (1986). Endogenous opioids and their receptors: Evidence for involvement in the postictal effects of electroconvulsive shock. *Ann. NY Acad. Sci.*, 462, 124–139.

Holden, R. R., Mendonca, J. D., & Mazmanian, D. (1985). Relation of response set to observed suicide intent. *Canad. J. Behav. Sci.*, 17(4), 359–368.

Holinger, P. C. (1987). *Violent deaths in the United States, 1900–1980: An epidemiologic study of suicide, homicide and accidents.* New York: Guilford.

Holinger, P. C. (1988). A prediction model of suicide among youth. *J. Nerv. Ment. Dis.*, 176(5), 275–279.

Holinger, P. C., & Offer, D. (1982). Prediction of adolescent suicide: A population model. *Amer. J. Psychiat.*, 139, 302–307.

Holinger, P. C., & Offer, D. (1984). Toward the prediction of violent deaths among the young. In Sudak et al. (Eds.), *Suicide among the young.* New York: Wright PSG.

Holinger, P. C., & Offer, D. (1991). Sociodemographic, epidemiologic, and individual attributes. In L. Davidson & M. Linnoila (Eds.), *Risk factors for youth suicide.* New York: Hemisphere.

Holinger, P. C., Offer, D., & Ostrov, E. (1987). Suicide and homicide in the United States: An epidemiologic study of violent death, population changes, and the potential for prediction. *Amer. J. Psychiat.*, 144(2), 215–218.

Hollander, E., Frenkel, M., Decaria, C., Trungold, S., et al. (1992). Treatment of pathological gambling with clomipramine. *Amer. J. Psychiat.*, 149(5), 710–711.

Hollander, M. H. (1988). Hysteria and memory. In H. M. Pettinati (Ed.), *Hypnosis and Memory.* New York: Guilford.

Hollin, C. R., & Trower, P. (Eds.). (1986). *Handbook of social skills training.* New York: Pergamon.

Hollingshead, A. B., & Redlich, F. C. (1958). *Social class and mental illness: A community study.* New York: Wiley.

Hollister, L. E. (1982). Plasma concentrations of tricyclic antidepressants in clinical practice. *J. Clin. Psychiat.*, 43(2), 66–69.

Hollister, L. E. (1986). Health aspects of cannabis. *Pharmacological Reviews*, 38(1), 1–20.

Hollister, L. E. (1986). Pharmacotherapeutic consideration in anxiety disorders. Annual Meeting of the American Academy of Clinical Psychiatrists (1985, San Francisco, CA). *J. Clin. Psychiat.*, 47(Suppl.), 33–36.

Hollister, L. E., & Csernansky, J. G. (1990). *Clinical pharmacology of psychotherapeutic drugs* (3rd ed.) New York: Churchill-Livingstone.

Hollon, S. D., & Beck, A. T. (1986). Research on cognitive therapies. In S. L. Garfield & A. E. Bergin (Eds.), *Handbook of psychotherapy and behavior change.* New York: Wiley.

Hollon, S. D., & Beck, A. T. (1994). Cognitive and cognitive-behavioral therapies. In A. E. Bergin & S. L. Garfiel (Eds.), *Handbook of psychotherapy and behavior change* (4th ed.). New York: Wiley.

Hollon, S. D., DeRubeis, R. J., Evans, M. D., Wiemer, M. J., et al. (1992). Cognitive therapy and pharmacotherapy for depression: Singly or in combination. *Arch. Gen. Psychiat.*, 49, 774–781.

Hollon, S. D., Evans, M. D., & De Rubeis, R. J. (1985). Preventing relapse following treatment for depression: The cognitive-pharmacotherapy project. In N. Schneiderman & T. Fields (Eds.), *Stress and coping* (Vol. 2). Hillsdale, NJ: Erlbaum.

Hollon, S. D., Shelton, R. C., & Davis, D. D. (1993). Cognitive therapy for depression: Conceptual issues and clinical efficacy. *J. Cons. Clin. Psychol.*, 61(2), 270–275.

Hollon, S. D., Shelton, R. C., & Loosen, P. T. (1991). Cognitive therapy and pharmacotherapy for depression. *J. Cons. Clin. Psychol.*, 59, 88–99.

Holman, T., Jensen, L., Capell, M., & Woddard, F. (1993). Predicting alcohol use among young adults. *Addictive Behaviors*, 18, 41–49.

Holmes, C. B. (1985). Comment on "Religiosity and U.S. suicide rates, 1972–1978." *J. Clin. Psychol.*, 41(4), 580.

Holmes, T. H., & David, E. M. (Eds.) (1989). *Life change, life events, and illness.* New York: Praeger.

Holmes, T. H., & Rahe, R. H. (1967). The social readjustment rating scale. *J. Psychosom. Res.*, 11, 213–218.

Holmes, T. H., & Rahe, R. H. (1989). The social readjustment rating scale. In T. H. Holmes & E. M. David (Eds.), *Life, change, life events, and illness:* Selected papers. New York: Praeger.

Holmes, V. F., & Rich, C. L. (1990). Suicide among physicians. In S. J. Blumenthal & D. J. Kupfer (Eds.), *Suicide over the life cycle: Risk factors, assessment, and treatment of suicidal patients.* Washington, DC: American Psychiatry Press.

Holroyd, J. C., & Brodsky, A. M. (1977). Psychologists' attitudes and practices regarding erotic and nonerotic physical contact with patients. *Amer. Psychol.*, 32, 843–849.

Holstein, J. A. (1993). *Court-ordered insanity: Interpretive practice and involuntary commitment.* New York: Aldine De Gruyter.

Holt, C. S., Heimberg, R. G., & Hope, D. A. (1992). Avoidant personality disorder and the generalized subtype of social phobia. *J. Abnorm. Psychol.*, 101(2), 318–325.

Holtzworth-Munroe, A., & Hutchinson, G. (1993). Attributing negative intent to wife behavior: The attributions of maritally violent versus nonviolent men. *J. Abnorm. Psychol.*, 102(2), 206–211.

Holzman, P. S. (1986). Quality of thought disorder in differential diagnosis. *Schizo. Bull.*, 12, 360–372.

Holzman, P. S., & Matthysse, S. (1990). The genetics of schizophrenia: A review. *Psychol. Science*, 1(5), 279–286.

Hong, L. K. (1984). Survival of the fastest: On the origin of premature ejaculation. *J. Sex Res.*, 20, 109–122.

Hooker, W. D., & Jones, R. T. (1987). Increased susceptibility to memory intrusions and the Stroop interference effect during acute marijuana intoxication. *Psychopharmacology*, 91(1), 20–24.

Hope, D. A., & Heimberg, R. G. (1993). Social phobia and social anxiety. In D. H. Barlow (Ed.), *Clinical Handbook of Psychological Disorders: A Step-by-Step Treatment Manual* (2nd ed.). New York: Guilford.

Hopson, J. L. (1986). The unraveling of insomnia. *Anthropol. Educ. Quart.*, 20(6), 42–49.

Horn, J. C., & Meer, J. (1987, May). The vintage years. *Psych. Today*, 76–77, 80–84, 88–90.

Horn, J. M., Loehlin, J. C., & Willerman, L. (1979). *Behav. Genetics, 9*(3), 177–207.

Horn, M. (1993, November). Memories lost and found. *U. S. News and World Report*, p. 52–63.

Horner, A. J. (1975). Stages and processes in the development of early object relations and their associated pathologies. *International Review of Psycho-Analysis, 2*, 95–105.

Horner, A. J. (1991). *Psychoanalytic object relations therapy.* Northvale, NJ: Hason Aronson.

Horney, K. (1937). *The neurotic personality of our time.* New York: Norton.

Horton, D. (1943). The functions of alcohol in primitive societies: A cross-cultural study. *Quart. J. Stud. Alcohol., 4*, 199–320.

Horton, P. C. (1992). A borderline treatment dilemma: To solace or not to solace. In D. Silver & M. Rosenbluth (Eds.), *Handbook of Borderline Disorders.* Madison, CT: International Universities Press, Inc.

House, J. S., Landis, K. R., & Umberson, D. (1988). Social relationships and health. *Science, 241*, (4865), 540–545.

Howard, K. I., Kopta, S. M., Krause, M. S., & Orlinsky, D. E. (1986). The dose-effect relationship in psychotherapy. *Amer. Psychol., 41*, 159–164.

Howe, A., & Walker, C. E. (1992). Behavioral management of toilet training enuresis, encopresis. *Pediatric Clinics of North America, 39*(3), 413–432.

Howells, J. G., & Guirguis, W. R. (1985). *The family and schizophrenia.* New York: International Universities Press, Inc.

Hser, Y., Anglin, D., & Powers, K. (1993). A 24-year follow-up of California narcotics addicts. *Arch. Gen. Psychiat., 50*, 577–584.

Hsu, L. K. G. (1980). Outcome of anorexia nervosa: A review of literature (1954–1978). *Arch. Gen. Psychiat., 37*, 1041–1046.

Hsu, L. K. G., Crisp, A. H., & Callender, J. S. (1992). Psychiatric diagnoses in recovered and unrecovered anorectics 22 years after onset of illness: A pilot study. *Comprehen. Psychiat., 33*(2), 123–127.

Hsu, L. K. G., Crisp, A. H., & Harding, B. (1979). Outcome of anorexia nervosa. *Lancet, 1*, 61–65.

Hsu, L. K. G., & Holder, D. (1986). Bulimia nervosa: Treatment and short-term outcome. *Psychol. Med., 16*, 65.

Hubbard, R. W., & McIntosh, J. L. (1992). Integrating suicidology into abnormal psychology classes: The revised facts on suicide quiz. *Teaching of Psychology, 19*(3), 163–166.

Hughes, C. W. et al. (1984). Cerebral blood flow and cerebrovascular permeability in an inescapable shock (learned helplessness) animal model of depression. *Pharm., Biochem. Behav., 21*(6), 891–894.

Human, J., & Wasem, C. (1991, March). Rural mental health in America. *Amer. Psychol., 46*, 232–239.

Humphreys, K., & Rappaport, J. (1993). From the community mental health movement to the war on drugs: A study in the definition of social problems. *Amer. Psychol., 48*(8), 892–901.

Humphry, D., & Wickett, A. (1986). *The right to die: Understanding euthanasia.* New York: Harper & Row.

Hunt, D., Lipton, D., Goldsmith, D., Strug, D., & Spunt, B. (1986). It takes your heart: The image of methadone maintenance in the addict world and its effect on recruitment into treatment. *Inter. J. Addic., 20*, 1751–1771.

Hunt, M. (1974). *Sexual behavior in the 1970s.* Chicago: Playboy.

Hunter, R., & MacAlpine, I. (1963). *Three hundred years of psychiatry.* Oxford: Oxford UP.

Huntington, D. D., & Bender, W. N. (1993). Adolescents with learning disabilities at risk: Emotional well-being, depression, suicide. *Journal of Learning Disabilities, 26*(3), 159–166.

Hurley, A. D., & Hurley, F. L. (1986). Counseling and psychotherapy with mentally retarded clients: I. The initial interview. *Psych. Aspects of Ment. Retardation Rev., 5*(5), 22–26.

Hurley, J. D., & Meminger, S. R. (1992). A relapse-prevention program: Effects of electromyographic training on high and low levels of state and trait anxiety. *Perceptual and Motor Skills, 74*(3, Pt. 1), 699–705.

Hurt, S. W., Clarkin, J. F., Munroe-Blum, H. et al. (1992). Borderline behavioral clusters and different treatment approaches. In J. F. Clarkin, E. Marziali, H. Munroe-Blum (Eds.), *Borderline personality disorder: Clinical and empirical perspectives.* The Guilford personality disorders series. New York: Guilford.

Hurt, S. W., Reznikoff, M., Clarkin, J. F. (1991). *Psychological assessment, psychiatric diagnosis, and treatment planning.* New York: Brunner/Mazel.

Hurwitz, T. D. (1974). Electroconvulsive therapy: A review. *Comprehen. Psychiat., 15*(4), 303–314.

Hutchings, D. F., Denney, D. R., Basgall, J., & Houston, B. K. (1980). Anxiety management and applied relaxation in reducing general anxiety. *Behav. Res. Ther., 18*(3), 181–190.

Hutchinson, R. L., & Little, T. J. (1985). A study of alcohol and drug usage by nine- through thirteen-year-old children in Central Indiana. *J. Alcohol & Drug Educ., 30*(3), 83–87.

Hutt, S. J., Hutt, C., Lee, D., & Ounstead, C. (1964). Arousal and childhood autism. *Nature, 204*, 908.

Hutton, E. L., Fleming, G. W. T. H. & Fox, F. E. (1941). Early results of prefrontal leukotomy. *Lancet, 2*, 3–7.

Huws, R. (1991). Cardiac disease and sexual dysfunction. *Sexual and Marital Therapy, 6*(2), 119–134.

Hwu, H. G., Yeh, E. K., & Chang, L. Y. (1989). Prevalence of psychiatric disorders in Taiwan defined by the Chinese Diagnostic Interview Schedule. *Acta. Psychiatr. Scandin., 79*, 136–147.

Hyde, A. P., & Goldman, C. R. (1992). Use of a multi-modal family group in the comprehensive treatment and rehabilitation of people with schizophrenia. *Psychosocial Rehabilitation Journal, 15*(4), 77–86.

Hyde, J. S. (1990). *Understanding human sexuality* (4th ed.). New York: McGraw-Hill.

Hyde, T. M., Casanova, M. F., Kleinman, J. E., & Weinberger, D. R. (1991). Neuroanatomical and neurochemical pathology in schizophrenia. In A. Tasman & S. M. Goldfinger (Eds.), *American psychiatric press review of psychiatry* (Volume 10). Washington, DC: American Psychiatric Press.

Hyler, S. E., & Spitzer, R. T. (1978). Hysteria split asunder. *Amer. J. Psychiat., 135*, 1500–1504.

Hyman, B. T., & Tanzi, R. E. (1992). Amyloid, dementia and Alzheimer's disease. *Current Opinion in Neurology and Neurosurgery, 5*, 88–93.

Hynd, G. W., Semrud-Clikeman, M., Lorys, A. R., Novey, E. S. et al. (1990). Brain morphology in developmental dyslexia and attention deficit disorder/hyperactivity. *Arch. Neurol., 47*(8), 919–926.

Iga, M. (1993). Japanese suicide. In A. A. Leenaars (Ed.), *Suicidology*. Northvale, NJ: Jason Aronson Inc.

Iivanainen, M., & Lahdevirta, J. (1990). Infectious diseases as causes of mental retardation and other concomitant neurological sequelae. *Australia & New Zealand Journal of Developmental Disabilities, 14*, 201–210.

Inglehart, R. (1990). *Culture shift in advanced industrial society.* Princeton, NJ: Princeton UP.

Ingrassia, M., & Beck, M. (1994, July 4). Patterns of abuse. *Newsweek*, pp. 26–33.

Insel, T. R., Ninan, P. T., Aloi, J., Jimerson, D., Skolnick, P., & Paul, S. M. (1984). Benzodiazepine receptors and anxiety in non-human primates. *Arch. Gen. Psychiat., 41*, 741–750.

Institute of Medicine [IOM]. (1989). *Research on children and adolescents with mental, behavioral, and developmental disorders.* Washington, DC: National Academy Press.

Ironson, G., Taylor, C. B., Boltwood, M., et al. (1992). Effects of anger on left ventricular ejection fraction in coronary artery disease. *American Journal of Cardiology, 70*(3), 281–285.

Irving, L. M. (1990). Mirror images: Effects of the standard of beauty on the self- and body-esteem of women exhibiting varying levels of bulimic symptoms. *J. Soc. Clin. Psychol., 9*(2), 230–242.

Ishii, K. (1991). Measuring mutual causation: Effects of suicide news on suicide in Japan. *Social Science Research, 20*(2), 188–195.

Iversen, L. L. (1975). Dopamine receptors in the brain. *Science, 188*, 1084–1089.

Iversen, L. L. (1965). *Adv. Drug Res., 2*, 5–23.

Iversen, S. D. (1989). Psychopharmacology. In J. Hobson (Ed.), *Abnormal states of brain and mind.* Boston: Birhauser.

Ivnik, R. J., Sharbrough, F. W., & Laws, E. R. Jr. (1987). Effects of anterior temporal lobectomy on cognitive function. *Journal of Clinical Psychology, 43*, 128–137.

Izard, C. E. (1977). *Human emotions.* New York: Plenum.

Jack, R. (1992). *Women and Attempted Suicide.* Hillsdale: Lawrence Erlbaum Associates, Publishers.

Jackson, J. S. (Ed.). (1988). *The Black American elderly: Research on physical and psychosocial health.* New York: Springer.

Jackson, J. L., Calhoun, K. S., Amick, A. A., Madever, H. M., & Habif, V. L. (1990). Young adult women who report childhood intrafamilial sexual abuse: Subsequent adjustment. *Archives of Sexual Behavior, 19*(3), 211–221.

Jacobs, B. L. (Ed.). (1984). *Hallucinogens: neurochemical, behavioral, and clinical perspectives.* New York: Raven Press.

Jacobs, B. L. (1987). How hallucinogenic drugs work. *American Scientist, 75*, 386–393.

Jacobs, D., & Klein, M. E. (1993). The expanding role of psychological autopsies. In A. A. Leenaars (Ed.), *Suicidology.* Northvale, NJ: Jason Aronson Inc.

Jacobs, R. (1993). AIDS communication: College students' AIDS knowledge and information sources. *Health Values, The Journal of Health, Behavior, Education, and Promotion, 17*(3), 32–41.

Jacobsen, L. K., Rabinowitz, I., Popper, M. S., Solomon, R. J., Sokol, M. S., & Pfeffer, C. R. (1994). Interviewing prepubertal children about suicidal ideation and behavior. *J. Amer. Acad. Child Adol. Psychiat., 33*(4), 439–452.

Jacobson, B., & Thurman-Lacey, S. (1992). Effect of caffeine on motor performance by caffeine-naive and -familiar subjects. *Perceptual & Motor Skills, 74*, 151–157.

Jacobson, E. (1971). *Depression.* New York: International Univ.

Jacobson, E. (1975). The psychoanalytic treatment of depressive patients. In E. J. Anthony & T. Benedek (Eds.), *Depression and human existence.* Boston: Little, Brown.

Jacobson, J. W., & Schwartz, A. A. (1991). Evaluating living situations of people with development disabilities. In J. L. Matson & J. A. Mulick (Eds.), *Handbook of mental retardation.* New York: Pergamon.

Jacobson, N. S. (1977). Problem-solving and contingency contracting in the treatment of marital discord. *J. Cons. Clin. Psychol., 45*, 92–100.

Jacobson, N. S. (1977). Training couples to solve their marital problems: A behavioral approach to relationship discord: I. Problem-solving skills. *Inter. J. Fam. Couns., 5*(1), 29–31.

Jacobson, N. S. (1977). Training couples to solve their marital problems: A behavioral approach to relationship discord: II. Intervention strategies. *Inter. J. Fam. Couns., 5*(2), 20–28.

Jacobson, N. S. (1984). A component analysis of behavioral marital therapy: The relative effectiveness of behavior exchange and problem solving training. *J. Cons. Clin. Psychol., 52*, 295–305.

Jacobson, N. S. (1989). The maintenance of treatment gains following social learning-based marital therapy. *Behav. Ther., 20*(3), 325–336.

Jacobson, N. S., & Addis, M. E. (1993). *Research on couple therapy: What do we know? Where are we going?* Submitted for publication.

Jacobson, N. S., & Margolin, G. (1979). *Marital therapy: Strategies based on social learning and behavior exchange principles.* New York: Brunner/Mazel.

Jacobson, N. S., Schmaling, K. B., & Holtzworth-Munroe, A. (1987). Component analysis of behavioral marital therapy: 2-year follow-up and prediction of relapse. *Journal of Marital and Family Therapy, 13*(2), 187–195.

Jacobson, N. S. et al. (1984). Variability in outcome and clinical significance of behavioral marital therapy: A re-analysis of outcome data. *J. Couns. Clin. Psychol., 52*(4), 497–504.

Jaegerman, M. (1993, February 4). Price Tag: Psychotherapy. *The New York Times*, p. C2.

Jaffe, J. H. (1985). Drug addiction and drug abuse. In Goodman & Gilman (Eds.), *The pharmacological basis of therapeutic behavior.* New York: Macmillan.

James, A. L., & Barry, R. (1980). A review of psychophysiology in child onset psychosis. *Schizo. Bull., 6*, 506–525.

James, W. (1890). *Principles of psychology* (Vol. 1). New York: Holt, Rinehart & Winston.

Jamison, K. R. (1987). Psychotherapeutic issues and suicide prevention in the treatment of bipolar disorders. In R. E. Hales & A. J. Frances (Eds.), *Psychiatric Update: American Psychiatric Association annual review* (Vol. 6). Washington, DC: American Psychiatric Press.

Janicak, P. G., Davis, J. M., Gibbons, R. D. et al. (1985). Efficacy of ECT: A meta-analysis. *Amer. J. Psychiat., 132*, 297–302.

Jannoun, L., McDowell, I., & Catalan, J. (1981). Behavioral treatment of anxiety is general practice. *Practitioner, 225*, 58–62.

Jannoun, L., Oppenheimer, C., & Gelder, M. (1982). A self-help treatment program for anxiety state patients. *Behav. Ther.*, *13*(1), 103–111.

Janowsky, D. S., & Davis, J. M. (1976). Methylphanidate, dextroamphetamine, and levamfetamine: Effects on schizophrenic symptoms. *Arch. Gen. Psychiat.*, *33*(3), 304–308.

Janowsky, D. S., El-Yousef, M. K., Davis, J. M., & Sekerke, H. J. (1972). A cholinergic-adrenergic hypothesis of mania and depression. *Lancet, 2*, 632–635.

Janowsky, D. S., El-Yousef, M. K., Davis, J. M., & Sekerke, H. J. (1973). Provocation of schizophrenic symptoms by intravenous administration of methylphenidate. *Arch. Gen. Psychiat., 28*, 185–191.

Jarvik, M. E., & Schneider, N. G. (1984). Degree of addiction and effectiveness of nicotine gum therapy for smoking. *Amer. J. Psychiat., 141*, 790–791.

Jaschke, V. A., & Spiegel, D. (1992). A case of probable dissociative disorder. *Bull. Menninger Clin., 56*(2), 246–260.

Jay, S. M., Elliot, C. H., Katz, E., & Siegel, S. E. (1987). Cognitive-behavioral and pharmacologic interventions for children's distress during painful medical procedures. *J. Cons. Clin. Psychol., 55*, 860–865.

Jefferson, J. W., & Greist, J. H. (1989). Lithium therapy. In H. I. Kaplan & B. J. Sadock (Eds.), *Comprehensive textbook of psychiatry V.* Baltimore: Williams & Wilkins.

Jefferson, L. (1948). *These are my sisters.* Tulsa, OK: Vickers.

Jemmott, J. B. (1985). Psychoneuroimmunology: The new frontier. *Amer. Behav. Scientist, 28*(4), 497–509.

Jemmott, J. B. (1987). Social motives and susceptibility to disease: Stalking individual differences in health risks. *J. Pers., 55*(2), 267–298.

Jemmott, J. B., & Locke, S. E. (1984). Psychosocial factors, immunologic mediation, and human susceptibility to infectious diseases: How much do we know? *Psychol. Bull., 95*, 78–108.

Jemmott, J. B., Borysenko, J. Z., Borysenko, M., McClelland, D. C., et al. (1983). Academic stress, power motivation and decrease in secretion rate of salivary immunoglobulin. *Lancet, 11*, 1400–1402.

Jenike, M. A. (1985). Monoamine oxidase inhibitors as treatment for depressed patients with primary degenerative dementia. *Amer. J. Clin. Psychiat., 142*(6), 763–764.

Jenike, M. A. (1990). Approaches to the patient with treatment-refractory obsessive compulsive disorder. *J. Clin. Psychiat., 51*(Suppl. 2), 15–21.

Jenike, M. A. (1991). Geriatric obsessive-compulsive disorder. *Journal of Geriatric Psychiatry and Neurology, 4*, 34–39.

Jenike, M. A. (1991). Management of patients with treatment-resistant obsessive-compulsive disorder. In M. T. Pato & J. Zohar (Eds.), *Current Treatments of Obsessive-compulsive Disorder.* Washington, DC: American Psychiatric Press.

Jenike, M. A. (1991). Obsessive-compulsive disorders: A clinical approach. In W. Coryell & G. Winokur (Eds.), *The Clinical Management of Anxiety Disorders.* New York: Oxford UP.

Jenike, M. A. (1992). New Developments in Treatment of Obsessive-Compulsive Disorder. In A. Tasman, & M. B. Riba (Eds.), *Review of Psychiatry* (Vol. 11). Washington, DC: American Psychiatric Press.

Jenkins, R. L. (1968). The varieties of children's behavioral problems and family dynamics. *Amer. J. Psychiat., 124*(10), 1440–1445.

Jenkins-Hall, K., & Sacco, W. P. (1991). Effect of client race and depression on evaluations by white therapists. *Journal of Social and Clinical Psychology, 10*(3), 322–333.

Jensen, J. P., Bergin, A. E., & Greaves, D. W. (1990). The meaning of eclecticism: New survey and analysis of components. *Professional Psychology: Research and Practice, 21*, 124–130.

Jimerson, D. C. (1984). Neurotransmitter hypotheses of depression: Research update. *Psychiat. Clin. N. Amer., 7*(3), 563–573.

Jimerson, D. C., Lesem, M. D., Kaye, W. H., Hegg, A. P. et al. (1990). Eating disorders and depression: Is there a serotonin connection? *Bio Psychiat., 28*(5), 443–454.

Joasoo, A., & McKenzie, J. M. (1976). Stress and the immune response in rats. *Inter. Arch. Allergy & Appl. Immun., 50*, 659–663.

Joffe, R. T., Singer, W., Levitt, A. J., & MacDonald, C. (1993). A placebo-controlled comparison of lithium and triiodothyronine augmentation of tricyclic antidepressants in unipolar refractory depression. *Arch. Gen. Psychiat., 50*, 387–393.

Johnson, C., & Maddi, K. L. (1986). The etiology of bulimia: Bio-psycho-social perspectives. *Ann. Adol. Psychiat., 13*, 253–273.

Johnson, C., & Wonderlich, S. A. (1992). Personality characteristics as a risk factor in the development of eating disorders. In J. H. Crowther, D. L. Tennenbaum, S. E. Hobfoll, & M. A. P. Stephens (Eds.), *The Etiology of Bulimia nervosa: The Individual and Familial Context.* Washington, DC: Hemisphere Publishing Corp.

Johnson, E. H., Gentry, W. D., & Julius, S. (Eds.) (1992). *Personality, elevated blood pressure, and essential hypertension.* Washington, DC: Hemisphere Publishing Corp.

Johnson, F. A. (1991). Psychotherapy of the elderly anxious patient. In C. Salzman & B. D. Lebowitz (Eds.), *Anxiety in the elderly.* New York: Springer.

Johnson, F. S., Hunt, G. E., Duggin, G. G., Horvath, J. S., & Tiller, D. J. (1984). Renal function and lithium treatment: Initial and follow-up tests in manic-depressive patients. *J. Affect. Dis., 6*, 249–263.

Johnson, M. R., Lydiard, R. B., Morton, W. A., Laird, L. K., Steele, T. E., Kellner, C. H., & Ballenger, J. C. (1993). Effect of fluvoxamine, imipramine and placebo on catecholamine function in depressed outpatients. *J. Psychiat. Res., 27*(2), 161–172.

Johnson, W. D. (1991). Predisposition to emotional distress and psychiatric illness amongst doctors: The role of unconscious and experiential factors. *British Journal of Medical Psychology, 64*(4), 317–329.

Johnson, W. G., Schlundt, D. G., Kelley, M. L., & Ruggiero, L. (1984). Exposure with response prevention and energy regulation in the treatment of bulimia. *Int. J. Eat. Dis., 3*, 37–46.

Johnson, W. R. (1981). Basic interviewing skills. In C. E. Walker (Ed.), *Clinical practice of psychology.* New York: Pergamon.

Johnson-Greene, D., Fatis, M., Sonnek, K., & Shawchuck, C. (1988). A survey of caffeine use and associated side effects in a college population. *Journal of Drug Education, 18*(3), 211–219.

Johnston, D. W. (1992). The management of stress in the prevention of coronary heart disease. In S. Maes, H. Levental,

& M. Johnston (Eds.), *International Review of Health Psychology* (Vol. 1). New York: Wiley.

Johnston, L. D., Bachman, J. G., & O'Malley, P. M. (1982). *Student drug use, attitudes and beliefs.* Washington, DC: National Institute on Drug Abuse.

Johnston, L. D., O'Malley, P. M., & Bachman, J. G. (1993). *National Survey Results on Drug Use from the Monitoring the Future Study, 1975–1992.* Rockville, Maryland: National Institute on Drug Abuse.

Jolly, J. B., & Dykman, R. A. (1994). Using self-report data to differentiate anxious and depressive symptoms in adolescents: Cognitive content specificity and global distress? *Cog. Ther. Res., 18*(1), 25–37.

Jonas, J. M., Coleman, B. S., Sheridan, A. Q., & Kalinske, R. W. (1992). Comparative clinical profiles of triazolam versus other shorter-acting hypnotics. *J. Clin. Psychiat., 53*(12, Suppl.), 19–31.

Jones, B., & Katz, N. (1992). Madness and addiction: Treating the mentally ill chemical abuser. *Journal of Health Care for the Poor and Underserved, 3*(1), 39–45.

Jones, D., Fox, M. M., Babigian, H. M. et al. (1980). Epidemiology of anorexia nervosa in Monroe County, NY, 1960–1976. *Psychosom. Med., 42*, 551–558.

Jones, D. M. (1985). Bulimia: A false self-identity. *Clin. Soc. Work J., 13*(4), 305–316.

Jones, J. M. (1990). A call to advance psychology's role in minority issues. *APA Monitor, 21*, p. 23.

Jones, M. (1994, April 25). The fallout of the burnout: The sad, sordid last days of Kurt Cobain. *Newsweek,* p. 68.

Jones, M. C. (1924). The elimination of children's fears. *J. Exp. Psychol., 7*, 382–390.

Jones, M. C. (1971). Personality antecedents and correlates of drinking patterns in women. *J. Cons. Clin. Psychol., 36*, 61–69.

Jones, M. C. (1968). Personality correlates and antecedants of drinking patterns in males. *J. Cons. Clin. Psychol., 32*, 2–12.

Jones, R. T., & Benowitz, N. (1976). The 30-day trip—clinical studies of cannabis tolerance and dependence. In M. C. Braude & S. Szara (Eds.), *Pharmacology of marijuana.* New York: Raven Press.

Jordan, B. K., Marmar, C. R., Fairbank, J. A., Schlenger, W. E., et al. (1992). Problems in families of male Vietnam veterans with posttraumatic stress disorder. *J. Cons. Clin. Psychol., 60*(6), 916–926.

Joseph, E. (1991). Psychodynamic personality theory. In K. Davis, H. Klar, & J. J. Coyle (Eds.), *Foundations of psychiatry.* Philadelphia: Saunders.

Jourard, S. M. (1971). *Self-disclosure.* New York: Wiley.

Joyce, C. (1988). Assault on the brain. *Psych. Today, 22*(3), 38–39, 42–44.

Joyner, C. D., & Swenson, C. C. (1993). Community-level intervention after a disaster. In C. F. Saylor (Ed.), *Children and Disasters.* New York: Plenum.

Juel-Nielsen, N., & Videbech, T. (1970). A twin study of suicide. *Acta Geneticae Medicae et Gemellologiae, 19*, 307–310.

Julien, R. M. (1985). *A primer of drug action* (4th ed.). New York: W. H. Freeman.

Julien, R. M. (1988). *A primer of drug action* (5th ed.). New York: W. H. Freeman.

Julius, S. (1992). Relationship between the sympathetic tone and cardiovascular responsiveness in the course of hyperten-

sion. In E. H. Johnson, E. D. Gentry, & S. Julius (Eds.), *Personality, elevated blood pressure, and essential hypertension.* Washington, DC: Hemisphere Publishing Corp.

Jung, C. G. (1909). *Memories, dreams, and reflections.* New York: Random House.

Jung, C. G. (1967). *The Collected Works of C. G. Jung.* Princeton, NJ: Princeton UP.

Jungman, J. (1985). De l'agir du toxicomane a l'agir du thérapeute [From the drug addict's acting out to the therapist's action]. *Information Psychiatrique, 61*(3), 383–388.

Kabat-Zinn, J. (1993). Meditation. In B. Moyers, *Healing and the Mind.* New York: Doubleday.

Kabat-Zinn, J., Massion, A. O., Kristeller, J., Peterson, L. G., et al. (1992). Effectiveness of a meditation-based stress reduction program in the treatment of anxiety disorders. *Amer. J. Psychiat., 149*(7), 936–943.

Kadushin, C. (1969). *Why people go to psychiatrists.* New York: Atherton.

Kafantaris, V., Campbell, M., Padron-Gayol, M. V., Small, A. M. et al. (1992). Carbamazepine in hospitalized aggressive conduct disordered children: An open pilot study. *Psychopharmacology Bulletin, 28*(2), 193–199.

Kagan, J. (1983). Stress and coping in early development. In N. Garmezy & M. Rutter (Eds.), *Stress, Coping, and Development in Children.* McGraw-Hill.

Kagan, J. (1989). Temperamental contributions to social behavior. Meeting of the American Psychological Association. *American Psychologist, 44*(4), 668–674.

Kagan, R. (1986). The child behind the mask: Sociopathy as a developmental delay. In W. Reid, D. Dorr, J. Walker, & J. Bonner (Eds.), *Unmasking The Psychopath.* New York: Norton.

Kahn, A. (1982). The moment of truth: Psychotherapy with the suicidal patient. In E. Bassuk, S. G. Schoonover, & A. D. Gill, *Lifelines.* New York: Plenum.

Kahn, R. S., Davidson, M., Siever, L., Gabriel, S., et al. (1993). Serotonin function and treatment response to clozapine in schizophrenic patients. *Amer. J. Psychiat., 150*(9), 1337–1342.

Kahn, R. S., Wetzler, S., Van Praag, H. A., et al. (1988). Behavioral indication of serotonergic supersensitivity in panic disorder. *Psychiatry Research, 25*, 101–104.

Kahneman, D., & Tversky, A. (1973). On the psychology of prediction. *Psych. Rev., 80*(4), 237–251.

Kahneman, D., Slovic, P., & Tversky, A. (Eds.). (1982). *Judgment under uncertainty: Heuristics and biases.* Cambridge: Cambridge UP.

Kaij, L. (1960). *Alcoholism in twins: Studies on the etiology and sequels of abuse of alcohol.* Stockholm: Almquist & Wiksell.

Kail, R. (1992). General slowing of information-processing by persons with mental retardation. *American Journal on Mental Retardation, 97*(3), 333–341.

Kalin, N. H. (1993, May). *The neurobiology of fear.* Scientific American, p. 94–101.

Kalinowsky, L. B. (1980). Convulsive therapies. In H. I. Kaplan, A. M. Freedman, & B. J. Sadock (Eds.), *Comprehensive textbook of psychiatry* (Vol. 3). Baltimore: Williams & Wilkins.

Kallman, W. M., & Feuerstein, M. J. (1986). Psychophysiological procedures. In A. R. Ciminero, K. S. Calhoun, & H. E. Adams, (Eds.), *Handbook of behavioral assessment* (2nd ed.). New York: Wiley.

Kaminer, Y. (1991). Adolescent substance abuse. In R. J. Frances & S. I. Miller (Eds.), *Clinical Textbook of Addictive Disorders.* New York: Guilford.

Kane, J. M. (1987). Treatment of schizophrenia. *Schizo. Bull., 13*(1), 133–156.

Kane, J. M. (1990). Treatment programme and long-term outcome in chronic schizophrenia. International Symposium: Development of a new antipsychotic: Remoxipride (1989, Monte Carlo, Monaco). *Acta Psychiatr. Scandin., 82*(385, Suppl.), 151–157.

Kane, J. M. (1992). Clinical efficacy of clozapine in treatment-refractory schizophrenia: An overview. *Brit. J. Psychiat., 160*(Suppl 17), 41–45.

Kane, M. T., & Kendall, P. C. (1989). Anxiety disorders in children: A multiple-baseline evaluation of a cognitive-behavioral treatment. *Behavioral Therapy 20* (4), 499–508.

Kanfer, F. H., & Philips, J. S. (1970). *Learning foundations of behavior therapy.* New York: Wiley.

Kanner, L. (1943). Autistic disturbances of affective contact. *Nerv. Child. 2,* 217.

Kanner, L. (1954). To what extent is early infantile autism determined by constitutional inadequacies? *Proceedings of the Association for Research in Nervous and Mental Diseases, 33,* 378–385.

Kanof, P. (1991). Neurotransmitter receptor function. In K. Davis, H. Klar, & J. T. Coyle (Eds.), *Foundations of psychiatry.* Philadelphia: Saunders.

Kaplan, H. I., & Sadock, B. J. (1989). Typical signs and symptoms of psychiatric illness. In H. I. Kaplan & B. J. Sadock (Eds.), *Comprehensive textbook of psychiatry* (Vol. 1, 5th ed.). Baltimore: Williams & Wilkins.

Kaplan, H. S. (1974). *The new sex therapy: Active treatment of sexual dysfunction.* New York: Brunner/Mazel.

Kaplan, H. S. (1977). Hypoactive sexual desire. *J. Sex & Marital Ther., 3,* 3–9.

Kaplan, H. S. (1979). *Disorders of sexual desire.* New York: Brunner/Mazel.

Kaplan, H. S. (1992). Does the CAT technique enhance female orgasm? *Journal of Sex and Marital Therapy, 18*(4), 285–291.

Kaplan, R. L., & Sadock, B. J. (1989). Psychiatric report. In H. I. Kaplan & B. J. Sadock (Eds.), *Comprehensive textbook of psychiatry* (Vol. 1, 5th ed.). Baltimore: Williams & Wilkins.

Kaplan, N. M. (1980). The control of hypertension: A therapeutic breakthrough. *Amer. Scientist, 68*(5), 537–545.

Kaplan, W. (1984). The relationship between depression and anti-social behavior among a court-referred adolescent population. Presented to the American Academy of Child Psychiatry, Toronto.

Karasu, T. B. (1986). The specificity versus nonspecificity dilemma: Toward identifying therapeutic change agents. *Amer. J. Psychiat., 143,* 687–695.

Karasu, T. B. (1992). The worst of times, the best of times. *Journal of Psychotherapy Practice and Research, 1,* 2–15.

Kardiner, A. (1977). *My analysis with Freud: reminiscences.* New York: Norton.

Karel, R. (1992, May 1). Hopes of many long-term sufferers dashed as FDA ends medical marijuana program. *Psychiatric News.*

Karno, M., & Golding, J. M. (1991). Obsessive compulsive disorder. In L. N. Robins, & D. A. Regier (Eds.), *Psychiatric Disorders in America: The Epidemiologic Catchment Area Study.* New York: Maxwell Macmillan International.

Karoly, P., & Lecci, L. (1993). Hypochondriasis and somatization in college women: A personal projects analysis. *Health Psychology, 12*(2), 103–109.

Karon, B. P. (1985). Omission in review of treatment interactions. *Schizo. Bull., 11*(1), 16–17.

Karon, B. P. (1988). Cited in T. De Angelis, "Resistance to therapy seen in therapists, too." *APA Monitor, 19*(11), 21.

Karon, B. P., & Vandenbos, G. R. (1981). *Psychotherapy of schizophrenia: The treatment of choice.* New York: Jason Aronson.

Kashani, J. H., Goddard, P., & Reid, J. C. (1989). Correlated of suicidal ideation in a community sample of children and adolescents. *J. Amer. Acad. Child. Adoles. Psychiat., 28,* 912–917.

Kashani, J. H., Husain, A., Shekim, W., Hodges, K., Cytryn, L., & McKnew, D. (1981). Current perspectives on childhood depression: An overview. *Amer. J. Psychiat., 138,* 143–153.

Kashden, J., Fremouw, W. J., Callahan, T. S., & Franzen, M. D. (1993). Impulsivity in suicidal and nonsuicidal adolescents. *J. Abnorm. Child Psychol., 21*(3), 339–353.

Kasl, S. V., & Cobb, S. (1970). Blood pressure changes in men undergoing job loss: A preliminary report. *Psychosom. Med., 32*(1), 19–38.

Kastenbaum, R. (1988). In moderation: How some older people find pleasure and meaning in alcoholic beverages. *Generations, 12*(4), 68–73.

Katerndahl, D. A., & Realini, J. P. (1993). Lifetime prevalence of panic states. *Amer. J. Psychiat., 150*(2), 246–249.

Kato, T., Takahashi, S., Shioiri, T., & Inubushi, T. (1993).Alterations in brain phosphorous metabolism in bipolar disorder detected by in vivo 31 P and 7 Li magnetic resonance spectroscopy. *Journal of Affective Disorder, 27,* 53–60.

Katz, R. J., Lott, M., Landau, P., & Waldmeier, P. (1993). A clinical test of noradrenergic involvement in the therapeutic mode of action of an experimental antidepressant. *Bio. Psychiat., 33,* 261–266.

Katz, S. E., & Levendusky, P. G. (1990). Cognitive-behavioral approaches to treating borderline and self-mutilating patients. *Bull. Menninger Clin., 54*(3), 398–408.

Katzman, R. (1981, June). Early detection of senile dementia. *Hosp. Practitioner,* 61–76.

Kaufman, A. S., & Harrison, P. L. (1991). Individual intellectual assessment. In C. E. Walker (Ed.), *Clinical Psychology: Historical and research foundations.* New York: Plenum.

Kaufman, M. Y. (1993, January 27). *'Chutzpah Therapy' for New Yorkers.* New York Times, p. B4.

Kaufman, C. L., & Roth, L. H. (1981). Psychiatric evaluation of patient decision-making: Informed consent to ECT. *Soc. Psychiat., 16*(1), 11–19.

Kay, D. W. K. (1972). *Br. J. Hosp. Med., 8,* 369.

Kaye, W. H., Weltzin, T. E., Hsu, L. G., & Bulik, C. M. (1991). An open trial of fluoxetine in patients with anorexia nervosa. *J. Clin. Psychiat., 52*(11), 464–471.

Kazdin, A. E. (1975). *Behavior modification in applied settings.* Homewood, IL: Dorsey.

Kazdin, A. E. (1975). Covert modelling, imagery assessment, and assertive behavior. *J. Cons. Clin. Psychol., 43,* 716–724.

Kazdin, A. E. (1977). Artifact, bias, and complexity of assessment: The ABCs of reliability. *J. Appl. Behav. Anal., 10,* 141–150.

Kazdin, A. E. (1977). The influence of behavior preceding reinforced response on behavior change in the classroom. *J. Appl. Behav. Anal., 10*(2), 299–310.

Kazdin, A. E. (1979). Advances in child behavior therapy. *Amer. Psychol., 34,* 981–987.

Kazdin, A. E. (1983). Failure of persons to respond to the token economy. In E. B. Foa & P. M. G. Emmelkamp (Eds.), *Failures in behavior therapy.* New York: Wiley.

Kazdin, A. E. (1986). Comparative outcome studies of psychotherapy: Methodological issues and strategies [Special Issue]. *J. Cons. Clin. Psychol., 54*(1), 95–105.

Kazdin, A. E. (1989). Childhood depression. In E. J. Mash & R. Barkley (Eds.), *Treatment of childhood disorders.* New York: Guilford.

Kazdin, A. E. (1990). Childhood depression. *J. Child Psychol. Psychiat. Allied Disc., 31,* 121–160.

Kazdin, A. E. (1993). Psychotherapy for children and adolescents: Current progress and future research directions. *Amer. Psychol., 48*(6), 644–657.

Kazdin, A. E. (1994). Methodology, design, and evaluation in psychotherapy research. In A. E. Bergin & S. L. Garfiel (Eds.), *Handbook of psychotherapy and behavior change* (4th ed.). New York: Wiley.

Kazdin, A. E. (1994). Psychotherapy for children and adolescents. In A. E. Bergin & S. L. Garfiel (Eds.), *Handbook of psychotherapy and behavior change* (4th ed.). New York: Wiley.

Kazes, M., Danion, J. M., Grange, D., Pradignac, A., et al. (1994). Eating behaviour and depression before and after antidepressant treatment: a prospective, naturalistic study. *J. Affect. Dis., 30,* 193–207.

Keane, T. M., Fairbank, J. A., Caddell, J. M., et al. (1989). Implosive (flooding) therapy reduces symptoms of PTSD in Vietnam combat veterans. *Behav. Ther., 20,* 245–260.

Kearney-Cooke, & Steichen-Asch, P. (1990). Men, body image, and eating disorders. In A. E. Andersen (Ed.), *Males with Eating Disorders.* New York: Brunner/Mazel.

Kebabian, J. W., Petzold, G. L., & Greengard, P. (1972). Dopamine-sensitive adenylate cyclase in caudate nucleus of rat brain and its similarity to the "dopamine receptor." *Proc. Nat. Acad. Sci.* (USA), 69, 2145–2149.

Keefe, F. J., Dunsmore, J., & Burnett, R. (1992). Behavioral and cognitive-behavioral approaches to chronic pain: Recent advances and future directions. *J. Cons. Clin. Psychol., 60,* 528–536.

Keen, E. (1970). *Three faces of being: Toward an existential clinical psychology.* By the Meredith Corp. Reprinted by permission of Irvington Publishers.

Keesey, R. E., & Corbett, S. W. (1983). Metabolic defense of the body weight set-point. In A. J. Stunkard & E. Stellar (Eds.), *Eating and its disorders.* New York: Raven Press.

Keith, S. J., Regier, D. A., & Rae, D. S. (1991). Schizophrenic disorders. In L. N. Robins & D. S. Regier (Eds.), *Psychiatric Disorders in America: The epidemiological catchment area study.* New York: Free Press.

Keller, M. B. (1988). Diagnostic issues and clinical course of unipolar illness. In A. J. Frances & R. E. Hales (Eds.), *Review of psychiatry* (Vol. 7). Washington, DC: American Psychiatric Press.

Keller, M. B., & Shapiro, R. W. (1982). "Double depression": Superimposition of acute depressive episodes on chronic depressive disorders. *Amer. J. Psychiat., 139*(4), 438–442.

Keller, R., & Shaywitz, B. A. (1986). Amnesia or fugue state: A diagnostic dilemma. *J. Dev. Behav. Pediatrics, 7*(8), 131–132.

Keller, S. E., Weiss, J., Schleifer, S. J., Miller, N. E., & Stein, M. (1981). Suppression of immunity by stress: Effect of a graded series of stressors on lymphocyte stimulation in the rat. *Psychosom. Med., 43,* 91.

Kelley, G. A. (1955). A theory of personality. New York: Norton.

Kelley, R. L., & Kodman, F. (1987). A more unified view of the Multiple Personality Disorder. *Soc. Behav. Pers., 15*(2), 165–167.

Kelly, I. W., Laverty, W. H., & Saklofske, D. H. (1990). Geophysical variables and behavior: LXIV. An empirical investigation of the relationship between worldwide automobile traffic disasters and lunar cycles: No relationship. *Psych. Rep., 67*(3, Pt.1), 987–994.

Kelly, I. W., Saklofske, D. H., & Culver, R. (1990). Aircraft accidents and disasters and full moon: No relationship. *Psychology: A Journal of Human Behavior, 27*(2), 30–33.

Kelly, J. B. (1982). Divorce: An adult perspective. In B. B. Wolman (Ed.), *Handbook of developmental psychology.* Englewood Cliffs, NJ: Prentice Hall.

Kelly, K. A. (1993). Multiple personality disorders: Treatment coordination in a partial hospital setting. *Bull. Menninger Clin., 57*(3), 390–398.

Kelsoe, J. R., Ginns, E. I., Egeland, J. A., Gerhard, D. S. et al. (1989). Re-evaluation of the linkage relationship between chromosome 11p loci and the gene for bipolar affective disorder in the Old Order Amish. *Nature, 342*(6247), 238–243.

Keltner, B. R. (1992). Caregiving by mothers with mental retardation. *Family and Community Health, 15*(2), 10–18.

Kemph, J. P., DeVane, C. L., Levin, G. M., Jarecke, R., & Miller, R. L. (1993). Treatment of aggressive children with clonidine: Results of an open pilot study. *J. Amer. Acad. Child Adol. Psychiat., 32*(3), 577–581.

Kempton, W., & Kahn, E. (1991). Sexuality and people with intellectual disabilities: A historical perspective. *Sexuality and Disability, 9*(2), 93–111.

Kenardy, J., Oei, T. P., & Evans, L. (1990). Hyperventilation and panic attacks. Austral. *New Zeal. J. Psychiat., 24*(2), 261–267.

Kendall, P. C. (1987). Behavioral assessment and methodology. In G. T. Wilson, C. M. Franks, P. C. Kendall, & J. P. Foreyt (Eds.), *Review of behavior therapy* (Vol. 11). New York: Guilford.

Kendall, P. C. (1990). Behavioral assessment and methodology. In C. M. Franks, G. T. Wilson, P. C. Kendall, & J. P. Foreyt (Eds.), *Review of behavior therapy: Theory and practice* (Vol. 12). New York: Guilford.

Kendall, P. C. (Ed.). (1990). *Child and adolescent therapy: Cognitive-behavioral procedures.* New York: Guilford.

Kendall, P. C. (1990). Cognitive processes and procedures in behavior therapy. In C. M. Franks, G. T. Wilson, P. C. Kendall, & J. P. Foreyt (Eds.), *Review of behavior therapy: Theory and practice* (Vol. 12). New York: Guilford.

Kendall, P. C., & Braswell, L. (Eds.). (1985). *Cognitive-behavioral therapy for impulsive children.* New York: Guilford.

Kendall, P. C., Chansky, T. E., Freidman, M., Kim, R., Kortlander, E., Sessa, F. M., & Siquelard, L. (1991). Treating anxiety disorders in children and adolescents. In P. C. Kendall (Ed.), *Child and adolescent therapy: Cognitive-behavioral procedures*. New York: Guilford.

Kendall, P. C., Kane, M., Howard, B., & Siqueland, L. (1989). *Cognitive-behavioral therapy for anxious children: Treatment manual*. Philadelphia: Temple Univ.

Kendall, P. C., & Kriss, M. R. (1983). Cognitive-behavioral interventions. In C. E. Walker (Ed.), *The handbook of clinical psychology: Theory, research, and practice*. IL: Dow Jones-Irwin.

Kendall, P. C., & Watson, D. (Eds.). (1989). *Anxiety and depression: Distinctive overlapping features*. San Diego: Academic.

Kendler, K. S. (1983). Computer analysed EEG findings in children of schizophrenic parents ("high risk" children): Commentary. *Integ. Psychiat., 1*(3), 82–83.

Kendler, K. S., Heath, A., & Martin, N. G. (1987). A genetic epidemiologic study of self-report suspiciousness. *Comprehen. Psychiat., 28*(3), 187–196.

Kendler, K. S., Heath, A., Neale, M., Kessler, R., & Eaves, L. (1992). A population-based twin study of alcoholism in women. *JAMA, 268*(14), 1877–1882.

Kendler, K. S., McGuire, M., Gruenberg, A. M., O'Hare, A., Spellman, M., & Walsh, D. (1993). The Roscommon Family Study. *Arch. Gen. Psychiat., 50,* 527–540.

Kendler, K. S., McGuire, M., Gruenberg, A. M., & Walsh, D. (1994). An epidemiological, clinical, and family study of simple schizophrenia in County Roscommon, Ireland. *Amer. J. Psychiat., 151*(1), 27–34.

Kendler, K. S., Neale, M. C., Heath, A. C., Kessler, R. C., & Eaves, L. J. (1994). A twin-family study of alcoholism in women. *Amer. J. Psychiat., 151*(5), 707–715.

Kendler, K. S., Neale, M. C., Kessler, R. C., Heath, A. C., et al. (1992). Generalized anxiety disorder in women: A population-based twin study. *Arch. Gen. Psychiat., 49*(4), 267–272.

Kendler, K. S., Ochs, A. L., Gorman, A. M., Hewitt, J. K., Ross, D. E., & Mirsky, A. F. (1991). The structure of schizotypy: A pilot multitrait twin study. *Psychiatry Research, 36*(1), 19–36.

Kennedy, J. L., Giuffra, L. A., Moises, H. W. et al. (1988). Evidence against linkage of schizophrenia to markers on chromosome 5 in a northern Swedish pedigree. *Nature, 336,* 167–168.

Kennedy, L. L. (1992). Partial Hospitalization. In A. Tasman & M. B. Riba (Eds.), *Review of Psychiatry: Vol. 11*. Washington, D.C.: American Psychiatric Press.

Kennedy, S. H., Kaplan, A. S., & Garfinkel, P. E. (1992). Intensive hospital treatments for anorexia nervosa and bulimia nervosa. In P. J. Cooper & A. Stein (Eds.), *Feeding Problems and Eating Disorders in Children and Adolescents*. Philadelphia, PA: Harwood Academic Publishers.

Kent, R. N., O'Leary, K. D., Diament, C., & Dietz, A. (1974). Expectation biases in observational evaluation of therapeutic change. *J. Cons. Clin. Psychol., 42*(6), 774–780.

Kernberg, O. F. (1976). Object-relations theory and clinical psychoanalysis. New York: Jason Aronson.

Kernberg, O. F. (1970). Factors in the psychoanalytic treatment of narcissistic personalities. *Journal of the American Psychoanalytic Association, 19,* 451–471.

Kernberg, O. F. (1984). Severe personality disorders. New Haven, CT: Yale UP.

Kernberg, P. F. (1989). Narcissistic personality disorder in childhood. *Psychiat. Clin. N. Amer., 12*(3), 671–694.

Kessler, R. C., McGonagle, K. A., Zhao, S., Nelson, C. B., Hughes, M., Eshleman, S., Wittchen, H. U., & Kendler, K. S. (1994). Lifetime and 12-month prevalence of DSM-III-R psychiatric disorders in the United States. *Arch. Gen. Psychiat., 51,* 8–19.

Kety, S. (1974). Biochemical and neurochemical effects of electroconvulsive shock. In M. Fink, S. Kety, J. McGaugh et al. (Eds.), *Psychobiology of convulsive therapy*. Washington, DC: Winston & Sons.

Kety, S. S. (1974). From rationalization to reason. *Amer. J. Psychiat., 131*(9), 957–963.

Kety, S. S. (1988). Schizophrenic illness in the families of schizophrenic adoptees: Findings from the Danish national sample. *Schizo. Bull., 14*(2), 217–222.

Kety, S. S., Rosenthal, D., Wender, P. H., Schulsinger, F., & Jacobsen, B. (1978). The biologic and adoptive families of adopted individuals who become schizophrenic: Prevalence of mental illness and other characteristics. In L. C. Wynne, R. L. Cromwell, & S. Matthysse (Eds.), The nature of schizophrenia: New approaches to research and treatment. New York: Wiley.

Kety, S. S., Rosenthal, D., Wender, P. H. et al. (1968). The types and prevalence of mental illness in the biological and adoptive families of schizophrenics. *J. Psychiat. Res., 6,* 345–362.

Kety, S. S., Rosenthal, D., Wender, P. H. et al. (1975). Mental illness in the biological and adoptive families of adopted individuals who became schizophrenic: A preliminary report based on psychiatric interviews. In R. R. Fieve, D. Rosenthal, & H. Brill (Eds.), Genetic research in psychiatry. Baltimore: Johns Hopkins Univ.

Keuthen, N. (1980). Subjective probability estimation and somatic structures in phobic individuals. Unpublished manuscript. State University of New York at Stony Brook.

Keys, A., Brozek, J., Henschel, A., Mickelson, O., & Taylor, H. L. (1950). The biology of human starvation. Minneapolis: Univ. Minnesota.

Khalsa, H., Shaner, A., Anglin, M., & Wang, J. (1991). Prevalence of substance abuse in a psychiatric evaluation unit. *Drug Alc. Dep., 28*(3), 215–223.

Khanna, R., Das, A., & Damodaran, S. S. (1992). Prospective study of neuroleptic-induced dystonia in mania and schizophrenia. *Amer. J. Psychiat., 149*(4), 511–513.

Khantzian, E. J. (1985). The self-medication hypothesis of addictive disorders: Focus on heroin and cocaine dependence. *Amer. J. Psychiat., 142*(11), 1259–1264.

Kiecolt-Glaser, J. K., Dura, J. R., Speicher, C. E., Trask, O. J., & Glaser, R. (1991). Spousal caregivers of dementia victims: Longitudinal changes in immunity and health. *Psychosom. Med., 53,* 345–362.

Kiecolt-Glaser, J. K., Garner, W., Speicher, C., Penn, G. M., Holliday, J., & Glaser, R. (1984). Psychosocial modifiers of immunocompetence in medical students. *Psychosom. Med., 46,* 7–14.

Kiecolt-Glaser, J. K., & Glaser, R. (1988). Psychological influences on immunity: Implications for AIDS. *Amer. Psychol., 43*(11), 892–898.

Kiecolt-Glaser, J. K., & Glaser, R. (1992). Psychoneuro-immunology: Can psychological interventions modulate immunity? *J. Cons. Clin. Psychol., 60,* 569–575.

Kiecolt-Glaser, J. K., Glaser, R., Shuttleworth, E. C., Dyer, C. S., Ogrocki, B. S., & Speicher, C. E. (1987). Chronic stress and immunity in family caregivers of Alzheimer's Disease victims. *Psychosom. Med., 49,* 523–535.

Kiecolt-Glaser, J. K., Ricker, D., Messick, G., Speicher, C. E., Garner, W., & Glaser, R. (1984). Urinary cortisol, cellular immunocompetency and loneliness in psychiatric patients. *Psychosom. Med., 46,* 15–24.

Kiecolt-Glaser, J. K., et al. (1991). Spousal caregivers of dementia victims: Longitudinal changes in immunity and health. *Psychosomatic Medicine, 53*(4), 345–362.

Kienhorst, C. W. M., Wolters, W. H. G., Diekstra, R. F. W., & Otte, E. (1987). A study of the frequency of suicidal behaviour in children aged 5 to 14. *J. Child Psychol. Psychiat. Allied Disc., 28*(1), 151–165.

Kiesler, C. A. (1992). U.S. Mental Health Policy: Doomed to fail. *Amer. Psychol., 47*(9), 1077–1082.

Kiesler, D. J. (1966). Some myths of psychotherapy research and the search for a paradigm. *Psychol. Bull., 65,* 110–136.

Kiev, A. (1972). Transcultural psychiatry. New York: Free Press.

Kiev, A. (1989). Suicide in adults. In J. G. Howells (Ed.), Modern Perspectives in the Psychiatry of the Affective Disorders. New York: Brunner/Mazel.

Kihlstrom, J. F. (1980). Posthypnotic amnesia for recently learned material: Interactions with "episodic" and "semantic" memory. *Cog. Psychol., 12*(2), 227–251.

Kihlstrom, J. F., Tataryn, D. J., & Hoyt, I. P. (1993). Dissociative disorders, In P. B. Sucker and H. E. Adams (Eds.) Comprehensive Handbook of Psychopathology (Second Edition). New York: Plenum.

Kilcourse, J., Gallagher-Thompson, D., Thompson, L. W., & Sheikh, J. (1991). The relationship between anxiety and depression in other adults. *J. Geriatric Psych.*

Kilmann, P. R., Sabalis, R. F., Gearing, M. L., Bukstel, L. H., & Scovern, A. W. (1982). The treatment of sexual paraphilias: A review of outcome research. *J. Sex Res., 18,* 193–252.

Kilmann, P. R., Wagner, M. K., & Sotile, W. M. (1977). The differential impact of self-monitoring on smoking behavior: An exploratory study. *J. Clin. Psychol., 33*(3), 912–914.

Kiloh, L. G. (1982). Electroconvulsive therapy. In E. S. Paykel (Ed.), *Handbook of affective disorders.* New York: Guilford.

Kilpatrick, D. G., Best, C. L., Veronen, L. J., Amick, A. E., Vileponteaux, L. A., & Ruff, G. A. (1985). Mental health correlates of criminal victimization: A random community survey. *J. Cons. Clin. Psychol., 53,* 866–873.

Kilpatrick, D. G., Saunders, B. E., Veronen, L. J., Best, C. L., & Von, J. M. (1987). Criminal victimization: Lifetime prevalence, reporting to police, and psychological impact. *Crime & Delinquency, 33,* 479–489.

Kimball, A. (1993). Nipping and tucking. In Skin Deep: Our national obsession with looks. *Psych. Today, 26*(3), 96.

Kimmel, D. C. (1988). Ageism, psychology, and public policy. *Amer. Psychol., 43*(3), 175–178.

Kimmel, E., & Kimmel, H. D. (1963). A replication of operant conditioning of the GSR. *J. Exp. Psychol., 65*(2), 212–213.

Kimzey, S. L. (1975). The effects of extended spaceflight on hematologic and immunologic systems. *J. Amer. Med. Women's Assoc., 30*(5), 218–232.

Kimzey, S. L., Johnson, P. C., Ritzman, S. E., & Mengel, C. E. (1976, Apr.). Hematology and immunology studies: The second manned Skylab mission. *Aviation, Space, & Environmental Medicine,* 383–390.

Kinard, E. M. (1982). Child abuse and depression: Cause or consequence? *Child Welfare, 61,* 403–413.

Kincel, R. L. (1981). Suicide and its archetypal themes in Rorschach record study of a male attempter. *Brit. J. Projective Psychol. & Pers. Study, 26*(2), 3–11.

King, C., Naylor, M., Hill, E., Shain, B., & Greden, J. (1993). Dysthymia characteristic of heavy alcohol use in depressed adolescents. *Bio. Psychiat., 33,* 210–212.

King, C. A., & Young, R. D. (1981). Peer popularity and peer communication patterns: Hyperactive vs. active but normal boys. *J. Abnorm. Child Psychol., 9*(4), 465–482.

King, D. J., Blomqvist, M., Cooper, S. J., Doherty, M. M. (1992). A placebo controlled trial of remoxipride in the prevention of relapse in chronic schizophrenia. *Psychopharmacology, 107*(2–3), 175–179.

King, G. A., Polivy, J., & Herman, C. P. (1991). Cognitive aspects of dietary restraint: Effects on person memory. *Inter. J. Eat. Dis., 10*(3), 313–321.

King, L. W., Liberman, R. P., & Roberts, J. (1974). An evaluation of personal effectiveness training (assertive training): A behavior group therapy. Paper presented at 31st Annual Conference of American Group Psychotherapy Association, New York.

King, M. B., & Mezey, G. (1987). Eating behaviour of male racing jockeys. *Psychological Medicine, 17,* 249–253.

King, N. J. (1993). Simple and social phobias. In T. H. Ollendick & R. J. Prinz (Eds.), Advances in clinical child psychology (Vol. 15). New York: Plenum.

King, N. J., Gullone, E., & Ollendick, T. H. (1992). Manifest anxiety and fearfulness in children and adolescents. *Journal of Genetic Psychology, 153*(1), 63–73.

King, N. J., Gullone, E., Tonge, B. J., & Ollendick, T. H. (1993). Self-reports of panic attacks and manifest anxiety in adolescents. *Behaviour Research and Therapy, 31*(1), 111–116.

King, R. D., & Raynes, N. V. (1967). Some determinants of patterns of residual care. First Congress of the International Association for the Scientific Study of Mental Deficiency.

King, T. I. (1992). The use of electromyographic biofeedback in treating a client with tension headaches. *American Journal of Occupational Therapy, 46*(9), 839–842.

Kinsey, A. C., Pomeroy, W. B., & Martin, C. E. (1948). Sexual behavior in the human male. Philadelphia: Saunders.

Kinsey, A. C., Pomeroy, W. B., Martin, C. E., & Gebhard, P. H. (1953). Sexual behavior in the human female. Philadelphia: Saunders.

Kinzie, J., Leung, P., Boehnlein, J., Matsunaga, D., et al. (1992). Psychiatric epidemiology of an Indian village: A 19-year replication study. *J. Nerv. Ment. Dis., 180*(1), 33–39.

Kipnis, D. (1987). Psychology and behavioral technology. *Amer. Psychol., 42*(1), 30–36.

Kirk, S. A., & Kutchins, H. (1992). The selling of DSM: The rhetoric of science in psychiatry. New York: Aldine De Gruyter.

Kirk, S. A., & Therrien, M. E. (1975). Community mental

health myths and the fate of former hospitalized patients. *Psychiatry, 38*(3), 209–217.

Kirkland, K., & Hollandsworth, J. G. (1980). Effective test taking: Skills-acquisition versus anxiety-reduction techniques. *J. Cons. Clin. Psychol., 48*(4), 431–439.

Kirmayer, L. J., Robbins, J. M., Dworkind, M., & Yaffe, M. J. (1993). Somatization and the recognition of depression and anxiety in primary care. *Amer. J. Psychiat., 150*(5), 734–741.

Kirmayer, L. J., Robbins, J. M., & Paris, J. (1994). Somatoform disorders: Personality and the social matrix of somatic distress. *J. Abnorm. Psychol., 103*(1), 125–136.

Kirsling, R. A. (1986). Review of suicide among elderly persons. *Psych. Rep., 59*(2, Pt. 1), 359–366.

Kivlaham, D. R., Marlatt, G. A., Fromme, K., Coppel, D. B., & Williams, E. (1990). Secondary prevention with college drinkers: Evaluation of an alcohol skills training program. *J. Cons. Clin. Psychol., 58,* 805–810.

Klaber, M. M. (1969). The retarded and institutions for the retarded. In S. B. Saranson & J. Doris (Eds.), *Psychological problems in mental deficiency.* New York: Harper & Row.

Klassen, D., & O'Conner, W. (1988). Crime, inpatient admissions and violence among male mental patients. *International Journal of Psychology and Law & Psychiatry,* (11), 305–312.

Klassen, D., & O'Conner, W. (1988). A prospective study of predictors of violence in adult mental health admissions. *Law and Human Behavior, 12,* 143–158.

Klausner, J. D., Sweeney, J. A., Deck, M. D., Haas, G. L., et al. (1992). Clinical correlates of cerebral ventricular enlargement in schizophrenia: Further evidence for frontal lobe disease. *J. Nerv. Ment. Dis., 180*(7), 407–412.

Kleber, H. D., & Gawin, F. H. (1987). "Cocaine withdrawal": In reply. *Arch. Gen. Psychiat., 44*(3), 298.

Kleber, H. D., & Gawin, F. H. (1987). "The physiology of cocaine craving and 'crashing'": In reply. *Arch. Gen. Psychiat., 44*(3), 299–300.

Kleber, H. D. et al. (1985). Clonidine in outpatient detoxification from methadone maintenance. *Arch. Gen. Psychiat., 42*(4), 391–394.

Klein, D. F. (1964). Delineation of two drug-responsive anxiety syndromes. *Psychopharmacologia, 5,* 397–408.

Klein, D. F., & Fink, M. (1962). Psychiatric reaction patterns to imipramine. *Amer. J. Psychiat., 119,* 432–438.

Klein, D. F., & Klein, H. M. (1989). The definition and psychopharmacology of spontaneous panic and phobia. In P. Tyrer (Ed.), Psychopharmacology of Anxiety. Oxford: Oxford UP.

Klein, D. F., Rabkin, J. G., & Gorman, J. M. (1985). Etiological and pathophysiological inferences from the pharmacological treatment of anxiety. In A. H. Tuma & J. Maser (Eds.), Anxiety and the anxiety disorders. Hillsdale, NJ: Lawrence Erlbaum Associates.

Klein, D. F., Ross, D. C., & Cohen, P. (1987). Panic and avoidance in agoraphobia. *Arch. Gen. Psychiat., 44,* 377–385.

Klein, D. F., Zitrin, C. M., Woerner, M. G., & Ross, D. C. (1983). Treatment of phobias: II. Behavior therapy and supportive psychotherapy. *Arch. Gen. Psychiat., 40,* 139–145.

Klein, R. G., Koplewicz, H. S., Kaner, A. (1992). Imipramine treatment of children with separation anxiety disorder: Special section: New developments in pediatric psychopharmacology. *J. Amer. Acad. Child Adol. Psychiat., 31*(1), 21–28.

Kleinman, J. E., Casanova, M. F., & Jaskiw, G. E. (1988). The neuropathology of schizophrenia. *Schizo. Bull., 14*(2), 209–216.

Klerman, G. L. (1984). Characterologic manifestations of affective disorders: Toward a new conceptualization: Commentary. *Integr. Psychiat., 2*(3), 94–96.

Klerman, G. L. (1984). History and development of modern concepts of affective illness. In R. M. Post & J. C. Ballenger (Eds.), Neurobiology of affective disorders. Baltimore: Williams & Wilkins.

Klerman, G. L., & Weissman, M. M. (1989). Increasing rates of depression. *JAMA, 261*(15), 2229–2235.

Klerman, G. L., & Weissman, M. M. (1992). Interpersonal psychotherapy. In E. S. Paykel (Ed.), Handbook of Affective Disorders. New York: Guilford.

Klerman, G. L., Weissman, M. M., Markowitz, J., Glick, I., Wilner, P. J., Mason, B., & Shear, M. K. (1994). Medication and psychotherapy. In A. E. Bergin & S. L. Garfiel (Eds.), Handbook of psychotherapy and behavior change (4th ed.). New York: Wiley.

Klerman, G. L., Weissman, M. M., Rounsaville, B., Chevron, E. (1984). Interpersonal psychotherapy of depression. New York: Basic Books.

Klimas, N., Morgan, R., Salvato, F., Van Riel, F., Millon, C., & Fletcher, M. A. (1992). Chronic fatigue syndrome and psychoneuroimmunology. In N. Schneiderman, P. McCabe, & A. Baum (Eds.), Perspectives in Behavioral Medicine: Stress and Disease Processes. Hillsdale, NJ: Lawrence Erlbaum Associates.

Klin, A. (1993). Auditory brainstem responses in autism: Brainstem dysfunction or peripheral hearing loss? *J. Autism Dev. Dis., 23*(1), 15–35.

Kline, N. S. (1958). Clinical experience with iproniazid (Marsilid). *J. Clin. Exp. Psychopath., 19*(1, Suppl.), 72–78.

Kline, N. S. (1973). A narrative account of lithium usage in psychiatry. In S. Gershon & B. Shopsin (Eds.), Lithium, its role in psychiatric research and treatment. New York: Plenum.

Kline, P. (1993). The Handbook of Psychological Testing. New York: Routledge.

Klingman, A., & Hochdorf, Z. (1993). Coping with distress and self harm: The impact of a primary prevention program among adolescents. *Journal of Adolescence, 15,* 121–140.

Klopfer, B., & Davidson, H. (1962). The Rorschach technique. New York: Harcourt, Brace.

Klosko, J. S., Barlow, D. H., Tassinari, R. B., & Cerny, J. A. (1990). A comparison of alprazolam and behavior therapy in the treatment of panic disorder. *J. Cons. Clin. Psychol., 58,* 77–84.

Kluft, R. P. (1982). Varieties of hypnotic interventions in the treatment of multiple personality. *Amer. J. Clin. Hyp., 24,* 230–240.

Kluft, R. P. (1983). Hypnotherapeutic crisis intervention in multiple personality. *Amer. J. Clin. Hyp., 26*(2), 73–83.

Kluft, R. P. (1984). Treatment of multiple personality disorder: A study of 33 cases. *Psychiat. Clin. N. Amer., 7*(1), 9–29.

Kluft, R. P. (Ed.). (1985). Childhood antecedents of multiple personality. Washington, DC: American Psychiatric Press.

Kluft, R. P. (1985). Hypnotherapy of childhood multiple personality disorder. *Amer. J. Clin. Hyp., 27*(4), 201–210.

Kluft, R. P. (1987). An update on multiple personality disorder. *J. Hosp. Comm. Psychiat., 38*(4), 363–373.

Kluft, R. P. (1987). The simulation and dissimulation of multiple personality disorder. *Amer. J. Clin. Hyp., 30*(2), 104–118.

Kluft, R. P. (1988). The dissociative disorders. In J. Talbott, R. Hales, & S. Yudofsky (Eds.), *Textbook of psychiatry.* Washington, DC: American Psychiatric Press.

Kluft, R. P. (1991). Multiple personality disorder. In A. Tasman & S. M. Goldfinger (Eds.), *American Psychiatric Press review of psychiatry* (Vol. 10). Washington, DC: American Psychiatric Press.

Kluft, R. P. (1992). Discussion: A specialist's perspective on multiple personality disorder. *Psychoanalytic inquiry, 12*(1), 139–171.

Knesper, D. J., Pagnucco, D. J. (1987). Estimated distribution of effort by providers of mental health services to U.S. adults in 1982 and 1983. *Amer. J. Psychiat., 144*(7), 883–888.

Knesper, D. J., Pagnucco, D. J., & Wheeler, J. R. (1985). Similarities and differences across mental health services providers and practice settings in the United States. *Amer. Psychol., 40*(12), 1352–1369.

Knesper, D. J., Wheeler, J. R., & Pagnucco, D. J. (1984). Mental health services providers' distribution across counties in the United States. *Amer. Psychol., 39*(12), 1424–1434.

Kobasa, S. C. (1979). Stressful life events, personality, and health: An inquiry into hardiness. *J. Pers. Soc. Psychol., 37*(1), 1–11.

Kobasa, S. C. (1982). Commitment and coping in stress resistance among lawyers. *J. Pers. Soc. Psychol., 42*, 707–717.

Kobasa, S. C. (1982). The hardy personality: Towards a social psychology of stress and health. In J. Suls & G. Sanders (Eds.), *Social psychology of health and illness.* Hillsdale, NJ: Erlbaum.

Kobasa, S. C. (1984). Barriers to work stress: II. The "hardy" personality. In W. D. Gentry, H. Benson, & C. J. de Wolff (Eds.), *Behavioral medicine: Work, stress and health.* The Hague: Martinus Nijhoff.

Kobasa, S. C. (1987). Stress responses and personality. In R. C. Barnett, L. Biener, & G. K. Baruch (Eds.), *Gender and stress.* New York: Free Press.

Kobasa, S. C. (1990). Stress resistant personality. In R. E. Ornstein, & C. Swencionis (Eds.), *The Healing Brain: A Scientific Reader.* Oxford, England: Pergamon Press.

Koegel, L. K., Koegel, R. L., Hurley, C., & Frea, W. D. (1992). Improving social skills and disruptive behavior in children with autism through self-management. *J. Appl. Behav. Anal., 25*(2), 341–353.

Koegel, R. L., Firestone, P. B., Kramme, K. W., & Dunlap, G. (1974). Increasing spontaneous play by suppressing self-stimulation in autistic children. *J. Appl. Behav. Anal., 7*, 521–528.

Koegel, R. L., & Rincover, A. (1977). Research on the difference between generalization and maintenance in extra-therapy responding. *J. Appl. Behav. Anal., 10*(1), 1–12.

Koenig, H., & Blazer, D. (1992). Epidemiology of geriatric affective disorders. *Clinics in Geriatric Medicine, 8*, 235–251.

Koenigsberg, H. W. (1993). Combining psychotherapy and pharmacotherapy in the treatment of borderline patients. In J. M. Oldham, M. B. Riba, & A. Tasman (Eds.), *Review of Psychiatry.* Washington, DC: American Psychiatric Press.

Kohn, P. M., Annis, H. M., Lei, H., & Chan, D. W. (1985). Further tests of a metamodel of youthful marijuana use. *Pers. & Individual Differences, 6*(6), 753–763.

Kohut, H. (1966). Forms and transformation of narcissism. *J. Amer. Psychoanal. Assoc., 14*, 243–272.

Kohut, H. (1977). *The restoration of the self.* New York: International Universities Press.

Kohut, H., & Wolf, E. S. (1978). The disorders of the self and their treatment: An outline. *Inter. J. Psychoanal., 59*(4), 413–425.

Kolb, B., & Whishaw, I. Q. (1980). *Fundamentals of human neuropsychology.* San Francisco: W. H. Freeman.

Kolb, B., & Whishaw, I. Q. (1990). *Fundamentals of human neuropsychology* (3rd ed.). San Francisco: W. H. Freeman.

Kolb, L. C. (1956). Psychotherapeutic evolution and its implications. *Psychiat. Quart., 30*, 1–19.

Kolb, L. C. (1992). "Research strategies for decoding the neurochemical basis of resistance to stress": Commentary. *Journal of Psychopharmacology, 6*(1), 11.

Kolff, C. A., & Doan, R. N. (1985). Victims of torture: Two testimonies. In E. Stover & E. O. Nightingale (Eds.), *The breaking of bodies and minds: Torture, psychiatric abuse, and the health professions.* New York: W. H. Freeman.

Kolodny, R., Masters, W. H., & Johnson, J. (1979). *Textbook of sexual medicine.* Boston: Little, Brown.

Kolodny, R., Masters, W. H., Kolodner, R. M., & Toro, G. (1974). Depression of plasma testosterone levels after chronic intensive marihuana use. *New Engl. J. Med., 290*(16), 444.

Komaroff, A. L., Masuda, M., & Holmes, T. H. (1986). The Social Readjustment Rating Scale: A comparative study of Negro, White, and Mexican Americans. *J. Psychosom. Res., 12*, 121–128.

Komaroff, A. L., Masuda, M., & Holmes, T. H. (1989). The Social Readjustment Rating Scale: A comparative study of Black, White, and Mexican Americans. In T. H. Holmes and E. M. David (Eds.), *Life Change, Life Events, and Illness.* New York: Praeger.

Kondziela, J. R. (1984). Extreme lithium intoxication without severe symptoms. *Hosp. Comm. Psychiat., 35*(7), 727–728.

Konig, P., & Godfrey, S. (1973). Prevalence of exercise-induced bronchial liability in families of children with asthma. *Arch. Diseases of Childhood, 48*, 518.

Konstantareas, M. M., Webster, C. D., & Oxman, J. (1979). Manual language acquisition and its influence on other areas of functioning in four autistic and autistic-like children. *J. Child Psychol. Psychiat. Allied Disc., 20*, 337–350.

Kootz, J. P., Marinelli, B., & Cohen, D. J. (1982). Modulation of response to environmental stimulation in autistic children. *J. Autism Dev. Dis., 12*, 185–193.

Kopelman, M. D. (1987). Amnesia: Organic and psychogenic. *Brit. J. Psychiat., 150*, 428–442.

Korchin, S. J. (1976). *Modern clinical psychology: Principles of intervention in the clinic and community.* New York: Basic Books.

Korchin, S. J., & Sands, S. H. (1983). Principles common to all psychotherapies. In C. E. Walker et al. (Eds.), *The handbook of clinical psychology.* Homewood, IL: Dow Jones-Irwin.

Korsten, M. A. et al. (1975). High blood acetaldehyde levels after ethanol administration. *New Engl. J. Med., 292*(8), 385–389.

Kosik, K. S. (1992). Alzheimer's disease: A cell biological perspective. *Science, 256*, 780–783.

Koson, D. F., & Dvoskin, J. (1982). Arson: A diagnostic study. *Bull. Am. Acad. Psychiat. Law, 10*, 39–49.

Korchin, S. J., & Sands, S. H. (1983). Principles common to all psychotherapies. In C. E. Walker et al. (Eds.), *The handbook of clinical psychology*. Homewood, IL: Dow Jones-Irwin.

Koss, M. P. (1990). The women's mental health research agenda: Violence against women. *Amer. Psychol., 45*(3), 374–380.

Koss, M. P. (1990, Aug.). Testimony. Senate Judiciary Committee.

Koss, M. P. (1992). The underdetection of rape: Methodological choices influence incidence estimates. *Journal of Social Issues, 48*(1), 61–75.

Koss, M. P. (1993). Rape: Scope, impact, interventions, and public policy responses. *Amer. Psychol., 48*(10), 1062–1069.

Koss, M. P., Dinero, T. E., Seibel, C., & Cox, S. (1988). Stranger and acquaintance rape: Are there differences in the victim's experience? *Psychol. Women Quart., 12*, 1–23.

Koss, M. P., & Harvey, M. R. (1987). *The rape victim*. Lexington, MA: Stephen Green.

Koss, M. P., & Harvey, M. R. (1991). *The rape victim: Clinical and community interventions*. Newbury Park, CA: Sage.

Koss, M. P., Koss, P., & Woodruff, W. J. (1991). Deleterious effects of criminal victimization on women's health and medical utilization. *Archives of Internal Medicine, 151*, 342–357.

Koss, M. P., Woodruff, W. J., & Koss, P. (1991). Criminal victimization among primary care medical patients: Prevalence, incidence, and physician usage. *Behavioral Sciences and the Law, 9*, 85–96.

Kosten, T. R. (1988). The symptomatic and prognostic implications of psychiatric diagnoses in treated substance abusers. *National Institute on Drug Abuse Research Monograph Series, 81*, 416–421.

Kosten, T. R., Rounsaville, B. J., Babor, T. F., Spitzer, R. L. et al. (1987). The dependence syndrome across different psychoactive substances: Revised DSM-III. *National Institute on Drug Abuse: Research Monograph Series, 76*, 255–258.

Kostlan, A. (1954). A method for the empirical study of psychodiagnosis. *J. Cons. Psychol., 18*, 83–88.

Kotses, H., Harver, A., Segreto, J., Glaus, K. D., et al. (1991). Long-term effects of biofeedback-induced facial relaxation on measures of asthma severity in children. *Biofeed. Self-Reg., 16*(1), 1–21.

Kovacs, M., Rush, A. J., Beck, A. T., & Hollon, S. D. (1981). Depressed outpatients treated with cognitive therapy or pharmacotherapy: A one-year follow-up. *Arch. Gen. Psychiat., 38*(1), 33–39.

Kraines, S. H., & Thetford, E. S. (1972). *Help for the depressed*. Springfield, IL: Thomas.

Kramer, F. M., Jeffery, R. W., Forster, J. L., & Snell, M. K. (1989). Long-term follow-up of behavioral treatment for obesity: Patterns of weight regain among men and women. *Inter. J. Obesity, 13*, 123–136.

Kramer, M. (1989, August 14). Cited in S. Begley, "The stuff that dreams are made of." *Newsweek*, p. 40.

Kramer, M. (1992). Cited in R. D. Cartwright, & L. Lamberg, "Crisis dreaming: Using your dreams to solve your problems." HarperCollins.

Kramer, M., Rosen, B. M., & Willis, E. M. (1973). Definitions and distributions of mental disorders in a racist society. In C. V. Willie, B. M. Cramer, & B. S. Brown (Eds.), *Racism and mental health*. Pittsburgh, PA: University of Pittsburgh Press.

Kramer, P. (1993). *Listening to Prozac—A Psychiatrist Explores Mood-Altering Drugs and the Meaning of the Self*. New York: Viking.

Krantz, D. S., & Glass, D. C. (1984). Personality, behavior, patterns, and physical illness: Conceptual and methodological issues. In W. D. Gentry (Ed.), *Handbook of behavioral medicine*. New York: Guilford.

Krantz, L. (1992). *What the Odds Are*. New York: Harper Perennial.

Kratochwill, T. R. (1992). Single-case research design and analysis: An overview. In T. R. Kratochwill, & J. R. Levin (Eds.), *Single-Case Research Design and Analysis: New Directions for Psychology and Education*. Hillsdale, NJ: Lawrence Erlbaum Associates.

Kratochwill, T. R., Mott, S. E., & Dodson, C. L. (1984). Case study and single-case research in clinical and applied psychology. In A. S. Bellack & M. Hersen (Eds.), *Research methods in clinical psychology*. New York: Pergamon.

Krauss, M. W., Seltzer, M. M., Goodman, S. J. (1992). Social support networks of adults with mental retardation who live at home. *Amer. J. Ment. Retard., 96*(4), 432–441.

Kreisman, D., Blumenthal, R., Borenstein, M., Woerner, M. et al. (1988). Family attitudes and patient social adjustment in a longitudinal study of outpatient schizophrenics receiving low-dose neuroleptics: The family's view. Meeting of the Society for Life History Research on Psychopathology (1984, Baltimore, Maryland). *Psychiatry, 51*(1), 3–13.

Kresin, D. (1993). Medical aspects of inhibited sexual desire disorder. In W. O'Donohue and J. Geer (eds.), *Handbook of sexual dysfunctions*. Boston: Allyn and Bacon.

Kriechman, A. M. (1987). Siblings with somatoform disorders in childhood and adolescence. *J. Amer. Acad. Child Adol. Psychiat., 26*(2), 226–231.

Kringlen, E. (1965). Obsessional neurosis: A long-term follow-up. *Brit. J. Psychiat., 111*, 709–722.

Kripke, D. F., & Robinson, D. (1985). Ten years with a lithium group. *McLean Hosp. J., 10*, 1–11.

Krishnan, K. R. R., Swartz, M. S., Larson, M. J., & Santoliquido, G. (1984). Funeral mania in recurrent bipolar affective disorders: Reports of three cases. *J. Clin. Psychiat., 45*, 310–311.

Kron, L., Katz, J. L., Gorzynski, & Weiner, H. (1978). Hyperactivity in anorexia nervosa: A fundamental clinical feature. *Comprehen. Psychiat., 19*(5), 433–440.

Krupp, P., & Barnes, P. (1992). Clozapine-associated agranulocytosis: Risk and aetiology. *Brit. J. Psychiat., 160*(suppl. 17), 38–40.

Krystal, H. (1968). *Massive psychic trauma*. New York: International Universities Press.

Kuch, K., & Cox, B. J. (1992). Symptoms of PTSD in 124 survivors of the Holocaust. *Amer. J. Psychiat., 149*(3), 337–340.

Kuehlwein, K. T., & Rosen, H. (Eds.) (1993). *Cognitive Therapies in Action*. San Francisco: Jossey-Bass Publishers.

Kuhn, R. (1958). The treatment of depressive states with G-22355 (imipramine hydrochloride). *Amer. J. Psychiat., 115*, 459–464.

Kuhn, T. S. (1962). *The structure of scientific revolutions*. Chicago: Univ. Chicago.

Kulick, A. R., Pope, H. G., & Keck, P. E. (1990). Lycanthropy and self-identification. *J. Nerv. Ment. Dis., 178*(2), 134–137.

Kumar, V. (1993). Editorial Commentary on two studies reporting controlled clinical trials of the use of tacrine in Alzheimer's disease. *Alzheimer's Disease and Related Disorders, 7*, 113.

Kuriansky, J. B. (1988). Personality style and sexuality. In R. A. Brown & J. R. Field (Eds.), *Treatment of Sexual Problems in Individual and Couples Therapy.* Costa Mesa, CA: PMA Publishing Corp.

Kurlander, H., Miller, W., & Seligman, M. E. P. (1974). *Learned helplessness, depression, and prisoner's dilemma.* Unpublished manuscript.

Kushner, H. L. (1985). Women and suicide and historical perspective. *Signs, 10*(3), 537–552.

Kushner, M. G., Riggs, D. S., Foa, E. B., & Miller, S. M. (1992). Perceived controllability and the development of posttraumatic stress disorder (PTSD) in crime victims. *Behav. Res. Ther., 31*(1), 105–110.

Kutcher, S., Kachur, E., Marton, P., Szalai, J., et al. (1992). Substance abuse among adolescents with chronic mental illnesses: A pilot study of descriptive and differentiating features. *Canad. J. Psychiat., 37*(6), 428–431.

Labbate, L. A., & Snow, M. P. (1992). Posttraumatic stress symptoms among soldiers exposed to combat in the Persian Gulf. *Hospital & Community Psychiatry, 43*(8), 831–833.

Labouvie, E. W., & McGee, C. R. (1986). Relation of personality to alcohol and drug use in adolescence. *J. Cons. Clin. Psychol., 54*(3), 289–293.

Lachman, S. J. (1972). *Psychosomatic disorders: A behavioristic interpretation.* New York: Wiley.

Lachner, G., & Engel, R. R. (1994). Differentiation of dementia and depression by memory tests: A meta-analysis. *J. Nerv. Ment. Dis., 182*(1), 34–39.

Lacks, P. (1984). Bender *Gestalt screening for brain dysfunction.* New York: Wiley.

Lader, M. (1992). Hazards of benzodiazepine treatments of anxiety. In G. D. Burrows, S. M. Roth, & R. Noyes, Jr., *Handbook of Anxiety* (Vol. 5). Oxford: Elsevier.

Lafferty, P., Beutler, L. E., & Crago, M. (1991). Differences between more and less effective psychotherapists: A study of select therapist variables. *J. Cons. Clin. Psychol., 57*, 76–80.

Lahey, B. B., Hartdagen, S. E., Frick, P. J., McBurnett, K., et al. (1988). Conduct disorder: Parsing the confounded relation to parental divorce and antisocial personality. *J. Abnorm. Psychol., 97*(3), 334–337.

Lahey, B. B., Piancentini, J. C., McBurnett, K., Stone, P., et al. (1988). Psychopathology in the parents of children with conduct disorder and hyperactivity. *J. Amer. Acad. Child and Adol. Psychiat., 27*(2), 163–170.

Lai, J. Y., & Linden, W. (1992). Gender, anger expression style, and opportunity for anger release determine cardiovascular reaction to and recovery from anger provocation. *Psychosom. Med., 54*, 297–310.

Laing, R. D. (1959). *The divided self: An existential study in sanity and madness.* London: Tavistock Publications.

Laing, R. D. (1964). *The divided self* (2nd ed.). London: Pelican.

Laing, R. D. (1967). *The politics of experience.* New York: Pantheon.

Lam, R. W., Berkowitz, A. L., Berga, S. L., Clark, C. M. et al. (1990). Melatonin suppression in bipolar and unipolar mood disorders. *Psychiat. Res., 33*(2), 129–134.

Lamb, H. R. (1979). Roots of neglect of the long-term mentally ill. *Psychiatry, 42*(3), 201–207.

Lamb, H. R. (1979). The new asylums in the community. *Arch. Gen. Psychiat., 36*(2), 129–134.

Lamb, H. R. (1982). *Treating the long-term mentally ill.* San Francisco: Jossey-Bass.

Lamb, H. R. (1988). When the chronically mentally ill need acute hospitalization: Maximizing its benefits. *Psychiat. Ann., 18*(7), 426–430.

Lamb, H. R., & Goertzel, V. (1977). The long-term patient in the era of community treatment. *Arch. Gen. Psychiat., 34*(6), 679–682.

Lambert, M. J., & Bergin, A. E. (1992). Achievements and limitations of psychotherapy research. In D. K. Freedheim (Ed.), *History of psychotherapy: A century of change.* Washington, DC: American Psychological Association.

Lambert, M. J., & Bergin, A. E. (1994). The effectiveness of psychotherapy. In A. E. Bergin, & S. L. Garfield (Eds.), *Handbook of psychotherapy and behavioral change* (4th ed.). New York: Wiley.

Lambert, M. J., & Hill, C. E. (1994). Assessing psychotherapy outcomes and processes. In A. E. Bergin & S. L. Garfiel (Eds.), *Handbook of psychotherapy and behavior change* (4th ed.). New York: Wiley.

Lambert, M. J., Shapiro, D. A., & Bergin, A. E. (1986). The effectiveness of psychotherapy. In S. L. Garfield & A. E. Bergin (Eds.), *Handbook of psychotherapy and behavioral change* (3rd ed.). New York: Wiley.

Lambert, M. J., Weber, F. D., & Sykes, J. D. (1993, April). Psychotherapy versus placebo. Poster presented at the annual meetings of the Western Psychological Association, Phoenix.

Lamberti, J. S., & Cummings, S. (1992). Hands-on restraints in the treatment of multiple personality disorder. *Hosp. Comm. Psychiat., 43*(3), 283–284.

Lancaster, N. P., Steinhert, R. R., & Frost, I. (1958). Unilateral electroconvulsive therapy. *J. Ment. Sci., 104*, 221–227.

Landau, P., & Paulson, T. (1977). Cope: A wilderness workshop in AT. In R. E. Alberti (Ed.), *Assertiveness: Innovation application, issues.* San Luis Obispo, CA: Impact.

Landesman-Dwyer, S. (1981). Living in the community. *Amer. J. Ment. Def., 86*(3), 223–234.

Landry, D., Zhao, K., Yang, G., Glickman, M., & Georgiadis, T. (1993). Antibody-catalyzed degredation of cocaine. *Science, 259*, 1899–1901.

Lang, A. R. (1983). Addictive personality: A viable construct? In P. K. Levison, D. R. Gerstein, & D. R. Maloff (Eds.), *Commonalities in substance abuse and habitual behavior.* Lexington, MA: Lexington.

Lang, P. J. (1985). The cognitive psychophysiology of emotion: Fear and anxiety. In A. H. Tuma & J. D. Maser (Eds.), *Anxiety and anxiety disorders.* Hillsdale, NJ: Erlbaum.

Lang, P. J., & Lazovik, A. D. (1963). Experimental desensitization of a phobia. *J. Abnorm. Soc. Psychol., 66*, 519–525.

Lang, P. J., Melamed, B. G., & Hart, J. D. (1970). A psychophysiological analysis of fear modification using an automated desensitization procedure. *J. Abnorm. Psychol., 76*, 220–234.

Langer, E. J. (1983). *The psychology of control.* Beverly Hills, CA: Sage.

Langer, S. Z., & Raisman, R. (1983). Binding of (3H) imipramine and (3H) desipramine as biochemical tools for studies in depression. *Neuropharmacology, 22,* 407–413.

Langevin, R. (1992). Biological factors contributing to paraphilic behavior. *Psychiat. Ann., 22*(6), 307, 309–314.

Langevin, R., Bain, J., Wortzman, G., Hucker, S., et al. (1988). Sexual sadism: Brain, blood, and behavior. *Annals of the New York Academy of Sciences, 528,* 163–171.

Langwieler, G., & Linden, M. (1993). Therapist individuality in the diagnosis and treatment of depression. *J. Affect. Dis., 27,* 1–12.

Lann, I. S., Moscicki, E. K., & Maris, R. (Eds.). (1989). *Strategies for studying suicide and suicidal behavior.* New York: Guilford.

Lanyon, R. I. (1984). Personality assessment. *Annu. Rev. Psychol., 35,* 667–701.

Lapierre, Y. D. (1991). Controlling acute episodes of depression. *International Clinical Psychopharmacology, 6*(Suppl. 2), 23–35.

Lapouse, R., & Monk, M. A. (1959). Fears and worries in a representative sample of children. *Amer. J. Orthopsychiat., 29,* 803–818.

Lapouse, R., & Monk, M. A. (1964). Behavior deviations in a representative sample of children. *Amer. J. Orthopsychiat., 29,* 803–818.

Laraia, M. T., Stuart, G. W., & Best, C. L. (1989). Behavioral treatment of panic-related disorders: A review. *Arch. Psychiat. Nursing, 3*(3), 125–133.

Largo, R. H., Pfister, D., Molinari, L., et al. (1989). Significance of prenatal, perinatal and postnatal factors in the development of AGA preterm infants at five to seven years. *Dev. Med. Child Neurol., 32,* 30–45.

Larsen, R. J. (1993). *Emotional regulation in everyday life: An experience sampling study.* Paper presented at the annual meeting of the American Psychology Association, Toronto.

Lasch, C. (1978). *The Culture of Narcissism: American Life in an Age of Diminishing Expectations.* New York: Norton.

Last, J. M., & Bruhn, A. R. (1985). Distinguishing child diagnostic types with early memories. *J. Pers. Assess., 49*(2), 187–192.

Laube, J. J. (1990). Why group therapy for bulimia? *Inter. J. Group Psychother., 40*(2), 169–1987.

Lawrence, C. (1987). An integrated spiritual and psychological growth model in the treatment of narcissism. *Journal of Psychology & Theology, 15*(3), 205–213.

Lawrence, G. H. (1986). Using computers for the treatment of psychological problems. *Computers in Human Behav., 2*(1), 43–62.

Lazarus, A. A. (1965). The treatment of a sexually inadequate man. In L. P. Ullman & L. Krasner (Eds.), *Case studies in behavior modification.* New York: Holt, Rinehart, & Winston.

Lazarus, A. A. (1971). *Behavior therapy and beyond.* New York: McGraw-Hill.

Lazarus, A. A. (1987). The need for technical eclecticism: Science, breadth, depth, and specificity. In J. K. Zeig (Ed.), *The evolution of psychotherapy.* New York: Brunner/Mazel.

Lazarus, R. S. (1990). Stress, coping, and illness. In H. S. Friedman (Ed.), *Personality and disease.* New York: Wiley.

Lazarus, R. S., & Cohen, J. B. (1977). Environmental stress. In I. Altman & J. F. Wohlwill (Eds.), *Human behavior and the environment: Current theory and research.* New York: Plenum.

Lazarus, R. S., & Folkman, S. (1984). *Stress, appraisal, and coping.* New York: Springer.

Leadbetter, R., Shutty, M. S., Pavalonis, D., Vieweg, V. (1992). Clozapine-induced weight gain: Prevalence and clinical relevance. *Amer. J. Psychiat., 149*(1), 68–72.

Leaman, T. L. (1992). *Healing the Anxiety Diseases.* New York: Plenum.

Lebegue, B. (1991). Paraphilias in U.S. pornography titles: "Pornography made me do it" (Ted Bundy). *Bulletin of the American Academy of Psychiatry and the Law, 19*(1), 43–48.

Lebell, M. B., Marder, S. R., Mintz, J., Mintz, L. I., Tompson, M., Wirshing, W., Johnston-Cronk, K., McKenzie, J. (1993). Patients' perceptions of family emotional climate and outcome in schizophrenia. *Brit. J. Psychiat., 162,* 751–754.

Ledoux, S., Choquet, M., & Manfredi, R. (1993). Associated factors for self-reported binge eating among male and female adolescents. *Journal of Adolescence, 16,* 75–91.

Lee, D. E. (1985). Alternative self-destruction. *Percep. & Motor Skills, 61*(3, Part 2), 1065–1066.

Lee, P. W. H., Lieh-Mak, Tu, K. K., & Spinks, J. A. (1993). Coping strategies of schizophrenic patients and their relationship to outcome. *Brit. J. Psychiat., 163,* 177–182.

Lee, T., & Seeman, P. (1980). Elevation of brain neuroleptic/dopamine receptors in schizophrenia. *Amer. J. Psychiat., 137,* 191–197.

Leenaars, A. A. (1989). *Suicide notes: Predictive clues and patterns.* New York: Human Sciences.

Leenaars, A. A. (1991). Suicide in the young adult. In A. A. Leenaars (Ed.), *Life span perspectives of suicide: Time-lines in the suicide process.* New York: Plenum.

Leenaars, A. A. (1992). Suicide notes, communication, and ideation. In R. W. Maris, A. L. Berman, J. T. Maltsberger, & R. I. Yufit (Eds.), *Assessment and prediction of suicide.* New York: Guilford.

Leenaars, A. A., & Lester, D. (1990). What characteristics of suicide notes are salient for people to allow perception of a suicide note as genuine? *Death Studies, 14*(1), 25–30.

Leenaars, A. A., & Lester, D. (1992). Facts and myths of suicide in Canada and the United States. *J. Soc. Psychol., 132*(6), 787–789.

Leff, J. (1992). Schizophrenia and similar conditions. *International Journal of Mental Health, 21*(2), 25–40.

Leff, J., & Vaughn, C. (1976, Nov.). Schizophrenia and family life. *Psychol. Today,* 13–18.

Lefkowitz, M. M., Eron, L. D., Walder, L. O., & Huesmann, L. R. (1977). *Growing up to be violent: A longitudinal study of the development of aggression.* New York: Pergamon.

Lehman, R. S. (1991). *Statistics and Research Design in the Behavioral Sciences.* Belmont, CA: Wadsworth.

Lehmann, H. E. (1967). Psychiatric disorders not in standard nomenclature. In A. M. Freedman, H. I. Kaplan, & H. S. Kaplan (Eds.), *Comprehensive textbook of psychiatry.* Baltimore: Williams & Wilkins.

Lehmann, H. E. (1985). Current perspectives on the biology of schizophrenia. In M. N. Menuck & M. V. Seeman. *New perspectives in schizophrenia.* New York: Macmillan.

Lehrer, P. M., Carr, R., Sargunaraj, D., & Woolfolk, R. L. (1993). Differential effects of stress management therapies in behavioral medicine. In P. M. Lehrer & R. L. Woolfolk (Eds.), *Principles and Practice of Stress Management* (2nd ed.). New York: Guilford.

Lehrer, P. M., & Woolfolk, R. L. (1993). *Principles and Practice of Stress Management* (2nd ed.). New York: Guilford.

Leitenberg, H., & Callahan, E. J. (1973). Reinforced practice and reduction of different kinds of fears in adults and children. *Behav. Res. Ther., 11*(1), 19–30.

Leitenberg, H., Rosen, J. C., Wolf, J., Vara, L. S., Detzer, M. J., & Srebnik, D. (1993). Comparison of cognitive-behavior therapy and desipramine in the treatment of bulimia nervosa. *Behav. Res. Ther., 32*(1), 37–45.

Leitenberg, H., Yost, L. W., & Carroll-Wilson, M. (1986). Negative cognitive errors in children: Questionnaire development, normative data, and comparisons between children with and without self-reported symptoms of depression, low self-esteem, and evaluation anxiety. *J. Cons. Clin. Psychol., 54*, 528–536.

Leland, H. (1991). Adaptive behavior scales. In J. L. Matson & J. A. Mulick (Eds.), *Handbook of mental retardation.* New York: Pergamon.

Lenzenweger, M. F., Cornblatt, B. A., & Putnick, M. (1991). Schizotypy and sustained attention. *J. Abnorm. Psychol., 100*(1), 84–89.

Leon, G. R. (1977). *Case histories of deviant behavior* (2nd ed.). Boston: Allyn & Bacon.

Leon, G. R. (1984). *Case histories of deviant behavior* (3rd ed.). Boston: Allyn & Bacon.

Leon, R. L., Bowden, C. L., & Faber, R. A. (1989). The psychiatric interview, history, and mental status examination. In H. I. Kaplan & B. J. Sadock (Eds.), *Comprehensive textbook of psychiatry* (Vol. 1, 5th ed.). Baltimore: Williams & Wilkins.

Leonard, B. E. (1992). Effects of pharmacological treatments on neurotransmitter receptors in anxiety disorders. In G. D. Burrows, S. M. Roth, & R. Noyes, Jr., *Handbook of Anxiety* (Vol. 5). Oxford: Elsevier.

Leonard, H. L., Lenane, M. C., Swedo, S. E., Rettew, D. C., et al. (1991). A double-blind comparison of climipramine and desipramine treatment of severe onychophagia (nail biting). *Arch. Gen. Psychiat., 48*(9), 821–827.

Lepine, J. P., Chignon, J. M., & Teherani, M. (1993). Suicide attempts in patients with panic disorder. *Arch. Gen. Psychiat., 50*, 144–149.

Lerner, H. D. (1986). Current developments in the psychoanalytic psychotherapy of anorexia nervosa and bulimia nervosa. *Clin. Psychologist, 39*(2), 39–43.

Lerner, H. D., & Lerner, P. M. (Eds.). (1988). *Primitive mental states and the Rorschach.* Madison, CT: Inter. Univ. Press.

Leroux, J. A. (1986). Suicidal behavior and gifted adolescents. *Roeper Rev., 9*(2), 77–79.

LeSage, J., & Zwygart-Stauffacher, M. (1988). Detection of medication misuse in elders. *Generations, 12*(4), 32–36.

Leshner, A. (1991). *Treatment. National Conference on Drug Abuse Research and Practice Conference Highlights.* Rockville, MD: NIDA.

Leshner, A. I., et al. (1992). *Outcasts on the main street: Report of the Federal Task Force on Homelessness and Severe Mental Illness.* Washington, DC: Interagency Council on the Homeless.

Lesieur, H. R., & Blume, S. B. (1991). Evaluation of patients treated for pathological gambling in a combined alcohol, substance abuse and pathological gambling treatment unit using the Addiction Severity Index. *British Journal of Addiction, 86*(8), 1017–1028.

Leslie, A. M., & Frifth, U. (1988). Autistic children's understanding of seeing, knowing and believing. *British Journal of Developmental Psychology, 6*, 315–324.

Lesse, S. (1988). The range of therapies with severely depressed suicidal patients. In S. Lesse (Ed.), *What we know about suicidal behavior and how to treat it.* Northvale, NJ: Jason Aronson Inc.

Lester, D. (1972). Myth of suicide prevention. *Comprehen. Psychiat., 13*(6), 555–560.

Lester, D. (1974). The effects of suicide prevention centers on suicide rates in the United States. *Pub. Hlth. Rep., 89*, 37–39.

Lester, D. (1985). Accidental deaths as disguised suicides. *Psych. Rep., 56*(2), 626.

Lester, D. (1985). The quality of life in modern America and suicide and homicide rates. *J. Soc. Psychol., 125*(6), 779–780.

Lester, D. (1989). *Can we prevent suicide?* New York: AMS Press.

Lester, D. (1991). Do suicide prevention centers prevent suicide? *Homeostasis in Health and Disease, 33*(4), 190–194.

Lester, D. (1991). The etiology of suicide and homicide in urban and rural America. *Journal of Rural Community Psychology, 12*(1), 15–27.

Lester, D. (1992). Alcoholism and drug abuse. In R. W. Maris, A. L. Berman, J. T. Maltsberger, & R. I. Yufit (Eds.), *Assessment and prediction of suicide.* New York: Guilford.

Lester, D. (1992). Suicide and disease. *Loss, Grief & Care, 6*(2–3), 173–181.

Lester, D. (1993). Suicidal behavior in bipolar and unipolar affective disorders: A meta-analysis. *J. Affect. Dis., 27*, 117–121.

Lester, D., & Yang, B. (1991). The relationship between divorce, unemployment and female participation in the labor force and suicide rates in Australia and America. *Austral. New Zeal. J. of Psychiat., 25*(4), 519–523.

Leszcz, M. (1992). Group psychotherapy of the borderline patient. In D. Silver & M. Rosenbluth (Eds.), *Handbook of Borderline Disorders.* Madison, CT: Inter. Univ. Press.

Letourneau, E., & O'Donohue, W. (1993). Sexual desire disorders. In W. O'Donohue & J. Geer (Eds.), *Handbook of sexual dysfunctions.* Boston: Allyn and Bacon.

LeUnes, A. D., Nation, J. R., & Turley, N. M. (1980). Male-female performance in learned helplessness. *J. Psychol., 104*, 255–258.

Levenkron, S. (1982). *Treating and overcoming anorexia nervosa.* New York: Scribner.

Levenson, J. L. (1985). Neuroleptic malignant syndrome. *Amer. J. Psychiat., 142*, 1137–1145.

Levenson, M. R. (1992). Rethinking psychopathy. *Theory and Psychology, 2*(1), 51–71.

Levin, B. L. (1992). Managed health care: A national perspective. In R. W. Manderscheid & M. A. Sonnenschein (Eds.), *Mental Health, United States, 1992.* Washington, D.C.: U.S. Department of Health and Human Services.

Levin, H., Chengappa, K. R., Kambhampati, R. K., Mahdavi, N., et al. (1992). Should chronic treatment-refractory akathisia be an indication for the use of clozapine in schizophrenic patients? *J. Clin. Psychiat., 53*(7), 248–251.

Levin, H. S., Mattis, S., Ruff, R. M., Eisenberg, H. M., Marshall, L. F., Tabaddor, K., High, W. M. Jr., & Frankowski, R. F. (1987). Neurobehavioral outcome following minor head injury: A three-center study. *Journal of Neurosurgery, 66,* 234–243.

Levin, S. (1968). Some suggestions for treating the depressed patient. In W. Gaylin (Ed.), *The meaning of despair.* New York: Aronson.

Levin, W. C. (1988, March). Age stereotyping: College student evaluations. *Res. on Aging,* 134–148.

Levine, M. D. (1975). Children with encopresis: A descriptive analysis. *Pediatrics, 56,* 412–416.

Levine, M. D. (1987). *How schools can help combat student eating disorders: Anorexia nervosa and bulimia.* Washington, DC: National Education Assoc.

Levine, M. D. (1988). Introduction to eating disorders: What the educator, health, and mental health professional need to know. Presentation at the Seventh National Conference on Eating Disorders of the National Anorexic Aid Society. Columbus, OH.

Levinson, D. J. (1977). Toward a conception of adult life course. In N. Smelser & E. H. Erikson (Eds.), *Themes of love and work in adulthood.* Cambridge, MA: Harvard UP.

Levinson, D. J. (1977). The mid-life transition. *Psychiatry, 40,* 99–112.

Levinson, D. J. (1984). The career is in the life structure, the life structure is in the career: An adult development perspective. In M. B. Arthur, L. Bailyn, D. J. Levinson, & H. Shepard, *Working with careers.* New York: Columbia Univ. School of Business.

Levinson, V. R. (1985). The compatibility of the disease concept with a psychodynamic approach in the treatment of alcoholism. Special Issue: Psychosocial issues in the treatment of alcoholism. *Alcoholism Treatment Quarterly, 2,* 7–24.

Levinson, D. J. (1986). Conception of adult development. *Amer. Psychol., 41*(1), 3–13.

Levis, D. J., & Carrera, R. N. (1967). Effects of 10 hours of implosive therapy in the treatment of outpatients: A preliminary report. *J. Abnorm. Psychol., 72,* 504–508.

Levitan, H. L. (1981). Implications of certain dreams reported by patients in a bulimic phase of anorexia nervosa. *Canad. J. Psychiat., 26*(4), 228–231.

Levitt, A. J., Joffe, R. T., Moul, D. E., Lam, R. W., Teicher, M. H., Lebegue, B., Murray, M. G., Oren, D. A., Schwartz, P., Buchanan, A., et al. (1993). Side effects of light therapy in seasonal affective disorder. *Amer. J. Psychiat., 150*(4), 650–652.

Levitt, E. E. (1989). *The clinical application of MMPI Special Scales.* Hillsdale, NJ: Erlbaum.

Levitt, R. (1975). *Psychopharmacology: A Biological Approach.* New York: Wiley.

Levor, R. M., Cohen, M. J., Naliboff, B. D., & McArthur, D. (1986). Psychosocial precursors and correlates of migraine headache. *J. Cons. Clin. Psychol., 54,* 347–353.

Levy, N. B. (1985). Conversion disorder. In R. C. Simons (Ed.), *Understanding human behavior in health and illness (3rd ed.).* Baltimore: Williams & Wilkins.

Levy, N. B. (1985). The psychophysiological disorders: An overview. In R. C. Simons (Ed.), *Understanding human behavior in health and illness (3rd ed.).* Baltimore: Williams & Wilkins.

Levy, S. M., & Roberts, D. C. (1992). Clinical significance of psychoneuroimmunology: Prediction of cancer outcomes. In N. Schneiderman, P. McCabe, & A. Baum (Eds.), *Perspectives in behavioral medicine: Stress and disease processes.* Hillsdale, NJ: Lawrence Erlbaum Associates.

Lewin, B. D. (1950). *The psychoanalysis of elation.* New York: Norton.

Lewinsohn, P. M. (1974). A behavioral approach to depression. In R. J. Friedman & M. M. Katz (Eds.), *The psychology of depression: Contemporary theory and research.* New York: Wiley.

Lewinsohn, P. M. (1974). Clinical and theoretical aspects of depression. In K. S. Calhoun, H. E. Adams, & K. M. Mitchell (Eds.), *Innovative treatment methods of psychopathology.* New York: Wiley.

Lewinsohn, P. M. (1975). Engagement in pleasant activities and depression level. *J. Abnorm. Psychol., 84,* 644–654.

Lewinsohn, P. M. (1975). The use of activity schedules in the treatment of depressed individuals. In C. E. Thoresen & J. D. Krumboltz (Eds.), *Counseling methods.* New York: Holt, Rinehart & Winston.

Lewinsohn, P. M. (1988). A prospective study of risk factors for unipolar depression. *J. Abnorm. Psychol., 97*(3), 251–284.

Lewinsohn, P. M., Antonuccio, D. O., Steinmetz, J. L., & Teri, L. (1984). *The coping with depression course.* Eugene, OR: Castalia.

Lewinsohn, P. M., & Arconad, M. (1981). Behavioral treatment of depression: A social learning approach. In J. F. Clarkin & H. I. Glazer (Eds.), *Depression: Behavioral and directive intervention strategies.* New York: Garland STPM.

Lewinsohn, P. M., Biglan, A., & Zeiss, A. M. (1976). Behavioral treatment of depression. In P. O. Davidson (Ed.), *The behavioral management of anxiety, depression and pain.* New York: Brunner/Mazel.

Lewinsohn, P. M., Clarke, G. N., Hops, H., & Andrews, J. (1990). Cognitive-behavioral treatment for depressed adolescents. *Behav. Ther., 21,* 385–401.

Lewinsohn, P. M., & Graf, M. (1973). Pleasant activities and depression. *J. Cons. Clin. Psychol., 41*(2), 261–268.

Lewinsohn, P. M., Rohde, P., Seeley, J. R., & Fischer, S. A. (1993). Age-cohort changes in the lifetime occurrence of depression and other mental disorders. *J. Abnorm. Psychol., 102*(1), 110–120.

Lewinsohn, P. M., Rohde, P., Teri, L., & Tilson, M. (1990, April). Presentation. Western Psychological Assoc.

Lewinsohn, P. M., & Shaffer, M. (1971). The use of home observations as an integral part of the treatment of depression: Preliminary report and case studies. *J. Cons. Clin. Psychol., 37,* 87–94.

Lewinsohn, P. M., Steinmetz, J. L., Larson, D. W., & Franklin, J. (1981). Depression related cognitions: Antecedent or consequence? *J. Abnorm. Psychol., 90*(3), 213–219.

Lewinsohn, P. M., Sullivan, J. M., & Grosscup, S. J. (1982). Behavioral therapy: Clinical applications. In A. T. Rush (Ed.), *Short-term psychotherapies for the depressed patient.* New York: Guilford.

Lewinsohn, P. M., Weinstein, M. S., & Shaw, D. (1969). Depression: A clinical-research approach. In R. D. Rubin & C. M. Franks (Eds.), *Advances in behavior therapy.* New York: Academic.

Lewinsohn, P. M., Youngren, M. A., & Grosscup, S. J. (1979). Reinforcement and depression. In R. A. Depue (Ed.), *The psychobiology of the depressive disorders.* New York: Academic.

Lewis, C. E., & Bucholz, K. K. (1991). Alcoholism, antisocial behavior and family history. *British Journal of Addiction,* *86*(2), 177–194.

Lewis, H. L., & MacGuire, M. P. (1985). Review of a group for parents of anorexics. Conference on Anorexia Nervosa and Related Disorders (1984, Swansea, Wales). *J. Psychiat. Res., 19,* 453–458.

Lewis, M. J. (1990). Alcohol: Mechanisms of addiction and re- inforcement. *Adv. Alcohol & Substance Abuse, 9,* 47–66.

Lewis, N. D. C., & Yarnell, H. (1951). Pathological firesetting (pyromania). *Nervous Mental Disorder Monographs, 82*(8).

Lewis-Fernandez, R., & Kleinman, A. (1994). *Culture, personality, and psychopathology, 103*(1), 67–71.

Lewontin, R. C., Rose, S., & Kamin, L. J. (1984). *Not in our genes.* New York: Pantheon.

Lewy, A. J., Ahmed, S., Jackson, J. M., & Sack, R. L. (1992). Melatonin shifts human circadian rhythms according to a phase-response curve. *Chronobiology International, 9*(5), 380–392.

Lewy, A. J., Sack, R. L., Miller, L. S., & Hoban, T. M. (1987). Antidepressant and circadian phase-shifting effects of light. *Science, 235,* 352–354.

Lewy, A. J., Wehr, T. A., Goodwin, F. K., Newsome, D. A., & Markey, S. P. (1980). Light suppresses melatonin secretion in humans. *Science, 210,* 1267–1269.

Lezak, M. (1976). *Neuropsychological assessment* (1st ed.). New York: Oxford UP.

Liberman, R. P. (1982). Assessment of social skills. *Schizo. Bull., 8*(1), 82–84.

Liberman, R. P. (1994). Treatment and rehabilitation of the se- riously mentally ill in China: Impressions of a society in transition. *Amer. J. Orthopsychiat., 64*(1), 68–76.

Liberman, R. P., & Corrigan, P. W. (1993). Designing new psy- chosocial treatments for schizophrenia. *Psychiatry, 56,* 238–253.

Liberman, R. P., & Eckman, T. (1981). Behavior therapy vs. in- sight-oriented therapy for repeated suicide attempters. *Arch. Gen. Psychiat., 38*(10), 1126–1130.

Liberman, R. P., & Raskin, D. E. (1971). Depression: A behav- ioral formulation. *Arch. Gen. Psychiat., 24,* 515–523.

Liberson, W. T. (1945). Time factors in electric convulsive therapy. *Yale J. Bio. Med., 17,* 571–578.

Libet, J., & Lewinsohn, P. M. (1973). The concept of social skill with special references to the behavior of depressed persons. *J. Consult. Clin. Psychol., 40,* 304–312.

Lichtenstein, E. (1980). *Psychotherapy: Approaches and applica- tions.* Monterey, CA: Brooks/Cole.

Lichtenstein, E., & Glasgow, R. E. (1992). Smoking cessation: What have we learned over the past decade? *J. Cons. Clin. Psychol., 60,* 518–527.

Lickey, M. E., & Gordon, B. (1991). *Medicine and Mental Illness: The use of drugs in psychiatry.* New York: W. H. Freeman.

Lidz, T. (1963). *The family and human adaptation.* New York: In- ternational Univ.

Lidz, T. (1973). *The origin and treatment of schizophrenic disorders.* New York: Basic Books.

Lidz, T., Cornelison, A., & Fleck, S. (1965). *Schizophrenia and the family.* New York: International Univ.

Lidz, T., Cornelison, A., Fleck, S., & Terry, D. (1957). The in- tra-familial environment of the schizophrenic patient: II. Marital schism and marital skew. *Amer. J. Psychiat., 114,* 241–248.

Lidz, T., Cornelison, A. R., Singer, M. T., Schafer, S., & Fleck, S. (1965). In T. Lidz, S. Fleck, & A. R. Cornelison (Eds.), *Schizophrenia and the family.* New York: International Univ.

Lidz, T., Miller, J. M., Padget, P., et al (1949). Muscular atro- phy and pseudologia fantastica associated with islet cell ade- noma of the pancreas. *Arch. Neurol. Psychiat., 62,* 304–313.

Lie, N. (1992). Follow-ups of children with attention deficit hyperactivity disorder. *Acta Psychiatr. Scandin., 85,* 40.

Lieberman, J. A. (1993). Prediction of outcome in first-episode schizophrenia. *J. Clin. Psychiat., 54*(3, suppl.), 13–17.

Liebowitz, M. Stone, M., & Turkat, I. D. (1986). Treatment of personality disorders. In A. Frances & R. Hales (Eds.), *Amer- ican Psychiatric Association Annual Review* (Vol. 5). Washing- ton, DC: American Psychiatric Press.

Liebowitz, M. R. (1992). Diagnostic Issues in Anxiety Disor- ders. In A. Tasman, & M. B. Riba (Eds.), *Review of Psychiatry* (Vol. 11). Washington, DC: American Psychiatric Press.

Liebowitz, M. R., Hollander, E., Schneier, F., Campeas, R., et al. (1990). Reversible and irreversible monoamine oxidase inhibitors in other psychiatric disorders. *Acta Psychiatr. Scan- din., 82*(Suppl. 360), 29–34.

Liebowitz, M. R., Schneier, F. R., Hollander, E., & Welkowitz, L. A., et al. (1991). Treatment of social phobia with drugs other than benzodiazepines. *J. Clin. Psychiat., 52*(Suppl), 10–15.

Lifton, R. J. (1973). *Home from the war: Vietnam veterans, neither victims nor executioners.* New York: Simon & Schuster.

Lindemann, J. E., & Matarazzo, J. D. (1990). Assessment of adult intelligence. In G. Goldstein & M. Hersen (Eds.), *Handbook of psychological assessment* (2nd ed.). New York: Pergamon.

Lindesmith, A. R. (1968). *Addiction and opiates.* Chicago: Al- dine.

Lindholm, C., & Lindholm C. (1981, Jul.). World's strangest mental illnesses. *Science Digest.*

Lindner, M. (1968). Hereditary and environmental influences upon resistance to stress. Unpublished doctoral dissertation, University of Pennsylvania.

Lindsay, D. S., & Read, J. D. (1993). Psychotherapy and mem- ories of childhood sexual abuse: A cognitive perspective. *Journal of Applied Cognitive Psychology.*

Lindsay, D. S., & Read, J. D. (1994). Psychotherapy and mem- ories of childhood sexual abuse: A cognitive perspective. *Journal of Applied Cognitive Psychology.*

Lindsay, W. R., Gamsu, C. V., McLaughlin, E., Hood, E. M. et al. (1987). A controlled trial of treatments for generalized anxiety. *Brit. J. Clin. Psychol., 26*(1), 3–15.

Lindstrom, E. M., Ohlund, L. S., Lindstrom, L. H., & Ohman, A. (1992). Symptomatology and electrodermal activity as predictors of neuroleptic response in young male schiz- ophrenic inpatients. *Psychiatric Research, 42*(2), 145–158.

Linehan, M. M. (1973). Suicide and attempted suicide: Study of perceived sex differences. *Perceptual and Motor Skills, 37,* 31–34.

Linehan, M. M., & Kehrer, C. A. (1993). Borderline personal- ity disorder. In D. H. Barlow (Ed.), *Clinical Handbook of Psy- chological Disorders: A Step-by-Step Treatment Manual* (2nd ed.). New York: Guilford.

Linehan, M. M., & Nielsen, S. L. (1981). Assessment of sui- cide ideation and parasuicide: Hopelessness and social desir- ability. *J. Cons. Clin. Psychol., 49*(5), 773–775.

Lingswiler, V. M., Crowther, J. H., & Stephens, N. A. (1989). Affective and cognitive antecedents to eating episodes in bulimia and binge eating. *Inter. J. Eat. Dis., 8*(5), 533–539.

Linnoila, V. M., & Virkkunen, M. (1992). Aggression, suicidality, and serotonin. *J. Clin. Psychiat., 53*(10, Suppl.), 46–51.

Linsky, A. S., Strauss, M. A., & Colby, J. P. (1985). Stressful events, stressful conditions and alcohol problems in the United States: A partial test of Bales's theory. *J. Studies on Alcohol, 46*(1), 72–80.

Linton, M. (1979, July). I remember it well. *Psych. Today.*

Linz, T. D., Hooper, S. R., Hynd, G. W., Isaac, W. et al. (1990). Frontal lobe functioning in conduct disordered juveniles: Preliminary findings. *Arch. Clin. Neuropsychol., 5*(4), 411–416.

Lipman, R. S. et al. (1986). Imipramine and chlordiazepoxide in depressive and anxiety disorders: I. Efficacy in depressed outpatients. *Arch. Gen. Psychiat., 43*(1), 68–77.

Lipowski, Z. J. (1980). *Delirium: Acute brain failure in man.* Springfield, IL: Thomas.

Lipowski, Z. J. (1987). Somatization: Medicine's unsolved problem. *Psychosomatics, 28*(6), 294–297.

Lipsky, M. J., Kassinove, H., & Miller, N. J. (1980). Effects of rational-emotive therapy, rational role reversal, and rational-emotive imagery on the emotional adjustment of community mental health center patients. *J. Cons. Clin. Psychol., 48*(3), 366–374.

Lipton, A. A., & Simon, F. S. (1985). Psychiatric diagnosis in a state hospital: Manhattan State revisited. *Hosp. Comm. Psychiat., 36*(4), 368–373.

Lipton, H. L. (1988). A prescription for change. *Generations, 12*(4), 74–79.

Lisansky-Gomberg, E. (1993). Women and alcohol: Use and abuse. *J. Nerv. Ment. Dis., 181*(4), 211–216.

Lissner, L., Odell, P. M., D'Agostino, R. B., Stokes, J., Kreger, B. E., Belanger, A. J., & Brownell, K. D. (1991). Variability of body weight and health outcomes in the Farmingham population. *New England Journal of Medicine, 324,* 1839–1844.

Litman, R. E. (1987). Mental disorders and suicidal intention. *Suic. Life-Threat. Behav., 17,* 85–92.

Little, K. B., & Shneidman, E. S. (1959). Congruences among interpretations of psychological test and amamnestic data. *Psychology Monographs, 73*(476).

Livesley, W. J., Schroeder, M. L., Jackson, D. N., & Jang, K. L. (1994). Categorical distinctions in the study of personality disorder: Implications for classification. *J. Abnorm. Psychol., 103*(1), 6–17.

Lloyd, G. G., & Lishman, W. A. (1975). Effect of depression on the speed of recall of pleasant and unpleasant experiences. *Psychol. Med., 5,* 173–180.

Lloyd, G. K., Fletcher, A., & Minchin, M. C. W. (1992). GABA agonists as potential anxiolytics. (1992). In G. D. Burrows, S. M. Roth, & R. Noyes, Jr., *Handbook of Anxiety* (Vol. 5). Oxford: Elsevier.

Locke, S., & Colligan, D. (1986). *The Healer Within.* New York: E. P. Dutton.

Loeb, A., Beck, A. T., & Diggory, J. (1971). Differential effects of success and failure on depressed and nondepressed patients. *J. Ner. Ment. Dis., 152*(2), 106–114.

Loebel, J. P., Loebel, J. S., Dager, S. R., Centerwall, B. S., et al. (1991). Anticipation of nursing home placement may be a precipitant of suicide among the elderly. *Journal of the American Geriatrics Society, 39*(4), 407–408.

Loeber, R. (1991). Antisocial behavior: More enduring than changeable? *J. Amer. Acad. Child Adol. Psychiat., 30,* 393–397.

Loewenstein, R. J. (1991). Psychogenic amnesia and psychogenic fugue: A comprehensive review. In A. Tasman & S. M. Goldfinger (Eds.), *American Psychiatric Press review of psychiatry* (Vol. 10). Washington, DC: American Psychiatric Press.

Loftus, E. F. (1993). The reality of repressed memories. *Amer. Psychol., 48,* 518–537.

Loge, D. V., Staton, R. D., & Beatty, W. W. (1990). Performance of children with ADHD on tests sensitive to frontal lobe dysfunction. *J. Amer. Acad. Child Adol. Psychiat., 23*(4), 540–545.

Logue, A. W. (1991). *The psychology of eating and drinking.* New York: W. H. Freeman.

Loney, J. (1981). Hyperkinesis comes of age: What do we know and where do we go? *Annu. Progress in Child Psychiat. Dev.,* 598–616.

Long, G. C., & Cordle, C. J. (1982). Psychological treatment of binge eating and self-induced vomiting. *Brit. J. Med. Psychol., 55,* 139–145.

Long, J. V., & Vaillant, G. E. (1984). Natural history of male psychological health: XI. Escape from the underclass. *Amer. J. Psychiat., 141,* 341–346.

Long, P., Forehand, R., Wierson, M., & Morgan, A. (1994). Does parent training with young noncompliant children have effects? *Behav. Res. Ther., 32*(1), 101–107.

Loomer, H. P., Saunders, J. C., & Kline, N. S. (1957). A clinical and phamacodynamic evaluation of iproniazid as a psychic energizer. *Amer. Psychiat. Assoc. Res. Rep., 8,* 129.

LoPiccolo, J. (1985). Advances in diagnosis and treatment of male sexual dysfunction. *J. Sex Marital Ther., 11*(4), 215–232.

LoPiccolo, J. (1990). Treatment of sexual dysfunction. In A. S. Bellak, M. Hersen, & A. E. Kazdin (Eds.), *Inter. handbook of behavior modification and therapy* (2nd ed.). New York: Plenum.

LoPiccolo, J. (1991). Post-modern sex therapy for erectile failure. In R. C. Rosen & S. R. Leiblum (Eds.), *Erectile failure: diagnosis and treatment.* New York: Guilford.

LoPiccolo, J. (1992). Paraphilias. *Nordisk Sexologi, 10*(1), 1–14.

LoPiccolo, J., & Friedman, J. R. (1988). Broad spectrum treatment of low sexual desire: Integration of cognitive, behavioral, and systemic treatment. In S. Leiblum & R. Rosen (Eds.), *Sexual desire disorders.* New York: Guilford.

LoPiccolo, J., Heiman, J. R., Hogan, D. R., & Roberts, C. W. (1985). Effectiveness of single therapists versus co-therapy teams in sex therapy. *J. Cons. Clin. Psychol., 53*(3), 287–294.

LoPiccolo, J., & Stock, W. E. (1987). Sexual function, dysfunction, and counseling in gynecological practice. In Z. Rosenwaks, F. Benjamin, & M. L. Stone (Eds.), *Gynecology.* New York: Macmillan.

Lorand, S. (1950). *Clinical studies in psychoanalysis.* New York: International Univ.

Lorand, S. (1968). Dynamics and therapy of depressive states. In W. Gaylin (Ed.), *The meaning of despair.* New York: Aronson.

Loranger, A. W., Sartoruis, N., Andreoli, A., Berger, P., et al

(1994). The International Personality Disorder Examination. *Arch. Gen. Psychiat., 51,* 215–224.

Losonczy, M. F. et al. (1986). Correlates of lateral ventricular size in chronic schizophrenia: I. Behavioral and treatment response measures. *Amer. J. Psychiat., 143*(8), 976–981.

Lovaas, O. I. (1987). Behavioral treatment and normal educational/intellectual functioning in young autistic children. *J. Cons. Clin. Psychol., 55,* 3–9.

Lovaas, O. I., Koegel, R. L., Schreibman, L. (1979). Stimulus overselectivity in autism: A review of research. *Psychol. Bull. 86*(6), 1236–1254.

Lovaas, O. I., Koegal, R., Simmons, J. Q., & Long, S. S. (1973). Some generalization and follow-up measures on autistic children in behavior therapy. *J. Appl. Behav. Anal., 6,* 131.

Lovaas, O. I., Schreibman, L., & Koegel, R. L. (1974). A behavior modification approach to the treatment of autistic children. *J. Autism Child. Schizo., 4,*111–129.

Lovaas, O. I., Schreibman, L., Koegel, R. L., & Rehm, R. (1971). Selective responding by autistic children to multiple sensory input. *J. Abnorm. Psychol., 77,* 211–222.

Love, S. R., Matson, J. L., & West, D. (1990). Mothers as effective therapists for autistic children's phobias. *J. Appl. Behav. Anal., 23*(3), 379–385.

Lovejoy, M. (1982). Expectations and the recovery process. *Schizo. Bull., 8*(4), 605–609.

Lovett, S., & Gallagher, D. (1988). Psychoeducational interventions for family caregivers: Preliminary efficacy data. *Behav. Ther., 19,* 321–330.

Lowenstein, L. F. (1989). The etiology, diagnosis and treatment of the fire-setting behavior of children. *Child Psychiat. Human Dev., 19*(3), 186–194.

Lubetsky, M. J. (1986). The psychiatrist's role in the assessment and treatment of the mentally retarded child. *Child Psychiat. Human Dev., 16*(4), 261–273.

Lubin, B. (1983). Group therapy. In I. B. Weiner (Ed.), *Clinical methods in psychology* (2d ed.). New York: Wiley.

Luborsky, L. (1973). Forgetting and remembering (momentary forgetting) during psychotherapy. In M. Mayman (Ed.), *Psychoanalytic research and psychological issues* (Monograph 30). New York: International Univ.

Luborsky, L. (1984). *Principles of psychoanalytic psychotherapy: A manual for supportive expressive treatment.* New York: Basic Books.

Luborsky, L., Singer, B., & Luborsky, L. (1975). Comparative studies of psychotherapies. *Arch. Gen. Psychiat., 32,* 995–1008.

Ludolph, P. S., Westen, D., Misle, B., Jackson, A., et al. (1990). The borderline diagnosis in adolescents: Symptoms and developmental history. *Amer. J. Psychiat., 147*(4), 470–476.

Lundholm, J. K., & Waters, J. E. (1991). Dysfunctional family systems: Relationship to disordered eating behaviors among university women. *Journal of Substance Abuse, 3*(1), 97–106.

Luntz, B. K., & Widom, C. S. (1994). Antisocial personality disorder in abused and neglected children grown up. *Amer. J. Psychiat., 151*(5), 670–674.

Lutgendorf, S. K., Antoni, M. H., Kumar, M., & Schneiderman, N. (1994). Changes in cognitive coping strategies predict EBV-Antibody titre change following a stressor disclosure induction. *J. Psychosom. Res., 38*(1), 63–78.

Lykken, D. T. (1957). A study of anxiety in the sociopathic personality. *J. Abnorm. Soc. Psychol., 55,* 6–10.

Lyman, J. L. (1961). Student suicide at Oxford University. *Student Medicine, 10,* 218–234.

Lyness, J. M., Conwell, Y., & Nelson, J. C. (1992). Suicide attempts in elderly psychiatric inpatients. *Journal of the American Geriatrics Society, 40*(4), 320–324.

Lynn, R. (1982). National differences in anxiety and extroversion. *Progress in Exp. Pers. Res., 11,* 213–258.

Lynn, S. J., & Frauman, D. C. (1985). Group psychotherapy. In S. J. Lynn & J. P. Garske (Eds.), *Contemporary psychotherapies: Models and methods.* Columbus, OH: Merrill.

Lynn, S. J., & Rhue, J. W. (1991). *Theories of hypnosis: Current models and perspectives.* New York: Guilford.

Lyon, K. A. (1992). Shattered mirror: A fragment of the treatment of a patient with multiple personality disorder. *Psychoanalytic Quarterly, 12*(1), 71–94.

Lyon, L. S. (1985). Facilitating telephone number recall in a case of psychogenic amnesia. *J. Behav. Ther. Exp. Psychiat., 16*(2), 147–149.

Lyons, L. C., & Woods, P. J. (1991). The efficacy of rational-emotive therapy: A quantitative review of the outcome research. *Clinical Psychology Review, 11,* 357–369.

Maas, J. W. (1975). Biogenic amines and depression: Biochemical and pharmacological separation of two types of depression. *Arch. Gen. Psychiat., 32*(11), 1357–1361.

Macciardi, G., Kennedy, J. L., Ruocco, L., Guiffra, L., et al. (1992). A genetic-linkage study of schizophrenia to chromosome 5 markers in a northern Italian population. *Bio. Psychiat., 31*(7), 720–728.

MacDonald, M. L., & Schnur, R. E. (1987). Anxieties and American elders: Proposals for assessment and treatment. In L. Michelson & L. M. Ascher (Eds.), *Anxiety and stress disorders: Cognitive behavioral assessment and treatment.* New York: Guilford.

Mace, N., & Rabins, P. (1991). *The 36-hour day* (2nd ed.). Baltimore: Johns Hopkins Univ.

MacFarlane, J. W., Allen, L., & Honzik, M. P. (1954). *A developmental study of the behavior problems of normal children between 21 months and 14 years.* Berkeley & Los Angeles: Univ. California.

MacHovek, F. J. (1981). Hypnosis to facilitate recall in psychogenic amnesia and fugue states: Treatment variables. *Amer. J. Clin. Hyp., 24*(1), 7–13.

Machover, K. (1949). *Personality projection in the drawing of the human figure.* Springfield, IL: Thomas.

MacLeod, C., Mathews, A., & Tata, P. (1986). Attentional bias in emotional disorders. *J. Abnorm. Psychol., 95,* 15–20.

Macpherson, R., & Collis, R. J. (1992). Tardive dyskinesia: Patients' lack of awareness of movement disorder. *Brit. J. Psychiat., 160,* 110–112.

Madden, D. J., Lion, J. R., & Penna, M. W. (1976). Assaults on psychiatrists by their patients. *Amer. J. Psychiat., 133,* 422–425.

Madden, J. S. (1984). Psychiatric advances in the understanding and treatment of alcohol dependence. *Alcohol and Alcoholism, 19,* 339–353.

Maddi, S. R. (1990). Issues and interventions in stress mastery. In H. S. Friedman (Ed.), *Personality and disease.* New York: Wiley.

Maddock, R. J., Carter, C. S., Blacker, K. H., Beitman, B. D., Krishnan, K. R. R., Jefferson, J. W., Lewis, C. P., & Liebowitz, M. R. (1993). Relationship of past depressive episodes to symptom severity and treatment response in panic disorder with agoraphobia. *J. Clin. Psychiat., 54*(3), 88–95.

Maddox, G. L. (1988). Aging, drinking and alcohol abuse. *Generations, 12*(4), 14–16.

Madianos, M. G., & Economou, M. (1988). Negative symptoms in schizophrenia: The effect of long-term, community-based psychiatric intervention [Special Issue]. *Inter. J. Ment. Hlth., 17*(1), 22–34.

Madianos, M. G., & Madianou, D. (1992). The effects of long-term community care on relapse and adjustment of persons with chronic schizophrenia. *International Journal of Mental Health, 21*(1), 37–49.

Magura, S., Grossman, J., Lipton, D., Siddiqi, Q., Shapiro, J., Marion, I., & Amann, K. (1989). Determinants of needle sharing among intravenous drug users. *Amer. J. Pub. Hlth., 79*, 459–462.

Maher, B. (1966). *Principles of psychopathology.* New York: McGraw-Hill.

Maher, B. A. (1974). Delusional thinking and perceptual disorder. *J. Indiv. Psychol., 30*(1), 98–113.

Maher, B. A., & Maher, W. B. (1994). Personality and psychopathology: A historical perspective. *J. Abnorm. Psychol., 103*(1), 72–77.

Maher, W. B., & Maher, B. A. (1982). The ship of fools. *Amer. Psychol., 37*(7), 756–761.

Maher, W. B., & Maher, B. A. (1985). Psychopathology: I. From ancient times to the eighteenth century. In G. A. Kimble & K. Schlesinger (Eds.), *Topics in the history of psychology* (Vol. 2). Hillsdale, NJ: Erlbaum.

Mahler, M. (1965). On early infantile psychosis: The symbiotic and autistic syndromes. *J. Amer. Acad. Child Psychiat., 4*, 554–568.

Mahler, M. (1974). Symbiosis and individuation: The psychological birth of the human infant. *Psychoanalytic Study Child, 29*, 89–106.

Mahler, M. (1979). On the first three subphases of the separation-individuation process. In *Selected Papers of Margaret Mahler,* Vol. 2. New York: Jason Aronson.

Mahoney, G., Glover, A., & Finger, I. (1981). Relationship between language and sensorimotor development of Down syndrome and nonretarded children. *Amer. J. Ment. Def., 86*(1), 21–27.

Mahoney, M. J. (1977). Some applied issues in self-monitoring. In J. D. Cone & R. P. Hawkins (Eds.), *Behavioral assessment: New directions in clinical psychology.* New York: Brunner/ Mazel.

Maier, S. F. (1984). Learned helplessness and animal models of depression. *Progress in Neuropsychopharm. & Bio. Psychiat., 8*(3), 435–440.

Maier, S. F., Laudenslager, M. L., & Ryan, S. M. (1985). Stressor controllability, immune function, and endogenous opiates. In F. R. Brush & J. B. Overmier (Eds.), *Affect, conditioning and cognition: Essays on the determinants of behavior.* Hillsdale, NJ: Erlbaum.

Main, M. (1989). Adult attachment classification system. In M. Main (Ed.), *Behavior and the development of representational models of attachment: Five methods of assessment.* New York: Cambridge UP.

Maj, M., Janssen, R., Starace, G., Zaudig, M., et al. (1994). Neuropsychiatric AIDS study, Cross-sectional Phase I. *Arch. Gen. Psychiat., 51*, 39–49.

Maj, M., Satz, P., Janssen, R., Zaudig, M., et al. (1994). WHO neuropsychiatric AIDS study, Cross-sectional Phase II. *Arch. Gen. Psychiat., 51*, 51–61.

Malamud, B. (1979). *Dublin's Lives.* Farrar Straus Giroux.

Malan, D. H. (1980). *Toward the validation of dynamic psychotherapy.* New York: Plenum.

Malcolm, A. H. (1990, Jun. 9). Giving death a hand. *New York Times,* A6.

Maletzky, B. M. (1974). "Assisted" covert sensitization in the treatment of exhibitionism. *J. Cons. Clin. Psychol., 42*(1), 34–40.

Maletzky, B. M. (1974). Behavior recording as treatment: A brief note. *Behav. Ther., 5*(1), 107–111.

Maletzky, B. M. (1977). Booster sessions in aversion therapy: The permanency of treatment. *Behav. Ther., 8*(3), 400–463.

Maletzky, B. M. (1980). Assisted covert sensitization. In D. J. Cox & R. J. Daitzman (Eds.), *Exhibitionism: Description, assessment, and treatment.* New York: Garland STPM.

Malinowski, B. (1927). *Sex and repression in savage society.* New York: Humanities.

Maller, R. G., & Reiss, S. (1992). Anxiety sensitivity in 1984 and panic attacks in 1987. *Journal of Anxiety Disorders, 6*(3), 241–247.

Malloy, P., Noel, N., Longbaugh, R., & Beattie, M. (1990). Determinants of neuropsychological impairment in antisocial substance abusers. *Addictive Behaviors, 15*(5), 431–438.

Maltsberger, J. T. (1991). The prevention of suicide in adults. In A. A. Leenaars (Ed.), *Life span perspectives of suicide: Time-lines in the suicide process.* New York: Plenum.

Maltz, W., & Holman, B. (1987). *Incest and sexuality: A guide to understanding and healing.* New York: Free Press.

Manderscheid, R., & Rosenstein, M. (1992). Homeless persons with mental illness and alcohol or other drug abuse: Current research, policy, and prospects. *Current Opinion in Psychiatry, 5*, 273–278.

Manderscheid, R. W., & Sonnenschein, M. A. (1992). *Mental health, United States, 1992.* Rockville, MD: U.S. Department of Health and Human Services.

Manley, A. (1992). Comorbidity of mental and addictive disorders. *Journal of Health Care for the Poor and Underserved, 3*(1), 60–72.

Mannuzza, S., Klein, R. G., Bessler, A., Malloy, P., & LaPadula, M. (1993). Adult outcome of hyperactive boys. *Arch. Gen. Psychiat., 50*, 565–576.

Manschreck, T. C. (1985). Delusional (paranoid) disorders. In H. I. Kaplan & B. J. Sadock (Eds.), *Comprehensive Textbook of Psychiatry* (4th ed.). Baltimore: Williams & Williams.

Marcus, B. F. (1989). Incest and the borderline syndrome: The mediating role of identity. *Psychoanalytic Psychology, 6*(2), 199–215.

Marcus, M. D., Wing, R. R., & Lamparski, D. M. (1985). Binge eating and dietary restraint in obese patients. *Addictive Behaviors, 10*, 163–168.

Marfo, K., & Kysela, G. M. (1985). Early intervention with mentally handicapped children: A critical appraisal of applied research. *Journal of Pediatric Psychology, 10*, 305–324.

Margo, A., Hemsley, D. R., & Slade, P. D. (1981). The effects of varying auditory input on schizophrenic hallucinations. *Brit. J. Psychiat., 139*, 122–127.

Margo, G. M., & Newman, J. S. (1989). Venesection as a rare form of self-mutilation. *Amer. J. Psycother., 43*(3), 427–432.

Margo, J. L. (1985). Anorexia nervosa in adolescents. *Brit. J. Med. Psychol., 58*(2), 193–195.

Margolin, G., & Weinstein, C. D. (1983). The role of affect in behavioral marital therapy. In M. L. Aronson & L. R. Wolbery (Eds.), *Group and family therapy 1982: An overview.* New York: Brunner/Mazel.

Margraf, J. (1993). Hyperventilation and panic disorder: A psychophysiological connection. *Adv. Behav. Res. Ther., 15*, 49–74.

Margraf, J., Barlow, D. H., Clark, D. M., & Telch, M. J. (1993). Psychological treatment of panic: Work in progress on outcome, active ingredients, and follow-up. *Behav. Res. Ther., 31*(1), 1–8.

Margraf, J., Ehlers, A., Roth, W. T., Clark, D. B., et al. (1991). How "blind" are double-blind studies? *J. Cons. Clin. Psychol., 59*(1), 184–187.

Maris, R. W. (Ed.). (1986). *Biology of Suicide.* New York: Guilford.

Maris, R. W. (1992). How are suicides different? In R. W. Maris, A. L. Berman, J. T. Maltsberger, & R. I. Yufit (Eds.), *Assessment and prediction of suicide.* New York: Guilford.

Maris, R. W. (1992). Methods of suicide. In R. W. Maris, A. L. Berman, J. T. Maltsberger, & R. I. Yufit (Eds.), *Assessment and prediction of suicide.* New York: Guilford.

Maris, R. W. (1992). Overview of the study of suicide assessment and prediction. In R. W. Maris, A. L. Berman, J. T. Maltsberger, & R. I. Yufit (Eds.), *Assessment and prediction of suicide.* New York: Guilford.

Markman, H. J., & Hahlweg, K. (1993). The prediction and prevention of marital distress: An international perspective. *Clinical Psychology Review, 13*(1), 29–43.

Marks, I. M. (1977). Phobias and obsessions: Clinical phenomena in search of a laboratory model. In J. Maser & M. Seligman (Eds.), *Psychopathology: Experimental models.* San Francisco: W. H. Freeman.

Marks, A. (1977). Sex differences and their effect upon cultural evaluations of methods of self-destruction. *Omega, 8*, 65–70.

Marks, I. M. (1969). *Fears and phobias.* New York: Academic.

Marks, I. M. (1986). Genetics of fear and anxiety disorders. *Brit. J. Psychiat., 149*, 406–418.

Marks, I. M. (1987). Comment on S. Lloyd Williams' "On anxiety and phobia." *J. Anx. Dis., 1*(2), 181–196.

Marks, I. M. (1987). *Fears, phobias and rituals: Panic, anxiety and their disorders.* New York: Oxford UP.

Marks, I. M. (1989). Behavioural psychotherapy for generalized anxiety disorder [Special Issue]. *Inter. Rev. Psychiat., 1*(3), 235–244.

Marks, I. M., & Gelder, M. G. (1967). Transvestism and fetishism: Clinical and psychological changes during faradic aversion. *Brit. J. Psychiat., 113*, 711–730.

Marks, I. M., & Tobena, A. (1990). Learning and unlearning fear: A clinical and evolutionary perspective. *Neuroscience and Biobehavioral Reviews, 14*(4), 365–384.

Marks, I. M., & Swinson, R. (1992). Behavioral and/or drug therapy. In G. D. Burrows, S. M. Roth, & R. Noyes, Jr., *Handbook of Anxiety* (Vol. 5). Oxford: Elsevier.

Marlatt, G. A. (1977). Behavioral assessment of social drinking and alcoholism. In G. A. Marlatt & P. E. Natha (Eds.), *Behavioral approaches to alcoholism.* New Brunswick, NJ: Rutgers Center for Alcohol Studies.

Marlatt, G. A. (1985). Controlled drinking: The controversy rages on. *Amer. Psychol., 40*(3), 374–375.

Marlatt, G. A., & Gordon, J. (Eds.). (1980). Determinants of relapse: Implications for the maintenance of behavior change. In P. Davidson & S. Davidson (Eds.), *Behavioral medicine.* New York: Brunner/Mazel.

Marlatt, G. A., & Gordon, J. R. (1985). *Relapse prevention: Maintenance strategies in the treatment of addictive behaviors.* New York: Guilford.

Marlatt, G. A., Kosturn, C. F., & Lang, A. R. (1975). Provocation to anger and opportunity for retaliation as determinants of alcohol consumption in social drinkers. *J. Abnorm. Psychol., 84*(6), 652–659.

Marlett, N. J. (1979). Normalization, integration and socialization. In J. P. Das & D. Baine (Eds.), *Mental retardation for special educators.* Springfield, IL: Thomas.

Marmar, C. R., Foy, D., Kagan, B., & Pynoos, R. S. (1993). An integrated approach for treating posttraumatic stress. In J. M. Oldham, M. B. Riba, & A. Tasman (Eds.), *Review of Psychiatry,* Vol. 12. Washington, DC: American Psychiatric Press.

Marmor, J. (1987). The psychotherapeutic process: Common denominators in diverse approaches. In J. K. Zeig (Ed.), *The evolution of psychotherapy.* New York: Brunner/Mazel.

Marquis, J. N., & Morgan, W. G. (1969). *A guidebook for systematic desensitization.* Palo Alto, CA: Veterans Admin. Hospital.

Marsden, C. D. (1986). Hysteria: A neurologist's view. *Psychological Medicine, 16*(2), 277–288.

Marsh, H. W., Richards, G. E., & Barnes, J. (1986). Multidimensional self-concepts: A long-term follow-up of the effect of participation in Outward Bound program. *Personality and Social Psychology Bulletin, 12*(4), 475–492.

Marshall, M. H. (1978). Anorexia nervosa: Dietary treatment and re-establishment by body weight in 20 cases studied on a metabolic unit. *J. Hum. Nutr., 32*, 349–357.

Marshall, W. L. (1979). Satiation therapy: A procedure for reducing deviant sexual arousal. *J. Appl. Behav. Annal., 12*, 10–22.

Marshall, W. L., & Lippens, K. (1977). The clinical value of boredom: A procedure for reducing inappropriate sexual interests. *J. Nerv. Ment. Dis., 165*, 283–287.

Marston, W. M. (1917). Systolic blood pressure changes in deception. *J. Exp. Physiol., 2*, 117–163.

Martin, D. (1972). *Learning-based client-centered therapy.* Monterey, CA: Brooks/Cole.

Martin, G., & Pear, J. (1988). *Behavior modification* (3rd ed.). Englewood Cliffs, NJ: Prentice Hall.

Martin, F. E. (1990). The relevance of a systemic model for the study and treatment of anorexia nervosa in adolescents [Special Issue]. *Canad. J. Psychiat., 35*(6), 496–500.

Martin, F. E. (1985). The treatment and outcome of anorexia nervosa in adolescents: A prospective study and five year follow-up. *J. Psychiat. Res., 19*(2–3), 509–514.

Martin, J. E. (1985). Anorexia nervosa: A review of the theoretical perspectives and treatment approaches. *Brit. J. Occupational Ther.*, *48*(8), 236–240.

Martin, P. R., & Welch, L. W. (1993). Psychopharmacologic treatment of memory disorders. In T. Yanagihara & R. C. Petersen (Eds.), *Memory Disorders: Research and Clinical Practice.* New York: Marcel Dekker.

Martin, W. T. (1984). Religiosity and U.S. suicide rates, 1972–1978. *J. Clin. Psychol.*, *40*(5), 1166–1169.

Martineau, J., Barthelemy, C., Jouve, J., Muh, J. P. (1992). Monoamines (serotonin and catecholamines) and their derivatives in infantile autism: Age-related changes and drug effects. *Developmental Medicine and Child Neurology, 34*(7), 593–603.

Marx, J., (1992). Boring in on beta-amyloid's role in Alzheimer's. *Science, 255,* 688–689.

Marzuk, P. M., Tardiff, K., Leon, A. C., Stajic, M., Morgan, E. B., & Mann, J. J. (1992). Prevalence of cocaine use among residents of New York City who committed suicide during a one-year period. *Amer. J. Psychiat., 149*(3), 371–375.

Maslow, A. H. (1967). Neurosis as a failure of personal growth. *Humanitas, 3,* 153–170.

Mason, B. J., Markowitz, J. C., & Klerman, G. L. (1994). Interpersonal psychotherapy for dysthymic disorders. In G. L. Klerman & M. M. Weissman (Eds.), *New applications of interpersonal psychotherapy.* Washington, DC: American Psychiatric Association.

Mason, J. W. (1968). A review of psychoendocrine research on the pituitary-adrenal cortical system. *Psychosom. Med., 30,* 576–607.

Mason, M. A., & Gibbs, J. T. (1992). Patterns of adolescent psychiatric hospitalization: Implications for social policy. *Amer. J. Orthopsychiat., 62*(3), 447–457.

Masters, W. H., & Johnson, V. E. (1966). *Human sexual response.* Boston: Little, Brown.

Masters, W. H., & Johnson, V. E. (1970). *Human sexual inadequacy.* Boston: Little, Brown.

Masterson, J. F. (1990). Psychotherapy of borderline and narcissistic disorders: Establishing a therapeutic alliance. *J. Pers. Dis., 4*(2), 182–191.

Matarazzo, J. D. (1972). *Wechsler's measurement and appraisal of adult intelligence* (5th ed.). Baltimore: Williams & Wilkins.

Matarazzo, J. D. (1984). Behavioral health: A 1990 challenge for the health sciences professions. In J. D. Matarazzo, S. M. Weiss, J. A. Herd, N. E. Miller, & S. M. Weiss (Eds.), *Behavioral health: A handbook of health enhancement and disease prevention.* New York: Wiley.

Matarazzo, J. D. (1992). Psychological testing and assessment in the 21st century. *Amer. Psychol., 47*(8), 1007–1018.

Mather, D. B. (1987). The role of antisocial personality in alcohol rehabilitation treatment effectiveness. *Military Medicine, 152*(10), 516–518.

Mathew, N. T. (1990). Advances in cluster headache. *Neurologic Clinics, 8*(4), 867–890.

Mathew, R., Wilson, W., Blazer, D., & George, L. (1993). Psychiatric disorders in adult children of alcoholics: Data from the epidemiologic catchment area project. *Amer. J. Psychiat., 150*(5), 793–796.

Mathew, R., Wilson, W., Humphreys, D., Lowe, J., & Weithe, K. (1993). Depersonalization after marijuana smoking. *Bio. Psychiat., 33,* 431–441.

Mathews, A. (1984). Anxiety and its management. In R. N. Gaind, F. I. Fawzy, B. L. Hudson, & R. O. Pasnau (Eds.), *Current themes in psychiatry* (Vol. 3). New York: Spectrum.

Mathews, A. (1985). Anxiety states: a cognitive-behavioural approach. In B. P. Bradley & C. T. Thompson (Eds.), *Psychological applications in psychiatry.* Chichester: Wiley.

Matson, J. L., & Gorman-Smith, D. (1986). A review of treatment research for aggressive and disruptive behavior in the mentally retarded. *Appl. Res. in Ment. Retardation, 7*(1), 95–103.

Matsuyama, S. S., Jarvik, L. F., & Kumar, V. (1985). Dementia: Genetics. In T. Arie (Ed.), *Recent advances in psychogeriatrics.* London: Churchill-Livingstone.

Matthys, W., Walterbos, W., Njio, L., & Van Engeland, H. (1988). Person perception of children with conduct disorders. *Tijdschrist voor Psychiatrie, 30*(5), 302–314.

Mattick, R. P., & Newman, C. R. (1991). Social phobia and avoidant personality disorder. *International Review of Psychiatry, 3*(2), 163–173.

Mattick, R. P., Peters, L., & Clarke, J. C. (1989). Exposure and cognitive restructuring for social phobia: A controlled study. *Behav. Ther., 20*(1), 3–23.

Maurer, D. W., & Vogel, V. H. (1978). *Narcotics and narcotic addiction.* Springfield, IL: Thomas.

Maurer, R. G., & Damasio, A. R. (1982). Childhood autism from the point of view of behavioral neurology. *J. Autism Dev. Dis., 12,* 195–205.

Mavissakalian, M. R. (1990). Sequential combination of imipramine and self-directed exposure in the treatment of panic disorder with agoraphobia. *J. Clin. Psychiat., 51*(5), 184–188.

Mavissakalian, M. R. (1993). Combined behavioral and pharmacological treatment of anxiety disorders. In A. A. Leenaars (Ed.), *Suicidology.* Northvale, NJ: Jason Aronson.

Mavissakalian, M. R., Hamann, M. S., & Jones, B. (1990). Correlates of DSM III personality disorder in obsessive-compulsive disorder. *Comprehen. Psychiat., 31*(6), 481–489.

Mavissakalian, M. R., Jones, B., & Olson, S. (1990). Absence of placebo response in obsessive-compulsive disorder. *J. Nerv. Ment. Dis., 178,* 268–270.

Mavissakalian, M. R., & Michelson, L. (1983). Tricyclic antidepressants in obsessive-compulsive disorder: Antiobsessional or antidepressant agents? *J. Nerv. Ment. Dis., 171*(5), 301–306.

Mavissakalian, M. R., & Michelson, L. (1986). Agoraphobia: Relative and combined effectiveness of therapist-assisted in vivo exposure and imipramine. *J. Clin. Psychiat., 47*(3), 117–122.

Mavissakalian, M. R., & Michelson, L. (1986). Two-year follow-up of exposure and imipramine treatment of agoraphobia. *Amer. J. Psychiat., 143*(9), 1106–1112.

Mavreas, V. G., Tomaras, V., Karydi, V., Economou, M. (1992). Expressed emotion in families of chronic schizophrenics and its association with clinical measures. *Social Psychiatry and Psychiatric Epidemiology, 27*(1), 4–9.

May, J. R. (1977). A psychophysiological study of self and externally regulated phobic thoughts. *Behav. Ther., 8,* 849–861.

May, P. R. A. (1968). *Treatment of schizophrenia.* New York: Science House.

May, P. R. A., & Simpson, G. M. (1980). Schizophrenia: Evaluation of treatment methods. In H. I. Kaplan, A. M. Freedman, & B. J. Sadock (Eds.), *Comprehensive textbook of psychiatry* (Vol. 3). Baltimore: Williams & Wilkins.

May, P. R. A., & Tuma, A. H. (1964). Choice of criteria for the assessment of treatment outcome. *J. Psychiat. Res., 2*(3), 16–527.

May, P. R. A., Tuma, A. H., & Dixon, W. J. (1981). Schizophrenia: A follow-up study of the results of five forms of treatment. *Arch. Gen. Psychiat., 38*, 776–784.

May, R. (1961). *Existential psychology.* New York: Random House.

May, R. (1967). *Psychology and the human dilemma.* New York: Van Nostrand Reinhold.

May, R. (1987). Therapy in our day. In J. K. Zeig (Ed.), *The evolution of psychotherapy.* New York: Brunner/Mazel.

May, R., Angel, E., & Ellenberger, H. F. (1958). *Existence: A new dimension in psychiatry and psychology.* New York: Basic Books.

May, R., & Yalom, I. (1989). Existential psychotherapy. In R. J. Corsini & D. Wedding (Eds.), *Current psychotherapies.* Itasca, IL: Peacock.

Mays, D. T., & Franks, C. M. (1985). *Negative outcome in psychotherapy and what to do about it.* New York: Springer.

McCabe, M. P., & Delaney, S. M. (1992). An evaluation of therapeutic programs for the treatment of secondary inorgasmia in women. *Archives of Sexual Behavior, 21*(1), 69–89.

McCabe, P. M., & Schneiderman, N. (1985). Psychophysiologic reactions to stress. In N. Schneiderman & J. T. Tapp (Eds.), *Behavioral medicine: The biopsychosocial approach.* Hillsdale, NJ: Erlbaum.

McCann, D. L. (1992). Posttraumatic stress disorder due to devastating burns overcome by a single session of eye movement desensitization. *J. Behav. Ther. Exp. Psychiat., 23*(4), 319–323.

McCarthy, M. (1990). The thin ideal, depression and eating disorders in women. *Behav. Res. Ther., 28*(3), 205–215.

McCarthy, P. R., Katz, I. R., & Foa, E. B. (1991). Cognitive-behavioral treatment of anxiety in the elderly: A proposed model. In C. Salzman & B. D. Leibowitz (Eds.), *Anxiety in the elderly.* New York: Springer.

McClelland, D. C. (1979). Inhibited power motivation and high blood pressure in men. *J. Abnorm. Psychol., 88*(2), 182–190.

McClelland, D. C. (1985). The social mandate of health psychology. *Amer. Behav. Scientist, 28*(4), 451–467.

McClelland, D. C. (1993). Motives and Health. In G. G. Brannigan & M. R. Merrens (Eds.), *The Undaunted Psychologist.* New York: McGraw-Hill.

McClelland, D. C., & Kirshnit, C. (1988). The effect of motivational arousal through films on salivary immunoglobulin. *Amer. Psychology & Health, 2*, 31–52.

McClelland, R. J., Eyre, D. G., Watson, D., Calvert, G. J. (1992). Central conduction time in childhood autism. *Brit. J. Psychiat., 160*, 659–663.

McCord, W., & McCord, J. (1960). *Origins of alcoholism.* Stanford, CA: Stanford UP.

McCormack, A., Rokous, F. E., Hazelwood, R. R., & Burgess, A. W. (1992). An exploration of incest in the childhood development of serial rapists. *Journal of Family Violence, 7*(3), 219–228.

McCoy, S. A. (1976). Clinical judgments of normal childhood behavior. *J. Cons. Clin. Psychol., 44*(5), 710–714.

McCrae, R. R. (1982). Age differences in the use of coping mechanisms. *J. Gerontology, 37*, 454–460.

McCurdy, & Daro, D. (1993). Current trends: A fifty state survey. National Committee for the Prevention of Child Abuse. Washington, DC: Authors.

McEachin, J. J., Smith, T., & Lovaas, O. I. (1993). Long-term outcome for children with autism who received early intensive behavioral treatment. *Amer. J. Ment. Retard., 97*(4), 359–372.

McElroy, L. P. (1992). Early indicators of pathological dissociation in sexually abused children. *Child Abuse and Neglect, 16*(6), 833–846.

McElroy, S. L., Hudson, J. L., Pope, H. G., & Keck, P. E. (1991). Kleptomania: Clinical characteristics and associated psychopathology. *Psychol. Med., 21*(1), 93–108.

McElroy, S. L., Hudson, J. I., Pope, H. G., Keck, P. E., et al. (1992). The DSM-III—R impulse control disorders not elsewhere classified: Clinical characteristics and relationship to other psychiatric disorders. *Amer. J. Psychiat., 149*(3), 318–327.

McEvoy, J. (1992). Fragile X syndrome: A brief overview. *Educational Psychology in Practice, 8*(3), 146–149.

McFall, M., Mackay, P., & Donovan, D. (1992). Combat-related posttraumatic stress disorder and severity of substance abuse in Vietnam veterans. *Journal of Studies on Alcohol, 53*(4), 357–363.

McFarlane, A. C. (1991). Posttraumatic stress disorder. *International Review of Psychiatry, 3*(2), 203–213.

McGhie, A. (1961). Disorders of attention and perception in early schizophrenia. *Brit. J. Med. Psychol., 34*, 103–116.

McGhie, A., & Chapman, J. S. (1961). Disorders of attention and perception in early schizophrenia. *British Journal of Medical Psychology, 34*, 103–116.

McGibbon, L., Handy, S., Ballard, C. G., & Silveira, W. R. (1991). "Anorexia nervosa in adolescents of Asian extraction": Comment. *Brit. J. Psychiat., 158*, 285.

McGlashan, T. H. (1986). Schizotypal personality disorder: Chestnut Lodge follow-up study: VI. Long-term follow-up perspectives. *Arch. Gen. Psychiat., 43*(4), 329–334.

McGlashan, T. H. (1988). A selective review of recent North American long-term follow-up studies of schizophrenia. *Schizo. Bull., 14*(4), 515–542.

McGlashan, T. H. (1992). The longitudinal profile of borderline personality disorder: Contributions from the Chestnut Lodge Follow-up study. In D. Silver & M. Rosenbluth (Eds.), *Handbook of Borderline Disorders.* Madison, CT: International Universities Press.

McGlothlin, W. H., Anglin, M. D., & Wilson, B. D. (1978). Narcotic addiction and crime. *Criminology: An Interdisciplinary J., 16*(3), 293–315.

McGrady, A., & Roberts, G. (1992). Racial differences in the relaxation response of hypertensives. *Psychosom. Med., 54*(1), 71–78.

McGrath, P. J., Stewart, J. W., Nunes, E. V., Ocepek-Welikson, K., et al. (1993). A double-blind crossover trial of imipramine and phenelzine for outpatients with treatment-refractory depression. *Amer. J. Psychiat., 150*(1), 118–123.

McGrath, T., Tsui, E., Humphries, S., & Yule, W. (1990). Successful treatment of a noise phobia in a nine-year-old girl with systematic desensitization in vivo. *Educational Psychology, 10*(1), 79–83.

McGuffin, P., & Thapar, A. (1992). The genetics of personality disorder. *Brit. J. Psychiat.*, *160*, 12–23.

McGuire, D. (1982). The problem of children's suicide: Ages 5–14. *Inter. J. Offend. Ther. Compar. Crimin.*, *26*(1), 10–17.

McGuire, P. K., Shah, G. M. S., & Murray, R. M. (1993). Increased blood flow in Broca's area during auditory hallucinations in schizophrenia. *The Lancet, 342*, 703–706.

McIntosh, J. L. (1987). Suicide: Training and education needs with an emphasis on the elderly. *Gerontol. & Geriatric Educ.*, *7*, 125–139.

McIntosh, J. L. (1991). Epidemiology of suicide in the U.S. In A. A. Leenaars (Ed.), *Life span perspectives of suicide*. New York: Plenum.

McIntosh, J. L. (1992). Epidemiology of suicide in the elderly. *Suic. Life-Threat. Behav.*, *22*(1), 15–35.

McIntosh, J. L. (1992). Methods of suicide. In R. W. Maris, A. L. Berman, J. T. Maltsberger, & R. I. Yufit (Eds.), *Assessment and prediction of suicide*. New York: Guilford.

McIntosh, J. L., Hubbard, R. W., & Santos, J. F. (1985). Suicide facts and muths: A study of prevalence. *Death Studies, 9*, 267–281.

McIntosh, J. L., & Santos, J. F. (1982). Changing patterns in methods of suicide by race and sex. *Suic. Life-Threat. Behav.*, *12*, 221–233.

McIntyre, I. M., Johns, M., Norman, T. R., & Armstrong, S. M. (1990). A portable light source for bright light treatment. *Sleep, 13*(3), 272–275.

McKenry, P. C., Tishler, C. L., & Kelley, C. (1982). Adolescent suicide: A comparison of attempters and nonattempters in an emergency room population. *Clin. Pediatr., 21*, 266–270.

McKenzie, S. J., Williamson, D. A., & Cubic, B. A. (1993). Stable and reactive body image disturbances in bulimia nervosa. *Behav. Ther.*, 195–207.

McKeon, J., McGuffin, P., & Robinson, P. (1984). Obsessive-compulsive neurosis following head injury: A report of four cases. *Brit. J. Psychiat., 144*, 190–192.

McLean, A., Temkin, N. R., Dikmen, S., & Wyler, A. R. (1983). The behavioral sequelae of head injury. *Journal of Clinical Neuropsychology, 5*, 361–376.

McLean, P. D., & Hakstian, A. R. (1979). Clinical depression: Comparative efficacy of outpatient treatments. *J. Cons. Clin. Psychol., 47*(5), 818–836.

McMahon, R. J., & Wells, K. C. (1989). Conduct disorders. In E. J. Mash & R. Barkley (Eds.), *Treatment of childhood disorders*. New York: Guilford.

McNally, R. J. (1986). Behavioral treatment of a choking phobia. *J. Behav. Ther. Exp. Psychiat., 17*(3), 185–188.

McNally, R. J. (1986). Preparedness and phobias: A review. *Psychol. Bull., 101*, 283–303.

McNally, R. J., & Lukach, B. M. (1991). Behavioral treatment of zoophilic exhibitionism. *J. Behav. Ther. Exp. Psychiat., 22*(4), 281–284.

McNeal, E. T., & Cimbolic, P. (1986). Antidepressants and biochemical theories of depression. *Psychol. Bull., 99*(3), 361–374.

McNeil, E. B. (1967). *The quiet furies*. Englewood Cliffs, NJ: Prentice Hall.

McNiel, D. E., & Binder, R. L. (1991). Clinical assessment of the risk of violence among psychiatric inpatients. *Amer. J. Psychiat., 148*(10), 1317–1321.

McQuiston, J. T. (1993, February 23). Suffolk mother's illness imperils son, judge rules. *The New York Times*, pp. B1, B2.

McShane, W., & Redoutey, L. J. (1987). Community hospitals and community mental health agencies: Partners in service delivery. Annual Meeting of the Association of Mental Health Administrators (1986, San Francisco, California). *J. Ment. Hlth. Admin., 14*(2), 1–6.

Mead, M. (1949). *Male and female: A study of the sexes in a changing world*. New York: Dell.

Meador, D. M., & Osborn, R. G. (1992). Prevalence of severe behavior disorders in persons with mental retardation and treatment procedures used in community and institutional settings. *Behavioral Residential Treatment*, 7(4), 299–314.

Mednick, S. A. (1971). Birth defects and schizophrenia. *Psych. Today, 4*, 48–50.

Meehl, P. E. (1951). *Research results for counselers*. St. Paul, MN: State Dept. Education.

Meehl, P. E. (1954). *Clinical versus statistical prediction: A theoretical analysis and a review of the evidence*. Minneapolis: Univ. of Minnesota.

Meehl, P. E. (1960). The cognitive activity of the clinician. *Amer. Psychol., 15*, 19–27.

Meehl, P. E., & Dahlstrom, W. G. (1960). Objective configural rules for discriminating psychotic from neurotic MMPI profiles. *J. Cons. Psychol., 24*, 375–387.

Megargee, E. I. (1991). Criminal behavior: Historical and research foundations. In C. E. Walker (Ed.), *Clinical psychology: Historical and research foundations*. New York: Plenum.

Mehrabian, A. (1972). *Nonverbal communication*. Chicago: Aldine-Atherton.

Mehta, M. (1990). A comparative study of family-based and patient-based behavioural management in obsessive-compulsive disorder. *Brit. J. Psychiat., 157*, 133–135.

Meibach, R. C., Mullane, J. F., & Binstok, G. (1987). A placebo-controlled multicenter trial of propranolol and chlordiazepoxide in the treatment of anxiety. *Current Therapeutic Research, 41*, 65–76.

Meichenbaum, D. H. (1972). Cognitive modification of test-anxious college students. *J. Cons. Clin. Psychol., 39*, 370–380.

Meichenbaum, D. H. (1972). Examination of model characteristics in reducing avoidance behavior. *J. Behav. Ther. Exp. Psychiat., 3*, 225–227.

Meichenbaum, D. H. (1974). *Cognitive behavior modification*. Morristown, NJ: General Learning.

Meichenbaum, D. H. (1974). Self instruction methods. In F. H. Kanfer & A. P. Goldstein (Eds.), *Helping people change*. New York: Pergamon.

Meichenbaum, D. H. (1975). A self-instructional approach to stress management: A proposal for stress inoculation training. In I. Sarason & C. D. Spielberger (Eds.), *Stress and anxiety* (Vol. 2). New York: Wiley.

Meichenbaum, D. H. (1975). Enhancing creativity by modifying what subjects say to themselves. *Amer. Educ. Res. J., 12*(2), 129–145.

Meichenbaum, D. H. (1975). Theoretical and treatment implications of development research on verbal control of behavior. *Canad. Psychol. Rev., 16*(1), 22–27.

Meichenbaum, D. H. (1975). Toward a cognitive of self control. In G. Schwartz & D. Shapiro (Eds.), *Consciousness and self regulation: Advances in research*. New York: Plenum.

Meichenbaum, D. H. (1977). *Cognitive-behavior modification: An integrative approach*. New York: Plenum.

Meichenbaum, D. H. (1977). Dr. Ellis, please stand up. *Couns. Psychologist*, 7(1), 43–44.

Meichenbaum, D. H. (1986). Metacognitive methods of instruction: Current status and future prospects. *Special Services in the Schools*, 3(1–2), 23–32.

Meichenbaum, D. (1993). Stress inoculation training: A 20-year update. In P. M. Lehrer & R. L. Woolfolk (Eds.), *Principles and Practice of Stress Management* (2nd ed.). New York: Guilford.

Meichenbaum, D. H. (1993). The personal journey of a psychotherapist and his mother. In G. G. Brannigan & M. R. Merrens (Eds.), *The Undaunted Psychologist: Adventures in Research*. New York: McGraw-Hill.

Meier, M. J. (1992). Modern clinical neuropsychology in historical perspective. *Amer. Psychol.*, 47(4), 550–558.

Meissner, W. W. (1987). The diagnosis of paranoid disorders. In F. Flach (Ed.), *Diagnostics and Psychopathology*. New York: Norton.

Melcher, J. (1988). Keeping our elderly out of institutions by putting them back in their homes. *Amer. Psychol.*, 43(8), 643–647.

Melges, F. T., & Swartz, M. S. (1989). Oscillations of attachment in borderline personality disorder. *Amer. J. Psychiat.*, 146(9), 1115–1120.

Melick, M., Logue, J., & Frederick, C. (1982). Stress and disaster. In L. Goldberger & S. Breznitz (Eds.), *Handbook of Stress*. New York: Free Press.

Meltzer, H. L. (1991). Is there a specific membrane defect in bipolar disorders? *Bio. Psychiat.*, 30, 1071–1074.

Meltzer, H. Y. (1987). Biological studies in schizophrenia. *Schizo. Bull.*, 13(1), 77–111.

Meltzer, H. Y. (1991). The mechanism of action of novel antipsychotic drugs. *Schizo. Bull.*, 17(2), 263–287.

Meltzer, H. Y. (1992). Dimensions of outcome with clozapine. *Brit. J. Psychiat.*, 160(suppl. 17), 46–53.

Meltzer, H. Y. (1992). Treatment of the neuroleptic-nonresponsive schizophrenic patient. *Schizo. Bull.*, 18(3), 515–542.

Meltzer, H. Y. (1993). Clozapine: A major advance in the treatment of schizophrenia. *The Harvard Mental Health Letter*, 19(2), 4–6.

Meltzoff, J., & Blumenthal, R. L. (1966). *The day treatment center: Principles, application and evaluation*. Springfield, IL: Thomas.

Meltzoff, J., & Kornreich, M. (1970). *Research in psychotherapy*. New York: Atherton.

Melville, J. (1978). *Phobias and obsessions*. New York: Penguin.

Mendels, J. (1970). *Concepts of depression*. New York: Wiley.

Mendels, J., & Cochrane, C. (1968, May supplement). The nosology of depression: The endogenous-reactive concept. *Amer. J. Psychiat.*, 124, 1–11.

Mendels, J., & Frazer, A. (1974). Brain biogenic amine depletion and mood. *Arch. Gen. Psychiat.*, 30(4), 447–451.

Mendelson, J., Weiss, R., Griffin, M., Mirin, S., Teoh, S., Mello, N., & Lex, B. (1991). Some special considerations for treatment of drug abuse and dependence in women. In R. Pickens, C., Leukefeld, & C. Schuster (Eds.), *Improving Drug Abuse Treatment*. Rockville, MD: National Institute on Drug Abuse.

Mendes-de-Leon, C. F. (1992). Anger and impatience/irritability in patients of low socioeconomic status with acute coronary heart disease. *Journal of Behavioral Medicine*, 15(3), 273–284.

Mendlewicz, J., Fleiss, J. L., & Fieve, R. R. (1972). Evidence for X-linkage in the transmission of manic-depressive illness. *JAMA*, 222, 1624–1627.

Mendlewicz, J., Linkowski, P., & Wilmotte, J. (1980). Linkage between glucose-6-phosphate dehydrogenase deficiency in manic depressive psychosis. *Brit. J. Psychiat.*, 137, 337–342.

Mendlewicz, J., Simon, P., Sevy, S., Charon, F., Brocas, H., Legros, S., & Vassart, G. (1987). Polymorphic DNA marker on X chromosome and manic depression. *Lancet 1*, 1230–1232.

Menke, J. A., McClead, R. E., & Hansen, N. B. (1991). Perspectives on perinatal complications associated with mental retardation. In J. L. Matson & J. A. Mulick (Eds.), *Handbook of mental retardation*. New York: Pergamon.

Menninger, K. (1938). *Man against himself*. New York: Harcourt.

Menninger, W. W. (1993). Management of the aggressive and dangerous patient. *Bull. Menninger Clin.*, 57, 209.

Menzies, R. G., & Clarke, J. C. (1993). A comparison of in vivo and vicarious exposure in the treatment of childhood water phobia. *Behav. Res. Ther.*, 31(1), 9–15.

Mercer, J. R. (1973). *Labeling the mentally retarded*. Berkeley, CA: Univ. California.

Merckelbach, H., Arntz, A., de Jong, P. (1991). Conditioning experiences in spider phobics. *Behav. Res. Ther.*, 29(4), 333–335.

Mermelstein, H. T., & Holland, J. C. (1991). Psychotherapy by telephone: A therapeutic tool for cancer patients. *Psychosomatics*, 32(4), 407–412.

Merrill, J., Milner, G., Owens, J., & Vale, A. (1992). Alcohol and attempted suicide. *British Journal of Addiction*, 87(1), 83–89.

Mersch, P. P., Emmelkamp, P. M., & Lips, C. (1991). Social phobia: Individual response patterns and the long-term effects of behavioural and cognitive interventions. A follow-up study. *Behav. Res. Ther.*, 29(4), 357–362.

Merskey, H. (1986). Classification of chronic pain: Descriptions of chronic pain syndromes and definitions of pain terms. *Pain*, 3, 226.

Merskey, H. (1992). The manufacture of personalities: The production of multiple personality disorder. *Brit. J. Psychiat.*, 160, 327–340.

Messer, A. A. (1985). Narcissistic people. *Med. Aspects Human Sex.*, 19(9), 169–184.

Messer, S. B., Tishby, O., & Spillman, A. (1992). Taking context seriously in psychotherapy research: Relating therapist interventions to patient progress in brief psychodynamic therapy. *J. Cons. Clin. Psychol.*, 60(5), 678–688.

Metalsky, G. I., Joiner, T. E., Jr., Hardin, T. S., & Abramson, L. Y. (1993). Depressive reactions to failure in a naturalistic setting: A test of the hopelessness and self-esteem theories of depression. *J. Abnorm. Psychol.*, 102(1), 101–109.

Meyer, B. C., & Weinroth, L. A. (1957). Observations on psychological aspects of anorexia nervosa: Report on a case. *Psychosom. Med.*, 19, 389.

Meyer, J. E. (1984). Die Therapie der Schizophrenie in Klinik und Praxis [Inpatient and outpatient treatment of schizophrenia]. *Nervenarzt*, 55(5), 221–229.

Meyer, R. E., Murray, R. F., Jr., Thomas, F. B. et al. (1989). *Prevention and treatment of alcohol problems: Research opportunities.* Washington, DC: National Academy.

Meyer, R. G. (1992). *Abnormal behavior and the criminal justice system.* New York: Lexington Books.

Meyer, V. (1966). Modification of expectations in cases with obsessional rituals. *Behav. Res. Ther., 4,* 273–280.

Meyer, V., Levy, T., & Schnurer, A. A. (1974). Behavioral treatment of OCD. In H. R. Beech (Ed.), *Obsessional states.* London: Methuen.

Michaelson, R. (1993). Flood volunteers build emotional levees. *APA Monitor, 24*(10), p. 30.

Michels, R. (1992). The borderline patient: Shifts in theoretical emphasis and implications for treatment. In D. Silver & M. Rosenbluth (Eds.), *Handbook of Borderline Disorders.* Madison, CT: International Universities Press.

Michelson, L. K., & Marchione, K. (1991). Behavioral, cognitive and pharmacological treatments of panic disorder with agoraphobia: Critique and synthesis. *J. Cons. Clin. Psychol., 59*(1), 100–114.

Mickalide, A. D. (1990). Sociocultural factors influencing weight among males. In A. E. Andersen (Ed.), *Males with Eating Disorders.* New York: Brunner/Mazel.

Miesel, A. (1989). *The right to die.* New York: Wiley.

Miklich, D. R., Rewey, H. H., Weiss, J. H., & Kolton, S. (1973). A preliminary investigation of psychophysiological responses to stress among different subgroups of asthmatic children. *J. Psychosom. Res., 17,* 1–8.

Miklowitz, D. J. (1994). Family risk indicators in schizophrenia. *Schizo. Bull., 20*(1), 137–149.

Miklowitz, D. J., & Goldstein, M. J. (1990). Behavioral family treatment for patients with bipolar affective disorder [Special Issue]. *Behav. Mod., 14*(4), 457–489.

Miklowitz, D. J., Goldstein, M. J., Nuechterlein, K. H., Synder, K. S. et al. (1988). Family factors and the course of bipolar affective disorder. *Arch. Gen. Psychiat., 45*(3), 225–231.

Miles, C. P. (1977). Conditions predisposing to suicide: A review. *J. Nerv. Ment. Dis., 164*(4), 231–246.

Millan, M. J., & Emrich, H. M. (1981). Endorphinergic systems and the response to stress. *Psychother. Psychosom., 36*(1), 43–56.

Millar, J. D. (1984). The NIOSH-suggested list of the ten leading work-related diseases and injuries. *J. Occupational Med., 26,* 340–341.

Millar, J. D. (1990). Mental health and the workplace: An interchangeable partnership. *Amer. Psychol., 45*(10), 1165–1166.

Miller, G. E., & Prinz, R. J. (1990). Enhancement of social learning family interventions for childhood conduct disorder. *Psychol. Bull., 108*(2), 291–307.

Miller, H. L., Coombs, D. W., Leeper, J. D. et al. (1984). An analysis of the effects of suicide prevention facilities on suicide rates in the United States. *Amer. J. Pub. Hlth., 74,* 340–343.

Miller, L. (1988). Neurocognitive aspects of remorse: Impulsivity-compulsivity-reflectivity. *Psychotherapy Patient, 5,* 63–76.

Miller, L. J. (1990). The formal treatment contract in the inpatient management of borderline personality disorder. *Hosp. Comm. Psychiat., 41*(9), 985–987.

Miller, N. E. (1948). Studies of fear as an acquirable drive. I. Fear as motivation and fear-reduction as reinforcement in the learning of new responses. *J. Exp. Psychol., 38,* 89–101.

Miller, N. E. (1969). Learning of visceral and glandular responses. *Science, 163,* 434–445.

Miller, N. S., & Giannini, A. J. (1990). The disease model of addiction: A biopsychiatrist's view. *J. Psychoact. Drugs, 22*(1), 83–85.

Miller, N. S., & Gold, M. S. (1990). Benzodiazepines: Tolerance, dependence, abuse, and addiction. *J. Psychoact. Drugs, 22*(1), 23–33.

Miller, N. S., Klahr, A. L., Gold, M. S., Sweeney, K. et al. (1990). The prevalence of marijuana (cannabis) use and dependence in cocaine dependence. *N.Y. St. J. Med., 90*(10), 491–492.

Miller, N. S., Mahler, J. C., & Gold, M. S. (1991). Suicide risk associated with drug and alcohol dependence. *Journal of Addictive Diseases, 10*(3), 49–61.

Miller, P. M., Ingham, J. G., & Davidson, S. (1976). Life events, symptoms, and social support. *J. Psychiat. Res., 20*(6), 514–522.

Miller, R. D. (1992). Need-for-treatment criteria for involuntary civil commitment: Impact in practice. *Amer. J. Psychiat., 149*(10), 1380–1384.

Miller, W. B. (1958). Lower class culture as a generating milieu of gang delinquency. *J. Soc. Issues, 14,* 5–19.

Miller, W. R. (1982). Treating problem drinkers: What works? *Behav. Ther., 5,* 15–18.

Miller, W. R. (1983). Controlled drinking, *Quart. J. Stud. Alcohol., 44,* 68–83.

Miller, W. R., & Dougher, M. J. (1984). Covert sensitization: Alternative treatment approaches for alcoholics. Paper presented at the Second Congress of the International Society for Biomedical Research on Alcoholism, Santa Fe.

Miller, W. R., & Hester, R. K. (1980). Treating the problem drinker: Modern approaches. In W. R. Miller (Ed.), *The addictive behaviors: Treatment of alcoholism, drug abuse, smoking, and obesity.* Elmsford, NY: Pergamon.

Miller, W. R., & Hester, R. K. (1986). Inpatient alcoholism treatment: Who benefits? *Amer. Psychol., 41,* 794–805.

Miller, W. R., Leckman, A. L., Delaney, H. D., & Tinchom, M. (1992). Long-term follow-up of behavioral self-control training. *Journal of Studies on Alcohol, 51,* 108–115.

Miller, W. R., & Seligman, M. E. (1975). Depression and learned helplessness in man. *J. Abnorm. Psychol., 84*(3), 228–238.

Millman, R. (1991). *Identification of dual diagnosis in drug abusers. National Conference on Drug Abuse Research and Practice: Conference Highlights.* Rockville, MD: NIDA.

Millon, T. (1969). *Modern psychopathology: A biosocial approach to maladaptive learning and functioning.* Philadelphia: Saunders.

Millon, T. (1981). *Disorders of personality.* New York: Wiley.

Millon, T. (1987). *Manual for the MCMI-II* (2nd ed.). Minneapolis, MN: National Computer Systems.

Millon, T. (1987). *Millon Clinical Multiaxial Inventory-II: Manual for the MCMI-II* (2nd ed.). Minneapolis, MN: National Computer Systems.

Millon, T. (1988). Personologic psychotherapy. *Psychotherapy, 25,* 209–219.

Millon, T. (1990). The disorders of personality. In L. A. Pervin

(Ed.), *Handbook of Personality Theory and Practice*. New York: Guilford.

Millon, T. (1990). *Toward a new personology*. New York: Wiley.

Millon, T., & Everly, G. S. (1992) *Personality disorders*. In R. Comer, *Abnormal psychology*. New York: W. H. Freeman.

Mills, M. C. (1985). Intervention strategies in a suicidal case. *Psych. Rep.*, *56*(3), 718.

Millstein, R. (1992). The national impact of alcohol and drug problems and HIV infection and AIDS among the poor and underserved. *Journal of Health Care for the Poor and Underserved*, *3*(1), 21–29.

Milner, B. (1971). Interhemispheric difference in the localization of psychological processes in man. *British Medical Bulletin*, *27*, 272–277.

Milner, B., Corkin, S., & Teuber, H. L. (1968). Further analysis of the hippocampal syndrome: 14-year follow-up study of H. M. *Neuropsychologica*, *6*, 215–234.

Mineka, S. (1985). Animal models of anxiety-based disorders: Their usefulness and limitations. In A. H. Tuma & J. Maser (Eds.), *Anxiety and the anxiety disorders*. Hillsdale, NJ: Erlbaum.

Mineka, S., Davidson, M., Cook, M., & Keir, R. (1984). Observational conditioning of snake fear in rhesus monkeys. *J. Abnorm. Psychol.*, *93*(4), 355–372.

Mineka, S., & Sutton, S. K. (1992). Cognitive biases and the emotional disorders. *Psychological Science*, *3*(1), 65–69.

Mineo, B. A., & Cavalier, A. R. (1985). From idea to implementation: Cognitive software for students with learning disabilities. *J. Learn. Dis.*, *18*(10), 613–618.

Minuchin, S. (1970). The use of an ecological framework in the treatment of a child. In J. Anthony & C. Koupernik (Eds.), *The child in his family*. New York: Wiley.

Minuchin, S. (1974). *Families and family therapy*. Cambridge, MA: Harvard UP.

Minuchin, S. (1987). My many voices. In J. K. Zeig (Ed.), *The evolution of psychotherapy*. New York: Brunner/Mazel.

Minuchin, S. (1992). *Family Healing*. New York: Free Press.

Minuchin, S. (1993, March). On family therapy: A visit with Salvador Minuchin. *Psych. Today*, *26*(2), pp. 20–21.

Minuchin, S., & Fishman, H. (1981). *Family therapy techniques*. Cambridge, MA: Harvard UP.

Minuchin, S., Rosman, B. L., & Baker, L. (1978). *Psychosomatic families: Anorexia nervosa in context*. Cambridge, MA: Harvard UP.

Miranda, J., & Persons, J. D. (1988). Dysfunctional attitudes are mood state dependent. Meetings of the Assoc. for Advancement of Behavior Therapy. *J. Abnorm. Psychol.*, *97*(1), 76–79.

Mirin, S. M., & Weiss, R. D. (1991). Substance abuse and mental illness. In R. J. Frances & S. I. Miller (Eds.), *Clinical Textbook of Addictive Disorders*. New York: Guilford.

Mirkin, M. P. (1985). The Peter Pan syndrome: Inpatient treatment of adolescent anorexia nervosa. *Inter. J. Fam. Ther.*, *7*(3), 205–216.

Mirsky, I. A. (1958). Physiologic, psychologic, and social determinants of the etiology of duodenal ulcer. *Amer. J. Digestional Diseases*, *3*, 285–314.

Mishkin, M. (1978). Memory in monkeys severely impaired by combined but not by separate removal of amygdala and hippocampus. *Nature*, *273*, 297–298.

Mishler, E., & Waxler, N. (1968). *Interaction in families: An experimental study of family process and schizophrenia*. New York: Wiley.

M.I.T. (1993). Cited in "Mental depression costs $43.7 billion, study shows. *The Daily News*, December 3, 1993.

Mitchell, J. E. (1989). Bulimia nervosa. In J. G. Howells (Ed.), *Modern perspectives in the psychiatry of the neuroses. Modern perspectives in psychiatry*, No. 12. New York: Brunner/Mazel.

Mitchell, J. E., & de Zwaan, M. (1993). Pharmacological treatments of binge eating. In C. G. Fairburn & G. T. Wilson (Eds.), *Binge eating: Nature, assessment, and treatment*. New York: Guilford.

Mitchell, J. E., Hatsukami, D., Goff, G., Pyle, R. L., Eckert, E. D., & Davis, L. E. (1985). Intensive outpatient group treatment for bulimia. In D. M. Garner & P. E. Garfinkel (Eds.), *Handbook of psychotherapy for anorexia nervosa and bulimia*. New York: Guilford.

Mitchell, J. E., & Pyle, R. L. (1985). Characteristics of bulimia. In J. E. Mitchell (Ed.), *Anorexia nervosa and bulimia: Diagnosis and treatment*. Minneapolis: Univ. Minnesota.

Mitchell, J. E., Pyle, R. L., Eckert, E. D., Hatsukami, D. et al. (1990). Bulimia nervosa in overweight individuals. *J. Nerv. Ment. Dis.*, *178*(5), 324–327.

Mitchell, J. E., Pyle, R. L., & Fletcher, L. (1991). The topography of binge eating, vomiting and laxative abuse. Inter. *J. Eat. Dis.*, *10*(1), 43–48.

Mitchell, J. E., Pyle, R. L., Miner, R. A. (1982). Gastric dilation as a complication of bulimia. *Psychosomatics*, *23*, 96–97.

Mitchell, J. E., Seim, H. C., Colon, E., & Pomeroy, C. (1987). Medical complications and medical management of bulimia. *Annals of Internal Medicine*, *107*, 71–77.

Mitchell, J. E., Specker, S. M., & de Zwaan, M. (1991). Comorbidity and medical complications of bulimia nervosa. *J. Clin. Psychiat.*, *52*(Suppl.), 13–20.

Mizes, J. S., & Arbitell, M. R. (1991). Bulimics' perceptions of emotional responding during binge-purge episodes. *Psych. Rep.*, *69*(2), 527–532.

Modell, J. G., Mountz, J. M., & Ford, C. V. (1992). Pathological lying associated with thalamic dysfunction. *J. Neuropsychiat. & Clin. Neurosci.*, *4*(4), 442–446.

Modestin, J., & Villiger, C. (1989). Follow-up study on borderline versus nonborderline personality disorders. *Comprehen. Psychiat.*, *30*(3), 236–244.

Modrow, J. (1992). *How to Become a Schizophrenic: The Case Against Bio. Psychiat.*, Everett, Washington: Apollyon Press.

Mohler, H., & Okada, T. (1977). Benzodiazepine receptor: Demonstration in the central nervous system. *Science*, *198*(4319), 849–851.

Mohler, H., Richards, J. G., & Wu, J.-Y. (1981). Autoradiographic localization of benzodiazepine receptors in immunocytochemically identified Y-aminobutyric synapses. *Proceedings of the National Academy of Sciences, U.S.A.*, *78*, 1935–1938.

Mohr, D. C., & Beutler, L. E. (1990). Erectile dysfunction: A review of diagnostic and treatment procedures. *Clin. Psychology Rev.*, *10*(1), 123–150.

Mohr, J. W., Turner, R. E., & Jerry, M. B. (1964). *Pedophilia and exhibitionism*. Toronto: Univ. Toronto.

Moller, H. J. (1990). Suicide risk and treatment problems in patients who have attempted suicide. In D. Lester (Ed.), *Current concepts of suicide*. Philadelphia: The Charles Press.

Mollerstrom, W. W., Patchner, M. A., & Milner, J. S. (1992).

Family violence in the Air Force: A look at offenders and the role of the Family Advocacy Program. *Military Medicine, 157*(7), 371–374.

Mollinger, R. N. (1980). Antithesis and the obsessive-compulsive. *Psychoanalytic Review, 67*(4), 465–477.

Monahan, J. (1978). Prediction research and the emergency commitment of dangerous mentally ill persons: A reconsideration. *Amer. J. Psychiat., 135*, 198–201.

Monahan, J. (1984). The prediction of violent behavior: Toward a second generation of theory and policy. *Amer. J. Psychiat., 141*, 10–15.

Monahan, J. (1992). Mental disorder and violent behavior: Perceptions and evidence. *Amer. Psychol., 47*(4), 511–521.

Monahan, J. (1993). Limiting therapist exposure to Tarasoff liability: Guidelines for risk containment. *Amer. Psychol., 48*(3), 242–250.

Monahan, J. (1993). Mental disorder and violence: Another look. In S. Hodgins (Ed.), *Mental disorder and crime.* Newbury Park: Sage Publications.

Monahan, J., & Davis, S. K. (1983). Mentally disordered sex offenders. In J. Monahan & H. J. Steadman (Eds.), *Mentally disordered offenders.* New York: Plenum.

Monahan, J., & Steadman, H. J. (Eds.). (1983). *Mentally disordered offenders.* New York: Plenum.

Monahan, J., & Walker, L. (Eds.). (1990). *Social science in law: Cases and materials* (2nd ed.). Westbury, NJ: Foundation Press.

Moneymaker, J. M., & Strimple, E. O. (1991). Animals and inmates: A sharing companionship behind bars. *Journal of Offender Rehabilitation, 16*(3-4), 133–152.

Monjan, A. A., & Collector, M. I. (1977). Stress-induced modulation of the immune response. *Science, 197*, 307–308.

Montagu, J. D., & Coles, E. M. (1966). Mechanism and measurement of the galvanic skin response. *Psychol. Bull., 65*, 261–279.

Montgomery, S. A., Bebbington, P., Cowen, P., Deakin, W., et al. (1993). Guidelines for treating depressive illness with antidepressants. *Journal of Psychopharmacology, 7*(1), 19–23.

Montgomery, S. A., Dufour, H., Brion S., Gailledreau, J. et al. (1988). The prophylactic efficacy of fluoxetine in unipolar depression. *Brit. J. Psychiat., 153*(3, Suppl.), 69–76.

Moody, H. (1969). Psychedelic drugs and religious experience. In R. E. Hicks & P. J. Fink (Eds.), *Psychedelic drugs.* New York: Grune & Stratton.

Moore, D. R., & Arthur, J. L. (1983). Juvenile delinquency. In T. Ollendick & M. Hersen (Eds.), *Handbook of child psychopathology.* New York: Plenum.

Moore, N. (1965). Behavior therapy in bronchial asthma: A controlled study. *J. Psychosom. Res., 9*, 257–276.

Moore, R., Brødsgaard, I., Berggren, U., & Carlsson, S. G. (1991). Generalization of effects of dental fear treatment in a self-referred population of odontophobics. *J. Behav. Ther. Exp. Psychiat., 22*(4), 243–253.

Moos, R. H., & Finney, J. W. (1983). The expanding scope of alcoholism treatment evaluation. *Amer. Psychol., 38*(10), 1036–1044.

Morales, A., Condra, M., Heaton, J. P. W., & Varrin, S. (1991). Impotence: organic factors and management approach. *Sexual and Marital Therapy, 6*(2), 97–106.

Moreno, I., Saiz, R. J., & Lopez, I. J. J. (1991). Serotonin and gambling dependence. *Human Psychopharmacology-Clinical-and-Experimental, 6*(Suppl), 9–12.

Morgan, A. H., & Hilgard, E. R. (1973). Age differences in susceptibility to hypnosis. *Inter. J. Clin. Exp. Hyp., 21*, 78–85.

Morgan, C. D., & Murray, H. A. (1935). A method of investigating fantasies: The Thematic Apperception Test. *Arch. Neurol. Psychiat., 34*, 289–306.

Morgan, H. G., & Russell, G. F. M. (1975). Value of family background and clinical features as predictors of long-term outcome in anorexia nervosa: Four-year follow-up of 41 patients. *Psychol. Med., 5*, 355–371.

Morley, S. (1989). Single case research. In G. Parry & N. W. Fraser (Eds.), *Behavioural and mental health research: A handbook of skills and methods.* Hove, UK: Erlbaum.

Morokoff, P. J. (1978). Determinants of female orgasm. In J. LoPiccolo & L. LoPiccolo (Eds.), *Handbook of sex therapy.* New York: Plenum.

Morokoff, P. J. (1988). Sexuality in premenopausal and postmenopausal women. *Psychol. of Women Quart., 12*, 489–511.

Morokoff, P. J. (1993). Female sexual arousal disorder. In W. O'Donohue and J. Geer (eds.), *Handbook of sexual dysfunctions.* Boston: Allyn and Bacon.

Morokoff, P. J., & Gillilland, R. (1993). Stress, sexual functioning, and marital satisfaction. *Journal of Sex Research, 30*(1), 43–53.

Morris, A., Cooper, T., & Cooper, P. J. (1989). The changing shape of female fashion models. *Inter. J. Eat. Dis., 8*(5), 593–596.

Morris, G. (1983). Acquittal by reason of insanity: Developments in the law. In J. Monahan & H. J. Steadman (Eds.), *Mentally disordered offenders.* New York: Plenum.

Morris, R. G., & Baddeley, A. D. (1988). Primary and working memory functioning in Alzheimer-type dementia. *Journal of Clinical Experimental Neuropsychology, 10*, 279–296.

Morris, R. J., & Kratochwill, T. R. (1983). *The practice of child therapy.* New York: Pergamon.

Morris, R. J., & Kratochwill, T. R. (1983). *Treating children's fears and phobias: A behavioral approach.* New York: Pergamon.

Morrison, J. R. (1980). Childhood hyperactivity in an adult psychiatric population: Social factors. *J. Clin. Psychiat., 41*(2), 40–43.

Morrison, J. (1989). Histrionic personality disorder in women with somatization disorder. *Psychosomatics, 30*(4), 433–437.

Morrissett, R., & Swartzwelder, S. (1993). Attenuation of hippocampal long-term potentiation by ethanol: A patch-clamp analysis of glutamergic and GABAergic mechanisms. *Journal of Neuroscience, 13*(5), 2264–2272.

Morrissette, D. L., Skinner, M. H., Hoffman, B. B., Levine, R. E., & Davison, J. M. (1993). Effects of antihypertensive drugs Atenolol and Nifedipine on sexual function in older men: A placebo-controlled, crossover study. *Archives of Sexual Behavior, 22*(2), 99–109.

Morse, S. J. (1982). A preference for liberty: The case against involuntary commitment of the mentally disordered. *Calif. Law Rev., 70*, 55–106.

Mortimer, J. A., van Duijn, C. M., Chandra, V., Fratiglioni, L., Graves, A. B., Heyman, A., Jorm, A. F., Kokmen, E., Kondo, K., & Rocca, W. A. (1991). Head trauma as a risk factor for Alzheimer's disease: A collaborative re-analysis of case-control studies. *International Journal of Epidemiology, 20*(Suppl.), 28–35.

Moses-Zirkes, S. (1992, October 10). Psychologists question anti-stalking laws' utility. *APA Monitor, 23*, p. 53.

Motley, M. T. (1988, January). Taking the terror out of talk. *Psych. Today, 22*(1), 46–49.

Motto, J. (1967). Suicide and suggestibility: The role of the press. *Amer. J. Psychiat., 124*, 252–256.

Motto, J. (1980). The right to suicide: A psychiatrist's view. In M. P. Battin & D. J. Mayo (Eds.), *Suicide: The philosophical issues.* New York: St. Martin's.

Motto, J. (1986). Clinical considerations of biological correlates of suicide. In R. W. Maris (Ed.), *Biology of suicide.* New York: Guilford.

Mowrer, O. H. (1939). A stimulus-response analysis of anxiety and its role as a reinforcing agent. *Psychol. Rev., 46*, 553–566.

Mowrer, O. H. (1939). An experimentally produced "social problem" in rats [Film]. Bethlehem, PA: Psychological Cinema Register, Lehigh Univ.

Mowrer, O. H. (1947). On the dual nature of learning: A reinterpretation of "conditioning" and "problem-solving." *Harvard Educ. Rev., 17*, 102–148.

Mowrer, O. H., & Mowrer, W. M. (1938). Enuresis: A method for its study and treatment. *Amer. J. Orthopsychiat., 8*, 436–459.

Muehlenhard, C. L., & Linton, M. A. (1987). Date rape and sexual aggression in dating situations: Incidence and risk factors. *J. Couns. Psychol., 34*(2), 186–196.

Mueser, K. T., Bellack, A. S., & Brady, E. U. (1990). Hallucinations in schizophrenia. *Acta Psychiatr. Scandin., 82*(1), 29–36.

Mueser, K. T., & Glynn, S. M. (1990). Behavioral family therapy for schizophrenia. In M. Hersen, R. M. Eisler, & P. M. Miller (Eds.), *Progress in behavior modification*, Vol. 26. Newbury Park, CA: Sage Publications.

Mueser, K. T., Yarnold, P. R., & Foy, D. W. (1991). Statistical analysis for single-case designs: Evaluating outcome of imaginal exposure treatment of chronic PTSD. *Behav. Mod., 15*(2), 134–155.

Mulkern, V. M., & Manderscheid, R. W. (1989). Characteristics of community support program clients in 1980 and 1984. *Hosp. Comm. Psychiat., 40*(2), 165–172.

Mullan, M., Crawford, F., Axelman, K., Houlden, H., Lilius, L., Winblad, B., & Lannfelt, L., (1992). A pathogenic mutation for probable Alzheimer's disease in APP gene at the N-terminus of Beta-amyloid. *Nature Genetics, 1*, 345–347.

Muller, P. (1983). Was sollen wir Schizophrenen raten: Medikamentose Langzeitpropylaxe oder Intervall behandlung? [What advice should be given to schizophrenic patients—long-term maintenance on neuroleptics or treatment at intervals?]. *Nervenarzt, 54*(9), 477–485.

Mullins, L. L., Olson, R. A., & Chaney, J. M. (1992). A social learning/family systems approach to the treatment of somatoform disorders in children and adolescents. *Family Systems Medicine, 10*(2), 201–212.

Munjack, D. J. (1984). The onset of driving phobias. *J. Behav. Ther. Exp. Psychiat., 15*, 305–308.

Munjack, D. J. (1984). The treatment of phenelzine-induced hypotension with salt tablets: Case report. *J. Clin. Psychiat., 45*, 85–90.

Munk, J. P., & Mortensen, P. B. (1992). Social outcome in schizophrenia: A 13-year follow-up. *Social Psychiatry and Psychiatric Epidemiology, 27*(3), 129–134.

Munsinger, H. (1975). The adopted child's IQ: A critical review. *Psychol. Bull., 82*, 623–659.

Murphy, D. L. (1989). Monoamine oxidase (MAO) inhibitors in psychiatric therapy. In J. Hobson (Ed.), *Abnormal states of brain and mind.* Boston: Birhauser.

Murphy, G. E. et al. (1979). Suicide and alcoholism: Interpersonal loss confirmed as a predictor. *Arch. Gen. Psychiat., 36*(1), 65–69.

Murphy, H. B. (1968). Cultural factors in the genesis of schizophrenia. In D. Rosenthal & S. S. Kety (Eds.), *The transmission of schizophrenia.* Elmsford, NY: Pergamon.

Murphy, J. B., & Lipshultz, L. I. (1988). Infertility in the paraplegic male. In E. A. Tanagho, T. F. Lue, & R. D. McClure (Eds.), *Contemporary management of impotence and infertility.* Baltimore: Williams & Wilkins.

Murphy, J. M. (1976, March). Psychiatric labeling in cross-cultural perspective: Similar kinds of disturbed behavior appear to be labeled abnormal in diverse cultures. *Science, 101*(4231), 1019–1028.

Murphy, J. M., Reede, J., Jellinek, M., & Bishop, S. (1992). Screening for psychosocial dysfunction in inner-city children: Further validation of the Pediatric Symptom Checklist. *J. Amer. Acad. Child Adol. Psychiat. 31*(6), 1105–1111.

Murphy, J. M., Sobol, A. M., Neff, R. K., Olivier, D. C., Leighton, A. H. (1984). Stability of prevalence: Depression and anxiety disorders. *Arch. Gen. Psychiat., 41*, 990.

Murphy, M., & Deutsch, S. I. (1991). Neurophysiological and neurochemical basis of behavior. In K. Davis, H. Klar, & J. T. Coyle (Eds.), *Foundations of psychiatry.* Philadelphia: Saunders.

Murphy, M., & Handelsman, L. (1991). Anxiety. In K. Davis, H. Klar, & J. Coyle (Eds.), *Foundations of psychiatry.* Philadelphia: Saunders.

Murphy, S., & Irwin, J. (1992). Living with the dirty secret: Problems of disclosure for methadone maintenance clients. *Journal of Psychoactive Drugs, 24*(3), 257–264.

Murphy, S. M. (1990). Rape, sexually transmitted diseases and human immunodeficiency virus infection. *International Journal of STD and AIDS, 1*, 79–82.

Murphy, S. M., Owen, R. T., & Tyrer, P. J. (1984). Withdrawal symptoms after six weeks' treatment with diazepam. *Lancet, 2*, 1389.

Murphy, S. M., Owen, R. T., & Tyer, P. (1989). Comparative assessment of efficacy and withdrawal of symptoms after six and twelve weeks treatment with diazepam or buspirone. *Brit. J. Psychiat., 154*, 529–534.

Murray, B. (1993). Human Nature: Attitudes and Age. *Psych. Today, 26*(2), 96.

Murray, H. A. (1938). *Explorations in personality.* Fairlawn, NJ: Oxford UP.

Murray, J. B. (1982). What is meditation? Does it help? *Genetic Psychol. Monographs, 106*(1), 85–115.

Murray, J. B. (1986). Psychological aspects of anorexia nervosa. *Genetic, Social & Genetic Psychology Monographs, 112*(1), 5–40.

Murray, J. D., & Keller, P. A. (1991, March). Psychology and rural America: Current status and future directions. *Amer. Psychol., 46*, 220–231.

Murray, K. (1993, May 9). When the Therapist is a Computer. *New York Times*, Section 3, p. 25.

Murrell, J., Farlow, M., Bernardino, G., & Benson, M. D. (1991). A mutation in the amyloid precursor protein associated with hereditary Alzheimer's disease. *Science, 254,* 97–99.

Murstein, B. I., & Fontaine, P. A. (1993). The public's knowledge about psychologists and other mental health professionals. *Amer. Psychol., 48*(7), 839–845.

Muuss, R. E. (1986). Adolescent eating disorder: Bulimia. *Adolescence, 21*(82), 257–267.

Myatt, R. J., & Greenblatt, M. (1993). Adolescent suicidal behavior. In A. A. Leenaars (Ed.), *Suicidology.* Northvale, NJ: Jason Aronson.

Naber, D., Holzbach, R., Perro, C., & Hippius, H. (1992). Clinical management of clozapine patients in relation to efficacy and side-effects. *Brit. J. Psychiat., 160*(supp. 17), 54–59.

Nace, E. P. (1992). Alcoholism and the borderline patient. In D. Silver & M. Rosenbluth (Eds.), *Handbook of Borderline Disorders.* Madison, CT: International Universities Press.

Nagy, J., & Szatmari, P. (1986). A chart review of schizotypal personality disorders in children. *J. Autism Dev. Dis., 16*(3), 351–367.

Nagy, L. M., Krystal, J. H., Charney, D. S., Merikangas, K. R., & Woods, S. W. (1993). Long-term outcome of panic disorder after short-term imipramine and behavioral group treatment: 2.9-year naturalistic follow-up study. *Journal of Clinical Psychopharmacology, 13*(1), 16–24.

Nagy, L. M., Morgan, C. A., III, Southwick, S. M., & Charney, D. S. (1993). Open prospective trial of fluoxetine for posttraumatic stress disorder. *Journal of Clinical Psychopharmacology, 13*(2), 107–113.

Nahas, G. G. (1984). Toxicology and pharmacology. In G. G. Nahas (Ed.), *Marijuana in science and medicine.* New York: Raven Press.

Narrow, W. E., Regier, D. A., Rae, D. S., Manderscheid, R. W., & Locke, B. Z. (1993). Use of services by persons with mental and addictive disorders: Findings from the National Institute of Mental Health Epidemiologic Catchment Area Program. *Arch. Gen. Psychiat., 50,* 95–107.

Nash, M. R., Hulsey, T. L., Sexton, M. C., Harralson, T. L., & Lambert, W. (1993). Long-term sequelae of childhood sexual abuse: Perceived family environment, psycho-pathology, and dissociation. *J. Cons. Clin. Psychol., 61,* 276–283.

Nathan, P. E., & Harris, S. L. (1980). *Psychopathology and society* (2nd ed.). New York: McGraw-Hill.

Nathan, P. E., & O'Brien, J. S. (1971). An experimental analysis of the behavior of alcoholics and nonalcoholics during prolonged periods of experimental drinking: A necessary precursor of behavior therapy? *Behav. Ther., 2,* 455–476.

Nathan, P. E., Titler, N. A., Lowenstein, L. W., Solomon, P., & Rossi, A. M. (1970). Behavioral analysis of chronic alcoholism. *Arch. Gen. Psychiat., 22,* 419–430.

National Alliance for the Mentally Ill (NAMI). (1994). Personal communication.

National Center for Health Statistics. (1988). *Vital statistics of the United States, 1985,* Vol. 2. Mortality. Washington, DC: Government Printing Office.

National Center for Health Statistics. (1988). *Vital statistics of the United States, 1986,* Vol. 2. Mortality. Washington, DC: Government Printing Office.

National Center for Health Statistics. (1989). *Vital statistics of the United States, 1987,* Vol. 2. Mortality. Washington, DC: Government Printing Office.

National Center for Health Statistics. (1990). *Vital statistics of the United States, 1987,* Vol. 2. Mortality. Washington, DC: Government Printing Office.

National Center for Health Statistics (1991). *Vital statistics of the United States* (Vol. 2): Mortality - Part A [for the years 1966–1988]. Washington, DC: U. S. Government Printing Office.

National Center for Health Statistics. (1993). *Advance report of final mortality statistics, 1991. Monthly Vital Statistics Report,* Vol 42(2), Hyattsville, MD: US Public Health Service.

National Commission on Children (1991). *Speaking of Kids: A national survey of children and parents.* Washington, DC: Author.

National Institute for Occupational Safety & Health. (1985). *Proposed national strategies for the prevention of leading work-related diseases and injuries.* (Pt. 1, NTIS No. PB87-114740). Cincinnati: Assoc. of Schools of Public Health/NIOSH.

National Institute for Occupational Safety & Health. (1988). *Proposed national strategies for the prevention of leading work-related diseases and injuries.* (Pt. 2, NTIS No. PB89-130348). Cincinnati: Assoc. of Schools of Public Health/NIOSH.

National Institute of Mental Health (NIMH) (1992). *Statistical Research Branch.* Unpublished estimate.

National Institute on Alcohol Abuse and Alcoholism (1991). *Alcohol Alert #11. Estimating the economic cost of alcohol abuse.* Rockville, MD: Author.

National Institute on Alcohol Abuse and Alcoholism (1991). *Alcohol Alert #14. Alcoholism and co-occurring disorders.* Rockville, MD: Author.

National Institute on Alcohol Abuse and Alcoholism (1992). *Alcohol Alert #15. Alcohol and AIDA.* Rockville, MD: Author.

National Institute on Alcohol Abuse and Alcoholism (1992). *Alcohol Alert #16. Moderate Drinking.* Rockville, MD: Author.

National Institute on Drug Abuse. (1985). *National household survey on drugs.* Washington, DC: Author.

National Institute on Drug Abuse. (1987). *Second triennial report to Congress on drug abuse and drug abuse research.* Washington, DC: Author.

National Institute on Drug Abuse (1990). *Substance abuse among blacks in the U.S.* Rockville, MD: Author.

National Institute on Drug Abuse (1990). *Substance abuse among Hispanic Americans.* Rockville, MD: Author.

National Institute on Drug Abuse (1991). *Annual Emergency Room Data, 1991.* Rockville, MD: Author.

National Institute on Drug Abuse. (1991). *Annual Medical Examiner Data, 1991.* Rockville, MD: Author.

National Institute on Drug Abuse (1991). *Third triennial report to Congress on drug abuse and drug abuse research.* Rockville, MD: Author.

National Institute on Drug Abuse (1992). *National Household Survey on Drug Abuse: Population Estimates 1991.* Rockville, MD: Author.

National Institute on Drug Abuse (1993). *National Household Survey on Drug Abuse: Highlights 1991.* Rockville, MD: Author.

National Institute on Drug Abuse (1993). *National survey results on drug use from monitoring the future study, 1975–1992.* Rockville, MD: Author.

National Institute on Drug Abuse (1993). *National survey results on drug use from monitoring the future study, 1975–1992,* Vol. II. Rockville, MD: Author.

National Victims Center. (1992, April). *Rape in America: A report to the nation.* Arlington, VA: Author.

Naylor, G. J., Dick, D. A., Dick, E. G., Moody, J. P. (1974). Lithium therapy and erythrocyte membrane cation carrier. P*sychopharmacology, 37*(1), 81–86.

Neiger, B. L., & Hopkins, R. W. (1988). Adolescent suicide: Character traits of high-risk teenagers. *Adolescence, 23*(90), 469–475.

Neisser, U. (1985, Sep.). Voices, glances, flashbacks. *Psych. Today,* 48–53.

Nelson, R. O. (1977). Assessment and therapeutic functions of self-monitoring. In M. Hersen, R. M. Eisler, & P. M. Miller (Eds.), *Progress in behavior modification.* New York: Academic Press.

Nelson, R. O. (1981). Realistic dependent measures for clinical use. *J. Cons. Clin. Psychol., 49,* 168–182.

Nemiah, J. C. (1984). In T. R. Insel (Ed.), *New Findings in Obsessive Compulsive Disorder.* Washington, DC: American Psychiatric Press. [7–6]

Nestadt, G., Romanoski, A. J., Brown, C. H., Chahal, R., et al. (1991). DSM-III compulsive personality disorder: An epidemiological survey. *Psychol. Med., 21*(2), 461–471.

Nestadt, G., Romanoski, A. J., Chahal, R., Merchant, A., Folstein, M. F., Gruenberg, E. M., & McHugh, P. R. (1990). An epidemiological study of histrionic personality disorder. *Psychol. Med., 29,* 413–422.

Neugarten, B. L. (1968). Adult personality: Toward a psychology of the life cycle. In B. L. Neugarten (Ed.), *Middle age and aging: Reader in social psychology.* Chicago: Univ. Chicago.

Neugebauer, R. (1978). Treatment of the mentally ill in medieval and early modern England: A reappraisal. *J. History of Behav. Sci., 14,* 158–169.

Neugebauer, R. (1979). Medieval and early modern theories of mental illness. *Arch. Gen. Psychiat., 36,* 477–483.

Neuman, P. A., & Halvorson, P. A. (1983). *Anorexia nervosa and bulimia: A handbook for counselors and therapists.* New York: Van Nostrand Reinhold.

Neuringer, C. (1974). Self and other appraisals by suicidal psychosomatic and normal hospital patients. *J. Clin. Cons. Psychol., 42,* 306.

Neuringer, C. (1976). Current developments in the study of suicidal thinking. In E. S. Schneidman (Ed.), *Suicidology: Contemporary developments.* New York: Grune & Stratton.

Newberger, E. H. (1983). The helping hand strikes again: Unintended consequences of child abuse reporting. *J. Clin. Child. Psychol., 12,* 307–311.

Newcomb, M. D., & Bentler, P. M. (1988). *Consequences of adolescent drug use: Impact on the lives of young adults.* Newbury Park, CA: Sage.

Newman, J. P., & Kosson, D. S. (1986). Passive avoidance learning in psychopathic and nonpsychopathic offenders. *J. Abnorm. Psychol., 95,* 257–263.

Newman, J. P., Kosson, D. S., & Patterson, C. M. (1987). Response perseveration in psychopaths. *J. Abnorm. Psychol., 96,* 145–149.

Newman, J. P., Kosson, D. S., & Patterson, C. M. (1992). Delay of gratification in psychopathic and nonpsychopathic offenders. *J. Abnorm. Psychol., 101*(4), 630–636.

Newman, M. E., Lerer, B., & Shapira, B. (1993). 5-HT-1A receptor mediated effects of antidepressants. *Progress in Neuro Psychopharmacoogy and Biological Psychiatry, 17*(1), 1–19.

Newsweek Poll. (1992, February 17). America seems to feel sound about self-esteem. *Newsweek,* p. 50.

Nezu, A. M. (1986). Efficacy of a social problem-solving therapy approach for unipolar depression. J. *Cons. Clin. Psychol., 54,* 196–202.

Nichols, M. P. (1984). *Family therapy: concepts and methods.* New York: Gardner Press.

Nichols, M. P. (1987). *The self in the system: Extending the limits of family therapy.* New York: Brunner/Mazel.

Nichols, M. P. (1992). *The power of family therapy.* New York: Gardner Press.

Nichter, M., & Nichter, M. (1991). Hype and weight. *Medical Anthropology, 13*(3), 249–284.

Nielsen, S. (1990). Epidemiology of anorexia nervosa in Denmark from 1973 to 1987: A nationwide register study of psychiatric admission. *Acta Psychiatr. Scandin., 81*(6), 507–514.

Nientimp, E. G., & Cole, C. L. (1992). Teaching socially valid social interaction responses to students with severe disabilities in an integrated school setting. *Journal of School Psychology, 30*(4), 343–354.

Nieto, E., Vieta, E., Lázaro, L., Gastó, C., et al. (1992). Serious suicide attempts in the elderly. *Psychopathology, 25*(4), 183–188.

Nigg, J. T., Lohr, N. E., Westen, D., Gold, L. J., et al. (1992). Malevolent object representations in borderline personality disorder and major depression. *J. Abnorm. Psychol., 101*(1), 61–67.

Nijinsky, V. (1936). *The diary of Vaslav Nijinsky.* New York: Simon & Schuster.

Niler, E. R., & Beck, S. J. (1989). The relationship among guilt, anxiety and obsessions in a normal population. *Behav. Res. Ther. 27,* 213–220.

Nisbett, R. E., & Ross, L. (1980). *Human inference: Strategies and shortcomings.* Englewood Cliffs, NJ: Prentice Hall.

Nitenson, N. C., & Cole, J. O. (1993). Psychotropic-induced sexual dysfunction. In D. L. Dunner (ed.), *Current psychiatric therapy.* Philadelphia: Saunders.

Nolen-Hoeksema, S. (1987). Sex differences in unipolar depression: Evidence and theory. *Psychol. Bull., 101*(2), 259–282.

Nolen-Hoeksema, S. (1990). *Sex differences in depression.* Stanford, CA: Stanford UP.

Nolen-Hoeksema, S., Girgus, J. S., & Seligman, M. E. (1992). Predictors and consequences of childhood depressive symptoms: A 5-year longitudinal study. *J. Abnorm. Psychol., 101*(3), 405–422.

Nolen-Hoeksema, S., Morrow, J., & Fredrickson, B. L. (1993). Response styles and the duration of episodes of depressed mood. *J. Abnorm. Psychol., 102*(1), 20–28.

Noonan, J. R. (1971). An obsessive-compulsive reaction treated by induced anxiety. *Amer. J. Psychother., 25*(2), 293–299.

Norcross, J. C., & Goldfried, M. R. (Eds.). (1992). *Handbook of psychotherapy integration.* New York: Basic Books.

Norcross, J. C., & Prochaska, J. O. (1984). Where do behavior (and other) therapists take their troubles? II. *Behav. Therapist, 7*(2), 26–27.

Norcross, J. C., & Prochaska, J. O. (1986). Psychotherapist heal thyself: I. The psychological distress and self-change of psychologists, counselors, and laypersons. *Psychotherapy, 23*, 102–114.

Norcross, J. C., Prochaska, J. O., & Farber, J. A. (1993). Psychologists conducting psychotherapy: New findings and historical comparisons on the psychotherapy division membership. *Psychotherapy, 30*(4), 692–697.

Norcross, J. C., Strausser, D. J., & Missar, C. D. (1988). The process and outcomes of psychotherapists' personal treatment experiences. *Psychotherapy, 25*, 36–43.

Norcross, J. C. et al. (1987). Presentation. Eastern Psychological Assoc.

Nordstrom, P., & Asberg, M. (1992). Suicide risk and serotonin. *International Clinical Psychopharmacology, 6*(Suppl 6), 12–21.

Norman, T. R., Judd, F. K., & Burrows, G. D. (1992). Long-term pharmacological management of panic disorder. In G. D. Burrows, S. M. Roth, & R. Noyes, Jr., *Handbook of Anxiety* (Vol. 5). Oxford: Elsevier.

Norris, P. A., & Fahrion, S. L. (1993). Autogenic biofeedback in psychophysiological therapy and stress management. In P. M. Lehrer & R. L. Woolfolk (Eds.), *Principles and Practice of Stress Management* (2nd ed.). New York: Guilford.

Norton, G. R., Dorward, J., & Cox, B. J. (1986). Factors associated with panic attacks in non-clinical subjects. *Behav. Ther., 17*, 239–252.

Norton, G. R., Rockman, G. E., Luy, B., & Marion, T. (1993). Suicide, chemical abuse, and panic attacks: A preliminary report. *Behav. Res. Ther., 31*(1), 37–40.

Novaco, R. W. (1975). *Anger control: The development and evaluation of an experimental treatment.* Lexington, MA: Heath.

Novaco, R. W. (1976). The functions and regulation of the arousal of anger. *Amer. J. Psychiat., 133*(10), 1124–1128.

Novaco, R. W. (1976). Treatment of chronic anger through cognitive and relaxation controls. *J. Cons. Clin. Psychol., 44*(4), 681.

Novaco, R. W. (1977). A stress inoculation approach to anger management in the training of law enforcement officers. *Amer. J. Comm. Psychol., 5*(3), 327–346.

Novaco, R. W. (1977). Stress innoculation: A cognitive therapy for anger and its application to a case of depression. *J. Cons. Clin. Psychol., 45*(4), 600–608.

Noyes, R. (1988). Beta adrenergic blockers. In C. G. Last & M. Hersen (Eds.), *Handbook of Anxiety Disorders* (1st ed.). New York: Pergamon.

Noyes, R. (1992). The outcome of panic disorder as influenced by illness variables and coexisting syndromes. In G. D. Burrows, S. M. Roth, & R. Noyes, Jr., *Handbook of Anxiety* (Vol. 5). Oxford: Elsevier.

Noyes, R., Anderson, D. J., Clancy, J., Crowe, R. R., Slyman, D. J., Ghoneim, M. M., & Hinrichs, J. V. (1984). Diazepam and propanolol in panic disorder and agoraphobia. *Arch. Gen. Psychiat., 41*, 287–292.

Noyes, R., Clancy, J., Crowe, R., Hoenk, P. R., & Slymen, D. J. (1978). The familial prevalence of anxiety neurosis. *Arch. Gen. Psychiat., 35*, 1057–1059.

Nuechterlein, K. H., Snyder, K. S., & Mintz, J. (1992). Paths to relapse: Possible transactional processes connecting patient illness onset, expressed emotion, and psychotic relapse. *Brit. J. Psychiat., 161*(suppl.18), 88–96.

Nunes, J. S., & Marks, I. M. (1975). Feedback of true heart rate during exposure in vivo. *Arch. Gen. Psychiat., 32*(7), 933–936.

Nunes, J. S., & Marks, I. M. (1976). Feedback of true heart rate during exposure in vivo: Partial replication with methodological improvement. *Arch. Gen. Psychiat., 33*(11), 1346–1350.

Nunn, C. M. (1992). Are double-blind controlled trials always necessary? *Human Psychopharmacology Clinical and Experimental, 7*(1), 55–57.

Nurnberger, J. I., Jr., & Gershon, E. S. (1984). Genetics of affective disorders. In R. M. Post & J. C. Ballenger (Eds.), *Neurobiology of mood disorders* (Vol. I, Frontiers of Clinical Neuroscience). Baltimore: Williams & Wilkins.

Nurnberger, J. I., Jr., & Gershon, E. S. (1992). Genetics. In E. S. Paykel (Ed.), *Handbook of Affective Disorders*. New York: Guilford.

Nutt, D. J. (1990). Selective ligands for benzodiazepine receptors: Recent developments. In N. N. Osborne (Ed.), *Current Aspects of the Neurosciences*. London: Macmillan.

Nutzinger, D. O., & de Zwaan, M. (1990). Behavioural treatment of bulimia (nervosa). In M. M. Fichter (Ed.), *Bulimia nervosa: Basic research, diagnosis and therapy*. Chichester: Wiley.

O'Brien, C. P., O'Brien, T. J., Mintz, J., & Brady, J. P. (1975). Conditioning of narcotic abstinence symptoms in human subjects. *Drug. Alc. Dep., 1*, 115–123.

O'Brien, E. (1993, Oct. 19). Expert sorts out the ways to chase the blues. *The Philadelphia Inquirer*, p. E5.

O'Connell, D. S. (1983). The placebo effect and psychotherapy. *Psychother. Theory Res. Prac., 20*(3), 337–345.

O'Connell, R. A., Mayo, J. A., Eng, L. K., Jones, J. S., & Gabel, R. H. (1985). Social support and long-term lithium outcome. *Br. J. Psychiat., 147*, 272–275.

O'Connor, D. (1979, October). Good girls and orgasm. *Newsweek.*

O'Connor, N., & Hermelin, B. (1991). Talents and preoccupations in idiot-savants. *Psychological Medicine, 21*(4), 959–964.

O'Farrell, T. J., Cutter, H. S., Choquette, K. A., Floyd, F. J., et al. (1992). Behavioral marital therapy for male alcoholics: Marital and drinking adjustment during the two years after treatment. *Behavior Therapy, 23*(4), 529–549.

O'Hare, T. (1992). The substance-abusing chronically mentally ill client: Prevalence, assessment, treatment and policy concerns. Social Work, 37(2), 185–187.

O'Leary, K. D., & Kent, R. (1973). Behavior modification for social action: Research tactics and problems. In L. A. Hamerlynck, L. C. Handy, & E. J. Mash (Eds.), *Behavior change: Methodology, concepts, and practice*. Champaign, IL: Research Press.

O'Leary, K. D., & Wilson, G. T. (1987). *Behavior therapy: Application and outcome* (2nd ed.). Englewood Cliffs, NJ: Prentice Hall.

O'Leary, K. M., Brouwers, P., Gardner, D. L., Cowdry, R. W. (1991). Neuropsychological testing of patients with borderline personality disorder. *Amer. J. Psychiat., 148*(1), 106–111.

O'Leary, K. M., Turner, E. R., Gardner, D., & Cowdry, R. W.

(1991). Homogeneous group therapy of borderline personality disorder. *Group, 15*(1), 56–64.

O'Malley, S., Jaffe, A., Chang, G., Schottenfeld, R., Meyer, R., & Rounsaville, B. (1992). Naltrexone and coping skills therapy for alcohol dependence. *Arch. Gen. Psychiat., 49*, 881–888.

O'Rourke, G. C. (1990). The HIV-positive intravenous drug abuser. Special Issue: HIV infection and AIDS. *Amer. J. Occupational Ther., 44*(3), 280–283.

O'Sullivan, G., & Marks, I. (1991). Follow-up studies of behavioral treatment of phobias and obsessive compulsive neuroses. *Psychiat. Ann., 21*(6), 368–373.

O'Sullivan, G., & Marks, I. M. (1991). Long-term outcome of phobic and obsessive-compulsive disorders after treatment. In R. Noyes, G. D. Burrows, & M. Roth (Eds.), *Handbook of Anxiety* (Vol. 4), Amsterdam: Elsevier Science Publishers.

O'Sullivan, G., Noshirvani, H., Marks, I., Monteiro, W., et al. (1991). Six-year follow-up after exposure and clomipramine therapy for obsessive compulsive disorder. *J. Clin. Psychiat., 52*(4), 150–155.

O'Sullivan, M. J., Peterson, P. D., Cox, G. B., & Kirkeby, J. (1989). Ethnic populations: Community mental health services ten years later. *American Journal of Community Psychology, 17*, 17–30.

Oakley-Browne, M. A. (1991). The epidemiology of anxiety disorders. *International Review of Psychiatry, 3*(2), 243–252.

Oberlander, E. L., Schneier, F. R., & Liebowitz, M. R. (1994). Physical disability and social phobia. *Journal of Clinical Psychopharmacology, 14*(2), 136–143.

Oei, T. P., Lim, B., & Hennessy, B. (1990). Psychological dysfunction in battle: Combat stress reactions and posttraumatic stress disorder. *Clin. Psychol. Rev., 10*(3), 355–388.

Offer, D., Ostrov, E., & Howard, K. I. (1981). The mental health professional's concept of the normal adolescent. *Arch. Gen. Psychiat., 38*(2), 140–152.

Office for Substance Abuse Prevention (1991). *Children of alcoholics: Alcoholism tends to run in families.* Rockville, MD: Author.

Office for Substance Abuse Prevention (1991). *College Youth.* Rockville, MD: Author.

Office for Substance Abuse Prevention (1991). *Crack cocaine: A challenge for prevention.* (Ed. R. Dupone). Rockville, MD: OSAP.

Office for Substance Abuse Prevention (1991). *Impaired Driving.* Rockville, MD: Author.

Ogles, B. M., Lambert, M. J., & Sawyer, D. (1993, June). The clinical significance of the NIMH Treatment of Depression Collaborative Research. Paper presented at the Annual Meetings of the Society for Psychotherapy Research, Pittsburgh.

Ogloff, J. R. P., Schweighofer, A., Turnbull, S. D., & Whittemore, K. (1992). Empirical research regarding the insanity defense: How much do we really know? In J. R. P. Ogloff (Ed.), *Law and psychology: The broadening of the discipline.*

Ohman, A. (1993). Stimulus prepotency and fear learning: Data and theory. In N. Birbaumer, & A. Öhman (Eds.), *The Organization of Emotion: Cognitive, Clinical, and Psychophysiological Perspectives.* Göttingen, FRG: Hogrefe & Huber.

Ohman, A., Erixon, G., & Lofberg, I. (1975). Phobias and preparedness: Phobic versus neutral pictures as continued stimuli for human autonomic responses. *J. Abnorm. Psychol., 84*, 41–45.

Ohman, A., & Soares, J. J. F. (1993). On the automatic nature of phobic fear: Conditioned electrodermal responses to masked fear-relevant stimuli. *J. Abnorm. Psychol., 102*(1), 121–132.

Okin, R. L., & Borus, J. F. (1989). Primary, secondary and tertiary prevention of mental disorders. In H. I. Kaplan & B. J. Sadock (Eds.), *Comprehensive textbook of psychiatry* (5th ed.). Baltimore: Williams & Wilkins.

Old Age Depression Interest Group (1993). How long should the elderly take antidepressants? A double-blind placebo-controlled study of continuation/prophylaxis therapy with dothiepin. *Brit. J. Psychiat., 162*, 175–182.

Olfson, M. (1992). Utilization of neuropsychiatric diagnostic tests for general hospital patients with mental disorders. *Amer. J. Psychiat., 149*(12), 1711–1717.

Olfson, M., & Klerman, G. L. (1993). Trends in the prescription of antidepressants by office based psychiatrists. *Amer. J. Psychiat., 150*(4), 571–577.

Olfson, M., Pincus, H. A., & Dial, T. H. (1994). Professional practice patterns of U. S. Psychiatrists. *Amer. J. Psychiat., 151*(1), 89–95.

Oliver, J. E. (1993). Intergenerational transmission of child abuse: rates, research and clinical implications. *Amer. J. Psychiat., 150*(9).

Ollendick, T. H., & King, N. J. (1991). Fears and phobias of childhood. In M. Herbert (Ed.), *Clinical child psychology: Social learning, development and behaviour.* Chichester, England: Wiley.

Olmos de Paz, T. (1990). Working-through and insight in child psychoanalysis. *Melanie Klein & Object Relations, 8*(1), 99–112.

Olmsted, M. P., Kaplan, A. S., & Rockert, W. (1994). Rate and prediction of relapse in bulimia nervosa. *Amer. J. Psychiat., 151*(5), 738–743.

Opdycke, R. A., Ascione, F. J., Shimp, L. A., & Rosen, R. I. (1992). A systematic approach to educating elderly patients about their medications. *Patient Education & Counseling, 19*(1), 43–60.

Opler, L. A., Caton, C. L. M., Shrout, P., Dominguez, B., & Kass, F. I. (1994). Symptom profiles and homelessness in schizophrenia. *J. Nerv. Ment. Dis., 182*(3), 174–178.

Oppenheim, R. C. (1976). Reactions to "Employing electric shock with autistic children." *J. Autism Child. Schizo., 6*, 291–292.

Oppenheim, S., & Rosenberger, J. (1991). Treatment of a case of obsessional disorder: Family systems and object relations approaches. *American Journal of Family Therapy, 19*(4), 327–333.

Orlebeke, J. F., Boomsma, D. I., Gooren, L. J. G., Verschoor, A. M., Van Den Bree, M. J. M. (1992). Elevated sinistrality in transsexuals. *Neuropsychology, 6*(4), 351–355.

Orloff, L. M., Battle, M. A., Baer, L., Ivanjack, L., Pettit, A. R., Buttolph, M. L., & Jenike, M. A. (1994). Long-term follow-up of 85 patients with obsessive-compulsive disorder. *Amer. J. Psychiat., 151*(3), 441–442.

Osgood, M. J. (1985). *Suicide in the elderly: A practitioner's guide to diagnosis and mental health intervention.* Rockville, MD: Aspen.

Osgood, M. J. (1987). Suicide and the elderly. *Generations, 11*(3), 47–51.

Ost, L. G., (1991). Acquisition of blood and injection phobia and anxiety response patterns in clinical patients. *Behav. Res. Ther.*, *29*(4), 323–332.

Osterweis, M., Solomon, F., & Green, M. (Eds.). (1984). *Bereavement: Reactions, consequences, and care. A report of the Institute of Medicine.* Washington, DC: National Academy Press.

Osterweis, M., & Townsend, J. (1988). *Understanding bereavement reactions in adults and children: A booklet for lay people.* Rockville, MD: U. S. Dept. Health and Human Services.

Otto, R. K. (1989). Bias and expert testimony of mental health professionals in adversarial proceedings: A preliminary investigation. *Behav. Sci. Law*, 7(2), 267–273.

Ottosson, J. O. (1960). Experimental studies of the mode of action of electroconvulsive therapy. *Acta. Psychiatr. Neurol. Scandin.*, *35*(145), 141.

Ottosson, J. O. (1985). Use and misuse of electroconvulsive treatment. *Bio. Psychiat.*, *20*(9), 933–946.

Ottosson, J. O. (1991). Is unilateral nondominant ECT as efficient as bilateral ECT? A new look at the evidence. *Convulsive Therapy*, 7(3), 190–200.

Overholser, J. C. (1992). Interpersonal dependency and social loss. *Personality and Individual Differences*, *13*(1), 17–23.

Overmier, J. B. (1992). On the nature of animal models of human behavioral dysfunction. In J. B. Overmier, & P. D. Burke (Eds.), *Animal Models of Human Pathology: A Bibliography of a Quarter Century of Behavioral Research 1967–1992.* Washington, DC: American Psychological Association.

Overstreet, D. H. (1993). The Flinders sensitive line rats: A genetic animal model of depression. *Neuroscience and Biobehavioral Review*, *17*, 51–68.

Overton, D. (1964). State-dependent or "dissociated" learning produced with pentobarbital. *J. Compar. Physiol. Psychol.*, *57*, 3–12.

Overton, D. (1966). State-dependent learning produced by depressant and atropine-like drugs. *Psychopharmacologia*, *10*, 6–31.

Owen, F., Crow, T. J., & Poulter, M. (1987). Central dopaminergic mechanisms in schizophrenia. *Acta Psychiatrica Belgica*, *87*(5), 552–565.

Owen, F., Crow, T. J., Poulter, M. et al. (1978). Increased dopamine receptor sensitivity in schizophrenia. *Lancet*, *2*, 223–226.

Owen, M. K., Lancee, W. J., & Freeman, S. J. (1986). Psychological factors and depressive symptoms. *J. Nerv. Ment. Dis.*, *174*(1), 15–23.

Owen, R. R., Gutierrez-Esteinou, R., Hsiao, J., Hadd, K., et al. (1993). Effects of clozapine and fluphenazine treatment on response to m-chlorophenylpiperazine infusions in schizophrenia. Arch. Gen. Psychiat., 50, 636–644.

Owens, R. G., Slade, P. D., & Fielding, D. M. (1989). Patient series and quasi-experimental designs. In G. Parry & N. W. Fraser (Eds.), *Behavioural and mental health research: A handbook of skills and methods.* Hove, UK: Erlbaum.

Owens, T. H. (1984). Personality traits of female psychotherapy patients with a history of incest: A research note. *J. Pers. Assess.*, *48*, 606–608.

Oyemade, U. J. (1989). *Parents and children getting a head start against drugs. Fact Sheet 1989.* Alexandria, VA: National Head Start Association.

Pace, T. M., & Dixon, D. N. (1993). Changes in depressive self-schemata and depressive symptoms following cognitive therapy. *Journal of Counseling Psychology*, *40*(3), 288–294.

Page, A. C. (1991). Simple phobias. *International Review of Psychiatry*, *3*(2), 175–187.

Pagelow, M. D. (1981). *Family violence.* New York: CBS Education.

Paget, K. D., Philp, J. D., & Abramczyk, L. W. (1993). Recent developments in child neglect. In T. H. Ollendick, & R. J. Prinz (Eds.), *Advances in clinical child psychology* (Vol. 15). New York: Plenum.

Painter, K. (1992, March 25). Drunken-driving casualties aren't the only victims of alcohol abuse. *USA Today*, p. 5D.

Palazzoli, M. S. (1974). *Self-starvation: From the intrapsychic to the transpersonal approach to anorexia nervosa.* London, England: Chaucer.

Palazzoli, M. S. (1985). Anorexia nervosa: A syndrome of the affluent society. *J. Strategic & Systemic Ther.* *4*(3), 12–16.

Pallis, D. J. et al. (1982). Estimating suicide risk among attempted suicides: I. The development of new clinical scales. *Brit. J. Psychiat.*, *141*, 37–44.

Palmblad, J., Cantell, K., Strander, H., Froberg, J., Karlsson, C., Levi, L., Grnstrom, M., & Unger, P. (1976). Stressor exposure and immunological response in man: Interferon-producing capacity and phagocytosis. *J. Psychosom. Res.*, *20*, 193–199.

Paniagua, F. A., Morrison, P. B., & Black, S. A. (1990, March). Management of a hyperactive-conduct disordered child through correspondence training: A preliminary study. *J. Behav. Ther. Exp. Psychiat.*, *21*, 63–68.

Papp, L. A., Coplan, J., & Gorman, J. M. (1992). Neurobiology of Anxiety. In A. Tasman, & M. B. Riba (Eds.), *Review of Psychiatry* (Vol. 11). Washington, DC: American Psychiatric Press.

Papp, L. A., & Gorman, J. M. (1993). Pharmacological approach to the management of stress and anxiety disorders. In P. M. Lehrer & R. L. Woolfolk (Eds.), *Principles and Practice of Stress Management* (2nd ed.). New York: Guilford.

Paradis, C. M., Freidman, S., Hatch, M., & Lazar, R. M. (1992). Obsessive-compulsive disorder onset after removal of a brain tumor. *J. Nerv. Ment. Dis.*, *180*(8), 535–536.

Pardes, H. (1989). Psychiatry, biological. In J. Hobson (Ed.), *Abnormal states of brain and mind.* Boston: Birhauser.

Paris, J. (1990). Completed suicide in borderline personality disorder. *Psychiat. Ann.*, *20*(1), 19–21.

Paris, J. (1991). Personality disorders, parasuicide, and culture. *Transcultural Psychiatric Research Review*, *28*(1), 25–39.

Paris, J., Nowlis, D., Brown, R. (1988). Developmental factors in the outcome of borderline personality disorder. *Comprehen. Psychiat.*, *29*(2), 147–150.

Parker, G. (1983). Parental 'affectionless control' as an antecedent to adult depression. *Arch. Gen. Psychiat.*, *48*, 956–960.

Parker, G. (1992). Early environment. In E. S. Paykel (Ed.), *Handbook of Affective Disorders.* New York: Guilford.

Parker, G., Hadzi-Pavlovic, D., Brodaty, H., Boyce, P., Mitchell, P., Wilhelm, K., Hickie, I., & Eyers, K. (1993). Psychomotor disturbance in depression: Defining the constructs. *J. Affect. Dis.*, *27*, 255–265.

Parker, G., Hadzi-Pavlovic, D., Wilhelm, K. et al. (1994).

Defining melancholia: Properties of a refined sign-based measure. *Brit. J. Psychiat.*, *164*, 316–326.

Parker, G., Roy, K., Hadzi-Pavlovic, D., & Pedic, F. (1992). Psychotic (delusional) depression: A meta-analysis of physical treatment. *J. Affect. Dis.*, *24*(1), 17–24.

Parker, N. (1991). The Gary David case. Austral. *New Zeal. J. Psychiat.*, *25*(3), 371–374.

Parker, P. E. (1993). A case report of Munchausen Syndrome with mixed psychological features. *Psychosomatics*, *34*(4), 360–364.

Parnas, J. (1988). Assortative mating in schizophrenia: Results from the Copenhagen high-risk study. *Psychiatry*, *51*(1), 58–64.

Parnas, J., Cannon, T. D., Jacobsen, B., Schulsinger, H., Schulsinger, F., & Mednick, S. A. (1993). Lifetime DSM-III-R diagnostic outcomes in the offspring of schizophrenic mothers. *Arch. Gen. Psychiat.*, *50*, 707–714.

Parnas, J., Jorgensen, A., et al. (1989). Pre-morbid psychopathology in schizophrenia spectrum. *Brit. J. Psychiat.*, *155*, 623–627.

Parnas, J., Schulsinger, F., Schulsinger, H., Mednick, S. A., & Teasdale, T. W. (1982). Behavioral precursors of schizophrenia spectrum: A prospective study. *Arch. Gen. Psychiat.*, *39*, 658–664.

Parnas, J. et al. (1982). Behavioral precursors of schizophrenia spectrum: A prospective study. *Arch. Gen. Psychiat.*, *39*(6), 858–884.

Pascal, G. R., & Suttell, B. J. (1951). *The Bender-Gestalt Test: Quantification and validity for adults.* New York: Grune & Stratton.

Patel, A. R., Roy, M., & Wilson, G. M. (1972). Self-poisoning and alcohol. *Lancet*, *2*, 1099–1103.

Patrick, C. J., Bradley, M. M., & Lang, P. J. (1993). Emotion in the criminal psychopath: Startle reflex modulation. *J. Abnorm. Psychol.*, *102*(1), 82–92.

Patrick, C. J., Cuthbert, B. N., & Lang, P. J. (1990). Emotion in the criminal psychopath: Fear imagery. *Psychophysiology*, *27*(Suppl.), 55.

Patterson, G. R. (1974). Interventions for boys with conduct problems: Multiple settings, treatments, and criteria. *J. Cons. Clin. Psychol.*, *42*, 471–481.

Patterson, G. R. (1977). Naturalistic observation in clinical assessment. *J. Abnorm. Child Psychol.*, *5*(3), 309–322.

Patterson, G. R. (1982). *Coercive family process.* Eugene, OR: Castalia.

Patterson, G. R. (1986). Performance models for antisocial boys. *American Psychologist*, *41*, 432–444.

Patterson, G. R., Capaldi, D., & Bank, L. (1991). An early starter model for predicting delinquency. In D. J. Pepler & K. H. Rubin (Eds.), *The development and treatment of childhood aggression.* Hillsdale, NJ: Erlbaum.

Patton, G. C., Johnson-Sabine, E., Wood, K., Mann, A. H. et al. (1990). Abnormal eating attitudes in London schoolgirls: A prospective epidemiological study: Outcome at twelve month follow-up. *Psychol. Med.*, *20*(2), 383–394.

Paul, G. L. (1967). The strategy of outcome research in psychotherapy. *Journal of Consulting Psychology*, *31*, 109–118.

Paul, G. L., & Lentz, R. (1977). *Psychosocial treatment of the chronic mental patient.* Cambridge, MA: Harvard UP.

Paul, S. M. (1988). Anxiety and depression: A common neuro-biological substrate? Symposia: Consequences of anxiety. *J. Clin. Psychiat.*, *49*(Suppl), 13–18.

Paul, S. M., Rehavi, M., Skolnick, P., Goodwin, F. K. (1984). High affinity binding of antidepressants to a biogenic amine transport site in human brain and platelet: Studies in depression. In R. Post & J. Ballenger (Eds.), *Neurobiology of mood disorders.* Baltimore: Williams & Wilkins.

Paurohit, N., Dowd, E. T., & Cottingham, H. F. (1982). The role of verbal and nonverbal cues in the formation of first impressions of black and white counselors. *J. Couns. Psychol.*, *4*, 371–378.

Paykel, E. S. (Ed.). (1982). *Handbook of affective disorders.* New York: Guilford.

Paykel, E. S. (1983). Methodological aspects of life events research. *J. Psychosomatic Res.*, *27*(5), 341–352.

Paykel, E. S. (1991). Stress and life events. In L. Davidson & M. Linnoila (Eds.), *Risk factors for youth suicide.* New York: Hemisphere.

Paykel, E. S., & Cooper, Z. (1992). Life events and social stress. In E. S. Paykel (Ed.), *Handbook of Affective Disorders.* New York: Guilford.

Paykel, E. S., Rao, B. M., & Taylor, C. N. (1984). Life stress and symptom pattern in outpatient depression. *Psychol. Medicine*, *14*(3), 559–568.

Payne, A. F. (1928). *Sentence completion.* New York: New York Guidance Clinics.

Payte, T. J. (1989). Combined treatment modalities: The need for innovative approaches. Third National Forum on AIDS and Chemical Dependency of the American Society of Addiction Medicine. *J. Psychoact. Drugs*, *21*(4), 431–434.

Peach, L., & Reddick, T. L. (1991). Counselors can make a difference in preventing adolescent suicide. School *Counselor*, *39*(2), 107–110.

Peachey, J. E., & Franklin, T. (1985). Methadone treatment of opiate dependence in Canada. *Brit. J. Addic.*, *80*(3), 291–299.

Pearce, J. (1977). Depressive disorder in childhood. *J. Child Psychol. Psychiat. Allied Disc.*, *18*(1), 78–82.

Pearlson, G. D. et al. (1984). Lateral ventricular enlargement associated with persistent unemployment and negative symptoms in both schizophrenia and bipolar disorder. *Psychiat. Res.*, *12*(1), 1–9.

Peck, M. (1982). Youth suicide. *Death Educ.*, *6*(1), 27–47.

Peele, S. (1989). *Diseasing of America: Addiction treatment out of control.* Lexington, MA: Lexington Books/D.C. Heath & Company.

Pekrun, R. (1992). Expectancy-value theory of anxiety: Overview and implications. In D. G. Forgays, T. Sosnowski, & K. Wrzesniewski (Eds.), *Anxiety: Recent developments in cognitive, psychophysiological, and health research.* Washington, DC: Hemisphere Pub. Corp.

Pekrun, R. (1992). The impact of emotions on learning and achievement: Towards a theory of cognitive/motivational mediators. *Applied Psychology: An International Review*, *41*(4), 359–376.

Pendery, M. L., Maltzman, I. M., & West, L. J. (1982). Controlled drinking by alcoholics? New findings and a reevaluation of a major affirmative study. *Science*, *217*(4555), 169–175.

Pendleton, L., Tisdale, M., & Marler, M. (1991). Personality pathology in bulimics versus controls. *Comprehen. Psychiat.*, *32*(6), 516–520.

Pennati, A., Sacchetti, E., & Calzeroni, A. (1991). Dantrolene in lethal catatonia. *Amer. J. Psychiat.*, *148*(2), 268.

Pennebaker, J. W., Colder, M., & Sharpi, L. K. (1990). Accelerating the coping process. *J. Pers. Soc. Psychol.*, *58*(3), 528–537.

Pepper, B., & Ryglewicz, H. (Eds.). (1982). *New directions for mental health services: The young adult chronic patient* (no. 14). San Francisco: Jossey-Bass.

Pericak-Vance, M. A., Bebout, J. L., Gaskell, P. C., Yamaoka, L. H., Hung, W. Y., Alberts, M. J., Walker, A. P., Bartlett, R. J., Haynes, C. A., & Welsh, K. A. (1991). Linkage studies in familial Alzheimer Disease: Evidence for chromosome 19 linkage. *American Journal of Human Genetics*, *48*, 1034–1050.

Perilstein, R. D., Lipper, S., & Friedman, L. J. (1991). Three cases of paraphilias responsive to fluoxetine treatment. *J. Clin. Psychiat.*, *52*(4), 169–170.

Perkins, D. O., Leserman, J., Gilmore, J. H., Petitto, J. M., & Evans, D. L. (1991). Stress, depression and immunity: Research findings and clinical implications. In N. Plotnikoff, A. Murgo, R. Faith, & J. Wybran (Eds.), *Stress and immunity*. Boca Raton: CRC Press.

Perlick, D., Stastny, P., Mattis, S., & Teresi, J. (1992). Contribution of family, cognitive and clinical dimensions to long-term outcome in schizophrenia. *Schizophrenia Research*, *6*(3), 257–265.

Perls, F. S. (1969). *Gestalt therapy verbatim.* Moab, UT: Real People.

Perls, F. S. (1973). *The Gestalt approach.* Palo Alto: Science Behav.

Perris, C. (1988). Decentralization, sectorization, and the development of alternatives to institutional care in a northern county in Sweden. In C. N. Stefanis & A. D. Rabavilis (Eds.), *Schizophrenia: Recent biosocial developments*. New York: Human Sci.

Perry, J. C. (1989). Dependent personality disorder. In American Psychiatric Association (Eds.), *Treatments of Psychiatric Disorders: A task force report of the American Psychiatric Association*. Washington, DC: American Psychiatric Press.

Perry, J. C. (1992). Problems and considerations in the valid assessment of personality disorders. *Amer. J. Psychiat.*, *149*, 1645–1653.

Perry, J. C., & Cooper, S. H. (1986). A preliminary report on defenses and conflicts associated with borderline personality disorder. *Journal of the American Psychoanalytic Association*, *34*(4), 863–893.

Perry, J. C., Herman, J. L., & Van der Kolk, B. A. (1990). Psychotherapy and psychological trauma in borderline personality disorder. *Psychiat. Ann.*, *20*(1), 33–43.

Perry, J. C., & Jacobs, D. (1982). Overview: Clinical applications of the amytal interview in psychiatric emergency settings. *Amer. J. Psychiat.*, *139*(5), 552–559.

Perry, S. (1990). Suicidal ideation and HIV testing. *JAMA*, *263*, 679–682.

Perry, S., Difede, J., Musngi, G., Frances, A. J., et al. (1992). Predictors of posttraumatic stress disorder after burn injury. *Amer. J. Psychiat.*, *149*(7), 931–935.

Perry, W., & Braff, D. L. (1994). Information-processing deficits and thought disorder in schizophrenia. *Amer. J. Psychiat.*, *151*(3), 363–367.

Perske, R. (1972). The dignity of risk and the mentally retarded. *Ment. Retardation, 10*, 24–27.

Persons, J. B. (1991). Psychotherapy outcome studies do not accurately represent current models of psychotherapy: A proposed remedy. *Amer. Psychol.*, *46*(2), 99–106.

Persson, C. (1972). Lithium prophylaxis in affective disorders: An open trial with matched controls. *Acta Psychiatr. Scandin.*, *48*, 462–479.

Pertschuk, M. J. (1977). Behavior therapy: Extended follow-up. In R. A. Vigersky (Ed.), *Anorexia Nervosa*. New York: Raven Press.

Pertschuk, M. J., Forster, J., Buzby, G., & Mullen, J. L. (1981). The treatment of anorexia nervosa with total parenteral nutrition. *Bio. Psychiat.*, *16*, 539–550.

Petersen, A. C., Compas, B., & Brooks-Gunn, J. (1991). Depression in adolescence: Implications of current research for programs and policy. Report prepared for the Carnegie Council on Adolescent Development, Washington, D.C.

Petersen, A. C., Compas, B. E., Brooks-Gunn, J., Ey, S., & Grant, K. E. (1993). *Depression in Adolescence. Amer. Psychol.*, *48*(2), 155–168.

Petersen, D. (1988). Substance abuse, criminal behavior, and older people. *Generations, 12*(4), 63–67.

Petersen, R. C. (1984). Marijuana overview. In M. D. Glantz (Ed.), *Correlates and consequences of marijuana use. NIDA Research Issues*, No. 34. Washington, DC: U.S. Department of Health and Human Service, U.S. Government Printing Office.

Peterson, C. (1993). Helpless behavior. *Behav. Res. Ther.*, *31*(3), 289–295.

Peterson, C., Colvin, D., & Lin, E. H. (1992). Explanatory style and helplessness. *Soc. Behav. Pers. 20*(1), 1–13.

Peterson, D. R. (1968). *The clinical study of social behavior.* New York: Appleton-Century-Crofts.

Peterson, L., & Roberts, M. C. (1991). Treatment of children's problems. In C. E. Walker (Ed.), *Clinical psychology: Historical and research foundations*. New York: Plenum.

Petrella, R. C., Benedek, E. P., Bank, S. C., & Packer, I. K. (1985). Examining the application of the guilty but mentally ill verdict in Michigan. *Hosp. Comm. Psychiat.*, *36*(3), 254–259.

Pettinati, H. M., & Rosenberg, J. (1984). Memory self-ratings before and after anticonvulsive therapy: Depression versus ECT-induced. *Bio. Psychiat.*, *19*, 539–548.

Pfeffer, C. R. (1984). Suicidal impulses of normal children. *Inter. J. Fam. Psychiat.*, *5*(2), 139–150.

Pfeffer, C. R. (1986). The suicidal child. New York: Guilford.

Pfeffer, C. R. (1988). Risk factors associated with youth suicide: A clinical perspective. *Psychiat. Ann.*, *18*(11), 652–656.

Pfeffer, C. R. (1990). Clinical perspectives on treatment of suicidal behavior among children and adolescents. *Psychiat. Ann.*, *20*(3), 143–150.

Pfeffer, C. R. (1993). Suicidal children. In A. A. Leenaars (Ed.), *Suicidology*. Northvale, NJ: Jason Aronson.

Pfeifer, M. P., & Snodgrass, G. L. (1990). The continued use of retractable invalid scientific literature. *JAMA*, *263*(10), 1420–1427.

Pfeiffer, S. I., & Nelson, D. D. (1992). The cutting edge in services for people with autism. *J. Autism Dev. Dis.*, *22*(1), 95–105.

Pfohl, B., Black, D. W., Noyes, R., Coryell, W. H., & Barrash, J. (1991). Axis I and axis II comorbidity findings: Implications for validity. In J. M. Oldham (Ed.), *Personality Disorders: New Perspectives on Diagnostic Validity*. Washington, DC: American Psychiatric Press.

Phares, E. J. (1979). *Clinical psychology: Concepts, methods, and profession*. Homewood, IL: Dorsey.

Phelan, J. (1976). *Howard Hughes: The hidden years*. New York: Random House.

Phelps, L., & Grabowski, J. (1993). Fetal Alcohol Syndrome: Diagnostic features and psychoeducational risk factors. *School Psychology Quarterly, 7*(2), 112–128.

Phillip, A. E., & McCulloch, J. W. (1966). The use of social indices in psychiatric epidemiology. *Brit. J. Preventive Soc. Med., 20*, 122–126.

Philipp, E., Willershausen-Zonnchen, B., Hamm, G., & Pirke, K. M. (1991). Oral and dental characteristics in bulimic and anoretic patients. *Inter. J. Eat. Dis., 10*(4), 423–431.

Phillips, D. P. (1982). The behavioral impact of violence in the mass media: A review of the evidence from laboratory and nonlaboratory investigations. *Sociol. Soc. Res., 66*, 387–398.

Phillips, D. P. (1983). The impact of mass media violence on U.S. homicides. *Amer. Sociological Rev., 48*, 560–568.

Phillips, D. P. (1994). Suic. Life-Threat. Behav.

Phillips, D. P., Lesyna, K., & Paight, D. J. (1992). Suicide and the media. In R. W. Maris, A. L. Berman, J. T. Maltsberger, & R. I. Yufit (Eds.), *Assessment and prediction of suicide*. New York: Guilford.

Phillips, D. P., & Ruth, T. E. (1993). Adequacy of official suicide statistics for scientific research and public policy. *Suic. Life-Threat. Behav., 23*(4), 307–319.

Phillips, K. A. (1991). Body dysmorphic disorder: The distress of imagined ugliness. *Amer. J. Psychiat., 148*(9), 1138–1149.

Phillips, K. A., McElroy, S. L., Keck, P. E., Pope, H. G., et al. (1993). Body dysmorphic disorder: 30 cases of imagined ugliness. *Amer. J. Psychiat., 150*(2), 302–308.

Phillipson, H. (1955). *The object relations technique*. London: Tavistock Publications.

Philpott, R. M. (1990). Affective disorder and physical illness in old age. *Inter. Clin. Psychopharm., 5*(3), 7–20.

Physicians' Desk Reference (48th ed.). (1994). Montvalle, NJ: Medical Economic Data Production Company.

Pickar, D., Owen, R. R., & Litman, R. E. (1991). New developments in pharmacotherapy of schizophrenia. In A. Tasman & S. M. Goldfinger (Eds.), *American psychiatric press review of psychiatry* (Volume 10). Washington, DC: American Psychiatric Press.

Pickens, R., & Fletcher, B. (1991). Overview of treatment issues. In R. Pickens, C. Leukefeld, & C. Schuster (Eds.), *Improving Drug Abuse Treatment*. Rockville, MD: National Institute on Drug Abuse.

Pierloot, R., Wellens, W., & Houben, M. (1975). Elements of resistance to a combined medical and psychotherapeutic program in anorexia nervosa. *Psychother. Psychosom., 26*, 101–117.

Pietrofesa, J. J. et al. (1990). The mental health counselor and "duty to warn." *J. Ment. Hlth. Couns., 12*(2), 129–137.

Pigott, T. A., Altemus, M., Rubenstein, C. S., Hill, J. L., et al. (1991). Symptoms of eating disorders in patients with obsessive-compulsive disorder. *Amer. J. Psychiat., 148*(11), 1552–1557.

Pillemer, K., & Finkelhor, D. (1988). The prevalence of elder abuse: A random sample survey. *Gerontologist, 28*, 51–57.

Pincus, H. A., Henderson, B., Blackwood, D., & Dial, T. (1993). Trends in research in two general psychiatric journals in 1969–1990: Research on research. *Amer. J. Psychiat., 150*(1), 135–142.

Pine, C. J. (1981). Suicide in American Indian and Alaskan native tradition. *White Cloud J., 2*(3), 3–8.

Pinel, P. A. (1962). *A treatise on insanity. History of medicine series* (Vol. 14). (Originally published, 1806).

Pinkston, E. M., & Linsk, N. L. (1984). Behavioral family intervention with the impaired elderly. *Gerontologist, 24*, 576–583.

Pithers, W. D. (1990). Relapse prevention with sexual aggressors. In W. L. Marshall, D. R. Laws, & H. E. Barbaree (Eds.), *Handbook of sexual assault*. New York: Plenum.

Pithers, W. D., & Cumming, G. F. (1989). Can relapses be prevented? Initial outcome data for the Vermont Treatment Program for Sexual Aggressors. In D. R. Laws (Ed.), *Relapse prevention with sex offenders*. New York: Guilford.

Plakun, E. M. (1991). Prediction of outcome in borderline personality disorder. *J. Pers. Dis., 5*(2), 93–101.

Plantes, M. M., Prusoff, B. A., Brennan, J., & Parker, G. (1988). Parental representations of depressed outpatients from a U.S. sample. *J. Affect. Dis., 15*, 149–155.

Plasse, T. F. et al. (1991). Recent clinical experience with dronabinol. *Pharmacology Biochemistry & Behavior, 40*, 695.

Platania-Solazzo, A., Field, T. M., Blank, J., Seligman, F., et al., (1992). Relaxation therapy reduces anxiety in child and adolescent psychiatric patients. *Acta-Paedopsychiatrica International Journal of Child and Adolescent Psychiatry, 55*(2), 115–120.

Plaut, V. L. (1983). Punishment versus treatment of the guilty but mentally ill. *Journal of Criminal Law and Criminology, 74*(2), 428–456.

Plotkin, R. (1983). Cognitive mediation in disciplinary action among mothers who have abused or neglected their children: Dispositional and environmental factors. Unpublished doctoral dissertation. Univ. Rochester.

Pogue-Geile, M. F. (1989). The prognostic significance of negative symptoms in schizophrenia. Symposium: Negative symptoms in schizophrenia (1987, London, England). *Brit. J. Psychiat., 155*(7, Suppl.), 123–127.

Pokorny, A. D. (1992). Prediction of suicide in psychiatric patients: Report of a prospective study. In R. W. Maris, A. L. Berman, J. T. Maltsberger, & R. I. Yufit (Eds.), *Assessment and prediction of suicide*. New York: Guilford.

Polcin, D. (1992). Issues in the treatment of dual diagnosis clients who have chronic mental illness. *Professional Psychology: Research and Practice, 23*(1), 30–37.

Polivy, J., & Herman, C. P. (1985). Dieting and bingeing: A causal analysis. *Amer. Psychol., 40*, 193–201.

Polk, W. M. (1983). Treatment of exhibitionism in a 38-year-old male by hypnotically assisted covert sensitization. *Inter. J. Clin. Exp. Hyp., 31*, 132–138.

Pollack, J. M. (1987). Relationship of obsessive-compulsive personality to obsessive-compulsive disorder: A review of the literature. *Journal of Psychology, 121*(2), 137–148.

Pollack, W. (1989). Schizophrenia and the self: Contributions of psychoanalytic self-psychology. *Schizo. Bull., 15*(2), 311–322.

Polster, M. (1987). Gestalt therapy: evolution and application. In J. K. Zeig (Ed.), *The evolution of psychotherapy.* New York: Brunner/Mazel.

Pomara, N., Deptula, D., Singh, R., & Monroy, C. (1991). Cognitive toxicity of benzodiazepines in the elderly. In C. Salzman & B. D. Lebowitz (Eds.), *Anxiety in the elderly.* New York: Springer.

Pomerleau, O. F., & Pomerleau, C. S. (1984). Neuroregulators and the reinforcement of smoking: Towards a biobehavioral explanation. *Neurosci. Biobehav., Rev., 8*(4), 503–513.

Pope, B. (1983). The initial interview. In C. E. Walker (Ed.), *The handbook of clinical psychology: Theory, research, and practice.* Homewood, IL: Dow Jones-Irwin.

Pope, H. G., Herridge, P. L., Hudson, J. I., & Fontaine, R. (1986). Treatment of bulimia with nomifensine. *J. Clin. Psychiat., 143,* 371–373.

Pope, H. G., & Hudson, J. I. (1984). *New hope for binge eaters: Advances in the understanding and treatment of bulimia.* New York: Harper & Row.

Pope, H. G., & Hudson, J. I. (1988). Is bulimia nervosa a heterogeneous disorder? Lessons from the history of medicine. *Inter. J. Eat. Dis., 7,* 155–166.

Pope, H. G., Hudson, J. I., & Jonas, J. M. (1983). Antidepressant treatment of bulimia: Preliminary experience and practical recommendations. *J. Psychiat., 140,* 554–558.

Pope, H. G., Hudson, J. I., & Jonas, J. M. (1983). Bulimia treated with imipramine: A placebo-controlled, double-blind study. *Amer. J. Psychiat., 140*(5), 554–558.

Pope, K. S., & Bouhoutsos, J. (1986). *Sexual intimacy between therapists and patients.* New York: Praeger.

Pope, K. S., & Tabachnick, B. G. (1993). Therapists' anger, hate, fear, and sexual feelings: National survey of therapist responses, client characteristics, critical events, formal complaints, and training. *Professional Psychology: Research and Practice, 24*(2), 142–152.

Pope, K. S., Tabachnick, B. G., & Keith-Spiegel, P. (1986). Sexual attraction to clients: The human therapist and the (sometimes) inhuman training system. *Amer. Psychol., 41*(2), 147–158.

Pope, K. S., Tabachnick, B. G., & Keith-Spiegel, P. (1987). Ethics of practice: The beliefs and behaviors of psychologists as therapists. *Amer. Psychol., 42*(11), 993–1166.

Pope, K. S., & Vetter, V. A. (1991). Prior therapist-patient sexual involvement among patients seen by psychologists. *Psychotherapy, 28*(3), 429–438.

Popper, C. W. (1988). Disorders usually first evident in infancy, childhood, or adolescence. In J. Talbott, R. S. Hales, & S. C. Yudofsky (Eds.), *Textbook of psychiatry.* American Psychiatric Press.

Poretz, M., & Sinrod, B. (1991). *Do you do it with the lights on?* New York: Ballantine Books.

Portegies, P., Enting, R. H., de Gans, J., Algra, P. R., Derix, M. M., Lange, J. M., & Goudsmit, J. (1993). Presentation and course of AIDS dementia complex: 10 years of following in Amsterdam & The Netherlands. *AIDS, 7*(5), 669–675.

Porter, S., Kelly, K. A., & Grame, C. J. (1993). Family treatment of spouses and children of patients with multiple personality disorder. *Bull. Menninger Clin., 57*(3), 371–379.

Posner, M. I., Early, T. S., Raiman, E., Pardo, P. J. et al. (1988). Asymmetries in hemispheric control of attention in schizophrenia. *Arch. Gen. Psychiat., 45*(9), 814–821.

Post, F. (1966). *Persistent persecutory states of the elderly.* Elmsford, NY: Pergamon.

Post, R. M., Ballenger, J. C., & Goodwin, F. K. (1980). Cerebrospinal fluid studies of neurotransmitter function in manic and depressive illness. In J. H. Wood (Ed.), *The neurobiology of cerebrospinal fluid,* Volume 1. New York: Plenum.

Post, R. M. et al. (1978). Cerebrospinal fluid norepinephrine in affective illness. *Amer. J. Psychiat., 135*(8), 907–912.

Poulson, R. L. (1990). Mock juror attribution of criminal responsibility: Effects of race and the guilty but mentally ill (GBMI) option. *Journal of Applied Social Psychology, 20*(19), 1596–1611.

Powell, G. E., & Lindsay, S. J. E. (1987). An introduction to treatment. In G. E. Powell & S. J. E. Lindsay (Eds.), *A handbook of clinical adult psychology.* Aldershot, England: Gower.

Powell, J., Bradley, B., & Gray, J. (1992). Classical conditioning and cognitive determinants of subjective craving for opiates: An investigation of their relative contributions. *British Journal of Addiction, 87*(8), 1133–1144.

Power, K. G., Jerrom, D. W. A., Simpson, R. J., et al. (1989). A controlled comparison of cognitive-behaviour therapy, diazepam, and placebo in the management of generalized anxiety. *Behav. Psychother., 17,* 7–14.

Power, K. G., Simpson, R. J., Swanson, V., Wallace, L. A., et al. (1990). A controlled comparison of cognitive-behaviour therapy, diazepam, and placebo, alone and in combination, for the treatment of generalized anxiety disorder. *Journal of Anxiety Disorders, 4*(4), 267–292.

Powers, P. S., Schocken, D. D., Feld, J., Holloway, J. D., et al. (1991). Cardiac function during weight restoration in anorexia nervosa. *Inter. J. Eat. Dis., 10*(5), 521–530.

Powis, T. (1990) Paying for the past: a brainwashing victim seeks compensation. *Macleans,* Mar. 19.

Prange, A. J. et al. (1970). Enhancement of imipramine by thyroid stimulating hormone: Clinical and theoretical implications. *Amer. J. Psychiat., 127*(2), 191–199.

Prange, A. J. et al. (1970). Use of a thyroid hormone to accelerate the action of imipramine. *Psychosomatics, 11*(5), 442–444.

Prange, A. J. et al. (1974). L tryptophan in mania: Contribution to a permissive hypothesis of affective disorders. *Arch. Gen. Psychiat., 30*(1), 56–62.

Prehn, R. A. (1990). Medication refusal: Suggestions for intervention. *Psychiat. Hosp., 21*(1), 37–40.

President's Commission on Mental Health. (1978). *Report to the President.* Washington, DC: GPO.

President's Committee on Mental Retardation. (1980, Dec.). *Report to the President, Mental Retardation: Prevention strategies that work.* Washington, DC: Office of Human Development Service.

Preskorn, S. H., & Fast, G. A. (1993) Beyond Signs and Symptoms: The Case Against a Mixed Anxiety and Depression Category. *J. Clin. Psychiat., 54*(Suppl. 1), 24–32.

Price, J. (1988). How to stabilize families: A therapist's guide to maintaining the status quo. *J. Strategic & Systemic Ther., 7*(4), 21–27.

Price, L. H. (1990). Serotonin reuptake inhibitors in depression and anxiety: An overview. *Ann. Clin. Psychiat., 2*(3), 165–172.

Price, L. H., Charney, D. S., Delgado, P. L., & Heninger, G. R. (1989). Lithium treatment and serotonergic union. *Arch. Gen. Psychiat., 46,* 13–19.

Price, L. H., Charney, D. S., Delgado, P. L., & Heninger, G. R. (1990). Lithium and serotonin function: implications for the serotonin hypothesis of depression. *Psychopharmacology, 100,* 3–12.

Price, R. W., Brew, B., Sidtis, J., Rosenblum, M., Scheck, A. C., & Cleary, P. (1988). The brain in AIDS: Central nervous system HIV-1 infection and AIDS dementia complex. *Science, 239,* 586–592.

Priebe, S., & Wildgrube, C. (1990). Expressed emotion and lithium prophylaxis. *Brit. J. Psychiat., 157,* 624.

Prien, R. F. (1978). Clinical uses of lithium—Part 1: Introduction. In T. B. Cooper, S. Gershon, N. S. Kline, & M. Schou, *Lithium: Controversies and unresolved issues.* Amsterdam: Excerpta Medica.

Prien, R. F. (1984). Five-center study clarifies use of lithium, imipramine for recurrent affective disorders. *Hosp. Comm. Psychiat., 35*(11), 1097–1098.

Prien, R. F. (1992). Maintenance treatment. In E. S. Paykel (Ed.), *Handbook of Affective Disorders.* New York: Guilford.

Prien, R. F., Balter, M. B., & Caffey, E. M. (1978). Hospital surveys of prescribing practices with psychotherapeutic drugs. *Arch. Gen. Psychiat., 35*(10), 1271–1275.

Prien, R. F., Caffey, E. M., Jr., & Klett, C. J. (1974). Factors associated with treatment success in lithium carbonate prophylaxis. *Arch. Gen. Psychiat., 31,* 189–192.

Prien, R. F. et al. (1984). Drug therapy in the prevention of recurrences in unipolar and bipolar affective disorders: Report of the NIMH Collaborative Study Group comparing lithium carbonate, imipramine, and a lithium carbonate-imipramine combination. *Arch. Gen. Psychiat., 41*(11), 1096–1104.

Priester, M. J., & Clum, G. A. (1992). Attributional style as a diathesis in predicting depression, hopelessness, and suicide ideation in college students. *Journal of Psychopathology and Behavioral Assessment, 14*(2), 111–122.

Primac, D. W. (1993). Measuring change in a brief therapy of a compulsive personality. *Psych. Rep., 72*(1), 309–310.

Prince, M. (1906). *The dissociation of a personality.* New York: Longmans, Green.

Prior, M. R., & Chen, C. S. (1975). Learning set acquisition in autistic children. *J. Abnorm. Psychol., 84,* 701–708.

Probsting, E., & Till, W. (1985). Suizidalitat und Arbeitslosigkeit [Suicidality and unemployment]. *Crisis, 6*(1), 19–35.

Prochaska, J. O. (1984). *Systems of psychotherapy.* Chicago: Dorsey.

Prochaska, J. O., DiClemente, C. C., & Norcross, J. C. (1992). In search of how people change. *American Psychologist, 47*(9), 1102–1114.

Prochaska, J. O., & Norcross, J. C. (1994). *Systems of psychotherapy: A transtheoretical analysis* (3rd ed.). Pacific Grove, CA: Brooks/Cole.

Prusiner, S. B. (1991). Molecular biology of prion diseases. *Science, 252,* 1515–1522.

Prusoff, B. A., Weissman, M. M., Klerman, G. L., & Rounsaville, B. J. (1980). Research diagnostic criteria subtypes of depression: Their role as predictors of differential response to psychotherapy and drug treatment. *Arch. Gen. Psychiat., 37*(7), 796–801.

Prussin, R. A., & Harvey, P. D. (1991). Depression, dietary restraint, and binge eating in female runners. *Addictive Behaviors, 16*(5), 295–301.

Puente, A. E. (1990). Psychological assessment of minority group members. In G. Goldstein & M. Hersen (Eds.), *Handbook of psychological assessment* (2nd ed.). Pergamon general psychology series, Vol. 131. New York: Pergamon.

Pueschel, S. M., & Goldstein, A. (1991). Genetic counseling. In J. L. Matson & J. A. Mulick (Eds.), *Handbook of mental retardation.* New York: Pergamon.

Pueschel, S. M., & Thuline, H. C. (1991). Chromosome disorders. In J. L. Matson & J. A. Mulick (Eds.), *Handbook of mental retardation.* New York: Pergamon.

Puig-Antich, J., Blau, S., Marx, N. et al. (1978). Prepubertal major depressive disorder: A pilot study. *J. Amer. Acad. Child Psychiat. 17,* 695–707.

Pulver, A. E., Carpenter, W. T., Adler, L., & McGrath, J. (1988). Accuracy of the diagnoses of affective disorders and schizophrenia in public hospitals. *Amer. J. Psychiat., 145*(2), 218–220.

Purcell, K., Brady, K., Chai, H., Muser, J., Molk, L., Gordon, N., & Means, J. (1969). The effect on asthma in children of experimental separation from the family. *Psychsom. Med., 31,* 144–164.

Purdon, C. L. (1992). Obsessional intrusive thoughts in normals: Are they a distinct cognitive phenomenon? Unpublished Master's thesis, University of New Brunswick, Fredericton, New Brunswick, Canada.

Pusakulich, R. L., & Nielson, H. C. (1976). Cue use in state-dependent learning. *Physiological Psychol., 4*(4), 421–428.

Putnam, F. W. (1985). Dissociation as a response to extreme trauma. In R. P. Kluft, *Childhood antecedents of multiple personality.* Washington, DC: American Psychiatric Press.

Putnam, F. W. (1985). Multiple personality disorder. *Med. Aspects Human Sexuality, 19*(6), 59–74.

Putnam, F. W. (1984). The psychophysiologic investigation of multiple personality disorder. *Psychiat. Clin. N. Amer., 7,* 31–40.

Putnam, F. W. (1988). The switch process in multiple personality disorder and other state-change disorders. *Dissociation., 1,* 24–32.

Putnam, F. W. (1992). Are alter personalities fragments of figments? *Psychoanalytic Inquiry, 12*(1), 95–111.

Putnam, F. W., Guroff, J. J., Silberman, E. K., Barban, L. et al. (1986). The clinical phenomenology of multiple personality disorder: Review of 100 recent cases. *J. Clin. Psych., 47*(6), 285–293.

Putnam, F. W., Zahn, T. P., & Post, R. M. (1990). Differential autonomic nervous system activity in multiple personality disorder. *Psychiat. Res., 31*(3), 251–260.

Pyle, R. L., Mitchell, J. E., Eckert, E. D., Hatsukami, D. et al. (1990). Maintenance treatment and 6-month outcome for bulimic patients who respond to initial treatment. *Amer. J. Psychiat., 147*(7), 871–875.

Quality Assurance Project. (1990). Treatment outlines for paranoid, schizotypal and schizoid personality disorders. *Austral. New Zeal. J. Psychiat., 24,* 339–350.

Quality Assurance Project. (1991). Treatment outlines for antisocial personality disorder. *Austral. New Zeal. J. Psychiat., 25,* 541–547.

Quality Assurance Project. (1991). Treatment outlines for avoidant, dependent and passive-aggressive personality disorders. *Austral. New Zeal. J. Psychiat., 25*(3), 311–313.

Quality Assurance Project. (1991). Treatment outlines for borderline, narcissistic and histrionic personality disorders. Austral. *New Zeal. J. Psychiat., 25*, 392–403.

Quevillon, R. P. (1993). Vaginismus. In W. O'Donohue & J. Geer (eds.), *Handbook of sexual dysfunctions.* Boston: Allyn and Bacon.

Quinsey, V. L., & Earls, G. M. (1990). The modificator of sexual preferences. In W. L. Marshall, D. R. Laws, & H. E. Barbaree (Eds.), *Handbook of sexual assault.* New York: Plenum.

Quitkin, F. M., Kane, J., Rifkin, A. et al. (1981). Prophylactic lithium with and without imipramine for bipolar I patients. *Arch. Gen. Psychiat., 38*, 902–907.

Qureshi, H., & Alborz, A. (1992). Epidemiology of challenging behaviour. *Mental Handicap Research, 5*(2), 130–145.

Rabins, P. V., Fitting, M. D., Eastham, J., & Zabora, J. (1990). Emotional adaptation over time in caregivers for chronically ill elderly people. *Age & Ageing, 19*, 185–190.

Raboch, J., & Faltus, F. (1991). Sexuality of women with anorexia nervosa. *Acta. Psychiatr. Scandin., 84*(1), 9–11.

Raboch, J., & Raboch, J. (1992). Infrequent orgasm in women. *Journal of Sex and Marital Therapy, 18*(2), 114–120.

Rachman, S. (1966). Sexual fetishism: An experimental analog. *Psych. Rec., 18*, 25–27.

Rachman, S. (1971). *The effects of psychotherapy.* Oxford: Pergamon.

Rachman, S. (1985). A note on the conditioning theory of fear acquisition. *Behav. Ther., 16*(4), 426–428.

Rachman, S. (1985). Obsessional-compulsive disorders. In B. P. Bradley & C. T. Thompson (Eds.), *Psychological applications in psychiatry.* Chichester, England: Wiley.

Rachman, S. (1985). The treatment of anxiety disorders: A critique of the implications for psychopathology. In A. Tuma and J. Maser (Eds.), *Anxiety and the anxiety disorders.* Hillsdale, NJ: Erlbaum.

Rachman, S. (1993). Obsessions, responsibility and guilt. *Behav. Res. Ther., 31*(2), 149–154.

Rachman, S., & deSilva, P. (1978). Abnormal and normal obsessions. *Behav. Res. Ther. 16*, 233–248.

Rachman, S., & Hodgson, R. J. (1974). Synchrony and desynchrony in fear and avoidance. *Behav. Res. Ther., 12*, 311–318.

Rachman, S., & Hodgson, R. (1980). *Obsessions and compulsions.* Englewood Cliffs, NJ: Prentice Hall.

Rachman, S., Hodgson, R., & Marks, I. M. (1971). Treatment of chronic obsessive-compulsive neurosis. *Behav. Res. Ther., 9*(3), 237–247.

Rachman, S., Hodgson, R., & Marzillier, J. (1970). Treatment of an obsessional-compulsive disorder by modelling. *Behav. Res. Ther., 8*, 385–392.

Rada, R. T. (1976). Alcoholism and the child molester. *Ann. NY Acad. Sci., 273*, 492–496.

Ragin, A. B., Pogue-Geile, M. F., & Oltmanns, T. F. (1989). Poverty of speech in schizophrenia and depression during inpatient and post-hospital periods. *Brit. J. Psychiat., 154*, 52–57.

Ragland, J. D., & Berman, A. L. (1991). Farm crisis and suicide: Dying on the vine? *Omega Journal of Death and Dying, 22*(3), 173–185.

Rahe, R. H. (1968). Life-change measurement as a predictor of

illness. *Proceedings of the Royal Society of Medicine, 61*, 1124–1126.

Raine, A. (1989). Evoked potentials and psychopathy. *International Journal of Psychophysiology, 8*(1), 1–16.

Raine, A. (1992). Sex differences in schizotypal personality in a nonclinical population. *J. Abnorm. Psychol., 101*(2), 361–4.

Raine, A., Lencz, T., Reynolds, G. P., Harrison, G., et al. (1992). An evaluation of structural and functional prefrontal deficits in schizophrenia: MRI and neuropsychological measures. *Psychiatry Research Neuroimaging, 45*(2), 123–137.

Raine, A., Sheard, C., Reynolds, G. P., & Lencz, T. (1992). Prefrontal structural and functional deficits associated with individual differences in schizotypal personality. *Schizophrenia Research, 7*(3), 237–47.

Ralston, P. A. (1991). Senior centers and minority elders: A critical review. *Gerontologist, 31*, 325–331.

Ram, R., Bromet, E. J., Eaton, W. W., & Pato, C. (1992). The natural course of schizophrenia: A review of first-admission studies. *Schizo. Bull., 18*(2), 185–207.

Ramey, C. T., & Ramey, S. L. (1992). Effective early intervention. *Mental Retardation, 30*(6), 337–345.

Ramirez, E., Maldonado, A., & Martos, R. (1992). Attributions modulate immunization against learned helplessness in humans. *J. Pers. Soc. Psychol., 62*(1), 139–146.

Ramm, E., Marks, I. M., Yuksel, S., & Stern, R. S. (1981). Anxiety management training for anxiety states: Positive compared with negative self-statements. *Brit. J. Psychiat., 140*, 397–373.

Rand, C. S., & Kuldau, J. M. (1991). Restrained eating (weight concerns) in the general population and among students. *Inter. J. Eat. Dis., 10*(6), 699–708.

Rand, C. S., & Kuldau, J. M. (1992). Epidemiology of bulimia and symptoms in a general population: Sex, age, race, and socioeconomic status. *Inter. J. Eat. Dis., 11*(1), 37–44.

Rapee, R. M. (1990). Psychological mechanisms underlying the response to biological challenge procedures in panic disorder. In N. McNaughton, & G. Andrews (Eds.), *Anxiety.* Dunedin, N. Z.: Otago UP.

Rapee, R. M. (1993). Psychological factors in panic disorder. *Adv. Behav. Res. Ther., 15*(1), 85–102.

Raphling, D. L. (1989). Fetishism in a woman. *J. Amer. Psychoanal. Assoc., 37*(2), 465–491.

Rapoport, J. L. (1989, March). The biology of obsessions and compulsions. *Scientific American*, 82–89.

Rapoport, J. L. (1991). Recent advances in obsessive-compulsive disorder. *Neuropsychopharmacology, 5*(1), 1–10.

Rapoport, J. L., Ryland, D. H., Kriete, M. (1992). Drug treatment of canine acral lick: An animal model of obsessive-compulsive disorder. *Arch. Gen. Psychiat., 49*, 517–521.

Rapoport, J. L., Swedo, S. E., & Leonard, H. L. (1992). Childhood obsessive compulsive disorder. *J. Clin. Psychiat., 53*(Suppl. 4), 11–16.

Rappaport, A. F., & Harrell, J. (1972). A behavioral exchange model for marital counseling. *Family Coordinator, 22*, 203–212.

Raskin, D. C. (1982). The scientific basis of polygraph techniques and their uses in the judicial process. In A. Trankell (Ed.), *Reconstructing the past: The role of psychologists in criminal trials.* Stockholm: Norstedt & Soners.

Raskin, M., Bali, L. R., & Peeke, H. V. (1980). Muscle

biofeedback and transcendental meditation: A controlled evaluation of efficacy in the treatment of chronic anxiety. *Arch. Gen. Psychiat.*, *37*(1), 93–97.

Raskin, M., Peeke, H. V. S., Dickman, W., & Pinkster, H. (1982). Panic and generalized anxiety disorders: Developmental antecedents and precipitants. *Arch. Gen. Psychiat.*, *39*, 687–689.

Raskin, N. H. (1975). Alcoholism or acetaldehydism. *New Engl. J. Med.*, *292*(8), 422–423.

Raskin, N. H., Hobobuchi, Y., & Lamb, S. A. (1987). Headaches may arise from perturbation of the brain. *Headache 27*, 416–420.

Raskin, N. J., & Rogers, C. R. (1989). Person-centered therapy. In R. J. Corsini & D. Wedding (Eds.), *Current psychotherapies.* Itasca, IL: Peacock.

Rathner, G., Bönsch, C., Maurer, G., Walter, M. H., & Söllner, W. (1993). The impact of a 'guided self-help group' on bulimic women: A prospective 15-month study of attenders and non-attenders. *J. Psychosom. Res.*, *37*(4), 389–396.

Rauchfleisch, U. (1992). The importance of different reference groups in the therapy of borderline patients. *Group Analysis*, *25*(1), 33–41.

Ray, O. S. (1983). *Drugs, society, and human behavior* (3rd ed.). St. Louis: Mosby.

Ray, O., & Ksir, C. (1993). *Drugs, society, & human behavior.* St. Louis: Mosby.

Rebert, W. M., Stanton, A. L., Schwarz, R. M. (1991). Influence of personality attributes and daily moods on bulimic eating patterns. *Addictive Behaviors*, *16*(6), 497–505.

Reda, M. A., Carpiniello, B., Secchiaroli, L., & Blanco, S. (1985). Thinking, depression, and antidepressants: Modified and unmodified depressive beliefs during treatment with amitriptyline. *Cog. Ther. Res.*, *9*(2), 135–143.

Redefer, L. A., & Goodman, J. F. (1989). Pet-facilitated therapy with autistic children. *J. Autism Dev. Dis.*, *19*(3), 461–467.

Redick, R. W., Witkin, M. J., Atay, J. E., & Manderscheid, R. W. (1992). Specialty mental health system characteristics. In R. W. Manderscheid & M. A. Sonnenschein (Eds.), *Mental Health, United States*, 1992. Washington, DC: U.S. Department of Health and Human Services.

Redmond, D. E. (1977). Alterations in the function of the nucleus locus coeruleus: A possible model for studies of anxiety. In I. Hanin & E. Usdin (Eds.), *Animal models in psychiatry and neurology.* New York: Pergamon.

Redmond, D. E. (1979). New and old evidence for the involvement of a brain norepinephrine system in anxiety. In W. E. Fann, I. Karacan, A. D. Pokorny, & R. L. Williams (Eds.), *Phenomenology and treatment of anxiety.* New York: Spectrum.

Redmond, D. E. (1981). Clonidine and the primate locus coeruleus: Evidence suggesting anxiolytic and anti-withdrawal effects. In H. Lal & S. Fielding, Psychopharmacology of clonidine. New York: Alan R. Liss.

Redmond, D. E. (1985). Neurochemical basis for anxiety and anxiety disorders: Evidence from drugs which decrease human fear or anxiety. In A. H. Tuma & J. Maser (Eds.), *Anxiety and the anxiety disorders.* Hillsdale, NJ: Erlbaum.

Reed, G. (1974). *The psychology of anomalous experience.* Boston: Houghton Mifflin.

Rees, L. (1964). The importance of psychological, allergic and infective factors in childhood asthma. *J. Psychosom. Res.*, *7*(4), 253–262.

Rees, W. D., & Lutkin, S. G. (1967). Mortality of bereavement. *British Medical Journal, 4*, 13–16.

Reese, R. M., & Serna, L. (1986). Planning for generalization and maintenance in parent training: Parents need I.E.P.s too. *Ment. Retardation*, *24*(2), 87–92.

Regier, D. A., Narrow, W. E., Rae, D. S., Manderscheid, R. W., Locke, B. Z., & Goodwin, F. K. (1993). The de facto US Mental and Addictive Disorders Service System: Epidemiologic Catchment Area prospective 1-year prevalence rates of disorders in services. *Arch. Gen. Psychiat.*, *50*, 85–94.

Reich, J. H. (1987). Sex distribution of DSM-III personality disorders in psychiatric outpatients. *Amer. J. Psychiat.*, *144*(4), 485–488.

Reich, J. H. (1990). Comparisons of males and females with DSM-III dependent personality disorder. *Psychiatry Research*, *33*(2), 207–214.

Reich, J. S., Yates, W., & Nduaguba, M. (1989). Prevalence of DSM-III personality disorders in the community. *Social Psychiatry & Psychiatric Epidemiology*, *24*(1), 12–16.

Reid, M. K., & Borkowski, J. G. (1987). Causal attributions of hyperactive children: Implications for teaching strategies and self control. *J. Educ. Psychol.*, *79*, 296–307.

Reid, R., & Lininger, T. (1993). Sexual pain disorders in the female. In W. O'Donohue and J. Geer (eds.), *Handbook of sexual dysfunctions.* Boston: Allyn and Bacon.

Reid, W. H., & Burke, W. J. (1989). Antisocial personality disorder. In American Psychiatric Association (Eds.), *Treatments of Psychiatric Disorders: A task force report of the American Psychiatric Association.* Washington, DC: American Psychiatric Press.

Reifler, B. V., Larson, E., Teri, L., & Poulson, M. (1986). Dementia of the Alzheimer's type and depression. *J. Amer. Geriat. Soc.*, *34*, 855–859.

Reik, T. (1989). The characteristics of masochism. *Amer. Imago*, *46*(2–3), 161–195.

Reis, B. E. (1993). Toward a psychoanalytic understanding of multiple personality disorder. *Bull. Menninger Clin.*, *57*(3), 309–318.

Reisman, J. M. (1991). *A history of clinical psychology* (2nd ed.). New York: Hemisphere Pub. Corp.

Reiss, S. (1985). The mentally retarded, emotionally disturbed adult. In M. Sigman (Ed.), *Children with emotional disorders and developmental disabilities.* New York: Grune & Stratton.

Reitan, R. M., & Wolfson, D. (1985). *The Halstead-Reitan Neuropsychological Test Battery: Theory and clinical interpretation.* Tucson, AZ: Neuropsychology.

Remington, G., Pollock, B., Voineskos, G., Reed, K., & Coulter, K. (1993). Acutely psychotic patients receiving high-dose Haloperidol therapy. *Journal of Clinical Psychopharmacology*, *13*(1), 41–45.

Renneberg, G., Goldstein, A. J., Phillips, D., Chambless, D. L. (1990). Intensive behavioral group treatment of avoidant personality disorder. *Behav. Ther.*, *21*(3), 363–377.

Report of the President's Commission on Mental Health. (1978). Washington, DC: GPO.

Repp, A. C., Barton, L. E., & Brulle, A. R. (1986). Assessing a least restrictive educational environment transfer through social comparison. *Educ. & Training of the Ment. Retarded*, *21*(1), 54–61.

Rescorla, R. A. (1988). Pavlovian conditioning: It's not what you think. *Amer. Psychol., 43*, 151–160.

Resick, P. A. (1987). Psychological effects of victimization: Implications for the criminal justice system. *Crime & Delinquency, 22*, 468–478.

Restak, R. M. (1979). The sex-change conspiracy. *Psych. Today, 20*, 20–25.

Reyna, L. J. (1989). Behavior therapy, applied behavior analysis, and behavior modification. In J. Hobson (Ed.), *Abnormal states of brain and mind.* Boston: Birhauser.

Reynolds, L. (1990). Drug-free after 30 years of dependence. *Aging, 361*, 26–27.

Rice, K. M., & Blanchard, E. B. (1982). Biofeedback in the treatment of anxiety disorder. *Clin. Psychol. Rev., 2*, 557–577.

Richards, C., & Lee, K. (1972). Social habilitation of the retarded. *Soc. Casework, 53*, 30.

Richelson, E. (1989). Antidepressants. In J. Hobson (Ed.), *Abnormal states of brain and mind.* Boston: Birhauser.

Richings, J. C., Khara, G. S., & McDowell, M. (1986). Suicide in young doctors. *Brit. J. Psychiat., 149*, 475–478.

Richman, J. (1991). Suicide and the elderly. In A. A. Leenaars (Ed.), *Life span perspectives of suicide: Time-lines in the suicide process.* New York: Plenum.

Richman, J. (1993). *Preventing elderly suicide: Overcoming personal despair, professional neglect, and social bias.* New York: Springer.

Richman, N. E., & Sokolove, R. L. (1992). The experience of aloneness, object representation, and evocative memory in borderline and neurotic patients. *Psychoanalytic Psychiatry, 9*(1), 77–91.

Rickels, K. (1978). Use of antianxiety agents in anxious outpatients. *Psychopharmacology, 58*(1), 1–17.

Rickels, K., & Schweizer, E. (1990). The clinical course and long-term management of generalized anxiety disorder. *Journal of Clinical Psychopharmacology, 10*(Suppl. 3), 101–110.

Rickels, K., Schweizer, E., Weiss, S., & Zavodnick, S. (1993). Maintenance drug treatment for panic disorder II. Short- and long-term outcome after drug taper. *Arch. Gen. Psychiat., 50*, 61–68.

Rietvald, W. J. (1992). Neurotransmitters and the pharmacology of the suprachiasmatic nuclei. *Pharmacological Therapy, 56*(1), 119–130.

Riggs, D. S., & Foa, E. B. (1993). Obsessive compulsive disorder. In D. H. Barlow (Ed.), *Clinical Handbook of Psychological Disorders: A Step-by-Step Treatment Manual* (2nd ed.). New York: Guilford.

Rimland, B. (1978). Inside the mind of the autistic savant. *Psych. Today, 12*, 68–80.

Rimland, B. (1988). Vitamin B6 (and magnesium) in the treatment of autism. *Autism Research Review International, 1*(4).

Rimland, B. (1990). Autistic crypto-savants. *Autism Research Review International, 4*(1), 3.

Rimland, B. (1992). Form letter regarding high dosage vitamin B6 and magnesium therapy for autism and related disorders. Autism Research Institute, publication 39E.

Rimland, B. (1992). Leominster: Is pollution a cause of autism? *Autism Research Review International, 6*(2), 1.

Rimm, D. C., & Litvak, S. B. (1969). Self-verbalization and emotional arousal. *J. Abnorm. Psychol., 74*(2), 181–187.

Rimm, D. C., & Masters, J. C. (1979). *Behavior therapy: Techniques and empirical findings* (2nd ed.). New York: Academic.

Ringuette, E., & Kennedy, T. (1966). *J. Abnorm. Psychol., 71*, 136–141.

Risch, S. C., & Janowsky, D. S. (1984). Cholinergic-Adrenergic balance in affective illness. In R. M. Post & J. C. Ballenger (Eds.), *Neurobiology of mood disorders* (Vol. I, Frontiers of Clinical Neuroscience). Baltimore: Williams & Wilkins.

Risch, S. C., Janowsky, D. S., & Gillin, J. C. (1983). Muscarinic supersensitivity of anterior pituitary ACTH and B endorphin release in major depressive illness. *Peptides, 4*(5), 788–792.

Ritchie, E. C. (1992). Treatment of gas mask phobia. *Military Medicine, 157*(2), 104–106.

Ritchie, G. G. (1968). The use of hypnosis in a case of exhibitionism. *Psychother. Theory Res. Prac., 5*, 40–43.

Roache, J. D., Cherek, D. R., Bennett, R. H., Schenkler, J. C., & Cowan, K. A. (1993). Differential effects of triazolam and ethanol on awareness, memory, and psychomotor performance. *Journal of Clinical Psychopharmacology, 13*(1), 3–15.

Roan, S. (1993, August 24). 900 Line for Sex Information to Feature Masters Touch. *Los Angeles Times*, p. E1.

Roazen, P. (1992). The rise and fall of Bruno Bettelheim. *Psychohistory Review, 20*(3), 221–250.

Robbins, D. R., & Alessi, N. C. (1985). Depressive symptoms and suicidal behavior in adolescents. *Amer. J. Psychiat., 142*(5), 588–592.

Roberts, A. R. (1979). Organization of suicide prevention agencies. In L. D. Hankoff & B. Einsidler (Eds.), Suicide: *Theory and clinical aspects.* Littleton, MA: PSG Publishing Company.

Roberts, A. R. (1990). *Crisis intervention handbook: Assessment, intervention, and research.* Belmont, CA: Wadsworth.

Roberts, C. F., Golding, S. L., & Fincham, F. D. (1987). Implicit theories of criminal responsibility. *Law and Human Behavior, 11*(3), 297–232.

Roberts, G. W., Gentleman, S. M., Lynch, A., & Graham, D. I. (1991). Beta-A4 amyloid protein deposition in brain after head trauma. *Lancet, 338*, 1422–1423.

Robertson, M. (1987). Molecular genetics of the mind. *Nature, 325*(6107), 755.

Robertson, M. (1992). *Starving in the Silences: An Exploration of Anorexia Nervosa.* New York: New York University Press.

Robertson, E. (1992). The challenge of dual diagnosis. *Journal of Health Care for the Poor and Underserved, 3*(1), 198–207.

Robin, M. W. (1992). Overcoming performance anxiety: Using RET with actors, artists, and other "performers." In W. Dryden & L. Hill (Eds.), *Innovations in rational emotive therapy.* Newbury Park, CA: Sage.

Robins, L. N., Locke, B. Z., & Regier, D. A. (1991). An overview of psychiatric disorders in America. In L. N. Robins, & D. A. Regier (Eds.), *Psychiatric disorders in America: The Epidemiological Catchment Area Study.* New York: Free Press.

Robins, L. N., & Przybeck, T. R. (1985). Age of onset of drug use as a factor in drug and other disorders. National Institute on *Drug Abuse: Research Monograph Series, 56*, 178–192.

Robins, L. N., & Regier, D. S. (1991). *Psychiatric Disorders in America: The epidemiological catchment area study.* New York: Free Press.

Robinson, L. H. (1988). Outpatient management of the suicidal child. In S. Lesse (Ed.), *What we know about suicidal behavior and how to treat it.* Northvale, NJ: Jason Aronson.

Robinson, N. M., & Robinson, H. B. (1970). *The mentally retarded child: A psychological approach.* New York: Wiley.

Robinson, N. M., & Robinson, H. B. (1976). *The mentally retarded child* (2nd ed.). New York: McGraw-Hill.

Robitscher, J., & Haynes, A. K. (1982). In defense of the insanity defense. *Emory Law J., 31,* 9–60.

Rodin, J. (1992). Sick of worrying about the way you look? Read This. *Psych. Today, 25*(1), 56–60.

Rodolfa, E. R., & Hungerford, L. (1982). Self-help groups a referral resource for professional therapists. *Professional Psychology, 13,* 345–353.

Rodriguez, O. (1986). Overcoming barriers to services among chronically mentally ill Hispanics: Lessons from the Project COPA evaluation. *Research Bulletin, 9*(1), Hispanic Research Center, Fordham University, Bronx, New York.

Roehrich, L. & Kinder, B. N. (1991). Alcohol expectancies and male sexuality: Review and implications for sex therapy. *Journal of Sex and Marital Therapy, 17*(1), 45–54.

Roesler, T. A., & McKenzie, N. (1994). Effects of childhood trauma on psychological functioning adults sexually abused as children. *J. Nerv. Ment. Dis., 182*(3), 145–150.

Roesler, & Greenfield, (Eds.). (1962). *Physiological correlation of psychological disorder.* Madison, WI: Univ. Wisconsin.

Rogers, C. R. (1951). *Client-centered therapy.* Boston: Houghton Mifflin.

Rogers, C. R. (1959). A theory of therapy personality, and interpersonal relationships as developed in the client-centered framework. In S. Koch (Ed.), *Psychology: A study of a science* (Vol. 3). New York: McGraw-Hill.

Rogers, C. R. (1961). *On becoming a person.* Boston: Houghton Mifflin.

Rogers, C. R. (Ed.). (1967). *The therapeutic relationship and its impact: A study of psychotherapy with schizophrenics.* Madison, WI: Univ. Wisconsin.

Rogers, C. R. (1987). Rogers, Kohut, and Erickson: A personal perspective on some similarities and differences. In J. K. Zeig (Ed.), *The evolution of psychotherapy.* New York: Brunner/Mazel.

Rogers, C. R., & Dymond, R. (1954). *Psychotherapy and personality change.* Chicago: Univ. Chicago.

Rogers, C. R., & Sanford, R. C. (1989). Client-centered psycho therapy. In H. I. Kaplan & B. J. Sadock (Eds.), *Comprehensive textbook of psychiatry* (Vol. 1, 5th ed.). Baltimore: Williams & Wilkins.

Rogers, J. A., & Centifanti, J. B. (1988). Madness, myths, and reality: Response to Roberta Rose. *Schizo. Bull., 14*(1), 7–15.

Rogers, J. C., & Holloway, R. L. (1990). Assessing threats to the validity of experimental and observational designs. *Family Practice Research Journal, 10*(2), 81–95.

Rogers, J. R. (1992). Suicide and alcohol: Conceptualizing the relationship from a cognitive-social paradigm. *J. Couns. Dev., 70*(4), 540–543.

Rogers, R. (1987). Assessment of criminal responsibility: empirical advances and unanswered questions. *Journal of Psychiatry & Law, 51*(1), 73–82.

Rogers, R., & Ewing, C. P. (1992). The measurement of insanity: Debating the merits of the R-CRAS and its alternatives. *International Journal of Law and Psychiatry, 15,* 113–123.

Rogler, L. H., Malgady, R. G., & Rodriguea, O. (1989). *Hispanics and mental health: A framework for research.* Malabar, FL: Krieger Publishing Company.

Rohsenow, D. J., Smith, R. E., & Johnson, S. (1985). Stress management training as a prevention program for heavy social drinkers: Cognition, affect, drinking, and individual differences. *Addic. Behav., 10*(1), 45–54.

Roll, M., & Theorell, T. (1987). Acute chest pain without obvious organic cause before age 40: Personality and recent life events. *J. Psychosom. Res., 31*(2), 215–221.

Rollin, H. R. (1980). *Coping with schizophrenia.* London: Burnett.

Rolls, B. J., Fedroff, I. C., & Guthrie, J. F. (1991). Gender differences in eating behavior and body weight regulation. *Health Psychology, 10*(2), 133–142.

Ronen, T. (1993). Intervention package for treating encopresis in a 6-year-old boy: A case study. *Behav. Psychother., 21,* 127–135.

Ronen, T., Wozner, Y., & Rahav, G. (1992). Cognitive intervention in enuresis. *Child and Family Behavior Therapy, 14*(2), 1–14.

Roose, S. S. (1991). Diagnosis and pharmacological treatment of depression in older patients. In W. A. Mayers (Ed.), *New techniques in the psychotherapy of older patients.* Washington, DC: American Psychiatric Press.

Root, M. P. (1990). Disordered eating in women of color [Special Issue]. *Sex Roles, 22*(7–8), 525–536.

Roper, G., Rachman, S., & Hodgson, R. (1973). An experiment on obsessional checking. *Behav. Res. Ther., 11,* 271–277.

Roper, M. (1992). Reaching the babies through the mothers: the effects of prosecution on pregnant substance abusers. *Law & Psychology Review, 16,* 171–188.

Roscoe, B., Martin, G. L., & Pear, J. J. (1980). Systematic self desensitization of fear of flying: A case study. In G. L. Martin and J. G. Osborne (Eds.), *Helping in the community: Behavioral applications.* New York: Plenum.

Rose, R. M. (1980). Endocrine responses to stressful psychological events. *The Psychiat. Clin. N. Amer., 3,* 251–276.

Rose, S. D. (1990). Group exposure: A method of treating agoraphobia. *Social Work with Groups, 13*(1), 37–51.

Rosen, E. F., Anthony, D. L., Booker, K. M., Brown, T. L., et al. (1991). A comparison of eating disorder scores among African American and White college females. *Bulletin of the Psychonomic Society, 29*(1), 65–66.

Rosen, J. C., & Gross, J. (1987). Prevalence of weight reducing and weight gaining in adolescent girls and boys. *Health Psychology, 6,* 131–147.

Rosen, J. C., & Leitenberg, H. (1982). Bulimia nervosa: Treatment with exposure and response prevention. *Behav. Ther., 13*(1), 117–124.

Rosen, J. C., & Leitenberg, H. (1985). Exposure plus response prevention treatment of bulimia. In D. M. Garner & P. E. Garfinkel (Eds.), *Handbook of psychotherapy for anorexia nervosa and bulimia.* New York: Guilford.

Rosen, W. G. (1991). Higher cortical processes. In K. Davis, H. Klar, & J. T. Coyle (Eds.), *Foundations of psychiatry.* Philadelphia: Saunders.

Rosenbaum, M. (1980). The role of the term schizophrenia in the decline of diagnoses of multiple personality. *Arch. Gen. Psychiat., 37*(12), 1383–1385.

Rosenbaum, M., & Berger, M. (Eds.). (1963). *Group psychotherapy and group function.* New York: Basic Books.

Rosenberg, H. (1993). Prediction of controlled drinking by alcoholics and problem drinkers. *Psychol. Bull., 113*(1), 129–139.

Rosenblatt, J. E. et al. (1979). The effect of imipramine and lithium on alpha and beta receptors binding in rat brain. *Brain Research, 160,* 186–191.

Rosenhan, D. L. (1973). On being sane in insane places. *Science, 179*(4070), 250–258.

Rosenman, R. H. (1990). Type A behavior pattern: A personal overview. *J. Soc. Behav. Pers., 5,* 1–24.

Rosenstein, M. J., Milazzo-Sayre, L. J., & Manderscheid, R. W. (1989). Care of persons with schizophrenia: A statistical profile. *Schizo. Bull., 15*(1), 45–58.

Rosenstein, M. J., Milazzo-Sayre, L. J., & Manderscheid, R. W. (1990). Characteristics of persons using specialty inpatient, outpatient, and partial care programs in 1986. In R. W. Manderscheid & M. A. Sonnenschein (Eds.), *Mental Health, United States, 1990.* DHHS Pub. No. (ADM)90-1708. Washington DC: GPO.

Rosenstock, H. A. (1985). Depression, suicidal ideation and suicide attempts in 900 adolescents: An analysis. *Crisis, 6*(2), 89–105.

Rosenthal, D. (Ed.). (1963). *The Genain quadruplets.* New York: Basic Books.

Rosenthal, D. (1970). *Genetic theory and abnormal behavior.* New York: McGraw-Hill.

Rosenthal, D. (1971). A program of research on heredity in schizophrenia. *Behav. Sci., 16*(3), 191–201.

Rosenthal, D. (1971). *Genetics of psychopathology.* New York: McGraw-Hill.

Rosenthal, N. E., & Blehar, M. C. (Eds.) (1989). *Seasonal affective disorders and phototherapy.* New York: Guilford.

Rosenthal, N. E., Jacobsen, F. M., Sack, D. A., Arendt, J., James, S. P., Parry, B. L., & Wehr, T. A. (1988). Atenolol in seasonal affective disorder: A test of the melatonin hypothesis. *Amer. J. Psychiat., 145,* 52–56.

Rosenthal, R. (1966). *Experimenter effects in behavioral research.* New York: Appleton-Century-Crofts.

Rosenthal, R., & Rubin, D. B. (1978). Interpersonal expectancy effects: The first 345 students. *Behavioral & Brain Sciences, 1*(3), 377–415.

Rosenthal, R. J. (1992). Pathological gambling. *Psychiat. Ann., 22*(2), 72–78.

Rosenthal, T., & Bandura, A. (1978). Psychological logical modeling: Theory and practice. In S. L. Garfield & A. E. Bergin (Eds.), *Handbook of psychotherapy and behavior change.* New York: Wiley.

Rosenzweig, S. (1933). The recall of finished and unfinished tasks as affected by the purpose with which they were performed. *Psychol. Bull., 30,* 698.

Rosenzweig, S. (1943). An experimental study of repression with special reference to need-persistive and ego-defensive reactions to frustration. *J. Exp. Psychol., 32,* 64–74.

Rosenzweig, S. (1987). Sally Beauchamp's career: A psychoarchaeological key to Morton Prince's classic case of multiple personality. *Genetic, Social, & General Psychology Monographs, 113*(1), 5–60.

Rosenzweig, S. (1988). The identity and idiodynamics of the multiple personality "Sally Beauchamp": A confirmatory supplement. *Amer. Psychol., 43*(1), 45–48.

Roskies, E., Seraganian, P., Oseasohn, R., Hanley, J. A., Collu, R., Martin, N., & Smigla, C. (1986). The Montreal Type A intervention Project: Major Findings. *Health Psychology, 5,* 45–69.

Rosmarin, P. (1989). Coffee and coronary heart disease: A review. *Progress in Cardiovascular Diseases, 32*(3), 239–245.

Ross, A. O. (1981). *Child behavior therapy: Principles, procedures and empirical basis.* New York: Wiley.

Ross, C. A., Anderson, G., Fleisher, W. P., & Norton, G. R. (1992). Dissociative experiences among psychiatric inpatients. *Gen. Hosp. Psychiat., 14*(5), 350–354.

Ross, C. A., & Gahan, P. (1988). Techniques in the treatment of multiple personality disorder. *Amer. J. Psychother., 42*(1), 40–52.

Ross, C. A., Kronson, J., Koenagen, S., Barkman, K., et al. (1992). Dissociative comorbidity in 100 chemically dependent patients. *Hosp. Comm. Psychiat., 43*(8), 840–842.

Ross, C. A., Miller, S. D., Bjornson, L., Reagor, P., Fraser, G. A., & Anderson, G. (1991). Abuse histories in 102 cases of multiple personality disorder. *Canad. J. Psychiat., 36,* 97–101.

Ross, C. A., Miller, S. D., Reagor, P., & Bjornson, L. et al. (1990). Structured interview data on 102 cases of multiple personality disorder from four centers. *Amer. J. Psychiat., 147*(5), 596–601.

Ross, C. A., Norton, G. R., & Wozney, K. (1989). Multiple personality disorder: An analysis of 236 cases. *Canad. J. Psychiat., 34*(5), 413–418.

Ross, D. M., & Ross, S. A. (1982). *Hyperactivity: Current issues, research and theory* (2nd ed.). New York: Wiley.

Ross, S. B. (1983). The therapeutic use of animals with the handicapped. *Inter. Child Welfare Rev., 56,* 26–39.

Ross, S. M., Gottfredson, D. K., Christensen, P., & Weaver, R. (1986). Cognitive self statements in depression: Findings across clinical populations. *Cog. Ther. Res., 10*(2), 159–165.

Rosse, R., Fay-McCarthy, M., Collins, J., Risher-Flowers, D., Alim, T., & Deutsch, S. (1993). Transient compulsive foraging behavior associated with crack cocaine use. *Amer. J. Psychiat., 150*(1), 155–156.

Rothbaum, B. O., Foa, E. B., Riggs, D. S., Murdock, T., & Walsh, W. (1992). A prospective examination of posttraumatic stress disorder in rape victims. *Journal of Traumatic Stress, 5*(3), 455–475.

Rothblum, E. D. (1992). The stigma of women's weight: Social and economic realities. *Feminism and Psychology, 2*(1), 61–73.

Rotheram, M. J. (1987). Evaluation of imminent danger for suicide among youth. Annual Meeting of the American Orthopsychiatric Assoc. *Amer. J. Orthopsychiat., 57*(1), 102–110.

Rotheram-Borus, M. J., Piacentini, J., Miller, S., Graae, F., & Castro-Blanco, D. (1994). Brief cognitive-behavioral treatment for adolescent suicide attempters and their families. *J. Amer. Acad. Child Adol. Psychiat., 33*(4), 508–517.

Rothman, D. (1985). ECT: The historical, social and professional sources of the controversy. In *NIH Consensus Development Conference: Electroconvulsive therapy.* Bethesda, MD: NIH & NIMH.

Rothschild, A. J. (1992). Disinhibition, amnestic reactions, and other adverse reactions secondary to triazolam: A review of the literature. *J. Clin. Psychiat., 53*(12, Suppl.), 69–79.

Rotter, J. B. (1954). *Social learning and clinical psychology.* New Jersey: Prentice Hall.

Rotter, M., Kalus, O., Losonczy, M., Guo, L., et al. (1991). Lateral ventricular enlargement in schizotypal personality disorder. *Bio. Psychiat.*, *29*, 182–185.

Rovner, S. (1993, April 6). Anxiety disorders are real and expensive. *Washington Post*, p. WH5.

Rowe, D. (1978). *The experience of depression.* Chichester: Wiley.

Rowe, J. W., & Kahn, R. L. (1987). Human aging: Useful and successful. *Science, 237*, 143–149.

Rowland, C. V. (1970). Anorexia nervosa: A survey of the literature and review of 30 cases. *Inter. Psychiat. Clinics*, 7(1), 37–137.

Roy, A. (1982). Suicide in chronic schizophrenics. *Brit. J. Psychiat., 141*, 171–177.

Roy, A. (1985). Early parental separation and adult depression. *Arch. Gen. Psychiat., 42*, 987–991.

Roy, A. (1985). Suicide in doctors [Special Issue]. *Psychiat. Clin. N. Amer., 8*(2), 377–387.

Roy, A. (1990). Possible biologic determinants of suicide. In D. Lester (Ed.), Current concepts of suicide. Philadelphia: The Charles Press.

Roy, A. (1992). Genetics, biology, and suicide in the family. In R. W. Maris, A. L. Berman, J. T. Maltsberger, & R. I. Yufit (Eds.), *Assessment and prediction of suicide.* New York: Guilford.

Roy, A. (1992). Suicide in schizophrenia. *International Review of Psychiatry, 4*(2), 205–209.

Roy, A., & Linnoila, M. (1986). Alcoholism and suicide. *Suic. & Life-Threat. Behav., 16*(2), 244–273.

Roy, A., Schreiber, J., Mazonson, A., & Pickar, D. (1986). Suicidal behavior in chronic schizophrenic patients: A follow-up study. *Canad. J. Psychiat., 31*(8), 737–740.

Roy-Byrne, P. P., & Wingerson, D. (1992). Pharmacotherapy of Anxiety Disorders. In A. Tasman, & M. B. Riba (Eds.), *Review of Psychiatry* (Vol. 11). Washington, DC: American Psychiatric Press.

Rozin, P., & Stoess, C. (1993). Is there a general tendency to become addicted? *Addictive Behaviors, 18*, 81–87.

Rozynko, V., & Dondershine, H. E. (1991). Trauma focus group therapy for Vietnam veterans with PTSD. *Psychotherapy, 28*(1), 157–161.

Rubonis, A. V., & Bickman, L. (1991). Psychological impairment in the wake of disaster: The disaster-psychopathology relationship. *Psychol. Bull., 109*, 384–399.

Ruderman, A. J. (1986). Dietary restraint: A theoretical and empirical review. *Psychol. Bull., 99*(2), 247–262.

Rudolph, J., Langer, I., & Tausch, R. (1980). An investigation of the psychological affects and conditions of person-centered individual psychotherapy. Zeitschrift fur Klinische Psychologie: *Forschung und Praxis, 9*, 23–33.

Ruedrich, S. L., Chu, C., & Wadle, C. V. (1985). The amytal interview in the treatment of psychogenic amnesia [Special Issue]. *Hosp. Comm. Psychiat., 36*(10), 1045–1046.

Runeson, B. (1989). Mental disorder in youth suicide: DSM-III-R Axis I and II. *Acta Psychiatr. Scandin., 79*(5), 490–497.

Rupert, P. A., & Schroeder, D. J. (1983). Effects of bidirectional heart rate biofeedback training on the heart rates and anxiety levels of anxious psychiatric patients. *Amer. J. Clin. Biofeed., 6*(1), 6–13.

Rush, A. J., & Watkins, J. T. (1981). Group versus individual cognitive therapy: A pilot study. *Cog. Ther. Res., 5*, 95–103.

Rush, A. J., Weissenburger, J., & Eaves, G. (1986). Do thinking patterns predict depressive symptoms? *Cog. Ther. Res., 10*(2), 225–235.

Russell, G. (1979). Bulimia nervosa: An ominous variant of anorexia nervosa. *Psychol. Med., 9*(3), 429–448.

Russell, G. (1981). The current treatment of anorexia nervosa. *Brit. J. Psychiat., 138*, 164–166.

Russell, R. J., & Hulson, B. (1992). Physical and psychological abuse of heterosexual partners. *Personality and Individual differences, 13*(4), 457–473.

Rutter, M. (1966). Prognosis: Psychotic children in adolescence and early adult life. In J. K. Wing (Ed.), *Childhood autism: Clinical, educational, and social aspects.* Elmsford, NY: Pergamon.

Rutter, M. (1968). Concepts of autism: A review of research. *J. Child Psychol. Psychiat. Allied Disc., 9*, 1–25.

Rutter, M. (1971). The description and classification of infantile autism. In D. Churchill, D. Alpern, & M. DeMeyer, *Infantile autism.* Springfield, IL: Thomas.

Rutter, M., & Bartak, L. (1971). Causes of infantile autism: Some considerations from recent research. *J. Autism Child. Schizo. 1*, 20–32.

Rutter, M., & Bartak, L. (1973). Special educational treatment of autistic children: A comparative study: I. Follow-up findings and implications for services. *J. Child Psychol. Psychiat. Allied Disc., 14*, 241–270.

Rutter, M., & Garmezy, N. (1983). Developmental psychopathology. In E. M. Hetherington (Ed.), *Handbook of child psychology: Socialization, personality, and social development* (Vol. 4). New York: Wiley.

Rutter, M., & Giller, H. (1983). *Juvenile delinquency: Trends and perspectives.* New York: Guilford.

Ryan, R. (1981, Apr. 3). Study shows wide abuse of elderly. *Philadelphia Inquirer.*

Rybarczyk, B., Gallagher-Thompson, D., Rodman, J., Zeiss, A. M., Gantz, F., & Yesavage, J. (1992). Applying cognitive-behavioral psychotherapy to the chronically ill elderly: Treatment issues and case illustrations. *Inter. Psychogeriatrics, 4*(1), 127–140.

Saccuzzo, D. P., & Schubert, D. L. (1981). Backward masking as a measure of slow processing in schizophrenia-spectrum disorders. *J. Abnorm. Psychol., 88*, 305–312.

Sachs, G. S., & Gelenberg, A. J. (1988). Adverse effects of electroconvulsive therapy. In A. J. Frances & R. E. Hales (Eds.), *American Psychiatric Press review of psychiatry* (Vol. 7). Washington, DC: American Psychiatric Press.

Sachs, R. G. (1986). The adjunctive role of social support systems. In B. G. Braun (Ed.), *The treatment of multiple personality disorder.* Washington, DC: American Psychiatric Press.

Sackeim, H. A. (1986). The efficacy of electroconvulsive therapy. *Ann. NY Acad. Sci., 462*, 70–75.

Sackeim, H. A. (1988). Mechanisms of action of electroconvulsive therapy. In A. J. Frances & R. E. Hales (Eds.), *American Psychiatric Press review of psychiatry* (Vol. 7). Washington, DC: American Psychiatric Press.

Sadock, B. J. (1989). Group psychotherapy, combined individual and group psychotherapy, and psychodrama. In H. I. Kaplan & B. J. Sadock (Eds.), *Comprehensive textbook of psychiatry* (Vol. 1, 5th ed.). Baltimore: Williams & Wilkins.

Sadock, V. A. (1989). Rape, spouse abuse, and incest. In H. I. Kaplan & B. J. Sadock (Eds.), *Comprehensive textbook of psychiatry* (Vol. 1, 5th ed.). Baltimore: Williams & Wilkins.

Safer, D. J., & Krager, J. M. (1984). Trends in medication therapy for hyperactivity: National and international perspectives. In K. D. Gadow (Ed.), *Advances in learning and behavioral disabilities* (Vol. 3). Greenwich, CT: JAI.

Safferman, A. Z., Lieberman, J. A., Kane, J. M., Szymanski, S., & Kinon, B. (1991). Update on the clinical efficacy and side effects of clozapine. *Schizo. Bull., 17*(2), 247–261.

Safferman, A. Z., & Munne, R. (1992). Combining clozapine with ECT. *Convulsive Therapy, 8*(2), 141–143.

Sagawa, K., Kawakatsu, S., Shibuya, I., Oiji, A. et al. (1990). Correlation of regional cerebral blood flow with performance on neuropsychological tests in schizophrenic patients. *Schizo. Res., 3*(4), 241–246.

Sahni, S. (1992). Heroin addiction and criminality. *Journal of Personality & Clinical Studies, 8*, 35–38.

Sakel, M. (1938). The pharmacological shock treatment of schizophrenia. *Nerv. Ment. Dis. Monograph Series, 62*, 136.

Sakheim, D. K., Hess, E. P., & Chivas, A. (1988). General principles for short-term inpatient work with multiple personality-disorder patients. *Psychotherapy, 24*, 117–124.

Salama, A. A. (1988). The antisocial personality (the sociopathic personality). *Psychiat. J. Univ. Ottawa, 13*(3), 149–151.

Sales, E., Baum, M., & Shore, B. (1984). Victim readjustment following assault. *J. Soc. Issues, 37*, 5–27.

Sales, E., Baum, M., & Shore, B. (1984). Victim readjustment following assault. *J. Soc. Issues, 40*(1), 117–136.

Salisbury, J. J., & Mitchell, J. E. (1991). Bone mineral density and anorexia nervosa in women. *Amer. J. Psychiat., 148*(6), 768–774.

Salkovskis, P. M. (1983). Treatment of an obsessional patient using habituation to audiotaped ruminations. *British Journal of Clinical Psychology, 22*, 311–313.

Salkovskis, P. M. (1985). Obsessional-compulsive problems: A cognitive-behavioural analysis. *Behav. Res. Ther., 23*, 571–584.

Salkovskis, P. M. (1989). Cognitive-behavioural factors and the persistence of intrusive thoughts in obsessional problems. *Behav. Res. Ther., 27*, 677–682.

Salkovskis, P. M., Clark, D. M., & Hackman, A. (1991). Treatment of panic attacks using cognitive therapy without exposure or breathing retaining. *Behav. Res. Ther., 29*(2), 161–166.

Salkovskis, P. M., & Westbrook, D. (1989). Behaviour therapy and obsessional ruminations: can failure be turned into success? *Behav. Res. Ther., 27*, 149–160.

Salovey, P., & Haar, M. D. (1990). The efficacy of cognitive-behavior therapy and writing process training for alleviating writing anxiety. *Cog. Ther. Res., 14*(5), 513–526.

Salzman, L. (1968). *The obsessive personality.* New York: Science House.

Salzman, L. (1980). *Psychotherapy of the obsessive personality.* New York: Aronson.

Salzman, L. (1985). Psychotherapeutic management of obsessive-compulsive patients. *Amer. J. Psychother., 39*(3), 323–330.

Salzman, L. (1989). Compulsive personality disorder. In *Treatments of Psychiatric Disorders.* Washington, DC: American Psychiatric Press.

Samelson, F. (1980). J. B. Watson's Little Albert, Cyril Burt's twins, and the need for a critical science. *Amer. Psycho., 35*, 619–625.

Sameroff, A. J., & Seifer, R. (1990). Early contributors to developmental risk. In J. E. Rolf, A. S. Masten, D. Cicchetti, K. H. Neuchterlein, & S. Weintraub (Eds.), *Risk and protective factors in the development of psychopathology.* New York: Cambridge UP.

SAMHSA News. (1993, Spring). *Agencies Improve Mental Health Services in Jails,* Vol. 1, No. 2. U. S. Dept. of Health and Human Services.

Sampath, G., Shah, A., Kraska, J., & Soni, S. D. (1992). Neuroleptic discontinuation in the very stable schizophrenic patient: Relapse rates and serum neuroleptic levels. *Human Psychopharmacology Clinical and Experimental, 7*(4), 255–264.

Sanchez-Canovas, J., Botella-Arbona, C., Ballestin, G. P., & Soriano-Pastor, J. (1991). Intervencion comportamental y analisis ipsativo normativo en un trastorno de ansiedad. [Behavioral intervention and ipsative-normative analysis in an anxiety disorder]. *Analisis y Modificacion de Conducta, 17*(51), 115–151.

Sander, F. M., & Feldman, L. B. (1993). Integrating individual, marital, and family therapy. In J. M. Oldham, M. B. Riba, & A. Tasman (Eds.), *Review of Psychiatry* (Vol. 12). Washington, DC: American Psychiatric Press.

Sanderman, R., & Ormel, J. (1992). De Utrechtse Coping Lijst (UCL): Validiteit en betrouwbaarheid [The Utrecht Coping List (UCL): Validity and reliability]. *Gedrag and Gezondheid Tijdschrift voor Psychologie and Gezondheid, 20*(1), 32–37.

Sanders, D. (1985). *The woman book on sex and love.* London: Joseph.

Sanders, D. (1987). *The woman report on men.* London: Sphere.

Sanderson, R. E., Campbell, D., & Laverty, S. G. (1963). An investigation of a new aversive conditioning treatment for alcoholism. *Quart. J. Stud. Alcohol., 24*, 261–275.

Sanderson, W. C., & Barlow, D. H. (1991). Research strategies in clinical psychology. In C. E. Walker (Ed.), *Clinical Psychology: Historical and research foundations.* New York: Plenum.

Sanderson, W. C., DiNardo, P. A., Rapee, R. M., & Barlow, D. H. (1990). Syndrome comorbidity in patients diagnosed with a DSM-III-R anxiety disorder. *J. Abnorm. Psychol., 99*(3), 308–312.

Sandler, J. & Sandler, A. M. (1978). On the development of object relations and affects. *Inter. J. Psychoanal., 59*, 285–296.

Sandler, M. (1990). Monoamine oxidase inhibitors in depression: History and mythology. *J. Psychopharm., 4*(3), 136–139.

Sandoval, J., Davis, J. M., & Wilson, M. P. (1987). An overview of the school-based prevention of adolescent suicide. *Special Services in the Schools, 3*(3–4), 103–120.

Sanford, R. C. (1987). An inquiry into the evolution of the client-centered approach to psychotherapy. In J. K. Zeig (Ed.), *The evolution of psychotherapy.* New York: Brunner/Mazel.

Sansone, R. A., Fine, M. A., & Dennis, A. B. (1991). Treatment impressions and termination experiences with borderline patients. *Amer. J. Psychother., 45*(2), 173–180.

Saposnek, D. T., & Watson, L. S. (1974). The elimination of the self-destructive behavior of a psychotic child: A case study. *Behav. Ther., 5*, 79–89.

Sarbin, T. R., & Coe, W. C. (1979). Hypnosis and psychopathology: replacing old myths with fresh metaphors. *J. Abnorm. Psychol.*, *88*(5), 506–526.

Sarrel, P. M., & Sarrel, L. J. (1989). Dyspareunia and vaginismus. In American Psychiatric Association, *Treatments for psychiatric disorders: A task force report of the American Psychiatric Association*. Volume 3, pp. 2291–2299. Washington, D.C.: American Psychiatric Association.

Satir, V. (1964). *Conjoint family therapy: A guide to therapy and technique*. Palo Alto, CA: Science & Behavior Books.

Satir, V. (1967). *Conjoint family therapy* (Revised Ed.). Palo Alto, CA: Science and Behavior Books.

Satir, V. (1987). Going behind the obvious: The psychotherapeutic journey. In J. K. Zeig (Ed.), *The evolution of psychotherapy*. New York: Brunner/Mazel.

Satz, P., & Baraff, A. (1962). Changes in relation between self concepts and ideal self-concepts of psychotics consequent upon therapy. *J. Gen. Psychol.*, *67*, 191–198.

Saunders, D. G. (1992). A typology of men who batter: three types derived from cluster analysis. *Amer. J. Orthopsychiat.*, *62*(2), 264–275.

Saunders, D. G. (1982). Counseling the violent husband. In P. A. Keller & L. G. Ritt (Eds.), *Innovations in clinical practice: A source book* (Vol. 1). Sarasota, FL: Professional Resource Exchange.

Saunders, J. C. (1963). Treatment of hospitalized depressed and schizophrenic patients with monoamine oxidase inhibitors: Including reflections on pargyline. *Ann. NY Acad. Sci.*, *107*, 1081–1089.

Saunders, R. (1985). Bulimia: An expanded definition. *Soc. Casework*, *66*(10), 603–610.

Savishinsky, J. S. (1992). Intimacy, domesticity and pet therapy with the elderly: Expectation and experience among nursing home volunteers. *Soc. Sci. Med.*, *34*(12), 1325–1334.

Saxe, L. (1991). Lying: Thoughts of an applied social psychologist. *Amer. Psychol.*, *46*(4), 409–415.

Saxe, G. N., van der Kolk, B. A., Berkowitz, R., Chinman, G., Hall, K., Lieberg, G., & Schwartz, J. (1993). Dissociative disorders in psychiatric inpatients. *Amer. J. Psychiat.*, *150*(7), 1037–1042.

Saxe, L., Dougherty, D., & Cross, T. P. (1985). The validity of polygraph testing: Scientific analysis and public controversy. *Amer. Psychol.*, *40*(3), 355–366.

Sayers, J. (1988). Anorexia, psychoanalysis, and feminism: Fantasy and reality. *J. Adolescence*, *11*(4), 361–371.

Sayette, M. A. (1993). An appraisal-disruption model of alcohol's effects on stress responses in social drinkers. *Psychol. Bull.*, *114*(3), 459–476.

Scarr, S., & Weinberg, R. A. (1977). Intellectual similarities within families of both adopted and biological children. *Intelligence*, *1*(2), 170–191.

Schachar, R. J., & Wachsmuth, R. (1990). Hyperactivity and parental psychopathology. *J. Child Psychol. Psychiat. Allied Disc.*, *31*, 381–392.

Schachter, S., & Singer, J. E. (1962). Cognitive, social, and physiological determinants of emotional state. *Psych. Rev.*, *69*, 379–399.

Schachter, S., & Wheeler, L. (1962). Epinephrine, chlorpromazine and amusement. *Journal of Applied Social Psychology*, *65*, 121–128.

Schacter, D. L. (1989). Autobiographical memory in a case of multiple personality disorder. *J. Abnorm. Psychol.*, *98*(4), 508–514.

Schacter, D. L., Glisky, E. L., & McGlynn, S. M. (1990). Impact of memory disorder on everyday life: Awareness of deficits and return to work. In D. Tupper & K. Cicerone (Eds.), *The Neuropsychology of Everyday Life*, Vol. 1: Theories and Basic Competencies. Boston: Marinus Nijhof.

Schanke, A. K. (1992). Mote med psykiatriens historie. Lombotomering belyst ved kasuistikk. [Encounter with the history of psychiatry: The case of a lobotomized patient.] *Tidsskrift for Norsk Psykologforening*, *29*(1), 16–31.

Schatzberg, A. T. et al. (1982). Toward a biochemical classification of depressive disorders: V. Heterogeneity of unipolar depressions. *Amer. J. Psychiat.*, *130*(4), 471–475.

Scheff, T. J. (1966). *Being mentally ill: A sociological theory*. Chicago: Aldine.

Scheff, T. J. (1975). *Labeling madness*. Englewood Cliffs, NJ: Prentice Hall.

Scheier, M. F., & Carver, C. S. (1985). Optimism, coping, and health: Assessment and implications of generalized outcome expectancies. *Hlth. Psychol.*, *4*(3), 219–247.

Schellenberg, G. D., Bird, T., Wijsman, E. M., et al. (1992). Genetic linkage evidence for a familiar Alzheimer's disease locus on chromosome 14. *Science*, *258*, 668–671.

Scherling, D. (1994). Prenatal cocaine exposure and childhood psychopathology: A developmental analysis. *Amer. J. Orthopsychiat.*, *64*(1), 9–19.

Schiavi, R. C., White, D., Mandeli, J., & Schreiner-Engel, P. (1993). Hormones and nocturnal penile tumescence in healthy aging men. *Archives of Sexual Behavior*, *22*(2), 207–216.

Schiele, B. C., & Brozek, J. (1948). Experimental neurosis resulting from semistarvation in man. *Psychosom. Med.*, *10*, 31–50.

Schiff, S. M. (1988). Treatment approaches for older alcoholics. *Generations*, *12*(4), 41–45.

Schildkraut, J. J. (1965). The catecholamine hypothesis of affective disorders: A review of supporting evidence. *Amer. J. Psychiat.*, *122*(5), 509–522.

Schleifer, S. J., & Keller, S. E. (1991). Depressive disorders and immunity. In N. Plotnikoff, A. Murgo, R. Faith, & J. Wybran (Eds.), *Stress and immunity*. Boca Raton: CRC Press.

Schlichter, K. J., & Horan, J. J. (1981). Effects of stress innoculation on the anger and aggression management skills of institutionalized juvenile delinquents. *Cog. Ther. Res.*, *5*(4), 359–365.

Schmauk, F. J. (1970). Punishment, arousal, and avoidance learning in sociopaths. *J. Abnorm. Psychol.* *76*(3, Pt. 1), 325–335.

Schmidt, F. L. (1992). What do data really mean? Research findings, meta-analysis, and cumulative knowledge in psychology. *Amer. Psychol.*, *47*(10), 1173–1181.

Schneider, R. H., Alexander, C. N., & Wallace, R. K. (1992). In search of an optimal behavioral treatment for hypertension: A review and focus on transcendental meditation. In E. H. Johnson, W. D. Gentry, & S. Julius (Eds.), *Personality, Elevated Blood Pressure, and Essential Hypertension*. Washington: Hemisphere Pub. Corp.

Schneiderman, L., & Baum, A. (1992). Acute and chronic stress and the immune system. In N. Schneiderman, P.

McCabe, & A. Baum (Eds.), *Perspectives in Behavioral Medicine: Stress and Disease Processes.* Hillsdale, NJ: Lawrence Erlbaum Associates.

Schneier, F. R., Johnson, J., Hornig, C. D., Liebowitz, M. R., et al. (1992). Social phobia: Comorbidity and morbidity in an epidemiologic sample. *Arch. Gen. Psychiat., 49*(4), 282–288.

Schneier, F. R., Spitzer, R. L., Gibbon, M., Fyer, A. J., et al. (1991). The relationship of social phobia subtypes and avoidant personality. *Comprehen. Psychiat., 32*(6), 496–502.

Schnurr, P. P., Friedman, M. J., & Rosenberg, S. D. (1993). Premilitary MMPI scores as predictors of combat-related PTSD symptoms. *Amer. J. Psychiat., 150*(3), 479–483.

Schoenberg, B., Kokmen, E., & Okazaki, H. (1987). Alzheimer's disease and other dementing illnesses in a defined United States population: Incidence rates and clinical features. *Ann. Neurol., 22,* 724–729.

Schoeneman, T. J. (1984). The mentally ill witch in textbooks of abnormal psychology: Current status and implications of a fallacy. *Profess. Psychiat., 15,* 299–314.

Scholing, A., & Emmelkamp, P. M. G. (1993). Cognitive and behavioral treatments of fear of blushing, sweating or trembling. *Behav. Res. Ther., 31,* 155–170.

Scholing, A., & Emmelkamp, P. M. G. (1993). Exposure with and without cognitive therapy for generalized social phobia: Effects of individual and group treatment. *Behav. Res. Ther. 31*(7), 667–681.

Schonfeld, L., & Dupree, L. (1990). Older problem drinkers — long-term and late-life onset abusers: What triggers their drinking? *Aging, 361,* 3–11.

Schopler, E. (1976). Toward reducing behavior problems in autistic childhood. *J. Autism Child. Schizo., 6,* 1–13.

Schopler, E. (1981). Autism in adolescence and adulthood. Proceeding of the 1981 International Conference on Autism, 16–21.

Schopler, E., & Hennike, J. M. (1990). Past and present trends in residential treatment [Special Issue]. *J. Autism Dev. Dis., 20*(3), 291–298.

Schover, L. R., Friedman, J., Weiler, S., Heiman, J. R., & LoPiccolo, J. (1982). A multi-axial diagnostic system for sexual dysfunctions: An alternative to DSM-111. *Arch. Gen. Psychiat., 39,* 443–449.

Schover, L. R., & Jensen, S. B. (1988). *Sexuality and chronic illness.* New York: Guilford.

Schover, L. R., & LoPiccolo, J. (1982). Treatment effectiveness for dysfunctions of sexual desires. *Journal of Sex and Marital Therapy, 8*(3), 179–197.

Schreiber, F. R. (1973). *Sybil.* Chicago: Regnery.

Schuckit, M. A., & Schuckit, J. J. (1991). In L. Davidson & M. Linnoila (Eds.), *Risk factors for youth suicide.* New York: Hemisphere.

Schuldberg, D., French, C., Stone, B. L., & Heberle, J. (1988). Creativity and schizotypal traits: Creativity test scores and perceptual aberration, magical ideation, and impulsive nonconformity. *J. Nerv. Ment. Dis., 176*(11), 648–57.

Schulz, P. M., et al. (1986). Diagnoses of the relatives of schizotypal outpatients. *J. Nerv. Ment. Dis., 174*(8), 457–463.

Schulz, R. (1994). Report. Psychosomatic Society.

Schulz, R., Visintainer, P., & Williamson, G. M. (1990). Psychiatric and physical morbidity effects of caregiving. *Journals of Gerontology, 45*(5), 181–191.

Schulz, S. C., Schulz, P. M., & Wilson, W. H. (1988). Medica-

tion treatment of schizotypal personality disorder. *J. Pers. Dis., 2*(1), 1–13.

Schut, J. (1992). From the folks who brought you the hot-tub. *Institutional Investor, 26,* p. 171.

Schwartz, A. J., & Whitaker, L. C. (1990). Suicide among college students: Assessment, treatment, and intervention. In S. J. Blumenthal & D. J. Kupfer (Eds.), *Suicide over the life cycle: Risk factors, assessment, and treatment of suicidal patients.* Washington, DC: American Psychiatry Press.

Schwartz, D. M., & Thompson, M. G. (1981). Do anorectics get well? Current research and future needs. *Amer. J. Psychiat., 138*(3), 319–323.

Schwartz, G. (1977). College students as contingency managers for adolescents in a program to develop reading skills. *J. Appl. Behav. Anal., 10,* 645–655.

Schwartz, G. E. (1977). Psychosomatic disorders and biofeedback: A psychobiological model of disregulation. In J. D. Maser and M. E. P. Seligman (Eds.), *Psychopathology: Experimental models.* San Francisco: W.H. Freeman.

Schwartz, G. E. (1982). Testing the biopsychosocial model: The ultimate challenge facing behavioral medicine? *J. Cons. Clin. Psychol., 50*(6), 1040–1053.

Schwartz, S., & Johnson, J. J. (1985). *Psychopathology of childhood.* New York: Pergamon.

Schwarz, J., & Lindner, A. (1992). Inpatient Treatment of male pathological gamblers in Germany. *Journal of Gambling Studies, 8*(1), 93–109.

Schwarz, K., Harding, R., Harrington, D., & Farr, B. (1993). Hospital management of a patient with intractable factitious disorder. *Psychosomatics, 34*(3), 265–267.

Schweizer, E., Rickels, K., Weiss, S., & Zavodnick, S. (1993). Maintenance drug treatment of panic disorder I. Results of a prospective, placebo-controlled comparison of alprazolam and imipramine. *Arch. Gen. Psychiat., 50,* 51–60.

Scola, P. S. (1991). Classification and social status. In J. L. Matson & J. A. Mulick (Eds.), *Handbook of mental retardation.* New York: Pergamon.

Scott, J. (1990, Jul. 25). Vertigo, not madness, may have tormented Van Gogh. *Los Angeles Times,* p. A14.

Scott, R. D., Fagin, L., & Winter, D. (1993). The importance of the role of the patient in the outcome of schizophrenia. *Brit. J. Psychiat., 163,* 62–68.

Scoville, W. B., & Milner, B. (1957). Loss of recent memory after bilateral hippocampal lesions. *Journal of Neurology, Neurosurgery, and Psychiatry, 20,* 11–21.

Seay, B. M., Hansen, H. F., & Harlow, H. F. (1962). Mother-infant separation in monkeys. *J. Child. Psychol. Psychiat., 3,* 123–132.

Seay, B. M., Hansen, E. W., & Harlow, H. F. (1965). Maternal separation in the rhesus monkey. *J. Nerv. Ment. Dis., 140,* 434–441.

Sederer, L. I. (1992). Brief Hospitalization. In A. Tasman & M. B. Riba (Eds.), *Review of Psychiatry:* Vol. 11. Washington, D.C.: American Psychiatric Press.

Sedvall, G. (1990). Monoamines and schizophrenia. International Symposium: Development of a new antipsychotic: Remoxipride. *Acta Psychiatr. Scandin., 82*(358, Suppl.), 7–13.

Sedvall, G. (1990). PET imaging of dopamine receptors in human basal ganglia: Relevance to mental illness. *Trends in Neurosci., 13*(7), 302–308.

Seeman, P., Lee, T., Chau Wong, M., & Wong, K. (1976). Antipsychotic drug doses and neurolaptic/dopamine receptors. *Nature*, *281*(5582), 717–718.

Segal, B. M. (1988). A borderline style of functioning: The role of family, society, and heredity: An overview. *Child Psychiat. Human Dev.*, *18*(4), 219–238.

Segal, S. P., Cohen, D., & Marder, S. R. (1992). Neuroleptic medication and prescription practices with sheltered-care residents: A twelve-year perspective. *Amer. J. Pub. Hlth.*, *82*(6), 846–852.

Segraves, R. T. (1988). Drugs and desire. In R. C. Rosen & S. R. Leiblum (Eds.), *Sexual desire disorders*. New York: Guilford.

Segraves, R. T. (1988). Hormones and libido. In R. C. Rosen & S. R. Lieblum (Eds.), *Sexual desire disorders*. New York: Guilford.

Seiden, R. H. (1981). Mellowing with age: Factors influencing the nonwhite suicide rate. *Inter. J. Aging and Human Devel.*, *13*, 265–284.

Seiden, R. H. (1969, December). *Suicide among youth: A review of the literature, 1900–1967*. NIMH Bulletin of Suicidology (Supplement), PHS Pub. No. 1971.

Seidman, L. J. (1990). The neuropsychology of schizophrenia: A neurodevelopmental and case study approach. *J. Neuropsychiat. & Clin. Neurosci.*, *2*(3), 301–312.

Seitz, P. F. D., & Molholm, H. B. (1947). Relation of mental imagery to hallucinations. *Arch. Neurol. Psychiat.*, *57*, 469–480.

Seligman, M. E. P. (1968). Chronic fear produced by unpredictable electric shock. *J. Compar. Physiol. Psychol.*, *66*, 402–411.

Seligman, M. E. P. (1971). Phobias and preparedness. *Behav. Ther.*, *2*, 307–320.

Seligman, M. E. P. (1975). *Helplessness*. San Francisco: W. H. Freeman.

Seligman, M. E. P. (1992). Wednesday's children. *Psych. Today*, *25*(1), 61.

Seligman, M. E. P., Abramson, L., Semmel, A., & Von Baeyer, C. (1979). Depressive attributional style. *J. Abnorm. Psychol.*, *88*, 222–247.

Seligman, M. E. P., Abramson, L., Semmel, A., & Von Baeyar, C. (1984). Depressive attributional style. *Southern Psychol.*, *2*(1), 18–22.

Seligman, M. E. P., Castellon, C., Cacciola, J., Schulman, P. et al. (1988). Explanatory style change during cognitive therapy for unipolar depression. *J. Abnorm. Psychol.*, *97*(1), 13–18.

Seligmann, J., Rogers, P., & Annin, P. (1994, May 2). The Pressure to Lose. *Newsweek*, p. 60–61.

Selkoe, D. J. (1992). Alzheimer's disease: New insights into an emerging epidemic. *Journal of Geriatric Psychiatry*, *25*(2), 211–227.

Selling, L. S. (1940). *Men against madness*. New York: Greenberg.

Selling, L. S. (1942). The psychiatric aspects of the pathological liar. *Nervous Child*, *1*, 335–350.

Selmi, P. M. (1983). *Computer-assisted cognitive-behavior therapy in the treatment of depression*. Unpublished doctoral dissertation. Illinois Institute of Technology. Chicago.

Selye, H. (1974). *Stress without distress*. Philadelphia: Lippincott.

Selye, H. (1976). *Stress in health and disease*. Woburn, MA: Butterworth.

Semans, J. H. (1956). Premature ejaculation: A new approach. *Southern Med. J.*, *49*, 353–357.

Senter, N. W., Winslade, W. J., Liston, E. H. et al. (1984). *Electroconvulsive therapy*. Bethesda, MD: NIH and NIMH.

Serban, G., & Gidynski, C. B. (1975). Differentiating criteria for acute chronic distinction in schizophrenia. *Arch. Gen. Psychiat.*, *32*(6), 705–712.

Servan-Schreiber, D. (1986). Artificial intelligence and psychiatry. *J. Nerv. Ment. Dis.*, *174*(4), 191–202.

Shader, R. I., & Greenblatt, D. J. (1993, May 13). Use of benzodiazepines in anxiety disorders. *The New England Journal of Medicine*, pp. 1398–1405.

Shadish, W. R., Montgomery, L. M., Wilson, P., Wilson, M. R., Bright, I., & Okwumakua, T. (1993). The effects of family and marital psychotherapies: A meta-analysis. *J. Cons. Clin. Psychol.*, *61*, 61.

Shaffer, D., & Fisher, P. (1981). Suicide in children and young adolescents. In C. F. Wells & I. R. Stuart (Eds.), *Self-destructive behavior in children and adolescents*. New York: Van Nostrand Reinhold.

Shaffer, D., & Gould, M. (1986). *A study of completed and attempted suicide in adolescents. Presented to the National Conference on Youth Suicide*. Oakland, CA.

Shafii, M., Carrigan, S., Whittinghill, J. R., & Derrick, A. (1985). Psychological autopsy of completed suicide in children and adolescents. *Amer. J. Psychiat.*, *142*(9), 1061–1064.

Shah, A. V., Parulkar, G. B., Mattoo, B., Bowalekar, S. K., et al. (1991). Clinical evaluation of buspirone and diazepam in generalized anxiety disorders. *Current Therapeutic Research*, *50*(6), 827–834.

Shamoian, C. (1991). What is anxiety in the elderly? In C. Salzman & B. D. Lebowitz (Eds.), *Anxiety in the elderly*. New York: Springer.

Shaner, A., Khalsa, M., Roberts, L., Wilkins, J., Anglin, D., & Hsieh, S. (1993). Unrecognized cocaine use among schizophrenic patients. *Amer. J. Psychiat.*, *150*(5), 758–762.

Shapiro, A. K., & Morris, L. A. (1978). The placebo effect in medical and psychological therapies. In S. L. Garfield & A. E. Bergin (Eds.), *Handbook of psychotherapy and behavior change* (2nd ed.). New York: Wiley.

Shapiro, D. A. (1982). Overview: Clinical and physiological comparison of meditation with other self-control strategies. *Amer. J. Psychiat.*, *139*(3), 267–274.

Shapiro, D. A., & Shapiro, D. (1983). Comparative therapy outcome research: Methodological implications of meta-analysis. *J. Cons. Clin. Psychol.*, *51*, 42–53.

Shapiro, S. (1993). cited in "Under the Couch." *Psych. Today*, *25*(2), p. 14.

Sharp, C. W., & Freeman, C. P. L. (1993). The medical complications of anorexia nervosa. *Brit. J. Psychiat.*, *162*, 452–462.

Shaunesey, K., Cohen, J. L., Plummer, B., & Berman, A. (1993). Suicidality in hospitalized adolescents: Relationship to prior abuse. *Amer. J. Orthopsychiat.*, *63*(1), 113–119.

Shavit, Y., & Martin, F. C. (1987). Opiates, stress, and immunity: Animal studies. *Ann. Behav. Med.*, *9*(2), 11–15.

Shaw, B. F. (1976). A systematic investigation of two psychological treatments of depression. *Dissertation Abstracts Inter.*, *36*(8-B), 4179–4180.

Shaw, B. F. (1977). Comparison of cognitive therapy and behavior therapy in the treatment of depression. *J. Clin. Psychol.*, *45*, 543–551.

Shaw, B. F., & Segal, Z. V. (1988). Introduction to cognitive theory and therapy. In A. J. Frances & R. E. Hales (Eds.), *American psychiatric press review of psychiatry* (Vol. 7). Washington, DC: American Psychiatric Press.

Shaw, D. M., Churchill, C. M., Noyes, R., & Loeffelholz, P. L. (1987). Criminal behavior and posttraumatic stress disorder in Vietnam veterans. *Comprehen. Psychiat.*, *28*(5), 403–411.

Shaw, P. (1979). A comparison of three behaviour therapies in the treatment of social phobia. *Brit. J. Psychiat.*, *134*, 620–623.

Shea, S. (1988). *Interviewing: The art of understanding.* Philadelphia: Saunders.

Shea, S. (1990). Contemporary psychiatric interviewing: Integration of DSM-III-R, psychodynamic concerns and mental status. In G. Goldstein & M. Hersen (Eds.), *Handbook of psychological assessment* (2nd ed.). New York: Pergamon.

Shedler, J., & Block, J. (1990). Adolescent drug use and psychological health: A longitudinal inquiry. *Amer. Psychol.*, *45*(5), 612–630.

Shedler, J., Mayman, M., & Manis, M. (1993). The illusion of mental health. *Amer. Psychol.*, *48*(11), 1117–1131.

Sheehan, D. V. (1982). Panic attacks and phobias. *New England Journal of Medicine, 307*, 156–158.

Sheline, Y., & Beattie, M. (1992). Effects of the right to refuse treatment medication in an emergency psychiatric service. *Hosp. Comm. Psychiat.*, *43*(6), 640–642.

Sheppard, M. A., Wright, D., & Goodstadt, M. S. (1985). Peer pressure and drug use: Exploding the myth. *Adolescence, 20*(80), 949–958.

Sher, K. J., & Trull, T. J. (1994). Personality and disinhibitry psychopathology: Alcoholism and antisocial personality disorder. *J. Abnorm. Psychol.*, *103*(1), 92–102.

Sheras, P., & Worchel, S. (1979). *Clinical psychology: A social psychological approach.* New York: Van Nostrand.

Sherer, M. (1985). Depression and suicidal ideation in college students. *Psych. Rep.*, *57*(3, Pt. 2), 1061–1062.

Sherfey, M. J. (1973). *The nature and evolution of female sexuality.* New York: Vintage.

Sherlock, R. (1983). Suicide and public policy: A critique of the "New Consensus." *J. Bioethics, 4*, 58–70.

Sherman, C. (1993). Behind closed doors: therapist-client sex. *Psych. Today, 26*(3), 64–72.

Sherman, L. W. (1992). *Policing domestic violence.* New York: Free Press.

Sherman, R., & Thompson, R. (1990). *Bulimia: A guide for family and friends.* Lexington, MA: Lexington.

Sherrington, C. S. (1906). *Integrative action of the nervous system.* New Haven, CT: Yale UP.

Shevitz, S. A. (1976). Psychosurgery: Some current observations. *Amer. J. Psychiat.*, *133*(3), 266–270.

Shi, J., Benowitz, N., Denaro, C., & Sheiner, L. (1993). Pharmacokinetic-pharmacodynamic modeling of caffeine: Tolerance to pressor effects. *Clin. Pharm. Ther.*, 53(1), 6–15.

Shiriqui, C. L., Bradwejn, J., Annable, L., & Jones, B. D. (1992). Vitamin E in the treatment of tardive dyskinesia: A double-blind placebo-controlled study. *Amer. J. Psychiat.*, *149*(3), 391–393.

Shneidman, E. S. (1963). Orientations toward death: Subintentioned death and indirect suicide. In R. W. White (Ed.), *The study of lives.* New York: Atherton.

Shneidman, E. S. (1973). Suicide notes reconsidered. *Psychiatry, 36*, 379–394.

Shneidman, E. S. (1979). An overview: Personality, motivation, and behavior theories. In L. D. Hankoff & B. Einsidler (Eds.), *Suicide: Theory and clinical aspects.* Littleton, MA: PSG Pub. Co.

Shneidman, E. S. (1981). Suicide. *Suic. Life-Threat. Behav., 11*(4), 198–220.

Shneidman, E. S. (1985). *Definition of suicide.* New York: Wiley.

Shneidman, E. S. (1987, Mar.). At the point of no return. *Psychol. Today.*

Shneidman, E. S. (1991). The key to suicide. In personal correspondence.

Shneidman, E. S. (1993). *Suicide as psychache: A clinical approach to self-destructive behavior.* Northvale, NJ: Jason Aronson.

Shneidman, E. S., & Farberow, N. (1968). The Suicide Prevention Center of Los Angeles. In H. L. P. Resnick (Ed.), *Suicidal behaviors: Diagnosis and management.* Boston: Little, Brown.

Shoham-Salomon, V. (1991). Introduction to special section on client-therapy interaction research. *J. Cons. Clin. Psychol., 59*, 203–204.

Shopsin, B., & Feiner, N. F. (1984). Serotonin and depression: A brief review. *Advances in Biological Psychiatry, 14*, 1–11.

Shtasel, D. L., Gur, R. E., Gallacher, F., Heimburg, C., et al. (1992). Gender differences in the clinical expression of schizophrenia. *Schizophrenia Research, 7*(3), 225–231.

Shuller, D. Y., & McNamara, J. R. (1980). The use of information derived from norms and from a credible source to counter expectancy effects in behavioral assessment. *Behav. Assess., 2*, 183–196.

Siegel, B. V., Buchsbaum, M. S., Bunney, W. E., Gottschalk, L. A., et al. (1993). Cortical-striatal-thalamic circuits and brain glucose metabolic activity in 70 unmedicated male schizophrenic patients. *Amer. J. Psychiatry., 150*(9), 1325–1336.

Siegel, K. (1988). Rational suicide. In S. Lesse (Ed.), *What we know about suicidal behavior and how to treat it.* Northvale, NJ: Jason Aronson.

Siever, L. J. (1981). Schizoid and schizotypal personality disorders. In J. R. Lion (Ed.), *Personality disorders—diagnosis and management.* Baltimore: Williams & Williams.

Siever, L. J. (1992). Schizophrenia spectrum personality disorders. In A. Tasman & M. B. Riba (Eds.), *American Psychiatric Press Review of Psychiatry* (Vol. 11). Washington, DC: American Psychiatric Press.

Siever, L. J., & Davis, K. L. (1991). A psychobiological perspective on the personality disorders. *Amer. J. Psychiat., 148*(12), 1647–1658.

Siever, L. J., Amin, F., Coccaro, E. F., Trestman, R. L., et al. (1993). CSF homonvanillic acid in schizotypal personality disorder. *Amer. J. Psychiat., 150*, 149–151.

Siever, L. J., Davis, K. L., & Gorman, L. K. (1991). Pathogenesis of mood disorders. In K. Davis, H. Klar, & J. T. Coyle, *Foundations of psychiatry.* Philadelphia: Saunders.

Siever, L. J., Keefe, R., & Bernstein, D. (1990). Eye tracking impairment in clinically-identified patients with schizotypal personality disorder. *Amer. J. Psychiat., 147*, 740–745.

Siever, L. J., Silverman, J. M., Horvath, T. B., et al. (1990). Increased morbid risk for schizophrenia-related disorders in relatives of schizotypal personality disordered patientes. *Arch. Gen. Psychiat., 47*(7), 634–640.

Sifneos, P. E. (1987). *Short term dynamic psychotherapy evaluation and technique* (2nd ed.). New York: Plenum.

Sifneos, P. E. (1992). *Short-term anxiety-provoking psychotherapy: A treatment manual.* New York: Basic Books.

Sigerist, H. E. (1943). *Civilization and disease.* Ithaca, NY: Cornell UP.

Silberman, E. K. et al. (1985). Dissociative states in multiple personality disorder: A quantitative study. *Psychiat. Res., 15*(4), 253–260.

Silver, J. M., & Yudofsky, S. C. (1988). Psychopharmacology and electroconvulsive therapy. In J. A. Talbott, R. E. Hales, & S. C. Yudofsky (Eds.), *The American Psychiatric Press textbook of psychiatry.* Washington, DC: American Psychiatric Press.

Silverman, K., Evans, S. M., Strain, E. C., & Griffiths, R. R. (1992). Withdrawal syndrome after the double-blind cessation of caffeine consumption. *The New England Journal of Medicine, 327*(16), 1109–1114.

Silverman, P. (1992). An introduction to self-help groups. In B. J. White & E. J. Madara (Eds.), *The self-help sourcebook: Finding & forming mutual aid self-help groups.* Denville, NJ: St. Clares-Riverside Medical Center.

Silverstein, B., Perdue, L., Peterson, B., & Kelly, E. (1986). The role of mass media in promoting a thin standard of bodily attractiveness for women. *Sex Roles, 14,* 519–532.

Silverstone, P. H. (1990). Low self-esteem in eating disordered patients in the absence of depression. *Psych. Rep., 67*(1), 276–278.

Silverstone, T., & Hunt, N. (1992). Symptoms and assessment of mania. In E. S. Paykel (Ed.), *Handbook of Affective Disorders.* New York: Guilford.

Simeon, J. G., Ferguson, H. B., Knott, V., Roberts, N., et al (1992). Clinical, cognitive, and neurophysiological effects of alprazolam in children and adolescents with overanxious and avoidant disorders. Special section: New developments in pediatric psychopharmacology. *J. Amer. Acad. Child Adol. Psychiat., 31*(1), 29–33.

Simhandl, C., & Meszaros, K. (1992). The use of carbamazepine in the treatment of schizophrenia and schizoaffective psychoses: A review. *Journal of Psychiatry and Neuroscience, 17*(1), 1–14.

Simmon (1990). Media and Market Study. In Skin Deep: Our national obsession with looks. *Psych. Today, 26*(3), 96.

Simon, R. (1987, January). Interview in Turkington, C., Treatment of depressed elderly could prevent silent suicides. *APA Monitor,* p. 13.

Simon, Y., Bellisle, F., Monneuse, M. O., Samuel-Lajeunesse, B., & Drewnowski, A. (1993). *Brit. J. Psychiat., 162,* 244–246.

Simons, L. S. (1989). Privatization and the mental health system: A private sector view. *Amer. Psychol., 44*(8), 1138–1141.

Simons, R. C. (1981). Contemporary problems of psychoanalytic technique. *J. Amer. Psychoanal. Assoc., 29*(3), 643–658.

Simpson, C. J., Hyde, C. E., & Faragher, E. B. (1989). The chronically mentally ill in community facilities: A study of quality of life. *Brit. J. Psychiat., 154,* 77–82.

Simpson, R. L., & Sasso, G. M. (1992). Full inclusion of students with autism in general education settings: Values versus science. *Focus on Autistic Behavior, 7*(3), 1–13.

Simpson, R. O., & Halpin, G. (1986). Agreement between parents and teachers in using the Revised Behavior Problem Checklist to identify deviant behavior in children. *Behav. Dis., 12*(1), 54–58.

Sines, L. K. (1959). The relative contribution of four kinds of data to accuracy in personality assessment. *J. Cons. Psychol., 23,* 483–495.

Singh, A., & Lucki, I. (1993). Antidepressant-like activity of compounds with varying efficacy at 5-HT receptors. *Neuropharmacology, 32*(4), 331–340.

Singh, G. (1981). The malignant neuroleptic syndrome (a review with report of three cases). *Indian Journal of Psychiatry, 23,* 179–183.

Sintchak, G., & Geer, J. (1975). A vaginal plethysmograph system. *Psychophysiology, 12,* 113–115.

Siomopoulos, V. (1988). Narcissistic personality disorder: Clinical features. *Amer. J. Psychother., 42*(2), 240–253.

Sipprelle, R. C. (1992). A Vet Center experience: Multievent trauma, delayed treatment type. In D. W. Foy (Ed.), *Treating PTSD: Cognitive-Behavioral Strategies. Treatment Manuals for Practitioners.* New York: Guilford.

Sizemore, C. C., & Huber, R. J. (1988). The twenty-two faces of Eve. *Individ. Psychol. J. Adlerian Theory Res. Prac., 44*(1), 53–62.

Sjostrom, R. (1973). 5-Hydroxyindole acetic acid and homovanillic acid in cerebrospinal fluid in manic-depressive psychosis and the effect of probenecid treatment. *Eur. J. Clin. Pharmacol., 6,* 75–80.

Skeels, H. M. (1966). Adult status of children with contrasting early life experiences: A follow-up study. *Monographs of the Society for Research in Child Development, 31*(105).

Skeels, H. M., & Dye, H. B. (1939). A study of the effects of differential stimulation on mentally retarded children. *Proceeding of the Amer. Assoc. of Mental Deficiency, 44,* 114–136.

Skinner, B. F. (1948). Superstition in the Pigeon. *J. Exp. Psychol., 38,* 168–172.

Skinner, B. F. (1957). *Verbal behavior.* Englewood Cliffs, NJ: Prentice Hall.

Skinner, B. F. (1989). *Recent issues in the analysis of behavior.* Columbus, OH: Merrill.

Skinner, H. A. (1984). Correlational methods in clinical research. In A. S. Bellack & M. Hersen (Eds.), *Research methods in clinical psychology.* New York: Pergamon.

Skoff, B. F., Mirsky, A. F., & Turner, D. (1980). Prolonged brainstem transmission time in autism. *Psychiat. Res., 2,* 157–166.

Slater, E., & Shields, J. (1969). Genetical aspects of anxiety. Special Publication No. 3. M. H. Lader (Ed.). *Brit. J. Psychiat.,* 62–71.

Sleek, S. (1994, April). Could Prozac replace demand for therapy? *APA Monitor, 25*(4), p. 28.

Slife, B. D., & Weaver, C. A. III. (1992). Depression, cognitive skill, and metacognitive skill in problem solving. *Cognition and Emotion, 6*(1), 1–22.

Sloane, R. B., Staples, F. R., Cristol, A. H., Yorkson, N. J., & Whipple, K. (1975). *Psychotherapy versus behavior therapy.* Cambridge, MA: Harvard UP.

Slovenko, R. (1992). Is diminished capacity really dead? *Psychiat. Ann., 22*(11), 566–570.

Small, J. G. (1985). Efficacy of electroconvulsive therapy in schizophrenia, mania, and other disorders, II: Mania and other disorders. *Convulsive Therapy, 1,* 271–276.

Small, M. A. (1992). The legal context of mentally disordered sex offender (MDSO) treatment programs. *Criminal Justice and Behavior, 19*(2), 127–142.

Smith, A. C. (1982). *Schizophrenia and madness.* London: Allen & Unwin.

Smith, A. L., & Weissman, M. M. (1992). Epidemiology. In E. S. Paykel (Ed.), *Handbook of Affective Disorders.* New York: Guilford.

Smith, D. (1982). Trends in counseling and psychotherapy. *Amer. Psychol., 37*(7), 802–809.

Smith, D. I., & Burvill, P. W. (1991). Relationship between alcohol consumption and attempted suicide morbidity rates in Perth, Western Australia, 1968–1984. *Addictive Behaviors, 16*(1–2), 57–61.

Smith, E., North, C., & Spitznagel, E. (1993). Alcohol, drugs, and psychiatric comorbidity among homeless women: An epidemiologic study. *J. Clin. Psychiat., 54*(3), 82–87.

Smith, I. L. (1983). Use of simulation in credentialing programs. *Profess. Practicing Psychol., 4,* 21–50.

Smith, J. E., Hillard, M. C., Walsh, R. A., Kubacki, S. R., et al. (1991). Rorschach assessment of purging and nonpurging bulimics. *J. Pers. Assess., 56*(2), 277–288.

Smith, J. E., Waldorf, A., & Trembath, D. L. (1990). "Single white male looking for thin, very attractive. . . "" *Sex Roles, 23*(11), 675–685.

Smith, J. H. (1974). The first lie. *Psychiatry, 31,* 61–68.

Smith, J. M., & Baldessarini, R. J. (1980). Changes in prevalence, severity, and recovery in tardive dyskinesia with age. *Arch. Gen. Psychiat., 37*(12), 1368–1373.

Smith, K. (1991). Comments on "Teen suicide and changing cause-of-death certification, 1953–1987." *Suic. Life-Threat. Behav., 21*(3), 260–262.

Smith, M. L., & Glass, G. V. (1977). Meta-analysis of psychotherapy outcome studies. *Amer. Psychol., 32*(9), 752–760.

Smith, M. L., Glass, G. V., & Miller, T. I. (1980). *The benefits of psychotherapy.* Baltimore: Johns Hopkins Univ.

Smith, R. E. (1988). The logic and design of case study research. *Sport Psychologist, 2*(1), 1–12.

Smith, S. (1991). Mental health malpractice in the 1990s. *Houston Law Review, 28,* 209–283.

Smith, S., O'Hara, B., Persico, A., Gorelick, D., Newlin, D., et al. (1992). Genetic vulnerability to drug abuse: The D2 dopamine receptor Taq I B1 restriction fragment length polymorphism appears more frequently in polysubstance abusers. *Arch. Gen. Psychiat., 49,* 723–727.

Smith, T. C., & Smith, B. L. (1986). The relationship between the WISC-R and WRAT-R for a sample of rural referred children. *Psychol. Schools, 23*(3), 252–254.

Smith, W. H. (1993). Incorporating hypnosis into the psychotherapy of patients with multiple personality disorder. *Bull. Menninger Clin., 57*(3), 344–354.

Smoller, J. W. (1986). The etiology and treatment of childhood. In G. C. Ellenbogen (Ed.), *Oral sadism and the vegetarian personality.* New York: Brunner/Mazel.

Smyer, M. A. (1989). Nursing homes as a setting for psychological practice: Public policy perspectives. *Amer. Psychol., 44*(10), 1307–1314.

Snow, E. (1976, Dec.). In the snow. *Texas Monthly Magazine.*

Snyder, C. R. (1955). Studies of drinking in Jewish culture. IV.

Culture and sobriety. A study of drinking patterns and sociocultural factors related to sobriety among Jews. *Quart. J. Stud. Alcohol., 16,* 263–289, 700–742.

Snyder, F. (1970). The phenomenology of dreaming. In L. Madlow & L. Snow (Eds.), *The Psychodynamic Implications of the Physiological Studies on Dreams.* Springfield, IL: C. C. Thomas.

Snyder, M. L. (1992). Unemployment and suicide in Northern Ireland. *Psych. Rep., 70*(3, Pt. 2), 1116–1118.

Snyder, S. (1976). Dopamine and schizophrenia. *Psychiat. Ann., 8*(1), 53–84.

Snyder, S. (1976). The dopamine hypotheses of schizophrenia: Focus on the dopamine receptor. *Amer. J. Psychiat., 133*(2), 197–202.

Snyder, S. (1977, Mar.). Opiate receptors and internal opiates. *Scientific American,* 44–56.

Snyder, S. (1977). Opiate receptors in the brain. *New England Journal of Medicine, 296,* 266–271.

Snyder, S. (1980). *Biological aspects of mental disorder.* New York: Oxford UP.

Snyder, S. (1984). Cholinergic mechanisms in affective disorders. *New Engl. J. Med., 311*(4), 254–255.

Snyder, S. (1986). *Drugs and the brain.* New York: Scientific American Library.

Snyder, S. (1991). Drugs, neurotransmitters, and the brain. In P. Corsi (Ed.), *The enchanted loom: Chapters in the history of neuroscience.* New York: Oxford UP.

Snyder, S., Burt, D. R., & Creese, I. (1976). The dopamine receptor of mammalian brain: Direct demonstration of binding to agonist and antagonist states. *Neuroscience Symposia, 1,* 28–49.

Snyder, W. V. (1947). *Casebook of non-directive counseling,* Boston: Houghton Mifflin.

Sobell, M. B., & Sobell, L. C. (1973). Alcoholics treated by individualized behavior therapy: One year treatment outcome. *Behav. Res. Ther., 11*(4), 599–618.

Sobell, M. B., & Sobell, L. C. (1973). Individualized behavior therapy for alcoholics. *Behav. Ther., 4*(1), 49–72.

Sobell, M. B., & Sobell, L. C. (1976). Second year treatment outcome of alcoholics treated by individualized behavior therapy: Results. *Behav. Res. Ther., 14*(3), 195–215.

Sobell, M. B., & Sobell, L. C. (1984). The aftermath of heresy: A response to Pendery et al.'s (1982) critique of "Individualized Behavior Therapy for Alcoholics." *Behav. Res. Ther., 22*(4), 413–440.

Sobell, M. B., & Sobell, L. C. (1984). Under the microscope yet again: A commentary on Walker and Roach's critique of the Dickens Committee's enquiry into our research. *Brit. J. Addic., 79*(2), 157–168.

Sohlberg, S., & Norring, C. (1992). A three-year prospective study of life events and course for adults with anorexia nervosa/bulimia nervosa. *Psychosom. Med., 54*(1), 59–70.

Sokol-Kessler, L., & Beck, A. T. (1987). Cognitive treatment of panic disorders. Paper presented at the 140th Annual Meeting of the American Psychiatric Assoc. Chicago.

Soloff, P. H. (1987). Neuroleptic treatment in the borderline patient: Advantages and techniques. *J. Clin. Psychiat., 48*(Suppl.), 26–30.

Solomon, G. F. (1969). Stress and antibody response in rats. *Inter. Arch. Allergy & Applied Immun., 35,* 97–104.

Solomon, M., & Murphy, G. (1984). Cohort studies of suicide.

In H. Sudak, A. Ford, & N. Rushforth (Eds.), *Suicide in the young*. London: PSG.

Solomon, R. L. (1980). The opponent-process theory of acquired motivation: The costs of pleasure and the benefits of pain. *Amer. Psychol., 35,* 691–712.

Solomon, R. L., Kamin, L. J., & Wynne, L. C. (1953). Traumatic avoidance learning: The outcomes of several extinction procedures with dogs. *J. Abnorm. Soc. Psychol., 48,* 291–302.

Soltys, S. M. (1992). Pyromania and firesetting behaviors. *Psychiat. Ann., 22*(2), 79–83.

Solyom, L., Freeman, R. J., & Miles, J. E. (1982). A comparative psychometric study of anorexia nervosa and obsessive neurosis. *Canad. J. Psychiat., 27*(4), 282–286.

Somasundaram, O., & Papakumari, M. (1981). A study on Down's anomaly. *Child Psychol. Quart., 14*(3), 85–94.

Sorokin, J. E., Giordani, B., Mohs, R. C., Losonczy, M. F. et al. (1988). Memory impairment in schizophrenic patients with tardive dyskinesia. *Bio. Psychiat., 23*(2), 129–135.

Sours, J. A. (1980). *Starving to death in a sea of objects: The anorexia nervosa syndrome*. New York: Jason Aronson.

Spaights, E., & Simpson, G. (1986). Some unique causes of Black suicide. *Psychology—A Quarterly Journal of Human Behavior, 23*(1), 1–5.

Spalter, A. R., Gwirtsman, H. E., Demitrack, M. A., & Gold, P. W. (1993). Thyroid function in bulimia nervosa. *Bio. Psychiat., 33,* 408–414.

Spanos, N. P. (1982). Hypnotic behavior: A cognitive, social psychological perspective. *Res. Communications in Psychol., Psychiat. & Behav., 7*(2), 199–213.

Spanos, N. P. (1986). Hypnosis and the modification of hypnotic susceptibility: A social psychological perspective. In P. L. N. Naish (Ed.), *What is hypnosis?* Philadelphia: Open Univ.

Spanos, N. P. (1986). Hypnotic behavior: A social psychological interpretation of amnesia, analgesia, and "trance logic." *Behav. Brain Sci., 9*(3), 449–467.

Spanos, N. P. (1986). More on the social psychology of hypnotic responding. *Behav. Brain Sci., 9*(3), 489–502.

Spanos, N. P. (1990). More on compliance and the Carleton Skill Training Program. *Brit. J. Exp. Clin. Hyp., 7*(3), 165–170.

Spanos, N. P. (1991). A sociocognitive approach to hypnosis. In S. J. Lynn & J. W. Rhue (Eds.), *Theories of hypnosis*. New York: Guilford.

Spanos, N. P. (1991). Imagery, hypnosis and hypnotizability. In R. G. Kunzendorf (Ed.), *Proceedings from American Assoc. for the Study of Mental Imagery 11th Annual Conference* (Washington, DC, 1989). New York: Plenum.

Spanos, N. P., & Coe, W. C. (1992). A social-psychological approach to hypnosis. In E. Fromm & M. R. Nash (Eds.), *Contemporary hypnosis research*. New York: Guilford.

Spanos, N. P., & D'Eon, J. L. (1980). Hypnotic amnesia, disorganized recall, and inattention. *J. Abnorm. Psychol., 89*(6), 744–750.

Spanos, N. P., Gwynn, M. I., & Stam, H. J. (1983). Instructional demands and ratings of overt and hidden pain during hypnotic analgesia. *J. Abnorm. Psychol., 92,* 479–488.

Spanos, N. P., Radtke-Bodorik, H. L., Ferguson, J. D., & Jones, B. (1979). The effects of hypnotic susceptibility, suggestions for analgesia and the utilization of cognitive strate-

gies on the reduction of pain. *J. Abnorm. Psychol., 88,* 282–292.

Spanos, N. P., Radtke-Bodorick, H. L., & Shabinsky, M. A. (1980). Amnesia, subjective organization and learning of a list of unrelated words in hypnotic and task-motivated subjects. *Inter. J. Clin. Exper. Hyp., 28*(2), 126–139.

Spanos, N. P. et al. (1980). Effects of social psychological variables on hypnotic amnesia. *J. Pers. Soc. Psychol., 38*(4), 737–750.

Sparr, L. F., Boehnlein, J. K., & Cooney, T. G. (1986). The medical management of the paranoid patient. *Gen. Hosp. Psychiat., 8*(1), 49–55.

Spear, N. E. (1973). Retrieval of memory in animals. *Psych. Rev., 80,* 163–194.

Spector, I. P., & Carey, M. P. (1990). Incidence and prevalence of sexual dysfunctions: A critical review of the empirical literature. *Archives of Sexual Behavior, 19*(4), 389–408.

Spiegel, D. (1992). Effects of psychosocial support on patients with metastatic breast cancer. *Journal of Psychosocial Oncology, 10*(2), 113–120.

Spiegel, D., Bloom, J. R., Kraemer, H. C., & Gottheil, E. (1989). The beneficial effect of psychosocial treatment on survival of metastatic breast cancer patients: A randomized prospective outcome study. *Lancet, 2,* 888.

Spiegel, R. (1965). Communication with depressive patients. *Contemp. Psychoanal., 2,* 30–35.

Spielberger, C. D. (1966). Theory and research on anxiety. In C. D. Spielberger (Ed.), *Anxiety and behavior*. New York: Academic Press.

Spielberger, C. D. (1972). Anxiety as an emotional state. In C. D. Spielberger (Ed.), *Anxiety: Current trends in theory and research* (Vol. 1). New York: Academic Press.

Spielberger, C. D. (1972). Conceptual and methodological issues in anxiety research. In C. D. Spielberger (Ed.), *Anxiety: Current trends in theory and research* (Vol. 2). New York: Academic Press.

Spielberger, C. D. (1985). Anxiety, cognition, and affect: A state-trait perspective. In A. H. Tuma & J. Maser (Eds.), *Anxiety and the anxiety disorders*. Hillsdale, NJ: Erlbaum.

Spiess, W. F., Geer, J. H., & O'Donohue, W. T. (1984). Premature ejaculation: Investigation of factors in ejaculatory latency. *J. Abnorm. Psychol., 93*(2), 242–245.

Spirito, A., Brown, L., Overholser, J., & Fritz, G. (1989). Attempted suicide in adolescence: A review and critique of the literature. *Clinical Psychology Review, 9,* 335–363.

Spitz, H. H. (1994). Lewis Carroll's formula for calendar calculating. *Amer. J. Ment. Retard., 98*(5), 601–606.

Spitz, R. A. (1945). Hospitalization: An inquiry into the genesis of psychiatric conditions of early childhood. In R. S. Eissler, A. Freud, H. Hartman, & E. Kris (Eds.), *The psychoanalytic study of the child* (Vol. 1). New York: International Universities Press.

Spitz, R. A. (1946). *Anaclitic depression. The psychoanalytic study of the child* (Vol. 2). New York: International Universities Press.

Spitzer, J. (1990). On treating patients diagnosed with narcissistic personality disorder: The induction phase. *Issues in Ego Psychology, 13*(1), 54–65.

Spitzer, R. L., & Fleiss, J. L. (1974). A reanalysis of the reliability of psychiatric diagnosis. *Brit. J. Psychiat., 125,* 341–347.

Spitzer, R. L., Skodol, A., Gibbon, M., & Williams, J. B. W. (1981). *DSM-III case book* (1st ed.). Washington, DC: American Psychiatric Press.

Spitzer, R. L., Skodol, A., Gibbon, M., & Williams, J. B. W. (1983). *Psychopathology: A case book.* New York: McGraw-Hill.

Spoov, J., Suominen, J. Y., Lahdelma, R. L., Katila, H., Kymalainen, O., Isometsa, E., Liukko, H., & Auvinen, J. (1993). Do reversed depressive symptoms occur together as a syndrome? *J. Affect. Dis., 27,* 131–134.

Spotts, J. V., & Shontz, F. C. (1983). Psychopathology and chronic drug use: A methodological paradigm. *Inter. J. Addic., 18*(5), 633–680.

Squire, L. R. (1977). ECT and memory loss. *Amer. J. Psychiat., 134,* 997–1001.

Squire, L. R., & Slater, P. C. (1978). Bilateral and unilateral ECT: Effects on verbal and nonverbal memory. *Amer. J. Psychiat., 135*(11), 1316–1320.

Squire, L. R., & Slater, P. C. (1983). Electroconvulsive therapy and complaints of memory dysfunction: A prospective three-year follow-up study. *Brit. J. Psychiat., 142,* 1–8.

Squires, R. F., & Braestrup, C. (1977). Benzodiazepine receptors in rat brain. *Nature, 266*(5604), 732–734.

Stack, S. (1981). Comparative analysis of immigration and suicide. *Psych. Rep., 49*(2), 509–510.

Stack, S. (1982). Suicide in Detroit 1975: Changes and continuities. *Suic. & Life-Threat. Behav., 12*(2), 67–83.

Stack, S. (1987). Celebrities and suicide: A taxonomy and analysis, 1948–1983. *Amer. Sociological Rev., 52,* 401–412.

Stahl, S. M. (1984). Regulation of neurotransmitter receptors by desipramine and other antidepressant drugs: The neurotransmitter receptor hypothesis of antidepressant action. *J. Clin. Psychiat., 45*(10, Sect. 2), 37–44.

Stahmer, A. C., & Schreibman, L. (1992). Teaching children with autism appropriate play in unsupervised environments using a self-management treatment package. *J. Appl. Behav. Anal., 25*(2), 447–459.

Stampfl, T. G. (1975). Implosive therapy: Staring down your nightmares. *Psych. Today, 8*(9), 66–68; 72–73.

Stampfl, T. G., & Levis, D. J. (1967). Essentials of implosive therapy: A learning theory-based psychodynamic behavioral therapy. *J. Abnorm. Psychol., 72,* 496–503.

Stanley, M. (1991). Post mortem studies of suicide. In L. Davidson & M. Linnoila (Eds.), *Risk factors for youth suicide.* New York: Hemisphere.

Stanley, M., Stanley, B., Traskman-Bendz, L., Mann, J. J., & Meyendorff, E. (1986). Neurochemical Findings in Suicide Completers and Suicide Attempters. In R. W. Maris (Ed.), *Biology of Suicide.* New York: Guilford.

Stanley, M., Virgilio, J., & Gershon, S. (1982). Tritiated imipramine binding sites are decreased in the frontal cortex of suicides. *Science, 216,* 1337–1339.

Stansfeld, S., & Marmot, M. (1992). Social class and minor psychiatric disorder in British civil servants: A validated screening survey using the General Health Questionnaire. *Psychol. Med., 22*(3), 739–749.

Starcevic, V. (1988). Diagnosis of hypochondriasis: A promenade through the psychiatric nosology. *Amer. J. Psychother., 42*(2), 197–211.

Stark, K. D., Rouse, L. W., & Livingston, R. (1991). Treatment of depression during childhood and adolescence: Cognitive-behavioral procedures for the individual and family. In P. C. Kendall (Ed.), *Child and adolescent therapy: Cognitive-behavioral procedures.* New York: Guilford.

Stark-Adamek, C. (1992). Sexism in research: The limits of academic freedom. *Women and therapy, 12*(4), 103–111.

Starker, S. (1988). Psychologists and self-help books: Attitudes and prescriptive practices of clinicians. *Amer. J. Psychother., 42*(30), 448–455.

Stattin, H., & Magnusson, D. (1980). Stability of perceptions of own reactions across a variety of anxiety-provoking situations. *Percept. & Motor Skills, 51,* 959–967.

Steadman, H., Monahan, J., Hartstone, E., Davis, S., & Robbins, P. (1982). Mentally disordered offenders: A national survey of patients and facilities. *Law & Human Behav., 6,* 31–38.

Steadman, H. J., Monahan, J., Robbins, P. C., Appelbaum, P., Grisso, T., Klassen, D., Mulvey, E. P., & Roth, L. (1993). From dangerousness to risk assessment: Implications for appropriate research strategies. In S. Hodgins (Ed.), *Mental Disorder and Crime.* New York: Sage Publications.

Steadman, H. J. (1993). *Before and after Hinckley: Evaluating insanity defense reforms.* New York: Guilford.

Steele, C. M., & Josephs, R. A. (1990). Alcohol myopia: Its prized and dangerous effects. *Amer. Psychol., 45*(8), 921–933.

Steen, S. N., Oppliger, R. A:, & Brownell, K. D. (1988). Metabolic effects of repeated weight loss and regain in adolescent wrestlers. *JAMA, 260,* 47–50.

Stefansson, C. G., & Wicks, S. (1991). Health care occupations and suicide in Sweden 1961–1985. *Social Psychiatry and Psychiatric Epidemiology, 26*(6), 259–264.

Steffenburg, S., Gillberg, C., Wellgren, L., Andersson, L. et al. (1989). *J. Child. Psychol. Psychiat., 30*(3), 405–416.

Steiger, H., & Houle, L. (1991). Defense styles and object-relations disturbances among university women displaying varying degrees of "symptomatic" eating. *Inter. J. Eat. Dis., 10*(2), 145–153.

Steiger, H., Puentes-Neuman, G., & Leung, F. Y. (1991). Personality and family features of adolescent girls with eating symptoms: Evidence for restricter/binger differences in a nonclinical population, *Addictive Behaviors, 16*(5), 303–314.

Stein, D. J., Hollander, E., Anthony, D. T., Schneier, F. R., et al. (1992). Serotonergic medications for sexual obsessions, sexual addictions, and paraphilias. *J. Clin. Psychiat., 53*(8), 267–271.

Stein, G., & Bernadt, M. (1993). Lithium augmentation therapy in tricyclic-resistant depression: A controlled trial using lithium in low and normal doses. *Brit. J. Psychiat., 162,* 634–640.

Stein, L. I. (1993). A system approach to reducing relapse in schizophrenia. *J. Clin. Psychiat., 54*(3 suppl.), 7–12.

Stein, M. B., Walker, J. R., & Forde, D. R. (1994). Setting diagnostic thresholds for social phobia: Considerations from a community survey of social anxiety. *Amer. J. Psychiat., 151*(3), 408–412.

Stein, Z., Susser, M., Saenger, G., & Marolla, F. (1972). Nutrition and mental performance. *Science, 178,* 708–713.

Steinberg, J. A. (1986). Clinical interventions with women experiencing the impostor phenomenon. *Women & Therapy, 5*(4), 19–26.

Steinberg, M. (1993). *Interviewer's guide to the Structured Clinical Interview for DSM-IV Dissociative Disorders.* Washington, DC: American Psychiatric Press.

Steinbrook, R. (1992). The polygraph test: A flawed diagnostic method. *New England Journal of Medicine, 327*(2), 122–123.

Steiner, H., Smith, C., Rosenkranz, R. T., & Litt, I. (1991). The early care and feeding of anorexics. *Child Psychiat. Human Dev., 21*(3), 163–167.

Steinglass, P., Tislenko, L., & Reiss, D. (1985). Stability/instability in the alcoholic marriage: The interrelationships between course of alcoholism, family process, and marital outcome. *Family Process, 24*(3), 365–376.

Steinmark, S. W., & Borkovec, T. D. (1974). Active and placebo treatment effects on moderate insomnia under counterdemand and positive demand instructions. *J. Abnorm. Psychol., 83*, 157–163.

Steketee, G. (1990). Personality traits and disorders in obsessive-compulsives. *Journal of Anxiety Disorders, 4*(4), 351–364.

Steketee, G., & Foa, E. B. (1987). Rape victims: Posttraumatic stress responses and their treatment. *J. Anx. Dis., 1*, 69–86.

Stellar, E. (1954). The physiology of motivation. *Psychol. Rev., 61*, 5–22.

Stengel, E. (1964). *Suicide and attempted suicide.* Baltimore: Penguin.

Stengel, E. (1974). *Suicide and attempted suicide* (2nd ed.). New York: Jason Aronson.

Stern, R. G., Mohs, R. C., Davidson, M., Schmeidler, J., et al. (1994). A longitudinal study of Alzheimer's disease: Measurement, rate, and predictors of cognitive deterioration. *Amer. J. Psychiat., 151*(3), 390–396.

Stern, R. S., & Cobb, J. P. (1978). Phenomenology of obsessive-compulsive neurosis. *Brit. J. Psychiat., 12*, 233–239.

Stewart, H. (1965). On keeping mental patients chronic. *Psych. Rep., 17*, 216–218.

Stewart, J. W., Mercier, M. A., Agosti, V., Guardino, M., & Quitkin, F. M. (1993). Imipramine is effective after unsuccessful cognitive therapy: Sequential use of cognitive therapy and imipramine in depressed outpatients. *Journal of Clinical Psychopharmacology, 13*, 114–119.

Stillion, J. M. (1985). *Death and the sexes: An examination of differential longevity, attitudes, behaviors, and coping skills.* Washington, DC: Hemisphere.

Stock, W. (1993). Inhibited female orgasm. In W. O'Donohue & J. Geer (eds.), *Handbook of sexual dysfunctions.* Boston: Allyn and Bacon.

Stoffelmayr, B. E., Benishek, L. A., Humphreys, K., Lee, J. A., et al. (1989). Substance abuse prognosis with an additional psychiatric diagnosis: Understanding the relationship. *Journal of Psychoactive Drugs, 21*(2), 145–152.

Stokes, T. E., & Osnes, P. G. (1989). An operant pursuit of generalization. *Behav. Ther., 20*(3), 337–355.

Stone, M. H. (1989). Schizoid personality disorder. In American Psychiatric Association (Eds.), *Treatments of Psychiatric Disorders: A task force report of the American Psychiatric Association.* Washington, DC: American Psychiatric Press.

Stonier, P. D. (1992). "Are double-blind controlled trials always necessary?": Response. *Human Psychopharmacology Clinical and Experimental, 7*(1), 57–60.

Stopa, L., & Clark, D. M. (1993). Cognitive processes in social phobia. *Behav. Res. Ther., 31*(3), 255–267.

Stoyva, J. M., & Budzynski, T. H. (1993). Biofeedback methods in the treatment of anxiety and stress disorders. In P. M. Lehrer & R. L. Woolfolk (Eds.), *Principles and Practice of Stress Management* (2nd ed.). New York: Guilford.

Strange, P. G. (1992). *Brain Biochemistry and Brain Disorders.* New York: Oxford UP.

Strassberg, D. S., Kelly, M. P., Carroll, C., & Kircher, J. C. (1987). The psychophysiological nature of premature ejaculation. *Archives of Sexual Behavior, 16*(4), 327–336.

Strassberg, D. S., Mahoney, J. M., Schaugaard, M., & Hale, V. E. (1990). The role of anxiety in premature ejaculation: A psychophysiological model. *Archives of Sexual Behavior, 15*(4), 251–157.

Strauss, J., & Ryan, R. (1987). Autonomy disturbances in subtypes of anorexia nervosa. *J. Abnorm. Psychol., 96*(3), 254–258.

Strauss, J. S. (1979). Social and cultural influences on psychopathology. *Annu. Rev. Psychol., 30*, 397–415.

Stravynski, A., & Greenberg, D. (1992). The psychological management of depression. *Acta Psychiatr. Scandin., 85*(6), 407–414.

Stravynski, A., Grey, S., & Elie, R. (1987). Outline of the therapeutic process in social skills training with socially dysfunctional patients. *J. Cons. Clin. Psychol., 55*(2), 224–228.

Stravynski, A., Marks, I., & Yule, W. (1982). Social skills problems in neurotic outpatients. *Arch. Gen. Psychiat., 39*, 1378–1384.

Streissguth, A. P., Aase, J. M., Clarren, S. K., Randels, S. P., LaDue, R. A., & Smith, D. F. (1991). Fetal alcohol syndrome in adolescents and adults. *JAMA, 265*, 1961–1967.

Strelau, J. (1992). Introduction: Current studies on anxiety from the perspective of research conducted during the last three decades. In D. G. Forgays, T. Sosnowski, & K. Wrzesniewski (Eds.), *Anxiety: Recent developments in cognitive, psychophysiological, and health research.* Washington, DC: Hemisphere Pub. Corp.

Stricker, G. (1992). The relationship of research to clinical practice. *Amer. Psychol., 47*(4), 543–549.

Strickland, B. R., Hale, W. D., & Anderson, L. K. (1975). Effect of induced mood states on activity and self-reported affect. *J. Cons. Clin. Psychol., 43*(4), 587.

Striegel-Moore, R. H., Silberstein, L. R., & Rodin, J. (1986). Toward an understanding of risk factors for bulimia. *Amer. Psychol., 41*(3), 246–263.

Striegel-Moore, R. H., Silberstein, L. R., & Rodin, J. (1993). The social self in bulimia nervosa: Public self-consciousness, social anxiety, and perceived fraudulence. *J. Abnorm. Psychol., 102*(2), 297–303.

Strober, M. (1981). The relation of personality characteristics to body image disturbances in juvenile anorexia nervosa: A multivariate analysis. *Psychosom. Med., 43*(4), 323–330.

Strober, M. (1981). The significance of bulimia in juvenile anorexia nervosa: An exploration of possible etiological factors. *Inter. J. Eat. Dis., 1*, 28–43.

Strober, M. (1983, May). Familial depression in anorexia nervosa. Paper presented at the meeting of the American Psychiatric Assoc. New York.

Strober, M. (1992). Family factors in adolescent eating disorders. In P. J. Cooper & A. Stein (Eds.), *Feeding Problems and Eating Disorders in Children and Adolescents.* Philadelphia: Harwood Academic Publishers.

Strober, M., & Bowen, E. (1986). Hospital management of the adolescent with anorexia nervosa. *Clin. Psychol., 39*(2), 46–48.

Strober, M., & Yager, J. (1985). A developmental perspective on the treatment of anorexia nervosa in adolescents. In D. M. Garner & P. E. Garfinkel (Eds.), *Handbook of psychotherapy for anorexia nervosa and bulimia*. New York: Guilford.

Stroebe, M., Gergen, M. M., Gergen, K. J., & Stroebe, W. (1992). Broken hearts or broken bonds: Love and death in historical perspectives. *Amer. Psychol., 47*(10), 1205–1212.

Strupp, H. H. (1989). Psychotherapy: Can the practitioner learn from the researcher? *Amer. Psychol., 44*, 717–724.

Strupp, H. H., & Binder, J. (1984). *Psychotherapy in a new key: Time-limited dynamic psychotherapy*. New York: Basic Books.

Strupp, H. H., Fox, R. A., & Lessler, K. J. (1969). *Patients view their psychotherapy*. Baltimore: Johns Hopkins Univ.

Stuart, R. B. (1969). Operant interpersonal treatment for marital discord. *J. Cons. Clin. Psychol., 33*, 675–682.

Stuart, R. B. (1975). Behavioral remedies for marital ills: A guide to the use of operant-interpersonal techniques. In A. S. Gurman & D. G. Rice (Eds.), *Couples in conflict: New directions in marital therapy*. New York: Jason Aronson.

Stuart, R. B. (1980). *Helping couples change: A social learning approach to marital therapy*. New York: Guilford.

Stuhr, U., & Meyer, A. E. (1991). Hamburg Short Psychotherapy Comparison Experiment. In M. Crago & L. Beutler (Eds.), *Psychotherapy research: An international review of programmatic studies*. American Psychological Association.

Stunkard, A. J. (1975). From explanation to action in psychosomatic medicine: The case of obesity. *Psychosom. Med., 37*, 195–236.

Stunkard, A. J., Sorenson, T. I. A., Hanis, C., Teasdale, T. W., et al. (1986). An adoption study of human obesity. *New England Journal of Medicine, 314*, 193–198.

Stunkard, A. J., & Wadden, T. A. (1992). Psychological aspects of severe obesity. *American Journal of Clinical Nutrition, 55*(Suppl.), 524–532.

Sturgeon, V., & Taylor, J. (1980). Report of a five-year follow-up study of mentally disordered sex offenders released from Atascadero State Hospital in 1973. Criminal Justice *J. Western State Univ., San Diego, 4*, 31–64.

Substance Abuse and Mental Health Services Administration. (1991). *National Household Survey on Drug Abuse, Highlights 1991*. Washington, DC: U.S. Department of Health and Human Services.

Suddath, R. L., Christison, G. W., & Torrey, E. F. (1990). Anatomical abnormalities in the brains of monozygotic twins discordant for schizophrenia. *New England J. of Medicine, 322*(12), 789–794.

Sudhalter, V., Cohen, I. L., Silverman, W., & Wolf-Schein, E. G. (1990). Conversational analyses of males with Fragile X, Down Syndrome, and autism: Comparison of the emergence of deviant language. *Amer. J. Ment. Retard., 94*, 431–441.

Sue, S. (1991). Ethnicity and culture in psychological research and practice. In L. Garnets, J. M. Jones, D. Kimmel, S. Sue, & C. Tavris (Eds.), *Psychological Perspectives on Human Diversity in America*. Washington, DC: American Psychological Association.

Sue, S. (1991). Ethnicity and culture in psychological research and practice. In J. D. Goodchilds (Ed.), *Psychological Perspectives on Human Diversity*. Washington, DC: American Psychological Association.

Sue, S., Zane, N., & Young, K. (1994). Research on psy-

chotherapy with culturally diverse populations. In A. E. Bergin & S. L. Garfield (Eds.), *Handbook of psychotherapy and behavior change*. New York: Wiley.

Suematsu, H., Ishikawa, H., Kuboki, T., & Ito, T. (1985). Statistical studies on anorexia nervosa in Japan: Detailed clinical data on 1,011 patients. *Psychother. & Psychosom., 43*(2), 96–103.

Suematsu, H., Kuboki, T., & Itoh, T. (1985). Statistical studies on the prognosis of anorexia nervosa. *Psychother. & Psychosom., 43*(2), 104–112.

Sugarman, A., Quinlan, D., & Devenis, L. (1981). Anorexia nervosa as a defense against anaclitic depression. *Inter. J. Eat. Dis., 1*, 44–61.

Suinn, R., & Richardson, F. (1971). Anxiety management training. A nonspecific behavior therapy program for anxiety control. *Behav. Ther., 2*, 498–510.

Sullivan, C. M., Tan, C., Basta, J., Rumptz, M., et al. (1992). An advocacy intervention program for women with abusive partners: Initial evaluation. *American Journal of Community Psychology, 20*(3), 309–332.

Sullivan, H. S. (1953). *The interpersonal theory of psychiatry*. New York: Norton.

Sullivan, H. S. (1954). *The psychiatric interview*. New York: Norton.

Sullivan, H. S. (1962). *Schizophrenia as a human process*. New York: Norton.

Sullwold, L., & Herrlich, J. (1992). Providing schizophrenic patients with a concept of illness: An essential element of therapy. *Brit. J. Psychiat., 161*(suppl. 18), 129–132.

Suls, J., & Rittenhouse, J. D. (1990). Models of linkages between personality and disease. In H. S. Friedman (Ed.), *Personality and disease*. New York: Wiley.

Sulser, F. (1983). Mode of action of antidepressant drugs. *J. Clin. Psychiat., 44*(5), 14–20.

Sulser, F., Vetulani, J., & Mobley, P. L. (1978). Mode of action of antidepressant drugs. *Biomed. Pharmacol., 27*(3), 257–261.

Sundberg, N. D., Tyler, L. E., & Taplin, J. R. (1973). *Clinical psychology: Expanding horizons* (2nd ed.). Englewood cliffs, NJ: Prentice Hall.

Suokas, J., & Lonnqvist, J. (1991). Selection of patients who attempted suicide for psychiatric consultation. *Acta Psychiatr. Scandin., 83*(3), 179–182.

Suomi, S. J. (1976). Factors affecting responses to social separation in rhesus monkeys. In G. Serban & A. Kling (Eds.), *Animal models in human psychobiology*. New York: Plenum.

Suomi, S. J., & Harlow, H. F. (1975). Effects of differential removal from group on social development of rhesus monkeys. *J. Child Psychol. Psychiat. Allied Disc., 16*, 149–158.

Suomi, S. J., & Harlow, H. F. (1977). Production and alleviation of depressive behaviors in monkeys. In J. D. Maser & M. E. P. Seligman (Eds.), *Psychopathology: Experimental models*. New York: W. H. Freeman.

Suomi, S. J., Harlow, H. F., & Domek, C. J. (1970). Effect of repetitive infant-infant separation of young monkeys. *J. Abnorm. Psychol., 76*, 161–172.

Suppes, T., Baldessarini, R. J., Faedda, G. L., & Tohen, M. (1991). Risk of recurrence following discontinuation of lithium treatment in bipolar disorder. *Arch. Gen. Psychiat., 48*(12), 1082–1088.

Surtees, P. G., & Barkley, C. (1994). Future imperfect: The

long-term outcome of depression. *Brit. J. Psychiat., 164*, 327–341.

Suter, S. (1986). *Health psychophysiology: Mind-body interactions in wellness and illness.* Hillsdale, NJ: Erlbaum.

Sutker, P. B., Allain, A. N., & Winstead, D. K. (1993). Psychopathology and psychiatric diagnoses of World War II Pacific Theater prisoner of war survivors and combat veterans. *Amer. J. Psychiat., 150*(2), 240–245.

Svartberg, M., & Stiles, T. C. (1991). Comparative effects of short-term psychodynamic psychotherapy: A meta-analysis. *J. Cons. Clin. Psychol., 59*, 704–714.

Svrakic, D. M. (1987). Pessimistic mood in narcissistic decompensation. *American Journal of Psychoanalysis, 47*(1), 58–71.

Svrakic, D. M. (1989). Narcissistic personality disorder: A new clinical systematics. *European Journal of Psychiatry, 3*(4), 199–213.

Svrakic, D. M. (1990). Pessimism and depression: Clinical and phenomenological distinction. *European Journal of Psychiatry, 4*(3), 139–145.

Svrakic, D. M. (1990). The functional dynamics of the narcissistic personality. *Amer. J. Psychother., 44*(2), 189–203.

Swanson, J., Holzer, C., Ganju, V., & Jono, R. (1990). Violence and psychiatric disorder in the community: Evidence from the epidemiological catchment area surveys. *Hosp. Comm. Psychiat., 41*, 761–770.

Swanson, J., Morrissey, J. P., Goldstrom, I., Rudolph, L., & Manderscheid, R. W. (1993, August). Demographic and diagnostic characteristics of inmates receiving mental health services in state adult correctional facilities: United States, 1988. Mental Health Statistical Note No. 209. Washington, D.C.: Department of Health and Human Services.

Swartz, L. (1985). Anorexia nervosa as a culture-bound syndrome. *Soc. Sci. Med., 20*(7), 725–730.

Swedo, S. E., Leonard, H. L., Rapoport, J. L., Lenane, M. C. et al. (1989). A double-blind comparison of clomipramine and desipramine in the treatment of trichotillomanio (hair pulling). *N. Engl. J. Med., 321*(8), 497–501.

Swedo, S. E., Pietrini, P., Leonard, H. L., Schapiro, M. B., et al. (1992). Cerebral glucose metabolism in childhood-onset obsessive-compulsive disorder: Revisualization during pharmacotherapy. *Arch. Gen. Psychiat., 49*(9), 690–694.

Swingle, C. (1993, July 26). Technophobia. *USA Today*, p. B1.

Swonger, A. K., & Constantine, L. L. (1983). *Drugs and therapy: A handbook of psychotropic drugs* (2nd ed.). Boston: Little, Brown.

Szapocznik, J., & Kurtines, W. M. (1993). Family psychology and cultural diversity: Opportunities for theory, research, and application. *Amer. Psychol., 48*(4), 400–407.

Szasz, T. (1991). The medicalization of sex. *Journal of Humanistic Psychology, 311*(3), 34–42.

Szasz, T. S. (1961). *The myth of mental illness: Foundations of a theory of personal conduct.* New York: Hoeber-Harper.

Szasz, T. S. (1963). *Law, liberty, and psychiatry.* Englewood Cliffs, NJ: Prentice Hall.

Szasz, T. S. (1963). *The manufacture of madness.* New York: Harper & Row.

Szasz, T. S. (1977). *Psychiatric slavery.* New York: Free Press.

Szasz, T. S. (1987). Justifying coercion through theology and therapy. In J. K. Zeig (Ed.), *The evolution of psychotherapy.* New York: Brunner/Mazel.

Szasz, T. S. (1991). The medicalization of sex. *Journal of Humanistic Psychology, 31*(3), 34–42.

Szatmari, P., & Jones, M. B. (1991). IQ and the genetics of autism. *J. Child Psychol. Psychiat. Allied Disc., 32*(6), 897–908.

Takanishi, R. (1993). The opportunities of adolescence—Research, interventions, and policy. *Amer. Psychol., 48*(2), 85–87.

Tallman, J. F. (1978). Research project. In S. Snyder, (1986). *Drugs and the brain.* New York: Scientific American Library.

Tanagho, E. A., Lue, T. F., & McClure, R. D. (1988). *Contemporary management of impotence and infertility.* Baltimore: Williams & Wilkins.

Tanay, E. (1992). The verdict with two names. *Psychiat. Ann., 22*(11), 571–573.

Tancer, M. E., Brown, T. M., Evans, D. L., Ekstrom, D. et al. (1990). Impaired effortful cognition in depression. *Psychiat. Res., 31*(2), 161–168.

Tanguay, P. E., & Edwards, R. M. (1982). Electrophysical studies of autism: The whisper of the bang. *J. Autism Dev. Dis., 12*, 177–183.

Tanzi, R. C., St. George Hyslop, P. H., & Gusella, J. T. (1989). Molecular genetic approaches to Alzheimer's disease. *Trends Neurosci., 12*(4), 152–158.

Tanzi, R. E. (1991). Gene mutations in inherited amyloidopathies of the nervous system. *American Journal of Human Genetics, 49*, 507–510.

Tapia, F. (1983). Current status of psychopharmacology and organic treatments. In C. E. Walker (Ed.), *The handbook of clinical psychology: Theory, research, and practice* (Volume II). Homewood, IL: Dow Jones-Irwin.

Taube, C. A. (1990). Funding and expenditures for mental illness. In R. W. Manderscheid & M. A. Sonnenschein (Eds.), *Mental Health, U.S., 1990.* DHHS #(ADM) 90-1708. Washington, DC: GPO.

Tavris, C. (1993). *Beware the incest-survivor machine.* New York Times Review of Books.

Taylor, C. B., Farquhar, J. W., Nelson, E., & Agras, S. (1977). Relaxation therapy and high blood pressure. *Arch. Gen. Psychiat., 34*, 339–342.

Taylor, E. A., & Stansfeld, S. A. (1984). Children who poison themselves. *Brit. J. Psychiat., 145*, 127–135.

Taylor, F., & Marshall, W. (1977). Experimental analysis of cognitive-behavioral therapy for depression. *Cog. Ther. Res., 1*, 59–72.

Taylor, J. R., & Carroll, J. L. (1987). Current issues in electroconvulsive therapy. *Psych. Rep., 60*(3, Pt. 1).

Taylor, R. (1975). *Electroconvulsive treatment (ECT): The control of therapeutic power.* Exchange.

Taylor, S., Koch, W. J., & McNally, R. J. (1992). How does anxiety sensitivity vary across the anxiety disorders? *Journal of Anxiety Disorders, 6*(3), 249–259.

Telch, C. F., & Agras, W. S. (1993). The effects of a very low calorie diet on binge eating. *Behav. Ther., 24*, 177–193.

Tellegen, A. (1985). Structures of mood and personality and their relevance to assessing anxiety, with an emphasis on self-report. In A. H. Tuma & J. Maser (Eds.), *Anxiety and the anxiety disorders.* Hillsdale, NJ: Erlbaum.

Telner, J. I., Lapierre, Y. D., Horn, E., & Browne, M. (1986).

Rapid reduction of mania by means of reserpine therapy. *Amer. J. Psychiat., 143*(8), 1058.

Telner, J. I., & Singhal, R. L. (1984). Psychiatric progress: The learned helplessness model of depression. *J. Psychiat. Res., 18*(3), 207–215.

Temoshok, L., Heller, B., Sagebiel, R., Blois, M., Sweet, D., Diclemente, R., & Gold, M. (1985). The relationship of psychosocial factors to prognostic indicators in cutaneous melanoma. *J. Psychosom. Res., 29,* 137–155.

Tenenbaum, J. (1983). ECT regulation reconsidered. *Mental Disability Law Reporter, 7,* 148–157.

Tennant, C. (1988). Psychological causes of duodenal ulcer. *Austral. N. Zeal. J. Psychiat., 22*(2), 195–202.

Teplin, L. A. (1990). The prevalence of severe mental disorder among male urban jail detainees: Comparison with the Epidemiologic Catchment Area Program. *Amer. J. Pub. Hlth., 80,* 663–669.

Teplin, L. A., Abram, K. M., & McClelland, G. M. (1994). Does psychiatric disorder predict violent crime among released jail detainees? *Amer. Psychol., 49*(4), 335–342.

Teri, L. (1982). The use of the Beck depression inventory for adolescents. *J. Abnorm. Child Psychol., 10*(2), 277–284.

Teri, L., & Lewinsohn, P. M. (1985). Group intervention for unipolar depression. *Behav. Ther., 8,* 109–123.

Teri, L., & Lewinsohn, P. M. (1986). Individual and group treatment of unipolar depression: Comparison of treatment outcome and identification of predictors of successful treatment outcome. *Behav. Ther., 17*(3), 215–228.

Teri, L., & Logsdon, R. (1991). Identifying pleasant activities for Alzheimer's disease patients: The pleasant events schedule-AD. *Gerontologist, 31,* 124–127.

Teri, L., & Reifler, B. V. (1987). Depression and dementia. In L. Carstensen & B. Edelstein (Eds.), *Handbook of clinical gerontology.* New York: Pergamon.

Terr, L. (1988). What happens to early memories of trauma? A study of twenty children under age five at the time of documented traumatic events. Annual Meeting of the American Psychiatry Association. *J. Amer. Academy Child Adol. Psychiat., 27*(1), 96–104.

Test, M. A., & Stein, L. I. (1978). Community treatment of the chronic patient. *Schizo. Bull., 4*(3), 350–364.

Thaker, G. K., Moran, M., Lahti, A., Adami, H., Tamminga, C. A., & Schulz, S. C. (1991). Pilot studies of schizotypal subjects. In C. A. Tamminga & S. C. Schulz (Eds.), *Schizophrenia Research.* New York: Raven Press.

Thapar, A., Davies, G., Jones, T., & Rivett, M. (1992). Treatment of childhood encopresis: A review. *Child Care, Health and Development, 18*(6), 343–353.

Theander, S. (1970). Anorexia nervosa. *Acta Psychiat. Scandin., (Suppl.),* 1–194.

Thigpen, C. H., & Cleckley, H. M. (1957). *The three faces of Eve.* New York: McGraw-Hill.

Thomas, C. S. (1984). Dysmorphophobia: A question of definition. *Brit. J. Psychiat., 144,* 513–516.

Thomas, P., & Goudemand, M. (1992). Seizure with low doses of clozapine. *Amer. J. Psychiat., 149*(1), 138–139.

Thompson, L. W., Gallagher, D., & Breckenridge, J. S. (1987). Comparative effectiveness of psychotherapies for depressed elders. *J. Cons. Clin. Psychol., 55,* 385–390.

Thompson, L. W., Gallagher, D., Nies, G., & Epstein, D. (1983). Evaluation of the effectiveness of professionals and nonprofessionals as instructors of "Coping with Depression" classes for elders. *Gerontologist, 23,* 390–396.

Thompson, M. S., & Conrad, P. L. (1977). Multifaceted behavioral treatment of drug dependence: A case study. *Behav. Ther., 8*(4), 731–737.

Thompson, P., Susan, K., & Turkat, I. D. (1988). Reactions to ambiguous stimuli among paranoid personalities. *Journal of Psychopathology and Behavioral Assessment, 10*(1), 21–32.

Thompson, R. A., & Sherman, R. T. (1993). *Helping athletes with eating disorders.* Champaing, IL: Human Kinetics Publishers.

Thompson, T. L. (1988). Psychosomatic disorders. In J. A. Talbott, R. E. Hales, & S. C. Yudofsky (Eds.), *Textbook of psychiatry.* Washington, DC: American Psychiatric Press.

Thompson, T. L., & Steele, B. F. (1988). The psychological aspects of pain. In R. C. Simons (Ed.), *Understanding human behavior in health and illness (3rd Ed.).* Baltimore: Williams & Wilkins.

Thorn, B. E., Shealy, R. C., & Briggs, S. D. (1993). Sexual misconduct in psychotherapy: Reactions to a consumer-oriented brochure. *Professional Research and Practice, 24*(1), 75–82.

Tice, D. (1990, Aug.). Presentation. Washington, DC: American Psychological Assoc.

Tice, D. (1992). Strategies for changing our emotional states. Conference presentation. American Psychological Association, Washington, DC.

Tien, H. C. (1975). Pattern of electrotherapy in Michigan. *Michigan Medicine, 74,* 251–257.

Tiller, J., Schmidt, U., Treasure, J. (1993). Compulsory treatment for anorexia nervosa: Compassion or coercion? *Brit. J. Psychiat., 162,* 679–680.

Tillich, P. (1952, Dec.). Anxiety, Religion, and medicine. *Pastoral Psychol., 3,* 11–17.

Tishler, C. L., & McKenry, P. C. (1982). Parental negative-self and adolescent suicide attempts. *Journal of the American Academy of Child Psychiatry, 21,* 404–408.

Tishler, C. L., McKenry, P. C., & Morgan, K. C. (1981). Adolescent suicide attempts: Some significant factors. *Suic. Life-Threat. Behav., 11*(2), 86–92.

Tobin, D. L., & Johnson, C. L. (1991). The integration of psychodynamic and behavior therapy in the treatment of eating disorders: Clinical issue versus theoretical mystique. In C. L. Johnson (Ed.), *Psychodynamic treatment of anorexia nervosa and bulimia.* New York: Guilford.

Tobin, S. (1990). Self psychology as a bridge between existential-humanistic psychology and psychoanalysis. *Journal of Humanistic Psychology, 30*(1), 14–63.

Todd, R. D. (1991). Fluoxetine in autism. *Amer. J. Psychiat., 148*(8), 1089.

Todd, T. C., & Stanton, M. D. (1983). Research on marital and family therapy: Answers, issues, and recommendations for the future. In B. B. Wolman & G. Stricker (Eds.), *Handbook of family and marital therapy.* New York: Plenum.

Tolstrup, K. et al. (1985). Long-term outcome of 151 cases of anorexia nervosa: The Copenhagen anorexia nervosa follow-up study. *Acta Psychiatr. Scandin., 71*(4), 380–387.

Tomasson, K., Kent, D., & Coryell, W. (1991). Somatization and conversion disorders: Comorbidity and demographics at presentation. *Acta Psychiatr. Scandin., 84*(3), 288–293.

Tomchek, L. B., Gordon, R., Arnold, M., Handleman, J. (1992). Teaching preschool children with autism and their normally developing peers: Meeting the challenges of integrated education. *Focus on Autistic Behavior, 7*(2), 1–17.

Torgersen, S. (1984). Genetic and nosological aspects of schizotypal and borderline personality disorders: A twin study. *Arch. Gen. Psychiatry., 41,* 546–554.

Torrey, E. F. (1988). *Nowhere to go: The tragic odyssey of the homeless mentally ill.* New York: Harper & Row.

Torrey, E. F. (1991). A Viral-Anatomical Explanation of Schizophrenia. *Schizo. Bull., 17*(1), 15–18.

Torrey, E. F., Wolfe, S. M., & Flynn, L. M. (1988). *Care of the seriously mentally ill: A rating of state programs* (2nd ed.). Washington, DC: Public Citizen Health Research Group and National Alliance for the Mentally Ill.

Torrey, E. F., Bowler, A. E., Rawlings, R., & Terrazas, A. (1993). Seasonality of Schizophrenia and Stillbirths. *Schizo. Bull., 19*(3), 557–562.

Toufexis, A. (1993). The personality pill. *Time,* Oct 11, 61–62.

Traskman, L., Asberg, M., Bertilsson, L., & Sjostrand, L. (1981). Monoamine metabolites in CSF and suicidal behavior. *Arch. Gen. Psychiat., 38,* 631–636.

Treaster, J. B. (1992, September 20). After hurricane, Floridians show symptoms seen in war. *New York Times.*

Treffert, D. A. (1989). *Extraordinary People: Understanding Savant Syndrome.* New York: Ballantine Books.

Trijsburg, R. W., & Duivenvoorden, H. J. (1987). Reactive-narcissistic character, obsessional personality and obsessive-compulsive behavior: A study of the validity of Sandler and Hazard typology. *British Journal of Medical Psychology, 60*(3), 271–278.

Tross, S., & Hirsch, D. A. (1988). Psychological distress and neuropsychological complications of HIV infection and AIDS. *Amer. Psychol., 43*(11), 929–934.

Trotter, R. J. (1985, Nov.). Geschwind's syndrome: Van Gogh's malady. *Psych. Today,* 46.

Trovato, F. (1987). A longitudinal analysis of divorce and suicide in Canada. *Journal of Marriage and the Family, 49,* 193–203.

Truax, C. (1963). Effective ingredients in psychotherapy: An approach to unraveling the patient-therapist interaction. *J. Couns. Psychol., 10,* 256–263.

Truax, C., Wargo, P., & Silber, L. (1966). Effects of group psychotherapy with high accurate empathy and nonpossessive warmth upon institutionalized female delinquents. *J. Abnorm. Psychol., 71,* 267–274.

Trujillo, K. A., & Akil, H. (1991). The NMDA receptor antagonist MK-801 increases morphine catalepsy and lethality. *Pharm. Biochem. Behav., 38*(3), 673–675.

Tryon, G. (1987). *Prof. Psychol., 17,* 357–363.

Tryon, G. S., DeVito, A. J., Halligan, F. R., Kane, A. S., et al. (1988). Borderline personality disorder and development: Counseling university students. *Journal of Counseling and Development, 67*(3), 178–181.

Tsai, L., Stewart, M., Faust, M., & Shook, S. (1982). Social class distribution of fathers of children enrolled in an Iowa autism program. *J. Autism Dev. Dis., 12,* 211–221.

Tsoi, W. F. (1992). Male and female transsexuals: a comparison. *Singapore Medical Journal, 33*(2), 182–185.

Tsuang, M. T. (1978). Suicide in schizophrenia, manics, depressives, and surgical controls: A comparison with general population suicide mortality. *Arch. Gen. Psychiat., 35*(2), 153–155.

Tsuang, M. T., Fowler, R. C., Cadoret, R. J., & Monnelly, E. (1974). Schizophrenia among first degree relatives of paranoid and nonparanoid schizoprenics. *Comprehen. Psychiat., 15*(4), 295–302.

Tsuang, M. T., Woolson, R. F., & Fleming, J. A. (1979). Long-term outcome of major psychoses: I. Schizophrenia and effective disorders compared with psychiatrically symptom-free surgical conditions. *Arch. Gen. Psychiat., 36*(12), 1295–1301.

Tucker, J. A., Vuchinich, R. E., & Schonhaut, S. J. (1987). Effects of alcohol on recall of social interactions. *Cog. Ther. Res., 11*(2), 273–283.

Tulkin, S. R. (1968). Race, class, and family and school achievement. *J. Pers. Soc. Psychol., 9,* 31–37.

Tulving, E., Risberg, J., & Ingvar, D. H. (1988). Regional cerebral blood flow and episodic memory retrieval. Presented at the Psychonomic Society Annual Meeting, Chicago.

Tulving, E., & Watkins, O. C. (1977). Recognition of failure of words with a single meaning. *Memory Cog., 5*(5), 513–522.

Tunnell, G. B. (1977). Three dimensions of naturalness: An expanded definition of field research. *Psychol. Bull., 84*(3), 426–437.

Tunstall, C. D., Ginsberg, D., & Hall, S. M. (1985). Quitting smoking. *Inter. J. Addict., 20,* 1089–1112.

Turk, D. (1975). Cognitive control of pain: A skills training approach for the treatment of pain. Unpublished master's thesis, Univ. Waterloo.

Turk, D. (1976). An expanded skills training approach for the treatment of experimentally induced pain. Unpublished doctoral dissertation, Univ. Waterloo.

Turkat, I. D., & Banks, D. S. (1987). Paranoid personality and its disorder. *Journal of Psychopathology & Behavioral Assessment, 9*(3), 295–304.

Turkat, I. D., Keane, S. P., Thompson-Pope, S. K. (1990). Social processing errors among paranoid personalities. *Journal of Psychopathology and Behavioral Assessment, 12*(3), 263–269.

Turkewitz, H., & O'Leary, K. D. (1981). A comparative outcome study of behavioral marital therapy and communication therapy. *J. Marital Fam. Ther., 7,* 159–170.

Turkington, C. (1987). Treatment of depressed elderly could prevent "silent suicides." *APA Monitor, 18,*(1), p. 13.

Turkington, C. (1992). Social variables tied to heart attack deaths. *APA Monitor, 23*(5), 44.

Turner, E., Ewing, J., Shilling, P., Smith, T., Irwin, M., Schuckit, M., & Kelsoe, J. (1992). Lack of association between an RFLP near the D2 dopamine receptor gene and severe alcoholism. *Bio. Psychiat., 31*(3), 285–290.

Turner, I. F., & Small, J. D. (1985). Similarities and differences in behavior between mentally handicapped and normal preschool children during play. *Child. Care Hlth. Dev., 11*(6), 391–401.

Turner, L. A., Althof, S. E., Levine, S. B., Bodner, D. R., Kursh, E. D., & Resnick, M. I. (1991). External vacuum devices in the treatment of erectile dysfunction: A one-year study of sexual and psychosocial impact. *Journal of Sex and Marital Therapy, 17*(2), 81–93.

Turner, S. M., Beidel, D. C., Borden, J. W., Stanley, M. A., et al. (1991). Social phobia: Axis I and II correlates. *J. Abnorm. Psychol., 100*(1), 102–106.

Turner, S. M., Beidel, D. C., Dancu, C. V., & Keys, D. J. (1986). Psychopathology of social phobia and comparison to avoidant personality disorder. *J. Abnorm. Psychol., 95*(4), 389–394.

Turner, S. M., Beidel, D. C., Long, P. J., & Greenhouse, J. (1992). Reduction of fear in social phobics: An examination of extinction patterns. *Behav. Ther., 23*(3), 389–403.

Turner, S. M., Beidel, D. C., & Nathan, R. S. (1985). Biological factors in obsessive-compulsive disorders. *Psychol. Bull., 97,* 430–450.

Turner, S. M., Hersen, M., & Bellack, A. S. (1977). Effects of social disruption, stimulus interference, and aversive conditioning on auditory hallucinations. *Behav. Mod., 1*(2), 249–258.

Twain, M. (1885). *The adventures of Huckleberry Finn.*

Tweed, J. L., Schoenbach, V. J., & George, L. K. (1989). The effects of childhood parental death and divorce on six-month history of anxiety disorders. *Brit. J. Psychiat., 154,* 823–828.

Tyor, P. L., & Bell, L. V. (1984). *Caring for the retarded in America: A history.* Westport, CT: Greenwood.

Tyrer, P. (1992). Anxiolytics not acting at the benzodiazepine receptor: Beta blockers. *Progress in Neuro Psychopharmacology and Biological Psychiatry, 16*(1), 17–26.

U. S. Bureau of the Census. (1988). *Statistical abstract of the United States* (108th ed.). Washington, DC: GPO.

U. S. Bureau of the Census. (1990). *Statistical abstract of the United States.* Washington, DC: GPO.

Uchoa, D. D. (1985). Narcissistic transference? *Revista Brasileira de Psicanalise, 19*(1), 87–96.

Uhde, T. W., Roy-Byrne, P. P., Vittone, B. J., Boulenger, J. P., & Post, R. M. (1985). Phenomenology and neurobiology of panic disorder. In A. H. Tuma & J. D. Maser (Eds.), *Anxiety and the anxiety disorder.* Hillsdale, NJ: Erlbaum.

Uhde, T. W., Siever, L. J., & Post, R. M. (1984). Clonidine: Acute challenge and clinical trial paradigms for the investigation and treatment of anxiety disorders, affective illness and pain syndromes. In R. M. Post & J. C. Ballenger (Eds.), *Neurobiology of mood disorders.* Baltimore: Williams & Wilkins.

Uhde, T. W., Siever, L. J., Post, R. M., Jimerson, D. C., Boulenger, J. P., & Buchsbaum, M. S. (1982). The relationship of plasma-free MHPG to anxiety and psychophysical pain in normal volunteers. *Psychopharma. Bull., 18,* 129–132.

Uhde, T. W., Stein, M. B., Vittone, B. A., et al. (1989). Behavioral and physiologic effects of short-term and long-term administration of clonidine in panic disorder. *Arch. Gen Psychiat., 46,* 170–177.

Uhde, T. W., Vittone, B. J., & Post, R. M. (1984). Glucose tolerance testing in panic disorder. *Amer. J. Psychiat., 14*(11), 1461–1463.

Uhde, T. W. et al. (1984). Fear and anxiety: Relationship to noradrenergic function. 14th Collegium Internationale Neuro-Psychopharmacologicum Congress (Florence, Italy). *Psychopathology, 17*(3, Suppl.), 8–23.

Uhde, T. W. et al. (1984). The sleep of patients with panic disorder: A preliminary report. *Psychiat. Res., 12*(3), 251–259.

Uhde, T. W. et al. (1985). Longitudinal course of panic disorder: Clinical and biological considerations [Special Issue]. *Progress in Neuro-Psychopharm. & Bio. Psychiat., 9*(1), 39–51.

Ullmann, L. P., & Krasner, L. (1975). *A psychological approach to abnormal behavior* (2nd ed.). Englewood Cliffs, NJ: Prentice Hall.

Uniform Crime Reports, 1990. (1991). Washington, DC: U. S. Department of Justice, U. S. Government Printing Office.

Ursano, R. J., Boydstun, J. A., & Wheatley, R. D. (1981). Psychiatric illness in U. S. Air Force Vietnam Prisoners of war: A five-year follow-up. *Amer. J. Psychiat., 138*(3), 310–314.

Vaillant, G. E. (1977). *Adaptions to life.* Boston: Little, Brown.

Vaillant, G. E. (1983). Natural history of male alcoholism: V. Is alcoholism the cart or the horse to sociopathy? *Brit. J. Addic., 78*(3), 317–326.

Vaillant, G. E. (1994). Ego mechanisms of defense and personality psychopathology. *J. Abnorm. Psychol., 103*(1), 44–50.

Vaillant, G. E., & Milofsky, E. S. (1982). Natural history of male alcoholism: IV. Paths to recovery. *Arch. Gen. Psychiat., 39,* 127–133.

Vaillant, G. E., & Milofsky, E. S. (1982). The etiology of alcoholism: A prospective viewpoint. *Amer. Psychol., 37,* 494–503.

Vaillant, G. E., & Perry, J. C. (1985). Personality disorders. In H. I. Kaplan & B. J. Sadock (Eds.), *Comprehensive Textbook of Psychiatry* (4th ed.). Baltimore: Williams & Wilkins.

Vaillant, P. M., & Antonowicz, D. H. (1992). Rapists, incest offenders, and child molesters in treatment: Cognitive and social skills training. *Inter. J. Offend. Ther. Compar. Crimin., 36*(3), 221–230.

Valenstein, E. S. (1973). *Brain Stimulation and motivation: Research and commentary.* Glenview, IL: Foresman.

Valenstein, E. S. (1986). *Great and Desperate Cures.* New York: Basic Books.

Valenti-Hein, D. C., Yarnold, P. R., & Mueser, K. T. (1994). Evaluation of the dating skills program for improving heterosocial interactions in people with mental retardation. *Behav. Mod., 18*(1), 32–46.

Valle, R. (1989). Cultural and ethnic issues in Alzheimer's disease family research. In E. Light and B. D. Lebowitz (Eds.), *Alzheimer's Disease treatment and family stress: Directions for research.* (DHHS Pub. #ADM 89-1569). Washington, DC: GPO.

Van Bourgondien, M. E., & Schopler, E. (1990). Critical issues in the residential care of people with autism. *J. Autism Dev. Dis., 20*(3), 391–399.

Van Dam, F. S., Honnebier, W. J., Van Zalinge, E. A., & Barendragt, J. T. (1976). Sexual arousal measured by photoplethysmography. *Behav. Engineering, 3*(4), 97–101.

Van de Castle, R. (1993). Content of Dreams. In M. A. Carskadon (Ed.), *Encyclopedia of Sleep and Dreams.* New York: Macmillan.

Van den Berg, J. H. (1971). What is psychotherapy? *Humanitas, 7*(3), 321–370.

Van Hasselt, V., Null, J., Kempton, T., & Buckstein, O. (1993). Social skills and depression in adolescent substance abusers. *Addictive Behaviors, 18,* 9–18.

van Hemert, A. M., Hawton, K., Bolk, J. H., & Fagg, J. (1993). Key symptoms in the detection of affective disorders in medical patients. *J. Psychosom. Res., 37*(4), 397–404.

Van Praag, H. M. (1977). The significance of dopamine for the mode of action of neuroleptics and the pathogenesis of schizophrenia. *Brit. J. Psychiat., 132,* 593–597.

Van Praag, H. M. (1978). *Psychotropic drugs: A guide for practitioners.* New York: Brunner/Mazel.

Van Praag, H. M. (1982). Depression, suicide and the metabolism of serotonin in the brain. *J. Affect. Dis., 4,* 275–290.

Van Praag, H. M. (1983). CSF 5-HIAA and suicide in non-depressed schizophrenics. *Lancet, ii,* 977–978.

Van Praag, H. M. (1983). In search of the action mechanism of antidepressants. 5-HTP/tyrosine mixtures in depression. *Neuropharmacology, 22,* 433–440.

Van Praag, H. M. (1984). Precursors on serotonin, dopamine, and norepinephrine in the treatment of depression. *Adv. Bio. Psychiat., 14,* 54–68.

Van Praag, H. M. (1986). Affective disorders and aggression disorders: Evidence for a common biological mechanism. In R. W. Maris (Ed.), *Biology of suicide.* New York: Guilford.

Van-Gent, E. M., & Zwart, F. M. (1991). Psychoeducation of partners of bipolar-manic patients. *J. Affect. Dis., 21*(1), 15–18.

Vandereycken, W., & Meermann, R. (1984). *Anorexia nervosa: A clinician's guide to treatment.* New York: de Gruyter.

Vanderlinden, J. & Vandereycken, W. (1989). *Overview of the family therapy literature.* In W. Vandereycken, E. Kog, & J. Vanderlinden (Eds.), *The family approach to eating disorders.* New York: PMA Publishing Corp.

Vanderlinden, J. & Vandereycken, W. (1991). Guidelines for the family therapeutic approach to eating disorders. *Psychotherapy and Psychosomatics, 56,* 36–42.

Varis, K. (1987). Psychosomatic factors in gastrointestinal disorders. *Ann. Clin. Res., 19*(2), 135–142.

Vatz, R., & Weinberg, L. (1993, January 10). Keno Krazy? *Washington Post,* p. C5.

Vaughan, K., Doyle, M., McConaghy, N., Blaszcznski, A. (1992). The relationship between relative's expressed emotion and schizophrenic relapse: An Australian replication. *Social Psychiatry and Psychiatric Epidemiology, 27*(1), 10–15.

Vega, W., & Rumbaut, R. (1991). Ethnic minorities and mental health. *Annual Review of Sociology, 17,* 351–383.

Veiel, H. O., Kuhner, C., Brill, G., & Ihle, W. (1992). Psychosocial correlates of clinical depression after psychiatric in-patient treatment: methodological issues and baseline differences between recovered and non-recovered patients. *Psychol. Med., 22*(2), 415–427.

Velamoor, V. R., Norman, R. M., Caroff, S. N., et al (1994). Progression of symptoms in neuroleptic malignant syndrome. *J. Nerv. Ment. Dis., 182,* 168–173.

Velleman, R., & Orford, J. (1993). The adult adjustment of offspring of parents with drinking problems. *Brit. J. Psychiat., 162,* 503–516.

Vellucci, S. V. (1989). Anxiety. In R. A. Webster & C. C. Jordan (Eds.), *Neurotransmitters, drugs and disease.* Oxford: Blackwell Scientific Publications.

Velten, E. (1968). A laboratory task for induction of mood states. *Behav. Res. Ther., 6,* 473–482.

Venter, A., Lord, C., Schopler, E. (1992). A follow-up study of high-functioning autistic children. *J. Child Psychol. Psychiat. Allied Disc., 33*(3), 489–507.

Verdoux, H., & Bourgeois, M. (1993). A comparison of manic patient subgroups. *J. Affect. Dis., 27,* 267–272.

Verfaellie, M., Cermak, L. S., Blackford, S. P., et al. (1990).

Strategic and automatic priming of semantic memory in alcoholic Korsakoff patients. *Brain and Cognition, 13*(2), 178–192.

Vernon, P. E. (1979). *Intelligence: Heredity and environment.* San Francisco: W. H. Freeman.

Vessey, S. H. (1964). Effects of grouping on levels of circulating antibodies in mice. *Proceedings of the Society of Exp. Bio. & Med., 115,* 252–255.

Vetter, H. J. (1969). *Language behavior and psychopathology.* Chicago: Rand McNally.

Victor, M., & Wolfe, S. M. (1973). Causation and treatment of the alcohol withdrawal syndrome. In G. Bourne & R. Fox (Eds.), *Alcoholism: Progress in research and treatment.* New York: Academic Press.

Vieira, C. (1993). Nudity in Dreams. In M. A. Carskadon (Ed.), *Encyclopedia of Sleep and Dreams.* New York: Macmillan.

Vieta, E., Nieto, E., Gasto, C., & Ciera, E. (1992). Attempted suicide by jumping. *European Psychiatry, 7*(5), 221–224.

Vieth, R. (1982). Depression in the elderly: Pharmacological considerations in treatment. *J. Amer. Geriatric Society, 30,* 581–586.

Viken, R. J. (1992). Therapy evaluation: Using an absurd pseudotreatment to demonstrate research issues. *Teaching of Psychology, 19*(2), 108–110.

Viney, W., & Zorich, S. (1982). Contributions to the history of psychology: XXIX. Dorothea Dix and the history of psychology. *Psych. Rep., 50,* 211–218.

Vitaliano, P., Maiuro, R., Ochs, H., & Russo, J. (1989). A model of burden in caregivers DAT patients. In E. Light & B. D. Lebowitz (Ed.), *Alzheimer's Disease treatment and family stress: Directions for research.* DHHS Pub. #ADM89-1569. Washington, DC: GPO.

Vitousek, K., & Manke, F. (1994). Personality variables and disorders in anorexia nervosa and bulimia nervosa. *J. Abnorm. Psychol., 103*(1), 137–147.

Vogele, C., & Steptoe, A. (1993). Anger inhibition and family history as modulators of cardiovascular responses to mental stress in adolescent boys. *J. Psychosom. Res., 37*(5), 503–514.

Volkmar, F. R., Carter, A., Sparrow, S. S., & Cicchetti, D. V. (1993). Quantifying social development in autism. *J. Amer. Acad. Child Adol. Psychiat., 32*(3), 627–632.

Volpe, B. T., & Hirst, W. (1983). The characterization of an amnestic syndrome following hypoxic ischemic injury. *Archives of Neurology, 40,* 436–440.

Volpicelli, J., Alterman, A., Hayashida, M., & O'Brien, C. (1992). Naltrexone in the treatment of alcohol dependence. *Arch. Gen. Psychiat., 49,* 876–880.

Von Korff, M., Nestadt, G., Romanoski, A. et al. (1985). Prevalence of treated and untreated DSM-III schizophrenia. *J. Nerv. Ment. Dis., 173,* 577–581.

Vonnegut, M. (1974, April). Why I want to bite R. D. Laing. *Harper's Magazine, 248*(1478), p. 90–82.

Vredenburg, K., Flett, G. L., & Krames, L. (1993). Analogue versus clinical depression: A critical reappraisal. *Psychol. Bull., 113*(2), 327–344.

Vredenburg, K., Krames, L., & Flett, G. L. (1985). Reexamining the Beck Depression Inventory: The long and short of it. *Psych. Rep., 56*(3), 767–778.

Wachtel, P. (1987). *Action and insight.* New York: Guilford.

Wadden, T. A., & Anderton, C. H. (1982). The clinical use of hypnosis. *Psychol. Bull., 91*(2), 215–243.

Wadden, T. A., Stunkard, A. J., & Liebschutz, J. (1988). Three-year follow-up of the treatment of obesity by very low calorie diet, behavior therapy, and their combination. *J. Cons. Clin. Psychol.*, *56*(6), 925–928.

Wade, T. C., Baker, T. B., & Hartmann, D. P. (1979). Behavior therapists' self-reported views and practices. *Behav. Ther.*, *2*(1), 3–6.

Wagman, M. (1980). PLATO DCS: An interactive computer system for personal counseling. *J. Couns. Psychol.*, *27*(1), 16–30.

Wagner, G., & Kaplan, H. S. (1993). *The new injection treatment for impotence.* New York: Brunner/Mazel.

Wahl, O. F., & Hunter, J. (1992). Are gender effects being neglected in schizophrenia research? *Schizo. Bull.*, *18*(2), 313–318.

Walburg, J. A. (1985). Verslaving en behandeling [Addiction and treatment]. *Gedragstherapie*, *18*(1), 7–17.

Walfish, S., Stenmark, D., Sarco, D., Shealy, J., et al. (1992). Incidence of bulimia in substance-misusing women in residential treatment. *Inter. J. Addic.*, *27*(4), 425–433.

Walker, E., & Lewine, R. (1990). Prediction of adult-onset schizophrenia from childhood home movies of the patients. *Amer. J. Psychiat.*, *147*, 1052–1056.

Walker, E., & Young, T. D., (1986). *A killing cure.* New York: Henry Holt.

Walker, L. E. (1979). *The battered woman.* New York: Harper & Row.

Walker, L. E. (1984). Battered women, psychology, and public policy. *Amer. Psychol.*, *39*(10), 1178–1182.

Walker, L. E. (1984). *The battered woman syndrome.* New York: Springer.

Wall, A. J. (1990). Group homes in North Carolina for children and adults with autism. *J. Autism Dev. Dis.*, *20*(3), 353–366.

Wallace, B. (1993). Cross-cultural counseling with the chemically dependent: Preparing for service delivery within a culture of violence. *Journal of Psychoactive Drugs*, *25*(1), 9–12.

Wallace, S. E. (1981). The right to live and the right to die. In S. E. Wallace & A. Eser (Eds.), *Suicide and euthanasia: The rights of personhood.* Knoxville, TN: Univ. Tennessee.

Wallen, J. (1992). A comparison of male and female clients in substance abuse treatment. *Journal of Substance Abuse Treatment*, *9*(3), 243–248.

Walsh, J. (1990). Assessment and treatment of the schizotypal personality disorder. *Journal of Independent Social Work*, *4*(3), 41–59.

Walsh, J., & Engelhardt, C. L. (1993). Myths about Dreaming. In M. A. Carskadon (Ed.), *Encyclopedia of Sleep and Dreams.* New York: Macmillan.

Walsh, R. (1992). Sociocultural perspectives on substance abuse disorders. *Amer. J. Psychiat.*, *149*(12), 1760–1761.

Walters, A. S., Barrett, R. P., & Feinstein, C. (1990). Social relatedness and autism: Current research, issues, directions. *Res. Dev. Dis.*, *11*(3), 303–326.

Waltzer, H. (1984). Suicide risk in young schizophrenics. *Gen. Hosp. Psychiat.*, *65*(3), 219–225.

Wanck, B. (1984). Two decades of involuntary hospitalization legislation. *Amer. J. Psychiat.*, *41*, 33–38.

Warah, A. (1993). Overactivity and boundary setting in anorexia nervosa: an existential perspective. *Journal of Adolescence*, *16*, 93–100.

Ward, D. A. (1985). Conceptions of the nature and treatment of alcoholism. *J. Drug Issues*, *15*(1), 3–16.

Ware, J. E. et al. (1984). Health and the use of outpatient mental health services. *Amer. Psychol.*, *39*(10), 1090–1100.

Waring, M., & Ricks, D. (1965). Family patterns of children who become adult schizophrenics. *J. Nerv. Ment. Dis.*, *140*(5), 351–364.

Warren, L. W., & Ostrom, J. C. (1988). Pack rats: World-class savers. *Psych. Today*, *22*(2), 58–62.

Wartenberg, A. A., Nirenberg, T. D., Liepman, M. R., Silvia, L. Y. et al. (1990). Detoxification of alcoholics: Improving care by symptom-triggered sedation. *Alcoholism: Clin. Exp. Res.*, *14*(1), 71–75.

Washton, A. M. (1987). Cocaine: Drug epidemic of the 80's. In D. Allen (Ed.), *The cocaine crisis.* New York: Pergamon.

Washton, A. M., & Stone-Washton, N. (1990). Abstinence and relapse in outpatient cocaine addicts. *J. Psychoact. Drugs*, *22*(2), 135–147.

Wasserman, I. M. (1984). Imitation and suicide: A reexamination of the Werther Effect. *Amer. Sociological Rev.*, *49*, 427–436.

Wasserman, I. M. (1992). The impact of epidemic, war, prohibition and media on suicide: United States, 1910–1920. *Suic. Life-Threat. Behav.*, *22*(2), 240–254.

Wasylenki, D. (1992). Psychotherapy of schizophrenia revisited. *Hosp. Comm. Psychiat.*, *43*(2), 123–128.

Waters, L. (1990). Reinforcing the empty fortress: An examination of recent research into the treatment of autism. *Educ. Studies*, *16*(1), 3–16.

Watkins, P. L., Clum, G. A., Borden, J. W., Broyles, S., et al. (1990). Imagery-induced arousal in individuals with panic disorder. *Cog. Ther. Res.*, *14*(1), 37–46.

Watkins-Duncan, B. A. (1992). Principles for formulating treatment with Black patients. *Psychotherapy*, *29*(3), 452–457.

Watson, C. G. (1987). Recidivism in "controlled drinker" alcoholics: A longitudinal study. *J. Clin. Psychol.*, *43*(3), 404–412.

Watson, C. G., & Buranen, C. (1979). The frequencies of conversion reaction symptoms. *J. Abnorm. Psychol.*, *88*(2), 209–211.

Watson, D., Clark, L. A., & Harkness, A. R. (1994). Structures of personality and their relevance to psychopathology. *J. Abnorm. Psychol.*, *103*(1), 18–31.

Watson, J. B. (1930). *Behaviorism* (Revised Edition). Chicago: The University of Chicago Press.

Watson, J. B., & Rayner, R. (1920). Conditioned emotional reaction. *J. Exp. Psychol.*, *3*, 1–14.

Waxer, P. (1974). Nonverbal cues for depression. *J. Abnorm. Psychol.*, *83*(3), 319–322.

Webster, R. L. (1991). Fluency enhancement in stutterers advances in self-regulation through sensory augmentation. In J. G. Carlson, & A. R. Seifert (Eds.), *International perspectives on self-regulation and health.* New York: Plenum.

Wechsler, H., Grosser, G. H., & Greenblatt, M. (1965). Research evaluating antidepressant medications on hospitalized mental patients: A survey of published reports during a five-year period. *J. Nerv. Ment. Dis.*, *141*, 231–239.

Wechsler, J. A. (1972). *In a darkness.* New York: Norton.

Wehmeyer, M. L. (1992). Self-determination and the education of students with mental retardation. *Education and Training in Mental Retardation*, *27*(4), 302–314.

Wehr, T. A., & Goodwin, F. K. (1981). Biological rhythms and psychiatry. In S. Arieti & H. K. H. Brodie (Eds.), *American handbook of psychiatry* (Vol. 7), New York: Basic Books.

Weidman, A. A. (1985). Engaging the families or substance abusing adolescents in family therapy. *J. Substance Abuse Treatment, 2*(2), 97–105.

Weinberg, J., & Levine, S. (1980). Psychobiology of coping in animals: The effects of predictability. In S. Levine & H. Ursin (Eds.), *Coping and health*. New York: Plenum.

Weinberg, J. R. (1977). Toward classifying psychoactive chemical use. *Amer. J. Drug & Alcohol Abuse, 4*(1), 77–90.

Weinberger, D. R. (1983). "Imaging of the brain: Aiding the search for physical correlates of mental illness": Comment. *Integ. Psychiat., 1*(4), 146.

Weinberger, D. R. (1991). Schizophrenia (Forward to Section I). In A. Tasman & S. M. Goldfinger (Eds.), *American psychiatric press review of psychiatry* (Vol. 10). Washington, DC: American Psychiatric Press.

Weinberger, D. R., & Kleinman, J. E. (1986). Observations of the brain in schizophrenia. In A. J. Frances & R. E. Hales (Eds.), *Psychiatry update* (Vol. 5). Washington, DC: American Psychiatric Press.

Weinberger, D. R. et al. (1982). Computed tomography in schizophreniform disorder and other acute psychiatric disorders. *Arch. Gen. Psychiat., 30*(7), 770–783.

Weiner, H. (1977). *Psychobiology and human disease.* New York: Elsevier.

Weiner, H. (1985). The psychobiology and pathophysiology of anxiety and fear. In A. H. Tuma & J. Maser (Eds.), *Anxiety and the anxiety disorders*. Hillsdale, NJ: Erlbaum.

Weiner, H., Thaler, M., Reiser, M. F., & Mirsky, I. A. (1957). Etiology of duodenal ulcer: I. Relation of specific psychological characteristics to rate of gastric secretion (serum pepsinogen). *Psychosom. Med., 19*, 1–10.

Weiner, I. W. (1969). The effectiveness of suicide prevention programs. *Ment. Hyg., 53*, 357–373.

Weiner, R. D. (1984). Does electroconvulsive therapy cause brain damage? *Behav. Brain Sci., 7*, 1–54.

Weiner, R. D. (1989). Electroconvulsive therapy. In H. I. Kaplan & B. J. Sadock (Eds.), *Comprehensive textbook of psychiatry* (Vol. 1, 5th ed.). Baltimore: Williams & Wilkins.

Weiner, R. D., & Coffey, C. E. (1988). Indications for use of electroconvulsive therapy. In A. J. Frances & R. E. Hales (Eds.), *American Psychiatric Press review of psychiatry* (Vol. 7). Washington, DC: American Psychiatric Press.

Weingartner, H., & Silberman, E. (1984). Cognitive changes in depression. In R. M. Post & J. C. Ballenger (Eds.), *Neurobiology of mood disorders*. Baltimore: Williams & Wilkins.

Weingartner, H., et al. (1984). Cognitive impairments in Parkinson's disease distinguishing between effort-demanding and automatic cognitive processes. *Psychiatry Res., 11*, 223–235.

Weingartner, H. J., Hommer, D., Lister, R. G., Thompson, K., & Wolkowitz, O. (1992). Selective effects of triazolam on memory. *Psychopharmacology, 106*, 341–345.

Weintraub, M., Segal, R. M., & Beck, A. T. (1974). An investigation of cognition and affect in the depressive experience of normal men. *J. Cons. Clin. Psychol., 42*, 911.

Weir, R. F. (1992). The morality of physician-assisted suicide. *Law, Medicine and Health Care, 20*(1–2), 116–126.

Weishaar, M. E., & Beck, A. T. (1992). Clinical and cognitive predictors of suicide. In R. W. Maris, A. L. Berman, J. T. Maltsberger, & R. I. Yufit (Eds.), *Assessment and prediction of suicide*. New York: Guilford.

Weisheit, R. A. (1990). Domestic marijuana growers: Mainstreaming deviance. *Deviant Behav., 11*(2), 107–129.

Weiss, D. E. (1991). *The Great Divide*. New York: Poseidon Press/Simon & Schuster.

Weiss, D. S., & Marmar, C. R. (1993). Teaching time-limited dynamic psychotherapy for posttraumatic stress disorder and pathological grief. *Psychotherapy.*

Weiss, D. S., Marmar, C. R., Schlenger, W. E., & Fairback, J. A., et al. (1992). The prevalence of lifetime and partial posttraumatic stress disorder in Vietnam theater veterans. *Journal of Traumatic Stress, 5*(3), 365–376.

Weiss, J. M. (1970). Somatic effects of predictable and unpredictable shock. *Psychosom. Med., 32*, 397–409.

Weiss, J. M. (1977). Ulcers. In J. D. Maser & M. E. P. Seligman (Eds.), *Psychopathology: Experimental models*. San Francisco: W. H. Freeman.

Weiss, J. M., Glazer, H. I., & Pohorecky, L. A. (1974). Neurotransmitters and helplessness: A chemical bridge to depression? *Psych. Today, 8*(7), 58–62.

Weiss, J. M., Glazer, H. I., & Pohorecky, L. A. (1976). Coping behavior and neurochemical changes: An alternative explanation for the original "learned helplessness" experiments. In G. Serban & A. Kling (Eds.), *Animal models of human psychobiology*. New York: Plenum.

Weiss, R. L., Hops, H., & Patterson, G. R. (1973). A framework for conceptualizing marital conflict, a technology for altering it, some data for evaluating it. In L. A. Hamerlynck, L. C. Handy & E. J. Mash (Eds.), *Behavior change: Methodology, concepts, and practice*. Champaign, IL: Research.

Weisse, C. S. (1992). Depression and immunocompetence: A review of the literature. *Psychol. Bull., 111*(3), 475–489.

Weissman, A. N., & Beck, A. T. (1978). Development and validation of the dysfunctional attitude scale. Paper presented at the 12th Annual Convention of the Assoc. for Advancement of Behavior Therapy. Chicago.

Weissman, M. M. (1974). The epidemiology of suicide attempts. *Arch. Gen. Psychiat., 30*, 737–746.

Weissman, M. M. (1984). *The psychological treatment of depression. Psychotherapy research: Where are we and where should we go?* New York: Guilford.

Weissman, M. M. (1988). The epidemiology of panic disorder. In A. J. Frances & R. E. Hales (Eds.), *American Psychiatric Press review of psychiatry* (Vol. 7). Washington, DC: American Psychiatric Press.

Weissman, M. M., & Boyd, J. H. (1984). The epidemiology of mental disorders. In R. M. Post & J. C. Ballenger (Eds.), *Neurobiology of mood disorders*. Baltimore: Williams & Wilkins.

Weissman, M. M., Bruce, M. L., Leaf, P. J., Florio, L. P., & Holzer, C. (1991). Affective disorders. In L. N. Robins & D. A. Regier (Eds.), *Psychiatric disorders in America: The Epidemiologic Catchment Area Study*. New York: Free Press.

Weissman, M. M., Fox, K., & Klerman, G. L. (1973). Hostility and depression associated with suicide attempts. *Amer. J. Psychiat., 130*(4), 450–455.

Weissman, M. M., & Klerman, G. L. (1985). Gender and depression. *Trends in Neurosci.*, *8*(9), 416–420.

Weissman, M. M., Myers, J. K., & Harding, P. S. (1978). Psychiatric disorders in a U. S. urban community. *Amer. J. Psychiat.*, *135*, 459–462.

Weissman, M. M., Myers, J. K., & Thompson, W. D. (1981). Depression and its treatment in a U. S. urban community—1975–1976. *Arch. Gen. Psychiat.*, *38*(4), 417–421.

Weissman, M. M. et al. (1979). The efficacy of drugs and psychotherapy in the treatment of acute depressive episodes. *Amer. J. Psychiat.*, *136*(4-B), 555–558.

Weissman, M. M. et al. (1981). Depressed outpatients: Results one year after treatment with drugs and/or interpersonal psychotherapy. *Arch. Gen. Psychiat.*, *38*, 51–55.

Weissman, M. M. et al. (1982). Short-term interpersonal psychotherapy (IPT) for depression: Description and efficacy. In J. C. Anchin & D. J. Kiesler (Eds.), *Handbook of interpersonal psychotherapy.* New York: Pergamon.

Weissman, M. M., et al. (The cross-national collaborative group) (1992). The changing rate of major depression: Cross-national comparisons. *JAMA*, *268*(21), 3098–3105.

Weizenbaum, J. (1966). ELIZA: A computer program for the study of natural language communication between man and machine. *Commun. Assoc. Comput. Machinery*, *9*, 36–45.

Weizman, R., & Hart, J. (1987). Sexual behavior in healthy married elderly men. *Archives of Sexual Behavior*, *16*(1), 39–44.

Wells, A. (1992). Cognitive therapy for anxiety and cognitive theories of emotion. In G. D. Burrows, S. M. Roth, & R. Noyes, Jr., *Handbook of Anxiety* (Vol. 5). Oxford: Elsevier.

Wells, K. C. (1985). Behavioral family therapy. In A. S. Bellack & M. Hersen (Eds.), *Dictionary of behavior therapy techniques.* New York: Pegamon.

Wells, K. C., & Biegel, D. E. (Eds.). (1991). *Family preservation services: Research and evaluation.* Newbury Park, CA: Sage.

Wells, K. C., Hersen, M., Bellack, A. S., & Himmelhoch, J. (1979). Social skills training in unipolar nonpsychotic depression. *Amer. J. Psychiat.*, *136*(10), 1331–1332.

Wells, M. C., Glickauf-Hughes, C., & Bruzzell, V. (1990). Treating obsessive-compulsive personalities in psycho-dynamic/interpersonal group therapy. *Psychotherapy*, *27*(3), 366–379.

Wells, M. E., & Hinkle, J. S. (1990). Elimination of childhood encopresis: A family systems approach. *J. Ment. Hlth. Couns.*, *12*(4), 520–526.

Wender, P. H., Kety, S. S., Rosenthal, D., Schulsinger, F., Ortmann, J., & Lunde, I. (1986). Psychiatric disorders in the biological and adoptive families of adopted and individuals with affective disorders. *Arch. Gen. Psychiat.*, *43*, 923–929.

Werner, P. D., Rose, T. L., & Yesavage, J. A. (1983). Reliability, accuracy, and decision-making strategy in clinical predictions of imminent dangerousness. *J. Consult. Clin. Psychol.*, *51*, 815–825.

Wernick, R. L. (1983). Stress inoculation in the management of clinical pain. In D. Meichenbaum & M. E. Jaremko (Eds.), *Stress reduction and prevention.* New York: Plenum.

Wertheim, E. H., & Poulakis, Z. (1992). The relationship among the General Attitude and Belief Scale, other dysfunctional cognition measures, and depressive of bulimic tendencies. *Journal of Rational Emotive and Cognitive-Behavior Therapy*, *10*(4), 219–233.

West, L. J. (1993). Reflections of the right to die. In A. A. Leenaars (Ed.), *Suicidology.* Northvale, NJ: Jason Aronson.

Westen, D. (1991). Cognitive-behavioral interventions in the psychoanalytic psychotherapy of borderline personality disorders. *Clinical Psychology Review*, *11*(3), 211–230.

Wester, J. M. (1991). Rethinking inpatient treatment of borderline clients. *Perspectives in Psychiatric Care*, *27*(2), 17–20.

Westermeyer, J. (1992). Schizophrenia and substance abuse. In A. Tasman, & M. B. Riba (Eds.), *Review of Psychiatry* (Vol. 11). Washington, DC: American Psychiatric Press.

Weston, S. C., & Siever, L. J. (1993). Biological correlates of personality disorders. *J. Pers. Dis.*, *Spring* (Suppl.), 129–148.

Wettstein, R. M. (1988). Psychiatry and the law. In J. A. Talbott, R. E. Hales & S. C. Yudofsky (Eds.), *American Psychiatric Press textbook of psychiatry.* Washington, DC: American Psychiatric Press.

Wettstein, R. M. (1989). Psychiatric malpractice. In A. Tasman, R. E. Hales, & A. J. Frances (Eds.), *American Psychiatric Press Review of Psychiatry* (Vol. 8). Washington, DC: American Psychiatric Press.

Wexler, D. B. (1976). *Criminal commitments and dangerous mental patients: Legal issues of confinement, treatment, and release.* DHEW Pub. No. (ADM) 76-28650, Rockville, MD.

Wexler, D. B. (1983). The structure of civil commitment. *Law & Human Behav.*, *7*, 1–18.

Wexler, D. B. (1988). Reforming the law in action through empirically grounded civil commitment guidelines. *Hosp. Comm. Psychiat.*, *39*, 402–405.

Weyerer, S., & Hafner, H. (1992). Epidemiologie psychischer Storungen [Epidemiology of mental disorders]. *Zeitschrift fur Klinische Psychologie*, *21*(1), 106–120.

Wheeler, D. L., Jacobson, J. W., Paglieri, R. A., & Schwartz, A. A. (1992). *An experimental assessment of facilitated communication.* Schenectady, NY: O.D. Heack/Eleanor Roosevelt Developmental Disabilities Services Office.

Whelan, J. P., & Houts, A. C. (1990). Effects of a waking schedule on primary enuretic children treated with full-spectrum home training. *Health Psychology*, *9*, 164–176.

Wherry, J. N., McMillan, S. L., & Hutchison, H. T. (1991). Differential diagnosis and treatment of conversion disorder and Guillain-Barre Syndrome. *Clinical Pediatrics*, *30*(10), 578–585.

Whipple, E. E., Webster, S. C., & Stratton, C. (1991). The role of parental stress in physically abusive families. *Child Abuse and Neglect: The International Journal*, *15*(3), 279.

White, B. J., & Madara, E. J. (Eds.) (1992). *The self-help sourcebook: Finding & forming mutual aid self-help groups.* Denville, NJ: St. Clares-Riverside Medical Center.

White, C. P., & Rosenbloom, L. (1992). Temporal-lobe structures and autism. *Developmental Medicine and Child Neurology*, *34*(6), 558–559.

White, G. D. (1977). The effects of observer presence on the activity level of families. *J. Appl. Behav. Anal.*, *10*(4), 734.

White, H. C. (1974). Self-poisoning in adolescents. *Brit. J. Psychiat.*, *124*, 24–35.

White, J. H., Hornsby, L. C., Boyleston, W. H., & Gordon, R. (1972). The treatment of Little Fritz: A modern-day little Hans. *Inter. J. Child Psychother.*, *1*(4), 7–23.

White, K., & Simpson, G. (1981). Combined MAOI-tricyclic antidepressant treatment: A reevaluation. *J. Clin. Psychopharm.*, *1*, 264–282.

White, L. (1964). Organic factors and psychophysiology in childhood schizophrenia. *Psychol. Bull.*, *81*, 238–255.

Whitehead, W. E. (1992). Biofeedback treatment of gastrointestinal disorders. *Biofeed. Self-Reg.*, *17*(1), 59–76.

Whitehorn, J. C., & Betz, B. J. (1975). *Effective psychotherapy with the schizophrenic patient.* New York: Jason Aronson.

Whiteside, M. (1983, Sep. 12). A bedeviling new hysteria. *Newsweek.*

Whiting, J. W. et al. (1966). *Six cultures series: I. Field guide for a study of socialization.* New York: Wiley.

Whitlock, F. A. (1967). The aetiology of hysteria. *Acta Psychiatr. Scandin.*, *43*(2), 144–162.

Whitlock, F. A., & Broadhurst, A. D. (1969). Attempted suicide and the experience of violence. *J. Biosoc. Sci.*, *1*, 353–368.

Whitman, T. L. (1972). Aversive control of smoking behavior in a group context. *Behav., Res. Ther.*, *10*, 97–104.

Whittaker, S., & Bry, B. H. (1992). Overt and covert parental conflict and adolescent problems: Observed marital interaction in clinical and nonclinical families. *Family Therapy, 19*(1), 43–54.

Whybrow, P. C., Akiskal, H. S., & McKinney, W. T. (1984). *Mood disorders: Toward a new psychobiology.* New York: Plenum.

Widiger, T. A. (1992). Categorical versus dimensional classification: Implications from and for research. *J. Pers. Dis.*, *6*, 287–300.

Widiger, T. A. (1993). The DSM-III-R categorical personality disorder diagnoses: A critique and an alternative. *Psychological Inquiry, 4*, 75–90.

Widiger, T. A., Corbitt, E. M., & Millon, T. (1992). Antisocial personality disorder. In A. Tasman & M. B. Riba (Eds.), *American Psychiatric Press Review of Psychiatry* (Vol. 11). Washington, DC: American Psychiatric Press.

Widiger, T. A., & Costa, P. T. (1994). Personality and personality disorders. *J. Abnorm. Psychol.*, *103*(1), 78–91.

Widom, C. S. (1991, Feb.). Presentation. American Assoc. for the Advancement of Science.

Wielawski, I. (1992, March 12). Mental patients overload county emergency system: Service cutbacks squeeze about 30,000 out of clinics and into 'revolving door' facilities. *Los Angeles Times*, p. A1.

Wiens, A. N. (1990). Structured clinical interviews for adults. In G. Goldstein & M. Hersen (Eds.), *Handbook of psychological assessment* (2nd ed.). New York: Pergamon.

Wiens, A. N., & Menustik, C. E. (1983). Treatment outcome and patient characteristics in an aversion therapy program for alcoholism. *Amer. Psychol.*, *38*(10), 1089–1096.

Wierson, M., Forehand, R. L., & Framne, C. L. (1992). Epidemiology and treatment of mental health problems in juvenile delinquents. *Adv. Behav. Res. Ther.*, *14*(2), 93–120.

Wiggins, J. S. (1973). *Personality and prediction: Principles of personality assessment.* Reading, MA: Addison-Wesley.

Wikan, U. (1991). *Managing turbulent hearts.* Chicago: University of Chicago Press.

Wilbur, C. B. (1984). Treatment of multiple personality. *Psychiat. Ann.*, *14*, 27–31.

Wilcox, J. A. (1990). Fluoxetine and bulimia. *J. Psychoact. Drugs*, *22*(1), 81–82.

Wilfley, D. E., Agras, W. S., Telch, C. F., Rossiter, E. M., Schneider, J. A., Cole, A. G., Sifford, L., & Raeburn, S. D. (1993). Group cognitive-behavioral therapy and group inter-personal psychotherapy for the nonpurging bulimic individual: A controlled comparison. *J. Cons. Clin. Psychol.*, *61*(2), 296–305.

Will, O. A. (1961). Paranoid development and the concept of self: Psychotherapeutic intervention. *Psychiatry, 24*(2), 16–530.

Will, O. A. (1967). Psychological treatment of schizophrenia. In A. M. Freedman & H. I. Kaplan (Eds.), *Comprehensive textbook of psychiatry.* Baltimore: Williams & Wilkins.

Willard, W. (1979). American Indians. In L. D. Hankoff & B. Einsidler (Eds.), *Suicide: Theory and clinical aspects.* Littleton, MA: PSG Publishing Company.

Willenbring, M., & Spring, W. (1988). Evaluating alcohol use in elders. *Generations, 12*(4), 27–31.

Williams, C. C. (1983). The mental foxhole: The VietNam veterans' search for meaning. *Amer. J. Orthopsychiat.*, *53*(1), 4–17.

Williams, R. B. (1977). Headache. In R. B. Williams, Jr. & W. D. Gentry (Eds.), *Behavioral approaches to medical treatment.* Cambridge, MA: Ballinger.

Williams, R. B. (1985). Biochemical factors in cardiovascular disease. In J. L. Houpt, R. Michels, J. O. Cavenar, Jr. et al. (Eds.), *Psychiatry* (Vol. 2). Philadelphia: JB Lippincott.

Williams, R. B. (1989). Biological mechanisms mediating the relationship between behavior and coronary heart disease. In A. W. Siegman & T. M. Dembroski (Eds.), *In search of coronary behavior.* Hillsdale, NJ: Erlbaum.

Williams, R. B. (1989). *The trusting heart: Great news about Type A behavior.* New York: Times Books.

Williams, R. B., Barefoot, J. C., Califf, R. M., Haney, T. L., et al. (1992). Prognostic importance of social and economic resources among medically treated patients with angiographically documented coronary artery disease. *JAMA, 268*(19), 2652.

Williamson, D. A., Cubic, B. A., & Gleaves, D. H. (1993). Equivalence of body image disturbances in anorexia and bulimia nervosa. *J. Abnorm. Psychol.*, *102*(1), 177–180.

Williamson, D. A., Gleaves, D. H., & Lawson, O. J. (1991). Biased perception of overeating in bulimia nervosa and compulsive binge eaters. *Journal of Psychopathology and Behavioral Assessment, 13*(3), 257–268.

Willner, P. (1984). Cognitive functioning in depression: A review of theory and research. *Psychol. Med.*, *14*(4), 807–823.

Wilson, G. T. (1978). Alcoholism and aversion therapy: Issues, ethics, and evidence. In G. A. Marlatt & P. E. Nathan (Eds.), *Behavioral approaches to alcoholism.* New Brunswick, NJ: Rutgers Center for Alcohol Studies.

Wilson, G. T. (1978). On the much discussed nature of the term "Behavior Therapy." *Behav. Ther.*, *9*, 89–98.

Wilson, G. T. (1987). Chemical aversion conditioning as a treatment for alcoholism: A re-analysis. *Behav. Res. Ther.*, *25*, 503–516.

Wilson, G. T. (1990). Clinical issues and strategies in the practice of behavior therapy. In C. M. Franks, G. T. Wilson, P. C. Kendall, & J. P. Foreyt (Eds.), *Review of behavior therapy* (Vol. 12). New York: Guilford.

Wilson, G. T. (1994). Behavioral treatment of obesity: Thirty years and counting. *Adv. Behav. Res. Ther.*, *16*, 31–75.

Wilson, G. T., & Fairburn, C. G. (1993). Cognitive treatments for eating disorders. *J. Cons. Clin. Psychol.*, *61*(2), 261–269.

Wilson, G. T., & Pike, K. M. (1993). Eating Disorders. In D. H. Barlow (Ed.), *Clinical Handbook of Psychological Disorders: A Step-by-Step Treatment Manual* (2nd ed.). New York: Guilford.

Wilson, G. T., Rossiter, E., Kleifield, E. I., & Lindholm, L. (1986). Cognitive-behavioral treatment of bulimia nervosa: A controlled evaluation. *Behav. Res. Ther., 24*(3), 277–288.

Wilson, M. R., Greene, J. H., & Soth, N. B. (1986). Psychodynamics of the adopted patient. *Adoption and Fostering, 10*(1), 41–46.

Wilson, R. S., Como, P. G., Garron, D. C., et al. (1987). Memory failure in Huntington's disease. *Journal of Clinical Experimental Neuropsychology, 9*, 147–154.

Wilson, S., & Maguire, F. (1985). Self-esteem and subjective effects during marijuana intoxication. Special Issue: Drugs: Euphoria and aphrodisia. *Journal of Drug Issues, 15*, 263–271.

Wilson, W. H., Diamond, R. J., & Factor, R. M. (1990). Group treatment for individuals with schizophrenia. *Comm. Ment. Hlth. J., 26*(4), 361–372.

Wilson, W. M. (1992). The Stanford-Binet: Fourth Edition and Form L-M in assessment of young children with mental retardation. *Mental Retardation, 30*(2), 81–84.

Wincze, J. P., & Lange, J. D. (1981). Assessment of sexual behavior. In D. H. Barlow (Ed.), *Behavioral assessment of adult disorders*. New York: Guilford.

Winfield, I., George, L. K., Schwartz, M., & Blazer, D. G. (1990). Sexual assault and psychiatric disorders among a community sample of women. *Amer. J. Psychiat., 147*, 335–341.

Wing, J. K. (1988). Coping with schizophrenia at home. In C. N. Stefanis & A. D. Rabavilas (Eds.), *Schizophrenia: Recent biosocial development*. New York: Human Sciences.

Wing, L. (1976). *Early childhood autism*. Oxford: Pergamon.

Wing, L. (1981). Social and interpersonal needs of autistic adolescents and adults. *Proceedings of the 1981 International Conference on Autism*, 294–312.

Wing, L., & Wing, J. K. (1971). Multiple impairments in early childhood autism. *J. Autism Child. Schizo., 1*, 256–266.

Winick, B. J. (1983). Incompetency to stand trial: Developments in the law. In J. Monahan & H. J. Steadman (Eds.), *Mentally disordered offenders*. New York: Plenum.

Winick, M., Meyer, K., & Harris, R. C. (1975). Malnutrition and environmental enrichment by early adoption. *Science*, 1173–1175.

Winick, M., Rosso, P., & Waterlow, J. (1970). Cellular growth of cerebrum, cerebellum, and brain stem in normal and marasmic children. *Experimental Neurology, 26*, 393–400.

Winokur, A. et al. (1980). Withdrawal reaction from long-term low-dosage administration of diazepam: A double-blind placebo-controlled case study. *Arch. Gen. Psych., 37*(1), 101–105.

Winslade, W. J. (1983). *The insanity plea*. New York: Scribner.

Winslade, W. J. (1988). Electroconvulsive therapy: Legal regulations and ethical concerns. In A. J. Frances & R. E. Hales (Eds.), *American Psychiatric Press review of psychiatry* (Vol. 7). Washington, DC: American Psychiatric Press.

Winslade, W. J., Liston, E. H., Ross, J. W. et al. (1984). Medical, judicial, and statutory regulation of ECT in the United States. *Amer. J. Psychiat., 141*, 1349–1355.

Winson, J. (1990, Nov.). The meaning of dreams. *Scientific American*, 86–96.

Winston, A., & Pollack, J. (1991). Brief adaptive psychotherapy. *Psychiat. Ann., 21*(7), 415–418.

Wirshing, W. C., Marder, S. R., Eckman, T. A., Liberman, R. P. (1992). Acquisition and retention of skills training methods in chronic schizophrenia outpatients. *Psychopharmacology Bulletin, 28*(3), 241–245.

Wise, T. N. (1985). Fetishism—etiology and treatment: A review from multiple perspectives. *Comprehen. Psychiat., 26*, 249–257.

Wise, T. N., Fagan, P. J., Schmidt, C. W., Ponticas, Y., et al. (1991). Personality and sexual functioning of transvestitic fetishists and other paraphilics. *J. Nerv. Ment. Dis., 179*(11), 694–698.

Wiseman, C. V., Gray, J. J., Mosimann, J. E., & Ahrens, A. H. (1992). Cultural expectations of thinness in women: An update. *Inter. J. Eat. Dis., 11*(1), 85–89.

Wisniewski, K. E., Wisniewski, H. M., & Wen, G. Y. (1985). Occurrence of neuropathological changes and dementia of Alzheimer's Disease in Down Syndrome. *Ann. Neurol., 17*, 278–282.

Witkin, M. J., Atay, J. E., Fell, A. S., & Manderscheid, R. W. (1990). Specialty mental health system characteristics. In R. W. Manderscheid & M. A. Sonnenschein (Eds.), *Mental health, United States* (DHHS Pub. No. ADM 90-1708). Washington, DC: GPO.

Wittchen, H. U. & Essau, C. A. (1993). Comorbidity and Mixed Anxiety-Depressive Disorders: Is there Epidemiological Evidence? *J. Clin. Psychiat., 54*(Suppl. 1), 9–15.

Wittchen, H. U., Essau, C., & vonZerssen, D. (1992). Lifetime and six-month prevalence of mental disorders in the Munich Follow-up Study. *European Archives of Psychiatry and Clinical Neuroscience, 241*(4), 247–258.

Wittrock, D. A., & Blanchard, E. B. (1992). Thermal biofeedback treatment of mild hypertension: A comparison of effects on conventional and ambulatory blood pressure measures. *Behav. Mod., 16*(3), 283–304.

Wixted, J. T., Morrison, R. L. & Bellack, A. S. (1988). Social skills training in the treatment of negative symptoms [Special Issue]. *Inter. J. Ment. Hlth., 17*(1), 3–21.

Wlazlo, Z., Schroeder-Hartwig, K., Hand, I., Kaiser, G., & Munchau, N. (1990). Exposure in vivo vs. social skills training for social phobia: Long term outcome and differential effects. *Behav. Res. Ther., 28*, 181–193.

Wolberg, L. R. (1967). *The technique of psychotherapy*. New York: Grune & Stratton.

Wolberg, L. R. (1987). The evolution of psychotherapy: Future trends. In J. K. Zeig (Ed.), *The evolution of psychotherapy*. New York: Brunner/Mazel.

Wolf, S., & Wolff, H. G. (1947). *Human gastric functions*. New York: Oxford Univ.

Wolfe, D. A., Edwards, B., Manion, I. & Koverola, C. (1988). Early intervention for parents at risk for child abuse and neglect: A preliminary investigation. *J. Cons. Clin. Psychol., 56*, 40–47.

Wolfe, D. A., Kaufman, D., Aragona, J., & Sandler, J. (1981). *The child management program for abusive parents*. Winter Park, FL: Anna.

Wolfe, J. K. L., & Fodor, I. G. (1977). Modifying assertive behavior in women: Comparison of three approaches. *Behav. Ther.*, *8*, 567–574.

Wolfe, S. M., Fugate, L., Hulstrand, E. P., Kamimoto, L. E. (1988). *Worst Pills Best Pills: The Older Adult's Guide to Avoiding Drug-Induced Death or Illness.* Washington, DC: Public Citizen Health Research Group.

Wolff, S. (1991). Schizoid personality in childhood and adult life I: The vagaries of diagnostic labeling. *Brit. J. Psychiat.*, *159*, 615–620.

Wolpe, J. (1958). *Psychotherapy by reciprocal inhibition.* Stanford, CA: Stanford UP.

Wolpe, J. (1969). *The practice of behavior therapy.* Oxford: Pergamon.

Wolpe, J. (1982). *The practice of behavior therapy* (3rd ed.). New York: Pergamon.

Wolpe, J. (1986). Misconceptions about behaviour therapy: Their sources and consequences. *Behaviour Change, 3*(1), 9–15.

Wolpe, J. (1987). The promotion of scientific psychotherapy: A long voyage. In J. K. Zeig (Ed.), *The evolution of psychotherapy.* New York: Brunner/Mazel.

Wolpe, J. (1990). *The practice of behavior therapy* (4th ed.). Elmsford, NY: Pergamon.

Wolpe, J. The case of Mrs. Schmidt [Transcript and record]. Nashville, TN: Counselor Recording and Tests.

Wolpe, J., & Lang, P. (1964). A fear-survey schedule for use in behaviour therapy. *Behav. Res. Ther., 2*, 27–34.

Wong, B. (1979). The role of theory in learning disabilities research: An analysis of the problem. *J. Learn. Dis., 12*, 19–29.

Wood, D., Del Nuovo, A., Bucky, S. F., Schein, S. F., & Michalik, M. (1981). Psychodrama with an alcohol abuser population. *U. S. Navy Medicine, 72*, 22–30.

Woodbury, M. M., DeMaso, D. R., & Goldman, S. J. (1992). An integrated medical psychiatric approach to conversion symptoms in a four-year-old. *J. Amer. Acad. Child Adol. Psychiat., 31*(6), 1095–1097.

Woodruff, R. A., Goodwin, D. W., & Guze, S. B. (1973). *Psychiatric diagnosis.* New York: Oxford UP.

Woodside, M. R., & Legg, B. H. (1990). Patient advocacy: A mental health perspective. *J. Ment. Hlth. Couns., 12*(1), 38–50.

Woodward, B., Duckworth, K. S., & Gutheil, T. G. (1993). The pharmacotherapist-psychotherapist collaboration. In J. M. Oldham, M. B. Riba, & A. Tasman (Eds.), *Review of Psychiatry* (Vol. 12). Washington, DC: American Psychiatric Press.

Woody, G., Luborsky, L., McLellan, A. T., & O'Brien, C. P. (1988). Psychotherapy for substance abuse. 50th Annual Scientific Meeting of the Committee on Problems of Drug Dependence. *National Institute on Drug Abuse Research Monograph Series, 90*, 162–167.

Woody, R. H., & Robertson, M. (1988). *Becoming a clinical psychologist.* Madison, CT: International Universities Press.

Wooley, S. C., & Wooley, O. W. (1979). Obesity and women— I. A closer look at the facts. *Women's Studies International Quarterly, 2*, 67–79.

Wooley, S. C., & Wooley, O. W. (1982). The Beverly Hills eating disorder: The mass marketing of anorexia nervosa. *Inter. J. Eat. Dis., 1*, 57–69.

Wooley, S. C., & Wooley, O. W. (1985). Intensive outpatient and residential treatment for bulimia. In D. M. Garner & P. E. Garfinkel (Eds.), *Handbook of psychotherapy for anorexia nervosa and bulimia.* New York: Guilford.

Woolfolk, R. L., Carr-Kaffashan, L., McNulty, T. F., & Lehrer, P. M. (1976). Meditation training as a treatment for insomnia. *Behav. Ther. 7*(3), 359–365.

Workman, E. A., & Short, D. D. (1993). Atypical antidepressants versus imipramine in the treatment of major depression: A meta-analysis. *J. Clin. Psychiat., 54*(1), 5–12.

World Health Organization (WHO). (1988, July 1). Correlates of youth suicide. Geneva: World Health Organization, Division of Mental Health.

Worth, D. (1991). A service delivery system model for AIDS prevention for women. In *National Conference on Drug Abuse Research and Practice Conference Highlights.* Rockville, MD: National Institute on Drug Abuse.

Wright, L. (1988). The Type A behavior pattern and coronary artery disease: Quest for the active ingredients and the elusive mechanism. *Amer. Psychol., 43*(1), 2–14.

Wright, L. S. (1985). High school polydrug users and abusers. *Adolescence, 20*(80), 852–861.

Wright, L. S. (1985). Suicidal thoughts and their relationship to family stress and personal problems among high school seniors and college undergraduates. *Adolescence, 20*(79), 575–580.

Wulsin, L., Bachop, M., & Hoffman, D. (1988). Group therapy in manic-depressive illness. *Amer. J. Psychother., 42*, 263–271.

Wurtman, J. J., & Wurtman, R. J. (1982). Studies on the appetite for carbohydrates in rats and humans. *J. Psychiat. Res., 17*(2), 213–221.

Wurtman, J. J. et al. (1981). Carbohydrate craving in obese people: Suppression by treatments affecting serotenergic transmission. *Inter. J. Eat. Dis., 1*(1), 2–15.

Wurtman, R. J. (1983). Behavioural effects of nutrients. *Lancet, i*, 1145–1147.

Wurtman, R. J., & Wurtman, J. J. (1984). Nutritional control of central neurotransmitters. In K. M. Pirke & D. Ploog (Eds.), *The psychobiology of anorexia nervosa.* Berlin: Springer-Verlag.

Yabe, K., Tsukahar, R., Mita, K., & Aoki, H. (1985). Developmental trends of jumping reaction time by means of EMG in mentally retarded children. *J. Ment. Def. Res., 29*(2), 137–145.

Yager, J. (1985). The outpatient treatment of bulimia. *Bull. Menninger Clin., 49*(3), 203–226.

Yalom, I. D. (1985). *The theory and practice of group psychotherapy* (3rd ed.). New York: Basic Books.

Yama, M., Fogas, B., Teegarden, L., & Hastings, B. (1993). Childhood sexual abuse and parental alcoholism: Interactive effects in adult women. *Amer. J. Orthopsychiat., 63*(2), 300–305.

Yang, B., Stack, S., & Lester, D. (1992). Suicide and unemployment: Predicting the smoothed trend and yearly fluctuations. *Journal of Socioeconomics, 21*(1), 39–41.

Yank, G. R., Bentley, K. J., & Hargrove, D. S. (1993). The vulnerability-stress model of schizophrenia: advances in psychosocial treatment. *Amer. J. Orthopsychiat., 63*(1), 55–69.

Yap, P. M. (1951). Mental diseases peculiar to certain cultures:

a survey of comparative psychiatry. *J. Ment. Sci., 97,* 313–327.

Yarock, S. (1993). Understanding chronic bulimia: A four psychologies approach. *American Journal of Psychoanalysis, 53*(1), 3–17.

Yates, A. (1989). Current perspectives of the eating disorders: I. History, psychological and biological aspects. *J. Amer. Acad. Child Adol. Psychiat., 28*(6), 813–828.

Yates, W. R., Petty, F., & Brown, K. (1988). Alcoholism in males with antisocial personality disorder. *Inter. J. Addic., 23*(10), 999–1010.

Yazici, O., Aricioglu, F., Gurvit, G., Ucok, A., Tastaban, Y., Canberk, O., Ozguroglu, M., Durat, T., Sahin, D. (1993). Noradrenergic and serotoninergic depression? *J. Affect. Dis., 27,* 123–129.

Yehuda, R., Southwick, S. M., & Giller, E. L. (1992). Exposure to atrocities and severity of chronic posttraumatic stress disorder in Vietnam combat veterans. *Amer. J. Psychiat., 149*(3), 333–336.

Yesavage, J., Brink, T. L., Rose, T. L., Lum, O., Huang, V., Adey, M. & Leirer, V. (1983). Development and validation of a geriatric depression screening scale: A preliminary report. *J. Psychiat. Res., 17,* 37–49.

Yontef, G. M., & Simkin, J. F. (1989). Gestalt therapy. In R. J. Corsini & D. Wedding (Eds.), *Current psychotherapies.* Itasca, IL: Peacock.

Yost, E., Beutler, L., Corbishley, A. M., & Allender, J. (1986). *Group cognitive therapy: A treatment approach for depressed older adults.* New York: Pergamon.

Young, A. M., & Herling, S. (1986). Drugs as reinforcers: Studies in laboratory animals. In S. R. Goldberg & I. P. Stolerman (Eds.), *Behavioral analysis of drug dependence.* Orlando, FL: Academic Press.

Young, J. E., Beck, A. T., & Weinberger, A. (1993). Depression. In D. H. Barlow (Ed.), *Clinical Handbook of Psychological Disorders: A Step-by-Step Treatment Manual* (2nd ed.). New York: Guilford.

Young, J. G., Kavanagh, M. E., Anderson, G. M., Shaywitz, B. A., & Cohen, D. J. (1982). Clinical neurochemistry of autism and associated disorders. *J. Autism Dev. Dis., 12,* 147–165.

Young, L. D., & Allin, J. M. (1992). Repression-sensitization differences in recovery from learned helplessness. *Journal of General Psychology, 119*(2), 135–139.

Young, M., Benjamin, B., & Wallis, C. (1963). Mortality of widowers. *Lancet, 2,* 454–456.

Young, R. C. & Klerman, G. L. (1992). Mania in late life: Focus on age at onset. *Amer. J. Psychiat., 149,* 867–876.

Young, T. J. (1991). Suicide and homicide among Native Americans: Anomie or social learning? *Psych. Rep., 68*(3, Pt. 2), 1137–1138.

Young, W. C., Young, L. J., Lehl, K. (1991). Restraints in the treatment of dissociative disorders: A follow-up of twenty patients. *Dissociation Progress in the Dissociative Disorders, 4*(2), 74–78.

Youngren, M. A., & Lewinsohn, P. M. (1980). The functional relation between depression and problematic interpersonal behavior. *J. Abnorm. Psychol., 89*(3), 333–341.

Youngstrom, N. (1990). Six offender types are identified. *APA Monitor, 21*(10), p. 21.

Youngstrom, N. (1992). Grim news from national study of rape. *APA Monitor, 23*(7), p. 38.

Youngstrom, N. (1992). Psychology helps a shattered L. A. *The APA Monitor, 23*(7), p. 1, 12.

Yudofsky, S., Silver, J., & Hales, R. (1993). Cocaine and aggressive behavior: Neurobiological and clinical perspectives. *Bull. Menninger Clin., 57*(2), 218–226.

Yuwiler, A., Shih, J. C., Chen, C., Ritvo, E. R. (1992). Hyperserotoninemia and antiserotonin antibodies in autism and other disorders. *J. Autism Dev. Dis., 22*(1), 33–45.

Zamichow, N. (1993, February 15). The Dark Corner of Psychology. *Los Angeles Times,* p. A1.

Zarit, S. H., Orr, N., & Zarit, J. M. (1985). *The hidden victims of Alzheimer's disease: Families under stress.* New York: New York Univ.

Zarr, M. L. (1984). Computer-mediated psychotherapy: Toward patient-selection guidelines. *Amer. J. Psychother., 38*(1), 47–62.

Zastowny, T. R., Lehman, A. F., Cole, R. E., & Kane, C. (1992). Family management of schizophrenia: A comparison of behavioral and supportive family treatment. *Psychiat. Quart., 63*(2), 159–186.

Zax, M., & Cowen, E. L. (1969). Research on early detection and prevention of emotional dysfunction in young school children. In C. D. Speilberger (Ed.), *Current topics in clinical and community psychology* (Vol. 1). New York: Academic.

Zax, M., & Cowen, E. L. (1976). *Abnormal psychology: Changing conceptions.* New York: Holt, Rinehart & Winston.

Zeiss, A. M., Lewinsohn, P. M., & Munoz, R. F. (1979). Nonspecific improvement effects in depression using interpersonal skills training, pleasant activity schedules, and cognitive training. *J. Cons. Clin. Psychol., 47,* 427–439.

Zeiss, A. M., Rosen, G. M., & Zeiss, R. A. (1977). Orgasm during intercourse: A treatment strategy for women. *J. Cons. Clin. Psychol., 45,* 891–895.

Zellner, D. A., Harner, D. E., & Adler, R. L. (1989). Effects of eating abnormalities and gender on perceptions of desirable body shape. *J. Abnorm. Psychol., 98*(1), 93–96.

Zerbe, K. J. (1990). Through the storm: Psychoanalytic theory in the psychotherapy of the anxiety disorders. *Bull. Menninger Clin., 54*(2), 171–183.

Zerbe, K. J. (1993). Selves that starve and suffocate: The continuum of eating disorders and dissociative phenomena. *Bull. Menninger Clin., 57*(3), 319–327.

Zerbe, K. J. (1993). Whose body is it anyway? Understanding and treating psychosomatic aspects of eating disorders. *Bull. Menninger Clin., 57*(2), 161–177.

Zerssen, D. et al. (1985). Circadian rhythms in endogenous depression. *Psychiatry Research, 16,* 51–63.

Zetin, M. (1990). Obsessive-compulsive disorder. *Stress Med., 6*(4), 311–321.

Zetin, M., & Kramer, M. A. (1992). Obsessive-compulsive disorder. *Hosp. Comm. Psychiat., 43*(7), 689–699.

Zettle, R. D., Haflich, J. L., & Reynolds, R. A. (1992). Responsivity of cognitive therapy as a function of treatment format and client personality dimensions. *J. Clin. Psychol., 48*(6), 787–797.

Ziegler, F. J., & Imboden, J. B. (1962). Contemporary conversion reactions: II. A conceptual model. *Arch. Gen. Psychiat.*, *6*(4), 279–287.

Zigler, E., & Hodapp, R. M. (1991). Behavioral functioning in individuals with mental retardation. *Annu. Rev. Psychol.*, *42*, 29–50.

Zigler, E., & Muenchow, S. (1979). Mainstreaming: The proof is in the implementation. *Amer. Psychol.*, *34*, 993–996.

Zigler, E., Taussig, C., & Black, K. (1992). Early childhood intervention: A promising preventative for juvenile delinquency. *Amer. Psychol.*, *47*(8), 997–1006.

Zilbergeld, B. (1978). *Male sexuality.* Boston: Little, Brown.

Zilboorg, G., & Henry, G. W. (1941). *A history of medical psychology.* New York: Norton.

Zill, N., & Schoenborn, C. A. (1990, November). *Developmental, learning, and emotional problems: Health of our nation's children, United States, 1988.* Advance Data: National Center for Health Statistics, Number 190.

Zimbardo, P. (1976). "Rational paths to madness." Presentation at Princeton University, Princeton, NJ.

Zimbardo, P. G., Andersen, S. M., & Kabat, L. G. (1981, June). Induced hearing deficit generates experimental paranoia. *Science, 212*(4502), 1529–1531.

Zimberg, S. (1978). Treatment of the elderly alcoholic in the community and in an institutional setting. *Addict. Dis., 3,* 417–427.

Zimmer, B., & Gershon, S. (1991). The ideal late life anxiolytic. In C. Salzman & B. D. Lebowitz (Eds.), *Anxiety in the elderly.* New York: Springer.

Zimmerman, M. (1994). Diagnosing personality disorders: A review of issues and research methods. *Arch. Gen. Psychiat., 51,* 225–245.

Zimmerman, M., & Coryell, W. (1989). DSM-III personality disorder diagnoses in a nonpatient sample: Demographic correlates and comorbidity. *Arch. Gen. Psychiat., 46*(8), 682–689.

Zohar, J., & Pato, M. T. (1991). Diagnostic considerations. In M. T. Pato & J. Zohar (Eds.), *Current Treatments of Obsessive-compulsive Disorder.* Washington, DC: American Psychiatric Press.

Zuckerman, M. (1978). Sensation seeking and psychopathy. In R. D. Hare & D. Schalling (Eds.), *Psychopathic behavior: Approaches to research.* New York: Wiley.

Zuger, A. (1993 July). The Baron strikes again. *Discover,* 28–30.

SOURCES OF ILLUSTRATIONS

■

Kreiner/Black Star; **277:** John Leongard; **278:** Callahan; **280:** Ron Haviv/SABA; **282:** Homer Sykes/Woodfin Camp & Associates; **284:** Harlow Primate Laboratory, University of Wisconsin; **287:** PEANUTS by Charles Schulz, © 1956 United Features Syndicate, Inc.; **293:** CALVIN AND HOBBES © 1993 Watterson; Universal Press Syndicate; **294:** The Dorthea Lange Collection, Oakland Museum; **303:** A. Knudsen/Sygma; **306:** Jerry Irwin; **Chapter 9, 310:** Paul Klee, *Voice from the Ether,* 1939, Victoria and Albert Museum/Art Resource New York; **312:** Chuck Fishman/Woodfin Camp & Associates; **320:** Phil Huber/Black Star; **325:** Will McIntyre/Photo Researchers; **332:** Gerd Ludwig/Woodfin Camp & Associates; **334:** Travis Amos; **Chapter 10, 342:** Frida Kahlo, *The Suicide of Dorothy Hale,* 1938–1939. Phoenix Art Museum, gift of anonymous donor; **344:** Grant Haller, *Seattle Post Intelligencer*/Sygma; **349:** Pressenbild/Adventure Photo; **354:** Ralf-Finn Hestoft/SABA; **357:** Karsh/Woodfin Camp & Associates; **358:** Steve Nickerson/Black Star; **360:** Greg Smith/SABA; **363:** John Kaplan/Media Alliance; **366:** H. Yamaguchi/Gamma-Liaison; **369:** Joel Gordon; **370:** Lawrence Migdale; **372:** Edward Abbott; **Chapter 11 376:** Boehringer Ingelheim International GmbH, photo Lennart Nilsson; **385:** Mary Evans Picture Library/Sigmund Freud Copyrights; **389(t):** J. James, Science Photo Library/Photo Researchers; **389(b):** Lester Sloan/Woodfin Camp & Associates; **392:** Lionel Cihes/Associated Press; **397:** Boehringer Ingelheim International GmbH, photo Lennart Nilsson; **398:** Frank Fournier/Woodfin Camp & Associates; **400:** Ted Spiegel/Black Star; **404:** Louis Psihoyos/Matrix; **405:** Sidney Harris; **407:** Ted Spagna; **Chapter 12, 410:** Wayne Thiebaud, *Confections,* 1962, Collection, Byron R. Meyer, San Francisco; **413:** B. Schiffman/Gamma-Liaison; **413(inset):** Steve Schapiro/Sygma; **415:** David Garner; **416:** Wallace Kirkland/*Life,* © Time Warner Inc.; **423(top):** Pierre August Renoir, *Seated Bather,* 1903–1906, Detroit Institute of the Arts, bequest of Robert H. Tannahill; **423(b):** Donna Terek, Michigan Magazine *(The Detroit News/Free Press);* **428:** Historical Research Center, Houston Academy of Medicine, Texas Medical Center Library; **429:** Richard Howard, © 1991 *Discover;* **431:** Michelle Bogre; **435:** Patt Blue; **437:** Patt Blue; **438:** James Wilson/Woodfin Camp & Associates; **Chapter 13, 442:** Joel Gordon; **445:** National Cancer Society; **448:** James Pozarik/Gamma-Liaison; **450:** John Chiasson/Gamma-Liaison; **452:** Tony O'Brian/Picture Group; **453:** Bettmann Archives; **457:** Charlie Steiner/JB Pictures; **461:** E.T. Archives; **466(l):** Richard E. Aaron/Sygma; **466(r):** Stephen Ellison/Shooting Star; **467:** James Aronovski/Picture Group; **468:** Vaughan Fleming/Science Photo Library/Photo Researchers; **471:** George Steinmetz; **472:** Andrew Savulich/New York Times Pictures; **478:** Steve Raymer/National Geographic Society; **Chapter 14, 482:** CHAGALL, Marc, *Birthday* [l'Anniversiare]. (1915) Oil on cardboard, 31¾ × 39¼". The Museum of Modern Art, New York. Acquired through the Lillie P. Bliss Bequest. Photograph © 1994 The Museum of Modern Art, New York; **494:** Joseph LoPiccolo; **498:** Gilbert Dupuy/Black Star; **500; 503:** Catherine Karnow/Woodfin Camp & Associates; **506:** Peter Yates/Picture Group; **507:** The Kobal Collection; **509:** Joel Gordon; **513(l):** The Bettmann Archive; **513(r):** David Levenson/Rex USA Ltd.; **514:** Marc Geller; **Chapter 15, 518:** Wölfli, Adolf. *St. Adolf Wearing Glasses, between the Two Giant Cities of Niess and Mia.* 1924. Collection de l'art brut, Lausanne; **522:** Kobal Collection; **525:** David Graham/Black Star; **529:** Oskar Diethelm Historical Library,

Cornell Medical College, New York Hospital; **533:** NYPL Performing Arts Research Center; **536:** Antoine Wiertz, *Hunger, Madness, Crime,* 1864, Royal Museum, Belgium; **538:** Julie Newdoll, Computer Graphics Laboratory, UCSF. © Regents University of California; **541:** National Institute of Mental Health; **546:** Courtesy of the artist, Gerald Scarfe and Tin Blue Ltd.; **Chapter 16, 550:** Jan Saunders van Hemessen, *The Surgeon,* 1530 Museo Nacional del Prado; **553:** Temple University Urban Archives, Philadelphia, Penn.; **554:** Bettmann Archives; **556(l):** Francisco Jose de Goya, *The House of the Insane,* Prado, Madrid/Art Resource New York; **556(r):** Museum of Modern Art Film Stills Archive; **559:** Museum of Modern Art Film Stills Archive; **563:** Lynn Johnson/Black Star; **570:** E. Fuller Torrey; **574:** Christopher Morris/Black Star; **576:** Andrew Holbrooke/Black Star; **Chapter 17 opener, 580:** Vincent van Gogh, *Portrait of a Patient,* 1889, Vincent van Gogh Foundation/Vincent van Gogh Museum, Amsterdam; **587:** Kobal Collection; **591:** Associated Press/Wide World Photos; **593(t):** Rob Nelson/Black Star; **593(b):** Sipa Press; **595:** Michael S. Yamashita/Woodfin Camp & Associates; **596:** Acikalin/Sipa Press; **597:** Kobal Collection; **603:** GARFIELD, Jim Davis © 1985 United Features Syndicate, Inc.; **607:** Joel Gordon; **610(t):** The Kobal Collection; **610(b):** Associated Press; **Chapter 18, 618:** Chagall, Marc. *I and the Village,* 1911. Oil on canvas, 6'3⅝" × 59⅝". The Museum of Modern Art, New York. Mrs. Simon Guggenheim Fund. Photograph © 1994 The Museum of Modern Art, New York; **622:** Thorensen; **623:** Associated Press/Wide World Photos; **624:** Dali, Salvador. *The Persistence of Memory* [Persistance de la memoire]. 1931. Oil on canvas, 9½" × 13". The Museum of Modern Art, New York. Given anonymously. Photograph © 1994 The Museum of Modern Art, New York; **628:** *People,* © 1989 Debra Lex; **630:** Kobal Collection; **634:** Ernest Hilgard, Stanford University; **636:** PEANUTS © 1977 United Features Syndicate, Inc.; **642:** Richard Falco/Black Star; **644:** Christopher Little/Outline; **Chapter 19, 648:** James Wilson/Woodfin Camp & Associates; **650:** Myrleen Ferguson/Tony Stone Worldwide; **654:** Arthur Pollock, *Boston Herald;* **655:** Janet Kelly/*Eagle-Times,* Reading, Pennsylvania; **656:** April Saul, *The Philadelphia Inquirer;* **657:** Paul Chesley/Tony Stone Worldwide; **658:** Edvard Munch, *The Dead Mother and the Little Girl,* Munch Museum, Oslo/Art Resource New York; **659:** Michael Amendolia/*The News Limited,* Sydney; **660:** Honoré Daumier, *Fatherly Discipline,* 1851. The Art Institute of Chicago, Arthur Heun Fund, 1952.1108; **665:** Michael Heron/Woodfin Camp & Associates; **667:** Tony Freeman/Photo Edit; **670:** Susan Young; **670:** The Eden Institute Foundation, Inc.; **675:** Nicholas Lisi/*Syracuse Newspapers;* **676:** *Newsweek,* E. Lee White; **679:** Photofest; **682:** Frank Varney; **687:** Joel Gordon; **Chapter 20, 692:** Graphische Sammlung Albertina, Vienna; **695:** Tom Moran; **696(t):** Mark Sennet/Onyx; **696(b):** Allen Horn/*Columbus Ledger-Enquirer;* **698:** Donna Ferrato/Black Star; **702:** Joel Gordon; **705:** Lloyd Fox, *The Philadelphia Inquirer;* **707:** Joel Gordon; **708:** B. Leonard Holman and Thomas C. Hill, Harvard Medical School; **712:** Dennis Selkoe, Harvard Medical School; **715:** Shara Leen; **717:** Michael Heron/Woodfin Camp & Associates; **720:** Lynn Johnson/Black Star; **Chapter 21, 724:** Otto Gleichmann, *Beams Collapse,* 1920, Sprengel Museum, Hanover; **727:** Associated Press/Wide World Photos; **732:** Stephen Ferry/Gamma-Liaison; **735:** *Milwaukee Sentinel*/SABA; **741:** John Ficara/Woodfin Camp & Associates; **742:** Conti Press/Claus Bergmann

NAME INDEX

SUBJECT INDEX